THE HACHETTE GUIDE TO FRANCE

Special thanks to :

- The French Government Tourist Board, French Government Tourist Offices in New York and London, French Ministry of Culture, French Ministry of Foreign Trade.
- Regional, departmental and local Tourist Authorities.

Originally produced and published in France as Guide Hachette France by **Hachette Guides Bleus.**
Editor : **Adélaïde Barbey.**
Executive editors : **Marie-Pierre Levallois** and **Dominique Ougier.**
Contributors : Danielle Blondy, Nicolas Boles, Brigitte Bouttin, Peter Inserra, Michel Lefèvre, Catherine Maîtrepierre, Béatrice Morin, Anne Ramirez, Alix Ratouis, Paulette Tepernowsky, John Tyler Tuttle.
First edition's authors : Jean-Jacques Fauvel, Florence Guibert, Bernard Hennequin, Hervé Juvin, Guy Michaud, Patrice Milleron, Jean Modot, François Monmarché, Christian Perrin, Duncan Richards, François Roboth, Jean Taverne, Françoise Vibert-Guigue.
Designer : **Pierre Faucheux,** APF.
Production : **Bernard Péronnet** and **Françoise Jolivot.**

First American Edition.
Revised and updated.

Translation first published in the United States by Pantheon Books, a division of Random House, Inc., New York, in 1985.

Library of Congress Cataloging — in — Publication Data.

Guide Hachette France. English.
The Hachette Guide to France.
Translation of : Guide Hachette France.

Includes index.
I. France--Description and travel--1975- --
Guidebooks. I. Hachette (Firm) II. Title.
DC16.G84713 1986 914.4'04838 85-43184
ISBN 0-394-74338-5 (pbk.)

Typeset by M.C.P. — Orléans
Manufactured in France by Aubin and Mame.

THE HACHETTE GUIDE TO FRANCE

PANTHEON BOOKS
NEW YORK

HOW TO USE THE GUIDE

The region

This guide is organised by region, within which the towns appear in alphabetical order. Each of the 28 regions is a geographical unit composed of several "departments" linked by landscape, culture, history, traditions.

1083

Alphabetical place-names index

To find a town or place of interest

Consult the index, **p. 1085**.
Blue numbers refer to sightseeing information.
Red numbers refer to practical information (hotels, restaurants, etc.).

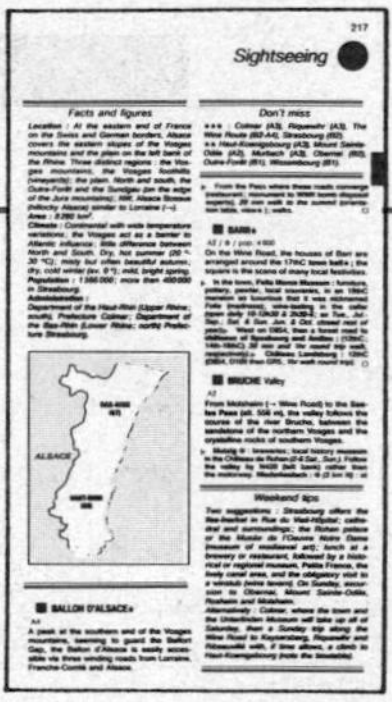
217

Sightseeing

Facts and figures

Don't miss

Weekend tips

To plan a journey and visit a region

Consult the general map, **pp. 8-9** and look up the regions to be visited.
Regions are listed in alphabetical order and are distinguished by a blue band on the edge of the page.

To find practical information

Châlons-sur-Marne · Nogent-sur-Seine 519

Pages dealing with practical information are distinguished in each region by a red band on the edge of the page. At the start of the red pages for each region, you will find the main information (tourist office, local festivities and events, addresses for holiday sports and activities, etc.).
Details of hotels, restaurants, camping sites appear under each town in this section.

To find out more

The geography, history, economy and architecture are discussed in **"The many faces of France"**, p. 13.

To prepare and organize your holidays

Consult the **"practical holiday guide"**, p. 43.

SYMBOLS AND ABBREVIATIONS

Alphabetical, by locality, in each region	RENNES
Sightseeing map reference	D2
Postal code	⊠ 35000
Telephone code	99
Tourist office or ***syndicat d'initiative*** address and map reference where applicable	(i) pont de Nemours (B2), ☎ 99.79.01.98.
Airport	✈ Saint-Jacques-de-la-Lande, 7 km SW. ☎ 99.50.41.13. *Air France Agency,* 7, rue de Bertrand, ☎ 99.63.09.09.
Railway station	SNCF (C4), ☎ 99.65.50.50.
Bus station	🚌 bd Magenta (B3-4), ☎ 99.30.87.80.

MAPS AND PLANS

- ≺ exceptional view
- ⛪ remarkable church
- ■ architecture worthy of interest
- ⌂ château
- ∴ archeological site
- ★ interesting
- ★★ remarkable
- ★★★ exceptional
- ------- hiking *(grande randonnée)* trail

Please note : maps in the guide vary in their scale, which is always indicated by the mention *échelle.* Unless otherwise stated, North is always upwards. **Towns name underlined** (<u>Quiberon</u>) **means specially recommended hotel or restaurant.**

- ☎ telephone
- ⊠ postal code
- (i) (or TO) Tourist office
- SNCF railway station
- 🚌 bus station
- ✈ airport
- ⛴ ferry line
- ♣ station verte (→ Rural holidays)
- ⚓ Spa (with dates of season)

- ⛷ Winter sports resort, with accessible altitudes
- P car-park
- ☼ view
- ♧ park or garden
- 🔔 quiet
- 🐕 no pets
- ♿ access for the disabled
- 🎾 tennis
- ⛳ golf
- ≋ swimming-pool

rm	room
L.F.	Logis de France hotel chain
SI	syndicat d'initiative (→ Information)
TO	tourist office
C.N.M.H.	National Monuments Board (→ Museums)
F.G.T.O.	French Government Tourist Office
S.N.C.F.	French National Railways Society

The → symbol indicates cross-referencing with another entry or section.

Prices

Restaurants : two prices given : the cheapest fixed-price meal ("menu") and average cost of a meal "à la carte" (appetizer, main course and dessert) including charge without wine.
Hotels : the price given is the average price for a double-bed room with bath.

Official hotel classification

★ and ★★	Simple but comfortable
★★★	Very comfortable
★★★★	First class hotel
★★★★ L	Luxury hotel

● Recommended hotel

Restaurant classification

◆	pleasant restaurant
◆◆	comfortable, pleasant surroundings
◆◆◆	refined surroundings, excellent reception and service
◆◆◆◆	exceptional surroundings, decor, reception and service

● Recommended restaurant

Contents

Regional Map-Index

NB : Regions as presented for the tourist's convenience in the guide may not always correspond to the official administrative regions.

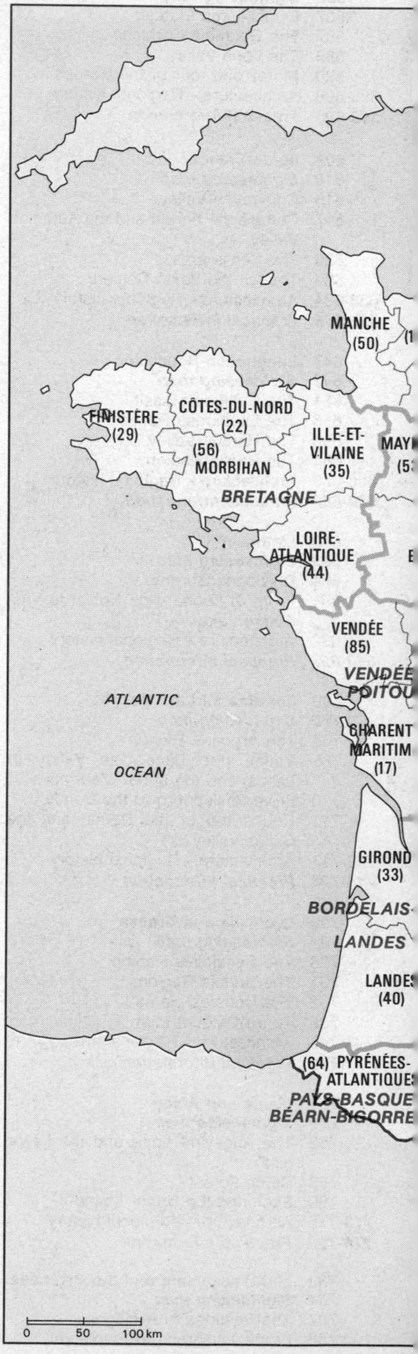

Index to place names : p. 1085 ▶

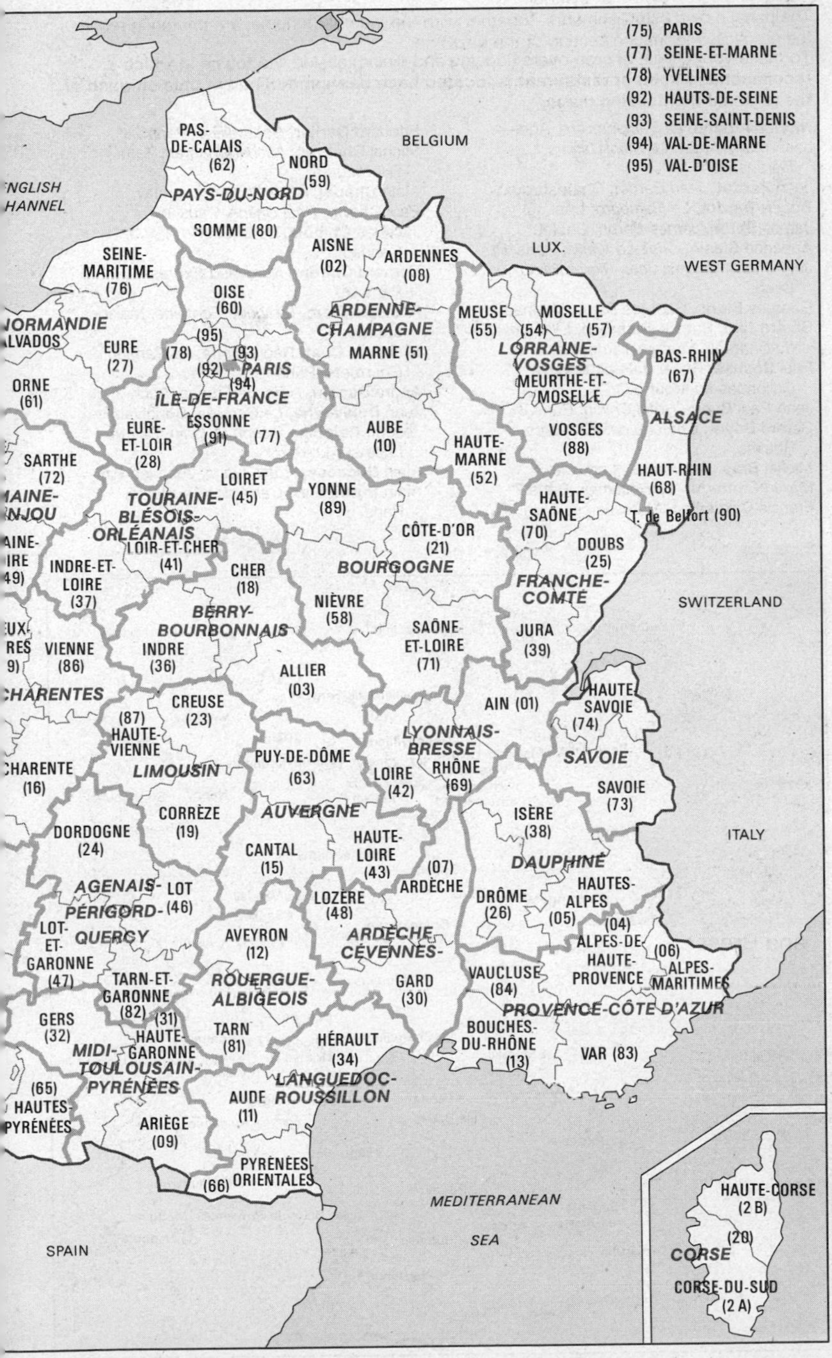

Gastronomy in the guide

Our gastronomy specialist **François Roboth and the following 122 top French chefs and restaurateurs** have selected their favorite restaurants from their own personal address books, indicated by the ● symbol.
The panel's own establishments, together with the member's name, are printed in red in the practical information section of the gazetteer.
To make your choice of stop-overs (lodging and dining) easier, **the towns in which a recommended hotel or restaurant is located have been underlined in blue on each of the regional Sightseeing maps.**

Nicolas **Albano,** *La Tamarissière,* Agde.
Jean-Marie **Amat,** *Le Saint-James,* Bordeaux.
Jean **Bardet,** *Jean Bardet,* Châteauroux.
Robert **Bardot,** *Le Flambard,* Lille.
James **Baron,** *James Baron,* Cholet.
Adrienne **Biasin,** *Chez La Vieille,* Paris 1er.
Jean-Pierre **Billoux,** *Jean-Pierre Billoux,* Dijon.
Georges **Blanc,** *Georges Blanc,* Vonnas.
Gérard **Blot,** Patrick **Michelon,** *L'Hostellerie du Château,* Fère-en-Tardenois.
Paul **Bocuse,** Roger **Jaloux,** *Bocuse,* Collonges-au-Mont-d'Or.
Jean-Paul **Bonin,** *Hôtel Crillon,* Paris 8e.
Gérard **Boyer,** *Château des Crayères,* Rheims.
Michel **Bras,** *Lou Mazuc,* Laguiole.
Martin **Cantegrit,** *Le Récamier,* Paris 7e.
Francis **Cardaillac,** Marssac-sur-Tarn.
Édouard **Carlier,** *Beauvilliers,* Paris 18e.
Michel **Chabran,** *Michel Chabran,* Tain-l'Hermitage.
Alain **Chapel,** *Alain Chapel,* Mionnay.
Paul **Chêne,** *Paul Chêne,* Paris 16e.
Jacques **Chibois,** *Hôtel Gray d'Albion,* Cannes.
Bernard **Chirent,** *Nord-Sud Express,* Paris 6e.
François **Clerc,** *La Vieille Fontaine,* Maisons-Laffitte.
Micheline **Coat,** Régis **Mahé,** *La Cantine des Gourmets,* Paris 7e.
André **Daguin,** *Hôtel de France,* Auch.
Jean **Delaveyne,** *Le Camélia,* Bougival.
Joseph **Delphin,** *Joseph Delphin,* Sainte-Luce-sur-Loire.
Alain **Ducasse,** *Hôtel Juana,* Juan-les-Pins.
Alain **Dutournier,** *Carré des Feuillants,* Paris 1er.

Henri **Faugeron,** *Faugeron,* Paris 16e.
Jean-Claude **Ferrero,** *Jean-Claude Ferrero,* Paris 16e.
Julien **Forêt,** *Julius,* Gennevilliers.
Bernard **Fournier,** *Le Petit Colombier,* Paris 17e.
Patrick **Fulgraff,** *Le Fer Rouge,* Colmar.
Pierre **Gagnaire,** *Pierre Gagnaire,* Saint-Étienne.
Francis **Garcia,** *Le Clavel,* Bordeaux.
André **Génin,** *Chez Pauline,* Paris 1er.
Claude **Giraud,** *Le Réverbère,* Narbonne.
Pierre and Jany **Gleize,** *La Bonne Étape,* Château-Arnoux.
Michel **Guérard,** Didier **Oudil,** *Les Prés et les Sources d'Eugénie,* Eugénie-les-Bains.
Paul, Jean-Pierre and Marc **Heaberlin,** *Auberge de l'Ill,* Illhaeusern.
Hubert, *Hubert,* Paris 1er.
Paul **Huyart,** *La Crémaillère,* Orléans.
Christian **Ignace,** *Le Petit Bedon,* Paris 16e.
Yann **Jacquot,** *Le Toit de Passy,* Paris 16e.
André and Jean-Paul **Jeunet,** *Le Paris,* Arbois.
Émile **Jung,** *Le Crocodile,* Strasbourg.
Michel **Kéréver,** *Le Duc d'Enghien,* Enghien-les-Bains.
Jean-Paul **Lacombe,** *Léon de Lyon,* Lyons.
Roger **Lamazère,** *Lamazère,* Paris 8e.
Jacques **Lameloise,** *Lameloise,* Chagny.
José **Lampreia,** *La Maison Blanche,* Paris 15e.
Pierre **Laporte,** *Le Café de Paris,* Biarritz.
François **Laustriat,** Pascal **Bouffety,** *Hôtel de Paris,* Moulins.
Gilbert **Le Coze,** *Le Bernardin,* Paris 17e.
Jacques **Le Divellec,** *Jacques Le Divellec,* Paris 7e.
Jean **Lenoir,** *Hostellerie Lenoir,* Auvillers-les-Forges.
Gaston and Patrick **Lenôtre,** *Le Pavillon Élysées,* Paris 8e, *Le Pré Catelan,* Paris 16e.
Paul **Le Quéré,** *Le Quéré,* Angers.
Bernard **Loiseau,** *La Côte d'Or,* Saulieu.
Michel and Jean-Michel **Lorain,** *La Côte Saint-Jacques,* Joigny.
Roland **Magne,** *Le Pactole,* Paris 5e.
Loïc **Martin,** *Le Paris,* Lille.
Jacques **Maximin,** *Le Chantecler,* Nice.
Roland **Mazère,** Alain **Scholly,** *Le Centenaire,* Les Eyzies.
Marc **Meneau,** *L'Espérance,* Saint-Père-sous-Vézelay.
Daniel **Météry,** *Le Lord Gourmand,* Paris 8e.
Philippe **Million,** *Million,* Albertville.
Jean and Paul **Minchelli,** *Le Duc,* Paris 14e.
Michel **Mioche,** *Hôtel Radio,* Chamalières.
Jean-Pierre **Morot-Gaudry,** *Morot-Gaudry,* Paris 15e.
Dominique **Nahmias,** *Olympe,* Paris 15e.
Guy **Nouyrigat,** *Pierre Traiteur,* Paris 1er.
Michel **Oliver,** *Le Bistrot de Paris,* Paris 7e.
Louis **Outhier,** *L'Oasis,* La Napoule.
Albert **Parveaux,** Jean-Pierre **Faucher,** *Castel Novel,* Varetz.
Michel **Peignaud,** *La Belle Époque,* Châteaufort.
Claude **Perraudin,** *L'Auberge Perraudin,* Paris 2e.
Claude **Peyrot,** *Le Vivarois,* Paris 16e.
Alain and Jacques **Pic,** *Pic,* Valence.
Mado **Point,** Guy **Thivard,** *La Pyramide,* Vienne.
Jean **Ramet,** *Jean Ramet,* Bordeaux.
Louis-Noël **Richard,** Jean-Michel **Bédier,** *Le Chiberta,* Paris 8e.
Joël **Robuchon,** *Jamin,* Paris 16e.
Michel **Rostang,** *Michel Rostang,* Paris 17e.
Guy **Savoy,** *Guy Savoy,* Paris 16e.
Claude **Scaviner,** *Le Manoir d'Hastings,* Bénouville.
Alain **Senderens,** *Lucas-Carton,* Paris 8e.
Claude **Terrail,** Dominique **Bouchet,** *La Tour d'Argent,* Paris 5e.
Raymond **Thuillier,** Jean-André **Charrial,** *L'Oustau de Baumanière,* Les-Baux-de-Provence.
Michel **Trama,** *L'Aubergade,* Puymirol.
Pierre and Michel **Troisgros,** *Frères Troisgros,* Roanne.
Éric **Trompier,** Gérard **Rouillard,** *La Marée,* Paris 8e.
Pierre and Sylvain **Vandenameele,** *La Poularde,* Houdan.
Lucien **Vanel,** *Vanel,* Toulouse.
Pierre **Vedel,** *Pierre Vedel,* Paris 15e.
Gérard **Veissière,** *Le Capucin Gourmand,* Nancy.
Roger **Vergé,** *Le Moulin de Mougins,* Mougins.
Gérard **Vié,** *Les Trois Marches,* Versailles.
Jean-Claude **Vrinat,** Claude **Deligne,** *Le Taillevent,* Paris 8e.

After Bernard Loiseau (Saulieu) in 1984, they have elected *ex aequo* winners of the
GRAND PRIX HACHETTE DES CUISINIERS DE FRANCE 1985
(The Hachette Grand Prix for French Chefs)
two chefs under 40:
JOËL ROBUCHON and GUY SAVOY

What a faultless career for **JOËL ROBUCHON,** born 7 April, 1945 in Poitiers. After being a cook's boy in his native city, he took his time to learn before settling, twenty years later, with his wife at the *Jamin* restaurant in Paris. Going from one establishment to another *(Berkeley, Concorde-Lafayette, Nikko...)* he worked with such prestigious masters as Jean Delaveyne, Charles Barrier and the late Marcel Trompier, demonstrating as much ability as modesty. Named Best Craftsman in France in 1976, his numerous honors place him in the forefront of great French chefs.

Born on 24 July, 1953 in Nevers, **GUY SAVOY**'s first experience in cooking came from a pastry-chef in Bourgouin who had studied with the great Bernachon. Fascinated, he undertook a rigorous apprenticeship with the famous Troisgros brothers in Roanne. Jean, the eldest whose premature death is greatly regretted, did not hesitate to say that he had been one of his most brilliant apprentices. The future would bear him out: *Lasserre* in Paris, *Le Lion d'Or* in Coligny, the *Oasis* in La Napoule, and Claude Verger's *Barrière de Clichy* where he succeeded his accomplice from Roanne, Bernard Loiseau. Married and father of two, he now has his own restaurant in Paris where a clientele of satisfied connaisseurs assure his success. F. R.

The many faces of France

A mini-encyclopaedia

France is not a country for short-cuts. The culture and atmosphere of the French nation have been developed through centuries of civilisation. This is a country that deserves to be savoured. And just as you may linger over a menu before you savour the superb cuisine of France, take time to plan a balanced itinerary that will allow you to sample the rich variety of pleasures France offers.

These introductory chapters have been designed to prepare you for your trip to France. They open up a number of perspectives that may be explored separately or together to give you an overall picture of each region, terrain and site, taking in the geology, climate, ecology, population, history, architecture, culture, technology and daily life. In this way, we hope to turn even the shortest excursion into an adventure, in which the unexpected and the spur-of-the-moment will play an equal role with thoughtful planning and pleasurable anticipation.

It is always a good idea to examine details in their proper context. Looking at the individual regions of France within the context of the French nation helps to explain their place in the entire scheme, as well as to define the distinctive features that set them apart. The regional differences, in turn, help to show how these various elements form a unified whole, with a distinctive identity among the countries of Europe. This unity in diversity springs from a twofold source in nature and in the history of the French people, whereby earth, air and water combine with human settlement and skill to create — and to offer you — a refined manner of living.

France is continuously on the move, and the far-reaching changes of recent years, here as elsewhere, have brought in their wake real risks to the traditional environment together with profound alterations to features once familiar. The latter part of this introduction will draw your attention to certain other developments that, while less immediately apparent, paradoxically seem to blend in with some of the most deep-rooted and characteristic traditions of the French people. These trends include the decentralisation of government, the premium placed on culture, and the pursuit of the quality of life.

Climate

Averages are only rough guides to the weather. France enjoys a moderate, temperate climate with a relatively limited temperature range. In winter, however, this range widens from west to east, and in summer it narrows from southeast to northwest. The seasons are more marked in eastern than in western France. Atlantic humidity, Siberian air masses in wintertime, summer anticyclones from the Azores, and the Mediterranean influence in the southeast result in **four major climate types.** In Brittany and Normandy to the west, the prevailing climate is oceanic : changeable with frequent rain, often overcast, but with winds that drive away the clouds. The winters are mild and the summers rather cool. The major trends are apparent, although modified by latitude, in the neighbouring regions : hotter summers with more sunshine in Aquitaine, more distinct seasons in the Parisian basin. All of eastern France, has a more continental climate, with more marked contrasts : cold winters, hot summers. The Mediterranean Midi is sunny and dry, with greater extremes : winds, autumn storms.

Sunshine

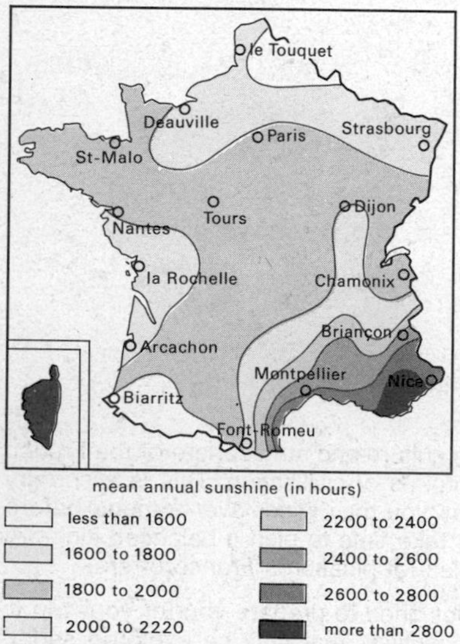

Summer temperatures

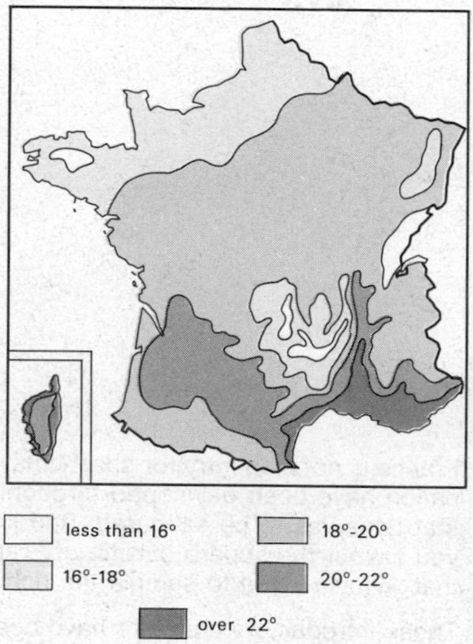

Winter temperatures

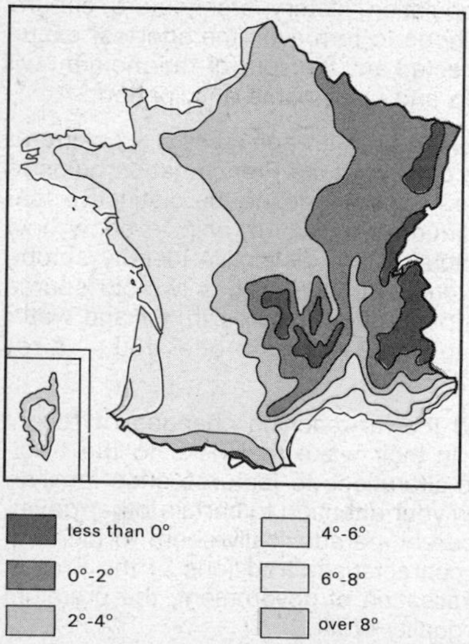

Mean annual rainfall

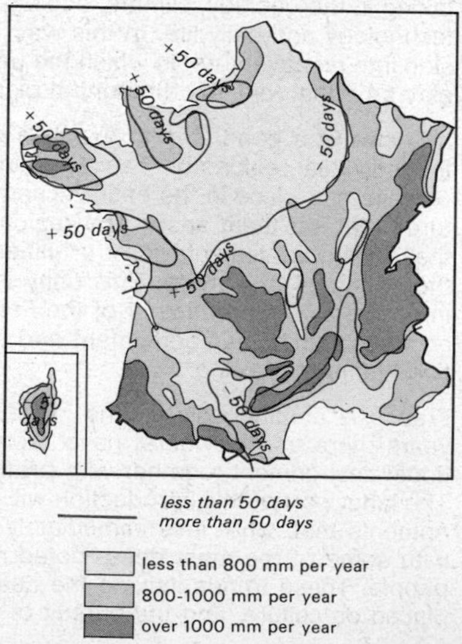

Altitude and exposure play a decisive role in the mountains. Temperatures fall and winters last longer the higher you go.

Terrain Water

Solidly bound to the European continent, and presenting a triple shoreline to the ocean, France is to some extent a crossroads and a summation of Europe : the terrain displays all the major features of the European contours, all the climates, and all the biological environments. This is the reason for the variety and diversity of the natural regions and landscapes where, at times, any European may with astonishment recognise some feature of his own country.

The Frenchman is the most complex crossbreed in Europe, mixing Nordic, Celtic and Mediterranean strains with untold others. Long after the supposed disappearance of regional identity, each region of France kept alive its individuality, its personality and its culture, beyond the reach of the all-powerful centralised state, safeguard of French harmony. In the long run, there are many different ways of being French, which is undoubtedly one of the distinctive features of the country.

The variety of the French **coasts** reflects the diversity of the map : the high, chalky cliffs of the Normandy and Picardy plateaux; the rocky shores of the old Breton massif; inlets hewn out of white limestone around Marseilles or of reddish porphyry in the Esterel; low, sandy shores on the maritime plains of Flanders, the Vendée, Roussillon, the Languedoc, and the Camargue. But there is more to water than the ocean. Water from sky and earth, channelled or untamed, marks the landscape everywhere.

France boasts one of the most extensive **canal networks** in Europe.

Relief map

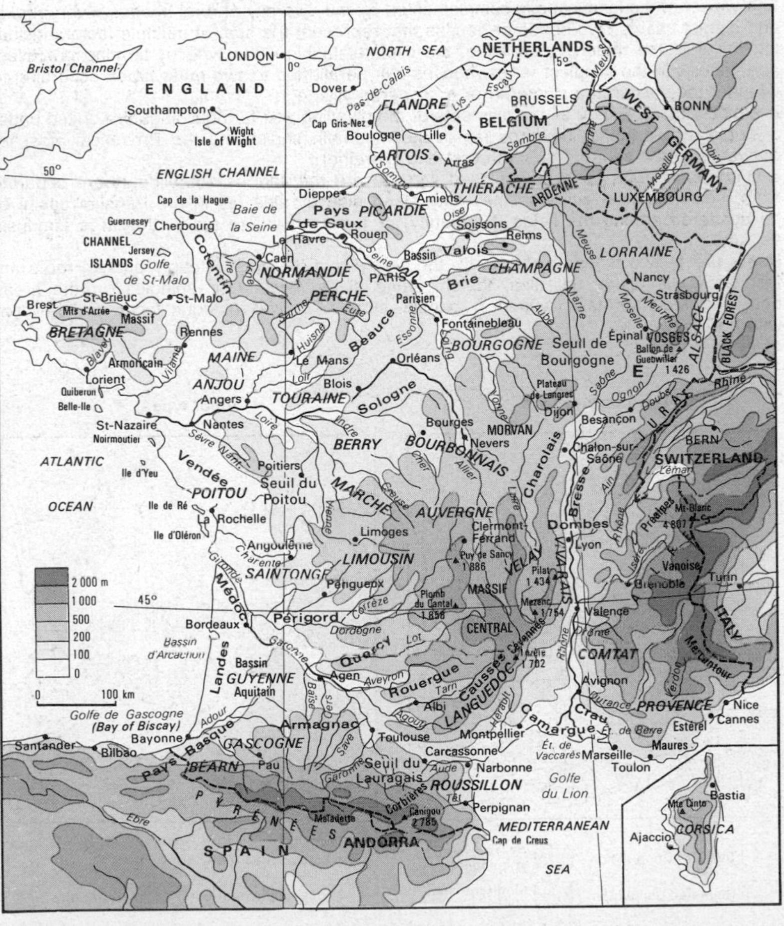

Landscapes

The variety of terrain, as well as of bioclimates, fosters a varied agriculture that makes France one of the foremost farming nations and the second most important worldwide exporter of agricultural products : 85 % of the territory yields live produce (59 % agricultural land, 26 % forest). The shape of French agricultural lands goes back virtually to the beginning of the nation's history and the Celtic colonisation. In the north and northeast, **open-field cultivatons** stretch out of sight, and the population clusters in large villages. In the **wooded landscapes** of the west and along the edges of the Massif Central, fields and pastures are criss-crossed by hedgerows, and the people live in hamlets or isolated farms. In the Mediterranean south, where arable land is scarce, farms are marked by mixed cropping, terraced hillsides, and irrigated flatlands; the villages are often perched on crags among arid hills.

Houses and villages

The variety of the landscape is complemented by the diversity of rural houses. Every region and district has its own house or houses that represent the sum of multiple factors including the soil, the materials available, the climate, fashion, the type of farming practised, and history. In the simplest terms, houses can be allotted to **two main types** according to whether they occur in a clustered or a scattered village :

- a block-house, where all the elements of the dwelling and farmbuildings are united under a single roof, whether upwards (as in the mountain chalet and the Provencal *mas*), or outwards (in the centre, the southwest and Lorraine);
- a farmstead with open or enclosed yard, where the various outbuildings are separate from the farmhouse, although they may stand side by side (as in the Parisian basin) or be scattered among the fields (Normandy) or in an enclosure (as in the large Limousin estates).

Roofs are of two types. In the north, the centre and the west, steeply pitched roofs are fashioned with slate, flat tiles, thatch, stone slabs *(lauzes)* or shingles. In the areas betraying Mediterranean influence, gentler slopes on two or four faces are covered with hollow tiles.

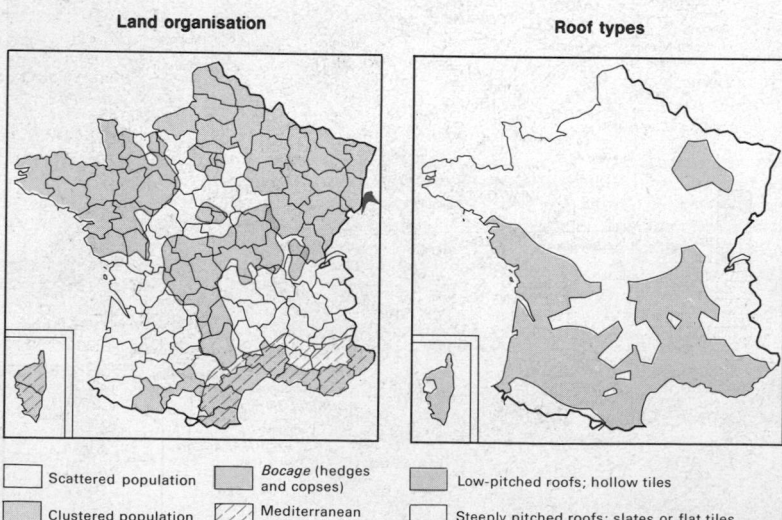

Land organisation

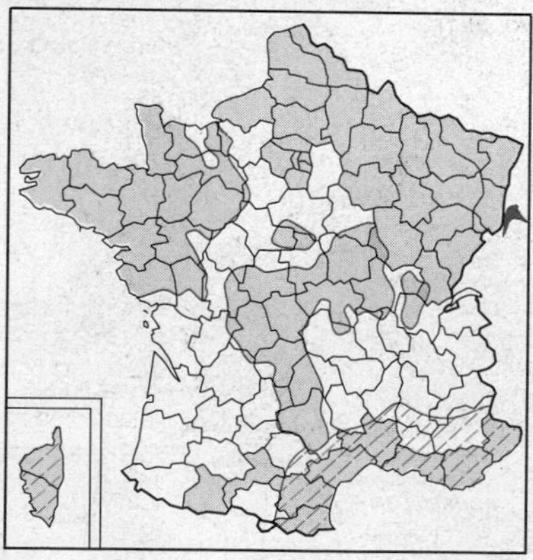

Roof types

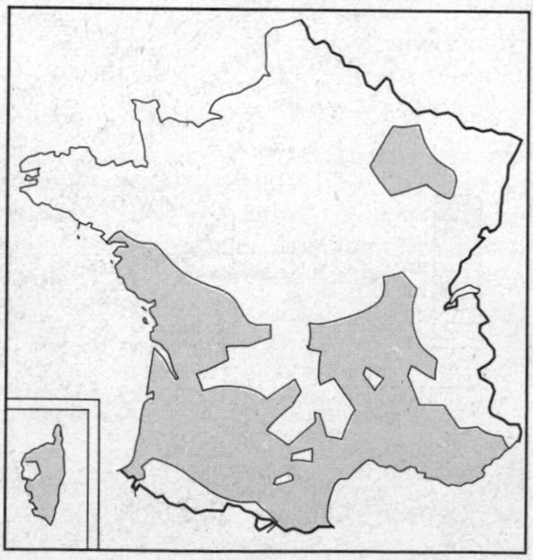

Forests

Forests

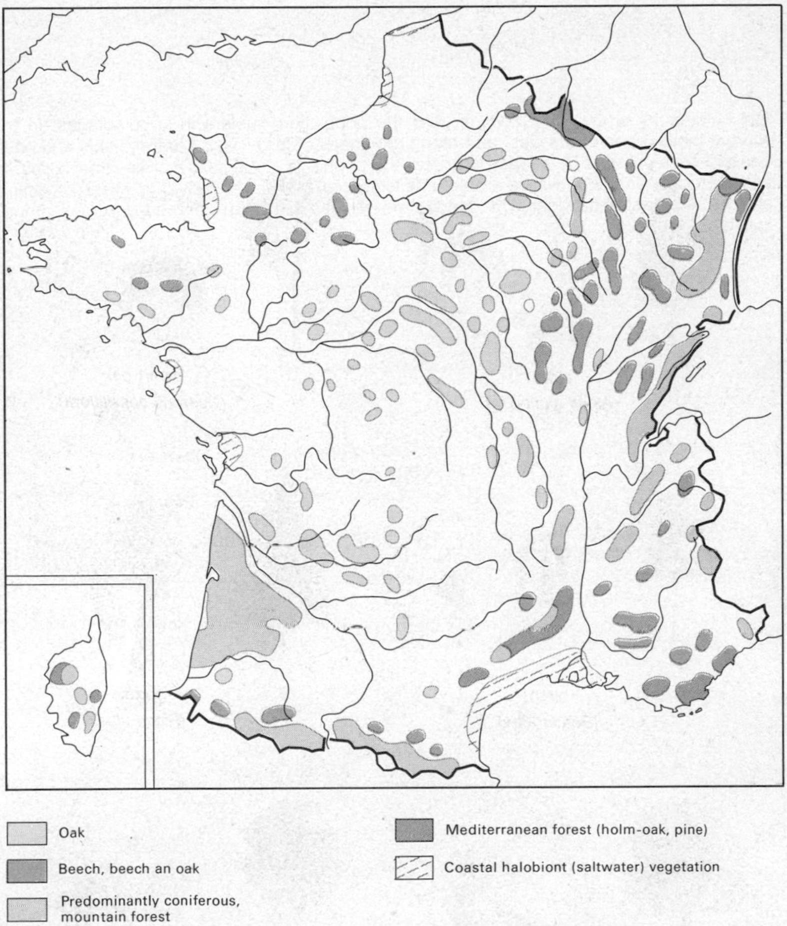

The natural landscape of France has not completely disappeared. The north, the east and the Parisian basin abound with temperate forest, where the predominant oak is mixed with birch, hornbeam, linden and ash. Beech grows in colder areas. The climate of Aquitaine fosters holm oak and umbrella pine. Land clearance in Brittany has encouraged the spread of broom, heather and gorse.

In the Mediterranean Midi, evergreens adapted to the aridity are trees with deep roots and persistent foliage; holm oak and aromatic scrub *(garrigue)* cover the limestone soil; cork oak and brush *(maquis)* grow in sandy areas. Pine, olive, wild almond and even horse-chestnut flourish together. Fire, pasture and building have made deep inroads into the Mediterranean forest, which now exists only in tattered remnants.

The mountain forests evolved according to altitude and climate levels. Beech and oak forests at 800-1 200 m are succeeded by conifers (fir, spruce, larch), which stop at about 2 000 m. There is nothing above the treeline except grasses and alpine plants. The general pattern varies, however, according to whether the aspect is a sunny southern slope or a cool, damp northern face. It is important, too, to realise that reforestation often changes the established balance, such as by the replacement of oak by beech and, especially, the spread of conifers. In fact, some forests, such as those in the Landes and Champagne areas, are completely artificial.

Forest trees

alder
(Alnus glutinosa)

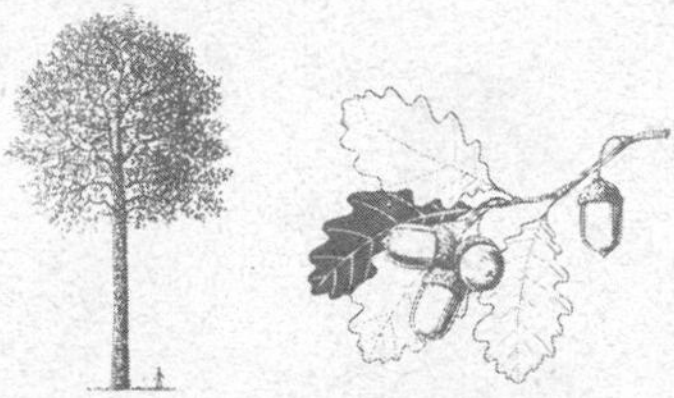

dwarf oak
(Quercus sessiliflora)

birch
(Betula alba)

spruce
(Picea alba)

hornbeam
(Carpinus betulus)

sycamore
(Acer campestre)

horse chestnut
(Castanea sativa)

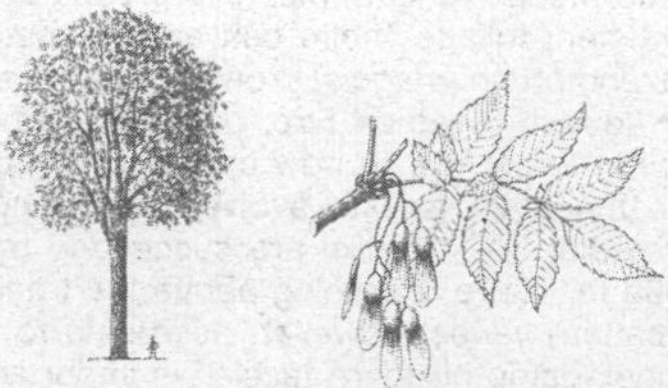

ash
(Fraxinus excelsior)

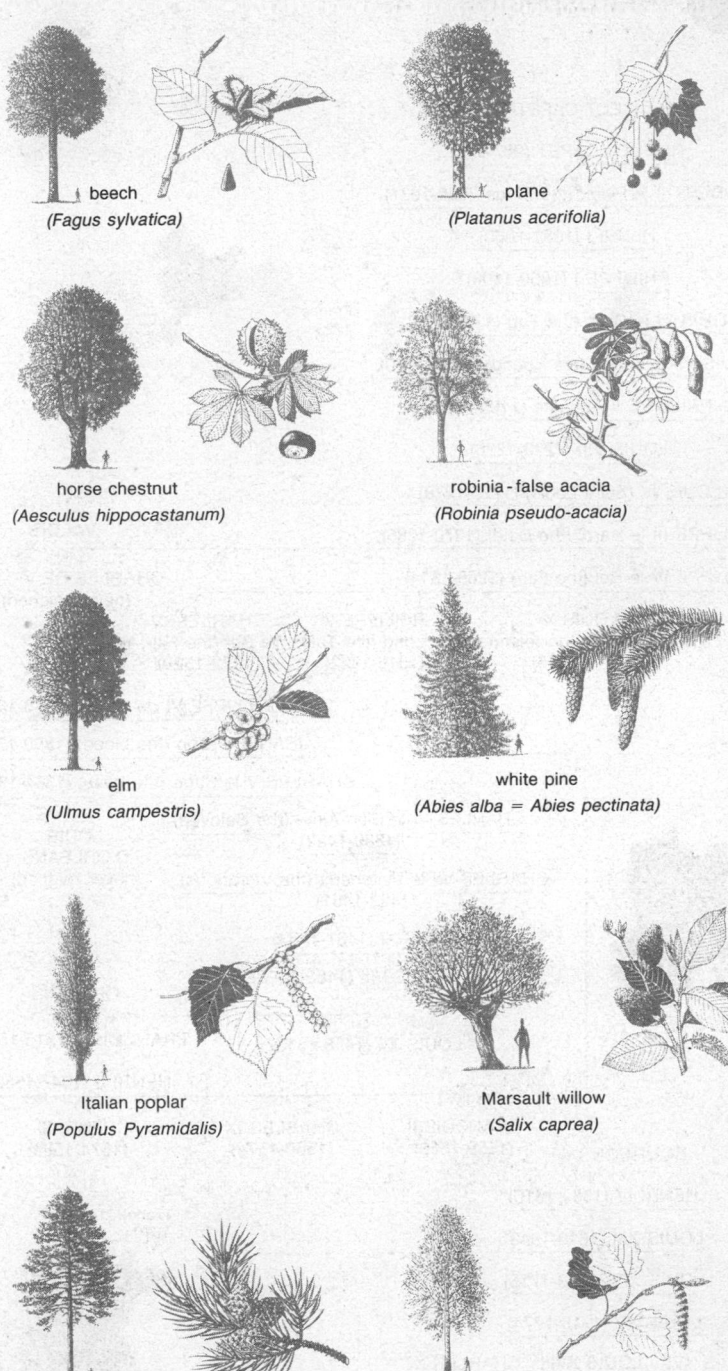

beech
(Fagus sylvatica)

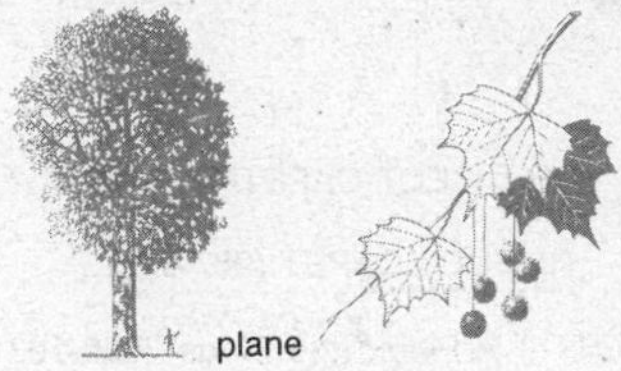

plane
(Platanus acerifolia)

horse chestnut
(Aesculus hippocastanum)

robinia - false acacia
(Robinia pseudo-acacia)

elm
(Ulmus campestris)

white pine
(Abies alba = Abies pectinata)

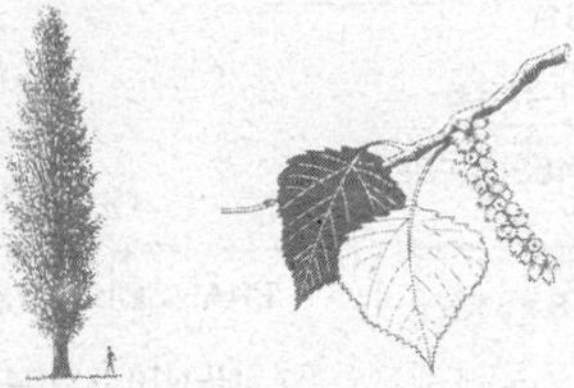

Italian poplar
(Populus Pyramidalis)

Marsault willow
(Salix caprea)

Laricio pine
(Pinus laricio)

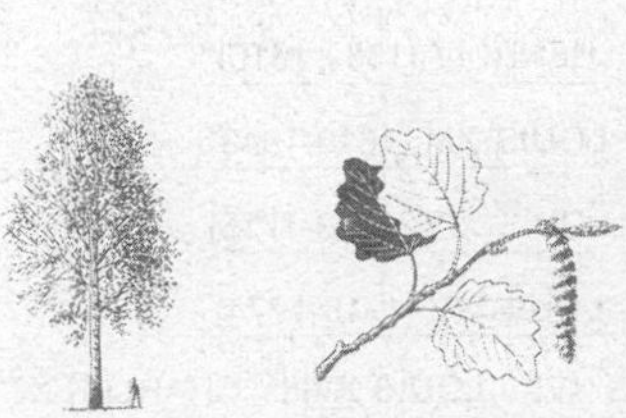

aspen
(Populus tremula)

Retrospective

THE DIRECT CAPETIAN LINE

France in 987

HUGUES CAPET (987-996)

ROBERT II le Pieux (the Pious) (996-1031)

HENRI I (1031-1060)

PHILIPPE I (1060-1108)

France in 1223

LOUIS VI le Gros (the Fat) (1108-1137)

LOUIS VII le Jeune (the Young) (1137-1180)

PHILIPPE II Auguste (1180-1223)

LOUIS VIII (1223-1226)

LOUIS IX (Saint Louis) (1226-1270)

PHILIPPE III le Hardi (the Bold) (1270-1285)

VALOIS

CHARLES DE VALOIS (never reigned)

PHILIPPE IV le Bel (the Fair) (1285-1314)

LOUIS X le Hutin (the Quarrelsome) (1314-1316)

PHILIPPE V le Long (the Tall) (1316-1322)

CHARLES IV le Bel (the Fair) (1322-1328)

PHILIPPE VI de Valois (1328-1350)

JEAN II le Bon (the Good) (1350-1364)

CHARLES V le Sage (the Wise) (1364-1380)

CHARLES VI le Bien Aimé (the Beloved) (1380-1422)

LOUIS D'ORLEANS (never reigned)

CHARLES VII le Victorieux (the Victorious) (1422-1461)

LOUIS XI (1461-1483)

CHARLES VIII (1483-1498)

ORLEANS

LOUIS XII (1498-1515)

FRANÇOIS I (1515-1547)

HENRI II (1547-1559)

FRANÇOIS II (1559-1560)

CHARLES IX (1560-1574)

HENRI III (1574-1589)

France in 1498

BOURBONS

HENRI IV (1589-1610)

LOUIS XIII (1610-1643)

LOUIS XIV (1643-1715)

LOUIS XV (1715-1774)

LOUIS XVI (1774-1793)

LOUIS XVIII (1814-1824)

CHARLES X (1824-1830)

France in 1610

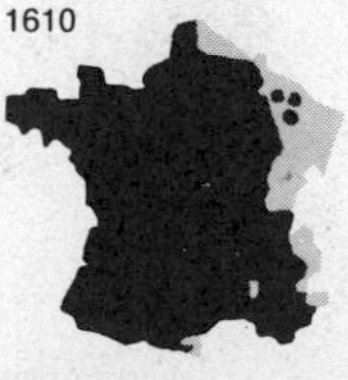

LOUIS-PHILIPPE (1830-1848)

The Rulers of France

France in 1789

1789 REVOLUTION
1790 The CONVENTION (21/9/1792-26/9/1795)
The DIRECTORY 1795-1799
1800
The CONSULATE 1799-1804
1810 NAPOLÉON I; FIRST EMPIRE 1804-1815
LOUIS XVIII/RESTORATION 1814/1815-1824
1820
CHARLES X (1824-1830)
1830
LOUIS-PHILIPPE/The JULY MONARCHY (1830-1848)
1840
LOUIS-NAPOLÉON BONAPARTE/SECOND REPUBLIC (10/2/1848-2/12/1852)
1850
NAPOLÉON III/SECOND EMPIRE (1852-1870)
1860
1870 The Paris COMMUNE

Heads of State : IIIrd Republic

1870 Adolphe THIERS 1871-1873
Marshall P. de MACMAHON 1873-1879
1880 Jules GRÉVY 1879-1887
Sadi CARNOT 1887-1894 (assassinated)
1890 Casimir PERIER 1894-1895
Felix FAURE 1895-1899
1900 Emile LOUBET 1899-1906
Armand FALLIÈRES 1906-1913
1910 Raymond POINCARÉ 1913-1920
Paul DESCHANEL 28/2-29/9/1920
1920 Alexandre MILLERAND 1920-1924
Gaston DOUMERGUE 1924-1932
1930 Paul DOUMER 1932 (assassinated)
1940 Albert LEBRUN 1932-1940
Marshall PÉTAIN Head of the French State 1940-1944
General Charles DE GAULLE President of the Provisional Government of the French Republic at Algiers, 1943; Paris, 1944; President of the Government of the French Republic 1946

Union of Nice and Savoy 1860

IVth Republic

1950 Vincent AURIOL 1946-1954
René COTY 1954-1958

Vth Republic

Charles DE GAULLE 1958-1969
1960 Georges POMPIDOU 1969-1974
1970 Valéry GISCARD D'ESTAING 1974-1981
1980 François MITTERRAND 1981

Heritage

The Norman invasions coincided with a period of weakness among French sovereigns and plunged France into a deep crisis. The **feudal system** grew out of the weakening of royal power and the dissolution of governmental structures that were the main results of this crisis. The feudal system was based on military authority. The feudal lords *(seigneurs)* made up a separate caste that ruled the greater part of the land, dominating the peasant population. The most powerful lords maintained their own courts and armies, and assumed the power that had been stripped from the kings : power to command, to punish, to tax and to make war. Gradually, however, the kings began to work their way into the feudal institutions and turn them to their own advantage, building a pyramid of power that culminated in the crown.

By virtue of its position between the Mediterranean and Barbarian worlds, France, the land of the Franks, became the cradle of a **new art** that originated in Romanesque art forms.

▶ e.g. Germigny-des-Prés, Crypts at Jouarre, Chartres, Auxerre, Choir of St. Philbert-de-Grandlieu

Beginnings

A state unique in Europe, France was formed by 10 centuries of centralised government that constituted a mould for national unity in a crossroads country where many races mingled. Cultural and human diversity were united under the strong presence of a central State and the influence of the capital.

The territory was populated in the **Palaeolithic Era** by bison- and reindeer-hunters seeking refuge in the Aquitainian basin during the last Ice Age. Notable sites from this era include Les Eyzies, Lascaux and Nas d'Azil. The **Neolithic Era** brought settled populations who cleared forests and established an agricultural economy. Colonisation proceeded slowly but steadily from 6 000BC (on the northeastern plains) until 2 000BC (in the mountain massifs). The use of copper and pottery began to spread at the same time. The remarkable megaliths of Brittany still stand as witnesses to these early peoples, and the lesser-known dolmens of the Midi are even more numerous. A population base was established in about 1 000BC with the arrival of the **Celts,** an Indo-European race who came from the east. France owes to them the principal features of the agrarian landscape. Settling down, the Celts established townships that were usually raised and fortified. The original Gallic civilisation rose and fell with the Celts. Their early burial mounds *(tumuli)* were succeeded by flat tombs in which urns containing the ashes of the dead were placed, hence the description of the period as "urn-field civilisation". Bronze and pottery crafts were perfected at this time. The Celtic civilisation was overlaid with the Roman imprint after the conquest by **Julius Caesar.** Celtic tongues were replaced by Latin; the Continental country of Gaul was transformed into a huge Mediterranean province. Over the agricultural foundations rose an urban civilisation that is still apparent at Arles, Autun, Fréjus, Lyons, Nîmes, Narbonne, Orange, Vaison and Vienne, among other sites. In the same way, the contributions of **Germanic invaders** were assimilated. Notable among these invaders were the Franks who, after being converted to Christianity, rebuilt Gallic unity during the Merovingian Era. Other important strains were those of the Arabs in southern France, and the Scandinavians who occupied modern-day Normandy in the 10thC.

The diversity of these origins mingled with the flow of immigration over the centuries, in no way impeded the growth of French unity, to which the Revolution of 1789 gave the decisive thrust.

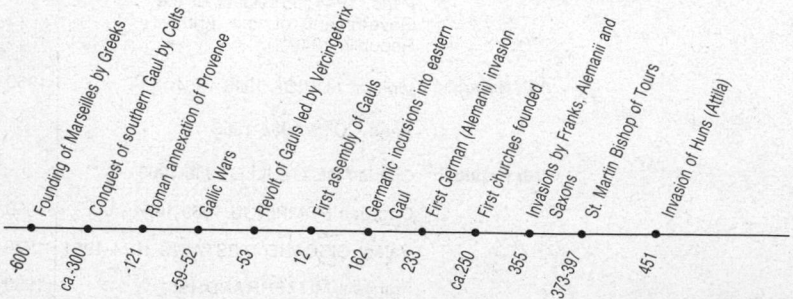

-600	Founding of Marseilles by Greeks
ca.-300	Conquest of southern Gaul by Celts
-121	Roman annexation of Provence
-59–52	Gallic Wars
-53	Revolt of Gauls led by Vercingetorix
12	First assembly of Gauls
162	Germanic incursions into eastern Gaul
233	First German (Alemanii) invasion
ca.250	First churches founded
355	Invasions by Franks, Alemanii and Saxons
373-397	St. Martin Bishop of Tours
451	Invasion of Huns (Attila)

Birth of a nation

Pépin le Bref (Pippin the Short) and his son Charlemagne (Charles the Great) united the western Germanic peoples of France, Germany and Italy under their sway and established the economic and social institutions of large domains, vassalage and serfdom. In 843, the Treaty of Verdun laid the foundations for the great Western states of the Middles Ages. Western France *(Francia occidentalis)* became a distinct entity. In 987, Hugues Capet was elected King of the Franks, although his power extended no farther than a small area around Paris. Only in the 13thC did the official title of King of France appear, reflecting a growing idea of nationhood that began to emerge during the Hundred Years' War against England.

Prehistoric and Gallo-Roman sites

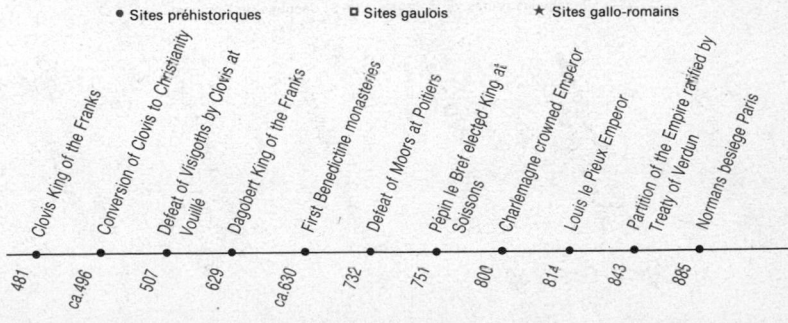

481	Clovis King of the Franks
ca.496	Conversion of Clovis to Christianity
507	Defeat of Visigoths by Clovis at Vouillé
629	Dagobert King of the Franks
ca.630	First Benedictine monasteries
732	Defeat of Moors at Poitiers
751	Pépin le Bref elected King at Soissons
800	Charlemagne crowned Emperor
814	Louis le Pieux Emperor
843	Partition of the Empire ratified by Treaty of Verdun
885	Normans besiege Paris

The Romanesque era

For the West, the years from 950 to 1200 were a period of continuous expansion that saw population growth, land clearance, technical advances, the rebirth of trade with fairs and pilgrimages, development of urban centres, and the peak of the Occitanian civilisation of Mediterranean France. Villages proliferated, and France became covered in a "white mantle of new churches". The 11thC was the gestation period for Romanesque art, which was derived from the Carolingian heritage enriched and transformed by new influences.

Principal Romanesque monuments

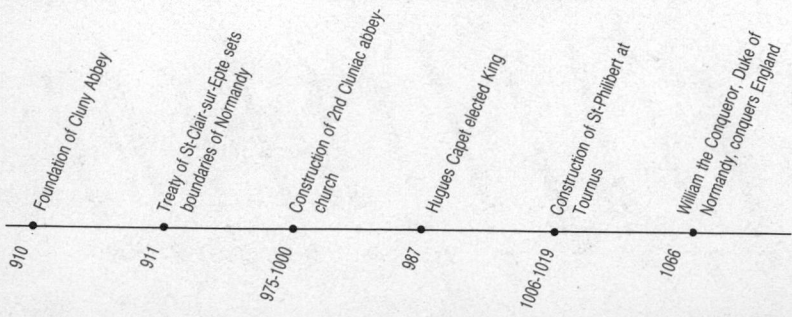

Principales routes du pèlerinage de St-Jacques-de-Compostelle

- 910 — Foundation of Cluny Abbey
- 911 — Treaty of St-Clair-sur-Epte sets boundaries of Normandy
- 975-1000 — Construction of 2nd Cluniac abbey-church
- 987 — Hugues Capet elected King
- 1006-1019 — Construction of St-Philibert at Tournus
- 1066 — William the Conqueror, Duke of Normandy, conquers England

The great innovation was **stone vaulting :** the semicircular barrel vault borne up by stout walls and sturdy pillars and supported on the outside by massive buttresses; the groined vault formed by barrel vaults intersecting at right angles; and the domed vault. The central nave, often hemmed in by side aisles, was crowned with a bell-tower and extended by an apse. Radiating chapels usually placed in the apse were built over a crypt designed to receive the relics of saints.

▶ e.g. St. Benoît-sur-Loire, Vézelay, Autun, Caen, Poitiers, Saintes, St. Nectaire, Issoire, Conques.

Sculpture turned the Romanesque churches and basilicas into picture books, where carvings on the capitals, around the arches and on the tympana above the doorways told the story of man from Genesis to Judgment Day. The schools of sculpture were especially outstanding in the **South,** for example around Toulouse, and in Burgundy.

Painting was an important art in the Romanesque period, although few traces remain. Roving schools of painters often depicted the themes of the Apocalypse or the Last Judgment.

▶ e.g. Saint-Savin, Tavant, Berzé-la-Ville.

Romanesque architecture reached its peak early in the **12thC.** Churches of a particular type or "family" were clustered in regions, such as the churches of Auvergne that spread from Notre-Dame-du-Port at Clermont-Ferrand, the hall-churches in Poitou, the domed churches of Aquitaine, the Provençal churches built in imitation of Roman monuments, and the churches of Burgundy. Many churches were built along the pilgrimage routes. Each displays the influence of the monastic order prevalent in the area : either sumptuous **Cluniac** or austere **Cistercian.**

▶ e.g. Cluny, Paray-le-Monial, Fontenay, Senanque, Le Thoronet.

Music was essentially liturgical. To the basic Gregorian chant, first written down in the 6thC, the 11thC monks at Jumièges added syllabic vocalisations, called tropes, that led eventually to the popular music of the 12thC troubadors.

At the same time, around the formal **literature** written in Latin there sprang up an oral literary tradition in the vernacular tongue, which marked the beginning of the Old French language. The themes had much in common with myths, as in all such traditions : whereas the lives of the saints were intended to glorify the great figures of Christianity (the Golden Legend), the early epic poems *(chansons de geste),* such as the *Chanson de Roland* and the *Chanson de Guillaume,* praised the deeds of heroes of the feudal world.

Church of St. Nectaire (Mid-12thC)

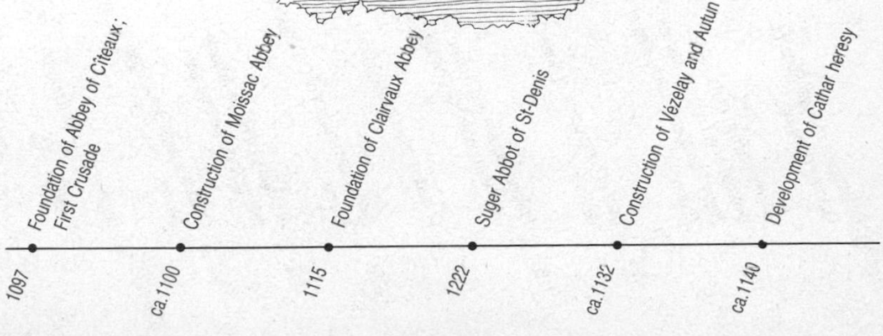

The Gothic age

The 12th-13thC was the great age of mediaeval France. The population burgeoned from 12 million to 20 million, old cities underwent renewal and new towns (such as the walled *bastides* of the Southwest) were built, trade thrived at the great fairs (e.g. Provins), and artistic and intellectual life flourished with the foundation of universities.

Gothic art was first and foremost a **northern** French style, whereas the Romanesque was a southern form. Moreover, Gothic art grew out of the cities, whereas Romanesque art was a rural development. Gothic fashion spread from Ile-de-France throughout Europe. Paris was one of the centres of the Western culture that was based on the Christian faith magnificently expressed in the Gothic cathedrals.

The 12thC was an age of experiment, first in Normandy and later in Île-de-France. The **13thC** was an age of achievement, which saw the construction of the four great cathedrals of Chartres, Rheims, Amiens, and Beauvais, together with the Sainte-Chapelle in Paris.

Principal Gothic monuments

- 1145 Construction of Royal Portal of Chartres Cathedral
- 1152 Eleanor (Aliénor) of Aquitaine, divorced from Louis VII, marries Henry Plantagenet, future King of England
- 1163 Start of construction of Notre-Dame de Paris
- 1190 Philippe-Auguste and Richard the Lion-Heart undertake Crusade
- 1204 Crusaders take Constantinople
- 1210 Start of construction of Cathedral of Rheims
- 1214 At Bouvines, Philippe-Auguste defeats Anglo-German alliance
- 1208 Crusade against the Albigensian heretics
- 1226-1270 Reign of St. Louis (Louis IX)

Rheims Cathedral (13thC)

New necessities, new techniques

Gothic art sprang from a technical innovation, **quadripartite vaulting,** in which pointed arches intersected on the diagonal to form a structural framework. This system, endlessly refined, freed architecture from old restrictions. Churches could be built higher, nearer to heaven, and opened up to light that would stream in like a divine manifestation. While this new art grew out of revolutionary technical progress, it was intended above all to express a new spirituality forged by exultant belief coupled with faith in man, and by fervour and serenity.

The faithful were welcomed at the cathedral doorways by statues that appeared profoundly human and reassuring : Christ triumphing over death, the Virgin-Mother, the saints.

Painting declined, replaced by **stained glass** windows that streamed with light to make translucent pictures outlined by a lacework of stone.

▶ e.g. Amiens, Bourges, Chartres, Laon, Le Mans, Notre-Dame and the Sainte-Chapelle in Paris.

A new music made its appearance along with the early cathedrals. **Polyphony** resounded first at Notre-Dame in Paris, and Adam de la Halle composed the musical Mysteries and Plays that foreshadowed by several centuries the light opera.

After the 13thC peak, Gothic architecture veered along an exuberantly decorative path. The 14thC Radiant Gothic, such as at Strasbourg and Metz, and the 15thC Flamboyant Gothic were distinguished by a profusion of curves, scrolls, lined vaulting, and brilliantly sculpted ornamentation. The Flamboyant style fourished especially around Normandy, Picardy, eastern France and, especially, Paris (St. Séverin).

Gothic art, symbolising growing northern French influence, came late to the **Midi,** which had been the homeground of the Romanesque style. The cathedral at Albi is the finest example of the Gothic style adapted to local conditions. In a region rife with heresy and independence movements, high brick walls and a tower-keep symbolised the power of the Church and opened up huge spaces for preaching.

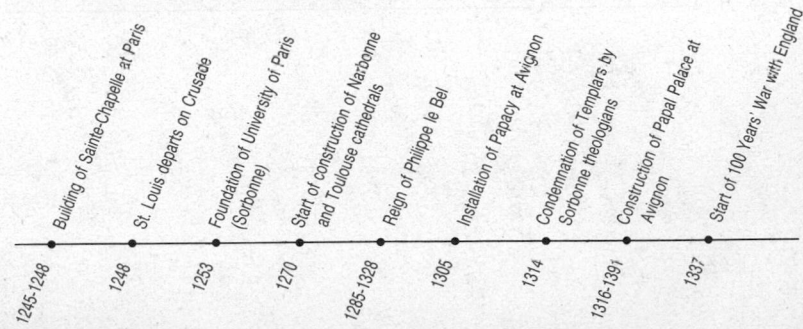

- 1245-1248 Building of Sainte-Chapelle at Paris
- 1248 St. Louis departs on Crusade
- 1253 Foundation of University of Paris (Sorbonne)
- 1270 Start of construction of Narbonne and Toulouse cathedrals
- 1285-1328 Reign of Philippe le Bel
- 1305 Installation of Papacy at Avignon
- 1314 Condemnation of Templars by Sorbonne theologians
- 1316-1391 Construction of Papal Palace at Avignon
- 1337 Start of 100 Years' War with England

From the Middle Ages to the Renaissance

After the dark period from the mid-14thC to the mid-15thC, which was marked in France by economic stagnation, the Hundred Years' War, famine and plague, the years from 1440 to 1515 were a time of renewal, restoration, and recovery. The country revived, and economy and trade burgeoned along with building, which took on the intensity of a "building fever". Many **city buildings** embellished during the period remain to this day.

▶ e.g. Jacques Cœur Mansion at Bourges, Cluny and Sens mansions and the churches of St. Séverin and St. Merri in Paris, Hospital *(hôtel-dieu)* at Beaune, Town halls *(hôtels de ville)* in Arras and St. Quentin, Courthouse *(palais de justice)* at Rouen.

Churches were rebuilt with new, exuberant and often opulent decoration abounding in scrolls and arabesques.

▶ e.g. Cathedrals at Bordeaux, Nantes, Tours, Church of Notre-Dame in Alençon, Abbey of Mont-St. Michel, St. Jacques tower in Paris; Cathedrals in Troyes and Rouen.

Castles began to lose their warlike appearance : keeps were turned into lookouts, galleries replaced covered ways, gables and mullioned windows replaced loopholes, and decoration began to slip in everywhere, right up to the mantel piece.

▶ e.g. Châteaux of Chambord, Pierrefonds, Langeais, Ussé, Chaumont.

In the 15thC, **sculpture** achieved independence and sculptors emerged from anonymity. The most renowned sculpture school grew up at the court of the Dukes of Burgundy. Subjects were invariably religious in inspiration : the Virgin and Child, the Virgin embracing the dead Christ, Death.

During the same two centuries, **painting** took an important step forward with the appearance of pictures worked on the easel. The late masterpieces of manuscript illumination are exemplified by the Book of Hours of the Duke of Berry *(Les Très Riches Heures de Jean Duc de Berry),* and mural painting achieved brilliance with the Dance of Death at Chaise-Dieu. The portrait (ca. 1360) of Jean le Bon (now in the Louvre Museum, Paris) marked the beginning of French portraiture. Painting blossomed under the dual influence of Flanders and Italy. The new flowering of French painting was epitomised in Provence by the Pietà of Avignon (now in the Louvre) and the Coronation of the Virgin by Enguerrand Quarton (at Villeneuve-lès-Avignon), and elsewhere by the portraits of Jean Fouquet and the works of the Moulins Master (at Moulins and Autun). Nevertheless, **tapestry** hangings remained the most important feature of decoration.

The Flemish Guillaume Dufay and Josquin Des Prés dominated the **musical scene.**

By the end of the 15thC, the kingdom was peaceful, and had been enlarged by the entry of Burgundy, Artois, Picardy, Anjou and Brittany into the royal fold. France was ready for the great adventure of the Renaissance.

From Plessis-les-Tours to Chambord, the châteaux of the Loire Valley offer a panoply of the development of French art in the 15thC and 16thC. The buildings illustrate the blending of late mediaeval traditions with new forms.

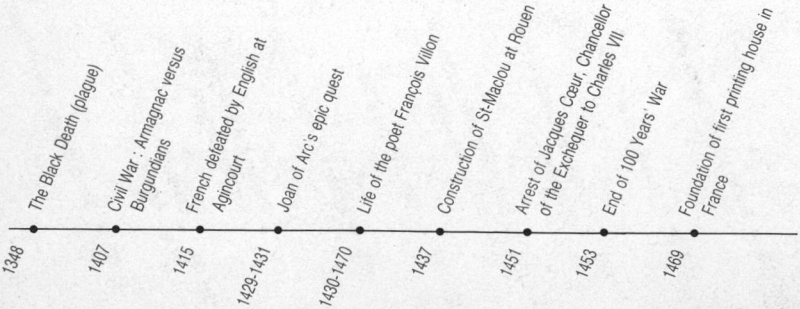

- 1348 — The Black Death (plague)
- 1407 — Civil War : Armagnac versus Burgundians
- 1415 — French defeated by English at Agincourt
- 1429-1431 — Joan of Arc's epic quest
- 1430-1470 — Life of the poet François Villon
- 1437 — Construction of St-Maclou at Rouen
- 1451 — Arrest of Jacques Cœur, Chancellor of the Exchequer to Charles VII
- 1453 — End of 100 Years' War
- 1469 — Foundation of first printing house in France

Albi Cathedral

Jacques Cœur Mansion (Bourges)

- 1472 — Construction of Château de Plessis-les-Tours; Jeanne Hachette rallies people of Beauvais besieged by Charles the Bold of Burgundy
- 1492 — First voyage of Christopher Columbus
- 1494 — First Franco-Italian War
- 1494-1553 — Life of the writer François Rabelais
- 1498 — Discovery of routes to the Indies; construction of Château de Blois
- 1515-1547 — Reign of François I, the "Father of Literature"; Leonardo da Vinci resides at Court

The Renaissance

The 16thC was a period of expansion for the economy and the population, stimulated by an influx of precious metals and distinguished by the development of the mercantile system together with the spread of printing.

The great fiefdoms were gradually absorbed by the Crown : Orleans in 1498, Brittany in 1532, the Bourbonnais, Auvergne and Manche in 1527. Territorial unification strengthened royal power. Central administration and royal justice were laid down : one king, one law. Governors and appointed commissioners, forerunners of the royal superintendents, represented the king in the provinces, and the Edict of Villers-Cotterets, which established the Civil State, made French the official language of the nation.

Humanists and courtiers

The religious civilisation that dominated the Middle Ages gave way to humanism that reflected a twofold return to fundamentals : to Christianity, with evangelism and the Protestant Reformation; and to Classicism, with Rabelais and the poets of the Pléiade group. Humanism, under Italian influence, bred a new kind of man, the courtier. A new society, secular and monarchical, assumed control of the country and affirmed its supremacy.

The Italian model

In 1494, Charles VIII, enthralled by the idea of rebuilding the Empire of Constantinople, embarked on the conquest of Naples, never dreaming that his foolish and disastrous venture would turn France upside down. Dazzled by the decoration of Italian palaces, Charles's warlords resolved to embellish their ancestral homes with the same wealth of ornament. The king led the way, luring a cohort of architects and artists back to France in his train. However, just as buildings continued to rise in Romanesque style right up to the High Gothic era, so the blossoming of the Italian style coincided with the **peak of Flamboyant Gothic.** Although decoration evolved, the construction remained that of the Middle Ages.

▶ e.g. St. Etienne-du-Mont, St. Germain-l'Auxerrois, and St. Eustache in Paris, small churches in the Vexin district, churches in Troyes and Brou, cathedral in Auch.

The Italian influence was already apparent before the wars with Italy, and permeated slowly. The Flamboyant style long remained alive, especially in Brittany and the North, but the hub of artistic life was on the banks of the Loire, where a new art and culture were developing around the life at Court. Absolute monarchy developed decisively under François I. The court had already become a tool of government; etiquette was fixed, royal ceremony and the nascent cult of monarchy transformed the nobles into courtiers. The great lords no longer had the means to call up private armies to do battle with the power of the King. They had, therefore, to submit, in exchange for which they were granted the appointments and revenues of the Court and the Church.

The sovereign and his followers launched the fashions. François I played the decisive part. Determined that his court should be no less dazzling than any in Italy, he extended invitations to artists such as Titian and Leonardo da Vinci. Leonardo, who died at Amboise in 1519, spent his last years as "First Painter, Engineer and Architect to the King". In the initial stage, only the **decorative elements** were clearly Italian. The early châteaux of the Loire blended mediaeval (layout, towers, roofs) and Renaissance (decoration, arcades, gardens) trends. At Amboise, Italian decoration supplanted the original Flamboyant Gothic. Blois, with its large windows and enclosed galleries, sealed the break with the Middle Ages. The style of Blois was soon echoed in the palace of the dukes of Lorraine at Nancy, the *hôtels de ville* in Dreux and Orléans, the Bureau of Finances in Rouen, and the château in Châteaudun. Chambord was the high point of attempts to sever the princely residence from its rough, feudal past.

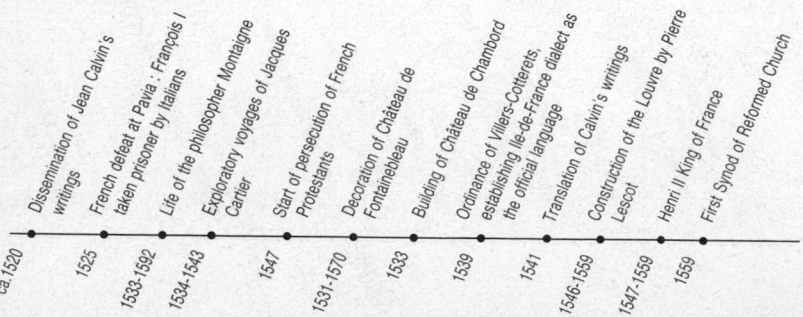

ca.1520	Dissemination of Jean Calvin's writings
1525	French defeat at Pavia : François I taken prisoner by Italians
1533-1592	Life of the philosopher Montaigne
1534-1543	Exploratory voyages of Jacques Cartier
1547	Start of persecution of French Protestants
1531-1570	Decoration of Château de Fontainebleau
1533	Building of Château de Chambord
1539	Ordinance of Villers-Cotterets, establishing Ile-de-France dialect as the official language
1541	Translation of Calvin's writings
1546-1559	Construction of the Louvre by Pierre Lescot
1547-1559	Henri II King of France
1559	First Synod of Reformed Church

▶ e.g. Ancy-le-Franc, Azay-le-Rideau, Fontaine-Henry, Le Lude, Beaugency, Montcontour, Assier, Puyguilhem, mansions in Toulouse.

The art of building was itself inspired by the lessons of the Italian Renaissance and, hence, by the strict architectural rules inherited from **Antiquity** : symmetry, harmony, balance. Architects adapted these rules to French traditions, bestowing originality on the art of the time, which prefigured Classicism. Anet is the model for such structures.

▶ e.g. Section of the Louvre Palace designed by Pierre Lescot and Jean Goujon (Paris), Anet, church in Gisors, the Gallery Bridge at Chenonceaux, Écouen.

Sculpture

The 16thC was a great age for French sculpture. Examples from the beginning of the century depict subjects typical of the preceding period, interpreted in the Italian manner. Important statuary from the time includes the tomb of the Duke of Brittany at Nantes, the tombs of Louis XII and Anne of Brittany in Saint-Denis, and numerous Virgins whose physical grace has the edge on their spirituality.

The rediscovery of Antiquity dictated the subjects of French sculpture for the next two centuries, when parks and palaces became populated by great mythological figures. Jean Goujon created the first models of this kind, examples of which can be seen in Écouen and in Paris in the Hôtel Carnavalet Museum, the Louvre, and the Innocents fountain. Pierre Bontemps was a more realistic sculptor (see his tomb for François I in Saint-Denis), and Germain Pilon, the Master of the Counter-Reformation, was already working in a near-Baroque idiom (tomb of Henri II and Catherine de Medici in Saint-Denis). In Lorraine, meanwhile, the works of Ligier Richier (Pietà d'Etain, skeletal monument in the church of St. Etienne in Bar-le-Duc) and the astounding cemetery at Marville, which constitues an outdoor museum, kept the great great Gothic lineage alive, as did the sculpted calvaries of Brittany.

Painting and Music

Italian mannerism triumphed in painting, as can be seen at the châteaux of Fontainebleau and Orion. The portrait painters Jean and François Clouet and Corneille de Lyon took their cue from Fouquet.

The mediaeval polyphonic tradition was carried on by the great masters Clément Jannequin and Roland de Lassus, among others.

Château de Chambord

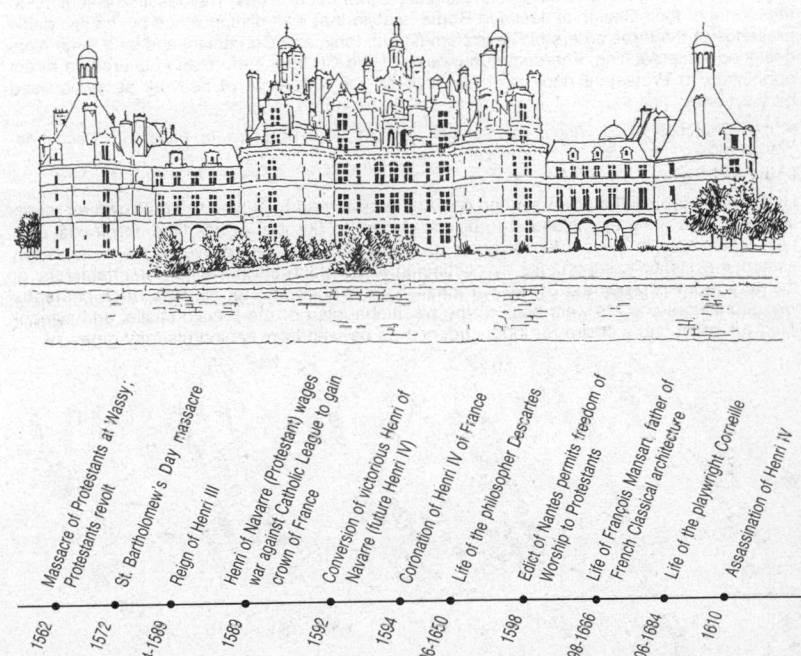

- 1562 — Massacre of Protestants at Wassy; Protestants revolt
- 1572 — St. Bartholomew's Day massacre
- 1574-1589 — Reign of Henri III
- 1589 — Henri of Navarre (Protestant) wages war against Catholic League to gain crown of France
- 1592 — Conversion of victorious Henri of Navarre (future Henri IV)
- 1594 — Coronation of Henri IV of France
- 1596-1650 — Life of the philosopher Descartes
- 1598 — Edict of Nantes permits freedom of Worship to Protestants
- 1598-1666 — Life of François Mansart, father of French Classical architecture
- 1606-1684 — Life of the playwright Corneille
- 1610 — Assassination of Henri IV

The Age of Louis XIII

The Wars of Religion sounded the knell of the Renaissance. These Wars, begun in 1562 during the Regency of Catherine de Médicis, were marked by atrocities, including the notorious St. Bartholomew's Day Massacre on 24 August 1572.

Henri III, assassinated in 1589, was eventually succeeded by Henri de Bourbon, the Protestant King of Navarre, who had to do battle for 5 years to achieve his coronation as **Henri IV** of France. Henri IV re-established religious peace with the Edict of Nantes, which permitted freedom of worship to Protestants, and reaffirmed the authority of the State. In Paris he laid the foundations for the rise of the urban middle class.

▶ e.g. Pont-Neuf, Place Dauphine, Place des Vosges and St. Louis Hospital in Paris, Henrichemont, the town built from the ground up by Sully, Minister to the King, Charleville.

Baroque

The conflicts of the late 16thC revealed a state of deep crisis, stemming from the first rupture between tradition and the modern spirit that revolted against the established rules. The conditions in Europe were translated into the new Baroque art form that was generated by the Counter Reformation. France did not completely escape this influence, and Classicism was reinstated only with the absolutism of Louis XIV, and then only within the court. The first half of the century was witness to the flowering of a much more heterogeneous art, strongly influenced both by the neighbouring countries and by popular traditions.

The more diversified style emerged also in poetry and most of all in the theatre, where a taste for decoration, illusion and metamorphosis reigned in the court ballet, the opera, and the pastoral plays, and held its own until the time of Corneille.

Between 1600 and 1660, many features of French culture became fixed in relation to the Baroque-Classical duality. French Baroque style retained a reserve and severity that were never really at odds with Classicism.

▶ e.g. Sully Mansion and the Luxembourg Palace in Paris, Blérancourt, Rennes Courthouse.

The Counter Reformation

The art of the Counter Reformation was the art of a dominant church, sure of itself and determined to impose a sovereign, organized, hierarchical order. The Jesuits disseminated the model of their Church of Jesus in Rome, a style that was distinguished by the invariable presence of the three orders of Classicism (Doric, Ionic and Corinthian) and by a large nave designed for preaching. The sumptuousness of the Counter Reformation church, in direct opposition to Protestant rigor, proclaimed it as the anteroom of heaven, as symbolised by the dome.

▶ e.g. Churches of St. Roch, St. Gervais, and St. Paul-St.-Louis in Paris, St. Vincent-de-Paul in Blois.

Louis XIII Style

Under Richelieu, all the powers in the country were forced to submit to the Crown as representative of a State that intended to be paramount in Europe. At this time, the feudal castles, testaments to the old feudal order to which Richelieu had delivered the death blow, assumed a symbolic importance by continuing to proclaim the power of the aristocracy at the very moment when the Crown had challenged it once and for all. New **brick châteaux** with stonework corners went back to the traditional plan of the French castle, and symbolised the aristocrat's desire for independence as he withdrew behind his lofty gateway.

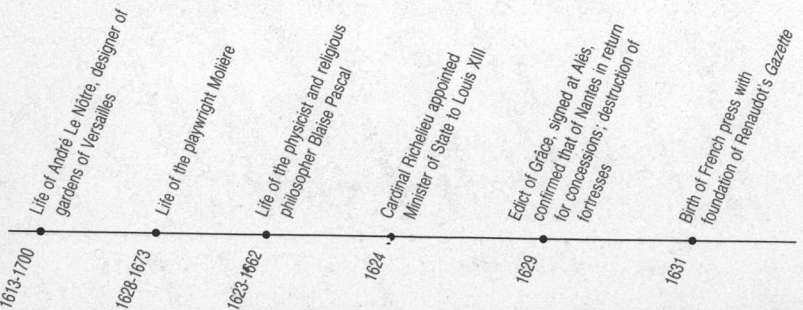

- 1613-1700 — Life of André Le Nôtre, designer of gardens of Versailles
- 1628-1673 — Life of the playwright Molière
- 1623-1662 — Life of the physicist and religious philosopher Blaise Pascal
- 1624 — Cardinal Richelieu appointed Minister of State to Louis XIII
- 1629 — Edict of Grâce, signed at Alès, confirmed that of Nantes in return for concessions; destruction of fortresses
- 1631 — Birth of French press with foundation of Renaudot's *Gazette*

▶ e.g. Vizille, Rosny, Grosbois, Balleroy.

During the reign of Louis XIII, who had little or no interest in city planning, architects working for the Church and for the great Ministers of State gradually consolidated a new mode; Mansart with Maisons-Laffitte, and Le Vau with Vaux-le-Vicomte, together fathered the Classical style.

▶ e.g. Richelieu, Brouage, Sorbonne chapel, Churches of St. Roch and Val-de-Grace, mansions in the Marais in Paris; Vaux-le-Vicomte.

French painting entered a period of eclipse before the creative explosion of the 1630s. The Flemish Pourbus the Younger was the official court painter, and minor Flemish masters carried out the decoration of Fontainebleau and the royal châteaux.

Château de Balleroy

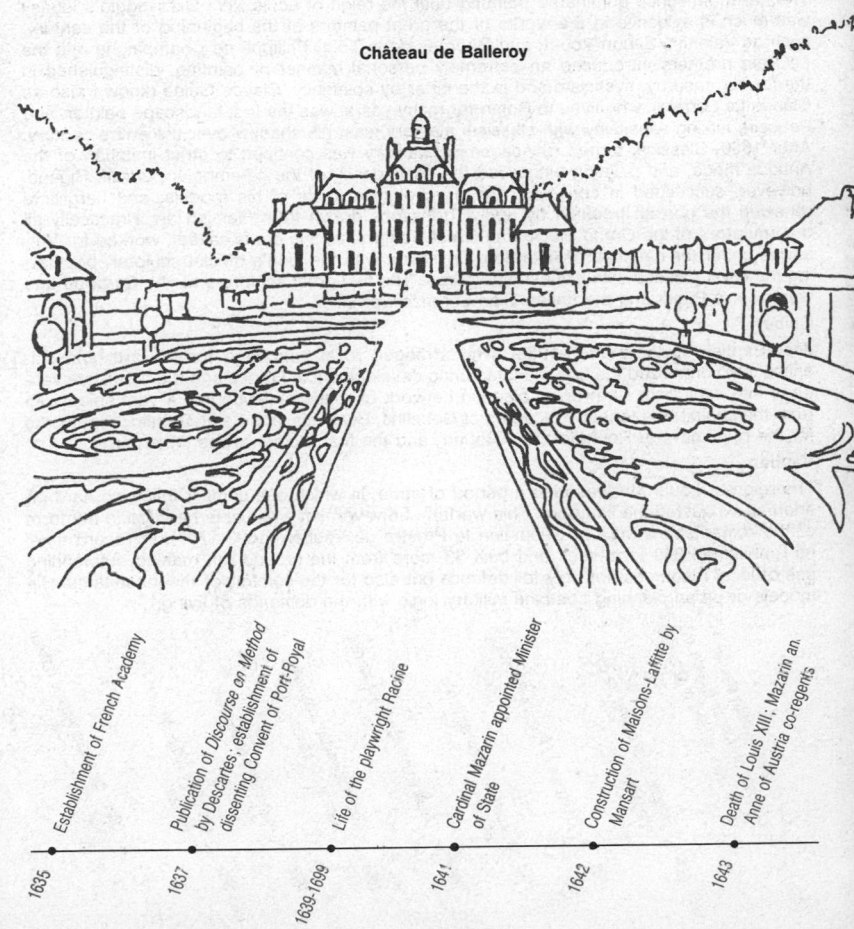

- 1635 — Establishment of French Academy
- 1637 — Publication of *Discourse on Method* by Descartes; establishment of dissenting Convent of Port-Royal
- 1639-1699 — Life of the playwright Racine
- 1641 — Cardinal Mazarin appointed Minister of State
- 1642 — Construction of Maisons-Laffitte by Mansart
- 1643 — Death of Louis XIII; Mazarin an[d] Anne of Austria co-regents

The Century of Louis XIV : Classicism

Cardinal Richelieu and Louis XIV, determined to re-establish the supremacy of royal authority, contributed a great deal to the success of Classicism. The order and progression of the straightforward ideas cherished by Cartesian rationalism, which was the philosophical underpinning of French Classicism, were ideally suited to the ceremonial and administrative absolutist government.

Versailles

After the Louvre and Vaux-le-Vicomte, which was designed by Le Vau, the palace of Versailles is the fullest expression of the order that was imposed everywhere in France, and that demonstrated the grandeur of the French monarchy to the rest of Europe. This theatrical assemblage of buildings, which was to fascinate the courts of Europe, was the temple of absolute monarchy. The château and the park, and even the town, were grouped around the Sun-King, representative of God on earth and answerable to Him alone. Strictness of form, majesty of proportions : the Academy ruled by the masterly hand of Le Brun fixed the rules of Classical order.

▶ e.g. Versailles, The Louvre, The Salpêtrière, The Institut, The Invalides, Place Vendôme, Place des Victoires (all in Paris).

Literature and the other arts were also dedicated to the sovereign, although here, Classicism prevailed only after having yielded to several endeavours inspired by Italian Baroque. The Italian influence dominated **painting** until the reign of Louis XIV; Caravaggio's legacy was much in evidence in the works of the great painters of the beginning of the century, such as Valentin, Simon Vouet, and Georges de la Tour. Philippe de Champaigne and the Le Nain brothers introduced an extremely personal manner of painting, distinguished in the former case by mysticism and in the latter by solemnity. Claude Gelée (known also as Claude Le Lorrain), who lived in Rome for many years, was the first landscape painter, and Poussin, mixing sensitivity with classical mastery, cast his shadow over the entire century. After 1660, Classical turned to Academic; statuary was confined to strict imitation of the Antique mode, and painting witnessed the ascendancy of the ceremonial portrait. Rigaud, however, succeeded in conveying the psychological traits of his models, and Largillière renewed the portrait tradition by applying lessons drawn from Flemish art. Practically all the **sculptors** of the *Grand Siècle* (the Great Century, as this era is called), worked for Versailles under the direction of Girardon. Coysevox was the king's official sculptor, populating the royal palaces with equestrian figures. The two great sculptors of the Baroque age were Pierre Puget and the Italian Gian Lorenzo Bernini.

Colbert

Jean-Baptiste Colbert (1619-1983), who arranged royal patronage for the arts and sciences, also organized the first manufacturing development in France and the first State ventures into capitalism : a proper, planned network of roads radiating like a vast spiderweb from the capital; the tapestry factories of Gobelins, Beauvais, and Saint-Gobain; ropeworks for the royal navy at Rochefort and Rouen; and the first factory towns (Villeneuve).

Vauban

The reign of Louis XIV was also a period of strife, in which one conflict following hard on another exhausted the kingdom. This warfare, however, left a valuable heritage in the form of the remarkable works of Sebastien le Prestre de Vauban (1633-1707). In record time, he redesigned 300 fortresses and built 33 more from the ground up, making outstanding use of local resources not only for defence but also for the comfort of the inhabitants. His models of urban planning combine military logic with the demands of living.

- 1646-1708 — Life of Jules Hardouin-Mansart, grandson of François Mansart and for 30 years architect of Versailles
- 1648-1653 — Frondist revolt against the co-Regents
- 1660 — Publication of Pascal's *Pensées*
- 1661 — Louis XIV assumes throne
- 1664 — Dissolution of Port-Royal convent
- 1665 — Colbert appointed comptroller-General of Finances
- 1674 — King resides at Versailles
- 1683-1764 — Life of the composer Jean-Philippe Rameau
- 1684-1721 — Life of the painter Antoine Watteau

▶ e.g. Bergues, Arras, Neuf-Brisach, Belfort, Fort-St. Vincent, Mont-Dauphin, Seynes-les-Alpes, Colmar, Entrevaux, Briançon, Château-Queyras, Port-Vendres, Montlouis, Socoa, Blaye, Saint-Martin-de-Ré, Belle-Ile.

The Tragic 17thC

It would a mistake to think of the 17thC as a period of static, sovereign immobility. In fact, Classicism represents only a short spell of balance and harmony in a century that was torn by struggles between opposing forces : tradition versus progress, libertinism versus rigidity. Members of the cultivated upper classes threw themselves violently and passionately into various religious movements and a form of stylized affectation known as "preciousness" *(préciosité).* Towards the end of Louis XIV's reign, a crisis of conscience, which waxed as the royal prestige waned, was focused on the quarrel that pitted those who continued to profess admiration for the ancient authors, the Latin language and the Classical spirit (typified by Boileau) against others who upheld the superiority of French and the spirit of modernism (Perrault and Fontenelle). The debate soon spread, and criticism of the established institutions (by such as La Bruyère, Fénelon and Vauban), the ideal of progress (Bayle) and claims for freedom of thought heralded the Age of Enlightenment.

Versailles

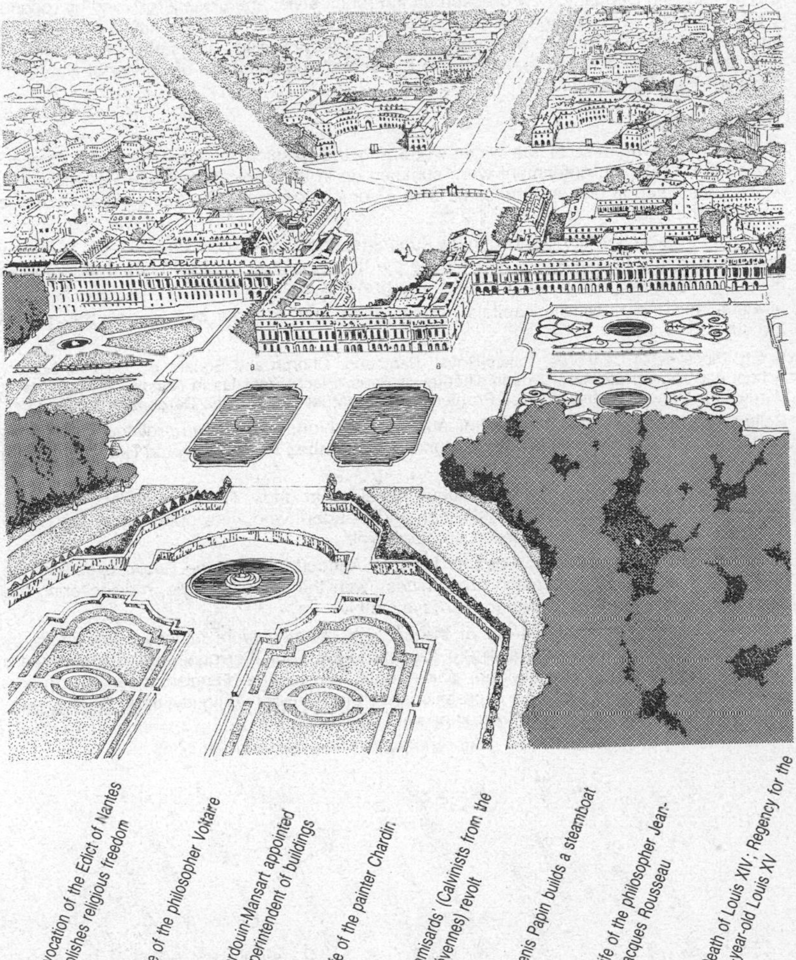

- 1685 — Revocation of the Edict of Nantes abolishes religious freedom
- 1694-1778 — Life of the philosopher Voltaire
- 1699 — Hardouin-Mansart appointed superintendent of buildings
- 1699-1779 — Life of the painter Chardin
- 1702-1704 — 'Camisards' (Calvinists from the Cévennes) revolt
- 1707 — Denis Papin builds a steamboat
- 1712-1778 — Life of the philosopher Jean-Jacques Rousseau
- 1715 — Death of Louis XIV; Regency for the 5-year-old Louis XV

The 18thC : Enlightenment

The Regency : salons and gallantry

The strictness of Louis XIV and the austerity that prevailed towards the end of his reign were abruptly succeeded by a joyous frivolity encouraged by an unprecedented economic boom that culminated in the development of major industry by the eve of the Revolution. "Live and enjoy!" was the motto of the day. **Paris** became the capital of pleasure, art and worldliness, the centre of taste and sophistication, as well as the nucleus of art in Europe. This was the age of gallantry, of dazzling receptions and salons where women reigned supreme. The **salons** fostered the spirit — formed by curiosity and the thirst for knowledge — of criticism and daring. Even more than in the days of Preciousness, love and the examination of feelings played the major role.

Construction flourished as never before or since. Châteaux, palaces and mansions changed in appearance, abandoning the rather theatrical grandeur of the previous century in favour of intimacy, gaiety and charm combined with luxurious comfort. The **salon** became the heart of the house, where the emphasis was on decoration; Baroque came back, by way of Italy and Germany, now dressed up in French style, and closely followed by rococo, grotto fantasies *(rocaille)* and the fashion for the exotic. This was the heyday of **gardens** and follies on the outskirts of the large cities, an age of dressing up as shepherdesses and cavorting in romantic ruins. Jean-Jacques Rousseau trumpeted the discovery of Nature as if it were Paradise regained.

The city of light

The growing awareness of the wider world and the passion for knowledge that characterised the Age of Enlightenment were summed up in the *Encyclopaedia* of Denis Diderot, which constituted at one and the same time a summation of politics and philosophy and a mirror of the age.

Concern for public welfare induced many superintendents, governors and prelates to endow their cities with public buildings that rivaled the finest palaces, and with city developments suited to the needs of a population that was growing apace.

In Paris and the provincial capitals, the gardens and squares built during this period are still renowned.

▶ e.g. Place de la Concorde, Palais-Royal, Pantheon, Church and Square St. Sulpice, Military School and Champ de Mars, Odeon Theatre in Paris, Place Stanislas in Nancy, city squares at Bordeaux, Rennes, Rheims, Peyrou Promenade at Montpellier, Fontaine Gardens in Nîmes.

Religious architecture was no less influenced by fashion. Abbeys and prelates' residences rivaled the palaces of the laity in luxuriousness. **Churches** were decorated like salons, with incrustations of marble and gilt.

In **sculpture,** the Baroque and the Antique remained at odds. The Baroque standard was upheld by Pigalle, Falconet, Pajou, Clodion and Houdon, who were opposed by the Coustou and Adam brothers, Bouchardon and Lemoyne.

Archaeological excavations at Pompeii brought Antiquity before the public eye, and the Louis XVI style managed to blend gracefulness with the Classical style, rediscovering the simplicity of straight lines, geometry and symmetry.

Watteau was the foremost **painter** of the century, imitated more or less successfully by Pater, Lancret, Boucher and Fragonard. Quentin de la Tour, Perronneau and Nattier were brilliant portraitists. While Chardin paid hommage to the Flemish tradition, Hubert Roberts's and Joseph Vernet's impressions of the ruins of Antiquity heralded the neo-Classicism that was later to reach fruition with David.

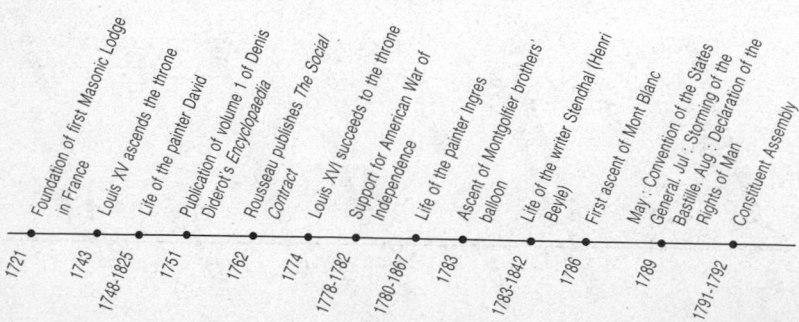

- 1721 Foundation of first Masonic Lodge in France
- 1743 Louis XV ascends the throne
- 1748-1825 Life of the painter David
- 1751 Publication of volume 1 of Denis Diderot's *Encyclopaedia*
- 1762 Rousseau publishes *The Social Contract*
- 1774 Louis XVI succeeds to the throne
- 1778-1782 Support for American War of Independence
- 1780-1867 Life of the painter Ingres
- 1783 Ascent of Montgolfier brothers' balloon
- 1783-1842 Life of the writer Stendhal (Henri Beyle)
- 1786 First ascent of Mont Blanc
- 1789 May: Convention of the States General. Jul: Storming of the Bastille. Aug: Declaration of the Rights of Man
- 1791-1792 Constituent Assembly

From the Revolution to the Republic

Three revolutions, two republics, two restorations, two empires : this was the laborious process that gave rise to modern France. Fraught with upheavals, the period nevertheless derived a certain unity from the class newly risen to power : the liberal middle class.

The 1789 Revolution : a decisive turning point

Ideas and criticism propounded by the philosophers, the example shown by the United States of America, the people's misery and a financial crisis culminated inevitably in the Revolution. Louis XIV's successors had attempted to cut back the allowances and privileges that were draining State resources, and to equalize the taxation burden in order to rectify the financial situation, but they encountered opposition from the upper classes, who wrested the Convention of the States General from the King in 1789. Under pressure from the Third Estate, events built up to a revolutionary explosion :

— 5 May : transformation of the States General into a Constituent Assembly
— 14 July : the storming of the Bastille, which symbolised Absolutism
— Night of 4 August : abolition of privilege : middle-class France took the place of the Old French aristocracy
— 26 August : Declaration of the Rights of Man, affirming the principle of equality
— 22 December : provinces replaced by administrative departments
— 22 September 1792 : the Convention elected by universal suffrage proclaimed the Republic.

The King's flight and arrest at Varennes set the seal on the monarchy's death warrant. The mobilisation of the European states against Revolutionary France similarly condemned the social revolution set in motion by Robespierre, and the Convention ended in the bloodshed of the Terror. Worn out, France yielded to dictatorship by a victorious general : Bonaparte.

The Napoleonic Era

Under the pretext of seeking to liberate Europe in the name of revolutionary principles, Napoleon Bonaparte, first Consul then Emperor of the French, led France into a series of wars and managed briefly to extend the power of France over almost all the Continent. Napoleon's epic venture will haunt the spirit of the French people and the poetic imagination for a long time to come. Foundering after Waterloo and the 100 Days that followed Napoleon's escape from Elba, the Napoleonic Empire left France impoverished but at the same time enriched by a soundly organised, centralized administration; the system of prefectures, the schools and civil code still attest to Napoleon's organizational genius.

The victorious states restored the Bourbon family to the throne of France. In 1830, however, a new revolution replaced Charles X with the liberal monarchy of Louis-Philippe. The Workers' Revolution of 1848 proclaimed the short-lived Second Republic, which lasted only until Napoleon's nephew became the second Emperor in 1852.

Empire Style

Neo-Classicism began in the reign of Louis XVI and achieved a peak with the First Empire. The taste for Antiquity reigned supreme; architecture boasted triumphal arches, colonnades, and the style of the Greek temple, as seen in the Church of the Madeleine, the Chamber of Deputies, and the Bourse (Stock Exchange) in Paris. In painting, **David** introduced the fashion for Roman costume and influenced all the painters of the era, including Isabey, Girodet, Gros, Gérard, and even Ingres.

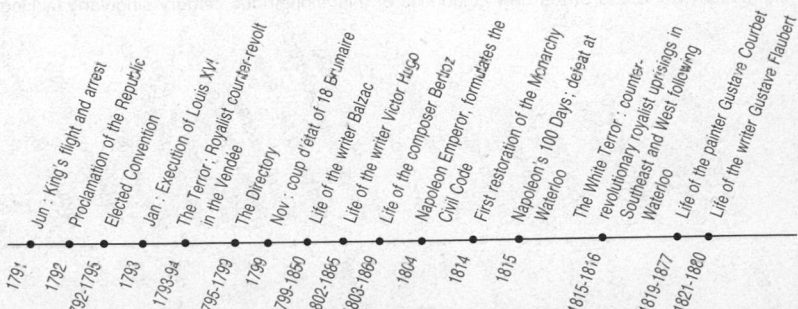

- 1791 — Jun : King's flight and arrest
- 1792 — Proclamation of the Republic
- 1792-1795 — Elected Convention
- 1793 — Jan : Execution of Louis XVI
- 1793-94 — The Terror; Royalist counter-revolt in the Vendée
- 1795-1799 — The Directory
- 1799 — Nov : coup d'état of 18 Brumaire
- 1799-1850 — Life of the writer Balzac
- 1802-1885 — Life of the writer Victor Hugo
- 1803-1869 — Life of the composer Berlioz
- 1804 — Napoleon Emperor, formulates the Civil Code
- 1814 — First restoration of the Monarchy
- 1815 — Napoleon's 100 Days; defeat at Waterloo
- 1815-1816 — The White Terror : counter-revolutionary royalist uprisings in Southeast and West following Waterloo
- 1819-1877 — Life of the painter Gustave Courbet
- 1821-1880 — Life of the writer Gustave Flaubert

19th Century France

Neither Louis XVIII nor Charles X managed to reconcile the traditional values of the Old Regime with the demands of the new spirit. After the 1830 revolution, Louis-Philippe's "middle-class monarchy" failed to show itself capable of striking a balance between social order and liberalism, and the revolution of 1848 finally put an end to the Bourbon monarchs.

In the light of the revolutionary and imperial years, the atmosphere of the middle-class France described by the novelist Honoré de Balzac seems stifling and lacking in grandeur. A yearning for adventure intensified by bitterness following the defeats of 1815 fostered the desire for an alternative among the younger generation.

Romanticism

The Romantic movement, filtering down from the Northern countries, marked a turning-point in European culture. It entered France at the beginning of the 19thC along with rupture and revolt : rupture with the Classical tradition and the worship of Antiquity, revolt against withering rationalism; rupture with the society of the time, revolt against convention and mediocrity. Revolt led naturally enough to escapism — escape into nature, back to the legendary Middle Ages, to exotic landscapes, into contemplation.

The watchword everywhere was freedom : in art, in the theatre, where drama ousted tragedy, and in painting, where first Géricault then Delacroix revolted against the Academic style. Painting became suffused with brilliant colour and subjective imagination.

From the Empire to the Republic

The 1848 Revolution ushered in the Second Republic but, after crushing the Workers' Movement during the events of June, the regime took a conservative turn before being abolished in the coup d'état staged by Louis-Napoléon Bonaparte on 2 December 1851. This nephew of the first Emperor restored the Empire on 2 December 1852 and assumed the name of Napoleon III.

The **Second Empire** was as important in terms of the economy as the 1789 Revolution had been in terms of politics : it brought France into the industrial age and provided remarkable economic growth. The ill-thought-out Franco-Prussian War of 1870, however, ended in disaster at Sedan and brought about the regime's downfall.

After 80 years of upheaval and revolution, France enjoyed a period of apparent stability under the **Third Republic,** during which the country amassed a vast colonial empire and passed important legislation that established fundamental freedoms as well as the first social welfare laws.

Starting with the Second Empire, it was no longer possible to refer to "an artistic movement"; rather, a series of successive and superimposed movements gave rise to debate about the very principles upon which modern humanism, art and poetry were founded.

The real winner of the Revolution was the Middle Class; in every regime it has been the Middle Class that has controlled political life and — especially since 1830 — has set the tone for society. A divorce was enacted between artist and public, between "sensitive souls" and "bourgeois society". The Romantic generation suffered through not being understood, but the dividing line was drawn bolder after 1850, and the history of art is punctuated with trials (Balzac, Flaubert, Zola, Manet) and rejections of artists (Courbet and the Realists, Manet and the Impressionists, the Fauvists, the Cubists, and so on).

The former aristocracy henceforth was to look only to the past, clinging to its rejection of the modern world and of the new celebrities of this "industrious century singularly lacking

1822-1895	Life of the scientist Louis Pasteur
1824	Charles X King
1830	Revolution deposes Charles X in favour of Louis-Philippe
1830-47	Conquest of Algeria
1840-48	Guizot government
1841-1919	Life of the painter Renoir
1844-1896	Life of the poet Verlaine
1848	Second Republic
1851	Coup d'état by Louis-Napoleon Bonaparte institutes Second Empire
1854-1891	Life of the poet Arthur Rimbaud
1857	The writer Charles Baudelaire publishes *Flowers of Evil*
1870-71	Franco-Prussian War; defeat at Sedan; fall of the Second Empire
1871	Paris Commune
1874	First Impressionist exhibition
1875	Proclamation of the Third Republic

in worthiness", who looked to models of the Old Regime for signals of their success and rise in society. This twofold movement fostered the most traditionalistic Academic art.

Architecture, more dependent than the other arts on financial conditions, erupted in a motley of borrowings; neo-Classicism, neo-Gothic, neo-Renaissance and neo-Romanesque styles sprang up. Nineteenth-century French architecture was primarily an eclectic, archival art, looking for its vocabulary in the history of France and the world. This was an age of archaeological summaries in the fine arts, of expeditions to Greece and Egypt, and of the discovery of historic monuments, notably by Eugène Viollet-le-Duc. Napoleon III's Louvre and Charles Garnier's Paris Opéra are the most remarkable examples of this composite style that mixed Renaissance ceilings with Louis XIII façades and Louis XV decoration.

Industrial architecture partly escaped the pervasive Academic influence by making use of the two great technical innovations of the age : iron and reinforced concrete. These materials were less in evidence in France, however, than in countries such as the United States and Germany. In Paris, an immense urban development programme was carried out in record time under the direction of Baron Haussmann.

▶ e.g. Courthouse, Stock Exchange and Fine Arts Museum in Marseilles, Opéra, Gare du Nord and Mayor's Office of the First Arrondissement, National Library (Bibliothèque) in Paris, Meunier chocolate factory in Noisiel.

"Rich" ornamentation proliferated to meet demands for decoration by wealthy industrialists and merchants. Furniture, metalwork, glassware, carpets, hangings and draperies from the period are snatched up today in the auction houses.

For a long time, **sculpture** provided an outlet for pretentious effusions, such as can be seen in the endless processions of caryatids supporting the fronts of residential properties and monuments to great men in public squares. The more original sculptors encountered great difficulty in becoming established. Jean-Baptiste Carpeaux was favoured by the patronage of the Imperial family. Auguste Rodin struggled alone against the world but finally dominated the last years of the century with his powerful genius, infused with Romanticism and coupled with incomparable technical mastery. Antoine Bourdelle, a follower of Rodin, produced a considerable body of work that — not entirely successfully — combined exuberant imagination with a return to the archaic Greek style. Aristide Maillol introduced an unadorned, serene simplicity, with sculpture that was close to the earth and embodied goddess-figures brimming with strength and grace.

Paris Opéra (1861)

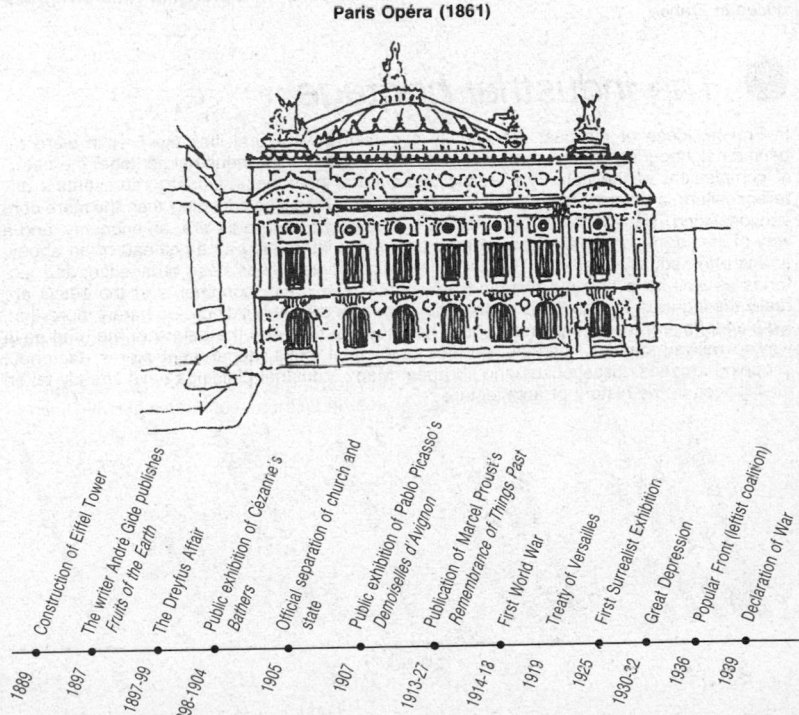

- 1889 Construction of Eiffel Tower
- 1897 The writer André Gide publishes *Fruits of the Earth*
- 1897-99 The Dreyfus Affair
- 1898-1904 Public exhibition of Cézanne's *Bathers*
- 1905 Official separation of church and state
- 1907 Public exhibition of Pablo Picasso's *Demoiselles d'Avignon*
- 1913-27 Publication of Marcel Proust's *Remembrance of Things Past*
- 1914-18 First World War
- 1919 Treaty of Versailles
- 1925 First Surrealist Exhibition
- 1930-32 Great Depression
- 1936 Popular Front (leftist coalition)
- 1939 Declaration of War

From Realism to Surrealism

Painting was undoubtedly the liveliest of the arts. In the course of a half-century, one school succeeded another, each venturing further than the last in the quest for form. Developments were made possible by the enthusiasm of a few rare art-lovers and dealers in paintings, but most of all by the courage of the painters, virtually alone in their questioning of accepted values.

Two main schematic trends evolved. Realism revolted against the conventional Academic view, reaching its peak and exhausting itself with the coming of Impressionism. From then, the painter's subjective imagination asserted itself through the most varied techniques.

Courbet was the master of Realism, which is not to say that his was not a highly personal vision of the world. He drew his inspiration from daily life, and the reproach generally addressed to him (that art should not impose ideas) was in fact aimed at **Realism,** this "aesthetic mistake", of which Daumier, Millet and Corot were also accused. Manet, also the subject of violent criticism, created an explosion in painting from 1865. He was the immediate forerunner of the **Impressionists** (Monet, Pissarro, Sisley), who sought to record visual sensation in its pure state. Renoir, Degas and Toulouse-Lautrec followed their own paths. Cézanne, Gauguin and Van Gogh, who overtook Impressionism, laid the foundations of modern painting, in which nature yielded to thought. Rather than breaking up form and volume, Cézanne emphasised them by contrasting colour and geometric shapes. To Gauguin, only the painter's soul mattered; art was an abstraction, a painting was music. Van Gogh was a visionary who expressed himself by means of colour.

Three movements arose directly out of the work of these painters : **Fauvism** (represented by Vlaminck, Derain, Dufy, Matisse), **Cubism** (Braque, Picasso) — which had the deepest influence on our view of the world, going beyond painting to turn the other arts upside down — and **Abstractionism,** which was not restricted to France.

In the 10 years from 1904 to 1914, from one revolution to another, works of art gained a sort of independence within the loose assembly of forms that made them, and active artists shed any specifically national character. Dada (Arp, Picabía, Duchamp), Surrealism (Masson, Tanguy, Chirico, Dali, Max Ernst) and Abstraction (Hartung, De Stael) played an important part in making art international. In addition, artists on the fringe — such as Douanier Rousseau, Bonnard, Rouault, Léger, Chagall, Giacometti and reformers such as Le Corbusier and Brancusi — produced images that ran counter to the art that was being produced in France.

The industrial heritage

In France, ideas of the past are usually associated with rural life; the French were far behind neighbouring countries in becoming interested in their industrial heritage, the natural complement of the country's artistic and cultural inheritance. Industry represents a different culture, a different beauty that is unexpected but no less engaging than the more conventional kind. The structures bequeathed by industry attest to an era, an economy, and a way of life; a mill or a blast furnace may be just as interesting as a château or an abbey, and is often equally beautiful. The very idea of monuments has been broadened, and factories as well have become historic monuments. The great monuments of the 19thC are really the legacies of industry and daily life, whereas official buildings are hardly more than jumbled leftovers from a bygone world. The house of God and the palace of the King gave way to railway stations, markets, bridges and canal locks, department stores, factories, shopping arcades, glasshouses and libraries. Many industrial buildings have already taken their places in the history of architecture.

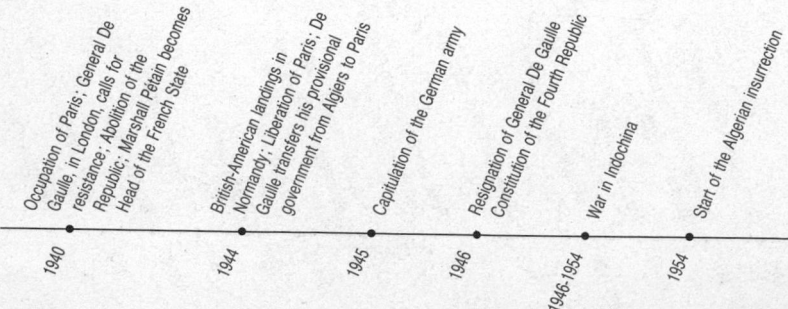

- 1940 — Occupation of Paris; General De Gaulle, in London, calls for resistance; Abolition of the Republic; Marshall Pétain becomes Head of the French State
- 1944 — British-American landings in Normandy; Liberation of Paris; De Gaulle transfers his provisional government from Algiers to Paris
- 1945 — Capitulation of the German army
- 1946 — Resignation of General De Gaulle Constitution of the Fourth Republic
- 1946-1954 — War in Indochina
- 1954 — Start of the Algerian insurrection

▶ e.g. Saltworks at Arc-et-Sénans, Ropeworks in Rochefort, mills in Villeneuve and Sedan, Creusot glassworks, Market place (Les Halles) and Gare du Nord in Paris, Garabit viaduct.

Other industrial buildings have been renovated and converted to cultural purposes.

▶ e.g. Lainé warehouses at Bordeaux, Tobacco factories at Nantes and Colmar, Match factory in Aix-en-Provence, Le Blan textile mills in Lille, Abattoir in Lyons.

Still other important industrial developments have been preserved.

▶ e.g. Sawmill at Saint-Sausan-le-Poterie, Meunier chocolate factory at Noisiel, Godin appliance factory at Guise, Industrial village at Fontaine-Daniel, Niderviller porcelain factory, Morlaix tobacco factory.

Several obsolete factories have been turned into museums that are to a certain extent responsible for maintaining the industrial landscape. The **working museums** *(écomusées)* are the industrial counterparts of nature parks, or of local and regional museums. The first examples at Creusot and Fourmies now have many imitators.

▶ e.g. Glass museum in a former crystal factory in Sars-Poteries, Woodworking museum in Felleries, Marble museum at Bellignies, Historical mining museum in an old mineshaft at Lewarde near Douai, Regional living museum at L'Isle-d'Abeau.

Architecture

The Modernist movement

The Modernist movement, which arose between the two World Wars and which was initiated in France by **Le Corbusier,** rejected all ties with tradition and aimed instead at finding original, rational solutions to problems posed by an environment for modern living. After 1945, while **Auguste Perret** applied his ideal of a grand, if rather academic, city plan to the rebuilding of Le Havre, Le Corbusier was belatedly setting down his dream of a "radiant city" *(cité radieuse)* at Marseilles (1947) and Nantes (1953) in projects that soon came to be questioned.

Although Le Corbusier continued to exert considerable influence, further developments in architecture favoured greater respect for nature and for the site in question (Marly-les-Grandes-Terres, 1955) and a greater variety of lines, volumes and decoration within the bounds of the space to be developed (as can be seen in certain of the new towns, such as Melun-Senart), as well as harmony with existing local architecture (the Châtaigniers development zone at Chambéry-le-Haut).

Post-modern architects

The years 1968-1970 represent a decisive turning-point in French architecture. Influenced by the theories of W. Benjamin, Umberto Eco, Duchamp and Deleuze, post-modern architects questioned the old idea of unity in an architectural work. Noting the failure of the ideas of the Modernist movement, they followed the method of "critical projects". According to these architects, a work should be "open", a mechanism in motion, with ambiguities, breaks, and surprises. Architecture should look not inwards but outwards, and be — like the city itself — an open book. Space should generate forms and, most of all, open areas, places for encounters and meetings. These ideas are embodied in the Labour Exchange *(Bourse de Travail)* in Saint-Denis, designed by R. Castro, who draws his inspiration from Piranesi (the 18thC Italian painter of imaginary architecture) and from "solid dynamics". A new generation (represented by O. Girard, A. Grumbach, and C. de Portzamparc, among others) is creating an architecture rife with reminiscence and allusions to the past, that keeps on evolving.

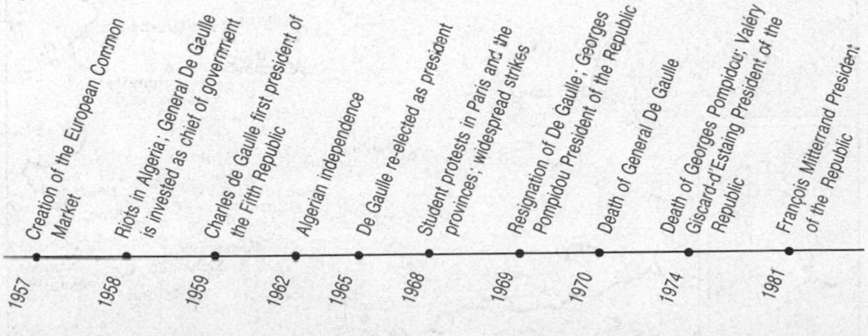
Creation of the European Common Market
1957
Riots in Algeria; General De Gaulle is invested as chief of government
1958
Charles de Gaulle first president of the Fifth Republic
1959
Algerian independence
1962
De Gaulle re-elected as president
1965
Student protests in Paris and the provinces; widespread strikes
1968
Resignation of De Gaulle; Georges Pompidou President of the Republic
1969
Death of General De Gaulle
1970
Death of Georges Pompidou; Valéry Giscard-d'Estaing President of the Republic
1974
François Mitterrand President of the Republic
1981

The plastic arts

The many French artists who emigrated to escape the ravages of 1939-1945 helped to make New York the world capital of art. Nevertheless, Paris has remained a major European art centre. As a result of the numerous art movements, international in scope, that have arisen and confronted one another in the past 40 years, the once-firm barrier between painting and sculpture has broken down, and experimentation has given rise to entirely new media that owe nothing to traditional art forms.

While the great painters, such as Braque, Léger, Matisse and Picasso continued their own explorations, the 1940s and 1950s saw conflict between figurative art and the renewal of abstraction, which was split into two contradictory trends :

▶ cold or geometric abstraction (Herbin, Govin, Domela, Magneli and Dewasne who, after the "Concrete Art" exhibition at Paris in 1945, joined forces at the *Salon des Réalités Nouvelles* from 1946 to 1957).

▶ lyrical or informal abstraction (Wols, Mathieu, Boyen, Soulages, Hartung).

▶ Neither "cold" nor "lyrical", the new School of Paris included painters as different as Poliakoff, Manessier, Bazaine, Estève, Lapicque, Tal-Coat, Vieira da Silva and de Stael.

▶ The Raw Art Company *(Compagnie de l'Art Brut),* founded in 1948 by Bernard Buffet and André Breton, focussed on all the marginal areas of art, thus preparing the ground for the unheard-of experiments of the 1950s and 1960s.

Pushing back the frontiers of art

Numerous groups have questioned the limits of art in the past 20 years.

▶ The Visual Art Research Group *(le Groupe de Recherche d'Art Visuel)* (1961-1968, with Le Parc, Vasarély, Morellet) investigated kinetic and optical art; the New Realists *(les Nouveaux Realistes)* (1960, with Klein, Arman, Tinguely, César, Christo, Niki de Saint-Phalle, Spoerri) declared themselves for a "technological humanism" with the use of actual space and objects.

▶ A politically involved art movement whose members were concerned with innovation of form appeared at the Young Painters' Salon in the late 1960s; their works often bore the mark of English or American pop art.

▶ The 1970s saw a further outbreak of the quarrel between figurative and abstract art, as represented by the "New Figuration" *(Nouvelle Figuration)* and "Support Surface" groups. At the same time, the most eclectic movements of "body art" and "conceptual art" declared that all of life was an art form.

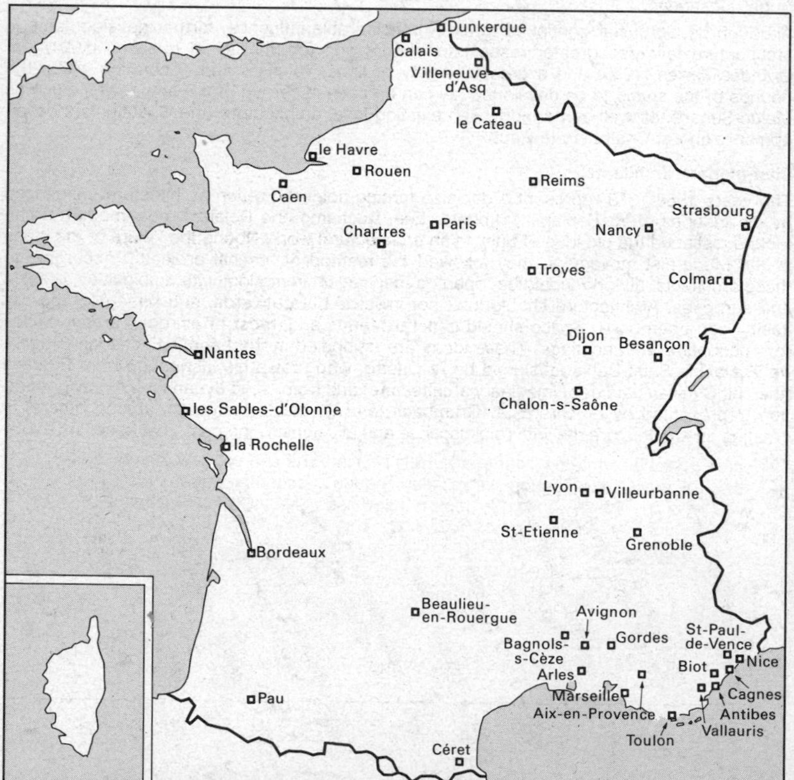

Practical holiday guide

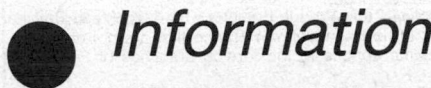

Information

Information at your fingertips

The French authorities take the tourist industry very seriously indeed, and every effort is made, not only at a national and international level to inform potential visitors of France's charms, but equally at a local level : the increasing availability of information and services has helped to attract holiday-makers from the traditionally overcrowded tourist spots into many lesser-known, but often far more authentic areas.

F.G.T.O.

The **French Government Tourist Office** in many cities abroad is without doubt the best source of information on the countless forms of holiday-making in France : whether the aim is to gain an overall view of available possibilities, or to gather specific information on a particular subject. Although the F.G.T.O. cannot actually book travel or accommodation (the F.G.T.O.U.K.'s *Gîtes de France Ltd.* service is an exception to this rule (→ Gîtes), staff go out of their way to provide all help necessary to enable potential visitors to decide, budget and plan their holiday arrangements. Available services vary from country to country and are far too numerous to list exhaustively. Anybody considering a holiday in France should first contact the F.G.T.O. (Callers are more than welcome but the telephone lines are often busy, and phone calls should be reserved for specific, priority enquiries. A letter is far more convenient, enclosing a stamped, addressed A4-format envelope if brochures are requested.)
The F.G.T.O. can provide lists of tour operators and travel agents specialising in every holiday field (together with the relevant brochures in many cases), and one-page summaries on specific subjects : travel for the disabled, inland waterways, country and farmhouse holidays, and many, many more. Another excellent initiative is the bilingual reservation form, a standard letter enabling visitors to make direct bookings with maximum precision. This aid, by no means limited to travel and accommodation, extends to every form of holiday activity. The **Agence Nationale pour l'Information Touristique** (A.N.I.T.) in Paris can provide every kind of advice the foreign visitor may require : accommodation, travel, special-interest holidays, useful addresses, etc. On a regional and departmental level the **associations, comités régionaux** or **Offices Départementaux du Tourisme** provide a postal information service (addresses : → relevant gazetteer section).

Loisirs-Accueil

These departmental booking organisations centralise accommodation vacancies (hotels, *gîtes,* campsites, etc.), sporting and special-interest activities available in their areas; there is usually no fee for reservations, and English-speaking staff are generally available for personal, postal or telephone bookings (addresses : → relevant gazetteer section).

Tourism offices and *syndicats d'initiative*

The most invaluable sources of information at a local level are the **Offices de Tourisme** ("TO" in this guide) and the **Syndicats d'Initiative** ("SI"), supplying information and advice of absolutely every kind : practical, cultural, leisure, accommodation and much more. Managed by competent local staff - volunteers in the smaller districts, professionals in the case of major centres - the TO and SI form a national network and thus are able to assist the visitor, not only with his stay in their area, but also to plan ahead. Personal, postal and telephone enquiries are welcome (addresses : → gazetteer section).

Visitors passing through Paris on their way to a particular region may want to pay a visit to the relevant *Maison de Province* (regional promotion centre) to pick up detailed information (also available by mail; addresses : → particular gazetteer section).

International tourism and travel show Visitors to Paris in February can plan their next French holiday at the *Village France :* this vast exhibit assembles all the regions of France for a prestigious international show at the C.N.I.T. exhibition hall at La Défense, the office-living complex just outside Paris proper.

Information

- **Agence Nationale pour l'Information Touristique,** 8 av. de l'Opéra 75001 Paris ☎ (1) 42.96.10.23 and 42.60.37.38.
- **Air France** and **U.T.A.** offices throughout the world can supply useful information on many aspects of holidaymaking in France that are not directly related to air-travel; the same applies to the foreign branches of French Railways **(S.N.C.F.).**
- **Treasure Tours International,** 15 rue de l'Arcade 75008 Paris ☎ (1) 42.65.05.69 and **Interséjours,** 4 rue de Parme 75009 Paris ☎ (1) 48.74.04.98; travel agents with a particularly wide experience in catering to foreign visitors.
- **Regional and departmental tourist offices, local tourist offices (TO) and *syndicats d'initiatives (SI) :*** → relevant gazetteer section.
- **Direction du Tourisme,** 17 rue de l'Ingénieur Robert Keller 75740 Paris Cedex 15 ☎ (1) 45.75.62.16; the **Service des Réclamations** handles complaints relating to the tourist trade.
- **French Government Tourist Offices** (F.G.T.O.) abroad :

Austria : Hilton Center 259 C Landstrasser Hauptstrasser 2A 1030 Wien ☎ (222) 75.70.62.
Belgium : 21 av. de la Toison-d'Or 1060 Brussels ☎ (2) 512.97.90.
Canada : 1840 Ouest rue Sherbrooke Montréal Qué H3H 1E4 ☎ (514) 931 3855; 1 Dundas Sté W. Suite 2405 Box 8 Toronto Ont. M5G 1Z3 ☎ (416) 593 4717.
Denmark : Frederiksberggade 28DK 1459 Copenhagen ☎ (1) 11.46.41.
West Germany : Westendestrasse 47 D6 Frankfurt/Main 1 ☎ (611) 75.20.29; Berliner Allee 26 D4 Dusseldorf ☎ (211) 803.75 or 76.
U.K. : 178 Piccadilly London W1V OAL ☎ (01) 493.65.94.
Greece : Air France, 4 Karageorgi Servias Athens ☎ (1) 32.80.501.
Italy : 5 via Sant' Andrea, 20121 Milan ☎ (2) 70.02.68; 93 via Veneto 00187 Rome ☎ (6) 48.35.65.
Japan : Landic 2 Akasaka Building 2-10-9 Akasaka Minatu-ku Tokyo 107 ☎ (3) 582 6965.
Netherlands : Prinsengracht 670 1017 KX Amsterdam ☎ (20) 24.75.34.
Portugal : Air France, Rua-Rodrigue Sampaio A8 Lisbon 2 ☎ (19) 56.24.61.
Spain : Gran Via 59 Madrid 13 ☎ (1) 241 8808; Gran Via 656 Barcelona 10 ☎ (3) 302 0582.
Sweden : Normalstorg 1 S III 46-Stockholm ☎ (8) 24.39.75/10.53.
Switzerland : 2 rue Thalberg 1201 Geneva ☎ (22) 32.36.10; Bahnhofstrasse 16 8022 Zurich ☎ (1) 211.30.85.
U.S.A. : 610 Fifth Av. New York 10020 ☎ (212) 757 1125; 645 North-Michigan Av. Suite 630 Chicago IL 60611 ☎ (312) 337 6301. World Trade Centre 103 2050 Sternmons Freeway P.O. Box 58610 Dallas TX 75258 ☎ (214) 742 7011; 9401 Wilshire Bvd. Beverly Hills CA 90212 ☎ (213) 272 2661; 360 Post St. San Francisco CA 94108 ☎ (415) 986 4161.

Getting to France

A number of organisations can supply further invaluable information for those planning a holiday in France, notably the **French Government Tourist Offices** (F.G.T.O.) abroad, which provide an extensive range of services for the would-be visitor (→ Information).

Air travel Every major airline flies to France — to Paris or to one of the country's several other international airports. Most airlines also offer package holidays and reductions for travel during certain periods or for a specified length of stay.

Air France offers the widest range of travel and holiday opportunities, and the national airline's booking offices are veritable information centres for travellers to France, offering assistance well beyond flight reservations.

Although many visitors arrive at airports near the principal holiday regions (Nice, Bordeaux, Toulouse and Lyons), Paris is the destination for the vast majority who arrive at Roissy-Charles de Gaulle Airport or at one of the two Orly terminals, Orly-South and Orly-West.

Roissy-Charles de Gaulle Airport is situated north of Paris on the A1 autoroute which connects with the Boulevard Périphérique (Paris's ring road) at Porte de la Chapelle or the Porte de Bagnolet (access ramps). Air France shuttle buses leave every 15 mins for the Centre International de Paris at **Porte Maillot** in western Paris, not far from the Champs Élysées. **Roissy-Rail** service provides trains every 15 mins to the **Gare du Nord** railway station in the north of Paris (30 mins journey) and on to the *Châtelet-Les Halles Métro* stop; this is by far the most reliable means of transport. The number 351 bus runs to the Porte de Bagnolet, the Porte de Vincennes and to the Place de la Nation, all in eastern Paris. The time required for travelling between Roissy and central Paris by road varies considerably according to the time of day : 30-40 mins are sufficient during slack periods, whereas during the rush-hour (7 : 30-10 & 4:30-7:30) the journey may take well over an hour.

Air France shuttle-buses run every 15 mins between the **Orly** terminals and the **Invalides** *aerogare* terminal in central Paris, with a request stop at Montparnasse (farther south). The number 215 bus runs to the Place Denfert-Rochereau in southern Paris. There is an excellent **Orly-Rail** train service (every 15 mins) to the **Gare d'Austerlitz** station in southeastern Paris and on to **Saint-Michel** and the **Gare d'Orsay** stations on the Seine's Left Bank. Travel time for the train is approximately 40 mins, whereas by road the time varies between 25 mins and 1 hr, according to the time of day. The Orly terminals are situated to the south of the city on the A6 autoroute, which connects with the Boulevard Périphérique at Porte d'Orléans and Porte d'Italie. Taxis are widely available at all three airports.

There are regular bus shuttles between Roissy-Charles de Gaulle Airport and the Orly terminals; the average journey takes approximately 75 mins, but passengers should allow at least 90 mins during the rush-hour.

For travellers in a hurry, or simply wishing to view Paris from the air (a stunning sight), there is now a **helicopter shuttle service** between Roissy and Orly airports, and from the airports to a heliport at the Porte de Sèvres in southern Paris (Métro : Place Balard). Private air services use the *zone d'aviation d'affaires* (business-flght zone) at **Le Bourget Airport** on the A1 autoroute north of Paris, before reaching Roissy. Air-taxis and private hire-craft are available here for every conceivable destination.

Air France Offices Abroad

- **U.K. :** 158 New Bond St. London W1 ☎ (01) 499 8611 ; **Heathrow Airport :** (01) 759 2311.
- **U.S.A. : (New York)** 666 Fifth Av ☎ (212) 841 7301 ; 1350 Ave. of the Americas ☎ (212) 841 7300 ; 888 Seventh Ave. ☎ (212) 247 0100 ; J. F. Kennedy Airport (212) 632 7200. **(Chicago and Midwestern regions)** John Hancock Center, 875 N. Michigan Ave. Mezzanine 60611 Chicago IL ☎ (312) 440.79.22 ; 22 South Michigan Ave. Chicago IL 60603 ☎ (312) 984 0200 ; O'Hare International Airport : (312) 686 4531. **(Los Angeles)** 510 West 6th St Suite 1128 Los Angeles CLA 90014 ☎ (312) 688 9200. Los Angeles Airport : (213) 6460028.
- **Canada :** 979 Ouest Bd. de Maisonneuve **Montréal** H3A 1M4 ☎ (514) 284 2825 ; Mirabel Airport : ☎ (514) 476 3838 ; 100 Sparks St. Trust Building **Ottawa** Ont ☎ (613) 236 0601 ; 2 Place Québec Suite 742 **Quebec** ☎ (418) 692 0733 ; 151 Bloor St West Suite 600 **Toronto** Ont ☎ (416) 364 0101 ; 700 West Georgia Suite 1120 **Vancouver** B.C. ☎ (604) 733 4151.

Other carriers

- **British Airways : U.K.** — (01) 897.40.00; **U.S.A.** — New York : (212) 687 1600; Chicago : (312) 786 1340; Los Angeles : (213) 748 2275; Washington D.C. (202) 393 5300;.
- **British Caledonian : U.K.** — (01) 293.278.90; **U.S.A.**-Houston : (713) 445 3501.
- **Capitol Air : U.S.A.** — (toll-free) (800) CAPITOL.
- **Pan American :** New York : (212) 687 2600 ; Chicago : (312) 332 4900 ; Los Angeles : (213) 670 7301 ; Washington D.C. : (207) 845 8000.
- **TWA : U.S.A.-New York :** (212) 290 2141; Chicago (312) 332 1118; Los Angeles : (213) 484 9319; Washington D.C. : (207) 737 7404 : **U.K.** (01) 636.40.90.
- **Airline reservations in Paris :** Air France : 45.35.61.61; Air Inter : 45.39.25.25 ; TAT (all domestic) : 46.87.35.53 ; UTA : 47.76.41.52 ; Air Canada : 47.42.21.21 : Alitalia : 42.56.65.00; British Airways : 47.78.14.14; British Caledonian : 42.61.50.21 ; Capitol Air : 47.55.87.62 ; El Al : 47.42.41.29 ; Iberia :

47.23.00.23; Japan Airlines : 42.25.85.05; KLM : 42.66.57.19; Lufthansa : 42.65.37.35; Pan Am : 42.66.45.45; Royal Air Maroc : 42.66.10.30; SAS : 47.42.06.14; Swissair : 45.81.11.01; Tunis Air : 42.61.82.40; Turkish Airlines : 47.42.60.85; TWA : 47.20.62.11; Varig : 47.20.03.33.

Information • **Roissy-Charles de Gaulle** Airport general enquiries : 48.62.22.80.
• **Orly-Sud/Orly-Ouest** general enq. : 48.84.32.10; Air France : 46.75.78.00; Air Inter : 46.87.12.12; Porte Maillot Terminal *(Centre International de Paris)* general enq. : 47.58.20.18.
• **Aerogare des Invalides Terminal** general enq. : 45.50.32.30.
• **Air France Offices :** 119 av. des Champs Élysées 75008 Paris ☎ (1) 45.35.61.61 and numerous other locations throughout the country (→ gazetteer section).
• **Helicopter shuttle :** Helifrance, Héliport de Paris ☎ 45.54.95.11.
• **Air-taxis and private hire :** Air Enterprise : 48.62.50.71; Darta Mercure : 48.62.54.54; Euralair : 48.38.92.73; Europe Falcon Service : 48.38.91.26.
• (→ France by air).

Rail France is linked into Europe's extensive railway system and can be reached by rail from such faraway destinations as Leningrad, Istanbul and even Vladivostock (→ France by rail).

Ferries The ferry boats that ply continously between England and France contribute to making the English Channel the world's busiest stretch of sea. The number of ferry services is such that only during the height of the holiday season - the last weekends in July and August, for example - will passengers encounter any difficulty in obtaining even last-minute reservations. There are ferries for rail, car and foot passengers (motorcycles, bicycles, coaches and trucks can be ferried, too); the choice of crossings is extensive, as is the choice of accommodation. The simplest and fastest crossing is certainly by the air-cushioned Hovercraft from Dover, (35 mins in good weather) fitted with standard airline-type seats. For longer crossings, such as the Southampton-Le-Havre night sailing, reclining armchairs and cabins are available; the traditional Dover-Calais ferryboat still provides 90 mins of sea-breezes (in good weather) for upper-deck passengers and duty-free drinking for those who prefer the warmth of the bar.

Information • Information and reservations can be obtained from most travel agents, or directly from the ferry companies : **Brittany Ferries** (Portsmouth/Plymouth Saint-Malo/Roskoff); ☎ : Saint-Malo enquiries, 99.56.68.40, (07) 52.18.21; reservations, 98.69.76.22; Roskoff enquiries, 98.69.76.33; Plymouth (07) 522.13.21; Portsmouth. Paris, c/o Paris Voyages, 11 rue de la Chaussée d'Antin 75009 Paris ☎ (1) 47.70.43.25.
• **Hoverspeed** (Dover-Calais/Boulogne) : Calais information and reservations ☎ (1) 21.96.67.10; Boulogne 21.30.27.26; Dover (03) 304.208.013, 4 rue de la Paix 75002 Paris ☎ (1) 42.60.36.48.
• **Sally-The Viking Line** (Ramsgate-Dunkirk); Dunkirk ☎ 28.68.43.44; Ramsgate enquiries (0843) 595566; reservations (0843) 595522.
• **Sealink** (British Rail & S.N.C.F.; Dover/Folkstone/Weymouth/Newhaven - Boulogne/Calais/Cherbourg/Dieppe/Dunkirk : 179 Piccadilly London W1V.OBA. ☎ (01) 493 4451; 12 bd de la Madeleine 75009 Paris ☎ (1) 42.61.85.40; enquiries and reservations in most major British Rail and S.N.C.F. booking offices.
• **Townsend-Thoresen** (Dover/Portsmouth-Calais/Cherbourg/Le Havre); Calais ☎ 21.34.41.90; Cherbourg 33.44.20.13; Le Havre 35.21.36.50; Portsmouth (0705) 755 521; Dover (0304) 223 605; London : 127 Regent's Street W.1., ☎ (01) 734 4431; Paris : 41 bd des Capucines 75002 Paris ☎ (1) 42.61.51.75.

Customs, passports and visas

Customs Visitors to France may import limited amounts of perfume, alcoholic drinks and tobacco free of import duty : details of these allowances are available in airports, rail and ferry terminals. These allowances are more generous for travellers arriving from E.E.C. countries (in addition to France : Belgium, Denmark, Greece, Ireland, Italy, Luxembourg, the Netherlands, Spain, West Germany, the United Kingdom).
Presents valued up to 1 400 FF (400 FF for persons under 15) may be brought into France duty-free by travellers from E.E.C. countries. Pre-

sents valued up to 300 FF (150 FF for persons under 15) may be brought into France duty-free by travellers from other countries.
Personal articles : all the usual portable personal requisites are allowed in duty-free.
Foreign currency is not subject to restrictions on entry; however, if more than 5 000 FF is to be re-exported, then a "declaration of entry" form should be completed on arrival and countersigned by the customs officer : this form will be requested on leaving France.
Animals under three months are forbidden to enter France; for those over this age, entry is limited to three animals, only one of which can be a puppy. Possession of an antirabies certificate (or a certificate stating that the animal's country of origin has been free of rabies for three years) is obligatory.
Importing gold is forbidden, except as personal jewellery.
Vehicles : The only vehicles subject to customs formalities on entry are new "mopeds" (peddle motorbikes) 50 cc^3. Automobiles, caravans, motor-homes, cycles and motor-cycles must be re-exported within six months, otherwise they become liable to import duty. During this period these vehicles must not be sold, lent or rented.
Value-Added Tax (V.A.T.) can be deducted from the price of goods bought in France : persons over 15, normally residing outside France and staying in the country for less than six months, can obtain this privilege by providing proof of identity at the time of purchase. The V.A.T. will either be deducted from the price of the article(s), or forwarded by the vendor on receipt of the sales docket, stamped at customs on exportation. The value of purchases from each vendor must be equal to at least 1 400 FF per article (or items making up an article, e.g., a three-piece suit or a dinner service) for E.E.C. residents and 800 FF for residents outside the E.E.C., regardless of the number of articles. Tobacco, foodstuffs, guns, medicine, gold and unset precious stones, as well as certain other categories of goods do not qualify for V.A.T. deduction.

Information

• **French Customs Information Centre,** 182, rue Saint-Honoré 75001 Paris ☎ (1) 42.60.35.90/42.61.56.02.

Passports and Visas

Visas are not required for U.S., Canada, U.K. and most Commonwealth nationals. However, a valid passport is required, although British subjects may use the simpler British Visitor's Passport or the new excursion pass, available from Post Offices. For stays of three months, a resident's permit *(carte de séjour)* is mandatory for foreign nationals. Apply to the nearest French consular service before departure or to the local préfecture once in France. (Non-E.E.C. nationals may be refused a resident's permit if they have entered the country as a tourist.) The E.E.C. resident's permit automatically allows the holder to take up employment in France; citizens of other countries must apply for a work permit — not easily granted at the present time, especially to applicants having entered the country as tourists.

France in 7, 15, or 21 days

Naturally, one week is too short a time to glimpse anything but a sampling of all that France has to offer. Nevertheless, a brief visit can form a rich mosaic of France's countryside and will certainly whet the appetite for a longer visit.
A 15-day itinerary opens up an enthralling variety of landscapes, architecture, traditions and cuisine which make France so attractive. Over 21 days the visitor is invited on a veritable *tour de France.*
Of course, France wouldn't be France without Paris, and all three itineraries start in the "City of Light" and continue onward to include both well-known and many lesser-known sites of interest for the visitor to this most delightful of countries.
Refer to the index at the end of this guide for the gazetteer pages describing places recommended in the itineraries.

7 days

— **Day 1 : Paris★★★ :** see the Eiffel Tower, the Champs Élysées and the Tuileries, and pay a quick visit to the masterpieces of the Louvre

Museum, Notre-Dame Cathedral and Ile-de-la-Cité; take a boat trip on the Seine in the evening.

— **Day 2 : Paris★★★ :** see the Madeleine Church and the Opéra, the stores along the *Grands Boulevards,* the district of Les Halles (lunch), then, stroll in the Marais Quarter before dining in Montmartre.

— **Day 3 :** Take the autoroute (A10 & A11) to **Chartres★★★** (visit the cathedral), then the N10 & D924 to **Blois★★ :** a walk around the town, lunch, then visit the château. Spend the afternoon driving along the **Loire Valley** from **Chambord★★★** to **Orléans★** before taking the autoroute back to Paris.

— **Day 4 :** Spend the morning visiting the château and the park at **Versailles★★★** before lunching and returning to **Paris★★★** to wander around the Left Bank, from the start of the Boulevard Saint-Germain to Montparnasse and the Latin Quarter.

— **Day 5 :** Take the **T.G.V.** high-speed train to **Mâcon** (1 h 41 mins!), hire a car (→ France by train) and spend a day in Burgundy; Romanesque art and architecture, history, wine and gastronomy. See the abbey at **Cluny★★,** then go on to **Tournus★★,** before taking the autoroute to **Beaune★★★** (lunch). Tour the region during the afternoon, arriving at **Dijon★★★** for dinner. Take a night-sleeper train to Marseilles.

— **Day 6 : Marseilles★★ :** a quick look around the town, then off by car to **Aix-en-Provence★★★** for a tour of the town and lunch. Take the autoroute to Le Luc then cross the Maures Massif (mountains) to **Saint-Tropez★★** for dinner and a night's rest.

— **Day 7 :** Visit Saint-Tropez, then take the cliff road (*Corniche de l'Esterel*★★) to **Cannes★★** (lunch). Tour the countryside back of the Riviera **(Côte d'Azur★★★)** and finish the day in **Nice★★,** where there are night trains to Paris, as well as an international airport.

15 days — **Days 1 & 2 : Paris★★★,** as above.

— **Day 3 : Versailles★★★** and **Paris★★★;** see Day 4 above.

— **Day 4 :** By car along the A13 autoroute to **Rouen★★★,** for a quick tour of the town (cathedral, Saint-Maclou church, Rue du Gros-Horloge and the old marketplace), then on again by autoroute to **Honfleur★★** (lunch). In the afternoon, visit **Deauville★, Cabourg, Arromanches** (reminiscences of the 1944 Normandy landings), **Bayeux★★** (cathedral and the Bayeux Tapestry). Spend the evening in **Caen★★★.**

— **Day 5 :** Spend the morning visiting Caen and Avranches before moving on to **Mont-Saint-Michel★★★** (visit and lunch). See **Saint-Malo★★★** and **Dinard** in the afternoon, then **Fréhel Cape★★★** before returning to **Dinan★★** for the evening.

— **Day 6 :** From Dinan drive to **Rennes★★** and **Angers★★** (château, tapestry museum; lunch), traverse the Loire Valley as far as **Tours★★** for a late afternoon visit and an evening's rest.

— **Day 7 :** Tour the Loire Valley, stopping to visit one of the châteaux **(Amboise★★, Chenonceaux★★★, Chaumont★★, Blois★★** or **Chambord★★★)** before returning to Paris on the A10 autoroute.

— **Days 8 & 9 :** Spend two days relaxing in **Paris★★★;** visit a few museums, parks and gardens, or the outlying quarters (or spend more time in the places that struck you during the first three days).

— **Day 10 :** Take a plane to **Bordeaux★★★,** hire a car; after a brief tour of the town, spend the day visiting the châteaux vineyards... and sample their wares!

— **Day 11 :** On by car through the **Dordogne Valley★★★** and the **Périgord Region,** through **Bergerac** to **Sarlat★★★** (gastronomic lunch); in the afternoon, make a detour to **Rocamadour★** and the chasm *(gouffre)* at **Padirac★★.** Spend the evening at **Figeac★.**

— **Day 12 :** From Figeac to **Villefranche-de-Rouergue★,** where the market is held in an old arcaded square; lunch at **Rodez★.** Drive via Sévérac-le-Château along the **Tarn Gorges★★★** before stopping for the night at **Florac.**

— **Day 13 :** Take the D9/D907 cliff road, the **Corniche des Cévennes★★★,** which winds through breathtaking scenery towards Anduze (where the bamboo grove is unique in Europe), then on to **Nîmes★★★.** After lunch and a tour of this ancient Roman town, finish the day at **Avignon★★★,** with its splendid Papal Palace.

— **Day 14 :** From Avignon, take the autoroute to **Aix-en-Provence★★★** for lunch and sightseeing. The autoroute then will take you across the

mountainous Maures Massif to **Saint-Tropez★★** in time for dinner.
— **Day 15 :** Saint-Tropez, **Nice★★;** see Day 7of the 7-day programme.

21 Days

— **Days 1, 2 and 3 : Paris★★★** and **Versailles★★★,** as above.
— **Day 4 :** Leave early by car for **Rheims★★★** A4 autoroute); visit the cathedral and a champagne cellar. Take the autoroute, then the N44 and N4 via Châlons-sur-Marne and **Toul★★** to **Nancy★★★,** a town rich in 18thC and Art Nouveau architecture; lunch in the Stainville area and visit Nancy itself in the afternoon. Travel on to Strasbourg via **Lunéville★★** and **Saverne.**
— **Day 5 :** Visit **Strasbourg★★★** and lunch in the charming Petite France Quarter. Drive along the **Alsace Wine Route★★★.** Finish the day with a tour of **Colmar★★★** and spend the night at **Mulhouse.**
— **Day 6 :** Visit one of Mulhouse's fine technical museums, then take the autoroute to **Beaune★★★** for lunch, sightseeing and dinner.
— **Day 7 :** Spend the day touring the **Burgundy** and **Beaujolais** regions : Beaune, **La Rochepot★★★, Tournus★★, Cluny★★** (lunch), and the **Mâconnals** Reglon. Spend the nlght In Lyons.
— **Day 8 : Lyons★★★;** see the Roman town and the old town *(Vieux Lyon),* test Lyons' reputation as a gastronomical haven...
— **Day 9 :** Lyons to **Grenoble** by autoroute, then drive along the **Route Napoléon★** (N85) to **Nice★★** (lunch in the **Gap** area, or detour to the shores of **Lake Serre-Ponçon★★**).
— **Day 10 :** Tour the **Côte d'Azur★★★** (Riviera) and its magnificent hinterland; visit **Monte-Carlo★★** and **Menton★★.** Drive along the **Grande Corniche★★** (breathtakingly beautiful cliff road); see **Vence★** and **Cannes★★.**
— **Day 11 :** Visit Cannes, drive along the **Corniche de l'Esterel★★,** then through **Saint-Tropez★★,** across the Maures Massif and along the autoroute to **Aix-en-Provence★★★.**
— **Day 12 :** Visit the Papal Palace in **Avignon★★★** in the morning, then leave for **Nîmes★★★.** After lunch in this ancient Roman town, drive along the **Corniche des Cévennes★★★** and admire the splendid scenery from this cliff road (D907 and D9). Spend the night in **Florac.**
— **Day 13 :** Head south across the flanks of **Mont Aigoual** via Le Vigan, the extraordinary natural amphitheatre of the **Cirque de Navacelles★★,** and **Saint-Guilhem-le-Désert.** Lunch at **Montpellier★★★** and visit the town before setting out for the coast and spending the night at **Sète★.**
— **Day 14 :** Visit Sète, **Béziers★, Fontfroide Abbey★★** and **Carcassonne★★★** (lunch). Take the autoroute to **Toulouse★★★** and visit the town in the late afternoon.
— **Day 15 :** Drive up to the **Périgord Region** via **Montauban★★** and **Cahors★,** with a detour toward **Rocamadour★** to the chasm *(gouffre)* at **Padirac★★** (lunch at Gramat or Alvignac). Tour the valleys of the **Dordogne★★★** and rivers **Vézère★★★** (see **Les Eyzies★★★**) before returning to **Sarlat★★★** for the night.
— **Day 16 :** After visiting Sarlat, see **Périgueux★** and **Brantôme★★** (lunch) before heading to **Poitiers★★★** via **Angoulême★★** (cathedral).
— **Day 17 :** Visit Poitiers in the morning, then take the autoroute toward the **Loire Valley.** Lunch at **Blois★★,** detour to see the château at **Chambord★★★,** then drive back down the valley to **Tours★★** via **Chaumont★★, Amboise★★** and, time permitting, **Chenonceaux★★★.**
— **Day 18 :** Visit Tours, then head through the **Loire Valley** and **Saumur★★** to **Angers★★;** visit the château and the tapestry museum. Drive on to **Rennes★★** via Châteaubriant.
— **Day 19 :** Drive from Rennes to **Caen★★★;** (reversing Day 5 of the preceding programme).
— **Day 20 : Caen** to **Paris;** (reversing Day 4 of the preceding programme).
— **Day 21 :** At your leisure in **Paris★★★.**

Hints

— Use the train-auto and fly-drive schemes offered by the French Railway (S.N.C.F.) and Air-Inter (→ France by train; France by plane).
— Book hotel rooms and restaurants well in advance in peak season.
— An after-dinner walk is one the most pleasant ways to gain an overall impression of a town.
— Consult the relevant gazetteer section of the guide for restaurant and museum closing days.

Emergencies

Throughout France, two telephone numbers are used to summon help in emergencies :
- **Police rescue** *(Police secours)* : 17.
- **Fire brigade** *(Sapeurs-Pompiers)* : 18.

These numbers are to a certain extent complementary, both police and firemen being equipped with emergency medical-treatment services, generally coordinated with SAMU *(Service d'Aide Médicale d'Urgence).*
E.E.C. residents should complete form CMI before departing for France : this will ensure subsequent reimbursement of any medical expenses incurred while on holiday. Full details from local health authorities. North American medical-insurance policies should be checked for terms of coverage when the holder is abroad.
Under French law, the police may hold suspects *incommunicado* for two consecutive 24-hour periods while investigations deemed necessary are made. Detainees are entitled to a doctor's visit and may refuse to reply to questions until they have conferred with a lawyer. After 48 hours, the police must charge or release the detainee, or apply to a magistrate for a prolongation of this *garde à vue* (literally, "keeping in sight"), which is only granted in exceptional circumstances.
Most police stations *(commissariats)* have at least one staff member who speaks a foreign language. Defence lawyers and interpreters are made available to detainees appearing before a magistrate.

Emergency telephone numbers are contained in each gazetteer section; these generally correspond to the SAMU services mentioned above and/or the local *gendarme* unit.

Some useful numbers for Paris and its suburbs :
- *SAMU* (emergency medical service) : ☎ (1) 45.67.50.50.
- Poisoning emergency centre (immediate advice : list of antidotes to every type of poisoning; emergency intervention, if necessary) : ☎ (1) 42.05.63.29.
- Serious burn wounds : Saint-Antoine Hospital : ☎ (1) 43.44.33.33. ext. 23.60.
- *S.O.S. Médecins* 24 hr visiting doctor service for which there is a fee. ☎ 43.37.77.77.
- All-night chemist : Dhéry, 84 av. des Champs-Élysées 75008 Paris ☎ (1) 45.62.02.41.
- *S.O.S. Dentistes* (emergency dental treatment after 8 pm and on Sundays and national holidays for which there is a fee. ☎ 43.37.51.00.

Money

The French monetary unit is the **franc,** subdivided into 100 **centimes.** Confusion may arise when the French talk in terms of "old" francs (which in fact correspond to the current centimes); prices are, however, always in "new" francs.
Currency-exchange facilities are available in most banks, all the major railway stations and airports, and at some major TO and SI locations. The rates obtained from these sources generally will be better than those offered by hotels, shops and restaurants. Some exchange facilities remain open until late at night and on Sundays and national holidays.

Major exchange offices — **Paris :** open all day : Union des Banques, 125 av. des Champs-Élysées 75008 ☎ (1) 47.20.77.19 (8:45-5 weekdays; 9:45-1 pm & 2-6 Sat. and Sun.).
— **Paris : railway stations :** Gare de Lyon, every day 6:30 am-11 pm; Gare d'Austerlitz 7 am-9 pm (closed Sun.); Gare Montparnasse, Mon.-Sat. 9-6; Sun 10-6; Gare Saint-Lazare, Mon-Fri 7 am-9 pm; Sat 9-6.
— **Major airports :** Roissy-Charles-de-Gaulle, every day, 6 am-11:30 pm; Orly, every day, 6:30 am-11:30 pm; Marseilles, every day, 8:30-7:30 (closes 11 am Sun.); Nice, every day, 8:30-7; Bordeaux, Mon.-Sat. 8:45-12:30 & 1-5.

Banks Banks in France are open from Monday to Friday from 9-4:30, and on Saturdays and days preceding national holidays from 9-noon. Some BRED bank branches in Paris and some suburban and provincial banks remain open all day on Saturdays, and close on Mondays. Most holiday resorts have banking facilities during the peak season.

Travellers' cheques

All major travellers' cheques are accepted by French banks; most hotels, shops and restaurants also accept this form of payment, although the exchange rate may not be especially advantageous.

Credit cards

The **Visa** card, which operates in France in conjunction with **Carte Bleue,** is by far the most widely accepted credit card. Not all hotels, restaurants (check before booking) and shops accept Diners Club and American Express cards, although both these organisations do have very extensive French networks (the American Express office behind the Opéra building in Paris provides a wide range of banking, credit card and other services for visitors).

• **Anti-theft advice :** As a general rule, take the same precautions with credit cards as with cash or travellers' cheques. After payment, make sure that it is your card which has been returned.
• In case of loss :
— Visa/Carte Bleue : ☎ (1) 42.77.11.90. American Express : ☎ (1) 47.08.31.21. Diners Club : ☎ (1) 47.23.78.05. Eurocard/Master Charge : ☎ (1) 43.23.46.46.

Post and telephone

The postal and telephone service in France is run by the same state-controlled organisation, *Poste et Télécommunications : PTT* (pronounce "pay tay tay" when asking directions). Most post offices are open on weekdays from 8 am-7 pm (smaller offices close for lunch between noon and 2 pm) and from 8-noon on Saturday. The main post office at 52 rue du Louvre 75001 Paris is **open 24 hours non-stop,** and telephone directories from all over the world can be consulted there. Letters can be sent ***poste restante*** to any French post office *(bureau de poste)* and can be collected for a small fee on proof of identity. The **maximum weight** for basic-rate, first-class letters is 20 gr. **Letterboxes** are painted bright yellow, and can always be found near tobacco stores *(tabacs),* where stamps are also sold.

Telephones

Direct-dialing is possible to anywhere in the U.K. and U.S.A. More and more call-boxes (phone booths) are equipped with modern instruments that allow direct-dialed international calls. Some *taxiphones,* that allow local calls only, often using a pre-purchased token *(jeton)* remain in *cafés* and restaurants. Hotels and restaurants are legally allowed to charge higher-than-standard rates for calls made by clients : the difference on international calls can be painfully steep.
Calls made to outside the locality are charged at the rate of one unit for a duration that varies according to the time of day and the destination (as short as three seconds for the U.S.A. during the day). These rates are displayed in post offices and call-boxes, and are contained in the telephone directory *(bottin).* A new system of **reduced-rate calls** has come into force in the EEC countries : 30 % reduction for calls made after 6:30 pm and 70 % for calls made after 11 pm and all day Sundays and national holidays. Reduced rates for the U.S.A. are in effect 10 pm-10 am (French time) and all day Sundays.
All the French phone numbers have been changed since Oct. 1985. Each number — Paris and regions — is now an 8-figure number.
— Paris, Hauts-de-Seine, Seine-Saint-Denis, Val-de-Marne: same number as before but preceded by 4; ex: 564.22.22 → 45.64.22.22.
— Ile-de-France, each number preceded by 6 (Seine-et-Marne, Essonne), or by 3 (Yvelines, Val-d'Oise).
— Departments, each number preceded by the code number; ex: (98) 85.04.32 → 98.85.04.32.
• When dialing a long-distance number from Paris: dial 16 before the 8-figure number.
• When making interdepartmental calls: do not dial 16, just the 8-figure number.
• When dialing Paris and Ile-de-France from departments: dial 16, then the code prefix (1) and the 8-figure number.
• When dialing from Paris to Ile-de-France: do not use 16, just the 8-figure number.

• To dial internationally, first dial 19, wait for the new tone then dial the code for the country, followed by the area code and the number. For **person-to-person** *(avec préavis)* [*avec avis d'appel*], or **booked** (call record; *avec avis d'appel*) [*avec préavis*], dial 10.

Telegrammes Can be sent from a post office, by phone (dial 14), or by telex. Telegrammes can also be registered (with signed delivery), with reply prepaid.

Hints — Use the full postal code on mail to avoid delays in delivery.
— Public call-boxes retain only the coins necessary for the duration of the call; unused coins are returned. Callers can thus "stock" the phone in advance : unused coins are returned (use 1-franc rather than 5-franc coins.
— Enquiries : concerning the postal system ☎ (1) 42.80.69.89. Directory (information) enquiries, Paris : 12. Provinces : 16 + 11 + 12; International : 19 + 33 + country and area code number.

Note — French telephone numbers are given in this guide in the form that the visitor will encounter throughout France, i.e. with periods separating the groups of numbers. When giving a phone number, for example, 43.29.12.24, **the French do not cite the individual digits;** instead, groups of digits are expressed in tens (e.g., *quarante-trois, vingt-neuf, douze, vingt-quatre*). If your French is not fluent, this can be very confusing; **ask for the number** *chiffre par chiffre* **(digit-by-digit).** This habit of expressing numbers in groups applies to postal codes, reference numbers, in fact, every situation in which numbers are used.

Children and young people

In general, children are well catered to in France, whether in terms of beach facilities (the children's magazine *Mickey* organises excellent beach-activity clubs throughout the summer in all the major resort centres; for a very reasonable fee, parents can leave their children all morning and all afternoon in the hands of experienced monitors), or in terms of holiday camps and specific leisure activities (→ below).

Restaurants The vast majority of establishments will provide simple dishes for children, or will allow children to share adult portions. There is no restriction on children entering premises licenced to sell alcoholic drinks, provided that they are accompanied by an adult.

Travel The restaurants situated along France's network of autoroutes offer facilities for children, including special menus and, in a number of cases, nappy (diaper) changing and bottle-warming rooms for travellers with babies. Similar services are available on some French trains, and under certain circumstances hostesses may be available to supervise children travelling alone (→ France by train). The major domestic airline, Air Inter, provides a wide range of facilities for children and babies. Children 4 years and more may fly unaccompanied : advance reservation is necessary. Further details from Air France offices or travel agents. A 50 % reduction in rail fares applies to children from 4-12 years, children from 2-12 years pay reduced rates for off-peak air travel (→ France by plane; France by train).

Camps In addition to the scouting movement, which organises summer camps on an international basis, a number of French-based organisations welcome English-speaking children at their holiday camps and villages :
— **Vacances-Loisirs,** 33, rue de Beaune, 75007 Paris ☎ (1) 46.45.04.16; for 9-12 year olds : workshops (pottery, etc.), ponies and a swimming pool on a model farm where children participate in daily tasks.
— **Loisirs de France,** 30, rue Godot-de-Mauroy, 75009 Paris ☎ (1) 47.42.51.81; 11 mountain or seaside holiday centres.
— **Fédération Nationale des Gîtes de France,** 35, rue Godot-de-Mauroy, 75009 Paris ☎ (1) 47.42.25.43; **U.K. :** Farm Holidays, 178 Piccadilly, London W1V 0AL ☎ 491.7622; children's holiday gîtes (→ Gîtes).
— **Centre Nautique de Rosbras-Brignau,** B.P. 3, 29116 Moëlan-sur-Mer ☎ 98.39.60.78; sailing for 8-14 year olds (basic French required).

— **Pierre et Vacances,** 74110 Morzine ☎ 50.74.04.46; children's mountain holiday village at Avoriaz (climbing, etc.).
— **Agriculture et Tourisme,** 9, av. Georges-V, 75008 Paris ☎ (1) 47.23.51.50; farm holidays for children.
— The regional **Loisirs-Accueil** organisations accept bookings for groups of 4 children (6-10 years) for farm holidays (→ Gazetteer section for addresses).

Hints

— *Europe with Children,* by Leila Hadley (750 p. NY 1972, revised 1984) : an excellent source of advice and information for travellers with children.

Young people

In addition to the traditional international organisations, such as the scouting movement or youth hostels, a number of lesser-known associations offer constructive holidays built around subjects ranging from computers and astronomy to pony-trekking and archeological excavations (considerable youth-orientated information is contained under the relevant subject headings of this guide).
The vast majority of special-interest holidays and instructional courses require basic French; beginners should not, however, be discouraged : the willingness to communicate is more important than the degree of proficiency.

Sources of Information

— Most French youth organisations affiliated with their foreign counterparts will generally be able to provide information on related activities in France.

— Among French sources the **C.I.D.J.** *(Centre d'Information et de Documentation de jeunesse)* is certainly the most extensive; it also provides a wealth of detailed leisure-activity information, classified according to subject and time of year. Visitors to C.I.D.J. centres may also consult a notices board (time-sharing, sales, swaps, etc.).
A second source of information is furnished by the **Directions Départementales du Temps Libre, de la Jeunesse et des Sports,** pioneers of such interesting schemes as P.A.J. and *Connaissance de France* (→ below).
The **O.T.U.** *(Organisation pour le Tourisme Universitaire)* organises and provides information about travel and holidays (including language courses) in France.

Travel

(→ France by train; France by plane.)
— Parents lending their cars to children on holiday in France should first check with their insurance company; restrictions or surcharges may apply.
— Hitch-hiking : (→ Getting to France).

Accommodation

Apart from the extensive youth-hostel network (→ relevant section), a number of organisations specialise in providing accommodation for young people. Among the most noteworthy are **A.J.F.** *(Accueil des Jeunes en France)* which runs three reception centres in Paris and guarantees accommodation for arriving young visitors on very short notice : **Gare du Nord** arrival hall ☎ (1) 42.85.86.19; 9:15-6:15 Mon.-Fri.; summer : 8:15-9:30, 7 days a week. **Hôtel de Ville,** 16, rue du Pont Louis-Philippe, 75004 Paris ☎ (1) 42.78.04.82; 9:30-6:30 Mon.-Fri.; summer : 9-7, 7 days a week; *Métro :* Hôtel de Ville or Pont Marie. **Beaubourg,** 119, rue St.-Martin, 75004 Paris ☎ (1) 42.27.87.80; open 9-7 Mon.-Sat.; *Métro :* Rambuteau or Hôtel de Ville or Châtelet-Les Halles. Group accommodation should be booked in advance through the main office : 12, rue des Barres, 75004 Paris ☎ 42.72.72.09.

U.C.R.I.F. *(Union des Centres de Rencontres Internationales de France),* 21, rue Béranger, 75003 Paris ☎ (1) 42.27.08.65; in association with international exchange organisations, U.C.R.I.F. offers a wide range of accommodation throughout France in well-equipped centres with a variety of activities. The aim is to promote international encounters, and language courses and conferences are thus a feature of many centres. In addition, some have swimming pools, tennis courts, skating rinks and other such facilities. A trilingual brochure giving full details is available from U.C.R.I.F. or F.G.T.O. An information and reservation centre is situated at the Gare du Nord in Paris ☎ (1) 48.74.68.69.

O.T.U. *(Office de Tourisme Universitaire),* offers single accommodation without prior reservation at 47 student centres located in 32 French cities.

Student cards, visas A wide range of reductions (cinema, theatre, etc.) are available to student card-holders; and check to be sure of card validity before leaving for France.
Non-E.E.C. nationals must obtain a visa before departure if their stay is likely to exceed three months.

Individual itineraries *Passeport vacances :* freedom of itinerary with accommodation in holiday and leisure centres (camps or dormitories with meals); details available from the U.F.C.V. *(Union française des centres de vacances).* The **P.A.J.** *(Points-Accueil-Jeunes)* scheme adopts a similar formula : 400 low-priced stopovers (list from *Directions Départementales du Temps Libre, Jeunesse et sports).*

Connaissance de la France *Getting to Know France* is a program of 10-day regional discovery sessions bringing together the French and visitors aged 16-35, organised by the **Ministère du Temps Libre, Jeunesse et sport.**

Sports **O.C.C.A.J.** and **U.C.P.A.** offer sports holidays for the 16-35 age group at more than 60 centres throughout France. Mountaineering, hiking, sailing, skiing, tennis and riding are just a few of the activities proposed. The travel agency **Terres d'Aventure** specialises in rambling (hiking) and nature activities and the **Nouvelles Frontières** travel agency offers a wide range of sports holidays (brochure available). The **Glénans** organisation is world-famous for its sailing holiday centres (→ Sailing).

Student exchanges One of the best ways for young people to learn a language and to get to know a culture and its present society. The list of exchange possibilities is endless, and the best source of information is certainly the cultural-affairs section of a local French Embassy or Consulate where information also is available on supporting grants to foreign students. Among the better-known organisations specialising in exchanges : **Franco-American Cultural Students Exchange,** 108 Westwood Bvd. Los Angeles CA 90024 ☎ (213) 208 5542; **Association for International Practical Training,** 217 American Bvd. Columbia MD 21044 ☎ (301) 997 2200; **Robertson's E.T.S.,** 44 Willoughby Rd. London NW3 ☎ (01) 435 4907; **Central Bureau for Educational Visits and Exchanges,** Seymour Mews House Seymour Mews London WIH 9PE ☎ (01) 486 5101 exchanges, some openings for paid employment (*Working Holidays* guide also available in bookshops).

General Information

- → **F.G.T.O.,** *France for Sports and Leisure,* a list of school travel operators is also available.
- **C.I.D.J.** *(Centre d'Information et Documentation de Jeunesse),* 101, quai Branly, 75015 Paris ☎ (1) 45.66.40.20. Provincial centres : Amiens, Besançon, Bordeaux, Caen, Cergy-Pontoise, Clermont-Ferrand, Dijon, Evry, Lille, Limoges, Lyons, Marseilles, Montpellier, Nancy, Nantes, Nice, Poitiers, Rennes, Strasbourg, Toulouse (addresses from town halls, SI or TO).
- **Ligue Française pour les Auberges de la Jeunesse,** 83, rue de Rennes, 75006 Paris, ☎ (1) 45.49.11.73.
- **Union Française des Centres de Vacances** (U.F.C.V.), 71-77, rue du Théâtre, 75015 Paris ☎ (1) 45.78.27.45; extensive range of student holiday services; English-language brochure.
Bureau des Voyages de la Jeunesse, 20, rue J.-J.-Rousseau, 75001 Paris ☎ (1) 42.36.88.18.

Scientific

- **A.N.S.T.J.** *(Association Nationale Sciences et Techniques Jeunesse),* 17, av. Gambetta, 91130 Ris-Orangis ☎ (1) 69.06.82.20; linked with the Paris science museum, *Palais de la Découverte.* **A.N.S.T.J.** is organising an experimental international summer camp (10 French- and 10 English-speaking participants) centred on miniature rocketry; high-school education required; details from **Bays Association,** Fortners House London WIX 1AB ☎ 734 6010; U.S. affiliates are currently being sought. **Mouvement Jeunes-Science,** 50, av. Bolivar, 75019 Paris ☎ (1) 42.05.61.21; laboratory clubs in Paris, Marseilles, Bordeaux and Dunkirk; foreign participation welcome. **Association Française d'Astronomie,** Observatoire du Parc Montsouris 17, rue E. Deutsche-de-la-Meurthe, 75014 Paris ☎ (1) 45.89.81.44; holiday courses at the Paris Observatory (from 8 yrs) or the one at Montpellier (from 14 yrs); affiliate membership required (national astronomic associations). **Fédération Nationale Microtel Club,** 9, rue Huymans, 75006 Paris ☎ (1) 45.44.70.23; computer initiation for those 16 and older. **École de Spéléologie** (spelunking school), 28, quai Saint-Vincent, 69001 Lyon ☎ 78.39.43.00.

Nature

- **Jeunes et Nature,** 129, bd Saint-Germain, 75279 Paris Cedex 06 ☎ (1) 43.26.19.26; holiday courses. **Concordia,** 27, rue du Pont-Neuf, 75001 Paris ☎ (1) 42.33.42.10; range of constructive activities from wildlife preservation to archaeology (→ relevant section heading); **C.O.L.I.N.A.T.** *(Comité de liaison pour les interassociations pour la nature et l'environnement),* 39, rue du Châteaudun, 75009 Paris ☎ (1) 45.26.70.06; coordinates activities of a number of interesting associations, as does **C.P.I.E.** *(Centre permanent d'initiation à l'environnement),* 2, rue Washington, 75008 Paris ☎ (1) 45.63.63.67. **Nature et Progrès,** 53, rue de Vaugirard, 75006 Paris ☎ 45.48.55.38; farmhouse instructional holidays; brochure available. **Leo-Lagrange Loisirs,** 17, rue de la Grande Batelière, 75009 Paris ☎ (1) 45.23.45.45. **Maisons des Parcs Naturels :** (→ National Parks and relevant gazetteer sections).

Sports

• **O.C.C.A.J.** *(Organisation centrale des camps et activités de jeunesse),* 11, rue de Vienne, 75008 Paris ☎ (1) 45.26.21.22; 43.87.06.59; **U.C.P.A.** *(Union nationale des Centres Sportifs de Plein Air),* 62, rue de la Glacière, 75013 Paris ☎ (1) 43.36.05.20. **Terres d'Aventure,** 3, rue Saint-Victor, 75005 Paris ☎ (1) 43.29.94.50. **Loisirs de France Jeunes,** 30, rue Godot-de-Mauroy, 75009 Paris ☎ (1) 47.42.51.81. → also relevant section headings.
U.K. : **School Travel Service,** 24 Culloden Rd. Enfield Middx ☎ (01) 363 8202; can arrange football matches in France for school groups.

Language courses

• The cultural departments of **French embassies** are able to provide details on officially-sponsored (university, etc.) language courses.
• **Alliance Française,** 101, bd Raspail, 75006 Paris ☎ (1) 45.44.38.28.
• **Comité d'Accueil** (French Ministry of Education), 166 Piccadilly, London W1V 9AJ ☎ (01) 493 2478; extensive range of language-course tours for all ages, groups and individuals.
• **Euro-Centre,** 13, passage Dauphine, 75006 Paris ☎ (1) 43.25.81.40; correspondents : Davies' School, 56 Ecclestone Square, **London** SW1V 1PQ ☎ (01) 834 4155. Euro-Centre, 26 Dean Park Road, **Bournemouth** BH1 1HZ ☎ (202) 24426. Columbia University, 505 Lewiston Hall, **New York,** NY 10027 ☎ (212) 280-3585. Language courses throughout the year (Paris); summer courses (Amboise).
→ **F.G.T.O.**

The disabled

The severely handicapped should contact one of the various specialised organisations, such as **C.N.F.L.R.H.** in France or **RADAR** in the U.K. (→ below), before planning holidays. For those who simply have difficulty in managing more than a few stairs, a few judicious advance enquiries, generally will ensure a trouble-free holiday.

The wheelchair symbol in this guide (♿) indicates hotels that are accessible to disabled people; however, specific requirements should be checked in advance. Suitable rooms may be limited, so early booking is advisable.

Hotels

The A.T.H. reservation centre (★, ★★ & ★★★hotels; ☎ (1) 48.74.88.51) provides information about access for the disabled.

The **Direction du Tourisme** (→ Information) can provide up-to-date lists of the facilities offered by various hotel networks as well as details of associations that offer holidays for the young disabled (physically or mentally handicapped); regional tourist offices also may be able to provide useful information in this respect.

Information

• **C.N.F.L.R.H.** *(Comité National Français de Liaison pour la Réadaptation des Handicapés),* 38 bd Raspail 75007 Paris ☎ (1) 45.48.90.13 : excellent source of information (some in English) on every aspect of activities for the disabled in France.
• **RADAR,** 25 Mortimer Street London WIN : specialist advice and an annual guide : *Holidays for the Physically Handicapped.*
• **Pauline Hephaistos Survey Projects** 39 Bradley Gardens London W13 : holiday guides (including some French regions) for the disabled.
• **Mobility International,** 2 Colombo Street London SE1 : publishes *Europe for the Handicapped Traveller* (No. 3-France).
• The **Agence Nationale pour l'Information Touristique,** 8 Av de l'Opéra 75001 Paris ☎ (1) 42.60.37.38 publishes a free brochure in French, "Touristes Quand Même" (Tourists Nevertheless), that contains invaluable information and addresses for the disabled tourist.

Press and radio

National press

In addition to *Le Monde* (considered as reflecting liberal, independent tendencies) and *Le Figaro* (firmly conservative), both known throughout the world, a number of other national dailies represent the spectrum of

French political outlook, from *l'Humanité* (Communist) to *Le Quotidien de Paris* (right-wing). The classified advertisement section of *Libération* (originally a rather anarchistic daily founded by late French intellectual Jean-Paul Sartre, now a highly successful "alternative" newspaper) contains a host of interesting offers for young people (flat-sharing, ride-sharing, and so forth). *Le Figaro* has the most extensive flat-rental advertisement section.

Regional press The regional publications provide, in addition to national and international news, a wealth of local information that is often of great interest to the tourist : concerts, festivals, the weather forecast, local produce prices, beach conditions and little bits of information that contribute to a successful holiday. Titles of the major regional newspapers are indicated in the relevant gazetteer sections.

English-language press Newsagents and *kiosks* in popular tourist resorts generally offer a wide selection of British newspapers and magazines during the peak season. The *International Herald Tribune,* edited in Paris, is widely available, even at smaller outlets as are the European editions of the *Financial Times* and the *Wall Street Journal.* The English-language monthly *Passion* is a source of information on Parisian events as well as news from New York City, Los Angeles and Montreal. Finally : as this guide went to press, a slimmed-down and more expensive *U.S.A. Today* went on sale in Europe.

Radio The opening of the FM waveband to local stations has considerably widened the variety of listening available to foreign visitors in France. The state-owned *France Inter* station (1829 m AM for national coverage; several regional FM stations) provides English-language news bulletins during the summer after the 9 am and 4 pm news broadcasts. *Inter's* special road-and-camping information service is available by telephone from 9 am to 6 pm at (1) 43.06.13.13 (also in English). At presstime KLOU-FM, a largely English-language station, was giving a 15-min news report each morning at 9 am.
A number of British radio stations can be heard in Northern France, particularly near the coast. American Forces Network program from West Germany also can be picked mainly up in eastern France.

Calendar, events

Calendar

The annual August holiday migration in France still remains a source of astonishment. A slight but definite improvement can be observed but July and August remain *the* holiday months. Nevertheless many regions now provide various seasonal activities and facilities in resort towns from early June through the end of September. A fifth week of paid vacation coupled with the spreading of school holidays has done much to ensure a reasonable flow of visitors to winter sports resorts.

Hints — If at all possible, avoid travelling on the following dates : 1 Aug.; 31 Aug. (to a lesser extent this applies to 1 and 31 July, and to the 15th of both these months); at the start or the end of school holidays (see below); on any national holiday close to the weekend.
— Motorists prepared to forsake the autoroutes and main highways can avoid the worst of France's traffic jams (→ Motoring).
— May, June, September and October are not only less crowded than July and August but considerably cheaper, too. Villa rental and package-holiday prices may fall by as much as 30-50 % and restaurant and local store prices return to normal levels. Autumn is a splendid season in the south and southwest of France, and the water of the Mediterranean is warm enough for even the most hesitant bather from the end of May onward.

Number of visitor/days (1 May-30 September)

- 6-9 million
- 9-13 million
- over 13 million

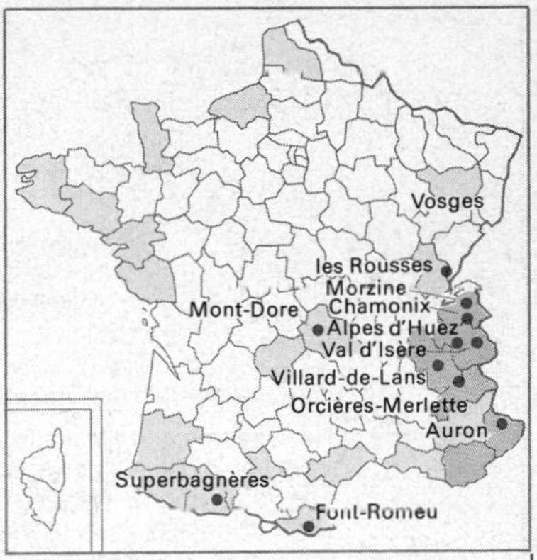

Number of visitor/days (1 October-15 April)

- 1,4-4 million
- over 4 million

School holidays, 1985

School holiday dates vary according to geographical zone. **Zone 1 :** Créteil, Paris, Versailles. **Zone 2 :** Bordeaux, Caen, Clermont-Ferrand, Grenoble, Lille, Montpellier, Nancy, Metz, Nantes, Nice, Rennes. **Zone 3 :** Aix, Marseilles, Amiens, Besançon, Dijon, Limoges, Lyons, Orléans, Tours, Poitiers, Rheims, Rouen, Strasbourg, Toulouse. The school calendar on Corsica is set independently.

- **Winter 86 :** zone 1, 6-17 Feb.; zone 2, 13-24 Feb.; zone 3, 20 Feb.-3 Mar.
- **Spring 86 :** zone 1, 25 Mar.-7 Apr.; zone 2, 28 Mar.-10 Apr.; zone 3, same.
- **Summer 86 :** zone 1, 28 Jun.-9 Sept.; zone 2, 27 Jun.-9 Sept.; zone 3, same.
- **All dates are inclusive. Future school holidays may be obtained from the Éducation Nationale** telephone service, (1) 45.50.10.00, or from F.G.T.O. offices.

National holidays, 1985

- New Year's Day: 1 Jan.; Easter Monday : 31 Mar.; Labour Day : 1 May; V.E. Day : 8 May; Ascension Day : 8 May; Whit Monday : 18 May; National (Bastille) Holiday : 14 Jul.; Assumption Day : 15 Aug.; All Saints Day : 1 Nov.; Armistice Day : 11 Nov.; Christmas Day : 25 Dec.; (Neither Good Friday nor Boxing Days are national holidays in France).

Cultural events

Few countries are as able as France to add exquisite surroundings to top-quality spectacles : sumptuous ballets in château courtyards, *sons et lumières* that bring ruins to life in an incomparable way, the subtle juxtaposition of contempory entertainment under Roman vaulting or the enchantment of a 300-strong choir in an antique amphitheatre on a warm Provençal night in Arles or Orange. The local press and tourist offices are excellent sources of information.

Festivals

The following map is necessarily limited to the principal festivals :
— **Music :** Aix-en-Provence (Jul.); Albi (Jul.-Aug.); Antibes (Jul.); Les Arcs (Jul.-Aug.); Besançon (Sep.); Bordeaux (May); Bourges; (May-Jun.); Carpentras (Jul.-Aug.); La Chaise-Dieu (Aug.-Sep.); Chartres (Jul.); Comminges (Jul.-Aug.); Cordes (Jun.-Sep.); Dijon (Jun.-Sep.); Divonne-les-Bains (Jun.-Jul.); Evian (May); Gannat (Jul.); Gourdon (Jul.-Aug.); Ile-de-France (May-Jun.); Lille (Oct.); Lorient (Aug.); Lourdes (Easter); Lyons (May-Jun. & Sep.); Menton (Aug.); Metz (Nov.);

■ Music □ Theatre ● Dance ○ Cinema

Main festivals

Mont-Saint-Michel (Jul.-Aug.); Nice (Jul.); Nîmes (Jun.-Jul.); Nohant (Jun.); Orange (Jul.); Paris (Jun.-Nov.); Poitiers (May); Pradès (Jul.-Aug.); Rheims (May); La Rochelle (Mar.-Apr.); Romans (Sep.); Saint-Céré (Aug.); Saintes (Jul.); Saint-Lizier (Sep.); Sceaux (Jul.-Oct.); Strasbourg (Mar. & June); Toulouse (Jun.-Jul.); Toulon (May-Jun.); Tours (May-Jul.); Vaison-la-Romaine (Jul.).

— **Dance :** Arles (Jul.); Bordeaux (May); Carpentras (Jul.-Aug.); Châteauvallon Toulon; (Jul.); Gannat (Jul.); Montpellier (Jun.); Paris (Sep.-Oct.); La Rochelle (Mar.-Apr.).

— **Theatre :** Aigues-Mortes (Aug.); Angers (Jun.); Avignon (Jul.); Bordeaux (May); Nancy (May); Paris (Jun.-Dec.); Quimper (Jul.-Aug.); La Rochelle (May-Jun.); Sarlat (Jul.-Aug.);

— **Cinema :** Avoriaz (Jan.); Cannes (May); Deauville (Sep.); Dinard (Sep.); La Rochelle (Mar.-Apr.).

Exhibitions Major festivals (e.g., Avignon and Sigma-Bordeaux) and exhibitions hold considerable interest. Details are usually published in the local press and are available at local TO and SI.

Information
- The **F.G.T.O.** can provide names of tour operators offering inclusive holidays to jazz festivals (Nice, Antibes and others) and opera festivals (Aix-en-Provence and Avignon) etc.
- *La France en Fête :* brochure published by the *Direction du Tourisme* 17, rue de l'Ingénieur Keller, 75740 Paris Cedex 15 ☎ (1) 45.75.62.16.
- ***Saison en Europe :*** Published by the *Association Nationale de Diffusion culturelle,* 5, rue Bellart, 75015 Paris ☎ (1) 47.83.33.58.
- TO and SI.
- The gazetteer sections of this guide.
- The French rock magazine **Rock'n Folk** (available at newsagents, also in New York and London) contains details of every form of rock, pop and folk concert programmed in France.

Festivities in France

Food and drink

Wine-harvest festivals, wine festivals (the "Trois Glorieuses" in Burgundy in Nov. with the world-famous **wine auctions** at the Beaune almshouse → Wine), **cider** in Normandy, **cheese** from the Champagne region to the Cantal; **beer** at Maubeuge; **sauerkraut** at Colmar or Brienne-le-Château; **boudin** (blood sausage or black pudding-the object of an eating contest) at Mortagne-en-Perche, **cherries** at Vieillevie (Cantal), **blueberries, melon, chestnuts** and even **herrings** at Séclin and Romerie in the North, **oysters** near Arcachon... and endless others.

Historical Festivities

In Mutzig (Alsace) every 13 July, the *sans-culottes* ("Republican rebels") lay siege to the Bastille, which capitulates amid feasting and fireworks the next day, **14 July,** all over France. Jugglers, fencers, and would-be troubadors are all part of the mediaeval festivals at Troyes, Langres (Jun.), Chinon (Aug.), Chénerailles (Jul.), and the feast of the **land of Cockaigne** at Saint-Félix-Laurageais in the Haute-Garonne (early Apr.).

Folklore

Songs and dances of yesteryear, costumes and ancient musical instruments are all on parade at Gannat (Allier, end-Jul.), Cannes, Marseilles, Nice, Dijon and Saint-Bictor (Allier), Salon-de-Provence, Arles. However, **Brittany** is indisputably the Mecca of Folklore : Bretons dance to the *biniou* (bagpipes) at *fest-noz* or *pardon* gatherings (→ the Brittany section of the gazetteer).

Traditions

Although *Mardi-Gras* and carnival are synonymous everywhere, revellers at Solesmes (Nord) are exposed to the antics of the *seringueux* (water-pistol bandits), who cheerfully spray unsuspecting bystanders. At Saint-Palais in the Basque country, tradition brings together woodcutters, tradesmen and other muscular specimens in various trials of strength (end Aug.). Other spectacular traditions include : ***corsos*** (processions of floats) at Carpentras, the ***Feria*** (feast-day) in Béziers, Spanish ***bravades*** (bull-running) in Saint-Tropez, ***corridas*** (bullfights) at Arles, Nîmes and Bayonne, and **cow-racing** in the Landes.

From the unusual to the bizarre

A selection from the endless list of events in this category must include the **Festival de l'Insolite** (weird books, films and exhibitions) at La Garde-Freinet (Var, May) and the **Festival de l'Étrange** (science-fiction and horror) at the Avoriaz ski-resort every winter. Mediaeval traditions make no concession to good taste : "hunchbacks" and the "blind" are pursued in Cassel (Nord) at Easter. Dragons and giants roam the streets of Denain and Maubeuge around this time. A glance at the gazetteer sections of this guide will provide you with a host of unusual festivities.

Carnivals

Nice and Lille are famous for their carnivals (→ gazetteer), but Chalon-sur-Saône, Limoux, and Dunkirk's sailors' carnival, are equally worthy of attention.

Religious events

The French calendar is still profoundly marked by religious traditions. Easter, Christmas, All Saints, Palm Sunday and many other traditional holy days give rise to celebrations, pilgrimages and processions.

Christmas

Midnight Mass on Christmas Eve is probably one of the most moving religious ceremonies encountered in France. The Nativity is enacted in a number of churches, such as the astonishing troglodyte church at Vals, in the Ariège region, or in the tiny village of Chamblac, in the Eure. In Provence, exquisite clay figures — *santons* — represent the Nativity, and the village of La Crémade in the Vaucluse is noted for its fine display.

Easter

In Perpignan during Easter Week, penitents parade huge sculptures around the town. At Saugues, in the Haute-Loire area, participants in the procession go barefoot and hooded. This same ambiance is encountered at Calvi, in Corsica; during the *Catenaccio* at Sartène (also in Corsica) a Christ, feet in chains, carries a local resident portraying the Cross through town. Mediaeval crucifixion *tableaux* are enacted in many localities. The Easter liturgy is still chanted in the Gregorian manner in a few abbeys, such as Saint-Benoît-sur-Loire. At Cargèse, in Corsica, the ceremony is that of the Greek Uniate Church.

Pardons Breton *pardons* (→ Brittany) are the occasion for much feasting; some remain deeply religious : Sainte-Anne-d'Auray, 25 Jul.; Folgoët, 7-8 Sep.; Tréguier, 19 May.

The regional gazetteer sections contain information on the major pilgrimages of each region. Among the better known are : Lourdes, La Salette, Lisieux, Sainte-Anne-d'Auray, Notre-Dame-de-la-Garde, Chartres, Orléans, Rocamadour, Le Puy and Paray-le-Monial. Lesser known, but worthy of interest, are the sailors' pilgrimage at Honfleur, Mont-Saint-Michel and Mont-Sainte-Odile (Bas-Rhin), the Joan-of-Arc pilgrimage at Domrémy and at Magnac-Laval (Haute-Vienne), a Whitsun pilgrimage.

Protestant ceremonies The Reformed Church organises a Desert Assembly every year on 1 Sep. at Mas-Soubeyran (or at the Temple of Anduze if the weather is bad) in the Cévennes.

Information

- **Centre d'Information et de Documentation Religieux** (C.I.D.R.), 6, place du Parvis-de-Notre-Dame, 75004 Paris ☎ (1) 46.33.01.01 (2:30-7).
- **Centre National Pastorale du Tourisme,** 4, Cité du Sacré-Cœur, 75018 Paris ☎ (1) 42.54.97.31.
- **Centre Pastorale du Tourisme de Paris,** 22, rue Chanoinesse, 75007 Paris ☎ (1) 43.29.37.73.
- **Consistoire Central Israélite de France et d'Algérie,** 17, rue Saint-Georges, 75009 Paris ☎ (1) 45.26.02.56.
- **Institut Musulman,** place du Puits de l'Ermite, 75005 Paris ☎ (1) 45.35.97.33.
- **Institut Saint-Serge** (Orthodox), 93, rue de Crimée, 75020 Paris ☎ (1) 48.74.15.08.
- **Fédération Protestante de France,** 47, rue de Clichy, 75009 Paris ☎ (1) 48.74.15.08.
- **SIP-Voyages,** agency specialising in religious theme tours and pilgrimages : 1, rue Garancière, 75006 Paris ☎ (1) 43.29.56.70.
- The **F.G.T.O.** in New York publishes an excellent brochure, *France for the Jewish Traveller.*

Sporting events

France can offer international-class sporting events of every type the year round; dates for 1985 events were not always available at the time of going to press : F.G.T.O. and Air France offices can provide up-to-date information.

Bullfighting Arles and Nîmes (Apr. to Oct.).

Cycling Paris-Nice (Mar.). Paris-Roubaix (early Apr.). Tour de France (Jul.). Grand Prix des Nations (end Sep.).

Football Championship from end Jul. through May, break in Dec. Matches on Tue. and Fri. French Cup Finals (Parc des Princes, 30 Apr.).

Golf French Open (May).

Horse-racing Prix du Président de la République (2nd half of Mar.). Grand Steeple-chase (3rd Sun. in Jun.). Grand Prix de Deauville (last Sun. in Aug.). Prix de l'Arc de Triomphe (1st Sun. in Jun.).

Motorcycling Le Touquet, Enduro des Sables (endurance race in the dunes; mid Feb.). - Grenoble, Ice-racing world championships (motor-racing on ice) - very spectacular - I and 9 Feb. 1986; European Grass-track championships in the Southwest - Apr. World Speed championships on the Paul Ricard circuit - 20 Jul.; 50th Bd d'Or (Golden Cup) - Sep.

Motor-racing Rally des 10 000 virages (Corsica, May). Grand Prix de Monaco (end May-early Jun.). Le Mans 24 Hour Race (Jun.). Paris-Dakar Rally (Jan.). Monte Carlo Rally (end Jan.).

Power-boating Rouen 24 Hour Race (30 Apr.-1 May). Paris 6 Hour Race (6 Oct.).

Rugby 5 Nation Tournament : France-Wales (19 Jan.). - France-Scotland (16 Feb.).
Running Figaro Cross-country Race (Paris, 2nd Nov.). Marathon de Paris (spring).
Skiing 30th Critérium des neiges at Val d'Isère (1st week in Dec.).
Tennis French international (Roland Garros Paris, May-Jun.).

Travel

France by plane

Flying offers the shortest routes and an **Air Inter** flight averages just an hour. From Ajaccio to Toulouse, from Brest to Strasbourg, Air Inter criss-crosses France with more than 50 routes linking major towns. Other destinations are offered by regional lines such as **T.A.T.** (Touraine Air Transport). With a broad possibility of reductions, **Air Inter** makes flying affordable on *vols blancs* and *vols bleus* ("white" and "blue" flights): under 25s, students under 27, retirement age, couples, families and groups can take advantage of reductions up to 50 %.

Air travel "à la carte"

Charter aircraft and helicopters operate out of the airports and aerodromes of most major towns (→ Getting to France - Air), and some offer regular excursions to or over places of interest such as the Loire châteaux, the vineyards of Burgundy or Mont-Saint-Michel. **Map Travel,** in particular, offers helicopter tours featuring luxury accomodation, gastronomic meals and transfers in chauffeur-driven limousines.

Hints

The "Carte Évasion" offers reductions on 400 Air Inter flights (incl. Corsica) and pays for itself in less than 2 round-trips.
— Some of T.A.T.'s and the minor companies' routes do not operate throughout the year : always check before planning air travel to or between minor towns.
— On routes covered by the T.G.V. and the faster expresses (→ France by Rail) always make a detailed comparison of the cost and convenience of rail and air travel.

Information

— **Air France,** ☎ (1) 45.35.61.61 or any of the numerous Air France agencies.
— **Air Inter,** ☎ (1) 45.39.25.25.
— **T.A.T.,** ☎ (1) 46.87.35.53 and eight regional offices (→ Gazetteer section); flights to winter sports resorts in season.
— **Air Limousin,** Limoges-Bellegarde airport, ☎ 55.00.11.84. Limoges, Brives and Agen to Paris, Nantes, Lyons, Nice and Marseilles.
— **Air Littoral,** Montpellier-Fréjorgues airport, ☎ 67.65.49.49. Main routes : Lyons-Pau-Biarritz ; Lyons-Perpignan ; Bordeaux-Nice ; Montpellier-Carcassonne-Nice ; Carcassonne-Toulouse ; Pau-Marseilles. International flights also to Milan, Valencia and Venice.
— **Air Vendée,** Nantes, Les-Bazinières-La-Roche-sur-Yonne, ☎ 51.62.31.65. Saint-Brieuc-Nantes ; Ile-d'Yeu-La-Roche-sur-Yonne ; Ile d'Yeu-Nantes.
— **Brittany Air International,** Morlaix-Ploujean aerodrome, ☎ 98.62.10.22. Rennes-Lyons-Nice and Rennes-Lyons-Marseilles in conjunction with Air Inter. Flights to London, Cork (Ireland) and Jersey from Rennes and Morlaix.
— **Lucas-Aigle-Azur,** Deauville-Saint-Gatien airport, ☎ 31.88.31.28. Deauville-Jersey and Deauville-London. Deauville-Lille and Deauville-Nice in the near future.
— **Air-Languedoc,** Albi-Le-Sequestre airport, ☎ 63.54.45.28. Clermont-Ferrand-Nice, Montpellier and Perpignan ; Montluçon-Toulouse via Clermont. Flights from Paris to the Southwest and Épinal.
— **Europe Aéro Service,** Rivesaltes-Perpignan airport, ☎ 68.61.11.83. Paris-Valence.
— **Montluçon Air Service,** Chamber of Commerce, ☎ 70.05.30.19. Montluçon-Clermont-Ferrand.
— **Air Jet,** Vaulx-en-Velin, ☎ 78.80.79.11. Orly, ☎ (1) 48.84.45.48. Avignon-Lyons.

— **Lance-Aviation,** Lognes-Torcy airport, ☎ 60.05.65.20.
— **Air Ardèche,** Aubenas Chamber of Commerce, ☎ 75.35.21.11.
— **Map Travel,** 3, rue du Tournon, 75006 Paris ☎ (1) 46.34.16.18. **U.S. correspondent :** Tour France, Fulton House, 345 N Canal St., Chicago IL 60606. Helicopter tours.

France by train

French railways have everything going for them as one of the most convenient ways of getting to, and exploring, France. A truly extensive network with increasingly modern rolling-stock and station facili-

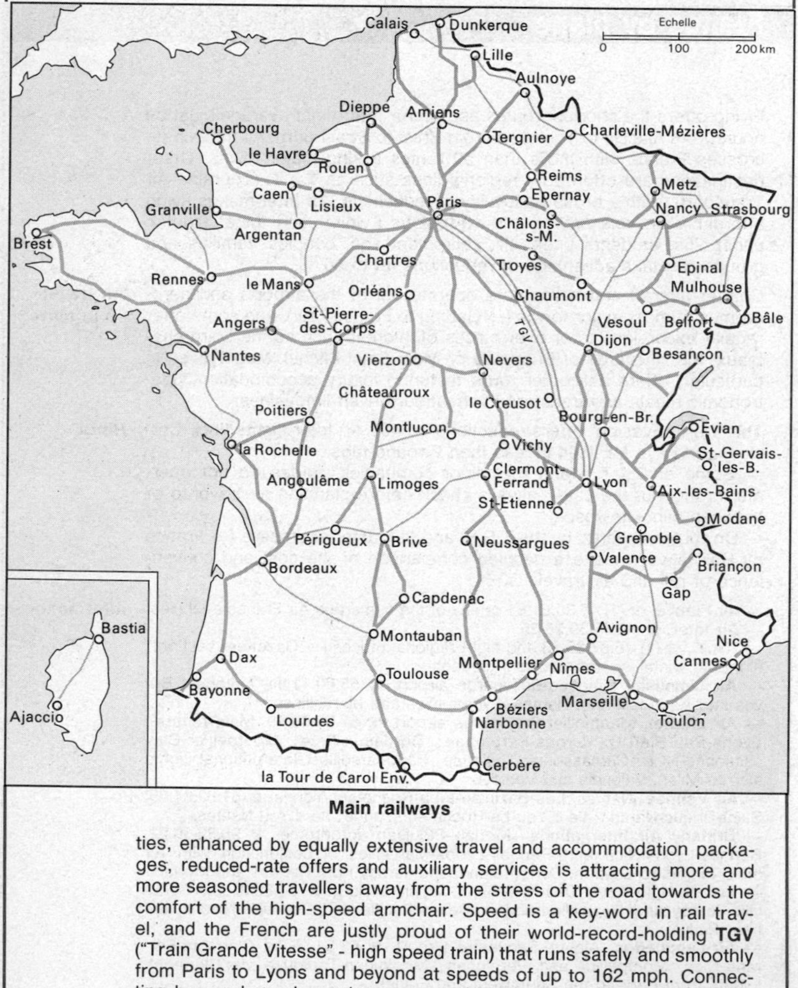

Main railways

ties, enhanced by equally extensive travel and accommodation packages, reduced-rate offers and auxiliary services is attracting more and more seasoned travellers away from the stress of the road towards the comfort of the high-speed armchair. Speed is a key-word in rail travel, and the French are justly proud of their world-record-holding **TGV** ("Train Grande Vitesse" - high speed train) that runs safely and smoothly from Paris to Lyons and beyond at speeds of up to 162 mph. Connecting bus and coach services are provided for out-of-the-way locations (excursions are often available to places of interest), and the car and bicycle hire schemes operating in a number of stations offer passengers complete freedom of movement on arrival at their destination. An interesting novelty : the wine road from Dijon to Beaune in just one day with the T.G.V.

Reservations

Tickets and seat reservations may be obtained outside France from rail-appointed travel agents, certain railway booking-offices, and from the overseas offices of French railways (Société Nationale des Chemins de Fer, hereafter referred to by the initials **S.N.C.F.**).

In France, reservations can be made at all the main railway stations, by personal application or by letter. Reservations open 2 months before departure date; written applications are accepted up to 6 months before this date. Reservations can be made by telephone during the 9 days preceding departure (1 month for couchettes and Motorail).
Advance bookings are necessary for : **TGV** notably; for **Motorail** travel (see below); and for the benefit of certain rates.

Unused tickets are refundable (a small fee is deducted) for up to 2 months after the expiration of the ticket.
— **Passengers with tickets purchased in France must validate their ticket before boarding the train** by using one of the automatic date-stamping machines *(composteurs)* provided at the platform entrance. Passengers failing to do so will be considered as travelling without a valid ticket and will be required to pay a supplementary fee.
— After a break of 24 hours or more in a journey, passengers must revalidate their ticket.
— This procedure does not apply to tickets purchased outside France.
— **Tickets can be purchased in the train itself** (from the itinerant *contrôleur,* or ticket collector), **but will be charged at the full applicable rate plus a small additional fee.**

Registered luggage

Three pieces of luggage (one weighing up to 40kg, the others up to 30kg) may be registered in advance from one station to another within France, and to and from certain stations abroad such as London Victoria. Registered luggage can be collected at the station of destination, and in many cases can be delivered to the door (enquire when booking).

Restaurant cars

The majority of main-line trains have restaurant facilities, or, more frequently, "Grill-Express" self-service cars. Drinks and sandwiches are sold from a trolley wheeled along the corridor. An interesting novelty : it is possible to taste the cuisine of a great French chef, Joël Robuchon, winner of the Hachette French Chef's Grand Prix 1985, in the specially-equipped first-class carriages of the Paris-Strasbourg line.

Overnight travel

Two types of sleeping accommodation are available for an extra fee to passengers holding ordinary rail tickets : Couchettes or sleeping-cars.
— Although last-minute couchette and sleeper reservation booths are provided at most stations, advance booking is strongly recommended; demand is well in excess of supply during the peak holiday periods.

The TGV

Lyons is now just 2 hours by rail from Paris, Geneva only 3hr 30, Marseilles 4hr 52 and Montpellier 4hr 47, thanks to the world's fastest train. Travel time can be considerably reduced on the whole southeastern network by using the TGV and the numerous local connections. Only a standard 1st- or 2nd-class ticket with advance booking is required (peak-day travel is subject to a supplement, as on most main-line trains). Reservations can be made, up to a few minutes before departure by using the computerised reservation machines provided at TGV stations.

On-board entertain ment

Trains currently singled out for entertainment are : **"Le Cévenol" :** Paris-Marseilles via the Auvergne and the Cévennes; **"L'Aubrac" :** Paris-Béziers via the Auvergne and the "Causses" plateaus; **"Le Ventadour" :** Lyons-Bordeaux via the Auvergne and Périgord; **"Le Thermal" :** Paris-Clermont-Ferrand; **"L'Alpazur" :** Nice-Geneva. **"Le Bocage" :** Paris-Granville. **"Le Trouvère" :** Paris-Calais. **"Le Valentré" :** Paris-Toulouse. **"Le Vert-Galant" :** Toulouse-Bayonne. **"Le Rouget-de-l'Isle" :** Strasbourg-Lyon. **"Le Paludier" :** Nantes-Bordeaux; enquire at S.N.C.F. offices in France or abroad, or at the F.G.T.O.

Motorail

Motorail services are available from **Calais** (the check-in is only a few minutes drive from the ferry terminal; combined ferry/Motorail tickets are available), **Boulogne, Dieppe, Lille** and **Amiens.** Destinations cover all the main holiday regions in southern and southwestern France, and reach on to Milan, Madrid and Lisbon. Advance booking is essential (book well in advance for peak-holiday travel). Motorcycles and bicycles are transported on all rail services within France : enquire at S.N.C.F. offices.

The disabled — Most stations now provide special facilities for the disabled (look for the international wheelchair symbol) : free wheelchairs, portable stairways, lifts, personnel to help in crossing the line, etc.
— The information desk in main-line stations can supply a French-language brochure listing facilities available for the disabled throughout the S.N.C.F. network.
— Passengers requiring the assistance of station personnel should arrive at the station well before departure time. (→ "The disabled")

Children — Children under 4 travel free of charge but are not entitled to separate seats of their own; together in a single couchette they pay only one half-price ticket and one couchette supplement at the normal price.
— Children from 4 to 11 pay half-price for a seat or couchette of their own (full couchette supplement). After the age of 12 children pay the same as adults.
— Under certain circumstances a hostess can accompany children of between the ages of 4 and 13 who are travelling alone. Ask for details of the **"Jeune Voyageur Service"** (young traveller's service) at S.N.C.F. offices.
— Some lines offer facilities (nursery corner, play-space, bottle-warmer points, special meals) for passengers travelling with young children or babies : ask for details of the ***Trains Familles*** (family trains) at S.N.C.F. offices.

Young people Reduced-price offers are available for young people on French and European railways :
— **Inter-rail pass :** one month's unlimited 2nd-class travel for the under-26s in 21 European countries, and half-price travel in the country of purchase (buy outside France). Applications for the Inter-rail pass must be made at least 5 days in advance. The "Inter-rail and ferry" card offers all the advantages of the "Inter-rail" card with in addition unrestricted travel on a certain number of maritime crossings.
— **"Carte-Jeune" :** half-price travel from 1 June to 30 September for those of 12-25 on 1 Jun. of the year of subscription on the entire S.N.C.F. network, provided all departures take place at off-peak times (***périodes bleues*** - consult the S.N.C.F. timetables). In the same period (Jun.-Sep.) a 50 % reduction on a return ticket on Sealink ferries between Dieppe and Newhaven, a 50 % reduction on a single on the railway network in Corsica and two free nights in the "Points d'Accueil Jeunes" (PAJ) youth hostels.

Senior citizens Men of 62 years and over and women of 60 years and over can purchase the **Carte Vermeil,** valid 1 year, which entitles them to the issue of tickets (valid 2 months) with a reduction of 50% on the basic fare. Holders of this card (but the men must be over 65) can obtain the **Rail-Europe S** card, which entitles the holder to reductions of 30-50% on the networks of 18 European countries.

Other reductions — The **Billet-Séjour** (holiday return) ticket offers a reduction of 25% on ordinary fares for return or circular journeys of more than 1 000 km (return included). The return journey may not be started until the 6th day after the outward journey.
For tickets bought in France, passengers must begin the journey during *période bleue* off-peak times; for tickets purchased in the U.K. the journey (on French territory) must commence on a Tuesday, Wednesday, Thursday or Saturday.
— Party tickets are available at reduced rates : 20% reduction for groups of more than 10 adults, 30% for more than 25. Group leaders may travel free in some cases.
— The 1st-class **Eurail** pass (valid 1, 2, or 4 weeks, 2 or 4 months) entitles the holder to rail travel on 18 European networks and provides attractive reductions on the cost of auxiliary services, notably on the Train-Auto rail/car-hire scheme in France. The 2nd-class **Eurail Youthpass** (valid 1 or 2 months) is issued to under-26s. Details from rail-appointed travel-agents or any European railway representative.
— The **France-Vacances** "rail-over" card is obtainable by non-residents of continental France and Corsica and is available for 7 days, 15 days

or 1 month. The card covers the whole S.N.C.F. network, including the TGV, but seat reservations and couchette supplements must be paid for. A host of bonus offers come with a France-Vacances card : free 1st-class return travel to and from Orly or Roissy-Charles-de-Gaulle airport for air travellers, free use of the Paris urban transport network, free entry to the Georges Pompidou National Art and Culture Centre and a highly attractive **free car-rental scheme for 1st-class card-holders** (1 day free rental for 7- and 15-day passes, 2 days for 1 month passes; four card-holders travelling together can thus obtain 4 days of free rental in a 7-day period). **Passports and proof of non-French residency** are required to purchase this pass, which can also be obtained in France from Roissy-Charles-de-Gaulle and Orly airports, Paris-Saint-Lazare, Nice, Strasbourg, Bordeaux, Lyons-Perrache, and Marseilles railway stations.
France-Vacances passes may also be purchased in conjunction with air tickets from Air-France offices overseas.

Train-Auto

Combined rail travel and car-rental, including special weekend hire, is offered at more than 2000 destinations by the **S.N.C.F.** in conjuction with **Budget.** Reservations can be made through travel agents or railway booking offices or at the **Bureau Central des Réservations,** 163, av. de Clichy, 75017 Paris, ☎ (1) 47.30.80.00.
The addresses of Budget car-rental centres are contained in each regional gazetteer section.

Bicycle rent

Over 220 stations now offer bicycle rentals, and this increasingly popular service is likely to be extended still further. Cycles can be hired by the half day, or the day; rates are generally reduced by 25% from the 3rd day onwards. In many cases cycles can be hired in one station and returned to another (→ Cycling Holidays). Enquiries and reservations at railway booking offices.

Holiday packages

An extensive range of holidays in France, including special interest (cookery, painting, etc.) and sports (skiing, golf, tennis) holidays are offered by the S.N.C.F. in conjunction with British Rail. Accommodation ranges from luxury hotels to self-catering rental flatlets and travel is by no means limited to rail; air travel is a feature of many of these holidays and passengers with their own cars are equally well catered to. Details from **French Travel Service,** Francis House, Francis Street, London SWIP IDE, ☎ : (01) 828 81 31/91 52.

Hints

— A careful study of the reductions and schemes offered by the S.N.C.F. will almost invariably lead to significant reductions in the price of your journey by rail. The off-peak rates are worthy of attention even for short trips within France.
— Timetables are available from all S.N.C.F. booking offices in France and abroad. Off-peak travel periods are marked in blue and peak periods in red.
— Not only is peak-period travel more expensive (in addition to the absence of reductions, main-line expresses are often subject to supplements), but the trains can be very crowded. For a more relaxing journey, avoid the main holiday migration times (→ "Calendar").
— Special stewards and hostesses (*personnel d'accueil,* welcome staff), wearing easily-recognisable orange uniforms, are available in main stations to inform and assist passengers.

Information

• Timetables and brochures covering everything that the rail and Motorail traveller could wish to know are available from :
• In the **U.K. :** French Railways Ltd, 179 Piccadilly, **London** W1V OBA, ☎ : (441) 493.97.31.
• In the **U.S. :** French National Railroads, Rockefeller Center, 610 Fifth Ave., **New York,** NY 10020, ☎ : (212) 582-2816; 360 Post Street on Union Square, **San Francisco,** CA 94102, ☎ : (415) 982-1993; 9465 Wilshire Blvd., **Beverly Hills,** CA 90212, ☎ : (213) 274-6934; 11 East Adams St., **Chicago** IL 60603, ☎ : (312) 427-8691; 2121 Ponce de Leon Blvd., **Coral Gables Miami** FL 33134, ☎ : (305) 445-8648.
• In **Canada :** French National Railroads, 1500 Stanley St., Suite 436, **Montréal,** Qué. H3A, 1R3, ☎ : (514) 288.82.55; 409 Granville St., Suite 452, **Vancouver,** B.C. V6C 1T2, ☎ : (604) 688.67.07.
• Each regional gazetteer section of this guide contains the telephone numbers of the relevant main-line stations.

Road signs

Road signs in France follow the now almost internationally standardised system of symbols; nevertheless certain signs may be unfamiliar to visiting drivers. A number of these signs are explained below. A more detailed summary of continental road signs may be obtained from motoring associations and road safety organisations: France's **La Prévention Routière** organisation runs information centres along main roads at peak holiday times.

Types of road sign

Danger
(e.g. slippery road)

Prohibition
(e.g. maximum speed limit)

End of prohibition
(e.g. end of maximum speed limit)

Obligation
(e.g. minimum speed limit)

End of obligation
(e.g. end of minimum speed limit)

Dip or hump in road (uneven road surface: CHAUSSÉE DÉFORMÉE)

One-way traffic

Two-way traffic

Intersection with priority to the right (PRIORITÉ À DROITE)

Intersection with priority to users of the major road (also indicated by an intersection sign bearing the words PASSAGE PROTÉGÉ)

Give way at intersection

Old form of "give way"

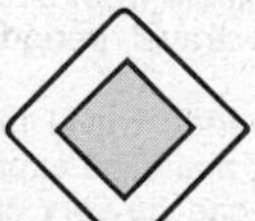

Priority road, even in the absence of other signs

End of priority road (generally on entering urban zones with right-hand priority)

Motoring

committee), 34, av. Marceau, 75008 Paris ☎ (1) 720.70.32.
- **Direction de Routes,** Ministère des Transports, 244, bd Saint-Germain, 75007 Paris ☎ (1) 544.39.93.
- **Prévention Routière** (the national road-safety oragnisation), av. Georges-Boillot, 91310 Linas-Montlhery ☎ (1) 901.20.03.

Driving in France The French drive on the right, and driving in France is basically subject to the rules that are gradually becomming standardised throughout Europe. The **right-hand priority** rule is however worthy of mention :

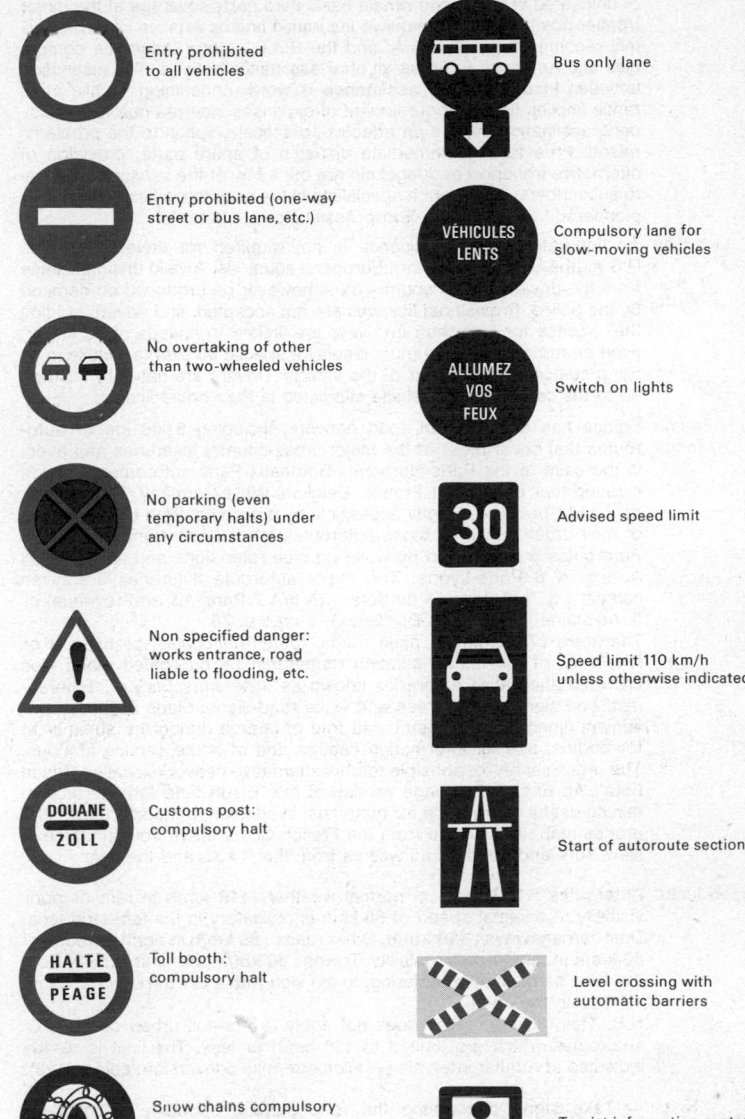

Entry prohibited to all vehicles

Bus only lane

Entry prohibited (one-way street or bus lane, etc.)

Compulsory lane for slow-moving vehicles

No overtaking of other than two-wheeled vehicles

Switch on lights

No parking (even temporary halts) under any circumstances

Advised speed limit

Non specified danger: works entrance, road liable to flooding, etc.

Speed limit 110 km/h unless otherwise indicated

Customs post: compulsory halt

Start of autoroute section

Toll booth: compulsory halt

Level crossing with automatic barriers

Snow chains compulsory (PNEUS NEIGE ADMIS: studded tyres allowed)

Tourist information centre

- **Association pour la Sécurité Routière,** 26, rue d'Enghien, 75010 Paris ☎ (1) 770.92.91.
- **Centre d'information sur les Autoroutes,** 276, bd Saint-Germain, 75007 Paris ☎ (1) 705.90.01.

English-speaking correspondents are generally available for enquiries.

Traffic must yield to vehicles coming from the right, whether at street junctions (even if the right-hand road is clearly the minor one) or at T and Y junctions. Only since I May 1984 has an amendment to this rule transferred **priority to the left on certain roundabouts.**

Insurance and assistance

Although the traditional Green Card international insurance certificate is no longer compulsory, drivers must ensure that their insurance covers driving in France (most European policies do so automatically). Drivers of uninsured vehicles can obtain basic third party coverage at the major frontier posts. A comprehensive insurance and assistance cover is warmly recommended. The A.A. and the R.A.C., motor insurance companies and American Express all offer assistance policies. The distinction between **insurance** and **assistance** is worth underlining : while insurance implies the reimboursement of expenses incurred due to an accident, assistance implies an effective, practical solution to the problems raised. Free towing, immediate dispatch of spare parts, provision of alternative transport and legal aid are but a few of the services available to subscribers. The French specialists in the assistance field, which they pioneered in France, are Europ Assistance (→ below).

Licences An international driving licence is not required for drivers from the U.S.A., the U.K. and Western European countries. A valid driving licence from the driver's home country must however be produced on demand by the police. Provisional licences are not accepted, and drivers holding their licence for less than one year are limited to speeds of 90 km/hr, even on motorways, and must display a special **90** sign (available in all filling stations) on the rear of the vehicle. Drivers are naturally restricted to the categories of vehicle stipulated in their home licence.

French roads France has an excellent road network, including 6 000 km of autoroutes that cover most of the major cross-country itineraries and even, in the case of the Paris-Narbonne-Bordeaux-Paris autoroutes, provide a round tour of most of France. Belgium, West Germany, Switzerland, Italy and Spain are directly accessible by autoroute. With the exception of their urban sections, these autoroutes are toll-operated.

Autoroutes are signalled by white on blue road-signs and are prefixed **A**, e.g. A 6 Paris-Lyons. The major autoroute itineraries are given names, e.g. "L'Autoroute du Soleil", (A 6/A 7 Paris-Aix-en-Provence) or "L'Aquitaine" (A 10 Paris-Bordeaux) → map p. 76.

There are 27 463 km of main roads, *routes nationales,* prefixed **N** or **RN.** Most of the major vacation routes can be duplicated along less crowded alternative itineraries known as *"itinéraires Bis"*, or *"Emeraudes"* and signalled by green and white road-signs. Maps of these convenient itineraries are distributed free of charge during the summer at toll-booths, special information centres and at some service stations. The organisation responsible for this alternative network is called "Bison Futé". An English-language version of the "Bison Futé" brochure, containing useful information for motorists, in addition to the alternative itineraries map, is available from the French Government Tourist Office in New York and London, as well as from the R.A.C. and the A.A.

Speed limits Autoroutes : **130 km/h** in normal weather; **110 km/h** in rain or poor visibility. A minimal speed of 80 kmh is obligatory in the left-hand lane. Dual carriageways : **110 km/h.** Other roads : **90 km/h** in normal weather; **80 km/h** in rain or poor visibility. Towns : **60 km/h** (this limit applies from the town name sign on entering, to the sign with a bar through the name on leaving the town).

N.B. The 130 km/h limit does not apply to non-toll urban sections of autoroutes which are limited to 110 km/h or less. The limit is clearly indicated at regular intervals (→ kilometre/mile conversion table p. 126).

Hints — Take signs concerning the road surface seriously : *"chaussée déformée"* (uneven road surface) can mean anything from crumbling macadam to distorted cambers or treacherous ruts in the road.

— Agricultural vehicles represent a regular hazard in rural areas, especially during the summer months; combine harvesters can emerge from unseen side tracks with no warning.

— Driving under the influence of **alcohol** is dealt with severely : driving after more than a couple of glasses of wine is a misdemeanor, while a few glasses more turns the offence into a crime. No breach of traffic regulations is required for prosecution, and random checks are lawful.

— Driving licence, insurance and vehicle registration papers must be available at all times for police inspection. Breaches of the French highway code can lead to stiff, on-the-spot fines.

— **By law, seat-belts** must be worn at all times by both driver and front-seat passenger. Rearseat belts, where fitted, must also be worn.

— **Children** under 10 years of age are prohibited from travelling in the front seat (unless the vehicle has no back seat).

— **Stop signs** must be strictly observed : the vehicle must come to a complete halt.

It is forbidden to stop on open highways unless you can park your vehicle off the road.

— **Overtaking** is forbidden on the brows of hills and wherever there is a continuous white line along the middle of the road or "no overtaking" restriction signs.

— If your vehicle is not equipped with **hazard warning lights** you must carry a **red warning triangle** in case of breakdowns.

— **Full or dipped headlights** must be used at night and in poor visibility; driving with sidelights is permitted in well-lit urban areas under the driver's responsibility. Yellow headlights are no longer compulsory, but beams must be adjusted for right-hand driving.

— **Horns** must not be used in built-up areas, except in genuine emergencies.

Breakdowns Emergencies

— There are **emergency telephone posts** every 2 km on motorways and on some major roads. The fixed towing fee is usually displayed on the post. There are 24 hr filling stations every 20 km on motorways.

— In case of breakdowns, always turn the **hazard warning lights** on, and if possible place a warning triangle 150 metres back up the road.

— French automobile manufacturers have a 24 hr breakdown service, the national centre will provide the location of the nearest local station : **Renault** (1) 42.52.82.82. **Citroën** (16) 05.05.24.24 (reverse charges). **Peugeot-Talbot** (1) 42.81.91.91.

Accidents

— If the accident is a minor one, with no physical injuries and no blatant breach of the law, the police or gendarmes may not intervene. The acknowledged practice is to fill out a *constat amiable* — a standard form. Two identical copies are filled out, and each driver signs the other's copy. Non-French speaking visitors should of course make sure that they know what they are signing : if any doubt subsists, then the police will have to be called in to make a report.

Car-rentals

France has an excellent fleet of rental-cars and all the major international agencies either operate in France or have reciprocal arrangements with French operators. **Fly-drive schemes** are available through all the major airlines including of course Air France and Air Inter (the main French domestic airline). French Railways also offer an especially attractive **train/car-rental scheme** ("Budget, Train-Auto") and include an amount of free car-rental for Ist class "France Vacances" pass-holders (→ France by train). Drivers must be at least 21 years of age, and often 25 to rent a car; some companies now insist on 3 years driving experience with a full licence no matter what the driver's age. Most companies have an upper age limit of 60 or 65 years.

Information

Rental-car addresses :

- **Hertz,** 27, rue Saint-Ferdinand, 75017 Paris ☎ (1) 45.74.59.33.
- **Avis,** 78, av. Pierre-Grenier, 92100 Boulogne ☎ (1) 46.09.92.12.
- **Europcar,** 42, av. de Saxe, 75007 Paris ☎ (1) 43.21.28.37.
- **Budget,** 21, rue du Départ, 75014 Paris ☎ (1) 42.29.50.50.
- **L.U.T.,** Total Station, porte d'Italie, 75013 Paris ☎ (1) 45.85.99.14.
- **Mattei,** 205, rue de Bercy, 75012 Paris ☎ (1) 43.46.11.50.

Europ Assistance

— In the **U.K. :** Europ Assistance, Europ Assistance House, 252 High St., Croydon, Surrey CRO 1NF, ☎ (01) 680 1234.

— In the **U.S. :** World Wide Services, 21000 Pennsylvania Ave. N.W., Suite 617, Washington, D.C. 20037, ☎ (202) 429-0655.

The following organisations can provide useful information concerning motoring on French roads :

- **Comité Interministériel à la Sécurité Routière** (inter-ministerial road-safety committee), 34, av. Marceau, 75008 Paris ☎ (1) 47.20.70.32.
- **Direction de Routes,** Ministère des Transports, 244, bd Saint-Germain, 75007 Paris ☎ (1) 45.44.39.93.
- **Prévention Routière** (the national road-safety organisation), 6, av. Hoche, 75008 Paris, ☎ (1) 42.67.97.17.
- **Association pour la Sécurité Routière,** 26, rue d'Enghien, 75010 Paris ☎ (1) 47.70.92.91.
- **Centre d'information sur les Autoroutes,** 3, rue Edmond-Valentin, 75007 Paris ☎ (1) 47.05.90.01.

English-speaking correspondents are generally available for enquiries.

A few distances between towns by the most rapid itineraries

	Amiens	Bayonne	Besançon	Bordeaux	Bourges	Brest	Caen	Cahors	Chamonix	Clermont-Fd	Dijon	Dunkerque	Grenoble	Le Havre	Lille	Limoges	Lyon	Le Mans	Marseille	Metz	Montpellier	Mulhouse	Nancy	Nantes	Nice	Nîmes	Orléans	Paris	Pau	Perpignan	Poitiers	Le Puy	Reims	Rennes	La Rochelle	Rodez	Rouen	St-Étienne	Strasbourg	Toulouse	Tours
Amiens																																								
Bayonne	918																																							
Besançon	556	885																																						
Bordeaux	728	184	698																																					
Bourges	379	596	328	412																																				
Brest	612	815	971	625	651																																			
Caen	240	771	645	581	366	372																																		
Cahors	743	349	697	212	386	785	647																																	
Chamonix	772	965	241	218	458	1094	865	727																																
Clermont-Fd	536	553	351	369	184	779	625	278	449																															
Dijon	459	825	102	682	245	874	548	566	264	288																														
Dunkerque	146	1064	590	874	518	754	382	886	821	681	538																													
Grenoble	713	816	291	655	385	1128	802	494	146	286	296	834																												
Le Havre	180	843	609	653	406	482	108	719	829	589	512	323	766																											
Lille	115	989	627	799	446	813	350	814	751	607	530	73	784	297																										
Limoges	542	410	499	220	192	600	453	194	630	181	436	687	467	570	613																									
Lyon	609	817	256	577	281	1024	698	441	241	208	192	730	104	662	680	389																								
Le Mans	349	620	578	430	230	402	151	496	697	383	481	453	735	223	420	302	630																							
Marseille	924	682	571	653	596	1339	1013	524	556	484	508	1046	314	977	995	664	315	946																						
Metz	359	1095	260	905	434	919	568	818	499	538	252	424	548	532	369	719	444	526	759																					
Montpellier	907	523	554	493	579	1131	996	365	442	361	491	1029	297	960	978	443	298	929	163	742																				
Mulhouse	607	1016	136	825	464	1098	772	795	309	482	229	677	426	736	617	626	382	705	698	253	681																			
Nancy	401	1022	202	832	395	961	610	767	443	489	201	494	497	574	423	594	393	568	708	56	691	183																		
Nantes	523	519	691	329	354	296	283	489	812	453	594	629	730	393	594	304	626	176	995	700	835	818	742																	
Nice	1080	842	727	813	784	1495	1169	712	479	640	664	1202	333	1133	1151	820	471	1102	188	915	323	680	864	1154																
Nîmes	860	574	505	544	530	1081	955	416	391	320	441	1001	248	917	931	500	249	804	121	698	51	631	642	795	281															
Orléans	265	650	392	460	106	545	271	459	559	307	295	410	549	304	336	265	444	138	760	441	743	519	372	299	916	627														
Paris	148	773	411	583	227	597	241	595	624	390	313	291	567	205	219	396	463	203	778	330	761	537	372	377	934	712	119													
Pau	931	107	990	190	554	815	771	258	876	574	862	1074	731	826	1002	362	734	603	593	1112	434	1116	1063	519	714	485	664	783												
Perpignan	1055	438	702	457	731	1095	1144	329	594	461	639	146	445	1108	1126	517	446	900	311	890	152	829	839	799	471	203	891	909	328											
Poitiers	483	414	534	230	187	472	151	313	749	300	432	626	612	406	554	119	508	183	783	665	546	661	707	176	971	609	211	335	420	640										
Le Puy	664	653	390	460	314	915	664	304	378	130	326	807	190	721	735	311	134	513	311	578	215	516	527	601	499	190	437	516	562	367	430									
Reims	170	907	317	717	348	731	380	736	538	487	283	264	575	344	213	530	471	337	786	188	769	436	230	511	942	724	253	141	924	917	476	605								
Rennes	494	626	723	436	385	244	176	595	850	514	625	639	879	286	565	378	775	153	1090	670	942	849	712	107	1246	957	296	348	626	906	282	666	482							
La Rochelle	619	370	670	186	324	442	429	336	847	568	568	762	710	542	690	217	606	319	811	801	617	797	843	146	999	752	347	471	376	643	136	528	612	253						
Rodez	757	437	587	330	407	840	702	118	584	227	523	900	422	830	828	249	331	551	372	775	178	713	724	544	532	251	514	609	348	272	368	206	714	650	439					
Rouen	115	811	544	622	318	498	124	687	749	524	447	258	701	88	227	504	596	195	912	419	895	671	461	371	1068	837	238	125	794	1043	378	641	231	302	510	742				
St-Étienne	668	703	315	519	274	891	757	382	300	150	251	813	137	721	739	330	59	489	334	503	317	441	452	618	490	268	386	522	606	465	450	78	530	643	718	284	655			
Strasbourg	515	1252	242	1062	570	1076	725	901	427	583	335	609	531	689	526	731	488	682	803	162	786	118	145	856	959	737	598	486	1157	934	767	622	345	827	903	819	623	547		
Toulouse	855	283	790	253	505	891	847	125	682	392	727	1000	533	919	926	313	534	696	399	978	240	917	927	595	559	291	578	709	194	204	446	490	843	702	439	154	817	412	1022	
Tours	380	538	504	348	150	484	233	414	608	301	407	525	536	305	451	220	431	82	757	557	855	631	484	195	913	621	112	234	521	818	101	431	368	235	237	469	273	423	713	614
Troyes	276	823	230	639	226	722	406	627	416	349	152	405	448	370	335	418	344	325	660	233	642	309	186	489	848	584	187	165	780	787	398	481	122	478	534	576	290	403	331	774	294

Through itineraries

See map page 72

Touring itineraries

Calais-Nice

The following seven itineraries are designed to take in some of France's most beautiful and authentic countryside. Although they are by no means the fastest routes, the sites encountered along the way should more than compensate for the extra time spent at the wheel. Use these itineraries in whole or in part to get from one town to another or to reach your holiday destination. Combine them, if you wish, to make up a 3-, 4- or 5-day tour. Graft your own detours on to them - the basic routes obviously cannot include everything that France has to offer you. Refer to the index for the place names cited; names of of regions are printed in bold type.

The North region : Calais - *D940* Boulogne★★ - *D119, D940* Le Touquet-Le-Crotoy - *D260, D94* Somme Valley and Abbeville★ - *D901, D218* Amiens★★ - *N29* Boves - *D935* Montdidier. **Ile-de-France :** Compiêgne★★ - *D973* Pierrefonds★ - *D936* La Ferté-Milon. **Ardenne, Champagne :** *D4, D973, D1* Château-Thierry★ - *N3* Épernay - Châlons-sur-Marne★ - *N44* Vitry-le-François - *D2,D396* Brienne - *D960* Troyes★★★ - *N71, D444* Chaource. **Burgundy :** *D444, D944*, Tonnerre★. Two alternative routes.

D965 Chablis★ - Auxerre★★ - *N6, D951* Vézelay★★ - *D957* Avalon★★ - *D10* Quarré-les-Tombes - *D20* Saulieu★ - *D980* Autun★★★ - *N80* Le Creusot - Montchanin - *D28* Saint-Gengoux-le-National - *D981* Cormatin★★ - Cluny★★ - *D980, N79* Berzé★ - Mâcon. **Lyonnais, Bresse**; *N79* Bourg-en-Bresse★ **or** *D905, D965* Tanlay★★★ - *D905* Ancy-le-Franc★★★ - Montbard-Fontenay★★★ - Tanlay★★★ - Alise-Sainte-Reine★ - *D9* Flavigny★★ - *D9, D26* Saint-Seine-l'Abbaye - *N71* Dijon★★★ - *D122, N74* Beaune★★★ - Chagny - *D981* Buxy - *D18* Sennecey - Tournus★★ - *D975* Cuisery. **Lyonnais, Bresse :** Bourg-en-Bresse★.

D979 Nantua★ - *D74, N84, D31* Ruffieux - Artemare - *D904* Virieu-Belley. **Savoie :** *N504* Chambéry★. **Dauphiné :** *N6* Saint-Laurent-du-Pont - *D520b* Saint-Pierre-de-Chartreuse (la Chartreuse★★) - *D512* Grenoble★★ - *N85* (route Napoléon★) Corps - Gap. **Provence-Côte d'Azur :** Sisteron★ - Digne - Castellanne★ - Grasse★ - Cannes★★ - Golfe-Juan - Nice★★.

Belgium-Hendaye

The North region : Valenciennes - *D13* Douai★ - *D42* Arras★★ - *N25* Doullens - Amiens★★. - **Ile-de-France :** *D210* Croissy-sur-C. - *D11, D149* Beauvais★★. **Normandy :** *D981* Gisors★ - *D181, D125* Les Andelys★ - *D313* Gaillon★ - *N15* Vernon★ - *D181* Pacy-sur-Eure - *D836* Ivry-la-Bataille. **Ile-de-France :** Anet★ - *D928* Dreux - *D929, D923* Maintenon★ - *D906* Chartres★★★ - *D921* Illiers - *D941, D955* Châteaudun. **Orléanais, Blésois, Touraine :** *N10* Vendôme★★ - Tours★★ - *D7* Villandry★★ - Azay-le-Rideau★★★ - *D751* Chinon★★. **Maine, Anjou :** Fontevraud★★ - Saumur★★. **Vendée, Poitou, Charente :** *N147* Thouars★ - *D938* Parthenay★ - *D949b* Secondigny - *D25* Coulonges-sur-l'Autize - *N745* Fontenay-le-Comte★ - *N148* Nieul-sur-l'Autize★ - *D24* Maillezais★ - *D15, D16* Courçon-d'Aunis - *N11* La Rochelle★★★ - *N137* Rochefort★★ - Saintes★★★ - *N150* Royan★ ferry across the Gironde. **Bordelais, Landes :** Soulac-sur-Mer★ - *N215* Saint-Vivier-Médoc - *D2* Pauillac-Bordeaux★★★ - *D10* Langon - *D932* Mont-de-Marsan - *D933* Saint-Sever★ - *D32* Dax★. **Basque country, Béarn, Bigorre :** *N124, N10* Bayonne★★ - Hendaye.

Cherbourg-Chamonix

Normandy : Cherbourg★ - *D101* Barfleur - *D902* Saint-Vaast - *D14, D913* Carentan - *N174* Saint-Lô - *D28* Tessy - *D21, D52* Vire - *D524, D924* Tinchebray - *D22* Domfront - *D908* Bagnoles-de-l'Orne★ - *D916, D218.* **Maine, Anjou :** Villaines-la-Juhel *D13, D16* Sillé-le-Guillaume -

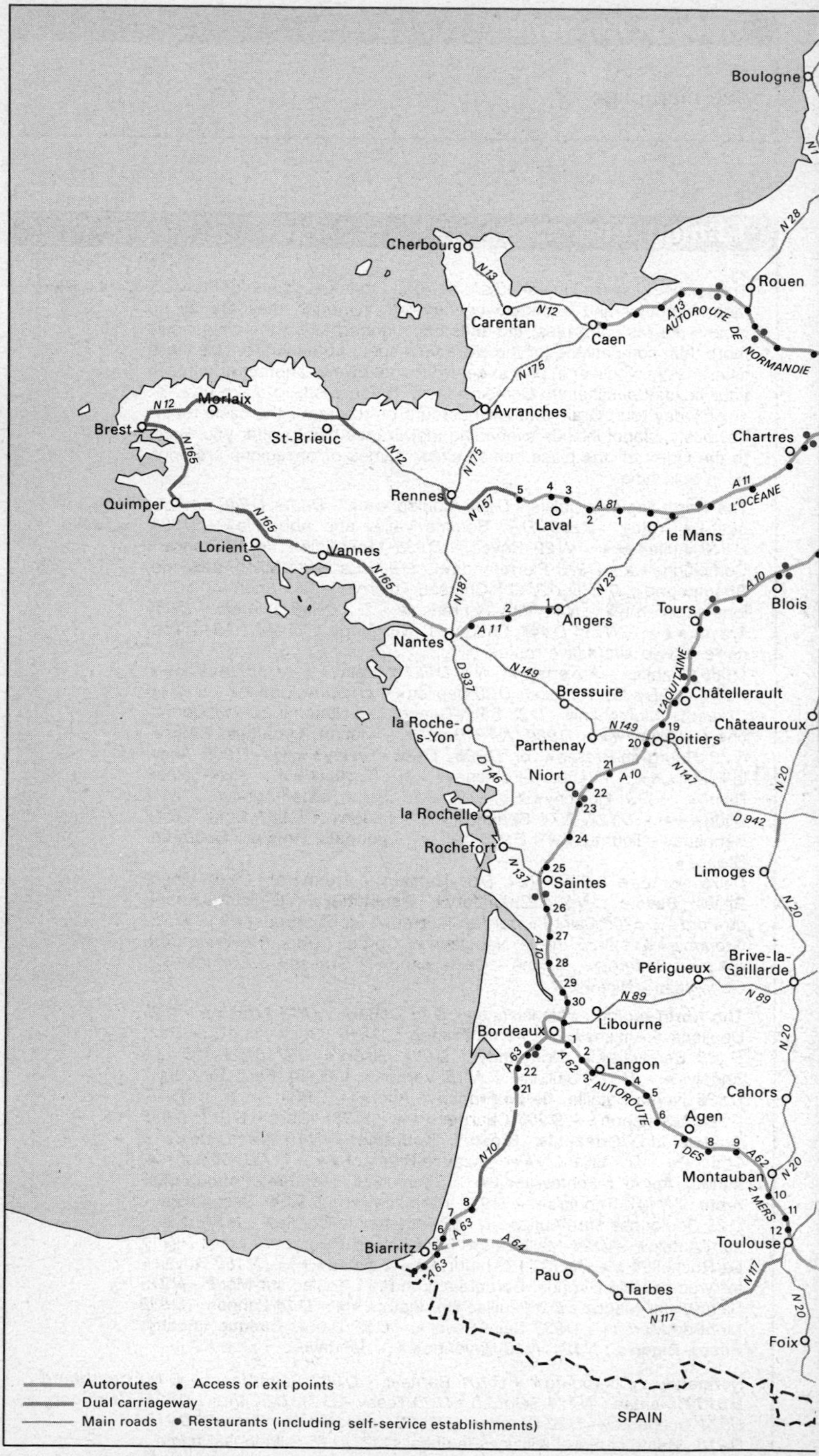
Boulogne
N1
N28
Rouen
Cherbourg
N13
Carentan
N12
Caen
A13
AUTOROUTE DE NORMANDIE
N175
Avranches
Morlaix
N12
Brest
St-Brieuc
N165
N12
N175
Chartres
Quimper
Rennes
N157
5 4 3
A81
2 1
Laval
A11
L'OCÉANE
le Mans
N165
Lorient
Vannes
N165
N187
N23
A10
Blois
Tours
2 1
Angers
A11
Nantes
D937
N149
Bressuire
L'AQUITAINE
Châtellerault
la Roche-s-Yon
N149
19
Châteauroux
Parthenay
20
Poitiers
21
A10
N147
Niort
22
23
N20
D746
la Rochelle
D942
24
Rochefort
N137
25
Saintes
Limoges
26
N20
27
A10
28
Périgueux
Brive-la-Gaillarde
29
30
N89
N89
Libourne
Bordeaux
1
A63
2
A62
N20
22
3
Langon
21
AUTOROUTE
4
5
Cahors
6
Agen
N10
7
DES
8
9
A62
Montauban
N20
2 MERS
10
11
8
7
6
A63
12
Toulouse
Biarritz
5
A64
A63
Pau
N117
Tarbes
N20
N117
Foix
Autoroutes
Access or exit points
Dual carriageway
Main roads
Restaurants (including self-service establishments)
SPAIN

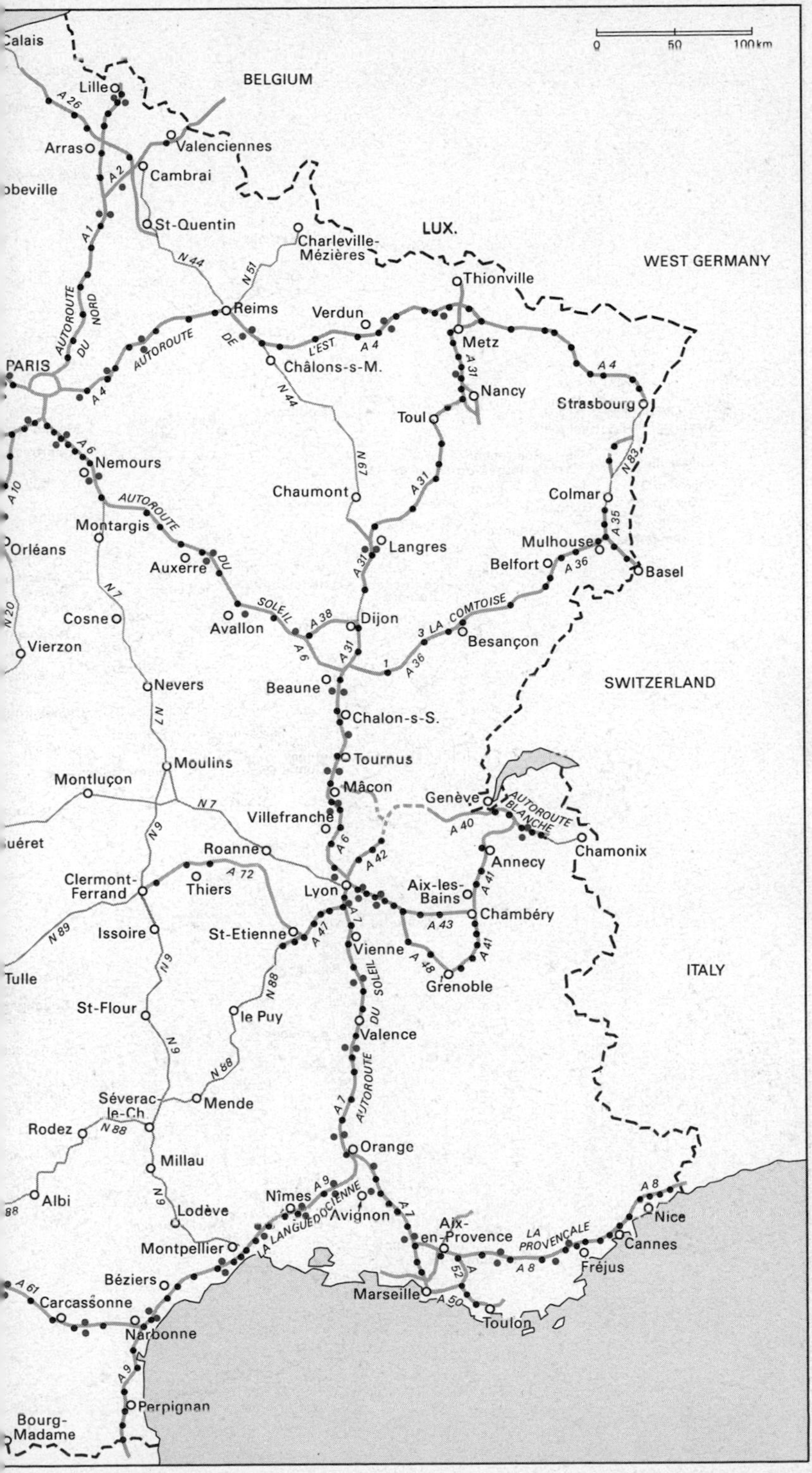
0 50 100 km
BELGIUM
LUX.
WEST GERMANY
SWITZERLAND
ITALY
Calais
Lille
Arras
Valenciennes
Cambrai
St-Quentin
Charleville-Mézières
Thionville
Reims
Verdun
Metz
Châlons-s-M.
PARIS
Nancy
Toul
Strasbourg
Nemours
Chaumont
Colmar
Montargis
Langres
Mulhouse
Orléans
Auxerre
Belfort
Basel
Cosne
Avallon
Dijon
Besançon
Vierzon
Nevers
Beaune
Chalon-s-S.
Tournus
Moulins
Montluçon
Mâcon
Genève
Villefranche
Chamonix
Roanne
Annecy
Clermont-Ferrand
Thiers
Lyon
Aix-les-Bains
Chambéry
Issoire
St-Etienne
Vienne
Grenoble
Tulle
St-Flour
le Puy
Valence
Séverac-le-Ch
Mende
Rodez
Orange
Millau
Albi
Nîmes
Avignon
Lodève
Aix-en-Provence
Nice
Cannes
Montpellier
Fréjus
Béziers
Marseille
Toulon
Carcassonne
Narbonne
Perpignan
Bourg-Madame
AUTOROUTE DU NORD
AUTOROUTE DE L'EST
AUTOROUTE DU SOLEIL
LA COMTOISE
AUTOROUTE BLANCHE
LA LANGUEDOCIENNE
LA PROVENÇALE
A 26
A 2
A 1
A 4
A 6
A 10
A 31
A 35
A 36
A 38
A 40
A 41
A 42
A 43
A 47
A 48
A 72
A 7
A 9
A 8
A 50
A 52
A 61
N 44
N 51
N 67
N 83
N 7
N 20
N 9
N 89
N 88

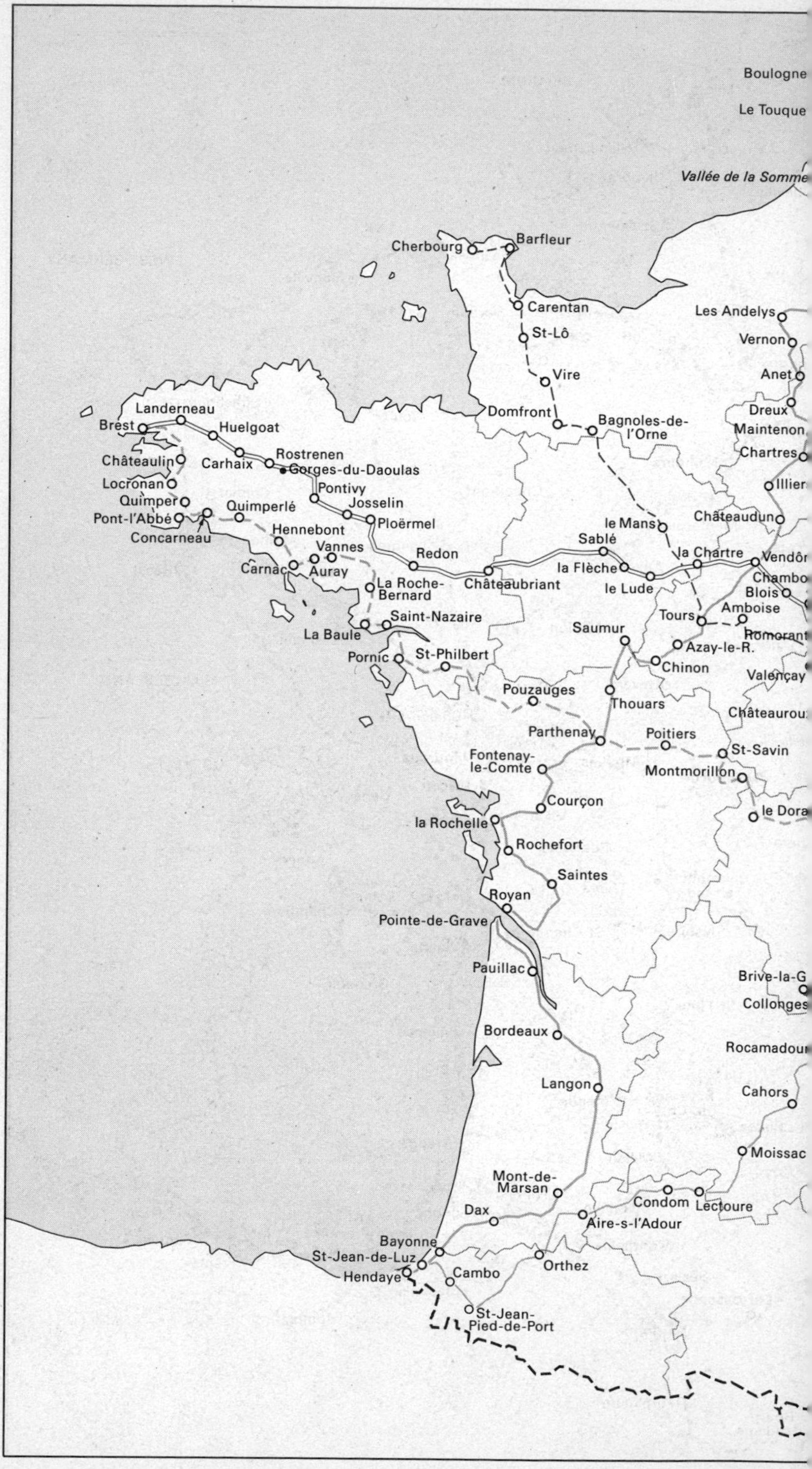
Boulogne
Le Touque
Vallée de la Somme
Cherbourg
Barfleur
Carentan
St-Lô
Vire
Les Andelys
Vernon
Anet
Dreux
Maintenon
Chartres
Illier
Domfront
Bagnoles-de-l'Orne
Landerneau
Brest
Huelgoat
Carhaix
Rostrenen
Gorges-du-Daoulas
Châteaulin
Locronan
Quimper
Pont-l'Abbé
Concarneau
Quimperlé
Pontivy
Josselin
Ploërmel
Hennebont
Vannes
Carnac
Auray
Redon
La Roche-Bernard
Châteaubriant
le Mans
Sablé
la Flèche
le Lude
la Chartre
Châteaudun
Vendôm
Chambo
Blois
Amboise
Romorant
Tours
Saumur
Azay-le-R.
Chinon
Valençay
Saint-Nazaire
La Baule
Pornic
St-Philbert
Pouzauges
Thouars
Châteauroux
Parthenay
Poitiers
St-Savin
Montmorillon
le Dora
Fontenay-le-Comte
Courçon
la Rochelle
Rochefort
Saintes
Royan
Pointe-de-Grave
Pauillac
Brive-la-G
Collonges
Bordeaux
Rocamadour
Langon
Cahors
Moissac
Mont-de-Marsan
Condom
Lectoure
Dax
Aire-s-l'Adour
Bayonne
St-Jean-de-Luz
Hendaye
Cambo
Orthez
St-Jean-Pied-de-Port

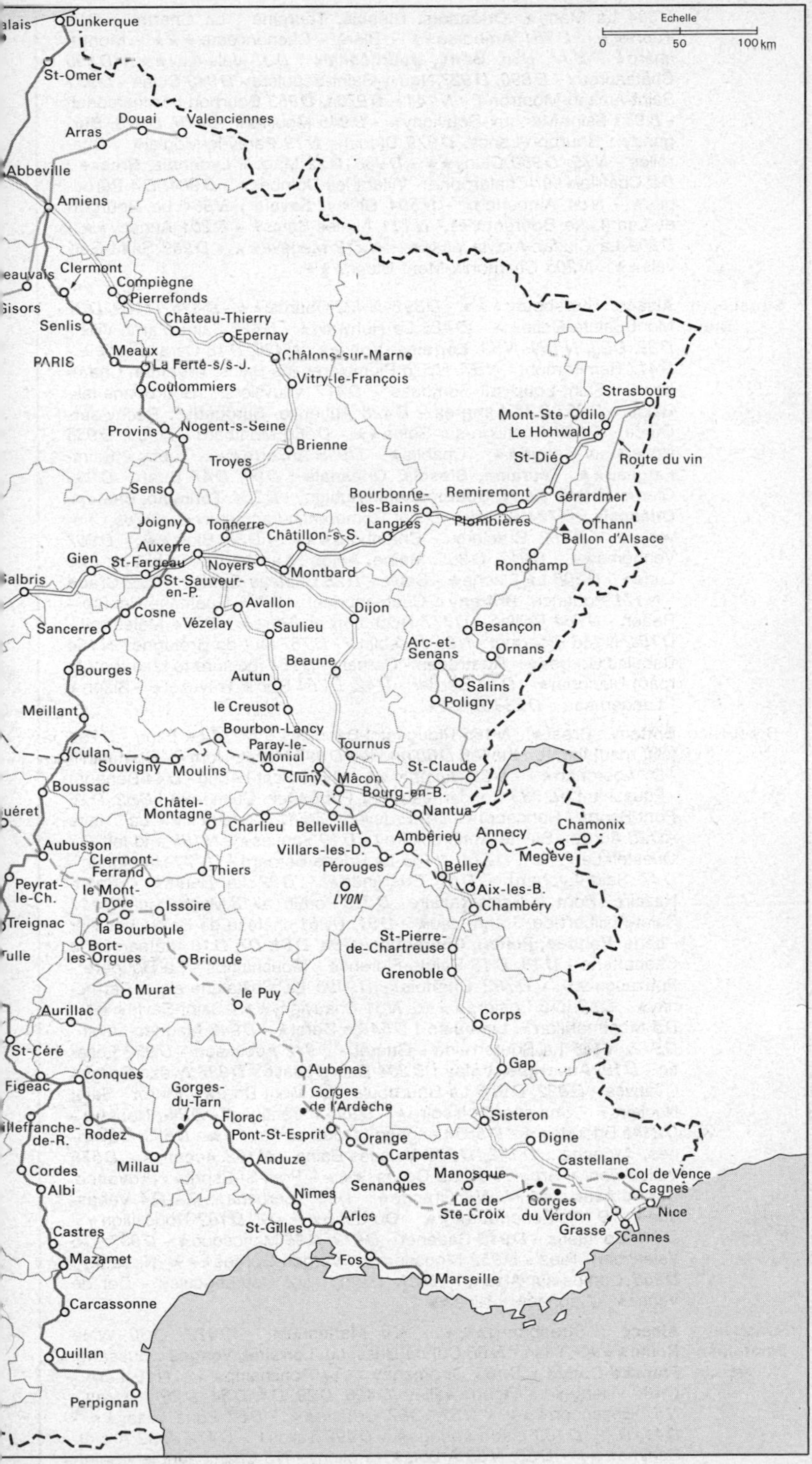
Echelle
0
50
100 km
Dunkerque
St-Omer
Douai
Valenciennes
Arras
Abbeville
Amiens
Clermont
Compiègne
Pierrefonds
Senlis
Château-Thierry
Epernay
Meaux
PARIS
La Ferté-s/s-J.
Châlons-sur-Marne
Vitry-le-François
Coulommiers
Strasbourg
Mont-Ste-Odile
Le Hohwald
Provins
Nogent-s-Seine
Brienne
St-Dié
Route du vin
Troyes
Sens
Bourbonne-les-Bains
Remiremont
Gérardmer
Joigny
Tonnerre
Langres
Plombières
Thann
Ballon d'Alsace
Châtillon-s-S.
Auxerre
Gien
St-Fargeau
Noyers
Montbard
Ronchamp
St-Sauveur-en-P.
Avallon
Dijon
Cosne
Vézelay
Besançon
Sancerre
Saulieu
Arc-et-Senans
Ornans
Beaune
Bourges
Autun
Salins
Poligny
Meillant
le Creusot
Bourbon-Lancy
Paray-le-Monial
Tournus
Culan
Souvigny
Moulins
Cluny
Mâcon
St-Claude
Boussac
Bourg-en-B.
Châtel-Montagne
Nantua
Charlieu
Belleville
Chamonix
Annecy
Ambérieu
Aubusson
Villars-les-D.
Megève
Clermont-Ferrand
Thiers
Pérouges
Belley
Peyrat-le-Ch.
le Mont-Dore
LYON
Aix-les-B.
Issoire
Chambéry
la Bourboule
Bort-les-Orgues
St-Pierre-de-Chartreuse
Brioude
Grenoble
Murat
le Puy
Aurillac
Corps
St-Céré
Gap
Aubenas
Conques
Figeac
Gorges-du-Tarn
Gorges de l'Ardèche
Florac
Sisteron
Rodez
Pont-St-Esprit
Orange
Digne
Millau
Anduze
Carpentas
Castellane
Cordes
Col de Vence
Albi
Senanques
Manosque
Nîmes
Lac de Ste-Croix
Gorges du Verdon
Cagnes
Nice
Arles
St-Gilles
Grasse
Cannes
Castres
Mazamet
Fos
Marseille
Carcassonne
Quillan
Perpignan

D 304 Le Mans★. **Orléanais, Blésois, Touraine :** La Chartre - *D 29* Tours★★ - *D 751* Amboise★★ - Bléré - Chenonceaux★★★ - Montrichard★ - *D 17, D35.* **Berry, Bourbonnais :** *D 37* Valençay★★ - *D 956* Châteauroux - *D 990, D 927* Neuvy-Saint-Sépulcre - *D 943* Culan - *D 951* Saint-Amand-Montrond - *N 144* - *D 978a, D 953* Bourbon-l'Archambault - *D 953* Saint-Menoux-Souvigny★ - *D 945* Moulins★ - *N 79, D 973.* **Burgundy :** Bourbon-Lancy. *D 979* Digoin - *N 79* Paray-le-Monial★ - Charolles - *N 79, D 980* Cluny★★ - *D 980, N 79* Mâcon. **Lyonnais, Bresse :** *D 2* Châtillon-sur-Chalaronne - Villars-les-Dombes★ - *D 904, D 4* Pérouges★ - *N 84* Ambérieux - *N 504* Bellay. **Savoie :** *N 504* Le Bourget-du-Lac (Lake Bourget★★) - *N 211* Aix-les-Bains★ - *D 201* Annecy★★ - *D 909* La Clusaz-Aravis pass★ - *N 212* Megève★★ - *D 909* Saint-Gervais★★ - *N 205* Chamonix-Mont-Blanc★★★.

Strasbourg-Brest — **Alsace :** Strasbourg★★★ - *D 392, N 422* Obernai★★ - *D 426, D 109, D 37* Mont-Sainte-Odile★★ - *D 426* Le Hohwald★ - *D 425* Saint-Martin-Villé - *D 39, D 23, N 159, N 59.* **Lorraine, Vosges :** *N 425, D 18* Gérardmer★★ - *D 417* Remiremont - *N 57, N 57b* Plombières-les-Bains. **Ardenne, Champane :** Saint-Loup-sur-Semouse - *D 417* Vauvillers - Bourbonne-les-Bains - *D 35, D 74* Langres - *D 428* Auberive. **Burgundy :** Recey-sur-Ource - *D 928* Châtillon-sur-Seine★★ - *D 980* Montbard - *D 905, D 956* Noyers-sur-Serein★★ - Chablis★ - *D 965* Auxerre★★ - Toucy - Saint-Fargeau★★. **Touraine, Blésois, Orléanais :** *D 90, D 47* Briare -*D 952* Gien★ - *D 940.* **Berry, Bourbonnais :** Aubigny - *D 924.* **Touraine, Blésois, Orléanais :** *D 724* Salbris - *D 724* Romorantin-Lanthenay★ - *D 765* Cheverny★ - *D 102* Bracieux - Chambord★★★ - *D 33* Blois★★ - *D 957* Vendôme★★ - *D 917, D 305.* **Maine, Anjou :** La Chartre-sur-le-Loir - Le Lude★ - *D 306* La Flèche★ - Sablé - *D 28* Château-Gontier - *D 22* Craon - *N 171* Pouance. **Brittany :** Châteaubriant - *D 775* Guémené-Penfao - Redon - *D 764* Peillac - *D 777* Rochefort-en-Terre★ - *D 774* Malestroit - *D 764, N 166* Ploermel - *N 24* Josselin★ - *D 767* Mur-de-Bretagne - *N 164* Daoulas Gorges★ - Rostrenen - Carhaix - *D 764* (be sure to take the old road) Huelgoat★ - *D 14* Berrier - *D 42, D 764* Roc'h-Trevezel★ - Sizun★ - Landerneau - *D 233* Brest★.

Brest-Nice — **Brittany :** Brest★ - *N 165* Plougastel-Daoulas★ - *D 770* Le Faou - *D 791* (cliff road) then on the left *D 60* and left *D 887* Menez-Hom★ - Châteaulin - *D 7* Locronan★★ - *D 39* Quimper★★ - *D 785* Pont-l'Abbé - *D 44* Bénodet - Fouesnant - *D 783* Concarneau★★ - Pont-Aven. Quimperlé - *D 62, D 26* Pont-Scorff - Hennebont - *D 9* Erdeven - *D 781* Carnac★★★ - La Trinité - *D 28* Auray - Sainte-Anne-d'Auray - *D 19* Vannes★ - *N 165* and left *D 7* Questembert - *D 1, D 774, N 165* La Roche-Bernard - *D 774* Herbignac - *D 47* Saint-Lyphard - *D 51* Guérande★ - *D 92* La Baule★ - Saint-Nazaire - Pont de Saint-Nazaire - *D 213* Pornic - *D 13* Machecoul - *D 117* Saint-Philibert-de-Grand-Lieu★ - *D 61, D 261* château de Bois-Chevalier - Légé. **Vendée, Poitou, Charentes :** *D 94, D 84, D7, D 18* château de la Chabotterie - *D 18, D 13* Sainte-Florence - Mouchamps - La Boupère - Pouzaugues★ - *D 752* Cheffois - *D 949b* La Châtaigneraie - Parthenay★ - *D 59, D 6* Poitiers★★★ - *N 51* Chauvigny★★ - Saint-Savin★★★ - *D 5* Montmorillon★. **Limousin :** *D 54* Le Dorat★ - *D 942* Magnac-Laval - *D 942, N 145* La Souterraine - Guéret - *D 942* Aubusson - *D 982* Felletin - *D 10.* **Auvergne, Velay :** *D 204* Bourg-Lastic - *D 987* Avèze Gorges - Tauves - *D 922, D 996* La Bourboule - Le Mont Dore★ - Murol - Saint Nectaire★ - Champeix - Issoire★ - *D 996* Parentignat - *D 34e* Nonette - *D 214e* Brioude★★ - *D 585* Langeac - *D 590* Le Puy★★★ - *D 535.* **Cévennes, Ardèche :** *D 122, D 578* Vals-les-Bains - *N 102* Aubenas - *D 579* Vallon-Pont-d'Arc - Ardèche Gorges★★★ - Pont-St-Esprit★. **Provence, Côte-d'Azur :** *D 994, N 7* Orange★ - *D 950* Carpentras★ - *D 4* Venasque★ - *D 177* Senanque★★★ - Gordes★★ - *D 2, D 102* Roussillon★ - *D 149* Bonnieux - *D 943* Cadenet - *D 973, N 96* Manosque★ - *D 907, D 6* Valensole - Riez - *D 952* Moustiers★ - Verdon Gorges★★★ (N. bank) - *D 955* Comps-sur-Artuby - *D 21, D 2211, D 2* Coursegoules - Col de Vence★ - Cagnes★ - Nice★★.

Strasbourg-Saint-Jean-de-Luz — **Alsace :** Strasbourg★★★ - *N 4* Marlenheim - *D 422, D 30* Wine Route★★★ - Than - *N 66* Col de Bussang. **Lorraine, Vosges :** Bussang. **Franche-Comté :** *D 465* Giromagny - *D 4* Ronchamp★★ - *N 19* Lure - *D 486* Villersexel - Ognon valley *(D 486, D 29, D 4, D 84, D 26)* - Voray - *N 57* Besançon★★★ - *N 57, D 67* Ornans★★ - *D 67* Loue valley★★ - *D 41, D 72, D 103* Lison springs★ - *D 492* Salins★ - *D 472, D 32* Arc-et-Senans★★★ - *D 32, N 83* Arbois★ - Poligny - *N 5* Champagnole - Saint-

Laurent-en-Grandvaux - *D 437* Saint-Claude. **Lyonnais, Bresse :** *D 436, D 936* Bourg-en-Bresse★ - Châtillon-sur-Chalaronne - *D 17* Belleville - *D 37* Beaujeu. **Burgundy :** *D 485* Chauffailles - *D 83, D 4* Charlieu★ - *D 87* Pouilly-sur-Loire. **Berry, Bourbonnais :** Châtel-Montagne. **Auvergne, Velay :** *D 7, D 49, D 122, D 201* Thiers★ - *N 89* Clermont-Ferrand★★ - *D 941* Pontgibaud - *D 986, N 89* Rochefort-Montagne - *D 74* Orcival★★ - *D 27, D 983* Le Mont-Dore★ - *D 996* La Bourboule - *D 922* Bort-Les-Orgues - *D 3* Riom - *D 62* Puy Mary - *D 680* Murat - *N 122* Le Lioran - Vic-sur-Cère - Aurillac. **Agenais, Périgord, Quercy :** *N 120, D 653* Souceyrac - Saint-Céré - Padirac★ - *D 673* Rocamadour★ - *N 20* Cahors★ - *D 953* Moissac★★★ - *N 113* Valence-d'Agenais. **Midi toulousain, Pyrénées :** *D 40, D 7* Lectoure★ - Condom★ - *D 931* Eauze - *N 124* Nogaro. **Bordelais, Landes :** Aire-sur-Adour★ - *D 2* Hagetmau - *D 933.* **Basque country, Béarn, Bigorre :** Orthez - Sauveterre-de-Béarn★ - Saint-Jean-de-Port★ - *D 918* Cambo - Espelette - Asain - Saint-Jean-de-Luz★.

Dunkerque-Perpignan or Marseilles

The North region : Dunkerque★ - *D 916* Bergues★ - *D 928* L'Erkelsbrugge - *D 226* Watten - *D 213* Saint-Omer★ - *D 928* Hesdin★ - Abbeville★ - *D 218* Somme valley - Amiens★★ - *D 210* Monsures. **Ile-de-France :** *D 11* Francastel - *D 151* Brèche valley - *D 15* Clermont - *N 16* Senlis★★★ - *N 330* Ermenonville★ - Meaux★ - *N 3* La Ferté-sous-Jouarre - *D 402* Coulommiers - *N 34, D 231* Provins★★. **Ardenne, Champagne :** *N 19* Nogent-sur-Seine - *D 951* La Motte-Tilly★. **Burgundy :** *D 439, D 939* Fleurigny★ - Sens★ - *N 6* Joigny★ - *D 955* Toucy - Saint-Sauveur-en-Puisaye - *D 955* Cosne-sur-Loire. **Berry, Bourbonnais :** Sancerre★ - Bourges★★★ - *N 76, D 953* Dun-sur-Auron - *D 10* Meillant★★ - Saint-Amand-Montrond - *D 951, D 997* Culan. **Limousin :** Boussac - Aubusson - *D 941, D 7* Peyrat-le-Château - *D 940* Eymoutiers - Treignac - Seilhac - *N 120* Tulle - *N 89* Brive - *D 38* Collonges-la-Rouge★★. **Agenais, Périgord, Quercy :** *D 940* Bretenoux★ - Saint-Céré - Lacapelle-Marival - *N 140* Figeac★. **Rouergue, Albigeois :** *D 901* Conques★★★ - Decazeville - Villefranche-de-Rouergue★★.
D 922 Cordes★★ - *D 600* Albi★★★ - *N 112* Castres★ - Mazamet. **Languedoc, Roussillon :** *D 118* Carcassonne★★★ - Quillan - *D 117* Perpignan★★.
D 901 Marcillac-Vallon★ - Rodez★ - *D 29, D 911* Millau - *D 907b* Tarn Gorges★★★. **Cévennes, Ardèche :** Florac - *D 907, D 9* Corniche des Cévennes (cliff road)★★★ - *D 907* Anduze★ - Nîmes★★★ - Saint-Gilles-du-Gard★★. **Provence, Côte-d'Azur :** *N 572* Arles★★★ - *N 570, D 36* (ferry), *N 268, N 568* Fos - Marseilles★★.

Coach and bus travel

Regular lines

Compared to neighbouring countries, France's bus and coach services seem underdeveloped at first sight, overshadowed as they are by an extensive, punctual rail network.

— In many outlying rural areas, the SNCF relies on buses to complete the rail service, and the resulting network provides access to just about every point on the map. Detailed timetables can be purchased from the SNCF.

Urban transport

The highly convenient Paris transport system allows passengers to use the same tickets or passes *(carte orange)* for either the bus or the métro (→ Paris gazetteer section). Tickets are sold on buses and all Métro stations. They are considerably cheaper if bought at the stations, in *carnets* of ten. A number of towns provide free or very low cost bus services; Lille, Marseilles and Lyons have métro services. Tipping taxi drivers is not obligatory, but appreciated. Normally this is no more than ten percent of the fare.
Urban transport guides are generally available at the local TO or SI.

Touring coaches

France's fleet of long-distance touring coaches has undergone considerable modernisation in recent years. Coach travel is certainly the most economical way to see France. Luxury coaches are by no means reserved for the use of travel agents and groups (→ "Organised travel").

Rail/Coach tours The SNCF publishes a guide ("indicateur") enabling visitors to compose over 1 300 rail and coach tours from over 100 different starting points throughout France. All the relevant fares are included in the guide.

Information • **L'Agetrans,** 2, av. Velasquez, 75008 Paris ☎ (1) 45.63.16.00; the coach operator's central organisation : enquiries and information.
• **SNCF** stations and offices : full information on both regular rail/coach links and excursions.
• The **RATP** (Paris Transport Authority) offers a wide range of excursions in the Paris-Ile-de-France area and beyond : Bureau des excursions, pl. de la Madeleine, 75008 Paris ☎ (1) 42.65.31.18. Two well-known private companies offer similar excursions : **Cityrama,** 4 pl. des Pyramides, 75001 Paris ☎ (1) 42.60.30.14. **Paris-Vision** 214, rue de Rivoli, 75001 Paris ☎ (1) 42.61.20.38.
• In provincial towns, the local **SI, TO** or **bus depot** ("Gare routière") can provide information on bus services and excursions.

A selection of coach excursion companies :

- **Caravelle Tours,** 12, rue Tronchet, 75008 Paris ☎ (1) 42.66.46.84. - **Cartour,** 10, rue Vignon, 75008 Paris ☎ (1) 42.66.14.90. - **Chantereau,** 3, bd de la République, 44000 Nantes ☎ 40.78.50.61. - **Citram,** 14, rue Fondoudège, 33000 Bordeaux ☎ 56.44.14.51. - **Europe Autocars,** 15, rue Poincaré-Thorigny, 77400 Lagny ☎ (1) 40.07.01.08. - **Lesage,** 9, av. Foch, 68100 Mulhouse ☎ 89.56.22.11. - **Terrien,** 1, allée de Turenne, 44003 Nantes ☎ 40.47.93.25. - **Tourisme Verney,** 14, rue de Lubeck, 75116 Paris ☎ (1) 45.53.66.33. - **Valadou-Mottet,** 73, La Canebière, 13001 Marseille ☎ 91.91.90.02; 31, rue Tronchet, 75008 Paris ☎ (1) 42.66.35.29.

• Certain hotel groups offer coach tours : **PLM, Etap** and **Arcade** have launched a "bus à la carte" scheme (overnight stops in 70 European towns). **Mapotel** and the **Relais du Silence** group offer regional and special interest tours. Enquiries to the relevant hotel group (→ Hotels).

Organised travel

Foreign tour operators now offer a range of packages that includes a tour for every taste and pocket, with an increasing emphasis on special interest holidays. Themes include regional exploration, gastronomy and wine-tasting, historical sites and monuments, and even guided tours of famous battlefields, including, of course, the Normandy D-Day beaches. A number of river cruises, horse-drawn caravan tours and, believe it or not, dog-sleigh holidays are now available. The French Travel Service, in conjunction with British Rail and French Railways (S.N.C.F.) offer a wide range of holidays with accommodation ranging from luxury hotels to bed and breakfast with French families. A number of organisations provide special interest tours of holidaymakers with their own car. **F.G.T.O.** offices everywhere can provide addresses, descriptions, and in many cases brochures of the various forms of package tours available. Some tour operators accept direct bookings, others deal only with registered travel agents.

French-based operators A considerable number of excellent packages are offered by French operators, generally through registered *(agréé)* travel agents.

Hints Always read the small print on package tour brochures : some surprises may still be found. A typical example is the quoting of prices "from..." *(à partir de);* the price in question is often for the minimum option, low-season package. Some French brochures, however, deliberately leave the price of meals rather vague, allowing for a certain flexibility in their clients' eating habits.
— Tour prices in France and abroad are almost always quoted for double room occupancy : single occupancy invariably involves an extra charge.
— There is a distinction between a courier *(accompagnateur)* and guide *(guide) :* the former is not expected to have a specialised knowledge of, for example, the history or the architecture of the region visited; he or she should, however, be thoroughly experienced in handling day-to-day problems and generally ensuring the smooth running of the tour. On the other hand, guides are the key to the success of a special interest tour and should be able to provide detailed specialist information on the theme in question.

Information • The French Railways, **(S.N.C.F.)** tourist service organises a number of interesting tours and excursions throughout France; prices include rail and coach travel and accommodation. Enquiries at any S.N.C.F. office or station or at S.N.C.F. agencies abroad (→ France by train).

● The **Caisse Nationale des Monuments historiques et des Sites** (the historical monuments board; → Museums), in conjunction with France-Voyages-Civilisations du Monde, 10, rue Auber, 75009 Paris, ☎ (1) 42.68.02.02, offers an annual selection of a dozen or so tours of historical interest sites, with highly qualified guides. Although the commentaries are in French (English commentaries can be provided by prior request for groups), English language booklets are available for each site.

● → **F.G.T.O.**

Hitch-hiking

The pros and cons of "thumbing it" are too well known to be debated here; however with a minimum of courtesy and respect, hitch-hiking is certainly far more than a mere means of transportation, especially for foreign visitors for whom the variety of human encounters provides a holiday bonus. A number of organisations specialise in bringing together drivers and passengers (passengers are generally asked to pay a registration fee and are expected to contribute in some way to the voyage: e.g. share the petrol costs), thus allowing the visitor to plan his or her itinerary.

Hints

— Hitch-hiking is strictly prohibited on motorways (but permitted on slip-roads and at toll-booths).

— Use common sense, taking into account both the motorist's convenience and security when choosing a spot to hitch from; **Le Manuel du Routard,** available in bookstores, contains a host of excellent advice and information for French-speaking hitch-hikers.

Addresses

● **Allostop,** 84, passage Brady, 75010 Paris, ☎ (1) 42.46.00.66. Bordeaux: ☎ 56.81.24.59. Cannes ☎ 93.38.60.88. Cholet ☎ 41.62.22.35. Lille ☎ 20.57.96.69. Lyons ☎ 78.42.38.29. Aix-en-Provence ☎ 42.38.37.51. Nantes ☎ 40.89.04.85. Rennes ☎ 99.30.98.87. Strasbourg ☎ 88.37.13.13. Toulouse ☎ 61.22.68.13.

● **Paris-Stop** 35, rue Jacob, 75005 Paris, ☎ (1) 42.60.42.09. Lyons, 29, rue Pasteur, ☎ 78.58.65.29.

Accommodation

Hotels

A word of **warning:** "hotel" has a variety of meanings in French. Endless confusion is caused by the term *hôtel particulier*: not a private hotel in the accepted English sense, but an often luxurious town house built (often some centuries ago) for the use of the wealthy or the aristocratic during their residence in the city. The *hôtel de ville* is the town hall, the *hôtel des ventes* the auction room, and the *hôtel des impôts* the tax centre. Naturally, none of these establishments will be inclined to accept paying guests...

Classification

There are approximately 17500 *hôtels de tourisme,* controlled and supervised on a national basis, and classified in **five categories** (used throughout this guide): *&** : Simple but comfortable hotel. *** : Very comfortable hotel. **** : First class hotel. ****(L) : Luxury hotel.

Several hundred hotels of all categories have been selected for this guide; **particularly recommended establishments** (amenities, quiet location, attentive service...) **are indicated by a ● symbol.** In 1986 numerous hotels will open with comfortable and inexpensive rooms for about 100 F a night per person.

Hotel chains

The whole range of hotel categories is covered by a number of hotel chains. In addition to the guarantees provided by these chains the visitor can identify in advance the "character" of the hotel concerned (a brief description of the better-known French chains is given below). A number of chains offer centralised reservation facilities; all publish an annual directory of their establishments (frequently available from F.G.T.O. offices).

Hints — Most summer and winter resort hotels offer special rates for *pension complète* (accommodation and full meals) or *demi-pension* (accommodation, breakfast and either lunch or dinner). A minimum stay of three nights is generally required and advance booking is naturally advisable.

— A legal distinction is made between an *acompte* - a simple down-payment, and *arrhes* - a deposit that may be witheld by the hotel in case of cancellation by the client, or reimbursed at 200 % should the hotel be responsable for the cancellation.

— Reservations made without a deposit should always be confirmed on the day if you intend arriving later than 7 pm, otherwise the hotel will have every right to re-let your room. In all circumstances, notify hotels of changes and cancellations as early as possible.

— Strange as this may seem to visitors, some small hotels have a fixed closing day. Family establishments with only one or two employees are unable to ensure full service on their staff's day off and although resident guests are assured of minimum services, the reception desk, and often the restaurant and bar remain closed.

— Strictly speaking, a hotel has no legal right to demand that short-term guests take their meals in the hotel. Nevertheless this custom is tolerated insofar as it is honestly formulated and can be explained by certain circumstances, notably in peak tourist season when the *hôtelier* can reasonably expect to find in the course of the day guests for all his rooms who will want to take their meals at the hotel.

— Advertised rates are generally quoted for a double room; few singles are available but a third bed can often be provided for around 30 % extra. Breakfast is rarely included in the basic room rate.

Reservations — Booking direct with France is an increasingly easy affair, thanks to direct-dialing facilities and the excellent reservation services offered by the regional **Loisirs-Accueil** (leisure welcome service) organisations (→ gazetteer sections under "Reservations"). Most services are free of charge and English is generally spoken. When booking by post, take advantage of the **F.G.T.O.** bilingual reservation form. F.G.T.O. offices can provide invaluable information and advice on hotels in France (→ Sources of Information).

The **Accueil de France** organisation in Paris and in a growing number of towns makes same-day bookings for personal callers only. Head office : 127, av. des Champs-Élysées, 75008 Paris; open Mon-Sat, 9 am-8 pm; Sun & nat hols : 9 am-6 pm. Provincial offices are generally open until 6 pm, later in summer (enquire at local TO or SI).

Information Associations of independent hotels :

- **Châteaux et demeures de tradition,** Demeure des Brousses, rue Mas-de-Brousses, 34000 Montpellier, ☎ 67.65.77.66; 64 stately establishments, mainly ***.
- **Châteaux-hôtels indépendents et hôtelleries d'atmosphère,** château de Pray, 37400 Amboise, ☎ 47.57.23.67; 120 hotels and 13 châteaux that accept paying guests (→ "Châteaux holidays"); ** to ****.
- **Châteaux en vacances,** B.P. 4, 78220 Viroflay-sur-Saône, ☎ 30.24.18.16.
- **France-Accueil,** 85, rue du Dessous-des-Berges, 75013 Paris, ☎ (1) 45.83.04.22; 149 traditional **& *** establishments, 12 new hotels in 1985 including the Hotel Solhotel in Cannes and the Hotel Aragon in Carcassonne. **U.K. reservations :** Minotels, 11 Palmeira Mansions, Hove, West Sussex BN3 2GA, ☎ (273) 731908.
- **Inter-Hotel,** Toulouse-Ramonville, 31520 Saint-Agne, ☎ 61.73.40.63; over 200 traditional ** to **** hotels. **U.K. reservations :** 35 Harrington Gardens, London SW7 4 JU ☎ 01.370.27.02.
- **Logis et Auberges de France,** 23, rue Jean-Mermoz, 75008 Paris, ☎ (1) 43.59.91.99; around 4600 * to *** establishments, generally family-managed and situated in the country, with a special emphasis on friendly service and regional cooking; annual guide (bookings direct with individual hotels).
- **Mapotel,** 3, rue de Ville-l'Evêque, 75008 Paris, ☎ (1) 42.66.41.74; 144 old-established town hotels, generally ***. **U.K. reservations :** Best Western Hotels, 26 Kew Road, Richmond, Surrey, ☎ (01) 940 9766. **U.S. reservations :** Best Western International H.Q., Best Western Way, P.O. Box 10203, Phoenix, AZ 85064, ☎ (800) 528 1234.
- **Petits Nids de France,** hôtel du Mouton Blanc, 59400 Cambrai, ☎ 27.81.30.16; 87 hôtels, mainly **.

● **Relais du Silence,** hôtel des Oiseaux, 38640 Claix, ☎ 76.98.35.79; around 200 *** and **** establishments where the accent, as the name suggests, is on calm and relaxation.

● **Relais et Châteaux,** 10, place de la Concorde, 75008 Paris, ☎ (1) 47.42.00.20; the showcase of the French hotel industry: 332 top-class establishments (including the "Relais Gourmands" restaurants); from *** to ****(L). **U.K. reservations :** (travel agents only) (1) 742 0020. **U.S. reservations :** David Mitchell & Co., 200 Madison Avenue, New York, NY 1016, ☎ (212) 696-1323.

● **Paris-Accueil,** 23, rue de Marignan, 75008 Paris, ☎ (1) 42.56.20.00. — **U.S. :** 630 Fifth Avenue-Suite 715, New York, N.Y. 10111 ☎ (212) 977-7171. If there is no more room at the hotel or if you are looking for a studio or an apartment in Paris or on the Côte d'Azur for a fairly brief period, this organisation proposes the 'hôtel chez le particulier' (hotel in someone's home) scheme. Normal housekeeping services are assured by the organisation.

French hotel chains :

● **Arcade,** 40, rue de l'Arcade, 75008 Paris, ☎ (1) 42.68.23.45; ** modern town-centre hotels with simplified yet quite adequate facilities.

● **Campanile,** 58, bd Gouvion-St-Cyr, 75017 Paris, ☎ (1) 47.57.11.11; around 80 ** establishments on the outskirts of major towns.

● **Climat de France,** B.P. 93, 91943 Les Ulis Cedex, ☎ 69.28.58.60; medium-sized ** establishments on the outskirts of major towns. **U.K. reservations :** The Voyage Organisation, 19 Catherine Place, London SW1 6DX, ☎ (01) 630 9061. **U.S. telephone reservations :** (703) 527-5410, or through any U.S. Climat hotel (Washington and Dallas areas).

● **Concorde,** 58, bd Gouvion-St-Cyr, 75017 Paris, ☎ (1) 47.58.12.25; 20 **, **** & ****(L) international-style hotels throughout France (6 in Paris). **U.K. reservations :** Thistle Hotels, co K.P.H., 5 De Vere Gardens, London SW7, ☎ (01) 938 1755 (groups : 937 8033). **U.S. reservations :** Marriot Supra-National Hotels, Omaha NE 58114, ☎ (tolll free); (800) 228-9290.

● **Frantel,** 12, rue Portalis, 75008 Paris ☎ (1) 42.68.22.88. Modern *** to ****(L) city-centre hotels where the accent is on traditional French hospitality and gastronomy. **U.K. reservations :** Utell International (U.K.), Banda House, Cambridge Grove, London W6 0LE, ☎ (01) 741 1588. **U.S. reservations :** 200 W 57th. Street, New York N.Y. 10017, ☎ (toll-free) : (800) 223 9862.

● **Ibis,** 6-8, rue du Bois-Briard, 91021 Evry Cedex ☎ 60.77.92.90; modern ** convenience hotels in or near towns. **U.K. & U.S. reservations :** see Novotel.

● **Mercure,** (ACCOR Group, 2, rue de la Mare-Neuve, 91021 Évry Cedex), ☎ 60.77.93.20; *** international-style convenience hotels similar to the related Novotels. **U.K. & U.S. reservations :** see Novotel.

● **Méridien,** 81, bd Gouvion-St-Cyr, 75017 Paris, ☎ (1) 47.57.15.70. ****(L) establishments in major towns and some holiday resorts; traditional French luxury in modern surroundings. **U.K. and U.S. reservations :** Air France Offices.

● **Novotel,** (ACCOR Group, with Mercure, Sofitel, Ibis); *** international-style hotels in or near major towns. **U.K. reservations:** Novotel International, 1, Short Lands, London W6, ☎ (01) 724 2140. **U.S. reservations:** Novotel International, 509 Madison Avenue, NY1022, ☎ (212) 752 7430.

● **P.L.M.-Etap,** 12, rue Portalis, 75008 Paris, ☎ (1) 42.68.22.88; *** to ****(L) in major towns and on the Riviera. **U.K. reservations :** Morris Assoc., 42 Chase Side, Enfield, Middx EN2 6NF, ☎ (01) 367 5175. **U.S. reservations :** Harry Jarvinen and Assoc., 1717 North Highland Av., Los Angeles CA 90028, ☎ (213) 462-6391.

Major international hotel chains operating in France :

● **Hilton Reservation Service,** Orly-Sud 267, 94544 Orly, ☎ 46.87.34.80. **U.S. :** (212) 564-7916; **U.K. :** (01) 631 1767.

● **Holiday Inn,** 61, rue de Malte, 75011 Paris, ☎ (1) 48.06.20.00. **U.S. :** (toll-free) (800) HOLIDAY; **U.K. :** (01) 722 7755.

● **Hyatt,** 120, av. des Champs-Élysées, ☎ (1) 45.62.47.10. **U.S. U.K.** - Inter Continental, 5, place de l'Opéra, 75009 Paris, ☎ (1) 42.68.13.80. **U.S. U.K.** - **Nikko,** 61, quai de Grenelle, 75015 Paris, ☎ (1) 45.75.62.62. **U.S. :** (toll-free) (800) 223 2094; **U.K.** (Top Rank Hotels) (01) 370 3484 - Nova Park, 53, rue François-1er, 75008 Paris, ☎ (1) 45.62.63.64. - **Sheraton,** 19, rue du Cdt-Mouchotte, 75014 Paris, ☎ (1) 320.15.51. **U.S.** (toll-free) (800) 325-3535; **U.K. :** (01) 636 66411 - **Trust House Forte,** 23, place Vendôme, 75001 Paris, ☎ (1) 42.61.10.65. **U.S. :** (12) 541-4400; **U.K. :** (01) 567 3444.

Self-Catering and rental accommodation

From self-contained "studio" flats to luxurious apartments, simple country cottages to genuine châteaux, the variety of self-catering accommodation available to visitors to France covers absolutely every need.

Foreign-based In both the U.K. and the U.S. a considerable number of agencies specialise in French holiday home rentals. Many of these provide services well beyond the simple rental arrangements : ferry bookings (often at reduced rates), overnight hotel reservations, air travel (with optional car-rental), etc. All offer comprehensive insurance schemes.
Lists of agencies, and in many cases brochures, are available from **French Government Tourist Offices.**

French estate agencies Since 1977, regulations require holiday homes rented through estate agents to be thoroughly inspected and to be classified in one of three categories : standard *(normal)*, comfortable *(confortable)* or luxury *(luxe)*. Rates are thus more or less standardised within these three categories, according to the law of supply and demand; very few cases of over-charging occur nowadays.
Insurance (including cancellation insurance) is widely available, and the agency fees rarely exceed 8-12 % of the rental.
The **F.N.A.I.M.** (one of the two French estate agents' federations; below) supervises rental operations, and will recommend suitable agencies according to the type of accommodation required... up to and including historical châteaux.

Other organisations **Loisirs-Accueil** (leisure welcome service), **T.O.'s** and **S.I.'s** all provide assistance in renting holiday homes; however, their workload prevents them from guaranteeing the exactitude of every particular description and the fairness of the rates demanded. The range of accommodation offered by these organisations is nevertheless quite vast, and always includes bargains that would be difficult to find through commercial agencies.

Direct rentals Although the best bargains of all are probably to be found in the small-ads sections of newspapers (particularly *Le Figaro*), this form of booking is best left to the more experienced - or adventurous - holidaymaker. Honest home-owners do of course exist but there is a definite tendency to over-estimate the rental value of villas in the popular resort areas; little legal recourse is available should disputes arise.

Exchanges Still in the developmental stage in France, accommodation exchanges are certainly the most inexpensive form of holiday, and frequently lead to the founding of long-lasting friendships (→ below for a selection of specialised exchange organisations).

Hints — Many owners and rental agencies still insist on a minimum one month rental during July and August, especially in resort areas (→ calendar). Elsewhere, and during the low season, two-week bookings are available; weekly rentals may occasionally be offered, although these often entail a surcharge. December is generally the latest reservation date if a wide range of choice is desired.
— A deposit will generally be required when dealing directly with a French agent or owner : → the "hotels" section for the distinction between *arrhes* and *acompte.*
— All gas and electricity charges must be settled before departure. Bottled butane gas is used extensively in rural areas : visitors should be prepared to replace empty bottles at the local concession (rarely more than a few minutes' drive away).
— In France, established organisations such as **Interhome, Vacances Lagrange,** or **Maeva,** and member agencies of the **F.N.A.I.M.** or the **F.F.P.I.C.** (→ below) offer the widest range of holiday homes and the best guarantees.
— Visitors seeking peace and quiet are advised to avoid peak-season apartment rentals in resort areas.
— When dealing directly with home-owners it is advisable to obtain the fullest possible description of the premises and amenities.
— SI and TO staff in the smaller rural districts often have first-hand knowledge of rental accommodation and will be pleased to supply information by telephone.
— **"Villages de Gîtes"** are becoming increasingly popular : independent accommodation (→ Gîtes) generally grouped around a central dining hall. The majority of these villages are managed by organisations such as V.V.T., V.A.L., O.C.C.A.J., etc. (→ Organised accommodation).

Information • **F.N.A.I.M.** (Fédération nationale des agents immobiliers), 129, rue du Faubourg-Saint-Honoré, 75008 Paris, ☎ (1) 42.25.24.26; list of registered agencies, descriptive catalogue and a telephone enquiry service called **"Allo Vacances"** (1) 42.21.75.75.

- **Interhome,** 14, av. Jean-Aicard, 75011 Paris, ☎ (1) 43.55.44.25; 15 000 villas, apartments and hotel rooms. **U.K. reservations** (also handles enquiries and reservations from the U.S.A.) : Interhome, 383 Richmond Road, Twickenham TW1 2EF, ☎ (01) 891.12.94.
- **Vacances-Lagrange,** 34, rue Pasquier, 75008 Paris, ☎ (1) 42.66.16.65; rental accommodation catalogue.
- **Maeva-locations,** 30, rue d'Orléans, 92200 Neuilly, ☎ (1) 47.45.17.21; rental accommodation catalogue.
- A number of **regular travel agents,** including Havas-Voyages and Frantour, offer standardised rental accommodation.

Accommodation exchange organisations :

- **Intervac,** 55, rue Nationale, 37000 Tours, ☎ 47.20.20.57. **U.K. representative :** Intervac G.B., 6 Siddals Lane, Allestree, Derby DE3 2DY, ☎ (0332) 55.89.31. **U.S. representative :** Vacation Exchange Club, 12006 11th Av., Unit 12, Youngtown, AZ 85363, ☎ (602) 972-2186.
- **Home Exchange International :** Vanessa Norgaard-Jensen, 82 Lyndhurst Way, London SE-155 AP, ☎ (01) 701.17.62. **U.S. representatives :** (West Coast) 22458 Ventura Bvd., Suite E, Woodland Hills, CA 91364, ☎ (318) 999-8990. (East Coast) Linda MacCall, 185, Park Row, Suite 14D, New York 10038, ☎ (212) 349-5340.
- **Home Interchange France,** 1, rue Ferruce, 84000 Avignon. 8 Hillside, Farningham, Kent DA40DD. (0322) 864 527.
- **Élysées-Concorde,** 9, rue Royale, 75008 Paris, ☎ (1) 42.65.11.99, telex 640 793 F; short term rentals of furnished and fully equiped apartments in Paris best areas. Studios to five bedroom flats available one week onwords.

Rural holidays

Stations vertes (lit. "green stations")

In addition to a basic natural attraction such as a lake, forest or river, *stations vertes* offer suitable accommodation facilities (hotel, registered camping site...), a minimum of leisure equipment (bathing facilities, tennis courts, youth club...), an efficient welcome service *(syndicat d'initiative, bureau de tourisme,* friendly shopkeeper, etc.) and a particular attention to all that meets the eye : floral decoration, cleanliness. *Stations vertes* are indicated in the gazetteer section of this guide by the symbol "♥".
A number of rural mountain villages have recently subscribed to a similar charter : *villages de neige de vacances.*

Pays d'accueil

The voluntary cooperation between adjacent local authorities has led to the creation of the *Pays d'accueil* system, (lit. "welcome region") where the various leisure facilities in a particular zone are coordinated by a responsible delegate. Visitors are thus offered a wide range of holiday activities, hiking and rambling trails, bicycle rental with signposted circuits, horse-riding, canoeing, arts and crafts exhibitions, etc. In many cases the purchase of an inexpensive pass provides access to all of these activities during the visitor's stay.
A wide range of suitable accommodation is, of course, offered in all cases.

Information

- **Association française des stations vertes de vacances,** Préfecture de la Sarthe, 72000 Le Mans.
- **Regional and departmental tourist organisations.**

Gîtes de France

A Gîte de France may be a small cottage or village house, a self-contained flat in a farmhouse (or a mill, manor, chalet, etc.) or a converted barn or outhouse. All provide low-cost, self-catering holiday homes in the heart of rural France.
Privately-owned, the overwhelming majority of gîtes are off the beaten track. The concept has been extended to a number of fields : ski-gîtes, children's gîtes, hikers', pony-trekkers' and cyclists' gîtes (the latter are very simple, providing the basic necessities for overnight stays); over 20 000 gîtes of one form or another are listed in France. The familial holiday gîte remains, however, by far the most popular.

Hints

— All have modern amenities such as electric light, running water and flush toilets but otherwise retain their rustic simplicity. Bed-linen is not provided.
— Minimum stay in peak season is always two weeks or one month.

Information

- **Fédération nationale des Gîtes ruraux de France,** 34, rue Godot-de-Mauroy, 75009 Paris, ☎ (1) 47.42.25.43; publishes an exhaustive annual guide.

— Information from F.G.T.O. offices, in particular in the U.K., where special booking facilities and an official handbook containing illustrated descriptions of 1800 selected gîtes are offered to members of Gîtes de France (£2.50 p.a.).
Members are also offered reduced-rate ferry crossings and overnight bookings at some Logis de France hotels (enquiries to Gîtes de France Ltd., address as F.G.T.O. → Sources of information).
● Reservations can be made through Loisir-Accueil offices (→ relevant gazetteer section).

Farmhouse holidays The emergence of a new breed of holidaymaker has coincided with a sustained effort on the part of French farmers and authorities to attract visitors to the "real" France and a wide range of farmhouse holidays now awaits the tourist seeking something more than the traditional "sea and sun". Although farms throughout France now participate in these schemes, the following regions are noteworthy for the number of possibilities available : Brittany, Normandy, Charentes and Poitou, Massif Central, Limousin, Périgord, Cévennes, Alps.

Camping "à la ferme" The simplest form of farm holiday : a maximum of 6 tent sites (pitches or emplacements) with adjacent sanitary facilities and a communal building for the occasional rainy day. The degree of contact with your hosts will vary from case to case but farm-grown produce is almost invariably available - camping and gastronomy are by no means incompatible!

Aires naturelles de camping A recent development : country sites, always near a farm or hamlet, that offer a maximum of 25 pitches.

Chambres d'hôte Bed and breakfast (in some cases dinner, too) in the farmhouse itself or in an adjacent building.

***Tables d'hôte* and farmhouse inns** An increasingly popular formula, simple in its originality : sharing the farm's menu of the day. While in a few isolated cases the line between a *table d'hôte* and an actual restaurant has become rather thin, guests are generally treated to authentic regional specialities, based on local produce prepared according to traditional recipes. A considerable number of excellent farms are reserved as stopovers for rambling and hiking circuits.

Special interest farm holidays In addition to exploring the environment and the ways of rural life, visitors are frequently offered specific activities such as cross-country skiing, horse-riding, cooking, wine-tasting and handicrafts.

Work on the farm A number of farms welcome help in harvesting, grape- and fruit-picking.

Children Farms in 33 departments offer *gîtes d'enfants* (→ Gîtes) for children from 5 to 13 yrs; groups never exceed a dozen or so and are welcomed by the farmer's children, their companions in the minor farmyard tasks (feeding and caring for the animals, etc.) and the games, walks and sports that are a feature of these *gîtes*. Children communicate with astounding ease, and rudimentary French is all that is generally necessary to ensure fast integration into the group.

Hints — July and August are not the best months for farmhouse holidays. Not only are they often fully-booked, but the harvest is in full swing and your hosts will rarely be available.
— In the low season, reduced rates apply to long-term reservations; short-term bookings (in some cases even for weekends) are also accepted.
— Advance notice is always required for both meals and accommodation : a phone call shortly before arriving is always appreciated.
— Farms and *gîtes* cannot provide the same services as hotels; your hosts are restricted by their every-day work and cannot revise their schedules to fit yours.

Holiday and weekend packages ● A number of tour operators and agencies offer all-inclusive farm holidays, among them :
● **Havas Voyage**
● **Voyage-conseil,** 26, quai de la Rapée, 75012 Paris, ☎ (1) 43.46.27.70.
● **V.V.T,** 38, bd. Edgar Quinet, 75014 Paris, ☎ (1) 43.20.13.66.
● **Hobby-Loisirs,** 8, rue de Milan, 75009 Paris, ☎ (1) 45.26.60.80.
● Further information from the **F.G.T.O.**

Information ● **Fédération des Gîtes ruraux de France et Maison du Tourisme Vert,** 35, rue Godot-de-Mauroy, 75009 Paris, ☎ (1) 47.42.25.43.

- **Agriculture et Tourisme,** 9, Av. George-V. 75008 Paris, ☎ (1) 47.23.51.50.; wide range of farm holidays and activities, exclusively through genuine farmers - no agencies or commercial organisations; annual guide "Bienvenue la Ferme" available by post for 45F.
- **Centre de Documentation et d'Information rurale,** 92, rue du Dessous-des-Berges, 75013 Paris, ☎ (1) 45.83.04.92.
- **Centre d'Information et de Documentation et de Jeunesse.** (→ Young people).
- The **F.G.T.O.**'s London office can provide a 250 page booklet "Accueil à la Campagne" listing *chambres d'hôtes, gîtes d'étape* and farmhouse camping and caravanning facilities (introduction in English; £3.50 inc. V.A.T. and postage).
- Local **TO** and **SI.**

Villages and clubs

The Club Méditerranée has become a household word in several languages, thanks to the club's pioneering work in providing totally carefree holidays with a remarkable absence of regimentation and where sport is a dominant theme.
The *village de gîtes* has become increasingly popular since its inception in the early seventies : *gîtes* clustered around a central leisure activity and restaurant centre; this inexpensive form of holiday offers the social atmosphere of a club, while allowing residents a high degree of independence. Naturally, as with all *gîte* holidays, the housework has to be done... Foreign-based tour operators now offer a range of holidays on an all-inclusive, "club" principle : lists are available from the F.G.T.O. in the U.S. and the U.K.
A number of French associations run excellent holiday villages, often with an accent on a particular sport or leisure activity.
Two other organisations are outstanding for their sports-orientated holiday villages : the **O.C.C.A.J.** (→ Young people), and **Vacances Auvergne-Limousin** (→ Winter sports).

Families

One of the pioneers in family-orientated holiday villages, **Leo Lagrande Loisirs,** 17, rue de la Grande-Batelière, 75009 Paris, ☎ (1) 45.23.45.45, still offers a wide range of holidays throughout France, with remarkable facilities. The same can be said of **Villages, Vacances, Familles,** 38, bd Edgar-Quinet, 75014 Paris, ☎ (1) 45.38.20.00.

Information

- **U.N.A.T.** (Union Nationale des Associations de Tourisme), 8, rue César-Franck, 75015 Paris, ☎ (1) 47.83.21.73; details of the facilities offered by the 150 member holiday associations.
- **Club Méditerranée,** Place de la Bourse, 75002 Paris, ☎ (1) 42.96.10.00; **U.S. :** Club Med Sales Inc., 3 East 54th St., 10019 New York, NY, ☎ (212) 750-1670. **U.K. :** 62, South Moulton St., London W1Y 1HH, ☎ (01) 409.0644.
- → Gîtes.

Château holidays

Châteaux-hôtels

Over 300 châteaux-hôtels are operated by three organisations : **Châteaux et demeures de tradition, Relais et Châteaux** and **Châteaux-hôtels indépendants et hostelleries d'atmosphères** (→ Hotels). **Les Grandes Étapes Françaises** offer 7 châteaux specially selected for their beauty and seclusion, where the accent is placed on individual attention.

Châteaux-hôtes

Châteaux-Accueil and **châteaux en Vacances** offer a network of authentic châteaux and manors where the owners are prepared to let one or two rooms and to share their table with their guests... who are naturally expected to adapt to the life of the château. A number of "châtelains" accept guests on a bed and breakfast basis — details are available from the relevant TO and SI.

Château camping

This recent initiative offers visitors camping facilities on the château estate, generally in parks of considerable beauty. **Castel-Camping** is the principal organisation involved, but information is also available from the regional TO.

Information

- **Château-Accueil,** brochure and information from **La Demeure historique,**

57, quai de la Tournelle, 75005 Paris, ☎ (1) 43.29.02.86 ; Vicomtesse de Bonneval, Présidente, **Château-Accueil,** 18210 Charenton-sur-Cher, ☎ 48.60.87.62 ; Mme A.-I. Ide, **Château-Accueil,** Saint-Maur-sur-Loir, 28800 Bonneval, ☎ 37.47.28.57.

- **Châteaux en Vacances,** B.P. 4, 78220 Viroflay, ☎ 30.24.18.16.
- **Castel-Camping,** château des Ormes, 35120 Épiniac, ☎ 99.48.10.19 ; 41 camp-sites in the shade of ancient towers...
- A number of ancient monuments and sites can be hired for receptions, seminaries, etc. : **Caisse Nationale des Monuments Historiques et des Sites** (C.N.M.H.S.), 62, rue Saint-Antoine, 75004 Paris, ☎ (1) 42.74.22.22.
- The **F.G.T.O.** can provide details of tour operators and agencies offering château holidays throughout France.

Youth Hostels

Conditions The Youth Hostel Association card, obtainable throughout the world (U.S. and U.K. → below) entitles the holder to the facilities provided by both French youth hostel organisations : the L.F.A.J. (300 hostels) and the F.U.A.J. (250 hostels). The length of stay may be limited to 3 or 4 nights during the peak season or in Paris, although a number of hostels offer longer stays with various activities (skiing and other sports, handicrafts, etc.) included in the price.

Information

- **F.U.A.J.** Fédération unie des auberges de jeunesse, 5, rue Mesnil, 75116 Paris, ☎ (1) 42.61.84.03.
- **L.F.A.J.** Ligue française pour les auberges de jeunesse, 83, rue de Rennes, 75006 Paris, ☎ (1) 45.49.11.73.
- **Youth Hostel Association,** 14 Southampton St., **London** WC2E 7H7, ☎ (01) 836 8541.
- **American Youth Hostel Inc.,** Travel Dept., 8th floor, 1332 1st St N.W., **Washington,** D.C. 20005, ☎ (2) 873-6161.
- **American Youth Hostels,** National Campus **Delaplane,** VA 22025.
- → Young people.

Camping and caravaning

The French were pioneers and France has more than 7 000 sites and parks.

Off-site camping Camping on private property is authorised only with the landowner's permission, but prohibited : on beaches, at the roadside, on sites designated for conservation *(classés)* by the Historical Monuments board, in nature parks and reserves, less than 200 m from water catchments (sumps) or less than 500 m from an historical monument.

Camping sites A minimum surface area per tent emplacement, or "pitch", is laid down : 90 m² (* and ** sites), 95 m² (***), 100 m² (****). Varying degrees of amenities are imposed according to the category. Sites also may be recognised and guaranteed by the F.F.C.C. *(Fédération Française de Camping-Caravaning),* the handbook of which lists more than 1 000.

Caravaning Caravans may be booked for the site in advance or can be towed to the chosen site (road regulations are similar to those in force in the U.K. : further information from the A.A., the R.A.C., the Touring Club of France, the Caravan Club of Great Britain and Ireland and, in the U.S.A., the A.A.A. and other car organizations). Officially-recognised sites must provide a minimum of 100 m² per caravan. A number of ski resorts offer camping sites which should always be booked well in advance (sites list available from the F.F.C.C.) (→ above).

Camping-cars A camping-car is subject to minor parking restrictions, especially in urban areas : always check with the local TO, SI or *gendarmerie.* The major car-hire companies (→ Motoring) offer camping cars ; L.U.T. and VALEM (see phone directory) specialise in these vehicles ; advance booking is essential.

Hints
— Advance booking is essential in the peak season.
— Five excellent camps operate within easy reach of Paris.
— Membership in a camping club or association is a distinct advantage and the International Camping Carnet (issued by national camping clubs and also by the R.A.C., A.A. and the Touring Club of France) is especially useful. In the U.S.A., check with the A.A.A.

— Numerous travel firms and operators at home offer all-inclusive camping and caravan holidays in France; sites are generally selected in the **** category and every aspect of the holiday is taken care of, down to the bottle opener : visitors need only pack their personal belongings. Brochures from F.G.T.O. offices.
— Camping equipment can be hired from British Rail and the S.N.C.F. at Newhaven and Dover, from Townsend Thoresen Ferries at Dover and Southampton, and Normandy Ferries at Southampton (→ Getting to France). A reduction of 25 % on the rental rate is offered to ferry users.

Information

Fédération Française de Camping-Caravaning, 78, rue de Rivoli 75004 Paris, ☎ (1) 42.72.84.08; **U.K. : F.F.C.C.,** 6 the Meadows Worlington Bury St Edmunds Suffolk IP288SH; coordinates 330 French clubs and associations; official guide to recognised camping sites : 8 400 sites, including seasonal farm locations and *caravaneige* sites; English supplement; (available by mail or from bookshops, including Hachette in London); list of clubs and associations.

- **Fédération Nationale de l'Hôtellerie de Plein-air** (open-air hotellery federation), 105, rue Lafayette, 75010 Paris, ☎ (1) 48.78.13.77.
- **Main French camping clubs :**
- **Camping Club de France,** 218, bd St. Germain, 75007 Paris, ☎ (1) 45.48.30.03.
- **Camping Club International de France,** 22, av. Victoria, 75001 Paris, ☎ (1) 42.36.12.40.
- **Campéoles,** (subsidiary of V.V.F.), 62, bd du Montparnasse, 75015 Paris, ☎ 45.49.21.12.
- **Vacances Mediterranéennes,** a new chain of camping sites. The group's flagship : Holiday Green at Fréjus (Var) with a 1000 m² swimming pool.
- **Groupement des Campeurs Universitaires de France,** 24, rue du Rocher, 75008 Paris, ☎ (1) 43.87.17.05.
- Two of the better known commercial guides to camping in France (available in bookshops) : **Michelin Camping Caravaning** (uses easily understood symbols); **Letts Campsite Guide** (in English).

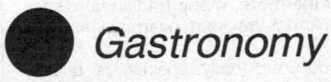

Gastronomy

Restaurants

To say that food is important to the French would be to understate the obvious. *La cuisine* is not just important; it is part of the national heritage. The occasional crisis that erupts in the rarified world of French gastronomy, in the process furnishing the media with lively copy, only provides further proof of the enduring vitality of food to the French. Where else in the world does a fall in the rating of a restaurant make headline news?

Restaurants... and other establishments

For most of us, France offers more ways of eating out probably than any other country in the world. A simple sandwich taken at a zinc *café* counter and accompanied by a glass of local wine can be memorable : there are ample establishments serving crispy *baguette* bread with delicious *saucisse* and other tasty fillings. The French response to *le fast food* is the ***croissanterie*** or ***briocherie,*** freshly-made pastries. For the best in take-away food, however, the traditional ***traiteur*** (delicatessen) or **charcutier** (prepared meats) provide a range of exceptional snacks and dishes, often including authentic regional specialities; some offer simple restaurant rooms. ***Boulangeries*** (bread and pastry shops) and ***pâtisseries*** (pastry only) are also a source of delicious snacks. France has almost as many pizzerias as Italy, and numerous **North African** or **Greek restaurants.** Even more exotic dishes are offered by the prevalent **Chinese** and **Vietnamese restaurants.** In the 13th arrondissement Paris now has the largest "Chinatown" of any European city. Inexpensive yet appetizing **French cooking** is to be had in innumerable *cafés* (look for the posted *plat du jour,* or daily special), ***brasseries*** (larger, more luxurious *cafés* that provide a wider range of dishes) and other modest restaurants.

For visitors travelling to and from their holiday destinations, the **autoroute restaurants,** now at least provide more-or-less acceptable fare for those unwilling to forsake the autoroute in search of a more rewarding country inn *(auberge).*

Restaurants this guide A wide selection of restaurants is provided in the gazetteer sections after each regional tourism description in this guide. Specialities, where mentioned, are subject to seasonal availability. Establishments preceded by a ● symbol have been singled out by a team of 121 top chefs and restaurant owners whose names are listed in the opening pages of this guide, together with the towns under which their own restaurants are mentioned (red type face) in the gazetteer sections. Their choice includes restaurants of every style and category, and is designed to provide an overall selection of the best in French gastronomy . The ♦ symbols are designed to convey the overall charm of a particular establishment : ♦ pleasant restaurant; ♦♦ comfortable, pleasant surroundings; ♦♦♦ refined surroundings, excellent reception and service; ♦♦♦♦ exceptional surroundings, decor, reception and service.

Mealtimes Although a number of Parisian restaurants remain open around the clock, lunch in France generally is served from 12:30-2 and dinner from 7:30-9/9:30. These hours may be considerably extended in the livelier districts or large towns and in some smaller resorts during the holiday season. People generally eat earlier in the provinces where opening and closing hours may be more restrictive. (The Midi Region is an exception; having dinner there at 10 pm is by no means unusual.)

Menu, *à la carte* and *plat du jour* By law restaurants must offer at least one fixed-price meal — the *menu,* which is more narrowly defined than in English. The term *table d'hôte* is rarely used in France, except in its strictest sense. (→ Farmhouse holidays). The service charge may be included. Wine (often a ***vin de pays*** local or regional wine, worth sampling) may be included, too. Drinking water (from the tap — *eau fraiche*) must be supplied free on request; The *menu* is far more economical than a meal compiled ***à la carte*** (*carte* can be a source of confusion for English-speaking visitors who know this French usage as a "menu"). Furthermore, many traditional dishes that require long preparation and cannot be kept overnight may be found on the menu.

For the same reasons, the *plat du jour* (daily special) is usually the most advantageous choice when ordering a meal *à la carte;* up to a dozen special dishes may be offered daily, according to the size of the establishment.

Hints — The service is generally slower in French restaurants than in their Anglo-Saxon counterparts; a long wait for a dish usually means that it is freshly prepared, rather than pre-cooked and reheated.

— Small restaurants offering a limited range of dishes may serve better, fresher fare than their similarly-priced competitors with extensive selections.

— The basic three-course fixed *menu* in a good, expensive restaurant is generally better, more economical than the de luxe *menu* ***(menu touristique*** or ***menu gastronomique)*** in a mediocre place. Naturally, the full de luxe *menu* in a high-quality establishment will be an exquisite experience.

— The cheese board is often a good indication of a restaurant's character : establishments offering a small selection of seasonal cheeses generally are preferable to those boasting a huge selection comprising all major varieties in various states of ripeness (→ Cheese).

Prices There is simply no such thing as an "average price" for a meal in France; the bill *(l'addition)* will vary considerably depending upon the choice of dishes, and even more, on the choice of wine. The prices used in the guide give a fair indication of the price range for each restaurant; however, the bill in an inexpensive one for a meal including, for instance, *foie gras* and oysters frequently will exceed the bill for the basic menu in a more expensive establishment.

Restaurants must by law clearly display their menus and prices (including the fixed-price *menu* outside the premises. The wine and drinks list ***(carte des vins)*** is not covered by this regulation; the vast majority of restaurants offer at least one or two low-priced regional wines *(vins de pays),* and rarely make exorbitant profits from château-bottled wines.

Cocktails ***(apéritifs)*** and liqueurs ***(digestifs)*** nevertheless often are considered a legitimate source of high-margin revenue (a glass of pre-WW II cognac can cost as much as the meal itself).
Increasingly, prices quoted include service charges ***(service compris, s.c.,*** or ***prix nets);*** otherwise expect to pay an additional **15 %.** Enquiries concerning prices are frowned upon only in inferior establishments....
Tips ***(pourboires),*** as opposed to service charges, are not compulsory, and should be given only in appreciation of particularly attentive service.

Types of cuisine

Descriptions of the various schools of French cuisine tend to leave readers in a state of acute perplexity : no two authors seem to agree on any one definition, let alone on the merits of the respective approaches. French restaurants and cuisine just do not fit into rigid categories, and the following descriptions are only meant to provide basic guidelines.

Grande cuisine

Also known as *haute cuisine,* this is the style of preparation that gave France a reputation as the gastronomical centre of the world. Said to have been imported, like much of what is ornate in French culture, from Italy, *grande cuisine* reached its zenith with chefs like Escoffier (one of the founders of London's Savoy Hotel). Today, it continues to attract gourmets from the world over. *La grande cuisine* invariably involves long, painstaking preparation, and often incorporates delicacies such as truffles, cognac, cream and wild mushrooms in extravagant sauces.

Nouvelle cuisine

In reaction to the extravagant approach of *grande cuisine, nouvelle cuisine* stresses the natural taste and freshness of ingredients, retained by light cooking. Free rein is given to the chef's imagination, resulting in previously unheard-of combinations of ingredients, a feature of this style. (Excesses of some young chefs have now practically disappeared). Considerable importance is attached to the presentation of *nouvelle cuisine,* the appearance of which often seems to have been inspired by Japanese arrangements.

Cuisine bourgeoise

Few restaurant *patrons* would actually describe their fare as *cuisine bourgeoise* (traditional cuisine) because the term seems to have taken on a rather derogatory meaning. Nevertheless, this is the description most frequently applied to the plain, everyday fare served in countless restaurants and hotels throughout France. *Daube, pot au feu* and *brandade* are all staple items on the *cuisine bourgeoise* menu. The result is generally delicious, and as long as the chef is competent and dedicated (most are), there is no reason why *cuisine bourgeoise* should lose by comparison with its currently more illustrious competitors.

Regional cuisine

In the beginning was the regional dish : simple, if often long in preparation, using widely available local ingredients. A number of regional dishes in fact have become standard fare in restaurants throughout France : *choucroute* (the Alsatian sauerkraut; the French say it is lighter and tastier than the German version), *bœuf bourguignon* (Burgundy-style beef stew made with red wine and onions), *confit* (pork, duck or goose cooked and preserved in its own fat, a speciality of the Southwest), *quiche lorraine* and many more. The variety of regional preparations is matched by the range of accompanying local wines and cheeses. A guide to culinary styles, wines, cheeses and specialties of each region can be found in the corresponding gazetteer section.

Paris... regional centre

Although Paris and the Ile-de-France region do not, as such, have a distinctive culinary style, every French region is represented among the restaurants of Paris, from the tiny café-restaurant, where the *patron* still receives supplies from his friends back home, to prestigious establishments considered to provide the best *cuisine régionale* in France.

The Southwest

Although Lyons, the Midi, and Alsace-Lorraine all lay claim to having the best cuisine in France, the Southwest probably has done more to encourage genuine appreciation of the culinary arts than any other region. Particularly worthy of mention is the T.E.R. *(Tourisme en Espace Rural)* scheme, where meetings are arranged between visitors and local producers, most of whom are willing to pass on traditional family recipes (→ below). The Southwest and the Pyrénées are also major centres for independently-operated cookery and gastronomy courses.

Associations and chains Several hotel groups are justly proud of their reputations for maintaining consistently high culinary standards; **Châteaux-Hôtels** and **Relais et Châteaux** (with their **Relais Gourmands** restaurants) are noteworthy examples in the luxury category, as is the **Sofitel** chain, with its team of top chefs. In the ★ and ★★ categories, the **Logis de France** group encourages members to offer traditional local cuisine, with the emphasis on value and quality (→ Hotels). ***Tables d'hôte, auberges rurales*** and ***fermes auberges*** also offer authentic local dishes at very reasonable prices (→ Farmhouse holidays). High standards are guaranteed by several associations of independant professionals, most of which, including the following three, publish brochures listing members :

- **Association des Maîtres Cuisiniers de France,** 40, rue Blanche, 75009 Paris ☎ (1) 45.26.99.39; more than 300 members.
- **Entente Nationale des Restaurateurs et Hôteliers de Métier,** c/o Pierre Alexandre 30128 Garons; more than 100 adherents.
- **Jeunes Restaurateurs de France,** c/o Marnier-Lapostolle, 91, bd Haussmann, 75008 Paris ☎ (1) 42.66.43.11; a growing organization of young chefs and restaurant owners, now numbering more than 120; brochure updated each spring and autumn.

Information

- Basic knowledge of French and an occasional reference to a dictionary open up the world of French food guides : the general press, from the national daily *Le Monde* down to the most parochial weekly, is an inexhaustible source of gastronomic reviews and information; the regional dailies are of particular interest to the holiday-maker in search of recommended addresses within a reasonable distance.
- Specialised magazines include *Plaisirs Gastronomie, Cuisine et Vins de France* and *Le Nouveau Guide Gault et Millau.*
- Each spring brings a crop of annual guides, and conversation turns to the changing fortunes of France's chefs and restaurants as dictated by gained and lost stars (or forks, chef's hats and various other symbols). **Gault et Millau** and **Michelin** still lead the field, and, among countless competitors, *Guide de l'Auto-Journal* is noteworthy for its emphasis on value. Also: the **Bottin-Gourmand** and the **Guide Annuel des Relais-Routiers.**
- Various gastronomic holidays - from gourmet tours with afternoon naps in the luxury coach to stays spent slaving over the proverbial hot stove - are available from U.S.A. and U.K. companies and agents; information from **F.G.T.O.** or local travel agents.
- Authentic cookery courses are available at the local level in every region of France; a selection of addresses is contained in each regional gazetteer section of the guide : the local TO or SI can also provide up-to-date information on these courses (booking facilities through Loisirs-Accueil).

Complaints (→ Hotels).

Cheese

The exact number of French cheeses is impossible to pin down. The standard reply, "one for every day of the year", is an underestimate because there are definitely well over 400 types. Cantal cheese is said to have been consumed more than 2 000 years ago, whereas Camembert was "invented" as recently as 1790. Cheese is served in France before the dessert course - pastries and sweetmeats "kill" the taste of wine that is considered as the indispensable complement to a good cheese. Although rules exist to be broken, asking for cheese after dessert, even with a glass of Port wine (not a French custom), is also asking for raised eyebrows. Becoming a true connaisseur of French cheese is a formidable task. The following information is aimed at encouraging visitors to venture beyond the traditional Bries and Roqueforts, excellent though they may be.

Categories

Cheese in France is made from the milk of cows, goats, or ewes (some varieties are also a blend of cow's and goat's milk). The three main categories are :

Fresh cream cheeses *(fromage frais) :* Some varieties have a very limited shelf-life, *(fromages blancs* and *petit suisse,* for example). They can be served sweet with sugar or fruit, or with herbs and salt, as a dip for raw vegetables or as a dressing for baked potatoes. Others keep longer and are generally more strongly flavoured, such as with herbs, garlic or pepper. Boursin from Normandy is the best known of the latter, although every region has its own *fromage frais.*

Pressed and hard cheeses *(pâtes pressées) :* Cooked varieties (Gruyère, Comté, Beaufort) are made from cow's milk, have firm rinds and are produced mainly in the East of France, although the North produces a range of harder cheeses, such as Mimolette. Uncooked types are also be made from goat's or ewe's milk (especially the Tomes or Tommes, produced throughout the South from the Alps to the Pyrénées). Cantal from the Auvergne region is the most famous cow's milk variety. These cheeses generally have thick, firm rinds, although some varieties have practically none.

Soft cheeses *(pâtes molles) :* Usually made from cow's milk, these cheeses account for more than one-third of national cheese production. Some have soft rinds formed by natural mould *(croûte fleurie);* others are washed *(lavée)* and have no rind. Of the former, among the most popular are Brie from the Ile-de-France, Camembert from Normandy and Carré de l'Est from Lorraine. It is worth mentioning that good Brie or Camembert should not be runny, which is a sign of inadequate drain-

ing or conservation. Munster from Alsace, Maroilles from Flanders and Reblochon from Savoy are well-known examples of washed varieties, the strong aroma of which belies a mild, almost sweet taste.
A fourth category is made up of varieties that do not fit into the first three : among these are the **blue cheeses** *(bleus),* which include the illustrious ewe's milk Roquefort (from the Rouergue Plateaus) and a number of other cow's, goat's and ewe's milk varieties *(bleu de Bresse, bleu d'Auvergne)* and the dozens of local **goat's milk cheeses,** of which the deliciously smooth Sainte-Maure (from Touraine) is probably the best introduction for the uninitiated before venturing into the more mature - and aromatic - *crottin* and other connoisseur's delights.

Seasons The advent of pasteurisation, coupled with modern stocking and distribution techniques, has eliminated many seasonal variations on availability and quality gourmets once had to consider in choosing suitable cheese. This is particularly true for cow's milk varieties, although authentic Bries and Camemberts made from unpasteurised farm milk (look for the label *fermier* or *au lait cru*) are not at their best in the summer, when the blue cheeses and the mountain varieties (Tome and Fourme) reach maturity. Nevertheless, seasons (mainly spring and autumn) still exist for many cheeses, particularly for local varieties of goat's and ewe's milk cheese : good restaurants and cheese shops adapt their stocks accordingly and generally are delighted to help a customer make a selection. The fact that one is sufficiently interested to ask about cheeses is always appreciated.

Which wines? Although cheese traditionally is consumed with red wines, certain varieties can safely be served with white wine : the Alsatian whites go well with Munster and with milder cheeses. Sipping a Sauternes with Roquefort is a well-known, if controversial, combination. The quite legitimate desire to stick to one wine throughout the meal should not take away from enjoying the cheese course if that wine happens to be a white. The cheese course should be accompanied by a wine at least as full-bodied as that served with the main course; some of the stronger cheeses will simply overpower the taste of finer wines. Don't choose, for instance, a ripe Roquefort when drinking vintage Médoc : a Brie or Camembert would be a sensible choice. Most goat's and ewe's milk cheeses go well with a full-bodied or medium *vin de pays :* e.g., Corbières or Minervois; a Côtes du Rhône will complement all but the mildest cheese.

Guaranteed origins Regulations laid down in 1966 define the production areas of several cheeses and set strict standards of quality. This *Appellation d'Origine* — similar to the *Appellation d'Origine Contrôlée* system for wine (→ below) — applies essentially to the following varieties : Eastern France and the Champagne District : Chaource, Maroilles and Munster; Jura and Franche-Comté : Bleu de Gex and Comté; Alps : Beaufort and Reblochon; Auvergne and Midi : Bleus des Causses and d'Auvergne, Cantal, Saint-Nectaire, Roquefort; Central France : Crottin de Chavignol, Selles-sur-Cher and Pouligny-Saint-Pierre; Ile-de-France : Bries de Meaux and de Melun; Normandy : Neuchâtel, Livarot, Pont-l'Évêque. Camembert has a label of its own : «V.C.N.» *(véritable Camembert de Normandie),* denoting a product made exclusively with milk from the Auge.

Information
- *Guide du fromage,* Pierre Androuet (Stock); the author both knows and loves his subject (not available in English).
- Local SI and departmental TO can provide details for visits to cheese producers (the Roquefort maturing cellars are particularly worth a visit). Ramblers in the Alps and the Auvergne hills may come across the chalets and huts where local farmers make their cheese; visitors generally are welcome. Cheese fairs, large and small, are held throughout France (the most famous are at Coulommiers in the Seine-et-Marne region and at Sancerre every spring, and at Chaource in the Aube every other October); → relevant gazetteer sections for further details.

Wine and Spirits

Although wine is produced everywhere in France with the exception of the extreme northwest of the country, seven major regions are generally singled out for attention : Champagne; Burgundy; Alsace; Val-de-

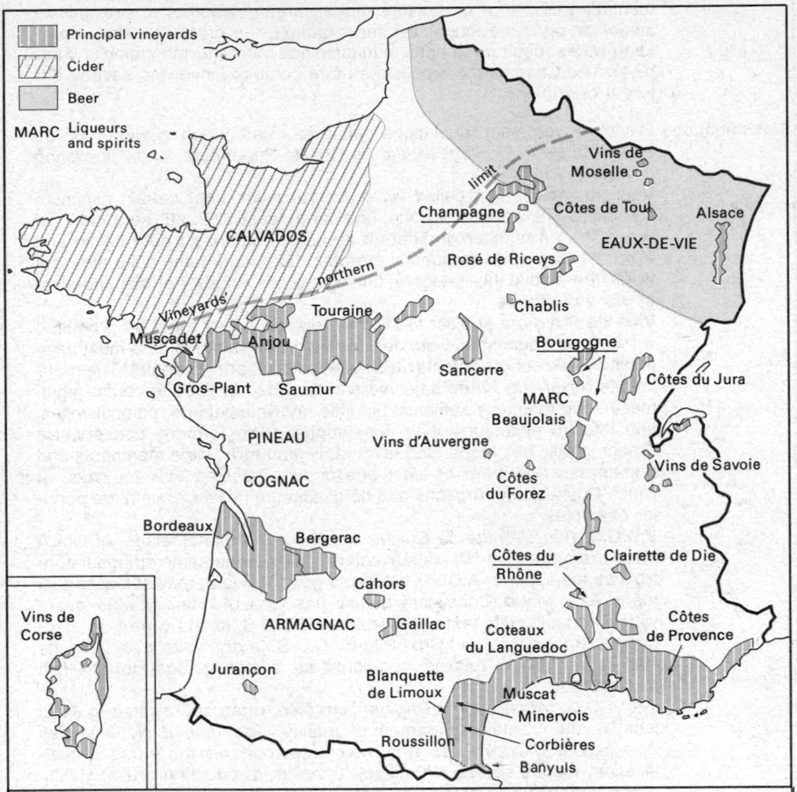

Loire (from Nantes through Touraine to Central France); Bordeaux and the Cognac, Armagnac and Béarn areas; Côtes du Rhône; Languedoc-Roussillon. Wine of excellent quality is also produced in Provence, Quercy (Cahors), the Jura, Corsica and Auvergne (→ gazetteer sections).

Quality

Wine quality is the sum of many factors : the variety of grape *(cépage)*, the soil *(terroir)*, climate, the wine-making process *(vinification)* and the competence of the grower-producer. The best-known grape varieties are Pinot Noir (red Burgundy and Champagne), Cabernet Sauvignon and Cabernet Franc, Merlot and Malbec (all of which can be used for red Bordeaux), and Chardonnay and Aligoté (white Burgundy). Beaujolais is made from the Gamay grape, which is also used in some red Burgundies. The white Sauvignon grape is widely cultivated throughout France, while Riesling, Traminer and Tokay grapes contribute significantly to Alsace's renowned whites. The Muscat variety provides dry white wine in Alsace and sweet wines elsewhere. The soil is a strong determinant of ultimate wine quality, so much so that a difference of only a few hundred yards between vineyards can separate a good wine from a great wine. Specialists recognize more than 200 basic combinations of grape and soil types that, together with the wine-making process and the climate, account for the wide differences in wines : red Burgundy and white Champagne are both made from the same black Pinot Noir grape.

Types of wine

White wine is not necessarily made from white grapes alone. With skins removed, red grapes or a red-and-white mix also can turn out white. The label of a wine fermented exclusively from white grapes will carry the term *blanc de blancs*. **Red** wine is produced from red grapes, using both the juice and the skin. **Rosé** is obtained from red grapes the skin of which is removed after a brief initial fermentation. The length of fermentation is one of the factors that determine whether a wine will be **sweet** or **dry** : the longer the fermentation, the dryer the wine. **Sparkling** wines result when bottling takes place before fermentation is complete. The Champagne process is more complex, involving several different operations.

Classifications French government regulations define four categories of wine : *Vin de table, Vin de Pays, Vin Délimité de Qualité Supérieure,* and *Appellation d'Origine Contrôlée.*

Vins de table (often called *vin ordinaire*) must meet certain minimum standards, including an alcohol level of at least 9.5°, but be a blend of wines from a number of different areas or countries : both Italian and North African wines frequently are used. Although some quite pleasant wines are sold in this category, finding them is a matter of trial and error or word of mouth.

Vins de Pays are subject to stricter controls : they must be produced within fixed boundaries from designated grape varieties, and must have a minimum alcohol content (which varies from north to south). The regulations governing *vin de pays* were established in 1964 to confer legitimacy upon the many authentic but little-known local and regional wines, and thus to encourage their consumption. The formerly conservative French public has responded favourably, and most wine merchants and restaurants now offer at least one or two selected *vins de pays,* of which Coteaux-de-l'Ardèche and Ile-de-Beauté (from Corsica) are popular examples.

V.D.Q.S. *(Vin Délimité de Qualité Supérieure)* regional wines, of which there are more than 60, are subjected to almost the same stringent controls as the superior A.C. (→ below); a good V.D.Q.S. may at least equal many A.C. wines. Consistent quality has won over many wine-lovers to the honest, fruity taste of Corbières V.D.Q.S. (a red wine from Languedoc-Roussillon), and Gros Plant V.D.Q.S. (a dry white wine from the Nantes region) is gaining popularity as a complement to shellfish and seafood.

The **A.O.C.** (*Appellation d'Origine Contrôlée,* often abbreviated to **A.C.**) label is the ultimate guarantee of quality. The *Institut National des Appellations d'Origine des Vins,* which also controls the V.D.Q.S. qualification, places severe restrictions upon the production areas, yields, grape varieties and processes associated with these wines. Although not every A.C. is necessarily a great wine, all the great French wines carry this label. As a general rule, the more precise the geographical location of the *appellation,* the finer the wine : an A.C. Châteauneuf-du-Pape (from a specified part of the Côtes-du-Rhône region) should be superior to an A.C. Côtes-du-Rhône. The addition of the *château* or *domaine* (estate) name to the label is usually a further guarantee, as is the address of the producer or *négociant* (wine wholesaler). The wines of Bordeaux are the exceptions to this rule; their labels are generally rather austere, and even the finest use only the *appellation* common to their area : Médoc, Margaux and Sauternes, for example. The order of growths (first, second and subsequent *crus* → Bordeaux), although obsolete in some cases, provides further information but may not always figure on the label. Each of the great Burgundy wines, on the contrary, has a distinct *appellation,* usually corresponding to a tiny tract of land known as a *climat* (→ Burgundy).

The simpler *appellation,* e.g., *A.C. Bordeaux supérieur* and *A.C. Beaujolais,* often preceded or followed by a brand name, cover blends of different wines from the same area, as well as those whose strict *appellation* is of insufficient commercial interest. These "generic" wines are usually reasonably priced and reliable. When no vintage *(millésime)* is mentioned on the label, the wine is a blend of several years. Restrictions imposed on the yields of defined *appellation* areas result in declassification of any excess production; this surplus often is sold under a generic *appellation,* as some substandard but still fine products of famous vineyards the reputations of which must be maintained at all costs. Enterprising restaurants and wine merchants seek out these bargains and consequently are able to offer customers astonishingly good wines at low prices.

Hints — Authentic *d'origine* wines always clearly display the term *Appellation d'Origine Contrôlée* (A.O.C.), *Appellation Contrôlée* (A.C.) or *Vin Délimité de Qualité Supérieure* (V.D.Q.S.) on the label; no reference is made

to the alcohol content. Genuine *vins de pays* specify the term in their name, e.g., *Vin du Pays de l'Aude,* or carry the mention *vin de pays* under the brand or grape variety.
— In the absence of A.O.C., A.C., V.D.Q.S. or *Vin de Pays,* phrases such as *Appellation d'Origine Simple, vin fin, mise en bouteilles dans nos chais* (bottled in our cellars) are generally meaningless in terms of quality and offer no particular guarantees, although some very acceptable wines use this sort of marketing jargon. The same applies to imposing brand names; always look for the official label of quality.
— It is beyond the scope of this guide to advise on tasting and choosing wines : when in doubt, don't hesitate to ask the wine merchant or, in a restaurant, the *sommelier* (wine waiter) to recommend a wine suited to your taste and budget.
— The list of vintages below is given as a guide, not an absolute rule. The quality of a vintage varies from area-to-area, and even within the same region. The wine-growers of Bordeaux are proud of their "microclimates", where a particular parcel of land may escape poor weather seriously affecting yield and quality of surrounding vineyards. Examples of variation include 1975, which was one of the very best years for Bordeaux but mediocre for Burgundies, and 1981, when the red Burgundies were as dismal as the whites were excellent. As for 1985, the unusually cold winter plus the drought at the end of the summer foretell reduced harvests, but good quality.
— Only the best years are bottled as vintage Champagne; non-vintage blends are carefully balanced to ensure consistent quality.

Recent Vintages

	Exceptional	Very Good	Good
Alsace	71, 76, 83	66, 67, 70, 73, 78	69, 75
Red Bordeaux	66,70,75,81,82,83	67, 71, 76, 78	73, 74, 79, 84
White Bordeaux	65, 75, 82	70, 71, 79, 81, 83	74,76,78,80
Red Burgundy	69, 76, 78	66, 71	70,72,79,82,83
White Burgundy		69, 70, 76, 78, 79, 82	66, 67, 71, 73, 74, 81, 84
Rhône Valley	78, 82	67, 70, 76, 83	71, 79, 80
Loire Valley		69, 71, 76, 81, 82	70, 77, 78
Champagne		71, 73	70, 75, 77, 78

Cognac, Armagnac and spirits

The wine that is distilled twice to obtain Cognac (→ Poitou-Vendée-Charente) comes from seven strictly-defined territories *(crus)* totalling less than 1 000 km² : Grande Champagne, Petite Champagne, Borderies, Fins Bois, Bons Bois, Bois Ordinaires and Bois à Terroir. The distilled spirit, which has an initial alcohol content of 68-70°, is left to age in oak or chestnut casks. It is then diluted with purest water to obtain an alcohol content of at least 40° (approximately 70 proof U.K.). **Grande Fine Champagne** is made only from Grande Champagne *cru* and **Fine Champagne** is a blend of Grande Champagne (50 % minimum) and Petite Champagne. Aging also influences the quality of cognac : **V.O., V.S.O.P.,** and **Réserve** are aged four years, **X.O., Extra, Napoléon** and **Vieille Réserve** five years.
Armagnac (→ Midi-Toulousain-Pyrénées) is distilled only once from wine from the area of Bas-Armagnac (the finest), Tenarèze (between Bas-Armagnac and Lot-et-Garonne) and Haut-Armagnac (considered by some to be slightly inferior). Armagnac is aged in oak casks and is age-graded according to a system nearly identical to the one used for Cognac.
Marc is distilled from the pulp that remains after grape pressing and is produced mainly in Burgundy, although a particularly delicious variety is made in the Champagne region.
Calvados is apple brandy that ranges in quality from a rather rough variety served at a *café* counter in tiny glasses (or often poured directly into black coffee), to a smooth, aged spirit taken as an after-dinner liqueur.

In addition to the conventional grades, restaurants and wine merchants usually offer vintage spirits and liqueurs, especially Armagnac, up to 100 years old.

Eau-de-Vie is the general term for brandy or spirits, but applies more particularly to the clear, dry fruit spirits produced in Eastern France. Pear, blueberry, cherry (kirsch) and raspberry are popular; these delicious *eaux-de-vies* are served chilled, often in frosted glasses.

Cocktails and *apéritifs*

The two most popular *apéritifs* in France are probably *Kir,* made of dry white wine (traditionally Burgundy Aligoté) with a dash of black currant liqueur, and *Pastis,* an aniseed and liquorice-based spirit usually diluted with 3-5 parts water. *Pernod* is similar to *pastis,* but contains no liquorice.

Many **wine-based aperitifs** are flavoured with essences such as *quinquina* (quinine or cinchona). Dubonnet, St.-Raphaël and Byrrh fall into this category.

Gentian-based aperitifs are widely appreciated, especially in their native Auvergne. Suze is by far the best known, with Avèze a close second.

Sweet wines such as Banyuls and Frontignan, often produced from Muscat grapes, are popular aperitifs in the Southwest and Languedoc-Roussillon regions; red or white Pineau de Charente is underrated outside its own region (→ gazetteer section) but can be a delicious aperitif when served chilled.

A point to remember : American-style martinis are pratically unknown outside international-class establishments; anyone ordering "a martini" is likely to be served the vermouth of that brand name. Instead, ask for "a gin martini" and indicate the proportions in sign language — with a cocktail-shaking gesture if you don't want ice cubes. (The French spell "olive" like the English and pronounce it, *oh-leave.* A cocktail *oignon* is said as *un-yon.*)

A selection of fairs and festivals

January : Saint-Vincent *tournante* in Burgundy (a wine-growers' festival held in a different village each year, and a major event : Mercurey ('85), Volnay ('86), Santenay ('87).

May : wine fairs at Guebwiller (Haut-Rhin), Mâcon and Sancerre.

June : "World Wine Week" in Bordeaux (trade only); Champagne fair at Troyes.

July : wine fairs at Arbois (Jura) and Ribeauvillé (Haut-Rhin).

August : wine fair at Pouilly-sur-Loire (Nièvre); wine-growers' festivals throughout the Cher region.

September : Champagne and wine fair at Bar-sur-Aube.

October : international wine and vineyard fair in Montpellier.

November : Sauvignon wine festival at Saint-Bris-le-Vineux (Yonne); **"Les Trois Glorieuses"** (three consecutive days of festivity over the weekend following November 11 in the Côte d'Or region of Burgundy : Saturday at the Chapître du Clos-Vougeot; Sunday at the Hospice de Beaune (a world-famous wine auction, the proceeds go to the upkeep of this still-functioning almshouse); Monday at Meursault. Another almshouse wine auction is held on the second Sunday before Easter at Nuits-Saint-Georges.

Countless other wine fairs and festivals are held throughout France, consult the relevant gazetteer section and local SI or TO for further details.

Information

- U.S.- and U.K.-based tour operators offer tours and holidays with wine as the central theme. Some offer serious studies in a particular growing area, others extended tours of the major vineyards. Wine-tasting is included in most packages and many also include gastronomic meals. Transportation is by air, coach or even barge, while accommodation ranges from luxury hotels to camping. Details from the **F.G.T.O.**
- Several organisations in Paris offer courses in oenology (the study of wine) and wine-tasting sessions : **Centre de documentation et de Dégustation du Vin,** 45, rue Liancourt, 75014 Paris ☎ (1) 43.27.67.21; **Académie du Vin,** cité Berryer, 25, rue Royale, 75008 Paris ☎ (1) 42.65.09.82; **École du Vin,** 61, rue Pierre-Charron, 75008 Paris ☎ (1) 45.27.19.94/92.40. **L'Invitation à Découvrir,** 6*bis,* Villa des Entrepreneurs, 75015 Paris ☎ 45.79.89.12.
- The gazetteer sections contain details of local wine-study courses; information also from local SI and TO.
- The Wine Museum *(Musée du Vin),* rue des Eaux, 75116 Paris, is a fascinating source of information on wine and viniculture.
- Wine can be purchased directly from a ***vigneron*** (grower). The ***négociant*** (specialised wholesaler), or ***négociant-éleveur*** (wholesaler-vineyard owner),

offers a wider range of products as well as very sound advice, as does the specialised ***marchand*** (merchant) in his ***cave*** (literally, cellar or vault). Around the vineyards themselves, ***coopératives*** (cooperative distribution centres) generally offer a wide range of authentic local wines.

Wines guides

- Hugh Johnson's Pocket Wine Book, Mitchell Beazley, London.
- New : the first real guide to the buying of wine : **U.S., The Hachette Guide to French Wines** (Alfred A. Knopf, Inc. New York), **U.K., Macdonald Guide to French wines** (Macdonald and Co, Londres); more than 5000 wines tasted and chosen from among all the appellations; for a complete knowledge of all vineyards, addresses of shops and wine bars, calendar of festivals, museums, etc. 816 intoxicating pages!

Holiday themes

Nature Parks and reserves

(see map p. 98)

National Parks

Six outstandingly beautiful national parks : Vanoise, Port-Cros, Pyrénées Occidentales, Cévennes, les Écrins and Mercantour now exist. Hunting is prohibited (except in the Cévennes park), the introduction of plant and animal species strictly controlled and building is not allowed. Visitors are accommodated in a "pre-park", where rural life is maintained and developed, whereas the heartland of the park itself may be designated a *réserve intégrale* where no human intervention is tolerated. Information centres, *maisons du parc* (lodges) and *portes du parc* (gatehouses) are situated at strategic points in and around the parks.

Nature Parks

In the nature parks, rural life is maintained and the pursuit of traditional skills and crafts is encouraged. 20 nature parks are currently in existence : Armorique; Brière; Brotonne Forest; Camargue; Corsica; Orient Forest; Haut-Languedoc; Landes de Gascogne; Lorraine; Lubéron; Marais poitevin (Poitou marshes); Val de Sèvres et Vendée; Montagne de Reims; Morvan; Normandy-Maine; Mont Pilat; Queyras; Saint-Armand-Raismes; Vercors; Volcans d'Auvergne; Vosges du Nord. Five more are planned : maritime Picardy; upper Chevreuse valley; Jura gessien; Audomarois-monts-de-Flandres et Boulonnais; Livradois-Forez.

Reserves

This term can cover anything from private initiatives of the more commercial variety to genuine nature reserves where fauna and flora are scrupulously respected.
Apart from the national parks, 63 defined areas are officially recognised as nature reserves. Conditions of access vary from one reserve to another.

Hints

— Park regulations must be respected : dogs are forbidden; in many cases visitors must not leave the established paths; fires are absolutely taboo.
— Camping is forbidden, except in specified zones of the nature parks.
— See the relevant gazetteer section for details of each region's flora, fauna and other points of interest.

Information

- The **F.G.T.O.** booklet "France for Sports and Leisure" lists parks and reserves of interest together with the various activities and specialties offered in each case. Further information may be obtained from regional and local tourist offices.

Nature Parks
Picturesque Regions
• Reserves (protected fauna and flora)

- **Société Nationale de Protection de la Nature :** 57, rue Cuvier, 75005 Paris ☎ (1) 47.07.31.95.
- **Direction de la Protection de la Nature,** Services des Parcs Nationaux, 14, bd du Général-Leclerc, 92524 Neuilly-sur-Seine ☎ (1) 47.58.12.12.
- **Fédération des Parcs Naturels de France,** 4, rue de Stockholm, 75008 Paris ☎ (1) 42.94.90.84.

Gardens

Every age has its gardens; they are the reflection of a civilization. Visiting gardens in France is a journey through time.

The mediaeval flora in the moat of the chateau at Angers (Maine-Anjou) evoke the *mille-fleurs* ("thousand flowers") of 15thC tapestries.

At Villandry (Touraine), labyrinths of boxwood trimmed in symbolic designs recreate a 16thC garden.

The flower-beds of Diane de Poitiers at Chenonceau (Touraine) are one of the first examples of Italian-style "embroidery" which was to reach its apogee at Vaux-le-Vicomte (Ile-de-France). This style, adopting the name 'à la française', was to become the symbol of French classicism. In the same region Versailles and Champs-sur-Marne are also fine examples.

In the 18thC, administrators in cities were to create garden promenades such as the Allées de Tourny in Bordeaux, the Parc de Blossac in Poitiers and the Peirou in Montpellier.

The advent of romanticism was to convert Europe to the Anglo-Chinese style of landscape gardens, called 'à l'anglaise'. At Ermononville and Malmaison (Ile-de-France) the intellectually-ordered flower-beds gave way to rolling countryside. In the Parc Monceau and the Bagatelle in Paris, reflecting pools are replaced by ponds and artificial lakes. The Retz desert near Marly (Ile-de-France) is studded with monuments ranging from an Egyptian pyramid to a Chinese pagoda, not to forget the Greek temple. This remains one of the most famous gardens of its type.
Compared with the Loire valley and the Ile-de-France, Provence offers a more Italianate style of garden with terraces and fountains. The region around Aix boasts numerous gardens from the 17th, 18th and 19thC, created around châteaux and country homes such as the Pavillon de l'Enfant, the Mignarde at Aix or the fountain gardens in Nîmes. The climate permitted the creation of exotic gardens such as those at Monaco and Eze.
Japan is present at the gates of Paris in the A. Kahn Gardens or at Monet's property in Giverny.
Instituted in the 19thC, botanical gardens enhance many cities, and today arboreta are increasingly common, that of the Domaine des Barres near Montargis (Loiret) meriting a detour.
In a class of its own, the unusual garden of the Postman Cheval in Hauterives (Dauphiné) transports the visitor into a strange universe, as individual as that of the Père-Lachaise cemetery in Paris or the new garden-cemeteries at Forcalquier.
Most parks and gardens remain open until dusk in summer. Some offer special attractions : boat rides, *son et lumière,* concerts or fountain spectacles.
Conceived as real works of art, some of these gardens look like museums and should be visited as such. Respect their beauty!

Information

- **Association des Parcs Botaniques de France,** 15 bis, rue de Marignan, 75008 Paris, ☎ (1) 43.59.74.11.
- **Maison de la Nature,** 9, quai du 4-Septembre, 92160 Boulogne, ☎ (1) 46.03.33.56.
- **Inspection Générale des Monuments Historiques,** 4, rue d'Aboukir, 75002 Paris, ☎ (1) 42.96.10.40.

Museums, monuments, exhibitions and classified sites

Despite wars and revolutions, France's heritage - historical, cultural, artistic and natural - still provides an inexhaustible source of discovery for the visitor. The UNESCO world patrimony selection retains no fewer than 12 sites in France : the Mont-Saint-Michel and its bay; Chartres cathedral; the château de Versailles; the Vézelay hill and basilica; the caves and their paintings in the Vézère valley including, of course, Lascaux; Fontainebleau Palace; the château de Chambord and its estate; Amiens cathedral; the antique theatre at Orange; the Roman and Romanesque monuments at Arles; Fontenay abbey; the Arc-et-Senans salt-mines. Literally thousands of sites and monuments of all kinds are classified (or are in the process of classification), as *monuments historiques* or are registered in the *inventaire supplémentaire.* The objective is always to perserve or to restore buildings and sites whenever they are threatened in any way.

New museums

Several museums of national importance have recently been established : the Modern Art Museums at Troyes and Dunkirk, the Customs Museum at Bordeaux, the Reine Mathilde tapestry museum at Bayeux, the *Musée du Nouveau Monde* (New World Museum) at La Rochelle, and the Art and History Museum at Saint-Denis. In Paris the project for the considerably extended "Grand Louvre" should reach completion in Dec. 1987, while the opening of the **musée d'Orsay** is scheduled for the end of 1986. The **Picasso Museum** opened in 1985, offering a matchless collection installed in the 17thC. Hôtel Salé in the heart of the Marais. **La Villette,** in the 19th arr. offers a glimpse of the year 2000 with its science and industrial museum which will open in March 1986.

Hints — Although, generally speaking, state museums are closed on Tuesdays and municipal museums on Mondays (Sunday opening is frequently encountered), **opening hours** are extremely variable : always consult the relevant gazetteer section of this guide. While larger museums in major towns may remain open throughout the day, provincial museums usually close between 12 and 2.

— The various sections of major museums such as the Louvre open and close at different times, according to the availability of guides. Schedules, including guided tour timetables, are always displayed and are available by telephone.

— It may always be possible to visit a museum or monument during the offseason, subject to prior appointment. Enquiries to the local SI or TO.

— Entry to museums is rarely free of charge, except to certain categories of visitors (children, the disabled...) and on certain days (Wednesdays : National museums; Sundays : Louvre Museum). National museums grant half-price admittance on Sundays, and to 18-25 year-olds and the over 65's. Other reductions are granted to groups, registered teachers, etc. (these reductions and exemptions apply only to State-owned museums, not to such attractions as the Eiffel Tower or wax-museums). Admission fees are usually extremely reasonable by international standards : often no more than 10 F.

— Flashes and tape recorders are forbidden in museums, as are cameras at temporary exhibitions.

Information

- **Direction des Musées de France,** palais du Louvre, 75001 Paris, ☎ (1) 42.60.39.26; publishes the review "Revue du Louvre et des Musées de France".
- **Caisse Nationale des Monuments Historiques et des Sites** (C.N.M.H.S.), hôtel de Sully, 62, rue Saint-Antoine 75004 Paris, ☎ (1) 42.74.22.22; publishes the excellent "Ouvert au public" : all the châteaux and classified sites open to the public, organises cultural voyages (→ Organised travel).
- **Fédération nationale des Associations de Sauvegarde des Sites et Ensembles monumentaux** (F.N.A.S.S.E.M.), 20, av. Mac Mahon 75017 Paris, ☎ (1) 42.67.52.00.
- **Vieilles Maisons Françaises,** 93, rue de l'Université 75007 Paris, ☎ (1) 45.51.07.12.
- **La Demeure Historique** 57, quai de la Tournelle 75005 Paris, ☎ (1) 43.29.02.85; publishes the review of the same name.
- **Association des Centres Culturels de Rencontre,** (address as C.N.M.H.S.), ☎ (1) 42.77.30.89; coordinates a number of interesting historical conference sites; publishes the review "Travées".
- **Répertoire des musées et collections publiques de France,** guide published by the assembly of the **Musées nationaux,** 10, rue de l'Abbaye 75006 Paris.
- See also **Pariscope,** the **Officiel des spectacles,** the **Officiel des Galeries, Art Info** (bulletin of information about the plastic arts). Enq. to the C.D.T. and the C.R.T.
- A number of foreign tour operators organise cultural, historical and architectural interest holidays (wide range of features, qualified guides, accommodation from châteaux to camping, etc.); information from the **F.G.T.O.**
- The brochure "France for sports and leisure" (available from the **F.G.T.O.**) contains an excellent list of unusual museums.
- → also Cultural events and Archaeological excavations.

Exhibitions In addition to the national galleries at the Grand Palais or the gallery of moden art at the Pompidou Centre, the museums and cultural centres of Paris regularly mount exhibitions. In Paris one should visit the art galleries which are concentrated around the École des Beaux Arts, the Pompidou Centre or the Champs-Élysées. In the provinces the museums, historic monuments and regional cultural centres also host exhibitions of a high standard, often allied to festivals and historically commemorative events.

Technical tourism Technical achievements have always been a source of fascination and as such, the Eiffel Tower, the Garabit viaduct in the Cantal, the Tancarville suspension bridge and the Donzère-Montdragon dam are unfailing attractions.

The future unfolded Examples of advanced technology, such as the nuclear power stations at Chinon or Paluel and the telecommunications centre at Plemeur-Boudou in Brittany, have begun to draw crowds of inquiring holiday-makers each summer. France offers a vast panorama of scientific interest sites, from the gigantic solar furnace at Odeillo, close to the ski slopes of Font-Romeu, to the Valbonne-Sophia-Antipolis centre near Antibes, dedicated to research into the relationship between man and science.

Industrial and archeology ecomuseums

This most recent form of archaeology consists of the study and conservation of various vestiges of the 19thC and early 20thC industrial society : not merely the factories themselves, but the lifestyles of the people concerned.
Since the early 70s this discipline has produced several flourishing ecomuseums : the museum at Creusot (Burgundy) which relates the history of a region in relation to crystal manufacturing and the founding of the Schneider mining "empire" for example. In northern France, a leading industrial region, ecomuseums preserve the history of the textile industry (Fourmies), crystal and glass manufacturing (Sars-Poteries), fine woodwork (Felleries, an authentic working watermill) and mining (Lewarde, near Douai, the pit-head is preserved just as it was left on the day it closed, complete with lamps, picks, and machinery).

museums of Mulhouse

Mulhouse has become the undisputed leader in the growing field of technical tourism and although the town authorities were not involved in the founding of the magnificent **Musée National de l'Automobile** (familiarly known as the *musée Schlumpf),* they were instrumental in the creation of the currently expanding railway museum (where one can simulate driving a T.G.V.). Nearing completion just across the road is the electrical museum. The reorganised printed fabrics museum now contains a section on the evolution of wallpaper from the 18thC to modern times.
Bordeaux also offers a range of interesting visits, not only to the vineyards but also to various factories.
Elsewhere, factory visits are generally available to recognised groups and only by prior demand.

Information

- Information on sites of technical interest and factory visits may be obtained from local and regional tourist organisations.
- → regional description section of this guide.

Antiques, "brocante" and auctions

Items ranging from priceless antique treasures to second-hand toothbrushes are offered for sale in an astounding variety of ways : through reputable dealers and *brocanteurs,* at antique and "brocante" fairs, flea-markets and auctions.

"Brocante"

Near-antiques, curios and second-hand goods in general (furniture, books, art, jewellery, rustic tools, etc.) all fall into this category and nearly every village seems to have a *brocanteur* nowadays. This diversity provides an endless source of bargains, real and imagined (the French for a bargain is *une occasion...* which can also mean merely "second-hand" - buyers beware !). Prices are almost always negotiable.

Antiques

Genuine antique dealers are to be found in all French towns, frequently grouped together in the same central quarter or in specific arcades. The most prestigious are gathered in Paris, Lyons, Strasbourg, Avignon, Grenoble, Toulouse, Nantes and on the Riviera. The better dealers are often recognised experts, able to provide guarantees or certificates of authenticity.

Auctions

Most French towns have an auction room *(hôtel des ventes)* presided by a certified auctioneer *(commissaire-priseur)* and details of sales and auctions are announced both in the local press and by poster. Goods are generally exhibited on the preceding day or the same morning and, with the exception of legally-enforced sales, reserve prices may be set by the seller or the auctioneer. Successful bidders carry their goods away as soon as they are paid for ; auctioneers' fees amount to 17.67 % on sums of up to 15 000 F, 13.22 % from 15 001 to 40 000 F, 11.15 % from 40 0001 to 300 000 F and 9.96 % thereafter.

Hints

— Furniture or objects described as "Louis XV" should date from the XVIIIC ; however, if preceded by **d'époque** or **de style,** the goods may be more recent copies.
— Antique furniture is frequently reconditioned or reassembled, may contain new or non-original elements and in the absence of a certifi-

cate of authenticity only your knowledge and intuition can be of any real guidance.

— The exportation of antiques (over 100 years old) and works of art whose value exceeds 10 000 F is subject to the issue of an export licence (the vendor is responsible for the application, which is only refused when the exportation in question is considered as depleting the national heritage). It is always wise, whatever the category of goods (genuine antiques or *brocante),* to insist on a detailed invoice for customs purposes.

Information

- For information on the Paris flea-markets see the gazetteer section.
- **Hôtel Drouot,** 9, rue Drouot, 75009 Paris, ☎ (1) 42.46.17.11; free estimates daily ex. Sunday; daily sales ex. August.
- The **Syndicat nationale des Antiquaires,** 11, rue Jean-Mermoz 75008 Paris, ☎ publishes the magazine "Art et Curiosités".
- Two publications, the **"Gazette de l'hôtel Drouot"** and **"Le Moniteur des Ventes",** 99, rue de Richelieu 75002 Paris, ☎ (1) 42.61.81.78. give details of major sales and auctions.
- **Guide Sotheby's - Le prix des choses,** gives current prices of 8 000 highly-prized objects (Lattès).
- **Almanach du Chineur,** a goldmine of information published by Hachette.

Crafts and Craftsmen

Craftsmanship and regional traditions

Several thousand craft workshops are spread around France, although a number of regions still maintain thriving traditional handicraft trades : lace at Alençon, in Brittany and the Velay; tapestry at Aubusson and Fromentines; stringed instruments at Mirecourt in Lorraine; stained glass at Troyes, Rheims and Chartres. The ancient glassworks at La Rochère in the Haute-Saône are still in activity; clogs are still made in the woodland areas of the Lozère, the Jura and Brittany; Limoges remains the enamel craft centre. Abundant sandstone deposits around La Borne, near Bourges, furnish the basis of a flourishing local production of crafted stoneware.

Courses

One of France's smallest and most isolated regions, the Rouergue, has become famous as a pioneer of handicraft courses. Blacksmiths, potters, weavers, embroiderers, painters, bookbinders and basket-workers : all open their workshops to would-be craftsmen, and many provide food and accommodation as well.

Information

- The **Centre Nationale d'Information et de Documentation sur les Métiers d'Art,** at the Decorative Arts Museum (10, rue de Rivoli, 75001 Paris, ☎ (1) 42.60.56.58 lists 1 700 courses (also listed in the F.G.T.O. booklet *France for Sports and Leisure)* and publishes *Le Courrier des Métiers d'Art* newsletter in addition to the magazine *Métier d'Art,* which contains useful addresses as well as articles on either particular crafts or regions (20, rue La Boétie, 75008 Paris).
- **L'Association pour le Développement de l'Animation Culturelle (A.D.A.C),** 27, quai de la Tournelle, 75005 Paris, ☎ (1) 43.26.13.54 lists courses organised by amateur associations.
- **Centre nationale des Jeunes Artisans,** 5, rue des Immeubles Industriels, 75011 Paris, ☎ (1) 43.73.86.83.
- **C.I.D.J.** (→ Young people)
- **Local and regional tourist organisations; Loisirs-Accueil;** (→ regional sections).

Different holidays

Walking and hiking

Sentiers de Grande Randonnée (major hiking trails)

For lovers of the great outdoors France offers over 35 000 km of hiking trails (G.R. : Grande Randonnée). The *Fédération Française de Randonnée pédestre - Comité Nationale des Sentiers de Grande Randonnée* marks out and maintains trails and publishes descriptions of the various itineraries ; points of interest, accommodation and provisionning can be found in *topo-guides* available in bookshops.
The major itineraries (GR) may follow historical traces, such as those of the Knights Templar in the Larzac or of the Compostela pilgrims in the Southwest. Seasoned hikers may even decide to cross France from one end to the other : GR5 runs from Luxembourg to Nice and the GR36 from Caen to Prades. The mountain region GR are the most difficult trails : the GR20 cross-Corsica trail (dangerous in parts yet much-frequented) ; GR54 & 541 in Oisans ; GR5 & 55, the extremely popular round tour of the Mont Blanc ; GR6 & 56 in the Queyras ; GR58, 541 & 10 across the Pyrénées.
All the *grande randonnée* trails are clearly marked with red and white markers.

Main hiking trails

***Randonnée du pays* and *petite randonnée* (ramble trails)** Less-ambitious hikers may be tempted by the red and yellow markers of the *randonnée du pays* or the yellow markers of the *petite randonnée* trails. The former generally wind around a specific scenic region before returning to the starting point; the lengths of the circuits vary considerably. The latter usually consist of one-day round-trips or point-to-point rambles (the Ile-de-France region offers a wide variety of short walking tours easily accessible from Paris). In most cases, local or regional tourist bodies are happy to provide information on points of interest along the trails and on the various activities available to the hiker.

Hints — Accommodation along the trails usually consists of *gîtes d'étapes* and may be difficult to book during peak seasons (e.g. summer for GR5 & 20 Mont Blanc route; weekends in the Ile-de-France).

Information
- The **F.G.T.O.** booklet "France for Sports and Leisure" contains a wealth of useful information for hikers : addresses, itineraries, etc.
- All *randonnée* trails are shown on the **I.G.N.** (Institut Géographique National) map nº 903 (scale 1/1 000 000) and on the more detailed "green series" (1/100 000) (1/50 0000 & 1/25 000) and *topo*, "red series" maps.
- **The Guide du Randonneur** published by the F.F.R.P. (→ below) contains invaluable information for French-speaking visitors. **160 topo-guides** are available in bookshops.
- **The Fédération Française de Randonnée Pédestre** and the **Comité Nationale des Sentiers de Grande Randonnée,** 8, avenue Marceau, 75008 Paris, ☎ (1) 47.23.62.32. **Ile-de-France section :** 64, rue de Gergovie, 75014 Paris, ☎ (1) 45.45.31.02. (For other regional sections see F.G.T.O. booklet). 160 topo-guides are published by the F.F.R.P.
- **Loisir-Accueil** offers "all-in" walking tours at certain reservation centres.

Riding and horse-drawn holidays

On horseback, or in a horse-drawn caravan *(roulotte)* or carriage *(calèche),* France offers a splendid variety of holidays for lovers of the quiet, rustic life.

Hints Trekking :
— Spring and autumn are the most enjoyable seasons for trekking.
— Riding and trekking are tiring; novices are advised to stick to a 4- or 5-day tour.
— Treks are usually organised, group activities, supervised by one or more highly experienced riders. Nevertheless, if you feel up to the challenge, there is nothing preventing you setting up your own trekking tour: the A. N. T. E. (→ below) is there to assist you.

Caravan or calèche — An hour spent with the hirer will reveal the secrets of driving - even downhill - and of tangle-free harnessing and un-harnessing. You will be provided with a basic handbook, a supply of oats and an outline of the route. Horse-drawn caravans are generally fitted out as more rustic versions of their motorised counterparts and a 4-5 day tour will rarely take in more than 60-70 km.
— *Calèches* are faster and more versatile - the horse may keep up a trot for several kilometers - but enforce a "return to civilisation" (in the form of a country hotel or *gîte d'étape ; → Gîtes)* each evening.

Information
- **Association Nationale pour le Tourisme Equestre (A.N.T.E.),** 15, rue de Bruxelles, 75009 Paris, ☎ (1) 42.81.42.82.
- F. G. T. O. offices can supply information on U. S. — and U. K. — based agencies offering horse-drawn holidays.

Cycling holidays

Unfortunately France is lagging behind her neighbours is terms of reserved cycle paths, only 3 000 km for an estimated 22 million bicycles: a lack that is at least partly compensated by the country's network of exquisite minor roads.

The handicapped The Vacances-Flok organisation arranges tandem tours for the blind. **Vacances-Flok,** 156, rue des Pyrénées, 75020 Paris, ☎ 636.91.91.

Hints

— Avoid major roads where drivers will only consider you as an intruder; don't ride abreast.

Rail and bicycle

— If you merely wish to sample the pleasures of cycling, or to discover a region from a different angle, the S.N.C.F. (French Railways) rents bicycles in 172 of its stations (tourist models; less than 50 F per day, 25 % reduction from the 3rd day). They may be hired at one station and returned to another. The R.E.R. provides a similar version of this service in the Paris area. Again in the Paris area, bicyles can be transported free of charge Wednesdays and weekends. Certain main lines also offer reductions: information is available in most stations.

Information

- The relevant gazetteer sections contain adresses of bicycle rental agencies throughout France.
- **S.N.C.F.**
- Bicycle rental in Paris:

Paris-Vélo: 2, rue du Fer-à-Moulin, 75005 Paris, ☎ (1) 43.37.59.22, métro Censier-Daubenton. **Bicy-Club de France:** 8, place de la Porte-Champerret, 75017 Paris, ☎ (1) 47.66.55.92, métro Porte de Champerret.

Inland waterways

Permits

Foreign visitors may sail and moor along the French coast and inland waterways for a period of 6 months in a single stretch or in broken periods) during any consecutive 12 months. During this time no permit is required unless such a permit be required in the country of ori-

Main inland waterways

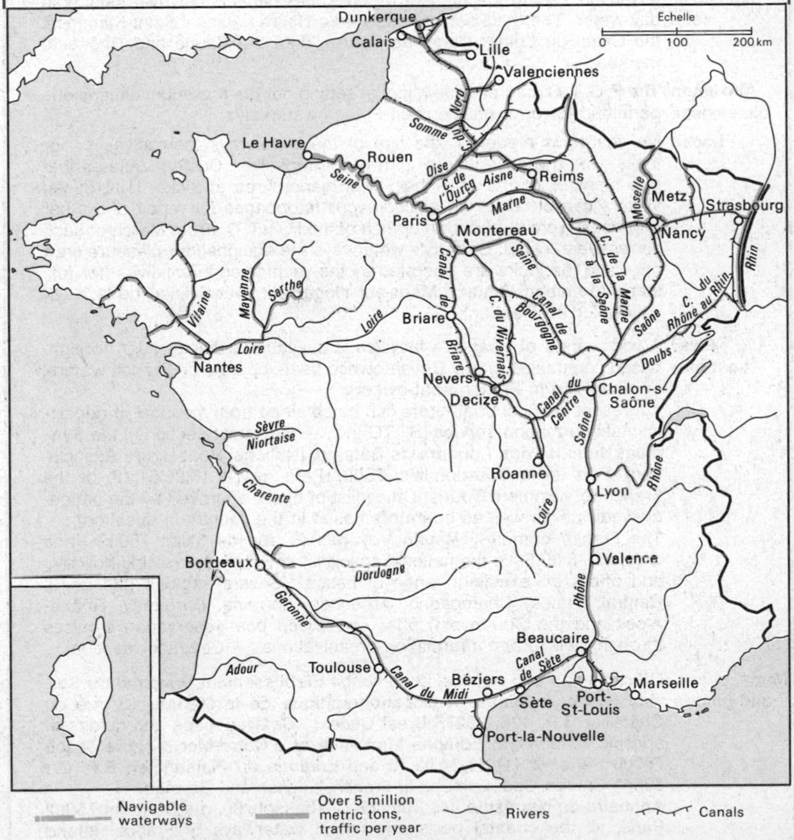

gin. Small yachts and motorboats under 24 m in length must have a Certificate of Registration, official ship's papers or the new British Small Ships Register. Ships owned by companies must have the official ship's papers. During your stay in France you may not lend, rent or use your boat for profitable gain; for business and for stays of more than 6 months, contact the French customs information center (→ Customs).

Health and Customs control Yachts from the U. K. sailing between France (incl. Corsica), Belgium and Holland require no maritime health declaration. This declaration should be obtained and certified from other ports of departure, and yachts arriving from areas of infection should have an international vaccination certificate covering all persons on board.
Duty-free goods and fuel are no longer available for pleasure craft (the allowance is the same as for tourist visitors). Yachts under 100 tons may be visited by French customs up to 20 km from the coast to inspect the ship's papers and list of stores.

The speed limit on rivers varies from 10 to 25 km/h, on canals and certain canalised rivers from 6 to 10 km/h and is fixed at 5 knots within 300 m of the shore in coastal waters. Navigation is prohibited in bathing areas.

Choice of inland water The Rhône is now completely canalised, but strong currents persist and pleasure craft should have adequate engine-power. (Information on navigation of the Rhône and Saône rivers: Service de la navigation, Quai de la Quarantaine 69321 Lyon Cedex 1.) The Rhine requires reserves of engine-power and attentive helmsmanship to manœuvre in the dense commercial traffic. The navigable stretches of the Loire are known for strong currents and difficult flood-waters.

Channel Mediterranean The Canal de Bourgogne is not recommended as a route to the Mediterranean, due to the number of locks; this canal is however ideal holiday water. The quickest route is via Le Havre - Paris - Saint-Mammès, the Canal du Loing, Canal du Centre, then the Saône and Rhône to the sea.

Maximum dimensions The F. G. T. O. can provide a leaflet setting out the maximum dimensions permitted for craft on the main French waterways.

Locks No charge is made for the use of the waterways themselves or for locks, with the exception of part of the Moselle. Custom dictates that one member of the crew help with manœuvres at locks. U. K.-based visitors can obtain a list of *chômages* (stoppages for repair and other purposes) from the London branch of the F. G. T. O. (from March of each current year . NB: Brittany's waterways are equipped for pleasure craft only, and the locks are operated by the yachtsmen themselves (for further information contact: Monsieur l'Ingénieur, Subdivision de la Navigation, 29190 Pleyben).

River boat-hire A wide range of boat-hire facilities is available, either through foreign-based companies (many British-owned fleets operate on French waters) or directly from French boat-owners.
Addresses of local boat-hirers can be obtained from the local or departmental information service (SI, TO etc., → Gazetteer sections), the **Syndicat National des Loueurs de Bateaux** (National Boat-Hirers Association), Port de la Bourdonnais, 75007 Paris, ☎ (1) 45.25.61.76, or the French Government Tourist Office (list of hirers approved by the national syndicate as well as operators based in the country in question).
The French company **Nautic Voyages** (8, rue de Milan 75009 Paris ☎ (1) 45.26.60.80 is the national specialist in waterway cruising holidays and offers an excellent range of bases. Several regions (the Loire, Central France, Champagne, Ardennes, Lorraine, Burgundy, Rhône-Alpes and the Southwest) offer centralised boat reservation services through their tourist information organisations (→ Gazetteer section).

Maps, charts and guides Official maps and nautical documents: **Établissement Principal du Service Hydrographique et Océanographique de la Marine,** 13, rue du Châtellier B.P. 426, 29275 Brest Cedex. Detailed maps and guides of specific waterways: **Éditions Maritimes et d'Outre-Mer,** 17, rue Jacob 75006 Paris, ☎ (1) 46.34.03.10 and **Éditions du Plaisancier,** B.P. 27, 69641 Caluire Cedex; maps in French, English and German.
Annuaire du Nautisme (les Éditions Chabassol), 30, rue Gramont 75002 Paris; all the coastal ports and inland waterways of France. **Inland**

Waterways of France (J. Liley-Stanford). **Through the French Canals** (Bristow Nautical).

Information

- F. G. T. O. leaflet.
- Inland waterways authority: **Office national de la Navigation,** 2 bd. Latour-Maubourg 75007 Paris, ☎ (1) 45.50.32.24, and regional offices. **Ministère des Transports** (waterways - "voies navigables"), 244 bd. Saint-Germain 75007 Paris, ☎ (1) 45.44.39.93. All information relating to inland waterways.
- **Ministère de la Mer, Bureau de la Plaisance,** 3 pl. de Fontenoy 75007 Paris, ☎ (1) 42.73.55.05; information relating to marine yachting.

Naturist holidays

Nudity is increasingly tolerated in holiday areas, but has no legal significance and may be reversed at anytime, especially if complaints are lodged.

Clubs

No such problems are encountered with France's 45 naturist holiday centres; the **F.F.N.'s** (Fédération Française de Naturisme) 225 associations are established in surroundings ranging from rustic camp-sites to vast beaches. Full list of sites available from the F.F.N.

Information

The spring editions of the French naturist publications contain an annual review of the various centres, activities, etc., and in certain cases list unofficial sites where nudism is tolerated. British and North American naturist magazines are also excellent sources of information concerning holidays in France.

- **"L'Officiel du littoral nudiste",** 1, rue du Petit-Bois, 44100 Nantes and at newsagents.
- **"La vie au soleil"** (recognised by the F.F.N.), 16, rue Drouot, 75009 Paris, ☎ (1) 45.23.52.00. **Fédération française de naturisme,** av. du Coq, 75009 Paris, ☎ (1) 42.80.10.35. Publications : "Guide naturiste Français"; "Naturisme informations" (newsletter).
- The **F.G.T.O.** can provide details of tour operators offering naturist holidays in France (camping, self-catering and central, centres, etc.).

Unusual holiday themes and courses

Details on a considerable number of sports and special themes are provided under the relevant section headings of this guide; however for the resolutely "different" holiday-maker the following selection may provide some original ideas.

Unusual Courses

Traditional paper-making courses are offered in the Bas-Rhin area, the construction of *épinettes* (virginals), the traditional regional musical instrument, is taught in the Vosges, **tap-dancing** lessons are offered at Aubenas and elsewhere, and courses in **Gregorian Chant** (prior experience required) at the abbeys of Aiguebelle and Senanque. "Spontaneous" musical instrument-making tuition is available at Aubigny-sur-Nère. Practical courses in **woodwork, wrought-iron work, automobile mechanics** and so on offered throughout France. Really bizarre courses (buyer beware!) include **gold-digging** and **conchyliculture** (mussel-breeding). Excellent courses in **"the safeguard of peasant traditions"** (compilation of folksongs, fables, fairy tales, etc. in the Vendée, Vienne, Haute-Vienne and Deux-Sèvres regions are organised by the **U.P.C.P.** at Pamproux).

New themes

Computer techniques are the subject of a wide range of courses and holidays offered all over France (→ Young people); following the continuing success of photo-safaris, pioneered by Val d'Isère, V.A.L. (→ organised holidays) offers courses in **the observation of migratory birds.** Gourmets can learn how to prepare **foie gras** and **confit de**

canard according to local recipes in the Southwest, and would-be oenologists (wine experts) are confronted with a vast choice of holiday activities. There is a regain of interest in a not-so-new form of holiday : the tours of **ancient monuments and buildings** organised by the Caisse des Monuments Historiques (the National Monuments board ; → Museums.) Two new courses are already much sought-after : off-track **four-wheel-drive motoring** counts over 60 clubs offering diverse adventures (Flaine, Vercours, Auvergne), while **survival courses** (Corsica and the Pyrénées ; contact Loisirs-Accueil) teach participants to fish without hooks, identify edible plants and generally live off the land.
Finally Jack London fans will definitely feel at home on a **dog-sleigh trekking** holiday in the snowy wilds of the Jura mountains (write to **AGAD,** les Bouchoux 39370 La Pesse).

Information

- The **F.G.T.O.** will generally be able to provide advice on unearthing unusual activities.
- A number of British and North American travel agents and tour operators offer specific activity holidays.
- Departmental and local **TO** offer the fullest information on unusual themes (reservations through Loisirs-Accueil → gazetteer section).
- The vast majority of major **ski-stations** provide an astounding range of specific activities during the summer months.
- **Treasure Tours international,** → Information. Special holiday themes for foreign visitors.
- For young people : **Club de Quatre Vents,** 1 rue Gozlin 75006 Paris, ☎ (1) 43.29.60.20. **L'Alliance Française,** 10 bd Raspail 75006 Paris, ☎ (1) 45.44.38.28.
Interséjours, 4 rue de Parme 75009 Paris, ☎ (1) 48.74.04.98.

Monastery retreats

Both short stays and longer retreats involve active participation in the monastery's community life and a modest financial contribution. Accommodation in monasteries and convents is offered by the Benedictine and Trappist orders, while the Carmelites provide convent accomodation in urban areas.

Information

- The **F.G.T.O.** can provide a list of monasteries and convents offering accommodation throughout France.
- **Centre d'Information et Documentation Religieux (C.I.D.R.),** ☎ (1) 46.33.01.01.
- **Guide des Monastères** : Editions Pierre Horay 1983 (available in bookshops).
- The offically-recognised International Zen Association has its headquarters in France, and organises summer courses (that include related activities such as Ikebana and Martial Arts), in addition to weekend sessions and regular Zen practice in dojos throughout France. **Association Zen International,** 17 rue des Cinq Diamants 75013 Paris ☎ (1) 45.80.10.00/08.87.

Cultural theme holidays

Photo and video courses

Arles is the most prestigious international photographic encounter : few events can rival with Arles' profusion of top names, exhibitions, instruction courses and debates. However, other equally valid courses exist throughout France. Nature studies and photo-safaris are also becoming increasingly popular.
Courses vary in their conditions : some provide all the necessary equipment. If you wish to use your own material, check that it is compatible with the course ; over-automated cameras are generally considered as poor instructional tools. Black and white courses invariably include on-site processing instruction ; if you work in colour, check that rapid processing facilities are available. The ground rule of nature photography is that ecology takes priority over technique : animals may be photographed but must be left in peace.

Information

- The availability of courses varies from year to year : French photo magazines (many available in the U.S. and the U.K) such as **Zoom, Photo** and **Photo-Reporter** contain details of courses and publish a full annual program in their spring issues.
- Tourist offices and the C.I.D.J. (→ Young people).

• **Images et Connaissances de la montagne,** B.P. 47 73150 Val-d'Isère, ☎ 70.06.00.03 (photo safaris). **O.R.E.P.A.G. Bretagne,** 9 pl. du Vally 22200 Guingamp ☎ 96.44.19.21; **C.R.E.P.A.G. Aquitaine,** B.P. 36 33036 Bordeaux, ☎ 56.81.78.40 (high quality instruction; French required).
• **Centre d'initiation à l'environnement,** La Maladrerie, 12100 Millau ☎ 65.61.06.57.
• **Rencontres internationales de la photographie** (Arles festival), 16, rue des Arènes, 13200 Arles, ☎ 90.96.76.06.

Music and dance

Over 700 educational courses based around music and dancing are offered each year all over France on many subjects. Some centres invite accomplished performers to share in the creation of a new work, occasional amateurs and even beginners, too.
The *colonies musicales* organised by both the **F.N.A.C.E.M.** and **"A Cœur Joie"** (high level of tuition) are particularly noteworthy, as are the **"Summer academy sessions"** organised at Les Arcs (this ski station also organises summer courses for the not-so-young), Nice, Vichy and Annecy.

Information

• The **Centre national d'action musicale,** 51 rue Vivienne 75002 Paris, ☎ (1) 42.33.38.24 : publishes a brochure containing details of just about everything available in this field in France. An adaptation of these details, specifically aimed at younger people, may be obtained from the **C.I.D.J.** (→ Young people).
• **Fédération Française de Danse A.C.E.C.,** 12 rue Saint Germain l'Auxerrois 75001 Paris, ☎ (1) 42.36.19.61. List of dance and body expression courses.
• **A Cœur Joie,** Les Passerelles 24 av. J. Masset 69009 Lyon, ☎ 78.83.19.61; choral and instrumental summer courses for 6-15 year olds.
• **La F.N.A.C.E.M.** Fédération Nationale d'Associations culturelles d'Expansion Musicale, 2 rue Rossini 75009 Paris, ☎ (1) 45.23.00.85 (foreign relations through : **Peter Owens,** 41 Burrows Road London NW10 5SL, ☎ 960.52.39 or cultural departments of French embassies); summer courses; courses for 4-17 year age group.
• **Jeunesses musicales de France** (conservatory-level tuition), 14 rue François Miror 75004 Paris, ☎ (1) 42.78.19.54.

Theatre and mime

Due to their very nature (especially continuing rehearsals) theatre and mime can hardly be considered as holiday activities. However, a few organisations (mainly youth clubs) offer occasional classes.

Information

• **Fédération Nationale de Compagnies de Théâtre et d'Animation,** 12 rue de la Chaussée d'Antin 75009 Paris ☎ (1) 45.23.36.46; coordinates numerous regional theatrical associations.
• Certain specialised leisure organisations may offer courses, e.g., **V.A.L.** *(Vacances Auvergne-Limousin).*
• The **C.I.D.J.** (→ Young people) has files on most youth-orientated activities.

Sporting holidays

Riding

The French school of horsemanship is considered to be mid-way between the Spanish and Viennese schools. In addition to the three Olympic disciplines of dressage, *concours complet* and jumping, mounted gymnastics are practised in France and polo is also played.

Equestrian events

Entertaining and instructive, a selection of equestrian contests and festivals must include: the **Féerie de Chantilly** (information ☎ (1) 42.96.20.01), the **Féria de Méjeanes** (in the Camargue region, ☎ 90.97.10.62), **La Haute École d'Arles** (same tel as Méjeanes) and, of course, the **Fête du Cheval** in Paris and the **grands concours hippiques (grand contests):** Maisons-Lafitte (Jun-Jul), Vichy and Deauville (Jul) and Fontainebleau (Sep). The **Société Hippique Française** (☎ (1) 45.00.85.74) can supply a complete calendar of quality events.

Information

• → Riding and horse-drawn holidays.
• F.G.T.O., TO and SI
• **Fédération Équestre Française** (the French Riding Federation) 164 rue du Faubourg St. Honoré 75008 Paris, ☎ (1) 42.25.11.22; 140 000 licenced members, hundreds of riding schools under the control of 23 regional leagues.

- **Poney-club de France** (for children), 15 rue Mesnil 75116 Paris, ☎ (1) 47.04.65.05.
- **"Guide des cavaliers 1984"** (Bastin-Lavauzelle; available in bookshops; professional and amateur equestrian activities).
- Equestrian monthlies **"Cheval Magazine", "l'Éperon", "l'Information Hippique", "Chevaux et cavaliers", "Poney Mon Ami".**

Tennis and squash

The total number of courts in France is estimated at over 17 000.

Young people The majority of most group courses are aimed at the 9-13 age-group. Information on these courses can be obtained from the **Association des Centres de Tennis pour jeunes** 69, av. Salvador Allende, 93290 Tremblay-les-Gonesse. ☎ 860.72.72.
Several organisations (U.C.P.A., O.C.C.A.J., → Young people) offer all-in tennis holidays for 18-35 year olds, accommodation is provided and other sporting and leisure activities are frequently included in the package.

Hint — Check the court reservation system as soon as (or even better, before) you arrive on holiday.

Information
- **F.F.T. (Fédération Française de Tennis),** Stade Roland Garros, av. Gordon Bennet, 75016 Paris, ☎ (1) 47.43.96.81. (enquiries in English welcome).
- **The various French tennis publications** (*Tennis Magazine, le Monde du Tennis, Tennis de France, Tennis Hebdo, Tennis Infos,* etc.) are among the best sources of information concerning the countless forms of tennis holidays available. The **F.G.T.O., Loisirs-Accueil** and local tourist offices can also assist you in your choice.
- **Forum Stages** 46, av. Kléber 75116 Paris, ☎ (1) 47.04.58.58 (tennis, but also music, dance, art, computers etc.; regularly welcome foreign participants). Courses in the Hautes-Alpes.
- **U.C.P.A., (Union Nationale des Centres Sportifs en Plein Air),** 62, rue de la Glacière, 75013 Paris, ☎ (1) 336.05.20.
- **O.C.C.A.J.,** 9, rue de Vienne 75008 Paris, ☎ (1) 42.94.21.21.
- **Club Méditerranée; Havas Voyages; Jet Tours.**
- **A.C.T.-J. Stages Gérard Pestre,** 60, av. Salvador-Allende, 93290 Tremblay les Gonesse, ☎ (1) 48.60.72.72. 2 000 places in 10 centres. Pilot departments : Haute-Loire, Puy-de-Dôme.
- **Tennis Forest Hill,** enquiries : 40, av. du maréchal-de-Lattre-de-Tassigny 92360 Meudon-la-Forêt, ☎ (1) 46.30.00.30; commercial organisation with 53 covered and 8 outdoor courts (also 13 squash courts) in the Paris area; extensive clubhouse facilities; organises tournaments, tennis lessons, "clinics", etc.; can provide courts on an hourly basis for transient visitors.
- **Fédération française de squash,** 45 *bis,* rue d'Aguessau, 92000 Boulogne Billancourt, ☎ (1) 46.05.27.32.

Golf

Instruction At the last count there were 141 golflinks in France, of which the most prestigious are : Saint-Cloud, Chantilly, Fontainebleau, Saint-Nom-la-Bretèche, Deauville, Biarritz, Mandelieu. The **F.F.G.** can provide a full list complete with details of access conditions for each course.

A wide range of instruction is available either on public (U.C.P.A.) or private (Jet-Tours, Club Méditerranée, etc.) links. Package golf + hotel holidays are extremely popular at Évian, Divonne, Tours, Biarritz, Le Touquet, Valbonne, Cannes, Deauville, La Baule and Cabourg.

Information
- **Fédération Française de golf,** 69, av. Victor Hugo, 75783 Paris Cedex 16, ☎ (1) 45.00.62.20.
- **"Golf en France" "Guide des terrains de golf Français"** (golf-courses and schools), Editions Person, 34, rue de Penthièvre, 75008 Paris, ☎ (1) 43.59.46.37.
- **F.G.T.O., SI, TO**
- Instruction and golfing holidays (selection) : **Gallia Voyages,** 12, rue Auber, 75009 Paris, ☎ (1) 42.66.07.24. **Golf Holidays,** Travia, 19, av. Victor Hugo, 75116 Paris, ☎ (1) 45.01.79.20.
- **U.C.P.A.** (Union National des Centres Sportifs en Plein Air; → Young people), **Jet Tours, Club Méditerranée.**
- → Gazetteer section.

Skiing and winter sports

France's ski resorts are recognised as the best in the world, in many cases with equipment and facilities years ahead of their competitors. The growing interest in cross-country skiing *(ski de fond)* has lured a number of skiers away from the major stations and into a host of picturesque villages. Rallies *(raids)* off the marked runs *(hors-piste)* and ski-trekking *(randonnée)*, invariably supervised by experienced instructors, are also increasingly popular.

Hints

— Alpine ski stations are generally situated over the 1500 metre mark.
— Insurance is essential. All specialist tour operators and travel agents offer insurance facilities when booking ski holidays.
— Ski runs are colour-graded according to difficulty : green = easy (beginners) ; blue = intermediate easy ; red = intermediate difficult ; black = very difficult (top-flight skiers only). Don't overestimate your skill...
— Take advantage of the different ski-passes offered in every station : (useful vocabulary : *téléphérique* : cable car ; *télésiège* : chair-lift ; *télé-ski* (more commonly *tire-fesses*) : Pomalift ; *œuf* or *gondole :* gondola).
— Everything a skier may need can be hired at the ski station.
— Never ski off the marked runs unless accompanied by a qualified guide or instructor. You may be held responsible for causing an avalanche.

Seasons

— If possible, book out of season (for school holidays, → calendar p. 56) ; the reductions are genuinely advantageous.

Main winter sports stations

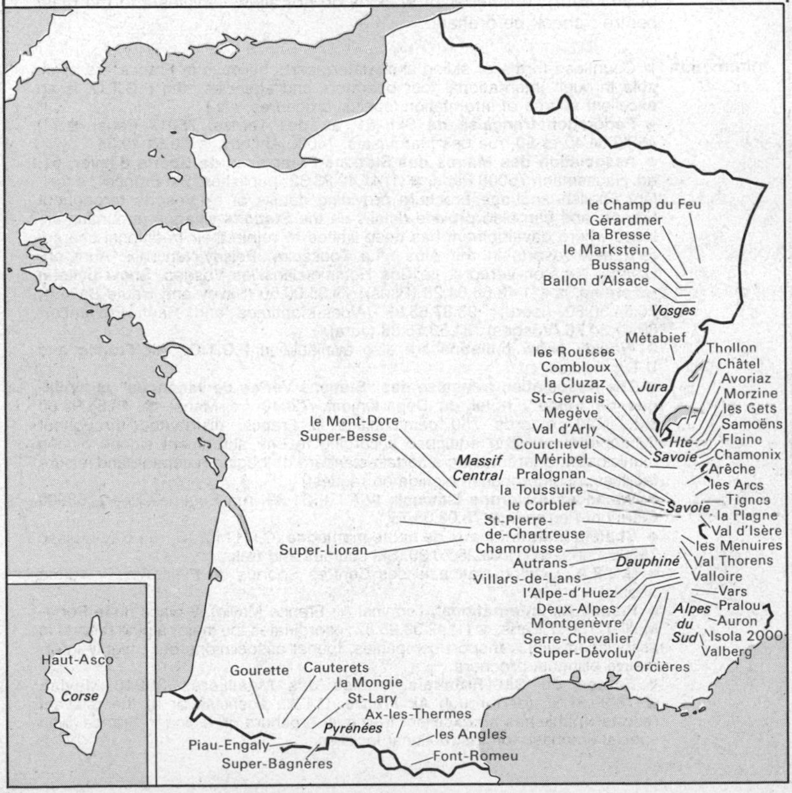

Ski-schools The vast majority of French ski instructors (over 8 000) are graduate members of the E.S.F. (Écoles du Ski Français). The E.S.F. reception office (in all of France's 207 resorts) will arrange individual or group instruction, on an hourly, daily or longer term basis. Peak season instruction (especially for groups) should be booked in advance; write to the Director of the E.S.F. in the relevant resort.

Children Children are exceptionally well catered to in every ski-station. Minimum age varies from 2 to 4 years according to the station.

Young people Various youth organisations (→ Young people) offer all-in winter-sports holidays; mountain-area Youth Hostels organise instructional courses, cross-country rallies, etc.

Accommodation Every taste (and pocket) is provided for, from the popular "studio" (one room self-catering rental appartment with a variable number of beds), to hotels, chalets, holiday villages and even specially equipped camping sites (→ Camping and caravaning).

Non-skiers The range of activities is practically unrivalled by any other form of holiday centre. Skating, bob-sleighing, mountain rambling, heated swimming pools, cinemas, discothèques, festivals and exhibitions.
In summer almost every kind of sport is offered. Of course, skiing is still possible (and delightful) in the higher altitude stations such as the Alpe d'Huez or Chamonix.

Travel No ski resort is more than 3hr30 travel from an airport, most a lot less; stations in the Haute-Savoie are generally within 80 km of Geneva airport. The S.N.C.F. provides rail services to the resort itself, or to the nearest railway station, where regular shuttle buses are available.
If you are travelling by car, chains or studded tires will be necessary (the latter are authorised from Nov. 15th to Mar. 15th with a speed limit of 90 km/hr); a number of stations do not allow vehicles into the main centre : check beforehand.

Information

- Countless forms of skiing and winter-sports holidays in France are available through international tour operators and agencies; the **F.G.T.O.** is an excellent source of information (special brochures, etc.).
- **Fédération française de Ski,** 81, av. des Ternes, 75017 Paris, ☎ (1) 45.72.64.40 et 50, rue des Marquisats, 74000 Annecy, ☎ 50.51.40.34.
- **Association des Maires des Stations Françaises de Sports d'hiver,** 61, bd. Haussmann 75008 Paris, ☎ (1) 47.42.23.32; publishes "Ski-France" : excellent English-language brochure providing details of ski resorts throughout France, and can also provide details on the **Stations villages** (mountain villages where development has been limited to retain their traditional character); new resorts in the Alps : La Toussuire, Peisey-Nancroix, Auris-en-Oisans, Lans-en-Vercors. Le Bon Homme dans les Vosges. **Snow bulletin recording,** ☎ (1) 42.66.64.28 (Paris); 79.35.00.50 (Savoy and Haute-Savoy); 76.54.30.80 (Isère); 93.87.63.99 (Alpes-Maritimes and Haute-Provence); 89.41.34.76 (Vosges); 81.53.55.88 (Jura).
- **Weekly snow bulletins** are also available in **F.G.T.O., Air France** and **U.T.A.** offices.
- **The Association française des "Stations Vertes de vacances" et "Villages de neige",** hôtel du Département, 72040 Le Mans, ☎ 43.84.96.00 ext. 3420, records 750 communities in France, distributed throughout 82 departments and equipped according to one agreement signed by the municipality, guaranteeing a certain standard of lodging reception and leisure facilities... comprehensive guide on request.
- **Vacances-Auvergne-Limousin** (V.A.L.), 31-33, rue Eugène-Gilbert, 63000 Clermont-Ferrand, ☎ 73.93.08.75.
- **Chalets internationaux de haute montagne** (C.I.H.M.), 15, rue Gay-Lussac 75005 Paris, ☎ (1) 43.25.70.90. Ski courses and treks.
- **U.C.P.A. :** Union Nationale des Centres Sportifs de Plein Air (→ Young people).
- **France Ski International,** Terminal Air France Maillot, 2 place de la Porte-Maillot, 75017 Paris, ☎ (1) 42.99.25.82; coordinates the major alpine resorts in association with transport companies, tourist associations etc.; highly informative bilingual brochure.
- **Écoles du Ski Français,** allée des Mitaillières 38240 Meylan ☎ 76.90.67.36 (or through Air France, U.T.A., agencies or at the relevant resorts); publishes an excellent tri-lingual brochure on skiing in France, with special emphasis on instructional facilities.

Mountaineering

The quality and variety of mountaineering facilities available in France are no doubt unrivalled in the world.

Hints

— The security aspect cannot be overstressed, as the annual list of accidents due to carelessness testifies.
— Check the weather and avalanche reports every day.

Instruction

Instruction and tuition at every level is available from the clubs and associations listed below.

Information

- **Fédération Française de la Montagne,** 20 bis, rue la Boétie, 75008 Paris, ☎ (1) 47.42.39.80. Information concerning all existing clubs and associations, including schools offering advanced courses for mountain guides and rescue workers (e.g. the world-famous **Compagnie des Guides de Chamonix**).
- **Club Alpin Français,** 9, rue la Boétie, 75008 Paris, ☎ (1) 47.42.38.46. A century of experience : activities ranging from conservation to hang-gliding; 130 chalets and shelters; alpine centres and climbing schools.
- **U.C.P.A.** (→ Young people), 62, rue de la Glacière, 75640 Paris Cedex 13, ☎ (1) 43.37.53.00 (for the 18-35 year age group); excellent centres at Chamonix-Argentière, La Bérarde, Pralognan, Monetier and Barèges.
- **Chalets Internationaux de haute-montagne,** 15, rue Gay Lussac, 75005 Paris, ☎ (1) 43.25.70.90. Excellent (and inexpensive) high-altitude courses in hiking, climbing and mountaineering for the 9-17 year age group.
- Further information (guides, equipment, etc.) from local S.I.

Speleology

France's calcareous massifs are the nearest thing to paradise for potholing (spelunking for U.S. readers) enthusiasts : Périgord and the Causses come to mind as the major speleological areas, but Haute-Provence, Charentes and the Pyrénées (home of the Gouffre de la Pierre St Martin, the world's deepest pothole at 1 332 m) should not be forgotten.
For the avid, but untrained, amateur of this underground world, guided tours of caves and grottos are offered throughout France. In the Lot, the Doubs, the Vercors and the Pyrénées speleologists devote themselves to this perilous and fascinating sport (→ National parks and reserves).

Information

- The **F.G.T.O.'s** booklet "France for Sports and Leisure" contains details of both regional potholing clubs and the better known guided speleological tours.
- The **Fédération Française de Spéléologie,** 130, rue St Maur, 75011 Paris, ☎ (1) 43.57.56.54 can provide lists of clubs offering initiation courses in speleology.

Motorcycling

Permits

Mopeds of less than 50 cc require no permit, and can be driven by persons over 14 years old. Motorcycles of less than 80 cc require the A1 permit for 16 year-old drivers. At 17 years you can only drive 125 cc of 13 CV maximum. Over 125 cc and 18 years old, you need the A Permit, up to 100 CV.

Rental

Small motorcycles and mopeds can be hired in most resort areas, enquire at the local SI.

Competitions

→ Sporting events.

Hints

— Motorcyclists are statistically an accident-prone group in France.
— **Helmets** are compulsory for both rider and passenger - the police or gendarmes will stop anyone disobeying this injunction.
— Only one passenger is allowed in motorcycle side-cars.
— Beware of treacherous road-surfaces : French shoulders are often anything but hard and the line between the shoulder and the road itself is frequently a mere sprinkling of gravel; many of the road-markings contain synthetic compounds that are very slippery when wet.

Information • **Fédération Française de Motocyclisme,** 74, av. Parmentier, 75011 Paris, ☎ (1) 47.00.94.40; supervises the 22 regional leagues, publishes an annual handbook of events, clubs, etc.
• **"France-Moto",** the F.F.M. official review.

Hunting and shooting

Although shooting is by far the most popular form of hunting, hunters also ride to hounds, and the ancient art of falconry is still practised.

Riding to the hounds The rules established by King François I still govern the hunt, whether for red deer, fallow deer or wild boar *(la grande vénerie)* or for roe deer, fox or hare *(la petite vénerie).* Visitors to Cheverny château can see one of France's most ancient and splendid hunts in exquisite surroundings. Local SI and TO can provide information on hunt days.

Shooting A hunting licence is required for shooting in France. Applicants must produce valid proof of identity, a temporary hunting insurance certificate issued by an insurance company recognised as operating on French territory, a hunting licence or equivalent (gun licence, etc.) issued in the applicant's home country, and two identity photographs. The fee is 150 FF. Under consideration is a new licence which would require both a written and a field test.

Visitors intending to hunt for more than two days, or more than twice in the year must pass the national examination (covering safety and nature preservation). Applicants must in addition produce valid proof of identity and a clean police record (or a certificate of good conduct issued by a competent local authority). U.S. nationals must have these documents certified by the nearest French consular office and they must be accompanied by a certified translation.

The basic fee for a hunting permit is 55 FF, plus variable additional fees according to the territory covered and the type of game.

Hunting ground that is not private property (in which case the owner's authorisation is necessary, and all game shot reverts to him) is allotted to hunting associations. Visitors must apply for at least temporary membership in order to hunt; some associations share all game shot among the hunters present during the shoot.

Travelling with guns Two shotguns with 200 cartridges each are allowed through French customs with no formalities other than the production of an invoice or equivalent certificate of origin.

Airlines vary in their attitudes to passengers travelling with guns and visitors should enquire in advance at the airline office.

All the usual types and bores of cartridges are widely available throughout France : almost every small town has its gunsmith.

The shooting season The season is generally open for 3-5 months from mid-September to late January or February. Information can be obtained from the local hunting association ("Association Communale de Chasse Agréée"); the departmental federation can supply lists of addresses.

Types of shooting The three types of game shooting practised in France are the conventional shoot with beaters; forest hunting, where the game is tracked down; and duck and other water-fowl shooting in marshes and estuaries.

Information • **Office National de la Chasse,** (National Hunting Office) 85 *bis,* av. de Wagram, 75017 Paris, ☎ (1) 42.27.81.75, supervises and coordinates the various hunter's federations, game reserves and experimental centres. The Office's priority is maintaining and encouraging France's valuable stock of game species.
• **Fédération Française de Tir** (French Marksmen's Federation), 16, av. du Président-Wilson, 75116 Paris, ☎ (1) 47.23.72.38; information on skeet shooting, pistol and rifle clubs.
• Museums : **National Hunting Museum** (Musée National de la Chasse), hôtel du Guénégaud, 60, rue des Archives, 75003 Paris, ☎ (1) 42.72.86.43. **Musée International de la Chasse,** Château de Gien, 45500 Gien, ☎ 38.67.24.11.
• A number of local events centred on hunting take place throughout France on the feast of the patron saint of hunting Saint Hubert's day, November 3. A hunting-horn festival and national dog show is held at Compiègne.

Fishing

Regulations in any particular locality or district are relatively straightforward, and are posted in the local mayoral office; the local fishing supply store is always the best source of information and in most cases issues the necessary permits. Advance information can be obtained from the local SI or TO.

Fishing rights

Angling water is classified in two categories : public *(libre)* and private *(close).* Although the owner's permission is all that is required to fish on private property (the catch reverts to the owner), all other water necessitates a permit issued by the association and payment of the annual fishing tax, valid throughout the country.

Fine and coarse fishing

Trout water is distinguished from coarse angling water and is termed category 1; all other water falls into category 2. A supplementary tax (in the form of a stamp) is required for category 1 water, and for spinning, live and dead-baiting elsewhere. Salmon fishing also requires an extra fee, as does authorised fishing during the closed season. Young people under 16 years of age are exempt from most of these regulations; however, they must pay the annual national fishing tax and are restricted to float-fishing.
Fishing is always **strictly forbidden in nature parks and reserves,** and near dams and locks.

Open seasons

As a general rule, category 1 water is closed from September/October to February/March. Category 2 water closes on the 2nd Tuesday in March and opens on the last Friday in April in the 25 southern and southeastern departments; elsewhere it closes on the Tuesday following April 15 and re-opens on the Friday following June 8.

Minimum sizes

Salmon under 50 cm in length, pike under 40 cm (except in category 1), and trout or char under 23 cm must be thrown back; regulations governing other species are posted at the mayoral office and in fishing supply stores.

Sea fishing

Amateur fishing is permitted all year round in French maritime waters. Fishing from the shore with a line or a small net requires no particular authorisation; only large nets are subject to regulations.
Fishing from boats, however, is regulated : a total of no more than 12 hooks on conventional lines, two *palangres* (lines suspended by floats) with a maximum of 30 hooks each, and two lobster pots.
Underwater fishing is subject to strict regulations. Snorkel-divers should enquire at the local port authority offices (or the municipal office in smaller resorts); scuba-divers are required to be members of a recognised club or to fill in a declaration at the nearest offices of the Affaires Maritimes; under no circumstances may any catch be sold (→ Skin-diving).

Information

● Secrétariat général du **Conseil Supérieur de la Pêche** (Higher Council of Fishing), 10, rue Péclet, 75015 Paris, ☎ (1) 48.42.10.00; enquiries, information and regulations. River-fishing only. Control over 250 000 km of French rivers.
● The departmental offices of the **Directions de l'Agriculture, de l'Équipement,** and **des Services de Navigation** can also supply fishing regulations.

Aquatic sports

The waterside

The water off all French beaches is tested at regular intervals throughout the summer season. The results of the tests (on 1700 beaches) must be displayed by the town hall of the locality concerned.
— At certain points on the Atlantic coast, tides and their attendant currents may make bathing dangerous for less experienced swimmers.
— The *Gendarmerie Nationale* maintains a network of lifeguard stations complete with helicopters; all major beaches and swimming sites are well-supervised.

— Whether on the Atlantic, the Channel or the Mediterranean coast, you are advised to bathe from a supervised beach; flags indicate the state of the sea : green for safe, orange for dangerous, red when bathing is prohibited.
— In a few specific areas, bathing shoes may be recommended as protection from sea-urchins (rocky coastlines) or *vives* (stingfish or weevers; Arcachon basin - low tide only). Local inhabitants will advise you.

Information
● Europe's first aquatic park is at Cap d'Agde (Hérault) : 10 acres of waterfalls, geysers, slides, etc., complete with a wave-generator.
● A full survey of beach pollution is published annually in the June edition of the French consumers' magazine "Que choisir" (available at newsagents).
● → also : Sailing and Windsurfing; Waterskiing; Diving; Children; Young people.

Sailing and wind-surfing
Almost every coastal resort and village has sailing facilities and often a club offering tuition.
Children are particularly well catered to during the summer months in the great majority of resorts. After a brief period of initiation children of 7 years and upwards are allowed out (under supervision) solo or in doubles in the Optimist, the basic instructional tool for young sailors. Most resort area clubs accept children on a weekly or fortnightly basis (tuition time varies considerably, but 4 hours per day is an average estimate); advance reservation is advisable, although not compulsory. Local **SI** and **TO** can provide information on tuition facilities available in their areas; parents are advised to ensure that the club is approved by the **Fédération Française de Voile** (the national sailing federation - see below).
The 420-class dinghy is still the most widely used craft both for instructional and pleasure purposes. A 2-week course, combining theory and practice, is usually quite sufficient to enable a novice to handle this type of craft with confidence in most circumstances.
It is forbidden to windsurf at a distance in excess of one nautical mile from the shore unless accompanied by a boat.
The **F.F.V.** offers a "carte voile" insurance scheme, covering rescue fees, third party and legal cost, etc. This scheme applies to both vessels and sail-boards.

Information
● **La Fédération Française de Voile** (French Sailing Federation), 55, av. Kléber, 75016 Paris, ☎ (1) 45.53.68.00; list of registered clubs and schools.
● **Les Glenans** schools are the old-established household name in sailing instruction, using rather military methods along the lines of the scouting movement; their results are beyond question, however : C.N.G., quai Louis-Blériot, 75781 Paris Cedex 16, ☎ (1) 45.20.01.40.
● A score of youth organisations offer sailing holidays (→ Young people).
● **U.C.P.A.** (Union Nationale des Centres sportifs de Plein Air), 62, rue de la Glacière, 75640 Paris Cedex 13, ☎ (1) 43.36.05.20; more than 800 boats in sailing centres throughout France.
● **Departmental tourist organisations** and local **TO** and **SI** can provide full information on sailing facilities in their particular area; reservations through **Loisirs-Accueil.**
● Sail-boards can be hired from practically any beach during the summer months; sailing dinghies are less often available for hire. If the local SI cannot recommend addresses, a few enquiries around the port and at the port authority offices will often prove fruitful.
● The **mairies** (municipal offices, in smaller resorts these may be housed in a single building) are mines of useful and necessary information for yachtsmen and wind-surfers : weather bulletins, tidal charts, regulations and restrictions, etc.
● The **Ministère de la Mer, Bureau de la Plaisance,** 3, place Fontenoy, 75007 Paris, ☎ (1) 42.73.55.05 provides information relating to seagoing navigation.
● A number of sailing clubs and regional federations are listed in the gazetteer sections of the guide.
● → **The waterside.**

Skin-diving
Underwater fishing requires a licence. It is illegal to fish with tanks.
Scuba-divers must be in possession of the relevant certificate (elementary : from 14 yrs, depths down to 20 m; 1st grade : depths down to 20 m, or 40 m with an instructor; 2nd grade : from 18 yrs, depths down to 40 m). Foreign certificates, delivered by affiliates of the C.M.A.S. (→ below), are acceptable (check that your insurance is valid for France). Some dream spots : Corsica (Propriano, Bonifacio, Calvi, Porto...), the Gulf of Morbihan, La Seyne-sur-Mer, Hyères, Sanary, Bandol and the whole Riviera.

Hint

— The ground rules (medical check-ups; never diving alone, etc.) of scuba-diving are international and apply even to the casual holiday-maker.

Information

- **C.M.A.S** (Confédération Mondiale des Activités Sub-aquatiques), 34 rue du Colisée 75008 Paris, ☎ (1) 42.25.60.42. Quarterly tri-lingual newsletter.
- **Fédération Française d'Études et de Sports Sous-marins,** 24 quai de Rive-Neuve 13007 Marseille, ☎ 91.33.99.31. Paris branch : as C.M.A.S. List of clubs and instructional courses; official annual; magazine : "Études et sports sous-marins".

A selection of organisations offering scuba instruction and holidays :
- **Océanide,** 4 bis rue Descombes 75017 Paris, ☎ (1) 47.63.12.72.
- **Odyssée,** 137 rue de Ranelagh 75016 Paris, ☎ (1) 42.88.82.66.
- **Subexplor,** 17 rue du Faubourg-Montmartre 75009 Paris, ☎ (1) 45.23.51.51.
- **Touring club de France, Jet Tours, Club Méditerranée.**

Canoe and kayak

The Fédération Française de Canoë-Kayak supervises a network of 550 clubs, regional committees and associations. Information on special sessions with specialised personnel can be obtained from the F.F.C-K.

Hints

Canoes and kayaks are considered as personal baggage at customs. Always consult a specialised map (F.F.C-K) : beware of dams and weirs. Discover the Ognon (Doubs), Orb (Hérault), Vézère, Dordogne, Ardèche, Ariège and Allier rivers.

Information

- **Fédération française de canoë-kayak,** 17 route de Vienne 69007 Lyon, ☎ 78.61.32.74. River guides and maps; annual guide : **"Vacances en canoë-kayak"** (schools, courses, etc.)
- **Canoë-Kayak Club de France,** 47 quai Ferber 94360 Bry-sur-Marne, ☎ (1) 48.81.54.26.
- **"Canoë-Kayak magazine",** 403 route de Poissy 78670 Villesnes-sur-Seine.

Water-skiing

Clubs throughout France - both on the coasts and inland — offer water-skiing instruction and ski and boat hire (list from F.F.S.N., → below). Skiing is generally restricted to well-marked channels and two people must always be aboard any boat towing a skier or skiers.

Information

- **Fédération française de ski nautique** (F.F.S.N.), 9 bd. Pereire 75017 Paris, ☎ (1) 42.67.15.66. Information (regulations etc.), list of clubs; magazine "Ski-Nautique".
- **Club Meditérranée** (water-skiing at most clubs).
- → Gazetteer section.

Surfing

Brittany and particularly the Atlantic coast are the prime surfing regions. Keen surfers are advised to bring all the necessary equipment (repairs, etc.); few surf shops exist away from major centres.

Fun...

Pedal boats *(pédalos)* and aqua-cycles *(vélo-pédalos)* can be hired from just about any beach in France.

Aerial sports and leisure

Private aviation

U.S. and U.K. pilot licences are valid worldwide, and a number of French aeroclubs rent small craft on a real flight-time basis (providing time spent on the ground is not unreasonable). The holiday possibilities open to pilot's licence holders are almost boundless...
Addresses of aeroclubs are given in the relevant gazetteer sections. Home civil aviation authorities can provide information on the use of French airfields, as can F.G.T.O.
Charts showing civil aviation fields in France are available in the U.K. from **A.O.P.A.** (Aircraft Owners and Pilots Association), 50A Cambridge St. London SW1 ☎ (1) 834 5631. These charts, called ICAO topographical maps in a set of seven, cover France and Corsica.
— Pilots arriving from abroad must use an airfield equipped with customs offices.

Information

- **Fédération Nationale Aéronautique,** 52, rue Galilée, 75008 Paris, ☎ (1) 720.39.75; full information about private aviation in France.

Hang-gliding

The regional gazetteer sections of this guide contain addresses and phone numbers of local hang-gliding centres. U.S. and U.K. hang-gliding licence-holders must apply in advance to the French Hang-gliding Federation (F.F.V.L. → below) to obtain certification of their licence.

Ultralight craft Visitors wishing to fly ultralights in France must either hold a regular pilot's licence or pass the French ultralight pilot's examination. While this involves only simple flight instruction and basic theory, the theory examination is in French...

At presstime there were 170 ultralight aviation clubs in France, all of which offer instruction. → The regional gazetteer sections for addresses of ultralight clubs.

A number of centres (about 140) are flourishing, and often specialising in instruction for teenagers. Glider pilot licences are internationally recognized. Addresses of gliding clubs are contained in the regional gazetteer sections (F.F.V.V. → below).

Information ● Hang-gliding : **Fédération Française de Vol Libre** (F.F.V.L.), 54 *bis,* rue de la Buffa, 06000 Nice, ☎ 93.88.62.89; coordinates regional leagues, including 64 instructional centres, 150 clubs and 12 000 adherents.

● Ultralight aviation : **Fédération Française de Planeurs et Ultra-Légers Motorisés** (F.F.P.U.L.M.), chemin de la Sacristie, 84140 Montfavet (near Avignon), ☎ 90.32.56.75.

● Gliding : **Fédération Française de Vol à Voile** (F.F.V.V.), 29, rue de Sèvres, 75006 Paris, ☎ (1) 45.44.04.78; full information on gliding in France.

● In conjunction with the F.F.V.V., **U.C.P.A.** *(Union Nationale des Centres Sportifs de Plein Air)* organizes instructional gliding holidays for young people : 62, rue de la Glacière, 75013 Paris, ☎ (1) 43.36.05.20.

Ballooning At the last count there were over 320 operational balloons in France. Licences are internationally recognised (if in doubt, check with the F.F.A.; → below).

Information ● **Fédération française d'Aérostation** (F.F.A.), 29, rue de Sèvres, 75006 Paris, ☎ (1) 45.44.04.78. List of various clubs and events (in French with special English page; price : 30 F).

● **Centre aérostatique de Coulommiers,** ☎ 64.03.23.07. (Balloon trips).

● **Association Picard de Sade-Balloon,** 2, square Th.-Judlin, 75015 Paris, ☎ (1) 48.32.05.80. (Balloon trips and even balloon hire!)

Parachuting There are 42 centres in France and the overseas departments. Disciplines range from simple drops to ram-air chuting and, for experts, freefall.

Foreign visitors with previous experience in parachuting should bring appropriate documentation (home association certificates, etc.) to ensure that they are able to practise at their accustomed level.

Information ● **Fédération Française de Parachutisme,** 35, rue Saint-Georges, 75009 Paris, ☎ (1) 48.78.45.00 coordinates the 23 regional leagues (every centre is operated under league supervision).

New Sports

For sportsmen with stamina under-water hockey is played in teams in swimming-pools and without oxygen cylinders. "Bobsleigh over the rapids" on the other hand is a sport for acrobats. Wet-suits and crash helmets are recommended.

Monoski should not pose any particular problems. But as with the numerous other new winter sports (bird-sail, winterstick and sail-skiing-windsurfing on snow) which can be practised in the Alps and the Pyrénées, the utmost caution is essential.

Boomerang, the Australian national sport, has met with great success, above all among the young. In France it is much practised in clubs.

Rafting consists of descending a river on a platform of tyres. A supervisor accompanies you. The passengers steer with the aid of oars. New in France, rafting only takes place on some rivers (Haut-Allier, Haute-Isère).

Information ● **Association française des nageurs en eau vive** (AFNEV), 21, rue des Garennes, 92140 Antony, ☎ (1) 46.51.12.93.

● **DEVPA** (white-water swimming), 25, av. Duquesne, 75007 Paris, ☎ (1) 46.44.51.49.

● **Hockey sous-marin,** 34, rue du Colisée, 75008 Paris, ☎ (1) 42.25.62.69.

● **Boomerang-Fan-Club** (Jacques Beslot), B.P. 77, Saumur, ☎ 41.67.22.93.

● **A.N. Rafting,** 38, rue d'Alsace, 92100 Clichy, ☎ (1) 47.37.08.77. On the Allier, Durance and Ubaye rivers, and mountain streams in the Pyrénées.

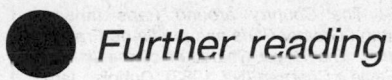

Further reading

Countless books have been written on France, and the following selection is necessarily incomplete. Some of the titles may be out of print, but remain valid sources, accessible second-hand through public libraries.

General

Chamberlain, Samuel : *Bouquet de France : An Epicurean Tour of the Provinces* (NY 1952). Delpel, Jean-Jacques : *Landmarks of France* (NY 1983). Editors of Gourmet Magazine : *Gourmet's France* (NY 1970). Hürliman, Martin : *France* (NY 1958). Jacobs, Michael and Paul Stirton : *The Knopf* (U.K. : *Mitchell Beasley*) *Traveller's Guide to Art : France* (NY/London 1984). Laurent, Jacques : *France* (NY 1983). Lichine, Alexis : *Guide to the Wines and Vineyards of France* (London 1979; NY 1984). Nicolson, Adam : *Long Walks in France* (NY 1983). Editors of Réalités : *The Châteaux of France* (London 1979; NY 1983). Root, Waverly : *The Food of France* (NY 1977). Stewart, J.I.M. : *A Villa in France* (London 1982; NY 1983). Wildman, Frederick S. : *A Wine Tour of France* (NY 1976). Zeldin, Theodore : *The French* (London 1983; NY 1984) (acclaimed by the French themselves as the definitive guide to the French people).

Paris

Paris Observed (Oxford) (NY/London 1977). *Paris* (Time-Life) (NY 1977). *The Great Houses of Paris* (Vendome/Hachette) (NY 1979). Alsop, Susan : *To Marietta from Paris,* 1945-1960 (NY 1975). Carzou, J.-M. : *Paris* (NY 1982). Chevalier, Maurice : *My Paris* (NY 1972). Cobb, Richard : *The Streets of Paris* (NY/London 1980). Evenson, Norma : *Paris : A Century of Change* (New Haven 1979). Gallet, Michel : *Stately Mansions : Eighteenth Century Paris Architecture* (NY 1972). Gajdusek, Robert : *Hemingway's Paris* (NY 1978). Jennet, Séan : *Paris* (NY 1973). Kane, Robert S. : *Paris A to Z* (Garden City NY 1974). Laclotte, Michel and Jean-Pierre Cuzin : *The Louvre* (NY/London 1983). Morton, Brian N. : *Americans in Paris : An Anecdotal Street Guide* (Ann Arbor 1984). Thompson, Ian Bentley : *The Paris Basin* (NY/London 1973). Shaw, Irwin : *Paris! Paris!* (NY 1977).

Agenais, Périgord Quercy

Daniel, Glyn Edmond : *The Hungry Archaeologist : A Travelling Guide to Caves, Graves and Good Living in the Dordogne and Brittany* (London 1963); *Lascaux and Carnac* (London 1955).

Alsace

Beyer, Victor : *Alsace* (Paris 1975). Gaertner, Pierre, and Robert Frederick : *The Cuisine of Alsace* (NY 1981). Shaw, Michael : *History, People and Places in Eastern France : Alsace, Lorraine and the Vosges* (Bourne End U.K. 1979).

Champagne, Ardenne

Forbes, Patrick : *Champagne : The Wine, the Land and the People* (Pomfret VT/London 1967).

Auvergne

Gorham, Peter : *Portrait of the Auvergne* (London 1975).

Berry, Bourbonnais

Maurois, André : *Lelia : The Life of George Sand,* tr. Gerard Hopkins (NY 1977).

Bordelais, Landes

Macdonald, Lyn : *Bordeaux and Aquitaine* (London 1976/NY 1977).

Brittany

Elsy, Mary : *Brittany and Normandy* (NY/London 1974). Hélias, Pierre-Jakez : *The Horse of Pride : Life in a Breton Village* (New Haven 1978). Millar, Ronald William : *A Time of Cherries* (London 1977). Spence, Keith : *Brittany and the Bretons* (London 1978).

Burgundy

Gunn, Peter : *Burgundy* (Mystic CT 1976). Lands, Neil : *People and Places in Burgundy* (Bourne End U.K. 1977). Speaight, Robert : *The Companion Guide to Burgundy* (London 1975).

Corsica

Balinger, William : *The Corsican* (NY 1974). Carrington, Dorothy : *Corsica : A Portrait of a Granite Island* (NY 1974). Hogg, Gary : *Corsica* (Reading MA 1973). Thompson, Ian Bentley : *Corsica* (North Pomfret VT 1971). Turnbull, Patrick : *Corsica* (NY 1976).

Dauphiné

Boell, Jacques : *High Heaven,* Introduction by François Mauriac (London 1947).

Ile-de-France	Bloch, Marc : *Ile-de-France : The Country around Paris* (Ithaca NY 1971). Brodrick, Alan Houghton : *Greater Paris and the Ile-de-France* (London 1952). Levron, Jacques : *The Royal Châteaux of the Ile-de-France* (Chicago 1965). Mâle, Émile : *Chartres* (NY 1983). Dubois, Jacques, and Jean d'Ormesson : *Versailles : A Garden in Four Seasons* (NY 1983), Van de Kamp, Gerald : *Versailles* (NY 1981).
Languedoc-Roussillon	Lands, Neil : *History, People and Places in Languedoc-Roussillon* (Bourne End U.K. 1976). Savage, Georges : *The Languedoc* (London 1975).
Lorraine, Vosges	→ Alsace.
Maine, Anjou	→ Touraine.
Midi Toulousain, Pyrénées	Battagel Arthur : *Pyrenees East : A Guide to the Mountains for Walkers and Climbers* (Goring, Berks. 1975); *Pyrenees West* (Goring, Berks. 1975). Gomez-Ibanez, Daniel Alexander : *The Western Pyrenees* (Oxford 1975).
Normandy	Gunn, Peter : *Normandy* (London 1975). Pitt, Derek William : *Portrait of Normandy* (London 1974). Roberts, Nesta : *The Companion Guide to Normandy* (London 1979; NY 1983). Robertson, Ian : *Loire Valley, Normandy, Brittany* (NY/London 1975). Whelpton, Barbara : *History, People and Places in Normandy* (Bourne End U.K. 1975).
Provence, Côte d'Azur	Brangham, Arthur Norman : *History, People and Places in Provence* (Bourne End U.K. 1976; NY 1978). Brown, Jamie : *The Lively Spirits of Provence* (Toronto 1974). Fisher, M.F.K. : *Two Towns in Provence* (NY 1983). Ford, Ford Madox : *Provence* (NY 1979). Jennet, Séan : *The Sun and Old Stones : A Tour through the Midi* (London 1961). Lyall, Archibald : *The Companion Guide to the South of France* (NY 1983; London 1979). Makin, Peter : *Provence and Pound* (Berkeley CA 1978). Pezet, Maurice : *This is Provence* (Oxford 1962). Phillips, G. Cecilia : *Letters from Provence* (London 1975). Turnbull, Patrick : *Discovering Provence* (London 1973); *The South of France* (NY 1972). Whelpton, Barbara : *Painters' Provence* (London 1970). Wylie, Lawrence W. : *Village in the Vaucluse* (Cambridge MA 1974).
Savoy	Cox, Eugene : *The Eagles of Savoy* (Princeton 1979).
Touraine, Blésois, Orléanais	Hibbert, Christopher : *Châteaux of the Loire* (NY 1982). Jeanbran, Hélène : *The Loire* (NY/London 1975). Martin-Demezil, Jean : *The Loire Valley and its Treasures* (Chicago 1970). Myhill, Henry : *The Loire Valley* (Boston/London 1978). Wade, Richard : *The Companion Guide to the Loire* (London 1979, NY 1983).
Vendée, Poitou, Charente	Spencer, Hubert : *Cognac Country* (London 1983).

Art and Architectural Terms

Ambulatory : passageway surrounding the choir.

Appareil : method of cutting and joining construction stones.

Apse or chevet : extreme eastern end of a church, beyond the choir, usually rounded in shape.

Archivolt : Arch surrounding an opening or doorway.

Art nouveau : decorative style that enjoyed great success just before WWI. Its characteristic curves were drawn from the supple shapes of stems and leaves.

Atlantes : male statue serving as a support (→ Caryatid).

Baroque : architectural style that began in 17thC Italy. Breaking with the formal strictness of Classicism, it maintained the basic elements but used them within an original framework of curves and counter-curves. The result was a monumental and sumptuous effect enhanced by richly sculpted and painted figures and brought to life by the play of light and shade.

Barrel vault : vault formed by a semicircular arch extended perpendicular; it is a broken vault if the arch is a broken arch.

Bastion : jutting construction at the corner of a fortification.
Bossage : method of arranging stone blocks so that they jut out from the surface of a façade.
Buttress : masonry block reinforcing a wall.
Caryatid : female statue serving as a support (→ Atlantes).
Chapter house : monks' common room opening on to the cloister.
Choir : part of the nave of a church reserved for singers during services.
Cintre : curve of a vault or arc.
Classical : the basic elements of Classical architecture were those of Greek and Roman Antiquity, and noted for symmetry and harmony, such as in the combination of pillars and lintel, or that of pillar and arch.
Corbelled structure : projection supported by corbels (justing stone-work).
Coursière : narrow walkway inside a wall.
Croisillon : arms of the transept on either side of the crossing.
Crossing : space at the intersection of nave and transept.
Curtain wall : stretch of wall between two rows of a fortification.
Doubleau : projecting arch under a barrel vault.
Entablature : topmost section of a building.
Flamboyant : last phase of the Gothic style, heavily ornamented with profuse curves and counter-curves, arcatures and stone lacework.
Flying buttress : external support abutting a structure and designed to resist the thrust of vaulting.
Germinate : divided into two identical parts.
Gothic : essentially religious architectural style predominant from the end of the 12thC until the Renaissance; churches in the form of the Roman cross were typified by ogival arches and vaulting, spacious, well-lighted side aisles surmounted by a gallery or triforium.
Groined vault : vault formed by the intersection of two vaults of equal size.
Hall-Church : church on a lengthwise plan with three naves of equal height.
Lintel : horizontal piece of stone or timber surmounting a rectangular opening.
Machicolation : opening between corbels supporting a parapet at the top of a fortification, used for defense.
Mullion : stone upright dividing a window.
Narthex : Vestibule at the church entrance, not to be confused with the porch that opens to the outside.
Nave : Central section of a church, between choir and western entrance.
Neo-Classicism : late-18thC architectural style inspired by Roman Antiquity.
Neo-Gothic : 19thC architectural movement that advocated a return to the Gothic style, opposed to the various Classically-inspired movements that had predominated since the Renaissance.
Ogive : diagonal arch supporting a vault.
Order : in Classical architecture, a grouping composed of column, capital, and architrave.
Orientation : placement of a church, with the choir towards the east in the direction of Jerusalem.
Oven vaulting : vault in the form of a quarter-sphere.
Pediment : section of the façade, usually triangular, placed on top of the entablature.
Pilaster : flattened column, in a wall but projecting from it.
Pilgrim church : church with side aisles extended into the ambulatory around the choir to accomodate large numbers of worshippers at places of pilgrimage.
Retable : architectural ornament above an altar; a painted panel in the final Gothic period.
Rococo : 18thC decorative style typified by a profusion of garlands, stucco-work and sculpture with graceful lines and delicate colouring.
Romanesque : 10thC and 11thC architectural style characterised by churches in the form of a Roman cross, with rounded arches and barrel vaulting.
Rood-screen : sculpted screen separating choir from nave.
Saddle-back : roof with double slope.
Side aisle : sections of a church on either side of the nave.
Stalls : seats for the clergy on either side of the choir.
Transept : Transverse section of a church, terminating the main nave and forming the symbolic cross-shape of the building.
Tympanum : panel above a church doorway, usually sculpted.

Menu guide

Agneau lamb.
Aiglefin haddock.
Aloyau sirloin of beef.
Amandes almonds.
Ananas pineapple.
Ancienne (à l') 'old style'.
Andouillette chitterling sausage.
Anglaise (à l') plain boiled.
Anguille eel.
Anis aniseed.
Araignée de mer spider crab.
Ballotine stuffed poultry or meat roll.
Bar or **Loup** sea-bass.
Barbue brill.

Basilic basil.
Basquaise Basque style: Bayonne ham, rice and peppers.
Bavette undercut of beef.
Béarnaise sauce with egg yolks, shallots, butter, white wine.
Bécasse woodcock.
Béchamel white sauce.
Beignets fritters.
Bercy wine and shallots sauce.
Beurre blanc butter, shallots, wine vinegar.
Beurre noir browned butter, vinegar, parsley.
Bigorneaux periwinkles.
Bisque shellfish soup.
Blanc (de volaille) white breast (of poultry).
Blanquette white stew.
Bœuf à la mode beef braised in red wine.
Bordelaise(e) Bordeaux style with shallots and red wine.
Boudin blood sausage (similar to black pudding).
Bouquet prawn.
Bourguignonne Burgundy style : red wine, onions, bacon..
Bourride white fish soup with *aioli*.
Brandade de morue salt cod with mashed potatoes and garlic.
Brochet pike.
Brochette shish-kebab of meat or fish.
Cabillaud cod.
Caen (à la mode de) cooked in Calvados and white wine.
Caille quail.
Calmars squid.
Canard duck.
Caneton duckling.
Cannelle cinnamon.
Carbonnade braised in beer.
Cassis blackcurrants.
Cassoulet casserole of beans, pork or goose or duck with sausage.
Cèpes boletus mushrooms.
Cerfeuil chervil.
Cerises cherries.
Cervelle brains.
Champignons mushrooms.
Chantilly whipped cream, sugar.
Charcuterie cold cut meats, sausage, pâté, etc.
Charolais beef.
Chasseur sauce with white wine, mushrooms, shallots.
Châtaignes (marrons) chestnuts.
Chausson pastry turnover .
Chevreuil roe-deer.
Chou cabbage.
Choucroute sauerkraut.
Chou-fleur cauliflower.
Citron lemon.
Citron vert lime.
Civet rich stew.
Cochon pig.
Cochonnailles pork products.
Colin hake.
Compote stewed fruit.
Confit(e) preserved or candied.
Coques cockles.
Coquillages shellfish.
Coquilles St. Jacques scallops.
Crème anglaise custard.
Cresson watercress.
Crevettes grises shrimps.
Croque Monsieur toasted cheese and ham sandwich.
Crudités raw vegetables.
Crustacés shellfish.
Daube stew (simmered in sealed recipient).
Daurade sea-bream.
Dinde turkey.
Doux (douce) sweet.
Échalotes shallots.
Écrevisses freshwater crayfish.
Entrecôte rib steak.
Épaule shoulder.
Escalope thin slice.
Escargot snail.
Estragon tarragon.
Farci(e) stuffed.
Faux-filet sirloin steak.
Fenouil fennel.
Feuilleté flaky pastry.
Flageolets kidney beans.
Flambé flamed.
Foie liver.
Foie gras fatted goose or duck liver.
Forestières with mushrooms.
Fraise strawberry.
Framboise raspberry.
Frites potato chips French fries.
Fromage cheese.
Fruits de mer seafood.
Fumé smoked.
Galette pancake or cake.
Gambas very large prawns.
Gâteau cake.
Gibier game.
Gigot leg of lamb.
Girolles mushrooms
Glacé iced, glazed.
Glace ice cream.
Gratin Dauphinois potatoes baked with cream and cheese.
Grenouille (cuisse de) frog leg.
Grillé(e) grilled.
Grive thrush.
Hachis minced.
Hareng herring.
Haricot bean.
Hollandaise sauce with butter, egg yolk and lemon juice.
Homard lobster.
Huîtres oysters.
Jambon ham.
Julienne finely sliced vegetables.
Lamproie lamprey.
Langouste spiny lobster or crawfish.
Langoustines Dublin Bay prawns.
Lapin rabbit.
Lard bacon.
Légume vegetable.
Lièvre hare.
Limande lemon sole.
Lotte burbot.
Madère madeira wine.
Magret breast (of duck or goose).
Maïs sweetcorn.
Maître d'hôtel butter and parsley (with lemon if served as a sauce).
Maquereaux mackerel.
Marcassin young wild boar.
Marchand de vin sauce with red wine, shallots.
Médaillon round cut.
Merlan whiting.
Mesclun blend of green salad varieties.
Meunière (à la) sauce with butter, parsley, lemon.
Mode (à la) in the manner of.
Moelle bone marrow.
Morilles edible wild mushrooms.
Mornay cheese sauce.
Moules marinières mussels steamed in white wine with shallots.
Mulet grey mullet.
Mûre mulberry or blackberry.
Myrtilles bilberries/blueberries.
Nage (à la) served in poaching stock.
Navarin stew.
Navet turnip.
Noix nuts or topside leg.
Normande (à la) Normandy style: with mushrooms, eggs and cream, often flamed in Calvados.

Œufs fried eggs.
Œufs brouillés scrambled eggs.
Oie goose.
Onglet flank of beef.
Oseille sorrel.
Oursins sea-urchins.
Pain bread.
Palmier (cœurs de) palm hearts.
Palombe wood pigeon.
Palourdes clams.
Pamplemousse grapefruit.
Pané(e) breaded.
Parmentier with potatoes.
Pastèque watermelon.
Pâtes (fraîches) pasta (fresh).
Paupiettes fine slices of meat or fish wrapped around a minced filling.
Pavé thick slice.
Pêche peach.
Perdreau partridge.
Périgueux sauce with truffles and Madeira wine.
Petits pois green peas.
Pieds de porc pig's feet.
Pigeonneau baby pigeon.
Pintade guinea-fowl.
Piperade omelette or scrambled eggs with Basque-style filling.
Piquante (sauce) sharp-tasting sauce.
Pissenlits dandelion salad.
Poché(e) poached.
Poêlé fried.
Poireau leek.
Poisson fish.
Poitrine breast.
Poitrine fumée smoked bacon (generally served in cubes).
Poivre pepper.
Poivrons sweet peppers.
Pommes apples.
Pommes de terre potatoes.
Porto port wine.
Potage thick soup.
Pot-au-feu meat and vegetables served in their broth.
Poularde hen.
Poulet chicken.
Praires small clams.
Printanièr(e) (à la) served with diced vegetables.
Profiteroles custard-filled pastry puffs.
Provençale (à la) Provençal style with tomatoes, garlic, olive oil, etc..
Pruneaux prunes.
Prunes plums.
Purée mashed.
Quenelles light dumplings of fish, poultry etc.
Quetsches small, purple plums.
Raclette melted cheese speciality.
Ragoût stew.
Raie skate or ray.
Raifort horseradish.
Raisin grape.
Rascasse scorpion fish.
Ratatouille casserole of aubergine, onions, courgettes, garlic, peppers and tomatoes.
Reines-Claude greengages.
Rillettes potted meat.
Ris sweetbreads.
Riz rice.
Rognons kidneys.
Rouget red mullet.
Sablés shortbread.
Salade Niçoise Mediterranean produce (tomatoes, olives, anchovy, tuna, etc.) in salad, with olive oil based French dressing.
Sang blood.
Sanglier wild boar.
Saucisse fresh sausage.
Saucisson dried, salami-style sausage.
Saumon salmon.
Sel salt.
Selle saddle.
Selon grosseur (S.G.) according to size.
Sorbet Water ice.
Tartare (steak) raw minced beef.
Tarte Tatin apple tart baked. "upside down" (browned on top).
Terrine baked minced meat or fish, served like pâté.
Thé tea.
Thon tuna fish.
Tournedos filet steak.
Tourte covered tart.
Tourteaux large crabs.
Truite trout.
Vacherin ice cream with meringue and cream.
Vapeur (à la) steamed.
Veau veal.
Velouté ingredients creamed to make a smooth sauce or soup.
Viande meat.
Vinaigre vinegar.
Vinaigrette French dressing.
Volaille poultry.
Vol au vent puff pastry case.

Weights and measures

WEIGHTS AND MEASURES: EQUIVALENCES

Weight

100 grammes	= 3.527 oz
1 kilo	= 2.205 lb
10 kilos	= 0.882 quater
1 tonne	= 1.102 short ton

Surface

1 m^2	= 1.197 sq. yard
1 km^2	= 0.386 sq. mile
1 hectare (ha)	= 2.47 acres

Length

1 millimeter (mm)	= 0.039 inch
1 centimeter (cm)	= 0.033 foot
1 meter (m)	= 1.094 yard
1 kilometer (km)	= 0.621 mile

Volume

1 cm^3	= 0.064 cu. inch
1 dm^3 (1 liter)	= 0.036 cu. foot
1 m^3	= 1.309 cu. yard

Liquids

1 litre	= 8.454 gills	1 litre	= 1.057 quart
1 litre	= 2.113 pints	1 litre	= 0.264 gallon

Temperature

ºC	ºF	ºC	ºF	ºC	ºF	ºC	ºF
100 =	212	90 =	194	80 =	176	70 =	158
60 =	140	50 =	122	40 =	104	37 =	98.6
30 =	86	25 =	77	20 =	68	15 =	59
10 =	50	5 =	41	0 =	32	— 5 =	23
— 10 =	14	— 20 =	— 4	— 30 =	— 22	— 40 =	40

Men's clothing

Suits:	U.S.A.	36	38	40	42	44	46	48
	Eur.	46	48	50	52	54	56	58
Shirts:	U.S.A.	14	14.5	15	15.5	16	16.5	17
	Eur.	36	37	38	39	41	42	43
Shoes	U.S.A.	6.5	7	8	9	10	10.5	11
	Eur.	39	40	41	42	43	44	45

Ladies' clothing

Blouses and cardigans:							
U.S.A.	32	34	36	38	40	42	44
Eur.	40	42	44	46	48	50	52
Suits and dresses:							
U.S.A.	10	12	14	16	18	20	
Eur.	38	40	42	44	46	48	
Socks and stockings:							
U.S.A.	8	8.5	9	9.5	10	10.5	
Eur.	0	1	2	3	4	5	
Shoes: U.S.A.	5.5	6	7	7.5	8.5	9	
Eur.	36	37	38	39	40	41	

Paris

When you arrive in Paris, whether it be your first visit or your hundredth, there is always the same thrill of pleasure. The Seine; the lovely grey of Notre-Dame; the long walls of the Louvre; the sweep of the Tuileries, the Concorde and the Champs-Élysées; distant Montmartre; and the dizzying height of the Eiffel Tower. Then, in the evening, the lights and the surging crowds. You probably knew it was like this, even before you saw it: the Paris of the Impressionists — sung, painted and filmed exactly as it is.

But there is a hidden side to this wonderful city. The Parisians have a tendency to keep it to themselves — Paris belongs to them, after all. It's a living city, full of oddities, unexpected pleasures and (sometimes) disappointments; above all, a place with a deep sense of history, which rarely degenerates into nostalgia. This is the Paris we have sought to reveal in this guide.

The sheer amount of sights and experiences offered by this unique city is such that the first-time visitor may feel overwhelmed, and at a loss for a starting point. This is why we have included a number of articles dealing with practical subjects in this chapter, in addition to the regular practical information section at the end. Sites of interest are described in alphabetical order, but are also grouped by district, or *quartier,* in the chapter's opening pages. A full page is devoted to travel, with a list of bus routes that take the visitor through some of Paris' most interesting areas : a novel and authentically Parisian way to see the city. One-, three- and eight-day itineraries are also suggested : naturally these can be modified and adapted to the visitor's own tastes...

Sightseeing

ARC DE TRIOMPHE★★

A1 / Place Charles-de-Gaulle. 8th, 16th, 17th arr. Métro and RER : Étoile-Charles-de-Gaulle. Bus : 22, 30, 31, 43, 52, 73, 83, 92. Access to the monument via underground passage at top of Ave. des Champs-Élysées.

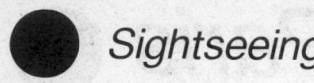

For over 150 years, the Arc de Triomphe in what is now the Place Charles-de-Gaulle has been a symbol of French patriotism; it also commemorates the heroes and the fallen of past wars. The colossal arch, built on the raised site of the former "Étoile de Chaillot" (Star of Chaillot) is the hub upon which twelve broad avenues converge like the spokes of a wheel. A project for a national monument was adopted during the Revolution, but construction did not start until 1806 when Napoléon approved Chalgrin's design for a triumphal arch "... except" (in his words), "for the embellishments, which are bad". The fall of the Empire put work on the Arc into abeyance for so long that it became a standing joke for Parisians. Finally, Louis-Philipppe inaugurated it, still unfinished, in 1836. The original plans called for the erection of a huge star or quadriga on the top of the building — an idea which has now been abandoned forever.

Don't miss

★★★ : *Champs-Élysées, Place de la Concorde, Jeu de Paume Museum, Invalides, Louvre Museum, Marais, Notre-Dame, Sainte-Chapelle, Eiffel Tower.*

★★ : *Arc de Triomphe, Beaubourg (Pompidou Centre), Musée d'Art Moderne de la Ville de Paris (Museum of Modern Art), Musée des Arts Décoratifs (Museum of Decorative Arts), Cluny Museum, Guimet Museum, Institut, Luxembourg, Montmartre, Army Museum, Carnavalet Museum, Rodin Museum, Opéra, Palais-Royal, Petit Palais, Place Vendôme, Place des Vosges, Saint-Germain-des-Prés, Île Saint-Louis, Basilica of Saint-Denis.*

★ : *Bois de Boulogne and the Bagatelle, Palais de Chaillot, La Défense, Faubourg Saint-Honoré, Les Halles, Palais de Justice (Law Courts), Panthéon, church of Saint-Eustache, church of Saint-Julien-le-Pauvre, church of Saint-Séverin, the Tuileries.*

▶ Nonetheless, the Arc de Triomphe, as it stands, is most impressive. Its massive proportions (50 m high by 40 m wide) combine with the vigour of its decorative reliefs to produce an effect of great power. The best-known of these reliefs is Rude's "La Marseillaise"★ (on the right, from the Champs-Élysées). An idea of the sheer scale of the building is given by the frieze of figures around its top, all of which are larger than life. The Arc may be unfinished, but it amply fulfills its role as a national symbol commemorating the glories of the Empire along with France's "Unknown Soldier", for whom a flame is kept constantly alight within the building by war veterans. Visitors, however, will probably prefer the view from the Arc's summit *(10-5)* to the wreaths, the flags and the ceremonies of Bastille Day (14th of July). **Panorama★** of the whole city, from the towers of La Défense to Montmartre and the Panthéon. □

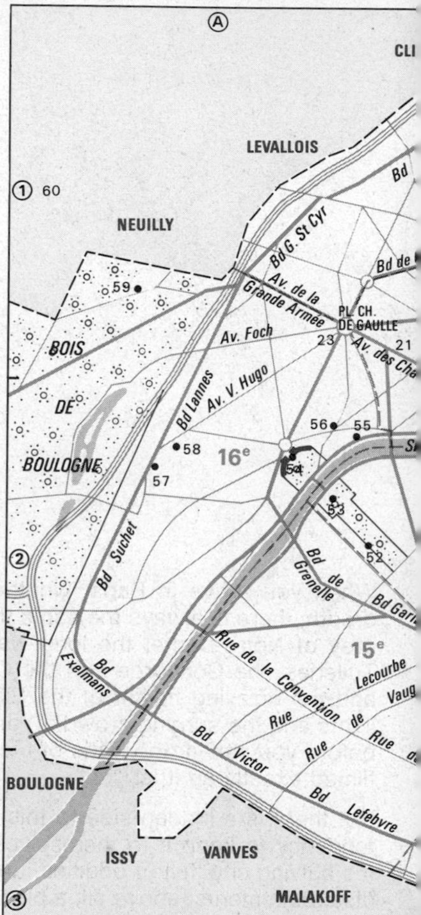

★★ 1 Arc de Triomphe - Place de l'Étoile A1
★★ 2 Museum of Modern Art A2
★★ 3 National Technical Museum B2
★★ 4 Museum of Popular Arts and Traditions A1
5 Buttes-Chaumont C1
★★ 6 Carnavalet Museum B2
7 Stock Exchange B2
8 Catacombs B3
★★ 9 Beaubourg B2
★ 10 Palais de Chaillot A2
11 Châtelet B2
★★ 12 Cluny Museum B2
13 Cognac-Jay Museum B1
★ 14 La Défense A1
★★ 15 Guimet Museum A2
★ 16 Les Halles B2
17 Hôtel de Ville B2
★★ 18 Île Saint-Louis B2
★★ 19 Institut B2

■ Musée d'**ART MODERNE DE LA VILLE DE PARIS**
(Museum of Modern Art)★★
Palais de Tokyo

A2 / 11, Avenue du Président-Wilson, 16th arr. Métro : Iéna, Alma-Marceau. RER : Pont de l'Alma. Bus : 32, 42, 63, 72, 80, 82, 92.

This museum has been completely refurbished since the National Museum's collections were moved to the Pompidou Centre, better adapted for exhibitions of contemporary art. The Museum of Modern Art now displays important cubist, fauvist and Paris school paintings, in the former Palais de Tokyo of the 1937 Universal Exhibition. Furthermore, the Centre National de la Photographie organizes many shows here.

▶ Matisse's famous triptych, "La Danse"★ is

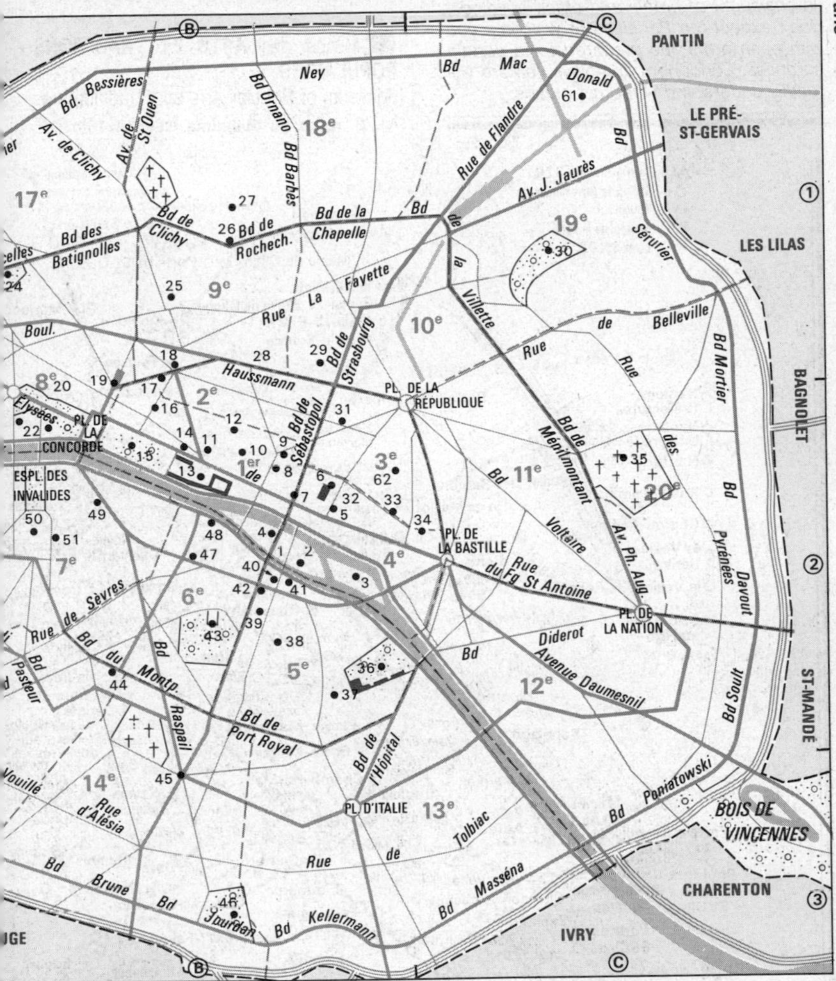

★★★ 20 Invalides B2
★★★ 21 The Louvre B2
★★ 22 Luxembourg (Palace and Gardens) B2
23 Madeleine B1
★ 24 Monceau Park B1
★★ 25 Montmartre B1
26 Montparnasse B2
27 Montsouris Park B3
★★★ 28 Notre-Dame B2
★★ 29 Opéra B1
★★ 30 Palais Royal B2
★★★ 31 Sainte-Chapelle B2
★ 32 Panthéon B2
★★ 33 Père Lachaise C1
★ 34 Petit and Grand Palais B2
35 Pigalle B1
★ 36 Jardin des Plantes B2
37 Latin Quarter B2
★★ 38 St Germain-des-Prés B2
★ 39 St Séverin B2
★★★ 40 Eiffel Tower B1
★★ 41 Tuileries B2
★★ 42 Place Vendôme B2
★ 43 Place des Victoires B2
★★ 44 Place des Vosges B2
★ 45 Champ de Mars A2
★★★ 46 Champs Élysées A1
★ 47 Faubourg St Germain B2
★ 48 Faubourg St Honoré B1
49 Grands Boulevards B1
★★★ 50 Marais B2
51 La Muette A1
52 Passy A1
★ 53 Île de la Cité B2
54 Advertising Museum B1
55 Parc de la Villette
56 Picasso Museum B2

Parisians

Parisians are no more hostile to visitors than other people. But sometimes they feel a trifle overwhelmed... their impression of not quite being at home in their own city is made more acute by a nagging fear that Paris is turning into a huge museum, with its last inhabitants slowly retreating before an onslaught of hotels and office buildings. Don't expect the Parisians to welcome you with open arms; be prepared for a certain hardness. Londoners and New Yorkers will readily understand what this means...

here, alongside Dufy's gigantic "Fée Electricité"★, one of the largest murals ever painted. ▶ There is still a whiff of scandal and provocation about the Museum of Modern Art : the ARC section (Animation-Research-Confrontation) organises demonstrations of contemporary art which are receptive to all the trends of the avant-garde. The plastic arts rub shoulders here with jazz and poetry; the result is sometimes "over-contemporary" — but always exciting *(10-5:30 or 8 Wed.; closed Mon.).* □

■ Musée des **ARTS ET TRADITIONS POPULAIRES**

(Museum of Popular Arts and Tradition)★★

A1, 6, route du Mahatma Gandhi, 16th arr.

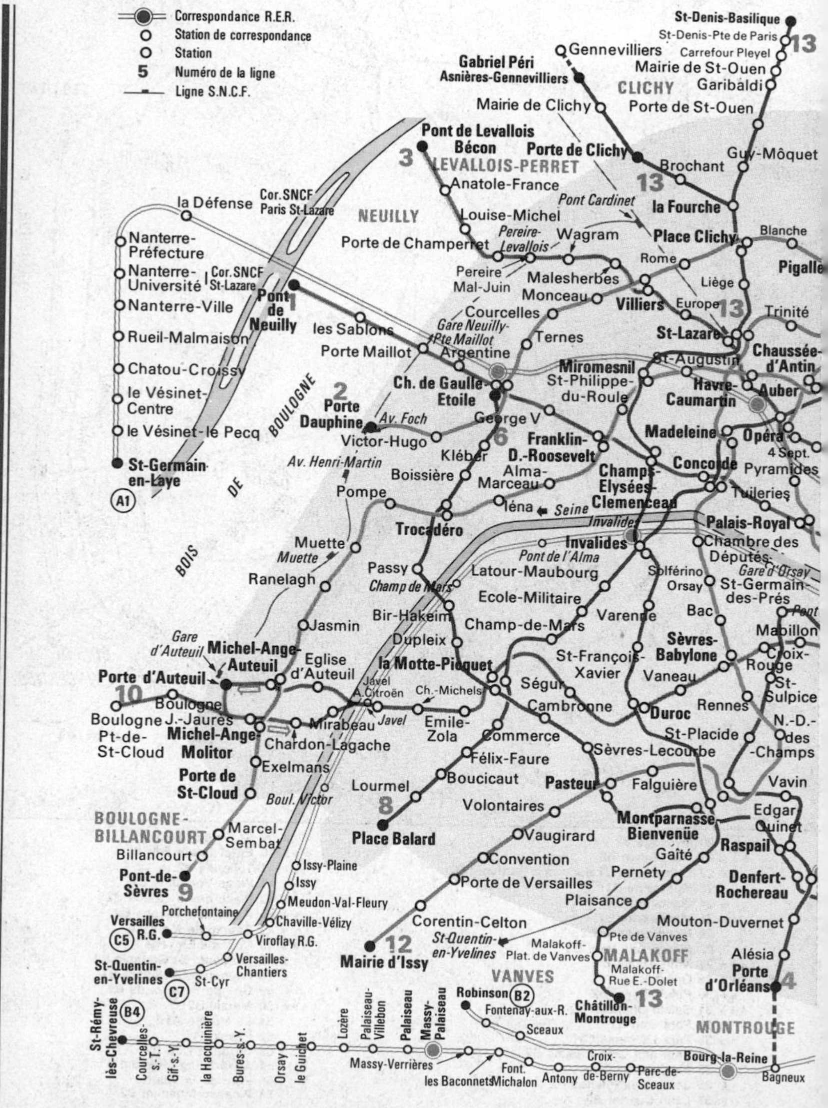

(Bois de Boulogne).
Métro : Porte Maillot, Sablons. Bus : 73, 33 Sat. and Sun.)

The aim of this highly individual museum is to breathe new life into the traditions of rural France, to display the wealth and variety of the nation's crafts, and to demonstrate the beauty and value of the tools and skills of an earlier time. The collection touches on every aspect of rural life; the games, entertainments and dances of provincial France all have their place here, along with traditional tools, utensils, crockery, pottery and a wide range of farm implements.

▶ Audio-visual montages have been assembled to deal with specific aspects of pre-industrial France, which, in this somewhat old and unfrequented museum, seems so far away. Recently an interesting attempt has been made to

Reservations

A general rule : if you want to be properly served at a good table, always reserve at restaurants. Renowned establishments are often booked up a week in advance — so make your arrangements ahead of time. The real cream (or the most fashionable) may even take three weeks to find you a table.

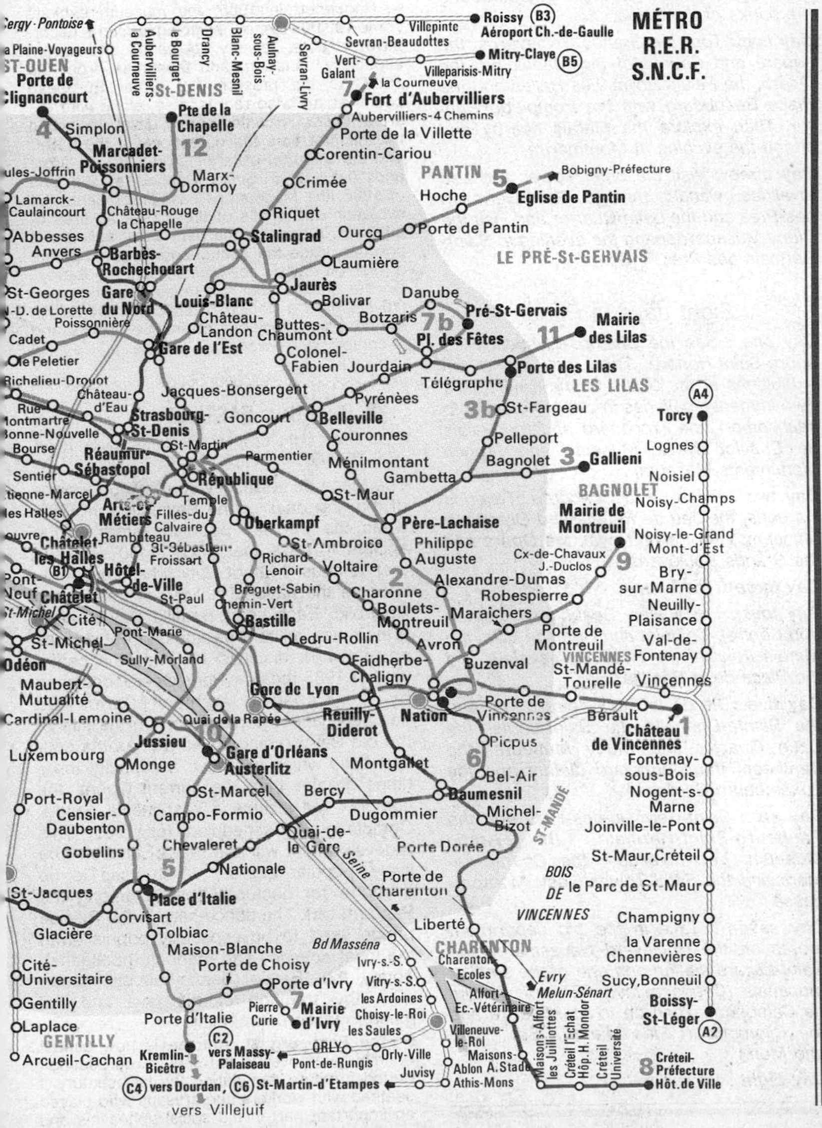

One day in Paris

In the morning : *visit the Île de la Cité, Notre-Dame and the Sainte-Chapelle, then on to the Louvre and the Tuileries. In the afternoon : tour the Champs-Élysées and the Arc de Triomphe, the Eiffel Tower and the Latin Quarter. Follow this with an evening stroll along the banks of the Seine or round Montmartre.*

Three days in Paris

Day one : *Visit the Champs-Élysées, Faubourg-Saint-Honoré, Place de la Concorde, the Louvre Museum, Notre-Dame and the Sainte-Chapelle. In the evening, walk along the banks of the Seine.*

Day two : *Tour the Grands Boulevards, the square and Church of the Madeleine, the Opéra, the Palais Royal, Les Halles and the Place Beaubourg with the Pompidou Centre. Then explore the Marais nearby and spend the evening at Montmartre.*

Day three : *Visit the Eiffel Tower and Les Invalides, wander through Saint-Germain-des-Prés and the Latin Quarter and visit the Cluny Museum; spend the evening in Saint-Germain-des-Prés.*

Eight days in Paris

Day one : *See the Champs-Élysées, Faubourg-Saint-Honoré. Then look round the exhibitions at the Grand or the Petit Palais (two immense galleries in close proximity to each other), the Trocadéro and the Palais de Chaillot (Naval Museum and French Monuments Museum).*

Day two : *Place de la Concorde, Tuileries Gardens, the Jeu de Paume and Orangerie Museums, the Palais Royal, the Opéra and the Grands Boulevards.*

Day three : *The Louvre.*

Day four : *Les Halles, Beaubourg (Pompidou Centre), Châtelet and Hôtel de Ville, the Marais (tour of the Hôtel Carnavalet), and the Place de la Bastille.*

Day five : *Île de la Cité, Notre-Dame and the Sainte-Chapelle, Île Saint-Louis, the Latin Quarter and Cluny Museum, the Panthéon, the Mouffetard district and the Luxembourg Gardens.*

Day six : *Saint-Germain-des-Prés and the Faubourg-Saint-Germain, the Rodin Museum, Les Invalides, the Champ-de-Mars and the Eiffel Tower. Last: Montparnasse.*

Day seven : *Take in the big department stores on the Boulevard Haussmann, the Saint-Lazare station and one of the smaller museums (Cognacq-Jay, d'Ennery, Nissim de Camondo). Then on to Montmartre and the Clignancourt Flea Market. (Sat., Sun. and Mon.)*

Day Eight : *Versailles.*

protect the oral heritage of the French countryside; fairy tales, legends, proverbs and songs are now being systematically collected and recorded *(10-5:15; closed Tue.).* □

■ Musée des **ARTS DÉCORATIFS** (Museum of Decorative Arts)★

Musée national des arts de la **Mode** (Museum of the Arts of Fashion)★
B2 / 107-109, rue de Rivoli, 1st arr. Métro : Palais-Royal, Tuileries. Bus : 21, 27, 39, 48, 68, 69, 72, 85.

The Museum of Decorative Arts was opened in 1905 in the Marsan Pavilion, rebuilt after the fire that destroyed the Tuileries Palace in 1871.

▶ Reopened in 1985, the museum exhibits some 100,000 pieces, including furniture, decorative objects, jewelry, *boiseries* (woodwork especially panelling) and tapestries, from the 15thC to the present day. Other European countries are also represented, along with the art of Islam. A contemporary gallery reuniting for the first time the collections of the 20thC and the Dubuffet gallery *(12:30-6:30; ex. Mon. and Tue.; 11-5 Sun.).* Opened at the end of 1985, the Museum of Fashion presents the evolution of the arts of dress over an area of 2000 m². Alongside the permanent collections one can trace the contemporary development of fashion day by day *(same hours as above).* On the ground floor the museum's bookshop *(10-7)* offers a choice of specialist works; in the boutique reeditions of antique objects and of contemporary works are on sale. □

■ Place de la **BASTILLE**

C2 / 4th, 11th, 12th arr. Métro : Bastille. Bus : 29, 65, 69, 76, 86, 87, 91.

The Place de la Bastille conjures up visions of the first days of the Revolution in 1789, when the Parisian populace stormed the ancient fortress that once stood here, on that famous 14th of July which has now become the national holiday of the French Republic. Each year, Bastille Day is celebrated with military parades, street dances and firework displays. ▶ Since the beginning of 1985 the new Paris Opéra, designed by the Canadian architect Carlos Ott has been under construction on the site of the old Bastille station. As well as the concert halls which will have a capacity three times greater than the current Opéra, the complex will include a vast media centre. Completion is scheduled for 1985. This redevelopment will add new distinction to a lively, popular *quartier* which used to be a centre for nocturnal revelry among the Paris riff-raff. The dance-halls in the Rue de Lappe used to be especially popular with the local *apaches* and *marlous* (hooligans). Today the "Balajo" dance-hall still keeps alive the tradition of the *java* and *bal musette* (accordeon balls).

▶ The **Faubourg St. Antoine** is now almost entirely given over to the sale of reproduction period furniture, but during the last century it seethed with workers and artisans who played an important part in the social upheavals and riots of 1830 and 1848. ▶ Looking at the slender **Colonne de Juillet** (July Column)★ crowned with its Spirit of Liberty, it requires a considerable effort of the imagination to visualise the massive eight-towered fortress demolished by the Revolution. The decision to eradicate the Bastille was actually made in 1784; the ancient prison, far from being a den of repression, was actually used as a depository for debauched young nobles, lunatics and inveterate pamphleteers like de Sade and Voltaire. Nonetheless, the crowd which stormed the Bastille on the 14th of July, 1789 made it into a revolutionary symbol; each year since, the celebration has taken on the carefree aspect of a huge party. On Bastille Day, the people of Paris still come out to dance in honour of one of the great legends of history. □

■ BOIS DE BOULOGNE★

A2 / 16th arr. between Neuilly and Boulogne. Métro : Porte-Maillot, Porte-Dauphine, Porte d'Auteuil, Sablons. Bus : 52, PC, 32, 63; 33 Sat. and Sun.; 244.

Who could ever describe the many faces of the Bois de Boulogne? At weekends, its two thousand-odd acres of woodland, grass sward and gardens are invaded by countless families : this is the "green lung" of western Paris. In the morning, people "come up" to the Bois from the Ranelagh and Passy areas, just as they did in the 19th century. To these are added the children from the smart areas of the 16th arr. and Neuilly, along with assorted nurses, joggers, and other lovers of green grass. And later on, in the evenings, the deeper undergrowth of the Bois is the scene of less innocent cavortings, despite the careful watch kept by the police. The former tradition of duelling is now gone forever, like the royal stag hunts which used to be held within an area blocked off by an immense wall extending between Neuilly and Auteuil.

▶ The Bois was ruthlessly cut down during the Revolution and again by the occupying British Army in 1815. Subsequently, it was rearranged according to Second Empire tastes as a park enlivened by lakes, **racecourses** (Auteuil and Longchamp) and a miniature railway track. On fine days, you can go boating on the lakes, which were designed by the engineer Alphand as part of a complicated network of watercourses fed by an artesian well. ▶ The miniature railway still carries children around the **Jardin d'Acclimatation** (Sablons crossroads; *9-dusk*), so called because various exotic creatures are acclimatised here to Paris temperatures : but children seem to prefer the goats, chickens and sheep of the "Farm" to the resident monkeys and parrots. The Jardin also has an extremely well-equipped and varied children's fun fair. ▶ "Papa Meilland", "Princess Ann" and "Sissi" are the stars of the **Bagatelle Park**★★ (Porte-de-Madrid crossroads); all three are species of rose. The rose gardens here are the most popular part of this much-loved park, landscaped around a splendid folly. The latter was built by the Count of Artois, who had a bet with the Queen of France that he could finish the job inside two months. The Count requisitioned all the stone and plaster available in Paris and had 900 labourers working round the clock; the Queen lost her wager. ▶ In the humid **Municipal Greenhouses** *(Serres du Fleuriste Municipal)* it's hard to believe that you are only a few metres above the roaring *Boulevard Périphérique* (ring road) and alongside the gigantic **Parc des Princes,** Paris' huge covered sports stadium which seats 50 000. The stadium was completed in 1974 : most weekends there is a top-class rugby or soccer match held here. ▶ The Bois has other sporting facilities (tennis courts at Roland-Garros, clay-pigeon shooting) along with a large number of restaurants. □

■ BUTTES-CHAUMONT

C1 / 19th arr. Métro : Buttes-Chaumont, Botzaris. Bus : 26.

With its sixty acres of rolling parkland, green enough to make a mockery of its name (*monts chauves* — literally, bald hills), the Buttes-Chaumont is perhaps Paris' most picturesque park. The place has a curious history : during the Middle Ages, it was the site of the dreaded Montfaucon gibbet, where public executions were held. Later, its plaster quarries became a refuge for thieves and brigands, and the scene of a battle fought in 1814 against the cossacks of the invading Russian Army. During the last days of the Communard uprising of 1871, the Buttes-Chaumont witnessed tragic fighting, but was subsequently transformed by the great urban planner Haussmann into a kind of fantasy garden. Haussmann made full use of the broken terrain, creating a lake with an island in the middle, crowned with a temple, along with waterfalls, caves and scree. The park also offers glorious views of Montmartre and the north of Paris.

▶ The Buttes-Chaumont Park straddles the twin quartiers of **Belleville** and **Ménilmontant,** which at one time were typically Parisian. After the war, they were taken over by a large North African population which was in turn forced out in recent years by massive construction projects. Édith Piaf and Maurice Chevalier would never recogise their beloved "Ménilmuche" these days. □

■ CARNAVALET Museum★★

B2 / 23, rue de Sévigné, 3rd arr. Métro : Saint-Paul, Chemin-Vert. Bus : 29, 69, 76, 96.

Four centuries of Paris life (1500-1900) are vividly displayed in this splendid Renaissance mansion, redesigned by Mansart in the 17thC and now a fit setting for the collections of the **Historical Museum of the City of Paris.** With originality, humour and relish, the Musée Carnavalet succeeds in making room for the ordinary daily life of the good citizens of Paris, alongside the great events that have marked the history of the capital. As an introduction to the history of Paris, this museum and its new annex in the **Hôtel Le Peletier de Saint-Fargeau** have no equal.

▶ Once the residence of Madame de Sévigné, the Carnavalet Museum has been conceived as a showpiece *(10-5:40; closed Mon.)*. Fine furniture (Regency, Louis XV and Louis XVI, *boise-*

Travelling in and around Paris

Paris street directions (whether given in this guide, or in advertisements, or by phone) usually include the arrondissement *(district) number and the name of the nearest Métro station. The twenty arrondissements of Paris are in the form of a clockwise spiral around the Hôtel de Ville. There are very few places in Paris which are further than four hundred metres from a Métro station. Métro stations can be located by their sign: a large capital M. At every entrance there is a large wallmap showing the entire underground network.*

Numbers of buildings are higher in proportion to their distance from the Hôtel de Ville and the Seine.

The Métro

Sixteen lines serve 273 stations on a network of nearly 200 kilometres. A line is indicated by its two terminals (e. g. Neuilly-Vincennes). Any given Métro platform is served by a single line, always passing in the same direction. This direction is shown by signs placed above the line, and the name of each station is marked clearly all along the platform.

A single ticket is valid for a journey anywhere on the inner Paris network, no matter how long it may be or how many line changes it may involve.

The Métro is open from 5 in the morning till 12:30 at night.

The bus

Bus lines are identifiable by their numbers. Up to 100, these lines serve central Paris; numbers over 100 operate in the suburbs. Detailed bus maps are obtainable in Métro stations and in the buses themselves.

All bus stops are by request. If you want to get on a bus, signal the fact to the driver. To get off, press the button marked arrêt demandé *(stop request) by the exit door.*

Buses differ from the Métro in that one or two tickets may be necessary, according to the length of the journey you envisage; the number of tickets is clearly indicated at bus-stops and in the bus itself. Buses operate between 7 am and approximately 8:30 pm. Certain lines continue into the night (12:30), and operate on Sundays and holidays.

The RATP (Paris Transport System) provides users with tickets enabling them to travel freely on all buses and Métro lines for periods of two, four and seven days at a time. This Paris Sesame *ticket has to be put through the slot in the Métro and RER (Express Regional Network) entry gates, but need only be shown to the driver as you enter the bus. Buy at any Métro station.*

... and a piece of advice. The best way to see Paris (and get off the beaten track) is by bus. Too many visitors never get out of the eight or nine central arrondissements, where they can go everywhere on foot, until they have to leave for the airport. They miss a multitude of other Parises, in which 75 % of Parisians live; these are the areas on the periphery of town, and they vary widely between popular and residential, hubbub and tranquility... Here are some bus lines which will take you over the frontiers into a different kind of Paris :

24 Saint-Lazare-Alfort (along the Seine).
29 Saint-Lazare-Porte de Montempoivre (Grands Boulevards).
30 Gare de l'Est-Trocadéro.
38 Gare de l'Est-Porte d'Orléans.
42 Gare du Nord-Balard (Concorde-Champ de Mars).
52 Opéra-Pont de Saint-Cloud (Faubourg Saint-Honoré-16th arrondissement).
58 Hôtel de Ville-Vanves (across the Latin Quarter).
60 Gambetta-Porte Montmartre (a little-known side of Paris in which the 19th and 20th centuries live side by side).
63 Gare de Lyon-La Muette (Left Bank).
69 Gambetta-Champ de Mars (Père-Lachaise, Bastille, Rue de Rivoli).
72 Hôtel de Ville-Porte de Saint-Cloud (Right Bank).
73 Gare d'Orsay-La Défense (Champs-Élysées, Neuilly).
82 Luxembourg-Neuilly (Montparnasse, Champ de Mars, Trocadéro).
87 Champ de Mars-Reuilly (Saint-Germain and the Left Bank).

The Carte orange *(orange card) is available to anyone, provided they produce an identity photo (passport size). This gives access to the bus and Métro network for one month (1st to 30th) and can save you a good deal of money if you plan to travel a lot within Paris. The* coupon jaune *(yellow coupon) gives the same unlimited transportation for one week (Mon.-Sun.). Buy them at any Métro station or* tabac.

Taxis

There are more than 15 000 taxis in Paris. Their prices include a basic charge (increased when the pick-up is made at a railway station or airport), a fare based on the length of the journey and marked on the taxi-meter beside the driver, and a small extra charge for bulky packages or cases. A special night fare goes into force between 10 pm and 6:30 am.

A suggestion : on your first night in town, take a taxi down the Right Bank of the Seine (Rive Droite) *from the Maison de la Radio to Bercy. An unforgettable first introduction to Paris!*

ries, gilt cabinet★★ painted by Le Brun), also period paintings, street scenes, shop signs, maps, and even an accurately-reconstructed café. □

The CATACOMBS

B3 / place Denfert-Rochereau, 14th arr. Métro and RER : Denfert-Rochereau. Bus : 38, 68.

An underground cemetery, which extends underneath an entire quarter of Paris, with tunnels running parallel to the streets on the surface : a veritable City of Death, the Catacombs can be entered through the E pavilion on the Place Denfert-Rochereau, a vestige of the old Barrière d'Enfer (Hell's Gate) in the city walls erected in 1784. They are really gigantic stone quarries used from 1785 as a dump for corpses from the cemetery of Les Innocents, near Les Halles, which had become so crowded that it was a permanent danger to public health.

▶ The mortal remains of some thirty generations of Parisians were deposited in the Catacombs ; some of the bones and skulls were laid out in geometrical patterns by anonymous agents with a taste for the maçabre. The visit is somewhat disturbing *(2-4, closed Mon. ; 9-11 & 2-4 Sat.)* though the future Charles X was evidently impervious to its horror when in 1787 he invited the ladies of the Court to dinner here. □

Palais de CHAILLOT★

A2 / 16th arr. Métro : Trocadéro. Bus : 22, 30, 32, 63, 74, 82.

Chaillot represents a vantage point over Paris, as well as a cluster of museums. The terraces of the Place du Trocadéro offer one of the loveliest views of the Left Bank; directly in front, the Eiffel Tower bestrides the Champ de Mars gardens, while in the background the École Militaire (Military Academy) carries the eye beyond to the distant skyscraper of Montparnasse. To the right, the modern tower blocks of the Front de Seine are grouped. It's a splendid sight and if you go to Chaillot in the summer, you won't be alone admiring it. Seen from the waterside, however, the steep bank of Chaillot has a strangely theatrical air, almost grandiose. The site caught the fancy of Napoléon III, who levelled its summit. The organisers of the Great Exhibition of 1878 were inspired to build a Moorish Palace here; their successors of 1937 constructed the present enormous building, the Palais de Chaillot, with two wings 200 m long, curving outward toward the Seine.

▶ The **Palais de Chaillot** is a prime example of the sober, somewhat cold architectural outlook of the 1930's. It now houses a huge **theatre,** made famous by Jean Vilar and the Théâtre National de Paris; a **Cinémathèque** (film library and archives), created by Henri Langlois (entrance Ave. A.-de-Mun); the **Naval Museum★★** (history of navigation : nautical instruments, *10-6; closed Tue. and holidays*); the **Musée de l'Homme★★** (Museum of Anthropology — human evolution and man's origins, *9:45-5:15; closed Tue.*); and the **Museum of French Monuments★★** (anthology of French sculpture, *9:45-12:30 & 2-5; closed Tue.*). All entrances are marked on the Place du Trocadéro. ▶ Below the Palais, in a cave built under the sloping gardens, is the **Aquarium★**; fresh water fish in somewhat hallucinatory surroundings *(10-6 daily)*. □

CHAMP-DE-MARS★

A2 / 7th arr. Métro : Ecole-Militaire, Bir-Hakeim ; RER : Champ-de-Mars. Bus : 28, 42, 49, 69, 80, 82, 87, 92.

The Champ-de-Mars used to be a training ground for military manœuvres, where the soldiers from the **École Militaire** (Military Academy; architect : Gabriel : completed 1773) were put through their paces before the king. Here the young Napoléon Bonaparte studied the art of war. The Revolution evicted the army and used the Champ-de-Mars for its own ceremonial purposes, such as the Fête de la Fédération on 14 July 1790, at which the king and no less than 300 000 people from all over France swore fidelity to the nation before General Lafayette. Parades, festivals and horse-races took place here before the great universal exhibitions of 1867 and 1889. The Eiffel Tower, which provoked the furious indignation of the local inhabitants while it was under construction, has since been a magnet for tourists — but the latter scarcely notice the gardens and the beautiful park with its shrubs, flowerbeds, puppet show, donkey-rides and children's playground. In fact, the Champ-de-Mars quietly retains something of the elegance bestowed upon it by the fine town houses nearby, in which the likes of Sacha Guitry and Paul Morand resided. □

CHAMPS-ÉLYSÉES★★★

A1 / 8th arr. Métro : Étoile, George-V, Champs-Élysées-Clemenceau, Concorde. RER : Étoile. Bus : 28, 30, 31, 32, 42, 49, 52, 73, 80, 83, 92.

Le Nôtre, who created the gardens at Versailles, was also responsible, in 1670, for laying out the wide avenue which prolongs the perspective from the Tuileries and the old Cours la Reine (Queen's Courtyard). Later, during the Second Empire, the Avenue des Champs-Élysées became the most fashionable haunt for high society. From the gardens with their resplendent flowerbeds, up to its splendid climax at the Arc de Triomphe, the Champs-Élysées is a micro-

Prices

French law obliges restaurants to show their prices on menus; hotels must display tarifs at their main entrances. So you won't have any nasty surprises where they are concerned. But beware of bars, discothèques and music halls : their prices bubble up like their champagne. And think twice before you sit down on a café terrace on any one of the main thoroughfares (Champs-Élysées, Grand Boulevards, Montparnasse or Saint-Germain) : the passing show is included in the price of your drink...

cosm of Paris. Luxury shopping arcades, overflowing café terraces, cinemas, shop windows full of *articles de Paris,* and drugstores keep the avenue in constant motion; while a few steps away are the world of high fashion (Ave. Montaigne, Rue François Premier), the shops of the Faubourg Saint-Honoré, and the private clubs of the Rue de Ponthieu.

▶ Before Le Nôtre planted his avenue of elms, there was nothing here but scrubland and marshes. Once lengthened and widened, the old Grand Cours became a meeting place for revolutionaries and ruffians, before developing into a site for theatres, puppet shows and gaming houses. In 1800, there were only six buildings on the Avenue; nor did it acquire its present aspect till a hundred years later. Office blocks, stores and cafés stretch from the Rond Point to the Étoile, whilst among the trees between the Rond Point and the Tuileries stand a number of theatres and restaurants. ▶ There are few monuments of note in this area, apart perhaps from the gaudy mansion of La Païva★ at No. 25, where the well known courtesan used to give her famous parties... and the "Lido", a monument of Paris nightlife which has serenely weathered both the vicissitudes of history and the challenge of the daring and modern "Crazy Horse" nearby. The present world-wide fame of the Champ-Élysées is largely due to the superb setting it provides as the centre of Paris-by-night. □

■ CHÂTELET

B2 / 1st arr. Métro and RER : Châtelet. Bus : 21, 24, 27, 38, 47, 58, 67, 69, 70, 72, 74, 75, 76, 81, 85, 96.

Around a 19thC fountain, the **Place du Châtelet** marks the convergence of the main north-south and east-west traffic through the capital, both on the surface and underground (two RER lines cross here).

▶ On the Square, the **Théâtre de la Ville** (Municipal Theatre) has been successfully modernised — though it retains the dressing room of the great tragic actress Sarah Bernhardt in its original condition, as a kind of intimate museum. The theatre itself was constructed by Davioud in 1862, like the **Théâtre Musical de Paris** (TMP) opposite. The latter used to be known as the Châtelet Theatre, and was renowned for its operetta productions; now ballet and opera have returned here. ▶ Close by is the **St. Jacques Tower★,** beloved of the Surrealists, which adds a touch of the unusual to this quartier as it submits to the daily nightmarish traffic jams. It was completed in 1522 as the bell-tower of the old church of St. Jacques-de-la-Boucherie, headquarters of a once-powerful corporation of butchers. The Revolution would have swept away the entire structure, had it not been for a gunsmith who used it as a shot-tower for making musket balls. □

■ Île de la CITÉ★

B2 / 1st and 4th arr. Métro : Cité. Bus : 21, 24, 27, 38, 47, 58, 70, 85, 96.

The Île de la Cité, often compared to a boat's hull carried by the Seine, is the original core from which Paris developed. Its inhabitants have to some extent departed; the great mass of the Palais de Justice now overshadows the island's few remaining Louis XIII houses, and its mediaeval buildings were long ago torn down by Haussmann. Nonetheless, the Île de la Cité remains the living heart of Paris. Here, 20 centuries ago, one of Julius Caesar's lieutenants first set up his headquarters close to a village inhabited by the Parisii...

▶ The **Pont Neuf★** spans the Seine and takes in the western (downstream) end of the Île de la Cité. This bridge is ill-named, because, far from being "Neuf" (new), it is the oldest bridge Paris can boast. It is also the best-loved, most painted, and most praised by poets. ▶ The statue of Henri IV, who inaugurated the Pont Neuf in 1607, dominates what is today the **Square du Vert-Galant,** a delightfully cool little garden on the tip of the island, much frequented on hot summer nights. ▶ The quiet **Place Dauphine★,** between two elegant Louis XIII buildings in brick and stone, was created in honour of the Dauphin. ▶ Enlarged under the Second Empire and at the turn of the century, the **Palais de Justice** (Law Courts)★ retains a considerable proportion of the original Gothic palace inhabited by the first twelve Capetian kings of France. Steer clear of the somewhat forbidding walls of the Quai des Orfèvres : more interesting is the **Quai de l'Horloge★,** to the north of the Palais. On this side, the façade is flanked by three round towers; on the left, the entrance to the **Conciergerie★★,** an imposing edifice which owes much of its mediaeval haughtiness to 19th century restoration *(10-5 daily).* Visit here the Prisoner's Gallery (cells occupied by Marie-Antoinette and Robespierre) and a small museum of the Revolution which occupies the chapel. The most remarkable aspect of this gaol-cum-palace, so laden with tragic memories, is the huge **Salle des Gens d'Armes★★,** with its four aisles (1315). ▶ At the corner of the Quai de l'Horloge and the Boulevard du Palais stands the massive square tower known as the "Tour de l'Horloge" (Clocktower). This has kept time for the people of Paris since 1334. ▶ From the boulevard, view the monumental Louis XVI façade which glowers over the Cour du Mai — this is the main public entrance to the Law Courts of the Palais de Justice. Constant comings and goings of lawyers, magistrates, and people with nothing better to do; tag along, and you will find yourself in the immense **Salle des Pas-Perdus,** the centre of the City's judicial life. Some of the courtrooms have retained fine elements of their original décor, notably the **Chambre Dorée** (Gilded Chamber) where Marie-Antoinette was condemned to death. Original *boiseries.* ▶ By now, you will probably be surfeited with gold leaf, stucco and pompous allegories — so take the passage to the left of the Cour du Mai to the breathtakingly lovely **Sainte-Chapelle★★★.** This is a masterpiece of Gothic art, built by Saint-Louis between 1246 and 1248 to house the relic of Christ's Crown of Thorns. Here the two superimposed naves give an impression of airy lightness, almost of fragility. The higher of the two seems to be a reliquary in itself, a jewel-box suffused with filtered light from the 13th and 14thC stained glass windows *(10-5).* ▶ At the exit of the Palais de Justice, the Rue de Lutèce leads through to the **Flower Market★,** one of the most picturesque spots in Paris, with its charm heightened by the gloomy surroundings : on one side, the Commercial Tri-

Paris, city of light

Every evening, the principal monuments of Paris are illuminated until one o'clock in the morning : the Invalides, École Militaire, Eiffel Tower, Palais de Chaillot and its fountains, Arc de Triomphe, Concorde, Louvre, Institut, Monnaie, Conciergerie, Notre-Dame, Hôtel-de-Ville, and certain great houses in the Marais.

bunal; on the other, the Hôtel Dieu (hospital); behind, the Préfecture de Police. ▶ From here, go back to the Place du Parvis-Notre-Dame and go down into the bizarre **Crypte Archéologique**★ *(10-12, 2-6 daily)*; exhibition of steles, reliefs, fragments of statues and inscritions which bring to life the Paris-that-existed-before-Paris, when the Île de la Cité was merely the site of a small village. ▶ At the upstream end of the island, see the moving **Mémorial de la Déportation**★★ (1962), commemorating those who were taken away to labour and concentration camps during World War II *(10-12 & 2-5 daily).* □

■ CLUNY Museum★★

B2 / 6, Place Paul-Painlevé, 5th arr. Métro : Saint-Michel, Odéon, Maubert-Mutualité. RER : Saint-Michel. Bus : 21, 24, 27, 38, 63, 85, 86, 87, 96.

On the ruined thermal baths of Lutetia, built by the Seine boatmen's corporation in the 2nd and 3rd centuries, the 14th century Abbots of Cluny raised a luxury Paris residence for their own use. On the initiative of A. de Sommerard, a prominent collector and antiquarian, the present building (15thC Flamboyant Gothic) was converted into a museum in 1844.

▶ In the Museum's pleasant and well-lit rooms *(9:45-12:30, 2-5:15; closed Tue.)* there is a fine exhibition of mediaeval ivories, reliquaries, altar-pieces, toys and miscellaneous objects in gold. ▶ **Tapestries** are among the Cluny Museum's most important exhibits, especially the famous "Dame à la Licorne"★★ (15thC); note also "La Vie Seigneuriale"★★ (16thC) and "L'Offrande du Cœur" (early 15thC). In addition, numerous 14th and 15thC statues. ▶ The large **Roman Pump Room** (Salle des Thermes Romains) is the only Roman construction in France which still retains its original arches. Display of archaeological remains, including part of the "Pilier des Nautes", the most ancient sculpture in Paris; the 21 heads of the kings of Judah★; and fragments of the statue columns of Notre-Dame which were dumped and lost during the Revolution, then dug up by workmen in the Rue de la Chaussée d'Antin in 1977. □

■ COGNACQ-JAY Museum

B1 / 25, Blvd. des Capucines, 2nd arr. Métro : Madeleine, Opéra. Bus : 20, 21, 27, 29, 42, 52, 53, 66, 68, 95.

Ernest Cognacq, founder of the La Samaritaine group of stores, created this museum of 18th century France in collaboration with his wife, Louise Jay. It was opened in 1929, foreshadowing the appearance of thoroughgoing American-style foundations endowed by private collectors. The Cognacq-Jay museum contains *boiseries*, precious objects, furniture, porcelain and miniatures, harmonising perfectly with paintings (Boucher, Chardin, Fragonard) and drawings (Watteau). Nothing is overdone or dull on any of the three floors; the impression is of constant decorative perfection and refinement, the hallmark of the great century of French taste *(10-5:40; closed Mon.).* □

Paris

Places of interest grouped according to quartier :

Île de la Cité (Conciergerie, Sainte-Chapelle, Notre-Dame Cathedral), Île Saint-Louis.

Champs-Élysées, Arc de Triomphe, Faubourg Saint-Honoré, Grand and Petit Palais, Musée d'Art Moderne de la Ville de Paris (Museum of Modern Art), Guimet Museum, Chaillot.

Concorde, Tuileries, the Jeu de Paume and Orangerie Museums, Musée des Arts Décoratifs (Museum of Decorative Arts), Louvre.

Palais-Royal, Opéra, Grands Boulevards and Passages Couverts (arcades), Place Vendôme, Madeleine, Cognacq-Jay Museum, Musée de l'Affiche et de la Publicité (Posters and Advertisements).

Châtelet, Les Halles, Beaubourg-Pompidou Centre, Hôtel de Ville, Saint-Eustache, Saint-Merri, Marais (Hôtel Soubise, Carnavalet Museum, Place des Vosges), Bastille.

Champ-de-Mars, Eiffel Tower, Invalides, Faubourg Saint-Germain, Rodin Museum, Saint-Germain-des-Prés, Institut.

Montparnasse, Catacombs, Luxembourg, Latin Quarter (Panthéon, Cluny Museum, Paris Mosque), Church of Saint-Séverin, Church of Saint-Julien-le-Pauvre, Jardin des Plantes (Botanical and Zoological Gardens).

Montmartre.

Other aspects of Paris; parks, gardens and city periphery :

Bois de Boulogne (Bagatelle), Passy-La Muette (Marmottan Musuem, Ennery Museum), Albert-Kahn Gardens, Museum of Popular Arts and Traditions.

Parc Monceau (Nissim de Camondo Museum, Cernuschi Museum), Buttes-Chaumont, Père-Lachaise, Vincennes.

Basilica of Saint-Denis.

La Défense.

■ CONCORDE★★★

B2 / 8th arr. Métro : Concorde. Bus : 24, 42, 52, 72, 73, 84, 94.

The Concorde bestrides two magnificent vistas : the Tuileries to the Champs-Élysées, and the Madeleine to the Palais Bourbon. It is also the largest unencumbered urban space in Paris. "Space" : the word is no exaggeration for this square, where even the heavy motor traffic seems to melt away into a harmonious setting which links the Seine, the carefully-ordered natural surroundings and the palace-like mansions designed by Gabriel.

▶ The Place de la Concorde owes its existence to the aldermen of Paris, who commissioned an equestrian statue of Louis XV and began to look for a place to put it; this the king supplied in 1759 by entrusting Gabriel with the reclamation of a marshy area close to the Tuileries. The architect conceived the Place Louis XV to match the surroundings, built the Ambassador's Mansions (now the Hôtel Crillon and the Navy Ministry) and surrounded the square with an octogonal moat which has now been filled in. The square was inaugurated in 1763. During the Revolution, the statue of Louis XV was removed and replaced by the guillotine, and the Place de la Concorde was confirmed in its present name under the July Monarchy. Louis-Philippe, who wished at all costs to avoid any suspicion of political symbolism, chose to erect the pink granite obelisk★ that stands there today, a gift from the government of Egypt. ▶ This obelisk was originally taken from the Temple of Rameses II at Thebes; it stands 23 metres high and is covered with hieroglyphs. Two high fountains play around its base. On the perimeter of the square are eight allegorical statues of the great towns of France. Where the Avenue des Champs-Elysées joins the Place de la Concorde you can see the famous rearing horses (Chevaux de Marly★★, 1719) by Coustou, installed here in 1795. At the Tuileries entrance are Coysevox's equestrian statues. Close by are the Orangerie and Jeu de Paume Museums, in the Tuileries Gardens. □

■ EIFFEL TOWER★★★

A2 / 7th arr. Métro : Bir-Hakeim. RER : Champ-de-Mars. Bus : 42, 69, 82, 87.

Everything has been said, and more, about this "superstar" of Paris tourist attractions, which attracts no less than 3 million visitors each year. The Universal Exhibition of 1889 instigated the building of an iron tower, as a symbol of the triumph of industrial civilisation. Gustave Eiffel, an engineer and specialist in metal construction techniques, was chosen, from 700 other competitors to make this idea a reality. The work lasted from January 1887 until the spring of 1889; 7 000 metric tonnes of iron, two and a half million rivets, 320 metres high... the figures make you dizzy, but perhaps the most astonishing fact of all is that not a single correction was made to the plans during construction, so perfect was Eiffel's final design.

▶ The Eiffel Tower today serves as a meteorological station and radio mast; every day its three levels are visited by thousands of people *(9:30 am-11 pm daily for the first and second levels, 9:30-8 daily for the top level).* Those who go straight to the summit are sometimes disappointed by clouds which obscure the stunning panorama★★★ over Paris; on cloudy days, therefore, the best view is to be had from the second level. Other, taller towers have been built in New York, Moscow and elsewhere. Nevertheless, this old lady of nearly a hundred, who bears her age lightly under forty tons of paint, still retains her power to fascinate. □

■ FAUBOURG SAINT-GERMAIN★

B2 / 7th arr. Métro : Invalides, Varennes, Chambres-des-Députés, Solférino, Rue-du-Bac. RER : Quai d'Orsay. Bus : 28, 49, 63, 69, 83, 84, 87, 94.

Between the Seine, the Invalides and the Boulevard Saint-Germain lies an elegant quarter which was first inhabited towards the end of the 17thC. As a result, the Faubourg Saint-Germain is a kind of life-size museum of the civil architecture which predominated in that era. On the site of an old game preserve, large numbers of fine houses were constructed in the early 18thC, which later became the homes of important functionaries and rich bourgeois during the Empire, before being turned into an immense complex of embassies and government ministries. Most were built along the same lines : two symmetrical façades enclosing a courtyard, which opens on the street through a decorated gateway. The main part of the building faces in the other direction, onto a park dotted with pavilions, balusters and fountains.

▶ The only two buildings here which are open to the public are the **Hôtel Biron,** now the Rodin Museum, and the **Hôtel de Salm**★ (1782, Museum of the Legion of Honour, 2 Rue de Bellechasse, *2-5; closed Mon.*). However, if you take a walk beginning at the antique shops and art galleries of the Quai Voltaire, taking in Rue du Bac, Rue de Beaune and Rue des St. Pères, you can get a sight of the *hôtels* of the **Rue de l'Université** (Nos. 17, 33, 60 and the Hôtel de Soyécourt★, 1707, No. 51), then the *hôtels* of the **Rue St. Dominique** (Hôtel de Brienne, No. 14; Hôtel de Broglie, No. 35; Hôtel de Sagan★, 1715, No. 57). Continue to the Quatre Saisons (Four Seasons) Fountain at No. 57, Rue de Grenelle, which leads to a group of 18thC houses (Nos. 70, 85, 87, 106-120, 140, 142). On either side of the **Hôtel Matignon** (1720), which is the Prime Minister's residence, the **Rue de Varenne** offers the Hôtel de Boisgelin★ (Italian Embassy), and other *hôtels* at Nos. 45, 47, 50, 56, 60, 73 and 75. At the end of the rue de Bourgogne stands the **Palais-Bourbon**★, now the Chamber of Deputies. This building dates from 1722, and was enlarged by the addition of the **Hôtel de Lassay**★★, a palace decorated with a number of allegories and statues. Frescoes by Eugène Delacroix in the library. □

■ FAUBOURG SAINT-HONORÉ★

B1 / 8th arr. Métro : St. Philippe-du-Roule. Bus : 28, 32, 42, 49, 52, 80, 83.

Between the Place Beauvau and the Rue Royale runs the Faubourg Saint-Honoré, which lays serious claim to be the international capital of *haute-couture* and luxury commerce. Here are the head-quarters of Lanvin, R. Gallet, Segoura (antiques), Courrèges, Gucci, Hermès, Ungaro, Ted Lapidus, Dior, Canta, Roger et Gallet... and on the Rue Royale round the corner are

Le Métro

On the 19th of July 1900, after only two years of work, the first line on the Metropolitan railway (designed by the government engineer Fulgence Bienvenüe) was inaugurated. Some Métro entrances still date from the turn of the century; conceived by Hector Guimard, they are characteristic of what was known as the "modern style" — Art Nouveau. By 1945, the network covered 145 km; nowadays it has reached nearly 200 km, with no less than 280 stations, and a number of suburban extensions under construction or at the planning stage. Every day, the Métro's 3500 carriages carry over 4 million travellers with clockwork reliability. The Express Regional Network (RER), operated jointly by the SNCF (National Railway Company) and the RATP (Paris Transport Network) connects the outlying Île-de-France region with the heart of the capital.

Christofle and the incomparable Maxim's. There's not much originality here, but plenty of willingness to respond to the universal criteria of quality and good taste. Today's Faubourg St.-Honoré is French good taste as viewed from the Persian Gulf... or from such multinational outfits as Cardin, Saint-Laurent, Dior and Chanel.

▶ Distinguished residences, built in the 18thC by financiers and businessmen of the period, punctuate the succession of boutiques : in the main, these are now foreign embassies. The British Embassy★ is at No. 39, in Pauline (Bonaparte) Borghese's former town house, amid a cluster or early 18thC mansions in various states of preservation. On the Place Beauvau, the *hôtel* built around 1760 for the Comte de Beauvau is now occupied by the Ministry of the Interior; but the Faubourg's best-known address is unquestionably No. 55-57 — the **Élysée Palace★★**, which originally belonged to Madame de Pompadour, became a public dance-hall during the Revolution, and is now (since 1873) the residence of the President of the French Republic. □

GEORGES-POMPIDOU CENTRE★★
(Beaubourg)

B2 / Rue Saint-Martin, 4th arr. Métro : Châtelet, Les Halles, Hôtel-de-Ville, Rambuteau. RER : Châtelet-Les Halles. Bus : 38, 47, 58, 67, 69, 70, 72, 74, 85, 96.

The Centre National d'Art et de Culture Georges Pompidou, better known as the Beaubourg or Pompidou Centre, was created at the behest of a former French President, Georges Pompidou (1969-1978). The aim of the Centre was to bring together in one place all the various trends in contemporary art forms with a view to acquainting the public at large with modern art and bringing creativity into the museum. This project, spurred on by France's rapid growth and prosperity during the early 1970's, has fulfilled its promise beyond all expectations. Despite the complaints of intellectuals and critics who call it a "gasworks", the Pompidou Centre (designed by architects Piano, Franchini and Rogers) is tremendously successful with the general public. At the time of writing, more than 50 million visitors have entered the strange transparent structure since its 1977 inauguration *(12-10 pm daily; 10-10, Sat. and Sun.; closed Tue.).*

▶ On the ground floor **piazza** level, the forum is dominated by a portrait of Georges Pompidou by Vasarely. Nearby are the reception and bookshop, next to the ***salles d'actualité*** (news rooms) of the Centre's library (reviews and recent publications), the CCI (Industrial Creation Centre), **children's workshops** and the **Atelier d'Aujourd'hui** (Workshop for Today). On the mezzanine above, the CCI organises original and sometimes rather shocking exhibitions which are a must for anyone interested in contemporary topics such as comic-strip art, the media, urban architecture. ▶ On the 1st, second and third floors, the **Public Information Library** (Bibliothèque Publique d'Information, BPI) displays books and periodicals and operates audio-visual equipment and cassettes in forty foreign languages. The BPI's total surface area, all of which is freely accessible, amounts to something like four acres of floor space.

▶ Part of the third floor, and the whole of the fourth floor is devoted to the works of artists born after 1865. This is the **National Museum of Modern Art★★★**, recently reorganised, which exhibits all the great names of the 20thC : Bonnard, Picasso, Pollock, Mathieu, etc. Works by Kandinsky, along with Matisse's bronzes and paintings by Max Ernst, the sculptures of Gonzalez and Miro, dominate a slightly uneven collection, which nonetheless demonstrates the fundamentally hesitant, questing nature of contemporary art. ▶ The fifth floor, which is the top, is the home of the **Cinémathèque** (film library and archives), along with certain temporary exhibitions, a bar and a restaurant. The **view** from here (40 m above ground level) is superb — the rooftops of all central Paris. ▶ All around the Pompidou Centre, the Piazza (once the **Plateau Beaubourg)** is now a pedestrian precinct. Bookshops, galleries and restaurants have replaced the former sordid haunts of the **Quartier de l'Horloge** (the Clock Quarter). The latter has become a modern building complex, almost a pastiche of the many styles that lurk behind the venerable facades of the **Rue St. Martin;** fittingly, somehow, a clockwork armed man emerges to do battle with a monster, at the stroke of every hour — over the shop of J. Monestier, Rue Bernard-de-Claivaux. Enter the Rue Quincampoix via Rue Rambuteau; fine 16th and 17thC town houses, beautifully restored, especially Nos. 14, 13, 12, 2-4. Note the wrought-iron balconies and high, sculpted doorways. Then take the narrow, mediaeval Rue des Lombards and continue along the Rue Saint-Martin to the church of St. Merri and the lively fountain designed by Jean Tinguely and Niki de Saint-Phalle (1938), above Pierre Boulez' IRCAM (Contemporary Musical and Acoustical Research Institute). □

GRAND PALAIS, PETIT PALAIS★

B2 / Petit Palais : Avenue Winston-Churchill. Grand Palais : Avenue Winston-Churchill, Avenue de Selves and Avenue Franklin-Roosevelt, 8th arr. Métro : Champs Elysées-Clemenceau. Bus : 28, 42, 49, 72, 73, 83.

Seasons

Holidays are generally associated with the summer, which is indeed an excellent time to see Paris, but not to meet Parisians, who leave the city "en masse" from July to September. This explains the summer closure of many of the most "Parisian" restaurants, not to mention the pastry-shops, bakers and charcutiers *(delicatessens) whose storefronts bear the cheerless sign* "fermé pour congés annuels" *(closed for annual holidays). Thankfully the sign always displays the addresses of the nearest counterparts open. Summer is a fine time for lovers of old stone and for wanderings in almost silent avenues. You can nod off for a siesta in a small Paris square or on a café terrace. But summer is no time for seeing the city at its liveliest. You should also consider that the less expensive hotels have no air-conditioning, which can be somewhat disagreeable when the weather gets really hot and heavy in August.*

Spring and autumn are sometimes thought of as off-seasons, but between them they share the favour of true lovers of Paris, with the city living at its customary tempo. Paris in spring is at its romantic best, the trees lining the broad avenues burst into green, and the cafés set out their tables on the pavement. In autumn the city exudes a more nostalgic feeling, the cantonniers *(road sweepers) languidly brush the fallen leaves into neat piles under the gaze of café patrons prolonging their tans in the warmth of the sun's last rays.*

A word of warning — avoid the periods of school holidays (in Oct.-Nov. and Mar.-Apr.) and the dates of the various salons *(trade exhibitions) when hotels are booked solid.*

Winter Paris is businesslike and bustling, the warmth leaves the streets for the comptoir *(bar) of the cafés and bistrots, with their nourishing midday* plat du jour *(dish of the day). The Christmas holidays bring another exodus, this time to the winter-sports resorts, although Christmas and New Year's eves are occasions for revelry, with every restaurant offering a special gastronomic feast at all-inclusive prices.*

The shopping periods in Paris are during the months of January and June, when the big sales are on. Real bargains can be had, notably in the big stores and the luxury boutiques. The latter are literally taken by storm on the first day of their sales dates announced in daily newspapers like Le Monde *and* Le Figaro*).*

The Grand Palais and Petit Palais stand on the site of the former gigantic Palais de l'Industrie, built for the 1900 Universal Exhibition. Both are now devoted to art exhibitions, even though the Grand Palais pays homage to technical science with its Palais de la Découverte (Discovery) Section. Both buildings with their immense glass windows (and the superb staircase of the Grand Palais) bear witness to the exuberance, even the excessiveness, of Art Nouveau at its zenith.

▶ The **Grand Palais** was for many years the accustomed venue for Paris's great commercial exhibitions. The huge facilities at the Porte de Versailles and La Défense have now taken over this function, and the Grand Palais is now devoted to art shows *(10-8 daily, 10-10 Wed.; closed Tue.).* The gigantic glass roof★★ which covers the hall is a masterpiece of Art Nouveau iron architecture. ▶ Behind the Grand Palais, on the Avenue Franklin-Roosevelt, is the **Palais de la Découverte★★** *(10-6, closed Mon. and nat. hols.),* displaying the various discoveries of modern science; interesting for both children and adults. Popularisation of knowledge is the rule here; the major attraction, a **planetarium,** offers a scaled-down version of the night sky, with 9000 stars swimming slowly across it. ▶ The **Petit Palais★** has now been transformed into a Fine Arts Museum by the City of Paris. It presents highly diverse collections relative to France in the 19thC : paintings by Delacroix, Géricault, Courbet, Monet, and Cézanne, along with a number of objects from the turn of the century. Also fine antiques and 18thC furniture. Frequent temporary exhibitions. *(10-5:40; closed Mon.).* □

■ The GRANDS BOULEVARDS

B1 / 1st, 2nd, 3rd, 8th, 9th and 10th arrs. Métro : Madeleine, Opéra, Richelieu-Drouot, Bonne-Nouvelle, Strasbourg-St. Denis. Bus : 20, 21, 22, 24, 27, 29, 38, 39, 42, 47, 48, 52, 67, 85, 95.

The Grands Boulevards, which were imposed by Haussmann on the old mediaeval Paris, became the focus of the city's life in the latter half of the nineteenth century when elegant society thronged to the Opéra, the Café de la Paix, and the surrounding shops and restaurants. The streets were lined with theatres right up to the edges of the Place de la République, and it was here that "café-concerts", the forerunners of the present music-halls, first emerged. Stars of the twenties and thirties like Piaf, Mistinguett and Maurice Chevalier began their careers in the "café-concerts" of the Grands Boulevards, yet the sad truth is that today they have lost much of their lustre.

▶ The **Boulevard de la Madeleine** and the **Boulevard des Capucines,** between the Café de la Paix and the Trois Quartiers department store, still maintain a certain tradition of luxury, even though the beautiful professional *marcheuses* (streetwalkers) of former times no longer walk here to disturb the mental serenity of Parisian males. ▶ Behind the Opéra, the **Boulevard Haussmann** becomes thoroughly dreary once it has passed the big department stores *(Grands Magasins)* and the vicinity of the St. Lazare railway station. The **Boulevard Malesherbes** peters out in the monotonously genteel 17th arrondissement. ▶ The real Grands Boulevards, which in the 19thC made a fine promenade all the way to the Place de la République, have now been wholly stripped of their original character by the proliferation of

Dress

Dress as you like, wherever you like, except:
— In first-class restaurants (especially top flight hotels). Here, city clothes (ties) are "de rigueur".
— Cabaret restaurants usually prefer clients to wear evening dress, though they do not always insist.
— When you go into that Parisian speciality, the private club, you'll be judged on your looks rather than on your clothes. The doorman will sum you up, along with your companions, according to his own mysterious standards. But remember that the hardest clubs to get into relax somewhat in summer. Dress correctly, but originality and a personal touch are more than acceptable. Lastly, a reservation made from a smart hotel is highly effective...

fast-food shops, couscous restaurants and other such establishments. ▶ Close by is the business quarter, huddled round the **Bourse★** (Stock Exchange), a somewhat severe Corinthian temple designed by Brongniart in 1825. This district passes into a deep sleep as soon as the offices close down in the evening, in contrast to the adjacent **Strasbourg-St. Denis** neighbourhood which seethes with lovers of Kung-Fu and pornographic movies. There is nothing especially Parisian about the crowds of tourists and seekers of doubtful pleasures around the **Porte St. Denis** and **Porte St. Martin,** but the *quartier* does still have one or two fine 19thC buildings such as the Porte St. Martin Theatre (1829), the Gymnase Theatre (38 Blvd. de Bonne-Nouvelle, 1820), the Variety Theatre (7 Blvd. Montmartre, 1807) and, coming back towards the Opéra, the *Opéra-Comique* (Blvd. des Italiens) or the **Maison Dorée,** on the corner of the Rue Laffitte (1839). □

■ GUIMET Musem★★

A2 / 6, Place d'Iéna, 16th arr. Métro : Iéna. Bus : 32, 63, 82.

The industrialist, musician and traveller Émile Guimet left his collections of Far-Eastern art to the state, when he died in 1884. Today they form the core of the newly renovated Guimet Museum, one of the richest exhibitions of Asiatic art on the planet *(9:45-12, 1:30-5:15; closed Tue. and nat. hols.).*

▶ Impressive **Cambodian statues★** at the museum's entrance set a religious tone that pervades most of the Cambodian and Southeast Asian works exhibited here, spanning the 6th to the 13thC. The contrast between these idealised and often enigmatic pieces and the **decorative objects** from Pakistan, Afghanistan and India, emphasises the myriad influences affecting this crossroads between East and West. The 11thC "Dancing Shiva"★, the "Flower Spirit" with its Greek overtones, and the 2ndC "King of the Snakes" are among the greatest masterpieces of the Indian subcontinent. For those who don't care for bronzes, hundred-armed goddesses and painted banners, there is the sumptuous collection of **porcelain and ceramics★★★,** which is unrivalled anywhere in the world for its sheer decorative richness, variety of subject-matter, and exquisite craftsmanship. □

■ Les HALLES★

B2 / 1st arr. Métro : Châtelet-Les Halles, Étienne Marcel. RER : Châtelet-Les Halles. Bus : 21, 29, 38, 47, 58, 67, 69, 70, 72, 74, 81, 85.

Les Halles are dead; long live Les Halles! Ever since the mid-19thC, when Baltard's glass-and-metal market buildings were constructed and Zola was writing his "Ventre de Paris" ("The Belly of Paris") about the area, the great Halles food and flower market at the centre of Paris had been slowly suffocating in an everlasting traffic jam. It continued to do so until the 1970's when the markets were moved to Rungis, well out of town on the main road to Orly Airport. Now the *quartier* is focussed on a

Paris hours

— Paris gets up late. Offices and banks don't open before 9:00; museums, luxury shops, antique dealers and art galleries often make you wait till 10. On the other hand, the city centre is far less crowded at this time than in the afternoon — so visit the big department stores from 9:30, the Faubourg Saint-Honoré from 10, and the Louvre from 9:45. Note : The Pompidou Centre (Place Beaubourg) does not open before 12 on weekdays.

Restaurants serve lunch from 12:30 to 1:30. Many shops, galleries and offices close down between 12:30 and 2, as do some museums.

Traffic (buses and taxis) gets congested in the centre of town from about 4:30 onwards. From 5 to 6:30, the Métro is crammed with people. Most museums and shops close at the same time as offices, between 5 and 6; banks, from 4 onwards. The main exhibition areas of the Louvre stay open till 8, and the Pompidou Centre can be visited till 10 pm.

Pause before you rush out to dinner! Small establishments serve from 7:30 onwards, grander ones wait till 8:30 or 9. Shows (opera, theatre and music-hall) generally start at 8 or 8:30, so if you're going to one, bow to the old Parisian tradition of dining out afterwards. The restaurants around the Champs-Élysées, the Grand Boulevards, Montmartre, Les Halles and Montparnasse specialise in these 10pm—midnight dinner services and some continue even later. Likewise, dinner is served at the big music-halls and cabarets from 10 onwards.

Paris nightlife begins very late. Bars, discothèques and private clubs open their doors around 10, but they don't move into top gear until midnight. The hour of decision is around 12:45, when the last Métros pass. After that anything can happen.

gigantic crater, where the markets used to stand — the largest urban project attempted in Paris since the Baron Haussmann.

▶ Today's Les Halles is an underground labyrinth, built over a railway station which is itself 25 metres below the surface. It includes some five thousand metres of streets and theatres, and a **shopping forum**★ filled with boutiques, stores and cinemas around a series of lively arcades. The forum is the work of two architects, Vasconi and Penchréac'h, who have taken care that abundant light should penetrate all four underground levels; glass arches, symbolising the modern Halles, echo the stone arches of the **Cathedral of Saint-Eustache** opposite (→), which represent Mediaeval and Renaissance Paris. Do not miss the **Holographie Museum** on level 1, 15-21 Grand Balcon *(11-7, Sun. and hols. 1-7).* ▶ On the corner of Rues Pierre-Lescot and Rambuteau, the municipality has created a **cultural centre** housing studios, exhibition halls, poetry workshop (Maison de la Poésie) and, above all, a cultural information service (SVP Culturel) supplying information from a computer bank. Apartments, a day-nursery and a garden which extends as far as the **Bourse du Commerce** (Commercial Stock Exchange) complete the setting, which is a popular meeting place for the young and the old avant-garde, as well as for artists, marginals and aggressive hooligans. ▶ This is not the least among the paradoxes that have attended the Les Halles project. In fact, the hub of Paris life has now been united with its historical centre — and to some extent this is the measure of its success. In the old streets of Les Halles *quartier,* with their mediaeval names, then around Gonjon's superb **Fontaine des Innocents**★★ (1549), a masterpiece of the Renaissance, you will find fashion boutiques, decorators shops, contemporary art galleries, and shops selling old slot machines and art deco objects. The old narrow houses, squeezed together by the centuries, have been heavily restored; Les Halles are fashionable these days. People come here to dine or drink in the American bars and restaurants; they listen to jazz and tango music in the vaulted 17thC cellars, or linger in the Rue St. Denis, with its more or less happy blend of fashion boutiques, sex shops, video clubs, secondhand stores and tawdry prostitutes. □

The "Grands Magasins"

Aristide Boucicaut's Bon Marché is the oldest department store in the world. It was described by no less a figure than Émile Zola; and up until 1960 enjoyed steady popularity. These days, however, the Bon Marché seems a trifle isolated and forlorn in its lonely Left Bank outpost. The real Grands Magasins, as the faithful know, are north of the Seine. First and foremost are the four stores of La Samaritaine, founded by Ernest Cognacq and rendered massively popular by successful advertising. These stores are of metal construction, very much an architectural vogue in the early years of this century; they offer virtually everything under the sun, not least a fine view of Paris from the roof terraces. On the same street (Rue de Rivoli) is the Bazar de l'Hôtel de Ville, better known as the BHV. This is a paradise for the do-it-yourselfer, and boasts that is sells more per square metre of floor space than any other store anywhere. The rival Galeries Lafayette and Grands Magasins du Printemps, on the Boulevard Haussmann, have a different approach : for millions of visitors every year, these two great department store symbolize Parisian luxury and elegance and constitute a major tourist attraction. The Printemps has the largest perfume counter in the world, whilst the Galeries offer the finest fashion department, along with museum-quality displays and endlessly inventive publicity, presentation and arrangement... The best-known names in ready-to-wear clothes, leather goods and perfumes are all represented here. Lastly, if you aren't put off by the milling crowds, don't miss the resplendent window displays at Christmas, when all the "Grands Magasins" surpass themselves! Their success is indisputable, so much so that no foreign competitor (with the sole exception of the much-appreciated British store, Marks and Spencer) has ever been able to gain a foothold in Paris.

■ HÔTEL DE VILLE

B2 / Place de l'Hôtel-de-Ville, 4th arr. Métro : Hôtel-de-Ville. Bus : 38, 47, 58, 67, 69, 70, 72, 74, 75, 76, 96. Group visits by request to : Accueil de la Ville de Paris, 49, Rue de Rivoli.

The Hôtel de Ville, headquarters of the mayor's administration, celebrated its centenary in 1982. This occasion was marked by a refurbishment of the former Place de Grève, now the Place de l'Hôtel-de-Ville, which stands in front. This pedestrians-only square was the setting for public executions in the Middle Ages; nowadays it shimmers with flowers and fountains, and below the surface is a huge car park. Jacques Chirac, first Mayor of Paris, was re-elected by a massive majority a few months after the Hôtel de Ville's centenary, a choice that confirmed the long tradition of Parisian opposition to the central government : Chirac is right of centre, in contrast to the current Mitterrand administration.

▶ The history of the Mairie de Paris (Municipal Authority) goes back to the reign of St. Louis, who in 1260 demanded of the people of Paris that they designate a Provost *(Prévôt)* and Aldermen. The latter deliberated in a salt-merchant's house on the Place de Grève, known as the "Parloir aux Bourgeois". A century later, in 1357, Provost Étienne Marcel bought the "Maison aux Piliers" on behalf of the City of Paris; subsequently greatly enlarged : first under François I, then during the July Monarchy, the building was totally demolished during the revolt of the Commune on the 24th of May 1871, then rebuilt according to a design by Ballu.

▶ The ornate façade of the Hôtel de Ville, with its Renaissance-style statues and decorations, was, for many years, roundly abused by Parisians; nowadays it is recognised for what it is, one of the greatest monuments of the 19thC. The ceremonial rooms inside (sumptuous, but highly impractical) now draw most of the critics' fire. □

■ INSTITUT★★

B2 / Quai Conti, 6th arr. Métro : Saint-Germain, Pont-Neuf. Bus : 24, 27, 39, 48, 58, 70, 95.

Under the Institut's august dome, the academicians brood over their interminable dictionary of the French language. Here also the hallowed sages of science and the arts meet in the learned assemblies of the Academy's five branches : Literature, Science, Fine Arts, Moral Science and Political Science.

▶ These five academies all occupy the serene **Palais de l'Institut de France★★,** designed by Louis Le Vau and completed after his death in 1691 by Lambert and d'Orbay. Before becoming the seat of the French Academy (founded by Richelieu in 1635), this building was occupied by the Collège des Quatre-Nations, as decreed by Cardinal Mazarin — who also bequeathed it his library. The present **Bibliothèque Mazarine** (Mazarine Library) possesses more than 5 000 000 volumes, manuscripts and precious incunabula, stored in its premises in the Tour de Nesle *(10-6; closed Sat. and Sun.).* Students and scholars now work in this tower, from which Queen Margot is said to have had her nightly lovers flung into the Seine. ▶ Close by, on the Quay, stands the **Hôtel de la Monnaie** (Mint)★ (1771-1777), a fine example of Louis XVI architecture (striking of medals; medal displays. *11-6; closed Mon.*). □

A word of warning

As in any other great city, it pays to stay alert in Paris. Even in broad daylight, be especially careful of your wallet, watch, jewelry or handbag when you take the Métro or visit any well-known tourist venue. Otherwise you may find yourself suddenly relieved of them. Likewise, it is best to avoid walking alone in the side-streets of the "bright lights" quarters late at night : Les Halles, the Grands Boulevards, Pigalle, Montmartre and the Champs-Élysées.

■ Les INVALIDES★★★

B2 / 7th arr. Métro : Invalides, Varenne, Latour-Maubourg. RER : Invalides. Bus : 28, 49, 63, 69, 82, 83, 92.

Founded by Louis XIV as a home for wounded veterans of his armies, Les Invalides contains the ashes of Napoleon the First. It also testifies to the military grandeur of France under the Empire and the post-revolutionary Republic. The facade, perhaps the finest in Paris, gives onto a majestic lawn-covered esplanade extending all the way to the banks of the Seine.

▶ Les Invalides is the work of two successive architects, Libéral Bruant and Hardouin-Mansart. The latter was responsible for the monumental general design of the building, especially the remarkable **dome★★** on the Place Vauban side, which took 25 years to build (1679-1706). ▶ A more fitting imperial mausoleum could scarcely be conceived for the **tomb of Napoleon I★,** which has lain in the crypt here since 1840 *(10-5 daily, 10-7 Jul.-Aug.)* when the ex-Emperor's body was brought back in triumph from St. Helena. His ashes are contained in six coffins inside an ornate red porphyry monument. Visitors file past in the golden half-light of the crypt, their minds no doubt filled with memories of Austerlitz and Waterloo... ▶ It is almost impossible to visit all of Les Invalides, with its 16 km of corridors. After the obligatory visit to the Dôme church, the royal church, the next stop should be the **church of St. Louis-des-Invalides★,** used by the soldiers. Once again, the former military splendours of France are evoked : tombs of great generals, Napoleonic memorabilia, remains of no less than 1417 standards captured from assorted enemies. The somewhat less warlike 17thC organ is one of the most beautiful in Paris. ▶ The two buildings of the **Musée de l'Armée** (Army Museum)★★ *(10-5 or 6 according to season)* enclose the courtyard. Although we may remain perplexed by the amount of ingenuity lavished on such killing machines as crossbows, arquebuses, muskets and guns, the artistry with which armour, weapons and artillery pieces were decorated is worthy of admiration. An ivory horn, or the sword of François I, and the "Sable and Silver" armour of Henri II★ are some of the pieces which display the almost casual mastery of bygone craftsmen and make 20thC soldiers' accoutrements seem thoroughly drab; but war, too, has become an industry. ▶ Lost in the garrets of the Invalides is a remarkable and most interesting **Plans-Reliefs Museum★** (relief maps; *10-4:30*). Here are 1/600 scale models of great cities and fortresses in France and abroad, ranging from Louis XIV to Napoleon III. These models were once classified military secrets; their precision is mind-boggling. A must for anyone interested in scale models. ▶ On Avenue Latour-Maubourg is the **Musée de l'Ordre de la Libération** *(2-5; closed Sun.)* devoted to the French Resistance, the Free French and the Deportation. □

■ JARDIN DES PLANTES★

(Botanical Gardens)

B2-C2 / 5th arr. Entrances : Place Buffon, Place Valhubert. Métro : Jussieu, Place Monge, Gare d'Austerlitz. RER : Gare d'Austerlitz. Bus : 24, 57, 61, 63, 65, 89, 91.

Created by Louis XIII as a "royal medicinal herb garden", and developed by the naturalists Fagon, Jussieu and (especially) Buffon, the Jardin des Plantes is today a haunt of children, students from the vicinity and retired people who wander under the aged trees or around the pits and aviaries of the zoo. In the 18th century this place was a centre for the fashionable aristocratic study of botany.

▶ Galleries devoted to mineralogy, entomology, palaeobotany, palaeontology and comparative anatomy... these names may make you a trifle languid, but the main gallery of the **Museum of Natural History★★** has a magic of its own, with its armies of skeletons and resplendent collections of minerals and butterflies. Some of the greatest names in world biology (Buffon, Daubenton, Cuvier) worked in this museum;

nonetheless, it became one of the poorest on earth, though its collections are among the richest. Now it has been renovated and restored, and at last can display its possessions in fit surroundings (57, rue Cuvier. *1:30-5; closed Tue.*). □

■ LATIN QUARTER

B2 / 5th and 6th arrs. Métro : Odéon, Saint-Michel, Maubert. RER : Luxembourg. Bus : 21, 24, 27, 38, 47, 58, 63, 67, 84, 85, 86, 87, 89, 96.

What ever happened to the Latin Quarter, where the students of Paris used to meet? Where are their universities and their learned professors? No one has spoken Latin there for years, and today the students themselves seems to be disappearing under the pressure of an unvarying cosmopolitan throng. The last protesters of 1968 have left, along with the last of the cobbles they used to hurl at the police; and the Fontaine St. Michel has been deserted by the street people who used to spend their time here. The small bars and bistrots have given way to Chinese restaurants, fast-food joints and pizza parlours. Even the Polytechnic Academy (École Polytechnique) has withdrawn to Massy-Palaiseau.

▶ From the **Odéon Theatre★** to the "heretical" skyscraper of the Faculty of Sciences (Jussieu), from the Place St. Michel to the Rue Mouffetard, the uniting factor for the Latin Quarter has been the Sorbonne. In the 12thC, Abelard rebelled against the ecclesiastical teachings of the Île de la Cité, and his students followed him across the river to found a new university; subsequently, in 1253, Robert de Sorbon opened a college which offered room and board to poor students. His name was extended to cover an institution grouping no less than four universities on the Left Bank, and the 10 000 students who flocked to the Sorbonne made Paris the intellectual capital of Christendom. Among the most renowned teachers here were St. Bonaventure, Albert le Grand, St. Thomas Aquinas and Malebranche. The Sorbonne was always a turbulent community, opposed to the royal authority; and by 1792 it had declined almost to the point of no return. Napoleon I breathed new life into it, but it was not until the Third Republic that a modern university was established, which the events of May 1968 fragmented into 13 multi-disciplinary universities scattered all over Paris and the suburbs.

▶ From the Carrefour de l'Odéon, one continues to the **Place Saint-Sulpice★★,** shaded by chestnut trees. In the centre is the monumental Fountain of the Four Bishops (1844), while to the east is the **Saint-Sulpice church★,** typical of the 17th and 18thC classical style with a reference to Antiquity *à la* Palladio. Sarvandoni undertook the famous façade whose towers were re-worked by Chalgrin. Inside, statues by Bouchardon, Pigalle; paintings by C. Van Loo and especially, the **chapelle des anges★** (angel's chapel, *1st on right*), decorated by Delacroix and on which he worked until his death in 1863.

▶ The Latin Quarter is today divided up by the Haussmann **boulevards of St. Michel** and **St. Germain.** Historically, its main artery was the **Rue St. Jacques,** which follows the lie of an old Gallo-Roman road. ▶ The Boulevard St. Michel, 1.5 km long, begins at Davioud's amazing Second Empire **fountain,** at the centre of the Place St. Michel and for years a great rallying point for Paris marginals. The latter have been drummed off the café terraces of the **St. André-des-Arts** and **îlôt St. Severin★** *quartier* by the progressive commercial banalisation of these ancient streets (fine 18thC houses★ at No. 29, Rue de la Parcheminerie, Rue de la Harpe, odd numbers, Rues des Grands-Augustins, Séguier, Gît-le-Cœur; also Nos. 47 and 42, Rue St. André-des-Arts). ▶ The atmosphere becomes duller in proportion to the growing number of boutiques; around the Sorbonne, however, a few "experimental" cinemas and bookshops maintain a token student presence. The **Sorbonne** itself, a gigantic barrack dating from 1900, deploys its 22 lectures theatres and scores of classrooms around a series of decorated corridors (frescoes and "kitsch" allegories). The main lecture theatre was embellished by Puvis de Chavannes. The only ancient part is the elegant **chapel★** (1635) with its domed façade dominating the Place de la Sorbonne. Inside, paintings by Philippe de Champaigne and Richelieu's tomb, by Girardon. ▶ **The Collège de France** on the Place Marcellin-Berthelot is dedicated to the impartial study of arts and sciences. The first stone of this building was laid by Louis XIII, though it was not completed until 1780. ▶ On the top of the "Montagne" Sainte-Geneviève, by the **Place du Panthéon** (→), the **church of Saint-Étienne-du-Mont★★** is dedicated to Geneviève, the saint who saved Paris (late 15thC; rood-screen, tombs of Pascal and Racine). Also the **Sainte-Geneviève Library,** with 1 700 000 volumes. The **Lycée Henri IV** (school) unfortunately bars the access to the remains of the Romanesque abbey of Sainte-Geneviève (kitchens, refectory, tower of Clovis, Library).▶ The **Place de la Contrescarpe,** behind the Lycée Henri IV, is very lively at night, with a mixture of tramps,

---

The canals

Once upon a time, one could float from La Villette to Meaux on a horse-drawn water coach... Those days are gone. All the same, the canals of Paris have mostly retained their curious setting, which made the unforgettable backdrop for Marcel Carné's great movie "Hôtel du Nord". The delightful Canal Saint-Martin gives the impression of being lost in Paris, as it wanders close by the roaring traffic of the Place de la République. The anachronistic pace of this waterway is regulated by the lazy barges churning slowly from lock to lock down to the Seine, behind the Ile Saint-Louis, under the Boulevard Richard Lenoir and the Place de la Bastille and past the new marina in the Bassin de l'Arsenal. Napoléon 1st realised the great dream of Henry IV when he opened his network of canals through the heart of Paris. Nowadays, more than 10 000 barges pass along the various waterways every year, using the Canal Saint-Martin, the Canal de l'Ourcq or the Canal Saint-Denis; all three meet at the immense Bassin de la Villette, with its wharves, warehouses and workshops. Trip round the canals : embarkation La Patache (→ Practical information). Bus : Quai Anatole France.

---

students and tourists. Innumerable restaurants and their cosmopolitain clientele are gradually forcing out the traditional inhabitants, who nowadays only manage to get together in the mornings for the provincial market★★ at the bottom of the **Rue Mouffetard.** ▶ The "Mouffe" is now an upscale neighbourhood but has managed to keep the feeling of a protected outpost, especially around the **church of Saint-Médard★.** This curious sanctuary is a blend of Flamboyant Gothic, Renaissance, 17thC and the fashionable Antique style of the 18thC. □

■ The **LOUVRE★★★**

B2 / 1st arr. Métro : Louvre, Palais-Royal. Bus : 21, 24, 27, 39, 48, 67, 69, 72, 74, 76, 81, 85, 95.

A former royal palace, transformed by the Revolution into a people's museum, which frankly lays claim to the title of "most beautiful museum in the world". Quite a challenge, this, to those responsible for the current "Grand Louvre" project which the Chinese-born American architect, I. M. Pei is in charge of. The museum will gradually recover the premises vacated by the Ministry of Economy and Finance, now transferred to Bercy from the Rue de Rivoli. Yet the Louvre's unrivalled collection of paintings and drawings, and the vast extent of the palace itself, give it every advantage.

▶ Seen from the Seine or the Tuileries Gardens, the largest building complex in Paris gives a false impression of unity; this is not far short of miraculous, since the Louvre took no less than eight centuries to reach its present state. First, the square fortress built by Philippe Auguste (1190), and Étienne Marcel's ramparts; then the "library" of Charles V, the château begun by Pierre Lescot for François I and Henry II, which was carried on by Catherine de Médicis and Henri II; then the finishing work done by Louis XIV. After this came the museum installed by the Revolution, which was enlarged under Napoléon; the 1871 burning of the Tuileries by the Communards; and finally André Malraux's restoration of the original moats (filled in during the transformation from fortress to palace) in 1965. The Louvre has never ceased to adapt and change. ▶ The Vieux (Old) Louvre (1660-1680) with its famous **colonnade★★** facing the Place du Louvre, surrounds the **Cour Carrée** (Square Courtyard)★ and continues along the Seine as far as the Pont du Carrousel. The western wing of the Cour Carrée is older; this structure is a masterpiece of the French Renaissance, with superb pediments. ▶ The Nouveau (New) Louvre spreads its wings around the Pont du Carrousel; its construction dates partly from Napo-

Art and antiques

The most prestigious antique dealers are located around the Quai Voltaire (B2; Métro : Bac), the Village Suisse (A2; Ave. de Suffren; Métro : La Motte-Picquet, closed Tue. and Wed.), *and the Faubourg St. Honoré (No. 54, Antique Market;* closed Sun.*). For Art Nouveau and Art Deco, Les Halles and the Village St. Paul (C3, Métro : Sully-Morland, 11-7;* closed Tue. and Wed.*), along with the plush Louvre des Antiquaires* (11-7; closed Mon.*) on the Place du Palais-Royal.*

Among the top art galleries, Artcurial, 9 ave. Matignon (B2; 11-7; closed Sun. and Mon.*) is a kind of contemporary art supermarket, with something to suit every taste and (almost) every pocket. Not so its neighbours : Bernheim-Jeune, 83, Rue du Faubourg Saint-Honoré; Maeght, 14, Rue de Téhéran; Marcel Bernheim, 35, Rue La Boétie; Wally Findlay, 2, Ave. Matignon. These galleries deal only in recognised — and expensive — artists. The Left Bank is more open to contemporary art : Berggruen, 70, Rue de l'Université; Isy Brachot, 35, Rue Guénégaud; Claude Bernard, 9, Rue des Beaux-Arts; Stadler, 51, Rue de Seine. These establishments deal in modern trends ranging from hyperrealism to the new figurative art. Among the many small galleries in the Beaubourg quartier, Daniel Templon, 30, Rue Beaubourg, stands out. For the experienced art lover, the best hunting ground is unquestionably the Nouveau Drouot auction rooms (9, Rue Drouot; tel. 42.46.17.11;* 11-6 daily*).*

Guimard and Art Nouveau

Best known as the designer of the famous floral motif of the Metro entrances (two survive complete, at the Porte Dauphine and Abbesses stations), the architect Paul Guimard (1867-1942) was the artist who most perfectly embodied the principles of Art Nouveau in Paris. Between 1890 and 1930, he built no less than twenty townhouses and buildings in the city, all of which were highly characteristic of a certain style and epoch. Most are concentrated in the 16th arrondissement and provide an excuse for a thoroughly original walk, beginning at the Castel Béranger, 14 Rue La Fontaine, Guimard's key work, 1895. Then to the group of buildings between 17 and 21 Rue La Fontaine, Rue Gros and Rue Agar; the Hôtel Mazzara, 60 Rue La Fontaine (1910). From here, take the Rue George Sand up to the Avenue Mozart to the house built by Guimard for himself at No. 122 (1922). The stylistic unity and sheer decorative skill involved in Guimard's work attest to a complete mastery of the techniques at his disposal. The Hôtel Jassède, at 41 Rue Chardon-Lagache and the Jassède building at 1 Rue Lancret are other examples. Notice the splendid ceramics in the former and the exuberant ironwork in the latter. Lovers of Art Nouveau will find other gems in different parts of Paris : for example, the Synagogue, 10 Rue Pavée (by Guimard), the Ceramic Hotel, 34 Avenue de Wagram (by Lavirotte); the building at 39 Rue Sheffer (by Herscher).

léon III and partly from the Third Republic, after the burning of the Tuileries (Flore and Marsan Pavilions). Between these two galleries, the gardens are dotted with Maillol's nude statues★, much beloved by photographers. □

▶ Louvre Museum *(9:45-5:15 or 6:30, according to the room; museum fully open Mon. and Wed.; closed Tue.)*

▶ For a quick look round the museum, take the following itinerary : at the main entrance *(entrée principale)* stay on the ground floor. See the **Parthenon friezes** and the **Venus de Milo** here (ancient Greek); then the **"Seated Scribe"** and the **Mastaba** (Ancient Egypt); after this, walk up to the 1st floor by the main staircase, for a look at the **Victory of Samothrace.** Then to the **Grande Galerie** (French paintings, "Mona Lisa", works by Rembrandt, Vermeer, Van Dyck, Titian and Caravaggio). Continue on to the **Galerie d'Apollon,** containing the **Crown Jewels.**

▶ The Louvre in detail

▶ It seems futile to attempt any kind of resumé of the Louvre's fabulous collections, of which the small proportion on view to the public is already enough to fill dozens and dozens of immense exhibition rooms. The best way to see the Louvre is the following : spend a half day looking over the principal masterpieces, and then come again in the days following to concentrate exclusively on certain departments. There are six of these, grouping objects broadly according to family.

▶ The **Ancient Greek** and **Roman pieces** *(ground floor)* which have recently been reorganised, are headed by the famous **Winged Victory of Samothrace★,** which was discovered in 1863. This statue stands at the top of a majestic staircase along with the armless **Venus de Milo★,** originally a gift to Louis XVIII. The "Venus" dates from the 2ndC BC. In a special room adjoining are several pieces from the Parthenon, notably the **Panathenian Frieze★.** Roman sculpture achieved an apotheosis with the creation of the **Captured Barbarian Princes★** and the **Apollo★.** ▶ Once known as the "Assyrian Museum", the department of **Oriental Antiquities** *(ground floor, Cour Carrée)* displays treasures from the Near East : **The Code of Hammurabi★,** a basalt stone bearing the laws of Babylon (1750 B.C.) ; **Frieze of Archers,** representing the King of Persia's bowmen (6thC BC); and **statue of the Commissary** (intendant) **Ebih-Il,** from the 3rd millennium BC, with eyes seeming to gaze on eternity. ▶ The **Ancient Egypt section** *(ground floor, basement and first floor, Cour Carrée)* has benefited from the prodigious discoveries made by Champollion and Marielle. Wide variety of figurines and jewelry; also statues like the colossal **Sphinx** and the famous **"Seated Scribe"★.** Fine sarcophagi and steles, along with an entirely reconstructed **Mastaba★,** or funeral chamber. ▶ **The Objets d'Art and Furniture department** *(1st floor, Cour Carrée)* offers an eclectic collection of furniture and objects from the Middle Ages to the 19thC. These include Roman reliquaries, ivories, enamelling, and snuff boxes. It would take hours and hours to give each object here the attention it deserves. Notice especially the lovely Boulle furniture; Marie Leszczynska's dressing case★, given to her in 1729; and, in the **Apollo Gallery★★★,** the **Crown Jewels** with the astonishing 137 carat "Regent" Diamond★, acquired by Philippe d'Orléans in 1717. ▶ The **Paintings section** is perhaps the best known part of the Louvre. *(1st floor, Grande Galerie, Aile de Flore, etc. 9:45-5, closed Tue.).* It seems to be perpetually undergoing reorganisation and contains works covering the development of European painting, from the 14th to the 19thC. French painting is represented by such masterpieces as the ***Pietà d'Avignon★, Watteau's Gilles*** and **Poussin's *Bergers d'Arcadie★.*** Nonetheless, the public seems to prefer works by the Italian masters, headed by Leonardo's ***Mona Lisa★*** ("La Joconde" in French), a veri-

The Louvre

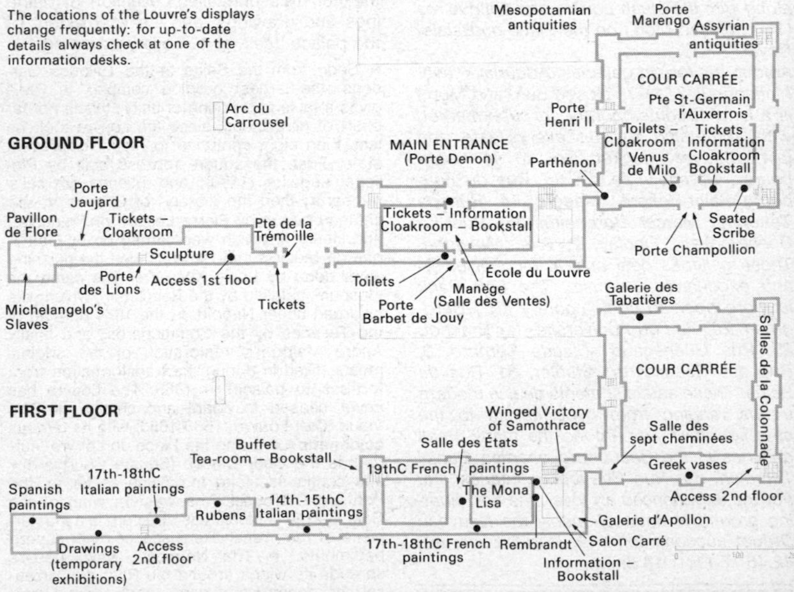

table superstar. This mysterious painting tends to overshadow Leonardo's other works in the Louvre, ***The Virgin of the Rocks*** and ***The Virgin, the Child Jesus and Saint Anne,*** but it should not distract too much attention from the lovely creations of Fra Angelico, Uccello, Titian and Raphael hanging nearby. The **Flemish and Dutch masters** offer a considerable contrast in style, represented by Van Eyck, Memling, Rubens, Rembrandt and above all, the fascinating Vermeer, to whose ***Lacemaker★*** *(Dentellière)* has now been added ***The Astronomer*** from the Rothschild collection. Lastly, the **Cabinet des Dessins** (Drawings department) offers constantly rotating exhibitions from its stock of 80 000 drawings. ▶ **Sculpture** is the last and perhaps the least-visited of the Louvre's sections; nonetheless, it contains Michelangelo's famous ***Slaves*** along with important works by Donatello, Jean Goujon, Germain Pilon and Carpeaux. □

■ LUXEMBOURG Gardens and Palace★★

B2 / 6th arr. RER : Luxembourg. Bus : 21, 27, 38, 58, 82, 84, 85, 89.

The Luxembourg Gardens, once so beloved of Marie de Médicis, is today a favourite haunt of students, intellectuals (from the surrounding left-bank quarter), joggers, tennis-players and generation after generation of children who come to see its venerable puppet theatre.

▶ After the assassination of Henri IV, his widow, Marie de Médicis, began building a palace (1615) in the gardens she had recently bought from François de Luxembourg and to which she constantly added. ▶ On the Rue de Tournon side, the **Palace★★,** designed by Salomon de Brosse, retains its original Florentine features. The building now houses the French **Senate** and was considerably modified in the 19thC. Haussmann was only prevented from destroying the Park by a petition signed by 12 000 people : as it was, the building of the Rue Auguste Comte reduced it to its present 60-odd acres. ▶ The Luxembourg is above all a highly civilised **park,** with its ponds, its terraces, its pretty **Fontaine Médicis** and its monument to Delacroix. Though it has lost its chair-attendants, the chairs are still there; alas, the park wardens are implacable about the hour of closing, which is exactly thirty minutes before sunset at all times of year. From the Luxembourg gardens by the Avenue de l'Observatoire or the Rue Gay-Lussac one reaches the Boulevard Port-Royal and the **Val-de-Grâce** military hospital★★ : the former monastery founded by Anne d'Autriche is one of the most remarkable architectural ensembles of the 17thC. Built to the design of F. Mansart, the dome is one of the finest examples of Roman Baroque in Paris. □

■ Church of La MADELEINE

B1 / Place de la Madeleine, 8th arr. Metro : Madeleine. Bus : 24, 42, 52, 84, 94.

The majestic, slightly ponderous Church of the Madeleine, with its temple facade and its plinth 24 steps high, is very much in tune with its smart location at the top of the Rue Royale. This is the core of Paris's luxury commercial area and the crux of the Grands Boulevards.

Jeu de Paume Museum

Place de la Concorde, in the Tuileries Gardens, 1st arr. Métro : Concorde. Bus : 24, 42, 52, 72, 73, 84, 94.

The museum is housed in a Second Empire orangery and owes its name to a tennis game played on its terrace by the son of Napoleon III. It contains a unique collection of Impressionist paintings from the period between 1860 and 1914. (9:45-5:15; closed Tue.)

The pictures are grouped in rooms which are either devoted to a single artist, or to an important collection. Two rooms are assigned to Degas : the first contains portraits ("Famille Belleli", "L'Artiste", "L'Absinthe"), and the second, some of the painter's famous dance motifs ("Fin d'Arabesque", "Danseuse au Bouquet", "Danseuses Bleues"). Manet also has two rooms for his paintings; among them are the famous "Déjeuner sur l'Herbe" (1863), which signalled the birth of Impressionism when first exhibited to a scandalised public at the Salon des Refusés. Above all, see "Le Balcon", "Olympia", and the various portraits. The best-represented painter at the Jeu de Paume is unquestionably Monet; see "Femmes au Jardin" (Salle Bazille), the two "Bassins aux Nymphéas" (Salle Caillebotte) and the five "Cathédrales de Rouen" (Salle Monet). Sisley, Pissarro and Boudin also figure alongside various Impressionist contemporaries, among whom Renoir stands out ("La Grenouillère", "Le Moulin de la Galette" (Salle Caillebotte) along with Van Gogh ("Hôpital Saint-Paul à Saint-Rémy", in the Salle Kaganovitch, "Eglise d'Anvers", Salle Gachet, "La Chambre Jaune", "L'Arlésienne" and "Self-portrait", Salle Gauguin) and Cézanne (several still-lifes, "L'Estaque", "La Maison du Pondy", "Les Baigneurs", Salle Cézanne). In 1986, the Jeu de Paume Collection will be taken across the Seine to its new home in the Orsay Museum.

▶ The church was begun by Napoléon I who wanted a temple dedicated to his Grand Army; but it was not completed until 1840. Designed by Vignon, the Madeleine has seen plenty of lavish weddings and funerals; nonetheless, it is the most secular of Parisian churches, with not a single cross to be seen on its pediment. □

■ Le MARAIS★★★

B-C2 / 3rd and 4th arr. Métro : Saint-Paul, Pont-Marie *(south side)*. Bastille, Chemin-Vert, Rambuteau *(north side)*. Bus : 20, 29, 38, 47, 65, 67, 69, 75, 76, 86, 87, 91, 96.

The twisting streets, magnificent private mansions, courtyards and ancient buildings of the Marais quarter cover some 300 acres of protected (*classé;* → museums) townscape. This *quartier* is really a huge museum of Paris, a living testimonial to the civil architecture of the 17thC. Not so long ago, it was on the brink of crumbling into ruin, but was saved *in extremis* by the Malraux Law of 1962, which led to a long and ultimately fruitful renovation of the Marais' forgotten treasures. Twenty years later, in the 1980's, accommodation here has become much sought after by wealthy Parisians just as it was in the days of Henri IV when aristocrats and burgers clustered around the Place Royale — now the Place des Vosges — and built themselves houses to match their wealth and ambition. The area is now considerably enlarged, stretching from the Church of St. Gervais to the Bastille and from the Seine to the Temple.

▶ A walk through the Marais

▶ Start at the Place de l'Hôtel de Ville; visit the **church of St. Gervais.** Then take **Rue François-Miron,** Rue de Jouy (Hôtel d'Aumont) and Rue du Figuier as far as the Seine (Hôtel de Sens). Walk upriver to the Arsenal and turn back into the Rue du Petit Musc (Hôtel de Mayenne) to Rue St. Paul. Then take Rue de Birague, which leads into the **Place des Vosges;** return via **Rue des Francs-Bourgeois (Hôtel Carnavalet)** and **Rue des Archives** (Palais Soubise, Billettes Cloister) to the **Hôtel de Ville** (→).

▶ The southern end of the Marais between Rue St. Antoine and the Seine is typical of old Paris. The church of **St. Gervais-St. Protais★** (16thC, pure Flamboyant Gothic), is a good starting point for a visit to this side of the quarter; its classical façade (1620) stands right behind the Hôtel de Ville. It was in this church that a German shell killed 51 people on Good Friday, 1918. ▶ Continuing down the **Rue François-Miron,** lovely houses of the precinct of St. Gervais (1732 : Nos. 2-14). No. 68 on this street is the **Hôtel de Beauvais★** (1655); No. 82, the Hôtel du President Hénault (1706). ▶ To the right is Rue de Fourcy, then Rue des Nonains d'Hyeres; on the right, **Hôtel d'Aumont★★** (1648); left, the rear façade of the **Hôtel de Sens★★,** heavily restored but still a fine example of 15thC architecture. This *hôtel* was the home of the eccentric Queen Margot; today, it houses the **Forney Library** *(1:30-8; closed Sun. and Mon.).* ▶ Close by the Quai des Célestins, a part of **Philippe Auguste's city wall** is still visible (Rue des Jardins-Saint-Paul). ▶ At the end of the quai is the Hôtel Fieubet, built by Mansart in 1678 but loaded with superfluous additions in the 19thC; likewise the mansion at No. 3, rue de Sully, now occupied by the **Library of the Arsenal.** This building still retains some rooms decorated in the style of Louis XIII, unchanged since the great finance minister Sully lived here *(10-5 daily; closed Sun.)* ▶ Via Rue du Petit-Musc, to the ancient and busily commercial **Rue St. Antoine,** the central artery of the Marais. At No. 17, the circular **Temple of St. Marie★,** built by Mansart in 1634; at No. 21, the Hôtel de Mayenne (1613) and the exceptionally graceful **Hôtel de Sully★★** at No. 62, built by Henry IV's great minister in 1624; today, beautifully restored, this building houses the Historic Monuments Board (C.N.M.H.S. → museums; information centre). Next to the Lycée Charlemagne, further on, is the **church of St. Paul-St. Louis★** (1627-1641), in the Jesuit style, rare in Paris. Madame de Sévigné used to come here to listen to the preacher Bourdalone's sermons. ▶ Coming from Rue St. Antoine, the northern end of the Marais is entered via the **Rue des Archives** *(to the right, off Rue de Rivoli).* No. 22, next to the Lutheran Church, is the mediaeval **Cloître des Billettes** (cloister), built in 1415; the only construction of its kind to be seen in Paris. ▶ At the intersection with the Rue des Francs-Bourgeois stands the **Hôtel Soubise★★** (1705-1709), where the National Archives are housed around a fine courtyard in the shape of a horseshoe. The superb apartments here are open to the public; these are occupied by the **Museum of French History** *(2-5 daily ex Tue.).* ▶ Behind this *hôtel* at No. 60 Rue des Archives, is the **Musée de la Chasse et de la Nature** (Hunting Museum) in the **Hôtel Guénégaud★** (1650), recently restored *(10-5:30 daily ex Tue. and hols.)* ▶ **Rue des Francs-Bourgeois** meets **Rue Vieille-du-Temple;** No. 87 of this street is the **Hôtel de Rohan★★,** also a depository for national archives. No. 47, the **Hôtel des Ambassadeurs d'Hollande,** dates from 1655; nearby, No. 31 Rue des Francs-Bourgeois is the **Hôtel d'Albret.** The proximity of these three great houses demonstrates the heavy concentration of aristocratic residences here during the 17thC. ▶ 14-16 Rue des Francs-Bourgeois is the **Hôtel Carnavalet★★** (→) former home of Mme de Sévigné; this architectural masterpiece faces the **Hôtel de Lamoignon★★** (history library) at 24 Rue Pavée... There are many others, too many to enumerate, which mark the apogee of civil architecture in France. A random choice might include the following : the **Hôtel Libéral-Bruant,** Place Thorigny, now the **Bricart de la Serrure Museum;** the **Hôtel Salé★★,** nearby, 5 Rue de Thorigny, built in 1656 by the seigneur de Fontenay, is now the **Picasso Museum★★** (→) where in superb surroundings the painter's personal collection is on display; the **Hôtel de Marle★,** 11 Rue Payenne. ▶ Rue des Francs-Bourgeois goes back to the **Place des Vosges★★** (→), the heart and origin of the Marais. This is where it all began : when Henry IV created this fascinating 127 m by 140 m square, he created a whole *quartier,* almost a whole town. The buildings here are uniform in design and the arcaded square is all but totally closed in on itself. The white stone and red brick of the masonry, tempered by dark blue slate roofing, gives an impression of purity and harmony. Victor Hugo lived at No. 6 Place des Vosges, the Hôtel de Rohan-Guéménée, between 1833 and 1848 and wrote some of his most famous works here. The house is now a **museum** dedicated to the great author *(10-5:30; closed Mon. and Tue.),* containing especially fine examples of his visionary and symbolist drawings. □

■ Parc MONCEAU★

B1 / 17th arr. Métro : Monceau. Bus : 30, 84, 94.

The Monceau park is the last remnant of the immense domain belonging to the Orléans family, which at one time covered a large proportion of the land on the western side of Paris. During the Second Empire, when so many of Paris's parks and green spaces were created, the Parc Monceau was landscaped in the English style by the architect Alphand, providing verdant views for the luxurious houses built on its perimeter by notables and favourites of the régime.

▶ Well worth a visit are Nos. 5 and 7, Rue Murillo, and No. 5 **Avenue Van-Dyck.** ▶ Just off the park are two quiet and intimate museums housed in fine specimens of 19thC

Paris mansions. At No. 7, **Avenue Velasquez,** the **Cernuschi Museum★** was donated to the City of Paris by the great collector of Far Eastern art, Henri Cernuschi, in 1896 *(daily 10-5:40; closed Mon. and hols.).* Considerably enlarged since then, notably with the addition of certain archaic pieces which are among the finest examples of their kind in the world. The upper floors contain objects ranging from the second century BC to the 15th and 16th centuries AD. On the ground floor, courses in calligraphy and temporary exhibition. ▶ At 63, Rue de Monceau, the Camondo family's collection from the French 18thC is now in the possession of the Union des Arts Décoratifs (Decorative Arts Union). The **Nissim de Camondo Museum★** *(10-12 & 2-5; closed Mon., Tue. and hols.)* exhibits bronzes, porcelain objects, Savonnerie carpets, furniture (some from the royal household) and *boiseries*. The former salons are decorated with 23 Aubusson carpets★. □

■ MONTMARTRE★★

B1 / 18th arr. Métro : Blanche, Abbesses, Pigalle, Anvers, Lamarck-Coulaincourt. Bus : 67, 30, 54, 80, 85, 95. A minibus service serves the Butte Montmartre, from the Place Pigalle to the Mairie of the 18th arr., Rue Ordener; funicular railway.

The Butte Montmartre has always been half dream and half reality, a mixture of the best and worst aspects of Paris. On the one hand, it is a mass of clichés and tourists; on the other, if you know how to choose the time and place, it can lead you to delightful discoveries. This ambiguity is the source of its strange fascination.

▶ Nothing in Montmartres's long history ever indicated that it would become a great centre for bohemianism and the arts. The *Mont,* which was once dedicated to the God Mercury, is 130 metres high, one metre taller than the Buttes Chaumont (129 m) and clearly dominating the Montagne Ste. Geneviève. During the reign of Charlemagne, it was named the "Mont des Martyrs", to commemorate the execution of St. Denis in 250 AD. In 1133, a Benedictine abbey was founded here by Queen Adelaïde of Savoy; the fields belonging to the abbey stretched out below, where the Grands Boulevards are now. Henri IV bombarded Paris from Montmartre's strategic heights; later, mills began to appear, as the land grew more heavily cultivated. Montmartre pancakes and wine were consumed in *cabarets* or taverns. The Butte began to acquire a bad reputation; libertine aristocrats built extravagant "follies" here, such as the Château des Brouillards, built by the Marquis de Pompignan in 1772. Then came the tragic events of 1815, when Montmartre put up a bloody resistance to the invading Cossacks. In 1871, hundreds of *Communard* rebels took refuge in the chalk mines of the Butte, where they were immured or blown up by the advancing Versaillais. To expiate their appaling massacre, the Third Republic erected the gigantic Basilica of Sacré-Cœur on the site. Even at this time, after Renoir and Van Gogh, unknown men of genius were beginning to converge on Montmartre from all over Europe : Van Dongen, Juan Gris, Picasso... the legend was born. At the beginning of 1914, Picasso was working on his "Demoiselles d'Avignon", and Cubism had been founded. Montmartre and the Bateau-Lavoir entered history as the birthplace of modern art. ▶ Like a theatre backdrop, Montmartre has its "street" side and its "garden" side. The street side is mainly the **Boulevard de Clichy,** the **Place Blanche** and the vanes of the **Moulin Rouge** which go round and round all night. Then there is **Pigalle,** with its sex-shops and sordid striptease joints (now being replaced by peep-shows and video-clubs); its vaguely unsavoury fauna, and its overpriced bars and cabarets. ▶ Leaving the bright lights of "Gay Paree" behind, the **Rue Lepic** with its lively market★ leads through to the "garden" side of Montmartre. ▶ The climb to the famous **Moulin de la Galette★** is a steep one; the latter was immortalised by Renoir, and is surrounded by houses from around 1900. Rue d'Orchampt leads down to the side of the Bateau-Lavoir at 5, Rue Ravignan, now demolished. ▶ On the other side of the Rue Lepic, **Avenue Junot** is surrounded by villas and gardens. ▶ In Rue des Saules, the **Lapin Agile Cabaret** still retains its rustic aspect; it stands at the foot of the famous Montmartre vineyards, where the grapes are harvested every year amid all the trappings of country folklore. ▶ At No. 12, Rue Cortot near the **Rue Saint-Vincent** (Aristide Bruant had a song about this street), is the **Vieux-Montmartre Museum** *(2:30-5:30 11-5 on Sun.; closed Tue.),* possibly the only museum in the world exhibiting a completely reconstructed old-fashioned bistro. ▶ At the top of the long **Rue du Mont-Cenis,** which dips down in a northward direction towards Clignancourt, stands the **Basilica of Sacré-Cœur★** built according to plans by the architect Abadie, between 1876 and 1919. The Basilica makes up for its relative lack of architectural interest by providing a matchless view of Paris from its terraces — or, even better, from its dome. ▶ It is unfortunate that the Sacré-Cœur sometimes distracts attention

Markets and flea markets

Markets play a considerable role in the life of a Paris quarter. Two of the most interesting are the excellently restored Marché Saint-Quentin (corner of Blvd. Magenta and Rue de Chabrol), and the Marché du Faubourg Saint-Martin (Rue Bouchardon). Both are covered markets, strongly characteristic of turn-of-the-century metal architecture. The open-air markets in Rue Lepic, Place Maubert, Rue Mouffetard, Rue de Buci, Blvd. Raspail (Métro Rennes) and Blvd. de la Muette are mostly for food. Place d'Aligre has a food market with a small flea market adjoining. The biggest flea market is in the northern edge of town, at the Porte de Clignancourt (Sat., Sun. and Mon.); *alas, few bargains are to be had there nowadays, since "real" antique dealers have moved in, paying high prices for sales locations. More in line with the flea market tradition (and more chancy, perhaps) are the "Puces du Montreuil" (small furniture, curios and bric-à-brac), the "Puces de la Porte de Vanves", and the "Puces du Kremlin-Bicêtre", in the inner suburbs* (Sat., Sun. am). *Note also the secondhand bookstands along the Seine, the flower market on the Ile de la Cité, and the stamp market* (Thur., Fri., Sat.) *in the gardens off the Champs-Élysées.*

Unusual museums : Musée du vin

The Wine Museum, sited in a former quarry under the ground, offers an initiation into the art of cultivating vines and the techniques of vinification (*Rue des Eaux, 16th arr.,* 10-6 daily).

from the lovely Romanesque Church of **Saint-Pierre-de-Montmartre★★,** the oldest sanctuary in Paris. There is doubt as to whether this structure embodies the remnant of a Gallo-Roman temple; however, its vaulted Gothic choir dates from 1147. A haven of coolness and peace, only a few steps away from the tourist frenzy of the **Place du Tertre★** with its cluttered café terraces, painters' easels and assembly-line artwork. All the same, if you come here on a spring or autumn morning, this all-too-famous little square regains some of its former village charm. ▶ The **Place du Calvaire** nearby is a veritable balcony over Paris, which can be both deserted and romantic at some hours. ▶ The steps, or the funicular, take you back down into the turmoil of the **Boulevard Rochechouart;** during the day, the famous Marché Saint-Pierre (cloth market) swarms with people from a different, almost Mediterranean Paris. □

■ MONTPARNASSE

B2 / 6th, 14th arrs. Métro : Montparnasse-Bienvenue, Gaité, Vavin. Bus : 28, 48, 58, 68, 82, 89, 91, 92, 94, 95, 96.

Montparnasse on the Left Bank, Montmartre on the Right. Their pasts are similar : dance-halls, rendez-vous for artists and exiles, who became famous. Here their names are Modigliani, Matisse, Henry Miller, Hemingway, Lenin and Trotsky. Then there is the immense crowd that throngs the many cinemas on the Boulevard du Montparnasse and its periphery, and the terraces of the Dôme and Coupole restaurants (once the headquarters of the avant-garde). The same crowd overflows into the *crêperies* (pancake bars) of the Breton quarter, the Rue Delambre, the Rue de la Gaieté and the Montparnasse station precinct. The Tour Montparnasse, beside the triple-galleried **commercial centre,** in a sense matches the Sacré-Cœur; both are equally decried, but for good or ill their silhouettes are part of the Paris skyline.

▶ At the foot of the giant **Tour Maine-Montparnasse** skyscraper (express lifts rising 200 metres in a few seconds; 56th and 59th floors, superb panorama of Paris★★, *9:30 am-11:30 pm daily*), is the capital's most modern mainline railway station, the **Gare Montparnasse.** Aspects of an earlier Montparnasse also survive in the vicinity : small avenues and courtyards, with green gardens and artists' studios. ▶ Southward, between the Plaisance and Alésia quarters, a former squatter's district has gradually been converted into modern building complexes, with a few older houses and villas gasping for air between them. ▶ To the west, the **Bourdelle Museum★** (16, Rue Bourdelle, 15th arr., *10-5:30; closed Mon.*) is housed in a characteristic artist's building, a tangle of *ateliers* (studios) piled with scale models, sketches and plaster casts left by the sculptor. ▶ Following the **Blvd. du Montparnasse** past the **church of Notre-Dame-des-Champs** (1876), you reach the **Blvd. Raspail** and Rodin's statue of Balzac, the centre of the artists' quarter between 1920 and 1940. ▶ In the little streets leading off this intersection, the lively atmosphere of the Boulevard quickly melts away. Cabarets and night clubs here do not stir till late at night, when the many artists' studios are lit up. ▶ At No. 100, Rue d'Assas is the **Zadkine Museum★** *(10-5:40 daily ex Mon.),* in the house occupied by the sculptor between 1928 and his death in 1967. Three hundred of his works have been assembled in the building and its small garden, which were first opened to the public in 1982. □

■ La MUETTE and PASSY

A2 / 16th arr. Métro : La Muette, Passy. Bus : 22, 32, 52, 63, PC.

An immense garden, on the edge of the Bois de Boulogne with its puppets and games; the delightfully old-fashioned Petite-Ceinture railway line, with its "provincial" station; fine villas hidden in protected alleyways behind larger buildings; the shops of Passy, and its bustling market — all these things make this riverbank quarter a kind of village within a town.

▶ The charming **Ranelagh Gardens** are laid out in the former park of a château lived in by Louis XV and Madame de Pompadour. The present château, hidden discreetly behind a screen of trees, was built at the beginning of the century by Baron de Rothschild. ▶ The resplendent **Marmottan Museum★★** (2, Rue Louis-Boilly, *10-6; closed Mon.*) is one of atmosphere. The lower floor is devoted to Impressionism; one can see Monet's "Les Nymphéas", which occupies an entire room. ▶ Discretion is also the hallmark of Balzac's house at No. 47, Rue Raynouard, where the writer used to come to escape his creditors. The resultant **Balzac Museum★***(10-5:30; closed Tue.)* looks like a country house, with its garden. Balzac was none too happy here, finding it suffocatingly hot in summer and freezing cold in winter. While endeavouring to pursue his somewhat intricate pleasures, and nursing his love for the Polish Mme. Hanska from afar, Balzac nonetheless contrived to finish the last section of his great "Comédie Humaine" in this house. His spartan workroom has been left in its original state, complete with the famous coffee pot. The other rooms are stuffed with the memorabilia of a restless life : portraits, manuscripts, letters and everday objects. ▶ The **Villa La Roche** (10, sq. du Dr Blanche), where the Le Corbusier foundation is located, illustrates the theories of the famous architect. □

■ The MOSQUE★

B2 / Place du Puits-de-l'Ermite, 5th arr. Métro : Monge. Bus : 24, 47, 57, 61, 63, 67, 89.

The Muslim community in Paris is very perceptible in the outlying quarters of Barbès and Belleville; all the same, the various Islamic institutions are grouped around the prestigious **Institute of Muslim Studies** *(Institut des Études Musulmanes),* facing the

Jardin des Plantes (Botanical and Zoological Gardens) (→).

▶ Built between 1922 and 1926 in the Moroccan style, the **Grand Mosque of Paris** *(10-12, 2-5:30; closed Fri. and Muslim holidays)* is decorated with a considerable eye to variety. The most diverse motifs in Islamic art have been used here, especially in the remarkable domed prayer hall. Many Parisians come to the *hammam* (baths) here, and greatly appreciate the cakes and mint tea available at the shops of the *souk*. Not far off are the **Arènes de Lutèce** (Rue Monge and Rue des Arènes), the heavily-restored remains of a Gallo-Roman amphitheatre which was destroyed in the 3rdC and rediscovered in the 19thC. An unusual place, much used by local schoolchildren as a sports area.

NOTRE-DAME★★★

B2 / 4th arr. Métro : Cité. Bus : 21, 24, 38, 47, 81, 85, 96.

World-famous masterpiece of the Middle Ages, perfect example of Gothic harmony. The Cathedral of Notre-Dame de Paris is more than a monument : it is a "history book", as Michelet has said. It should be visited at different hours of the day, for a full appreciation of the architecture of light embodied in the Gothic nave. Notre-Dame swarms perpetually with visitors, though it takes on a more authentic character during great religious ceremonies or organ recitals. The great organists of Europe come here to play the massive instrument installed in 1730 and rebuilt by Cavaillé-Coll during the 19th century *(free concert, Sun. pm).*

Great contemporary projects and monuments

Since the massive building works inspired by the Universal Exhibitions (the Eiffel Tower and the Palais de Chaillot), Paris has seen very few large scale public projects. The Unesco Building (1955-1958 : Place de Fontenoy, 10-12, 3-5) or the Maison de Radio France (1952-1963) are about the only major works carried out in the 1950's. The arrival of international style architecture changed everything during the mid-60's with the advent of the Maine-Montparnasse complex (→), the La Défense quarter (→), Front de Seine, along with shops and office buildings. The aggressively modern Beaubourg Centre (→) was completed a little earlier than Les Halles Forum (→); between them, these two projects changed the face of the historic centre of Paris. Demolition work at the Bastille station, La Villette and the Bercy warehouse area has cleared the way for a new covered bicycle stadium (vélodrome) *and sports centre, as well as a new facility for the Ministry of the Economy; the La Villette site is to be turned into a large park, with cultural amenities and theatres. These projects should transform the northern and eastern districts of Paris, which have long been neglected.*

Unusual museums : the Grevin waxworks

1982 was the centenary year of this museum of historical scenes and waxworks. A new ensemble devoted to 19th century Paris and its spectacles *(shows) has now been opened in Les Halles under the same auspices* (*10, Blvd. Montmartre, 9th arr.* 1-7 daily, *and Forum des Halles, level 1, 1st arr.* 10:30-8 daily).

▶ The name of Maurice de Sully is closely associated with the construction of Notre-Dame; after commencing the works, he directed them for thirty three years until the completion of the choir and transept around 1200. Four more stages of construction had yet to be undertaken before France's largest cathedral was finally completed at the end of the 14th century. From that time onward, Notre-Dame has witnessed many great events : Saint-Louis' lying-in-state (1270); the solemn conversion of Henry IV (1594); the crowning of Napoléon I as Emperor (1804); the singing of the Victory Te Deum (1945); the funeral of General de Gaulle, attended by chiefs of state from all over the world (1970). Notre-Dame's historical importance is matched by its architecture as the symbol of Paris. All Gothic religious art was deeply infuenced by it, to the farthest outposts of Europe. The architects Jean de Chelles and Pierre de Montreuil endowed their cathedral with simplicity and harmony, and proportions of 130 m long, 48 m wide and 35 m high from floor to roof. ▶ The **west façade,** enclosed by two massive square towers (69 m high) is divided into three levels : at the base stands the great doorway★★, with on the left a carved Virgin, in the centre the Last Judgment, and on the right, Saint Anne. This is surmounted by the **Gallery of Kings** (their heads have been replaced; some of the originals, knocked off by the Revolutionaries in 1793, are now in the Cluny Museum). Above them is the great rose window, 9.6 m in diameter, itself

Unusual museums : Musée d'Ennery

The Musée d'Ennery is an "atmospheric" museum, one among many others in Paris. The difference here is that the atmosphere is a very strong one, since the collections are entirely devoted to Far Eastern art, and plenty of it : the rooms are so crammed with statues and objects that their quality is almost submerged. The best items are doubtless the netsukés *and* kogos, *skilfully worked buttons and boxes illustrating everyday scenes in the 17th and 18th centuries. The sense of detail and decorative precision shown in these objects makes each one a work of art in itself, and gives the Musée d'Ennery its particular distinction as a museum of miniature art* (*59, Ave Foch, 16th arr.* Thu. and Sun., 2-5 only).

topped by an open gallery joining the two towers *(access to towers 10-4:30)*. ▶ The **lateral façades** and **the apse** have three levels backing on to each other; the apse itself is supported by flying buttresses with a span of 15 m. The 90-m spire was replaced by Viollet-le-Duc in 1860. ▶ The **interior** of Notre-Dame *(8-6:30 ex during services)* is composed of five naves, lit by three great rose windows★★ which still have their original 13th century stained glass. The side chapels contain 17th and 18thC paintings. ▶ The wooden choir stalls date from the 18thC; behind them is a magnificent screen decorated with a series of bas-reliefs★★ in polychrome stone. On the right, in the chancel, is the entrance to the Treasury, which displays gold plate, cameos of the various Popes, and a Palatine cross including a fragment of the True Cross. The **archeological crypt** *(10-5)* displays objects discovered during the construction of the underground parking garage. ▶ Behind Notre-Dame, several parcels of the mediaeval street network disturbed by the Baron Haussmann are still visible. Rue Massillon, Nos. 4-8, fine 17th and 18thC homes; Rue Chanoinesse, Nos. 22 and 24, odd-looking canon's houses; finally, on the Rue de la Colombe, part of the Gallo-Roman defensive works built around the Île de la Cité. □

■ OPÉRA★★

B1-2 / Place de l'Opéra, 9th arr. Métro : Chaussée d'Antin, Opéra. RER : Auber. Bus : 20, 21, 22, 27, 29, 42, 52, 57, 53, 66, 95.

Built at the behest of Napoleon III, the Paris Opéra boasts that it is the most important example of 19thC theatre architecture. Since the foundation of the Royal Academy of Music by Louis XIV, Paris had had nothing but temporary theatres, which were frequently destroyed by fire. The Second Empire bequeathed to Paris the great opera house it had always dreamed of, in the heart of Haussmann's new quarters.

▶ The original project for the Opéra was devised by Charles Garnier. It was opposed by the Empress Eugénie, who condemned the plans for their lack of style. The architect replied that they were "... in the style of Napoleon III, Madame". The period of construction lasted for 15 years, and incorporated a number of new construction techniques, especially the use of iron; work was interrupted by the Commune's insurrection and a series of financial difficulties. The building was finally inaugurated on the 5th of January 1875 by Marshal de Mac-Mahon; as of 1881, electric lights replaced the gaslights; and by 1964 Chagall's frescoes covered the ceiling of the opera house. Originally conceived for the social crowds of the Second Empire, the Opéra apportions more space to its public areas and salons than it does to the theatre itself. ▶ The sumptuous marble and onyx staircase★, the grand foyer★ with its mosaic-covered roof and the gigantic six-ton chandelier in the theatre bear witness to an omnipresent concern for display. This is particularly true of the ornate façade, with a replica of Carpeaux's famous sculpured group, "La Danse". ▶ Lovers of opera and ballet will not overlook the little **Opéra Museum** *(10-5 daily ex Mon.)* in the West Pavilion, where designs, maquettes, decor and costumes recreate the magic of past productions mounted in the "Palais Garnier". □

■ ORSAY Museum★

The Orsay Museum is scheduled to open by the end of 1987 in what was formerly a railway station designed by Victor Laloux in 1900. Works and documents tracing the evolution of the arts and French society from 1848 to 1914 will be presented in the new galleries created by the Italian architectural designer Gae Alenti. ▶ The museum will consist of 3 exhibition floors : the first, on the level of the old tracks, will cover the period 1848-70; the next floor, 1870-1914; the top floor will be devoted to the Impressionists. Special areas will consider Charles Garnier and the Paris Opéra, Hector Guimard, Baron Haussmann, and in addition the city planning of 1900. The press, books and posters of the time will also be dealt with. □

■ PALAIS-ROYAL★★

B2 / 1st arr. Métro : Palais-Royal. Bus : 21, 27, 29, 39, 48, 67, 69, 72, 74, 81, 95.

The Palais-Royal is a marvellous, timeless enclave, set apart from the surrounding city, which seems to retain something of the 18thC which so loved it. Oddly, Parisians do not know it very well, though foreigners seem to be fully alive to its charm. Built by Richelieu between 1629 and 1642, it was at first a "Palais-Cardinal", for it was here that Louis XIII's great minister lived and died. It became the Palais-Royal when the young Louis XIV moved in, with Anne of Austria.

▶ The regent Philippe of Orléans turned the Palace and **gardens**★★ into a venue for his famous (and still scandalous) parties. After the destruction by fire of the Opéra close by, the Palace had to be reconstructed in 1763. The future Philippe-Égalité was so short of money to do this that he built **galleries** all round the gardens, which he rented to tradesmen, along with apartments in the upper stories. A second fire in 1781 destroyed the theatre on the site of today's **Comédie Française.** The Palais-Royal's bad reputation attracted crowds of common people; it was in the gardens that Camille Desmoulins called the populace to arms on the 13th of July 1789. Subsequently, the Palais Royal's gambling dens and cafés made it a haunt of men-about-town and dandies. Even Napoléon I, who installed the Council of State on the premises, failed to restore its former dignity. But fashion succeeded where authority had failed : the 19th century Paris crowd preferred the Grands Boulevards or the new *quartiers* to the Palais-Royal, and the gardens regained a tranquillity that has remained ever since. ▶ Behind the double portico of the Galerie d'Orléans, which separates the courtyard from the garden, the long galleries house a series of strange little shops selling military decorations, curios and lead soldiers. □

■ The PANTHÉON★

B2 / Place du Panthéon, 5th arr. Métro : Cardinal-Lemoine. RER : Luxembourg. Bus : 21, 24, 27, 38, 84, 85, 89.

The Panthéon is a lay temple dedicated to the great Republican figures. The Republic is sometimes a generous builder (witness the ardor of the "Marseillaise" bas-relief on the Arc-de-Triomphe) but in this case it has chosen coldness and austerity to represent the virtues of its great men *(10-12 & 2-4).*

▶ The history of the Panthéon is hardly one of airy gaiety. Soufflot, the architect of what was then the church of Sainte-Geneviève, died of grief after seeing that his building was fissuring progressively as its dome was raised. The church had hardly been completed when it was turned into a Republican temple, by vote of the Constituent Assembly, in order to "receive the great men of the epoch of French liberty" Mirabeau was the first to enter it, followed by Voltaire, Rousseau and Marat. Some of the great men became less great after their Revolution : Mirabeau and Marat were constrained to leave the premises, but the Third Republic installed Victor Hugo, Jean Jaurès and Gambetta. The day after his election, President François Mitterrand paid a visit to the building into which André Malraux had received the ashes of Jean Moulin, the Resistance hero, and where the frescoes of Puvis de Chavannes are in perfect harmony with the solemn, funereal atmosphere. □

■ PASSAGES DES GRANDS BOULEVARDS

B2 / 2nd arr. Métro : Bourse, Richelieu-Drouot, Rue Montmartre. Bus : 20, 29, 31, 48, 67, 68, 74, 85.

On the margins of the congested Grands Boulevards (→), are 19th century galleries and covered arcades which offer highly interesting walks; they can be found all over, from the Palais-Royal to the Faubourg St. Denis. With their anachronistic decoration, daring metal-and-glass roofs, old-fashioned shops and tea salons, the "Passages" survive at one remove from the commercial mainstream. Some have been restored and given a new lease on life; others have become a trifle sordid and dilapidated. The oldest, such as the Passage des Panoramas (Blvd. Montmartre, opened in 1808) witnessed all the fashionable crowds of the Restoration; figures like Balzac and Chopin used to frequent their shops and restaurants.

▶ The most beautiful gallery in Paris is probably the **Galerie Vivienne★**, which is broad and airy, with monumental decor and elegant paving. Fashion boutiques and tea shops have given this *passage* new life. By contrast, the **Passage Véro Dodat★** (1826), the **Passage Choiseul** and the **Passage Jouffroy** (→ box, "Musée Grévin") are devoted to old books, workshops or ... neglect. ▶ Not far from the Grands Boulevards, several galleries have opened in the Rue St. Denis. Most of these do a roaring down-market trade. The **Passage du Caire** is a headquarters for the wholesale cloth trade; originally created as a memorial to Napoleon's Egyptian campaign, it has now lost much of its former charm. The **"Passages du Grand Cerf"** and **"du Bourg-l'Abbé"**, on the other hand, have contrived to preserve their original 19thC decor. □

Unusual museums :
Public Health Museum
(Musée de l'Assistance publique)

In a fine 17thC aristocratic mansion, a display of ten centuries of medical history, bizarre instruments, anecdotes and curiosities. (47 Quai de la Tournelle, 5th arr. 10-5; closed Mon, Tue. and hols.).

■ PÈRE-LACHAISE Cemetery★★

C2 / 20th arr. Métro : Gambetta, Père-Lachaise. Bus : 26, 61, 69, 76.

The 125 acres of the Père-Lachaise Cemetery are half burial ground, half museum of 19thC sculpture. It is also a much-appreciated green area, full of tall trees *(7:30 or 8:30-5 or 6, according to season).*

▶ Many of France's most famous figures are buried in Père-Lachaise Cemetery; the place itself is remarkable for its staggering variety of monuments, ranging from the ridiculous to the sublime. Opened in 1803 by the Municipality, Père-Lachaise is not unmarked by the publicity surrounding the legendary tomb of Héloise and Abélard - but it has also had its authentically tragic moments. On the 28th of May 1871, the last 147 Communard insurgents were lined up and shot here against the **Mur des Fédérés** (Unionist's Wall); every year on the first of May, the procession of trade unionists comes to render them symbolic homage. □

■ PICASSO Museum★★

B2 / 5, rue de Thorigny, 3rd arr. Métro : St-Sébastien Froissard. Bus : 20, 29, 65, 96.

Inaugurated in September 1985, the Picasso Museum is housed in the Hôtel Salé, built in 1656 by Aubert de Fontenay, the collector of taxes on salt (hence the nickname "Salted Mansion"). The classical-styled building, superbly restored, is in keeping with the painter's preference for old residences; 6000 m^2 were cleared, and Diego Giacometti, the sculptor's brother, created the furniture and light fixtures *(daily 9:45-5:15 ex Tue, Wed till 10 p.m.).*

▶ This exceptional collection, comprised of 203 paintings, 158 sculptures, more than 3000 drawings and prints, collages and ceramics, was assembled according to a French law which permits payment of inheritance taxes with art works. Furthermore, Jacqueline Picasso contributed the painter's personal collection (paintings and drawings by Renoir, Cézanne, Rousseau, Derain, Braque, Matisse, Miró). The whole, unique in the world, permits a vast overview of the work of one of the century's greatest artists. □

■ Musée de la PUBLICITÉ (Advertising Museum)

B2 / 18, rue de Paradis, 10th arr. Métro : Gare de l'Est, Château d'Eau. Bus : 32, 39, 48.

The extraordinary development and expansion of advertising, from the early days of lithographed placards to modern posters, radio spots and TV commercials. This unique museum chronicles the precursors of the industry, along with its often neglected masters, whose talents have brightened the walls of city buildings over the years. Collection constantly being added to *(12-6; closed Tue.).* Posters by Toulouse-Lautrec, Mucha, Erté, Jacno, Colin and Morvan; also fine protest work from 1968 and a mine of cinema and TV publicity footage. Finally, notice the building itself, formerly the store for the Faïenceries de Choisy-le-Roi; in the courtyard and interior, very fine ceramic panels. □

■ RODIN Museum★★

B2 / 77, rue de Varenne, 7th arr. Métro : Varenne. Bus : 69, 87.

The splendid **Hôtel Biron,** built in 1730 to plans by the architect Gabriel, was originally lent to Rodin in exchange for a donation of his work and collections.

▶ The Rodin Museum is now installed in the surroundings where Rodin lived and worked between 1908 and his death in 1917. It is really a museum-cum-garden, offering a delightful open setting for the sculptor's creations. Here are represented all the phases of Rodin's development, from his youth (around 1875) to his evolution toward modern art in 1895, and his subsequent maturity, covering the years from 1900 onwards. Among the famous works in the museum are : "The Kiss"★★, an astonishing Balzac series, "The Thinker"★, maquettes for the "Bourgeois de Calais"★★, plasters and studies. The collections left by Rodin are of considerable interest : they include Monet ("Paysage de Belle-Isle"), Renoir, and two of Van Gogh's most celebrated canvases, "Le Père Tanguy"★★ and "The Harvesters"★★ *(10-5:30; closed Tue.).* □

■ Church of SAINT-EUSTACHE★

B2 / Rue Rambuteau, 1st arr. Métro : Les Halles. RER : Châtelet-Les Halles. Bus : 67, 74, 85.

This formidable stone building (1530-1640) has dominated Les Halles' skyline since the demolition of the old market. Its architecture is remarkably unified (considering that the work continued for over a century), the best of Renaissance style combining with the most sophisticated Gothic techniques.

▶ Saint-Eustache is only a church, despite its cathedral proportions. It was altered by Colbert, the parish benefactor (whose imposing tomb stands in a chapel behind the choir), then renovated by Baltard in the 19thC (façade); but its main tradition is musical. Rameau is buried here; Berlioz created and performed his Te Deum (1855) at Saint-Eustache, and Liszt gave a recital of his "Messe de Gran". The organ has been heavily restored; today, with its 8000 pipes and broad variety of tones, it is one of the largest instruments of its kind in Paris. □

■ SAINT-GERMAIN-DES-PRÉS★★

B2 / 6th arr. Métro : Saint-Germain-des-Prés. Bus : 39, 48, 63, 70, 86, 87, 95, 96.

More than just a church, more than just a *quartier,* Saint-Germain-des-Prés is heavily associated with the 1950's, when it was a centre for artists and intellectuals. Boris Vian's trumpet-playing, Juliette Greco's songs, the existentialists and the jazz cellars of Saint-Germain made the area's name, along with its famous cafés (the "Flore" and the "Deux Magots") and the venerable Brasserie Lipp. Places are hard to come by in these establishments, especially at Lipp, which is intensely exclusive at lunch and dinner times.

▶ Amid the turmoil, the **church of Saint-Germain-des-Prés**★★ stands behind its massive bell-tower porch (12thC), which has recently been cleaned. This building, though it has frequently been restored and repaired, constitutes the most important vestige of what used to be the oldest and most brilliant abbey in Paris. Saint Germain himself, who was bishop of Paris, inspired King Clovis to build a basilica on the Left Bank of the Seine in the year 545. The abbey that soon grew up around it took the name of Saint-Germain, and the foundations of the present church were laid in about the year 1000. The Romanesque nave is balanced by the early Gothic traits of the choir; the large paintings by H. Flandrin hanging here are somewhat aggressively 19thC. ▶ On the Rue de l'Abbaye side is the tomb of King Casimir of Poland (17thC) and a statue of St. François-Xavier by G. Coustou. ▶ Also nearby, but seeming a hundred miles from the bustle of the **Blvd. Saint-Germain,** is the tiny **Place Fürstenberg**★, with the air of a backward provincial town square. Nothing here but a lamp post and four catalpas on a small round island in the middle of an 18thC street. A few art galleries : No. 6 was **Delacroix's studio** until his death in 1863 *(museum, 9:45-5:15; closed Tue.).* That's all : yet, for many this little square on the former abbey courtyard is one of the most enchanting spots in all Paris. □

■ Church of SAINT-JULIEN-LE-PAUVRE★

B2 / Rue Saint-Julien-le-Pauvre, 5th arr. Métro : Maubert-Mutualité, Saint-Michel, Cité. RER : Saint-Michel. Bus : 21, 24, 27, 38, 47, 63, 85, 86, 87, 96.

The church of Saint-Julien-le-Pauvre has the air of a humble country church that has somehow wandered into one of the noisiest *quartiers* of Paris. The simplicity of this ancient sanctuary, which was once a shrine for pilgrims on their way to Santiago de Compostela, is a powerful contrast to the lavishness of the other great Parisian churches.

▶ Built in the 12thC, the church bears the scars of an eventful history. The style is halfway between Romanesque and Gothic; squat, without flying buttresses, St.-Julien nestles in the shadows of its little **square.** Each year, concerts of ancient and modern music are held here, particularly during the Paris summer festival. Saint-Julien-le-Pauvre owes allegiance to the Graeco-Byzantine church (closely akin to Greek Orthodox). ▶ Nearby is another sanctuary of a different kind. On the Rue de la Bûcherie, *Shakespeare and Company* is the temple of Anglo-Saxon literature in Paris, where everyone who was anyone in the small world of 20thC letters came to drink tea under the bookshelves. □

■ Île SAINT-LOUIS★★

B2 / 4th arr. Métro : Cité, Hôtel-de-Ville, Pont-Marie. Bus : 24, 47, 67, 86, 87.

When people from the Île Saint-Louis go across one of the bridges that connect the island with the rest of town, they say they're "going to Paris". The Île is indeed a world apart, as every visitor immediately realises.

▶ Originally the Île Saint-Louis was two islands; they were joined together and developed just before the mid-17thC. The most beautiful houses date from this time (**Hôtel Chenizot★,** 51 Rue St. Louis-en-l'Île : **Hôtel Lauzun★,** 17 Quai d'Anjou : **Hôtel Lambert★,** close by the Pont Sully). Nonetheless, it is the whole ensemble, rather than the individual buildings, which is important. Go down the **Quai d'Anjou,** the **Quai d'Orléans** (Nos. 6, 8, 20 and 22) and the **Quai de Bourbon.** With its glorious views★★ of the Cité, the Seine and the Left Bank, the Île Saint-Louis has managed to preserve its charm, in the face of the restaurants and *brasseries* which would wreck it if they could. Unfortunately, the great houses here are defended with similar ferocity and, with the exception of the sumptuous Hôtel de Lauzun, they are almost impossible to visit. *(Visits to the latter are organised by the Centre d'Accueil de la Ville de Paris, 29 rue de Rivoli.)* ▶ **Rue Saint-Louis-en-l'Île** is the best introduction to the island's special private atmosphere. No. 21, the **church of Saint-Louis★** (1656-1725) is in the Baroque Jesuit style. The chapels contain a fine selection of Italian paintings. But the street's most popular monument is unquestionably No. 31, which is Berthillon, the ice-cream shop; one of the best in Paris. □

■ Church of SAINT-MERRI

B2 / 78 Rue Saint-Martin. 4th arr. Métro : Châtelet, Hôtel-de-Ville. Bus : 21, 38, 47, 58, 69, 70, 72, 74, 75, 76, 85, 96.

The first period of the Renaissance in France (1515-1550) witnessed the building of a number of mansions between the Hôtel de Ville and the Rue Saint-Martin, which espoused the decorative principles of antiquity, as imported from Italy. Religious architecture, notwithstanding, remained faithful to the patterns set out during the golden age of Flamboyant Gothic; and it was as a Gothic church that Saint-Merri was planned. The 18thC to some extent bastardised it, with the copious addition of stucco and pompous motifs. This superimposed decoration has a certain advantage, all the same — looking at it, we may imagine what the vanished choir of Notre-Dame might have looked like. □

■ Church of SAINT-SÉVERIN★

B2 / Rue des Prêtres-Saint-Séverin. 5th arr. Metro : Saint-Michel. Bus : 21, 23, 27, 38, 47, 63, 81, 85, 86, 87, 96.

At the centre of this pedestrian precinct, with its mediaeval street-names (La Huchette, La Bûcherie, Le Chat-qui-Pêche) and pavement artists, the lovely nave of the **church of Saint-Séverin** broods over the galleries of a 15thC charnel house (labelled a "cloister").

▶ Built between 1414 and 1520, than extended in 1670, Saint-Séverin boasts a singular marvel : the astonishing column in its ambulatory, which is a masterpiece of Flamboyant Gothic, with arches fanning out in the form of palm fronds from its summit. The technical perfection and complexity of this ensemble marks the watershed of several centuries of architectural development. Saint-Séverin's other claim to fame is its magnificent organ (used by composers Saint-Saëns and Fauré) with many parts dating from the 18thC. Frequent organ concerts are held here. Also, stained glass★ (15th and 16thC) and modern windows by Bazaine. □

■ TUILERIES Gardens★★

B2 / 1st arr. Métro : Concorde, Palais-Royal, Tuileries. Bus : 21, 24, 27, 39, 48, 68, 69, 72, 81, 95.

The Tuileries Gardens offer one of the most delightful walks in Paris, along the Seine, from the Louvre to the Concorde; a distance of about one kilometre. The terraces beside the river, the garden with its pools and fountains, the merry-go-rounds and children's playgrounds, cover a site where the grim palace of the Kings of France once stood, until it was burned down by the Communard insurgents in 1871.

Unusual Museums : Musée Baccarat

Also known as the Crystal Museum, this little establishment has been set up next to the salesrooms of the Baccarat company, rue de Paradis (No. 30, 10th arr. 9-5; closed Sun.*), in the street which is the commercial centre for the glass and porcelain industries. The Musée Baccarat offers a unique demonstration of the French glassworker's art, as practised by a company that has existed since the 18thC and has worked for all the great families of Europe, from the Romanovs to the Hapsburgs. On display are some of Baccarat's most beautiful creations : giant candelabras, flagons, bowls, beakers, and glasses, in every colour and style. This exhibition will make you view the other shop windows in the quartier with a decidedly jaundiced eye...*

▶ First, take a stroll round the **Carrousel Gardens,** past Napoléon I's small triumphal arch and the bronzes by Maillol; then walk the whole way along the terraces on the Seine side. ▶ At the top end of the Tuileries (Place de la Concorde) are the **Orangerie★★** which houses the Walter-Guillaume collection *(9:45-5:15, closed Tue.)* and **Jeu de Paume Museums★★** (→). Both date from the Second Empire and are undergoing renovation, preparatory to the collections' inclusion in the Orsay Museum. □

Paris-on-the-Seine

Paris was born of a river; today the city counts no less than 33 bridges across the Seine. The oldest is the Pont Neuf, and the newest are the two spans of the Boulevard Périphérique (ring-road). Two recent reconstructions have been the Pont de l'Alma (with its famous Zouave statue, by whose feet and knees the flood-levels of the Seine are popularly measured), and the Pont des Arts, restored in 1984. The traditional clochards *(tramps) may still sleep under the arches on both sides of the river, but many have been driven away by the bankside expressway. There is, finally, no sense in visiting Paris without taking a walk or a boat-trip along the Seine.*

■ Place **VENDÔME★★**

B2 / 1st arr. Métro : Pyramides, Tuileries. Bus : 24, 42, 52, 84, 94.

Between the arcades of the Rue de Castiglione and the **Rue de la Paix,** the Place Vendôme opens out like a theatre set, starring the Ritz Hotel, Cartier, Van Cleef, Boucheron and others. This is the centre of the world of expensive jewelry and luxury products; the square itself is one of the most balanced and harmonious of the great squares built in honour of the Sun King, Louis XIV, an equestrian statue of whom once stood here — before the Revolution.

▶ Jules Hardouin-Mansart designed the Place Vendôme according to the requirements of Louvois and Louis XIV; the king and his minister were concerned for their future prestige, but they also had an eye for an excellent real-estate operation. The rigorous facades of the Place Vendôme, with their clear-cut horizontal lines, were completed in 1715 : the idea was that rich buyers could lay out their houses behind them just as they liked. Louis XIV's statue was knocked down during the Revolution, and replaced by Napoléon I with a tall column in his own honour. When the Bourbons returned after Waterloo, they appropriated this to themselves by crowning it with their emblem, the *fleur-de-lys.* Louis-Philippe put back the statue of Napoleon I; the Commune then pulled the whole thing down, at the instigation of the painter Courbet — and down it remained, for a few months. The unfortunate artist was condemned to put it up again at his own expense; the business ruined him, but it is to Courbet that we owe the present column and, at its top, the statue of Napoléon in Roman costume. □

Who runs Paris ?

The City of Paris is both a commune *and a* département. *Its 2200000 inhabitants are administered by a Mayor, who is elected by the 163 members of the Council of Paris. This council is both a municipal and a general governing body; it is elected by universal suffrage every six years. The Mayor of Paris shares his powers with a Prefect of Police. The same system prevails in each one of the twenty sub-mayoral districts of the capital, with a total of 326 district councillors* (conseillers d'arrondissements) *elected by universal suffrage. These, in turn, elect the mayors of their own* arrondissements.

■ Place des **VICTOIRES★**

B2 / 1st and 2nd arr. Métro : Bourse. Bus : 20, 21, 29, 39, 48, 67, 74, 85.

Designed like the Place Vendôme by Jules Hardouin-Mansart in honour of Louis XIV, the Place des Victoires was abandoned in the 19thC to merchants and tradesmen who installed shop windows in the beautiful 1700 facades.

▶ The Restoration replaced its equestrian statue of Louis XIV, but the whole spirit of the Place des Victoires was considered irretrievably lost when the Rue Étienne Marcel was driven through in 1883. Fortunately, a concerted renovation project has now restored the Place to its former glory; it has become a centre for high fashion and luxury ready-to-wear clothes.
▶ Nearby is the **church of Notre-Dame-des-Victoires,** founded by Louis XIII and built in the 17th and 18thC. More interesting, perhaps, than the bust of Lully (1702) or the fine *boiseries* in the choir, are the ex-voto tablets that cover the church's walls — there are more than 30000! □

Shopping in Paris

Most visitors to Paris see it as the capital of French luxury commerce, fashion and the art of good living. Yet Paris owes a lot to talented foreigners living here, who have become some of its greatest creators : Japanese and Italians for fashion and luxury goods, Greeks for jewelry, even Englishmen for wines! As to fashion, you will always find in Paris the great names of the past, the severe, the outrageous, the avant-garde, haute-couture and ready-to-wear, along with the traditional fashion strongholds like the Faubourg St. Honoré, Place des Victoires, Boulevard des Capucines, St-Germain-des-Prés and Les Halles. One piece of advice : if you want to save time, go straight to see "what people are wearing" in the two leading department stores, Printemps and Galeries Lafayette. See also the list of good shopping addresses in the pages following.

■ **LA VILLETTE**

C1 / ® / 19th arr. Métro : Porte de la Villette. Bus : 60.

The 55 hectare park which occupies the site of the former slaughterhouses, constructed in 1866, of which survives the Mérindols★ Grande Halle (250 m long, 81 m wide, 25 m high), is the object of one of the greatest urban projects of our time. In 1986 there is scheduled the opening by stages of the Museum of Science, Technology and Industry which will house permanent and temporary exhibitions, a planetarium, a discovery centre for children, a media centre and a centre of education; the "Géode", a highly polished sphere of stainless steel, 36 m in diameter, containing a hemispherical spectacle-hall, equipped with a 1000 m² screen, was opened in 1985 *(11-6:30, Tue., Thu., Sun.; 11-11:30, Wed., Fri., Sat., closed Mon.)*; Music City will comprise a conservatoire, an Instrument Museum, a centre of education and research and concert halls for both classical and modern music, of which the "Zenith" is already in operation. The park of 30 hectares, crossed by the Ourcq canal, will be enlivened by fountains, follies for games, restaurants and a centre for children.

Suburbs

■ ALBERT KAHN Gardens★

9, Quai du 4-Septembre, Boulogne-Billancourt. Métro : Pont-de-Saint-Cloud. Bus : 52, 72.

The Albert Kahn Gardens (Jardins Albert Kahn) are as filled with contrasts as the life of the turn-of-the-century adventurer for whom they are named. Extraordinary juxtaposition of pinewoods, rock garden, orchard, English park, Japanese garden; astonishingly varied collection of flowers from all over the world. A veritable garden museum. *(9:30-12:30 & 2-6; 15 Mar.-15 Nov.)*. Note : the paper houses, the tea pavilion where sometimes on Sunday at 4 the traditional ceremony is performed. Alongside the **House of Nature,** the first of its kind established in an urban situation, organises activities for young people and exhibitions (1, rue des Abondances). The photographic and cinematographic library shows different films belonging to the Albert Kahn collection (10, quai du 4 Septembre).

■ La DÉFENSE★

Pont de Neuilly, Puteaux. Métro : Pont de Neuilly; RER : La Défense. Bus : 73.

The largest agglomeration of offices in Europe, and France's largest commercial centre, La Défense was originally designed some fifteen years ago as a kind of Paris Manhattan, built in the old quarters of Puteaux, Nanterre and Courbevoie.

▶ La Défense has its commercial centre, Exhibition Halls (Palais des Expositions★ - Centre National des Industries et des Techniques) and headquarters of giant companies. But of late it has also become a pleasant place to walk about. The areas around the skyscraper towers have been converted to pedestrian precincts, and special efforts have been made to maintain an atmosphère of constant animation. This is supplied by the *CNIT's* exhibitions (computer science, domestic arts, boat show, etc.), along with jazz and classical music concerts in summer. There are also art exhibitions devoted to young contemporary artists. Streams of water, a musical fountain, sculptures and (shortly) a monumental gateway complete this gigantic project, which is now a vital component of the arterial route running out westwards from the Concorde and the Étoile. □

■ Château de MALMAISON★★★ and de BOIS-PRÉAU★

® / R.E.R. La Défense, then 158A bus.

A temporary residence of Napoléon during the Consulate, and later, Empress Josephine's retreat, Malmaison and its "annex", the Bois-Préau, offer a marvelous example of Empire-style decoration : furniture, paintings, memorabilia *(10-12 & 1:30-4:30 or 5)*. In the **park★**, rose garden. ▶ 3 km S. : ponds of Saint-Cucufa. □

■ MEUDON

® / SNCF (Montparnasse station); R.E.R. line C; 136, 169, 179 buses.

On the edge of its **forest** (wooded parks, play areas), at the foot of the terrace of its former château (*8:30-5:30 or 6;* **view★★** of Paris) and its **Observatory,** Meudon is a residential town. **Historical museum** (11, rue des Pierres) and **Rodin museum,** annex of the one in Paris, with the sculptor's tomb (19, av. Rodin, *Sat. and Sun., 1:30-5*). □

■ SAINT-CLOUD

® / SNCF (Saint-Lazare station); 52, 72, 144, 175 buses.

Terraced above Boulogne, Saint-Cloud has lost its château, but the **park★★** remains, where joggers mix with strollers. Steep paths lead down to the spectacular Grande Cascade (view★). Accessible by car, the Grand Parc spreads out towards the W. ▶ Beyond the **ponds of Ville d'Avray,** the Fausses-Reposes woods cover the heights between Vaucresson and Versailles. At the edge of Vaucresson, the **Butard pavilion** is a former hunting lodge of Louis XV. □

■ Basilica of SAINT-DENIS★★★

Métro : Saint-Denis Basilique. SNCF : all lines from Paris-Nord, except Crépy-en-Valois. Bus : 153, 155, 156, 170, 177.

Formerly an abbey church, the Basilica of Saint-Denis is one of the earliest examples of Gothic Art. The 13thC nave and transept are attributed to Pierre de Montreuil. The narthex (1130-1140) under the towers of the façade marks the first use of the Gothic pointed arch in a large building. Hence the Basilica of St.-Denis is a prelude to the extraordinary flowering of Gothic art in the centuries that followed, though it is visited more for its historical associations than for its architecture.

▶ Legend has it that Saint Denis, after his decapitation in 250, walked all the way up to the north of Paris, head in hands, to be buried there. Here an abbey was founded in 775. Following the example of King Dagobert and Hugues Capet, the Kings of France adopted the habit of having themselves buried in the basilica, which at intervals for over a thousand years resounded with the cry "Le Roi est mort, vive le Roi!" ("The King is dead, long live the King!"). During the Revolution, the royal tombs were desecrated and the statues mutilated; the treasury, which was the richest in all Christendom, was sold or melted down. For better or worse, Louis XVIII restored the basilica, of which he proved to be the last occupant. □

■ SCEAUX

® / R.E.R. line B; 128, 188, 194, 197, 297 buses

Colbert's château was destroyed, replaced by a replica which houses the **Île-de-France Museum** (*9-12 & 4-8, closed Tue.*; artistic and historical collections, exhibitions). The park, very "Grand Siècle", is intact; see the Grand Canal and the Octogone cascades, the Aurora pavilion (17thC), designed by Perrault, and the Hanover pavilion (18thC) which becomes a concert hall in summer. □

■ SÈVRES

® / Métro Pont de Sèvres

On the edge of the Saint-Cloud park, the **National Ceramics Museum★** retraces the history of this technique — and this art — from its origins to the present *(9:30-12 & 1:30-5:15, closed Tue.)*; Islamic and Chinese pieces, works from Delft, Nevers and, of course, Sèvres. □

■ Forest and Château of **VINCENNES**

C3 / Avenue de Paris, Vincennes. Métro : Château-de-Vincennes. Bus : 46, 56, 86.

The forest to which Saint Louis used to come to give judgement sitting under an oak-tree was cleared well before the Bois de Boulogne, at the beginning of the 18th century. The present facilities, lakes and rides of the Bois de Vincennes were organised during the Second Empire.

▶ The **zoological gardens★** *(9-5:30 or 6 in summer)* and **flower gardens** *(parc floral : 9:30-6:30)* attract many visitors from the eastern areas of Paris, as do the many grassy areas and sports grounds of the Bois de Vincennes. ▶ Not far from the flower gardens stand the forbidding walls of the **Château de Vincennes★,** surrounded by moats. This was originally the mediaeval palace of the Valois kings, and was embellished by Le Vau in the 17thC. After this it endured two centuries of military occupation, begun under Napoléon I, which almost completely obliterated the ancient stronghold. Recent restoration work has saved the ensemble, which is in two parts. The first *(10-5),* at the foot of the keep, is composed of the Sainte-Chapelle and various 15th and 16thC buildings. The second is the royal residence, constructed by order of Mazarin in 1654; here the pavilions of the king and queen face each other, perfect examples of classical elegance. □

● *Brief history*

53 BC-451 AD During the Gallic Wars, Caesar's army discovered a small township named **Lutetia** on what is now the Île de la Cité; it was inhabited by a small tribe called the **Parisii.** ● The Romans established themselves there, building a new town on the left bank of the river; with traffic thriving the Seine boatmen's corporation acquired an importance that lasted for ten centuries. ● **Saint Denis,** bishop of the town, converted the Parisii to Christianity, but was beheaded on the Butte Montmartre in the year 250. Two centuries later, **Sainte Geneviève,** a shepherdess from Nanterre, rallied the Parisians in their successful resistance to Attila's invading Huns (451).

5th-10thC **Clovis** was the first Christian chieftain of the whole of Gaul; he chose Paris as his capital and died there in 511. His successors extended and beautified the city. **King Dagobert** was buried at Saint-Denis. ● **Charlemagne** preferred Rome and Aix-la-Chapelle to Paris — his descendents signally failed to defend the city against the Norman onslaught. Paris was once more reduced to a small island town during the siege of 885-886.

10th-15thC

With the arrival of the Capetian kings on the throne of France, Paris once more became a centre of political power. Its mercantile prosperity favoured the Seine's right bank, which was low-lying and marshy; **Les Halles** (central markets) were founded in 1137, and remained on the same site for more than eight hundred years. ● The churches and royal palace of the Île de la Cité were joined in the 12thC by the **Cathedral of Notre Dame,** which was begun in 1163. The City's subsequent development obliged **King Philip Augustus** to build a defensive rampart, culminating in the fortress of the **Louvre** (1190). ● The left bank once more entered the picture with the foundation of the **University.** Meanwhile, the reputation of Paris was spreading. Saint Louis and Philippe le Bel built the **Sainte Chapelle** and extended the royal palace on the Île de la Cité. The population soon surpassed 200 000 and Paris became a focus for political, religious, economic and intellectual power. ● The revolt led by the ambitious merchant-provost Étienne Marcel created a deep and lasting suspicion of the subversive Paris populace in the minds of the French monarchs. Subsequently, the city was brought to the brink of ruin by the **Hundred Years' War.**

16th-18thC

Louis XII established the first grand rules for urban development; François I then tackled the reconstruction of the Louvre Palace, widened streets and forced the municipality to build a **Hôtel de Ville** (town hall) worthy of Paris. His reign marked the beginning of a veritable renaissance, during which the city acquired immense **intellectual prestige.** The Wars of Religion broke out in 1572, and eventually led to the devastation of part of the city. Henry IV quickly rebuilt it after his conversion to Catholicism, leaving, with the able assistance of Sully, a lasting testimonial to his concern for urban planning. Private promoters followed the King's example, and new ***quartiers*** sprang up all around (Île St. Louis, Faubourg Montmartre, Faubourg St. Germain, Faubourg St. Honoré, with the various mansions built by Mansart) along with religious foundations (Val-de-Grâce) spearheading the reaction against Protestantism. ● Louis XIV cared little for Paris after the **Fronde insurrections;** despite the triumphal arches he erected in the city (Porte St. Denis and Porte St. Martin) and the Paris squares built around his statue (Place des Victoires, Place Vendôme), the Sun King preferred his palace of Versailles, designed by Hardouin-Mansart, Le Brun and Le Nôtre. ● The 18th century was a period of unprecedented **economic growth.** For the first time, private houses were built with an eye to real comfort : Louis XV set about a number of major building projects within Paris (Place de la Concorde, Panthéon, Saint-Sulpice, École Militaire). On the eve of the Revolution, the population of Paris had increased to around 650 000. ● The Revolution left no buildings of note. On the contrary, its influence was mainly destructive; after the Bastille, many convents, churches and aristocratic mansions were pulled down. More seriously in terms of the future, the parks belonging to the nobility and the religious orders were annexed for other purposes — thus Paris was deprived of all its green spaces.

19thC

Napoléon turned Paris into the **capital** of his empire. His **organisational genius** was applied to the city's roads, drains and water supply, as well as to major public building projects like the Arc de Triomphe at the Carrousel, the Arc de Triomphe at the Étoile, the Stock Exchange (Bourse) and the Madeleine. ● Napoléon's ambitious street-widening projects were not realised till the arrival of **Haussmann** during the **Second Empire.** Meanwhile, apartment blocks and buildings swelled the faubourgs of Paris northward and eastward; these became hotbeds of revolution in 1830 and 1848. ● Napoléon III collected a remarkable team of planners to **reorganise Paris.** In the space of 15 years, he created a modern city. Broad boulevards pierced through the tangled alleys of former ages (Saint-Michel, de Sébastopol, de Strasbourg, de Magenta, Voltaire, Diderot, Saint-Germain, Malesherbes and Haussmann). The Baron Haussmann made it possible to get around Paris; and Alphand, with his green parks and gardens, made it possible to breathe (Parc Monceau, Buttes-Chaumont, Bois de Vincennes and Bois de Boulogne). At this period, the city swallowed up its faubourgs and inner suburbs, Auteuil, Passy, La Chapelle, Belleville, Bercy, Grenelle and Vaugirard. ● The **Commune,** a socialist/anarchist insurrection among the Paris populace, was bloodily repressed in May 1871 following Napoléon III's defeat by the Prussians at Sedan. The advent of the Third Republic saw a resumption of the capital's expansion. The Basilica of Sacré-Cœur (Montmartre) was built at this time, with construction in steel enjoying an immense vogue. **The Eiffel Tower,** steel's unrivalled showpiece, appeared in 1889. Development was also underway beneath the surface; drains, water pipes and electricity cables were laid. The first **Metropolitan Railway** (Métro) line opened in 1900.

20thC

The turn of the century, the ***Belle Époque*** to which a few Métro stations and buildings still bear witness, was quickly submerged in the 1914-1918 War. Paris emerged from this holocaust, only to plunge immediately into profound political and economic crisis. Concrete was used for the first time as a building material (Champs-Élysées Theatre) whilst the first low-rent apartment buildings significantly failed to relieve an acute **housing shortage.** ● During the **German Occupation** (June 1940-August 1944), a time of strict rationing, fear and Gestapo raids was offset by glittering and provocative night-life and real intellectual and artistic creativity. After the resistance uprising of the 19th and 20th August 1944, General Philippe Leclerc's tank division at last entered Paris on the 24th. ● Once it had been liberated by Allied forces, Paris undertook an intense effort of **reconstruction** and **modernisation.** The 1950's witnessed a crop of somewhat featureless buildings, and it was only in the 1960's that the "International" architectural style (glass, steel and aluminium) made its first appearance. (Unesco building, Maison de la Radio, Maine-Montparnasse complex, Palais des Congrès). ● In 1964, an **administrative rearrangement** separated Paris with its twenty arrondissements from "Greater Paris", which included 280 *communes* and a population of almost 10 million people living outside the Boulevard Périphérique (ring-road). Traffic and supply problems led to the demolition of the iron-structured Halles de Baltard (Central Market) in 1970, and to the controversial opening of the Seine bank expressways (Voies Express). ● In 1977, for the first time in history, Paris elected a **mayor.** Among the major problems he is facing at the present time are the growing depopulation of the city, the soaring cost of living accomodation, and the proliferation of offices. All these factors are gradually pushing Parisians into the suburbs. At the same time, the city administration must wrestle with the difficulties of coordinating ambitious state projects with the wishes of the people of Paris.

Practical information

Paris at a glance

☎ 1 ⊠ 75000

ℹ *Office de Tourisme de Paris,* 127, av. des Champs-Élysées, 75008, ☎ (1) 47.23.61.72. Open daily high season 9 am-10 pm (Sun 9 am-8 pm) ; low season, 9 am-8 pm (Sun 9 am-6 pm). Gare du Nord Office : ☎ (1) 45.26.94.82, at the international train arrival area. Gare de l'Est Office : arrival hall, ☎ (1) 46.07.17.73. Gare de Lyon Office : "Grandes Lignes" exit area, ☎ (1) 44.43.33.24. Gare d'Austerlitz Office : ☎ (1) 45.84.81.70, "Grandes Lignes" arrival area. Offices open daily ex Sun. Queues in summer can be lengthy !

Maison d'information culturelle de la Ville de Paris : 1, rue Pierre-Lescot, 75001, ☎ (1) 42.33.75.54 (automatic answering service). Open daily ex Sun from 10 am to 8 pm. All enq on cultural activities in Paris.

Paris Informations Loisirs : 24-hour service, ☎ (1) 47.20.94.94. In English : ☎ (1) 47.20.88.98. Deutsch : ☎ (1) 47.20.57.58.

Bureau d'Accueil de la Ville de Paris, 29, rue de Rivoli, ☎ (1) 42.77.15.40 (ex Sun).

Embassies and consulates : *American Embassy,* 2, av. Gabriel, 75008, ☎ (1) 42.96.12.02, the Consulate is at 2, rue St-Florentin, 75008 ; *British Embassy,* 35, rue du Faubourg-St-Honoré, 75008, ☎ (1) 42.66.91.42, the *Consulate* is at 105-109 ; *Canadian Embassy,* 35, av. Montaigne, 75008, ☎ (1) 47.23.01.01 or (1) 47.23.52.20 ; *Irish Embassy,* 4, rue Rude, 75016, ☎ (1) 45.00.20.87.

Further information : the most detailed sources of information for the visitor are the weeklies *Une semaine de Paris-Pariscope, l'Officiel des Spectacles, 7 à Paris,* which come out on Wed and are sold at all news-stands ; these weekly publications provide full information on theatres, shows, cinemas, concerts, exhibitions, festivals, etc., along with practical information and leisure centres. The monthly English language newspaper *Passion* is also an excellent source of information on Parisian events and topics.

Guided tours : the C.N.M.H.S. (National Monuments Board ; → Monuments and Museums) organises daily lectures and visits in Paris. Enq : 63, rue Saint-Antoine, 75004, ☎ (1) 48.87.24.14, and in numerous daily newspapers. Independent lecturers and associations ; see the forementioned weeklies and daily newspapers. Special tours for children : *Paris-Baskets,* ☎ (1) 42.77.23.31.

Post Office : *Central Post Office,* 52, rue du Louvre, ☎ (1) 42.33.71.60. Open all night.

Banks : open daily ex Sat, Sun and nat hols. Some foreign exchange offices open on Sat. Banks close at noon on days preceding nat hols, and all day on nat hols.

Foreign exchange offices : open every day at : Gare de Lyon, ☎ (1) 43.41.52.70 (7 am to 11 pm) ; 125, av. des Champs-Élysées, ☎ (1) 47.20.77.19 (8:45 am to 5:15 pm ; Sat and Sun from 10:30 am to 1 pm and 2-4 pm). Open daily ex Sun : 117, av. des Champs-Élysées, ☎ (1) 47.23.27.22 (9 am to 8 pm). Open Mon to Sun : Gare de l'Est, ☎ (1) 42.06.51.97, 7 am to 9 pm. Gare du Nord, ☎ (1) 42.80.11.50 (6:30 am to 10 pm). Gare d'Austerlitz, ☎ (1) 45.84.91.40 (7 am to 9 pm). Gare Saint-Lazare, ☎ (1) 43.87.72.51 (7 am to 9 pm). Porte Maillot, ☎ (1) 47.58.22.05 (9 to 12:30 and 1:45 to 4).

American Express, 11, rue Scribe, 75009, ☎ (1) 42.66.09.99 (9 to 5 Mon-Sat) ; *Thomas Cook,* 2, place de la Madeleine, ☎ (1) 42.60.33.20.

Maps : Paris, plans Neufs G T 1/12 500 (Éd. Gabelli) ; Michelin plan.

Audio-guide : cassettes for Paris visitors, for sale at the Paris Tourism Office, at the Centre Pompidou, in leading department stores, and at record shops and certain book-shops.

S.O.S. : *SAMU* (Emergency Medical Service) Paris, ☎ (1) 45.67.50.50. *S.O.S. Médecins,* ☎ (1) 47.07.77.77. *SAMU* **Hauts-de-Seine,** ☎ (1) 47.41.79.11. *SAMU* **Val-de-Marne,** ☎ (1) 42.05.51.41. *Poisoning Emergency Centre,* ☎ (1) 42.05.63.29. *Police,* ☎ 17. *Lost and found,* 36, rue des Morillons, 75015, ☎ (1) 45.31.14.80.

Weather forecast : ☎ (1) 45.55.91.90.

✈ *Charles-de-Gaulle/Roissy-en-France,* 25 km N, ☎ (1) 48.62.22.80. *Air France :* information, ticket sales and bookings, ☎ (1) 45.35.61.61. *Air Inter :* information, bookings, ☎ (1) 45.39.25.25. Access : R.E.R. line B, direction *Roissy-Rail,* trains at approx 15 min intervals. R.A.T.P. bus nº 350 Gare de l'Est and Gare du Nord ; nº 351 departure pl. de la Nation. Air France buses : terminal porte Maillot, departure every 15 min. *Orly-Sud* and *Ouest,* 14 km S, ☎ (1) 48.84.32.10. Access : R.E.R. line C, direction *Orly Rail ;* trains at approx 15 min intervals until 9 pm. R.A.T.P. bus nº 215, departure pl. Denfert-Rochereau ; 183A, departure porte de Choisy, and 285, departure porte d'Italie, dir. Savigny-sur-Orge, which passes through the airport. Air France buses, Invalides terminal ; departure every 12 min.

SNCF (French Railways) Gare du Nord, northern region, ☎ (1) 42.80.03.03. Gare de l'Est, eastern region, ☎ (1) 42.08.49.90. Gare de Lyon, south-east region, ☎ (1) 43.45.92.22. Gare d'Austerlitz, south west region, ☎ (1) 45.84.16.16. Gare Montparnasse, western region, ☎ (1) 45.38.52.29. Gare Saint-Lazare, western region, ☎ (1) 45.38.52.29. *S.N.C.F. Central Enq. Office :* ☎ (1) 42.61.50.50.

Metro : R.A.T.P. Central Enquiries Office : 53, quai des Grands-Augustins, 75006, ☎ (1) 43.46.14.14. Maps of the urban and regional express network are posted and distributed at all stations. The first trains run from 5 am or 5:30 am for the regional express network (R.E.R.), and from 5:30 am for the urban metro. The last trains leave the terminus at between 12:30 am and 1 am according to the line, all trains being scheduled to arrive at their final destinations by 1:15 am. Apart from the Charenton-Écoles — Créteil sections (line nº 8) and carrefour Pleyel — Saint-Denis (line nº 13), cost of the Metro ticket (1st or 2nd class) is fixed, independent of the length of the journey or the number of changes of line.

R.E.R. : The Regional Express Network comprises three lines : Line A : Saint-Germain-en-Laye-Boissy-Saint-Léger or Marne-la-Vallée. Line B : Saint-Rémy-lès-Chevreuse or Robinson-Châtelet-Roissy or Mitry-Claye. Line C : Saint-Quentin-en-Yvelines-Dourdan, Massy or Étampes.

City bus service : The map of the city bus network is posted on Metro station quays, bus shelters and main bus stations. Except for the « PC » line (Petite Ceinture - inner ring-road), the lines are numbered. Tariff : 1 2nd class Metro ticket for 1 or 2 section trips, 2 Metro tickets for any trips exceeding 2 sections. Special tariffs for the PC line.

Tourist passes : these allow an unlimited number of trips for 2, 4 or 7 day periods on all R.A.T.P. lines (Metro, R.E.R., buses), and are sold in 50 metro stations, in Paris railway stations and at the Paris Tourism Office. If you are staying a while in Paris, it might be worth buying an "orange card", allowing unlimited travel for a calendar month on the R.A.T.P. networks or a "yellow card" valid Mon-Sun, within the allocated zones. The R.A.T.P. also proposes "orange card coupons", valid for one day.

Taxis : a few of the many taxi service numbers : ☎ (1) 47.39.33.33, (1) 42.03.99.99, (1) 42.05.77.77, (1) 42.70.41.41.

Driving in Paris : Do not use your car in Paris unless it's absolutely necessary ; traffic is extremely dense, with numerous traffic jams. Parking places, if there are any, must be paid for. It is thus preferable to use public transport and to leave your vehicle at one of the many car-parks at the "portes de Paris" (the main entrances to the city on the ring-road, the Boulevard Périphérique).

Car-hire : *Budget* train + auto, 4, av. Franklin-Roosevelt, 75008, ☎ (1) 42.25.79.89 ; Gare St-Lazare, ☎ (1) 42.85.88.00, ext 2744 ; Gare de l'Est, ☎ (1) 42.03.96.31, ext 11506 ; Gare du Nord, ☎ (1) 42.80.63.63, ext 11842 ; Gare de Lyon, ☎ (1) 43.43.14.52 ; 10, rue de Bercy, 75012, ☎ (1) 43.07.50.43 ; Gare d'Austerlitz, ☎ (1) 45.84.14.18, ext 11343 ; Gare Montparnasse, ☎ (1) 45.38.52.19, ext 11433, and 21-23, rue du Départ, 75014, ☎ (1) 43.21.56.50 ; Porte Maillot : 71, bd Gouvion-St-Cyr, 75017, ☎ (1) 45.72.11.13 ; 51, rue Marx-Dormoy, 75018, ☎ (1) 46.07.93.05 ; Paris-La Défense : Quatre Temps Commercial Centre, pl. de la Patinoire, ☎ (1) 47.78.43.44 ; Orly-Ouest aérogare, ☎ (1) 48.84.46.08/56.08 ; aérogare de Roissy I, ☎ (1) 48.62.50.56/57 ; aérogare de Roissy II, ☎ (1) 48.62.50.58/59 ; Rueil, 78, av. Paul-Doumer, ☎ (1) 47.49.72.74.

Aerial views of Paris : Paris-Hélicoptère, héliport de Paris, ☎ (1) 45.54.12.55 ; Métro Balard.

Paris by bus : *France Tourisme Paris Vision,* 214, rue de Rivoli, 75001, ☎ (1) 42.60.30.01 and 42.60.31.25. *Cityrama Rapid-Pullman,* 4, pl. des Pyramides, 75001, ☎ (1) 42.60.30.14.

Excursion on the Seine : *bateaux-mouches (Seine launch service) :* pont de l'Alma, 75007, ☎ (1) 42.25.96.10. *Bateaux parisiens/Tour Eiffel,* pont d'Iéna, 75007, ☎ (1) 45.51.33.08. *Vedettes (launches) du Pont-Neuf,* pont Neuf, 75001, ☎ (1) 46.33.98.39. *Nautic Croisières,* quai du Point-du-Jour, pont de Boulogne, 92100 Boulogne, ☎ (1) 46.21.48.15. *Vedettes de Paris et de l'Ile-de-France,* port de Suffren, 75007, ☎ (1) 47.05.71.29.

Bicycle-hire : cottage next to the *Relais du Bois,* 9, rue de la Faisanderie, 75116, Wed, Sat, Sun and hols ; daily Jul-Aug ; or *Locations Vertes,* bois de Vincennes and bois de Boulogne, ☎ (1) 42.37.39.10.

On the Paris canals : *Patache Eautobus,* a 3 hour morning excursion, leaving from the quai Anatole-France (Metro : Solférino) to the Villette basin, up the Seine and the canal St-Martin ; vice versa in the afternoon, daily ex nat hols from May to Nov. Booking essential : ☎ (1) 48.74.75.30. *Canauxrama :* from the Villette basin (Metro : Jean-Jaurès) to the Arsenal port (Metro : Bastille) ; the canal de l'Ourcq, from Paris to Meaux. Bookings : from 9 am to 1 pm, ☎ (1) 46.24.86.16.

Markets : *Saint-Ouen flea-market,* Sat, Sun and Mon from 9 am to 7 pm. *Montreuil flea-market :* Sat and Sun. *Flower-market :* daily ex Sun from 8 am to 7 pm. *Stamp and post-card market :* Thu, Sat, Sun and nat hols from 9 am to 6:30 pm, angle av. Marigny and av. Gabriel, near the Champs-Élysées roundabout.

Auction rooms : *Nouveau Drouot,* 9, rue Drouot, 75009, ☎ (1) 42.46.17.11. Daily ex Sun from 11 am to 6 pm.

Major department stores : open from Mon to Sat, from 9:30 am to 6:30 pm ; *Bazar de l'Hôtel de Ville,* 52, rue de Rivoli, 75004, ☎ (1) 42.74.90.00. *Bon Marché,* 38, rue de Sèvres, 75007, ☎ (1) 42.60.33.45. *Galeries Lafayette,* 40, bd Haussmann, 75009, ☎ (1) 42.82.34.56. *Printemps,* 64, bd Haussmann, 75009, ☎ (1) 42.85.22.22. *Samaritaine,* 19, rue de la Monnaie, 75001, ☎ (1) 45.08.33.33. *Trois Quartiers,* bd de la Madeleine, opposite the Madeleine, 75001, ☎ (1) 42.60.39.30.

Cultural events : **Apr-May** : *Paris Poetry Festival ; Traditional Arts Festival.* **Jun** : *Mozart Festival.* **May-Jul** : *Ile-de-France Festival.* **Jun-Jul** : *festival du Marais.* **Summer** : *Festival estival de Paris ; Festival de l'Orangerie de Sceaux.* **Sep-Dec** : *Paris International Dance Festival ; Autumn Festival.* **Sep** : *Paris Chamber Music Festival.* **Oct** : *Jazz Festival.* **Nov** : *Paris International Festival of Fantastic and Science Fiction Films.*

Other events : these are many and varied, including such events as the Foire de Paris, the Salon du Prêt-à-Porter and the Paris Marathon. For all info contact the hostesses at the mairie de Paris, ☎ (1) 42.76.40.40. Lists of these events can be found in the brochures published by the Paris Tourist Office and the Ville de Paris, and in the weeklies *Pariscope, L'Officiel des Spectacles,* etc.

Room and board with a Paris resident : the Paris Tourism Office proposes up to 500 rooms with residents in Paris and the suburbs, ranging from single bed-rooms with toilet facilities to independent one-room flats with bath-room, suitable for 2 or 3 persons.

Lodging for young people : *U.C.R.I.F., (→ Young people),* 20, rue J.-J.-Rousseau, 75001, ☎ (1) 42.36.88.18. *A.J.F.,* 12, rue des Barres, 75004, ☎ (1) 42.72.72.09.

⛺ ★★★*Paris-Ouest-Bois de Boulogne,* rte du Bord-de-l'Eau (500 pl.), ☎ (1) 45.06.14.98. *Paris-Issy-les-Moulineaux* (48 pl.), ☎ (1) 46.38.07.66. ★★★*Le Tremblay-Champigny-sur-Marne* (308 pl. ; access N4, A4), ☎ (1) 42.83.38.24.

Hotels and restaurants

PARIS 1st

Hotels :

★★★★(L) ***Ritz,*** 5, pl. Vendôme, 75001, ☎ (1) 42.60.38.30. Tx 220262, 670112. AE, DC, Euro, Visa. 163 rm, 42 apart. P ♨ ♿ The favourite residence of Chanel and E. Hemingway, in the most prestigious square in Paris, 1 900. Rest. ● ♦♦♦♦ ***l'Espadon.*** Excellent fare. ♿ Gilbert Le Gay creates classic cooking for a great hotel. Spec. : *assiette de petits hors-d'œuvre Escoffier, raviolis de fruits de mer mousse à la cresson, canette de Barbarie, pêches au vin d'orange,* 250-500.

★★★★(L) ***Meurice,*** 228, rue de Rivoli, 75001, ☎ (1) 42.60.38.60. Tx 230673. AE, DC, Euro, Visa. 160 rm, 32 apart. P ♿ View over the Tuileries Gardens, 1 600. Rest. ♦♦♦ 220-310.

★★★★(L) ***Intercontinental,*** 3, rue de Castiglione, 75001, ☎ (1) 42.60.37.80. Tx 220114. AE, DC, Euro, Visa. 500 rm including 27 apart. ♨ ♿ Garnier's historic façades, 1 650. Rest. ♦♦ ***la Rôtisserie Rivoli*** ♿ 270-310, and ♦♦ ***le Café Tuileries,*** 120-210. Discotheque.

★★★★(L) ***Lotti,*** 7, rue de Castiglione, 75001, ☎ (1) 42.60.37.34. TX 240066. AE, DC, Euro, Visa. 130 rm, 2 apart. ♿ Calm and perfect, discreet service, 1 500. Rest. ♦♦ and grill-room ♦ 210-320.

★★★★***Castille,*** 37, rue Cambon, 75001, ☎ (1) 42.61.55.20. 76 rm ♿ 980. Rest. ♦♦ ***Relais Castille*** ♿ 150-200.

★★★★***Saint-James et Albany,*** 202, rue de Rivoli, 75001, ☎ (1) 42.60.31.60, Tx 213031. AE, DC, Euro, Visa. 208 rm, 3 apart. ♨ View of the 18 thC Hôtel de Noailles, 660. Rest. ♦♦ ***le Noailles,*** 100-180.

★★★★***Mayfair,*** 3, rue Rouget-de-l'Isle, 75001, ☎ (1) 42.60.38.14. Tx 240037. AE, DC, Euro, Visa. ♿ 720.

★★★***Molière,*** 21, rue Molière, 75001, ☎ (1) 42.96.22.01. 32 rm, 3 apart. 350.

★★★***Brighton,*** 218, rue de Rivoli, 75001, ☎ (1) 42.60.30.03. Tx 217431. 70 rm 415.

★★***Agora,*** 7, rue de la Cassonnerie, 75001, ☎ (1) 42.33.46.02. 28 rm In the heart of Les Halles, 300.

★★***Ducs de Bourgogne,*** 19, rue du Pont-Neuf, 75001, ☎ (1) 42.33.95.64. Visa. 49 rm ♿ 260.

★***Le Palais,*** 2, quai de la Mégisserie, 75001, ☎ (1) 42.36.98.25. 22 rm on the Seine 175.

Restaurants :

♦♦♦♦ ***Le Grand Véfour,*** 17, rue de Beaujolais, 75001, ☎ (1) 42.96.56.27. AE, DC, Euro, Visa P ♿ closed 29 Jul-27 Aug, Sat and Sun. The historically-classified decor has been freshened up, and the impressive ballet of waiters and maître d'hôtel enhances chef Signoret's lighter cooking. One still expects Raymond Oliver to come pay his respects, 320-450.

● ♦♦♦ ***Carré des Feuillants,*** 14, rue de Castiglione, 75001, ☎ (1) 42.96.67.92. Alain Dutournier's longtime dream of a beautiful, classy restaurant has at last come true. (He still supervises ***le Trou Gascon*** which is now managed by his competent, charming wife.) Here it is something else, and he does his at most to satisfy his stylish clientele, 350-400.

● ♦♦♦ ***Le Mercure Galant,*** 15, rue des Petits-Champs, 75001, ☎ (1) 42.97.53.85. closed Sat noon, Sun and hols. Good service in an extremely elegant dining-room. Spec : *feuilleté de langoustines,* 170-210.

● ♦♦♦ ***Gérard Besson,*** 5, rue Coq-Héron, 75001, ☎ (1) 42.33.14.74. DC, Visa ♿ closed 3 weeks Jul, 2 weeks year-end, Sat and Sun. Very good cooking, refined service, 120-310.

● ♦♦♦ ***Pierre Traiteur*** (Guy Nouyrigat), 10, rue de Richelieu, 75001, ☎ (1) 42.96.09.17. AE, DC, Visa ♿ closed Sat, Sun and Aug. In this Parisian institution, Guy Nouyrigat, and his team prepare marvellous Auvergne specialities : *terrines, jambon persillé, foie gras, estofinade Rouergate, bœuf ficellé* and pleasant Loire wines, 220-310.

● ♦♦♦ ***Hubert,*** 25, rue de Richelieu, 75001, ☎ (1) 42.96.48.07. Tx 210311. AE, Visa P ♿ closed Sun, Mon. Thanks to Hubert, the 1900's decor and modern cooking go well together, and the menu is constantly being improved. Good cheeses and light desserts, 150-280.

♦♦♦ ***Prunier-Madeleine,*** 9, rue Duphot, 75001, ☎ (1) 42.60.36.04. AE, DC, Euro, Visa. ♿ Spec. : *langouste au basilic, salade Prunier,* 200-300.

● ♦♦ ***Le Globe d'Or,*** 158, rue St-Honoré, 75001, ☎ (1) 42.60.23.37. Gérard Constiaux and wife Christiane will soon have gourmets running to try their good southwest cooking, 170-260.

● ♦♦ ***A la Grille Saint-Honoré,*** 15, pl. du Marché-St-Honoré, 75001, ☎ (1) 42.61.00.93. AE, Visa ♿ closed Sat and Sun. Christine and Bernard Charretton's traditional restaurant featuring the good cooking of D. Cassagne. A daily special for 145. Spec : *raviolis de crabe beurre blanc et herbes, filet de dorade grillé aux légumes frits, pot-au-feu "à la Grille",* 145-240.

● ♦♦ ***Les Bouchôleurs,*** 34, rue de Richelieu, 75001, ☎ (1) 42.96.06.86. Closed Sat, Sun noon, 3 weeks in spring, 1 week in mid-Aug. The true *moule de bouchots* from L'Aiguillon-sur-Mer, in the Vendée region, is served in all its delicious forms, 120-210.

♦♦ ***La Main à la Pâte,*** 35, rue Saint-Honoré, 75001, ☎ (1) 42.36.64.73. AE, DC, Visa ♿ closed Sun. Good Italian cooking, served until late evening. Spec : *carpaccio, jardinet des Quatre Pâtes,* 80-200.

● ♦♦ ***Chez Pauline,*** 5, rue Villedo, 75001, ☎ (1) 42.96.20.70. Visa. 4 weeks Jul, 1 week end-year, Sat eve and Sun. André Genin adds light dishes to the solid traditional ones. Excellent Beaujolais wines. Spec : *raie au chou nouveau, bœuf bourguignon,* 250-310.

● ♦♦ ***Pharamond,*** 24, rue de la Grande-Truanderie, 75001, ☎ (1) 42.33.06.72. AE, DC, Visa P closed Jul, Sun and Mon noon. Authentic *Belle Époque* setting. Normandy specialities, 90-170.

● ♦♦ ***Chez la Vieille,*** 37, rue de l'Arbre-Sec, 75001, ☎ (1) 42.60.15.78 closed Sat, Sun, lunch noon only. Very few tables (booking necessary) to discover and appreciate Adrienne Biasin's authentic, generous cooking prepared in limited space : *pot au bœuf, bœuf gros sel, rognons, côte de veau, faux-filet, tomates farcies.* If you are starving, unlimited helpings of hors-d'œuvres and desserts, 150-230.

♦♦ ***Ruc-Univers,*** pl. du Théâtre-Francais, 75001, ☎ (1) 42.60.31.57. AE, DC, Euro, Visa. Open till 1:30 am ; the ideal place to sup after the show. Spec : *filet de sole au coulis de poivron rouge, aiguillette de canard de Barbarie vallée d'Auge,* 100-140.

♦♦ ***Le Caveau des Chevillards,*** 1, rue St-Hyacinthe, 75001, ☎ (1) 42.61.19.74. AE, DC, Visa ; closed Sat noon and Sun. Good value-for-money fare in magnificent vaulted dining-rooms, 100-180.

♦♦ ***Escargot Montorgueil,*** 38, rue Montorgueil, 75001, ☎ (1) 42.36.83.51. AE, DC, Euro, Visa closed 1 week 15 Aug, 1 May, 1 Jan, Mon and Tue. A stunning setting ; six snail specialities, and the *Montorgueil turbot*, 180-280.

♦♦ ***Chez Clovis,*** 33, rue Berger, 75001, ☎ (1) 42.33.97.07. AE, Visa ♿ closed Aug and Sun. Traditional *cuisine bourgeoise*, 70-120.

♦♦ ***Pavillon,*** 9, rue Coquillière, 75001, ☎ (1) 42.36.22.00. AE, DC, Euro, Visa ♿ Alsatian regional dishes ; 12 different sorts of *choucroute*, 160.

● ♦ ***La Barrière Poquelin,*** 17, rue Molière, 75001, ☎ (1) 42.96.22.19. AE, DC, Visa ; closed 1-20 Aug, Sat noon and Sun. Delightful decor for M. Guillaumin's fine light cooking : Spec : *Lapin aux navets Barrière, escalope de cervelle aux épinards*, 130-300.

● ♦ ***Porte du Bonheur,*** 8, rue du Mont-Thabor, 75001, ☎ (1) 42.60.55.99. AE, DC, Euro, Visa ♿ One of the best Chinese restaurants in Paris. Fine, subtle dishes ; if you go in a group, order a Chinese banquet from Mr. Chong, 55-150.

♦ ***Au Pied de Cochon,*** 6, rue Coquillière, 75001, ☎ (1) 42.36.11.75. AE, DC, Visa ♿ "New-look" for this institution which never closes, 120-200.

♦ ***La Vigne,*** 30, rue de l'Arbre-Sec, 75001, ☎ (1) 42.60.13.55. In this old Halles bistro, a young woman offers solid, traditional cooking. Spec : *œufs en meurette à la moelle, magret de canard à l'orange, onglet de bœuf à l'auvergnate*, 115-140.

♦ ***La Ferme Irlandaise,*** 30, pl. du Marché-St-Honoré, 75001, ☎ (1) 42.96.02.99. Irish stew and good Irish meats, 80-130.

♦ ***La Fermette du Sud-Ouest,*** 31, rue Coquillière, 75001, ☎ (1) 42.36.73.55. Visa closed Sun and Aug. Good, rich cooking from Périgord, 80-200.

♦ ***Joe Allen,*** 30, rue Pierre-Lescot, 75001, ☎ (1) 42.36.70.13. Spec : American salads, apple-pies, 100-130.

♦ ***Yakitori,*** 34, pl. du Marché-St-Honoré, 75001, ☎ (1) 42.61.03.64. Delicious and inexpensive Japanese shish kabob, 40-60.

PARIS 2nd

Hotels :

★★★★(L) ***Westminster,*** 13, rue de la Paix, 75002, ☎ (1) 42.61.57.46. AE, DC, Euro, Visa. 102 rm, 18 apart. P ♿ Almost next-door to the Opéra, 1250. Rest. ♦♦♦ ***Céladon*** ♿ closed Aug, Sat and Sun, 180-350.

● ★★★★***Edouard VII,*** 39, av. de l'Opéra, 75002, ☎ (1) 42.61.56.90. Tx 680217. AE, DC, Visa. 95 rm, 5 apart. P ♿ 760.

★★★***Ascot Opéra,*** 2, rue Monsigny, 75002, ☎ (1) 42.96.87.66. 36 rm, 650.

★★★***Favart,*** 5, rue Marivaux, 75002, ☎ (1) 42.97.59.83. (1) 42.97.53.34. Tx 213126. 38 rm ♿ 380.

★★★***Métropole-Opéra,*** 2, rue de Gramont, 75002, ☎ (1) 42.96.91.03. Tx 212276. AE. 52 rm ♿ An old hotel renovated, 380.

★★***Nouveau Monde,*** 98, rue de Cléry, 75002, ☎ (1) 42.33.22.37. 48 rm, 250.

Restaurants :

♦♦♦ ***Drouant,*** 18, rue Gaillon, 75002, ☎ (1) 47.42.56.51. closed 15-31 Aug. Spec : oysters and fish, *suprême de turbot chamery, noisette de chevreuil à la Diane*, 160-300.

● ♦♦ ***La Corbeille,*** 154, rue Montmartre, 75002, ☎ (1) 42.61.30.87. ♿ closed 25 Dec-1 Jan, 1 week at Easter, Sat, Sun, hols. The rendez-vous of busy exacting stockbrokers and businessmen. Enjoyable dinners prepared by the talented J.-P. Cario. Spec : *profiteroles d'escargots et terrine de légumes façon Denis, bœuf à la ficelle sauce olivette*, 140-300.

♦♦ ***Le Vaudeville,*** 29, rue Vivienne, 75002, ☎ (1) 42.33.39.31. AE, DC, Visa. ♿ A beautiful old-fashioned tavern, 105-150.

♦♦ ***Au Lyonnais,*** 32, rue Saint-Marc, 75002, ☎ (1) 42.96.65.04. AE, DC, Visa. ♿ closed Sun. Cooking from the Lyons region, 100-130.

● ♦♦ ***Le Petit Coin de la Bourse,*** 16, rue Feydeau, 75002, ☎ (1) 45.08.00.08. closed Sat and Sun. The inexhaustible Claude Verger runs this gourmet branch of the stock market, 100-180.

● ♦♦ ***Auberge Perraudin*** (Claude Perraudin), 164, rue Montmartre, 75002, ☎ (1) 42.36.71.09. AE, DC, Visa ; closed Sun. Such discretion in the restaurant of this disciple of the Troisgros brothers and Paul Bocuse. Claude Perraudin has a setting equal to his talent. Spec : *terrine de foie gras* (take-away), *saumon aux écrevisses, gigue d'agneau en chevreuil*, 120-310.

♦ ***L'Amanguier,*** 110, rue de Richelieu, 75002, ☎ (1) 42.96.37.79. AE, DC, Visa ; closed 1 May. Spec : *estouffade à la menthe en cassolette.* Winter garden, and patio, 80-100.

♦ ***Hollywood Savoy,*** 44, rue Notre-Dame-des-Victoires, 75002, ☎ (1) 42.36.16.73. AE, DC, Euro, Visa. Closed Sat noon. American specialities, 80-120.

♦ ***Au Duc de Richelieu,*** 110, rue de Richelieu, 75002, ☎ (1) 42.96.38.38. ♿ closed 28 Jul-1 Sep, Sun. Sandwiches with regional products, *andouillettes*, wide selection of Beaujolais, 55-140.

♦ ***Dow-Jones,*** 6, rue Saint-Marc, 75002, ☎ (1) 42.36.63.09 ♿ closed 10-20 Aug, Sat and Sun eve. Improving cooking for this fashionable spot, 80-200.

♦ ***L'Izard,*** 17, rue Saint-Augustin, 75002, ☎ (1) 42.61.02.13. closed Sat noon, Sun. Specialities from the southwest : *foie gras, confit*, fish, 120-200.

♦ ***Krake's,*** 9, rue d'Aboukir, 75002, ☎ (1) 42.36.57.68. The Swedish snacks are very popular with journalists. Calmer in the eve. Smoked fish, hamburgers, Swedish bread and cakes, 80-130.

♦ ***Dona Flor,*** 10, rue Dussoubs, 75002, ☎ (1) 42.36.46.55. closed Mon. The meeting-place for Brazilians in Paris from 8 pm-2 am, 120-210.

PARIS 3rd

Hotels :

★★★***Little Palace Hotel,*** 4, rue Salomon-de-Caus, 75003, ☎ (1) 42.72.08.15. 59 rm ♿ 250. Rest. ♦ 70-100.

★★***Roubaix,*** 6, rue Greneta, 75003, ☎ (1) 42.72.89.91. (1) 42.72.76.27. AE, DC, Visa. 53 rm, 210.

★***Grand Hôtel Arts-et-Métiers,*** 4, rue Borda, 75003, ☎ (1) 48.87.73.89. 35 rm ♿ 155.

Restaurants :

● ♦♦ ***Ambassade d'Auvergne,*** 22, rue du Grenier-Saint-Lazare, 75003, ☎ (1) 42.72.31.22. Visa ; closed Sun. The excellent cooking offerred by the Petrucci family and staff is a passport to Auvergne. Spec : *charcuterie, saucisse fraîche, aligot, soupe aux choux*, 230-250.

♦ ***L'Ami Louis,*** 32, rue du Vertbois, 75003, ☎ (1) 48.87.77.48. Closed Jul-Aug, Mon, Tue, Solid, traditional fare, 120-260.

PARIS 4th

Hotels :

★★★***Deux Iles,*** 59, rue St-Louis-en-l'Ile (île Saint-Louis), 75004, ☎ (1) 43.26.13.35. 17 rm Lovely 17 thC mansion, 500.

★★★***Lutèce,*** 65, rue St-Louis-en-l'Ile (île Saint-Louis), 75004, ☎ (1) 43.26.23.52. 23 rm 485.

★★★**Saint-Merry,** 78, rue de la Verrerie, 75004, ☎ (1) 42.78.14.15. 13 rm, 400.
★★**Célestins,** 1, rue Charles-V, 75004, ☎ (1) 48.87.87.04. 15 rm, 260.
★★**Place des Vosges,** 12, rue de la Birague, 75004, ☎ (1) 42.72.60.46. AE, DC, Euro, Visa. 16 rm, 275.

Restaurants :
♦♦♦ ***Chez Benoît,*** 20, rue Saint-Martin, 75004, ☎ (1) 42.72.25.76. Closed Aug, Sat and Sun, 150-210.
♦♦♦ ***Les Ursins dans le Caviar,*** 3, rue de la Colombe, 75004, ☎ (1) 43.29.54.20. Closed Sun, eve only (dinner, supper). The new French cooking, 150-300.
● ♦♦ ***Au Quai des Ormes,*** 72, quai de l'Hôtel-de-Ville, 75004, ☎ (1) 42.74.72.22. Visa ♿ closed Sat, Sun, 5-31 Aug. The Masraffs keep their numerous customers happy. Spec : *dos de st-pierre grillé, poêlée de langoustines aux artichauts,* low-calorie specials, 140-200.
● ♦♦ ***Domarais,*** 53 *bis,* rue des Francs-Bourgeois, 75004, ☎ (1) 42.74.54.17 closed 12 Aug-2 Sep, 1 week in winter, Sat noon, Sun, Mon noon. Surprising decor in a 15thC chapel under an 18thC cupola. The young Patrice Bougerol is earning compliments with his enjoyable cooking. Spec : *estouffade d'escargot à l'ail doux, saumon à la moelle de bœuf,* 110-200.
♦♦ ***Coconnas,*** 2 *bis,* pl. des Vosges, 75004, ☎ (1) 42.78.58.16. AE, DC, Visa ♿ closed 15 Dec-15 Jan, Mon and Tue, 160-300.
● ♦♦ ***Le Tourtour,*** 20, rue Quincampoix, 75004, ☎ (1) 48.87.82.48. Simple cooking at honest prices, a stone's throw from the Beaubourg centre. Real theatre in the vaulted cellar after 10 pm, 75-125.
♦♦ ***La Guirlande de Julie,*** 25, pl. des Vosges, 75004, ☎ (1) 48.87.94.07. closed Sun, Mon and Feb. An attractive, reasonably-priced restaurant in a charming setting, 80-140.
♦♦ ***Bofinger,*** 5, rue de la Bastille, 75004, ☎ (1) 42.72.87.82. AE, DC, Euro, Visa ♿ 1900 setting, seafood, *choucroute,* 120-160.
♦♦ ***Au Franc Pinot,*** 1, quai Bourbon (île Saint-Louis), 75004, ☎ (1) 43.29.46.98. AE, DC, Euro, Visa ; closed Sun and Mon. Bernard Meyruey's excellent dishes are served in the vaulted basement rooms of this 17thC restaurant ; wine-tasting at the counter, 120-210.
♦♦ ***Chez Julien,*** 1, rue du Pont-Louis-Philippe, 75004, ☎ (1) 42.78.31.64. Closed 10 Aug-3 Sep, Sun, Mon. A new nightlife for this former bakery. Reasonable menu, 110-200.
♦♦ ***Le Monde des Chimères,*** 69, rue St-Louis-en-l'Isle (île Saint-Louis), 75004, ☎ (1) 43.54.45.27. closed Sun and Sep. New cooking : Spec : *filet de bar sauce foie gras, tartare de saumon frais,* 120-280.
♦ ***Jo Goldenberg,*** 7, rue des Rosiers, 75004, ☎ (1) 48.87.20.16. The meeting-place for the Parisian Jewish community, 80-130.
♦ ***Au Rendez-vous des Amis,*** 10, rue Ste-Croix-de-la-Bretonnerie, 75004, closed Mon noon, 50-90.

PARIS 5th

Hotels :
★★★**Sélect Hôtel,** 1, pl. de la Sorbonne, 75005, ☎ (1) 46.34.14.80. 70 rm 600.
● ★★**Collège de France,** 7, rue Thénard, 75005 ☎ (1) 43.26.78.36. AE. 29 rm 320.
★★**Esmeralda,** 4, rue Saint-Julien-le-Pauvre, 75005, ☎ (1) 43.54.19.20. Tx 270105, 19 rm 280.
★★**Carmes,** 5, rue des Carmes, 75005, ☎ (1) 43.28.78.40. 42 rm 140.
★★**Maxim Hôtel,** 28, rue Censier, 75005, ☎ (1) 43.31.16.15. 37 rm, 260.
★★**Trois Collèges,** 16, rue Cujas, 75005, ☎ (1) 43.54.67.30. Tx 206034. AE, DC, Visa. 4 rm 300.
★**Grand Hôtel Saint-Michel,** 19, rue Cujas, 75005, ☎ (1) 46.33.65.03. 62 rm, 150.

Restaurants :
● ♦♦♦♦ ***La Tour d'Argent,*** 15-17, quai de la Tournelle, 75005, ☎ (1) 43.54.23.31. AE, DC, Visa P ♿ closed Mon In his superb decor, the still young and untiring Claude Terrail, Lord of the "*Tour*", is not resting on his laurels. He supervises everything for his demanding customers while, in the kitchen, Dominique Bouchet prepares all perfectly. Here a duck does not "die for nothing" : *canard au sang, canard Marco Polo...* but also *gigot de sept heures, curry de homard aux légumes.* The little wine and vineyard museum is a must, opposite the "Comptoir de la Tour" (sale of wines), 120-260.
● ♦♦♦ ***Miraville,*** 25, quai de la Tournelle, 75005, ☎ (1) 46.34.07.78. AE, DC, Visa ; closed Sun. Spec : *filet d'agneau sous croûte de sel, crêpes soufflées à la liqueur,* 130-240.
● ♦♦♦ ***Dodin-Bouffant,*** 25, rue Frédéric-Sauton, 75005, ☎ (1) 43.25.25.14. DC, Visa P ♿ closed Aug, end-of-year, Sat, Sun. The traditions of the great J. Manière live on ; saltwater vivarium for shellfish. Spec : *fricassée de morue à la provençale, estouffade d'agneau, ragoût de canard et de ris de veau.* Unbeatable value, 180-300.
● ♦♦♦ ***Duquesnoy,*** 30, rue des Bernardins, 75005, ☎ (1) 43.54.21.13. AE, Visa ♿ closed Sat, Sun and Aug. Classical, but constantly evolving cooking. Spec : *fondants de pieds de porcs truffés, terrine fondante de canard, agneau rôti, gratin d'artichauts,* 160-250.
● ♦♦♦ ***Auberge de la Bûcherie,*** 41, rue de la Bûcherie, 75005, ☎ (1) 43.54.78.06. AE, DC ♿ closed Mon (Jul-Aug). B. Bosque offers an excellent cellar and dishes to match. Spec : *chou farci aux langoustines,* 130-250.
● ♦♦ ***Le Pactole,*** 44, bd Saint-Germain, 75005, ☎ (1) 46.33.31.31 and 43.26.92.28. Visa ♿ closed Sun, Sat noon. Good cooking from Roland Magne, and his young team. Nice service, flowers and a warm welcome from Noëlle. Beautiful terrace in warm weather. Spec : *filet de daurade à l'ail doux, faisan aux choux vinaigrette de truffes, filet de bœuf surprise,* 155-250.
● ♦♦ ***L'Ambroisie,*** 65, quai de la Tournelle, 75005, ☎ (1) 46.33.18.65. AE, Visa ♿ closed Feb school hols, 10-31 Aug, Sun and Mon. There are only nine dining-tables in this excellent restaurant, where the privileged clientele can taste dishes such as *queue de bœuf braisée en crépines, mousse de poivrons au coulis de tomates, millefeuille aux fruits,* 150-300.
♦♦ ***Le Coupe-Chou,*** 11, rue de Lanneau, 75005, ☎ (1) 46.33.68.69. AE, Visa P closed Sun noon. Very "left bank" setting and clientele, 155-220.
♦♦ ***Villars-Palace,*** 6, rue Descartes, 75005, ☎ (1) 43.26.39.08. AE, DC, Euro, Visa P closed Sat noon. The montagne Sainte-Geneviève graced with deliciously prepared offerings from the sea, 170-260.
♦♦ ***Auberge des Deux Signes,*** 46, rue Galande, 75005, ☎ (1) 43.25.46.56. AE, DC, Euro, Visa ; closed Sun and hols. Solid Auvergne-style fare, along with fish and seafood, 170-240.
● ♦ ***Balzar,*** 49, rue des Écoles, 75005, ☎ (1) 43.54.13.67. Visa. closed Aug, end-of-year hols and Tue. Solid home-style fare in a superb setting. Spec : bœuf gros sel on Sat, *foie de veau niçoise,* 90-130.
● ♦ ***Salut l'Artiste,*** 22, rue Cujas, 75005, ☎ (1) 43.54.01.10. AE, DC, Visa ♿ closed Sun, Aug. Paul Chêne has reason to be pleased with

Paris

his children : their restaurant is enjoyable and prices honest, 150-200.

● ♦ ***Vivario,*** 6, rue Cochin, 75005, ☎ (1) 43.25.08.19 closed 25 Dec-1 Jan Sun, Mon. True Corsican cooking and wines in a friendly atmosphere, 150-200.

● ♦ ***Chez Toutoune,*** 5, rue de Pontoise, 75005, ☎ (1) 43.26.58.81. Visa ; closed Sun, Mon, 15 Aug-15 Sep. "Toutoune" keeps busy making bread and *andouillettes.* Unique menu is a bargain, 85.

♦ ***Abélard,*** 1, rue des Grands-Degrés, 75005, ☎ (1) 43.25.16.46. AE, DC, Visa closed Feb, Tue. Behind a classified façade, a young couple worth following. Spec : *panaché de poissons au safran,* 85-200.

♦ ***Chez René,*** 14, bd Saint-Germain, 75005, ☎ (1) 43.54.30.23 ♿ closed 26 Jul-3 Sep, Sat and Sun. Good, solid bistro-style cooking, 110-180.

♦ ***Le Bouquet du Port,*** 4, bd de Port-Royal, 75005, ☎ (1) 47.07.08.99. AE, DC, Euro, Visa ; closed 5 Aug-3 Sep, Sun noon, Mon. Fish, oysters, seafood, live lobsters, 100-250.

♦ ***L'Estrapade*** (M. Chastillon), 15, rue de l'Estrapade, 75005, ☎ (1) 43.25.72.58. Closed Sat noon, Sun 7-23 Aug. Simple, pleasant meals in this small, extremely reasonable restaurant, 80-125.

♦ ***La Criée,*** 15, rue Lagrange, 75005, ☎ (1) 43.54.23.57. Fish specialities, 60-110.

♦ ***Le Sunset,*** 35, quai de la Tournelle, 75005, ☎ (1) 43.25.44.42. Subdued lighting for intimate suppers. Modern cooking, 80-210.

Le Petit Prince, 12, rue de Lanneau, 75005, ☎ (1) 43.54.77.26. open eve. Left bank atmosphère, 60-120.

PARIS 6th

Hotels :

● ★★★★(L) ***Guy-Louis Duboucheron,*** 13, rue des Beaux-Arts, 75006, ☎ (1) 43.25.27.22. Tx 270870. AE, DC, Visa. 27 rm The jet-set clientele simply refers to this place as "the hotel", as though it were the only one worth mentioning. Perhaps the most beautiful bar in Paris, 700. Rest. ♦♦♦ suppers, closed Aug, 220-310.

● ★★★★***Relais Christine,*** 3, rue Christine, 75006, ☎ (1) 43.26.71.80. 51 rm Ⓟ Former 16 thC cloister, 650.

★★★★***Littré,*** 9, rue Littré, 75006, ☎ (1) 45.44.38.68. Tx 203852. AE, Euro, Visa. 100 rm Comfortable and classic, 560. Rest. ♦♦ 120-210.

★★★★***Victoria,*** 6, rue Blaise-Desgoffes, 75006, ☎ (1) 45.44.38.16. Tx 270557. AE, Visa. 113 rm A small grand hotel, 610. Rest. ♦♦ ♿ 120-150.

★★★★***Lutetia-Concorde,*** 45, bd Raspail, 75006, ☎ (1) 45.44.38.10. AE, DC, Euro, Visa. 300 rm, 17 apart. One of the largest hotels on the Left Bank, 1 200. Rest. ● ♦♦♦ ♿ ***le Paris.*** Commander Jacky Fréon (Joël Robuchon's co-pilot at *les Célébrités*) and staff offer you an excellent gourmet voyage in the beautiful dining-room decorated by Slavik and Sonia Rykiel. Spec : *langoustines aux 3 brunoises, filet d'agneau au curry, filet de bar homardine,* 170-270.

● ★★★***Saints-Pères,*** 65, rue des Saints-Pères, 75006, ☎ (1) 45.44.50.00. Tx 205424. 40 rm ♿ In the middle of Saint-Germain, 1 000.

★★★***Abbaye Saint-Germain,*** 10, rue Cassette, 75006, ☎ 45.44.11.52. 45 rm A former convent, 650.

★★★***Madison Hôtel,*** 143, bd Saint-Germain, 75006, ☎ 43.29.72.50. AE, Visa. 57 rm ♿ Charming hotel with view of St-Germain-des-Prés, 450.

★★***Balcons,*** 3, rue Casimir-Delavigne, 75006, ☎ 46.34.78.50. Euro, Visa. 55 rm ♿ 250.

★***Verneuil,*** 36, rue Dauphine, 75006, ☎ 43.26.85.34. 29 rm, 160.

Restaurants :

● ♦♦♦ ***Lapérouse,*** 51, quai des Grands-Augustins, 75006, ☎ 43.26.68.04. AE, DC, Euro, Visa ♿ closed 1 May, Sat noon. A classified setting (with the famous "private salons" of the "*Belle Époque*") L. Bicheron takes care of everything. His Japanese chef Maeda cooks French dishes : *tourte de volaille, consommé de rougets marinés avec du foie gras, tartare de saumon et dorade, ris de veau aux langoustines,* 190-350.

● ♦♦♦ ***Jacques Cagna,*** 14, rue des Grands-Augustins, 75006, ☎ 43.26.49.39. AE, Visa ; closed 24 Dec-2 Jan, Aug, Sat and Sun. The highest quality and comfort, with discretion to match. Spec : *salade de homard breton et de foie de canard tiède, pétoncles en coquille fumet crémé au caviar Serruga,* 190-280.

● ♦♦♦ ***Brasserie Lipp,*** 151, bd Saint-Germain, 75006, ☎ 45.48.53.91. Closed Jul, 1 Nov, 25 Dec, Easter and Mon. The most discreet of the great young chefs will delight you in his exquisite contemporary setting. Spec : *pétoncles en coquille crémées au caviar,* great and modest wines, 185-400.

♦♦♦ ***Relais Louis XIII,*** 8, rue des Grands-Augustins, 75006, ☎ 43.26.75.96. AE, DC, Euro, Visa ; closed Sun, Mon noon, 1-9 Jan and 27 Jul-25 Aug. Subtle, inventive cooking under magnificent old beams. Spec : fish, *chartreuse de bar aux langoustines à l'aneth,* 180-350.

● ♦♦ ***Nord-Sud Express,*** 15, rue Princesse, 75006, ☎ 43.26.90.22. Jean Castel is one of the "Kings of the Night" of Paris. Bernard Chirent is the efficient, brilliant, discrete chef trained by the Troisgros brothers. The result is excellent cuisine. Take-away service, 170-200.

● ♦♦ ***O Brasil,*** 10, rue Guénégaud, 75006, ☎ 43.54.98.56. Private restaurant club open until 2 am. Authentic Brazilian music and cooking. *Feijoada* as in Rio, 100-180.

♦♦ ***Allard,*** 41, rue Saint-André-des-Arts, 75006, ☎ 43.26.48.23. DC, Visa ♿ closed Aug, end-of-year hols, Sat and Sun. Good traditional fare, 110-210.

♦♦ ***Les Arêtes,*** 165, bd du Montparnasse, 75006, ☎ 43.26.23.98. Closed Sat noon and Mon. A complete selection of ever fresh, tasty seafood dishes. 120-170 noon, 160-250 eve.

● ♦♦ ***La Petite Cour,*** 8, rue Mabillon, 75006, ☎ 43.26.52.26. Visa ; closed 15 Dec-15 Jan, Sun and Mon in winter. Yet another haunt of the Oliver family, this time directed by Stéphane, the youngest son. Light cooking, prepared by a French-trained Japanese cook : *tartare de thon frais, lapereau aux pâtes fraîches* served in a Napoléon III setting. Beautiful terrace in summer, 130-250.

● ♦♦ ***L'Apollinaire,*** 168, bd Saint-Germain, 75006, ☎ 43.26.50.30. AE, DC, Euro, Visa closed 18 Dec-3 Jan. Fish specialities, 90-220.

● ♦♦ ***Le Chat Grippé,*** 87, rue d'Assas, 75006, ☎ 43.54.70.00. Closed Aug, Sat noon, Mon. Interesting menu, *truite de mer à l'oseille,* 80-280.

● ♦♦ ***Chez Gramond,*** 5, rue de Fleurus, 75006, ☎ 42.22.28.89. Visa ; closed 31 Jul-3 Sep, Sun. The gourmet's annex to the neighboring Senate. Spec : *civet de lièvre* in season, fish, 220-330.

● ♦♦ ***L'Épicurien,*** 11, rue de Nesles, 75006, ☎ 43.29.55.78. Closed Sun. An enjoyable moment in this small flowered restaurant, 120-210.

● ♦♦ ***La Foux,*** 2, rue Clément, 75006, ☎ 43.25.77.66 ♿ closed Sun, Christmas and nat hols. A favourite editors' haunt, with the best in Lyons-style cooking prepared by A. Guini : *pieds de mouton, gras double, tablier de sapeur.* At noon on Sat the chef and his wife serve a delicious *casse-croûte niçois.* Excellent Beaujolais wines, 120-210.

● ♦♦ ***Joséphine (Chez Dumonet),*** 117, rue du Cherche-Midi, 75006, ☎ 45.48.52.40. Solid, honest cooking in a very handsome 1900's bistro. Exceptional wine, 220-300.

● ♦♦ ***Guy,*** 6, rue Mabillon, 75006, ☎ 43.54.87.61. Closed 10-20 Aug, Sun, noon ex Sat. Brazil and its specialities : samba, *feijoda,* carioccas and pretty girls, especially Sat noon, 140-200.

● ♦♦ ***Grégoire Xavier,*** 80, rue du Cherche-Midi, 75006, ☎ 45.44.72.72. AE, Visa closed 1-25 Aug, Sat eve, Sun. Small rooms with lots of flowers for the excellent cooking of Xavier Grégoire who, after *le Toit de Paris,* now has his own restaurant. Astonishing 100 F menu. Spec : *salade de rougets, ris de veau à la graine de moutarde,* 110-220.

● ♦♦ ***Le Petit Zinc,*** 25, rue de Buci, 75006, ☎ 43.54.79.34. Spec : *foie frais, confit de canard,* fish and seafood, 110-130.

● ♦♦ ***Le Muniche,*** 27, rue de Buci, 75006, ☎ 46.33.62.09. AE, DC, Euro, Visa. Open until 3 am ; the Layrac brothers serve such good, solid dishes as a lavish *choucroute au confit, boudin aux châtaignes.* Take-aways, oysters, 110-130.

♦♦ ***Brasserie Lutetia,*** 45, bd Raspail, 75006, ☎ 45.44.38.10. A very popular large, recently renovated restaurant, 100-160.

♦♦ ***La Grosse Horloge,*** 22, rue St-Benoît, 75006, ☎ 42.22.22.63, 45.48.28.12. AE, DC, Visa. Spec : fish, *foie gras de canard maison,* 70-180.

♦♦ ***La Closerie des Lilas,*** 171, bd du Montparnasse, 75006, ☎ 43.52.21.68. AE, DC, Visa Ⓟ ♿ Pricey, but a must for those who want to be "in" on the Paris world of arts and letters ; the "real" intellectuals queue up to eat at the brasserie, 230-500.

● ♦ ***Le Caméléon,*** 6, rue de Chevreuse, 75006, ☎ 43.20.63.43. Closed Sep, Sun, Mon, hols. Good meat, enjoyable wines - happiness at low prices, thanks to the Faucher family, 150.

● ♦ ***La Porte Fausse,*** 72, rue du Cherche-Midi, ☎ 43.22.20.17. closed Sun, Mon, 1 week in Easter, Aug, 1st week Sep. *Tourte de blettes, pâtes fraîches, ravioli, pissaladière, sardines à la sauge, poche de veau farcie* and many other genuine Nice specialities prepared by Jeanine Louis, an authentic "Niçoise", 100-210.

♦ ***Le Palanquin,*** 12, rue Princesse, 75006, ☎ 43.29.77.66. Visa ♿ closed Sun. Vietnamese specialities, 65-120.

♦ ***Procope,*** 13, rue de l'Ancienne-Comédie, 75006, ☎ 46.33.69.71. closed Jul, 100-180.

♦ ***Aux Charpentiers,*** 10, rue Mabillon, 75006, ☎ 43.26.30.05. AE, DC ; closed 20 Dec-2 Jan, Sun. Moderately-priced meals in a real bistro, 80-110.

♦ ***Polidor,*** 41, rue Monsieur-le-Prince, 75006, ☎ 43.26.95.34. Closed Sun, Mon and 25 Jul-1 Aug. Family-style meals at reasonable prices, 40-70.

PARIS 7th

Hotels :

● ★★★★(L) ***Pont-Royal*** (Mapotel), 7, rue de Montalembert, 75007, ☎ (1) 45.44.38.27. Tx 270113. AE, DC, Euro, Visa. 80 rm, 5 suites Ⓟ ♿ The most literary bar in Paris, in the heart of the editors' quarter, 1 020. Rest. ♦♦ ***les Antiquaires,*** closed Aug and Sun. Spec : *magret de canard au confit d'oignons,* 150-200.

★★★★(L) ***Sofitel-Bourbon,*** 32, rue Saint-Dominique, 75007, ☎ (1) 45.55.91.80. Tx 250019. AE, DC, Euro, Visa. 112 rm, 4 apart. Ⓟ ♿ A charming modest-sized hotel, 950. Rest. ● ♦♦♦ ***le Dauphin*** ♿ 180-280.

★★★★***Montalembert,*** 3, rue Montalembert, 75007, ☎ (1) 45.48.68.11. 60 rm ♿ Surrounded by antique shops, 900.

★★★***L'Académie,*** 32, rue des Saints-Pères, 75007, ☎ (1) 45.48.36.22. Tx 205650. AE, DC, Euro, Visa. 34 rm, 420.

★★★***Cayré,*** 4, bd Raspail, 75007, ☎ (1) 45.44.38.88. Tx 270577. AE, DC, Euro, Visa. 130 rm Ⓟ ♿Calm close to St-Germain, 700.

★★★***Saint-Simon,*** 14, rue St-Simon, 75007, ☎ (1) 45.48.35.66. 34 rm A former private mansion, 600.

★★★***Verneuil Saint-Germain,*** 8, rue de Verneuil, 75007, ☎ (1) 42.60.24.16. Tx 205650. AE, Visa. 26 rm ♿ 360.

★★★***Quai Voltaire,*** 19, quai Voltaire, 75007, ☎ (1) 42.61.50.91. 33 rm ♿ Oscar Wilde and Wagner were once guests here ; exceptional view of the Louvre and Seine, 300.

★★★***Thoumieux,*** 79, rue St-Dominique, 75007, ☎ (1) 47.05.49.75. 10 rm, 350. Rest. ♦♦♦ closed Mon. A neighbourhood institution spruced up, 50-150.

★★★***Université,*** 22, rue Université, 75007, ☎ (1) 42.61.09.39. 28 rm 500.

★★★***Varenne,*** 44, rue de Bourgogne, 75007, ☎ (1) 45.51.45.55. AE. 24 rm invaded by deputies during sessions at the nearby Palais-Bourbon, 335.

★★★***Résidence Élysées-Maubourg,*** 35, bd de Latour-Maubourg, 75007, ☎ (1) 45.56.10.78. Tx 206227. AE, DC, Euro, Visa. 30 rm, 500.

● ★★***Solferino,*** 91, rue de Lille, 75007, ☎ (1) 47.05.05.54. Visa. 34 rm closed 22 Dec-3 Jan, The charm of a small hotel, 265.

★★***Résidence Latour-Maubourg,*** 150, rue de Grenelle, 75007, ☎ (1) 45.51.75.28. 12 rm 300. Rest. 60-85.

★★***Vaneau,*** 85, rue Vaneau, 75007, ☎ (1) 45.48.25.09. DC, Euro, Visa. 52 rm ♿ 270.

Restaurants :

● ♦♦♦♦ ***Jacques Le Divellec,*** 107, rue de l'Université (Fabert road corner), 75007, ☎ (1) 45.51.91.96. AE, DC, Visa ♿ closed Sun and Mon. Jacques Le Divellec's restaurant in Paris is a success. Fresh fish spec's in a sea-blue setting : *huîtres frémies, langoustines au foie gras, pâtes fraîches à l'encre de seiche,* 170-400.

♦♦♦♦ ***Le Jules Verne,*** tour Eiffel, 2nd floor (direct elevator service), 75007, ☎ (1) 45.55.20.04 (reservations necessary). The most stunning aerial view in Paris, in a harmonious grey and black decor designed by Slavik. Cooking improving gradually. Piano-bar, 170-400.

● ♦♦♦ ***Bistrot de Paris,*** 33, rue de Lille, 75007, ☎ (1) 42.61.16.83 ♿ closed Sat noon and Sun. In spite of his success in the media, Michel Oliver still takes the time to supervise his restaurant with talent and competence for starving fashionable Parisians. Spec : *côte de bœuf rôtie,* superb wines, 220-250.

● ♦♦♦ ***La Ferme Saint-Simon,*** 6, rue de Saint-Simon, 75007, ☎ (1) 45.48.35.74. Visa ♿ closed 2-26 Aug, Sat noon and Sun. Superb cooking and excellent desserts prepared by Francis Vandehende. Spec : *duo d'oursins en demi-glace, grillandine de homard,* 150-270.

● ♦♦♦ ***La Cantine des Gourmets,*** 113, av. de la Bourdonnais, 75007, ☎ (1) 47.05.47.96. AE,

DC, Visa ⚲ closed Sun and Mon. Micheline Coat's charming welcome, and a cosy, comfortable setting to make you better appreciate Régis Mahé's great light cooking. Spec : *galette de pigeon au foie gras, st-pierre en Barigoule, aileron de raie aux câpres,* 200-280.

● ♦♦♦ ***Le Récamier*** (Martin Cantegrit), 4, rue Récamier, 75007, ☎ (1) 42.22.51.75. DC, Euro, Visa ; closed Sun. The competent Martin Cantegrit takes care of everything : his beautiful, discreet terrace, the fresh produce bought at Rungis, and his prestigious choice of dishes. Solid meals for editors, politicians and regular customers. Spec : fish, *bœuf bourguignon, foie de veau à l'auvergnate, terrine de champignons des bois,* 300-350.

♦♦♦ ***Le Galant Verre,*** 12, rue de Verneuil, 75007, ☎ (1) 42.60.84.56. AE, DC, Euro, Visa ♿ closed Sat noon and Sun. Warm, comfortable setting. Spec : *jarret de veau aux pâtes fraîches,* 180-250.

♦♦♦ ***Chez les Anges,*** 54, bd Latour-Maubourg, 75007, ☎ (1) 47.05.89.86. AE, DC, Euro, Visa ♿ closed Sun eve and Mon. Burgundy and its rich cooking. Fine wines, 160-300.

♦♦♦ ***La Bourgogne,*** 6, av. Bosquet, 75007, ☎ (1) 47.05.96.78. AE, DC, Visa ; closed Sat noon and Sun. Lionel Lesage continues the Julien family's tradition of rich cooking with the same chef. Spec : *ris de veau aux morilles,* 250-350.

● ♦♦ ***Florence,*** 22, rue du Champ-de-Mars, 75007, ☎ (1) 45.51.52.69. AE, Visa ; closed Jul, Sun and Mon. The Fayet brothers offer good fresh pasta and excellent Italian-style cooking, 70-220.

● ♦♦ ***Quai d'Orsay,*** 49, quai d'Orsay, 75007, ☎ (1) 45.51.58.58. AE, DC, Euro, Visa ♿ closed Sun, Christmas and 2-25 Aug. Warm ambiance and fashionably crowded for chef Bigeard's excellent seasonal cooking, 150-280.

● ♦♦ ***La Sologne,*** 8, rue de Bellechasse, 75007, ☎ (1) 47.05.98.66. AE, DC, Visa ; closed Aug, Sat, Sun. Game in season, 95-210.

● ♦♦ ***Labrousse,*** 4, rue Pierre-Leroux, 75007, ☎ (1) 43.06.99.39 ♿ After the luxury of ***le Grand Véfour*** where he was chef, the calm of a small, almost provincial, street for Yves Labrousse and his fine cooking. Spec : *langue d'agneau lie de ravigote, salmis de pintade aux girolles,* 125-250.

● ♦♦ ***Tan Dinh,*** 60, rue de Verneuil, 75007, ☎ (1) 45.44.04.84. Closed Sun and 15-31 Aug. The most Parisian Vietnamese restaurant ; one of the best-stocked wine-cellars in Paris, 120-250.

● ♦♦ ***Chez Françoise,*** aérogare des Invalides, 75007, ☎ (1) 47.05.49.03. AE, DC, Visa ♿ closed Sun eve, Mon and Aug. A dining-room for the nearly National Assembly, whence throngs the cohort of famished ministers and deputies. *Foie gras frais d'oie, filet de barbue à la mousse de truite, pigeons à la crème de petits pois,* 100-170.

♦♦ ***Relais Saint-Germain,*** 190, bd Saint-Germain, 75007, ☎ (1) 42.22.21.35. Spec : *saumon cru au citron et au poivre vert, marquise au chocolat.* Excellent value-for-money, 80-150.

♦♦ ***La Flamberge,*** 12, av. Rapp, 75007, ☎ (1) 47.05.91.37. closed 8 Aug-8 Sep, Sat noon and Sun. Spec : *salade de feuilles de chêne,* desserts, 300-350.

♦♦ ***Cantegril,*** 73, av. de Suffren, 75007, ☎ (1) 47.34.90.56. AE, DC, Euro, Visa ⚲ ♿ closed Sun eve and Mon. Spec : *salade de concombres au chèvre tiède, feuilleté de foie de morue aux champignons thaïlandais, profiteroles à la brouillade de crabes mixés,* 140-200.

● ♦ ***Au Pied de Fouet,*** 45, rue de Babylone, 75007, ☎ (1) 47.05.12.27. Closed Sat eve, Sun, 27 Jul-31 Aug, 22 Dec-2 Jan, 23 Mar-1 Apr. More *à la mode* than ever. Very good and still inexpensive. Martial has not abandoned his bar, his cousin is still at the piano, and his wife provides a very warm welcome. Perhaps the best pastries in Paris, 100-120.

● ♦ ***Le Bistrot 28,*** 28, rue de l'Exposition, 75007, ☎ (1) 47.05.80.39. Closed Sat noon, Mon, 10-25 Aug, 20 Dec-5 Jan. A delightful little restaurant in a calm street. Good fare at reasonable prices, 120-210.

♦ ***Aux Fins Gourmets,*** 213, bd St-Germain, 75007, ☎ (1) 42.22.06.57. Good and inexpensive, 80-130.

♦ ***L'Œillade,*** 10, rue de Saint-Simon, 75007, ☎ (1) 42.22.01.60. AE, DC, Visa ; closed Sun. Catherine and Evelyne are with it. It's feminine, good and inexpensive. Spec : *terrine, bavette, haddock au poivre vert,* 100-120.

PARIS 8th

Hotels :

● ★★★★(L) ***Bristol,*** 112, rue du Faubourg-Saint-Honoré, 75008, ☎ (1) 42.66.91.45. Tx 280961. AE, DC, Euro, Visa. 200 rm, 45 apart. Ⓟ ♨ ⚲ ▭ A discreet palace looking over an 18thC cloister ; greatly appreciated by its international clientele, 2 400. Rest. ♦♦♦ ***le Bristol*** ❄ Excellent fare. Spec : *escalope de turbot au sauterne, salade landaise au mesclun, pigeon de Bresse étuvé en feuille de chou,* 200-600.

● ★★★★(L) ***Crillon*** (Concorde, Relais et châteaux), 10, pl. de la Concorde, 75008, ☎ (1) 42.96.24.24. Tx 290204, 290241. AE, DC, Euro, Visa. 195 rm, 48 apart. ⚘ ♿ A waft of aristocracy continues to haunt Gabriel's palace (1760) with its famous columns, 2 000. Rest. ● ♦♦♦♦ Jean-Paul Bonin and his team bring talent and art to their cooking, served in this superb grand hotel setting. Delicious light dishes : *artichaut frais aux truffes, rognons poêlés au miel d'acacia,* 315-450. Grill ♦♦ ***l'Obélisque.*** Sonia Rykiel's feminine decor, light cooking, 120-210.

● ★★★★(L) ***Claridge Bellman,*** 37, rue François-Ier, 75008, ☎ (1) 47.23.54.42. Tx 641150. AE, DC, Visa. 42 rm ❄ A palace with splendid old furnishings, where the friendly atmosphere comes as an agreeable surprise, 875. Rest. ♦♦♦ ***Relais Bellman,*** closed Sat, Sun and Aug. Spec : *ravioles Royans, papillote de barbue à l'étuvée de poireaux, pavé grillé aux champignons de bois,* 220-350.

● ★★★★(L) ***Warwick,*** 5, rue de Berri, 75008, ☎ (1) 45.63.14.11. Tx 642295. AE, DC, Euro, Visa. 50 rm including 4 suites ♿ New but in the grand tradition, 1 400. Rest. ♦♦♦ ***la Couronne*** ♿ closed 5-26 Aug and nat hols, 175-230.

● ★★★★(L) ***California*** (Mapotel), 16, rue de Berri, 75008, ☎ (1) 43.59.93.00. Tx 660634. AE, DC, Euro, Visa. 188 rm, 5 suites ♿ Right next to the Champs-Élysées, 970. Rest. ♦♦ closed Sat, Sun, 120-210.

● ★★★★***Atala,*** 10, rue Chateaubriand, 75008, ☎ (1) 45.62.01.62. 49 rm ♨ ⚲ ♿ A garden in the middle of Paris, 650. Rest. ♦♦ ♿ 150-210.

★★★★(L) ***Plaza-Athénée,*** 25, av. Montaigne, 75008, ☎ (1) 47.23.78.33. Tx 650092. AE, DC, Visa. 218 rm, 44 apart, closed 15-31 Dec Ⓟ ♿ 1 800. A favourite celebrities' haunt, Rest. ♦♦ ***Relais Plaza,*** 200-300, and ♦♦♦ ***le Régence Plaza.*** Excellent cooking. Spec : *soufflé de homard Plaza, trois mignons mousseline de légumes, salade d'artichauts au haddock.* One of the finest examples of culinary renewal in the grand hotels, 300-500.

★★★★(L) ***George V,*** 31, av. George-V, 75008, ☎ (1) 47.23.54.00. Tx 650082, 290776. AE, DC, Euro, Visa. 298 rm, 38 apart., Grand tradition. Superb furnishings, 1 990. Rest. ♦♦♦ ✗ ***les Princes.*** Good fare. Spec : *filet en croûte George V, noisette d'agneau George V.* Outstanding wine selection, 380-450.

★★★★(L) ***Frantel Windsor,*** 14, rue Beaujon, 75008, ☎ (1) 45.63.04.04. Tx 650902. AE, DC, Euro, Visa. 135 rm ⛱ Great comfort, 950. Rest. ● ♦♦♦ ***le Clovis,*** ☎ (1) 45.61.15.32 ♿ closed Aug, Sat, Sun, hols. Spec : *fondant de légumes de Provence et ses petits rougets de roche, croûte de st-pierre à la crème d'oseille,* 125-300.

★★★★(L) ***Lancaster,*** 7, rue de Berri, 75008, ☎ (1) 43.59.90.43. Tx 640991. AE, DC, Euro, Visa. 67 rm, 10 apart. ⛱ An excellent hotel near the Champs-Élysées, 1 400. Rest. ♦♦ closed Sat eve and Sun eve, 160-300.

★★★★(L) ***Royal Monceau,*** 37, av. Hoche, 75008, ☎ (1) 45.61.98.00, (1) 45.63.38.93. 220 rm ⛱ 📺 Comfortable and enjoyable, 1 600. Rest. ● ♦♦♦♦ ***le Jardin,*** merits its name, and the fresh cooking of the Basque chef Biscay is spring-like. Spec : *gelée tremblante d'écrevisse au dill, mignon de veau câpres et anchois,* good wines, 240-300 ♦♦♦ ***Le Carpaccio,*** luxurious Italian cooking at soaring prices, 200-500.

★★★★(L) ***Nova-Park Élysées,*** 51, rue François-Iᵉʳ, 75008, ☎ (1) 45.62.63.64. 75 rm, 6 apart. Ⓟ 📺 ♿ 2 300. Rest. ♦♦♦ ***les Élysées,*** 300-450 ♦ ***Le Bistrot des Poètes,*** 110-210.

★★★★***Castiglione,*** 40, rue du Faubourg-Saint-Honoré, 75008, ☎ (1) 42.65.07.50. Tx 240362. AE, DC, Euro, Visa. 114 rm, In the midst of the great *couturiers,* 990. Rest. ♦♦ 150-200.

★★★★***Napoléon,*** 40, av. de Friedland, 75008, ☎ (1) 47.66.02.02. Tx 640609. AE, DC, Euro, Visa. 140 rm, Close to the Arc de Triomphe, 950. Rest. ♦♦♦ ***Baumann-Étoile,*** 170-230.

★★★★***Astor l'Horset,*** 11, rue d'Astorg, 75008, ☎ (1) 42.66.56.56. 128 rm ⛱ ♿ 600. Rest. ♦♦ ***la Table de l'Astor.*** Spec from the southwest, 100-200.

★★★★***Bedford,*** 17, rue de l'Arcade, 75008, ☎ (1) 42.66.22.32. Tx 290506. Visa. 147 rm, 12 apart. ♿ 570. Rest. ♦♦ ♿ ***le Relais Victoria,*** 130-210.

★★★★***Royal-Hôtel,*** 33, av. de Friedland, 75008, ☎ (1) 43.59.08.14. Tx 280965. AE, DC, Euro, Visa. 57 rm ✗ 655.

★★★★***Royal Malesherbes,*** 24, bd Malesherbes, 75008, ☎ (1) 42.65.53.30. 102 rm, 700. Rest. ♦♦ ♿ 85-130.

★★★★***Royal-Alma,*** 35, rue Jean-Goujon, 75008, ☎ (1) 42.25.83.30. AE, Visa. 84 rm ✗ ♿ 700. Rest. ♦♦ 200-280.

★★★***Franklin,*** 19, rue Buffault, 75008, ☎ (1) 42.80.27.27. Tx 640988. AE, DC, Euro, Visa. 64 rm ⛱ ♿ 530. Rest. ♿ closed Sat, Sun, hols, 85-220.

★★★***Montaigne,*** 6, av. Montaigne, 75008, ☎ (1) 47.20.92.28. Tx 630410. AE, DC. 31 rm ✗ ♿ 650.

★★★***Bradford,*** 10, rue Saint-Philippe-du-Roule, 75008, ☎ (1) 43.59.24.20. 48 rm ✗ Traditional, 400.

★★★***Powers,*** 52, rue François-Iᵉʳ, 75008, ☎ (1) 47.23.91.05. Tx 642041. AE, Visa. 57 rm, 540.

● ★★★***Résidence Saint-Honoré*** (Mapotel), 214, rue du Faubourg-Saint-Honoré, 75008, ☎ (1) 42.25.26.27. Tx 640524. AE, DC, Euro, Visa. 91 rm ♿ 525.

★★★***Newton-Opéra,*** 11 *bis,* rue de l'Arcade, 75008, ☎ (1) 42.65.32.13. Tx 280340. AE, DC, Visa. 31 rm, 280-495.

★★***Ceramic Hôtel,*** 34, av. de Wagram, 75008, ☎ (1) 42.27.20.30. Tx 260717. AE, DC. 60 rm. An Art Deco hotel with an astonishing ceramic-covered façade, 290.

★★***Élysée,*** 12, rue des Saussaies, 75008, ☎ (1) 42.65.29.25. 32 rm, 275.

● ★★***Folkestone,*** 9, rue de Castellane, 75008, ☎ (1) 42.65.73.09. 32 rm, 320.

★★***Royal Colisée,*** 7, rue du Colisée, 75008, ☎ (1) 43.59.32.40, 43.59.71.51. Visa. 37 rm, 275.

Restaurants :

● ♦♦♦♦ ***Taillevent,*** 15, rue Lamennais, 75008, ☎ (1) 45.63.39.94. Closed 9-16 Feb, 26 Jul-24 Aug, Sat and Sun. A temple of French cooking managed by J.-C. Vrinat with cooking by Claude Deligne. Great wines at modest prices. Early booking recommended, 350-450.

● ♦♦♦♦ ***Lasserre,*** 17, av. F.-D.-Roosevelt, 75008, ☎ (1) 43.59.53.43 ✗ closed 3 Aug-1 Sep, Sun and Mon. The valiant René Lasserre deserves particular mention for his important services rendered to great French cooking. Maîtres d'hôtel, sommeliers and a roof which opens. Spec : lobster Newburg, *pigeon André Malraux,* 400-600.

● ♦♦♦♦ ***Lamazère,*** 23, rue de Ponthieu, 75008, ☎ (1) 43.59.66.66. AE, DC, Euro, Visa Ⓟ ✗ closed Aug and Sun. Roger Lamazère's magic cooking to delight gourmands. Spec : *foie gras, truffes, confit,* 400-500.

● ♦♦♦♦ ***Le Pavillon Élysée,*** 10, av. des Champs-Élysées, 75008, ☎ (1) 42.65.85.10. AE, DC, Visa Ⓟ 🌳 closed Sat, Sun, Aug. G. Lenôtre's dream come true : a luxurious gourmet spot on the Champs-Élysées with the staff of Pré Catelan supervised by Patrick Lenôtre. On the ground floor, *les Jardins de l'Élysée* mixes modern cooking and traditional dishes at lower prices. Spec : *foie gras,* caviar, salmon, 300-550.

● ♦♦♦♦ ***Chiberta,*** 3, rue A.-Houssaye, 75008, ☎ (1) 45.63.77.90. AE, DC, Visa ♿ closed Aug, Sat, Sun and nat hols. Beautiful modern decor by Jean Dives. L. Noël Richard is pleased to offer his satisfied customers Jean-Michel Bedier's exceptional cooking : *bavarois de saumon, marbré de rougets,* great desserts and Burgundy wines, 300-420.

♦♦♦♦ ***Maxim's,*** 3, rue Royale, 75008, ☎ (1) 42.65.27.94. Closed Sun. Pierre Cardin imposes his style while the chef Menant and his fine brigade make a serious effort. The mayonnaise (with caviar, of course) is taking. Let the feast begin ! 500-700 or more. On the 1st floor, lunch and suppers. Nearby in the rue St-Honoré : ***Minim's.*** The prices are, too, 200.

♦♦♦♦ ***Ledoyen,*** carré des Champs-Élysées, 75008, ☎ (1) 42.66.54.77 Ⓟ ♿ closed 2 Aug-3 Sep, Easter, Mon and Sun. Tie obligatory. Spec : *fricassée de poissons à la provençale, mignon d'agneau poêlé aux corolles de courgettes et de tomates avec galette de pommes dauphin, surprise Ledoyen aux fraises des bois,* 320-450.

♦♦♦♦ ***Laurent,*** 41, av. Gabriel, 75008, ☎ (1) 42.25.00.39. AE, DC Ⓟ 🌳 ✗ ♿ closed Sat, Sun and nat hols. The pearl of the Golden Triangle is the Champs-Élysées gardens. Marc Pralong is making sparks. Spec : lobster salad, *côte de bœuf écossais « Angus » ;* great wines. Economize with the 300-franc menu. A la carte, 500 or more.

● ♦♦♦ ***Lucas-Carton,*** 9, pl. de la Madeleine, 75008, ☎ (1) 42.65.22.90. Visa ✗ ♿ closed Fri, Sat noon and Sun. In a historically-classified decor with superb lemon wood worked by Majorelle (1856-1926), the highly-talented Alain Senderens's inventive light cooking : *asperges meunière, canard Apicius, gâteau de riz,* superb wines. A feast for a minimum of 580 F. On the 1st floor : private clubhouse, 450-500.

● ♦♦♦ ***Fouquet's,*** 99, av. des Champs-Élysées, 75008, ☎ 47.23.70.60. AE, DC, Visa ♿ closed 20 Jul-20 Aug. They have come... they are all there ! A meeting place for show business and the cinema. The warm welcome of Maurice Casanova, the good cooking of P. Ducroux, the beautiful terrace, the Champs-Élysées, Paris... 160-300.

● ♦♦♦ ***La Marée*** (Relais gourmand), 1, rue Daru, 75008, ☎ 47.63.52.42. Closed Sat, Sun. Quality remains the main characteristic of this restaurant specialised in fish. The competent and lively Éric Trompier, does the cooking assisted by his mother and Gérard Rouillard (M.C.F.) : *rougets grillés,* oysters, seafood, *turbot à la moutarde.* Great cellar, 300-400.

♦♦♦ ***Copenhague,*** 142, av. des Champs-Élysées, 75008, ☎ 43.59.20.41 ⚒ closed Aug and Sun. Danish and Scandinavian specialities, 130-180.

♦♦♦ ***Au Petit Montmorency,*** 5, rue Rabelais, 75008, ☎ 42.25.11.19. Visa ⚒ closed Aug, Sat and Sun. Spec : *foie gras au caramel poivré,* 220-310.

♦♦♦ ***Marius et Janette,*** 4, av. George-V, 75008, ☎ 47.23.41.88. AE, Visa ♿ Fish and seafood in a fishing club decor by Slavik. Expensive, 300-400.

♦♦♦ ***Le Marcande,*** 52, rue de Miromesnil, 75008, ☎ 42.65.19.14. AE, DC, Visa ♒ closed 9 Aug-2 Sep, Sat and Sun. Spec : *pavé de saumon au caviar d'aubergines, coq au vin froid en gelée,* 170-350.

● ♦♦ ***Chez Vong*** (M. Vong), 27, rue du Colisée, 75008, ☎ 43.59.77.12. AE, DC, Visa 🅿 ♿ closed Sun. A chic Chinese restaurant with a Hollyvood decor. Refined dishes, with excellent *dim-sum* (steam-cooked foods), 130-210.

● ♦♦♦ ***La Fermette Marbeuf 1900,*** 5, rue Marbeuf, 75008, ☎ 47.23.31.31. AE, DC, Euro, Visa. Dressed in 1900's green ceramic, the *Fermette* is prettier and younger than ever. The good, subtle cooking of G. Isaac is worthy of the setting and permits the sly farmer Jean Laurent to attend to the very last detail, 120-200.

● ♦♦♦ ***Lord Gourmand,*** 9, rue Lord-Byron, 75008, ☎ 45.62.66.06. AE, Visa ; closed Sat, Sun, nat hols, Aug and 1 week at Christmas. Very few chefs have as brilliant a prize-list as Daniel Météry, a pupil of the Troisgros brothers, Paul Bocuse, Michel Guérard. The lessons have paid off to the delight of his regular customers. Spec : *bar à la vapeur en vinaigrette, souris d'agneau, tourte tiède aux pommes et abricots,* 150-250.

● ♦♦ ***La Barrière des Champs,*** 18, av. F.-D.-Roosevelt, 75008, ☎ 45.62.08.37. Closed Sat, Sun. One of Claude Verger's most gourmet *Barrières,* 150-280.

● ♦♦ ***Tong Yen*** (Mme Luong), 1 *bis,* rue Jean-Mermoz, 75008, ☎ 42.25.04.23. AE, DC, Visa. ♿ A well-frequented fashionable spot where Pierre Perret satisfies his customers. Good Chinese specialities, 200-250.

● ♦♦ ***La Dariole de Paris,*** 49, rue du Colisée, 75008, ☎ 42.25.66.76. AE, DC, Visa ; closed Sat, Sun and nat hols. Seasonal menus in a Napoléon III decor. Spec : *salade de caille, pigeon rôti aux cèpes.* On the ground floor, a small bistro, 100-250.

● ♦♦ ***L'Espace,*** 1, av. Gabriel, 75008, ☎ 42.66.11.70. AE, DC, Visa ; closed Sat noon. ♿ High-class crowds are guaranteed at the daily receptions of the untiring Jacques Collart who knows Paris society perfectly. Buffets, daily specials, inexpensive wines, 130-200.

● ♦♦ ***Le Grenadin,*** 46, rue de Naples, 75008, ☎ 45.63.28.92. Closed 2 weeks in Aug, Sat, Sun. The young Patrick Cirotte is a chef to follow. Spec : *lapin rôti jus à l'ail, ragoût de langoustines aux artichauts violets,* 120-250.

● ♦♦ ***Hédiard,*** 21, pl. de la Madeleine, 75008, ☎ 42.66.09.00. AE, DC, Visa ; closed Sun ♿ To prevent you from dying of hunger or thirst. Rest. 200, caterer, food shop and wine cellar.

♦♦ ***Prunier-Élysées,*** 25, av. des Champs-Élysées (in the arcade), 75008, ☎ 45.62.26.51. ♒ ♿ Seafood specialities. Reasonably-priced menu. Terrace, 150-220.

● ♦♦ ***Chez Modeste,*** 8, rue Miromesnil, 75008, ☎ 42.65.20.39. J.-P. Coffe is unique ! His clientele, his good dishes and modest wines direct from the vineyards, 150-260.

♦♦ ***Baumann-Marbeuf,*** 15, rue Marbeuf, 75008, ☎ 47.20.11.11. Good meat, 120-210.

♦♦ ***Le Drugstorien,*** 1, av. Matignon, 75008, ☎ 43.59.38.70. The Publicis chain's very good restaurant. Spec : *foie gras frais maison, sole à la ciboulette,* 120-210.

♦♦ ***La Ligne,*** 30, rue Jean-Mermoz, 75008, ☎ 42.25.52.65. AE, DC, Visa ; closed 5-31 Aug, 25-31 Dec, Sat, Sun. Spec : *fricassée de canette de Challans aux pêches fraîches, poêlon de langoustines et pétoncles au safran,* 170-220.

♦♦ ***Olsson's,*** 62, rue Pierre-Charon, 75008, ☎ 45.61.49.11. AE, Visa ; open daily 12-12. In an upper-floor apartment with enormous mirrors, Sweden in your plate : salmon, herring, 150-250.

● ♦ ***Savy,*** 23, rue Bayard, 75008, ☎ 47.23.46.98. Closed Sat, Sun and Aug. Auvergne-inspired fare, which is good, simple, and not too expensive : *choux aveyronnais, farçou, jambonneau aux lentilles,* 120-210.

♦ ***La Maison de la Vigne et du Vin,*** 21, rue François-Ier, 75008, ☎ 47.20.59.42. A lovely restaurant dedicated to wine, with cooking by the Layrac brothers, 120-210.

♦ ***Le Bistrot des Champs,*** 18, av. F.-D.-Roosevelt, 75008, ☎ 45.62.08.37. AE, Visa. ♿ Chic bistro for customers in a hurry. Spec : *tête de veau, magret de canard aux pêches,* 70-200.

♦ ***Le Colisée,*** 44, av. des Champs-Élysées, 75008, ☎ 42.25.44.50. Piano-bar atmosphere. Fish and seafood specialities, 120-210.

♦ ***L'Alsace,*** 39, av. des Champs-Élysées, 75008, ☎ 43.59.44.24. ♿ open non-stop. Food is improving, 110-150.

♦ ***Grand Pub de Lady Hamilton,*** 82, av. Marceau, 75008, ☎ 47.20.20.40. A good English-style pub, 120-210.

♦ ***Théâtre des Mathurins,*** 36, rue des Mathurins, 75008, ☎ 42.65.98.00. Friendly cafeteria open daily 'til midnight, 80-130.

PARIS 9th

Hotels :

● ★★★★(L) ***Scribe,*** 1, rue Scribe, 75009, ☎ 47.42.03.40. 217 rm, 5 apart. and 6 duplex. ♿ Napoléon III façade. Grand tradition, 1 400. Rest. ● ♦♦♦ ***les Muses,*** ♿ closed Sat, Sun and eve in Aug. A refined setting for thoroughly classical dishes prepared by the young P. Aracil. Spec : *baudruche de fruits de mer à la crème légère, poulet de Bresse en pot-au-feu,* 300-450. ♦♦ ***Le Jardin des Muses.*** Coffee shop with low-calorie specials, 100.

● ★★★★(L) ***Grand Hôtel,*** 2, rue Scribe, 75009, ☎ 42.68.12.13. Tx 220875. AE, DC, Euro, Visa. 583 rm, 12 suites ♿ Luxurious salons designed by Garnier. Across from the Opéra, 1 250. Rest. ♦♦♦ ***le Patio*** (noon only) ⚒ ♿ closed Aug, 210-320. ♦♦ ***Café de la Paix.*** In the tradition of supper after the show, 250-330.

★★★***Bergère Mapotel,*** 34, rue Bergère, 75009, ☎ 47.70.34.34. Tx 290668. AE, DC, Euro, Visa. 125 rm ⚒ ♿ The charm of an interior garden, 500.

★★★**Monterosa,** 30, rue La Bruyère, 75009, ☎ 48.74.87.90. Tx 650697. AE, DC, Visa. 34 rm 🛎 ♿ 240.
★★★**Aston,** 12, cité Bergère, 75009, ☎ 47.70.52.46. Tx 280025. 40 rm 🛎 ♿ 410.
★★**La Bruyère,** 35, rue La Bruyère, 75009, ☎ 48.74.03.69. AE, Visa. 31 rm, 200.
★**Royal Médoc,** 14, rue Geoffroy-Marie, 75009, ☎ 47.70.37.33. Tx 660063. AE, DC, Euro, Visa. 41 rm 🚫 400.

Restaurants :
● ◆◆◆◆ ***L'Opéra,*** 5, pl. de l'Opéra, 75009, ☎ (1) 42.68.12.13 ❄ ♿ closed Aug. Chef Gil Jouanin belongs among the greats. Under Charles Garnier's ceilings, classified historical monuments, fine traditional cooking, large wine selection, 300-400.
◆◆◆ ***Relais des Capucines,*** 12, bd des Capucines, 75009, ☎ (1) 42.68.12.13 ♿ Fast service, 150-200.
◆◆◆ ***Auberge Landaise,*** 23, rue Clauzel, 75009, ☎ (1) 48.78.74.40. AE, DC, Visa Ⓟ ♿ closed Aug, Sun. Spec : *foie gras chaud aux raisins, cassoulet,* 150-200.
● ◆◆ ***Ty Coz,*** 35, rue Saint-Georges, 75009, ☎ (1) 48.78.42.95. AE, DC, Visa ; closed Sun, Mon. An hommage to seafood, with 20 years of tradition, 200-250.
● ◆◆ ***Le Grand Café,*** 4, bd des Capucines, 75009, ☎ (1) 47.42.75.77. AE, DC, Visa ; open non-stop. « Belle Époque ». Seafood and good cooking, 180-200.
◆◆ ***Charlot,*** 12, pl. Clichy, 75009, ☎ (1) 48.74.49.64. AE, DC, Visa. Fish and seafood specialities, 220-310.
◆◆ ***Pagoda,*** 50, rue de Provence, 75009, ☎ (1) 48.74.81.48. Visa ; closed Sun in Aug. Chinese cooking. Spec : *canard laqué, pinces de crabes frites,* 120-210.
◆◆ ***Le Petit Riche,*** 25, rue Le Pelletier, 75009, ☎ (1) 47.70.68.68. AE, Visa ; closed 10-31 Aug and Sun. Improved cooking in this 1880's setting. Recommended spec : *petit salé, bœuf gros sel, foie de veau,* Loire wines, 100-200.
◆◆ ***Savoie-Bretagne,*** 21, rue St-Lazare, 75009, ☎ (1) 48.78.91.94. Closed 15 Jul-15 Aug, Sat, Sun, hols. Exclusively fresh produce, *charcuterie* and home-made desserts, 180-200.
◆◆ ***Le Square,*** 6, sq. de l'Opéra-Louis-Jouvet, 75009, ☎ (1) 47.42.78.50. Visa. ♿ A meeting-place of actors. And a few women, 95-200.

PARIS 10th

Hotels :
★★★★**Chamonix,** 8, rue d'Hauteville, 75010, ☎ (1) 47.70.19.49. 35 rm 🚫 600.
★★★**Pavillon l'Horset,** 38, rue de l'Échiquier, 75010, ☎ (1) 42.46.92.75. Tx 641905. AE, DC, Euro, Visa. 91 rm ♿ 425.
★★★**Gare du Nord,** 33, rue de Saint-Quentin, 75010, ☎ (1) 48.78.02.92. Tx 642415. AE, Euro, Visa. 49 rm 🚫 390.
★★**Frantour-Château-Landon,** 1-3, rue de Château-Landon, 75010, ☎ (1) 42.41.44.88. Tx 214761. AE, DC, Euro, Visa. 161 rm ♿ 305.
★★**Apollo,** 11, rue de Dunkerque, 75010, ☎ (1) 48.78.04.98. Tx 648895. AE. 45 rm, 300.
★★**Europe,** 98, bd Magenta, 75010, ☎ (1) 46.07.25.82. Euro, Visa. 36 rm 🚫 190.
★★**Vieille France,** 151, rue Lafayette, 75010, ☎ (1) 45.26.42.37. 50 rm 🚫 ♿ 230. Rest. ◆ closed Sun, 40-80.
★**France,** 57, rue des Petites Écuries, 75010, ☎ (1) 42.46.39.70. 40 rm 🚫 105.
★**Chabrol,** 46, rue de Chabrol, 75010, ☎ (1) 47.70.10.77. 25 rm, 150.

Restaurants :
● ◆◆ ***Au Châteaubriant,*** 23, rue de Chabrol, 75010, ☎ (1) 48.24.58.94. AE, Visa 🛎 🚫 ♿ closed 27 Jul-27 Aug, Sun, Mon. For more than 10 years, the skilled Guy Bürrli, former chef of J. Forno, has cooked pasta and offers excellent Italian cooking, 250.
● ◆◆ ***Brasserie Flo,*** 7, cour des Petites-Écuries, 75010, ☎ (1) 47.70.13.59. AE, DC, Visa ; closed 1-28 Aug. This 1900's restaurant is also owned by J.-P. Bucher ; excellent brasserie-style cooking. Book by phone to avoid queuing at the bar, 100-140.
● ◆◆ ***La Petite Tonkinoise,*** 56, rue du Faubourg-Poissonnière, 75010, ☎ (1) 42.46.85.98. Visa Ⓟ closed Aug-15 Sep, 24 Dec-5 Jan, Sun, Mon. Excellent Vietnamese cooking, 120-210.
◆◆ ***Louis XIV,*** 8, bd Saint-Denis, 75010, ☎ (1) 42.08.56.56. AE, DC, Visa Ⓟ ♿ closed 1 Jun-1 Sep, Mon, Tue. Superb fish and seafood dishes, and game in season. Traditional *grande cuisine,* 220-310.
◆◆ ***Le Paillon,*** 4, cour des Petites-Écuries, 75010, ☎ (1) 45.23.02.77. Visa ; closed Aug, Sun, Mon. Dishes with a southern flavour. Spec : *aïoli, bourride, daube aux cèpes et pâtes fraîches,* 170-210.
◆◆ ***Chez Michel,*** 10, rue de Belzunce, 75010, ☎ (1) 48.78.44.14. AE, DC, Visa Ⓟ closed 1-25 Aug, 15 days in Feb, 25 Dec, Fri, Sat. Spec : *salade de langoustines aux kiwis,* 200-320.
◆◆ ***Julien,*** 16, rue du Faubourg-Saint-Denis, 75010, ☎ (1) 47.70.12.06. AE, DC, Visa ♿ closed Jul. One of the most delightful "links" in J.-P. Bucher's chain. Good cooking in a *brasserie* whose success ensures its continuation. Expect an hour wait standing and 20 min seated during peak times, 100-180.
● ◆ ***Pinocchio,*** 49, rue d'Enghien, 75010, ☎ 47.70.01.98. AE, DC, Visa ; closed Sat noon, Sun and 31 Jul-30 Aug. All possible kinds of pasta. Excellent, simple Italian cooking, 55-165.
◆ ***Le New-Port*** (MM. Martin and Pion), 79, rue du Faubourg-Saint-Denis, 75010, ☎ (1) 42.46.81.59. Closed Sat noon and Mon. English-style fish restaurant, with a few places at the bar. Perfectly fresh fish, with a glorious platter of seafood, 120-210.

PARIS 11th

Hotels :
★★★★**Holiday Inn,** 10, pl. de la République, 75011, ☎ (1) 43.55.44.34. Tx 210651. AE, DC, Euro, Visa. 333 rm, 8 suites Ⓟ ♿ Modern comfort behind an historic facade, 970. Rest. ◆◆ ♿ 125-250.
★★★**Le Méridional,** 36, bd Richard-Lenoir, 75011, ☎ (1) 48.05.75.00. 36 rm, 400.
★★**Du Nord et de l'Est,** 49, rue de Malte, 75011, ☎ (1) 47.00.71.70. 44 rm 🚫 220.
★★**Royal-Voltaire,** 53, rue Richard-Lenoir, 75011, ☎ (1) 43.79.75.67. AE, Visa ; 55 rm, 230.

Restaurants :
● ◆◆◆ ***A Sousceyrac,*** 35, rue Faidherbe, 75011, ☎ (1) 43.71.65.30. AE, Visa ; closed 1-31 Aug, 1 week (Easter), Sat, Sun. Spec : game, *lièvre à la royale, foie gras.* Weight-watchers, stay away ! Good desserts, and a good, inexpensive wine selection, 120-220.
● ◆◆ ***Le Chardenoux,*** 1, rue Jules-Vallès, 75011, ☎ (1) 43.71.49.52. AE, Visa Ⓟ In an authentic 1900's bistro, Alain Morel invites you to discover his excellent professional cooking. Spec : *pudding à la moelle,* seasonal produce, 210-250.
● ◆◆ ***Le Grand Méricourt,*** 22, rue de la Folie-Méricourt, 75011, ☎ (1) 47.00.43.87. Closed

12 Aug-9 Sep, 1 week in winter, Sun, Mon noon. J.-C. Charles Adib, the sympathetic and dynamic owner, watches over everything. Fresh cuisine according to the market. Spec : *cassoulet,* 200.
● ♦♦ ***Le Péché Mignon,*** 5, rue Guillaume-Bertrand, 75011, ☎ (1) 43.57.02.51. Visa ; closed Aug, 1 week school hols in Feb, Sun, Mon. Spec : *panaché de poissons aux raviolis de St-Jacques, fricassée de ris et rognon de veau au sauternes,* 150-210.
● ♦♦ ***Le Repaire de Cartouche,*** 8, bd des Filles-du-Calvaire, 75011, ☎ (1) 47.00.25.86. Visa Ⓟ ♿ closed 25 Jul-24 Aug, Sat, Sun and nat hols. Dishes from the Southwest ; rich and well served, 70-210.
● ♦♦ ***Chez Philippe*** (M. Serbource), 106, rue de la Folie-Méricourt, 75011, ☎ (1) 43.57.33.78. Ⓟ closed Sat, Sun and Aug, nat hols. Delightful family and associates, directed by the warm and competent Philippe Serbource, offer fine, rich specialities from the Southwest. Good wines, 200.
● ♦ ***Astier,*** 44, rue J.-P.-Timbaud, 75011, ☎ (1) 43.57.16.35. closed 9 Aug-2 Sep, 25 Dec-1 Jan, Sat, Sun. It's good ! It's a bistro ! It's not expensive ! The menu changes daily, and Michel Picquart knows his wines, 80-95.

PARIS 12th

Hotels :
★★★***Paris-Lyon Palace*** (Inter-Hôtel), 11, rue de Lyon, 75012, ☎ (1) 43.07.29.49. 128 rm ♿ 420. Rest. ♦♦ ***le Relais de la Méditerranée,*** 120-180.
★★★***Azur,*** 5, rue de Lyon, 75012, ☎ (1) 43.43.88.35. Tx 670038. AE, Visa. 64 rm, 355.
★★★***Modern-Hôtel Lyon,*** 3, rue Parrot, 75012, ☎ (1) 43.43.41.52. Tx 230369. AE, Visa. 53 rm ⚘ Calm and modern comfort, 360.
★★***Jules Cesar,*** 52, av. Ledru-Rollin, 75012, ☎ (1) 43.43.15.88. Tx 670945. 48 rm ⚘ 180.
★***Aveyron,*** 5, rue d'Austerlitz, 75012, ☎ (1) 43.07.86.86. AE, Visa. 3 rm ⚘ 170.

Restaurants :
● ♦♦♦ ***Au Pressoir,*** 257, av. Daumesnil, 75012, ☎ (1) 43.44.38.21. Visa ; closed Aug, Easter school hols, Sat and Sun. The freshened-up setting highlights Henri Seguin's pleasant cooking : *rougets à la purée de cresson, lapereau farci aux cèpes, mesclun aux oreilles de porc.* The charming and competent Mme Seguin takes care of the service, 270-300.
♦♦♦ ***Le Train Bleu,*** 20, bd Diderot, gare de Lyon, 1st Floor, 75012, ☎ (1) 43.43.09.06. Tx 220064. AE, DC, Euro, Visa ♿ Historically classified 1900's setting. Cooking from the Lyons and Forez regions, 180-220.
● ♦♦ ***Le Trou Gascon,*** 40, rue Taine, 75012, ☎ (1) 43.44.34.26. Ⓟ closed 15 Aug-15 Sep, Sat and Sun. Now an annex of Alain Dutournier since he opened on rue Castiglione. His charming wife manages efficiently. Good country cooking. Southwest spec : *jambon de pays, conflit de canard à la galette de cèpes, ravioles au foie gras,* good Bordeaux wines and choice of armagnacs, 250-320.
♦♦ ***La Gourmandise,*** 271, av. Daumesnil, 75012, ☎ 4 (1) 43.43.94.41 Ⓟ ♿ closed 15-31 Aug, Sat noon, Sun. Alain Denoual's efforts are praiseworthy ; we must encourage him. Spec : *cabillaud à la compote d'aubergines, magret de canard aux navets nouveaux,* 130-200.
♦♦ ***La Petite Alsace,*** 4, rue Taine, 75012, ☎ (1) 43.43.21.80. Closed Sat noon, Sun, Mon and Aug. Strasbourg cooking at Paris's doorstep, 150-200.

PARIS 13th

Hotels :
★★***Gobelins,*** 57, bd Saint-Marcel, 75013, ☎ (1) 43.31.79.89. 45 rm, 300.
★★***Résidence des Gobelins,*** 9, rue des Gobelins, 75013, ☎ (1) 47.07.26.90. AE, Visa. 32 rm ⚘ 290.
★★***Véronèse,*** 5, rue Véronèse, 75013, ☎ (1) 47.07.20.90. 66 rm ⚘ 150.

Restaurants :
● ♦♦ ***Le Petit Marguery,*** 9, bd de Port-Royal, 75013, ☎ (1) 43.31.58.59. AE, DC, Euro, Visa ; closed Sun, Mon and Aug, 23 Dec-2 Jan. Bravo to the Cousyn brothers for their good humor and fine cooking. Spec : *champignons des bois,* game in season, 230.
● ♦♦ ***Tikoc,*** 13, pl. de Vénétie, av. de Choisy, 75013, ☎ (1) 45.84.21.00 ⚘ ♿ The family-like cabaret of the Asian community. Dinner and show, just like in Hong Kong or Singapore. Spec's *à la vapeur,* 200.
● ♦♦ ***Oui-Tiens, les Olympiades,*** 103, rue de Tolbiac, 75013, ☎ (1) 45.85.98.30. A big brasserie in the middle of the Chinese quarter, with the French welcome of the proprietor, Pierre Luong. Steam-cooked specialities *(dim-sun)* at reasonable prices, 50-80.
● ♦♦ ***Les Vieux Métiers de France,*** 13, bd Auguste-Blanqui, 75013, ☎ (1) 45.88.90.03, (1) 45.81.07.07. AE, DC, Euro, Visa ; closed Sun, Mon. Spec : *cocotte d'oursins, sauté de langoustines maraîchères,* 140-300.
♦♦ ***Chinatown Olympiades,*** 44, av. d'Ivry, 75013, ☎ (1) 45.84.72.21. Chic, but reasonable prices, 120-210.
● ♦ ***Hawaï,*** 87, av. d'Ivry, 75013, ☎ (1) 45.86.91.90. Visa ♿ closed Thu. The chic Asian brasserie. Vietnamese spec : *nems, raviolis,* grilled pork and chicken, 70-100.
♦ ***Chez Jacky,*** 109, rue du Dessous-des-Berges, 75013, ☎ (1) 45.83.71.55. Spec : *foie gras armagnac maison, queue de langoustine tiède au pamplemousse,* 200.
♦ ***Sing-Sing,*** 100, av. d'Ivry, 75013, ☎ (1) 45.82.93.07/08. Vietnamese spec's, 80-130.
♦ ***Le Traiteur,*** 28, rue de la Glacière, 75013, ☎ (1) 43.31.64.17. AE, DC, Euro, Visa ♿ closed 15 Dec-10 Jan, Sat, Sun. French regional cooking, 140-210.

PARIS 14th

Hotels :
★★★★(L) ***P.L.M. Saint-Jacques,*** 17, bd Saint-Jacques, 75014, ☎ (1) 45.89.89.80. 797 rm Ⓟ ♿ Close to Montparnasse, 1 100. Rest. ♦♦ ***Café Français,*** closed Aug. Regional dishes, 150-220.
★★★★(L) ***Montparnasse Park Hotel,*** 19, rue du Cdt-Mouchotte, 75014, ☎ (1) 43.20.15.51. Tx 200135, 203518. AE, DC, Euro, Visa. 950 rm including 35 apart. Ⓟ ⚘ ⚘ ♿ All the advantages of the new, 995. Rest. closed 4-31 Aug. ♦♦ ***la Ruche,*** 120-200 ; ♦♦ ***le Montparnasse 25,*** 190-230.
★★★***Aiglon,*** 232, bd Raspail, 75014, ☎ (1) 43.20.82.42. AE, Visa. 50 rm, 8 suites Ⓟ ⚘ Convenience in a 1925 building, 350.
★★***Châtillon Hôtel,*** 11, sq. de Châtillon, 75014, ☎ (1) 45.42.31.17. 31 rm ⚘ closed Aug, 190.
★★***Carlton Palace,*** 207, bd Raspail, 75014, ☎ (1) 43.20.62.94. Tx 200183. Visa. 63 rm ♿ 280.
★★***Moulin Vert,*** 74, rue du Moulin-Vert, 75014, ☎ (1) 45.43.65.38. AE, DC, Visa. 28 rm, 290.

Restaurants :
● ♦♦♦ ***Le Duc*** (Jean and Paul Minchelli), 243, bd Raspail, 75015, ☎ (1) 43.20.96.30 ♿

closed Sat, Sun, Mon. Fresh fish feast by Jean and Paul Minchelli. An annex in Geneva, another in the Seychelles : shellfish, *loup cru en vessie tartare, sole au vinaigre,* seafood, 300-450.

♦♦♦ ***Les Armes de Bretagne,*** 108, av. du Maine, 75014, ☎ (1) 43.20.29.50. AE, DC, Euro, Visa ♿ closed Sun eve and Mon, 4-26 Aug, 1 week beg Jan and beg May. Rich, refined, and costly. Hot oyster dishes, *bar en croûte, cassolette de langouste,* 120-250.

♦♦♦ ***Le Dôme,*** 108, bd du Montparnasse, 75014, ☎ (1) 43.35.25.81. AE, DC, Visa ; closed Mon. Excellent fish and seafood served in this famous setting, redecorated by Slavik, 160-220.

● ♦♦ ***Auberge de l'Argoat*** (M. Goareguer), 27, av. Reille, 75014, ☎ (1) 45.89.17.05. Closed Aug, Sun, Mon. First place goes to Brittany cooking, with such dishes as the *andouille de Guéméné aux poissons de la côte,* 140-200.

● ♦♦ ***Lous Landés,*** 157, av. du Maine, 75014, ☎ 45.43.08.04. Visa. An abundance of flowers and paintings, and Jean-Pierre's piano add to the excellent Landaise cooking of the valiant Georgette Descat. Spec. : *macaronade de coquillages, foie gras en papillote, garbure,* 150-300.

♦♦ ***Provost,*** 1, rue de Coulmiers, 75014, ☎ (1) 45.39.85.99. AE, Visa Ⓟ ♿ closed Aug, Sat, Sun and nat hols, 250-280.

♦♦ ***Le Flamboyant,*** 11, rue Boyer-Barret, 75014, ☎ (1) 45.41.00.22. closed Aug, Sun eve, Mon and Tue noon. The best Antilles restaurant in Paris, 150-250.

♦♦ ***Zeyer,*** 234, av. du Maine, 75014, ☎ (1) 45.40.43.88. Brasserie, 120-190.

● ♦♦ ***Gérard et Nicole,*** 6, av. J.-Moulin, 75014, ☎ (1) 45.42.39.56. AE, Visa Ⓟ closed 15 Jul-15 Aug, Sat and Sun. Finally in a setting which pleases them and their customers, Gérard and Nicole continue to offer a warm welcome and very good cooking. Spec : *saumon aux feuilles de lard, feuilleté de pigeon à la sauce betterave,* Loire wines, 230-290.

♦♦ ***La Chaumière Paysanne,*** 7, rue Léopold-Robert, 75014, ☎ (1) 43.20.76.55. AE, DC, Euro, Visa ⛱ closed 15 Jul-20 Aug, Sun, Mon noon. Didier Bondu's good dishes change frequently. Spec : *langouste tiède aux truffes,* 150-220.

● ♦ ***La Cagouille*** (G. Allemandou), 89, rue Daguerre, 75014, ☎ (1) 43.22.09.01 ♿ closed Sun, Mon and 26 Jul-3 Sep. The best and undoubtedly cheapest fish bistro in Paris. The proprietor spends his nights at Rungis, awaiting daily shipments from the coast ! Spec : *moules brûle-doigts, rougets grillés, drôle de petite friture* which varies according to the ocean harvest ; a magnificent selection of cognacs, 120-210.

● ♦ ***Chez Fernand,*** 11, rue G.-Saché, 75014, ☎ (1) 45.43.65.76. AE, Visa ♿ closed Sun. The proprietor makes his own bread, butter and *charcuterie,* and prepares his delectable *camemberts,* 100-250.

♦ ***La Coupole,*** 102, bd du Montparnasse, 75014, ☎ (1) 43.20.14.20. Visa ♿ closed Aug. Good, simple fare in a 1925 setting, which draws a varied and ever-numerous clientele, 100-160.

● ♦ ***Au Feu Follet*** (Mme Bihourd), 5, rue Raymond-Losserand, 75014, ☎ (1) 43.22.65.72 ♿ closed Sat noon, Sun, 20 Jul-20 Aug. A friendly little restaurant, where the proprietress is hard at work in the kitchen. *Bœuf mode* and *brandade de morue* served long into the evening, 100-135.

♦ ***L'Assiette,*** 181, rue du Château, 75014, ☎ (1) 43.22.64.86. Closed Aug, 1 week in May, Sat noon and Mon. Only 5 tables to sample the Southwest spec's, 120-210.

♦ ***Olympic Entrepôt,*** 5, rue de Pressensé, 75014, ☎ (1) 45.41.06.17. For movie buffs and fans of honest family-style cooking, 80-130.

♦ ***Les Petites Sorcières,*** 12, rue Liancourt, 75014, ☎ (1) 43.21.95.68. Closed Aug, 1 week at Christmas, Sat noon, Sun. Good, simple fare and friendly service, 150.

PARIS 15th

Hotels :

★★★★(L) ***Hilton International Paris,*** 18, av. Suffren, 75015, ☎ (1) 42.73.92.00. Tx 200955. AE, DC, Euro, Visa. 79 rm, 29 apart. ⚘ Ⓟ ⛱ ⛌ ♿ View of the Seine near the Eiffel Tower, 1 100. Rest. ♦♦♦♦ ⚘ ♿ ***le Toit de Paris*** (closed 27 Jul-28 Aug, Sun eve only). The top of the Hilton offers a splendid view of the capital, 235-325. Rest. ♦♦ ⛌ ***le Western,*** 155-220 ; ♦ ***la Terrasse*** (coffee-shop), 100-140.

★★★★(L) ***Sofitel Paris,*** 8-12, rue Louis-Armand, 75015, ☎ (1) 45.54.95.00. Tx 200432. AE, DC, Euro, Visa. 635 rm ⚘ Ⓟ ⛱ ▭ ♿ At the city limits, a contemporary palace with its own panoramic swimming pool, 1 000. Rest. ♦♦♦ ***le Relais de Sèvres*** ♿ closed Aug, Sat and Sun, 180-280.

★★★★(L) ***Nikko,*** 61, quai de Grenelle, 75015, ☎ (1) 45.75.62.62. Tx 260012. AE, DC, Euro, Visa. 777 rm, 9 suites Ⓟ ⛱ ▭ ⛌ ♿ The ultramodern masterpiece of the newly constructed Seine waterfront, 900. Rest. ● ♦♦♦ ♿ ***les Célébrités.*** Joel Robuchon's brilliant culinary traditions perpetrated masterfully by his gifted friend and successor, Jacques Sénéchal. Spec : *tête de veau aux herbes, fricassée de ris et rognons.* Magnificent desserts in a spacious, modern setting, 245-475.

★★★***Suffren la Tour,*** 20, rue Jean-Rey, 75015, ☎ (1) 45.78.61.08. Tx 204459. AE, DC, Euro, Visa. 407 rm ⚘ Ⓟ ♨ ♿ Modern, close to the Eiffel Tower, 410. Rest. ♦♦ ♿ closed Aug, 150-210.

★★***Pacific Hôtel,*** 11, rue Fondary, 75015, ☎ (1) 45.75.20.49. Tx 201346. Euro. 66 rm. Small and classic, 230.

Restaurants :

● ♦♦♦ ***Olympe*** (Dominique Nahmias), 8, rue Nicolas-Charlet, 75015, ☎ (1) 47.34.86.08. AE, DC, Visa ; closed 29 Jul-21 Aug, 22 Dec-2 Jan, Mon. Eve only ex Thu. Dominique Nahmias's charm and competence for high quality cooking. Fashionable Parisian and international clientele, 300-450.

● ♦♦♦ ***Morot-Gaudry,*** 6, rue de la Cavalerie, 75015, ☎ (1) 45.67.06.85. Visa ⚘ closed Sat, Sun. In the "open sky", with a superb view on the roofs of Paris and the Eiffel tower from the beautiful terrace on warm days, J.-P. Morot-Gaudry's good cooking with good wines, 230-350.

● ♦♦♦ ***Le Pfister,*** 1, rue du Dr-Jacquemaire-Clemenceau, 75015, ☎ (1) 48.28.51.38 ♿ closed Sat noon, Sun and Aug, Sep and hols. Hushed opulence in a calm street ; Catherine and Philippe offer a celestial *feuilleté d'endives au roquefort, rillettes de saumon, ragoût de tête de veau, mijoté aux légumes, feuilleté aux prunes et à la canelle.* Reasonably-priced wines, 130-250.

♦♦♦ ***Bistro 121,*** 121, rue de la Convention, 75015, ☎ (1) 45.57.52.90. AE, DC, Euro, Visa ♿ closed 14 Jul-20 Aug, 23 Dec-1 Jan, Sun eve and Mon. Spec : *foie gras sous la cendre, lièvre à la royale,* 185-300.

● ♦♦ ***Pierre Vedel,*** 19, rue Duranton, 75015, ☎ (1) 45.58.43.17 Ⓟ ⛌ ♿ closed Sat and Sun from 9 Jul to 8 Aug. In this restaurant, Pierre Vedel has kept the tradition of good Sète region cooking. He shares his time between sports and cooking : *bourride,* fish, but also *tête de veau Vaugirard, côte de bœuf ;* pleasant and low-priced wines, 200-300.

● ♦♦ ***L'Aquitaine,*** 54, rue de Dantzig, 75015, ☎ (1) 48.28.67.38. AE, DC, Euro, Visa ; closed

Sun, Mon. Seven competent women under the direction of Christiane Massia prepare dishes inspired by the Southwest. Spec : *foie gras,* meat from Chalosse, regional wines, 230-300.

● ♦♦ ***Chez Maître Albert,*** 8-10, rue de l'Abbé-Groult, 75015, ☎ (1) 48.28.36.98. AE, DC, Euro, Visa. closed Sat noon. Artists from the Beaux-Arts exhibit while Mr. Civel serves little masterpieces. Spec : *bouillabaisse en filets, escalope de saumon frais Maître Albert,* 170-210.

● ♦♦ ***Le Clos de la Tour,*** 22, rue Falguière, 75015, ☎ (1) 43.22.34.73. AE, DC, Euro, Visa ; closed Aug, Sat noon, Sun. Small, selective menu, 150-220.

● ♦♦ ***Courrège,*** 2, rue de Langeac, 75015, ☎ (1) 48.42.55.26. Closed Sun. Good cooking, 120-210.

● ♦♦ ***La Petite Bretonnière,*** 2, rue de Cadix, 75015, ☎ (1) 48.28.32.39. AE, Visa ♿ closed 5 Aug-2 Sep, 24 Dec-7 Jan, Sat noon, Sun. Southwest spec's : *foie gras frais au torchon, terrine de St-Jacques aux artichauts* (in season), 100-155.

● ♦♦ ***La Renardière,*** 12, rue Falguière, 75015, ☎ (1) 43.20.39.78. Visa ♿ closed Aug, Sat, Sun. A delightful restaurant run by a conscientious young couple. An astonishing set menu of southwestern fare for a mere 120 F. Truffles in season, 120-180.

● ♦♦ ***Napoléon et Chaix*** (M. Pousse), 46, rue Balard, 75015, ☎ (1) 45.54.09.00. Closed Jul, 2 weeks in Sep, Sat noon and Sun. Unsophisticated, enjoyable, varied meals, 150-240.

● ♦♦ ***La Maison Blanche*** (José Lampreia), 82, bd Lefèvre, 75015, ☎ (1) 48.28.38.83 ♿ closed Sat noon, Sun and Mon. In a few years, the friendly and talented José Lampreia has become the fashionable customers' "darling". Thanks to the quality of his cooking, he is now part of our jury. Light dishes, reasonable prices, 130-320.

● ♦♦ ***La Gauloise*** (M. Aphécetche), 59, av. de La Motte-Picquet, 75015, ☎ (1) 47.34.11.64. AE, Visa ❀ ♿ closed Sat and Sun, 220-310. It's worth trying out the next-door annex, *la Gitane,* at the pleasant, inexpensive bistro-kitchen.

● ♦♦ ***Aux Trois Horloges*** (M. Pons), 73, rue Brancion, 75015, ☎ (1) 48.28.24.08. AE, DC, Euro, Visa. Real *pied-noir* cooking in the great tradition of the late Mimi de Guyotville, well-prepared by her son Bernard. *Couscous, paëlla, méchoui,* 200. Home catering service.

● ♦♦ ***Le Restaurant du Marché,*** 59, rue de Dantzig, 75015, ☎ (1) 48.28.31.55, (1) 45.32.26.88. The Massia family's first restaurant. Excellent spec's from the Landes : meat from Chalosse, regional wines, 200-250.

♦♦ ***Aux Senteurs de Provence,*** 295, rue Lecourbe, 75015, ☎ (1) 45.57.11.98 ♿ closed 26 Jul-25 Aug, 28 Mar-7 Apr, Sun, Mon. Spec : *bouillabaisse aïoli, bourride,* 160-190.

♦♦ ***Le Croquant,*** 28, rue Jean-Maridor, 75015, ☎ (1) 45.58.50.83. AE, DC, Visa ♿ closed Aug, Sun, Mon. To be encouraged for the reasonable prices. Spec : *filets d'anguilles en brouet de madiran, magret de canard Mulard à la purée de cèpes,* 110-240.

♦♦ ***L'Oyonnade,*** 38, rue Sébastien-Mercier, 75015, ☎ (1) 45.79.42.98. Visa ♿ closed 3-27 Aug, 24 Dec-1 Jan, Sat noon, Sun. Marius Chanat's star offering is his *civet d'oie.* Other good dishes : *remoulade de pieds de veau, andouillette à la moutarde,* live oysters and lobsters, 135-200.

● ♦ ***Le Volant,*** 13, rue B.-Dussanne, 75015, ☎ (1) 45.75.27.67. Visa ; closed Aug, Sat noon and Sun. The quarter frequented by competition racing drivers. Simple, tasty dishes under the direction of the ex-driver proprietor, G. Houel. Superb meats and *pommes G. Houel,* 180-200.

● ♦ ***Le Caroubier*** (M. Michel), 8, av. du Maine, 75015, ☎ (1) 45.48.14.38. Closed Sun eve and 15 Jul-21 Aug. Excellent *couscous,* prepared in all possible ways. Good *merguez* and *pastillas,* 120-210.

● ♦ ***Moulin de la Boulange*** (M. Chanrion), 70, rue de Vouillé, 75015, ☎ (1) 48.28.81.61. AE, DC, Euro, Visa ; closed Sat and Sun. The "Ragoûgnasse Prize" brings luck to Jean Chanrion : his mill is never empty while the wheel turns on Beaujolais and Coteaux du Lyonnais. Good *charcuterie,* 120-150.

● ♦ ***Le Tout Alger,*** 364, rue de Vaugirard, 75015, ☎ (1) 45.32.78.26. Closed Sun, Mon and Aug. *Couscous, paëlla, brochettes, merguez,* 80-180.

● ♦ ***La Gitane,*** 53 *bis,* av. La Motte-Picquet, 75015 ☎ (1) 47.34.62.92. Visa ♿ closed Sun and 1 May. Attractive bistro setting, 80-110.

♦ ***L'Amanguier,*** 51, rue du Théâtre, 75015, ☎ (1) 45.77.04.01. Closed 1 May, 80-110.

♦ ***Le Pacifico,*** 50, bd du Montparnesse, 75015, ☎ (1) 45.48.63.87. Closed 25 Dec-1 Jan, Mon noon. For the "Chicanas" and Mexican spec's : *tacos, enchiladas, guacamole,* 80-120.

PARIS 16th

Hôtels :

★★★★(L) ***Raphaël,*** 17, av. Kléber, 75016, ☎ (1) 45.02.16.00. Tx 610356. AE, DC, Euro, Visa. 87 rm, 4 suites ♿ Rather showy ; fashionable clientele, 1 000. Rest. ♦♦ closed Sun, 180-200.

★★★★***Résidence du Bois*** (Relais et châteaux), 16, rue Chalgrin, 75016, ☎ (1) 45.00.50.59. 20 rm ⚘ ♨ Napoléon III residence, 975.

★★★★***Baltimore,*** 88 *bis,* av. Kléber, 75016, ☎ (1) 45.53.83.33. Tx 611591. AE, DC, Euro, Visa. 119 rm ♿ Chic but in perfect taste. Ideal for business men, 1 000. Rest. ● ♦♦♦ ***l'Estournel,*** closed Sat, Sun and Aug. Enjoyable fare, 185-310.

★★★★***Alexander,*** 102, av. Victor-Hugo, 75016, ☎ (1) 45.53.64.55. Tx 610373. 62 rm ⚘ ❀ 660.

★★★***Farnese,*** 32, rue Hamelin, 75016, ☎ (1) 47.20.56.66. 37 rm ❀ Calm near the pl. V.-Hugo, 400.

★★★***Muette,*** 32, rue de Boulainvilliers, 75016, ☎ (1) 45.25.13.08. AE, DC, Visa. 13 rm ⚘ closed Aug. Former 18thC mansion, 360.

★★★***Régina de Passy,*** 6, rue de la Tour, 75016, ☎ (1) 45.24.43.64. 62 rm ❀ 340.

★★★***Résidence Impériale,*** 155, av. Malakoff, 75016, ☎ (1) 45.00.23.45. AE, DC, Euro, Visa. 30 rm, 300.

★★★***Victor Hugo*** (Mapotel), 19, rue Copernic, 75016, ☎ (1) 45.53.76.01. Tx 630939. AE, DC, Euro, Visa 🅿 ♿ Lovely rms, winter garden, 450.

★★***Keppler*** (Inter-Hôtel), 12, rue Keppler, 75016, ☎ (1) 47.20.65.05. Tx 620440. AE, Euro. 48 rm ❀ 240.

★★***Exelmans,*** 73, rue Boileau, 75016, ☎ (1) 42.24.94.66. 53 rm ❀ ♿ 260.

★★***Villa d'Auteuil,*** 28, rue Poussin, 75016, ☎ (1) 42.88.30.37. 17 rm, Quiet little hotel, 195.

Restaurants :

● ♦♦♦♦ ***Faugeron*** (Henri Faugeron ; Relais gourmand), 52, rue de Longchamp, 75016, ☎ (1) 47.04.24.53. ❀ closed Aug, end Dec, Sat and Sun. Henri Faugeron successfully blends Corrèze regional recipes with modern light ones : *truffes, foie gras,* mushrooms, *côte de veau gratinée,* interesting selection of low-priced wines, 185-440.

● ♦♦♦♦ ***Jamin*** (Joël Robuchon), 32, rue de Longchamp, 75016, ☎ (1) 47.27.12.27. 🅿 ❀

closed Jul, Sat and Sun. Joël Robuchon, our last year's prize-winner (*ex-aequo* with G. Savoy), is still the leader of the great young French chefs. In a new setting, assisted by his charming wife and an efficient staff, his preparations have reached the highest standards : *raviolis de langoustines, morue fraîche aux aromates, agneau rôti en croûte de sel,* great wines, 350-450. Early booking is highly recommended.

● ♦♦♦♦ ***Le Pré Catelan,*** rte de Suresnes, bois de Boulogne, 75016, ☎ (1) 45.24.55.28. Tx 614983. AE, DC, Visa. Ⓟ ♨ ♘ ♿ closed Feb, Sun eve and Mon. Gaston Lenôtre, a "flying" man and a real "band master", still takes time for his restaurant, a beautiful little paradise in the woods... very near Paris, 480-550.

● ♦♦♦♦ ***Jean-Claude Ferrero,*** 38, rue Vital, 75016, ☎ (1) 45.04.42.42. AE, DC, Visa. ♨ ♘ ♿ closed 15 Aug-1 Sep, 24 Dec-5 Jan, Sat and Sun. In his beautifully-restored private mansion, J.-C. Ferrero's mushroom spec's, exceptional menus, 350-450.

● ♦♦♦♦ ***Le Vivarois,*** 192, av. Victor-Hugo, 75016, ☎ (1) 45.04.04.31. AE, DC, Visa. Ⓟ ♨ ♿ closed Aug, Sat and Sun. We are pleased to welcome Claude Peyrot, a talented and brilliant chef, to our jury. An ultra-modern decor for traditional cooking based on market-fresh produce. Spec : *huîtres chaudes au curry, pâté de canard F. Point, pied de porc farci aux légumes et aux truffes, coq ivre de pommard,* good wines, 250-310.

● ♦♦♦ ***Guy Savoy,*** 28, rue Duret, 75016, ☎ (1) 45.00.17.67. ❄ ♿ closed Sat and Sun. In spite of his award of the "Grand Prix Hachette des Cuisiners 1985" (*ex-aequo* with Joël Robuchon), Guy Savoy has remained simple. He now makes an even greater effort to satisfy his demanding customers, delighted with his light, refined preparations, and progress is constant, 290-400.

● ♦♦♦ ***Le Toit de Passy*** (Yann Jacquot), 94, av. Paul-Doumer, 75016, ☎ (1) 45.24.55.37. Visa. ⚘ Ⓟ ♿ closed Sat noon, Sun, nat hols, 22 Dec-5 Jan. Above the roofs of Paris, a small gourmet's paradise. Modern decor with a terrace for Yann Jacquot's good cooking. Spec : *blancs de poireaux à la vinaigrette de truffes, rognon de veau rôti entier, poulet de Bresse à la crème d'estragon,* 170-300.

● ♦♦♦ ***Le Petit Bedon,*** 38, rue Pergolèse, 75016, ☎ (1) 45.00.23.66. AE, DC, Visa ; closed Sat, Sun, and Aug. Thanks to Jean Dives, who has beautifully redecorated this pleasant restaurant, Christian Ignace can now devote himself to his simple but great cooking. Prices have not increased. Spec : *tourte au frais, homard cocotte,* 250-300.

● ♦♦♦ ***Prunier Tratkir,*** 16, av. Victor-Hugo, 75016, ☎ (1) 45.00.89.12. AE, DC, Visa. ♿ closed 1 May, Mon and Tue. A restaurant-fish-shop since 1925 ; traditions continue, seafood dishes being the speciality of the house, 220-320.

● ♦♦♦ ***Jenny Jacquet,*** 136, rue de la Pompe, 75016, ☎ (1) 47.27.50.26. Visa. ❄ ♿ closed Feb hols, Aug, Sat and Sun. Dishes and wine from the Loire region, prepared by the proprietor himself. Spec : *mousseline de brochet au beurre blanc,* 180-220.

● ♦♦♦ ***Paul Chêne,*** 123, rue Lauriston, 75016, ☎ (1) 47.27.63.17. AE, DC, Visa ; closed Sat, Sun and Aug. Paul Chêne is, thanks to his steady and inspired cooking, one of the greatest ambassadors of French cooking. Spec : *beignets de brandade à la rouille, merlan frit en colère,* game in season, 220-310.

♦♦♦ ***Pavillon des Princes,*** 69, av. de la Porte-d'Auteuil, 75016, ☎ (1) 46.03.31.63. AE, DC, Visa. An enjoyable restaurant near the bois de Boulogne, 220-350.

♦♦♦ ***Michel Pasquet,*** 59, rue La Fontaine, 75016, ☎ (1) 42.88.50.01. AE, DC, Visa ; closed Sat noon and Sun. Spec : *panaché de salade aux langoustines et au filet d'oie mariné, desserts,* 260-300.

♦♦♦ ***La Grande Cascade,*** bois de Boulogne, 75016, ☎ (1) 45.06.33.51. AE, DC, Euro, Visa. ⚘ Ⓟ ♘ ♿ closed 20 Dec-20 Jan, noon and eve 15 May-15 Oct ; noon only the rest of the year. A pastoral setting for an extremely Parisian restaurant, 190-350.

♦♦♦ ***Le Chandelier,*** 4, rue P.-Valéry, 75016, ☎ (1) 47.04.55.22. AE, DC, Visa. ♘ closed Jewish hols, Fri and Sat eve May to Sep. A luxurious kosher restaurant in an 18thC mansion, run by the Beth-Din of Paris. Light cooking, 200-300.

♦♦♦ ***Le Moï,*** 7, rue Gustave-Courbet, 75016, ☎ (1) 47.04.95.10. Closed Aug and Mon. Vietnamese dishes for Parisian clientele, 160-260.

♦♦♦ ***Île de Kashmir,*** quai de Billy, across from 32, av. de New-York, 75016, ☎ (1) 47.23.77.78, 47.23.50.97. Tx 649108. AE, Euro, Visa, closed 26-31 Dec. Two floating restaurants : the *Lotus* and the *Jardin de Shalimar.* Thousand-and-One-Nights decor for this Indian cooking from Kashmir, 200-300.

♦♦♦ ***Ramponneau,*** 21, av. Marceau, 75016, ☎ (1) 47.20.59.61. AE, DC, Visa ; closed Aug, 280-300.

● ♦♦ ***Brasserie le Stella*** (M. Guerlet), 133, av. Victor-Hugo, 75016, ☎ 47.27.60.54. Closed Aug and 1 week Feb. An attractive, highly fashionable brasserie ; the proprietor buys his wines directly off the property, 160-210.

♦♦ ***Conti*** (M. Fayet), 72, rue Lauriston, 75016, ☎ (1) 47.27.74.67. Visa ; closed Sat, Sun, nat hols and Aug. Excellent Italian spec's, 250-300.

♦♦ ***Le Grand Chinois,*** 6, av. de New-York, 75016, ☎ (1) 47.23.98.21. AE, DC ; closed 1-26 Aug and Mon. The heights of Chinese cooking, 80-120.

♦♦ ***Le Vieux Galion,*** 10, allée du Bord-de-l'Eau, 75016, ☎ (1) 45.06.26.10. AE, DC, Visa ♿ Spec : fish and shellfish, in a boat-restaurant anchored in the Seine, 150-300.

♦ ***Chalet des Iles,*** lac Inférieur, bois de Boulogne, 75016, ☎ (1) 42.88.04.69. DC, Visa ; closed 15 Sep-15 Apr. The country at your doorstep. Unfortunately, the weather is unpredictable, 150-210.

PARIS 17th

Hotels :

★★★★(L) ***Concorde La Fayette,*** 5, pl. du Gal-Kœnig, 75017, ☎ (1) 47.58.12.84. Tx 650892, 650905. AE, DC, Euro, Visa. 1 000 rm, 25 apart. Ⓟ ♿ A very modern complex, dotted with boutiques, conference rooms, theatres, accommodation and restaurant facilities, 1 300. Rest. ♦♦ ♿ ***l'Arc-en-Ciel,*** 150-210 ; ♦♦♦ ***l'Étoile d'Or.*** Spec : *effeuillé de raie bouclée aux herbes potagères, beuchelle Ed. Nignon,* 220-310 ; ♦ ***les Saisons*** (coffee-shop), 120-210. Panoramic bar on the 33rd floor.

★★★★(L) ***Méridien Paris,*** 81, bd Gouvion-Saint-Cyr, 75017, ☎ (1) 47.58.12.30. 1 027 rm, 16 apart. Ⓟ Modern complex near the Porte Maillot, 1 000. Rest. ♦♦ ***le Clos Longchamp,*** 150-230 ; ♦♦ ***le Yamato*** (Japenese dishes), 80-140 ; ♦ ***la Beaujolaise,*** 80-130 ; ♦ ***Arlequin*** (coffee-shop), 70-120.

★★★★***Splendid Étoile,*** 1 *bis,* av. Carnot, 75017, ☎ (1) 47.66.41.41. Tx 280773. AE, DC, Euro, Visa. 57 rm, 3 apart. ⚘ ♘ ❄ ♿ View of the Arc de Triomphe, 650. Rest. ♦♦ ♿ closed 3-26 Aug, Sat and Sun, 220-310.

★★★***Belfast,*** 10, av. Carnot, 75017, ☎ (1) 43.80.12.10. 59 rm ⚘ 🅿 ♿ Near the Arc de Triomphe, 360.

★★★***Monceau Élysées,*** 108, rue de Courcelles, 75017, ☎ (1) 47.63.33.08. 29 rm, 350.

★★★***Mercedes l'Horset,*** 128, av. de Wagram, 75017, ☎ (1) 42.27.77.82. Tx 660751. AE. 37 rm ♿ 330.

★★***Résidence Villiers,*** 68, av. de Villiers, 75017, ☎ (1) 42.27.18.77. AE, DC, Euro, Visa. 28 rm, 255.

Restaurants :

● ♦♦♦♦ ***Michel Rostang*** (Relais gourmand, Relais et châteaux), 20, rue Rennequin, 75017, ☎ (1) 47.63.40.77. Visa ; closed 26 Jul-26 Aug, Sat noon, Sun. The restaurant is becoming more and more beautiful, which makes you further appreciate Michel Rostang's cooking and his wife's charming welcome. Spec : *soufflé léger de homard, tarte chaude aux escargots,* good wine selection, 270-450.

● ♦♦♦ ***La Barrière de Clichy,*** 1, rue de Paris, 92110 Clichy, ☎ (1) 47.37.05.18. AE, DC, Visa ; closed Sat noon, Sun. Claude Verger has just turned over his last restaurant to the young chef Yves Le Galles who is talented and favours fish which he prepares perfectly, 250-300.

● ♦♦♦ ***Le Bernardin,*** 18, rue Troyon, 75017, ☎ (1) 43.80.40.61. AE, Visa ; closed Sun, Mon and Aug. A pleasant setting where Gilbert Le Coze takes care of his starving regulars. Fresh fish selected nightly at Rungis (the largest fishing port in France), 350-450.

● ♦♦♦ ***Ma Cuisine,*** 18, rue Bayen, 75017, ☎ (1) 45.72.02.19. AE, DC, Visa 🅿 ♿ closed Sun. A new setting to enhance the meat and fish dishes prepared by Alain Donnard. Glorious desserts, 250-310.

● ♦♦♦ ***Chez Georges,*** 273, bd Pereire, 75017, ☎ (1) 45.74.31.00. Closed Aug. Open till 11 pm. The leg of lamb is carved before you in the dining-room once a week. Dishes on the other days include : *train de côte de bœuf,* memorable fresh chips. The cellar is well looked after by the proprietor, Roger Mazarguil, 120-210.

● ♦♦♦ ***Le Manoir de Paris,*** 6, rue P.-Demours, 75017, ☎ (1) 45.74.61.58. AE, DC, Visa ; closed 5 Jul-5 Aug, Sat, Sun. Francis Vendehende *(la Ferme St-Simon)* and his chef, P. Groult, give a daily demonstration of their competence and talent in this charming restaurant. Spec : *morue fraîche aux anchois, langoustines aux courgettes,* fine wines, impeccable service, 150-300.

● ♦♦ ***Le Petit Colombier,*** 42, rue des Acacias, 75017, ☎ (1) 43.80.28.54. Visa 🅿 ♿ closed Sat and Sun noon, 25 Dec-3 Jan, 25 Jul-17 Aug. Bernard Fournier, the untiring and competent "President" (of Parisian chefs) does not forget his profession and his pleasant small country-style inn. Spec : *foie de veau, terrine de mousserons à la julienne de truffes,* selected wines at reasonable prices, 160-310.

● ♦♦ ***Chez la Mère Micnel,*** 5, rue Rennequin, 75017, ☎ (1) 47.63.59.80. Visa ♿ closed Aug, Sat, Sun, hols. The conservatory of *beurre blanc* perpetuated by M. Gaillard in his authentic little bistro, 150-230.

● ♦♦ ***Paul et France,*** 27, av. Niel, 75017, ☎ (1) 47.63.04.24. AE, DC, Visa ❀ closed 14 Jul-15 Aug, Sat and Sun. Members of the Paris-St-Germain football club and G. Romano's other clients are delighted. The boss always has a good story to tell, and his cooking flirts with the summits. Excellent fresh produce, 110-250.

● ♦♦ ***Chez Laudrin,*** 154, bd Pereire, 75017, ☎ (1) 43.80.87.40. AE, Visa ♿ closed 24 Mar-1 Apr, Sat and Sun. Solid cooking and good wines (billed according to amount consumed) are offered by Jacques Billaud, ably seconded by the young chef Benoît Teillet. Spec : *pétoncles farcies, bourride de baudroie, bavette* and delicious chips, 250.

♦♦ ***L'Écrevisse,*** 212 *bis,* bd Pereire, 75017, ☎ (1) 45.27.17.60. AE, DC, Visa ♿ closed Aug, 25 Dec-1 Jan, Sat and Sun. Spec : *mousse de St-Jacques au homard et au beurre de ciboulette, selle d'agneau farcie au pistou,* 220-310.

● ♦♦ ***Dessirier,*** 9, pl. du Mal-Juin, 75017, ☎ (1) 43.80.50.72. DC, Visa 🅿 ♿ closed 20 Jul-20 Aug. Recently taken over by the extremely rigorous Alain Robinet. Delectable oysters, and beaujolais and sancerre of equal quality, 250-350.

● ♦♦ ***Apicius,*** 122, av. de Villiers, 75017, ☎ (1) 43.80.19.66. Closed 8-24 Aug, Sat, Sun. In a handsome new decor, J.-P. Vigato demonstrates the talent which marked his start. Spec : *tête de veau remoulade, ragoût de homard et de turbot à l'ail,* modest, enjoyable light wines, 150-250.

● ♦♦ ***La Braisière,*** 54, rue Cardinet, 75017, ☎ (1) 47.63.40.37. Closed Sat noon, Sun. Good cooking from the Breton B. Vaxelaire. Spec : *braisière de canard, poêlée de lotte,* 120-230.

● ♦♦ ***Lajarrige,*** 16, av. de Villiers, 75017, ☎ (1) 47.63.25.61. Visa ; closed 4 Aug-1 Sep, Sat noon, Sun. Musketeer J.-C. Lajarrige receives you in his 17thC setting. Regional cooking by E. Marrottat, a student of André Dagoin. Spec : *foie gras en papillote à l'émincé de homard, cuisse de canard confite et fumée,* 100-200.

● ♦♦ ***La Petite Auberge,*** 38, rue Laugier, 75017, ☎ (1) 47.63.85.51, (1) 47.63.85.81. DC, Visa ; closed Aug, Sun, Mon. Go discover the fine cooking of Léo Harbonnier. Spec : *turbot Camille Renault, millefeuille,* 115-230.

● ♦♦ ***Le Relais d'Anjou,*** 15, rue de l'Arc-de-Triomphe, 75017, ☎ (1) 43.80.43.82. DC, Visa ; closed Aug, Sat noon, Sun. Excellent Angevine cooking. Spec : *charlotte de crabe et d'avocat au coulis de tomate,* 170-230.

● ♦♦ ***La Soupière,*** 154, av. de Wagram, 75017, ☎ (1) 42.27.00.73. AE, Visa ; closed 8-24 Aug, 20-28 Dec, Sat, Sun. Soups prepared by C. Thuillart are excellent, especially the peach. Good menu at 130. Spec : *salade de raie aux perce-pierres, jarret de veau au vinaigre,* 130-200.

● ♦♦ ***Verger Pereire,*** 275, bd Pereire, 75017, ☎ (1) 45.74.33.32. C. Verger returns to his first love. *Prix fixe* menu includes a *faux-filet grillé sauce anchoïade* and excellent chips, 80-130.

● ♦♦ ***La Toque,*** 16, rue de Tocqueville, 75017, ☎ (1) 42.27.97.75. Visa ♿ closed 14 Jul-15 Aug, Christmas hols, Sat and Sun. Alain Donnard gives the full measure of his ability. Spec : *bœuf à la ficelle, paillard de veau,* 250-300.

● ♦♦ ***La Barrière de Neuilly,*** 275, bd Pereire, 75017, ☎ (1) 45.74.33.32. Verger cooking at its least expensive, with the same everpresent concern for quality, and the famous fine tart made to order, 150-260.

● ♦♦ ***La Côte de Bœuf,*** 4, rue Saussier-Leroy, 75017, ☎ (1) 42.27.73.50. AE, DC, Visa ; closed Sat, Sun, 1 week Easter, 3-31 Aug and Christmas hols. A superb joint of beef, along with excellent dishes inspired by Fernande Allard, the chef's mentor for twelve years, 120-210.

♦♦ ***Baumann-Ternes,*** 64, av. des Ternes, 75017, ☎ (1) 45.74.16.66 ♿ Alsatian specialities, 90-180.

♦♦ ***Brasserie Lorraine,*** pl. des Ternes, 75017, ☎ (1) 42.27.80.04. Oyster and seafood vivarium, 130-210.

♦♦ ***Guyvonne,*** 14, rue de Thann, 75017, ☎ (1) 42.27.25.43. Closed 24 Dec-5 Jan, 14 Jul-4 Aug, Sat and Sun. Carefully-prepared dishes made to measure, and served in the calm of the parc Monceau, 220-310.

♦♦ **Le Santenay,** 75, av. Niel, 75017, ☎ (1) 42.27.88.44. closed 30 Jul-16 Aug, Sun eve and Mon. An extensive choice of classical dishes ; highest quality fare prepared by the chef Francis Vallot, 220-310.
♦♦ **Chez Léon,** 32, rue Legendre, 75017, ☎ (1) 42.27.06.82. DC, Visa ; closed Aug, Sat, Sun. A neighbourhood institution adopted by Parisians. Spec : *foie gras maison,* fish *au beurre blanc,* game in season, 120-170.
♦♦ **La Coquille,** 6, rue du Débarcadère, 75017, ☎ (1) 45.74.25.95, (1) 45.72.10.73. Visa ; closed Aug, 25 Dec-1 Jan, Sun, Mon. C. Lausecker continues the fine tradition of Paul Blache's cooking. A festival of seafood, 170-230.
♦♦ **Les Cyprès,** 40, rue des Dames, 75017, ☎ (1) 43.87.86.19. AE, Visa ; closed Aug, Sat noon, Sun. Enjoyable cooking by Marie-Laure Watrinelle. Fish, 45-130.
♦♦ **Epicure 108,** 108, rue Cardinet, 75017 ☎ (1) 47.63.50.91. Closed Sun, Mon. Seasonal menu with fresh produce. Try the "menu élégant", 150-200.
♦♦ **Sormani,** 4, rue du Gal-Lanrezac, 75017, ☎ (1) 43.80.13.91 ⚘ closed 1-25 Aug, 1 week at Easter, 25 Dec-1 Jan, Sat, Sun. In a setting of blue velvet, Pascal Fayet offers you the finest Italian gourmet festival in Paris. Accept recommendations. Pasta, *raviolis, carpaccio,* ham, *rougets* sublime ! Great chiantis, 150-250.
● ♦ **Le Beudant,** 97, rue des Dames, 75017, ☎ (1) 43.87.11.20. Closed 15-30 Jan, Sat noon, Sun. It's quite small, but you'll appreciate the excellent regional cooking. Spec : *salade de moules, poulet au vinaigre,* Loire wines, 200-300.
♦ **Le Beau Manoir,** 16, rue Brey, 75017, ☎ (1) 46.22.92.02. Closed Sun. A pleasant, inexpensive meal just across from the Étoile. Spec : *choucroute de poissons,* 80-130.

PARIS 18th

Hotels :
● ★★★★**Mapotel Terrass,** 12, rue Joseph-de-Maistre, 75018, ☎ (1) 46.06.72.85. Tx 280830. AE, DC, Euro, Visa. 108 rm, 19 apart. A remarkable view of Paris from the upper floors, 590. Rest. ♦♦ **le Guerlande,** 80-260.
★★★**Résidence Montmartre,** 10, rue Burcq, 75018, ☎ (1) 46.06.45.28. 46 rm in a typical Vieux-Montmartre street, 230.
★★**Capucines-Montmartre,** 5, rue A.-Briant, 75018, ☎ (1) 42.52.89.80. 31 rm, 180.
★★**Prima Lepic,** 29, rue Lepic, 75018, ☎ (1) 46.06.44.64. AE, DC ⚘ 38 rm, 185.
★★**Royal Montmartre,** 68, bd de Clichy, 75018, ☎ (1) 46.06.22.91. 51 rm ♿ 155. Brasserie **le Chat Noir,** 50-80.

Restaurant :
● ♦♦♦♦ **Beauvilliers** (Édouard Carlier), 52, rue Lamarck, 75018, ☎ (1) 42.54.19.50, (1) 42.54.54.42. Visa ⚘ ♿ closed 1-15 Sep, Sun, Mon noon. Let the feast begin ! is Édouard Carlier's motto. He welcomes you in his beautiful Montmartre restaurant as if you were a surprise guest. Superb fresh bouquets, refined cooking. Green terrace in nice weather, 260-450.
♦♦♦ **Les Fusains,** 44, rue Joseph-de-Maistre, 75018, ☎ (1) 42.28.03.69. Visa ♿ closed Sun, Mon and Sep, Eve only. Spec : *feuilleté léger de petits-gris et champignons des bois, aiguillettes de canard au miel et au vinaigre, gratin de fruits rouges au champagne,* 220-310.
● ♦♦ **Clodenis,** 57, rue Caulaincourt, 75018, ☎ (1) 46.06.20.26. AE, DC, Visa ; closed Sun. The second "great" restaurant at the Butte. Spec : game in season, *foie gras de canard, turbot aux algues, gibiers,* 130-170.
♦♦ **Les Chants du Piano,** 3, rue Steinlen, 75018, ☎ (1) 46.06.37.05. AE, DC, Visa. Closed 1-15 Feb, 15-31 Aug, Sun, Mon. Michel Derbane's recital for gourmands : *cigale de mer et cresson de fontaine au basilic, suprêmes de pigeonneau « Mozart »,* 200-300.
♦♦ **Grandgousier,** 17, av. Rachel, 75018, ☎ 43.87.66.12. AE, DC, Euro, Visa 🅿 ♿ closed a week in Aug, Sat, Sun. Good home cooking, with a modern touch, 110-220.
♦♦ **La Crémaillère 1900,** 15, pl. du Tertre, 75018, ☎ (1) 46.06.58.59. AE, DC ⚘ A picturesque 1900's brasserie, 160-210.
♦ **Le Bateau-Lavoir,** 8, rue Garreau, 75018, ☎ (1) 46.06.02.00. Good food at honest prices, 60-130.

Paris

PARIS 19th and 20th

Hotels :
★★**Parc,** 1, pl. A.-Carrel, 75019, ☎ (1) 42.08.08.37. 51 rm ♨ ⛱ 250.
★★**Pyrénées Gambetta,** 12, av. du Père-Lachaise, 75020, ☎ (1) 47.97.76.57. 30 rm ⛱ 265.
★★**Unic-Hôtel,** 6, rue du Pont-de-l'Eure, 75020, ☎ (1) 43.61.93.10. 34 rm ♿ closed Aug, 230.

Restaurants :
♦♦♦ **Relais des Pyrénées,** 1, rue du Jourdain, 75020, ☎ (1) 46.36.65.81. AE, DC, Euro, Visa ; closed Aug, Sat. Spec : *piperade, garbure, saumon frais au champagne, poulet basquaise sauté,* 220-310.
♦♦ **Au Cochon d'Or,** 192, av. Jean-Jaurès, 75019, ☎ (1) 46.07.23.13. AE, DC, Euro, Visa 🅿 ♿ Spec : beef, fish, 240-310.
♦♦ **Le Petit Pré,** 1, rue Bellevue, 75019, ☎ (1) 42.08.92.62. Closed Sat, Sun. An attractive little rustic bistro at the heights of Belleville. Spec : *mousse de poireaux aux gambas, blanquette de turbot aux raviolis de légumes, crêpière de Pierre-Jean,* 120-210.
♦♦ **La Chaumière,** 46, av. Secrétan, 75019, ☎ (1) 46.07.98.62. AE, DC, Euro, Visa ; closed Aug and Sun. Spec : *tartare de langue de veau, barbue à la crème d'oursin,* 70-150.
♦ **Dagorno,** 190, av. Jean-Jaurès, 75019, ☎ (1) 46.07.02.29. AE, DC, Euro, Visa ♿ closed Sat. Spec : home-smoked salmon, *foie gras de canard maison,* 165-230.

BOULOGNE-BILLANCOURT

Paris 10 ☎ 1 ✉ 92100

Restaurants :
● ♦♦ **La Bretonnière,** 120, av. J.-B.-Clément, ☎ (1) 46.05.73.56. AE, DC, Visa. ♿ closed Sat, Sun. Marc Laurens intends to freshen up the Breton style setting, a good initiative ! Classic cooking, 130-300.
● ♦♦ **La Petite Auberge Franc-Comtoise,** 86, av. J.-B.-Clément, ☎ (1) 46.05.67.19, 46.05.22.35. ♿ closed 4 Aug-1 Sep, Sun, hols. The calm of the Franche-Comté next to the Seine and the bois de Boulogne. Spec : *potée jurassienne,* seafood, Arbois wines, 130-250.
♦♦ **Au Comte de Gascogne,** 89, av. J.-B.-Clément, ☎ (1) 46.03.47.27. ♨ ⛱ ♿ closed Aug, Sat, Sun, hols, 300-420.

CHENNEVIÈRES-SUR-MARNE

Paris 17 ☎ 1 ✉ 94430

Restaurant :
♦♦ **L'Écu de France,** 31, rue de Champigny, ☎ (1) 45.76.00.03. ⚟ 🅿 ♨ ⚘ closed 1-8 Sep, Sun eve and Mon. Terrace overlooking the river, 120-210.

CLICHY

Paris 6.5 ☎ 1 ⊠ 92110

Restaurant :

● ♦♦ ***La Bonne Table,*** 119, bd Jean-Jaurès, ☎ (1) 47.37.38.79. Closed Sep, Sun and Mon. Simple fish and shellfish dishes prepared by the proprietress. Other spec : *boudin de saumon, chou farci aux St-Jacques, bourguignon de lotte,* 120-220.

COURBEVOIE

Boulogne 10, Paris 10 ☎ 1 ⊠ 92400

Restaurants :

● ♦♦ ***Helodini,*** 46, bd de Verdun, ☎ (1) 43.33.53.09. Closed 15 Aug-1 Sep, Sun. Excellent seafood specialities prepared by J.-P.-Crème : *lotte au miel de framboise, rascasse au cidre, raie grillée sauce roquefort,* 120-200.

♦♦ ***Les Trois Marmites,*** 215, bd St-Denis, ☎ (1) 43.33.25.35. closed 28 Mar-9 Apr, 4 Aug-2 Sep, Sat, Sun. Fish and mushrooms according to season : *rougets à la moelle, bar aux cèpes, boudin de campagne aux reinettes,* 100-200.

GENNEVILLIERS

Paris 11 ☎ 1 ⊠ 92230

ℹ 117, av. G.-Péri, ☎ (1) 47.99.33.92.

Hotel :

★★★***Julius,*** 6, bd Camélinat, ☎ (1) 47.98.79.37. Visa. 20 rm, 450. Rest. ● ♦♦♦ Ⓟ ♿ closed Sat noon, Sun. Julien Forêt, alias Julius, oversees everything. Light, inspired cooking based on fresh produce. Spec : *boudin de chou vert, aiguillette de canette à la confiture d'oignons,* 190-300.

LEVALLOIS-PERRET

Paris 8 ☎ 1 ⊠ 92300

Restaurants :

● ♦♦ ***Le Jardin,*** 9, pl. J.-Zay, ☎ (1) 47.39.54.02. AE, DC, Visa. Ⓟ ♿ closed Sat, Sun and 10 Aug-10 Sep. The country at your doorstep. The setting is as enjoyable as the light cooking. Spec : *morue fraîche à l'aigre-doux, fricassée de poulet au safran,* 120-200.

● ♦♦ ***Pointaire,*** 46, rue de Villiers, ☎ (1) 47.57.44.77. DC, Visa. ♿ closed Sat noon, Sun. A culinary institution with a youthful zest. Friendly service from the Albert family. Spec : *carbonnade flamande* and the indispensable *beuchelle tourangelle,* 120-210.

♦♦ ***Gouvain,*** 11, rue Louis-Rouquier, ☎ (1) 47.58.51.09. Closed Sat, Sun. A bakery from the turn-of-the-century has been transformed into a plush restaurant. The menu changes weekly. Spec : *mousse d'artichauts aux langoustines, turbot poêlé à la crème de ciboulette,* 150-175.

♦ ***Au Petit Poucet,*** 1, bd de Levallois, ☎ (1) 47.38.61.85. Visa. closed 15-31 Jan, Sat eve, Sun. New-wave country inn, 120-180.

LIVRY-GARGAN

Paris 19 ☎ 1 ⊠ 93190

ℹ pl. Hotel-de-Ville, ☎ (1) 43.30.61.60.

Restaurants :

● ♦♦ ***Auberge Saint-Quentinoise,*** 23, av. de la République, ☎ (1) 43.81.13.08. closed Sun eve and Mon. Michel Nicoleau is an excellent chef and now, in his own restaurant, he gives full measure of his ability. Spec : *homard à l'anis et à l'ail doux.* 125-300.

♦ ***La Petite Marmite,*** 8, bd de la République, ☎ (1) 43.81.29.15. Closed 5-aug-1 Sep, Feb school hols. Simple fare in an enjoyable little inn. Spec : fish, grilled meats, 110-220.

NEUILLY-SUR-SEINE

Paris 8 ☎ 1 ⊠ 92200

Hotels :

★★★★***Club Méditerranée,*** 58, bd Victor-Hugo, ☎ (1) 47.58.11.00. Tx 610971. AE, DC, Visa. 345 rm Ⓟ ♿ Spacious rooms. Ideal for seminars, 840. Rest. ● ♦♦ ♿ A lavish buffet reminiscent of Club Méditerranée holiday meals, with daily special dessert, and as much wine as you like, 170.

★★***Parc,*** 4, bd du Parc, ☎ (1) 46.24.32.62. Tx 613689. 71 rm, 240.

Restaurants :

● ♦♦♦ ***Jacqueline Fénix,*** 42, av. Ch.-de-Gaulle, ☎ (1) 46.24.42.61. Visa. ♿ closed Aug, end Dec, Sat and Sun. A delightful reception in J. Fénix's very feminine restaurant. Spec : *poissons cuits aux algues, jambon à l'os aux choux,* 260-350.

● ♦♦ ***Bouvier,*** 1, pl. Parmentier, ☎ (1) 46.24.11.19. ♿ closed 1-20 Aug, Sat (Oct-Apr), Sun. An agreeable stop for Yves Bouvier's Lyonnais cooking : *quenelles, anguille rôtie,* pheasant Louis XIV (in season), 180-250.

● ♦♦ ***La Tonnelle Saintongeaise,*** 32, bd Vital-Bouhot, ☎ (1) 46.24.43.15. ♿ closed 15 Aug-15 Sep, Feb school hols, Easter, Sat, Sun. A delightful spot next to the water with a terrace in summer. Regional spec's : *chaudrée, cagouilles, lapereau au pineau,* 150-200.

● ♦♦ ***Le Manoir,*** 4, rue de l'Église, ☎ (1) 46.24.04.61. AE, Visa. ♿ closed Sat, Sun eve and 26 Jul-26 Aug. Light fare prepared under the proprietor's watchful eye : *ragoût de canard aux écrevisses, filet de sole aux pâtes fraîches* and delicious wines from the Loire, 220-310.

♦♦ ***Carpe Diem,*** 10, rue de l'Église, ☎ (1) 46.24.95.01. Closed Aug, Sat noon, Sun, 150-220.

♦♦ ***Sébillon,*** 20, av. Ch.-de-Gaulle, ☎ (1) 46.24.71.31. Excellent leg of lamb, 120-210.

♦♦ ***La Rascasse,*** 10, av. de Madrid, ☎ (1) 46.24.05.30. AE, DC, Visa ; closed hols, Sat and Sun. Fish dishes, 320-450.

♦♦ ***Jarrasse,*** 4, av. de Madrid, ☎ (1) 46.24.07.56. AE, DC, Visa. ♿ closed 15 Jul-31 Aug, Sun eve and Mon, 250-350.

♦ ***Focly,*** 10, rue P.-Chatrousse, ☎ (1) 46.24.43.36. AE, Visa ♿ closed end Aug, 60-500.

♦ ***Pizza Livio,*** 6, rue de Longchamp, ☎ (1) 46.24.81.32 closed Aug and end-of-year hols, 105-130.

♦ ***Le Martin-Pêcheur,*** 79, bd Bourdon, ☎ (1) 46.24.05.85. Fashionable barge-restaurant, 120-210.

♦ ***L'Amanguier,*** 12, av. de Madrid, ☎ (1) 47.45.79.73. Closed 1 May, 80-110.

ORLY

Paris 16 ☎ 1 ⊠ 94396

Hotels :

★★★***Hilton International Orly,*** ☎ (1) 46.87.33.88. Tx 250621. AE, DC, Euro, Visa. 380 rm Ⓟ ♿ 650. Rest. ♦♦ ***la Louisiane,*** 200-250 ; ♦ ***le Café du Marché,*** 100-150.

Restaurant :

♦♦♦ ***Maxim's,*** aérogare d'Orly-Ouest, ☎ (1) 46.87.16.16. Tx 201389. AE, Visa Ⓟ ♿ 190-310.

Le PRÉ-SAINT-GERVAIS

Paris 7 ☎ 1 ⊠ 93310

Restaurant :

● ♦♦ ***Le Pouilly-Reuilly,*** 68, rue André-Joineau, ☎ (1) 48.45.14.59. AE, DC, Visa Ⓟ closed Aug, Sun and nat hols. A genuine bistro with good solid food prepared by the proprietor. *Poulet sauté aux écrevisses, œufs en meurette, rognons de veau dijonnaise.* The proprietress takes care of the wine, 120-150.

ROISSY-EN-FRANCE

Paris 26 ☎ 1 ⊠ 95500 Gonesse

✈ *Roissy-Charles-de-Gaulle,* ☎ (1) 38.64.20.76. *Air France,* ☎ (1) 38.64.16.65. *Air Inter,* ☎ (1) 35.39.25.25.

R.E.R., line B.

Car-hire : *Budget* train + auto Roissy I, ☎ (1) 38.62.50.56 and 57, Roissy II, ☎ (1) 38.62.50.58 and 59.

Hotels :

★★★***Sofitel,*** aéroport Charles-de-Gaulle, ☎ (1) 38.62.23.23. 375 rm Ⓟ ▭ ⚲ 500. Free bus service to terminals. Panoramic restaurant ♦♦ 130-200. Brasserie and pizzeria, 80-130.

★★★***Holiday Inn,*** 54, rue de Paris, ☎ (1) 39.88.00.22. 250 rm Ⓟ ❀ ♿ Free bus service to terminals. Spacious, functional rooms, 500. Rest. 120-210.

★★***Arcade Roissy,*** 10, rue du Verseau (S.N.C.F.-R.E.R. station), ☎ (1) 38.62.49.49. 360 rm Ⓟ 350. Rest. ♦ 120-200.

Restaurant :

♦♦♦♦ ***Maxim's,*** at the air terminal 1, ☎ (1) 38.62.24.16. Spec : *terrine de pigeon, poulet de Bresse,* 160-300.

RUEIL-MALMAISON

Paris 15 ☎ 1 ⊠ 92500

Restaurants :

♦♦♦ ***El Chiquito,*** 126, av. Paul-Doumer, ☎ (1) 47.51.00.53 Ⓟ ♨ ♿ closed Aug, Sat, Sun. Spec : *gigot de mer aux pâtes fraîches, blanc de barbue, mousseline de légumes coulis homard,* 250-280.

♦♦ ***Relais de Saint-Cucufa,*** 114, rue Gal-Miribel, ☎ (1) 47.49.79.05. AE, DC, Visa Ⓟ ♿ closed 15-31 Aug, Sun eve, Mon eve and Wed, 150-250.

SAINT-OUEN

Paris 7 ☎ 1 ⊠ 93400

ℹ pl. de la République, ☎ (1) 42.54.77.36.

Hotel :

★***Alhambra,*** 23, rue E.-Renan, ☎ (1) 42.54.06.22. closed Aug, 30 rm ❀ 80.

Restaurant :

● ♦♦ ***Coq de la Maison Blanche,*** 37, bd Jean-Jaurès, ☎ (1) 42.54.01.23. AE, Visa. Ⓟ ♿ closed week-ends of 14 Jul, 15 Aug, Sun eve and Wed eve. A gastronomical institution in this big suburb at Paris's threshold. Varied fare, with a new speciality every day. Not to mention the *boudin froid,* the *terrine de filets de harengs* and the famous *coq au vin.* Remarkable wine selection, 120-250.

La VARENNE-SAINT-HILAIRE

Paris 16 ☎ 1 ⊠ 94210

ℹ 63, av. du Bac, ☎ (1) 42.83.84.74.

Hotel :

Saint-Maur, ⊠ 94100 :

★★★***Winston,*** 119, quai Winston-Churchill, ☎ (1) 48.85.00.46. Tx 231400. AE, DC, Visa. 24 rm Ⓟ 310.

Restaurant :

● ♦♦♦ ***La Bretèche,*** 171, quai de Bonneuil, ☎ (1) 48.83.38.73. ♿ closed Sun, Mon, Aug. Max Lamoureux and his wife Christiane provide delightful service to match the superb fare served on the banks of the Seine (you dine in the garden in summer) : *foie gras macéré aux sauternes, bar poché à l'huile de noix,* capital desserts and magnificent cellar, particularly well-stocked with burgundy wines, 220-310.

VINCENNES

Paris 6 ☎ 1 ⊠ 94300

ℹ 11, av. de Nogent, ☎ (1) 48.08.13.00.

Hotel :

★★***Donjon Vincennes,*** 22, rue du Donjon, ☎ (1) 43.28.19.17. 28 rm, closed 1 week Feb, Aug, 180.

Restaurant :

♦ ***Au Petit Bourguignon,*** 46, av. du Gal-de-Gaulle, ☎ (1) 43.28.05.27. Ⓟ ♿ closed Aug, Sun and Mon, 70-130.

● Recommended addresses

Multistore Hachette-Opéra

6, bd des Capucines, 75009, ☎ (1) 42.65.83.52. open daily 10 am-1:30 am. Open since the beginning of the year, the first French *Multistore* covers 6 000 square meters, and offers shopping and leisure facilities unlike those of any other store. A well-lit, restful setting for sales departments specialised in communications, with highly competitive prices for video and laser-music equipment, compact records, and new electronic appliances, a video club, a computer club open to children, a diffusion centre equipped with giant television screen, an extensive newspaper and magazine department (1 000 French and foreign publications), a literature department (15 000 works), tobacconist's, grocery and caterer's stores, and two inexpensive restaurants : ***l'Opéra,*** with its plush decor and view of the palais Garnier, club atmosphere with varied cocktails, a large buffet with hors-d'œuvres, salads, cold dishes, and grills, and ***la Place,*** for rapidly-served light meals in a friendly, informal atmosphere.

Music-halls and cabarets : *Alcazar,* 62, rue Mazarine, 75006, ☎ (1) 43.29.02.20. Ⓟ An entirely new show, setting and atmosphere, thanks to J.-M. Rivière's long-awaited return to the Alcazar. ***Crazy Horse Saloon,*** 12, av. George-V, 75008, ☎ (1) 47.23.32.32. Alain Bernardin's extraordinary nude revues are justifiably rated amongst the world's best. ***Don Camillo,*** 10, rue des Saints-Pères, 75007, ☎ (1) 42.60.25.46. A tradition of dinners and shows ensured by the entertainers of today and tomorrow. ***Folies-Bergères,*** 32, rue Richer, 75009, ☎ (1) 42.46.77.11. A huge theatre (seats 1 600) for lasting memories of Paris night-life. ***Lido,*** 116 *bis,* av. des Champs-Élysées, 75008, ☎ (1) 45.63.11.63. A perfectly organised show with astonishing stage machinery, lavish costumes, and of course the famous Blue-Bell Girls, ensuring the Lido's glittering reputation. ***Michou,*** 80, rue des Martyrs, 75018, ☎ (1) 46.06.16.04. Michou, famed as "the only show that really colours Paris nights", with the *Michettes,* the best transvestite show in town. ***Moulin-Rouge,*** pl. Blanche, 75009, ☎ (1) 46.06.00.19. The most famous "dance floor" in Paris. ***Paradis Latin,*** 28, rue du Cardinal-Lemoine, 75005, ☎ (1) 43.25.28.28. Closed Tue. Former Alcazar impresarios and artists with stage machinery worthy of the Châtelet Theatre. Show for children on Wed afternoon.

Clubs, discotheques : ***Adison Square Gardel,*** 23, rue du Cdt-Mouchotte, 75014, ☎ (1) 43.21.54.58. From the genteel 5 pm "tea and dance-floor" to the Fri night American style. ***Cherry Lane,*** 8, rue des Ciseaux, 75006, ☎ (1) 43.26.28.28. Left bank disco, young, often foreign clientele. ***Caveau de la Huchette,*** 5, rue de la Huchette, 75005, ☎ (1) 43.26.65.05. A jazz institution. ***Club 79,*** 79, av. des Champs-Élysées, 75008, ☎ (1) 47.23.68.75. ***Chez Castel,*** 15, rue Princesse, 75006, ☎ (1) 43.26.90.22. As private as it is famous. ***Élysées-Matignon,*** 2, av. Matignon, 75008, ☎ (1) 42.25.73.13. Oil kings, show-biz Parisians, the high-fashion world... a luxury haunt. ***Keur Samba,*** 79, rue La Boétie, 75008, ☎ (1) 43.59.03.10. African music ; one of Paris's liveliest night-spots. ***La Main Jaune,*** pl. de la Porte-de-Champerret, 75017, ☎ (1) 47.63.26.47. Disco dancing... on roller-skates ! ***Le Palace,*** 8, rue du Faubourg-Montmartre, 75009, ☎ (1) 42.46.10.87. Still one of the most "in" night-spots in Paris, which continues to attract both local roughnecks and the Paris jet-set. ***Regine's Club,*** 49, rue de Ponthieu, 75008, ☎ (1) 43.59.21.60. A brilliant night-life capital. ***La Scala,*** 188 *bis,* rue de Rivoli, 75001, ☎ (1) 42.61.64.00. A huge discotheque, where the dancers vibrate to an electronic setting and light shows. ***Apocalypse,*** 40, rue du Colisée, 75008, ☎ (1) 42.25.11.68. ***Apoplexy,*** 45, rue François Ier, 75008, ☎ (1) 47.23.70.72. ***Bains-Douches,*** 7, rue du Bourg-l'Abbé, 75003, ☎ (1) 48.87.34.40. Crowds guaranteed. Rest. ♦♦ Food for fashionable night-owls, 200. ***Bus Palladium,*** 4, rue Fontaine, 75009, ☎ (1) 48.74.54.99. ***L'Écume des Nuits,*** 81, bd Gouvion-St-Cyr (hôtel Méridien), 75017, ☎ (1) 47.58.12.30. ***Le Garage,*** 41, rue de Washington, 75008, ☎ (1) 45.63.21.27. ***New-Morning,*** 79, rue des Petites-Écuries, 75010, ☎ (1) 45.23.51.41. Jazz, nothing but good jazz. ***La Resserre aux Diables,*** 94, rue St-Martin, 75010, ☎ (1) 42.72.01.73. Restaurant-rock club complex, 120-210. ***Utopia Jazz Club,*** 79, rue de l'Ouest, 75014, ☎ (1) 43.27.27.36. One of the last clubs of progressive jazz. ***Royal,*** 2, rue des Italiens, 75009, ☎ (1) 48.24.43.88. "Retro" dancing with orchestra for aging couples. Young on Tue eve.

Restaurants open non-stop :

♦ ***La Nouvelle Gare,*** 49, bd Vincent-Auriol, 75013, ☎ (1) 45.84.74.29. Closed Sun. For hungry performers and cab-drivers. Spec : *pâtés, filets de hareng.*

♦ ***La Tour de Montléry (Chez Denise),*** 5, rue des Prouvaires, 75001, ☎ (1) 42.36.21.82. The nocturnal restaurant of les Halles.

♦ ***Robert Vattier,*** 14, rue Coquillère, 75001, ☎ (1) 42.36.51.60. Turn-of-the-century decor.

♦ ***Au Duc de Richelieu,*** 110, rue de Richelieu, 75002, ☎ (1) 42.96.38.38. Wine by the glass, snacks until 5 am ex Sun.

Tea-rooms : ***Ladurée,*** 16, rue Royale, 75008, ☎ (1) 42.50.21.79 ; extremely elegant decor ; delicious macaroons. ***Le Flore-en-l'Ile,*** 42, quai d'Orléans, 75004, ☎ (1) 43.29.88.27. ***Le Jardin de Thé,*** 10, rue Brise-Miche, 75004, ☎ (1) 42.74.35.26 ; near IRCAM and Beaubourg ; excellent tarts. ***Le Lys d'Argent,*** 90, rue Saint-Louis-en-l'Ile, 75004, ☎ (1) 46.33.37.39. ***Pandora,*** 24, passage Choiseul, 75002, ☎ (1) 42.97.56.01. ***Fanny Tea,*** 20, pl. Dauphine, 75001, ☎ (1) 43.25.83.67. ***Photo-galerie,*** 2, rue Christine, ☎ (1) 43.29.01.76. ***Cador,*** 2, rue de l'Amiral-Coligny, 75001, ☎ (1) 45.08.19.18. View of the Louvre Colonnade. ***Pons,*** 2, pl. Ed.-Rostand, ☎ (1) 43.29.31.10 ; overlooking the Luxembourg Gardens.

Cakes and pastries : ***Le Nôtre,*** 51, av. V.-Hugo, 75016, ☎ (1) 45.01.71.71 ; ***Dalloyau,*** 101, rue du Fg-St-Honoré, 75008, ☎ (1) 43.59.18.10. ***Christian Constant,*** 26, rue du Bac, 75007, ☎ (1) 42.96.53.53 ; lemon meringue tarts, chocolate biscuits.

Ices : ***la Sorbetière,*** 12, rue Gustave-Courbet, 75016, ☎ (1) 45.53.26.91. ***Glacier de France,*** 48 *bis,* av. d'Italie, 75013, ☎ (1) 45.80.23.75. ***Raïmo,*** 59, bd de Reuilly, 75012, ☎ (1) 43.43.70.17. ***Baggi,*** 38, rue d'Amsterdam, 75009, ☎ (1) 48.74.01.39. ***Le Bac à Glaces,*** 109, rue du Bac, 75007, ☎ (1) 45.48.87.65. ***Jean Saffray,*** 18, rue du Bac, 75007, ☎ (1) 42.61.27.63. ***Berthillon,*** 31, rue St-Louis-en-l'Île, 75004, ☎ (1) 43.54.31.61.

Wine bars :
average meal : 100-150.

♦ ***Bernard Pontonnier,*** 19-21, rue des Fossés-Saint-Jacques, 75005, ☎ (1) 43.26.80.18. Closed Sat, Sun, Aug. In the heart of the Latin quarter, the most popular university wine bar in Paris. Reasonable prices. Touraine, champigny, beaujolais, sandwiches with Landes ham and a delicious camembert de Sainte-Mère-Église.

♦ ***Taverne Henri IV*** (Robert Cointepas), 13, pl. du Pont-Neuf, 75001, ☎ (1) 43.54.27.90. Closed Sat, Sun, Aug, Christmas, Easter, nat hols. Beaujolais, Touraine and Muscadet wines, regional products as sandwiches or snacks.

♦ ***Le Sauvignon*** (Henri Vergne), 80, rue des Saints-Pères, 75007, ☎ (1) 45.48.49.02. Closed Sun, Aug. A veritable institution, despite its several square meters of floor space. The feminine prêt-à-porter clientele comes here for the finest sandwiches in Paris, and for the Beaujolais, Bordeaux, and Sancerre wines.

♦ ***Ma Bourgogne*** (Louis Prin), 133, bd Haussmann, 75008, ☎ (1) 45.63.50.61. Closed Sat, Sun, Aug. Remarkable value for money and Louis Prin's unequalled warm welcome. Brasserie and restaurant at noon in a bar that stocks genuine Beaujolais and Burgundy wines, purchased and bottled by the proprietor.

♦ ***La Cloche des Halles*** (Serge Lesage), rue du Coq-Héron, 75003, ☎ (1) 42.36.93.89. Closed Sun. Good wines (brouilly, fleurie, aloxe corton), and quiche, ham on the bone.

♦ ***Le Rubis*** (Albert Prat), 10, rue du Marché-Saint-Honoré, 75001, ☎ (1) 42.61.03.34. Closed Sat, Sun, Aug. Good, reasonably-priced beaujolais.

♦ ***La Tartine*** (Jean Bouscarel), 24, rue de Rivoli, 75004, ☎ (1) 42.72.76.85. Closed Tue, Aug. The regular clients fully appreciate the extensive selection of good wines, the strongly-flavoured cheeses and the *crottins de Sancerre.*

♦ ***Le Rallye*** (Bernard Peret), 6, rue Daguerre, 75014, ☎ (1) 43.22.57.05. Closed Sun, Mon, 14 Jul-15 Sep. Beaujolais, sancerre and touraine at the counter. Take-aways and fine sandwiches.

♦ ***La Tassée d'Argent*** (Pierre Bourdut), 21, av. Gabriel-Péri, 94100 Saint-Maur, ☎ (1) 48.83.00.14. Cooking prepared by the proprietor (noon only). A complete selection of Beaujolais wines.

♦ ***Le Val d'Or*** (Géraud Rongier), 28, av. Franklin-Roosevelt, 75008, ☎ (1) 43.59.95.81. Closed Sun. Brasserie and restaurant at noon. Terrines and home-cured ham on the bone. All Beaujolais wines and superb aloxe corton.

♦ ***Chez Serge*** (Serge Cancé), 7, bd Jean-Jaurès, 93400 Saint-Ouen, ☎ (1) 42.54.06.42. Closed Sun. The proprietor cooks at midday while Serge serves in the dining-room. Eve until 9 pm, packed with regular clients. Beaujolais, bourgogne, champagne.

♦ ***Relais Beaujolais*** (Laurent Pagadoy), 3, rue Milton, 75009, ☎ (1) 48.78.77.91. Closed Sun, Aug. Small restaurant (luncheons, dinners). A tiny counter frequented by the locals. Beaujolais, Loire wines.

♦ ***La Royale*** (Roger Aygalenq), 80, rue de l'Amiral-Mouchez, 75014, ☎ (1) 45.88.38.09. Closed Sun, Aug. Restaurant with a daily special at noon. The proprietor offers advice for those wishing to taste Touraine and Beaujolais wines.

♦ ***Le Rallye*** (Antoine Deconquand), 267, rue du Fg-Saint-Martin, 75010, ☎ (1) 46.07.22.83. Closed Sun, Aug. Auvergne *charcuterie.* Daily special prepared by the proprietress at noon. All varieties of Beaujolais. Take-aways.

♦ ***Au Père Tranquille*** (Jean Nouyrigat), 30, av. du Maine, 75015, ☎ (1) 42.22.88.12. Closed Sun, Mon. A true wine club, not always accessible to the general public. Priority is given to Touraine wines. A number of tables reserved for the regular clients ; beautiful terrace in summer. Daily special at noon.

♦ ***J.-P. Chastang,*** 8, av. A.-Briand, 92160 Antony, ☎ (1) 46.66.01.14. Closed Wed, Sun, Aug. The mother does the cooking and the son looks after the wines : beaujolais, bordeaux, *charcuterie* from the Rouergue and Lot regions.

♦ ***Jacques Melac,*** 42, rue Léon-Frot, 75011, ☎ (1) 43.70.59.27. Closed Sun, Mon, hols, Jul. Good wines and snacks at the counter.

♦ ***Le Millésime,*** 7, rue Lobineau, 75006, ☎ (1) 46.34.22.15. Closed Sun. Quality French wines, and occasionally less convincing wines from elsewhere. Gypsy guitarist in the evenings.

♦ ***Gaîté Bar,*** 7, rue Papin, 75003, ☎ (1) 42.72.79.45. This bar proves that wine-tasting has a great future ; an inimitable setting. Beaujolais, Bordeaux wines.

♦ ***La Boutique des Vins,*** 31-33, rue de l'Arcade, 75008, ☎ (1) 42.65.27.27. Closed Sat, Sun and Aug. One of the most recent wine bars, and the first run by a woman who prepares a different dish of the day for every meal. Wine by the glass, by the bottle, and to take-away.

♦ ***Le Pain et le Vin,*** 1, rue d'Armaillé, 75017, ☎ (1) 47.63.88.29. Annex of the *Toques Gourmandes* (Fournier, Dutournier, Faugeron, Morot-Gaudry). Dish of the day, wine by the glass and by the bottle, sandwiches, fresh *charcuterie,* open noon-2 am.

♦ ***La Cave Drouot,*** 8, rue Drouot, 75009, ☎ (1) 47.70.83.38. Closed Sun. Daily special and wines at the counter, rigorously selected by the proprietor J.-P. Cachau. Auction room atmosphere. Beaujolais, bordeaux, côtes-du-Rhône, madiran.

♦ ***Le Petit Bacchus*** (J.-M. Picard), 13, rue du Cherche-Midi, 75006, ☎ (1) 45.44.01.07. Closed Sun and Mon. Now flying under Steven Spurrier's English banner. *Charcuterie,* cheese, pastries, and wine by the glass or take-away.

♦ ***Le Soleil d'Austerlitz,*** 18, bd de l'Hôpital, 75005, ☎ (1) 43.31.39.36. Visa ; closed Aug, Sat. Excellent wines at the counter, *tartines,* daily special.

♦ ***Le Café Parisien,*** 15, rue d'Assas, 75006, ☎ (1) 45.44.41.44. Closed 15 days in Aug, 1 week in winter, eve, Sun. Mon. Excellent regional wines, a daily special, and a view of traffic and the prettiest girls in Paris.

♦ ***Le Mâconnais,*** 10, rue du Bac, 75007, ☎ (1) 42.61.21.89. Closed Sat noon, Sun. Beaujolais, *charcuteries.*

♦ ***Vin sur Vin,*** 20, rue de Montessuy, 75007, ☎ (1) 47.05.14.20. Closed Sun. Under the shadow of the Eiffel tower, in a calm street. Tastings and food served 11 am-11 pm. Don't let word get out : this is a real little restaurant with a talented young chef. Excellent food and 120 wines to sample.

♦ ***Le Blue Fox,*** cité Berryer, 75008, ☎ (1) 42.65.08.47. Numerous tourists. Fashionable and expensive.

♦ ***Bistrot du Sommelier,*** 97, bd Haussmann, 75008, ☎ (1) 42.65.24.85. Closed 25 Dec-1 Jan, Sat eve, Sun. Selection of wines direct from the proprietors.

♦ ***L'Œnothèque,*** 20, rue St-Lazare, 75009, ☎ (1) 48.78.08.76. Visa ; closed Sat, Sun, hols. Intelligent cooking which enhances the wines being tasted.

♦ ***La Devinière,*** 70, rue Alexandre-Dumas, 75011, ☎ (1) 43.73.22.97. Visa ; closed 5 Aug-5 Sep, Sun, Mon. Rabelais would be pleased : good selection of Loire wines, *tartines* and plates.

♦ ***La Winstub,*** 11, av. de la Grande-Armée, 75017, ☎ (1) 45.00.13.21. Solid food at low prices and a magnificent selection of Alsatian wines, *cervelas, roll-mops, jambonneau.*

♦ ***Aux Négociants,*** 27, rue Lambert, 75018, ☎ (1) 46.06.15.11. Closed 15 Jul-15 Aug, 25 Dec, 1 Jan, Sat, Sun. Good Beaujolais and Bourgueil wines, low-priced daily specials.

♦ ***Les Caves Angevines,*** 2, pl. Léon-Deubel, 75016, ☎ (1) 42.88.88.93. Well-chosen wines bottled by the *patron.* Six tables for his wife's delicious daily specials.

English book shops : *Brentano's,* 37, av. de l'Opéra, 75002, ☎ (1) 42.61.52.50. ***Galignani,*** 224, rue de Rivoli, 75001, ☎ (1) 42.60.76.07. ***Shakespeare & Co.,*** 37, rue de la Bûcherie, 75005. ***W. H. Smith,*** 248, rue de Rivoli, 75001, ☎ (1) 42.60.37.97.

Wine cellars and depots : *la Galerie des Vins,* 201, rue Saint-Honoré, 75001, ☎ (1) 42.61.81.20. ***Lucien Legrand,*** 1, rue de la Banque, 75002, ☎ (1) 42.60.07.12. ***Vintage Sélection,*** 17, rue Ferdinand-Duval, 75004, ☎ (1) 42.74.53.92. ***René Sinard,*** 43, rue Poliveau, 75005, ☎ (1) 47.07.22.91. ***Steven Spurrier,*** 25, rue Royale, 75008, ☎ (1) 42.65.92.40. ***Georges Dubœuf,*** 25, rue Marbœuf, 75008, ☎ (1) 47.20.71.23. ***L'Œnophile,*** 30, bd Voltaire, 75011, ☎ (1) 47.00.69.45. ***Cave des Gobelins,*** 56, av. des Gobelins, 75013, ☎ (1) 43.31.66.79. ***Réserve et Sélection,*** 119, rue du Dessous-des-Berges, 75013, ☎ (1) 45.83.65.19 (depot). ***Divinord,*** 10, rue Morice, 92110 Clichy, ☎ (1) 47.30.30.56 (depot). ***Caves de Passy,*** 3, rue Duban, 75016, ☎ (1) 42.88.85.56. ***Centre de Distribution des Vins de Propriétés,*** 13, bd Ney, 75018, ☎ (1) 42.09.61.50. ***Gambrinus,*** 13, rue des Blancs-Manteaux, 75004, ☎ (1) 48.87.81.92. ***King Henry,*** 44, rue des Boulangers, 75005, ☎ (1) 43.54.54.37. ***La Carte des Vins,*** 8 *bis,* bd R.-Lenoir, 75011, ☎ (1) 43.38.74.99. Tasting on the premises. ***Kayyam,*** 8, pl. Félix-Éboué, 75012, ☎ (1) 43.43.39.71. ***Caves Lepic,*** 19, rue Lepic, 75018, ☎ (1) 46.06.18.50. ***Ma Cave,*** 105, rue de Belleville, 75019, ☎ (1) 42.08.62.95. ***Cave Jean Mermoz,*** 25, rue Jean-Mermoz, 75006, ☎ (1) 42.56.07.49. For all objects to do with wine : ***Lescène-Dura,*** 63, rue de la Verrerie, 75004, ☎ (1) 42.72.08.74.

Pianos-bars :

♦ ***Le Montana,*** 28, rue St-Benoît, 75006, ☎ (1) 45.48.93.08. From midnight 'til 6, snacks and jazz.

♦ ***Le Clair de Nuit,*** 9, rue Deparcieux, 75014, ☎ (1) 43.20.25.54. Closed noon. For small hungers and large thirsts at night, 120-210.

Beer :

♦ ***Le Trappiste,*** 4, rue St-Denis, 75001, ☎ (1) 42.33.08.50.

♦ ***Le Manneken Pis,*** 4, rue Daurou, 75002, ☎ (1) 47.42.85.03.

♦ ***La Gueuze,*** 19, rue Soufflot, 75005, ☎ (1) 43.54.63.00.

♦ ***L'Académie de la Bière,*** 88 *bis,* bd de Port-Royal, 75005, ☎ (1) 43.54.66.65.

♦ ***La Taverne de Nesles,*** 32, rue Dauphine, 75006, ☎ (1) 43.26.38.36.

♦ ***Pub Saint-Germain,*** 17, rue de l'Ancienne-Comédie, 75006, ☎ (1) 43.29.38.70.

♦ ***Le Bar de la Marine,*** 59, bd du Montparnasse, 75006, ☎ (1) 45.48.27.70.

♦ ***Bar (belge) du New Store,*** 63, Champs-Élysées, 75008, ☎ (1) 42.25.96.16.

♦ ***Au Général La Fayette,*** 52, rue La Fayette, 75009, ☎ (1) 47.70.59.08.

♦ ***La Taverne Kronenbourg,*** 24, bd des Italiens, 75009, ☎ (1) 47.70.16.64. Brasserie 11 pm-3 am.

♦ ***La Taverne de la Bière,*** 15, rue de Dunkerque, 75010, ☎ (1) 42.85.12.93.

Video-bars :

Le Look, 49, rue Saint-Honoré, 75001, ☎ (1) 42.33.44.98. Reasonably-priced drinks, pleasure for the eyes guaranteed.

Hall-Catraz, 72, rue Quincampoix, 75003, ☎ (1) 42.71.39.02. Very *à la mode :* salads and giant screen.

Le Studio, 15, rue Quincampoix, 75004, ☎ (1) 42.78.73.90. Video, billiards, restaurant, lots of noise.

Le Casablanca, 41, rue Quincampoix, 75004, ☎ (1) 42.78.82.69. Video, electronic games, small sandwiches.

Gastronomy, fine foods, caterers, specialities :

Battendier, 8, rue Coquillière, 75001, ☎ (1) 42.36.95.50. Charcutier-caterer, take-aways (Mme de Gaulle's favourite caterer !). ***Verlet,*** 256, rue Saint-Honoré, 75001, ☎ (1) 42.60.67.39. The oldest tea and coffee house in Paris. Tasting and sales. ***La Maison des Foies Gras,*** 9, rue Danièle-Casanova, 75001, ☎ (1) 42.61.42.36. ***Paul Corcellet,*** 46, rue des Petits-Champs, 75002, ☎ (1) 42.96.51.82. The most exotic fine food-stuffs. ***Legrand,*** 1, rue de la Banque, 75002, ☎ (1) 42.60.07.12. Traditional fine foods. Excellent wines. ***Le Car St-Honoré,*** 3, rue Gomboust, 75001, ☎ (1) 42.61.52.04. Selected poulty, game in season. ***Coesnon,*** 30, rue Dauphine, 75005, ☎ (1) 43.54.35.80. One of the best *charcutiers* in Paris. ***Boutique Layrac,*** 27, rue de Buci, 75006, ☎ (1) 43.25.17.72. Open until 3 am. Regional produce, take-away dishes. ***Poilâne, Lionel,*** 8, rue du Cherche-Midi, 75006, ☎ (1) 45.48.42.59. Always a queue to buy the rye bread, *croissants, tartes aux pommes.* ***Poilâne, Max,*** 87, rue Brancion, 75015, ☎ (1) 48.28.45.90. Good bread is a family affair. ***Pétrossian,*** 18, bd de Latour-Maubourg, 75007, ☎ (1) 45.51.59.73. The Parisian Mecca for caviar and smoked salmon. ***Bon Marché,*** 38, rue de Sèvres, 75007, ☎ (1) 42.60.33.45. The best grocery store among the large department stores. ***Fauchon,*** 26, pl. de la Madeleine, 75007, ☎ (1) 47.42.60.11. An impressive array of produce, with prices to match the house's very high reputation. ***Hédiard,*** 21, pl. de la Madeleine, 75008, ☎ (1) 42.66.44.36. Specialised in exotic fruits, jams and fruit jellies ; good wines straight from the properties. ***Androuet,*** 41, rue d'Amsterdam, 75008, ☎ (1) 48.74.26.93. Fine cheeses to savour there or take-away. ***Cantin Christian,*** 2, rue de Lourmel, 75015. A great master of cheese who upholds tradition. ***A l'An 2000,*** 82, bd des Batignolles, 75017. Open until 1 am. *Charcuterie* caterer ; take-away dishes.

Fashion addresses : ***Giorgio Armani,*** 31, rue du Four, 75006. ***Azzedine Alaia,*** 60, rue de Belle-chasse, 75007. ***Anne-Marie Béretta,*** 24, rue Saint-Sulpice, 75006. ***Cacharel,*** 34, rue Tronchet, 75008, and Forum des Halles. ***Pierre Cardin Diffusion,*** 185, bd Saint-Germain, 75006. ***Castelbajac,*** 31, pl. du Marché-Saint-Honoré, 75001. ***Cerruti 1881,*** 15, pl. de la Madeleine (women), and 1, rue Royale (men). ***Chanel,*** 21, rue Cambon, 75008. *Chloé,* 3, rue de Gribeauval, 75007, and rue du Fg-Saint-Honoré, 75008. ***Dior,*** 15, av. Montaigne, 75008. ***Dorothée Bis,*** 10, rue Tronchet, 75008. ***Givenchy,*** 3, av. George-V, 75008. ***Issey Miyaké,*** 201, bd Saint-Germain, 75006. ***Emmanuelle Khanh,*** 2, rue de Tournon, 75006. ***Kenzo,*** Jungle Jap, 3, pl. des Victoires, 75008. ***Lanvin,*** 22, rue du Fg-Saint-Honoré, 75008. ***Guy Laroche,*** 30, rue du Fg-Saint-Honoré. ***Mic-Mac,*** 13, rue de Tournon, 75006. ***Thierry Mugler,*** 10, pl. des Victoires, 75001. ***Per Spook,*** 18, av. George-V, 75008. ***Nina Ricci,*** 17, rue François-Ier, 75008. ***Sonia Rykiel,*** 6, rue de Grenelle, 75006. ***Saint-Laurent Rive Gauche,*** 6, pl. Saint-Sulpice, 75006, and 38, rue du Fg-Saint-Honoré, 75008. ***Élisabeth de Senneville,*** 3, rue de Turbigo, 75001. ***Angelo Tarlazzi,*** 67, rue du Fg-Saint-Honoré, 75008. ***Chantal Thomass,*** 5, rue du Vieux-Colombier, 75006, and Forum des Halles. ***Ventilo,*** 27 *bis,* rue du Louvre, 75001.

Chic and inexpensive : Most of the top designers have boutiques and warehouses where they sell models from previous years for half-price. ***Courrèges,*** 7, rue de Turbigo, 75001. ***Rodier,*** 11, bd de la Madeleine, 75001. ***Pierre Cardin,*** 11, bd de Sébastopol, 75001. ***Pierre d'Alby,*** 60, rue de Richelieu, 75002. ***Givenchy,*** 3, av. George-V, 75008. ***Nina Ricci,*** 39, av. Montaigne, 75008. ***Dorothée Bis Stock,*** 76, rue d'Alésia, 75014. ***Mic-Mac,*** 13, rue Laugier, 75017. ***Cacharel Stock,*** 171, rue de Belleville, 75019 ; 114, rue d'Alésia, 75014. ***Paris-Nord Diffusion*** (Daniel Hechter Depot), 62, rue de Pelleport, 75020. ***Emmanuelle Khanh,*** 6, rue Pierre-Lescot, 75001. Most of the sales depots are situated near the rue Saint-Placide (75006), and in the 10th, 15th and 16th arrondissements. The main sales depot is the ***Réciproque,*** 95, rue de la Pompe, 75016.

Shoes : ***Walter Steiger,*** 49, rue du Fg-Saint-Honoré, 75008. ***Stéphane Kélian,*** 62, rue des Saints-Pères, 75007. ***Laurent Mercadal,*** 3, pl. des Victoires, 75001. ***Accessoire,*** 6, rue du Cherche-Midi, 75006. ***Gli Rossetti,*** 54, rue du Fg-Saint-Honoré. ***Bally,*** 11, bd de la Madeleine, 75001 ; 12, rue du Four, 75006. ***Charles Jourdan,*** 62, rue de Rennes, 75006. ***Maud Frizon,*** 83, rue des Saints-Pères, 75006. ***Pucci Verdi,*** 40, rue de Verneuil, 75007. ***Sacha,*** 24, rue de Buci, 75006. ***Weston,*** 124, av. des Champs-Élysées, 75008.

Saddlers : ***la Bagagerie,*** 12, rue Tronchet, 75008, 41, rue du Four, 75006. ***Céline,*** 6, av. Victor-Hugo, 75008. ***Fred,*** 6, rue Royale, 75008. ***Gucci,*** 27, rue du Fg-Saint-Honoré, 75008. ***Hermès,*** 24, rue du Fg-Saint-Honoré, 75008. ***Lancel,*** 8, pl. de l'Opéra, 75008. ***Vuitton,*** 78, av. Marceau, 75008.

The Agenais, Périgord and Quercy Regions

Art and man have their roots here in the Cro-Magnon past. In Périgord and Quercy there are traces of history dating back for tens of thousands of years : the history of the earth, where slow drops of water patiently carved out the famous rock shelters, and the history of man himself. In the world-famous limestone caves and grottos, the paintings left by prehistoric man float eerily among stalactites and stalagmites. Some of these paintings show the landscape we can see today, a landscape of fertile valleys basking in the shadow of great limestone plateaus known as *"causses"* are alive with spiny, sweet-smelling shrubs.

This landscape, with its many quick-flowing rivers and streams is astonishingly diverse : there are hundreds of castles and churches, stone sentinels bearing witness to heroic and crueller times marked by religious wars and harshly-repressed peasant revolts. This very beautiful region is also fragile and poor, and has suffered more than any other from the rural exodus. The rural architecture of Périgord and Quercy is justly famous, and throughout the ages the inhabitants have made excellent use of the region's good stone.

Périgord is a paradise for gourmets, renowned for its fattened poultry, *foie gras,* truffles, boletus mushrooms and nuts, not to mention the excellent wine of Cahors, popular both in France and abroad for hundreds of years. A hint : perhaps the best and most memorable meals are to be had in Périgord's many picturesque villages.

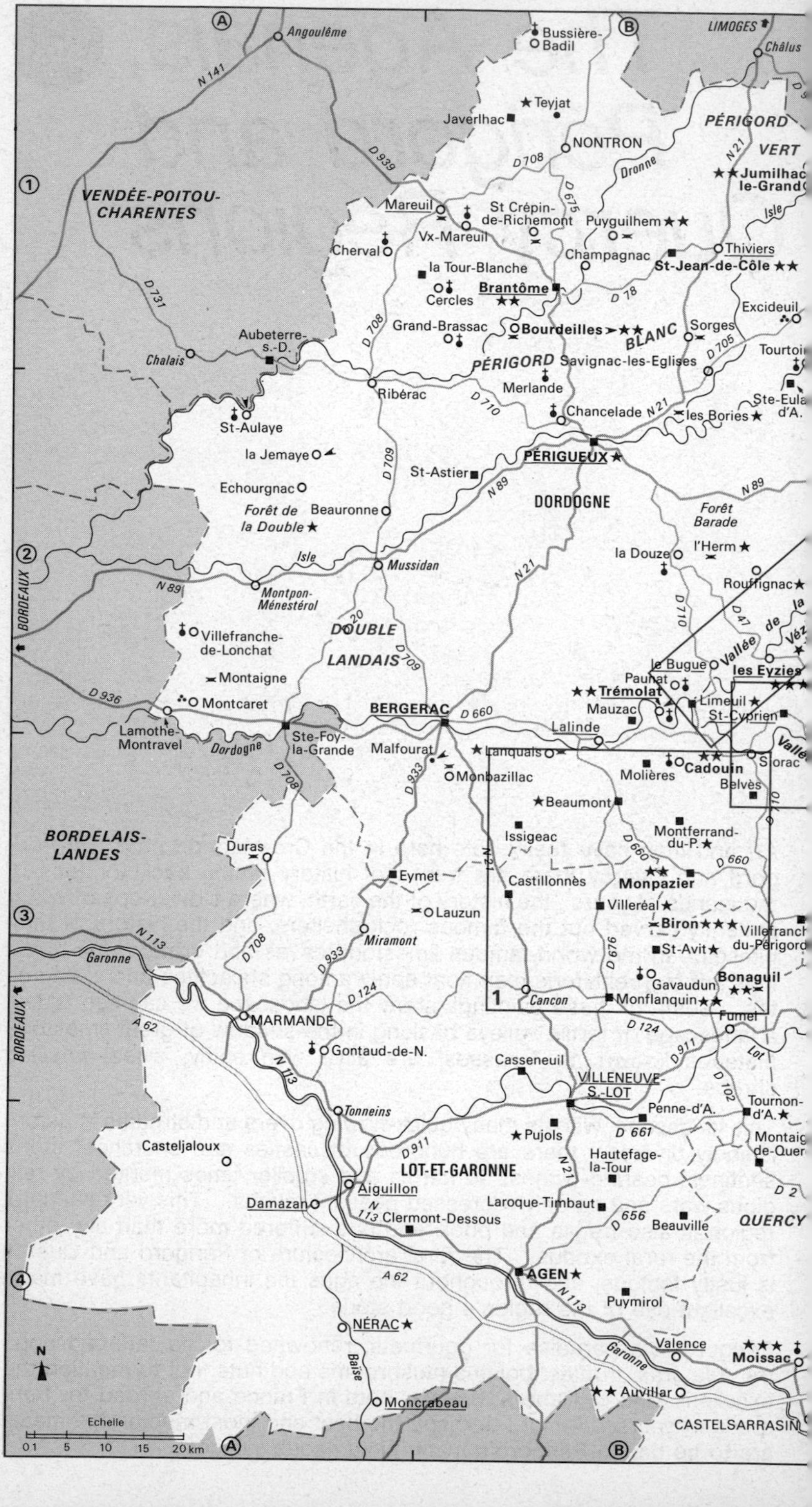
A
B
1
2
3
4
Angoulême
N 141
LIMOGES
Châlus
Bussière-Badil
Teyjat
Javerlhac
NONTRON
PÉRIGORD VERT
D 939
D 708
Dronne
N 21
Jumilhac-le-Grand
VENDÉE-POITOU-CHARENTES
Mareuil
St Crépin-de-Richemont
D 675
Puyguilhem
Isle
Vx-Mareuil
Cherval
Champagnac
Thiviers
la Tour-Blanche
St-Jean-de-Côle
D 731
Cercles
Brantôme
D 78
Excideuil
D 708
Grand-Brassac
Bourdeilles
BLANC
Sorges
Aubeterre-s.-D.
PÉRIGORD
Savignac-les-Eglises
D 705
Tourtoirac
Chalais
Ribérac
Merlande
Ste-Eulalie-d'A.
D 710
Chancelade
N 21
les Bories
St-Aulaye
PÉRIGUEUX
la Jemaye
D 709
St-Astier
Echourgnac
N 89
DORDOGNE
N 89
Forêt de la Double
Beauronne
Forêt Barade
BORDEAUX
Isle
la Douze
l'Herm
Mussidan
N 21
N 89
Montpon-Ménestérol
Rouffignac
D 710
D 47
D 20
DOUBLE
Villefranche-de-Lonchat
LANDAIS
D 709
Vallée de la Vézère
le Bugue
les Eyzies
Montaigne
Paunat
D 936
Trémolat
Limeuil
Montcaret
BERGERAC
D 660
Mauzac
St-Cyprien
Lamothe-Montravel
Dordogne
Ste-Foy-la-Grande
Lalinde
Malfourat
Lanquais
Vallée
Siorac
D 708
Monbazillac
Molières
Cadouin
Belvès
D 933
Beaumont
D 710
BORDELAIS-LANDES
Issigeac
Montferrand-du-P.
D 660
Duras
N 21
D 660
Eymet
Castillonnès
Monpazier
Villeréal
Lauzun
Biron
Villefranche-du-Périgord
N 113
Miramont
St-Avit
Garonne
D 708
D 933
D 676
Gavaudun
Bonaguil
D 124
1
Cancon
Monflanquin
Fumel
A 62
MARMANDE
D 124
Lot
BORDEAUX
Gontaud-de-N.
D 911
Casseneuil
D 102
N 113
VILLENEUVE-S.-LOT
Tonneins
Penne-d'A.
Tournon-d'A.
D 661
Pujols
Casteljaloux
D 911
N 21
Hautefage-la-Tour
Montaigu-de-Quercy
LOT-ET-GARONNE
Aiguillon
D 2
Damazan
Laroque-Timbaut
N 113
D 656
Clermont-Dessous
Beauville
QUERCY
A 62
AGEN
N 113
Puymirol
NÉRAC
Valence
Garonne
Moissac
Baïse
Auvillar
Moncrabeau
Echelle
0 1 5 10 15 20 km
CASTELSARRASIN
N

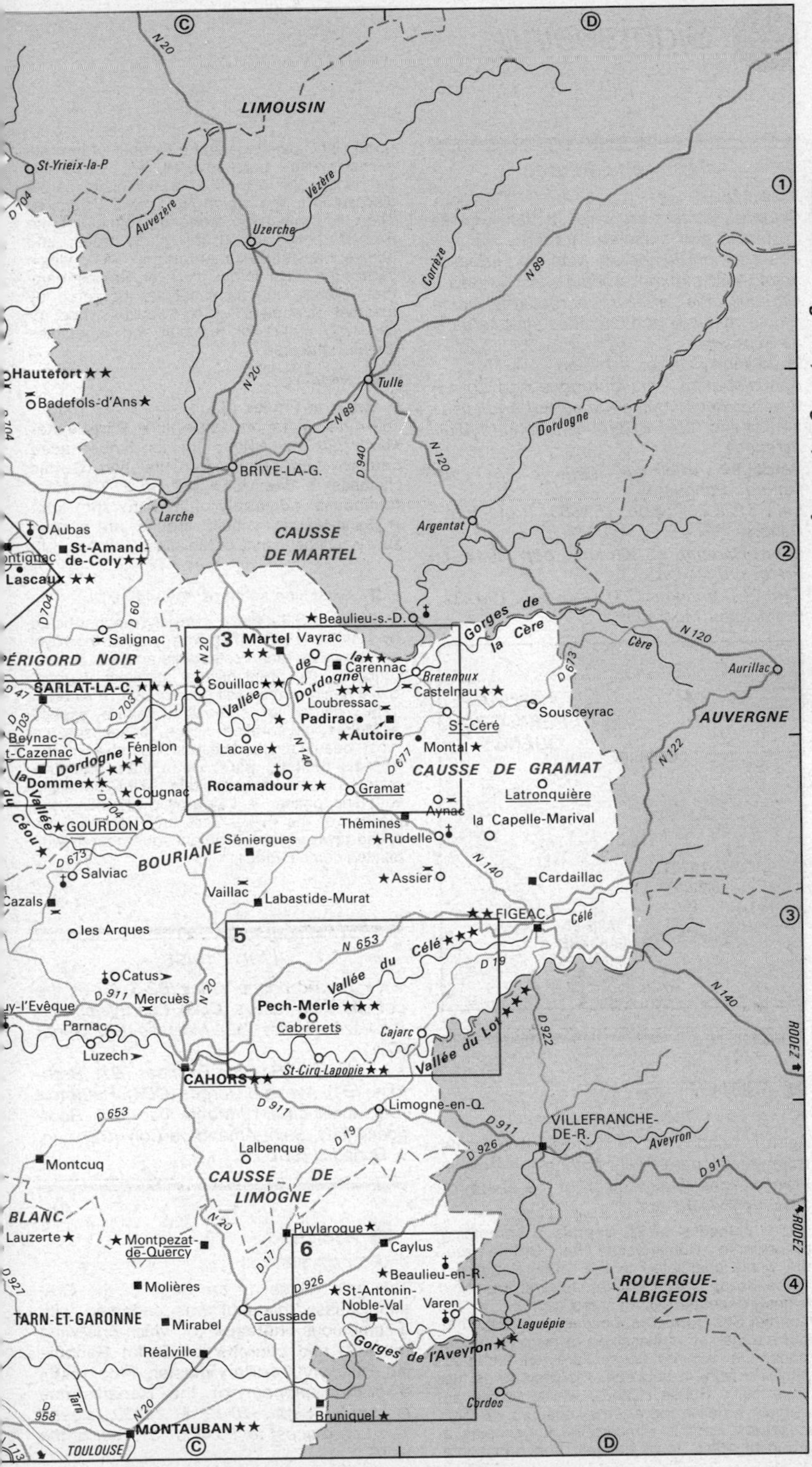

LIMOUSIN
St-Yrieix-la-P
Auvezère
Vézère
Uzerche
Corrèze
N 89
N 20
Tulle
Hautefort ★★
Badefols-d'Ans★
Dordogne
BRIVE-LA-G.
D 940
N 120
Larche
CAUSSE DE MARTEL
Argentat
Aubas
St-Amand-de-Coly★★
Montignac
Lascaux ★★
Salignac
PÉRIGORD NOIR
★Beaulieu-s.-D.
Gorges de la Cère
3
Martel
Vayrac
Vallée de la Dordogne★★★
Carennac
Bretenoux
Castelnau★★
Cère
N 120
Aurillac
SARLAT-LA-C.★★
Souillac★★
Loubressac
Padirac
★Autoire
St-Céré
Sousceyrac
AUVERGNE
Beynac-et-Cazenac
Fénelon
Dordogne
Domme★★
Lacave★
Montal★
CAUSSE DE GRAMAT
N 122
Rocamadour★★
Gramat
Latronquière
★Cougnac
Aynac
la Vallée du Céou★
★GOURDON
Thémines
la Capelle-Marival
Séniergues
★Rudelle
BOURIANE
Salviac
★Assier
N 140
Cardaillac
Vaillac
Labastide-Murat
Cazals
★★FIGEAC
Célé
les Arques
5
N 653
Vallée du Célé★★★
D 19
Catus
Mercuès
Pech-Merle★★★
Cabrerets
Puy-l'Evêque
Parnac
Luzech
Cajarc
Vallée du Lot★★★
D 922
RODEZ
CAHORS★★
St-Cirq-Lapopie★★
D 911
Limogne-en-Q.
VILLEFRANCHE-DE-R.
Aveyron
D 653
Lalbenque
D 926
Montcuq
CAUSSE DE LIMOGNE
BLANC
Lauzerte★
★Montpezat-de-Quercy
Puylaroque★
6
Caylus
★Beaulieu-en-R.
ROUERGUE-ALBIGEOIS
Molières
★St-Antonin-Noble-Val
Varen
TARN-ET-GARONNE
Mirabel
Caussade
Laguépie
Gorges de l'Aveyron★★
Réalville
Tarn
Cordes
Bruniquel★
MONTAUBAN★★
TOULOUSE

Sightseeing

Facts and figures

Area : *23 379 km²*
Climate : *winters are cold on the causses* (plateaux) *and summers are hot; the valleys are more temperate than the plateaus; spring and autumn are the most pleasant seasons, the latter is particularly calm. (Some châteaux and churches shut as early as September).*
Population : *approx 1 million.*
Administration : *the Dordogne and Lot-et-Garonne departments are part of Aquitaine; the Lot and Tarn-et-Garonne belong to Midi-Pyrénées.*
Dordogne : *9 060 km²; pop. 385 772; Prefecture : Périgueux.*
Lot : *5 228 km²; pop. 159 663; Prefecture : Cahors.*
Lot-et-Garonne : *5 360 km²; pop. 304 491; Prefecture : Agen.*
Tarn-et-Garonne : *3 731 km²; pop. 196 232; Prefecture : Montauban.*

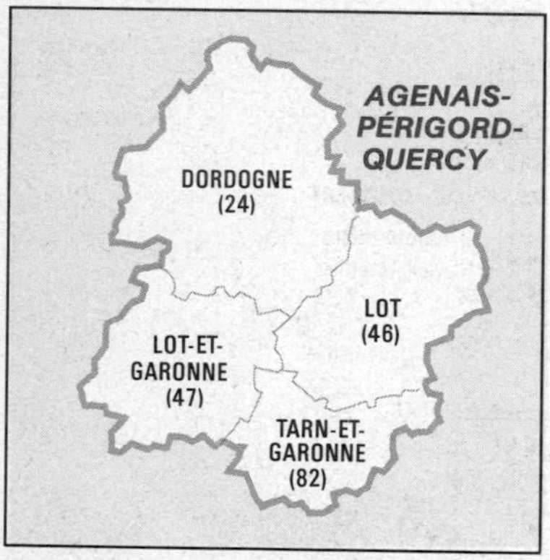

AGEN★

B4 / ® / pop. 32 893 (Lot-et-Garonne)

Agen is famous for its prunes; also for its rugby team, perennially among the best in France. Agen retains much of the charm of a past provincial era.

▶ The **cathedral of St. Caprais** is something of a mixture - Romanesque choir, Gothic nave, the whole completed in the 16thC - but the Romanesque *chevet* is beautiful and the choir is finely decorated with carved capitals. ▶ The **Quartier des Cornières,** between the cathedral and the market, is classified of historic importance; the restored houses are half-timbered with brickwork in between; the prettiest is the Seneschal's House (13thC), which serves as a show window for Agen's museum. ▶ The **museum★** itself is remarkable. It occupies a group of 16thC town houses, and has some good 18thC paintings and a number of Impressionist works - but above all, five Goyas and the famous Venus du Mas, a Hellenistic marble discovered in the region *(10-12 & 2-6; closed Tue.).* ▶ Promenade along the banks of the river Garonne among the plane trees, and admire the 19thC **canal-bridge★** (A1), which carries the canal across the river. Downstream, the Garonne and its canal are bordered by a forest of poplars, which supplies wood for *cageots* - crates for the fruit and vegetables grown in the area. □

▶ Nearby

▶ **Manor of Prades** *(8 km on Valence road) :* 16th-17thC *(visit on request).* ▶ **Port-Sainte-Marie** *(20 km NW) :* for its timber-faced houses (15th-18thC) and its two Gothic churches. ▶ **Beauville★** *(26 km E) :* fortified farmhouse admirably suited to the site. ▶ **Saint-Maurin :** built around an ancient abbey, a dependency of Moissac. □

▶ Excursion south of Agen *(40 km)*

▶ **Château d'Estillac★ :** largely reconstructed by Montluc (1502-1577), who headed the royal armies against the Protestants and was a forerunner of the great military architect Vauban. Still a family home *(visit on request).* ▶ **Aubiac,** 12thC church of somewhat severe aspect. ▶ **Moirax,** old fortified village; possesses the most beautiful Romanesque church★ in the Agenais region : pure, clean lines, faithfully restored; remarkable capitals; 17thC panelling with fine patina. ▶ **Layrac★** overlooking the junction of the rivers Gers and Garonne; arcaded town square; Romanesque church with painted dome (18thC). □

Don't miss

★★★ The Dordogne Valley (B2-3, C2-3), the Lot and Célé valleys (CD3), Les Eyzies and the Vézère Valley (B2), Moissac (B4), Sarlat (C2).
★★★ Auvillar (B4), the Bastides (B1), Brantôme (B1), Aveyron Gorges (CD4), Hautefort (C2), Jumilhac (B1), Montauban (C4), Rouffignac (B2), Saint-Amand-de-Coly (C2).
★ Bonaguil (B3).

ASSIER★

D3 / pop. 863 (Lot)

This little village on the edge of the Gramat Causse (plateau) was endowed with a sumptuous **château★** (of which one wing remains) and **church★** by Galiot Genouillac (Henry IV's artillery master, 1465-1546), a *grand seigneur* of the Renaissance *(1 Jun-30 Sept., 10-12 & 2-6:30, closed Tue.; on request tel 65.40.57.31, rest of the year).* □

Weekend tips

Spend a Friday evening at Sarlat and the rest of the weekend in the valleys of the Dordogne, the Lot and the Célé, with a stopover in Cahors. The caves at Pech Merle and Font de Gaume are truly worth a detour.

■ AUVILLAR★★

B4 (Tarn-et-Garonne)

A sleepy, magical village overlooking the river Garonne. The **market building,** with bulbous columns and rounded arches, is strongly reminiscent of Tuscany. Auvillar was formerly a great producer of faience.

□

■ BARADE Forest

B2 (Dordogne)

Between Rouffignac and Montignac in the country of the 17thC rebel, Jacqou le Croquant (→). Classic Périgord countryside : groves of trees following hill contours, grassy valleys and stony plateaus perfumed by heather, broom and gorse.

▶ D31 runs along the Barade Forest between Rouffignac (→) and Thenon ; for walkers, GR36 serves this purpose. The TO has signposted a path along the route taken by Jacqou, but it is enough to see Fanlac, where he spent his childhood, and the Château de l'Herm, which he burned down. ▶ **Fanlac** is deserted but remains an archetypal Périgord village, with ochre houses, a square, bordered by the church (12th-17thC) and the squire's house. ▶ Deep in the woods, abandoned, gloomy and austere, stands the **château de l'Herm** (15thC), home of the wicked Lord of l'Herm in Le Roy's novel *(Jun.-Sep.)*.

□

Prunes and plum trees

Prunes have been part of the French diet for almost 1 000 years. Introduced from Persia by returning Crusaders, and planted in the valley of the Lot by the tireless monks of Clairac, the plum tree was one of the earliest and most successful of agricultural "speculations", since the fruit could easily be preserved by drying. The name of Agen has become synonymous with prunes, not simply because they are grown nearby but also because it has been the principal point of dispatch for other regions. Faced with competition from California, the growers between Agen and Villeneuve-sur-Lot have modernised their operations and modern hillside orchards are one of the dominant features of the landscape.

The BASTIDES of PERIGORD★★

▶ Round-trip *(approx 130 km, full day).* B3 *(see map 1)*

The *bastides,* sited apparently at random all over this gentle countryside, are charming, old-world surprises for travellers in Périgord. They were built during the Franco-English wars of the 13thC and have prospered ever since; today they form an important network of market towns throughout SW Aquitaine. *Bastides* were fortified walled towns inhabited by freemen. All were built according to the same plan : a rectangular grid with streets at right angles centred on a large, arcaded square. The church was usually fortified and played the role of keep.

▶ **Belvès** (pop. 1 652) : a fortified town (but not a *bastide*) at the entry to the Pays au Bois, a broad, wooded plateau. Mediaeval and Renaissance houses; 15thC covered market; 12thC keep; Benedictine church (13th-15thC); Belfry (15thC). Centre for the marketing of walnuts. ▶ **Monpazier**★★★ ® (pop. 533) : the most perfect of all the *bastides.* Founded in 1284 by Pierre de Gontaut, Monpazier controlled one of the area's main highways on behalf of Edward I of England, Duke of Aquitaine. Superb arcaded square. 16thC covered market with embossed roof, and church with carved doorway of same period. ▶ **Biron**★★★ **:** high on its *pech* (limestone outcrop), the huge **castle** of Biron controlled a wide area of the Agenais and Périgord. Biron was built by 14 generations of the Gontaut-Biron family (barons of Périgord under the English dukes of Aquitaine), combining every style from the 12thC to the 18thC in a charming blend. Double chapel★ (Flamboyant Gothic) and Renaissance loggia★; vistas of pretty green Valleys *(1 Feb.-15 Dec., closed Tue., 9:30-11:30 & 2-6; Jul.-Aug., 9-12 & 2-6).* The village nestles below. ▶ Down through the woods of the Lède Valley to **Saint-Avit**★**,** classic Périgord houses and Romanesque chapel. ▶ **Gavaudun :** a rugged keep above the gorges of the Lède *(3-7, 1 Jul.-15 Aug. and Sun.),* remains of almshouse and 14thC Templars Commandery. ▶ Beyond **Montagnac-sur-Lède** (Romanesque and Gothic church), the landscape changes, the forest vanishes, the horizon broadens, the plain undulates with fruit trees and grain fields. The walnut gives way to the plum and the grape, the houses are longer and lower; tiled roofs predominate : this is the Agenais Region. ▶ **Monflanquin**★★ (pop. 2 356) : *bastide* built by the French (1279), with arcaded square, stone façades (some decorated), and half-timbered houses in side streets. Poultry market on Thursdays and, on Saturdays and Tuesdays in summer, a small market for farm produce. ▶ **Villeréal**★ (pop. 1 340) : another French-built *bastide* (1269). Covered market : wooden pillars (14thC) with 16th-17thC upper story. Fortified church. ▶ **Castillonnès** (pop. 1 400) : French *bastide* (1259) on a spur above the valley of the Dropt, like Villeréal and Monpazier. ▶ **Issageac** (pop. 686) between Dropt and Dordogne, plum and vineyard country. This mediaeval town was an ecclesiastical dependency of Sarlat. Late Gothic church (early 16thC), summer residence of the Bishops of Sarlat (17thC) and 16th-17thC Provost's house. Gothic house in the main street; pigeon loft and outside staircase. ▶ **Bardou,** between Issigeac and Beaumont, has a church with wall belfry (12thC) and 15th-17thC manor. ▶ **Beaumont** ® (pop. 1 300) was the principal English *bastide* (1272), built in the shape of an H in honour of England's Henry III. The main square, rebuilt along with the covered market in the 18thC, is incomplete, but the fortified church★ (13th-14thC) is full of character. ▶ **Saint-Avit-Sénieur**★ is the offshoot of a 12thC Benedictine abbey (mineral collection; *15 Jul.-15 Aug., 3-6).* The church is rugged, massive and military in aspect; it is, nevertheless, rather beautiful. Both the site and the buildings are classified monuments. A pretty winding road by the river runs directly to Montferrand (→). ▶ **Molières :** a little country *bastide* begun by the English but never finished. ▶ **Cadouin**★★ is a modest village sheltered by an oversized church, surrounded by chestnut-tree-covered hills. Ruins of a Cistercian abbey here exemplify the best of regional architecture. The first monks cleared the forest of Bessède and founded the villages in the vicinity. A piece of the Holy Shroud brought from Antioch attracted crowds of pilgrims, and a lovely church was built to receive them (1154). The cloister mingles Flamboyant Gothic and Renaissance styles and contains some highly realistic sculptures *(1 Feb.-15 Dec., closed Tue., 9:30-11:30 & 2-6; Jul.-Aug., 9-12 & 2-6).* The other abbey buildings (17thC) have been greatly altered. Covered market, as in Montferrand. ▶ **Montferrand-du-Périgord**★ straggles up the hill, crowned by the remains of a fortress (12th-15thC). Renaissance houses, 16thC covered market and Romanesque church in the cemetery. □

1. Tour of the Bastides

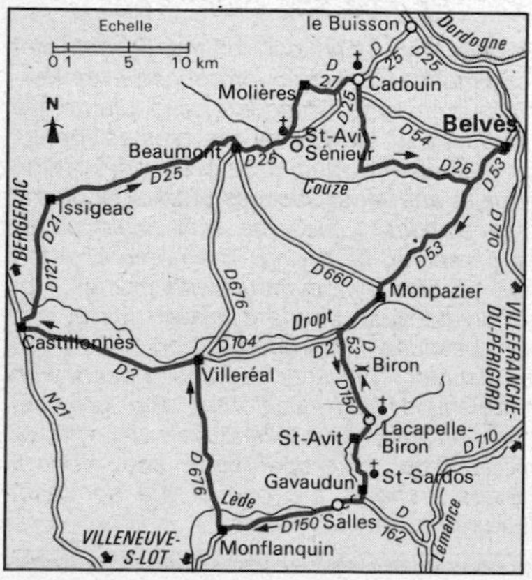

The walnut

The walnut tree, introduced by the Romans, grows throughout the region, following the banks of the Dordogne and its tributaries. It grows only in chalky soil and gives way to chestnut and pine where rock or clay predominates. The biggest walnut plantation in Europe is at Doissat, near Belvès (→), together with a museum devoted to walnuts (Musée de la Noix). *The Dordogne is France's leading producer of walnuts; walnut wood is much prized for use as veneer and in general cabinet making.*

■ BEAULIEU-EN-ROUERGUE★

D4 (Tarn-et-Garonne)

The former Cistercian abbey (12thC and 17thC) has been perfectly restored and is now a contemporary art centre (exhibitions in summer; *10-12 & 2-6 Apr.-Sep. closed Tue.)* ▶ The **château de Cas** at Espinas is a former Templar Commandery *(5 km SW; 2-7 Sat., Sun. and hols., Apr.-Oct.).* □

■ BEAUMONT-DE-LOMAGNE

24 km S. of Castelsarrasin B4 / ® (Tarn-et-Garonne)

Capital of white garlic, Beaumont-de-Lomagne is equally known for its equestrian events. Streets, squares, half-timbered houses and, especially ▶ the medieval market (14thC.) and ▶ the church in meridional Gothic style are worthy of a stop. □

▶ Nearby

▶ In the church of **Bouillac** (14 km SE) the treasury of the former Cistercian abbey of Grand-Selve (13thC.)
▶ **Gramont** (→ Lectoure, Midi-Toulousain). □

■ BERGERAC

B2-3 / ® / pop. 28 617 (Dordogne)

On the banks of the Dordogne where it enters the plain, Bergerac has always been a port, a ford and a cross-roads. It is also the capital of southern Périgord. Today little remains of Bergerac's commercial importance or its intellectual activity as the capital of Protestantism. There are a few timbered houses, here and there a Renaissance dormer window, but the winding, narrow streets of the old port and the wide, straight avenues in the centre of town retain a certain charm.

▶ The **Récollets Cloister** (Renaissance and 18thC galleries) houses the offices of the Bergerac Regional Wine Council. ▶ In a bend of the Rue du Château there is a pretty balustraded balcony; **Rue de l'Ancien Pont** boasts a 14thC house, Louis XIII (1601-1643) building and the Maison Peyrarède, known as the Château Henri IV (1553-1610). ▶ The town hall, formerly the Convent of the Dames de la Foi, houses the **Tobacco Museum**★ *(Musée du Tabac)* : bright and lively, this display provides a wealth of information on the major SW product *(9-12 & 2-6, closed Sun. am and Mon. am low season).* □

■ The BERGERAC Region

A2 (Dordogne)

The lush valley of the Dordogne opens out below Bergerac, spreading into the Bordelais and the Midi-Agenais regions. The landscape is crowded with orchards of peach, pear and apple. Vineyards cover the hillsides, changing colour with the seasons (→ Monbazillac). □

■ BONAGUIL★★

B3 (Lot-et-Garonne)

The **castle** of Bonaguil, the "mad castle" ("château fou" : its defensive sophistication borders on paranoia), is fascinating as the quintessence of later feudal architecture.

▶ The castle stands alone, perched on a forbidding outcrop between two wooded valleys, representing a last futile challenge to the centralised power of French monarchs. It was built when the châteaux of a more easy-going world were already appearing along the banks of the Loire *(guided tours hourly from 10 am and 3 pm; out of season : Sun. only, 3 pm; closed Jan.-Feb. Tel (58) 36 57 27).* □

▶ Nearby

▶ **Sauveterre-la-Lémance**★ feudal castle of the Kings of England and Dukes of Aquitaine, built on the lines of Welsh fortresses. □

Romanesque art

Both Périgord and Quercy were regions originally dominated by Romanesque architecture. They eventually developed along different lines, to some extent for political reasons but principally because of the rivalry between the Cistercian and Cluniac monastic orders. Périgord, within the orbit of the Comte de Poitiers, *remained an island of architectural purity, thanks largely to the influence of the Cistercian monks. Quercy, on the other hand, drew its inspiration from Toulouse and the art of Languedoc, developing a style of monumental sculpture of which Moissac is the finest example. The majority of important ecclesiastical buildings in Quercy belonged to the Cluniac Order. Their all-embracing mentality differed profoundly from the austere aesthetic and spiritual concepts of the Cistercians. However, the church designs of both orders were always based on a single nave, even in the largest buildings; this led to the development of cupolas as a modification of vaulted roofs and rendered the architecture of the region distinctive.*

■ BRANTÔME★★

B1 / ® / pop. 2 100 (Dordogne)

The river Dronne runs merrily around the town; on the opposite bank stands an abbey, home to the writer Brantôme (1540-1614), courtier, soldier and one-time escort of Mary, Queen of Scots. ▶ Like Périgueux cathedral, the church was restored by the architect Abadie; fine 11thC bell-tower, 17thC and 18thC convent buildings. The crudely-carved (16thC) caves are the setting for the Brantôme Dance Festival. An angled bridge leads to the **monks' garden** ★ with benches dating from the Renaissance. Charm and culinary renown. ▶ Don't miss the **château de Richemont** (16thC; *7 km NW; 15 Jul.-31 Aug.; closed Fri. and 15 Aug.)* □

▶ Trip around Brantôme★★ (approx 50 km, half-day)

▶ **Brantôme.** ▶ **Champagnac-de-Belair** ® : a well-known restaurant in an old oil-pressing mill beside the river. ▶ The Cistercian **Abbey of Boschaud**★ (1163) has been restored by the MH (historical monuments board) and the younger members of the Club du Vieux Manoir voluntary organisation *(15 Jul.-15 Aug.; 9-12 & 2-7).* ▶ The **château de Puyguilhem★★** is on a par with many châteaux of the Loire. The sculpture and decoration of its monumental chimneys were probably done by local craftsmen. *(9:30-11:30 & 2-5 or 6; closed Tue. and 15 Dec.-1 Feb.).* ▶ **Villars :** the Grotte (cave) de Cluzeau contains cave paintings contemporary with those of Lascaux (→) *(15 Jun.-15 Sep., 9-12 & 2-7; out of season Sun. and nat. hols.)* **Saint-Jean-de-Côle★★,** another village masterpiece on the banks of the river; Gothic bridge, mill, faded gold and brown tiles and pot-bellied houses straight out of the Middle Ages. Around the enormous square : interesting church with figured capitals (12thC), Renaissance cloister, covered market and the château de Marthonie (15th-16thC; *Jul.-Aug. 10-12 & 2-7*). Museum : Musée du Vieux St. Jean. ▶ Pretty road along the river Col which flows around the ruins of the **castle of Bruzac** (15thC). ▶ **Saint-Pierre-de-Côle** huddles around a poorly restored Romanesque church. ▶ The château at **La Chapelle-Faucher,** perched atop a cliff over the river, was devastated by fire. Crude Romanesque church in the village. ▶ Between Brantôme and Bourdeilles flows the **Dronne★,** bordered by poplar and walnut trees. The river passes beneath impressive cliffs pocked with shelters hollowed out by prehistoric man. ▶ **Bourdeilles★★** ® (pop. 728) : Ravishing site. The river flows under a Gothic bridge. The seigneurial mill projects over the river like the prow of a boat, and the château itself stands hard by, anchored to an enormous rock shelf; this was a 13th-15thC fortress, later a Renaissance palace designed by a sister-in-law of Brantôme; antique furnishings★ *(1 Feb.-15 Dec., closed Tue., 9-11:30 & 2-6; Jul.-Aug., daily; Oct., closed first week).* □

■ CAHORS★

C3 / ® / pop. 20 774 (Lot)

A remarkable site on a loop of the river Lot, surrounded by wild, bare hills. Twenty centuries of history are represented in this little capital of one of the most rural departments in France. The town is cosy and affable, a little sleepy, but its people are fond of life. Cahors is especially proud of Léon Gambetta (1838-82), the founder of Occitanian Radicalism. Visit on market days *(Wed. or Sat.)* when town meets country on the square in front of the cathedral.

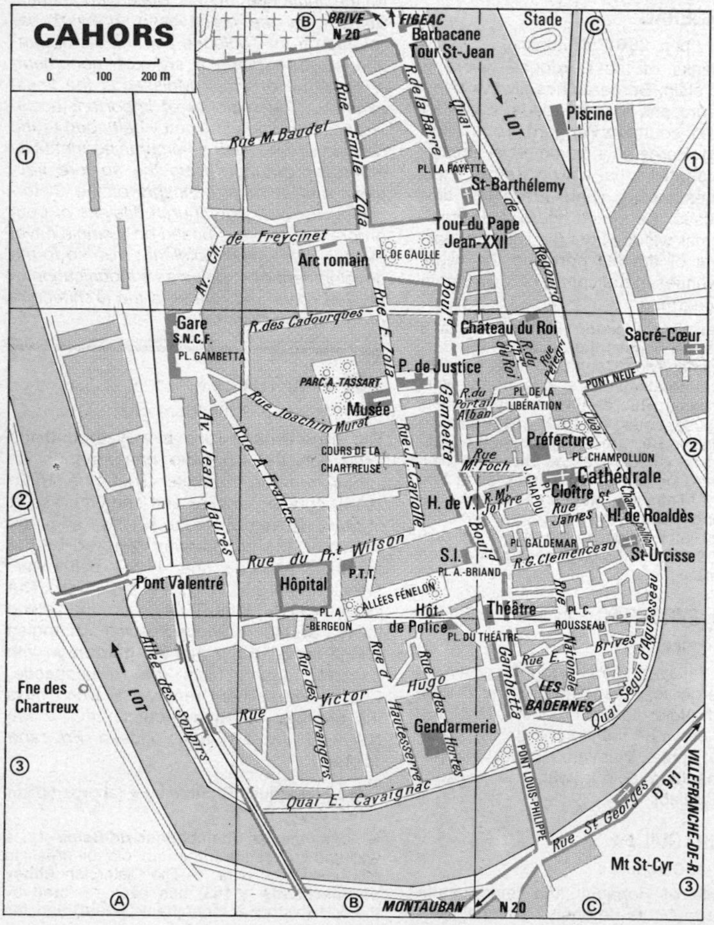

The wine of Cahors

Cahors wine was brought back into fashion by the late President Pompidou and the Comte de Montpezat, Prince Consort to Queen Margrethe of Denmark. In the Middle Ages, wine from Cahors (one of the most ancient wine-producing centres in France) was widely exported, even as far as Russia. It is born of the union of the Lot Valley and the Causse Plateau; classified A.O.C. (→ Wine) since 1971, and ever more widely appreciated; fortunately, production is now on the increase. This is a wine for keeping (4 or 5 years); dark and heady. 1978 was an exceptional year.

▶ **Pont Valentré★★** (bridge; A2) is the principal monument in Cahors. Built at the time of the Franco-English wars, a prime example of a fortified mediaeval bridge (14thC). ▶ The **cathedral★** bell-tower keep (11th-12thC) dominates the pink-tiled roofs of the old town. Its massive façade was added in the 14thC and the **Romanesque tympanum★,** similar to Moissac's and already showing hints of Gothic design, was moved to the north side near the Prefecture (the 18thC Episcopal Palace). On the south side, the 16thC **cloister** has satirical sculptures in the style of Cadouin (→) and paintings in 16thC Italian style. ▶ NE from the cloister, pretty Renaissance decor in the former **Archdeaconry of St. Jean.** ▶ The **Badernes sector★** (S; C3) is now being restored. During the great days of the 13thC this was the commercial centre of Cahors and today it is still a lively and picturesque area. ▶ The **Hôtel de Roaldès** on the Place Henri IV (C2) was probably decorated by the cathedral sculptors (ca. 1500). ▶ The upper quarter of the town, **Soubirous,** where Catholics and Protestants once clashed, was the site of the university, founded by Pope John XXII (ca. 1244-1334; last Pope at Avignon and native of Cahors), and closed in the 18thC. One of the towers of the **Collège Pellegri** (15thC) is still standing, masked by modern buildings. ▶ If you go up towards the **church of St. Barthélemy** (14thC), you will see many architectural details from the 13thC, 14thC and 17thC; next to the church the stocky **Tower of Pope John XXII** is a remnant of the former Duèze Palace, built by the Pope's brother and never finished (14thC). ▶ The **Diane Gate** on the Place Thiers bears vestiges of the old Roman Baths. ▶ North of the town, standing watch over the Lot, are the 15thC Barbican and the Tour (tower) St. Jean, outside the walls (B1). The museum in the old Episcopal Palace honours the famous men of Cahors, Pope John XXII, the poets Clément Marot (1493-1544) and de Magny (ca. 1530-1561), Gambetta himself *(high season; closed Sun.).* ▶ The walk to **Mont Saint-Cyr★** rewards the visitor with a view over the whole town.

Also... ▶ **Château de Roussillon** *(3 km N)* : a mediaeval fortress containing a small museum of rural life in Quercy *(summer, groups only; 2-7; closed Tue.).* □

▶ Round-trip of the Cahors vineyards *(107 km from Cahors to Bonaguil via the lower valley of the Lot; sign-posted on each bank, but the right bank carries much more motor traffic).* No more cliffs but plenty of bends in the river, with villages perched on hills or by the water's edge, their Romanesque churches and châteaux surveying the vineyards from above. ▶ **Cahors.** ▶ From **Mercuès** ® onward (Château of the Bishops of Cahors now a hotel), the vine is predominant. ▶ **Parnac :** headquarters of the Winegrowers' Cooperative. ▶ **Luzech** is a small industrial centre, superbly sited; the mediaeval village is clustered at the keep; behind is the hill of Impernal, one of the numerous possible sites of the Roman town of *Uxellodunum.* ▶ **Puy-l'Évêque** ®, another production centre for Cahors wine, is a fortified town in a natural amphitheatre by the Lot; Gothic church (sculptures) which was part of the town's defence system, opposite a 13thC keep (view). ▶ 15thC frescos in the church at **Martignac** *(4 km N).* ▶ The country here is more level and roofs are lower : this is the Agenais Region. ▶ Return to **Bonaguil★★** (→) along a lovely road through **Duravel** (11thC church with figured capitals and archaic crypt) and **Montcabrier,** 13thC *bastide* with an attractive church. □

■ CAUSSADE

C4 / ® / pop. 6 132 (Tarn-et-Garonne)

Former Protestant stronghold, latterly a hat-making centre. Hôtel de Maleville (17thC mansion; *visit on request Apr.-Nov. ex Sun. and Mon.*). ▶ Three *bastides* nearby : **Réalville** *(7.5 km S),* **Mirabel** *(6.5 km W of Réalville)* and **Puylaroque★** *(13 km NE).* □

■ CÉOU Valley★

C3 (Lot)

Between Quercy and Périgord, from the **Causse de Gramat** (→) to the **château de Castelnau** (→) in the Dordogne, this valley provides one of the most agreeable walks imaginable. The Céou is, in fact, a stream winding beneath poplars through a plain chequered with crops and studded with villages. □

■ CÈRE Gorges

D2 (Lot)

The Cère is a minor tributary of the Dordogne, rising in the Plomb du Cantal; between **Laroquebrou** and the **château de Castelnau** (→) the Cère plunges through wild and wooded rocks. Its course is followed by the railway and by GR652, a trail through oak and beech along the hilltops. □

Strawberries

For many years the Dordogne has been France's main source of strawberries. Plastic cold frames have appeared in almost all the woods in the area as a last hope for this sparse, acid-soiled countryside.

■ DORDOGNE PÉRIGOURDINE★★★

(Perigord sector of the Dordogne Valley)

▶ From Souillac to Badefols-sur-Dordogne *(90 km, full day)*
B2-3 / C2-3 *(see map 2)*

The river curves slowly around high limestone cliffs; villages and châteaux face one another across the river, and rich crops spread away over the plain.

▶ The Dordogne rises in the Puy de Sancy (alt. 1 886 m), and enters Périgord-Dordogne at Cazoulès, downstream from **Souillac** (→). ▶ Just after the charming church in **Carsac** (Romanesque, ogive vaulting from the 16thC) on the right bank, the road runs above the river bend known as the **Cingle de Montfort★.** The 15thC castle (heavily restored) is perched on a bluff high above the river; village with stone-tiled roofs at cliff-foot. ▶ **Cénac** crouches below the *bastide* of Domme. The church is not typical of Périgord but its 12thC *chevet* is very fine; carved corbels and capitals. ▶ **Domme★★** ® : here everything is exceptional - the site, the view from the Barre, terrace, the quality of the architecture, the colour of the stone. This is a French *bastide* (1383) built on an irregular plan to accommodate the terrain. 13thC ramparts, 17thC covered market, 16thC governor's house on the square, stalactite caves *(open Apr.-Sep.).* ▶ Starting from Domme, visit the town of **La Roque-Gageac** ®, a former inland port, built right against the cliffs. ▶ **Marquayssac** is a 17thC château-belvédère opposite those of **Lacoste** (19thC) and **Castelnau** (12thC and 15thC). ▶ **Beynac-et-Cazenac★★** ® is a gem : the village is built over a lovely bend in the river, and the **castle** - one of the *Four Baronies of Périgord* - sits atop the cliff; this was once (13th-16thC) a formidable fortress, despite its idyllic setting; 13th-18thC decoration; 14thC frescos *(1 Mar.-15 Nov., 10-12 & 2:30-6:30, 4:30 low season).* ▶ Beyond Beynac, the valley reveals more beautiful scenery; the left bank is recommended. ▶ The river flows past the **château de Fayrac** (14th-17thC) and through an experimental walnut plantation. ▶ **Les Milandes :** the country château (end 15thC, much restored) of the Caumont family; made famous when purchased by the late American singer-dancer Josephine Baker *(visits Palm Sun.-15 Oct., 9-12 & 2-6).* ▶ At **Berbiguières,** the 17thC château is hidden behind high walls. ▶ **Saint-Cyprien** ® spreads along a hillside. Pretty houses surround the church (12thC bell-tower keep) former abbey (16thC) occupied by the State Tobacco Board *(Régie des Tabacs).* North of the village on a wooded hill is the lovely restored **château de Fages;** superb site; view. ▶ Another château (15thC-17thC) above **Mouzens** *(10-12 & 3-6, 15 Jul.-30 Aug.).* ▶ At **Limeuil** the road rejoins the valley of the Vézère. ▶ Superb route towards **Trémolat** (→) and **Badefols-sur-Dordogne★** ®, a protected *(classé)* site (→ Monuments). □

■ DORDOGNE QUERCYNOISE★★★

(Quercy sector of the Dordogne Valley)

▶ From Souillac to Saint-Céré *(60 km, half-day)*
C2 *(see map 3)*

As in Périgord, narrow passes give way to luxuriant meadows, dominated by villages and hilltop châteaux. The country is well-watered and peaceful, planted with alders, poplars and tobacco.

▶ **Souillac** (→). ▶ At the end of the Pinsac bridge is the **château of La Treyne** (17thC), built on a rock above the river; at the junction of the Dordogne and the green-banked Ouysse is **Belcastel château** (14thC and 19thC), with an incomparable view *(visit the terrace in summer only).* ▶ Stalactite caves at **Lacave** ® *(Palm Sun.-end Sep.).* ▶ Good view over **Meyronne** (former residence of the Bishops of Tulle), and **Saint-Sozy.** ▶ **Creysse** is superb. Interesting Romanesque church with twin apses from different periods. ▶ View over the **Cirque de Montvallon** (natural amphitheatre) from the **Calvaire** (wayside cross) **de Copeyre;** visible on another loop of the river are the château de Mirandol (16thC), the bell-tower of Floirac (18thC) and, in the distance, the Puy d'Issolud, another possible site of *Uxellodunum.* **Martel★★,** on the *causse* (plateau) to the north is charming. The entire town centre is classified, with numerous 14thC, 15thC and 16thC houses; the Town Hall and Raymondie Palace, (14thC; *Jul.-Aug., p.m.*); 13thC Mint; covered markets (18thC); fortified Gothic church with Romanesque tympanum. ▶ **Carennac★★** ®, a delightful, brown-tiled town, grew up around the priory where the author François Fénelon (1651-1715) was abbot. The 15th-17thC château stands above the island-studded river. The doorway★ of the church (12thC, 15thC) echoes the motifs of Moissac (→); satirical carvings on

2. **Dordogne River in Périgord**

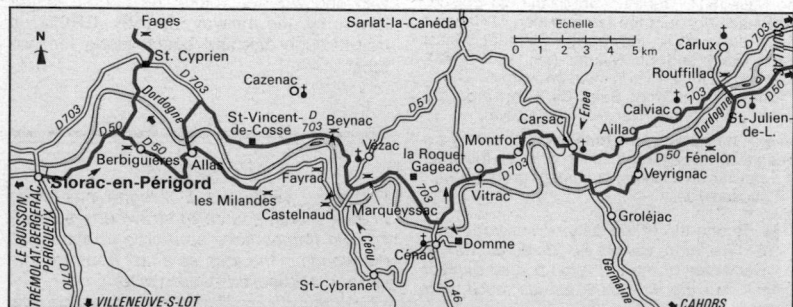

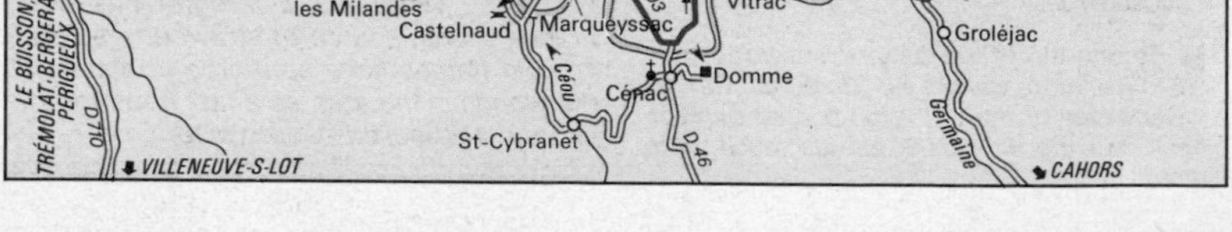

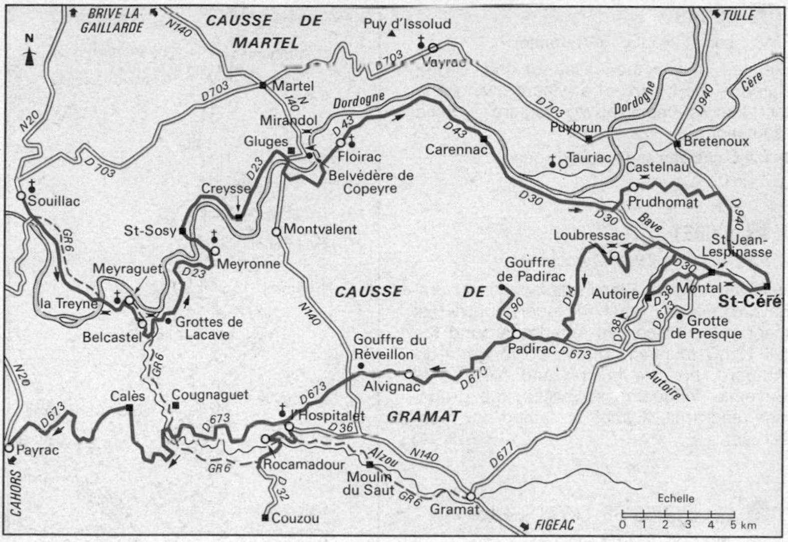

3. Dordogne River in Quercy

the capitals, 16thC statues and 15thC murals. Gothic cloister with Romanesque gallery. The village contains numerous Renaissance vestiges. ▶ The formidable red bulk of the **château de Castelnau-Bretenoux★** on a wooded hillock dominates all the surrounding valleys *(30 Jun.-14 Sept., 10-1 & 2-7)* ▶ At its foot is the village of **Prudhomat,** scattered among the greenery. ▶ **Bretenoux** is a former *bastide* founded by the Lord of Castelnau. ▶ **Saint-Céré** (→). □

■ DOUBLE Forest★

A2 (Dordogne)

This is true forest country★, in contrast to the nearby Landes region, where trees are farm cultivated; many of the streams that wind beneath oak and pine have been dammed to make ponds. This ancient forest long had a reputation as the haunt of wolves and fantasy or maleficent creatures; the ponds spread malaria and even animals had rheumatism. Drained, improved and planted with pines, the region now resembles the Sologne, south of Orléans. There are few villages, but a sprinkling of half-timbered farmhouses and hamlets on the dryer slopes. For walkers, this is a poetic landscape and for bird-watchers, a treasure trove.

▶ **Échourgnac** is the capital of the Double; important fairs, almost unchanged since the last century, are held here four times a year. The broad **Etang** (pool) **de la Jemaye★** has now become a leisure centre. ▶ Don't miss **Saint-Astier★** on the edge of the forest. Here, at the end of autumn, farmers and merchants spread coloured umbrellas over the squares, and crowds come to buy poultry, *foie gras* and truffles for the Christmas and New Year festivities. A massive church and bell-tower (15thC) dominate the whole town and overlook the valley of the river **Isle**. Several houses have kept Renaissance elements - turrets, half-timbering. The industrious SI organises short hiking tours, excursions to churches and châteaux and visits to local quarries. ▶ The area is richly supplied with fire clay; tilemakers working in the traditional manner have replaced the 19thC potters. □

Perigord gastronomy

Plump poultry, Boletus mushrooms (cêpes), *truffles : Périgord is justly famous as a gastronomic paradise. A few marvellous dishes have made its reputation :* foie gras, *omelette with truffles or with* cêpes, confit *(goose or duck cooked and preserved in its own fat) served with sorrel or* pommes sarladaises *(potatoes cooked in goose fat),* salade aux noix *(salad garnished with walnuts) and* cabécou *(goat cheese); these make up the traditional menu in all the area's restaurants. Sometimes there may be* tourin *(garlic soup),* tourtières *(pies),* coq au vin *or* au verjus *(juice of white grapes),* les farcies *(stuffed poultry, goose neck, hare). Unfortunately, lazy cooks tend to rely on the can-opener and the Périgord reputation rather than following the traditional recipes. Apart from a few great restaurants, you will find your best meals in unpretentious village inns or farms.*

There are good local wines to go with the meal : Coteaux de Bergerac, Monbazillac *with the* foie gras, Côtes de Duras *and* Côtes de Buzet *(1979 and 1982 were very good years) and the neighbouring* Cahors.

DURAS

A3 / pop. 1 245 (Lot-et-Garonne)

Situated above the valley of the Dropt, Duras is the centre of a wine-growing district that is beginning to acquire a solid reputation.

▶ 17thC château and arcaded square. □

EYMET

A3 / ® / pop. 2 945 (Dordogne)

Visit this ancient French *bastide* on Thursday, market day, when the local country folk meet in the Place des Arcades around the tall 17thC fountain. This is no longer truly Périgord, but the humps and hillocks of Guyenne, kingdom of tobacco, the grapevine and fruit. Eymet is famed for conserves. □

Les EYZIES-DE-TAYAC★★★

B2 / ® / pop. 858 (Dordogne)

The science of prehistory originated in this village, between holm oak-covered cliffs at the confluence of the Vézère and the Beune. The first drawing of a mammoth was discovered here along with the first skeleton of Cro-Magnon Man, 30 000 years old.

▶ The **National Prehistory Museum★★★** *(9:30-12 & 2-6; closed Tue.)*, an essential introduction to the prehistoric sites of Périgord. ▶ The **fortress church★** of **Tayac** (12thC; Limousin doorway) was built by the monks of Paunat. ▶ Le Roc de Tayac (troglodyte dwellings) houses a **speleological museum** *(May-Sep.)*. ▶ The cave of **Font de Gaume★★★** *(9-11 & 2-3, May-Sep.; 10-11 & 2-3 Sep.-May, closed 25 Nov.-26 Dec., Tue. and nat. hols.; also closes when the number of visitors exceeds 700)* : this is the most beautiful collection of polychrome cave paintings open to the public in France. ▶ The cave of **Combarelles** *(same hours and conditions as above)* contains France's most important collection of rock engravings. ▶ The **Abri du Cap Blanc** has a lifesize bas-relief of horses★ (permission to view from the hamlet of La Grèze). ▶ The **Grand Roc Cave** above the river Vézère in the **Laugeries Cliffs** (prehistoric remains) is famous for its coral-like mineral deposits. □

▶ Prehistoric Périgord : valley of the Vézère River★★★ *(see map 4)*

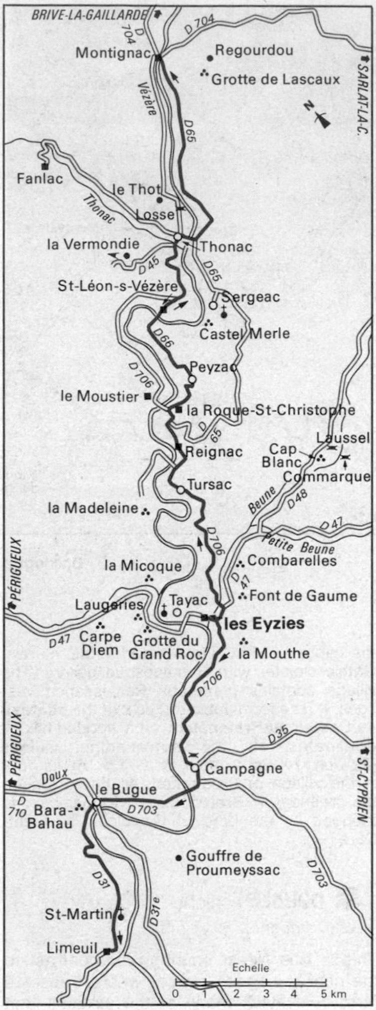

4. Valley of the Vézère

During the past 100 years, 25 caves, 150 sites and thousands of vestiges have been found in the Vézère Valley, demonstrating man's persistent presence in these white cliffs; the place is a sort of Cro-Magnon version of Egypt's Valley of the Kings. □

▶ South of Les Eyzies *(16 km)*

▶ The road follows the left bank of the Vézère. ▶ **Campagne** ® **:** the 15thC castle is over-restored, but the site, with the stream, wash-house and wall-belfryed church (12th-15thC), is very pretty. ▶ **Le Bugue** ® : between hills and river, (spoiled by heavy traffic). ▶ The engravings in the **Bara-Bahau Cave** are hard for non-experts to decipher *(8:30-12:30 & 1:30-7 high season; closed Tue. am)*. ▶ The **Gouffre de Proumeyssac** *(Palm Sun.-30 Sep., 8-12 & 2-6)* offers impressive cave scenery. ▶ The hilltop road to Limeuil has broad views over the valley and the hills. ▶ **Limeuil★,** on the hilltop where the Vézère joins the Dordogne, is a former fortified town turned inland port. It is now one of the Périgord's most charming villages. ▶ The country chapel of **Saint-Martin-de-Limeuil** (in the cemetery) is an endangered masterpiece. □

▶ North of Les Eyzies *(approx 30 km)*

On the right bank, the site of **La Madeleine** has given its name to the Higher Paleolithic culture of the Lascaux artists. ▶ **Tursac :** church with a row of cupolas and bell-tower keep. Fortified house at **Reignac.** ▶ **La Roque-Saint-Chris-**

tophe, a long, natural *corniche* (ledge) that once served as a rampart. In the cliff is a **troglodyte village** with a 15thC chapel and a feudal castle. At **Pas du Miroir,** there are five levels of habitation occupied since the Gallo-Romans *(Palm Sun.-15 Sep., 10-12 & 2-6).* ▶ On the other bank, the **Moustier** site has given its name to a stone-working period. ▶ **Peyzac :** 14thC chapel in the cemetery. ▶ **Saint-Léon-sur-Vézère★ :** delightful village by the river; stone-roofed church and two châteaux (14thC and 16thC). On the other bank, **Sergeac** has stone-roofed houses around a 13thC manor, the remains of a Templar Commandery and an astonishing 13th-14thC fortress church. Viewpoint at **Castel-Merle.** ▶ **Thonac : Thot Prehistoric Centre** on the wooded hillside *(4 km)* : introduction to Prehistory *(9-12 & 2-6; out of season : Sun. nat. and school hols.).* ▶ West of Thonac, superb village of **Plazac★** and **Côte de Jor★** bank (viewpoint). ▶ To see the **château de Losse★** (16thC; 1 Jul.-15 Sep.) on a rock above the green river, follow the left bank. ▶ **Montignac** ®, astride the river, was just another inland port (galleried houses on the quays) before it became famous with the discovery of **Lascaux** (→). ▶ The tour of prehistoric Périgord would not be complete without a visit to **Rouffignac** (→). □

■ FIGEAC★★

D3 / ® / pop. 10 500 (Lot)

Once a Protestant refuge, Figeac still has the air of a lively town of the Middle Ages, when it was a trading centre and staging post for pilgrims to Compostela. The town is now undergoing intensive restoration.

▶ There are few monuments here other than the **Mint** (dedicated to Champollion, decipherer of the Rosetta Stone, born at Figeac in 1790) constructed in local 13thC style : arcades forming a covered market, columned windows and open gallery beneath a flat roof. ▶ The **church of St. Sauveur,** a Benedictine abbey church (12th-14thC) was completely remodelled in the 17thC and 19thC; 13thC chapter-house with 17thC polychromed wood. ▶ Something interesting in every street : the great arcades in front of ancient shops, half-timbering and corbelled upper stories, soft-hued brickwork. ▶ Place Carnot is a former market-place; the Rue Gambetta full of ogives, the Rue Colomb, which was the town's aristocratic street in the 17thC, and the Rue Boutaric are full of antique shops. ▶ Fine restoration of the **Enclos des Carmes.** ▶ **Champollion Museum** *(15 Jun.-15 Sept., 10-12 & 2:30-6:30).* ▶ The **Aiguilles de Figeac** are 13thC obelisks planted S and W of the town. ▶ **Cardaillac** ® *(11 km NW)* was a fortified village, home of one of the most powerful feudal families in Quercy, and a Protestant refuge. □

■ GOURDON★

C3 / ® / pop. 5 096 (Lot)

Gourdon's high hill can be seen from 20 km around. It is the principal town of a green, wooded district, the **Bouriane.** The old town has been spring-cleaned; its stonework now rivals that of Sarlat (→).

▶ The prettiest square is framed by the 17thC town hall, overlooking covered arcades; there is also a powerful Languedoc Gothic church. ▶ 360° view from the site of the château (destroyed). □

Also... ▶ **Cougnac Caves★** *(3 km N)* : decorated with Magdalenian paintings, very similar to those of Pech Merle (→) *(Palm Sun.-1 Nov., 9-11 & 2-5:30; Jul.-Aug., 9-6:30).* □

▶ South of Gourdon : La Bouriane region. Round trip *(approx 80 km; half-day)*

This is a hidden land, all hills, hollows, meadows, streams and woods. Ruined feudal buildings litter the limestone peaks, and many villages have pretty Romanesque churches bearing witness to the vigour of rural life at the end of the 11thC. ▶ **Gourdon.** ▶ In the **Céou Valley** are the ruins of the Cistercian **Abbaye Nouvelle** (new abbey). ▶ **Salviac :** a village reminiscent of the Midi : 14thC stained glass★ in the church; **Lacoste Manor** (13th16thC). ▶ **Cazals★:** above the valley of the Masse. ▶ The **château de Montcléra** was remodelled in the 16thC. ▶ The churches in **Arques** and **Saint-André-des-Arques** owe much to the Franco-Russian sculptor Zadkine, who discovered the frescos in the latter and had the former restored. ▶ **L'Herm** is a delightful village; the priory at **Goujounac★** ® is overrun by vegetation. ▶ **Catus** in the Vert Valley was once a fortified town and has an 11thC priory. ▶ The beautifully aged church at **Rampoux** is marred by clumsily-restored frescos. □

■ GRAMAT

C3 / ® / pop. 3 828 (Lot)

The principal town in the Gramat *causse* (plateau), on the banks of the Alzou. Important sheep fairs are held here. ▶ A wildlife park★ shows the animals of the region at liberty *(pm only, low season).*

▶ On the Figeac road : **Beaulieu Hospice,** almshouse for pilgrims to Compostela; **Thémines** (covered market★); **Rudelle** and its fortress church★; **Le Bourg** early 12thC Romanesque church. ▶ At the other end of the *causse,* **La Bastide-Murat** was the home of Joachim Murat (1767-1815; marshal under Napoléon; small museum, *1 Jul.-15 Sept., 10-12 & 2-6, closed Tue.*); important fairs are held here. ▶ Beautiful villages nearby : **Vaillac, Soulomès, Montfaucon, Séniergues.** □

■ The GRAMAT Causse (Plateau)

CD3 (Lot)

The Causse de Gramat is the largest and wildest of the *causses* in the Lot area. It is scarred by the canyons of the Alzou and the Ouysse where a number of mills still can be seen. This is a mountain landscape, swept by a remorseless wind, with here and there a drystone hut or sheepfold. In the clearings, a few grey houses with brown-tiled roofs huddle around fortified churches.

▶ To the E, a remarkable site : the **Desert of La Braunhie★.** □

■ HAUTEFORT★★

C1-2 / pop. 1 035 (Dordogne)

The grand **château de Hautefort** *(Palm Sun.-All Saints day, 9-12 & 2-7; rest of the year, Sun. and hols., 2-5)* is surrounded by an enormous park. Recently restored after a fire in 1968.

▶ The château is built on a spur overlooking broad woodlands and heath country. Two famous people lived in this château : the warrior-troubadour Bertrand de Born in the 12thC, and much later Marie de Hautefort, a mistress of Louis XIII and hostess of a famous 17thC literary *salon.* ▶ The architecture of the **village church** recalls that of the château. □

▶ Nearby

▶ **Badefols-d'Ans★** *(6 km S) :* on the edge of the Périgord, this feudal castle was enlarged in the 15thC and 18thC. Church with cupolas (12thC). □

■ JUMILHAC-LE-GRAND★★

B1 / pop. 1 450 (Dordogne)

This village is in fact part of the Limousin region and centres around a vast market place (famous at the turn of the century for pig fairs).

▶ The **château,** hanging over the **Gorges de L'Isle,** is straight out of a fairy-tale, bristling with towers, belfries and pepperpot turrets (note the herringbone ridge tiles). Various portions of the building date from the 14th-18thC *(Easter-Nov., Sun. 2-6; Jul.-Aug. 10-12 & 2-6:30).* ▶ The **church** was once the castle chapel. □

■ The LANDAIS Region

A2 (Dordogne)

The Landais is a region of former forest and marsh, through which the Lidoire runs. In the 19thC, sea pine encroached on the heath and ousted the native deciduous forest, until the region looked very much like the neighbouring Landes (→). Forest clearing has now created vineyards and arable land. □

■ LANQUAIS★

B3 (Dordogne)

A tiny village (market, interesting grainstore) with a superb unfinished **château,** now very dilapidated. Feudal keep and Renaissance structure by the same masons responsible for the Louvre in Paris *(9-11:30 & 2-5 or 6 Apr.-Oct.; closed Thu.).*

▶ On the other bank of the Dordogne, feudal castle of **Baneuil** *(1 Jul.-20 Sep., 10-12 & 3-6; closed Sun.).* □

■ LASCAUX★★

C2 (Dordogne)

The famous cave discovered in 1940 has been closed to the public for the past 20 years. The 1 500 drawings and paintings could only be saved by such measures. Recently an astonishing facsimile, Lascaux II★★, was opened; it was created over 10 years by artists using the same methods as the painters of the Palaeolithic era. *(10-6; closed Tue. and winter; enquire at local TO.)* □

■ LAUZERTE★

C4 / ® / pop. 1 700 (Tarn-et-Garonne)

A *bastide* on a hill. Square houses with flat roofs currently undergoing restoration.

▶ NE, **Barguelonne Vale,** pretty villages. ▶ **Montcuq★** old fortified village, capital of the **Quercy Blanc Region,** white as the limestone of the plateaus; in the little valleys, a wide variety of crops. On the hillside, the *chasselas* grape predominates. □

■ LIMOGNE Causse (Plateau)

C3-4 (Lot)

Fields of lavender and a *maquis* (heath) of holm-oak and aromatic plants in hot sun on stone give the *causse* a Mediterranean atmosphere. Dolmens, little stone huts, local architecture, and here and there a mill, a well, or a washhouse are reminders of an active community in this region.

▶ The capital, **Limogne,** is right in the middle of the *causse,* the crossroads and centre of the truffle industry. ▶ **Lalbenque** ® : site of the biggest market in the district. □

■ Valleys of the LOT and the CÉLÉ★★★

▶ Round-trip *(160 km from Cahors to Cahors, full-day).*

CD3 *(see map 5)* (Lot)

These narrow slots between golden cliffs separate the *causses* of Gramat and Limogne. The road follows them with difficulty and at each bend you may discover a château, a fortress church or a village perched on high like an eagle's eyrie.

▶ **Cahors.** ▶ At Vers, **Notre Dame de Velles :** pretty apse with rustic corbels. ▶ The Célé and Lot rivers region at **Conduché.** ▶ The writer André Breton (1896-1966; founder of Surrealism) spent his summers in **Saint-Cirq-Lapopie★★** ® (pop. 179), and compared its charms to the poetry of Rimbaud. Renaissance church and charming museum in the château de la Gardette. ▶ **Castle of Cénevières★** *(10-12 & 2-6; closed Tue.; 1 Apr.-30 Sep., 1 Oct.-31 Mar., closed at 5) :* overlooking the Lot, this feudal fortress was transformed during the Renaissance. Opposite, troglodyte village of **La Toulzanie.** ▶ **Calvignac :** on the edge of the cliff overlooking **Larnagol.** ▶ **Carjac** ® was once an inland port : seamen's chapel; charming holiday spot. ▶ 8 km from Cajarc, there is a remarkable but unknown site called **Le Saut-de-la-Mounine.** ▶ **Montbrun★** ®, clusters high around its fortress. ▶ **Laroque-Toirac :** 15thC château *(19 Jul.-19 Sep.).* ▶ The warlike church of **Saint-Pierre-Toirac** (11th-12thC, fortified 14th-15thC) looks like a feudal keep. ▶ Return to **Figeac** (→) across the *causse.* ▶ The châ-

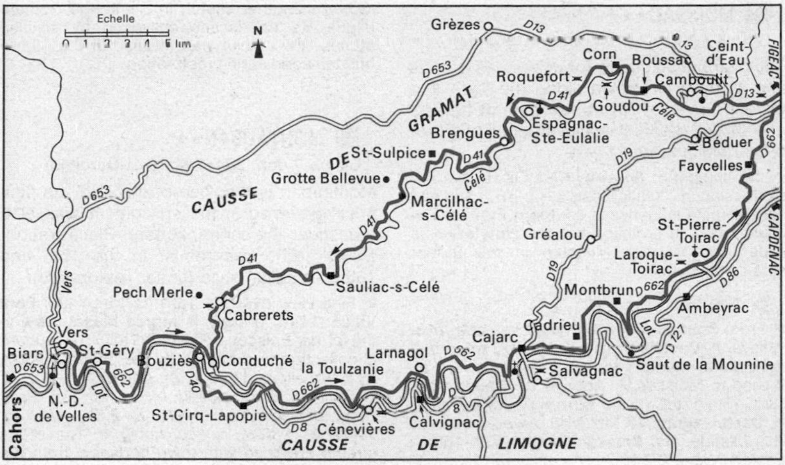

5. Valleys of the Lot and the Célé

teaux of **Ceint d'Eau** (15thC) and **Béduer** (13thC) have been much restored. ▶ After **Boussac,** the Célé disappears into a canyon and narrow gorges alternate with cropland. ▶ **Espagnac-Sainte-Eulalie★,** on the edge of the *causse,* its pointed roofs grouped around a priory, (17th-18thC). The principal sight here is the church (12th-14th-15thC); 14thC tombs and remarkable gilded woodwork (17thC). ▶ **Marcilhac-sur-Célé★** was a rich Benedictine abbey; magnificent ruins. The Romanesque portion has not been rebuilt but the Gothic part is in use as a church (frescos). In a nearby valley, Bellevue cave (view of the village). ▶ **La Pescalerie** is one of the most delightful sites in the region. ▶ **Cabrerets** ® : through the valley of the Sagne★ (a little ecological paradise), to the **Pech-Merle Caves★★★,** a beautiful Paleolithic sanctuary. Open to the public; remarkable site, very instructive museum *(Palm Sun.-end Oct. and by appt. off-season.).* □

■ MAREUIL

B1 / pop. 1 215 (Dordogne)

One of the outposts of the province and one of the four Baronies of the ancient Province of Périgord. Unusually, the **castle** is built in the plain, completely surrounded by moats; Flamboyant Gothic chapel *(2-6, Easter to All Saints' day, daily; low season, Sun and hols. only).* □

▶ Nearby

▶ A number of châteaux provide excellent destinations for walks, though most are not open to the public : ▶ **Beaulieu** *(3 km, very near the Riberac road).* ▶ **Beauregard** *(3 km along a path on the left of the Riberac road).* ▶ **Repaire** *(2 km on the first road left from the Ribérac road).* Several pretty churches nearby : ▶ **Vieux Mareuil** ® *(5 km E; D939);* 13thC Romanesque church fortified in the 14thC. ▶ **Cherval** *(10 km SW; D708) :* fortress church with four cupolas★. ▶ **Cercles** *(10 km S D99) :* part of an old priory; figured capitals (12thC) on west door. ▶ On a neighbouring bluff, fine houses reminiscent of the Renaissance in **La Tour Blanche★ :** 10thC keep; 17thC manor.

Also... ▶ **Château des Bernardières** (14thC, 15thC and 17thC; *Jul.-Sep., 10-12 & 2-6),* near Champaux *(10 km E).* □

■ MARMANDE

A3 / ® / pop. 17 758 (Lot-et-Garonne)

The main agricultural centre of the Garonne Valley, which vies with the Loire Region for the title of "the garden of France". The landscape here is often compared to that of Tuscany in Italy.

▶ On the Agen road : ▶ **Le Mas-d'Agenais :** covered market and Rembrandt painting in the Benedictine church. ▶ **Clairac,** along the Lot where, in the 16thC, the Benedictines pioneered tobacco and prunes, now the principal crops of the region (museum). ▶ **Gontaud-de-Nogaret.** □

Truffles

The truffle is a black mushroom, strongly yet delicately flavoured, growing in chalky soil and generally beneath oak trees. Truffle hunting (cavage) *is seasonal from November to March and since the 'black diamond of haute cuisine' grows underground, truffle hunters use trained dogs or (more rarely) sows to help them in their efforts. One oak may yield up to 2 kilos of truffles; the best are found late in the season. Périgord markets around 4 tons of truffles a year out of a national total of 15 tons; the markets in the Lot, especially at Lalbenque (Tue. during Jan. and Feb.) are much the best source both for quantity and quality. Research has not yet discovered the secret of growing this marvellous and extremely valuable mushroom, but a 25-acre experimental truffle farm has been established near Coly. Visit the Truffle Museum at Sorges on N21 between Périgueux and Thiviers (pm only; closed Tue.).*

MOISSAC★★★

B4 / ® / pop. 11 410 (Tarn-et-Garonne)

The distribution centre for *chasselas* grapes and all the fruit grown along the Tarn and Garonne rivers. The **abbey church** here is one of the greatest achievements of European religious art.

▶ Its **majestic doorway★★★** is a perfect expression of Cluniac ideals (→ p.467) and had considerable influence in southern France. The church itself is ordinary, but the **cloister★★** is superb. ▶ Moissac Museum in the former abbot's residence. □

▶ Nearby

▶ From **Boudou** *(7 km W)* view over both river valleys. ▶ **Castelsarrazin** *(8 km S) :* important agricultural market; former *bastide,* priory attached to Moissac. ▶ **Abbaye de Belleperche** (12th-13th-17thC; *6 km S from Castelsarrasin).* ▶ **Castelsagrat** *(13 km NW) :* well-preserved little *bastide,* and **Brassac Castle** (13th-15thC; *Easter-1 Nov., 2-7:30*). □

MONBAZILLAC

B3 / ® / pop. 837 (Dordogne)

Monbazillac produces wine as famous as Sauternes and both have suffered from the current preference for dry wines. ▶ The Renaissance **château** belonging to the winemaking cooperative is now a museum *(9-12 & 2-6).* One room is consecrated to wine, another devoted to Protestantism, equally important to local people. ▶ The **vineyards** cover the surrounding hills (30 km^2). Planted by monks at the end of the 11thC, they blossomed under the influence of Bergerac merchants and exiled Protestants. This fertile agricultural region marks the transition from the Dordogne to the opulent Bordelais Region. Even the more ordinary houses have handsome, dignified façades, and the Roman-tiled roofs projecting over their verandahs echo this feeling. Farms and smallholdings are sprinkled throughout the area, and the market towns, with their population of independent growers, are focal points of the region. □

▶ Nearby

▶ **Sainte-Foy-la-Grande** *(25 km W),* astride the Dordogne, was a French *bastide* (arcaded square) and Protestant stronghold. ▶ **Montcaret★** *(13 km W) :* Gallo-Roman mosaics and Romanesque church (the capitals are re-used Gallo-Roman sculptures). ▶ **Saint-Michel-de-Montaigne** *(4 km NW) :* in the centre of the Montravel vineyards, (velvety *demi-sec* wines). The château where Montaigne lived was destroyed by fire and rebuilt during the 19thC, but the **library tower** where he wrote his *Essays* (1580-1585) is the original. *(9-12 & 2-7; closed Mon., Tue. am and 6 Jan.-6 Feb.).* ▶ In the north of the Dordogne, vineyards give way to small fields, orchards and tobacco plantations. ▶ **Montpeyroux** *(6 km N).* ▶ The U-shaped château of Montecoulon (17th-18thC) makes a pretty picture with the neighbouring church and its beautiful apse in Saintonge Romanesque. ▶ **Carsac-de-Gurson** *(6 km N) :* a pretty church in similar style. Ruins of feudal castle at Gurson. ▶ **Saint-Martin-de-Gurson** *(2 km) :* another church in Saintonge Romanesque, its flat façade enlivened by stylised arches; the *chevet* was fortified in the 15thC, but damaged during restoration. □

•

MONTAUBAN★★

C4 / ® / pop. 53 147 (Tarn-et-Garonne)

Montauban is the rose of the Midi, its pink brick gleaming in the sunlight. It was also a *bastide;* the central square, Place Nationale★★ (B2), was rebuilt in the 17th and 18thC in Italian style (under restoration).

▶ Fine view over the Tarn (B2) from the **Pont Vieux** (14thC bridge). ▶ **Ingres Museum★★** in the former Episcopal Palace (17thC) : exceptional collection bequeathed by the painter; works by Bourdelle and Desnoyer. *(Palm Sun. - 1 July, 1 Sept.-15 Oct., closed Mon.; 16 Oct.-Palm Sun., closed Sun.; 10-12 & 2-6; July-Aug. 10-12 & 1:30-6, closed hols.)* ▶ Numerous streets are lined with town houses★ from the French Classical period. ▶ A rare classical **cathedral,** gleaming white in this town of pink brick, symbolises the Counter-Reformation against the Protestant heresy; Montauban was the capital of the "Protestant Republic" of the Midi. Inside, a painting by Ingres, "Le vœu de Louis XIII". ▶ One private town residence, the **Hôtel Lefranc-de-Pompignan** (17th-18thC) is a fine example of Montalbanais architecture *(visits : ask at the SI).* ▶ West of the town is a fertile plain watered by the Tarn and the Garonne; good land shimmering with heat in the summers at the foot of landscape is changing, and industry is starting to oust agriculture as the area's economic mainstay. ▶ **Natural history and Prehistoric Museum** *(10-12 & 2-6, closed Mon., Sun. am and hols.)* across from the Ingres Museum; also **Soil Museum** *(Tue., Fri., 10-12 & 2-6).* Rose garden in Chambord park, near the municipal pool. □

MONTPEZAT-DE-QUERCY★

C4 / ® / pop. 1 412 (Tarn-et-Garonne)

Montpezat is built on a ridge along the edge of the Limogne Causse and owes its treasures to a dynasty of outstanding prelates, the des Prés.

▶ Arcaded square; Languedoc Gothic church : 16thC Flemish tapestries and beautiful statue of the Virgin. □

Also... ▶ Church at **Saux** *(4 km NW)* deep in the woods and decorated with murals (15thC). **Castelnau-Montratier★** *(12 km NW)* former fortified town on a hill. □

NÉRAC★

A4 / ® / pop. 7 270 (Lot-et-Garonne)

Domaine of the d'Albrets, the family of Henry IV, Nérac, situated on the banks of the delightful Baïse river, was a European Humanist centre, later a hotbed of the Reformation.

▶ **Museum** in the only remaining wing (15thC) of the old **château :** interesting documentation on life in Nérac. ▶ 1780 **church** by Victor Louis, architect of the Palais Royal in Paris. ▶ Gothic bridge; attractive walk along the Garenne; mediaeval area (*petit* Nérac); château de Bournac (16thC). □

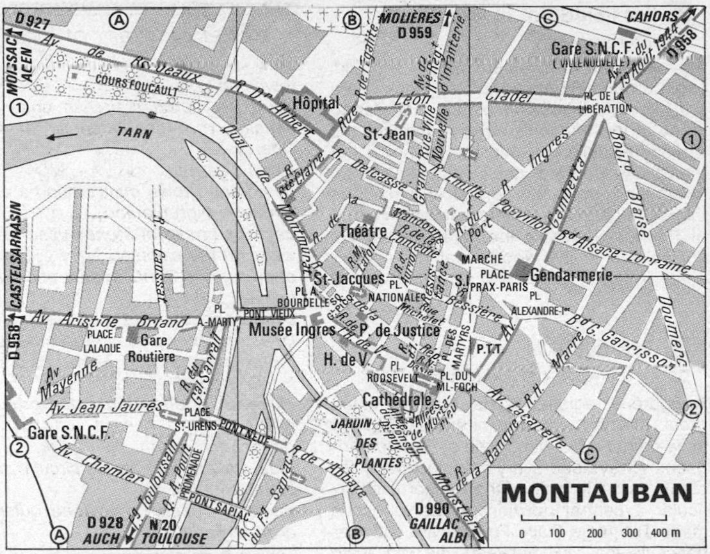

▶ Nearby

▶ Fortified mill★ and Gothic bridge at **Barbaste** *(6 km NW).* ▶ Another mill S of **Lavardac.** ▶ **Château de Xaintrailles★** *(12 km NW) :* on the edge of the Landes forest (→ Bordelais-Landes). ▶ *Bastides :* **Vianne★** *(9 km N),* **Francescas** ® *(10 km SE),* **Mézin** *(13 km SW).* ▶ **Poudenas★** ® *(17 km SW) :* **château** where Henry IV used to hunt *(10-6, Jul.-Aug.)* ▶ **Château de Buzet-sur-Baïse** *(15 km N),* surrounded by the *Côtes de Buzet* vineyards. ▶ 12 km S, **Moncrabeau** ® is celebrated locally for its liars and storytellers. □

NONTRON

B1 / ® / pop. 4 000 (Dordogne)

A beautiful site between two ravines. 18thC château. View over the Bandiat Valley. □

▶ Nearby

▶ Explore the valley of the Bandiat and the old smithies that give a special character to this small district; at **Javerlhac** ® *(10.5 km W),* everybody speaks Occitan, the ancient dialect of the south. The 13thC church, the 15thC castle with its dovecote, the mill and the willows combine to create a beautiful rustic landscape. ▶ Romanesque chapel at **Saint-Robert** *(16 km NW)* has one of the finest bell-towers in the region. ▶ The **Teyjat Grotto** is decorated with remarkable Magdalenian rock carvings. ▶ Leisure centre on the **Saint-Estèphe Lake** ®, in woods strewn with rocky outcrops *(10 km N).* ▶ **Bussière-Badil** *(15 km W) :* on the borders of the Périgord and Charente regions, with a fine Romanesque church mingling the architectural characteristics of both regions. Reminiscent of Cadouin (→ Bastides), but the west porch and the south tympanum are decorated with carvings. □

The NONTRONNAIS Region

B1 (Dordogne)

This is Périgord Vert - called green, for its ubiquitous grass and chestnut trees. A centre for the manufacture of barrels, baskets and other functional items. The westerly wind carries a tang of Brittany, blowing across the heather and over the massive granite rocks (Roc Branlant, Roc Poperdu). This is an outpost of the Limousin, with a more boisterous climate than elsewhere in Périgord and more lakes and rivers. Don't miss Chalard Waterfall *(Saut du Chalard).* □

Gouffre de PADIRAC (Chasm)★★

C2 *(see map 3)* (Lot)

The most famous chasm in France, plunging onto the heart of the Causse de Gramat.

▶ The river running through the Gouffre joins the Dordogne at Montvalent, but its source is still unknown. Visit the Gouffre by boat; the water's surface is smooth and unruffled. *(spring hols. to Oct., 9-12 & 2-6; 8-12 & 2-7 in Jul.; 8-7 Aug.).* □

Tobacco

The valleys of the Garonne, the Dordogne and the Lot rivers are France's main tobacco regions. This crop was introduced at Clairac at the beginning of the 17thC, and has adapted well. The tall wooden drying sheds are familiar sights in the landscape. All tobacco here is bought by the State. Under the Third Republic, numerous politicians in the southwest ensured local support through this arrangement.
A difficult crop to raise, tobacco provides a regular income for many, but requires so much work that the return is scarcely worthwhile.

The **PÉRIGORD BLANC** Region

AB2 (Dordogne)

Aquitaine and the western part of the Midi begin around Ribérac and Périgueux. Here are riverside limestone plateaus similar to those of the Sarladais region - the Isle, the **Auvézère,** the **Loue** and the **Dronne** - but the valleys are wider, the slopes gentler, the farms more opulent. The middle reaches of the Isle extend into a different region south of Périgueux, where the little hamlets are so isolated in the woods that the country seems overrun by oak and chestnut. □

PÉRIGUEUX★

B2 / ® / pop. 35 400 (Dordogne)

A vigorous regional capital that has made great efforts to restore its old buildings (now comparable with those at Sarlat). Périgueux always had everything necessary for status as the kingpin of the Périgord, in particular a central position, where all roads meet. The huge Place Francheville (B2; car park) is the link between the old town around the cathedral (C2) and the lower town (A2), with vestiges of the Gallo-Roman town *Vesona*. Visitors keen on archaeology should begin here and climb up the streets of Saint-Front. Otherwise, head for the cathedral and the classified historical *(classée)* area, especially on Wednesday or Saturday (market days) when all the little squares have a holiday air.

Vesona, Gallo-Roman capital of the Pétrocores (inhabitants of Roman Périgord) was, to judge by the excavations, a rich city with luxurious villas. An amphitheatre for 30 000 people was dismantled to build ramparts in the 3rdC, together with a huge temple of which only the **Vesone Tower** (B3), formerly the *Cella* or Holy of Holies, remains. The Gallo-Roman city was succeeded by two rival cities, each behind ramparts : the city of the count and the bishop (built on the ancient ruins of Vesona) and the town of the merchants and artisans. The Quartier Saint-Front is still the dynamic heart of Périgueux, and the old buildings along the winding streets are gradually being restored. The cathe-

A brief glossary of local terms

barri *or* ***barry*** *: a settlement outside the town walls.*

bolet *: a porch staircase under an overhanging roof characteristic of houses in Quercy.*

casal *: garden.*

castelnau *: town built around a castle.*

causse *: high plateau.*

cayroux *: heap of stones used to make low walls on the causse.*

chartreuse *: 18thC aristocratic house (local usage).*

cingle *: bend in the river; by extension, the limestone precipice on the outer curve.*

cloup *: depression in the* causse, *usually fertile ground.*

cluzeau *: shelter dug in the ground or into a cliff.*

garissade *: heath, scrub oak.*

igue *: aven, pothole or circular pit in limestone country.*

pech *or* ***puech*** *: limestone outcrop or hill around Sarlat.*

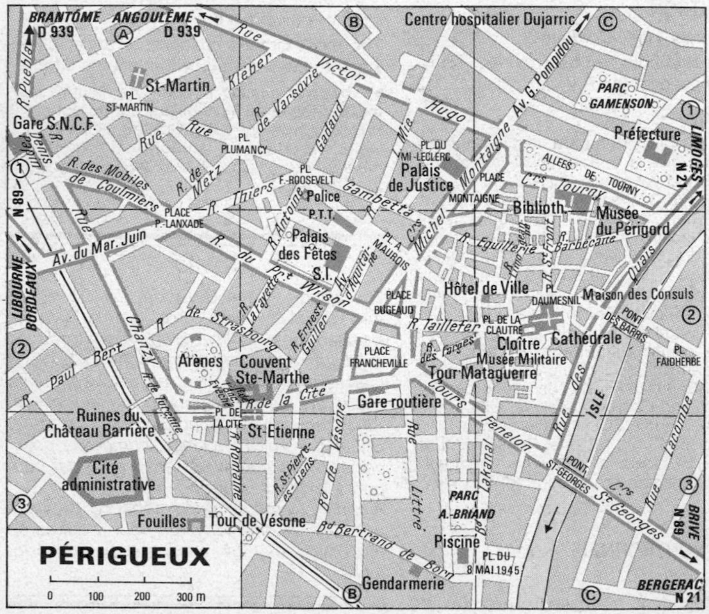

dral is spectacular and somehow anachronistic, seeming to belong more to the 19thC than to the 12thC. In Renaissance times, merchants built their houses along the banks of the Isle. The modern town has grown out from the wide 18thC boulevards and rather dreary developments around the station.

▶ The **church of St. Etienne** (B2-3) was long a cathedral and the model for numerous diocesan churches with cupolas; it is a good example of Périgord Romanesque, spare and stern, even if the nave is a 17thC reconstruction. ▶ At the back of the **Place Francheville** (B2), which was once a sort of no-man's-land between the two rivals, the **Mataguerre Tower** (end 15thC), the last of the 28 towers that fortified the bourgeois town of Saint-Front. ▶ The preserved area has been admirably restored (pedestrian precinct). ▶ On the **Place de la Clautre,** in front of the cathedral façade formed by the original 10th-11thC church, is a bustling open-air market *(Wed., Sat.).* ▶ The **Cathedral of St. Front** (C2) is the greatest of cupola churches, its grandiose dimensions inspired by Venice with five oriental-style cupolas and belltowers dreamed up in the late 19thC by Abadie, architect of Sacré Coeur in Paris. ▶ Many 15thC and 16thC private houses *(hôtels particuliers)* in the **old town★** (preservation area) : — Rue Aubergerie : No. 8, Hôtel de Sallegourde (15th-16thC); No. 11, Hôtel d'Abzac de Ladouze (15thC); No. 20 (17thC); No. 23 (15thC); — No. 7 Rue de la Constitution, Hôtel Gamensan★ (end 15thC); — Nos. 1-3-5 Rue Limogeanne : 3 Renaissance *hôtels;* — No. 1 Rue de la Sagesse : Renaissance staircase★. — No. 17 Rue Eguillerie : maison Tenant (14th-15thC). — Rue de la Miséricorde : Renaissance staircase★ (No. 2), Nos. 4 and 7, interesting doors (15th and and 17thC); — Rue du Plantier : 17th and 18thC *hôtels.* ▶ **Les Allées Tourny** (1743) separate the old town from the new town that developed along the Bordeaux road before the arrival of the railway (1856). ▶ The **Périgord Museum** (C1) is excellent for regional archaeology★. Important section on prehistory, complementing the Eyzies Museum (→). Gallo-Roman finds, popular arts and traditions *(10-12 & 2-5; closed Tue.).* ▶ On the **quays** (C2) with the best view of the cathedral and the old town : Hôtel de Lur (mid-16thC), Maison des Consuls (15thC), Maison Lambert (early 16thC) and, on the other side, the old Moulin du Chapitre (chapter house mill). □

▶ Nearby

▶ **Chancelade★** ® *(6 km W) :* admirably restored Romanesque abbey in deep woodland. Cupola church partly rebuilt in the 17thC (14thC frescos and painting by Georges de la Tour, 1593-1652). Abbey buildings around a pretty garden *(15 Jun.-15 Sep., 2-6);* 15thC fermenting room where exhibitions and concerts are held in summer; stables and workshops (17thC) fortified mill (15thC); Bourdeilles apartments (15th-17thC); abbot's apartments (18thC). On the other side of the square, tiny Romanesque chapel★. A late Magdalenian tomb was found at Chancelade. ▶ The priory of **Merlande★** *(6 km N)* was founded by the monks of Chancelade in a clearing of Feytaud Forest. The Romanesque church was fortified in the 16thC. Remarkable carved capitals. To one side, the prior's house. ▶ **Bassillac** ® *(9 km E) :* in a loop of the Isle, mill and château of Rognac; Romanesque church. ▶ **Antonne-et-Trigonant** ® *(12 km, Limoges road) :* **château des Bories★** on a terrace above the Isle, a typical 15thC Périgord manor *(10-12 & 2-7, Jul.-Aug.).* Château d'Escoire (18thC). ▶ **Le Change** *(15 km E) :* At a bend in the Auvézère, Romanesque church, two châteaux, interesting bridge with cutwaters and mill. ▶ **Agonac** *(15.5 km N) :* fortified Romanesque church with cupolas (11th-13thC); 15thC manor. ▶ **Château de Jaillac** *(17 km N) :* feudal fortress, frequently remodelled *(2-7, Jul.-Oct.; closed Tue. and Thu.).* □

■ RIBÉRAC

A2 / ® / pop. 4 290 (Dordogne)

No grand monuments, simply a charming site, a good fishing river, green valleys, woods full of birds and the soft sky of Aquitaine. The Charentes Region lies in the far distance. □

▶ Nearby

▶ **Saint-Privat-des-Prés** *(12 km W) :* fortified church★ with the same façade, copied from the nearby Saintonge Region, as Saint-Martin-de-Gurson (→ Monbazillac). ▶ **Saint-Aulaye** *(10 km from Saint-Privat),* another *bastide* on a hill rising out of the Dronne, a little to one side, another Saintonge-style church★ with figured capitals. ▶ On the Brantôme (→) road is the fortified church of **Grand Brassac** *(20 km)* with characteristic line of cupolas; 16thC sculptures reused on the N. doorway. □

Caves

There are innumerable caves in this country of limestone cliffs. Many contain calcite deposits (stalactites and stalagmites) formed by the continuous interaction of the limestone with water. These caves were too damp for prehistoric man to live in, but some of them probably served as sanctuaries. Apart from the famous Lascaux Cave, now closed, the most beautiful are at Font de Gaume, Rouffignac, and Pech Merle in Quercy.

■ ROCAMADOUR★★

C3 / ® / pop. 795 (Lot)

Inseparable from Padirac (→) and much like it. This village, built into the cliff beneath a comic-opera château, boasts its charms on billboards and road signs. After so much publicity, *"le deuxième site de France"* (the second most-visited site in France) might easily be disappointing. However, the site★★ itself is remarkable (see it from the Hospitalet Road), while the seven sanctuaries of Rocamadour have a number of treasures, in particular two 12thC frescos. These sanctuaries were frequented by pilgrims on their way to Compostela, although their origins go back to pagan times *(guided tour Jun.-Sep. and spring school hols.).* ▶ View★ over the town, the canyon and the *causse* from the château terrace. □

▶ Nearby

▶ **Hospitalet :** Grotte des Merveilles (Cave of Marvels) is decorated with figures like those in Pech Merle (→ Vallée du Lot) but much deteriorated *(1 Jul.-31 Oct., 9-8).* ▶ The road★ to **Calès** ® on the edge of the *causse* follows the meandering Alzou and leads to the **Moulin de Cougnaguet**★ (14thC mill) on the river. ▶ Lovely walks to the sources of the Ouysse★ *(3 hr round-trip),* the biggest underground river in the region, and to the **Gorges of Alzou**★, marked by old mills *(3 hr round-trip on GR 6).* □

■ ROUFFIGNAC Caves★★

B2 (Dordogne)

A pantheon of prehistory with 11 km of galleries and more than 200 rock carvings, half depicting mammoths *(Palm Sun.-1 Nov., 10-11:30 & 2-5; 9-11:30 & 2-6, 1 Jul.-15 Sep.; Sun. only low season).*

▶ In the village of Rouffignac only the Renaissance **church**★ escaped destruction by the Nazis. □

▶ Nearby

▶ **Plazac**★ *(6 km E) :* a touching cemetery surrounds the Romanesque church with its beautiful square bell-tower (16thC frescos); the presbytery is the former 14thC Episcopal Palace. ▶ View from the **Côte de Jor**★ (steep bank) over the Vézère Valley (→). □

■ SAINT-AMAND-DE-COLY★★

C2 / pop. 300 (Dordogne)

The former abbey church of the Augustinian canons, perhaps the most beautiful church in the Périgord, rises out of the woods of Sarlat.

▶ This building was originally intended as a fortress with gate-house, keep, fortification and ramparts. ▶ The village it protected is now empty but remains beautiful with its ochre walls and stone-tiled roofs. The buildings are now being restored and exhibitions and concerts are staged here in summer. □

■ SAINT-ANTONIN-NOBLE-VAL★

C4 / ® / pop. 1 870 (Tarn-et-Garonne)

Located on the banks of the Aveyron between the Quercy and Rouergue regions, the sun-bleached roofs of this small village recall those of the Midi. Between the quay and the Town Hall★ (12thC; small prehistory museum) you will find a mediaeval town★ of merchants' houses from the 13thC, 14thC and 15thC. □

▶ Nearby

▶ **Varen**★ **:** fortified château (14th-15thC) and church (12thC); ▶ **Verfeil**★ **:** old village and covered market; ▶ **Beaulieu Abbey**★ (→). ▶ **Bosc Cave** *(Grotte du Bosc; Easter-Oct.).* ▶ A pretty road running north up the **valley of the Bonnette**★ will bring you to two beautiful villages : **Caylus**★, a mediaeval township with fortified church, 14thC market and feudal keep, and **Lacapelle Livron**★, a former Templar Commandery between the Causse de Limogne (→) and the army training ground of the Espagots. □

▶ Aveyron Gorges★★
Round-trip *(34 km; approx 3 hr)*
CD4 *(see map 6)*

Downstream from **Saint-Antonin** the river abruptly penetrates the **Causse**; a *corniche* (cliff road) follows it closely and hillside villages appear. ▶ **Penne**★ balanced on the cliff with a notable fortress. ▶ **Bruniquel**★ **:** Gothic houses and château. ▶ South of Bruniquel in the **Vère Vale** are other fine fortified villages, while to the east stretch the tall oaks of the **La Grésigne Forest**★, which for years supplied the French navy with timber. Beyond Bruniquel, the valley opens out into a plain. ▶ **Montricoux** is the last of the hill villages, with corbelled and half-timbered houses along the right bank, guarded by a 13thC Templars' keep. □

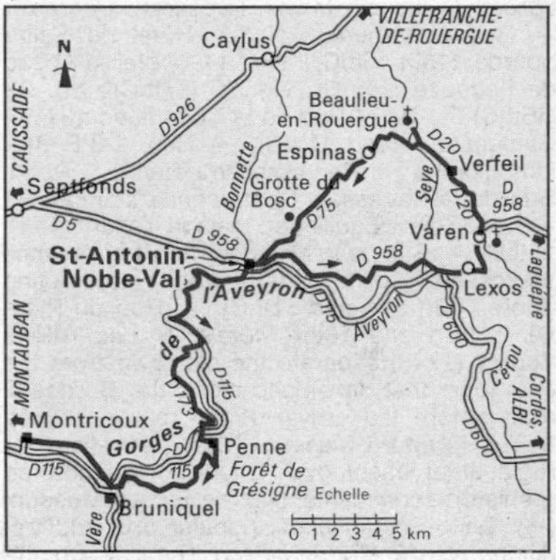

6. Aveyron Gorges

■ SAINT-CÉRÉ

D2 / ® / pop. 4 210 (Lot)

Picturesque old houses with wooden facings (15th, 16th and 17thC) and, in the background, the towers of St. Laurent (12th and 15thC) where Jean Lurçat (1892-1966; tapestry artist influenced by Cézanne) had his workshop; tapestry exhibition in the casino. □

▶ Nearby

▶ **Ségala** is a mountainous region stretching east to join the Auvergne. ▶ The **château de Montal**★ *(1.5 km W)* is a great Renaissance work. *(Easter-Oct., 9:30-12 & 2-6, 9:30-12 & 3-7 Aug., closed Sat. ex Jul.-Aug.).* □

▶ Tour of the Merveilles area *(20 km)*
C2 *(see map 3)*

▶ **Saint-Céré.** ▶ **Grotte de Presque :** "the cave of columns" *(la grotte des colonnes; Apr.-Oct.).* ▶ **Autoire**★★, a fairy-tale village at the mouth of the **Autoire Gorges**★, is as discreet and perfect as Rocamadour is brash. ▶ **Loubressac**★, fortified village at the uppermost junction of three valleys. The **château** (15th-17thC) is, in fact, an overgrown manor house. □

■ SARLAT★★★

C2 / ® / pop. 10 627 (Dordogne)

The Renaissance and the Middle Ages still live in this town, one of the rare sites in France to remain intact since the 17thC; and on this account entirely restored by the Historical Monuments Board *(CNMHS)*. At one time girdled with ramparts, it has kept its heart-shaped ground plan and is divided in two by *la traverse*, the busy commercial Rue de la République. Sarlat is the capital of France for walnuts and *foie gras*, as any shop window in the old town will confirm. On Saturdays, there is a market in the Place de la Grande Rigaudie and, once a month, a fair that attracts people from miles around. On other days, this square serves as a car park. The entire eastern part has already been restored and is brought to life by the TO *(evenings, Easter-15 Sep.)*.

▶ **Place du Peyrou** (B2) : surrounded by the Renaissance façade of the former Episcopal buildings now used as a theatre, by old shops with bow-fronted windows and by the Cathedral of St. Sacerdos, a blend of 16th-17thC architecture. The **Hôtel La Boétie,** where the writer Étienne La Boétie (1530-63) was born, is also located on the square. ▶ **La Chapelle des Pénitents Blancs** (White Penitents' Chapel; B2) is purest Romanesque architecture. ▶ The Penitents' garden is a former cemetery with an enigmatic **light-tower** (*lantorne des morts*; C2). ▶ The charm of Sarlat lies in its coherent style, the elegance of even its humblest houses, its ochre tones and its stone roofs, rather than in its monuments. Note the **Renaissance houses** on Rue de la Salamandre and Rue Landry. ▶ At the back of a garden is the former **Présidial** (Tribunal of Justice) crowned with a curious turreted lantern tower. ▶ The **Place de la Liberté**, now given over to luxury shops, is an extension of the Place du Marché (Market Square) and the Place du Marché Aux Oies (Goose Market Square), which overflow into it on Saturdays with cages of ducks and geese, fresh goose liver or mushrooms, according to season. In summer a theatre festival takes over this square. **Maleville House★** *(Hôtel de Maleville)* has two very different façades; it is, in fact, three houses run together and remodelled in the 16thC by a finance official of Henry IV,

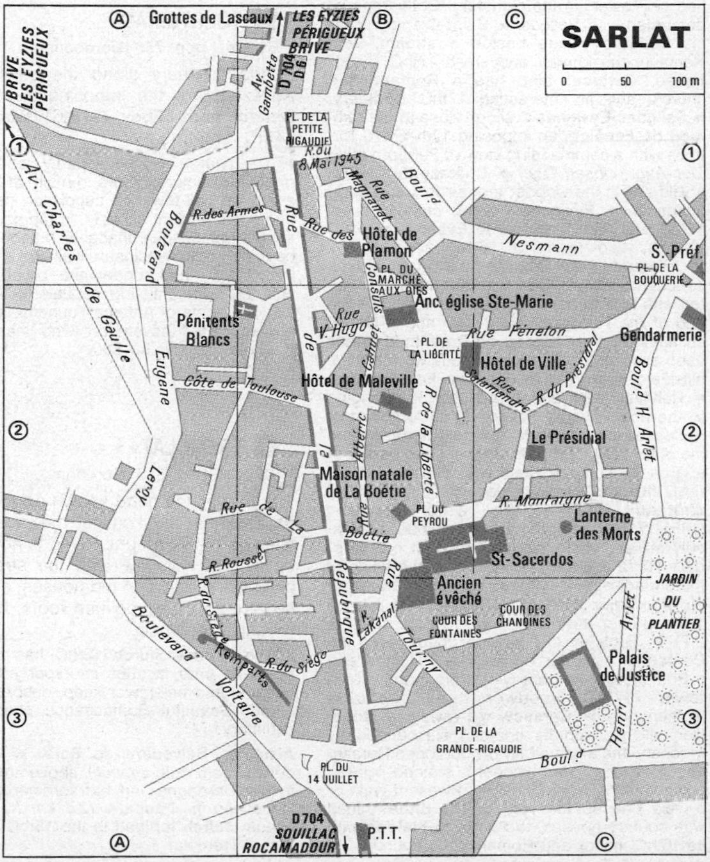

hence the portraits of the king and his mistress Gabrielle d'Estrées (1573-99). Town Hall (17thC); church of Sainte-Marie (14th-16thC); Gisson House (*Hôtel de Gisson;* 16thC). ▶ All the **mansions** in the **Rue des Consuls★** are worthy of mention; the street of a perfect example of urban architecture of the 16th-17thC. ▶ The western sector (B2) has not yet been restored, and is therefore ignored by tourists and business alike; it has the flavour of old towns, full of bustling, chaotic and unreconstructed streets. Here are Récollets Convent (Rue Rousseau) and Ste Claire Convent★ (Rue de la Boétie, *Jul.-Aug., 9-12 & 2-6*), built in the 17thC. □

■ Around SARLAT

▶ Round trip *(68 km; approx half-day; see map 2)* (Dordogne)

Sarlat is the ideal departure for exploring the **Périgord Noir** region, a country of round hills covered in oak woods, chestnut groves and pine forests, and where the finest stone-roofed houses are to be found.

▶ Sarlat. ▶ **Temniac :** The chapel of Notre-Dame, in the simple Périgord style of the 12thC, on a superb site. **Château** ruins *(10-12 & 2-6 or 7).* ▶ **Saint-Geniès :** Romanesque church with broad stone-tiled roof; 16thC fortified bell-tower; in the cemetery, Gothic chapel decorated with frescos. ▶ **Saint-Crépin :** classic Périgord village beside a stream, with Romanesque church and small 17thC manor house. **Carlucet** also has a Romanesque church, and an interesting 17thC cemetery. ▶ **Salignac-Eyvignes** ® clings close to the **château de Fénélon,** an imposing 12th-17thC fortress with a commanding view of Périgord Noir. *(Jul.-Aug.; closed Tue.).* ▶ **Château du Claud :** a wild site in the woods; stone roofs and great character. ▶ **Eyvigues :** 16thC manor house, 12thC and 16thC church. ▶ **Eybènes :** 12thC church, two manors (16thC and 18thC). ▶ **Orliaguet :** small Romanesque church in typical countryside. ▶ **Carlux :** little squares planted with lime trees, a fortress in ruins since the end of the Hundred Years' War and a Gothic chimney. S, the **château de Rouffilhac** ® has been over-restored, but the site is wonderful, a hillside of evergreen oaks above the Dordogne. ▶ **Calviac :** 12th and 15thC church belonging to the abbey where Sacerdos, patron saint of Sarlat, was a monk. ▶ **Sainte-Mondane :** on the other bank of the Dordogne in the centre of a large agricultural estate with classified historic 17thC farm buildings, you will find the 15thC **château★** where the writer Fénélon (1651-1715) was born; it has retained a markedly military character (collection of old cars; *daily 10-12 & 2-6 or 7).* View over the vales of the Sarladais. ▶ **Veyrignac :** on the left bank of the Dordogne, with a little church and a large château over the river *(1 Jul.-15 Sep. 10-12 & 2-7).* ▶ **Groléjac** ® : a wide bridge over the Dordogne, a manor house, old buildings and a Romanesque church with a big, square bell-tower (17thC woodwork and *repoussé* leatherwork). ▶ **Carsac★ :** a ravishing stone-tiled village, with its château surrounded by greenery and a beautifully proportioned Romanesque church (but modern stained glass; ogive vaulting from 16thC). ▶ Pleasant walk or bicycle ride up the **vale of the Enea★** lined with country houses, to **Sainte-Nathalène** with its 16thC manor and Romanesque church.

Also... ▶ **Saint-André-d'Allas** *(4.5 km W of Sarlat) :* on a rock above the Allas is a large 18thC (Louis XV) château. The rustic church at **Allas** with its wall-belfry and stone roof was remodelled in the 15thC, whereas the church at **Saint-André,** also stone-tiled, was rebuilt in the 16thC. In the hamlet of **Bussiéral,** the **huttes gauloises** of **Breuil★** are an intriguing collection of drystone huts.

▶ For tourists, the region around Sarlat is identified by its stone roofs, its châteaux, its winding rivers (→ Dordogne) and its caves on the Vézères (→ Eyzies), with limestone hills crowned by dark green oaks and the rich lowlands full of walnut trees, tobacco plantations, orchards... and flocks of geese. □

■ SOUILLAC

C2/ ® / pop. 4 062 (Lot)

The town itself has little character, but the **doorway** of the **abbey church★★,** mutilated and then rebuilt inside the church, is a major work of Southern Romanesque art, very close in style to Moissac (→). Tobacco warehouse in the former 18thC abbey. □

■ TOURTOIRAC

B1 / ® / pop. 756 (Dordogne)

In the greenery along the banks of the Auvézère are the imposing remains of a **Benedictine abbey** (11thC), girdled with 14thC ramparts.

▶ The church has been partly rebuilt; of the original structures there remain the transept, a square bell-tower, a cupola on pendentives and some ancient capitals. In the garden★ is a small Romanesque chapel with acoustic chambers, part of the enclosure wall, the abbey building (17thC) and, under the presbytery, the chapter, with amusing capitals. ▶ Tourtoirac was the home of Antoine Tounens, an obscure lawyer turned adventurer who made himself King of Patagonia in 1860. □

■ TRÉMOLAT★★

B2 / ® / pop. 543 (Dordogne)

The horseshoe bend known as the **"Cingle de Trémolat"★★,** one of the most famous sites on the Dordogne River, is now a yacht basin. The village★ with the stream tumbling along between the houses, and manor houses with their pointed roofs, has a thoroughly French air.

▶ The **fortress church** (12thC) has much character, its bare façades interspersed with buttresses, and bell-tower keep, decorated in the 18thC. Beautiful Romanesque chapel in the cemetery.

Also... ▶ **Belvédère de Sors★★** *(54 km E, downstream from Limeuil),* above another bend in the Dordogne; an extraordinarily peaceful landscape. ▶ **Paunat★** *(2.5 km N) :* Romanesque **church** fortified in the 15thC; similar to that of Trémolat. □

Jacquou le Croquant

French television serialised a novel by Eugène le Roy (1836-1907), whose fictional hero Jacquou le Croquant *(Jimmy the Bumpkin) has become synonymous with the Périgord. Jacquou was the son of a peasant who died in the ship galleys, under the oppressive Lord of l'Herm. Raised by the village priest of Fanlac, Jacquou later led peasants in a successful revolt, culminating in destruction of the Château de l'Herm.*

■ VILLEFRANCHE-DU-PÉRIGORD★

B3 / ® / pop. 800 (Dordogne)

Villefranche is an isolated *bastide* village with an arcaded square and a covered market (early 19thC) on heavy pillars, overlooking a minor tributary of the Lémance and surrounded by wooded hills in the heart of the 100 km^2 forest of pine, oak and chestnut stretching between the Périgord and the Quercy regions. □

▶ Nearby

▶ **Besse** *(8 km N) :* delightful grouping of 16th-17thC château and stone-tiled fortified church; the porch is a rare example of Romanesque sculpture in the Périgord. □

■ VILLENEUVE-SUR-LOT

B3-4 / ® / pop. 23 730 (Lot-et-Garonne)

A *bastide* (→) that expanded over the fertile plain, where fruit of all kinds, especially plums, grow in abundance.

▶ The classic checkerboard pattern is clearly apparent around the arcaded square where the market is still held. Good view over the town and houses on the quay from the Pont-Vieux (Old Bridge; 13thC). Small local museum. □

▶ Nearby

▶ **Pujols★** ® with Renaissance houses; ▶ **Casseneuil :** former inland port on the Lède; ▶ **Penne d'Agenais** *(8 km E) :* perched high above the Lot; ▶ **Hautefage-la-Tour★** *(10 km S from Penne) :* as fine as any Tuscan village; ▶ **Laroque-Timbaut :** old houses huddled around the covered market. **Frespech★** *(5 km) :* miniature fortified village. ▶ Caves at **Lestournelles** and **Fontirou.** □

Architecture

Périgourdine house

The Périgord and Quercy regions have some of the loveliest rural architecture in France. This is due not only to the fine golden limestone of Sarlat and the paler variety from the Quercy, but also to the fact that the area is well away from the major highways, and has largely escaped industrialisation. ● In Quercy, houses tend to be tall and solid, with a view to bringing together all activity under a single, flat-tiled roof. The staircase is generally outside, protected by a porch or *bolet,* where visitors are greeted. The elegant and elaborate dovecote is an indispensable feature, a vital source of fertilizer since there is practically no stock raising in the region. In the Périgord, dovecotes are rare, as they were long a privilege of the nobility. This was not the case in the Quercy, which was always a region of small landowners. ● Nowhere in France were more feudal châteaux built than in the Périgord. They were invariably sited in the centre of the holding, which was divided

Dovecote

Quercynoise house

into tenant farms. The villages are grouped at the foot of the châteaux, upon which they used to depend almost entirely. ● The great variety of houses in the Périgord matches the land's extensive use. *Périgord Vert*, where stock raising predominates, favoured

Agenais farmhouse

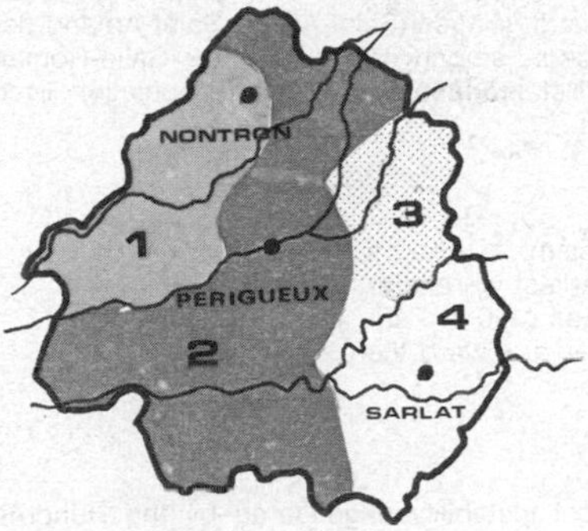

Distribution of roof types: 1. hollow tiles; 2. hollow or flat tiles; 3. flat tiles or slates; 4. flat tiles or *lauzes* (wooden shingles).

the stable-barn of the Limousin Region and the low slate-tiled roof with two pitched sides. The Bergerac country and the plain of the Garonne show a preference for barns with broad overhanging eaves. In the Double area, by contrast, the soil is poor and stone is rare; here houses are small, with half-timbered cob walls, and working buildings are detached from the farmhouses. In the area around Sarlat the single unit returns, and the roofing design contributes much to the area's beauty. ● Other typical forms are the troglodyte valley dwelling-half-cave-in the Périgord; and the small drystone hut, the *gariote* or *casèle* of the Quercy. ● In the plain of the Garonne, houses are long and low, with a clear separation between accommodation and working sections; the roofs are of Mediterranean type, with overhanging eaves that make it possible to carry out some domestic activities in the open. The construction material is poor : clay brick or cob, or a mixture of the two. Pigeons thrive in dovecotes; outbuildings, ovens, wells, mills and washhouses are still in good condition. Rural civilisation remains strong in these parts.

Gariote on the Causse

● *Brief regional history*

27 BC - ca. 350 AD Under the Emperor Augustus, the **Romans** introduced the walnut, the chestnut and the grapevine to the Aquitaine Region. They also gradually developed urban life. The regional capitals were then *Vesona* (Périgueux), *Aginnum* (Agen) and *Divona* (Cahors). ● As a result of successive invasions, the population diminished and the forest took over the land once more. Périgord was completely covered with forest : the Limousine forest to the north, that of the Double to the west, and the Forests of Sarlat, Belvès and Bessède in the south. ● **Hermits** were attracted to these uninhabited regions, leaving their names on a number of towns and villages (Saint-Astier, Saint-Amand-de-Cloy, Saint-Avit-Sénieur, among others). Former Gallo-Roman villas became the first **monasteries** and the population lived largely in the valleys.

12thC Population growth and the spread of monasticism. ● Abbeys were usually founded in deep woodland; the earliest were later rebuilt. ● The number of **Romanesque churches** (400 in Périgord; 200 in Quercy) bears witness to this renewal toward the end of the 12thC, somewhat later than elsewhere.

13thC The constant political instability engendered by the Hundred Years' War (1335-1445), in fact, began as early as 1154 with the marriage of Eleanor of Aquitaine to Henry II of England. ● In 1259 the **Treaty of Paris** between Louis IX of France (St. Louis) and the Duke of Aquitaine, Henry III of England, divided the region. Henry III received Saintonge, the Agenais, a part of the Limousin, the Périgord and Quercy. The treaty turned the area into a frontier region, constantly **ravaged by war.** ● Instability affected the artistic development of Aquitaine; it was cut off from new trends and remained resolutely turned to the past. ● However, intermittent warfare permitted the construction of castles, fortifications (including fortified churches) and a new and original form of town planning, the ***bastides.*** These were the new towns of the 13thC that today still are basic to the urban network in the southwest. Montauban was the first *bastide.*

16thC The 16thC was a period of **renaissance** in every sense. The reconquest of the territory by the kings of France was accompanied by reconstruction or completion of unfinished projects. ● It was at this period that Gothic architecture made its first timid appearance in religious buildings; however, Périgord and Quercy remained aloof from the **classical influence** that was spreading through France. ● Similarly, the rebuilt châteaux, which reached into the hundreds, kept their mediaeval structure and essentially defensive aspect; the Hundred Years' War gave way to clashes of the Protestant Reformation and the innumerable popular uprisings that tore apart 17thC Périgord.

End 16thC Under the aegis of Margaret of Navarre and her daughter, Jeanne d'Albret, Aquitaine and western Périgord rallied massively to the Protestant cause. ● From 1570 to 1590, war was continuous. Bergerac, Sainte-Foy-la-Grande and Montauban became bastions of the **Reformation**, while Périgueux and Cahors were strongholds of the Catholic Holy League *(Sainte-Ligue).* ● In opposition to the mood of fanaticism that gripped both sides, the great writer Montaigne retired to his estate near Monbazillac to work on his *Essays.*

17thC In the Périgord, land of great estates, the dominant agricultural system was that of sharecropping, as reflected by the castles, positioned in the centre of landholdings. ● Between 1635 and 1685, **peasant rebellions** succeeded one another from year to year. Peasants of Protestant and Catholic factions rose against heavy taxation, landowners and army levies, attacking châteaux and attempting to organise general uprisings, only to be crushed by the armed retainers of the landowners.

18thC The end of the Monarchy *(Ancien Régime)* was marked by a brief industrial expansion : metalworking in Périgord (the Nontronnais Region), and textile industries in Montauban and Agen. ● The central administration, or its representatives, helped to develop the towns of Périgueux and Montauban. ● In the countryside, the principle of **speculative mixed crops** took root and today is typical of the southwest : grapevines, fruit (prunes, walnut), tobacco, fattened geese and so on. ● **The French Revolution** created the Department of the Dordogne, an area that corresponded almost exactly to the boundaries of the ancient Province of Périgord. Through the purchase of church lands, the urban *bourgeoisie* became integrated with the ancient landowning aristocracy, who preserved the greater part of their possessions. The basic system of great estates and tenant farmers remained the same, and, with the acquisition of political power, the gentry also acquired control. The lord of the manor simply became the elected representative.

19thC The beginning of the Second Empire in 1852 coincided with the apogee of rural civilisation. Population density reached its maximum. ● Grape-growing was highly labour-intensive, and was extended mainly through forest clearance at the instigation of the great landowners. The **phylloxera crisis** that ruined the grapevines was a shattering disaster, precipating a massive rural exodus. ● Between 1886 and 1921, three-quarters of the population left the land, but the towns did not benefit in any real sense. ● Peasants and rural craftsmen, deprived of their markets, left for manufacturing centres; the gentry departed for well-placed administrative posts in Paris.

20thC After the loss of its work force (depopulation was further aggravated by the massive losses in WWI), Périgord vegetated and has only recently begun a successful agricultural revolution. Certain regions have not yet been touched and the contrast between carefully cultivated valleys and the plateaus covered in light woodland and scrub is very marked. ● The Lot and Dordogne are still regions from which people tend to emigrate : today there are hardly more inhabitants in these areas than there were in Roman times.

Practical information

The region

Information : Dordogne (Périgord) : *Comité Départemental de Tourisme* (C.D.T.), 16, rue du Pdt-Wilson, 24000 Périgueux, ☎ 53.53.44.35. **Lot :** *C.D.T.*, Chambre de Commerce, 46000 Cahors, ☎ 65.35.07.09. **Lot-et-Garonne :** *C.D.T.*, B.P. 158, 47005 Agen, ☎ 53.66.14.14. **Tarn-et-Garonne :** O.T., Hôtel des Intendants, pl. Foch, 82000 Montauban, ☎ 63.63.31.40. In Paris : *Maison du Périgord,* 30, rue Louis-le-Grand, 75002, ☎ 47.42.09.15 ; *Maison du Lot-et-Garonne,* 15-17, passage Choiseul, 75002, ☎ 42.97.51.43.

Bookings : *Loisirs-Accueil (L.A.) :* **Dordogne,** 16, rue du Pdt-Wilson, 24000 Périgueux, ☎ 53.53.44.35 ; **Lot,** 430, av. Jean-Jaurès, 46000 Cahors, ☎ 65.22.55.30 ; **Tarn-et-Garonne,** Hôtel des Intendants, pl. Foch, 82000 Montauban, ☎ 63.63.31.40.

Maps : *Michelin :* n°s 72, 75, 79, 1/200 000. *I.G.N. :* n°s 47, 48, 49, 56, 57, 58, 64, 1/100 000, and 110, 111, 114, 1/250 000.

S.O.S. : Dordogne : *SAMU* (Emergency Medical Service), ☎ 53.08.81.11. **Lot :** *SAMU,* ☎ 65.30.01.01. **Lot-et-Garonne :** *SAMU,* ☎ 53.96.39.39. **Tarn-et-Garonne :** *SAMU,* ☎ 63.04.03.80. *Poisoning Emergency Centre :* Toulouse, ☎ 61.49.33.33 ; Bordeaux, ☎ 56.96.40.80.

Weather forecast : Dordogne, ☎ 56.34.34.73 ; **Lot,** ☎ 65.41.00.14 ; **Lot-et-Garonne,** ☎ 53.96.34.04 ; **Tarn-et-Garonne,** ☎ 63.03.00.66.

Farmhouse holidays : numerous accommodation possibilities, including rural gîtes, camping, farmhouse-inns. List of addresses at the T.O., *Loisirs-Accueil* and *Relais Dép. des Gîtes Ruraux :* **Dordogne,** 16, rue du Pdt-Wilson, 24000 Périgueux, ☎ 53.53.44.35 ; **Lot,** Chambre d'Agriculture, 46000 Cahors, ☎ 65.22.55.30 ; **Lot-et-Garonne,** Chambre d'Agriculture, 1, rue du Pechabout, 47000 Agen, ☎ 53.96.44.99 ; **Tarn-et-Garonne,** enq T.O.

Festivals : May : *Concerts* in Chancelade-Périgueux. **May-Jun :** *Dance Festival* in Brantôme ; *Spring Music Festival* in Marmandais. **Jul :** *Dance Festival* in Brantôme ; *International Folk Festival* in Casseneuil ; *Jazz Festival* in Montauban. **Mid-Jul :** *Music* at *La Rougerie,* in Sarlat. **End Jul :** *Périgord « Noir » Music Festival* in Saint-Léon-sur-Vézère. **Jul-Aug :** *Theatre* in Sarlat ; *Chamber Music* in Saint-Amand-de-Coly ; *Music and theatre* in Lanquais ; *Jazz Festival* in Souillac ; *dance* in Biron ; *Music Week* in Clairac ; **Aug :** *Festival du Quercy « Blanc », music* in Saint-Céré.

Events : May : *horse fair* in Montclar-du Quercy. **Jul :** *foires à la brocante (antiques and bric-à-brac)* in La Mothe-Montravel and Belvès ; *international horse races* in Le Bugue. **Aug :** *Foire des Fouineurs (antiques, bric-à-brac), Bourse des Vieux Papiers illustrés (market of old illustrated newspapers & magazines)* in Thiviers ; *Marché d'antan (antiques)* in Nontron. **Jul-Aug :** *"Liars' Festival" and Face-making World Champion-ships* at Moncrabeau.

Markets : principal markets for *foie gras* and truffles (from Nov to end-Feb) : Bergerac (Wed and Sat), Cahors (Sat), Excideuil (Thu), Lalbenque (Tue), Limogne (Tue and Fri), Lisle (Tue), Mussidan (Sat), Périgueux (Wed and Sat), Ribérac (Fri), Sarlat (Sat), Sauzet (Thu), Terrasson (Thu), Thenon (Tue), Thiviers (Sat), Tocane-Saint-Apre (Mon), Valence-d'Agen (Tue), Vergt (Fri).

Rambling and hiking : the region is traversed by numerous G.R. tracks (n°s 4, 636, 646, 64, 46, 65, 651, 652), which may also be used as bridlepaths, particularly on the Quercy *causses* (plateaus). Enq : **(Dordogne, Lot, Tarn-et-Garonne).** *Comité départemental des Sentiers de Grande Randonnée,* résidence Vésuna, 7, impasse Vésone, 24000 Périgueux.

Riding holidays : lists of riding centres and gîtes are available at T.O. and *Associations de Tourisme équestre départementales. A.T.E. Aquitaine,* ☎ 59.38.48.16 **(Lot-et-Garonne).** *A.T.E. Midi-Pyrénées,* ☎ 63.63.05.72 **(Tarn-et-Garonne).** *A.T.E.* ***Lot,*** B.P. 103, 46002 Cahors, ☎ 65.35.07.09. *A.T.E.* ***Dordogne,*** T.O. in Périgueux.

Horse-drawn holidays : *Loisirs-Accueil,* **Dordogne** and **Lot :** *Les Attelages d'Armagnac,* Domaine de Cézaou, 47170 Mezin, ☎ 53.65.70.61. *Les Roulottes de l'Agenais,* 47370 Cazideroque, ☎ 53.71.72.65. *Hobby Voyages,* 8, rue de Milan, 75009 Paris, ☎ 45.26.60.80, 42.80.04.96, 42.80.42.82.

Cycling holidays : *Comité départemental de Cyclotourisme et Cyclo-Assistance,* 51, rue J.-Mermoz, 24000 Chamiers, ☎ 53.09.08.22. **Lot :** *Comité départemental de Cyclotourisme,* av. de la Dordogne, 46600 Martel, ☎ 65.37.30.82. **Tarn-et-Garonne :** 12 clubs, enq T.O.

Instructional courses : Dordogne : *beginners' course on the preparation of* foie gras : Mme Delpeuch, la Borderie, Chavagnac, 24120 Terrasson, ☎ 53.50.10.24. *Préparation of pork dishes :* Mme Dubois, Peyrenègre-Ladornac, 24120 Terrasson, ☎ 53.50.04.24. *Gastronomy of the Périgord region :* Royal-Vézère, 24260 Le Bugue, ☎ 53.06.20.01. *Jams :* Mme Manet, Moulin du Panissal, Auriac-du-Périgord, 24290 Montignac, ☎ 53.50.86.42. *Walnuts and chestnuts :* Mme Lagrange, Lafargue-Villars, 24530 Champagnac-de-Belair, ☎ 53.54.81.31. *Œnology* (wine courses) in Bergerac. *Beginners' instructional courses in* trufficulture (one-day course), Maison de la truffe, 24420 Sorges, ☎ 53.05.90.11. **Tarn-et-Garonne :** *beginners' course in the preparation of* foie gras *and* confits, M. André Pochat, les Vignes-de-Brassac, 82190 Bourg-en-Visa, ☎ 63.94.24.30.

Farm work : *Direction Départementale de l'Agriculture* ***Dordogne,*** pl. Francheville, 24000 Périgueux, ☎ 53.09.84.54. *Dir. Dép. Agriculture* ***Lot,*** pl. de la Gare, 46000 Cahors, ☎ 65.35.44.76. *Dir. Dép. Agriculture* ***Lot-et-Garonne,*** Cité Administrative, 47000 Agen, ☎ 53.66.26.41.

Children : riding courses at the farm, *Poney Club du Quercy Blanc* (Loisirs-Accueil, **Lot**). Holidays on the farm : *Agriculture et Tourisme,*

9, av. George-V, 75008 Paris, ☎ 47.23.55.40. *Poney Club de la Marsale,* 47300 Villeneuve-sur-Lot, ☎ 53.70.68.75. Sports holidays : *Open-air sports centre,* 47110 Le Temple-sur-Lot, ☎ 53.01.08.33.

Golf : Périgueux-Marsac (9 holes) ; Bon-Encontre-Capitouls (9 holes).

Canoeing : *Ligue Aquitaine de la F.F.C.K.,* 184, rue Pasteur, 33000 Bordeaux-Cauderan ; *C.D.T.* **Lot,** *M.J.C. de Cahors,* B.P. 42, ☎ 55.35.06.43. *Safaraid,* 46140 Albas, ☎ 65.31.27.04. *Comité dép. de Canoë de Dordogne,* 24130 Le Fleix. *Comité départemental de canoë-kayak* at Agen, ☎ 53.66.25.99. Excursions on the Dronne, *Loisirs-Accueil* **Dordogne.**

Potholing and spelunking : *Comité Dép.,* **Dordogne :** c/o M. Vidal, 7, rue de la Cité, 34000 Périgueux, and M. Raffeneur, Espinières-sur-Orniac, 46330 Cabrerets, ☎ 65.31.32.17 or 65.31.26.73.

Hunting and shooting : *Féd. Dép. des Chasseurs :* **Dordogne,** 4, rue Arago, 24000 Périgueux, ☎ 53.08.75.38 ; **Lot** : 22, rue Brives, 46000 Cahors, ☎ 63.35.13.22. **Lot-et-Garonne** : 111, bd de la Liberté, 47000 Agen, ☎ 53.47.05.44. **Tarn-et-Garonne** : 4, rue Denfert-Rochereau, 83000 Montauban, ☎ 63.03.46.51.

Fishing : *Féd. Dép. des Associations de Pêche et de Pisciculture :* **Dordogne :** 31, rue Wilson, 24000 Périgueux, ☎ 53.53.44.21 ; **Lot :** 40, bd Gambetta, 46000 Cahors, ☎ 65.35.50.22 ; **Lot-et-Garonne :** cité administrative, 47000 Agen, ☎ 53.66.30.36 ; **Tarn-et-Garonne :** 160, fg Toulousain, 82000 Montauban, ☎ 63.63.01.77.

Towns

AGEN

Toulouse 114, Bordeaux 139, Paris 735
B4 ✉ 47000

ℹ 107, bd Carnot (B2), ☎ 53.47.36.09.

✈ La Garenne, 3 km SW, ☎ 53.96.21.77.

SNCF ☎ 53.66.50.50, 53.66.01.63.

Car-hire : *Budget* train + auto, 7, av. du Gal-de-Gaulle, ☎ 53.47.26.68, at the station, ☎ 53.60.50.50, and at the airport.

Hotels :
● ★★★***Résidence des Jacobins*** (L.F.), 1 *ter,* pl. des Jacobins (A2), ☎ 53.47.03.31. 16 rm Ⓟ ♨ ♘ ♿ 180.
★★***Atlantic,*** 133, av. J.-Jaurès (C2), ☎ 53.96.16.56. AE, DC, Euro, Visa. 30 rm Ⓟ ♿ closed Aug and a week at Christmas, 200.
★★***Le Quercy*** (L.F.), 10, rue de la Grande-Horloge, ☎ 53.66.35.49. Visa. 12 rm ♿ closed Aug and Sun, 130. Rest. ♦ Spec : *truite rosée au beurre de vinaigre, mousseline de St-Jacques au coulis de poisson, confit de canard aux cerises de vin,* 55-104.

Bon-Encontre, ✉ 47240, 5 km E :
● ★★★***Château de St-Marcel*** (Châteaux-hôtels), ☎ 53.96.61.30. AE, DC, Euro, Visa. 12 rm Ⓟ ♨ ♘ ♿ closed Sun. This riverside residence, set in the midst of a park, once belonged to the Count de Montesquieu (one of France's greatest 16thC writers), 280. Rest. ♦♦ closed Sun, 75-150.
● ★★***Sxandra,*** ☎ 53.96.37.02. 38 rm Ⓟ ♨ ♘ ♿ closed Feb and 1 week in Nov. A quiet place except on Sat when there is a « café-théâtre » representation, 180.
★★***Parc*** (L.F.), rue de la République, ☎ 53.96.17.75. Visa. 10 rm Ⓟ ♨ ♘ 180.
★★***La Rigalette,*** vallon de Vérone, ☎ 53.47.37.44. AE, DC, Visa. 9 rm Ⓟ ♨ ♘ ♿ closed 20-31 Dec, Sun eve (ex summer) and Mon, 150. Rest. ♦♦ 100-240.

Colayrac, ✉ 47450, 5 km W :
★★***La Corne d'Or*** (L.F.), ☎ 53.47.02.76. Tx 560800. AE, DC, Visa. 14 rm ⚟ Ⓟ closed 15 Jul-15 Aug, Sat and Sun eve, 180. Rest. ♦♦ ♿ Spec : fish and shellfish, 90-180.

Galimas, ✉ 47340 Laroque-Timbaut, 11 km N on the RN21 :
★★★***La Sauvagère,*** ☎ 53.95.60.39. Tx 560800. AE, DC, Euro, Visa. 12 rm Ⓟ ♨ ♘ closed Sun eve low season and Sun noon high season, 270. Rest. ♦ 55-145.

Youth hostel : rue Léo-Lagrange, cité Léon-Blum, rte de Cahors, ☎ 53.66.18.98.

⛺ ★★★*Municipal Leclerc* (62 pl.), ☎ 53.96.85.48.

Restaurants :
♦♦ ***Aéroport,*** La Garenne, ☎ 53.96.38.95. closed Sat and Sun eve, nat hol eves and Aug. *Cuisine du terroir* (regional specialities), 180.
♦ ***Le Voltaire,*** 36, rue Voltaire, ☎ 53.47.27.01. closed Sat noon and Sun. Regional spec, 60-105.
♦ ***L'Absinthe,*** 29 *bis,* rue Voltaire, ☎ 53.66.16.94. Visa. ♿ closed Sat noon and Sun, 1-15 Aug. An interesting address, 150.

Bon-Encontre :
● ♦♦ ***La Table de Cœur,*** rte de Cassou, ☎ 53.96.10.73. DC. closed Feb, Sun eve and Mon. A warm welcome in this delightfully hospitable restaurant. Simple, thoroughly enjoyable fare in an atmosphere of good humour and gaiety. Spec : *feuilleté de cervelle de veau au caramel de citron, suprême de volaille de Bresse aux pruneaux, amandes et sésame grillés,* 138-300.

Puymirol, 16 km E :
● ♦♦♦ ***L'Aubergade,*** Michel Trama (M.C.F.), 52, rue Royale, ☎ 53.95.31.46. AE, Visa. closed Mon ex Jul-Aug and nat hols. An exquisite 18thC house with a lovely garden. Maryse welcomes you, and husband Michel Trama, a talented cook, is a part of our grand prix jury. His cooking is generous and superb : *mignons de saumon aux jaunets, feuillets d'agneau aux truffes du pays, millefeuille de nougatine glacée.* Pleasant côtes du Bulet (Château Bouchet) wines, 100-250

Manifestations : *Gravel fair* in Jun, *Pine fair* in Sep.

Guided visits : ℹ (Jul-Aug).

AIGUILLON

Agen 30, Mont-de-Marsan 83, Paris 704
11 km S of Tonneins, A4 ✉ 47190

ℹ rue Bazin, ☎ 53.79.62.58.

SNCF ☎ 53.79.64.60.

Hotel :
● ★★***Les Cygnes*** (L.F.), rte de Villeneuve, ☎ 53.79.60.02. 17 rm ⚟ Ⓟ ♨ closed 21 Dec-28 Jan, 27 Apr-5 May and Sat ex Jul-Aug, 180. Rest. ♦♦ 120-210.

⛺ ★★★*Municipal* (75 pl.), ☎ 53.79.61.43.

Event : *regional produce fair* in Aug.

BEAUMONT

Bergerac 29, Périgueux 68, Paris 583
B3 ⊠ 24440

ⓘ mairie, 15 Jun-15 Sep, ☎ 53.61.30.24.

Hotel :
★***Voyageurs,*** ☎ 53.22.30.11. 10 rm. closed 1 Jan-28 Feb and 1 Oct-30 Nov, 180. Rest. ♦ 120-210.

Chambres d'hôtes : *château de Régagnac* (Château-Accueil), ☎ 53.22 42.98. 5 rm Ⓟ closed Nov and Feb, 180. Rest. services only if ordered ahead, 120-210.

⛺ ★★★***Les Remparts*** (470 pl.) ☎ 53.22.40.86.

BEAUMONT-DE-LOMAGNE

Montauban 36, Toulouse 57, Paris 692
25 km SW of Castelsarrasin, B4 ⊠ 82500

Hotel :
★***Commerce*** (L.F.), 58, rue Mal-Foch, ☎ 53.02.31.02. DC, Euro, Visa. 14 rm ♿ closed 20 Dec-15 Jan, Sun eve and Mon, 130. Rest. ♦ ♿ Regional cooking, 40-120.

⛺ ★★★*Municipal du Lac* (100 pl.), ☎ 63.65.26.43.

BERGERAC

Périgueux 47, Bordeaux 92, Paris 555
B2-3 ⊠ 24100

ⓘ 99, rue Neuve-d'Argenson, ☎ 53.57.03.11.

✈ Roumanières, 5 km SE, ☎ 53.57.00.09.

SNCF ☎ 53.57.26.71, 53.57.72.79.

Car-hire : *Budget* train + auto, at the station, ☎ 53.57.15.27.

Hotels :
★★★***Mounet-Sully*** (Châteaux-hôtels), 1 km N, rte de Mussidan, ☎ 53.57.04.21. 10 rm Ⓟ closed Nov-May. This historic residence of France's great 19thC actor, Mounet-Sully, offers a park setting, a magnificent cloister and theatre, and a beautifully-decorated interior, 280.
● ★★***Cyrano,*** 2, bd Montaigne, ☎ 53.57.02.76. AE. 11 rm Ⓟ closed 28 Jun-12 Jul, 2-27 Dec, 155. Rest. ♦♦ closed Sun eve (low season) and Mon. Traditional recipes with a modern touch. Spec : *salade de lapin confit aux pointes d'asperges, mignon de veau et son ris aux morilles, suprême de pigeonneau aux morilles,* 60-180.
● ★★***Bordeaux*** (Inter-Hôtel, L.F.), 38, pl. Gambetta, ☎ 53.57.12.83. Tx 550412. AE, DC, Euro, Visa. 42 rm Ⓟ ♿ closed 20 Dec-30 Jan, 200. Rest. ♦ 65-190.
★★***Commerce*** (France-Accueil ; L.F.), 36, pl. Gambetta, ☎ 53.27.30.50. AE, DC, Euro, Visa. 30 rm, closed 16-31 Mar, 195. Rest. ♦ closed Sun eve (low season), 65-125.
★★***Europ-Hôtel,*** 20-22, rue Petit-Sol, ☎ 53.57.06.54. 22 rm Ⓟ 175.
★★***La Flambée*** (L.F.), rte de Périgueux, 3 km, ☎ 53.57.52.33. 21 rm Ⓟ ♿ closed 15-30 Jun, 1-20 Jan, Sun eve and Mon from 1 Nov to 30 Mar, 190. Rest. ♦♦ ♿ closed Sun eve and Mon, 120-210.

Monbazillac, ⊠ 24240 Sigoulès, 7 km S :
★★***Relais de la Diligence,*** rte d'Eymet, ☎ 53.58.30.48. 8 rm closed 24 Jun-10 Jul, Tue eve and Wed low season, 100. Rest. ♿ 80-130.

Saussignac, ⊠ 24240 Sigoulès, 17 km SW :
★★***Relais*** (L.F.), ☎ 53.27.92.08. 18 rm Ⓟ closed Feb, 15-30 Nov and Mon low season, 180. Rest. ♦ ♿ 80-130.

⛺ ★★*La Pelouse* (470 pl.), ☎ 53.57.06.67.

Events : *Easter fair* and *Saint-Martin's fair* (Nov).

Sports and leisure activities : parachuting : *Centre École de Parachutisme Sportif,* aérodrome de Bergerac-Roumanières. Archery : *Compagnie d'Arc du Périgord,* ☎ 53.57.16.33. Fishing : *Gaule Bergeracoise,* ☎ 53.57.13.71.

Recommended : *flea-market :* in Old Bergerac, 1st Sun of each month. *Hôtel des Ventes (auctions) :* pl. Gambetta, ☎ 53.57.38.16.

BEYNAC-ET-CAZENAC

Sarlat 11, Périgueux 64, Paris 551
Vallée de la Dordogne, B2
⊠ 24220 Saint-Cyprien

SNCF ☎ 55.39.00.08.

Hotels :
● ★★***Bonnet*** (L.F.), ☎ 53.29.50.01. 22 rm Ⓟ closed 15 Oct-31 Mar, 180. Rest. ♦ Pleasant stopover on the banks of the Dordogne, 80-160.

Vézac, 2 km S :
● ★★★***L'Oustal de Vézac,*** ☎ 53.29.54.21. 16 rm Ⓟ ♿ closed 1 Nov-Easter, 260.

⛺ Vézac : ★★★*les Deux Vallées* (80 pl.), ☎ 53.29.53.55 ; ★*la Cabane* (33 pl.), ☎ 53.29.52.28.

BRANTÔME

Périgueux 27, Angoulême 58, Paris 483
B1 ⊠ 24310

ⓘ pavillon des Gardes de l'Abbaye, ☎ 53.08.80.52 (high season).

Hotels :
● ★★★★***Moulin de l'Abbaye*** (Relais et châteaux), ☎ 53.05.80.22. 12 rm Ⓟ closed 3 Nov-8 May. Old restored mill on the banks of the Dronne River, 500. Rest. ● ♦♦♦♦ closed Mon. Régis Bulot is in Courchevel in the winter and in the Périgord in the summer : *salade du Moulin aux gésiers, manchon de canard confit, mignon de veau aux gousses d'ail,* 150-300.
★★★***Chabrol,*** 57, rue Gambetta, ☎ 53.05.70.15. AE, DC, Visa. 20 rm Ⓟ closed 17 Nov-13 Dec, Feb hols, Sun eve and Mon low season, 250. Rest. ♦♦ 85-250.
Auberge du Soir, 6, rue Georges-Saumande, ☎ 53.05.82.93. AE, DC, Visa. 9 rm, closed 10 Jan-28 Feb, Mon (1 Oct-30 Mar), 100. Rest. ♦ ♿ 55-110.

Champagnac-de-Belair, ⊠ 24530, 6 km NE :
● ★★★★(L) ***Moulin du Roc*** (Relais et châteaux), ☎ 53.54.80.36. 12 rm Ⓟ ♿ closed 18 Nov-20 Dec and 15 Jan-15 Feb, 400. Rest. ● ♦♦♦ ♿ closed Tue and Wed noon. Spec : *foie gras poêlé à la ciboulette, pigeon aux choux verts, flan à l'orange,* 210-320.

Bourdeilles, 10 km SW :
● ★★★***Les Griffons,*** le Pont, ☎ 53.05.75.61. AE, DC, Euro, Visa. 10 rm Ⓟ ♿ closed 15 Sep-30 Apr. 16thC building, 220. Rest. ♦♦ ♿ 90-195.

⛺ ★★*Municipal* (56 pl.), ☎ 53.05.75.24 ; *Municipal Fonseigner,* Bourdeilles (35 pl.), ☎ 53.05.74.17.

Recommended : *conserverie d'oie,* Montplaisir (prepared goose products), ☎ 53.54.83.14.

Le BUGUE

Sarlat 32, Périgueux 41, Paris 528
B2 ⊠ 24260

ⓘ hôtel de ville, ☎ 53.06.20.48 (high season).

SNCF ☎ 53.06.20.05.

Hotels :
● ★★★***Royal Vézère*** (Mapotel), pl. de l'Hôtel-de-Ville, ☎ 53.06.20.01. 53 rm closed 10 Oct-30 Apr, 310. Rest. ♦♦ ***l'Albuca*** closed Wed noon and Thu noon. Spec : *tourain blanchi, cassoulet périgourdin*, 95-250.

Campagne, 4 km S :
★★***Du Château,*** ☎ 53.06.23.50. 18 rm closed 15 Oct-31 Mar, 170. Rest. ♦ 50-100.

★★*Municipal le Port* (135 pl.), ☎ 53.06.24.60.

Sports : Horse-racing club : *Parc Royal Vézère*, ☎ 53.06.21.67.

CABRERETS

Cahors 33, Brive 101, Paris 593
Célé Valley, C3 ⊠ 46330

Hotels :
● ★★***Grottes*** (L.F.), ☎ 65.31.27.02. closed 10 Oct-1 Apr, 155. Rest. ♦ closed Sat noon, 55-100.
At the Pescalerie Fountain, 2 km on the Figeac road :
● ★★★***La Pescalerie*** (Relais et châteaux), ☎ 65.31.22.55. 10 rm closed 1 Nov-1 Apr. 17thC manor. 400. Rest. ♦♦ Traditional regional cooking, 120-210.

Marcilhac-sur-Célé, ⊠ 46610, 15 km NE :
Touristes, ☎ 65.40.65.61. 4 rm, 100. Rest. 80-130.

CAHORS

Montauban 61, Agen 92, Paris 595
C3 ⊠ 46000

ℹ pl. A.-Briand (B2), ☎ 65.35.09.56, and Valentré Bridge, ☎ 65.35.13.15 (Jul-Aug).

✈ Cahors-Lalbenque, ☎ 65.21.00.48.

SNCF (A2), ☎ 65.35.27.44, 65.35.20.41.

Car-hire : *Budget* train + auto, rte de Toulouse, ☎ 65.35.15.95, and at the station, ☎ 65.35.27.44.

Hotels :
★★★***La Chartreuse*** (L.F.), fg St-Georges (C3), ☎ 65.35.17.37. 34 rm closed 24 Dec-1 Jan, 180. Rest. ♦♦ closed Mon, 120-210.
★★★***France*** (L.F.), 252, av. J.-Jaurès (B2), ☎ 65.35.16.76. 79 rm closed 23 Dec-2 Jan, 180.
★★★***Terminus,*** 5, av. Ch.-Freycinet (B1), ☎ 65.35.24.50. AE, Visa. 30 rm 230. Rest. ● ♦♦♦ ***le Balandre.*** closed 2 weeks in Feb, 10 days in Jun. Gilles and his charming wife have returned to this family restaurant, closed for more than 20 years. Light and inventive cooking served in authentic 1900's *Belle Époque* ambiance. One to watch. Very good choice of Cahors wines, 75-180.
★★★***Wilson,*** 72, rue Wilson (B2), ☎ 65.35.41.80. 36 rm 260.
★***Palx*** (L.F.), 30, pl. St-Maurice, ☎ 65.35.03.40. 22 rm closed Sun and 15 Dec-15 Jan, 100. Rest. ♦ 50-150.

Labéraudie, 3 km NW :
★***Le Clos Grand*** (L.F.), ☎ 65.35.04.39. Visa. 21 rm 130. Rest. ♦ closed end Sep-end Jun, Fri eve and Sat, 60-100.

Mercuès, ⊠ 46090, 7 km NW :
★★★★(L) ***Château de Mercuès,*** ☎ 65.20.00.01. AE, DC, Euro, Visa. 45 rm closed 1 Nov-Palm Sunday, 1 500. Rest. ♦♦ ***l'Aigle d'Or*** closed early Nov-Palm Sun. Chef : Hervé Guérin. Spec : *petites salades châtelaines, escalope de foie gras au château de Haute-Serre, magret de canard au cassis*, 155-250.

Caillac, ⊠ 46140 Luzech, 11 km NW :
★★***Relais des Champs*** (L.F.), ☎ 65.30.92.35. 22 rm closed early Nov-early Mar, 260. Rest. closed Mon, 80-130.
★***Chez Nadal*** (L.F.), ☎ 65.30.91.55. 18 rm closed early Nov-early Mar and Mon, 100. Rest. ♦ 120-210.

Vers, ⊠ 46090, 15 km NE :
★***Les Chalets*** (L.F.), ☎ 65.31.41.53. 7 rm closed 11 Nov-1 Mar, Mon eve and Tue, 140. Rest. ♦ 50-150.
★***La Truite Dorée,*** ☎ 65.31.41.51. 18 rm. closed Fri and Sat, 100. Rest. ♦ 80-130.

★★*Municipal Saint-Georges* (50 pl.), ☎ 65.35.04.64.

Restaurants :
● ♦♦ ***La Taverne,*** 41, rue Delpech (B-C2), ☎ 65.35.28.66. closed 15 Nov-10 Dec, Sun eve and Mon. The hosts are a dynamic young couple, Renée and Patrick Lannes, who propose seemingly endless forms of *confit, foie gras* and truffles. Traditional cuisine with a new touch. An impressive selection of good Cahors wines, 230-310.
♦♦ ***Le Sénéchal du Quercy,*** St-Henri, N20, ☎ 65.35.52.97. closed 15-28 Feb and Wed, 55-170.
♦ ***Marie-Colline,*** 173, rue Clemenceau (C2), ☎ 65.35.59.96 closed Sun and Mon eves and 1-15 Sep. Vegetarian cooking, 80-130.

Lamagdelaine, 7 km E :
♦♦♦ ***Chez Marco,*** ☎ 65.35.30.64. AE, DC, Visa closed last week in Oct, 15 Jan-1 Mar, Sun eve and Mon low season, 100-200.

Montat, 8.5 km on the D47 :
♦♦ ***Les Templiers,*** ☎ 65.21.01.23. Visa closed Sun eve and Mon, Feb, 1-12 Jul. 12thC commandery. Spec : fish, 80-200.

Douelle, 12 km W :
♦♦ ***Marine,*** ☎ 65.20.02.06. Visa. closed two weeks in Oct, two weeks in Apr, Tue. Spec : fish and seafood, 120-210.

Saint-Médard, 18 km NW :
♦♦ ***Le Gindreau,*** ☎ 65.36.22.27 closed Tue eve, Wed, Mon (Jul-Aug), 3 Nov-19 Mar. Spec : *ris de veau, foie gras, assiette du pêcheur*, 100-260.

Sports and leisure activities : *M.J.C.*, impasse de la Charité, B.P. 42, ☎ 65.35.06.43, proposes canoe and kayak excursions on the Lot, the Célé and the Dordogne ; guided tours, lectures on potholing (spelunking), prehistory and local history ; rambles (hiking) ; typical Quercy meals, with tasting of Cahors wines.

Bicycle hire : *Éts Combes*, 117, bd Gambetta, ☎ 65.35.06.73.

Recommended : Pastries : *Larguille*, 21, bd Gambetta, ☎ 65.35.09.86. Local products : *Sudreau*, 91, bd Gambetta. Gastronomy, handicrafts : *la Tour du Pape Jean XXII*, 3, bd Gambetta, ☎ 65.35.39.52.

CAJARC

Cahors 51, Aurillac 90, Paris 609
D3 ⊠ 46160

SNCF ☎ 65.34.65.37.

Restaurant :
Montbrun, 9 km NE :
♦♦ ***Ferme de Montbrun,*** ☎ 65.40.67.71. AE. closed Wed ex summer and 15 Jan-1 Mar. Modern, regional cooking, 95-180.

CANCON

Agen 48, Cahors 81, Paris 595
B3 ⊠ 47290

Hotel :
Monviel, 10.5 km on the D124 :
★★★★**Château de Monviel** (L.F. ; Relais et châteaux), ☎ 53.01.71.64. Tx 560800. AE, DC, Visa. 8 rm 17thC residence, closed early Jan-end Mar, 350. Rest. ♦♦ closed Wed eve (ex guests), 100-200.

★★*Municipal du Lac* (33 pl.), ☎ 53.01.61.59.

CASTELJALOUX

Agen 55, Mont-de-Marsan 73, Paris 691
23 km S of Marmande, A3 ⊠ 47700

SNCF ☎ 53.93.00.45.

Hotels :
★★**Cordeliers** (L.F.), 1, rue des Cordeliers, ☎ 53.93.02.19. Euro, Visa. 26 rm 180.
★★**Cadets de Gascogne,** pl. Gambetta, ☎ 53.93.00.59. AE, DC, Euro, Visa. 15 rm closed 15-30 Nov, 160. Rest. ♦ 60-150.
Vieille Auberge, 11, Posterne, ☎ 53.93.01.36. 4 rm closed Sun eve and Mon, 1st week in Mar, 3rd week in Jun, last three weeks in Oct, 130. Rest. ♦ Spec : *aiguillettes de canard aux pruneaux, côtelette de volaille alexandrine,* 80-130.

★★*Municipal* (66 pl.), ☎ 53.93.00.24.

CAUSSADE

Montauban 22, Cahors 39, Paris 634
C4 ⊠ 82300

rue de la République (high season).

SNCF ☎ 63.63.50.50, 63.43.10.21.

Hotels :
● ★★**Larroque,** av. du 8-Mai, ☎ 63.93.10.14. Euro, Visa. 28 rm closed 31 Dec-31 Jan, Sat noon and Sun eve low season, 135. Rest. ♦♦ Regional cooking, 60-200.
★★**Dupont,** 25, rue des Récollets, ☎ 63.93.05.02. Euro, Visa. 31 rm closed Nov, first week in May, Fri eve and Sat low season, 150. Rest. ♦ 55-100.

★★★*La Piboulette* (100 pl.), ☎ 63.93.09.07.

DAMAZAN

Marmande 30, Agen 38, Paris 698
13 km W of Clermont-Dessous, A4 ⊠ 47160

Hotel :
● ★★**Canal** (L.F.), ☎ 53.79.42.84. 20 rm 110. Rest. ♦♦ 65-120.

★★*Du Lac* (66 pl.), ☎ 53.79.42.98.

Wines (Côtes de Buzet) : *Vignerons réunis,* Buzet-sur-Baïse, ☎ 53.79.44.30.

DOMME

Cahors 52, Brive 64, Paris 552
C3 ⊠ 24250

50, pl. de la Halle, ☎ 53.28.37.09 (high season).

Hotel :
★★**L'Esplanade** (L.F.), ☎ 53.28.31.41. AE. 20 rm closed Mon, Feb and Nov, 250. Rest. ♦ 80-180.

★★*La Croix des Prés* (33 pl.), ☎ 53.28.30.18 ; ★★*le Perpetuum* (85 pl.), ☎ 53.28.35.18.

EYMET

Bergerac 25, Périgueux 72, Paris 579
A3 ⊠ 24500

château, ☎ 53.58.81.60.

Hotel :
★**Château,** 9, rue du Couvent, ☎ 53.23.81.35. 10 rm closed 1-25 Oct, 100. Rest. ♦ Simple, tasty cooking, 45-80.

★★*Municipal* (33 pl.), ☎ 53.23.80.28.

Les EYZIES-DE-TAYAC

Sarlat 21, Périgueux 45, Paris 532
B2 ⊠ 24620

pl. de la Mairie, ☎ 53.06.97.05 (1 Apr-30 Oct).

Hotels :
● ★★★**Centenaire** (Roland Mazère and Alain Scholly) [Relais et châteaux], ☎ 53.06.97.18. Tx 541921. AE, DC, Euro, Visa. 31 rm closed 4 Nov-Apr, 250. Rest. ● ♦♦♦ closed Tue noon. The Mazère and Scholly couples are a superb family success story. The restaurant has continued to grow more agreeable every year, and the cooking, which pays due regard to the Périgord gourmand, is steadily approaching a state of perfection. Spec : marvelous *foie gras, feuilleton de ris de veau, pot-au-feu avec mique, tourtière de volaille, brick de fruits,* 120-320.
● ★★★**Cro-Magnon** (Mapotel), ☎ 53.06.97.06. Tx 570637. AE, DC, Visa, Euro. 27 rm closed 13 Oct-end Apr, 400. Rest. ♦♦♦ 100-280.
★★★**Les Glycines,** ☎ 53.06.97.03. AE, Visa. 25 rm closed 15 Oct-23 Mar, 250. Rest. ♦♦ Spec : *salade d'encornets au fenouil à l'huile de piment doux, escalope de saumon braisée à la julienne de cèpes, gratin Sarladais aux truffes et au confit,* 90-120.
★★**Centre** (L.F.), ☎ 53.06.97.13. Visa. 18 rm closed 15 Nov-1 Mar, 160. Rest. ♦♦ Spec : *assiette périgourdine, tournedos nouveau, soufflé aux noix,* 65-150.
★★**Roches** (L.F.), ☎ 53.06.96.59. 20 rm closed Nov-20 Mar, 180.
★★**Le Moulin de la Beune,** ☎ 53.06.94.33. 20 rm closed Nov-Mar, 180.

Tamniès, 12 km W. :
★★**Laborderie** (L.F.), ☎ 53.29.68.59. Euro. 25 rm closed 15 Nov-15 Mar, 180. Rest. ♦♦ 55-105.

★★★*le Mas de Sireuil* (100 pl.), ☎ 53.29.68.06 ; ★★*le Pech Denissou* (100 pl.), ☎ 53.06.95.84 ; ★★*la Rivière* (65 pl.), ☎ 53.06.97.14 ; ★★*L'Étang Joli* (33 pl.), ☎ 53.06.96.62.

FIGEAC

Cahors 69, Brive 92, Paris 584
D3 ⊠ 46100

pl. Vival, ☎ 66.34.06.25.

SNCF ☎ 66.34.10.37.

Car-hire : *Budget* train + auto, at the station, ☎ 66.34.10.37.

Hotels :
● ★★★**Carmes,** enclos des Carmes, ☎ 66.34.20.78, Tx 520794. AE, DC, Euro, Visa. 32 rm closed 15 Dec-2 Jan, Sat and Sun (Oct-May), 250. Rest. ♦♦♦ One of the best restaurants in Quercy, 85-200.
★★**Bains** (L.F.), 1, rue du Griffoul, ☎ 66.34.10.89. Euro, Visa. 21 rm closed 15 Dec-15 Mar, 200.

Loupiac, ⊠ 12700 Capdenac, 8 km on the D22 :
★★**Belle Rive,** pont de la Madeleine, ☎ 66.64.62.14. AE, DC, Visa. 11 rm closed 15 Nov-23 Mar, Sat low season, 140. Rest. ♦ 40-115.

Cardaillac, 10 km N on the N140 and D18 :
★**Chez Marcel,** ☎ 66.40.11.16. 6 rm. Closed Mon (low season) and 13-26 Oct, 150. Rest. ♦♦ Country-style cooking, 50-80.

⛺ ★★★*Les Carmes* (60 pl.), ☎ 66.34.08.56 ; ★★★*Le Lido* (85 pl.), ☎ 66.34.12.58.

Sports : *Club Hippique de la Châtaignorio (riding club),* ☎ 66.34.14.37.

Bicycle hire : Mme Barriac, 4 *bis,* pl. aux Herbes, ☎ 66.34.10.03.

GOURDON

Cahors 46, Brive 66, Paris 558
C3 ✉ 46300

ℹ allées de la République, ☎ 65.41.06.40.

SNCF ☎ 65.41.02.19.

Car-hire : *Budget* train + auto, rte du Vigan, ☎ 65.41.10.24, and at the station, ☎ 65.41.02.19.

Hotels :
★★★***Bissonier,*** 51, bd des Martyrs, ☎ 65.41.02.48. AE, DC, Euro, Visa. 26 rm P ♿ closed Dec and Fri eve (low season), 160. Rest. ♦ ***la Bonne Auberge,*** 48-160.
● ★★***Bourianne,*** pl. du Foirail, ☎ 65.41.16.37. 22 rm P ♿ closed 1 Jan-15 Mar, 200. Rest. ♦ closed Sun eve and Mon low season, 58-200.
★★***Promenade,*** bd Galliot-de-Genouilhac, ☎ 65.41.05.41. 15 rm P 120.

⛺ ★★★*Municipal « Écoute s'il Pleut »,* (110 pl.), ☎ 65.41.06.19.

Sports : *Cyclo-Club,* pl. de l'Ancienne-Gendarmerie.

GRAMAT

Figeac 35, Cahors 56, Paris 549
C3 ✉ 46500

ℹ pl. de la République, ☎ 65.38.73.60.

SNCF ☎ 65.38.71.27.

Car-hire : *Budget* train + auto, at the station, ☎ 65.38.71.27.

Hotels :
● ★★★***Lion d'Or,*** 8, pl. de la République, ☎ 65.38.73.18. Visa. 15 rm P ♿ closed 15 Dec-15 Jan and Mon low season, 280. Rest. ♦♦ ♿ Classical dishes from the Quercy region, along with new inventions, 60-180.
★★***Centre*** (L.F.), pl. de la République, ☎ 65.38.73.37. 15 rm P ♿ closed Feb hols and Sat low season, 180. Rest. 80-130.

Rignac, 4.5 km NW on the Martel road :
★★★***Château de Roumégouse*** (Relais et châteaux), ☎ 65.33.63.81. AE, DC, Visa. 14 rm P closed 15 Nov-1 Apr, 320. Rest. ♦♦ ♿ closed Tue noon, 105-200.

LACAPELLE-MARIVAL

Cahors 65, Tulle 82, Paris 569
21 km NW of Figeac, D3 ✉ 46120

ℹ château, ☎ 65.40.81.11 (high season).

Hotel :
★★***Terrasse,*** ☎ 65.40.80.07. AE, DC, Euro. 23 rm P closed 20 Dec-1 Apr, 180. Rest. ♦♦ 50 150.

⛺ ★★*Municipal Bois de Sophie* (65 pl.), ☎ 65.40.82.59.

Sports : *Classes Vertes d'Équitation* (riding school), château d'Aynac, ☎ 65.38.93.16.

LACAVE

Brive 49, Cahors 63, Paris 540
C2-3 ✉ 46200 Souillac

Hotels :
Calès, 4 km S :
★★***Pagès,*** ☎ 65.37.95.87. 15 rm P ♿1/2 pension high season, closed 1-29 Oct and Tue, 160. Rest. ♦ closed 3 Jan-3 Feb and Tue, 45-200.
★***Le Petit Relais*** (L.F.), ☎ 65.37.96.09. DC, Visa. 9 rm. closed Sat noon, 100. Rest. ♦ ♿ 35-85.

Farmhouse-inn : *le Bougayrou,* ☎ 65.37.87.20.

LALBENQUE

Cahors 23, Montauban 30, Paris 646
C4 ✉ 46230

SNCF ☎ 65.37.62.07.

Hotels :
★★★***L'Aquitaine,*** on the N20, ☎ 65.21.00.51. 44 rm P ♿ closed 24 Dec to 8 Jan and Sun eve low season, 180.

Concots, ✉ 46260 Limogne-en-Quercy, 15 km NE :
Auberge du Mesnil, le Bourg, ☎ 65.31.51.96. Visa. 5 rm P ♿ closed Dec-Jan, 90. Rest. ♦ 50-155.

Recommended : truffle market, Tue.

LALINDE

Bergerac 22, Périgueux 59, Paris 576
6 km W of Mauzac, B2 ✉ 24150

ℹ ☎ 53.61.08.55.

SNCF ☎ 53.61.04.39.

Hotels :
★★***Résidence,*** rue du Pr-Testut, ☎ 53.61.01.81. 11 rm P ♿ closed 30 Sep-15 May, 140.
★★***Château*** (L.F.), 1, rue de Verdun, ☎ 53.61.01.82. DC, Visa. 9 rm closed 15 Nov-1 Mar and Fri, 145-180. Rest. ♦♦ ♿ 55-160.

Badefols-sur-Dordogne, 5 km E :
★***Lou Cantou*** (L.F.), ☎ 53.22.50.36. 12 rm P closed Oct-Mar, 100. Rest. ♦ ♿ 80-130.

Mauzac, 6 km E :
★★★***La Métairie*** (Relais et châteaux), ☎ 53.22.50.47. AE, Euro, Visa. 11 rm P ♿ closed 1 Jan-22 Mar, Tue and Wed (15 Oct-1 Jan), 365. Rest. ♦♦ closed Tue, 90-200.

⛺ ★★*Le Moulin de la Guillou* (100 pl.), ☎ 53.61.02.91.

Restaurant :
Saint-Capraise-de-Lalinde, 4 km W :
● ♦♦ ***Le Relais St-Jacques,*** pl. de l'Église, ☎ 53.23.22.14. Visa. closed 15 Jan-1 Feb, Mon eve and Tue eve ex 15 Jul-15 Aug. Attentively prepared fare in a setting of beguiling modesty. Spec : *escalope de foie de canard chaud au monbazillac, salade de gésiers confits, noisette d'agneau aux échalotes en chemise et au jus,* 50-150.

Sports and leisure activities : open-air leisure centre, *Moulin de la Guillou,* ☎ 53.61.02.91. Beginners' and seasoned sportsmens' courses : canoeing, archery, climbing, swimming, tennis.

LATRONQUIÈRE

Aurillac 45, Cahors 85, Paris 574
28 km N of Figeac, D3 ✉ 46210

ℹ mairie, ☎ 65.40.26.62 (high season).

Hotel :
● ★★★***Tourisme,*** ☎ 65.40.33.60. 30 rm P closed Oct-May, 200. Rest. ♦♦ Spec : *pâté de foie de canard truffé maison, escargots en coquilles « vieille mode », pièce de bœuf au jus de truffe,* 75-150.

LAUZERTE

Montauban 37, Agen 52, Paris 635
C4 ✉ 82110

Hotel :
Cazes-Mondenard, 7 km SE :
★***L'Atre,*** pl. de l'Hôtel-de-Ville, ☎ 63.94.68.67. 10 rm, closed 4-19 Apr and 15-29 Nov, 100. Rest. 40-100.

MAREUIL

Brantôme 20, Limoges 86, Paris 494
B1 ✉ 24340

Hotel :
Vieux-Mareuil, 5 km SW :
● ★★★***Auberge de l'Étang Bleu*** (France-Accueil), ☎ 53.60.92.63. AE, DC, Euro, Visa. 11 rm P A natural bathing lake in a 49-acre park, closed 15 Dec-15 May and Mon (ex 1 Jun-30 Sep), 185. Rest. ♦♦ ♿ 80-210.

⛺ ★★★*L'Étang Bleu,* Vieux-Mareuil (165 pl.), ☎ 53.56.62.63.

MARMANDE

Agen 58, Bordeaux 89, Paris 684
A3 ✉ 47200

ℹ pl. Clemenceau, ☎ 53.64.32.50.

✈ Vizareil, 3 km E, ☎ 53.64.26.36.

SNCF ☎ 53.64.29.23.

Car-hire : *Budget* train + auto, at the station, ☎ 53.64.23.36.

Hotels :
★★***Capricorne*** (L.F.), rte d'Agen, ☎ 53.64.16.14. AE, DC, Euro, Visa. 33 rm P ♿ closed 2 weeks end-of-year hols, 170. Rest. ♦ ☎ 53.64.56.12, 60-200.
★***Auberge de Guyenne,*** 9, rue Martignac, ☎ 53.64.01.77. Euro, Visa. 16 rm P closed 15 Dec-15 Jan, Sun eve and Mon (ex 15 Jun-15 Sep), 150. Rest. ♿ 50-85.

⛺ ★★*Municipal* (75 pl.), ☎ 53.64.63.05.

MOISSAC

Montauban 29, Agen 43, Paris 657
B4 ✉ 82200

ℹ pl. Durand-de-Bredon, ☎ 63.04.01.85 (high season).

SNCF ☎ 63.04.01.61.

Hotels :
★★★***Moulin de Moissac*** (Mapotel), pl. du Moulin, ☎ 63.04.03.55. 57 rm P 400. Rest. ♦♦ ♿ Discotheque, Quick-service restaurant, 80-130.
★★***Chapon Fin,*** pl. des Récollets, ☎ 63.04.04.22. AE, DC, Euro, Visa. 32 rm P closed 1 Nov-7 Dec and Mon, 190. Rest. ♦ closed Mon, 60-150.

⛺ ★★★*L'île de Bidounet* (140 pl.), ☎ 63.32.29.96.

MONCRABEAU

Agen 41, Mont-de-Marsan 82, Paris 732
12 km S of Nérac, A4 ✉ 47600 Nérac

Hotel :
● ★★***Phare*** (L.F.), ☎ 53.65.42.08. AE, Visa. 7 rm closed 10 Feb-2 Mar, 15-31 Oct and Tue, 160. Rest. ● ♦ Copious regional cooking, good value. Spec : *gâteau de cèpes aux noix, écrevisses flambées à l'armagnac, feuilleté aux fruits de saison,* 55-155.

⛺ ★★★*Municipal* (150 pl.), ☎ 53.65.42.11.

Event : *Fête de l'Académie des Menteurs* (Liars' Academy festival) in Aug.

MONPAZIER

Bergerac 45, Périgueux 79, Paris 565
B3 ✉ 24540

ℹ pl. Centrale, ☎ 53.61.60.38 (high season).

Hotels :
★★***Londres,*** ☎ 53.22.60.64. AE, DC, Euro, Visa. 10 rm closed Nov-Easter and Mon low season, 100.
★***France,*** 21, rue St-Jacques, ☎ 53.22.60.06. Euro, Visa. 14 rm, 70. Rest. ♦ closed Wed, 45-100.

⛺ ★★★*Moulin de David* (100 pl.), Gaujac, ☎ 53.22.65.25.

MONTAUBAN

Toulouse 53, Auch 86, Paris 656
C4 ✉ 82000

ℹ Ancien Collège, 2, rue du Collège (B-C2), ☎ 63.63.60.60.

✈ 2 km NE, ☎ 63.03.26.93.

SNCF (A2), ☎ 63.63.50.50, 63.63.05.14.

Car-hire : *Budget* train + auto, at the station, ☎ 63.63.19.15.

Hotels :
★★★***Ingres*** (Mapotel), 10, av. Mayenne (A2), ☎ 63.63.36.01. Tx 520319. AE, DC, Euro, Visa. 34 rm P ♿ 260.
★★***Midi*** (L.F. ; Inter-Hôtel), 12, rue Notre-Dame (B2), ☎ 63.63.17.23, Tx 531705. AE, DC, Euro, Visa. 48 rm P ♿ 230. Rest. ♦♦ ♿ closed Jan, 62-160.
★★***Prince Noir*** (L.F.), pl. Prax-Paris (C2), ☎ 63.63.10.10, Tx 520362. Euro, Visa. 33 rm P ♿ Flower-decorated terrace, 160.
★★***Orsay,*** opposite train station (A2), ☎ 63.63.00.57, Tx 520362. AE, DC, Euro, Visa. 20 rm P ♿ closed 29 Apr-20 May, Sun and Mon noon, 200. Rest. ● ♦♦ ***la Cuisine d'Alain.*** On the way up. Spec : *poêlée de langoustines aux poireaux, civet de cuisse de canard, saumon grillé avec sa peau, riz impératrice,* 75-200.

Montbeton, ✉ 82290 La Ville-Dieu-du-Temple, 5 km W :
★★★***Les Coulandrières*** (Mapotel), rte de Castel-Sarrasin, ☎ 63.03.18.09. Tx 520200. AE, Visa. 21 rm P ♿ 260. Rest. ♦♦ closed Sun eve and Mon noon low season, 120-210.

Restaurants :
♦ ***Le Ventadour,*** 23, quai Villebourdon, ☎ 63.63.34.58. AE, DC, Euro, Visa. P ♿ closed Sat noon, Sun, nat hols, 1 week in Feb and 3 weeks in Aug. Spec : *onglet du berger, civet de cèpes au vin de Cahors,* 80-140.
♦ ***Le Pitzou,*** 24, rue de la Comédie (B1), ☎ 63.63.02.83. Visa. Spec : *fromage chaud aux cèpes, ragoût de St-Jacques et de grenouilles, foies gras aux pointes d'asperges,* 80-130.
♦ ***Delmas,*** 10, rue Michelet (B2), ☎ 63.63.03.74. AE, DC, Euro, Visa. ♿ closed Sun eve, Mon and 4 Aug-2 Sep. Spec : *poulet aux morilles,* 60-180.
♦ ***Au Chapon Fin,*** 1, pl. Saint-Orens (A2), ☎ 63.63.12.10. closed Fri eve and Sat, 28 Jun-28 Jul. Classic cooking, 50-190.

Recommended : *Pâtisserie Robert Marty* (pastries), 70, rue Léon-Cladel, ☎ 63.03.46.52. *Laplace,* 52, rue de la Résistance, ☎ 63.63.06.08 : chocolates, icecreams and tea. *Coop Confidou,* Z.I. (Industrial Zone), ☎ 63.01.01.90 : pruneaux. *Market,* esplanade Prax-Paris, Sat a.m.

MONTIGNAC

Brive 38, Périgueux 47, Paris 497
C2 ✉ 24290

ℹ pl. B.-de-Born, ☎ 53.51.82.60 (high season).

Hotels :
★★★★***Château de Puy Robert,*** 2 km on the D5, ☎ 53.51.89.24. 15 rm closed 20 Oct 5 Mar, 500. Rest. ♦♦♦ The latest of the fine Relais Albert Parveaux. An exquisite small château summoning up the era of Napoléon III. In the heart of the Périgord Noir Region, with a view on the Vézère River, and near the famous Lascaux caves (where you can visit an exact replica of the original). Light, contemporary preparation of regional specialities, 200-300.
★★★***Relais Soleil d'Or,*** 16, rue du 4-Septembre, ☎ 53.51.80.22. 38 rm closed Dec, end Feb-early Mar and Sat (Nov-Mar), 180. Rest. ● ♦♦ Refined regional gastronomy, 120-210.
★***Lascaux,*** 109, av. J.-Jaurès, ☎ 53.51.82.81. AE, DC. 17 rm closed Sun eve and Mon (in winter), Nov and Feb, 100. Rest. ♦ Spec : *foie gras frais, caneton aux figues, charlotte de fruits au coulis de framboises,* 80-130.
Le Lardin-Saint-Lazare, ✉ 24570 Condat, 11 km NE :
★★***Sautet*** (L.F.), ☎ 53.51.27.22. AE, Visa. 38 rm ♿ closed 20 Dec-20 Jan, Sat and Sun from Oct to Easter, 205. Rest. ♦♦ 45-120.
⛺ ★★*Le Bleufond* (80 pl.), ☎ 53.51.83.95.
Restaurants :
Castel-Merle, 10 km S :
♦ ***Auberge de Castel-Merle,*** ☎ 53.50.70.08. Euro, Visa. closed 1 Nov-1 Apr (ex Sun) and Mon. Classic meals of the Périgord region, 55-105.
Condat-sur-Vézère, 11 km NE :
● ♦ ***L'Aérodrome,*** ☎ 53.51.27.80. AE, Euro, Visa. ♿ closed Mon and 2 weeks in Feb. An unpretentious restaurant with a wonderfully warm welcome and delightful atmosphere, 80-130.

MONTPEZAT-DE-QUERCY

Cahors 29, Montauban 34, Paris 625
C4 ✉ 82270
ℹ RN 20, ☎ 63.02.05.65 (high season).
SNCF ☎ 63.02.07.16.
Hotel :
● ★***Depeyre,*** rue de la République, ☎ 63.02.08.41. AE, DC. 7 rm ♿ closed 3-18 Jan, Mon and Tue eve high season, 150. Rest. ● ♦ Spec : *filet de sandre au vin rouge à l'étuvée de poireaux, aiguillette de dinde aux morilles brunes ;* excellent pastries, 70-235.

NÉRAC

Agen 30, Bordeaux 124, Paris 719
A4 ✉ 47600
ℹ hôtel de ville, ☎ 53.65.00.54.
SNCF ☎ 53.65.00.34.
Hotels :
★★***Château*** (L.F.), 7, av. Mondenard, ☎ 53.65.09.05. 20 rm. closed 1-31 Oct, 180. Rest. ♦ ♿ closed Sun eve and Mon noon low season, 55-120.
★★***Albret*** (L.F.), 40, allées d'Albret, ☎ 53.65.01.47, Tx 560800. 15 rm. closed Sep, 1st week in Mar and Mon low season, 150. Rest. ♦ 45-160.
Restaurants :
Francescas, 10.5 km SE on the D232 :
♦ ***Le Pot aux Roses,*** 3, Grande-Rue, ☎ 53.65.41.59. AE, Euro, Visa. ♿ closed 18 Jun-10 Jul, 15-30 Nov and Wed. Spec : *escalope de saumon au beurre battu citronné, salade de queues d'écrevisses aux pêches blanches, aiguillettes de canard gras au poivre vert et zestes d'orange,* 50-105.
Poudenas, ✉ 47170 Mézin, 17 km SW :
● ♦♦ ***Auberge la Belle Gasconne,*** ☎ 53.65.71.58. AE, DC, Euro, Visa. ♿ closed 1-7 Dec, 15-31 Jan, Sun eve and Mon ex Jul-Aug. Good, refined local specialities cooked by Madame Gracia : *tourte aux légumes, terrine de chipirons,* goose, duck. Home-made pastries and jams, 120-210. Products for sale (by mail, too).
⛺ ★★*Municipal* (33 pl.), ☎ 53.65.14.26.

NONTRON

Périgueux 49, Limoges 69, Paris 477
B1 ✉ 24300
ℹ pl. du Champ-de-Foire (high season).
Hotels :
★★***Grand Hôtel*** (L.F.), 3, pl. A.-Agard, ☎ 53.56.11.22. Visa. 26 rm ♿ closed 15-31 Jan and Sun eve (Nov-Feb), 180. Rest. ♦ 120-210.
Javerlhac, 11 km NW :
★***Auberge des Tilleuls*** (L.F.), av. de la Gare, ☎ 53.56.30.12. Euro. 8 rm 55. Rest. ♦ ♿ 45-90.
Saint-Saud-Lacoussière, ✉ 24470 St-Pardoux-la-Rivière, 17 km E :
Auberge du Vieux Moulin, pont de la Macque, ☎ 53.56.97.26. AE, Visa. 8 rm On the banks of the Dronne river, 200. Rest. ♦ half-pension high season, 60-140.
Restaurant :
Saint-Estèphe, 9 km N :
♦ ***Gérard Dutin,*** ☎ 53.56.83.24. AE, Euro. ♿ closed 15 Oct-1 Nov and Tue. A menu of specialities from the Périgord region, 80-130.

PÉRIGUEUX

Brive 73, Angoulême 85, Paris 530
B2 ✉ 24000
ℹ av. d'Aquitaine, ☎ 53.53.10.63 ; *T.O.,* 16, rue Wilson, ☎ 53.53.44.35.
✈ Bassillac, ☎ 53.53.41.08.
SNCF (A1), ☎ 53.09.50.50, 53.08.23.00.
🚌 pl. Francheville, ☎ 53.08.76.00.
Car-hire : *Budget* train + auto, opposite the station, ☎ 53.08.69.55, and at the airport.
Hotels :
● ★★★***Bristol,*** 37, rue Antoine-Gadaud (B1), ☎ 53.08.75.90, Tx 540131. Visa. 28 rm 185.
★★★***Domino*** (Inter-Hôtel), 21, pl. Francheville (B2), ☎ 53.08.25.80. 37 rm ♿ 250. Rest. ● ♦ Spec : *mignonnette de foie de canard au poivre, ragoût d'écrevisses aux pâtes fraîches,* 70-200.
★★***Périgord*** (L.F.), 74, rue V.-Hugo (B1), ☎ 53.53.33.63. 21 rm closed 1 Nov and Shrove Tue (Easter week), 100. Rest. ♦ 80-130.
Annesse-et-Beaulieu, ✉ 24430 Razac-sur-l'Isle, 4 km SW :
★★***Château de Lalande*** (Châteaux-hôtels ; L.F.), ☎ 53.54.52.30. DC, Euro, Visa. 22 rm closed 15 Nov-15 Mar and Wed low season, 250. Rest. ♦♦ ♿ 58-200.
Chancelade, ✉ 24650, 5 km NW :
★★***Pont de la Beauronne,*** ☎ 53.08.42.91. AE, Visa. 24 rm closed 20 Sep-19 Oct, Sun eve and Mon noon, 100. Rest. ♦ closed Sun eve and nat hols eves, 80-130.
Bassilac, ✉ 24330, 6 km W :
★★***Château de Rognac,*** ☎ 53.54.40.78. 12 rm closed 1 Nov-Palm Sunday, 225. Rest. ♦ 70-100.

Antonne-et-Trigonant, ✉ 24420 Savignac-les-Églises, 10 km NE :
★★**Hostellerie la Charmille,** Laurière, ☎ 53.06.00.45. Visa. 18 rm closed Mon, 100. Rest. ♦ 80-130.

Périgueux-Boulazac : ★★*Barnabé* (80 pl.), ☎ 53.53.41.45 ; Périgueux-Lesparat : ★*de l'Isle* (100 pl.), ☎ 53.53.57.75.

Restaurants :
● ♦♦♦ **L'Oison,** 31, rue Saint-Front (C2), ☎ 53.09.84.02. AE, DC, Visa. closed 15 Feb-15 Mar, Sun eve and Mon ♿ Excellent value. Spec : *foie gras de canard mi-cuit, panaché de poissons au beurre d'aromates,* 95-300.
♦♦ **La Flambée,** 2, rue Montaigne, ☎ 53.53.23.06. An interesting address : lobsters vivarium, fish, 85-200.

Sports : *Étrier Périgourdin,* domaine Borie-Petit, ☎ 53.53.61.48.

Bicycle hire : 41 *bis,* cours Saint-Georges, ☎ 53.53.31.56.

Recommended : Antiques : salesroom, 32, rue Gadaud, ☎ 53.53.11.15. Numerous antique dealers in the old quarter. *Foie gras : Pierre Champion,* 21, rue Taillefer.

PUY-L'ÉVÊQUE

Cahors 31, Sarlat 58, Paris 600
C3 ✉ 46700

ℹ mairie, ☎ 65.36.33.81.

Hotels :
● ★★**Bellevue** (L.F.), pl. de la Truffière, ☎ 65.21.30.70. 15 rm closed 15 Nov-15 Mar, Sun eve and Mon low season, 165. Rest. ♦♦ 50-140.
★**Henry** (L.F.), ☎ 65.21.32.24. AE, DC, Euro, Visa. 22 rm Ⓟ 100. Rest. ♦ closed Sun eve, 80-130.

★★*Municipal de la Plage* (100 pl.), ☎ 65.30.81.45.

Sports : hire of bicycles, canoes and kayaks ; *Safaraid,* pl. du Rampeau, ☎ 65.36.30.39.

Wines (Cahors) : M. Delgoulet, château Chambert, Flousors ; M. Balder ; M. Bernede.

RIBÉRAC

Périgueux 37, Angoulême 58, Paris 503
A2 ✉ 24600

ℹ pl. du Gal-de-Gaulle, ☎ 53.90.03.10 (high season).

Hotel :
★★**France** (L.F.), 3, rue M.-Dufraisse, ☎ 53.90.00.61. AE, Euro, Visa. 19 rm 145. Rest. ♦ ♿ 50-120.

★*La Dronne* (100 pl.), ☎ 53.90.03.10.

Recommended : foie gras : *charcuterie Raynaud,* rue du 26-Mars ; *Maison Dumonteil,* 35, rue du 26-Mars.

ROCAMADOUR

Brive 55, Cahors 59, Paris 545
C3 ✉ 46500 Gramat

ℹ Grande-Rue, ☎ 65.33.62.59 (Easter-30 Sep).

SNCF ☎ 65.33.63.05.

Hotels :
★★★**Château** (L.F.) and ★★**Relais Amadourien,** rue de la Corniche, ☎ 65.33.62.22. Tx 521871. AE, DC. 58 rm Ⓟ ♿ closed 4 Nov-31 Mar, 180. Rest. ♦♦ 80-130.
★★★**Beau Site et Notre-Dame** (Mapotel), rue Roland Lepreux, ☎ 65.33.63.08. Tx 520421. AE, DC, Euro, Visa. 55 rm Ⓟ closed 9 Nov-end Mar, 240. Rest. ♦♦ **Jehan de Valon.** Spec : *salade de jambon de canard fumé et gésiers confits, poêlée d'agneau à la fleur de moutarde et flan d'aubergines, foie de veau au vinaigre de cidre et aux raisins,* 70-180.
★★**Sainte-Marie,** pl. des Shenais, ☎ 65.33.63.07. Visa. 22 rm Ⓟ closed 3 Nov-end Mar, 10 days in Oct, 162. Rest. ♦ 45-87.

Alvignac, 8 km E :
★★★**Grand Hôtel Palladium,** ☎ 65.33.60.23. AE, DC, Visa. 25 rm Ⓟ closed 15 Aug-1 May, 210. Rest. ♦♦ closed Mon noon. Quercy regional specialities, 65-180.

★★*Le Relais du Campeur* (100 pl.), ☎ 65.33.63.28.

La ROQUE-GAGEAC

Sarlat 13, Périgueux 60, Paris 552
Dordogne Valley, C3 ✉ 24250 Domme

Hotels :
★★**Belle Étoile,** ☎ 53.29.51.44. 16 rm Ⓟ closed 15 Oct-1 Apr, 130. Rest. ♦ 65-120.
★★**Périgord,** rte de Vitrac, 3 km, ☎ 53.28.36.55. AE, DC, Visa. 40 rm Ⓟ 190. Rest. ♦ ♿ 60-90.

★★★*Beau Rivage* (190 pl.), ☎ 53.28.32.05 ; ★★*Verte Rive* (60 pl.), ☎ 53.28.30.04.

SAINT-CÉRÉ

Brive 54, Cahors 76, Paris 546
D2 ✉ 46400

ℹ pl. de la République, ☎ 65.38.11.85.

Hotels :
★★★**Coq-Arlequin** (L.F.), 1, bd du Dr-Roux, ☎ 65.38.02.13. 30 rm Ⓟ closed 1 Jan-1 Mar and Mon low season, 235. Rest. ♦♦ 65-160.
★★★**France,** av. Maynard, ☎ 65.38.02.16. Visa. 27 rm closed 15 Oct-1 Jun, 250. Rest. ♦ ♿ 60-150.
★★**Parc,** av. J.-Mouliérat, ☎ 65.38.17.29. 24 rm Ⓟ closed Dec, Fri eve and Sat low season, 135-180. Rest. ♦ ♿ 50-100.

Sousceyrac, ✉ 46190, 16 km E :
● ★**Au Déjeuner de Sousceyrac,** ☎ 65.33.00.56. AE, DC, Visa. 14 rm, closed Sat and 1 Nov-1 Apr, 125. Rest. ♦♦ Pleasant setting, good value, 55-120.

★★★*Municipal de Soulhol* (200 pl.), ☎ 65.38.12.37.

SAINT-CIRQ-LAPOPIE

Cahors 33, Figeac 45, Paris 628
C3 ✉ 46330

Hotels :
★**Auberge du Sombral,** ☎ 65.31.26.08. 10 rm, closed 15 Nov-15 Feb, 150. Rest. ♦♦ ♿ closed Tue eve and Wed, 55-180.
Pelissaria (L.F.), ☎ 65.31.25.14. 6 rm Ⓟ closed 3 Nov-1 Apr, 170. Rest. ♦ eve only, 100.

Pradines, ✉ 46000 Cahors, 3 km on the D42 :
★**Causse,** ☎ 65.31.24.16. Visa. 9 rm Ⓟ 115.

★★*La Truffière* (33 pl.), ☎ 65.31.24.16.

Restaurant :
Saint-Martin-Labouval, 7 km E :
♦♦ **La Batellerie,** La Toulzanie, ☎ 65.31.28.25. closed Tue and 1 Oct-1 Apr, 120-210.

SAINT-CYBRANET

Sarlat 16, Cahors 54, Paris 555
Dordogne Valley, C3 ✉ 24250

Hotel :
★**Le Relais Fleuri,** ☎ 53.28.33.70. 7 rm Ⓟ closed 31 Oct-Easter, 110. Rest. ♦ 55-85.

⩓ ★★★*Le Céou* (65 pl.), ☎ 53.28.32.12 ; ★★*les Cascades du Lauzel* (60 pl.), ☎ 53.28.32.26.

Sports : *Aquatic sports centre* (canoe and kayak hire) ; climbing instruction centre.

Recommended : Antique dealer : P. Versteegh, pl. de l'Église.

SAINT-CYPRIEN

Sarlat 21, Périgueux 54, Paris 541
B2 ⊠ 24220

ℹ ☎ 53.29.20.39.

Hotels :
● ★★★***L'Abbaye*** (France-Accueil), rue de l'Entrepôt, ☎ 53.29.20.48. AE, DC, Euro, Visa. 19 rm 🅿 ♨ ⛱ ♿ closed 4 Nov-15 Mar, 200-320. Rest. ♦♦ 65-230.
★★***Terrasse*** (L.F.), pl. Jean-Landignac, ☎ 53.29.21.69. Visa. 16 rm ♿ closed 2 Nov-1 Mar, 205. Rest. ♦ 65-155.

Siorac, ⊠ 24170 Belvès, 8 km SW :
★★★***Scholly*** (L.F.), ☎ 53.28.60.02. AE, DC, Visa. 32 rm 🅿 ♨ ⚲ closed 15 Jan-15 Feb, 230. Rest. ♦♦ Traditional cooking, 85-230.

⩓ ★★★*Municipal du Garrit* (90 pl.), ☎ 53.29.20.56.

SALIGNAC-EYVIGNES

Sarlat 19, Brive 34, Paris 527
C2 ⊠ 24590

Hotel :
★***La Terrasse,*** pl. de la Poste, ☎ 53.28.80.38. Euro. 13 rm, closed 5 Nov-1 Apr, 150. Rest. 45-100.

SARLAT

Brive 51, Périgueux 66, Paris 539
C2 ⊠ 24200

ℹ pl. de la Liberté, ☎ 53.59.27.67.

SNCF ☎ 53.59.00.21.

Hotels :
● ★★★***Salamandre,*** rue de l'Abbé-Surguier, ☎ 53.59.35.98. AE, DC, Euro, Visa. 23 rm ♿ closed 31 Oct-15 Apr, 250.
★★★***La Madeleine,*** 1, pl. de la Petite-Rigaudie, ☎ 53.59.12.40, Tx 550689. AE, DC, Euro, Visa. 22 rm. closed 1 Jan-10 Mar, 11 Nov-31 Dec, 275. Rest. ♦♦ ♿ 65-200.
★★★***Hoirie*** (Relais du Silence), 2 km S, ☎ 53.59.05.62. 15 rm 🅿 ♨ ⚲ 🎾 closed 15 Dec-15 Mar, 250. Rest. Spec : *émincé de magret à la fleur de pêche,* 100-160.
★★***St-Albert*** (L.F.), 10, pl. Pasteur, ☎ 53.59.01.09. AE, DC, Euro, Visa. 52 rm 🚭 closed Sun eve and Mon low season, 180. Rest. ♦♦ ♿ Regional cooking. Spec : *tourin blanchi, cou d'oie farci sauce Périgueux, truffes sous la cendre, ris de veau aux girolles,* 70-130.
★★***Mairie,*** 13, pl. de la Liberté, ☎ 53.59.05.71. AE, Visa. 11 rm ⚘ closed 15 Nov-1 Apr, 135.
● ★***La Verperie,*** allée des Acacias, ☎ 53.59.00.20. 15 rm ⚘ 🅿 ♨ ⚲ closed 20 Dec-1 Feb, 145. Rest. ♦ 🚭 ♿ closed Sun low season, 65-115.

On the Eyzies road, 3 km, at the place known as Argentouleau :
● ★★★***Hostellerie de Meysset*** (Châteaux-hôtels), ☎ 53.59.08.29. AE, DC, Visa. 21 rm + 6 apts ⚘ 🅿 ♨ ⚲ ♿ closed Oct-Easter, 260. Rest. ♦♦ 120-210.

Vitrac, 7 km S :
★★***Plaisance,*** ☎ 53.28.33.04, le Port. AE, Visa. 38 rm 🅿 ♨ 🎾 closed 17 Nov-1 Feb, 145. Rest. ♦ ♿ closed Fri eve and Sat noon low season, 55-130.

Groléjac, ⊠ 24250 Domme, 11 km SE :
★★***Le Grillardin,*** ☎ 53.28.11.02. AE, Euro. 14 rm 🅿 ♨ 🚭 100. Rest. ♦ 80-130.

Youth hostel : 15 *bis,* av. de Selves, ☎ 53.59.14.20.

⩓ ★★★★*Les Périères* (90 pl.), ☎ 53.59.05.84 ; ★★★★*les Grottes de Roffy* (125 pl.), ☎ 53.59.15.61 ; St-André-d'Allas, 10 km W : ★★★★*Moulin du Roch* (160 pl.), ☎ 53.59.20.27 ; ★★★★*les Granges,* Groléjac, 11 km SE (135 pl.), ☎ 53.28.11.15.

Restaurant :
Caudon-de-Vitrac, 8 km S :
● ♦ ***La Ferme,*** ☎ 53.28.33.35. ⚘ ⚲ ♿ closed Oct and Mon. Spec : *soupe de haricots, omelette aux truffes,* 55-120.

Sports : canoeing, riding : *Centre Hippique Fournier Sarlouève,* Ferme des Bories, ☎ 53.59.15.83. *Cyclotourisme Sarladois,* 10, bd Nessmann, ☎ 53.59.00.74.

Recommended : *Aux Armes du Périgord,* 1, rue de la Liberté, ☎ 53.59.19.12 : truffles. *Boutique Rougier,* rue des Consuls : *foie gras.*

SAVIGNAC-LES-ÉGLISES

Brive 62, Limoges 84, Paris 476
20 km NW of Périgueux, B2 ⊠ 24420

Hotels :
★★★★***Parc*** (Relais et châteaux), rue Sylvain-Bordas, ☎ 53.05.08.11, Tx 570335. AE, DC, Euro, Visa. 14 rm 🅿 ♨ ⚲ 🚭 closed 15-28 Oct, 450. Rest. ♦♦♦ 🚭 ♿ closed 3 Jan-1 Mar and Tue low season. Spec : *huîtres chaudes au jus de truffes, salade tiède de langoustines et de homard au beurre d'oranger, aiguillette de canette de Barbarie sauce au vin de noix.* Booking advisable, 155-330.

Sarliac-sur-l'Isle, 4 km S :
★***Chabrol,*** ☎ 53.06.01.35. 12 rm ♨ ⚲ closed 15-30 Sep. Simple, good fare, 90. Rest. ♦ 45-150.

⩓ ★★*Du Moulin* (33 pl.), ☎ 53.05.00.54.

SOUILLAC

Brive 37, Cahors 66, Paris 529
C2 ♥ ⊠ 46200

ℹ 9, bd Malvy, ☎ 65.37.81.56.

SNCF ☎ 65.32.78.21.

Car-hire : *Budget* train + auto, at the station, ☎ 65.32.78.21.

Hotels :
★★★***Les Granges Vieilles*** (L.F.), rte de Sarlat, ☎ 65.37.80.92. 11 rm 🅿 ♨ ⚲ 🚭 closed Nov, 300. Rest. ♦♦ 70-160.
★★★***Puy d'Alon,*** av. J.-Jaurès, ☎ 65.37.89.79. AE. 11 rm 🅿 ♨ ⚲ ♿ closed 15 Oct-15 Apr, 210.
★★***Ambassadeurs*** (L.F.), av. du Gal-de-Gaulle, ☎ 65.32.78.36. 28 rm 🅿 ♨ 🚭 closed 28 Sep-28 Oct, a week in Jan, Feb hols, Fri eve and Sat ex Jul-Sep and nat hols, 185. Rest. ♦♦ ♿ Regional cooking, 45-135.

Rouffilhac, ⊠ 24370 Carlux, 13 km W :
★★***Aux Poissons Frais,*** ☎ 65.29.70.24. 21 rm ⚘ 🅿 ♨ ⛱ 🎾 closed 30 Sep-1 Nov, 170. Rest. ♦♦ 50-125.

Cressensac, ⊠ 46600 Martel, 17 km N :
★★***Chez Gilles*** (L.F.), ☎ 65.37.70.06. AE, Euro, Visa. 25 rm 🅿 ♿ closed Feb and Wed, 180. Rest. ♦ 120-210.

⩓ ★★★★*La Paille Basse* (220 pl.), ☎ 65.32.73.51 ; ★★*Ombrages de la Dordogne* (80 pl.), Rouffilhac, 13 km W, ☎ 65.29.70.24.

Recommended : *charcuterie Maury,* 13, rue de la Halle, ☎ 65.37.83.12.

THIVIERS

Périgueux 37, Limoges 64, Paris 457
B1 ⊠ 24800

ℹ pl. Mal-Foch, ☎ 65.55.12.50 (1 Jun-20 Sep).

SNCF ☎ 53.55.00.21

Hotels :
★★★***France et Russie,*** 51, rue Gal-Lamy, ☎ 65.55.17.80. 11 rm Ⓟ 🌳 220.

Mavaleix, 11 km N on the N21 :
● ★★★***Château de Mavaleix*** (Châteaux-hôtels), on the N21 by private access road, ☎ 53.52.82.01, Tx 570523. Euro, Visa. 30 rm, closed 3 Jan-7 Feb Ⓟ 🌳 ⛱ ♞ 57-acre park alongside a river (hunting and fishing), 300. Rest. ♦♦♦ 70-200. Instructional courses in the preparation of *foie gras.*

La Coquille, ⊠ 24450, 15 km N on the N21 :
★★***Les Voyageurs*** (L.F.), 12, rue de la République, ☎ 53.52.80.13. AE, DC, Visa. 10 rm Ⓟ 🌳 closed Nov-end Mar, 165. Rest. ♦♦ ♿ 80-170.

TONNEINS

Agen 41, Bordeaux 106, Paris 701
A4 ⊠ 47400

SNCF ☎ 53.79.00.60.

Hotel :
★★***Parc*** (L.F.), ☎ 53.79.30.30. AE, DC, Euro, Visa. 17 rm Ⓟ 🌳 ⛱ ♞ In an 18thC residence, 180. Rest. ♦ ♞ closed Sun eve, 120-210.

⛺ ★★*Municipal Robinson* (53 pl.), ☎ 53.79.02.28.

Sports : *UST Kayak,* 22, quai Barre, ☎ 53.84.52.22.

TOURTOIRAC

Périgueux 37, Brive 55, Paris 472
B1 ⊠ 24390 Hautefort

Hotels :
★★***Voyageurs*** (L.F.), ☎ 53.51.12.29. AE, DC, Visa. 11 rm Ⓟ 🌳 ♞ ♿ closed Jan, 180. Rest. 45-100.

Sainte-Orse, 8 km S :
France, pl. de la Mairie, ☎ 53.05.24.22. 10 rm 🌳 ⛱ closed Christmas school hols, 75. Rest. ♦ 35-100.

⛺ ★*Municipal* (16 pl.), ☎ 53.50.42.17.

TRÉMOLAT

Bergerac 34, Périgueux 54, Paris 639
B2 ⊠ 24150 Saint-Alvère

Hotel :
● ★★★***Le Vieux Logis*** (Relais et châteaux), ☎ 53.22.80.06, Tx 541025. AE, DC, Euro, Visa. 19 rm Ⓟ 🌳 ⛱ ♿ A 16thC vine-covered residence, 495. Rest. ♦♦♦ ♿ Choice fare at reasonable prices, 75-200.

⛺ ★★★*Centre nautique* (30 pl.), ☎ 53.22.81.18.

Sports : *aquatic sports centre.*

VALENCE

Montauban 46, Cahors 66, Paris 760
26 km SE of Agen, B4 ⊠ 82400

SNCF ☎ 53.39.50.75.

Hotel :
★★***Tout Va Bien,*** 35-37-39, rue de la République, ☎ 63.39.54.83. AE. 22 rm ⚟ Ⓟ ⛱ closed Jan, 145. Rest. ♦ 65-160.

⛺ ★★*Municipal* (33 pl.), ☎ 63.39.50.88.

Restaurant :
● ♦♦ ***La Campagnette,*** rte de Cahors, ☎ 63.39.65.97. Ⓟ 🌳 ⛱ ♿ closed Mon eve and Tue, 8-23 May and 8-20 Sep. Good value for money. Spec : *assiette 3 salades aux 3 foies de canard, magret de canard aux échalotes confites,* 120-210.

VAYRAC

Brive 33, Cahors 92, Paris 526
10 km E of Martel, C2 ♥ ⊠ 46110

SNCF ☎ 65.32.40.28.

Hotels :
★***Modern Hôtel,*** ☎ 65.32.50.53. 15 rm (and 24 rm-annex) 🌳 closed Oct and Sat, 110. Rest. ♿ 45-145.

Carennac, 7 km SE :
★***Fénelon*** (L.F.), ☎ 65.38.67.67. Visa. 22 rm ⚟ Ⓟ closed 1 Feb-10 Mar, 130. Rest. ♦ closed Fri and Sat noon, 50-125.

⛺ ★★*Les Granges* (200 pl.), ☎ 65.32.46.58.

VILLEFRANCHE-DU-PÉRIGORD

Cahors 40, Périgueux 85, Paris 584
B3 ⊠ 24550

ℹ mairie, ☎ 53.29.91.44.

SNCF ☎ 53.29.94.55.

Hotels :
★★***Commerce,*** ☎ 53.29.90.11. 29 rm, closed 1 Dec-1 Mar, 180. Rest. ♦♦ 80-130.

Goujounac, ⊠ 46250, 12 km SE :
Host. de Goujounac, ☎ 65.36.68.67. 7 rm, closed Oct and Mon low season, 100. Rest. ♦ Regional cooking, 80-130.

VILLENEUVE-SUR-LOT

Agen 29, Cahors 75, Paris 614
B3-4 ⊠ 47300

ℹ bd de la République, ☎ 53.70.31.37.

SNCF ☎ 53.70.00.35.

Hotels :
★★★***Parc*** (Mapotel), 13, bd de la Marine, ☎ 53.70.01.68, Tx 550379. AE, Visa. 42 rm Ⓟ ⛱ ♿ With flower-covered terrace, 215. Rest. ♦♦ ♿ closed Mon low season, 68-180.
★★***Résidence,*** 17, av. L.-Carnot, ☎ 53.70.17.03. 18 rm Ⓟ 🌳 ⛱ closed 10 Dec-15 Jan, 100.
★★***Glacier*** (L.F.), 23, rue A.-Daubasse, ☎ 53.70.70.14. 30 rm ⛱ ♿ 100. Rest. snacks, closed Mon, 80-130.
★***L'Espoir,*** 5, pl. de la Marine, ☎ 53.70.71.63. 9 rm Ⓟ ⛱ closed 20 Dec-10 Jan, 115.

Pujols, 4 km SW :
● ★★★***Les Chênes*** (Bel-Air), ☎ 53.49.04.55. AE, DC, Euro, Visa. 21 rm ⚟ Ⓟ 🌳 ⛱ ♿ closed 25 Nov-2 Dec, 24 Feb-4 Mar, 250.

Youth hostel : Cité Rieurs.

⛺ *Municipal de Rooy* (50 pl.), ☎ 53.70.24.18.

Restaurants :
Pujols :
● ♦♦ ***Auberge de la Toque Blanche,*** ☎ 53.49.00.30. AE, DC, Euro, Visa. Ⓟ 🌳 ⛱ ♞ ♿ closed Sun eve and Mon low season, Feb school hols, 23 Jun-8 Jul. Good regional produce from the neighbouring market, 95-210.

Teysset, ⊠ 47380 Monclar, 20 km W, D667 and D13 crossroads :
♦♦♦ ***Le Teysset,*** ☎ 53.79.95.56. AE, Visa. Ⓟ 🌳 ⛱ closed Thu and Fri noon and 15 Jan-1 Mar, 80-130.

Recommended : *la Maison du Pruneau d'Agen,* 5, porte de Paris, ☎ 53.70.30.86.

Alsace

Between the Vosges forest and Germany lies Alsace, perhaps the most unusual of all the French provinces. Even the French tourist sometimes feels as if he has entered a foreign country : landscape, architecture, lifestyle and even language (a Germanic dialect mixed in some parts with French to create a picturesque blend known as *"frangermal"*) are different from those he has left behind. But the hospitality of the inhabitants quickly dispels any feeling of strangeness. The Alsatian has always been conscious of his region's position as a hub of European civilization and despite his fight to retain his individuality and annexations by the region's powerful neighbor, he has remained open to the outside.

The picturesque streets of Colmar, studded with museums, churches and charming old buildings, combine cosmopolitan bustle with quiet provincial charm. Strasbourg has the jovial atmosphere of its wine bars or *winstubs,* the famous cathedral of Notre-Dame, Gothic splendor in delicately worked pink sandstone, and the prestige associated with the presence of the European Parliament. The half-timbered houses of the region contribute a great deal to the charm of its villages. The countryside is densely populated and most of the inhabitants live in villages, where each house is separated from its neighbors by a narrow passageway.

Alsace is famous too for its cuisine : sausages, black puddings, *foie gras,* vegetable and fruit tarts, the famous *choucroute* (sauerkraut), based on chopped cabbage marinated in brine, but differing subtly from one town to another, and the region's excellent white wines.

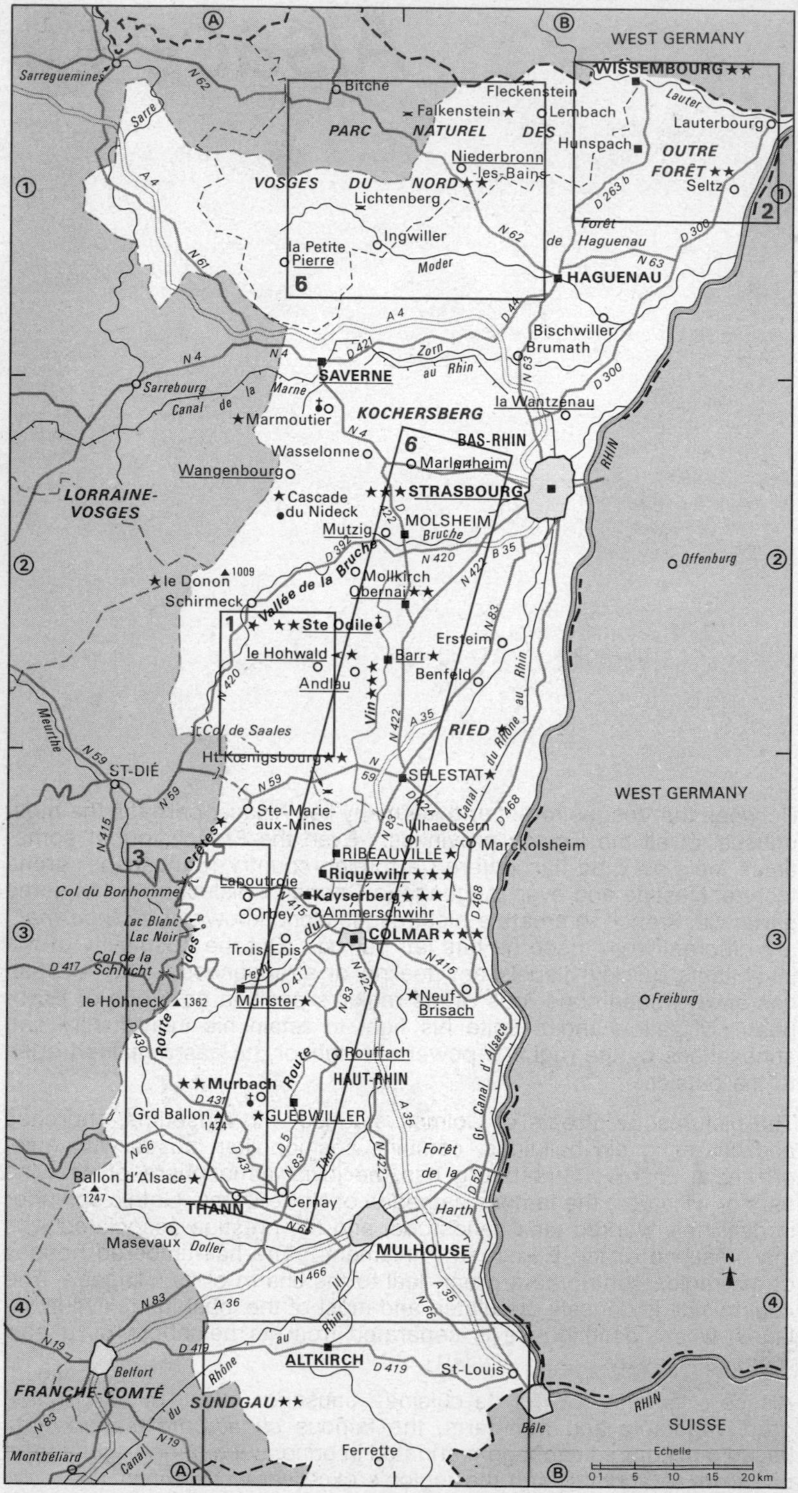
WEST GERMANY
WISSEMBOURG★★
Lauter
Lauterbourg
OUTRE FORÊT★★
Seltz
Bitche
Fleckenstein
Falkenstein★
Lembach
PARC NATUREL DES VOSGES DU NORD★★
Hunspach
Niederbronn -les-Bains
Lichtenberg
Ingwiller
la Petite Pierre
Moder
Forêt de Haguenau
HAGUENAU
Sarreguemines
Sarre
Bischwiller
Brumath
Zorn
SAVERNE
Sarrebourg
Canal de la Marne au Rhin
la Wantzenau
Marmoutier
KOCHERSBERG
BAS-RHIN
Wasselonne
Marlenheim
Wangenbourg
STRASBOURG
Cascade du Nideck
LORRAINE-VOSGES
MOLSHEIM
Mutzig
Bruche
Offenburg
le Donon
1009
Mollkirch
Vallée de la Bruche
Schirmeck
Obernai★★
Ste Odile
Ersteim
le Hohwald
Barr★
Benfeld
Andlau
Route du Vin
Col de Saales
RIED
Meurthe
Ht.Kœnigsbourg★★
SÉLESTAT★
ST-DIÉ
WEST GERMANY
Ste-Marie-aux-Mines
Route des Crêtes★
Canal du Rhône au Rhin
Ilhaeusern
Marckolsheim
RIBEAUVILLÉ★
Riquewihr★★★
Col du Bonhomme
Lapoutroie
Kayserberg★★★
Orbey
Ammerschwihr
Lac Blanc
Lac Noir
COLMAR★★★
Trois-Epis
Col de la Schlucht
Fecht
le Hohneck
1362
Munster★
Neuf-Brisach
Freiburg
Rouffach
HAUT-RHIN
Gr. Canal d'Alsace
★★Murbach
Grd Ballon
1424
GUEBWILLER
Forêt de la Harth
Thur
Ballon d'Alsace★
1247
Cernay
THANN
Masevaux
Doller
MULHOUSE
Ill
N
Belfort
ALTKIRCH
St-Louis
FRANCHE-COMTÉ
SUNDGAU★★
RHIN
Bâle
SUISSE
Montbéliard
Ferrette
Echelle
0 1 5 10 15 20 km

Sightseeing

Facts and figures

***Location :** At the eastern end of France on the Swiss and German borders, Alsace covers the eastern slopes of the Vosges mountains and the plain on the left bank of the Rhine. Three distinct regions : the Vosges mountains, the Vosges foothills (vineyards); the plain. North and south, the Outre-Forêt and the Sundgau (on the edge of the Jura mountains); NW,* Alsace Bossue *(hillocky Alsace) similar to Lorraine (→).*
***Area :** 8 280 km².*
***Climate :** Continental with wide temperature variations; the Vosges act as a barrier to Atlantic influence; little difference between North and South. Dry, hot summer (20 °-30 °C); misty but often beautiful autumn; dry, cold winter (av. 0 °); mild, bright spring.*
***Population :** 1 566 000; more than 400 000 in Strasbourg.*
Administration :
*Department of the **Haut-Rhin** (Upper Rhine; south), Prefecture Colmar; Department of the **Bas-Rhin** (Lower Rhine; north) Prefecture Strasbourg.*

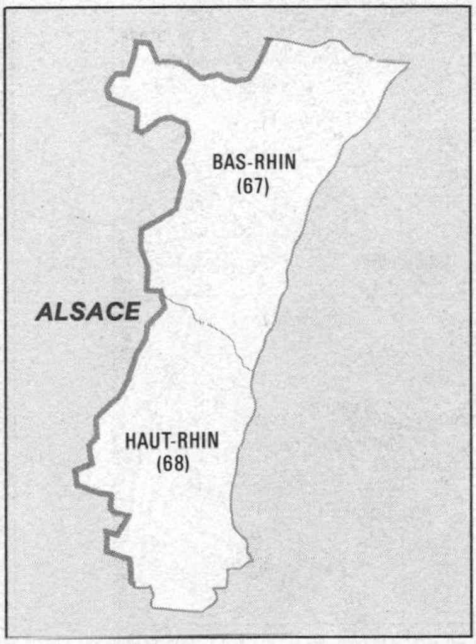

■ BALLON D'ALSACE★

A4

A peak at the southern end of the Vosges mountains, seeming to guard the Belfort Gap, the Ballon d'Alsace is easily accessible via three winding roads from Lorraine, Franche-Comté and Alsace.

Don't miss

★★★ : Colmar (A3), Kaysersberg (A3), Riquewihr (A3), Strasbourg (B2), The Wine Route (B2-A4).
★★ Haut-Koenigsbourg (A3), Mount Sainte-Odile (A2), Murbach (A3), Obernai (B2), Outre-Forêt (B1), Sundgau (A4), Northern Vosges (A-B1), Wissembourg (B1).

▶ From the Pass where these roads converge (restaurant; monument to WWII bomb disposal experts), *20 min walk to the summit* (orientation table, view★); walks. □

■ BARR★

A2 / ® / pop. 4 600 (Bas-Rhin)

On the Wine Road, the houses of Barr are arranged around the 17thC **town hall★ ;** the square is the scene of many local festivities.

▶ In the town, **Folie Marco Museum :** furniture, pottery, pewter, local souvenirs, in an 18thC mansion so luxurious that it was nicknamed *Folie* (madness); wine-tasting in the cellar *(open daily 10-12:30 & 2:30-6; ex Tue., Jul.-Sep.; Sat. & Sun. Jun. & Oct. closed rest of year).* ▶ West on D854, then a forest road to **châteaux of Spesbourg and Andlau :** (12thC; 14th-16thC) *30 min and 1hr round trip walk, respectively).* ▶ **Château Landsberg :** 12thC (D854, D109 then GR5; *1hr walk round trip*).

■ BRUCHE Valley

A2 (Bas-Rhin)

From Molsheim (→ Wine Road) to the **Saales Pass** (alt. 556 m), the valley follows the course of the river Bruche, between the sandstone of the northern Vosges and the crystalline rocks of southern Vosges.

▶ **Mutzig** ® : breweries. Follow the valley by

Weekend tips

Two suggestions : Strasbourg offers the flea-market in Rue du Vieil-Hôpital; cathedral and surroundings; the Rohan palace or the Musée de l'Oeuvre Notre Dame (museum of mediaeval art); lunch at a brewery or restaurant, followed by a historical or regional museum, Petite France, *the lively canal area, and the obligatory visit to a* winstub *(wine tavern). On Sunday, excursion to Obernai, Mount Sainte-Odile, Rosheim and Molsheim.*
Alternatively : Colmar, where the town and the Unterlinden Museum will take up all of Saturday, then a Sunday trip along the Wine Road to Kaysersberg, Riquewihr and Ribeauvillé with, if time allows, a climb to Haut-Koenigsbourg (note the timetable).

N420 (left bank) rather than the motorway. **Niederhaslach :** ® *(3 km N) :* at the edge of a forest, a 13th-14thC **abbey** showing influence of Strasbourg cathedral; stained glass window; tomb; 18thC stalls. ▶ **Guirbaden** *(7 km S) :* ruined castle on a rock; important fortress until the 17thC; view★. ▶ **Schirmeck** ® : summer and winter resort; capital of the valley; the textile industry replaced by engineering; **historical museum** *(2-7, Sun., hols. in season);* walks. Excursion to **Donon** ® : (alt. 1 009 m; *12 km drive & 15 min walk*) view★★★, via **Grandfontaine :** old **iron mine** open to the public *(2-6, Sat., Sun.).* ▶ **Struthof :** the only **WWII concentration camp** in France held 40 000 prisoners, of whom 10 000 were exterminated; huts, barbed-wire enclosure, watchtowers, gas-chamber; museum *(10-12 & 2-6 in summer; pm ex Tue. in winter);* National Deportation Cemetery. ▶ **Fouday** and neighbouring **Waldersbach :** museum in Protestant presbytery *(2-6 Wed., Fri., Sat., Sun. Easter-Sep.; 2-5 Sat., Sun. Nov.-Easter);* regional memories of Jean-Frédéric Oberlin (1740-1826), local pastor and philanthropist. □

■ COLMAR★★★

A3 / ® / pop. 63 700 (Haut-Rhin)

A popular French illustrator known as Hansi (a leader of French Resistance during WWI) was born in Colmar. The charm of this typical Alsatian town inspired his art. Capital of the Haut-Rhin department, Colmar is a busy city with a constant flow of business and tourism.

▶ Leave your car near the Champs-de-Mars (A-B2) under the protection of General Rapp, sculpted (like New York's Statue of Liberty) by Frédéric Bartholdi, and enter the **old town** by the Rue des Augustins. ▶ **Place du Marché aux Fruits** (fruit market square) : pink sandstone façade of the **Conseil Souverain d'Alsace★** (Supreme Council of Alsace, 1765 now a lawcourt) and Kern house with scrolled gable. ▶ **Krutenau district** (B3) : follow Rue St. Jean (house of the Knights of St. John, showing Italian influence); from the bridges over the river Lauch, views of flowered balconies and weeping willows; this area, known as **"Little Venice"★★,** is illuminated at night. ▶ Between the Lauch and the old Customs House is the **tanners' district,** (BC2) : the restored elegance of this flower-laden old quarter makes a pleasant backdrop to modern life. **Ancienne Douane★★** Old Customs House (15th-16thC) : the municipal magistrates and town council used to meet on the first floor; a passage through the building leads to the **Grande-Rue★** (main street; B2) with interesting houses (No. 15, Maison des Arcades 1606) and the Protestant **church of St. Mathieu :** choir-screen★, 14th-15thC stained glass; behind the church, Louis XV façade of the former hospital. ▶ Rue des Marchands (B2) **half-timbered houses★★** and mansions : **Pfister House★★** at the corner of Rue Mercière (1537; frescos, oriel window, galleries); Nos. 32, 34, 38, 44, 48; at No. 30, **Bartholdi Museum** (sculptor's work;

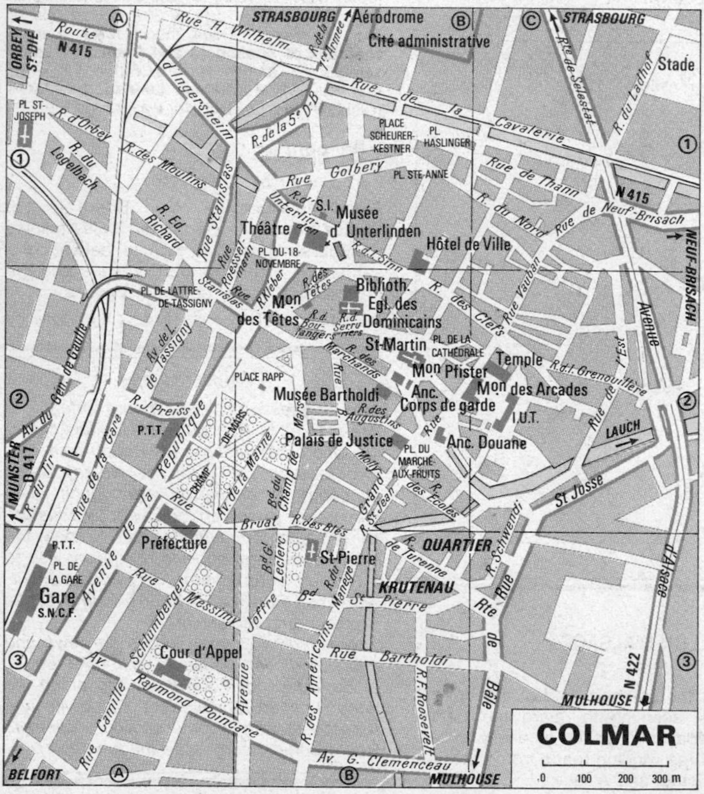

local history; *10-12 & 2-6, Apr.-Oct.; Sat., Sun. rest of year);* Rue Schongauer, the **Maison du Cygne★** (House of the Swan). ▶ Former **Guard-house** (1575; B2) and other old houses line the cathedral square; the cathedral is the former **collegiate church of St. Martin★★** (13th-14thC; sculptures on the E and S doorways; 19thC choir stalls★). ▶ **Dominican church★★** (B2) : nave, typical Rhineland Gothic; 14thC stained glass windows★; 1473 **Virgin with Rose Bush★★★** *(10-6, 23 Mar.-15 Nov.).* **Maison des Têtes★★** (17thC), in the street of the same name. ▶ **Unterlinden Museum★★★ :** (B1; *9-12 & 2-6 or 5 in winter; closed Tue., hols. out of season*) Unterlinden (under the lime trees), a Dominican convent from the 13thC to 1790 now a superb museum; **cloister★;** archaeology, mediaeval and Renaissance sculpture, stained glass windows, mediaeval paintings (Martin Schongauer altarpiece★★, Nativity★; **Issenheim altarpiece★★★** →), **modern art, Alsatian folk art** (furniture, iron-work, toys, winepresses). □

■ GUEBWILLER

A3/ ® / pop. 11 080 (Haut-Rhin)

Three churches, three styles : three ages in the history of Guebwiller, an industrial town (textiles, engineering) at the entrance to the Lauch valley, once controlled by the abbey of Murbach.

▶ **Church of Notre-Dame★★ :** 18thC French neo-Classical structure, now a Protestant church; Baroque choir★ (stalls★) showing Austrian influence. ▶ **Dominican church★ :** Gothic, mediaeval frescos; concerts. **Florival Museum :** art and local history displays in the church *(1 May-30 Oct., weekdays ex Tue., 2-5, weekends and hols. 10-12 & 2-5; 1 Nov.-30 Apr., weekends, hols. only, same hours).* ▶ Church of **St. Léger★** : oldest in town (12th-13thC), Romanesque façade★, doorway★ and nave; Gothic choir. ▶ 16thC town hall (Hôtel de Ville). □

▶ Nearby

▶ **Lauch Valley★** (Guebwiller) : called "Florival" (Vale of Flowers) for its floral charm. The ridge road leads to **Buhl** ® : 15thC altarpiece★ in neo-Romanesque church; then to **Lautenbach :** restored Romanesque church, portico★, Baroque pulpit★★, Gothic cloister. ▶ **Ungersheim** (8 km SE) : the Upper Alsace Ecomuseum displays about twenty peasant houses which recreate an Alsatian village. *(Jun.-21 Sep., daily 10-8; 22 Sep.-21 Dec., 10-7; 22 Dec-May, 11-5 on request.)* □

■ HAGUENAU

B1 / ® / pop. 38 000 (Bas-Rhin)

This mediaeval town on the river Moder is the gateway to Northern Alsace.

▶ Activity is centred on the pedestrian precinct around the **Grande-Rue** (main street) : 18thC houses on the Place d'Armes. ▶ **Church of St. Georges★ :** built over 5 centuries; Romanesque nave, Flamboyant Gothic vaulting and tabernacle★ in the choir; 15thC altarpiece in the right transept. ▶ **Alsatian Museum★ :** furniture, shop signs, tools, costumes, folk art *(8-12 & 2-6; Sat., Sun. 2-5 closed Tue.).* ▶ **Library** (early 20thC) : historical museum of archaeology, coins *(9-12 & 3-6; weekends 3-5:30; closed Tue.).* ▶ **Church of St. Nicolas :** 14th-15thC; statues, furnishings. □

▶ Nearby

▶ N of town : **Haguenau Forest,** the largest in Alsace (137 km^2; pine, oak, hornbeam and beech). At the edge of the forest, church of **Walbourg★** (15thC). ▶ **Soufflenheim** *(14 km E)* : pottery industry, as at Betschdorf (→ Outre-Forêt). ▶ **Sessenheim** *(4 km farther)* : place of pilgrimage for admirers of the German poet Johann Wolfgang von Goethe (1749-1832), who stayed here long enough to have an affair with the daughter of the pastor in 1770-71; Protestant church; Goethe memorial *(9-12 & 2-7).* ▶ **Marienthal** ® *(5.5 km SE) :* site of pilgrimage to the Virgin since the 12thC. ▶ **Pfaffenhofen :** *(14 km W)* centre of peasant revolts in 1525; **museum of folk art★★** *(2-5, Wed., Sat., Sun.);* Bertrand Uberech distillery *(visits by request, tel. 88.07.70.33.* ▶ **Morsbronn-lès-Bains** ® *(11 km N) :* thermal spa, leisure park.

■ HAUT-KOENIGSBOURG★★

A3 ® (Haut-Rhin)

▶ Remodelled to suit the German Kaiser Wilhelm II at the beginning of the 20thC; a feudal fortress behind triple ramparts; several rooms with 15th-16thC furnishings; weapons; festival hall★; chapel, forge, mill; **view★★.** ▶ **Oedenbourg** *(200m W) :* ruins of **castle** (12th-13thC).

■ The HOHWALD Region★

▶ Round trip *(59 km, half-day)*

A2 *(see map 1)* (Bas-Rhin)

The land of the cherry-flavoured liqueur kirsch (Val de Villé; visit to the distilleries in Bassemberg, Steige and on the "kirsch route", D 39), and the heart of central Vosges; a tour through the range of Vosges landscapes.

▶ **Villé** : tourist centre at the junction of several valleys *(signposted hikes).* **Albé,** 1 km N : traditional houses; **museum of Val de Villé** *(2:30-6 Sun. Wed., Sat. in summer).* ▶ The road climbs to Kreuzweg Pass (alt. 768 m; view★), then drops to **Hohwald★★** ® : attractive summer and winter resort with scattered villas and chalets between alt. 600 m and 1 100 m; walks (Hohwald waterfall★★, 45 min; Ungersberg summit, 2hr). ▶ The road climbs

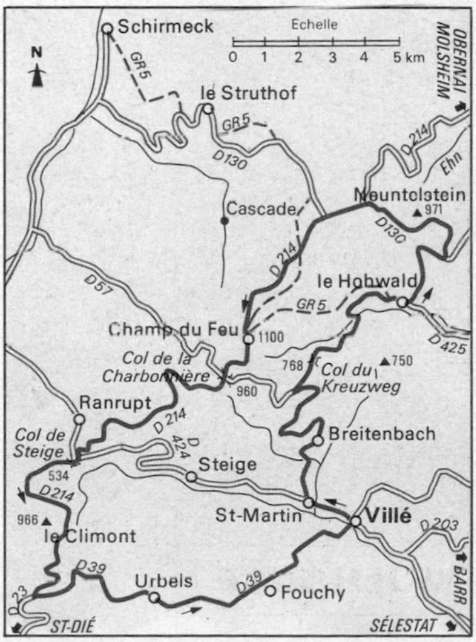

1. Hohwald region

the side of **Neuntelstein** (alt. 971 m; view★★). Leave right D310 to Struthof (→ Bruche Valley). ▶ **Champ du Feu** plateau★ : downhill and cross-country skiing; view★★ from the lookout tower. ▶ Other lookouts on the way down to **Steige Pass** (alt. 534 m). ▶ **Urbeis :** country town at the foot of Bilstein castle ruins.

■ The KOCHERSBERG Region

A-B2 (Bas-Rhin)

Kochersberg, once the granary of Strasbourg, is a rich agricultural region NW of the city; cereals, tobacco and hops trained on high trellises create a distinctive chequered landscape.
▶ **Truchtersheim :** local **museum** *(Sun. 2:30-6).* ▶ **Wasselonne** ® : on the edge of the Kochersberg; mediaeval remains and old houses. ▶ **Hohatzenheim,** *(16 km NE) :* Romanesque church★. □

■ MARMOUTIER★

A2 / ® / pop. 2 000 (Bas-Rhin)

Benedictine monastery founded in the 6thC; Rhineland Romanesque abbey-church **façade**★★ (1150); Gothic nave with 18thC choir; Louis XV stalls★; 18thC organ (concerts). Small **museum** in the village *(1 May-30 Sept., Sun., 10-12 & 2-7).* □

Tobacco in Alsace

Tobacco is grown south of Strasbourg in the Ried, and in the Kochersberg. Alsace is the most important producer in France, after Bergerac. Blond Virginia varieties are being grown increasingly to replace brown tobacco. The crop is processed in Obernai at the HQ of SEITA, the French state tobacco monopoly (visits Jun.-Sep.). *Cigars and cigarillos are produced at the Strasbourg factory* (morning visits Mon. to Fri.). *A "tobacco road" runs through the growing areas.*

■ MULHOUSE

A4 / ® / pop. 113 700 (Haut-Rhin)

The town and district of Mulhouse (total pop. ca. 250 000) can be seen from the top of the Tour de l'Europe (Tower of Europe; C2). Traditional industries include textiles and potash mining *(NW of town).* Dynamic cultural life includes music, theatre, dance, museums.

▶ **Hôtel de Ville**★ (1552; B2); historical museum *(10-12 & 2-5 or 6, closed Tue.; Thu.*

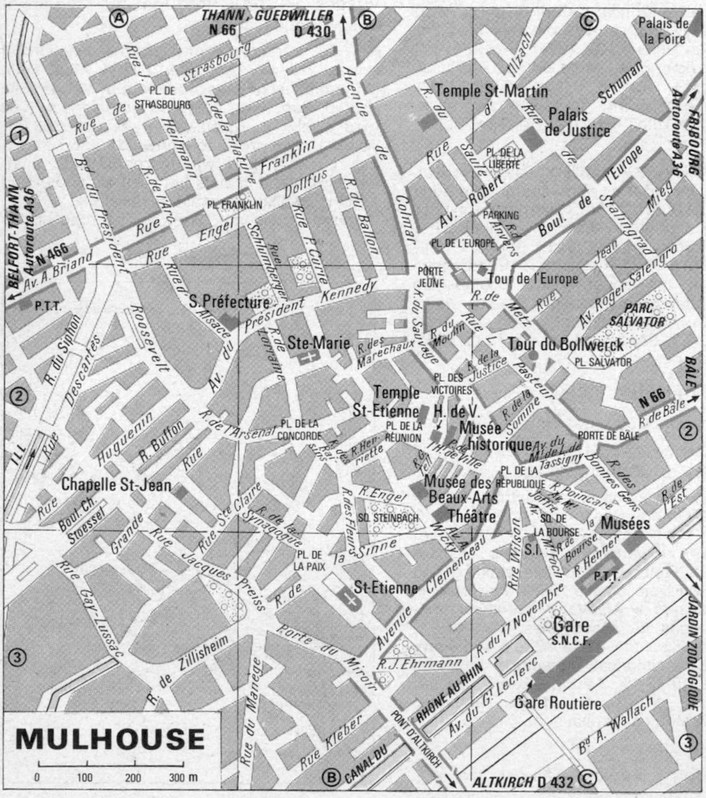

8:30 pm-10:30 pm); ▶ Protestant **church of St. Etienne :** 14thC stained glass★. **Fine Arts Museum** and Lapidary Museum in the chapel of St. Jean (murals) ▶ **Fabric Printing Museum★★ :** (C3; *10-12 & 2-6 closed Tue. and hols)* no fewer than ten million samples from which manufacturers still derive inspiration; techniques and motifs since the 18thC; demonstration of machinery *(Mon. & Wed. am)*. ▶ **Musée du Chemin de Fer** (Railway Museum)★★★; *(1 Apr.-30 Sep., 9-6; 1 Oct.-31 Mar., 10-5; closed hols)* signposted from the Belfort road; the largest railway museum in Europe; small-scale models, miniature network; exceptional items on 860 m of rails in the great hall; first European steam locomotive; Napoleon III's private car decorated by the 19thC architect Eugène Viollet-le-Duc (1814-79); carriages from the great European express trains; locomotive "Pacific 231"; posters; platform equipment, accessories. ▶ Annex with **Musée du Sapeur-Pompier** (Firemen's Museum) : equipment, uniforms and vehicles from 18thC to present day. ▶ **National Automobile Museum★★★** (192, avenue de Colmar; *11-6, closed Tue.)* The Schlumpf brothers' collection of 440 European cars of all periods, in working order; 122 Bugattis, including two of the six Royales from the Molsheim Bugatti works; Mercedes, Hispano-Suiza, Rolls-Royce, Peugeot, Citroën, Panhard, Renault, as well as famous racing cars. □

▶ Nearby

▶ To the E, the dense **Hardt Forest** (hornbeam, oak). **Ottmarsheim** *(11 km)* **: octagonal Romanesque church★★** inspired by the 11thC Imperial chapel at Aix-la-Chapelle (Aachen). ▶ **Ensisheim** *(14 km N)* : town hall★ and Renaissance houses. □

The wines of Alsace

The vineyards of Alsace cover a total of 110 km² fragmented into about 12 000 holdings. The wines are classified not by grades within district of origin, as in the rest of France, but rather according to the seven permitted grape varieties, plus an eighth wine blended from a selection of the seven. Varieties are : Sylvaner, fruity, light and fresh; Riesling, fruity, delicately perfumed; Gewürztraminer, flowery, spicy and elegant; Muscat d'Alsace, dry, the ideal aperitif; Tokay (Pinot Gris), opulent and full; Pinot Blanc, rounded and balanced; Pinot Noir, dry, fruity red or rosé. The eighth, Edelzwicker, combining several varieties, is the white wine for everyday consumption. All the wines of Alsace, in distinctive slender bottles, are consumed young and cool.

■ MUNSTER Valley★

A3 (Haut-Rhin)

A valley watered by the Fecht and dotted with farm-inns where you can sample *tourte* (pies) and the celebrated Alsace cheeses.

▶ **Soultzbach-les-Bains :** spa, table waters; flowers; church and 15thC chapel inside the ramparts. ▶ **Gunsbach :** on the left bank of the Fecht; **house of Albert Schweitzer** (1875-1965), doctor, musician, winner of the Nobel Peace Prize (museum, *9-12 & 2-6;* **African art museum,** *weekdays 2-5, 15 Jul.-15 Sep.)*; ecumenical church, used by both Catholics and Protestants. ▶ **Munster** ® (pop. 5 000) : grew around a 7thC abbey; ideal stopover; signposted walks; covered market and town hall; weaving factory; spa. ▶ **Muhlbach** ® : Log Transport (Schlitte) Museum *(7 Jul.-1 Sep., 3-6)*. Farther on, after **Metzeral :** walk to the **lakes of Fischboedle and Schiessrothried** *(1 hr & 2 hr walk, respectively, round trip)*. □

▶ Nearby

▶ 11 km from Munster, via winter resort of Hohrodberg **Linge Pass★ :** battlefield with trenches and 1915 memorial. ▶ **Lake Vert :** *(14 km via Schlucht pass road, then right)*. □

Storks

The Alsatians are attached to these birds, the emblem of their province, and were extremely concerned when only three pairs of storks returned to Alsace for the summer of 1981. The main reasons for this disappearance seem to be the draining of marshes and winter-time hunting in Africa. The Alsatians are attempting to rebuild the population by mating wild birds with storks reared in captivity; the baby storks migrate as do their wild forebears. There are several "stork parks" in Alsace, the main one at Kintzhzeim (→ Wine Road).

■ MURBACH★★

A3 (Haut-Rhin)

Abbey church of pink sandstone amid the valley greenery, although damaged (nave destroyed in the 18thC), the most beautiful Romanesque church in Alsace.

▶ Hermits lived at the site before the abbey was founded in 727. A century later its influence extended to the Palatinate (West Germany) and Switzerland. The abbots of Murbach, always from the higher nobility, were Princes of the Holy Roman Empire. The abbey was sacked during the French Revolution (1789). ▶ Choir and transept, flanked by two towers framing the square apse, are decorated with blind arcades and pierced with semicircular bays. □

■ NEUF-BRISACH★

B3 / ® / pop. 2 200 (Haut-Rhin)

A fortress built in the late 17thC by Louis XIV's military engineering genius Sebastien de Vauban (1633-1707). Neuf (new) Brisach faces Vieux (old) Brisach on the opposite river bank, once Austrian, now German.

▶ An octagonal **enclosure★★** with canals, bastions and forts surrounds the symmetrical town centred on the place d'Armes (church of St. Louis, altarpiece★). Two of the four gates still remain; in the Belfort Gate, the **Vauban museum** *(9-11 & 2-5 closed Tue.;* model★ of the town). □

▶ Nearby

▶ **Rhine island** leisure area near the **Vogelgrün** lock (view★; motel, camp-site, swimming

Alsace

pool); industrial area to N. ▶ **Rhine tourist train** *(Sun. and nat. hols., Jun.-Sep.)* to Marckolsheim. □

■ NIEDERBRONN-LES-BAINS

B1 / ® / pop. 4 440 (Haut-Rhin)

Two springs gave rise to the town; both Celts and Romans bathed in the waters (municipal museum : *on request, tel. 88.09.17.00).* Good base for excursions in the Northern Vosges (→); Alsace's only casino.

▶ Walks; parks and gardens in the town; **Wasenbourg castle** (15thC; *1 hr walk; view*); Ziegenberg; Celtic campsite *(NW, 1 hr).* □

▶ Nearby

▶ **Vieux-Windstein castle** *(7 km N)* : 1212, partly hollowed out of the rock; 500 m away, **Nouveau-Windstein castle** (1340); 10 km away *(still on D53)* ruins of **Wineck** and **Schoeneck castles.** ▶ **Reichshoffen** *(3 km SE).* □

■ OBERNAI★★

A-B2 / ® / pop. 9 440 (Bas-Rhin)

At the foot of Mount Sainte-Odile, on the Wine Road. **Place du Marché★ :** the heart of town; old houses behind ruined ramparts; **corn market★** (Halle aux Blés); 16thC town hall; Renaissance well★ . The town was the 7thC birthplace of Ste. Odile (patron of Alsace), and a member of the 14thC Decapol (→ Brief Regional History). Active industries are located outside the town walls. □

■ ORBEY

A3 / ® / pop. 3 140 (Haut-Rhin)

Orbey, like the neighbouring commune of **Lapoutroie** ®, is an ideal stopover for peace and quiet and country walks (Grand Faudé *45 min;* Pierre-du-Loup *20 min;* Noirmont *3 km + 15 min;* Tête-du-Faux *2 hr).*

▶ The **Orbey Valley (Orbey, Fréland, Lapoutroie, Hachimette, Le Bonhomme** and **Labaroche**), has been a French-speaking enclave since the 16thC; Munster cheese production centre. ▶ **Lakes Noir** and **Blanc :** *(8 km and 10 km)* pleasant, among firs and rocks; the lakes, linked by a force-feed duct, produce 60 000 kW/hr; water from the first lake is pumped back into the second during off-peak periods. □

■ The OUTRE-FORÊT Region★★

Round trip (approx 75 km, full day)
B1 *(see map 2)* (Bas-Rhin)

In the extreme NE of France, between Wissembourg and the forest of Haguenau, this borderland of cultivated hillsides has often been a battle-ground; here and there can be seen the structures of the **Maginot Line** (→). Today, the villages are peaceful and flowery, with half-timbered houses (18th-19thC) in tidy streets. In this devoutly Protestant area with long-standing traditions, regional costumes are still occasionally worn.

The Alsatian dialect

Alsatian is neither a variation of French nor a separate language, but a distinct Germanic dialect, spoken by all generations. There are many local variations, especially from north to south : a person from the Sundgau could more easily understand someone from Basle in Switzerland than a fellow Alsatian from Wissembourg. The Alsatian dialect is continually being enriched and transformed; where French words predominate, it is the picturesque and widespread Frangermal. *An extensive literature in the dialect includes poetry and plays; colourful use of Alsatian can be heard at the satirical reviews performed by Germain Muller at his Strasbourg cabaret, the Barabli. Works in French and German also co-exist.*

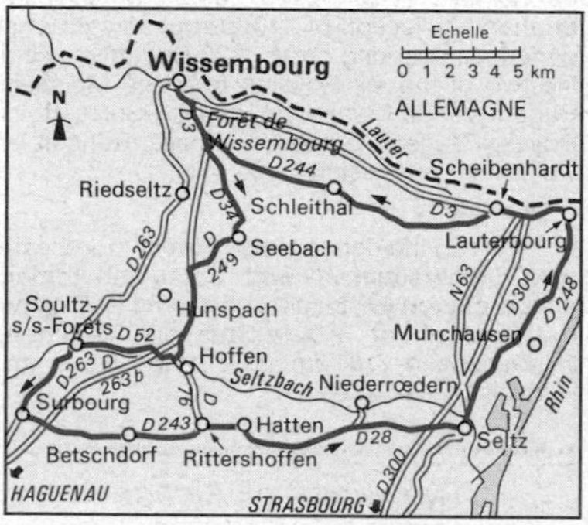

2. Outre-Forêt region

▶ **Seebach★** (formerly Oberseebach and Niederseebach) : one of the first villages on the itinerary, with traditional houses among less distinctive buildings. ▶ **Hunspach★★★ :** the most uniform village, with sloping streets leading to public buildings grouped in the square. ▶ **Schoenenbourg★★** *(2 km E)* : on the Maginot Line (open weekends). ▶ **Hoffen★★★ :** town hall with wooden columns. ▶ **Soultz-sous-Forêts :** belonged to the powerful Rohan-Soubise family in the 18thC. **Merkwiller-Pechelbronn** *(4 km W)* : thermal spa once exploited for oil (museum : *3-5, Sun. Jul.-Aug.).* ▶ **Surbourg :** Rhenish Romanesque church★, the abbey that once stood here. ▶ **Betschdorf★ :** pottery (blue decoration on a grey ground) in shops and workshops on the main street (museum, Rue Kuhlendorf : *1 May-30 Jun., Sep. 2-5, closed Mon.; 1 Jul.-30 Aug., Sun., hols., 10-12 & 2-5);* 15thC frescos in the church; half-timbered houses. ▶ **Kuhlendorf** *(2 km N)* : church. ▶ **Hatten :** entirely destroyed in 1945. ▶ **Seltz :** Roman in origin; tourist centre with shore, sailing, ferry across the Rhine. On the right of the road to **Munchhausen** and **Mothern :** marshy forest area, with unusual flora and fauna now fast disappearing. ▶ **Lauterbourg** ® : (pop. 2 460) once fortified by Vauban. ▶ **Schleital :** one-street village with houses lined up for 4 km. □

■ RIBEAUVILLÉ★

A3 / ® / pop. 4 600 (Haut-Rhin)

Modest but attractive town on the Upper Rhine, once headquarters of the itinerant musicians' guild. The **Grande-Rue** (main street) is straddled by the **Tour des Bouchers★** (Butchers' tower 13th-16thC); flower-decked fountains and carefully restored houses; Gothic church (organ casing★); small **museum** in the town hall (silver and silver-gilt goblets), unfortunately rarely open. □

▶ Nearby

▶ Three castles : 45 min walk to **castle of St Ulrich★** (12th-14thC, once the residence of the powerful Ribeaupierre family); opposite, ruins of **Girsberg castle,** or "Petit Ribeaupierre"; another 15 min walk to the **castle of Haut-Ribeaupierre** (Altenkastel; 13thC; 15thC keep★); view★. ▶ From Ribeauvillé, good roads to Sainte-Marie-aux-Mines and, via Aubure, to **Fréland Pass,** in the heart of the Vosges. □

■ The RIDGE Road★ (Route des Crêtes)

▶ From Cernay to the Bonhomme Pass *(77 km)*

A3-4 *(see map 2)* (Haut-Rhin)

Partly built during WWI to serve the Front, the ridge road is now the main tourist route in the Upper Vosges, with views of the hillside fields (Hautes Chaumes), and pine and beech woods. Roads and footpaths connect, and farm-inns are dotted along the way.

▶ **Cernay** ® (pop. 10 300) : badly damaged during the two World Wars, now an industrial and wine-making centre at an important crossroads; 13thC town gate; stork park; Doller Valley tourist steam-train *(at the level crossing on D66, Sun. and nat. hols., May-Oct., daily ex Mon. and Tue. in Jul.-Aug.; 1hr round trip to Sentheim; info. tel. 89.82.88.48).* ▶ Leaving **Mount Molkenrain** (alt. 1 125 m) on the left, the road winds up to **Vieil-Armand★★ :** site of an 8-month battle in 1914-15; National Monument; cemetery; from the summit, view★ over the battlefield. **Ballon de Guebwiller★★** ® (Grand Ballon Mountain, alt. 1 424 m) : highest point of the Vosges *(15 min hike to the top, view★★)*; Diables Bleus (Blue Devils) monument to Hunters' Battalions; signposted paths (e.g., Ballon lake). ▶ **Le Markstein** ® : a renowned summer and winter resort; starting point for hikes (road★★ to the valley of the Lauch and Guebwiller). ▶ **Hahnenbrunnen Pass** (alt. 1 180 m) : from the farm, view★ over the the Fecht Valley. **Herrenberg Pass** (alt. 1 186 m) : to the right, **Mount Rainkopf** (alt. 1 304 m). ▶ **Mount Honeck** (alt. 1 362 m) : 1.5 km access road; orientation table at one of the best **panoramas** in the Vosges. ▶ **Schlucht Pass :** winter sports and excursion centre; highest pass in the mountains (alt. 1 139 m) **Haut-Chitelet** *(2 km SE) :* alpine garden *(Jun.-Oct.).* ▶ To the right, paths, views over the **lakes (Vert, Noir, Blanc); Calvaire Pass** (alt. 1 134 m). ▶ The road descends to the **Bonhomme Pass** (alt. 949 m), Franco-German border in 1871. To the right, road down to **Le Bonhomme** ® (can also be reached via **Bagenelles Pass★,** *11 km detour*).□

■ RIQUEWIHR★★★

A3 / ® / pop. 1 040 (Haut-Rhin)

This town is described as a "pearl" among the vineyards that surround it. For several centuries it was the property of the eccentric dukes of Wurtemberg. Houses built by wine-growers in the 16th and 17thC, like the rest of the town, are exceptionally well-preserved. Riquewihr produces excellent Riesling.

▶ The houses are built against the rectangular **fortifications.** The town offers many treasures for the eye : **oriel windows,** sculpted galleries, doorways, **fountains** and wells, yards and passages, shop signs, and flowers everywhere from May to Oct. The **main street** (Rue du Général de Gaulle) leads from the town hall to the **Dolder★** (13thC gate; small museum, as also in the Tour des Voleurs (Thieves' Tower); *9-12 & 1:30-6 Sat., Sun., Easter-1 Nov.; daily Jul.-Aug.),* and the Obertor, gate of the second enclosure. ▶ Château of the Wurtemberg-Montbéliard : (16thC) now an attractive historical **Museum of the French Post, Telegraph**

3. Ridge road (Route des Crêtes)

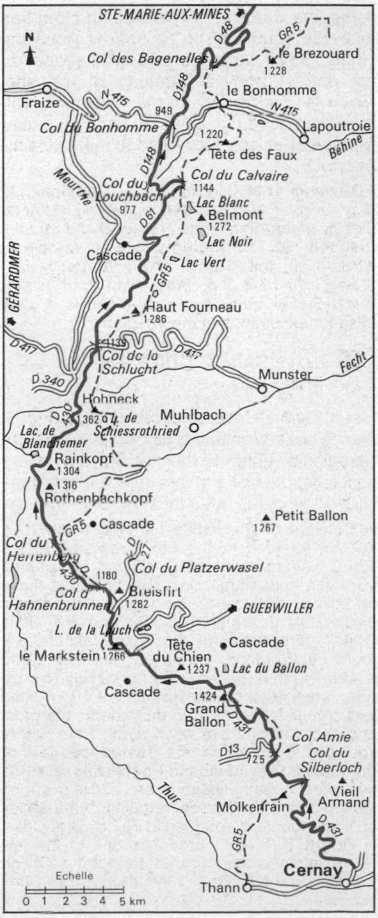

The Issenheim altarpiece

The Colmar museum is the most popular French museum outside of Paris, largely because of the altarpiece painted by Mathias Grünewald (1460-1528), for the Issenheim hospital chapel. The sick were shown scenes from the altarpiece appropriate to the phases of the liturgical calendar, or the sections carved by the contemporary Nicolas de Haguenau. According to chroniclers of the time, the impact of the work was therapeutic.
The subjects portrayed are mediaeval in character, but the use of form and colour shows Renaissance influence.

and Telecommunications (PTT) office : documents, costumes, models from early times to the present day *(10-12 & 2-6, 3-7 Sun.; closed Tue. ex. Jul.-Aug., Sun., hols, 10-12 & 3-6).* □

SAINTE-MARIE-AUX-MINES

A3 / ® / pop. 6 530 (Haut-Rhin)

Although mines supplying silver, lead, copper, cobalt and arsenic gave the town its name, the weaving of fine woolen cloth has been the source of its prosperity since the 18thC. Small factories and workshops do not detract from the beauty of the site, which is a widening of the Liepvrette valley. Passage to Lorraine has become easier with the opening of the road tunnel to Saint-Dié *(toll)*.

▶ **Museum of Mining and Local Traditions** *(30 Rue Wilson; 10-12 & 2-6 Jul.-Aug.).* Mineral Exhibition and Exchange *(1st weekend in Jul.).* **Disused St. Barthélemy silver mine★★,** worked in the 16thC *(Whit-Sunday; Jul.-5 Sep.; 10-12 & 2-6, Sun., Mon. of Whitsun, 2 last Sun of Jun.).* ▶ Sainte-Marie is a good base for excursions in the Vosges. □

Mount SAINTE-ODILE ★★

A2 / ® (Bas-Rhin)

Mount-Sainte-Odile, the patronal shrine of Alsace, was probably a sacred place before Christianity entered the region. Its history and location make it not just a pilgrimage site for the pious but a must on any itinerary.

▶ **Convent of Ste. Odile :** a Roman site (alt. 761 m) founded in the 8thC, restored in the 12thC; devastated many times, reoccupied from the mid-19thC on. The buildings have no special distinction, apart from the chapels of the Holy Cross (11th-12thC) and Ste. Odile (12thC; 8thC tomb of the saint); almshouse. From the terraces, **view★★★** over the plain. ▶ **Mur Païen★** (pagan wall) : originally Bronze Age, remodelled by the Romans, a 10 km long wall completely enclosing the mount; the most apparent remains are near D426, from where you can also reach the ruined **castles of Birkenfels, Dreysteim** and **Hagelschloss.** ▶ Via the road to Saint-Nabor : Ste. Odile's spring *(600 m away)*; farther on, remains of the abbey of Niedermunster, founded in 707 by Ste. Odile. ▶ **Ottrott** ® *(8 km)* : produces one of the few red Alsatian wines; **tourist train** from Ottrott to Rosheim *(16 km; 1 hr round trip Sun., Jul.-Sep.).* □

SAVERNE

A1 / ® / pop. 10 480 (Bas-Rhin)

When in 1770, Goethe (→ Sessenheim) was invited to the palace of Cardinal de Rohan, he was astonished by the luxury of the stables. Goethe's surprise suggests the splendour of the "Alsatian Versailles", surrounded today by a town that was for 5 centuries the property of the Rohan family.

▶ On the banks of the Marne-Rhine canal (pleasure craft), flowered paths lead to the most beautiful façade of the **palace★★,** built in red sandstone in the late 18thC in neo-Classical style. Place du Général de Gaulle : more austere, but still elegant *(10-12 & 3-5, Sun. and nat. hols.; 2:30-6 daily ex. Tue., 15 Jun.-15 Sep.).* ▶ Old houses near the town hall in the **Grande-Rue** (main street). ▶ **Rose garden** (1 300 varieties) on the bank of the river Zorn *(9-12 & 2-7, Jun.-Sep.; Rose Festival Jun.);* **botanical garden** *(3.5 km NW via N4; 9-6 Jun.-Sep.).* □

▶ Nearby

▶ W of Saverne : ruined **castle of Haut-Barr★** (12th-16thC, "the Eye of Alsace"), and Géroldseck, attractive sites facing the plain. Not far from Haut-Barr : restored optical telegraph installed by the engineer Claude Chappe (1763-1803) in 1794 (museum). From the ruins, GR53 takes hikers south towards the summit of Mount Brotschberg (*30 min*; 531 m), then to the ruins of **Ochsenstein castle** *(3 hr 30).* ▶ Church of **St. Jean-Saverne :** *(5 km;* worth a visit) Romanesque building (only remains of Benedictine abbey) with 18thC gate-tower; inside, 16thC tapestries. ▶ Artzwiller inclined plane → Sarrebourg, Lorraine. □

SÉLESTAT★

A-B3 / ® / pop. 15 400 (Bas-Rhin)

An old city supposed to have been founded by a giant. It was a residence of Charlemagne, later part of the Holy Roman Empire and a member of the Decapol (→ Brief Regional History). From the Middle Ages, Sélestat was renowned for its university and school of Humanism in the 15th-16thC.

Ste. Odile

Odile was born in the 7thC, the blind daughter of a cruel duke of Alsace who had hoped for a son and wanted the infant killed. Spirited away from the court by a nurse, Odile recovered her sight when she was baptised in a convent in the Jura mountains. She came back to Alsace and miraculously escaped the marriage planned for her by her father, now reconciled to having a daughter and hoping to profit from the fact. The father eventually became resigned to the Divine Will as interpreted by Odile, and had a convent built for her. The flood of aspirants drawn by Odile's faith necessitated a second convent, which was built below the first (Niedermunster). Odile was canonised in the 11thC by the Alsatian Pope Leo IX; in 1946 she was proclaimed patron saint of Alsace.

▶ **Humanist Library★★ :** books from the 7thC on : manuscripts, incunabula and works of art. (B1; *9-12 & 3-5; closed Sat. am and Sun.).* ▶ **Church of St. Georges :** Gothic (13th 15thC); ancient and modern stained glass, Renaissance pulpit★. Nearby, **abbey church of Ste. Foy★★ :** (C1) one of the finest Romanesque churches in Alsace despite 19thC restoration. ▶ Walk through the winding streets in the heart of the town to admire towers, old houses and sculpted doorways, with boulevards following the line of the ancient fortifications. □

▶ Nearby

▶ **Ebermunster** *(8 km NE) :* domed **abbey church** in the middle of the Alsatian plain; this Austrian Baroque sanctuary (1719) replaced a church destroyed during the Thirty Years' War; gold, stucco, frescos, curves and counter-curves form a theatrical monument. ▶ **Benfeld** *(11 km farther on) :* main centre for Alsatian tobacco (festival end Aug.); town hall with 16thC Jack-o'-the-Clock. ▶ Not far from the Rhine in **Marckolsheim** *(15 km SE) :* **Maginot Line** pill-box, now a memorial museum with Sherman tank, Soviet cannon *(9-12 & 2-6, Sun. and nat. hols.; daily 15 Jun.-15 Sep.; closed 15 Nov.-15 Mar.);* **Rhine tourist train** (→ Neuf-Brisach). □

■ STRASBOURG★★★

B2 / ® / pop. 252 200 (400 000 with surrounding area) (Bas-Rhin)
See plan on following page

Strasbourg is irrigated by the two arms of the Ill river and the canals that flow into it. It is a city with two identities, one European and international, the other Alsatian and full of provincial charm. Under the lofty vaults of the cathedral, on the flowery quays of Petite France where picturesque 16thC houses line the canals, or in the warm atmosphere of a wine tavern where the tantalising smell of ham baked in a crust mingles with the bouquet of a glass of Edelzwicker, past and present blend in harmonious well-being.

▶ **Place Kléber** (C3) : a popular meeting place disfigured by unattractive shopfronts; even the **Aubette★,** an 18thC guardhouse, has been defaced. A better starting point for a walking tour is **place Gutenberg** (C3; carpark; TO in the Renaissance **Chamber of Commerce★★★**). ▶ **Rue Mercière :** half-timbered houses, leads to the cathedral : in front, the **Pharmacie du Cerf** (pharmacy of the stag; 1268)★★ and **Kammerzell House★★** (1589). ▶ **Cathedral of Notre-Dame★★★ :** 142 m spire; red sandstone façade of Gothic lacework; statuary (right doorway : Tempter and Foolish Virgins★★★); beautiful side doors; at 12:30 enter by the South door (tympanum of the Virgin★★) and see the **astronomical clock★★** (16thC) in operation in the transept. Inside, Romanesque foundations have been re-used (choir over the 11thC crypt), but the architecture and decoration are pure Gothic; 14thC stained glass★; Pillar of the Last Judgement★★; 15thC pulpit★, baptismal fonts and altarpiece; 17thC tapestries of the Life of the Virgin exhibited in the nave in May and June (C3; *8-11 & 1-7, ex. during services; son et lumière at 9 pm in French, 8 pm in German 15 Apr.-30 Sep.;* 330 steps to the top of the tower; view★★). ▶ **Place du Château** (C3; tourist mini-train) : 18thC Jesuit college, now a secondary school. **Palais Rohan★ :** palace of the Prince-Archbishops, built by Armand Cardinal de Rohan-Soubise in 1732 (façade★★★ on the Ill river); mediaeval and Renaissance houses of the Oeuvre-Notre-Dame. ▶ **Museums of the Palais Rohan : State Apartments★★; Fine Arts★★** (Italian paintings; El Greco, Goya, Flemish masters, 18thC French school); **Decorative Arts** (ceramics by the celebrated 18thC Hannong family of potters); **Archaeology★** *(10-12 & 2-6, 1 Apr.-Sep.; Sun., weekdays pm, closed Tue. rest of year).* ▶ **Museum of the Oeuvre-Notre-Dame★★★ :** *(same hours)* art and documents from the 11thC to the 17thC relating to the cathedral; stained glass, paintings, furniture, religious art. ▶ Nearby, three more museums *(same hours) :* the **Historical Museum★★,** in the old Grande Boucherie (C3; military collections; relief map of the city); **Museum of Modern Art★,** in the **Ancienne Douane★** (Old Customs House; C3); across the Ill, the **Alsatian Museum★★★** (C4), in three old houses, interior decoration popular arts and traditions. Quai des Bateliers : (D3) : **Cour du Corbeau★★,** 14th-16thC hostelry. ▶ Past the **Church of St. Thomas★** (C3) : the Protestant cathedral (Gothic) tomb of Maréchal de Saxe by the 18thC scupltor Pigalle★★. **Petite France** district★★★ (B3) : half-timbered houses with galleries overhanging the Ill; **covered bridges★** with towers; dam. ▶ **St. Pierre-le-Vieux** (B3) : two churches in one, Catholic (15thC paintings★★) and Protestant (choir-screen★). **Grand'Rue** (16thC and 18thC houses) or Rue du 22 Novembre (B-C3) leads back to the city centre; Church of **St. Pierre-le-Jeune** (C2). Rest of the visit by car. ▶ **Place Broglie** (C2) :

Alsace cuisine

"... one of the regions of Europe where my mouth watered the most", wrote the 18thC gastronomist Jean-Antheime Brillat-Savarin (1755-1826) about Alsace. The food is very rich, and pork products (charcuterie) *abound : saveloy (served as a salad with Gruyère cheese), liver sausages, Strasbourg sausages, black pudding, and Alsatian* foie gras *(livers of specially -fed geese) served in a pastry crust or with veal or bacon added, as a paté. The farm-inns of the Munster valley serve a typical local meal : onion tart* (tourte), sauerkraut, *Munster cheese and rhubarb or apple pie. The traditional* baeckaoffe *is a particularly fortifying dish of potatoes baked slowly (formerly in the baker's oven) with pork, beef and mutton marinated in wine. Around Strasbourg, a tart called* flammenkueche *is usually made with onion, less often with fresh fruit. Sauced dishes (stews, chicken braised in Riesling) are often accompanied by egg noodles. Also served with Riesling is a freshwater fish stew called the* matelote, *made with fish from the Ill or the Rhine; fried carp is traditional in the Sundgau. Springtime asparagus is the speciality of Hoerdt, north of Strasbourg. To finish the meal, a favourite dessert : the* kugelhopf, *a yeasty raisin cake followed by another Alsatian specialty,* eau-de-vie *(brandy) flavoured with fruit or berries.*

town hall★ and surrounding area (civic offices, officers' club, rue Brûlée) reveal the prosperity of Strasbourg in the 18thC. ▶ A century later, the Administration moved to the other side of the Ill, around the **place de la République** (D2), built by the Germans : Palais du Rhin (Rhine Palace), library, music conservatory, theatre, post office. ▶ The 20thC appears farther on : synagogue at the **Contades Park★** (D1), **Radio House** (D1 ; 1961), **Music and Congress Palace** (N of Radio House ; 1975). ▶ Opposite the **Orangery Park★★** (F1 ; zoo, farm, well-known

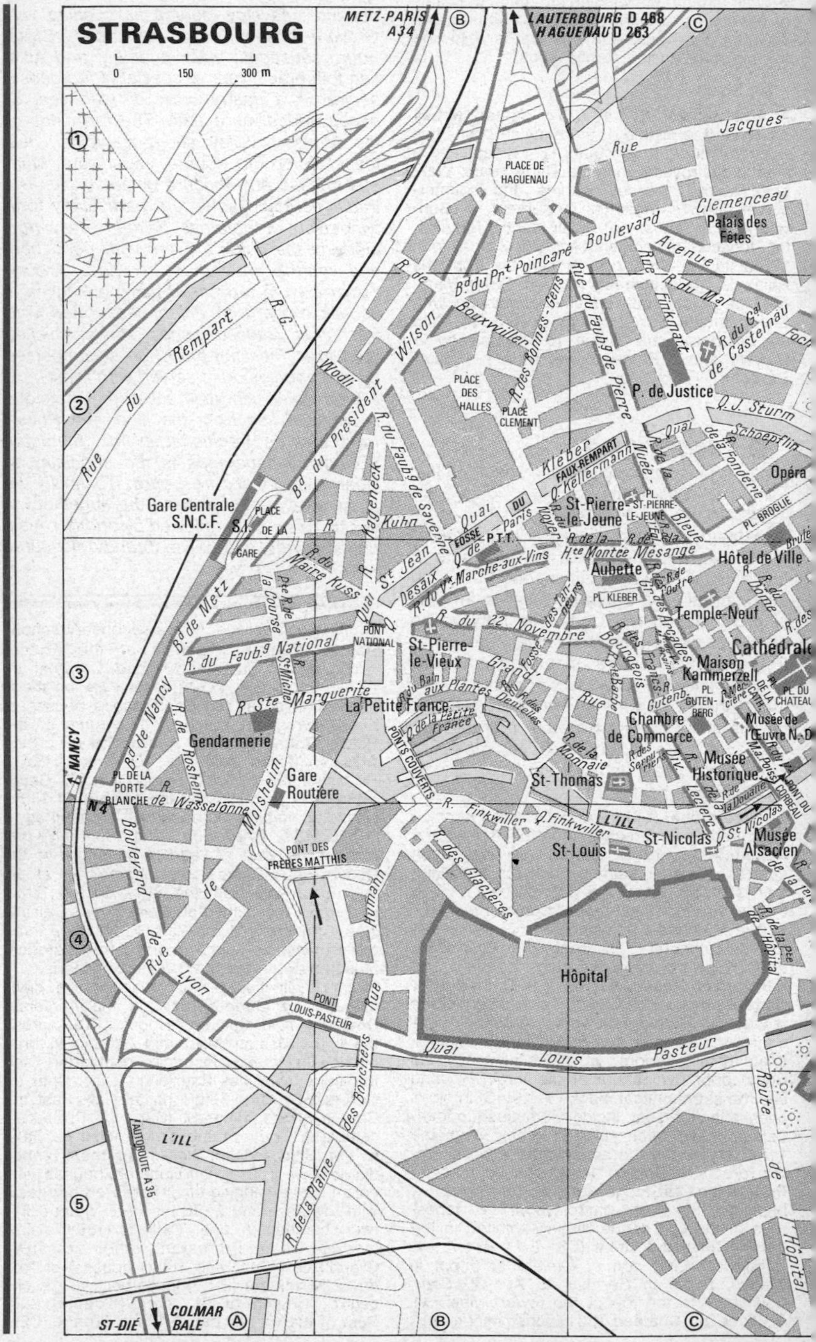

restaurant, Josephine Pavillion), the **Palais de l'Europe★★** : (1977) the Council of Europe, sessions of the European Parliament, and offices *(9-12 & 2:30-5; tel. in advance 88. 61.49.61 ext. 3033).* ▶ Near the University : **zoological museum★** (E3; *2-6, Wed. and Sun. 10-12 & 2-6; closed Tue. Oct.-May).* ▶ **Boat trips** (landing stages by the Rohan Palace and Dauphine Promenade → ®; *Apr.-Oct.)* : 3 hr cruise on the Rhine, visit to **Free Port of Strasbourg,** the most important river port in France after Paris. □

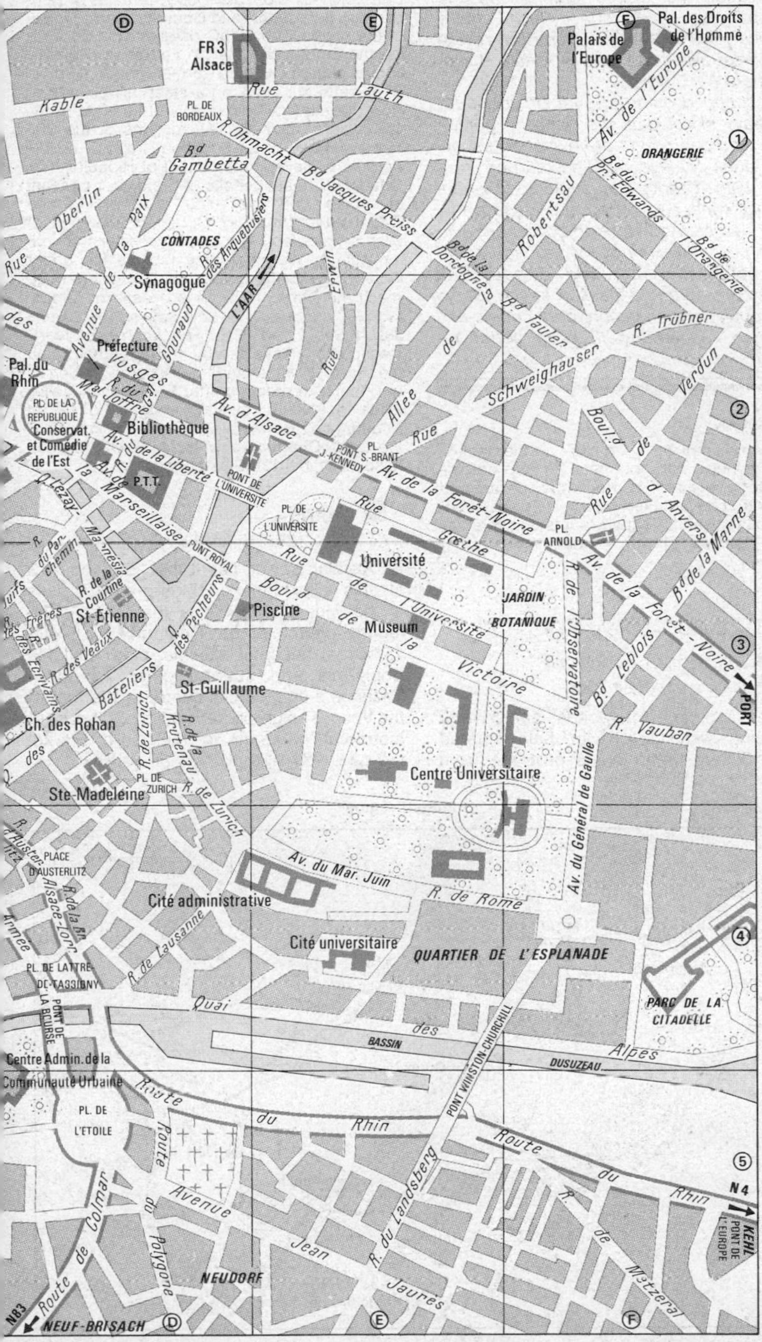

Sauerkraut

There are so many ways to prepare sauerkraut, *the pride of Alsatian cuisine, that the name should be written in the plural. In general, the pickled cabbage is the same; what makes the dishes different is the accompanying* charcuterie, *which differs from one town to another. Here is a recipe from Hansi, illustrator and Alsatian Resistance hero (→ Colmar) :*
"Fry a chopped onion in suet or goose-fat in a heavy skillet until the onion is golden brown. Add one pound of unwashed sauerkraut; *cook for five minutes, stirring constantly with a fork; add a glass of good, dry white wine, a chopped apple and a few juniper berries. Add stock to cover, put a lid on the pot, and simmer for 2-3 hours. An hour before serving, add a pound of smoked brisket and a glass of kirsch. Serve on a hot platter with bacon, pork cutlets and sausages.* Sauerkraut *is even better reheated."*

▶ Nearby

▶ **La Wantzenau** ® *(12 km NE) :* on the bank of the Ill; popular with gourmets. ▶ Two notable agricultural regions : N, **Hoerdt** is the asparagus centre (served everywhere in Apr. & May); S, cabbage used for sauerkraut is cultivated as far as **Eschau** (11thC **Romanesque abbey** church★★). □

■ The SUNDGAU Region★★

▶ Round trip *(110 km; full day)*

A-B4 *(see map 4)* (Haut-Rhin)

Southern country, of ponds and rivers, abounding with carp, with half-timbered houses where bread-ovens protrude from the walls; peaceful and not much visited, it attracts those who like quiet country-side, fishing and reflective walks.

▶ **Altkirch** ® : a modest town (pop. 6 120) over the Sundgau; an old house on the Place de l'Hôtel de Ville is the **Sundgau Museum** (archaeology and popular traditions; *(3-5:30 Sun.; daily ex Mon. Jul.-Sep.);* remains of ramparts. ▶ **Ballersdorf** and **Gommersdorf :** typical of the region with 18thC peasant houses. Follow the Grumbach Valley. ▶ **Feldbach : Romanesque church★★** of a former priory (12thC). ▶ **Ferrette** ® : site★ on a steep hill below two ruined castles *(10 min walk)* on the edge of the Swiss Jura, near the few remains of the **Cistercian abbey of La Lucelle** *(11 km S, on the border).* ▶ Beyond the chapel of Hippoltskirch, **Oltingue** is characteristic of Sundgau : **peasant museum★** *(3-6 Tue., Thu., Sat.; 11-12 and 2:30-6 Sun., 15 Jun.-1 Oct.; 2-5 Sun. rest of year, closed Jan., Feb.).* ▶ **Bouxwiller :** church furnishings. **Werentzhouse :** cross the upper Ill valley (beautiful houses at **Grentzingen**) to reach the site★ of the ruined castle of **Landskron** *(30 min walk; 10-12 & 2-6, or 10-7; Sun., Jul.-15 Sep.; Wed., Sat., Sun. am rest of year);* macaque monkeys nearby. ▶ **Hagenthal :** near the Basle (Switzerland) golf-course, which is on French territory; crafts. ▶ Thalbach Valley leads to Altkirch; typical Sundgau houses at **Knoeringue, Berentzwiller,** and *(4 km N of the road),* **Obermorschwiller.** ▶ Saint-Morand : hospital chapel 12thC sarcophagus. □

■ THANN

A4 / pop. 7 780 (Haut-Rhin)

An Alsatian saying has it that "Strasbourg's steeple is the highest, Fribourg-en-Brisgau's is the widest, Thann's is the finest." **Collegiate church of St. Thiébaut★★ :** (14th-15thC) a beautiful steeple plus sculpted doorways and stained glass windows. Thann is a commercial centre at the foot of the Vosges : sign-posted walks; old houses; **historical museum** in the Corn Market *(10-12 & 2:30-6:30, 15 May-30 Sep.).* □

4. Sundgau region

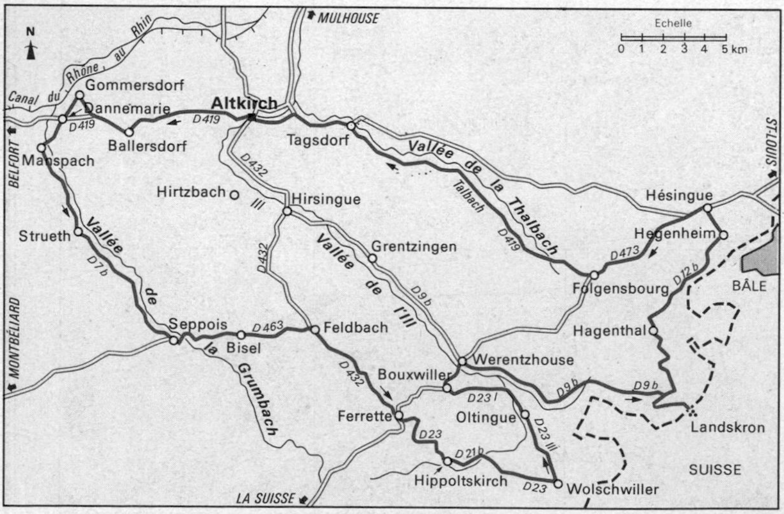

The wine tavern

The wine tavern is an institution - associated especially with Strasbourg - that is indispensable for getting to know Alsace. The proprietor often serves wine from his own vineyard. A popular meeting place at the end of the afternoon and in the evening, with the warm atmosphere of a wood-lined room, where a ham baked in a pastry crust, a knuckle of pork with horseradish or an onion tart will bring out the best in a young wine. Each tavern has a loyal group of regulars who meet at the stammtisch *(regulars' table); this is the place of honour where the proprietor may invite you to join in (→ practical info. Strasbourg).*

■ Les **TROIS ÉPIS** (The Three Spires)

A3 / ® (Haut-Rhin)

At only 15 km from Colmar, this is a notable excursion centre for the Vosges and the Colmar region; the health resort was entirely rebuilt after 1945. □

■ Northern **VOSGES** Region★★

▶ Round trip *(approx 172 km; 1 or 2 days)*

A-B1 *(see map 5)* (Bas-Rhin)

Across the Vosges massif and the **Northern Vosges Nature Park** with a detour through the Moselle department. Romantic landscapes and ruins in forests where folklore is part of daily life.

▶ **Niederbronn-les-Bains** (→) : on the right, forest road to **Wintersberg★.** ▶ **Falkenstein castle★★ :** *(15 min walk)* ruins; **Lake Hanau★** (shore, woods) near the **Waldeck** ruins (site★). ▶ **Zinsel Valley :** lakes and woods. ▶ **Offwiller : museum** of popular art in half-timbered house *(Sun. pm, 2-6 Jul.-Sep.).* ▶ **Lichtenberg :** hilltop castle once owned by the counts of Hanau, renovated by Vauban in the 17thC *(9-12 & 1:30-6 Mar.-Nov.);* the village is a summer resort. ▶ **Bouxwiller :** capital of Hanau-Lichtenberg county, but the Revolution destroyed most traces of the past; Renaissance town hall★ (museum *8-12 & 2-6 closed Jan.-Apr.);* old houses. ▶ **Neuwiller-lès-Saverne :** square in front of the mediaeval abbey **church** (18thC façade and steeple); inside, 15thC **tapestries★★★** (story of Ste. Adelphe) in an **upper chapel★★** (11thC; *Sun. am, ask at the presbytery).* Protestant 13thC collegiate church of Ste. Adelphe behind the abbey. **Weitersweiller** *(3.5 km N) :* 15thC frescos in church; fossil and mineral museum *(9-12 & 2-6).* ▶ A winding forest road (animal park) leads to **La-Petite-Pierre★★** ® : picturesque village; 13th and 17thC château; regional nature park centre; **Museum of the Seal of Alsace** *(10-12 & 2-6 daily May.-Sep., closed Mon.; 1 Oct.-31 Dec., Sat. 2-6, Sun. 10-12 & 2-6; 1 Jan.-26 Feb., Sun. 2-6).* ▶ **Wingen-sur-Moder :** Lalique crystalworks. Meisenthal : **Glass and Crystal Museum** *(2-6 in summer, Sun. Apr.-May and Sep.-Oct.).* **Saint-Louis-lès-Bitche :** displays at former royal glassworks (founded 1767). **Lemberg.** ▶ **Bitche** ® (pop. 7 860; Moselle Department) : mediaeval fortress turned into a citadel★ by Vauban (museum; *9-12 & 2-6 Feb.-Oct., closed Mon.).* Along the mountain

5. Northern Vosges

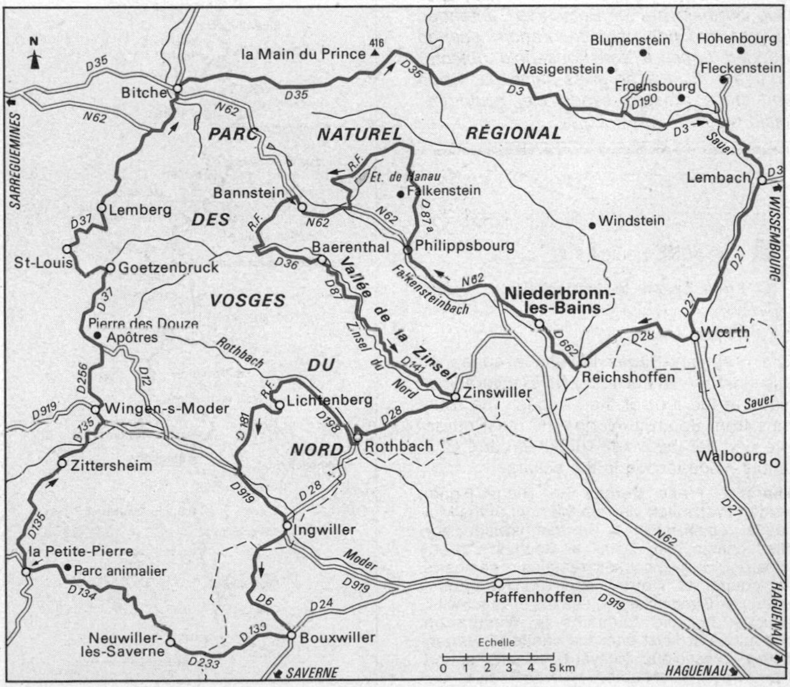

road, several mediaeval ruins in the woods to the left : **Lutzelhardt, Wasigenstein★, Petit-Arnsberg, Froensbourg★** (paths). ▶ A road leads to semi-underground **Fleckenstein★★** : museum *(8-7 Apr.-Oct.)*; beyond, path to **Hohenbourg castle.** ▶ 1 km S of **Lembach** ® : **limekiln★★** of the **Maginot Line** recently opened to the public; visit to the underground installations *(8-6, May-Oct.)*. ▶ **Woerth** ® : château of the Counts of Hanau; museum of 1870-71 Franco-Prussian war *(2-5, Apr.-Oct.)*; battlefields nearby (Reichshoffen). □

■ WANGENBOURG

A2 / ® / pop. 230 (Bas-Rhin)

Evergreen forests, game-filled woods, meadows, waterfalls and mediaeval fortresses.

▶ **Wangenbourg castle :** a stone's throw from the town centre, 13thC fortifications, keep destroyed by Swedish troops in 1663. Walks : SW, **Schneeberg** peak (alt. 960 m; panorama★); N, **Obersteigen** : 13thC **priory;** S along D218, **Nideck : castle** and **waterfall★★; Hohenstein, Birkenvald** and **Freudeneck castles.** □

Alsatian crafts

Alsace abounds in folklore, and tradition is not lost on the souvenir industry. At times it can be difficult to distinguish true from false, authentic from imitation. Nevertheless, you can trust craftsmen and shops bearing the sign Souvenir de France - Alsace Authentique. *Notable among the crafts of Alsace are the brightly coloured pottery of Soufflenheim and the grey-and-blue earthenware of Betschdorf, intended for use and not mere decoration; painted wooden furniture and household objects; printed cloth; folk art glass paintings; wood and stone (Vosges sandstone) sculpture; inlaid wood.*

■ The WINE Route★★★

▶ From Thann to Marlenheim *(120 km; 2 days)*

B2-A4 *(see map 6)*

The prettiest villages in Alsace appear in this itinerary, on flowering, vine-covered hillsides at the foot of the Vosges. The route runs from South to North; the most attractive part lies between Turckheim and Châtenois. Wine-tasting in the cellars.

Thann (→) and **Cernay** (→ Ridge Road). ▶ After **Wattwiller,** view on the right of the Mulhouse potash basin. ▶ **Hartmannswiller :** fortified church, old castle. ▶ **Soultz★ :** pretty square town hall, houses, remains of ramparts. W, chapel of Notre-Dame of Thierenbach (site★). ▶ **Guebwiller** (→) : castle in **Orschwihr;** houses and old fountains in **Westhalten.** ▶ **Soultzmatt :** just after the **castle of Wagenbourg,** prestigious vineyard; mineral spring; Romanesque steeple. ▶ **Rouffach★** ® :

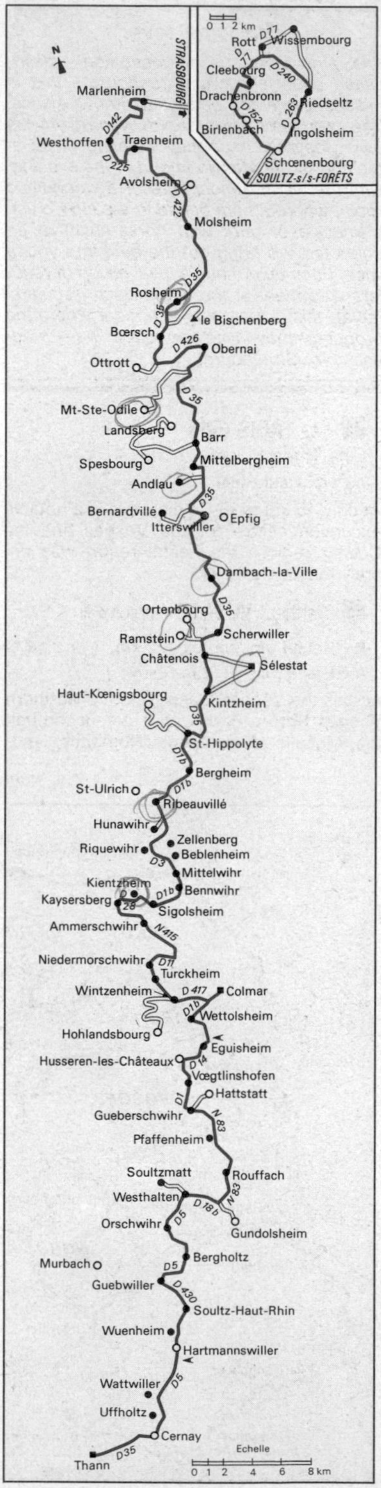

6. Wine route

St. Louis crystal

From the 15thC on, numerous glassworks were established south of Bitche, where fuel was plentiful. In about 1782, lead crystal (previously an English process) began to be made in the royal glassworks at Saint-Louis-lès-Bitche. The superior product obtained with the new technique assured the prosperity of the factory and surrounding workshops. The techniques used in glass- and crystal-making are virtually identical; the raw materials of crystal are silica, potash and lead oxide.

(pop. 4900) "Witches' Tower" crowned by a stork's nest; 12th-14thC **church of Notre-Dame★★;** mediaeval and Renaissance square★★ **(place de la République);** museum in the wheat market; on the way out of town, 19thC Issenbourg castle. ▶ **Hattstatt :** church, town hall. **Gueberschwihr :** old houses, Romanesque bell-tower. ▶ **Husseren-les-Châteaux :** start of the Road of the Five Castles — the three **towers** of **Eguisheim, Hohlandsbourg** (view★), and **Pflixbourg** (supposedly haunted by a White Lady); all date from the 13thC. ▶ **Eguisheim★** ® : walk around the ramparts; old houses; remains of castle and church doorway. ▶ **Colmar** (→). ▶ **Turckheim★★** ® : three gates, a square; and the last town-crier in Alsace still calls the hours *(at 10 pm, from May to the grape harvest).* **Niedermorschwihr★** ® : houses with oriel windows Romanesque bell-tower. ▶ **Kaysersberg★★★ :** charming village (pop. 2710, ®), banners flying from the castle opposite the **fortified bridge★★** over the river Weiss; 16th and 17thC houses, Renaissance town hall★, **church★** (12th and 15thC); gilded wood **altarpiece★★; birthplace of Albert Schweitzer** (→ Soultzbach-les-Bains); small **museum** *(10-12 & 2-6 daily Easter, 2 May-31 Oct.).* **Kientzheim** ® : castle with **vineyard museum** *(10-12 & 2-6 Jul.-Oct.);* 16thC tombstones in the church. ▶ **Sigolsheim :** church★ (1200) escaped destruction in 1944; National War Cemetery. **Bennwihr :** modern church. **Mittelwihr** ® : wines. ▶ **Riquewihr** (→). ▶ **Hunawihr :** fortified church surrounded by 14thC fortifications; stork park, deer park *(Apr.-Oct.).* ▶ **Ribeauvillé** (→). ▶ Road from **Bergheim** (mediaeval towers, gates and fortifications) **Thannenkirch** ® *(7 km) :* summer resort. ▶ **Saint-Hippolyte** ® : houses, fountain, red wine. ▶ **Kintzheim :** on the Sélestat road leisure park *(Wed., Sat., Sun., 15 Sep.-end Oct.; daily, Jun.-15 Sep.)* and **Centre de Réintroduction de la Cigogne★** (stork preserve); *10-12 & 2-6 Apr.-Oct., closed Sun. am; Wed. Sat. and Sun. in good weather in autumn).* At the château on the Haut-Koenigsbourg road : **falconry displays★★** *(2-5, Apr.-Oct.; Wed., Sat., Sun. in autumn).* Farther on; Montagne des Singes (Monkey Mountain nature park *10-12 & 2-6, Apr.-Oct.).* ▶ **Châtenois,** towers gates and old buildings. ▶ Scherwiller : excursion to **Ramstein and Ortenbourg★★ castles** (1 hr 15 walk). ▶ **Dambach-la-Ville★ :** vine-growing, knitwear; circular ramparts (gates, wooden houses). NE, **Epfig :** Romanesque chapel of St. Marguerite★★. ▶ **Andlau★** ® : **church★★** of an abbey founded by St. Richarde (11thC crypt, Romanesque frieze★★, doorway★★). ▶ After **Barr** (→) and **Obernai** (→), the vines are less dense. **Boersch :** gates and square★ ▶ **Rosheim★ :** typical Alsatian Romanesque **church★★★** (outside sculpture, apse, Rhenish-style capitals); town gates; 12thC Maison du Païen, oldest house in Alsace; **tourist train** to Ottrott *(Sun., nat. hols., Jul.-Aug., 1 hr).* ▶ **Molsheim** ® : (pop. 6990) once site of the *Bugatti* motor factory; ramparts; stork park. **Metzig★ :** Renaissance museum *(2-6, Sat. and Sun.; closed Oct.-Mar.).* **Altorf** *(E) :* Romanesque and Baroque church. ▶ **Avolsheim :** 11th-12thC chapel of St. Ulrich, among the oldest in the province, and, a bit further, the church of **Dompeter,** in the middle of the cemetery. ▶ **Traenheim. Westhoffen :** Rosenbourg castl; cherry festival in June. **Wangen★ :** fountain festival (wine flows free) in July. **Marlenheim :** rosé wines; Friend Fritz's Wedding Festival *(Aug.).* These are the last villages on the Wine Road, which continues to the small vineyard south of Wissembourg (→). □

Alsace

■ WISSEMBOURG★★

B1 / ® / pop. 7340 (Bas-Rhin)

Flowery quays, gardens on the ramparts, and brown-tiled roofs lend colour to Wissembourg.

▶ Stroll along the Lauter through the **Bruch★★ district** to **Anselmann Quay★** (Renaissance houses), or past the **Maison du Sel★** (salt house, 1450). ▶ 18thC town hall; **Hôpital Stanislas,** residence of ex-king Stanislas Leszczynski of Poland, whose daughter Maria was married to Louis XV in 1725. ▶ **church of St. Pierre-et-St. Paul★ :** (W) Gothic with Romanesque tower; frescos; stained glass; furnishings. ▶ **Westercamp Museum★** in a 16thC mansion in the N of town : historical collections, furniture, old kitchen, wine-press *(10-12 & 2-5 closed Sun., hols., Wed. and Jan.).* □

▶ Nearby

▶ **Altenstadt★,** *(1 km E) :* 11th-12thC Romanesque church. ▶ S of Wissembourg, **Cleebourg vineyard :** Tokay, Pinot blanc. □

The Maginot Line

André Maginot (1877-1932), French Minister of War in 1930, was the main promotor of a system of fortifications that eventually bore his name. The Maginot Line was intended to defend the NE borders of France between Stenay and St Louis. Built amid much controversy between 1930 and 1940; it is a technically remarkable underground network of blockhouses, pill-boxes and tunnels. The only parts above ground are metal observation and firing points designed to make best use of the terrain. Troops lived on the Line like submarine crews. It has been said that the Maginot Line "remains an outstanding example of the inadequacy of a military tool in a given strategic situation", because it gave priority to static defence at a time when aircraft and tanks controlled troop mobility. Outflanked from the West and cut off from the South, in June 1940 the defenders of the Maginot Line could put up only a feeble resistance (→ Outre-Forêt and Northern Vosges).

Brief regional history

Up to the 9thC

Alsace has distinct geographical characteristics, but little historical identity before the Roman era. The Celtic inhabitants established important market-towns and sanctuary cities. ● Fortified border towns built during the **Pax Romana,** following the conquest by Julius Caesar (58BC) when the vine was introduced, emphasised the territory's position as a border state. The agricultural and trading system that grew in response to the demands of the garrisons laid the foundations for the **economy** that remains the basis of prosperity to this day. ● Christianity began to take root during the Roman era. A troubled period marked by successive invasions of **Germans** (Alemanni) and Huns (453) was finally ended in 596 with the conquest of **Clovis,** king of the Franks. The name Alsace appeared for the first time in the 7thC : its origin is uncertain but at that time it was used to indicate the independent duchy of Alsace.

9thC-11thC

Under Frankish protection, the church prospered and the **Carolingian Renaissance** gave rise to magnificent buildings, including the bishop's palace at Strasbourg and Murbach abbey. As Charlemagne's empire crumbled, the two counties of Nordgau and Sundgau replaced the Duchy of Alsace. ● Two sons of Louis the Debonair, Charles and Louis, allied themselves against their brother Lothar in the **Oath of Strasbourg** (842), the earliest historical text known to have been written in Romance and Germanic languages. ● In 870, Charles conceded Alsace to Louis, and the territory remained under the sway of the **Holy Roman Empire** until 1648.

12thC-14thC

The feudal era in Alsace culminated in the "**Hohenstaufen Century",** which ended with the death of the Emperor Frederick II in 1250. During this period trade thrived, towns expanded and **Romanesque art** and architecture flourished. ● Many fortified towns united to form boroughs. In 1354, Haguenau, Wissembourg, Obernai, Rosheim, Sélestat, Colmar, Turckheim, Kaysersberg, Munster and Mulhouse (later to unite with the Swiss cities) formed a cooperative alliance known as the **Decapol** ("ten cities"); trade with the Rhineland enabled Strasbourg to remain independent. ● During the Hundred Years' War only minor incidents disturbed the peace, by virtue of the region's relative remoteness from the English territories in France.

14thC-16thC The later Middle Ages were marked by religious intensity and municipal pride. The magnificent spire was erected on Strasbourg cathedral, and the Issenheim altarpiece was created. In 1434, the German Gutenberg (1400-68) moved to Strasbourg, where he worked until 1448 on his "secret process" that, as the printing press, was soon to revolutionise the world. As the **Renaissance** dawned, Alsace was pledged to the Dukes of Burgundy; the tyranny of their bailiff, Pierre de Hagenbach, brought about revolt. ● The bloodily suppressed peasants' revolt was followed by the **"peasants' war"** (1525) in which 40 000 died. ● During these upheavals, humanist thought and the **Protestant Reformation** took root; Strasbourg was an intellectual centre. Many buildings from this era are still standing.

17thC-18thC As a border territory, Alsace was a pawn in the political struggles between the Great Powers. During the **30 Years' War** (17thC), a request for French aid was answered by annexation of a substantial region. With the **Treaty of Westphalia,** France took possession of the Austrian territories in Alsace. The feeble influence of the Holy Roman Empire was extinguished after 1679 defeat of the Imperial forces by the French commanders Turenne and Condé; in 1681, Strasbourg recognised French sovereignty. Strasbourg continued to flourish as the meeting place of the Latin and Germanic worlds; during the Enlightenment, art, trade and industry thrived. ● Strasbourg's French identity was confirmed in 1792 during the Revolution, when a young military engineer, Rouget de l'Isle, composed the "War Song for the Army of the Rhine" that, after its adoption by the Marseilles Volunteers, became known as the *Marseillaise* — now the French national anthem.

19thC-20thC When the armies of the Coalition against Napoleon occupied Alsace (1814-1818), there was no question of annexation. ● However, after the defeat of 1870 (Franco-Prussian War), when the citizens of Strasbourg maintained heroic resistance for 45 days, the region was "Germanised" and French identity suppressed. ● During **WWI,** almost 20 000 Alsatians joined the French army to avoid being pressed into the German army for service on the Russian front. In 1918 Alsace was liberated from German occupation. ● In **1940** Alsace was once more annexed. From 1942 on, many Alsatians were forced to serve in the German army. The Resistance was active despite the threat of the Struthof concentration camp. The French General Leclerc liberated Strasbourg in November 1944. ● Since the end of WWII Alsace has remained in the forefront of the **European movement,** still a crossroads and meeting place for trade and culture.

Architecture

Outre-Forêt

The attractive Alsatian domestic architecture is preserved in the towns and villages, where many traditional houses date from the 16th, 17th and 18thC. ● The communes, "municipal republics", are proud of their beautiful public buildings such as town halls, markets and towers that attest to their prosperity. ● In many cities, such as Strasbourg, Wissembourg and Haguenau, mansions were built during the 18thC. The 20thC German occupation left characteristically grandiose constructions, including the railway station and the place de la République at Strasbourg. ● In the densely populated Alsatian countryside, dwellings are usually clustered, except in a few valleys of the Vosges. If the villages seem cramped, rural houses, by contrast, are never semi-detached, but are separated by passages forming either "street-villages" or "cluster-villages". Gables are always turned towards the street. The family quarters and outbuildings may be under a single roof, or around three sides of an open yard, with the fourth side giving on to the street. In vineyard areas, the ground floor is a stone cellar and the house is higher than elsewhere. ● Half-timbered walls, covered in rough-cast, are built on the stone foundations or ground floor. Upper floors are often corbelled. The roofs are steep, often with an overhang, and the gable-ends have pivoting skylights; roofing is a flat brown "beaver-tail" tile. ● Richly decorated balconies, wooden galleries, or oriel windows of wood or stone signify prosperity. The complex patterns of half-timbering sometimes incorporate magical symbolism. The characteristics are similar for half-timbered houses in both town and country, although stone is used more often in the towns. ● The *stube* is the living room, warmed by a stove, in a corner of the building. In this main room, the walls are usually wainscotted, and the master of the house often has a private alcove. One corner of the *stube* serves as an oratory; another may be the workshop. The kitchen, on the other side of the stove wall, is used only for preparing the meals, which are eaten in the *stube*. The bread oven often protrudes from the outer wall (Sundgau). A hall and another small room heated by the kitchen complete the ground floor. The first floor consists of bedrooms, the largest of which corresponds to the *stube*. The usual pantry above the kitchen is now often converted into a bathroom.

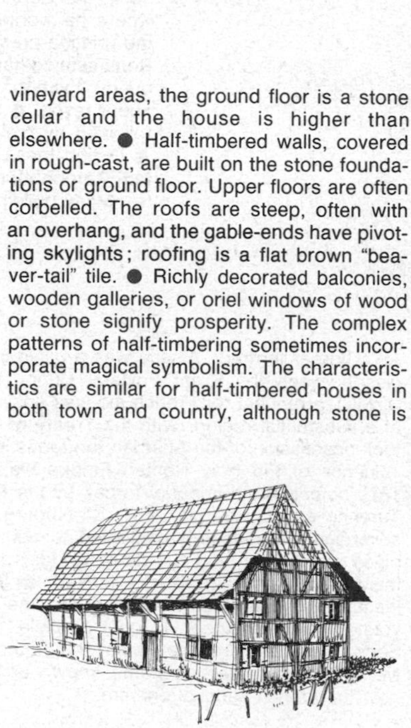

Sundgau

Vineyard areas

Practical information

The region

Information : Bas-Rhin : *Office Départemental du Tourisme* (O.D.T.), 9, rue du Dôme, 67000 Strasbourg, ☎ 88.22.01.02. **Haut-Rhin :** *Association Départementale du Tourisme,* 68020 Colmar, ☎ 89.23.21.11. In Paris : *Maison de l'Alsace,* 39, av. des Champs-Élysées, 75008, ☎ (1) 42.25.93.42. *Dir. Rég. du Temps Libre, Jeunesse et Sports,* 17, rue Goethe, 67083 Strasbourg Cedex, ☎ 88.61.62.01. *Dir. Rég. des Affaires Culturelles,* palais du Rhin, 3, pl. de la République, 67082 Strasbourg Cedex, ☎ 88.32.28.37.
Attention : Good Friday and Dec 26 are nat hols in Alsace.

Maps : *Michelin,* n°s 57, 62, 66 and 87 1/200 000. *IGN,* nº 104 1/250 000, nº 12 and 31 1/100 000.

S.O.S. : Bas-Rhin : *SAMU :* Emergency Medical Service, ☎ 88.33.33.33. **Haut-Rhin :** ☎ 17. *Poisoning Emergency Centre,* ☎ 88.35.41.03.

Weather forecast : Bas-Rhin : ☎ 88.78.23.23. **Haut-Rhin :** ☎ 89.56.68.68.

Farmhouse, rural "gîtes" chambres d'hôtes and farmhouse-inns : enquiries : *Relais Départemental du Tourisme Rural du* ***Bas-Rhin,*** Maison de l'Agriculture, 103, rte de Hausbergen, 67300 Childikheim, ☎ 88.62.45.09. *Chambre d'Agriculture du* ***Haut-Rhin,*** 4, rue de l'Est, 68005 Mulhouse Cedex, ☎ 89.45.84.25. *Gîtes Ruraux du Haut-Rhin* (Farmhouse gîtes) ☎ 89.46.22.12.

Holiday villages : in Albé, Plaine, Saales (Enq at the **Bas-Rhin** O.D.T.).

Camping : approx 90 camp-sites and many possibilities for farmhouse camping ; list of sites and enquiries : O.D.T. **Bas-Rhin** and Association départementale du Tourisme du **Haut-Rhin.**

Festivals and events : May : *street festival* Huningue ; *Colmar antique fair ; candlelight concerts in* Sainte-Marie-aux-Mines ; *Mulhouse international fair.* **Jun : 1st Sun in Jun,** *Dorlisheim wine fair ;* **2nd Sun in Jun,** *rose festival* in Saverne ; **1st fortnight in Jun,** *Kougelhopf fair (traditional dessert),* in Ribeauvillé ; **2nd and 3rd weeks in Jun,** *Strasbourg music festival ;* **Early Jul,** *cherry festival in* Uffoltz ; **13 Jul,** *grand défilé des Sans-Culottes (celebration of the 1789 French Revolution)* in Mutzig ; *woodsmen's competition* in Saint-Pierre-Bois ; **end Jul :** *Ribeauvillé wine fair.* **Early Aug :** *handicrafts festival* in Masevaux ; **1st Sun in Aug,** *mountain festival* in Grandelbruch. **Jul-Aug :** *Nautical jousting on the Ill,* Mon., Fri., 8:30 pm. **End Aug-early Sep :** *choucroute day* in Colmar. **Early Sep :** *hops celebration* in Haguenau ; *fiddlers' festival* in Ribeauvillé ; **1st Sun in Sep,** *beer fountain* in Mutzig ; **end Sep,** *Brumath onion fair ; grape harvest festival* in Niedermorschwihr. **End Sep-early Oct,** *autumn cloth festival* in Sainte-Marie-aux-Mines. **2nd Sun in Oct :** *grand grape festival* in Molsheim ; **3rd Sun in Oct,** *grape harvest festival* in Obernai. **Dec,** *Strasbourg Christmas fair.*

Alsace wine : tasting is the only way to really choose one's wine ; list of producers and cellars at the S.I. and T.O. or at the *Centre d'Information du Vin d'Alsace (C.I.V.A.),* 12, av. de la Foire-aux-Vins, 68003 Colmar, ☎ 89.41.06.21.

Scenic railways : *Rhine tourist railway* (C.F.T.R.), Neuf-Brisach-Marckolsheim. From Jul-Sep, Sun and nat hols ; — *Vallée de la Doller.* Departure from Cernay or Sentheim. Sun and nat hols, and daily ex Mon and Tue in Jul-Aug. Duration : 1 hr ; — *Rosheim-Ottrott :* Sun and nat hols in Jul-Aug. Duration : 1 hr ; return trip.

Hiking and Rambling : numerous possibilities for "walking holidays", thanks to the chalets and refuges on the Vosges Massif. Enquiries : *Club vosgien,* Comité central, 4, rue de la Douane, 67000 Strasbourg, ☎ 88.32.57.96. *Amis de la Nature-Strasbourg,* 9, rue de Sainte-Marie-aux-Mines, 67300 Schiltigheim ; — Mulhouse, M.-F. Stein, 11, rue Chopin, 68100 Mulhouse, ☎ 89.42.55.90.
The *Club vosgien,* the biggest tourism association in Eastern France, aims to develop pedestrian tourism in natural parks and regions, in terms of historical monuments, etc. This association is highly active in the maintenance and setting up of public walkways, and publishes guides and maps, scale ranging from 1/50 000 to 1/25 000. Other possibilities : crossing of the Vosges mountains on foot : *T.O.* and *S.I.* in Sainte-Marie-aux-Mines, ☎ 89.58.80.50. The Northern Range on foot : *Relais Départemental du Tourisme Rural,* Maison de l'Agriculture, 103, rte de Hausbergen, 67300 Childikheim, ☎ 88.62.45.09.

Riding holidays : list of riding centres and gîtes, veterinarians and blacksmiths, available at the **Bas-Rhin** O.D.T. and at the Association départementale du Tourisme du **Haut-Rhin.** Further information : *Association Alsacienne de Tourisme Equestre,* 78, rue d'Oberhardt, 68000 Colmar, ☎ 89.79.38.48 ; I.G.N. maps show bridle paths.

Cycling holidays : *O.D.T.* **Bas-Rhin ;** *Association Départementale du Tourisme du* ***Haut-Rhin.*** *Fédération Française de Cyclotourisme,* ligue d'Alsace de Cyclotourisme, M.-P. Wanner, 1, rue F.-Kuhllmann, 68000 Colmar.

River and canal cruises : discover Alsace by travelling up the Marne canal to the Rhine. Enquiries and bookings : *O.D.T.* ***Bas-Rhin ;*** *Assn. Dép. du Tourisme du* ***Haut-Rhin.***

Handicraft courses : sculpture-model-making (Colmar) ; weaving (Schirmeck, Kurtzenhouse, Wintzeldeld, Sainte-Marie-aux-Mines) ; pottery (Betschdorf, Wintzfeld) ; polychrome painting (Wingen-sur-Moder) ; spinning and natural dyes (Sainte-Marie-aux-Mines) ; wickerwork (Kurtzenhouse) ; copper enamelling (Kurtzenhouse) ; silk painting (Wintzeld). Enquiries : *O.D.T.* ***Bas-Rhin*** and *Assn. Dép. du Tourisme du* ***Haut-Rhin.***

Peasant Cookery Courses : Bas-Rhin : Lembach, Marlenheim, Mutzig, Niederbronn-les-Bains, Obersteigen, Strasbourg. **Haut-Rhin :** Jungholtz, Thierenbach. Enrolments : *Relais Dép. du Tourisme Rural,* Maison de l'Agriculture, 103, rte de Hausbergen, 67300 Childikheim, ☎ 88.62.45.09.

Other courses : nature and environmental discovery courses, *Centre Permanent d'Initiation à l'Environnement Régional d'Alsace* (C.P.I.E.),

36, rue de Sélestat-Muttersholtz, 67600 Sélestat, ☎ 88.85.11.30 (also exhibitions and applied research).

Children : for all information about children's holidays (music, sports, farm holidays, etc.) and children's activities throughout the year, consult the *Centre d'Information Jeunesse Alsace* (C.I.J.A.), 7, rue des Écrivains, 67000 Strasbourg, ☎ 88.37.33.33. *Direction Rég. Temps Libre-Jeunesse and Sports.*

Tennis : *Ligue Régionale,* 52, rue de l'Espérance, 68120 Pfastatt.

Golf : Bas-Rhin : Strasbourg, Illkirch-Graffenstaden (18 holes). **Haut-Rhin** : Chalampé, golf de l'Ile-du-Rhin (18 holes).

Aquatic sports : Haut-Rhin : *Club Nautique du Rhin-Colmar,* M.-F. Hausherr, 1, rue Principale, 68000 Houssen, ☎ 89.23.59.02. *Cercle de Voile-Mulhouse,* M. Schreiber, 22a, rte de Jungholtz, 68360 Soultz, ☎ 89.76.82.81. *Cercle de Yachting à Voile des Trois Frontières Village Neuf,* Mme Willig, 41, rue du Rhin, 68300 Saint-Louis, ☎ 89.69.80.82. **Bas-Rhin** : *Assn. "Plaisir",* 9, rue du Gal-Gouraud, 67000 Strasbourg, ☎ 88.35.69.69.

Winter sports : resorts : col des Bagenelles, ballon d'Alsace, le Bonhomme, Champ du Feu, Cote 1000, Dolleren, Donon, le Frenz, Gaschney, Grand-Ballon, Grendelbruch, le Hohwald, Markstein, Saales, la Schlucht, Schnepfenried, Tanet, Trois-Fours, Wangenbourg-Egenthal. Cross-country skiing : *Centre École de Ski de Fond,* 67000 Strasbourg, ☎ 88.97.33.57. Cross-country skiing possibilities in Champ du Feu, Donon, Grendelbruch, la Petite-Pierre, Plaine, Saales, Wangenbourg-Egenthal. Cross-country instructional courses from Dec to Mar : M.-C. Benistant, Schoultzbach farm, nº 283, 68370 Orbey-Pairis, ☎ 89.71.28.02. *Ski trek across the Vosges mountains* : S.I. Sainte-Marie-aux-Mines. "Forfait Hautes-Vosges" : S.I. de Munster. Cross-country ski schools : *S.U.A. Tourisme et Propagande, Chambre d'Agriculture du Haut-Rhin,* 4, rue de l'Est, 68055 Mulhouse Cedex, ☎ 89.45.84.25.

Flying, gliding, etc. : enq : *O.D.T.* ***Bas-Rhin;*** *Association Dép. du Tourisme du* ***Haut-Rhin;*** S.I. and T.O. in Colmar, Mulhouse, Oberbruck, Haguenau, Sarre-Union, Saverne, Sélestat, Strasbourg, Hang-gliding : *Association Dép. du Tourisme du* ***Haut-Rhin.***

Hunting and shooting : local legislation on hunting is fairly restrictive. Enquiries at the féd. dép. **Bas-Rhin** : Résidence Lafayette, 5, rue Staedel, 67000 Strasbourg, ☎ 88.79.12.77. **Haut-Rhin** : 2, av. A.-Wicky, 68100 Mulhouse, ☎ 89.45.60.28.

Fishing : *Féd. Dép. des Associations de Pêche et de Pisciculture du* ***Bas-Rhin,*** 2, rue de Nomeny, 67000 Strasbourg, ☎ 88.34.51.86. *Féd. Dép. des Associations de Pêche et de Pisciculture du* ***Haut-Rhin,*** 29, rue de Colmar, 68200 Mulhouse, ☎ 89.59.06.88.

● Towns

ALTKIRCH

Mulhouse 20, Belfort 35, Paris 529
A4 ⊠ 68130

ℹ pl. Xavier-Jourdain, ☎ 89.40.02.90 (high season).

SNCF ☎ 89.40.96.44.

Hotels :

★***Ottié-Baur,*** 9, rue de-Lattre-de-Tassigny, ☎ 89.40.93.22. 13 rm ☼ Ⓟ ≋ ⊘ closed 24 Jun-16 Jul, a week in Oct and Carnival, Mon eve and Tue, 145. Rest. ● ◆◆ Spec : fried carp, 45-140. 3.5 km W on the D 419 :

★★***Auberge Sundgovienne*** (L.F.), ☎ 89.40.97.18. AE, DC, Euro, Visa. 31 rm Ⓟ ≋ ⚘ ⊘ ♿ closed Xmas-1 Feb, 170. Rest. ◆ closed Mon and Tue noon. Good simple fare, 50-145.

Hirtzbarch, ⊠ 68118, 4 km S :

⛺ ★★*Les Acacias* (80 pl.), ☎ 89.40.95.96.

AMMERSCHWIHR

Colmar 7, Saint-Dié 49, Paris 508
4.5 km E of Kaysersberg, A3 ⊠ 68770

Hotels :

★★***Aux Armes de France,*** 1, Grand'Rue, ☎ 89.47.10.12. Tx 880666. AE DC, Euro, Visa. 10 rm ⊘, 400 closed Wed and Thu noon. 6-30 Jan. Rest. ● ◆◆ Things are going pretty well at Gaertner's. Alsace wines by the litre, 140-350.

★★***A l'Arbre Vert*** (L.F.), 7, rue des Cigognes, ☎ 89.47.12.23. 13 rm ⊘ closed 10 Feb-25 Mar, 26 Nov-10 Dec and Tue, 180. Rest. ◆ Good regional dishes in a traditional Alsace setting, 80-130.

★***Aux trois Merles*** (L.F.), 1, rue de la 5ᵉ-D.B., ☎ 89.78.24.35. 22 rm Ⓟ ≋ ⊘ closed 1 Dec-4 Jan and Mon, 180. Rest. closed Mon and Tue in Winter, 60-130.

Recommended : *Jean Schaetzel wine-cellars,* 3, rue de la 5ᵉ-D.B, ☎ 89.47.11.39.

ANDLAU

Colmar 40, Strasbourg 40, Paris 526
2 km SW of Barr, A2 ⊠ 67140 Barr

ℹ pl. de la Mairie, ☎ 88.08.22.57.

Hotels :

★★★***Kastelberg*** (L.F.), rue du Gal-Kœnig, ☎ 88.08.97.83. 28 rm Ⓟ ⚘ ⊘ 180. Rest. closed Tue, Nov-Easter, 120-210.

★***Au Canon*** (L.F.), 2, rue des Remparts, ☎ 88.08.95.08. Euro. 10 rm Ⓟ closed Nov-Apr, 180. Rest. ◆◆ closed Feb, 19-26 Nov Mon eve and Tue, 90-130.

Restaurant :

◆◆◆ ***Au Bœuf Rouge,*** 6, rue du Dr-Stoltz, ☎ 88.08.96.26. closed 28 Dec-31 Jan, Wed eve and Thu, 100-200. ◆ *Winstub du Bœuf.*

BARR

Strasbourg 35, Colmar 39, Paris 493
A2 ⊠ 67140

ℹ pl. de l'Hôtel-de-Ville, ☎ 88.08.94.24.

SNCF ☎ 88.08.90.15.

Hotels :

★★***Maison Rouge*** (L.F.), 1, av. de la Gare, ☎ 88.08.90.40. 13 rm Ⓟ closed 1 Feb-15 Mar and Mon, 180. Rest. ◆◆ 80-130.

★★***Château d'Andlau,*** 113, vallée Saint-Ulrich, rte de Sainte-Odile, 2 km W, ☎ 88.08.96.78. 26 rm ☼ Ⓟ ≋ ⚘ ⊘ 150.

Mittelbergheim, 2 km S :

★***Winstub Gilg*** (L.F.), 1, rue Rotland, ☎ 88.08.91.37. 11 rm Ⓟ ⊘ closed 10 Jan-8 Feb, 26 Jun-7 Jul, 150. Rest. ◆ closed Tue eve and Wed, 115-175.

Itterswiller, 6 km S :

★★★***Arnold,*** rte du Vin, ☎ 88.85.50.58. Tx 870550. AE, DC, Visa. 28 rm ☼ Ⓟ ⚘ ⊘ closed 24 Jan-12 Feb, 250. Rest. ● ◆◆ closed

Sun eve and Mon low season. Traditional table in the grand style : *choucroute royale, noisette de marcassin aux airelles, filet de sandre au Riesling,* 90-120.

Chambres d'hôtes. *Maison Ruff,* in Heiligenstein, 1.5 km N, ☎ 88.08.10.81.

⛺ ★★*Wepfermatt* (70 pl.), ☎ 88.08.02.38.

Restaurant :

♦ ***Caveau Folie Marco,*** 30, rue du Dr-Sultzer, ☎ 88.08.91.06. closed May, Mon eve and Tue, 80-130.

Recommended : *Wantz wine-cellars,* 3, rue des Vosges, in Mittelbergheim, 2 km S, ☎ 88.08.91.43.

BITCHE

Sarreguemines 34, Strasbourg 74, Paris 427
A1 ✉ 57230 (Moselle)

ℹ porte de Strasbourg, ☎ 87.96.00.13 (high season).

SNCF ☎ 87.06.00.18.

Hotel :

★★***Strasbourg*** (L.F.), 24, rue Teyssier, ☎ 87.96.00.44. 10 rm Ⓟ closed 22 Aug-15 Sep, Feb hols, Sun eve and Mon, 100. Rest. ♦ Good simple dishes, 80-130.

⛺ ★★★*Hasselfurth* (120 pl.), ☎ 81.96.05.18.

BRUMATH

Haguenau 11, Saverne 30, Paris 468
17 km N of Strasbourg, B2 ✉ 67170

SNCF ☎ 88.51.10.11.

Hotel :

★★***A l'Ecrevisse*** (M.C.F.), 4, av. de Strasbourg, ☎ 88.51.11.08. Euro, Visa. 21 rm Ⓟ ♿ closed 14 Jul-7 Aug, Mon eve and Tue, 180. Rest. ● ♦♦ In this superb house, home for the Orth family since 1780, excellent crayfish and *selle de chevreuil* in season, 120-155.

Restaurant :

Mommenheim, ✉ 67670, 6 km NW :

♦♦ ***Manoir de la Tour St.-Georges,*** 165, rte de Brumath, ☎ 88.51.61.78. AE, DC, Euro Ⓟ closed Mon and Tue eve, 40-200.

CERNAY

Mulhouse 19, Colmar 36, Paris 531
A4 ✉ 68700

ℹ 1, rue Latouche, ☎ 89.75.50.35. (high season).

SNCF ☎ 89.75.40.02.

Hotels :

★***Bellevue*** (L.F.), 10, rue Mal-Foch, ☎ 89.75.40.15. Visa. 12 rm Ⓟ closed 20 Dec-20 Jan and Sun, 170. Rest. ♦ 35-70.

★***Hostellerie d'Alsace*** (L.F.), 61, rue Poincarré, ☎ 89.75.59.81. 11 rm Ⓟ closed 18 Dec-9 Jan, 180. Rest. ♦ closed Sun eve and Mon, 80-130.

Uffoltz, 1 km N :

★★***Frantz*** (L.F.), 41, rue de Soultz, ☎ 89.75.54.52. 50 rm Ⓟ 180. Rest. ♦ closed 3 Jan-25 Jan and Mon, 80-130.

★★***Auberge du Relais,*** 35, rue de Soultz, ☎ 89.75.56.19. Visa. 24 rm Ⓟ closed 14 Dec-7 Jan and Fri, 170. Rest. ♦ closed Oct-Easter, 40-80.

⛺ ★★★★*Les Acacias* (145 pl.), ☎ 89.75.56.97.

COLMAR

Strasbourg 71, Nancy 148, Paris 531
A3 ✉ 68000

ℹ 4, rue d'Unterlinden (B1) ☎ 89.41.02.29.

✈ Houssen, 3 km N., ☎ 89.23.31.23.

SNCF (A3), ☎ 89.24.50.50., 89.23.17.00.

🚌 S.N.C.F. railway station.

Car-hire : *Budget* train + auto, at the airport and at the station, ☎ 89.23.17.17.

Hotels :

★★★***Champ-de-Mars*** (P.L.M., Etap, Frantel), 2, av. de la Marne (A2), ☎ 89.41.54.54. Tx 880928. AE, DC, Euro, Visa. 75 rm Ⓟ 275.

★★★***Terminus Bristol*** (Mapotel), 7, pl. de la Gare (A3), ☎ 89.23.59.59. 70 rm ♿ 580. Rest. ● ♦♦♦ ***le Rendez-vous de Chasse.*** Attractive table, good food. Spec. : fish, seafood, game in season, 220-310.

★★***Fecht*** (L.F.), 1, rue de la Fecht, ☎ 89.41.34.08. 39 rm Ⓟ ♿ 260. Rest. ♦ closed Sun eve and Mon, 100-250.

★★***Majestic*** (L.F.), 1, rue de la Gare (A2), ☎ 89.41.45.19. 40 rm Ⓟ ♿ closed Sun, Mon, eve, 15 Dec-10 Jan, 180. Rest. 120-210.

★★***Hostellerie le Maréchal,*** 4-6, pl. des Six-Montagnes-Noires, ☎ 89.41.60.32. AE, DC, Visa. 40 rm Ⓟ ♿ closed 5 Jan-21 Feb, 250. Rest. ♦♦ ♿ 70-160.

★★***Kempf,*** 1, av. de la République (A-B2), ☎ 89.41.21.72. 25 rm closed Wed, 200. Rest. ♦♦ ♿ 95-110.

★***Beau Séjour*** (L.F.), 25, rue du Ladhof (C1), ☎ 89.41.37.16. 30 rm closed 16-26 Dec, Sun (low season), 180. Rest. closed Sun and Mon noon, 80-130.

★***Rapp,*** 16, rue Berthe-Molly (B2), ☎ 89.41.62.10. 14 rm, closed 25 Jun-10 Jul, 1 Dec-5 Jan and Wed. Rest. ♦ closed Mon.

A la Truite, 57, rte de Neuf-Brisach (C1), ☎ 89.41.46.25. AE, DC, Visa. 7 rm, closed Feb, 75. Rest. closed Mon and Thu eve, 40-55.

Horbourg, 4 km E :

★★***Romains*** (Inter-Hôtel), 13, rte de Neuf-Brisach, ☎ 89.23.46.46. Tx 880294. Visa. 63 rm Ⓟ closed 22 Dec-10 Jan, 195. Rest. closed Sat and Mon noon, 60-80.

★★***Cerf*** (L.F.), 9, Grand'Rue, ☎ 89.41.20.35. 27 rm Ⓟ closed 15 Jan-1 Mar, Mon, Sun eve low season, 185. Rest. ♦♦ ♿ 60-120.

Wettolsheim, 4.5 km SW :

★★★***Auberge du Père Floranc*** (Relais du Silence), 9, rue Herzog, ☎ 89.41.39.14. AE, DC, Visa. 32 rm Ⓟ closed 30 Jun-15 Jul, 10 Nov-13 Dec, 185. Rest. ● ♦♦ ♿ Calm in the middle of a beautiful park surrounded by vineyards. The Florancs cook as a family. Spec. : *foie gras de l'auberge,* game in season, 75-230.

Bischwihr, ✉ 68230 Muntzenheim, 6 km E :

★★***Relais du Ried*** (L.F.), 3, Grand'Rue, ☎ 89.47.47.06. 60 rm Ⓟ ♿ closed 15 Dec-15 Feb, 180. Rest. ♦ 120-210.

Youth Centre, *M.J.C.,* 17, rue Schlumberger, ☎ 89.41.26.87.

Youth Hostel, 7, rue Sint-Niklaos, ☎ 89.41.33.08.

⛺ ★★★*III* (100 pl.), ☎ 89.41.15.94.

Restaurants :

● ♦♦♦ ***Schillinger,*** 16, rue Stanislas (A2), ☎ 89.41.43.17. ♿ closed 11 Jul-5 Aug, Sun eve and Mon, ex nat hols. Excellent regional cuisine with a modern flair, 220-310.

● ♦♦♦ ***Au Fer Rouge,*** 52, Grand'Rue (B2), ☎ 89.41.37.24. AE, DC, Visa ♿ closed 6-28 Jan, 28 Jul-6 Aug, Sun eve and Mon. Paul Bocuse, Claude Peyrot and Jacques Pic are happy to welcome among the Hachette great cooks world, the young Patrick Fulgraff, one of their former trainees. Today, in his beautiful Alsacian house where his mother takes care of

Alsace

service, he proposes a superb cuisine with a nice mixture of flavours : *pied de porc truffé aux lentilles, homard et grenouilles au chou rave à la ciboulette,* and lots of good other things ; great Alsacian wines, 120-350.

♦♦ ***Maison des Têtes,*** 19, rue des Têtes (B2), ☎ 89.24.43.43. AE, DC, Visa. closed 15 Jan-15 Feb, Sun eve and Mon, 80-150.

♦♦ ***Meistermann,*** 2a, av. de la République (A2), ☎ 89.41.26.35. AE, DC, Euro, Visa ♿ closed 15 Nov-1 Dec, Wed low season, 120-210.

♦♦ ***Unterlinden,*** 2, rue Unterlinden (B1), ☎ 89.41.18.73. AE, DC. closed 2-20 Jan, Sun and Tue eve, 60-120.

● ♦ ***S'Parisser Stewwele,*** 4, pl. Jeanne-d'Arc, ☎ 89.41.42.33. closed Tue, 8-20 Feb and last week of Jun and Nov. Winstub in a 16thC listed house, regional dishes, 90-130.

Guided tour of the old town in a mini-train from Jun to Oct. Enq & bookings at the T.O.

Recommended : *Pâtisserie du Musée,* 3, rue des Têtes, ☎ 89.23.34.72. *Léonard Helmstetter,* cake-shop, 11, rue des Serruriers, ☎ 89.41.27.78. *Clergue,* cake-shop and tearoom, 21, pl. de la Cathédrale (B2), ☎ 89.41.82.60. Charcuterie : *Woelfflé,* 10, rue de la Semm, ☎ 89.41.28.54. *Kempf,* 21, rue des Clerf (B-C2), ☎ 89.41.32.07. *Martin-Jund wine-cellar,* 12, rue de l'Ange, ☎ 89.41.58.72. Foie gras : *Schillinger,* 16, rue Stanislas, ☎ 89.41.43.17.

EGUISHEIM

Mulhouse 39, Belfort 71, Paris 518
6 km S of Colmar, A3 ✉ 68420 Herrlisheim

Hotels :

★★★***Auberge Alsacienne,*** 12, Grand'Rue, ☎ 89.41.50.20. 20 rm closed 15 Dec-1 Feb and Tue. 🅿 180. Rest. ♦♦ ♿ (eve only) closed Mon, 120-210.

★***A la Ville de Colmar*** (L.F.), 1, pl. Ch.-de-Gaulle, ☎ 89.41.16.99. 7 rm closed 1-15 Sep and Wed, 180. Rest. ♦ 80-130.

⛺ ★★***Municipal*** (100 pl.), ☎ 89.23.19.39.

Restaurant :

● ♦♦ ***Caveau d'Eguisheim,*** 3, pl. du Château, ☎ 89.41.08.89. DC ♿ closed 15 Jan-1 Mar, last week in Jun, Wed eve and Thu. Fine cuisine by one of Paul Bocuse's trainees. Spéc. : *grenouilles au riesling,* 105-200.

Recommended : Wine merchant, caves *Hertz,* 1, porte des Chevaliers, ☎ 89.41.81.61 ; caves *Sorg,* 8, rue Stumpf, ☎ 89.41.80.85.

ERSTEIN

Colmar 49, Saint-Dié 68, Paris 511
24 km S of Strasbourg, B2 ✉ 67150

SNCF ☎ 88.98.00.06.

Hotels :

★★***Motel Au Brochet,*** 94, rue du Gal-de-Gaulle, ☎ 88.98.03.70. AE, Euro, Visa. 31 rm 🅿 ♿ 145. Rest. ♦ 75-100.

Sand, ✉ 67230 Benfeld, 6 km S :

★★***Hostellerie la Charrue*** (L.F.), 4, rue du 1er-Décembre, ☎ 88.74.42.66. 26 rm 🅿 closed 10-23 Feb, Christmas, 170. Rest. ♦ ♿ closed Sun eve and Mon, 60-120.

Rhinau, ✉ 67230 Benfeld, 14 km SE :

★★***Bords du Rhin,*** 10, rte du Rhin, ☎ 88.74.60.36. 15 rm 🅿 closed 15 Jan-15 Feb, Mon eve, Tue, 180. Rest. ♦ 80-130.

⛺ Rhinau : ★★★*Ziegelhof* (100 pl.), ☎ 88.74.60.45. ★★*Wagelrott* (100 pl.), ☎ 88.98.13.51.

Restaurant :

Rhinau, ✉ 67230 Benfeld, 14 km SE :

♦♦ ***Vieux Couvent,*** 6, rue des Chanoines, ☎ 88.74.61.15. closed Feb school hols, 8-31 Jul, Christmas, New Year's Day, Tue eve and Wed, 120-210.

FERRETTE

Belfort 47, Colmar 79, Paris 546
A4 ✉ 68480

ℹ hôtel de ville, ☎ 89.40.40.01.

Hotels :

★★***La Bonne Auberge*** (L.F.), 5, rue Léon-Lehmann, ☎ 89.40.40.34. AE, DC, Euro, Visa. 20 rm 🅿 closed Jan, Feb, Mon and Tue until 4 pm, 100. Rest. ♦♦ ♿ 80-130.

Felseneck (L.F.), 42, rue du Château, ☎ 89.40.41.54. DC, Euro, Visa. 10 rm closed 22 Dec-15 Jan, Sun eve and Mon, 110. Rest. ♦ ♿ 30-130.

Le GRAND BALLON

Mulhouse 40, Colmar 48, Paris 528
A3 ✉ 68760 Willer sur Thur

Hotels :

★***Grand Ballon*** (L.F.), ☎ 89.76.83.35. 20 rm 🅿 closed 15 Nov-15 Dec, 115. Rest. ♦ ♿ 55-160.

Goldenmatt, rte des Crêtes, ☎ 89.82.32.86. 15 rm 🅿 ♿ closed 20 Nov Easter. 200. Rest. ♦ 75-160.

GUEBWILLER

Colmar 26, Belfort 53, Paris 548
A3 ✉ 68500

ℹ 5, pl. St-Léger, ☎ 89.76.10.65.

SNCF ☎ 89.46.50.50.

Hotels :

★★***Lac*** (L.F.), rue de la République, ☎ 89.76.63.10. Euro, Visa. 44 rm 🅿 150. Rest. ♦ ♿ closed Mon. Good basic fare, 35-50.

Soultz, ✉ 68360, 3 km SE :

★★***Belle Vue,*** 28, rte de Wuenheim, ☎ 89.76.95.82. DC, Euro, Visa. 7 rm 🅿 closed Fri, 150. Rest. ♦ 55-100.

Buhl, ✉ 68530, 3 km NE :

★★***A la Vigne*** (L.F.), 141, rue Florival, ☎ 89.76.92.99. Visa. 12 rm 🅿 closed Jan and Mon low season, 100. Rest. ♦ ♿ 80-130.

Murbach, ✉ 68530 Buhl, 5.5 km N :

★★★***Hostellerie St-Barnabé*** (L.F.), 25, rue de Murbach, ☎ 89.76.92.15. 29 rm, closed 2 Jan-1 Mar and Mon. 🅿 180. Rest. ♦♦ 80-130.

Jungholtz, 7 km S :

● ★★★***Résidence les Violettes*** (L.F., Relais du Silence), Thierenbach, ☎ 89.76.91.19. 12 rm 🅿 260. Rest. ♦♦♦ closed Mon eve and Tue. Renowned cuisine, 120-210.

★★***Auberge de la Ferme*** (L.F.), Thierenbach, ☎ 89.76.93.01. 13 rm 🅿 150. Rest. ♦♦ ♿ Good fare (farm produce), 70-120.

★***Biebler*** (L.F.), 2, rue de Rimbach, ☎ 89.76.85.75. AE, DC, Euro, Visa. 12 rm 🅿 closed Fri, 95. Rest. ♦♦ Simple, enjoyable meals, 50-130.

Hartmannswiller, 7 km S :

★★***Meyer*** (L.F.), 49, rue de Cernay, ☎ 89.76.73.14. 18 rm 🅿 180. Rest. ♦ 80-130.

Recommended : Mme Halterbach, 8, rue Verdun, painted wooden furniture.

HAGUENAU

Strasbourg 32, Sarreguemines 75, Paris 477
B1 ✉ 67500

ℹ 1, pl. Joseph-Thierry, ☎ 88.73.30.41.

SNCF ☎ 88.93.77.05.

Hotels :

★★*Europ-Hôtel,* 15, av. du Prof. R. Lorioho, ☎ 88.93.58.11. Tx 880566. AE, DC, Euro, Visa. 55 rm P ♨ ♿ closed Sat and Sun eve, 180. Rest. 120-210.

Marienthal, 5.5 km S :

★★*Hermitage,* 4, pl. de la Basilique, ☎ 88.93.87.46. Euro, Visa. 17 rm P ♿ closed Feb school hols, 100. Rest. closed Sun eve and Mon, 80-130.

Å★★*Les Pins* (70 pl.), ☎ 88.93.90.57.

Restaurants :

♦♦ ***Taverne Barberousse,*** 8, pl. Barberousse, ☎ 88.73.31.09. AE, DC, Euro, Visa ♨ ♿ closed 22 Jul-10 Aug, Feb school hols, Sun eve and Mon, 40-130.

Drusenheim, ☒ 67410, 16 km E :

♦♦♦ ***Auberge du Gourmet,*** 707, rte de Herrlisheim, ☎ 88.63.30.60. P ♨ closed 15 Jul-15 Aug, Tue eve and Wed, 120-210.

Attractions : ***le Nautiland,*** 8, rue des Dominicains, ☎ 88.73.49.59.

HAUT-KŒNIGSBOURG

Colmar 27, Saint-Dié 44, Paris 432
A3 ☒ 68590 Saint-Hippolyte

Hotels :

Thannenkirch, 7 km SW :

★★*Touring* (L.F.), 43, rte du Haut-Kœnigsbourg, ☎ 89.73.10.01. 34 rm P ♿ closed 15 Nov-15 Mar, 180. Rest. ♦ 60.

★★*Auberge la Meunière* (L.F.), 38, rue Ste-Anne, ☎ 89.73.10.47. Visa. 15 rm P ♨ closed 30 Nov-15 Mar and Wed, 155. Rest. ♦ ♿ 70-95.

See also Saint-Hippolyte.

Le HOHWALD

Saint-Dié 46, Strasbourg 47, Paris 495
A2 88 ☒ 67140 Barr

Winter sports holiday village.

ℹ ☎ 89.08.30.90.

Hotels :

● ★★★*Grand Hôtel* (Inter-Hôtel), rue Principale, ☎ 89.08.31.03. 74 rm P ♨ closed 10 Nov-20 Dec, 5 Jan-beg. Feb, 180. Rest. ♦♦ 120-210.

★★*Marchal,* ☎ 88.08.31.04. Visa. 17 rm P ♨ closed 5 Nov-20 Dec, 5-15 Mar and Tue, 180. Rest. ♦♦ 75-90.

At the col de Kreuzweg, 5 km SW :

★*Zundelkopf* (L.F.), ☎ 88.08.30.41. 22 rm P closed 9-20 Mar, 20 Oct-30 Nov, 370. Rest. pension only.

At the col de la Charbonnière, 9 km SW :

★★*Charbonnière* (L.F.), ☎ 88.08.31.17. Euro, DC. 20 rm P ♨ 190. Rest. ♦ ♿ 65-100.

Å ★★★★*Municipal* (100 pl.), ☎ 88.08.30.90.

ILLHAEUSERN

Saint-Dié 51, Strasbourg 60, Paris 521
17 km NE of Colmar, A3 ☒ 68150 Ribeauvillé

Hotel :

● ★★★*La Clairière,* rte de Guémar, ☎ 89.71.80.80. 25 rm P ♿ closed 1 Jan-1 Mar, Mon eve and Tue, in Nov, Dec, Mar, 400.

Chambres d'hôtes : Mme René Jehl, 57, rue du 25-Janvier, ☎ 89.71.83.76. 6 rm.

Restaurant :

● ♦♦♦♦ ***Auberge de l'Ill,*** rue de Collonges, ☎ 89.71.83.23. AE, DC, Visa ♨ ♿ closed 27 Jan-28 Feb, 30 Jun-10 Jul, Mon eve and Tue in summer and Mon and Tue in winter. The Haeberlin family is faithful to its motto : "Tradition et qualité". Jean-Pierre is the untiring ambassador, while, in the kitchen, his brother Paul assures perfect preparation. His son Marc innovates while respecting the principles which make this pleasant stop on the banks of the Ill one of the great restaurants of France. Spec : *homard à la chinoise, pigeonneau en pot-au-feu,* exceptional wine cellar, 250-400.

KAYSERSBERG

Colmar 11, Saint-Dié 46, Paris 504
A3 ☒ 68240

ℹ 44, rue Gal-de-Gaulle, ☎ 89.47.10.16.

Hotels :

★★★*Remparts* (L.F.), 4, rue de la Flieh, ☎ 89.47.12.12. AE, Euro, Visa. 31 rm P ♨ 230.

★★★*Chambard,* 13, rue du Gal-de-Gaulle, ☎ 89.47.10.17. AE, DC, Euro, Visa. 20 rm P ♨ closed 1-20 Mar, 1-15 Dec, 400. Rest. ● ♦♦ ♿ closed Sun eve, Mon. Two dining rooms for the good cooking of P. Irmann. Spec : *boudin de foie gras, turbot au gingembre,* riesling, tokay, 120-210.

★★*Arbre Vert* (L.F.), 1, rue Haute-du-Rempart, ☎ 89.47.11.51. 24 rm closed 15 Nov-15 Dec, 15-28 Feb and Mon low season, 180. Rest. ♦♦ 80-130.

Kientzheim, 3 km E :

★★*Hostellerie Schwendi* (L.F.), 2, pl. Schwendi, ☎ 89.47.30.50. 7 rm P closed 15 Nov-1 Apr and Wed, 175. Rest. ♦ 60-80.

★★*Hostellerie de l'Abbaye d'Alspach* (L.F.), 2-4, rue Foch, ☎ 89.47.16.00. 20 rm P ♨ closed 6 Jan-9 Feb, 170. Rest. ♦♦ eve only, 120-210.

Å ★★★★*Municipal* (100 pl.), ☎ 89.47.14.47.

Restaurant :

♦♦ ***Au Lion d'Or,*** 66, rue du Gal-de-Gaulle, ☎ 89.47.11.16. DC, Visa ♿ closed 10 Jan-20 Feb, 1st week July, Tue eve and Wed, 70-130.

Recommended : charcuterie : *J.-L. Bruxer,* 107, rue du Gal-de-Gaulle, ☎ 89.78.23.19.

LAPOUTROIE

Colmar 19, Saint-Dié 37, Paris 496
4.5 km N of Orbey, A3 ☒ 68650

Hotels :

● ★★*Les Alisiers* (L.F.), 3 km S, ☎ 89.47.52.82. Visa. 15 rm P ♨ closed 15 Nov-15 Dec, 80. Rest. ♦ closed Mon eve and Tue, 185.

★★*Faudé* (L.F.), 28, rue du Gal-Dufieux, ☎ 89.47.50.35. Euro, Visa. 27 rm P ♨ closed 3-15 Mar, 12 Nov-1 Dec, 160. Rest. ♦ ♿ closed 15 Nov-15 Dec, 60-105.

Le Bonhomme, 5 km W :

★★*Poste* (L.F.), rue du 3e-Spahi, ☎ 89.47.51.10. Euro, Visa. 21 rm P ♨ closed 15 Nov-15 Dec, 170. Rest. ♦ closed Tue eve and Wed, 60-90.

★*Lion d'Or,* 68, rue Principale, ☎ 89.47.51.18. Visa. 12 rm P closed 5-end Nov and Wed eve, 100. Rest. ♦ 45-95.

Å ★★*Le Clos des Biches* (70 pl.), ☎ 89.47.50.86.

Recommended : cheese shop (munster) *Haxaire,* 18, rue Gal-Dufieux, ☎ 89.47.50.76.

LAUTERBOURG

Haguenau 41, Strasbourg 63, Paris 528
B1 ☒ 67630

SNCF ☎ 88.54.60.00.

Hotel :
★***Au Cygne,*** 1, rue du Gal-Mittelhauser, ☎ 88.94.80.59. 7 rm, closed Jul, Tue eve and Wed, 100. Rest. ◆ 80-130.

Restaurant :
◆◆◆ ***A la Poële d'Or,*** 35, rue du Gal-Mittelhauser, ☎ 88.94.84.16. AE, DC Ⓟ closed 9-30 Jan, Tue, Fri noon, 110-250.

LEMBACH

Haguenau 24, Strasbourg 56, Paris 495
19 km NE of Niederbronn, B1 ☒ 67510

ⓘ 45, rue de Bitche, ☎ 88.94.43.81.

Hotels :
★★***Vosges du Nord,*** 59, rte de Bitche, ☎ 88.94.43.41. 8 rm Ⓟ 🚫 ♿ closed 20 Aug-15 Sep, Mon and Tue, 100.

Niedersteinbach, 8 km W :
● ★★***Cheval Blanc*** (L.F.), 27, rte de Bitche, ☎ 88.09.25.31. Euro, Visa. 31 rm ☼ Ⓟ 🌳 🔇 🚫 🏊 🎾 closed 1-15 Dec, 20 Jan-1 Mar, 160. Rest. ◆ ♿ Good simple fare, 60-95.

Obersteinbach, 10 km W :
★***Anthon,*** 45, rue Principale, ☎ 88.09.25.01. Euro. 7 rm Ⓟ 🌳 ♿ closed 2 Jan-1 Feb, Mon and Tue, 150. Rest. ◆ ♿ Excellent meals. Spec : *foie gras frais, filet de turbotin au beurre d'orange,* 65-150.

⛺ ★★★*Fleckenstein* (250 pl.), ☎ 88.94.40.38.

Restaurant :
● ◆◆ ***Auberge du Cheval Blanc,*** 4, rue de Wissembourg, ☎ 88.94.41.86. Visa Ⓟ 🚫 closed end Aug. early Sep, Feb hols Mon and Tue. The Mischlers' opulent cuisine is equal to the 1740 décor. Spec : *feuilleté de grenouilles à l'oseille, filets de sole au pinot.* 40 000 bottles in the wine cellar, 220-310.

Gimbelhof, 10 km N :
Gimbelhof Farm, ☎ 88.94.43.58. Euro ☼ Ⓟ 🌳 🔇 8 rm. closed 15 Nov-25 Dec, Mon and Tue, 65. Rest. ♿ Spec : frogs legs, 45-85.

MARLENHEIM

Saverne 19, Strasbourg 20, Paris 465
4.5 km SE of Wasselone, A2 ☒ 67520

ⓘ pl. Kaufhaus, ☎ 88.87.75.80.

Hotels :
★★***Hostellerie du Cerf,*** 30, rue du Gal-de-Gaulle, ☎ 88.87.73.73. AE, DC, Visa. 19 rm Ⓟ 🌳 ♿ closed Mon and Tue, 240. Rest. ● ◆◆ ♿ Very good dishes. *Suprême de sandre au pinot noir sur lit de pâtes fraîches, poitrine et cuisses de poularde rôties aux légumes nouveaux caramélisés,* 150-260.
★★***Hostellerie Reeb*** (L.F.), 2, rue du Dr-Schweitzer, ☎ 88.87.52.70. 35 rm Ⓟ 🌳 🚫 closed 7-31 Jan and Tue, 180. Rest. ◆◆ 120-210.

Farmhouse gîte : *Schmitt,* in Soultz-les-Bains, 6.5 km S, ☎ 88.38.21.09.

Restaurant :
◆◆ ***Auberge du Kronthal,*** 2, rue du Kronthal, ☎ 88.87.50.25. Euro, Visa Ⓟ 🌳 ♿ closed 10 Jul-10 Aug, 23-28 Dec, Sun eve and Mon. Spec : *canard à l'orange,* 50-150.

MARMOUTIER

Saverne 6, Strasbourg 33, Paris 452
A2 ☒ 67440

Hotels :
Birkenwald, 4 km S :
★★***Vosges,*** 59, rue Principale, ☎ 88.70.61.06. Euro, Visa. 14 rm Ⓟ 🌳 🔇 closed 8-31 Jan, 125. Rest. ◆ ♿ closed Mon eve and Tue, 45-85.
★★***Au Chasseur*** (L.F.), 8, rue du Cimetière, ☎ 88.70.61.32. Visa. 25 rm Ⓟ 🌳 🔇 🚫 ♿ closed 18 Sep-10 Oct, 1-20 Feb, Sun eve and Mon, 170. Rest. ◆ ♿ 40-120.

MASEVAUX

Belfort 23, Colmar 57, Paris 521
A4 ☒ 68290

ⓘ 36, Fossé-Flagellants, ☎ 89.82.41.99 (high season).

Hotels :
★***A l'Aigle d'Or*** (L.F.), pl. G.-Clemenceau, ☎ 89.82.40.66. 9 rm Ⓟ 🚫 closed 3-28 Jan, 15 Sep-10 Oct, Mon eve and Tue, 100. Rest. ◆ 120-210.

Sewen, 8 km SW :
★★***Vosges*** (L.F.), 38, Grand'Rue, ☎ 89.82.00.43. 22 rm ☼ Ⓟ 🌳 🔇 closed 15-31 Jan, 15 Oct-30 Nov., Sun eve and Tue (low season), 140. Rest. ◆ closed Tue eve and Wed, 70-150.
★***Au Relais des Lacs,*** 30, Grand'Rue, ☎ 89.82.01.42. DC, Visa. 16 rm ☼ Ⓟ 🌳 🔇 closed 6 Jan-15 Feb, 27 Aug-11 Sep, 180. Rest. ◆ ♿ closed Tue eve and Wed, 120-210.

⛺ ★★★*Municipal* (60 pl.), ☎ 89.82.42.90.

MOLSHEIM

Strasbourg 27, Lunéville 94, Paris 474
A-B2 ☒ 67120

ⓘ hôtel de ville, ☎ 88.38.52.00, and Caveau de la Metzig (high season).

SNCF ☎ 88.38.14.31.

Hotels :
★★★***Diana,*** pont de la Bruche, ☎ 88.38.51.59, Tx 890559. AE, DC, Euro, Visa. 44 rm ☼ Ⓟ 🌳 🔇 ♿ 205. Rest. ◆◆ 85-170.
★★Centre (L.F.), 1, rue St-Martin, ☎ 88.38.54.50. DC. 29 rm Ⓟ 🌳 🔇 130.
★***Au Cheval Blanc*** (L.F.), 5, pl. de l'Hôtel-de-Ville, ☎ 88.38.16.87. 13 rm. Rest. ◆◆ closed Feb.

⛺ ★★*Municipal* (100 pl.), ☎ 88.38.11.67.

MONT-SAINTE-ODILE

Strasbourg 42, Colmar 52, Paris 501
A2 ☒ 67530 Ottrott

Hotels :
★***Mont Sainte-Odile,*** ☎ 88.95.80.53. 130 rm ☼ Ⓟ 🚫 closed 15-30 Nov and 7-20 Jan, 100. Rest. ◆ 80-130.

Ottrott, 8 km N :
★★★***Beau Site,*** 1, rue du Gal-de-Gaulle, ☎ 88.95.80.61, Tx 870445. AE, Euro, Visa. 14 rm Ⓟ 🚫 250. Rest. ◆◆◆ ♿ closed Sun eve and Mon. Opulence and tradition. Spec : game in season, fish, 150-160.
● ★★***Hostellerie des Châteaux*** (L.F., Relais du Silence), 11, rue des Châteaux, ☎ 88.95.81.54, Tx 870439. AE, Euro, Visa. 37 rm ☼ Ⓟ 🌳 🔇 ♿ closed 3 Jan-3 Feb and Tue low season, 200. Rest. ◆◆ ♿ Spec : *foie gras d'oie maison, loup de mer au fumet d'alisier,* 75-160.
★★***Le Moulin*** (L.F.), rte de Klirgerthal, ☎ 88.95.87.33, Tx 870445. AE, Euro, Visa. 21 rm ☼ Ⓟ 🌳 🔇 ♿ 230. Rest. ◆ ♿ 80-130.

MULHOUSE

Colmar 41, Strasbourg 118, Paris 537
A1 ✉ 68100

ℹ 9, av. Foch (C2-3), ☎ 89.45.68.31, and at the musée de l'automobile, 192, av. de Colmar, 9:30-5, all year.

✈ Bâle-Mulhouse, 27 km SE, ☎ 89.69.00.00. *Air France Agency,* 7, av. Foch, ☎ 89.46.10.18.

SNCF (C3), ☎ 89.46.50.50., 89.45.62.83.

🚌 av. du Gal-Leclerc (C3), ☎ 89.45.36.56.

Car-hire : *Budget* train + auto, 7, av. Mal-Foch, ☎ 89.56.11.00 ; Mulhouse airport.

Hotels :
★★★***Europe,*** 11, av. du Mal-Foch, ☎ 89.45.19.18. Tx 881720. DC, Euro, Visa. 50 rm ♿ 250.
★★★***Bristol*** (Mapotel), 18, av. de Colmar (B1), ☎ 89.42.12.31. 50 rm P ♿ closed 24 Dec-2 Jan, 180.
★★***Musée,*** 3, rue de l'Est (C2), ☎ 89.45.47.41, Tx 881188. DC, Euro, Visa. 44 rm P ⚘ closed 20 Dec-5 Jan, 210.
★★***Wir,*** 1, porte de Bâle (C2), ☎ 89.56.13.22. Tx 881720. Euro, Visa. 40 rm ♿ 185. Rest. ♦♦ closed 15 Jun-15 Jul and Mon, 25-60.
★***Le Paon d'Or*** (L.F.), 13, av. de Colmar (B1), ☎ 89.45.34.41. 25 rm, closed 15 Jan-15 Feb and Fri, 180.

Youth hostel, 37, rue d'Illberg, ☎ 89.42.63.28.

⛺ ★★★*Ill* (200 pl.), ☎ 89.06.20.66.

Restaurants :
♦♦ ***Auberge Alsacienne du Parc Zoologique,*** 31, av. de la 9e-D.I.C., ☎ 89.44.26.91. AE, Visa, Euro P ⚘ closed Feb, Mon eve and Sun, 120-210.
♦♦ ***Le Belvédère,*** 80, av. de la 1re-D.-B., ☎ 89.44.18.79. AE, DC, Euro, Visa. closed Feb hols, Mon eve and Tue, 120-210.
♦♦ ***Aux Caves du Vieux Couvent,*** 23, rue du Couvent, ☎ 89.46.28.79. closed Sun and Mon, 80-130.
♦♦ ***Musée de l'Automobile,*** 192, av. de Colmar, ☎ 89.42.22.48. Visa ✂ ♿ closed 1-15 Jan, Mar. For old car buffs who don't want to stop looking. *Choucroutes,* 90-130.

Steinbrunn-le-Bas, ✉ 68440 Habsheim, 8.5 km S :
● ♦♦♦ ***Moulin du Kaegy,*** ☎ 89.81.30.34. AE P ⚘ ♿ closed 15 Jul-1 Aug/15 Dec-15 Jan, Sun eve and Mon 16thC mill. Evocative menus : "Feast - Tradition - Today". Spec. : *foie d'oie confit à l'ombre, fricassée d'asperges, carottes primeurs et pleurotes, grosse sole au beurre de gingembre,* 200-360.

Recommended : pâtisserie-salon de thé *Carlos,* 26, rue E.-Dolfus, ☎ 89.42.16.06.

MUNSTER

Colmar 19, Strasbourg 89, Paris 463
A3 ♥ ✉ 68140

ℹ pl. de la Salle-des-Fêtes, ☎ 89.77.31.80.

SNCF ☎ 89.77.34.17.

Hotels :
★★***La Cigogne*** (L.F.), 4, pl. du Marché, ☎ 89.77.32.27. Visa. 10 rm ✂ closed 16-29 Jun, 24 Nov-14 Dec, Tue eve and Wed, 165. Rest. ♦♦ ✂ 60-110.
★★***Au Val St-Grégoire*** (L.F.), 5, rue St-Grégoire, ☎ 89.77.36.22. 28 rm P ⚘ ♿ closed 4-25 Jan, 4-22 Dec and Fri, 150. Rest. ♦ 80-100.

Luttenbach, 3 km SW on the D10 :
● ★★***Au Chêne Voltaire,*** rue Voltaire, ☎ 89.77.31.74. Visa. 19 rm P ⚘ ✂ closed 3-15 Mar, 15 Nov-15 Jan, 140. Rest. ♦ 50-80.
★***Le Chalet,*** 85, rue de la Mairie, ☎ 89.77.38.33. 18 rm P ⚘ ✂ closed 2 Jan-1 Feb and Tue low season, 140. Rest. ♦ 40-70.

Mulbach, ✉ 68380 Metzeral, 4 km SW :
★★***Perle des Vosges*** (L.F.), 22, rue de Gaschney, ☎ 89.77.61.34. 25 rm P ✂ closed 3 Jan-2 Feb, 180. Rest. ♦ closed Wed low season, 180-130.

Soultzbach-les-Bains, ✉ 68230 Turckheim, 6 km E :
★***Saint-Christophe*** (L.F.), 4, rue de l'Église, ☎ 89.71.13.09. DC, Visa. 10 rm P ⚘ closed Jan and Wed, 150. Rest. pension, half-pension.

Hohrodberg, 7.5 km N :
★★***Roess*** (L.F.), 16, rte du Linge, ☎ 89.77.36.00. 24 rm ✂ closed 4 Nov-18 Dec, 160. Rest. ♦ 70-105.
★***Beau Site,*** Hohrod, ☎ 89.77.31.55. Visa. 13 rm P ⚘ closed 6 Nov-20 Dec, 5-20 Jan and Wed noon, 130. Rest. ♦ 125 (half-pension) - 170 (full-pension).

⛺ ★★★*Municipal* (205 pl.), ☎ 89.77.31.08.

MUTZIG

Strasbourg 28, Saint-Dié 65, Paris 477
3 km W of Molsheim, A-B2 ✉ 67190

SNCF ☎ 88.38.13.06.

Hotel :
★★***Hostellerie de la Poste*** (L.F.), 4, pl. de la Fontaine, ☎ 88.38.38.38. Visa. 19 rm ✂ 180. Rest. ♦ ♿ 80-130.

Restaurant :
● ♦♦ ***Auberge alsacienne Au Nid de Cigognes,*** 25, rue du 18-Novembre, ☎ 88.38.11.97. closed Tue eve and Wed. For good traditional fare, 50-150.

NEUF-BRISACH

Colmar 16, Strasbourg 72, Paris 467
B3 ✉ 68600

ℹ 6, pl. d'Armes, ☎ 89.72.56.66 (high season), and mairie, ☎ 89.72.51.68 (low season).

SNCF ☎ 89.72.51.02.

Hotels :
★★***Soleil*** (L.F.), 6, rue de Bâle, ☎ 89.72.51.28. AE, DC, Euro, Visa. 25 rm, closed Sun eve and Mon, 100. Rest. ♦♦ ♿ 120-210.
★★***Cerf,*** 11, rte de Strasbourg, ☎ 89.72.56.03. Euro, Visa. 30 rm ✂ closed 24 Dec-15 Jan, 195. Rest. ♦ 45-150.

Biesheim, 3 km N :
★★***Aux Deux Clefs*** (L.F.), 50, Grand'Rue, ☎ 89.72.51.20. DC, Euro, Visa. 24 rm P ⚘ ✂ closed 1-24 Jan, 180. Rest. ♦ ♿ 80-130.

Volgelgrun, 4 km E :
★★***Motel Européen,*** Ile du Rhin, ☎ 89.72.51.57. AE, DC, Visa. 23 rm P ⚘ ✂ ✂ ♿ closed Feb and Christmas, 200. Rest. ♦ closed Mon, 85-180.

Andolsheim, 10.5 km NW :
★★★***Soleil*** (L.F.), 1, rte de Colmar, ☎ 89.71.40.53. AE, DC. 17 rm P ⚘ ✂ closed Feb and Wed eve, 170. Rest. 85-180.

Artzenheim, ✉ 68320 Muntzenheim, 11 km N :
★★***Auberge d'Artzenheim*** (L.F.), 30, rue du Sponeck, ☎ 89.71.60.51. AE, DC, Euro, Visa. 10 rm P ⚘ ✂ ✂ closed 15 Feb-15 Mar, 145. Rest. ● ♦♦ ♿ closed Mon eve and Tue. The

Hüssers' restaurant is known for its quality and low prices. Spec. : fresh frogs, *pâté en croûte, vacherin glacé,* Alsatian wines, 70-120.

⛺ ★★★*Ile du Rhin* (265 pl.), ☎ 89.72.57.95, in Biesheim ; ★★*Vauban* (135 pl.), ☎ 89.72.54.25.

NIEDERBRONN-LES-BAINS

Haguenau 21, Strasbourg 53, Paris 449
B1 ⊠ 67110

ⓘ hôtel de ville, ☎ 88.09.17.00.

SNCF ☎ 88.09.01.08.

Hotels :
★★★***Grand Hôtel*** (Inter-Hôtel), 16, av. Foch, ☎ 88.09.02.60. Tx 890151. AE, DC, Visa. 60 rm Ⓟ 🌳 🏊 🎾 ♿ 400. Rest. ◆◆ 120-210.
★★***Bristol,*** 4, pl. de l'Hôtel-de-Ville, ☎ 88.09.61.44. AE, DC, Euro, Visa. 28 rm Ⓟ ♿ 200. Rest. ● ◆◆ ♿ closed Jan, Tue eve and Wed. Enjoyable light cooking. Spec : *terrine de poularde au foie gras, saumon au vinaigre de Xérès, râble de lapereau,* 60-100.
★★***Muller*** (L.F.), 16, av. de la Libération, ☎ 88.09.70.00. AE, DC, Visa. 16 rm Ⓟ 🌳 🏊 closed Jan, 160. Rest. ◆ ♿ closed Sun eve, Mon, 40-60.

⛺ ★★*Heidenkopf* (70 pl.), ☎ 88.09.08.46.

Restaurant :
◆◆◆ ***Parc,*** pl. des Thermes, ☎ 88.09.68.88. AE, DC, Visa. closed Feb and Tue, 120-210.

OBERHASLACH

Strasbourg 40, Saint-Dié 55, Paris 477
16 km W of Molsheim, A-B2 ⊠ 67190 Mutzig

ⓘ mairie, ☎ 88.50.90.15.

Hotels :
★★***Aux Ruines du Nidek*** (L.F.), 2, rue de Molsheim, ☎ 88.50.90.14. DC, Euro, Visa. 15 rm Ⓟ 🌳 closed 15 Nov-16 Dec, 1-15 Mar, Tue eve, Wed, 180. Rest. ◆ closed Tue eve and Wed, 50-60.
Urmatt, 4 km S :
★★***Poste*** (L.F.), 74, rue du Gal-de-Gaulle, ☎ 88.91.40.55. AE, DC, Visa. 13 rm Ⓟ 🚫🐕 closed 18 Nov-2 Dec, 11-24 Mar, Mon, 170. Rest. ◆◆ closed Mon, 60-100.

⛺ ★★*Luttenbach* (100 pl.), ☎ 88.50.90.62.

OBERNAI

Strasbourg 30, Colmar 45, Paris 485
A-B2 ⊠ 67210

ⓘ chapelle du Beffroi, ☎ 88.95.64.13.

SNCF ☎ 88.95.52.54.

Hotels :
● ★★★***Parc*** (L.F., Relais du Silence), 169, rue du Gal-Gouraud, ☎ 88.95.50.08. Tx 870615. Visa. 34 rm ⚟ Ⓟ 🌳 🏊 250. Rest. ● ◆◆◆ ⚟ ♿ closed Sun eve and Mon, 1 Dec-1 Jan, 22 Jun-7 July. For 30 years, Marc Wucheretson and his chef, Boschaefer, have respected tradition. Fresh market produce, 190-200.
★★★***Le Grand Hôtel,*** rue Dietrich, ☎ 88.95.51.28. AE, DE, Euro, Visa. 24 rm, closed 9-25 Feb, 15 days in Nov, Sun eve and Mon, 210. Rest. ◆ 🚫🐕 95-150.
★★***Hostellerie la Diligence*** (L.F.), 23, pl. de la Mairie, ☎ 88.95.55.69. 50 rm closed 22 Nov-15 Dec, 180. Rest. ◆◆ ♿ Tue low season and Wed, 120-210.
★★***Vosges,*** 5, pl. de la Gare, ☎ 88.95.53.78. 15 rm Ⓟ 🚫🐕 closed 10-31 Jan, 155. Rest. ◆ 🚫🐕 closed 3 weeks in Jan, 2 weeks in Jun, Mon in Summer, Sun eve and Mon from Nov-Jun, 55-175.

⛺ ★★*Municipal* (150 pl.), ☎ 88.95.61.31.

Restaurants :
◆ ***A l'Étoile,*** 6, pl. de l'Étoile, ☎ 88.95.50.57. closed 1-15 Dec, 20 Jan-5 Feb and Wed, 120-210.
◆ ***La Halle aux Blés,*** pl. du Marché, ☎ 88.95.56.09. AE, Visa ♿ Authentic Alsatian decoration, 80-130.

Recommended : *pâtisserie-chocolaterie Urban,* 82, rue du Gal-Gouraud, ☎ 88.95.58.90.

ORBEY

Colmar 20, Saint-Dié 42, Paris 500
A3 ⊠ 68370

ⓘ mairie, ☎ 89.71.30.11.

Hotels :
★★***Motel Bois-le-Sire*** (L.F.), 20, rue Ch.-de-Gaulle, ☎ 89.71.25.25. Euro. 34 rm ⚟ Ⓟ 🚫🐕 closed 5-31 Jan, 180. Rest. ◆ closed Sun eve and Mon, 95-130.

Basses-Huttes, 5 km SW :
★★***Wetterer,*** ☎ 89.71.20.28. Visa. 18 rm Ⓟ 🌳 🏊 🚫🐕 closed 10 Nov-15 Dec and Wed, ex Jul-Aug, 170. Rest. ◆◆ 🚫🐕 85.

⛺ ★★*Municipal* (65 pl.), ☎ 89.71.20.07.

La PETITE-PIERRE

Haguenau 40, Strasbourg 59, Paris 431
A1 ⊠ 67290 Wingen sur Moder

ⓘ ☎ 88.70.44.30.

Hotels :
● ★★***Auberge d'Imsthal*** (L.F., Relais du Silence), rte forestière d'Imsthal, ☎ 88.70.45.21. 19 rm ⚟ Ⓟ 🌳 🏊 🚫🐕 closed 25 Nov-15 Dec, 190. Rest. ◆ 🚫🐕 ♿ closed Mon eve and Tue, 50-140.
★★***Lion d'Or*** (L.F.), 15, rue Principale, ☎ 88.70.45.06. DC, Visa. 35 rm ⚟ 🌳 🏊 🚫🐕 📺 🎾 ♿ closed 5 Jan-15 Feb, 210. Rest. ◆ closed Wed eve and Tue, 120-210.
★★***Vosges*** (L.F.), 30, rue Principale, ☎ 88.70.45.05. Euro, Visa. 30 rm ⚟ Ⓟ 🌳 🏊 ♿ closed 12 Nov-12 Dec, 260. Rest. ◆ closed Tue eve and Wed, 120-210.
★***Vieux Moulin,*** ☎ 88.70.17.28. Euro, Visa ⚟ 🌳 ♿ closed 11 Nov-26 Dec, 100. Rest. ◆◆ ♿ closed Mon eve and Tue, 55-120.

Wingen-sur-Moder, 10 km N :
★★***Wen*** (L.F.), 1, rue Principale, ☎ 88.89.71.01. DC, Euro, Visa. 19 rm Ⓟ 🌳 🏊 closed 2 Jan-7 Feb, 145. Rest. ◆ closed Tue eve and Wed, 40-75.

RIBEAUVILLÉ

Colmar 15, Strasbourg 62, Paris 524
A3 ⊠ 68150

ⓘ Grand'Rue, ☎ 89.73.62.22, and at the mairie, ☎ 89.73.60.26.

SNCF ☎ 89.73.60.20.

Hôtels :
● ★★★★(L) ***Clos St-Vincent*** (Relais et châteaux), rte de Bergheim, ☎ 89.73.67.65. Visa. 11 rm ⚟ Ⓟ 🌳 🏊 ♿ closed end Nov-1 Mar, 600. Rest. ◆◆◆ closed Tue and Wed. Fine food and wines. Spec : *émincé de lapin aux choux, foie chaud de canard aux noix,* 110.
★★***Cheval Blanc*** (L.F.), 122, Grand'Rue, ☎ 89.73.61.38. Euro, Visa. 25 rm Ⓟ 🌳 🏊 ♿ closed 1 Dec-1 Feb and Mon, 455. Rest. ◆ ♿ 40-80.
★★***Les Seigneurs de Ribeaupierre,*** 11, rue du Château, ☎ 89.73.70.31. 10 rm 🏊 closed 30 Nov-28 Feb. In a 17thC residence, 390.
★***Vosges*** (L.F.), 2, Grand'Rue, ☎ 89.73.61.39. 14 rm 🚫🐕 closed 15 Jan-15 Mar, 23 Nov-1 Dec,

100. Rest. ● ♦♦ closed Mon eve and Tue. Refined, delicious dishes from Joseph Matter. Spec : *saumon au beurre de verveine, poulet de Bresse au riesling,* 110-230.

Ostheim, 6 km E :
★★***Au nid des Cigognes*** (L.F.), 2, rte de Colmar, ☎ 89.47.91.44. Visa. 50 rm closed 15 Feb-25 Mar, Sun eve and Mon in Winter, 200. Rest. ♦ ♿ closed Sun eve and Mon, 45-100.

⛺ ★★★★*Pierre de Coubertin* (300 pl.), ☎ 89.73.66.71 ; ★*Trois Châteaux* (100 pl.), ☎ 89.73.60.26.

Restaurant :
Zum Pfifferhuss, 14, Grand'Rue, ☎ 89.73.62.28 closed 15 Feb-15 Mar, 1st week in July, Wed and Thu, 100-120.

Recommended : *John,* cake and pastry shop, 58, Grand'Rue. *Jean-Paul Mette,* spirits, 9, rue des Tanneurs, ☎ 89.73.65.88.

RIQUEWIHR

Colmar 13, Saint-Dié 46, Paris 529
A3 ✉ 68340

ℹ rue du Gal-de-Gaulle, ☎ 89.47.80.80 (high season).

Hotels :
★★***Auberge du Schoenenbourg,*** 2, rue de la Piscine, ☎ 89.47.92.28. Visa. 25 rm Ⓟ ♿ closed 13 Jan-14 Feb, Wed eve and Tue, 200 Rest. ● ♦♦ Shady garden overlooking vineyards, everything to please. Spec : *soufflé de saumon au sabayon truffé, tournedos en croûte.* Fine wines, 75-230.
★★***Le Riquewihr,*** rte de Ribeauvillé, ☎ 89.47.83.13. AE, DC, Euro, Visa. 49 rm Ⓟ 210.

Zellenberg, 1 km E :
★★***Au Riesling*** (L.F.), 93, rte du Vin, ☎ 89.47.85.85. 36 rm Ⓟ ♿ closed Nov-Mar, Sun eve and Mon, 180. Rest. ♦ 120-210.

⛺ ★★★★*Intercommunal* (100 pl.), ☎ 89.47.90.08.

Restaurants :
♦♦ ***L'Écurie,*** cour des Cigognes, ☎ 89.47.92.48. closed 1 Dec-1 Mar, Sun eve and Mon, 120-210.
♦ ***Au Tire-Bouchon,*** 33, rue du Gal-de-Gaulle, ☎ 89.47.92.58. AE, Visa ♿ closed 12 Nov-15 Dec, Mar, Tue eve and Wed low season. Pleasant country inn setting, 40-60.

Mittelwihr, ✉ 68630, 3 km SE :
♦♦ ***A la Couronne d'Or*** (L.F.), 19, rte du Wine, ☎ 89.47.90.47. DC, AE, Euro, Visa ♿ closed Jan, Sun eve and Mon. Fish specialities, 120-210.

Recommended : *Mittnacht-Klack wine cellars,* 8, rue des Tuileries, ☎ 89.47.92.54. In Mittelwihr : *Gocker wine-merchant,* 24, rue de Riquewihr, ☎ 89.47.88.02. *Schaller wine-merchant,* 5, rue des Merles.

ROUFFACH

Mulhouse 28, Belfort 60, Paris 529
15 km S of Colmar, A3 ✉ 68250

SNCF ☎ 89.49.60.09.

Hotels :
● ★★★★***Château d'Isenbourg*** (Relais et châteaux), ☎ 89.49.63.53. Tx 880819. Visa. 40 rm Ⓟ ♿ closed 5 Jan-7 Mar, 650. Rest. ● ♦♦♦ *les Tommeries,* Good classical fare. Perfect service in a panoramic dining-room. Spec : *viennoise de turbot à la moutarde de Meaux,* 185-300.

Bollenberg, 6 km SW, ✉ 68111 Westhalten :
★★***Bollenberg*** (France-Accueil), ☎ 89.49.62.47. Tx 880896. AE, DC, Euro, Visa. 50 rm Ⓟ ♿ 225. Rest. ♦ ***Au Vieux Pressoir,*** ☎ 89.49.60.04 ♿ closed Christmas, 1 Jan, 100-130.

Recommended : Soultzmatt, ✉ 68570, 3 km W : *Boesch wine-merchants,* 4, rue du Bois.

SAALES

Saint-Dié 20, Strasbourg 69, Paris 472
20 km SW of Schirmeck, A2 ✉ 67420

ℹ ☎ 88.97.70.26.

SNCF ☎ 88.97.70.12.

Hotels :
★★***Roche des Fées*** (L.F.), rue de l'Église, ☎ 88.97.80.90. AE, DC, Euro, Visa. 20 rm Ⓟ closed 1 Jan-15 Feb, 129. Rest. ♿ 80-130.

Colroy-la-Roche, 11 km NE :
● ★★★★***Cheneaudière*** (Relais et châteaux), ☎ 88.97.61.64. Tx 870438. AE, DC, Euro, Visa. 28 rm Ⓟ ♿ closed 15 Jan-1 Mar, 480. Rest. ♦♦♦ ♿ 180-230.

⛺ ★*Municipal* (30 pl.), ☎ 88.97.70.26.

Recommended : *la Chenaudière,* spirits, Colroy-la-Roche, ☎ 88.97.61.64.

SAINT-HIPPOLYTE

Colmar 20, Saint-Dié 45, Paris 504
9 km SW of Sélestat, A-B3 ✉ 68590

Hotels :
★★★***Munsch Aux Ducs de Lorraine*** (L.F.), 16, rte du Vin, ☎ 89.73.00.09. AE, DC, Visa. 44 rm Ⓟ ♿ closed 10 Jan-1 Mar, 1-17 Dec and Mon, 260. Rest. ♦♦ 120-210.
★★***A la Vignette*** (L.F.), 66, rte du Vin, ☎ 89.73.00.17. 16 rm, closed 1 Dec-31 Jan and Tue, 160. Rest. ♦ 75-120.

Recommended : in Orschwiller, ✉ 67600, 2 km N : *Engel* Vineyard, 1, rte du Vin.

SAINT-LOUIS

Mulhouse 31, Belfort 62, Paris 557
B4 ✉ 68300

SNCF ☎ 89.67.50.50.

Hotels :
★***National*** (L.F.), 71, rue de Bâle, ☎ 89.67.20.32. 23 rm Ⓟ closed 15 Sep-15 Oct and Mon, 100. Rest. ♦ 80-130.

Ronspach-le-Haut, ✉ 68220 Hegenheim, 14 km W :
★★***Le Relais du Sundgau*** (L.F.), 2, rue de l'Église, ☎ 89.68.00.35. 13 rm closed 15 Jan-15 Feb, 180. Rest. ♦ closed Tue eve and Wed, 120-210.

SAINTE-MARIE-AUX-MINES

Saint-Dié 23, Colmar 34, Paris 411
A3 ✉ 68160

ℹ 1, pl. de la Gare, ☎ 89.58.80.50, and 158, rue de-Lattre-de-Tassigny, ☎ 89.58.74.04 (high season).

Hotels :
★★***Cromer*** (L.F.), 185, rue de-Lattre-de-Tassigny, ☎ 89.58.70.19. Tx 880666. AE, DC, Euro, Visa. 40 rm Ⓟ closed 17 Nov-18 Dec, 17 Feb-18 Mar, Sun eve, Mon, 155. Rest. ♦ 60-100.

Sainte-Croix-aux-Mines, 3 km E :
★***Central,*** 41, rue Maurice-Burrus, ☎ 89.58.73.27. AE, Euro, Visa. 9 rm closed 15 Feb-1 Mar, 15 Jun-1 Jul, Sun eve and Mon, 145. Rest. ♦ Spec : *estoufinade de fruits de mer,* 120-160.

Youth hostel : 21, rue Reber, ☎ 89.58.75.74.

SAVERNE

Strasbourg 39, Luneville 80, Paris 446
A1 ⊠ 67700

ℹ château des Rohan, ☎ 88.91.80.47 (in summer), and mairie, ☎ 88.91.18.52.

SNCF ☎ 88.91.16.72.

Hotels :
★★***Chez Jean*** (L.F.), 3, rue de la Gare, ☎ 88.91.10.19. DC, Euro, Visa. 23 rm Ⓟ & closed 1-10 Sept, 25 Dec-10 Jan, 200. Rest. ♦ closed Sun eve and Mon, 45-125.
★★***Fischer*** (L.F.), 15, rue de la Gare, ☎ 88.91.19.53. DC, Euro. 19 rm Ⓟ closed 21 Dec-12 Jan, 26 Apr-9 May, Fri eve, Sat, 155. Rest. & closed Fri eve and Sat, 40-80.

Youth hostel, château des Rohan, ☎ 88.91.14.84. closed 1-15 Feb, 1-15 Nov.

Ⓐ ★★★*Municipal* (100 pl.), ☎ 88.91.35.65.

Restaurant :
Landersheim, 12 km on the D41 :
● ♦♦ ***Auberge du Kochersberg,*** rue de Saessolsheim, ☎ 88.69.91.58. AE, DC, Euro, Visa. & closed 18 Feb-5 Mar, 28 Jul-21 Aug, Sun eve, Tue and Wed. In this "Adidas" annex, the team of A. Roth and P. Klipfel plays and wins. Spec : *foie gras maison, raviolis aux queues d'écrevisses,* 140-220.

SCHIRMECK

Saint-Dié 40, Strasbourg 49, Paris 499
A2 ⊠ 67130

ℹ ☎ 88.97.00.02.

Hotels :
★★***Neuhauser*** (L.F.), Les Quelles, ☎ 88.97.06.81. AE, DC, Visa. 10 rm closed Wed, 12-30 Nov, 15-30 Jan, 160. Rest. ♦ 75-150.
★★***La Rubanerie*** (L.F.), La Claquette-Rothau, ☎ 88.97.01.95. AE, DC, Visa. 16 rm Ⓟ & 205. Rest. ♦ & 130.

Col du Donon, 10 km NW :
★★***Donon*** (L.F.), col du Donon by Grandfontaine, ☎ 88.97.20.69. 20 rm Ⓟ & closed 20 Nov-20 Dec, 1-10 Mar and Tue low season, 160. Rest. ♦ 80, 130.

Natzwiller, 10 km SE :
★***Auberge Metzger,*** 70, rue Principale, ☎ 88.97.02.42. 10 rm Ⓟ & closed 15 Nov-5 Dec and Mon, 125. Rest. ♦ 40-70.

Ⓐ ★★*Municipal* (50 pl.), ☎ 88.97.01.61.

SÉLESTAT

Colmar 22, Strasbourg 47, Paris 508
A-B3 ⊠ 67600

ℹ pl. de la République (B2), ☎ 88.92.02.66.

SNCF (A2), ☎ 88.82.50.50.

Hotel :
★★***Vaillant,*** pl. de la République (B2), ☎ 88.92.09.46. AE, Visa. 47 rm Ⓟ & 180. Rest. ♦ & closed end Oct-early Apr, Sun eve and Mon low season, 50-150.

Ⓐ ★★***Les Cigognes*** (50 pl.), ☎ 88.92.03.98.

Restaurants :
● ♦♦ ***Jean-Frédéric Edel,*** 7, rue des Serruriers, ☎ 88.92.86.55. AE, DC, Euro, Visa. closed 1-10 Jan, Tue noon and Wed. An interesting establishment in which J.-F. Edel, a student of Jean Delaveyne, upholds family tradition. Menu decided by the market. Spec : *palette fumée aux pommes sautées, saumon poêlé aux blinis,* 140-220.

♦ ***A la Vieille Tour,*** 8-10, rue de la Jauge, ☎ 88.92.15.02 & closed 1-17 Jul, Sun eve and Mon. Spec : *cassolette aux foies de volailles et raisins blonds, mignons de veau aux courgettes et concombres, assiette délice des îles,* 55-150.

Recommended : *Sontag cake and pastry shop,* 1, rue du 17-Novembre, ☎ 88.92.02.53.

STRASBOURG

Nancy 145, Metz 162, Paris 486
B2 ⊠ 67000

ℹ Palais des Congrès, av. Schutzenberger (not on the D1 map), ☎ 88.35.03.00. Other addresses : 10, pl. Gutenberg (C3), ☎ 88.32.57.07 ; pl. de la Gare (A2), ☎ 88.32.51.49 ; Pont de l'Europe, 5 km E, ☎ 88.61.39.23.

✈ Strasbourg-Entzheim, 11 km SW, ☎ 88.78.40.99.

✈ *Air France Agency,* 15, rue des Francs-Bourgeois, ☎ 88.32.99.74.

SNCF (A2), ☎ 88.22.50.50., 88.32.07.51.

🚌 place d'Austerlitz and pl. de l'Étoile.

Car-hire : *Budget,* train + auto, 21, rue Déserte, ☎ 88.32.13.90. Strasbourg-Entzheim airport, ☎ 88.68.94.08.

Hotels :
★★★★(L) ***Hilton,*** av. Herrenschmidt, ☎ 88.37.10.10. AE, DC, Euro, Visa. 253 rm and apts Ⓟ & 400. Rest. ● ♦♦ ***la Maison de Bœuf.*** Michou, the chef, is a master of simplicity : *saumon et lotte fumés maison,* fish, grilled meats, 220-310.
★★★★(L) ***Terminus-Gruber*** (Mapotel), 10, pl. de la Gare (A2), ☎ 88.32.87.00. 78 rm Ⓟ & closed 22 Dec-6 Jan, 100. Rest. ♦♦♦ 220-310.
● ★★★***France,*** 20, rue du Jeu-des-Enfants (B3), ☎ 88.32.37.12. Tx 890084. AE, DC, Euro, Visa. 70 rm Ⓟ 380.
● ★★★***Orangerie,*** 58, allée de La Robertsau, ☎ 88.35.10.69. 25 rm Ⓟ 180.
● ★★★***Rohan*** (Château et demeures de tradition), 17-19, rue du Maroquin, ☎ 88.32.85.11. Tx 380324. 36 rm 375.
★★★***Hannong,*** 15, rue du 22-Novembre, ☎ 88.32.16.22. Tx 890551. AE, DC, Euro, Visa. 70 rm Ⓟ closed 20-27 Dec, 350. Rest. ♦♦ Wyn'Bar, enjoyable and rapid ; good selection of wine by the glass, 150.
★★★***Monopole-Métropole,*** 16, rue Kuhn (B2), ☎ 88.32.11.94. Tx 890366. AE, DC, Euro, Visa. 98 rm Ⓟ & closed Christmas-1 Jan, 210.
★★★***Villa d'Est,*** 12, rue J.-Kablé, ☎ 88.36.69.02. Tx 890020. AE, DC, Euro, Visa. 32 rm Ⓟ closed 23 Dec-2 Jan, 290.
● ★★***Europe,*** 38, rue du Fossé-des-Tanneurs (B3), ☎ 88.32.17.88. Tx 890220. AE, DC, Euro, Visa. 60 rm & 180.
● ★★***Gutenberg,*** 31, rue des Serruriers (C3), ☎ 88.32.17.15. 50 rm & closed 1st week in Jan, 185.
★★***Carlton,*** 15, pl. de la Gare (A2), ☎ 88.32.62.39. Tx 880400. 67 rm & 180. Rest.
★★***Rhin,*** 7-8, pl. de la Gare (A2-3), ☎ 88.32.35.00. Tx 880466. Euro, Visa. 63 rm & closed 20 Dec-2 Jan, 200.
★★***Suisse-Horloge astronomique,*** 2-4, rue de la Râpe, ☎ 88.35.22.11. 25 rm 230. Rest. ♦ closed 15 Dec-15 Jan, Mon and Tue noon, 75-100.
★★***Union,*** 8, quai Kellermann (C2), ☎ 88.32.70.41. 60 rm & closed 25 Dec-1 Jan, 180.
★***Michelet,*** 48, rue du Vieux-Marché-aux-Poisson (C3), ☎ 88.32.47.38. 16 rm 140.

★***Victoria,*** 7-9, rue du Maire-Kuss (A-B3), ☎ 88.32.13.06. 37 rm, 120.

Reichstett, ⊠ 67460 Souffelweyersheim, 9 km N :

★★★***A l'Aigle d'Or,*** 5, rue de la Wantzenau, ☎ 88.20.07.87. AE, DC, Visa. 18 rm 🅿 ♿ 260.

★★***Paris*** (L.F.), 2c, rue du Gal-de-Gaulle, ☎ 88.20.00.23. Visa. 16 rm 🅿 closed 5-31 Aug, 180. Rest. ♦ 80-130.

Youth hostel (F.U.A.J.), 9, rue de l'Auberge-de-Jeunesse, ☎ 88.30.26.46.

Farmhouse gîte : *Diemer,* in Breuschwickersheim, ⊠ 67112, 11 km W, ☎ 88.96.02.89.

⛺ ★★★★*Montagne Verte* (200 pl.), ☎ 88.30.25.46 ; ★★★*Baggersee* (250 pl.), ☎ 88.39.03.40.

Restaurants :

● ♦♦♦♦ ***Crocodile*** (Relais gourmand) ; ***Émile Jung,*** 10, rue de l'Outre (C3), ☎ 88.32.13.02. AE, DC, Euro. ❄ closed 7 Jul-6 Aug, 21 Dec-2 Jan, Sun and Mon. In their pretty establishment, E. Jung and his charming wife do honour to the reputation of welcome and quality of the Alsatian table. A happy marriage of region and tradition, 220-310.

● ♦♦♦ ***Buerenhiesel,*** 4, parc de l'Orangerie, ☎ 88.61.62.24. AE, DC. ⚘ ⛵ closed 20 Feb-5 Mar, 7-21 May, Christmas, 1 Jan, Tue eve and Wed. A highly-reputed bastion of nouvelle cuisine, 170-230.

♦♦♦ ***Valentin Sorg,*** 6, pl. de l'Homme-de-Fer (B3), ☎ 88.32.12.16. AE, DC, Visa. ❄ ⛵ ♿ closed 15-28 Feb, 15-30 Aug, Sun eve and Tue. Remarkable view of the town ; classical menu, 130-260.

♦♦ ***Maison Kammerzell,*** 10, pl. de la Cathédrale (C3), ☎ 88.32.42.14, Tx 890221. AE, DC, Euro, Visa. 180-220.

♦♦ ***Zimmer-Sengel,*** 8, rue du Temple-Neuf (C3), ☎ 88.32.35.01. AE, DC, Visa ♿ closed Aug, Sat and Sun, 140-195.

♦♦ ***Au Gourmet sans Chiqué,*** 15, rue Ste-Barbe, near pl. Kléber (C3), ☎ 88.32.04.07. AE, DC, Visa ♿ closed Sun and Mon noon. Period style, 120-180.

♦♦ ***Maison des Tanneurs,*** 42, rue du Bain-aux-Plantes (B3), ☎ 88.32.79.70. AE, DC ♿ closed 26 Jun-9 Jul, 22 Dec-23 Jan, Sun and Mon. The most beautiful half-timbered house in la Petite France. Good food. Spec : *choucroute, matelote,* 220-310.

♦♦ ***Restaurant de l'Orangerie,*** parc de l'Orangerie, bd du Pdt-Édouard (F1), ☎ 88.61.36.24. Visa, AE ❄ 🅿 ⚘ ⛵ ♿ closed Mon. Good value, 45-130.

● ♦ ***A l'Arsenal,*** 11, rue de l'Abreuvoir, ☎ 88.35.03.69. AE, Euro, Visa, closed 15 Jul-15 Aug, 15-30 Jan, Sat and Sun. Alsace cuisine with a modern touch. Excellent value. Spec : *salade de choucroute aux cervelas rôtis, veau au raifort,* 40-90.

♦ ***Gutenberg,*** 8, pl. Gutenberg (C3), ☎ 88.32.82.48. AE, DC, Visa, 80-130.

♦ ***Ami Schutz,*** 1, Ponts-Couverts (B3), ☎ 88.32.76.98. Visa, closed Sun eve and Mon. Regional specialities, 110-150.

Schiltigheim, ⊠ 67300, 6 km N :

● ♦♦ ***La Table Gourmande,*** 43, rte du Gal-de-Gaulle, ☎ 88.83.61.67. AE, DC, Visa ♿ closed 24 Dec-2 Jan, end Jul-mid Aug, Sun and Mon noon. Spec : *daube de turbot au vin du Médoc,* 120-210.

Pfulgriesheim, ⊠ 67370 Truchtersheim, 10 km NW :

● ♦♦ ***Bürestuebel,*** 8, rte de Lampertheim, ☎ 88.20.01.92 ♿ closed Mon and 18-31 Aug. Eve only. Authentic Alsace-style cooking in a half-timbered dining-room with a polychrome ceiling : *tarte flambée au feu de bois,* black pudding, *palets de pommes de terre.* Regional brandies and wines. Take-away service, 70-80.

Brasseries :

● ***A l'Ancienne Douane,*** 6, rue de la Douane (C3-4), ☎ 88.32.42.19 AE ❄ ♿ One of the last of Strasbourg's great brasseries, in an establishment on the banks of the Ill which dates back to 1358. Extremely varied, reasonably-priced meals. Spec : *choucroute, sandre à la strasbourgeoise, foie gras,* 55-95.

● ***Au Rocher du Sapin,*** 6, rue du Noyer (B2), ☎ 88.32.39.65 ♿ closed Sun (and Mon in summer), 30-100.

● ***Au Romain,*** 6-8, rue du Vieux-Marché-aux-Grains (C3), ☎ 88.32.08.54. AE, DC, Euro, Visa ♿ closed Sun eve and Mon. Spec : *choucroute garnie, matelote aux quatre poissons,* 35-120.

● ***Bague d'Or,*** rue de l'Église (C2), ☎ 88.32.47.42 ♿ closed Sat eve, Mon and a week before Easter, 40-60.

Au Dauphin, 13, pl. de la Cathédrale (C3), ☎ 88.32.86.95. AE, DC, Euro, Visa ♿ closed Feb, Sun eve and Mon, 90-150.

Wine-bars :

● ***S'Burjerstuewel, Chez Yvonne,*** 10, rue du Sanglier, ☎ 88.32.84.15. AE, DC, Visa, closed 14 Jul-10 Aug, Christmas-1 Jan, Sun and Mon noon, 80-130.

● ***Le Clou,*** rue du Chaudron, ☎ 88.32.11.67. Eve only, closed Sun and nat hols, 90-100.

● ***Au Coin des Pucelles,*** rue des Pucelles (D3), ☎ 88.35.30.85. Eve only, closed Sun, 80-130.

● ***Pfifferbriader,*** 9, pl. du Marché-aux-Cochons-de-Lait, ☎ 88.32.15.43 ♿ closed Aug and Sun, 35-80.

● ***Strissel,*** 5, pl. de la Grande-Boucherie, ☎ 88.32.14.73. Visa, closed 7-31 Jul, Feb hols, Sun eve and Mon, 40-80.

Guided tours : of the town daily at 10am and 9pm ex Sun and Mon eve in Jul-Aug, on foot. Departure from the T.O. Visit old Strasbourg in a minitrain, commentary provided by a guide, from end Mar to 31 Oct. Bookings : pl. de la Cathédrale, ☎ 88.30.20.24.

Boat trips : floodlit evening cruises up the Ill river, launch trips on the Ill, from Apr to Oct. Embarkation points : château des Rohan, ☎ 88.32.75.25 ; promenade Dauphine, ☎ 88.32.49.15, ext 276. It is advisable to book ahead.

Events : nautical tournaments on the Ill, 2 eves weekly in Jul and Aug in front of the Rohan Palace.

Night-clubs : *l'Astronautus,* rue de Londres, ☎ 88.61.03.82. *Le Charlie's,* pl. des Halles, ☎ 88.22.32.22. *Le Flore,* 7, rue Hannong, ☎ 88.22.53.57.

Recommended : cakes and pastries, iced sweets, tea-room, *Christian :* 10, rue Mercière, ☎ 88.22.12.70 ; and 12, rue de l'Outre, ☎ 88.32.04.41. *Beyler tea-room,* 5, pl. de la Cathédrale, ☎ 88.32.73.66. Bakery : *Au Vieux Strasbourg,* 10, rue de la Division-Leclerc, ☎ 88.32.00.88. Charcutier-traiteur *Kirn,* 19, rue du 22-Nov., ☎ 88.32.16.10, and pl. Gutenberg, ☎ 88.22.13.13. *Frick Lutz,* 16, rue des Orfèvres, ☎ 88.32.60.60. Fine wines : *la Sommelière* (Mr. Kaus), 1, rue du Fossé-des-Tailleurs, ☎ 88.32.78.59. Coffee : *Reck,* 37, rte de Colmar, ☎ 88.34.62.41. *La Boutique du Foie Gras,* 6, rue Friesé, ☎ 88.32.28.42. *Les 12 Apôtres,* rue Mercière ; 125 labels of beer. Alsatian costumes, embroidery : 11 *bis,* quai Turckheim.

Les TROIS-ÉPIS

Colmar 12, Saint-Dié 54, Paris 519
A3 ⊠ 68410

ℹ ☎ 89.49.80.56.

Hotels :

★★★★(L) ***Le Grand Hôtel*** (Mapotel), ☎ 89.49.80.65. Tx 880229. AE, DC, Euro, Visa. 48 rm ⚘ P ♨ ⛰ ▭ ♿ 550. Rest. ♦♦♦ ♿ 250.

★★★***Marchal*** (LF), ☎ 89.49.81.61. Visa. 40 rm ⚘ P ♨ ⛰ ✗ closed 5 Dec-15 Jan, 340. Rest. ♦♦ ✗ ♿ 80-165.

★★***La Croix d'Or*** (L.F.), ☎ 89.49.83.55. 12 rm ⚘ P ⛰ closed 2 Jan-4 Feb and Wed, 300. Rest. ♦ 80-130.

TURCKHEIM

Colmar 7, Saint-Dié 55, Paris 514
A3 ⊠ 68230

SNCF ☎ 89.27.06.37.

Hotels :

★★***Deux Clefs*** (L.F.), 3, rue du Conseil, ☎ 89.27.06.01. AE, Visa. 49 rm ♨ ♿ 240. Rest. ♦♦ ♿ closed 1 Jan-1 Feb, Thu and Fri noon, 70-100.

★★***Vosges,*** 1, pl. de la République, ☎ 89.27.02.37. Tx 880294. Visa. 32 rm P ♨ closed 31 Dec-1 Apr, 180. Rest. ♦ ✗ closed Thu noon, 60-85.

Niedermorschwihr, 2 km N :

★★***L'Ange*** (L.F.), 125, rue des Trois-Épis, ☎ 89.27.05.73. Euro. 10 rm ♨ closed Jan-24 Mar, 180. Rest. ♦ closed Tue eve and Wed low season, 80-130.

Restaurant :

Niedermurschwihr, 2 km N :

♦ ***Caveau du Morakopf,*** 7, rue des Trois-Épis, ☎ 89.27.05.10. closed 1-15 Jul, 1-15 Dec, Sun, 120-210.

⛺ ★★★★*Municipal* (130 pl.), ☎ 89.27.02.00.

WANGENBOURG

Saverne 20, Strasbourg 41, Paris 464
A2 ⊠ 67710

ℹ 47, rue du Gal-de-Gaulle, ☎ 88.87.32.44 (Jul-Aug).

Hotels :

● ★★***Parc Hôtel*** (L.F.), rue du Gal-de-Gaulle, ☎ 88.87.31.72. 34 rm ⚘ P ♨ ⛰ ✗ ▭ 🎾 closed 4 Nov-22 Dec, 200. Rest. ♦♦ 65-100.

★***Scheidecker Fruhauff,*** 35, rue du Gal-de-Gaulle, ☎ 88.87.30.89. 26 rm P ♨ ⛰ closed 12 Nov-20 Dec and Tue, 170. Rest. ♦ 50-100.

Engenthal, 2 km N :

★★***Vosges*** (L.F.), 5, rue de Steigenbach, ☎ 88.87.30.35. DC. 11 rm ⚘ P ♨ 190. Rest. ♦ ⚘ closed Tue eve and Wed low season, 75-85.

⛺ ★*Essi* (40 pl.), ☎ 88.87.32.44.

La WANTZENAU

Haguenau 27, Saverne 45, Paris 483
12 km NE of Strasbourg, B2 ⊠ 67610

ℹ pont international de Gambsheim, 8 km NE, ☎ 88.96.44.08.

SNCF ☎ 88.96.20.16.

Hotels :

● ★★★***Moulin de La Wantzenau*** (Relais du Silence, Moulin Étape), 27, rte de Strasbourg, ☎ 88.96.27.83. AE, DC, Euro, Visa. 20 rm ⚘ P ♨ ⛰ 210. Rest. ● ♦♦ ♿ closed 6-20 Jan, 26 Jun-21 Jul, Sun eve and Thu. Very good restaurant. Spec : *poussin « mère Clauss », matelote au vin blanc,* 115-220.

Gambsheim, ⊠ 67760, 6 km NE :

★★***Europ Stop Relais,*** rte du Rhin, ☎ 88.96.43.33. AE, DC, Euro, Visa. 22 rm P ♨ ⛰ closed 15-30 Aug and Sat, 180. Rest. ♦ ♿ closed Sat noon, 80-130.

Restaurants :

♦♦ ***A la Barrière,*** 3, rte de Strasbourg, ☎ 88.96.20.23. AE, DC P ♿ closed 15 Aug-5 Sep, Wed eve and Thu. Good fare, 165-200.

♦♦ ***J. Schaeffer,*** 1, quai des Bâteliers, ☎ 88.96.20.29. AE, DC. closed 15-30 Jul, Sun eve and Mon, 95-170.

♦♦ ***Zimmer,*** 23, rue des Héros, ☎ 88.96.62.08. AE, DC, Euro, Visa ♨ ♿ closed 1-16 Aug. Spec : *matelote au riesling, salade gourmande au foie gras,* 80-155.

WASSELONNE

Saverne 14, Strasbourg 25, Paris 460
A2 ♥ ⊠ 67310

ℹ pl. du Gal-Leclerc, ☎ 88.87.17.22 (high season).

Hotel :

★***Au Saumon,*** 69, rue du Gal-de-Gaulle, ☎ 88.87.01.83. AE, DC, Visa. 18 rm P ♨ closed 15-30 Jun, Sun eve low season and Mon, 100. Rest. ♦ ⛰ ♿ 80-130.

⛺ ★★*Municipal* (100 pl.), ☎ 88.87.00.08.

WISSEMBOURG

Strasbourg 64, Sarreguemines 80, Paris 509
B1 ⊠ 67160

ℹ hôtel de ville, ☎ 88.94.14.55.

SNCF ☎ 88.94.00.44.

Hotels :

★★***Au Cygne*** (L.F.), 3, rue du Sel, ☎ 88.94.00.16. Euro, Visa. 16 rm P ✗ closed Feb and three weeks in Jul, 200. Rest. ♦♦ ♿ closed Wed and Thu noon, 100.

★★***A la Cave de Cleebourg*** (L.F.), rte de Lobsann-Rott, ☎ 88.94.52.18. Visa. 20 rm ⚘ P ♨ ⛰ ♿ closed 15 Dec-15 Jan, Sun eve and Mon, 100. Rest. ♦ 80-130.

★★***L'Ange,*** 2, rue de la République, ☎ 88.94.12.11. Visa. 8 rm, closed 15 Jan-15 Feb, 1-15 Jul, Sun eve and Mon, 100. Rest. ♿ 80-130.

WŒRTH

Strasbourg 47, Sarreguemines 66, Paris 485
10 km E of Niederbronn, B1 ⊠ 67360

ℹ 2, rue du Moulin, ☎ 88.09.30.21.

Hotels :

★***Belle Vue,*** 43, Grand'Rue, ☎ 88.09.31.44. 12 rm ⚘ P ♨ ✗ closed Sep, 100. Rest. ♦ ♿ closed Mon, 80-130.

Morsbronn-les-Bains, 5 km S :

★★***Beau Séjour,*** 3, rte de Haguenau, ☎ 88.09.42.55. 40 rm P ♨ ▭ ♿ closed 20 Dec-1 Jan, 155. Rest., 50-100.

★★***A la Vignette,*** 24 c, rte de Haguenau, ☎ 88.09.30.50. 30 rm P ♨ ✗ closed Jan, Thu and Sun eves, 125.

The Ardèche and Cévennes Regions

The region is built on three kinds of rock and stone — granite, limestone and schist — which have formed three different cultures and civilizations; two peoples who were enemies for many years, but who now share the same destiny.

Schist underlies mountain torrents, rugged peaks and chestnut trees and has given birth to a freedom-loving society characterized by religious dissent. The pink and grey granite of the high crests provides a backdrop to the breeding of hardy animals able to withstand storms and snow. The great limestone plateaus, or *causses,* swept by wind and clouds, are the home of sheep and wool, crosses and religious rebels. Hardworking and rebellious Cévennes, poor and pious Lozère, and unlike either of them, the wine-growing country with its individualist and anti-clerical tradition.

Despite their differences, these regions complement each other. Highlanders have always been drawn to the plain, towards the distant horizon of the sea. The Cévennes mountains surge up from the *garrigue* over the ochre villages of the vineyards, like waves emerging from purple mist. With its sharp peaks and steep, narrow valleys it is an austere, almost haughty country, both fierce and fragile, intimidating and fascinating.

At the edge of the purple plains, bordering the saltmarshes, is Aigues-Mortes, a walled city at the edge of the Rhône delta. Saint Louis wanted to make it the major port of the Levant, but nature defeated his efforts and Aigues-Mortes became instead a prison for Protestants in the 17th and 18th centuries. The visitor can still read their names and sentences — some exceeding fifty years' imprisonment — in the register of the Constance tower.

Nîmes is a postcard dream of the south — sun and aniseed aperitifs, markets under the plane trees, pines and cypresses, fountains and squares still impregnated with the memory of its Roman past.

The region's gorges and plateaus are perfect for hiking and canoeing, and its hundreds of underground caverns and rivers attract many speleologists. The great peaks and cliffs have been carved and sculpted over the centuries into fantastic and eery shapes. The Cévennes *corniche,* or winding roadway, passes through one of the most rugged landscapes in France — in spring its sharp peaks and weathered rocks are softened by cherry blossom and narcissus.

Sightseeing

Facts and figures

Location : *South of the Massif Central Mountains*
Area : *16 545 km²*
Climate : *Varied, depending on relief, latitude and proximity to the sea.*
Sunny Mediterranean climate on the coastal plain; Mont Aigoual, only 70 km from the sea, is one of the wettest places in France, and often foggy; the Lozère region suffers long snowy winters; the causses (plateaus) have mountain winters and Mediterranean summers; the Cévennes mountains benefit from a coastal climate with occasional heavy rain and storms.
Population : *894 140*
Administration :
Department of the ***Ardèche,*** *Prefecture : Privas; Department of the* ***Gard,*** *Prefecture : Nîmes; Department of the* ***Lozère,*** *Prefecture : Mende.*

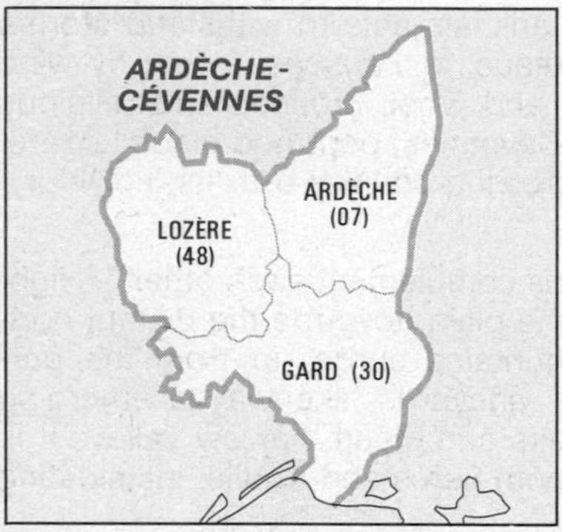

Don't miss

★★★ *Tarn and Jonte Gorges (A2/3), Aigoual Massif (A3), Mont Lozère (B2), Grandes Causses (A3), Ardeche Gorges (C2), Mont Mézenc (B1), Cévennes Corniche (B3), Nîmes (C4), Gard Aqueduct (C3).*
★★ *Cèze Gorges (B/C3), Vivarais Corniche (B2), Thines (B2), La Garde-Guérin (B2), Aigues-Mortes (B4), Uzès (C3), Orgnac Aven (C2), Beaume Gorges (C2), Mont Gerbier de Jonc (B1), Rhone Valley (C1-C4).*

■ MONT AIGOUAL★★★

(Gard)

▶ Round trip *(32 km from Mayrueis to the meteorological station at Aigoual; approx 1 hr.)*

Mont Aigoual is the highest point in the Cévennes; to the south, the Hérault Valley

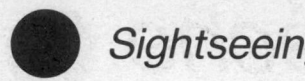

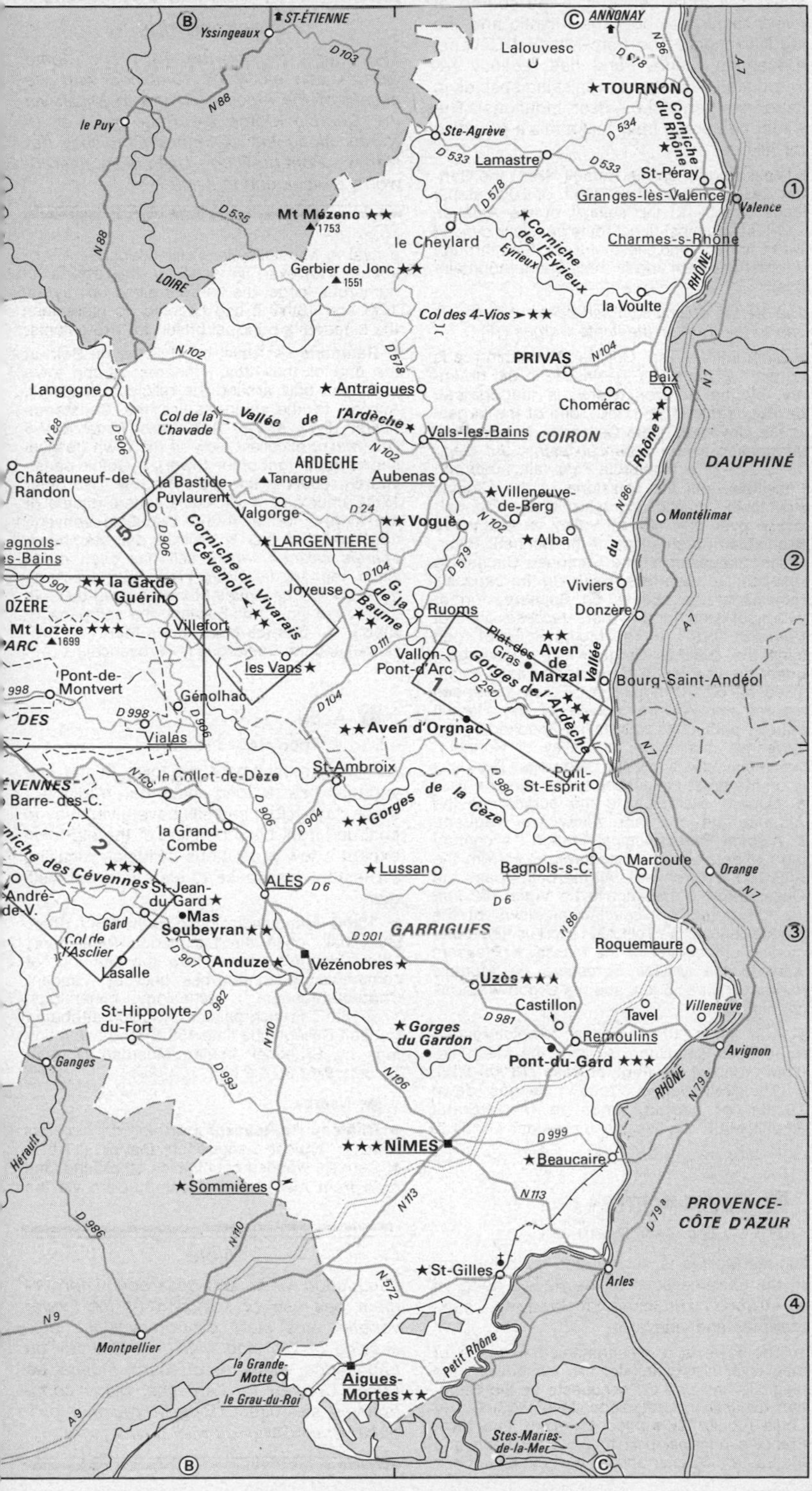
B
ST-ÉTIENNE
Yssingeaux
D 103
N 88
le Puy
C
ANNONAY
Lalouvesc
D 578
N 86
A 7
★TOURNON
Corniche du Rhône
Ste-Agrève
D 534
D 533
Lamastre
D 533
St-Péray
Granges-lès-Valence
Valence
1
D 578
Mt Mézeno ★★
1753
D 535
N 88
le Cheylard
★Corniche de l'Eyrieux
Eyrieux
Charmes-s-Rhône
Gerbier de Jonc ★★
1551
LOIRE
RHÔNE
la Voulte
Col des 4-Vios ★★
D 578
N 102
PRIVAS
N 104
Baix
N 7
Langogne
★ Antraigues
Chomérac
N 88
Col de la Chavade
Vallée de l'Ardèche★
Vals-les-Bains
COIRON
D 906
N 102
Rhône★★
DAUPHINÉ
Châteauneuf-de-Randon
ARDÈCHE
Tanargue
Aubenas
la Bastide-Puylaurent
★Villeneuve-de-Berg
N 86
Valgorge
D 24
★★ Voguë
Montélimar
5
D 906
Corniche du Vivarais Cévenol
★ LARGENTIÈRE
N 102
★ Alba
du
Bagnols-les-Bains
D 104
D 579
2
D 901
★★ la Garde Guérin
Joyeuse
G. de la Baume ★★
Viviers
LOZÈRE
Ruoms
Donzère
Mt Lozère ★★★
1699
Villefort
Plat. des Gras
★★ Aven de Marzal
A 7
PARC
D 111
Vallon-Pont-d'Arc
Gorges de l'Ardèche ★★★
Vallée
les Vans★
1
D 290
Bourg-Saint-Andéol
D 998
Pont-de-Montvert
Génolhac
D 104
DES
D 998
D 906
★★ Aven d'Orgnac
Vialas
N 7
St-Ambroix
N 106
le Collet-de-Dèze
D 980
Pont-St-Esprit
CÉVENNES
Barre-des-C.
D 906
D 904
★★Gorges de la Cèze
la Grand-Combe
2
★★★
Corniche des Cévennes
Marcoule
★ Lussan
Bagnols-s-C.
Orange
St-André-de-V.
St-Jean-du-Gard★
ALÈS
D 6
N 7
D 6
Mas Soubeyran★★
Gard
D 981
GARRIGUES
N 86
3
Col de l'Asclier
D 907
Anduze★
Vézénobres★
Roquemaure
Lasalle
Uzès★★★
D 982
Castillon
Tavel
Villeneuve
St-Hippolyte-du-Fort
N 110
D 981
★ Gorges du Gardon
Remoulins
Avignon
Ganges
Pont-du-Gard ★★★
D 999
N 106
RHÔNE
N 79a
Hérault
D 999
★★★ NÎMES
★ Beaucaire
★ Sommières
N 113
N 113
D 986
N 110
PROVENCE-CÔTE D'AZUR
D 79a
★ St-Gilles
Arles
N 572
4
N 9
Montpellier
Petit Rhône
la Grande-Motte
Aigues-Mortes★★
le Grau-du-Roi
A 9
Stes-Maries-de-la-Mer
B
C

appears 1 000m below. It is the source of rivers running to both the Atlantic and the Mediterranean. The Parc National Cévenol (Cévennes Nature Park) has recently re-introduced a number of vanishing species in its forests (red and roe deer, mouflons). The winter pasturage trails make this a paradise for hikers.

▶ **Valleraugue,** on the Hérault river : the **Sentier des "4 000 marches"** (path of 4 000 steps) leads directly to the summit of the Aigoual, shortest and most direct route *(full day; difficult walk),* first through chestnut trees, then through a forest of beech and fir trees (more mountainous).

The standard excursion can be combined with one to the Tarn or the Jonte Gorges (→).

▶ **Meyrueis** (→ Tarn Gorges). ▶ Hairpin roads up the Causse Noir (→). Nestled in the greenery, by the Bétuzon river★, is the **château de Roquedols** (15th-17thC), one of the largest in the Cévennes : the Cévennes Nature Park information centre *(mountain paths; Jul.-Sep., 10-12 & 3-7).* ▶ **Monjardin Pass** (alt. 1 090 m) : transition from the limestone of the Causse Noir to the granite and schist of the Aigoual; view★ over the Trévezel Valley. ▶ **Abîme de Bramabiau :** resurgence of the Bonheur River, which disappears in the Camprieu Causse to reappear as waterfalls *(visit).* On the *causse :* remains of the **abbaye du Bonheur,** former overnight stop for travellers *(access on foot from the GR62).* ▶ The Mount Souquet road joins the **Dourbie Gorges★★** (→ Rouergue) under the fir trees. ▶ **Serreyrède Pass★★** (alt. 1 300 m) on the ridge-line : E, an enormous natural amphitheatre, source of the Hérault (narrow path to the waterfall) overlooked by the Cévennes mountains; W, valley of Bonheur, which disappears into the peat bogs. The pass is on the great Languedoc winter pasture trail. ▶ Superb excursion to the summit of the Aigoual, but mist and snow are frequent. ▶ **Aigoual Meteorological Station :** a century old : orientation table; **panorama★★** from the Alps to the Pyrennees. All the paths pass the Observatory. ▶ Descent to **Le Vigan** *(32 km)* via L'**Espérou** ® : spectacular views of the Mediterranean. ▶ This ski-resort is the communications centre for the Massif. ▶ Pleasant walk to the Maison Forestière de Montals *(forestry centre; 5 km)* and the Orgon waterfall (25 min).

▶ From the top of the Aigoual, the picturesque but difficult **Cabrillac** road joins the Meyrueis-Florac road at the **Perjuret Pass** *(13 km NW).* ▶ The **Valleraugue** road★ plunges down 20 km of hairpin bends to the Hérault amphitheatre : fir, beech and chestnut woods. □

AIGUES-MORTES★★

C4 / ® / pop. 4 475 (Gard)

Aigues-Mortes is surrounded by ramparts, at the extreme point of the Rhône delta, in a strange landscape of lagoons, salt-marshes and vineyards.

▶ The town is a well-preserved example of mediaeval military architecture, symbolising the religious and political conquests of the Capetian dynasty in Languedoc. In the 13thC, St. Louis (Louis IX) wanted to make this town France's principal port to the Holy Land and the Eastern Mediterranean; it would have been a rival to Marseilles in a still-independent Provence. However, in spite of the efforts of numerous kings, the harbour silted up; by the 17th and 18thC it had become no more than the kingdom's principal prison for Protestants.

▶ **Ramparts★★ :** built by Philippe the Bold at the end of the 13thC; the rest of the town had been built around the religious buildings. Access to the ramparts via the **Constance Tower** *(9-12 & 2-6, Apr.-Sep.; 10-12 & 2-5 Oct.-Mar) :* excellent view of the town (festival shows at the foot of the tower). ▶ Gothic parish **church** rebuilt in the 17th-18thC. ▶ Two other 17thC churches. ▶ St. Louis square (statue of the king) : former 17thC Capuchin convent, now exhibition hall. ▶ Visit the **salt-marshes★** *(marais salants),* where salt has been made since the Middle Ages *(Tue.-Fri.; Jul.-Aug., from the TO at Aigues-Morte or Grau-du-Roi).* Listel rosé vineyards between the salt-pans.
Also... ▶ **Saintes-Marie-de-la-Mer** (→ Provence) and the **Camargue** (→ Provence). □

Weekend tips

The round trip of the Tarn and Jonte Gorges can easily be combined with the ascent of the Aigoual. Return to Millau via the Dourbie Gorge (→ Rouergue), or to Nîmes along the Cévennes Corniche; but Nîmes - Pont-du-Gard - Uzès is an itinerary worth a week-end in itself.

ALÈS

B3 / ® / pop. 44 345 (Gard)

Alès, the most important town in the Cévennes, has a long industrial tradition : these days, cloth and silk have given way to coal and iron. Little remains of the old town except a few prestigious buildings recalling Protestant resistance to state-imposed religion.

▶ 18thC Meridional Gothic **cathedral;** 18thC town hall, once the Languedoc Parliament; 18thC bishop's palace, now the chamber of commerce; prison-fortress built by Vauban. **Château-museum :** archaelogy, mineralogy, 17th-18thC French painters, triptych attributed to Jean Bellegambe (late 15thC) and two paintings by Brueghel. **Mining Museum** *(1 Apr.-30 Sep. 9-11:30 & 2-6).* □

▶ Nearby

▶ **Château de Rousson★** *(10 km on Aubenas road) :* typical Languedoc manor (17thC). ▶ Densely-wooded countryside all around; the road from Alès to Saint-Jean-du-Gard via the

Wine

Languedoc wines have undergone improvement because of selection of the grape varieties and more control over the processing of vine and wine. Try Côteaux du Languedoc, Costières du Gard, Muscat de Lunel, Côteaux de l'Ardèche. Many cooperatives sell direct. Biggest regional producer : Les Salins du Midi (Listel rosé).

Uglas Pass★ is like a tunnel through oaks and chestnuts (30 km). ▶ **Vézénobres**★ *(11 km S)* : beautiful village; remains of ramparts; Romanesque houses; feudal ruins; Louis XV château hidden in the trees. ▶ **Grotte de la Cocalière** *(25 km N; Palm Sunday to end Oct. 9-12 & 2-6)* : cave pearls and hanging discs (rock formations). □

ANDUZE★

B3 / ® / pop. 2790 (Gard)

Anduze has an old tradition of Protestant independence.

▶ **Protestant church,** one of the largest in France, on the central square opposite the **clock-tower** (1320) and a 17thC château. ▶ The **old quarter**★ was the craftsmen's district until the 19thC; many 17thC houses; 15thC covered market; **fountain-pagoda** (1648) in green and yellow tile - the same colour as Anduze pottery. □

▶ Nearby

▶ From Anduze to Saint-Jean-du-Gard via Mas-Soubeyran *(25 km)*

▶ **Bambouseraie de Prafrance**★ (bamboo plantation) : botanical garden like a Far Eastern jungle *(Mar.-Nov., 9-12 & 2-7; Jul.-Aug., 9-7)*. ▶ **Générargues** ® : fork to the Gardon de Mialet in a narrow **canyon**★. ▶ **Les Mas-Soubeyran**★★ was one of the centres of French Protestantism : **Désert Museum** dedicated to the Cévennes resistance to State-imposed religion *(Mar.-Nov., 9:30-12 & 2:30-6)*. ▶ Picturesque cul-de-sac leads to the **Trabuc grotto**★ : lake and interesting formations *(9:30-12 & 2-6, Jun.; Jul.-Aug., 9-7; Easter-Oct., Sun.)*. ▶ Return to Luziers cross-roads. ▶ **Pont des Abarines**★ (bridge over the Gardon de Mialet). ▶ **Saint-Jean-du-Gard**★ ®, the other gateway to the Cévennes; built along the Gardon in a valley of vines and olive trees : 17thC bridge. Some 20 spinning factories here were still working at the end of the 19thC; today, it is a major tourist centre. Market on Tuesdays; concerts at the church; exhibitions at the town hall; **Musée des Vallées Cévenoles** *(regional history museum, 15 Jun.-15 Sep., 9:30-12:30 & 3-7, closed Mon. and Sun. morning; 16 Sept.-14 Jun., Sun. only 2:30-6:30)*. ▶ The clock-tower is all that remains of the Benedictine priory. □

ANNONAY

C1 / ® / pop. 20085 (Ardèche)

In the 15thC, the leather and wool industries made use of the Deûme and Canse rivers at Annonay. In the 17thC, they were joined by the paper industry (Montgolfier, Canson).

▶ Annonay was built in the narrow Deûme gorge (old bridge) : 19thC factories currently being modernised. ▶ Château; monument to the Montgolfier brothers who made the first balloon ascent here in 1783. ▶ **César Filhol Museum** behind the town hall (15 rue Béchetoille; *Wed., Sat., Sun., 2-6; daily in summer*) : art, folklore, Montgolfier brothers memorabilia); Christ★ in the church of Veyrine (17thC). □

▶ Nearby

▶ *(6 km NE)* **Peaugres** ® : **safari park** *(summer 9:30-6; winter 11-5:30)*. ▶ **Terney Dam** : lake surrounded by cedars. ▶ *(5 km N)* **Boulieu** : fortified town. ▶ **Serrières** ®, river-harbour on the Rhône *(15 km NE)* : museum *(weekends and hols. Easter-31 Oct., 3-6)*. ▶ Romanesque church★ at **Champagne** : cupola vaulting★; carved tympanum and lintels; 15thC stalls. ▶ **Quintenas** . 12th-14thC fortified church; *(10 km S)*, chapel of Notre-Dame d'Ay above the Ay gorge *(7 km, then 4km)*. □

▶ Round trip through the upper Vivarais *(approx 120 km; full day)*

Annonay. ▶ *Corniche* (cliff road) above the Canse gorge. ▶ **Péreandre rock** (40 m) above the stream. ▶ S of **Saint-Vallier,** the **Rhône Pass** is particularly spectacular : ruins of **Arras** and **Serves.** ▶ **Vion** : striated capitals in the church. ▶ **Hermitage vineyards** on the opposite bank. ▶ **Tournon**★ ®, opposite Tain-Hermitage : beautiful town; the oldest **lycée** (school) in France (1536; rebuilt in the 18thC); 17thC Jesuit chapel★ where symbolist poet Mallarmé taught; 15th-16thC **château** where the son of François I died in childhood; small museum *(1 Apr.-31 May 2-6; 1 Sep.-31 Oct. 2-5; summer 10-12 & 2-6)*; terraces★★ overlooking the Rhône. Flamboyant Gothic church : 16thC frescos and triptych; 17thC organ. ▶ Bridge over the Doux (14th-18thC). ▶ *Corniche* to Lamastre along the **Doux gorges**★. ▶ **Small steam train**★ between Tournon and Lamastre along the bottom of the valley *(tel : 78.28.83.34)*. ▶ **Boucieu-le-Roi** : 13th-16thC church. ▶ **Lamastre** ® : small industrial town and renowned gastronomic site; rebuilt Romanesque church above the old quarter of Macheville. ▶ Louvesc *corniche* : views over the watershed between the Doux and Eyrieux valleys. ▶ **Château de Rochebloine** : panorama over the upper Doux valley★, with the Alps on the horizon. ▶ **Buisson Pass** (reconstructed miniature Ardèche village; view) : winding road to the right to **Pailharès** and Romanesque church at **Saint-Félicien** *(detour 25 km if returning via Faux Pass)*. ▶ **Lalouvesc** ® : mountain resort in pine woods above the **Ay gorges**; 19thC basilica of St. François-Régis (museum). ▶ Modest Romanesque church at **Veyrines** *(6 km from Satillieu)*. ▶ Return to **Annonay.** □

The Cévennes-Ardeche cuisine

The Cévennes, a poor region of Protestant traditions, is not really a gastronomic area, and simply makes use of local produce (trout, game and charcuterie*). Chestnuts were long the staple food of the region, and* marrons glacés *(crystallised chestnuts) are still a speciality of the Ardèche. A local cheese of interest is the Pélardon, a round goat cheese; try the sharp tasting Clinton wine. In the Lozère,* tripoux *(tripe), game and mushrooms are traditional, together with cheese and charcuterie (as in the Rouergue and Auvergne). On the Languedoc plain, cooking has a Mediterranean character, based on olives, fish and seafood. It is also, like the Ardèche, a fruit, salad and vegetable area (Remoulins cherries, Eyrieux peaches). At Aigues-Mortes, the sandy soil grows good asparagus. The most popular dishes are* brandade *(salt cod creamed with mashed potatos and garlic) and* boeuf à la gardiane *(the recipe for this stew is a closely-kept secret among families of the area).* Brasucades *(grilled mussels) and* sardinade *(sardines grilled on vine-cuttings) are popular tourist dishes.*

■ ARDÈCHE Gorges★★★

▶ From Vallon to Saint-Martin *(48 km; 2 hr)*
C2 *(see map 1)*

Rock, water, sun, wind, light and silence : unsullied nature. Perched on top of the cliff and overlooking the tourist road, the Ardèche Gorges follow the river 200 m below for a distance of 32 km. Discover the grandiose spectacle of nature untouched and untamed — a paradise for climbing, canoeing and camping in caves. Numerous viewpoints have been constructed allowing one to admire the silken curves of the river from the edge of the Gras plateau, above the towering cliffs, sculpted in a myriad of forms, and innumerable grottoes sparkling in the sun. The Ardèche is an excellent region for speleologists and potholers (spelunkers).

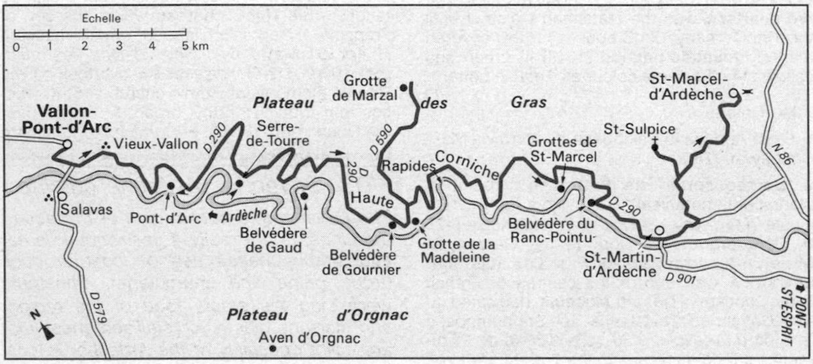

1. Ardèche Gorges

▶ **Vallon-Pont-d'Arc** ® : busy tourist centre. ▶ Two keeps overlook the entrance to the canyon between the Gras Plateau and the Orgnac Aven Plateau; easy parking *(lock car doors)* : viewpoints at Serre de Tours, Gaud, La Madeleine, Les Templiers. ▶ **Pont-d'Arc★ :** huge natural stone arch across the river *(beach, canoe hire)*. ▶ After Pont-d'Arc, the canyon is really spectacular. ▶ **La Madeleine grotto :** classic karst cave with wide variety of stalactites and stalagmites *(daily Apr.-Oct., 9:30-12 & 2-6:30)*. ▶ **Saint-Martin-d'Ardèche** ®, in the Côtes du Rhône vineyards, is the other tourist centre for the region.

Also... ▶ Marzal cave★★ on the **Gras plateau★** (→ Villeneuve-de-Berg) : entrance through the ceiling; museum of the underground world *(Mar.-Nov., Sat., Sun. only 9-12 & 2-6; 9-7 in summer)*. Nearby, "Prehistoric Zoo"★ (prehistoric animals recreated lifesize). ▶ **Orgnac Plateau,** covered with evergreen oak : **Orgnac Aven,** one of the most spectacular underground labyrinths with gigantic formations in sparkling colours *(Mar.-15 Nov., 9-12 & 2-6)*. ▶ **Forestière Aven** is quite different, with extremely delicate formations *(1 Apr.-30 Sep. daily 10-7)*. Acclimatization laboratory for cavernicolous animals, unique in Europe. □

■ Upper ARDECHE Valley★

▶ From La Chavade Pass to Aubenas *(43 km; approx. 3 hr)*
B2

The Ardèche river drops 1 000 m in the space of a few miles; small stone bridges and, after Thueyts, black basalt rock.

▶ **La Chavade Pass★** (alt. 1 271 m) on the watershed between the Atlantic and the Mediterranean slopes. The river rises in the nearby **Mazan forest :** numerous mountain paths; ruins of 12thC abbey. ▶ The Aubenas road runs along the mountain side : views★ over the gorge. Mediterranean influence in the villages : vines are trained up the walls. ▶ Ruins of the Montlaur château. ▶ **Malbos :** pretty mediaeval **bridge** at the foot of the former mining village of **Mayres.** ▶ **Thueyts** ® : fruit-growing village on a lava outflow from the **Gravenne de Montpezat** volcano★ *(2 hr 30 excursion to the north)*; view over the lava field and the Devil's Bridge *(Pont du Diable; marked path; approx. 1 hr 30)*. ▶ **Neyrac-les-Bains** ® : small spa, volcanic waters. ▶ **Château de Ventadour** at the entrance to **Pont-de-Labeaume.** ▶ The road runs through chestnut woods and past abandoned spinning factories. ▶ **Vals-les-Bains** (→). ▶ **Aubenas** (→). □

■ AUBENAS

C2 / ® / pop. 13700 (Ardèche)

Aubenas has the charm of a large Provençal village : Saturday market held on the château square, old-fashioned shops in faded colours and a splendid view over the river.

▶ Good view of the town from the south : old ramparts round the town centre, the many-coloured château roofs and the St. Benoît Dome. Take a short walk through the arcaded streets and see the gargoyles and mullioned windows of the old houses. ▶ The strategic position of the 12thC **castle** gave it control over the region : rebuilt in the 17thC, now the town hall; 15thC spiral staircase; 16thC gallery in a courtyard★; 1750 Grand Staircase; 18thC decor; terrace overlooking the valley *(Jul.-Aug., 10-12 & 3:30-6:30 closed on Sun. pm; Easter-1 Nov., Sat. 3-6 and Sun. 10-12)*. ▶ The **St. Benoît Dome★** is an elegant Italianate 17thC building; the mausoleum of the Maréchal d'Ornano, Lord of Aubenas, who was involved in all the plots against Cardinal Richelieu; he died in the Vincennes prison in Paris (exhibitions of religious art; *same hours*). □

▶ Nearby

▶ **Vals-les-Bains** ® *(5 km N)* : delightful old-fashioned spa. ▶ The **Volane Valley** runs between the lava fields of the Aizac volcanos. ▶ **Antraigues★** ® *(10 km N from Vals),* at the junction of three rivers. ▶ **Castle of Boulogne★** (14thC, *18 km N*) : abandoned. ▶ **Jastres** viewpoint *(7.5 km W).* ▶ **Largentière★** ® *(20 km SW) :* a mediaeval silver mining town, that now extracts lead and zinc; astonishing site : pink-tiled roofs at the bottom of the Ligne gorge, overlooked by 12thC castle ruins and the impressive Law Courts (Palais de Justice) which look like a Greek temple; the bishop's **castle** is now an almshouse. **Récollets Gate,** remains of the ramparts, leads into the old town★ : narrow streets and stone steps. Gothic church with Flamboyant chapels and 19thC spire; 15thC Hôtel de Ville (town hall) and arcaded square. ▶ All the villages in the area were fortified to defend the mines : **Chassiers★** has a fortified church (14thC) and a 14th-16thC château. ▶ **Montréal :** 13th-16thC keep. ▶ **Sanilhac** *(W) :* 15thC château. ▶ Farther up, the **Brizon Tower** (orientation table and panorama★) used to communicate by signals with the Loubaresse tower in the Baume valley. □

▶ Through the Ardèche Valley★ *(from Aubenas to Vallon-Pont d'Arc 40 km, 2-3 hr)*

▶ Soft fertile hills of vineyards, orchards, and southern-looking villages. In central Ardèche, there are villages in green pastures between the cliffs, or nestled on the edge of the plateau. ▶ **Sauveplantade★ :** delightful 12thC Romanesque church. ▶ **Rochecolombe★, Lagorce★.** ▶ **Voguë★★ :** feudal castle, rebuilt in the 17thC *(Jul.-Aug., 10-12 & 2-6, Sun. 3-6; Mar.-Nov., Sun. only; closed Nov.-Mar.)* info, Aubenas town hall. ▶ **Balazuc★ :** old fortified village in grey stone. ▶ **Ruoms★** ®, fortified town at the mouth of three gorges; the old centre★ is worth restoring : ramparts; Romanesque church (mosaic in volcanic stone), Gothic houses. ▶ N, the **Ruoms Pass★** is one of the great natural curiosities in the region. ▶ Another pass through the **Beaume Gorges★★,** where the river drops 1500 m in 40 km; past the beautiful village of **Labeaume★,** you must go on foot. ▶ The lower **Chassezac Valley★** is typically Mediterranean with vineyards stretching out of sight; cypress and olive trees. ▶ Don't miss the **Mas de la Vignasse★,** where writer Alphonse Daudet lived; his parents were wealthy silk merchants (Daudet museum and agronomy museum in the former silk-worm rearing building; *1 May-1 Oct., daily 9-12 & 2-6:30*). ▶ **Vallon-Pont-d'Arc** (→ Ardèche gorges). □

BAGNOLS-SUR-CÈZE

C3 / ® / pop. 17780 (Gard)

Life in the old town known and loved by the painter Renoir was drastically altered by the development of the modern Marcoule district, but the ancient *bastide* is still there, and the Place des Arcades★ (square) is being restored.

▶ Small **museum** created by painter Albert André, friend of the Impressionists, with an important collection of modern art *(10-2 & 2-6; closed Tue.) :* good collection of Renoirs, 19thC Lyonnais school, Besson collection of figurative painters : Pignon, de Koninck, Cueco. ▶ Rue Crémieux and neighbouring streets : dilapidated town **mansions** still worth seeing. □

▶ Nearby

▶ **Marcoule,** most important plutonium production centre in France (viewpoint and exhibition). ▶ Lovely villages on a hilltop among the Côtes du Rhône vineyards : **Laudun** *(9 km SE) :* Gothic church transformed in the 17thC. ▶ **Château de Lascours,** E, (16thC). ▶ On the edge of the Gard forest★ : **Saint-Laurent-des-Arbres :** fortified Romanesque church and much-restored château; **Saint-Victor-la-Coste★.** □

▶ Down the **Cèze Valley★★** *(From Bagnols to Les Vans 66 km, half day)*

▶ **La Roque-sur-Cèze★ :** Romanesque church; château; ▶ Downstream, the spectacular **Sautadet waterfall★.** ▶ **Cornillon★ :** Romanesque church among the remains of the castle and fortification wall (view★). ▶ **Goudargues★** ®, former site of a Benedictine abbey : canal, wash-house, fountains, remains of three churches including the former **abbey church★,** one of the most remarkable Romanesque buildings in the Gard Department (nave restored in the 17thC, vaulting and doorway in the 19thC). ▶ Dry heath country on the plateau. ▶ The road runs above the **Cèze Gorges★** *(access on foot).* ▶ **Barjac** is a tourist centre for the Ardèches gorges : 17thC church; château; old houses. ▶ **Saint-Paul-le-Jeune,** old mining village north of the Cévennes Valley. ▶ Through the **Païolive woods** before reaching **Les Vans** (→). □

BEAUCAIRE★

C4 / ® / pop. 13000 (Gard)

On the banks of the Rhône, at the foot of an impressive keep, opposite the castle of Tarascon (→ Provence). In the 18thC, this was an important textile town.

Sign-posted tour of the town starting from the castle. ▶ The triangular keep built into the rock and the Romanesque chapel (dismantled in the 17thC) are the only remains of the fortifications; viewpoint★. ▶ **Vignasse Museum :** archaeological and historical collections in the château buildings *(10:15-12 & 2-6; tel 66.59.47.61).* ▶ **Rue de la République :** 17th and 18thC mansions. ▶ Place de la République : arcades and French Classical mansions; the ground floors were used as warehouses. ▶ Franciscan church of St. Paul (15thC). ▶ Sunday market in front of the late 17thC **Hôtel de Ville★** (town hall), copied from the Lunaret mansion in Montpellier (→). ▶ Church of **Notre-Dame des Pommiers★** (1744) by Franque, the architect of Avignon; the re-utilised Romanesque frieze★ was inspired by St. Gilles (→); inside : 18thC furnishing; pictures by Parocel). □

▶ Nearby

▶ Abbey of **Saint-Roman-l'Aiguille★** *(5 km NW)* on the cliff above the Rhône; fortified in the 17thC *(visit Sun. pm).* ▶ **Villeneuve-lès-Avignon** (→ Provence). ▶ The Nîmes road runs through the **Costières-du-Gard** vineyards : circuit, follow arrows starting at the Costières house on the Générac road. □

CÉVENNES Corniche★★★

▶ From Saint-Jean-du-Gard to Florac *(50 km)*
B3 *(see map 2 following page)*

▶ **Saint-Jean-du-Gard** (→ Anduze). ▶ Winding road up through the pine forest, running along the crest of the mountains. ▶ **Saint-Roman-de-Tousque** is the only village between Saint-Jean and Le Pompidou, a stopover on the winter pasture route from Languedoc, and a former

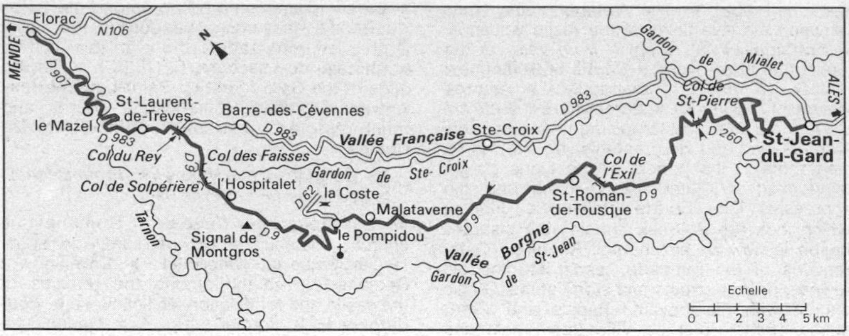

2. Cévennes Corniche

Cévennes nature park

Created in 1970, in an area seriously depopulated by rural exodus, this is the largest of the nature parks, and the only inhabited one : 840 km² at the centre of the park cover the Cévennes and Lozère uplands (Mount Lozère, Bougès, Aigoual, Lingas and the Méjean causse). There are 120 landholdings, 52 administrative communes and 117 hamlets in the Gard and Lozère regions; these are sustained by a total population of barely 500 people. The periphery of the park consists mainly of the Cévennes causses, which are more thickly populated : 2280 km², with 41000 inhabitants.

The park management provides agricultural and sheepfarming advice and guidance, and ensures that the inhabitants participate in the protection of the environment, through the maintenance of footpaths and hiking trails, farm holidays, sale of local produce etc.

There is an ecological museum at Mount Lozère with exhibitions, events, monument restoration etc. The park has the same rules as the other French nature parks (→ p. 102), with special status for the inhabitants. Fauna and flora are protected and several species have been re-introduced (red and roe deer, grouse, griffon vulture, golden eagle, beaver). Seven different information centres welcome visitors : Florac, Villefort, Pont-de-Montvert, Meyrueis, Saint-Jean-du-Gard, Le Vigan, Génolhac. 750 km of GR paths, 500 km of horse-riding paths, 200 km of ski-trails (all with stopover cabins) run through the park. Half-day hikes are indicated on the information sheets.

post-relay on the Gévaudan road. Two roads lead out of it, one to the pretty village of **Saumane,** in the Borgne Valley, and the other to **Sainte-Croix-Vallée-Française.** ▶ **Le Pompidou,** at the foot of the **Can de l'Hospitalet** mountain (superb view from the top over the Saint-Jean river, the Borgne Valley, and the Gardon de Sainte-Croix river - Vallée Française) : Romanesque chapel of **Saint-Flour-du-Pompidou★** in the old cemetery; 16thC side chapels; concerts in summer. ▶ The Gardon de Sainte-Croix river starts at the **Faïsses Pass** (alt. 1 018 m); to the north, the Can Noire. ▶ Romanesque church in **Barre-des-Cévennes,** to the East. ▶ The road follows the Tarnon to Florac; schist and limestone houses; hump-backed bridge at the entrance to Florac (→). □

▶ The **Vallée Française,** along the Gardon de Sainte-Croix river, is typical of the Cévennes. Silk-worm breeding was once a major industry in the region. Today, young farmers are trying to revive the abandoned hamlets. ▶ **Sainte-Croix-Vallée-Française :** school in the 12th-17thC château; Romanesque church; stone bridge. ▶ **Moissac :** ruins of the château and of the church destroyed during the Camisards war (Protestant resistance to State-imposed religion); Protestant church of **La Boissonnade★** in an old Romanesque church; pélardon cheese-making. ▶ **Pont-Ravagers :** small local museum. ▶ The 14thC tower of **Saint-Étienne-Vallée-Française** once communicated with the one at Lancize. □

■ COIRON Plateau

C2 (Ardèche)

Created by lava from the Massif Central mountains, a volcanic plateau between Privas (→) and Aubenas (→) : black cliffs, low houses of dark stone, stretches of grassland and many streams.

▶ **Balmes de Montbrun★** *(13 km N from Saint-Jean-le-Centenier)* : cliffs riddled with volcanic caves. ▶ The dykes of **Rochemaure★** ®, by the Rhône, and the giant rocks of **Chenavari★** are the extreme limits of the lava field. ▶ The villages★ are built both of black basalt and white stone : ▶ **Saint-Jean-le-Sentenier, Mirabel, Saint-Laurent-sous-Coiron** (panoramas across the Cévennes). □

■ EYRIEUX Corniche and Gorges★

▶ Round trip from La Voulte to Saint-Agrève *(74 km; half day)*

C1 (Ardèche)

A scenic road on the high Ardèche plateaus among the chestnut trees and the spruce. At its foot, the vineyard-covered Eyrieux Valley, best seen in spring when the peach and cherry trees are in bloom.

▶ **La Voulte-sur-Rhône** ® : small industrial town on the Rhône by the reservoir of the Loriol dam :

enormous Renaissance château (damaged in 1944); in the chapel, pretty ornamentation *(ask at the SI, Jun.-Oct., closed Sun. and nat. hols.).* Remains of ramparts around the old town (15th-16thC houses). ▶ **Saint-Symphorien-sous-Chomerac,** wickerwork museum *(1 May-15 Oct., 10-7; low season on request, tel. 75.65.02.07).* ▶ **Saint-Laurent-du-Pape :** surrounded by orchards. ▶ **Fortress of Pierre-Gourde★,** impressive views over the Rhône, the Ventoux, the Vivarais ridges and Mount Mézenc *(11 km N from Saint-Laurent on a winding road).* ▶ The **Eyrieux Corniche★** is breathtaking : many viewpoints over the valley and the mountain ridges. The road climbs towards Le Cheylard, above the gorges. ▶ **Pont-de-Chervil :** Gothic bridge over the river. ▶ **Le Cheylard** ®, between Gerbier de Jonc and Mount Mézenc. ▶ Beautiful road going up to Saint-Agrève : views down to the Saint-Julien Valley, and up to the Gerbier de Jonc, Mount Mézenc and the Suc de Sara; hike *(1/2 hr)* up to the feudal ruins of **Rochebronne castle★** (site), among pine trees, juniper and heather. ▶ **Saint-Agrève :** small mountain resort in the high pastureland on the **Boutières** Massif★; many walks and hikes. ▶ Tourist **train** from Saint-Agrève to Dunières (→ Leisure information, Auvergne). □

■ FLORAC★

A2 / ® / pop. 2 104 (Lozère)

A small frontier town between the Huguenot (Protestant) areas and the fortresses of the Papal States; also a crossroads between the Cévennes mountains and the limestone region of the Tarn gorges. With a combination of mountain and Mediterranean climates, Florac is ideally situated to be the HQ of the Cévennes Nature Park.

▶ Built at the foot of the **Méjean** (→), by the bed of the Tarnon river. ▶ Protestant church and market-place *(Sat.)* mark the town centre. ▶ Good view from the bridge of the source of the Pêcher river. ▶ **Château :** at the top of the town (keep rebuilt in 17thC); HQ of the Cévennes Nature Park (introduction to the park; annual exhibitions; *8-12:30 & 2-8*).
Also see 1583 convent with carved façade. □

▶ From Florac, direct ascent of the Aigoual possible via the Tarpoul Gorges★ *(difficult road),* or descent to Saint-Jean-du-Gard (→ Anduze) via the Borgne Valley, Saumane and the narrow Estréchure defile. □

■ Pont du GARD (Gard Aqueduct)★★★

C3 / ® (Gard)

This 2000 year-old Roman structure, reproduced in countless posters and calendars, is one of France's best-preserved Roman monuments.

▶ The Pont du Gard spans the Gardon gorge 49 m above water-level, and is 275 m long. The top tier, smallest of the three, carries the pipeline supplying Nîmes with 20 000 m³ of water per day from a catchment area some 50 km away. The stone architecture is still as beautiful as when it was first built.

Also... ▶ **Remoulins** ®, the cherry capital : Romanesque church transformed into the town hall; French Classical parish church; Romanesque church at Saint-Bonnet on the Nîmes road. ▶ **Villeneuve-lès-Avignon★★** (→ Provence). ▶ *16 km NE,* the famous **Tavel** ® vineyards (rosé) □

■ LA GARDE-GUÉRIN★★

B2 *(See map 3)* (Lozère)

The village, right on the edge of the Chassezac gap★, is a classified site. It was formerly a fortress guarding the Régordane, the ancient road linking Nîmes to the Auvergne. In the 10thC this was a dangerous route, because the local robber barons habitually captured travellers and held them for ransom. Eventually, the Bishop of Mende took control of the situation by giving these brigands official duties, including the protection of travellers, for which they received a toll. La Garde-Guérin was made their official headquarters.

▶ These robber barons were known as *Seigneurs pariers,* i.e. equals in power and privilege; there were 27 of them. Today, their tall houses (14thC), the sheepfolds, and the square keep of the castle (11th-13thC) can be seen inside the ramparts. Fine capitals in the Romanesque chapel.

Also... ▶ Attractive Romanesque churches at **Prévenchères** (12th-15thC; *9 km N*) and **Puylaurent** *(10 km W from Prévenchères).* □

■ Mont GERBIER DE JONC★★

B1 (Ardèche)

Volcanic Mont Gerbier de Jonc — similar views to Mont Mézenc (→) — stands like a dome on the Cévennes ridge : one of the sources of the Loire river... But the mountain where France's longest river starts looks bone dry. It is anybody's guess which of the streamlets running out of the surrounding heath is the true source....

▶ From **Estables,** the road follows the ridge-line between the Loire and Rhône, running through forests with views on both sides. It winds round the upper **Bonnefoy Valley** (remains of the Bonnefoy Charter-House), among spruce forests (raspberry and blueberry bushes). Easy climb of the Gerbier de Jonc *(10-20 min).* ▶ **Isarlès Lake** *(25 km W) :* crater-lake surrounded by peaks and forests: swimming, wind-surfing. ▶ To the S *(15 km, then 1 hr round trip) :* **Ray Pic** waterfalls. ▶ Beautiful route (view★★) from Gerbier de Jonc to Aubenas by **Usclades-et-Rieutord** ® and through the **Pal Pass,** around the **Suc de Bauzon★** (lava outcrop). ▶ Small Romanesque church at **Saint-Cirgues-en-Montagne.** *Corniche* above the **Fontolière Gorges★.** ▶ Back in the **Ardèche Valley** (→) at **Pont-de-Labeaume** *(50 km).* □

■ LANGOGNE

B2 / ® / pop. 4 025 (Lozère)

An austere, mountainous, sheep breeding region. ▶ The town centre is clearly marked by the five round towers of the ramparts, and the square clock-tower. ▶ Romanesque **church★** with Gothic façade; Cistercian ground-plan; interesting capitals. ▶ Close by : late Gothic houses (17thC) and superb covered market★. □

▶ Nearby

▶ Beautiful walk in the Mercoire forest *(S)* to the **Mercoire abbey** (13th-17thC). ▶ **Châteauneuf-de-Randon** *(21 km SW)* overlooking the valley of Boutaresse, is the main cattle market in the area; on the square (Place du Champ de Foire) : statue of Constable Du Guesclin (→ Brittany) who died during the siege of Châteauneuf in 1380. Remains of ramparts. ▶ The road to La Bastide-Puylaurent *(20 km S)* follows the meandering upper **Allier River★.** □

Blizzard bells

At over 1 000 m altitude, the Lozère has a mountain climate and the main season is a long, cold and snowy winter. When the wind rises in furious gusts, the only hope for the traveller is the guidance of the "blizzard-bell" with its continuous ringing. During the last century, each village had its own bell-tower for bad weather, but also for celebrations, since the church was so far away, down in the valley...

■ Mont **LOZÈRE★★★**

B2 (Lozère)

This a bare granite peak projecting above the Cévennes Mountains, overlooking extensive peat-bogs and closely-cropped turf strewn with granite rocks.

▶ The Saint-John's Hospitallers (or Knights of Malta) owned thousands of acres on the Lozère; their **commandery** (at the hamlet of **l'Hôpital,** near Pont-de-Montvert) is on the territory of the **Ecomusée de Lozère★,** an outdoor museum which illustrates the agro-pastoral past of the mountain. Two old farms are examples of traditional architecture : Mas Camargues and Mas Troubat. ▶ One of the highest points (alt. 1 680 m) is **Cassini Peak,** near the source of the Tarn river★ : in fine weather, the view stretches from the volcanic mountains of southern Auvergne (Chaîne des Puys) to the Alps and Mount Ventoux, and from the Languedoc plain to Canigou. □

▶ Trip around Mont Lozère *(160 km; full day)*

B2 *(see map 3)*

▶ **Pont-de-Montvert,** on the upper reaches of the Tarn river, was an important Calvinist centre; 17thC bridge; clock-tower and old houses; **Ecomusée information centre.** ▶ From Pont-de-Montvert to **Le Bleymard,** via the Finiels Pass★ (alt. 1 541 m) : wind-swept rocky pasture land and woods. ▶ **Croix de Berthel Pass.** ▶ Beautiful views over the Cévennes along the ridge road★ (route des Crêtes) leading to Alès via **Portes★** (14th-17thC château). ▶ **Vialas** ® is almost Mediterranean; one of the few remaining Protestant churches (17thC); former lead mine. ▶ **Génolhac** ®, on the Régordane road (→ La Garde-Guérin); 17thC houses; church with 11thC tower; Cévennes Nature Park information centre. ▶ From Génolhac to Villefort the road climbs 1 000 m through chestnut, oak and beech woods, to emerge among upland pastures and pine trees. ▶ **Villefort** ® was a fortified town; 14th and 16thC houses; Nature Park centre. ▶ **Reservoir** on the Altier River outside town; **château de Castanet** (1578; *exhibitions*). The road from Villefort to Mende along the valleys of the Altier and Lot Rivers replaces the mule-track along the passes (GR68). ▶ **Altier :** 17thC church, Romanesque nave; castle ruins; views★. ▶ On the opposite bank, **château du Champ,** rebuilt during the Romantic period. ▶ La Prade fortified farm. ▶ **Les Tribes Pass** (alt. 1 131 m), highest point on the trip; separating the Altier and the Lot rivers running respectively to the Mediterranean and the Atlantic. ▶ **Le Bleymard** has an Auvergne look. ▶ **Saint-Jean-du-Bleymard :** former Benedictine priory; Romanesque church and fortified 13thC farm. ▶ **Château du Tournel** (12thC). ▶ **Saint-Julien-du-Tournel★ :**

3. Mont Lozère

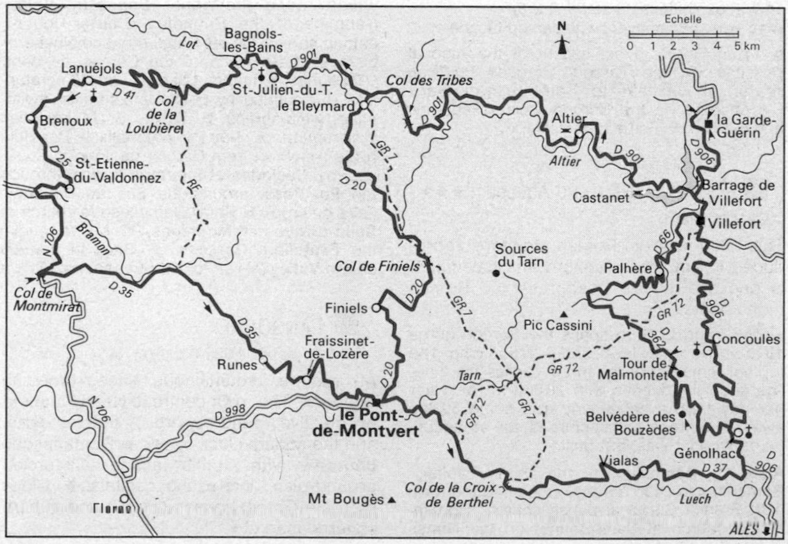

Romanesque church★. ▶ **Bagnols-les-Bains** ® : miniature spa; 18th-19thC façade on the spa buildings. ▶ Return to Mende (→) along the river, or detour to **Lanuejols :** Gallo-Roman mines; 3rdC funeral monument★; Auvergnat Romanesque church★; 16thC fountain. ▶ **Balsièges,** at the foot of the Lion rock : typical Lot village with fish-scale tiling. ▶ **Montmirat Pass,** between the Lot and Tarn valleys : view over the Cévennes and the Aigoual. ▶ Serpentine road; excellent view over **Florac** (→). Beautiful route along the Tarn, to Pont-de-Montvert. □

The MARGERIDE Region★

A2 (Lozère)

This abandoned and unpopulated region of dark pine forests, granite and porphyry, heather and pasture-land, is made for lovers of open spaces and unspoilt nature.

▶ The mountain was once divided into vast land-holdings but the forests and pasture-land were too heavily taxed for farmers to exploit satisfactorily : this explains the low population and the scarcity of villages. Ironically, the southern plateau was known as the **Plateau du Palais du Roi**★ (plateau of the King's Palace). □

MARVEJOLS★

A2 / ® / pop. 6 000 (Lozère)

Three fortified gates still guard this town, rebuilt by Henry IV after the destruction of the Wars of Religion (16thC; statue). 17thC houses recall the prosperous merchants who sold the wool and cloth produced by the shepherd families of the Margeride and the Gévaudan. □

▶ Nearby

▶ Two Romanesque churches : **Chirac** *(5.5 km S)* and former Benedictine abbey of **Monastier** ® in the Colagne Valley★ *(6 km S).* ▶ **Gévaudan Park** *(10 km N)* at Sainte-Lucie : European animals, especially wolves *(Easter-Oct., 10-6).* ▶ Near **Moulinet Lake**★ *(17 km NW),* **château de La Baume**★ has surprisingly luxurious ornamentation by Montpellier artists (early 18thC; *10-12 & 2-6, 15 Jun.-15 Sep.; 2-5 rest of year, closed Tue.*). □

MÉJEAN Causse★★

A3 *(See map 4)* (Lozère)

The highest of the Grands Causses (plateaus); only 13% is cultivated, 10% is forest land, and the remainder is bare : sheep grazing to the E, and wood to the W : follow the grazing trails using the brochure provided by the Méjean Association (in local *mairies*) to discover the beauty of the *causse,* and understand the shepherds' life and the local stone architecture. Here and there, dolmens and carved stone crosses; birds of prey wheel in the sky. Good view over the Park from the **Can de l'Hospitalet**★ mountain.

▶ The **Armand aven**★★ is the most spectacular site, an enormous underground cavern : rock formations include a "forest" of 400 stalagmites *(Easter-Palm Sunday).* ▶ Villages on the *causse* : **Hyelzas** (rural museum), **La Parade** (13thC church, old mill), **Drigas, Hures** (Romanesque churches★). Views over the gorges from **Hourtous Rock** (by the Tarn) and **Saint-Pierre-des-Tripiers** (on the Jonte). □

Peat-bogs

Peat-bogs develop on flinty soil in cold, wet regions like the Lozère. As the water stagnates, a carpet of moss appears; sphagnum, or peat-moss, grows vertically and dies from the base, while continuing to grow above water-level; other species take root, including bog-myrtle, cotton-grass, and sundew (an insect eating plant).

MENDE★

A2 / ® / pop. 12 100 (Lozère)

Mende is very much a country town : pasture-land is close by, and at this stage the Lot river is just a little trout stream with cows grazing on its banks. You can smell the mountain air and the pine forest.

▶ Capital of the Lozère Department, a tiny cathedral town : narrow streets with old corbelled houses, stone doorways with wooden doors, elaborate staircases, 15th and 16thC oriel windows on the façades; pretty fountains. ▶ **Cathedral of St. Pierre**★★, a Catholic watchtower over the nearby Protestant areas : begun in the 15thC by Pope Urban V (native of the region), it took nearly five centuries to build : the two great Flamboyant doorways were installed at the beginning of the 20thC. View over the old town★ from the two 16thC towers; inside : 17thC stalls, woodwork and altars, organ, tapestries and parts of choir-screen. ▶ **Ignon-Fabre museum :** regional folk art and archaeology *(10-12 & 2-5, closed Sun.).* ▶ In the former Carmelite convent (Rue de l'Ange) exhibition and sale of Lozère craft-work. ▶ Rue Notre-Dame : 13thC former synagogue; see courtyard. ▶ **Tour des Pénitents** (tower) : remains of 12thC rampart, 17thC chapel. ▶ 16thC **bridge**★ over the Lot. □

Mont MÉZENC★★

B1 (Ardèche)

Between the Velay (→ Auvergne) and Vivarais regions, the Mézenc volcano, the Meygal (NW) and Coiron (→) Massifs form a long volcanic chain from the Loire to the Rhône. To the east, by the Rhône, erosion has eaten deeply into the chain, forming the Boutières Amphitheatre and numerous valleys; to the west, by the Loire, the peaks are more gently rounded and covered with rich pasture.

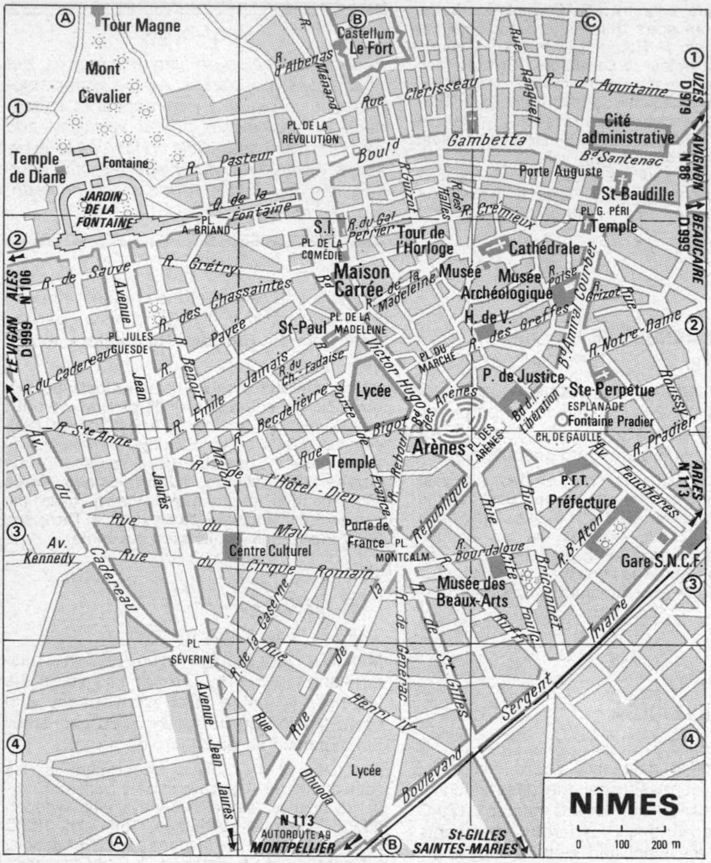

▶ **Estables** (→ Auvergne, Velay) : cross-country skiing in winter; ascent of Mont Mézenc *(2.6 km by car to Croix-des-Boutières, then 15-20 mins on foot).* There are two peaks to the Mézenc, separated by a valley : the higher *(S)* overlooks the Alps and the Massif Central.

▶ See the hamlets of **Moudeyres** (→ Auvergne, Velay ®) and **Laussonne** *(8 km and 11 km NE from Estables) :* tall houses roofed with thatch.

□

■ NÎMES★★★

C4 / ® / pop. 140 000 (Gard)

For the northerner, Nîmes is the archetypal Southern town : sun, *pastis* (anis - flavoured liquor), markets under the plane trees, pines and cypresses, fountains and squares where venerable Romans nod to you graciously. The monuments are beautiful and photogenic; in the evening you might imagine yourself in Italy or Spain.

▶ *Guided tours with the CNMHS (National Monuments Board ; → p. 00) in summer ; comprehensive ticket for the Roman monuments : 9-12 & 2-5 or 7 according to season.*

Nîmes was a major city under the Romans, at the cross-roads of the Domitian Way between Arles and Narbonne and the Régordane Way to the mountains. The Emperor Augustus made Nîmes a showplace of the Roman Empire. Later, the city was to be the scene of bitter struggles between the Protestant and Republican merchants and the Royalist Catholic working classes during the Revolution. Since the Protestants were forbidden to hold public office, they channelled their energies into trade, and quickly dominated the wool and silk industry in the Cévennes. Nîmes is one of the three or four towns which claim to have supplied Levi Strauss with the cloth to make his first blue jeans (denim : *de Nîmes*).

▶ **Esplanade** (C2) : the main thoroughfare of the town. Two steps away is the **Roman arena**★★ (corridas), slightly smaller than the arena at Arles : four entrances, two superimposed arcaded stories of 60 arches, and 24 000 seats arranged in thirty-four tiers; from the Middle Ages to the 18thC it was developed into housing for some 2 000 people. ▶ 500 m away is the **Maison Carrée**★★ (square house, B2), a Roman temple to the grandsons of the Emperor Augustus which may have formed part of the forum. Carved entablature supported by columns spaced at varying intervals. Inside : **antiquities museum**★ of discoveries from the same period as the temple : mosaics, marble statue of Apollo★, bronze head of Apollo★, eagle frieze in Augustan Empire style, a Venus reassembled from 103 fragments. ▶ Go down the residential **Quai de la Fontaine★** along the canal to the delightful **Fountain Gardens★★** (Jardins de la Fontaine; A1-2) : a masterpiece of 18thC garden planning, around the ruins of the first Roman buildings, including the **Temple of Diana★** (2ndC) and the Nemausus spring. ▶ Through the alleys of cedar and pine walk up to the **Magne Tower★,** remains of the Roman ramparts (A1; panorama★ over the town, the Cévennes, and Ventoux as far as the Pyrénées). ▶ Flea-market *(Sun.)* and Monday market under the nettle trees of Blvd. Gambetta (B1). ▶ Blvd. Amiral Courbet (C2) : the main avenue in Nîmes with shops, cafés and inexpensive restaurants; on the right hand side : **Porte Auguste,** city gate built in 16BC as part of the Roman ramparts; Protestant church (former Dominican church; 17thC); **archaeological museum★** in the former church of the Jesuit college (17thC chapel) : ancient civilisations from the early Iron Age to the end of the Roman occupation; the necessary background for understanding the Nîmes of Classical times; Grésan warrior★, frieze from Nagès★, mosaic of Bellepheron killing the Chimaera; Natural History Museum in same building *(10-12 & 2-5, 1 Oct.-Palm Sunday; 3-7 in summer, closed Sun. am).* ▶ **Place aux Herbes** (C2) : Romanesque house; cathedral and former bishop's palace. The **cathedral of St. Castor★** (C2) was rebuilt in the 19thC in Romano-Byzantine style. 11thC façade : upper frieze★ of the Creation (Romanesque and 17thC). The former bishop's palace★ (17thC) houses the Music Conservatory and the **Museum of Old Nîmes** *(same hours as above)* : Folk art including local forms of bull-fighting; beautiful silk shawls★; traditional furniture★; ceramics. ▶ Wander through the narrow streets of **mediaeval Nîmes,** around the cathedral : upper class houses (16th-17th-18thC), fashionable shops (pedestrian zone).

Also... ▶ **Fine Arts Museum★** Rue Cité-Foulc (C3; *9-12 & 2-5 or 4 in winter; closed Tue.*) : temporary exhibitions of various painters. ▶ Extraordinary **aqueduct★★** built by the Romans ca. 19BC to bring water to the city, snaking through 50 km of rugged countryside from the Eure springs near Uzès (→) : a masterpiece of Roman civil engineering like the Pont du Gard *(guided tours, ask at SI).* □

▶ Nearby

▶ **Gardon gorges★,** between **Dions** and the **Gard aqueduct** (→). The river Gard runs through a narrow canyon high cliffs overlooked by the GR6; many caves. ▶ View★ over the gorges from the Uzès road by **Saint-Nicolas bridge★** (13thC) and the priory of **Saint-Nicolas-de-Campagnac★** (half-farm, half-fortress; 12th-13thC). □

■ Causse NOIR

A3

Surrounded by the rivers Tarn, Jonte and Dourbie, this is the smallest of the Grands Causses (plateaus).

▶ W : dark forests (hence the name; noir = black), hills, sinkholes and choked *avens* (caves); SW : landscapes like ruined towns around Montpellier-le-Vieux; E : sheepfolds and flocks. □

■ PRIVAS

C1-2 / ® / pop. 10 638 (Ardèche)

The capital of the Ardèche was an important Protestant centre, destroyed by royal troops in 1629. Only three years later it was rebuilt.

▶ Close to Mont Toulon, above the Ouvèze river (17thC stone bridge), and facing the Coiron plateau. ▶ **Agricultural Museum of the Verdus★** *(5 km S)* in a country inn *(Mr. Clair, tel : 75.64.27.40, every day in summer).* ▶ Pretty village at **Coux** *(3 km E)*; **Jaubernie Caves :** shelter for Protestants in the 16th-17thC *(3.5 km E, then 30 mins on foot).*

Also... ▶ **Pranles** *(15 km N)* : Museum of Protestant Vivarais in the house of Pierre and Marie Durand, 17thC martyrs *(10-12 & 2:30-6:30, 15 Jun.-15 Sep.; Palm Sunday - 1 Nov., weekends only 10-12 & 2-6)*; interesting example of a Cévennes farm.

▶ From Privas to Vernoux-en-Vivarais via the Dunière gorges *(40 km; approx. 3 hr)*

Spectacular winding mountain road and *corniche* above the valleys; nice views of terraced hillsides and isolated hamlets. ▶ **Privas.** ▶ Between **Moulin-à-Vent** and **Ollières-sur-Eyrieux** : road through chestnut trees. ▶ Turn right on the La Voulte road, to **Dunière** at the entrance to the **gorges**; up to the ruins of the **château de Tourette★ :** impressive keep in untouched setting. ▶ **Vernoux-en-Vivarais.** □

▶ From Privas to Aubenas via the **Escrinet Pass★** ® (alt. 788 m) : beautiful road; mountain panoramas. □

▶ From Privas to Gerbier-de-Jonc on the **Quatre Vios** (Four Winds) **Pass** road★★ : one of the most spectacular in Upper Vivarais. □

Local vocabulary

Bajanat : *chestnut soup*
Bancel : *terrace (syn. : faïsse, traversier, accol)*
Béal, béalière : *irrigation canal*
Cade : *juniper*
Cadi : *coarse woollen cloth*
Calade : *stony soil*
Clapas : *heap of rocks in limestone country*
Clède : *chestnut drying shed*
Clinton : *light sharp Cévennes wine*
Gardons : *Cévennes rivers, many of the tributaries of the Gard river*
Gardonnade : *flooding Gardons*
Gavache, gavot : *pejorative nickname for mountain-dwellers*
Magnan : *silk-worm*
Magnanerie : *silk-worm hatchery*
Mas : *traditional rural house or farm*
Mazet : *rustic shelter erected for celebrations*
Pelous : *prickly outer husk of the chestnut*
Quartier : *group of mas and hamlets in the same valley; basis of social organisation in the Cévennes*
Raïol : *nickname for inhabitant of the Cévennes; according to popular etymology, "faithful to the king" (roi); in fact, means mountain-dweller*
Serre : *narrow saw-edged ridge between deep valleys; typical of the Cévennes*
Valat : *lateral valley*

The **RHÔNE** Corniche★★

▶ From Tournon to Saint-Péray *(26 km)*

C1

Between Tournon (→) and Valence (→ Dauphiné), there is a series of beautiful landscapes as the valley narrows; the Rhône *corniche* (cliff road) gives excellent views over the river, the orchards in the plain, and the Vercors mountains on the horizon.

▶ **Tournon.** ▶ Steep climb along the cliff edge : Doux Gorges to the west. ▶ **Saint-Romain-de-Lerps** ® : two orientation tables pin-point 13 departments. Above **Saint-Péray** is the eagle's nest castle of **Crussol**★, 200 m above the plain *(one hour round trip : narrow road, then path) :* impressive 12thC ruins. Below, on the river-bank, 17thC **château de Châteaubourg.** □

The **RHÔNE** Valley★★

▶ From La Voulte to Pont-Saint-Esprit *(65 km; half day)*

C2

This was one of the great North-South highways of European civilisation. Every stop-over became a town, and in the wake of the merchants came ideas, art, new customs... and wars. The hill-top villages with their towers and crenellations recall old rivalries. Each rock carries a fortress, as in the Rhine Valley. Over the ages, the river boatmen were the mainspring of valley life - until the arrival of the railway and the construction of the great dams which tamed the river. Today, the Rhône Valley is an industrial and commercial centre with factories, warehouses, refineries and nuclear power stations. Fortunately, the orchards and vineyards are only a few miles away.

▶ **La-Voulte-sur-Rhône** (→ Eyrieux). ▶ **Baix** ®, downstream from the Loriol dam. ▶ **Cruas**★ on the banks of the river canal : remarkable Romanesque **abbey church**★ (Lombard influence; 11thC mosaic; one pre-Romanesque crypt with fine capitals★, one Gothic crypt); 12th-16thC fortified chapel and fortress built by the monks; access through Mediaeval streets. ▶ **Meysse :** Mediaeval town centre. ▶ **Mélas :** Romanesque chapel. ▶ **Rochemaure :** feudal castle★ (13th-16thC); **Pic de Chenavari :** volcanic dyke on a basalt base★ (views★ from the top, *45 min round trip*). ▶ **Viviers**★ C2 / ® (pop. 3290) : former episcopal city on a rock above the river : traditionally, the *Midi* (the South of France) begins here. The rounded roof-tiles, steeply sloping streets and balconies of wrought-iron give the place a Provençal look. At the entrance to the lower town, the Bishop's palace, the Hôtel de Roqueplane and the Dominican chapel of Notre-Dame du Rhône form a charming 18thC group; the **old town**★★ takes you straight back to the Middle-Ages. The Place de l'Ormeau★ is overlooked by the superb cathedral apse★★ (12thC, rebuilt 17th-18thC); the tower in front seems to be a fortified gateway from an earlier period; remarkable **Renaissance house** (Maison des Chevaliers) on the Place de la République; wrought-iron balconies in the Grand'-Rue; view of the Rhône and the Alps from the esplanade. ▶ Beyond Viviers, the Rhône runs through the **Donzère defile**★. Viewpoint above the **Donzère-Mondragon** complex (canal, electricity generating station, Pierrelatte nuclear power station). ▶ **Saint-Baume Gorges**★ to the W : villages of **Saint-Montant**★ and **Larnas,** each with a typical Vivarais Romanesque church. ▶ **Bourg-Saint-Andéol** ® (pop. 7665) by the banks of the Rhône : view from the quays, plane trees, church towers and ramparts of the episcopal palace. **Church of St. Andéol** (12thC chevet★) partially rebuilt in 18thC; 2ndC Gallo-Roman sarcophagus, said to be that of St. Andéol; Adoration of the Magi (primitive, Portuguese); French Classical mansions; convents; Renaissance loggia of the **Hôtel Nicolaï**. 10 min SW, **Tournes fountain,** with Gallo-Roman bas-relief dedicated to Mithras. ▶ **Pont-Saint-Esprit**★ C3 / ® (pop. 8135) : grew around a **bridge**★ (*pont :* bridge) dedicated to the Holy Spirit, one of the four such on the Rhône. On the terrace★ above the river are three churches : St. Saturnin (15thC), the Baroque chapel of the Penitents★ (17thC) and the former church of St. Pierre, in French Classical style (17thC); monumental staircase leading to the quay. Renaissance house at the foot of the bridge. Remains of Vauban's citadel and the former collegiate church (15thC). P. Raymond Museum (archaeology and local traditions; *10-12 & 2-6; closed Tue.)*

Also... ▶ The **Charterhouse of Valbonne**★ *(10 km W) :* set in a forest of oak and beech, roofed with varnished tiles★, a perfect example of French Classical monastic architecture; built on a Mediaeval ground-plan; superb Baroque church. And of course, the gorges of the Ardèche (→) and the Cèze (→). □

SAINT-GILLES-DU-GARD★

C4 / ® / pop. 10850 (Gard)

The modern town is a crossroads, but the old Saint-Gilles on the hillside has kept its character.

▶ The 12thC abbey church of St. Gilles was damaged during the Wars of Religion (16thC); after the Revolution, only the triple **doorway**★★ and magnificent west façade were left. The general restoration carried out in the 17thC was clumsy, but the façade is a marvel, inspired by Classical architecture and, in turn, frequently copied in Languedoc and Provence. The theme illustrated is the Passion of Christ. ▶ The triple-vaulted **crypt** houses the tomb of St. Gilles. ▶ The **spiral staircase** of the north bell-tower was an obligatory part of the curriculum for apprentice stonemasons. ▶ Covered market like the old Baltard markets of 19thC Paris. ▶ Small museum in much-restored Romanesque house. □

SAUVETERRE Causse★★

A2

The most northerly of the great *causses,* and also the most wooded : the west of the plateau is a natural forest of oak, beech and fir ; a further 12000 acres have been planted.

▶ **Sauveterre** ® is one of the main villages of the *causse;* farms are usually scattered. Typical Sauveterre dormer-windows. ▶ Fortified farm of **Choisal** (17thC). ▶ **La Canourgue** ® has lost some of its character but the narrow streets around the church have been restored : modest cob-walled houses, vaulted street-passages, fountains. It was once a weaving village, producing coarse woollen cloth. Benedictine church★ (11th-14thC; pink and white sandstone mosaic; 18thC statues). Small Gallo-Roman museum : ceramics from Banassac, like Millau an important pottery centre in the 1st, 2nd and 3rdC. ▶ Beautiful road★★ from **Chanac** (château of the Bishops of Mende; 13thC church, Gothic bridge) and Boyne, on the Tarn; particularly spectacular from **Le Massegros,** by the Point Sublime★★★ on the Tarn Gorges. □

■ SOMMIÈRES★

B4 / ® / pop. 3 000 (Gard)

Beautiful and somewhat neglected, near the stony hills where Lawrence Durrell found the same light and olive trees as in Greece.

▶ On the banks of the Vidourle, Sommières is a former stronghold : elegant French Classical mansions★ round an arcaded square★ behind the dismantled ramparts. On the hill, castle ruins; remains of the Roman bridge under the one in use.

Also... ▶ **Château de Villevieille★★** *(2 km)* : a harmonious blend of several periods (12th, 16th, 18thC); Louis XIII furniture; small Gallo-Roman museum; summer concerts *(Jul.-15 Sep., 2-7:30; Sun. off-season).* ▶ Charming cypress-flanked Romanesque chapel at **Saint-Julien-de-Salinelles★** *(5 km N; concerts in summer).* □

▶ The Silk route★ *(approx. 65 km; half day)*

N of Sommières are the southern Cévennes : vines, olive trees, pine woods, holm-oak and mastic in the fields; charming towns showing the influence of the Midi. These were weaving towns but the handsome silk factories are now deserted.

▶ **Sommières.** ▶ On the edge of the cliff. **Sauve★** : from the old bridge, nice view of the village; since the Middle Ages, speciality of pitchforks made from hackberry wood. ▶ Surrounded by vineyards, **Saint-Hippolyte-du-Fort★** : Mediterranean atmosphere, but typical Cévennes houses (17th-18thC), large Protestant church, Louis XIV fort, silk factories. The Margaride winter pasture trail starts from Saint-Hippolyte : today it is a hiking trail through the **Asclier Pass** (panorama★★), Aire de Côte, Can de l'Hospitalet and Florac. ▶ The road through **Monoblet** and **Saint-Félix-de-Pallières** (two pretty villages) is more difficult than the direct route, but the landscapes are typical of the Cévennes although the vegetation is Mediterranean. Silkworm breeding is being revived in Monoblet. ▶ **Ganges** (→ Languedoc). ▶ **Le Vigan★** ®, at the foot of the Aigoual (→) : Place du Quai and Place d'Assas (lime trees and fountains) are the town's social centres; walk in the Promenade des Chataigniers (park) by the former ramparts. The **Cévenol Museum** recalls the prosperous period of silk production *(10-11:30 & 2-6:30, Apr.-Oct., closed Tue. and Sat., ex. Jul.-Aug.; off-season, Wed. only).* □

■ TARN★★★ and JONTE★★ Gorges

▶ From Florac to Millau *(84 km; half day)*

A2-3 *(see map 4)*

The Tarn Gorges have long been a major tourist attraction, but the few villages and the dramatic landscape have remained unspoilt. The many caves in the area served as refuges for Protestants, Catholics and aristocrats at different times in history.

The road follows the bottom of the gorge between the coloured cliffs of the Sauveterre and Méjean *causses* (plateaus). Flourishing vegetation *(boat-trips Easter-Sep., from La Malène to Les Baumes amphitheatre).*

4. Tarn Gorges

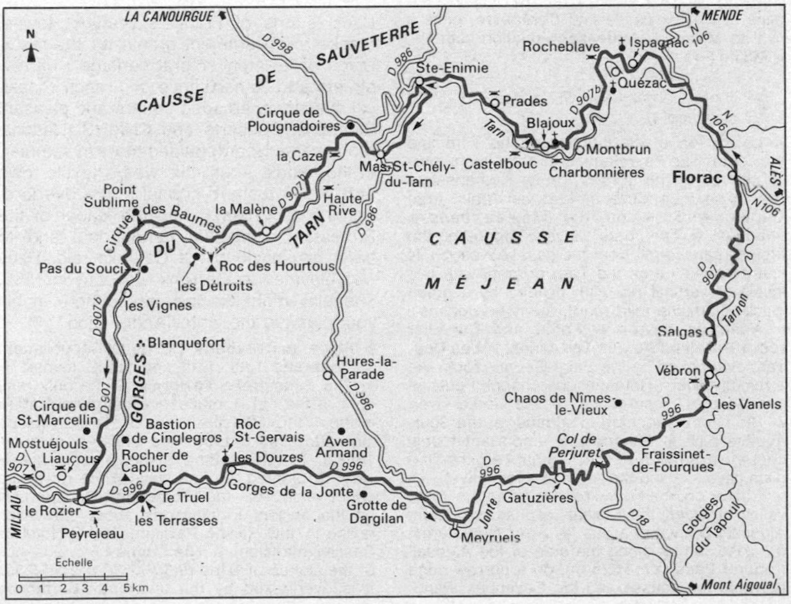

▶ **Florac** (→). ▶ **Ispagnac★,** fortified in the 15thC : bridge; Romanesque church and Benedictine priory; Gothic houses; 17th-18thC château. ▶ Gothic **bridge★** near **Quézac★;** large 14th-16thC church. ▶ The canyon begins at **Molines.** ▶ **Rocheblave** manor (16thC). ▶ Another 16thC château below **Montbrun bridge.** ▶ Viewpoint above **Castelbouc★★.** ▶ **Prades :** village and 16thC château. ▶ **Sainte-Énimie** ®, in a pretty setting at the mouth of the ravine : narrow cobbled streets, terraced slopes, 14thC Romanesque church, small regional museum; above, 13thC Benedictine priory, Romanesque chapel. ▶ **Mas-Saint-Chély,** beside a waterfall : 12thC Romanesque church (Gothic doorway); houses with Renaissance decoration. ▶ **Pougnadoires** Amphitheatre★. ▶ **La Caze** château (15th-17th-19thC) : now a hotel ®. ▶ **Hauterive★,** on the opposite bank. ▶ **La Malène** ®, where two ravines meet : a stone bridge links it to the left bank, overlooked by the hair-pin bends of the Méjean road★★ (spectacular); 15thC château-hotel; Romanesque church; marvellous excursions to the Hourtous rock★★ and Point Sublime★★★. (*Departure for the boat-trip*★★★). ▶ The Tarn runs over rapids and through **Les Détroits★** (series of narrows), and into **Les Baumes amphitheatre★★.** ▶ **Pas du Souci,** overlooked by the **Aiguille rock.** ▶ **Les Vignes** ®, where the valley broadens. ▶ The Sévérac road (→ Rouergue) leads to the **Point Sublime★★★,** fabulous view over the canyon and the *causse* (plateau) *(13 km, including 5 km tight bends).* ▶ **La Sourde rock :** view over Pas du Souci. ▶ From Vignes to Le Rozier, the canyon straightens out : marvellous rock formations such as the **Bastion de Cinglegros** on the left bank. ▶ The Sauveterre cliffs widen to form the **Saint-Marcellin amphitheatre.** ▶ **La Muse bridge** (500 m upstream from the junction with the Jonte river) leads to Le Rozier where the Promenade de la Jonte begins (see below). ▶ Towards Millau, the road is less spectacular; the Tarn leaves the gorges after it joins the Jonte. ▶ Pretty Mediaeval villages of **Liaucous** and **Mostuéjouls** (12-17thC château). ▶ Two views over the valley : the ruins of **Caylus** castle and **Compeyre,** once a rival to Millau. ▶ **Aguessac,** junction with N9. ▶ **Millau** (→). □

▶ Jonte Gorges★★★ *(56km; approx. 2 hr)* A3 *(see map 4)*

▶ **Le Rozier,** at the junction of the Tarn and the Jonte : like **Peyreleau,** one of the main tourist centres of the gorges; pretty Romanesque church near La Muse bridge; view-point from **Capluc rock★★** on the Méjean *causse (45 mins).* ▶ The Jonte canyon, separating the Méjean *causse (N)* from the *causse* Noir *(S),* is just as beautiful as the Tarn gorges, with two levels of vertical red cliff, divided by a green glacis. *Corniche* (cliff road), many viewpoints : ▶ **Vase de Sèvres** ▶ **Fabié and Curvelier rocks** ▶ **Belvédère des Terrasses.** ▶ **Les Douzes,** overlooked by the Saint-Gervais rock, like a ruined tower : Romanesque chapel. Fontaine des Douzes, resurgence of the Jonte river. ▶ The river disappears in summer at the Sourguettes mill. ▶ **Meyrueis** ®, important tourist centre : excursion to the Aigoual (→), the Dargilan cave (→) and the Armand aven (cave) (→). ▶ Further on, the Florac road runs up the Jonte valley between the Méjean *causse* and Mont Aigoual; cultivated areas. ▶ After **Gatuzières,** the road climbs along the side of the Aigoual. **Perjuret Pass** (alt. 1 028 m), on a narrow ridge between the causse and the Cévennes. Panorama over the Cévennes and the Lozère. Aigoual road to the S; **Nîmes-le-Vieux★** road to the N; spectacular rocks around Veygalier. ▶ The road runs down into the Lozère : open horizons, grass-covered slopes and woods. ▶ **Fraissinet-de-Fourques** (bridge). ▶ Limestone cliffs. ▶ **Les Vanels :** down the Tarnon to Florac (→). □

The Garrigues

The Garrigues form the last plateau between the causses *and the coastal plain. These low limestone plateaus stretch around the SE of the Massif Central mountains, limited by the plain of the Vistre (S), the Cévennes (N) and the Ventoux (E). Clumps of holm-oak alternate with stony areas of aromatic herbs : thyme, savory, laurel, rosemary and lavender, and of course, kermes oak (*garric *which gives the area its name). The Protestants used to worship in the valleys, when their religion was outlawed; the textile workers built their* mazets *(→ local vocabulary) in the shade of the cyprus and almond trees. The perfume and dyeing industries find their raw materials here; the sheep graze on buckthorn and honeysuckle, and provide fertiliser for the vineyards. Near the towns the land is cultivated, but the surroundings are left wild (woods).*

There are more dolmens in the Garrigues than anywhere else in France, as well as the dry-stone huts known as capitelles *in Languedoc. The beautiful Uzès-Nîmes road crosses this unusual sun-drenched landscape, where it is always summer.*

UZÈS★★★

C3 / ® / pop. 7 826 (Gard)

Uzès is one of France's prettiest towns, thanks to government grants for the restoration of its architectural heritage : narrow streets and Renaissance or French Classical mansions, arcaded square and pleasant fountains. Concerts and CNMHS (National Monuments Board) guided tours in summer. In the Middle Ages, this was a textile town and a Protestant citadel : its overlord, Antoine de Crussol, was the leader of the Protestant armies in Languedoc, and to bring him back to the Catholic fold, Uzès was elevated to the rank of Duchy in 1565. The playwright Racine stayed here in his youth, as did the writer André Gide.

▶ **Place aux Herbes★** (pl. de la République) : arcades and 16th, 17th and 18thC mansions. ▶ **The Fenestrelle Tower★★** is the only remnant of the old Romanesque cathedral, rebuilt in the 17thC after the Wars of Religion (paintings attributed to Simon de Châlons, Avignon, 16thC). The 17th-18thC bishop's residence is very dilapidated. ▶ Fine view of the town and countryside from the **Promenade Racine,** built on the ancient fortifications above the Alzon ravine (17thC Racine Pavilion). 19thC Hôtel de Castille (mansion). ▶ **The Duché★★ :** residence of the Dukes of Uzès *(9:30-12:30 & 2:30-6:30).* It is overlooked by the enormous **Bermonde**

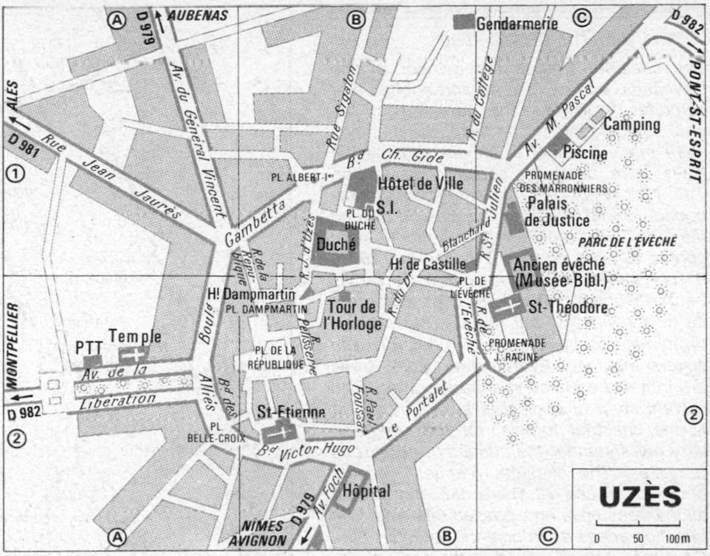

Tower square keep, (11thC); in the courtyard, Renaissance façade. Inside : Louis XV and Louis XVI furniture. ▶ 18thC Hôtel de Ville (town hall). ▶ 3rdC crypt on the Place du Duché. ▶ The tour de l'Horloge (Clock-tower, 11thC), representing the power of the church; opposite, the Tour du Roi. ▶ Renaissance Hôtel Dampmartin (mansion). ▶ French Classical church of **St. Étienne★ :** trefoil ground-plan and curved façade (18thC).

Also... ▶ Stud-farm (Alès road), and Agricultural and Locomotion Museum at Arpaillargues *(4.5 km W, 9-12 & 2-7, closed Mon.).* □

▶ Nearby

▶ The woods and orchards in the countryside around Uzès alternate with the former vine-growing villages, now active holiday resorts. Nearly all of them have a château or pretty church. ▶ **Saint-Siffret★ :** hilltop village around a Templar castle and attractive church *(4 km W).* ▶ **La Capelle** and ▶ **Masmolène** *(15 km NE)* each have a château. ▶ **La Bastide-d'Engras** *(12 km NE) :* feudal castle. ▶ **Argilliers :** typical Languedoc château remodelled in the 18thC by the Baron de Castille in neo-Classical style. ▶ Picturesque hermitage at **Collias** on the Gardon river *(5 km S).* Superb hilltop village of **Lussan★** ® overlooking the Garrigue *(17 km NW)* and **Guidon du Bouquet rock** (alt. 629 m) between Uzès and Alès (view★ of the region). □

■ LES VANS★

B2 / ® / pop. 2 580 (Ardèche)

Between Upper and Lower Ardèche, Les Vans is a tourist centre : bright stone houses, square, fountains, 17thC church. □

▶ Nearby

▶ The Vans region is attractively situated at the foot of the Cévennes; the **Chassezac Valley** changes character as it runs from the schist of the Cévennes to the limestone of the Vivarais. ▶ **Païolive woods★** is a natural curiosity : immense labyrinth with amazing formations in a tumble of rocks and trees; numerous marked paths. ▶ Nearly all the surrounding villages have a pretty church and interesting architecture. ▶ Don't miss **Naves★** *(2.5 km SW),* nor ▶ **Brahic** in the little Gagnière valley *(7 km SW).* ▶ **Joyeuse★** ® *(15 km NE),* former stronghold and trading place between the valley and the mountain : château of the Duc de Joyeuse; 17thC church; old town centre. □

■ VILLENEUVE-DE-BERG★

C2 / ® / pop. 2 083 (Ardèche)

This former bastide (13thC) is situated between the basalt plateau of Coiron and the limestone of the Gras - two very different landscapes.

▶ It was once the juridical capital of the Vivarais and still has beautiful 17thC mansions from this period. Cistercian church rebuilt in the 17thC; panorama over the Vivarais. ▶ Small museum in the farm-school at **Le Pradel** *(5 km N; closed for work).* ▶ **La Villedieu** *(6 km) :* small museum of the bizarre, Bayssac quarter *(year-round, daily).* □

▶ Nearby

▶ S from Villeneuve : **Gras Plateau★.** ▶ **Saint-Maurice-d'Ibie,** ▶ **Saint-Andéol-de-Berg,** ▶ **Les Salelles.** ▶ **Alba** *(13 km E),* was a Roman town; 11th-16thC keep. Opposite, Mediaeval village of **La Roche★.** Farther S, another hill-village : **Saint-Thomé★** (ramparts, remains of two châteaux and 15thC cloister). □

■ VIVARAIS CÉVENOL Corniche★★

▶ La Bastide to Les Vans *(45 km)*
B2 *(see map 5 following page)*

Less traffic than on the Cévennes *corniche* (cliff road), with beautiful views in a changing landscape, running from the mountains to the lower plateau.

The bread tree

The chestnut tree is the symbol of the Cévennes, source of food and shelter. For centuries, it provided the staple diet of the area's inhabitants. In addition, the saplings were made into barrel staves and mature trees were used for construction timber. The history of the Cévennes is closely bound up with this tree; it appeared around the 12thC with the Benedictine monks, and spread to such an extent that in the 16thC it had become a mono-culture. It grows best between 500 m and 800 m on acid granite or schist soils, but never on limestone. From Alès to Le Vigan, the chestnut tree covers the land. Every three years, trees are trimmed and young shoots grafted. The current state of neglect is a serious threat to the chestnut forests, for they degrade very quickly under the attacks of numerous parasites. The chestnut reaches maturity between 35 and 70 years old, and almost all the trees have now passed this limit. The question arises as to how the forests of the Cévennes can be saved in the face of the ever-spreading gorse - a plant that tourists love, but which, as the Cevenol saying goes, 'smells of death'?

▶ **La Bastide-Puylaurent :** brought into existence by the railway. ▶ **Trappe-de-Notre-Dame-des-Neiges :** R.L. Stevenson stayed here on his "Travels with a Donkey". ▶ **Saint-Laurent-les-Bains :** small spa. ▶ The route crosses the **Borne Ravine,** then runs through the **Chap del Bosc forest.** ▶ **Montselgues** was a dependency of the Benedictine Abbey of Monastier, which played an important role in developing the mountain area; Romanesque church★. ▶ **Thines** (see below), appears on its rocky outcrop. ▶ After **Peyre,** the Mediterranean climate leaves its mark : chestnut trees replace firs, and vineyards are more common. ▶ Turn towards **Chambonas** ® and its château, down a very winding road running through marvellous villages clustered around their churches : **Saint-Jean-de-Pourcharesse★, Faugères, Payzac, Brès,** surrounded by miles of terraced hillsides. ▶ On the twisting road from Les Vans to La Bastide, take the detour to **Thines★★ :** isolated village with an outstanding church; a stop-over for pilgrims between Le Puy and Provence; stone-tiled roofs, multicoloured stonework, and carved ornamentation inspired by St. Gilles (→). The most beautiful part is the chevet, built of red-sandstone and white limestone. ▶ **Pied-de-Borne :** lovely site at the junction of three gorges. The generating station is the key element in the Chassezac complex. ▶ Delightful Romanesque chapel at **Sainte-Marguerite-Lafigère.** ▶ This narrow sloping valley is covered in chestnut trees and irrigated by a very sophisticated system installed in the 19thC. The best illustration of the extraordinary work of the Cévennes farmers. ▶ Romanesque church at **Saint-Jean-Chazorne.** ▶ **Beaumes :** Romanesque chapel and small bridge. ▶ The **Roujanel dam** has transformed the mountain stream into a peaceful lake. ▶ **Alzons,** in the heart of the chestnut woods. ▶ **La Bastide.** □

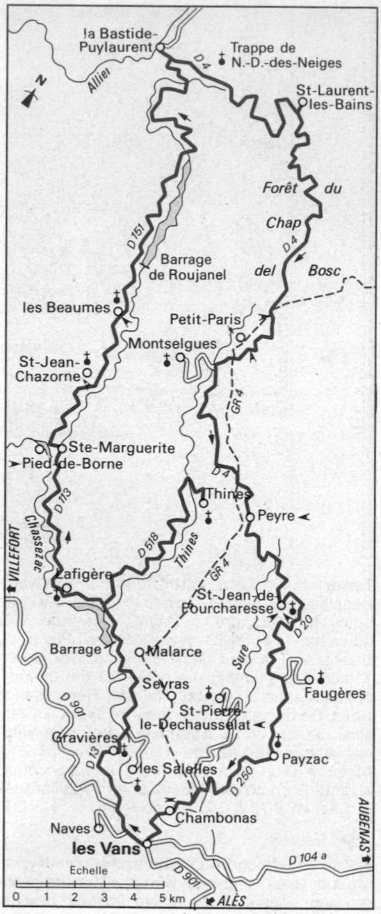

5. Vivarais Cévenol Corniche

Architecture

The *mas* (rural stone-built houses) of the Cévennes are usually grouped in hamlets; from the outside, there is little to be seen except narrow windows. Inside, they are astonishingly complex, having been extended according to the needs of the family. At the foot of the house, the out-buildings include the drying-room for chestnuts, the cheese cellar and press, the store-house and the stables. On the upper-floor are the living quarters. Under the roof is the silk-worm hatchery, used as a hay-barn in winter.

The *mas* is built with local stone, black or brown, and roofed with stone or terra-cotta tiles, depending on altitude. Decoration is always in cut-stone. Agricultural land includes cultivated land, chestnut woods, spring and autumn pasturage, and the summer hay fields. ● In the Languedoc Plain and the Lower Vivarais, the houses are adapted to vine-growing, and hence are more outward-looking : there is always a balcony with over-hanging roof outside the main room; as in all rural houses, this is the kitchen. Beneath are the stables and the cellar, usually vaulted. On the top floor is the hay-loft, also used as a barn or silk-worm hatchery. Building stone is pink sandstone in the Les Vans region, limestone on the Gras plateau, and black basalt round Coiron. ● On the limestone *causse,* rock lies close to the surface and is used for everything, from walls to roofs : every farm has its own quarry. Wood is rare and beams are replaced by stone vaulting. Houses are built in folds of the *causse,* sheltered from the prevailing winds. All the farm buildings are under one roof on various levels; these farms are often very large, since there is no shortage of space or stone.

Cévennes region

On the Sauveterre Causse

● *Brief regional history*

The Romans The Romans conquered the region in 121BC. Under Emperor **Augustus** (27-14BC), **Nîmes** became one of the showpieces of the Roman Empire, for the benefit of the colonists and retired veterans of his Egyptian campaigns against Anthony and Cleopatra. Beaucaire, Uzès, Anduze and Le Vigan were also founded by the Romans. ● Roman cultural influence made a profound and lasting impression on the country's language, customs and infra-structure. Roman first names are still common in Nîmes and in the Cévennes.

11th-13thC ● Convents and abbeys (principally **Benedictine**) were the major instruments of development in the area. The Knights Hospitallers of Lozère extended their influence throughout the Gévaudan area. Vineyards regained the importance they had under the Gallo-Romans, and **chestnut trees** started to spread throughout the Cévennes. Trade expanded : the fair of St. Gilles became a major annual trading event. ● Unlike the Midi-Toulousain (→), the Languedoc area remained firmly Catholic; it was made part of the **Royal Domain,** and with the stewardships of Beaucaire (created 1229) and Aigues-Mortes (1246) formed a defensive zone to counteract the effects of the heretical tendencies of the South. ● Guillaume de Grimoard, born at Bougès, became Pope Urban V in 1362.

The Reformation Together with the Roman influence, the **Protestant Reformation** constitutes the major cultural event in the region. Directly or indirectly, the Reformation affected every sector of society and every part of the region, even including neighbouring areas such as Gévaudan and Rouergue, which remained Catholic. Protestantism spread along trade-routes down the Rhône Valley and into the mountains; the combination of Protestantism and a strongly **latinised rural population** is typical of Languedoc, and was to influence its development. Protestants, also known as Huguenots or Camisards, hastened the spread of Northern French culture, since they were completely divorced from their Catholic neighbours, having different feast days, first names, meals and cultural orientation, taking the Bible as their cultural basis, while the Catholics emphasised processions, rituals and crosses. ● There was soon a vigorous **Catholic reaction,** leading to the foundation of numerous missions. ● The Revocation of the Edict of Nantes signalled the start of religious persecution, and popular Protestant resistance remains firmly rooted in local memory; finally, in July 1702, the **Camisards** revolted against State-imposed religion. ● During the **Revolution,** the Protestants were on the side of the Republic, while the counter-revolutionary Catholics supported the Church and Crown. ● Under the 3rd Republic (1870-1940), this division acquired a new look : the Protestant areas always voted to the left, while the Catholics remained firmly legitimist. This cultural difference is still visible today.

18th-19thC

The **local economy was at its height** in the 18thC, when the valleys of the Cévennes produced a large proportion of French silk. ● During the **first industrial revolution,** the Péchiney factories were built at Salindres, near Alès, developing an important steel industry around the coal-mines and stimulating the building of one of the first railway lines (La Grand-Combe to Beaucaire). ● The wine trade also benefitted from new means of transport, and more acres of **vineyards** were planted; this was the period of great **trade-fairs** at Beaucaire, Barre-des-Cévennes and Alès. ● In the middle of the 19thC, the traditional economy of the area was hit by silk-worm disease, which was not overcome until Pasteur's discoveries later in the century. Around the same period, Phylloxera destroyed the vines, and a fungus attacked the chestnut trees. Re-development of the **vineyards** at the end of the century was paralleled by the appearance of great estates and an emphasis on monoculture. Languedoc became a wine factory.

Today

At the beginning of the 20thC, disquieting signs began to appear : competition from artificial textiles, poor wine sales, the coal crisis and the fall in agricultural prices, followed by the blood-bath of WWI. In the back country, disaster was not far off; silk producers and factories closed, and the coal mines too were threatened. The **rural exodus** accelerated, and by 1970 there were only 500 inhabitants in the Cévennes Nature Park. ● But while the back country was dying slowly, the coast was undergoing development : major engineering projects on the Rhône, irrigation helping the expansion of fruit production, and the growth of the tourist industry. ● Today, there are **encouraging** signs of growing interest in preserving the cultural and agricultural identity of the region. Steps have been taken to encourage traditional activities including silk production and goat-breeding, together with country holidays that spread the benefits of the tourist industry inland.

Practical information

The region

Information : Languedoc-Roussillon : *Comité régional de Tourisme* (C.R.T.), 12, rue Foch, 34000 Montpellier, ☎ 67.60.55.42. **Rhône-Loire :** C.R.T., 5, pl. de la Baleine, 69005 Lyon, ☎ 78.42.50.04. **Ardèche :** *Comité départemental de Tourisme* (C.D.T.), 8, cours du Palais, 07002 Privas Cedex, ☎ 75.64.04.66. **Gard :** C.D.T., 3, pl. des Arènes, B.P. 122, 30011 Nîmes Cedex, ☎ 66.21.02.51. **Lozère :** *Office départemental de Tourisme* (O.D.T.), pl. Urbain-V, B.P. 4, 48002 Mende Cedex, ☎ 66.65.34.55. In Paris, *Maison de la Lozère,* 4, rue Hautefeuille, 75006, ☎ 43.54.26.64. In Lyon : *Maison de la Lozère,* 9, rue du Plat, 69002 Lyon, ☎ 78.38.28.23.

Bookings : *Loisirs-Accueil Lozère,* B.P. 4, 48002 Mende Cedex, ☎ 66.65.34.55.

Maps : *Michelin,* nos 76, 77, 80, 81, 83 at 1/200 000. *I.G.N.,* nos 49, 50, 51, 52, 58, 59, 65, 66 at 1/100 000.

S.O.S. : Ardèche : ☎ 17. **Gard :** *S.A.M.U.* (Emergency Medical Service), ☎ 66.67.00.00. **Lozère :** ☎ 17. *Poisoning Emergency Centres :* Montpellier, ☎ 67.63.24.01, and Grenoble, ☎ 76.42.42.42. *Ocean Rescue :* ☎ 66.51.43.09 (headquarters at Port-Camargue).

Weather forecast : Ardèche, ☎ 75.01.83.50. **Gard,** ☎ 66.26.08.88.

Rural gîtes, chambres d'hôtes, farmhouse accomodation : Ardèche : *Relais dép. des Gîtes de l'Ardèche,* C.D.T., 8, cours du Palais, B.P. 221, 07002 Privas Cedex, ☎ 75.64.04.66 (enq), and 75.64.04.66 (bookings). **Gard :** *Gîtes ruraux du Gard,* S.D.T.R. at C.D.T., ☎ 66.21.02.51. **Lozère :** *Relais Agriculture et Tourisme,* Chambre d'Agriculture, 1, av. du Père-Coudrin, 48000 Mende, ☎ 66.65.26.77.

Holiday villages : → practical holiday information.

Camping : approx 280 campsites ; lists available at each C.D.T.

Festivals : Apr : *Lussas Cinema Festival.* **Jul :** *Uzès Festival Nights ; Alès Young Theatre Festival ; Jazz Festival* in Nîmes ; *Summer Festival* in St-Thomé. **Jul-Aug :** *International Summer Festival* at the charterhouse in Villeneuve-lès-Avignon ; *Theatre Festival* in Aigues-Mortes ; *Classical Music Festival* in Vigan ; *musical evenings* at the château de Villevieille ; *Nîmes Folk Festival.* **Aug :** *Theatre and Poetry Festival* in Valvignères ; *concerts* in Annonay.

Other events : *Féria de Pentecôte* in Nîmes. **Mid-July :** *festival of Violets* at Sainte-Eulalie ; **end of July :** *Festival of Olives* at Les Vans. **Aug :** *annual festival of peasant art* in Les Vans. **Mid-July-end of Aug :** *the festival of Jousters* at Serrière and **end of August :** *the festival of Onions.* **Early Sep :** *Protestant gathering* in Mialet, at musée du Désert. *Féria des Vendanges* in Nîmes. *Wine festival* at Saint-Péray. **Mid-Nov :** *festival of Chestnuts* at Privas ; **end of Nov :** *wine festival* at Conas.

Scenic railways : *Vivarais Railway,* Tournon-Lamastre line : Sun and nat hols, Apr-Oct, several days weekly during high season. Enq and bookings : Société C.F.T.M., 8, rue d'Algérie, 69001 Lyon, ☎ 78.28.83.34. *Le Transcevenol,* the Cévennes steam-powered locomotive, from Anduze to St-Jean-du-Gard, runs May-Oct. Enq and bookings : ☎ 66.85.13.17, or T.V.C. gare, 30270 St-Jean-du-Gard.

National and nature parks : *Cévennes National Park :* information service in Florac, ☎ 66.45.01.75 and 66.45.10.60 (summer). In Jul-Aug an office is open at the château de Florac along with six other information centres : Pont-de-Montvert, Meyrueis, Saint-Jean-du-Gard, Le Vigan, Génolhac and Villefort. The Cévennes National Park publishes leaflets called *Sentiers de découverte des paysages* (Discovering Country Trails), which provide interesting maps and descriptions. *Gévaudan Nature Park,* in Sainte-Lucie, NE of Marvejols, ☎ 66.32.09.22. Exhibition organised by the *Chambre des Métiers de la Lozère* in Jul-Aug.

Rambling and hiking : the region is traversed by GR trails 4, 6, 7, 42, 44, 427, 420, 60, 65, 66, 68, 67, 72 and 73 (topoguides). *Assn. de Tourisme de Randonnée Languedoc-Roussilon* (A.T.R.), 12, rue Foch, 34000 Montpellier, ☎ 67.66.24.19. *Eric Recolin, mas de l'Alouette,* Avèze, ☎ 67.81.05.88 ; *les Pierres Sauvages,* at Allègre, ☎ 66.85.78.22. *Comité de Coordination des Randonnées non-motorisées,* 8, cours du Palais, 07002 Privas Cedex, ☎ 75.64.04.66 (hiking, horseback, riding, biking, canoeing, cross-country, skiing : see the *Guide to Walking and Rambling*). The *Gard C.D.T.* publishes a brochure which describes approx 28 short and medium-distance hikes. The *Association des Randonnées en Cévennes et Vivarais largentiérois (R.C.V.L.)* has published a descriptive guide which presents all the different aspects of the region, and can be purchased at the *Largentière S.I.,* ⊠ 07110. The *Mende S.I.* provides a list of associations which propose hiking and rambling ideas and the *Cévennes National Park* publishes particularly informative documentation.

Riding holidays : *Comité gardois de Tourisme équestre et de Loisirs,* 3, pl. des Arènes, B.P. 122, 30011 Nîmes Cedex. *Le Beaucent,* 30190 Vic-St-Anastasie, ☎ 66.81.00.98. Enq concerning riding *gîtes,* horse hire and trails at the Cévennes National Park information service, château de Florac. *Assn. régional pour le Tourisme équestre et l'équitation de loisirs en Cévennes, Roussillon et Languedoc,* M. Ségui, 14, rue des Logis, Loupian, 34140 Mèze, ☎ 67.43.82.50. *Lozère C.D.T.,* ☎ 66.65.34.55.

Cycling holidays : the *Gard Conseil Général* has published a brochure listing approx 20 circuits (available at each C.D.T.).

River and canal cruises : houseboat hire on the Rhone Canal in Sète : *Nautic Voyages,* marina, 30220 Aigues-Mortes, ☎ 66.51.04.34 ; *Camargue Cruisers,* 30800 St-Gilles, ☎ 66.87.22.66.

Children : *Assn. lozérienne mutuelle d'Animation et de Formation agricole,* 10, cité des Carmes, 48000 Mende, ☎ 66.65.18.30, and

Assn. d'Accueil en milieu rural de la Basse-Ardèche, M. Dutruit, hameau des Salelles, 07170 St-Maurice-d'Ibie, ☎ 75.37.84.10, propose holidays for children in rural family homes. The *Poney Club de la Blaquière,* 30430 Saint-Privat-de-Champclos, ☎ 66.60.53.43, organises riding courses for children over 8 years old.

Tennis : enq. at the ℹ

Golf : Nîmes, rte de Saint-Gilles (18 holes), ☎ 66.70.10.01.

Motoring and motorcycling : Ledenon circuit, 20 km from Nîmes, ☎ 66.37.15.31 and 66.37.18.38.

Aquatic sports : centres : Camboux Lake, at Sainte-Cécile-d'Andorge, ☎ 66.34.06.57 and at the Sénechas Dam, near Bessèges, ☎ 66.25.00.01 ; Ponaut Lake, ☎ 67.56.66.42 ; Villefort Lake. Cruises, boat races at the *Ecole de Mer,* Port-Camargue, 30240 Le Grau-du-Roi, ☎ 66.51.43.09. Nautical Club of Langogne, ☎ 66.69.21.26.

Canoeing : Ardèche : *Comité dép. de Canoë-kayak,* M. Aymard, Grand-Rue, 07190 Saint-Sauveur-de-Montagut. *Le Tourbillon :* M. Houlière, ch. de Saint-Privat, 30210 Collias, ☎ 66.81.85.54 ; paddling school, beginners' and advanced courses. List of clubs and canoe-hire centres at the C.D.T. Canoe trip down the Ardèche and the Tarn : see the C.D.T.

Potholing and spelunking : *Comité dép. de spéléo en Ardèche :* enq at the C.D.T. ; underground safari in the Trabuc Cave, enq : *S.C.M.S.,* B.P. 121, 34003 Montpellier, ☎ 67.89.79.12.

Climbing : *Club Alpin Français,* 14, rue F.-Pelloutier, 30000 Nîmes. *Ardèche escalade* at Pradons (Mr. Termine), ☎ 75.39.61.56.

Winter sports : *Assn. ardéchoise des Centres-écoles et Foyers de ski de fond,* M. Duvert, 07510 St-Cirgues-en-Montagne. *Ski Club mendois,* ☎ 66.65.02.69. The **Ardèche** and **Lozère** C.D.T. publish brochures which provide lists of resorts and propose various ski holiday possibilities. **Gard :** Espérou/Prat-Peyrot resorts, ☎ 67.82.22.78, and Mas de la Barque, ☎ 66.48.80.26.

Parachuting : *Centre régional de Parachutisme Provence-Méditerranée,* aérodrome, 30150 Pujaut, ☎ 90.25.19.20.

Ballooning : *Freefall* at Annonay, 16, pl. des Cordeliers.

Hunting and shooting : enq at *Féd. dép. des chasseurs.* **Ardèche :** 5, av. C.-Faugier, 07000 Privas, ☎ 75.64.30.53 ; **Gard :** 21, rue Dhuoda, 30000 Nîmes, ☎ 66.84.01.65 ; **Lozère :** 16, bd Soubeyran, 48000 Mende, ☎ 66.65.04.44.

Fishing : the *Féd. de Pêche et de Pisciculture de l'Ardèche,* 12, bd de la République, 07100 Annonay, ☎ 75.33.26.20, publishes a fishing and tourism map. **Gard :** *Féd. dép. des Assn. de Pêche et de Pisciculture,* 8, rue Sully, 30000 Nîmes, ☎ 66.67.56.29. **Lozère :** *Féd. dép. de la Pêche,* av. Paulin-Daudé, 48000 Mende, ☎ 66.65.36.11. C.D.T., ☎ 66.65.34.55.

● Towns

AIGUES-MORTES

Montpellier 29, Nîmes 41, Paris 749
B4 ✉ 30220

ℹ pl. Saint-Louis, ☎ 66.51.95.00 (high season), and mairie, ☎ 66.51.83.10 (low season).

SNCF ☎ 66.51.99.78.

Hotels :
● ★★★***Les Remparts,*** 6, pl. d'Armes, ☎ 66.53.82.77. AE, DC, Euro, Visa. 19 rm Ⓟ ♨ ♿ closed 2 Jan-28 Feb. Beautiful, tastefully-furnished 18thC building, 310. Rest. ♦♦♦ closed 10 Nov-1 Mar and Mon, 100-200.
★★★***Saint-Louis,*** 10, rue de l'Amiral-Courbet, ☎ 66.53.72.68. 23 rm Ⓟ ♨ closed Jan and Feb, 210. Rest. ♦♦ closed Wed low season, 80-230.

⛺ ★★★★*Petite Camargue* (350 pl.), ☎ 66.51.84.77.

Restaurants :
♦♦ ***Les Arcades,*** 23, bd Gambetta, ☎ 66.53.81.13 ♿ closed 2-18 Jan, Mon (ex Jul-Aug). The old stones and P. Merquiol's cuisine are authentic, 85-150.
● ♦ ***La Camargue,*** 19, rue de la République, ☎ 66.53.86.88. AE, DC, Euro, Visa. ♨ closed 5 Jan-7 Feb, Mon and noon ex Sun. Gypsy guitar players settled in a superb old Camarguais house. Good régional cooking, 80-130.
♦ ***Le Minos,*** 7, pl. Saint-Louis, ☎ 66.53.83.24 ♿ Priority is given to fish specialities, 120-210.

ALÈS

Nîmes 44, Montpellier 70, Paris 709
B3 ✉ 30100

ℹ 3, rue Michelet, ☎ 66.52.21.15, and pl. G.-Péri, ☎ 66.52.80.04 (high season).

SNCF ☎ 66.23.50.50, 66.30.12.43.

Car-hire : *Budget* train + auto, pl. de la Gare, ☎ 66.86.37.57, and at the station, ☎ 66.30.12.43.

Hotels :
★★★***Grand Hôtel,*** 17 *bis,* pl. G.-Péri, ☎ 66.52.19.01. Euro. 43 rm Ⓟ ♿ 180. Rest. ♦♦ closed 15 Nov-Easter, Sun and Sat eve low season, 80-130.
★★★***Orly,*** 10, rue d'Avejan, ☎ 66.52.43.27. AE, DC, Euro, Visa. 43 rm Ⓟ ♿ closed 1-15 Jan, 220.

St-Hilaire-de-Brethmas, ✉ 30560, 3 km S on the N106 and D280 :
★★***Écusson*** (L.F.), rte de Nîmes, ☎ 66.30.10.52. 26 rm Ⓟ ♨ ♿ 180.

La Favède, Les Salles-du-Gardon, ✉ 30110 La Grand-Combe, 15 km N :
● ★★★***L'Auberge Cévenole*** (L.F. ; Relais du Silence), ☎ 66.34.12.13. Euro. 18 rm Ⓟ ♨ ♿ closed 2 Nov-30 Mar, 250. Rest. ♦♦ ♨ ♿ Spec : *escargots à la cévenole, petit chausson cévenol,* 130-180.

⛺ ★★*Châtaigniers* (76 pl.), ☎ 66.52.53.57. Allègre, ✉ 30500 St-Ambroix : ★★★*Château de Boisson* (90 pl.), ☎ 66.85.65.61 ; ★★★*Domaine des Fumades* (100 pl.), ☎ 66.85.70.78.

Restaurant :
♦ ***Le Clou de Girofle,*** 58, rte de Saint-Martin, ☎ 66.86.22.46. ♿ closed Jan and Sun, 120-210.

ANDUZE

Alès 13, Nîmes 47, Paris 722
B3 ✉ 30140

ℹ plan de Brie, ☎ 66.61.98.17 (high season).

SNCF ☎ 66.52.53.57.

Hotels :
★★***Porte des Cévennes,*** ☎ 66.61.99.44. AE. 18 rm P closed 1 Nov-31 Mar, 170. Rest. ♦ closed Sun noon, 50-110.

Générargues, 3.5 km N on the D129 :
★★★***Trois Barbus,*** ☎ 66.61.72.12. AE, DC, Euro, Visa. 36 rm P ♿ closed 3 Oct-15 Mar and Mon. Restful setting, 280. Rest. ♦♦ 120-200.

⛺ ★★★*Les Fauvettes* (60 pl.), ☎ 66.61.72.23 ; ★★★*Malhiver* (102 pl.), ☎ 66.61.76.04 ; 3 campsites ★★ (total 500 pl.) ; Mialet : ★★*la Rouquette* (133 pl.), ☎ 66.85.32.97 ; ★★*les Plans* (230 pl.), ☎ 66.85.32.46.

Restaurant :

Mialet, 10 km NW :
♦♦ ***Auberge du Fer à Cheval,*** ☎ 66.85.32.80. closed 2 Jan-20 Mar, Sun eve and Mon low season and from Oct, open only Fri, Sat and Sun. Village atmosphere. Spec : *pelardon chaud et sa petite salade, feuilleté aux champignons sauvages, daube de sanglier aux marrons,* 60-130.

Recommended : *Chez Daniel Girard,* antique dealer, Nîmes road, leaving the town. *Charcuterie Dhombre,* pl. du Château. *La Vitrine Cévenole,* rte de St-Jean-du-Gard. *Poterie d'Anduze,* rte de St-Jean-du-Gard, ☎ 66.61.80.86.

ANNONAY

Saint-Étienne 43, Valence 53, Paris 575
C1 ✉ 07100

ℹ 5, bd de la République, ☎ 75.33.24.51.

SNCF ☎ 75.33.31.24.

Hotels :

Davezieux, 3 km NE :
★★***Siesta,*** ☎ 75.33.07.90. AE, DC, Visa. 46 rm P ♿ closed Jan and Sat low season, 180. Rest. ♦ 120-210.

St-Marcel-lès-Annonay, 7.5 km W on the D82 :
★***Auberge du Teruay*** (L.F.), barrage du Ternay (dam), ☎ 75.67.12.03. AE, DC, Euro, Visa. 7 rm P closed mid-Jan to mid-Feb and Mon ex Jul-Aug, 100. Rest. ♦ 40-100.

Restaurants :
● ♦♦ ***Le Château*** (A.R.C.), 2, montée du Château, ☎ 75.32.19.78. AE, DC, Visa. closed 3 weeks in Jan and Mon. 18thC structure, 75-250.
Marc et Christine Julliat, 29, av. Marc-Seguin, ☎ 75.33.46.97, 85-220.

Farmhouse-inn : *le Miron,* Saint-Marcel-lès-Annonay, ☎ 75.33.35.78 ♿ ⛺ and sale of farm produce. Open weekdays if requested, 100.

ANTRAIGUES

Privas 42, Le Puy 79, Paris 817
C2 ✉ 07530

ℹ ☎ 75.38.72.46 - 75.38.70.10 (mairie).

Hotel :

Laviolle, 7 km N on the D578 :
★***Plantades*** (L.F.), ☎ 75.38.71.58. 10 rm P ♿ closed 5 Nov-15 Dec, 100. Rest. 50-80.

Restaurants :
♦♦ ***Lo Podello,*** ☎ 75.38.71.48. AE. P closed Jun-Oct and Thu (low season). Rustic setting (former castle), and permanent exhibition of paintings. Tasty Ardèche cooking, 110-230.
● ♦ ***La Brasucade,*** La Plage, ☎ 75.38.72.92. closed Tue, open only Sat and Sun from Oct to Apr. An unbelievably inexpensive menu. Permanent painting exhibition, 70.
♦ ***La Remise,*** ☎ 75.38.70.74. P ♿ closed Fri and Sun eve (ex summer), Nov. Typical Ardèche gastronomical fare ; regional produce which varies according to the season and local wines, 70-120.

AUBENAS

Privas 30, Le Puy 91, Paris 633
C2 ✉ 07200

ℹ pl. Airette, ☎ 75.35.24.87.

SNCF ☎ 75.35.01.67.

Hotels :
● ★★***Pinède*** (L.F.), rte du camping des Pins, ☎ 75.35.25.88. Visa. 32 rm P ♿ closed 15 Dec-20 Jan and Mon noon, 195. Rest. closed Mon, 70-95.
★★***Orangerie,*** 7, allées de la Guinguette, ☎ 75.35.30.42. AE. 17 rm P 180.
★***Auberge des Pins,*** 95, rte de Vals, ☎ 75.35.29.36. 8 rm P closed 1 Oct-31 Nov and Sat eve Sun in winter, 170. Rest. 55-85.

L'Escrinet (Pass), 14 km NE, on the N104 :
● ★★***Le Panoramic l'Escrinet*** (L.F.), ☎ 75.87.10.11. AE. 20 rm P ♿ closed 16 Nov-15 Mar and Sun eve (ex Jul-Aug), 230. Rest. ♦ closed Sun eve and Mon noon. Book ahead, 90-250.

⛺ ★★*Pins* (200 pl.), ☎ 75.35.18.15.

Recommended : *les Halles,* rue Pradal, ☎ 75.35.07.07 ; Ardèche produce (fruits, vegetables, *charcuterie*). *Marrons glacés d'Aubenas,* ch. de Bourgneuf, ☎ 75.35.13.39 (glazed chestnuts, other chestnut specialities).

AUMONT-AUBRAC

Mende 42, Le Puy 91, Paris 535
A2 ✉ 48130

SNCF ☎ 66.31.80.30.

Hotels :
★★★***Grand Hôtel Prouhèze,*** 2, rte du Languedoc, ☎ 66.42.80.07. AE, DC, Euro, Visa. 30 rm P ♿ closed Nov-Feb, Sun eve and Mon ex school hols, 300. Rest. ● ♦♦ An attractive, good stop in the heart of Gévaudan where the owner is the chef. Spec : *escargots aux cèpes, galette d'agneau en arlequin au vin de noix, médaillon de porcelet à l'estragon,* 70-220. A wine list with more than 500 *crus.*
★★★***Chez Camillou,*** ☎ 66.42.80.22. AE, Euro, Visa. 41 rm P ♿ closed 1 Nov-20 Dec, 150. Rest. ♦ 50-100.

⛺ ★★*Municipal* (100 pl.), ☎ 66.42.80.02.

BAGNOLS-LES-BAINS

Alès 93, Le Puy 95, Paris 594
21 km E of Mende, A2 ✉ 48190

(May-Oct), ☎ 66.47.60.02.

ℹ ☎ 66.47.64.79.

Hotels :
● ★★***Commerce,*** ☎ 66.47.60.07. Euro, Visa. 28 rm P closed Nov-1 Apr and Sun eve, Mon low season, 150. Rest. ♦ ♿ Good, basic fare, 55-100.
★★***Modern Hôtel,*** ☎ 66.47.60.04. Euro, Visa. 18 rm P closed 3 Nov-30 Jan ex Christmas, 130. Rest. ♦ ♿ 50-100.
★★***Pont,*** 7, pl. du Pont, ☎ 66.47.60.03. Visa. 28 rm P closed 20 Oct-Feb, 140. Rest. ♿ 50-80.

⛺ ★★*Municipal* (100 pl.), ☎ 66.47.64.79.

BAGNOLS-SUR-CÈZE

Avignon 33, Alès 50, Paris 659
C3 ✉ 30200

ℹ Mont-Cotton, esplanade, ☎ 66.89.54.61.

SNCF ☎ 66.23.50.50.

Hotels :
● ★★★★***Château de Coulorgues,*** rte d'Avignon, ☎ 66.89.52.78. AE, DC, Euro, Visa. 23 rm Ⓟ ♨ ♘ ▭ ♪ ♿ closed 15 Jan-15 Feb, Sun eve and Mon low season. Very pleasant setting, 400. Rest. ◆◆ ✂ closed Sun eve and Mon, 125-240.
★★***Valaurié,*** rte de Nîmes, ☎ 66.89.66.22. Euro, Visa. 22 rm ⚘ Ⓟ ♨ ✂ closed 15 Dec-15 Jan, Sun eve and Mon, 175.

Goudargues, ⊠ 30630. 15 km NW on the D980 :
★★***Commerce,*** quai du Canal, ☎ 66.82.20.68. Euro. 50 rm ⚘ Ⓟ ♨ ♘ ♿ 200. Rest. ◆ ✂ 50-120.

⛺ ★★★*Genêts d'Or* (95 pl.), ☎ 66.89.58.67.

Restaurant :
Connaux, ⊠ 30330, 8.5 km S on the N86 :
● ◆◆ ***Maître Itier,*** N86, ☎ 66.82.00.24. AE. Ⓟ ♨ ✂ ♿ closed 1-16 Feb, 15-30 Jun, Sun eve and Mon. A beautiful inn, where the cooking is delightfully simple and the setting lovely; fish soup *aux petits légumes,* 120-210.

Farmhouse-inn : *Venepean,* 5 km on the RN86 and RD148, ☎ 66.89.65.16. Grilled meats and poultry cooked over a wood fire.

BAIX

Montélimar 20, Privas 20, Paris 595
11 km E of Chomérac, C2 ⊠ 07210 Chomérac

Hotel :
● ★★★★(L) ***La Cardinale et Résidence*** (Relais et châteaux, Relais du Silence), ☎ 75.85.80.40, Tx 346143. AE, DC, Euro, Visa. 17 rm ⚘ Ⓟ ♨ ♘ ▭ closed 3 Jan-15 Feb. Stately residence on the banks of the Rhône River, 595-800. Rest. ◆◆ closed 15 Nov-30 Mar, 160-300.

Restaurant :
Fonts-du-Pouzin, ⊠ 07250 Le Pouzin, 8.5 km NW on the N86 and N104 :
◆◆ ***La Marcanterie,*** rte de Privas, ☎ 75.63.88.84. DC, Visa. Traditional stone house. Ⓟ ♨ closed Mon, 120-210.

BEAUCAIRE

Nîmes 24, Avignon 25, Paris 710
C4 ⊠ 30300

ℹ 6, rue de l'Hôtel-de-Ville, ☎ 66.59.26.57.

SNCF ☎ 66.59.10.27.

Hotels :
★★★***Les Vignes Blanches*** (Inter-Hôtel), rte de Nîmes, ☎ 66.59.13.12, Tx 480690. Visa. 62 rm Ⓟ ♨ ▭ ♿ closed 15 Oct-15 Mar, 260. Rest. ◆◆ 120-210.
● ★★***Les Doctrinaires*** (Châteaux-Hôtels), quai du Gal-de-Gaulle, ☎ 66.59.41.32. Euro, Visa. 34 rm Ⓟ ♨ ♘ ♿ 18thC building, 240. Rest. ◆◆ closed Sun eve low season, 80-150.
★★***Le Robinson*** (L.F.), rte de Comps, ☎ 66.59.21.32. 30 rm Ⓟ ♨ ♘ ▭ ♪ ♿ closed Feb, 190. Rest. ◆ 45-100.

⛺ ★★*Le Rhodanien* (80 pl.), ☎ 66.59.25.50.

BOURG-SAINT-ANDÉOL

Montélimar 28, Privas 55, Paris 630
14 km S of Viviers, C2 ⊠ 07700

ℹ pl. Champ-de-Mars, ☎ 75.54.54.20.

SNCF ☎ 75.04.50.70.

Hotels :
★★***Prieuré,*** quai Madier-de-Montjau, ☎ 75.54.50.97. AE, Visa. 10 rm Ⓟ Former priory, 100.
★★***Moderne,*** pl. Champ-de-Mars, ☎ 75.54.50.12. AE, Euro. 21 rm Ⓟ ♨ closed Nov-Mar, 150. Rest. ✂ ♿ closed Sat noon and Sun eve, 55-110.

⛺ ★★★*Camp du Lion* (140 pl.), ☎ 75.54.53.20.

Farmhouse-inn : *la Vachère,* 2 km, ☎ 75.54.58.68. ♿ closed Mon. Spec : *salmis de pintade, criques ardéchoises,* 80-130.

La CANOURGUE

Mende 47, Rodez 67, Paris 580
A2 ✿ ⊠ 48500

ℹ ☎ 66.32.83.67 (high season), and at the mairie, ☎ 66.32.81.47.

Hotels :
● ★★***Commerce,*** ☎ 66.32.80.18. Visa. 32 rm Ⓟ ♨ ♘ ♿ closed 1 Dec-1 Feb, Fri eve and Sat low season, 170. Rest. 45-80.

Banassac, 2 km W :
★★***Relais de la Motte,*** ☎ 66.32.81.72. 10 rm Ⓟ closed 1 Sep-30 Jun, 150.

⛺ ★★*Le Moulin* (50 pl.), at Banassac, ☎ 66.32.83.30.

Farmhouse-inn : *le Muscadel,* 2 km, ☎ 66.32.81.89. Ⓟ ♨ ✂ ♿ Book ahead.

CHARMES-SUR-RHÔNE

Valence 11, Privas 28, Paris 579
8 km N of La Voulte, C1 ⊠ 07800 La Voulte

ℹ ☎ 75.62.44.36.

Hotels :
★★***Vieille Auberge*** (L.F.), ☎ 75.60.80.10. AE, DC, Visa. 7 rm Ⓟ closed 2 weeks in Jan, 3 Aug-3 Sep, Sun eve and Wed, 180. Rest. ● ◆◆ ♿ Enjoy the light *nouvelle cuisine* in this 17thC vaulted dining-room with its beautiful fireplace, 80-130.

La Voulte :
★★***Musée*** (L.F. ; France-Accueil), ☎ 75.62.40.19. Euro, Visa. Ⓟ 15 rm. closed 1 Feb-1 Mar, Sat (Oct-Apr), 165. Rest. 65-100.

Le CHEYLARD

Privas 48, Le Puy 77, Paris 604
21 km SW of Lamastre, C1 ⊠ 07160

Hotel :
★***Voyageurs,*** 2, rue du Temple, ☎ 75.29.05.88. AE, DC, Visa. 17 rm, closed Feb school hols, 22 Sep-15 Oct and Sun eve, 140. Rest. ✂ closed Sun eve low season, 50-80.

⛺ *La Chèze* (120 pl.), ☎ 75.29.09.53.

Le COLLET-DE-DÈZE

Alès 32, Mende 80, Paris 706
17 km NW of La Grand-Combe, B3 ⊠ 48160

Hotels :
★***Le Vieux Moulin,*** ☎ 66.45.52.62. AE, DC, Euro, Visa. 14 rm Ⓟ closed 15 Dec-15 Jan and Wed (low season), 100. Rest. 80-130.

Saint-Julien-des-Points, 8 km NE :
★★***Les Cévennes,*** ☎ 66.45.51.48. AE, DC, Euro, Visa. 14 rm ♿ 100. Rest. 80-130.

Farmhouse-inn : *Pennens Bas,* 48240 Saint-Frezale-de-Ventalon, 8 km, ☎ 66.45.52.45. Ⓟ ♨ Book ahead, 100.

L'ESPÉROU

Mende 85, Alès 95, Paris 654
10 km S mount Aigoual, A3 30570 Valleraugue

Hotel :
★★***Source,*** ☎ 67.82.60.35. 10 rm Ⓟ ♘ ✂ closed Oct, Christmas Day, Easter Sun and 15 days in Jun, 180. Rest. ◆ 50-80.

FLORAC

Mende 39, Alès 71, Paris 611
A2-3 ✉ 48400

ℹ av. J.-Monestier, ☎ 66.45.01.14.

Hotels :
★★**Grand Hôtel du Parc,** 47, av. Jean-Monestier, ☎ 66.45.03.05. AE, DC, Visa. 58 rm P closed 1 Dec-15 Mar, Sun eve and Mon low season. Half-pension obligatory during high season, 180. Rest. ♦ Regional cooking, 50-130.
★**Gorges du Tarn,** ☎ 66.45.00.63. 31 rm closed 1 Oct-1 May, 170.

Cocurès, 5 km NE :
La Lozérette, ☎ 66.45.06.04. 17 rm P closed 30 Sep-31 May, 130. Rest. closed Sun noon (Jun and Sep), 60-110.

★★*La Tière* (35 pl.), ☎ 66.45.01.14 ; ★★*Municipal* (130 pl.), ☎ 66.45.00.53.

Farmhouse-inn : *Blajoux,* in Quézac, 12 km NW on the N107 and 107 *bis,* ☎ 66.48.51.95. Book ahead.

GÉNOLHAC

Alès 37, Nîmes 81, Paris 618
B2 ✉ 30450

ℹ mairie, ☎ 66.61.10.55.

SNCF ☎ 66.61.10.35.

Hotel :
★**Mont Lozère,** 13, av. de la Libération, ☎ 66.61.10.72. Euro. 15 rm P closed Nov-Feb and Tue (low season), 130. Rest. ♦ 50-120.

GRANGES-LÈS-VALENCE

Privas 39, Saint-Étienne 90, Paris 562
C1 ✉ 07500

Hotels :
★★**Alpes-Cévennes,** 641, av. de la République, ☎ 75.44.61.34. AE, Euro. 28 rm P closed 6-26 Aug, 29 Dec-5 Jan, 160.

Saint-Péray, ✉ 07310, 4 km W on the N532 :
★★**Bains** (L.F.), ☎ 75.40.30.13. AE, DC, Euro, Visa. 35 rm P closed 20 Dec-23 Jan, 200. Rest. 65-110.

Soyons, ✉ 07130 St-Péray, 6 km S on the N86 :
★★★**Musardière,** ☎ 75.60.83.55. AE, DC, Euro, Visa. 12 rm P 2 ha closed 20 Dec-10 Jan, 350. Rest. ♦ closed Sat noon, 100-220.

Saint-Romain-de-Lerps, ✉ 07130 Saint-Péray, 12 km NW on the N532 and D287 :
★★★★(L) **Le Château du Besset** (Relais et châteaux), ☎ 75.58.52.22. Tx 345261. AE, DC, Visa. 10 rm P 15thC castle. closed 26 Oct-28 Mar, 2 200. Rest. ● ♦♦♦ Regal fare to match the setting ; two beautiful dining-rooms. Spec : *salade Ardéchoise aux langoustines, tartare de daurade rose au caviar,* 250-300.

Restaurants :
● ♦♦ **Auberge des Trois Canards** (L.F.), 565, av. République, ☎ 75.44.43.24. AE, DC, Visa P 120-210.

Châteaubourg, ✉ 07130 St-Péray, 10 km N on the N86 :
● ♦♦♦ **Château,** ☎ 75.40.33.28. AE, DC, Visa. P closed Sun eve, Mon, 10 Jan-10 Feb, 16-26 Aug. Spec : *médaillons de lotte à la crème d'herbes, goujonnette de soles, magret de canard aux baies de cassis,* 100-220.

Le GRAU-DU-ROI

Montpellier 26, Nîmes 47, Paris 756
B4 ✉ 30240

ℹ bd du Front-de-Mer, ☎ 66.51.67.70.

SNCF ☎ 66.51.40.93.

Hotels :
★★**Nouvel Hôtel,** quai Colbert, ☎ 66.51.43.54. 21 rm closed Oct-Easter, 180.
★★**Les Acacias,** 21, rue de l'Égalité, ☎ 66.51.40.86. Visa. 27 rm closed 30 Oct-22 Mar, 180. Rest. closed 12 Oct-22 Mar, 50-125.
★★**Splendid,** 15, bd du Front-de-Mer, ☎ 66.51.41.29. 27 rm 200. Rest. ♦ 120-210.

Port-Camargue, 3 km S :
● ★★**Le Spinaker,** pointe du Môle, ☎ 66.51.54.93. Euro, Visa. 20 rm P closed 6 Jan-14 Feb, 16-27 Nov, Mon eve, 300. Rest. ♦ closed Sun eve and Mon, 115-250.

★★★★*L'Éden* (400 pl.), ☎ 66.51.49.81 ; ★★★★*Abri de Camargue* (300 pl.), ☎ 66.51.54.83 ; ★★★★*Le Boucanet* (436 pl.), ☎ 66.51.47.48.

JOYEUSE

Privas 52, Mende 97, Paris 655
B2 ✉ 07260

ℹ ☎ 75.39.56.76.

Hotels :
★★**Cèdres** (L.F.), ☎ 75.39.40.60. DC, Euro. 40 rm P closed 15 Oct-15 Apr, 250. Rest. 50-130.
★**Couronne** (L.F.), ☎ 75.36.61.67. 18 rm P 100. Rest. ♦ Family cooking, 80-130.

Rosières, 1.5 km NE on the N104 :
★**Cévennes** (L.F.), ☎ 75.39.52.07. Euro, Visa. 14 rm P 100. Rest. ♦ 80-130.

Chandolas-Maisonneuve, ✉ 07230, 13 km S on the N104 and D208 :
★★**Relais de la Vignasse** (L.F.), ☎ 75.39.31.90 and 75.39.04.66. 15 rm P closed 15 Oct-15 Mar, 210. Rest. ♦ 70-210.

★★★*Le Sous-Perret* (75 pl.), ☎ 75.39.50.54 ; Rosières : *Blajoux farmhouse campsite,* alongside a stretch of water (bathing and fishing).

Restaurant :
Laurac-en-Vivarais, ✉ 07110 Largentière, 6 km NE on the D212 :
Auberge des Piles (L.F.), ☎ 75.36.85.75. 8 rm P open only Jul-Aug, 75. Rest. ♦ open noon only ex Jul-Aug, 80-130.

Farmhouse-inns : *les Granges,* 1 km from Rosières, ☎ 75.39.50.38. 6 rm P Spec : *caillettes, daube, charcuterie. Maison de Chalençon,* in Lablachère, ☎ 75.36.60.28. Spec : *confits, charcuterie and foie gras ; Les Marronniers,* in Montréal, 6 km NE on the D212, ☎ 75.36.82.54, farm produce for sale.

LALOUVESC

Yssingeaux 43, Privas 83, Paris 559
27 km N of Lamastre, C1 ✉ 07520

ℹ ☎ 75.67.84.20.

Hotels :
★★**Beau Site** (L.F.), ☎ 75.67.82.14. AE. 33 rm closed 1 Oct-1 Apr, 220. Rest. 70-150.
★★**Monarque** (L.F.), ☎ 75.67.80.44. AE, DC. 20 rm P closed 15 Oct-1 May, 200. Rest. ♦ 60-115.

Satillieu, ✉ 07290, 11 km NE on the D578 :
★★**Gentilhommière** (France-Accueil ; L.F.), ☎ 75.34.94.31, Tx 345548. AE, DC, Euro, Visa.

41 rm P ♨ ⛰ ▭ ⛳ ♿ 300. Rest. ♦♦ closed 1 Nov-1 Apr, 80-110.

⛺ ★★*Granjeon*, Satillieu (100 pl.), ☎ 75.34.96.64.

LAMASTRE

Valence 40, Privas 56, Paris 583
C1 ✉ 07270

ℹ av. Boissy-d'Anglas, ☎ 75.06.52.86.

Hotels :
★★★***Midi Barattéro,*** pl. Seiguobos, ☎ 75.06.41.50. AE, Euro, Visa. 20 rm P ♨ ♿ closed 15 Dec-1 Mar, Sun eve and Mon (ex Jul-Aug and nat hols), 240. Rest. ● ♦♦ *Salade tiède aux foies de canard et champignons des bois, soufflé glacé aux marrons,* 140-250.
★★***Commerce*** (L.F.), ☎ 75.06.41.53. DC, Euro. 23 rm P ♨ ⛰ ✗ closed 1 Nov-end Feb, 210. Rest. ♦ ✗ 60-160.

Urbilhac, 2 km W on the D533 :
★★***Château d'Urbilhac,*** Vernoux road, ☎ 75.06.42.11. 14 rm ⚘ P ♨ ⛰ ▭ closed 1 Oct-1 May. Antique furniture, 300. Rest. ♦♦ 120-190.

Desaignes, ✉ 07570, 7 km W on the D533 :
★***Voyageurs*** (L.F.), ☎ 75.06.61.48. Visa. 20 rm P ♨ ⛰ ⛳ closed 30 Sep-15 Mar, 110. Rest. ✗ 50-100.

⛺ ★★*Municipal* (130 pl.), ☎ 75.06.44.33.

LANGOGNE

Le Puy 42, Mende 50, Paris 551
B2 ✉ 48300

ℹ 15, bd des Capucins, ☎ 66.69.01.38 (high season).

SNCF ☎ 66.69.10.80.

Hotels :
★★***Voyageurs,*** 9, av. Joffre, ☎ 66.69.00.56. Visa. 14 rm P closed 15 Dec-22 Jan and Sun low season, 150. Rest. ♦ ✗ ♿ 50-110.
★***Gaillard,*** av. du Pont-de-l'Allier, ☎ 66.69.10.55. 20 rm P closed 1 Dec-1 Apr, 80. Rest. ⚘ ✗ closed Sun eve (1 Feb-1 Jun), week-end (15 Sep-1 Dec), 40-80.

Youth hostel : Auroux, 15 km on the D26, ☎ 66.69.45.40.

⛺ ★*Municipal* (100 pl.), ☎ 66.69.10.33.

LARGENTIÈRE

Aubenas 16, Alès 60, Paris 649
B2 ✉ 07110

SNCF ☎ 75.39.11.29.

Hotel :
Valgorge, 19 km NW :
● ★★***Tanargue*** (L.F.), ☎ 75.93.68.88. AE. 25 rm ⚘ P ♨ ⛰ ♿ closed 5 Jan-5 Mar, 200. Rest. 80-160.

LASALLE

Alès 30, Nîmes 42, Paris 739
B3 ✉ 30460

Hotel :
★★***Les Camisards,*** 51, rue de la Croix, ☎ 66.85.20.50. AE, DC, Euro, Visa. 20 rm P ♨ ♿ closed 20 Nov-Apr, 180. Rest. ♦ 80-130.

⛺ ★★*Val de la Salendrinque* (75 pl.), ☎ 66.85.24.57.

Recommended : the *S.I.C.A.*, Cevennes regional produce, on the road leading out of the village.

LUSSAN

Alès 29, Nîmes 42, Paris 713
C3 ✉ 30580

Hotel :
● ★★***Auberge de la Treille,*** Andabiac, ☎ 66.72.90.26. 10 rm P ⛰ ▭ 170. Rest. ♦ ♿ 75-105.

Restaurant :
Roux, about 2 km N on the D787 :
♦ ***Auberge de la Valcroze,*** ☎ 66.72.90.73. ⚘ P ♨ ⛰ closed Nov-Apr, Mon and Tue. Superb village setting, 70-180.

La MALÈNE

Mende 41, Millau 42, Paris 601
A2-3 ✉ 48210 Sainte-Énimie

ℹ ☎ 66.48.53.44.

Hotels :
★★★***Manoir de Montesquiou*** (Châteaux-hôtels), ☎ 66.48.51.12. DC. 12 rm ⚘ P ♨ ⛰ closed end Oct-1 Apr, 250. Rest. ● ♦♦♦ ♿ 20thC cooking in a 15thC setting ; good regional specialities : *médaillon de ris de veau à la crème de laitue,* 40-170.

La Caze, 5.5 km NE on the D907 *bis* :
● ★★★★***Château de la Caze,*** ☎ 66.48.51.01. 20 rm P ♨ ⛰ ✗ closed 15 Oct-1 May. 15thC castle with a 120-acre park, 550. Reputable rest. ♦♦♦ Spec : freshwater crayfish *(écrevisses),* trout, 200-250.

⛺ ★*Le Clos* (70 pl.), ☎ 66.48.51.24.

MARVEJOLS

Mende 29, Rodez 85, Paris 558
A2 ✉ 48100

ℹ av. de Brazza (Jul-Aug), ☎ 66.32.02.14.

SNCF 66.32.00.10.

Hotels :
★★***Gare et des Rochers,*** ☎ 66.32.10.58. AE, DC, Euro. 30 rm ⚘ P ⛰ ♿ closed 15 Jan-15 Feb and Sat (low season), 170. Rest. ♿ 50-100.

Monastier, 10 km S :
★***Les Ajustons,*** 2.5 km S of intersection N9 and N88, ☎ 66.32.70.35. Euro, Visa. 28 rm ⚘ P ⛰ closed Sat and Sun in winter, 100. Rest. ♦ 40-100.

Restaurant :
♦♦ ***Viz Club,*** rte du Nord, ☎ 66.32.17.69. AE, DC, Visa. P ♨ ⛰ ✗ ♿ Louis XIII dining-room. Spec : *escalope de brochet au poivre vert, paupiettes de canard à l'ananas,* 50-120.

⛺ ★*Municipal* (35 pl.), ☎ 66.32.00.45.

MENDE

Le Puy 92, Rodez 108, Paris 573
A2 ✉ 48000

ℹ 16, bd du Soubeyran, ☎ 66.65.02.69.

✈ Brenoux, 4 km SE, ☎ 66.65.14.61.

SNCF (C1), ☎ 66.65.00.39/66.65.15.37.

Hotels :
● ★★★***Lion d'Or*** (Mapotel), 12-14, bd Britexte (C2), ☎ 66.49.16.46. AE, DC, Euro, Visa. 40 rm P ♨ ⛰ ▭ ♿ closed 15 Nov-15 Mar, 310. Rest. ✗ ♿ closed Sun and Mon noon, 80-180.
● ★★***Urbain V,*** 9, bd Th.-Roussel (A1), ☎ 66.49.14.49. AE, Euro, Visa. 59 rm P ♿ closed 15 Dec-7 Jan, 220. Rest. ✗ ♿ closed 1 Dec-2 Jan and Sun, 60-100.
★★***France*** (L.F.), 9, bd L.-Arnault (B1), ☎ 65.00.04. Visa. 27 rm P ⛰ ♿ closed 15 Dec-early Feb, 180. Rest. ♦♦ ♿ closed Sun eve and Mon low season. Simple, tasty meals, 60-135.

Ardèche, Cévennes

Rieutort-de-Randon, ✉ 48700 Saint-Amans, 18 km N :
★***Plateau du Roy*** (Relais du Silence), N106, ☎ 66.47.33.03. 17 rm P closed 30 Dec-15 Mar, 200. Rest. ♦ ♿ 40-120.

⛺ ★★*Sirvens* (70 pl.), ☎ 66.65.16.93 ; *Tivoli* (35 pl.), ☎ 66.65.00.38.

Guided tours : C.N.M.H.S. (Jul-Sep : 11 am and 5 pm ex Sun ; Oct-Jun : 3 pm Wed ; departs from front of the cathedral).

Recommended : *Coopérative des artisans et paysans de Lozère,* rue de l'Ange, ☎ 66.65.01.57.

MEYRUEIS

Millau 42, Mende 57, Paris 628
A3 ✉ 48150

ℹ rue de l'Horloge, ☎ 66.45.60.33 (high season), and mairie, ☎ 66.45.62.64.

Hotels :
● ★★★***Renaissance*** (Inter-Hôtel), ☎ 66.45.60.19. AE, DC, Visa. 20 rm Remarkable interior furnishings, 260. Rest. ♦♦ Good regional cooking. Spec : *godireau de truite aux écrevisses, musquette au miel,* 180.
★★***Europe,*** pl. d'Orléans, ☎ 66.45.60.05. Visa. 38 rm P closed Oct-Apr, 180. Rest. ♦ ♿ 80-130.
★★***France*** (L.F.), ☎ 66.45.60.07. Visa. 46 rm ♿ closed Oct-Apr, 130. Rest. ♦ 65-100.
1.5 km E on the D57 :
● ★★★***Château d'Ayres*** (Châteaux-Hôtels, Relais du Silence), ☎ 66.45.60.10. AE, DC. 23 rm P closed 2 Nov-29 Mar. 12thC Benedictine monastery. Extremely comfortable rooms, 350. Rest. ♦♦ 110-165.

⛺ ★★★*Capelan* (80 pl.), ☎ 66.45.60.50 ; ★★*le Pré de Charlet* (70 pl.), ☎ 66.45.63.65 ; ★★*Champ d'Ayres* (70 pl.), ☎ 66.45.60.51.

Farmhouse-inns : *Ayres,* ☎ 66.45.60.71 ; *les Hérans,* Hures-la-Parade, 12 km N on the N586, ☎ 66.45.61.42 ; *le Buffre,* Hures-la-Parade, ☎ 66.45.61.84.
See also Peyreleau (Rouergue, Albigeois).

NASBINALS

Mende 59, Saint-Flour 59, Paris 549
A2 ✉ 48260
1 180-1 450 m

Hotels :
● ★***Route d'Argent*** (behind the church), ☎ 66.32.50.03. 20 rm, 90. Rest. ● ♦ ♿ Authentic rustic fare, solid and varied, 50-70.
Recoules-d'Aubrac, 4 km N on the D12 :
★★***Relais d'Aubrac,*** pont de Gournier, ☎ 66.32.52.06. 18 rm P ♿ closed Oct and 15 Nov-15 Dec, 100. Rest. ♦ ♿ 40-90.

NÎMES

Avignon 43, Montpellier 51, Paris 712
C4 ✉ 30000

ℹ 6, rue Auguste (B1-2), ☎ 66.67.29.11.

✈ Nîmes-Garons, 6 km S, ☎ 66.20.12.40. *Air France Agency,* ☎ 66.20.12.55.

SNCF (C3), ☎ 66.23.50.50, 66.29.44.95.

Car-hire : *Budget* train + auto, 3, rue de La Cité-Foulc, ☎ 66.67.28.94 ; at the airport, ☎ 66.20.12.55 ; at the station, ☎ 66.67.82.20.

Hotels :
● ★★★★***Impérator*** (Mapotel), quai de la Fontaine (A2), ☎ 66.21.90.30, Tx 490635. AE, DC, Visa. 61 rm closed 15 Jan-15 Feb. Luxuriously restored old hotel with indoor garden, 260. Rest. ● ♦♦ ♿ *l'Enclos de la Fontaine* ♿ In the heart of a residential area, near historic ruins. Large dining room, terrace and garden. Chef Martial Nocquard, who apprenticed with J. Robuchon and Guy Legay, prepares admirable fare. Spec : *saint pierre au vin vieux, aiguillettes de canette rosée,* 110-300.
★★★***Cheval Blanc,*** 1, pl. des Arènes (C3), ☎ 66.67.20.03, Tx 481856. AE, DC, Euro, Visa. 47 rm, 260. Rest. ♦♦ ♿ 120-210.
★★★***Tuileries,*** 22, rue Roussy, ☎ 66.21.31.15. 12 rm P ♿ 300. Meals served in rooms.
★★***Louvre,*** 2, square de la Couronne (C2), ☎ 66.67.22.75, Tx 480218. AE, DC, Euro, Visa. 35 rm and 5 apt. P ♿ Renovated old private hotel, 270. Rest. ♦ 70-175.
★★***Midi et Provence,*** 5, square de la Couronne (C2), ☎ 66.67.28.64, Tx 480846. AE, DC, Euro, Visa. 33 rm P ♿ 190. Rest. 80-130.
On the Garons airport road at Caissargues, ✉ 30230 Bouillargues :
★★★***Les Aubuns,*** ☎ 66.70.10.44. 30 rm P ♿ 260.

⛺ ★★★*Domaine de la Bastide* (230 pl.), ☎ 66.38.09.21.

Restaurants :
♦♦ ***Au Cocotier,*** 15, rue P.-Sémard, ☎ 66.67.83.29. Euro, Visa. closed Aug and Sun. Exotic specialities, 80-150.
♦♦ ***Le Lisita,*** 2, bd des Arènes, ☎ 66.67.29.15. AE, DC, Visa. ♿ closed Aug, Sat and Sun eve, 80-150.
Jardin d'Adrien, 11, rue de l'Enclos-Rey (C1), ☎ 66.21.86.65. ♿ Seafood, *filet de loup,* 80-130.
Garons, ✉ 30128, 12 km SE :
♦♦ ***Alexandre,*** ☎ 66.70.08.99. P closed 15 Aug-1 Sep, Sun eve, Mon and Tue noon. Renowned cooking. Spec : *tournedos Frédéric Mistral.* Book ahead, 180-320. With 5 rm.

Guided tours : C.N.M.H.S. (1 Jul-15 Sep : 9:30 and 10:30) enq ℹ

PONT-SAINT-ESPRIT

Nîmes 59, Avignon 60, Paris 647
C3 ✉ 30130

ℹ La Citadelle, av. Pasteur, ☎ 66.39.13.25.

SNCF ☎ 66.39.09.87.

Hotel :
★★***Le Vieux Moulin*** (L.F.), ☎ 66.39.18.44. Visa. 9 rm P 130. Rest. ♦ ♿ 50-120.

Chambres d'hôtes : *la Cantarelle,* Saint-Paulet-de-Caisson, 4.5 km, ☎ 66.39.17.67.

⛺ ★★*Municipal* (50 pl.), ☎ 66.39.10.18.

Recommended : *Brocante de Haute-Provence/Malbec,* rte de Saint-Paulet-de-Caisson (3 km).

PRIVAS

Montélimar 33, Le Puy 118, Paris 603
C1-2 ✉ 07000

ℹ 1, av. Chomérac, ☎ 75.64.33.35.

SNCF ☎ 75.64.11.87.

Hotels :
★★★***Chaumette,*** av. Vanel, ☎ 75.64.30.66. DC, Euro, Visa. 35 rm P ♿ 210. Rest. ♦ closed Sat 15 Jun-15 Sep, 60-100.
Ollières-sur-Eyrieux, ✉ 07360, 19 km N :
★★***Auberge de la Vallée*** (L.F.) Bas Pranles, ☎ 75.66.20.32. Euro, Visa. 8 rm P closed 1 Feb-15 Mar, 17-23 Sep, Sun eve and Mon low season ex nat hols, 250. Rest. ♿ 70-210.

⛺ ★★*Municipal d'Ouvèze* (166 pl.), ☎ 75.64.05.80.

Farmhouse-inn : *musée agricole* in Verdus, ☎ 75.64.27.40. closed week-days in winter.

REMOULINS

Nîmes 20, Alès 49, Paris 692
3 km E from the Gard Bridge, C3 ⊠ 30210

ℹ Pont-du-Gard, ☎ 66.37.00.02.

SNCF ☎ 66.37.13.42.

Hotels :
★★***Moderne,*** pl. des Grands-Jours, ☎ 66.37.20.13. AE, DC, Euro, Visa. 25 rm Ⓟ ♿ closed 19 Oct-17 Nov and 1 week Feb school hols, Sat low season, 130. Rest. ● ♦ ♿ Good, simple, inexpensive meals, 40-120.

Pont du Gard, 3 km W on the N100 :
★★★***Le Vieux Moulin,*** left bank, ☎ 66.37.14.35. AE, DC, Euro, Visa. 17 rm Ⓟ closed 11 Nov-15 Mar, 270. Rest. ♦♦ closed Mon noon and Tue noon, 70-120.
★★***Le Colombier,*** rte de Nîmes, ☎ 66.37.05.28. Euro. 12 rm Ⓟ ♿ closed Dec-1 Jan and Wed low season, 200. Rest. ♦♦ ♿ 70-150.

Castillon-du-Gard, 4 km NE on the D19 and D228 :
● ★★★★(L) ***Le Vieux Castillon*** (Relais et châteaux), ☎ 66.37.00.77. Tx 490946. Visa. 35 rm Ⓟ ♿ closed 2 Feb-10 Mar. In the heart of an authentic mediaeval village, 940. Rest. ♦♦♦ 210-320.

Estézargues, ⊠ 30390 Aramon, 9 km E on the N100 and D235 :
★★***La Fenouillère,*** on the N100, ☎ 66.57.03.08. Ⓟ closed 30 Oct-30 Mar, 150. Rest. for hotel guests only, 50-130.

Rochefort-du-Gard, ⊠ 30650, 10 km NE on the N100 and D976 :
★★***Mas de la Rouvette*** (L.F.), rte d'Orange, ☎ 90.31.73.11. Visa. 18 rm Ⓟ closed 20 Jan-28 Feb and Tue, 200. Rest. ♦ ♿ 80-150.

Saze, ⊠ 30650 Rochefort-du-Gard, 10.5 km E on the N100 and D287 :
★★***Le Mas de Valiguière,*** La Fontaine-du-Buis, ☎ 90.31.73.04. AE, Visa. 10 rm Ⓟ ♿ closed 1-15 Jan, Thu, 200.

Ⲁ ★★★★*La Soubeyranne* (200 pl.), ☎ 66.37.03.21 ; ★★★*Sousta* (300 pl.), ☎ 66.37.06.57 ; ★★*Camp-Plage du Pont-du-Gard* (80 pl.), ☎ 66.37.03.00.

ROQUEMAURE

Avignon 16, Nîmes 45, Paris 672
C3 ⊠ 30150

Hotels :
★★***Château de Cubières*** (Châteaux-hôtels), rte d'Avignon, ☎ 66.50.14.28. Visa. 19 rm Ⓟ ♿ Beautiful 18thC residence in park setting, 250. Rest. ♦ closed 15 30 Nov, 20 Feb-20 Mar and Tue, 60-165.

Sauveterre, 6 km S on the N580 :
● ★★***Hostellerie de Varenne,*** pl. St-Jean, ☎ 66.82.59.45. 15 rm Ⓟ 150. Rest. ♦ ♿ closed Jan, Feb, Mon, Tue and 1st week of Nov, 105-200.

Restaurant :
Sauveterre :
● ♦♦ ***La Crémaillère,*** N580, ☎ 66.82.55.05. AE, Visa. Ⓟ ♿ closed 1-15 Feb, 1-12 Aug, Mon eve, Tue eve and Wed. A beautiful country inn, with simple, varied meals. Spec : *assiette Crémaillère, filet de bœuf en chemise,* 70-180.

RUOMS

Aubenas 24, Alès 52, Paris 656
C2 ⊠ 07120

ℹ pl. de la Mairie, ☎ 75.93.91.90.

Hotels :
★***Savel,*** rte des Brasseries, ☎ 75.39.60.02. 15 rm Ⓟ closed 1 Dec-1 Mar, Sun eve (winter), and Mon (ex high season), 100. Rest. 80-130.

Sampzon, 5 km S on the N579 and D161 :
● ★★***Château de Sampzon,*** ☎ 75.39.67.14. 12 rm Ⓟ ♿ closed Oct-Easter, 260. Rest. ♦ ♿ dinner only, closed week days in winter, and Wed (high season), 120-210.

Grospierres, 7.5 km SW on the D111 :
● ★★★★***Caléou,*** domaine de Rouret, ☎ 75.93.60.00. Tx 345478. AE, DC, Euro, Visa. 117 rm Ⓟ ♿ closed 21 Dec-21 Jan, 430. Rest. ♦ ♿ 130-200.

Ⲁ ★★★*Chapoulière* (100 pl.), ☎ 75.39.64.98 ; ★★★*Grand Terre* (200 pl.), ☎ 75.39.64.94 ; ★★★*la Plaine* (62 pl.), ☎ 75.39.65.83 ; ★★★*Mas du Barry* (80 pl.), ☎ 75.39.67.61 ; ★★*Municipal* (100 pl.), ☎ 75.39.62.38.

SAINT-AMBROIX

Alès 19, Aubenas 55, Paris 688
B3 ⊠ 30500

Hotel :
Courry, 6 km NW :
● ***Auberge Croquembouche*** (L.F.), ☎ 66.24.13.30. Euro. 5 rm Ⓟ closed Wed low season. Peaceful setting, 230. Rest. ♦♦ ♿ 75-150.

Youth hostel : *les Pierres Sauvages,* mas d'Allègre, ☎ 66.85.78.22. Closed Jan.

Restaurant :
Sauvas, ⊠ 07460 Saint-Paul-le-Jeune, 9 km NW :
♦♦ ***La Cocalière,*** ☎ 75.39.81.34. DC, Visa Ⓟ ♿ closed Feb and Wed. Spec : *truite soufflée à la mousse de brochet, blanc de turbot à la moutarde ancienne,* 120-210.

SAINT-CHÉLY-D'APCHER

Mende 48, Le Puy 85, Paris 525
10 km N of Aumont-Aubrac
A2 ⊠ 48200

ℹ bd Guérin-d'Apcher (high season), ☎ 66.31.03.67.

SNCF ☎ 66.31.00.16.

Hotels :
★***Lion d'Or,*** 132, rue T.-Roussel, ☎ 66.31.00.14. Visa. 30 rm Ⓟ ♿ closed 20 Dec-15 Jan, 100. Rest. ♦ Good basic fare, 80-130.

La Garde, 9 km on the N9 :
★★***Rocher Blanc,*** ☎ 66.31.90.09. Visa. 21 rm Ⓟ closed 1 Dec-5 Jan, 110. Rest. ♦ ♿ 50-80.

Ⲁ ★★*Municipal* (80 pl.), ☎ 66.31.03.24.

Event : mineral and fossil market in Aug.

SAINT-GILLES-DU-GARD

Nîmes 19, Montpellier 57, Paris 732
C4 ⊠ 30800

ℹ Maison Romane, ☎ 66.87.33.75 (high season).

SNCF ☎ 66.87.32.83.

Hotels :
★★***Le Cours,*** 10, av. F.-Grifeuille, ☎ 66.87.31.93. AE, DC, Visa. 26 rm closed 22 Dec-1 Feb, 170. Rest. ♿ Spec : *bœuf à la gardiane* and *riz créole,* 45-110.
La Rascasse, 16, av. F.-Grifeuille, ☎ 66.87.42.96. 5 rm Ⓟ 150. Rest. ♦♦ closed Wed ♿ 70-200.

Ⲁ ★★★*La Chicanette* (100 pl.), ☎ 66.87.28.32.

SAINT-JEAN-DU-GARD

Alès 27, Nîmes 61, Paris 736
B3 ✉ 30270

ℹ av. R.-Boudon, ☎ 66.85.32.11 (high season).

Hotels :
★★***L'Oronge*** (L.F., A.R.C.), 103, Grand-Rue, ☎ 66.85.30.34. AE, DC, Euro, Visa. 38 rm Ⓟ closed 2 Jan-1 Apr, Sun eve and Mon low season. 17thC post-house, 250. Rest. ♦ 50-160.

Les Plantiers, ✉ 30122, 20 km W :
★***Valgrand*** (L.F.), ☎ 66.83.92.51. 8 rm ⁂ ♧ closed 1 Oct-1 Jun, 110.

⛺ ★★★*La Forêt* (60 pl.), ☎ 66.85.37.00 ; ★★*la C.A.M.* (200 pl.), ☎ 66.85.32.06 ; ★★*les Sources* (100 pl.), ☎ 66.85.38.03.

Recommended : Grand-Rue : antique shop at No. 158 ; lambskin garments at No. 129 ; and wrought-iron work at No. 113.

SAINT-MARTIN-D'ARDÈCHE

Avignon 70, Privas 74, Paris 653
Ardèche Gorges, C2-3
✉ 07700 Bourg-St-Andéol

ℹ pl. du Champ-de-Mars, ☎ 75.54.54.20.

Hotel :
Saint-Marcel-d'Ardèche, 6.5 km on the D201 :
Auberge de la Source, ☎ 75.04.65.66. 4 rm ⁂ Ⓟ ♧ ⛰ ♿ closed 15 Jan-15 Mar, 180. Rest. ♦ Provençal specialities, 80-130.

⛺ ★★★*Le Moulin* (200 pl.), ☎ 75.04.66.20 ; ★★*Municipal* (70 pl.), ☎ 75.04.65.25.

Restaurant :
Saint-Marcel-d'Ardèche :
Échiquier, ☎ 75.98.70.81. ⁂ terrace overlooking the Ardèche River ♿ closed Tue and Oct, 45-90.

Market : local produce and handicrafts (Sun, high season).

Recommended : canoe hire : *Lafet*, rte des Gorges, ☎ 75.04.62.17 ; *Raoux*, le Village, ☎ 75.04.67.00.

SAINTE-ÉNIMIE

Mende 28, Millau 56, Paris 599
Tarn Gorges A2-3 ✉ 48210

ℹ mairie, ☎ 66.48.50.09 (high season).

Hotels :
★★***Burlatis,*** rue de la Combe, ☎ 66.48.52.30. Visa. 18 rm ⛰ ✂ closed 1 Oct-30 Apr, 190.
★★***Commerce,*** ☎ 66.48.50.01. AE, Euro, Visa. 20 rm ⁂ Ⓟ closed early Oct-Easter school hols. Private beach on the Tarn River, 150. Rest. 60-100.

⛺ ★★Outdoor leisure centre/*base de plein air,* (80 pl.), ☎ 66.48.53.55.

Farmhouse-inn, camping and riding : *la Périgouse,* 8 km from Sainte-Énimie, ☎ 66.48.53.71. Rooms and table d'hôte : *Mativet,* Montbrun, 7 km on the D907, ☎ 66.45.04.74. Book ahead.

SERRIÈRES

Vienne 28, Saint-Étienne 54, Paris 520
15 km NE of Annonay, C1 ✉ 07340

ℹ quai Jules-Roche, ☎ 75.34.06.01.

Hotels :
★***Schaeffer,*** ☎ 75.34.00.07. AE. 12 rm Ⓟ ♧ ✂ closed 2-30 Jan, Mon eve, Tue, 130. Rest. ✂ 85-140.

Peaugres, 7 km SW on the N82 :
★***Bon Gîte*** (L.F.), ☎ 75.34.80.44. 11 rm Ⓟ ♧ 150. Rest. ♿ closed 17 Jan-3 Mar and Sat (1 Nov-Easter), 55-80.

Recommended : wine *coopérative de Saint-Désirat-Champagne,* ☎ 75.34.22.05.

SOMMIÈRES

Montpellier 28, Nîmes 28, Paris 740
B4 ✉ 30250

ℹ 1, pl. de la République, ☎ 66.80.99.30.

SNCF ☎ 66.80.96.63.

Hotel :
● ★★★***Auberge du Pont-Romain*** (Châteaux-hôtels), 2, rue Émile-Jamais, ☎ 66.80.00.58. AE, DC, Visa. 14 rm ⁂ Ⓟ ♧ ⛰ 🎾 ♿ closed 15 Jan-15 Mar, 250. Rest. ♦♦ ♿ closed Wed. Preserves for sale, 130-190.

⛺ ★★★*International Club,* at Mus (50 pl.), ☎ 66.35.07.06 ; ★★*Municipal* (60 pl.), ☎ 66.80.93.10.

Restaurant :
● ♦♦♦ ***Enclos Montgranier,*** rte de Gallargues-le-Montueux, ☎ 66.80.92.00. AE, DC, Euro. ♿ closed Sun eve and Mon, Jun, 15-30 Nov, 15-end Apr. One of the most beautiful restaurants in France. A former hunting lodge now excellently restored. Everything seems to have got back onto the right track at the *Enclos.* You are welcomed by the Destenay family, and a young chef, trained by Senderens, prepares the wholesome fresh produce of the Languedoc. An enchanting setting and very reasonable prices : *flan à la truffe fraîche du village* (when in season), *noix de baudroie à la crème de favouilles et pâtes fraîches, carré d'agneau de Nîmes.* A fine selection of wines of the Languedoc, 100-240.

Recommended : Traditional-style preserves from the Auberge du Pont-Romain.

TAVEL

Avignon 14, Nîmes 39, Paris 681
C3 ✉ 30126

ℹ mairie, ☎ 66.50.04.10.

Hotels :
★★★***Auberge de Tavel,*** voie Romaine, ☎ 66.50.03.41. AE, DC, Euro, Visa. 11 rm ♧ ⛰ ▭ closed Feb, Mon low season. Pleasant terrace, 300. Rest. ♦♦ 100-240.
★***Hostellerie du Seigneur,*** ☎ 66.50.04.26. Euro. 7 rm. Ⓟ ✂ closed 15 Dec-15 Jan. 16thC residence, 120. Rest. ♦ 70-120.

Le TEIL

Privas 28, Aubenas 37, Paris 611
6 km W of Montélimar, C2 ✉ 07400

ℹ pl. Sémard, ☎ 75.49.10.46.

SNCF ☎ 75.49.00.13.

Hotel :
Rochemaure, 4 km N :
★★***Les Genêts*** (L.F.), ☎ 75.49.07.05. Visa. 40 rm Ⓟ ♧ closed Christmas hols, 180. Rest. ***l'Auberge,*** ☎ 75.49.12.69. ♿ 80-130.

⛺ ★★*Municipal* (71 pl.), ☎ 75.52.13.27.

Restaurant :
♦♦ ***Ardéchois,*** 34, rue H.-Barbusse, ☎ 75.49.21.39. Visa. closed 30 Jun-15 Jul, Mon, Sat noon and Sun eve, 80-180.

THUEYTS

Privas 50, Le Puy 72, Paris 651
Ardèche Valley, B2 ✉ 07330

Hotels :
★★**Nord** (L.F.), ☎ 75.36.40.38. 27 rm Ⓟ closed 1 Oct-1 Apr, Tue (low season), 170. Rest. 80-130.
★★**Platanes,** ☎ 75.93.78.66. 26 rm Ⓟ ♿ closed 3 Nov-Feb, 180. Rest. 65-150.

Neyrac-les-Bains, ⊠ 07380 Lalevade, 4 km E on the N102 :
★**Levant,** ☎ 75.36.41.07. 20 rm Ⓟ closed Jan-Feb and Sun eve low season, 180. Rest. 80-130.

Jaujac, ⊠ 07380 Lalevade, 9.5 km SE on the N108 and D5 :
★**Caveau** (L.F.), ☎ 75.93.22.29. AE. 20 rm Ⓟ closed 15 Dec-1 Mar, 160. Rest. 55-100.

Δ ★★*De Belos* (67 pl.), ☎ 75.36.44.35.

TOURNON

Valence 18, Saint-Étienne 75, Paris 550
C1 ⊠ 07300

ℹ imm. la Tourette, ☎ 75.08.10.23.

SNCF ☎ 75.08.31.87.

Hotels :
★★★**Paris** and **Château** (L.F.), 12, quai Marc-Seguin, ☎ 75.08.01.11 and 75.08.60.22. Tx 345156. AE, DC, Euro, Visa. 36 rm Ⓟ ♿ closed Feb, 1-15 Nov, Sat and Sun (low season), 220. Rest. ♦♦ ♿ 80-140.
★★**Manoir,** 226, rte de Lamastre, ☎ 75.08.20.31. AE, DC, Visa. 10 rm Ⓟ closed 30 Sep-15 Mar, 160.

Restaurant :
Paradisio, ☎ 75.08.07.77. AE, DC, Visa. ♿ 80-130.

Δ ★★★*Municipal* (100 pl.), ☎ 75.08.05.28 ; ★★★*Manoir* (80 pl.), ☎ 75.08.02.50 ; ★★*Foulons* (70 pl.), ☎ 75.08.22.72 ; ★★*Sables* (100 pl.), ☎ 75.08.20.05.

Recommended : wines, *J.-L. Chave* vineyards, ⊠ 07300 Mauves.

USCLADES-ET-RIEUTORD

Aubenas 46, Le Puy 50, Paris 556
15 km S of Le Gerbier de Jonc, B1
⊠ 07510 Saint-Cirgues

Hotel :
★**Ferme de la Besse,** ☎ 75.38.80.64. 18 rm Ⓟ Rustic setting, closed 31 Oct-22 Déc. Charge for skiing, 130. Rest. ♦ 80.

Farmhouse-inn : *Sablouze,* ☎ 75.38.80.93. With gîte and chambre d'hôte ; cross-country skiing on farm property ; local fare (booking necessary during high season), 100.

UZÈS

Nîmes 25, Avignon 38, Paris 707
C3 ⊠ 30700

ℹ pl. du Duché (B1), ☎ 66.22.68.88.

🚌 enq ☎ 66.22.12.52.

Hotels :
★★★**Entraigues,** 8, rue de la Calade (BC-2), ☎ 66.22.32.68. DC, Visa. 18 rm Ⓟ closed 2 Jan-3 Feb, 300. Rest.-grill ♦♦ closed Tue, 75-150.

Arpaillargues, 4.5 km W :
● ★★★**Marie d'Agoult** (Châteaux-hôtels, Relais du Silence), château d'Arpaillargues, ☎ 66.22.14.48, Tx 490415. Visa. 25 rm Ⓟ ♿ closed 15 Oct-15 Mar. 17th-18thC residence, once inhabited by Marie d'Agoult, Liszt's companion. Superb interior furnishings, 700. Rest. ♦♦♦ closed Wed low season. Spec : *médaillon de lotte au safran, parfait de banane aux violettes, filets de morue fraîche « à la d'Uzès »,* 150-250.

Δ ★★★*Mas Fran Val* (50 pl.), ☎ 66.22.27.62 ; ★★*Municipal* (66 pl.), ☎ 66.22.11.79.

Restaurant :
Alibi, 1, pl. Dampmartin, ☎ 66.22.01.32. ♿ closed Wed. Former mansion of the Count of Dampmartin (15thC). Good jazz concerts, 80-130.

Guided tours : C.N.M.H.S. (13 Jun-19 Sep ; 10 am and 4 pm). Enq ℹ

VALLON-PONT-D'ARC

Montélimar 57, Privas 63, Paris 633
C2 ⊠ 07150

ℹ ☎ 75.37.04.01.

Hotel :
Manoir de Raveyron, rue Henri-Barbusse, ☎ 75.88.03.59. Visa. 11 rm closed 1 Oct-early Mar, Wed (Mar and Apr). Set amid trees, 150. Rest. ♦ 55-110.

Δ ★★★*Beau Rivage* (100 pl.), ☎ 75.88.03.54 ; ★★★*Arc-en-ciel* (100 pl.), ☎ 75.88.04.65 ; ★★★*Plage Fleurie* (150 pl.), ☎ 75.88.01.15 ; ★★★*Roubiné* (135 pl.), ☎ 75.88.04.56 ; ★★★*Provencal* (315 pl.), ☎ 75.88.00.48 ; ★★★*Mondial* (250 pl.), ☎ 75.88.00.44 ; 8 campsites★★ (690 pl.).

Recommended : canoe hire : addresses available at T.O.

VALS-LES-BAINS

Privas 34, Le Puy 87, Paris 636
C2 ⊠ 07600

☎ 75.37.46.68.

ℹ 12, av. Farincourt, ☎ 75.37.42.34.

SNCF ☎ 75.37.40.06.

🚌 ☎ 75.37.44.62.

Hotels :
★★★**Bains,** ☎ 75.37.42.13 and 75.94.65.55. AE, DC, Visa. 55 rm Ⓟ ♿ closed 5 Oct-20 May, 400. Rest. ♦♦ 120-210.
★★★**Vivarais** (Mapotel), ☎ 75.94.65.85. Tx 345866. AE, DC, Euro, Visa. 40 rm Ⓟ closed 15 Nov-31 Dec, Sun eve and Mon low season, 330. Rest. ♦ 95-200.
● ★★**Europe** (L.F.), 86, rue Jean-Jaurès, ☎ 75.37.43.94. AE, DC, Euro, Visa. 35 rm, closed 15 Oct-20 Apr, 220. Rest. ♦ ♿ Spec : *lotte aux morilles, comtassot (gâteau à la crème de marron),* 85-120.

Farmhouse-inn : *Mas de la Pierre,* St-Andéol-de-Vals, 7.5 km N on the D257, ☎ 75.37.56.12. closed during the week in winter. Regional cooking.

Les VANS

Alès 43, Privas 66, Paris 670
B2 ⊠ 07140

ℹ ☎ 75.37.24.48.

Hotels :
★**Cévennes,** ☎ 75.37.23.09. 16 rm Ⓟ closed 15-30 Jan, 1-8 May, 15-30 Oct, Sun eve and Mon, 80. Rest. ♦ ♿ 70-120.

Chambonas, 2 km N :
● ★★**Château du Scipionnet** (Châteaux-hôtels, Relais du Silence, L.F.), ☎ 75.37.23.84. Tx 345790. Euro. 26 rm, 3 apt Ⓟ ♿ closed 15 Oct-15 Mar. Quaint Napoléon III castle alongside a river in a superb park, 360. Rest. ♦ ♿ 130-200.

⛺ ★★*Châtaigniers,* Chambonas (85 pl.), ☎ 75.37.25.18.

Farmhouse-inn : *la Pomponnette,* Les Armas-le-Haut, ☎ 75.37.22.83. Honoré offers royal service to clients in this old Saracen post-house.

VIALAS

Alès 41, Mende 77, Paris 650
8 km W of Génolhac, B2
⊠ 48220 Le Pont-de-Montvert

ℹ mairie, ☎ 66.61.00.05.

Hotel :
★★***Chantoiseau,*** rte du Haut, ☎ 66.41.00.02. 15 rm. closed 2-31 Jan, Tue eve and Wed. Beautiful 17thC Cévennes building, 160. Rest. ● ♦♦♦ The chef is also a poet and the wine waiter. Cévennes regional produce. Cooking classes in season, home-made preserves to take away.

Le VIGAN

Montpellier 63, Millau 72, Paris 774
A3 ⊠ 30120

ℹ ☎ 67.81.01.72.

SNCF ☎ 67.81.03.01.

Hotels :
Le Rey, ⊠ 30570, 5 km E on the D999 :
★★***Château du Rey,*** ☎ 67.82.43.08. DC, Visa. 12 rm Ⓟ ♿ closed Mon low season and 30 Nov-1 Apr. 18thC castle, 260. Rest. ♦♦ ☎ 67.82.43.08. ♿ 120-210.

Pont-d'Hérault, ⊠ 30570 Valleraque, 6 km E on the D999 :
★★***Maurice,*** ☎ 67.82.40.02. Visa. 18 rm Ⓟ closed 23 Dec-1 Feb, 200. Rest. ♦ ♿ 140-210.

Aulas, 7 km NW on the D48 and D190 :
★★***Mas Quayrol*** (Châteaux-hôtels), ☎ 67.81.12.38. DC. 16 rm Ⓟ closed 10 Oct-23 Mar, 250. Rest. ● ♦ ♿ In the heart of the countryside with a stunning view over the foothills of the Cévennes : *champignons des bois, escargots, viandes grillées et fumées en potée, morilles au vin jaune flambées à la fine champagne, truite en papillote à la façon du chevrier,* 105-200.

⛺ ★★★*Val d'Arre* (120 pl.), ☎ 67.81.02.77.

Les VIGNES

Millau 31, Mende 53, Paris 620
Tarn Gorges, A2-3 ⊠ 48210 Sainte-Énimie

Hotel :
★★***Gévaudan,*** ☎ 66.46.81.55. 18 rm Ⓟ closed 15 Sep-15 Jun, 180. Rest. 80-130.

⛺ ★★*Beldoire* (100 pl.), ☎ 66.48.82.79.

VILLEFORT

Mende 59, Le Puy 91, Paris 600
B2 ⊠ 48800

ℹ rue de l'Église, ☎ 66.46.80.26.

SNCF 66.46.80.03.

Hotels :
★★***Balme*** (L.F.), pl. du Portalet, ☎ 66.46.80.14. 23 rm Ⓟ closed 11 Nov-31 Jan, Sun eve and Mon low season, 180. Rest. ● ♦♦ The food is good, the helpings are generous and it's not at all expensive. Michel and Micheline pull out all the stops to give satisfaction : *pied de veau farci aux girolles, épaule d'agneau cuite dans le foin* and, on request, *la grande soupe d'orge perlée aux 5 viandes,* 60-130.
★★***Nord,*** ☎ 66.46.80.12. 20 rm, 100. Rest. 80-130.

⛺ ★★*Le Petit Paradis* (35 pl.), ☎ 66.46.80.26.

VIVIERS

Montélimar 11, Privas 41, Paris 623
C2 ⊠ 07220

ℹ RN86, ☎ 75.52.77.00.

Hotels :
★★***Provence*** (L.F.), ☎ 75.52.60.45. 10 rm. closed 20 Dec to mid-Feb, Sun eve, Mon low season, 100. Rest. 80-130.
★***Relais du Vivarais,*** ☎ 75.52.60.41. Ⓟ closed 20 Dec-20 Jan, 100. Rest. ♦ ♿ 80-130.

⛺ ★★★★*Rochecondrie* (80 pl.), ☎ 75.52.74.66 ; ★★*Roqueplane* (70 pl.), ☎ 75.52.64.43.

Auvergne

The awe-inspiring volcanic relief of Auvergne, with its giant massifs and mountain chains, have long given it a reputation for isolation and self-sufficiency. This citadel in the very heart of France has often been described as the museum of a past and a tradition long stripped of their original dynamism. But modern communications have triumphed over geographical and climatic barriers, and commerce and tourism have further opened up a region which possesses attractions rivalling the better-known beauty spots of France. Many of Auvergne's sons and daughters have "emigrated" to the large cities, particularly Paris, where they opened up little corner cafés and bars, selling wood and domestic coal as profitable sidelines.

Auvergne has five of the ten leading thermal resorts in France, and excels in country holidays : trekking in the Cantal mountains, pony-trekking, country inns and camping on farms, amidst lakes, splendid scenery and mountains. Auvergne also boasts excellent ski resorts, attracting skiers from all over France and Europe. Cross-country skiing at Mont-Dore, Super-Besse and Super-Lioran is perhaps the greatest drawcard, although downhill skiing is also popular.

Auvergne is the site of one of the most original and important schools of Romanesque art in France — here 12th-century architecture and sculpture show perhaps their most personal expression. Castles and country houses, popular traditions and crafts and the gastronomic specialties of Auvergne further explain its popularity with tourists. The region is noted for its cheeses : Cantal, Auvergne blue, creamy Saint-Nectaire, and a number of goat cheeses, the best-known being the *cabecou* of Salers and Aurillac. Sausages, salami and the famous Auvergne ham find willing buyers all over France, and the local wines provide an earthy and very palatable accompaniment.

The capital, Clermont-Ferrand, is an important automobile manufacturing center, specializing in tyres. It has always been a meeting place for inhabitants and tourists alike, a busy, lively city with more than a drop of southern blood in its veins, and blessed with many fine buildings including a number of well-preserved Gothic and Renaissance dwellings.

Sightseeing

Facts and figures

Location : *in the centre of France covering most of the Massif Central. A number of rivers rise in its mountains and flow down to the Atlantic and the Mediterranean.*
Area : *18 700 km^2*
Climate : *Auvergne has a reputation for harsh weather especially in winter, when the temperatures drop sharply and the mountains are covered in snow. Spring temperatures vary from one extreme to the other; summer tends to be heavy and hot, although higher up the mountains the air is refreshing; autumn is usually the best season of the year.*
Population : *967 000, mainly in Puy de Dôme and Clermont-Ferrand.*
Administration : *Department of the* ***Cantal,*** *Prefecture : Aurillac; Department of the* ***Haute-Loire,*** *Prefecture : Le Puy; Department of the* ***Puy-de-Dôme,*** *Prefecture : Clermont-Ferrand.*

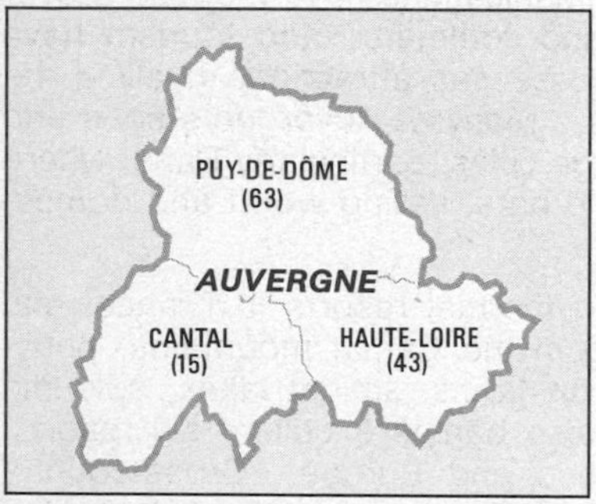

■ AIGUEPERSE

B1 / ® / pop. 2740 (Puy-de-Dôme)

Former capital of the Duchy of Montpensier, a modest linear town in the centre of the rich agricultural region of Limagne.

▶ **Sainte Chapelle★,** built in 1475 by Louis I of Bourbon-Montpensier (*Louis le Bon,* 1402-1486); excellent 14thC statues. ▶ Hôtel de Ville (17thC) : belfry with jack o' the clock (animated clock). ▶ 13th-14thC church (rebuilt nave) with 15thC **"Mourning of the Dead Christ"** (wood polychrome group) and remnants of frescos. □

Don't miss

★★★ : *La Chaise-Dieu (BC2), Le Puy (C3), Puy-de-Dôme (A1).*
★★ : *Brioude (B2-3), Clermont-Ferrand (B1), Puy Mary (A3), Salers (A3), Garabit Viaduct (B3), Truyère Gorges (B3).*

▶ Nearby

▶ Above **Chaptuzat** *(3 km NW)*, château de la Roche★ on the edge of the plateau (view★), 11th-12thC fortress rebuilt in the 15th-16thC *(9-12 & 2-7)*. ▶ **Montpensier** *(3 km NE)* : a tiny

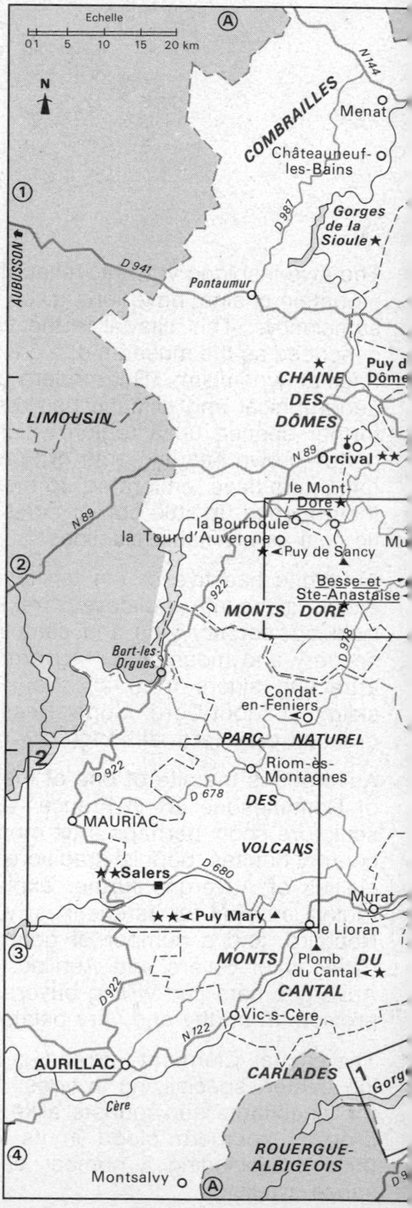

village despite the historical splendour of the family that bore its name, hidden away among vineyards at the foot of a butte (view★). **Effiat,** 0 km farther, has a pretty Louis XII château★; don't miss the Grand Salon. *(9-12 & 2-7, daily Jun.-Sep., Sat., Sun. and nat. hols. Mar.-May and Oct.-Nov.)*; 1 km farther on **château de Denone** 16thC *(2-7 Easter school hols. and Jul.-Aug.)*; in the 12thC church at **Biozat,** figured capitals★ and 15thC frescos. From here, return to Aigueperse via **Saint-Genès-du-Retz** (Romanesque church). ▶ **Artonne** *(5.5 km SW)* with a Romanesque church in part, dating to the 10thC. At **Saint-Myon,** church★ with a superb apse. □

■ ALLIER Gorges

▶ From Vieille-Brioude to Monistrol-d'Allier *(63 km, approx 2 h 30)*
B3

The fish-filled river Allier runs over rocks and gravel, snaking its way between mountains speckled with ancient villages perched on hillsides.

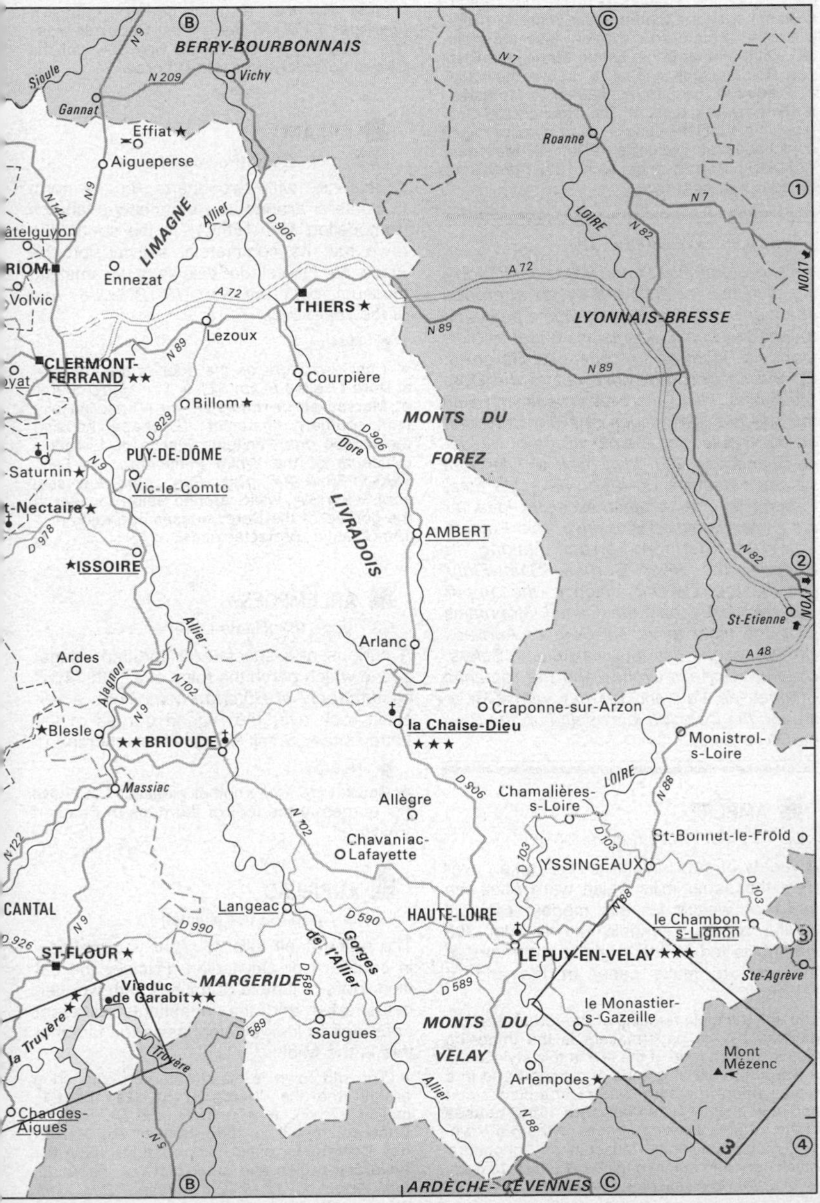

▶ **Vieille-Brioude.** ▶ **Saint-Ilpize :** a typical valley village, ranged along an escarpment, with a modest church and a ruined castle. ▶ **Blassac :** 11th-12thC church with 14thC frescos. ▶ **Lavoûte-Chilhac,** on a peninsula linked to the left bank by a 15thC bridge; important 18thC buildings from a former Benedictine monastery; 15thC church (see treasure room, *8 or 9-12 & 2-6 or 7).* ▶ **Saint-Cirgues :** 15thC frescos★ in the church choir; 10 km W, on the **Ally Plateau** are a number of windmills, including one still in working order. ▶ Frescos, sculptures or architecture make almost every church in the valley worth stopping for : **Aubazat, Arlet** *(off the road)* **Peyrusse, Langeac** (pop. 4733 ®; small capital of this region; ancient houses). **Chanteuges** is a pretty village clustering around an old priory (see the cloister). On the other bank, **Sainte-Marie-des-Chazes** Romanesque chapel. ▶ Leave the valley at **Prades** ® (basalt colonnades) to **Monistrol-d'Allier** by the ruins of the Rochegude Château, in a superb setting★; nearby, more basalt colonnades at Escluezis; 9 km N, **Mercoeur Château :** Renaissance, with 12th-14thC keep (prison; *visit possible*). □

Weekend tips

Visiting Clermont-Ferrand will take all morning, and can be followed by an afternoon spent driving up the Puy-de-Dôme peak and touring the Dôme Mountains; return to Clermont via Royat or the plateau of Gergovie. On the second day, drive out to the Dore Mountains, climb the Sancy peak and visit the spa and ski villages of Mont Dore and La Bourboule; see the old village of Besse-en-Chandesse and drive back to Clermont via Saint-Nectaire or, if you have the time, through Issoire. Another excellent idea for a summer weekend is to drive from Puy-en-Velay to Clermont-Ferrand, taking in Brioude, the Allier Gorges, Saint-Flour (lunch), the Garabit Viaduct, the upper Truyère Valley and the Cantal Mountains (stay the night at Vic-sur-Cère or Aurillac). On the second day tour via Anjony, Salers, Mauriac, Bort-les-Orgues and the romantic Château de Val; end the day with a drive around the Dore Mountains and up the Puy-de-Dôme peak.

■ AMBERT

C2 / ® / pop. 8026 (Puy-de-Dôme)

A variety of small industries has taken over from the paper mills which were once the focus of wealth for this modest regional capital of the Livradois; more than 300 watermills fed by the streams and rivers of the area to make paper at the end of the 16thC.

The only tangible remains of the fortunes accumulated by the papermakers is the imposing Gothic **church** (one of the few in this style in the Auvergne), built of granite at a period and in a region where the norm was *pise* (a clay, stone and mud mix). ▶ Numerous **15th-16thC houses** in the narrow, twisting streets of the old town. ▶ Circular town hall. Museum of Agricultural machinery and steam engines *(15 Jun.-15 Sep., 9-12 & 2-6; low season on request).* □

▶ Nearby

▶ **Richard de Bas Mill★** *(4 km E).:* a perfect example of the paper-mills of yesteryear, with manufacturing processes dating to the 14thC and a whole floor of stretched lines open to the wind to dry the sheets (*9-12 & 2-6 Jul.-Aug. 9-8;* museum, history of paper). From the mill you can take a pleasant trip through the **Forez Mountains** *(55 km; approx. 2 hr),* taking D996 to the left; a good run over Pradeaux Pass to **Saint-Anthème,** a little summer resort and winter-sports centre. Go N up the valley of the Ance River by D139 to reach the **Grand Genèvrier,** where the mountain farm of Coq Noir has been transformed into a museum celebrating *Fourme,* a local country cheese★ *(tastings; 1 Jul.-15 Sep.).* Past Supeyres Pass (alt. 1366 m), view★ on the way down of the **Cirque de Valcivières** (steep hollow). □

■ ARLANC

BC2 / pop. 2300 (Puy-de-Dôme)

A little city with two hearts; in the north it clusters around a Romanesque church (remodelled 15th-16thC); in the south, the town has its commercial activity; on the Place de l'Hôtel de Ville is a lacemaking museum *(daily Jul.-Sep. 10-12 & 3-6; rest of the year : 3-6).* □

▶ Nearby

▶ 13thC ironwork on the door of the church★ at **Dore-l'Église** *(4 km SE).* ▶ The 15thC church of **Marsac-en-Livradois** *(7 km N)* has an evident southern character; S, chapel housing the Musée des Pénitents Blancs du Livradois (Museum of the White Penitents; *Jun.-Sep., 9:30-11:30 & 2-6; Sat., Sun., Mon. low season*). 9 km SW, walks around **Saint-Sauveur** in the gorges of the Dore; houses and ruins of a 15thC castle; protected site★. □

■ ARLEMPDES★

C3 / pop. 182 (Haute-Loire)

A curious and spectacular fortified village, above which perch the ruins of a 12th-14thC castle *(apply at Hôtel du Manoir)* on a volcanic rock over the rugged gorges of the Loire : site★. Small Romanesque church. □

▶ Nearby

▶ **Goudet** *(10 km),* another pleasant site above the gorges at the foot of the ruins of Beaufort Castle. □

■ AURILLAC

A3 / ® / pop. 33197 (Cantal)

The name itself tells you that you are now in southern or Occitanian, France; the flat tiled roofs, a jumble of houses with wooden balustrades and the inhabitants' different approach to life : all emphasize the fact that this is the Midi.

▶ The old town is clearly marked, clustering around the the **church of St. Géraud** (C1; mainly 17thC). ▶ 400 m N, the **St. Etienne Château,** rebuilt in 1880, houses the **Maison des Volcans★ :** exhibitions on volcanos in the Auvergne region and other parts of the world. *(Jul.-Aug., 10-12 & 2-7; closed Sun. am;*

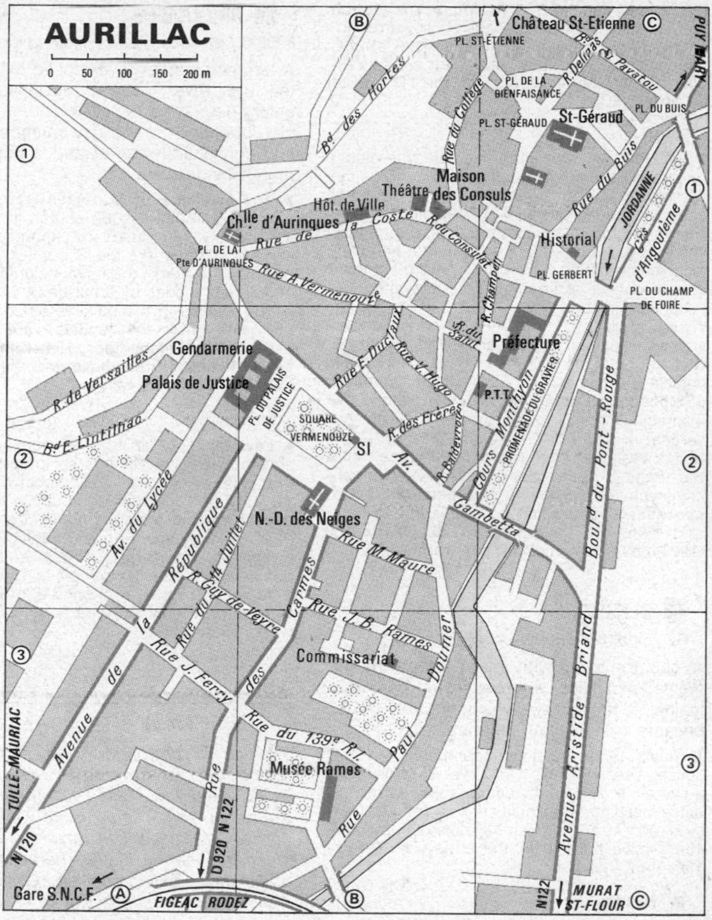

Sep.-Jun. 9-12 & 2-6; closed Sun.). ▶ The 16thC Maison des Consuls★ (B1) is today given over to the **Musée du Vieil Aurillac** the old city *(10-12 & 2-6; closed Tue., Sun. and nat. hols.).* ▶ On Place Gerbert (Gerbert was a former monk of St. Géraud and first French Pope as Sylvester II in 999), is the wax museum *(Historial;* C1; *daily 2-7).* View★ upstream from the neighbouring bridge of old houses bordering the Jordanne. ▶ 17thC Flemish tapestries★ in the **Palais de Justice** (law courts; A-B2; *9-12 & 2-6; closed Sun.).* ▶ In the church of Notre Dame des Neiges (B2; 14th-16thC) : 17thC Black Virgin. ▶ **Rames Museum★** (B3; *2nd floor, 10-12 & 2-6; closed Sun. am; Tue. and nat. hols.)* : exhibition on life in the Cantal Region; **Parieu Museum** *(3rd floor, same hours)* : Fine Arts. □

▶ Nearby

▶ **Château de Conros,** 4 km S of **Arpajon-sur-Cère** ® *(4 km SW),* old feudal manor, housing a museum of arts and traditions of Cère Valley *(14 Jul.-Aug., 2-7).* ▶ **Route des Crêtes★** (ridge road), NE, above the right bank of the Jordanne River; views★; continue down into the **Mandailles Valley★★** before climbing to Puy Mary peak. ▶ **Laroquebrou** *(25 km W)* : on the right bank of the Cère below feudal ruins; 14thC church; small archaeological collection at the *mairie;* 16thC Messac Château *(visit on request).* 5 km upstream, the **Saint-Etienne-Cantalès** dam turns the Cère into a 12 km long lake (view★). □

■ BILLOM★

B2 / pop. 4 164 (Puy-de-Dôme)

A few small industries and an important position in the garlic and spice markets haven't yet restored its mediaeval importance : at that time it had 5 000 inhabitants, and was, in the 13thC, an important university town with more than 2 000 students.

▶ A number of beautiful **old houses** still survive from the period of glory and prosperity : see the **Corporation of Butchers** (trade guild), and the Dean's House (16thC; Rue des Boucheries), the **Chapter House** (façade of the old university, 1447), the 16thC houses of the Échevin (magistrate) and the Bailli (bailiff). ▶ The **church** has a remodelled Romanesque choir, surrounded by 12thC **grillwork★**; in a chapel, 14thC frescos★; 11thC crypt★; in the left aisle: frescos and sculptured group of the "Burial of Christ" (15thC). □

▶ Nearby

▶ **Chauriat** *(7 km NW)* has an interesting Auvergnat Romanesque church★; note the remarkable mosaïc work on the S transept gable; figured capitals. ▶ The capitals of the church in **Espirat** *(4 km from Billom)* are no less interesting. ▶ **Ravel** *(12 km NE)* has a fine château rebuilt during 17th-18thC on the remains of a mediaeval fortress: 18thC apartments★, paintings *(Easter-1 Nov., 10-12 & 2-7)*; 2.5 km W, the church of **Moissat-Bas** has a wooden shrine★ sheathed in copper (13thC); 5 km S, **Glaine-Montaigut**: Romanesque church with notable capitals. ▶ 5 km SE of Billom: remains of **Montmorin Castle** (12thC) on a hilltop; the main building has been turned into an Auvergnat museum *(2-7 daily Jul.-Oct., Sat.-Sun. rest of year)*; return to Billom making the round trip through **Saint-Dier-d'Auvergne** (Romanesque church); 5 km S, **château des Martinanches,** 15th-16thC *(2-7 daily 15 Jun.-15 Sep.)* and ruins of the **château de Mauzun★** (12th-16thC; *10 min climb*; panorama). □

BLESLE★

B2 / pop. 851 (Haute-Loire)

A country town with many stone monuments, indicating a prosperous past due mainly to an abbey which, in the 16thC, became a chapter of canonesses.

▶ Ruins of fortifications and massive 13thC square keep★, 14thC bell-tower★, remains of a church. ▶ The Romanesque **abbey church★,** dates back to Carolingian times; stalls, treasure room★. ▶ The town hall now occupies the 15thC main building of the abbey. ▶ Several 15th-16thC houses. □

▶ Nearby

▶ **Massiac** ® *(9 km S)*: country holiday centre; 15thC church with beautiful 15thC reliquary Virgin. ▶ **Léotoing** *(16 km NE)*: 11thC chapel decorated with 15thC murals; ruins of 13thC château, large cylindrical keep overlooking the gorges★ of the Alagnon River; a little to the N, at the opening of the gorge, **Lempdes** has an original semicircular market hall on Doric pillars; 6 km farther on, the church of **Saint-Gervazy** has a Romanesque statue of "The Virgin Enthroned"★★, without doubt the most beautiful in the Puy-de-Dôme. □

La BOURBOULE

A2 / ® / pop. 2403 (Puy-de-Dôme)

A well-known spa resort (specialising in the relief of asthma, skin disorders and allergies), with all attendant leisure facilities.

▶ **Grands Thermes**: a sort of pseudo-Byzantine palace. ▶ On the opposite bank of the Dordogne River, **Fenestre Park★,** departure point for a cable-car up to **Charlannes Plateau** *(closed Oct.-15 Dec.; also accessible by road: 7 km)*; a pleasant wooded park overlooking the valley of the Dordogne. ▶ N of the resort, excursion *(7 km by car and 1/2 hr on foot)* to **Banne d'Ordanche** (alt. 1 515 m; panorama★). □

BRIOUDE★★

B2-3 / ® / pop. 7 854 (Haute-Loire)

A terraced market town above the valley of the Allier River; once an ecclesiastical seigniory (feudal estate) of considerable financial importance. It is today an important veal and agricultural market and a popular salmon-fishing centre.

▶ The **Basilica★ of St. Julien** (11th-12thC) is the biggest Romanesque church in Auvergne, its majesty reinforced by impressive polychrome stone work; the S porch★ retains its original metalwork; the nave, heightened in the 13thC, is preceded by a narthex★ with Romanesque frescos in the gallery; other frescos in the nave, where the capitals★ are not to be missed; 16thC stone floor; 15th-16thC statues. ▶ Old houses; from the terrace of the town hall, view★ over the valley. □

▶ Nearby

▶ **Lavaudieu** *(10 km SE)*: Romanesque abbey church; the nave still has an important group of frescos★ from the 14thC; sober cloister *(10-12 & 2-5 or 6),* with wooden upper floor, leads directly into the refectory (12thC fresco). Small museum of popular arts and traditions. ▶ 5 km farther on, **Domeyrat**: Romanesque church; dominated by the ruins of a 15thC castle. ▶ **Auzon,** 12 km N, was once a fortified town; Romanesque church: see south porch★ and works of art inside. □

Skiing in Auvergne

Thanks to prolonged and ample snow during the winter months, the Auvergne Region and the Massif Central mountains are remarkably well-suited to winter sports, and excellent facilities have been installed since the early 1950's. There are a number of alpine skiing centres, but the emphasis is on cross-country skiing, at cosy family resorts. Mont-Dore, Super-Besse and Super-Lioran are the main centres in Auvergne, popular with the French as well as with visitors. But Chastreix-Sancy, Chambon-les-Neiges and Saint Anthème (22 km from Ambert) are also well-frequented. At Alberoche-Collandres and La Bourboule-Charlannes a start has been made with ski-trekking.

La CHAISE-DIEU★★★

BC2 / ® / pop. 953 (Haute-Loire)

At the heart of an immense forested area, a few scantily populated hamlets; as its name — literally, the throne of God — indicates, this was once the seat of an influential abbey: one of its former monks became Pope.

▶ **Church of St. Robert★★**: superb 15thC Gothic edifice, built at the order of Pope Clement VI, with a majestic interior with a Flamboyant Gothic choir screen★ (15thC); 17thC organ case; important works of art in the choir

(9 or 10-12 & 2-5 or 7; closed Tue. Nov.-May) : tomb of Clement VI★ (d. 1353); 156 Gothic stalls★; early 16thC tapestries★★; 15thC mural of the *"Danse Macabre"*★ in N side aisle. ▶ S, only two galleries of the **cloister** remain. Over the apse, **Clémentine Tower** looks like a fortified keep. ▶ Next to the cloister, the convent buildings (17th-18thC) house the **Historial** (wax museum, *Jun.-Sep. 9-12 & 2-7)* and the **"Echo Room"** (two people in opposite corners with their backs turned can talk quietly together). ▶ Old houses. □

▶ Nearby

▶ **Saint-Claude Signal** (peak, *1 km E;* alt. 1 112 m; view★). ▶ **Malaguet Lake** *(10 km S)* in the heart of a pine forest. ▶ **Craponne-sur-Arzon** ® *(19 km E)* : summer resort and mechanised lacemaking centre; 16thC church, with Romanesque tower for belfry; old houses and remains of fortifications. □

■ CHÂTEAUNEUF-LES-BAINS

12 km S. of Menat, A1 / ® / pop. 374 (Puy-de-Dôme)

Tiny mineral water spa on both banks of the Sioule River; a trout fisherman's paradise.

▶ Shady park of Sequoias; porphyry (crystalline) rocks on the right bank, granite on the left. □

▶ Nearby

▶ **Sioule Gorges★,** towards Ébreuil (→ Berry); to one side, **Menat :** Romanesque church, very much restored in the 19thC but still preserving carved capitals★ with leaves, interlacings and animals, and a 15thC cloister gallery. ▶ **Saint-Gervase-d'Auvergne** *(8 km W)* : 15thC church with Romanesque apse; from there, visit the **Viaduc des Fades★** (viaduct; *10 km S*) : built in 1908, the highest in France (132.5 m above the river Sioule). □

■ CHÂTELGUYON

B1 / ® / pop. 4 588 (Puy-de-Dôme)

About 100 m above the plain of Limagne on a spur of the Puys Mt. chain, this is a health resort for those with digestive problems.

▶ The old town is centred around the church (modern frescos) to the N; **spa★** in the park on either side of the Sardon River, with pine-covered **Chalusset Hill** to the S; from the top, view over the Puys, Limagne and Forez mountains. □

▶ Nearby

▶ **Château de Chazeron★** *(3 km W)* : overlooking the west bank of the Sardon : 16th-17thC building with 14thC keep *(May-Sep 3-6).* From there, tour the foothills of the Puys Mountains *(50 km, approx. 2 hrs)* via **Manzat** (Renaissance woodwork in church), *Gour de Tazenat* (a perfectly circular crater lake), Charbonnières-les-Vieilles, **Combronde** (18thC town hall), **Davayat** (Louis XIII-style château; *May-15 Oct.10-12 & 2-7; Sat. and Sun. pm rest of year*) and **Saint-Bonnet** (12th-14thC church). ▶ **Enval** *(3.5 km S) :* at the exit from the gorges *(15 mins on foot),* where the Ambène River comes down in a chain of miniature cascades; farther on, **Volvic** and **Tournoël château** (→ Volvic). □

■ CHAUDES-AIGUES

B3-4 / ® / pop. 1 267 (Cantal)

A fortified city in times past, now cautiously developing into a health resort; very much a leader in matters of energy saving, thanks to its hot springs (70-82°C). The majority of buildings have long enjoyed hot water and central heating at very low cost.

▶ 15thC church. ▶ Each of the eight districts of the town has a niche sheltering a statue of its patron saint. ▶ Château de Couffour (14thC, restored) to the S. ▶ 4 km NW, château de Montvallat, of solid granite with corner towers (16th-17thC). □

▶ Tour of the Truyère Gorges★★ *(122 km; half day; see map 1)*

▶ Leave Chaudes-Aigues by the Garabit road (D13). ▶ From the **Belvédère du Cheylé,** view★ over the cirque de Mallet (steep hollow) and the lake created on the Truyère River by the Grandval Dam; views all the way to **Auriac.**

1. Tour of the Truyère Gorges

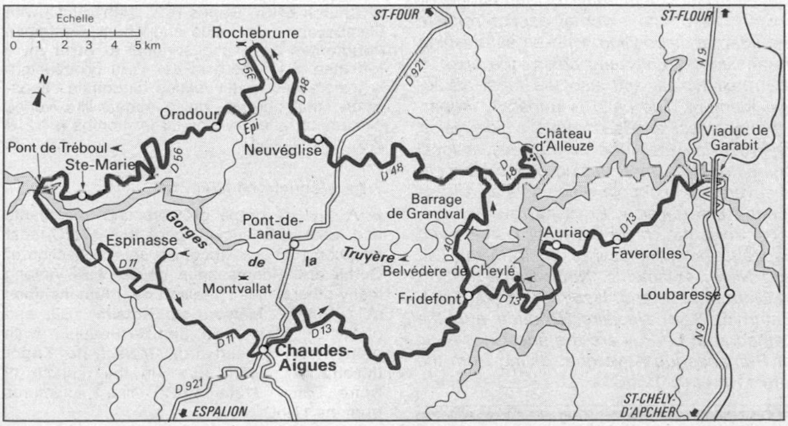

Auvergne

Here, descend via **Faverolles** (craft exhibition at the Compagnons du Buffadou; château de Chassan 14th-18thC, *Jul.-Sept., 2:30-7)* to the **Garabit Viaduct★★** ® with a superb 564 m arch, by Gustave Eiffel (1884); carrying the Paris-Béziers road 90 m above the water. At **Loubaresse** *(7 km S)* is the Eco-musée de la Margeride on an old farm; nearby, château de Pompignac (14thC; *15 Jul.-early Aug.*) overlooking the Arcomie Valley ▶ Return as far as Fridefont to see the **Grandval Dam★,** an impressive structure with vaults 85 m high which backs up the waters of the Truyère for 27 km. ▶ Ruins of the **château d'Alleuze★** (13thC) on the edge of a cliff. ▶ Through Lavastrie and Neuvéglise to the **château de Rochebrune★** (15thC; 13thC keep; *Easter-Oct., 2:15-5:45; closed Tue.).* ▶ Superb drive along D56. ▶ Hamlet of **Sainte-Marie :** modest church with stained glass windows by Jean Cocteau. ▶ At **Tréboul** Bridge, continue along the lower part of the gorge (in Rouergue) : wonderful scenery; you may wish to go on to the **Belvédère du Vézou** (view★), or even the **château de Bohal★** (13thC; *12.5 km N of Pierrefort; visit on request; tel : 73 40 82).* ▶ Return to Chaudes-Aigues with a detour to **Espinasse** *(3.5 km round trip),* built on a spur (view★). □

■ CHAVANIAC-LAFAYETTE

B3 / pop. 425 (Haute-Loire)

American-owned by the Lafayette Memorial Trust, which has carefully restored the 1701 château, birthplace of the famous general (1757-1834) who fought for American independence. Wax museum and Franco-American memorabilia *(10-12 & 2-7).* □

Romanesque Auvergne

During the Romanesque period, Auvergne gave birth to one of France's most original and most important regional "schools". The churches of this period are sober and severe, with a powerful beauty as ageless and uncompromising as the mountains that surround them. Built of sandstone or volcanic lava, the external aspect reflects the internal disposition, with an astonishing impression of unity and poise; the apse is the most typical and also the most attractive element. The nave is generally separated by massive pillars from the side aisles, on which are set lofts or galleries, a local characteristic. The crossing of the transept is covered by a cupola which acts as a base for the bell-tower, while a narrow ambulatory circles the choir. The vigorously-carved capitals show subjects taken from the Old and New Testaments. Notre-Dame-du-Port in Clermont-Ferrand, Issoire, Orcival, Saint-Saturnin, Saint Nectaire, Brioude and the cathedral at Le Puy are the finest flowering of Romanesque Auvergne, dating from the late 11th-early 12thC.

■ CLERMONT-FERRAND★★

B1 / ® / pop. 151 092 (Puy-de-Dôme)

Clermont has a very staid appearance (the town of Volvic and its quarries are not far away), but it is by no means dreary. It came late to industrialisation (the principal industry is tyre manufacture, developing after the automobile at the end of the last century). But it is now and has always been the hub of the region, where the Auvergnat people living in the mountains meet those from the plain, and where health-resort visitors come on excursions. For this is a town full of bustle with a definite flavour of the Midi Region.

▶ **Place de Jaude** (B2) is the link between old and new Clermont city, with cafés, theatre and shopping centre and, as is fitting, a statue of the Gaulish hero Vercingetorix (Bartholdi, 1902). ▶ The classic church of **St. Pierre des Minimes** has elegant 18thC woodwork in the choir. ▶ **Rue des Chaussetiers** has been renovated and is now a pedestrian street leading past ancient houses (No. 3, Hôtel Savaron, 1513) to the **cathedral★** (C1; 13th-14thC; facade and spires 19thC). This is an elegant Gothic building, with a light and graceful interior due to extremely slender pillars made possible by using solid basalt stone. 13th-14thC stained glass, frescos of the same period in radiating chapels. From the transept, paid access to Bayette Tower; panorama★ . ▶ Other beautiful old houses in **Rue Pascal** (No. 4, Hôtel de Chazerat) and **Rue du Port★.** ▶ **Notre Dame du Port★★,** excellent example of Auvergnat Romanesque (11th-12thC) with superb choir and figured capitals★★ which are among the most beautiful in the region. ▶ Place de la Poterne, the **Ambroise Fountain★** (1515) in Volvic stone. ▶ **Rue des Gras** (B1-2), interesting houses and a 16thC *hôtel particulier* (mansion) housing the **Ranquet Museum** (history of the town, *objets d'art,* including mediaeval sculpture; *10-12 & 2-5 or 6; closed Mon. and nat. hols.*). ▶ Nearby, the St. Pierre Market and the narrow streets make an agreeable stroll (Rue de la Boucherie).

Also... ▶ **Bargoin Museum** (C3; *10-12 & 2-5 or 6; closed Mon. and nat. hols.*) : prehistoric and Gallo-Roman archaeology, paintings and sculpture. ▶ **Lecoq Museum** *(same hours) :* natural history, interesting regional collections. Opposite, **Lecoq Garden★** (7 acres) where a fortified 15th-16thC gate has been re-erected. ▶ **Church of St. Genès** (C2; 14th-15thC) with Flamboyant Gothic side chapels. ▶ **Fontaines Petrifiantes** (petrifying springs) at Saint Alyre (off map, B1) where in the Peru grotto highly mineralised water leaves carbonate deposits on small objects, which appear like ivories or cameos after two or three months *(9-12 & 2-6; 8-7 Jul.-Aug.).* □

▶ Montferrand *(3 km NE)*

▶ A city of grape growers and merchants and, until the beginning of the 17thC, seat of a court of law. Incomparable collection of **Gothic and Renaissance houses★.** ▶ Among many others, see : **Maison de l'Annonciation** (A1; 16thC), **Maison du Notaire** (B2, end of 15thC), **Maison du Sire de Beaujeu** (with pretty Henri II courtyard), **Maison de l'Apothicaire** (B1; 15thC). ▶ In the church of Notre Dame (13th-14thC), fine sculptures from the 17thC. □

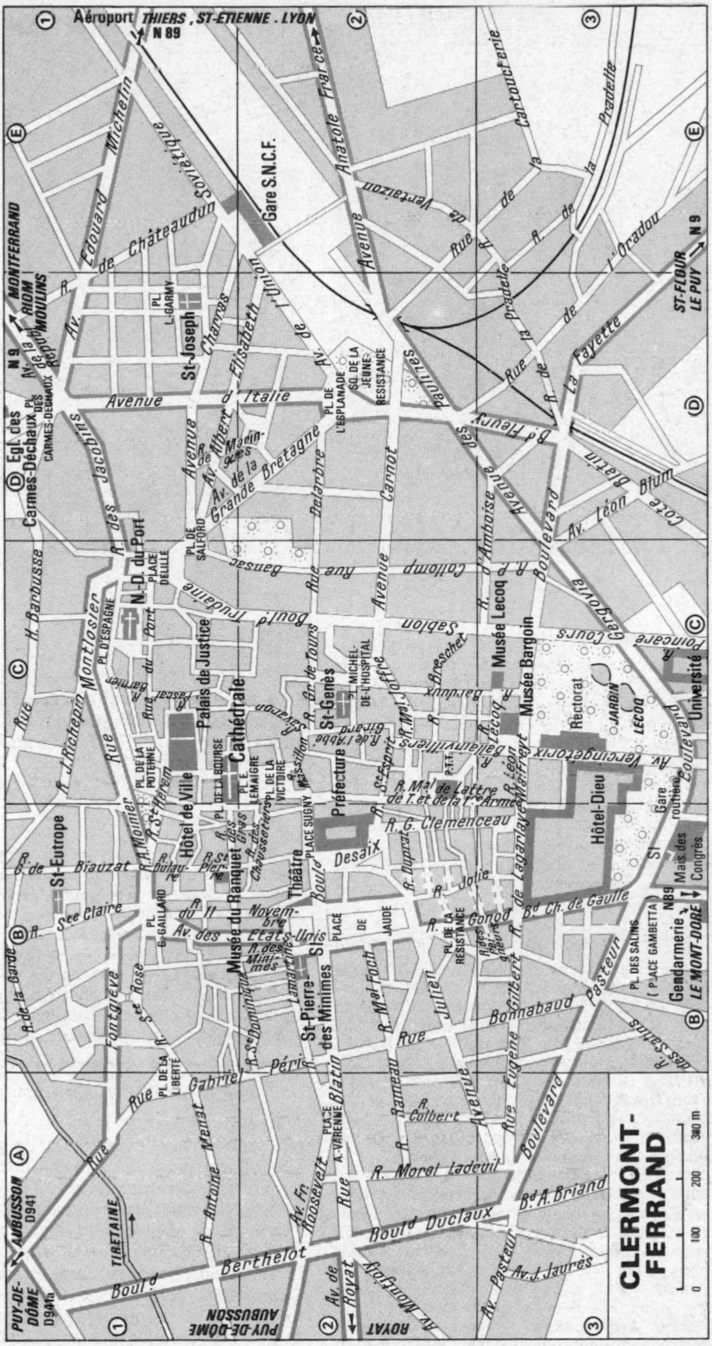

▶ Chamalières ® *(1.5 km W)*

▶ Industrialised (iron and steel, paper) long before Clermont, and now its residential annex, halfway between the Auvergnat capital and the hot-spring spa at Royat (→).

▶ The narthex and nave of the church go back to Carolingian times; lovely choir with ambulatory, 12th-13thC.

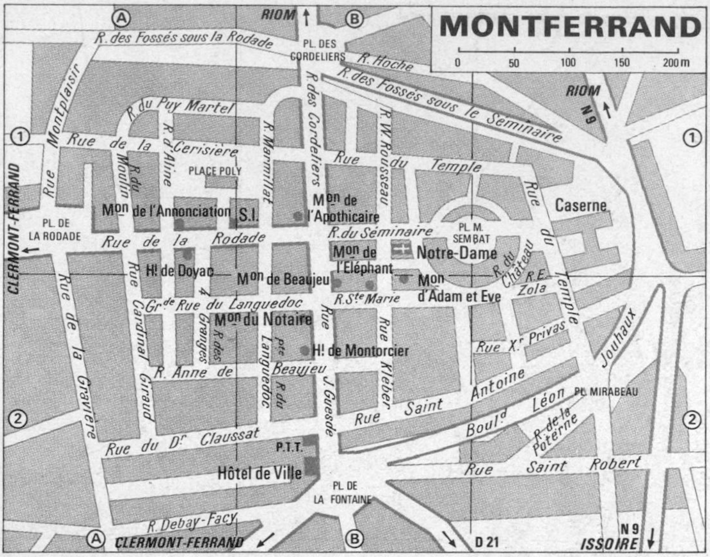

▶ Nearby

▶ **Royat** (→) and the Puy de Dôme peak. ▶ N of the village, the **Côtes de Clermont** (view★ of the town), where some theories site the Gallic stronghold of Gergovie. ▶ **Gergovie** *(14 km S)* : a monument vigorously recalls the Gauls' dubious victory over Caesar; overlooking the black basaltic village of the same name (called Merdogne until the last century), this basalt plateau has not yielded any convincing proof of the events reputed to have occurred there; but it's a good story — and the view is marvellous★. □

▶ **Tour of Serre Mt.** *(approx 60 km; 2hr30)*
Leave Clermont by the N89 and D3 to the south; **Opme,** a truly archaic hamlet, dominated by its château★, a fortress in volcanic rock, 11th-13thC, with 17thC main building. Near **Chanonat,** the château de la Bâtisse (15th-18thC); gardens, apartments★ *(May-Sep. 10-12 & 2-7; Sat. and Sun. 2-6 rest of year).* From **Crest** (13th-15thC church, remains of fortifications and tower; view★), descend to the valley of the Veyre R. and cross the Gothic bridge at **Saint-Amand-Tallende.** The church★★ of **Saint-Saturnin★** expresses the spirit of monastic poverty; its bell-tower served as a model for many others in the Auvergne. 15thC *Pietà* in the crypt. Imposing 14th-15thC château *(Easter-1 Nov., 9-7);* remains of ramparts. 2 km SW, the **abbey of Notre Dame de Randol** (1971) : geometric architecture★, startling in this calm nook of the gorges of the Monne. **Aydat Lake★,** retained by a wall of lava, is surrounded with pleasant forest. Return to Clermont by D145 across the Serre Mountain by a (views), then by the N89. 9 km NW of the lake is the **château de Montlosier** (near Randanne), administrative centre of the *Volcans d'Auvergne* nature park (→) : exhibition and models of volcanic activity, audiovisuals *(15 Jun.-30 Sep., 10-12:30 & 2-7).* □

■ CONDAT

A2 / pop. 1 568 (Cantal)

In a delightful basin of meadows surrounded by wooded hills, Condat's first summer villas were built by successful travelling salesmen from the linen trade, a traditional regional activity. □

▶ Nearby

▶ Few vestiges remain of the 12thC Cistercian abbey of **Féniers** *(3 km S)* which was rebuilt in 1686. ▶ **Montboudif** *(6 km NW)* is the village birthplace of Cantal school-teacher's son Georges Pompidou (1911-74; President of France 1969-74). ▶ **Égliseneuve-d'Entraigues** *(12 km NW),* up the pretty valley of the Rhue; small Romanesque church, rustic and full of character with interesting capitals; *Maison des Fromages d'Auvergne★*

Is Gergovie at Gergovie?

The plateau known as Gergovie is too beautiful for anyone to doubt that it could be the site of the seeming victory of the Gallic cavalry over Caesar's legions (→ p.301), but despite searches made on the plateau since the reign of Napoleon III, and after close analysis of Caesar's own writings, there is still great uncertainty among specialists. Other neighbouring sites which were also fortified Gallic strongholds have good claims to be considered the site of that epic, if inconclusive, victory. Among them : the Plateau des Côtes, to the north of Clermont-Ferrand. The controversy has not been resolved, and modern-day Gaul remains divided upon the question...

(regional cheeses exhibition : audiovisuals; tools; tastings; *15 Jun.-30 Sep. 10, 11, 14, 15, 16, 17, 18, daily).* **Rhue Valley★**, downstream *(32 km to Bort-les-Orgues,* → Limousin), by a corniche (cliff road) through the Maubert Forest. □

■ ISSOIRE★

B2 / ® / pop. 15383 (Puy-de-Dôme)

A small island of urban life inhabited mainly by technicians in a predominantly rural region; this ancient city is an important industrial centre, producing 50 % of France's aluminium; it is also the site of a Soviet-made hydraulic press, capable of forging parts under 65000 tons pressure.

▶ The old town remains a captive of its ancient fortifications, long since disappeared; narrow streets and old buildings, one of which, the *Maison des Échevins,* houses the **Historial** (a wax museum) retracing the city's past *(10-7 or 2:30-7).* ▶ In the town centre, the **church of St Austremoine★★** (12thC) is a worthy example of the Romanesque art and architecture in the Auvergne region; clumsy restorations effected during the last century; look instead at the scope and imagination of the design and the quality of the architectural detail. Apse★★ remarkable for its architecture and ornamentation; crypt★★, fresco★ of the "Last Judgement" (15thC) in the narthex. □

▶ Nearby

▶ **Parentignat** ® *(4 km SE)* has a classic 17thC château richly furnished with pieces from the French Regency and Louis XV periods; paintings★; *(2-6, May-Jun., Sun. and nat. hols.; 15 Jun.-20 Sep., daily ex Wed.).* ▶ At **Nonette** *(7 km S of Parentignat);* ruins★ of a 14thC château on a conical spur; admirable view★ over the valley; in the village, remains of ramparts, ancient houses and 11th-16thC church housing 14thC Christ figure★ of great quality (only the bust remains). 6 km E of Nonette, graceful Romanesque church at **Mailhat** (12thC) is decorated in a vigorous, even earthy style. ▶ **Usson** *(12 km E),* the flank of a basalt peak bearing a statue (1892) of the Virgin, offers a fine view; old houses, 12th-14thC church, remains of the château where Queen Margot, wife of Henri IV, was exiled from 1585-1605 for "conduct unbecoming of a Queen", a surprising reason when we consider the license permitted at the court (Henri is known to the French as *Vert Galant,* kindly translated as a man who doesn't know his years with women). □

▶ Around the Couzes *(approx 110 km; 1/2 day)*

▶ From Issoire, go up the valley of the Couze de Pavin. ▶ At the entrance to **Perrier,** a vertical flow of basalt has been pierced to produce artificial grottos. ▶ In **Saint-Floret,** remains of 13thC château (Gothic hall; 14thC frescos); on a rock, the church of Chastel with 15thC frescos. ▶ **Saurier :** site★, a mediaeval bridge and fortified gates. Farther on, the **Courgoul Gorges,** through which runs the Couze de Valbeleix; follow the road to Besse-en-Chandesse for a few miles for **Moulin Neuf,** where there is small Auvergnat museum of 19thC rural tools and traditions *(Jun.-Sep. 9-12 & 2-7),* and a little farther on the **Jonas★,** 60 artificial grottos dug out at some unknown, possibly prehistoric, period, much used and fortified during the Middle Ages *(15 May-Sep. 9-12 & 2-7; Sun. pm rest of year).* ▶ **Compains;** Romanesque church with elegant Gothic choir. ▶ **Saint Alyre ès-Montagne,** where you rejoin the valley of the Couze d'Ardes (or Vallée des Rentières★) with spectacular basalt rock structures; rare 13thC graveyard lantern. ▶ **Ardes-sur-Couze** is the former capital of this modest duchy; in the church the main altar (17thC) includes eight 15thC painted bas-reliefs on wood; stone *Pietà,* paintings, all 15thC. ▶ **Saint-Germain-Lembron,** amid vineyards; 6 km NW, fine Renaissance château★ at **Villeneuve,** decorated with 16th-17thC frescos illustrating tales and fables *(Apr.-Sep. 10-12 & 4-6; closed Tue.; Oct.-Mar., 10-12 & 3-5; closed Tue. and Wed.).* □

■ Le LIORAN

A3 / ® / pop. Laveissière, 623 (Cantal)

At the end of one of the oldest road tunnels in France (1839), this simple hamlet has grown into the winter sports resort of **Super-Lioran** ®, created in 1963 to take advantage of one the Auvergne's best alpine skiing locations. □

▶ Nearby

▶ **Cère Pass** (alt. 1285 m; *45 mins on superb road;* views), from here an easy ascent to the Puy de Lioran (1368-m peak; *15 mins).* ▶ **Plomb du Cantal★** (alt. 1858 m; *2-3 hr ascent, 1hr15-1hr30 descent; or 50 mins there and back by cable car from Super-Lioran),* second highest peak in the Massif Central after Sancy; remarkable panorama★★. ▶ **Alagnon Valley★,** towards Murat; 1.5 km from Lioran on the right, buron de Belles-Aigues (shepherd's hut for making cheese); cheese-making *(15 Jun.-15 Sep., 10-12:30 & 2:30-7).* □

Auvergne

Emigration from the Auvergne

Thanks to the dynamism of Clermont-Ferrand, the population of the Puy-de-Dôme department has increased steadily over recent decades. But the country around the Puy-de-Dôme has for centuries been a region of emigrants, albeit temporary ones for the most part, who leave the centre of France to seek their fortunes in Paris, in the cities on the coast, or even farther afield. The picture of the bougnat, *the coal-merchant with a modest bar supplying wood coal and fuel for his neighbourhood, was long associated with expatriate Auvergnats who left an agriculturally inhospitable region to try their chances elsewhere, ultimately to return home to the region of their birth. Many have taken their ambition further, and the Auvergne has bred numerous influential politicians. Somehow, whatever heights they scale, they seldom seem to forget their homeland; among the long list of names there are no less than three Presidents of the Republic - Paul Doumer, Georges Pompidou and Valéry Giscard d'Estaing.*

MAURIAC

A3 / ® / pop. 4 776 (Cantal)

The enormous cattle markets held twice a month hardly seem to dent the calm of this pleasant country town, its black basalt houses contrasting sharply with the surrounding greenery.

Despite archaeological restoration, **Notre-Dame-des-Miracles Basilica★** (12thC) has kept its charm : carved Ascension (mutilated) on the tympanum; in the apse, very freely-inspired corbel work; inside, walnut statue of the Virgin★ (12thC); to which the church owes its name. ▶ **Sainte Mary Puy** *(NW, 15 min)* : grassy knoll with broad view over the plains of Cantal and Corrèze. □

▶ Nearby

▶ On the road to Bort-les-Orgues (→ Limousin), stop at the site★ of the **Charlus ruins** *(18 km)* and at **Ydes-Bourg** *(22 km)*, where the Romanesque church★ has some interesting 12thC bas-reliefs under the porch, with delightfully-carved corbelling of ribald faces; 2.5 km E, **Saignes :** pretty summer resort. □

▶ Around the Puy Mary peak *(150 km approx 1 day; see map 2)*

▶ From Mauriac, follow D681 south. ▶ Before **Ally,** château de la Vigne★, roofed with stone; built in 1450 with added *logis* from the 18thC *(Jul.-Aug. 2:30-7)*; 6 km N, in a remarkable setting★ above the gorges of the Auze River is **Brageac★ ;** the church, although restored, is well worth a look (capitals, bases of columns, small treasure room); nearby, former abbey chapel with fine stone roof and large tower. ▶ **Saint Martin-Valmeroux :** old town with attractive market buildings and turretted houses (15th-16thC). ▶ A pleasant ride down the valley of the Maronne : site★ of the château de Palemont (15thC); 2 km S, **Fontanges** (15thC church). ▶ **Salers (→).** ▶ The road★ to Neronne Pass runs along a corniche (cliff road) over basalt escarpments above pastures and shepherds' nuts before reaching the upper valley and the steep hollow, **Cirque du Falgoux★.** ▶ From the **Pas de Peyrol** (alt. 1 589 m), easy climb up the **Puy Mary★★** (alt. 1 787 m; 25 mins) : spectacular view of the nearer valleys, separated by narrow ridges. After **Eylac Pass** (alt. 1 500 m) view of the Impradine Valley, which runs down towards Dienne and Murat (→). ▶ From the **Serres Pass** (alt. 1 364 m) there is an oblique view of the valley of Cheylade before the road goes hairpinning down. Church at **Cheylade :** wooden panelling★ consisting of 1 428 small, painted panels (18thC); waterfalls★ nearby. Site★ of the chapel of Font-Saint (alt. 1 250 m), a very important place of Marian pilgrimage. ▶ The stone-roofed houses of **Apchon** are typical of the region; castle ruins *(10-min climb)*, oblique view★ over the valley. ▶ **Riom-ès-Montagne** ® : important dairy centre where a large cattle market is held on St. Michael's day *(29 Sep.)*; figured capitals★ in the 11thC choir of the church; *maison de la Gentiane et de la flore★* (gentian and flora; *15 Jun.-15 Sep., 10-12:30 & 2:30-7 ex Tue*). ▶ Several ruined châteaux around **Trizac,** and the *Cases de Cotteughe,* remains of what are said to be Gallic houses. ▶ Remarkable *Pietà* in the church at **Auzers;** castle★ with stone roofing (14th-15thC; *Jul.-15 Sep., 2-6:30)*. ▶ **Moussages :** church housing the most beautiful Romanesque statue in Upper Auvergne, Notre Dame de Claviers★★. From here, reach the end of Falgoux Valley★ via the château de Chanterelle (17thC). ▶ **Anglards-de-Salers :** Romanesque church of Limousin Region influences; château de la Trémolière (15thC; *Jul.-Aug. 4:30-7*) : good collection of Aubusson tapestries★ (16thC). □

2. Round the Puy Mary

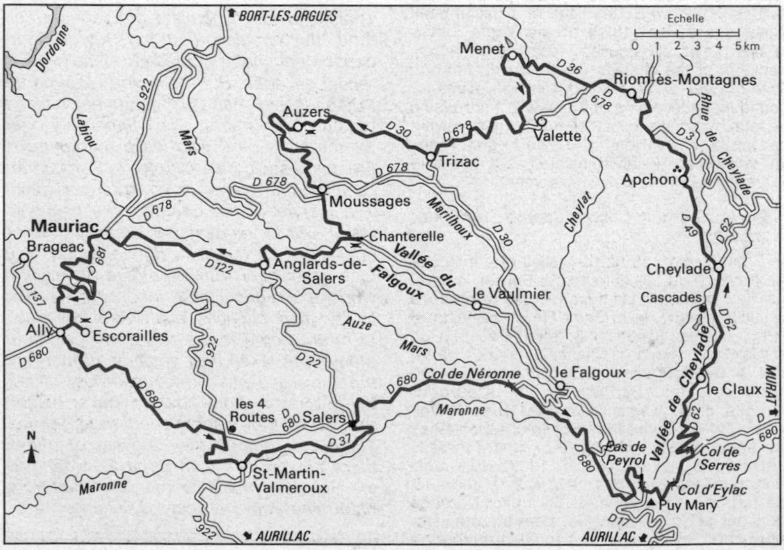

MÉZENC Massif

▶ Round trip from Monastier-sur-Gazeille to Le Puy *(103-120 km; half day)*
C3-4; *see map 3*

Pure air, cool streams, gentle slopes, superb pastures, easy walks and wonderful views.

▶ **Le-Monastier-sur-Gazeille** (pop. 2 093) traces its ancestry to an abbey founded in the 7thC; remains include a remodelled 12thC church (polychrome, treasure room★) and, behind it, the former castle of the abbey (14th-17thC), a massive construction in black basalt. ▶ A detour to **Moudeyres★** ® is a must: thatched roofs, and the Perrel brothers' farm, restored to create the atmosphere of 18thC rural life *(Jul.-15 Sep. 9-2 & 3-7, ex Wed.).* ▶ **Les Estables**: excellent for cross-country skiing; starting point for the **Mézenc** Massif (alt. 1 753 m; *by Croix de Peccata, 3 km, then 20 mins on foot; by Croix des Boutières, 2.5 km, then 15 mins*) : from the top of the Mézenc (→ Ardèche, Cévennes), broad horizons★★ - as far as the Alps in good weather. ▶ Only the priory remains of the former **Bonnefoy charterhouse**; superb wooded site★; 7 km farther, is **Gerbier de Jonc Mt** (→ Cévennes; *20-min climb;* view) : at its foot, a monument to the sources of the Loire River. ▶ Snaking down the E flank of the Mézenc River, the road gives views of the **Boutières region,** with sharper peaks and deeper valleys running down to the Rhône. ▶ After **Fay-sur-Lignon,** take a short turn around St. Front Lake, through **Saint-Front** to **Maziaux★,** a hamlet where stone tiling still strongly rivals thatched roof. ▶ Romanesque churches at **Saint-Julien-Chapteuil,** musée Jules Romains *(Jul.-Aug. on request tel. 71.08.70.14)* and **Saint-Pierre-Eynac.**

MONISTROL-SUR-LOIRE

C2-3 / pop. 5 438 (Haute-Loire)

This former secondary residence of the bishops of Puy 2 km from the Loire River is now a little industrial township in the development area of Saint-Étienne. Romanesque church enlarged in the 17thC; former 17thC episcopal château *(hospice)*; with its old gardens form a terrace above the gorges of the Bilhard (waterfalls; views over the Loire Valley). □

▶ Nearby

▶ **Saint-Didier-en-Velay** *(10 km E)* : Museum of Arts and Crafts of the Massif Central (collection of wheels and ploughs; *Jul.-Aug., 3-6; closed Mon.).* ▶ From **Bas-en-Basset,** climb to the ruined château of Rochebaron (14th-15thC; entrance free; view); 8 km W, the **château de Valprivas** (15th-16thC; court of honour with Italian-influenced decoration; *10-12 & 3-6).* ▶ Via **Beauzac** *(11 km SW;* Romanesque-Gothic church★) and **Retournac,** overlooking the Loire, go up the river valley to **Chamalières-sur-Loire** (Romanesque church★), and from here through **Roche-en-Régnier** to the foot of a volcanic peak surmounted by a feudal keep (view); continue N to **Chalençon★,** an ancient village on a splendid site★ with mediaeval keep, 12thC chapel, old houses, bridge from the Middle Ages; cultural activities in summer.□

MONT DORE★

A2 / ® / pop. 2 394 (Puy-de-Dôme)

The thermal springs of Mont Dore, forgotten like so many others since Roman days, began their return to fashion at the beginning of the 18thC. But this resort of repentant smokers and victims of respiratory ailments is also an important winter sports centre. The lavishly-equipped slopes at Sancy offer a wide choice of trails for skiers at all levels.

▶ The **spa★** was considerably enlarged at the end of the last century and totally renovated some years ago; it has now reached monumental proportions. Gallo-Roman ruins on view *(guided tours in season; closed Sun. and nat.*

3. Mezenc Massif

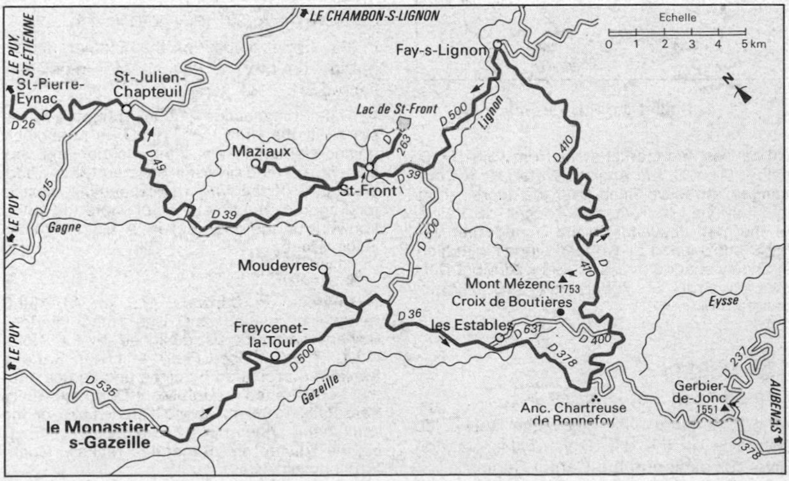

hols.). ▶ Many walks; reception room at Pic du Capucin (peak, *8 mins by cable-car and 35 mins on foot:* alt. 1 463 m; panorama★); big waterfall SE, 45 mins-1 h; waterfalls at Queureilh (site★) and Saut du Loup *(3 hr round trip).* ▶ **Puy de Sancy**★★ (S; *4 km by road, 5 mins in cable-car and 20 mins on foot);* the summit (alt. 1 886 m) is the highest in the Massif Central; fantastic view★★. □

▶ Around the Puy de Sancy *(approx 80 km; 1/2 -1 day; see map 4).*

▶ Go to La Bourboule and take the D88 to the left. ▶ Overlooking the hamlet of Vendeix-Haut is **Roche Vendeix,** a solid block of basalt with ruins of a fortress; *(access in a few minutes)* fine panoramic view. ▶ A pleasant drive down the D88; here make a rapid detour *(12 km round trip)* to the Roc Courlande (alt. 1 577 m; view) and the resort of **Chastreix-Sancy.** ▶ At **Chastreix,** Gothic church (13th-14thC). ▶ **Super-Besse** ® is a resort built in 1961, departure point for a cable car over the valley of Chaudefour★ to reach the Puy de la Perdrix (alt. 1 824 m; view). ▶ From the D978/D149 crossroads there are excursions to **Lake Pavin★,** one of the most typical circular crater lakes in the Auvergne, surrounded by steep basalt walls below the Puy de Montchal (alt. 1 411 m; *30 mins;* wide view); at **Notre-Dame-de-Vassivière** *(10 km round trip),* a chapel of 1515 with a Black Virgin, still an important centre of pilgrimage *(2 Jul. and Sun. after 21 Sep.).* ▶ **Besse-en-Chandesse** (pop. 1 860) ® : a dairy-farming centre : Saint-Nectaire cheese is made here) and a winter and summer resort; church★ with Romanesque nave and figured capitals; market building; old château; Rue de la Boucherie with

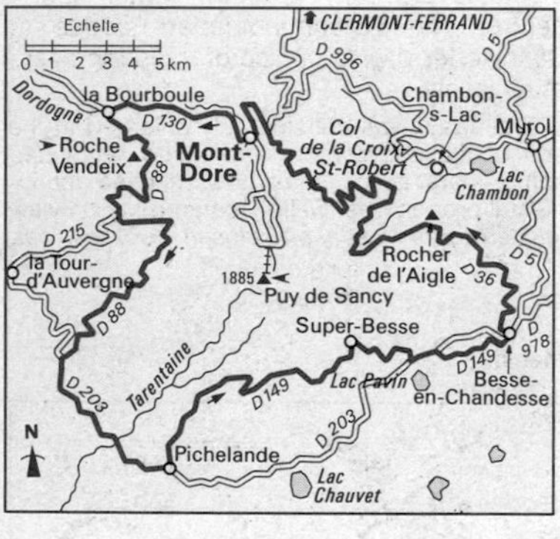

4. Round the Puy de Sancy

old houses and market stalls from 15th-16thC; belfry; 3 km S, the Anglard Waterfall. ▶ **Courbanges,** attractive lintels over the doors; shortly after, view★ from the Rocher de l'Aigle. ▶ The road descends to the **Chaudefour Valley★,** surrounded by wooded slopes with high, strangely-shaped peaks. ▶ Back to Mont Dore over the Croix St. Robert Pass (alt. 1 425 m; panorama★). □

MURAT

A3 / ® / pop. 2 813 (Cantal)

A good summer base below the Rocher de Bonnevie on the left bank of the Alagnon River for exploring the Cantal Region.

▶ **Maison Rodier** (16thC) and **Maison Tallandier** (15thC) in the heart of the old town; in the neighbouring church (15thC, remodelled) is a Black Virgin, said to have been brought back from Palestine by Louis IX. ▶ NW, the **Rocher de Bonnevie** *(30-min climb)* is the pedestal for a colossal cast-iron Virgin; view★ over the town and valley. ▶ From the opposite side of the valley, **Bredons** *(1 hr round trip; 2.5 km road)* has a lovely site★ for its church★ on a turf-covered terrace; Romanesque edifice, Renaissance stalls, Baroque altarpiece and a small treasure room. □

▶ Nearby

▶ **Château de Massebeau,** with two principal buildings flanked by machicolated towers (with openings for dropping molten lead, stones, etc.) and roofed in stone *(20 Jul.-end Aug., 10-12 & 2-4).* ▶ Château d'Anterroches, 15thC keep overlooking the Lioran road. ▶ **Dienne** *(10 km N)* is a robust mountain village on one of the roads to Peyrol Passe (→ Mauriac, Puy Mary circuit); remarkable capitals with *naïf* carvings bear witness to a vigorous popular art; the church also houses a strikingly realistic 13thC wooden Christ figure. ▶ Magnificent view★ over Murat from Laveissenet *(6 km S).* □

MUROL

A2 / ® / pop. 624 (Puy-de-Dôme)

The château★ (14th-15thC), an irregular dodecahedron, is mounted on a basalt formation; muted, red-hued lava blocks used in its construction add to the romantic ambience of this ruin *(Jun.-Sep. 10-12 & 2-7; Sun. only low season).* □

▶ Nearby

▶ **Lake Chambon** *(2 km SW),* a marvellous 140-acre lake with beach bordered by meadows and pine woods. Above to N, the Dent du Marais, a sheer cliff face, also called the Saut de la Pucelle (Virgin's Leap). ▶ **Chambon-sur-Lac** ®, little Romanesque church partly buried by silt from the Couze River. ▶ Mont Dore (→). ▶ Saint-Nectaire (→). □

ORCIVAL★★

A2 / ® / pop. 381 (Puy-de-Dôme)

In the upper valley of the Sioulet, stock-rearing country; a key site for mediaeval sacred art.

▶ The Romanesque (12thC) **church★★,** restored in the 15thC and 19thC, is remarkably homogeneous; inside, light, slender and very elegant, a seated silver-gilt covered 12thC wooden statue of the Virgin★★; beautiful capitals (one figured); enormous crypt; note the 13thC ironwork on the door leaves. ▶ Gothic houses in the village. □

▶ Nearby

▶ **Château de Cordès★** *(2.5 km N),* 15thC remodelled in the 17thC with 18thC interiors. Bowers and arbours designed by Le Nôtre *(10-12 & 2-6; closed Feb.).* ▶ 11 km S, **Lake Servière** surrounded by pines and spruce. Farther south on the road to Mont-Dore, the **Guéry Pass** (alt. 1 264 m) above Guéry Lake of the same name; 500 m away : viewpoint overlooking the **Tuilière and Sanadoire rocks★,** gigantic phonolitic dykes. □

■ Le PUY★★★

C3 / ® / pop. 29 024 (Haute-Loire)

In the centre of a natural amphitheatre ringed by volcanic mountains, dotted with unusual rock formations, each serving as the pedestal for a statue or monument, Le Puy, capital of the Velay area, is foremost a religious centre, owing its origins to an important Marian Order pilgrimage.

▶ The **Place du Breuil** (AB3) is the heart of the modern town, with cafés, a market and municipal offices; S is Vinay. ▶ At the rear of the garden is the **Crozatier Museum** (A3) : archaeology, fine arts, regional arts and traditions; above all, see the lace room★; *(10-12 & 2-4 or 6; closed Tue. and Feb.).* ▶ The old town still has many **mediaeval Gothic and Renaissance houses :** don't miss (B2) Rues Porte-Aiguière, Chaussade, du Collège, Pannessac and others. ▶ The **cathedral★★** (11th-12thC) is an exceptional building, with cupolas over the nave and bold construction : the steep street (actually a stairway) passes right under the church, between doorways with 12thC leaves. Note 13thC frescos; 11thC frescos in the left transept and the gallery; in a relics chapel *(visit with* **Cloister** *daily ex Tue., 9-12 & 2-6)* is a large 15thC fresco; the room next door is the treasure room. Romanesque **cloister★★** *(same hours).* The Porche du For★ overlooks the square of the same name from the right transept (view over the town), beside the 16thC bishop's palace. From the left transept, the Porche St. Jean leads to an 11thC baptistry adjoining the prior's house. ▶ N of the cathedral, the chapel of the Penitents (coffered painted ceiling, 1630; important pictures by local painters, 18thC). ▶ **Corneille Rock** (B1), 130 m above the Place du Breuil offers a good view of the town and its environs *(9 or 10 to 5,6,7 or 8; closed Tue. low season and Dec.-Jan., ex school hols. and Sun. pm);* the view from the crown of an enormous statue of Notre Dame de France (1860) is equal. ▶ A little way out of the centre, the 14th-15thC **Gothic church of St. Laurent** (A1); nearby the **Centre d'Initiation à la Dentelle de Puy** (lacemakers at work, exhibition; *week days only).* ▶ Perched on an 85-m volcanic dyke is the 10th-12thC **church of St. Michel d'Aiguilhe★** (B1); with a polychrome façade★ of Eastern inspiration *(9 or 10-12 & 2-6 or 7, ex. Christmas and 1 Jan., 15 Mar.-Oct.; winter school hols., pm only);* important fragments of paintings, probably 10thC. □

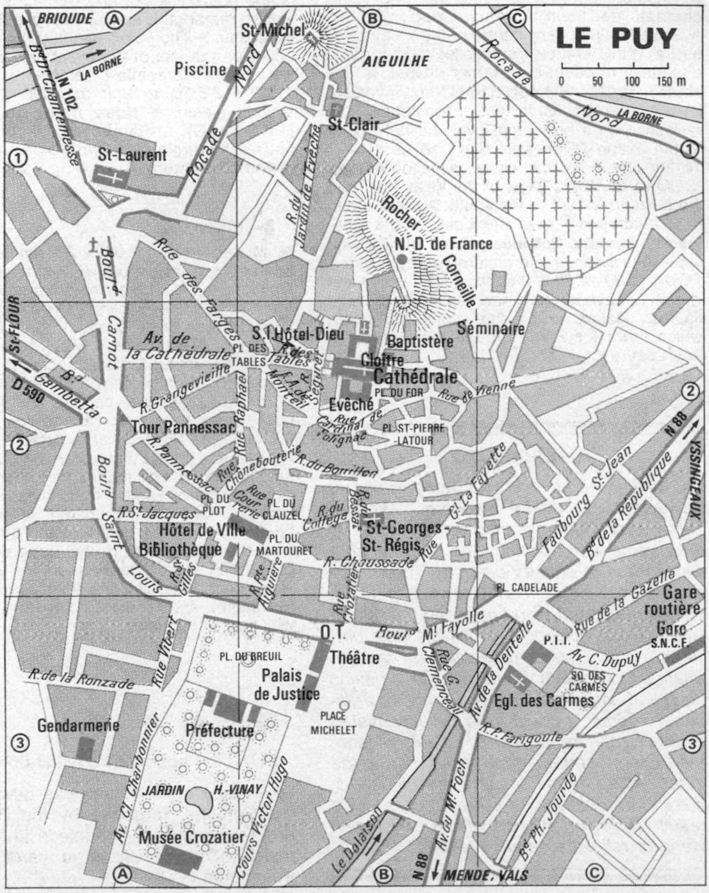

▶ Nearby

▶ **Espaly Saint-Marcel** *(1.5 km W)* is dominated by two volcanic rock formations one of which bears the remains of a château and the other a number of pious but unattractive constructions, and a gigantic statue of St. Joseph *(entry fee;* diorama); from the terrace, view of Le Puy and the basalt colonnades known as the **Orgues d'Espaly.** ▶ SW of Puy, basalt **Mons Plateau,** with steep flanks partially enclosed by a loop of the Loire River. Near **Coubon,** the châteaux de **Volhac** *(15 Jun.-15 Sep., 2-8; closed Tue.)* and the **Daniel Tower,** a 14thC square keep to which has been added a Renaissance *logis (Jul.-Sep., Tue., Wed., Thu. 4-6);* 3.5 km S, the château de Poinsac (16th-18thC); return to Puy via **Bouzols** (another château, 12th-13thC, partially in ruins). ▶ **Saint-Germain-Laprade** *(11 km),* little Romanesque church with fortified bell-tower. □

▶ Around the châteaux of Velay *(50 km; approx half day)*

▶ At **Polignac,** on an enormous flat-topped basalt formation, reinforced by a 13thC wall, rest the remains of a 14thC château★ *(May-Sep., 9:30 or 10-12 & 2-5:30 or 7),* powerful keep 32-m high (view★); church partially Romanesque, 12th and 14thC frescos; 3 km E: 16thC fortified house at **Cheyrac** with curious painted decoration *(high season, by appt.).* ▶ Another imposing fortress, the 14th-16thC **château de Saint-Vidal** *(Jul.-Aug., 4-6:30).* ▶ **Saint-Paulien,** early centre of the Velay area, has a 12thC church, remodelled and fortified and small museum in a former chapel. ▶ The **château de Rochelambert** (16thC) sober volcanic rock structure, is, in fact, a romantic 16thC residence on a pretty site over the right bank of the Borne River *(Mar.-Sep., 10-12 & 4-6);* 14 km NW, from the castle ruins of **Allègre** *"Gallows of Allègre"* view of the Velay Mts. and the Mézenc Massif to the south. ▶ On a steep rock outcropping over the Loire is the **château de Lavoûte-Polignac** (rebuilt 19thC), with superb furnishings and picture gallery *(Easter-1 Nov.; 9:30-12:30 & 2-6:30);* 1 km farther, the church of **Lavoûte-sur-Loire** has a 13thC Christ figure★. Return to Le Puy along the Loire, which flows for 9 km through the **Gorges of Peyredeyre★.** □

Lacemaking

The delicate craft made its appearance in Puy and Velay during the 16thC. Women began very young, working with a needle or on a frame with bobbins. The craft became widespread in country districts. The manufacturer, a businessman in town, organised the distribution of work, provided the thread (linen, wool, silk, gold or silver) and patterns, which were renewed as fashion changed. Although underpaid, lacemaking played an important economic role as additional income; it could even be essential in times of scarcity. No doubt for this reason, the trade prospered in the region during the 17thC, aided by the Jesuit, François Régis, a stubborn defender of social causes; as a result, an important part of the production went for religious ornamentation.

■ RIOM★

B1 / ® / pop. 18901 (Puy-de-Dôme)

Riom holds itself aloof on its butte like a magistrate in court; lofty facades and monumental fountains recall the past of this city of lawyers, sculpted into the sombre stone of Volvic, black as the rich soil of the Limagne plains.

▶ **The church of St. Amable,** heavily restored, has a nave and transept in the purest Auvergne Romanesque style, and a Gothic choir; in the sacristy are wooden panelling from 1687 and a collection of chasubles. ▶ In the **Rue de l'Horloge** there are a number of old *hôtels particuliers* (private mansions; 3,7,15,19,21,28,22,20,4); note No.12, the **Hôtel Guimoneau★** *(closed Sun. and Aug.)* the staircase of which is decorated with an Annunciation; opposite is a Gothic and Renaissance belfry. ▶ In the Rue de l'Hôtel de Ville are other mansions (**Maison des Consuls★,** 1527) and the Hôtel de Ville (town hall; 18thC restored). The 1st floor houses a small museum *(week days only).* ▶ The **Mandet Museum,** in a 17thC mansion *(daily ex Tue., 10-12 & 2-4:30 or 5:30),* is principally devoted to painting (Flemish and Dutch schools; 17thC Italian and Spanish; 18thC French). ▶ The **Auvergne Museum** *(same hours; closed end Oct.-early Nov.)* provides a remarkable exhibition of popular arts and traditions. ▶ The *Palais de Justice* (Law Courts) occupies the site of the ducal palace, of which the **Sainte Chapelle★** remains (14thC; *10-11:30 & 2-5:30, ex Sun. and nat. hols.;* 15thC stained glass). ▶ **Notre Dame du Marthuret** (14th-15thC) : Flamboyant Gothic *façade* houses a "Virgin with Bird"★★, a masterpiece of 14thC sculpture. □

▶ Nearby

▶ **Mozac** (pop : 3080, *1.5 km W)* has an interesting abbey church★ (Romanesque nave, Gothic choir and transept), particularly good figured capitals★★ and a treasure room★ (12thC shrine of St. Cadmin); 2 km farther, the church at **Marsat** has a Black Virgin★ of the 12thC. ▶ 9 km E : 11th-12thC church★ at **Ennezat** stands as a prototype of Romanesque art in the Auvergne (see capitals and 15thC frescos). From here you can go for a walk in the **Limagne** Plain, an area carpeted with alluvial silt, and so flat that water flows very slowly among willows and populars; a sharp contrast with the nearby ragged mountains. **Maringues,** partially Romanesque church, lovely wooden tanneries★ on the banks of the Morge; view over the Limagne from the Butte de Montgaçon. Push on to **Randan** on the edge of a fine forest, returning via **Villeneuve-les-Cerfs** (dovecote) and **Thuret;** 11th-12thC church★ with figured capitals. □

■ ROYAT

B1-2 / ® / pop. 4094 (Puy-de-Dôme)

Like many spas, Royat was developed by the Romans, forgotten by the Barbarians and resurrected by Napoléon III during the mid-19thC. Specialises in cardio-vascular treatments.

Where do all the bilberries go?

Although other regions of France claim myrtilles - *known to English-speakers as bilberries, blueberries, whortleberries, huckleberries and so on - as their local speciality, in the Auvergne their production has always been regarded as an essential factor of the rural economy. Several hundred tons of* myrtilles *are picked each year : Courtière, not far from Thiers, has specialised in the distribution of these succulent little berries, which have the advantage of growing almost everywhere without any special attention. Their abundance encourages casual picking and use as a culinary extra by the local population. A large part of the production is exported to Switzerland, Germany and Britain.* Myrtilles *are also widely used in the pharmaceutical industry (opthalmology, circulatory disorders) and, of course, in jams.*

▶ Pleasant walks in the **Parc Thermal** (spa), typical architecture. Nearby, the **Grotte du Chien** (Dog's Grotto) *(15 Apr.-Sep., 9-12 & 2-6)*... but don't take your dog - there's a layer of carbon dioxide close to the ground and it won't get enough air. ▶ Uphill, the old town stands around the **church★** (12thC, fortified 13thC) built onto a priory (much remodelled); 10thC crypt. ▶ 150 m along on the banks of the Tiretaine River, a **stonecutter's workshop** *(mid-Jun.-Sep., 9:30-12 & 2-6; closed Sun. and nat. hols.).* □

▶ Nearby

▶ Walks through three gorges opening W on the Royat Valley. ▶ The best excursion is to **Puy de Dôme★★** ® *(6-km toll road),* on whose flanks the ruins of a Gallo-Roman Temple of Mercury have been unearthed. The summit (alt. 1 465 m), highest peak in the chain of the Puys, towers nearly 1 000 m over Clermont; vast and unrivalled panorama★★★. Close by, information office of Volcans d'Auvergne regional nature park (*15 Jun.-15 Sep., daily 10-12:30 & 2:30-7;* exhibitions). □

■ SAINT-CERNIN

A3 / pop. 1 271

On the slopes above the Doire River, a large village very typical of the Cantal area; Romanesque church with massive wall-belfry; in the choir, 15thC wood panelling and stalls. □

▶ Nearby

▶ **Château d'Anjony★** *(7.5 km E),* 15thC with high keep comprised of four towers close together; at the foot, graceful 17thC addition. *(Palm Sunday-1 Nov., 2-6:30)*; frescos in **Tournemire** church. ▶ **Saint-Chamant** *(10.5 km NE)* has beautiful painted 15thC stalls★ in its church; 17th-18thC château with 15thC keep *(15 Jun.-15 Sep., 9-7).* ▶ Salers (→). □

■ SAINT-FLOUR★

B3 / ® / pop. 9 148 (Cantal)

Once the capital of Haute (upper) Auvergne. The look of this old town with its fortress-like presence, perched on a basalt terrace 100 m above the valley of the Lander, confirms the pride felt by inhabitants who willingly proclaim themselves "the most Auvergnat of the Auvergne".

▶ Picturesque streets lined with 16thC town houses (Rue des Lacs, Rue Marchande) run from the Allées Pompidou to the Place d'Armes. ▶ 15thC **cathedral** has the dour lines of a real fortress; 17th-18thC paintings; Fragments of murals; large 13thC wooden Christ figure★, the black *Bon Dieu Noir.* ▶ In the former episcopal palace (17thC), is the Hôtel de Ville (town hall) and the **Haute Auvergne Museum** (archaeology, mediaeval art, folklore; *9-12 & 2-6; closed Sat. and Sun. Oct.-May).* ▶ Left of the cathedral, the former Maison Consulaire (16thC; *Jul.-Aug., 9-12 & 2-7)* now housing the Douet Decorative Arts Museum. □

▶ Nearby

▶ Walks through the **Lander Gorges** *(SE).* ▶ **Sailhant Waterfall** *(8 km, plus 10 mins on foot) :* at the foot of a château (restored), return via **Roffiac :** little Romanesque church★, former chapel of a château, now in ruins. ▶ **Villedieu** *(5.5 km S) :* church (1363) with handsome doorway (ironwork and knocker) and carved stalls. ▶ **Les Ternes** *(12 km SW),* 15thC church, château★ (15th-16thC, restored, *Jul.-Aug. 2-7; closed Sun.).* ▶ Many dolmens and *menhirs* on the **Planèze,** a wind-swept plateau 1 000 m above sea level. □

■ SAINT-NECTAIRE★

B2 / ® / pop. 650 (Puy-de-Dôme)

Despite the still-existing famous *fromage* called *Saint-Nectaire,* this is no longer a cheese market, but a spa (kidney treatments) linked by a string of villas and hotels to a small mountain town.

▶ **Saint-Nectaire-le-Haut :** 12thC **church★★** of modest but perfectly harmonious proportions, the epitome of Auvergnat Romanesque, with 103 capitals, including 6 with figures in the choir; remarkable treasures on view in the left transept. ▶ **Saint-Nectaire-le-Bas** looks like other spas; visit the **Fontaine pétrifiante** (fossilizing spring; *8:30-12 & 2-7 in summer; 9:30-12 & 2-6, ex Mon. low season*). □

▶ Nearby

▶ **Puy de Mazeyres** (*3 km E;* 919 m; view, especially). ▶ **Châteauneuf Caves** *(NW; 1 hr round trip)*; on the flank of the Puy also called Châteauneuf, nine artificial caves served as a fortress during the Norman invasions. ▶ **Maison de Sailles** *(1.5 km N) :* an old farm turned into a museum of domestic traditions *(daily Jul.-Aug.; pm only in Jun. and Sep.).* ▶ **Couze de Chambon Valley :** downstream by **Saillant** (waterfall) to **Montaigut-le-Blanc,** fortified town with mediaeval appearance at the foot of the ruins of a 13th-15thC château, and **Champeix★,** surrounded by vineyards, village with a profusion of old houses (see the upper town or *Marchidial*). ▶ Murol (→) and Lac Chambon. □

Auvergne cuisine

Auvergne culinary specialities are simple and hearty, shunning pretention. Traditional produce, regionally grown for centuries, predominates, almost as if foods imported into Europe from faraway places had not yet penetrated the Massif Central. Similarly, the culinary traditions, although differing from area to area, mostly remain solidly based on long and very gentle simmering. Thus, traditional soups (cabbage-based) and stews blend local produce, to which are added different preparations of lentils, chestnuts or mushrooms. Among the meats, charcuterie *excels :* rissoles, fricandeaux, saucissons, *and, of course, the famous Auvergne ham.* Charolais *beef is a speciality, and the celebrated cheese of Salers is another bovine product not to be missed. The delicately flavoured mutton of the region appears in dishes such as* gigot brayaude *(larded, cooked with white wine and herbs), and in* tripou d'Auvergne *made from tripes and paunch. Then, there is poultry, game in season (hare, venison, boar, pheasant, partridge, quail...) and lake fish (trout, char, even salmon — which fortunately have been protected and flourish around Langeac). However lavish your meal, it is inconceivable to skip the cheese course (→ box), nor that it should end without locally-grown fruit, possibly in a* tarte *or a* clafoutis *(flan). To eat as they do in Auvergne, remember to have some tasty rye bread with your meal, and a local wine - even if the wine list is not the equal of other regions in scope and prestige; certainly, you should try* Boudes, Châteaugay, Corent, Dallet, Madargue, *or* Saint Pourçain, *from the Allier; and finally, let us not omit the* Gentiane, *as* apéritif, *and the* Marc d'Auvergne *or* Prunelle du Velay *as a* digestif *to complete the meal.*

■ SALERS★★

A3 / ® / pop. 470 (Cantal)

On a superb site overlooking the valley of the Maronne, Salers was from the 15thC the seat of the *bailliage* (administrative region) of Haute-Auvergne. This official role made the town's fortune, and the remains of ramparts, the sober walls of volcanic rock, stone roofs and sombre doorways still give an impression of aristocratic luxury behind the facade of a country town. Whether a city the size of a village, or a village with the pretensions of a city, Salers is one of the most attractive places in the Auvergne.

▶ The **church★** (15th-16thC) in the lower town houses a polychrome Holy Sépulchre★ of 1495, two paintings attributed to the Spaniard José Ribera and five 17thC Aubusson tapestries. ▶ Among the beautiful buildings in the upper town on the **Grande-Place★** (Place Tyssandier d'Escous) and nearby, see the **Maison du Bailliage** (15thC; *10-12 & 2-6; closed Tue., Jan. and Feb.*), the **Hôtel de Bargues** (16th-17thC; *Apr.-Sep. 10-12 & 4-7; closed 5 pm in Oct.*), the **Maison de la Ronade** (end 14th-early 15thC; *visit on request*) and the **Maison des Templiers★** (*Aug., 10-12 & 2-6*; exhibition of cheesemaking and folklore). ▶ From the **Promenade de la Barouze,** 250 m above the valley of the Maronne, view★ E over the Puy Violent Peak. □

▶ Nearby

▶ Around the Puy Mary peak (→ Mauriac). ▶ Down the **valley of the Maronne :** Palemont and Saint-Martin-Valmeroux (→ tour of the Puy Mary); **Saint-Eulalie** (church); fine ruins of château de Branzac; **Saint-Christophe-les-Gorges** (site★ of Romanesque chapel of Notre-Dame-du-Château); **Saint-Martin-Cantalès** (hexagonal 12thC bell-tower); Bertrande Gorges; **Saint-Illide** (16thC woodwork in church); return via Saint-Cernin (→). □

■ SAUGUES

B3 / pop. 2 497 (Haute-Loire)

One of the strongholds of the Gévaudan region. Today this is a market town for the northern part of the Margeride Mountains (→ Cévennes) and a summer resort.

▶ **Church** with Romanesque gatetower, 12thC Virgin enthroned, 15thC *Pietà;* treasure room. ▶ Huge 12th-13thC keep, the **Tour des Anglais,** with forestry museum. Holy Thursday (Easter Week penitents' procession). □

▶ Nearby

▶ **Esplantas** *(7 km S),* pretty hill village with granite houses and ruins of a 14thC château. ▶ 28 km W, **Mont Mouchet** was a bulwark of the WWII Resistance; monument to the *Maquis* (partisans); Mont Mouchet Museum in neighbouring forester's lodge *(15 May-Oct., 9-12:30 & 1:30-8).* □

■ THIERS★

B1 / ® / pop. 16 820 (Puy-de-Dôme)

Congesting the gorges of the Durolle are factories and workshops, some old and blackened, others freshly painted, defining this town of steps and zig-zagging streets.

The cheeses of Auvergne

"Auvergne is one huge cheese-board!" exclaims a promotional poster, disputing this title with France itself! For good reason : Cantal *(fresh or aged), especially from Salers, the blue-veined* bleu d'Auvergne *and* fourme d'Ambert *(taking its name from the moulds used to shape the cheese) and the smooth and creamy* Saint-Nectaire *are known to all gourmets. Other names should be added to these well-known cows-milk cheeses :* fourme de Montbrison, fourme de Saint-Anthème, Saingorlon, Murol, *and* Gaperon à l'ail *(with garlic), as well as a number of goats-milk cheeses such as* Cabecou, *from the Salers and Aurillac areas.*

Thiers has for centuries provided France's eating implements (70% of the national production, one-quarter for export).

▶ A few old houses in the Rue Conchette, leading to the **Terrasse du Rempart** (B3; panorama★). ▶ More old houses in the Rue du Bourg and the **Place du Pirou**; see Maison (also called Château) du Pirou (15thC, restored; SI); temporary exhibitions on local history and folklore; No.11 on the street of the same name, the *Maison des Sept Péchés Capitaux* (House of the Seven Deadly Sins). ▶ In the Rue de la Coutellerie★ see No. 12 and 14; at No. 21, known as *La Maison de l'Homme de Bois* ("The Wooden Man's House", 15thC), knife-grinding and polishing workshops have been reconstituted as an annex to the **Maison des Couteliers**★ (Cutlery House No.58, *Jun.-Sep. daily ex Sun., 10-12 & 2-6:30; Oct.-May, daily ex Sun. and Mon., 2-6)*. Workshops and large collections of cutlery and associated tableware. ▶ Church of St. Genès (11thC, much restored) has 12thC frescos in the choir and cupola. ▶ From the church of St. Roch to the church at Le Moûtier (A4; 12thC; disfigured 19thC; capitals★), go down the **Durolle Valley**★, with a number of series of factories exploiting the many falls in the river. □

▶ Nearby

▶ **Saint-Rémy-sur-Durolle** *(8.5 km NE)* near a pool in a lovely location★. ▶ **Château d'Aulteribe** *(14 km SW)*, an old mediaeval house "enriched" in the 19thC with troubadour decorations; good collections *(9 or 10-12 & 2-5 or 6, daily; closed Tue.)*. ▶ **Courpière** *(15 km S)* : Romanesque Virgin★ and Holy Sepulchre in the 15thC church; 2.5 km N, **château de la Barge** (16th-18thC; *early Jul.-end Sep., 2-5)*; 7 km NE, **Vollore Ville,** an old town on a fine site★ : 17thC château in the shadow of a 12thC keep, housing souvenirs of Lafayette and the American War of Independence *(Jul.-5 Sep., 2-7)*. ▶ **Lezoux** ® *(16 km W)*, an important ceramics centre during the Gallo-Roman period; traces of more than 200 kilns; municipal ceramics museum *(Jul.-Aug. 2:30-6 ex Mon.; open Sun. and Mon. Easter-Whitsun; Sun. only Jun. and 1-15 Sep.)*; very rich collection, including the Mithras Vase★. □

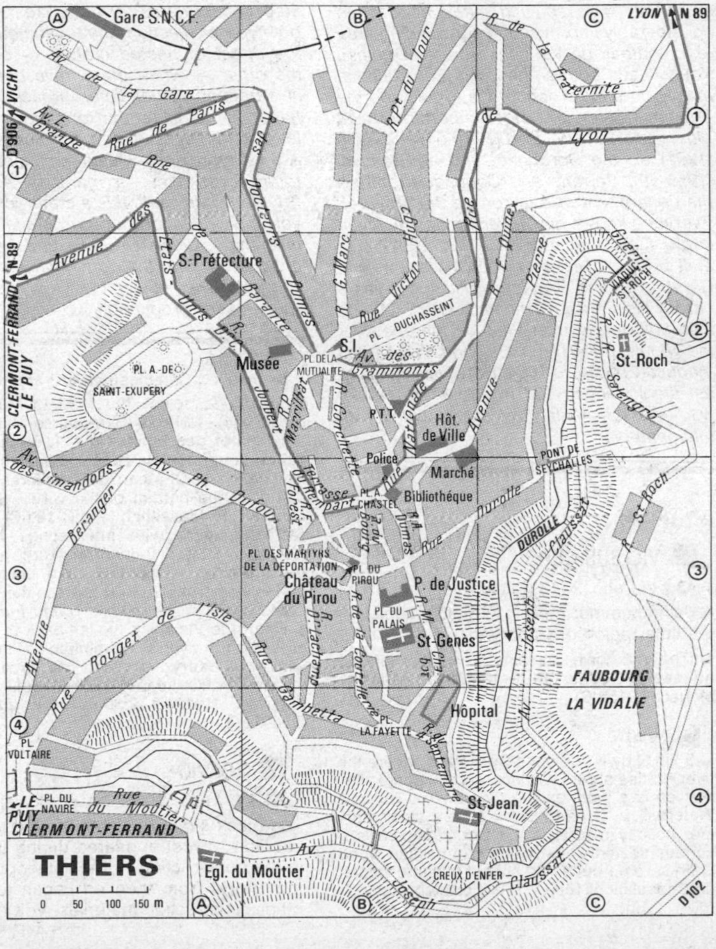

■ VIC-LE-COMTE

B2 / ® / pop. 3 787 (Puy-de-Dôme)

In a region of hillocks where the Allier River winds through the Limagne Plain; Middle Ages stronghold and capital of the County of Auvergne.

▶ **Sainte Chapelle★,** built in 1510, serves as the choir of a 19thC church; Italian altarpiece of 1520, 17thC stalls and a painting on wood from the 15thC. □

▶ Nearby

▶ Imposing dimensions of ruined **château de Buron** *(5 km S).* ▶ **Château de Montfleury** *(2 km N)* : large 13th-18thC country mansion (furniture; collection of horse-drawn carriages; *15 Jun.-15 Sep. 10-12 & 2-7*); 4 km farther on, 12thC **château de Busséol** *(15 Jun.-15 Sep.; 10-12 & 2-7)*; view★ over the area. □

Dams and bridges in Auvergne

! *From the 19thC on, it was evident that the valleys slicing into the Auvergne countryside were ideal for hydroelectric projects; some say the resulting lakes have often considerably improved the surrounding area (e.g. château de Val near Bort-les-Orgues). You will see both arched and gravity dams, mainly on the Dordogne, the Sioule and the Truyère rivers : the most important are at Marèges (1931-35), Bort (1946-54) and Aigle (1951) on the Dordogne, and at Grandval (1955-59), Sarrans and Couesque (both in the department of Aveyron on the Truyère). Everyone knows his Tower; but many fewer know that Gustav Eiffel (1832-1923) also built bridges. His best known viaduct is at Garabit, on the Truyère, built some years before his Parisian landmark (1882-84). He also built the Rouzat Viaduct, the one over the Sioule (Allier) in 1869, and the Tardes Viaduct (Creuse) in 1884. However, the highest steel viaduct, 132 m above the Sioule, was built by Vialard at the beginning of this century.*

■ VIC-SUR-CÈRE

A3 / ® / pop. 2 113 (Cantal)

A rising summer resort; long ago, capital of the little region of Carladès.

▶ The old town contains a number of **old houses** including that of the Princes of Monaco★ (15thC). □

▶ Nearby

▶ 3 km N by N122 is the **Cère Pass,** where the river hurtles abruptly from a narrow gorge; farther on is a path leading *(30 mins)* to Roucole Waterfall. ▶ **Thiézac** *(6 km N)* is a small summer holiday resort; in the Gothic church is a curious seated Christ figure★ in painted wood (16thC); on a butte, the chapel of Notre-Dame-de-Consolation (16thC; 17thC painted vaulting). □

Hot baths and volcanos

The Auvergne is a truly spectacular region, shaped in the fierce volcanic activity of the tertiary era after the shock of the geological upheaval which created the Alps. Several volcanic massifs piled on top of each other over some 30 million years; the gigantic mass of the Cantal, which is, in fact, an enormous, eroded volcanic cone, probably reached 75 km in circumference and some 3 000-m high. The next act was the appearance of the Dore, Cézallier and Aubrac peaks and those of Mégal and Mézenc of Velay, some 12 million years ago. The second phase of the phenomenon, which, comparatively speaking, occurred only yesterday, was relatively minor in size; the Devès chain, and the Puys (or Dômes) developed during the quarternary era some 50 000 years ago, in a burst of volcanic activity which continued until about 5 000 BC, resulting in a chain 30-km long from north to south and 3 to 4 km wide. But the Puy is not ordinary volcano; the giant of the chain, it is a massive pyramid dominating some 60 extinct craters. Volcanos like this, Stromboli-type or ejection cones, sometimes give the effect of nested craters — one inside the other — when there have been several eruptions; other times breached craters have split to allow the formation of rugged lava fields spreading over several miles. A third type, solid-walled explosion craters, today form lakes, or marshes. As for the Puy de Dôme itself, it is a crater-less Pelean volcano which produced "domite", a clear lava that solidified rapidly and here accumulated to form the dome, while elsewhere characteristic volcanic dykes, necks or spines were produced.

▶ Around Carladès *(65 km; approx 3 h)*

▶ From Vic, follow the road to Mur-de-Barrez (D 54). ▶ From Curebourse Pass, up to the **Rocher des Pendus** (alt. 1 068 m; view★). ▶ **Jou-sous-Monjou,** Romanesque church with wall-belfry. ▶ **Château de Cropières★,** dilapidated, at the bottom of the valley. ▶ But the **château de Messilhac** (14thC-16thC) is in perfect condition, with interestings furnishing (Jul.-early Sep., 2-6:30) ▶ Turn around to reach **Carlat** at the foot of a basalt formation★ once crowned by a fortress that was later razed by Henri IV *(20-min round trip)*; view★. ▶ Return to Vic along the left bank of the Cère, crossing the river at **Polminhac :** 12thC church with wall-belfry; château de Pesteils with square 14thC keep★ (14thC-15thC frescos; *Jul.-Aug. 10-12 & 2:30-6; May, Jun., Sep., 2:30-5:30*). □

■ VOLVIC

B1 / ® / pop. 3 936 (Puy-de-Dôme)

The black stone of Volvic is hard and solid, yet light; it first appeared during the 13thC in the construction of the cathedral at Clermont, and from then on began to replace other construction materials. Volvic became the major source of building stone, hence the rather severe appearance of towns in the vicinity.

▶ The **Maison de la Pierre** (Stone House), at the entrance to underground quarries, displays the volcanic origins of Volvic rock (andesite) and the often wretched lives of the quarry workers of former times, together with uses of the quarried stone *(guided tours every 45 mins; 10-11:30 & 2:15-6; closed Tue., 15 Mar.-15 Nov.; take warm clothing).* ▶ Nearby, bottling plant for Volvic mineral water *(May-Sep.; 9-12 & 2:30-6:30; closed Sun. and Mon. am and nat. hols.).* ▶ Romanesque choir with ambulatory in the church. Capitals★. ▶ From the town hall, 20-min ascent to Notre-Dame-de-la-Garde (panorama★). From here, a good path *(20 mins, or 2 km by road from the town)* leads to the **château de Tournoël**★★ (13thC), dismantled by Cardinal Richelieu; pretty 15thC turreted staircase, chapel, keep, superb cylindrical tower 32-m high (marvellous view; *Easter-Oct., 9-12 & 2-7; closed Tue.).* ▶ Near Les Goulots *(1.2 km after the station, which is 6 km from Volvic)* : the **Maison du Miel**★ (Honey House) shows the life of a bee-keeper *(May-Sep. 2-6:30 daily; Sun. only 2-5:30 rest of year).* ▶ 7 km SE, **Châteaugay,** dominated by a powerful square keep★ of the château (14th-16thC; *10-12 & 2-7*); tasting of Côtes d'Auvergne wines). □

YSSINGEAUX

C3 / ® / pop. 6718 (Haute-Loire)

A modest town that lives from meat-curing and sub-contracting for industries in the Saint-Étienne area.

▶ The town hall occupies the Former Gothic (14thC) living quarters of a old château. ▶ W, a 922 m butte provides a view over the area *(15-min walk).* □

▶ Nearby

▶ **Puy de Glavenas** *(6 km, plus 15 mins on foot)* : a flat-topped-mountain; 2 km NE, the château de Mortessagne (15thC). ▶ **Versilhac** *(9 km NE),* museum of local and art traditions *(Jul.-Aug.; 2:30-6; closed Tue.);* nearby, two dams on the Lignon (view★ from Lavalette), which source of Saint-Étienne's water supply. ▶ E, pleasant summer resorts in unspoiled countryside : **Montfaucon-en-Velay, Saint-Bonnet-le-Froid** ®, **Tence** ® and **Le Chambon-sur-Lignon** ® : (arts and crafts museum : agricultural tools and *techniques; Jul.-Aug., Mon.-Fri. 3-6, Sat.-Sun. 2-6; closed Tue.*). ▶ S, the **Massif du Meygal,** bristling with volcanic cones and dykes. Their clear-cut silhouettes overlook lava-shingled roofs of the little villages; leaving the forest, there is a view from the peak of Grand Testavoyre, (alt. 1436 m); more spectacular the view from **Queyrières**★★. □

● Architecture

Building materials in the Auvergne Region are usually schist (layered rock) or sandstone, but very often, especially near Volvic or Fontfreyde, dark lava, and from area-to-area a grey, brown or red-hued somewhat crystalline stone. *Torchis* — cob, or mud-

Near Brioude

wall construction — is seldom found. ● Houses, rarely isolated are generally loosely clustered in villages and hamlets. They usually face southeast, where possible protected by a fold in the ground or a curtain of trees, and near a water supply. In the coldest districts, if exterior protection is wanting, the most exposed wall is often backed on the inside with one of a loose drystone.● The chimney is always an important element, heating the *oustau,* or living room;

In the Haut-Loire region

the hearth is enormous, often large enough to allow a man to stand upright. Windows are small and generally on the least exposed side of the house. ● Another form of insulation is provided by locating the living quarters above ground level, with access by a staircase.● Roofs are steeply pitched in the

In South Cantal

high country, becoming flatter at lower altitudes, especially on the southern slopes of the Massif Central. Here, hollow tile replaces the flat kind, and the more traditional stone or thatched roofing gives way to less-vulnerable slate. ● Although there is a certain similarity in construction, local variants are more frequent further away from the central mountains, taking on the character-

"Jasserie" in the Puy-de-Dôme region

istics of other regions at the borders of the Auvergne. ● Finally, there are many isolated shepherds' cottages, usually single-storey with tiny windows and doorways, such as the *jasseries* of the Puy de Dôme, and the *burons* where cheese is made in Cantal or the Forez. The latter are simply built because they are used only seasonally.

Near Murat

Brief regional history

Up to 1stC BC. There was human life in the Auvergne Region even before the Cantal volcano became extinct, apparently going back some two million years. The Chilhac deposits (near Brioude, Haute-Loire), appear contemporary with the middle Villafranchian epoch; the largest palaeolithic deposits in the Auvergne date, however, from the **Magdalenian era** (15 000-8 000 BC). ● The **Neolithic era** (megaliths) was succeeded by the various **metal-working periods,** during which the **Celtic invasions** occurred. ● Towards 800 BC the **Arvernes** - pastoral nomads - settled the plains of the Allier River and neighbouring mountains. Their dominance rapidly extended from the Rhine to the Atlantic, and in 124 BC they annexed the territory of the *Vellaves* (Velay). But this was the Arvernian Empire's last effort. For in 121 BC King Bituit was defeated by the Roman armies, and the resistance of Vercingetorix, culminating in the victory of the Gallic cavalry at Gergovie before Bituit's final defeat at Alesia, was not sufficient to save the Gauls from Roman domination.

1st-5thC **Rome** attached Auvergne to the **Province of Aquitaine,** and immediately began to build roads and baths; agricultural development was encouraged, and Lezoux became an important producer of ceramics. ● Toward the middle of the 3rdC, Christian colonies came to be established in urban centres, notably Austremoine, Nectaire, Mary, Genès, Florus and Julien. Although the invasion of the Visigoths widely spread the Arian heresy, Christianity and the long-standing influence of Roman civilisation retained its hold, largely due to personalities such as Sidonius Apollinaris, man-of-letters and Bishop of Clermont (where he died in 487).

6th-13thC However, despite its nominal attachment to the Duchy of Aquitaine under both Frankish and Carolingian rule, Auvergne was fragmented by private wars between warrior overlords, each with his fortress or other stronghold. **Churches and monasteries** continued to prosper and the poor sought their protection. Influential religious figures include Gerbert, former monk at Aurillac, who became Pope Sylvester II in 999; Robert de Turlande, who introduced Benedictine rule in 1043, later to have immense influence, and Urban II, who urged the First Crusade at the Council of Clermont in 1095. This period (11th-12thC) also saw the major achievements of **Auvergnat Romanesque architecture** (→ box). In 1169, the Bishop of Puy became Count of Velay, to the detriment of Guillaume d'Auvergne. ● The King of France supported the power of the church, benefitting from it to establish his influence in the region, and eventually uniting the County of Auvergne with the French crown, under Philippe Auguste. ● The bourgeoisie at this period grew rich from the wool trade, and during the 12th and 13thC obtained a number of communal charters giving them limited local autonomy.

14th-17thC

Toward the middle of the 14thC, during the Hundred Years' War, the "Black Death" - bubonic plague - brought a **new wave of desolation.** Jean, Duke of Berry (1340-1416), uncle of King Charles VI (1380-1422), received the Auvergne and made Riom one of his sumptuous residences. However, the province fell prey to pillaging by English soldiers and various irregulars who roamed the country during the Hundred Years' War; the exactions of these mercenaries led to the revolt of the Tuchins (1378-85), put down by the Duke of Berry. The Duke's heiress married Jean de Bourbon, whose family kept the Auvergne for over a century until the treason of the constable Charles III in 1527, and the return of the province to the crown. ● From the end of 15thC with the uneasy return of peace, there had been a slow move toward economic growth : cutlery at Thiers, fulling mills at Saint-Flour and Aurillac and lace in the towns of Velay. This renewal of trade benefitted the bourgeoisie, whose interests were upheld by the crown as a check on the ambitions of the nobility. ● Around 1530, the introduction of the **Protestant Reformation** began to make its influence felt dramatically at all levels of society. Henri IV and the Edict of Nantes calmed matters for a while, but the regency of Marie de Médicis brought a return to religious intolerance. Additionally, the increase in taxes during the Thirty Years' War led to popular uprisings; and because Richelieu was not effective in quelling disturbances in the area, Louis XIV held the *Grands Jours d'Auvergne* in 1665-66, during which the parliament in Paris, from which the Auvergne parliament derived its authority, reorganised affairs of the region.

18th-20thC

Despite good management by royal adminstrators Auvergne underwent a period of general shortages at the beginning of the 18thC; overpopulation in the mountain regions led to temporary emigration to other parts of France. Politically, the **French Revolution and the Empire** found little enthusiasm in the Auvergne Region, where the mountains became the natural refuge of non-conformists. ● At the time of the restoration of the monarchy in 1814, daily life in the Auvergne was characterised by the privileged position held by local dignitaries in a society which remained largely rural and agricultural, despite a number of industrialised localities such as Thiers and Clermont-Ferrand, where a rubber products factory was established in 1832. ● By the time of Napoleon III and the **Second Empire** (1852), labour was beginning to emigrate definitively from the region. The phylloxera blight which wiped out the vineyards of the province aggravated the situation, and, despite the popularity of spas and thermal waters (for fashionable as well as medicinal reasons), emigration rose to a level which the increasing industrialisation of other areas was not able to absorb. ● After World War I, which again reduced available agricultural manpower, then the crisis years of the 1930's, the 20thC began to offer hope to this impoverished region : electrification schemes on the Truyère and in the upper Dordogne rivers, the creation in 1964 of the *Société pour la mise en valeur de l'Auvergne et du Limousin.* Since the presidencies of Auvergne natives Georges Pompidou and Valéry Giscard d'Estaing, serious efforts have been made to break the region's isolation by pushing a motorway network through to Clermont-Ferrand, and opening of new airport at Aulnat.

Practical information

The region

Information : *Comité régional du Tourisme* (C.R.T.), 45, av. Julien, B.P. 395, 63011 Clermont-Ferrand Cedex, ☎ 73.93.04.03. **Cantal** : *Comité départemental du Tourisme Cantalien* (C.D.T.), Préfecture, 15000 Aurillac, ☎ 71.48.53.54. **Haute-Loire** : *Comité Départemental du Tourisme* (C.D.T.), Hôtel du Département, av. Charles-de-Gaulle, 43000 Le Puy, ☎ 71.09.26.05. **Puy-de-Dôme** : *Comité départemental du Tourisme et du Thermalisme,* 69, bd Gergovia, 63038 Clermont-Ferrand Cedex, ☎ 73.93.84.80. *Direction Régionale du Temps Libre, Jeunesse et Sports,* 8, pl. de Regensburg, 63000 Clermont-Ferrand, ☎ 73.35.09.56. In Paris : *Maison de l'Auvergne,* 194 *bis,* rue de Rivoli, 75001, ☎ 42.61.82.38.

Bookings : *Loisirs-Accueil Cantal,* B.P. 8, 15000 Aurillac, ☎ 71.48.53.54.

Maps : *Michelin,* nos 73, 76, 91, 1/200 000. *I.G.N.* nos 42, 43, 48, 49, 50, 57, 58, 59, 1/100 000.

Local and regional press : *l'Éveil de la Haute-Loire, la Montagne, le Progrès Renouveau.*

S.O.S. : **Cantal** : *SAMU,* Emergency Medical Service, ☎ 71.48.45.45 and 17. **Haute-Loire** : *Samu* : 71.02.02.02. **Puy-de-Dôme** : *S.M.U.R.,* 73.27.33.33. *Poisoning Emergency Centre* : Clermont-Ferrand, ☎ 73.27.33.33.

Weather forecast : **Cantal** : ☎ 71.63.67.48. **Haute-Loire,** ☎ 71.08.66.96. **Puy-de-Dôme** : ☎ 73.92.28.49.

Farmhouse and chambres d'hôtes : enq at the *Relais départementaux.* **Cantal** : préfecture, 15006 Aurillac, ☎ 71.48.53.54. **Haute-Loire** : 4, av. Charles-de-Gaulle, 43000 Le Puy-en-Velay, ☎ 71.09.26.05. **Puy-de-Dôme** : 69, bd Gergovia, 63000 Clermont-Ferrand, ☎ 73.93.84.80.

Holiday villages : see practical holiday information.

Camping : approx 230 camp-sites. List at the C.R.T.

Festivals and events : **Maundy Thursday** : *Procession of the Penitents* in Saugues, Paulhaguet, in Puy-en-Velay and in Puy-Valcivières. **Jun-Aug** : *International Folk Festival of Spas* at La Bourboule, Châtelguyon, Le Mont-Dore, etc. **Jul** : *concerts* at Vollore. **14 Jul** : *Tourist Festival* in Olliergues. **End Jul** : *Le Velay International Folk Festival* in Brives-Charensac, Le Puy-en-Velay, Saint-Didier-en-Velay, Sainte-Sigolène, in Monastier-sur-Gazelle. *Music Festival* at Thiers. **Jul-Aug** : *Festival of French music* in La Chaise-Dieu. **Aug** : *Lanobre International Folk Festival. Festival of the Shepherds* in La Font-Sainte. *Artistic and cultural Festival* at Saint-Germain-l'Herm. **15 Aug** : *procession* in Notre-Dame du Puy. **Early Sep** : *National Fair* at Clermont-Ferrand.

Sporting events : **Jun** : Issoire *French Bowls Championships.* Saint-Eloy-les-Mines. **Aug** : *National scrambling* at Ambert. *French Hill-Climb Motor-racing Championships* at Mont-Dore. *International Hill-Climb Motor-racing* at Châtelguyon. **End of Aug** : *Festival of Free fall* at Puy-de-Dôme.

Scenic railways : *la Galoche, small tourist train* in Velay-Vivarais, Dunières-St-Agrève (37 km). From May to Oct, Sun and nat hols ; from 15 Jul to end Aug, Sun and Wed. Enq : M. Granger, 7, impasse de l'Onzonnière, 42290 Sorbiers, ☎ 77.90.26.90, and *Direction des Chemins de fer régionaux,* chemin du Badet, 42100 St-Étienne, ☎ 77.25.45.01. *Tour of the Cantal region by train : 265 km in a special railcar which crosses 16 valleys. Duration : 10 to 12 h.* Enq and bookings : S.N.C.F. station master, Traveller's Commercial Service, 15000 Aurillac, ☎ 71.48.25.55 or 71.48.08.56.

Rambling and hiking : Auvergne is one of France's best regions for rambling and hiking, being traversed by G.R.'s numbers 3, 30, 33, 330, 4, 40, 41, 400, 412, 441, 65, 7 (topoguides). Le *Chamina,* 5, rue Pierre-le-Vénérable, 63000 Clermont-Ferrand, ☎ 73.92.82.60, publishes numerous pedestrian guides and itineraries, together with the yearly updated list of gîtes and relais. Chamina also organises a number of hikes with guides. Further enq : *Assn. de Randonnée pédestre du Cantal,* château Saint-Étienne, 15000 Aurillac, ☎ 71.48.49.09. *Comité départemental de la Randonnée,* préfecture de la **Haute-Loire,** 43000 Le Puy, ☎ 71.09.24.12, ext 319. *Assn. pour la pratique des Sports de Plein air* (A.P.S.-P.A.), 17, pl. Lafayette, 43100 Brioude, ☎ 71.50.00.70.

Riding holidays : Enq : *A.R.T.E. Velay-Auvergne,* 5, rue de la Gazelle, 43000 **Le Puy,** ☎ 71.09.17.48 ; Chamina, see below. List of riding centres at the C.D.T.

Cycling holidays : *Chamina,* 5, rue Pierre-le-Vénérable, 63000 Clermont-Ferrand, ☎ 73.92.82.60, proposes 15 itineraries departing from the « le Cévenol » S.N.C.F. line, and currently being published ; circuits with guides : tour of the Auvergne lakes (7 days). The *Tour cycliste du Puy-de-Dôme* (Jul) is an event open to ail. Enq : M.B. Gounel, 62 *bis,* rue de l'Oradou, 63000 Clermont-Ferrand, ☎ 73.91.63.99. There are numerous organised touristic cycling circuits. Enq : *Ligue Auvergne-Velay de Cyclotourisme,* 27, rue des Chandiots, 63100 Clermont-Ferrand, ☎ 73.25.29.03. M. Charles Rolland, president of the groupe cyclotouriste, les Bouleaux, bât E, b3, av. Foch, 43000 Le Puy, ☎ 71.09.49.65.

Handicraft courses : lace-making, basket-making, the making of straw chair-bottoms, copper-work, etc : *Maison de l'Artisanat,* Bilhac-Polignac, 43000 Le Puy, ☎ 71.09.50.94. Calligraphy, artistic binding, beginners' courses in traditional building techniques : *Assn. « Château-Rocher »,* Saint-Rémy-de-Blot, 63440 Saint-Pardoux, ☎ 73.85.53.00. The making of lace squares : enq : Mme Chometon, Saint-Bonnet-le-Chastel, 63630 Saint-Germain-l'Herm, ☎ 73.72.50.49. Beginners' courses in weaving, macramé, lace-making with a spindle, in an old farm in the Libradois mountains : M. Sauvage, « la Fontaine des Thiolles », 63630 Saint-Germain-l'Herm, ☎ 73.72.02.16.

Children : "riding holidays" : Montcelet riding farm, Saint-Gervazy, 63340 Saint-Germain-Lembron, ☎ 73.96.44.51 ; Zanières riding centre, 63420 Ardes-sur-Couze, ☎ 73.71.84.30. Sailing instruction for beginners in Gournon, from 2 until 6 pm. Enq : *Direction Départementale du Temps Libre, Jeunesse et Sports,* cité administrative, rue Pélissier, 63034 Clermont-Ferrand Cedex, ☎ 73.92.42.68.

Tennis : enq at the ℹ

Golf : courses in Royat (9 holes) and Le Mont-Dore (9 holes), Chambon-sur-Lignon (4 holes), in Orcines (14 holes).

Motoring and motorcycling : *Ligue motocycliste régionale d'Auvergne,* 1, rue J.-Prugnard, 63100 Cébazat, ☎ 73.24.00.83. *Moto-club d'Auvergne,* 40, bd Charles-de-Gaulle, 63000 Clermont-Ferrand, ☎ 73.93.19.84.

Aquatic sports : numerous stretches of water. Enq : C.D.T. and *Club des Sports de Clermont-Ferrand,* 19, av. de la Libération, ☎ 73.93.93.59.

Diving : *Club de Plongée Aurillacois,* M. Souloumiac, les Landes du Bex, 15130 Arpajan-sur-Cère, ☎ 71.62.83.70. *Club Arverne de Plongée* (ex Aug), M. Dondainas, 23, rue A.-Fallières, 63000 Clermont-Ferrand, ☎ 73.37.37.44. *Club de Plongée Sous-Marine Clermontois,* 18, pl. Sugny, 63000 Clermont-Ferrand, ☎ 73.92.53.99. *Club Vellave de Plongée,* Coopérative d'habitat rural, bd Bertrand, 43000 Le Puy-en-Velay ☎ 71.09.28.01.

Canoeing : Auvergne offers numerous and varied possibilities for canoeing. *Ligue Auvergne de Canoë-Kayak,* M. J. Mougin, pl. de la République, 63800 Cournon, ☎ 73.84.81.33.

Potholing and spelunking : *Société Aurillacoise de Spéléologie,* 38, av. Milhaud, 15000 Aurillac. *Groupe Spéléologique Auvergnat,* mairie, 63170 Aubière.

Climbing-mountaineering : *Club Alpin Français,* 3, rue Mal-Joffre, salle nº 7, 63000 Clermont-Ferrand, ☎ 73.92.16.37. *Groupe des alpinistes gaulois,* 40, av. A.-Elisabeth, 63000 Clermont-Ferrand, ☎ 73.26.50.75.

Winter sports : cross-country skiing : the entire central Massif can be safely crossed on skis, thanks to excursions organised by *Chamina,* 5, rue P.-le-Vénérable, 63000 Clermont-Ferrand, ☎ 73.92.82.00. Enq concerning winter sports resorts at the T.O.

Hang-gliding : *Féd. Française de Vol à Voile Libre,* Ligue du Centre, M. Verdier, 41, rue de Madargue, 63200 Riom, ☎ 73.83.06.84. *Assn. de Vol Libre d'Auvergne,* M. A. Molia, 20, av. J.-Jaurès, 63400 Chamalières, ☎ 73.35.32.84. *École de Vol Libre du Velay,* M. G. Maniglier, Les Sources, 1, rue Estaunié, 43000 Le Puy, ☎ 71.09.68.01 (from 8 to 9 am). *Les Ailes de Plomb du Cantal,* M. Dourel, allée de la Promenade, 15800 Le Puech-Vic-sur-Cère, ☎ 71.47.56.56. *Centre d'école d'Auvergne,* aérodrome de la Pêche, 32, rue Henri-Chas, 43000 Le Puy-en-Velay, ☎ 71.09.09.44.

Gliding : Velay gliding centre, ☎ 71.09.64.33. Aéroclub de Brioude, M.J.C. Brun, ☎ 71.50.04.67. Gliding centre, aéro-club P. Herbaud, 63500 Issoire, ☎ 73.89.16.62.

Parachuting : *Para-Club,* Mlle Auberger, 38, av. Mozart, 15000 Aurillac, ☎ 71.64.24.03. Aérodrome Le Puy/Loudes, M. Dursapt, 2, rue de Sébastopol, 43300 Langeac, ☎ 71.77.11.41.

Hunting and shooting : enq at the *Féd. dép. des Chasseurs.* Cantal : 14, allée du Vialenc, ☎ 71.48.62.66. **Haute-Loire :** 17, bd A.-Clair, ☎ 71.09.10.91. **Puy-de-Dôme :** 42, rue Morel-Ladeuil, ☎ 73.93.76.27.

Fishing : enq at the *Féd. dép. des Assn. de Pêche et de Pisciculture.* Cantal : 14, allée du Vialenc, ☎ 71.48.19.25. **Haute-Loire :** 12, av. du Mal-Foch, ☎ 71.09.09.44. **Puy-de-Dôme :** 65, rue Oradou, ☎ 73.91.42.33.

Towns

AIGUEPERSE

Clermont-Ferrand 31, Montluçon 74, Paris 359
B1 ✉ 63260

SNCF ☎ 73.63.60.35.

Hotels :

★***Hostellerie Blondeau*** (L.F.), ☎ 73.63.61.78. Euro, Visa. 21 rm Ⓟ closed 1 Nov-15 Dec, 120. Rest. ♿ 120-150.

★***Le Marché,*** pl. de la Halle, ☎ 73.63.61.96. Visa. 20 rm Ⓟ closed Oct and Wed eve, 150. Rest. ♿ 50-130.

AMBERT

Le Puy 74, Clermont-Ferrand 78, Paris 436
C2 ✉ 63600

ℹ 4, pl. de l'Hôtel-de-Ville, ☎ 73.82.01.55, and pl. G.-Courtial, ☎ 73.82.14.15 (high season).

SNCF ☎ 73.82.09.60, 73.92.50.50.

Hotels :

★★***Livradois,*** 1, pl. du Livradois, ☎ 73.82.10.01. AE, DC, Euro, Visa. 14 rm Ⓟ closed 3-10 Jan, 15 Nov-15 Dec, Sun eve and Mon, 190. Rest. ♦♦ Good traditional meals, including the *médaillon de lotte au vinaigre de cidre, escalopines de saumon frais grillées au beurre de ciboulette, aiguillettes de canard au miel au porto,* 100-210.

★***Chaumière*** (L.F.), 41, av. Mal-Foch, ☎ 73.82.14.94. AE, DC, Euro, Visa. 15 rm Ⓟ closed 1-29 Apr, 1-13 Sep, 150. Rest. ♦ closed Sat and Sun eve, 60-100.

★***Dore*** (L.F.), 58, av. Mal-Foch, ☎ 73.82.00.58. DC, Euro, Visa. 12 rm Ⓟ closed 2 Jan-1 Feb, 140. Rest. closed Mon eve, 40-90.

⛺ ★★*Trois Chênes,* rte du Puy (120 pl.), ☎ 73.82.34.68.

Restaurant :

La Chaulme, ✉ 63660, 22 km E on the N496 until Saint-Anthème then D67 :

● ♦ ***Le Creux de l'Oulette*** (L.F.), ☎ 73.95.41.16. Euro, Visa. Ⓟ closed 20 Nov-20 Mar ex Feb school hols, Tue eve and Wed. A charming little Auvergne restaurant, simple and attractive, and famous for its *charcuterie maison.* Prices accessible to all, 40-100. With 11 rm.

AURILLAC

Brive 98, Clermont-Ferrand 160, Paris 546
A3 ✉ 15000

ℹ pl. du Square (B2), ☎ 71.48.46.58.

✈ *Aurillac-Tronquières,* ☎ 71.63.56.98.

SNCF (A3), ☎ 71.48.50.50, 71.45.50.50, 71.48.10.12.

Car-hire : *Budget* train + auto, at the station, ☎ 71.48.09.23, and at the airport.

Hotels :

● ★★★**La Thomasse,** 40, rue du Dr-Mallet (A3), ☎ 71.48.26.47. AE, DC, Euro, Visa. 22 rm 🅿 ♨ ♿, 230.

★★★**Grand Hôtel de Bordeaux** (L.F., Mapotel), 2, av. de la République (A2-3), ☎ 71.48.01.84. Tx 990316. AE, DC, Euro, Visa. 37 rm 🅿 ♿ closed 20 Dec-19 Jan. A warm welcome, 280.

★★**Ferraudie,** 15, rue Bel-Air, ☎ 71.48.72.42. DC, Euro, Visa. 22 rm 🅿 ♿ 250.

★★**Univers,** 2, pl. P.-Sémard (A3), ☎ 71.48.24.57. 43 rm 🅿 ♨ ♿ 220. Rest. ♦ 80-130.

⛺ ★★★*L'Ombrade* (200 pl.), ☎ 71.48.28.87.

Restaurant :

♦♦ **La Reine Margot,** 19, rue G.-de-Veyre (A2-B3), ☎ 71.48.26.46. Euro, Visa. ♿ closed Mon. A must for gourmets and enthusiasts of regional fare : *ris de veau aux cèpes, cœur de filet au poivre, filet de turbot « Reine Margot ».* Friendly service, 65-200.

Recommended : *pain paillé, tourtes* (local breads and savoury tarts), *Rondet,* 12, rue des Frères. Sweetmeats at *Vernande,* 16, rue des Frères. Cakes and pastries, sweets, *Favre,* rue des Carmes (Auvergne tourte).

BESSE-ET-SAINT-ANASTAISE

Clermont-Ferrand 51, Mauriac 82, Paris 437
A2 ✉ 63610

Super-Besse : 1 350 m-1 850 m

ℹ pl. Gd-Mèze, ☎ 73.79.52.84.

Hotels :

★★★**Mouflons,** rte de Super-Besse, ☎ 73.79.51.31. Visa. 50 rm 🅿 ♨ closed 25 Sep-31 May. Comfortable, well-situated establishment, 220. Rest. ● ♦♦ ♿ True regional fare in the heart of Auvergne, thanks to Antoine Sachapt's light, skillful cooking : *saumon de fontaine aux champignons sylvestres, feuilleté de grenouilles aux escargots et aux cèpes ;* Auvergne cheeses ; good local wines, 80-180.

★★**Gazelle,** rte de Compains, ☎ 73.79.50.26. Euro, Visa. 30 rm 🅿 ♨ closed 15 Sep-20 Dec, after Easter-early Jun, 310. Rest. pension only.

★★**Petite Ferme** (L.F.), Le Fau, ☎ 73.79.51.39. 32 rm 🅿 ♨ ♿ closed 20 Apr-20 May, 20 Sep-1 Nov and week-end only from 1 Nov to 20 Dec, 180. Rest. 80-130.

★★**Levant** (L.F.), ☎ 73.79.50.17. Visa. 15 rm 🅿 ♨ closed 15 Apr-1 Jun, 20 Sep-20 Dec, 140. Rest. 60-90.

★**Clos** (L.F.), rte du Mont-Dore, ☎ 73.79.52.77. 25 rm 🅿 ♨ closed 25 Apr-15 Jun, 30 Sep-20 Dec, 100. Rest. 80-130.

Super-Besse (1 350 m), 7 km W :

★★★**Gergovia,** 1, rue M.-Gauthier, ☎ 73.79.60.15. 53 rm closed 11 Apr-12 Jun, 4 Oct-17 Dec. Comfortable, well-furnished chalet, 240. Rest. Spec : *truite à l'auvergnate,* 80-130.

★★**Sabrina,** ☎ 73.79.60.02. 46 rm closed 15 Apr-20 Dec, 130. Rest. 50-120.

⛺ ★*Bois de Gravière* (125 pl.), ☎ 73.79.52.05.

Sports : fishing (mountain river or lake) : in Pavin, sailing school, Hermines lake.

Bicycle hire : garage *Fabre,* ☎ 73.79.51.10.

La BOURBOULE

Clermont-Ferrand 53, Mauriac 70, Paris 439
A2 850-1 500 m. 2 May-30 Sep, ☎ 73.81.02.92. ✉ 63150

ℹ pl. de l'Hôtel-de-Ville, ☎ 73.81.07.99.

SNCF ☎ 73.81.03.64.

Hotels :

★★**Aviation** (L.F.), rue de Metz, ☎ 73.81.09.77. Visa. 50 rm 🅿 closed 15-30 Apr, 1 Oct-20 Dec, 180. Rest. ♿ 50-100.

★★**International,** av. d'Angleterre, ☎ 73.81.05.82. Tx 990332. AE, DC, Euro, Visa. 16 rm closed 20-30 Apr, 3 Nov-18 Dec. In the 42-acre Fenestre park. Warm welcome, 180. Rest. 75-100.

★★**Les Fleurs** (L.F.), av. Guéneau-de-Massy, ☎ 73.81.09.44. 24 rm 🅿 ♨ closed 1 Oct-15 Jan, Mar, Jul-Aug : half-board only.

★★**Parc,** quai Mal-Fayolle, ☎ 73.81.01.77. AE, DC, Euro, Visa. 54 rm 🅿 closed 25 Sep-15 May, 170. Rest. ♿ 70-90.

★**Baigneurs,** quai de la Libération, ☎ 73.81.07.66. 33 rm 🅿 ♿ closed Easter-early May, 30 Sep-25 Dec, 120. Rest. 80-130.

★**Pavillon** (L.F.), av. d'Angleterre, ☎ 73.81.01.42. DC. 26 rm ♨ ♿ closed 20 Sep-15 May, 120. Rest. ♿ 50-70.

★**Poste,** bd G.-Clemenceau, ☎ 73.81.09.66. 50 rm 🅿 closed 30 Sep-10 Oct. Opposite the spa, 130. Rest. ♿ 50-70.

Auberge de Tournebride, rte de Murat-le-Quaire, ☎ 73.81.01.91. 🅿 ♨ 8 rm, closed Mon low season ex school hols and nat hols, 14-21 Apr, 150. Rest. ♿ 70-150.

⛺ ★★★*Les Clarines,* 920 m (100 pl.), ☎ 73.81.02.30 ; ★★*les Cascades,* 850 m (165 pl.), ☎ 73.81.10.20 ; ★★*le Piquetou,* rte de la Tour (80 pl.), ☎ 73.95.03.02.

Natural camping grounds : 4 km from the station, 63950 Saint-Sauves, ☎ 73.81.17.08 ; Murat-le-Quaire, ☎ 73.81.01.59.

Casino : ☎ 73.81.25.24. closed 15 Sep-15 May.

BRIOUDE

Le Puy 60, Clermont-Ferrand 70, Paris 456
B2-3 ✉ 43100

ℹ 3, bd Dr-Devins, ☎ 71.50.05.35.

SNCF ☎ 71.50.11.51.

Hotels :

★★**Brivas** (L.F., Inter-Hôtel), rte du Puy, ☎ 71.50.10.49. AE, DC, Euro, Visa. 30 rm 🅿 ♨ closed 18 Nov-28 Dec, Fri eve and Sat noon (15 Oct-15 Mar). Pleasant building set in a flower-filled garden ; view over the Livradois mountains, 225. Rest. ♦ Good service, 60-120.

★★**Hôtel Moderne** (L.F.), 12 av. Victor-Hugo, ☎ 71.50.07.30. AE, DC, Euro, Visa. 17 rm 🅿 closed 1 Jan-15 Feb, Sun eve Mon noon (ex in season), 235. Rest. ● ♦ **Marius** ♿ Quality fare in an elegant setting. Spec : *saumon frais aux gousses d'ail confites, magret de canard au Xérès,* delicious desserts, 120-210.

★**Chaumine,** 13, av. de la Gare, ☎ 71.50.14.10. 17 rm, closed 10-31 Jan, Sun eve (winter), 150.

⛺ ★★*La Bageasse* (85 pl.), ☎ 71.50.07.70.

Restaurant :

♦ **Julien,** 7, rue d'Assas, ☎ 71.50.00.03. Euro, Visa. Closed Sun eve and Mon. Family-style cooking in a traditional setting. Spec : *saumon grillé au beurre blanc* and home-cured salmon, 45-80.

Events : mid-Aug, *bric-à-brac and second-hand fair.* End Aug-early Sep, *local festivities.*

La CHAISE-DIEU

Le Puy 41, Saint-Étienne 79, Paris 469
B2 ✉ 43160

(1 080 m), 15 Dec-15 Apr

ℹ pl. de la Mairie, ☎ 71.00.01.16.

Hotels :
★★*Au Tremblant* (L.F.), ☎ 71.00.01.85. 28 rm Ⓟ closed 1 Dec-1 Apr, 190. Rest. ♿ Spec : *coquelet au vin,* 55-100.
● ★★*L'Écho et l'Abbaye* (L.F.), pl. de l'Écho, ☎ 71.00.00.45. AE, Euro, Visa. 11 rm closed 5 Nov-1 Apr. In the one-time abbey refectory, 190. Rest. 60-115.
★★*Le Vénéré,* de la Tour lake, 2 km on the D906, ☎ 71.00.01.08. 18 rm Ⓟ closed 30 Sep-1 Apr, 180. Rest. eve only, 80-130.

★★*Les Sapins* (33 pl.), ☎ 71.00.01.57.

Events : last Sun in Jul, *local festivities ;* Jul-Aug : *Festival of music.*

CHAMBON-SUR-LAC

Clermont-Ferrand 37, Mauriac 93, Paris 435
3 km W of Murol, A2 ⊠ 63790 Murol

Chambon-des-Neiges (1 250-1 800 m).

Hotels :
★★*Bellevue,* ☎ 73.88.61.06. 25 rm Ⓟ closed 1 Oct-1 Feb, Mar, 140. Rest. closed 10 Oct-1 Feb. View of the mountain and lake, 50-90.
★★*Lac,* ☎ 73.88.60.17. 13 rm Ⓟ closed end Sep-Easter ex Feb hols, 180. Rest. ♦ ♿ 80-130.
★★*Grillon,* ☎ 73.88.60.66. Euro, Visa. 20 rm Ⓟ closed 1 Nov-26 Dec (ex school hols), 140. Rest. 50-110.
★★*Bonne Hôtesse,* ☎ 73.88.61.03. Euro. 9 rm Ⓟ closed 30 Oct-15 Apr, 100. Rest. 50-90.

Youth hostel : Voissières, 1.5 km, closed Oct, ☎ 73.88.61.12.

★★★*Le Pré Bas* (130 pl.), ☎ 73.88.63.04 ; ★★★municipal *les Bombes* (50 pl.), ☎ 73.88.61.21.

Restaurant :
♦ *Beau Cottage,* ☎ 73.88.62.11. Ⓟ closed 1 Oct-1 Dec, 50-110. With 14 rm.

Le CHAMBON-SUR-LIGNON

Le Puy 46, Saint-Étienne 62, Paris 582
C3 ⊠ 43400

ⓘ pl. du Marché, ☎ 71.59.71.56.

Hotels :
★★★*Bel Horizon* (L.F.), chemin de Molle, ☎ 71.59.74.39. 19 rm Ⓟ ♿ closed 25 Sep-15 Oct, 250. Rest. closed Wed noon, 60-80.
★★*Central,* Le Carrefour, ☎ 71.59.70.67. 25 rm Ⓟ closed 28 Sep-20 Oct, Mon eve and Tue low season. Traditional establishment in the middle of the village, 170. Rest. ♦ Copious, family-style meals. Spec : *saumon à l'oseille, crêpe Central, gratin dauphinois,* 50-140.

Barandons, 3.5 km on the D157 and D185 :
● ★★*Clair Matin* (L.F.), Les Barandons, ☎ 71.59.73.03. AE, DC, Euro, Visa. 30 rm Ⓟ closed 5-20 Jan, 1-15 Mar, 20 Nov-20 Dec. A pleasant halt in a breath-taking setting, 210.

Tence, ⊠ 43190, 8.5 km N by D103 :
★★*Grand Hôtel* (Relais du Silence), rue d'Annonay, ☎ 71.59.82.76. 16 rm Ⓟ closed 1 Dec-1 Feb, Sun eve and Mon, 290. Rest. ♦ Traditional cooking by P.M. Placide, one of R. Vergé's former pupils : *foie gras chaud aux cèpes, myrtillade de canard,* 110-300.

★★★★*Les Hirondelles* (50 pl.), ☎ 71.59.73.84 ; ★★*le Lignon* (130 pl.), ☎ 71.59.72.86.

Events : 1st Sun in May, *daffodil festival ;* 2nd Sun in Sep, *local festivities.*

CHÂTEAUNEUF-LES-BAINS

Clermont-Ferrand 49, Montluçon 55, Paris 375
12 km S of Menat, A1
⊠ 63390 Saint-Gervais-d'Auvergne

2 May-30 Sep, ☎ 73.86.67.49.

ⓘ ☎ 73.86.67.86.

SNCF Saint-Gervais-Châteauneuf, 8 km, ☎ 73.85.71.85.

Hotels :
★*Château,* ☎ 73.86.67.01. 38 rm closed 30 Sep-10 May, 130. Rest. ♿ 50-120.
★*Pergola* (L.F.), ☎ 73.86.67.95. 9 rm closed 30 Sep-1 May, 100. Rest. 50-105.

★★*Le Got* (55 pl.), ☎ 73.86.67.85 ; Saint-Gervais-d'Auvergne (7 km) : farmhouse gîte and camping, Le Fél, ☎ 73.85.72.25. Fishing.

Farmhouse-inn : Saint-Pardoux, ⊠ 63440, 11 km NE on the D122 and D50 : *les Labbis,* Pouzols, ☎ 73.97.45.56. Good regional fare ; tasty and tastefully served.

CHÂTELGUYON

Clermont-Ferrand 20, Montluçon 75, Paris 378
B1 ⊠ 63140

3 May-15 Oct, ☎ 73.86.00.08.

ⓘ parc municipal, ☎ 73.86.01.17.

SNCF ☎ 73.86.00.29.

Hotels :
● ★★★★*Splendid* (Mapotel), 5-7, rue d'Angleterre, ☎ 73.86.04.80. AE, DC, Visa. 93 rm Ⓟ near the spa ; an attractive, renovated residence in a sheltered park, closed 15 Oct-25 Apr, 480. Rest. ♦♦ ♿ Delicious omelettes, 120-210.
★★★*International,* rue Punett, ☎ 73.86.06.72. Visa. 68 rm closed 30 Sep-2 May, 250. Rest. 90-120.
★★★*Paris,* 1, rue du Dr-Levadoux, ☎ 73.86.00.12. 62 rm ♿ closed 5 Oct-20 Nov and 30 Mar-24 Apr and Sun eve, 230. Rest. ♦ ♿ Superb fare ; excellent value, 70-140.
★★*L'Univers,* 37, av. Baraduc, ☎ 73.86.02.71. AE, Euro, Visa. 42 rm ♿ closed 15 Dec-15 Jan, and Sun eve and Mon (Oct-Apr), 140. Rest. ♿ 80-140.
★★*Thermalia,* 20, av. Baraduc, ☎ 73.86.00.11. 49 rm ♿ closed 1 Oct-1 May. Ideally situated in the middle of the spa area, 180. Rest. 120-210.
★★*Beau Site,* 2, rue du Chalusset, ☎ 73.86.00.49. 31 rm Ⓟ closed 30 Sep-1 May, 175. Rest. 60-110.
★★*Hirondelles,* 16, av. des États-Unis, ☎ 73.86.09.11. AE, Visa. 50 rm Ⓟ closed 10 Oct-20 Apr, 180. Rest. 50-100.
★*Bellevue,* 4, rue A.-Punett, ☎ 73.86.07.62. 40 rm closed 5 Oct-25 Apr, 180. Rest. 80-130.
★*Chante-Grelet,* av. Gal-de-Gaulle, ☎ 73.86.02.05. 35 rm Ⓟ ♿ closed 11 Oct-24 Apr, 100. Rest. 90-170.

1 km on the Saint-Hubert road :
★★*Le Manoir Fleuri,* rte du Château-de-Chazeron, ☎ 73.86.01.27. 15 rm Ⓟ closed 10 Oct-25 Apr. Set in the heart of the countryside, 160. Rest. ♦ ♿ closed Feb, 80-160.

★★★*Clos de la Balanède* (250 pl.), ☎ 73.86.02.47 ; ★★*la Croze,* Saint-Hippolyte (200 pl.), ☎ 73.86.01.88. Natural camping ground, Le Court-Loubeyrat (6 km), ☎ 73.86.64.31.

Restaurant :
♦♦ ***La Grilloute,*** 33, av. Baraduc, ☎ 73.86.04.17. Visa. ♿ closed Tue (ex nat hols) and 15 Oct-15 May. Delicious Auvergne charcuteries, excellent *terrines* and *truite aux chanturgues*, 80-130.

CHAUDES-AIGUES

Rodez 87, Aurillac 94, Paris 522
B3 ✉ 15110
(1 May-17 Oct), ☎ 71.23.51.06/71.23.52.21.
ⓘ 1, av. G.-Pompidou, ☎ 71.23.52.75.

Hotels :
★★***Beau Séjour,*** 9, av. G.-Pompidou, ☎ 71.23.52.37. Euro. 47 rm Ⓟ ♿ closed Fri eve and Sat low season ex school hols and 15 Nov-1 Mar, 170. Rest. ♿ 50-130.
★★***Valette,*** 29, pl. du Gravier, ☎ 71.23.52.43. Euro. 45 rm Ⓟ closed 15 Oct-1 May, 200. Rest. 50-100.
★★***Aux Bouillons d'Or,*** 10, quai du Remontalou, ☎ 71.23.51.42. 12 rm ♿ closed 1 Dec-1 Mar, Tue (15 Oct-1 May), 180. Rest. ● ♦♦ ♿ Reasonably-priced, quality fare. Good, simple cooking at reasonable prices by J. M. Cornut. - Spec : *palette d'agneau et sa mousse de navet raves, jarret de porc demi-sel à la potée de légumes,* 80-180.
★***Mairie*** (L.F.), 1, pl. de la Mairie, ☎ 71.23.52.54. Euro, Visa. 15 rm Ⓟ closed 2 weeks in Dec, Sat eve and Sun eve (15 Oct-15 Mar), 110. Rest. ♿ 40-110.
⛺ ★★*Le Couffour* (170 pl.), ☎ 71.23.57.08.

CLERMONT-FERRAND

Moulins 96, Saint-Étienne 150, Paris 390
B1 ✉ 63000
ⓘ 69, bd Gergovia (B3), ☎ 73.93.30.20, and pl. de Jaude (B2 ; high season).
✈ Clermont-Ferrand-Aulnat, 6 km, ☎ 73.91.71.00.
Air France Agency, at the airport, B.P. 16, ✉ 63510 Aulnat, ☎ 73.91.84.84.
SNCF (E2), ☎ 73.92.50.50, 73.30.11.67, 73.30.10.00.
🚌 bd Gergovia, ☎ 73.93.13.61.

Car-hire : *Budget* train + auto, Auvergne Location, 45, av. d'Italie, ☎ 73.91.82.59, at the station, ☎ 73.30.11.60, and at the airport.

Hotels :
★★★***Frantel,*** 82, bd Gergovia (B3), ☎ 73.93.05.75. Tx 392658. AE, DC, Euro, Visa. 124 rm Ⓟ ♿ 410. Rest. ● ♦♦ ***la Rétirade.*** closed Sat noon and Sun. Good meals in a comfortable setting. Spec : *marinade de saumon et sandre, picattas de lotte au pistil de safran, duo de caille en pot-au-feu.* Worthy Auvergne wines, 130-210.
★★★***Colbert*** (Mapotel), 19, rue Colbert (A2), ☎ 73.93.25.66. AE, DC, Euro, Visa. 70 rm Ⓟ 280.
★★★***Lyon,*** 16, pl. de Jaude (B2), ☎ 73.93.32.55. Visa. 34 rm Ⓟ 230. Rest. 35-130.
★★***Albert-Élisabeth,*** 37, av. A.-Élisabeth (D1), ☎ 73.92.47.41. AE, Visa. 40 rm Ⓟ 180.
★★***Minimes*** (Inter-Hôtel), 10, rue des Minimes (B2), ☎ 73.93.31.49. AE, DC, Euro, Visa. 28 rm Town centre, 180.
★★***Midi*** (L.F.), 39, av. de l'Union-Soviétique (E1), ☎ 73.92.44.98. Visa. 39 rm, 180. Rest. closed Mon, 80-130.
★★***Floride II,*** cours R.-Poincaré (C3), ☎ 73.37.30.20. AE, DC, Euro, Visa. 30 rm Ⓟ 180.
★★***Régina,*** 14, rue Bonnabaud (B2), ☎ 73.93.44.76. 27 rm, 150.
★***Beaulieu,*** 13, av. des Paulines (D3) ☎ 73.92.46.99. 16 rm Ⓟ 110.
★***Foch,*** 22, rue du Mal-Foch (B2), ☎ 73.93.48.40. Euro. 19 rm closed 26 Dec-5 Jan, 100.

Chamalières, ✉ 63400 :
★★★***Europe,*** 29, av. de Royat, ☎ 73.37.61.35. DC. 33 rm Ⓟ ♿ 250.
★★***Chalet fleuri,*** 37, av. Massenet, ☎ 73.35.09.60. Visa. 40 rm Ⓟ 170. Rest. 80-120.

Puy-de-Dôme, ✉ 63870 Orcines, 15 km W :
● ★★***Le Dôme*** (L.F.), ☎ 73.91.49.00, 10 rm closed Oct-8 May, 180. Rest. ♦♦ ♿ 80-130.

Youth hostel, 55, av. de l'Union-Soviétique, ☎ 73.92.26.39.
⛺ ★★★*Chanset,* Ceyrat, 6 km on N89 (210 pl.), ☎ 73.61.30.73.

Restaurants :
♦♦ ***Truffe d'Argent,*** 17, rue Lamartine (B2), ☎ 73.93.22.42. AE, DC, Euro, Visa. Closed Sat noon. Enjoyable meals in an attractive setting (excellent *terrine de grives*), 90-200.

Chamalières, 1 km O :
● ♦♦ ***Radio*** (Michel Mioche), 43, av. Pierre-Curie, ☎ 73.30.87.83. AE, DC, Euro, Visa. Ⓟ ♿ closed Sun eve, Mon noon. Hotel closed Jan-Feb. Michel Mioche, a former pupil of J. Delaveyne from Bougival, proposes good dishes halfway between traditional dishes and new specialities : *filet d'agneau au beurre de coriandre,* 220-310. With 27 rm.

Durtol, ✉ 63830, on the D941A :
● ♦♦♦ ***L'Aubergade,*** rte de la Baraque, ☎ 73.37.84.64. Visa. Ⓟ closed Sun eve, Mon, 1-21 Mar, 1-21 Sep. One of the best restaurants in the area ; expert, imaginative cooking, and excellent value. Spec : *turbot à la crème d'estragon, rognon de veau entier roti à l'étouffée,* 90-160.

At the col de Ceyssat, 14 km E on the Puy-de-Dôme road and the D68 :
● ♦♦ ***Auberge des Muletiers,*** ☎ 73.87.11.18. ♿ closed Sun eve, Mon, 23 Dec-6 Jan. Delightful, friendly, rustic inn. Specialities from south-west : *cassoulet, aiguillettes aux cèpes, palombe, gibier,* 60-150.

Flea-market : 1st Sat of each month.

Bicycle hire : *Mazeyrat,* 3, bd Gergovia, ☎ 73.91.44.74.

Recommended : *Vieillard,* chocolate-confectioner, 13, rue Pascal. *Quinty,* cheese, halle Saint-Pierre.

Sightseeing : from 15 Jun to 15 Sep, daily, information ⓘ

CRAPONNE-SUR-ARZON

Saint-Étienne 60, Paris 470
19 km E of La Chaise-Dieu, B-C2 ✉ 43500
ⓘ La Grenette, bd du Nord, ☎ 71.03.23.14.
SNCF ☎ 71.03.20.10.

Hotels :
Pontempeyrat, 6 km ENE :
★***Au Grandgousier*** (L.F.), 3, pl. de la Grenette, ☎ 71.03.21.90. Visa. 9 rm, closed 1st week Sep, 21 Oct-15 Nov, and Mon (low season), 110. Rest. ♿ 40-130.
★★***Mistou*** (L.F. ; Relais du Silence), ☎ 77.50.62.46. AE, Visa. 25 rm Ⓟ closed Tue eve and Wed (ex Summer), 11 Nov-4 Mar, 175. Rest. 90-160.

Farmhouse gîte and camping : 8 km, Le Maisonny-Saint-Georges-Lagricol, ☎ 71.03.25.87.
⛺ ★★★★*Parc des Sports* (14 pl.), ☎ 71.00.23.09.

Auvergne

GARABIT

Mende 71, Aurillac 88, Paris 502
B3 ⊠ 15390 Loubaresse

SNCF Loubaresse, ☎ 71.73.70.55.

Hotels :
★★***Beau Site*** (L.F.), on the N9, ☎ 71.23.46.34. Euro. 20 rm P ♿ closed 6 Nov-1 Apr. View over the viaduct and lake, 170. Rest. 40-90.
★★***Garabit*** (L.F.), ☎ 71.23.42.75. Euro. 48 rm P closed 1 Nov-1 Apr, 220. Rest. 50-150.
★★***Viaduc*** (L.F.), ☎ 71.23.43.20. 20 rm P closed 1 Nov-1 Apr, 170. Rest. 40-100.

Anglards-de-Saint-Flour (825 m) :
★★***Panoramic,*** Le Bioset, ☎ 71.23.40.24. Euro, Visa. 30 rm P ♿ closed 3 Nov-23 Mar. Superb site. View over the lake, 160. Rest. ♿ 40-80.

Chambres d'hôtes : La Bessoir-de-Lair : Mme Valaix, ☎ 71.73.71.71 (also farmhouse-inn) ; M., Mme André, ☎ 71.73.71.01.

Farmhouse-inn : *les Compagnons de Buffadou,* Faverolles, ☎ 71.23.40.84.

ISSOIRE

Clermont-Ferrand 37, Le Puy 93, Paris 423
B2 ⊠ 63500

ⓘ pl. Gal-de-Gaulle, ☎ 73.89.15.90.

SNCF ☎ 73.89.22.48, 73.89.20.06.

Hotels :
★★***Floride*** (L.F.), rte de Solignat, ☎ 73.89.04.25. AE, DC, Euro, Visa. 17 rm P closed 16 Dec-15 Jan, 180. Rest. 800 m from the hotel ; closed Mon, 80-130.
★***Pariou*** (L.F.), 18, av. Kennedy, ☎ 73.89.22.11. Euro, Visa. 29 rm P closed 22 Sep-15 Oct, Christmas and end-of-year hols, Sat and Sun (ex Jul-Aug), 140. Rest. ♦ Pleasant meals. Flower-laden terrace. Spec : *truite aux amandes, tripous d'Aurillac,* 50-90.

Parentignat, 4 km SE on the D996 :
★★***Tourette*** (L.F.), ☎ 73.55.01.78. Euro, Visa. 31 rm P closed 5 Nov-1 Dec, Fev, Fri eve, 50-150.

Restaurant :

Montpeyroux, ☎ 63730, 13 km N :
● ♦♦♦ ***Auberge de Tralume*** (Châteaux-hôtels), ☎ 73.96.60.09. AE, DC, Euro, Visa. P closed Sun eve and Mon low season. In the heart of the Auvergne country, simplicity and refinement in a beautiful 13thC house set in a listed site : *terrine de canard chaude, filet de turbot à la moutarde,* 110-300. With 4 rm, 260.

LANGEAC

Le Puy 41, Mende 95, Paris 485
B3 ⊠ 43300

ⓘ pl. Hôtel-de-Ville, ☎ 71.77.05.41.

SNCF ☎ 71.77.05.63.

Hotels :
Prades, 13 km SE on the N585 and D48 :
● ★***Chalet de la Source,*** rte de Langeac, ☎ 71.74.02.39. 17 rm P Trout fishing in this agreeable stop-over, closed 1 Oct-1 May, 220. Rest. Good cooking : *escalope de saumon au cerfeuil, étuvée de pintade au xérès,* 70-180.

Reilhac, 2 km N, on the D585 :
★***Val d'Allier,*** ☎ 71.77.02.11. 10 rm P closed 1 week in Jun, 1 week during end-of-year hols, 130. Rest. ♦ ♿ closed Sat (Oct-Apr). Spec : *parfait de foie de volaille, tourte de saumon,* 50-70.

Chambres and table d'hôtes : M. Simon, Lestival, ☎ 71.77.04.99.

★★*Le Prado* (133 pl.), ☎ 71.77.05.01.

Events : *feu de la St-Jean* (Jun), *St-Gal traditional festival* (1st Sun Jul).

LEZOUX

Clermont-Ferrand 27, Moulins 100, Paris 393
B1 ⊠ 63190

SNCF ☎ 73.73.10.53.

Hotels :
★★***Les Voyageurs,*** pl. de la Mairie, ☎ 73.73.10.49. 10 rm closed 15 Sep-20 Oct, 10-17 Feb, Sun eve and Mon, 160. Rest. ♦ Spec : *foie gras de canard frais et sa chiffonnade à l'huile de noix,* 80-190.

Bort-l'Étang, 8 km SE on the D223 and D115 :
★★★★***Château de Codignat*** (Relais et châteaux), ☎ 73.68.43.03. Tx 990606. AE, DC, Euro, Visa. 14 rm P closed 1 Oct-1 Apr. An excellent welcome in this stunning 15thC castle, 840. Rest. ♦♦♦ closed Tue, Thu noon (ex nat hols). Spec : *morue à la bohémienne, cassolette de ris de veau,* 220-310.

Riding : Les Cavaliers arvernes, Les Bradoux, 63120 Sermentizon, ☎ 73.53.11.38.

Le LIORAN

Saint-Flour 37, Aurillac 39, Paris 507
A3 ⊠ 15300 Murat

Super-Lioran, 1 250 m-1 850 m

ⓘ ☎ 71.49.50.08.

SNCF ☎ 71.49.50.05.

Hotels :
★***Auberge du Tunnel*** (L.F.), ☎ 71.49.50.02. DC, Euro. 18 rm P closed 1 May-1 Jun, 1 Oct-21 Dec, 140. Rest. ♦ ♿ Good regional cooking : *potée auvergnate, tripous cantaliens,* 50-130.

Super-Lioran, 2 km SW on the D67 :
★★★***Grand Hôtel Anglard et du Cerf,*** ☎ 71.49.50.26. 38 rm P closed 23 Apr-30 May, 12 Jun-1 Jul, 30 Sep-20 Dec. View of the Cantal mountains, 240. Rest. ♦♦ Spec : *foie gras du chef,* pastries, 80-170.
★★***Remberter et Saporta,*** ☎ 71.49.50.28. Euro. 32 rm P ♿ closed 20 Apr-15 Jun, 15 Sep-20 Dec. Full board only in winter, 170. Rest. 80-130.
★***Rocher du Cerf,*** ☎ 71.49.50.14. 11 rm P closed 15 Apr-29 Jun, 10 Sep-19 Dec. Set amidst the pine trees at the foot of the Cantal slopes. Pension oblig. in winter, 200. Rest. ♦ Good regional dishes, 50-90.

Laveissière, 6 km NE :
★★***Le Vallagnon*** (L.F.), rte de Murat, N122, ☎ 71.20.02.38. 30 rm P ♿ closed 5 Nov-3 Dec, Mon (Apr and May), 180. Rest. ♿ closed Mon (Oct-early Dec), 80-130.
★***Bellevue*** (L.F.), ☎ 71.20.01.22. 23 rm P closed 15 Sep-1 Jun (ex school hols and weekend). Well situated, 110. Rest. 45-70.

MASSIAC

Saint-Flour 30, Clermont-Ferrand 80, Paris 460.
B3 ⊠ 15500

ⓘ rue de la Paix, ☎ 71.23.07.76.

SNCF ☎ 71.23.02.69.

Hotels :
★★***Mairie*** (L.F.), rue A.-Chalvet, ☎ 71.23.02.51. 27 rm P closed 15 Nov-15 Dec and Mon low season, 180. Rest. 80-150.

★★*Poste,* av. de Clermont-Ferrand, ☎ 71.23.02.01. AE, Euro, Visa. 36 rm Ⓟ mini-golf ♿ closed 6 Nov-19 Dec and Wed (ex summer), 180. Rest. ♿ 50-130.

⛺ ★★*L'Allagnon* (85 pl.), ☎ 71.23.03.93.

MAURIAC

Aurillac 56, Tulle 70, Paris 486
A3 ✉ 15200

ℹ pl. G.-Pompidou, ☎ 71.68.01.85.

SNCF ☎ 71.68.01.21.

Hotels :
★★***Central*** (L.F.), 4, rue de la République, ☎ 71.68.01.90. Euro, Visa. 34 rm ♿ closed 10-30 Nov, 180. Rest. ♦ Good service, 80-130.
★★***Écu de France,*** 6, av. Ch.-Périé, ☎ 71.68.00.75. Visa. 26 rm closed Sun and Mon noon low season, 31 Dec-10 Mar, 210. Rest. 60-140.

⛺ ★★★*Coste Mauve* (70 pl.), ☎ 71.68.08.73 ; ★★*la Roussille* (100 pl.), ☎ 71.68.06.99.

Le MONT-DORE

Clermont-Ferrand 47, Mauriac 73, Paris 437
A2 ✉ 63240

1 050 m-1 846 m

(15 May-30 Sep), ☎ 73.65.05.10.

ℹ av. du Gal-Leclerc, ☎ 73.81.18.88.

SNCF ☎ 73.65.04.74, 73.65.00.02.

Hotels :
★★★***Panorama,*** 27, av. de la Libération, ☎ 73.65.11.12. Visa. 40 rm Ⓟ closed 10 Apr-15 May, 30 Sep-20 Dec, 240. Rest. 90-150.
★★***Cascades,*** av. G.-Clemenceau, ☎ 73.65.01.36. Visa. 23 rm Ⓟ ♿ closed 1 Oct-20 Dec, 2 Apr-15 May, 180. Rest. ♦ 60-100.
★★***Oise*** (L.F.), 35, av. de la Libération, ☎ 73.65.04.68. 50 rm Ⓟ closed 15 Apr-15 May, 30 Sep-20 Dec, 205. Rest. ♿ 70-120.
★★***Nouvel Hôtel,*** rue J.-Moulin, ☎ 73.65.11.34. DC, Visa. 64 rm ♿ closed 15 Apr-10 May, 10 Oct-18 Dec, 180. Rest. ♿ 50-100.
★ ***Mon Clocher*** (L.F.), 5, rue Sauvagnat, ☎ 73.65.05.41. 32 rm. closed 30 Mar-15 May, 30 Sep-25 Dec, 140. Rest. Spec : *escalope de veau à la fondue de poireaux,* 40-110.

At the foot of the Sancy mountain, 4 km on the D983 :
● ★★***Puy Ferrand*** (Relais du Silence), ☎ 73.65.18.99. AE, Euro, Visa. 42 rm Ⓟ ♿ closed 15 Apr-15 May, 25 Sep-15 Dec. Near the ski-lifts, in the middle of nature, 170. Rest. ♦ Spec : *saumon à l'oseille, filet de sandre aux mousserons, fricassée de volailles,* 90-180.

9 km N on the D983 :
★★***Auberge du Lac de Guéry*** (L.F.), ☎ 73.65.02.76. 11 rm Ⓟ closed Easter-1 Jun, end Sep-26 Dec. Cross-country skiing, 180. Rest. 80-130.

Youth hostel, rte de Sancy, ☎ 73.65.03.53.

⛺ ★★*Domaine de la Grande Cascade* (60 pl.), ☎ 73.65.06.23 ; ★★*les Crouzets* (250 pl.), ☎ 73.65.21.60.

Restaurant :
● ♦ ***La Belle Époque,*** 1, rue Sauvagnat, ☎ 73.65.07.68. AE, DC, Euro, Visa. Closed Wed (ex Jul-Aug) and 25 Oct-30 Nov. Good cooking. Spec : *charlotte de grenouilles aux blancs de poireaux,* 100-200.

Farmhouse-inns : *le Pistounet,* ☎ 73.65.00.67. *Ferme de l'Angle,* ☎ 73.65.02.11.

Casino, 12, rue Meynadier, ☎ 73.65.00.58. closed Oct-Nov, Apr-May.

MONTSALVY

Figeac 57, Rodez 60, Paris 581
35 km S of Aurillac, A3-4 ✉ 15120

ℹ mairie, ☎ 71.49.20.10.

Hotels :
★★***Nord*** (L.F., Inter-Hôtel), ☎ 71.49.20.03. AE, Euro, Visa. 30 rm Ⓟ closed 2 Jan-15 Mar. Warmth and confort, 130. Rest. ♦ ♿ Spec : *foie gras entier au sauternes,* 60-150.
★***Auberge Fleurie*** (L.F.), pl. du Barry, ☎ 71.49.20.02. AE, DC, Euro, Visa. 18 rm. A pleasant rustic home ; annex 1 km away, with 5-acre park, 130. Rest. ♦ closed 1 Nov-1 Mar. Good regional dishes : *tripous, omelettes aux cèpes, truite aux lardons, clafoutis au caramel et aux cerises,* 40-100.

⛺ ★★*La Grangeotte* (50 pl.), ☎ 71.49.20.10.

Farmhouse-inns : *Aubesfeyre,* Junhac, ☎ 71.49.22.70. *Sunezergues,* ☎ 71.49.92.01. *Lacaze,* Lacapelle-del-Fraysse, ☎ 71.62.55.07.

MOUDEYRES

Le Puy 25, Aubenas 63, Paris 541
13 km ENE of Monastier-sur-Gazeille, C3-4
✉ 43480 Laussonne

Hotel :
★★***Auberge le Pré Bossu*** (Châteaux-hôtels, Relais du Silence, L.F.), ☎ 71.05.10.70. AE, Visa. 11 rm Ⓟ closed 11 Nov-Easter ex school hols, 160. Rest. ♦ ♿ 100-200.

MURAT

Saint-Flour 25, Aurillac 51, Paris 491
A3 ✉ 15300

ℹ av. Dr-Mallet, ☎ 71.20.09.47, and hôtel de ville, ☎ 71.20.03.80.

SNCF ☎ 71.20.07.20.

Hotels :
★★***Messageries,*** 6, av. de la République, ☎ 71.20.04.04. AE, Visa. 24 rm Ⓟ closed 15 Nov-15 Dec, and Sat, 170. Rest. ♦ ♿ Good regional cooking, 60-130.
★***Bredons,*** 6, av. de la République, ☎ 71.20.08.66. Euro, Visa. 18 rm Ⓟ closed 1 Nov-20 Dec, 130. Rest. 50-80.

⛺ ★★*Stalapos* (85 pl.), ☎ 71.20.01.83.

Farmhouse-inn : Dieune, M. Meyniel, ☎ 71.20.80.60.

MUROL

Clermont-Ferrand 37, Mauriac 96, Paris 433
A2 ✉ 63790

ℹ mairie and pl. Coudert, ☎ 73.88.62.62.

Hotels :
★★***Parc,*** ☎ 73.88.60.08. 39 rm Ⓟ closed Oct-1 May (ex Feb hols, Easter), 220. Rest. 80-130.
★★***Pins*** (L.F.), rue de Levat, ☎ 73.88.60.50. 31 rm Ⓟ closed 30 Sep-15 Apr, 150. Rest. 45-90.

Groire, 0.5 km E on the D146 :
★★***Dômes,*** ☎ 73.88.60.13. 37 rm Ⓟ closed 15 Sep-1 Jun (ex Feb hols, Easter), 180. Rest. ♿ 60-130.

Auvergne

Beaune-le-Froid, 4 km NW, alt. 1 000 m :
★**Relais des Montagnes,** ☎ 73.88.61.48. Visa. 12 rm closed 30 Sep-1 Feb, Mar, 120. Rest. Lavish fare, 40-90.

★★★*La Ribeyre,* Jassat, Saint-Victor-la-Rivière, (100 pl.), ☎ 73.88.61.50 ; ★★*la Plage,* lac Chambon (450 pl.), ☎ 73.88.60.27 ; ★★*la Rivière,* rte de St-Nectaire (40 pl.), ☎ 73.88.60.95 ; ★★municipal *André-Auserre* (350 pl.), ☎ 73.88.60.46.

Bicycle hire : M. J.-L. Rebouffat, rte de la Plage, ☎ 73.88.63.08.

ORCIVAL

Clermont-Ferrand 27, Mauriac 84, Paris 416
A2 ⊠ 63210 Rochefort-Montagne

Hotels :
★**Les Bourelles,** ☎ 73.65.82.28. 7 rm closed Oct and Apr ex school hols Easter, 100.
★**L'Ajasserie d'Orcival,** ☎ 73.21.21.54. Visa. 14 rm closed Oct-Easter (ex school hols), 120.

★★*Étang de Fléchat* (65 pl.), ☎ 73.65.82.96 ; ★*Ferme des Planchettes* (65 pl.), ☎ 73.21.22.75.

Restaurant :
♦ **Cantou** (A.F.), ☎ 73.21.22.07. Copious, family style meals, 80-120. With 8 rm.

Le PUY

Saint-Étienne 78, Mende 92, Paris 516
C3 ⊠ 43000

pl. du Breuil (B3), ☎ 71.09.38.41 ; and 23, rue des Tables (B2), ☎ 71.09.27.42. Opened in Jul and Aug.

SNCF (C3), ☎ 71.02.75.05, 71.02.50.50.

Le Puy-Loudes, ☎ 71.08.62.28.

cour de la gare S.N.C.F. (B3), ☎ 71.09.25.60.

Car-hire : *Budget* train + auto, at the station, ☎ 71.09.38.82, and at the airport.

Hotels :
★★★**Chris'tel,** 15, bd A.-Clair (A3), ☎ 71.02.24.44. Euro, Visa. 30 rm 210. Rest. ♦♦ **le Chavagnac.** closed Fri eve and Sat noon low season and 15 Dec-15 Jan, 50-100.
★★★**Régina,** 34, bd Fayolle (B3), ☎ 71.09.14.71. Tx 990971. AE, DC, Euro, Visa. 40 rm 270. Rest. 80-180.
★★**Bristol,** 7, av. Foch (B3), ☎ 71.09.13.38. AE, DC, Euro, Visa. 33 rm closed school hols, 100. Rest. Regional specialities : *potée auvergnate,* 80-130.
★**Grand Cerf** (L.F.), 3, av. Ch.-Dupuy (C3), ☎ 71.09.05.51. Euro, Visa. 13 rm. closed Mon (10 Oct-Easter), 100. Rest. 60-100.

Blavozy, ⊠ 43540, 6 km E, on the N88 :
★★**Moulin de Barette,** pont de Sumène, ☎ 71.03.00.88. Euro, Visa. 42 rm closed 15 Jan-15 Feb, 240. Rest. ♦ 60-160.

★★★*Bouthezard* (83 pl.), ☎ 71.09.55.09, RN102. Sun before Easter-15 Oct.

Restaurants :
♦♦ **Bateau Ivre,** 5, rue Portail-d'Avignon (B2), ☎ 71.09.67.20. Euro, Visa. Closed 1-17 Jul, Mon, Sat noon and Sun. Quality fare in a hushed atmosphere. Spec : *ris de veau aux morilles,* 70-130.
♦♦ **Sarda,** 12, rue Chênebouterie (A2), ☎ 71.09.58.94. Visa. closed 13 Oct-10 Nov, Sun eve and Mon. Rest. decorated with two 17thC frescoes, set in an 18thC building, 60-190.

Recommended : Velay liqueurs and apéritifs : *la Verveine du Velay,* fg St-Jean, ☎ 71.05.68.11. Velay raspberry liqueur and sloe gin : *Tour Pannessac,* ☎ 71.09.06.57. Cakes and pastries : *le Bergerac,* 43, pl. du Breuil, ☎ 71.09.05.72. Auction rooms : 10, bd de la République, ☎ 71.09.03.85.

RIOM

Clermont-Ferrand 15, Moulins 81, Paris 375
B1 ⊠ 63200

16, rue du Commerce (B2), ☎ 73.38.59.45.

SNCF (C2), ☎ 73.38.20.14.

Hotel :
★**Caravelle,** 21, bd de la République (A1), ☎ 73.38.31.90. Visa. 28 rm, 100.

Restaurant :
● ♦♦ **Les Petits Ventres,** 6, rue A.-Dubourg (A1), ☎ 73.38.21.65. AE, Euro, Visa. closed 25 Aug-22 Sep, 2-10 Jan, Sat noon, Sun eve and Mon. Light dishes : *blanquette de turbot, carré d'agneau à la moutarde,* 80-160.

Sightseeing : from 15 Jun to 15 Sep, Mon, Thu, Fri at 3:15. Information T.O.

RIOM-ES-MONTAGNES

Mauriac 36, Aurillac 94, Paris 494
A3 ⊠ 15400

pl. Gal-de-Gaulle, ☎ 71.78.07.37.

SNCF ☎ 71.78.00.66.

Hotels :
★**Panoramic** (L.F.), ☎ 71.78.06.41. 11 rm closed 15 Sep-15 Jun (ex Feb), 100. Rest. 80-130.
★**Modern** (L.F.), opposite the station, ☎ 71.78.00.13. Euro. 32 rm. closed 15 Dec-15 Jan, Sun low season and school hols, 120. Rest. ♦ 80-100.

★★★*Le Sedour* (176 pl.), ☎ 71.78.05.71.

ROYAT

Clermont-Ferrand 4, Montluçon 95, Paris 393
B1-2 ⊠ 63130

(1 Apr-31 Oct), ☎ 73.35.80.16, 73.35.80.28.

pl. Allard, ☎ 73.35.81.87.

SNCF 73.35.80.68, 73.30.11.93.

Hotels :
★★★**Métropole,** bd Vaquez, ☎ 73.35.80.18. Euro. 76 rm closed 1 Oct-30 Apr, 380. Rest. ♦♦ 100-120.
★★**Royal Hôtel Saint-Mart,** 6, av. de la Gare, ☎ 73.35.80.01. 61 rm closed 30 Sep-1 May, 300. Rest. ♦ 120-240.
★★**Richelieu,** 3, av. A.-Rouzaud, ☎ 73.35.86.31. 60 rm. closed 10 Oct-15 Apr, 200. Rest. 70-90.

★★★★*L'Oclède,* rte de Gravenoire (90 pl.), ☎ 73.35.91.05.

Restaurants :
● ♦♦♦ **Belle Meunière,** 25, av. de la Vallée, ☎ 73.35.80.17. AE, DC, Euro, Visa. closed 2 weeks in Feb, 2 weeks in Nov (school hols), Sun eve and Wed low season. Refined, classical cooking in a splendid restaurant. The first-class produce and preparation fully justify the rather expensive menu, 130-250. With 11 rm.
♦♦♦ **Le Paradis,** av. de Paradis, ☎ 73.35.85.46. AE. closed Jan-10 Feb, Sun eve, Mon. Spec : *terrine maison au foie gras frais, noisette d'agneau Paradis, suprême de blanc de turbot soufflé et sa fine quenelle,* 110-150.

♦♦ ***Écu de France,*** 1, av. J.-Agid, ☎ 73.35.81.81. closed Sun eve, Tue eve and Wed low season, 70-150. With 5 rm.
♦♦ ***Royal-Restaurant*** (L.F.), bd J.-B.-Romeuf, ☎ 73.35.82.72. AE, Euro, Visa. closed 15 Jan-15 Feb, Sun eve and Mon low season. A worthwhile stopping place, with such delectable treats as the superbe *lotte au pistil de safran,* excellent local cheeses and enchanting sweets, 100-150. With 14 rm.

Casino municipal, ☎ 73.35.80.81.

SAINT-BONNET-LE FROID

Saint-Étienne 58, Le Puy 62, Paris 580
34 km E of Yssingeaux, C3
⊠ 43290 Montfaucon

Hotel :
★★***Auberge des Cimes*** (L.F.), ☎ 71.59.93.72. AE, DC, Euro, Visa. 12 rm P closed 1-28 Dec, Mar, Sun eve and Mon, 120. Rest. ♿ 65-200.

Event : *cèpes* fair in Nov (fine, highly sought-after mushrooms).

SAINT-DIDIER-EN-VELAY

Saint-Étienne 25, Le Puy 58, Paris 544
38 km NW Yssingeaux, C2 ⊠ 43140

Hotel :
★***Auberge du Velay,*** Grand-Place, ☎ 71.61.01.54. 8 rm, 160. Rest. ♦ In this 17thC country inn you will taste : *crème de lentilles au saumon, magret de canard,* 70-260.

SAINT-FLOUR

Aurillac 76, Le Puy 92, Paris 490
B3 ⊠ 15100

ℹ 2, pl. d'Armes, ☎ 71.60.14.41.

SNCF ☎ 71.60.03.37.

Hotels :
Upper town :
★★***Europe,*** 12-13, cours Spy-des-Ternes, ☎ 71.60.03.64. Euro, Visa. 45 rm P ♿ closed Dec, Jan and Feb. Well situated. Half-pension oblig. during high season, 200. Rest. ♦ Good service. Spec : *chou farci, pounti, steak de canard au vieux vinaigre, potée auvergnate,* 50-140.
★★***Grand Hôtel des Voyageurs,*** 25, rue du Collège, ☎ 71.60.34.44. AE, DC, Euro, Visa. 38 rm P closed 15 Oct-1 Apr, 190. Rest. ♦ Good traditional Auvergne cooking : *terrine de poisson au coulis d'écrevisses,* 50-130.

Lower town :
★★★***Étape,*** 24, av. de la République, ☎ 71.60.13.03. 33 rm P ♿ closed Oct-Dec, Sun eve and Mon low season, 180. Rest. 60-200.
★★***Nouvel Hôtel-Bonne Table*** (L.F.), av. de la République, ☎ 71.60.05.86. AE, DC, Euro, Visa. 48 rm P ♿ closed 1 Nov-1 Mar, 180. Rest. ♦ Regional dishes : *potée, tripous, truffades,* 80-170.
★★***Saint-Jacques,*** 6, pl. de la Liberté, ☎ 71.60.09.20. Visa. 30 rm P closed Nov-5 Jan, Fri eve and Sat noon low season, 200. Rest. 80-150.
★***Éventail,*** 7, av. de la République, ☎ 71.60.14.07. 20 rm P ♿ closed 1 Oct-25 May, 130. Rest. 45-100.

Ⴤ ★★★*Les Orgues,* upper town (105 pl.), ☎ 71.60.14.41 ; ★★*le Lander,* lower town (50 pl.), ☎ 71.60.14.41.

Restaurant :
Saint-Georges, 5 km E :
♦ ***Au Rendez-vous des Pêcheurs,*** Bout du Monde, ☎ 71.60.15.84. P ♿ Attractive Auvergne inn with affordable local specialities *(potée, tripous, farinette),* 35-60. With 16 rm.

SAINT-NECTAIRE

Clermont-Ferrand 43, Mauriac 102, Paris 428
B2 ⊠ 63710

(25 May-30 Sep), ☎ 73.88.50.01.

ℹ parc des Grands-Thermes, ☎ 73.88.50.86 (high season), and mairie, ☎ 73.88.50.41.

Hotels :
★★***Paix*** (L.F.), ☎ 73.88.50.20. 27 rm P closed 30 Sep-25 May, 150. Rest. 65-85.
★★***Savoy,*** ☎ 73.88.50.28. 32 rm P closed 22 Sep-23 May, 180. Rest. for hotel guests only, 80-130.
★★***Hermitage,*** ☎ 73.88.50.17. 45 rm P closed 30 Sep-25 May, 130. Rest. 60-100.

Ⴤ ★★★*Oasis* (80 pl.), ☎ 73.88.52.68 ; ★★*Hutte des Dômes,* at Saillant (60 pl.), ☎ 73.88.50.22.

Farmhouse-inn : Freydefond, 5 km NW, Mme et M. Rassion, ☎ 73.88.52.76 ; agreeable setting and famous St-Nectaire cheese.

SALERS

Mauriac 19, Aurillac 49, Paris 505
A3 ⊠ 15410

ℹ pl. Tissandier-d'Escous, ☎ 71.40.70.68, and mairie, ☎ 71.40.72.33.

Hotels :
★★***Bailliage*** (L.F.), ☎ 71.40.71.95. Euro. 35 rm P ♿ closed 12 Nov-20 Dec, 180. Rest. Well prepared, copious *tripous* and *potée,* 80-110.
★***Remparts*** (L.F.), ☎ 71.40.70.33. Visa. 18 rm ♿ closed Oct, 5-30 Nov. Well situated, 180. Rest. ♦ Pension only. Equally good service and fare ; unforgettable *petites galettes au beurre de Salers,* 80-100.

Le Theil, ⊠ 15140 Saint-Martin-Valmeroux, 6 km SW on the D35 and D37 :
★★***Hostellerie Maronne*** (Relais du Silence), ☎ 71.69.20.33. Euro. 20 rm P ♿ closed 3 Nov-20 Mar, 180. Rest. eve only, 80-130.

Ⴤ ★★*Le Mouriol* (43 pl.), ☎ 71.40.73.09.

Farmhouse-inn : Mme Geneix, in Récusset (11 km E, in the upper Maronne valley), ☎ 71.40.73.55.

THIERS

Clermont-Ferrand 45, Lyons 137, Paris 387
B1 ⊠ 63300

ℹ pl. du Pirou (B3), ☎ 73.80.10.74, and pl. de la Mutualité (B2 ; high season).

SNCF ☎ 73.80.19.62.

Hotels :
★***Nouvel et Grand Hôtel,*** rue Prosper-Marilhat (B2), ☎ 73.80.00.61. 20 rm 180.

Pont-de-Dore, ⊠ 63920 Peschadoires, 6 km SW:
★***Avenue,*** av. de la Gare, ☎ 73.80.10.14. Visa. 15 rm P closed 26 Dec-10 Jan, Sun eve, 130. Rest. closed Sun eve and Mon noon, 60-130.

Ⴤ ★★*Le Moutier,* Le Breuil (33 pl.), ☎ 73.80.37.71.

Restaurant :
Pont-de-Dore :
♦♦ ***Chez la Mère Dépalle,*** ☎ 73.80.10.05. Euro, Visa. P ♿ Spec : *poulet crémé aux morilles, grenouilles à la provençale, écrevisses à la nage,* 80-210. With 10 rm.

La TOUR-D'AUVERGNE

Mauriac 57, Clermont-Ferrand 60, Paris 446
13 km S of La Bourboule, A2 ⊠ 63680
1 220-1 380 m

ℹ mairie, ☎ 73.21.50.12 (high season).

Hotels :
★***Lac*** (L.F.), rte de Bort-les-Orgues, ☎ 73.21.52.19. 12 rm (annex : 6 supp. rm) P closed 1 Oct-15 Dec, 155. Rest. 50-90.
★***Reine Margot,*** pl. de la Mairie, ☎ 73.21.50.96. AE, Euro, Visa. 18 rm, closed 15 Apr-15 May, 15 Oct-15 Nov, 120. Rest. ♿ 35-80.

VIC-LE-COMTE

Clermont-Ferrand 24, Le Puy 105, Paris 414
B2 ⊠ 63270

SNCF ☎ 73.39.92.18.

Restaurant :
Longues, 4 km NW :
● ♦♦ ***Le Comté,*** ☎ 73.39.90.31. Euro, Visa. P closed Mon eve, Tue and Feb. A wide selection of regional dishes ; good, solid food, with varying menus according to season, 90-200.

VIC-SUR-CÈRE

Aurillac 21, Saint-Flour 55, Paris 525
A3 ⊠ 15800

ℹ av. Mercier, ☎ 71.47.50.68.

SNCF ☎ 71.47.51.74.

Hotels :
● ★★***Bains*** (Relais du Silence), 9-11, av. de la Promenade, ☎ 71.47.50.16. 38 rm P closed 14 Apr-5 May, 13 Oct-24 Dec, 180. Rest. ♦ Spec : *terrine de truite saumonée, magret de canard au poivre vert,* 80-170.
★★***Beauséjour,*** av. André-Mercier, ☎ 71.47.50.27. Euro. 75 rm P ♿ closed 1 Oct-15 May, 200. Rest. ♿ 50-80.
★★***Family*** (L.F.), rue Émile-Duclaux, ☎ 71.47.50.49. Euro, Visa. 39 rm P ♿ closed 1 Oct-Christmas school hols, 140. Rest. ♦ ♿ Family-style regional cooking : *chou farci, potée, tripous,* 40-70.
★★***Bel Horizon*** (L.F.), ☎ 71.47.50.06. 24 rm P closed mid-Nov-mid-Dec, 180. Rest. 80-180.
★★***Auberge des Monts,*** ☎ 71.47.51.71. Visa. 26 rm P closed 30 Sep-1 May ex Feb, 180.

Pailherols, 14 km SW :
★***Auberge des Montagnes,*** ☎ 71.47.57.71. 11 rm P closed Oct and Sat (Nov-Feb), 100. Rest, 50-95.

Curegourse Pass, 6 km SE on the D54 :
Å ★★★★*Pommeraie* (50 pl.), ☎ 71.47.54.18 ; ★★★*Allée des Tilleuls* (250 pl.), ☎ 71.47.51.04.

Bicycle hire : *Angelvy,* ☎ 71.47.51.84 (by the day and by the week).

VOLVIC

Clermont-Ferrand 20, Montluçon 83, Paris 382
B1 ⊠ 63530

SNCF ☎ 73.33.51.71.

Hotels :
Tournoël, 1 km N :
La Chaumière (A.F.), ☎ 73.33.50.37. 6 rm P closed low season and Tue, 90. Rest. closed week-ends, 40-90.

Luzet, 3 km :
★***Rose des Vents*** (L.F.), ☎ 73.33.50.77. DC, Euro. 28 rm P 180. Rest. ♿ closed Mon noon, 80-130.

Å ★*Municipal* (50 pl.), ☎ 73.33.50.38.

Event : end May, pilgrimage at Notre-Dame-de-la-Garde.

YSSINGEAUX

Le Puy 27, Saint-Étienne 51, Paris 570
C3 ⊠ 43200

Hotels :
★★***Hôtel du Cygne,*** 8, rue d'Alsace-Lorraine, ☎ 71.59.01.87. 18 rm P closed 28 Aug-2 Oct, 20 Dec-10 Jan, Sun eve and Mon, 150. Rest. ♦♦ 60-150.
★★***Voyageurs*** (L.F.), 5, pl. de la Victoire, ☎ 71.59.06.54. AE, Euro, Visa. 11 rm, closed Oct, Thu eve, Fri (low season), 180. Rest. 80-130.

Å ★★*Choumouroux* (50 pl.), ☎ 71.59.01.13.

The Basque Country, Béarn and Bigorre

Perhaps the most striking thing about the Pyrénées is their aura of coolness and greenery. The word mountain usually conjures up images of gravel and scree, silence and vast stretches of empty land — but these mountains are as green and lush as any idyllic painter's landscape. The far-off bluish haze of the high peaks melts into the watercolor tints of the Labourd region, and the countryside is full of bubbling streams and rivers running through valleys large and small. Other mountains have rivers — this country has a whole glossary of special terms for its waterways to translate all possible variations in size, speed and color.

On the road from Mont-de-Marsan to Pau, the traveller can stop to watch the peaks of the Pyrénées rearing up like a crenellated fortress over the low plains of Aquitaine. Everywhere, sea, mountains and sky converse before the Pyrénées come to a head in one last masterful surge near the Spanish border.

The clear sky of Bayonne floats over the sharp spires of the cathedral. Biarritz, once a simple fishing village enriched by whale-hunting, is now a center of tourist attraction whose perfect climate also draws an increasing number of retired people.

Despite the differences between the Basque country and the Béarn region, these two regions, with their strong centuries-old traditions, live in perfect harmony in the shadow of the Atlantic Pyrénées. Bigorre, too, has its own special personality, its own history and traditions as befits the native land of Henry IV, born in Pau in 1553. Bigorre's prestige is increased by the four million visitors and tourists who each year come to Lourdes, the town where the Virgin Mary appeared to a young village girl named Bernadette and left behind the miraculous springs. Here the infirm and the healthy bathe together; piety and rosary beads, plastic statuettes and tourist buses coexist peacefully in the shadow of the Pyrénées.

Sightseeing

Facts and figures

***Location** : the Pays Basque (the Basque Country), the Béarn and Bigorre regions cover the western one-third of the Pyrenean Chain and the river valleys flowing into the Adour, which is the chain's northern limit.*
***Area** : 12 110 km^2.*
***Climate** : in general, sunny; however, the western Pyrénées are affected by their proximity to the ocean. The Pays Basque is known for mild autumns, but also for summer showers. Frequent heavy rain keeps summer temperatures low, even in Bigorre.*
***Population** : approx. 766 000.*
***Administration** : The Pyrénées-Atlantiques Department (prefecture : Pau) is part of the economic region of Aquitaine, whereas the Hautes-Pyrénées Department (prefecture : Tarbes) is part of the Midi-Pyrénées economic region.*

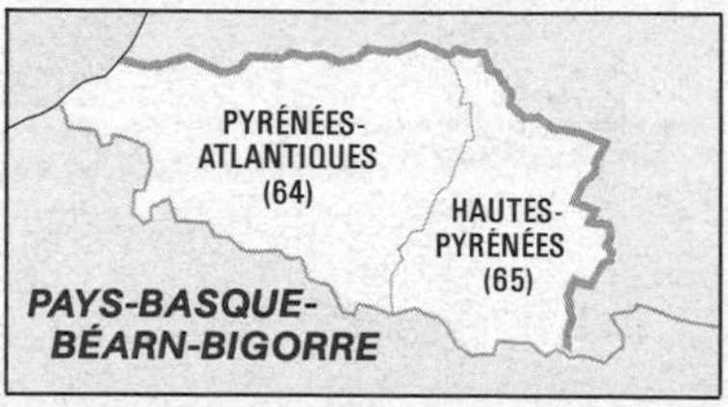

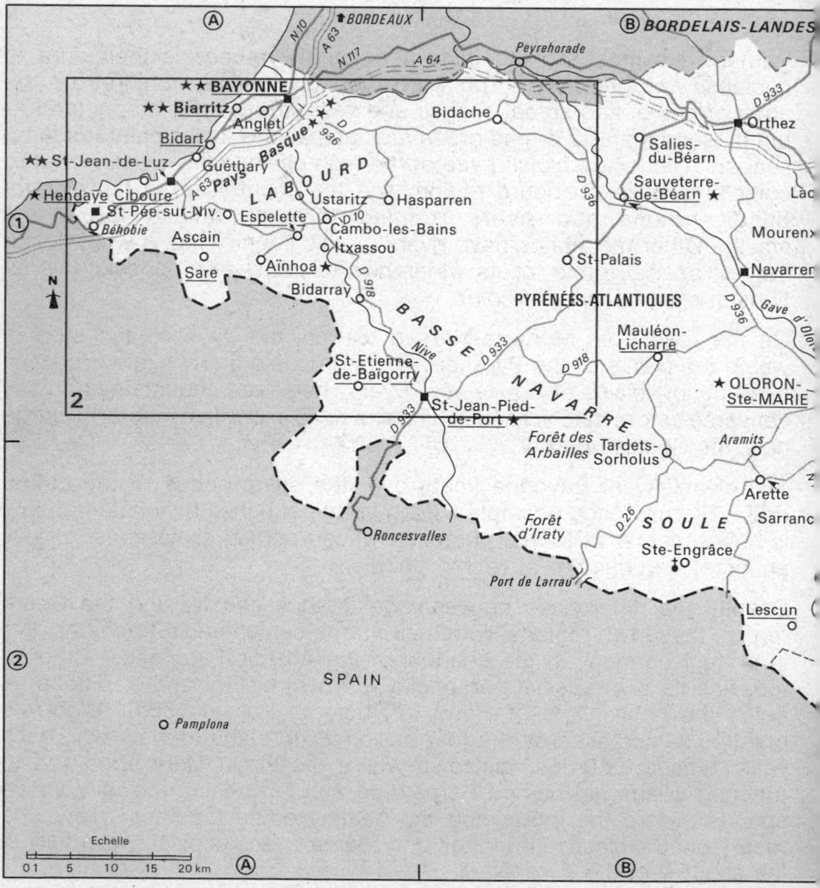

Don't miss

★★★ : Basque Country (A1), Cavarnie Valley (C2), High Passes of the Pyrénées circuit (C2), ★★ : Arreau and the upper valley of the Aure (D2), Laruns and the Ossau Valley (C2), Pau (C1), Saint-Jean-de-Luz (A1), Western Pyrénées National Park (C2).

■ ARETTE-PIERRE-SAINT-MARTIN

B2 / ® / pop. 1 120 (Pyrénées-Atlantiques)

Arette (alt. 1 650 m), westernmost winter resort in the Pyrénées (open also in summer, hikes and rambles) forms a kind of balcony on Anie Peak (alt. 2 504 m).

▶ **Pierre-Saint-Martin Pass** *(3 km SW;* alt. 1 760 m; *open mid-May-mid-Oct.).* Near the **gouffre de la Pierre-Saint-Martin** (world's deepest pothole, more than 1 760 m; *inaccessible to the public*), a ceremony has taken place every 13th of July since 1375 : the shepherds of Barétous pay a tribute of three heifers to their Spanish neighbours from Roncal in exchange for grazing rights. □

Leave Bayonne or Biarritz, explore Bidache, Salies and Sauveterre-de-Béarn, Château de Laàs, Barcus (lunch), Saint-Engrâce and Mauléon-Licharre. Stopover at Saint-Jean-Pied-de-Port. Next day, visit the Aldudes, Cambo, Saint-Pée and Sare (lunch), then Rhune and Saint-Jean-de-Luz. A visit to Lourdes (full day) could be rounded off by an excursion to Cauterets and the Gavarnie natural amphitheatre.

■ ARGELÈS-GAZOST★

C2 / ® / pop. 3 460 (Hautes-Pyrénées)

Argelès (alt. 465 m), a spa specialising in the relief of skin diseases and rheumatism, is set in a lush valley where the rivers Cau-

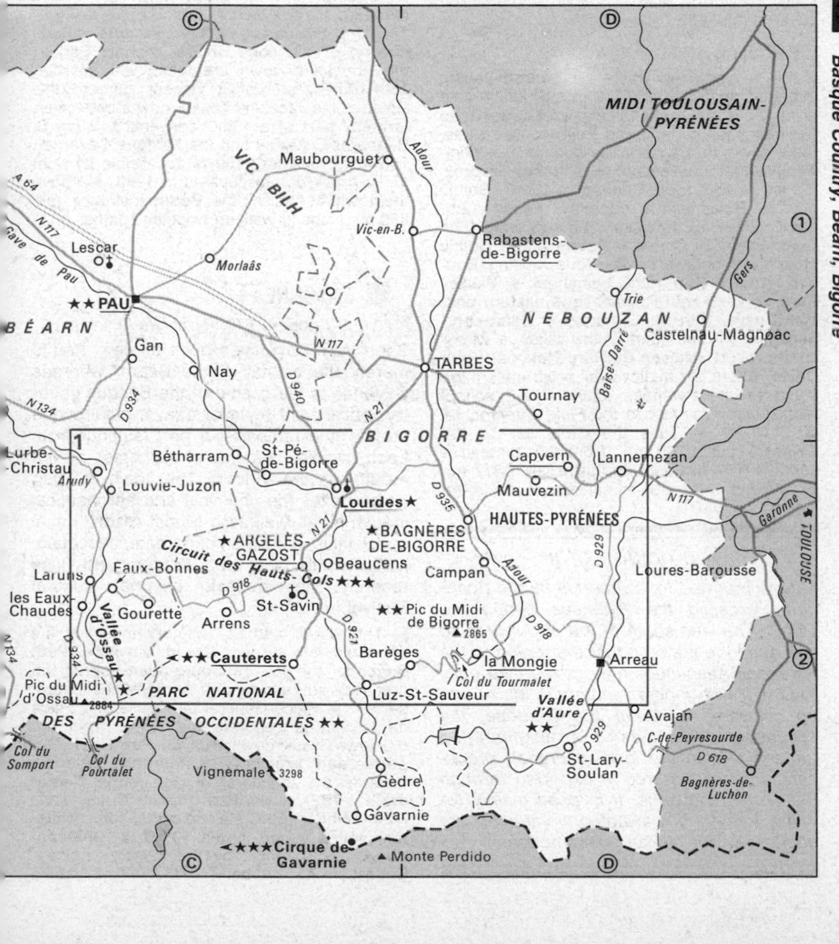

terets and Gavarnie combine to form the Haut Gave de Pau (upper reaches of the river). Mild, sunny climate; mineral springs on extensive grounds. □

▶ Argelès Valley

▶ **Saint-Savin** ® : 12thC monastery on the site of a Gallo-Roman camp; fortified **Romanesque church★** (organ casing 1557, museum of religious art in the Chapterhouse); view over the houses. The 12thC **château d'Arcizans-Avant** ®, above the town, has commanded the Auzun and Saint Savin valleys since the 12thC *(daily pm Jul.-21 Sep.; Sun. and school hols. pm Apr.-Oct.).* ▶ **Pierrefitte-Nestalas :** at the exit of the Luz and Cauterets gorges; 16th-18thC houses. ▶ **Beaucens** ® : Musée des Aigles★ (Falconry Museum, *daily pm Apr.-Oct.*). ▶ 20 km drive E on the Hautacam mountain road. □

■ ARREAU and the Upper Valley of the Aure★★

D2 / ® / pop. 820

Once the principal town for four valleys, at the junction of the rivers Aure and Louron. Walks.

▶ Church of **St. Exupère :** 16thC houses (especially noteworthy, Maison du Lys (Lily) near the covered market).

▶ Nearby

▶ 7 km along the **Neste de Louron valley,** overshadowed by the 3130 m high snow-covered Gourgs Blancs Peak to **Loudervielle** (Romanesque church) and **Peyresourde Pass,** then down to Bagnères-de-Luchon (→ Midi-Toulousain-Pyrénées). ▶ **Aure Valley** *(approx. 70 km round trip).* **Cadéac :** 16thC Gothic church, Romanesque doorway, ruined 12th-13thC tower. ▶ **Ancizan : church** with 1554 Entombment of Christ. ▶ **Bazus-Aure :** Gothic church with noteworthy keystone vaulting. **Bourisp :** church (late 16thC paintings). ▶ **Vieille-Aure :** church with Romanesque eastern end, 16thC nave, 15th-16thC murals. ▶ **Saint-Lary-Soulan** ® : in the heart of the valley, a winter sports resort; **Maison du Parc National** (Park Office) offers an audiovisual program on the fauna of the Pyrénées *(daily during school terms, or by request to the Field Director, tel 62.39.40.91).* ▶ Take the cable car to **Pla d'Adet** ® (alt. 1700 m) : from that plateau a gondola runs to **Soum de Matte** (alt. 2377 m). Excursions on foot or by car, especially in the vicinity of **Orédon Lakes★** (alt. 1850 m) and **Cap-de-Long★★** (alt. 2160 m) the largest dam in the Pyrénées. From the lodge (Châlet-Refuge), interesting walks through the **Néouvielle Nature Reserve★** (23 km²), next to the National Park; or climb up Long Peak (alt. 3194 m; guide essential), the highest peak in the French Pyrénées. ▶ Upstream of Saint-Lary the road runs through the **resort** and **plateau of Aragnouet :** Romanesque former chapel of the Hospitallers (warrior-monks who guarded the pilgrimage routes) on one of the roads to the Spanish shrine of St. James of Compostela. From here, reach the winter sports centre of **Piau-Engaly** (alt. 1880-2380 m) and the **Bielsa tunnel** into Spain. □

The golden grain

Maize, imported from America by the Spaniards, crossed the Pyrénées during the 17thC. The land south of the Adour was so well suited to the crop that the region of the Pyrénées Atlantiques now grows little else. Although with modern methods, maize can be cultivated north of the Garonne, the Pyrénées Atlantiques and neighbouring Landes remain the leading French producers. Part of the crop is exported through the port of Bayonne. It is used mainly for cattle fodder, but sweetcorn varieties are also grown for human consumption.

■ BAGNÈRES-DE-BIGORRE★

D2 / ® / pop. 9850 (Hautes-Pyrénées)

Bagnères (alt. 550 m) offers a range of interests : thermal springs (sulphur, calcium, iron and other mineral waters), a summer resort, industrial weaving, slate and marble quarries. Other activities include the manufacturing of equipment for the aviation, railway and electrical industries; flower festival in summer.

▶ Casino, **spa facilities** and the **Salies Museum** *(daily ex. Tue. and Sun. in season; Thu. and Fri. out of season;* fine arts, natural history) at the edge of the Thermal Park★; the houses in town are faced with marble; 15th-16thC church of St. Vincent; ruined 12thC cloister; the Jacobins Tower, now a bell-tower, formerly part of a 15thC convent. ▶ 2 km S, Bagnères Gateway and the **Médous Caverns :** 760 m of galleries; 160 m accessible by boat *(daily Apr.-Oct.),* discovered in 1948. ▶ Above the town to the W, the **Bédat lookout★** (alt. 880 m), a one hr walk on woodland paths. □

■ BAYONNE★★

A1 / ® / pop. 42970 (Pyrénées-Atlantiques)

Seen from Bayonne's point of view, Pau is merely the capital of the Béarn, whereas Bayonne is the capital of the Basque country. An ancient town of quays, picturesque streets and ramparts, a port (sulphur from Lacq, maize, cement, phosphates) at the mouth of the Adour. The town is also a centre for the chemical and aeronautical industries as well as a tourist resort. Local specialities include smoked ham, chocolate, nougat with pine nuts *(touron)* and (less recently) the namesake bayonet; cultural festival in August.

▶ The Adour and its tributary the Nive cut the town into three : **Grand Bayonne, Petit Bayonne** and the **Faubourg-Saint-Esprit;** the first two are surrounded by formidable ramparts★. ▶ Place Général de Gaulle and Place de la Liberté separate the Adour from the old town; walk down **Rue du Port-Neuf** (B2; pedestrian precinct; restaurants) and up towards the cathedral. ▶ **Ste Marie Cathedral★ :** (B2) in Northern French Gothic style (13th-14thC); 16thC stained glass, 13thC **cloister;** spires added in the 19thC. ▶ **Château-Vieux :** (B2) rebuilt by the military engineer Sébastien de Vauban (1633-1707) in 1680,

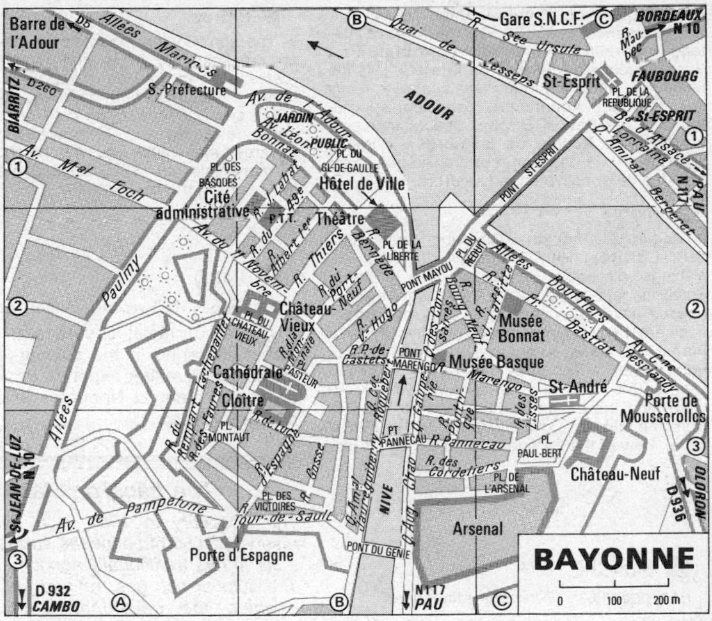

occupies the NW corner of the fortifications, incorporating mediaeval defensive walls. ▶ **In Petit Bayonne, Bonnat Museum★** of collections donated by the painter Léon Bonnat (1833-1922) (C2; 15th-19thC paintings, drawings, antiquities; *daily ex. Tue. and nat. hols.*); **Basque Museum★★** in a 16thC house (B2; regional art, Basque folklore; *daily ex. Sun. and nat. hols.*). Near the 17thC Mousserolles Gateway, **Château Neuf** C3; 15th-17thC. ▶ On the right bank of the Adour, at 9 Amiral Bergeret Quay, **Izarra Distillery** for the local liqueur *(visits tel. 59.55.09.45)*. ▶ Visits to the **port** : *enquire at Chamber of Commerce tel. 59.25.75.75.* In summer, cruises on the river Adour (Société Nautique, Mousserolles Quay *tel. 59.59.21.93*). □

▶ Nearby

▶ **Ustaritz** ® *(13 km S)* : capital of Labourde until 1790, on the left bank of the Nive; the Seminary of St. François-Xavier has played an important role in preserving the Basque language. □

■ BIARRITZ★★

A1 / ® / pop. 26 650 (Pyrénées-Atlantiques)

Biarritz, Anglet and Bayonne form a vast urban agglomeration separated by green spaces; it is difficult to say where one town ends and another begins. Biarritz was long a simple fishing village to which the whaling industry brought a degree of prosperity, but starting with the second Empire (ca. 1850) wealthy Europeans flocked to spend their leisure time near the Villa Eugénie, built for the wife of Napoléon III. Soon they commissioned architects to build residences in the surrounding areas. Later, the gentle winter climate attracted the retired, who now represent about 20 % of the population. The two casinos, three beaches (Côtes des Basques, Port Vieux and Grande Plage) and outdoor activities (underwater fishing, surfing, wind surfing) make Biarritz equally popular with tourists.

▶ Start exploring the town from **Place Georges Clemenceau,** a busy square near the **Place Bellevue** and the **Summer Casino** (Casino d'Été). North of the **Municipal Casino** and the **Grande Plage** (main beach) is the former Villa Eugénie, now the Palais Hotel; farther on, the

Pyrenean flora and fauna

The Western Pyrénées National Park (Park National des Pyrénées Occidentales) *protects countless specimens of native fauna, of which the Pyrenean bear is probably the most intriguing. There is little likelihood of finding yourself face-to-face with one, as only about 30 are in existence. There are, however, about 1 500 isard (Pyrenean mountain goat, the park's symbol) as well as lynx, civet, marten, ermine, marmot and other species. The park shelters many varieties of birds : Egyptian vulture, griffon vulture, golden eagle, bearded vulture and sparrow hawk. Smaller birds include ptarmigan (similar to the Scottish grouse), capercaillie, water ouzel, and others. The rivers abound with char and several species of trout. Flora include blue iris, rhododendron, jonquil, asphodel, turk's cap lily, anemone, and scented daphne, as well as alpine varieties such as gentian, edelweiss, ramondia, Pyrenean buttercup, and dwarf plants such as catch-fly and Pyrenean willow.*

almost equally old **Hotel Miramar,** now a salt-water treatment centre. ▶ On the **Atalaye Plateau** separating the fishing port from Port Vieux beach is the **Musée de la Mer★** (Marine Museum) : ancient and modern seafaring *(daily 9-7 Jul.-Aug.).* **Aquarium★ :** principal species found in the Bay of Biscay. Spectacular promontory, the **Rocher de la Vierge★** (Virgin's Rock). ▶ View★ the length of the Basque coast from the perspective on the seafront. □

▶ Nearby

▶ **Anglet** ® : industrial Bayonne meets residential Biarritz; 16thC church, 17th-18thC furnishings; distinctive Basque wooden galleries. Since the late 19thC, many imposing weekend houses have been built. The principal attractions are 4 km of sandy beach and the Chiberta Forest (170 acres; footpaths, bridle paths, lake, golf course). ▶ The other side of the Négresse Quarter (Biarritz railway station), between Mouriscot and the ocean, is **Ilbaritz.** ▶ 5 km SW, from the **Bidart** ® cliffs (chapel of the Madeleine), view of the Pyrénées and the Bay of Biscay. □

BIDACHE

B1 / pop. 1 015 (Pyrénées-Atlantiques)

This village overlooking the valley of the Bidouze between Béarn and Navarre was once the independent fiefdom of the Gramont family, one of the most illustrious in France.

▶ 16thC **church.** Ruined **château de Gramont★,** parts of which date from the 16thC *(daily ex. Tue., Mar.-Sep.).*

▶ Nearby

▶ **Château de Guiche** *(7 km NW) :* rebuilt in the 18thC, was also the property of the Dukes of Gramont *(same hours);* ruined 13thC keep. ▶ View★ over the Adour Valley and the Pyrénées from **Miremont Ridge** *(6 km W).* ▶ **Labastide-Clairence** *(15 km SW :* a walled town founded in 1312, with typical roofs of the region; also a Gothic church fitted in the 17th-18thC with Basque-style wooden galleries.) □

CAUTERETS★★

C2 / ® / pop. 1 110 (Hautes-Pyrénées)

Cauterets and the neighbouring valleys are among the leading Pyrenean winter sports and excursion areas. Cauterets is also a spa, with 11 sulphur-rich springs. The 16thC author Rabelais, the 18th-19thC statesman Talleyrand, the 19thC authors Chateaubriand, George Sand, and Flaubert, and the turn-of-the-century actress Sarah Bernhardt were among the famous visitors.

▶ In the town centre, Place Clemenceau is built over the river Cauterets; at the heart of the left bank is the **Casino Esplanade.** The **Cauterets Museum** is also the **HQ of the Western Pyrénées National Park** (exhibitions of flora, fauna, insects, geology, ecology). On the right bank, a path above the park leads to the Bains (Baths) de la Raillère and the **Cascades de Lutour★** (waterfalls). □

▶ Nearby

▶ The surrounding mountain woods are ideal for cross-country hikes and rambles. ▶ SW *(paths; road to the Pont d'Espagne)* **Jeret valley★★ :** waterfalls★ at **Cérisey,** the Pas de l'Ours and Boussès. From the Pont d'Espagne continue along the **Marcadeau valley** or towards **Lake Gaube★★,** with the snowy peaks of Vignemale (alt. 3 298 m) and the adjacent mountains in the background. □

LACQ

B1 / pop. 710 (Pyrénées-Atlantiques)

A thicket of metal towers and pipelines, flames flickering in the sulphur-laden air : the sulphur is either exported or used in the aluminium plant at Noguères and in other chemical plants. □

The Lacq gas lake

The discovery in 1951 of a natural gas reservoir 3 550 m below the surface caused a stir in this traditionally agricultural region. The sulphur-rich gas, refined at Lacq, has enabled the development of industry throughout the region. To visit the refinery, tel. 59.60.07.78. Gas not required locally is piped throughout France. The 300 billion m^3 reserve is expected to run out before the end of this century.

▶ Nearby

▶ After **Mourenx** ® *(2 km SW) :* a new town created in 1957-61 ; (lookout and orientation table), the countryside soon sheds the industrial air of Lacq; the Gave de Pau and surrounding villages have a traditional appearance. ▶ **Monein** *(13 km S) :* vineyards, orchards on a road to Compostela; largest Gothic church in Béarn (15th-16thC, 12thC tympanum). ▶ **Château de Morlanne★ :** *(21 km NE);* 18thC furnishings, paintings; *(pm daily Mar.-Oct.)* was used in the 14thC to defend Béarn's northern border. The village church (14thC bell-tower; 17th-18thC furnishings) was also part of the defences. □

LARUNS and the Ossau Valley★★

C2 / ® / pop. 1 465 (Pyrénées-Atlantiques)

Laruns, in the Valentin Valley (→ High Pyrenean Passes), is the best place to begin a visit to the upper valley of the Gave d'Ossau, where many mountain village traditions are still maintained.

▶ Annual folklore festival *(15 Aug.)* in the main square; the inhabitants don traditional Béarnais costume. Walks. ▶ **Béost :** *(1.5 km NE)* a charming mountain village; Romanesque church★, enlarged in the 15thC.

▶ Ossau Valley★★ *(approx 60 km round trip).*

▶ **Eaux-Chaudes :** a spa in a narrow, wooded gorge; excellent base for excursions.

▶ Gorges de Bitet★ : pleasant walks, **Miegebat** hydroelectric station. ▶ **Gabas :** the Bious and the Brousset meet here to form the Gave d'Ossau; **Maison du Parc National** (Park Office) provides information on mountain ecology; life at high altitudes *(daily pm 15 Jun.-15 Sep. or by request to the Field Director, tel. 59.05.32.13).* Climbs and excursions in the mountains (guide essential); lakes★ Bious, Ayous; **Midi d'Ossau Peak** (alt. 2 885 m; panorama★★). ▶ The cable car at **Sagette** (winter sports), between Gabas and Lake Fabrèges, takes you to the **Artouste★ tourist train** *(15 Jun.-15 Sep.),* the highest in Europe. After about 10 km, **Lake Artouste★** (alt. approx. 2 000 m). From here, climb **Balaïtous** (guide; alt. 3 146 m). ▶ Splendid view of the surrounding peaks from **Pourtalet Pass★★** on the Spanish border (alt. 1 792 m). □

■ LOURDES★

C2 / ® / pop. 17 620 (Hautes-Pyrénées)

A sleepy hamlet and former stronghold of the County of Bigorre, Lourdes, in 1858, saw its destiny change in the Massabielle Cave where Bernadette Soubirous, then a 14-year-old peasant girl claimed to have had several visions of the Virgin Mary. Four million visitors and pilgrims now make their way to Lourdes each year; the pious and the ailing from all over the world contribute to the town's incongruous admixture of bustle, contemplation and commerce.

▶ The **Processions Esplanade** (A1) passes close to the **underground Basilica of St. Pius X★** (capacity 20 000) built in 1958 for the Centenary of the Visions. ▶ **Basilica of the Rosary :** the lower church, in neo-Byzantine style (1885), is set beneath a neo-Gothic Basilica (1876); remarkable pipe organ. Pilgrims crowd around the lower church to collect water from taps next to the **Massabielle Cave.** Farther on are baths for immersing the sick. In the Prairie de la Grotte (Cave forecourt), a slideshow called "*Un jour, Bernadette...*" is shown in megavision on six screens *(daily until 8:30 pm in season).* ▶ Above the basilica, the **chemin du Calvaire** (road to Calvary) leads past a spur; view★. ▶ **Museum of Petit Lourdes :** (68 Avenue Peyramale) model of the town in 1858 *(daily in season).* ▶ Rue de la Grotte (B2) leads to the **Gemmail Museum of Sacred Art** (N° 72, *daily Palm Sunday to 15 Oct.*) and the **Wax Museum** (N° 87 *daily Mar.-Oct.; until 9:30 pm in season).* ▶ The **Boly Mill** on Rue Bernadette-Soubirous (B1) is the birthplace of Ste Bernadette *(daily Easter to 15 Oct.).* ▶ The **Municipal Hospice** (C1) displays mementoes of Bernadette, who spent some time there in retreat before entering a convent at Nevers, where she died in 1879. Rue des Petits Fossés, the *cachot* (lock-up) (B1, *daily; closed am in winter)* was the humble home of the Soubirous at the time of the visions. At 38 Rue de la

Pelota

There is hardly a Basque village that does not have a pelota *wall* (fronton). *The better organised, including some in the Béarn, also have indoor* frontons *called* trinquets, *or courts for* jaï alaï, *with a wall on the left. The game is played by two teams of three. The numerous variations include* chistera, cesta punta, joko garbi *and* remonte, *for which the* pelotari *(players) use* chistera *(a narrow, curved basketwork racket) strapped to their wrists.*

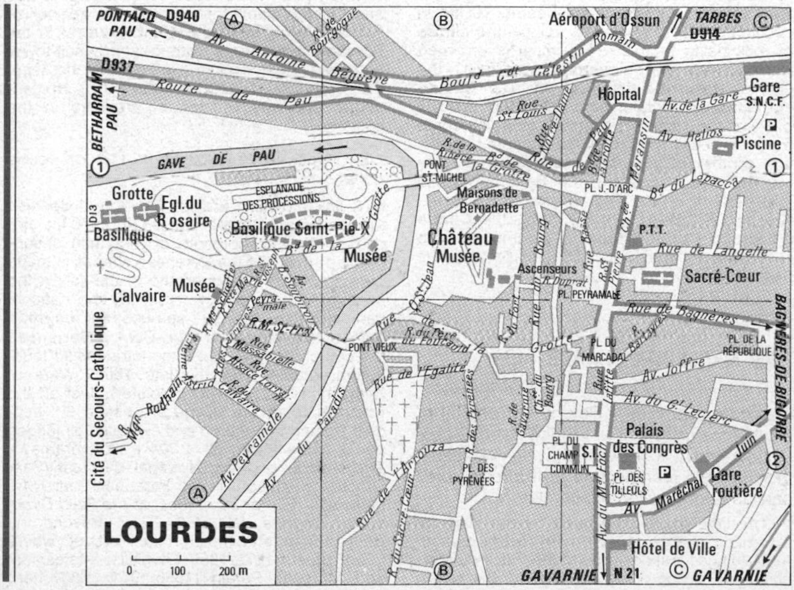

Grotte and 14 Rue du Fort, films are shown on the life of Saint Bernadette *(daily in season).* ▶ **Château of the Counts of Bigorre :** (B1) 11thC, 14thC keep, over-restored in the 19thC, with the **Pyrenean Museum** *(daily Apr.-Oct.);* history of Lourdes; Basque, Béarn and Bigorre folklore; natural history). ▶ 1.5 km S, cable-car to **Béout** (alt. 700 m); farther on, cable railway to **Jers Peak** (alt. 900 m); views★. ▶ 2 km NW : **Lake Lourdes** in a charming setting. ▶ **Bartrès** *(4 km N) :* the sheep farm (Maison de Lagüe) where Bernadette lived during her childhood. □

■ LUZ-SAINT-SAUVEUR

C2 / ® / pop. 1 160 (Hautes-Pyrénées)

Luz is a mountain spa above the Saint-Sauveur Gorge *(season from May to Oct.).* Access from here to beautiful sites around Gavarnie (see below), Barèges or Tourmalet (→ High Passes of the Pyrénées).

▶ **Romanesque church★ :** late 12thC, with 14thC surrounding wall, formerly part of a Hospitallers' Commandery; **museum** of religious art, archaeology, ethnography *(open on request daily pm ex. Sat. and Sun., tel 62.92.81.75).* ▶ **Maison de la Vallée** (cultural centre) : various exhibitions and events. ▶ Spa (alkaline sulphur springs) in the upper area of Saint-Sauveur. ▶ Winter sports centre at **Luz-Ardiden** (alt. 1 700-2 200 m; *12 km NW*). □

▶ Gavarnie Valley *(approx 40 km round trip)*

▶ **Pont Napoléon** (bridge) crosses 65 m above the river in the Saint-Sauveur Gorge★. ▶ The hydroelectric station at **Pragnères** is the largest in the Pyrénées *(visits in summer).* ▶ From **Gèdre** ® at the junction of the Gavarnie and the Héas, you can go up the Héas valley to the **Cirque de Troumouse** (natural amphitheatre)★★, less well known but just as impressive as that at Gavarnie. ▶ **Gavarnie** ® (alt. 1 360 m) : beyond the **Chaos de Coumely** (rockfall), the best base for excursions on foot, horse or donkey to the **Cirque★★★** *(approx. 2hr).* This magnificent amphitheatre, 10 km in circumference, is formed by concentric circles of rock rising to 1 200-1 500 m. It is crowned with glaciers and numerous waterfalls; the Grande Cascade★ falls 240 m. The **Botanical Gardens** contain more than 400 species of Pyrenean plants, almost half of which come from the locality. Among the mountain walks and climbs *(guide often essential),* the **Tantes Peak** (alt. 2 322 m), the **Boucharo Pass** (alt. 2 270 m; *on the Spanish border road),* the **Brèche de Roland** (alt. 2 807 m), the **Cirque d'Estaubé** and the **Cirque de Troumouse** (also called the **Pimené,** alt. 2 801 m) provide the best views★★. □

■ MAULÉON-LICHARRE

B1 / ® / pop. 4 310 (Pyrénées-Atlantiques)

Mauléon, in a wide valley, is the capital of Soule (one of the three French Basque provinces) and a town with thriving traditions, including the manufacture of the rope-soled canvas shoes called espadrilles.

▶ The little town, dominated by the ruins of a fortified château (view), has several beautiful buildings; arcades around the Place du Marché. At N° 9 Rue du Jeu de Paume, the **Andurain Manor★** (16th-18thC furniture; *Jul.-15 Sep. ex. Thu. Sun. and nat. hols. am*). ▶ Ruins of the **château de Mongaston** *(10 km N) :* 16thC; *(daily ex. Wed. Jul.-Sep.).* ▶ **Aussurucq** *(10 km SW) :* a good base for walks in the Arbailles or Soule woods (numerous paths). □

▶ Saison Valley★★ *(approx 80 km round trip)*

▶ **Gotein :** the church has a Virgin and Child of Spanish origin. ▶ **Tardets-Sorholus** ® : a *bastide* (fortified town) of 1280; several of the surrounding villages have Romanesque churches. ▶ **Licq-Athérey :** recreational facilities, including : trout-fishing, jeep racing in the mountains, hang gliding, walks and pigeon shoots. ▶ Higher up, the junction where the valleys of Larrau and Uhaïtxa meet to form the Saison; continuing up the Uhaïtxa you come to the narrow **Kakouetta Gorges★** *(Jul.-Aug.;* potholing/spelunking exhibition at the entrance), the **Ehujarre Ravine★** (trails), and the village of **Sainte-Engrâce,** its 11th-12thC Romanesque church★ one of the most interesting in the region (carved decoration; 18thC Spanish altarpiece), on a pilgrim road to Compostela. Beyond, GR 10 leads to the **Holcarté Crevasses** *(access difficult).* ▶ Paths to the winter pastures throught **Larrau** (14thC church); walks in the **Iraty and St. Joseph woods** (pigeon shooting in autumn). □

■ OLORON-SAINTE-MARIE★

B1 / ® / pop. 12 237 (Pyrénées-Atlantiques)

The ancient Basque town called *Iluro,* at the junction of the Aspe and the Ossau, is now know as Oloron and linked with the episcopal city of Sainte-Marie. High points of the year are the May and September agricultural fairs. Town industries also include household linen, Basque bérets and chocolate. Biennial international folklore festival in Aug.

▶ From place Mendiondou at the centre of town between the bridges over the rivers Aspe and Ossau, climb through the old **quarter of Sainte-Croix** (15thC and 18thC houses) to the **Romanesque church,** with its sturdy bell-tower and keep; view. ▶ On the left bank of the Aspe, the **Cathedral :** (rebuilt 13th-14thC) Romanesque doorway; sculpture; treasury in the sacristy. □

▶ Aspe Valley★★ *(approx 110 km round trip)*

▶ A link between French Béarn and Spanish Aragon via the Somport pass (alt. 1 630 m), and one of the last holdouts of mountain sheep-farming; much of the Pyrenean cheese is made here; towards the upper end of the valley, the flora and fauna are protected by the national park. ▶ **Saint-Christau :** spa used for the treatment of skin disorders *(Apr.-Oct.).* ▶ **Sarrance :** the church is a 14thC Premonstratensian foundation, rebuilt after the late 16thC Wars of Religion (17thC two-story cloister). Just off the Somport road, the village of **Lescun** ® : huddled around the church and enclosed by jagged peaks (**Anie Peak,** alt. 2 504 m; panorama★). The **Maison du Parc National d'Estaut** (Park Office) : exhibition on the Pyrenean bear *(11-7 daily, Jul.-Aug. or by request to the Field Director at Bedous, tel. 59.34.70.87.* Beyond the Pont d'Enfer and the Fort de Portalet, where Léon Blum (1872-1950; socialist statesman) and Marshall Pétain (1856-1951; WWI hero who led the pro-Nazi Vichy government during during WWII) were imprisoned, is **Urdos,** the last village before the **Somport Pass** (Customs post). Somport was known to the Romans as *Summus Portus* (High Gate); it was used by the Arabs as a gateway to Europe in the mediaeval epic poem, the *Chanson de Roland.* □

■ ORTHEZ

B1 / ® / pop. 11 540 (Pyrénées-Atlantiques)

Vines, maize and livestock are raised in the surrounding area. Orthez is an important market town *(every Tue.)* where poultry, *foie gras (Nov. to Feb.)* and *jambon de Bayonne* (smoked, air-cured ham) are the specialities. Furniture is also manufactured in the town.

▶ The Counts of Folx-Béarn favoured this fortified town in a strategic position. A humpbacked **bridge★** (13th-14thC) with a central tower crosses the Gave de Pau; the remains of the concentric fortifications around the **Moncade keep** lie to the north of the town. **Church of St. Pierre** (13th-14thC) was also part of the defence system. In Rue du Bourg Vieux, old houses and mansions, including one said to have belonged to Jeanne d'Albret, Protestant Queen of Navarre from 1555 to 1572 and mother of Henry IV of France. □

▶ Nearby

▶ **Sault de Navailles** *(10 km NE) :* ruins of the château overlook tracks that were once pilgrim and trading routes as well as trails to the winter pastures. **Bellocq** *(15 km NW) :* 13thC fortified town; remains of the Château of the Viscounts of Béarn. ▶ **Salies-de-Béarn** ® *(17 km W) :* in the **Saleys Valley,** a spa, 15thC church, old bridge and houses. □

■ PAU★★

C1 / ® / pop. 90 020 (Pyrénées-Atlantiques)

English travellers in the 19thC discovered the delightful seasons of late autumn and almost nonexistent winter in Pau. The largest town close to the mountains, Pau is the regional capital of the Pyrénées-Atlantiques, a university town, an important army base and an agricultural market centre. During recent decades, this former capital of the Béarn has received an economic boost from the exploitation of natural gas deposits at Lacq (→).

▶ **Château★** (A3; *daily 15 Apr.-15 Oct.*) : built on a spur in the 12thC, enlarged in the 13th-14thC, completely remodelled in the 19thC; **National Museum** (tapestries, furniture, memorabilia of Henri IV [see box]; **Béarnais Museum** (prehistory, archaeology, natural sciences, ethnography). Opposite is the General Council, formerly the **Parliament of Navarre.** ▶ The **Boulevard des Pyrénées★★** (late 19thC) overlooks the 200 Chamerop (dwarf) palms of the Joantho gardens and offers an exceptional view in clear weather over 150 km of the moun-

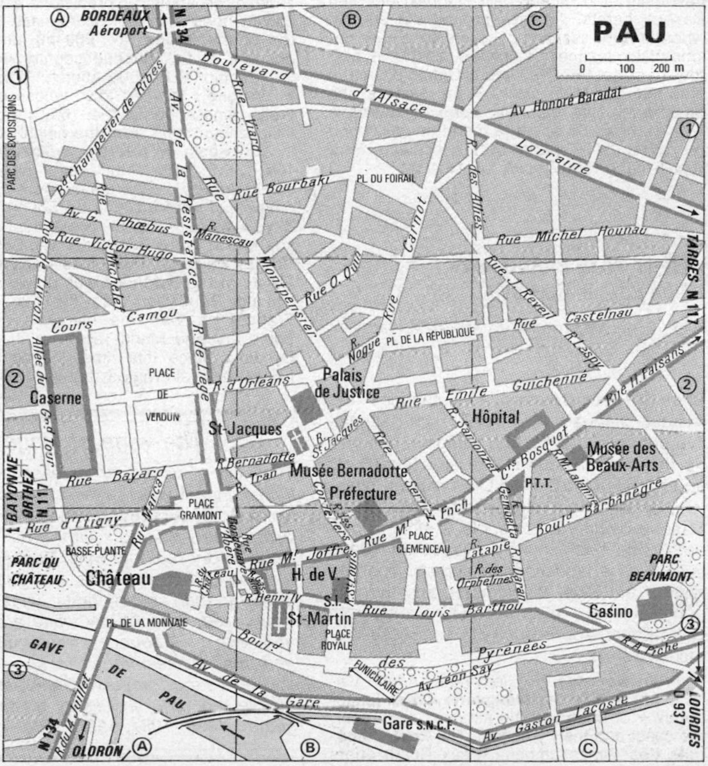

tain chain. ▶ The boulevard runs past the Place Royale (statue of Henri IV) to end at **Beaumont Park★**, a 30-acre English garden around the casino *(open all year).* **Fine Arts Museum★** (C2, Rue Mathieu Lalanne; *closed Tue.*) : 17th-20thC European paintings. ▶ **Place Clemenceau** (Palais des Pyrénées conference centre) and the surrounding streets from the busy town centre, with banks, hotels, restaurants and shops. ▶ **Bernadotte Museum** : in the 18thC Maison Balagué (B2; *closed Mon. and Jan.*), birthplace in 1763 of Napoléon's General Bernadotte, who became (1818) King Charles XIV-Jean of Sweden. ▶ From here, walk through the old streets of the restored Hédas Quarter, full of attractive restaurants and shops, to reach the château and the **Tour de la Monnaie,** formerly the government mint. □

▶ Nearby

▶ **Jurançon** ® : on the left bank of the Gave de Pau, the name given to the wine of the region; visit the wine cooperative at **Gan** ®, *tel. 59.21.57.03, 8 km away.* ▶ **Lescar★** ® *(8 km NW) :* was a bishopric from the 6thC until the French Revolution. The kings of Navarre were buried in the **cathedral★★;** Romanesque eastern end (sculpted corbels); inside, capitals (partly reworked in the 17thC and 19thC), 12thC mosaic in the choir. In the former Bishop's Residence, the **Musée Béarnais;** opposite the cathedral, 14thC **Fort Esquirette;** view★ of the Pyrénées from the neighbouring terrace. In the lower town, **church of St. Julien,** rebuilt in the 17thC. Lescar is a major maize-growing centre; the Agricultural Cooperative *(Coopérative Agricole)* is open to visitors, *tel. 59.32.84.46.* ▶ **Nay** ® *(18 km SE) :* local products are cow-bells and sheep-bells *(sonnailles)* and Basque berets. Arcades around the square, where a Renaissance house is said to have belonged to Jeanne d'Albret (→ box); the bell-tower of the 15thC southern Gothic church is built into the town walls. 3 km away on the other bank, the medieval **keep** of **Coarraze** where Henri IV spent a carefree childhood (→ box); other parts of the château were rebuilt in the 18thC *(open Jul.-15 Aug.).* □

■ Le PAYS BASQUE★★★ (The Basque Country)

▶ From Bayonne to Biarritz *(approx 205 km, 2-3 days)*

A1 *(see map 2)*

The Basque Country encompasses the Atlantic seaboard (75 % of French Basques live between Biarritz and Hendaye), as well as the mountainous inland area stretching southwest of the Gave d'Oloron to the Spanish border. The distinctive character of the Basque country and people is most apparent in the back-country villages and deep valleys. The landscape is superb. The valleys of the Nive, the Aldudes and the Saison (Soule) are described in itineraries from Saint-Étienne-de-Baïgorry (→) and Mauléon-Licharre (→).

▶ From **Bayonne** (→) leave the Adour Valley and climb to the **Mouguerre Cross** (panorama★★ of the town, the mouth of the Adour, the coast and the Pyrénées). The **Route Impériale des Cimes** (Imperial Peak Road) offers splendid views. **Cambo-les-Bains** ® : a spa and winter resort best viewed from the terrace in front of the church, which is in traditional Basque style (17thC altarpiece). The Emperor Napoléon III, his wife the Empress Eugénie and the actress Sarah Bernhardt were among the habitual clients. **Villa Arnaga★ :** 1.5 km W on the Bayonne Road, where the poet Edmond Rostand (1619-55, author of the verse drama *Cyrano de Bergerac*) lived; garden, museum. ▶ The **Isturitz and Oxocelhaya★ Caves** are just off the road between Isturitz and Saint-Martin-d'Arberoue (*visits;* traces of prehistoric habitation). ▶ **Garris :** charming church in village of Basque houses. ▶ **Saint-Palais** ® : annual Basque Festival in summer at this crossroads of former pilgrimage routes to Compostela. ▶ **Osquich Pass :** (alt. 392 m) separates the provinces of Soules and lower (Basse) Navarre : view over Béarn.

▶ **Saint-Jean-le-Vieux** and **Saint-Jean-Pied-de-Port** (→). ▶ **Saint-Étienne-de-Baïgorry** (→). ▶ Before reaching **Bidarray** ® you reach Pont d'Enfer (Hell's Bridge); Nive Gorges, (trout fishing). ▶ From **Itxassou** ® (pretty church) to the opening of Pas de Roland (mountain pass), from where you can reach **Mont Urzumu★** and **Artzamendi** (difficult road; alt. 926 m; panorama★). ▶ **Espelette** ® : a typical Basque village★ with 17thC wooden galleries in the church and discus-shaped tombstones dating from the 13thC. Winter, *pottoks* fair (Basque ponies). ▶ **Aïnhoa★** ® : one of the most typical Basque villages in Labourdes; Romanesque church, 17thC houses, ▶ **Sare★** ® : at the foot of Saint-Ignace Pass, attractive village, church with 17th-18thC galleries; from here, you can reach the Sare Forest (11 km²; pigeon shooting in autumn); prehistoric caves. A cog railway goes from the Saint-Ignace Pass to the top of the **Rhune** (alt. 900 m), best vantage point★★ in the Basque country. ▶ **Ascain★** ® : traditional Basque church, 17thC houses. ▶ **Urrugne :** fortified town whose church (entirely remodelled in the 16thC) borrows the Guipuzcoan style from the neighbouring province in Spain. ▶ Nearby, **château d'Urtubie :** 16th-18thC, with 14thC keep *(daily pm mid-Jul.-mid-Sep.);* panorama★ from the pilgrim chapel of Notre-Dame-de-Socorri. ▶ **Hendaye★** ® : rises steeply above the River Bidassoa, which forms the border with Spain. On the **Île des Faisans** in the middle of the river, the Treaty of the Pyrénées was drawn up in 1659 (linking Roussillon and the Cerdagne with France) as was the marriage contract of Louis XIV and Maria-Teresa of the Hapsburg Dynasty. Since that time, the control of the island has alternated between France and

The wine of kings

The king of wines, or at least the wine of kings since it was served at the baptism of Henri IV, is **Jurançon :** *white, dry or sweet, firm, clean-tasting, with little perfume. Another dry regional wine,* **Pacherenc** *from the Vic-Bilh region, has a higher alcohol content than most table wines. Béarn wines, red, rosé or dry white are pleasant and have a full bouquet;* **Irouléguy** *rosé, red and the occasional white should be savoured young. People who enjoy an uplifting, simple red wine should try* **Madiran.** *Good years : 1975, 1981, 1982, 1983.*

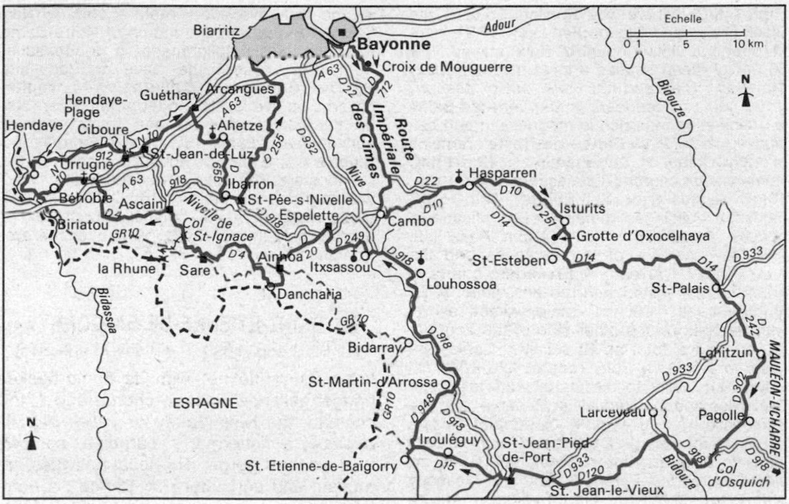

1. Tour of the Basque Country

Spain every six months. In the town, the St. Vincent church (16th-17thC) has a beautiful 12thC crucifix. ▶ To the north, the seaside resort of **Hendaye-Plage** and the coast road of the **Corniche des Basques★**. ▶ **Socoa :** one of the great Atlantic surfing beaches. ▶ **Ciboure** and **Saint-Jean-de-Luz** (→). ▶ **Guéthary** ® : view★ NE as far as Biarritz; remodelled 17thC church. ▶ **Saint-Pée-sur-Nivelle★** ® : on the edge of an 18 km² forest; old houses, galleried Basque church, remains of a 16thC château with keep dating from 1403. □

■ High Passes of the PYRÉNÉES★★

▶ Round trip from Lourdes *(approx 280 km, 2-3 days)*

C2 *(see map 1)*

Several valleys north from the **Western Pyrénées National Park :** Gave d'Ossau, Arrens, Cauterets and Gavarnie, which make up the Gave de Pau, the Adour and the Neste d'Aure. They are linked by high passes at Aspin, Tourmalet, Soulor and Aubisque, whose names and gradients are well known to followers of the *Tour de France,* the annual cycle race, the town of Lourdes is a gateway to these valleys and passes.

▶ **Lourdes** (→). ▶ Bagnères-de-Bigorre (→). ▶ **Beaudéan :** 16thC church, bell-tower with noteworthy timber structure. Drive up the **Lesponne Valley★** along D29 to Chiroulet, and from there on foot to **Lake Bleu★.** ▶ **Campan** ® : 16thC church; 18thC woodwork; 16thC covered market. ▶ **Asté :** 16thC church; remains of 13thC fortress; keen walkers can climb the Casque de Lhéris (alt. 1 595 m; view). ▶ **Escaladieu★ :** Cistercian abbey (1142) where the Counts of Bigorre were buried; chapterhouse; church rebuilt in the 17thC. ▶ **Mauvezin** ® : view of the Pyrénées from the former **fortress**

2. High passes of the Pyrénées

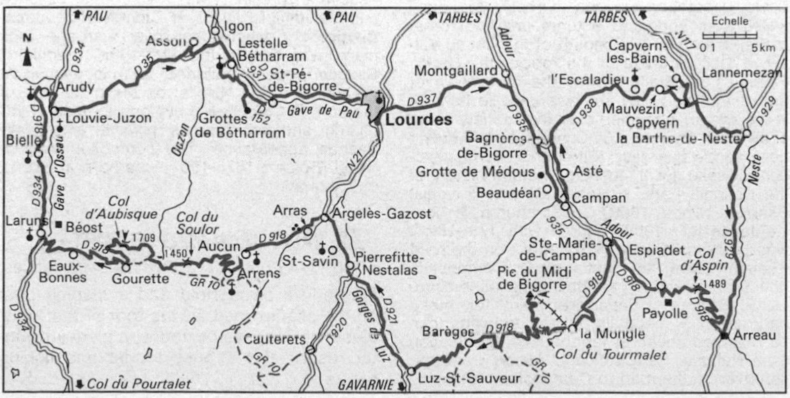

(10th-14thC), where the English Edward the Black Prince and Gaston Fébus (1331-91, gentle poet and violent count of Foix) stayed. The 36 m-high keep houses a local museum *(daily May-Sep.; Sun. and nat. hols. out of season; group visits by request).* ▶ **Capvern-les-Bains** ® : mineral springs rich in magnesium and calcium sulphate. ▶ **La Barthe-de-Neste :** remains of 12thC keep. ▶ **Sarrancolin★ :** 12th-13thC Romanesque church (Renaissance choir stalls; 13thC reliquary of St. Ebons; 12th-15thC monastic buildings; remains of fortifications, houses. ▶ **Arreau** (→). ▶ **Aspin Pass** (alt. 1490 m) views★★ of the Pyrénées and the Aure Valley (→ Arreau). ▶ **Espiadet :** quarry of green marble veined with red and white. ▶ **La Mongie** ® (alt. 1800 m) : major winter resort; with Barèges on the other side of the Tourmalet, offering a total of 40 ski lifts. Cable-cars *(Dec. to end Apr.)* from **Taoulet** (alt. 2340 m; views★★); walks to the Garet waterfall, Lake Gréziolles and the Néouvielle Reserve, and the Aure valley (→ Arreau). ▶ **Tourmalet Pass :** (alt. 2115 m) site★★; a toll road *(1 Jul.-10 Oct.)* leads to **Midi du Bigorre Peak** (alt. 2865 m; view★★★ of the Pyrénées and the Gascony plain); observatory, Geophysical Institute (visits) established in 1880. ▶ **Barèges** ® : (alt. 1220 m) sports resort and spa (alkaline sulphur springs). Cable-car from Lienz Plateau (alt. 1600 m; skiing); cable railway to Airé Peak (alt. 2418 m). ▶ **Luz-Saint-Sauveur** (→) leads to the natural amphitheatres of Gavarnie and Troumouse. **Luz Gorge** opens into the valleys of Pierrefitte-Nestalas and Argelès-Gazost (→ Argelès). **Arras-en-Lavedan** ® : château de Castelnau d'Azun with wall and ruined keep (13th-15thC). ▶ **Aucun :** Romanesque church extended with the addition of a Gothic sanctuary. ▶ **Arrens** ® : church surrounded by a 15thC crenellated wall. Arrens is a gateway to the national park, along the Gave d'Arrens valley; it is a base for many walks and climbs to high mountain lakes. The isards (Pyrenean mountain goats) are unfortunately still prey to unscrupulous hunters. ▶ **Soulor Pass★** (alt. 1450 m), **Pyrénées corniches** (cliff roads) and **Litor Amphitheatre** (sites★★) lead up to the **Aubisque Pass** (alt. 1710; panorama★★). ▶ **Gourette** ® : (alt. 1400 m) oldest winter resort in the Pyrénées, with 25 ski runs and numerous lifts, one of which goes to Pène Blanque (alt. 2550 m), from where you can continue to the **Ger Peak** (alt. 2613 m; view★★). ▶ **Valentin Valley** with woods and waterfalls★, links Gourette to **Eaux-Bonnes** ® : (alt. 750 m) mineral springs with chloride, sulphur and trace metals; 12thC Romanesque church with rather ribald decoration on the corbels. Mountain walks from spring to autumn (marked forest paths). ▶ **Laruns** (→), mouth of the Ossau Valley. ▶ Horses graze at the foot of the Benon Plateau near **Bielle :** once the main town of the valley; the valley archives used to be kept in the *sagrari* (chamber) over the sacristy in the 15th-16thC church; 16thC houses. ▶ **Arudy :** near marble quarries; 15th-16thC church; Maison d'Ossau (local museum), natural history of the National Park. ▶ **Sainte-Colome :** typical Béarnais village, 16thC Gothic church. ▶ **Louvie-Juzon** ® : 15thC church with 17th-18thC woodwork decoration. ▶ **Mifaget :** on the road through Ossau to Santiago de Compostela (the Spanish shrine), a 12thC almshouse chapel. ▶ **Bruges :** departure point for steep and arduous mountain hikes; lodgings can be reserved ahead at farmhouses (information from National Park Offices). **Asson :** another stopover on the road to Compostela; château; church with five-sided eastern end. ▶ Near **Lestelle-Bétharram** ® : church of Notre-Dame, a 17thC place of pilgrimage; a bridge dating from 1687 crosses the Gave de Pau; site. ▶ The **Bétharram Caverns★★ :** vaulted caverns on five levels; underground river (boat on the lake), cable-car and tourist train in summer *(daily, Easter-mid-Oct.).* ▶ **Saint-Pé-de-Bigorre** ® : a halt on the pilgrimage road to Compostela. The abbey (founded in the 11thC) was burnt during the late 16thC Wars of Religion; vestiges of the original church next to another built in the 17thC; view over the area from the Gave de Pau. □

■ SAINT-ÉTIENNE-DE-BAÏGORRY★

A1 / ® / pop. 1690 (Pyrénées-Atlantiques)

From Saint-Étienne, with its hump-backed bridge, galleried Basque church and 17thC château, the **Nive Valley** or *vallée des Aldudes★*, a fisherman's paradise, narrows to a wooded gorge. The local activities are tourism and agriculture. ▶ **Banca :** a hamlet, formerly a copper-smelting centre. **Aldudes :** an autumn rendez-vous for hunters, out for the migrating pigeons that fly up through the valley and over Spain. □

■ SAINT-JEAN-DE-LUZ★★

A1 / ® / pop. 12920 (Pyrénées-Atlantiques)

Saint-Jean-de-Luz is a relatively new town, whose finest hours came in the 17thC with a Treaty of the Pyrénées and the marriage of Louis XIV. A whaling-station since the 11thC, Saint-Jean is today a tuna-fishing port. In winter, the anchovy fleet takes over (the cannery is the leading French producer). Seaside resort with casino.

▶ The **Place Louis XIV,** with its bandstand and café terraces, overlooks the quay where the tuna fleet is moored. Next to the town hall (1657), the **château Lohobiaque** (1635) was Louis XIV's residence during his marriage solemnities (memorabilia; furniture; *daily ex. Sun. pm, 8-15 Jun. and Jul.-21 Sep.*). ▶ Maria Teresa, future Queen of France, stayed in a mansion along the quay. ▶ The **Barre Quarter,** between the Place, the quay and the raised dyke along the edge of the beach, was once the shipowners' district; it is now partly a pedestrian precinct with restaurants, galleries and fashionable shops. ▶ **Church of St. Jean-Baptiste★ :** where the royal marriage took place, was built in the 14th-15thC (traditional Basque wooden galleries, altarpiece★). ▶ At the mouth of the Nivelle, on the other side of the port, is **Ciboure★** ®, whose fortified 16thC church and old houses give it a typically Basque appearance. The composer Maurice Ravel *(Bolero;* 1875-1937) was born at No. 12 on the quay. □

■ SAINT-JEAN-PIED-DE-PORT★

A-B1 / ® / pop. 1770 (Pyrénées-Atlantiques)

Formerly a stronghold and a staging post on the pilgrim road, at the foot of the "port" (pass) of Roncevaux; today, a pleasant winter resort, and a busy tourist and fishing centre.

Henry IV

The son of Jeanne d'Albret, heiress to the throne of Navarre, and Antoine de Bourbon, was born at Pau in 1553. The tradition that his proud grandfather brushed a clove of garlic and a drop of Jurançon over the newborn's lips, like his cradle that was said to have been a tortoise-shell, is part of the colourful legend surrounding the king and his time. In Béarn, tales are still told of his carefree country childhood at the château de Coarraze, and of his lifelong romance with the beautiful Corisande de Guiche. When Henri succeeded to the throne of France in 1589, Navarre became part of France. Despite the devastation wrought by the bitter Wars of Religion during the reign of Henri IV, he was a popular monarch, remembered today for having wished : "A chicken in every pot". He died in 1610.

▶ Ramparts surround the 17thC area around the **Rue d'Espagne,** which runs north to the **old bridge** on the Nive (view★). The Rue de la Citadelle, lined with 16th and 17thC red sandstone houses, runs N through the upper town★ surrounded by 15thC walls. Near the bridge, the church of the Assumption, rebuilt in the 18thC with a 16thC doorway. Almost opposite, in Rue de l'Église, the former almshouse is now a **Museum of Basque Pelota.** Beyond the 15thC house known as the bishops' prison *(Prison des Évêques)* you reach the St. Jacques gateway on the way up to the 17thC **citadel;** valley view. ▶ On the edge of the old town, the France gateway opens on to an avenue lined with bustling sidewalk cafés. □

▶ Nearby

▶ Upstream from Saint-Jean, the valley of the Petite Nive becomes the **Défilé de Valcarlos★** (pass) marking the border with Spain. ▶ Along the valley of the Nive itself you can go up to the excursion centre of **Béhérobie** *(13 km).* ▶ Down the Laurhibar Valley SE, you come to the 12thC Romanesque church of Saint-Sauveur and *(approx. 30 km)* the **Iraty Forest** (23 km^2) : flora and fauna; footpaths, bridle-paths and cross-country skiing. ▶ Finally, from **Saint-Jean-le-Vieux** (red sandstone church; Romanesque doorway, 17th-18thC galleries), you can follow GR65, one of the most trodden of the former pilgrim routes to Compostela, which runs parallel to D933. It passes through **Osterbat and Harambels** (Chapel of St. Nicolas★), which were also pilgrim halts. □

■ SAUVETERRE-DE-BÉARN★

B1 / ® / pop. 1 668 (Pyrénées-Atlantiques)

An 11thC viscount of Béarn granted a charter of independence to this delightful city on the road to Compostela. The name is pronounced locally as *Sauveté.*

▶ Beautifully situated on an escarpement overlooking the Gave d'Oloron, Sauveterre has retained parts of its mediaeval walls and the ruins of the 12th-13thC **château de Montréal,** as well as an arch of a fortified bridge. From the terrace of the church, with its 12th-13thC bell-tower keep, view★ over the Pyrénées; 16thC **château de Nays.** □

▶ Nearby

▶ **Château de Laàs** *(8 km E;* 1 775) : furniture and works of art from the Middle Ages to the early 19thC; gardens *(Jul.-Sep.; Sat. and Sun. Mar-Jun.).* ▶ **Navarrenx** ® *(18 km SE)* : 16thC **ramparts** (St. Antoine Gateway; 15thC church); the world salmon-fishing championship is held in the Gave d'Oloron every year between Mar. and Jun.-Jul.; a good departure point for cross-country treks with pack ponies. The town is a regional centre for furniture production. □

Local vocabulary

Gascon, the spoken dialect of Béarn and Bigorre, belongs to the Occitan (Provençal) *linguistic group; there are many variants from valley to valley. Basque, however, is not a Latin language, and its origins are still unknown. The following terms refer to life in the mountains; Basque words are indicated by (ba).*

aigue, aygue : *water*
arriu : *stream*
bielle : *region or village*
case : *house, home, farm*
cayolar, cuyala, cujala, kayolar *(ba) : isolated shepherd's hut*
cesta punta *(ba) :* pelota *played in a* jaï alaï
chistera *(ba) : wickerwork and chestnut basket used for playing* pelota
chori *(ba) : bird*
gave, nive : *mountain stream or river*
jaï alaï *(ba) : indoor* pelota *court with the wall on the left*
labrit : *Pyrenean mountain sheep dog*
maysou : *house*
pech, pouy, poudge : *hill, hillock, mound*
plan : *flat ground, pasture*
pottok *(ba) : wild pony from the Pyrénées*
port : *col, pass*
saloir : *cheese-ripening shed*
soum : *summit*
trinquet *(ba) : outdoor* pelota *court*
uri *(ba) : rain*
yoko garbi *(ba) : "open game",* pelota *played on an improvised outdoor court*

■ TARBES

D1 / ® / pop. 54 055 (Hautes-Pyrénées)

The rich soil here is drained by the upper valley of the Adour; wheat and maize are cultivated, and lush grass provides pasture for the National Stud. Tarbes is the major agricultural market of the region, as well as an industrial centre (electricity from generating stations in the mountains; engineering and chemical industries). High-level technical schools have been established in the area.

▶ The main thoroughfares of the town meet at the **Place de Verdun** (B2), where townspeople gather in the evenings. Rues Brahauban and

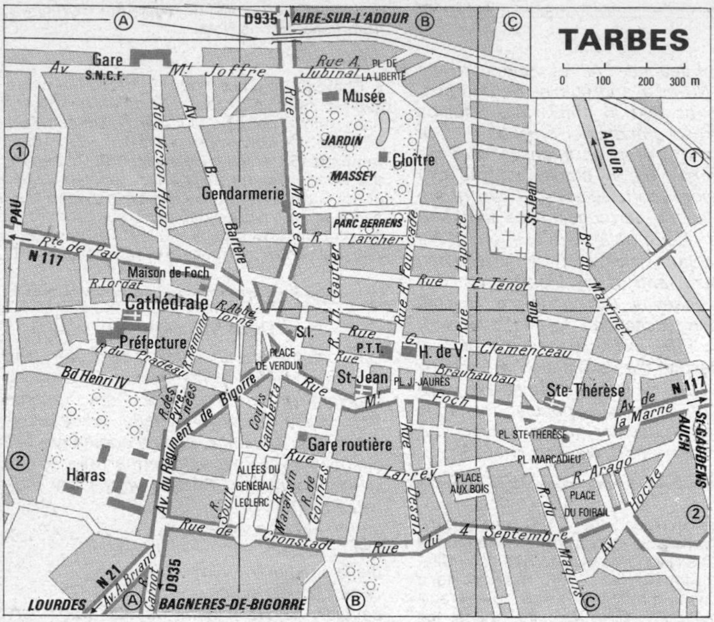

Maréchal Foch are shopping centres. ▶ Main attraction is the **Massey Garden**★ (B1), one of the the most beautiful parks in SW France, with mediaeval architectural vestiges (capitals from Trie-sur-Baïse, Gothic cloister from Saint-Séver-de-Rustan →), as well as an 1850 villa in Italian style, with art collections and a **Museum of Cavalry and Horses** *(daily ex. Mon., Tue and nat. hols).* **Birthplace of Maréchal Foch** (1851-1929 WWI hero) at Nº 2 Rue de la Victoire, a Louis XV mansion (*daily ex. Tue. and Wed.;* memorabilia). ▶ **Cathedral of Notre-Dame-de-la-Sède :** (A2) 12thC structure with Gothic ogive vaulting added in the 14thC; 18thC furnishings. ▶ The *Haras National* (National Stud Farm)★ : (A2) some of the finest stallions in France *(visit park and stables daily pm ex. Tue., Jul.-Feb.).*

▶ Nearby

▶ **Château Montaner**★ *(15 km NW in the Atlantic Pyrénées) :* on a site fortified as early as the 11thC; transformed by Gaston Fébus (→ Hauts Cols des Pyrénées), 40 m high keep, polygonal brick surrounding wall in brick *(Sat. and Sun. pm Apr.-Sep., or by appt. with the organisation Pierres et Vestiges (Stones and Traces) 64110 Jurançon, tel. 59.32.37.39).* In the village church, 15th-16thC frescoes. ▶ **Saint-Séver-de-Rustan :** *(25 km NE)* remains of a Benedictine abbey; the cloister has been reassembled at Massey Gardens at Tarbes, together with capitals from the 15thC collegiate church of **Trie-sur-Baïse** ® *(30 km NE),* much of which is now in the Cloisters division of the Metropolitan Museum of Art in New York; remains of the 13thC fortified town. □

■ The **VIC-BILH** Region

C1

An agricultural region best known for the Madiran vineyards, first planted during the Gallo-Roman period. The area includes numerous valleys that run more or less parallel between the Gave de Pau and the Adour.

▶ **Morlaàs :** on the edge of the Vic-Bilh *(12 km NE from Pau on D943),* one of the leading towns in mediaeval Béarn. The church was part of a Cluniac priory founded in the 11thC and rebuilt between the 14th and 16thC. ▶ The Romanesque church at **Sévignacq-Thèze** *(7 km NW from D943, between Morlaàs and Lembeye)* was also rebuilt in the 15thC; wall

Basque cuisine

Jambon de bayonne *is prized far and wide. Traditionally, this ham is cured simply by being rubbed with salt. Fried with eggs or used in cooking Basque style, it is delicious. Chocolate was introduced into France Europe by way of Bayonne in 1670. The mouth-watering fattened goose or duck livers* (foie gras) *are equally good* au naturel *or as* confits *(preserved in their own fat).* Garbure *is a delectable thick green vegetable soup. Fish dishes make free use of tunny, sea bream, turbot and whiting; specialities are fried sardines with egg yolk, fish stew* (matelote) *and* chipirones *(baby squid) served in various ways. Salmon from the mountain streams* (saumon des gaves)*, particulary the Adour, is exquisite. Ewe's milk cheese is excellent as, for the sweet tooth, is* touron *(rich marzipan, with nuts).*

belfry; Romanesque sculptures in the doorway, much mediaeval detail. ▶ **Lembeye** *(32 km NE from Pau)* : 16thC church (Flamboyant Gothic doorway), visit the Madiran wine-making co-operative, *tel. 59.68.10.93.* □

VIC-EN-BIGORRE

C-D1 / ® / pop. 5 065 (Hautes-Pyrénées)

Vic is a typical mediaeval walled town *(bastide)*, and provides an excellent centre for exploring the Adour valley.

▶ Nearby

▶ **Rabastens-de-Bigorre** ® *(8 km E)* : a walled town founded in the 14thC near the Alaric Canal, the name of which is derived from the Visigothic occupation of the area in the 5thC; large Gothic church. ▶ **Maubourget** ® *(9 km N)* : the church, near the extensive market-place, was formerly part of an 11thC Benedictine priory. ▶ **Madiran** *(21 km N)*: 12thC Romanesque apse and crypt in the church; Benedictines were also established here, where they contributed significantly to the development of the vineyards. ▶ Nearby is **Castelnau-Rivière-Basse** *(23 km N from Vic)* : former stronghold overlooking the Adour valley (ruined 13thC keep; Gothic church with massive gate tower). ▶ **Mazères** *(2 km E in the plain)* : a Romanesque church fortified in the 15thC. □

WESTERN PYRÉNÉES NATIONAL PARK★★

C2

The park, created in 1967, covers 457 km^2 at an altitude of 1 070-3 300 m. It includes the high valleys of Aspe, Ossau, Azan, Cauterets, Barèges and Aure. At the southern boundary it crosses the border to become the Spanish national park of Ordesa. A great variety of plant and animal species are protected here. The aims of the park include not only the protection of flora and wildlife, but also the encouragement of mountain traditions and rural economies. Guided walks slanted towards ecology, fauna and flora, and history, start from the valleys; information available from the various park offices *(Maisons du Parc)* or the Regional HQ at Tarbes. □

Ostabat and the pilgrimage to Compostela

In the Middle Ages, pilgrims who took the road to Compostela in thousands crossed the Pyrénées over the principal passes of Somport and Bentarte (Ronceveaux or Roncesvalles, where Charlemagne's legendary General Roland met his death in 778.), which had been well known to the Romans. Inns, shelters and almshouses built by religious and lay communities marked the route. Ostabat, at the foot of the Pyrénées and Saint-Jean-Pied-de-Port (at the foot of the pass) were important meeting points. Ostabat is now a small village on the old road, the line of which is still traced by GR65. The pilgrimage waned from the 16thC onwards, when the Wars of Religion added yet more hazards to a road already beset by highwaymen and adventurers.

Architecture

The traditional Basque house, the *etché,* is architecturally the most interesting in the three regions of Bigorre, Béarn and the Pays Basque. Three variations on the structure correspond to the Labourd, Basse Navarre and Soule regions. White-washed and spacious, facing the south, the house is

Basque house

usually timber-framed; the ridge of the shallow tiled roof is offset, giving asymmetrical slopes. In Navarre, houses often have wooden balconies and, above the doors, lintels carved with inscriptions. ● In Béarn, houses vary with the altitude; the higher, the more austere the houses and the steeper the roofs, with slate instead of tiles. In the mountains, the houses are grouped in hamlets; the family quarters are sandwiched between the stables (which give natural heat) and a big attic (which insulates the roof). ● The same features are found in houses in Bigorre. In Lower Bigorre, houses

Béarn house

resemble those in neighbouring Armagnac, whereas in the mountains, structures generally have thick walls, smaller doors and windows, and central gables.

Bigorre mountain house

Brief regional history

Prehistory-Roman occupation The Pyrénées have been inhabited since the earliest prehistoric times. By the Neolithic Era, a linguistic and ethnic identity had been established. The principal resources were agricultural and pastoral, based mainly on stock rearing.

1st-9thC The arrival of **Roman troops** drove the local population into the western mountains; Roman influence weighed most heavily around *Beneharnum* (Lescar), which, together with *Iluro* (Oloron), became the seat of a bishopric soon after the establishment of Christianity (6th-7thC). ● The Visigoths, who assumed the region in the 5th-7thC, were replaced in the 9thC by the Frankish Emperor Charlemagne.

9th-15thC The Carolingian Dynasty was in turn overthrown by the 9thC Norman invaders, but control of the free-spirited mountain population was at best nominal, and the inhabitants of the former Roman Province of *Novempopulanie* paid little more than lip-service to historical developments. ● The Viscounty (Vicomté) of Béarn, created in 820, moved the regional capital from Lescar *(Beneharnum)* to Morlaàs. The states of Soule, Bigorre and Labourd were established between the 9th and the 11thC. ● Political control of the region was complicated by the 1154 marriage of Eleanor of Aquitaine (divorced wife of the French Louis VII) to Henri II Plantagenet of England, which gave the English a hold on Eleanor's dowry territories in SW France. The regions of Labourd, Soule and Bigorre came under English rule, and Bayonne developed into an important port. ● In 1290, the Counts of Foix were granted Béarn and began a **policy of neutrality** — especially under Gaston Fébus in the 14thC — that resulted in the formation of an independent Béarn state. The English were driven out of western France at the conclusion of the Hundred Years' War (early 15thC). At the end of the 15thC, the Albret family assumed the crown of Navarre, a kingdom straddling both sides of the Pyrénées. The Protestant Albrets, who established a new capital at Pau, tended to the French side, and the Catholic rulers of Spain (Ferdinand and Isabella) confiscated Upper Navarre at the beginning of the 16thC.

16th-18thC Henri of Navarre, heir to Jeanne d'Albret, Queen of Navarre, succeeded to the throne of France as Henri IV in 1589, uniting his old and new kingdoms (1607) along with the three northern Basque provinces of Soule, Labourd and Bigorre. In 1620 Henri's son, Louis XIII, created the **Parliament of Navarre,** which conferred a degree of autonomy on the region. In 1659, during the reign of Louis XIV, the **Treaty of the Pyrénées** finally ratified the union. ● Maize was introduced during this period from America by way of Spain. Trade developed with the Spanish Americas and the French West Indies. Chocolate, which first arrived through Bayonne, was a popular import.

19th-20thC In 1790, the Départements of Hautes (Upper) and Basses (Lower) Pyrénées were created; administrative centres were established at Tarbes and Pau. ● During the 19thC Spain's decline and the loss of its Empire destabilised the economy of the region, which depended entirely on agriculture, lacking as it did the raw materials (iron, coal) necessary for industrialisation. ● Tourism was the salvation of the area, economically stagnant despite the revival of trade relations with South America. The English, who occupied Bayonne at the fall of Napoléon (1814) favored Pau as a winter resort; Biarritz and the Basque coast were "launched" by Napoléon III and his wife the Empress Eugénie in the latter half of the 19thC. The introduction of the railway and the institution of the pilgrimage to Lourdes further stimulated this economic revival. ● The two World Wars, the economic crisis of the 1930s and the effects of the Spanish Civil War halted the tourist boom. After WWII, possibilities were enlarged with the discovery of natural gas at Lacq and the development of hybrid maize strains. Today, Bayonne and Pau account for half the population of the Atlantic Pyrénées. Together with Tarbes, Pau is an industrial centre of the SW, and Bayonne remains an important port and tourist centre.

Practical information

The region

Informations : *Comité Régional de Tourisme* (C.R.T.) *Aquitaine,* 24, allées de Tourny, 33000 Bordeaux, ☎ 56.44.48.02. **Midi-Pyrénées :** *C.R.T. Midi-Pyrénées,* 12, rue Salambô, 31200 Toulouse, ☎ 61.47.11.12. **Pyrénées-Atlantiques :** *Comité Départemental de Tourisme* (C.D.T.), Parlement de Navarre, rue Henri-IV, 64000 Pau, ☎ 59.83.92.37. **Béarn :** *(C.D.T.),* building des Pyrénées, 64000 Pau, ☎ 59.32.84.32. ext. 45-10. **Pays basque :** B.P. 247, 64108 Bayonne Cedex, ☎ 59.59.28.77. **Hautes-Pyrénées :** *Comité Départemental de Tourisme* (C.D.T.), 6, rue Eugène-Ténot, 65000 Tarbes, ☎ 62.93.03.30. In Paris : *Maison des Pyrénées,* 15, rue St-Augustin, 75002, ☎ 42.61.58.18.

Maps : *Michelin* n°s 78, 85 1/200 000. *I.G.N.* n°s 69, 70 1/100 000 ; n° 113 1/250 000.

Local and regional press : *la Dépêche du Midi, l'Éclair Pyrénées, la République des Pyrénées, Sud-Ouest.*

S.O.S. : Pyrénées-Atlantiques : *SAMU* (Emergency Medical Service), ☎ 59.27.15.15 (Pau) ; 59.63.33.33 (Bayonne). **Hautes-Pyrénées :** *SAMU* ☎ 62.34.44.44. *Poisoning Emergency Centre :* ☎ 56.96.40.80 (Bordeaux) ; 61.49.33.33 (Toulouse).

Weather forecast : Pyrénées-Atlantiques : ☎ 59.27.50.50 (Pau) ; ☎ 59.22.03.30 (Bayonne) ; *Ocean Search and Rescue :* ☎ 59.59.82.00. *Road and snow conditions :* ☎ 59.39.16.04 and 56.96.33.33. **Hautes-Pyrénées :** ☎ 62.34.77.77 and 62.34.44.18.

Farmhouse gîtes and chambres d'hôtes : Pyrénées-Atlantiques : *Association Départementale des Gîtes Ruraux,* Maison de l'Agriculture, 124, bd Tourasse, 64000 Pau, ☎ 59.80.19.13. **Hautes-Pyrénées :** *Relais Dép. des Gîtes Ruraux,* 22, pl. du Foirail, 65000 Tarbes, ☎ 62.34.52.82.

Farmhouse accommodation : numerous possibilities (camping, chambres d'hôtes, etc.). Enq : *Assn. Dép. Agriculture et Tourisme,* 124, bd Tourasse, 64000 Pau, ☎ 59.02.33.44.

Camping : approx. 250 camp-sites. The *"Camping et Caravaning Pyrénées-Atlantiques"* guide is available at the *T.O.* and *S.I.*

Festivals and events : Mar : *Week of Occitan Culture* in Tarbes. **Easter :** *Festival of Music and Religious Art* in Lourdes, Tarbes and Saint-Savin. **May :** *Jazz Festival* in Tarbes. **Jun :** Pau *Theatre Festival.* **Jul :** *Pyrénées Folk Festival* in Oloron-Sainte-Marie ; *Sailing and Surfing Film Festival* in Biarritz. **Aug :** *International Festival of Basque Folklore* in Bayonne ; *Basque Festival* in Saint-Palais. *Cheese fair* in Loures-Barousse ; *Cartoon Festival* in Anglet. **Sep :** *International Bridge Festival* in Biarritz ; *Session of the Maurice Ravel International Academy of Music* in Saint-Jean-de-Luz ; *September Music Festival* on the Basque Coast (concerts in numerous towns).

Scenic railways : *the Artouste scenic railway* leads from the upper station of the telecabin line to the Artouste lake (55 mn trip), daily mid-Jun-end Sep, ☎ 59.05.36.99. *Rhune rack railway :* from the Saint-Ignace pass to the Rhune summit, 1 Jul-30 Sep daily, Easter hols, 1 May-30 Jun, 1 Oct-15 Nov : Sat, Sun and nat hols with departures at 10 am and 3 pm. *Avré Funicular railway in Barèges.* Enq : ☎ 62.92.68.19 and 62.92.68.26.

Technical tourism : *Bayonne Port installations ;* enq : C.C.I. Bayonne, 50, allées Marines, B.P. 115, 64102 Bayonne Cedex, ☎ 59.55.84.08. *Fromagerie des Chaumes (local cheese producer)* in Jurançon, 155, av. Rauski, ☎ 59.06.17.20. *Distillerie Izarra,* 9, quai Bergeret, 64108 Bayonne, ☎ 59.55.09.45.

National and nature parks : *parc national des Pyrénées-Occidentales,* rte de Pau, 65013 Tarbes-Ibos, ☎ 62.93.30.50. *Assn. des Amis du parc national des Pyrénées,* 20, rue Samonzet, 64000 Pau, ☎ 59.27.15.30. The National Park Centres in Etsaut, Gabas, Arrens, Cauterets and Saint-Lary, propose a different exhibition in each valley, together with all documents published by the park.

Rambling and hiking : maps *I.G.N.* parc national des Pyrénées 1/25 000. Pays basque-Soule, Pays basque Ouest Labourd and Béarn parc national au 1/50 0000. The G.R.10 crosses the region, linking the Atlantic and the Mediterranean (topoguide). For all rambles, hikes and courses, practical information at the : *C.I.M.E.S. Pyrénées (Centre d'Information Montagnes et Sentiers),* 3, sq. Balagué, 09200 St-Girons, ☎ 61.66.40.10 ; every morning ex Wed *Assn. des Amis du parc national des Pyrénées,* hiking rambling club, 32, rue Samonzet, 64000 Pau, ☎ 59.27.15.30. *Assn. Départementale des Sentiers d'Excursion,* 83, av. des Lauriers, 64000 Pau. Mr. and Mme Dotter, mountain guides, organise circuits with accommodation, enq : 65200 Sainte-Marie-de-Campan, ☎ 62.91.82.26. The Pyrénées on foot : *Pyrenaica-Estaing,* 65400 Argelès-Gazost, ☎ 62.97.20.36. The "unknown Pyrénées" on foot : J.-P. Datcharry, Gavarnie, 65120 Luz-Saint-Sauveur, Rambling in Béarn : *C.R.T. Aquitaine.* Certain *T.O.* or *S.I.* publish brochures on rambles near their towns.

Riding holidays : *Association Départementale de Randonnées Équestres,* Escos, 64270 Salies-de-Béarn, ☎ 59.38.40.16.

Cycling holidays : numerous clubs. Enq : *Ligue Adour-Pyrénées,* M. J.-J. Labadie, 4, rue R.-Aznard, Lons, 64140 Billère, ☎ 59.32.45.40. A guide, "Cycling holidays in Béarn" is available at the *S.I.* and *O.T.* The *O.T.* in Luz-Saint-Sauveur, ⌧ 65120, ☎ 62.92.81.60, organises one-week cycling courses.

Handicraft courses : enq : *C.R.T. Aquitaine* and *C.D.T. Pyrénées-Atlantiques.* Pottery, weaving in Pau, fabric painting in Bayonne, weaving in Louhossoa. Enq : *C.D.T. Pyrénées-Atlantiques.* Reupholstery, poster design at Tarbes (youth club).

Other courses : canoeing, gourmet tours, cross-country skiing (*C.D.T.* **Pyrénées-Atlantiques**) ; climbing (Pyrénées Ski and Mountain Service), 9, pl. de la Mairie, 65400 Argelès-Gazost, ☎ 62.90.31.99. Mountain ecology : J.-R. Jaheny, mairie de Génos, 65510 Loudenvielle. Mountain discovery course : Guy Maillé, c/o M. et Mme Desmarais, quartier de la Coutellerie, 65240 Arreau, ☎ 62.98.64.73 ; *Maison de la Découverte Pyrénéenne*, 3, rte de Tarbes, 65200 Bagnères-de-Bigorre, ☎ 62.95.45.20. Funboard in Saint-Jean-de-Luz : *U.C.P.A.*, 62, rue de la Glacière, 75013 Paris, ☎ 43.36.05.20.

Golf : 18 hole courses in Anglet, Biarritz, Ciboure, Lannemezan, Pau-Billère, Saint-Jean-de-Luz.

Tennis : see S.I.

Jai alai (pelota) : *Féd. française de Pelote Basque*, rue du Sous-Lieutenant-Iribarne, 64100 Bayonne, ☎ 59.22.22.34.

Aquatic sports : *Assn. Nautique de Biarritz*, port des Pêcheurs, ☎ 59.24.11.41. Surfing and wind-surfing : *Bidassoa Surfing-Club*, 8, rue de la Forêt, 64700 Hendaye, ☎ 59.20.14.35. *Biarritz Surfing-Club*, 78, av. Kennedy, ☎ 59.23.10.05.

Scuba diving : *Centre de Plongée de la Côte Basque*, rue des Usines, Ciboure, 64500 Saint-Jean-de-Luz.

Canoeing : *Comité Départemental de canoë-kayak des Hautes-Pyrénées*, cité du Clauzier, B2, 65000 Tarbes, ☎ 62.93.76.61. *U.S.S. Canoë-Kayak*, Sauveterre-de-Béarn, ☎ 59.38.57.58.

Potholing-spelunking : *Assn. Dép. d'Études et de Recherches Spéléologiques*, centre Pilar, 125, av. J.-Mermoz, 64140 Billère, ☎ 59.32.13.85. *Centre International de spéléologie des Pyrénées-Atlantiques*, La Pierre-Saint-Martin.

Climbing-mountaineering : *Club Pyrénéiste Jurançonnais*, 12, rue J.-P.-Toulet, ☎ 59.06.22.86. *Ski-Montagne-Services-Pyrénées*, 8, pl. de la Mairie, 65400 Argelès-Gazost, ☎ 62.90.31.99.

Winter sports : *Assn. Dép. de Ski de Fond des Pyrénées-Atlantiques*, Parlement de Navarre, rue Henri-IV, 64000 Pau, ☎ 59.83.12.37. *Assn. Pays d'Accueil en vallée de Baretous*, 64570 Aramits, ☎ 59.34.60.76.

Gliding and hang-gliding : *Delta-Club du Labourd*, 109, bd de la Mer, 64700 Hendaye. *École Pyrénéenne de vol libre (Pyrénées gliding school)*, 65240 Vieille-Louron, ☎ 62.99.68.55 ; enq and enrollments : Central Reservation, 65590 Borderes-Louron, ☎ 62.98.64.12.

Hunting and shooting : enq at the *Féd. Dép. des Chasseurs*. **Pyrénées-Atlantiques** : rue Jean-Zay, 64000 Pau, ☎ 59.84.31.55. **Hautes-Pyrénées** : 6, rue G.-Clemenceau, 65000 Tarbes, ☎ 62.34.53.01.

Fishing : *Féd. des Assn. de Pêche des Pyrénées-Atlantiques*, 29, rue A.-Briand, 64000 Pau, ☎ 59.02.38.27. The *Féd. Dép. des A.P.P.*, *Féd. Dép. de Pêche*, résidence Bigerrions, bd Martinet, 65000 Tarbes, ☎ 62.36.62.09, publishes a brochure which lists the federal fishing reserves and associations, and dates for the season. Sea fishing : *Yacht-Club Adour Atlantique*, Fishing Section, av. de l'Adour, 64600 Anglet, ☎ 59.63.16.22. World salmon-fishing championships in Navarrenx. Enq : *S.I.* Navarrenx, ☎ 59.34.10.22.

Towns

AINHOA

Bayonne 26, Pau 124, Paris 798
A1 ⊠ 64790

Hotels :
● ★★★***Argi-Eder*** (Mapotel), ☎ 59.29.91.04. Tx 570067. AE, DC, Euro, Visa. 36 rm closed 15 Nov-1 Apr, Sun eve and Wed, 410. Rest. ♦♦ ♿ Well-known restaurant, 130-270.
★★★***Ithurria*** (Châteaux-hôtels), ☎ 59.29.92.11. AE, DC, Visa. 28 rm P closed 22 Nov-23 Dec, 3-23 Jan, Tue eve and Wed, 260. Rest. ● ♦♦♦ Good fare. In this historically-classified residence, good meals on the road to Compostela. Spec : *louvine grillée, foie gras, saumon sauvage*. Good Bordeaux wines, 110-250.
★★***Oppoca***, ☎ 59.29.90.72. 12 rm P closed end Dec-Mar and Tue low season. Rest. ♦♦ Spec : fillet steak from the Labourd region, *terrine de St-Jacques*, 80-150.
⛺ ★★★*Xokoan* (33 pl.), ☎ 59.29.90.26.

ANGLET

Bayonne 3, Pau 110, Paris 775
A1 ⊠ 64600
ℹ 1, av. de la Chambre-d'Amour, ☎ 59.03.77.01.
✈ Biarritz-Parme, 3 km SW, ☎ 59.23.90.67.

Hotels :
● ★★★***Golf et Chiberta*** (Inter-Hôtel), 104, bd des Plages, ☎ 59.63.88.30. Tx 550637. AE, DC, Euro, Visa. 75 rm P ♿ 440. Rest. ♦ ♿ closed Sun eve in winter, 180-250.
★***Parc***, 57, av. de la Chambre-d'Amour, ☎ 59.03.82.61. 22 rm, closed 31 Oct-15 Mar P ♿ 110. Rest. 55-120.

Brindos lake, 3 km SW :
★★★★***Château de Brindos*** (Relais et châteaux), ☎ 59.23.17.68. Tx 541428. AE, DC, Euro, Visa. 16 rm P ♿ closed Jan and Mon, 650. Rest. ♦♦♦ Very good fare, 150-220.

Youth hostel : rte des Vignes, quartier Chiberta, ☎ 59.03.85.01.

⛺ ★★★*Parme* (200 pl.). ☎ 59.23.03.00.

ARCIZANS-AVANT

Oloron 20, Pau 53, Paris 838
B2 ⊠ 64570
(La Pierre-St-Martin) 1 500-1 650-2 000 m

Hotels :
★***Salies***, ☎ 59.34.61.03. 21 rm P closed 15 Nov-1 Dec, 100. Rest. ♦ closed Tue, 40-100.

Lanne, 64570 Aramits, 5 km NW :
★***Lacassie*** (L.F.), ☎ 59.34.62.05. 10 rm P closed Mon, 150. Rest. ♦ 45-120.

ARGELÈS-GAZOST

Tarbes 33, Pau 53, Paris 838
C2 (1 Jun-30 Sep) ⊠ 65400
ℹ pl. de la Mairie, ☎ 62.97.00.25.
SNCF ☎ 62.97.00.28.

Hotels :
● ★★***Miramont***, bd des Pyrénées, ☎ 62.97.01.26. 29 rm P closed Oct-25 Dec, 120. Rest. ♦ closed Mon. Good value for money, 80-150.
★★***Bernède*** (L.F.), 31, rue Mal-Foch, ☎ 62.97.06.64. Tx 531040. AE, DC, Euro, Visa.

40 rm P closed mid-Oct-mid-Dec and Mon, 200. Rest. ♦ 45-180.
★★**Cimes** (L.F.), pl. Ourout, ☎ 62.97.00.10. AE, Euro. 26 rm P ♿ closed Nov-Dec, 150. Rest. ♦ 40-120.
★**Bon Repos** (L.F.), 13, rue du Stade, ☎ 62.97.01.49. 20 rm P ♿ closed 10 Oct-20 May ex Easter and Feb hols, 140. Rest. ♦ ♿ 50-80.
★**Nord,** 22, av. Gal-Leclerc, ☎ 62.97.08.84. 20 rm P closed Oct, 70. Rest. ♦ closed Mon, 50-100.

Ayzac-Ost, 2 km N :
★★**Val du Bergons,** rte de Lourdes, ☎ 62.97.08.76. 16 rm P closed Nov and Mon, 130. Rest. ♦ 45-170.

Saint-Savin, 3 km S on the D101 :
★★**Panoramic** (L.F.), ☎ 62.97.08.22. AE, Visa. 22 rm P closed mid-Oct-Mar, 155. Rest. ♦ 55-180.

Arras-en-Lavedan, 3 km SW on the D918 :
★**Auberge de l'Arragnat** (L.F.), ☎ 62.97.14.23. 18 rm P ♿ closed Oct-Mar, 80. Rest. ♦ 40-150.

Arcizans-Avant, 5 km S :
★**Le Cabaliros,** ☎ 62.97.04.31. 9 rm P closed 6-21 Jan, 70. Rest. ♦ 50-130.

Agos-Vidalos, 5 km NE :
★★**Chez Pierre d'Agos,** ☎ 62.97.05.07. 54 rm P ♿ 130. Rest. ♦ 40-130.

Ⅹ Arras-en-Lavedan, 3 km SW : ★★*l'Idéal* (40 pl.), ☎ 62.97.03.13 ; ★★*le Pircoulet* (40 pl.), ☎ 62.97.02.11 ; Arcizans-Avant, 5 km S : ★★*le Lac* (66 pl.), ☎ 62.97.01.88 ; Agos-Vidalos, 5 km NE : ★★★*la Tour* (120 pl.), ☎ 62.97.08.59 ; ★★*la Châtaigneraie* (65 pl.), ☎ 62.97.07.40.

Ski-Montagne-Service-Pyrénées : 8, pl. de la Mairie, ☎ 62.90.31.99 (skiing in spring, hiking, etc.).

ARREAU

Bagnères-de-Luchon 32, Tarbes 57, Paris 895
D2 ✉ 65240

ℹ pl. du Monument, ☎ 62.98.63.15.

SNCF ☎ 62.98.64.23.

Hotels :
● ★★**Angleterre** (L.F.), rte de Luchon, ☎ 62.98.63.30. 20 rm P closed 1 Oct-20 Dec, 180. Rest. ♦ 80-130.

Guchen, ✉ 65440 Acizans-Avant, 5 km S :
★**Pyrénées,** ☎ 62.39.50.03. Visa. 19 rm closed May-Jun, Oct-Christmas, 95. Rest. ♦ 30-70.

Héches, 65250 La Barthe-de-Neste, 13 km N :
★**Host. de la Neste,** rue de la Gare, ☎ 62.98.83.05. 15 rm P closed Nov and Mon, 90. Rest. ♦ ♿ 45-120.

Ⅹ ★★★*Refuge International* (65 pl.), ☎ 62.98.63.34 ; Guchen, 5 km S : ★★*le Lavedan* (35 pl.), ☎ 62.39.50.21.

ASCAIN

Bayonne 27, Pau 135, Paris 800
6 km SE of Saint-Jean-de-Luz, A1 ✉ 64310

ℹ mairie, ☎ 59.54.00.84.

Hotels :
● ★★★**L'Hacienda,** N618, 2 km NW, ☎ 59.54.02.47. Visa. 26 rm P closed Oct-7 Apr, 315. Rest. ♦♦ 90-190.
● ★★**Rhûne,** ☎ 59.54.00.04. 27 rm P (Annexe) closed 1 Nov-1 Feb, 240. Rest. ♦ 80-130.

Ⅹ ★★★*Zelaia* (170 pl.), ☎ 59.54.02.36.

AVAJAN

Bagnères-de-Luchon 24, Tarbes 65, Paris 903
8 km SE of Arreau, D2 ✉ 65240 Arreau

ℹ mairie, ☎ 62.99.67.72.

Hotel :
★**Relais d'Avajan,** ☎ 62.99.67.08. 10 rm P 90. Rest. ♦ 35-80.

Ⅹ ★★*Le Hourgade* (50 pl.), ☎ 62.99.68.33.

BAGNÈRES-DE-BIGORRE

Tarbes 21, Saint-Gaudens 57, Paris 826
D2 (all yr), ☎ 62.95.00.23. ✉ 65200

ℹ pl. La Fayette, ☎ 62.95.01.62.

SNCF ☎ 62.95.01.19.

Hotels :
★★★**La Résidence,** ☎ 62.95.03.97. Visa. 40 rm P closed 15 Oct-1 Apr, 250. Rest. ♦ 70-130.
★★**Frascati et Parc** (L.F.), bd Carnot, ☎ 62.95.21.14. Visa. 18 rm P ♿ closed Nov-Apr, 150. Rest. ♦ 55-120.
★**Bellevue La Reine,** lacets des Thermes, ☎ 62.95.24.58. 20 rm P closed end Oct-Apr, 170.
★**France,** 7, bd Carnot, ☎ 62.95.08.16. 21 rm P closed Nov-Feb, 115.
★**Petites Vosges,** 17, bd Carnot, ☎ 62.95.28.31. 8 rm closed Oct-Nov and Jan, 75. Rest. ♦ 45-70.
★**Tivoli,** rue P.-Noguès, ☎ 62.95.07.64. 22 rm ♿ closed Oct-Apr, 120. Rest. ♦ 80-130.

Farmhouse gîte, natural camp-site : J. Pujo, Orignac, 5 km from Bagnères-de-Bigorre on the RN117 and the D925, 938 and 120, ☎ 62.95.48.18.

Ⅹ ★★★*Les Tilleuls* (100 pl.), ☎ 62.95.26.04 ; ★★★*les Fruitiers* (100 pl.), ☎ 62.95.25.97 ; ★★*les Palomières* (40 pl.), ☎ 62.95.59.79.

Event : *flower festival* in Aug.

Casino, pl. des Thermes, ☎ 62.95.20.42.

Bicycle hire : M. Couture, rue Mal-Foch, ☎ 62.95.03.93.

BARÈGES

Lourdes 38, Tarbes 58, Paris 863
D2 ✉ 65120 Luz-Saint-Sauveur

(Jun-Sep), ☎ 62.92.68.02 1 250-2 350 m.

ℹ mairie, ☎ 62.92.68.19.

Hotels :
★★**Europe,** ☎ 62.92.68.04. Visa. 53 rm closed 6 Apr-7 Jun, 23 Sep-21 Dec, 180. Rest. ♦ ♿ 60-130.
★**Grand Bivouac,** ☎ 62.92.67.91. 20 rm. closed 15 Apr-10 May, 140.

Ⅹ ★★*La Ribère* (50 pl.), ☎ 62.92.76.91.

BAYONNE

Pau 107, Bordeaux 184, Paris 773
A1 ✉ 64100

ℹ pl. de la Liberté (B1-2), ☎ 59.59.31.31.

✈ Biarritz-Bayonne-Anglet, ☎ 59.23.90.67.

SNCF (C1), ☎ 59.55.50.50, 59.55.11.88.

Car-hire : *Budget* train + auto, quai A.-Sala (B-C2), ☎ 59.55.16.77, and station, ☎ 59.55.50.50.

Hotels :
★★★**Agora,** av. J.-Rostand (B3), ☎ 59.63.30.90. Tx 550621. AE, DC, Euro, Visa. 110 rm P 250. Rest. ♦ 70-100.

★★★**Capagorry** (Mapotel), 14, rue Thiers (B2), ☎ 59.25.48.22. Tx 540376. AE, DC, Euro, Visa. 48 rm Ⓟ ♿ closed 22 Dec-2 Jan, 260.
★★**Basses-Pyrénées,** 1, pl. des Victoires (B3), ☎ 59.59.00.29. Tx 541435. AE, DC, Euro, Visa. 50 rm Ⓟ ♿ 170. Rest. ♦ 50-80.
★★**Aria,** Saint-Frédéric, 117, rte de Pau, ☎ 59.55.22.70. Tx 541320. AE, DC, Euro, Visa. 84 rm Ⓟ ♿ closed 15 Dec-10 Jan, 185. Rest. ♦ closed Sat and Sun noon, 50-70.
★**Les Arceaux,** 26, rue Port-Neuf, ☎ 59.59.15.53. 17 rm, 100. Rest. ♦ 80-130.

Mouguerre, 6 km on the D936 :
★★**Kuluska** (L.F.), ☎ 59.31.83.60. 10 rm closed 1-15 Feb and Sun eve, 150. Rest. closed Fri and Sun eve, 50-130.

Ʌ ★★★★*La Chêneraie* (170 pl.), ☎ 59.55.01.31.

Restaurants :
♦♦ ***Euzkalduna,*** 61, rue Panneceau (B-C3), ☎ 59.59.28.02. Closed 1 week Jan, 19 May-4 Jun, 15 days Oct, Mon noon, every eve ex Sat all year ex Jul-Aug (closed Sun eve only). Spec : fish soup, omelette with sweet peppers, 110-130.
♦ ***Chistera,*** 42, rue du Port-Neuf, ☎ 59.59.25.93. AE, DC, Euro. ♿ closed 15 Oct-15 Nov and Tue low season, 45-110.

Urt, 10 km :
● ♦♦ ***La Galupe,*** pl. du Port, ☎ 59.56.21.84. ♿ closed Tue, Wed, 15 Jan-end Feb. A charming little inn in a delightful setting, 120-210.

Guided tours : *C.N.M.H.S.* (1 Jul-15 Sep ex Sun), enq at ⓘ

Excursions : boat trip on the Adour, embarkation quai Mousserolles, av. du Cdt-Resplandy (C2), ☎ 59.59.21.93.

Events : in Aug, *festival, bullfights ; ham fair* in early Apr.

Bric-à-brac and second-hand market : every Fri am.

Bicycle hire : *Loca Sport,* 48, allées Marines, ☎ 59.25.67.64. *Nivadour :* av. du 11-Novembre, ☎ 59.59.24.60.

Recommended : *Auction rooms,* 22, av. Dubrocq, ☎ 59.59.88.73. Chocolates and *tourons* (regional sweetmeats) : *Barrère,* under the arcades of the rue Port-Neuf.

BEAUCENS

Tarbes 41, Pau 61, Paris 846
8 km SE of Argelès-Gazost, C2
☒ 65400 Argelès-Gazost

⚓ (May-Oct), ☎ 62.97.04.01.

Hotels :
★★**Thermal** (L.F.), ☎ 62.97.04.21. 32 rm Ⓟ ♿ closed 1 Oct-1 Jun, 180. Rest. ♦ 55-110.
★**Vallauris,** ☎ 62.97.04.22. 18 rm Ⓟ closed Oct-Easter, 85. Rest. ♦ 40-100.

Ʌ ★★*Le Viscos* (100 pl.), ☎ 62.97.05.45.

BIARRITZ

Pau 115, Bordeaux 184, Paris 780
A1 ☒ 64200

ⓘ sq. d'Ixelles (C2), ☎ 59.24.20.24.

✈ Biarritz-Bayonne-Anglet, 4 km SE, ☎ 59.23.90.67.
Air France Agency, Parme — airport, ☎ 59.23.93.82.

SNCF ☎ 59.55.50.50, 59.23.58.95, 59.23.58.97.

Car-hire : *Budget* train + auto, 4, rue du Helder, ☎ 59.24.70.91 ; Biarritz airport, ☎ 59.24.17.80, and at the station, ☎ 59.24.15.40.

Hotels :
★★★★(L) ***Miramar,*** av. de l'Impératrice, ☎ 59.24.85.20. Tx 540831. AE, DC, Euro, Visa. 126 rm Ⓟ 750. Rest. ● ♦♦♦ Enjoyable fare in comfortable modern surroundings with a view of the ocean. Spec : *salade de homard, magret aux fruits,* dietetic specialities, 190-280.
★★★★(L) ***Palais,*** 1, av. de l'Impératrice (C1), ☎ 59.24.09.40. Tx 570000. AE, DC, Euro, Visa. 140 rm Ⓟ ♿ open 1 May-30 Oct, 1 400. Rest. ● ♦♦♦♦ ♿ In one of the last great Napoléon III luxury hotels, the cuisine is worthy. Spec : *filets de rougets aux haricots verts, homard à la compote de poivrons,* 200-300.
● ★★★★**Eurotel,** 19, av. de la Perspective (A2), ☎ 59.24.32.33. Tx 570014. AE, DC, Visa. 60 rm closed 31 Oct-1 Dec, Sun eve and Mon noon, 590. Rest. ● ♦♦♦ Quality cooking served on the top floor overlooking one of the most beautiful views in the world, 130-180.
● ★★★**Windsor** (Inter-Hôtel), Grande Plage (C1), ☎ 59.24.08.52. AE, DC, Euro, Visa. 37 rm closed 11 Nov-20 Mar, 350. Rest. ♦ 80-150.
★★★**Plaza,** av. Edouard-VII (C1), ☎ 59.24.74.00. Tx 570048. AE, DC, Euro. 60 rm Ⓟ ♿ 470. Rest. ♦♦ ♿ 120-210.
★★★**Regina et Golf,** 52, av. de l'Impératrice (C1), ☎ 59.24.09.60. Tx 541330. AE, DC, Visa. 50 rm Ⓟ closed 15 Oct-15 May, 380. Rest. 120-210.
● ★★**Atalaye,** plateau de l'Atalaye (A2), ☎ 59.24.06.76. DC, Visa. 25 rm Ⓟ closed 30 Oct-30 Mar, 270.
★★**Beaulieu,** 3, pl. du Port-Vieux (A2), ☎ 59.24.23.59. 28 rm, closed Nov-Mar, 190. Rest. ♦ closed end Sep, 55-90.
★★**Edouard VII,** 21, av. Carnot, ☎ 59.24.07.20. Visa. 15 rm, closed 31 Oct-1 Mar, 195. Rest. ♦ 70-100.

Arcangues, 7 km S :
★★**Marie-Eder,** rte de St-Pée, ☎ 59.43.05.61. 8 rm Ⓟ closed 6-30 Oct, and Tue low season, 210.

Ʌ ★★★*Splendid* (135 pl.), ☎ 59.23.01.29 ; ★★★*Biarritz* (267 pl.), ☎ 59.23.00.12. Arcangues, 7.5 km S : ★★*Aldabenia* (80 pl.), ☎ 59.23.72.25.

Restaurants :
● ♦♦♦♦ ***Café de Paris*** (Pierre Laporte), 5, pl. Bellevue, ☎ 59.24.19.53. AE, DC, Visa. closed 5 Jan-16 Mar and Mon low season. In a lovely, flowered setting, P. Laporte cooks for your greatest happiness. Spec : *terrine de rougets, louvine de ligne en chemise, steak de canard,* festival of desserts, home-made bread, wonderful selection of Bordeaux, 250-300.
● ♦♦ ***Relais de Parme,*** at the airport, ☎ 59.23.93.84. AE, DC, Visa ♿ closed Sat. The branch of the *Café de Paris.* P. Laporte's excellent cooking in an enjoyable setting. ***Silver Flight,*** snack-bar, 200-250.
● ♦ ***Auberge de la Négresse,*** 10, bd de l'Aérodrome, ☎ 59.23.15.83. Euro. ♿ closed 4 Oct-early Nov and Mon. Fashionable bistro, simple, hearty fare. Spec : *boudin aux pommes, langoustines grillées,* 90-110.
● ♦ ***Alambic,*** 5, pl. Bellevue, ☎ 59.24.53.41. closed 5 Jan-5 Feb and Mon low season. Prepared by P. Laporte's team, hors d'œuvre table, steaks, daily specials. Young ambiance, low prices, 100-130.

Guided tours : enq at the ⓘ

Events : Easter, *festivals and galas, antique dealer's salon, folklore ;* Aug, *cow running, international horse racing.*

Institut de Thalassothérapie Louison-Bobet, av. de l'Impératrice, ☎ 59.24.20.80.

Rhumatology, post-surgical re-education, fitness... **Thermes Marins (ocean spas) :** rue de Madrid, ☎ 59.24.13.80.

Bicycle hire : 16, av. Jaulerry, ☎ 59.24.13.64. 10, av. de la Marne, ☎ 59.24.06.31.

Casino : pl. Bellevue, ☎ 59.24.11.22.

Recommended : *Dodin-Garrigue,* cake and pastry cook, 7, rue Gambetta (B2), ☎ 59.24.16.37. *Tourons* (regional sweetmeats) : *Daranatz,* 12, rue Mal-Foch, ☎ 59.24.21.91. Chocolatiers : *Mirmont,* 3, rue Mazagran ; *Henriet,* av. Edouard-VII. Gourmet shop : *Arosteguy,* 5, rue Victor-Hugo. Coffee : *Moka Fina,* next to les Halles. *Auction rooms,* 6, rue du Centre. ☎ 59.24.21.88.

BIDARRAY

Bayonne 36, Pau 122, Paris 807
15 km S of Cambo-les-Bains, A1 ⊠ 64780

Hotels :
★★***Pont d'Enfer,*** ☎ 59.37.70.88. 18 rm P closed Nov-Feb, 220. Rest. ♦ Good simple fare, 75-150.
★***Erramundeya,*** ☎ 59.37.71.21. 10 rm P closed 30 Nov-1 Mar and Tue ex Jul-Aug, 120. Rest. ♦ 50-100.
★***Noblia,*** ☎ 59.37.70.89. Visa. 16 rm P ♿ 100. Rest. ♦ 45-80.

BIDART

Bayonne 14, Pau 121, Paris 786
A1 ⊠ 64210

ℹ Grande Plage (high season), ☎ 59.54.93.85.

SNCF ☎ 59.54.92.91.

Hotels :
● ★★★***Bidartea*** (Mapotel), 3 km on the N10, ☎ 59.54.94.68. 30 rm P ♿ closed Nov-Mar, 340. Rest. ♦ 120-170.
★★***Ypua,*** rte de la Chapelle, ☎ 59.54.93.11. Euro. 12 rm P closed Nov, Feb and Mon low season, 120. Rest. ♦ 65-120.
★***Elissaldia,*** pl. Sauver-Atchoarena, ☎ 59.54.90.03. 20 rm P 75. Rest. 55-120.
★***Itsas-Mendia,*** ☎ 59.54.90.23. 18 rm P closed 15 Oct-1 Mar, 180. Rest. ♦ 60-120.
★***Pénélope Enia,*** av. du Château, ☎ 59.23.00.37. Visa. 21 rm P ♿ closed 30 Oct-1 May, 110. Rest. ♦ 50-60.

⛺ ★★★★*Le Ruisseau* (300 pl.), ☎ 59.23.54.56 ; ★★★*Itsasoa la Mer* (200 pl.), ☎ 59.26.52.21.

CAMBO-LES-BAINS

Bayonne 19, Pau 113, Paris 791
A1 ⊠ 64250

ℹ parc St-Joseph, ☎ 59.29.70.25.

SNCF ☎ 59.55.50.50, 59.25.71.24.

Hotels :
★★★***Errobia,*** av. Chanteclerc, ☎ 59.29.71.26. Visa. 15 rm P closed Nov-Apr, 210.
Louhossoa, 8 km SE :
★***Trinquet,*** ☎ 59.93.32.54. AE, DC, Euro, Visa. 18 rm P ♿ closed Jan, 160. Rest. ♦ closed Tue low season, 50-130.

⛺ ★★★*Ur-Hégia* (120 pl.), ☎ 59.29.72.03.

CAMPAN

Tarbes 28, Saint-Gaudens 64, Paris 833
D2 ⊠ 65200 Bagnères-de-Bigorre

ℹ ☎ 62.95.35.01.

Hotels :
★***Beauséjour,*** ☎ 62.95.35.30. 22 rm closed Nov, 90. Rest. ♦ 40-80.
Val d'Arizes, ☎ 62.95.35.04. 7 rm 140. Rest. 45-90.

Sainte-Marie-de-Campan, ⊠ 65710, 6 km SE :
★★***Chalet-Hôtel,*** ☎ 62.91.85.64. 24 rm P closed 15 Apr-15 May and 30 Sep-15 Dec, 140. Rest. ♦ 55-120.
★***Deux Cols,*** ☎ 62.91.85.60. 20 rm P closed Oct-Dec, Apr-May, 135. Rest. ♦ 45-90.

Payolle, 16 km SE :
★★***Arcoch,*** ☎ 62.91.85.76. 20 rm P ♿ closed 15 Oct-1 Dec and May, 150. Rest. ♦ 65-250.

⛺ ★★★*Orée des Monts* (90 pl.), ☎ 62.91.83.98 ; ★★*les Bulanettes* (50 pl.), ☎ 62.95.85.90 ; ★★*le Layris* (50 pl.), ☎ 62.95.35.34.

CAPVERN-LES-BAINS

Bagnères-de-Bigorre 20, Tarbes 27, Paris 832
D2 (May-Oct), ☎ 62.39.00.02 ⊠ 65130

ℹ ☎ 62.39.00.46.

SNCF ☎ 62.39.03.82.

Hotels :
● ★★★***Laca,*** rte de Mauvezin, ☎ 62.39.02.06. Tx 521929. AE, DC, Euro, Visa. 60 rm P ♿ closed mid-Oct-Apr, 290. Rest. ♦ 80-370.
★★***Lac Saint-Martin,*** RN117, ☎ 62.39.04.13. Visa. 20 rm P ♿ closed 1 Dec-31 Mar, 190. Rest. ♦ 65-170.
★★***Paris*** (Inter-Hôtel), ☎ 62.39.00.15. AE. 50 rm, closed Oct-Apr, 180. Rest. ♦ 65-120.
★★***Poste et Victoria,*** bd des Marronniers, ☎ 62.39.00.27. AE, DC, Euro, Visa. 29 rm P 180. Rest. 50.
★***Bellevue*** (L.F.), rte de Mauvezin, ☎ 62.39.00.29. 34 rm P ♿ closed Oct-Apr, 275. Rest. ♦ 55-75.

Mauvezin, 5 km SW :
★***Auberge de l'Arros,*** Escaladieu, ☎ 62.39.05.05. 12 rm P 85. Rest. ♦ 40-130.

⛺ ★★*Bel Air* (44 pl.), ☎ 62.39.00.35.

CASTELNAU-MAGNOAC

Tarbes 45, Toulouse 94, Paris 846
16 km E of Trie-sur-Baise, D1 ⊠ 65230

ℹ mairie, ☎ 62.99.80.62.

Hotel :
★***Dupont*** (L.F.), ☎ 62.99.80.02. 25 rm, 100. Rest. ♦ 80-130.

CAUTERETS

Tarbes 50, Pau 70, Paris 855
C2 1 500-2 000 m ⊠ 65110

(May-Oct), ☎ 62.92.51.60.

ℹ pl. de la Mairie, ☎ 62.92.50.27.

Hotels :
● ★★★***Bordeaux,*** 23, rue de Richelieu, ☎ 62.92.52.50. Tx 521425. AE, DC, Visa. 26 rm P ♿ closed 15 Apr-15 May and 4 Oct-15 Dec, 250. Rest. ♦ ♿ 90-200.
● ★★★***Trois Pics,*** av. Leclerc, ☎ 62.92.53.64, Tx 530337. AE, DC, Euro, Visa. 30 rm P ♿ closed Nov-mid-Dec, end Apr and Wed in winter, 255. Rest. ♦ 65-150.
● ★★***Etche Ona,*** 20, rue Richelieu, ☎ 62.92.51.43, Tx 530337. AE. 35 rm, closed 15 Apr-4 May and 30 Sep-15 Dec, 170. Rest. 65-140.
★★***Rotonde*** (L.F.), 38, rue Richelieu, ☎ 62.92.52.68. 22 rm, closed Nov-mid-Dec, 140. Rest. ♦ 50-75.
★***Astoria,*** av. du Mamelon-Vert, ☎ 62.92.53.77. 14 rm closed Oct-mid-Dec and May, 120.
★***Centre et Poste*** (L.F.), 11, rue de Belfort, ☎ 62.97.52.69. 40 rm ♿ closed 30 Sep-20 Dec, 15 Apr-6 May, 130. Rest. ♦ 55-100.

La Fruitière, 5 km S :
★**Fruitière** (L.F.), vallée du Lutour, ☎ 62.92.52.04. AE, Visa. 8 rm ⚟ Ⓟ ⛰ ♿ closed 1 Oct-15 May, 120. Rest. ♦ ♿ closed Sun eve, 50-110.

⛺ ★★★*Mamelon Vert* (100 pl.), ☎ 62.92.51.56 ; *les Bergeronnettes* (50 pl.), ☎ 62.92.50.69 ; *les Glères* (100 pl.), ☎ 62.97.52.34.

Casino, esplanade des Œufs, ☎ 62.92.52.14.

Recommended : cakes, pastries and sweets : *l'Avalanche,* La Raillière, ☎ 62.92.52.97. Crêperie : *le Royalty,* 9, esplanade des Œufs, ☎ 62.92.52.24.

CIBOURE

Bayonne 23, Pau 130, Paris 795
1.5 km W of Saint-Jean-de-Luz, A1
☒ 64500 Saint-Jean-de-Luz

Hotel :
★★**La Caravelle,** bd P.-Benoît, ☎ 59.26.18.05. 16 rm ⚟ ♿ 1 Nov-1 Mar, 155. Rest. ♦ ✂ ♿ 60.

Restaurants :
♦♦ **Chez Mattin,** 51, rue E.-Baignol, ☎ 59.47.19.52. AE, Visa ♿ closed Jan and Mon, 80-130.
● ♦ **Dominique,** quai M.-Ravel, ☎ 59.47.29.16. Visa ✂ ♿ closed Mon and Sun eve, 130-200.

EAUX-BONNES

Pau 43, Tarbes 75, Paris 828
C2 ☒ 64400 Laruns

⚕ (15 May-30 Sep), ☎ 59.05.34.02.

ℹ ☎ 59.05.33.08.

Hotels :
★★**Poste** (France-Accueil), rue L.-Barthou, ☎ 59.05.33.06. AE, DC, Euro, Visa. 20 rm ⚟ closed Easter-mid-May, 1 Oct-20 Dec, 180. Rest. ♦ ⚟ 55-150.
★**Abadie** (France-Accueil), rue L.-Barthou, ☎ 59.05.34.03. AE, DC, Euro, Visa. 20 rm, closed Easter-May, 1 Oct-20 Dec, 140. Rest. 55-100.
★**Richelieu et Thermes,** rue du Dr-Creignoux, ☎ 59.05.34.10. Visa. 24 rm Ⓟ closed end Sep-15 Dec, end Apr-15 May, 50. Rest. ♦ 120.

Casino municipal : ☎ 59.05.31.30.

ESPELETTE

Bayonne 20, Pau 119, Paris 790
A1 ☒ 64250 Cambo-les-Bains

Hotel :
● ★★**Euzkadi** (L.F.), ☎ 59.29.91.88. 28 rm ⁂ closed 15 Nov-15 Dec, 1 week during winter school hols, Mon and Tue, off-season, 140. Rest. ♦ ♿ The conservatory of good Basque dishes thanks to André Darraïdou. Spec : *ttoro, axoa, pipérade, tripoxa,* 55-90.

Restaurant :
♦ **Pottoka,** ☎ 59.29.90.92 ♿ closed 25-31 Oct, 1-15 Feb and Mon, 45-100.

Events : *pottok fair,* end Jan, *capsicum fair* in Oct.

GAN

Oloron 25, Lourdes 38, Paris 793
8 km S of Pau, C1 ☒ 64290

Hotel :
★**Hostellerie de l'Horizon,** ☎ 59.21.58.93. 11 rm Ⓟ ⁂ ⛰ ♿ 140. Rest. ♦ 60 85.

Recommended : *Jurançon Cooperative Wine-Cellar,* 53, av. Henri-IV, ☎ 59.21.57.03.

GAVARNIE

Bagnères-de-Bigorre 67, Tarbes 71, Paris 876
C2 ☒ 65120 Luz-Saint-Sauveur

⛷ 1 400-2 500 m

ℹ mairie, ☎ 62.92.48.26.

Hotels :
★★**Cimes,** ☎ 62.92.48.13. Euro, Visa. 13 rm ✂ closed Nov, 170. Rest. ♦ 45-200.
★**Astazou,** ☎ 62.92.48.07. 14 rm, closed Sep-Feb, 90. Rest. ♦ 45-100.
★**Taillon,** ☎ 62.92.48.20. 24 rm ⚟ Ⓟ ⛰ ✂ closed 15 Oct-20 Dec, 100. Rest. ♦ ♿ 45-100.
★**Voyageurs,** ☎ 62.92.48.01. 21 rm Ⓟ ⁂ closed Nov-Dec, Easter and Whitsuntide, 125. Rest. ♦ 45-120.

Gèdre, 8 km N :
★**Brèche de Roland,** ☎ 62.92.48.54. 19 rm Ⓟ ⁂ ⛰ ♿ closed 15 Oct-20 Dec, end Apr, 160. Rest. ♦ 50-120.
★**Pyrénées** (L.F.), ☎ 62.92.48.51. 20 rm Ⓟ closed 15 Nov-15 Dec, 170. Rest. ♦ 55-100.

⛺ ★★*Le Relais d'Espagne* (40 pl.), ☎ 62.92.47.70.

GOURETTE

Pau 51, Tarbes 67, Paris 836
C2 ⛷ 1 400-2 400 m ☒ 64440

ℹ high season, ☎ 59.05.12.17.

Hotels :
★★**Boule de Neige,** ☎ 59.05.10.05. 18 rm ⚟ ⛰ ✂ closed 1 Sep-20 Dec, Easter-10 Jul, 190. Rest. ♦ closed in summer, 60-150.
★★**Pène-Blanque** (Inter-Hôtel), ☎ 59.05.11.29. 20 rm ⚟ closed 1 Sep-20 Dec, 190. Rest. ♦ 55-150.
★**Glacier,** ☎ 59.05.10.18. Visa. 10 rm, closed 15 Apr-1 Jul, end Aug-15 Dec, 100. Rest. ♦ 40-90.

GUÉTHARY

Bayonne 15, Pau 123, Paris 789
A1 ☒ 64210 Bidart

ℹ pl. de la Mairie, ☎ 59.26.56.60.

SNCF ☎ 59.26.50.41.

Hotels :
★★★**Briketenia,** rue de l'Empereur, ☎ 59.26.51.34. AE, Visa. 22 rm ⚟ Ⓟ ⁂ ✂ ♿ closed 30 Oct-15 Dec, Tue, 220. Rest. ● ♦♦♦ ♿ The Ibarboure brothers' gastronomic festival. Spec : excellent fishermen's menu, *bar à la vapeur,* 90-190.
★★**Pereria,** ☎ 59.26.51.68. 30 rm ⚟ Ⓟ ⁂ ⛰ closed 1 Nov-1 Mar, 175. Rest. ♦ 55-100.

HASPARREN

Bayonne 24, Pau 103, Paris 797
A1 ☒ 64240

ℹ pl. St-Jean (high season), ☎ 59.29.62.02.

Hotel :
★★**Tilleuls,** pl. de Verdun, ☎ 59.29.62.20. Euro. 12 rm Ⓟ ✂ closed 7-28 Oct, 145. Rest. ♦ ✂ closed Fri eve, Sat, Sun eve (ex hols), 60-95.

⛺ ★★★*Chapital* (100 pl.), ☎ 59.29.62.94.

Events : cow running in the streets during Jul.

HENDAYE

Bayonne 32, Pau 141, Paris 807
A1 ☒ 64700

ℹ 12, rue des Aubépines, ☎ 59.20.00.34.

SNCF ☎ 59.55.50.50, 59.20.70.09.

Car-hire : *Budget* train + auto, 107, bd de-Gaulle, ☎ 59.20.79.04, and at the station, ☎ 59.20.70.11.

Hotels :

★★★***Lilliac,*** rd-pt de la Plage, ☎ 59.20.02.45. AE, DC, Euro, Visa. 23 rm ♿ 230.

★★★***Paris,*** rd-pt de la Plage, ☎ 59.20.05.06. DC, Visa. 39 rm Ⓟ closed 1 Oct-Whitsun, 235.

● ★★***Pohoténia,*** rte de la Corniche, ☎ 59.20.04.76. Visa. 42 rm Ⓟ closed Jan, 140. Rest. ♦ closed Sun eve low season, 80-150.

★★***Larramendy Baita,*** bd de la Mer, ☎ 59.20.04.68. 12 rm Ⓟ ♿ closed 15 Oct-24 Mar, 130. Rest. ♦ 80-130.

● ★***Gitanilla*** (L.F.), 52, bd Gal-Leclerc, ☎ 59.20.04.65. AE, DC, Euro, Visa. 9 rm 95. Rest. ♦♦ closed 15 Oct-end Nov, Sun eve and Mon. Simple and good. Spec : steaks, *chipirons,* 80-150.

★***Chez Antoinette,*** pl. Pellot, ☎ 59.20.08.47. 24 rm Ⓟ closed end Sep-1 Jun, 95. Rest. ● ♦ Spec : *pantxeta d'agneau, magret de canard,* 80-100.

Biriatou, 4 km SE :

● ★★***Bakea,*** ☎ 59.20.76.36. AE, DC, Euro, Visa. 15 rm Ⓟ ♿ closed 30 Sep-15 May, 220. Rest. ● ♦♦ In this large chalet, no drop in quality, only the prices rise. Spec : *foie gras,* grilled lobster, *brochette de rognons,* 90-220.

⛺ ★★★*Acacias* (120 pl.), ☎ 59.20.78.76 ; ★★*Abaya* (160 pl.), ☎ 59.20.03.77.

Casino : *Hendaye Plage,* ☎ 59.20.04.79.

ITXASSOU

Bayonne 24, Pau 118, Paris 795
4 km S of Cambo-les-Bains, A1
✉ 64250 Cambo-les-Bains

Hotels :

★★***Fronton*** (L.F.), pl. du Fronton, ☎ 59.29.75.10. DC, Visa. 15 rm Ⓟ closed 1 Jan-15 Feb and Tue, 175. Rest. ♦ ♿ 45-130.

★***Txistulari,*** on the D918, ☎ 59.29.75.09. 17 rm Ⓟ ♿ closed 20 Dec-15 Jan, 95. Rest. ♦ 50-100.

Farmhouse gîte, chambres d'hôtes : *Arosteya,* ☎ 59.29.98.28

LANNEMEZAN

Tarbes 35, Auch 66, Paris 840
D1 ✉ 65300

ℹ pl. de la République, ☎ 62.98.08.31.

SNCF ☎ 62.98.00.49.

Car-hire : *Budget* train + auto, at the station, ☎ 62.98.00.49.

Hotels :

★★***Pyrénées*** (France-Accueil), rue Diderot, rte de Tarbes, ☎ 62.98.01.53. AE, DC, Euro, Visa. 31 rm Ⓟ ♿ closed 1-30 Nov, 180. Rest. ♦ ♿ 55-180.

★***Hostellerie du Pont d'Espagne,*** 12, rue du 8-Mai-1945, ☎ 62.98.01.52. 10 rm Ⓟ 80. Rest. ♦ 40-60.

Galan, ✉ 65330, 10 km N :

★***Arcades*** (L.F.), ☎ 62.99.77.55. 10 rm, 100. Rest. ♦ 80-130.

Saint-Laurent-de-Neste, ✉ 65150, 12 km SE :

★***La Plantade*** (L.F.), on the RN117, ☎ 62.39.76.73. 10 rm Ⓟ closed Sat and Sun low season, 90. Rest. ♦ 45-70.

Aventignan, ✉ 65660, 16 km SE :

★***Grottes de Gargas,*** ☎ 62.99.02.38. 8 rm Ⓟ closed end Sep-1 Apr, 90. Rest. ♦ closed Wed low season, 40-100.

Fairs : 2nd Tue in Oct, *horse fair ;* 1st Wed in Dec, *horse and mule fair.*

LARUNS

Pau 37, Tarbes 71, Paris 822
C2 ✉ 64440

Hotels :

★★***Ossau,*** pl. de la Mairie, ☎ 59.05.30.14. Visa. 12 rm. closed 1 week in May, 115. Rest. ♦ closed Tue low season, 55-100.

★***Le Lorry,*** quartier Boilaa, ☎ 59.04.31.22. Visa. 20 rm Ⓟ closed Nov, 95. Rest. ♦ 55-110.

⛺ ★★★*Les Gaves* (60 pl.), ☎ 59.05.32.37.

Events : *Ossau valley festivals* (traditional mountain festivals), 15 Aug ; *cheese fair* in Oct.

LESCUN

Oloron 36, Tarbes 110, Paris 854
18 km S of Sarrance, B2 ✉ 64490

Hotel :

● ★★***Pic d'Anie,*** ☎ 59.34.71.54. 21 rm closed 20 Sep-1 Apr, 150. Rest. ♦ 70-165.

LESTELLE-BÉTHARRAM

Lourdes 16, Pau 23, Paris 811
C2 ✉ 64800

Hotels :

★★***Central,*** 2, av. de Bétharram, ☎ 59.61.27.18. AE, Visa. 10 rm ♿ closed mid-Oct-mid-Nov, Tue and Wed, 100. Rest. ♦ 45-110.

★***Le Vieux Logis,*** rte des Grottes, 3 km, ☎ 59.61.34.40. Euro. 14 rm Ⓟ closed Dec-Mar. Rest. ♦ 45-140.

⛺ ★*Du Saillet* (50 pl.), ☎ 59.61.29.07.

LOURDES

Bayonne 143, Toulouse 169, Paris 824
C2 ✉ 65100

ℹ pl. du Champ-Commun (B-C2), ☎ 62.94.15.64.

✈ Tarbes-Ossun, 10 km NE, ☎ 62.34.42.22.

SNCF (C1), ☎ 62.94.35.36, 62.94.10.47, 62.34.35.36.

🚌 av. du Mal-Juin (C2).

Car-hire : *Budget* train + auto, at the station, ☎ 62.94.35.36, and at the airport.

Hotels :

● ★★★★***Grand Hôtel de la Grotte*** (Mapotel), 66-68, rue de la Grotte (B2), ☎ 62.94.58.87. Tx 531937. AE, DC, Euro, Visa. 84 rm Ⓟ ♿ closed end Oct-end Mar, 430. Rest. ♦♦ 90-250.

★★★★***Gallia et Londres,*** 26, av. B.-Soubirous (A1), ☎ 62.94.35.44. Tx 521424. AE, DC, Visa. 90 rm Ⓟ ♿ closed 20 Oct-20 Apr, 600. Rest. ♦♦ 80-180.

★★★★***Impérial,*** 3, av. du Paradis (A2), ☎ 62.94.06.30. Tx 530802. AE, DC, Euro, Visa. 100 rm ♿ closed mid-Oct-end Apr, 420. Rest. ♦♦ 95-150.

● ★★★***Auberge Provençale*** (Inter-Hôtel), 4, rue Baron-Duprat (B-C2), ☎ 62.94.31.34. Tx 520257. AE, DC, Euro, Visa. 62 rm ♿ 300. Rest. ♦♦ 70-85.

● ★★★***Espagne*** (Mapotel), 9, av. du Paradis (A2), ☎ 62.94.50.02. Tx 520066. AE, DC, Euro, Visa. 92 rm Ⓟ ♿ closed mid-Oct-mid-Apr, 300. Rest. ♦♦ 80-250.

● ★★★***Excelsior*** (Mapotel), 83, bd de la Grotte (B1), ☎ 62.94.02.05. Tx 520343. AE, DC, Euro, Visa. 80 rm Ⓟ ♿ closed Easter, 240. Rest. ♦♦ 80-200.

★★★**Ambassadeurs,** 66, bd de la Grotte (B1), ☎ 62.94.32.85. Tx 570317. AE, DC, Euro, Visa. 49 rm closed Nov-mid-Mar, 310. Rest. ♦ 80-145.
★★★**Christina,** 42, av. Peyramale (A2), ☎ 62.94.26.11. Tx 531062. AE, DC, Euro, Visa. 265 rm closed end Oct-early Apr, 265. Rest. ♦ 70-110.
★★★**Gave,** 28, av. Peyramale (A2), ☎ 62.94.90.11. Tx 521435. AE, Visa. 60 rm closed Oct-Easter, 305. Rest. ♦ 75.
★★**Albret,** 21, pl. du Champ-Commun (C2), ☎ 62.94.75.00. Euro, Visa. closed Jan and Mon (Nov-Mar), 165. Rest. ● ♦♦ ***Taverne de Bigorre,*** 40-140.
★★**Beauséjour,** 16, av. de la Gare (C1), ☎ 62.94.38.18. AE, Visa. 44 rm closed Nov-Apr, 200.
★★**Lutetia,** 19, av. de la Gare (C1), ☎ 62.94.22.85. Tx 521702. AE, DC, Euro, Visa. 47 rm closed 5 Jan-6 Feb and 3-10 Mar, 205. Rest. ♦ 45-130.
★★**Majestic,** 9, av. Maransin (C1), ☎ 62.94.27.23. AE, DC, Euro, Visa. 36 rm closed 15 Oct-15 Apr, 180. Rest. ♦ 55-90.
★**Auberge Maurice Prat,** av. A.-Béguère (A1), ☎ 62.94.01.53. 15 rm closed 15 Dec-1 Mar and Mon low season, 210. Rest. ♦♦ Good basic dishes, 55-100.
★**Caravelle,** 60, av. A.-Marqui, ☎ 62.94.02.63. 12 rm closed Oct-Easter, 180.
★**Printemps,** 27, bd de la Grotte (B2), ☎ 62.94.24.77. AE, DC, Euro, Visa. closed Oct-Easter, 170. Rest. ♦ 45-65.

Adé, 5 km N :
★★**Virginia,** ☎ 62.94.66.18. Euro, Visa. 42 rm closed 25 Dec-1 Jan, 240. Rest. ♦ 60-150.

Lamarque-Pontacq, 65380 Ossun, 10 km NW :
★★**Béarn-Bigorre,** ☎ 62.53.57.55. 18 rm closed 20 Oct-7 Apr, 150. Rest. ♦ 55-110.

Ⴀ ★★★★*Plein Soleil* (50 pl.), ☎ 62.94.40.93 ; ★★★*de Sarsan* (65 pl.), ☎ 62.94.43.09 ; ★★*Anclades* (100 pl.), ☎ 62.94.10.37 ; ★★*l'Arrouach* (65 pl.), ☎ 62.94.25.75 ; ★★*la Scierie* (75 pl.), ☎ 62.94.29.24 ; ★★*Moulin du Monge* (66 pl.), ☎ 62.94.28.15.

Leisure activities : Lourdes lake, 3 km on the Pau road, ☎ 62.94.26.50. Surfing, yachting, pedal boats, etc.

LOURES-BAROUSSE

Bagnères-de-Luchon 29, Tarbes 59, Paris 814
24 km SE of Lannemezan, D2 ☒ 65370

ⓘ rte Nationale, ☎ 62.99.21.30.

SNCF Loures-Barbazan, ☎ 62.99.20.24.

Hotels :
★★**Hostellerie des Vallées,** ☎ 62.99.20.34. 18 rm closed 1 Nov-28 Feb, 155. Rest. ♦ closed Sun eve and Mon low season, 60-150.
Source, ☎ 62.99.21.24. 18 rm closed Oct-Apr, 100. Rest. ♦ 80-130.

Event : cheese fair in Aug.

LOUVIE-JUZON

Pau 26, Tarbes 60, Paris 811
3 km S of Arudy, C2 ☒ 64260 Arudy

Hotels :
★★★**La Forestière,** rte de Pau, ☎ 59.05.62.28. Euro, Visa. 15 rm 235. Rest. ♦ 70-150.
★★**Dhérété,** rue Gambetta, ☎ 59.05.61.01. 18 rm closed 5 Oct-1 Dec and Mon low season, 140. Rest. ♦ 50-100.

LURBE-SAINT-CHRISTAU

Pau 42, Tarbes 81, Paris 827
9 km S of Oloron-Sainte-Marie, B1
☒ 64660 Asasp-Issor

(Apr-Oct), ☎ 59.39.40.04.

Hotels :
★★★**Résidence du Parc,** ☎ 59.34.40.04. Tx 550656. 43 rm closed Nov-Mar, 310. Rest. ♦♦ 70-130.
★★**Vallées,** ☎ 59.34.40.01. 20 rm closed 11 Jan-25 Mar, 150. Rest. ♦ 40-70.

LUZ-SAINT-SAUVEUR

Lourdes 31, Bagnères-de-Bigorre 47, Paris 856
C2 ☒ 65120

ⓘ pl. du 8-Mai, ☎ 62.92.81.60.

Hotels :
★★**Europe** (L.F.), on the D921, ☎ 62.92.80.02. AE. 25 rm closed 11 Sep-14 Jun, 170.
★**Chardons Bleus** (L.F.), ☎ 62.92.80.06. 22 rm 150.
★**Remparts** (L.F.), ☎ 62.92.81.70. 12 rm. closed May and 1 Oct-20 Dec, 100. Rest. ♦ Pension only.

Esquièze-Sère, 2 km N :
★★**Montaigu** (L.F.), ☎ 62.92.81.71. Euro, Visa. 23 rm closed 30 Sep-20 Dec, 165. Rest. ♦ 50-150.
★★**Londres,** ☎ 62.92.80.09. 30 rm closed 30 Apr-15 Jun, 190. Rest. ♦ 45-100.
★**Terminus,** ☎ 62.92.80.17. 18 rm Open school hols (Christmas, Feb and Easter) and 1 Jun-20 Sep, 100. Rest. ♦ 80-130.

Farmhouse gîte and chambres d'hôtes : J. Castagne-Cloze, rue de Lanne, ☎ 62.92.81.19. fishing, farm produce for sale.

Ⴀ ★★*Saint-Bazerque* (66 pl.), ☎ 62.92.80.83 ; Esquièze-Sère : ★★★*International* (135 pl.), ☎ 62.92.82.02.

Mountain discovery tours : guides and escorts propose a number of mountain hikes and rambles. Enq : *Maison de la Montagne,* ☎ 62.92.87.28.

MAUBOURGUET

Tarbes 26, Auch 62, Paris 788
9 km N of Vic-en-Bigorre, D1 ☒ 65700

ⓘ mairie, ☎ 62.96.30.09.

SNCF ☎ 62.96.31.56.

Hotels :
★★**Au Fer à Cheval,** 173, av. des Pyrénées, ☎ 62.96.42.88. AE, DC, Euro, Visa. 8 rm closed 15 Sep-15 Oct, 115. Rest. ♦ Spec : *foie frais aux pommes,* 45-110.
★**France,** allée Larbanès, ☎ 62.96.30.10. 19 rm, 105. Rest. ♦ 40-100.

Farmhouse-inn, farmhouse camping, chambres d'hôtes : canoeing, water-skiing on the river, tennis. Pony promenades for children. Farm produce, *confits* and *foie gras.* Enq : R. Larrieu, Labatut-Rivière (5 km NE), 65700 Maubourguet, ☎ 62.96.46.28.

Fair : 1st Tue in May, *livestock fair.*

MAULÉON-LICHARRE

Bayonne 77, Pau 63, Paris 817
B1 ☒ 64130

ⓘ 12, rue J.-B.-Heugas, ☎ 59.28.02.37.

SNCF 59.28.07.80.

Hotels :
● ★★***Hostellerie du Château*** (L.F.), 25, rue de la Navarre, ☎ 59.28.19.06. 35 rm Ⓟ closed 15 Jan-20 Feb, 160. Rest. ♦ 80-130.
★★***Bidegain,*** 13, rue de la Navarre, ☎ 59.28.16.05. AE, DC, Visa. 30 rm Ⓟ closed end Nov, 15 Dec-15 Jan, Fri eve and Sun eve, 180. Rest. ♦ ♿ 45-120.

Barcus, 14 km SE :
★★***Ilhareguy*** (L.F.), ☎ 59.28.90.80. 12 rm Ⓟ closed Nov, 100. Rest. ♦ 80-130.
★***Chilo,*** ☎ 59.28.14.79. 12 rm Ⓟ closed 15 Sep-15 Oct and Mon, 100. Rest. ♦ 80-130.

⛺ ★★*Du Saison* (30 pl.), ☎ 59.28.18.79.

La MONGIE

Bagnères-de-Bigorre 25, Lourdes 47, Paris 851
D2 ✉ 65200 Bagnères-de-Bigorre

1 800-2 400 m

ℹ (Nov-May), ☎ 62.91.93.05.

Hotels :
● ★★★***Mandia,*** ☎ 62.91.93.49. Tx 521424. AE, DC, Visa. 50 rm Ⓟ ♿ closed Easter-mid-Dec, 500. Rest. Full pension ♦♦ 70-150.
● ★★★***Sol Y Neou*** (L.F.), ☎ 62.91.93.22. Tx 521424. AE, DC, Visa. 36 rm closed end Apr-15 Dec, 260. Rest. ♦ 65-100.
● ★★***Crête Blanche,*** ☎ 62.91.92.49. AE. 30 rm closed end Apr-15 Dec, 210. Rest. ♦ 70-100.

MOURENX

Orthez 20, Pau 26, Paris 790
B1 ✉ 64150

Hotel :
★★***Béarn,*** 3, av. Ch.-Moureu, ☎ 59.60.02.98. 21 rm Ⓟ ♿ closed Sun eve and Mon, 170. Rest. ♦ 50-90.

⛺ ★★*Municipal* (85 pl.), ☎ 59.60.07.23.

NAVARRENX

Oloron 22, Bayonne 90, Paris 800
B1 ✉ 64190

ℹ pte St-Antoine (high season) and mairie, ☎ 59.34.10.22.

Hotel :
● ★★***Commerce,*** ☎ 59.66.50.16. 32 rm, closed 1 Jan-15 Feb, end Oct and Mon ex Jul-Aug, 135. Rest. ♦ 50-120.

Event : *World Salmon Fishing Competition* in Mar, Apr and Jul. Enq at ℹ

NAY

Lourdes 25, Bayonne 125, Paris 805
18 km SE of Pau, C1 ✉ 64800

Hotels :
★★***Chez Lazare*** (L.F.), quartier Labassères, Arros-Nay, ☎ 59.61.05.26. 7 rm Ⓟ closed 1-17 Aug, 155. Rest. ♿ closed Sun and noon, 65-80.
★★***Voyageurs*** (L.F.), 12, pl. Marcadieu, ☎ 59.61.04.69. 22 rm ♿ closed Nov, 155. Rest. ♦ 45-95.
★***Béarn,*** 6, cours Pasteur, ☎ 59.61.02.38. 8 rm Ⓟ closed 1-8 Oct, 90. Rest. ♦ closed Sun low season, 40-60.

OLORON-SAINTE-MARIE

Pau 33, Bayonne 99, Paris 818
B1 ✉ 64400

ℹ pl. de la Résistance, ☎ 59.39.98.00.

SNCF ☎ 39.00.61.

Hotels :
● ★★***Béarn,*** 4, pl. Georges-Clemenceau, ☎ 59.39.00.99. AE, DC, Euro, Visa. 26 rm Ⓟ closed Feb and Sun low season, 220.
★★***L'Auberge*** (L.F.), 9, rue Carérot, ☎ 59.39.43.78. AE, Visa. 14 rm, 160. Rest. ♦ closed Sat noon, 45-95.
★★***Paix,*** 24, av. Sadi-Carnot, ☎ 59.39.02.63. 24 rm Ⓟ 160.

Féas, 64570 Aramits, 8 km SW :
★***Forgerie du Beau Site,*** ☎ 59.39.24.87. Euro. 10 rm Ⓟ closed 15 Nov-15 Dec, 80. Rest. closed Wed low season, 35-170.

⛺ ★★*Municipal* (110 pl.), ☎ 59.39.11.26 ; Féas : ★★*Vieux Moulin* (50 pl.), ☎ 59.39.81.18.

Event : *livestock fair* on 1 May.

ORTHEZ

Dax 37, Pau 41, Paris 777
B1 ✉ 64300

ℹ rue des Jacobins, ☎ 59.69.02.75.

SNCF ☎ 59.30.50.50, 59.69.93.24, 59.69.93.24.

Hotel :
★***Voyageurs,*** av. G.-Moutet, ☎ 59.69.02.29. 10 rm 130. Rest. ♦ closed Sun and noon, 60-85.

⛺ ★★*Source* (65 pl.), ☎ 59.69.02.75.

Restaurant :
♦♦ ***Auberge Saint-Loup,*** 20, rue du Pont-Vieux, ☎ 59.69.15.40. Visa ♿ closed 15-30 Jun, 15-30 Oct, Mon and noon every day ex Sun. Spec : *mousseline de St-Jacques au coulis d'écrevisses et cresson,* 100-140.

PAU

Bordeaux 190, Toulouse 194, Paris 785
C1 ✉ 64000

ℹ pl. Royale (B3), ☎ 59.27.27.08.

✈ *Pau-Uzein,* 10 km N, ☎ 59.27.97.44.

SNCF (B3) ☎ 59.30.50.50, 59.28.86.08.

Car-hire : *Budget* train + auto, 70, rue d'Étigny, ☎ 59.32.04.59 ; at the airport, ☎ 59.24.70.91, 59.24.17.80, and the station, ☎ 59.27.59.42.

Hotels :
● ★★★***Continental*** (Mapotel), 2, rue Mal-Foch (B3), ☎ 59.27.69.31. Tx 570906. AE, DC, Euro, Visa. 100 rm Ⓟ ♿ 350. Rest. ♦♦ 80-170.
★★★***Bristol,*** 3, rue Gambetta (C2-3), ☎ 59.27.72.98. Tx 570929. AE, DC, Euro, Visa. 26 rm Ⓟ 240.
★★★***Montpensier,*** 36, rue Montpensier (B2), ☎ 59.27.42.72. Tx 570929. AE, DC, Euro, Visa. 24 rm Ⓟ ♿ 165.
★★★***Paris,*** 80, rue E. Garet (C2), ☎ 59.27.34.39. Tx 541595. AE, DC, Euro, Visa. 41 rm Ⓟ ♿ 320.
★★***Bourbon,*** 12, pl. Clemenceau (B3), ☎ 62.27.53.12. Tx 541965. AE, DC, Euro, Visa. 33 rm ♿ 150.
★★***Commerce*** (Inter-Hôtel), 9, rue du Mal-Joffre (B3), ☎ 62.27.24.40. Tx 540193. AE, DC, Euro, Visa. 50 rm Ⓟ 210. Rest. ♦ closed Sun, 60-120.
★★***Europe,*** 9, pl. Clemenceau (B3), ☎ 62.27.73.40. AE, DC, Euro, Visa. 33 rm Ⓟ closed 24 Dec-2 Jan, 215.
★★***Colbert,*** 1, rue Manescau (A1), ☎ 62.32.52.78. 21 rm Ⓟ closed Sep-1 Oct, 160. Rest. ♦ 40-85.
★***Bernard,*** 7, rue de Foix (B3), ☎ 62.27.40.28. 21 rm, closed 24 Dec-1 Jan, 135.

Gelos, ✉ 64110 Jurançon, 1 km S :

★★**Le Bourbail** (L.F. ; Relais du Silence), ☎ 62.21.54.60. Visa. 20 rm 🅿 ♨ ♿ 200. Rest. ♦ ♿ closed 22 Dec-20 Jan and Sat, 80-130.

Lescar, ✉ 64230, 7 km NW :
★★★**Le Bilaa,** chemin de Lons, ☎ 62.81.03.00. Tx 541856. AE, Visa. 80 rm 🅿 ♨ ♿ 210.

Ousse, ✉ 64230 Bizanos, 9.5 km E :
★★**Pyrénées,** ☎ 62.81.71.51. AE, Euro, Visa. 22 rm 🅿 ♨ ♿ closed Nov, Sat and Sun eve low season, 170. Rest. ♦ ♿ 55-100.

Soumoulou, ✉ 64420, 17 km E :
★★**Béarn** (France-Accueil), 18, rue Las-Bordes, ☎ 62.04.60.09. AE, DC, Euro. 13 rm 🅿 ♨ closed 15 Jan-15 Feb, Mon and Sun eve low season, 175. Rest. ♦♦ 50-160.

⛺ ★★★*Plaine des Sports et des Loisirs* (70 pl.), ☎ 62.02.30.49 ; ★★★*les Sapins* (35 pl.), ☎ 62.02.34.21.

Restaurants :
● ♦♦♦ **Chez Pierre,** 16, rue L.-Barthou (B3), ☎ 62.27.76.86. AE, DC, Euro, Visa ♿ closed 11-26 Feb, and Sun. For hearty appetites... and others. Spec : *garbure, cassoulet,* fresh salmon, *canard aux truffes fraîches.* Bordeaux, local wines, 180-220.
● ♦♦♦ **Patrick Jourdan,** 14, rue Latapie (B3), ☎ 62.27.68.70. AE, DC, Visa ; closed Sat noon and Sun. An excellent gourmet's stop. Spec : *fin ragoût de fruits de mer, pigeon rôti en bécasse aux choux, feuilleté léger aux fruits rouges.* Jurançon wines, 135-180.
♦♦ **Saint-Jacques,** 9, rue du Parlement, ☎ 62.27.58.97. AE, Euro, Visa ♿ closed 15-28 Feb, 2 weeks in Jul, Sat noon and Sun, 50-140.
♦♦ **Pyrénées,** pl. Royale (B3), ☎ 62.27.07.75. AE, DC, Euro, Visa ; closed mid-Aug and Sun, 70-150.

Jurançon, 2 km S :
● ♦♦ **Ruffet,** ☎ 62.06.25.13. AE, DC ♿ closed Aug, early Jan, Sun eve and Mon. A lovely good traditional inn. Spec : *feuilletés, pigeonneau flambé,* good local wines, 70-180.

Events : *Automobile Grand Prix* in May ; *horse races* in autumn. *Traditional festivals* in Jurançon, in August.

Markets : local produce on Sat. Bric-à-brac and second-hand market every Sat, and Sun.

Casino, parc de Beaumont, ☎ 62.27.06.92.

RABASTENS-DE-BIGORRE

Tarbes 19, Auch 54, Paris 824
D1 ✉ 65140

ℹ mairie, ☎ 62.96.60.22.

SNCF ☎ 63.33.72.14.

Hotels :
● ★**Platanes** (L.F.), pl. du Centenaire, ☎ 62.96.61.77. 6 rm ♿ closed Sun eve, 90. Rest. ♦ 45-150.
★**Chez Yvonne** (L.F.), ☎ 62.96.60.20. 10 rm 🅿 closed early May, 15 Oct-10 Nov, Sun eve and Fri, 75. Rest. ♦ 40-100.

Farmhouse camping, farm riding centre : *Domaine de Florence,* Bazillac, ☎ 62.96.82.97.

SAINT-ÉTIENNE-DE-BAIGORRY

Bayonne 51, Pau 114, Paris 822
11 km W of St-Jean-Pied-de-Port, B1 ✉ 64430

ℹ pl. de la Mairie (closed Feb), ☎ 59.37.43.11.

Hotels :
★★★**Le Trinquet-Arcé,** ☎ 59.37.40.14. Visa. 24 rm 🅿 ♨ closed Nov-Mar, 290. Rest.
● ♦♦ A great restaurant on the banks of the Nive. Regional fare. Spec : *foie gras aux truffes, omelette aux cèpes, civet de marcassin à l'Irouléguy,* 120-190.
● ★★**Panoramique Cortea,** quartier Occos, D15, ☎ 59.37.41.89. Visa. 20 rm 🅿 ♨ closed 15 Nov-15 Mar, 240. Rest. ♦♦ ♿ 100-180.
★**Manechenea,** ☎ 59.37.41.68. Euro. 10 rm 🅿 ♨ ♿ closed 20 Nov-1 Mar, 70. Rest. ♦ ♿ 50-100.

⛺ ★★*Irouléguy* (70 pl.), ☎ 59.37.43.96.

Wines of the Irouléguy region : cooperative wine-cellar, ☎ 59.37.41.33.

SAINT-JEAN-DE-LUZ

Bayonne 21, Pau 128, Paris 793
A1 ✉ 64500

ℹ pl. Mal-Foch, ☎ 59.26.03.16.

SNCF ☎ 59.26.02.08.

✈ Biarritz-Parme, 16 km NE, ☎ 59.23.90.67.

Car-hire : *Budget* train + auto, at the station, ☎ 59.26.02.08.

Hotels :
★★★★(L) **Chantaco,** Chantaco gulf, ☎ 59.26.14.76. Tx 540016. AE, DC. 28 rm. Beautiful Spanish-style residence in a peaceful setting 🅿 ♨ ♿ closed Oct-Easter, 600. Rest. ♦♦ 120-180.
★★★**Madison,** 25, bd Thiers, ☎ 59.26.35.02, Tx 540140. AE, DC, Euro, Visa. 25 rm ♿ 235.
★★★**Goélands,** 6, av. Etcheverry, ☎ 59.26.10.05. Visa. 45 rm 🅿 closed 15 Dec-15 Feb, 255. Rest. ♦ closed 1 Oct-Easter, 70-95.
★★★**Plage,** 33, rue Garat, ☎ 59.51.03.44. Euro, Visa. 35 rm 🅿 ♿ closed 15 Oct-1 Apr, 245. Rest. ♦ ♿ 50-150.
★★**Commerce,** 3, bd du Cdt-Passicot, ☎ 59.26.31.99, Tx 540518. 36 rm, 220.
★★**La Fayette** (L.F.), 18-20, rue de la République, ☎ 59.26.17.74. AE, DC, Euro, Visa. 19 rm. closed Jan, 200. Rest. ♦ ♿ Terrace, 55-155.
★**Jardin,** 5, rue Loquin, ☎ 59.26.05.51. 14 rm ♿ closed 31 Oct-10 Mar, 130. Rest. ♦ open 1 Jun-30 Sep. Half-pension only.

⛺ ★★★*Chibaou-Berria* (220 pl.), ☎ 59.26.11.94 ; ★★★*Inter-Plages* (100 pl.), ☎ 59.26.24.78 ; ★★★*Itsas-Mendi* (300 pl.), ☎ 59.26.56.50 ; ★★*Maya* (115 pl.), ☎ 59.26.54.91 ; ★★*Plage Soubelet* (115 pl.), ☎ 59.26.51.60.

Restaurants :
♦ **Au Chipiron,** 4, rue Etchegaray, ☎ 59.26.03.41. AE ♿ Terrace, closed 2 Jan-1 Feb and Mon, 55-110.
♦ **Ostatua,** 25, rue de l'Église, ☎ 59.26.47.22. AE, Visa ; closed Sun eve and Mon low season, Mon noon high season. Seafood specialities, 80-180.
♦ **Le Petit Grill Basque,** 4, rue St-Jacques, ☎ 59.26.80.76 ♿ closed 20 Dec-20 Jan, 5-15 May and Fri, 50-80.

Guided tours : enq at ℹ

Events : *midnight mass, Basque Christmas service ; tuna festival* in Jul, *Ttoro festival* in Sep.

Casino, 75, rue Gambetta, ☎ 59.26.00.41.

Bicycle hire : *Cycles Ado,* 7, av. Labrouche, ☎ 59.26.14.95.

Recommended : chocolate : *Paries,* 15, rue Gambetta ; Basque linen : *Lparralde,* rue Gambetta.

SAINT-JEAN-PIED-DE-PORT

Bayonne 54, Pau 103, Paris 825
A-B1 ⊠ 64220

ⓘ pl. du Marché, ☎ 59.37.03.57.

SNCF ☎ 59.37.02.00.

Hotels :
★★★***Continental,*** 3, av. Renaud, ☎ 59.37.00.25. AE, DC. 22 rm Ⓟ closed 15 Nov-1 Apr, 230.
● ★★***Pyrénées,*** 19, pl. Ch.-de-Gaulle, ☎ 59.37.01.01. 31 rm ♿ closed 3-26 Jan, 1-20 Dec, Mon eve and Tue, 220. Rest. ● ♦♦♦ Excellent fare. Pleasant terrace setting. Spec : *foie gras frais de canard poché et servi au naturel, pigeon rôti à l'ail doux et raviolis aux cèpes*, 95-250.
★★***Etche Ona,*** 15, pl. Floquet, ☎ 59.37.01.14. 13 rm closed 5 Nov-15 Dec and Fri ex school hols, 135. Rest. ● ♦♦ ♿ Tasty, inventive cooking from J.-L. Ibargaray. Spec : *St-Jacques aux cèpes, foie de canard aux pommes, soufflé à l'Izarra.* Jurançon wines, 65-180.
★***Ramuntcho*** (L.F.), 1, rue de France, ☎ 59.37.03.91. DC. 17 rm Ⓟ closed Jan, 115. Rest. ♦ closed Wed, 55-110.

Esterençuby, 8 km SE :
★★***Artzain-Etchea,*** ☎ 59.37.11.55. 16 rm Ⓟ ♿ closed 2 Jan-10 Feb, 110. Rest. ♦ closed Wed, dinner only, 30-90.
● ★★***Sources de la Nive,*** ☎ 59.37.10.57. 12 rm Ⓟ ♿ closed Jan, 90. Rest. ♦ 45-100.

Event : *cheese fair* in Aug.

Recommended : distillery *Brana.*

SAINT-LARY-SOULAN

Bagnères-de-Luchon 44, Tarbes 69, Paris 907
D2 830-2 380 m ⊠ 65170

ⓘ ☎ 62.39.40.29, 62.39.50.81.

Hotels :
★★***Grand Hôtel Mir,*** rte d'Arreau, ☎ 62.39.40.03. 26 rm Ⓟ closed Apr-May, Oct-Nov, 170. Rest. ♦ 60-100.
★★***Lou Périgord,*** Cadeilhan Trachère, ☎ 62.98.44.49. 22 rm Ⓟ closed 15 Apr-15 Dec, 100. Rest. ♦ 80-130.
★★***Terrasse Fleurie,*** ☎ 62.39.40.26. Tx 520360. AE. 28 rm Ⓟ closed 15 Apr-15 May, 15 Sep-15 Dec, 230.

Guchan, 4 km N :
★***Moderne*** (L.F.), ☎ 62.39.50.10. 24 rm Ⓟ closed Nov, 150.

Le Pla d'Adet, 13 km on the D123 :
★★***Christiania,*** ☎ 62.98.44.42. 24 rm closed 15 Apr-15 Dec, 225. Rest. ♦ 80-130.

Ⲁ ★★★★*Municipal* (100 pl.), ☎ 62.39.41.58.

SAINT-PALAIS

Bayonne 54, Pau 80, Paris 801
B1 ⊠ 64120

ⓘ pl. de l'Hôtel-de-Ville, ☎ 59.38.71.78.

SNCF ☎ 59.38.72.58, 46.22.12.66.

Hotels :
Larceveau, 15 km SW :
★***Espellet,*** ☎ 59.37.81.91. 21 rm Ⓟ closed Feb-Mar, 100. Rest. ♦ 40-100.
★***Trinquet,*** ☎ 59.37.81.57. Visa. 10 rm Ⓟ closed 15 Nov-1 Dec, 80. Rest. ♦ closed Mon low season, 35-100.

Ⲁ ★★★★*Ur-Alde* (80 pl.), ☎ 59.38.72.01.

Event : *Basque Festival* in Aug.

SAINT-PÉ-DE-BIGORRE

Lourdes 10, Pau 31, Paris 816
C2 ⊠ 65270

ⓘ mairie, ☎ 62.41.80.07.

Hotel :
★★***Pyrénées,*** av. Gal-de-Gaulle, ☎ 62.41.80.08. AE, Visa. 42 rm Ⓟ closed Jan, 125. Rest. ♦♦ 45-150.

Ⲁ ★★*La Grotte aux Fées* (65 pl.), ☎ 62.41.81.63 ; ★★*les Rives du Gave* (35 pl.), ☎ 62.41.80.29.

SAINT-PÉE-SUR-NIVELLE

Bayonne 19, Pau 131, Paris 791
12 km W of Espelette, A1 64310 Ascain

Hotels :
★★***Bonnet,*** Ibarron, 1.5 km, ☎ 59.54.10.26. Tx 541104. AE, DC, Euro, Visa. 60 rm Ⓟ closed 3 Nov-6 Dec, 150. Rest. ♦ ♿ 65-140.
★★***Bichta-Eder,*** ☎ 59.54.21.14. 26 rm Ⓟ ♿ closed Tue, 140. Rest. ♦ 50-100.
★***Fronton,*** Ibarron, ☎ 59.54.10.12. AE, DC. 16 rm Ⓟ ♿ closed 15 Jan-15 Feb and Wed low season, 90. Rest. ♦♦ ♿ Terrace and winter garden. Spec : *langoustines aux cèpes, turbot aux moules et poivrons, St-Jacques au magret,* 80-180.
★***Nivelle*** (L.F.), rue Principale, ☎ 59.54.10.27. 38 rm Ⓟ closed Jan and Feb, 100. Rest. ♦ closed Mon low season. A data-processor transformed into a cook. Spec : *piballes* in season, 80-130.

Ⲁ ★★★*Goyetchea* (100 pl.), ☎ 59.54.11.68.

SALIES-DE-BÉARN

Dax 36, Bayonne 54, Paris 787
B1 (all yr), ☎ 59.38.10.11 ⊠ 64270

ⓘ 4, bd St-Guily, ☎ 59.38.00.33.

SNCF ☎ 59.38.08.02.

Hotels :
★★***Blason,*** 6, pl. J.-d'Albret, ☎ 59.38.00.53. 27 rm Ⓟ closed Jan, 110. Rest. ♦ 45-80.
★***Les Chênes,*** bd de Paris, ☎ 59.38.12.05. 14 rm Family pension, 100.
★***Larquier,*** 9, rue des Salines, ☎ 59.38.10.43. 20 rm Ⓟ ♿ closed 30 Sep-15 Mar, 330 (with pension). Rest. ♦ 55-80.

Puyôo, 64270 Salies, 9 km N :
★★***Voyageurs,*** RN117, ☎ 59.38.10.98. Euro, Visa. 15 rm Ⓟ closed Sun eve and Mon, 135. Rest. ♦ ♿ closed 3-20 Feb, 23 Dec-2 Jan, Mon and Sun eve. Pleasant simple cooking, 55-120.

Youth hostel : stade Al Cartero, ☎ 59.38.03.66.

Ⲁ ★★★*Mosqueros* (60 pl.), ☎ 59.38.12.94 ; ★*Al Cartero* (20 pl.), ☎ 59.38.29.11.

Restaurant :
♦♦ ***La Terrasse,*** rue Loumé, ☎ 59.38.09.83 ♿ closed Christmas, Easter and Mon, 60-100.

Casino, bd St-Guily, ☎ 59.38.05.95.

SARE

Bayonne 35, Pau 137, Paris 807
9 km W of Ainhoa, A1 ⊠ 64310 Ascain

Hotels :
● ★★★***Arraya,*** ☎ 59.54.20.46. Euro, Visa. 20 rm Ⓟ closed 1 Nov-15 May, 230. Rest. ● ♦♦ The Fagoaga/Ducasse team gambles and wins in this provincial haven of calm. Delicious regional cooking : *pavé de bœuf au fumet de cèpes avec pruneaux farcis au foie gras, pastiza.* Local and Spanish wines, 90-220.

★★**Picassaria,** 2 km, Lehembiscay quarter, ☎ 59.54.21.51. 28 rm 🅿 closed 30 Nov-Mar and Wed ex Jul-Aug, Sep, 130. Rest. ♦ ♿ 60-120.
★**Lastiry,** pl. du Fronton, ☎ 59.54.20.07. 23 rm. closed Nov-Easter, 130. Rest. ♦ 40-120.
★**Poste,** ☎ 59.54.20.06. 9 rm 🅿 closed Tue low season, 95. Rest. ♦ 40-80.

⛺ ★★*Petite Rhûne* (35 pl.), ☎ 59.54.21.51.

SAUVETERRE-DE-BÉARN

Dax 45, Bayonne 62, Paris 795
B1 ✉ 64390

SNCF ☎ 59.38.52.63.

Hotel :
● ★**A Boste** (L.F.), rue L.-Bérard, ☎ 59.38.50.62. AE, Visa. 10 rm 🅿 closed 15 Oct-15 Nov, Sun eve and Mon low season, 130. Rest. ♦ Pleasant simple meals, 45-200.

⛺ ★★*Gave* (100 pl.), ☎ 59.38.53.30.

TARBES

Auch 73, Toulouse 154, Paris 805
D1 ✉ 65000

ℹ pl. de Verdun (B2), ☎ 62.93.36.62.

✈ Tarbes-Ossun-Lourdes, 9 km SW, ☎ 62.34.42.22.

SNCF (A1), ☎ 62.37.50.50.

🚌 pl. au Bois (B2), ☎ 62.93.31.21.

Car-hire : *Budget* train + auto, at the station, ☎ 62.34.28.74, and at the airport, ☎ 62.24.70.91 and 62.24.17.80.

Hotels :
● ★★★**Président** (Mapotel), 1, rue Gabriel-Fauré (A2), ☎ 62.93.98.40. Tx 530522. AE, DC, Euro, Visa. 57 rm 🅿 ♿ 320. Rest. ♦♦ 80-160.
★★★**Foch,** 18, pl. de Verdun (B2), ☎ 62.93.71.58. AE, Visa. 30 rm 🅿 ♿ closed 20-31 Jul, end Dec and Sun eve, 210.
★★★**Henri IV,** 7, av. B.-Barère (A1), ☎ 62.34.01.68. AE, DC, Euro, Visa. 24 rm 🅿 ♿ 230.
★★**Béarn-Bigorre,** 6 *bis*, av. de la Marne (C2), ☎ 62.93.23.33. Tx 520888. AE, DC, Euro, Visa. 38 rm 🅿 ♿ 190.
★★**Martinet,** 13, bd Martinet, ☎ 62.37.96.30. Euro, Visa. 24 rm 🅿 ♿
★★**Normandie,** 33, rue Massey (B1), ☎ 62.93.08.47. 21 rm 🅿 ♿ 150.
★★**Terminus,** 42, av. Joffre (A1), ☎ 62.93.00.33. Visa. 32 rm, 185. Rest. ♦ closed Sep and Sat, 45-105.
★**Carillon,** 5, pl. Marcadieu (C2), ☎ 62.93.29.18. 15 rm, closed Mon low season, 100. Rest. ♦ 45-80.
★**Fontaine,** 2, rue J.-Pellet, ☎ 62.93.37.95. AE, DC, Euro, Visa. 10 rm, closed Sun, 90. Rest. ♦ 35-80.
★**L'Isard,** 70, av. Mal-Joffre (A1), ☎ 62.93.06.69. AE, Euro, Visa. 7 rm closed Feb, Sat noon and Sun eve, 110. Rest. ♦ ♿ Spec : *filet de truite aux écrevisses, fricassée d'anguilles au madiran, tournedos sauté au foie frais de canard,* 45-170.

Laloubère, ✉ 65310, 3 km S :
★**Tilleuls** (L.F.), ☎ 62.93.19.66. 11 rm 🅿 closed Sep, 70.

Odos, 65310 Laloubère, 4 km S :
★★★**Concorde** (Inter-Hôtel), RN21, ☎ 62.93.51.18. Tx 530194. AE, DC, Euro, Visa. 42 rm 🅿 255. Rest. ♦ 55-120.
★**Bellevue,** 34, rte de Lourdes, ☎ 62.93.19.29. 11 rm 🅿 closed Mon, 90. Rest. ♦ 55-110.

Ibos, 5 km W :
★★**La Chaumière du Bois,** rte de Pau, ☎ 62.31.02.42. AE, DC, Euro, Visa. 11 rm 🅿 ♿ closed 1 week in Apr, 2 weeks in Feb, end Dec-early Jan, 240. Rest. ♦♦ Regional dishes. Meat cooked over a wood fire, 65-150.

Juillan, ✉ 65290, 5 km SW :
★★**L'Aragon** (Inter-Hôtel), ☎ 62.93.99.33. AE, Visa. 14 rm 🅿 closed 1-28 Jan, 155. Rest. ♦ closed Sun eve and Mon, 55-190.

Louey, 65290 Juillan, 8 km SW :
★**Relais de la Ferme,** ☎ 62.93.68.27. 17 rm 🅿 closed Jan, Mon and Sun eve low season, 95. Rest. ♦ ♿ 50-160.

Chis, 65800 Aureilhan, 9 km NE :
★★**Ferme de St-Ferréol** (L.F.), ☎ 62.36.22.15. AE, DC, Euro, Visa. 22 rm 🅿 ♿ closed Fri and Sun eve, 180. Rest. ♦♦ closed Sat noon and Sun eve, 55-150.

Youth hostel : 6, quai de l'Adour, ☎ 62.93.31.59.

Restaurants :
● ♦♦ **La Caravelle,** at the airport, 5 km SW 65290 Juillan, ☎ 62.32.99.96. AE, DC, Visa. 🅿 ♿ Spec : *œuf Caravelle au foie de canard frais et truffes, coquilles Saint-Jacques et ris d'agneau en habit vert,* 125-200.
● ♦♦ **L'Amphitryon,** 38, rue Larrey, ☎ 62.34.08.99. AE, DC, Visa. ♿ closed 5-19 Aug, Christmas week, Sat noon and Sun. Spec : *émincé de saumon cru au coulis d'huîtres, magret de canard au gros sel,* 130-220.
● ♦ **Buffet de la Gare,** 21, av. du Mal-Joffre (A1), ☎ 62.93.16.22. AE, Visa ; closed Sat. An impeccable dining-room, without a trace of the usual chilly railway buffet atmosphere, 40-130.

Events : *Tarbes and Bigorre exhibition fair* in May ; *festival de Sainte-Thérèse,* pl. Marcadieu, in Oct ; *grand fair* on the 3rd Sun in Jun.

Markets : bric-à-brac and second-hand market in the halle Marcadieu on the 1st Sat of each month.

TARDETS-SORHOLUS

Oloron 27, Bayonne 90, Paris 830
B1-2 ✉ 64470

ℹ administrative centre, ☎ 59.28.50.26.

Hotel :
★★**Gave,** ☎ 59.28.53.67. Euro, Visa. 14 rm 🅿 closed 15 Nov-1 Mar, Sun eve and Mon low season, 200. Rest. ♦ 60-150.

TOURNAY

Tarbes 18, Saint-Gaudens 46, Paris 823
16 km NE of Bagnères-de-Bigorre, D2 ✉ 65190

ℹ mairie, ☎ 62.35.70.26.

SNCF ☎ 62.35.71.63.

Hotel :
★**Moderne,** ☎ 62.35.70.30. 24 rm closed Oct and Fri eve ex Jul-Aug-Sep, 90. Rest. ♦ ♿ 50-90.

⛺ ★★*Municipal* (33 pl.), ☎ 62.35.76.05.

TRIE-SUR-BAÏSE

Tarbes 30, Auch 48, Paris 813
D1 ✉ 65220

ℹ mairie, ☎ 62.35.51.38.

Hotel :
★**Tour,** ☎ 62.35.52.12. Visa. 11 rm 🅿 closed 2-14 Jun and 1-11 Oct, 150. Rest. closed Mon noon, 45-110.

⛺ ★*Municipal* (33 pl.), ☎ 62.35.50.21.

Events : *horse races* in Aug ; *annual* foie gras *competition* in mid-Dec.

USTARITZ

Bayonne 12, Pau 119, Paris 784
7 km NW of Cambo-les-Bains, A1 ✉ 64480

ℹ mairie, ☎ 59.93.00.44.

SNCF ☎ 59.93.00.35.

Hotel :
★***Arretz,*** ☎ 59.31.00.25. 8 rm closed 4 Oct-5 Apr, 95.

⛺ ★★*Kapito-Harri* (50 pl.), ☎ 59.31.00.44.

VIC-EN-BIGORRE

Tarbes 17, Auch 62, Paris 788
C-D1 ✉ 65500

ℹ rue Mal-Foch, ☎ 62.96.81.33.

SNCF ☎ 62.96.71.64.

Hotels :
★★***Baloc,*** rte de Bordeaux, ☎ 62.96.73.95. Euro, Visa. 21 rm Ⓟ 115. Rest. ♦ closed 9 Oct-1 Nov. Spec : *foie gras frais aux pêches,* 40-100.
★★***Tivoli*** (L.F.), pl. Gambetta, ☎ 62.96.70.39. Visa. 24 rm, closed 1-15 Jan, 1-15 Sep, 105. Rest. ♦ closed Mon, 40-150.

Farmhouse gîte : Nouilhan (5 km), ☎ 62.96.74.96. Farm produce for sale. 500 m away.

⛺ ★★*Municipal* (22 pl.), ☎ 62.96.71.38.

The Berry and Bourbonnais Regions

This largely unknown region, set in the middle of France, is a harmonious combination of many of the country's features : immense wheatfields, alternating forests and pastureland, grassy mountain slopes irrigated by hundreds of little streams, ponds and forests, narrow, snaking valleys and pebble-strewn hills. Berry Bourbonnais has borrowed aspects from all its neighbours and it is often hard to say exactly where the region begins or ends. But there is a spiritual unity nonetheless, composed of calm and moderation, a natural tendency towards balance in art and in all the details of daily life. Here are churches and châteaux, half-timbered houses, gorges, country paths, scenic panoramas — but all in moderation : a few masterpieces and hundreds of minor treasures to discover at every turn of the path.

The magnificent cathedral of Bourges rises up above the tiled roofs of its parish huddled on a slight rise in the plain of Champagne. Despite the industrial and urban bustle of the newer part of the city, the narrow, winding streets of the old town have retained much of their charm. The writer George Sand, who spent 41 years of her life in Nohant, and was revered by the local people both for her charity and her genius, described Bourges cathedral as "a blend of the delicate and the colossal, both gracious and untamed, simultaneously heavy and airborne." Many consider it the most beautiful cathedral in France.

The Benedictine abbey of Fontgombault, founded in the 11th century, still resounds to the purity of Gregorian chant, and the countryside is dotted with Romanesque and Gothic churches. Near the border with Auvergne is Vichy, with its Belle Époque architecture, where jaded colonials used to come to recover their dissipated health and restore their dwindling fortunes at the casino.

Bourbonnais and Berry may not figure among the most famous wine-producing regions of France, but there are excellent local vintages, mainly white : Sancerre, a fruity dry white sauvignon, with a palatable red counterpart; Quincy, Reuilly, Pouilly — especially Pouilly Fumé — and a host of others. The region is famous for its goat cheeses, the best-known being the round *crottin* of Chavignol and the ash-covered *pyramides* of Valençay and Levroux. Regional cooking is hearty, but far from plain, featuring delicious stews of game and chicken, meat pies and *patés* — recipes simmered and perfected over the centuries in the low-roofed farmhouses of this harmonious region.

Sightseeing

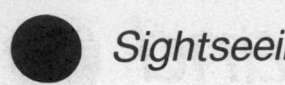

Facts and figures

Location : *geographical centre of France.*
Area : *21 400 km^2.*
Climate : *mixture of continental and coastal influences; quite cold in winter, with late springs, pleasant summers and autumns that are usually long and sunny.*
Population : *943 000.*
Administration : *departments : Allier, Prefecture Moulins; Cher, Prefecture Bourges; Indre, Prefecture Châteauroux.*

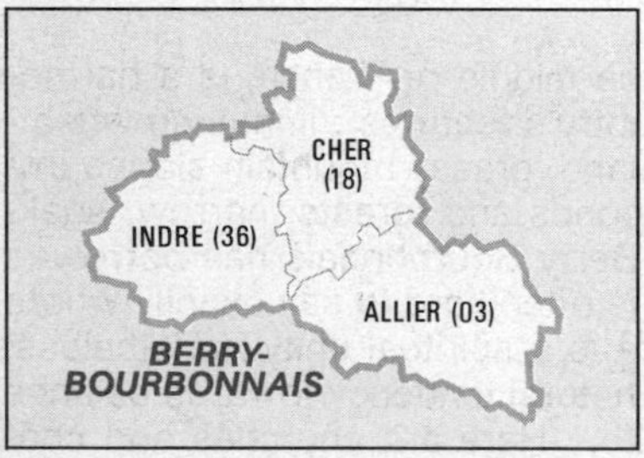

Weekend tips

Starting from Moulins, where you can find an excellent lunch, a Saturday afternoon itinerary will take you to beautiful churches at Souvigny and Saint-Menoux; continue through Bourbon-l'Archambault to Ygrande (stopover in the forest of Tronçais). On Sunday, to Ainay-le-Vieil and the country around Saint-Amand-Montrond : Drevant, Noirlac, the Château de Meillant.

ARGENTON-SUR-CREUSE

A2 / ® / pop. 6 141 (Indre)

Charming houses with wooden porches on the banks of the river Creuse.

▶ SI in a lovely old house not far from the **Vieux Pont** (Old Bridge)★; view★ over the river and the town. ▶ On the far side of the bridge, a 15thC house and the **chapel of St. Benoît** (Virgin and Child, 1485). □

▶ Nearby

▶ **Prunget**★ *(8 km NE) :* the **donjon** (keep), a large square 14thC tower, nearby those at **Mazières**★ and **La Chaise-Saint-Éloi.** ▶ **Saint-Marcel** ® *(2 km N) :* on the site of a Gallo-Roman town called *Argentomagus;* artifacts in the museum *(15 Jun-15 Sep, 10-12 & 2-6:30; Sun pm or daily on request rest of year);* remains of frescos in 12th-15thC church; crypt (pre-Romanesque chancel) and treasury★.

▶ **Chazelet** *(12 km SW) :* a 15thC château. 10 km farther lies **Saint-Benoît-du-Sault :** mediaeval houses★ on a granite spur; fortified gateway (14thC); Romanesque church. **Roussines** *(3 km N) :* vaulting in the church is decorated with 15thC paintings. □

ARGY★

A2 / pop. 687 (Indre)

A square keep bracketed by four 14thC turrets and a gallery with Renaissance decoration make the **château**★ worth a visit *(exterior only, 9-12 & 2-6);* exhibition of 19thC agricultural implements in outbuildings. □

AUBIGNY-SUR-NÈRE

B1 / ® / pop. 5 693 (Cher)

14thC ramparts, **wooden houses** (15th-

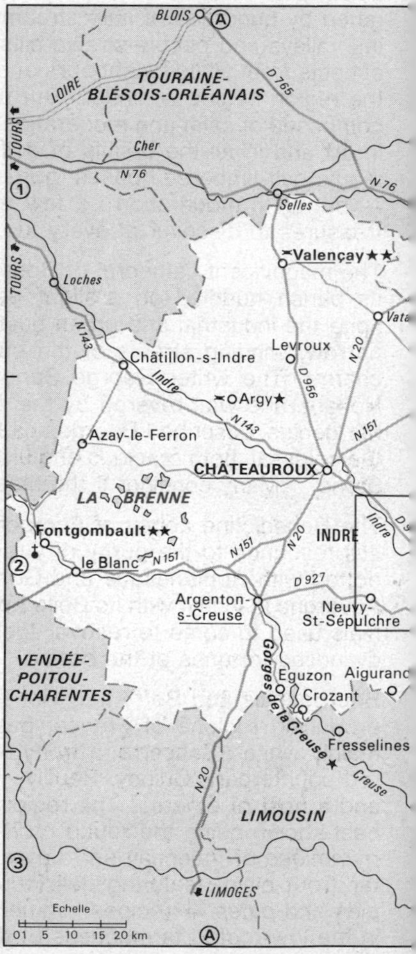

16thC); Maison du Bailli (magistrate's house)★ near the (12th-15thC) church (16thC choir stalls). □

▶ Nearby

▶ **Argent-sur-Sauldre** *(10 km N)* : 15thC church; 18thC château with 15thC towers. ▶ **Blancafort** *(9 km NE)* : 15thC church with an interesting timbered gate-tower; 15th-17thC château★ with a formal French garden and a large park *(Jan.-Mar., 4 Nov.-Dec., 2-4, closed Tue.; Apr.-Jun., Sep.-3 Nov., 10-12 & 2-7, closed Tue. Jul.-Aug., 10-12 & 2-7).* ▶ **Château de la Verrerie**★ ® *(10 km SE)* : by a lake on the river Nère; the Scottish family of Stuart (not the royal Stuarts) rebuilt it in the 15th-16thC; graceful Italian courtyard, furniture, tapestries; chapel *(daily, 10-12 & 2-7, 15 Feb-15 Nov).* □

Valley of the **BESBRE**

▶ From Lapalisse to Dompierre *(36 km; 90 km with detours; half-day)*

C2-3

The valley contains a surprising number of châteaux.

Don't miss

★★★ *Bourges (B1), Nohant Vic (B2)*
★★ *Fontgombault (A2), Meillant (B2), Noirlac (B2), Sancerre (D1), Valençay (A1), Vichy (C3).*

▶ Lapalisse (→). ▶ Château de Gléné : 4 km away, remodelled in 18thC (14thC towers). ▶ **Cindré** : 18thC château, Château de Puyfol : 3 km S, 15th-16thC. ▶ Pass Château du Verger (left) and Château de la Pouge (right) and continue to **Chavroches**★ : ruins of a 13thC fortress surround a 15thC building. ▶ **Château du Vieux-Chambord**★ : a square keep with turrets (13thC) towers over the 14thC-16thC château. ▶ **Jaligny-sur-Besbre** : large Renaissance château; poultry market on Wednesdays. ▶ Near Chapeau, 10 km WNW from Vaumas : Château de la Cour (15th-16thC), a typical Bourbonnais structure with diapered black and red brick *(exterior visits all year).* ▶ **After Vaumas** (15thC church with wooden porch), the 15thC **Château de Beauvoir**★ : gardens *(daily)* and a 17thC façade. ▶ **Château de Toury**★ : a miniature fortress in pink granite (15thC); hunting museum

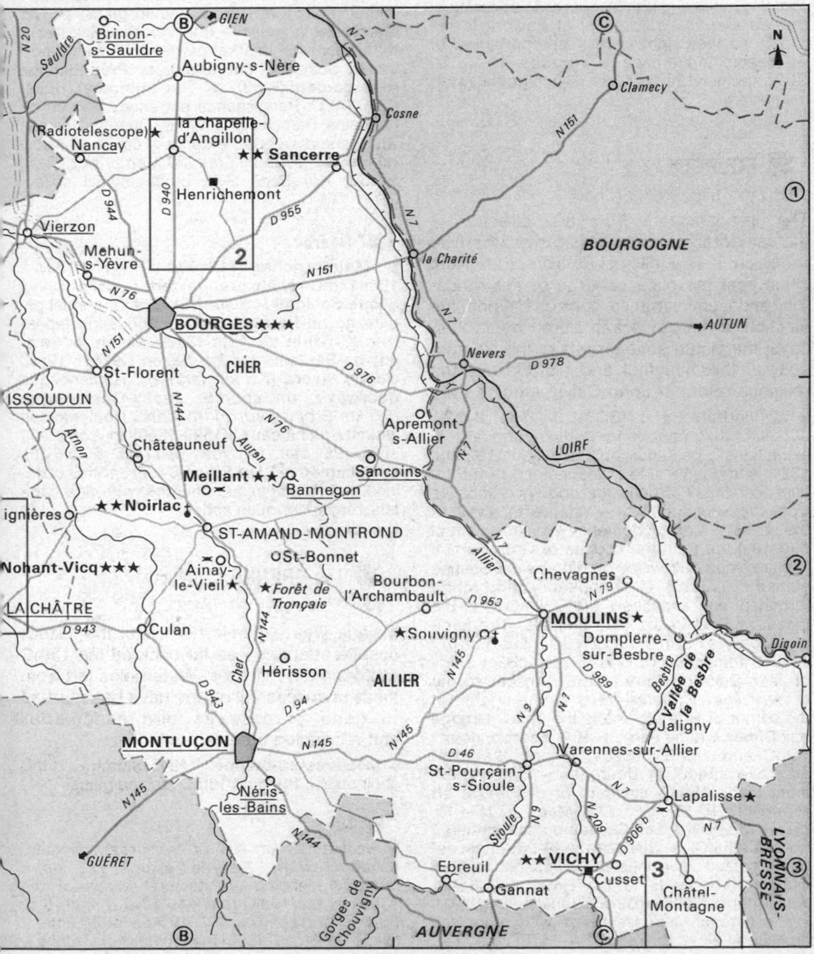

(Apr.-Oct., Sat., Sun and nat. hols., 10-12 & 2-6). ▶ **Dompierre-sur-Besbre** ® : the largest town in the valley; **Abbey of Sept Fons** *(4 km N)* Trappists, *audio-visual show only.* **Beaulon** *(7 km N from Sept-Fons) :* regional museum *(Sun. and nat. hols. Jun-Sep, 3-7).* □

BOURBON-L'ARCHAMBAULT

C2 / ® / pop. 2 550 (Allier)

A spa whose origins lie in Celtic times; subsequently the seat of the Bourbons, who eventually became the largest royal family in Europe.

▶ Opposite the spa, the **Logis du Roi** (King's Lodgings) : built in 1645, now housing the SI and the Augustin-Bernard Museum of regional history, folk arts and costume. *(15 Apr-15 Oct, 3-6).* ▶ Three of the 14thC **castle's** 24 towers★ remain; steps by the lake down to a rather disfigured 14thC fortified mill; view of the massive **Quiquengrogne Watchtower** (1317), remains of the external fortifications. □

▶ Nearby

▶ **Saint-Menoux** *(9 km E) :* a beautiful Romanesque church★ (12thC), carved decoration, capitals and frieze; choir★; stonework in the 11thC narthex (entrance); sarcophagus of St. Menoux in the choir. ▶ **Ygrande** *(10 km W-SW) :* another 12thC church★ (octagonal 14thC bell-tower). □

BOURGES★★★

B1 / ® / pop. 80 379 (Cher)

The first landmark from any direction is the cathedral, standing watch over the tiled roofs on a low hill rising from the plain. Once past the plain suburbs of this industrial and administrative centre, beyond the junction of the Yèvre and Auron rivers, discover the picturesque streets of the old section; in this beautiful and historic city the religious reformer John Calvin studied law.

▶ **Cathedral★★★ :** (BC3; *8-12 & 2-6:30, Jul.-Aug., 6-7*), famous for its five doorways, is exceptionally beautiful; built between 1192 and 1324, with double side-aisles instead of a transept; carvings★ around the doorways (scenes from the Old and New Testaments, lives of the saints, a Last Judgment★★ on the central doorway) are from the apogee of Gothic art; a Romanesque doorway★ on either side. Stained glass★★ (13thC) in ambulatory and choir (prophets and apostles); 14thC window in the façade; 16thC in the side chapels. The large crypt *(daily ex Sun am 9 or 10-12 & 4-5 or 6) :* 1543 Entombment of Christ; recumbent effigy of Jean Duke of Berry (15thC). Access to the N tower (view★; *same hours as the crypt*). On the corner of Rue Molière is the 13thC **Grange aux Dîmes**★ (tithe barn). ▶ **Rue Bourbonnoux :** 15thC and 16thC houses, among the most attractive streets in Bourges. ▶ **Hôtel Lallemant** (early 16thC) museum of decorative art *(Apr.-Oct. 10:15-5:15; Oct.-Mar. 10:15-4:15, closed Mon.).* ▶ **Place Gordaine :** half-timbered houses (15thC). ▶ **Rue Mirabeau :** (B2; pedestrian) gabled dwellings. ▶ Passage to Rue Branly which leads to the **Hôtel des Échevins** (Council House) (B2)★ : Renaissance building, octagonal staircase tower with bracketed arches. ▶ Next to (rebuilt in 1520), the **Maison de Pellevoysin,** a 15thC Gothic mansion in stone, surrounded by half-timbered houses; courtyard at N° 3 Rue Cambournac. ▶ **Hôtel Cujas**★ : built in 1515; it has an interior courtyard and corbelled turrets, and now houses the **Berry Museum**★★ (prehistory, antiques, folk art and traditions : *10-11:30 & 2-5:30; closed Tue.).* ▶ **Palais de Justice** (courthouse) : (A3) 17thC convent built by Jules Hardouin-Mansart (the 18thC architect who worked for 30 years on the Palace of Versailles; → Ile-de-France). ▶ **Palais Jacques Cœur**★★ (B3) : situated on Gallo-Roman fortifications, which are partly visible. Jacques Coeur (→ box) built the palace in 1443-51; it is a superb example of Gothic civil architecture *(9-11:15 & 2:15-5:15; closed nat. hols.).* ▶ On Rue des Armuriers (16thC house at the corner of Rue d'Auron), the **Prefecture** (B4 : 18thC), which incorporates part of the 15thC ducal palace where Louis XI was born. ▶ Follow the Rue du 95°-de-Ligne (11thC **doorway**★ at the corner of the Rampe Marceau), past the **Cultural Centre** (Maison de la Culture,1964) to the **Archepiscopal Gardens** (Jardins de l'Archevêché)★ (B-C4; view★ of the cathedral), in front of the town hall (hôtel de ville, 17thC). □

▶ **Also...** ▶ The **church of St. Bonnet** (C2) : 16thC choir; 15th-16thC stained glass. ▶ The **Marais de la Voiselle** (the Voiselle Marshes) : the "water rats" (market gardeners) use flat-bottomed boats to get about. ▶ **Prés-Fichaux rose garden** (B1-2). ▶ The **Infirmary** (Hôtel-Dieu) (A2) : Renaissance entrance; Maison de La Reine Blanche (the White Queen's House) with carved wooden exterior (16thC). ▶ **Natural History Museum** *(Jan.-30 March, Oct.-Dec., 2-5:30; Apr.-Sept. 2-6),* ornithological collection. □

▶ Nearby

▶ **Maubranches** *(12 km E on N151) :* 15th-17thC château★ *(exterior visits only).* **Sainte-Solange** *(4.5 km NE) :* site of annual pilgrimage on Easter Monday; Aubusson tapestries (1704) in the 12th-13thC church. ▶ **Savigny-en-Septaine** *(14 km SE on D976) :* 12thC church. **Avord** *(7.5 km farther) :* Romanesque doorway★ on church. **Jussy-Champagne** *(5.5 km S of Avord) :* 11th-12thC Romanesque church★; château★ (1590-1650) in Louis XIII style *(25 Mar.-15 Nov., 9-11:45 & 2-6:30).* ▶ **Plaimpied** *(11 km SE on D106) :* 15thC buildings and Romanesque church★ with fine capitals, remainder of an abbey. □

The BRENNE Marshes

A2

Malaria was endemic here until the 19thC, despite attempts - as far back as the 13thC - to drain the marshes. Waterholes left from these unsuccessful efforts have been turned to good purpose as bird sanctuaries and recreation areas.

▶ **Mézières-en-Brenne :** 14thC church★, 15thC choir stalls; 14th and 16thC stained glass. □

▶ Nearby

▶ **Paulnay** *(6 km NW of Mézières) :* Romanesque church★. **Azay-le-Ferron**★ *(12 km) :* **château** blending architectural styles of the 15thC to the 19thC *(daily 10-12 & 2-4:30, 5 or 6; closed Wed, Thu, Fri, ex Apr-Sep);* Empire (Napoléon 1, ca. 1800) furnishings★; gardens. □

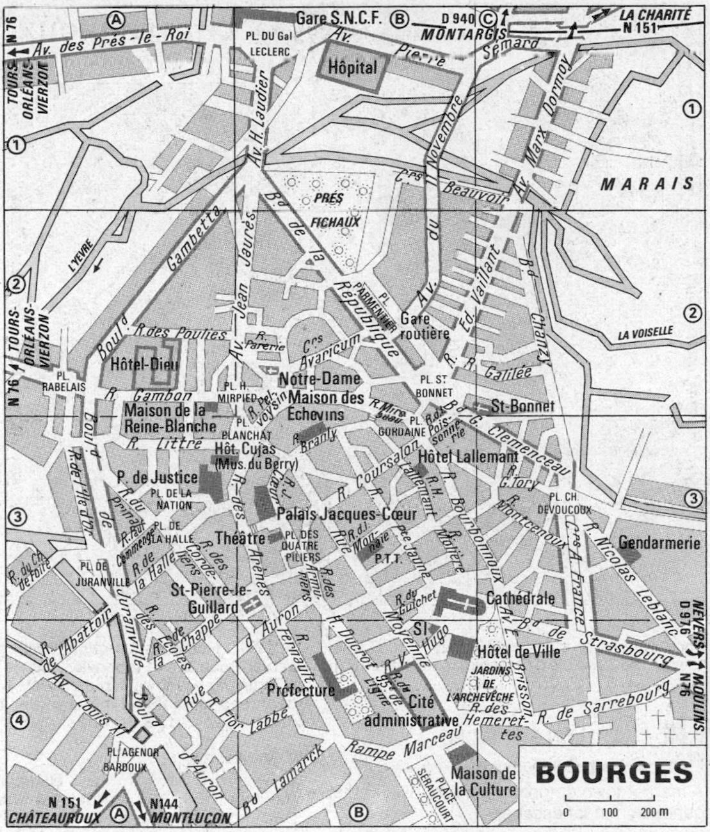

■ CHÂTEAUNEUF-SUR-CHER

B2 / pop. 1 663 (Cher)

Château★ (16th-17thC), Renaissance carving in the courtyard; French Regency, Louis XIV and Louis XVI furniture (ca. 1650-1790); antique copper kitchenware★; zoo park *(daily 10-12 & 4-7 Apr-Oct; 2-6:30 rest of year).* □

▶ Nearby

▶ **Lignières** *(16 km SW)* : château★ rebuilt in 1660 *(exterior visits, 9-6; closed Wed).* **Château du Plaix** : museum of folk art and traditions (costumes; *Sun 3-8, 24 Jun.-29 Sept.*). □

■ CHÂTEAUROUX

A2 / ® / pop. 53 967 (Indre)

See map on the following page

Manufactory of the "Gitane", the French cigarette made from black tobacco, with an aroma more like that of a cigar. SEITA (the French tobacco monopoly) produces more than 30 million/day in this town (named after the 15thC Château Raoul) on the banks of the river Indre. View★ from the Pont-Neuf.

▶ **Museum** *(daily ex Mon. 9:30-12 & 4-6 Jun.-Sept.; 2-5 rest of year;* archaeology, Napoleonic memorabilia, fine arts, local folklore). ▶ **Déols :**

Jacques Cœur

Jacques Cœur (cœur : heart) was without doubt the greatest financier of his age. Born in modest circumstances at Bourges in 1395, he demonstrated a gift for commerce and built an immense fortune, becoming expert in trade with the East. His wealth was such that he was able to support the State of France out of his own pocket after the Treaty of Troyes ceded most of northern France to the English in 1420. Charles VII appointed Cœur minister of finance in 1436, and in 1441 ennobled him. He carried out important commissions for the king and won fame and honours, but his success and magnificent mode of living aroused jealousy at the court, leading to downfall and imprisonment in 1451. Inspired by his motto, "To the valiant Heart, nothing is impossible", he escaped from France and entered the service of the Pope, who put him in command of a fleet against the Turks. He died at Chios in Greece in 1456.

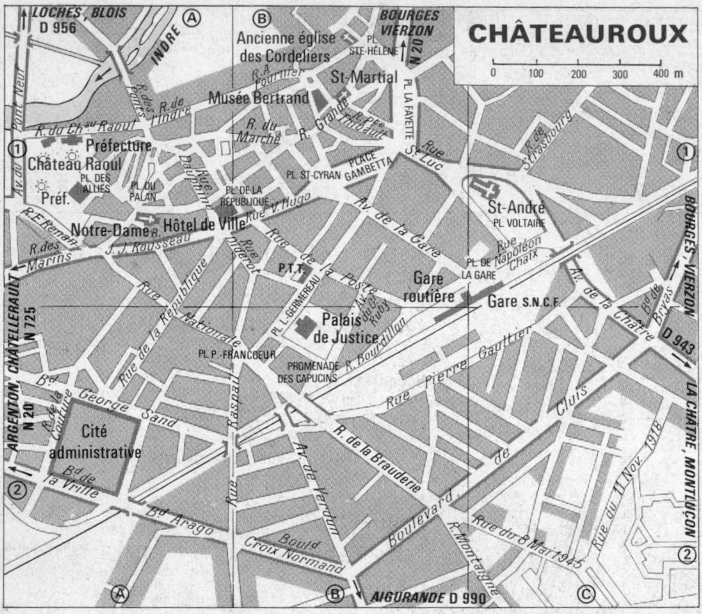

once the site of a powerful abbey; 12thC bell-tower; 3rdC marble sarcophagus in the church crypt. □

■ CHÂTILLON-SUR-INDRE

A1 / ® / pop. 3 560 (Indre)

A market town on one of the rare hills in this generally flat landscape.

George Sand

George Sand was born Aurore Dupin, the great-granddaughter of the Maréchal de Saxe (brilliant military commander in the service of Louis XV). In 1808, at the age of five, after the sudden death of her father, Aurore was taken to live at Nohant with her grandmother. She married the Baron Dudevant, a man of gloomy disposition, but often found a chance to slip away to dances with the villagers at La Châtre, sometimes even accompanying poachers on their rounds. Throughout 40 years of upheavals, Nohant remained her safe harbour, and she drew extensively on her childhood haunts to add colour and depth to her writings. At Nohant she entertained the cultural elite of her day, including Liszt and Marie d'Agoult, Delacroix, Balzac, Chopin, Flaubert, Turgenev and many others.

George Sand (the pen-name she adopted with her first novel) remained close to the peasant friends of her childhood, providing both financial and medical help (she studied anatomy and herbal medicine). At her death in 1876, she was mourned throughout the countryside.

▶ 12thC Romanesque **church** with graphically carved capitals★ (doorway, pillars in nave, columns in windows and arcades). ▶ The mantled **keep** is all that remains of the 11th-12thC castle *(9 or 10-12 & 2-4 or 7).* □

▶ Nearby

▶ Near Clion *(6.5 km SE)* : château de l'**Isle-Savary**★ (15thC). ▶ **Palluau-sur-Indre** *(12 km SE)* : 12th-15thC château (restored; illuminations *Jul.-Aug.; visits Apr.-Dec., daily ex Tue. 10-12 & 4-6*); 12th-16thC church with stained glass, stalls, statuary★ from 16thC. □

■ La CHÂTRE

B2 / ® / pop. 5 142 (Indre)

Little changed since the novelist George Sand (→ box) wrote about it more than a century ago : square tower, remains of the seigneurial castle, and a gate-tower serving as belfry and porch for the church.

▶ Tower : now the **Museum of George Sand and the Vallée Noire** (Black Valley) *(daily ex Thu. and Sun. am.; 9:30-11:30 & 4-5:30, Apr.-15 Oct.; Wed., Sun. and nat. hols. 3-6 rest of year)* : life and work of the writer; ornithological collection; view★ from the tower. □

▶ La Vallée Noire (Black Valley) : George Sand territory *(round trip, sign-posted; approx. 85 km; half-day; see map 1)*

▶ **Nohant**★★★ ® : a centre of the Romantic movement, and a memorial to George Sand (→ box). The large 18thC mansion surrounded by greenery was home to the writer for more than 40 years *(9 or 10-11:45 & 2-4 or 6; closed Tue., nat. hols. and Wed, ex Apr.-Sep.).* ▶ **Vic** : Romanesque church★ (11th-12thC) has exceptional 12thC frescos★★ that were saved by the efforts of George Sand. ▶ A little off the route, **Saint-Chartier** ® : 15thC château, where every July an international gathering of lutenists and bellringers is held. ▶ **Verneuil-sur-Igneraie :** a village of potters. ▶ **Berthenoux :** large Romanesque church with sculpted capitals★; 18thC *trompe-l'oeil* (illusory, literally "fool-the-eye") paintings. ▶ **Thévet-Saint-Julien :** church of St. Martin (12thC); frescos★★ more beautiful than those at Vic. ▶ Château du Magnet (15th-16thC). ▶ **Lys-Saint-Georges :** 15thC castle★ surrounded by moats; ruined 12thC keep. ▶ **Neuvy-Saint-Sépulchre :** named for the circular church★ (late 11th-12thC) modelled on that of the Holy Sepulchre in Jerusalem. ▶ **Château de Sarzay**★ **:** massive 14thC keep *(daily ex Tue., 10-12 & 2-7 Apr.-Sep.).* ▶ **Château de Montgivray :** once the property of Solange, daughter of George Sand; campsite in the park. □

▶ South of La Châtre *(round trip approx. 60 km; 2 hr 30)*

▶ **Chassignoles :** bell-tower on the church. ▶ **Saint-Denis-du-Jouhet :** 12th-13thC stained glass in the choir. ▶ **Crevant :** above the church doorway, 15thC bas-relief (Adoration of the Magi). ▶ **Saint-Sévère-sur-Indre :** charming market square (1696 covered market★; 1543 stone cross). ▶ **La Motte-Feuilly :** church (15th-16thC), remarkable recumbent effigy (1521) of Charlotte d'Albret whose château★ (14th-15thC) stands by the lake. □

1. George Sand territory

■ CREUSE Gorges★

▶ From Argenton to Fresselines *(62 km; half-day)*

A2

There is no single, continuous road running the length of the Creuse Valley. Numerous dams that have halted the flow of rushing streams by no means detract from the natural beauty of the area.

▶ **Argenton-sur-Creuse** (→). Drive up the right river bank past **Menoux** ® : old church, the interior covered with brightly coloured paintings★ of Hell and Paradise by the Columbian painter Carasco (1976). ▶ View★ over the valley from Chocats. ▶ **Gargilesse**★ **:** old gateway with two towers; ancient château; church★ (12thC) with some of the finest capitals★★ in Berry; in the crypt, 13th-15th-16thC frescos; Villa Algira : once George Sand's, now a museum *(Easter-30 Sept., 9:30 or 10-12 or 12:30 & 2 or 2:30-6 or 7).* ▶ Near Pommiers : *(7 km from Gargilesse)* **château du Châtelier**★ (15th-16thC; *exterior visits 9-12 & 2-5, closed Sat, Sun and nat hols, Sep-Mar*). ▶ View of the valley from the ruined **Château de Châteaubrun** (13thC). ▶ Éguzon : the dam forms a lake★ 15 km long on the Creuse; panorama★ from the viewing-area (access by D45A). 11 km E of the dam, **château de Breuil-Yvain** (15th-18thC : *exterior visits Aug.-15-Sept., 9-12 & 2-6*). ▶ **Éguzon :** castle ruins. ▶ **Crozant**® : near the southern end of the lake, ruins of an 11th-15thC fortress *(entrance fee; Easter-Oct.).* ▶ From **Fresselines,** between the Grande and the Petite Creuses, it is a 15-min walk to the junction of the two streams : site★. □

■ CULAN

B2 / ® / pop. 1 055 (Cher)

▶ 13th-15thC **castle**★ with rare wooden galleries on the towers; well-appointed interior, tapestry collection★ (15th-17thC); *(9-11:30 & 2-5, 6:30 in season; closed Wed. ex in season).* □

▶ Nearby

▶ **Vesdun** *(6.5 km E) :* claimed by some as the exact centre of France, a lively village with many exhibitions and events. **Saint-Désiré** *(5 km S from Vesdun) :* Romanesque church (11th-12thC) enhanced by the use of pink and ochre sandstone; eastern end, crypt. ▶ **Châteaumeillant** *(12 km W) :* a small market town surrounded by vineyards (sign-posted route), producing V.D.Q.S (government classification as *"Vins Délimités de Qualité Supérieure"*, i.e. not top-grade, but pleasant to drink and often good value) white, red and *rosé* wines; the 12thC church of St.-Genès is noteworthy for six apsidal chapels on each side of the choir, graphically carved capitals. Émile Chenon Museum : archaeological museum in 14th-16thC house *(10-12 & 2-6, 15 Jun.-15 Sep.).* ▶ **Saint-Jeanvrin** *(5 km NE) :* Romanesque church by a lake. ▶ **Châtelet** *(12 km from Châteaumeillant) :* another beautiful Romanesque church. □

■ ÉBREUIL

C3 / ® / pop. 1 224 (Allier)

▶ This town grew up around an abbey whose 18thC buildings are now a hospital (collection of pharmacist's jars★). ▶ The church is Auvergne Romanesque; 12thC statues★ in the narthex, frescos★ in the gallery. □

▶ Nearby

▶ **Saint-Quentin-sur-Sioule** *(4 km SW) :* 12th-13thC castle incorporating a 10thC Romanesque chapel *(Jul-Sep, 10-12 & 2-7).* ▶ **Gannat** ® *(10 km E) :* 12th-14thC castle, now a museum *(Jun.-Sep., 3-7; closed Mon) :* gospel★ with 10th-12thC bindings; crafts, etc.; the Gothic church incorporates a Romanesque building (capitals★). ▶ From **Vicq** *(4 km N; Romanesque church),* go to see the church★ at **Veauce** (11thC, eastern end★), also the 14th-15thC château, poorly restored *(10:30-12 & 2:30-6; closed 5 Dec.-5 Jan.; son et lumière show in summer).* ▶ NE on D350 **Château de Rochefort**★ (13th-15thC; *4 km*). □

▶ **Sioule Gorges** *(18 km to Pont-de-Menat).*

▶ D915 climbs to a cliff road above the left river bank before droppping to the foot of a 13thC château and village of **Chouvigny**★, also the name of the most beautiful part of the Gorges.★ ▶ Continue to **Pont de Menat,** a mediaeval hump-backed bridge close to the ruined **Château-Rocher** (11thC, refortified in 13thC; *Jun.-Sep., 9-12 & 2-7; Nov.-Apr., 4-5).* ▶ The excursion into Auvergne can be extended to Châteauneuf-les-Bains (→ Auvergne). □

■ FONTGOMBAULT★★

A2 / pop. 267 (Indre)

▶ The abbey **church**★ (11th-12thC, 19thC nave) is an important centre of Gregorian chant *(mass at 10:15, vespers at 6 daily, 5 Sun and feasts);* splendid Romanesque choir★★ with double side aisles and ambulatory with three radiating chapels; capitals★ with carved foliage; 15thC convent buildings. ▶ **Le Blanc** ® *(8 km SE) :* view★ from the upper town; bell-tower of St-Génitour; ornithological museum *(1st and 3rd Sat, Jun-Sep, 3-6).* □

■ HAUT BERRY (Upper Berry)

▶ *From La Chapelle-d'Angillon to Saint-Martin-d'Auxigny (approx. 50 km; 2 hr 30)*
B1 *(see map 2)*

From the Paris-Bourges road, which runs straight through the Sologne, the gentle hills of Boischaut can be seen to the east as you approach the Pays-Fort and the district of Sancerre. Hedges, copses and thickets between stands of forest are steadily being cleared for open-field cultivation.

▶ **La Chapelle-d'Angillon :** 15thC church, old houses; Château de Béthune, 17thC mansion, 11thC keep *(Jan.-31 Dec. 9-12 & 2-6, closed Sun.).* **Henrichemont** was started by the Duke of Sully (Prime Minister to Henri IV) but never completed; there are no important buildings in the town. ▶ **La Borne :** a clay subsoil provides building material for half-timbered houses, as well as raw material for the local potters★, who for the past 20 years have been reviving a craft that brought renown to La Borne for more than three centuries. ▶ **Morogues :** the church (14thC) has a 15thC wooden canopy★; old houses. **Château de Maupas** (15thC, much restored) : important collection of ceramic plates★, mainly from Nevers and Moustiers *(23 March-13 Jul., 9 Sept.-15 Oct.; 2-7, Jun. 11-12 & 2-7; 14 Jul.-8 Sept., 11-12 & 2-6).* ▶ **Aix d'Angillon** church has a 12thC Burgundian choir. ▶ **Château de Menetou-Salon** (remodelled in 19thC; *Apr.-Oct., 10-12 & 2-6 ex. Tue.*); 15thC tapestries and, in the outbuildings, a collection of old cars. The local white wine is excellent. ▶ Get back on the road to Bourges at **Saint-Martin-d'Auxigny.** ▶ **Saint-Palais** *(3 km N) :* 12th-13thC church and grape-press (15thC). □

2. Tour of Upper Berry

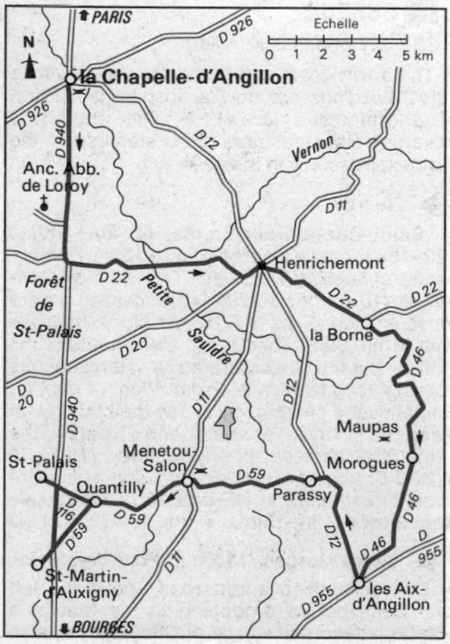

■ ISSOUDUN

B2 / ® / pop. 15 166 (Indre)

An ancient stronghold at the confluence of two rivers on the edge of the plateau.

▶ The **belfry**★ (12th-14thC) was formerly part of the city gate, and is flanked by two towers of unequal size. ▶ **Tour Blanche**★ (White Tower) : cylindrical keep 27 m high, built by Richard the Lion-Heart (King of England, 1189-99; his territory included all of western France); panorama★ as far as Bourges *(38 km).* ▶ **Church of St-Cyr :** 16thC stained-glass★ in the choir. ▶ **Museum** in the former Hospice St.-Roch (almshouse; *10-12 & 2-7 daily; closed Tue.) :* fine buildings, dispensary★ (379 pharmacist's jars in Nevers earthenware); chapel with two (originally four) 16thC carved Trees of Jesse★ (genealogies of Christ). □

▶ Nearby

▶ **Charost** *(12 km NE) :* 19thC château (remains of 13thC keep), Romanesque church, **château de Castelnau**★ : *(4 km NE)* 16thC. **Chezal-Benoît** *(17 km SE) :* only the nave remains of the 12thC abbey church (carved foliage on capitals★); the 18thC abbey buildings now house a psychiatric hospital. □

■ LAPALISSE★

C3 / ® / pop. 3 673 (Allier)

A cross-roads town best known for the **château**★ de La Palice : the main building of this Italianate Renaissance château (15th-16thC) is built against the original 11th-13thC castle and a Gothic chapel; inside, paintings, furnishings★ from Renaissance to Empire, Flemish 15thC tapestries★★ *(Palm Sunday-1 Nov., 9-12 & 2-6; closed Tue. ex Jun.-Sept.).* □

▶ Nearby

▶ **Saint-Gérand-le-Puy** *(9 km W) :* 12thC church with 13thC frescos; 5 km N from here are the spectacular ruins of the château de **Montaigu-le-Blin** (14thC; restoration in progress; *visits during school hols.*). In the town hall, small historical museum *(open Sun pm in summer).* ▶ **Montaiguët-en-Forez : *(15 km E),*** 15thC city gate and castle *(exterior visits daily).* □

■ LEVROUX

20 km N of Châteauroux
A2 / ® / pop. 3 126 (Indre)

▶ 13thC **church**★ built on the ruins of the Roman governor's palace; 15thC statues and

Berry and Bourbonnais cuisine

Simple country cooking which makes the most of local produce. Apparent simplicity however, masks skills developed throughout generations in farmhouse kitchens. Not everyone can make a successful oyonnade *(chicken in a sauce combining eau-de-vie, wine); braised chicken Berry-style (with the blood and liver of the bird) or a* poulot en barbouille *(*barbouille *means daub and tells you that this is the sort of chicken you want to eat with your fingers). Chicken is also prepared with* verjuice *(unsweetened grape-juice) and in pies.* Patés *and meat pies with crackling are also popular. Both Berry and Bourbonnais claim to have invented the* sanciau, *a cross between a pancake and an omelette, which may be sweet or savoury. Other regional specialties are* paupiettes au bouillon *(meat "olives" braised in wine),* tête de veau berrichonne *(braised head of veal), excellent local beef, and game of many kinds from the woods of Berry. The Indre and Cher valleys provide goat's milk cheese, among which the charcoal-dusted* "pyramides" *of Valençay and Levroux are famous, as are the* "crottins" *of Chavignol.*

organ casing★. ▶ Near the church, wooden houses and tiled gateway (Porte de Champagne; 1435-1506). □

▶ Nearby

▶ **Château de Bouges** *(9 km NE)* : 18thC building, furniture★; park; in the outbuildings, collection of saddles, harness★ and horse-drawn carriages *(daily 9 or 10-12 & 4-6, Apr-Oct; closed Tue ex Jul and Aug; Wed pm Sat and Sun rest of year).* ▶ **Villegongis**★ *(9 km S)* : 16thC château, architecture and decoration similar to Chambord (→), although on a lesser scale *(exterior visits free).* □

■ MEHUN-SUR-YÈVRE

B1 / ® / pop. 7 178 (Cher)

Once the favourite of Jean, Duke of Berry (→ Brief regional history), Mehun today is a small industrial center for porcelain and ceramics.

▶ A tower★ of the 14thC château houses a **museum** *(10-12 & 2-7:30 ex Tue. Jul.-Aug.; Sun. Jun. and Oct., Apr. Mon. and weekends only, 10-12 & 2:30-5:30).* ▶ 16thC Porte de l'Horloge (Clock Gate). ▶ 11thC-12thC church. ▶ Visits to porcelain factory. □

■ MOUNTAINS of the Bourbonnais

▶ Round trip from Châtel-Montagne *(approx. 90 km; half-day)*
C3 *(see map 3)*

▶ **Châtel-Montagne :** unusually well-preserved 12thC Romanesque church★★; 15thC houses. ▶ Drive to **Mayet-de-Montagne** and up the Sichon Valley. ▶ **Glozel :** a hamlet famous for prehistoric discoveries whose authenticity has been the subject of controversy (museum :

3. The Bourbonnaise Mountains

daily ex Sun and nat. hols. out of season). ▶ Near **Ferrières :** Grotte des Fées (fairy cavern; *2 km downstream*); 15thC château de Chappes (restored; *2 km N*); chapel squeezed into a crack in the rock known as Pierre Encize *(2 km upstream).* ▶ **Rocher Saint-Vincent** (Saint-Vincent's Rock) is 40 min. on foot from **Lavoine** (clog-making). ▶ **Puy de Montoncel** (alt. 1,287 m; view★), a 2 hr hike. ▶ The valley of Boen leads to a ford at La Chaux, 2 km from the **Rocher de Rochefort** (view★). ▶ Hill road along the Monts de la Madeleine (hills) to La Trapière at the foot of the **Pierre du Charbonnier** (alt. 1 031 m, panorama★). ▶ A little way off the route *(1.5 km to Biefs, then 30 mins on foot)* is the **Pisserotte waterfall.** □

■ MONTLUÇON

B2-3 / ® / pop. 51 765 (Allier)

See plan on following page

Until the 19thC this was a very small town perched on a hill. The opening of the Berry Canal and the development of local coal-mines rapidly industrialized and greatly enlarged the town.

▶ Grand'Rue (B2; numerous 15th-16thC houses) leads to the 15thC **church of Notre-Dame** (B-C2; 15thC statues★). ▶ Château of the dukes of Bourbon (B2; 15th-16thC, much restored), houses the **Musée de la Vielle** (hurdy-gurdy museum; *15 Mar.-15 Oct., 10-12 & 2-6; ex Tue.; 16 Oct.-14 Mar., 2-6 ex Mon and Tue)* : hurdy-gurdies★ and ceramics; archaeology; history; folklore. From the terrace, view★ over the city. ▶ **Church of St. Pierre :** Romanesque and 15thC; 16thC statues and wooden 15thC crucifix. ▶ Every Saturday, flower market in the streets of Old Montluçon. □

▶ Nearby

▶ **Domérat** ® *(6 km NW)* : Romanesque church with 11thC crypt. ▶ **Huriel** *(6 km farther)* : 12thC church. Two 15thC towers and a magnificent square keep (105 steps; view★; *8:30-6 ex Sat. and Sun.*), are all that remains of the castle ▶ **Magnette** *(5 km N)* : a warehouse and a barge are the main attractions at the museum of water transport on the Berry canal *(end Jul.-early Sep., Sat., Sun. and 15 Aug. 2-8).* □

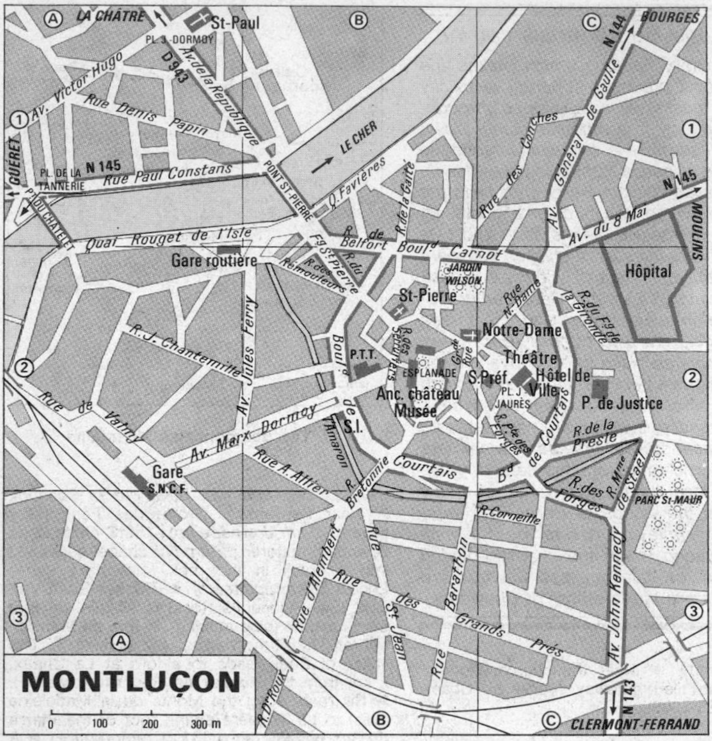

■ MOULINS★

C2 / ® / pop. 25 548 (Allier)

At the end of the 15thC, Moulins became the capital of the Duchy of Bourbon and was for a while a centre of cultural activity.

▶ Rue d'Allier (B2) : the busiest street, lined with 15thC and 16thC mansions. ▶ Rue de l'Horloge : **bell-tower** (1455) topped with a gallery and a 16thC belfry; mechanical figures (the Jacquemart family) strike the hours and quarters. ▶ Left of the tower, **rue des Orfèvres★** (goldsmiths' street); half-timbered houses. Rue and Place de l'Ancien Palais : a 15thC mansion is now the **Museum of Folklore and Old Moulins** (Musée du Folklore et du Vieux Moulins; history; *daily ex Thu.; 9-12 & 3-6:30*). ▶ **Cathedral** (B1) : in the 19thC, a pseudo-Gothic nave was grafted onto the late 15thC Flamboyant Gothic choir; stained glass★ in the apse; treasury-room *(daily 9-12 & 2-6; closed Tue. out of season)* with triptych★★★ (1498-1501) by the Moulins Master (→ box), portraying Anne of France (daughter of Louis XI) and her husband Pierre, Duke of Bourbon, donors of the painting; also a beautiful triptych by the Flemish painter Joss Van Cleve (16thC). ▶ Only the 15thC Tour Mal Coiffée and a Renaissance pavilion remain of the Château (**Museum of Art and Archaeology :** *10-12 & 2-5 or 6 daily; closed Tue.*). ▶ Rue F. Péron and Rue de Paris; handsome old mansions. Continue to the school chapel (*lycée*, A-B1) to see the **mausoleum of Henri II de Montmorency★★** (1652). ▶ See also the Cours Anatole France and Jean Jaurès (B-C1) : avenues lined with typical Bourbonnais mansions decorated with diapered black and red brick. □

The Moulins Master

The most important late-15thC French painter long remained anonymous, although his work was often favourably compared to that of his Italian contemporaries Leonardo da Vinci, Bellini and Perugino.

After much research, art experts and historians have recently agreed that he was almost certainly Jean Hey, a painter of Flemish origin. Born around 1450 and active from 1480 to 1501 (date of his masterpiece, the Moulins triptych), he was employed at the court of the dukes of Bourbon in 1490; his portraits of several members of the ducal family are now in the Louvre Museum in Paris. The museum at Autun in nearby Burgundy cherishes a superb Nativity *by this master painter.*

▶ Nearby

▶ **Yzeure** *(1 km E) :* Romanesque church with 11thC crypt; small historical museum of the Bourbonnais *(closed Sat. Sun. and nat. hols., and am Nov-Mar).* ▶ **Allier Valley** upstream to **Châtel-de-Neuvre :** Romanesque churches at **Chemilly, Besson, Châtel-de-Neuvre** (site★, view over the valley and the Monts de la Madeleine), **Bessay-sur-Allier** and **Toulon-sur-Allier;** 13thC and 15thC castles at Bressolles (châteaux du Lys; *no visits*); near **Besson,** castles of Ris (14th-15thC), Rochefort (ruins), Vieux Bostz (15th-16thC) and Fourchaud★ (14thC;

one of the best preserved fortresses in Bourbonnais).

▶ **Allier Valley,** downstream : château d'Avrilly (16thC, much restored); **château du Riau** (15th-17thC), near 1584 barn with exquisite keel-form timberwork★ *(3-6 ex Tue. Apr.-Sept.; 2-7 ex Sun. rest of year)*; N from Villeneuve-sur-Allier, the **Arboretum de Balaine**★ (botanical park specialising in trees; est. 1804; *2-7 May-Oct; closed Tue. and Fri.)*. □

■ NANÇAY★

B1 / ® / pop. 790 (Cher)

Charming village in the Sologne region with a castle (15th-16thC, much restored), woods, lakes and a population of craftsmen. It is also a radio-astronomy station, with a giant mirror★ (200 x 40 m; *4 km N; parking*). □

■ NÉRIS-LES-BAINS

B3 / ® / pop. 12801 (Allier)

A spa since pre-Roman days, when the Gauls made use of the healing properties of the hot springs.

▶ Roman remains at the **Rieckotter Museum.** *(5-7 daily; closed Sun. and nat. hols., May-Sept.)* in the spa buildings. ▶ Romanesque **church** (11th-12thC) and octagonal bell-tower roofed with chestnut shingles, built on top of Gallo-Roman remains; nearby, Merovingian burial ground. □

■ SAINT-AMAND-MONTROND

B2 / ® / pop. 12770 (Cher)

On Wednesdays and Saturdays, lively market in the heart of the old town.

▶ In a 15th-16thC building, **St.-Vic Museum** *(10-11:30 & 2-6 ex Sun. am. and Mon. and Tue. am.)*; history, folk art of Berry. ▶ Close by is the church of St. Amand (11th-13thC). □

▶ Nearby

▶ **Noirlac abbey**★★ *(5 km N)* : founded in 1136, one of the most beautiful and best-preserved Cistercian abbeys; 12thC church of perfect simplicity and balance, Gothic cloister★ (13th-14thC), chapterhouse (12thC), storeroom, refectory, dormitory *(daily 10-12 & 2-5 or 6; closed Tue. 1 Oct.-31 Dec.)*. ▶ **La Celle :** romanesque church with Carolingian carvings set in the façade. ▶ **Meillant :** castle★★ (rebuilt 15th-16thC), mediaeval western façade contrasts with the exuberant Renaissance east side and the Tour du Lion, a tower famed for its decoration of interlaced "C"s and the lead lion that stands at its head; furnishings *(daily 9-11:45 & 2-5, 6:45)*. **Dun-sur-Auron** *(13 km N of Meillant)* : Tour de l'Horloge (clocktower) and old houses; 12th-15thC church. ▶ **Thaumiers** ®, *(10 km SE from Dun)* : the château, an elegant 18thC building, is now a hotel. ▶ **Ainay-le-Vieil** ® *(10 km S of Saint-Amand)* : château★★ is worth a special trip; Renaissance building surrounded by walls and towers, encircled by moats *(10-12 & 2-7, daily closed Tue. am.,*

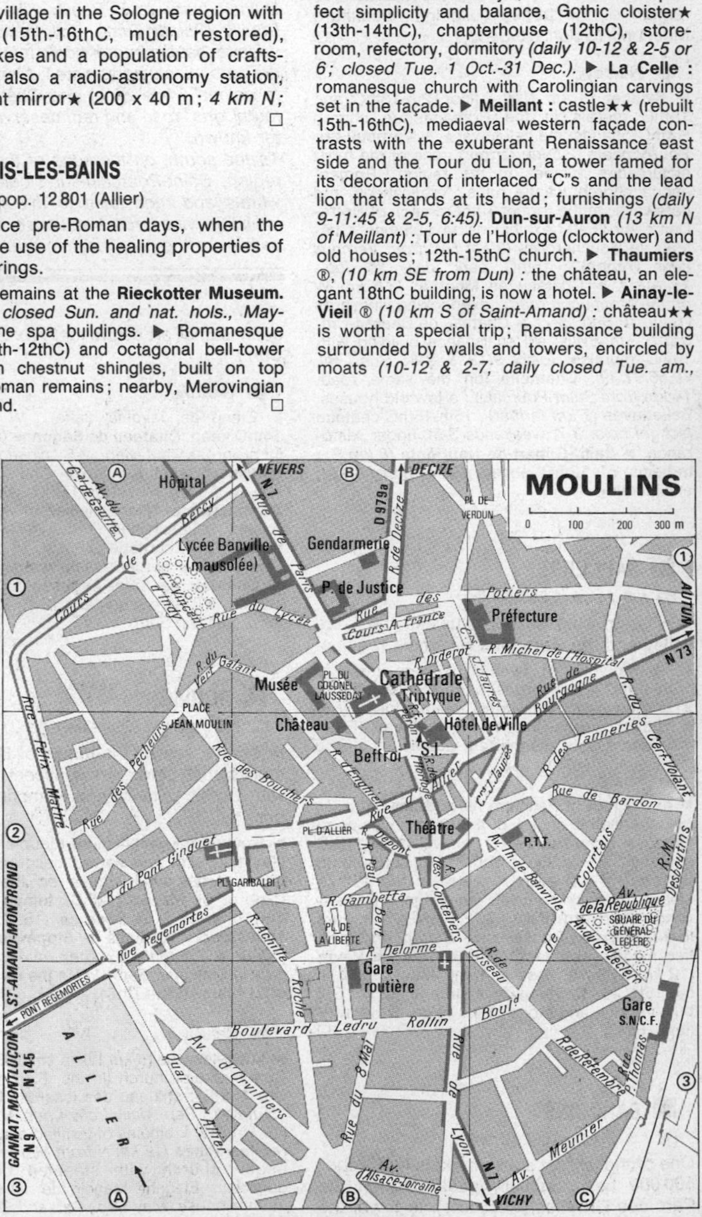

7 Feb.-31 Mar. and Nov.-Jan). ▶ **Drevant** : a flowery village between Saint-Amand and Ainay : excavations of a Roman theatre. □

SAINT-POURÇAIN-SUR-SIOULE

C2-3 / ® / pop. 5433 (Allier)

The town grew around the 11thC Romanesque abbey church (15thC carved choir stalls), which was rebuilt several times between the 14th and the 19thC. A 15thC bell-tower and several half-timbered houses remain of the abbey buildings. Viticulture Museum *(15 Jun.-10 Sept.).* □

▶ Nearby

▶ **Saulcet** *(3 km NW)* : fine 12th-13thC and 15thC murals in the Romanesque church (14thC); handsome bell-tower★. ▶ **Verneuil-en-Bourbonnais** *(2.5 km farther)* : one of the most picturesque villages in the region; Romanesque church, castle ruins, fortifications and gateways; at the former 10thC church of Notre-Dame-sur-l'Eau, exhibitions in summer. Château de Boucherolles (*9 km NW from Verneuil near* **Tréban**) : 16thC, park *(daily 15 Jun.-15 Aug.).* ▶ Château de **Montfan** *(3.5 km W on the Montluçon road)* : overlooking vineyards *(1 Jul.-10 Sep., 3-7).* ▶ Château de **Chareil-Cintrat** *(7 km SW)* : a Renaissance building with 16thC murals★ *(daily 9-12 & 2-6; Sun., tel. 70.56.91.39),* **Chantelle** (on the same road, *14 km from Saint-Pourçain*) : a few old houses, **Bellenaves** *(7 km farther)* : 15th-16thC château *(school hols, 3-7, weekends 3-5),* under restoration. ▶ **Saint-Gilbert-de-Neuffonts** *(8 km S)* : remains of 12thC abbey (*Palm Sun-1 Nov*; exhibitions). □

SANCERRE★★

B1 / ® / pop. 2286 (Cher)

A wine-growing district, between the Loire valley and the Berry and Nivernais regions.

▶ A network of twisting streets (several 15th-16thC houses) runs to the **Tour des Fiefs,** a striking cylindrical 15thC keep. Close by is a 19thC pseudo-Renaissance château. From the Caesar Gate, magnificent view★. □

▶ Nearby

▶ At the foot of Sancerre hill is **Saint-Satur** ®; only the Gothic choir★ of the church was completed. ▶ **Sens-Beaujeu** *(11 km W)* : 16th-17thC château (with additions from 1810), **château du Boucard** *(4 km away)* : rebuilt in the 16thC; severe exterior conceals an elegant Renaissance courtyard *(daily 10-12 & 2-6, 7).* ▶ **Jars** *(5 km farther)* : Renaissance church, and fortified mediaeval manorhouse. ▶ **Tour de Vèvre** *(12 km SW)* : a massive 12thC keep rebuilt in the 15thC. ▶ **Château de la Grange** *(12 km S)* : built in brick and stone in the reign of Henri IV (late 16thC). □

SANCOINS

B2 / ® / pop. 3667 (Cher)

One of the largest cattle markets in Europe; 500000 head annually pass through the Parc des Grivelles (saleyards). In town, the Jean Baffier art centre *(daily ex Sat. pm and Sun.).* □

▶ Nearby

▶ Étang de Javoulet (lake) : W, ruins of a 14thC keep, **Château de Sagonne** (restorations in progress; *Jul.-Sep. 2-6; closed Mon*) with remains of another keep. ▶ Château de Gros-souvre *(7 km N)* : 12th-17thC. Along D76 to **Apremont-sur-Allier :** mediaeval village; in the château outbuildings (15th-17thC), display of horse-drawn carriages *(7 Apr.-15 Sep. 2-6 ex Tue.)*; flower garden *(same hours; 10-12 am).* ▶ **Château de Saint-Augustin** *(8.5 km SE)* : 18thC; 87 acre zoo-park *(2-6, school hols, Wed, Sat and Sun).* □

Wines

Berry and Bourbonnais, although not among the top-ranked wine-producing districts, produce several highly-esteemed wines, whites for the most part.
Best known is white Sancerre — fruity and very dry — made from the Sauvignon grape; the finest come from Bué and Chavignol. There is also a fresh and lively red Sancerre. Good years for Sancerre rouge : 1962, 64, 66, 69, 70, 71, 73, 76, 78, 83.
Quincy (very dry), Reuilly (like Sancerre), Pouilly (Pouilly-Fumé, still fresh and light, despite having more body than Sancerre) are also widely appreciated. Menetou-Salon (a golden white wine) and Châteaumeillant (both "gris" rosé and red) deserve to be better known.
To the south, on the edge of the Auvergne region, Saint-Pourçain-sur-Sioule produces whites and reds (akin to the spicy Beaujolais) in vineyards traditionally claimed to date from the pre-Christian era.

SOUVIGNY★

C2 / ® / pop. 1929 (Allier)

Priory chosen by the dukes of Bourbon as their burial place : magnificent church★★ with Gothic exterior and Romanesque interior.

▶ Noteworthy architecture (double side-aisles, elevation with fine carved decoration) : **capitals★,** ornamental arches on the supposed tomb of St. Mayeul (12thC), **tombs of Louis II and Charles I of Bourbon** (15thC). ▶ 16th-18thC priory buildings. ▶ **Stonework Museum** *(10-12 & 3-6, daily ex Tue, Jul-Aug; Sat, Sun only in May Jun, Sep, Oct)* in the former church of St-Marc (12th-17thC). □

▶ Nearby

▶ **Autry-Issards** *(5 km W)* : a small Burgundian-Romanesque church (inside, Flemish painting, late 15thC); château des Issards (15th-19thC; *15 Jun.-15 Sep., daily from 4 pm).* ▶ **Le Montet** *(18 km SW)* : remains of fortified church, **Buxières-les-Mines** *(12 km N from Montet)* : Romanesque church with steepled bell tower; doorway. Elegant Manoir de la Condemine (manor house, *May-Sep., Sat. and Sun. 2-7*). □

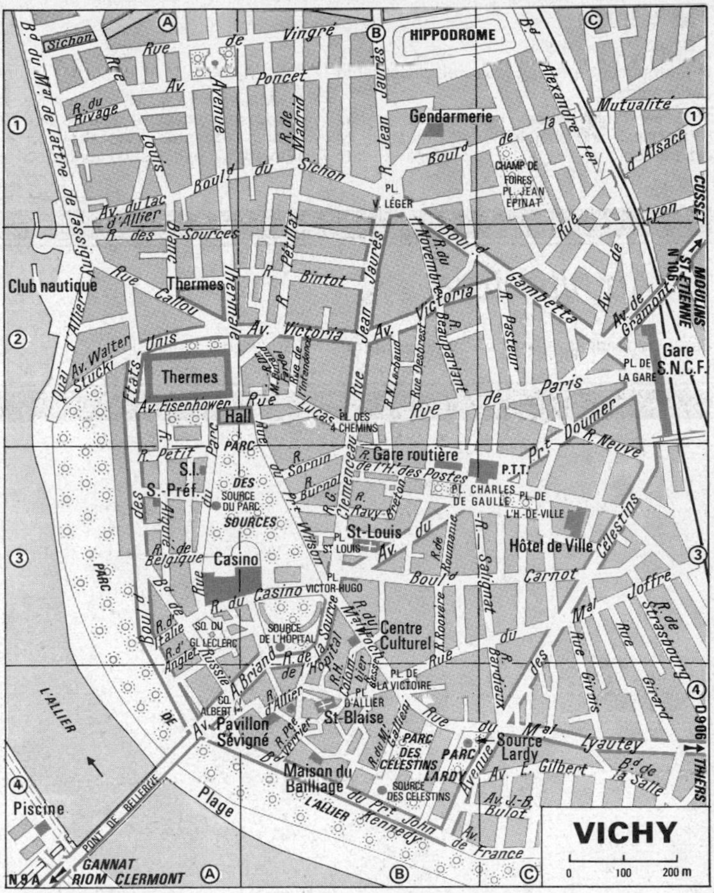

■ TRONÇAIS Forest★

B2 / ® (St. Bonnet-Tronçais).

Beautiful, dense forest 105 km² in area; avenues through stands of oak (70 %) and beech. Replanted by Jean-Baptiste Colbert (1619-1683; Louis XIV's prime minister).

▶ Picnic areas, camping grounds, lakes with leisure facilities. Numerous walks; take the routes past the **300 year-old oaks** (some over 35m high and 3.5 m in circumference). ▶ S, **Hérisson** ® : a charming village in the shadow of a ruined 13th-14thC castle (panorama). □

■ VALENÇAY★★

A1 / ® / pop. 3 139 (Indre)

The **château★★** presents a uniform architectural style, even though construction spanned more than 200 years.

▶ French Regency, Louis XVI and Empire furnishings in the apartments *(15 Mar-15 Nov, daily 9-11:15 & 2-6:15).* ▶ Animals roam the park *(open all year 9-12 & 2-7).* ▶ In the outbuildings : **Automobile Museum,** 50 models★ from 1898-1945; *same hours as the park.* □

■ VICHY★★

C3 / ® / pop. 30 554 (Allier)

This health resort preserves the charm that drew fashionable clients long before the turn of the century; it is equipped with up-to-date leisure and sports facilities; casino; attractive gardens; antique shops; luxurious hotels.

▶ **Maison du Bailliage,** or Chastel Franc, (magistrate's court; B4, 1531) displays art and archaeology collections; near the church Saint-Blaise, the Centre for Archaeological Research has exhibits on the history of Vichy (2 Rue Porte de France; *in season, Sat 2-6*). ▶ The **spa buildings** (A2) can be visited on certain afternoons in season and a Missionary Museum, 18 Avenue Thermale *(May-Sep., daily ex Mon. 3-6).* □

▶ Nearby

▶ **Cusset** ® *(3 km E) :* an industrial suburb; houses of Charles VII and Louis XI (both 15thC) and other old houses; historical museum in the Tour Prisonnière (prison tower final remains of 15thC fortifications; *May-Sep., Wed., Sat., Sun. 3-7*). ▶ **Billy** *(15 km N) :* at the foot of a rock crowned with the ruins of a 13th-14thC fortress *(pm Jun.-15 Sep.).* □

VIERZON

B1 / ® / pop. 34 886

Industrial centre for agricultural implements and ceramics.

▶ Several old houses near the town hall (17th-18thC) and church (17thC); museum of old Vierzon. □

▶ Nearby

▶ **Massay** (*10 km SW,* N20) : a fine 12th-14thC church and extensive remains of a Benedictine abbey (chapter, storehouse, dormitory, 12th-13thC ; exhibits and concerts in summer). □

● *Architecture*

See surrounding regions : Touraine, Burgundy, Auvergne, Limousin.

Brief regional history

Before 52BC

Two Celtic tribes (the Biturigi) inhabited the Berry and Bourbonnais regions after immigrations of the 8thCBC. The territory of the northern Biturigi extended as far as Bourges (Avaric), reputedly the most beautiful city in Gaul, while the southern kingdom of Arverne was based in Gergovia, and included part of the Allier Plain.

52BC-10thC

When Gaul was partitioned in 27BC, the region was included in the province of Aquitaine, with Avaric as its capital. The Romans developed the countryside and built roads. Thermal springs (Vichy, Néris) prospered from rich clients. When Christianity began to spread during the 3rdC, **Bourges** became the Metropolitan See for the dioceses of Aquitaine. ● In 270 Germanic tribes began to invade, but neither the Franks nor the Visigoths reached Berry-Bourbonnais in sufficient numbers to impose their authority. ● The Duchy of Aquitaine, constituted in 614, remained independent of the Frankish Merovingian kings until the reign of Pepin the Short (761). The region was finally broken up by the development of the feudal system in the 10thC.

10thC-13thC

The former **county of Bourges** was divided into two principal seigneuries : the **viscounty of Bourges,** which was sold to the king of France in 1101 and elevated to the status of duchy; and the **viscounty of Déols,** which remained under Aquitaine until conquered by Philippe Auguste at the end of the same century. ● The seigneury of **Bourbonnais,** based around Bourbon-l'Archambault, was formed at the same period, and prospered through marriages, legacies and the king's favour.

14thC-15thC

The most famous Duke of Berry was **Jean** (1340-1416), third son of Jean le Bon (John the Good), and brother of King Charles V. He surrounded himself with an elegant court and patronized the arts. Some of the most exquisite manuscript miniatures of the Middle Ages were created on his order, including the famous book of hours, the **"Très Riches Heures du Duc de Berry"** (now in the Condé Museum, Château de Chantilly). ● Bourges was an important mediaeval centre of artistic achievement. King Charles VII of France resided there, and Bourges remained his capital, thanks to the financial aid of Jacques Coeur (→ box), until Joan of Arc in 1428 rallied the French to drive out the occupying English. ● The Bourbon dukes who made **Moulins** the capital at the end of the 15thC lived in luxury.

16thC to the present day

King François I, humiliated by the splendid court of Charles III, **Duke of Bourbon,** sequestrated some of the duke's possessions. In retaliation, Charles joined forces with Holy Roman emperor Charles Quint, and played a decisive role in defeating the French at Pavia. This provoked François I to attach all Bourbon estates to the crown on the death of Charles in 1527. Berry followed in 1601; since that time the Berry and Bourbonnais regions have formed an integral part of France.

Practical information

The region

Information : *Comité Régional de Tourisme Auvergne* (C.R.T.), 45, av. Julien, B.P. 395, 63011 Clermont-Ferrand, ☎ 73.93.04.03. *C.R.T. Val de Loire,* 10, rue du Colombier, B.P. 2412, 45032 Orléans Cedex, ☎ 38.62.68.48. **Allier :** *Office régional du Tourisme et du Thermalisme,* 35, rue Belle-Croix, 03400 Yzeure, ☎ 70.44.41.57. **Cher :** *Comité Départemental de Tourisme* (C.D.T.), préfecture, pl. M.-Plaisant, 18014 Bourges Cedex, ☎ 49.70.71.72, ext 446. **Indre :** *C.D.T.,* bus station, rue Bourdillon, 36000 Châteauroux, ☎ 54.22.91.20.

Maps : *Michelin,* nos 64, 65, 68, 69, 73, 1/200 000. *I.G.N.,* nos 26, 27, 34, 35, 36, 42, 43, 1/100 000.

S.O.S. : Allier : ☎ 17. **Cher :** *SAMU* (emergency medical service), ☎ 48.65.15.15. **Indre :** *S.M.U.R.,* ☎ 54.27.01.64. *Poisoning Emergency Centre :* Tours, ☎ 47.66.15.15. Clermont-Ferrand, ☎ 73.27.33.33.

Weather forecast : Allier : Montluçon, ☎ 70.28.03.50 ; Moulins : ☎ 70.44.44.44 ; Vichy : ☎ 70.32.34.59. **Cher :** ☎ 48.50.15.91. **Indre :** ☎ 54.34.05.13.

Rural gîtes and chambres d'hôtes : enq at the *Relais départementaux des gîtes ruraux.* **Allier :** Chambre d'Agriculture, 60, cours J.-Jaurès, 03000 Moulins, ☎ 70.44.42.88. **Cher :** 10, rue de la Chappe, 18000 Bourges, ☎ 48.24.14.95, ext 445/446. **Indre :** Chambre d'Agriculture, 24, rue des Ingrains, B.P. 307, 36006 Châteauroux Cedex, ☎ 54.22.20.07.

Camping : approx 140 sites : list at the C.D.T. and S.I.

Festivals and events : Feb : *wine fair* at Saint-Pourçain-sur-Sioule. **Apr :** *Spring Carnival* in Vierzon. **End Apr.-mid-Sep :** *Été de Noirlac.* **May :** *Fête de la Louée* in Vesdun. **Jul :** *grape festival* in Verdigny. **Jul-Aug :** *fête des ânes (donkey fete)* in Garigny ; *ancestral fete of the bargemen of the Loire* in Saint-Satur. *Wizards' Fair* in Bué ; *French Wines Fair* in Sancerre. **Sep :** *Slide-show Festival* in Vichy. **Sep-Oct :** *Autumn Days* in Moulins. **Oct :** *Orval fairs* in Saint-Amand-Montrond.

Rambling and hiking : the region is traversed by the G.R.31, 41, 412 (topoguides). Enq : *Délégué Dép. du Comité National des Sentiers de G.R.,* M. Vurpillot, 33, rue Mozart, 18000 Bourges, ☎ 48.24.67.96 ; Mlle Guinard, 14, pl. de la République, 03000 Moulins, ☎ 70.44.00.61.

Riding holidays : *Comité Départemental pour le Tourisme Équestre du* ***Cher*** (riding centre), La Rongère, Saint-Éloy-de-Gy, 18110 Saint-Martin-d'Auxigny, ☎ 48.25.43.97. *Direction Départementale Temps Libre, Jeunesse et Sports,* 27, rue L.-Mallet, 18014 Bourges Cedex, ☎ 48.50.48.48. **Allier,** contact M. Humbert, 6, rue Berthelot, 03000 Moulins, ☎ 79.44.01.63.

Cycling holidays : *Comité Dép. de Cyclotourisme,* M. Sarrazin, 21, rue Darcin, 03300 Cusset, ☎ 70.98.64.44 and 70.98.01.51, ext 397. *Dir. Dép. Temps Libre, Jeunesse et Sports,* 27, rue Louis-Mallet, 18014 Bourges Cedex, ☎ 48.50.48.48. *Délégation Dép. du Cyclisme de l'****Allier,*** M. Gazur, pl. de la Mairie, 03500 Saint-Pourçain-sur-Sioule.

River and canal cruises : cruise on canals of the region : *Loire Line,* L'Équerre, 18320 Marseille-les-Aubigny, ☎ 48.76.48.01.

Children : riding course in Boischaut, Pony-club de Puyferrand, 18170 Le Châtelet-en-Berry, ☎ 48.56.31.52. Pony-club : château de la Roche, rte de Graçay (children's leisure centre), Anjouin, 36210 Châbris.

Tennis : enq at the ℹ

Golf : Nassigny (9 and 18 holes), Vichy (18 holes), Hérisson (9 holes).

Aquatic sports : on the St-Bonnet and Pirot lakes, ☎ 70.67.50.01 ; Sault, ☎ 70.51.50.03 ; Goule, ☎ 70.66.60.77 ; Vichy, ☎ 70.98.71.94.

Lakes : Cher : Argent-sur-Sauldre, ☎ 38.87.64.72, Bessais-le-Fromental, ☎ 48.60.75.93, Bourges/Plainpied/Givaudins, ☎ 48.70.19.32, Mareuil-sur-Arnon, ☎ 48.59.92.87, Sidiailles, ☎ 48.56.71.30. **Indre :** Chabris, ☎ au ℹ 54.40.04.18, Eguzon, enq at ℹ ☎ 54.47.43.69. Linge : enq at the mairie, ☎ 54.28.02.07, Vendœuvres.

Canoeing : *Ligue Auvergne de Canoë-Kayak,* M. Y. Lecaude, 32, rue C.-Péguy, 63800 Cournon, ☎ 73.84.71.30.

Hang-gliding : *Aéroclub de Moulins-Montbeugny,* ☎ 70.20.04.56. *Union Aéronautique du Centre,* 18000 Bourges, ☎ 48.50.41.83. *Aéro-club d'Issoudin,* ☎ 54.21.21.27. *Aéroclub* at Le Blanc, ☎ 54.37.06.97.

Parachuting : *Centre Aéroparachutiste,* M. Eskenazi, aérodrome de Lapalisse, 03120 Lapalisse, ☎ 70.99.18.03.

Winter sports : ski resorts at La Loge-des-Gardes, 03250 Le Mayet-de-Montagne, ☎ 70.56.41.87 ; La Font-Blanche, 03250 Le Mayet-de-Montagne, ☎ 70.56.40.66. Enq : S.I. of the Montagne Bourbonnaise, *Maison de la Montagne Bourbonnaise,* 03250 Le Mayet-de-Montagne, ☎ 70.41.75.24. Cross-country skiing in Saint-Nicolas-des-Biefs, Lavoine, La Loge-des-Gardes.

Hunting and shooting : enq at the *Féd. Dép. des Chasseurs.* **Allier :** 6, av. V.-Hugo, 03000 Moulins, ☎ 70.44.07.71. **Cher :** 9, pl. de la Nation, 18000 Bourges, ☎ 48.24.28.46. **Indre :** 11, rue Belle-Isle, 36000 Châteauroux, ☎ 54.22.15.98.

Fishing : Allier : *Féd. Dép. de Pêche et Pisciculture,* impasse des Martyrs, 03000 Moulins, ☎ 70.46.34.29. **Cher :** *Féd. de Pêche,* 59, rue Barbès, 18000 Bourges, ☎ 48.50.53.07. **Indre :** *Féd. Dép. de la Pêche,* 19, rue des États-Unis, 36000 Châteauroux, ☎ 54.34.59.69.

Towns

AIGURANDE

Guéret 35, Châteauroux 48, Paris 316
26 km SW of La Châtre, B2 ⊠ 36140

SNCF ☎ 54.30.30.36.

Hotels :
★***Berry,*** rue Grande, ☎ 54.30.30.38. 9 rm closed Oct, Fri (low season), 160. Rest. ♦ Fish specialities, 120-210.
★***Relais de la Marche*** (L.F.), pl. du Champ-de-Foire, ☎ 54.30.31.58. 7 rm closed Nov, Fri (low season), 100. Rest. ♦ Spec : frogs' legs and fresh-water crayfish (écrevisse), 80-130.

Events : Tue of Whitsuntide : *pilgrimage to Notre-Dame de la Bouzanne. Fresh water crayfish fair,* last Sun in Aug.

ARGENTON-SUR-CREUSE

Châteauroux 31, Limoges 94, Paris 302
A2 ⊠ 36200

ℹ hôtel de Scévolle, ☎ 54.04.05.30.

SNCF ☎ 54.24.15.72.

Hotels :
★★***Cheval Noir*** (L.F.), 27, rue Auclert-Descottes, ☎ 54.04.00.06. Visa. 35 rm closed Sun eve, Jan, 210. Rest. ♦ 80-130.
★★***Manoir de Boivilliers,*** 11, rue Moulin-de-Bord, ☎ 54.24.13.88. Visa. 15 rm closed 21 Dec-2 Jan, 180.
★***France*** (L.F.), 8, rue J.-J.-Rousseau, ☎ 54.24.03.31. AE, DC, Visa. 16 rm closed 15 Nov-15 Dec, 160. Rest. ♦ closed Tue and Sat low season, 80-130.
Chez Maître Jean, 67, av. Rollinat, ☎ 54.24.02.09. Visa. 7 rm closed 15-30 Oct and 1-15 Feb, 65. Rest. ♦ closed Wed, 50-100.

Saint-Marcel, 2 km N on the N20 :
★★***Prieuré*** (L.F.), rte de Châteauroux, ☎ 54.04.05.19. Euro, Visa. 12 rm closed Mon, Feb, 145. Rest. ♦ 40-100.

Le Pèchereau, 2.5 km SE on the D48 :
★★***Moulin du Vivier,*** le Vivier, by D48, ☎ 54.24.03.23. 14 rm closed Mon and Sun eve, 20 Jan-28 Feb, 135.

Menoux, 5 km SE, on the D48 :
★***Petit Roy,*** 6, rue Le Bourgoin, ☎ 54.47.87.09. Euro, Visa. 8 rm 80. Rest. ♦ closed Wed, 45-130.

▲ ★★★*Les Chambons* (35 pl.), ☎ 54.04.15.26.

Restaurant :
Tendu, 9 km on the N20 :
● ♦♦ ***Moulin des Eaux Vives,*** ☎ 54.24.12.25. AE, DC, Euro, Visa. daily until 10 pm ; closed Mon (ex Jul-Aug) ; book ahead for weekends. An old mill with a terrace overlooking the water. Spec : *salade de chavignol chaud* and *tournedos au chablis,* 65-125.

Recommended : Gargilesse : blacksmith : *S. Bachelier,* ☎ 54.47.83.28 ; wood sculpture : *la Damielle,* A. Bonithon, ☎ 54.47.80.97 ; cabinet-maker : *G. Dorangeaon,* ☎ 54.47.85.26 ; pottery, *F. Baudat,* ☎ 54.47.86.28.

AUBIGNY-SUR-NÈRE

Bourges 46, Orléans 75, Paris 181
B1 ⊠ 18700

ℹ mairie, ☎ 48.58.00.09.

SNCF ☎ 48.58.04.89.

Hotels :
★★***Château de la Verrerie*** (Château-accueil), 10 km on the D89, ☎ 48.58.06.91. DC. 7 rm in the park of the château ; closed 1 Dec-1 Apr, 550. Rest. ♦♦ closed 20 Oct-14 Jun, Tue. Spec : *terrine de foie de volaille aux truffes,* home-made tarts, 70-100.
★★***Chaumière*** (L.F.), 1, pl. Paul Lasnier, ☎ 48.58.04.01. AE, DC, Visa. 16 rm 140. Rest. ♦ ♿ Rustic setting. Spec : *escargots au sancerre, poulet en barbouille,* 60-130.

Youth hostel : Parc des Sports, ☎ 48.58.00.09.

▲ ★★*Parc des Sports* (100 pl.), ☎ 48.58.02.37.

Restaurant :
♦***Auberge de la Fontaine,*** 27, av. Charles-de-Gaulle, ☎ 48.58.02.59. closed 1-21 Oct, 25 Dec-1 Jan, Sun eve and Mon. In a typical setting, Paulette Massé (A.R.C.) is cooking for your great pleasure, 50-130.

Bicycle hire : M. Barré, rue Charbon, ☎ 48.58.00.29.

BANNEGON

Bourges 42, Nevers 57, Paris 269
24 km E-NE of Saint-Amand-Montrond, B2
⊠ 18210 Charenton-du-Cher

Hotels :
● ★★★***Auberge du Moulin de Chaméron*** (L.F., Moulin-Etape, Relais du Silence), 3 km SE on the D76, ☎ 48.60.75.80. Visa. 12 rm ♿ closed 4 Nov-15 Mar and Thu. The 18thC mill provides a ravishing setting, 300. Rest. ♦♦ 100-230.

Thaumiers, 5 km NW on the D41 :
Château de Thaumiers (Château-Accueil), ☎ 48.60.87.62. 5 rm and 2 suites in this delightful 18thC residence closed 15 Nov-31 Mar, 400.

Le BLANC

Châteauroux 60, Poitiers 60, Paris 300
A2 ⊠ 36300

ℹ pl. de la Libération, ☎ 54.37.05.13 (high season), and hôtel de ville, ☎ 54.37.23.40.

SNCF ☎ 54.37.07.01.

Hotels :
● ★★***Domaine de l'Étape*** (Châteaux-hôtels), rte de Belâbre, ☎ 54.37.18.02. AE, DC, Euro. 21 rm 130 ha riding, 235. Rest. 60-80.
★***Promenade*** (L.F.), 36, rue St-Lazare, ☎ 54.37.48.80. Euro, Visa. 21 rm 200. Rest. ♦ closed Sun eve and Mon, 75-90.

▲ ★★*Municipal Isle-d'Avant* (100 pl.), ☎ 54.37.02.21.

Events : mid-Feb : *Saint-Valentine's fete.* Early Sep : *pilgrimage of the Saints.* Nov : *Saint-Martin's Fair.*

Recommended : enamelled jewellery : *A. Jubard,* Les Chezeaux, rte d'Avant, ☎ 54.37.32.17 ; sculpture and pottery : *F. Taillandier,* 16, quai Aubépin, rte de Bélabre, ☎ 54.37.17.94.

BOURBON-L'ARCHAMBAULT

Moulins 48, Nevers 51, Paris 291
C2 (all yr), ☎ 70.67.07.88 ⊠ 03160

ℹ 1, pl. des Thermes, ☎ 70.67.09.79 (high season).

Hotels :
★★***Thermes,*** av. Ch.-Louis-Philippe, ☎ 70.67.00.15. 22 rm Ⓟ ♨ closed Nov-21 Mar, 195. Rest. ♦♦ ⚘ ⚘ ♿ Traditional cooking : *foie gras, noix de lotte florentine,* 65-125.
★★***Grand Hôtel Villa des Fleurs*** (L.F.), 2, bd des Solins, ☎ 70.67.09.53. 26 rm Ⓟ ♨ ⚘ ♿ Rustic setting, 125. Rest. ♦ Spec : *magret de canard au calvados,* 40-110.
★***Acacias,*** av. Ch.-Louis-Philippe, ☎ 70.67.06.24. 25 rm, closed end Jan-15 Mar, 130. Rest. ♦♦ ♿ closed Mon eve (high season) and Sun (low season). Spec : delicious, tender Charolais beef, and a superb *ris de veau aux morilles,* 120-170.

⛺ ★★*Parc de Bignon* (157 pl.), ☎ 70.67.08.83.

Restaurant :
♦ ***L'Oustalet,*** av. E.-Guillaumin, ☎ 70.67.01.48. Euro, Visa. Ⓟ closed 15-31 Oct and 1-8 Mar, Fri and Sun eve (low season), 70-110.

Casino des Thermes, ☎ 70.67.07.88.

BOURGES

Châteauroux 67, Orléans 106, Paris 227
B1 ✉ 18000

ⓘ pl. E.-Dolet (B4), ☎ 48.24.75.33 (closed Sun low season).

SNCF (B1), ☎ 48.65.50.50 and 48.70.10.52.

🚌 Le Prado (A3), ☎ 48.24.36.42.

Car-hire : *Budget* train + auto, 259, av. du Gal.-de-Gaulle, ☎ 48.24.99.97, and at the station, ☎ 48.70.10.52.

Hotels :
★★***D'Artagnan,*** 19, pl. Séraucourt (B4), ☎ 48.24.67.51. AE, DC. 73 rm Ⓟ closed 10-30 Oct, 230. Rest. ♦ ♿ closed Mon 80-130.
★★***Grand Argentier,*** 9, rue Parerie (B2), ☎ 48.70.84.31. AE, DC, Visa. 14 rm ⚘ closed 21 Dec-31 Jan, 205. Rest. ♦ ♿ closed Mon and Sun eve. Copious family-style fare and warm service, 70-100.
★★***Tilleuls,*** 7, pl. de la Pyrotechnie (C4), ☎ 48.20.49.04. 29 rm Ⓟ ♨ ⚘ 180.
★★***Monitel*** (Inter-Hôtel), 73, rue Barbès, ☎ 48.50.23.62. Visa. 48 rm Ⓟ ♿ closed 24 Dec-New Year's Day, 200. Rest. ***la Braisière,*** 70-110.
★★***Saint-Jean,*** 23, av. M.-Dormoy (C1), ☎ 48.24.13.48. Tx 782026. Euro, Visa. 24 rm Ⓟ ♿ closed Feb, 135.

Youth hostel : 22, rue Henri-Sellier, ☎ 48.24.58.09.

⛺ ★★*Municipal* (75 pl.), ☎ 48.20.16.85.

Restaurants :
● ♦♦♦ ***Jacques Cœur,*** 3, pl. J.-Cœur (B3), ☎ 48.70.12.72. AE, DC, Visa. ♿ closed 24 Dec-2 Jan, 14 Jul-12 Aug, Sat and Sun eve. The fine traditions of this house are perfectly reflected in chef François Bernard's excellent regional cooking : *poulet en barbouille, coquilles Saint-Jacques sautées, profiterolles au chocolat ;* wines from the Cher region, 140-220.
♦♦ ***Ile d'Or,*** 39, bd Juranville (A3), ☎ 48.24.29.15. AE, DC, Euro, Visa. ♿ closed 1-17 Sep, 15 Feb-3 Mar, Sun and Mon noon, 80-160.
● ♦♦ ***Au Sénat,*** *6 bis*-8, rue de la Poissonnerie (B2-3), ☎ 48.24.02.56. Visa. ♿ closed Fri eve, Sat noon. Good, old-style cooking in the heart of the old town : *poulet en barbouille, terrine maison, magret de canard au sancerre,* 50-100.

Bicycle hire : *Loca-Bourges,* rue E.-Vaillant, ☎ 48.24.52.46.

Recommended : ceramic craftwork : *M. Levêque,* 9, av. E.-Renan, ☎ 48.20.07.92. Enamelled jewellery : *Boutique des Artisans,* 89, rue d'Auron, ☎ 48.24.59.66. Cake-shop and tea-room : *Aux Trois Flûtes,* 13, rue Bourbonnoux, ☎ 48.24.24.28. Confectioner's shop : *Maison des Forestines,* B.P. 108, 3, pl. Cujas (A-B3), ☎ 48.24.00.24. Delicious praline-filled sweets.

BRINON-SUR-SAULDRE

Orléans 57, Bourges 64, Paris 188
18 km NW of Aubigny-sur-Nère, B1
✉ 18410 Argent-sur-Sauldre

Hotel :
★★***Solognote*** (L.F., Relais du Silence), Grande-Rue, ☎ 48.58.50.29. AE. 10 rm Ⓟ ♨ ⚘ ♿ closed 10 Feb-6 Mar, 21 May-5 Jun, 11-25 Sep, 200. Rest. ♦♦ closed Tue eve and Wed. Choice regional dishes in a charming rustic inn. Spec : *salade tiède de Saint-Jacques, petit salé de canard en potée,* 105-230.

⛺ ★Municipal *de la Sauldre* (27 pl.), ☎ 48.58.50.28.

Event : last Sun in May : *Rose Fête,* Argent-sur-Sauldre.

Bicycle hire : Argent-sur-Sauldre, M. G. Serre, pl. du Marché, ☎ 48.73.60.04.

CHÂTEAUROUX

Bourges 67, Guéret 89, Paris 269
A2 ✉ 36000

ⓘ pl. de la Gare, ☎ 54.34.10.74.

SNCF (B-C1), ☎ 54.27.50.50, 54.34.44.17, 54.34.18.51.

🚌 (B1), ☎ 54.22.13.22.

Car-hire : *Budget* train + auto, at the S.N.C.F. station, ☎ 54.34.18.51.

Hotels :
★★★***Élysées,*** 1, rue J.-J.-Rousseau, ☎ 54.34.82.69. AE, DC, Euro, Visa. 17 rm ♿ closed Sun, 300. Rest. ● ♦♦♦ closed 1-20 Feb, 25 Nov-4 Dec, Mon, Sun eve (1 Oct-30 Jun) and noon (1 Jul-30 Sep). Spec : *civet de homard breton et de petits crustacés,* 140-320.
★★***Faisan*** (L.F.), 78, av. de la Gare (B1), ☎ 54.27.06.58. Tx 750839. AE, DC, Euro, Visa. 68 rm, 180. Rest. ♦ ♿ 50-120.
★★***Parc,*** 148, av. de Paris (B1), ☎ 54.34.36.83. 27 rm Ⓟ ♨ closed Nov and Sat (1 Dec-1 May), 135. Rest. ♦ Family-style cooking, good wines, 50-120.

Coings, 36130 Déols, 5 km N on the N20 :
★★***Relais Saint-Jacques*** (Inter-Hôtel), RN 20, ☎ 54.22.87.10. AE, DC, Visa. 46 rm Ⓟ ♨ ⚘ ♿ 180. Rest. ♦ 120-210.

⛺ ★★★★Municipal *du Rochat* (100 pl.), ☎ 54.34.26.56.

Restaurants :
● ♦♦♦ ***Jean Bardet,*** 1, rue J.-J.-Rousseau (A1), ☎ 54.34.82.69. Closed Sun eve and Mon in summer, Sun in winter. You will share the satisfaction of Jean Bardet's friends, the actors J. Carmet and G. Depardieu. His inventive and refined cooking puts him among our great chefs jury. His wife, Sophie, assisted by a young wine-waiter, both take care of the harmony of dishes and wines. Let yourself be tempted : the *homard aux gésiers confits* and its glass of Banyuls wine is one of the greatest moments, 140-350.
♦ ***L'Escargot,*** 7, rue Jean-Jaurès (B1), ☎ 54.22.06.75. Euro, Visa. ⚘ ♿ closed Mon, 50-110.

Events : early May : *spring fair and congress of Culinary Art* (gastronomy days). Mid-Sep : *annual fair,* with fun-fair, exhibition-fair floral floats parade.

Recommended : pottery : *B. François,* 33, rue Sagot. Wood sculpture : *J. Loyrette,* ☎ 54.27.11.44 (by appt.). Jewellery, *D. Prudhomme,* 11, rue Cazala, ☎ 54.34.03.11.

CHÂTILLON-SUR-INDRE

Châteauroux 67, Blois 76, Paris 256
A1 ✉ 36700

ℹ 81, rue Grande, ☎ 54.38.70.96.

SNCF ☎ 54.38.71.63.

Hotel :
★***Auberge de la Promenade,*** 88, rue Grande, ☎ 54.38.71.95. AE, DC, Visa. 10 rm P ♿ closed Sun eve, 100. Rest. ♦ 50-125.

⛺ ★★Municipal *la Menetrie* (45 pl.), ☎ 54.38.75.44.

La CHÂTRE

Châteauroux 36, Montluçon 62, Paris 301
B2 ✉ 36400

ℹ square G.-Sand, ☎ 54.48.22.64 (high season).

SNCF ☎ 54.48.00.06.

Hotels :
★★***Notre-Dame*** (L.F.), pl. Notre-Dame, ☎ 54.48.01.14. AE, DC, Euro, Visa. 17 rm P closed 24 Dec-2 Jan, 175.
★★***Commerce,*** 9, pl. du Marché, ☎ 54.48.00.25. 12 rm closed 23 Sep-23 Oct and Mon, 100.
★★***Lion d'Argent,*** 2, av. du Lion-d'Argent, ☎ 54.48.11.69. Tx 751222. AE, Euro, Visa. 26 rm P 130. Rest. ♦ 65-135.

Saint-Chartier, 8 km NE :
● ★★***Vallée Bleue*** (Châteaux-hôtels), rte de Verneuil, ☎ 54.31.01.91. Visa. 15 rm P closed Jan, Thu (low season), 190. Rest. ♦ ♿ 85-145.

⛺ ★★Municipal *Solange Sand,* Montgivray (100 pl.), ☎ 54.48.11.09.

Restaurant :
♦ ***Poste,*** 10, rue Basse-du-Mouhet, ☎ 54.48.05.62. AE, DC, Euro, Visa. ♿ closed 10-30 Sep, 25 Dec-1 Jan, Sun eve and Mon, 65-170.

Event : Aug : *dog fair.*

CHEVAGNES

Nevers 74, Vichy 74, Paris 314
18 km E of Moulins, C2 ✉ 03230

Hotel :
★***Cheval Blanc,*** rte Nationale, ☎ 70.43.40.15. Euro. 18 rm P ♿ closed 1 Dec-10 Feb. Alongside the river, 120. Rest. ♦ 50-80.

Farmhouse-inn : *domaine les Boudants,* Paray-le-Frésil. Spec : cheese *soufflé, coq au vin, gâteau de foie de volaille* (chicken liver).

CROZANT

Guéret 40, Châteauroux 63, Paris 334
10 km S of Eguzon, A2-3
✉ 23160 Saint-Sébastien

Hotel :
★***Lac*** (L.F.), pont de Crozant, 1 km E on the D72 and D30, ☎ 55.89.81.96. 10 rm P closed Oct-1 May, 180. Rest. ♦ ♿ 80-130.

⛺ ★★*Le Fontbonne* (33 pl.), ☎ 55.89.80.34.

Restaurant :
♦ ***Auberge de la Vallée,*** ☎ 55.89.80.03. Closed 2 Jan-2 Feb, Mon eve and Tue, 40-160.

CULAN

Guéret 68, Châteauroux 69, Paris 302
B2 ✉ 18270

Hotel :
★***Poste,*** Grande-Rue, ☎ 48.85.66.57. 14 rm P ♿ closed 5 Jan-15 Feb and Mon, 145. Rest. ♦ 40-100.

⛺ ★*La Guinguette* (35 pl.), ☎ 48.56.64.41.

Recommended : handicrafts : decorative objects, *M. Prudhomme,* rue du Château, ☎ 48.56.63.91. Silk painting : *M. Cl. Baramin,* Lavret, Saint-Maur, ☎ 48.56.74.24 (also organises instructional courses).

CUSSET

Moulins 54, Clermont-Ferrand 62, Paris 351
3 km E of Vichy, C3 ✉ 03300

ℹ 2, rue Saturnin-Arloing, ☎ 70.31.39.41.

Hotels :
★★***Globe,*** 1, rue Pasteur, ☎ 70.97.82.31. AE, DC, Euro, Visa. 25 rm P 180. Rest. ♦ ♿ closed Fri eve, 1-15 Mar, 50-120.

Creuzier-le-Neuf, 5.5 km N on the N209 :
★***Bon Accueil*** (L.F.), les Combes, rte de Paris, ☎ 70.98.06.01. Euro, Visa. 6 rm P closed 20 Jan-20 Feb and Wed, 65. Rest. ♦♦ ♿ 36-85.

⛺ ★*Montbeton* (19 pl.), ☎ 70.31.82.88.

Restaurant :
♦♦ ***Taverne Louis XI,*** near the church, ☎ 70.98.39.39. ♿ closed Feb hols, 3-27 Oct, Sun eve and Mon, 120-210.

DOMPIERRE-SUR-BESBRE

Moulins 32, Vichy 59, Paris 327
19 km N of Jaligny-sur-Besbre, C2 ✉ 03290

SNCF ☎ 70.34.55.76.

Hotels :
★***L'Olive*** (L.F.), rue de la Gare, ☎ 70.34.51.87. 11 rm P ♿ closed 15 Nov-15 Dec, 130. Rest. ♦ closed Fri, 50-80.
★***Paix*** (L.F.), pl. du Commerce, ☎ 70.34.50.09. 10 rm closed 25 Oct-15 Nov, Sun eve and Mon, 100. Rest. 80-130.

⛺ ★★*Municipal* (66 pl.), ☎ 70.34.55.57.

ÉBREUIL

Montluçon 58, Moulins 66, Paris 360
C3 ✉ 03450

ℹ hôtel de ville, ☎ 70.90.71.33.

Hotel :
★★***Commerce*** (L.F.), ☎ 70.90.72.66. 22 rm closed Oct and Mon (ex Jul-Aug), 180. Rest. ♦ ♿ 80-130.

⛺ ★★★★*La Filature* (50 pl.), ☎ 70.90.72.01 ; ★★Municipal *les Nières* (33 pl.), ☎ 70.90.71.33.

GANNAT

Clermont-Ferrand 40, Moulins 56, Paris 349
C3 ✉ 03800

ℹ pl. Rantian, ☎ 70.90.17.78 (high season).

Hotels :
★***L'Agriculture,*** 3, pl. Rantian, ☎ 70.90.00.17. Euro, Visa. 28 rm P ♿ closed Mon (low season), 90. Rest. 45-130.

★**La Paix,** 18, av. de la République, ☎ 70.90.01.64. 12 rm Ⓟ closed Mon, 80. Rest. ♿ 45-75.
Hôtel du Château (France-Accueil), 9, pl. Rantian, ☎ 70.90.00.88. Visa. 10 rm Ⓟ 100. Rest. ♦ 80-130.

⛺ ★★*Municipal* (66 pl.), ☎ 70.90.12.16.

ISSOUDUN

Châteauroux 29, Bourges 38, Paris 243
B2 ✉ 36100

ℹ pl. du Dr-Guilpain, ☎ 54.21.13.23.

SNCF ☎ 54.21.01.54.

Hotels :
★★★**France Commerce** (L.F.), 3, rue P.-Brossolette, ☎ 54.21.00.65. Tx 751422. AE, DC, Euro, Visa. 25 rm Ⓟ ♨ 🌳 ♿ closed 31 Jan-4 Mar, 240. Rest. ♦ **les Trois Rois** ♿ closed Sat (15 Oct-15 Mar), 50-130.
★**Berry,** 88, rue P.-Brossolette, ☎ 54.21.20.51. 16 rm Ⓟ 🌳 ♿ closed school hols and Sun eve in winter, 140.

⛺ ★*Municipal* (30 pl.), ☎ 54.21.14.59.

Restaurant :
● ♦♦♦♦ **Auberge la Cognette,** 2, bd de Stalingrad, ☎ 54.21.21.83. AE, DC, Visa. ♿ closed 6-22 Jan, 19 Aug-10 Sep, Sun eve and Mon ex nat hols. A. Nonnet's excellent cooking in this inn Balzac used to stop at. Spec : *poulet en barbouille, ragoût d'écrevisses aux petits légumes, foie de veau au miel et citron,* 120-330.

Events : Apr : *wine fair.*

LAPALISSE

Moulins 50, Clermont-Ferrand 79, Paris 344
C3 ✉ 03120

ℹ pl. Ch.-Bécaud, ☎ 70.99.08.39 (high season).

Hotels :
★★**Galland,** 20, pl. de la République, ☎ 70.99.07.21. DC, Euro. 8 rm Ⓟ closed 2-31 Jan, Wed, 200. Rest. ♦ 50-150.
★**Bourbonnais,** 1, pl. du 14-Juillet, ☎ 70.99.04.11. 11 rm Ⓟ ♨ closed 15 Mar-1 Apr, 1 Dec and Mon, 130. Rest. ♦ ♿ closed Sun and Mon, 80-160.
★**Lion des Flandres,** 40, rue Roosevelt, ☎ 70.99.06.75. 7 rm Ⓟ 🐕 closed 15-30 Dec, 15-30 Jan, last week of Jun and Mon, 125. Rest. ♦♦ ♿ Friendly service ; a variety of good, solid dishes. Spec : *rognon de veau flambé, ris de veau aux gyromitres,* 55-140.

Son et lumière : every eve in summer.

LEVROUX

Blois 76, Châtellerault 96, Paris 257
20 km N of Châteauroux, A2 ✉ 36110

Hotel :
★★**Cloche** (L.F.), 3, rue Nationale, ☎ 54.35.70.43. Visa. 30 rm Ⓟ 🐕 ♿ closed 1-28 Feb, Mon eve and Tue, 160. Rest. ♦ 50-140.

⛺ *Municipal* (35 pl.), ☎ 54.35.70.54.

Bicycle hire : *A.D.E.L.,* 2, rue Traversière, ☎ 54.35.64.87.

Recommended : original leatherwork, chests : *J. Le Blanc,* av. J.-Jaurès, ☎ 54.35.82.86.

MEHUN-SUR-YÈVRE

Bourges 17, Châteauroux 61, Paris 226
B1 ✉ 18500

ℹ pl. du 14-Juillet, ☎ 48.57.35.51 (high season).

SNCF ☎ 48.57.30.22.

Hotel :
★**Croix-Blanche,** 164, rue Jeanne-d'Arc, ☎ 48.57.30.01. Visa. 20 rm Ⓟ ♨ closed 20-30 Sep, 20 Dec-20 Jan, Sun eve and Mon, 170. Rest. 🐕 ♿ 50-90.

⛺ ★★*Municipal* (35 pl.), ☎ 48.57.33.08.

Recommended : handicrafts : porcelain decoration, *J. Debesson,* 157 *bis,* rue A.-Brému, ☎ 48.57.41.34.

MONTLUÇON

Clermont-Ferrand 91, Bourges 93, Paris 320
B2-3 ✉ 03100

ℹ 1 *ter,* av. Marx-Dormoy (B2). ☎ 70.05.05.92.

SNCF (A2), ☎ 70.05.05.50.

🚌 quai Rouget-de-Lisle (A1-2), ☎ 70.05.39.97.

Car-hire : *Budget* train + auto, at the station S.N.C.F., ☎ 70.28.29.30.

Hotels :
★★★**Château Saint-Jean** (Château-hôtels), St-Jean Park, rte de Clermont-Ferrand, ☎ 70.05.04.65. AE, DC, Euro, Visa. 8 rm Ⓟ ♨ 🌳 ♿ Historical residence converted into a restaurant-hotel, 350. Rest. ♦♦♦ 125-200.
★★**Univers,** 38, av. Marx-Dormoy (A2), ☎ 70.05.33.47. AE, DC, Euro. 53 rm Ⓟ 175.
★★**Gare,** 42, av. Marx-Dormoy (A2), ☎ 70.05.44.22. 21 rm Ⓟ closed Christmas and 1 Jan, 180.
★★**Bomotel,** 2, rte du Moulin, 2 km WSW on the N145, ☎ 70.05.76.22. 20 rm Ⓟ ♨ 🌳 closed Mon, 180. Rest. ♦ ☎ 70.05.62.93. closed 15-30 Oct and Mon, 80-130.
★**Celtic,** 1, rue Corneille (C3), ☎ 70.05.28.79. 27 rm. closed Sun, 95.
★**Hostellerie du Théâtre,** 1, rue de la Croix-Verte, ☎ 70.05.07.27. Euro, Visa. 7 rm 🌳 closed 5-25 Jul, 23 Dec-3 Jan, 110. Rest. ♦ closed Sun, 45-70.

Domérat, ✉ 03410, 3.5 km WNW on the N145 :
★★**Novelta** (L.F.), rte de Guéret, ☎ 70.03.34.88. Euro, Visa. 40 rm Ⓟ 🌳 🐕 220. Rest. ♦ 🐕 ♿ closed Sun eve. Family-style cooking ; good value, 70-105.
● ★★**Saint-Victor,** rte de Bourges, 7.5 km on the N144, ☎ 70.28.80.64 and 70.28.83.59. 28 rm Ⓟ ♨ 🌳 ♿ 170. Rest. ♦ Spec : *coq au vin d'Auvergne,* 50-80.

Hérisson, 18.5 km NE on the N144 and D3 :
Château de la Roche-Othon (Château-Accueil), ☎ 70.06.80.31 or 70.05.19.54. DC, Euro, Visa. 3 rm ✳ Ⓟ ♨ 🌳 15th-16thC fortress. closed 1 Dec-31 Mar, 395. Rest. 90-280.

Youth hostel : *le Moulin de Nerdre,* rte de Clermont-Ferrand, ☎ 70.05.41.32.

⛺ ★★*Municipal* (33 pl.), ☎ 70.05.39.53.

Restaurants :
♦♦ **Grenier à Sel,** 10, rue Notre-Dame (C2), ☎ 70.05.53.79. AE, DC, Euro, Visa. ♿ closed 1 Jul-15 Aug, Mon and Sun eve. Refined regional cooking in a 17thC setting, 100.
♦♦ **Ducs de Bourbon,** 47, av. Marx-Dormoy (A2), ☎ 70.05.22.79. AE, DC, Euro, Visa. ♿ closed Sun eve and Mon. Classic cooking in a Louix XVI-style dining-room, 75-125.

MOULINS

Clermont-Ferrand 96, Bourges 98, Paris 294
C2 ✉ 03000

ℹ pl. de l'Hôtel-de-Ville, ☎ 70.44.14.14.

SNCF (C3), ☎ 70.46.50.50, 70.44.23.73.

🚌 av. Mal-de-Lattre-de-Tassigny (B3), ☎ 70.44.06.31.

Car-hire : *Budget* train + auto, 59, rue de Lyon, ☎ 70.20.13.65 ; at the S.N.C.F. station, ☎ 70.44.23.73.

Hotels :

★★★***Paris*** (Relais et châteaux), 21, rue de Paris (B1), ☎ 70.44.00.58. Tx 394853. AE, DC, Euro, Visa. 27 rm Ⓟ ♿ 490. Rest. ● ♦♦♦ ✂ ♿ closed Sun eve and Mon noon (1 Sep-15 Jul). In this beautiful house, François Laustriat and his chef Pascal Bouffety propose excellent traditional Bourbonnais cooking. Spec : *salade bourbonnichonne de filet de charolais, foie de canard à la "Gros Michel", noisettes d'agneau aux rouelles de pied de cochon,* 130-280.

★★★***Moderne*** (Inter-Hôtel), 9, pl. J.-Moulin (A1-2), ☎ 70.44.05.06. Tx 990740. 44 rm Ⓟ ♨ ♿ 190. Rest. ♦ closed 4 Nov-8 Dec, 60-90.

● ★★***Parc*** (L.F.), 31, av. Gal.-Leclerc (C2), ☎ 70.44.12.25. 30 rm Ⓟ closed 1-15 Oct, 23 Dec-7 Jan, 180. Rest. ♦ closed Sat. Clients are well looked after in this good, simple restaurant, with reasonably-priced fare, 65-140.

★***L'Agriculture,*** 15, cours V.-d'Indy (A1), ☎ 70.44.08.58. 24 rm Ⓟ closed 1-10 Oct, 130.

Coulandon, 6 km W on the D945 :

● ★★***Le Chalet*** (L.F. ; Relais du Silence), ☎ 70.44.50.08. DC, Euro, Visa. 21 rm ☼ Ⓟ ♨ ☘ closed 16 Nov-32 Jan and Sun in winter. Attractive chalet in an immense park with a lake, 215. Rest. ♦ dinner only, 60-90.

Villeneuve-sur-Allier, ⊠ 03460, 13 km N on the N7 :

Château du Riau (Château-Accueil), ☎ 70.43.30.74. Ⓟ ☘ 2 rm + 1 suite in this 15th-16thC castle, 330.

⛺ ★*Plage* (66 pl.), ☎ 70.44.19.29.

Restaurants :

● ♦♦ ***Jacquemart,*** 10, place de l'Hôtel-de-Ville, ☎ 70.44.32.58. Closed 3-17 Aug, 14-20 Apr, 21 Dec-5 Jan, Sun eve and Mon. 17thC house. The chef "Louis", a fine former disciple of Alain Seuderens offers good dishes : *tresse de sole à la gousse de vanille, tournedos au roquefort fermier,* 100-220.

♦♦ ***Des Cours,*** 36, cours J.-Jaurès (C2), ☎ 70.44.32.56. AE, DC, Visa. ♿ closed 1-15 Jul, 20-31 Dec and Tue, 120-210.

Bressolles, 4.5 km S on the N9 :

♦♦ ***Le Bateau Ivre,*** ☎ 70.44.48.00. Euro Ⓟ ♿ Good food in a pleasant atmosphere. Spec : *salade de Saint-Jacques vinaigrette framboise, saumon au coulis de tomates,* 75-145.

Bicycle hire : *Au Cyclo,* 31, rue d'Allier, ☎ 70.46.01.99.

Recommended ; *Galerie des Artisans,* hôtel de Moret, rue d'Allier, ☎ 70.46.78.34.

NANÇAY

Bourges 36, Châteauroux 68, Paris 201
B1 ⊠ 18330 Neuvy-sur-Barangeon

Hotels :

● ★★★***Auberge les Meaulnes,*** ☎ 48.51.81.15. AE, DC, Visa. 9 rm ♨ ☘ closed 30 Jan-1 Mar. Stunning residence with period furnishings, 305. Rest. ♦♦♦ ♿ closed Tue (low season, ex nat hols). Quality fare, 170-210.

Vouzeron, 6 km SE :

● ★★★***Relais de Vouzeron*** (Châteaux-hôtels), ☎ 48.51.61.38. AE, DC, Visa. 8 rm Ⓟ ♨ ☘ closed Aug, Sun eve, Mon, 260. Rest. ♦♦ ♿ closed Sun eve and Mon. Spec : *rillettes de saumon, gâteau aux framboises,* 120-210.

⛺ ★★*Les Pins* (70 pl.), ☎ 48.51.81.80.

Recommended : *Galerie Sophie et Gérard Capazza,* grenier de Villabre, ☎ 48.51.80.22 : painting, engraving, sculpture, crafted fabrics, stained glass, clothing, jewellery, and more.

NÉRIS-LES-BAINS

Montluçon 8, Clermont-Ferrand 83, Paris 327
B3 ♥ ⊠ 03310

♆ (2 May-23 Oct), ☎ 70.03.10.39.

ⓘ carrefour des Arènes, ☎ 70.03.11.03.

Hotels :

● ★★***Parc des Rivalles,*** 7, rue Parmentier, ☎ 70.03.10.50. 32 rm Ⓟ ♨ ☘ Near the spa, closed 30 Sep-1 May, 165. Rest. ♦ ✂ ♿ Overlooking the park, 70-200.

★★***Garden*** (L.F.), 12, av. Marx-Dormoy, ☎ 70.03.21.16. 16 rm Ⓟ ♨ ☘ closed 25 Oct-25 Nov, 1st week in Jan and Fri eve (1 Dec-1 May), 180. Rest. ♦ 80-130.

★***Centre*** (L.F.), 10, rue du Capt.-Migat, ☎ 70.03.10.74. 24 rm ♨ ♿ closed 30 Sep-2 May, 100. Rest. 50-60.

⛺ ★★★*Municipal* (65 pl.), ☎ 70.51.17.59.

Casino, 2, bd des Arènes, ☎ 70.03.10.32.

NOHANT-VIC

Châteauroux 30, Montluçon 68, Paris 250
B2 ⊠ 36400

Hotel :

★***Petite Fadette,*** ☎ 54.31.01.48. 15 rm Ⓟ ☘ closed Jan, Tue (16 Sep-31 Mar), 140. Rest. 70-110.

Son et lumière : spectacle at the castle (summer).

Event : Jun, *Festival des Fêtes Romantiques de Nohant* (concerts).

SAINT-AMAND-MONTROND

Bourges 44, Montluçon 49, Paris 271
B2 ♥ ⊠ 18200

ⓘ pl. de la République, ☎ 48.96.16.86.

SNCF ☎ 48.96.04.50.

Hotels :

★★***Poste,*** 9, rue de la Poste, ☎ 48.96.27.14. Visa. 24 rm Ⓟ ☘ closed 18 Nov to end-Dec and Mon (ex nat hols), 165. Rest. ♦ 60-130.

★***Croix d'Or*** (L.F.), 18, rue du 14-Juillet, ☎ 48.96.09.41. Visa. 17 rm ✂ 150. Rest. closed Fri eve low season, 50-125.

Orval, 5 km N :

★***Pont du Cher,*** 2, av. de la Gare, ☎ 48.96.00.51. 13 rm ☼ Ⓟ closed 21 Oct-21 Nov, Mon and Sun eve, 110. Rest. ♦♦ ♿ Spec : *saumon à l'oseille, coquelet au sang,* 60-110.

Ainay-le-Vieil, 11 km SE :

★***Crémaillère*** (L.F.), pl. de l'Église, ☎ 48.96.02.95. 8 rm Ⓟ ✂ ♿ closed 15 Jan-15 Feb and Fri, 100. Rest. 80-130.

Youth hostel : *Foyer des Jeunes Travailleurs,* 38, rue de la Brasserie, ☎ 48.96.07.70.

⛺ ★★Municipal *de la Roche* (100 pl.), ☎ 48.96.09.36.

Restaurant :

♦♦ ***Bœuf Couronné,*** 86, rue Juranville, ☎ 48.96.42.72. Ⓟ ♿ closed Tue noon and Wed, 45-100.

Event : *wine fair,* 3rd week-end in Mar.

Bicycle hire : M. Legras, 51, av. Jean-Jaurès, ☎ 48.96.01.70.

SAINT-BONNET-TRONÇAIS

Montluçon 43, Moulins 58, Paris 283
B2 ⊠ 03360

Hotel :
★★***Le Tronçais*** (L.F.), ☎ 70.06.11.95. 12 rm 🅿 closed Dec-Feb, Sun eve and Mon (low season), 180. Rest. ♦ ♿ closed Mon. 80-130.

⛺ ★★★*Champ Fossé* (120 pl.), ☎ 70.06.11.30.

Bicycle hire : *Association du Pays de Tronçais,* ☎ 70.67.56.89. Rural centre *(foyer rural),* ☎ 70.06.11.15.

SAINT-POURÇAIN-SUR-SIOULE

Moulins 31, Clermont-Ferrand 65, Paris 325
C3 ⊠ 03500

ℹ bd Ledru-Rollin, ☎ 70.45.32.73 (high season).

SNCF ☎ 70.45.31.20.

Hotels :
★★***Les Deux Ponts*** (France-Accueil, L.F.), îlot de Tivoli, ☎ 70.45.41.14. AE, DC, Euro, Visa. 27 rm 🅿 closed 15 Nov-20 Dec and 1-15 Mar. Alongside the river, 170. Rest. ♦ closed Sun eve and Mon (ex nat hols from 1 Oct to 1 Jun), 50-180.
★★***Chêne Vert*** (L.F.), 35, bd Ledru-Rollin, ☎ 70.45.40.65. AE, DC, Euro, Visa. 35 rm 🅿 closed 5 Jan-7 Feb, 1-10 Oct, 170. Rest. ♦ ♿ closed Tue and Wed noon (ex Jul-Aug). Classic dishes : *coussinet de saumon aux crustacés, éventail d'agneau au jus à la purée d'échalote ;* good wines (saint-pourçain), 70-180.
★***Globe,*** 11, rue M.-Berthelot, ☎ 70.45.30.42. 15 rm 🅿 ♿ closed mid-Oct to mid-Nov and Mon (Oct-Jun), 100. Rest. 80-130.

⛺ ★★★*Île de la Ronde* (50 pl.), ☎ 70.45.45.43 ; *la Moutte* (33 pl.), ☎ 70.45.91.94.

Event : end Aug : *wine fête.*

Bicycle hire : M. Marchant, Bayet, ☎ 70.45.31.62.

SANCERRE

Bourges 46, Nevers 50, Paris 204
B1 ⊠ 18300

ℹ mairie, ☎ 48.54.00.26.

Hotels :
★★***Rempart*** (L.F.), rempart des Dames, ☎ 48.54.10.18. AE, DC, Visa. 12 rm 125. Rest. ♦ ♿ 60-130.
★★***Panoramic,*** rempart des Augustins, ☎ 48.54.22.44. AE. 57 rm ♿ 215.
● ★***Saint-Martin,*** ☎ 48.54.28.03. 23 rm 100. Rest. ♦ 80-130.

Saint-Satur, 4 km NE :
L'Étoile, 2, quai de Loire, ☎ 48.54.12.15. 11 rm 🅿 closed 15 Nov-1 Mar, Wed, 140. Rest. ♦♦ ♿ Good cooking of the Sancerre region ; the best Sancerre and Pouilly wines of the region, 80-185.
★***Le Laurier,*** 29, rue du Commerce, near the pl. du Marché, ☎ 48.54.17.20. Visa. 10 rm 🅿 closed Sun eve and Mon low season, 130. Rest. ● ♦♦ Very good Verdigny sancerre red wine. Spec : *jambonnette de lapin safranée aux pâtes fraîches, quenelle de brochet au coulis d'écrevisses,* 50-150.
Saint-Thibault, 5 km NE on the D955 and D4 :
L'Auberge, 37, rue Jacques-Combes, ☎ 48.54.13.79. AE, DC, Visa. 🅿 6 rm. closed 11 Nov-10 Dec, 15 days in Mar, Mon eve and Tue. Rest. ♦♦ ♿ Spec : *ficelle Auberge, coq au vin.* Excellent red Sancerre wine from Verdigny, 50-90.

Restaurants :
♦ ***Auberge Alphonse Mellot,*** 16, pl. de la Halle, ☎ 48.54.20.53. Visa. ♿ closed Jan and Wed. Spec : omlets, hams and goat cheese. Pleasant wines. 80-130.
Chavignol, 3 km SW :
♦ ***La Treille,*** ☎ 48.54.12.17. Visa. closed Jan-Feb, Tue eve and Wed (ex Jul-Aug). Simple dishes in the goat cheese region, 50-80.
Saint-Thibault, 5 km NE on the D955 and D4 :
♦ ***Saint-Roch,*** quai de Loire, ☎ 48.54.01.79. Visa. closed 15 Dec-1 Mar and Mon. Barge restaurant, 120-210.

Events : 1st week-end in May : *goat-cheese fête.* 1st week-end in Jun : *wine fair* (presentation of Sancerre wines). Last Sun in Jul, in Verdigny : *grape festival.* 1st Sun in Aug, in Bué : *wizards' fair.* Last week-end in Aug : consecrated to the wines of France.

Recommended : honey produce : *J.-P. Senée,* farmer, av. de Verdun, ☎ 48.54.09.00. Handicrafts : *la Poterie de Sancerre,* 3, pl. de la Halle, ☎ 48.54.10.34.

SANCOINS

Nevers 39, Bourges 51, Paris 265
B2 ⊠ 18600

Hotels :
● ★★★***Donjon de Jouy*** (Châteaux-hôtels), 4 km SW on the D41, ☎ 48.74.56.88. 38 rm 🅿 260. Rest. ♦♦ Spec : *pavé de charolais aux champignons, saumon à la crème,* 120-210.
★★***Parc,*** 8, rue M.-Audoux, ☎ 48.74.56.60. 12 rm 180.

SOUVIGNY

Moulins 12, Montluçon 55, Paris 306
C2 ⊠ 03210

SNCF ☎ 70.43.61.47.

Hotels :
★***Poste*** (L.F.), 20, rue de la Verrerie, ☎ 70.43.61.52. 15 rm 🅿 closed Wed (low season), 180.
Auberge des Tilleuls, pl. Saint-Eloi, ☎ 70.43.60.70. 3 rm. closed 1-15 Oct, 1-15 Feb, Mon eve and Tue, 140. Rest. ♦ 80-130.

VALENÇAY

Châteauroux 43, Blois 55, Paris 235
A1 ⊠ 36600

ℹ rte de Blois, ☎ 54.00.04.42 (high season).

SNCF ☎ 54.00.12.34.

Hotels :
● ★★★★***Espagne*** (Relais et châteaux), 9, rue du Château, ☎ 54.00.00.02. Tx 751675. AE, Euro, Visa. 18 rm 🅿 ♿ closed 15 Nov-15 Mar. A delightful old residence with a gloriously calm, flower-filled inner courtyard-terrace, 700. Rest. ♦♦♦ Impeccable service and superb fare : *terrine aux cinq légumes, coquelet à la crème de ciboulette, noisettes d'agneau à l'estragon,* 160-200.
★★***Lion d'Or*** (L.F.), ☎ 54.00.00.87. AE, DC, Visa. 15 rm 🅿 160. Rest. ♦ ♿ closed 1 Jan-15 Feb, Mon, 50-135.

Rooms at the farm : *la Petite Vernelle,* ☎ 54.00.17.73. Vineyards, produce for sale.

Restaurant :
♦ ***Chêne Vert,*** 55, rte Nationale, ☎ 54.00.06.54. closed 5-25 Jun, 5 Dec-15 Jan, Sun eve and Sat (low season). Friendly service ; good game dishes with sauces during hunting season, 40-115.

Son et lumière : at the castle (Jul and Aug).

Recommended : enamelled stoneware, *Monique Legrand,* Launay, on the D13, D25 and D35.

VARENNES-SUR-ALLIER

Moulins 30, Clermont-Ferrand 73, Paris 324
11 km E of Saint-Pourçain, C3 ⊠ 03150

SNCF ☎ 70.45.05.04.

Hotels :
★★***Nouvel Hôtel*** (L.F.), 20, av. de la Gare, ☎ 70.45.00.06. Visa. 26 rm P 150. Rest. ♦ closed Wed, 50-130.

Les Cailloux, 2 km SE on the N7 :
★★***Auberge de l'Orisse*** (L.F.), ☎ 70.45.05.60. 23 rm P closed 1 Jan-1 Feb, 21-29 Oct. Comfortable residence in a park setting, 200. Rest. ♦♦ closed Sun eve and Mon noon (low season). Inventive cooking : *cœur de filet aux huîtres, carré d'agneau au miel,* 120-210.

Saint-Loup, 5.5 km on the N7 :
★★***Route Bleue*** (F.A., L.F.), ☎ 70.45.07.73. AE, DC, Euro, Visa. 22 rm P closed 2 Nov-15 Mar. Comfortable hotel, 150. Rest. ♦♦ 80-130.

⛺ ★★★★*Château de Chazeuil* (60 pl.), ☎ 70.45.00.10 ; ★★★*les Plans d'Eau* (83 pl.), ☎ 70.45.01.55.

Restaurant :
Saint-Loup, 5.5 km N on the N7 :
♦♦ ***La Locaterie,*** ☎ 70.45.13.90. P closed 29 Nov-30 Dec, Tue eve and Wed. Excellent food, 95-270.

VICHY

Moulins 57, Clermont-Ferrand 59, Paris 351
C3 (Bellerive-sur-Allier) ⊠ 03200

(Mar-Dec), ☎ 70.98.95.37.

i 19, rue du Parc (A3), ☎ 70.98.71.94.

✈ Vichy/Charmeil, 6 km N, ☎ 70.32.34.09.

SNCF (C2), ☎ 70.98.41.06.

pl. C.-de-Gaulle (B3), ☎ 70.98.41.33.

Car-hire : *Budget* train + auto, 6, rue de Paris, ☎ 70.98.41.06 ; at the station, ☎ 70.98.47.19.

Hotels :
Spa centre :
★★★★***Aletti Thermal Palace,*** 3, pl. Aletti (near the casino, A3), ☎ 70.31.78.77. DC, Euro. 57 rm closed 1 Oct-15 May. The only truly period-style palace in Vichy ; excellent service ; bridge club, 420.
★★★★***Pavillon Sévigné,*** 10, pl. Sévigné (A4), ☎ 70.32.16.22. Tx 990393. AE, DC, Euro, Visa. 40 rm 600. Rest. ♦♦♦ closed Mon and Sun eve (low season only), 145-240.
★★★***Paix,*** 13, rue du Parc (A3), ☎ 70.98.20.56. Visa. 80 rm closed 30 Sep-2 May, 260. Rest. ♦♦ 120-210.
★★★***Régina,*** 4, av. Thermale (A2), ☎ 70.98.20.95. Visa. 90 rm closed Oct-2 May, 320. Rest. ♦ 100-140.
★★***Cloche d'Argent,*** 2, rue d'Angleterre (A3), ☎ 70.92.22.88. 50 rm closed 15 Oct-15 May, 180. Rest. ♦ 80-130.

Old town and south spa area :
★★★***Ermitage du Pont-Neuf,*** 5, sq. Albert-Ier (A4), ☎ 70.32.09.22. 65 rm P closed 30 Sep-5 May, 260. Rest. ♦ 120-210.

Town centre :
★★***Carnot*** (L.F.), 24, bd Carnot (B3), ☎ 70.98.36.98. 28 rm Family-run hotel, 170. Rest. 75-130.
★★***Gallia,*** 12, av. Doumer (B3), ☎ 70.31.86.66. AE, Visa. 72 rm closed 10 Nov-1 Mar, 180. Rest. 75-125.

Bellerive-sur-Allier, 2 km SW, left bank :
★★★***Marcotel,*** rue de la Grange-aux-Grains, ☎ 70.32.34.00. Tx 990665. AE, DC, Visa. P closed 15-29 Dec, 420. Rest. ♦ closed Sun eve (low season) and Mon noon, 120-210.
★★★***Le Bellerive,*** rte d'Hauterive, ☎ 70.32.02.55. 122 rm P Alongside the Allier River, 180.
★★***Chez Mémère,*** chemin de Halage, ☎ 70.32.35.22. 10 rm P closed 10 Sep-10 May. On the banks of the Allier River, 165. Rest. ♦♦ closed every day noon ex Sun. Carefully prepared dishes, 120-160.
★★***Résidence,*** rue de la Grange-aux-Grains, ☎ 70.32.37.11. 114 rm P 175.

Abrest, 4 km S on the D906 :
★***La Colombière*** (L.F.), rte de Thiers, ☎ 70.98.69.15. DC, Visa. 4 rm P closed 15 Jan-15 Feb, Sun eve and Mon, 175. Terraced garden. Rest. ♦ 70-125.

Youth hostel : 19, rue du Stade, ☎ 70.32.25.14.

Restaurants :
● ♦♦♦ ***Violon d'Ingres,*** 5, rue du Casino, ☎ 70.98.97.70. closed 2 Jan-15 Feb. Tue and Wed noon (low season). A delightful restaurant for health-cure "escapees" from the spa. Jacques Muller also offers lighter fare for delicate constitutions. Spec : *salade de pigeon au foie gras, noisette d'agneau à la crème d'ail,* 220-310.
♦♦ ***Grillade Strauss,*** 5, pl. J.-Aletti (A3), near the casino, ☎ 70.98.56.74. closed Mon (low season), 31 Dec-31 Jan. In the nice warm atmosphere of this villa where memories of Napoleon III and of G. Hilmer, the former chief, are still alive : *œuf en meurette, tripes à la mode de Rouen,* good grilled meat for serious customers, 120-260.
♦♦ ***Rotonde du Lac,*** bd Mal-de-Lattre-de-Tassigny, at the yacht-club, ☎ 70.98.72.46. AE, DC, Euro, Visa. P closed Feb and Mar, 150-300.
♦♦ ***Rossini,*** 6, bd du Sichon, ☎ 70.98.54.66. Euro, Visa. P closed Mon. Rich fare, 50-135.

Rhue, 03300 Creuzier-Le-Vieux, 5 km N on the N209 :
♦ ***La Fontaine,*** ☎ 70.31.37.45. AE, DC, Euro, Visa. P closed 22 Dec-8 Feb, Tue eve and Wed. Country house with fireplace. Good, simple dishes at reasonable prices, 50-90.
Charmeil, 8 km N :
♦ ***La Musarde,*** ☎ 70.32.06.76. P closed 24 June-2 Jul, 25 Nov-5 Dec, and Mon. Piastra family's good cooking : *andouillette, saucisson chaud de grenouilles,* 120-210.

Bicycle hire : M. Marchand, 13-15, allée Mesdames, ☎ 70.31.87.10. *Établissements Brière,* 48, bd Gambetta, ☎ 70.31.52.86. M. Gayet, 8, rue Source-de-l'Hôpital, ☎ 70.32.12.37.

VIERZON

Châteauroux 58, Orléans 79, Paris 210
B1 ✉ 18100

ⓘ pl. Gabriel-Péri, ☎ 48.75.20.03.

SNCF ☎ 48.75.08.61.

Car-hire : *Budget* train + auto, at the station, ☎ 48.75.06.14.

Hotels :
● ★★★***Sologne,*** rte de Châteauroux, 2 km SW, ☎ 48.75.15.20. 24 rm Ⓟ ♨ 200.
★★★***Continental,*** 104 *bis,* av. E.-Vaillant, ☎ 48.75.35.22. DC, Visa. 36 rm Ⓟ ♿ 240. Rest. closed Aug, Sat eve and Sun. Snack, eves only, 80-130.
★★***Terminus et Bordeaux,*** pl. de la Gare, ☎ 48.75.00.46. Visa. 42 rm Ⓟ 130.

Saint-Hilaire-de-Court, 7 km SW on the N20 :
★★★***Château de la Beuvrière*** (Châteaux-hôtels), ☎ 48.75.08.14, 48.75.14.63. AE, DC, Visa. 5 rm Ⓟ ♨ closed Jan and Feb. Private residence which receives guests, 240. Rest. ♦♦ 100-200.

Youth hostel, pl. de la République, ☎ 48.75.30.62.

Ⓐ ★★*Bellon-Plage* (80 pl.), ☎ 48.75.49.10 ; ★★*le Crot,* Saint-Hilaire-de-Court (35 pl.), ☎ 48.75.10.54.

Restaurant :
♦♦♦ ***Mataffan,*** 7, rue Porte-aux-Bœufs, ☎ 48.75.00.63. Ⓟ ♨ closed Aug, Sun eve and Mon. Spec : *pot-au-feu au confit de canard, coq au sang.* Good local wines, 120-210.

Event : early Sep : *fair-exhibition,* pl. de la Libération.

Bicycle hire : *Clerice-Vierzon 2-Roues,* 8, rue Voltaire, ☎ 48.75.30.30.

The Bordelais and Landes Regions

A triangular-shaped region with a wide stretch of coast as its hypotenuse, infinite beaches of fine sand and a hinterland containing the largest forest in France, dotted with large, tranquil lakes fringed with pinetrees. Along the valleys of the Gironde, the Garonne and the Dordogne lie great stretches of vineyards, where almost half of France's best wines are produced. We could divide the region in two : to the east is Entre-Deux-Mers — "between two seas" — named for the great ocean tides which swell the Garonne and the Dordogne; the fertile cornfields and pastureland of Bazardais, the forests of Albret, and the farmlands of Marsan and Chalosse with their hot springs. To the west, the ocean and wine-growing Médoc, with its industry and summer tourism; the Arcachon basin, famous for its oysters; Buch and Born — army, petrochemicals and tourism, and the resorts along the southernmost part of the coast, which live on fresh air and holiday-makers.

The city of Bordeaux is both an ocean and river port, with installations stretching along one hundred kilometres — oil tankers, cargo ships, shipyards and barges all have their appointed places. The city also boasts magnificent 18th-century administrative and private buildings, beautiful churches and cathedrals and many fine museums, including the Centre Jean Moulin, a Resistance museum and centre of documentation on the Second World War.

Bordeaux wines grow in an area of 1 000 square kilometres, producing 500 million bottles a year, and including the most famous vintages in the world : Château-Lafite-Rothschild, Château-Latour, Château Margaux, Château-Mouton-Rothschild, Château-Haut-Brion and Château Yquem. Médoc is a country of châteaux, ranging from simple farm buildings to genuine castles and grandiose mansions built by the *chartrons,* merchants of English descent who still dominate the Bordeaux wine-trade. And to accompany the wine there is the excellent cooking of the region : eels and oysters, lamb from the salty meadows of Pauillac, goose — and duck — liver *pâtés* and rich *confit* from the Landes region and the excellent, yellow, corn-fed poultry for which the region is famous.

Sightseeing

Facts and figures

Area : *The Gironde (10 626 km²) and the Landes (9 364 km²) are the two largest French departments, together forming a region of 20 090 km².*
Population : *1 425 000; 1 127 000 in the Gironde, 297 500 in the Landes.*
Climate : *Mild with a warm, early spring. In this season, the Côte d'Argent (Silver Coast) fully deserves its name when a barely perceptible haze softens contours and colours the seascape. Beautiful days are frequent in autumn, the time of the grape-harvest. Winter, mild on the coast, is hardly more severe inland.*
Administration : *The Gironde and the Landes belong to the Aquitaine region.* ***Gironde*** *Department, prefecture : Bordeaux;* ***Landes*** *Department, prefecture : Mont-de-Marsan.*

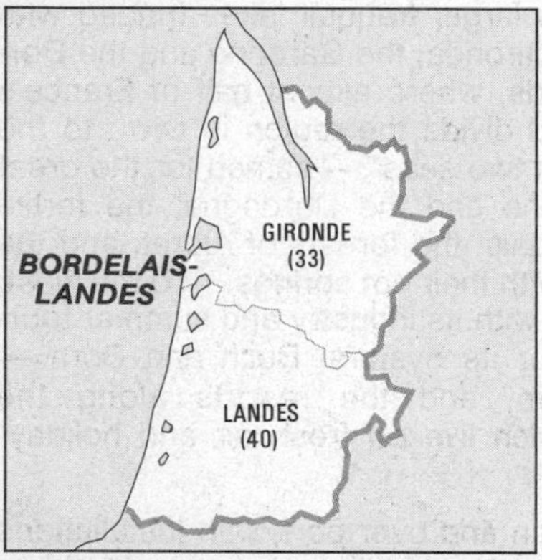

Don't miss

★★★ : *Bordeaux (B2), Saint-Emilion (B2), The Bazas Region (B2).*
★★ : *Courant d'Huchet (A3), Entre-Deux-Mers Region (B2), Garonne Valley (B2), the Grandes Landes Region (A-B3), the Marensin Region (A3), the Médoc Region (A1), Saint-Macaire (B2), Sabres (A3), the Sauternais Region (B2).*

■ ARCACHON Basin★

▶ From Arcachon to Cap Ferret *(approx 70 km, half day)*

A2 *(see map 4, Landes coast)*

The Arcachon Basin is the only wrinkle in an otherwise straight coastline. It is connected to the ocean by a narrow channel partially obstructed by sand but never entirely blocked, unlike other adjacent basins that have become inland lakes.

▶ **Arcachon★** ® : marine and forest resort, villas; Thiers jetty at the centre of the town's seafront offers views of the Ile aux Oiseaux (an island bird sanctuary) and the entire sea-basin to the N; **Aquarium Museum** *(daily, Easter to 1 Nov.)* ▶ 9 km S beyond **Pyla-sur-Mer** ® is the **Pilat Dune,** rising to a height of about 115 m; shining white sand constantly transformed by the wind. The Dune has been growing for over 100 years. ▶ **La Teste** ® : oyster farming and fish reservoirs by the landing stage. **La Hume★** *(3 km NE) :* another small oyster harbour, zoological park and village craftwork. ▶ **Gujan-Mestras** ® : the principal oyster-breeding centre in the basin, a port of tile-roofed cabins; a picturesque place, with channels full of *pinnaces* (the local type of small fishing vessel) and oyster boats. ▶ **Le Teich :** small town near the Eyre delta; **ornithology reserve,** local and migrating species *(daily visits in season).* ▶ **Facture :** large pinewood conversion factory. The route continues through **Audenge, Taussat-les-Bains, Andernos-les-Bains** ®, the Arcachon Basin's number two resort, and finally **Arès.** At **Lège,** a small road goes through the pines to the wild **Grand-Crohot beach** (bathing sometimes dangerous). Between Lège and Cap-Ferret, several oyster ports; then, at **Cap Ferret★** ®, luxurious villas scattered among the pines; a tall lighthouse (52 m high, 258 steps) marks the entrance of the basin (from the top, magnificent view). Farther on from Lège, itinerary continues along the **Landes coast** (→) to Grave Point. □

■ The BAZAS Region★★

▶ Round trip from La Réole to Roaillan *(approx 60 km, half day)*

B2 *(see map 2)*

Rolling countryside, in which maize production is gradually encroaching on vineyards. Agricultural enclave bordered to the S and W by the Landes Forest.

▶ From **La Réole (Garonne valley** →) to **Auros** *(15 km SW),* gateway to the Bazadais (Bazas region). 4 km NW, remains of 14thC Cistercian **Abbey of Le Rivet.** ▶ The capital of the Bazadais, **Bazas** ® : on high ground overlooking the small and narrow valley of the Beuve. Above the russet rooftops soars the elegant nave of the **cathedral of St. Jean★,** facing a broad arcaded square. This cathedral is one of the most beautiful Gothic edifices of Aquitaine; built in 1233, partially remodelled in the 16thC and 17thC; beautiful **façade★,** three doorways (13thC) with mediaeval statuary. Christ in the central doorway, flanked by the Virgin Mary (right doorway) and St. Peter (left doorway); fine figured arches. Although rebuilt after the Huguenot damage, the **nave** retains its original Gothic character; in the choir, Louis XV altar in polychrome marble. To the right of the cathedral, pleasant terraced **garden** overlooking the

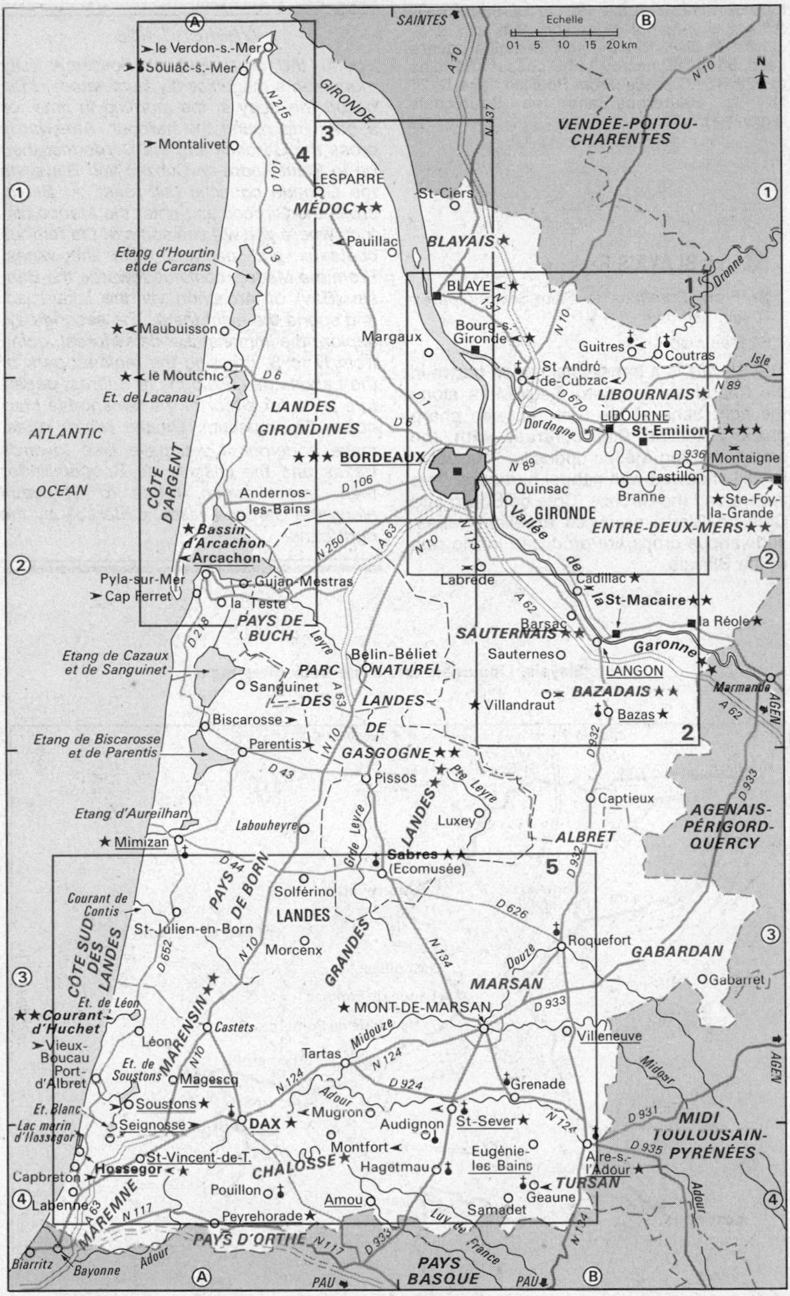

Beuve valley. Nearby, **Porte Gisquet** (gateway), with two 15thC towers; ancient ramparts. ▶ **Beaulac :** take the road out towards Préchac. To the right, small road to **fortified mill** (15thC) at Cossarieu, at the entry to the **Ciron gorges,** full of greenery, difficult access. ▶ **Préchac** has an original Romanesque church, remodelled 15thC (apse★, capitals). ▶ **Uzeste** *(6 km N) :* former Gothic **collegiate church**; apse, shrine of Pope Clement V (who was born in this region); in the *chevet* chapel, beautiful Virgin of the same period. ▶ **Villandraut★ :** birthplace of Pope Clement, who built the town's imposing château, typical of 14thC lowland fortifications *(daily).* **Roaillan :** Romanesque church. Nearby, **Roquetaillade château★** built in early 14thC by Cardinal de la Mothe (nephew of Clement V); interior restored and decorated by Viollet-le-Duc in the 19thC *(Jul.-Sept., daily 9:30-12 & 2-7; out of season, Sun. pm, 2-6; closed 15 Dec.-15 Jan.)* very beautiful square keep, 35 m tall; nearby 14thC chapel and ruins of 12th-13thC castle. From Roaïllan, take D125 NW to Sauternes and the Sauternais region (→). □

■ The **BLAYAIS** Region★

▶ From Bordeaux to Saint-Savin *(approx 70 km, half-day)*

B1 *(see map 1)*

The Blayais is a transitional region between the Charentes and Entre-Deux-Mers along the right bank of the Gironde, with sharp chalk outcrops that contrast with the smooth, rolling Médoc opposite. The coast is well endowed with natural harbours. This zone along the Gironde (Côte de Bourg and Côte de Blaye) produces excellent wines, and various crops are produced in the rest of the Blayais.

Weekend tips

Spend the first night at Bordeaux (city monuments magnificently illuminated); then be on the quay in the morning in time for a boat trip round the harbour. Afterwards cross the Garonne and the Dordogne, then on to Saint-André-de-Cubzac and Blaye via the Gironde corniche (hill road). At Blaye, cross the Gironde and enter the Médoc district, where you will see some of the famous châteaux and perhaps taste the wines. From the Médoc, continue towards the Bassin (Bay) of Arcachon via the lake road, and spend the night there. The second day, explore the immense Landaise forest, going from N to S, crossing the regional park of the Landes de Gascogne to Sabres, departure point for a tour of the remarkable Mar-quèze Eco-museum. *On the return route, make a detour if you have time towards Bazas and the château de Roquetaillade; then, from Langon, return to Bordeaux along the Garonne valley, preferably by the right bank.*

1. Blayais, Libournais and Entre-Deux-Mers region

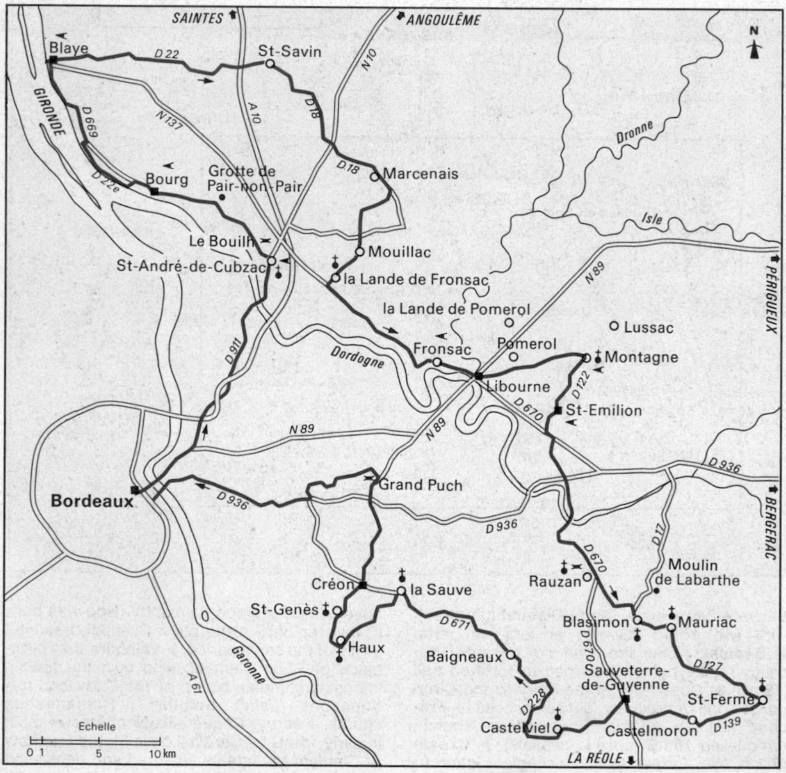

▶ From **Bordeaux** (→) along the right bank to the Dordogne via the Cubzac viaduct, built by Eiffel in 1882. ▶ **St. André-de-Cubzac :** church with Romanesque apse, raised and fortified in the 15thC. **Château de Bouilh,** 2 km N in the heart of the wine country : built in 1787 but not finished, by Victor Louis, architect of the Grand Theatre of Bordeaux *(Thu., Sat., Sun. pm May-Sep.);* wine-tasting room and cellar *(open Mon.-Fri.).* ▶ **Saint-Gervais :** fortified Romanesque church. ▶ **Prignac :** to the right, road to the **Pair-non-Pair grotto** in a limestone slope of the Moron valley, which later joins the Dordogne; inside, paintings from the Aurignacian period. ▶ **Bourg★ :** suspended on the edge of a limestone cliff, this fortified city possesses remains of a 13thC enclosure and several old houses. In the upper city, the *District* terrace offers a superb view of the Gironde. To the W, the **Citadelle château,** 17thC; former residence of the Archbishops of Bordeaux, built over a maze of galleries now used as cellars. On the approach to the hill, the **Gironde corniche** (hill road) provides splendid views of the river; beyond Bayon, the route goes past cliffs riddled with galleries and cave dwellings. **Blaye★★** ® : because of its strategic position on the Gironde, long an active harbour. Impressive fortifications : **citadel** with streets, squares and gardens that have remained unchanged for centuries; convent and cloister (1610); remains of old fortified castle, birthplace of the troubadour Jaufré Rudel; ancient ruins of the St. Romain basilica; according to tradition, the crypt contains the body of the Chevalier Roland, killed fighting the Moors at the legendary battle of Ronceval. The ancient house of the Master-at-Arms, now the Blayais Museum of Art and History *(daily).* ▶ **Saint-Christoly-de-Blaye :** Romanesque church. ▶ **Saint-Savin :** remains of Saujan château. ▶ From Saint-Savin, D18 turns SW towards the **Libournais** region. □

Vineyards of Bordeaux

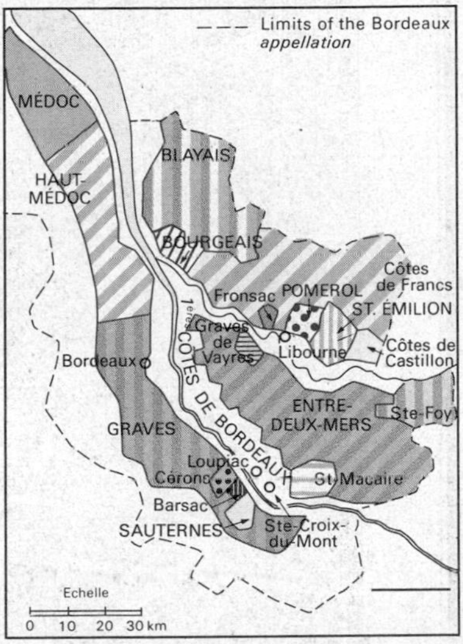

■ BORDEAUX★★★

B2 / ® / pop. 208 200 (Greater Bordeaux pop. 620 000) (Gironde)

See plan on following pages

Bordeaux is the great tidal port of the Gironde river. Thanks to innovative town planning imposed by the *Intendants Royaux* (administrators), the city's 18thC architecture remains an impressive whole. The quays fronting the river form a broad crescent, hence the nickname *port de la lune* (moon port) and the coat of arms of Bordeaux, a silver crescent and blue waves.

▶ The town's unique 18thC character is exemplified by the Place de la Comédie (Comedy Square) at its centre and the **Grand Theatre★** (C2-3), built between 1773 and 1780 by Victor Louis. To the S, the Rue Ste. Catherine, commercial centre of Bordeaux, links the Place de la Comédie with the **Porte d'Aquitaine** (1755); to the NW stretch the Allées de Tourny, 200 ft. wide. ▶ The **Quinconces Esplanade** (C2) built 1818-28 on the site of the château Trompette, forms a semicircle as far as the 130 ft high **Girondins monument** (1895), topped by its statue of Liberty. Also, immense statues of Montaigne and Montesquieu and, on the quayside, columns (1829) with allegorical figures representing Commerce and Navigation. Nearby, the **public gardens** (B-C1), 25 acres laid out by Tourny in 1746-56, a favourite promenade for the people of Bordeaux. Contains

Bordeaux wines

The Bordelais is the world's largest group of vineyards producing fine wines, with an output of more than 100 million gallons per year. That means about 500 million bottles, from an area covering something like 250 000 acres. Unlike Burgundy, Bordeaux has no system of classification by quality, only a set of local classifications that have no common standard. Of these, the most famous is the classification of the Médoc châteaux, organised in 1855 during the reign of Napoleon III by the Bordeaux Chamber of Commerce, and based on the prices the wines had brought during the previous 100 years. Thus, wines were classified as First (premier), *second, third, fourth or fifth growths* (crus). *To these were added* Crus Exceptionels, Crus Bourgeois Supérieurs, Crus Bourgeois *and later* Crus Artisans *and* Crus Paysans. *The old list still holds good today. The original four first growth châteaux (Lafite-Rothschild, Latour, Margaux and Haut-Brion) were joined in 1973 by château Mouton-Rothschild. Only one Sauternes has a premier cru (first growth) title :* Château Yquem. *Most of the other* crus classés *(classified growths) are concentrated in the communes of Saint-Estèphe, Pauillac, Saint-Julien and Margaux, all on the deep gravelly soil of the Gironde's south bank. To these should be added this century's classifications of the Graves, Saint-Emilion and Pomerol areas, each with its own first and second growths.*

the **Museum of Natural History** *(pm daily closed Tue.).* ▶ Rue Ferrère (C1), the former Lainé warehouses now contain the CAPC **Contemporary Art Museum** *(11-7, closed Mon.)* which is enhanced by remarkable 19thC architecture. ▶ The **Gallien Palace** (B2) : 3rdC Roman amphitheatre, the only remains of ancient Burdigala, as the Romans called the city; farther on, **St. Seurin church★,** original edifice of the 12th-15thC, one of the city's oldest sanctuaries. A modern façade hides the 12thC porch; crypt from the 11thC, sarcophagi

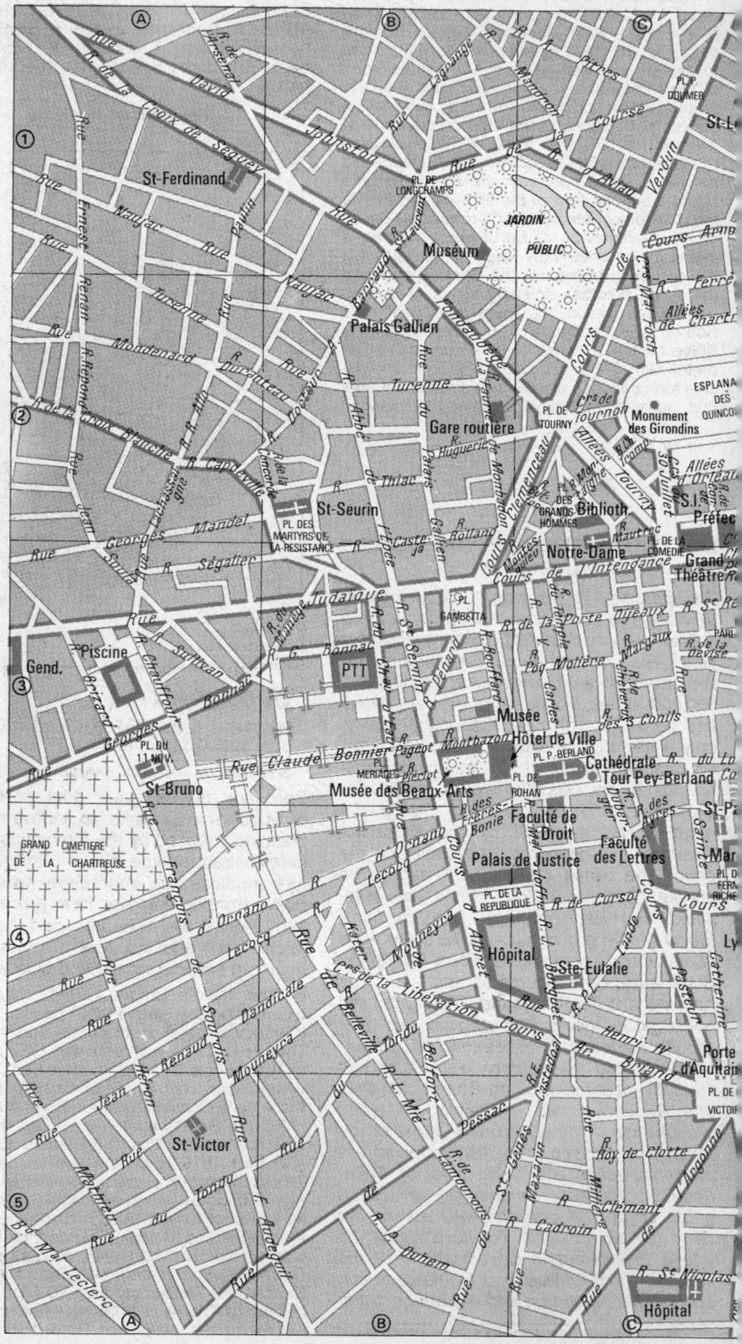

and Merovingian remains. ▶ **Place Gambetta** (B3), the city's loveliest square, has a pleasant garden surrounded by Louis XV houses. ▶ Elegant stores stretch along the **Cours de l'Intendance,** smart shopping precinct. (The closest equivalent to *Cours* in English is mall.) To the left of Rue Martignac is the **church of Notre-Dame** (C2-3), 17thC ; former Dominican chapel, fine example of the "Jesuit" style (French Baroque). ▶ On Place Pey-Berland (C3) is the **Jean Moulin Centre :** Museum of the Resistance coupled with a documentation centre on WWII

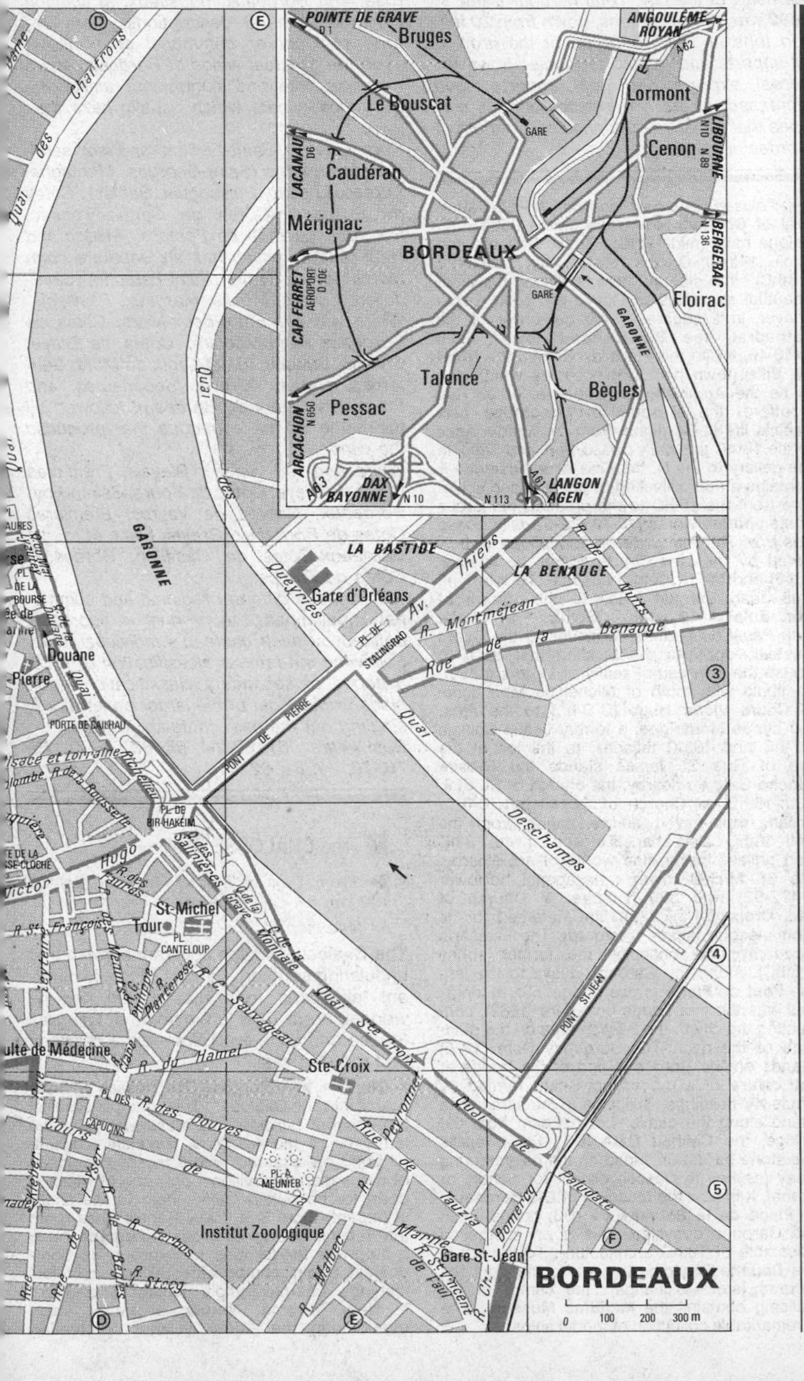

The harbours of Bordeaux

Bordeaux is a port for both ocean and river; its installations cover approximately 100 km from the port of Verdon at the mouth of the Gironde to the barge-wharves situated in the heart of the city. Total harbour traffic in 1982 was 17 million tons, down from 20 million tons in 1981, because of the drop in oil imports and related products; however, cereal exports and coal imports have increased, as have the miscellaneous cargoes that constitute the principal strength of Bordeaux shipping.

(pm; closed Sat., Sun. and nat. hols.). **Cathedral of St. André★★ :** two spires 250ft. tall; unique nave (mid-12thC); Gothic transept and choir (14thC). On the N side, the royal door (13thC) : the statuary here is among the most beautiful examples of Gothic art. Next to the *chevet,* in a square, is the bell-tower of the cathedral, the **Pey-Berland tower,** built 1440-46. ▶ On the Place de Rohan, the **Hôtel de Ville** (town hall; B3) occupies what used to be the Archbishop's residence. At 39 Rue Bouffard, the **Museum of Decorative Arts** depicts life in Bordeaux from the Middle Ages to the 18thC *(pm daily closed Sun. and Tue.).* In the gallery to the N, the **Fine Arts Museum★★** contains a rich collection of painting and sculpture from the 15thC to the present; numerous contemporary works *(10-12 & 2-6; daily closed Tue.).* ▶ The **Place de la République** is bordered by the Law Courts (Palais de Justice, 1846) and the St. André hospital. To the right, Rue Jean Burguet leads to the **church of Ste. Eulalie,** 12th-16thC Gothic. From here, Rue Paul-Louis-Lande continues to the Cours Pasteur, opposite the building that used to house the Bordeaux Faculty of Letters (1886); vestibule with tomb of Michel de Montaigne. ▶ **Cours Victor Hugo** (C-D4) : to the right, the **Lycée Montaigne,** a former Jesuit College (17thC and 19thC façade); to the left at the top of Rue St James stands the **Grosse Cloche Gate★ :** nearby, the **church of St. Eloi,** 13th-15thC. ▶ **Church of St. Michel** (D4), a broad, triple-naved edifice dating from the 14th-16thC : aisle chapels closed off with 18thC iron grilles; inside, fine works of art. Nearby, the **St. Michel tower :** hexagonal belltower (1472-92) with 330 ft spire. ▶ **Church of Ste. Croix** (E4-5), 12th-13thC : famed for its Romanesque façade (restored). The Fine Arts Academy now occupies the former abbey (18thC). Along the Garonne quays to the left, the **Pont de Pierre** (stone bridge, 501 m long); this was the first bridge built here (1882), connecting the city to the *bastide* area on the other side of the river. The Burgundy Gate (1775) stands on the Bordeaux end of the bridge at the centre of a graceful crescent formed by Louis XV buildings. Buildings in the same style stand along the quays. Downstream from the bridge, the **Cailhau Gate** (D3; 1495) recalls the stone ballast unloaded on the neighbouring quay (*cailhau* is Gascon dialect for pebble or stone). It is now the **Museum of Old Bordeaux.** ▶ **Place de la Bourse★★★** (D3) opens on to the Garonne quayside. This is an interesting ensemble of 18thC architecture. To the left is the **Douane** (customs house), to the right the **Bourse** (stock-exchange); the centre of the building contains the **Maritime Museum,** with a remarkable collection of model ships. □

Appellations

There are seven appellations : *Bordeaux, Bordeaux clairet (hence the English claret), Bordeaux rosé, Bordeaux supérieur, Bordeaux supérieur clairet, Bordeaux supérieur rosé, and Bordeaux mousseux. In addition to these general descriptions, there are forty regional or communal appellations; even the greatest wines of Bordeaux share these* appellations contrôlées, *unlike the Burgundy wines, which usually have their own.*

Red wines : Saint-Émilion and six satellite appellations *(Saint-Georges, Montagne, Parsac, Lussac, Puisseguin, Sables); Côtes de Fronsac, Côtes de Canon-Fronsac, Pomerol, Lalande de Pomerol, Médoc and Haut-Médoc, which has six separate communal* appellations *(Saint-Estèphe, Saint-Julien, Listrac, Moulis, Margaux, Pauillac).*

White wines : Entre-deux-Mers, Côtes de Bordeaux-Saint-Macaire, Côtes de Blaye, Cérons, Loupiac, Saint-Croix du Mont, Sauternes, Barsac, Graves Supérieures, and Premières Côtes de Bordeaux followed by the name of the commune that produced the wine.

White and red wines : Blayais, Premières Côtes de Blaye, Côtes de Bourg, Sainte-Foy-Bordeaux, Graves de Vayres, Premières Côtes de Bordeaux, Graves blanc et rouge, Bordeaux-Côtes de Castillon, Bordeaux-Côtes de France.

Within these different regional and communal appellations, *the product is rigorously defined by each château's individual label. Following the famous classification of 1855, a series of secondary classifications took place within most of the larger* appellations, *singling out the best châteaux in each.*

Best years : 61, 62, 64, 66, 67, 70, 71, 75, 76, 78, 79, 81, 82.

■ The **CHALOSSE** Region★

▶ From Dax to Mont-de-Marsan *(approx 130 km, full day)* (Landes)

A4 *(see map 5)*

The Chalosse Region covers the green and undulating southern Landes, a totally different landscape from that of the heavily-wooded north. This is the home of *foie gras* (goose and duck liver), free-range chickens and milk-fed veal.

▶ **Dax** (→). ▶ At **Pontonx** D10 crosses the river Adour into the Chalosse. This road passes first through the *barthes,* low meadows along the left bank of the Adour. ▶ **Poyanne :** beautiful Louis XV château, with a façade composed of five separate pavilions, only one of which is open to the public *(daily);* next to the chapel (recent) there is a lovely Renaissance room that retains its original decor. ▶ **Laurède,** once a stopover for pilgrims to Santiago de Compostela, Spain; church with striking rococo furnishings (marble pulpit, lectern and altar). ▶ Near **Mugron, Nerbis,** a pretty village overlooking the Adour valley : interesting church, partly 11thC. ▶ At **Montaut,** remains of mediaeval fortifications, with a church backed up against them; two naves, one 14thC, the other 15thC. ▶ **Saint-Sever★** ®, which straddles the Adour valley, was built around an important Benedictine abbey (10thC); the abbey church★ (11thC) was damaged by Protestants during the 16thC, but retains the original capitals; the presbytery and the *hôtel de ville* (town hall) now occupy parts of the former monastic building. The church of the Jacobins is another former abbey church, with an especially beautiful cloister; now under restoration after a long period of use as a grain market. To the S of Saint-Sever, take the narrow road to **Audignon :** church★, bell-tower-porch, Romanesque apse. ▶ Country holiday resort of **Hagetmau** ® : this town is known for chair manufacturing. On the outskirts, the **crypt** of St. Girons is the only vestige of the 12thC abbey which was built around the sepulchre of this saint who evangelised SW France. Inside : beautifully sculpted capitals. ▶ From Hagetmau, go E along D2 to **Samadet,** famous for the pottery made here between 1732 and 1840. See the house of the Abbé de Roquépine, founder of the industry; small museum *(daily).* ▶ Beyond Samadet lies the pleasant enclave of **Tursan,** which produces a fine wine classified "VDQS" (*Vin Délimité de Qualité Supérieure;* → Wine); its capital, **Geaune** ®, was a *bastide* (→) built by a Genoese seneschal for Edward II of England; the town's church (Languedoc-Gothic, 15thC) has a large bell-tower-porch. ▶ **Aire-sur-l'Adour★** ® : founded during the Roman conquest; 11thC cathedral, later remodelled (beautiful furnishings from the 18thC). In the **Mas d'Aire** suburb, south of this small market town, is the original Romanesque church of Ste. Quitterie, elegantly remodelled : crypt with magnificent 6thC sarcophagus★ in marble, carved with biblical scenes. ▶ From Aire, continue up the Adour valley taking N124 towards Mont-de-Marsan. **Grenade-sur-Adour,** a former *bastide* built in the 14thC, church completely redone in the 18thC, except for the *chevet.* On the other bank of the Adour, above the village of **Larrivière,** is the old chapel of St. Savin, built in the 11thC with large stones taken from the Adour; now dedicated to Notre-Dame of Rugby! ▶ Between Grenade and Mont-de-Marsan, detour towards **Bascons** fortified church *(3 km N from Grenade).* At **Bostens,** N of the village : chapel (15thC) Notre-Dame de la Course Landaise, where participants in the local sport of bull-running can solicit the protection and assistance of the Virgin Mary. The *Courses Landaises* are akin to the annual Pamplona bull-running; young heifers race the *écarteurs* (dodgers) who try to avoid being butted or trampled. **Mont-de-Marsan** (→) □.

■ DAX★

A3-4 / ® / pop. 18650 (Landes)

Dax (the name derives from the Latin *aquae* - "waters") is today the second-most important thermal spa in France after Aix-les-Bains. Ever since the visit of the Roman Emperor Augustus in the 1stC, Dax has attracted visitors to its hot springs; combined with mud from the Adour (the celebrated *dacquoise* or *peloïde*), they work wonders for the health.

▶ From the old **bridge** (B1) over the Adour, there is a beautiful view of the town, framed by the green islands of the **Parc Théodore-Denis** (C1 : Roman arenas) upstream, and the **Parc des Baignots** downstream. At the end of the Parc des Baignots are the mud basins. ▶ On **Place Thiers** (B1) is a statue of the navigator and mathematician Charles de Borda. Below, mists rise above the **Fontaine Chaude** (B2)

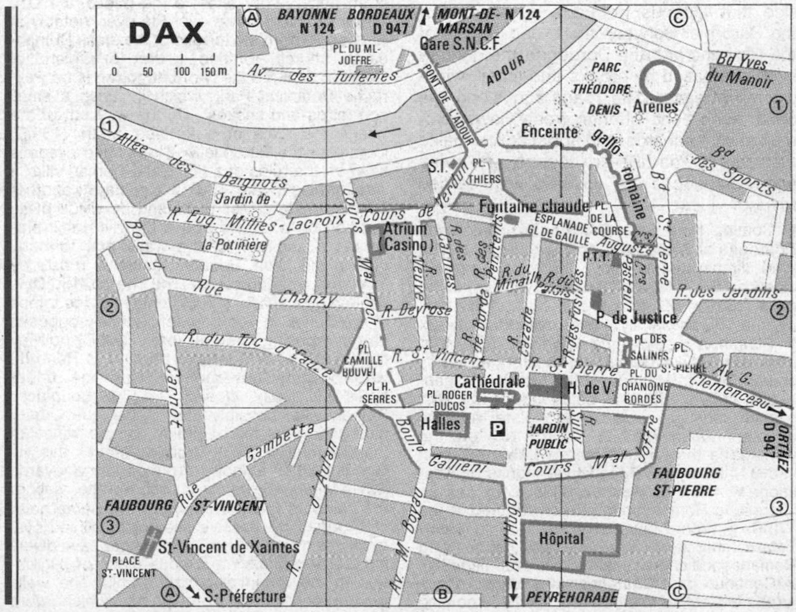

(hot springs daily produce a 400 cm^3 metres of water at a constant 64°C. ▶ Above the Théodore-Denis park are the remains of **Gallo-Roman fortifications** (C1) from the 4thC, almost entirely destroyed in the last century and converted into a promenade under the plane trees. ▶ The **cathedral★** of Dax (B2) was rebuilt in the 17thC in the French Classical style and afterwards restored : however, the Apostles doorway (13thC) of the former Gothic sanctuary still remains, while inside the church there are 16th-17thC stalls, 18thC furniture and paintings from the 17thC and 18thC ▶ In the St-Martin-d'Ages mansion (17thC, Rue Cazade) is the **Borda museum** (archaeology, arts and traditions of the Landes; *Apr.-Oct. 2-7, Mon.-Fri.; Nov.-Mar. 2-7, Tue., Wed., Thurs.; closed nat. hols.).* ▶ The **church of St. Vincent-de-Xaintes** (A3; 19thC) has a Gallo-Roman mosaic in the choir. □

▶ Nearby

▶ On the right bank of the Adour is **Saint-Paul-lès-Dax** ®. The **church** has a decorated Romanesque *chevet★* (frieze★ in marble: bestiarv and religious scenes) running above arcatures, with figured capitals. ▶ **Berceau-de-Saint-Vincent-de-Paul** (Cradle of St. Vincent), 7 km NW from Dax was the saint's birthplace. On the church square, by the large oak where Vincent kept his father's flock, is the house in which he was born (visit daily). ▶ **Oeyreluy** *(5 km S of Dax) :* the doorway of the village church here is decorated with interesting pre-Romanesque sculpture. □

ENTRE-DEUX-MERS Region★★

▶ From Saint-Émilion to Bordeaux *(approx 130 km, full day)*

B2 *(see map. 1)*

The fast roads leading NE and E of Bordeaux give little idea of the charming countryside that extends from the right bank of the Garonne. Between the broad valleys of the Garonne and the Dordogne the country is criss-crossed by brooks and small, winding mill-streams. The roads run along the crest, each bend offering fresh views over meadows, orchards and tobacco or maize plantations. The hills are topped with trees and their slopes are covered with serried rows of vines.

▶ Coming from **Saint-Emilion** (→), cross the Dordogne at **Saint-Jean-de-Blaignac** ®. ▶ The road climbs steeply above the valley, passing close by the village of **Rauzan,** with imposing ruins (13th-14thC) of a feudal castle long held by the Duras family; fine cylindrical keep. ▶ **Blasimon :** below the town, on the other bank of the river Gamage is the former abbey church of St. Maurice (12th-13thC). Romanesque façade and wall-belfry; doorway with elegant carvings, ruins of the cloister and the chapter house (12thC). 2 km NE on the Gamage is the fortified **mill** of **Labarthe,** built in the 14thC by the Benedictine monks of Blasimon. ▶ 4 km E, **Mauriac.** This town has an interesting Romanesque church fortified in the 14thC. ▶ From Mauriac, rejoin D127 to **Saint-Ferme :** church, ancient Benedictine abbey with Romanesque *chevet* (inside : sculpted capitals). ▶ Continue past **Castelmoron-d'Albret,** a picturesque fortified town on rocky hillside coming out at **Sauveterre-de-Guyenne,** a *bastide* built in 1281 by Edward I of England : broad arcaded square and four town gateways. ▶ 8 km SW, **Castelvieil,** on its hill, boasts a 12thC church with an S doorway in perfect Saintonge Romanesque style. ▶ **Saint-Brice.** ▶ Today, the site of the great forest *(silva major)* that gave its name to the little village of **La Sauve★★** is cloaked with vineyards; it was cleared by Benedictine monks from the **abbey** founded here by St. Gérard in 1079. The imposing ruins★ of the church and monastic buildings clearly show the importance of this religious establishment on the route of the pilgrims to Compostela. On a neighbouring hilltop is the parish **church of St. Pierre :** Gothic style (early 13thC); square apse adorned on the outside with four very fine statues; inside, interesting 16thC frescos. ▶ From La Sauve, slight detour towards **Haux** (*8 km S;* another Saintonge Romanesque church, with sculpted doorway) and **Saint-Genès-de-Lombaud,** N of Haux. The church has been a shrine for pilgrims to the Black Virgin since the 13thC; doorway with amusing sculptures. ▶ **Créon,** heart of the Entre-Deux-Mers region : former *bastide* built in the early 14thC; arcaded square. ▶ 10 km N stands the **fortified castle of Grand Puch,** 14thC, a well-preserved example of mediaeval military architecture. ▶ Bordeaux (→). □

The GARONNE Valley★★

▶ From Bordeaux to La Réole *(approx 70 km, half-day)*

B2 *(see map 2)*

Upstream from Bordeaux, the Garonne valley narrows rapidly. On the right bank are the limestone hills of **Entre-Deux-Mers** (→). The vineyards here produce both red and white wines and have the appellation *Premières Côtes de Bordeaux.*

▶ **Bordeaux** (→). ▶ From **Floirac,** where there is an observatory open to the public, the D10 offers excellent views over the river, notably at **Bouliac** ® (from the terrace of the small Romanesque church, fortified in the 15thC) and at **Quinsac** ®. ▶ To the N of **Langoiran** is La Peyruche Botanical Park, which includes a small zoo (birds and snakes). On the way out of the village the ruins of a fortified castle (13thC) loom over the Garonne. ▶ **Rions :** this village is sited on the ruins of a rich Gallo-Roman villa; it was fortified in the 14thC. ▶ **Cadillac★,** another *bastide* made easier to defend by virtue of its position on a hillside above the river, still preserves a segment of the walls that formerly girdled the town. Beautiful gateway *(Porte de Mer)* and arcaded square.The church (15thC) is flanked by a chapel (1606) containing the tombs of the Dukes of Epernon. Immediately opposite is the imposing **château** (early 17thC) built by the first Duke of Epernon, a friend of Henri III, who became governor of Guyenne under Louis XIII *(daily, closed Tue.).* ▶ **Loupiac :** Roman villa, possibly that of the poet Ausonius, who was full of praise for the wines of the Garonne. ▶ **Saint-Croix-du-Mont :** this village is built on a knoll surrounded by vineyards (white wines). From the church terrace, view of the valley of the Garonne and the Sauternais; cliff formed by massive piles of fossilized oyster shells from the late Tertiary Age; cave dwellings. ▶ **Verdelais :** a famous place of pilgrimage to the Virgin since the 14thC. The walls of the church of Notre-Dame, which were

Bordeaux cuisine

Bordeaux and its region, well known as the world capital of wine, also enjoy superb food; the two are inseparable. First, there are the sea and its products : plentiful fish, oysters from the Arcachon basin (gravettes *are the youngsters) served at any hour with bread, butter and small sausages. The Gironde and Its tributaries provide lamprey, shad, and eel, sometimes even caviar-bearing sturgeon, though this is rare. For gourmets, there is salt-meadow lamb from Pauillac and, in season, mushrooms* à la bordelaise *(cooked in oil with parsley and garlic); shallots and wine, are used for other dishes* à la bordelaise, *including the famous* entrecôte *steak, grilled for preference over vine prunings. Other marvellous products of the Bordeaux area are* foie gras *(goose and duck livers),* confit *(any meat preserved in its own fat) and* magret *(the fresh breast meat of a goose or duck), and excellent 'yellow' chicken* (poulet jaune) *raised on high quality maize only. You can sometimes find* ortolan *(a small bird fattened on millet), although it is a protected species. Salmon can still be caught in the Adour and Gaves Réunis. Excellent beef from Saint-Vincent de Tyrosse.*

2. Garonne valley, Bazadais and Sauternais regions

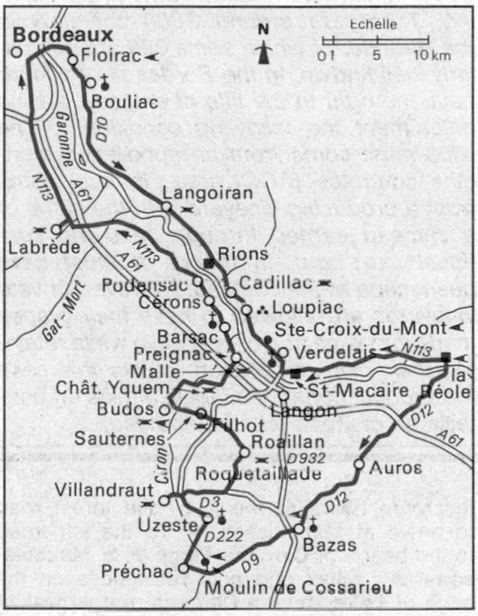

rebuilt after the Religious Wars, are covered with ex-voto plaques. In the cemetery is the grave stone of the painter Henri de Toulouse-Lautrec, who died aged 37 in a nearby château. From the Calvary hill, the view is similar to that of neighbouring Malagar, described by the writer François Mauriac (1883-1970), who lived 1 km from the village. ▶ Opposite **Langon** ®, an important wine centre on the right bank of the Garonne, is **Saint-Macaire★★** ®, named after a 6thC bishop. This town is built on limestone rock overlooking the right bank of the river; its three fine fortified gateways lead into a charming and intact mediaeval city. A labyrinth of cool, narrow streets centres on the long **Place du Mercadieu** (partly 15thC), which is surrounded by beautiful houses resting on arcades *(couverts).* One of these houses, a post-house in the time of Henry IV, has been made into the **Postal Museum of Aquitaine** : history of the postal service from the Renaissance to the 20thC *(May-Oct. 10 to 12 & 2 to 6 daily; out of season, Sun. only).* St. Sauveur church : panoramic terrace, former Benedictine abbey (12th-14thC) : in the dome of the apse, **paintings** (14thC) include the Apocalypse of St. John. ▶ **La Réole★** ® : this was a strategic position during the Roman era. Church of St. Pierre : Benedictine monastery built in the 10thC, abbey church rebuilt in the late 18thC. The monastic buildings open on to a terrace (view). To W, the château includes the remains of an English fortress. Perhaps the most intriguing monument in La Réole, at the highest part of the city, is the ancient *Maison Communale* (12thC), one of the rare Romanesque edifices still remaining in Aquitaine, composed of a hall on the ground floor and the *Salle des Echevins* (aldermen's hall) on the first floor. S of La Réole, beyond the Garonne valley, is the **Bazadais** region (→). □

■ The **GRANDES LANDES** Region★★

▶ From Mont-de-Marsan to Lit-et-Mixe *(approx 100 km, full day)*

A-B3 *(see map 3 following page)*

The Grandes Landes Is an Immense expanse of forest. It is entirely artificial : most of the forest was planted in the last century. The forester remains indispenable : there is no natural equilibrium in the area and if it were left to nature, scrub would gain the upper hand, the sand dunes would start to move, ponds would silt up, and marshes would return due to lack of drainage.

▶ **Mont-de-Marsan** (→) : take the road straight through the forest to **Garein :** factory where pine by-products are processed. ▶ 28 km NE, **Luxey** ® : a former processing plant for resin products open to the public *(same hours as the Eco-musée de Marquèze).* ▶ At **Sabres** ® make a point of seeing the beautiful Renaissance doorway to the church; also the tall arcaded bell-tower. Leave your car at the station if you want to go to the Marquèze - the train is the only way to get there. ▶ The **Eco-musée de Marquèze★★ :** one of the principal attractions of the **Landes de Gascogne regional park★★ ;** situated 5 km NE of Sabres, Marquèze is a clearing in the heart of the forest, a new museum of faithfully reconstructed 19thC village life in the once-numerous small agricultural communities of the Grandes Landes (horses, watermill, barn, chicken houses; *mid-Jun to mid-Sep. daily. end Mar. to mid-Jun and mid-Sep. to end Oct., Sat., pm Sun. and nat. hols.; closed beginning Nov. to Mar.)* ▶ **Solférino,** on the road to Mimizan : the former model village founded by Napoleon III in 1857 during his intensive afforestation of the Grandes Landes. Small museum *(daily) :* souvenirs and memorabilia. ▶ **On the road from Solférino to**

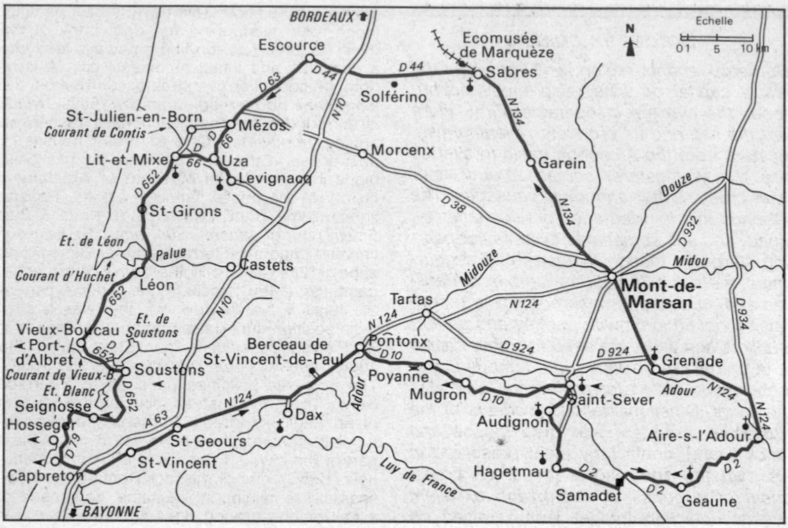

3. Grandes Landes region

Escource, the forest gives way in places to intensively cultivated maize fields. ▶ The forest continues from Escource to **Mézos** ® : church, fortified bell-tower (14thC). ▶ From Mézos, leaving **Saint-Julien-en-Born** ® to the right, the road continues to **Uza,** a village buried in the greenery next to a small lake formed by the Vignac River; remarkable old statues (painted wood) in the church. ▶ 5 km SE, **Levignac★** : another valley formed by the Vignac : traditional Landais half-timbered houses; remarkable 14thC fortified church : wooden vaulting with naif 18thC fresco by local artists; Renaissance doorway installed in the 18thC. ▶ **Lit-et-Mixe,** D652 runs N towards Mimizan (→), or S towards the *étangs* (ponds) of **Marensin** (→). □

■ The **LANDES GIRONDINES** Coast★

▶ From Lège to the Pointe de Grave *(approx 130 km, full day)*

A1-2 *(see map 4)*

From the Arcachon Basin to the Pointe de Grave stretches an endless beach of fine sand, backed by dunes. Behind it, other dunes have disappeared under the immense pine forests. The white sand beaches, inland lakes and pines stretch south as far as the mouth of the Adour.

▶ From Lège, at the top of the **Arcachon Basin,** head north towards **Le Porge,** a village receded several times because of the advancing dunes. ▶ From **Lacanau,** a small market-town set in the heart of the pine forest with a beautiful 18thC church, the route leads you to the charming resort of **Moutchic** ® which extends to the shore of the vast **Lacanau lake,** the windsurfers' paradise. Water-skiers have their own stretch of water at **Pitrot Lake** very close-by. ▶ Beyond Moutchic, the road runs along-side the very handsome golf-course at Ardilouse, an exceptional links, before reaching the ocean. On entering **Lacanau-Océan** ®, the large bathing resort of the "Médoc Atlantique", the route bears to the N by the forest road to arrive at Maubuisson. ▶ To the left, road to the beach of **Carcans-Plage** ®. ▶ **Maubuisson★** ® : villas and new residences on the edge of **Lake Hourtin-Carcans,** the largest of the Landes lakes (15 000 acres, 19 km long and 3-4 km wide), bordered with marshes to the N and SE; the west bank consists of high, pine-covered dunes. Pleasant open-air centre at **Bombannes.** ▶ **Hourtin** ® : sailing, canoes, kayaks. The road then crosses a marsh in the direction of **Hourtin-Plage** (beach), for which development is planned. ▶ **Pin-Sec,** deserted beaches popular with naturists. ▶ **Montalivet-les-Bains** ® : excellent swimming; France's first naturist beach was opened here in 1950. ▶ **Soulac-sur-Mer★** ® : exceptional and safe family beach on the ocean; formerly an impor-

Châteaux in the Bordeaux region

Châteaux *are obviously not unique to the Bordeaux region, but here the name takes on a special meaning linked to the production of wine rather than the style of the building. There are around 3 000* châteaux *in the Gironde, of which some 300 are particularly well known. In the Bordeaux region, to have the right to the title of* château, *a wine must meet the following conditions : The wine must come from an* appellation d'origine controlée *(AOC) area; it must come from a producing vineyard with the name of a château earned through past and continual use; and, in theory, it must have been made at the château. However, private vineyards are allowed to have their grapes made into wine at a cooperative while retaining their own* appellation, *but in this case the product cannot be labelled* mise en bouteille au château *(château-bottled).*

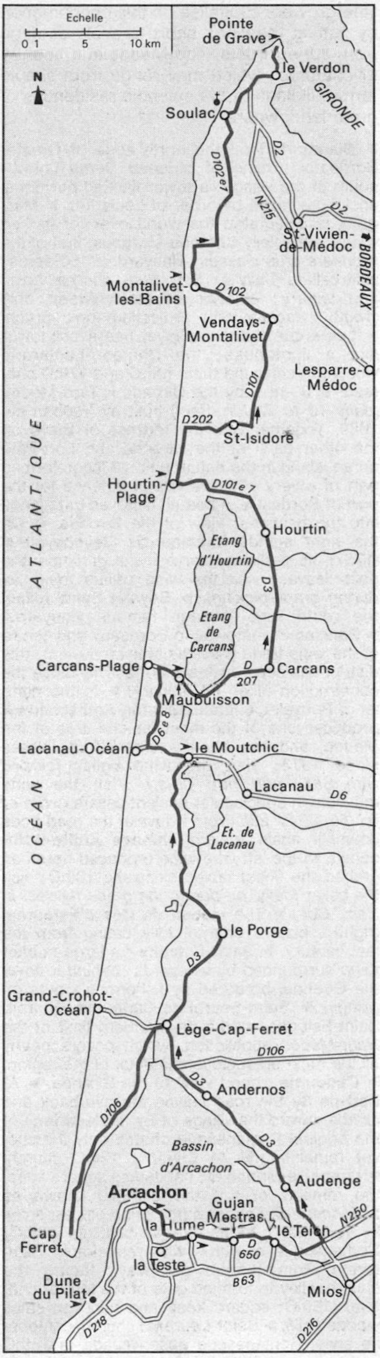

4. Landes Girondines coast

tant harbour on the Gironde, which has gradually silted up since the 16thC; **Notre-Dame-de-la-Fin-des-Terres basilica**★ was engulfed by the dunes in 1757. A century later it was unearthed : a fine example of Romanesque architecture, with Saintonge-style apse, and Poitou-style nave; in the interior, beautifully figured capitals depicting the burial of Ste. Véronique at Soulac; polychrome wood statue of Notre-Dame de la Fin des Terres. ▶ **Le Verdon-sur-Mer,** to the N of Soulac : a deepwater **port** for tankers and container ships. ▶ Still farther N, a pine-covered dune marks the **Pointe de Grave** at the entrance to the Gironde Estuary. On the sea wall at the site of the American landings in 1917, is a plaque commemorating the departure of La Fayette to the United States. Pointe de Grave may be reached all the year round from **Royan** (→ Charentes). In season, a ferry carries visitors to the **Cordouan lighthouse** *(approx 8 km from Pointe de Grave;* the building dates from the Renaissance; superb view). □

■ The **LIBOURNAIS**★

▶ From Saint-Savin to Saint-Emilion *(approx 60 km half day)*

B2 *(see map 1)*

After the Medoc, this is the next most important wine-growing region of the Bordelais. On both sides of the Isle Valley, and on the right bank of the Dordogne, there is a succession of famous wine-producing districts. From the W to the E : Canon Fronsac, Fronsac, Pomerol and Lalande-de-Pomerol, coupled with Saint-Emilion and its satellite *appellations.* These districts constitute a vast area, exclusively producing red wines. They are nearly as famous as the competing wines from the Médoc, although not distinguished by the same illustrious classification.

▶ D18 from **Saint-Savin** to the eastern edge of the **Blayais** (→) to **Marcenais :** 13thC Romanesque Templar church. ▶ **Mouillac :** Romanesque church enlarged in the 16thC. ▶ **Lalande-de-Fronsac :** Romanesque church decorated with superb carved tympanum (Apocalypse of St. John). ▶ Beautiful views of the valley of the Dordogne, especially from the hill-fort of **Fronsac;** below, in the village, there is a Romanesque church. ▶ **Libourne** ® is a former English *bastide,* of which the old ramparts have been replaced by a shady promenade. The town borrows its name from the seneschal Roger de Leyburn who founded it in the 13thC. The harbour here for wine boats from Saint-Emilion and Pomerol dates from when lighters came down on the current to meet larger ships entering with the tide. Libourne still has an important role in the wine trade. From the long stone bridge there is an excellent view of the city. Where the Dordogne and the Isle rivers meet, the **Grand-Port tower** (14thC) controls access to the old harbour. The heart of the city is a large arcaded square, very lively during market days. The *Hôtel de Ville* was rebuilt in 1910 : inside is a **museum** of archaeology along with a picture gallery containing works by René Princeteau, one of Toulouse-Lautrec's masters. ▶ Beyond Libourne, a list of prestigious names : **Pomerol, Château Pétrus, Néac,** and finally **Montagne-Saint-Emilion,** with its Romanesque church, much restored. ▶ **Saint-Émilion** (→). □

■ The MARENSIN★★

▶ From Lit-et-Mixe to Dax *(approx 100 km full day)*

A3 *(see map 3)*

This country covers the southern section of the Landes coast. Afforested in the 19thC, sparsely populated except in the seaside resorts. The Marensin is dotted with ponds which drain off to the ocean through the dunes.

▶ **Lit-et-Mixe,** where the **Grandes Landes** (→) meet the coastal strip. ▶ **Saint-Girons,** 5 km W : Romanesque, fortified church; immense beach of very fine sand. ▶ **Léon** ® : picturesque Landais half-timbered houses around the church. ▶ **Lake Léon** *(2 km W) :* a paradise for fishermen and windsurfers, and the departure point for boat trips down the capricious **Courant d'Huchet Stream★★★,** through beautiful greenery with rare hibiscus amid the alders, tamarisk and willows *(ask at the Bureau des Bateliers, the boatmen's office, tel 58.48.75.39).* ▶ **Moliets :** rustic houses among cork-oaks. 3 km W, limitless sandy beach. W and S of the village, **Moliets and Prade ponds,** both easily accessible. ▶ **Vieux-Boucau** ® : once the busy **Port d'Albert,** at the mouth of the Adour; today an active tourist resort on the banks of a 180-acre lake. ▶ The route follows the **Courant de Vieux-Boucau.** ▶ **Soustons★** ® : founded in the 14thC by the English (its name comes from the English south town), small bustling centre (corks, plastic, wood) of an agricultural region (asparagus, maize, chicken); alley of plane-trees to **Soustons pond,** fringed with rushes. ▶ **Tosse : Romanesque church,** square tower and 12thC apse. ▶ Several kilometres of pinewoods separate the old town of **Seignosse** ® from Penon, a brand-new seaside resort. ▶ **Hossegor★** ® grew around a lake in the forest before expanding to the ocean. Fine villas in the Basque-Landais style, set in the middle of the pine woods contrast oddly with the modern buildings of Hossegor. **Capbreton** ® : situated at the mouth of the Adour; as early as the 10thC it was an important maritime city, its sailors going as for as the north American coast in search of whales. The church tower served as a landmark to navigators, who have venerated the Pietà in the porch since the 15thC; today a large marina has been built where the Bourret and Boudigau rivers meet. The beach here is safe and well protected from ocean swells. ▶ **Saint-Vincent-de-Tyrosse** ® : cattle-breeding centre. ▶ **Dax** (→). □

■ The MÉDOC Region★★

▶ Circuit Bordeaux to Bordeaux *(approx 150 km full day)*

A1 *(see map 5)*

Bathed in a special light, the vine-growing Médoc is geographically different from the rest of the Bordeaux region. Its narrow, enclosed valleys provide a wide variety of growing conditions. There is a local saying that the wine is best when the grape "sees" the water (i.e. the Gironde), but this is by no means the case with the great *Premiers Crus.* The stony Médoc soil retains the warmth of the sun well into the night; the vine-growers capitalise on this phenomenon by cutting the vines short to avoid damage from spring frosts. The Médoc is a country of châteaux, which may range from simple farm buildings to the splendid residences of great landowners.

▶ **Blanquefort** on the north edge of Greater Bordeaux : ruins of **château Duras** (14thC) south of the village; a tower-flanked polygonal enclosure razed by order of Louis XIII. ▶ **Margaux** is celebrated the world over for its red wines, especially **Château-Margaux,** first of the *premiers crus classés;* vineyard of 150 acres; visit cellars *(daily ex Sat., Sun., and nat hols.)* and winery; exterior of the **château** only (1802) : façade with projecting Ionic porch. ▶ **Lamarque** (ferry to Blaye) has a bell-tower like a lighthouse; the Château-Lamarque vineyards surround their 13thC and 17thC château. ▶ 3 km E by the Gironde is **Fort-Médoc** *(daily 10 to 7, Jun.-Sep.)* built by Vauban ca. 1689. Together with the fortress of Blaye on the other bank of the Gironde and Fort-Paté on an island in the estuary, Fort-Médoc formed part of a very effective line of defence for the port of Bordeaux. A beautiful carved gate leads into the bastions; view of the Gironde. ▶ On the right stands **château de Beychevelle★** (1757), its pediment carved with garlands and palm leaves; visit the wine cellars *(daily ex during grape-picking).* ▶ Beyond **Saint-Julien,** the route runs through famous vineyards. ▶ **Pauillac** ® : gateway to Bordeaux and centre of the wine trade (*visit the* Maison du Vin); this district has seen a renewal of activity since the construction of an oil refinery. ▶ In the hamlet of Pouyalet, **château Mouton-Rothschild★★** produces one of the most famous *crus* of the Médoc, and has been a *premier cru classé* since 1973; visit the wine cellar *(closed Sun.,Sat., and nat. hols.).* Visit the wine museum in spectacular ancient cellars *(write or tel (56) 59 22 22).* From Pouyalet the road goes downhill again toward **château Lafite-Rothschild,** to the left; the wine produced here has graced the finest tables since the 18thC; visit the cellar *(daily, ex during the grape harvest in Sep., Oct.)* ▶ The **manoir de Cos d'Estournel** (right) : bizarre oriental folly dating from the last century. ▶ **Saint-Estèphe :** a large market town surrounded by vineyards; behind it flows the Gironde, bordered by fishermen's huts on pilings. ▶ **Saint-Seurin-de-Cadourne,** N from Saint-Estèphe, marks the northern limit of the *Haut-Médoc* appellation, which covers nearly all the most prestigious châteaux of the region. ▶ **Cadourne :** good view of the Gironde. ▶ At **Port-de-By** the road leaves the riverbank and climbs toward the village of **By.** ▶ **Begadan :** of the original Romanesque **church** only the chevet remains . ▶ At **Civrac : 12thC church.** ▶ **Lesparre-Medoc** ® : handsome square keep, the remains of a 14thC château known as *L'Honneur de Lesparre* (the pride of Lesparre). ▶ **Vertheuil :** former abbey building, 18thC; Romanesque church★ with remarkable Saintonge Romanesque doorway; facing the church, alley to fortified gate of the former château (15thC; square keep and ruins on small wooded hill). ▶ **Saint-Laurent :** church, composite style, Romanesque apse, façade of 14thC and spire of 16thC. ▶ **Listrac :** known for its Haut-Médoc wine. ▶ At **Moulis,** Romanesque church★ : sculpted corbels, apse, figured capitals inside, fortified chamber above the transept crossing. ▶ **Avensan :** in the church, Romanesque apse, interesting 15thC *bas-reliefs* in the altar piece. ▶ At **Castelnau-de-**

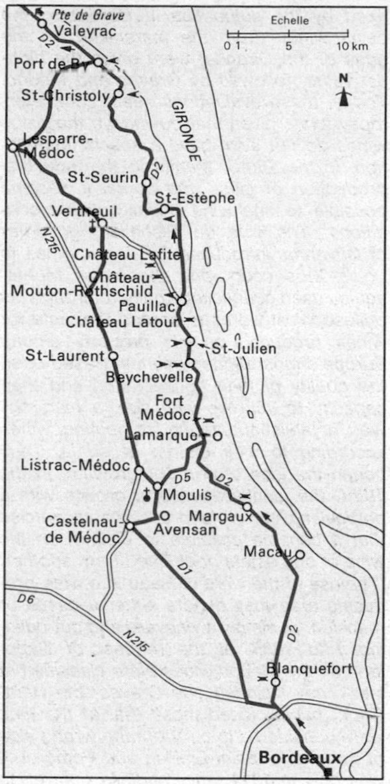

5. Médoc region

Médoc : church (15thC); stained glass of the same period and several carved wood panels of the 17thC. ▶ Bordeaux (→). ☐

■ MIMIZAN★

A3 / ® / pop. 7 410 (Landes)

Two roads from either side of the river link this small town to the seaside resort of Mimizan-Plage. Until the 17thC there was an active harbour here, the *Segosa* of the Roman era, which finally disappeared under the moving sand dunes.

▶ The stabilisation of the dunes at the end of the 18thC enabled the **bell-tower★** of a former Benedictine abbey church to be saved; magnificent Romanesque doorway (12thC); tympanum (Adoration of the Three Kings). Around the **abbey** were four stone pyramids *(garluch)*, only one of which remains. They marked the limits of the old sanctuary, where fugitives or the oppressed could find inviolable safety. To the W of the old **bell-tower,** the Papeteries de Gascogne paper mill : documentation room *(pm, season only).* ☐

▶ Nearby

A pleasant road links Mimizan to **Parentis-en-Born** ® : *(18 km NE)* fine views of **Aureilhan lake,** and its larger neighbour at **Parentis et Biscarrosse;** derricks of the last of the Parentis oil wells. The Esso-Rep group, which holds the well concession, has a permanent exhibition in the village of Parentis. *(Apr.-Oct. 9-12 & 2-6 daily ex Tue.)* ▶ **Biscarrosse** ® : *(10 km NW from Parentis)* renewed activity since the creation of the Landes testing centre for the aerospace industry. ☐

■ MONT-DE-MARSAN★

B3 / ® / pop. 27 330 (Landes)

Situated at the junction of the Douze and Midou rivers, which together form the Midouze. This is the administrative centre of the Landes, with a busy military aircraft testing centre on the outskirts. Particularly lively in mid-July, during the *Fête de la Madeleine,* with *Courses Landaises* and *Corridas.*

▶ Behind the square of the *Hôtel de Ville* (town hall), you can **see** picturesque 18thC houses straddling the Ruelle des Arceaux. ▶ The **Lacataye keep :** only vestige of a 14thC castle built by Gaston Phoebus, Count of Béarn, now transformed into a **Fine Arts museum★** dedicated to two local sculptors, Charles Despiau and Robert Wiérick *(9h30-12 & 2-6 daily, closed Tue.).* Nearby is a former **Romanesque chapel** overlooking the Midou, well restored. It houses the **Dubalen Museum** of prehistory and natural science *(9h30-12 & 2-6, closed Tue.).*

■ PEYREHORADE★

A4 / ® / pop. 3 090 (Landes)

Peyrehorade, capital of the **Orthe region,** faces Bayonne rather than the wooded Landes or Chalosse areas. Its name means *pierced stone* and it stands on the banks of the *Gaves Réunis,* a tributary of the Adour formed by the mountain streams *(gaves)* of Pau and Oloron.

▶ At the foot of a hill crowned by the keep of the ruined **château d'Apremont★** is a small village around the **château Montréal★** (late 16thC), built by the viscounts of Orthe. This is a large building flanked by four round towers, with remarkable entrance gates. Behind it, a pleasant shady walk along the banks of an artificial lake fed by the Gaves ; small **port** for pleasure-craft. ☐

▶ Nearby

▶ **Arthous abbey★ :** 3 km SW, built by Premonstratensian monks in 1160, a stopover on one of the pilgrim roads to Santiago de Compostela : Romanesque church; apse with remarkable exterior decoration; **archaeology museum** in former monastic building *(daily).* ▶ **Sorde-l'Abbaye★★** *(3 km SE from Peyrehorade) :* on the pilgrim road between the Landes and the Pyrénées, which was successively travelled by Neolithic man, the Roman legions, Charlemagne's troops and the pilgrims of St. James. The village developed around an abbey built on the foundations of a large 4thC Gallo-Roman villa; it later became a fortified *bastide* (13thC); remains of ramparts. **Church** with Romanesque apse and doorway; Gothic transept and nave; in the choir, fragments of a mosaic (11thC, hunting scenes). Nearby, the 16thC **abbot's house** with polygonal turret, built on the site of a Gallo-Roman spa; foundations and fragments of mosaic. Other abbey remains : part of a cloister; a long subterra-

History of the vineyard

It seems that vineyards were planted in the Graves and Saint-Émilion areas by the Romans when they occupied the region around 50BC. The Elder Pliny mentions the wines of Burdigala (Bordeaux) and in the 4thC the poet Ausonius praised the wines of the Garonne valley. As with all the great French vineyard regions, the history of the Bordelais is related to the development of large agricultural estates by the monasteries, which contributed greatly to their prosperity. The marriage of the future Henry II of England to Eleanor of Aquitaine (1152) resulted in the English ascendancy over Aquitaine, which led to the Hundred Years' War, some 2 centuries later. This was the beginning of an exceptionally prosperous period for Bordeaux wines because of the strong English appreciation of their clairet, *or claret. This prosperity lasted until the beginning of the 13thC, when the production of the Aunis vineyards farther north was sent directly from La Rochelle to Flanders and England, but the conquest of Aunis (now part of the Charente Maritime department) by Louis VIII in 1224 eventually closed this route, and the Bordeaux wines regained the English market. To insure their delivery in London, the English fitted out a wine fleet numbering 300 ships in 1370. To satisfy the demands on the other side of the Channel, Bordeaux asked for help from producers in neighbouring regions : Bergerac, Gaillac, Moissac, Cahors, Agen and even Toulouse. To protect themselves from possible competition, they obtained important privileges and tax deductions from the King of England. These were abolished by Charles VII after France reconquered Guyenne, but later re-established by the shrewd Louis XI.*

Although Bordeaux appears to have been the wine-making capital of the civilised world during the Middle Ages, the region had yet to become pre-eminent in terms of quality. At that time a wine's geographical origins were not considered important and the idea of classification by growth was unknown. In the same way that Châteauneuf-du-Pape was used to improve Burgundy wines, the red wines of Gaillac and the black wine of Cahors were frequently used to give body to the lighter clarets of Bordeaux. The Bordeaux wineries showed their gratitude to the Gaillac producers by allowing them privileges that prohibited Cahors and Bergerac winemakers from competing.

In the 17thC, land ownership progressively passed to parliamentary aristocrats, recently ennobled and financially more sound than the old landowning families. The land they accumulated was made into large vineyards, notably in the Médoc. However, even at that time, the Bordeaux vineyards produced only young wine that aged poorly. In 1647, when prices for red wines were fixed by the authorities in Bordeaux, the palus *wines (from the marshland on the edge of the Gironde) were given the highest value, followed by Graves and Médoc. Today, these evaluations seem completely topsy-turvy, given that nowadays the palus wines do not even have a special appellation. In the 18thC, thanks to the industrial production of glass and corks, it became possible to age wine under suitable conditions. The Duc de Richelieu, governor of Guyenne, introduced Bordeaux wines to Louis XV's court, and the writer Montesquieu used connections gained through his philosophical works to spread the taste for wines produced on his property among Europe's most refined palates. Based upon the quality of their conservation and their capacity to improve with age, a hierarchy was established among competing wines according to their district of origin. Thus began the idea of* crus, *or growths. In the 19thC the identification of a growth with a particular piece of land became so precise that it became possible to distinguish the wine of one estate or château from another. (The use of the word* château *in a wine-producing area may denote either a castle or mansion, or simply a vineyard and out-buildings.) In 1885, at the request of Napoleon III, the Médoc wines were classified at last. They included one Graves, the Haut-Brion, but excluded those that at the time were considered to be "from the wrong side of the river" - Saint-Émilion and Pomerol. It was only in 1911, after endless quarrelling and litigation, that the limits of the Bordeaux wine region became those of the Gironde department. In contrast with the 19thC, the practice of bottling wine at its vineyard of origin became generalised after 1925, encouraged by merchants who were thus able to be sure of the quality of the wine they bought. Today, however, only 10% of the producers within the* Appellation Contrôlée *of the Bordeaux region, created in 1936, bottle their own wine. The production of Bordeaux wines currently varies between 90 and 100 million gallons per annum. One-third of this is white, and the total represents about half the entire French production of* Appellation Contrôlée *wines.*

nean gallery (1710) by the stream (once used as a cellar and fishpond). ▶ **Cagnotte** ® *(8 km NE) :* Romanesque **church,** formerly the mausoleum of the Vicomtes d'Orthe; interesting funerary monuments. □

■ SAINT-ÉMILION★★★

B2 / ® / pop. 3010 (Gironde)

In the hills above the Dordogne basin, this vineyard village is one of the most beautiful sites of France and one of the strangest, for its golden limestone buildings are rooted in a network of subterranean galleries. The Gallo-Roman poet Ausonius praised the site. In the 8thC, the Breton monk Émilion made his hermitage in one of the numerous grottoes, and later a community of Benedictine monks founded a monastery. The village and its ramparts grew up around this foundation. During the Revolution, Saint-Émilion was the last refuge of the unfortunate Girondins (→ *Brief regional history*).

▶ N, the **Dominican wall,** ruins of a convent outside the walls; two of the town gates; considerable remains of the ramparts; remains of Romanesque and Gothic houses. ▶ Enter the town by Rue Gaudet; a road leads off to the **convent of the Cordeliers** (Franciscan friars); square, 14thC cloister *(daily).* The **Porte de la Cadène** leads to the centre of the town : picturesque **Place du Marché** (market square), closed by a rocky wall with pierced windows lighting a **church** quarried out of **solid rock** *(guided tours : ask at SI).* A beautiful doorway (14thC) leads to this large and unique subterranean church built by the monks (9th-12thC) out of several caves. On the cliff, the **bell-tower** (12thC and 16thC) seems isolated from the rest of the church. ▶ From the Place du Marché, visit the **catacombs** *(ask SI) :* former charnel house with cemetery on the cliff. ▶ At the end of the square : angular apse (13thC) of the **Trinité chapel** *(visits, ask at SI),* above the **hermitage** of **Saint-Émilion** (see the *furniture* cut in the rock); a spring rises in the oratory. ▶ Behind the Trinité chapel, an alley leads to the **château du Roi :** massive 13thC keep. Another steep alley links the Place du Marché with the **Place des Créneaux,** which is surrounded by the monastery buildings : bell-tower of the underground church. Also see the Collegiate Church's beautiful 14thC **cloister** with its Gothic arcades. W of the former **deanery** (office of the SI) is the **Chapter chapel** (13thC). Go round the chapel to the former **Maison de l'Abbé;** small **museum** *(daily).* ▶ The **collegiate** church, which was built in the 12thC, replaced the underground church : Romanesque nave, Gothic gate-tower, choir and transept. □

■ The **SAUTERNAIS** Region★★

▶ From Roallan to Bordeaux *(approx 70 km, half-day)*

B2 *(see map 2)*

Region of sweet white wines (Sauternes and Barsac). Pretty winding roads between vine-covered hillsides dotted by châteaux. The Sauternes wines of five communes are obtained from a special (natural) process : the grapes are picked in an advanced state of ripeness when they have been attacked by the tiny fungus that causes *pourriture noble,* noble rot. This causes the grapes to diminish in size while their sugar content increases, giving the resultant wine a unique flavor.

▶ W from **Roaillan,** D125 crosses the wooded region up to the **Bazadais** (→), then suddenly enters the Sauternais vineyards, where even the smallest plot of land is reserved for the precious grapes. ▶ Not far from **Sauternes** (partly Romanesque church) is the winery of **château Filhot** (19thC), neo-Classical style; taste the wines of the vineyard. ▶ On the other bank of the Ciron, on the western limit of Sauternes, is **Budos :** ruins of the 14thC fortified château. ▶ **Château Yquem** occupies a site at the top of the slope *(admission free to the estate and interior courtyard of the château);* built in the early Renaissance and remodelled in the 17thC, it stands in the centre of a vineyard that produces the most prestigious and the most expensive of the great *crus* of Sauternes : each vine produces only one glass of wine annually. ▶ On the road to the Garonne Valley, see the ravishing **château de Malle★★,** Classical style (early 17thC), with French gardens; inside, rare furniture, good paintings *(late Mar.-mid Oct. daily closed Wed, 3 to 7).* ▶ **Barsac** ® : one of the five wine-making communes with the Sauternes appellation; the church with three naves dates from the early 17thC (inside 18thC furniture). ▶ Around **Cérons** ®, a very ancient port on the Garonne, an *A.C.* wine is produced that is close to Sauternes : Romanesque church with interesting carvings on the doorway. ▶ Across the **Graves region,** the vineyards extend all along the left bank of the Garonne up to Bordeaux. ▶ **Labrède** ® : beautiful Romanesque church façade : Montesquieu was born in 1689 at the **château de Labrède★** *(mid-Mar.-mid Nov. 9:30-11:30 & 2:30-5:30 daily, closed Tue.; out of season 2:30-5 Sat., Sun. only : closed mid-Dec-end Jan.).* Montesquieu also designed the park of the fortified manor, 13thC and 15thC. Visit the salons and the writer's bedroom and library. ▶ **Bordeaux** (→). □

Architecture

● Half-timbered walls in the Bordelais-Landes tend to be filled with cob or brick, then covered with a light-coloured roughcast that leaves the wooden framework visible. The Landes house is usually a single story with a hayloft under a double-sloped and round-tiled roof. The loft opens onto the front of the building, which usually has a gallery-verandah. This verandah sometimes extends across the full width of the building.

Landes house

Arcaded house, right bank of Garonne river

● On the right bank of the Garonne, numerous small cities *(bastides)* remain faithful to the old checkerboard construction plan, with right-angled streets leading off a central square of arcaded galleries. ● Apart from these small towns, the vineyard region of Bordeaux is not densely populated.

Gironde peasant's house

Brief regional history

10th-1stC BC In the first millennium BC, **Iberians** from Spain established themselves between the Garonne and the Pyrénées. ● Invading **Celts** subsequently pushed them back to the mountains in the 6thC and 5thC. ● In 56 BC **Publius Crassus,** Julius Caesar's lieutenant, fought a victorious campaign against the Celts in the Aquitaine basin.

1st-4thC AD In the 1stC AD, **Roman colonisation** was in full swing in the area. Prosperous Gallo-Roman **villas** were built throughout Aquitaine at this time. ● The 4thC saw the flowering of a brilliant cultural **elite** that included the poet and grammarian Ausonius (309-394) and **St. Paulinus of Nole,** bishop and poet, born in 353.

5th-8thC The great barbarian **invasions** began in the 5thC, reaching a climax when the **Visigoths** forced the Emperor **Honorius** to cede them an empire in the SW with Toulouse as its capital. In the early 6thC, however, the Frankish king **Clovis** defeated the Visigoth **Alaric**; this led to the absorption of Aquitaine into the Frankish kingdom. ● At the end of the century, the **Vascons** (Iberians who had not been colonized by Rome) came down from their Pyrenean fortresses and systematically ravaged the region. ● However, in the mid-7thC an alliance between the Vascons and the Aquitaines led to the restoration of the Kingdom of Toulouse now ruled by the **Dukes of Aquitaine.** ● The Saracens invaded Aquitaine in 729; Duke **Eudes** sought help from **Charles Martel** (viceroy of the king of the Franks) who crushed the Arab invading force at Poitiers (732). ● **Charles Martel** occupied the entire Bordeaux region when in 735 Duke **Hunald,** son of Eudes, refused to recognise his suzerainty. Martel's son, **Pépin le Bref,** the first king of the Carolingian Dynasty, completed the conquest of Aquitaine in 759. ● In 780 Charlemagne made Aquitaine a kingdom for his son Louis the Pious and entrusted **Guilhem,** Count of Toulouse, with the defence against Muslim invaders.

9th-12thC In 817 **Louis the Pious** made his son Pépin Viceroy of Aquitaine. ● But in the 10thC anarchy spread and the country broke up for a time into numerous **independent baronies.** ● A period of relative security in the 11thC favoured the expansion of **monastic foundations,** which cleared the land and increased agricultural development. **Pilgrims** flocked to the shrine of St. James of Compostela in Spain, and various religious orders established numerous hostelries along the roads they travelled. ● In 1036 the Duchy of Gascony was amalgamated with the **Duchy of Aquitaine,** now ruled by the **Counts of Poitiers.** ● In 1137, **Eleanor of Aquitaine,** sole heiress and daughter of Duke Guillaume X, married the King of France, **Louis VII,** who repudiated her in 1152. She then married **Henry Plantagenet,** heir to the English throne (who already possessed Anjou, Touraine, and Normandy), bringing him a priceless dowry. ● In 1169, Henry ceded Aquitaine to his son, **Richard the Lionheart.**

12th-15thC The death of Richard the Lionheart in 1199, followed by Eleanor's death in 1204, began a period of instability; **King John,** Richard's younger brother, was unable to maintain power in his distant duchy. ● But in the mid-13thC the Gascon **stewards** appointed by **King Henry III** achieved a return to order with the help of the Church. The King of England granted the Gascon towns important **freedoms** to consolidate his control. ● The period of peace that followed brought about **changes in the patterns of rural population**; from 1250 to 1350 numerous walled towns (*bastides* →) were built. ● At the beginning of the Hundred Years' War, the **Black Prince,** Duke of Aquitaine and son of Edward III of England, defeated the French at Poitiers in 1356. ● His death in 1376 led to the emergence of the **Guyenne parliament** and the **city government of Bordeaux** as the real centres of power in the region. ● In 1451 Bordeaux recognised the suzerainty of the French king, but the following year rallied to an English army sent by **Henry VI.** ● At the battle of **Castillon** (1453) **Charles VII** defeated the English and ended 3 centuries of English domination. He cancelled all the special privileges of Bordeaux, but in 1462, **Louis XI,** an adroit politician, re-established the Parliament with all its former liberties.

16th-17thC

Francis I, who ascended the throne of France in 1515, set about **strengthening the monarchy** by progressive **centralisation** of the power of the state. ● From 1550 the reformed (Protestant) religion made numerous converts; **religious wars** raged, in spite of the peace-making efforts of **Michel de Montaigne,** mayor of Bordeaux from 1581-1585. The Edict of Nantes (1598) promulgated by **Henry IV** (a native of Aquitaine), re-established religious peace. ● In 1685, the Revocation of the Edict of Nantes by **Louis XIV** provoked a major **emigration** of the Huguenots (the Protestant middle class).

18thC

The 18thC saw the **reconciliation** of Bordeaux with the monarchy. It was also a period of great **economic expansion;** vineyards and maize cultivation prospered, and new land was cleared for cultivation. At the same time the wine trade with England was on the increase, as was the slave trade, to the profit of Europe and North America. New industries also began to appear in Aquitaine. ● At this time the Royal Intendants (administrators) were profoundly transforming Bordeaux; **Montesquieu,** whose ideas on the separation of powers inspired the legislators of 1791, was a member of the Guyenne Parliament. ● In 1787 this regional parliament, in refusing to register the royal edicts, signalled general dissatisfaction with the monarchy. ● During the Revolution that followed in 1789, the National Assembly at Paris voted for the administrative division of France into **departments** in order to abolish provincial privileges and special rights. ● In 1792, the Revolutionary moderates were nicknamed *Girondins* because their best speakers came from the Bordeaux (Gironde) region. When property seized during the Revolution was sold off, the **urban bourgeoisie** acquired large land-holdings, at the expense of the former aristocratic landowners.

19th-20thC

Under Napoleon's Empire, the **continental blockade** organised by Great Britain ruined Bordeaux's maritime trade. After the restoration of the Bourbons, politicians of the region (Decazes, Lainé, Martignac) were **liberals** and **moderates,** and the July Monarchy (Louis-Philippe, 1830-48) was easily accepted. ● The Second Empire (Napoleon II, 1852-70) was a period of great **economic change.** The **Landes of Gascony** were systematically developed, and landowners preferred to cultivate vineyards rather than less profitable cereals. ● In 1870, the advent of the Third Republic was enthusiastically welcomed in Aquitaine but shortly afterwards **phylloxera** destroyed the vineyards. This catastrophe stimulated a massive **rural exodus,** only surpassed by the shattering effects on population caused by the First World War. ● Since WWI, successive French governments have sought to encourage **industrial development** in the area. At the same time, **agriculture** has undergone a **revolution :** the grape no longer monopolizes the land. Other crops, especially maize, vegetables and fruit, have developed well.

Practical information

The region

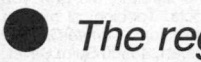

Information : Aquitaine : *Comité Régional du Tourisme* (C.R.T.), 24, allées de Tourny, 33000 Bordeaux, ☎ 56.44.48.02 ; **Gironde :** *Comité Départemental du Tourisme* (C.D.T.), 21, cours de l'Intendance, 33080 Bordeaux Cedex, ☎ 56.52.61.40 ; **Landes :** *C.D.T.,* 22, rue V.-Hugo, 40011 Mont-de-Marsan, ☎ 58.75.38.67.

Bookings : *Loisirs-Accueil Gironde,* 21, cours de l'Intendance, 33080 Bordeaux, ☎ 56.52.61.40.

Youth information : *C.I.D.J.,* 5, rue Duffour-Dubergier, 33000 Bordeaux, ☎ 56.48.55.80.

Maps : *Michelin,* n°s 75 and 78 1/200 000 and regional map n° 234 ; *I.G.N.,* n°s 55 and 62 1/100 000.

Local and regional press : *Sud-Ouest, la France-Nouvelle République.*

S.O.S. : Gironde : *SAMU* (Emergency Medical Service), ☎ 56.96.70.70. **Landes :** *SAMU,* ☎ 58.75.44.44 (Mont-de-Marsan) and 58.75.44.44 (Dax). *Poisoning Emergency Centre :* ☎ 56.96.40.80. *Ocean rescue centre :* ☎ 56.52.26.23., 56.52.26.24., or 56.59.82.00.

Weather forecast : Gironde : ☎ 56.34.26.74. ; **Landes,** ☎ 58.75.28.44.

Rural gîtes and chambres d'hôtes : Gironde : *Relais Régional,* Tauriac, 33710 Bourg sur Gironde, ☎ 56.68.40.02 ; **Landes :** Cité Galliane, 40000 Mont de Marsan, ☎ 58.75.15.62, and Loisirs-Accueil for reservations in certain gîtes.

Holiday villages : see practical holiday information.

Camping : more than 200 camp sites. Enq : *Syndicat de l'Hôtellerie de Plein Air,* 12, cours du 30-Juillet, 33080 Bordeaux. *Syndicat des Propriétaires and Gestionnaires des Terrains de Camping,* 38, cours du Mal-Joffre, 40100 Dax, ☎ 58.74.08.03.

Festivals : Apr : *Music Festival Week* in Saint-André-de-Cubzac, Albret Musical (Apr-Aug), ☎ 58.58.43.08. **May :** *music in Bazadais, May Music Festival* in Bordeaux, ☎ 56.90.91.60, ext 1259 and ☎ 47.05.40.42. **Jun :** *Music Season* in the Guîtres Abbey (Jun-Sep), ☎ 57.49.12.74, *Abbey Festival,* ☎ 58.92.02.07. **Jul :** *Jazz Festival* in Andernos, *Festival de Labastide-d'Armagnac* (until 15 Sep), ☎ 58.44.81.65, *Pyla Music Weeks* (Jul-Aug). **Aug :** *Chalosse Musical Monuments,* ☎ 58.73.71.93. **Sep-Oct :** *Autumn Music Festival* in the Orthe region. **Oct :** Music in Eysines, ☎ 56.28.03.33. *Autumn Music Festival* in Bazas. **Nov :** painting exhibition in La Réole, *SIGMA* in Bordeaux (contemporary art works).

Sporting events : mid-Mar : *coastal regatta* in Cagnotte. **Apr :** *cow-running* in Amou and Pomarez. **Whitsun :** *regattas* in Pauillac. **14 Jul :** *Haute-Lande marathon* (race on stilts). **Aug :** *Cesta Punta international tournament* in Hossegor. **Dec :** *international show jumping* in Bordeaux.

Exhibitions and trade fairs : Feb : *Salon des Antiquaires* in Bordeaux. **Apr :** *Exhibition Fair* in Biscarosse. **May :** *flower festival* in Cadillac, Saint-Justin *grand fair,* Bordeaux *international fair.* **Jun :** *wine fete* in Carcans-Maubuisson. **Jul :** Lesparre *wine fair.* **Aug :** *pony and draught horse fair* in Saubusse, *honey fair* in Pissos, *wine fair* in Sainte-Croix-du-Mont, *oyster fair* in Gujan-Mestras. **Sep :** Ousse-Suzan *grand fair* (St-Michel). **Oct :** *Radio, Television, Electroacoustic and Audiovisual Show* in Bordeaux.

Rural and traditional festivals and fairs : Feb : *Carnival* in Saubusse. **Mar :** *Fatted oxen parade* in Bazas. **Jun :** *fête de la Jurade* in Saint-Émilion. **May-Sep :** *summer festival* in Soustons. **Jun-Sep :** *summer festival* in Vieux-Boucau. **Jul :** *pine festival* in Tarnos, *traditional festival* in Saint-Vincent-de-Tyrosse. **Aug :** *jeux floraux* (flower show) in Contis, *traditional festival* in Hagetmau, Dax, Roquefort, Pomarez, Soustons, Saint-Sever and Arcachon. **Sep :** *festival of the new season's wine* in Cadillac, Barsac-Sauternes. **Oct :** *fêtes des vendanges* (grape harvest fetes) in Pouillon. **24 Dec :** *feu de la Torelle* in Cap-Breton.

Scenic railways : Guîtres-Marcenais line, ☎ 56.39.10.78, or 56.49.00.89 ; Sabres-Marqueze line runs on Sat, Sun and nat hols from Apr to Oct and daily from 15 Jun to 20 Sep. Labouheyre-Marqueze-Sabres line : Sun and nat hols from 1 Jun to 15 Sep ; A.B.A.C., 40630 Sabres, ☎ 58.07.52.99.

Technical tourism : *Journées Rencontres de Tourisme* in a rural setting ; the programme includes a visit to a wine cellar or store-house, an apiculture course for beginners, a visit to a pine processing mill, a demonstration in the tapping of pine resin, and a visit to a *foie gras* cooperative : enq *Service Social Spécialisé de la Caisse Mutuelle Sociale Agricole,* rte de Bayonne, 40000 Mont-de-Marsan, ☎ 58.75.44.88. *Caves du Pain de Sucre,* 33710 Bourg sur Gironde, on the scenic road to Blaye.

Rambling and hiking : topoguides (G.R.6) 662/65. The Mont-de-Marsan Prefecture, ☎ 58.75.84.40, ext 433, provides useful information on the indicated trails in the Landes Nature Park. Numerous short hikes : bookings at *Gironde Loisirs-Accueil* and the *C.D.T.* Landes, ☎ 56.20.20.53, for the C.R.A.P.A circuits. Numerous other possibilities at the *C.A.F. Sud-Ouest,* 17, cours Xavier-Arnozan, 33000 Bordeaux, ☎ 56.52.26.80, and *Dir. Dép. Jeunesse and Sports Gironde,* ☎ 56.52.13.52 ; *Landes,* ☎ 58.75.52.22. Orientation courses : *Comités Départementaux Gironde,* ☎ 56.60.31.01, and *Landes,* ☎ 58.75.46.66, ext 234.

Riding holidays : Gironde : *Association Régionale de Tourisme Équestre* (A.R.T.E.), domaine de Volcelest, 33830 Joué-Belin, ☎ 56.88.02.68, and *Ligue Régionale de la Féd. Franc. d'Équitation,* 51, quai de Queyries, 33100 Bordeaux-Bastide, ☎ 56.56.01.38. **Landes :** A.D.T.E.,-Chambre d'Agriculture, 40000 Mont-de-Marsan, ☎ 58.75.15.62. *Comité Dép. Hippique Landais,* Esalat, rte de Tercis, 40100 Dax, ☎ 58.74.13.00, and *C.D.T. Landes :* these organizations give information on the excursion possibilities, itineraries and lodgings. For "carriage holidays", contact ☎ 58.07.66.04 in Luxey, 40430 Sore.

Cycling holidays : the *Comité Dép. de Cyclotourisme des Landes* proposes twenty-five 50-100 km itineraries and a number of permanent circuits ; enq : 12, rue Gabriel-Fauré, 40990 Saint Paul lès Dax, ☎ 58.74.27.52, and Préfecture de Mont-de-Marsan, ☎ 58.75.38.67. In the Gironde region : bookings *Loisirs-Accueil,* ☎ 56.52.61.40.

River and canal cruises : Bordeaux wine cruises on the Garonne and Dordogne rivers and the Midi canal : bookings : *Loisirs-Accueil* Gironde, ☎ 56.52.61.40, and enq *C.D.T.* Gironde, ☎ 56.90.92.24.

Instruction courses : the *Dir. Dép. du Temps Libre,* ☎ 58.75.52.22, organises sailing courses and scenic bicycle tours of the **Landes** region. Free instruction sports courses for beginners (May-Jun-Sep-Oct) organised by the *Dir. Régional du Temps Libre,* ☎ 56.24.33.33.

Children : courses organised by the *Dir. Dép. du Temps Libre,* ☎ 58.75.52.22, and *Dir. Régionale,* ☎ 56.24.33.33.

Golf : Bordeaux-Lac (9 holes) ; Arcachon (18 holes) ; Bordeaux-Caudéran (18 holes) ; Bordeaux-Cameyrac (18 holes) ; Lacanau (18 holes) ; Mont-de-Marsan (9 holes) ; Hossegor (18 holes).

Aquatic sports : sailing, wind-surfing : for information concerning sailing schools and regattas, contact the *Ligue Régionale de Voile :* AC du Sud-Ouest, 8, pl. des Quinconces, Bordeaux, ☎ 56.44.22.92, *Yacht-Club Landais,* av. de Bordeaux, 40150 Hossegor, ☎ 58.43.66.82, and *C.D.T. Landes.*

Surfing : *Féd. Franç. de Surf et de Skate,* Comité de Tourisme et des Fêtes, Cité administrative, av. Édouard-VII, 64250 Biarritz, ☎ 56.24.52.50.

Speed-sailing : Féd. Franç. : 96, rue Etchenique, 33200 Bordeaux, ☎ 56.02.09.81.

Canoeing : *Ligue Régionale,* 184, cours Pasteur, 33200 Bordeaux-Cauderan, ☎ 56.08.23.15. Possibility in Gironde ou the Lège, the Ciron, the Dropt, the Eyre, the Jalle, the Larrit. Landes : streams of Contis, of Ste-Eulalie and of Muchet on the Douze, the Gorbas, the Leyre and the Luy. C.D.T. Landes and Gironde will give you information about schools. Topological map of the rivers of the Landes region : *Comité Dép. de Canoë-Kayak,* 8, rue Guibert, 40500 Saint Sever, ☎ 58.76.00.51.

Potholing and spelunking : *Comité Spéléo de Gironde,* hôtel des Sociétés Savantes, 71, rue du Loup, 33000 Bordeaux.

Cow running : *Féd. Franç. de Course Landaise,* 2, rue des Archers, 40100 Dax, ☎ 58.74.70.10, and *C.D.T. Landes.*

Flying, gliding and parachuting : flying : *Union Régionale,* 79, av. du Mal-Leclerc, 33200 Sainte Foy la Grande, ☎ 56.46.15.82 ; gliding : *Ligue Régionale,* 10, cours Alsace-Lorraine, 33000 Bordeaux, ☎ 56.44.22.81, and *Association Aéronautique Aquitaine,* ☎ 56.21.75.57 ; parachuting : *Ligue Régionale de Prachutisme Sportif d'Aquitaine,* stade Vangermez, 33140 Villenave-d'Ornon. **Gironde :** La Teste, ☎ 56.66.09.72 ; Soulac, ☎ 56.59.84.50. **Landes :** Biscarosse, ☎ 58.78.10.69.

Hunting and shooting : *Fédération Dép. des Chasseurs de Gironde,* 82, quai des Chartrons, 33000 Bordeaux, ☎ 56.29.24.45. *Féd. Dép. des Chasseurs des Landes,* 151, av. G.-Clemenceau, B.P. 172, 40130 Dax Cedex, ☎ 58.74.38.69.

Fishing : enq at the *Féd. dép. des Assoc. de Pêche et Pisciculture* (F.D.A.P.P.). **Gironde :** 299, cours de la Somme, 33800 Bordeaux, ☎ 56.92.59.48. **Landes :** pl. A.-Briand, 40400 Tartas, ☎ 58.73.43.79. Sea fishing : quartier des Affaires maritimes, *Direction des Aff. Marit. du Littoral Sud-Ouest,* 3, rue Fondaudège, 33000 Bordeaux, ☎ 56.52.10.71, and *Affaires Maritimes,* at the port, 33120 Arcachon, ☎ 56.83.06.47.

● Towns

AIRE-SUR-L'ADOUR

Mont-de-Marsan 31, Pau 49, Paris 736
B4 ⊠ 40800

ⓘ pl. Ch.-de-Gaulle (high season), ☎ 58.76.64.70.

SNCF ☎ 58.76.64.65.

Hotel :

● ★★**Commerce** (L.F.), 3, bd des Pyrénées, ☎ 58.76.60.06. Euro. 20 rm Ⓟ closed 2-20 Jan, Mon, 180. Rest. ♦♦ Highly reputed, closed Mon, Sun eve. Spec : *foie de canard aux pommes, confit de canard aux cèpes,* 120-210.

⛺ ★★*Les Ombrages de l'Adour* (100 pl.), ☎ 58.76.64.70.

Restaurant :

Geaune, ⊠ 40320, 13 km W :

♦ **Frande,** rue Gourgues, ☎ 58.44.51.18. With rm ♿ Good value for money, 80-130.

See also Riscle (Midi-Toulouse region).

Leisure activities : canoe trip down the Adour river, M. Bourrec, bd Lamothe, ☎ 58.76.67.88.

AMOU

Mont-de-Marsan 47, Pau 49, Paris 737
A4 ⊠ 40330

ⓘ mairie, ☎ 58.89.00.22.

Hotel :

● ★★**Commerce,** pl. de la Poste, ☎ 58.89.02.28. AE, DC, Euro, Visa. 20 rm Ⓟ closed Nov and Mon in winter, 135. Rest. ♦♦ Spec : *foie gras aux raisins, confit,* 45-80.

Farmhouse gîte : *les Pins,* in Castel-Sarrazin, 4 km N, ☎ 58.89.30.31.

Bicycle-hire : M. Capdeville, ☎ 58.57.02.99. M. Larrey, ☎ 58.57.02.26.

ANDERNOS-LES-BAINS

Bordeaux 46, Mont-de-Marsan 118, Paris 627
35 km NE of Arcachon, A2 ⊠ 33510

ⓘ 33, av. Gal-de-Gaulle, ☎ 56.82.02.95.

Hotel :

★★**Le Coulin,** 3, av. d'Arès, ☎ 56.82.04.35. Visa. 11 rm Ⓟ closed 1 Jan-1 Feb and Mon, 180. Rest. ♦ ♿ Good basic fare, 45-80.

⛺ ★★★*Pleine Forêt* (210 pl.), ☎ 56.82.17.18.

Event : jazz festival in Jul.

ARCACHON

Bordeaux 64, Bayonne 181, Paris 653
A2 ⊠ 33120

ⓘ quinconces de la Gare, ☎ 56.83.01.69.

SNCF ☎ 56.83.88.88.

Car-hire : *Budget* train + auto, at the station, ☎ 56.83.08.28.

Hotels :
★★★★***Arc Hôtel,*** 89, bd de la Plage, ☎ 56.83.06.85. AE, DC, Visa. 30 rm P 710.
★★★***Les Ormes,*** 1, rue Hovy, ☎ 56.83.09.27. Tx 570503. Visa. 24 rm P 400. Rest. ♦♦ ♿ 120-210.
★★★***Richelieu,*** 185, bd de la Plage, ☎ 56.83.16.50. Tx 540043. AE, DC, Visa. 42 rm P ♿ closed Nov-mid-Mar, 180. Rest., 80-130.
★★★***Roc Hôtel,*** 202, bd de la Plage, ☎ 56.83.05.01. Tx 570503. 33 rm ♿ closed early Oct-Easter, 400. Rest. ♦ 80-130.
★★★***Les Vagues,*** 9, bd de l'Océan, ☎ 56.83.03.75. Tx 570503. AE, DC, Visa. 21 rm P closed Nov-Feb, 260. Rest. ♦♦ (eve only), 120-210.
★★★***Point France,*** 1, rue Grenier, ☎ 56.83.46.74. Tx 570503. AE, DC, Euro, Visa. 34 rm ♿ closed 15 Nov-1 Mar, 450.
★★***Gascogne,*** 79, cours Héricart-de-Thury, ☎ 56.83.42.52. Tx 570503. AE, DC, Visa. 38 rm ♿ 190. Rest. ♦ 70-120.
★★***Lamartine,*** 28, av. Lamartine, ☎ 56.83.95.77. Tx 550422. AE, Visa. 31 rm P ♿ closed 1 Nov-1 Mar, 250.

Moulleau, 5 km SW :
★★***Les Buissonnets,*** 12, rue L.-Garros, ☎ 56.22.53.89. 7 rm closed 1-31 Oct, 220. Rest. ♦ ♿ Spec : seafood, *magret de canard,* 65-140.

⛺ ★★*Les Abatilles* (240 pl.), ☎ 56.83.24.15.

Restaurants :
♦♦ ***Boron,*** 15, rue Pr-Jolyet, ☎ 56.83.29.96. closed Dec, Wed low season. Spec : *huîtres en civet au vin d'entre-deux-mers,* 120-210.
♦♦ ***Chez Yvette,*** 59, bd Gal-Leclerc, ☎ 56.83.05.11. ♿ closed 2 Jan-9 Feb. Spec : seafood, 160.
♦ ***Bayonne,*** 9, cours Lamarque, ☎ 56.83.33.82. AE P ♿ closed 30 Sep-Easter, 80-130.
♦ ***Café de Bordeaux,*** 39, bd Mal-Leclerc, ☎ 56.83.05.18. With 10 rm. Good value for money, 80-130.

Event : basin festival 15 Aug.

Casino, 210, bd de la Plage, ☎ 56.83.16.66.

Leisure activities : *promenade en pinasse* (flat-bottomed boat) in the Arcachon basin (enq O.D.T.).

Recommended : *la Maison des Produits Régionaux,* aire de repos de Cestas, Arcachon motorway (Bernard Lafon's regional preserves).

BARSAC

Bordeaux 38, Bergerac 80, Paris 634
8 km NW of Langon, B2 ✉ 33720 Podensac

Hotels :
● ★★★***Le Château de Rolland,*** on the N113 (Châteaux-Hôtels), ☎ 56.27.15.75, AE, DC, Visa. 8 rm P 220. Rest. ♦♦ ♿ Good fare, 95-220.

Farmhouse-inn, chambres and tables d'hôtes : *château de Broustaret,* à Rioms, 9 km NW, ☎ 56.27.06.53.

⛺ ★*Les Vignes* (50 pl.), ☎ 56.27.19.34.

Recommended : *Confrérie Vineuse et Dégustation (wine-tasting association) :* château Gravas, ☎ 56.27.15.20.

BAZAS

Bordeaux 59, Agen 85, Paris 653
B2 ✉ 33430

ℹ pl. de la Cathédrale, ☎ 56.25.00.02.

Hotels :
● ★★★***Relais de Fompeyre,*** rte de Bayonne, ☎ 56.25.04.60. Tx 550684. AE, DC, Visa. 32 rm P ♿ 255. Rest. ♦ 65-110.
★★***Saint-Sauveur*** (L.F.), 14, cours du Gal-de-Gaulle, ☎ 56.25.12.18. 10 rm P closed Jun and Sun ex Jul-Aug, 180.

Farmhouse-inn : *Piquetuge,* Gajac, 6 km E, ☎ 56.25.10.62.

Event : *promenade des bœufs gras* (parade of fatted oxen) in Mar.

BISCARROSSE

Bordeaux 72, Mont-de-Marsan 87, Paris 661
A2 ✉ 40600

ℹ 19 *ter,* av. de la Plage, in Biscarrosse-Plage, 9.5 km NW, ☎ 58.78.20.96.

Hotels :

Ispe, 6 km N :
★★***La Caravelle,*** ☎ 58.78.02.67. 11 rm P ♿ closed Oct-1 Feb, 200. Rest. ♦ ♿ closed Mon ex Jun to Sep, 70-160.

La Plage, ✉ 40520 Biscarosse-Plage, 9 km NW :
★★***La Forestière*** (L.F.) av. du Pyla, ☎ 58.78.24.14. Visa. 34 rm P ♿ Pension, 300. Rest. ♦ closed Nov and Fri, 55-160.
★***Auberge Régina,*** 2, av. de la Libération, ☎ 58.78.23.34. 11 rm P ♿ closed 1 Sep-1 Apr, Wed noon 1 Apr-1 Jun, 210. Rest. 55-100.

⛺ ★★★*De la Rive* (345 empl.), ☎ 58.78.12.33.

Bicycle-hire : *Éts Brogniez,* ☎ 58.78.13.76.

BLAYE

Bordeaux 51, Saintes 76, Paris 545
B1 ♥ ✉ 33390

ℹ allées Marines, ☎ 57.42.02.45 (high season).

SNCF ☎ 57.92.50.50.

Hotels :
● ★★***La Citadelle*** (Châteaux-Hôtels), a remarkable setting in the Blaye citadel, ☎ 58.42.17.10. Tx 540127. AE, DC, Visa. 21 rm P 210. Rest. ♦♦ 70-150.
★★***Bellevue,*** 2, cours du Gal-de-Gaulle, ☎ 58.42.00.36. AE, Euro, Visa. 24 rm closed 18 Dec-5 Jan, Sat low season, 100. Rest. ♦ 80-130.

⛺ ★★*La Citadelle* (30 pl.), ☎ 58.42.00.20.

BORDEAUX

Agen 139, Bayonne 184, Paris 583
B2 ✉ 33000

ℹ 12, cours du 30-Juillet (C2), ☎ 56.44.28.41.

✈ Bordeaux-Mérignac, 10 km W, ☎ 56.34.84.84.
Air France Agency, 29, rue Esprit-des-Lois (C2), 33077 Bordeaux Cedex, ☎ 56.44.64.35. Airport, ☎ 56.34.32.32.

SNCF Saint-Jean station (F5), ☎ 56.92.50.50., 56.92.76.56.

🚌 rue La Raurie-de-Monbadon (B2).

Car-hire : *Budget* train + auto, S.N.C.F. station, Saint-Jean, ☎ 56.91.65.50/56.91.20.65, and Bordeaux-Mérignac airport, ☎ 56.47.30.50.

Hotels :

★★★★***Frantel,*** 5, rue R.-Lateulade (A-B3), ☎ 56.90.92.37. Tx 540565. AE, DC, Euro, Visa. 196 rm Ⓟ ♿ 400. Rest. ♦♦ ***le Mériadeck.*** Spec : *noix de st-jacques au sauternes, émincé de lapereau aux champignons des bois et graine de moutarde,* 120-210.

★★★***Terminus*** (Mapotel), Saint-Jean station (F5), ☎ 56.92.71.58. Tx 540264. AE, DC, Euro, Visa. 80 rm Ⓟ ♿ 260. Rest. ♦♦♦ 120-210.

● ★★★***Sèze,*** 23, allée de Tourny (C2), ☎ 56.52.65.54. AE, DC, Visa. 25 rm, 280.

★★★***Grand Hôtel et Café de Bordeaux,*** 3-5, pl. de la Comédie (C2-3), ☎ 56.90.93.44. Tx 541658. AE, DC, Euro, Visa. 98 rm Ⓟ ♿ 410.

★★★***Français,*** 12, rue du Temple (C3), ☎ 56.48.10.35, Tx 550587. AE, DC, Visa. 36 rm ♿ 260.

★★★***Normandie,*** 7, cours du 30-Juillet (C2), ☎ 56.52.16.80. Tx 570481. AE, DC, Euro, Visa. 100 rm ♿ 250.

★★★***Majestic,*** 2, rue de Condé (C2), ☎ 56.52.60.44. Visa. 50 rm Ⓟ ♿ 240.

★★★***Royal Médoc,*** 3-5, rue de Sèze (C2), ☎ 56.81.72.42. Tx 660053. 45 rm 260.

★★***Atlantic,*** 69, rue E.-Leroy (E5), ☎ 56.92.92.22. AE, Visa. 36 rm Ⓟ closed 22 Dec-2 Jan, 200.

★★***Continental,*** 10, rue Montesquieu (C2-3), ☎ 56.52.66.00. Visa. 51 rm Ⓟ ♿ 180.

★★***Vieux Bordeaux,*** 22, rue du Cancéra (C3), ☎ 56.48.07.27. AE, Visa. 11 rm 18thC furnishings, 150.

Pessac, ⊠ 33600, 5 km SW :

★★★★***La Réserve*** (Relais et châteaux), 74, av. du Bourgailh, ☎ 56.07.13.28. Tx 560585. AE, DC, Euro, Visa. 20 rm Ⓟ closed 31 Oct-31 Mar, 510. Rest. ● ♦♦ ♿ A 7 ha park and a lake with swans for the other gourmand address of the Flourens family (Rest. *Dubern*), 180-300.

★★★***Royal Brion,*** 10, rue du Pin-Vert, ☎ 56.45.07.72. AE, DC. 26 rm Ⓟ ♿ closed 23 Dec-mid-Jan, 260.

Saint-Médard-en-Jalles, ⊠ 33160, 14 km NW :

★★***La Chaumière,*** 141, av. du Gal-de-Gaulle, ☎ 56.05.07.64. Visa. 20 rm Ⓟ ♿ 120. Rest. ♦ closed Sun eve and Mon and eve nat hols, 65-140.

La House, Canéjean, ⊠ 33610 Cestas, 15 km SW on the RN10 :

★★***La Palombière,*** ☎ 56.89.17.52. Visa. 20 rm Ⓟ ♿ 70-160. Rest. ♦ 190.

Salaunes, ⊠ 33160, 19 km NW :

★★★***Les Ardillères,*** ☎ 56.05.20.70. 40 rm Ⓟ 6 ha 260. Rest. ♦♦ ***la Bombarde,*** 120-210.

Youth hostel : 22, cours Barbey (E5), 33000 Bordeaux.

Restaurants :

● ♦♦♦ ***Jean Ramet,*** 7 et 8, pl. Jaurès (D2), ☎ 56.44.12.51. Visa. Ⓟ ♿ closed Sat, Sun. Efficiently helped by his charming wife and young team, this brilliant student of the Troisgros brothers and Michel Guérard treats you, according to his whim and the day's market, to classic or modern dishes. Spec : *foie gras de canard au caramel,* lamprey, *bar au médoc.* Excellent pastries. Fine cellar, 220-310.

● ♦♦♦ ***Dubern*** (Relais gourmand), 42, allée de Tourny (C2), ☎ 56.48.03.44. AE, DC, Euro, Visa Ⓟ A magnificent listed hotel masterfully directed by R. Flourens. Spec : *magret au foie gras, écrevisses au sainte-croix,* a fine list of bordeaux wines excellently advised by the president of master-sommeliers, H. Valverde. Downstairs : *l'Estaminet :* piano-bar, chic young people, low prices, 240-300.

● ♦♦♦ ***La Chamade,*** 20, rue Piliers-de-Tutelle (D3), ☎ 56.48.13.74. AE. closed Sun noon from 14 Jul-15 Aug. A fine 18thC cellar for inspired cuisine. Spec : *salade de poissons à l'huile de noix, gâteau de carottes à l'orange,* 125-200.

● ♦♦♦ ***Christian Clément,*** 58, rue Pas-St-Georges (C3), ☎ 56.81.01.39. AE, DC. ♿ closed Sat noon, Sun nat hols and 10-31 Aug. An excellent cuisine executed in a masterful manner by a former cook at Sanderen's we had forgotten. Spec : *filets de rougets au foie gras frais à l'acidulé, escalopes de rognons de veau panés au cumin.* Good wine cellar, 230-250.

● ♦♦♦ ***Clavel,*** 44, rue Ch.-Domercq (F-E5), ☎ 56.92.91.52. ♿ closed 14 Jul-1 Aug. Here hides a modest but great chef, inventor and poet. For Francis Garcia, « Cooking from the heart is the one that touches souls ». Charming welcome from Géraldine Garcia. Spec : *gratin d'huîtres au foie gras, pot-au-feu de canard,* dessert festival, 220-310.

● ♦♦ ***Le Rouzic,*** 34, cours Chapeau-Rouge (C-D3), ☎ 56.44.39.11. AE, DC, Visa. ♿ closed Sat and Sun noon (summer) and Sat noon and Sun (winter). Calm, refinement and quality for Michel Gautier's excellent cuisine. Spec : *feuilleté léger de queues de langoustines aux morilles et ris de veau,* lamprey. Fine wine cellar. *Le Bolchoï,* upstairs : for folklore, Russian cooking and 25 kinds of vodka, 220-310.

● ♦♦ ***Bistrot de Bordeaux,*** 10, rue Piliers-de-Tutelle (D3), ☎ 56.52.92.32. AE, Visa. ♿ closed Sat and Sun. Daily specials and good wines served by the glass or by the bottle, 120-210.

♦♦ ***Le Buhan,*** 28, rue Buhan (D4), ☎ 56.52.80.86. AE, DC. closed Mon (winter), 80-250.

● ♦♦ ***Philippe,*** 1, pl. du Parlement (C3), ☎ 56.81.83.15. AE, DC, Visa, closed Sun, Mon, Aug. For quality fish. Spec : seafood platter, *escalope de bar aux raisins frais,* 220-310.

● ♦ ***La Tupina,*** 6, rue Porte-de-la-Monnaie, ☎ 56.91.56.37 ♿ closed Sun and nat hols. Authentic SW cuisine : *mignons de canard vinaigrette échalote, brochette de cœurs de canard grillés,* 120-210.

♦ ***Le Chef,*** 57, rue Huguerie (B2), ☎ 56.81.67.07. Visa. ♿ closed Sun eve, Mon, 80-130.

♦ ***L'Ombrière,*** 14, pl. du Parlement (C3), ☎ 56.44.82.69. AE, DC, Visa. ♿ closed Sun, Mon and Aug. Period setting, 120-210.

♦ ***Le Péché Mignon,*** 6, rue du Temple (C3), ☎ 56.44.60.37, closed Sat and Sun. Fish dishes, 80-130.

Bègles, ⊠ 33130 Bègles-Dorat :

♦♦ ***Erbia,*** 1, rte de Courréjean, ☎ 56.85.88.87. Visa. Ⓟ ♿ closed 15 Jul-15 Aug, nat hols, Sat noon and Sun. An ARC cook specialized in regional cooking : lamprey, *chipirons, coquilles st. jacques* when in season, 220-310.

Bouliac (rt bank), ⊠ 33270 Floirac, 9 km SE :

● ♦♦♦ ***Saint-James*** (Relais gourmand), pl. Camille-Hosteins, ☎ 56.20.52.19 closed 15 Jan-28 Feb. From « la Haut » as J.-M. Amat's beautiful house has been named by Bordelais people, we have a view over Bordeaux ! This allows us to appreciate more the delicate and inventive cuisine. Spec : *fondant d'aubergines au cumin, filets d'anguilles simplement sautés aux baraganes ;* superb desserts and bordeaux wines, 100-300.

♦♦ ***Auberge du Marais,*** 22, rte Latresne, ☎ 56.20.52.17 Ⓟ ♿ closed Wed, Feb school hols and Aug. Seasonal cuisine, 120-210.

La Prade, ⊠ 33650 Labrède, 11 km S :

♦♦ ***Le Bocage,*** ☎ 56.20.20.68. closed Feb, Sun eve and Mon low season. Spec : *huîtres chaudes* *au carry de Madras à fondu de foie gras, magret grillé au cassis et aux airelles,* 120-210.

See also Quinsac.

Guided tours : enq ℹ

Entertainment : *Grand Théâtre de Bordeaux,* pl. de la Comédie (C2-3), *Centre d'Animation Culturelle de l'Ouest Aquitain,* pl. de la République, at Saint-Médard-en-Jalles, ☎ 56.05.09.53.

Event : *May Music Festival,* information and bookings at the Grand Théâtre, ☎ 56.90.91.60.

Recommended : *Hôtel des Vins,* 106, rue Abbé-de-l'Épée (B2), ☎ 56.48.01.29 ; sampling and sales of bordeaux wines, carafes, museum. *Cellier des Chartrons,* 41, rue Borie (D1), ☎ 56.29.72.91. *M. Mazauque,* 10, rue des Bahutiers (D3), ☎ 56.52.94.14, engraver ; glasses for bordeaux wines engraved to order. *Saunion,* chocolate confectioner, 56, cours G.-Clemenceau (B3-C2), ☎ 56.48.05.75. *F. Chabrette,* home-made *foie gras,* Le Mouréou, Cabanac, 33650 Labrède, 30 km S of Bordeaux, ☎ 56.20.24.87.

BRANNE

Bordeaux 32, Bergerac 55, Paris 616
8 km SW Saint-Émilion, B2 ✉ 33420

ℹ mairie, ☎ 57.84.52.33.

Hotel :
★★***France*** (L.F.), 7, pl. du Marché, ☎ 57.84.50.06. 15 rm Ⓟ ♨ ✈ closed Oct, 180. Rest. ♦ closed Tue low season, 120-210.

CAPBRETON

Bayonne 18, Mont-de-Marsan 84, Paris 756
A4 ✉ 40130

ℹ av. G.-Pompidou, ☎ 58.72.12.11.

Hotels :
★★***Atlantic,*** 75, av. de-Lattre-de-Tassigny, ☎ 58.72.11.14. 53 rm Ⓟ ♨ ⛱ ▭ closed 1 Oct-15 May, 190. Rest. ♦ ✈ closed 15-31 May and 15-30 Sep, 100.
★★***Miramar,*** bd du Front-de-Mer, ☎ 58.72.12.82. AE, Euro. 43 rm ⁘ Ⓟ ✈ ♿ closed Oct-Apr, 230. Rest. ♦ 65-170.
★★***Océan*** (L.F.), 95, bd G.-Pompidou, ☎ 58.72.10.22. AE, DC, Euro. 45 rm ⁘ Ⓟ ✈ closed 10 Oct-15 Mar, 180. Rest. ♦♦ ♿ closed Tue low season, 50-120.

⛺ ★★★*La Civelle* (600 pl.), ☎ 58.72.15.11.

Restaurant :
♦♦ ***La Sardinière,*** 87, av. G.-Pompidou, ☎ 58.72.10.49. AE, DC ⁘ Ⓟ closed 12 Nov-12 Dec, 130-160.

Bicycle-hire : beach arcades.

CAP-FERRET

Bordeaux 71, Mont-de-Marsan 148, Paris 653
A2 ✉ 33970

ℹ pl. du Marché, ☎ 56.60.63.26.

Hotels :
★★***Dunes,*** 119, av. de Bordeaux, ☎ 56.60.61.81. 13 rm Ⓟ ⛱ ♿ closed 25 Sep-Easter, 155.
★***Pins,*** 25, rue des Fauvettes, ☎ 56.60.60.11. 14 rm ♨ ✈ closed 16 Oct-1 Jun, 230.

⛺ ★★★*Les Sables d'Or* (230 pl.), ☎ 56.60.62.73.

CASTETS

Dax 22, Bayonne 57, Paris 714
A3 ✉ 40260

ℹ ☎ 58.89.44.79.

Hotel :
★***Côte d'Argent,*** rte de Léon, ☎ 58.89.40.33. 12 rm Ⓟ ♨ ⛱ ✈ closed 1 Nov-1 Apr, 100. Rest. 60-130.

⛺ ★★★*Le Galan* (210 pl.), ☎ 58.89.43.52.

Farmhouse gîtes : *Lelanne,* ☎ 58.89.41.89 ; *Jouand'Herm,* 5 km S, ☎ 58.89.42.17.

CASTILLON-LA-BATAILLE

Bergerac 43, Bordeaux 49, Paris 544
B2 ✉ 33350

ℹ mairie, ☎ 57.40.00.06.

SNCF ☎ 56.40.00.28.

Hotel :
★★***Bonne Auberge,*** 12, rue du 8-Mai-1945, ☎ 57.40.11.56. AE, DC, Visa. 10 rm ♿ closed 1-21 Nov, Sat noon and Mon, 130. Rest. ♦ Regional products, 60-160.

⛺ ★★*La Pelouse* (45 pl.), ☎ 57.40.04.22.

Table d'hôtes and riding centre : *Blanzas,* ☎ 57.49.00.85.

Farmhouse gîte : *le Bourg,* 9 km SE, in Gensac, ☎ 57.40.42.25.

COUTRAS

Bordeaux 49, Périgueux 77, Paris 585
B1 ✉ 33230

ℹ mairie, ☎ 57.49.04.60.

SNCF ☎ 57.49.00.85.

Hotel :
Rolland, 6 km NE :
★★★***Auberge la Rollandière,*** ☎ 57.49.11.63. 9 rm ⁘ Ⓟ ♨ ⛱ ▭ closed 1 Apr-1 May and Mon low saison, 200. Rest. ♦ ♿ 30-100.

⛺ ★★*Municipal Frais Rivage* (50 pl.), ☎ 57.49.12.00.

DAX

Bayonne 50, Bordeaux 142, Paris 736
A3-4 ⚓ (t.a.) ✉ 40100

ℹ pl. Thiers (B1), ☎ 58.74.82.33.

SNCF ☎ 58.74.50.50., 58.74.38.75.

Car-hire : *Budget* train + auto at *Hendaye Auto Rental.* Esplanade Gal-de-Gaulle, res. La Néhé, ☎ 58.74.58.00, or at the station, ☎ 58.74.38.75.

Hotels :
● ★★★***Parc*** (Mapotel), 1, pl. Thiers (B1), ☎ 58.74.86.17. Tx 540481. AE, DC, Visa. 40 rm Ⓟ 260. Rest. ♦♦♦ ✈ ♿ closed 15 Dec-15 Jan, 120-210.
★★★***Splendid,*** 2, cours de Verdun (B1-2), ☎ 58.74.59.30. Tx 540085. AE, DC, Euro. 180 rm ⁘ ♨ closed 27 Nov-1 May, 270. Rest. ♦♦ 80-130.
★★★***Grand Hôtel,*** bd des Sports (C2), ☎ 58.74.84.58. Tx 540516. 138 rm Ⓟ ♨ ⛱ ▭ 200. Rest. ♦♦ ♿ 120-210.
★★★***Regina,*** bd des Sports (C1), ☎ 58.74.84.58. 131 rm Ⓟ ♨ ⛱ ♿ closed 4 Dec-3 Mar, 140. Rest. ♦♦ 120-210.
★★***Miradour,*** av. E.-Millies-Lacroix (A2), ☎ 58.74.98.86. Tx 540085. AE, DC. 120 rm ⁘ Ⓟ ♨ ♿ 180. Rest. ♦ 80-130.

★★***Les Écureuils,*** rue de la Croix-Blanche, ☎ 58.90.07.71. 52 rm 🅿 ♨ ♿ closed Dec-Mar, 180.
★★***Gare,*** pl. de la Gare (B1), ☎ 58.74.21.91. AE, Visa. 20 rm 🅿 ♨ 180. Rest. ♦ 80-130.
★***Nord*** (L.F.), 68, av. Saint-Vincent-de-Paul, ☎ 58.74.19.87. 19 rm 🅿 ♨ closed 20 Dec-6 Jan, 80.

Saint-Paul-lès-Dax, ✉ 40990, 2 km N :
★★***Relais des Thermes,*** av. Mal-Foch, ☎ 58.91.64.37. DC, Visa. 20 rm 🅿 ♨ closed 23 Dec-31 Jan and Mon low season. Half-board only in high season, 180. Rest. ♦ 80-130.

Restaurants :
● ♦♦ ***Bois de Boulogne,*** ☎ 58.74.23.32. 🅿 ♨ ♿ closed Sun eve, Mon and Oct. Subtle fish grills seasoned with herbs and *foie frais de canard grillé ;* delicious fare in an equally ravishing setting, 45-130.
♦♦ ***Relais des Plages,*** Saint-Paul-lès-Dax (3 km SE on the D947), ☎ 58.74.08.86. With rm 🅿 ♿ closed mid-Nov-mid-Dec and Mon, 120-210.
♦ ***Richelieu,*** 13, av. Victor-Hugo (B3), ☎ 58.74.81.81. AE, DC, Euro, Visa. With 20 rm ♨ ♿ Good value for money. Spec : *homard à la Marensine,* 80-210.

Casino : cours de Verdun (B1-2), ☎ 58.74.21.35.

Bicycle-hire : *Escoubeyron et Lucchi,* ☎ 58.74.29.92.

Recommended : *J. Lasserre, foie gras* and *confits,* Pouillon, 15 km SE, ☎ 58.98.24.90. Retail sales and shipping.

EUGÉNIE-LES-BAINS

Mont-de-Marsan 26, Pau 53, Paris 743
B4 ✉ 40320 Geaune

⚕ (1 Apr-31 Oct), ☎ 58.58.19.01.

ℹ ☎ 58.58.15.37.

Hotel :
● ★★★★***Les Prés et les Sources d'Eugénie*** (Relais et Châteaux), ☎ 58.51.19.01. Tx 540470. AE, DC. 35 rm. Beautiful Second Empire residence 🅿 ♨ closed Nov-1 Mar, 500. Rest. ● ♦♦♦♦ We do not have to introduce Michel Guérard, one of the masters of French cuisine. His cuisine is the best of SW France. Each of his creations is unique and masterfully executed by the faithful and talented Didier Oudil. Christine is the hostess of this veritable paradise. When you read this, new delightful dishes will have been added to their *carte,* 320-450.

Restaurants :
♦ ***Bistrot d'Eugénie,*** rue René-Vielle, ☎ 58.51.19.07. With rm ♿ closed 2 weeks in Feb and 2 weeks in Dec. Good value for money, 120-210.
♦ ***Lalanne,*** rue René-Vielle, ☎ 58.51.19.17 🅿 ♨ ♿ closed Nov-Mar, 60-130.

Gîte, farmhouse-inn : *Pigon,* Vieille-Tursan, 8.5 km W, ☎ 58.58.16.51.

GUJAN-MESTRAS

Bordeaux 54, Mont-de-Marsan 115, Paris 644
10 km E of Arcachon, A2 ✉ 33470

ℹ 41, av. de-Lattre-de-Tassigny, ☎ 56.66.12.65.

SNCF ☎ 56.66.00.68.

Hotels :
★★***La Guérinière,*** ☎ 56.66.08.78. 25 rm 🅿 ♨ 260. Rest. ♦♦ 120-210.
★***Il Bacio,*** 8, av. de-Lattre-de-Tassigny, ☎ 56.66.12.12. 17 rm ♨ ♿ closed 1 Oct-1 Dec, 1-28 Feb and Wed low season, 140. Rest. ♦ 70-110.

Event : oyster fair in Aug.

Leisure activities : excursion in a *pinasse* (flatbottomed boat) from the port.

Recommended : *oyster tasting : Beynel-Daney,* av. de la Gare, port du Canal, ☎ 56.66.00.37. *Orvart,* port de Larros, ☎ 56.66.01.04.

HAGETMAU

Mont-de-Marsan 29, Pau 57, Paris 716
B4 ✉ 40700

ℹ ☎ 58.79.33.14.

SNCF ☎ 58.79.33.30.

Hotels :
★★***Auberge Lacs d'Halco*** (Relais du Silence), ☎ 58.79.56.56. Visa. 23 rm 🅿 ♨ ♿ 180. Rest. ♦ 80-130.
★***Le Jambon,*** 27, rue Carnot, ☎ 58.79.32.02. AE, Visa. 9 rm 🅿 ♨ closed Jan and Mon low season, 160. Rest. 60-170.
★***Relais Basque,*** 1, rue Pascal-Duprat, ☎ 58.79.30.64. Euro, Visa. 6 rm ♨ closed Sun eve, 80. Rest. 45-85.

⛺ ★★★★*Municipal des Loussets* (25 pl.), ☎ 58.79.33.14.

Farmhouse-inn and chambres d'hôtes : *César,* 2 km on the N133. ☎ 58.76.41.45.

HOSSEGOR

Bayonne 20, Bordeaux 167, Paris 716
A4 ✉ 40150

ℹ pl. Pasteur, ☎ 58.43.72.35.

Hotels :
★★★***Beauséjour,*** av. du Tour-du-Lac, ☎ 58.43.51.07. 45 rm 🅿 ♨ ♿ closed 17 Sep-6 Jun, 310. Rest. ♦ (eve only), 115-150.
★★★***Mercédès,*** av. du Tour-du-Lac, ☎ 58.43.52.23. 40 rm 🅿 ♨ closed 11 Sep-15 Jun. Full board only in high season, 300. Rest. ♦♦ 100.
● ★★***Huîtrières du Lac,*** 1187, av. du Touring-Club, ☎ 58.43.51.48. 9 rm 🅿 closed end Nov-1 Mar and Wed low season, 160. Rest. ♦ ♿ Private oyster bed, fish and seafood. Good value for money, 100-170.
★★***Ermitage*** (L.F.), allée des Pins-Tranquilles, ☎ 58.43.52.22. 12 rm 🅿 ♨ closed 20 Sep-30 Mar, 190. Rest. ♦ (eve only), 180.
★★***Plage,*** ☎ 58.43.50.12. 30 rm closed 17 Sep-1 Jun, 250. Rest. ♦ Half-board only, 80.

Casino : av. P.-Lahary, ☎ 58.43.51.59.

HOURTIN

Lesparre 17, Bordeaux 62, Paris 555
20 km NE of Maubuisson, A1
✉ 33990

ℹ pl. de l'Église, ☎ 56.41.65.57.

Hotel :
★★***Le Dauphin,*** av. du Lac, ☎ 56.41.61.15. Visa. 20 rm ♨ ♿ closed Nov and Mon, 210. Rest. ♦ 55-75.

⛺ ★★★*La Côte d'Argent,* Hourtin-Plage (750 pl.), ☎ 56.41.60.25.

LABENNE

Bayonne 13, Mont-de-Marsan 83, Paris 756
5 km S of Capbreton, A4 ✉ 40530

ℹ ☎ 59.31.40.99.

SNCF ☎ 59.31.40.15.

Hotel :
★★***Européen,*** ☎ 59.31.41.49. 24 rm 🅿 ♨ closed 15 Jan-1 Mar, 100. Rest. ♦ 80-130.

⛺ ★★★***La Mer*** (300 pl.), ☎ 59.31.42.09.

LACANAU-OCÉAN

Lesparre 52, Bordeaux 59, Paris 592
12 km SW of Maubuisson, A1 ☒ 33680

ℹ pl. de l'Europe, ☎ 56.03.21.01.

Hotel :
★★***Étoile d'Argent*** (L.F.) pl. de l'Europe, ☎ 56.03.21.07. 19 rm Ⓟ ♨ closed 11 Nov-1 Jan, 120. Rest. 45-105.

⛺ ★★★*Les Grands Pins* (545 pl.), ☎ 56.03.20.77.

Casino : bd de la Plage, ☎ 56.03.22.98.

LANGON

Bordeaux 46, Bergerac 79, Paris 641
B2 ☒ 33210

ℹ allée Jean-Jaurès, ☎ 56.62.34.00.

SNCF ☎ 56.63.32.83.

Hotel :
● ★★***Lion d'Or-Claude Darroze,*** 95, cours du Gal-Leclerc, ☎ 56.63.00.48. AE, DC, Euro, Visa. 16 rm Ⓟ ♨ closed 10 Oct-10 Nov, Sun eve and Mon, 250. Rest. ● ♦♦♦ ♿ Highly reputed restaurant. Spec : *lamproie de Gironde,* game (hunting season), Graves wines, 150-250.

⛺ ★★*Municipal des Allées Marines* (50 pl.), ☎ 56.63.06.57.

Farmhouse gîte : *la Grange,* ☎ 56.25.32.20, Villandraut, ☒ 33730, 15 km SW.

Chambres and tables d'hôtes : *les Berdicots,* ☎ 56.25.30.79, Villandraut, 15 km SW.

LÉON

Dax 28, Bayonne 52, Paris 728
A3 ☒ 40550

ℹ rue de la Poste, ☎ 58.48.74.40.

Hotel :
★***Lac,*** at the lake, 2 km NW, ☎ 58.48.73.11. 16 rm ☀ Ⓟ ⛵ 🐕 ♿ closed Oct-25 Mar, 130. Rest. ♦ 50-110.

⛺ ★★★★*Lou Puntaou* (720 pl.), ☎ 58.48.74.30.

LESPARRE-MÉDOC

Royan 38, Bordeaux 63, Paris 577
A1 ☒ 33340

ℹ pl. de la Mairie (été), ☎ 56.41.05.02.

SNCF ☎ 56.41.06.67.

Hotel :
★***Paris,*** 16, cours du Gal-de-Gaulle, ☎ 56.41.00.22. Visa. 10 rm Ⓟ ♨ ♿ closed Feb hols, 120.

Restaurant :
♦♦ ***La Mare aux Grenouilles,*** rte de Soulac, ☎ 56.41.03.46. AE, DC, Visa. ☀ Ⓟ ♨ ♿ closed Mon low season, 60-80.

Recommended : Bégadan, 7 km N : *Wine producers cooperative. Cave Saint-Jean,* ☎ 56.41.50.13. *Château la Tour de By,* ☎ 56.41.51.53. *Château Patache d'Aux,* ☎ 56.41.50.18. Blaignan, 4 km E : *Château la Tour Haut Cassan,* ☎ 56.41.04.77.

LIBOURNE

Bordeaux 31, Périgueux 90, Paris 577
B2 ☒ 33500

ℹ pl. A.-Surchamp, ☎ 57.51.15.04.

SNCF ☎ 57.51.11.80., 57.51.41.50.

Car-hire : *Budget* train + auto, at the station, ☎ 57.51.41.50.

Hotels :
★★★***Loubat,*** 32, rue de Chanzy, ☎ 57.51.17.58. AE, Visa. 45 rm Ⓟ ♨ ⛵ ♿ 220. Rest. ♦♦ On the Wine route, 60-200.
★★***Gare,*** 43, rue de Chanzy, ☎ 57.51.06.86. 11 rm Ⓟ ♨ closed Nov, 180. Rest. ♦ ♿ closed Sun.

⛺ ★★*Le Ruste* (100 pl.), ☎ 57.51.01.54.

Restaurant :
● ♦ ***Le Landais,*** 15, rue des Treilles, ☎ 57.74.07.40 ♨ ⛵ ♿ Good value for money in this country restaurant run by an excellent chef, 40-85.

Recommended : *wine-tasting association : Hospitaliers de Pomerol,* château de Tailhas, ☎ 57.51.26.02. *Château-Latour,* ☎ 57.51.75.55. Fronsac, 2 km SW : Fronsac, *Château Canon de Breur,* ☎ 57.51.30.60. Saint-Michel-de-Fronsac, 6 km, *Château la Rivière,* ☎ 57.24.98.01.

LUXEY

Mont-de-Marsan 43, Bordeaux 77, Paris 660
B3 ☒ 40430 Sore

Hotel :
★★***Relais de la Haute Lande,*** ☎ 58.08.02.30. Visa. 10 rm Ⓟ ♿ closed mid-Jan-mid-Feb and Mon low season, 100. Rest. ♦♦ Good fare. Spec : *salmis de palombes, cèpes à la bordelaise,* 120-210.

Leisure activities : *Horse-drawn caravans,* Mme Salicettei, attelages de la Haute-Lande, l'Arbousière, ☎ 58.07.66.04.

MAGESCQ

Dax 16, Bayonne 45, Paris 728
A3 ☒ 40140 Soustons

ℹ ☎ 58.41.52.62.

Hotel :
● ★★★***Relais de la Poste,*** ☎ 58.47.70.25. AE, DC. 12 rm Ⓟ ♨ ⛵ 🐕 📺 🎾 closed 11 Nov-24 Dec, Mon eve and Tue, 300. Rest. ● ♦♦ ♿ Landaise cuisine by the Cousseau brothers for our greatest delight. Spec : *soles aux cèpes, saumon frais sauvage grillé béarnaise,* 200-300.

Restaurant :
● ♦ ***Le Cabanon,*** ☎ 58.47.71.51. Tx 540660. AE, Euro. Ⓟ ♨ ⛵ 🐕 ♿ closed 30 Sep-30 Oct, Sun eve and Mon. In this former Landaise farm, Françoise Hauff respects regional cooking. Spec : *pigeonneau de Magescq au cognac* (she also does the cooking just next door at the *Grange aux Canards*), 60-180.

MAUBUISSON

Lesparre 37, Bordeaux 58, Paris 580
A1 ☒ 33121 Carcans

ℹ rte de l'Océan, ☎ 56.03.31.16.

Hotel :
★★***Lac,*** ☎ 56.03.30.03. 39 rm ☀ Ⓟ closed Nov-Feb. Rest. 🐕 70-110.

⛺ ★★★***Le Pin Franc,*** Carcans, 6 km E (45 pl.), ☎ 56.03.33.57.

MIMIZAN

Mont-de-Marsan 75, Bordeaux 114, Paris 702
A3 ☒ 40200

ℹ av. M.-Martin, Mimizan-Plage, ☎ 58.09.11.20.

Hotels :
Mimizan-Bourg :
★★***Taris,*** 19, rue de l'Abbaye, ☎ 58.09.02.18. AE, Euro, Visa. 23 rm Ⓟ ♨ 🐕 160. Rest. ♦ 🐕 closed Oct-Mar.

Bordelais, Landes

Mimizan-Plage :
● ★★★**Côte d'Argent,** av. M.-Martin, ☎ 58.09.15.22. AE, DC, Euro, Visa. 40 rm ⚘ 🅿 ♧ ✗ ♿ 340. Rest. ♦♦ 110.
★★**Mermoz** (L.F.), 16, av. du Courant, ☎ 58.09.09.30. AE, DC, Euro, Visa. 18 rm ⚘ ⚘ ♧ ✗ closed 15 Sep-15 Jun, 250. Rest. ♦ 80-150.
★★**Parc** (L.F.), 6, rue des Papeteries, ☎ 58.09.13.88. Visa. 16 rm 🅿 ⚘ closed mid Dec-Jan, Fri eve and Sat low season, 180. Rest. ♦ 80-130.
★**Au Bon Coin du Lac,** 34, av. du Lac, ☎ 58.09.01.55. 12 rm ⚘ 🅿 ⚘ ♧ ✗ closed Feb-1st Apr. Rest. ● ♦ closed Sun eve and Mon. A delicious cuisine in an ordinary decor : *salade de l'échassier landais, panaché de poisson au beurre de cerfeuil,* 220-310.

⛺ ★★★★*Marina* (630 pl.), ☎ 58.09.12.66.

Casino, ☎ 58.09.05.02.

MONTALIVET-LES-BAINS

Lesparre 21, Bordeaux 85, Paris 537
A1 ✉ 33930 Vendays

ℹ ☎ 56.41.30.12.

Hotel :
★**Marin,** av. de l'Océan, ☎ 56.41.32.07. 14 rm ✗ 150. Rest. ♦ ♿ closed low season, 80-130.

Restaurant :
♦♦ ***Clef des Champs,*** rte de Vendays, 5 km SE, ☎ 56.41.71.11. Visa. 🅿 ⚘ ♧ ♿ closed Nov-Feb, noon Jul-Aug and Tue ex Jul-Aug. Spec : *aiguillette de canard au vin de Médoc,* Médoc-style eel, and regional disches, 120-210.

MONT-DE-MARSAN

Pau 80, Bordeaux 126, Paris 721
B3 ✉ 40000

ℹ 22, rue Victor-Hugo, ☎ 58.75.38.67.

SNCF ☎ 58.75.37.69., 58.75.37.69.

Hotel :
★★**Richelieu** (L.F.) rue Wlérick, ☎ 58.06.10.20. Tx 550238. AE, DC, Euro, Visa. 70 rm 🅿 ♧ ♿ 165. Rest. ♦ closed 12-20 Jan, 60-130.

Restaurant :
Saint-Médard, 3 km E :
♦ ***Zanchettin,*** 1565, av. de Villeneuve, ☎ 58.75.19.52 🅿 ⚘ ♿ closed 3 weeks Feb and 3 weeks Aug, Sun eve and Mon, 80-130.

Bicycle-hire : M. Camiade, ☎ 58.75.28.60.

MORCENX

Mont-de-Marsan 39, Bordeaux 110, Paris 700
A3 ✉ 40110

SNCF ☎ 58.07.84.18.

Hotel :
★★**Bellevue,** 2, rue Carnot, ☎ 58.07.85.07. 24 rm 🅿 ⚘ ♧ closed Christmas hols, Fri eve, 180. Rest. ♦ closed Fri eve, Sat and Sun eve, 80-130.

⛺ ★★★*Le Clavé* (50 pl.), ☎ 58.07.83.11.

PARENTIS-EN-BORN

Bordeaux 74, Mont-de-Marsan 78, Paris 676
A2-3 ✉ 40160

ℹ pl. des Marronniers, ☎ 58.78.43.60.

Hotel :
Gastes, 7 km SW :
★**L'Estanquet,** ☎ 58.78.42.00. AE, DC, Visa. 🅿 ⚘ ♧ closed Nov-May and Tue ex Jul-Aug, 90. Rest. ● ♦♦ Georgette and her daughter "Papette" prepare very rich, varied dishes for the hearty eater, 50-210.

⛺ ★★*Essi* (130 pl.), ☎ 58.78.42.27.

Restaurant :
♦♦ ***Poste,*** 12, av. du 8-Mai, ☎ 58.78.40.23 🅿 ✗ ♿ closed end Nov and Sun eve. Good value for money, 120-210.

Bicycle-hire : M. Thomas, ☎ 58.78.40.79.

PAUILLAC

Bordeaux 42, Toulouse 295, Paris 625
A-B1 ✉ 33250

ℹ ☎ 56.59.03.08.

SNCF ☎ 56.92.50.50.

Hotel :
★★**France et Angleterre,** quai Albert-de-Pichon, ☎ 56.59.01.20. AE, Visa. 15 rm 🅿 ⚘ ♧ ♿ closed in winter, 180. Rest., 120-210.

Farmhouse gîte and riding gîte : Castelnau-Médoc, ✉ 33480, 21 km S, *Pomeys,* ☎ 56.58.24.85.

Recommended : *Wine producers' cooperative,* ☎ 56.59.26.00 ; *Château Lafite-Rothschild,* ☎ 56.59.01.04 ; *Château Pichon-Longueville,* ☎ 56.59.19.40 and 56.59.00.82. 20 km S : Margaux : *Château Margaux,* ☎ 56.88.70.28 ; *Château Pouget* (Cantenac), ☎ 56.88.30.58. 18 km S : Moulis, *Château Moulin à Vent,* ☎ 56.58.15.79. 11 km N : Saint-Estèphe, *Château Cos d'Estournel,* ☎ 56.59.25.50.

PEYREHORADE

Dax 23, Bayonne 36, Paris 770
A4 ✉ 40300

ℹ pl. Sablot, ☎ 58.73.00.52.

SNCF ☎ 58.73.03.38.

Hotels :
★**Central** (L.F.), pl. Aristide-Briand, ☎ 58.73.03.22. AE, DC, Visa. 10 rm 🅿 closed Sun eve and Mon ex Jul-Aug, 120. Rest. ● ♦♦ ♿ A real gourmand paradise. Pleasant and varied menu, 50-160.

Port-de-Lanne, 7 km NW :
★★**La Vieille Auberge** (L.F.), ☎ 58.89.16.29. 9 rm 🅿 ⚘ ♧ ▭ ♿ closed 30 Sep-28 Jun, 230. Rest. ● ♦♦Dinner only. This early 18thC inn has kept its genuine furniture. Spec : *foie gras à l'ancienne, aiguillettes de canard au vin de fleur,* 100-150.

Cagnotte, 7.5 km NE par D29 :
★★**Boni** (L.F.), ☎ 58.73.03.78. DC, Euro. 10 rm 🅿 ⚘ ♧ ▭ closed 1 Dec-28 Feb and Mon eve low season, 130. Rest. ● ♦♦ ♿ closed Sun eve and Mon low season. In the open country, the good cuisine of Annie Demen. Very nice dining-room in an old bake-house, 50-130.

Labatut, 10 km E :
★**Auberge du Bousquet** (L.F.), carrefour du Maou, on RN117, ☎ 58.98.18.24. AE, DC, Visa. 6 rm 🅿 ⚘ ♿ closed Mon eve and Tue, 1 Oct-Jan, 120. Rest. ● ♦♦ A late 18thC former post-house, now presided over by a chef who trained at the famous Trou Gascon. Spec : *canard confit en salade, magret de canard, bavaroise aux kiwis et ses 3 coulis.* Local wines, 50-160.

Farmhouse gîte and farmhouse-inn : *L'Oustaou,* Cauneille, 3 km E, ☎ 58.73.07.43.

PYLA-SUR-MER

Bordeaux 65, Bayonne 181, Paris 654
4 km SW of Arcachon, A2 ✉ 33115

ℹ mairie, rd-pt du Figuier, ☎ 56.22.53.83.

Hotels :

★★★***La Guitoune,*** 95, bd de l'Océan, ☎ 56.22.70.10. AE, DC, Euro, Visa. 25 rm Ⓟ closed 11 Nov-20 Dec, 1 jan-15 Feb, 380. Rest. ♦♦ ♿ Spec : grilled fish and *bouillabaisse,* 120-250.

★★***Beau Rivage,*** 16, bd de l'Océan, ☎ 56.22.01.82. 20 rm closed Oct-Apr, 180.

★★***La Corniche,*** 52, av. L.-Gaume, ☎ 56.22.72.11. 15 rm closed 23 Oct-23 Mar, Wed, low season, 250. Rest. ♦♦ 80-130.

★★***Oyana,*** 52, av. L.-Gaume, ☎ 56.22.72.59. 17 rm closed 1 Oct-Mar, 200. Rest. ♦ 70-100.

⛺ ★★★*La Dune* (335 pl.), ☎ 56.22.72.17.

Restaurant :

♦♦ ***Les Embruns,*** 65, bd de l'Océan, ☎ 56.22.50.67. AE, Visa ♿ Fish and seafood dishes ; good value, 120-210.

QUINSAC

Libourne 35, Bergerac 90, Paris 591
15 km SE of Bordeaux (right bank), B2
☒ 33360 Latresne

Hotel :

Esconac, 1 km NW :
★★***A La Varenne,*** ☎ 56.21.31.15. 12 rm Ⓟ ♿ closed Jan and Wed, 250. Rest. ♦♦ Regional dishes, 80-130.

Restaurant :

♦♦ ***Robinson,*** 2 km SE, on the D10, ☎ 56.21.31.09 Ⓟ ♿ closed Oct and Tue, 120-210.

Recommended : *Wine producers' cooperative,* ☎ 56.20.86.09.

La RÉOLE

Bordeaux 66, Agen 77, Paris 660
B2 ☒ 33190

ℹ pl. de la Libération (summer), ☎ 56.61.13.55.

SNCF ☎ 56.61.00.56.

Hotel :

★★***Centre,*** rue A.-Caduc, ☎ 56.61.02.64, AE. 12 rm Ⓟ closed 24 Dec-5 Jan, 120. Rest. ♦ closed Sun and noon, 50-100.

⛺ ★★***Le Rouergue*** (60 pl.), ☎ 56.61.10.11.

Table d'hôtes : *les Barthes,* Mongauzy, 6 km E, ☎ 56.61.70.39.

Chambres and table d'hôtes : *château de Beysserat,* Monségur, ☒ 33580, 13 km NE, ☎ 56.61.61.65.

Recommended : *Christian Planton,* Pondaurat, ☎ 56.61.22.27 (wicker handicrafts).

SABRES

Mont-de-Marsan 35, Bordeaux 93, Paris 682
A-B3 ☒ 40630

Hotel :

★★***Auberge des Pins*** (L.F.), rte de la Piscine, ☎ 58.07.50.47. Visa. 14 rm Ⓟ closed 15 Jan-15 Feb, Sun eve and Mon, 190. Rest. ♦ ♿ 55-160.

⛺ ★★*Les Cigales* (30 pl.), ☎ 58.07.50.18.

SAINT-CIERS-SUR-GIRONDE

Saintes 57, Bordeaux 71, Paris 527
B1 ☒ 33820

Hotel :

★★***Les Callonges,*** ☎ 57.42.63.97. Visa. 15 rm Ⓟ ♿ closed 10 Dec-15 Jan, 1st week Sep, 140. Rest. ♦ closed Mon, 40-100.

SAINT-ÉMILION

Bordeaux 39, Bergerac 56, Paris 611
B2 ☒ 33330

ℹ pl. des Créneaux, ☎ 57.24.72.03.

SNCF ☎ 57.24.72.12.

Hotels :

★★★★***Hostellerie de Plaisance,*** pl. du Clocher, ☎ 57.24.72.32. AE, DC, Euro, Visa. 12 rm Ⓟ ♿ 260. Rest. ♦♦♦ Regional cooking. Spec : *magret de canard aux orties, feuilleté aux pommes tièdes,* 120-210.

★★***Auberge de la Commanderie,*** rue des Cordeliers, ☎ 57.24.70.19 Ⓟ closed 15 Dec-15 Feb, 190. Rest. ♦ closed Tue, 70-170.

⛺ ★★★*La Barbanne* (70 pl.), ☎ 57.24.75.80.

Restaurant :

● ♦♦ ***Logis de la Cadène,*** pl. du Marché-au-Bois, ☎ 57.24.71.40 Open noon only ; closed 15-30 Jun, 1-15 Sep, 1 week Oct and Mon. Clean country house. Shady terrasse. Good wines on the list and in all the sauces, 50-140.

Recommended : *Galerie Jean Guyot* (potter), rue Guadet. *Wine-tasting association : Château Figeac,* ☎ 57.24.72.26. Lussac, 10 km N : *château Ausone,* Maison Vauthier, ☎ 57.51.19.22.

SAINT-JULIEN-EN-BORN

Mont-de-Marsan 68, Bayonne 76, Paris 712
18 km S of Mimizan, A3 ☒ 40170

ℹ ☎ 58.42.89.80.

Hotels :

★★***Le Neptune,*** Contis-Plage, ☎ 58.42.85.28. 16 rm Ⓟ closed 15 Sep-1 Jun, 195.

★***Le Pré Fleuri,*** rte de Mézos, ☎ 58.42.80.09. 10 rm Ⓟ 100.

Restaurant :

Mézas, 6 km E :
♦♦ ***Boucau,*** ☎ 58.42.61.38. AE, DC Ⓟ ♿ closed Sep-Mar, Sun eve and Mon low season, 45-200.

SAINT-MACAIRE

Bordeaux 49, Bergerac 76, Paris 641
B2 ☒ 33490

ℹ Le Prieuré, ☎ 56.63.34.52.

Hotel :

★***Arts*** (L.F.), allée des Tilleuls, ☎ 56.63.07.40. Visa. 9 rm Ⓟ closed Wed low season, 150. Rest. ♦ 55-140.

Farmhouse-inn and chambres d'hôtes : *le Roy,* Verdelais, ☎ 56.63.25.26.

SAINT-SEVER

Mont-de-Marsan 17, Pau 69, Paris 740
B3-4 ☒ 40500

ℹ pl. Tour-du-Sol (high season), ☎ 58.75.00.10.

SNCF ☎ 58.76.00.45.

Hotels :

● ★★***Le Relais du Pavillon,*** quartier Péré, ☎ 58.76.20.22. AE, DC, Euro, Visa. 14 rm Ⓟ closed Sun eve low season, 200. Rest. ♦ Spec : *foie gras, brochette gourmande.* Wines from the property, 80-200.

★***France et Ambassadeurs,*** pl. Cap-du-Pouy, ☎ 58.76.00.01. 22 rm, closed Oct, Sun eve and Mon, 90. Rest. ● ♦ Good value for money. Goose and duck specialities, 120-210.

Farmhouse gîte : *le Coum,* Fargues, 7 km E, ☎ 58.45.10.94.

Entertainment : at the abbaye des Jacobins, rue Lamarque, ☎ 58.76.01.38.

SAINT-VINCENT-DE-TYROSSE

Dax 24, Bayonne 25, Paris 745
A4 ⊠ 40230

SNCF ☎ 58.77.03.53.

Hotels :
★★***Côte d'Argent,*** rte d'Hossegor, ☎ 58.77.02.16. 22 rm P ♨ ♿ 180. Rest. ♦ please check closing dates (hotel guests only), 80-130.
★***Touristes,*** av. Nationale, ☎ 58.77.03.28. 10 rm P ♨ closed and Sat Nov-Jan, 150. Rest. ♦ 50-130.

Restaurant :
● ♦♦ ***Le Hittau,*** ☎ 58.77.11.85. AE, DC, Euro, Visa P ♨ closed 15 Feb-15 Mar, Sun eve and Mon. Renowned local cuisine in an old sheepfold, 85-260.

Riding gîte : *Cibade,* Saint-André-de-Saignanx, 14.5 km S, ☎ 58.56.13.30.

Recommended : *Ets Labeyrie, foies gras, magrets,* St-Geours-de-Mareme, 7 km NE.

SAINTE-FOY-LA-GRANDE

Périgueux 64, Bordeaux 70, Paris 642
B2 ⊠ 33220

ℹ pl. Gambetta, ☎ ① 57.46.00.26.

SNCF ☎ 57.92.50.50.

Hotels :
★★★***Grand Hôtel,*** 117, rue de la République, ☎ 57.46.00.08. AE, DC, Euro, Visa. 17 rm P ♨ closed 9-25 Jan and Oct, Sun eve and Mon, 280. Rest. ♦♦ ♿ 60-175.
★★***Victor Hugo,*** 101, rue Victor-Hugo, ☎ 57.46.18.03. AE, Euro, Visa. 12 rm P closed 1 week in Feb, 1 week in Sep, Sun and Mon noon, 180. Rest. 65-130.
★***Vieille Auberge,*** 10, rue Pasteur, ☎ 57.46.04.78. 7 rm closed 12-30 Apr, 16-30 Oct, Sun eve and Mon, 100. Rest. ♦♦ 50-150.

Ⓐ ★★★Municipal *La Tuilerie* (65 pl.), ☎ 57.46.13.84.

Farmhouse gîte : *les Girards,* Pellegrue, ⊠ 33790, 18 km SW, ☎ 57.61.32.06.

SANGUINET

Bordeaux 59, Mont-de-Marsan 93, Paris 648
13 km NE of Biscarrosse, A2 ⊠ 40460

Hotel :
★***Les Eaux qui Rient,*** av. Ch.-Castets, ☎ 58.78.61.15. 11 rm ♨ closed 1 Nov-30 Mar, 160. Rest. 70-150.

Ⓐ ★★★★*Lou Broustaricq* (555 pl.), ☎ 58.78.62.62 ; ★★*Lac* (233 pl.), ☎ 58.78.61.94.

SEIGNOSSE

Bayonne 27, Mont-de-Marsan 79, Paris 751
A3-4 ⊠ 40510

ℹ av. des Lacs, ☎ 58.43.32.15.

Hotel :
● ★***La Soleillade*** (L.F.), in the town, ☎ 58.72.80.38. 7 rm P ♨ ♿ closed end Sep-1 Jun, 180. Rest. ● ♦♦ closed Tue (Jun-Sep). Beautiful house located between the sea and the woods, managed by E. Lesparre : *confit de porc et de canard, daube de St-André,* 80-130.

SOULAC-SUR-MER

Lesparre 30, Bordeaux 94, Paris 517
A1 ⊠ 33780

ℹ pl. du Marché, ☎ 56.59.86.61.

SNCF ☎ 56.59.85.56.

Hotel :
★★***Molière,*** ☎ 56.09.82.69. Euro. 17 m P ♨ ♿ closed 1 Jan-30 Apr, 1 Oct-31 Dec. Half-board only in high season, 200.

Ⓐ ★★★★*Palace* (550 pl.), ☎ 56.09.80.22.

Casino : ☎ 56.09.82.74.

SOUSTONS

Dax 28, Bayonne 41, Paris 738
A3 ⊠ 40140

ℹ mairie, ☎ 58.41.52.62.

Hotels :
★★★***Pavillon Landais,*** 26, av. du Lac, ☎ 58.48.04.49. AE, DC, Visa. 8 rm P ♨ closed 22 Dec-1 Mar, Sun eve and Mon from May to Oct, 210. Rest. ● ♦ Next to the lake, a peaceful gourmet stop. Spec : duck, *foie gras, saumon de l'Adour,* 100-160.
● ★★***Bergerie,*** av. du Lac, ☎ 58.48.01.43. Visa. 12 rm P ♨ closed Oct, 200. Rest. ♦ (guests only), 80-130.
★★***Château Bergeron,*** rue Vicomte, ☎ 58.41.58.14. Visa. 17 rm P ♨ closed mid-Oct-1 Jun. Pension only high season, 180. Rest. ♦ (guests only), 80-130.

Ⓐ ★★★★*L'Airial* (400 pl.), ☎ 58.48.02.48. See also Magescq.

Bicycle-hire : M. Nicolas, ☎ 58.48.01.10.

La TESTE

Bordeaux 59, Bayonne 176, Paris 648
4 km S of Arcachon, A2 ⊠ 33260

ℹ pl. J.-Hameau (high season), ☎ 56.66.55.49.

SNCF ☎ 56.66.29.70.

Hotel :
★★***Basque*** (L.F.), 36, rue du Mal-Foch, ☎ 56.66.26.04. 8 rm ♨ closed Oct-mid-Nov, Sun eve and Mon low season, 180. Rest. ♦ 80-130.

Recommended : oyster tasting : *Cameleyre,* port de La Teste, ☎ 56.66.27.94.

VIEUX-BOUCAU-LES-BAINS

Dax 36, Bayonne 38, Paris 746
A3 ⊠ 40480

ℹ port d'Albret, ☎ 58.48.13.47.

Hotels :
★***Côte d'Argent,*** rue Principale, ☎ 58.48.13.17. 45 rm P closed Oct-15 Nov, 100. Rest. ♦ closed Mon low season. Spec : *salmis de palombes,* 80-130.
★***La Marenne,*** av. de la Plage, ☎ 58.48.12.70. AE, Visa. 38 rm P ♨ ♿ closed Nov-Apr, 100. Rest. 80-130.

Ⓐ ★★★*Municipal les Sablières* (410 pl.), ☎ 58.48.12.29.

VILLENEUVE-DE-MARSAN

Mont-de-Marsan 17, Pau 70, Paris 715
B3 ⊠ 40190

Hotels :
● ★★★***Europe*** (L.F.), pl. Forail, ☎ 58.45.20.08. Visa. 15 rm P ♨ 180. Rest. ♦ ♦ Robert Garrapit is a well-known figure in the Landes and his cooking is in his image. Spec : *salade de cèpes aux aiguillettes d'oie, tourtière aérienne.* A large cellar of armagnac and bordeaux, 220-310.
● ★★***Darroze,*** ☎ 58.45.20.07. AE, Visa. 38 rm P ♨ ♿ 180. Rest. ● ♦♦♦ ♿ One of Pierre Perret's favorite gastronomic stops, 120-210.

Brittany

Brittany is a region with a personality both strong and mysterious. For Brittany is several regions in one and diversity is the rule, in language and landscape alike. The natural parks of Brière and the salt marshlands of Guérande cover 70 square kilometres of low-lying land drained by canals and a multitude of channels. The inhabitants — who occupy the higher-lying islands — live from fishing, hunting, peat — and reed-gathering and animal-breeding. The ancient fortified city of Concarneau now lives from trawler fishing and tourism. Along the Emerald Coast, the infinite variations of sea-green reflections and a succession of capes, bays, rocks, cliffs and estuaries lead to Saint-Malo, with its ramparts and narrow streets, and Cap Fréhel. Dinand preserves its character as a favourite holiday spot for Post-Victorian English aristocrats — sporting luxurious villas with Mediterranean gardens of fig trees, palms and camellias. Brest is a naval base and the most important nuclear submarine base in France. Nantes is a busy port and the largest city in Western France, but it is also worth a visit for its shady avenues, its cathedral, its massive buildings. The imposing city of Rennes is the administrative capital of the region and possesses many fine museums and dwellings.

Popular traditions, such as *Fest Noz,* the nocturnal festival marking the successful completion of collective activities, the medieval *pardons* which only Brittany has kept alive, the saints still remembered for their miraculous powers of healing, the strange musical instruments played only here and the unusual language of *brezhoug* spoken by 800 000 people in the south—— all contribute to Brittany's very special, individual character. The region's healthy, outdoor attractions and its great seafaring traditions make it one of France's most popular holiday spots.

Sightseeing

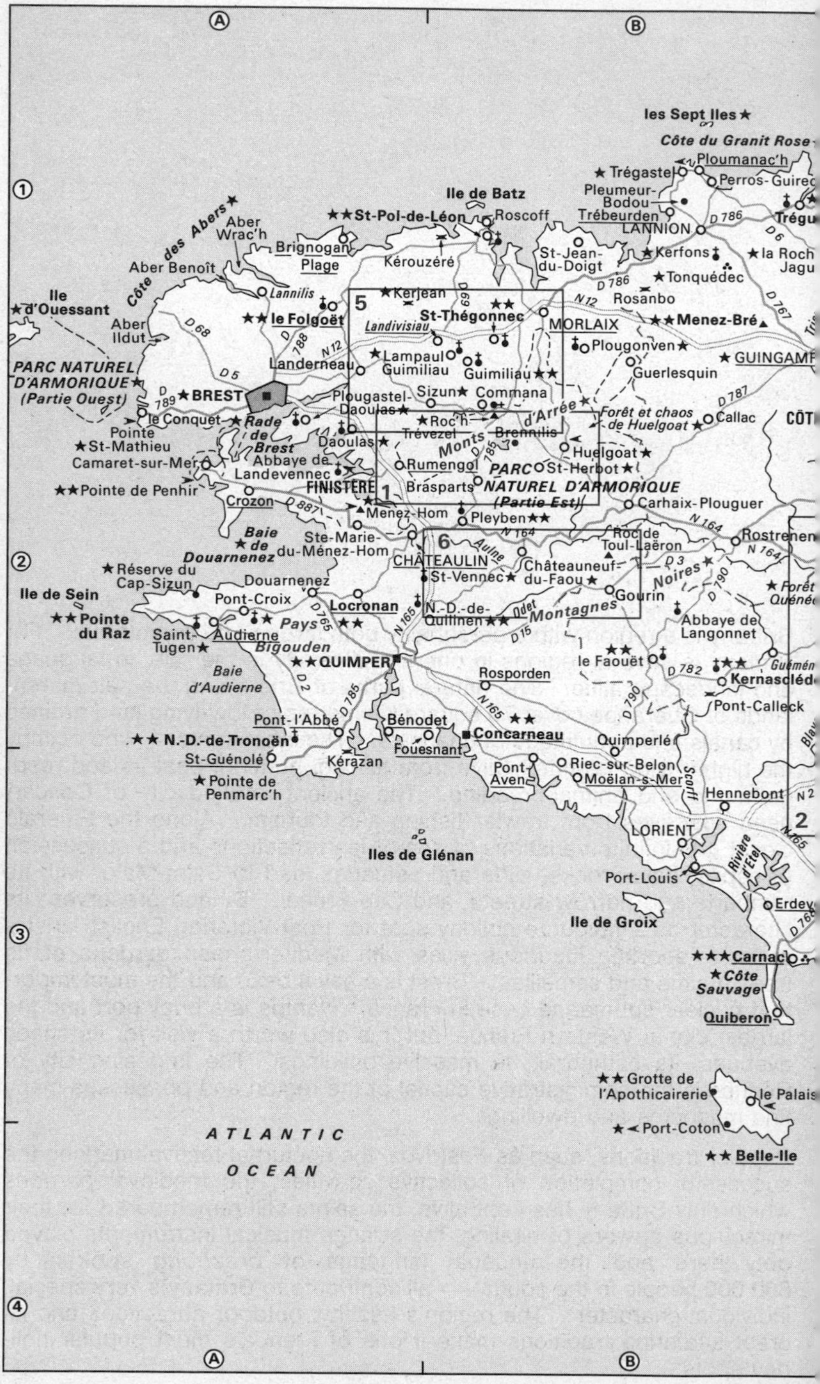

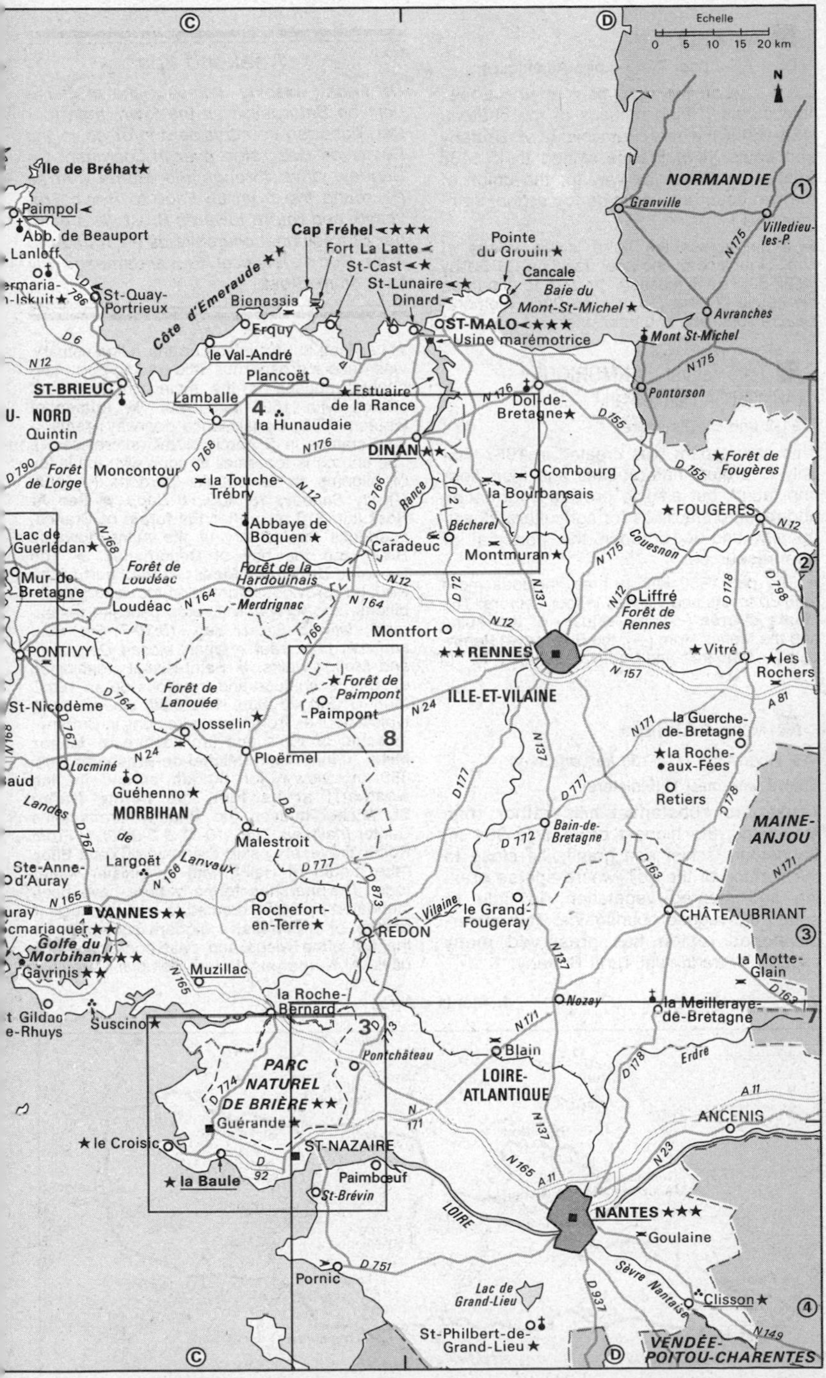
Echelle
0 5 10 15 20 km
N
C
D
NORMANDIE
1
2
3
4
7
8
Granville
Villedieu-les-P.
N 175
Avranches
Mont St-Michel
Pontorson
Ile de Bréhat★
Paimpol
Abb. de Beauport
Lanloff
ermaria-
-Iskuit★
D 786
St-Quay-Portrieux
Côte d'Emeraude★★
Cap Fréhel★★★
Fort La Latte
St-Cast★
St-Lunaire★
Dinard
Pointe du Grouin★
Cancale
Baie du Mont-St-Michel★
Bignassis
Erquy
le Val-André
ST-MALO★★★
Usine marémotrice
D 6
N 12
ST-BRIEUC
Plancoët
Estuaire de la Rance
N 176
Dol-de-Bretagne★
Lamballe
la Hunaudaie
U- NORD
Quintin
D 768
DINAN★★
D 155
Forêt de Fougères
D 790
Forêt de Lorge
Moncontour
la Touche-Trébry
Combourg
la Bourbansais
FOUGÈRES
D 766
Rance
D 2
Abbaye de Boquen★
Bécherel
Lac de Guerlédan★
N 168
Caradeuc
Montmuran★
Couesnon
N 175
Forêt de Loudéac
Forêt de la Hardouinais
Mur-de-Bretagne
Loudéac
N 164
Merdrignac
D 72
N 137
Liffré
Forêt de Rennes
D 178
D 798
Montfort
PONTIVY
★★RENNES
Vitré
les Rochers
Forêt de Paimpont
Forêt de Lanouée
Paimpont
N 24
ILLE-ET-VILAINE
N 157
A 81
St-Nicodème
D 764
Josselin★
D 767
Locminé
Ploërmel
la Guerche-de-Bretagne
N 171
la Roche-aux-Fées
Baud
Guéhenno★
MORBIHAN
Landes de Lanvaux
D 8
D 177
D 777
Retiers
Bain-de-Bretagne
D 772
MAINE-ANJOU
Malestroit
Ste-Anne-d'Auray
Largoët
D 873
C 163
N 165
VANNES★★
Rochefort-en-Terre★
Vilaine
le Grand-Fougeray
CHÂTEAUBRIANT
Golfe du Morbihan★★
Gavrinis★★
REDON
Muzillac
la Motte-Glain
la Roche-Bernard
Nozay
la Meilleraye-de-Bretagne
Suscinio★
Gildas-de-Rhuys
Pontchâteau
Blain
Erdre
PARC NATUREL DE BRIÈRE★★
D 774
LOIRE-ATLANTIQUE
A 11
Guérande★
ANCENIS
le Croisic
ST-NAZAIRE
N 23
la Baule
D 92
Paimbœuf
St-Brévin
LOIRE
NANTES★★★
Goulaine
D 751
Pornic
Lac de Grand-Lieu
D 937
Sèvre Nantaise
Clisson★
St-Philbert-de-Grand-Lieu★
N 149
VENDÉE-POITOU-CHARENTES

Brittany

Sightseeing

ANCENIS

D3-4 / ® / pop. 7 263 (Loire-Atlantique)

Small city on the right bank of the Loire; light industry. Fine remains of the château (15th-17thC) where François II of Brittany and Louis XI of France signed their 1468 treaty that paved the way for the union of the two countries *(visits during school summer hols.)*.

▶ 3 km across the Loire is the village of **Liré,** birthplace of the poet Joachim Du Bellay (1522-60); small museum devoted to him in an old house *(9-12 & 2-6; closed Sun.;* memorabilia, regional arts and traditions). □

Parc naturel d'ARMORIQUE★ (ARMORICA Nature Park)

A1-2 and B2 (Finistère)

This nature park was created in 1967, not only to protect natural sites and their flora and fauna, but also to provide information and research facilities for agricultural development and to broaden the potential of rural resources.

▶ The park, 650 km² in area, includes more than 30 towns and villages in four sectors: The **Monts d'Arrée** (→), the estuary of the Aulne and the Menez Hom (→), the **Roscanvel Peninsula** (→ **Camaret**) and **Ouessant Island** (→). □

Monts d'ARRÉE★

▶ Round trip *(110-130 km, one day)*

AB2 *(see map 1)* (Finistère)

These are substantial hills rather than mountains, the highest being only 384 m. Sandstone, schist and granite lie close to the surface of the soil, where sparse grazing and stunted vegetation do little to soften the rugged countryside. This underdeveloped region has preserved many aspects of traditional, rural Brittany.

Weekend tips

On Friday evening, take a plane to Quimper; on Saturday, visit the town, then tour the Bigouden countryside and/or go to the Pointe du Raz; stop over in Locronan. On Sunday, drive through the Monts d'Arrée (→ round trip from Le Faou to Roc'h Trévezel), and return towards Brest via a number of traditional churchyards (→ round trip from Roc'h Trévezel to Landerneau). Fly back from Brest.

▶ Le **Faou** ® : far inland on the Aulne estuary, was once a prosperous little trading port (merchants' houses in the main street); 16thC church with 1628 bell-tower. ▶ **Rumengol** (church 1536; Renaissance doorway; remarkable statues in S porch; 17thC altarpieces★). The church is too small to cope with the influx of pilgrims to its popular *pardons* (→ box) *(Trinity Sunday, 15 Aug., 8 Sep.)*. ▶ **Pen Ar Hoat** (alt. 210 m) : after the **forest of Cranou,** overlooks the estuary of the Aulne, towards Brest and the bay of **Douarnenez.** ▶ The **Domaine de Menez Meur :** at the heart of the Park (→) provides information for visitors (exhibitions, zoo, *crêperie* (Breton pancake restaurant); *daily 15 Jun.-15 Sep., 10:30-7; Sat., Sun. and nat. hols. rest of year; closed Dec., Jan. and Mon.*); walks. ▶ **Saint-Rivoal :** exhibition of rural techniques and traditions on an 18thC farm *(1 Jun.-15 Sep. 1:30-6:30, closed Tue.)*, typical houses from various regions in Brittany; museum of tools and architecture. ▶ **Menez Mikel (Mont Saint-Michel-de-Brasparts;** alt. 380 m; view★ for 60 km around in fine weather); at its foot, the **Ferme (farm) St. Michel** houses the Brittany Craftsmen's Center *(daily ex. Tue., 10-12 & 2-6:30)*. ▶ From **Roc'h Trévezel★**, skirt the bowl of **Yeun Ellez** ("the mouth of Hell"), with its sinister winter fogs. The marshes formerly here have been inundated by a lake created to cool the nuclear reactor of **Brennelis,** a modern substitute for the will o'the wisps and peat bogs of earlier days. At **Kerbérou :** former Templar Comman-

1. Monts d'Arrée

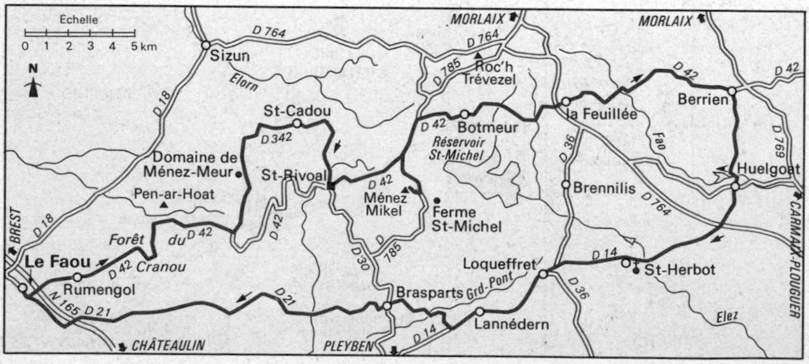

dery. ▶ **Huelgoat★** ® : one of the most beautiful sites in inland Brittany, between a 1.5 km² lake and a forest★★ with granite rocks, streams and luxuriant undergrowth; 16thC church and chapel of Notre-Dame-des-Cieux; endless possibilities for walks in the Chaos du Moulin (rockfall)★ or to the Pierre Tremblante (Shivering Stone), the Ménage de la Vierge Cavern, the Artus Cavern, La Mare aux Sangliers (Wild Boar Pond), the Gouffre★ (sinkhole of the Rivière d'Argent). ▶ Outside the **chapel of Saint Herbot★★** (15th-16thC), an elaborate figured cross★ (1571). Statues of the Apostles in the porch (1498), square 15thC tower and small ossuary. Fine furnishings (carved wood chancel★ (16thC), stalls, altarpieces, stained glass (1556). ▶ Interesting furnishings in the churches of **Loqueffret** (16thC), **Brennilis** (end of 15thC) and **Lannédern** (porch, 1662; cross and ossuary of 17thC in the cemetery). ▶ **Brasparts** churchyard (→) is typical : church (1551) with Renaissance porch★ (1589), Calvary★ with Pietà, and ossuary with two figures of *Ankou* (Death) at the corners. □

AUDIERNE

A2 / ® / pop. 3094 (Finistère)

This pretty lobster port has a fine beach and provides access to the **Île de Sein** (→).

▶ You will see lobster traps piled at the watergate. Rue du Môle, **La Chaumière Bretonne** *(Jun.-Sep. 9 or 10-7 or 8).* □

▶ Nearby

▶ 4.5 km W : the **chapel of Saint Tugen★** (1535), 17th-18thC furnishings. ▶ **Pont-Croix :** a little town with ancient paved alleys. Church of Notre-Dame de Roscudon, rebuilt 15thC; 13thC nave; S porch★ and bell-tower with 67 m stone steeple. ▶ **Plozévet** ® (15th-16thC) : Romanesque arcades; chapel of La Trinité★ (16thC, *1 km N*), fine statuary. □

AURAY

C3 / ® / pop. 10185 (Morbihan)

An unpretentious town on the banks of the Loch, where the tide comes 12 km inland.

▶ The church of St. Gildas (1641) mixes styles, with a preference for the Renaissance (side porch). ▶ Through the Place de la République (Hôtel de Ville, late 18thC), and down the Rue du Père Eternel (stalls★ in the chapel) to the Promenade du Loch★ overlooking the river and the estuary. ▶ From here, visit **St. Goustan quarter★** across a 17thC stone bridge : 15thC half-timbered houses★ by the old port. □

Don't miss

★★★ *Cap Fréhel (C1), Carnac (B3), Nantes (D4), Saint-Malo (D1), Gulf of Morbihan (C3).*

★★ *Belle Ile (B3-4), Brière Nature Park (C3-4), Concarneau (B2), Côte d'Émeraude (Emerald Coast) (CD1), Côte du Granit Rose (Pink Granite Coast) (B1), Dinan (CD2), Le Folgoët (A1), Guimiliau (B1), Locmariaquer (C3), Locronan (A2), Menez Bré (B1), Notre-Dame de Quilinen, Notre-Dame de Tronoën (A2), Pen Hir Point, Pleyben, Quimper (A2), Raz Point (A2), Rennes (D2), Saint-Pol de Léon (AB1), Saint-Thégonnec (AB1), Tréguler (B1), Vannes (C3).*

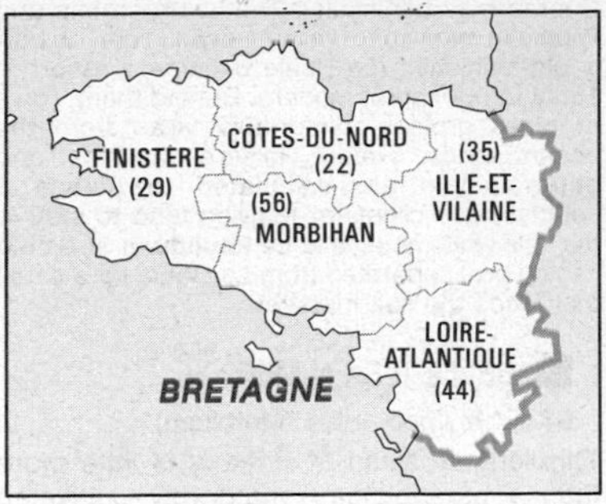

Facts and figures

Location : *At the westernmost point of France, a 250 km long peninsula whose breadth varies from 75 to 150 km, separating the English Channel from the Atlantic Ocean.*

Area : *34077 km².*

Climate : *Maritime, thus variable. Generally clement, due to the influence of the Gulf Stream. Bracing on the coast, with little frost, even inland; few really hot spells (mean summer temperatures between 18 and 25 °C), but high rate of sunshine (2000 hours per year : as much as the Mediterranean Coast).*

Population : *3349183.*

Administration : ***Côtes-du-Nord*** *Department, Prefecture Saint-Brieuc.* ***Finistère*** *Department, Prefecture Quimper.* ***Ille-et-Vilaine*** *Department, Prefecture Rennes.* ***Loire-Atlantique*** *Department, Prefecture Nantes.* ***Morbihan*** *Department, Prefecture Vannes.*

▶ Nearby

▶ **Sainte-Avoye** *(4.5 km SE) :* 16thC chapel with choir screen★ (1554) in carved wood. ▶ The bridge at **Bono** *(6 km from Auray)* gives a fine view of the port, where the principal occupation is raising oyster spat. ▶ **Sainte-Anne d'Auray** ® *(6 km NE; pilgrim influx, 15-16 July);* neo-Renaissance basilica; behind, former Carmelite convent with 17thC cloister; treasury and ex-votos★ *(daily 10-12 & 2-6, 1 Jul.-30 Sep.; Sun. and Wed. only in May-Jun.).* Gallery of Breton religious art (statues; same hours). Near the Breton War Memorial (1932), the La Fontaine Museum (dolls in Breton costumes); wax museum *(1 Apr.-30 Oct., 8-8);* Nicolazic House (mobilier). Nicolazic Gallery, display case of processional banners. □

LA BAULE★

C4 / ® / pop. 14688 (Loire-Atlantique)

The most popular seaside resort in Brittany, on a par with Royan and Biarritz, the other major resorts on the Atlantic Coast. La Baule claims to have the most beautiful beach in Europe.

▶ A broad promenade with flower gardens flourishing in the mild climate starts at **Porni-**

chet ®, created 20 years ago on the edge of an 8 km crescent of fine sand (the **Côte d'Amour,** Guérandaise peninsula). The luxury hotels and imposing mansions vary in style from quaintly old-fashioned (La Baule became a resort in 1880) to up-market modern. Behind them, rows of pines protect comfortable villas from the ocean winds. Hotels, leisure facilities and entertainment are calculated to please a sophisticated clientele; families tend to stay in the little white houses at **Le Pouliguen** ®, an old fishing port separated from La Baule by a canal that feeds the salt marshes. □

BELLE-ÎLE-EN-MER★★

B3-4 / ® / pop. 4191 (Morbihan)

This largest island of Brittany is little more than a bare plateau stubbornly cultivated by its inhabitants. Its many valleys protect crops from waves that thunder against the cliffs. Some of the beaches are dangerous, but the remoteness of Belle-Île attracts many visitors.

▶ **Le Palais :** a port fortified during the 1st and 2nd Empires (ca. 1800; ca. 1860). Citadel (museum) dating from 1572 *(free entrance; 9-6).* □

▶ Tour of the island *(57 km; an easy day; take care when walking near the edge of the cliffs).*

▶ Start from **Sauzon,** a little fishing port; go to **Poulains Point**★ at the northernmost tip of the island; **L'Apothecairerie Cave**★★, a natural marvel; after a quick visit to **Port Donnant** (cliffs★) and a brief stop at the **Grand Phare** (lighthouse; panorama★; *1 Jul.-15 Sep. 9:30-12:30 & 2-6;* 256 steps; 85 m above sea level), see the rock needles★★ at **Port-Coton.** Via **Bangor** and **Locmaria** (superb ex-voto model in the church) you can reach lilliputian **Port-Maria** on the eastern tip of the island. Return to Le Palais along the beach (Les Grands Sables). □

BÉNODET

B2 / ® / pop. 2286 (Finistère)

The population increases to around 30000 in summer; the site★★ (picture-postcard marina on the Odet Estuary) and lush vegetation are very attractive. Marvellous views from the lighthouse, the banks of the Odet and the **Pont de Cornouaille** (Cornwall Bridge). □

BIGOUDEN Region

A2 (Finistère)

Typical Breton countryside around Pont-l'Abbé, mixing tradition (the tall white caps of the women) and modernity (tractors and market gardening, tourism and rows of identical little white houses).

▶ **Pont-l'Abbé** (A2 / ® / pop. 7729) is 6 km upriver. The **Bigouden Museum**★ in a round 15thC tower by a lake *(1 Jun.-30 Sep., daily, 9-12 & 2-6:30; closed Sun. and nat. hols.) :* costumes and headdresses. ▶ Church (1383, two rose windows★) near shady walk on right bank. ▶ **Kerlever** (5 km NE), Cornouaille botanical garden *(in season, 10-12 & 2-6).* □

▶ Round trip along the coast *(43 km, 2 1/2 hr).*

▶ Follow D2. The pretty Bigouden farm at **Kervagégan** has been transformed into an eco-museum. ▶ **Kérazan Manor** (16th-18thC) in a park; 18th-19thC furniture, 16th-20thC paintings and drawings *(1 Jun.-15 Sep.; 10-12 & 2-6; closed Tue.).* ▶ **Loctudy** ® (pop. 3560) : an ideal seaside resort for children. The church★ is one of the most beautiful Romanesque buildings in Brittany; the port (fishing, pleasure craft) faces **L'Île-Tudy,** a fishing port on the end of a narrow peninsula. ▶ Busy little ports along the coast : **Lesconil** ® (sardines and langoustines), **Lechiagat** and **Le Guilvinec** (third most active fishing port). ▶ The church★ at **Penmarc'h** is a fine example of Flamboyant Gothic Breton architecture (1508). ▶ The **Eckmühl lighthouse** (64 m, 1897) on the tip of Penmarc'h is one of the most powerful in France; superb view *(1 May-15 Sep., 10-12 & 2-7; pm only rest of year).* ▶ **Saint-Guénolé** ® : a coastal and deep sea fishing port; to the N, the sea boils around the rocks; **museum of prehistory** *(10-12 & 2-6, Jun.-Sep.),* surrounded by megaliths; reconstructed burial chambers inside. ▶ Dolmens, menhirs, and cromlechs (→ box) line the road to **Plomeur** ® (18thC church). ▶ **Château de Kernuz** (now a hotel) stands in a park, and possesses a 15thC guardroom. □

▶ Round trip inland *(approx. 50 km; 3 hr)*

▶ Tour of the churches and chapels : **Tréminou**★ (15thC; Calvary in the form of a pulpit); **Saint-Jean-Trolimon** (16thC, rebuilt); **Notre-Dame de Tronoën**★★ (15thC; Calvary★★ on the heath, prototype of the Breton Calvaries). ▶ **Plonéour-Lanvern :** surrounded by churches and chapels; chapels of Languivoa (14th-16thC) and Lanvern (16thC); churches at **Tréguennec** (15th-16thC; stained glass, altarpieces, beams), **Trégoat** (15thC) and **Peumerit** (13thC); ruined chapel at **Languidou**★ (13thC). The manor houses are hardly less numerous : manor farm at Minven (16thC door), fortified manor at **Penquelenec; Trévilit Manor**★ (15thC; *exterior visit only*). □

The BLAVET River

▶ From Mur-de-Bretagne to Pluvigner *(148 km, full day).*

BC 2-3 *(see map 2)* (Côtes-du-Nord - Morbihan)

A dark, peaceful river running through quiet countryside, with here and there a grove of trees or a clump of golden furze among the potato fields that stretch to Pontivy.

▶ An interesting route from north to south through the centre of Brittany. ▶ **Mur-de-Bretagne** ® (pop. 2165) on a hilltop, 17thC chapel surrounded by old oaks; 2 km W, **Lake Guerlédan**★ (4 km², boat trips); wooded banks; producing since 1929 electricity in the Blavet Gorges. ▶ Through the rock-strewn **Poulancre Gorges** to **Saint-Gilles-Vieux-Marché** (lakes, menhirs) and **Saint-Mayeux** (Calvary surrounded by old yews in the cemetery). D76 runs from here along the ridge line; views. ▶ In **Laniscat,** furnishings and wheel of bells in the church (1691); continue to the **Daoulas Gorges**★, with almost vertical schist formations *(in summer,* mineralogical exhibition). ▶ Ruins of the Cistercian **abbey of Bon Repos** near an old, ivy-covered bridge (doorway, 18thC buildings, remains of 13thC chapel). ▶ Delightful walks in the woodlands around **Forges-des-Salles.** ▶ GR34 runs through the **forest of**

Quénécan★, a beautiful itinerary along the south bank of the lake, with a steep rock wall on the opposite side; by car to the bay at **Sordan**; view from the dam. ▶ The Tree of Jesse (genealogy of Christ) is often represented in Breton churches : at **Saint-Aignan** (12thC), carved; St. Mériadec Chapel (16thC), **Stival,** in a stained glass window. ▶ After **Pontivy** (→) and environs, leave the Blavet : **Quelven,** depopulated by a rural exodus, an old village that is still crowded every 15 August at the *pardon* (→ box), on one of the rare days when the sides of an Opening Virgin in the Notre-Dame chapel (15th-16thC) are unfolded to reveal 12 bas-reliefs of Christ's Passion. ▶ The road zig-zags back to the Blavet at **Rimaison** (remains of château). ▶ The chapel of **Saint-Nicodème★** is of remarkable proportions (46 m bell-tower); built in 1537 in Flamboyant Gothic style; furnishings. Nearby, a consecrated fountain (1608). ▶ **Saint-Nicolas-des-Eaux** ® : on the

2. The Blavet river

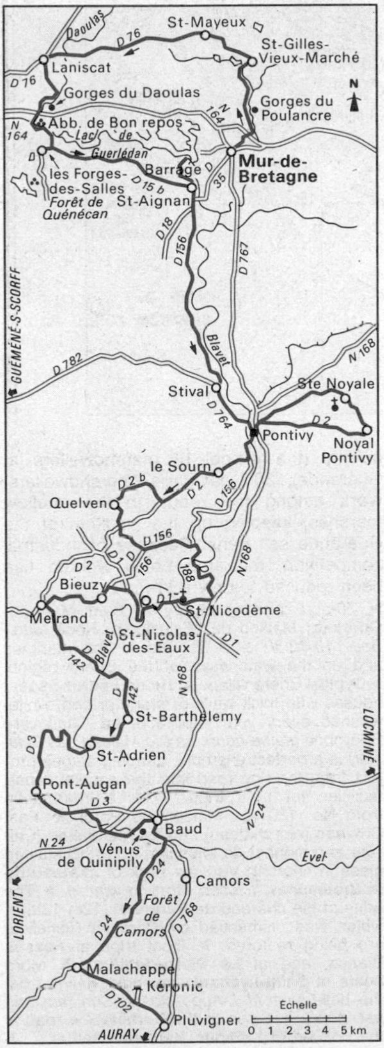

banks of the Blavet Canal, old granite houses, some with thatched roofs. ▶ The road follows the river in a tight bend around **La Couarde "peninsula"** : view★ of both sides of the valley; La Trinité chapel (15th-16thC) at **Castennec;** old hermitage of St. Gildas at the foot of the hamlet. ▶ **Bieuzy :** church retaining 16thC beams and stained glass; Renaissance houses with wells; 16thC fountain. ▶ **Melrand :** typical old inland Brittany village with granite houses (several from the Renaissance); 200 m from the church, unusual Calvary★ (18th-19thC). ▶ The road criss-crosses the Blavet through neatly-tended countryside where thatched roofs are still common; menhirs (3.5-m and 5-m high) at **Saint-Barthélemy;** the water from the fountains at the **chapel of Saint-Adrien** (15thC) is reputed to cure stomach pains. Visit the **château de Villeneuve-Jacquelot** and the exhibition of regional arts and traditions in the Poul Fétan Museum at **Quistinic;** catch your breath in refreshing **Pont Augan.** ▶ Before you reach **Baud** ® (pop. 4 962; 16thC church), visit the statue known as the **Vénus de Quinipily,** which gave the local clergy sleepless nights for centuries in their struggle to overcome popular superstition and the cult that surrounds the goddess. ▶ Choice of walks in the **forest of Camors** (beech, megaliths). ▶ The Château de Kéronic (16thC; *private*) is worth a detour on the way to **Pluvigner** (many chapels). □

BRÉHAT island★

C1 / ® / pop. 511 (Côtes-du-Nord)

An island 1.5 by 3.5 km, 10 mins from Arcouest Point among scattered reefs and islets; jagged coastline, no cars allowed (a few tractors only). Camellias and hydrangeas, mimosa and rose laurel brighten the gardens; roads wind through heather to bays and creeks inhabited by guillemots and cormorants, curlews and seagulls, where fishermen bring in lobster, king prawns and crab. □

BREST★

A2 / ® / pop. 160 355 (Finistère)

Brest successfully disguised its post war development as well as its military-industrial activities; it is not a tourist town in the traditional sense, but its superb roadstead, the romantic names of streets and bistros and the mild climate attract numerous visitors, in addition to admirers of the French Navy.

▶ Brest, originally a Roman military outpost, became an important port under Cardinal Richelieu (1631). During WWII it was France's principal naval dockyard; it became a German submarine base, as a result of which the port was heavily bombed. After the D-Day landings in 1944 (see Normandy), a devastating siege of 43 days obliterated the town centre.

▶ **Museum** *(B3; 10-11:45 & 2-6:45; closed Tue.)* : paintings from the 17th, 18th and 19thC; Dutch, Flemish and Italian schools; school of Pont-Aven. ▶ The **Recouvrance Bridge★** (AB3) has an 87 m centre span which rises 29 m in 2 min 28 sec. View★ of the Penfeld and the **arsenal buildings** (visits for French citizens only). ▶ In La Motte-Tanguy Tower (16thC; A3) is the **Old Brest Museum** *(daily Jul.-Aug., 10-12 & 2-7; Jun. and Sep., 2-7; Thu.)* military history; dioramas. The **Naval Museum** is in the

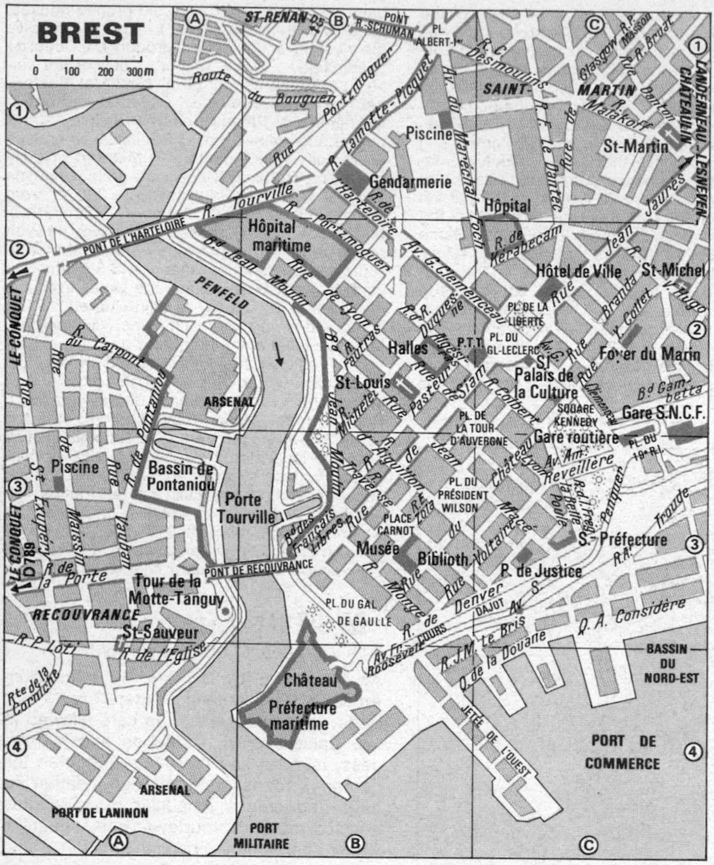

15th-16thC **château** (B4; *daily ex. Tues.; 9:30-11:30 & 2-5*). ▶ From the Cours (avenue) Dajot (B4-C3) on the south side of the ramparts (built in 1683 by Louis XIV's military engineer Sebastien de Vauban), view★★ of the harbour.□

■ BRIÈRE Nature Park★★ and GUÉRANDE Salt Marshes★

▶ From Montoir-de-Bretagne to Guérande *(96-138 km, full day)*
C3-4 *(see map 3)* (Loire-Atlantique)

The Grande Brière is a 200 km² peat bog drained by numerous ditches. The inhabitants of the 21 communes in the area own the marshes collectively, as they have done since the letter of patent of the Duke of Brittany, François II, signed in 1461. The people live by netting fish, wildfowling, stock-rearing and the sale of peat and reeds, supplemented by boat trips and other tourist activities. Today, however, these are only secondary livelihoods; many are employed in the dockyards at Saint-Nazaire or the workshops at Trignac.

Not far from the summer excitement of the Côte d'Amour (5 km from la Baule), which shows signs at present of an increased activity (the school of marshdwellers at Guérande), 300 *paludiers* (marshdwellers) work among the reeds in the shallow marshes, keeping up the tradition of the Guérande salt pans. Because of industrial competition, the area being worked has been reduced to only 8 km².

▶ 70-acre bird sanctuary at **Saint-Malo-de-Guersac;** Maison de l'Eclusier at **Rosé** *(Jun.-Sep. 10-12:30 & 3-7)* : life in the marshes and on the waterways of the Brière region. ▶ Typical Brière village at **Île de Fédrun :** squat houses with thick walls of stone or cob, whitewashed every year. No. 308, La Chaumière Briéronne *(same hours as the Maison de l'Eclusier)* is a perfect example. Landing stages project from the ring road into the parallel canal; facilities for boat trips. Visitor's information from No. 180 (La Maison du Parc). ▶ Past **Crossac** (old château) and **La Madeleine** (Calvary and menhir), to **Missillac** ® (16thC stained glass in church); visit the park of **château de la Bretesche**★ *(closed Mon. in winter).* ▶ The ruins of the **château de Ranrouët** (12th-13thC), which was dismantled by Cardinal Richelieu, are being restored. ▶ Boat trips at **Fossés Blancs,** and at **La Pierre-fondue;** ▶ More boats at **Saint-Lyphard;** splendid view★ from the bell-tower *(Jul.-Aug; closed Sun. am and nat. hols.).* ▶ Close to the **Kerhinet**★★ road is the dolmen of **Kerbour.** Kerhinet itself is a village-museum (inn; museum : *same hours as the Maison de l'Eclusier*); traditional Brière houses. **Bréca** and **La Chaussée Neuve :** boat trips, views★ over La Brière. Through **Guérande** (→) to **château de Careil★ ;** Renaissance façades in the courtyard *(20 Mar.-30 Sep., 10:30-12 & 2:30-7:30; candlelight visits Wed. and Sat. at 9:30 pm, 15 Jun.-30 Aug.)*. ▶ **Kervalet** is a marvellous little marshdwellers' village.

▶ **Saillé :** Maison des Paludiers offers an introduction to the world of the salt marshes; costumes, furnishings, tools, explanatory models *(1 Jul.-15 Sep., 10-12 & 2-7; pm only in Jun.)*.

▶ **Batz-sur-Mer** (Batz is pronounced "Ba") : 15th-16thC church with unusual carved keystones; view★ over saltings from the tower (1677; 60 m; *15 Jun.-31 Aug.*); *(see the Saltworks or Marshdwellers Museum)*. ▶ Pretty road around the point at **Croisic** (→); squat salt barns in wood or stone, their walls supported by buttresses, line the road. Drive or walk carefully along this low dyke between tidal reservoirs and mud flats to explore the marshes. ▶ **La Turballe .** a sardine port linked by a lovely road to **Piriac-sur-Mer** (13thC crypt under the church; attractive old houses); extensive view★ of the coast from **Castelli Point.** □

■ CALLAC

B2 / pop. 2 957 (Côtes-du-Nord)

Formerly a horse-breeding centre *(visit the stud farm)*, now a poultry- and pig-breeding community; Breton spaniels are also a local concern.

▶ 200 km of trout river within a radius of 15 km. Church★ (14th-16thC; 15thC porch) at **Plourac'h** *(10.5 km W)*. 7 km S : **Duault Forest,** studded with megaliths. 16thC stained glass in the churches of **Duault** *(6.5 km S)*, **Locarn**

3. Brière Nature Park

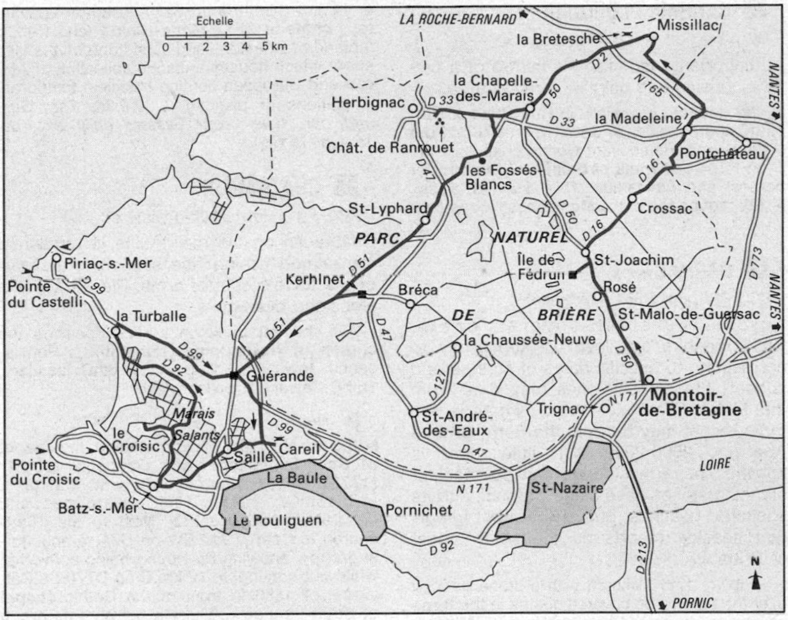

Megaliths

Megaliths date from the Neolithic Era and the Bronze Age (4500-2000 BC). They are not restricted to Brittany, but are so numerous here that most of the names used to describe them are Breton words. A dolmen (stone table), apparently a group burial chamber, consists of a corridor with a circular vault, sometimes covered with earth (tumulus) or rocks (cairn); some have no terminal chamber. Menhirs (standing stones) vary in size; the largest known (now broken) was found at Locmariaquer; it stood 20.3-m tall and weighed 350 tons. Menhirs occur both alone and grouped in cromlech (stone rings) or in rows (→ Carnac).

(13.5 km S; treasury★) and **Maël Pestivien** *(13.5 km E)*. ▶ Church★ at **Bulat-Pestivien** *(9 km NE; Pardon* (→) on Sun. after 8 Sep.), Renaissance; bell-tower (66 m), porch and sacristy (carved frieze of the *Dance of Death*); 16thC Calvary★ in **Pestivien** cemetery. □

■ CAMARET-SUR-MER

A2 / ® / pop. 3 064 (Finistère)

France's leading source of langoustes; a pleasant town protected by a 600 m natural dyke on which stand the chapel of Notre-Dame de Rocamadour (16th-17thC) and the Château Vauban (1689) naval and historical museum *(daily Jun.-Sep.)*.

▶ 1 km W, **rows of menhirs** (143 altogether) at **Lagat Jar;** 2 km W, Toulinguet Point (lighthouse, fort, caves); 3 km SW, **Pen Hir Point★★,** a 70 m sheer cliff with the enormous rocks of the Tas de Pois extending out to sea; a magnificent and popular site. ▶ View★★ over Brest Channel and roadstead from the Pointe des Espagnols on **Roscanvel Peninsula,** covered with gorse, small forts and army training grounds. □

■ CANCALE

D1 / ® / pop. 4 693 (Ille-et-Vilaine)

Oysters are the main product of Cancale : *creuses* (concave shell) are the most numerous; *plates* (flat shells) are less common; *pieds de cheval* (shaped like horses, hooves) are rare. The seafront★ is a long line of restaurants looking across to Mont-Saint-Michel Bay (25 km).

▶ **Views★** from three headlands linked by GR34. Another view from the church tower *(15 Jun.-15 Sep.; ticket from SI);* next door, house with carved woodwork. □

■ CARHAIX-PLOUGUER

B2 / ® / pop. 9 100 (Finistère)

An important market in tne centre of a cattle — raising and dairy — farming area.

▶ **Old houses,** especially in Rue Brizeux (SI); 16thC church tower. ▶ 3 km NE on D787 : **Pont Gaulois** and Flamboyant Gothic chapel; 8 km E on N164 : **chapels of Saint-Eloi** (*pardon* for horses) and **Lansalaün** (1528 stained glass). ▶ SW : round trip of the Montagnes Noires (→). □

■ CARNAC★★★

B3 / ® / pop. 3 964 (Morbihan)

Across the scrub-covered heath, 2 935 menhirs are lined up apparently to correspond to specific dates of sunrise and sunset; the oldest stones may date from the Middle Neolithic Period, whereas the most recent may be from the Early Bronze Age (ca. 2500-2000 BC); little more is known. These mysterious and spectacular standing stones have made Carnac, with its sheltered beaches, one of the most important seaside resorts on the south coast of Brittany.

▶ In town, 17thC **church** with a stone canopy over the porch; the covered beams in the three naves are decorated with paintings★. **Miln-le-Rouzic Museum :** prehistory collection (a new museum opened in 1985 : prehistory collection, *daily ex. Tues., 10-12 & 2-5).* Nearby, the **St. Michel Tumulus★,** a large burial chamber from 3000 BC *(daily Apr.-Sep.),* surmounted by a chapel (view★). ▶ From the Plouharnel road, a turning which runs alongside the lines of standing stones; **Menec Alignments★★** (1 099 menhirs in 11 lines 1 167 m long, starting from a cromlech of 70 menhirs); **Kermario Alignments★** (1 029 menhirs in 10 rows 1 120 m long); **Kercado Tumulus** *(Easter and Jun.-Sep.);* **Kerlescan Alignments★** (594 menhirs in 13 rows of 880 m); return to Carnac via the **Moustoir Tumulus.** The region is dense with megaliths (signposted) : dolmens at Kériaval, Mané Kérioned and Runesto (Plouharnel - Auray road), the dolmens at **Rondossec, Crucuno,** Mané Groac'h, **lines of menhirs at Kerzhero** (1 129 menhirs; Plouharnel-Erdeven road). ▶ Services in Gregorian chant at the Benedictine abbeys of Ste. Anne and St. Michel in **Kergonan.** ▶ **La Trinité-sur-Mer** ® : a pleasant fishing port and yacht harbour on the Crash Estuary, considered for a decade the centre of open-sea racing (oyster beds; view★ from the bridge). □

■ CHÂTEAUBRIANT

D3 / ® / pop. 14 415 (Loire-Atlantique)

▶ The **château★** is in two parts : Vieux Château (11th, 13th and 15thC), with 13thC entrance, 12th-13thC chapel and 15thC main building attached to a large square keep; and Château Neuf (Renaissance, 1533-39, restored); the parts are linked by a gallery to a lodge with projecting bays that shelters a staircase *(daily 15 Jun.-15 Sep., 9-12 & 2-7, closed* Mon.). ▶ 15th-16thC houses. ▶ In the Faubourg (suburb) of Béré (take the Rennes road) : 11thC **church★** with wooden 15thC porch, three 17thC altarpieces and a 14thC Virgin. □

▶ Nearby

▶ 17 km SE, through Saint-Julien-de-Vouvantes : **château de La Motte-Glain★** (end 15thC), a blend of limestone and sandstone on the lake shore which houses a unique collection of African and European hunting trophies, temporary exhibitions of painting *(2:30-6:30, Sat., Sun. and nat. hols. from Easter; daily ex Tue. 15 Jun.-15 Sep.).* □

■ CHÂTEAULIN

AB2 / ® / pop. 6 102 (Finistère)

Châteaulin on the river Aulne is renowned for salmon fishing; the salmon forms part of the town's coat of arms. Pleasant walks along the riverbanks.

▶ On the left bank on a rocky peak is the **church of Notre-Dame** (15th-16thC); Renaissance tower; 1722 porch; 16thC ossuary, 15thC Calvary. Excellent view. □

▶ Nearby

▶ 6.5 km N : overlooking the Aulne, the **chapel of Saint-Sébastien★** with octogonal sacristy (1772), in a churchyard with Calvary★ (mid-16thC); inside, 18thC altarpieces and decorated rood beam. ▶ Next to the 16thC church in **Cast** *(7 km SW on D7)* , a sculptural group★ showing St. Hubert being converted while out hunting. ▶ 12 km S on D770 : a Calvary★ of 1556 in front of the Gothic **chapel of Saint-Vennec★,** where a polychrome group depicts Ste. Gwen (Ste. Blanche) with three breasts to feed her sons, St. Gwenolé, St. Jacut and St. Vennec. □

■ CLISSON★

D4 / ® / pop. 5 032 (Loire-Atlantique)

Two rivers meet at the foot of an old château. Local economy depends on uranium and livestock.

▶ The town was levelled during the French Revolution of 1798 and rebuilt in an oddly Italianate style. ▶ Opposite the **Pont de la Vallée** (Valley Bridge, 14thC) across the Sèvre is a staircase leading through the pedestrian precinct **(wood-framed covered market★)** to the **château★** *(9-12 & 2-6 or 7; closed Tue.);* a bridge across the moat leads to the 15thC entrance; the western part (to the right as you enter) was built in the 15thC by François II, last Duke of Brittany. The eastern half dates from the 13th and 14thC; 16thC additions reinforce it to the south. □

Salmon

The rivers of Brittany were once so full of salmon that numerous apprenticeship contracts did not allow employers to serve the fish more than three times a week. The position today is very different : in 1982, France imported 2 200 tons of salmon from Norway. Efforts are being made by various organisations to clean the rivers and rebuild the salmon leaps. Together with anti-pollution campaigns and the establishment of experimental salmon farms in the Trégor area, these steps are slowly improving the situation. Investment is heavy and it takes 4 years for a salmon to grow to full size.

▶ Nearby

▶ 7.5 km NW, near the Sèvre, stained glass in the church at **Monnières** depicts the surrounding vineyards. ▶ The Pierre Abélard Museum, at **Pallet** on the opposite bank : arts and traditions of the vineyard and tasting of muscadet and gros-plant *(May-Nov., Sat. Sun. and nat. hols., 2:30-6:30).* ▶ 9 km N : **Vallet** specialises in Muscadet wine. 3 km further : the **château La Noë de Bel-Air :** a Palladian villa of 1836 in an English-style park *(exterior visit on request).* □

■ COMBOURG

D2 / ® / pop. 4 763 (Ille-et-Vilaine)

The **château★** is a 14th-15thC fortress, remodelled in Romantic style between 1876-1900; the machicolated towers can be seen through the trees.

▶ The writer Chateaubriand (1768-1848) passed his childhood here; memorabilia *(park and château 9-12 Mar.-Nov.; château only 2-5:30; closed Tue.).* ▶ 5 km E : **château de Lanrigan** (15th-16thC), Flamboyant Gothic with flanking turrets in grey granite *(park only, Jun.-Sep., 8 12 & 2-7).* ▶ At **Dingé,** 7 km S of Lanrigan, **Ville-André Manor** *(exterior only, 8-12 & 2-8; closed Sun.),* a rectangular granite building with square turrets. 18 km E., **château de la Ballue** (17thC), remarkable Baroque gardens★★ and, inside the château, collections concerning gardens *(10-12 & 2:30-5:30 in Jul.-Aug., closed Tue.).* □

■ CONCARNEAU★★

B2 / ® / pop. 18 225 (Finistère)

This ancient city combines tourism with trawler fishing. The boats return every 10 to 15 days from the waters off Scotland, Ireland or the African coast; Concarneau boasts the third largest fresh-fish landings and the biggest tuna catch in France.

▶ The **Ville Close** (Walled Town)★★; fortified in the 13th-14thC, 300 m long; illuminated on summer evenings. This little island was given new granite ramparts★ in the 16thC and was further fortified in the 17thC by Vauban *(sentry-walk open Easter-30 Sep., 9-7).* ▶ Narrow alleys open off Rue Vauban, which is lined with souvenir shops. **Musée de la Pêche** (Fisheries Museum : *daily 9:30-8:30 Jul.-Aug., 10-12:30 & 2:30-6 out of season*) : 47 aquariums, models and displays of the history and commercial activity of the town. ▶ Another sea-oriented exhibition at the **Marinarium** *(15 Jun.-15 Sep. 10-12 & 2-6:30)* in front of the yacht harbour, at Port de la Croix. On the north side of the inner harbour, the **fish auction** *(Criée)* where tons of fish are unloaded, starting at 10 pm; the *Criée* gets into full swing around 7 am, although nowadays the procedure is automated and much less noisy than it used to be. ▶ 1.5 km N of the town centre on the La Forêt Bay is the seaside resort of **Les Sables Blancs.** ▶ 5 km S : good views from **Cabellou Point;** elegant villas in the woods. ▶ At the exit from the town : **château de Kériolet,** built in 1870 in late-15thC style. □

▶ Nearby

6 km SE, **château de la Chapelle-aux-Elitzméens** (15th-17thC), dovecote intact, collection of antique lace *(daily, May-Oct.).*

▶ 70 mins away by boat *(tel. 98.97.01.44; in summer, service also from Beg Meil and Bénodet, tel. 98.57.00.14),* the **Glénan Islands** form an archipelago of 9 small islands, one of which boasts an impressive fort (18thC), while the others offer a bird sanctuary, a lighthouse and, especially, a well-known nautical centre.

■ LE CONQUET

A2 / ® / pop. 2 011 (Finistère)

This fishing port, weekend resort for the people of Brest and point of embarquation for boats to Ouessant (→), maintains a radio station that broadcasts weather reports and messages to the fishing fleet.

▶ View★ of the coast and the islands from **Kermorvan Point.** From **Renards Point,** you can see the beams from 13 lighthouses. ▶ 4 km away, **Saint-Mathieu Point★** view; ruins of a large 13thC abbey. □

■ CÔTE DES ABERS★

(Abers Coast)

▶ From Le Conquet to Brignogan *(approx 120 km, full day)*

A1 (Finistère)

The banks of the estuaries, with rounded cliffs covered in pale heather, are less steep than in the north; the creeks and beaches are popular with shell and seaweed collectors.

▶ Via **Ploumoguer** (Cohars Manor E) as far as the sandbanks at Porsmoguer; **Corsen Point** (view★, *1 km on foot)* is the westernmost outcrop of continental France. ▶ **Plouarzel** (*4 km E;* polychrome Pietà in church) has the tallest menhir in France (12-m high). ▶ **Brélès** overlooks the Aber Ildut; 16th-18thC church with St. Isidore in Breton costume accompanied by angels playing bagpipes. ▶ 11 km from Brélès, the museum of local history at **Saint-Renan** *(daily, Jul.-Aug.).* ▶ Beyond **Aber-Ildut,** at the mouth of the estuary, the village of **Melon** lives by seaweed harvesting. ▶ Menhirs, chapels and manor houses ring the resort of **Porspoder.** ▶ Near **Kersaint** and **Portsal,** a cliff road *(corniche)* runs past **château de Trémazan** (12th-15thC). ▶ 3 km from **Ploudalmézeau :** church at **Lampaul-Ploudalmézeau** with a Renaissance bell-tower★ and porch. ▶ Cross the Aber Benoît to **Sainte Marguerite Peninsula** to visi **Aber Wrac'h★** : a lobster and king prawn fishing port in a ring of reefs and islets. ▶ **Plouguerneau :** in a region notorious in the 16-17thC for ship plunderers and wreckers. ▶ **Kerlouan :** an important chicory-growing centre; drive through to reach the sea at **Brignogan-Plage** ® : sandy beaches and rock outcrops; 5.5 km S behind a sandbank : the church★ of **Goulven.** □

■ CÔTE D'ÉMERAUDE★★

(Emerald Coast)

CD1 (Ille-et-Vilaine)

This part of the North Brittany coast is named for the infinite variety of green shades reflected by the sea. From Grouin Point, to Val-André, a succession of capes and bays with rocks, inlets, cliffs, estuaries, beaches and islets, not to mention Saint-Malo and Cape Fréhel.

▶ Eastern sector, Saint-Malo to Cancale *(23 km; approx 1hr30).*

▶ Leave **Saint-Malo** (→) via Paramé and the beach at **Minihic** (18thC fort reused by the Germans). ▶ **Rothéneuf :** 300 carved rocks★, a masterpiece of naïf art by a local priest, the Abbé Fouré (early 20thC); marine aquarium; 500 m S from the church, **Limoëlou Manor★,** once the property of Jacques Cartier (1491-1557; discovered Canada in 1534), restored and refurnished *(exhibition daily pm; closed Tue. in season; Sat. pm and Sun. pm rest of year).* ▶ The harbour of Rothéneuf is an enclosed bay that almost entirely empties at low tide; above it stands the **Malouinière de Lupin★** (1692, private mansion). ▶ Beyond the **Du Guesclin Inlet** *(anse)* (site★, beach, 1758 island fort) and Verger Beach), is **Grouin Point★,** a 49 m high rocky crest with a superb view, from Mont-Saint-Michel and the Cotentin Peninsula to Cape Fréhel; pretty coast road back to Cancale (→). □

▶ West sector from Dinard to Val André *(87 km; full day)* (Côtes-du-Nord)

▶ Leave **Dinard** (→) on the road to **Saint-Lunaire★,** where Claude Debussy composed *La Mer;* Décollé Point : one of the best views★ on the coast; charming old church in the town. ▶ After **La Garde-Guérin Point** (view★), to **Saint-Briac** at the entrance to the Frémur, which drains at low tide (view★ of the estuary from the bridge). ▶ At **Lancieux** (family beach★) the road leaves the coast briefly. ▶ Water-tower at **Ploubalay** (1970; 54 m; lift; *9 to midnight Apr.-Sep.; Sat. pm, Sun. and nat. hols. Oct.-Nov.) :* terrace with the most beautiful view★★ in the region. ▶ Between two deep bays that dry out at low tide is the long **Saint-Jacut** Peninsula. ▶ Cross the estuary of the Arguenon (view downstream of mussel beds) and, at the foot of Notre-Dame du Guildo, throw pebbles to hear the "ringing stones" ring. ▶ **Saint-Cast-le-Guildo★** ®, a gracious resort with one of the most attractive beaches in North Brittany; pleasant walks to Saint-Cast and La Garde Points. ▶ **Matignon :** home town of the family that built the Matignon Palace in Paris, now the residence of France's Prime Minister. The big event here is the Wednesday market; *galettes* (buckwheat cakes) and sausage are sold on street corners (the *Café-Charcuterie Samson* is particularly good). ▶ Salt-meadow *(pré-salé)* sheep graze around the deep bay at Le Frênaye, which you must skirt to see Fort La Latte and Cape Fréhel (→). ▶ The beaches of **Pléherel-Plage** and **Sables-d'Or-les-Pins★** ® are widely known for silky sand and pine woods. ▶ Reach Val-André (→) by **Erquy,** a little port specialising in *coquilles St. Jacques* (scallops). □

Breton bonnets

Breton bonnets are essential items in the traditional feminine costume. They have developed over 2 centuries; fortunately, with the aid of folklore, tourism and nostalgia, they have not totally disappeared, and it is even said that the bonnets in the Bigouden region are now three times as high as they were in the 1930s. However that may be, they are dazzling evidence of the embroidery skills of women who maintain the old traditions throughout Brittany. The museums at Dinan and Pont-l'Abbé have extremely fine collections.

■ LE CROISIC★

C4 / ® / pop. 4 365 (Loire-Atlantique)

Next to La Baule and the Côte d'Amour, the port of Le Croisic is more involved with fishing (sardines, prawns, oysters and mussels) than with tourism.

▶ The picturesque **port★** is separated by little islands, called *jonchères,* into a number of basins. It was reshaped in the 18thC and is surrounded by **houses** of the period, stretching between two moles created with ballast left by boats loading salt from the nearby marshes. The **Aquarium of the Côte d'Amour★** *(10-8, Jul.-Sep.; 10-12 & 2-7 remainder of year; closed Mon. and last 2 weeks in Jan.) :* more than 3 000 shells, in addition to live specimens from all over the world. Nearby, the Town Hall (end 16thC) has a small naval museum *(Jun.-Sep., 10-12 & 3-7; closed am Mon. and Thu.).* Flamboyant Gothic church (1494-1507) with 56 m tower. □

▶ Nearby

▶ Besides the trip to Guérande (→) and salt marshes (→ Brière), take a trip around **Croisic Point;** a *corniche* runs along the cliffs of the **Grande Côte.** □

■ CROZON Peninsula

A2 (Finistère)

This sparse extension of Brittany projects into the Atlantic at the mercy of the heavy seas. Corn is grown wherever shelter can be found. At the base of the peninsula, the bald mountain of Ménez Hom (→) is similar of many others found further inland. On the tip is Camaret (→), with lobster boats sheltered behind one of the innumerable headlands. The peninsula is a microcosm of Brittany.

▶ **Crozon-Morgat*** ® (Morgat is the port) lives more from tourism than from sardine fishing; a superb beach★, admirably sheltered and surrounded by cliffs, together with attractive sites in the vicinity, makes it a popular resort. Near the beach are the **Grottes Marines★** (sea-caves), some accessible only by boat. **Dinan Point** *(6 km W-SW) :* a mass of rocks (known as the Château de Dinan) resembling a ruined

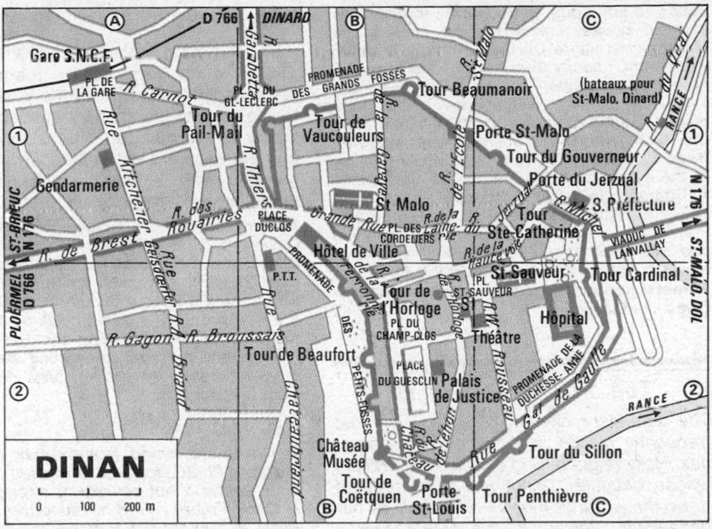

castle, linked to land by two natural bridges. Close by, Les Korrigans★ caves can be reached only during the season of spring tides *(guide essential)*; **Cap de la Chèvre★★ :** no less impressive with 100 m sandstone-and-quartz cliffs. ▶ In **Crozon** itself, the church has an altarpiece★ dating from 1602, with 400 carved and painted wooden figures, full of vigour and expression. □

■ DINAN★★

CD2 / ® / pop. 14 157 (Côtes-du-Nord)

Dinan is fortified and crenellated, girdled with ramparts, paved with cobblestones and full of old houses. It is built almost entirely of light grey granite, and the houses do not seem austere. Window-boxes and gardens, the deep green valley of the Rance with its little yacht marina, together with a busy country market make this an extremely attractive town.

▶ In the heart of town, the Place des Cordeliers (B1), the Rue de l'Apport and the **Place des Merciers★** have retained **timber houses★.** Close by, the Church of St. Malo (choir and transept from 1490, remainder rebuilt in the 19thC), and the former convent of the Cordeliers (private school; restored 15thC cloister; *visit during school hols.*). Opposite is the lively market. ▶ The steep **Rue du Jerzual★★** (C1), lined with 16thC houses occupied by craftsmen, runs down to the 14th-15thC port of the same name and continues into Rue du Petit Fort, equally steep and quaint, with craft workshops and crêperies. Continue on to the **port** (Gothic bridge) where the sails woven nearby used be shipped to Saint-Malo. ▶ **Basilica of St. Sauveur** (C2) : an interesting mixture of styles; Romanesque (façade and right half of the nave; 12thC), Flamboyant Gothic, and Renaissance. The heart of Du Guesclin (14thC Constable of France and probably its ablest leader during the Hundred Years' War) is buried here. Around the *chevet* (eastern end), is the Jardin Anglais★ (English garden; view★); tour of the ramparts. ▶ Almost opposite the SI (C1), in the Kératry Mansion★ (1559), are the **Tour de l'Horloge** (clock tower; end 15thC; *Jul.-Aug. 10-12 & 2-6; closed Sun.)* and a former stone mason's workshop. ▶ **Castle★★ :** a handsome oval keep (1382) standing 34 m high astride the ramparts; inside is a museum of life in Dinan through the ages *(daily 9-12 & 2-7 In summer; shorter hours, closed Nov. and Tue. out of season) :* bonnets and regional costumes; view★ from the platform; at the foot of the ramparts, Petits Fossés Promenade★. □

▶ Nearby

▶ **Léhon★** *(2 km S) :* fine church★, formerly a priory chapel (tombs, tablets and funerary statues from 13th, 14th and 15thC); 15thC refectory and remains of 17thC cloister. Walks along the Rance. ▶ **Valley of the Argentel** (40 mins on foot along Rue St. Malo, C1), shady site with fountain. ▶ 2 km N : ruins of 16thC **château de la Garaye.** ▶ **Aublette** *(3 km W) :* automobile museum *(daily Jun.-Sep. 3-6).* □

▶ Round trip through the Rance and Arguenon regions *(approx 160 km; one long day)*
See map 4 on following page

▶ Dinan. ▶ On the road from **Pleslin,** with one of the rare lines of menhirs in Upper Brittany, watch for charming manor house of Bois de La Motte (16th-17thC). 500 m from the Dinan road, near a farm : ruins of a Roman **temple of Mars;** more interesting Roman remains can be found at **Corseul** (Jardin des Antiques, museum in the town hall). ▶ **Pléven :** a pretty village near **Vaumadeuc Manor★** (15thC, now a hotel) and ruins of the 14thC **château de la Hunaudaie★ ;** a surprising fortress in this quiet countryside. ▶ **Saint-Esprit-des-Bois :** a farm-museum displaying various aspects of Breton life. ▶ **Jugon-les-Lacs** : an ideal country holiday spot between a lake (upstream) and a reservoir (downstream). ▶ **Mégrit :** churchyard. ▶ Massive Romanesque church in **Yvignac.** ▶ After **Caulnes,** you can see *(but not visit)* the **château de Couëlan★** and, beside a lake that supplies drinking water to Rennes, the 15thC château de Beaumont. ▶ Beyond **Saint-Pern** (18thC château) : **Caradeuc★ :** an extensive French Classical country house; French gardens★ (8 am-8 pm). ▶ **Bécherel :** fortifications and old houses; close by, the **château de Montmuran,** where Du Guesclin was knighted (12th-14thC; *hourly from 2 until 7 and every 1/2 hour on Sun.; open Sat. and Sun. 2-6 from 1 Nov. to Easter);* 500 m away : the Flamboyant Gothic Church★ (15th-16thC) of **Les Iffs,** with nine 16thC stained-glass windows. **Hédé** ® : walks in the Vallée des Moulins (valley of the mills) and along the Ille-et-Rance canal. ▶ **Château de la Bourbansais**★ : aristocratic 14th and 17thC residence with 18thC interiors; French park; zoo *(3-6, 15 Jun.-15 Sep.; Sun. and nat. hols. rest of year).* ▶ If you have time left, take a short detour in the **Coëtquen Forest**★ to see the ruins of a château and **La Chesnaie Manor.** □

The drowned city of Ys

The legendary city of Ys (or Is) is most frequently placed in the Bay of Douarnenez. Here reigned King Gradlon (or Grallon) whose daughter Dahut (or Ahès) brought down the wrath of heaven on the city by her debauchery. Warned in time by St. Guénolé, abbot of Landevennec, Gradlon was able to escape on horseback, but his daughter, riding behind him, was swallowed by waves that engulfed the city.

It is possible that this famous legend had its origins in a real event and that a relatively important city existed near Douarnenez or close by, which was destroyed by a tidal wave around the 4th or 5thC. Alternatively, it may refer to the progressive subsidence of the coast, which still continues in the Gulf of Morbihan.

■ DINARD

D1 / ® / pop. 10 016 (Ille-et-Vilaine)

The English aristocracy made Dinard fashionable at the end of the Victorian Era. In the turn-of-the-century atmosphere, the luxury hotels have an old-fashioned charm and the villas are set in Mediterranean-style gardens with fig-trees, palms, camellias, tamarisks and other exotic trees.

▶ Stroll around the **Écluse Beach**★ and the Casino (B2). It is almost obligatory to take a walk along the **Clair de Lune Promenade**★ (B3-C2), which runs past the **Sea Museum and Aquarium** *(Pentecost Sunday to 30 Sep., 10-12 & 2-6; 7 pm Sun. and nat. hols).* ▶ View★ from the Vicomté (via C3) over the Rance, Saint-Servan, and the **tidal generating station** *(8:30 am-8 pm; entry on the left bank downstream from the lock).* □

▶ Boat trips

▶ **Cézembre Island** *(approx 4 hr round trip, including 2hr30 stopover; in season only) :* take your swimsuit but beware of strong currents. ▶ **Cape Fréhel** (→) *(3 hr round trip, in season only).* ▶ **Trip up the Rance**★ to Dinan *(2hr30 to Dinan; the return journey depends on the tide and is not always possible the same day).* Excursion through a valley winding among green banks dotted with little ports; the fishermen have yielded to boating enthusiasts since the construction of the dam. □

■ DOL-DE-BRETAGNE★

D2 / ® / pop. 4 974 (Ille-et-Vilaine)

A long street that broadens as it descends the hill, lined with **houses**★ dating back to the 11th and 12thC (Nos 17 and 18) and 13thC (No 27, antique shop★).

4. The Rance and Arguenon regions

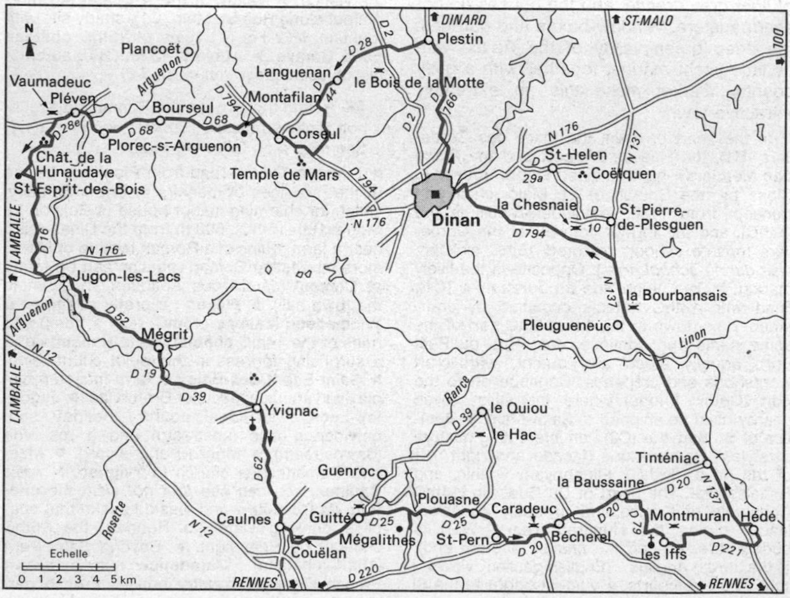

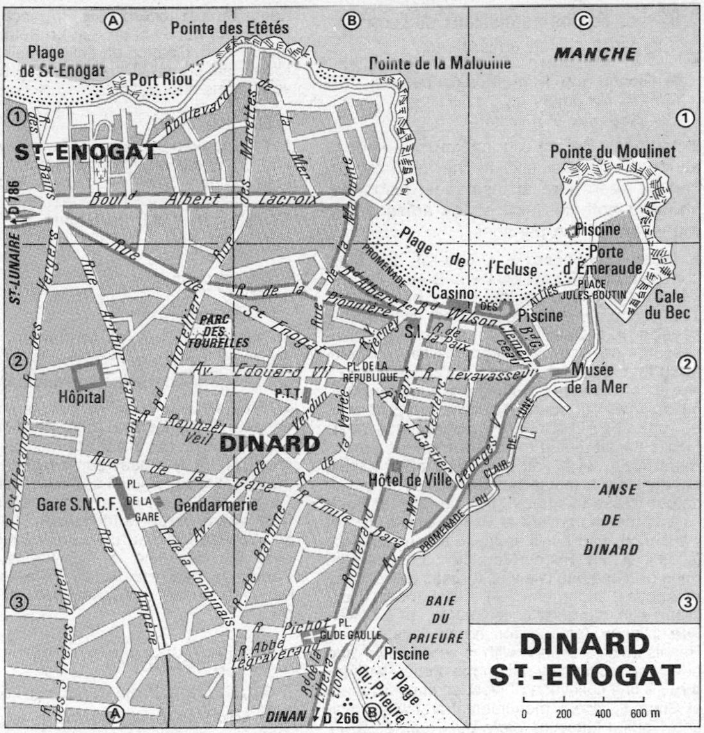

▶ The **cathedral★** attests to the religious importance of the city during the High Middle Ages; the kings of Brittany made it the religious capital of the country despite Papal objections. It is a majestic 13thC Gothic edifice, more Norman than Breton in style, with an elegant south porch and a noteworthy 13thC window★ in the choir. ▶ Opposite, the historical museum★ *(Easter-30 Sep., 9:30-5:30).* ▶ To the East : the **Douves Promenade** follows the ramparts (view★ over the marshes and Mont Dol). □

▶ Nearby

▶ **Mont Dol** *(4 km N)* : site of a mythical combat between St. Michael and the Devil; magnificent view over the Marais (marsh) where the legendary forest of Scissy was engulfed by the sea in the 8th and 9thC. The land was progressively reclaimed through the efforts of monks from the 12thC on; it was dried out for good after the 18thC, and is now extremely fertile. ▶ Continue to the coast *(5 km farther)* where villages such as **Le Vivier-sur-Mer** shelter with mills behind a dyke : panoramic views★ over the bay of Mont-Saint-Michel. ▶ Through **Epiniac** (16thC bas-reliefs in the church) to see the outside of **château de Landal** (15th-19thC) in a romantic setting of woods and lakes; return via Ormes (similar attractions) or detour via the church of Broualan : a faithful 15thC rendering of the bas-Breton style. ▶ 10 km SW on the edge of a lake : remains of the Benedictine **Le Tronchet Abbey** with a monumental 17thC cloister; the nearby **Mesnil Forest** is ideal for walks : châteaux, dolmens, and other diversions. □

■ DOUARNENEZ

A2 / ® / pop. 17 813 (Finistère)

Deep in a bay★ where the legendary city of Ys (→ box) is said to lie beneath the waves, the fishing port of Douarnenez rivals Guilvinec as the third French tuna fishing port. Expansion around **Tréboul** has given the town an interest in tourism.

▶ Between the new port and Rosmeur Harbour, visit the **Maritime Museum** and the **fish auction** *(criée),* opposite. Boat Museum, on the banks of the river of Port-Rhu. ▶ In town : chapels of Ste. Hélène (Flamboyant Gothic) and St. Michel (17thC). ▶ The 16th-17thC church in the Plouaré District has a 45-m bell-tower (16thC). ▶ View★ from the viaduct to **Tréboul,** set above the harbour, and stretching towards rocky Leydé Point (*3 km;* view★) along Les Sables Blancs beach. □

▶ Nearby

▶ In **Kerlaz** *(5 km E),* 16th-17thC church with ossuary and lacy spire. Return to **Pouldavid** (14th-16thC church; 16thC painted panelling inside) through **Le Juch** (in the church, Annunciation in recesses with painted shutters, old stained glass). ▶ 11 km W : inside the Flamboyant Gothic church★ at **Confort,** a wheel of bells said to restore speech to the dumb. 2 km from here : the open-air pulpit and consecrated fountain in front of the chapel of **Notre-Dame de Kérinec** (13th-14thC). □

Les **Enclos paroissiaux** du Léon (The parish churchyards of Léon)

▶ Round trip from Morlaix *(approx 107-121 km, full day)*
AB1 *(see map 5)* (Finistère)

Traditional Breton churchyards (→ box), although not exclusive to the Léon region, can be seen here at their most elaborate, showing both the skill of the artisans and the wealth of the parishes.

▶ **Saint-Thégonnec** ® : one of the most complete; 17thC ossuary★★ in Breton Renaissance style; Calvary of 1610; doorway of 1587; church (16th-17thC) with noteworthy panelling★. ▶ **Guimiliau :** unusual size and richness for so small a village; Calvary★★ with more than 200 statuettes; 17thC church with a wealth of carved furnishings. ▶ **Lampaul-Guimiliau :** without doubt the most richly-decorated church★ in Brittany; polychrome altarpieces★★ attributed to joiners from the French Royal Navy. ▶ If you have time after visiting **Landivisiau** ® (cattle market; naval air base), detour to see the 16th-17thC church★ at **Bodilis** and the churchyard at **Saint-Servais;** return via Brézal, with a mill opposite a ruined church (site★). ▶ **La Roche-Maurice :** beneath the ruins of a château (view★), a rustic churchyard. ▶ Above Landerneau (→) : little-known **Pencran,** with expressive sculptures. ▶ **La Martyre :** once famous for horse fairs, has a Renaissance ossuary with a well-known and oddly menacing caryatid on the corner. ▶ **Ploudiry :** a fine collection of wooden statues; more at **Sizun★,** also a monumental archway. River and Fishing Museum *(daily, Jul.-Aug., 11:30-7).* ▶ **Ker Hoad :** the **mills,** now a museum, demonstrate the many uses of water in traditional rural economies *(Apr.-June, daily 2-6; July-15 Sept., 11-7; 16 Sep.-end Oct., Sun. 2-6).* ▶ **Commana :** an interesting churchyard; the ornate altarpieces★ in the church illustrate "rustic Baroque". From here, visit the dolmen at **Mougau.** ▶ Continue along the foot of Roc'h Trévezel (→ Monts d'Arrée) and through **Plounéour Ménez** (churchyard) to reach the former Cistercian abbey church at **Le Relecq** (Romanesque and Gothic, partially rebuilt), returning to Morlaix via **Pleyber-Christ** (churchyard; carved beams and stalls). □

▶ Also...

▶ **Plougonven** *(12 km SE from Morlaix) :* fine and complete churchyard; vibrant carved figures on the Calvary★. Others at Plében (→) and Sainte-Marie du Ménez Hom (→ Ménez Hom), to name only the largest. □

ÉTEL Estuary

B3 (Morbihan)

A miniature Gulf of Morbihan; the south coast is strewn with many islets that offer challenging obstacles to windsurfers.

▶ The estuary is barred at its mouth by a sandbank, the Barre d'Étel, which causes dangerous currents; visible in high seas. ▶ **Étel** (pop. 2 699) is a busy sardine-and-tuna-fishing port as well as a small bathing resort. ▶ **Saint-Cado :** *(5 km N),* on a peninsula linked to an islet with a partly Romanesque chapel (site★). ▶ Highway crosses the **Lorois Bridge;** view★ over the coastline. ▶ 8.5 km N from Étel, **Plouhinec :** surrounded by megaliths; Romanesque church★ at **Merlevenez,** 4 km farther on. □

LE FAOUËT★★

B2 / ® / pop. 3 185 (Morbihan)

The town is built around a large square with a covered market★★ (end 16thC; timber construction on granite pillars). □

▶ Nearby

▶ Several superb chapels (15th-16thC) in nearby hamlets are worth a visit, not only for their artistic qualities but also for the sites★ on which they stand : **Sainte-Barbe** *(3 km NE by road; more pleasant on foot)* in Baroque set-

5. Parish churchyards

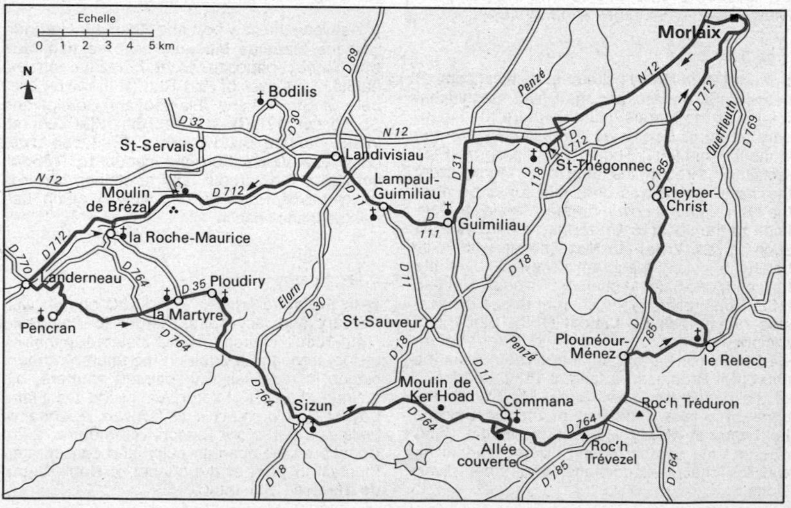

ting (oratory, main building, bell and staircase); **Saint-Fiacre** *(3 km S)* with a wall belfry and lacy choirscreen★★ (1480); the choirscreen at **Saint-Nicolas** *(8.5 km E)*, dating from the Renaissance, is a masterpiece of naïf art; the chapel of **Saint-Sébastien** is also worth a visit *(5.5 km N)*; carved beams show a saraband danced by demons in court costume. **Saint-Jean** *(3.5 km W from Saint-Nicolas)* rustic, with a touching Pietà. ▶ 11 km N : the **Langonnet Abbey** (rebuilt 18thC) has a 13thC chapterhouse. ▶ 13 km S : site★ of the **Rochers du Diable** (Devil's Rocks), a tumble of huge boulders among greenery overlooking the Ellé River. □

■ LE FOLGOËT★★

A1 / pop. 2 826 (Finistère)

One of Brittany's most important pilgrimages, dating from the 14thC, brings the main square (Grand'Place) to life every 7-8 September.

▶ The Flamboyant Gothic **church of Notre-Dame★★,** built 1422-60, began the fashion for scalloped windows and doorways. Inside : fine statues; 15thC altars; beautiful rose window (choir); kersantite (regional stone) choirscreen, once polychrome. Close to the presbytery, in a turreted 16thC manor house, the pilgrim hostel (1929 neo-Gothic) is the setting for the **Folgoët Museum** (religious art; reproduction of the bedroom of Anne of Brittany (15thC). ▶ 2 km NE : **Lesneven** (pop. 7 087) : an important cattle and pig market; old houses and pretty 1678 cloister. The **Léon Museum,** which has just opened. ▶ 4.5 km SE : close to Ploudaniel, **Trébodennic Manor** (16thC restored 1880; *8-12 Apr.-Sep.*). □

■ FOUESNANT

B2 / ® / pop. 5 430 (Finistère)

Famous for its cider, and the girls' head-dresses at the Fête des Pommiers (apple festival, 3rd Sun. in July), the town is close to the coastline of rocks and beaches. Romanesque church★ (nave, transept). □

Traditional Breton costume

For the men, bragou braz *(baggy trousers),* chupen *(jacket) and round hat; for women, a bodice laced over a linen blouse and a wide gathered skirt covered by an apron, topped with a neckerchief and bonnet. Traditional country costumes were very similar throughout western France, and did not vary much in Brittany itself. Only after the Revolution did the stratification of rural society, with imitation of the gentry and wealthy townsfolk, lead to the development of regional styles, influenced by the variety of goods supplied by travelling salesmen. These regional differences became part of local folklore. Breton costumes (extremely fine collection in the Ecomusée at Montfort) tell about the taste and character of the Breton people, their creativity and their desire for self-expression.*

Traditional Breton churchyards

Until the end of the 15thC, the churchyard was only an enclosure around the church, a transitional zone between the sacred and the secular. Here, processions began and ended at the the foot of a Calvary, which sometimes served as a pulpit. On pardon days, stalls of various kinds were erected against the outside wall. The dead were buried in the church, and later transferred to a building outside, known as the reliquary. During the 16thC, this was replaced by a larger ossuary that also served as a mortuary chapel. Later still, epidemics and population growth caused the tombs to be moved into the churchyard. Parishioners themselves took care of the churchyard, which had become a symbol of community life. In the 17thC, economic expansion enabled them to indulge in extravagant expenditure, often with one eye on their neighbours' activities : churchyards were elaborated with continual rebuilding and the addition of ornate decoration. Craftsmen and artists of great talent were frequently engaged.

▶ Nearby

▶ **La Forêt-Fouesnant** ® *(3.5 km E)* : country holidays, golf; site★★. ▶ **Beg Meil** ® *(6 km S)*, surrounded by greenery, with inlets and a broad beach; view★ over the bay, Concarneau *(regular 30 min crossings in season)* and the Glénan Islands. To either side of **Mousterlin Point** stretch long, uncluttered beaches. □

■ FOUGÈRES★

D2 / ® / pop. 25 131 (Ille-et-Vilaine)
see map following page

A centre of the French shoe industry and an important cattle market, one of the most modern in Europe (every Friday in the Parc de l'Aumaillerie). For the tourists, the walled town and castle are perhaps the most interesting features.

▶ From the **Place aux Arbres★** (A2), with shady, flowered terraces, a good view★ of the 14th-16thC Hôtel de Ville (town hall), the Gothic Church of St-Léonard (15th-16thC) and the castle, set against the Nançon Valley. ▶ 51 Rue Nationale is **La Villéon Museum** (Impressionist painter; *Apr., May, Jun., Sep., weekends and hols.; Jul.-Aug., daily 2-7*). ▶ **Castle★★** (A1; 12th-15thC) : on a rocky outcrop at the bottom of the valley, an apparently impregnable fortress, with 13 towers. It was nevertheless captured and recaptured a number of times. The interior has been turned into an open-air theatre; guided tour of the sentry-walk and some of the towers *(9, 10, 11, 2, 3, 4, 5 or 6, Mar.-Oct., closed Tue. off season; Sat. and Sun. only in Nov.; Sun. only in Feb.).* **Shoe Museum** *(same hours of opening as the castle).* Near the entrance is the **Maison des Artisans** (artisans' centre, local crafts). ▶ **Church of St. Sulpice** (15th-18thC) : at the foot of the

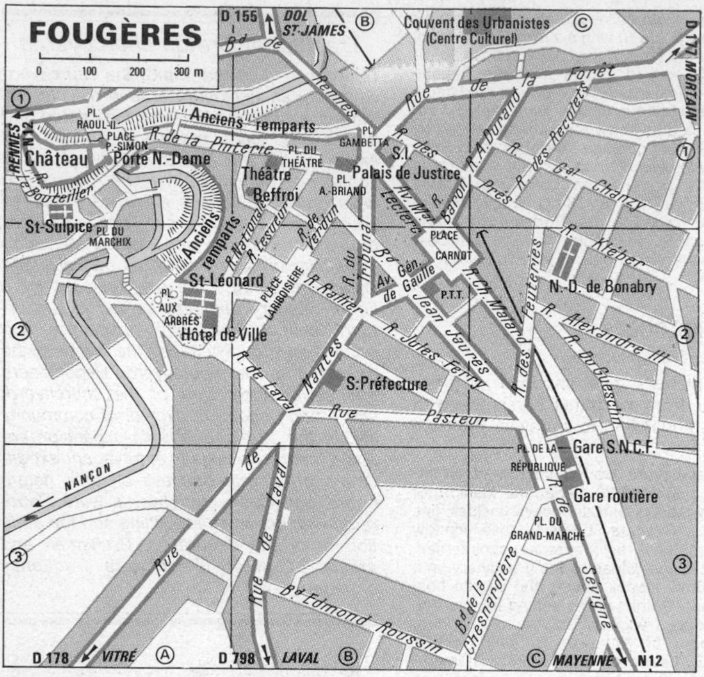

fortress, has two big altarpieces carved in the granite wall itself; Louis XV (18thC) furnishings; a village priest was burnt at the stake because of suspicions aroused by the twisted spire. Many **old houses** in the neighbouring Marchix quarter (A2). To the N, the Urbanist Convent (17thC) has been converted into a cultural centre. □

▶ Nearby

▶ To the west stretches the **Coglès** region, with streams, old mills and pleasant valleys. At **Saint-Brice-en-Coglès :** two handsome châteaux (Le Rocher Portail, 17thC and La Motte; *no visits*). Farther south is the **château La Haye** (15th-17thC; *exterior visit only*) at **Saint-Hilaire-des-Landes;** the **château de Belinaye** (18thC; *on request, 8-12 & 2-6; closed Sat. and Sun. Mar.-Oct., Sun. rest of year*) can be seen at **Saint-Christophe-de-Valains.** ▶ 20 km SW : **Saint-Aubin-du-Cormier,** a strategic promontory between the Ille and Couesnon rivers, site of the dramatic defeat of the Breton army by the French that marked the end of independent Brittany. The ruins of the 12th-15thC castle are still struggling, but against ivy now. □

■ Cape FRÉHEL★★★

C1 / ® (Côtes-du-Nord)

A windswept plateau 70 m above the waves, with walls of red granite. The view is most impressive from the sea (boats from Saint-Malo and Dinard); on a clear day you can see as far as the island of Jersey in the English Channel.

▶ The **Grande Fauconnière★** is sugar-loaf hill on the right, where thousands of herring gulls, guillemots, kittiwakes and cormorants nest. Like the treeless, gorse-grown plateau itself (the **Lande de Fréhel**), it is a classified nature reserve. ▶ 3 km E : **Fort La Latte★** (14th-19thC) stands on an isolated rocky knoll *(Jun.-Sep., school hols.; 10-12:30 & 2:30-6:30; tel 96.41.40.31).* □

■ GRAND-FOUGERAY

D3 / pop. 2 032 (Ille-et-Vilaine)

A frontier town between Brittany and Anjou; partly Romanesque church. The park surrounds the only tower left of a fortress captured from the English by Du Guesclin and his soldiers, who disguised themselves as woodcutters to perform this notable feat of arms. □

▶ Nearby

▶ Châteaux and manors are plentiful throughout the region, especially to the west, along the banks of the Vilaine. Near **Guipry,** N, you can visit the 17th-18thC château des Champs★ *(9-12 & 2-6, 10 Jul.-20 Aug.).* ▶ Farther S, the Vilaine runs past **Langon,** whose partly Romanesque church has a 12thC fresco; the chapel appears oiginally to have been a Gallo-Roman sanctuary dedicated to Venus; a damaged fresco shows the goddess rising from the waves. Ste. Agathe, patron saint of nursing mothers, has taken her place. Close to the town are 28 menhirs, said to be girls who were turned to stone for missing the evening service. □

■ GROIX Island

B3 / ® / pop. 2 605 (Morbihan)

The Sorcière Island is 45 mins by ferry from Lorient, Enez or Groarc'h. It is a flat undulating plateau, girdled with cliffs rising out of the sea. A tunafish on the church steeple replaces the traditional rooster as a weather vane (to draw attention to the importance of tuna-fishing at the beginning of the century).

To the south, a beautiful section of coast looks out to sea; walks along the headland and to the local landmark known as the Trou d'Enfer; return to Port Saint-Nicolas.

▶ **Port Judy,** Groix Historical and Ethnographic Museum *(in season, daily 9:30-12:30 & 3-7; out of season, 10-12:30 & 2-5 ex Mon.),* the centre of an ecomuseum spread out over the island highlights its heritage; a discovery path connects the main sites. □

■ GUÉRANDE★

C3-4 / ® / pop. 9 475 (Loire-Atlantique)

The old city huddles behind almost intact ramparts that serve as wind-breaks; the cobbled streets come to life for the Saturday market.

▶ Tour of the granite **ramparts★** (14th-15thC) to see the six towers and four gateways, one of which, the Porte St. Michel (E, with massive machicolated towers), now houses the **Musée du Vieux Guérande★** (local historical museum; *Easter - 30 Sep., 9-12 & 2-7*) : furniture, costumes★, Le Croisic ceramics (1602-1734), model of the saltmarshes. ▶ The **church★** *(Friday organ concerts in summer)* has been frequently remodelled but retains its Flamboyant Gothic structure; amusing rustic capitals and interesting furnishings (tombs, altarpieces, statues); 17th-18thC houses. □

▶ Nearby

▶ **Côte-d'Amour, Guérandaise Peninsula and Brière Nature Park :** salt marshes. □

■ LA GUERCHE-DE-BRETAGNE

D2-3 / pop. 4 075 (Ille-et-Vilaine)

The square on the west side is almost as large as the town itself; 12th-15thC church with amusing carvings in the stalls; old pillared houses in and around the Place de la Mairie. □

▶ Nearby

▶ 3 km NW of Rétiers : the **Roche aux Fées (Fairies' Rock),** 22 m long, is one of the largest megalithic monuments in France. ▶ 16 km NW : the **château de Monbouan** (18thC), with its balustrades reflected in a little lake *(15 Jul.-31 Aug., 9-12 & 2-6);* 3 km farther : the church at **Louvigné-de-Baix** has stained-glass windows★ (1542) that are among the oldest of their kind in Brittany. □

■ GUINGAMP

B1 / ® / pop. 9 519 (Côtes-du-Nord)

Once a thriving cloth market, the city has recaptured some of its former prosperity through successful cattle and pig farming in the district.

▶ Old houses around the Renaissance fountain in the central square; close by, an imposing half-Gothic, half-Renaissance **basilica★** with a Black Virgin whose *pardon,* celebrated with fireworks on the first Saturday night in July, draws enormous crowds. □

▶ Nearby

▶ The carvings on the beams in the chapel of Notre-Dame, at **Grâces,** *(3 km W)* warn of the evils of alcohol. ▶ Celtic harps are manufactured at **Plouisy,** *(4 km NW).* ▶ **Bourbriac,** *(11.5 km S) :* a large village of granite houses. ▶ 7 km SE from Bourbriac is **Plésidy :** the 15th-16thC Toul Al Gollet Manor★ *(vis. on written request).* ▶ Towards Saint-Brieuc, **Châtelaudren** is known for apples and the brown trout from the Leff River; in the cemetery chapel, more than 120 15thC wooden panel paintings, early "cartoon strips" illustrating the Old and New Testaments and the legends of Ste. Marguerite and St. Fiacre. □

■ HENNEBONT

B3 / ® / pop. 13 103 (Morbihan)

▶ The **church** is a Flamboyant Gothic building dating from 1513, with a 72 m spire. ▶ Remnants of the ramparts around the **walled town★** (Bro Erec'h gate, 15thC, flanked by massive towers); pretty gardens at the foot of the walls. Botanical gardens at Kerbihan. ▶ Large **stud-farm** on the grounds of the former abbey of la Joie *(visits in summer, 10, 11, 2 and 4).* □

▶ Nearby

▶ Modern (1958) church at **Kervignac,** 6 km S. ▶ **Lochrist,** (4 km NE) : Workers' Museum★ of the Hennebont Forges *(Tue. Wed., Thu. 9-12 & 2-5 or 6, Fri. 9-12, Sat., Sun., 2-6).* □

■ JOSSELIN★

C2 / ® / pop. 2 740 (Morbihan)

The best-known picture postcard of inland Brittany shows pleasure craft at the foot of this formidable castle with tall, pointed towers and soaring walls.

▶ The **castle★★,** on a sheer rock over the river Oust, is the very image of a mediaeval fortress *(Easter-1 Jun. : Wed., Sun. and nat. hols. 2-6; June and 1st fortnight Sep. : daily 2-6; Jul.-Aug. : daily 10-12 & 2-6; closed in winter).* Within the walls is a long, low building★★ (1490-1505) facing a courtyard, richly decorated in the style of the period. The 19thC interior★★ owes its warmth and charm to the fact that the Rohan family still lives here. In the stables (separate entrance), the Old Doll Museum presents the Rohan private collection *(1 May-30 Sep. 10-12 & 2-6, closed Mon.; 1 Oct.-15 Nov. and 1 Feb.-30 Apr., Wed., Sat., Sun. and hols. 2-6).* ▶ The rest of the town lives up to the castle : charming **16th and 17thC houses,** many half-timbered, with caryatids or carved woodwork. ▶ The Flamboyant Gothic **church★** has pinnacled buttresses, gargoyles and a series of gables pierced with large windows. □

▶ Nearby

▶ **Ploërmel** ® : a crossroads town that was much fought over in the 14th and 16thC. The ramparts have been converted into houses. The 16thC Renaissance and Flamboyant Gothic church★ has a carved N doorway★ and 16thC stained glass.★ At Le Mennais college, a 19thC astronomical clock. □

■ KERNASCLÉDEN

B2 / pop. 434 (Morbihan)

The murals★★ in the Gothic chapel (1420-64) are among the most beautiful collections of French 15thC painting : scenes from the Life of the Virgin and the Childhood of Christ, *Dance of Death (Danse Macabre)*, depiction of Hell. Their evocative character, composition and range of colours show great artistic skill. □

■ LAMBALLE

C2 / ® / pop. 10 078 (Côtes-du-Nord)

Capital of Penthièvre before Guingamp, now a market town and the summer gateway to the beaches at Val-André, Erquy and Les Sables d'Or.

▶ **Old houses** line the Place du Martrai, including the Maison du Bourreau (executioner's house), now used by the SI and housing a small **museum** *(15 Jun.-15 Sep. ex Tue., 10-12 & 2:30-6:30)*. ▶ A steep street runs up to the Collegiate church (13th-15thC) and the surrounding shady walk. ▶ Large **stud-farms** *(daily 2-4:30, Sun. and nat. hols.; 9-4:30 15 Jul.-15 Sep.; 9-12 & 2-4:30 rest of year)*. In the distance the attractive **church of St. Martin**★ (11thC arcades; carved 1519 wooden porch). ▶ 23 km S : in Cistercian solitude, the **Boquen Abbey**★ (12thC church, restored). □

■ LANDERNEAU

A1 / ® / pop. 15 531 (Finistère)

An inland town linked to the sea by the river Elorn, prospering from cloth and leather in the 16th-17thC (old houses); today trade centres around meat, milk and cauliflowers.

▶ **De Rohan Mansion**★ (9, pl du General de Gaulle), now a tea shop; in golden granite with slate shingles, one of the loveliest buildings in the old town; see also the de Léon Quay. The **Pont de Rohan**★ (bridge; best view from upstream) and Rue St. Thomas (left bank). ▶ Church of St. Thomas (16thC). ▶ 6.5 km N : **Trémaouézan** has a 15thC church with porch★ that was its gallery. ▶ E : round trip of the Breton churchyards (→). □

■ LANNION

B1 / ® / pop. 17 228 (Côtes-du-Nord)

Where the valley of the river Léguer turns into an estuary, close to the resorts of the Côte de Granit Rose (Pink Granite Coast; → Perros Guirec), this old country town does its best to profit from the presence of the National Telecommunications Research Centre.

▶ **Old houses** on the Place du General Leclerc, corbelled, slate-roofed or decorated with caryatids; near the Church of St. Jean (16th-17thC) visit the Romanesque **church of Brélévenez**★ (12th-13thC, remodelled). □

▶ Nearby

▶ 2.5 km W : **Loguivy** has a charming churchyard. ▶ **Le Yaudet** *(7.5 km W)* : a little port at the mouth of the Léguer; pretty site★; unusual Nativity in the church. ▶ 10 km N : the **Pleumeur-Bodou** space communications station *(guided tours : 9-11 or 12 & 1:45 or 2-4:45 or 6, Easter-15 Oct.; closed Tue. ex Jun.-Aug.)*; the key attraction is the 50 m tall Dacron dome (Radome) housing one of the antennae. □

▶ Round trip to Tonquédec and Rosanbo *(approx 60 km, 1/2 day)*.

▶ On the road to Pouaret (D11) and a number of small roads to the left, you can see : the

Brittany cuisine

Food in Brittany depends more on quality and freshness than on a tradition of haute-cuisine*; all the vegetables are locally grown, and fish or seafood will have been caught the same day. In earlier times, the inland Bretons ate mainly cereals and vegetables; meat (in stews or* charcuterie*), was for feast days; fish was eaten only by the coastal population.*

More recently, a number of traditional preparations have made their way outside Brittany, among them the Kauteriad *(or* Côtriade*), a fish soup quite unlike* bouillabaisse, *and the* Kouign, *of which the best known variety is the* Kouign Amân *(with butter), a sweet fried cake of wheat flour, eggs and honey.* Crêpes *(pancakes made with wheat flour) and* galettes *(a thick variety made with buckwheat) were usually eaten plain or with butter or, in Upper Brittany, with eggs or grilled sausages. Other ways of serving them are recent inventions, but nonetheless delicious.*

Brezoneg : the Breton language

The birth of the Breton language can be schematised as follows :

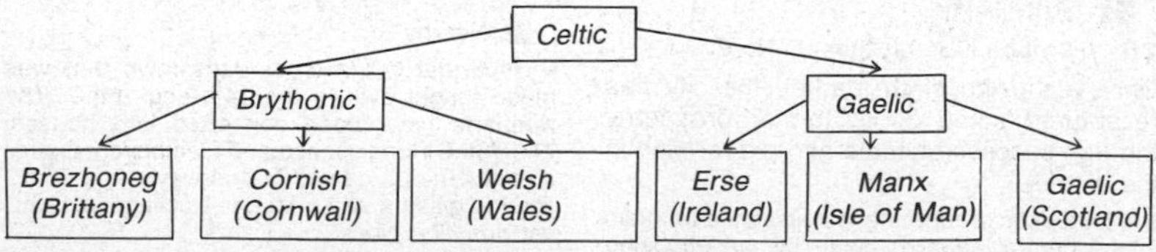

Brezhoneg includes four different dialects : Cornouaillais, Léonard, Trégorrois, and Vannetais, the last of which differs considerably from the others.

Brezhoneg was forcibly forbidden by the French authorities, even in sermons and schools. As recently as 1960 in certain areas, any child caught speaking Breton had a horseshoe or a clog hung around his neck as a mark of shame.

Nowadays, the language is openly spoken by some 800 000 people west of a line from Paimpol to Vannes.

ruins of château de Coat Frec (16thC); the **chapel at Kerfons★** (1559, polychrome wood choirscreen★), in a charming valley; the imposing ruins of the feudal **château de Tonquédec★** (14th-16thC); the **château de Kergrist★** *(9-12 & 2-6)*, and the **Chapelle des Sept Saints** (Seven Saints' Chapel), built on a dolmen, and a pilgrims' shrine for both Catholics and Muslims on the 4th Sun. in July. ▶ After **Plouaret** (old houses, 16thC church), the **château de Rosanbo★**, a severely aristocratic 15thC residence, enlarged in the 17thC. Interesting furnishings *(2-6, 3-18 Apr.; week-ends, 24 Apr.-30 Jun.; daily 10-12 & 2-6, 1 Jul.-6 Sep.)*. ▶ Return via Saint-Michel-en-Grève (→ below). □

▶ **Armorique Cliff Road** *(Corniche) (24 km to Locquirec)*

▶ The Morlaix road is especially attractive past **Saint-Michel-en-Grève** ® along the 5-km beach of the Lieue de Grève; it continues along the **Corniche de l'Armorique★★** that skirts **Plestin-les-Grèves** (Lesmaës manor, early 16thC, *early Aug.-mid-Sep. 2-6*) to provide an infinite variety of views over the sea, the cliffs, the shoreline and the rocks, finally reaching **Locquirec** (panel paintings in the church, 1712). □

■ LANVAUX Region

C3 (Morbihan)

This was long one of the poorest areas of Brittany, a wilderness whose inhabitants eked out a living as woodchoppers and lumberjacks and expressed their resentments as *chouans*, royalist rebels who attempted to turn back the Revolutionary tide.

▶ Clumps of pine and holly, tufts of spiky heather and broom have a tenuous hold on the soil where sparse trees only rarely add up to a forest worthy of the name. Forests occur, however, in the west at Floranges and Lanvaux, where the remains of a Cistercian abbey can be seen near **Bieuzy-Lanvaux.** ▶ At **Grand-Champ,** religious treasury★ in the porch of the 12th-16thC church. ▶ Near **Plumelec** (Kerangat château and arboretum), the hamlet of **Cadoudal,** birthplace of a regional hero, the Chouan conspirator known as Cadoudal, who was executed on Napoleon's orders in 1804; national parachutists' museum. ▶ **Sérent** (16thC church, museum) is in an interesting area : **Lizio,** a village of granite houses where craftsmen and women flock to a reunion held annually on the 2nd Sun. in Aug.; **Saint-Guyomard,** 15thC château de Brignac, megaliths; **Trédion,** with a lakeside château★; **château de Crévy** at **La Chapelle-Caro** which houses a collection of costumes★ from the 18thC to present *(10-2 & 4-6:30 in season; Wed., Sat., Sun. pm. off season)*. ▶ Near Elven, the striking ruins of the old **fortress of Largoët** (keep), *(son et lumière in season)*★. ▶ **Malestroit** (pop. 2 502) on the river Oust, picturesque old dwellings around a 12th-14thC church; **Saint-Marcel** *(4 km W)* : a stronghold of the WWII Resistance (museum of the Occupation and the Resistance, *Jun.-Sep., 10-5; Oct.-May, 10-6)*. □

■ LOCMARIAQUER★★

C3 / ® / pop. 1 279 (Morbihan)

Like Carnac (→), this holiday resort is close to numerous megaliths; boat trips to the Gulf of Morbihan (→).

Place names

The following prefixes and suffixes will help you understand the origins of a number of place-names :

*— **ar** : in front of (can also be an article)*
*— **bihan** : small*
*— **braz** : big or large*
*— **coat, goat, hoat, hoet** : wood (Argoat, the woodland or the inland)*
*— **coz, goz, koz** : old*
*— **dol** : table or plateau (the Mont Dol)*
*— **his** : long*
*— **illis** : church*
*— **kemper** : river junction (Quimper, Quimperlé)*
*— **ker** : village, hamlet*
*— **kroaz** : cross, cross-roads*
*— **lann** : hermitage, consecrated ground*
*— **loc, log, log** : cell, consecrated site*
*— **manac'h** : monk*
*— **men** : stone*
*— **meur** : vast, big*
*— **minihy** : monastery*
*— **mor** : sea (Mor-bihan, small sea; Ar-mor, country of the sea)*
*— **pénity** : place of penance, hermit's retreat*
*— **pl, pleu, plou, plu, ploe, plé, poul** : former parish territory under the protection of a Breton saint; most of the time the prefix is followed by the name of the saint but there are exceptions, i.e. Plougastel, Plancoët.*
*— **relec** : relics*
*— **roc'h** : rock*
*— **toul** : hole*
*— **tre, trève, tref** : subdivision of plou*
*— **ty** : house, residence*

▶ Dolmens at Kercadoret and Kervérès, Mane-Réthual★ and Mane-Lud; decorated chambers at the **Table des Marchands★★** (one of the most famous) and in the Pierres Plates★; broken menhir at **Men-er-Hroëc'h,** formerly one of the largest in the world (20.3 m, 347 tons); tumulus at Mané-er-Hroëc'h; dolmen at Kerlut. ▶ View★ over the Gulf of Morbihan and the sight from **Kerpenhir Point.** □

■ LOCRONAN★★

A2 / ® / pop. 704 (Finistère)

It is rare to find such architectural quality and unity so well preserved. Locronan, formerly a city of weavers and textile merchants, is now thriving due to tourism.

▶ The granite Renaissance houses (16th-17thC) around the well in the **town square★★** have elegant pediments above dormer windows. ▶ Stained glass★ (end 15thC) in the apse of the **church★** (same period; *closed 12:30-1:30*). On the right, in the **Pénity Chapel,** a Burial of Christ (16thC naïf masterpiece), and the 15thC tomb of St. Ronan. ▶ On the second Sunday in July participants in the *pardon* make their way in a great procession to the top of the Montagne de Locronan (alt. 289 m; view★) : this is the *Petite Troménie* (*tro minihy*, procession around the monastery); every 6th year (1989), a longer route is used and the procession is called the *Grande Troménie.* □

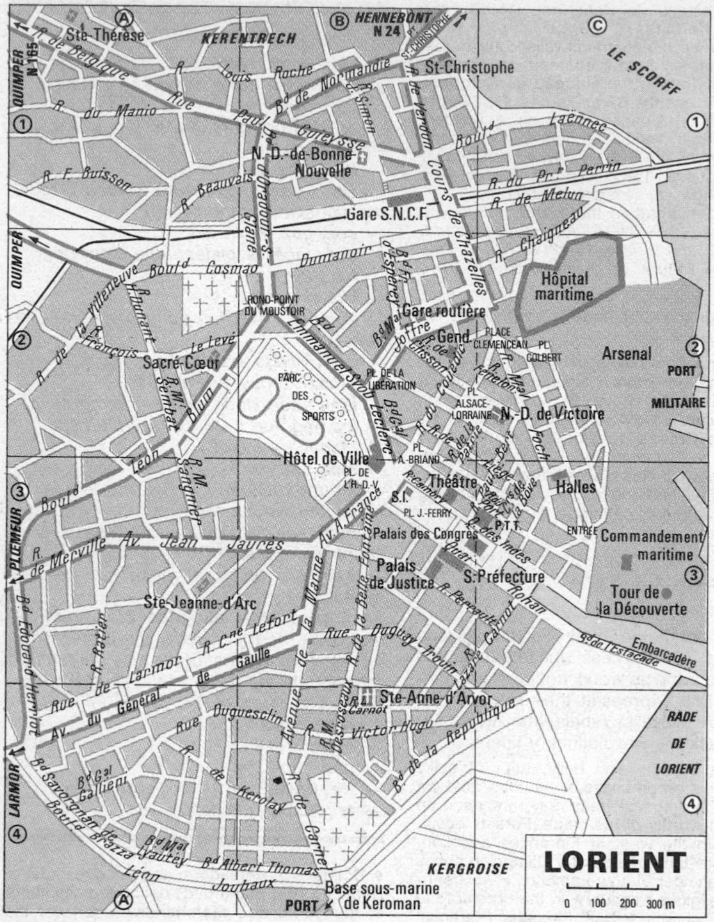

▶ Nearby

▶ 4 km NW : **Moëllien Manor** (17thC, *now a hotel*). ▶ 8 km W, **Sainte-Anne-la-Palud** ®, where the *pardon* is one of the most famous *(last Sun. in Aug.)*. ▶ 8,5 km : **Ploéven,** charming 16thC church (17thC painted panels). □

■ LORIENT

B3 / ® / pop. 64 675 (Morbihan)

Three centuries ago, the newly-created French East India Company (Compagnie des Indes), needing more warehouses and dockyards, founded the Port de l'Orient (Port of the East). Since then, Lorient has always lived by and from the sea. After being devastated in WWII, the town has been completely rebuilt.

▶ Between the town hall (B2-3) and the church of Notre-Dame de la Victoire (C2), a broad pedestrian precinct is centred around the lively **Place Aristide-Briand.** ▶ Only French citizens may visit the **arsenal,** which specialises in repair and construction of small- and medium-sized vessels. ▶ **Port de Keroman** was built for the fishing fleet in 1919-27; best seen in early morning. □

▶ Nearby

▶ 6 km S : **Larmor Plage** ® : two lovely beaches; 16thC church; the figures on the Flemish-inspired polychrome wooden altarpiece are full of life; 15th-16thC frescos. West of Larmor, the tranquil coastline is dotted with ports that double as family resorts. ▶ On the opposite bank of the estuary of the Scorff and the Blavet is **Port-Louis★** ® (pop. 3700). This former fortified town was protected by the château de Kerso, on the headland; the city, with its 17thC ramparts, has a **citadel★★** that juts into the roadstead (16th-17thC; *1st Jun.-30 Sep. 10-7; May and Oct. 10-5; ex. Tues. and 15 Nov.-15 Dec.*). Compagnie des Indes Museum; Atlantic Museum. □

■ MENEZ BRÉ★★

B1 (Côtes-du-Nord)

This peak (alt. 302 m) is high enough to give a view★ of the sea.

▶ 8 km W : **Belle-Isle-en-Terre** is surrounded by woods, hills and ravines. In this beautiful setting, the Breton wrestling championships are held on the 3rd Sun. in July. 15 km N : the **chapel of Locmaria** has an early 16thC choir-screen★, as has the church of the same period in **Loc Envel.** □

Musical instruments

The most typically Breton instrument is the ***bombarde,*** *a sort of short oboe with a penetrating sound, which intones the melody, sets the rhythm and leads the dance. It is accompanied by the* ***biniou koz*** *(old biniou). This is probably the nearest instrument to the old cornemuse, known in many European countries, which began to evolve in the 15thC, turning into the veuze in the region around Nantes. It is a cousin of the Scottish bagpipes, which were adopted at the beginning of this century in Brittany under the title of* ***biniou braz*** *(big biniou). The bardic* ***harp*** *has 30 metal strings, whereas the Celtic harp has 32 gut strings. Thanks to musician Alan Stivell, these neglected instruments are being heard once more. The* ***vielle,*** *or hurdy-gurdy, although not of Breton origin, is well known in Upper Brittany. The* ***violin*** *is found only in Ille-et-Vilaine, where it has gradually replaced the biniou since the 19thC.*

■ MENEZ HOM★

A2 (Finistère)

The last heights of the Montagne Noire deserve special mention in a list of vantage points : panorama★ over the Bay of Douarnenez, the Brest roadstead and the Aulne estuary.

▶ 16thC chapel of **Sainte-Marie du Ménez Hom,** with three altarpieces★; spiral columns are wreathed with vine branches in typical Breton exuberance. ▶ Near **Saint-Nic** (16thC church), the chapel of St. Côme and St. Damien has a cross-timbered interior and wall beams (mid-17thC) carved with rustic flower and animal motifs. Close by : the beaches of **Pentrez-Plage** and Lieue de Grève. ▶ **Landévennec,** on the last loop of the Aulne before it reaches the estuary near Brest, guards the remains of an abbey founded by St. Guénolé (5thC ; site★); a small museum recounts the history of the abbey, installed in 1958 in neighbouring buildings. ▶ Over the Terénez Bridge, at the end of the *corniche* (cliff road) of the same name (views★), to **Trégarvan :** Musée de l'Ecole Rurale (rural schools museum : *Jul.-Aug. 2-6, closed Tue.*). □

■ MONCONTOUR

C2 / pop. 1 015 (Côtes-du-Nord)

On a promontory girdled with ramparts and greenery, flower-decked shops and fine old houses, some in granite, others in wood.

▶ **St. Mathurin Church :** six magnificent stained-glass windows★ (1520-49, Flemish influence). ▶ On the hill opposite : château des Granges (18thC, 13thC tower). ▶ 2 km S : the **chapel of Notre-Dame-du-Haut** with statues of seven healing saints *(pardon 15 Aug.).* ▶ 5.5 km E : **château** and lake of **La Touche-Trébry★,** 16thC *(daily, ex Sun. and nat. hols. 2-6).* ▶ Near **Hénon** *(6 km NW),* Le Colombier Manor (15th-17thC) in a romantic setting *(visit by request).* ▶ Numerous other manors and **châteaux** in the area, including **La Houssaye** *(12 km NW),* in a large park *(20 Jul.-31 Aug., closed 15 Aug., 10-12 & 3-7).* □

■ Les MONTAGNES NOIRES★

(the Black Mountains)

▶ Round trip *(127 km, full day)*
B2 *(see map 6)* (Finistère)

Not so high as the Monts d'Arrée (→), with wooded valleys and winding roads. Trout and salmon in the rivers.

▶ **Carhaix-Plouger** (→). Leaving the Gourin road at **Port-de-Carhaix** and passing the unusual Calvary★ at **Kerbreuden** (15thC), you arrive at **Saint-Hernin** churchyard (16th-17thC, ossuary 1697, Calvary). ▶ Almost on the ridge of the Montagnes Noires is the chapel of Saint-Hervé★, protector of horses. ▶ **Gourin** hosts the annual 1st of May *bagadou* championship, an annual affirmation of Celtic customs, with lively music and wrestling. In the church

6. Montagnes Noires (Black Mountains)

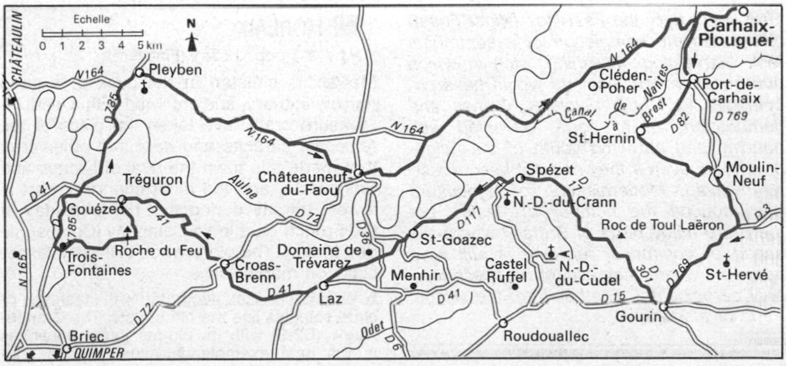

Healers and protecting saints

Guardian saints and healers, making up for the almost total lack of doctors, occupied an important place in popular religion, and pardons (→ box) drew great crowds to the saints' sanctuaries. A random selection of the saints and their special talents : Alar and Noyale protect horses; Cornély and Herbot, horned beasts; Briac cures nervous ailments; Cado helps the deaf; Guirec helps girls to find a husband; Egarec cures ear infections; Gurloës, gout; Hervé is visited for scalp infections and protects against fear; Ivy guards new-born children, especially their eyes. Livertin and Tujanne cure headaches; Mamert relieves stomachaches; Méen takes care of the insane; Tugen looks after rabies cases; Vennec helps rheumatism; and the Virgin is good for any complaint.

(17thC), 15thC Pietà. Several slate quarries in the vicinity. ▶ The **Toul Laëron Rock,** 326 m high, gives a wide view over the region. ▶ The **chapel of Notre-Dame du Crann★** (1535; *1 km from Spézet*) has a charming exterior; inside, the original stained glass★ (1548), evidently inspired by German engravings, shows the extent of Brittany's cultural awareness at this period. ▶ In the heart of the **forest of Laz★,** the **Domaine de Trévarez★** *(1-6 ex Tue., May-Sep.; Sat., Sun. and nat. hols. 2-6 in Apr., Oct., Nov.; Sun. and nat. hols. rest of year)* provides wonderful walks through its 185 acres of camellias, azaleas and rhododendrons. ▶ As you leave the forest, there is a fine view over the bell-tower-studded landscape of the Aulne Valley and the Monts d'Arrée. Calvary★ in the cemetery. ▶ Pretty winding road to **Tréguron** (chapel), **Gouézec** (16thC stained-glass Passion★ in the church), and **La Roche du Feu** (alt. 281 m; panorama). ▶ One 16thC fountain is left at the **Trois Fontaines Chapel;** Calvary, fine woodwork, gallery, carved beams, statues). ▶ After **Pleyben** (→), which is worth a prolonged visit, the return trip is shorter. ▶ Stop at **Châteauneuf-du-Faou,** on top of a hill over the Aulne; immense panorama★ over the Montagnes Noires. ▶ **Cléden-Poher;** 15thC church; woodwork, ossuary, elegant Calvary. □

The Fest Noz

Fifty years ago, the Fest Noz (Night Feast) celebrated the completion of a communal task (harvesting, threshing, etc.) in which two, three or four hamlets would have cooperated for several weeks. Games and competitions of all sorts alternated with dancing and attracted youth of the neighbourhood, even if they had not been directly involved. Modernisation of agriculture has reduced the number of "fests", but there are many parts of Brittany where the sense of communal rejoicing is still alive and well, where they accept no spectators, only participants...whether from the village, Paris or elsewhere.

■ MONTFORT

D2 / pop. 4378 (Ille-et-Vilaine)

This is a country-holiday resort with remains of ramparts and a 14thC keep from the mediaeval town.

▶ The **museum** *(Ecomusée; closed Sat. and Sun. in summer)* has a fascinating collection★ of country costumes (originals, and scale reproductions on dolls). □

▶ Nearby

▶ **Château de Montauban★** *(15 km NW, closed Tue.)* : at the edge of the forest; 5 km onwards : the **Manor of the Louverie** (17thC; *Jul.-Aug.; closed Sun. and nat. hols.*). From here, continue to **Saint-Méen-le-Grand** and see the 13th-14thC **church.** ▶ 6.5 km W : **Iffendic** (15thC church with 1547 stained glass), not far from the Étang de Trémelin (lake; leisure centre). ▶ 10 km S : in **Monterfil,** the annual Upper-Brittany music competition *(end Jun.)* is accompanied by enthusiastic festivities. □

■ MONT-SAINT-MICHEL

"Le Couesnon par sa folie
A mis le Mont en Normandie"

«By the boundary river's decree,
Mont-Saint-Michel's in Normandy! (→)»

■ Gulf of MORBIHAN★★★

C3

Mor Bihan (the "little sea") is sprinkled with isles and islets at water level which are sometimes accessible on foot at low tide. The bay is almost closed by the Rhuys (→) and Locmariaquer (→) peninsulas. Wind surfers, sailing boats, tourist excursions and the ferries to the larger islands can be glimpsed between the white houses and the little gardens with their clumps of trees.

▶ The **Île d'Arz★** ® is an island only 3 km long; partially Romanesque church. ▶ **Île aux Moines★★,** somewhat longer, is covered with pinewoods; many charming sites; see the Château de Guéric, the road along the ridge (views★ over the bay), Pen Hap Point, etc. ▶ **Île de Gavrinis** *(access from* **Larmor Baden** ® *in 15 min; daily 15 Jun.-15 Sep.)* has a tumulus★★ (8 m high, 100 m circumference); an astonishing size, with esoteric signs engraved on the walls; further south, the **Islet of Er Lanic** has two cromlechs, one of which is visible only at low tide. The bay was formed when the ground subsided after the prehistoric era. □

■ MORLAIX

B1 / ® / pop. 19541 (Finistère)

Morlaix is situated at the back of a deep narrow estuary, and crowned with a viaduct. Pleasure craft have taken the place of the *feluccas,* caracks and *nefs* and other craft that made this town the rival of Nantes and Saint-Malo, and the most important port in lower Brittany during the 18thC heyday of the French East India Company (Compagnie des Indes). The old town is still lively, especially on market days.

▶ Wooden houses decorated with statuettes or slate shingles line the old streets. The **Grande-Rue★** (B2-3) with its old-fashioned boutiques is the best example. ▶ Allow a good hour

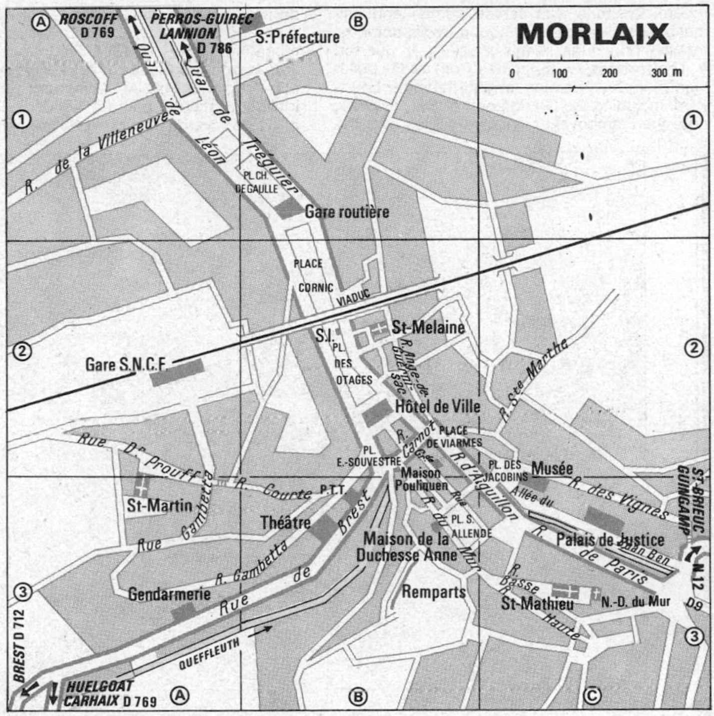

for exploring; see the *Maison de la Duchesse Anne* (Duchess Anne's house; B3, end of 15thC); carved wooden staircase inside. **Museum** (C2-3; *9-12 & 2-6; closed Tue.*), paintings of the French, Italian and Dutch schools, and some modern works but particularly good on rural life in times past. Church of St. Melaine (B2, 1489). □

▶ Nearby

▶ **Carantec** ® *(15 km N)* : very much a family resort, reached by a lovely *corniche* (cliff road)★. ▶ Enjoyable excursion along the right bank *(48 km round trip)* beginning at the **château de Keranroux** (18thC; *visit on request*), following the coastline to the **Cairn de Barnenez★**, a large stone tumulus with eleven funerary chambers *(9-12 & 2-6; Jun.-Sep.)* and continuing to the magnificent red rocks at Primel Point★, near **Primel-Trégastel;** return via **Plougasnou** (16thC church), **Saint-Jean-du-Doigt,** site of an important *pardon* on 23/24 June (15th-16thC church; see the treasure room; 1691 fountain; 1577 chapel), and **Lanmeur** (pre-Romanesque crypt beneath the church; chapel of Kernitron with Romanesque doorway, nave and transept). ▶ SW : tour of traditional churchyards (→). □

■ NANTES★★★

D4 / ® / pop. 247 227 (Loire-Atlantique)
See plan on following pages

Nantes is the principal city in western France, the link between the Atlantic and the rest of the country; during the days of Brittany's autonomy, Nantes was its capital city. Today it is a town of shady courtyards, alleyways and boulevards; it has a cathedral, a château, massive towers and balconied mansions. The busy port takes ships of up to 20 000 tons.

▶ Pedestrian precinct of **old streets** around the **church of Sainte-Croix** (D3; 17thC); 15th-16thC timbered houses (SI in the former Apothecaries' Hall; 16thC); others, more

Pardons

Pardons *were a common feature throughout mediaeval France, but only in Brittany has the name been preserved, along with the meaning of this somewhat original celebration : a sort of communal pilgrimage during which a participant receives forgiveness (pardon) for his sins, in the form of indulgences. Whether they are patron saints of a parish, or merely venerated in some small chapel, the Virgin, St Anne and other important saints are the focal points of these processions, as are a number of Breton and Celtic saints (not all of whom are recognized by the Roman Catholic Church). Many are held in reverence as much for their healing powers as for their spiritual help. Mass, vespers, processions and thanksgivings are the usual constituents of the ceremony itself. Breton* pardons *are full of religious devotion and contemplation, which does not prevent them ending in general celebration around tents and open-air stalls.*

recent, in stone with carved human and animal heads. Second-hand shops, *croissanteries*, fashion boutiques in this most lively quarter. ▶ The **fortress★★** (E2) dates from 1466; buildings of various periods around the inner courtyard, including the Grand Logis ★(SW; Gothic); note the Flamboyant pinnacled gables over the dormer windows, in contrast with the severe mass of the building. 12thC keep, with three museums *(daily, 10-12 & 2-6; closed Tue. ex Jul.-Aug.)* : the **Musée d'Art Populaire Régional★** (Regional Folk Art Museum : the five Breton départments, plus La Vendée), the **Musée d'Art Décoratif** (Decorative Art Museum : furni-

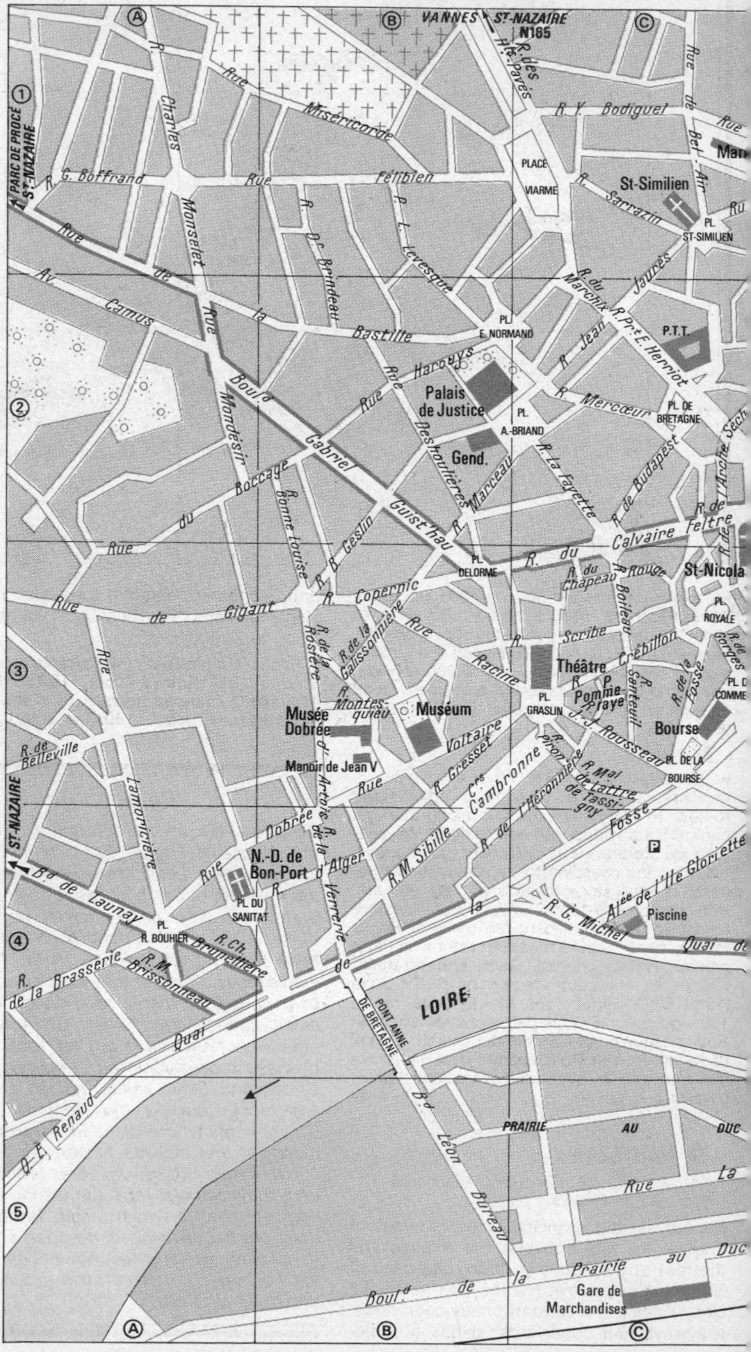

ture, lace, 16thC Rhodes ceramics), and the **Naval Museum** ("Musée des Salorges"). ▶ The **cathedral★** (E2) is still undergoing renovation after a fire in 1971. This superb, soaring Gothic building (begun in 1434) has 15thC carvings on the inner façade; tomb of François II★★ by Michel Colombe, Brittany's greatest sculptor. ▶ On the south side of the cathedral, see the **Psalette,** former 16thC chapter-house; on the north side, the 15thC Gate of St. Pierre. Remains of the Gallo-Roman surrounding wall have been uncovered nearby. ▶ **Musée des Beaux-Arts★★★** (Fine Arts Museum; E1; *daily ex Tue. and nat. hols.,*

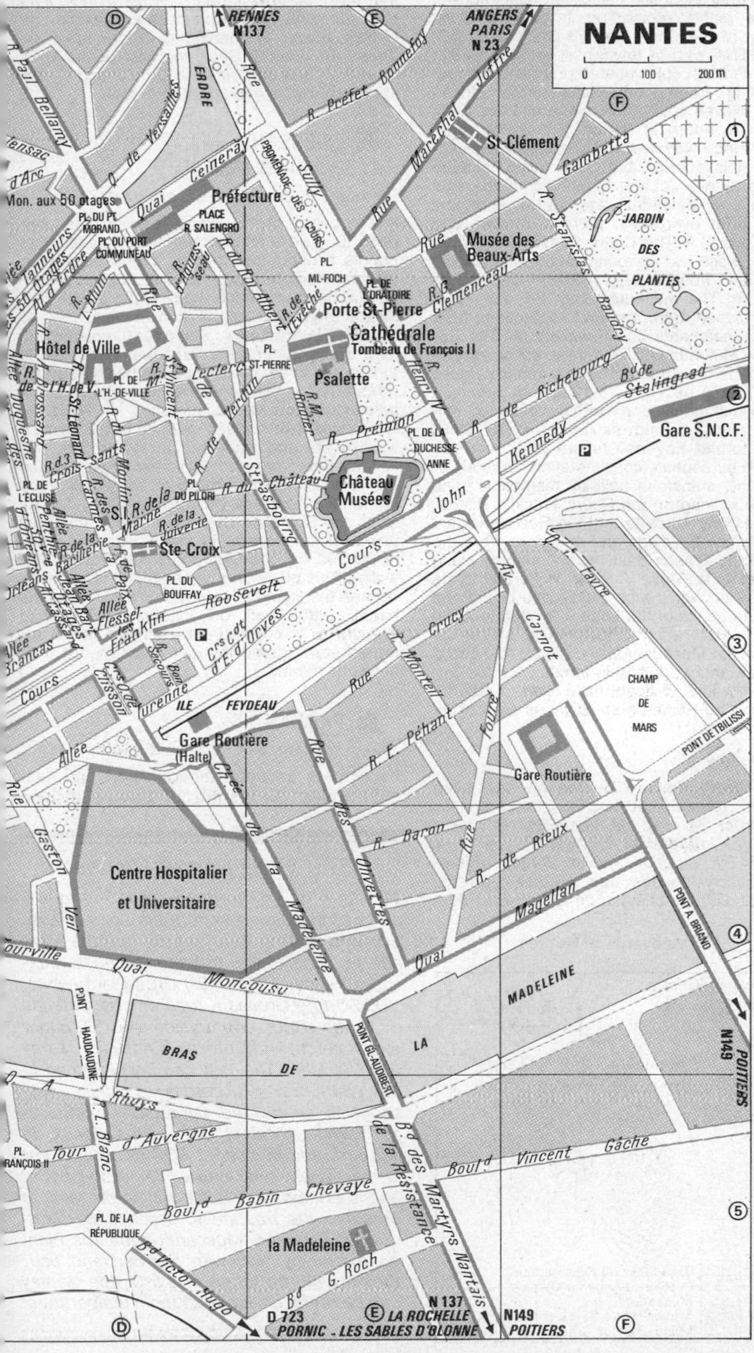

9:15-12 & 2-6 or 5 out of season); excellent French, Flemish and Italian paintings (three major works by Georges de La Tour, two paintings by Monet; Rubens, Tintoretto, Guardi, and an anonymous Florentine triptych); a number of contemporary works. ▶ **Jardin des Plantes★** (botanical gardens; F1-2), has marvellous magnolias and camellias; glass houses of rare plants recall French colonial days. ▶ West of the Cours des 50 Otages (D1-2-3) is the **18thC part of town,** built with the wealth gained through colonial enterprise and triangular trading : trade goods exchanged for African slaves, slaves sold in Louisiana and the Antilles, and a return to Nantes with sugar cane. ▶ **The Place Royale★** (C3) is one of the centres of this quarter, but don't miss **Passage Pommeraye★★** (at the beginning of the Rue Santeuil), a delightful late 19thC shopping arcade with staircases, mirrors, statues and plaster work. ▶ **The Cours Cambronne★** (B3; to the west) is surrounded by magnificent 18th-19thC houses with pilasters and balustrades. ▶ The **museum** *(daily 2-6 and Wed. 10-12; closed Mon. and Fri.);* collections from Nantes' merchants and travellers. ▶ The **Dobrée★★ Museum** occupies three buildings, one of which is the former Bishop's country house (15thC; *daily ex Tue., 10-12 & 2-6) :* antiquities, Romanesque and Gothic treasures, religious paintings and sculptures 15th-16thC. ▶ The former **Feydeau Island** (D3), now surrounded by asphalt, consists almost entirely of **mid-18thC mansions** built by merchants; fine façades looking on the Cours Franklin Roosevelt, the Allée Turenne and the Rue Kervégan. ▶ Other fine buildings and mansions from the time of the French East India Company along the **Quai de la Fosse** (A-B-C4). ▶ Further to the west : view over the port, Beaulieu Island and the south banks of the Loire from **Sainte-Anne Butte;** nearby, a 19thC townhouse is now the **Jules Verne Museum** *(daily ex Tue., 10-12:30 & 2-5) :* life and work of this famous Nantes writer, who would no doubt have liked to visit the neighbouring **Planetarium** *(daily ex Mon., Tue. and Sun. am).* □

▶ Nearby

▶ The **Erdre Valley★** *(to the N),* best seen by boat (promenade and luncheon cruises *leave from 24 Quai de Versailles, D1; daily Apr.-Aug.; information for rest of year : tel 40.20.24.50; duration approx 3hr30*). Numerous country houses can be seen on the trip, including the château de la Gâcherie (right bank, 15thC, much restored). ▶ The banks of the Loire★, upstream : a narrow road running along a dyke (good restaurants), parallels the south bank as far as **Champtoceaux** (in Anjou; *3 km from Nantes;* see the Promenade de Champalud★). Off the road, château of **Goulaine★** (15th-16thC), last château on the Loire, the furthest downstream *(visits to the interior, Jun.-Sep.),* conservatory★★ of exotic butterflies, unique in continental Europe *(daily ex. Tues., 16 Jun.-15 Sep., the rest of the year, Sat., Sun. and nat. hols., 2:30-6:30)* and church at **Loroux-Bottereau** (13thC frescos). □

7. Vineyards of Nantes

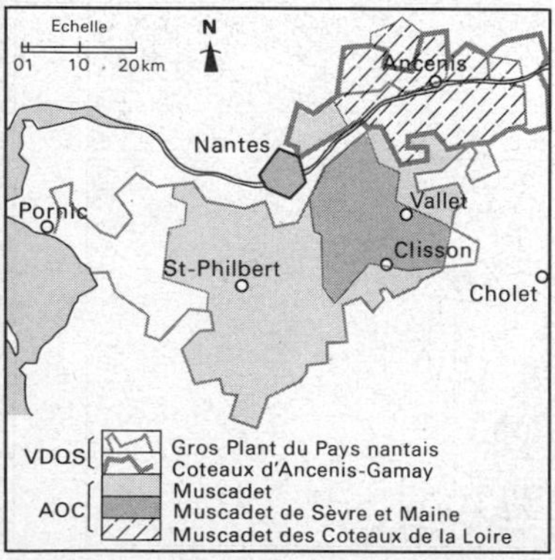

■ OUESSANT Island★

A1 / pop. 1 255 (Finistère)

Pleasant in summer; severe winters.

▶ The centre of this island community is **Lampaul.** Its granite houses with their blue shutters huddle around the church; in the neighbouring cemetery, a mausoleum (1668) houses little wax crosses, each made when a man was lost at sea. The cross, known as "Croix de Broëlla" (*Bro:* country; *Ela:* return) replaced the man during funeral rites and was deposited in a reliquary in the church, before being solemnly transferred to this collective memorial. ▶ In the hamlet of **Niou Huella,** *(barely 1 km W)* is the *Ecomusée,* two houses devoted to the island's way of life and traditions *(daily ex Tue., 11-7, May-Sep.; pm and Sun. rest of year) :* see the furniture, made entirely of shipwreck wood (there are no trees on the island). ▶ To the west, the **Phare de Créac'h** is one of the most powerful lighthouses in the world (theoretical range 200 km; the foghorn can be heard 18 km away). This black and white-striped tower symbolises the island's identity. ▶ Walk across the heath : little black or white sheep, attached in pairs to low windbreaks shaped like three-armed stars, graze the salt grass (hence their delicious meat). □

■ PAIMPOL

C1 / ® / pop. 8 367 (Côtes-du-Nord)

Paimpol is an unpretentious port and seaside town, the centre of the cod-fishing

The vineyards of Nantes

126 km² of vineyards, in the S and SE parts of the Department of the Loire-Atlantique and spilling over slightly into the Vendée and the Maine-et-Loire, produce Muscadet (white, AOC.; 12°) Gros Plant (white, VDQS; 11°) Grolleau, rosé or gris, extends over the Retz countryside (VDQS under examination) and Coteaux d'Ancenis-Gamay (VDQS; 12°). The last can be produced in red, white or rosé according to choice. Muscadet is subdivided by regions : Muscadet Sèvre-et-Maine, Muscadet Coteaux de la Loire, and Muscadet AOC. Muscadet sur lie *has spent only one winter in the barrel and is bottled early while still on the lees, to preserve the freshness, delicacy and bouquet of the wine. Muscadet and Gros Plant go extremely well with seafood and fish; they should be taken at 8.5°C; the Gamay can be drunk chilled or at room temperature.*

industry in the second half of the 19thC : **Musée Municipal de la Mer** (Municipal Maritime Museum : *daily 1 Apr.-15 Sep., 10-12 & 3-7*). ▶ At the gates of the town is the **Abbey of Beauport★** *(guided tours at Easter, Whitsun and 1-Jul.-20 Sep., 9-12:30 & 2-7)*; important 13thC remains (see the chapter and the *salle au Duc*). □

▶ Nearby

▶ **Arcouest Point★★** *(6 km N)*; boats for Bréhat Island (→) leave from the foot : marvellous view of the island and the reef-strewn sea. From both sides of the highway between Paimpol and Arcouest, little roads run towards the shore, where tiny ports are hidden among the hollyhocks, the broom and the pinewoods. ▶ **Loguivy-de-la-Mer** *(5 km N)* is one of them, a king prawn fishing port by the mouth of the Trieux (view from the heath). ▶ Fine walks along the coast to the south. ▶ Good view of the Trieux Estuary from the bridge at **Lézardrieux** ® *(5 km W)*. □

▶ Round trip to Lanleff and Kermaria *(28 to 40 km, 2 hr)*.

Take the Lanvollon road for 9.5 km, reaching **Lanleff** on your right : a curious circular ruin known as the **Temple de Lanleff,** attributed successively to the Romans, Gauls and Templars, is in fact a church, almost certainly 11thC, built on the plan of the Holy Sepulchre in Jerusalem. ▶ The **chapel of Kermaria an Iskuit★** (House of Mary, restorer of health) dates principally from the 14th and 15thC; attractive porch and collection of interesting murals (end of 15thC); see the terrifying Danse Macabre★★ (47 pictures accompanied by naive captions, expressing the haunting presence of Death, the Great Leveller) : numerous sculptures★. ▶ **Lanloup** (16thC church) is only 2 km from the shore where, according to legend, the first Celtic immigrants from Britain landed in the 5thC. The site is marked by the tiny port of **Bréhec-en-Plouha.** ▶ **Bilfot Point,** 4 km from **Plouézec :** fine view over the islands in the Bay of Paimpol and, in the distance, Bréhat. □

Forest of PAIMPONT★

▶ Round trip to Plélan Le Grand *(signposted; 66 km; 1/2 day)*
C2 / ® / *(see map 8)* (Ille-et-Vilaine)

The largest of Brittany's forests (70 km²) is only a remnant of the great forest of **Brocéliande,** mentioned in the legends of King Arthur and his knights. The forest covered the whole of central Armorica (Brittany), and was reputedly the scene of some of the adventures of the knights of King Arthur's Round Table. This magnificent forest site today includes no fewer than 14 lakes. Further information available from the TO of Brocéliande (Plélan town hall).

▶ The **château de Brocéliande,** in Norman style, and the **château at Le Pas du Houx,** are set on either side of a lake. Both date from early this century. ▶ The 15th-19thC **château de Comper** *(exterior visit Easter-Oct., ex Wed. and Thu. Rest of year, ex Sat. and Sun.)*, stands silhouetted between three lakes. ▶ The ivy-covered château du **Rox** backs onto the forest. ▶ **Tréhorenteuc** has a church unusually "restored" some years ago by a parish priest, an amateur of legends and symbols. The **Val**

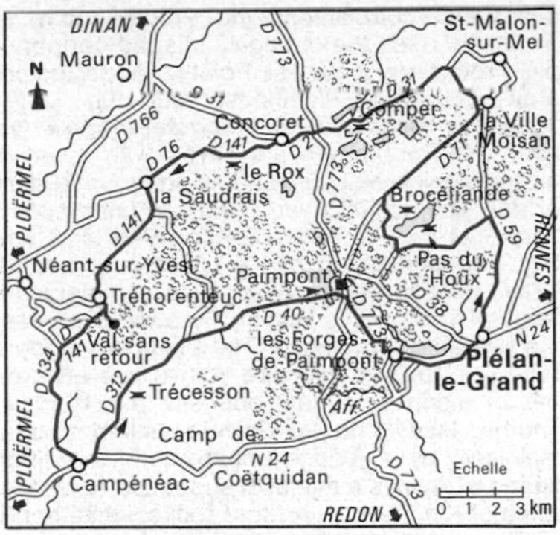

8. Forest of Paimpont

Sans Retour (the Valley of No Return) is a rocky ravine reached from the foot of a little 16thC manor; here, according to the Arthurian legend, the wizard Merlin is still held captive in a prison of air... ▶ Looking down from the road you can see the **château de Trécesson★,** an austere and unusual castle in brown rock. ▶ **Paimpont** ®, in a large clearing by a lake★, owes its origin to an abbey; 17thC building (temporary exhibitions in season) and large 13thC church. ▶ **The Paimpont Forges** used to produce steel of the highest quality from local iron ore and charcoal. All that is left today among the ancient trees by the two lakes are two small châteaux (modern), two chapels, and the remains of the workshops and furnace. □

PERROS-GUIREC★

B1 / ® / pop. 7 497 (Côtes-du-Nord)

Despite the crowds that fill its forty hotels and flock to the beaches and casino, this, the second largest resort on the North Brittany Coast, has not succumbed to expansionism. Excellent harbour, strange rock formations and elegant 1900's-era houses.

▶ Sheltered by the Castle Point (Pointe du Château), **Trestrignel beach★** is lined with villas, some of extravagant size; near the beach at **Trestraou★** is the Palais des Congrès (Congress Hall), Seawater Institut de Cure Marine (Cure Institute) and the Yachting Centre. Superb views of Tomé Island, reefs and islets from the Sentier des Douaniers (excisemen's path), which links the two beaches and continues west towards Ploumanac'h *(1 hr from Trestraou)*. □

▶ Nearby

▶ **Les Sept Îles** (the Seven Islands) *(boat trips 15 Jun.-15 Sep., approx 2 hr, tel 96.23.22.47)* are some 4.5 km off the coast. The main island is the **Île aux Moines**; lighthouse and 1720 fort. The remainder, in particular the **Île Rouzic** (to seaward) and the **Ile Malban,** are now bird sanctuaries *(no visits)* where gulls, cormorants, guillemots and especially puffins, gannets, oyster catchers and petrels can be seen in the distance.

▶ La Côte de Granit Rose★★ (Pink Granite Coast), from Perros Guirec to Trébeurden *(18 km)*.

After Perros, the road runs past the chapel of Notre-Dame de Clarté (1445, *Pardon* 15 Aug.; panorama★ from neighbouring orientation table) and cuts across the **Ploumanac'h** ® peninsula : see the strangely shaped coppery-pink rocks on Squewel Point★, a protected area; 500 m W, lighthouse *(Jul.-Aug., 2-5).* ▶ Similar rocks around **Trégastel-Plage★** ®; near Coz-Porz beach are caves with a small archaeological museum and an aquarium *(Easter and May holidays,* weekends *and nat. hols.; Jun.-Sep. daily 2-6:30, Jul.-Aug., 9-8).* ▶ 3 km S : **Trégastel-Bourg** has a 16thC church and 17thC ossuary, surrounded by a cemetery. In front of it stands a menhir, known locally as the "Menhir of Virility". ▶ The Pleumeur-Bodou road (→ Lannion) will take you to see a number of menhirs; almost opposite this road is another leading to **Île Grande,** linked to the mainland by a bridge; nearby on the little **island of Aval** is a megalith supposed to be the tomb of King Arthur. ▶ More rocks, white sand and a *corniche* (cliff road) overlooking islands and peninsulas at **Trébeurden,** ® a large family resort. □

■ PLEYBEN★★

B2 / pop. 3 897 (Finistère)

The parish churchyard here has the same structure and richness as those of the Léon region, testifying to the creativity of Breton art and the wealth of the farmers who made up the parish councils in the 16th and 17thC.

▶ Even before you reach the entrance (1725) you will be struck by the **Calvary★★,** (mid 16thC and later additions); one of the most impressive of its kind. ▶ The Flamboyant Gothic **ossuary** houses pieces of stonework and statues; exhibitions in summer. ▶ The Flamboyant Gothic **church★** (1564) contrasts with the solidity of the Renaissance bell-tower. Timberwork★ from late 16thC; beams carved with rustic, macabre or burlesque scenes; interesting furniture and numerous old statues. □

■ PLOUGASTEL-DAOULAS★

A2 / ® / pop. 9 611 (Finistère)

Renowned for its strawberries and its gentle climate, in the centre of a wide peninsula jutting into the Brest roadsteads; panoramic views. The town has one of the most beautiful **Calvaries★★** (1602) in the region, with more than 150 figures.

▶ 10 km E from Plougastel : Daoulas★ has a Romanesque church next to monastic buildings of great elegance (12thC cloister); a rare and beautiful example of Romanesque architecture in Finistère. ▶ 7 km SE of Daoulas : don't miss the little-known **chapel** of **Notre-Dame de Lorette;** curious Calvary★, like a stylised anchor. □

■ PONT-AVEN

B3 / ® / pop. 3 295 (Finistère)

Best known for its associations with the painter Paul Gauguin. He first stayed here in 1886 and soon attracted a group of young painters, subsequently known as the School of Pont-Aven, who followed him some three years later to Le Pouldu.

▶ **Municipal Museum** *(1 Apr.-30 Sep.)* temporary exhibitions of regional painters. ▶ Former **Mill** (15thC), Breton furniture and décor *(Jul.-15 Sep.).* ▶ Pleasant walks along the **banks of the Aven** to the south; château de Hénan (*4 km;* 15th-16thC), fine site above the estuary. ▶ **Port-Manec'h** ® *(10 km S),* site★ at the mouth of the Aven. ▶ 4.5 km E : **Riec-sur-Bélon** ® owes its fame to exquisite oysters and a famous restaurant. □

■ PONTIVY

C2 / ® / pop. 14 224 (Morbihan)

The old town and its 15thC château have a distinctly Breton character; the new town dates from 1805 and was built on almost military lines at the orders of Napoleon.

▶ In the heart of old Pontivy are the **Place du Martray★,** the Rue du Pont and the Rue du Fil, lined with old 15th-16thC houses. 16thC Flamboyant Gothic church. ▶ The **château de Rohan★** (15thC fortress; *15 Apr.-15 Oct., 10-12 & 2-6; 2-4 out of season; closed Tue., Wed. and every morning rest of year; closed Nov.-Dec. Temporary exhibitions);* set on a hillside, with outer fortifications intact. ▶ 17th-18thC bourgeois houses in the Rue de Lourmel. □

▶ Nearby

▶ Naif statues in the porch of the 15th-16thC church at **Noyal-Pontivy** *(7 km E).* ▶ 2 km further on, **Sainte-Noyale** is the scene of a *Pardon* for horses *(last Sun. in June).* Fine religious buildings★ : oratory, fountain, ornate cross, Flamboyant Gothic chapel (painted 17th C panelling★). ▶ Excursions in the valley of the Blavet (→). □

■ PORNIC

C4 / ® / pop. 8 709 (Loire-Atlantique)

This small natural port at the end of a deep inlet is a cosy seaside resort and capital of the Jade coast. The port★ is the most attractive area with sailing boats at the foot of the 13th-14thC castle and its surrounding greenery; its tiled roofs give it a slightly Mediterranean air. □

▶ Nearby

▶ **Bourgneuf-en-Retz** *(15 km SE) :* at the back of a wide sandy bay; museum of the Retz area (Pays de Retz Musée; *9-12 & 2-5, Jun.-Sep.; closed Tue.; Wed., Sat., Sun. only out of season).* ▶ **Saint-Gildas Point** (*NW;* panorama★) marks the end of the rocky coast; from here to the mouth of the Loire (Fort de Mindin → near Saint-Nazaire), the **Jade Coast** (Côte de Jade) becomes a 16-km long, gently sloping beach, lined with pine-covered dunes. Principal resorts : **Tharon-Plage, Saint-Brévin-les-Pins,** ® which offers a sudden air of Provence, with its dunes, 8 km of beach and lovely stretch of pine after the bridge at Saint-Nazaire ®. **Mindin** is part of Saint-Brévin; a fort of 1861 is now a small Naval Museum (models, temporary exhibitions; *3-6:30 daily, Easter hols. and 15 May-15 Sep.; Sat. and Sun. from Easter to 15 May*). □

■ QUIBERON

B3 / ® / pop. 4 812 (Morbihan)

Quiberon is a tourist town on a peninsula (normal population 7 000) which receives more than 100 000 visitors each year. This is the Côte Sauvage (Wild Coast) : Quiberon and its beach, sheltered by Belle-Île; Port Haliguen, Saint-Pierre and Kerhostin face inland across the bay.

▶ At the entrance to the peninsula, **Le Galion Ship Museum,** dedicated to the art of shell design *(15 Apr.-30 Sep., 9:30-12:30 & 2-7:30).* ▶ **Trip around the peninsula .** 10.5 km to Port Blanc. ▶ The *corniche* starts at **Port-Haliguen :** at the SE end of the peninsula, Conguel Point provides a lovely view of the bay, Houat and Belle-Île. Return past Quiberon via **Goulvars Point** (Thalassotherapy Institute founded in 1964 by Louison Bobet, legendary *Tour de France* cyclist) and follow the **Côte Sauvage★,** a long succession of rugged cliffs, pierced by caves, arches and tunnels filled with the din of wind and sea. □

QUIMPER★★

A2 / ® / pop. 60 162 (Finistère)

This former capital of Cornouaille has prospered in the 20thC, whilst preserving its Breton character and atmosphere.

▶ The **cathedral of St. Corentin★** (B1, *8-11:45 & 1:45-6:30*) is dedicated to the city's patron saint. The 13th-15thC building shows the different phases of Breton Gothic architecture; between the two spires (19thC), the legendary King Gradlon watches over the town he founded after the destruction of his city of Ys (→). Inside, numerous tombs and effigies; don't miss the splendid stained glass★ (end 15thC). ▶ In the former bishop's palace (Gothic and Renaissance) is the **Musée Départemental Breton** (Brittany Museum; *closed until summer '86, important renovation work in process*); wood-carvings, tombstones, traditional interior and costumes★ from Cornwall; free admission to the gardens. ▶ The **Musée des Beaux Arts** (Fine Arts Museum) in the Hôtel de Ville *(9:30-12 & 2-6:30, 1 May-15 Sep.; 9:30-12 & 2-6, 16 Sep.-30 Apr.; closed Tue. and nat. hols.)* is one of the richest provincial museums : Flemish and Dutch 17thC paintings and superb canvasses by the School of Pont-Aven. ▶ NW from the square, walk through the Rue Elie Fréron and the neighbouring streets with their appetising names : Rue du Sallé, Place au Beurre (butter), Rue des Boucheries (butchers), Venelles du Poivre (pepper) and du Pain Cuit (baked bread); the **old houses** along these streets become more numerous in the **Rue Kéreon★** opposite the cathedral façade. ▶ Fine view over the old town from the wooded hill of Mont Frugy (B2), on the left bank of the Odet; pleasant walks. ▶ 500 m downstream from the town centre is the **Locmaria** Quarter (A2), where Quimper began; Romanesque church★ (11th-12thC). Since the 17thC Locmaria has been a centre of ceramics production with an international reputation : **Faïenceries HB-Henriot** *(visit Mon.-Fri. 9-11:30 & 2-5:30)*; 500 m towards Bénodet : **Faïencerie Keraluc** *(visit Mon.-Fri., 8-12 & 2-6).* 16thC church in the Kerfeunteun District *(1 km N);* 1550 stained glass★. □

▶ Nearby

▶ Downstream, the **Odet** widens into an attractive estuary★★ lined with numerous châteaux among rhododendron, camellias, and Virginia tulip trees; this is a trip to make by boat *(daily service May-Sep.; 1 hr 15 from Quimper to Bénodet).* ▶ 6.5 km E, **Ergué Gabéric :** in the church, 16thC stained glass window of the Passion; 3.5 km further on : chapel of Notre-Dame de Kerdévot, excellent example of 15thC Cournish architecture, with late 15thC Flemish altarpiece★. ▶ 12.5 km N : there is a remarkable pyramidal Calvary of 1550 in front of the chapel of **Notre-Dame de Quilinen★★** (16thC; 1520 Descent from the Cross). □

QUIMPERLÉ

B2-3 / ® / pop. 11 697 (Finistère)

Here, the Ellé and Isolde rivers meet to form the Laïta, which meanders down to the sea *(14 km S);* wonderful walks along its banks. At Pentecost, Quimperlé celebrates the *Pardon de Toulfoën* (a feast day for birds).

▶ From the cloister buildings of the former 17thC Abbey on the **Place Nationale,** good view of the Church of Sainte-Croix (rotunda; rebuilt 19thC). One of the three apses dates from 11thC; crypt with interesting capitals; finely-carved stone Renaissance altarpiece★ (1541) behind the entrance door. ▶ To the

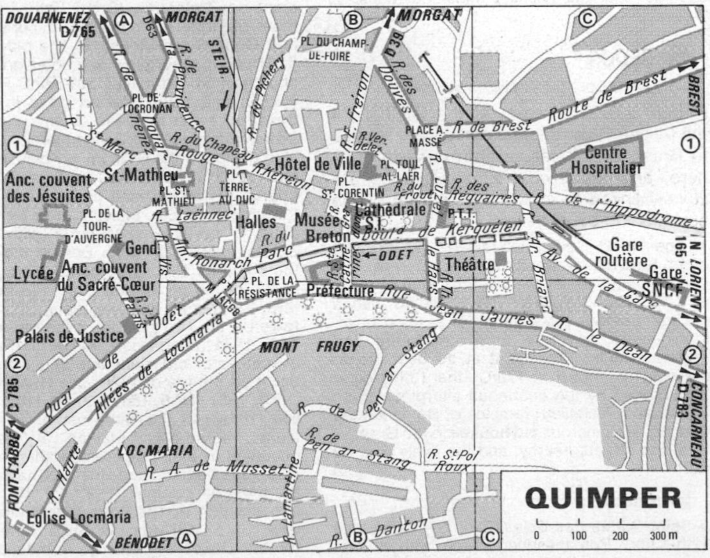

north, the aristocratic **Rue de Brémond d'Ars** runs through the old town, bordered by ancient houses; in the Rue Dom Morice, opposite the ruins of the church of St. Colomban, see the 15thC **Maison des Archers** (archer's house; small museum; history and local traditions: *Jul.-Aug.; closed Sun. and nat. hols.*). ▶ Across the Isole, climb the steep old-fashioned Rue Savary to the **Place St. Michel** in the heart of the upper town; square-towered church (13thC nave, square 15thC choir) with Flamboyant Gothic north porch. □

▶ Nearby

▶ **Le Pouldu** ®, at the mouth of the Laïta, is a pleasant town which still remembers the period (1889-94) when Gauguin and his friends used to stay here. □

RAZ Point★★

A2 / ® (Finistère)

A long rocky spur beaten by the waves and swept by the wind, a marvel to be visited outside the holiday season, or when poor weather has discouraged visitors...

▶ Go past the enormous car-park *(paying)*, the shopping centre and the semaphore, for a **view★★** of the Point and its reefs, the lighthouse (le Phare de la Vieille) and, 12 km out, the Île de Sein. ▶ A path runs around the Point *(non-slip soles recommended, guide advised)*; see the sinkhole **(Enfer de Plogoff)** and other chasms. ▶ The **Baie des Trépassés★** (beach; when druids died, they were taken by boat from here to the Île de Sein for burial; according to some, the drowned city of Ys is here (→ box). From the opposite end, you can reach the **Pointe du Van★★,** no less impressive but with fewer facilities, and the Pointe de Brézellec. ▶ **Cléden-Cap-Sizun** ®: church with 1550 bell-tower★ and Renaissance porch. ▶ As you go towards Douarnenez, make a detour to see the **Réserve Ornithologique du Cap Sizun★** (bird sanctuary; *10-12 & 2-6, 15 Mar.-31 Aug.*) on the Catel-ar-Roch promontory; with luck and binoculars, you can see interesting species such as razor-billed auks, puffins and shags. □

REDON

C3 / ® / pop. 10252 (Ille-et-Vilaine)

Redon is a small town at the junction of the Vilaine River and the canal from Nantes to Brest. Only pleasure craft pass through here, and the town's light industries are closely linked to agricultural activity of the surrounding countryside.

▶ The 14thC Gothic bell-tower★ (67 m high) of **St. Sauveur** overlooks the town centre. The church lost 25 m of nave in a fire; what remains is a fine 12thC Romanesque building with a second (central) bell-tower: it is a squat building despite its three arcaded stories and rounded angles. To see it at its best, go to the cloister, rebuilt in 17thC; the 13thC choir is darkened by the enormous altarpiece given by Cardinal Richelieu; remains of Romanesque frescos. ▶ Numerous **old houses** in the Grande-Rue, the streets nearby, and the lively Rue du Port. □

▶ Nearby

▶ **Saint-Gildas-des-Bois** *(17 km S)*: handsome 12th-13thC Romanesque church with central bell-tower. ▶ 15 km W, near Béganne: the **château de l'Estier,** a fine mediaeval manor house (14th-15thC, enlarged 17thC); no fewer than 24 chimneys! *(2-7, 1 Jul.-15 Sep.; closed Tue.)*; 4 km on: **château de Lehélec** (16th-18thC) with an austere façade of red schist and granite *(2-7 on Sun., 15 May-15 Jun.; daily ex Tue., Jul.-Aug.)*; small rustic museum in the out-buildings. □

RENNES★★

D2 / ® / pop. 200390 (Ille-et-Vilaine)

This ancient city was partially rebuilt after a catastrophic fire in 1720. The French classic architecture of the period contrasts stongly with the appearance of other Breton towns: nothing Celtic or regional about it, but very suitable for a Breton Parlement that wanted to affirm its independence in the face of an absolute monarch. Nonetheless, the area around the cathedral and the Rue Saint-Georges maintain a mediaeval look.

▶ **Place de la République** (B2) overlooking the river Vilaine is the heart of the town. The Palais du Commerce, an imposing building in the style of Louis XIV, was built between 1886 and 1932. ▶ The **Hôtel de Ville★** (1732-62, arch. Jacques Gabriel) is in the purest Louis XV style, with two pavillions linked by a central block to form a horseshoe, and topped by a bell-tower. See the monumental staircase and the 18thC tapestries in the south pavillion; opposite is the **theatre** (1856). ▶ The **Place du Parlement★** is surrounded by classical façades, also by Gabriel. The fourth side is occupied by the **Palais de Justice** (courthouse)★ designed by Salomon de Brosse and built (1618-54) for the Parlement de Bretagne. The façade is typical of Rennes: grey granite, with white stone for the upper stories. Inside, the decoration★★ (by painters who also worked in Versailles) dates from the reign of Louis XIV. Ask the Concierge de la Cour (the official court attendant) to show the Assize Court, (Salle des Assises - panelling), the Civil Court (Première Chambre Civile - paintings) and the Grand'-Chambre du Parlement de Bretagne★ (Great Hall of the Parliament of Brittany - panelling, decorated ceiling and Gobelin tapestries). ▶ The old houses in the **Rue St. Georges★** are noteworthy. ▶ The church of St. Germain (15th-16thC Flamboyant Gothic) has 16thC stained glass in the south transept. ▶ Art Nouveau ceramics in the 1926 **swimming pool** by Emmanuel Le Ray, who also designed the Halle de la Poissonnerie (fish market; 1912; rue de Nemours, B3). ▶ The **church of Notre-Dame** (B-C1), also known as the church of Ste. Mélaine, is a former abbey church; partly Romanesque with charming cloister gallery of 1683. Behind the church is the colourful Thabor Garden. ▶ Enjoy the lively bustle of the pedestrian streets (Rues Le Bastard, La Fayette and Nationale, B2), then walk towards the old town near the **cathedral** (A2; 1787-1844; altarpiece★, Antwerp 1520), where a number of **old mansions** and **wood houses** escaped the fire of 1720; see Rue St. Sauveur (Nº 3, 1557; Nº 5, 18thC) to the left of the basilica (18thC) of the same name. Rue St. Guillaume, the so-called Maison Du Guesclin★, is occupied by the Ti Coz restaurant. See also the Rue de la Psalette and Rue du Chapitre, one of the most handsome, (Nº 22, 20, 18, 11, 8, and especially 6). ▶ The **Porte Mordelaise** (Mordelaise Gate; A2) was the city's State Entrance for the Dukes of Brittany. Astride an ancient

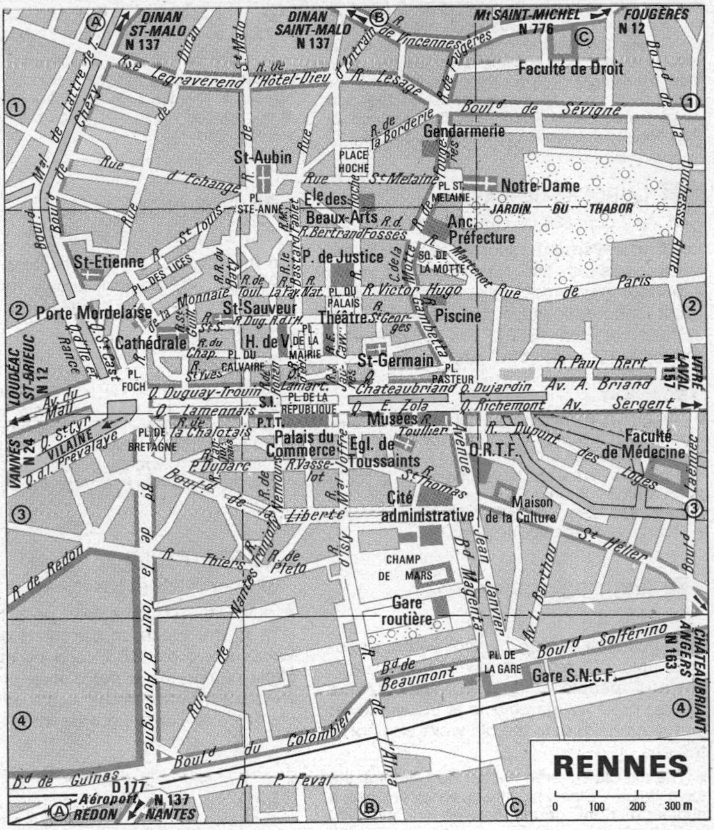

street, this gateway, entirely restored, was once part of the city ramparts (15thC). ▶ Du Guesclin is reputed to have entered his first tournament in the **Place des Lices;** lined with tall houses (mostly 17thC), it is now a thriving marketplace. ▶ In the Rue St. Michel and Rue du Champ-Jacquet, there are pretty half-timbered houses. ▶ On the left bank, see the Palais des Musées (B3; two museums; *daily ex Tue., 10-12 & 2-6*) : the **Musée de Bretagne** (Brittany Museum : pre-history, history, art, ethnology, costumes★, furniture; lively setting) is the best introduction to a trip around Brittany *(daily 10-12 & 2-6);* the **Musée des Beaux-Arts** (Fine Arts) is one of 15 great regional museums created in Year IX of the French Revolution (1801); don't miss the Newborn Child★★ by Georges de La Tour, canvasses by the painters of the School of Pont-Aven, the regional artists' room, and the Rennes ceramics (17th-19thC). ▶ In the **Maison des Métiers** (B3, Champ de Mars), exhibitions and sale of regional crafts. □

▶ Nearby

▶ **Rennes Forest** *(9-15 km NE) :* 30 km² of oaks, a pleasant picnic place for those who do not care for the famous restaurant in **Liffré** ®; half-way between Rennes and the forest is the Musée Automobile de Bretagne (Brittany Automobile Museum : 80 vehicles in running order from 1895 to 1925; *daily ex Tue. 9-12 & 4-6*). ▶ In the valley of the Vilaine, downstream from Rennes, is the site★ of the **Moulin du Boël** (mill; *17 km S, right bank*). On the other bank, pleasant walks along the GR 39. ▶ **Châteaugiron** *(16 km SE);* imposing remains of a castle★ with moats, walls and ivy-covered keep (12th-13thC); main buildings date from the 17th-18thC (restored). Pretty houses in the town. □

■ RHUYS Peninsula

C3 (Morbihan)

This low peninsula which shelters the Gulf of Morbihan from the wind, has recently developed a number of yacht harbours, created the resort of Le Crouesty, and built a highway : this is perhaps a way of protecting the remainder.

▶ At the base of the peninsula, the **château de Kerlévenan** (end 18thC) is surprisingly Italianate. ▶ **Sarzeau** ® (pop. 4 443) is surrounded by campsites; near the church (1626) are a number of granite houses★ (17th-18thC) with decorated dormer windows. ▶ The **château de Suscinio**★ has been restored and made into a museum *(out of season 9:30-12 & 1:30-7 ex. Tues., Sat. and Sun.; 1 Apr.-30 Sept. daily; closed Feb.)*. However, to preserve its well-known silhouette, the roofs were not altered. This superb fortified building (13th-15thC) was once the residence of the Dukes of Brittany. ▶ Partially Romanesque church at **Saint-Gildas-de-Rhuys** (12thC capitals, 11th-18thC tomb-stones) housing one of the largest treasure rooms★ in Brittany *(5-7, Sun. 4-6).* ▶ The 20 m high **tumulus of Tumiac** or Butte de César, beside the road, gives a splendid view over the bay and the ocean. ▶ Another view from the Pointe du Petit Mont above the developing town of **Kerjouanno** and the port of **Le Crouesty.** ▶ The shady little harbour of **Port-Navalo** ® overlooks the neck of the bay. □

LA ROCHE-BERNARD

C3 / ® / pop. 838 (Morbihan)

La Roche-Bernard, situated on a headland★, was, in the 17thC, a moderately important naval dockyard. Today, it is a yacht harbour, linked to the sea by the lock at the Arzal Dam (1970; *7 km downstream*). Attractive 15th and 16thC wooden houses. □

▶ Nearby

▶ 16 km W, **Pénestin :** an unpretentious seaside resort where the coastline alternates between beaches and cliffs. ▶ 14 km NW is the **château de Branféré,** surrounded by a park; zoo★ with 1 000 animals in semi-liberty *(9-12 & 2-6:30, Apr.-Sep., or 5:30, 16 Sep.-14 Nov).* ▶ Boat trips on the Vilaine River. □

ROCHEFORT-EN-TERRE★

C3 / pop. 613 (Morbihan)

In a beautiful setting of rocks and woodland, this old fortified town is filled with cheerful people, *crêperies,* and antique shops; there are geraniums at the windows, and more flowers in the old wells and horse troughs.

▶ The the old covered market now houses the town hall. ▶ Close by, the main street has a number of **17thC granite houses,** one of which is flanked by a pentagonal corbelled turret. Others, even more delightful, stand around an old well in a tiny square. ▶ The **church** dates from the 12thC but was rebuilt during 16th-17thC; interesting furnishings (stalls, 1592 and altarpiece of painted stone, 1610). ▶ The **castle** is only a heap of ruins (view★) with the exception of the out-buildings, rebuilt stone by stone with material from other ruined castles and now refurbished to make a museum *(11-12 & 2-6, June-15 Sep.; Sun. and nat. hols. only rest of year).* □

▶ Nearby

▶ **Questembert** ® (*10 km SW;* pop. 4 900) : several 16th and 17thC houses with carved façades, fine timber-built market★ of 1675. □

ROSCOFF

B1 / ® / pop. 3 787 (Finistère)

This old port became a health-spa centre in 1899 and later, a seaside resort. It is surrounded by market gardens and has regained its youth since local growers established the Brittany Ferries line to export their onions and import tourists!

▶ The Gothic **church** has an over-decorated bell-tower; the wooden ceiling and monumental carved wood altarpiece are more interesting. ▶ **Aquarium★** *(2-7, last Sat. in Mar.-31 May; 10-12 & 2-7, Jun.-15 Sep.; Sun. and nat. hols., 2-6 16, Sep.-31 Oct.).* □

▶ Batz Island

(15-min crossing hourly; extra sailings in summer)

▶ Flat, ringed with beaches and reefs that appear at low tide; an exceptionally gentle climate. Specialises in market gardening and seaweed gathering. □

ROSPORDEN

B2 / ® / pop. 6 752 (Finistère)

On the edge of a 110-acre lake formed by the Aven; the church, largely rebuilt in the 17thC, has a 14thC bell-tower with very pure lines. □

▶ Nearby

▶ 9 km W : **Saint-Yvi** has a beautiful parish churchyard★ planted with old yew trees; church and calvary (16thC), ossuary (15thC) and fountain. ▶ 14 km NW : **Scaër** is famous for its Breton wrestling *(last Sun. in Aug.);* 15thC figured cross in front of the church. □

ROSTRENEN

B2 / pop. 4 391 (Côtes-du-Nord)

A quiet little country town on a hill, with a lake to the south, in the heart of Brittany. Walks along the GR37 and by the Nantes-Brest canal; the canal cutting crosses the watershed between the Aulne and the Blavet rivers at Glomel, not far from here. □

▶ Nearby

▶ 6 km SW : the **Manor of Coatcouraval** (15thC), in a woodland setting *(Jul.-Aug.).* ▶ 9 km N : **Kergrist-Moëlou** is worth a detour for its 16thC Flamboyant Gothic church, surrounded by aged yew trees, with a 1578 Calvary (damaged). ▶ 11 km E, **Gouarec** ®; schist houses by the junction of the river Blavet and the Nantes-Brest canal : 4 km S : the chapel of Notre-Dame de la Croix at **Plélauff** has a choir-screen★ whose paintings are masterpieces of naïf art. ▶ 14 km NE, **Saint-Nicolas-du-Pélem :** beside the church (1470 stained glass) is the St. Nicholas Fountain, one of the most charming you could find; in the vicinity of the town, you will see pretty chapels, megaliths and rocky outcrops; at **Toul-Goulic,** the Blavet goes briefly underground. En route, **Lanrivain :** 15thC ossuary, 16thC Calvary★ □

SAINT-BRIEUC

C1-2 / ® / pop. 51 399 (Côtes-du-Nord)

On a headland between the Goët and Gouédic rivers, formerly a quiet market town, the seat of a bishopric, a stopover in the Tro Breiz (→ box), a small fishing port. Under the pressures of immigration from the countryside and recent industrialisation, Saint-Brieuc is changing fast.

▶ The town centre with its narrow streets is very lively. ▶ The 14th-15thC **cathedral** (rebuilt in 18th and 19thC) has an unusually austere appearance for so important a sanctuary, due to the two tower-like mediaeval keeps. ▶ The neighbouring streets have a number of fine **old**

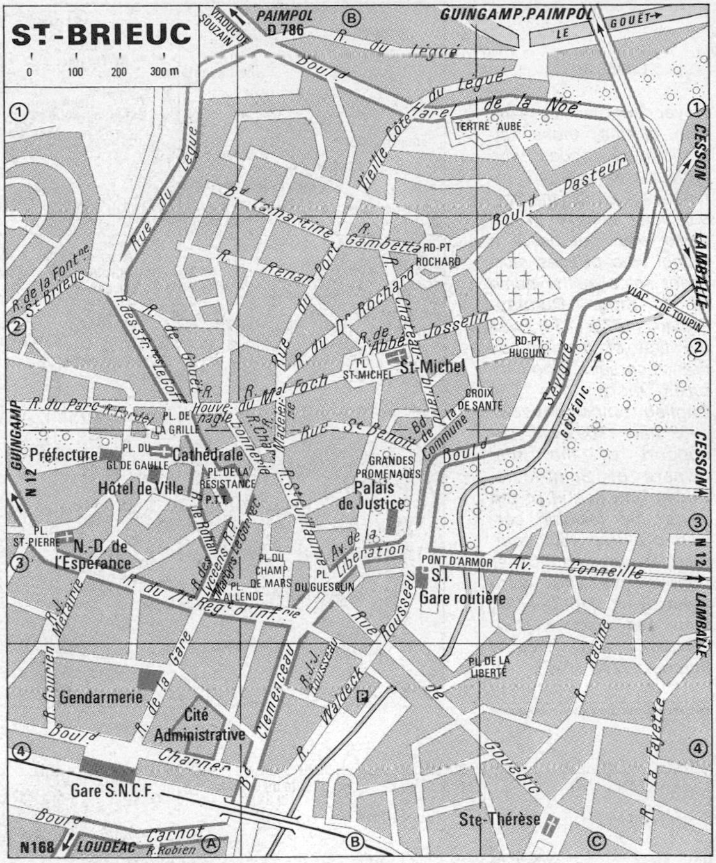

timber-fronted houses, often carved, as in the Rue Fardel (A2). ▶ Fine **views** from many points around the headland : the **Rond-Point Huguin** (C2) overlooking the Gouédic Ravine (pleasant walks). The Tertre Aubé★ (BC1), surveys the Gouët Valley, the port and the bay. □

▶ Nearby

▶ 3.5 km NE is the **Cesson Tower,** a ruined 14thC keep dominating the mouth of the Gouët. ▶ **Roselier Point** (*8.5 km NE;* view★ over the bay) is reached through **Le Légué** (port of Saint-Brieuc) and Saint-Laurent-de-la-Mer; a pleasant road continues to **Les Rosaires beach,** surrounded by cliffs. ▶ 19 km SW : **Quintin**★ is a charming ancient town above a lake; 15thC gate, 16th-18thC houses and the 17th-18thC wings of an uncompleted château. 2 km S : the park of the **château de Robien** (18thC). □

The Tro Breiz

The Tro Breiz was a pilgrimage that every Breton was supposed to accomplish once in his life. The custom arose at an unknown date, probably around 1200, and died out during the Wars of Religion (1562-1598). The pilgrims visited the tombs of the seven saints who founded the first seven bishoprics in Brittany : Samson at ***Dol,*** *Malo at* ***Saint-Malo,*** *Brieuc at* ***Saint-Brieuc,*** *Tugdual at* ***Tréguier,*** *Pol-Aurélien at* ***Saint-Pol-de-Léon,*** *Corentin at* ***Quimper*** *and Patern at* ***Vannes.*** *At the rate of about 20 km a day, the circuit of the country took each pilgrim approximately one month.*

■ SAINT-MALO★★★

D1 / ® / pop. 47 324 (Ille-et-Vilaine)

It is almost impossible to believe that Saint-Malo was totally rebuilt in its present form after WWII. The ramparts and narrow streets of the Ville Close (walled city) are lined by houses in the severe style of the 17th and 18thC, and it is very easy to imagine the place as it was in the days of the great sailing ships.

▶ The best place for an overall view of Saint-Malo is the **Esplanade Saint-Vincent** (E1). To the W is the ancient walled city, proud of its history; to the N and NW lies the seaside resort with beach, hotels, casino and Palais des Congrès. To the E and SE you can see the port with its busy trade in cod and coal; S, behind the yacht harbour, are the wooded heights of Saint-Servan and the estuary of the Rance, gateway to the high seas... ▶ The **castle**★ is a mighty pentagonal fortress flanked by round

Corsairs

Never confuse corsairs with pirates, those unscrupulous rogues who looted and pillaged for their own profit; the corsair may behave in the same way, but he is a patriot who pillages merchant ships in the name of his King... ***Duguay-Trouin*** *(1673-1736) was the first of the famous French corsairs, who captured more than 300 English ships between 1689 and 1709, with the support of the ship owners of Saint-Malo. During one period of ten years, the Malouin corsairs captured 3800 commercial vessels. Other famous corsairs were* ***Jean Bart*** *(1650-1732, born and died in Dunkerque) and* ***Robert Surcouf*** *(1773-1827).*

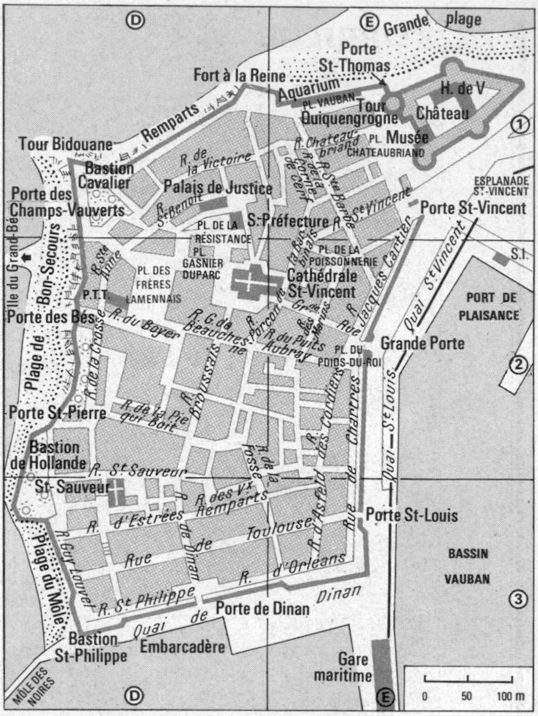

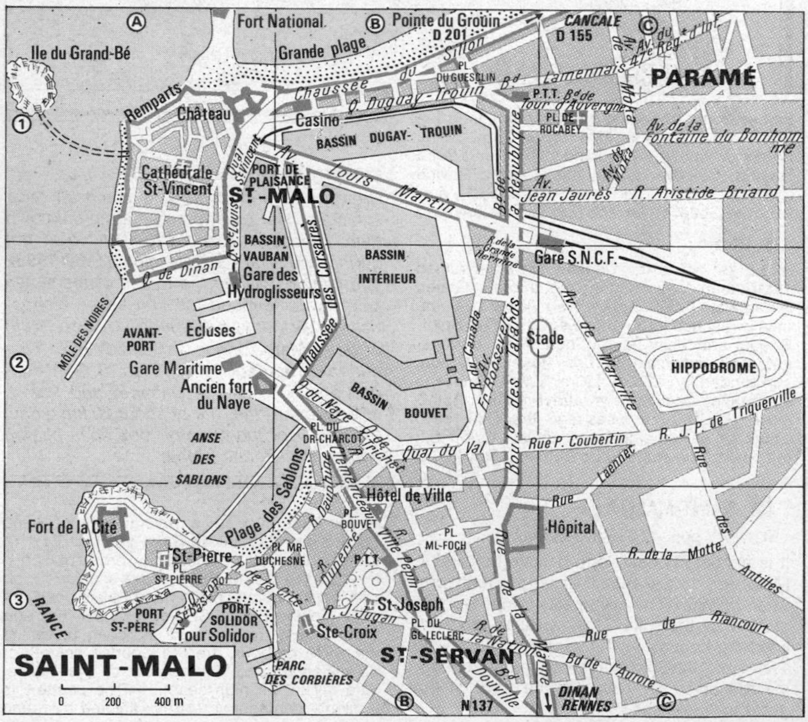

towers, now housing the townhall and the **City Museum** *(10-12 & 2-6, 1 June-30 Sep.)* : history of the town and its great men. Also in the castle is the **Galerie Quiquengrogne** *(Easter-15 Sep., 9-11:45 & 2-6; open 30 mins earlier am and pm Jul.-Aug.)* : wax museum of the town's famous men including Cartier (1491-1557), discoverer of Canada and Chateaubriand. ▶ **Tour of the ramparts★★** for a series of splendid views over the sea and its islets : at high tide the waves beat on the ramparts; at low tide you can reach the **islands of Grand Bé** (A1 ; Chateaubriand's tomb), **Petit Bé** and **Fort National** (*guided tour,* view★ of the Ville Close). ▶ Wander around the pedestrian precinct inside the ancient **walled city★;** souvenirs, antiques, curiosities, café, *crêperies...* ▶ The **cathedral★** (D-E2) is a contrast in styles where every century is represented, from the 12th to 18thC; modern stained-glass windows in blazing colours. ▶ **Aquarium** in the ramparts (Place Vauban; E1 ; *every day*); opposite, **Exotarium** *(combined tickets).* ▶ The **Pointe de la Cité** (A3) is crowned by a fort (1759), rebuilt during the German occupation (*exterior visit only;* orientation table). The **Corniche d'Aleth★** (path; pedestrians only; view★) runs around the point. ▶ The **Solidor Tower★** (1382; there are in fact three towers) houses the **Musée International des Long-Cours Cap-Horniers,** illustrating the lives of the seamen who sailed ocean-going three-masters around Cape Horn *(guided tours at 2, 3:15 and 4:30, Jan.-Mar. and Oct.-Dec; at 10:30, 2, 3:30 and 5, Apr.-14 Jun. and 15-30 Sep.; at 10:30, 11, 2, 2:30, 3:30, 4, 5, 15 Jun.-14 Sep.).* ▶ Excellent **view** over the estuary from the path round Corbières Park (B3; *8 am-8 pm*). ▶ **Paramé** (C1) is the seaside resort of Saint-Malo; walk along the wave-battered sea-wall (view★). □

▶ Nearby

▶ As from Dinard (→), boat trips to Cézembre Island, Cape Fréhel and Dinan. ▶ The Côte d'Émeraude (Emerald Coast; →) E of Saint-Malo is a short but indispensable walk. ▶ Around Saint-Malo, many 18thC *Malouinières* (mansions built by the sea-traders of the period), all on the same pattern; only one is open to visitors : the **château du Bosq★** *(7 km S on the N137 and a narrow road on the right).* □

■ SAINT-NAZAIRE

C4 / ® / pop. 68 947 (Loire-Atlantique)
See plan following page

This harbour was built a century ago for ships too large to enter Nantes. It was destroyed during WWII, when it served as a German submarine base. The town is now the leading French naval dockyard (70 % of national production) and a major commercial port.

▶ Everything here converges on the **port★★** where a **viewing terrace** has been built above the old submarine pens (C3; *9:30-7:30; Jul.-Aug. : 9:30-12 & 2-6 ex Mon. in Jun. and 1-15 Sep.*). View over the outer port, protected by two 500 m jetties and the Saint-Nazaire Basin (550 m x 160 m); the submarine base is still intact and this 10-acre concrete rectangle is now used by industry; you can also see the Penhoët Basin (1100 x 230 m) and surrounding shipyards. The skilled workforce and high performance equipment can build tankers of up to 500 000 metric tonnes. A sizeable proportion of their output today consists of motors, compressors, boilers and equipment for nuclear power-plants and aerospace (avions, jet aviation). ▶ The town has been rebuilt on a generous scale; the most interesting architectural achievement is the **Salle Omnisport★** (1975; sports stadium) where an enormous concrete shell, roofed with plastic-coated steel cable stands in the middle of the sports ground. □

▶ Nearby

▶ **Donges,** 16.5 km E, is the third largest oil port in France; see the refineries with flares at night. The modern **church** has a monumental Calvary★ on the façade, inspired by Breton traditions. ▶ **Montoir de Bretagne,** 8 km away, the foremost methane port of Europe, completes this industrial complex. ▶ From the **Saint-Nazaire Bridge★** (1965; 3 356 m; 60 m above the Loire; *toll*) you have a wide view★ over the town and the estuary. □

■ SAINT-PHILBERT-DE-GRAND-LIEU★

D4 / pop. 4 182 (Loire-Atlantique)

Red tiles instead of slates, white tufa instead of granite... Muscadet or Gros Plant white wines instead of cider. Nevertheless, the Retz region has been part of Brittany since the year 851.

▶ In 815 the monks of Noirmoutier, fleeing the Normans, founded an abbey a few kilometres from a marsh-bordered lake in this remote spot. The **church★** is still there, a rare example of Carolingian architecture, with pillars based alternately on stone and brick, and a crypt containing the 7thC sarcophagus of St. Philbert. 16th-17thC priory and monastic buildings. □

▶ Nearby

▶ **Machecoul** (15 km SW) : old houses and ruins of the 14thC castle of Gilles de Retz, the valiant companion at arms of Joan of Arc; he later became one of history's worst criminals, the inspiration for Perrault's "Bluebeard". ▶ 19 km S, in Legé : **château de Bois-Chevalier★** (1655; *1 Apr.-31 Oct., 9-12 & 2-7*). □

■ SAINT-POL-DE-LÉON★★

AB 1 / ® / pop. 7 998 (Finistère)

Lacy stonework and a pointed bell-tower set among cultivated fields... This is a region famous for its artichokes and other vegetables, and also for the flowers, shrubs, and conifers grown for replanting in private gardens.

▶ The chapel of **Notre-Dame du Kreisker★★** (14thC; *summer, 10-11:30 & 1:30-5:30, 12-6 the rest of the year*) is of astonishing size; the 15thC bell-tower★★ is 77 m high, with an openwork spire flanked by pinnacles which has been much copied in the region. ▶ **Old houses** in the street leading to the **cathedral★★** (13th-16thC; *8-11:45 & 1:30-7:30*), a sober Gothic edifice showing signs of Norman influence. Inside, see the 15th and 16thC stained glass, the Renaissance organs, the carved stalls (1512) and the unusual *Etagères de la Nuit* behind the left-hand stalls : these are small chapel-shaped reliquaries containing skulls. ▶ The Hôtel de Ville is in the former bishop's palace (18thC). ▶ The **Promenade du Champ de la Rive** (riverside walk) ends at a Calvary where there is an excellent view over the estuary of the Penzé and its islets. The port of Pempoul and the Sainte-Anne beach are at the head of a shallow bay. □

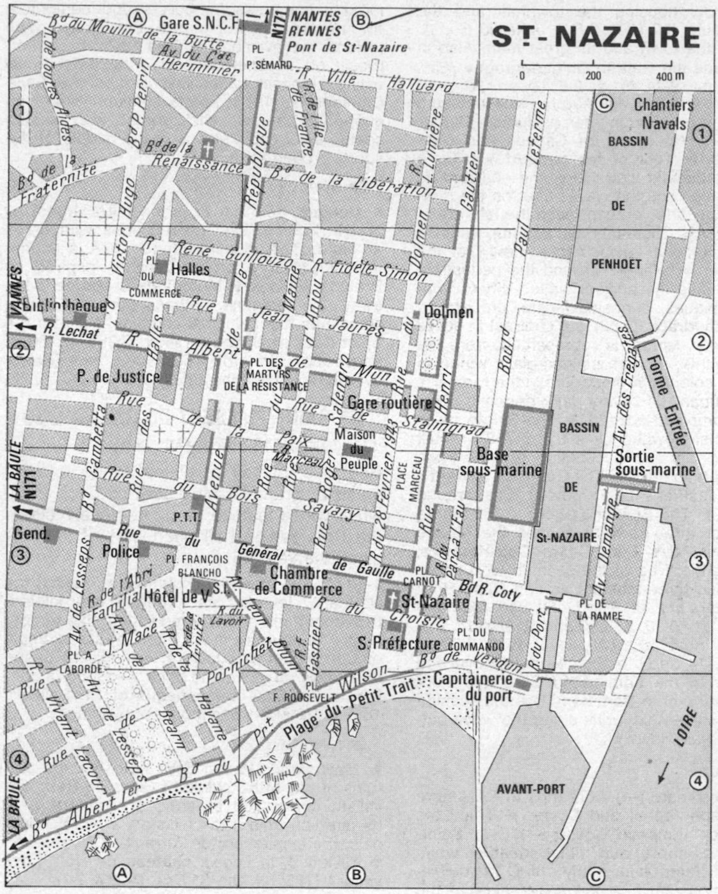

▶ Round trip of the châteaux in Léon *(65 km approx).*

▶ Take the road from **Saint-Pol** to Plouescat; after crossing the Landivisiau road, you drive alongside a crenellated wall *(right)* surrounding the Manor of Pontplancoët; further on, is the Manor of Kerautret, on the left. ▶ The **château de Kérouzéré★** *(exterior visit only, 1 Jul.-15 Sep.)* is one of the region's best examples of 15thC military architecture. ▶ 1 500 m from Cléder, the château de **Tronjoly** is an elegant Renaissance mansion *(exterior visit only).* ▶ Leaving **Plouescat** ®, a town specialising in garlic and shallots (see the *cohue* - 16thC covered market), take the D30 which passes the château de Maillé (1570) towards Kerjean. A short detour to the left takes you to see *(from the road only)* the spectacular ruins of the château de Kergornadeac'h, near a lake in the middle of the woods. ▶ **Kerjean★★** is one of the finest 16thC Breton châteaux *(9-12 & 2-6 Apr.-Sep.; to 5 rest of year; closed Tue.).* This luxurious mansion is surrounded by fortifications, reflecting both the uncertainty of the times and the independent spirit of wealthier Bretons. In the chapel, see the beautiful chestnut-panel vaulting and the carved beams; in the rooms that have been restored, 16th and 17thC Breton furniture of interest. ▶ Through **Berven** (15th-16thC church★ in a churchyard with Renaissance gateway), to **Tréflaouénan** (in the church, decorated nave panelling showing fourteen scenes from the Life of Christ); ruins of the **Manor of Créac'h Ingar** (15thC, under restoration, *free admission*). □

■ SAINT-QUAY-PORTRIEUX

C1 / ® / pop. 3 399 (Côtes-du-Nord)

A family seaside resort with beaches, facilities and a good location.

▶ Beaches and cliffs, sand and rocks, paths among the gorse and pines, stretching along the coast which seems to be a continuous holiday area from **Binic** (museum) through **Etables-sur-Mer** ® and Saint-Quay, to **Portrieux.** □

▶ Nearby

▶ 9 km SW : chapel of **Notre-Dame de la Cour★** (15thC) with stained glass★ in the apse, illustrating the Life of the Virgin in eighteen scenes *(guided tour, 8-8, Jul.-Sep.).* □

■ Île de SEIN

A2 / ® / pop. 504

The highest point on the island, 8 m above sea-level. This flat 140-acre rock has no trees, no springs (the inhabitants rely on rainwater), a few cows, and some potatoes or other vegetables grown in the shelter of low stone walls. The houses huddle along narrow streets barely 2 m wide. A fierce current rushes between the mainland and this wind-swept island. The only resources are scallops, lobsters, and other sea-food. □

■ TRÉGUIER★★

B1/ ® / pop. 3 400 (Côtes-du-Nord)

▶ **Cathedral of St. Tugdual★★ :** one of the most beautiful 14th-15thC Gothic buildings in Brittany *(Easter-end Sep., 9-12 & 2-7)*; inside, see the carved choir-stalls and the neo-Gothic tomb of St. Yves, a very popular saint, whose *pardon* on May 19 attracts thousands. In the north transept is the entry to the treasure room and the 15thC cloister★ *(admission charged).* □

▶ Nearby

▶ 2 km S : **Minihy-Tréguier** is the birthplace of St. Yves (1253-1303); 15thC church. ▶ **Pleubien** *(9 km NE)* in the centre of a peninsula; seaweed gathering. ▶ 7 km N : **Plougescrant;** fantastically-shaped rocks; chapel of St. Gonéry, with an astonishing bent spire covered with lead; panelling with naïf paintings★. ▶ All along the Tégor coast★ are little resorts surrounded by rocks, reefs, islets and inlets : **Port Blanc** ® , **Trestel** and **Trévou-Tréguignec** ® ▶ 11 km SE, **château de la Roche-Jagu★ :** a fortified mansion of the 14th and 15thC surrounded by greenery above the left bank of the Trieux *(daily 1 Jul.-15 Sep.; Sun. and nat. hols. only May-Jun. and 15 Sep.-31 Oct.).* □

■ LE VAL-ANDRÉ

C1 / ® / pop. 3 801 (Côtes-du-Nord)

2 km from the town of **Pléneuf,** a century-old resort by a marvellous beach. Yacht harbour at Dahouët (site★).

▶ 6 km NE, **château de Bienassis★** (1620) : a fine mansion in pink sandstone with double moats (15th-17thC) and French formal gardens *(8 Jun.-15 Sep., ex. Sun. and nat. hols. 10:30-12:30 & 2-6:30).* □

■ VANNES★★

C3 / ® / pop. 45 397 (Morbihan)

A quiet country town at the back of the Gulf of Morbihan. Charming old buildings and narrow twisting streets, flower-beds at the base of the ramparts.

▶ Starting from the **port** (B3) Rue Le Pontois is probably the best way to approach the old city : **ramparts★** studded with towers and gateways, formal French garden, old wash houses on the Ruisseau de Rohan (Rohan Brook), all of which are illuminated on summer evenings. The view★ is even more beautiful from the Garenne Promenade. ▶ You reach the *chevet* of the cathedral through the **Porte Prison** (B2; 15thC, machicolated tower). Around the cathedral, old buildings★ house many antique shops and boutiques : Rue Saint-Guenhaël is the most typical. ▶ The **cathedral★,** principally 15th and 16thC, has a Flamboyant Gothic north doorway with Renaissance recesses; inside is the tomb of St. Vincent Ferrier (tapestries of

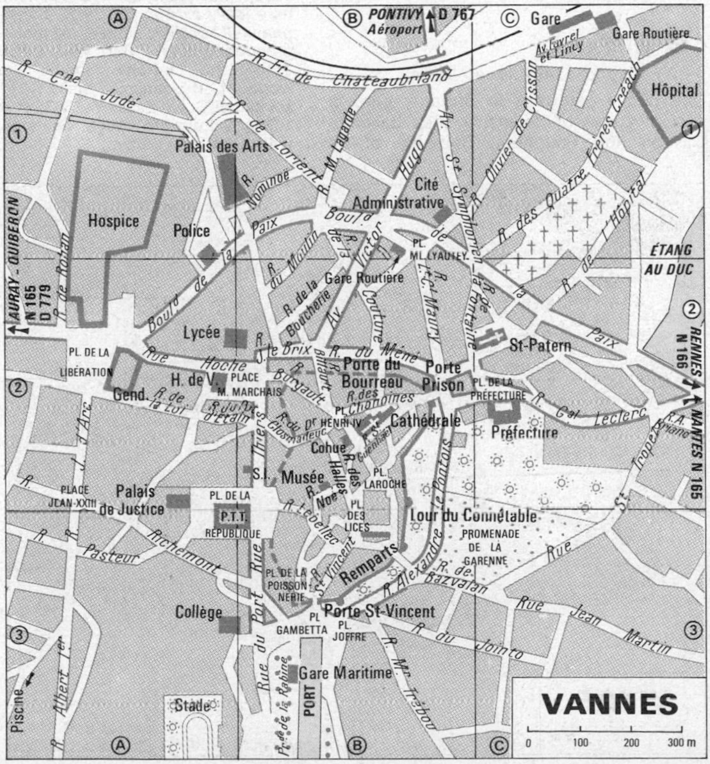

his miracles); chapels with altarpieces, statues and paintings; don't miss the treasury★ in the former chapterhouse. ▶ Opposite the cathedral is the **cohue** (12th-14thC covered market) looking on old houses; on the first floor, a Fine Arts Museum. ▶ Place Henri IV, Rue Salomon and Rue des Halles in the pedestrian precinct are also lined by fine **old houses.** ▶ In the château Gaillard (1400, former seat of the Parliament of Brittany), is the **Museum of Archeology** *(daily ex Sun., 9:30-12 & 2-6),* especially rich in pre-historic finds★ from the Gulf of Morbihan. ▶ Close by, in the Place Valancia, is the Maison de Vannes, decorated with two carved wood grotesques. ▶ In the Louis XIV-style Hôtel de Limur (Rue Thiers, B2) is the TO. At N° 1 of the same street, near the port, is the Gulf and Sea Museum. ▶ Interesting and important **Aquarium** (the second-most in Europe) at the end of the bridge : species from the Gulf, the tropical coral reefs and the great lakes of Africa *(daily 9-12 & 1:30-6:30; Jun., Jul., Aug. 9-9).* ▶ 5 km S, **Conleau island** ® lovely shady spot with pine trees, where people go to eat oysters. Regular boat service to the Ile d'Arz. □

▶ Nearby

▶ 9 km SW the **Pointe d'Arradon★** ® gives a good view of the many islands and inlets in the Gulf of Morbihan (→). ▶ In **Saint-Avé** *(4 km NE)* chapel of Notre-Dame du Loc★ : figured cross with carved alabaster panels (15thC). ▶ 15 km E **château du Plessis-Josso★** (14th-16thC) : vast manor house with ramparts, towers, mill and pond *(10 Jul.-30 Aug., pm).* 4 km further on : the 18thC **château de Trémohar-en-Berric** has kept its 14th-15thC fortified out-buildings *(visit on request 1 Jul.-15 Sep., 9-12 & 2:30-6).*□

■ VITRÉ★

D2 / ® / pop. 13491 (Ille-et-Vilaine)

One of the gateways to Brittany, Vitré is part of a line of defensive sites between Clisson and Fougères. Because of its defensive role, Vitré has acquired an impressive castle and a ring of ramparts; with quaint narrow streets and old houses the town looks much like a mediaeval woodcut.

▶ Enter the **old city** by the **Rue d'Em-Bas** lined, like the **Rue Baudrairie★,** with ancient houses. ▶ The pride of the city is the **castle★★** (A1; 14th-15thC; *1 Jul.-30 Sep., daily 10-12 & 1:30-6; 1 Oct.-31 Mar., 10-12 & 2-5:30, closed Tue., Sat., Sun., Mon. am.; 1 Apr.-30 June 10-12 & 2-5:30, closed Tue.*), a perfect example of mediaeval military architecture. Built on a triangular plan with three broad round towers, it opens onto the square through a gatehouse, itself flanked by several towers and today housing the town hall and a museum. ▶ The **church of Notre-Dame** (B1, 15th-16thC) is very characteristic of Flamboyant Gothic in Upper Brittany : southern façade is studded with gables and pinnacles, while an outside 15thC pulpit recalls the important role played by the Church in the public life of those days; ask in the sacristy to see the series of 32 Limousin enamels★ (1544). ▶ Walk down the Rue Notre-Dame (old houses) and the neighbouring streets to the Place de la République where the **Promenade du Val** starts, and continues along the N and E **ramparts★.** □

▶ Nearby

▶ From the **Rachapt** District (A1; 15thC chapel of St. Nicolas with 16thC frescos) you can walk up to the **Tertres Noirs** *(15 min)* : view★ over town and castle. ▶ 6 km SE : the **château des Rochers-Sévigné★** (16th-17thC) would still look familiar to the Marquise de Sévigné (1626-1696), who wrote some of her famous letters here *(daily ex Sun. am; 9-12 & 2-6).* ▶ **Champeaux** *(9 km NW);* square, old granite houses★ grouped around a 1601 well, and a collegiate 15th-16thC church★; inside Renaissance works of art : canopied stalls (1530-35), mausoleum of Guy d'Espinay (1553), stained glass; 1.5km S from the village, **château d'Espinay** (14th-16thC; *no visitors*). □

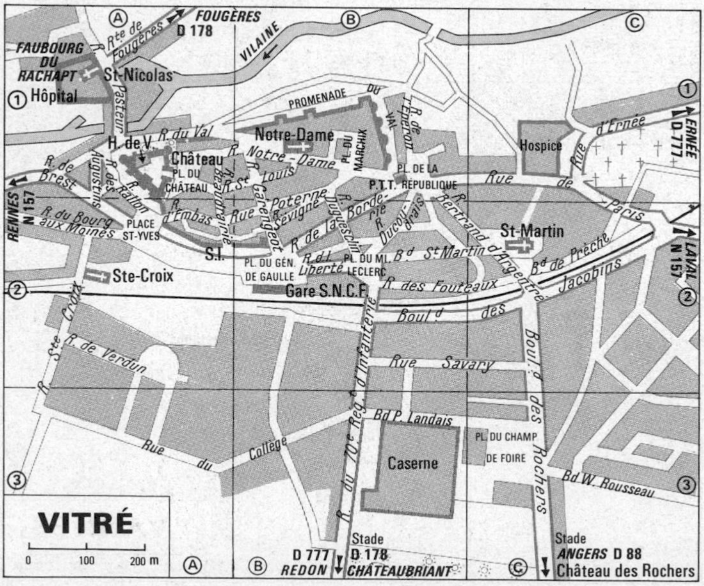

Architecture

The typical Breton house is built in granite or schist, and roofed with slate (formerly hatch). ● It usually faces south, with few openings in the façade; the low outline and sombre colour blend into the surroundings. Two other general characteristics : chimneys on the gables and a central ridgeline. ● In Finistère, gables tend to overlap the

Côtes-du-Nord

roof and the walls are faced in stone; there is sometimes a second storey, with an exterior staircase protected by an overhang, and/or a wing running back at right-angles to the main building (Monts d'Arrée). ● In Morbihan, the house is long and low with an exterior staircase and the roof overlapping the gables; openings are arched. The same style is found around Pontivy. ● Houses on the northern coast often have an upper floor and are built of fieldstone. They may consist

Brière

of a single long building (Dol and Fougères) or of several buildings a round a courtyard (Trégor). ● Many cob and timber houses are still to be seen between Rennes and Merdrignac. ● The thatched cottages

Monts d'Arrée

Morbihan

of Brière are also cobbuilt; the reed thatch is curved around the loft window. The façade is periodically whitewashed. A variety of smaller outbuildings of the same proportions prolong the gable walls or are built opposite, outlining an open courtyard. ● South of the Loire, the houses take on a southern look with shallow, hollow-tiled roofs and more numerous openings, frequently framed in brick. There is usually an upper storey. ● The manorhouse is another traditional form of architecture in Brittany. Throughout the region it is much the same : a large house set around a paved courtyard, with high chimneys and at least one

Rennes Basin

tower or pointed turret. However, Breton manor houses are by no means identical. Depending on the region, the period, and the wealth of the builder, they vary from the big farm, where the only external decoration is around the main door, to the small fortress, and from the elegant country mansion to the real château. ● There is more unity of style in the timber-clad houses found in large and small towns all over Brittany : this type of construction has a long history, because woodwork and carpentry were always encouraged by the naval dockyards.

Brief regional history

4500-2000 BC Successive waves of colonists came from the Iberian Peninsula, bringing the enigmatic **Megalithic Civilisation** whose traces can be seen throughout the region. Trade began across the English Channel.

4thC BC-9thC AD **Celts** came from **Central Europe** to settle on the island of Great Britain; around 350 BC five great tribes settled in Brittany (Armorica); the naval defeat of the Veneti tribe, which occupied the area around the Gulf of Morbihan, opened the way for the **Romans** (56 BC). ● In about 460 AD, the Celts of Great Britain, driven out by the Angles and the Saxons, migrated to **Armorica** (Brittany); legend has it that they crossed the Channel in "stone troughs" with their chiefs, usually priests or monks. With the retreat of the Gallo-Romans, the Celts organised themselves into independent principalities. ● In the east of Brittany the key towns of Vannes, Rennes and Nantes remained part of the Kingdom of the Franks.

9th-12thC The Carolingians, unable to conquer Brittany, attempted to increase their influence through **Nominoë,** a Breton chief who subsequently proclaimed himself **King of Brittany** and turned against the Carolingians. He and his successors established the boundaries where they remain today. ● Norman invasions and internal rivalries left Brittany in a state of anarchy for a century. At the beginning of the 10thC Alain le Grand and his grandson Alain Barbe Torte expelled the Normans and reunified the country. Brittany suffered from periodic internal conflicts but enjoyed relative peace and independence from France, developing its own social and administrative organisation.

The struggles between the Franch royal house of Capet and the rival Plantagenets (Kings of England) increased **French influence** in the Duchy of Brittany, and after 1250 its Dukes became vassals of the King of France. ● Brittany developed a thriving international sea trade and grew increasingly independent until Charles VIII of France crushed the Bretons at the battle of Saint-Aubin du Cormier (1488).

1491-1532 **Anne de Bretagne,** heiress of François II, the last Duke of Brittany, was compelled to marry first Charles VIII then, after Charles's death, his successor Louis XII. Her attempts to preserve Brittany's independence within the framework of the French kingdom were only partially effective. The marriage of her daughter Claude to the future King of France (François I) put an **end to self-determination in Brittany.**

16th-19thC The **Parlement de Bretagne,** the regional administrative body, was always careful to preserve its few remaining privileges. The ports and shipbuilding industry flourished and coastal Brittany grew rich during the period of colonial and commercial expansion. ● The liberal ideals of the French Revolution were at first welcomed, but unpopular measures passed by the Revolutionary Government of the Convention (military conscription, religious intolerance) gave rise to the **Chouannerie,** the revolt of the Bretons.

19th-20thC Arrival of the railway brought competition from industrialised areas and hastened the region's economic decline, simultaneously encouraging emigration. ● To the problems of a neglected region were added the ravages of WWII, and Brittany had to wait until 1968 before modernising its agriculture and emerging from a state of virtual isolation. Since then, the development of maritime and tourist activities together with increasing industrialisation, has given impetus to economic growth.

Practical information

The region

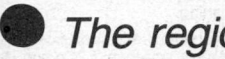

Information : *Délégation Régionale au Tourisme,* 3, rue d'Espagne, B.P. 2275, 35022 Rennes Cedex, ☎ 99.50.11.15. **Côtes-du-Nord :** *Comité Départemental du Tourisme* (C.D.T), 1, rue Chateaubriand, 22000 Saint-Brieuc, ☎ 96.61.66.70. **Finistère :** C.D.T., 6, rue René-Madec, 29000 Quimper, ☎ 98.95.28.86. **Ille-et-Vilaine :** C.D.T., 1, rue Martenot, 35032 Rennes Cedex, ☎ 99.02.97.43. **Loire-Atlantique :** C.D.T., 34, rue de Strasbourg, 44035 Nantes Cedex, ☎ 40.89.50.77. **Morbihan :** C.D.T., Hôtel du Département, B.P. 400, 56009 Vannes Cedex, ☎ 97.54.06.56. In Paris : *Maison de la Bretagne,* Maine-Montparnasse shopping centre, 75737, ☎ 45.38.73.15. Well-stocked bookshop.

Bookings : *Loisirs-Accueil **Ille-et-Vilaine*** (L.A.), 1, rue Martenot, 35000 Rennes, ☎ 99.02.97.41. *Loisirs-Accueil **Loire-Atlantique*** (L.A.), 34, rue de Strasbourg, 44000 Nantes, ☎ 40.89.50.77.

Maps : *Michelin* 1/200 000 nº 230 for the over-all region, or nºs 58, 59, 63 and 67. *I.G.N.* 1/250 000 nº 105 ; 1/100 000, nºs 13, 14, 15, 16 and 24.

S.O.S. : Côtes-du-Nord, *Samu,* ☎ 96.94.40.15. **Finistère,** *Samu,* ☎ 98.46.11.33. **Ille-et-Vilaine,** *Samu,* ☎ 99.59.16.16. **Loire-Atlantique,** *Samu,* ☎ 40.48.35.35. **Morbihan,** *Samu,* ☎ 97.54.22.11. Poisoning Emergency Centre : Rennes, ☎ 99.59.22.22. Nantes, ☎ 40.48.38.88.

Weather forecast : Sud-Finistère : ☎ 98.94.00.69. Brest : ☎ 98.84.63.00. Morlaix : ☎ 98.88.34.04. **Ille-et-Vilaine :** ☎ 99.31.90.00. Nantes : ☎ 40.75.86.87. **Morbihan :** ☎ 97.84.83.44.

Rural gîtes, chambres d'hôtes and farmhouse camping : enq and reservations at the Relais départementaux : **Côtes-du-Nord,** 5, rue Baratoux, 22000 Saint-Brieuc, ☎ 96.61.82.79. **Finistère,** 5, allée Sully, 29332 Quimper Cedex, ☎ 98.95.75.30. **Ille-et-Vilaine :** *C.D.T.* Ille-et-Vilaine. **Loire-Atlantique,** 46 *bis,* rue des Hauts-Pavés, 44024 Nantes Cedex, ☎ 40.76.39.90. **Morbihan,** 11, pl. Mal-Joffre, B.P. 78, 56400 Auray, ☎ 97.56.48.12.

Holiday villages : see practical holiday information.

Camping : 1 140 sites ; listed in the *C.D.T.*

Festivals and events : end Apr, *Festival of traditional arts,* in Rennes. **Whitsun :** *Toulfoen Folk Festival,* in Quimperlé. **May :** *le mai breton,* in Saint-Brieuc. **From Jun to Sep,** *festival de La Roche-Jagu.* **Jun :** *concours de musique gallèse,* in Monterfil : *festival de Brocéliande,* in Paimpont. **Early Jul,** *festival de création bretonne,* in Rennes. **2nd Sun in Jul :** *fête des brodeuses (embroidery festival),* in Pont-l'Abbé. **Mid-Jul :** *Breton Dance Festival* in Guingamp ; *les Tombées de la Nuit,* in Rennes ; *festival des Temps Anciens,* in Monterfil. **3rd Sun in Jul :** *fête des pommiers,* in Fouesnant. **End Jul :** *grandes fêtes de Cornouaille,* in Quimper. **End Jul-mid-Aug :** *abbey festival,* in Redon. **Jul-Aug :** *Classical music Festival,* in Locronan. **Early Aug :** *Celtic festival,* in Lorient ; *theatre and dance festival,* in Hédé. **15 Aug :** *Grandes Fêtes d'Arvor,* in Vannes. **3rd Sun in Aug :** *fête des filets bleus,* in Concarneau. **End Aug-early Sep :** *fête de la jeunesse et de la mer (fete of youth and the sea),* in Dinard. **3rd Sun in Aug :** *grande fête des menhirs,* in Carnac. **In summer :** *International Festival of Arts and Popular Traditions,* at Nantes. **Nov :** *Rock music,* in Rennes.

Pardons (traditional religious feast-days → box) : 2nd Sun in May in Quintin, *Pardon Notre-Dame de Délivrance.* **End May :** Kerity-Paimpol, *Pardon Sainte-Barbe ;* Tréguier, *Pardon Saint-Yves.* **Trinity Sun :** Rumengol, *Pardon Notre-Dame de Rumengol ;* La Trinité-Porhoet, *Pardon de la Trinité.* **End Jun** in Le Faouët, *Pardon Sainte-Barbe.* **1st Sun in Jul** in Guingamp, *Pardon Notre-Dame de Bon Secours.* **2nd Sun in Jul** in Locronan, *la Troménie.* **25 and 26 Jul** in Sainte-Anne-d'Auray, *Pardon de Sainte-Anne.* **End Jul :** Guérin, *Notre-Dame du Méné Guen ;* Saint-Quay-Portrieux, *Pardon de Sainte-Anne ;* Vieux-Marché, at the chapelle des Sept-Saints, *Islamic Christian pilgrimage.* **15 Aug :** Rochefort-en-Terre, *Pardon Notre-Dame de la Tronchaye ;* Perros-Guirec, *Pardon Notre-Dame de la Clarté.* **Last Sun in Aug** in Plonevez-Porzay, *Pardon de Sainte-Anne-la-Palud.* **1st Sun in Sep** in Le Folgoet, *Pardon Notre-Dame.* **8 Sep** in Josselin, *Pardon Notre-Dame du Roncier.* **15 Sep** in Carnac, *Saint-Cornély,* Pontivy, *Notre-Dame de la Joie.* **20 Sep** in Saint-Jean-Trolimon, *Pardon Notre-Dame-Tronoën ;* Plouha, *Pardon de Kermaria-en-Isquit.*

National and nature parks : *Parc naturel régional d'Armorique,* Balaneg-Huella Saint-Éloi, 29224 Daoulas, ☎ 98.21.90.69. *Parc naturel régional de Brière,* Administrative Centre, 180, île de Fédrun, 44720 Saint-Joachim, ☎ 40.88.42.72.

Rambling and hiking : 4 500 km of marked tracks. The GR34, 37, 38 and 39 cross Brittany, along with two alternative routes on the GR341 and 347 (topoguides). *L'Association Bretonne des Relais et Itinéraires* (A.B.R.I.), 3, rue des Portes-Mordelaises, 35000 Rennes, ☎ 99.31.59.44, 10, rue Lafayette, 44000 Nantes, ☎ 40.73.91.69, and 33, rue Félix-Le-Dantec, 29200 Brest, ☎ 98.46.18.39, provide appropriate gîtes for hikers.

Riding holidays : 3 700 km network. *Association Régionale pour le Tourisme Équestre en Bretagne* (A.R.T.E.B.), 1, rue Gambetta (afternoon), 56300 Pontivy, ☎ 97.25.31.36. *Fédération des Sports Équestres* for the Finistère : M. Le Couriand, Paul Morvan, Clerguer, 56620 Pont-Scorff. *C.D.T.* at Vannes for the **Loire-Atlantique.** Caravan holidays in the parc d'Armorique and the Arrée mountains : enq *C.D.T.* Quimper.

Cycling holidays : *L.A.* **Ille-et-Vilaine ;** other enq : A.B.R.I. Rennes, ☎ 99.79.36.26. See also Brest, 33, rue Félix-Le-Dantec, ☎ 98.46.18.39, and Nantes, 3, pl. Saint-Pierre, ☎ 40.48.24.20. The *C.R.T. des Pays de la Loire* organises cycling tours in the **Loire-Atlantique** area. **Morbihan :** *Comité Départemental du Cyclotou-*

risme, rue Guillaume-le-Bartz, 56000 Vannes, ☎ 97.63.19.00.

River and canal cruises : Brittany is doted with 600 km of navigable waterways. For boat hire, enq at the *Comité de Promotion Touristique des Canaux Bretons et Voies Navigables de l'Ouest,* 3, rue des Portes-Mordelaises, 35000 Rennes, ☎ 99.79.36.26.

Handicraft courses : a vast selection, including cookery (château-hôtel de Coatguelen, at Pléhédel : see Paimpol).

Tennis : enq ℹ

Golf : Côtes-du-Nord : Saint-Quay-Portrieux, *golf des Ajoncs d'Or* (18 holes) ; Perros-Guirec (18 holes) ; Pleumeur-Bodou, *golf Saint-Samson* (18 holes) ; Sables-d'Or-Frehel, *golf des Sables-d'Or-les-Pins* (9 holes) ; Saint-Cast-Le Guildo, *golf de Pen-Guen* (9 holes). **Finistère :** La Forêt-Fouesnant, *golf de Quimper et de Cornouaille* (9 holes) ; Landernau, *golf de Lann-Rohou* (18 holes). **Ille-et-Vilaine :** Dinard, *golf de Dinard* (18 holes) ; Rennes, *golf Saint-Jacques-de-la-Lande* (9 holes). **Morbihan :** Ploërmel, *golf Saint-Laurent* (18 holes). **Loire-Atlantique :** La Baule, *golf La Baule-Saint-André-les-Eaux* (18 holes) ; *de la Bretesche* (18 holes).

Sailing : list of sailing clubs and schools at the *Ligue Haute-Bretagne* (for the **Ille-et-Vilaine** and Côtes-du-Nord), 1, rue des Fours-à-Chaux, 35260 Cancale, and at the *Ligue Armor* (for **Finistère**), 2, cours de la Bôve, 56100 Lorient ; *C.D.T.* Nantes (for the **Loire-Atlantique**) and Société anonyme de Gestion du Morbihan, 26, rue Jeanne-d'Arc, 56000 Vannes, ☎ 97.63.42.00.

Wind-surfing : Instructional courses at La Baule ; reservations, *L.A.* in Nantes.

Water skiing : *Ligue de Bretagne de Ski Nautique,* B.P. 99, 49303 Cholet.

Scuba diving : enq at the *Comité Régional Bretagne-Normandie de la Fédération Française d'Étude des Sports sous-marins,* 78, rue Ferdinand-Buisson, 44600 Saint Nazaire ; same address for scuba fishing.

Canoeing : fully-equipped aquatic sports centres throughout the navigable waterways. *Comité de Promotion Touristique des Canaux Bretons et des Voies Navigables de l'Ouest,* 3, rue des Portes-Mordelaises, 35000 Rennes Cedex, ☎ 99.79.36.26 ; in Morbihan, the *Comité Départemental de Canoë-Kayak,* 14, rue du Blavet, 56650 Lochrist, ☎ 97.36.09.05.

Hunting and shooting : enq at the *Fédérations Départementales de Chasse,* 19, rue de Brest, 22000 Saint-Brieuc, ☎ 96.33.15.92 ; 178, rue Antrain, 35000 Rennes, ☎ 99.63.20.21 ; 13, bd François-Blancho, 44005 Nantes, ☎ 40.89.59.25 ; rue Cap.-Jude, 56000 Vannes, ☎ 97.47.10.32.

River fishing : 10 000 km of rivers and canals open to the public. *Fédérations Départementales des Associations de Pêche :* **Côtes-du-Nord :** B.P. 242, 22000 Saint-Brieuc, ☎ 96.33.23.26 ; **Finistère :** 1, rue Poher, 29000 Quimper, ☎ 99.55.16.61 ; **Ille-et-Vilaine :** 149, rue d'Antrain, 35000 Rennes, ☎ 99.63.03.95 ; **Loire-Atlantique :** 80, rue Hector-Berlioz, 44005 Nantes, ☎ 40.59.38.01 ; **Morbihan :** mairie de Ploërmel, ☎ 97.63.10.92. And *Fédération des Associations de Pêche et de Pisciculture du Morbihan :* Pisciculture de Gouarnais, 56000 Saint Avétel, ☎ 97.60.70.18.

Sea fishing : enq at the *Comité Régional de Bretagne-Vendée,* Pont-Roux, Le Yaudet, 22300 Ploumiliau, ☎ 96.38.31.42.

● Towns

ANCENIS

Nantes 42, Rennes 102, Paris 342
D3-4 ✉ 44150

SNCF ☎ 40.96.21.30.

Hotel :

★★***Val de Loire*** (L.F.), rte d'Angers, ☎ 40.96.00.03. AE, DC, Euro, Visa. 30 rm Ⓟ ♨ ♘ ♿ 180. Rest. closed Sat (1 Oct-30 Apr), 60-140.

AUDIERNE

Quimper 35, Brest 75, Paris 591
A2 ✉ 29113

ℹ pl. de la Liberté, ☎ 98.70.12.20.

⛴ ferry service to the île de Sein, ☎ 98.70.13.78.

Hotels :

● ★★★***Goyen,*** pl. Jean-Simon, ☎ 98.70.08.88, Tx 940195. 34 rm ⚘ Ⓟ closed 15 Nov-15 Dec, 260. Rest. ● ♦♦♦ closed Mon (ex Jul, Aug and nat hols). Spec : *délice de sole au sancerre, civet de homard,* 320-450.

★★***Roi Gradlon*** (L.F.), 3, av. M.-Brusq, ☎ 98.70.04.51. Visa. 20 rm Ⓟ ♨ closed Dec-Feb, 180. Rest. ✂ 120-210.

Near the pointe du Raz, 14 km W, on the D784 :
★★***Baie des Trépassés*** (L.F.), ☎ 98.70.61.34. 27 rm ⚘ Ⓟ ♘ closed 15 Nov-1 Mar, 210. Rest. ⚘ ♿ On the sea-side, a good spot for sea produce, 60-160.

⛺ ★★*Kerhuon* (50 p.), ☎ 98.70.10.91 ; ★★*Kérivoas* (20 empl.), ☎ 98.70.26.86.

Restaurants :

♦ ***Dunes,*** 3, rue Ampère, ☎ 98.70.01.19. With 22 rm Ⓟ ♨ closed Mon low season, 120-210.

Cleden-Cap Sizun, 10 km W :
L'Étrave, pl. de l'Église, ☎ 98.70.66.87. closed 30 Sep-20 Mar, Wed. Lobster and delicious fish, low prices.

AURAY

Vannes 18, Quimper 98, Paris 474
C3 ✉ 56400

ℹ pl. de la République, B.P. 403, ☎ 97.24.09.75.

SNCF ☎ 97.24.02.02., 97.24.00.06.

⛴ launch service to Locmariaquer, Port-Navalo, *Green launches* at the port.

Car-hire : *Budget* train + auto, at the station, ☎ 97.24.02.02.

Hotels :

★***Gare et Voyageurs,*** av. de Gaulle, ☎ 97.24.00.18. AE, Visa. 18 rm Ⓟ ♨ closed Oct-15 Nov, 180. Rest. ♿ closed Tue low season, 80-130.

Sainte-Anne-d'Auray, 6 km NE :
★★***Myriam,*** 37, rue du Parc, ☎ 97.57.70.44. 30 rm Ⓟ ♨ ♿ closed 15 Sep-Easter, Mon eve and Tue (May-Jun), 180.

La BAULE

Nantes 74, Rennes 136, Paris 445
C4 ✉ 44500

ℹ 9, pl. de la Victoire, ☎ 40.24.34.44.

✈ Saint-Nazaire-Montoir, 22 km E, ☎ 40.22.35.06.

SNCF ☎ 40.60.13.20., 40.60.01.97.

pl. de la Victoire, ☎ 40.66.50.50.

Car-hire : *Budget* train + auto, at the S.N.C.F. railway station, ☎ 40.60.22.37.

Hotels :
★★★★(L) ***L'Hermitage,*** esplanade F.-André, ☎ 40.60.37.00, Tx 710510. AE, DC, Visa. 230 rm P closed Oct-Apr, 1 500. Rest. ● ♦♦♦ The lively Yves le Haour and the competent François Sierra are associated for your pleasure : *tartare de bar au jus de truffes,* 120-210.
★★★★ (L) ***Castel Marie-Louise*** [Relais et Châteaux], espl. Casino, ☎ 40.60.20.60, Tx 700408. AE, DC, Euro, Visa. 31 rm P closed Jan, 1 050. Rest. ● ♦♦ The ocean in your plate : *gelée de raie à l'oseille, marinière de palourdes et de fraise de veau,* 115-220.
★★★***Alizés*** (L.F.), 10, av. de Rhuys, ☎ 40.60.34.86, Tx 710050. AE, DC, Visa. 32 rm P 280. Rest. ♦ open only Jul-Aug, 120-210.
★★***Palmeraie*** (L.F.), 7, allée des Cormorans, ☎ 40.60.24.41. AE, DC, Euro, Visa. 23 rm closed Oct-Apr, 250. Rest. ♦ 90-110.
★★***Pavillon des Fleurs,*** 13, av. Pierre-Percée, ☎ 40.60.20.86. Visa. 27 rm P closed Nov-Mar, 180. Rest. ♦ 80-130.
★★***Concorde,*** 1, av. Concorde, ☎ 40.60.23.09. 42 rm P closed 20 Oct-25 Mar, 285.

Le Pouliguen, ✉ 44510, 3 km W :
★***Beau Rivage*** (L.F.), 11, rue Jules-Benoît, ☎ 40.42.31.61. 54 rm P closed Sep-Easter, 180. Rest. 80-130.

⛺ ★★★★*Pré du Château Careil,* Guérande road (43 pl.), ☎ 40.60.22.99 ; ★★★*Caravaning l'Éden* (105 pl.), ☎ 40.60.03.23 ; ★★*Ajoncs d'Or* (200 pl.), ☎ 40.60.33.29. Pornichet : ★★★*Bugeau* (170 pl.), ☎ 40.61.02.02 ; *Bel Air* (230 pl.), ☎ 40.61.10.78 ; *Forges* (170 pl.), ☎ 40.61.18.84. Le Pouliguen : ★★*Mouettes* (230 pl.), ☎ 40.42.10.29 ; ★*Clein,* rue de Kerlis (100 pl.), ☎ 40.42.10.29.

Restaurants :
♦♦♦ ***Espadon,*** 2, av. de la Plage, 5th floor of the résidence du Golfe, ☎ 40.60.05.63. AE, DC, Visa P Panoramic dining-room. Spec : *cassolette de belons, rougets au basilic ou à l'émincé de concombre,* 220-310.
♦ ***Pergola,*** 147, av. des Lilas, ☎ 40.24.57.61. AE, Visa. closed 1 Jan-28 Feb and Wed, 80-120.
♦ ***Ankou,*** 38, av. de l'Étoile , ☎ 40.60.22.47. AE, Visa closed Jan, Mon and Tue noon (low season), 150-210.

Casino, ☎ 40.60.20.23 P closed 15 Sep-1 Jun. Rest. ♦♦ ***le Bistingo,*** closed noon, 220-310. Rest. ♦ ***la Trattoria,*** 210-300.

BELLE-ÎLE-EN-MER

B3-4 ✉ 56360 Le Palais

ℹ Le Palais, quai Bonnelle, ☎ 97.31.81.93.

⛴ 4 to 10 daily service according to season, 45 mn from Quiberon, ☎ 97.31.80.01 (book car passage in high season).

Hotels :
★★★★***Castel Clara*** (Relais et Châteaux), in Port-Goulphar, ☎ 97.31.84.21. AE, Visa. 47 rm and 10 apts P closed 1 Jan-15 Mar, 600. Rest. ● ♦♦ 120-210.
★★★***Cardinal,*** in Sauzon, at Cardinal Point, ☎ 97.31.61.60, Tx 730750. 85 rm P closed Oct-Apr, 650. Rest. ♦ 130-280.
★★★***Manoir de Goulphar,*** Bangor, ☎ 97.31.80.10, Tx 730750. 52 rm P closed Nov-Mar. 280. Rest. ♦ 120-210.

Youth Hostel : pointe de Taillefer, ☎ 97.31.64.28.
Restaurant :
♦ ***La Forge,*** Cosquet, route de Goulphar, ☎ 97.31.51.76. AE, Euro, Visa P closed Nov-Mar. Spec : *feuilleté de langoustines à l'anis et au basilic,* 85-150.

BÉNODET

Quimper 16, Lorient 71, Paris 556
A-B2 ✉ 29118

ℹ 51, av. de la Plage, ☎ 98.57.00.14.

⛴ daily ferry service to the Glénan islands in Jul-Aug.

Hotels :
● ★★★***Gwell-Kaer,*** 3, av. de la Plage, ☎ 98.57.04.38. Visa. 24 rm P closed 2-25 Jan and 10 days in Oct, Sun eve and Mon (low season and nat hols), 345. Rest. 70-150.
★★★***Kastel Moor,*** ☎ 98.57.05.01, Tx 941182. 22 rm P closed Nov-Easter, 260.
★★★***Ker Moor,*** ☎ 98.57.04.48. 70 rm P closed Oct-Easter, 260. Rest. ♦ 120-210.

Sainte-Marine, ✉ 29120 :
★***Jeanne d'Arc,*** 52, rue de la Plage, ☎ 98.56.32.70. 8 rm P 180. Rest. ♦ Spec : *panaché de poissons à l'émincé de choux, beurre de poivrons rouges, sole à l'effiloché de poireaux et son beurre d'ortie,* 120-210.

⛺ ★★★★*Letty* (500 pl.), ☎ 98.57.04.69 ; ★★★*Pointe Saint-Gilles* (476 pl.), ☎ 98.57.05.37 ; ★★*Plage* (300 pl.), ☎ 98.57.00.55.

Île de BREHAT

C1 ✉ 22870 Paimpol

⛴ from Arcouest Point, in 10 mins ; numerous daily trips (at approx half-hourly intervals in summer), ☎ 96.20.82.30 ; from Saint-Quay-Portrieux in 1 hr 30 (Jun-Sep), ☎ 96.20.00.66.

Hotel :
★★***Vieille Auberge*** (L.F.), Le Bourg, ☎ 96.20.00.24. 15 rm closed Nov-Easter, 100. Rest. (pension).

BREST

Quimper 71, Rennes 244, Paris 597
A2 ✉ 29200

ℹ pl. du Gal-Leclerc (C2), ☎ 98.44.24.96.

✈ Guipavas, 9 km NE, ☎ 98.84.61.49.

⛴ Daily service with Ouessant, in 2 hours, ☎ 98.80.24.68. Cruises and excursions. Camaret, les Tas de Pois and l'île de Sein, le Conquet, the Molène and d'Ouessan islands.

SNCF (C2), ☎ 98.80.50.50., 98.80.71.02.

pl. Franklin-Roosevelt (C2-3), ☎ 98.44.50.24.

Car-hire : *Budget* train + auto : at the S.N.C.F. railway station, ☎ 98.80.50.50, and 8, quai de la Douane, ☎ 98.44.70.60.

Hotels :
★★★***Continental,*** square de la Tour-d'Auvergne (B-C2), ☎ 98.80.50.40, Tx 940575. AE, DC, Visa. 75 rm ♿ 260. Rest. ♦ closed Sat noon and Sun, 80-130.
★★***Bellevue,*** 53, rue Victor-Hugo (C2), ☎ 98.80.51.78. 26 rm ♿ 180.

Restaurants :
♦♦♦ ***Frère Jacques,*** 15 *bis,* rue de Lyon, ☎ 98.44.38.65. AE, Euro. closed 29 Jul-11 Aug, Sat noon, Sun. Spec : *blanquette de coquilles Saint-Jacques au cresson, bisque de tourteaux à la crème,* 80-200.
♦♦ ***Poulbot,*** 26, rue d'Aiguillon, ☎ 98.44.19.08. AE, DC, Euro, Visa ♿ closed end Aug-early Sep, 1 week Feb, Sat noon and Sun, 70-185.

Youth hostel : Gaston-Ramon, Queliverzan, ☎ 98.45.07.60.

BRIGNOGAN-PLAGE

Brest 37, Quimper 87, Paris 594
A1 ⊠ 29238

ℹ rue Gal-de-Gaulle, ☎ 98.83.41.08.

Hotels :
● ★★***Castel Régis,*** pl. du Garo, ☎ 98.83.40.22. Euro. 10 rm Ⓟ ♿ closed Oct-Easter, 260. Rest. ♦♦ ♿ closed Wed noon. Light, classic cuisine which makes full use of all fish and seafood from the area, 120-210.

Plouidern, ⊠ 29260 Lesnevin, 6 km S par D770
★★***Butte,*** 10, rue de la Mer, ☎ 98.83.10.54. DC, Visa. 15 rm Ⓟ closed 1 Jan-8 Feb, Sun eve and Mon, 180. Rest. ♿ 120-210.

⛺ ★★*Keravezan* (250 pl.), ☎ 98.83.41.65.

BUBRY

Lorient 34, Vannes 53, Paris 481
18 km NW of Baud, C3 ⊠ 56310

Hotel :
★★***Coët Diquel,*** ☎ 97.51.70.70. Euro, Visa. 20 rm Ⓟ ♿ closed 1 Dec-15 Mar, 270. Rest. ♦ 75-150.

CAMARET-SUR-MER

Quimper 64, Brest 66, Paris 594
A2 ⊠ 29129

ℹ pl. Kléber, ☎ 98.27.93.60 (high season).

Hotels :
★★***France*** (L.F., les Hôtes bretons), at the port, ☎ 98.27.93.06. DC, Visa. 22 rm Ⓟ closed 15 Nov-1 Apr, Fri low season and school hols, 180. Rest. ♦ ♿ 120-210.

⛺ ★★★*De Lambézen* (83 pl.), ☎ 98.27.91.41.

CANCALE

Dinan 34, Avranches 59, Paris 396
D1 ⊠ 35260

ℹ rue du Port, ☎ 99.89.63.72 (high season).

Hotels :
★★***Continental*** (L.F.), at the port, ☎ 99.89.60.16. Euro, Visa. 20 rm closed 11 Nov-28 Mar, 300. Rest. ♦ closed Mon, 100-200.
★★***Pointe du Grouin*** (L.F.), ☎ 99.89.60.85. 17 rm Ⓟ closed 1 Oct-1 Apr and Tue eve, 230. Rest. ♦♦ 90-230.

Saint-Méloir-des-Ondes, ⊠ 35350, 6 km SW :
★★***De la Gare*** (L.F.), ☎ 99.89.10.46. 58 rm Ⓟ closed 15 Nov-15 Jan, 200. Rest. ● ♦♦ Countryside peace, not far from the sea. Excellent menus, reasonable prices and a priority to desserts, 120-210.

⛺ ★★★*Port-Mer* (83 pl.), ☎ 99.89.63.17 ; ★★*Bel Air* (280 pl.), ☎ 99.89.64.36 ; ★★*Pointe du Grouin* (165 pl.), ☎ 99.89.63.79.

Restaurants :
● ♦♦ ***De Bricourt,*** 1, rue Du-Guesclin, ☎ 99.89.64.76. Euro, Visa ♿ closed Tue, Wed, Dec-Mar. Local seafood - oysters and shellfish - have prime place on the menu, along with the salt-meadow mutton and lamb specialities. Advance booking indispensable, 100-210.
♦ ***Cancalais,*** 12, quai Gambetta, ☎ 99.89.61.93. Euro, Visa ♿ closed 8-31 Jan and 15-30 Nov, 130.

CARANTEC

Morlaix 15, Brest 71, Paris 553
10 km SE of St-Pol-de-Léon
B1 ⊠ 29226

ℹ pl. Ch.-de-Gaulle, ☎ 98.67.00.43.

Hotel :
★***La Falaise,*** Kélenn beach, ☎ 98.67.00.53. Euro. 26 rm Ⓟ closed 18 Sep-Easter, 130. Rest. ♦ 55-105.

⛺ ★★★*Mouettes* (140 pl.), ☎ 98.67.02.46 ; ★★*Méneyer* (58 pl.), ☎ 98.67.00.13.

CARHAIX-PLOUGUER

Guingamp 48, Brest 86, Paris 505
B2 ⊠ 29270

ℹ rue Brizeux, ☎ 98.93.04.42. Feb-Oct (closed Sun).

Hotel :
★★***Gradlon*** (Inter-hôtel), 12, bd de la République, ☎ 98.93.15.22. AE, DC, Euro, Visa. 44 rm Ⓟ ♿ 260. Rest. ♦ closed Sat noon and Sun eve, 80-130.

Restaurant :
♦♦ ***Auberge du Poher,*** Port-de-Carhaix, 6,5 km SW, ☎ 98.99.51.18. Euro, Visa Ⓟ ♿ closed Mon and Feb, 80-130.

CARNAC

Vannes 31, Lorient 37, Paris 487
B3 ⊠ 56340

ℹ av. des Druides, ☎ 97.52.13.52.

Hotels :
★★★★***Diana,*** 21, bd de la Plage, ☎ 97.52.05.38. Visa. 33 rm Ⓟ closed Oct-Mar, 500. Rest. ♦ ♿ 110-210.
★★***Alignements*** (L.F.), 45, rue Saint-Cornely, ☎ 97.52.06.30. 27 rm closed 22 Sep-5 May, 220. Rest. ♦ closed noon, 60-120.
★***Genêts,*** 45, av. Kermario, ☎ 97.52.11.01. 33 rm Ⓟ closed 30 Sep-29 Mar, 15 Apr-1 Jun, 230. Rest. ♿ 85-150.

See also Plouharnel.

⛺ ★★★★*Grande Métairie* (352 pl.), ☎ 97.55.71.47 ; ★★★★*Menhirs,* rte D119 (400 pl.), ☎ 97.52.94.67 ; ★★*Beaumer* (100 pl.), ☎ 97.52.93.52.

Leisure activities : Kermario Zoo.

Recommended : *Gouzer,* ☎ 97.52.07.37 (oysters).

CHÂTEAUBOURG

Rennes 21, Laval 53, Paris 330
15 km W of Vitré, D2 ⊠ 35220

SNCF ☎ 99.00.31.13.

Hotels :
★★★***Ar Milin,*** ☎ 99.00.30.91. 33 rm P ♨ ⛰ ⛳ ♿ closed 22 Dec-6 Jan. A mill in a park setting, 240. Rest. ♦♦ 120-170.
★★***Pen'Roc*** (L.F.), La Peinière, at 6 km, ☎ 99.00.33.02. 15 rm P ♨ ⛰ closed Nov, 200. Rest. closed Sun eve, 70-170.

CHÂTEAUBRIANT

Rennes 55, Nantes 70, Paris 355
D3 ✉ 44110

ℹ 40, rue du Château, ☎ 40.81.04.53.

SNCF ☎ 40.81.10.52.

Hotel :
★★★***Ferrière*** (Châteaux-hôtels, France-Accueil), rte de Nantes, ☎ 40.28.00.28. AE, DC, Euro, Visa. 25 rm ⚘ P ♨ 18thC castle in a 7 acre park, 190. Rest. ♦♦ ♿ 70-155.

CHÂTEAULIN

Quimper 29, Brest 47, Paris 551
A2 ♥ ✉ 29150

ℹ quai Cosmao (high season), ☎ 98.86.02.11.

SNCF ☎ 98.86.00.52.

Hotels :
★★***Bon Accueil*** (L.F.), Port-Launay, 2 km, ☎ 98.86.15.77. Euro, Visa. 59 rm ⚘ P ♨ ≈ ♿ closed Jan, Sun eve and Mon, 200. Rest. ♦ closed Mon, 60-150.
Auberge des Ducs de Lin, rte de Quimper (1.5 km), ☎ 98.86.04.20. Euro. 6 rm ⚘ P ♨ ≈ closed Sun eve and Mon low season, 200. Rest. ♦ ♨ ♿ Spec : salmon, 75-190.

Plomodiern, ✉ 29127, 12 km NW by D887 and D47 :
★★***Motel Relais Pors Morvan,*** ☎ 98.81.53.23. 8 rm ♨ ⛰ ⛳ 220.

Restaurant :
Lopérec, ✉ 29117, 12.5 km N :
● ♦ *Auberge Bretonne,* 7, rue de l'École, ☎ 98.73.05.03 ♿ closed eve, Sat and Aug. Booking necessary. In a new style Brittany setting, Marie Avan cooks simple dishes, fresh fish, meat with delicious buttered potatoes, home-made sorbets. Jean Avan proposes good and great wines at reasonable prices, 70-170.

CLISSON

Nantes 28, Cholet 33, Paris 377
D4 ♥ ✉ 44190

ℹ 1, pl. du Minage, ☎ 40.78.02.95.

Hotel :
★***Auberge de la Cascade,*** rte de Nantes-Poitiers, ☎ 40.78.02.41. 10 rm ⚘ P ♨ ⛰ ≈ closed 1-15 Oct, Sun eve, 140. Rest. 50-180.

⛺ ★★*Municipal* (65 pl.), ☎ 40.78.35.14.

Restaurant :
● ♦♦ ***La Bonne Auberge,*** 1, rue Olivier-de-Clisson, ☎ 40.78.01.90. Visa ♿ closed 15-28 Feb, 15-24 Aug, Sun eve, Mon, and nat hols. Good, refined cuisine, 70-170.

COMBOURG

Dinan 24, Rennes 37, Paris 369
D2 ♥ ✉ 35270

ℹ *Maison de la Lanterne,* pl. Albert Parent, ☎ 99.73.13.93.

SNCF ☎ 99.73.00.43.

Hotels :
★★***Château et Voyageurs,*** 1, pl. Chateaubriand, ☎ 99.73.00.38, Tx 740802. AE, DC, Euro, Visa. 33 rm P ♨ ♿ closed 15 Dec-20 Jan, Sun eve and Mon (low season), Mon noon (high season), 200. Rest. ♦♦ ⚘ 60-130.
★★***Lac*** (L.F.), 2, pl. Chateaubriand, ☎ 99.73.05.65. AE, DC, Euro, Visa. 30 rm ⚘ P ♨ closed 1-30 Oct, 210. Rest. closed Fri and Sun eve low season, 65-150.

CONCARNEAU

Quimper 24, Lorient 52, Paris 543
B2 ✉ 29110

ℹ pl. J.-Jaurès, ☎ 98.97.01.44.

SNCF ☎ 98.97.00.66.

Hotels :
★★★★***Belle Étoile*** (Châteaux-hôtels, Relais du Silence), Cabellou beach, ☎ 98.97.05.73. AE, DC, Euro, Visa. 29 rm ⚘ P ♨ ⛰ ⛳ closed 15 Nov-Mar, 550. Rest. ♦♦♦ Fish specialities, 150-240.
★★★***Ty Chupen Gwenn,*** 23, Sables-Blancs beach, ☎ 98.97.01.43. Visa. 15 rm ⚘ ♨ ⛰ closed 1 Dec-5 Jan, Sat eve and Sun low season, 300.
★***Bonne Auberge*** (L.F.), Cabellou beach, ☎ 98.97.04.30. 16 rm ⚘ P ♨ ⛰ closed 15 Sep-22 Jun, 180. Rest. 50-85.

Trégunc, ✉ 29128, 6 km E :
★★***Grandes Roches*** (L.F.), ☎ 98.97.62.97. 21 rm ⚘ P ♨ ⛰ closed 30 Nov-15 Jan and Mon. In an old farmhouse, 195. Rest. ♦ ≈ ♿ 55-120.

Youth hostel : pl. de la Croix, ☎ 98.97.03.47.

⛺ ★★★*Cabellou* (100 pl.), ☎ 98.97.10.40 ; ★★★*les Prés Verts* (150 pl.), ☎ 98.97.09.74 ; ★★*Lanadan* (100 pl.), ☎ 98.97.17.78 ; Trégunc : ★★★*Pendruc* (170 pl.), ☎ 98.97.66.28 ; ★*Loc'h Ven* (200 pl.), ☎ 98.97.68.00.

Restaurants :
● ♦♦♦ ***Galion,*** 15, rue Saint-Guénolé, in the Ville Close, ☎ 98.97.30.16. AE, Euro, Visa ♿ closed 18-27 Nov, end Jan-early Mar, Sun eve and Mon. A restaurant known for its fish specialities prepared by Goam'ach, 140-260.
● ♦♦ ***Douane,*** 71, av. Alain-le-Lay, ☎ 98.97.30.27. Visa ♿ closed Feb and Sun. Fish arrives directly from the port to Mr. Peron who cooks with talent and competence, 120-210.
♦♦***Coquille,*** 1, rue de Moros, ☎ 98.97.08.52. AE, Euro, Visa ⚘ ♿ closed 20 Dec-20 Jan, Sun eve and Mon, 70-180.

Le CONQUET

Brest 24, Morlaix 84, Paris 536
4 km N of Saint-Mathieu Point, A2
✉ 29217

Hotel :
★★***Pointe Sainte-Barbe,*** ☎ 98.89.00.26. DC, Euro, Visa. 33 rm ⚘ over the sea P ⛰ closed Jan, 235. Rest. ♦ ≈ closed Mon, 65-200.

⛺ ★★*Presqu'île de Kermorvan* (66 pl.), ☎ 98.89.01.64 ; ★★*le Theven* (300 pl.), ☎ 98.89.06.90.

Le CROISIC

Vannes 75, Nantes 84, Paris 455
C4 ✉ 44490

ℹ pl. de la Gare.
SNCF ☎ 40.23.00.68.

Hotel :
★★***Nids*** (L.F.), 83, bd Gal-Leclerc, Port-Lin, ☎ 40.23.00.63. Visa. 28 rm ⚘ ♨ ⛰ ♿ closed Oct-Mar, 190. Rest. ♦ 60-160.

⛺ ★★*Océan* (260 pl.), ☎ 40.23.07.69; ★★*Stella Maris,* Castouillet beach (185 pl.), ☎ 40.23.03.71; ★★*Paradis,* Castouillet beach (100 pl.), ☎ 40.23.07.89; Batz-sur-Mer: ★★★*de la Govelle* (50 pl.), ☎ 40.23.91.63; ★★*Municipal* (400 pl.), ☎ 40.23.91.71.

Restaurant:
♦ ***Bretagne,*** 11, quai de la Petite-Chambre, at the port, ☎ 40.23.00.51. Visa ♿ closed Nov-Feb and Tue eve, Wed, 120-210.

CROZON-MORGAT

Quimper 55, Brest 57, Paris 585
A2 ✉ 29160

ℹ bd de la Plage, Morgat (high season), ☎ 98.27.07.92 and 98.27.21.65.

Hotels:
★★***Moderne*** (L.F.), 61, rue Alsace-Lorraine, ☎ 98.27.00.10. Euro, Visa. 34 rm Ⓟ ♨ 200. Rest. ♦ 55-130.

Le Frêt, 5.5 km:
★★***Hostellerie de la Mer,*** ☎ 98.27.61.90. Visa. 26 rm ⚘ ♨ ⚘ closed Oct-Mar, 220. Rest. ♦ ⚘ ♿ 80-215.

⛺ ★★★*Plage de Goulien* (90 pl.), ☎ 98.27.17.10; ★★*Pen Ar Menez* (200 pl.), ☎ 98.27.12.36.

Restaurant:
● ♦♦ ***Le Roof,*** bd de la France-Libre, ☎ 98.27.08.40. closed 6-11 Nov and Mon low season. A boat-style decor, and excellent fish specialities: *pavé de lotte au concombre, turbot grillé au beurre blanc,* 120-210.

DINAN

Rennes 51, Avranches 67, Paris 393
D2 ✉ 22100

ℹ *Maison du Tourisme* (hôtel Keratry), 6, rue de l'Horloge (B2), ☎ 98.39.75.40.

✈ Dinard-Pleurtuit, 16 km N, ☎ 99.46.18.46.

⛴ Dinan-Dinard launch crossing (over the Rance), ☎ 99.46.10.45 and 96.39.18.04 (daily during high season).

SNCF ☎ 96.39.22.39., 96.39.00.78.

🚌 pl. Ducros (B1).

Hotels:
● ★★★***Avaugour*** (L.F.), 1, pl. du Champ-Clos (B2), ☎ 96.39.07.49, Tx 950415. AE, DC, Euro, Visa. 27 rm ♨ ♿ 260. Rest. ♦♦ ♿ Flower garden above the ramparts. Good cooking served by a young and efficient team, 120-210.
★★***Marguerite*** (L.F.), 29, pl. Du-Guesclin (B2), ☎ 96.39.47.65. AE, DC, Euro, Visa. 19 rm. closed Jan, Sun eve and Mon (low season), 200. Rest. ♦♦ 60-170.

Youth hostel: Moulin de Méen, vallée de la Fontaine-des-Eaux, ☎ 96.39.10.83.

Restaurant:
♦♦ ***Caravelle,*** 14, pl. Duclos (B1), ☎ 96.39.00.11. AE, DC ♿ closed Oct-Whitsun and Wed low season. Behind the plain façade hides a good restaurant, 110-250.

Farmhouse-inn: Trevron, 10 km on the D78, ☎ 96.83.56.89. Spec: *canard aux navets* and *potée campagnarde.*

Handicrafts: numerous workshops, rue du Jerzual.

Crêperie:
Des Artisans, 6, rue du Petit-Fat (C1), ☎ 96.39.44.10.

DINARD

Rennes 72, Saint-Brieuc 68, Paris 413
D1 ✉ 35800

ℹ 2, bd Féart, ☎ 99.46.10.18.

✈ Dinard-Pleurtruit, 7 km S, ☎ 99.46.18.46.

⛴ Dinard-Saint-Malo launch service. Departure point for the Chausey Islands, Cape Fréhel, Bréhat Island, the Channel Islands: *Vedettes Blanches, Vedettes Vertes,* ☎ 99.46.10.45.

Hotels:
★★★★***Grand Hôtel,*** 46, av. George-V (C2), ☎ 99.46.10.28, Tx 740522. AE, DC, Euro, Visa. 100 rm ⚘ Ⓟ ♨ ♿ closed Nov-Easter, 700. Rest. ♦♦ ⚘ 140-240.
★★★★***Reine Hortense,*** 19, rue de la Malouine (B1), ☎ 99.46.54.31. AE, DC, Visa. 10 rm ⚘ Ⓟ ♨ ⚘ closed 15 Nov-1 Apr, 700.
★★***Vieux Manoir,*** 21, rue Gardiner, ☎ 99.46.14.69. AE, DC, Euro, Visa. 26 rm Ⓟ ♨ ⚘ ⚘ ♿ closed 15 Oct-1 Apr, 280.
★***Sables*** (L.F.), pl. du Calvaire, ☎ 99.46.18.10. 42 rm Ⓟ ♨ ⚘ ♿ closed 15 Oct-1 Apr, 160. Rest. ♦ 55-80.

⛺ ★★★★*La Ville Mauny* (174 pl.) ☎ 99.46.94.73; ★★★★*Prieuré* (100 pl.), ☎ 99.46.20.04.

Restaurants:
La Gougeonnais, ✉ 35780 La Richardais:
♦♦ *Le Petit Robinson,* ☎ 99.46.14.82. AE, DC, Euro, Visa. closed 15 Nov-15 Dec, 15 days in Feb, Tue eve and Wed, 70-140.
♦***Le Glacier,*** plage de l'Écluse, ☎ 99.46.54.39. Euro. ⚘ ♿ closed 1 Nov-1 Apr. A good choice of grilled meat and excellent ice-creams, 80-130.

DOL-DE-BRETAGNE

Saint-Malo 24, Rennes 54, Paris 373
D1-2 ✉ 35120

ℹ hôtel de ville, ☎ 99.48.15.37.

SNCF ☎ 99.48.00.86.

Hotel:
★★***Le Logis de la Bresche-Arthur,*** 36, bd Deminiac, ☎ 99.48.01.44. AE, DC, Euro, Visa. 24 rm Ⓟ ♨ ♿ closed 1 Nov-1 Dec, 210. Rest. ♦ 65-140.

⛺ ★★*Municipal* (66 pl.), ☎ 99.48.14.68.

DOUARNENEZ

Quimper 22, Brest 74, Paris 578
A2 ✉ 29100

ℹ rue du Dr-Mével, ☎ 98.92.13.35. closed Sun. Guided tour during high season.

✈ Quimper-Pluguffan, 21 km SE, ☎ 98.94.01.28.

SNCF ☎ 98.92.00.88.

Hotels:
★★***Auberge de Kerveoc'h*** (L.F.), rte de Kerveoc'h, ☎ 98.92.07.58. Visa. 14 rm Ⓟ ♨ closed Nov-Mar (ex school hols), 180. Rest. ♦ ♿ 80-130.
★★***Grand Hôtel de la Plage,*** Tréboul, ☎ 98.74.00.21. 102 rm ⚘ Ⓟ ♨ ♿ closed 2 Nov-14 Mar. Private beach, 180 (half board only). Rest. ♦ ⚘ ♿ 80-130.

⛺ ★★*Ferme de Kerleyou* (70 pl.), ☎ 98.74.03.52.

ERDEVEN

Lorient 28, Vannes 32, Paris 488
15 km NW of Carnac, B3 ✉ 56410 Etel

Hotels :
● ★★★★***Château de Keraveon*** (Châteaux-hôtels), 1.5 km on D105, NW, ☎ 97.55.34.14, 20 rm P 18thC castle. closed 15 Sep-Apr, 640. Rest. ♦♦♦ 160-300.
★★***Auberge du Sous-Bois*** (L.F., France-Accueil), rte du Pont-Lorois, ☎ 97.55.34.31, 22 rm P ♿ closed 15 Oct-1 Apr, 180. Rest. ♦ 120-210.

⛺ ★★*Les Sept Saints* (200 pl.), ☎ 97.55.52.65.

Le FAOU

Brest 30, Quimper 41, Paris 562
2 km W of Rumengol, A2 ✉ 29142

ℹ 10, rue du Gal-de-Gaulle, ☎ 98.81.90.44.

Hotel :
★★***Relais de la Place,*** 7, pl. de la Mairie, ☎ 98.81.91.19. Euro. 38 rm closed 15 Sep-15 Oct and 1-10 May, Fri eve and Sat low season, 180. Rest. ♦ ♿ Spec : seafood, 120-210.

Le FAOUËT

Lorient 40, Quimper 51, Paris 508
B2 ✉ 56320

ℹ ☎ 97.23.08.37.

Hotel :
★***Croix d'Or,*** 9, pl. Bellanger, ☎ 97.23.07.33. Euro. 16 rm P closed 17 Dec-15 Jan, Sat low season, 100. Rest. ♿ 80-130.

La FORÊT-FOUESNANT

Quimper 16, Lorient 55, Paris 546
7 km NE of Concarneau, B2 ✉ 29133

ℹ 2, rue du Port, ☎ 98.56.94.09 (high season) and 98.56.96.57 (low season).

Hotels :
● ★★★★***Manoir du Stang*** (Châteaux-hôtels), at 1.5 km N on the D783, ☎ 98.56.97.37. 28 rm P ♿ closed 20 Sep-10 May. A 16thC mansion, beautifully furnished in a nice country setting with a park and a pool, 450. Rest. ♦♦♦ 210-300.
★★***Espérance*** (L.F.), ☎ 98.56.96.58. 30 rm P closed 10 Oct-Apr, 170. Pension in high season. Rest. ♦ 50-140.

⛺ ★★★★*Saint-Laurent,* at Kerléven (300 pl.), ☎ 98.56.97.65 ; ★★★*Pen-ar-Steir* (103 pl.), ☎ 98.56.97.75 ; ★★*Kerantérec* (210 pl.), ☎ 98.56.98.11 ; ★★*Saules* (110 pl.), ☎ 98.56.98.57.

FOUESNANT

Quimper 15, Lorient 59, Paris 549
10 km NW of Concarneau, B2 ✉ 29170

ℹ rue Kérourgué, ☎ 98.56.00.93 (high season).

Hotels :
★★***Pointe de Mousterlin*** (L.F.), ☎ 98.56.04.12. 48 rm P closed 21 Sep-26 May, 200. Rest. ♦♦ 60-155.
★***Armorique*** (L.F.), 33, rue de Cornouaille, ☎ 98.56.00.19. Euro. 14 rm P closed Oct-Apr and Mon, 210. Rest. ♦ 60-105.

Beg-Meil, 6 km S :
★★***Thalamot*** (L.F.), 4, le Chemin-Creux, ☎ 98.94.97.38. AE, Euro, Visa. 35 rm closed Oct-May, 180. Rest. 80-130.

⛺ ★★★*Grand Large,* Mousterlin (300 pl.), ☎ 98.56.04.06.

Restaurant :
♦♦***L'Huîtrière,*** 2.5 km on the Saint-Évarzec road, ☎ 98.56.06.62 P ♿ closed 1 Aug-1 Jul. Eve only. Spec : lobster, seafood, 115-300.

FOUGÈRES

Rennes 48, Laval 48, Paris 322
D2 ✉ 35300

ℹ pl. A.-Briand, ☎ 99.94.12.20.

SNCF ☎ 99.99.01.40.

Hotels :
★★***Mainotel*** (Beauce), rte de Paris, N12, ☎ 99.99.81.55, Tx 730956. Visa. 50 rm P ♿ 180. Rest. ♦ closed Sun eve, 120-210.
★***Commerce*** (L.F.), pl. du Grand-Marché, ☎ 99.94.40.40. Visa. 23 rm P closed Christmas and Sun low season, 180. Rest. ♦ ♿ 80-130.

Louvigné-du-Désert, ✉ 35420, 16 km N :
★★***Manoir*** (L.F., France-Accueil), pl. Ch-de-Gaulle, ☎ 99.98.53.40. 20 rm P ♿ closed 15 Feb-1 Mar and Mon (low season). Rest. closed Sun eve and Mon (low season).

Youth hostel : 11, rue Beaumanoir, ☎ 99.99.22.06.

⛺ ★★★*Municipal* (90 pl.), ☎ 99.99.40.81 ; ★★*le Relais Breton* (55 pl.), ☎ 99.99.27.70.

Recommended : *maison des Artisans d'Art,* rue de la Fourchette, 7 Jun-15 Sep, 9-12 and 2-7.

GOUAREC

Pontivy 28, Loudéac 37, Paris 474
12 km E of Rostrehen, B2 ✉ 22570

Hotel :
★★***Blavet*** (L.F.), RN164 *bis,* ☎ 96.24.90.03. 15 rm P closed 22-29 Dec, 3 Feb-3 Mar, Sun eve and Mon ex Jul-Aug. Country-style furniture, 140. Rest. ♦♦ 50-130.

⛺ ★★★*Municipal* (100 pl.), ☎ 96.24.90.22.

Île de GROIX

B3 ✉ 56590

ℹ 4, rue Gal-de-Gaulle, ☎ 97.05.81.75.

⛴ several trips daily between Lorient and Port-Tudy (45 min crossing). Bookings indispensable for motorists in summer, ☎ 97.21.03.97.

Hotel :
★★***Ty Mad,*** Port-Tudy, ☎ 97.05.80.19. Visa. 12 rm P closed Nov-Mar ex Christmas hols, 180. Rest. ♿ 120-210.

Youth hostel : batterie du Méné, ☎ 97.21.41.87.

⛺ ★★★*Les Sables Rouges* (120 pl.), ☎ 97.05.81.32 ; ★*Fort du Méné* (45 pl.), ☎ 97.05.80.15.

GUÉRANDE

Vannes 65, Nantes 77, Paris 450
C3-4 ✉ 44350

Hotel :
★★***Roc Maria,*** 1, rue des Halles, ☎ 40.24.90.51. Visa. 9 rm closed Nov-Mar, 15thC dwelling, 180.

Restaurants :
♦♦ ***La Collégiale,*** 63, fg Bizienne, ☎ 40.24.97.29. AE, DC. ♿ closed 1 week Xmas, Feb, Tue and Wed noon, 170-250.
♦ ***Le Chat Botté,*** 7, fg Bizienne, ☎ 40.24.93.06., 80-130.

GUIDEL

Lorient 12, Vannes 68, Paris 504
12 km S of Quimperlé, B2-3 ⊠ 56520

ℹ mairie, ☎ 97.65.98.05.

Hotels :
★★★***Châtaigneraie,*** ☎ 97.65.99.93, 10 rm ⁂ P ⁂ ⁂ ⁂ ♿ 250.
★★***Fusils de Palmero,*** on the rte de Moelan-sur-Mer, ☎ 97.65.98.02. Visa. 8 rm P ⁂ In a pine forest, 180.

⛺ ★★*Bas Pouldu* (265 pl.), ☎ 97.65.98.05.

GUINGAMP

Saint-Brieuc 31, Morlaix 53, Paris 484
B1 ⊠ 22200

ℹ pl. du Vally, B.P. 29, ☎ 96.43.73.89.

SNCF ☎ 96.43.70.53.

Car-hire : *Budget* train + auto, at the S.N.C.F. station, ☎ 96.43.89.48.

Hotels :
★★***Le Goéland,*** rte de Corlay, ☎ 96.21.09.41. Visa. 28 rm P ⁂ ⁂ ♿ closed 20 Dec-5 Jan, 155.

Louargat, ⊠ 22450, 14 km O by ancient RN12 :
★★***Manoir du Cleuziou,*** ☎ 96.43.14.90, 25 rm P ⁂ ⁂ ⁂ ⁂ ♿ closed 15 Nov-15 Mar, 260. Rest. ● ♦♦ In a 17thC manoir, A. Le Rest proposes you his excellent cuisine : *salade de homard au basilic, soupière de St-Jacques et langoustines,* 120-210.

Farmhouse gîte : *E. et G. Page,* 10 km (5 pers.), fishing.

Youth hostel : Centre d'hébergement du Vally, 7 et 9, pl. du Vally, ☎ 96.44.19.21.

Events : Fêtes de la Saint-Loup (Breton dances), 3rd week of Aug.

HÉDÉ

Rennes 23, Dinan 29, Paris 371
15 km S of Combourg, D2 ⊠ 35630

Hotels :
★★***Hostellerie du Vieux Moulin*** (L.F.), ☎ 99.45.45.70. DC, Visa. 14 rm P ⁂ closed 15 Dec-31 Jan, Sun eve and Mon, 150. Rest. ♦ 65-180.

Tinténiac, ⊠ 35190, 5 km NW :
★★***Voyageurs*** (L.F.), rue Nationale, ☎ 99.68.02.21. Euro. 16 rm P ⁂ ⁂ closed 15 Dec-15 Jan, Sun eve and Mon, 200. Rest. ⁂ ♿ 40-130.

Restaurant :
♦♦ ***La Vieille Auberge,*** RN137, ☎ 99.45.46.25. AE, DC. ⁂ ♿ closed 26 Aug-4 Sep, 4 Feb-4 Mar, Sun eve, Mon, 120.

HENNEBONT

Lorient 10, Vannes 46, Paris 487
B3 ⊠ 56700

ℹ pl. du Mal-Foch, ☎ 97.36.24.52.

SNCF ☎ 97.36.20.08.

Hotels :
● ★★★★***Château de Locguénolé*** (Relais et châteaux), rte de Port-Louis, ☎ 97.76.29.40, Tx 950636. AE, DC, Euro, Visa. 38 rm ⁂ P ⁂ ⁂ ⁂ ⁂ ⁂ ♿ closed 15 Nov-1 Mar. Park on a riverside, hunting and fishing on the Blavet, a 12 rm-annex even quieter in Kernavien, ☎ 97.76.29.22, 700. Rest. ● ♦♦♦♦ Delightful service by the Sablière family who welcomes customers as they would for a private dinner. Refined cuisine by Michel Gaudin, light sauces, fresh fish. Excellent desserts, nice cellar, 250-450.

★★***Auberge du Toul Douar*** (L.F.), ☎ 97.36.24.04. Visa. 32 rm P ⁂ ⁂ closed 2 weeks in Feb, Fri eve, Sun eve, Mon noon (1 Nov-1 Apr), 100. Rest. ♿ 120-210.

⛺ *Blavet* (60 pl.), ☎ 97.36.24.09.

Recommended : Kervignac, 6 km S, *crêperie Hent Er Mor,* 30, av. des Plages, ☎ 97.65.77.17.

HUELGOAT

Morlaix 29, Quimper 56, Paris 527
B2 ⊠ 29218

ℹ 14, pl. Aristide-Briand, ☎ 98.99.72.32.

Hotels :
★***An Triskell,*** rue des Cieux, ☎ 98.99.71.85. 11 rm ⁂ P ⁂ ⁂ ⁂ ♿ closed 15 Nov-15 Dec, 130.
★***Auberge de la Truite,*** Locmaria-Berrien, ☎ 98.99.73.05. 7 rm ⁂ P ⁂ ⁂ closed Jan, Sun eve, Wed am. Breton furnishings and decor, 180. Rest. ♦ Quality and tradition, 220-310.

⛺ ★★*Fao* (100 pl.), ☎ 98.99.71.55.

Leisure activities : excursions in horse-drawn carriages, Locmaria-Berrien station.

Recommended : folklore cabaret 2.5 km from Huelgoat, *le Temps des Cerises.*

JOSSELIN

Loudéac 34, Vannes 42, Paris 422
C2 56120

ℹ pl. Congrégation, ☎ 97.22.36.43.

Hotel :
★★***Château*** (L.F.), 1, rue Gal-de-Gaulle, ☎ 97.22.20.11, 36 rm ⁂ of the castle P closed Feb and Mon, 195. Rest. ♦ 50-150.

LAMBALLE

Saint-Brieuc 21, Rennes 81, Paris 431
C2 ♥ 22400

ℹ 2, pl. Martray, ☎ 96.31.05.38 (high season).

SNCF ☎ 96.31.00.56.

Car-hire : *Budget* train + auto : at the S.N.C.F. station, ☎ 96.31.00.56.

Hotels :
★★★*Angleterre* (L.F.), 29, bd Jobert, ☎ 96.31.00.16, Tx 950750. AE, DC, Euro, Visa. 22 rm P ⁂ closed Sun eve and Mon noon (Oct-Apr ex nat hols), 200. Rest. 60-130.
● ★★***Manoir des Portes*** (Relais du Silence), La Poterie, ☎ 96.31.13.62. 16 rm P ⁂ ⁂ ♿ closed Feb and Mon, 260. Rest. ♦♦ closed Mon and Sun eve ex Jul-Aug, 120-210.

⛺ *Municipal* (35 pl.), ☎ 96.31.00.61.

Restaurant :
Ponts-Neufs, 11 km NW :
♦♦♦ ***Lorand-Barre,*** les Ponts-Neufs, ☎ 96.32.78.71. AE, DC ⁂ ⁂ closed 1 Dec-1 Mar, Sun eve and Mon. The most famous restaurant in the *brioche* region, 380.

Leisure activities : Kerrozen racecourse.

LAMPAUL-PLOUARZEL

Le Conquet 15, Brest 29, Paris 616
2 km S of Aber Ildut, A1 ⊠ 29229

Restaurant :
♦♦♦ ***Auberge du Kruguel,*** 7, rue de la Mairie, ☎ 98.84.01.66. AE, Euro P ⁂ ⁂ ⁂ closed Wed, Thu noon and Sun eve, Sep and 3 weeks Feb. Excellent fish, 130-200.

LANDERNEAU

Brest 20, Quimper 62, Paris 580
A1 ☒ 29220

ⓘ pont de Rohan, ☎ 98.85.13.09.

✈ Guipavas, 12 km W.

SNCF ☎ 98.85.00.30.

Hotel :
★★***Clos du Pontic*** (L.F.), rue du Pontic, ☎ 98.21.50.91. Visa. 32 rm P ♨ ♘ ♿ 195. Rest. ♦ closed Sat noon, Sun eve, Mon, and Christmas school hols, 70-155.

Restaurant :
Roche-Maurice, 5 km by D 712 :
♦ ***Auberge du Vieux Château,*** Grand-Place, ☎ 98.20.40.52. Euro. Eve on request only, closed 2-20 Nov, 1-20 Mar, 65-90.

LANDIVISIAU

Brest 38, Quimper 72, Paris 584
A-B1 ☒ 29230

ⓘ rue G.-Clemenceau, ☎ 98.68.03.50.

SNCF ☎ 98.68.00.04.

Hotel :
Saint-Thégonnec ☒ 29223, 12 km E on old RN 12 :
★***Auberge St-Thégonnec*** (L.F.), 6, pl. de la Mairie, ☎ 98.79.61.18. Euro, Visa. 7 rm ♨ closed Dec-1 Feb, Mon eve, Tue, 130. Rest. ● ♦♦ You must discover Alain Le Coz' excellent cuisine. Pleasant service by his wife. Varied menus with very reasonable prices. Home smoked fish, *terrine d'artichauts à la mousse d'avocats, pot-au-feu du pêcheur, homards grillés,* 70-210.

LANNION

Morlaix 38, Saint-Brieuc 63, Paris 515
B1 ☒ 22300

ⓘ quai d'Aiguillon, ☎ 96.37.07.35. closed Sat pm and Mon am during low season.

SNCF ☎ 96.37.03.01.

✈ Lannion-Servel, 3 km N, ☎ 96.37.42.92.

Car-hire : *Budget* train + auto, at the S.N.C.F. station, ☎ 96.37.04.59.

Hotels :
Ploulec'h, 8 km W :
★***Genêts d'Or,*** Le Yaudet, ☎ 96.35.24.17. Visa. 15 rm P ♨ closed 15 Jan-15 Feb, Sun eve and Mon low season, 100. Rest. ⚘ ♿ 80-130.

Saint-Michel-en-Grève, 11 km SW :
★★***Plage*** (L.F.), ☎ 96.35.74.43. 38 rm ☼ ♿ closed 3 Jan-1 Mar, 100. Rest. ♦ 80-130.

Farmhouse gîte : *J. et L. Jacob,* 4 km on the D 786 (15 pers.), ☎ 96.37.06.33.

Youth hostel : 6, rue du 73ᵉ-Territorial, ☎ 96.37.91.28. Rambling and hiking, bicycle hire.

⛺ ★★★*Beg-Léguer* (200 pl.), ☎ 96.48.75.20.

LARMOR-BADEN

Vannes 14, Lorient 50, Paris 472
On the Gulf of Morbihan, C3 ☒ 56790

Hotels :
★★***Auberge Parc Fétan*** (L.F.), ☎ 97.57.04.38. AE, DC, Euro, Visa. 23 rm P ♨ closed early Nov-25 Mar, 225. Rest. ♦ ♿ closed 15 Oct-1 Apr, 60-120.

★***Isles,*** ☎ 97.57.03.31. Visa. 19 rm ☼ P ♨ ♿ closed Oct-Apr, 120. Rest. 55-105.

⛺ ★★*Ker-Eden* (100 pl.), ☎ 97.57.05.23.

LESCONIL

Quimper 29, Lorient 87, Paris 576
8 km S of Pont-l'Abbé, A2 ☒ 29138

ⓘ rue Pasteur, ☎ 98.87.86.99.

Hotel :
★★***Plage,*** ☎ 98.87.80.05, Tx 941200. AE, DC, Euro, Visa. 30 rm ☼ P ♿ closed Nov-Feb, Sun eve and Mon low season ex weekends and nat hols. Rest. ♿ 120-210.

⛺ ★★*Dunes* (102 empl.), ☎ 98.87.81.78.

LIFFRÉ

Rennes 17, Fougères 30, Paris 352
D2 ☒ 35340

Hotel :
La Quinte, 2 km SW by N 12 :
★★***Reposée,*** ☎ 99.68.31.51. 25 rm ☼ P ♨ ♘ ⚲ ♿ In a big park, quiet and peace a few minutes from Rennes, 200. Rest. ♦ closed Mon noon, 75-210.

Restaurant :
● ♦♦♦ ***Lion d'Or,*** 8, rue de Fougères, ☎ 99.68.31.09. AE, Euro, Visa P ♨ ♘ closed Mon and Tue noon. Michel Kerever cooks at *Duc d'Enghien* but still supervises his team which has remained here and which is managed by his young son.

LOCMARIAQUER

Quiberon 31, Vannes 32, Paris 487
C3 ☒ 56740

ⓘ pl. de la Mairie, ☎ 97.57.33.05.

Hotel :
★★***Relais de Kerpenhir,*** ☎ 97.57.31.20. 16 rm ☼ P ♨ ⚘ ♿ closed Oct, 180. Rest. 80-130.

⛺ ★★*Kerpenhir* (115 pl.), ☎ 97.57.31.92 ; ★★*Locker* (65 pl.), ☎ 97.57.32.74.

LOCRONAN

Quimper 17, Brest 63, Paris 567
A2 ☒ 29136 Plogonnec

ⓘ pl. de la Mairie, ☎ 98.91.70.14 (high season).

Hotels :
★★***Fer à Cheval,*** rte du Bois-de-Nevet, 1 km SW on the D 63, ☎ 98.91.70.67. AE, DC, Euro, Visa. 35 rm P ♨ ♘ ♿ 260. Rest. ♦ ⚘ 80-120.
★***Prieuré*** (L.F.), 11, rue du Prieuré, ☎ 98.91.70.89. 15 rm P ♨ ♘ ⚘ ♿ closed 1 Oct-2 Nov and Mon low season, 200. Rest. ♦ ♿ 60-140.
See also Plonévez-Porzay.

LOCTUDY

Quimper 26, Lorient 84, Paris 574
6 km SE of Pont-l'Abbé, A2 ☒ 29125

ⓘ pl. de la Mairie, ☎ 98.87.53.78.

Hotels :
★★***Rafiot,*** on the port, ☎ 98.87.42.57. 9 rm ☼ closed Oct and Sun (low season), 180. Rest. 80-130.

⛺ ★★*Kergall* (100 pl.), ☎ 98.87.45.93 ; ★★*Mouettes* (60 pl.), ☎ 98.87.43.51.

LORIENT

Quimper 64, Rennes 147, Paris 496
B3 ⊠ 56100

ⓘ pl. Jules-Ferry (B3), ☎ 97.21.07.84.

✈ Lann-Bihoué, 6 km NW, ☎ 97.82.32.93.

⛴ regular service to Pen-Mané, Larmor, Kernével, Port-Louis and île de Groix, ☎ 97.21.03.97.

SNCF (B1), ☎ 97.21.21.04., 97.21.08.23.

🚌 bd Mal-Joffre (B2), ☎ 97.21.02.48.

Car-hire : *Budget* train + auto, at the S.N.C.F. station, ☎ 97.21.21.04.

Hotels :
★★★***Bretagne,*** 6, pl. de la Libération (B2), ☎ 97.64.34.65. AE, DC, Euro, Visa. 34 rm Ⓟ 240. Rest. ♦ ♿ closed Sun, 24 Dec-21 Jan, 80-205.
★★★***Richelieu Mapotel,*** 31, pl. Jules-Ferry (B3), ☎ 97.21.35.73. 58 rm ♿ 260. Rest. ♦ closed Sun, 120-210.
★★***Cleria,*** 27, bd Franchet-d'Esperey (B2), ☎ 97.21.04.59. AE, Visa. 36 rm Ⓟ 190.

Larmor-Plage, ⊠ 56260, 6 km S :
★★***Beau Rivage*** (L.F.), plage de Thonlhars, ☎ 97.65.50.11. AE, DC, Visa, Euro. 18 rm Ⓟ closed Nov-Dec, 180. Rest. ♦ ♿ closed Sun eve and Mon, 220-310.

⛺ ★★*Municipal* (65 pl.), ☎ 97.37.34.98 ; Larmor-Plage : ★★*Phare* (175 pl.), ☎ 97.65.53.22.

Restaurants :
♦♦ ***Pic'Assiett,*** 2, bd Franchet-d'Esperey (B2), ☎ 97.21.18.29. Visa, 60-160.
♦ ***Le Poisson d'Or,*** 1, rue Maître-Esvelin, ☎ 97.21.57.06. AE, DC, Euro, Visa Ⓟ ♿ closed 1-15 Nov and Feb school hols, Sat noon and Sun. Enjoyable cooking, 120-210.
♦ ***Les Arcades,*** 11, bd Franchet-d'Esperey, ☎ 97.21.17.42. AE, DC, Euro, Visa ♿ closed Sun, 120-210.

Guided visits : Quay, fishing port, military port, submarine base, stops at Larmor and Hennebont, info at ⓘ

Recommended : *crêperie St-Georges,* 14, rue P.-Bert, ☎ 97.64.28.11.

LOUDÉAC

Saint-Brieuc 41, Rennes 85, Paris 436
C2 ⊠ 22600

ⓘ gare routière, ☎ 96.28.00.34.

SNCF ☎ 96.28.00.29.

Hotel :
★★***Voyageurs*** (L.F.), 10, rue Cadelac, ☎ 96.28.00.47. AE, DC, Euro, Visa. 32 rm Ⓟ ♿ closed 20 Dec-10 Jan, 180. Rest. ♿ closed Fri eve and Sat (low season), 120-210.

Chambres d'hôtes : *Ferme Chauvel,* Ville-aux-Veneurs, 9 km on the G.R. 34.

Farmhouse gîtes : *Ferme de Saint-Leunec,* Merdrignac, ⊠ 22230, on the D 793. *Ferme de Loscouet-sur-Meu,* 13 km on the N 164.

⛺ ★*Municipal* (75 pl.), ☎ 96.28.14.92.

Restaurant :
♦***Auberge du Cheval Blanc,*** pl. de l'Église, ☎ 96.28.00.31. Euro, Visa ♿ closed 15 Sep-15 Oct, Mon, 45-105.

MISSILAC

Vannes 53, Nantes 61, Paris 427
8 km WNW of Pontchâteau, C3
⊠ 44160 Pontchâteau

Hotel :
★★★***Golf de la Bretesche*** (Châteaux-hôtels), ☎ 40.88.30.05 and 40.88.31.85. 27 rm Ⓟ closed Feb. Superb setting on a 13 hectare pond, 250. Rest. ♦ 120-210.

MOËLAN-SUR-MER

Lorient 25, Quimper 45, Paris 517
10 km SW of Quimperlé, B3 ⊠ 29116

ⓘ rte des Moulins, ☎ 98.96.67.28.

Hotel :
● ★★★★***Auberge des Moulins du Duc*** (Relais et châteaux), 2 km NNW, bordering the Belon, ☎ 98.39.60.73, Tx 940080. AE, DC, Euro, Visa. 27 rm Ⓟ ♿ closed 30 Nov-1 Apr, 400. Rest. ● ♦♦ In a 16thC mill, the Japanese chef Torigaï devotes his talent to great French cuisine, 120-210.

⛺ ★★*Ile Percée* (65 pl.), ☎ 98.56.98.92 ; ★★ *Tal ar Moor,* at Kerfany-les-Pins (66 pl.), ☎ 98.71.01.43.

MORLAIX

Brest 60, Quimper 82, Paris 536
B1 ⊠ 29210

ⓘ pl. des Otages (B2), ☎ 98.62.14.94. closed Sun.

✈ Morlaix-Ploujean, ☎ 98.62.16.09.

SNCF (A2), ☎ 98.88.08.88., 98.88.55.00.

🚌 (B1)

Car-hire : *Budget* train + auto, at the S.N.C.F. station, ☎ 98.88.06.43.

Hotels :
★★***Fontaine,*** Z.A. la Boissière, dual carriageway, rte de Lannion, ☎ 98.62.09.55, Visa. 35 rm Ⓟ ♿ 220.
★★***An Ty Korn,*** pl. de l'Église, ☎ 98.67.72.72. 7 rm closed 23-30 Mar, 15-30 Sep, Sun eve and Mon, ex Jul and Aug. Rest. Seafood cooked simply.

Saint-Antoine-Plouezoch, ⊠ 29252, 6 km N :
★★***Menez,*** ☎ 98.67.28.85. 10 rm Ⓟ ♿ closed 11 Sep-23 Oct, Sun eve and Mon low season, 155.

Plounerin, ⊠ 22780, 23 km E on old RN 12 :
★★***Relais de Bon Voyage,*** ☎ 98.38.61.34. 3 rm Ⓟ closed 7 Jan-2 Feb, Tue noon and Wed, 200. Rest. ● ♦♦ P. Fer — a former pupil of G. Thivard's — proposes a fine and inventive "sea" cooking, 90-230.

Youth hostel : 3, rte de Paris, ☎ 98.88.13.63.

⛺ ★*Vierge Noire,* Ploujean (35 pl.), ☎ 98.88.38.96.

Restaurants :
Plouigneau, ⊠ 29234, 10 km on N 112 :
♦♦***Auberge de Pen-ar-c'hra,*** 29, rue Nationale, ☎ 98.67.70.02. AE, Visa ♿ closed Nov, and Sun eve, Mon (low season). Spec : seafood, 80-130.

Bicycle hire : *Le Gall Henri,* 1, rue du Callac, ☎ 98.88.60.47.

Recommended : *Crêperie Grall,* 6, rue au Fil, ☎ 98.88.50.81 ; *Roc'Hellon,* at Plouigneau : huge "madeleine" cakes.

MUR-DE-BRETAGNE

Loudéac 21, Quimper 98, Paris 458
C2 ⊠ 22530

ⓘ pl. de l'Église, ☎ 96.28.51.32.

Hotel :
★★**Auberge Grand'Maison,** 1, rue Léon-Le-Cerf, ☎ 96.28.51.10. AE. 15 rm. closed 25 Sep-25 Oct, school hols Feb, Sun eve and Mon (ex Jul-Aug), 200. Rest. ● ♦♦ Excellent cuisine at reasonable prices, 130-275.

Farmhouse-inn and chambres d'hôtes : *Manoir de Saint-Peran,* Glomel, 33 km on N 164 (Rostrenen) and D 3, ☎ 96.29.60.04.

⛺ ★★**Rond-point du Lac** (133 pl.), ☎ 96.26.01.90.

MUZILLAC

Vannes 25, Nantes 85, Paris 428
25 km SE of Vannes, C3 ✉ 56190

ℹ mairie, ☎ 97.41.66.25.

Hotels :
★★**Auberge de Pen Mur** (L.F.), 20, rte de Vannes, ☎ 97.41.67.58. AE, DC, Euro. 24 rm Ⓟ 200. Rest. ♦♦ 65-175.

Pointe de Penlan, 4 km S by D 5 :
★★★★**Château de Rochevilaine** (Relais et châteaux), ☎ 97.41.69.27, Tx 950970. AE, DC, Euro, Visa. 28 rm on the coast Ⓟ ♿ closed 1-15 Nov, 400. Rest. ● ♦♦ Traditional Brittany cuisine by P. Caillaut, 220-310.

⛺ ★★*Guérandière,* Billiers, 3 km S (150 pl.), ☎ 97.41.64.83.

NANTES

Angers 89, Rennes 107, Paris 377
D4 ✉ 44000

ℹ pl. du Change (D2), ☎ 40.47.04.51.

✈ Château-Bougon, 10 km SW, ☎ 40.75.80.00. *Air France Agency,* immeuble Neptune, pl. Neptune, ☎ 40.47.12.33.

SNCF (F2), ☎ 40.50.50.50., 40.74.63.65.

Champ-de-Mars (D3).

excursions on the Endre, see ℹ

Car-hire : *Budget* train + auto, 26, Pré-Gauchet, ☎ 40.89.26.94, at the station, ☎ 40.48.09.09, and at the airport, ☎ 40.75.30.78.

Hotels :
★★★★(L) **Sofitel,** rue A.-Millerand (on Beaulieu island), ☎ 40.47.61.03. Tx 710990. AE, DC, Euro, Visa. 99 rm Ⓟ ♿, 450. Rest. ♦♦ **la Pêcherie** and **le Café de Nantes.** closed Sat, Sun and nat hols ♿ 80-250.
★★★**Astoria,** 11, rue de Richebourg (C2), ☎ 40.74.39.90. 45 rm Ⓟ ♿ closed Aug, 250.
★★★**Mapotel Central,** 4, rue du Couëdic (D3), ☎ 40.20.09.35. 143 rm ♿ 260. Rest. ♦ 120-210.
★★**Grand Hôtel de Paris,** 2, rue Boileau, ☎ 40.48.78.79. Visa. 58 rm Ⓟ ♿ closed Christmas-New Year's Day, 175.

Orvault, ✉ 44700, 7 km NW on the D42 :
★★★★**Domaine d'Orvault** (Relais et châteaux), ☎ 40.76.84.02, Tx 700450. AE, DC, Euro, Visa. 30 rm Ⓟ ♿ 450. Rest. ♦♦♦ ♿ closed Mon noon, 140-300.

Haute-Goulaine, ✉ 44115, 10 km SE :
★★★**La Lande Saint-Martin** (Inter-Hôtel), ☎ 40.06.20.06. AE, DC, Euro, Visa. 42 rm Ⓟ 220. Rest. ♦♦ ♿ closed Sun eve, 60-150.

Les Sorinières, ✉ 44400, 12 km S :
● ★★★★**Abbaye de Villeneuve** (Relais et châteaux), ☎ 40.04.40.25, Tx 710451. AE, DC, Euro, Visa. 14 rm and 3 apt Ⓟ In an 18thC Cistercian abbey, 700. Rest. ♦♦ ♿ closed Wed. Spec : *petit pâté de sandre aux concombres et ciboulette, émincé de bar aux courgettes,* 110-260.

⛺ ★★★★*Val de Cens,* on the D69 (200 pl.), ☎ 40.74.47.94.

Restaurants :
● ♦♦♦ **Maraîchers,** 21, rue Fouré (E-F3), ☎ 40.47.06.51. AE, DC, Visa. Ⓟ ♿ closed Aug and Sat noon, Sun and Mon, 220-310.
♦♦♦ **Esquinade,** 7, rue Saint-Denis (D2), ☎ 40.48.17.22. DC, Visa. ♿ closed 10-31 Jul, Sun eve, Mon and Thu eve, 120-210.
♦♦ **Relais Saint-Yves** (at the station, F2), ☎ 40.74.79.60. AE, DC, Visa. ♿ closed Sat eve and Sun, 120-210.
♦♦ **La Cigale,** 4, pl. Graslin, ☎ 40.89.34.84. Classic cuisine in a 19thC setting. Rest. 100-120.
♦♦ **Nantais,** 161, rue des Hauts-Pavés (not on the B1 map), ☎ 40.76.59.54. Visa. Ⓟ ♿ closed Aug, 1-15 Jan, eve ex Sat and Sun, 80-110.

Saint-Julien-de-Concelles, ✉ 44115, 12 km E :
♦♦ **Clémence,** at la Chebuette, ☎ 40.54.10.18. AE, DC, Visa. Ⓟ ♿ closed Sun eve and Mon. Where the tradition of "white butter", invented by C. Paraud at the end of the last century, is kept carefully, 120-210.
♦♦ **Mon Rêve,** le Bois-Moreau, rte de Champteaux, ☎ 40.03.55.50. AE, DC, Visa. Ⓟ closed Sun eve. Service in a pretty garden in nice weather. Spec : *poisson, grenouilles, écrevisses, foie de veau au vinaigre de muscadet,* 100-190.

Bellevue, ✉ 44470 Sainte-Luce-sur-Loire, 9 km E :
● ♦♦♦ **Delphin** (Joseph Delphin), ☎ 40.49.04.13. AE, DC, Euro, Visa Ⓟ closed Sun eve, Mon, 1 Aug-1 Sep, Christmas school hols. Well-indicated from Bellevue bridge, J. Delphin's small and pretty restaurant on the side of the Loire is now more accessible. Festival of fresh sea fish and riverfish : marvellous smoked salmon, *royale de homard, estouffade de turbot au muscadet, ragoût de saumon frais.* Very nice cellar, 145-300.

Saint-Jean-de-Boiseau, ✉ 44640 Le Pellerin, 15 km W by D723-D58 :
● ♦♦ **Enclos de la Cruaudière,** ☎ 40.65.66.10. Visa. Ⓟ ♿ closed Aug, Sun and Mon. G. Durand proposes varied and imaginative cooking, 200.

Farmhouse-inn : *la Barre Peinte,* Le Cellier, ✉ 44850, 20 km on the N23, ☎ 40.25.40.07. Spec *pigeonneaux au muscadet,* 35-75.

Recommended : *foie gras* and smoked salmon for sale at the Delphin Rest. *Maraîchers ; chocolats Gautier,* 9, rue Fosse, and 18 B, av. Émile-Boissier.

PAIMPOL

Saint-Brieuc 45, Morlaix 72, Paris 496
C1 ✉ 22500

ℹ pl. de la République, ☎ 96.20.83.16. closed pm low season.

SNCF ☎ 96.20.81.22.

Hotels :
● ★★★**Barbu,** Arcouest Point, ☎ 96.55.85.98. 18 rm of the sea Ⓟ ♿ closed 15 Nov-15 Feb, 300. Rest. ♦ 115-200.
★★★**Repaire de Kerroch** (Châteaux-hôtels), 29, quai Morand, ☎ 96.20.50.13. AE, DC, Euro, Visa. 7 rm ♿ closed 5 Jan-5 Feb, Mon eve and Tue, 290. Rest. ♦♦ Spec : seafood, 125-250.

Lézardrieux, ✉ 22740, 5 km W :
★★★**Relais Brenner** (Relais et châteaux), ☎ 96.20.11.05. 32 rm Ⓟ ♿ closed Nov-Feb, Sun eve, Mon (low season), 260. Rest. ♦ Spec : seafood, 220-310.

Pléhédel, ⊠ 22290 Lanvollon, 7 km S on D7 :
● ★★★***Château-hôtel de Coatguelen,*** ☎ 96.22.31.24. AE, DC, Euro, Visa. 16 rm 510. Rest. ● ♦♦♦ closed 5 Nov-1 Mar, Mon noon and Tue noon. Traditional Brittany cooking in a magnificent castle, 130-340.

Youth hostel : château de Keraoul, ☎ 96.20.83.60.

Farmhouse gîte : *ferme le Goaster,* Kerbourg Kerloury, 2 km ; sea within 800 m.

⚠ ★★*Cruckin* (100 pl.), ☎ 96.20.78.47 ; Lézardrieux : ★★*Municipal* (70 pl.), ☎ 96.20.17.22.

Restaurants :
♦♦ ***Vieille Tour,*** 13, rue de l'Église, ☎ 96.20.83.18 closed 15 Nov-10 Dec, Feb, Tue eve, Wed (ex school hols), 70-190.
♦♦ ***Cotriade,*** quai Dayot, ☎ 96.20.81.08 closed 15 Nov-15 Mar, Tue and Wed (ex Jul-Aug), 120-210.

PAIMPONT

Rennes 40, Dinan 54, Paris 390
C2 ⊠ 35380

ⓘ Office touristique de Brocéliande at the mairie of Plélan, ☎ 99.06.86.17.

Hotel :
Manoir du Tertre, 4 km on the route de Beignon, ☎ 99.07.81.02. Visa. 8 rm closed Tue. 16thC manor, 140. Rest. 70-130.

Bicycle hire : ☎ 99.06.83.03.

PERROS-GUIREC

Morlaix 50, Saint-Brieuc 74, Paris 526
B1 ⊠ 22700

ⓘ 18, pl. de l'Hôtel-de-Ville, ☎ 96.23.21.15, and pl. du Centre, Ploumanach (in summer), ☎ 96.23.06.63.

✈ Lannion-Servel, 9 km S, ☎ 96.37.42.92.

Hotels :
★★★***Grand Hôtel de Trestraou,*** bd Joseph-Le Bihan, ☎ 96.23.24.05. 70 rm 300. Rest. ♦ 60-120.
★★★***Morgane*** (L.F.), 46, av. du Casino, ☎ 96.23.22.80. AE, DC, Euro, Visa. 28 rm closed 30 Oct-1 Apr, 230. Rest. ♦ 75-150.
★★★***Printania,*** 12, rue des Bons-Enfants, ☎ 96.23.21.00. AE, DC, Euro, Visa. 39 rm closed Christmas, New Year, 280. Rest. ♦ closed Sun and Mon noon (in winter), 120-210.
★★***Feux des Îles*** (L.F.), 53, bd Clemenceau, ☎ 96.23.22.94. Visa. 15 rm closed 15 Oct-15 Nov, Sun eve and Mon (low season), 180. Rest. ♦ 120-210.
★★***France*** (Relais du Silence), 14, rue Rouzig, ☎ 96.23.20.27. 30 rm closed 15 Nov-5 Feb, Sun eve and Mon noon (low season), 200. Rest. closed 3 Nov-10 Mar, Sun eve and Mon, 80-140.
★***Ker Ys*** (L.F.), 12, rue du Mal-Foch, ☎ 96.23.22.16. Visa. 30 rm closed 1 Oct-15 Feb, Tue (low season), 100. Rest. 80-130.
★***Verger,*** pl. de la Chapelle, ☎ 96.23.23.29. 18 rm closed 15 Dec-15 Jan and Mon, 100. Rest. 80-130.

Ploumanach, ⊠ 92700, 5 km W :
● ★★***Rochers*** (L.F.), chemin de la Pointe, ☎ 96.23.23.02. AE. 16 rm, closed end Sep-end Mar. On the shore, 260. Rest. ♦ closed Wed low season, 120-210.
★***Sternes,*** ☎ 96.91.03.38. AE, Euro, Visa. 20 rm 200.
★***Roch'Hir,*** 124, rue Saint-Guirec, ☎ 96.23.23.24. 24 rm closed 15 Sep-1 May, 75.

⚠ ★★★*Claire-Fontaine,* rue du Pont-Hélé (180 pl.), ☎ 96.23.03.55 ; ★★★*Trestraou,* av. du Casino (180 pl.), ☎ 96.23.08.11 ; Ploumanach : ★★★★*Ranolien* (450 pl.), ☎ 96.23.19.41.

Restaurants :
♦♦♦ ***Homard Bleu,*** bd Le Bihan, plage de Trestraou, ☎ 96.23.24.55. Euro, Visa. closed 4 Jan-5 Feb, 60-210.
♦ ***Crémaillère,*** 13, pl. de l'Église, ☎ 96.23.22.08. AE, DC, Euro, Visa. closed 15 Feb-15 Mar and Mon. Spec : *ragoût de homard au champagne,* 75-220.

Casino de la Côte de Granit : plage de Trestraou, ☎ 96.23.02.51 (Easter-mid-Oct).

Palais des Congrès, plage de Trestraou, ☎ 96.23.21.99.

PLANCOËT

Dinan 17, Saint-Brieuc 47, Paris 410
17 km NW of Dinan, C-D2 ⊠ 22130

ⓘ ☎ 96.84.10.48.

SNCF ☎ 96.31.64.64.

Hotels :
★★★***Manoir de Vaumadeuc*** (Châteaux-hôtels), Pleven, 11 km SW, ☎ 96.84.46.17. 9 rm closed 3 Jan-15 Mar, 400. Rest. ♦♦ 120-210.
★★***Chez Crouzil*** (L.F.), ☎ 96.84.10.24. AE, DC, Euro, Visa. 14 rm closed Sun eve and Mon (1-15 Oct, 1-15 Jan), 170. Rest. ● ♦♦ Good fish. A dynamic team prepares light, inventive dishes with market-fresh produce and vegetables from the neighbouring garden, 70-205.

Farmhouse gîte : *J. Robert,* Halouze, ☎ 96.84.12.37.

PLOËRMEL

Vannes 46, Saint-Brieuc 87, Paris 410
C2-3 ⊠ 56800

ⓘ pl. Lamennais, ☎ 96.74.02.70.

SNCF ☎ 96.74.05.35.

Hotel :
★***Commerce*** (L.F.), 70, rue de la Gare, ☎ 97.74.05.32. Visa. 19 rm closed 2-22 Jan, Sun eve and Mon low season, 140. Rest. ● ♦♦ ***Reberminard.*** After Rennes, the Cruaud brothers opened their second restaurant here : *bavarois d'avocat au crabe, suprême de colin au foie gras,* 55-140.

⚠ ★★★*Belles Rives,* alongside the Étang au Duc (lake) ; aquatic sports centre (135 pl.). ☎ 97.74.01.22.

PLONÉVEZ-PORZAY

Quimper 21, Brest 62, Paris 565
4 km N of Locronan, A2 ⊠ 29127 Plomodiern

ⓘ ☎ 98.92.53.57.

Hôtels :
● ★★***Manoir de Moëllien*** (Châteaux-hôtels, Relais du Silence), ☎ 98.92.50.40. 10 rm closed Jan-21 Mar, 11 Nov-15 Dec and Wed low season. A mansion built in 1642 set in the Porzay countryside, nicely furnished rooms, pleasant cooking and good value, 220. Rest. ♦♦ 60-150.

Sainte-Anne-La-Palud, 4 km NW :
★★★★***Plage*** (Relais et châteaux), ☎ 98.92.50.12. 30 rm ⚘ Ⓟ ⛰ ⛵ ▭ ♿ closed 10 Sep-1 Apr, 580. Rest. ♦♦ ⚘ Spec : *homard, bar fumé*, 140-260.

Plomodiern, 7 km N :
★★***Pors Morvan,*** ☎ 98.81.53.23. Visa. 12 rm ⚘ Ⓟ ⛰ ⛵ ⚘ ⚘ closed Nov-Easter, 180. Crêperie ♿ closed low season ex eve and nat hols, 80-130.

⛺ ★★★*Kervel* (250 pl.), ☎ 98.92.51.54 ; ★★*Treguer-Plage* (333 pl.), ☎ 98.92.51.91 ; ★★*le Porzay* (80 pl.), ☎ 98.92.50.51 ; ★★*Sainte-Anne* (100 pl.), ☎ 98.92.51.17.

PLOUESCAT

Brest 43, Quimper 95, Paris 572
6 km NE of Folgoët, A1 ✉ 29221

ⓘ ☎ 98.69.62.18.

Hotels :
★★***La Caravelle*** (L.F.), 20, rue du Calvaire, ☎ 98.69.61.75. 16 rm ⚘ Ⓟ 180. Rest. ♦ ♿ 80-130.
★***Baie du Kernic*** (L.F.), rte de Brest, ☎ 98.69.63.41. Visa, Euro. 17 rm Ⓟ ⛰ ♿ closed 2 Nov-5 Dec, Mon low season, 100. Rest. 80-130.
★***L'Azou,*** 8 *bis*, rue du Gal-Leclerc, ☎ 98.69.60.16. 8 rm. closed 25 Sep-25 Oct, end Feb-early Mar, Tue and Wed noon, 180. Rest. ♦ ♿ A varied menu and very good wines.

⛺ ★★*Pors-Meur* (88 pl.), ☎ 98.69.63.16 ; ★*Poulfoën* (88 pl.), ☎ 98.69.81.80.

Restaurant :
Cléder, 5 km W on the D10 :
● ♦♦ ***Temps de Vivre,*** 9, rue de l'Armorique, ☎ 98.69.42.48 ⚘ closed 2-13 Feb, Wed eve (ex Jul-Aug) and Mon, 120-210.

PLOUGASTEL-DAOULAS

Brest 11, Quimper 62, Paris 593
A2 ✉ 29213

ⓘ ☎ 98.40.34.98.

Hotel :
★★***Kastel Roc'h*** (Inter-Hôtel), 29N, Roch Kerezen, ☎ 98.40.32.00 and 98.40.32.54. AE, DC, Euro, Visa. 45 rm Ⓟ ⛰ ⛵ ▭ closed Sun 12-6, 180.

⛺ ★★*Clé des Champs* (57 pl.), ☎ 98.40.36.14 ; ★★*Saint-Jean* (100 pl.), ☎ 98.40.32.90.

Restaurant :
♦♦ ***Chevalier de l'Auberlac'h,*** ☎ 98.40.54.56. AE, DC, Euro, Visa. Ⓟ ⛰ ⛵ ♿ closed 1-22 Oct, Sat noon, Sun eve and Mon, 130-280.

PLOUHARNEL

Vannes 30, Lorient 34, Paris 486
3 km NW of Carnac, B3 ✉ 56720

SNCF ☎ 97.52.01.05.

Hotel :
★★***Chez Michel*** (L.F.), av. de l'Océan, ☎ 97.52.31.05. 24 rm Ⓟ ⛰ closed 27 Nov-15 Feb and Wed low season, 185. Rest. 50-85.

⛺ ★★*Sables Blancs* (565 pl.), ☎ 97.52.00.25 ; ★★*Goélands* (80 pl.), ☎ 97.52.31.92 ; ★*Bois d'Amour* (200 pl.), ☎ 97.52.35.39.

Restaurant :
♦♦ ***Auberge de Kérank,*** rte de Quiberon, ☎ 97.52.35.36. Visa. ⚘ Ⓟ ⛰ ⛵ private beach ♿ closed Mon (winter) and Jan, 90-180.

Recommended : *Kercroc,* ☎ 97.52.01.09 (oysters).

PLOZEVET

Quimper 25, Brest 92, Paris 580
10 km SE of Audierne, A2
✉ 29143 Plogastel-Saint-Germain

ⓘ ☎ 98.58.30.73.

Hotels :
★★***Moulin de Brenizenec,*** rte de Pont-l'Abbé, towards Audierne, ☎ 98.58.30.33. 10 rm Ⓟ ⛰ closed Oct-1 Nov and 1 Nov-Easter, open only on request, 265.

Pouldreuzic, 6.5 km SE :
★★★***Ker Ansquer*** (L.F.), Labadan, 2 km on the D40, ☎ 98.54.41.83. 11 rm ⚘ Ⓟ ⛰ ⛵ ⚘ ♿ closed 30 Sep-11 May (ex Easter), 195 (1/2 pension only).
★★***Breiz-Armor,*** ☎ 98.54.40.41. 23 rm ⚘ Ⓟ ⛰ ♿ closed 2 Jan-1 Mar (open week-ends ex Jan-Feb), 180. Rest. ♦ 70-155.

⛺ ★★*Cornouaille* (100 pl.), ☎ 98.58.30.81.

PONT-AVEN

Quimper 32, Lorient 38, Paris 527
B3 ✉ 29123

ⓘ ☎ 98.05.04.70.

Hotels :

Raguenès-Plage, ✉ 29139 Névez, 12 km SW :
★★***Men Du,*** rue des Îles, ☎ 98.06.84.22. 15 rm ⚘ Ⓟ ⛰ ⛵ closed 30 Sep-Easter, 175.
★★***Chez Pierre*** (L.F.), ☎ 98.06.81.06. 23 rm Ⓟ ⛰ closed 30 Sep-Easter and Wed (Jun-Sep), 180.

Port-Manech, ✉ 29139 Névez, 13 km S :
★★***Ar Moor,*** ☎ 98.06.82.48. 36 rm ⚘ Ⓟ ⛰ closed 30 Sep-1 Apr, 230. Rest. ♦ 80-200.

⛺ ★★*Roz-Pin,* rte de Névez (600 pl.), ☎ 98.06.03.13.

Restaurants :
● ♦♦♦ ***Moulin de Rosmadec,*** alongside the Aven, ☎ 98.06.00.22 ⛰ ⚘ ♿ closed 15 Oct-15 Nov, 12 days in Feb and Wed. A classic menu with delicious seafood in a beautiful Breton restaurant, 220-310.
● ♦♦ ***La Taupinière,*** 4 km on the D783, rte de Concarneau, ☎ 98.06.03.12. AE, DC, Euro, Visa. ⚘ ♿ closed 6-16 Mar, 15 Sep-15 Oct, Mon eve and Tue. Charm and good cooking in this nice thatched cottage. Spec : *langoustines géantes grillées au feu de bois, filets de rougets,* 120-210.

See also Riec-sur-Belon.

PONTIVY

Vannes 52, Saint-Brieuc 64, Paris 460
C2 ✉ 56300

ⓘ pl. A.-Briand, ☎ 97.25.04.10 (high season).

SNCF ☎ 97.25.00.20.

Hotel :
★★***Martin*** (L.F.), 1, rue Leperdit, ☎ 97.25.02.04. Visa. 30 rm Ⓟ ⛰ closed 15 Dec-15 Jan, Sun (low season), 180. Rest. ♿ 80-130.

Saint-Nicolas-des-Eaux, ✉ 56150, 12 km SW :
★★***Vieux Moulin*** (L.F.), ☎ 97.51.81.09. 12 rm ⚘ Ⓟ ⛰ ⛵ closed Feb, Sun eve and Mon low season, 200. Rest. ♿ 60-105.

⛺ ★*Le Douric,* Toulboudou (35 pl.), ☎ 97.25.00.33.

PONT-L'ABBÉ

Quimper 20, Lorient 78, Paris 568
A2 ⊠ 29120

ℹ château, ☎ 98.87.24.44.

Hotels :
★★***Château de Kernuz*** (Châteaux-hôtels), ☎ 98.87.01.59. Euro. 10 rm Ⓟ ♧ closed 1 Oct-31 Mar. 16thC castle, 220. Rest. ♦♦ ♿ closed Mon, 60-90.

Plomeur, 6 km SW :
★★***Ferme du Relais Bigouden*** (L.F.), Pendreff-en-Plomeur, ☎ 98.58.01.32. 16 rm Ⓟ ♧ ♿ 180. Rest. 3 km away, closed end Oct, Dec-15 Jan, 50-100.

Restaurants :
♦♦ ***Le Relais de Ty Boutic,*** 3 km, rte de Peumarc'h, ☎ 98.87.03.90. AE, Visa. Ⓟ ♿ closed 1-15 Sep, Tue eve and Wed. A wide choice of dishes, 120-210.

Plobannalec, ⊠ 29138 Lesconil, 6 km S by D102 :
● ♦♦ ***Petit Kéroulé,*** ☎ 98.82.22.55 Ⓟ ♧ ♿ closed 1-24 Nov, Mon eve and Tue low season. J.-P. Stephan cooks excellent fish and shellfish, 220-310.

⛺ ★★*Châtaigniers,* Kerseoch (100 pl.), ☎ 98.87.11.90 ; ★★*Écureuils* (130 pl.) ; ☎ 98.87.03.39 ; Plomeur, ★★*Moulin* (80 pl.), ☎ 98.58.18.93 ; ★★*Pointe de la Torche* (155 pl.), ☎ 98.58.62.82.

PORNIC

Nantes 51, La Roche-sur-Yon 79, Paris 428
C4 ⊠ 44210

ℹ pl. du Môle, ☎ 40.82.04.40.

SNCF ☎ 40.82.00.06.

Hotel :
★★***Sablons,*** ☎ 40.82.09.14. Visa. 30 rm Ⓟ ♧ ✂, 180. Rest. ♦ ✂ ♿ 120-210.

⛺ ★★*Madrague* (400 pl.), ☎ 40.82.06.73 ; ★★*Boutinardière* (235 pl.), ☎ 40.82.05.68 ; ★★*Bleuets* (170 pl.), ☎ 40.82.11.07 ; ★★*Source* (100 pl.), ☎ 40.82.04.37.

Casino : quai Leray, ☎ 40.82.26.87.

PORNICHET

Nantes 71, Rennes 133, Paris 442
Adjacent to La Baule, C4 ⊠ 44380

ℹ pl. Aristide-Briand, ☎ 40.61.08.92.

Hotel :
★★★***Sud Bretagne*** (L.F.), 42, bd de la République, ☎ 40.61.02.68. AE, DC, Euro, Visa. 34 rm ♧ closed 15 Oct-15 Mar, 260. Rest. ♦♦ 200-250.

⛺ ★★★*Bugeau* (170 pl.), ☎ 40.61.02.02 ; *Bel Air* (230 pl.), ☎ 40.61.10.78 ; *Forges* (170 pl.), ☎ 40.61.18.84.

Boat hire : Pornichet-La Baule new port.

Casino : bd des Océanides, ☎ 40.61.05.48.

PORT-LOUIS

Lorient 19, Vannes 47, Paris 503
B3 ⊠ 56290

⛴ ferries for Lorient, Groix and Gâvres.

Hotel :
★★★***Avel Vor*** (L.F., France-Accueil), 25, rue Locmalo, ☎ 97.82.46.59. 20 rm ✂ ♿ closed 10 Nov-10 Jan, 260. Rest. ♦ 75-215.

⛺ ★★*Remparts* (135 pl.), ☎ 97.82.47.16.

PORT-NAVALO

On the gulf of Morbihan, C3 ⊠ 56640 Arzon

ℹ ancient station, ☎ 97.41.31.63.

Hotel :
★***Ruys,*** 28, bd de la Rade, ☎ 97.41.20.01. 14 rm Ⓟ ♧ closed Oct-1 Apr, 180. Rest. ♦ 80-130.

Restaurant :
♦ ***Escarpolette,*** 13, av. Gal-de-Gaulle, ☎ 97.41.26.25 ♧ closed 15 Nov-1 Apr and Thu, 80-130.

Le POULDU

Lorient 23, Quimper 59, Paris 514
15 km S of Quimperlé, B3 ⊠ 29121

ℹ bd de l'Océan (high season), ☎ 98.96.93.42.

Hotels :
★★★***Castel Treaz,*** ☎ 98.39.91.11. 24 rm Ⓟ ♧ closed Sep-Jun, 230.
★★***Bains,*** ☎ 98.39.90.11. 49 rm ✂ ♿ closed Sep-Apr, 180. Rest. ✂ ♿ 80-130.
★★***Quatre Chemins*** (L.F.), ☎ 98.39.90.44. Euro, Visa. 38 rm Ⓟ ♧ closed 15 Sep-Jun, 215. Rest. ♦ 70-150.

⛺ ★★*Les Embruns* (200 pl.), ☎ 98.39.91.07.

Le POULIGUEN

Nantes 76, Rennes 138, Paris 447
Adjacent to La Baule, C4 ⊠ 44510

ℹ port Sterwitz, ☎ 40.42.31.05.

SNCF ☎ 40.60.51.35.

Hotels :
★★***Grand Hôtel Neptune,*** 17, quai Jules-Sandeau, ☎ 40.42.30.99. 44 rm, closed 30 Sep-1 Feb. ♧ ♿ 170. Rest. ♦ 80-130.
★***Beau Rivage*** (L.F.), 11, rue Jules-Benoît, ☎ 40.42.31.61. 38 rm Ⓟ ♿ closed Sep-Easter, 180. Rest. 80-130.

⛺ ★★*Mouettes* (230 pl.), ☎ 40.42.10.29 ; ★*Clein,* rue de Kerlis (100 pl.), ☎ 40.42.43.99.

Restaurant :
♦♦ ***Voile d'Or,*** av. de la Plage, ☎ 40.42.31.68. AE, Visa. Ⓟ closed 15 Nov-15 Dec, Tue eve and Wed low season, 120-210.

QUÉDILLAC

Dinan 26, Rennes 40, Paris 392
27 km S of Dinan, C-D2
⊠ 35290 Saint-Méen-le-Grand

Hotel :
★★***Rance*** (L.F.), ☎ 99.07.21.25. AE, DC, Euro, Visa. 14 rm Ⓟ ♧ ♿ closed Jan, Sun eve, 180. Rest. ♦ ✂ Spec : *barbue à l'oseille, confit de canard aux cèpes,* 120-210.

QUESTEMBERT

Vannes 27, Rennes 88, Paris 424
10 km WSW of Rochefort-en-Terre, C3 ⊠ 56230

SNCF ☎ 97.26.11.05.

Hotel :
★★★★***Bretagne*** (Relais et châteaux), 13, rue Saint-Michel, ☎ 97.26.11.12. AE, Visa. 6 rm Ⓟ closed Sun eve, Mon, 3 Jan-15 Mar, 430. Rest. ● ♦♦♦ ♿ Light, inventive cooking, 200-390.

QUIBERON

Vannes 46, Lorient 49, Paris 502
D0 ⊠ 56170

🛈 7, rue de Verdun, ☎ 97.50.07.84, and Saint-Pierre (⊠ 56510), ☎ 97.50.07.84.

SNCF ☎ 97.50.07.07.

ferry service to Belle-Île, 45 mn (in high season book car passage), ☎ 97.31.80.01. For Houat and Hoedic (2 and 2 1/2 hours), ☎ 97.50.06.90.

Hotels :
★★★★***Sofitel Diététique,*** ☎ 97.50.20.00, Tx 691320. AE, DC, Euro, Visa. 76 rm over the sea P closed 2 Jan-1 Feb, 900. Rest. ♦ 200-320.
★★★★***Sofitel Thalassa,*** pointe de Goulvars, ☎ 97.50.20.00, Tx 691320. AE, DC, Euro, Visa. 113 rm P closed Jan-Feb, 940. Rest. ♦♦ 175-360.
★★★***Ker Noyal*** (L.F.), ☎ 97.50.08.41. AE, Visa. 92 rm P closed 25 Oct-20 Mar, 260. Rest. ♦ 120-210.
★★***Navirotel*** (L.F.), ☎ 97.50.16.52, Tx 950358. AE, DC, Euro, Visa. 21 rm over the sea P closed Jan-Feb, 180. Rest. ♦ closed Tue (Oct-Dec, Feb-Mar), 120-210.
★★***Plage,*** Saint-Pierre (L.F.), ☎ 97.30.92.10. Visa. 41 rm P closed 5 Oct-25 Mar, 15 Apr-1 May, 300. Rest. ♦ 80-140.
★★***Petite Sirène,*** 15, bd de la Mer, ☎ 97.50.17.34. AE, DC, Visa. 14 rm P closed 1 Nov-20 Mar, 195. Rest. ♦ Full board only in high season, 60-150.
★***Océan*** (L.F.), 7, quai de l'Océan, ☎ 97.50.07.58. 35 rm P closed Nov-Easter, 150. Rest. 55-90.
★***Deux Mers,*** av. Surcouf, Saint-Pierre, ☎ 97.52.33.75. 27 rm P closed 1 Oct-31 Mar, 130. Rest. ♦ 50-85.
Parc Tehuen, 1, rue des Tamaris, ☎ 97.50.10.26. 24 rm P closed Oct-15 May, 100. Rest. 80-130.

Youth hostel : 45, rue du Roch-Priol, ☎ 97.50.15.54.

⛺ ★★★*Joncs du Roch,* rue de l'Aérodrome (110 pl.), ☎ 97.50.24.37 ; ★★★*Park et Lann,* Saint-Pierre (135 pl.), ☎ 97.50.24.93 ; ★★*Penthièvre,* Saint-Pierre (665 pl.), ☎ 97.52.33.86 ; ★★*Goviro* (200 pl.), ☎ 97.50.13.54 ; ★★*Bois d'Amour* (335 pl.), ☎ 97.50.13.52 ; ★★*Conguel* (165 pl.), ☎ 97.50.19.11 ; ★★*le petit Rohu,* Saint-Pierre (165 pl.), ☎ 97.50.27.85 ; ★★*De Kerthogtin,* Saint-Pierre (150 pl.), ☎ 97.30.95.25 ; ★★*Do-mi-si-la-mi* (100 pl.), ☎ 97.50.22.52.

Restaurants :
♦♦ ***Relax,*** 27, bd de Castéro, ☎ 97.50.12.84. AE, DC, Visa. P closed 20 Nov-2 Feb, Mar and Sun eve (low season), 50-120.
● ♦ ***Goursen,*** 10, quai de l'Océan, ☎ 97.50.07.94. AE, Visa. closed 15 Nov-1 Apr (ex Feb school hols and Easter) and Tue. Fish, glorious fish... freshly caught in the nearby ocean, and prepared in a dozen excellent ways ; delicious, reasonably priced dishes, 200.
Taverne, Pontivy, ☎ 97.30.91.61. closed end Sept-begin Mar. Spec : grilled lobster, 120-210.

Casino : *Ker Braz.*

Recommended : *Confiserie Le Roux,* 18, rue du Port-Maria, for its famous caramels , *Viviers de Portivien,* Saint-Pierre, ☎ 97.30.93.81 (king prawns, lobster, crab).

QUIMPER

Brest 72, Vannes 115, Paris 556
A2 ⊠ 29000

🛈 rue du Roi-Gradlon (B1), ☎ 98.95.04.69. Guided tour of the old quarters.

✈ Pluguffan, 6 km SW, ☎ 98.94.01.28.

SNCF (C2), ☎ 98.90.50.50., 98.90.26.21.

🚌 2, bd de Kerguelen (B1), ☎ 98.95.02.36.

launches to Bénodet, Loctudy and the Glénan Islands.

Car-hire : *Budget* train + auto, at the station, ☎ 98.90.50.50, ☎ 98.52.04.87, and at the airport.

Hotels :
★★★***Griffon,*** 131, rte de Bénodet, 2 km S, ☎ 98.90.33.33, Tx 940063. AE, DC, Euro, Visa. 50 rm P 250. Rest. ♦ ☎ 98.90.03.30. closed Sun (low season), 65-180.
★★***Tour d'Auvergne*** (L.F.), 13, rue des Réguaires (B-C1), ☎ 98.95.08.70, Tx 941100. Visa. 45 rm P closed 17 Dec-10 Jan, 180. Rest. closed Sat eve, Sun (Oct-Easter), 120-210.

⛺ ★★★★*Orangerie de Lanniron* (100 pl.), ☎ 98.90.62.02.

Restaurants :
♦♦♦ ***Capucin Gourmand,*** 29, rue des Réguaires, ☎ 98.95.43.12. closed 15 Aug-1 Sep, Feb school hols and Mon, 100-160.
♦♦ ***Ferme et Océan,*** 19, rue Sainte-Thérèse, ☎ 98.90.08.32. Visa. P closed Mon, 120-210.
♦♦ ***Tritons,*** allées de Locmaria, ☎ 98.90.61.78 closed Mon and Sep. Enjoyable fare. Spec : *gratin fruits de mer, confit de canard ;* good value for money, 75-100.

Sports : horse races in Aug.

Event : Cornwall Festival : the 4th Sun in Jul.

Guided visits : of old quarter, 15 Jun to 15 Sep ; all year with reservation, enq 🛈

Bicycle hire : *Locavélo,* M. Hénaff, 107, av. de Ty-Bos, ☎ 98.53.30.04.

Recommended : *Au Costume Breton,* 11, rue Madec (dolls, hats, regional headdresses).

QUIMPERLÉ

Lorient 21, Quimper 46, Paris 511
B2-3 ⊠ 29130

🛈 pont de Bourgneuf, ☎ 98.96.04.32 (high season).

SNCF ☎ 98.39.24.24.

Hotels :
★★★***Hermitage,*** 2 km S on the D49, ☎ 98.96.04.66. Visa. 22 rm P closed 1 Nov-1 Apr, 250. Rest. ♦♦ ***Au Relais du Roch,*** ☎ 98.96.12.97. closed 20 Dec-Early Jan, Feb school hols and Mon, 65-130.
★***Europe,*** 32, bd de la Gare, ☎ 98.96.00.02. 23 rm P 145. Rest.

RENNES

Nantes 107, Brest 244, Paris 348
D2 ⊠ 35000

🛈 pont de Nemours (B2), ☎ 99.79.01.98.

✈ Saint-Jacques-de-la-Lande, 7 km SW, ☎ 99.50.41.13. *Air France Agency,* 7, rue de Bertrand, ☎ 99.63.09.09.

SNCF (C4), ☎ 99.65.50.50., 99.65.18.65.

🚌 bd Magenta (B3-4), ☎ 99.30.87.80.

Car-hire : *Budget* train + auto, 2, bd Solférino, ☎ 99.30.32.51, at the station, ☎ 99.30.45.96, and at the airport.

Hotels :
★★★**Frantel,** 1, rue du Cap.-Maignan (B4), ☎ 99.31.54.54. AE, DC, Euro, Visa. 140 rm ♿ closed Sun, 380. Rest. ♦♦ **la Table Ronde.** closed Sat noon and Sun, 125-230.
★★★**Président,** 27, av. Janvier (C3), ☎ 99.65.42.22. AE, DC, Euro, Visa. 34 rm Ⓟ ♿ 240.
★★**Astrid,** 32, av. Louis-Barthou (C4), ☎ 99.30.82.38. AE, Euro, Visa. 30 rm ♿ 180.
★★**Garden,** 3, rue Duhamel, ☎ 99.65.45.06, Tx 730772. AE, Visa. 22 rm ♿ 180.
★**Nemours,** 5, rue de Nemours (B3), ☎ 99.79.23.85. AE, DC, Euro, Visa. 22 rm closed 15 Jul-15 Aug, 110.

Noyal-sur-Vilaine, ⊠ 35530, 6 km E :
★★**Forges** (L.F.), 22, av. du Gal-de-Gaulle, ☎ 99.00.51.08. 11 rm Ⓟ closed 18 Feb-4 Mar, 8-28 Jul, Sun eve, 170. Rest. ♦ 60-155.

⛺ ★★*Gayeulles,* on the RN12 (100 pl.), ☎ 99.36.91.22.

Restaurants :
● ♦♦ **Palais,** 6, pl. du Parlement-de-Bretagne (B2), ☎ 99.79.45.01. AE, DC, Euro, Visa. ♿ The best restaurant in Rennes. Light and inventive cooking : *saint-pierre et sole en sauce claire, petites salades épicuriennes,* 150-220.
● ♦♦ **Le Piré,** 18, rue du Mal-Joffre, ☎ 99.79.31.41, Ⓟ closed Sat noon and Sun. Mr. Angelle proposes simple but refined cooking : *salade de foie gras, ris de veau au citron vert.*
● ♦♦ **Reberminard,** 67 *ter,* bd de La Tour-d'Auvergne (A4), ☎ 99.30.19.71. closed 1-15 Jan, Mon. Varied and refined dishes, 55-130.
♦♦ **Ouvrée,** 18, pl. des Lices (A2), ☎ 99.30.16.38. AE, DC, Euro, Visa. ♿ 16thC listed house, 90-150.
♦♦ **Ti-Coz,** 3, rue Saint-Guillaume (A2), ☎ 99.79.33.89. DC, Euro, Visa. closed 9-19 Aug, Sun (low season), Sat and Sun (Jul-Aug), 100-225.
♦♦ **Escu de Runfão,** 5, rue du Chapitre (A2), ☎ 99.79.13.10. AE, Visa. ♿ closed Sat noon, Sun eve and Mon noon, 120-210.

RIEC-SUR-BELON

Lorient 33, Quimper 37, Paris 523
4.5 km E of Pont-Aven, B3 ⊠ 29124

ⓘ ☎ 98.06.97.65.

Hotel :
★**Chez Mélanie,** pl. de l'Église, ☎ 98.06.91.05. AE, DC. 7 rm Ⓟ closed 15 Nov-15 Dec, Jan, 190. Rest. ♦♦ ♿ closed Tue, 100-200.

⛺ ★★*Belon* (150 pl.), ☎ 98.06.90.58.

Restaurant :
★★**Kerland,** on the D4, pont du Guilly, ☎ 98.06.42.98. Visa. Ⓟ ♿ closed 15 Feb-10 Mar, Sun (winter), 95-190.

La ROCHE-BERNARD

Vannes 40, Nantes 70, Paris 441
C3 ⊠ 56130

ⓘ hôtel de ville, ☎ 99.90.60.51.

Hotels :
★★**Auberge Armor-Vilaine** (L.F.), Peaule, 9 km NW, ☎ 99.42.91.03. Euro, Visa. 21 rm Ⓟ closed 15 Dec-15 Jan, Sun eve and Mon (ex Jul-Aug), 150. Rest. ♦ 50-160.
★★**Auberge Bretonne,** ☎ 99.90.60.28. AE, DC, Euro, Visa. 7 rm Ⓟ closed 1 Nov-1 Dec, Thu and Fri until 4 pm, 170. Rest. ● ♦ ♿ 85-170.

⛺ ★★*Municipal* (65 pl.), ☎ 99.90.60.13.

Recommended : *Doyenné de Lanvaux, foie gras de canard.*

ROSCOFF

Morlaix 28, Brest 62, Paris 565
B1 ⊠ 29211

ⓘ chapelle Sainte-Anne, rue Gambetta, ☎ 98.69.70.70.

boats for Batz Island (15 mn), ☎ 98.61.79.66. Connections with Plymouth, 8 hr by *Brittany Ferries,* and Roscoff-Cork in 10 hr, ☎ 98.69.07.20.

SNCF ☎ 98.69.70.20.

Hotels :
★★★**Brittany,** ☎ 98.69.70.78, Tx 940397. Visa. 19 rm Ⓟ ♿ 350. Rest. 120-210.
★★★**Regina,** 1, rue Ropars-Morvan, ☎ 98.61.23.55. Visa. 50 rm closed Sep-May, 180.
★★★**Gulf Stream** (L.F.), Marquise de Kergariou, ☎ 98.69.73.19. Visa. 32 rm Ⓟ closed Oct-Mar, 180. Rest. ♦ ♿ 120-210.
★★**Bellevue** (L.F.), rue Jeanne-d'Arc, ☎ 98.61.23.38. 23 rm Ⓟ closed Sep-May, 180. Rest. ♦ 120-210.
★**Bains,** ☎ 98.61.20.65. Visa. 60 rm Ⓟ closed Oct-Mar, 100. Rest. 80-130.

⛺ ★★*Manoir de Kerestat* (100 pl.), ☎ 98.69.71.92 ; ★★*Per'haridy* (200 pl.), ☎ 98.69.70.86.

ROSPORDEN

Quimper 22, Lorient 47, Paris 538
13 km NE of Concarneau, B2 ⊠ 29140

ⓘ ☎ 98.59.27.26.

SNCF ☎ 98.59.20.15.

Hotels :
★★**Bourhis,** ☎ 98.59.23.89. AE, DC, Euro, Visa. 27 rm Ⓟ ♿ closed 15 Feb-8 Mar, 15 Nov-1 Dec, Sun eve and Mon low season, 270. Rest. ● ♦ Seafood prepared by Mme Bourhis, 65-230.
★**Gai Logis** (L.F.), rte de Quimper, ☎ 98.59.22.38. Euro, Visa. 18 rm Ⓟ ♿ closed 15 Feb-15 Mar, Sat low season, 150. Rest. ♦ 50-170.

SABLES-D'OR-LES-PINS

Saint-Brieuc 39, Rennes 95, Paris 445
8 km SW of cap Fréhel, C1 ⊠ 22240 Fréhel

ⓘ pl. des Fêtes, ☎ 96.41.42.40.

Hotels :
★★**Ajoncs d'Or,** allée des Acacias, ☎ 96.41.42.12. 75 rm Ⓟ closed end Sep-early May, 260. Rest. ♦ 70-195.
★★**Diane** (L.F.), allée R.-Brouard, ☎ 96.41.42.07 and 96.41.42.19. 42 rm Ⓟ ♿ closed 20 Sep-Easter, 270.
★**Pins,** allée des Acacias, ☎ 96.41.42.20. Euro, Visa. 22 rm Ⓟ closed mid-Oct-mid-Mar, 85. Rest. 60-125.

Cap Fréhel :
★**Relais de Fréhel,** 2 km S on the D16, ☎ 96.41.43.02. 13 rm Ⓟ ♿ closed 5 Nov-Feb ex Christmas and Feb hols, 180. Rest. ♦ 80-130.

⛺ Cap Fréhel : ★*Grèves d'En Bas* (100 pl.), ☎ 96.41.43.34 ; *Pont de l'Étang* (1 000 pl.), ☎ 96.41.40.45.

SAINT-BREVIN-LES-PINS

Nantes 57, Vannes 90, Paris 434
C1 ⊠ 44250

ⓘ 10, rue de l'Église, ☎ 40.27.24.32.

Hotels :
★★***Grand Hôtel du Casino et de la Plage,*** bd de l'Océan, ☎ 40.27.20.05. Visa. 40 rm ⚟ Ⓟ ♒ ♿ closed Oct-Mar, 200. Rest. ♦ 60-160.
★***Débarcadère*** (L.F.), ☎ 40.27.20.53. AE, DC, Euro, Visa. 17 rm ⚟ Ⓟ ♒ ⛱ closed 15 Oct-1 Feb, Sun eve low season, 200. Rest. 60-210.
★***Kayak*** (L.F.), 119, av. Mal-Foch, ☎ 40.27.22.37. 11 rm Ⓟ ♒ ♿ closed 1 Nov-28 Apr, 150. Rest. 45-95.

Youth hostel : allée Jeunesse, ☎ 40.27.25.27.

⛺ ★★★*Vieux Logis de Neuvillette* (15 pl.), ☎ 40.27.46.80 ; ★★*Pierre Attelée* (600 pl.), ☎ 40.27.80.32 ; ★★*Rochelets* (300 pl.), ☎ 40.27.40.25 ; ★★*Farandole* (200 pl.), ☎ 40.27.92.95 ; ★★*Pierre Couchées* (250 pl.), ☎ 40.27.85.64.

Casino : ☎ 40.27.21.51.

SAINT-BRIEUC

Rennes 99, Quimper 139, Paris 452
C2-3 ⊠ 22000

ⓘ *Pavillon du Tourisme,* 7, rue Saint-Gouéno, ☎ 96.33.32.50 and 96.33.42.29.

✈ Saint-Brieuc-Trémuson, 3 km W, ☎ 96.94.61.11.

SNCF (A4), ☎ 96.94.50.50., 96.94.04.79.

🚌 rue Waldeck-Rousseau (B3), ☎ 96.33.33.52.

Car-hire : *Budget* train + auto, at the S.N.C.F. station, ☎ 96.94.00.77.

Hotels :
★★***Alexandre Ier,*** 19, pl. Du-Guesclin (B3), ☎ 96.33.79.45. AE, DC, Euro, Visa. 43 rm Ⓟ ♒ ♿ closed 23 Dec-10 Jan, 180.
★★***Chêne Vert*** (L.F.), Saint-Laurent-de-la-Mer intersection, ☎ 96.74.63.20. AE, DC, Euro, Visa. 52 rm Ⓟ ♒ ⛱ ♿ squash. closed 20 Dec-6 Jan, 210. Rest. ♦ closed Sat and Sun noon, 60-110.
★★***Mon Hôtel,*** 19, rue Jean-Métairie (A3), ☎ 96.33.01.21. Visa. 48 rm Ⓟ ♒ 🚫 ♿ closed 1 week in Feb, 180.

Youth hostel : *Ty Coat,* rue A.-Daudet, ☎ 96.61.91.87. Cycle tours.

⛺ ★★*De Brezillet* (200 pl.), ☎ 96.61.29.33.

Restaurants :
● ♦♦ ***Vieille Tour,*** 75, rue de la Tour, Plérin (3 km N), ☎ 96.33.10.30 ⚟ ⛱ 🚫 ♿ closed 15-20 Jun, 23 Dec-3 Jan, Sat noon and Sun. The view over Saint-Brieuc bay and its small fishing craft is yet another reminder that here, fish is king ! 120-280.
● ♦ ***Aiguade,*** 46-48, rue de Gouët, ☎ 96.33.56.44. closed early Jul and Christmas, Sun and nat hols. An exquisite mixture of innovation and tradition, 120-210.

SAINT-CAST-LE-GUILDO

Saint-Brieuc 50, Rennes 87, Paris 435
C1 ⊠ 22380

ⓘ ☎ 96.41.81.52.

SNCF Lamballe station, 30 km.

Hotels :
★★★***Ar Vro*** (L.F.), 8, bd de la Plage, ☎ 96.41.85.01. AE, DC, Euro, Visa. 47 rm ⚟ Ⓟ ♒ ⛱ closed 9 Sep-5 Jun, 300. Rest. ♦ 120-240.
★★***Dunes,*** rue Primauguet, ☎ 96.41.80.31. Visa. 27 rm ⚟ Ⓟ ♒ 🚫 🎾 closed 3 Nov-20 Mar, 200. Rest. ♦ 90-175.
★***Angleterre et Panorama*** (L.F.), 01, rue de la Fosserole, ☎ 96.41.91.44. 38 rm Ⓟ ♒ 📺 🎾 closed Sep-Jun, 85. Rest. ♦ 🚫 Spec : seafood, 60-135.

Pen-Guen, 2 km :
★★***Pins,*** bd de l'Arguenon, ☎ 96.41.93.81. Visa. 32 rm ⚟ Ⓟ ♒ ⛱ closed 20 Sep-1 Apr, 180. Rest. ♿ 🚫 Spec : seafood, 80-130.

Farmhouse gîte, chambre and table d'hôtes : *Ferme du Fraîche,* Pléboulle, ⊠ 22550, 11 km on the D786, ☎ 96.41.13.04.

⛺ ★★★*Des Mielles* (100 pl.), ☎ 96.41.03.60 ; ★★*Ferme de Pen Guen* (300 pl.), ☎ 96.41.92.18 ; ★★*la Clôture* Goudeoir (100 pl.), ☎ 96.41.80.18.

Guided tours : enq ⓘ

SAINT-GUÉNOLÉ

Quimper 34, Lorient 92, Paris 582
Near Penmarc'h Point, A3 ⊠ 29132 Penmarc'h

ⓘ pl. A.-Dupany, ☎ 98.58.79.05, 96.58.10.79.

Hotels :
★★***Mer,*** 184, rue Péron, ☎ 98.58.62.22. AE, DC, Euro, Visa. 17 rm Ⓟ closed 1-15 Feb, 15 Oct-25 Nov, Sun eve and Mon low season, 180. Rest. ● ♦ 🚫 ♿ An out-of-this-world place facing the Ocean where you can find good, solid cooking : *homard à la bigoudine cuit aux algues,* 120-210.
★★***Moguerou*** (L.F.), rue Lelay, ☎ 98.58.62.16. 24 rm ⚟ Ⓟ ♒ 📺 closed Dec-Jan, 100. Rest. ♦♦ 120-210.

SAINT-MALO

Avranches 66, Rennes 69, Paris 411
D1 ⊠ 35400

ⓘ at the marina (E2), ☎ 99.56.64.48.

✈ Dinard-Pleurtuit, 17 km SW

⛴ Dinan by the Rance ; excursions to Cézembre Island, cap Fréhel, Chausey Islands, ☎ 99.56.68.40 and 99.81.61.46 ; regular service to Portsmouth on the *Brittany Ferries,* ☎ 99.56.68.40. Excursions to the Channel Islands by hydrofoil, ☎ 99.56.42.29, 99.40.94.95, 99.56.61.46.

SNCF (C2), ☎ 99.56.08.18., 99.56.15.53.

🚌 esplanade Saint-Vincent (E1).

Car-hire : *Budget* train + auto, at the S.N.C.F. station, ☎ 99.56.08.18.

Hotels :
★★★***Central Mapotel,*** 6, Grande-Rue (E2), ☎ 99.40.87.70, Tx 740802. AE, DC, Euro, Visa. 46 rm Ⓟ ♿ 360. Rest. ♦ closed 3 Jan-15 Feb, Sun eve and Mon in winter, 120.
★★★***Élisabeth*** (Châteaux-hôtels), 2, rue des Cordiers, ☎ 99.56.24.98. AE, DC, Visa. 17 rm ♿ 350.
★★★***Valmarin*** (Châteaux-hôtels, Relais du Silence), quartier Saint-Servan, 7, rue Jean-XXII, ☎ 99.81.94.76. AE, Visa. 10 rm Ⓟ ♒ ⛱ closed 19 Jan-28 Feb and Sun eve 1 Oct-19 Jan, 450.
★★***France et Chateaubriand,*** 1, rue Chateaubriand, ☎ 99.56.66.52. AE, DC, Euro. 80 rm ⚟ ♿ 240. Rest. ♦ closed 11 Nov-1 Apr, 85-120.
★***Annick,*** 13, rue du Boyer (D2), ☎ 99.40.88.57. Visa. 10 rm ⚟ ⛱ closed 1 Dec-15 Jan, 80. Rest. closed Wed, 45-100.
★***Porte St-Pierre*** (L.F.), 2, pl. du Guet (D2), ☎ 99.40.91.27, 29 rm ⚟ closed 15 Nov-1 Feb and Mar, 170. Rest. ♦ ♿ 60-150.

Youth hostel : av. du R.-P.-Humbricht, ☎ 99.40.29.80.

⛺ ★★*Cité d'Aleth,* Saint-Servan (400 pl.), ☎ 99.81.60.91 ; ★★*Nielles,* bd de Rothéneuf (95 pl.), ☎ 99.40.26.35 ; ★★*Ilots,* Rothéneuf (130 pl.), ☎ 99.56.41.36.

Restaurants :
♦♦♦ ***Métairie de Beauregard,*** Saint-Servan, rte de Rennes, ☎ 99.81.37.06. AE, DC, Visa. 1 Sep-15 Jun. The grilled lobster, *foie gras de canard,* and *boudin de barbue* are fitting dishes in this elegant manor setting, 150-280.
♦♦ ***Duchesse Anne,*** 5, pl. Guy-La Chambre, ☎ 99.40.85.33 ♿ closed Dec-Jan and Wed. Spec : *foie gras,* sole fillets, 150-250.
♦ ***Gilles,*** rue de la Pie-qui-Boit (D2), ☎ 99.40.95.25. closed 12 Nov-6 Dec, 1-15 Mar, Thu and Sun eve low season, 65-95.

Leisure activities : casino, sailing.

SAINT-NAZAIRE

Nantes 62, Rennes 124, Paris 433
C4 ✉ 44600

ℹ pl. de l'Hôtel-de-Ville (A3), ☎ 40.22.40.65.

✈ Montoir, 7 km NE, ☎ 40.22.46.03.

SNCF (A1), ☎ 40.66.50.50., 40.66.51.68.

🚌 17, rue Henri-Gautier (B2), ☎ 40.22.21.07.

Car-hire : *Budget* train + auto, 1, rue du Cdt-l'Herminier, ☎ 40.22.06.77, 40.22.22.30, station, ☎ 40.22.57.87, and Saint-Nazaire airport.

Hotels :
★★★***Berry,*** 1, pl. de la Gare (B1), ☎ 40.22.42.61. AE, DC, Euro, Visa. 27 rm ⚘ P 🌳 ♿ closed 2 Dec-2 Jan, 340. Rest. ♦♦ 65-100.
★★***Dauphin,*** 33, rue Jean-Jaurès, ☎ 40.66.59.61. AE, Visa. 20 rm, 180.
★***Galathé,*** 97, bd Albert-Ier (A4), ☎ 40.70.18.15. 12 rm ⚘ P 🌳 closed Mon, 100.

⛺ ★★★*L'Ève* (404 pl.), ☎ 40.45.92.65 ; ★★*les Jaunais* (70 pl.), ☎ 40.45.92.60.

SAINT-POL-DE-LÉON

Morlaix 20, Brest 58, Paris 557
A-B1 ✉ 29250

ℹ pl. de l'Évêché, ☎ 98.69.05.69.

SNCF ☎ 98.69.14.55.

Restaurant :
♦♦ ***Pomme d'Api,*** 49, rue Verderel, ☎ 98.69.02.92 ♿ closed 30 Oct-15 Mar, Sat noon and Tue. Nice Brittany-style setting, fire-place and oak beams, 80-130.

SAINT-QUAY-PORTRIEUX

Saint-Brieuc 21, Guingamp 28, Paris 472
C1 ✉ 22410

ℹ opposite the casino, ☎ 96.70.40.64.

⛴ boats to Bréhat island, ☎ 96.70.40.64.

Hotels :
★★★***Ker Moor,*** 13, rue du Pdt-Le Senecal, ☎ 96.70.52.22, Tx 950729. AE, DC, Visa. 28 rm P 🌳 🎾 closed 15 Nov-15 Feb, Sun eve and Mon (low season), 180. Rest. ♦ ♿ 120-210.
★★***Gerbot d'Avoine*** (L.F.), 2, bd du Littoral, ☎ 96.70.40.09. Euro. 26 rm ⚘ P 🌳 closed 6-24 Jan, 23 Nov-12 Dec, Sun eve and Mon low season, 200. Rest. ♦ ⚘ ♿ 60-100.
★***Modern'Hôtel,*** 3, rue Adj.-Chef-Cadot, ☎ 96.70.40.97. Visa. 37 rm P 🌳 ♿ 100. Rest. ♦ 120-210.

Étables-sur-Mer, ✉ 22680, 3 km S :
★★★***La Colombière,*** bd du Littoral, ☎ 96.70.61.64. Visa. 5 rm ⚘ P 🌳 closed 15 Nov-1 Dec, 260. Rest. ♦♦ ♿ closed Tue (low season), 220-310.

⛺ ★★★*Bellevue* (200 pl.), ☎ 96.70.41.84 ; Étables-sur-Mer, 4 km S : ★★★*Abri Côtier* (140 pl.), 96.70.61.57.

Restaurant :
Étables-sur-Mer :
♦♦ ***La Colombière,*** bd du Littoral, ☎ 96.70.61.64 5 rm. ⚘ 🌳 closed end Nov. 15 Jan-early Feb, 260. Rest. ♦♦ ♿ closed Tue (low season), 220-310.

SARZEAU

Vannes 22, Nantes 110, Paris 463
On the Gulf of Morbihan, C3 ✉ 56370

ℹ ☎ 97.41.82.37.

Hotels :
Chaumière de la Mer, ☎ 97.41.71.84. 14 rm P 🌳 closed 30 Sep-1 Apr, 100. Rest. 80-130.
Le Tour-du-Parc, 9 km E :
★★***Croix du Sud,*** ☎ 97.67.30.20. 27 rm 🌳 🎾 ♿ closed Sun eve and Mon low season, 180. Rest. ♦ 120-210.

⛺ ★★★★*Madone* (380 pl.), ☎ 97.41.70.64 ; ★★★*Kersial,* rte de Saint-Jacques (110 pl.), ☎ 97.41.75.59.

Île de SEIN

A2 ✉ 29162

⛴ 1 hr trip to Audierne ; daily service (3 in Jul-Aug) ex Wed, ☎ 98.70.02.37 or 38.

Restaurant :
♦♦ ***Auberge des Senans,*** on the port, ☎ 98.70.90.01, 60-170.

TRÉBEURDEN

Morlaix 48, Saint-Brieuc 72, Paris 524
11 km S of Trégastel, B1 ✉ 22560

ℹ pl. Crech-Hery (daily ex Sun), ☎ 96.23.51.64.

✈ Lannion-Servel, 8 km SE.

⛴ sea excursions, ☎ 96.23.51.64.

Hotels :
● ★★★***Ti Al Lannec*** (L.F., Relais du Silence, Châteaux-hôtels), allée de Mezo Guen, ☎ 96.23.57.26, Tx 740656. AE, Visa. 24 rm ⚘ P 🌳 closed 15 Nov-15 Mar, 400. Rest. ♦ closed Mon noon, 220-310.
★★★***Manoir de Lan Kerellec*** (Relais et châteaux), allée centrale de Lan Kerellec, ☎ 96.23.50.09, Tx 741172. AE, DC, Visa. 11 rm ⚘ P 🌳 closed Nov-15 Mar, 500. Rest. ● ♦♦ ♿ closed Mon noon low season. Wonderful manor, superb service and cooking : *feuilleté de langoustines et petit-gris, saint-pierre au cidre et sa fricassée de pommes,* 220-310.
★***Potinière,*** Tresmeur beach, ☎ 96.23.50.43. 13 rm ⚘ P 🌳 closed end Sep-Apr, 100. Rest. ♿ closed Wed low season, 50-150.

Youth hostel : Pors Toëno, corniche de Goas-Treiz, ☎ 96.23.52.22. Riding instruction and sailing courses.

⛺ ★★★*Armor-Loisirs,* Pors Mabo (120 pl.), ☎ 96.23.52.31 ; ★★★*Hostiou Kerdual* (35 pl.), ☎ 96.23.54.86 ; ★★★*Espérance,* Penvern (50 pl.), ☎ 96.23.95.35.

TRÉGASTEL-PLAGE

Morlaix 52, Saint-Brieuc 76, Paris 528
D1 ✉ 22730

ℹ pl. Sainte-Anne, ☎ 96.23.88.67.

✈ Lannion-Servel, 8 km S.

Hotels :
★★★**Belle Vue** (L.F.), rue des Calculots, ☎ 96.23.88.18. Euro, Visa. 33 rm ⚟ Ⓟ ⅏ closed Oct-Easter, 310. Rest. ♦ ♿ 100-220.
★★**Bains,** rue du Gal-de-Gaulle, ☎ 96.23.88.09. DC, Visa. 30 rm ⚟ Ⓟ ⅏ ♿ closed Oct-Apr, 180.
★★**Beau Séjour** (L.F., Inter-Hôtel), Coz-Pors beach, ☎ 96.23.88.02. AE, DC, Euro, Visa. 20 rm ⚟ Ⓟ closed Oct-Mar, 200. Rest. ♦ 75-170.

⛺ ★★★*Golven,* Kerlavos Bay (160 pl.), ☎ 96.23.87.77 ; ★★*Tourony* (100 pl.), ☎ 96.23.86.61.

TRÉGUIER

Guingamp 36, Saint-Brieuc 60, Paris 511
B1 ✉ 22220

ℹ mairie, ☎ 96.92.30.19.

Hotels :
★★**Kastel Dinec'h** (L.F.), ☎ 96.92.49.39. Visa. 15 rm Ⓟ ⅏ ♿ closed 15-27 Oct, 1 Jan-1 Mar, Tue eve and Wed, 210. Rest. ✾ 220-310.

Farmhouse gîte : *Ferme Guillou-Trohadiou,* Trédarzec, 2 km, ☎ 96.35.36.81.

Trévou-Tréguignec, ✉ 22660 Trélévern, 1 km NW :
★**Trestel-Bellevue,** rte de Trestel, ☎ 96.23.71.44. 14 rm ⚟ Ⓟ ⅏ ♿ closed Sep-Easter, 180. Rest. ♦ shellfish, 80-130.

Port-Blanc, ✉ 22710 Penvénan, 11 km NW :
★**Grand Hôtel** (L.F.), bd de la Mer, ☎ 96.92.66.52. 30 rm ⚟ Ⓟ ⅏ ♿ closed 15 Nov-1 Mar, 180. Rest. ♦ 80-130.

⛺ Trévou-Tréguignec, 13 km NW : ★★★*Mât* (70 pl.), ☎ 96.23.71.52 ; ★★★*Anciennes Dunes* (120 pl.), ☎ 96.23.76.09.

TREMBLAY

Fougères 23, Rennes 42, Paris 345
16 km S of Pontorson, D2
✉ 35460 Saint Brice en Coglès

Hotel :
★★★**Roc Land,** La Lande, ☎ 99.98.20.46. Visa. 19 rm Ⓟ ⅏ ✾ closed 15-28 Feb, 15-30 Oct, Sat eve, Sun eve and Mon, 230. Rest. ♦♦ ♿ 80-150.

La TRINITÉ-SUR-MER

Vannes 30, Lorient 41, Paris 485
4.5 km from Carnac, B3 ✉ 56470

ℹ cours des Quais, ☎ 97.55.72.21 (high season).

Hotels :
★★**Le Rouzic,** 17, cours des Quais, ☎ 97.55.72.06. AE, Euro, Visa. 32 rm ⚟ closed 15 Nov-15 Dec, 220. Rest. ♦ ♿ closed Sun eve and Mon low season, 80-100.
★**Panorama, le Congre,** St-Philibert, ☎ 97.55.00.56. 25 rm Ⓟ ⅏ closed Oct-Mar, 190. Rest. 75-150.

⛺ ★★★*Baie* (185 pl.), ☎ 97.55.73.42 ; ★★★*Plijadur* (100 pl.), ☎ 97.52.72.05.

Restaurant :
♦♦ **Azimut,** 1, rue du Men-Dû, ☎ 97.55.71.88. Visa. Ⓟ ⅏ closed Sun eve and Mon (winter), Dec-Feb, 100-170.
♦♦ **Les Hortensias,** ☎ 97.55.75.11 ⚟ ⅏ closed 1 Mar-31 Nov, Sun eve and Mon in low season. Reasonably priced cooking in a beautiful blue granite house facing the port : *salade de rougets et de girolles, gigotin de lapereau à la crème de thym,* nice desserts, 100-170.

Le VAL-ANDRÉ

Saint-Brieuc 29, Dinan 43, Paris 436
16 km N of Lamballe, C2 ✉ 22370 Pléneuf

ℹ arcades du Casino, B.P. 25, ☎ 96.72.20.55 or 96.72.93.03 in Pléneuf.

Hotels :
★★**Grand Hôtel du Val-André,** rue Amiral-Charner, ☎ 96.72.20.56. Visa. 39 rm ⚟ Ⓟ ⅏ ♿ closed 1 Nov-1 Mar, 220. Rest. ♦ ✾ closed end Sep-1 May, 120-210.
★★**Petit Prince et** ★**France** (L.F.), 4, rue Pasteur, ☎ 96.72.22.52. DC, Visa. 55 rm Ⓟ ⅏ closed Nov-Mar, Sun eve and Mon, half-board only in high season, 180.
★**Grand Hôtel des Bains,** 7, pl. du Gal-de-Gaulle, ☎ 96.72.20.11. 26 rm ⚟ Ⓟ closed end Sep-Easter, 100. Rest. 80-130.

⛺ ★★*Salines de Mercœur* (133 pl.), ☎ 96.72.95.09 ; ★★*Monts Colleux* (300 pl.), ☎ 96.72.95.10.

Restaurant :
● ♦♦ **Cotriade,** at the port of Piégu, ☎ 96.72.20.26. DC ⚟ closed Mon eve, Tue and 15 Dec-16 Jan. Spec : seafood, especially shellfish ; talented, original cooking, 100-280.

VANNES

Rennes 106, Quimper 116, Paris 456
C3 ✉ 56000

ℹ 29, rue Thiers (B2), ☎ 97.47.24.34.

✈ Meucon, 10 km NE, ☎ 97.60.78.79.

⛴ Gulf of Morbihan, Houat and Hoëdic, embarcation at Rabine and Pont-Vert, *Vedettes vertes,* ☎ 97.63.79.99. *Navisspace,* ☎ 97.63.79.99 : gastronomic cruises, dinner-cruises in candlelight.

SNCF (C1), ☎ 97.42.50.50.
97.54.11.48.

Car-hire : *Budget* train + auto, at the S.N.C.F. station, ☎ 97.54.12.36.

Hotels :
★★★**Manche Océan** (Inter-Hôtel), 31, rue Colonel-Maury (B2), ☎ 97.47.26.46. AE, Visa. 42 rm Ⓟ ♿ 215.
★★★**Marebaudière,** 4, rue Aristide-Briand (C2), ☎ 97.47.34.29. AE, DC, Euro, Visa. 40 rm Ⓟ ⅏ ♿ closed 19 Dec-7 Jan, Sun eve low season, 260.
★**De Clisson,** 11, rue Olivier-de-Clisson (C1), ☎ 97.54.13.94. 12 rm Ⓟ closed 15 Dec-5 Jan, 150.
★**Verdun,** 10, av. de Verdun (not on the C2 map), ☎ 97.47.21.23. Visa. 24 rm Ⓟ closed Dec-15 Jan and Sun afternoon, 180.

Conleau Peninsula, 4.5 km SW :
★★**Roof** (L.F.), ☎ 97.63.47.47. AE, DC, Euro, Visa. 11 rm ⚟ Ⓟ ✾ closed Mon-Jan-mid-Feb, 230. Rest. ♦ ♿ closed Mon low season, 80-200.

Arz Island, ✉ 56840 :
★**Escale,** at the pier, ☎ 97.44.32.15. 11 rm ⚟ ✾ closed Sep-Apr, 125. Rest. ♦ ♿ 50-90.

Arradon Point, ⊠ 56610 :
★★***Vénètes,*** ☎ 97.26.03.11. 12 rm ⚟ ✈ closed Oct-Easter and Mon (ex high season), 300. Rest. ♦ 85-190.

⛺ ★★★*Conleau,* 3 km (290 pl.), ☎ 97.63.13.88.

Restaurants :

● ♦♦ ***Le Lys,*** 51, rue du Mal-Leclerc, ☎ 97.47.29.30. closed Sun eve in winter and Mon. Good cooking in a nice atmosphere, 90-180.

♦♦ ***Épée,*** 2, rue J.-Le Brix (B2), ☎ 97.47.10.11. AE, Visa ♿ closed Sun, 45-110.

Leisure activities : Ocean and tropical aquarium, Ferme des Marais, ☎ 97.42.74.93.

VITRÉ

Rennes 36, Nantes 118, Paris 311
D2 ⊠ 35500

ℹ pl. Saint-Yves (A1), ☎ 97.75.04.46.

SNCF ☎ 97.75.00.47.

Hotel :

★★***Petit Billot,*** 5, pl. Mal-Leclerc (B2), ☎ 97.75.02.10. Euro. 22 rm ✈ closed 15 Dec-15 Jan, Fri eve and Sat noon, 200. Rest. ♦ 60-110.

Market : every monday.

Burgundy

It is sometimes difficult to ascertain where Burgundy begins and where it ends : its borders are vague and it encloses a multitude of different regions. There is Celtic, rugged Morvan, the romanesque and mystical tradition of its medieval abbeys, the sensuality of the Côte-d'Or and the magnificent city of Dijon. For tourists, its major attractions are just as diverse. For many, Burgundy is first and foremost the prestigious domain of the great wines from the 210 square kilometres of vineyards along the purple and gold banks of the river. More than 150 of these produce wine bearing the coveted *A.O.C.* label. It is divided up into some 5 000 separate vineyards producing wine of the most varied nature, depending on the particular microclimate, soil and exposure. The most famous burgundies come from the Côte d'Or with its two great vineyards, the Côte de Nuits and the Côte de Beaune.

For others, Burgundy represents a soil fertilized by mediaeval faith, the site of Romanesque architecture's finest masterpieces : Vézelay, Autun, and Cluny, and the modest country churches of Brionnais and Mâconnais. In 910 Bernon founded a Benedictine abbey on the banks of the Grosne, and Cluny very quickly became the center of mediaeval Catholicism. Its abbots enjoyed an influence greater than that of popes and kings. Two centuries after it was founded, Cluny had 1 200 brother and sister houses throughout Europe.

For still others, Burgundy is a mosaic of landscapes, generous and severe by turns, studded with forests, waterways and canals. Dotted too with the imposing châteaux of feudal lords and the cultivated noblemen of the Age of Enlightenment. Burgundy has traditionally been a place of exchanges and encounters, of summer holidays and weekend escapades; hunting, fishing, sporting activities and cultural marvels, excellent cooking and specialities which flavor the whole of French cuisine : snails, Dijon mustard, gingerbread, cassis blackcurrant liqueur and the famous *kir* — an aperitif of white wine and cassis.

The capital city, Dijon, houses the splendid palaces of Burgundian aristocracy, a Fine Arts Museum testifying to the genius of the Flemish artists who lived and painted here under the patronage of the Great Dukes, and a bevy of churches and private mansions.

Sightseeing

Facts and figures

Location : *East of the centre of France, a crossroads and passage way on the North-South axis.*
Area : *31 582 km²*
Population : *1 596 000*
Climate : *temperate; colder in Morvan; wet in the mountains; very sunny west of Dijon. Winter often cold but clear; variable spring; summer often wet; mild, clear autumn (vine harvest), the most beautiful season in Burgundy.*
Administration :
— Departement of **Côte d'Or,** *Prefecture Dijon;*
— Departement of **Nièvre,** *Prefecture Nevers;*
— Departement of **Saône-et-Loire,** *Prefecture Mâcon;*
— Departement of **Yonne,** *Prefecture Auxerre.*

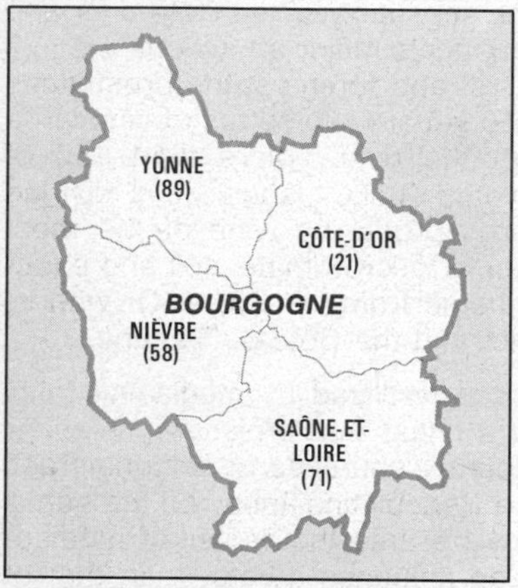

Don't miss

★★★ : *Ancy-le-Franc (B1), Autun (B3), Beaune (C3), Dijon (C2), Fontenay (B2), Tanlay (B1), Vézelay (A2)*
★★ : *Anzy-le-Duc (B4), Auxerre (A1), Avallon (B2), Brancion (C4), Brionnais region (B4), Bussy-Rabutin (B2), Châteauneuf (B3), Châtillon-sur-Seine (B1), Clos-de-Vougeot (C2), Cluny (B4), Cormatin (C4), The Vineyard Road (C2-3), Cousin Valley (B2), Cure Valley (A-B2), Flavigny (B2), Morvan Nature Park (B3), Nevers (A3), Noyers (B2), Pontigny (A1), La Rochepot (B3), Saint-Fargeau (A2), Saint-Thibault (B2), Semur-en-Auxois (B2), Solutré (C4), Sully (B3), Tournus (C4), Souzon Valley (C2).*

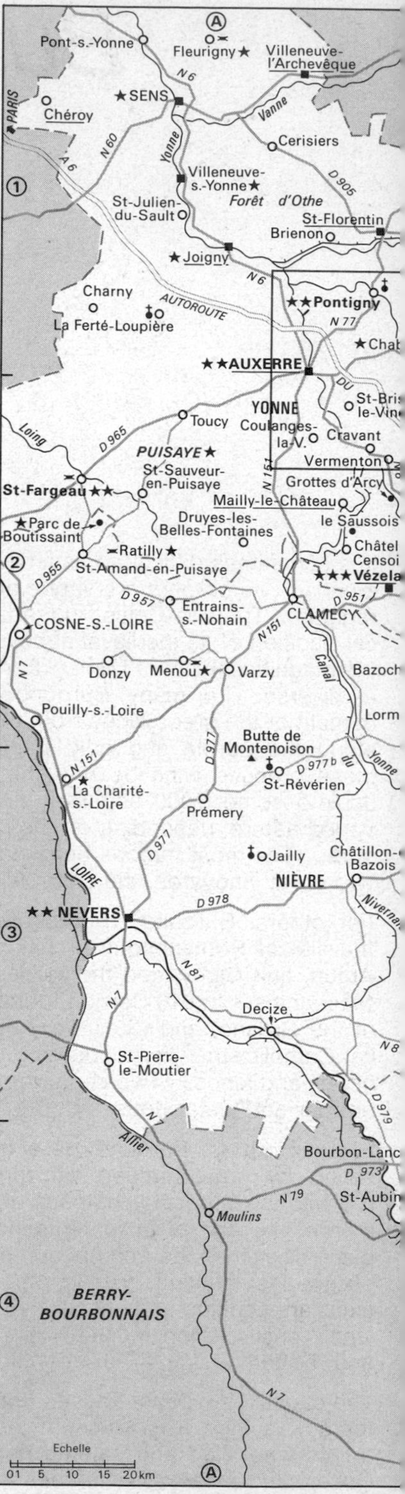

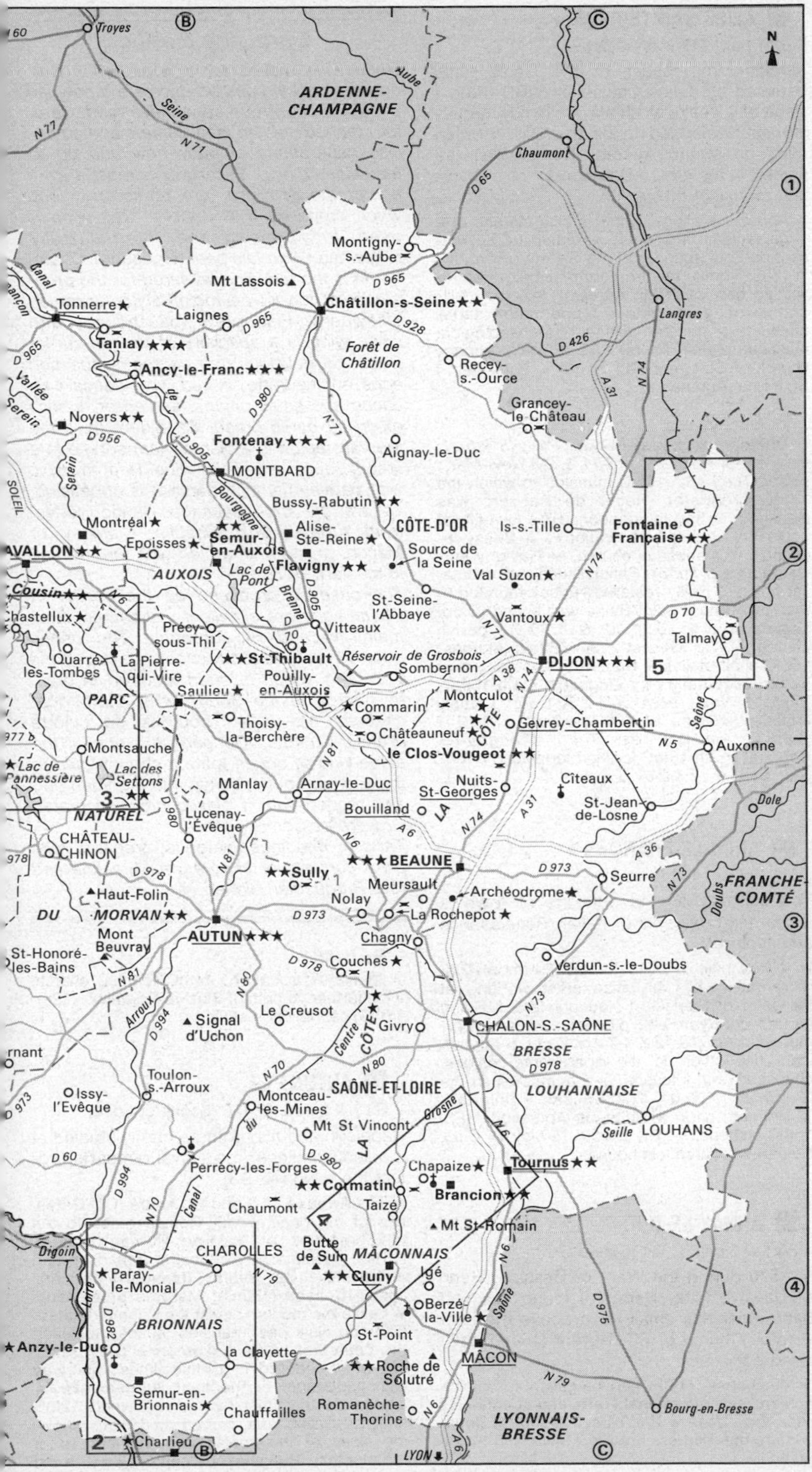
Troyes
ARDENNE-
CHAMPAGNE
Aube
Seine
N 71
N 77
Chaumont
D 65
Montigny-
s.-Aube
Mt Lassois
D 965
Châtillon-s-Seine ★★
Tonnerre ★
Laignes
D 965
D 928
Forêt de
Châtillon
Tanlay ★★★
Ancy-le-Franc ★★★
Recey-
s.-Ource
D 426
Langres
A 31
N 74
Grancey-
le-Château
Vallée
Serein
Noyers ★★
D 956
D 980
N 71
Fontenay ★★★
Aignay-le-Duc
D 905
MONTBARD
Bourgogne
SOLEIL
Bussy-Rabutin ★★
CÔTE-D'OR
Is-s.-Tille
Fontaine
Française ★★
Montréal ★
Epoisses ★
★★ Semur-
en-Auxois
Alise-
Ste-Reine ★
Source de
la Seine
AVALLON ★★
AUXOIS
Lac de
Pont
Flavigny ★★
Val Suzon ★
N 74
Cousin ★★
Brenne
D 905
St-Seine-
l'Abbaye
Vantoux ★
D 70
Chastellux ★
Précy-
sous-Thil
Vitteaux
N 71
Talmay
Quarré-
les-Tombes
La Pierre-
qui-Vire
★★ St-Thibault
Réservoir de Grosbois
Sombernon
DIJON ★★★
5
PARC
Saulieu ★
Pouilly-
en-Auxois
A 38
N 74
Montculot
Commarin
Thoisy-
la-Berchère
Châteauneuf ★
CÔTE
Gevrey-Chambertin
Saône
N 5
Auxonne
Montsauche
N 81
le Clos-Vougeot ★★
Lac de
Pannessière
Lac des
Settons
3
Manlay
Arnay-le-Duc
Nuits-
St-Georges
Cîteaux
NATUREL
D 980
Lucenay-
l'Évêque
Bouilland
LA
A 31
St-Jean-
de-Losne
Dole
A 6
N 74
CHÂTEAU-
CHINON
N 6
A 36
D 978
N 81
★★ Sully
★★★ BEAUNE
D 973
Seurre
N 73
FRANCHE-
COMTÉ
Doubs
Haut-Folin
Meursault
Archéodrome ★
DU
MORVAN ★★
Nolay
La Rochepot ★
D 973
Mont
Beuvray
AUTUN ★★★
Chagny
St-Honoré-
les-Bains
D 978
Couches ★
Verdun-s.-le-Doubs
N 81
N 80
N 73
Arroux
D 994
Signal
d'Uchon
Le Creusot
CÔTE
Centre
Givry
CHALON-S.-SAÔNE
BRESSE
D 978
N 80
N 70
Toulon-
s.-Arroux
SAÔNE-ET-LOIRE
LOUHANNAISE
D 973
Issy-
l'Evêque
Montceau-
les-Mines
du
Mt St Vincent
Grosne
LA
N 6
Seille
LOUHANS
D 60
Perrecy-les-Forges
D 980
Chapaize ★
Tournus ★★
D 994
★★ Cormatin
Brancion ★★
Canal
N 70
Chaumont
Taizé
4
Mt St-Romain
Digoin
CHAROLLES
Butte
de Suin
MÂCONNAIS
★ Paray-
le-Monial
N 79
★★ Cluny
Igé
N 6
Loire
Berzé-
la-Ville ★
Saône
D 975
BRIONNAIS
St-Point
D 982
★ Anzy-le-Duc
la Clayette
MÂCON
★★ Roche de
Solutré
N 79
Semur-en-
Brionnais ★
Chauffailles
Romanèche-
Thorins
N 6
Bourg-en-Bresse
LYONNAIS-
BRESSE
2
★ Charlieu
A 6
LYON
B
C
1
2
3
4
N

ALISE-SAINTE-REINE★

B2 / pop. 717 (Côte-d'Or)

Vercingetorix, leader of the Gauls, was defeated by Julius Caesar in 52BC after a siege of 6 weeks at **Alésia,** a site now generally acknowledged to be the Gallo-Roman ruins on **Mount Auxois.** The village was named in the 4thC AD in honour of a Christian martyr of the region.

▶ Above the village, which is also the site of a large regional hospital established by St. Vincent-de-Paul (founder of the Sisters of Charity) in 1660, Roman theatre, forum, temples; Merovingian basilica *(10-6, Apr.-Oct. 9-7 summer);* statue of Vercingetorix; orientation table **(view★).** ▶ In the village : archaeological museum *(same hours);* St. Reine's spring; church of St. Léger (7th-11thC) ▶ Early Sep. : St. Reine pilgrimage. □

▶ Nearby

▶ **Château de Bussy-Rabutin★★ :** *(5 km N; 9-11 & 2-5, Apr. Oct.; 10-11 & 2-3 Nov.-Mar.; closed Tue.)* 15th-16thC mansion to which the 17thC proprietor, Roger de Rabutin, was banished for having lampooned the love-life of Louis XIV; painted decoration★. ▶ **Bussy-le-Grand :** Romanesque church. ▶ **Flavigny-sur-Ozerain★★** *(7 km S) :* Renaissance and mediaeval houses, partly restored; abbey founded in the 7thC, where Saint Reine was buried (Carolingian crypt★; *8-11:30 & 1:30-5*); parish church of St. Genest (13th-15thC; statues; 15thC choir stalls). ▶ Numerous châteaux near **Venarey-les-Laumes : Grignon★** (11th-16thC; *Easter-1 Nov.; from Jul. 2:30-6:30*); **Lantilly** (18thC), "château of 100 windows" *(10-12 & 2-6:30; Apr.-Oct. ex. Tue.).* **Marigny-le-Cahouët :** 12th-16thC fortified farmstead *(Wed., Sat., Sun., 9-12 & 2-6).* □

ANCY-LE-FRANC★★★

B2 / pop. 1 188 (Yonne)

The **château** on the outskirts of town is a charming example of Italian Renaissance architecture.

▶ It was built in 1546 for the Clermont-Tonnerre family by an Italian artist working at the court of François I : quadrilateral building around **courtyard★★;** pilasters, alcoves, dormer-windows *(10-12 & 3-7 Apr.-Oct.).* ▶ Magnificent decoration in the apartments, salons, chapel, library, kitchens, and **murals★★** in the "Pharsale" and "Sacrifices" galleries. ▶ 125 acre park. ▶ **Nuits-sur-Amançon** *(SE) :* 16thC château *(9-12 & 2-6:30, 15 May-15 Oct.).* **Ravières :** church, old houses. □

ARNAY-LE-DUC

B3 / ® / pop. 2 334 (Côte-d'Or)

In 1570 during the Wars of Religion, Henri of Navarre (later Henri IV) fought his first battle near this small town above the river Arroux. Church of St. Laurent (15th-16thC; restored).

▶ Almshouse : (17thC) now a gallery for exhibition and sale of **regional crafts and specialities** *(Apr.-Oct. 10-12 & 2-6, closed Mon.).* ▶ Bonaventure-des-Perriers Square : town hall, turreted house. □

Burgundy cuisine

Good wine makes for a good table. Burgundian cooking and produce are renowned even in a country of superlative food. Carefully tended soil, an ideal climate and countless generations of know-how add up to matchless dining. Escargots, *almost a symbol of the province, are particulary good when prepared with Chablis. Red wine is used for braising the internationally renowned Charolais beef* (en daube). *Chambertin is the red wine favoured for the preparation of* coq-au-vin, *too often poorly served elsewhere. Fish stew* (pauchouse) *with white wine is a specialty of Verdun-sur-le-Doubs. A delicious first course is poached eggs* en meurette, *in red wine sauce with bacon and small onions, served on a slice of grilled garlic bread.* Saupiquet *from the Morvan region is a dish of ham served in a cream sauce with white wine. Ham in aspic with parsley* (jambon persillé) *is appetising, as are the tripe sausages* (andouillettes) *from Arnay-le-Duc, Chablis, Clamecy or Mâcon, grilled and served with the aromatic mustard of Dijon.*

The cheeses produced on the border of Champagne are excellent : Chaource, Soumaintrain and St. Florentin. The undisputed king of Burgundy cheeses is the strong Époisses, which is often matured in brandy (marc). *In the South, firm, sharp goat cheeses are called* boutons de culotte *(trouser buttons). Gougère is a ring of the same kind of dough* (pâte à choux) *used to make cream puffs, baked into a golden ring and topped with a glazed crust of grated Gruyère or Comté cheese.*

Tarts or puddings (clafoutis) *prepared with black-currants or cherries make a fine end to a Burgundian dinner.*

▶ Nearby

▶ **Manlay** *(12 km E) :* 14thC fortified church. 4 km farther, church of **Bard-le-Régulier :** (12th-13thC) carved choir stalls. □

AUTUN★★★

B3 / ® / pop. 22 156 (Saône-et-Loire)

Napoleon and his brothers briefly studied at the Jesuit college; mediaeval ramparts protect the town (A2-B3).

▶ The **Arroux★** (A1) and **St. André** (C1) **Gates,** two of the original four Roman gates to the city; remains of a large Roman **theatre** (15 000 spectators) overlooking a stadium and artificial lake (C2). Nearby, **Bonaparte** (formerly Jesuit) **College** (17thC); Marbres promenade. ▶ Leave the modern city at the Champ de Mars (B2) and walk past mansion façades to reach the **cathedral of St. Lazare★★★** (B3) : early 12thC, remodelled in Gothic times; doorway with **tympanum of the Last Judgement★★★** signed on the lintel by the renowned 12thC sculptor Gislebertus, carved medallions showing signs of the zodiac and the labours of the months); Romanesque **capitals★★★** in the nave (some, replaced by copies, are displayed in the chapterhouse); third chapel on left, martyrdom of St. Symphorien by Ingres; view★ from the bell-tower. ▶ **Rolin Museum★★ :** on the other side of St. Louis Square, Recumbent Eve★★★ by Gislebertus; 15thC Virgin of Autun★★ (polychrome stone); Nativity★★★ by the Master of Moulins *(9-12 & 2-6:30; 15 Mar.-Sep.; 10-12 & 2-4, Oct.-15 Mar.; closed Sun. am, Tue.).* ▶ Chapel of St. Nicolas (B1) : garden, **lapidary museum** *(info. at Rolin Museum).* ▶ Rue St. Antoine (B2-3) : **natural history museum.** □

Alésia

The local Gaulish tribe of Edueni at first collaborated with the occupying Romans, but in 52BC joined other Gaulish peoples to overthrow Julius Caesar. At the hill-fort of Bibracte (→ Beuvray) Vercingetorix was appointed leader, and decided to mount the attack in the Upper Seine valley. Defeated, the Gauls fled to Mount Auxois at Alésia, where, after a siege by the Roman legions, they were forced to surrender. Vercingetorix was taken to Rome to be exhibited at Caesar's triumph and executed 6 years later. Archaeological research has confirmed the descriptions given in Caesar's "Gallic Wars".

Weekend tips

Full Saturday morning at Dijon, then following the Vineyard Road to Beaune, and stop for the night at Tournus or Cluny. Early morning drive to Autun, then Saulieu (where you should have lunch). Continue to Avallon and Vézelay, and end the day at Auxerre. If you are taking the train, go to Laroche-Migennes (direct lines).

▶ Nearby

▶ **Temple of Janus** at the city gates *(between D978 and D980 N)*; **Couhard Rock** *(D120 S)*; **Cross of Liberation** lookout *(D256)*; **Briscou waterfall** and **Planoise Forest** *(D120 and D287).* ▶ **Château Montjeu** *(5 km S)* : splendid park. ▶ **Château Sully★★** (B3) : superb 16th-18thC edifice with skewed corner towers *(exterior visits 8-6 Palm Sunday to Oct.).* □

▶ Round trip to Mount Beuvray★ *(approx 80 km in the South of the Morvan Nature Park)*

▶ West from Autun via N81, take D3 to right. **Château Monthelon :** 15thC. ▶ La grande Verrière : **Morvan Mineral Museum** *(2-6 Sat., Sun., nat. hols. and school hols. Mar.-Oct.).* ▶ **Saint-Léger-sous-Beuvray :** at the foot of Mount Beuvray (alt. 821 m; *one-way road*) : chestnut cultivation. **Bibracte :** Gaulish hill-fort and capi-

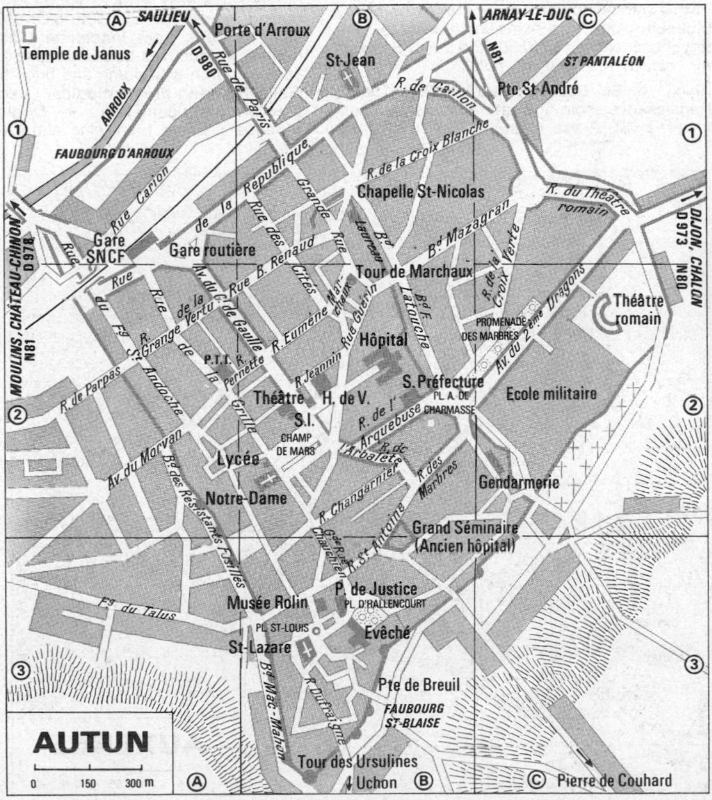

tal of the Edueni (→ Alesia) (view★★). ▶ Beyond the source of the Yonne river, through Saint-Prix Forest *(D18, D500)*, **Haut-Folin peak** (alt. 901 m), the highest point in Morvan. ▶ Return to Autun via Canche Gorge and D78. □

■ AUXERRE★★

A1-2 / ® / pop. 41 164 (Yonne)

Auxerre, in a beautiful site★ on the left bank of the Yonne, has been a thriving commercial centre since the Gallo-Roman era.

▶ Walk from the quays through the old quarter towards the **cathedral of St. Étienne★★** (B2) : flamboyant Gothic façade (damaged 13th-14thC sculptures★ on doorways), **stained glass★★** (16thC rose windows in the transept, 13thC windows in the ambulatory). 11thC **crypt★★,** with 11th-13thC **frescos★★** (Christ on a white horse); Treasury of illuminated manuscripts, enamels, ivories *(9-12 & 2-6).* ▶ **St. Germain abbey church★ :** founded in the 6thC; Gothic structure (13th-15thC); remains of 6thC abbey; elements of the 12thC Romanesque cloister were found in the 18thC buildings now used as a cultural centre (exhibitions). Two levels of **Carolingian crypts★★★ :** ancient (850AD) **frescos★★** depicting the life and martyrdom of St. Stephen *(9-11:30 & 2-5:30 ex. Tue and nat. hols.);* numerous tombs including that of St. Germain, 5thC bishop of the city. ▶ Rue de Paris leads to the central squares of **Surugue** (A2) and **Hôtel-de-Ville** (B2) connected by **Rue de l'Horloge★ :** fine buildings; 15thC clock tower. ▶ **Leblanc-Duvernoy Museum** (A2) : in a mansion; tapestries, pottery, historical items *(10:30-12 & 2-6 or 5 in winter; closed Tue. and nat. hols).*

Also... ▶ **St. Eusèbe church** (A2) : 15thC; Renaissance choir, fine Late-Romanesque bell-tower. ▶ **St. Pierre church** (B2) : 16th-17thC. ▶ Paul Bert nature conservatory (Blvd Vauban, A1; *daily*). ▶ **Museum of Art and History :** at the Coche d'Eau Mansion on Marine Quay (B1; temporary exhibition). □

■ The AUXERROIS Region

▶ Round trip from Auxerre *(105 km, full day)*

A1-2 *(see map 1)*

▶ **Auxerre** (→). ▶ Beyond the A6 motorway interchange, **Appoigny** ® : 13th-16thC church★, Renaissance choirscreen. ▶ **Seignelay :** timber-built covered **market★;** Church of St. Martial (15th-16thC). ▶ **Pontigny★★ :** Romanesque **church** (108 m long) with Gothic (ogival) arches, second daughter foundation (built in 1114) of the abbey of Citeaux (→ Côte de Nuits); 17thC choir stalls★; an important mediaeval abbey that provided refuge for three exiled Archbishops of Canterbury : Thomas Becket from 1164 to 1166, Stephen Langton (1208-1213) and Edmund Rich (venerated here where he died in 1240, as St. Edme). ▶ **Ligny-le-Chatel :** church with Romanesque nave, Renaissance choir. ▶ **Chablis★** ® : where a renowned white wine is produced; **wine cellar** in the former chapel of the 13thC infirmary (Hôtel-Dieu); S of town, **churches of St. Martin** (13thC) and the partly Romanesque **St. Pierre.** ▶ Via **Chitry** (fortified church), **Saint-Bris-le-Vineux** (church 13th-16thC; 16thC fresco and furniture), and **Irancy** (old houses), through the Yonne vineyards (lower Bourgogne); before the phylloxera crisis (→ box, "Wines of Burgundy") this was a more important wine-producing region than the Côte d'Or. Wines were sent to Paris from **Vincelotte** (13thC storehouse). ▶ **Escolives-Sainte-Camille** ® : Romanesque church with porch and brick bell-tower; Gallo-Roman archaeological excavations, Merovingian cemetery. ▶ **Coulanges-la-Vineuse :** where both wine and cherries are

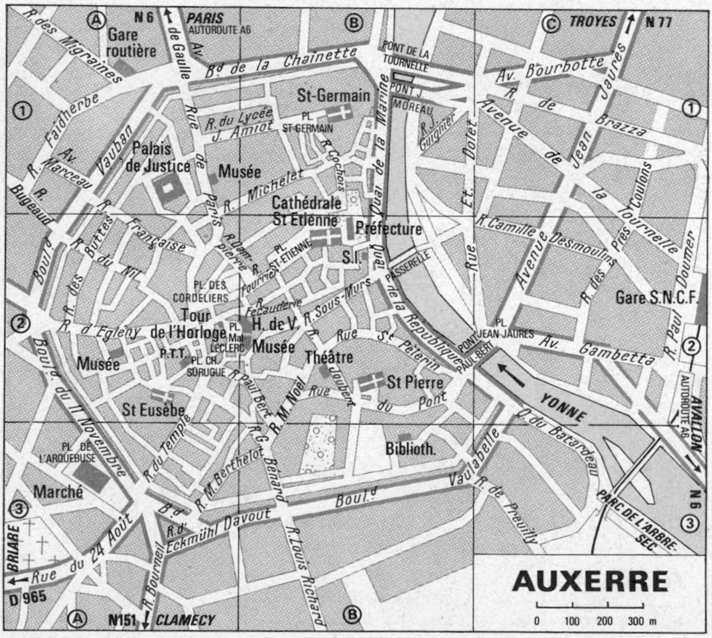

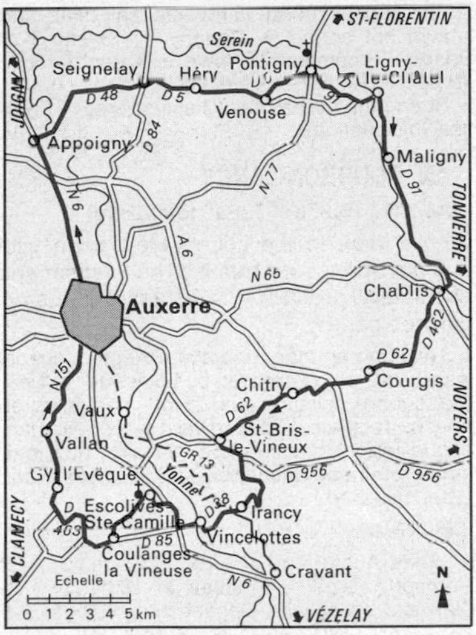

1. Auxerrois region

produced. ▶ **Gy-l'Evêque :** ruined church, 12thC bell-tower still standing. ▶ **Vaux** ® : a favourite of anglers; an excellent restaurant draws gourmets from Auxerre; attractive porch on the church. □

■ AVALLON★★

B2 / ® / pop. 8 904 (Yonne)

Reach Avallon via the valley of the river Cousin (→ below) to discover this ancient town at its most picturesque. Sensible planning has placed the modern development of Avallon far enough from the old town to preserve the charm promised by the sight of its ivy-covered ramparts and weathered watchtowers.

▶ Behind the **ramparts★ :** Petite-Porte promenade; Fort-Mahon and Fontaine-Neuve streets; numerous 15th-17thC houses line the main street (Rue Aristide Briand). ▶ Near the 15thC **Sires de Domecy mansion,** the **church of St. Lazare★ :** the two 12thC **doorways★★,** although damaged, are beautifully carved; inside, figured capitals, statuary in the nave. ▶ Left, past the 15thC **tour de l'Horloge** (clock-tower), **Avallon museum :** geology and local archaeology, paintings, engravings, goldsmith's work *(Easter school hols., 2:30-6:30, ex. Tue.; 15 Jun.-15 Sep. 10-12 & 3-7, ex. Tue.; closed Mon. in Jun.).* ▶ Near Place Vauban : former post house, now a prestigious restaurant; beginning of the commercial part of town *(market days; Thu. & Sat. am).* ▶ Chaumes Park : *(via Lyon road, then right;* swimming pool) panorama over the town. □

▶ The Cousin Valley★★ *(38 km round trip; approx half-day)*

▶ 6 km down the Saulieu road, turn right towards Magny and **Moulin-Cadoux** (D75), to cross the Cousin river. ▶ **Marrault :** a rural setting by a pond; ivy covered chapel, 18thC château, small inn. ▶ D10 runs down to the valley (D427), below the walls of Avallon. **Cousin-le-Pont :** glass-works. Beautiful riverside road amid trees, numerous water mills turned into restaurants. ▶ **Pontaubert** ® : the mediaeval Hospitallers of St. John of Jerusalem controlled this "bridge-town" on the Vézelay (→) pilgrimage road : **church★** in perfect 12thC Burgundian Romanesque style (14th and 16thC statues). ▶ **Vault-de-Lugny :** moated castle★ (partly 15thC); church with 70m-long 16thC **fresco★** of Christ's Passion. ▶ Return via **Annéot** (12th-15thC church), D128 and D166. □

■ BEAUNE★★★

C3 / ® / pop. 20 207 (Côte-d'Or)

Beaune is the wine-trading centre of Burgundy, but also one of France's most charming towns, with a wealth of historical and artistic treasures.

▶ **Hôtel-Dieu★★★ :** mediaeval infirmary, in continuous use as a hospital from its founding in 1443 until 1971; part of it still serves as a home for the aged. The splendid **courtyard★★** is often photographed as a symbol of Burgundy

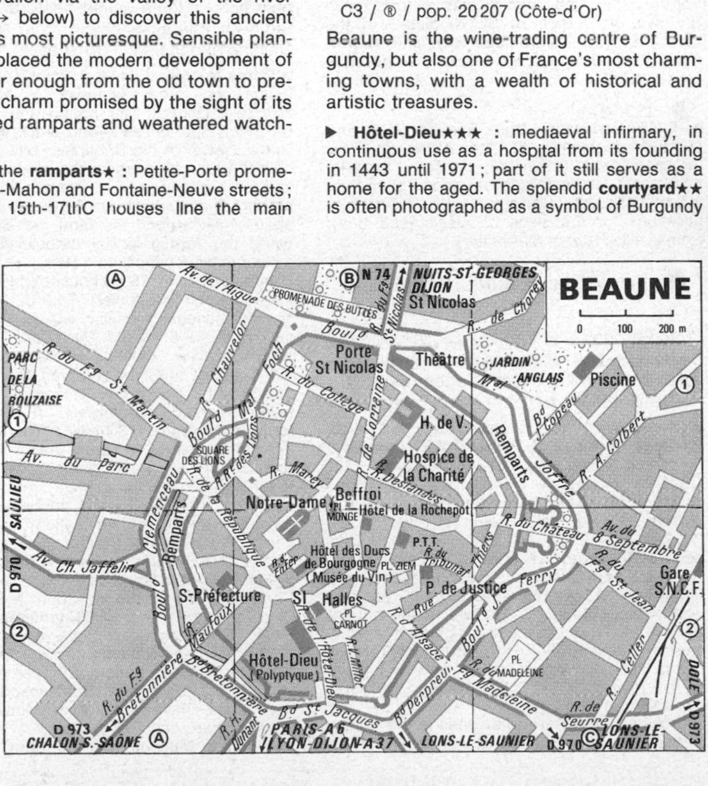

(glazed-tile roof, turrets and dormer-windows, galleries, wrought-iron well). The mediaeval decoration and furniture are preserved in the infirmary proper (52 m long; polychrome timber vaulting). A polyptych of the **Last Judgement★★★** (Roger Van der Weyden, 1443) formerly in the infirmary and now displayed in the museum, is a masterpiece of primitive Flemish painting. **Pharmacy★** (pewter and ceramics); habits worn by the nursing nuns until 1961 (window in courtyard); tapestries and furniture *(9-6:40 in season; 9-11 & 2-5 rest of year).* ▶ **Mansion of the Dukes of Burgundy★ :** (B2) among other old houses and mansions, built in the 14th, 15th and 16thC, has two wooden galleries, now the **Burgundy Wine Museum★★** *(9-12:30 & 2-5:45)* vine-growing techniques, history of the vineyard, tools, bottles, paintings and sculptures, contemporary tapestries; fermentation room *(son et lumière* show, *Thu., Fri., Sat.,; info. at SI).* ▶ **Collegiate Church of Notre-Dame★ :** 14thC porch, Romanesque nave reminiscent of Autun (→); choir remodelled in the 13thC, side-chapels added later (frescos; sculpture; 15th-16thC paintings); 15thC silk and wool **tapestries** depicting **the Life of the Virgin★★** exhibited behind the altar; eastern end of the church★ (from outside). ▶ Around Place Monge : interesting mansions, such as the 16thC la Rochepot Mansion (B2). ▶ Not far from there is a former orphanage founded in the 17thC **(Hospice de la Charité;** *temporarily closed***).** ▶ In the Town Hall (former Ursulines Convent; 17thC, **Museum of Fine Arts :** archaeology, history, painting and **Etienne-Jules Marey** (1830-1904) **collection :** Marey invented chronophotography, *(Apr.-Nov. 9-12 & 2-5:30 ex. Tue.).* ▶ Stroll the streets to discover the many old houses of Beaune, before visiting the Saint-Nicolas district, north of town. ▶ **Church of St. Nicolas :** in the vineyard area, 12thC doorway and tower, 15thC wooden porch; the rest of the church is mostly 13thC. □

▶ Nearby

▶ Easily accessible from Beaune (D18 and D23; or highway A6), the **Archéodrome★** (archaeological information centre) : models, documents, outdoor reconstructions of prehistoric and Gaulish dwellings, tombs, Roman fortifications for the siege of Alésia (see box), Roman villa *(10-8 or 6 in winter).* □

■ The Côte de BEAUNE Region★★

C3

From Serrigny N to Santenay S, the Côte de Beaune is one of the most densely cultivated and — square metre for square metre — most valuable tracts of land in the world.

▶ **Serrigny :** 18thC château, beautiful farm. ▶ **Aloxe-Corton** and **Pernand-Vergelesses :** great red wines. **Savigny-les-Beaune★** ® : 12thC Romanesque bell-tower; 15th-18thC church; 17th and 18thC **château★** with cellars, stables, motor-cycle museum of 250 models *(9-12 & 2-6);* Louis XIV pavilion, French gardens. ▶ **Pommard :** old houses, château (14thC cellars). **Volnay :** château. (Both great red wine names). ▶ **Auxey-Duresses :** both red and white wines. **Meursault** ® : site of the annual *Paulée* (→ Trois Glorieuses); 15th-18th-19thC château, glazed-tile roof. ▶ **Saint-Romain** *(6 km) :* summertime exhibition of local history in the town hall. ▶ **Puligny-Montrachet** and **Chassagne-Montrachet :** revered as the sources of the finest white wines in the world. ▶ **Santenay** ® : château at the foot of cliffs (15thC keep); 13th-15thC church; salt and lithium hot spring. ▶ **Chagny** ® *(15 km S of Beaune) :* commercial town and gastronomic stopover; Romanesque elements in the church. ▶ Round trip of the Côte (illuminations, → Practical Information). □

■ BOURBON-LANCY

A4 / ® / pop. 6507 (Saône-et-Loire)

With a view to the Loire valley, town with five hot springs for treating rheumatism and circulatory problems; substantial industry; casino; park.

▶ Near the springs, **Hospice d'Aligre :** chapel with 17thC pulpit donated by Louis XIV. ▶ Near the square, picturesque 16thC half-timbered house, fountain, clock-tower. ▶ N., Romanesque former church of St. Nazaire, now **museum of local antiquités** *(4-7 ex. Mon. and Wed., Jul.-Sep.)* □

▶ Nearby

▶ **Saint-Aubin-sur-Loire★★** *(6.5 km S past Germigny forest) :* **château** in 18thC French Classical style, with elegant outbuildings *(2-5 ex. Tue. Jul.-Sep.).* ▶ **Signal du Mont** (alt. 469 m; *7 km W from Bourbon-Archambault) :* **view** to the Auvergne peaks in clear weather. ▶ **Ternant** *(18 km N) :* church with two Flemish sculpted wood **triptychs★★** (1432-1435; *9-6 or 4 in winter*). □

■ The BRIONNAIS Region★★

▶ Round trip *(approx 127 km, full day)*

B4 *(see map 2)*

Between the Loire and the wooded Mâconnais hills, a litttle-visited pastoral area dotted with churches dating from the era of Cluniac expansion (11th-12thC).

▶ **Paray-le-Monial** ® (→). ▶ **Saint-Yan :** Romanesque choir and bell-tower. ▶ **Montceaux-l'Étoile :** Church with noteworthy Ascension on the tympanum★★★ and lintel. ▶ **Anzy-le-Duc★ :** jewel of the Brionnais; bell-tower★★ ; church★★★, supposedly the model for Vézelay (→); **carvings★★★** (tympanum, capitals) among the earliest in Burgundy; frescoed apse; walk around the farm *(no entry)* occupying the former priory outbuildings to see more primitive tympanum (11thC). ▶ **Marcigny :** commercial town, 15thC houses; partly Romanesque church (bell-tower); Tour du Moulin (Mill Tower) museum with fine woodwork (statues, ceramics : *2-6 closed Dec.-Jan.).* ▶ **Semur-en-Brionnais★** : château where St. Hugues, a 12thC abbot of Cluny (→) was born; remains of late-12thC church★★ : octagonal 13thC bell-tower; carved doorway★★. ▶ **Saint-Christophe-en-Brionnais** *(8 km NE) :* Thursday morning cattle market. ▶ **Saint-Julien-de-Jonzy :** tympanum★★ (Last Supper and Christ Washing the Disciples' Feet, on the lintel); mid-12thC bell-tower★ and doorway★★ (partly damaged during the Revolution); view★ from behind the church. ▶ **Iguerande :** on the banks of the Loire, figured capitals★ in the church. ▶ **Fleury-la-Montagne :** tympanum★ depicting Christ, the Virgin and St. John. ▶ **Charlieu★** (→ Lyonnais-Bresse) ▶ **Châteauneuf :** hillside site★; Romanesque church★ overlooking old bridge; Château Bauchet (partly 16thC). **Saint-Maurice-lès-Châteauneuf** (D8) : cemetery chapel with bell-tower and Romanesque eastern end. ▶ **La Clayette** ® (pron. "clette") : small market town; moated castle★★ (14th-19thC); **Automobile Museum★** in the 15thC out-build-

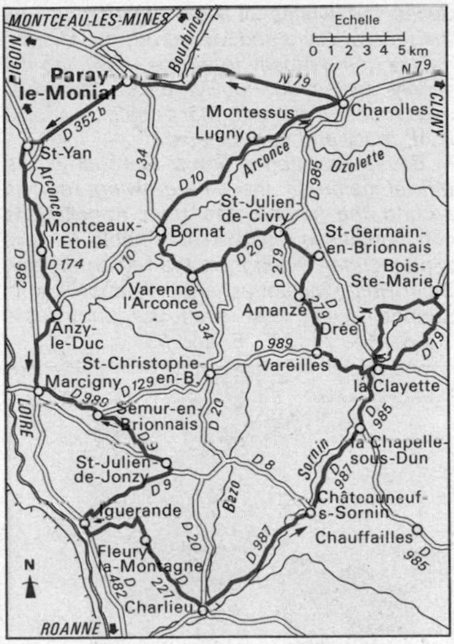

2. Brionnais region

ings *(9-12 & 2-7 ex. Sun., Easter-1 Nov.; 2-6 ex. Sat., Sun. rest of year)*, an annex of the larger museum at **Chaufailles** ® *(7 km E; same hours)*. ▶ **Bois-Sainte-Marie :** one of the oldest (11thC) churches★ in the Brionnais; side tympanum; capitals; unusual ambulatory. ▶ **Château Drée★★ :** (17thC) among trees at the end of a beautiful walk. ▶ **Vareilles :** Romanesque bell-tower. ▶ **Saint-Germain-en-Brionnais :** solid country church. ▶ **Varenne-l'Arconce :** bell-tower; decoration carved from hard local sandstone. ▶ Beyond Château Montessus, **Charolles** ® : cattle market and centre of the Charollais; remains of the château of the counts of Charollais; museum of the works of a local sculptor, René Davoine (1888-1962; *closed Tue.)*. ▶ Paray-le-Monial (→). □

CHALON-SUR-SAÔNE

C3 / ® / pop. 57 967 (Saône-et-Loire)

An important market since the Middle Ages, where each year before the carnival (Mardi Gras), the "cold" fair attracts trappers from all over France, and fur-buyers from all over the world, to trade in pelts.

▶ On the island in the Saône, the **Hospital** (C2) : 16thC refectory★; 15thC Doyenné Tower, formerly near the Cathedral, rebuilt here in 1907 *(visits Wed., Sat. and Sun., Apr.-Oct.)*. ▶ On the right bank of the river, 18thC Messageries Mansion housing the **Nicéphore Niepce Museum★★ :** Scientist and inventor of photography (1765-1833), born and died at Chalon; equipment, heliography, daguerreotypes, contemporary photographs (B2; *9:30-11:30 & 2:30-5:30 ex. Tue. and nat. hols.*). ▶ Cathedral of St. Vincent (C1) : Romanesque transept, Gothic apse, Renaissance chapels, 19thC façade; among half-timbered houses. ▶ **Denon museum★** (B2) : archaeology (Gallo-Roman bas-relief★) ethnology (lighterage, craftwork), paintings (16thC altarpiece, pre-Impressionists) *(9:30-12 & 2-5:30 ex. Tue. and nat. hols.)*. ▶ **The House of Wines** of the Chalonnaise Region *(N, N6)* and an important **rose garden** (Plaine Saint-Nicolas) round off Chalon's attractions. ▶ On the left bank of the Saône, **Saint-Marcel :** Cluniac Romanesque priory church commemorating a regional martyr; the philosopher Peter Abelard (b.1079) died here in 1148.□

The CHALONNAISE Region★

C3

W of Chalon-sur-Saône, the Chalonnais region (Côte) extends N and S of Mercurey between the districts of Beaune and Mâconnais. The vineyards produce red and white wines of great quality.

▶ **Chassey-le-Camp** *(SW of Châgny) :* "camp" refers to a Neolithic hillfort. ▶ **Rully** ® *(W of D981) :* 13th and 15thC fortress★ with large towers and square keep *(Sat., Sun., Apr.-Oct.)*; white wines. ▶ **Mercurey** ® : red wine tastings.

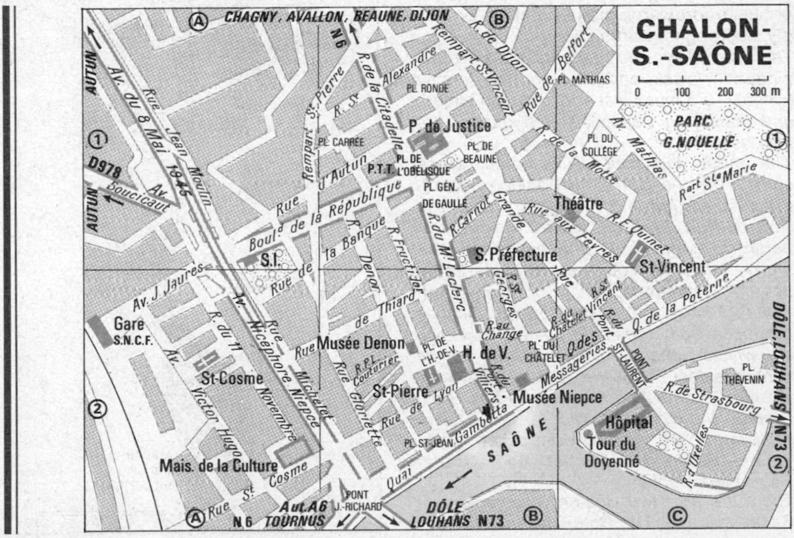

Burgundy wines

The Romans found vines already flourishing when they conquered Burgundy, but Burgundian wines came into their own during the Middle Ages. The Cluniac and Cistercian monks systematically cultivated and improved vines while, at the same time, improving techniques of fermentation and aging. Many vineyards today yielding excellent wines originated as dependencies of abbeys.

Burgundian vineyards cover a total of 52 500 acres, of which 38 000 are entitled to the superior status of A.O.C. (controlled place-name of origin). Nearby 5 000 growers cultivate plots that are called "climats". There may be as many as 50 climats in a single "place of origin" but it is essential to bear in mind that in Burgundy, more than anywhere else, quality counts above quantity. Plots as small as a single row of vines may change hands for fabulous sums.

Like all the vineyards in France, those of Burgundy were completely laid waste during the 19thC by the American vine louse, Phylloxera vastatrix, which destroyed the vines at the root. Phylloxera was finally overcome by grafting French vines onto the root stocks of resistant American varieties, but only after an appalling toll had been exacted of French vine-growers and workers in related industries.

The finest Burgundian wines are described as appelations communales (of community origin). Wines of lesser quality are appelations régionales (of regional origin, i.e. less specific), including wines that are defined not by locality but by some other peculiarity, such as Bourgogne aligoté (a white Burgundy wine made from aligoté grapes) or Bourgogne passe-tout-grains ("pass all berries" i.e., a red made from a mixture of grape varieties).

Others may be described as Bourgogne ordinaire (ordinary), grand ordinaire or simply Bourgogne (Burgundy).

The two widely used grape varieties are the pinot noir (black) and the pinot chardonnay (white). To a much lesser extent, the aligoté and (mainly in Beaujolais) the gamay are also used.

The most illustrious Burgundian wines come from the Côte-d'Or ("golden coast"), which is divided into two main areas. The Côte de Nuits produces superb reds (Chambertin, Clos-de-Bèze, Bonnes-mares, Musigny, Clos-de-Vougeot, Grands-Échézeaux, Romanée-Conti, Romanée-Saint-Vivant, Richebourg). The Côte de Beaune produces both reds and whites, including the whites generally acknowledged as the very greatest by wine lovers; the reds include Corton-Charlemagne and Les Bressandes; the whites are Montrachet, Chevalier-Montrachet, Bâtard-Montrachet, Bienvenues-Bâtard-Montrachet and Criots-Bâtard-Montrachet.

There are also two vine-growing regions in Saône-et-Loire. The Côte Chalonnaise produces the whites of Rully, Montagny and the reds of Givry and Mercurey; the Mâconnais is home mostly to whites, including the widely acclaimed Pouilly-Fuissé. The reds and rosés from the Mâconnais are also light, fruity and very pleasant.

In Basse Bourgogne (lower Burgundy), the official name of the vine-growing regions around the Yonne, the term appellations communales is reserved for Chablis (always white). Other wines from the region (Irancy, Saint-Bris, Vincelottes) are only appellations régionales. The best recent Burgundy years are 61, 69, 71, 76, 78, and 83.

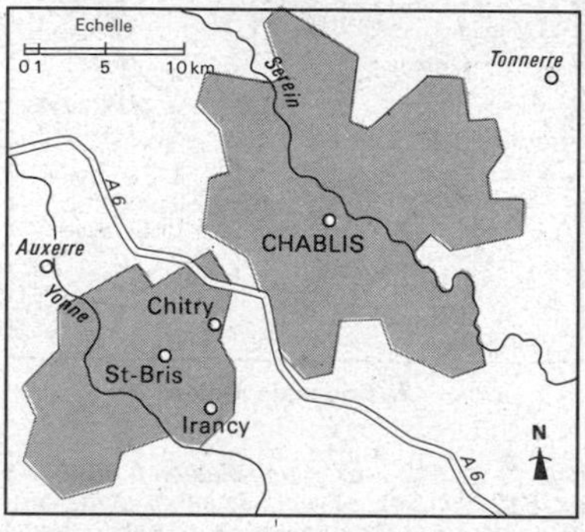

Vineyards of upper and lower Burgundy

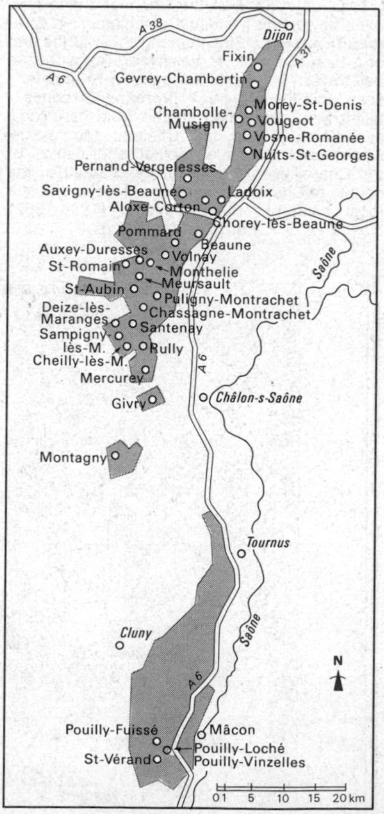

▶ **Château Germolles★** : 13th-14thC *(10-12 & 2-6 ex. Tue.; Aug.-15 Sep.)*. ▶ **Givry** *(D981)* : commercial town and red wine centre; 18thC layout; monumental gates, fountains, covered markets, church★. ▶ **Buxy★** : mediaeval fortifications, old houses, Romanesque church; white wine tastings. ▶ S of **La Ferté** Forest, a Louis XIII abbey building and farm remain from the first daughter foundation of Citeaux (→ Côtes de Nuits). ▶ **Saint-Martin-de-Laives★** *(7 km farther, above the A6 motorway)* : 11thC **church.** In same direction, **Sennecy-le-Grand** : Romanesque church. ▶ **Saint-Julien** *(1 km S* : church 11th-12thC.). □

La CHARITÉ-SUR-LOIRE★

A3 / ® / pop. 6416 (Nièvre)

Pilgrims on the road from Vézelay to the Spanish shrine of St. James of Compostela were entitled to stop for a night's board and lodging at the Cluniac abbey, which thereby earned the name of "Charity on the Loire".

▶ On the banks of the Loire (view★ from the bridge), La Charité surrounds the remains of the abbey. The **church★★**, despite the destruction of the first bays of the nave, remains a splendid example of Cluniac architecture. St. Croix tower was part of the 12thC façade (tympanum); nave rebuilt in the 18thC; choir and transept★ 11th-12thC; capitals; outside, chevet (eastern end)★★. ▶ Museum of local mediaeval archaeology *(3-6; Jul.-Aug. 10-12 & 3-6; closed Tue.)*. □

▶ Nearby

▶ **Pouilly-sur-Loire** ® *(13 km N)* : centre of a sign-posted route around a white wine region.

CHÂTEAU-CHINON

B3 / ® / pop. 2463 (Nièvre)

The town motto says "Small town, great renown"; on a hillside once inhabited by Gauls, good base for excursions to the Morvan Nature Park (→).

▶ From the château promenade, view★ over the Morvan and the Yonne Gorges; climb **Calvaire ridge** (butte) (view★★). ▶ Rue St Christophe, **Morvan Costume and Folklore museum★,** with memorabilia of Napoleon III *(Wed., Sat., Sun., 2:30-6 May-Oct.)*. □

▶ Nearby

▶ To the N, Morvan lakes (→). ▶ **Château Besne** (12 km W) : 12th-15thC *(Tue., Thu., Sat., Apr.-Sep.)*. Beyond **Châtillon-en-Bazois** : mediaeval château *(am ex. Tue. Jul-Aug.)*. ▶ Along D978 E, then at **Arleuf** by D177 to the **Anost Forest★** : signposted trails not far *(20 km)* from **Anost:** wild-boar reserve and look-out at **Notre-Dame-de-l'Aillant** *(alt. 625 m)*. **Cussy-en-Morvan** *(7.5 km farther)* : site★. □

CHÂTILLON-SUR-SEINE★★

B1 / ® / pop. 7963 (Côte-d'Or)

The Seine flows under the Perthuis-au-Loup bridge in a city that retains a great deal of charm despite extensive damage inflicted in 1940.

▶ Town life is centred around Rue Maréchal de Lattre-de-Tassigny and the Place de la Résistance. Tourists flock to the **museum★★** (7 Rue du Bourg; *9-12 & 2-6 or 5 in winter, 7 in summer; closed am out of season)*. In the Renaissance Philandrier★ mansion : archaeological collection (Gallo-Roman domestic objects, tools) including the **Vix Treasure,** unearthed in 1953 in the burial mound of a Gaulish noblewoman, the prize exhibit a **bronze urn** dating from the 6thC BC, 1.64 m high, 208 kg, with a magnificent frieze; also gold and silver jewellery (diadem★★). ▶ Left on Rue du Bourg, overlooking the town near the château ruins, **Church of St. Vorles★★** : 10thC Romanesque, built of small stones and stone tiles, 13thC bell-tower; 16thC Holy sepulchre in spare interior. ▶ Nearby, pleasant walk to the **source of the Douix★** at the foot of a rocky slope. □

▶ Nearby

▶ **Vix** *(7 km NW)* : small village at the foot of **Mount Lassois,** remembered for the treasure (see above) unearthed near the hill-fort; Church of St. Marcel, partly Romanesque. ▶ SE, the 85 km² **Châtillon Forest** (oak, beech, conifers); 18 km of forest road; via D928, another forest route to **Marots lakes** and **Val des Choues abbey** ruins. ▶ Down the **Seine** and **Coquille valleys** (N71) past remains of 14thC castle at Brémur then (D32 and D954) to **Aignay-le-Duc** *(33 km from Châtillon)* : Gothic church with 16thC altarpiece. **Etalante** *(5 km farther)* : **source of the river Coquille★. Duesme** *(4 km from Aignay)* : remains of 14thC château; waterfall. **Quemigny-sur-Seine** : 18thC château. Farther west to **Jours-les-Baigneux** : Renaissance château *(Easter and school hols. ex. Tue.)*. ▶ **Montigny-sur-Aube** (extreme N of Côte d'Or, *22 km NE*) : 16thC château. ▶ In a small valley between two forests, ruined abbey of **Molesmes** *(24 km NW; 2-7, Mar.-Oct.)* : the first abbey of the Cistercian order (1098), which exerted profound effects on both architecture and religious thought. □

CLUNY★★

B-C4 / ® / pop. 4734 (Saône-et-Loire)

William the Pious, Duke of Aquitaine, founded the Benedictine monastery here on the banks of the Grosne in 910. Cluny quickly became the most famous and powerful abbey in Christendom; its abbots — Odon, Mayeul, St. Hugues and Peter the Venerable — at times surpassed popes and kings in influence. Numerous country churches, in a rustic but accomplished Romanesque style, remain from this period. Two centuries after its foundation, Cluny had spawned 1200 daughter-abbeys throughout Europe. The abbey church, still a magnificent building, was systematically demolished in 1798 after the Revolution.

▶ The city grew up around the abbey *(reached by D15 to E)*; remains of the **ramparts** can still be seen. ▶ Place du 11 août : **stables of St. Hugues** *(summer exhibitions)*; opposite, the Gothic façade of the **abbey** (over-restored in the 19thC) *(10-12 & 2-5, 9-12 & 2-6 in summer)*; most of the existing buildings were reconstructed in the 18thC; they frame the cloister facing the gardens (School of Arts and Crafts, national thoroughbred stud-farm; *9-11 & 2-5)*, shadowed by the 62m-high octagonal **Clocher de l'Eau Bénite★★** (Holy-Water bell-tower) and the clock-tower (Tour de l'Horloge). With the Gothic **Bourbon chapel,** these are the only remains of the **abbey church**

The high-speed express

The TGV (Train à Grande Vitesse) is a newcomer to the Burgundy countryside; fortunately, the track is less obtrusive than a motorway. Now in service over the whole route, TGV trains run at up to 270 km/h, linking Paris to Montchanin in 1 hr 26, to Dijon in 1 hr 36 and to Mâcon in 1 hr 41. Weekends in Burgundy are now easier. Technical innovations include fully automated signalling to the driver's cabin and high-speed power cut-off by pantographic switch. Wheel deformation at the tolerance limit of 3/10 mm occurs only after 300000 km, compared with 50000 km for an ordinary train.

of St. Pierre-St. Paul. The scope of the original can be imagined from the fact that these great structures once formed a single crosspiece of one of the two transepts. This church, built between 1088 and 1130, was 177 m long, with five naves, five bell-towers and 301 windows; for several centuries it was the largest church in Christendom. ▶ At the rear of the gardens in the 13thC **Farinier** (flour store) are the figured **capitals★★★** from the choir : Adam & Eve, Abraham's sacrifice, beekeepers, seasons, musical modes, and many others, all carved in 1095. ▶ Right, on leaving the abbey, Rue A. K. Conant follows the line of the former nave : the two square Baraban towers mark the former façade. ▶ Farther along on the right, in a 15thC abbey building, the **Ochier Museum★ :** sculptures and souvenirs of the abbey; local history; work by the painter Pierre Prud'hon (1758-1823) who was born at Cluny *(10-12 & 2-4 or 6:30 in summer : closed 20 Dec.-15 Jan.).* ▶ Nearby, the former 15thC **abbey palace,** now the town hall. ▶ 12th and 13thC **houses;** Hôtel de la Monnaie : exhibitions; 13thC **church of Notre-Dame** (pretty parvis with fountain); late Romanesque **church of St. Marcel★** (1159; bell-tower★★). Then to the land of the poet Alphonse de Lamartine (1790-1869) (→ Mâcon), or the Cluny area towards Tournus (→). □

▶ Nearby

▶ **Azé caves** *(12 km E) :* underground river; prehistoric museum *(9-12 & 2-7, Palm Sunday-1 Oct.).* ▶ **Grosne Valley** (→ between Tournus and Cluny). **Suin Ridge** *(21 km W from Cluny) :* 592m-high; view★★. **Pézanin Arboretum** *(13 km S) :* 45 acres of exotic trees. **Chaumont** *(8 km NW) :* Renaissance and 19thC **château,** neo-Gothic; 17thC stables★. □

COSNE-SUR-LOIRE

A2 / ® / pop. 12463 (Nièvre)

Small town on the Loire, shopping centre on N7, **museum;** river boats *(10-12 & 1-7 ex. Mon. and Tue., 15 Jun.-15 Sep.).* **Church of St. Agnan :** former Cluniac priory (Romanesque apse and doorway. ▶ **Saint-Père :** *(2 km E) :* 12th-16thC Commandery of Villemoison (Knights-Templars' residence; *Sat. pm in summer*). □

▶ Nearby

▶ **Cadoux farm** *(11 km N on N7) :* exhibition of country traditions in summer. Farther on, view (left) of the **Belleville-sur-Loire Nuclear Centre** under construction. ▶ At the gates of **Donzy** ® *(17 km E)* is **Donzy-le-Pré :** 12thC tympanum of the Cluniac priory is considered a masterpiece of Burgundian Romanesque sculpture. **Château de La Motte-Josserand** *(4 km N) :* a mediaeval fortress remodelled in the 17thC *(10-12 & 2-6, Apr.-Oct.).* SE, the forests of Donzy and Bellary. □

Le CREUSOT

B3 / ® / pop. 32309 (Saône-et-Loire)

Le Creusot, Montchanin and Montceau-les-Mines : an industrial conglomeration (urban pop. 120000) that has much to interest tourists. The substantial remains of 17th and 18thC industry have contributed greatly to understanding the developments that paved the way for the industrial revolution.

▶ Iron was exploited south of the Morvan from the Middle Ages; the 17thC discovery of extensive coal seams permitted large-scale development in the form of steel mills and other industries dependent on readily available fuel, such as ceramics and glass-making. ▶ **Château de la Verrerie :** the name commemorates the former glassworks transferred to Creusot in 1787 and continuing throughout the 19thC under the aegis of the renowned St. Louis and Baccarat crystal manufacturers (→ Vosges). From 1834 to 1970, the château was the home of the Schneider family, whose steel mills enlarged the town and its factories several times over during the 19thC and first half of the 20thC. It is now a **Museum of local and industrial history** offering courses and exhibitions *(2-6 ex. Mon.).* □

▶ Nearby

▶ In summer *(Jun.-Sep.),* the Museum offers displays at various locations, including a mine entrance at **Blanzy** *(16 km S),* lock-keeper's house at **Ecuisses** *(9 km SE),* school-house at **Montceau-les-Mines (→)** *(info. from Château de la Verrerie).* ▶ **Saint-Sernin-du-Bois** *(7 km N) :* keep and partly Romanesque priory near a reservoir. ▶ **Couches** ® *(16 km NE; D1) :* **château** belonged to Marguerite of Burgundy, widow of Charles d'Anjou, King of Naples and Sicily, and brother of St. Louis (13thC); 11thC keep, 13thC wall. In the village : 15th and 16thC church; old houses. ▶ **Signal d'Uchon** *(18 km W of Le Creusot) :* alt. 681 m, orientation table, one of the best vantage points on the massif. □

CURE Valley★★

▶ From Cravant to Chastellux *(85 km, full day)*
A-B2

Ideal for weekends away from Paris (2 hr away) : river, meadows and woods, caves, Vézelay.

▶ The Cure and Yonne rivers meet at **Cravant** and join the Seine, near Paris. A stopover for loggers with timber from the forests; Renaissance church; old houses. ▶ **Accolay :** (left bank) 12thC church. ▶ **Vermenton** ® : large market-village; church, 12thC towers. ▶ **Arcy-sur-Cure** ® : **caves★,** visit the Large Grotto with mineral formation; lake *(9-12 & 2-6, Mar.-Nov.);* stroll on the riverbank. ▶ **Saint-Moré :** caves, Gallo-Roman ruins of Nora; wall, tower. ▶ After **Sermizelles,** leave N6 for D951 on the left. ▶ **Asquins :** at the foot of the

Vézelay hill (→). ▶ **Saint-Père-sous-Vézelay (→ Vézelay).** ▶ **Pierre-Perthuis** : ruined mediaeval castle; modern bridge over the **Cure Gorges (site★★)**; old hump-backed bridge. ▶ Leave the Cure for a detour to **Bazoches;** the military engineer Sébastien de Vauban (1633-1707) is buried in the church (his heart is in the Invalides Museum in Paris); 12th-15thC **castle★.** ▶ Via D127, **Cure** (site★) and D20, reach **Chastellux** (→ round trip of the Morvan Lakes). □

DECIZE

A3 / ® / pop. 7 437 (Nièvre)

Decize is a charming town on an island at the junction of the Aron and the Loire, where the Nivernais canal ends.

▶ **Church of St. Aré :** 11thC, over a 7thC Merovingian crypt dedicated to St. Aré, Bishop of Nevers. □

DIJON★★★

C2 / ® / pop. 140 942 (Côte-d'Or)

Dijon is an elegant, busy city, former capital of the Grand Dukes of Burgundy who brought the finest artists of Flanders to adorn it. It is a cross-roads, where all the Burgundian regions converge.

Between the train station (A2; near Arquebuse gardens and Natural History Museum) and the town centre, **Place Darcy** (A2) : heart of Dijon; 18thC Guillaume gate and Darcy garden with fountains. ▶ Left of the lively **Rue de la Liberté :** market district; **Rue des Forges** lined with exquisite houses (nos. 52, 56, 40 (Aubriot Mansion★★), 38, 34) leading to **Place de la Libération★★** (B2) 1690, designed, by Jules Hardouin-Mansart (1647-1708), who succeeded his grandfather as Royal Architect at Versailles). ▶ Courtyard of Honour of the **Grand Duke's Palace★★** (now the Town Hall) opens onto the square; staircase★★, 18thC State Room. Right of the courtyard, passageway to bar courtyard : Bar tower (14thC) flanked by Renaissance Bellegarde stairway. ▶ The **Fine Arts Museum★★★** (B2) : one of the richest in France *(10-6 ex. Tue.; some rooms are closed at midday)*; partly in the 15thC ducal kitchens★, near the sculpture collection of works of the sculptors François Rude (1784-1855) and François Pompon (1855-1933), born at Dijon. In the Guards' Hall★, the remarkable 15thC **tombs★★★** of Philippe le Hardi and Jean sans Peur; carved and painted **altarpieces** illustrate the golden age of Flemish art. Important painting collections include : Flemish Primitives, Dutch Masters (Teniers, Hals, Rubens); Italian (Lotto, Veronese, Tintoretto, Tiepolo); French 17th-18thC (Champaigne, Rigaud, Mignard); 19thC (Géricault, Delacroix, Corot, Monet, Vuillard); 20thC (Delaunay, de Staël, Messagier, Vieira da Silva) and many others. ▶ Behind the Ducal Palace, **Place des Ducs** (B2), with old houses : **Verrerie and Chouette streets** are lined with houses and mansions from the 15th to the 17thC (**Voguë Mansion★** with glazed-tile roof; B2). ▶ **Church of Notre-Dame★★ :** façade with fine Gothic arches; the nave is a beautiful example of Burgundian Gothic (1210-1240); in the right transept, 13thC Black Virgin. Outside, bell-tower : Jack-o'-the-Clock with his wife and children (the Jacquemart family) strikes the hours. ▶ **Lantenay Mansion★★** (1759; B1) : now administrative offices; in the street, 18thC mansions. ▶ **Church of St. Michel★** (B2) : behind a Renaissance façade, a Flamboyant Gothic building. ▶ **Lantin Mansion** (17thC) : now **Magnin Museum,** retains most of its furniture; paintings (Hieronymus Bosch : Christ Crowned with Thorns★; Vouet; Gros; *9-12 & 2-6, closed Tue.).* ▶ Many houses and mansions dating from the 16th-18thC in Rue Vauban (No. 21 : Liégard Mansion★★), Rue de l'Amiral Roussin, Rue du Petit Potet, Rue Berbissey, Place Bossuet. ▶ **Palais de Justice** (Courthouse) in the former Parliament of Burgundy (B2) : Renaissance doorway; ceiling★ in the 17thC court of assizes. ▶ Past the churches of St. Jean (15thC) and St. Philibert★ (12th; 16thC spire), the **cathedral★ of St. Bénigne** (A2) : a glazed-tile roof on the Gothic former abbey church (1280-1314); the circular **crypt★★★** is in fact the Romanesque basilica built by Abbot Guillaume of Volpiano (10thC); pre-Romanesque capitals★★★. ▶ **Archaeological Museum★★** in the 12thC dormitory of the former abbey; on the ground floor, Gallo-Roman votive statues★★ found at the source of the Seine; on the first floor, Romanesque and Gothic sculpture *(9-12 & 2-6; 9:30-6 in summer; closed Tue.).* ▶ At the W exit from town, former **Champmol Charterhouse,** now a psychiatric hospital, built by Philippe le Hardi; burial site of the Dukes of Burgundy, destroyed during the Revolution. The only remains are : chapel **doorway★** (1390) and **Puits de Moïse★★** (Moses Well), base of a Calvary (scene of Christ's death) by the 14thC master-sculptor Claus Sluter (the original polychrome stressed the realism of the masterpiece). ▶ Out of town, **Lake Kir** (beach, leisure centre, sailing, restaurant) named after a canon and mayor of Dijon who favoured the drink of white wine enlivened by black-currant liqueur *(cassis)* named Kir in this honour.

Also... ▶ **Museum of Burgundian life** (17, rue Sainte-Anne, B3; *temporary exhibits only*). ▶ **Museum of Religious Art :** (No. 15 Rue Ste. Anne; B3) goldsmiths' work, textiles *(9-12 & 2-6, closed Tue. and nat. hols.).* ▶ **Hospital Museum :** in 17thC hospital (15thC chapel), works of art, illuminated manuscripts related to the 14thC founding of the hospital. □

▶ Nearby

▶ **Mount Afrique (***10 km SW;* alt. 600 m) : park view★. ▶ **Rouvres-en-Plaine** *(14 km SE) :* Cistercian Gothic church (13thC) with sculptures by Sluter and treasury. ▶ Narrow road along the **Souzon Valley★** ® *(NW; D996 and D7; or GR7 and GR2) :* 1790 **château de Vantoux★.** □

▶ Ouche Valley★

From Dijon to Bligny *(47 km; half-day)*

▶ The highway and the Bourgogne canal run through this valley in the Dijon countryside. ▶ Beyond **Velars-sur-Ouche** ® turn right at **Fleury-sur-Ouche,** towards the **château de Lantenay** (18thC; *Thu., 1st and 3rd Sun. in month, Apr.-Oct.).* ▶ **Pont-de-Pany** ® : left, road to 18thC **château de Montculot★.** ▶ Before **Saint-Victor-sur-Ouche,** ruins of Marigny castle on the right. ▶ **La Bussière-sur-Ouche :** remains of 13thC Cistercian abbey *(10-12 & 3-6, 15 Jun.-15 Sep. ex. Tue. and Sun. am).* ▶ Beyond the motorway viaduct at **Pont-d'Ouche,** the valley ends just past **Bligny-sur-Ouche** (Gothic church with Romanesque doorway; tourist-train). □

■ FONTENAY Abbey★★★

B2 (Saône-et-Loire)

The 12thC monastic reformer St. Bernard of Clairvaux laid down stringent rules for his builder-monks. The abbey he founded here illustrates the virtuosity of Romanesque architecture within the Cistercian strictures on austerity and sobriety, where nothing should distract from prayer; the beauty of the buildings springs entirely from the fundamental design and materials.

▶ The abbey was begun in about 1120. Behind the entrance building (15thC upper floor) left, not far from the dovecote, the **church★** (1140-1147) : simple doorway; the pillars and arches of the nave draw the eye to the choir and square apse (12thC floor tiling); the Virgin★ of Fontenay (13thC) stands in the left transept. Opposite, staircase to the dormitory (chestnut beams★) and the entrance to the chapterhouse ▶ This leads to the **cloister★★** with massive yet elegant arcades. Up to 300 monks and lay-brothers at a time lived in the abbey. ▶ Through the prison (the monks had rights of justice on abbey lands) to the forges, restored like the rest of the buildings, at the beginning of this century. The abbey was used as a paper mill after the Revolution (1789) until 1906 *(guided tours every hour or half-hour, Jul.-Aug.; 9-12 & 2 or 2:30-6).* □

■ JOIGNY★

A1 / ® / pop. 9 644 (Yonne)

Gateway to Burgundy on the river Yonne, Joigny is a stopover for shopping and excellent dining.

▶ Park on the quay, then walk to the church of **St. Thibault★** (15thC Flamboyant Gothic; Flemish paintings; 14thC Smiling Virgin★) or of **St. Jean** (Renaissance; 13thC tomb of a countess of Joigny) among half-timbered houses. ▶ North of town, remains of ramparts; from D20, view over the town. □

▶ Nearby

▶ **Saint-Cydroine** church (11th-12thC Romanesque; *4 km E) :* octagonal bell-tower, near **Laroche-Migennes** (train-station). ▶ **La Ferté Loupière** *(18 km SW) :* church with late-15thC mural **dance of death★★. Bontin** *(6 km S) :* 17thC **château,** residence of Sully, minister to Henry IV *(10-12 & 2-6, Jul.-Aug.).* □

Wet nurses

Miraculous springs and prayers were often invoked by Burgundian women to ensure the plentiful flow of milk necessary to find employment as wet nurses. Some women lived with well-to-do families, whereas others fostered city babies in their own homes in a system that all too often degenerated into the notorious baby-farming industry of the 19thC. Agents used to travel the Morvan countryside to recruit wet nurses whom they would send to Paris. Orphanages were founded in the Morvan to receive foundlings from Paris; several still in existence cope today with the sad flow of urban children in need of care.

LOUHANS

C3-4 / ® / pop. 6 923 (Saône-et-Loire)

On the left bank of the Saône, a charming town with arcaded main street, old houses and handsome 18thC infirmary (pharmacy★). Renowned markets for cattle, pigs and poultry. □

MÂCON

C4 / ® / pop. 39 866 (Saône-et-Loire)

The curved tile roofs of Mâcon (birth-place of Lamartine) suggest that the Midi is not far away. A busy commercial town on the right bank of the Saône, and an important wine centre (wine sales in May).

▶ Near the prefecture, **Old St. Vincent★** (C2) : narthex (porch) of a Romanesque church destroyed in 1795. ▶ **Ursulines Museum** (B2) : archaeology (Solutré (→) excavations), ethnography, art (Dutch, Flemish and French paintings, contemporary art; *10-12 & 2-6, closed Tue. and Sun. am*). ▶ On the other side of La Barre and Sigorgne streets (main thoroughfares), **Lamartine Museum** (B2) : 19thC furniture and art; mementoes of Lamartine *(2-5 ex. Tue., May-Oct.)*. ▶ Place aux Herbes : wooden house (D-C1). □

▶ Nearby

▶ **Saint-André-de-Bâgé★** *(9 km W)* : 11thC church with octagonal bell-tower in a small cemetery, interesting capitals. ▶ On the southern edge of the Department, **Romanèche-Thorins** *(14 km S)* in the renowned Moulin-à-Vent wine-producing region of Beaujolais; Guillon Museum of Crafts *(Sun. and nat. hols.)*. □

▶ Lamartine territory

Round trip from Mâcon *(approx 64 km, half-day)*

▶ Distinctive silhouette of **Solutré Rock★★** *(9 km W* : alt. 495 m), where prehistoric men chased wild horses over the cliff; the site abounds in prehistoric remains and has lent its name to the Solutrean Era (18 000-15 000BC). ▶ **Pouilly** ® and **Fuissé** are joined in the name of a great white wine; **Chasselas** has given its name to a variety of table grapes. ▶ Via Grand Vent Pass and D22 (leisure centre on Lake Saint-Point) to **Saint-Point★** : château, Romanesque church and funerary chapel of Lamartine and his family *(10-12 & 2-6, ex. Sun. am and Wed.)*. ▶ **Berzé-le-Châtel★** : triple-walled mediaeval castle *(D22, N79)*. 2 km farther, **Berzé-la-Ville** : monk's chapel★, Cluniac 12thC former priory church; **murals★★** *(9:30-12 & 2-6, Palm Sunday-1 Nov.)*. ▶ On the other side of the valley, **Milly-Lamartine★** (Romanesque church) : village where the poet stayed in his childhood; **château de Pierreclos★** (rebuilt 17thC), mentioned in Lamartine's work. ▶ Cross the valley again to **château de Montceau** : summer residence of the Lamartine family in the middle of their vineyards.

MONTBARD

B2 / ® / pop. 7 707 (Côte-d'Or)

Between the Brenne river and the Burgundy canal, the town was once home to Dukes of Burgundy (Jean sans Peur spent his youth here). It was the birthplace of the cele-

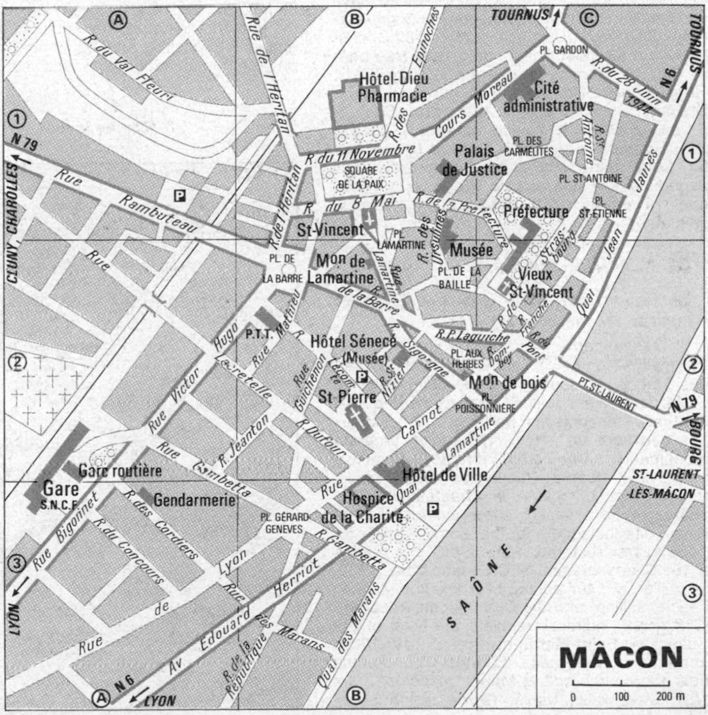

brated 18thC naturalist Georges-Louis Leclerc de Buffon (1707-1788).

▶ Place Buffon : the mansion of the naturalist had direct access to the **chateau park★**, which he remodelled; archaeology and history **museum** (mediaeval and 19th-20thC sculpture; local painters); Buffon's study; 13thC St. Louis and Aubépin towers *(8-12 & 2-6 Apr.-Oct., or 4:30 Nov.-Mar.; closed Tue.).* ▶ In town, **fine arts museum** (Rue Piron; *2:30-5, Apr.-Dec.; out of season ask at the Town Hall).* □

▶ Nearby

▶ **Buffon Forges★★** *(6 km NW via D905 then left) :* 18th industrial centre; exhibits on steel-making in Burgundy *(2:30-6, Jun.-Sep., closed Tue).* ▶ **Vausse** *(20 km W, between the forests of St. Jean and Châtel-Gérard) :* 12thC former Cistercian priory; cloister. □

■ MONTCEAU-LES-MINES

B3-4 / ® / pop. 26 949 (Saône-et-Loire)

A 19thC industrial town bred from the coal-mines of Blanzy, part of the Le Creusot complex.

▶ Two branches of the Le Creusot Museum (→) *(school hols)* recall an earlier life : the school house (37 Rue Jean-Jaurès, *last Sun. of month, 3-7*); and, at **Blanzy** *(3 km NE),* St. Claude mine-shaft (Rue du Bois-Clair, *Sun. 3-7*). □

▶ Nearby

▶ **Gourdon** *(7 km SE, D980) :* hilltop village with Romanesque church★, frescos and carved capitals. **Mont-Saint-Vincent** ridge *(8 km farther;* alt. 603 m) : view★★ sometimes as far as the Alps; 11th-12thC Romanesque church in the village with transverse barrel-vaulted nave and small archaeological museum. ▶ **Bissy-sur-Fley** *(28 km E, D90 and D28) :* 15thC castle where the poet Pontus de Thiard was born in 1521. ▶ **Perrecy-les-Forges** *(17 km SW) :* 12thC church; in the upper narthex★★, Le Creusot Museum exhibit *(Sat. and Sun. 3-7 Jun.-15 Sep.).* ▶ **Toulon-sur-Arroux** *(20 km W) :* Romanesque church and old bridge, not far from there, a Buddhist community and pagoda at the **château de Plège. Issy-l'Évêque** *(16 km W) :* 11th-12thC church, frescos, capitals. □

■ MORVAN Lakes★★

▶ Round trip from Quarré-les-Tombes *(approx 134 km, full day)*

B2-3 *(see map 3)*

Quarré-les-Tombes ® : named after the numerous sarcophagi found near the church, which posed a mystery until it was discovered that 6th-9thC stonemasons working at local quarries had kept up a thriving trade in funerary monuments. S **Duc Forest :** forest roads, hiking trails; deer reserve; Roche des Fées (Fairies' rock); Pérouse rocks★. ▶ **Chastellux★ :** the **château★**, in a superb site★ overlooking the Cure, has belonged to the same family for 1 000 years; restored in the 19thC, but retains a 15thC appearance. ▶ **Crescent Dam** (1930, 14 million m³, 407 acres : hydroelectric station; beach; sailing) and the **Chaumecon Reservoir** (333 acres) indirectly regulate the level of the Seine. ▶ **Saint-Martin-du-Puy :** 14th-18thC **château de Vésigneux. Lormes :** panoramas near the church and at Mount Justice *(1.5 km N);* view★; walks. Narvau Gorge, Goulot pond.

▶ Across the Yonne channel, 15th-17thC **château de Chassy** *(4-7 Jul.-Aug.).* ▶ **Pannesière-Chaumard Reservoir★ :** the biggest in Morvan (1950, 85 million m³), 1 284 acres; hydroelectric station; aquatic sports). **Ouroux-en-Morvan** *(8 km NW).* ▶ Despite numerous man-made tourist attractions, **Lake Settons★★** remains beautiful; the reservoir (1861, 21 million m³, 887 acres; aquatic sports) regulates the level of the Yonne. ▶ **Montsauche** ® : a mountain village (alt. 650 m). **Savault** *(5 km W) :* crafts in summer. Just off the road, **Saut de Gouloux :** waterfall running into the Cure; site★★. ▶ **Saint-Brisson :** park office (→ Nature Park); resort for hiking and angling. ▶ **Dun-les-Places :** on the other side of the Breuil-Chenue forest, nature trail and angling. ▶ **Saint-Agnan :** the 350 acre **lake** is little frequented despite an attractive shore. ▶ **Saint-Marie-de-la-Pierre-qui-Vire** (Balanced Rock) : at the Benedictine **abbey** founded in 1850, the monks publish informative books on Romanesque art (Zodiaque series); exhibits *(weekday mass at 9:30; Sun. at 10).* ▶ **Saint-Léger-Vauban :** birthplace of the military architect Sébastien de Vauban, who is buried in Bazoches (→ Cure Valley); exhibits *(2:30-7, Jul.-Aug.).* □

■ MORVAN Nature Park★★

B2-3 / ®

A region once renowned in Paris for two essential resources : timber floated down the Cure and Yonne rivers, and wet nurses. A wet, hilly, thickly wooded region (beech, hornbeam, oak, and conifers on the hilltops) that today is France's main source of Christmas trees.

▶ The nature park created in 1970 comprises 1 730 km² overlapping four Burgundy departments. The park has fostered redevelopment of the human and natural resources of the region; ample signposting and equipment encourage environmental exploration and nature-related

3. Morvan lakes

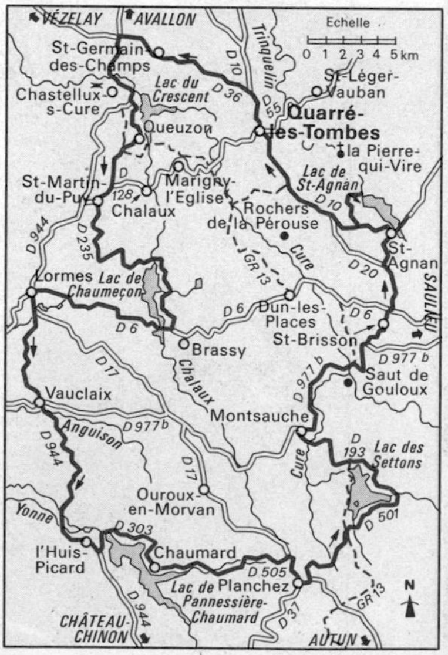

activities. ▶ The **Maison du Parc** (office) at Saint-Brisson (→ Morvan lakes) is in a 19thC lakeside mansion, with information, exhibits, activities; essential stop; Résistance museum *(D6; 9-12 & 2-6).* □

■ NEVERS★★

A3 / ® / pop. 44 700 (Nièvre)

Nevers is situated in a bend on the right bank of the river Loire.

▶ The town is centred on **Place Carnot** (B2) (Rue St. Martin, **Chapel of Ste. Marie** with Louis XIII façade★) and **Rue du Commerce** (C2; partly pedestrian; 15thC belfry). ▶ Near the Prefecture, 1612 **church of St. Pierre★** (C1) and 18thC **Paris Gate.** ▶ **Church of St. Étienne★★** (C1) Cluniac Romanesque, late 11thC; noteworthy eastern end. ▶ **Ducal Palace★** (B2) : now the Courthouse; 15th-16thC; combining mediaeval strength with Renaissance delicacy (stairway, dormer-windows, chimneys). ▶ **Cathedral of St. Cyr-et-Ste. Julitte** (B3) : an apse at either end of the nave; west end, Romanesque over an 11thC crypt (excavated 6thC baptistery); east end, 13thC Gothic nave; 15thC chapels. ▶ Rue St. Genest, **Municipal Museum** (A3) : **faïence collection★★** from Nevers and elsewhere; ivories, enamels, glass, modern painting *(10-12 & 2-6 closed Tue. and Jan.).* ▶ On the 12thC ramparts, **Croux gate★★** (A3; 14thC) : lapidary museum, Roman era, Romanesque *(daily 2-8 in season; in winter Wed., Sat., Sun. only).* From there, one can walk as far as the Loire along the particulary well preserved collection of ramparts.

Also... ▶ **St. Gildard Convent** (A1) where Bernadette Soubirous (→ Lourdes) lived as a nun from 1860 to 1879; her embalmed body lies in a glass casket in the chapel. ▶ **Church of Ste. Bernadette** (*N on map;* Blvd de Lattre-de-Tassigny) contemporary architecture (1966). □

▶ Nearby

▶ **Pougues** *(11 km NW)* : at one time a thermal spa on the banks of the Loire. ▶ **Guérigny** (*14 km N;* on the way, two châteaux near **Urzy**) 18thC château and state forges. **Marzy** *(4.5 km W)* : 12thC Romanesque church (bell-tower★); local ethnographic museum in town hall. **La Machine :** Mine museum *(Jun.-Sept., closed Tue., 10-12 & 3-7; Oct.-May, Sat. and Sun., 2-6).*

▶ Between the Loire and Allier rivers *(75 km round trip, half-day)*

▶ Near the **Bec d'Allier** *(D976, SW),* where the Allier meets the Loire, **château du Marais** (14th-16thC) and **Guétin canal-bridge** (the Loire canal flows over the Allier after a series of three locks). ▶ Farther south, 13thC fortress at **Meauce,** and *(via D134)* ruined Cluniac priory at **Mars-sur-Allier** (12thC church). ▶ **Saint-Pierre-le-Moutier** ® *(A3, via D108) :* old houses (Renaissance; 12th-15thC church). ▶ Via N7 north, then right by the **château de Villars** (14th-15thC), **Saint-Parize-le-Châtel :** church over a Romanesque crypt (capitals★); 2 km away, golf course and motor racing track at **Magny-Cours** ® (race-driving school). ▶ From **Rozemont** (*D133;* remains of 13thC fortress), D13 leads back to Nevers via **Chevenon** (14thC castle) along the Loire canal; on the opposite bank, **Imphy** Forges. □

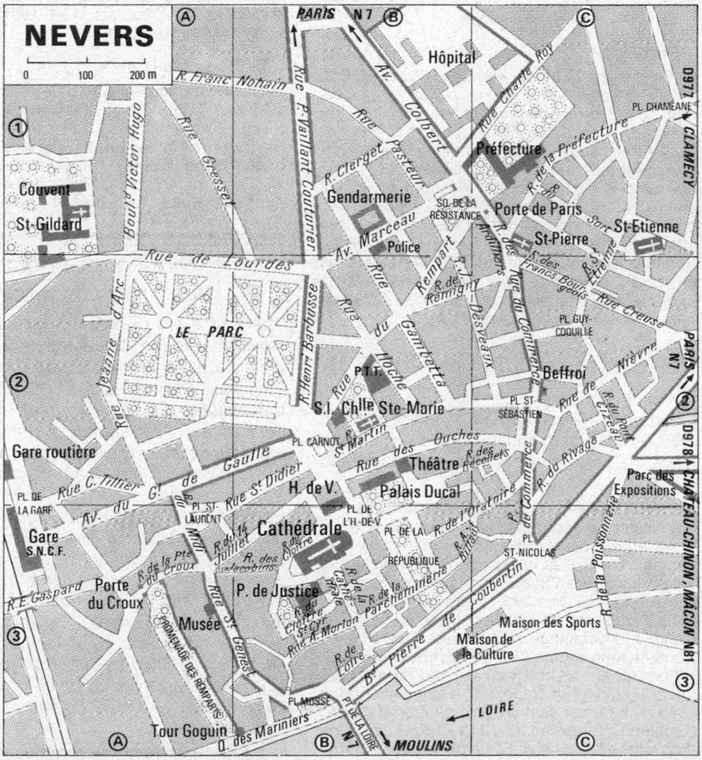

Nevers ceramics

Louis de Gonzagues, Duke of Nevers, brought artisans and craftsmen from Italy to improve the local industries of fine enamel and spun glass. In 1580, he invited the Conrade brothers, three master potters, to instruct local craftsmen in techniques of art pottery. The distinctive style of Nevers ware rapidly caught on and, by the mid-17thC, 12 workshops were employing 1 800 potters. Faïence (named for Faenza in Italy, where it originated) is a brittle, porous compound of clay, sand and limestone marl, fired first at 750°-900°C, then glazed with tin salts and lead oxide and refired at a lower temperature.

The characteristic Nevers decoration is a blue background overpainted by hand with white and yellow. In the 18thC, figured Nevers ware was decorated with scenes from everyday life, Revolutionary symbols and military scenes; "Chinese" (chinoiserie) *designs enjoyed popularity. With industrialisation, transfer designs and mass production, output has declined since the 19thC.*

■ NOLAY

B3 / ® / pop. 1 582 (Côte-d'Or)

Below walls, among meadows and vineyards : 14thC covered **markets★** roofed with stone tiles; in the church, bell-tower with 16thC jack-o'-the-clock.

▶ Nearby

▶ **Cirque du Bout du Monde★** (World's End natural amphitheatre) *(5 km N; D111)* : **Cormot** limestone **escarpments** overlooking the Tournée river (rock-climbing). ▶ **La Rochepot★★** ® : above trees and vineyards, beautiful **château,** birthplace of Philippe Pot (1428; his tomb is in the Louvre Museum in Paris), ambassador of the Grand Dukes of Burgundy; château was restored during the 19thC on the 12th and 15thC remains; Renaissance wing; furniture and works of art in several rooms *(10-12 & 2-6, Palm Sunday-1 Nov. closed Tue.)*. In the village, Romanesque church (12thC capitals; Renaissance bell-tower). □

■ The côte de NUITS Vineyards★★

C2-3

Great wine names appear at every turn on the Côte de Nuits road through a region that rivals the Côte de Beaune for prestige and quality.

▶ From **Chenôve** ®, at the S exit of Dijon (→), the hillsides are covered with vine rows, often in walled enclosures (the *clos* of many vineyard names). The Dukes of Burgundy maintained an estate here; the **Cuverie des Ducs★** (fermenting room) still has two huge wine presses (13thC originals or 15thC copies; *8-12 & 2-7 daily*). ▶ **Marsannay :** rosé wines. ▶ **Fixey :** Romanesque church with glazed-tile bell-tower. ▶ **Fixin** ® : known both for wine and for a statue, the "Awakening of Napoleon" commissioned in 1846 by a former captain of the Imperial guard; Napoleonic museum *(9-12 & 2-5, 7 in summer, closed Tue. and Fri. am)*. ▶ **Chambertin** and Clos-de-Bèze : great wines. **Gevrey** ® : 10thC castle★ rebuilt in the 13thC *(10-12 & 2-6, 15 Apr.-15 Nov.; 10:30-12 & 2:30-4:30 rest of year; closed Sun. am)*; church with Romanesque doorway. **Collonges-lès-Bévy :** 17th-18thC **château** *(2-6 Jul.-Sep.)*. W, D31 follows the **Lavaux valley.** ▶ **Morey-Saint-Denis** ®, **Chambolle-Musigny, Vougeot :** famous vineyards and great red wines. **Château du Clos Vougeot★★ :** built by Cistercian monks in 1551, stands in their vineyards *(9-11:30 & 2:30-5:30; closed 20 Dec.-5 Jan.)*; nearby, 12thC wine store and 13thC fermenting room (wine presses); today the château is the headquarters of the promotional brotherhood of the Chevaliers du Tastevin (see box). ▶ **Gilly** *(1 km E)* : 15th-17thC **château,** former residence of Cistercian abbots *(daily)*. ▶ The **Vosne-Romanée** holdings include Romanée-Conti, the rarest and most expensive of red wines (less than 5 acres of vineyard). ▶ **Nuits-Saint-Georges** ® : once a Gallo-Roman township, now a prosperous Burgundian village; archaeological museum in the 17thC clock-tower (Gallo-Roman and Merovingian exhibits; *2-6 daily Jul.-Sept.; Sun. only May, Jun.)*; Romanesque church in the cemetery. ▶ **Cussigny** *(6 km S)* : 17th-18thC **château** *(10-12 & 2-6, Aug.-15 Sep.)*. □

▶ Nearby

▶ **Cîteaux Abbey** *(12 km E)* : founded in 1098, visited by St. Bernard (→ Fontenay) in 1112; nucleus of the dynamic expansion of the Cistercian order (more than 1 000 abbeys throughout Christendom by the 13thC) advocating rigorous application of the Benedictine rule, in reaction to the laxity of Cluny (→); reformed again in the 18thC, the Order has since been known as the Trappists; 15th-18thC buildings, audiovisual presentation. □

▶ The Côte-Hinterland

▶ **St. Vivant Abbey** (at **Curtil-Vergy,** *8 km via D25 and D35)* 10thC ruins; signposted trails. **Reulle-Vergy** *(1 km farther)* : Church of St. Saturnin; **museum of folk arts and crafts of the Upper Côtes★** *(Sun. 2-6 and daily Jul.-15 Sep.*; nature trail). Beyond, between **Ternant** and **Rolle :** two dolmens *(D104b)*. ▶ Via

Three days of glory (les Trois Glorieuses)

The first event of these great days in mid-November is the annual meeting of a wine-promotion organisation, the Confrérie du Tastevin (Brotherhood of Winetasters) at the château Clos de Vougeot. New members of the Confraternity are initiated with many speeches, toasts, songs and bottles of Burgundy. The second, on the following day, is the wine auction at the Hospices de Beaune (→). The administration of the Hospices (founded as a charity hospital) auctions the wine from its estates according to ancient tradition. Buyers come from all over the world, and prices serve as benchmarks for the greatest wines. The third and final glorious day is the La Paulée banquet the next day at Meursault : the participating vineyard owners bring bottles of wine and a literary prize — of 100 bottles of Meursault — is awarded.

D25 (Serrée Valley), cultivation of blackcurrants and raspberries near **Arcenant,** then Pertuis Valley. ▶ **Bouilland** ® *(22 km from Nuits via D25 then left on D2, or 16 km from Beaune) :* charming site★, many walks; ruins of Ste. Marguerite abbey; rock Percée (pierced); La Vieille valley. □

■ OTHE Forest

A1

Forested massif between Sens and Troyes (→ Ardenne, Champagne), dotted here and there by apple and cherry orchards; vestiges of prehistoric habitation.

▶ Today crossed by the TGV line (→), the region offers numerous resorts and excursion centres such as **Dixmont** (13th-16thC church), **Cerisiers** (partly 12thC church), **Arces, Vaudeurs** ®, and the many villages in the Vanne, Yonne and Armançon valleys (→ Sightseeing). □

■ The OUANNE Valley

▶ Round trip from Ouanne to Charney *(38 km, approx 2hr)*

A2

Favoured by Parisians as a weekend retreat, this valley irrigated by the Ouanne river (D950) still has an unspoilt rustic charm.

▶ **Ouanne** *(26 km SW from Auxerre).* ▶ **Toucy** ® (A2; pop. 2 665) : home town of the lexicographer Pierre Larousse (1817-1875); shopping centre; church rebuilt 16thC; two 12thC defensive towers. ▶ **Villiers-Saint-Benoît : regional museum of folk art★★** displaying interior of an 18thC Puisaye home; 12th-16thC Burgundian sculpture; Auxerrois and Puisaye ceramics *(10-12 & 2-6 ex. Tue.; closed 15 Dec.-15 Jan.).* ▶ **Charny** ® : agricultural and market town (Joigny → *27 km*). □

■ PARAY-LE-MONIAL★

B4 / ® / pop. 11 312 (Saône-et-Loire)

Paray-le-Monial is a religious centre and an important market town; the Romanesque basilica of Sacré-Cœur has been a focus of Roman Catholic devotion since the 17thC.

▶ On the banks of the Bourbince, **abbey church of Notre-Dame★★** (now the basilica) built between 1090 and 1110 in golden stone; two towers flank the doorway; beautiful **eastern end★★★** with octagonal tower at the transept crossing : inside; slender columns, capitals, 15thC fresco; the plan resembles that of the now demolished church of Cluny. ▶ Annual pilgrimage to **relics** of 17thC Ste. Marguerite-Marie Alacoque *(9-12 & 2-7, Mar.-Oct.;* park, diorama). ▶ Place Guignaud : Renaissance **Town Hall★,** 16thC St. Nicolas Tower. ▶ Rue de la Paix, **Hiéron Museum★** of Religious Art : 12thC tympanum★ from Anzy-le-Duc; paintings (Italian, French, Flemish) on the theme of the Eucharist *(2-7 or 4 in winter).*

▶ Nearby

▶ **Château** (18thC) **de Digoine★★** *(16 km NE) :* can be seen from D128 or, on the other side of the Centre Canal, D974. ▶ **Digoin** ® *(12 km NW) :* a paradise for anglers at the junction of the Arroux, Loire, Arconce and Bourbince rivers, and the intersection of several canals. Ceramics Centre : techniques, exhibits of Digoin ceramics and others *(2-6 ex. Sun.).* □

Monks

The landscape of Burgundy, a treasury of Romanesque architecture, was in large part fashioned by monks. Between the 10th and 13thC, offshoots of the Burgundian motherhouses of Cluny and Cîteaux diffused the monastic principles defined by St. Benedict in the 6thC throughout the Western world. The Cluniac foundations sought to proclaim the glory of God through splendid churches and influential abbots. The Cistercians on the other hand, formed by St. Bernard in the 12thC, assumed the simplicity and rigor of the original monastic Rule. The foundation of Cîteaux in 1092 marked the beginning of Cluny's decline.

■ POUILLY-EN-AUXOIS

B2 / ® / pop. 1 396 (Côte-d'Or)

A road transport intersection in S Auxois near the Burgundy canal, which passes through a tunnel. Church of **Notre-Dame-Trouvée** (14th-15thC) with miraculous statue. □

▶ Nearby

▶ **Chailly-sur-Armançon** *(6.5 km W) :* 12thC remains; 16thC fortified house. ▶ **Grosbois Reservoir** *(11 km N) :* fishing. ▶ **Thoisy-le-Désert** *(3.5 km S) :* 14thC spire on the church. ▶ **Châteauneuf★★** ® *(10 km SE) :* above the canal and motorway A6 (site★), a picturesque village★ sheltered by a castle (12th-15thC; *10-12 & 2-4 or 6, closed Tue.*); ramparts : 14th-16thC houses. ▶ **Commarin** *(5 km from Châteauneuf) :* on the edge of the village, 17th-18thC château★ flanked by 15thC towers (tapestries, 18thC furniture; *10-12 & 2-6 ex. Tue., Palm Sunday-1 Nov.*). □

■ PRÉMERY

A3 / pop. 2 603 (Nièvre)

On the banks of the Nièvre, in the heart of a wooded massif, the 14th-17thC **château** that once belonged to the counts of Nevers : Gothic collegiate church. □

▶ Nearby

▶ **Giry** *(4.5 km N) :* 12th-15th-18thC **château** *(10-12 & 2-5, Jul.-Oct. ex. Tue.).* ▶ **Montenoison Butte** *(8.5 km NE) :* feudal ruins and panorama. **Saint-Révérien** *(13 km NE) :* **church★** with Romanesque apse (capitals★). ▶ **Champallement** *(N) :* 15thC castle and Gallo-Roman site of **Compierre. Brinon-sur-Beuvron** *(8 km farther) :* 13th-17thC moated castle. ▶ **Saint-Saulge** *(17 km SE) :* Gothic church over a Romanesque crypt. **Jailly** *(4 km W) :* Romanesque church. □

■ The PUISAYE Region★

A2

A region of woods, meadows, ponds and hedges often mentioned by the writer Colette (1873-1954) who was born in Saint-Sauveur. The clay soil gave rise to a pottery-making tradition as long ago as the Middle Ages.

▶ **Saint-Sauveur-en-Puisaye** (A2; pop. 1 149) : capital of the region; old streets, birthplace of Colette (Rue des Vignes), 12th-16thC church; 11 km NE, site of the **Battle of Fontenoy,** where Charles the Bald was defeated by his brother Lothaire in 841. ▶ **Treigny :** the church is referred to as the "cathedral of Puisaye" : pottery exhibit in the Canons' House (Maison du Chanoine). ▶ **Ratilly★ :** 13thC feudal castle; pottery workshop, courses; contemporary art exhibits in summer *(10-12 & 2-6).* ▶ **Saint-Armand-en-Puisaye** (A2; pop. 1 314) : pottery workshops; Renaissance château. ▶ **Saint-Fargeau :** old houses; Gothic and Renaissance church (stalls, triptych, 15thC Pietà); 15thC clock-tower; and 15th-17thC **château★★,** a pink brick, slate-roofed pentagon flanked by fat towers; here, Madame de Montpensier (La "Grande Mademoiselle"), first cousin to Louis XIV, was exiled for her persistent involvement in anti-government plots (La Fronde; → pp. 00); the 17thC composer Jean-Baptiste Lully worked here as a kitchen helper and before becoming court composer to Louis XIV (*10-12 & 2-7;* equestrian museum : son et lumière show some summer evenings). Beyond the park *(4 km SE),* **Bourdon Reservoir★** (beach, sailing). Farther *(10 km, D185)* at **Boutissaint, St. Hubert Animal Park★ :** red and roe deer, bison; camera safari courses; riding excursions. ▶ 20 km NE from **Saint-Fargeau** *(D90),* **Rogny-les-Sept-Ecluses :** gigantic 17thC step-locks on the dried-out Briard canal. □

SAINT-FLORENTIN

A1 / ® / pop. 6 757 (Yonne)

Close to the Champagne region (→ Ardennes-Champagne), Saint-Florentin is a pleasant stopover above the Armançon river and the Burgundy canal. Saint-Florentin and Soumaintrain cheeses are produced in this area.

▶ **Church★★ :** 15th-17thC **stained glass★** (The Creation); nave and chapel with Renaissance decoration; choirscreen and statues by sculptors of the Champagne school. □

▶ Nearby

▶ **Brienon-sur-Armançon** *(8 km W) :* collegiate church (16thC choir★); round 17thC wash-house★. □

SAINT-HONORÉ-LES-BAINS

B3 / ® / pop. 831 (Nièvre)

This thermal spa for the treatment of asthma and respiratory problems, on the edge of the Morvan Nature Park, is a pleasant place to stay; walks, excursions. □

▶ Nearby

▶ **Vandenesse castle★** *(6 km W) :* 15thC towers. ▶ **La Bussière : 15thC castle.** ▶ **Moulin-Engilbert** *(11 km N) :* cattle-market; old houses around the Gothic church. ▶ **Commagny** *(2 km SW) :* priory with 12thC church, 15thC buildings. ▶ **Limaton** and **Brinay** *(6 km and 11 km W) :* 14th-17thC and 13thC castles. ▶ Above the Roche Valley, **Larochemillay★** *(18 km E) :* 18thC **château** at the foot of Mount Beuvray (→ Autun).

The race for the ring

Each year, on the Sunday closest to 31 May, the whole of Sémur-en-Auxois turns out for the race for the ring. The 2275 m horse race, which has been held annually since 1639, is said to date back even further, to the return of a Crusader-Lord of Saumur, who returned from Jerusalem bearing a ring that he had acquired in the belief that it was the Virgin's wedding ring. The prizes are always the same : a golden ring engraved with the arms of the town, a gold-embroidered scarf, and a pair of gloves.

SAINT-SEINE-L'ABBAYE

C2 / pop. 309 (Côte-d'Or)

Early 13thC church, Romanesque in appearance, constitutes the remains of the abbey that once was the source of the village's prosperity; choirscreen; paintings, 18thC stalls. Attractive fountains, including "La Samaritaine" (1715). □

▶ Nearby

▶ **Source of the Ignon** (rebuilt 16thC manor house at **Poncey-sur-l'Ignon;** *Sat., Sun. am)* and the **Seine★** *(10.5 km NW),* maintained by the City of Paris; close by, Gallo-Roman excavations of a temple to the goddess Sequana (divinity of the Seine). ▶ **Frolois★ :** *(7 km farther)* former **fortress** in a picturesque site★ *(daily 2-6 ex. Tue., Jun.-Oct. and Easter school hols.; Sat., Sun. and Mon., Apr.-May).* □

The SAÔNE Valley

C3-4

From Franche-Comté (→), the Saône runs through a pleasant valley, past small towns (fishing; shores; sailing); from N to S, D20, D976.

▶ **Pontailler-sur-Saône** (→ along the Vingeanne). ▶ **Auxonne** ® (C2; pop. 7 121) : a town of character, on the Dijon-Dole road; 16thC **Comté Gate;** 15thC Town Hall; Gothic **church of Notre-Dame** (Romanesque tower; 15th-16thC statues); 15thC château with **Bonaparte museum** (Napoleon served here as a lieutenant of artillery; *2:30-4:30 ex. Thu.*) and arsenal built by Vauban (→ Bazoches). ▶ **Saint-Jean-de-Losne** ® (C3; pop. 1 476) : small craft port at the mouth of the Burgundy canal and close to the Rhône-Rhine canal junction; 15th-16thC church. ▶ **Seurre** ® (C3; pop. 2 694) : 16thC family home of the preacher and writer Jacques-Bénigne Bossuet (1624-1704), now an **environmental museum of the Saône★** (geology, history, ethnology; *10-12 & 2:30-6, Jul.-Aug.*); 17thC hospital. ▶ **Verdun-sur-le-Doubs** ® (C3; pop. 1 139) : at this junction of two rivers the specialty is *pôchouse* (→ Eating in Burgundy); **Grain and Bread Museum** (Musée du Blé et du Pain, Rue du Pont-St. Jean; *3-7, Sat., Sun.*); old houses. ▶ **Terrans★** *(21.5 km W of Verdun)* 18thC **château.** ▶ **Pierre-de-Bresse** *(3 km farther) :* 17thC château; **Bresse environmental museum** (the N of this region is part of Burgundy; *2-6 ex. Tue.*); lakes. □

■ SAULIEU★

B2 / ® / pop. 3 084 (Côte-d'Or)

Countless pilgrims and travellers over the ages have halted at Saulieu, gateway to the Morvan (→). Writers François Rabelais (ca. 1490-1553) and the 17thC Marquise de Sévigné (1626-1696) stopped at Saulieu and praised the quality of the food and wine. Mme de Sévigné confessed to having been tipsy for the first time in her life and made an expiatory offering to the local church. Saulieu is still today a gastronomic attraction.

▶ **Basilica of St. Andoche★★;** (12thC) on a charming square; noteworthy figured **capitals** (Flight into Egypt★, Christ and Mary Magdalene, Hanging of Judas) in the Romanesque nave (rebuilt 1704); 14thC stalls. ▶ Next door, **museum** of archaeology, local history, rural crafts and traditions, religious art, sculpture by Pompon (→ Dijon); *(9:30-12:30 & 2-8 or 6 in winter; closed Tue.).* ▶ SE of town, 15thC church of St. Saturnin. □

▶ Nearby

▶ **La Roche-en-Brénil** (12 km N) : 16th-18thC **château★.** ▶ **Thoisy-la-Berchère** *(10 km E) :* 15thC **château** built over a feudal manor (Renaissance façade). **Mont-Saint-Jean★** *(6.5 km NE) :* **site★** and old village (ramparts, Romanesque church over crypt, mediaeval houses, château). ▶ **Menessaire** *(11 km S) :* 12th-17thC **château** with glazed-tile roof *(9-6, Jul.-Aug.).* □

■ SEMUR-EN-AUXOIS★★

B2 / ® / pop. 4 619 (Côte-d'Or)

Approached from the West, the spire and mediaeval towers of the town suddenly appear on a spur on the river Armançon.

▶ The 14thC Sauvigny Gate leads along the Rue de la Liberté (elegant buildings) to the heart of the old town. ▶ **Church of Notre-Dame★★ :** Burgundian Gothic, 13thC transept and choir; 14th-15thC chapels, tympanum on N doorway; 14thC stained-glass; 15thC entombment of Christ; furnishings. ▶ View from the ramparts. ▶ **Municipal Museum** in former Dominican convent (Rue J. J. Collenot) : sculpture, paintings, archaeology, natural sciences *(daily 2-6, Wed. and Fri. 10-12 Jul.-Aug.).* ▶ Orle d'Or Tower : remains of 14thC keep. □

▶ Nearby

▶ **Lake Pont** *(4 km S) :* shore, sailing. ▶ **Thil :** 9th-12thC castle, 14thC collegiate church, both damaged in the late-16thC Wars of Religion; site★★ *(15 km S)* is a landmark on A6 motorway. ▶ **Bourbilly** *(9 km SW) :* 14thC castle★ restored in the 19thC (Venetian chandeliers) in the valley of the Serein *(10-12 & 3-6, ex. Sun., Easter-1 Nov.);* Madame de Sévigné (→ Saulieu) stayed here, and at the **château d'Époisses★ :** 11th, 16th and 18thC; double fortifications with moats, dovecote, interior decoration and furniture *(11.5 km E of Semur; 10-12 & 3-6; exterior visits 9-5 or 7).* Époisses produces a cheese praised by the 18thC gastronomist Jean-Anthelme Brillat-Savarin (1755-1826) as the "king of cheeses". □

■ SENS★

A1 / ® / pop. 27 900 (Yonne)

Sens, 1 hr 15 from Paris on the banks of the Yonne, is the point where Ile-de-France, Gâtinais, Champagne and Burgundy meet. The history of the town reaches back to the Romans.

▶ **Cathedral of St. Étienne★★ :** earliest of the great Gothic cathedrals (1130-1164), site of the wedding of St. Louis (Louis IX) and Marguerite de Provence. The **nave** looks Romanesque, but the **transepts** (15th-16thC) are Flamboyant Gothic; the outer doorways lost their carvings during the Revolution; Renaissance belfry on the S tower. Inside : rose windows in the transepts; **stained glass windows★★** from 12thC (ambulatory) to 16thC; 18thC choir enclosure gate; **mausoleum★** of the Dauphin Louis de Bourbon (1729-1765), only son of Louis XV and father of Louis XVI; **Treasury★★** *(temporarily closed)* is one of the richest in France : textiles, ivories, ornaments, liturgical objects. ▶ Right of the cathedral, 13thC **Synod Palace★ :** restored by the 19thC architect Eugène Viollet-le-Duc (1814-1879), roofed with glazed-tiles, now museum of stonework, tapestries and furniture *(9-12 & 2-6 or 4, closed Tue.).* Renaissance and 18thC buildings nearby. ▶ Opposite, covered market in 19thC ironwork; close by, neo-Renaissance Town Hall of 19thC. ▶ Among old mansions, **Municipal Museum** place de la République : Gallo-Roman inscriptions; archaeology, mediaeval sculpture, 17th-19thC paintings *(9-12 & 2-6 or 5, closed Tue.).*
Also... ▶ **Strolls** near the former **ramparts** (remains *S of town centre;* base built with re-used Roman stones). ▶ **Old houses** in Rue Jean Cousin. ▶ **Church of St. Jean** at former hospital : Champenois Gothic style. Farther on, **church of St. Savinien :** partly 11thC. □

▶ Nearby

▶ On the Gâtinais Plateau W, **Chéroy** ® *(22 km) :* 13thC tithe-barn; 6 km farther, château de Vallery (→ Ile-de-France). ▶ **Pont-sur-Yonne** ® *(12 km NW) :* 13th and 15thC church; old bridge. ▶ **Fleurigny★** *(15 km NE) :* mediaeval **château** with Renaissance additions; chapel with coffered ceiling *(Apr.-15 Sep., 2:30-5:30 Sat., Sun. and nat. hols.; daily ex. Wed. in Aug.).* □

■ SEREIN Valley★

▶ From Auxerre to Avallon *(approx 90 km; full day)*

A1

From **Auxerre** (→), reach the Serein river at Pontigny, and follow it to Chablis (*D91* → Auxerrois). ▶ From **Chablis,** D45 follows the Serein. ▶ **Pailly-sur-Serein :** Flamboyant Gothic church. ▶ Just after **Annay-sur-Serein :** 16thC **Château de Moutot.** ▶ **Noyers-sur-Serein★★** (B2; pop. 837) : fortified mediaeval town, 15th-16thC half-timbered houses; place de l'Hôtel-de-Ville★; 15thC church; 13thC rampart E of town. ▶ **L'Isle-sur-Serein** *(D96) :* island in the river (B2); remains of 15thC castle, old houses. ▶ **Montréal★** *(D11) :* early 12thC Gothic **church★★** on hilltop; carved choir stalls★★ (1526), 14th-16thC statues and furnishings; view★. Nearby *(NE),* **Talcy :** Romanesque church. **Thizy :** 13thC castle. **Pizy :** 15thC fortified farmstead. ▶ SW, **Avallon** (→). □

■ TILLE Valley

C2

In the north of Burgundy the river Tille runs through thickly wooded countryside S towards the Saône.

▶ **Grancey-le-Château :** on the edge of the Côte-d'Or; old city gate, 17th-18thC château★. ▶ **Villey-sur-Tille** and **Crecey-sur-Tille :** castle ruins. ▶ **Is-sur-Tille** ® : two Renaissance houses; 14th church. ▶ **Courtivron** *(13 km W) :* 14th-18thC **château** *(exterior visits 14 Jul.-1 Sep.);* village between the forest of Mouloy and Is-sur-Tille. ▶ **Til-Châtel :** old houses, 12thC **church★** (doorway and tympanum; capitals★). ▶ **Lux :** 16thC château *(Sun. am Jun. and Sep.; daily Jul.-Aug.).* ▶ **Selongey.** □

■ TONNERRE★

B1 / ® / pop. 6 007 (Yonne)

A well-placed trading town on the banks of the Armançon and the Bourgogne canal.

▶ In the lower town, a spring, the **Fosse Dionne★★,** runs into a pool used as a public laundry, before joining the Armançon. ▶ Former **hospital :** founded in 1293 by Marguerite of Burgundy (→ Couches), infirmary★ 80 m long; timber vault★; tomb of Marguerite; tomb of Louvois★, Count of Tonnerre (minister to Louis XIV); Entombment of Christ★, a masterpiece of 15thC Burgundian sculpture *(10-11:30 & 2-5:30 ex. Tue., Jun.-15 Sep.).* ▶ In town, **Uzès Mansion★** (1533) : now a savings bank; birthplace in 1728 of the notorious Chevalier d'Eon, brilliant soldier and diplomat, who was condemned to exile in London and not permitted to re-enter France unless wearing female dress (his preferred garb in any case); at his death in London in 1810 he was shown to be unequivocally male. Municipal Museum of local history *(Wed., Sat. 2-5).* Collegiate church of St. Pierre : 14th and 16thC (furnishings). □

▶ Nearby

▶ **Tanlay★★★** *(9.5 km E) :* **château** (1643-1648) down a lime-tree walk, through a 1630 pavilion to a formal courtyard, then the buildings; left, protected by the moat, another pavilion (Portail Neuf); beyond, the Court of Honour and the main building. Inside : Grand Gallery decorated with illusionist paintings; furniture; 16thC school of Fontainebleau (→ Ile-de-France) fresco *(9:15-11:30 & 2:15-5:15 ex. Tue., Palm Sunday-1 Nov.).* □

■ TOURNUS★★

C4 / ® / pop. 7 338 (Saône-et-Loire)

A stopover on the main road S to the Mediterranaen, rich in Romanesque architecture.

▶ Fleeing the Normans, monks from Noirmoutier (→ Poitou, Vendée, Charentes) settled here with relics of St. Philibert (9thC) and rebuilt the 300 year-old abbey. The **church★★★ :** 9thC façade; 10thC crypt and ground floor of the narthex; 11th and 12thC nave and choir; three 12thC towers. Past the **narthex** (1st floor; 11thC chapel of St. Michel★) the **nave** has sturdy pillars and unusual transverse barrel vaulting. The **choir★** and chapels are in accomplished Romanesque style. ▶ To the side of the church : abbey buildings around the cloister *(summer exhibitions).* ▶ Place de l'Abbaye (old houses); **Perrin de Puycousin museum :** domestic interiors, furniture, costumes *(9-12 & 2-6 closed Tue.).* ▶ Farther south, a street and **museum** named for the painter **Jean-Baptiste Greuze** (1725-1805), who was born here (paintings, archaeology; *9:30-12 & 2-6:30 closed Tue. and Sun. am).* ▶ S of town, Church of Ste. Madeleine★ : 12th, 15thC nave and Renaissance chapel. □

■ Between TOURNUS and CLUNY★★

▶ Round trip from Tournus *(95 km; full day)*

C4 *(see map 4)*

▶ **Tournus** (→). ▶ **Ozenay** and **Martailly-lès-Brancion** ® : 10th-14thC castle. Detour recommended to **Cruzille** *(6 km S) :* museum of Burgundian rural craft tools *(9-11:30 & 1:30-6:30, Easter-Oct.).* Then road right towards **Brancion★★** : mediaeval village beneath a 10th-14thC castle; houses, market; on the spur (view★★), attractive 12thC Romanesque **church★★** (with stone tiles; Gothic murals). Below and opposite, **La Chapelle-sous-Brancion :** partly Romanesque church. ▶ **Chapaize★ :** 11thC church with 12thC chapels; bell-tower★★ appears at the end of a straight run through the forest. NE, **Lancharre :** ruin of Romanesque abbey. ▶ **Chissey-lès-Mâcon :** capitals★ in 13thC church. ▶ View★★ from **Mount Saint-Romain** (alt. 579 m); **Blanot Caves** below *(Mar.-Nov. 9-12 & 1:30-7).* ▶ **Blanot :** very narrow roads; 12thC Romanesque church, 14thC priory buildings. ▶ **Azé Caves** (→ Cluny). ▶ **Donzy-le-Pertuis** : 11thC church. ▶ **Cluny** (→). D981 runs by the Grosne river. ▶ **Taizé :** œcumenical religious community made up of men of many Christian denominations from all over the world; Romanesque church★ in the village. ▶ **Ameugny :** Romanesque church. ▶ **Cormatin :** Renaissance **château★★** (1600) with exceptional interior decoration, paintings, furniture *(10-12 & 2:30-7 Jun.-Sep.).* ▶ Beyond **Malay** (Romanesque church), possible detour to **Sercy** (15thC château) and **Saint-Gengoux-le-National** (Romanesque church, château, old houses), to the N. ▶ Return via D215 and Chèvres Pass. □

■ VARZY

A2 / pop. 1 475 (Nièvre)

Former residence of the bishops of Auxerre. **Museum** of archaeology, sculpture, religious art, furniture, ceramics *(10-12 & 2-6, Oct.-Mar.).* Church of St. Pierre (13th-14thC), statues and Renaissance triptychs.□

▶ Nearby

▶ La-Chapelle-Saint-André *(6 km NW) :* 13thC and Renaissance **Corbelin Manor. Menou** *(10 km W) :* 17thC **château★; 18thC entrance gates. ▶ **Entrains-sur-Nohain** *(18 km NW) :* Gallo-Roman dig, museum *(3-7, Jul.-Aug.).* ▶ In **Champlémy** *(10 km S) :* 14th-16thC, near the source of the Nièvre. □

■ VÉZELAY★★★

A2 / ® / pop. 582 (Yonne)

Vézelay is a Romanesque masterpiece that has been designated by UNESCO as an international treasure. Founded in 878, the abbey of Vézelay (harboring relics of Christ's disciple St. Mary Magdalene) became a major place of pilgrimage in its own right, but was also an important stopover on the pilgrim road to the Spanish shrine of St. James of Compostela.

▶ Stroll from place du Champ de Foire (fairground, now the carpark) up winding streets to

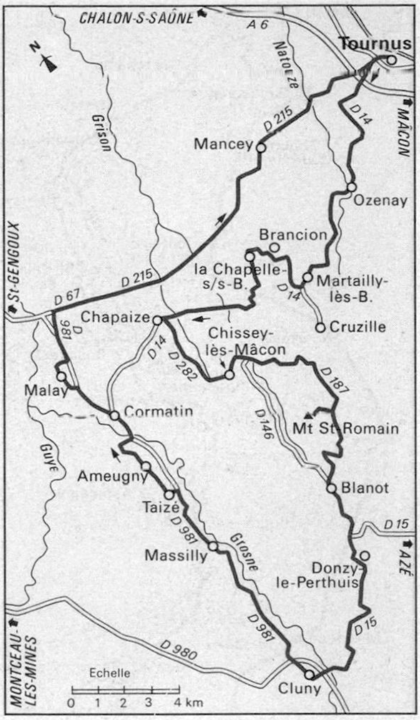

4. Between Tournus and Cluny

the **basilica of Ste. Madeleine★★★** on the hilltop. **Tympanum★★★** in the narthex (Christ in Glory; Apostles); luminous nave (1120-1140), the arches in two contrasting light shades of stone; pillars, graphic **capitals★★★** (nearly 100, including the Mystic Mill, Moses and St. Paul, St. Eustache, the Golden Calf, Adam and Eve); early Gothic choir (1185). The abbey declined after the 16thC and the church had been abandoned when the 19thC restorer Viollet-le-Duc (→ Sens) undertook to rebuild it. Concerts and illuminations in summer. ▶ Right of the basilica, chapterhouse and cloister (restored); remains of abbey buildings. ▶ In the former dormitory, **lapidary museum★** (sculpture unearthed during restoration; exhibits, *15 Jun.-15 Sep., 10-12:30 & 3-7 closed Mon.).* ▶ Rampart walk. At the eastern end of the basilica, terraced garden (view★). Numerous old houses, often over huge vaulted halls where pilgrims stayed. □

▶ Nearby

▶ **Saint-Père-sous-Vézelay** ® : at the foot of the hill, efforts are being made to reintroduce vines; 13th-15thC Gothic **church★★** with tall spire and elaborate porch; elegant interior architecture, combining Champenois and Burgundian influences. Close by, **Archaeological Museum of Fontaines Salées :** finds from the Gallo-Roman site *(3 km SE)* in the Cure Valley (→) *(9:30-12:30 & 2:30-6:30, Mar.-Nov. ex. Wed.; daily Easter-Sep.).* □

■ VILLENEUVE-L'ARCHEVÊQUE

A1 / ® / pop. 1 234 (Yonne)

In the Vanne Valley (which sends drinking water via an aqueduct to Paris), Villeneuve (New Town) was founded in 1163 by an

Romanesque art

Romanesque art in Burgundy ranges from the simple structure of Saint-Voles (Châtillon-sur-Seine) and churches in the villages of the Mâcon, Brionnais and Cluny regions, to the virtuoso techniques of Tournus and the splendour of Vézelay.
Burgundian Romanesque was long labelled as one "school" typified by certain buildings and decorations, and exemplified by the style of the Cluniac monastic order, which in turn displayed influence from 10th and 11thC Lombard masonry styles. In fact, there were many styles of Romanesque architecture in Burgundy. The ribbed vaulting of Vézelay, presumably modelled on that of Anzy-le-Duc, was an important landmark in construction style. The Cistercians adopted the Gothic ogival arch at a very early date. Under the influence of St. Bernard of Clairvaux, the Cistercian builders substituted technical perfection and rigorous design for decoration and ornament.

archbishop of Sens. St. Louis came here to receive Christ's supposed Crown of Thorns, brought from the East, which he later housed in the Sainte-Chapelle in Paris.

▶ 13th-14thC **church :** Gothic doorway★; 16thC Entombment of Christ showing Champenois influence. ▶ Walks in the Othe forest (→). □

■ VILLENEUVE-SUR-YONNE★

A1 / ® / pop. 4 980 (Yonne)

Created from scratch in 1163 as a royal residence by King Louis VIII, the town was originally called Villefranche-le-Roy. A pleasant centre for excursions to the Othe Forest (→), and a week-end resort.

▶ At either end of Rue Carnot, a handsome gate (13th and 16thC). Opposite an 18thC posthouse, **Church of Notre-Dame :** Renaissance **façade★★,** Gothic nave, stained glass from 13th to 16thC, 16thC Entombment of Christ. ▶ **Saint-Julien-du-Sault** *(7 km S) :* church with 13thC and Renaissance stained glass; old houses : steep walk to the hill-top chapel of Vauguillan with a view over the Yonne Valley. □

■ Along the river VINGEANNE★

▶ Round trip from Pontailler-sur-Saône *(approx 66 km, full day)*

C3 *(see map 5)*

Parallel with the Marne-Saône canal, the Vingeanne flows through a little-frequented valley to the extreme NE of Burgundy, on the edge of Franche-Comté (→).

▶ **Pontailler-sur-Saône :** at the foot of Mount Ardoux, a hill rising gently from the plain. ▶ **Talmay :** 18thC **château** with 13thC keep; Louis XV style embellished in the "Chinese" fashion of the mid-18thC; furnishings *(3-4:30 Jul. Aug. closed Mon.).* ▶ The road crosses and re-crosses the canal before reaching **Beaumont-sur-Vingeanne :** 1724 folly★ visible from the street *(no visits).* ▶ On the other bank, château de **Rosières★,** fortified, 15th-17thC;

painted ceiling★. ▶ **Saint-Seine-sur-Vingeanne :** Romanesque church, 16th-18thC château. Farther on, **Mornay :** 16thC château. ▶ The road passes a beautiful wash-house on the left before reaching **Fontaine-Française :** Henri IV defeated the Spaniards and the Catholic League here in 1595; 18thC lakeside **château★** where the 18thC luminaries Voltaire, Rousseau, Madame de Staël and Madame Récamier all stayed *(2-6, Jul.-Aug. closed Tue. and Thu.).* ▶ **Bèze :** fortified town with towers, church, 13thC houses; source of the river Bèze in caverns *(Apr., and Oct.; Sat., Sun.; May-Sep. daily ex. Mon. and Tue. am).* ▶ **Mirebeau** ® : stopover town; 13th and 16thC church.

■ VITTEAUX

B2 / 1 097 (Côte-d'Or)

At a point where the river Brenne is joined by several streams, Vitteaux is a pretty town with old houses, Gothic market and church (15thC organ loft, stalls). □

▶ Nearby

▶ **Posanges★★** *(3 km N) :* feudal castle, recently restored; four 15thC towers. ▶ **Church of Saint-Thibault★★ :** a "stone shrine"; 13thC doorway on tympanum, late-15thC carved doors (Life of St. Thibault; choir★ with 14thC vaulting; carved and painted altarpiece★★ (Virgin and Child, same period). □

■ The YONNE Valley

A2

The Yonne rises near Château-Chinon in the Morvan region, and runs into the Pannesière-Chaumard reservoir (→ Morvan Lakes). It runs through a valley parallel to the Nivernais canal before widening near Auxerre to join and augment the Seine.

▶ **Montreuillon Aqueduct** (152 m long) carries water from the Yonne channel across the river to the canal. ▶ **Marcilly :** 15thC castle. **Lantilly** *(S of Corbigny) :* 15th and 17thC castle with moats, keep and furnished rooms *(3-6 ex. Tue.; Jul.-Aug.).* ▶ **Corbigny** (B3; pop. 1 997) : Flamboyant Gothic church; market town. ▶ Nearby, **château de Chitry :** 16th-18thC; Italian gallery *(2-6, 15 Jun.-1 Oct.),* **château de Villemoulin** *(6 km NE) :* 16thC *(11-6 Apr.-Oct.).* ▶ **Tannay** ® : a white wine village W of the valley, **château Pignol** 17thC; and St. Léger church (13th-16thC). ▶ Farther, on the right bank, **Metz-le-Comte★** ridge : Romanesque church. ▶ **Clamecy** ® (A2; pop. 5 590) : busy town between the Yonne and Mount Beuvron; old houses; 12th-14thC church of St. Martin; **museum** in the Bellegarde Mansion (Rue Bourgeoise; regional ethnography, archaeology, painting; *10-12 & 2:30-5:30, May-15 Oct. closed Tue.).* ▶ **Coulanges-sur-Yonne :** (A2) stopover; E, 4 km along the right bank, 15thC **château Faulin.** ▶ 12 km W, partly destroyed château of **Druyes-les-Belles-Fontaines** (12thC; *3-6, 1 Jul.-15 Sep.).* ▶ **Châtel-Censoir :** site★; road to Vézelay (→); **church★** with Romanesque

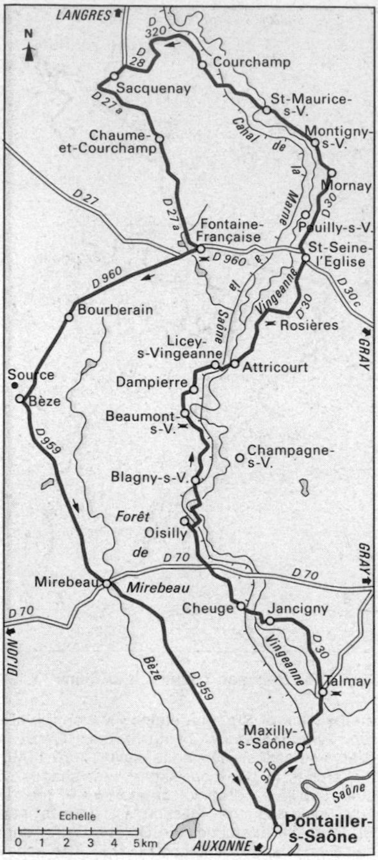

5. Along the river Vingeanne

choir, crypt 16thC nave. ▶ Saussois Rocks★ : rock-climbing school above the canal; **Mailly-le-Château** ® : site; old bridge. ▶ **Cravant :** junction of the Yonne and the Cure rivers (→ Cure valley). □

Snails or escargots?

Helix pomatia, the vineyard snail, has declined in numbers since the turn of the century because of sulfate spraying and the use of fertilisers. It is a large snail that was eagerly consumed in Roman times. Its greatest popularity, however, was probably achieved during the 19thC. Snails are still on tables throughout France, and production can hardly satisfy demand despite artificial rearing. Imports from Eastern Europe fill the gaps left by Burgundian snail breeders.

Architecture

In the Auxerrois region

The Burgundy landscape is criss-crossed by stone walls, mostly dry-built, occasionally secured by narrow lines of mortar. The colour varies from region to region : pearl-grey walls are built of stone from the marble-limestone quarry at Comblanchien S of Nuits-Saint-Georges; in Morvan and around Autun, steel-grey granite is more common. Near the Bresse region, in the plain, timber and clay are the usual building materials. ● In the N of Burgundy, massive, rectangular houses are built of trimmed stone. The detached main building has two stories under a four-sided roof. The traditional stone tiles are increasingly rare, replaced now by flat clay tiles. ● The stone used in the Auxerrois is whitish, and houses are usually built on top of cellars with an entrance beneath the outside staircase. ● In the Auxois, stable, barn and family quarters are under the same roof. Buildings in the "mountain" hinterland differ hardly at all from those of the surrounding areas. ● By contrast, the vineyard areas give priority to a cellar that has an entrance sheltered by a staircase leading to the family living level. An overhanging roof protects the building. Space is precious in the region, and village houses are crowded together. Richer landowners over the years have built comfortable middle-class houses with several stories, elaborate entrances and dormer-windows. Roofs are sometimes in glazed tile. ● Throughout the Mâconnais, the vine-growers' houses often have a Mediterranean look, with rounded terracotta tiles and first-floor galleries running the length of the façade behind the roof overhang. Stone in the area is pink or russet, and the houses are the most beautiful in Burgundy. The Morvan region is more rugged, and the villages resemble those of the mountains. Thatch was once commonly used for roofing. Today, the granite houses are more often roofed with slate. The houses are more scattered in this well watered and woody region; timber is often used to build extensions to houses.

In the Nivernais region

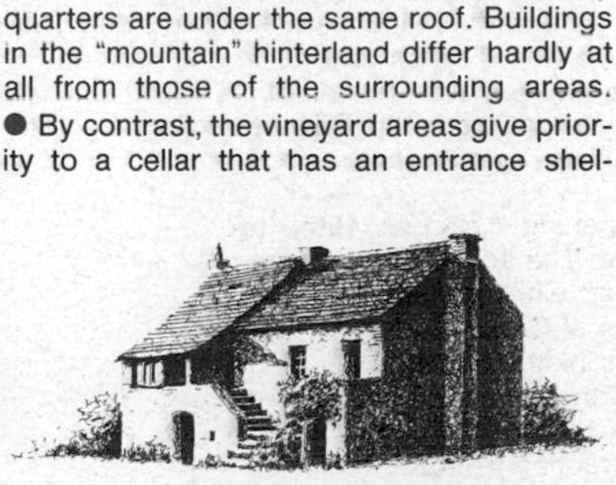

Wine grower's house

Master's house

In the Mâconnais region

Burgundy

Brief regional history

Prehistory to Roman Era

Prehistoric man left traces throughout Burgundy, from the inhabited caves at Arcy to the horse graveyard at Solutré rock. ● The arrival of the Romans encouraged trade and permitted many **Celtic settlements,** including Autun, to grow from trading posts into full-fledged cities. ● The **final Gaulish revolt** against the Roman colonisers was crushed by Julius Caesar's legions at **Alésia** in 52BC. **Christianity,** introduced during the Roman era, took root despite repeated checks with every Barbarian **invasion.** The ancient churches at many sites (St. Symphorien at Autun, Ste. Reine at Alise) commemorate Christians were who martyred there during this era.

5th-14thC

In 470, the **Burgundians,** fleeing the Huns, swept from the shores of the Baltic down into the Rhône valley and settled in the regions corresponding to modern-day Burgundy and Provence. ● The neighbouring **Franks** occupied Burgundy in 534. A long period of conflict following the death of the Frankish Emperor Charlemagne in 814 resulted in the territory's **being divided** into an eastern (left bank of the Saône) and a western (right bank) region. ● The eastern region, ruled by Charlemagne's grandson Lothaire, eventually became the **County of Burgundy,** whereas the western, ruled by Lothaire's enemy and brother Charles the Bald, became the **Duchy of Burgundy.** Beginning in the 11thC, the feudal system fragmented Burgundy, like most of Europe, into fiefdoms controlled by local warlords. The **establishment of large religious foundations** during this era (Vézelay in 867, Cluny in 910) played a vital role in the development of agriculture and viticulture, which laid a solid foundation for trade and prosperity. ● Burgundian Romanesque Art flourished in the ecclesiastical buildings erected from the late 10th to early 13thC.

14th-18thC

In the latter part of the 14thC, **Jean le Bon** (John the Good), King of France, settled the Duchy of Burgundy on his fourth son, **Philippe le Hardi** (Philip the Bold). Philippe promptly married Margaret of Flanders, heiress to the County of Burgundy, in one stroke consolidating vast territories and founding a dynasty of Grand Dukes whose power surpassed that of the Kings of France. ● The power of Burgundy was maintained by the three successors (father to son) of Philippe, who were **Jean sans Peur** (the Fearless), **Philippe le Bon** (the Good), and the bellicose **Charles le Téméraire** (the Bold). Following Charles's inglorious death (his corpse, ravaged by wolves, was dragged from a frozen pond) during his siege of Nancy, his daughter Marie was granted part of the Duchy as dowry on her marriage to Maximilian von Hapsburg, while the rest of the Burgundian territories — Burgundy proper, the Mâconnais, Auxerrois and Charollais — reverted to the French crown in the person of Charles's rival, **Louis XI.** From the first half of the 17thC until the Revolution, Burgundy was ruled by the Princes de Condé (→ Ile-de-France : Chantilly) as royal Governors.

19thC to present

The modern era in Burgundy began with the opening (1794) of the Centre Canal linking the Saône and the Loire. The advent of this simplified freight transport system coincided with the first large-scale exploitation of vast iron-ore deposits at Creusot. To this day, Burgundy remains an area of limitless historical interest whose balanced economy thrives, on the one hand, from agricultural production, and on the other, from heavy industry that has been developed judiciously without detracting from the rural and pastoral charm of the region.

Practical information

The region

Information : *Délégation régionale au Tourisme* (D.R.T.), 55, rue de la Préfecture, 21041 Dijon Cedex, ☎ 80.55.24.10. *Comité régional de Tourisme,* same address. — **Côte-d'Or :** *Association départementale de Tourisme,* 55, rue de la Préfecture, 21041 Dijon Cedex, ☎ 80.73.81.81. — **Nièvre :** *Association départementale de Tourisme,* préfecture, 58019 Nevers, ☎ 86.57.80.25. — **Saône-et-Loire :** *Association départementale de Tourisme,* Conseil général, 71025 Mâcon, ☎ 85.38.21.00. — **Yonne :** *Association départementale de Tourisme,* Maison départementale du Tourisme, 1 et 2, quai de la République, 89000 Auxerre, ☎ 86.52.26.27.

Maps : *Michelin,* nos 61, 65, 66, 69, 70 (73), at 1/200 000. *I.G.N.,* nos 8, 9, 11, 21, 27, 28, 29, at 1/250 000 (tourist map series), nos 36, 37, 43, 44, at 1/100 000 (tourist map series), map of the Morvan nature park.

Local and regional press : *le Bien Public, l'Yonne Républicaine, le Courrier de Saône-et-Loire.*

S.O.S. : Côte-d'Or : *Medical Emergency Centre* (SMUR) Dijon, ☎ 80.41.12.12 ; *Poisoning Emergency Centre* Dijon, ☎ 80.41.12.12. **Nièvre :** *SAMU* (Emergency Medical Service), ☎ 86.59.22.00 ; *Poisoning Emergency Centre* Lyons, ☎ 78.54.14.14. **Saône-et-Loire :** *Medical Emergency Centre* (SMUR) Chalon-sur-Saône, ☎ 85.48.85.00, and Mâcon, ☎ 85.34.33.00 ; *Poisoning Emergency Centre* Lyons, ☎ 78.54.14.14. **Yonne :** *Medical Emergency Centre* (SMUR) Auxerre, ☎ 86.46.45.67 ; *Poisoning Emergency Centre* Paris, ☎ 42.05.63.29.

Rural Gîtes and chambres d'hôtes : enq : *Relais départementaux des Gîtes ruraux :* **Côte-d'Or,** 42, rue de Mulhouse, 21000 Dijon, ☎ 80.66.81.25 ; **Nièvre,** 6, pl. Chaméane, 58005 Nevers Cedex, ☎ 86.36.01.51 ; **Saône-et-Loire,** A.D.T.R., bd Dunant, 71010 Mâcon Cedex, ☎ 85.38.50.66 ; **Yonne,** Service Promotion rurale, 14 *bis,* rue Guynemer, 89000 Auxerre, ☎ 86.46.47.48.

Camping : 154 sites and 14 farmhouse camping sites : enq C.D.T.

Festival and event (→ also wine) : **Feb-Mar :** *Carnival* in Chalon-sur-Saône. **Mar :** *Spring fair* in Dijon. **Sun before Palm Sunday :** *Almshouse wine sale* in Nuits-Saint-Georges. **May :** *Sale of antiques and bric-à-brac* in Dijon, *Fair of French wines* in Mâcon. **Sun preceding 31 May ;** *Course des chausses* in Semur-en-Auxois, and **31 May :** *Course de la bague.* **May-Jun :** *Antiques show* in Tournus. **Jun :** *Summer music festival* in Dijon. *Fête de la batellerie* in Saint-Jean-de-Losne. **25 Jun :** *Foire chaude des sauvagines et de la récupération.* **Jul :** *Festival des nuits de Bourgogne ;* Autun *Morvan music festival ;* Clamecy, *water tournament.* **Jul-Aug :** *Estivades* in Dijon. **15 Aug :** *Water tournament* in Coulanges-sur-Yonne. **Aug :** *les Grandes Heures de Cluny, Wine Fair* in Pouilly-sur-Loire. *Horse racing* in Vitteaux. **Sep :** in Dijon *International Folklore Festival* and *Fêtes de la vigne.* **Sep-Oct :** *Nivernais music festival* in Nevers. **End Oct :** *Chestnut fair* in Saint-Léger-sous-Beuvray, *International Gastronomy Fair* in Dijon. **Nearest Sun to 11 Nov :** *Fête du sauvignon* in Saint-Bris-le-Vineux. **End Nov :** *les Trois Glorieuses :* this is a major 3-day wine festival in a principal wine-growing area. Sat, *le Chapitre* at the Clos de Vougeot, Sun, *Vente des Hospices* in Beaune (a world-famous wine auction at the Beaune Almshouse → Wine), and Mon, the *Paulée de Meursault.* **4th Sun in Nov :** *Wine Festival* in Chablis.

Exhibitions and trade fairs : fairs and markets of livestock, horses and bovines ; **Dec :** *Agricultural show* in Nevers. **Sat and Sun :** *Charolais cattle show and festival* in Saulieu. **Every second Tue of each month :** *Livestock market* in Corbigny. **10 Feb :** *Livestock fair* in Fours. **Every Thu :** *Livestock market* in Saint-Christophe-en-Brionnais ; **every Mon :** *Market of Bresse poultry* in Louhans.

Son et lumière : Côte-d'Or : *circuit de la Côte de Nuits, circuit de la Côte de Beaune ;* enq : O.T./S.I. Beaune, ☎ 80.22.24.51. O.T./S.I. Dijon, ☎ 80.43.42.12. *Son et lumière at the Hotel of the Dukes of Burgundy :* enq O.T. in Beaune, in the **Yonne** region, *grand spectacle historique* in Saint-Fargeau ; enq : *Association des Amis de Saint-Fargeau,* ☎ 86.74.05.67.

Visits to vineyards and cellars : enq : *Comité interprofessionnel de la Côte-d'Or et de l'Yonne pour les vins d'appellation contrôlée de Bourgogne,* rue Henri-Dunant, 21200 Beaune, ☎ 80.22.21.35. *Comité interprofessionnel des Vins de Bourgogne et du Mâconnais :* B.P. 113, Maison du Tourisme, 71000 Mâcon, ☎ 85.38.20.15.

Scenic railway : *le train des pêcheurs* ("fishermen's train"), Dijon-Bligny traversing the Ouche valley ; enq : *C.F.V.O. station,* ☎ 80.20.14.49.

National and nature parks : *nature park of the Morvan region ;* enq : *Maison du Parc,* Saint-Brisson, 58230 Montsauche, ☎ 86.78.70.16. One-day excursions in the Morvan ; enq : *Ecotour,* résidence le France, 2, av. Colbert, 58000 Nevers, ☎ 86.61.56.78. Inclusive holidays *Chaîne hôtelière du Morvan,* le Relais des Lacs, Planchez-en-Morvan, 58230 Montsauche, ☎ 86.78.41.68.

Rambling and hiking : Burgundy is traversed by the G.R. 7 from Nolay to Beaujeu, the G.R. 13 Ile-de-France-Bourgogne passes through the Morvan area, and the G.R. 137, a transverse axis between the G.R. 13 and the G.R. 7, links Nolay and Autun (topoguides).

Riding holidays : enq : *A.R.T.E. Bourgogne-Morvan,* 9, Grande-Rue, 89120 Charny, ☎ 86.63.67.25.

Horse-drawn wagon or caravan : *les Cavaliers de la nature,* Marcy, 58210 Varzy, ☎ 86.29.40.19. **Wild West style covered wagon :** *Bourgogne Buissonnière,* B.P. 1, 21820 Labergerment-les-Seurre, ☎ 80.21.00.16/80.21.10.58.

Cycling holidays : enq : *Bicy-club de France,* 8, pl. de la Porte-de-Champerret, 75017 Paris, ☎ 47.66.55.92, and *Ligue régionale de Bour-*

gogne, 8, rue du Tillor, 21000 Dijon. Bicycle hire : train + bike in numerous S.N.C.F. stations. **Nièvre** : *Comité départemental de Cyclo-tourisme,* rue Émile-Zola, 58260 La Machine, ☎ 86.50.84.73.

River and canal cruises : Burgundy, Nivernais, Centre, Yonne, and Saône canals, and canal which runs lateral to the Loire. Enq : *Association Régionale de Défense et de Promotion des Voies navigables de Bourgogne,* 1-2, quai de la République, 89000 Auxerre, ☎ 86.52.26.27.

Instruction al courses : Oenology, enq : *Maison des Vins,* prom. Ste-Marie, 71100 Chalon-sur-Saône, ☎ 85.41.64.00.

Young people : enq *C.R.I.,* 1, bd Champollion, 21000 Dijon, ☎ 80.71.32.12.

Golf : Mâcon (15 holes). Chalon-sur-Saône (18 holes). Norges-la-Ville (9 holes). Magny-Cours (9 holes). Savigny-sous-Clairis (9 holes).

Tennis : *Comité départemental,* 28, rue de Nièvre, 58700 Premery.

Aquatic sports : sailing : Pannessière, Settons and Saint-Aignan lakes. Water skiing : Settons lake, Branlasses aquatic-sports centre.

Canoeing : in the Morvan, La Cure and Le Chalaux areas, with the Chameçon lake station. Enq : *Canoë-club de Clamecy* and ℹ in Clamecy.

Climbing : *Club Alpin Français,* 5, rue de Strasbourg, 71100 Chalon-sur-Saône, ☎ 85.48.91.21, and Mâcon, 7, rue des Cordiers, 71000 Rock-climbing in the **Yonne** region, at Saussois rock, 25 km S of Auxerre ; in the **Nièvre** region, at Surgy rock, N of Clamecy ; in the **Côte-d'Or** region, on the Saffres cliffs near Vitteaux ; and in **Saône-et-Loire** at the famous Solutré rock.

Potholing and spelunking : in Chablis, enq mairie and in Dijon *Centre Social Balzac,* rue Balzac, 21000 Dijon, ☎ 80.32.58.46.

Flying, gliding and ballooning : ballooning, enq : *The Bombard Society,* hôtel de la Poste, 3, bd Clemenceau, 21100 Beaune, ☎ 80.22.51.61 until 15 Nov, and 80.22.08.11 as of 15 Nov. Balloon ascents, enq : 1 to 30 Apr, *Centre aérostatique de Bourgogne,* 8, rue Jules-Merey, 21200 Beaune, ☎ 80.22.21.03, and from 1st Apr to 31 Jan, M. Pierre Bonnet, résidence du Lac, Les Hêtres, 21200 Beaune, ☎ 80.22.62.25. Other flying activities : **Nièvre,** Cosnes-sur-Loire, Nevers, aérodrome de la Sangsue, ☎ 86.57.03.92.

Hunting and shooting : *Fédérations départementales des chasseurs.* **Côte-d'Or :** 47, rue Verrerie, 21000 Dijon, ☎ 80.32.19.19. **Nièvre :** rte du Terrain de karting, 58000 Nevers, ☎ 86.61.27.91. **Saône-et-Loire :** *Maison de l'Agriculture,* bd Henri-Dunant, 71000 Mâcon, ☎ 85.38.32.37. **Yonne :** 19, rue Moreaux, 89000 Auxerre, ☎ 86.51.06.44.

Fishing : *Fédérations départementales des Associations de Pêche et de Pisciculture.* **Saône-et-Loire :** 334, résidence du Parc, rue Claude-Debussy, 71000 Mâcon, ☎ 85.38.38.52 ; **Côte-d'Or :** 9, rue A.-Comte, 21000 Dijon, ☎ 80.30.85.20 ; **Nièvre :** bât. 2, les Pâtis, rue du Commerce, 58000 Nevers, ☎ 86.61.18.98. **Yonne :** 9 *bis,* av. Marceau, 89000 Auxerre.

Towns

ARCY-SUR-CURE

Autun 28, Dijon 57, Paris 290
B3 ♥ ✉ 21230

ℹ 15, rue St-Jacques, ☎ 80.90.11.59.

SNCF ☎ 80.41.50.50.

Hotels :

★★★***Chez Camille,*** 1, pl. É.-Herriot, ☎ 80.90.01.38. AE, DC, Euro, Visa. 12 rm P closed 10-30 Jan, 250. Rest. ● ♦♦ ♿ Spec : *tartare de saumon frais à l'aigrelette, croûte de filet de bœuf aux truffes,* 90-220.

★***Terminus*** (L.F.), 2, rue de l'Arquebuse, ☎ 80.90.00.33. AE, Visa. 12 rm P closed 6 Jan-6 Feb and Wed, 100. Rest. ♦ 80-130.

Restaurant :

Relais Saint-Jacques, 27, rue Saint-Jacques, ☎ 80.90.07.33. P ♿ closed Oct, 80-130.

AUTUN

Chalon-sur-Saône 53, Dijon 85, Paris 293
B3 ✉ 71400

ℹ 3, av. Charles-de-Gaulle (B2), ☎ 85.52.20.34.

SNCF (A1), ☎ 85.52.73.65, 85.52.28.01.

Hotels :

★★★***Vieux Moulin,*** porte d'Arroux (B1), ☎ 85.52.10.90. AE, DC, Visa. 18 rm P closed 10 Dec-1 Mar, Sun eve and Mon (low season), 220. Rest. ♦♦ ♿ 110-170.

★★***Tête Noire*** (L.F.), 1-3, rue de l'Arquebuse (B2), ☎ 85.52.25.39. Visa. 20 rm P closed Mar, Sat eve low season, 180. Rest. ♦ closed Fri eve and Sat, 55-100.

★***France,*** pl. de la Gare (A1), ☎ 85.52.14.00. 23 rm P 150.

Clef des Champs, rte de Château-Chinon, opposite the aerodrome, ☎ 85.52.12.30. Euro. 10 rm P closed 16 Jan-28 Feb, Sun eve and Mon, 90. Rest. ♦♦ *Aiguillette de canard au vin rouge et miel,* 95-200.

⛺ ★★★*Municipal du Pont-d'Arroux* (104 pl.), ☎ 85.52.10.82.

Restaurant :

♦ ***Chalet Bleu,*** 1, rue du Bourg, ☎ 85.52.25.16. ♿ closed 3 Jun-3 Jul, Sun eve and Tue. Very good, unsophisticated cooking ; remarkable value for money, 80-130.

Events : *Jul Music in Morvan,* enq ℹ

Aerial sports : *aéroclub du Morvan,* aérodrome de Bellevue, ☎ 85.52.14.14.

AUXERRE

Sens 57, Dijon 148, Paris 168
A1-2 ✉ 89000

ℹ 1-2, quai de la République (B2), ☎ 86.52.06.19.

✈ Auxerre-Branches, ☎ 86.53.02.89, 86.53.02.65.

SNCF Auxerre-Saint-Gervais (C2), ☎ 86.46.50.50, 86.46.93.94, 86.46.95.06, 86.46.96.15.

Car-hire : *Budget* train + auto, at the S.N.C.F. station, ☎ 86.52.28.34.

🚌 rue des Migraines (A1), ☎ 86.46.90.66.

Hotels :

★★★***Maxime,*** 2, quai de la Marine (B1), ☎ 86.52.14.19. AE, DC, Euro, Visa. 25 rm P 375. Rest. ♦♦ 130-210.

★★**Clairions,** av. Worms, ☎ 86.46.85.64. Tx 800039. AE, Euro, Visa. 62 rm Ⓟ ♨ ♘ ▭ ♿ 190. Rest. ♦♦ 60-140.

★★**Normandie,** 41, bd Vauban (A1), ☎ 86.52.57.80. AE, DC, Euro, Visa. 48 rm Ⓟ ♨ ♘ ⚘ ♿ 175.

★★**Pont Paul-Bert,** 4, av. Gambetta (C2), ☎ 86.46.90.26. 17 rm Ⓟ ♨ closed Sat pm and Sun, 180. Rest. ♦ 80-130.

Escolives-Sainte-Camille, ⊠ 89290, 10 km S :
★★**Galaxie,** « la Cour Barrée », ☎ 86.53.60.55. Euro, Visa. 17 rm Ⓟ ♨ ♘ ▭ ♿ closed 23 Dec-2 Jan and Sun (only in winter), 180. Rest. ♦ 100-130.

⛺ ★★★*Municipal* (220 pl.), ☎ 86.52.11.15.

Restaurants :

♦♦♦ **Le Jardin Gourmand,** 56, bd Vauban (A1), ☎ 86.51.53.52. AE, DC, Euro, Visa. Ⓟ ♨ ♿ closed 15 Aug-7 Sep, 15-31 Dec, Tue and Wed. Spec : *foie gras, ris et rognons de veau aux pleurotes,* 95-240.

♦♦ **Saint-Hubert,** 3, rue de la Poterne, ☎ 86.52.10.57. Tx 800997. Euro, Visa. ⚘ Simplicity and quality : *puits d'escargots au chablis, estouffade de bœuf,* 40-110.

Vaux, ⊠ 89290, 6 km S :
● ♦♦ **La Petite Auberge,** 2, pl. du Passeur, ☎ 86.53.80.08. Visa. ⚘ ⚘ ♿ closed 24 Dec-1 Jan, 1-15 Jul, Sun eve, Mon and nat hols. Comfort and refinement for cooking full of Burgundy's flavours, 95-150.

Chevannes, 8 km SW :
● ♦♦ **La Chamaille,** ☎ 86.41.24.80. AE, DC, Visa. ⚘ Ⓟ ♨ ♘ ♿ closed 5 Feb-5 Mar, 1-10 Sep, 23-30 Dec, Tue eve, Wed and Sun eve. An old farmhouse on the waterside in the open country. Market fresh produce cuisine, 100-200.

Appoigny, ⊠ 89380, 10 km N :
● ♦♦♦ **Relais Saint-Fiacre,** rte de Paris, RN6, ☎ 86.53.21.80. AE, DC, Euro, Visa. Ⓟ ♨ ▭ closed 7-20 Jan, Sun eve and Mon. Burgundy region in your plate and in your glass, 95-250.

Flea-market : 2nd Sun of each month, 7 am to 2 pm, pl. Saint-Nicolas.

Boat-hire : *Pro Aqua, Péniche-hôtels,* marina, ☎ 86.46.96.77.

Recommended : *Goussard Chocolatier,* 3, pl. Ch.-Surugue, ☎ 86.52.04.25. *Hôtel des ventes,* 21, av. Pierre-Larousse, ☎ 86.52.17.98, every Fri, pm.

AUXONNE

Dole 16, Dijon 32, Paris 345
C2-3 ♥ ⊠ 21130

ⓘ bd Pasteur, ☎ 80.36.34.46.

SNCF ☎ 80.41.50.50, 80.37.30.31.

Hotel :

★★**Corbeau** (L.F.), 1, rue de Berbis, ☎ 80.31.11.88. AE, DC, Euro, Visa. 10 rm ⚘ closed 22 Dec-27 Jan and Sun eve (1 Sep-31 May), 140. Rest. ♦ closed Mon and Sun eve low season, 60-130.

⛺ ★★★*Arquebuse* (100 pl.), ☎ 80.37.34.36.

AVALLON

Auxerre 51, Dijon 105, Paris 225
B2 ♥ ⊠ 89200

ⓘ high season : 24, pl. Vauban, ☎ 86.34.14.19, and pl. Saint-Lazare, ☎ 86.34.09.12 ; low season : mairie, ☎ 86.34.13.50.

SNCF ☎ 86.46.50.50, 86.34.01.01, 86.34.09.22.

Hotels :

★★★★ **Poste** (Relais et châteaux), 13, pl. Vauban, ☎ 86.34.06.12. Tx 351806. AE, DC, Visa. 20 rm Ⓟ ♨ ♘ ♿ closed 1 Dec-15 Jan, 25 Mar-5 Apr, Wed and Thu noon, 470. Rest. ♦♦♦ Spec : *matelote de sandre à l'épineuil, poussin sauté aux effluves de moutarde et citron vert,* 170-300.

★★★**Relais Fleuri** (L.F.), RN6, motorway exit A6, ☎ 86.34.02.85. Tx 800084. AE, Euro, Visa. 48 rm Ⓟ ♨ ▭ ♿ 240. Rest. ● ♦♦ In the open country, good cooking, low prices : *turbotin beurre blanc, jambon à l'os au vin rouge,* 80-140.

● ★★**Vauban,** 53, rue de Paris, ☎ 86.34.36.99. 26 rm Ⓟ ♨ ♿ closed 16 Nov-8 Dec, 260.

★**Parc** (L.F.), pl. de la Gare, ☎ 86.34.17.00. Visa. 27 rm Ⓟ ♨ closed 15 Dec-15 Jan and Sun, 100. Rest. 50-90.

Les Capucins, 6, av. Paul-Doumer, ☎ 86.34.06.52. Visa. 10 rm Ⓟ ♨ closed 15 Dec-15 Jan, Tue eve and Wed, 70. Rest. ● ♦♦ ♿ Spec : *gâteau de lapereau en gelée de chablis,* 80-170.

Pontaubert, 4 km W :
★★**Fontaine,** Grande-Rue, ☎ 86.34.02.87. AE, Euro, Visa. 9 rm Ⓟ ♨ ♘ closed 15 Nov-8 Dec and Mon low season, 165.

● ★★**Moulin des Templiers,** vallée du Cousin, ☎ 86.34.10.80. 14 rm ⚘ a water-side setting Ⓟ ♨ ♘ closed 1 Jan-15 Mar and 1 Nov-31 Dec, 220.

★★**Fleurs** (L.F.), ☎ 86.34.13.81. Visa. 7 rm Ⓟ ♨ ♘ closed 30 Jan-1 Mar, 10 days in Oct, Wed, Thu noon low season, 165. Rest. ♦ ♿ 75-125.

Cousin Valley, 5 km S :
★★★**Moulin des Ruats** (Châteaux-hôtels), ☎ 86.34.07.14, 86.34.10.11. AE, DC, Euro, Visa. 20 rm ⚘ Ⓟ ♨ ♘ closed 30 Oct-2 Mar, Mon and Tue noon low season, 260. Rest. ♦♦ ♿ Spec : *truite au bleu, salade du Moulin,* 155-200.

⛺ ★★★*Sous-Roche* (100 pl.), ☎ 86.34.10.39.

Restaurants :

● ♦♦♦ **Le Morvan** (M.C.F.), 7, rte de Paris, ☎ 80.34.18.20. AE, DC, Euro, Visa. Ⓟ ♨ ♿ Terrace, closed Mon and Sun eve, 6 Jan-6 Feb, 15-30 Nov, 5-25 Jan. Good country cooking adapted to today's tastes : *escargots aux noisettes et chablis, escalope de ris de veau à l'oseille,* 110-170.

Sainte-Magnance, 14 km SE :
● ♦ **La Chênevotte,** N6, ☎ 80.33-14-79. Ⓟ ♨ ♘ closed Tue eve and Wed. Friendly family atmosphere. Spec : meat and poultry grilled over wood fire, 55-100.

BEAUNE

Chalon-sur-Saône 30, Dijon 45, Paris 316
C3 ⊠ 21200

ⓘ rue de l'Hôtel-Dieu (B2), ☎ 80.22.24.51, 80.22.26.05, and A6 motorway, aire de Beaune-Merceuil, 21190 Meursault, ☎ 80.21.46.43, 80.21.46.78.

SNCF (C2), ☎ 80.41.50.50, 80.22.80.56, 80.22.13.13, 80.22.14.99.

Hotels :

● ★★★★**Le Cep,** 27, rue Maufoux (A2), ☎ 80.22.35.48. 21 rm Ⓟ ♨ ♘ closed 30 Nov-22 Mar, 500.

★★★★**Poste,** bd Clemenceau (A2), ☎ 80.22.08.11. AE, DC, Visa. 25 rm Ⓟ ♨ closed 18 Nov-28 Mar, 550. Rest. ● ♦♦♦ A great Bourguignon cooking institution : *rognons à la moutarde, salade d'écrevisses,* great Burgundy wines, 220-310.

★★★**Central** (L.F.), 2, rue Victor-Millot (B2), ☎ 80.24.77.24. Tx 350690. Visa. 22 rm, closed end Nov-end Mar and Wed, 230. Rest. ♦♦ ♿ closed Wed low season, 90-210.
★★★**Closerie** (L.F.), 61, rte de Pommard, ☎ 80.22.15.07. Tx 351213. AE, DC, Visa. 30 rm P closed 24 Dec-31 Jan and Sun (low season), 260.
● ★★**Grillon** (L.F.), 21, rte de Seurre (C2), ☎ 80.22.44.25. AE, DC, Visa. 18 rm P closed 15 Jan-15 Feb, eve, 190. Rest. ♦ closed Wed, 65-110.
★★**Home,** 138, rte de Dijon (B1), ☎ 80.22.16.43. Visa. 20 rm P ♿ Ivy-covered, 220.
★★**Auberge Bourguignonne,** 4, pl. Madeleine (C2), ☎ 80.22.23.53. AE, Visa. 8 rm closed 22 Dec-21 Jan, first week of Jun and Mon, 180. Rest. ♦ ♿ Traditional cooking, 75-160.
★★**Bourgogne,** 27, av. Charles-de-Gaulle (off map via B2), ☎ 80.22.22.00. Tx 350666. AE, DC, Euro, Visa. 120 rm P ♿ closed 18 Nov-1 Apr, 210. Rest. ♦♦ 85-140.
★★**Bretonnière,** 43, fg Bretonnière (A2), ☎ 80.22.15.77. 21 rm P ♿ 180.

Montagny-lès-Beaune, 1 km S :
★★**Les Genièvres,** ☎ 80.22.37.74. AE, Visa. 19 rm P ♿ closed Dec-Jan, 170.

Savigny-lès-Beaune, 6 km N :
★★**Ouvrée,** rte de Bouilland, ☎ 80.21.51.52. 22 rm P ♿ 180. Rest. ♦♦ 80-180.

Chorey-lès-Beaune, 8 km NE :
★★★★(L) **L'Ermitage de Corton,** rte de Dijon, ☎ 80.22.05.28. 4 apts. closed 15 Jan-15 Feb, Sun eve and Mon, 770. Rest. ● ♦♦♦ In the heart of vineyards, velvet and gold are still the setting for a wiser A. Parra's (M.C.F.) cooking. Spec : *persillé de Bourgogne, émincé de volaille à l'aligote,* an astonishing choice of desserts, 220-310.

Ʌ ★★★★*Les Cent Vignes* (120 pl.), ☎ 80.22.03.91.

Restaurants :
♦♦♦ **Les Gourmets,** 17, rue Monge (B1), ☎ 80.22.15.99, 80.22.13.67. AE, Visa. ♿ 120-210.
♦♦♦ **Relais de Saulx,** 6, rue Louis-Véry, ☎ 80.22.01.35. ♿ closed Mar, last week of Aug, Sun eve and Mon. Spec : *fricassée de volaille de Bresse à la crème d'ail, éventail de magret de canard à la poivrade de cidre,* 70-170.
● ♦♦ **Alain Billard,** 3, rue Nicolas-Rolin, ☎ 80.22.64.20. AE, Euro, Visa. ♿ closed 20 Dec-31 Jan, Sun eve and Mon. Pleasant cooking, fine cellar. Spec : *cassolette d'escargots aux herbes fines, ravioles de langoustines,* 120-210.
● ♦♦ **Jacques Lainé,** 10-12, bd Foch, ☎ 80.24.76.10. AE, DC, Euro, Visa. P 90-250.
♦♦ **Auberge St-Vincent,** pl. de la Halle (B2), ☎ 80.22.42.34. AE, DC, Euro, Visa. closed 1-31 Dec and Sun eve low season. Good traditional cooking in an old home, 100-175.
♦ **Au Petit Pressoir,** 15, pl. Fleury, ☎ 80.22.07.31. AE, DC, Visa, closed Tue eve and Wed. Spec : *pintadeau au bourgogne et lard fumé,* 70-160.

Chorey-lès-Beaune :
Le Bareuzai, rte Beaune-Dijon RN74, ☎ 80.22.02.90. AE. P ♿ Terrace. closed 1 Jan-15 Feb. Luxurious cooking, 65-220.

Vignoles, 4 km E :
● ♦♦ **Au Petit Truc,** pl. de l'Église, ☎ 80.22.01.76. closed 9-18 Apr, 5-20 Aug. Mon and Tue. Fine, home cooking, in the true family tradition, 320-450.

Son et lumière : at the Hotel of the Dukes of Burgundy (B2).

Excursions in horse-drawn carriages : enq ℹ ☎ 80.22.24.51.

Bicycle hire : *Cycles Bouillot,* 18, fg Saint-Nicolas, ☎ 80.22.36.37.

Tours of wine-cellars : *cave des Batistines,* pl. de la Madeleine, ☎ 80.22.09.05 ; *Reine Pédauque,* 2, fg Saint-Nicolas, ☎ 80.22.23.11 ; *cave du Bourgogne,* 28, rue Sylvestre-Chauvelot, ☎ 80.22.18.34.

Recommended : *Wine Market,* rue Nicolas-Rolin, ☎ 80.22.27.69, 21200 Beaune ; unlimited tasting. *Confiserie A. Bouché,* 1, pl. Monge, ☎ 80.22.10.35, for *burgondines, grumelles* and *pâtes de fruits.*

BOUILLAND

Dijon 44, Autun 55, Paris 304
16 km N of Beaune C3
☒ 21420 Savigny-lès-Beaune

Hotel :
★★★**Vieux Moulin,** ☎ 80.21.51.16. AE, DC, Visa. 8 rm P closed 15 Dec-1 Jan and Wed eve, 220. Rest. ● ♦♦ ♿ closed Wed and Thu noon. Spec : *lasagnes de truite de mer et choux au chèvre frais, pigeonneau de Cussigny rôti aux fèves fraîches,* 130-270.

BOURBON-LANCY

Moulins 36, Autun 62, Paris 312
A4 ☒ 71140

10 May-30 Sep

ℹ pl. d'Aligre, ☎ 85.89.18.27.

SNCF ☎ 85.38.50.50.

Hotels :
★★**Raymond** (L.F.), 8, rue d'Autun, ☎ 85.89.17.39. DC, Euro, Visa. 20 rm P closed 26 Mar-2 May, 15 Nov-5 Dec, Fri eve and Sat noon (ex Jul-Aug), Sun eve (Nov-May), 170. Rest. ♦ ♿ 60-220.
★**Poste** (L.F.), 19, av. Gal-de-Gaulle, ☎ 85.89.00.31. Visa. 16 rm P closed Mon low season, 100. Rest. ♦ ♿ 80-130.

Ʌ ★★★*Saint-Prix* (128 pl.), ☎ 85.89.14.85.

Casino des Thermes, ☎ 85.89.09.04.

CHABLIS

Auxerre 19, Dijon 135, Paris 184
A1 ☒ 89800

SNCF ☎ 86.46.50.50.

Hotel :
★**L'Étoile,** 4, rue des Moulins, ☎ 86.42.10.50. Euro. 16 rm P closed 15 Dec-1 Feb, Mon and Tue noon, 180. Rest. ♦ ♿ 60-160.

Event : 4th Sun in Nov, *wine festival.*

Recommended : *Chablis 82, domaine Rottiers-Clotilde,* rue Auxerroise, 89800 Chablis. *Vins Henri Laroche,* 10, rue Auxerroise, ☎ 86.42.14.30.

CHAGNY

Beaune 15, Mâcon 75, Paris 331
C3 ☒ 71150

ℹ rue des Halles. High season, ☎ 85.87.25.95 ; low season, ☎ 85.87.13.54.

SNCF ☎ 80.93.50.50, 85.87.16.95.

Hotels :
★★★**Lameloise,** 36, pl. d'Armes, ☎ 85.87.08.85. Visa. 25 rm P closed 10 Dec-9 Jan, 7-25 Jul, Wed and Thu noon, 420. Rest.

● ♦♦♦♦ ♿ Jacques Lameloise is the wisest and the most discrete of the great cooks. With his family's efficient assistance, he prepares an excellent Burgundian cooking and a light and modern one. It is a perfect combination. Great Burgundy wines in the cellar, 300-500.
★★**Capucines,** (L.F.) 30, rte de Chalon, ☎ 85.87.08.17. Visa. 15 rm 🅿 ♿ closed 20 Dec-4 Jan, Mon and Sun eve, 170. Rest. ♦ 65-175.
★★**Château de Bellecroix** (L.F., Relais du Silence, Châteaux-hôtels), RN6, ☎ 85.87.13.86. AE, DC, Visa. 14 rm 🅿 closed 24 Dec-25 Jan and Wed, 260. Rest. ♦ ♿ 120-210.
★★**La Ferté** (ex **Nouvel Hôtel**), 11, bd de la Liberté, ☎ 85.87.07.47. Visa. 14 rm 🅿 ♿ 195.

Rully, 5 km S :
★★**Rully,** RN6, ☎ 85.87.89.69. 57 rm 🅿 ♿ closed 27 Nov-2 Jan, 180. Rest. ♦ closed noon ex Sun, 80-130.

⛺ ★★★Municipal *Pâquier-Fané* (85 pl.), ☎ 85.87.21.42.

Aerial sports : *Dirigeables de Bourgogne,* terrain de Champforgueil, enq M. Michel Arnould, ☎ 85.49.45.84.

CHALON-SUR-SAÔNE

Dijon 69, Lyons 126, Paris 340
C3 ✉ 71100

ℹ square Chabas, bd de la République (A1), ☎ 85.48.37.97.

SNCF (A2), ☎ 85.48.28.37, 85.48.09.12, 85.93.50.50.

Car-hire : *Budget* train + auto, 34, av. V.-Hugo (A2), ☎ 85.48.52.61 and at the station, ☎ 85.48.09.12.

Hotels :
★★★**Royal Hôtel** (Mapotel), 8, rue du Port-Villiers (B2), ☎ 85.48.15.86. Tx 801610. AE, DC, Euro, Visa. 50 rm 🅿 ♿ 360. Rest. ♦♦ closed Sun and Mon noon low season, 120-210.
★★★**Saint-Georges** (Inter-Hôtel), 32, av. Jean-Jaurès (A2), ☎ 85.48.27.05. Tx 800330. AE, DC, Euro, Visa. 48 rm 🅿 ♿ 270. Rest. ● ♦♦ Quality fare : *feuilleté d'escargots de Bourgogne, loup au vin rouge,* 80-250.
★★★**Saint-Régis** (Mapotel), 22, bd de la République (A1), ☎ 85.48.07.28. Tx 801624. AE, DC, Euro, Visa. 40 rm 🅿 ♿ 265. Rest. ♦♦ closed Sat noon, Sun and 21 Dec-21 Jan, 85-185.
★★**Nouvel Hôtel** (L.F.), 7, av. Boucicaut (A1), ☎ 85.48.07.31. 27 rm 🅿 150.
★★**Saint-Jean,** 24, quai Gambetta (B2), ☎ 85.48.45.65. 25 rm ♿ 175.
★★**Aux Vendanges de Bourgogne** (L.F.), 21, rue du Gal-Leclerc (B1-2), ☎ 85.48.01.90. AE, DC, Visa. 21 rm 🅿 ♿ 130.

Lux, 3 km S :
★★**Charmilles,** rue de la Libération, ☎ 85.48.58.08. Visa. 32 rm 🅿 ♿ 180. Rest. closed 15 Feb-15 Mar, 80-130.

Youth hostel : av. Léon-Blum, ☎ 85.46.62.77. 96 beds.

⛺ ★★★*La Butte,* Saint-Marcel (92 pl.), ☎ 85.48.26.86.

Restaurants :
♦♦♦ **Le Bourgogne,** 28, rue de Strasbourg (C2), ☎ 85.48.89.18. Euro, Visa, closed 28 Nov-4 Dec and Sun eve. Excellent, reasonably priced cooking in a 17thC wine-cellar. Spec : *barbue à la fondue d'échalotes, canette à la lie de vin,* 70-150.
● ♦♦ **Luc Pasquier,** pl. de la Gare (A2), ☎ 85.48.29.33. AE, DC, Visa. ♿ closed Sun eve and Mon. As years go by, Luc Pasquier confirms his talent : *bisque d'écrevisses, pigeonneaux de Bresse au jus de truffes,* 65-215.
♦♦ **Marche,** 7, pl. St-Vincent, ☎ 85.48.62.00. DC, Visa. in the old town. closed 15 Aug-15 Sep, Sun eve and Mon, 65-160.
♦ **Ripert,** 31, rue Saint-Georges, ☎ 85.48.89.20. Visa. closed Sun and Mon, 4-23 Aug, 25 Dec-31 Jan and 1 week in Apr. In the heart of the old town ; delicious dishes which vary according to the market, 65-100.

Events : end Feb-early Mar, *Carnival,* enq : Comité des Fêtes, salle Marcel-Sembat, ☎ 85.43.08.39.

Aerial sports : ballooning at the *aéroclub de Bourgogne,* ☎ 85.46.08.48.

La CHARITÉ-SUR-LOIRE

Nevers 24, Auxerre 95, Paris 216
A3 ✉ 58400

ℹ 49, Grande-Rue, ☎ 85.70.16.12.

SNCF ☎ 85.61.50.50, 85.70.03.02.

Hotels :
★★**Grand Monarque,** 33, quai Clemenceau, ☎ 85.70.21.73. AE, DC, Visa. 9 rm 🅿 180. Rest. ♦♦ closed Wed, 120-210.
★**Terminus,** 23, av. Gambetta, ☎ 85.70.09.61. 10 rm 🅿 closed 23 Dec-20 Jan, 175. Rest. ♦ 55-115.

⛺ ★★*La Saulaie* (50 pl.), ☎ 85.70.00.83.

Recommended : *Confiserie du Prieuré,* 11, pl. des Pêcheurs, ☎ 85.70.01.81.

Guided tours : see ℹ

CHARNY

Montargis 35, Auxerre 49, Paris 150
27 km W of Joigny, A1 ✉ 89120

SNCF ☎ 86.46.50.50, 86.63.61.14.

Hotel :
★**Cheval Blanc** (L.F.), pl. de l'Ancienne-Mairie, ☎ 86.63.60.66. Visa. 9 rm 🅿 ♿ closed Tue eve and Wed, 15 Feb-10 Mar, 100. Rest. 80-130.

⛺ ★★Municipal *le Pâtis* (50 pl.), ☎ 86.63.63.56.

CHAROLLES

Mâcon 55, Autun 75, Paris 409
B4 ✉ 71120

ℹ couvent des Clarisses, ☎ 85.24.05.95.

SNCF ☎ 85.38.50.50, 85.24.12.41.

Hotels :
★★**France,** 3, av. de la Gare, ☎ 85.24.06.66. 12 rm ♿ closed 15 Dec-Jan, 200. Rest. ♦ closed Sun ex Jul-Aug, 80-130.
★★**Moderne,** 14, av. de la Gare, ☎ 85.24.07.02. AE, DC, Visa. 18 rm 🅿 ♿ closed 24 Dec, Sun eve and Mon noon low season, 155. Rest. ♦♦ Spec : *terrine de foies de volailles,* 70-220.

Saint-Bonnet-de-Joux, ✉ 71220, 14 km NE :
★**Val de Joux,** ☎ 85.24.72.39. Visa. 10 rm 🅿 closed 20 Dec-1 Feb, 1-15 Jul, Mon, 120. Rest. ♦♦ ♿ 45-100.

⛺ ★★*Municipal* (60 pl.), ☎ 85.24.04.90.

Folklore evenings : Jul-Aug and Sep ; enq ℹ

Recommended : *la Maison du Charolais,* RN79, ☎ 85.24.00.46. Regional produce and handicrafts for sale. Daily *charolais* afternoon tea at 3 pm.

CHÂTEAU-CHINON

Autun 36, Nevers 66, Paris 287
B3 ⊠ 58120

ℹ ☎ 86.85.06.58.

Hotel :
★★**Au Vieux Morvan,** 8, pl. Gudin, ☎ 86.85.05.01. Euro. 23 rm closed 15 Nov-11 May and Fri, 170. Rest. ◆ ♿ closed 15 Nov-15 Jan and Fri, 55-150.

⛺ ★*Du Pertuy d'Oiseau* (70 pl.), ☎ 86.85.15.05.

CHÂTILLON-SUR-SEINE

Auxerre 83, Dijon 84, Paris 248
B1 ♥ ⊠ 21400

ℹ pl. Marmont, ☎ 80.91.13.19.

SNCF ☎ 80.41.50.50, 80.91.08.29.

Hotels :
★★★**Côte-d'Or,** rue Ch.-Ronot, ☎ 80.91.13.29. AE, DC, Euro, Visa. 11 rm Ⓟ closed 15 Dec-15 Jan, Sun eve and Mon (ex Jul-Aug), 230. Rest. ◆◆ 65-175.
★★**Sylvia Hôtel,** 9, av. de la Gare, ☎ 80.91.02.44. Visa. 21 rm Ⓟ ♿ closed Feb, 165.

⛺ ★★★*Essi* (66 pl.), ☎ 80.91.03.05.

Guided tours : see ℹ

Leisure activities : park 12 km from Châtillon-sur-Seine, Marcenay Lake.

CHAUFFAILLES

Mâcon 68, Lyons 88, Paris 442
13 km S of La Clayette, B4 ♥ ⊠ 71170

ℹ Le Château, ☎ 85.26.07.06.

SNCF ☎ 85.38.50.50, 85.26.04.05.

Hotel :
★★**Paix** (L.F.), pl. de la République, ☎ 85.26.02.60. 19 rm Ⓟ closed Nov-25 Mar, 230. Rest. ◆◆ Excellent cooking : *cuisse de canard marinée en cocotte,* 120-210.

CHÉROY

Sens 22, Auxerre 67, Paris 104
A1 ⊠ 89690

Restaurants :
◆◆ **La Tour d'Argent,** 3, pl. de la Concorde, ☎ 86.88.53.43. Visa. ♿ closed 15 Jan-15 Feb, 9-15 May, Mon and Tue (open noon Jul-Aug), 60-150.

Saint-Valérien, ⊠ 89150, 8 km E :
● ◆ **Le Gâtinais,** 22, rue de la République, ☎ 86.88.62.78. closed Tue, Wed, 1-22 Sep/1-22 Feb. A restaurant which provides a warm welcome and family-style cooking from the South-West for Burgundians and others : *foie gras, sardines en escabèche, champignons en saison,* 120-210.

CLAMECY

Nevers 69, Dijon 142, Paris 211
A2 ♥ ⊠ 58500

ℹ high season : rue du Grand-Marché, ☎ 86.27.02.51 ; low season : ☎ 86.27.16.70.

SNCF ☎ 86.46.50.50.

Hotels :
★**Auberge Au Bon Accueil,** 3, rte d'Auxerre, ☎ 86.27.06.32. Visa. 10 rm Ⓟ closed 15 Dec-Jan, Mon eve and Tue, 120. Rest. ◆ 65-160.
★**Hostellerie de la Poste,** pl. Émile-Zola, ☎ 86.27.01.55. Euro, Visa. 17 rm Ⓟ closed 20 Dec-20 Jan, 20 Jun-1 Jul, 1 May and Mon, 150. Rest. ◆ ♿ 50-125.

Tannay, ⊠ 58180, 13 km SE :
★**Gare** (L.F.), ☎ 86.29.87.51. Visa. 18 rm Ⓟ closed 1-25 Oct, 1-15 Feb and Mon, 100. Rest. ◆ ♿ 80-130.

⛺ ★★*Du Pont Picot* (70 pl.), ☎ 86.27.05.97.

River and canal cruises : on the Nivernais canal, *N.F. navigation,* La Plage, 58500 Clamecy, ☎ 86.27.25.98, 45.54.89.81.

La CLAYETTE

Mâcon 57, Lyons 97, Paris 240
B4 ⊠ 71800

Hotel :
★★**Poste et Dauphin** (L.F.), 17, rue Centrale, ☎ 85.28.02.45. AE, DC, Visa. 15 rm Ⓟ closed 22 Dec-15 Jan, Fri, Sat and Sun eve (ex during high season), 180. Rest. ◆ 65-180.

⛺ ★★*Les Bruyères* (100 pl.), ☎ 85.28.09.15.

CLUNY

Mâcon 25, Chalon-sur-Saône 52, Paris 391
B4 ⊠ 71250

ℹ 6, rue Mercière, ☎ 85.59.05.34.

SNCF ☎ 85.38.50.50, 85.59.07.72.

Hotels :
● ★★★**Bourgogne,** pl. de l'Abbaye, ☎ 85.59.00.58. AE, DC, Visa. 18 rm. Opposite the abbey. Ⓟ ♿ closed 15 Nov-8 Mar, Tue eve (low season), 300. Rest. ◆◆ closed Tue and Wed noon (low season). Quality fare. Spec : *foie gras,* 100-250.
★★**Moderne,** pont de l'Étang, ☎ 85.59.05.65. AE, DC, Visa. 15 rm Ⓟ closed 4 Nov-1 Dec, Sun eve and Mon (low season), 200. Rest. ◆◆ ♿ Excellent cooking, 80-190.
★**Abbaye** (L.F.), av. de la Gare, ☎ 85.59.11.14. 18 rm Ⓟ closed 1 Dec-28 Feb, Sun eve, 155. Rest. ◆ closed Mon noon and Sun eve, 65-90.

⛺ ★★★Municipal *Saint-Vital,* rue des Griottes (90 pl.), ☎ 85.59.08.34.

Events : in Aug *"les Grandes Heures"* five concerts in the abbey cloister. Art exhibitions throughout the summer at the Écuries Saint-Hugues and at the Hôtel de la Monnaie.

COSNE-SUR-LOIRE

Nevers 52, Auxerre 84, Paris 188
A2 ⊠ 58200

SNCF ☎ 86.61.50.50, 86.28.05.12.

Hotels :
★★**Grand Cerf,** 43, rue Saint-Jacques, ☎ 86.28.04.46. Visa. 21 rm Ⓟ closed 10 Dec-10 Jan, Sun eve, Mon, 140.
★★**Vieux Relais** (L.F.), 11, rue Saint-Aignan, ☎ 86.28.20.21. AE, DC, Visa. 11 rm Ⓟ closed Feb, 180. Rest. ◆ ♿ closed Wed, Fri noon (season), Wed (low season), 80-130.
★**Saint-Christophe,** pl. de la Gare, ☎ 86.28.02.01. Visa. 15 rm Ⓟ closed Feb and Fri, 80. Rest. ◆ ♿ closed Fri, 50-100.

⛺ ★★★Municipal *Ile de Cosne* (200 pl.), ☎ 86.28.27.92.

Restaurant :
◆◆ **La Panetière,** 18, pl. Pêcheries, ☎ 86.28.11.70. ♿ closed 1-15 Sep and Feb hols, 80-130.

Le CREUSOT

Autun 29, Mâcon 90, Paris 378
B3 ⊠ 71200

ℹ 1, rue du Mal-Foch, ☎ 85.55.02.46.

SNCF ☎ 85.93.50.50, 85.80.25.55, 85.55.24.77.

Car-hire : *Budget* train + auto, at the S.N.C.F. station, ☎ 85.55.24.77 ; and (T.G.V.), ☎ 85.78.03.46 ; and Montchanin station, ☎ 85.78.10.47.

Hotels :

Le Breuil, ⊠ 71670, 3 km NE :
★★***Moulin Rouge,*** rte de Montcoy, ☎ 85.55.14.11. AE, DC, Visa. 37 rm closed 20 Dec-10 Jan, Fri and Sun eve, 210. Rest. ♦♦ ♿ 120-210.

Couches, ⊠ 71490, 15 km NE :
★***Trois Maures*** (L.F.), pl. de la République, ☎ 85.49.63.93. 10 rm Ⓟ closed 15 Feb-15 Mar and Mon, 115. Rest. ♦ ♿ 45-90.

DECIZE

Nevers 34, Autun 78, Paris 274
A3 ⊠ 58300

ℹ mairie, ☎ 86.25.03.23.

SNCF ☎ 86.61.50.50, 86.25.08.53.

Hotel :
★***Agriculture*** (L.F.), 20, rte des Moulins, ☎ 86.25.05.38. 18 rm Ⓟ closed 1-15 Oct and Sun (winter), 140. Rest. ♿ 80-130.

⛺ ★★★★*Municipal les Halles* (208 pl.), ☎ 86.25.14.05.

Boat-hire : *Camping-Nautic,* 4, rue Morambeau, 71670 Le Breuil, ☎ 85.55.21.10, 85.55.22.16. *Champvert-Plaisance,* port de la Copine, B.P. 37, 58300 Decize, ☎ 86.25.00.35.

Guided tours : see ℹ

DIGOIN

Autun 67, Mâcon 80, Paris 360
B4 ⊠ 71160

ℹ 8, rue Guilleminot, ☎ 85.53.00.81.

SNCF ☎ 85.38.50.50, 85.53.12.61, 85.53.17.39.

Hotels :
★★***Diligences et Commerce*** (L.F.), 14, rue Nationale, ☎ 85.53.06.31. AE, DC, Euro, Visa. 10 rm Ⓟ closed 4 Nov-4 Dec, 2-12 May and Tue, 120. Rest. ♦ Spec : *ris de veau en papillote,* 75-250.
★★***Gare,*** 79, av. du Gal-de-Gaulle, ☎ 85.53.03.04. AE, DC, Visa. 15 rm Ⓟ ♿ closed Jan and 1 week in Jun, 260.

Geugnon, ⊠ 71130, 16 km NE :
★★***Le Relais Bourguignon*** (L.F.), 47, rue de la Convention, ☎ 85.85.25.23. AE, DC, Euro, Visa. Ⓟ closed 1 week in Feb, 3 weeks in Aug, Sun eve and Mon, 120. Rest. ♦♦♦ ♿ Spec : *salade bressane aux foies de volailles sautés,* 70-150.

⛺ ★★★*Municipal de la Chevrette* (100 pl.), ☎ 85.53.11.49.

DIJON

Auxerre 148, Lyons 192, Paris 313
C2 ⊠ 21000

ℹ pl. Darcy (A2), ☎ 80.43.12.12.

✈ Longvic-Dijon, 7 km SE ; Air France Agency, 7, pl. Darcy (A2), ☎ 80.30.10.48.

SNCF (A1) ☎ 80.41.81.35, 80.41.50.50, 80.43.52.56.

🚌 (C2)

Car-hire : *Budget* train + auto, at the S.N.C.F. station, ☎ 80.45.30.60, 80.43.52.56.

Hotels :
★★★★***Cloche,*** 14, pl. Darcy (A2), ☎ 80.30.12.32. Tx 350498. AE, Euro, Visa. 80 rm with 4 apts Ⓟ ♿ closed Jan-3 Feb, 600. Rest. ● ♦♦♦♦ A new start for J. P. Billoux and his wife. There will be more customers but be sure that this brilliant chef will not fall asleep in his beautiful vaulted cellar. Delicate and inventive cooking, 220-350.
● ★★★***Chapeau Rouge*** (Mapotel), 5, rue Michelet (A-B2), ☎ 80.30.28.10. Tx 350535. AE, DC, Euro, Visa. 33 rm 460. Rest. ♦♦♦ ♿ 140-220.
★★★***Europe,*** 4, rue Audra (B2), ☎ 80.30.78.08. 28 rm Ⓟ 220.
★★★***Jura,*** 14, av. Mal-Foch (A2), ☎ 80.41.61.12. Tx 350485. AE, DC, Euro, Visa. 75 rm Ⓟ ♿ closed 20 Dec-15 Jan, 250.
★★★***Morot et Genève,*** 17, av. Mal-Foch (A2), ☎ 80.43.40.01. AE, Visa. 86 rm Ⓟ ♿ 180. Rest. ♦♦ 80-130.
● ★★***Jacquemart,*** 32, rue Verrerie (B2), ☎ 80.73.39.74. Visa. 32 rm closed 5-25 Feb, 140.
★★***Allées,*** 27, cours Gal-de-Gaulle (B3), ☎ 80.66.57.50. 37 rm Ⓟ ♿ closed 1-15 Aug, Feb school hols, 150.
★★***Chambellan,*** 92, rue Vannerie (B2), ☎ 80.67.12.67. AE, DC, Euro, Visa. 20 rm closed 20 Dec-4 Jan, 170.
★★***Nord,*** pl. Darcy (B2), ☎ 80.30.58.58. Tx 351554. AE, DC, Euro, Visa. 24 rm, closed 23 Dec-14 Jan, 200. Rest. ♦♦ 90-150.
★★***Poste,*** 5, rue du Château (B2), ☎ 80.30.51.64. Tx 351225. AE, DC, Visa. 60 rm Ⓟ 195. Rest. ♦ ***Grand Café,*** 75-130.
★★***Saint-Bernard,*** 7 *bis,* rue Courtépée, ☎ 80.30.74.67. 19 rm Ⓟ ♿ 180.

Chenove, ⊠ 21300, 2 km S :
★★★***L'Escargotière,*** 96, rte de Beaune, ☎ 80.52.15.35. 30 rm Ⓟ ♿ 180. Rest. ♦ closed sun, 80-130.

Talant, ⊠ 21240, 4 km W :
★★★***La Bonbonnière,*** 24, rue des Orfèvres, near the church, ☎ 80.57.31.95. Euro, Visa. 20 rm Ⓟ ♿ 190.

Youth hostel : 1, bd Champollion, ☎ 80.71.32.12.

⛺ ★★*Municipal du Lac* (249 pl.), ☎ 80.43.54.72.

Restaurants :
♦♦♦ ***Le Pré aux Clercs et Trois Faisans,*** 13, pl. de la Libération (B2), ☎ 80.67.11.33. AE, DC, Euro, Visa. ♿ closed Tue and Sun eve, 110-210.
● ♦♦ ***Chez Thibert,*** 23, rue Crébillon, ☎ 80.30.52.34. DC, Visa. ♿ closed Sun and Mon noon. Extraordinary dishes prepared by an imaginative young chef : *bouillon d'escargots ; filets de poisson en paupiette au caramel,* 75-200.
● ♦♦ ***Le Rallye,*** 39, rue Chabot-Charny (B2), ☎ 30.67.11.55. AE, DC, Visa. ♿ closed 14 Febearly Mar, 14 Jul-early Aug, Sun and nat hols. Good cooking supervised by Francis Minot, 120-210.
♦♦ ***Breuil,*** 1, rue de la Chouette (B2), ☎ 80.30.18.10. AE, DC, Visa, Euro, closed Mon eve, Tue and Jan. Refined cooking in an old house in the heart of the city, 85-230.
♦♦ ***Les Œnophiles,*** 18, rue Sainte-Anne, ☎ 80.30.73.52. Tx 351681. AE, DC, Euro, Visa. Ⓟ ♿ closed Sat noon and Sun, nat hols, Aug, school hols in Feb. Wine-cellar museum in a historical residence, 95-270.
♦♦ ***Le Vinarium,*** 23, pl. Bossuet, ☎ 80.30.36.23. AE, DC, Visa, closed 8-23 Feb, Mon noon and Sun eve, 80-150.

● ◆ ***Le Chabrot,*** 36, rue Monge, ☎ 80.30.69.61. Visa. 🐦 ♿ closed Sun and Mon noon. Spec : *foies de volailles au vin rouge, saumon grillé,* 60-250.

Marsannay-la-Côte, ⊠ 21160, 6 km S :
● ◆◆ ***Les Gourmets,*** 8, rue du Puits-de-Têt, ☎ 80.52.16.32. AE, DC, Visa. 🌳 ♿ closed Jan, Mon eve and Tue. A refined decor for perfectly prepared, excellent cooking : *ris de veau au coulis d'asperges, noisettes d'agneau aux morilles,* 85-200.

Plombières-lès-Dijon, 6 km NW :
◆◆ ***Le Cygne,*** Kir lake, ☎ 80.41.02.40. DC. ☀ 🅿 🌳 🐦 ♿ closed Sun eve, Mon and Feb, 70-150.

Velars-sur-Ouche, ⊠ 21370 Plombières-lès-Dijon, 12 km W :
◆◆ ***Auberge Gourmande,*** rue de la Cude, ☎ 80.33.62.51. Visa. 🅿 🌳 🐦 ♿ closed Sun eve and Mon (low season). Spec : *coq au vin, turbot grillé sauce béarnaise,* 80-160.

Events : *Estivades,* dance, theatre, music from 1 Jul-13 Aug. Jul-Aug *Festival des nuits de Bourgogne.*

River and canal cruises : Barge-hôtel "Duc de Bourgogne", marina, ☎ 80.41.51.99.

Bicycle hire : *Cycles Pouilly,* 3, rue de Tivoli, and 3, rue Sysley, ☎ 80.66.61.75. *Rousseau,* 3, place Notre-Dame, ☎ 80.30.91.52.

DONZY

Nevers 49, Auxerre 65, Paris 205
A2 ❦ ⊠ 58220

ℹ mairie, ☎ 80.39.30.28.

Hotel :
★★***Ermitage Hôtel,*** rue Gal-Leclerc, ☎ 80.39.30.62. Visa. 20 rm ☀ 🌳 160. Rest. ◆ closed Fri low season, 80-160.

⛺ ★★*Municipal* (33 pl.), ☎ 80.39.30.28.

GEVREY-CHAMBERTIN

Beaune 27, Dole 62, Paris 315
13 km S of Dijon, C2 ⊠ 21220

ℹ pl. de la Mairie, ☎ 80.34.38.40.

SNCF ☎ 80.41.50.50, 80.34.30.59.

Hotels :
★★★***Terroirs*** (L.F.), 28, rte de Dijon, ☎ 80.34.30.76. AE, DC, Euro. 15 rm 🅿 🌳 ♿ closed 20 Dec-10 Jan, 230.
★★★***Grands Crus,*** rte des Grands-Crus, ☎ 80.34.34.15, 24 rm 🅿 🌳 🐦 closed 2 Dec-15 Feb, 260.

Fixin, 2 km N :
★★***Chez Jeannette*** (L.F.), 7, rue Noisot, ☎ 80.52.45.49. AE, DC, Euro, Visa. 11 rm 🐦 Terrace. closed 25 Dec-25 Jan and Thu. Friendly service, 105. Rest. ◆ 60-150.

Morey-Saint-Denis, 4 km S :
★★***Castel Très Girard,*** ☎ 80.34.33.09. AE, DC, Visa. 12 rm 🅿 🌳 🐦 ♿ 160. Rest. ◆◆ 75-180.

Restaurant :
● ◆◆◆ ***La Rôtisserie du Chambertin,*** rue des Grands-Crus, ☎ 80.34.30.02. AE. closed Feb, 30 Jul-13 Aug, Sun eve and Mon. Life goes on, Pierre Menneveau manages with courage this nice stop-over, 220-310.

IS-SUR-TILLE

Dijon 21, Langres 47, Paris 318
C2 ⊠ 21120

ℹ rue Charbonnel, ☎ 80.95.24.03.

SNCF ☎ 80.41.50.50, 80.95.06.88.

Hotel :
★***Lion d'Or,*** 29, rue du Gal-Bouchu, ☎ 80.95.11.44. 15 rm 🅿 closed 15 Aug-15 Sep and Mon, 100. Rest. ♿ 80-130.

⛺ ★★*Des Capucins* (33 pl.), ☎ 80.95.02.08.

JOIGNY

Auxerre 27, Sens 30, Paris 148
A1 ⊠ 89300

ℹ bus station, quai Dagobert, ☎ 86.62.11.05.

SNCF ☎ 86.46.50.50, 86.62.07.66.

Hotels :
● ★★★★***A la Côte St-Jacques*** (L.F., Relais et châteaux), 14, fg de Paris, ☎ 86.62.09.70. Tx 801458. AE, DC, Visa. 33 rm ☀ 🅿 🌳 🏊 ♿ closed 5 Jan-28 Feb, 350. Rest. ● ◆◆◆◆ Michel Lorain and his wife are well-assisted by the young and talented Jean-Marc who has just become a member of our jury. The restaurant is always getting more beautiful : *salade de cèpes et foie gras, dos de saumon sauvage en vessie,* 140-360.
★★★***Modern'Hôtel*** (L.F. ; Mapotel), av. Robert-Petit, ☎ 86.62.16.28. Tx 801693. AE, DC, Visa. 22 rm 🅿 🌳 🏊 closed 25 Nov-15 Dec, 260. Rest. ● ◆◆ ♿ Good traditional recipes, 170-250.
★***Paris-Nice*** (L.F.), rd-pt de la Résistance, ☎ 86.62.06.72. Visa. 10 rm 🅿 🌳 closed Jan and Mon, 180. Rest. ◆ ♿ 75-140.

La Celle-Saint-Cyr, ⊠ 89970, 10 km W :
★★***Auberge de la Fontaine aux Muses*** (L.F.), ☎ 86.73.40.22. 14 rm 🅿 🐦 🚫🐕 🏊 🎾 closed Mon and Tue noon, 220. Rest. ● ◆◆ 120-210.

⛺ ★★*Municipal* (60 pl.), ☎ 86.62.07.55.

Boat-hire : *Locaboat Plaisance,* quai du Port-au-Bois, ☎ 86.62.06.14.

LOUHANS

Chalon-sur-Saône 40, Dijon 83, Paris 380
C3-4 ⊠ 71500

ℹ av. du 8-Mai-1945, ☎ 85.75.05.02.

SNCF ☎ 85.93.50.50, 85.75.12.35.

Hotel :
★***Cheval Rouge*** (L.F.), 5, rue d'Alsace, ☎ 85.75.21.42. Euro, Visa. 13 rm 🅿 closed 12 Dec-4 Jan, Sun eve and Mon, 90. Rest. ◆ 50-80.

⛺ ★★Municipal *la Chapellerie* (51 pl.), ☎ 85.75.19.02.

Market : Bresse poultry market every Mon.

MÂCON

Chalon-sur-Saône 58, Lyons 68, Paris 396
C4 ⊠ 71000

ℹ 187, rue Carnot (B2), ☎ 85.38.06.00.

✈ Charnay, 3 km SW, ☎ 85.34.15.15.

SNCF (A3), ☎ 85.95.50.50 ; gare T.G.V. Mâcon-Loché, ☎ 85.38.50.50, 85.34.62.39, 85.38.21.87, 85.38.44.48.

Car-hire : *Budget* train + auto, at the S.N.C.F. station, ☎ 85.38.44.48. T.G.V., ☎ 85.34.62.39, and 53, rte de Lyon, ☎ 85.34.80.00.

Hotels :
★★★***Mapotel Bellevue,*** 416-420, quai Lamartine (B2), ☎ 85.38.05.07. Tx 800837. AE, DC, Euro, Visa. 30 rm ☀ 🅿 ♿ 400. Rest. ◆◆ Spec : *goujonnette de lotte aux petits légumes,* 100-180.
★★***Genève*** (L.F.), 1, rue Bigonnet (A3), ☎ 85.38.18.10. Tx 351934. AE, DC, Euro, Visa. 62 rm 🅿 🌳 ♿ 220. Rest. ◆ 75-130.

★★**Promenade** (L.F.), 266, quai Lamartine (B2), ☎ 85.38.10.98. AE, DC, Visa. 21 rm, closed 15 Dec-1 Jan and Wed low season, 200. Rest. ♦ 55-120.
★★**Terminus,** 91, rue V.-Hugo (A2), ☎ 85.39.19.11. Tx 351938. AE, DC, Euro, Visa. 48 rm 🅿 ♘ ♿ 250. Rest. ♦ 60-130.
★★**Nord,** 313, quai Jean-Jaurès (C1), ☎ 85.38.08.68. AE, Visa. 21 rm ⚘ 135.

Igé, ✉ 71960 Pierreclos, 11 km SE :
● ★★★★**Château d'Igé** (Relais et châteaux), ☎ 85.33.33.39. 14 rm ⚘ 🅿 ♘ A delightful former post-house, closed 5 Nov-15 Mar, 580. Rest. ♦♦♦ ⚘ Lovely decor, 130-210.

Solutré, ✉ 71960 Pierreclos, 10 km W :
★★**Relais de Solutré,** ☎ 85.37.82.67. Visa. 32 rm 🅿 ♘ ♿ 260. Rest. ♦ 80-130.

⛺ ★★★Municipal *les Varennes* (200 pl.), ☎ 85.38.16.22.

Restaurants :
♦♦♦ **Auberge Bressane,** 114, rue du 28-Juin, ☎ 85.38.07.42. AE, DC, Visa. ♿ Spec : *feuilleté d'escargots à la crème d'ail,* 120-210.
● ♦♦ **Au Rocher de Cancale** (C1-2), 393, quai Jean-Jaurès, ☎ 85.38.07.50. AE, DC, Euro, Visa, closed 2-16 Jan, 10-22 Jul, Sat noon, Sun eve and Mon. Salt-water vivarium, *le gâteau de foie blond au sabayon de langoustines,* 65-180.
♦♦ **Pierre,** 5-9, rue Dufour (B2), ☎ 85.38.14.23. ♿ closed Sun eve and Mon, 60-100.
● ♦ **Saint-Laurent,** 1, quai Bouchacourt, Saint-Laurent-sur-Saône, ☎ 85.38.32.03. AE, Visa. ♿ closed Sun eve and Mon, 1-15 Dec. Unsophisticated food, but good quality. Spec : *poissons, blanc de volaille,* 120-210.

Events : in May, *National Fair of French Wines ;* 1st Sun in Sep, *Fête de la Vigne et des Vins mâconnais (Mâcon wine and vine festival).* Enq ℹ ☎ 85.38.06.00.

Market : every Sat morning, regional market, promenade Lamartine.

Aerial sport : *aéroclub du Mâconnais,* Mâcon-Charnay, ☎ 85.34.18.54.

Recommended : *Mâcon Wine Specialist,* 484, av. de-Lattre-de-Tassigny, ☎ 85.38.36.70. Wine-tasting and sales, regional meals.

MAILLY-LE-CHÂTEAU

Clamecy 22, Auxerre 30, Paris 205
A2 ✉ 89660 Châtel-Censoir

Hotel :
★★**Castel** (L.F., Relais du Silence), pl. de l'Église, ☎ 86.40.43.06. Euro, Visa. 12 rm ⚘ ♘ ♿ closed 15 Nov-1 Jan, Tue eve and Wed low season, nat hols, 220. Rest. ● ♦ Luxuriance and calm ; an ideal atmosphere for savoring fish : *escargots aux noisettes,* 70-150.

⛺ ★★*Pré du Roi* (50 pl.), ☎ 86.40.44.85.

MERCUREY

Chalon-sur-Saône 13, Autun 40, Paris 350
12 km NW of Givry, C3 ✉ 71640 Givry

Hotel :
★★★**Hostellerie du Val d'Or** (L.F.), ☎ 85.47.13.70. Visa. 12 rm ⚘ 🅿 ⚘ ⚘ closed 25 Aug-5 Sep, 8 Dec-5 Jan, Mon, Tue noon (15 Mar-15 Nov), Sun eve (15 Nov-15 Mar), 230. Rest. ♦ Very good cooking, 75-230.

Recommended : grower-vendor, *Jeannin-Naltet,* sale of Mercurey red and rare white at the property.

MEURSAULT

Autun 42, Dijon 47, Paris 324
8 km S of Beaune, C3 ✉ 21190

SNCF ☎ 80.21.23.75.

Hotels :
★★**Motel Au Soleil Levant,** 5, rte de Volnay, ☎ 80.21.23.47. 35 rm ♘ ♿ 170. Rest. ♦ closed 20 Nov-20 Dec, 50-100.
★★**Centre** (L.F.), 4, rue de-Lattre-de-Tassigny, ☎ 80.21.20.75. AE, DC, Euro, Visa. 7 rm, closed 20 Nov-5 Dec, 145. Rest. ♿ 75-100.

⛺ ★★★*Grappe d'Or* (115 pl.), ☎ 80.21.22.48.

Restaurants :
♦♦ **Relais de la Diligence,** 23, rue de la Gare, ☎ 80.21.21.32. AE, DC. 🅿 ♿ closed Jan, Tue eve and Wed, 50-100.

Auxey-Duresses, 1.5 km W :
♦♦ **La Crémaillère,** ☎ 80.21.22.60. ⚘ ♿ closed 1 Feb-10 Mar, Mon eve and Tue. Spec : *cassolette d'escargots bourguignonne, dodines de caneton aux cinq poivres,* 120-210.

MONTBARD

Auxerre 73, Dijon 81, Paris 237
B2 ⚘ ✉ 21500

ℹ Pavillon, rue Carnot, ☎ 80.92.03.75. Low season, mairie, ☎ 80.92.01.34.

SNCF ☎ 80.41.50.50.

Hotels :
★★**Côte-d'Or,** 26, rue Carnot, ☎ 80.92.01.77. Tx 920177. 17 rm 🅿 ♿ 170. Rest. ♦ ♿ 50-120.
★★**Écu** (L.F.), 7, rue Auguste-Carré, ☎ 80.92.11.66. DC, Euro, Visa. 24 rm 🅿 ♘ 200. Rest. ♦♦♦ ♿ 70-200.

⛺ ★★★★*Municipal* (53 pl.), ☎ 80.92.21.60.

Restaurant :
♦♦♦ **Le Saint-Rémy,** 2, rte de Dijon, ☎ 80.92.13.44. AE, DC, Visa. ♿ closed eves ex Sat, 23 Dec-29 Jan, Mon. Spec : *pâté de truite,* 60-150.

MONTCEAU-LES-MINES

Autun 42, Mâcon 68, Paris 384
B3-4 ✉ 71300

ℹ 1, pl. de l'Hôtel-de-Ville, ☎ 85.57.38.51.

SNCF ☎ 85.93.50.50, 85.57.14.15.

Car-hire : *Budget* train + auto, at the S.N.C.F. station, ☎ 85.57.14.15.

Hotels :
★★★**Commerce,** 70, quai Jules-Chagot, ☎ 85.57.34.18. AE, DC, Euro, Visa. 32 rm 🅿 ♿ 160. Rest. ♦♦ 60-170.
★**Lac,** 58, rue de la Loge, ☎ 85.57.18.22. 20 rm ⚘ 🅿 ⚘ ♘ ⚘ 105.

Aquatic sports : 2 lakes ; Plessis : sailing and wind-surfing ; La Sorme : sailing.

Aerial sports : *aéroclub du Bassin minier,* aérodrome à Pouilloux, 71320 Saint-Vallier, ☎ 85.79.10.83.

MONTSAUCHE (Settons lake)

Autun 45, Nevers 90, Paris 277
B3 ✉ 58230

Hotels :
★★**Grillons** (L.F.), 4 km, ☎ 86.84.51.43. 16 rm ⚘ 🅿 ⚘ ♘ ♿ closed 15 Dec-15 Mar, 180. Rest. ♦ 55-140.

Moux, 14 km SE :
Beau Site, ☎ 86.76.11.75. 26 rm ⊞ Ⓟ ⚘ closed 18 Dec-8 Jan, Sun eve and Mon eve from 15 Nov to 15 Mar, 105. Rest. ♦ 45-100.

Planchez-en-Morvan, 9 km S :
★★***Relais des Lacs,*** ☎ 86.78.41.68. AE, DC, Visa. 36 rm Ⓟ ⚘ ♿ closed 15 Nov-15 Dec, Jan, 100. Rest. ♦ ♿ closed Wed low season, 120-210.

⛺ ★★★*Plage du Midi* (190 pl.), ☎ 86.84.51.97 ; ★★*Branlasses* (56 pl.), ☎ 86.84.51.98.

MORVAN Nature Park

B23

ⓘ *Maison du Parc,* Saint-Brisson, 58230 Montsauche, ☎ 86.78.70.16.

Holiday village : Saint-Agnan, 58230 Montsauche, ☎ 86.78.72.00, enq *Fédération Léo-Lagrange,* 58, rue La Fayette, 75009 Paris, ☎ 45.23.45.45, or *Ligue française de l'Enseignement,* 7, bd Saint-Denis, 75014 Paris, ☎42.71.29.30.

Accomodation for young people : *Chalet refuge de Breuil,* Morvan Regional Nature Park, ☎ 86.78.72.34. 34 beds all year round.

Rambling : 100 km of G.R.13, 220 km Tour of the Morvan by the Great Lakes, 10-day circuit with marked trails and 10 overnight gîtes. 300 km of short treks.

NEVERS

Moulins 54, Dijon 188, Paris 240
A3 ✉ 58000

ⓘ 31, rue des Remparts, ☎ 86.59.07.03.

SNCF ☎ 86.36.25.00.

Car-hire : *Budget* train + auto, at the station, ☎ 86.57.36.21 ; and 2, av. Colbert, ☎ 86.61.56.78.

Hotels :
★★★***Diane*** (Mapotel), 38, rue du Midi (A3), ☎ 86.57.28.10. Tx 801021. AE, DC, Euro, Visa. 30 rm Ⓟ closed 21 Dec-27 Jan, 480. Rest. ♦♦ closed Sun eve and Mon (Oct-Easter), 320.
★★★***P.L.M. Loire,*** quai de Médiné, ☎ 86.61.50.92. 60 rm Ⓟ ♿ 380. Rest. ♦♦♦ closed 15 Dec-15 Jan and Sat, 120-210.
● ★★***Château de la Rocherie,*** RN7, Varennes-Vauzelles, ☎ 86.57.26.79. AE, DC, Visa. 15 rm Ⓟ closed 1-31 Jan and Tue, 240. Rest. ♦♦ ♿ 120-210.
★★***Folie*** (L.F.), rte des Saulaies, ☎ 86.57.05.31. Euro, Visa. 23 rm Ⓟ closed 15 Dec-8 Jan, 155. Rest. ♦ bar, grill-room, closed Fri, 55-110.
★★***Auberge Sainte-Marie,*** 25, rue du Petit-Mouësse, ☎ 86.61.10.02. Visa. 17 rm Ⓟ closed 20 Jan-26 Feb, 1-8 Jul, Mon, Sun eve (1 Sep-15 Jul), 125. Rest. 45-110.
★***Morvan*** (L.F.), 28, rue du Petit-Mouësse, ☎ 86.61.14.16. 11 rm Ⓟ closed Tue eve, Wed, 1-15 Jan, 1-21 Jul, 95. Rest. ♦ ♿ 75-170.
★***Villa du Parc,*** 16 *ter*-18, rue de Lourdes (A2), ☎ 86.61.09.48. 28 rm ♿ 115.
Auberge de la Porte-du-Croux, 17, rue de la Porte-du-Croux (A3), ☎ 86.57.12.71. AE, DC, Euro, Visa. 3 rm Ⓟ closed 10 Aug-2 Sep, Sun and Fri eve, 115. Rest. ♦♦ Expert cooking ; fish fresh from La Rochelle, 90-170.

Magny-Cours, ✉ 58470, 12 km S :
★★***La Renaissance,*** ☎ 86.58.10.40. AE, DC, Euro. 10 rm Ⓟ closed end Jan-early Mar, 1-7 Jul, Sun eve and Mon, 220. Rest. ● ♦♦ ♿ Excellent fare : *rognon de veau entier aux échalotes confites, filet de Charolais à la crème et aux morilles,* 170-330.

Bona, ✉ 58330 Saint-Saulze, 23 km NE :
★***La Réunion,*** ☎ 86.58.63.71. 7 rm ♿ closed 8 days in Feb, 100. Rest. ♦ closed Mon (winter) Claude Perraudin features market fresh produce, 120-210.

⛺ ★★*Municipal* (70 pl.), ☎ 86.57.56.95.

Canal cruises : cruises on the Nivernais canal, enq préfecture, 58019 Nevers, ☎ 86.57.80.25, ext 387.

Boat-hire : *Caravanauti,* RN7, le Paradis, 58640 Varennes, ☎ 86.57.20.20.

NOLAY

Beaune 20, Mâcon 90, Paris 315
5 km W of La Rochepot, B-C3 ✉ 21340

ⓘ M. Jean Grillot, rue Saint-Pierre, ☎ 80.21.70.86 ; or mairie, ☎ 80.21.73.00.

Hotels :
★***Chevreuil*** (L.F.), pl. de l'Hôtel-de-Ville, ☎ 80.21.71.89. AE, DC, Euro, Visa. 9 rm Ⓟ closed Dec and Wed low season, 80. Rest. ♿ 50-100.
★***Sainte-Marie*** (L.F.), 38, rue de la République, ☎ 80.21.73.19. AE, DC, Visa. 12 rm, closed 3 Jan-3 Feb and Mon low season, 100. Rest. ♦ ♿ 80-130.

La Rochepot, 5 km E :
★***Relais du Château*** (L.F.), ☎ 80.21.71.32. Visa. 12 rm Ⓟ closed end Nov-mid Mar, 100. Rest. ♦♦ ♿ 80-130.

⛺ ★★*Municipal,* rte de Couches (70 pl.), ☎ 80.21.73.00.

NUITS-SAINT-GEORGES

Beaune 17, Dijon 22, Paris 322
C3 ✉ 21700

ⓘ *Maison du Tourisme,* ☎ 80.61.22.47.

SNCF ☎ 80.41.50.50, 80.61.05.84, 80.61.10.80.

Hotels :
★★★***Côte-d'Or,*** 37, rue Thurot, ☎ 80.61.06.10. AE, DC, Euro, Visa. 7 rm closed Sun eve and Wed, 1-25 Aug, 15 days in Jan, 450. Rest. ● ♦♦♦ ♿ Lightness and refinement are the characteristics of Jean Crotet's cooking. Fine cellar, 280-320.
★★★***Gentilhommière,*** 13, rte de la Serrée, CD25, ☎ 80.61.12.06. Tx 350401. AE, Euro. 20 rm. Former hunting lodge Ⓟ ♿ closed 1-20 Jan, 215. Rest. ♦♦ closed Mon, 55-170.

Events : Sun before Palm Sunday : *wine sale at the Almshouse,* enq mairie, ☎ 80.61.12.54.

Recommended : wine, M. Jayer, Magny-les-Villers.

PARAY-LE-MONIAL

Mâcon 68, Autun 79, Paris 372
B4 ✉ 71600

ⓘ pl. de la Poste, ☎ 85.81.10.92.

SNCF ☎ 85.38.50.50, 85.81.07.97, 85.81.13.25.

Hotels :
★★***Trois Pigeons,*** 2, rue Dargaud, ☎ 85.81.03.77. Euro, Visa. 33 rm Ⓟ closed Dec-Feb, 160. Rest. ♦♦ 70-160.
★★***Aux Vendanges de Bourgogne*** (L.F.), 5, rue Denis-Papin, ☎ 85.81.13.43. AE, Euro, Visa. 14 rm Ⓟ closed 6 Feb-10 Mar, Sun eve and Mon noon, 160. Rest. ♦ ♿ 55-165.
★***Nord*** (L.F.), 45, av. de la Gare, ☎ 85.81.05.12. Visa. 15 rm Ⓟ closed 24 Dec-26 Jan and Sat low season, 120. Rest. 50-110.

Vitry-en-Charolais, 2 km W :
★★★**Motel le Charolais,** RN79, ☎ 85.81.03.35. Tx 801801. AE, Visa. 20 rm Ⓟ ♿ Small lake, 205. Rest. grill, 60 100.

⛺ ★★★Municipal *le Pré Barret* (57 pl.), ☎ 85.81.05.05.

Events : *Pèlerinages du Sacré-Cœur* end Jun-early Jul. In Oct, the Sun following the 16, *procession pour la Fête de Ste-Marguerite-Marie* ; enq Dir. des Pèlerinages, Paray-le-Monial, ☎ 85.81.11.72.

Aerial sport : *aéroclub du Charolais,* ☎ 85.81.08.19.

PONT-SUR-YONNE

Sens 12, Auxerre 69, Paris 108
A1 ✉ 89140

SNCF ☎ 86.46.50.50, 86.67.15.87.

Hotels :
★★**Hostellerie de l'Écu** (L.F.), 3, rue Carnot, ☎ 86.67.01.00. AE, DC, Visa. 8 rm Ⓟ closed 6 Jan-6 Mar, 150. Rest. ♦ ♿ closed Mon eve and Tue ex Jul-Aug. An enjoyable meal in a relaxed atmosphere, 70-140.
Auberge du Kilomètre 99, 1, rue Mal-Leclerc, ☎ 86.67.00.40. Euro, Visa. 5 rm Ⓟ closed Thu, 105. Rest. ♦♦ 60-130.

⛺ ★★Municipal *de l'Ile d'Amour* (100 pl.), ☎ 86.67.03.62.

POUILLY-EN-AUXOIS

Dijon 42, Autun 45, Paris 273
B2 ✉ 21320

SNCF ☎ 80.41.50.50.

Hotels :
★★★**Motel du Val Vert,** rte d'Arnay-le-Duc, ☎ 80.90.82.34. Euro, Visa. 30 rm Ⓟ ♿ 280.
★**Bassin** (L.F.), ☎ 80.90.83.98. 7 rm Ⓟ closed 15 Sep-15 Oct, 24 Dec, 1 Jan, Mon and Sun eve, 105. Rest. ♦ ♿ 40-85.

Châteauneuf, 10 km SE :
★★**Hostellerie du Château** (L.F., Relais du Silence), ☎ 80.33.00.23. AE, Euro, Visa. 11 rm closed 15 Nov-15 Mar, Mon eve and Tue low season, 180. Rest. ♦♦ Spec : *médaillons de lotte au vinaigre de framboises, poulet de grain aux morilles,* 95-160.

Sainte-Sabine, 9 km SE :
★★**Château,** ☎ 80.33.02.01, 80.33.02.04. 50 rm Ⓟ 100. Rest. ♦ ♿ 80-130.

⛺ ★★*Municipal* (70 pl.), ☎ 80.90.85.44.

Boat-hire : *Burgundy Line,* 9, rue Bellenot, 21320 Pouilly-en-Auxois, ☎ 80.90.70.97.

POUILLY-SUR-LOIRE

Nevers 37, Bourges 59, Paris 203
A2 ✉ 58150

ℹ rue Waldeck-Rousseau, ☎ 86.39.12.55.

SNCF ☎ 86.61.50.50, 86.39.13.33.

Hotels :
★★★**L'Espérance,** 17, rue René-Couard, ☎ 86.39.10.68. 4 rm Terrace looking out over the vineyards and the Loire. closed 7-20 Dec, Jan, Mon and Sun eve low season, 220. Rest. ♦♦ Spec : *écrevisses au pouilly, émincé de bar au vinaigre xérès, lapin en gelée,* 220-310.
★★**Bouteille d'Or** (L.F.), 3 *bis,* rue de Paris, ☎ 86.39.13.84. 31 rm, closed 15 Jan-15 Feb, 1 week in Oct, and Fri low season, 160. Rest. ♦♦ ♿ 65-180.
★★**Relais Fleuri** (L.F.), ☎ 86.39.14.15. Euro, Visa. 9 rm over the Loire Ⓟ closed 15 Nov-15 Dec, Wed eve and Thu low season, 150. Rest. ♦♦ ♿ 50-150.

⛺ ★★*Malaga,* on the banks of the Loire (100 pl.), ☎ 86.39.14.54.

Restaurant :
♦ ***La Vieille Auberge,*** hameau de Charenton, ☎ 86.39.17.98. Ⓟ closed Wed. Delightful cooking in an old residence, 75-145.

QUARRÉ-LES-TOMBES

Avallon 19, Auxerre 72, Paris 236
B2 ✉ 89630

Hotels :
★★**Nord et Poste** (L.F.), 25, pl. de l'Église, ☎ 86.32.24.55. 35 rm, 185. Rest. ♦ ♿ Spec : *parfait de foie blond de canard tiède aux champignons noirs, cuisse de canard braisée au miel et vinaigre de framboise,* 65-130.
★**Brizards** (L.F.), ☎ 86.32.20.12. Visa. 26 rm Ⓟ ♿ closed 2 Jan-2 Feb, 180. Rest. ♦ 80-130.

ROMANÈCHE-THORINS

Mâcon 17, Lyons 56, Paris 411
17 km S of Mâcon, C4
✉ 71570 La Chapelle-de-Guinchay

SNCF ☎ 85.35.50.18.

Hotels :
★★★**Maritonnes,** ☎ 85.35.51.70. AE, DC, Euro, Visa. 20 rm Ⓟ closed 15 Dec-25 Jan, 1 week in Jun, Sun eve (Oct-Jun), and Mon, 300. Rest. (M.C.F.) ♦♦ ♿ Spec : *grenouilles sautées, fricassée de volaille aux morilles,* 130-240.
★★**Commerce,** ☎ 85.35.51.82. AE, Visa. 14 rm Ⓟ closed Tue eve, Wed and Feb, 100. Rest. ♦ ♿ 80-130.

Recommended : *Vins Georges Dubœuf,* ☎ 85.35.51.13.

SAINT-FLORENTIN

Auxerre 31, Sens 44, Paris 174
A1 ✉ 89600

SNCF ☎ 86.46.50.50/86.35.02.74.

Hotels :
★★★**Grande Chaumière** (L.F.), 3, rue des Capucins, ☎ 86.35.15.12. AE, DC, Visa. 10 rm Ⓟ closed 20 Dec-20 Jan, 1-8 Sep and Wed, 280. Rest. ♦ 80-240.
★**Est,** 7-9, fg Saint-Martin, ☎ 86.35.10.35. Visa. 25 rm Ⓟ ♿ closed Feb, Wed eve and Sat low season, 180. Rest. ♦ 80-130.

Venizy, 5.5 km N :
● ★★**Moulin des Pommerats** (L.F. ; Châteaux-hôtels), ☎ 86.35.08.04. DC, Euro, Visa. 16 rm Ⓟ ♿ closed Sun eve and Mon low season, 320. Rest. ● ♦♦ The mill is near a trout-fishing river. Spec : *gambas flambées au marc, rognon sauté à la moutarde,* 95-220.

⛺ ★★*Plage* (150 pl.), ☎ 86.35.08.13.

SAINT-HONORÉ-LES-BAINS

Moulins 66, Nevers 67, Paris 307
B3 ✉ 58360

(27 Mar-30 Sep), ☎ 86.30.73.27.

SNCF ☎ 86.30.84.57.

Hotels :
★★★**Bristol Thermal,** 16, rue Joseph-Duriaux, ☎ 86.30.71.12. 62 rm Ⓟ ♿ closed 26 Sep-30 Apr, 180. Rest. ♦♦ 80-130.
★★**Henry Robert,** 47, av. Gal-d'Espeuilles, ☎ 86.30.72.33. AE, Euro, Visa. 14 rm Ⓟ closed Jan-Feb and from Mon to Sat noon (Oct-Mar), 175. Rest. ♦ 70-130.

★★***Morvan,*** 9, av. Jean-Mermoz, ☎ 86.30.74.44. AE, DC, Visa. 48 rm 🅿 ♨ ♿ closed 26 Sep-25 Mar, 100. Rest. ♦ 80-130.

⛺ ★★★*Des Bains* (100 pl.), ☎ 86.30.73.44 ; ★★*Bonneau* (33 pl.), ☎ 86.30.76.00.

Casino : ☎ 86.30.70.99.

SAINT-JEAN-DE-LOSNE

Dole 22, Dijon 32, Paris 345
C3 ✉ 21170

ℹ ☎ 80.29.05.44.

SNCF ☎ 80.41.50.50, 80.29.05.64.

Hotel :
★***Saônotel,*** 27, rue du Château, ☎ 80.29.04.77. Euro, Visa. 13 rm ☀ 🅿 ⛰ ♿ closed 1 Nov-7 Dec and Wed, 145. Rest. ♦ 40-80.

⛺ ★★*Les Herlequins* (67 pl.), ☎ 80.29.05.44.

Events : Jun, *fête de la batellerie.*

River cruises : water bus on the Saône, enq *Croisières françaises,* la Gare d'Eau, 21170 Saint-Jean-de-Losne, ☎ 80.29.18.80/80.29.10.48.

Boat-hire : *Plaisance et Tourisme fluvial,* Saint-Usage, 21170 Saint-Jean-de-Losne, ☎ 80.29.11.06. *Saône Line,* 21170 Saint-Jean-de-Losne, ☎ 80.29.12.86.

SAINT-PIERRE-LE-MOUTIER

Nevers 23, Moulins 31, Paris 263
A3 ✉ 58240

SNCF ☎ 86.61.50.50/86.68.40.35.

Restaurant :
♦♦ ***La Vigne - le Relais Gastronomique,*** rte de Decize, ☎ 86.37.41.66. ☀ 🅿 ⛰ ♿ closed Mon eve, Tue and Feb. In the grand culinary tradition : *terrine au foie gras de canard, cassolette de lotte à la russe,* 105-220.

⛺ ★★*Municipal* (40 pl.), ☎ 86.37.42.09.

SANTENAY

Beaune 18, Autun 45, Paris 335
5 km W of Chagny, C3 ✉ 21590

🍇 ♨ all year round

ℹ high season : *Centre thermal,* ☎ 80.20.62.32 ; low season, *casino,* ☎ 80.20.61.00.

SNCF ☎ 80.41.50.50, 80.20.60.50.

Hotel :
★★***Santana*** (Mapotel), av. des Sources, ☎ 80.20.62.11. Tx 350190. AE, DC, Euro, Visa. 65 rm 🅿 ♨ ⛰ 220. Rest. ♦ ***les Vendangeurs,*** 90-120.

⛺ ★★*Municipal* (100 pl.), ☎ 80.20.60.32.

Casino : ☎ 80.20.61.00.

Recommended : *vins André Monnot,* grower-vendor, in Dezize-les-Maranges, 4 km W.

SAULIEU

Autun 41, Dijon 73, Paris 252
B2 ✉ 21210

🍇 Saulieu and Précy-sous-Thil touristic region.

ℹ rue d'Argentine, ☎ 80.64.00.21, and mairie, ☎ 80.64.09.22.

✈ Saulieu-Liernais.

SNCF ☎ 80.41.50.50, 80.64.05.32.

Hotels :
● ★★★★***Côte-d'Or*** (Relais et châteaux), 2, rue d'Argentine, ☎ 80.64.07.66. AE, DC, Euro, Visa. 24 rm 🅿 closed 17 Nov-7 Dec, 1-15 Mar, Tue and Wed noon low season, 500. Rest. ● ♦♦♦♦ Bernard Loiseau, prizewinner of the "Grand Prix Hachette des Cuisiniers de France" is winning his challenge. The new rooms and apartments are superb, and his cooking remains one of the best and most inventive in France : *saint-pierre rôti aux carottes Vichy, cuissot de lapin dans son jus aux choux, gâteau au chocolat amer ;* the cellar is of the same high standard, 210-450.
● ★★***Poste*** (L.F., Inter-Hôtel), 1, rue Grillot, ☎ 80.64.05.67. Tx 350540. AE, Visa. 48 rm 🅿 ♿ 190. Rest. 95-200.
★★***Renaissance*** (L.F.), 7, rue Grillot, ☎ 80.64.08.72. AE, DC, Euro, Visa. 13 rm 🅿 closed 5 Jan-5 Feb, Mon eve and Tue low season and school hols, 130. Rest. ♦ 60-120.
★***Borne Impériale*** (L.F.), 14-16, rue d'Argentine, ☎ 80.64.19.76. AE, Visa. 7 rm 🅿 closed 15 Nov-15 Dec, Mon eve and Tue, 180. Rest. ● ♦ ♿ Classical cooking of quality : *jambon aux morilles à la crème, escargots de Bourgogne,* 120-210.
★***Lion d'Or,*** 7, rue Courtépée, ☎ 80.64.16.33, 80.64.00.33. Visa. 10 rm ♨ closed Jan, 180. Rest. ♦ closed Sun eve and Mon (low season), 80-130.

⛺ ★★*Du Perron* (70 pl.), ☎ 80.64.16.19.

Events : Sat and Sun following 15 Aug. *Charolais Cattle Show and Festival,* enq mairie, ☎ 80.64.09.22.

Recommended : Baker, *Dechaume,* 42, rue du Marché.

SEMUR-EN-AUXOIS

Avallon 42, Dijon 81, Paris 250
B2 🍇 ✉ 21140

ℹ 2, pl. Gaveau, ☎ 80.97.05.96.

SNCF ☎ 80.97.11.04.

Hotels :
★★***Côte-d'Or*** (L.F.), 3, pl. Gaveau, ☎ 80.97.03.13. AE, DC, Visa. 15 rm 🅿 closed 10 Jan-20 Mar and Wed, 164. Rest. ♦ ♿ 55-140.
★***Gourmets,*** 4, rue Varenne, ☎ 80.97.09.41. Visa. 15 rm 🅿 ♨ ♿ closed 15 Nov-1 Jan and Tue, 140. Rest. ♦ 60-120.

Pont-et-Massène, 4 km S :
★★***Lac*** (L.F.), ☎ 80.97.11.11. DC, Visa. 23 rm 🅿 ⛰ 🐕 closed 15 Dec-1 Feb, 180. Rest. ● ♦ ♿ closed Sun eve and Mon low season. In the open country, a pleasant stopover, 80-130.

Family holiday homes : 10, rue du Couvent, ☎ 80.97.07.08.

Youth hostel : 1, rue du Champ-de-Foire, ☎ 80.97.10.32.

Village and gîtes : V.V.F. Flée, ☎ 80.97.12.99.

⛺ ★★*Du Lac,* Pont-et-Massène, 4 km S (120 pl.), ☎ 80.97.01.26.

Restaurant :
♦♦ ***La Cambuse,*** pl. Notre-Dame, 8, rue Févret, ☎ 80.97.06.78. AE, DC, Euro, Visa. ♿ closed 15 Nov-15 Mar and Tue. Regional dishes in an enjoyable atmosphere, 75-160.

Events : Sun preceding 31 May, *course des chausses.* 31 May, *Fête de la Bague* (horse races), enq ℹ

SENS

Auxerre 57, Troyes 65, Paris 119
A1 ⊠ 89100

ℹ pl. Jean-Jaurès, ☎ 86.65.19.49.

SNCF ☎ 86.46.50.50, 86.65.05.25, 86.65.06.44.

Car-hire : *Budget* train + auto, at the station, ☎ 86.65.05.25, and rte de Lyon, ☎ 86.65.04.14.

Hotels :
★★★***Paris et Poste*** (Mapotel), 97, rue de la République, ☎ 86.65.17.43. AE, DC, Euro, Visa. 32 rm P 🌳 Flowered terrace, 260. Rest. ♦♦ 100-250.
★★***Croix Blanche*** (L.F.), 9, rue V.-Guichard, ☎ 86.64.00.02. Visa. 24 rm P 🌳 🛁 185. Rest. ♦ 🐕 ♿ closed Fri eve and Sat, 60-110.
★★***Résidence René-Binet,*** 20, rue René-Binet, ☎ 86.95.21.50. Euro, Visa. 33 rm P 🛁 closed Sun eve (1 Oct-31 Mar), 160.

Villeroy, 5.5 km W :
★★***Relais de Villeroy,*** rte de Nemours, ☎ 86.88.81.77. AE, DC, Visa. 8 rm P 🌳 closed 3-24 Aug, 22 Dec-4 Jan, Sun eve and Mon, 170. Rest. ♦ ♿ 100-200.

Soucy, 7 km NE :
★***Auberge du Regain,*** rte de Nogent, ☎ 86.86.64.62. 7 rm P 🌳 🛁 closed 25 Aug-1 Oct, Sun eve and Mon, 200. Rest. ♦♦ ♿ Set menu only, 75-105.

⛺ ★★Municipal *Entre-deux-Vannes,* rte de Lyon (85 pl.), ☎ 86.65.64.71.

Restaurants :
♦♦ ***Auberge de la Vanne,*** 176, rte de Lyon, ☎ 86.65.13.63. AE, Euro, Visa. P ♿ A water-side setting, closed 15 Dec-10 Jan, Fri eve and Sat. Spec : *demi-caneton au poivre vert,* 65-140.
♦♦ ***Palais,*** 18, pl. de la République, ☎ 86.65.13.69. Visa. 🐕 ♿ closed 2-16 Jan and Mon, 60-150.
♦ ***Cathédrale,*** 11, pl. de la République, ☎ 86.65.17.79. closed 20-30 Mar, 20-31 Oct, Mon eve and Tue, 55-115.

SEURRE

Beaune 26, Dijon 39, Paris 339
C3 ⊠ 21250

SNCF ☎ 80.41.50.50.

Hotel :
★★***Castel*** (L.F.), 20, av. de la Gare, ☎ 80.20.45.07. Visa. 22 rm ⚘ 🐕 ♿ closed 2 Jan-15 Feb and Mon, 180. Rest. ♦♦ 65-140.

⛺ ★★*La Piscine* (190 pl.), ☎ 80.21.15.92 ; ★★*De la Raie Mignot* (33 pl.), ☎ 80.21.14.61.

Boat-hire : *Bourgogne Buissonnière,* B.P. 1, 21820 Labergement-lès-Seurre, ☎ 80.21.10.58, 80.20.44.30.

SOMBERNON

B-C2 ⊠ 21540

ℹ ☎ 80.33.40.01.

Hotels :
★★***Le Sombernon*** (L.F.), rue Ferdinand-Mercuzot, ☎ 80.33.41.23. 16 rm ⚘ P closed 15 Jan-15 Feb and Wed, 180. Rest. ♦ ♿ 80-130.

Pont-de-Pany, ⊠ 21410, 10 km E :
★***Pont de Pany,*** RN905, ☎ 80.23.60.59. 16 rm P 🌳 ♿ closed Jan-Feb and Wed, 100. Rest. ♦♦ 120-210.

TONNERRE

Auxerre 35, Troyes 57, Paris 200
B1 ⊠ 89700

ℹ pl. Marguerite-de-Bourgogne, ☎ 86.55.14.48.

SNCF ☎ 86.55.16.99.

Hotel :
● ★★★★***L'Abbaye Saint-Michel*** (Relais et châteaux), montée Saint-Michel, ☎ 86.55.05.99. Tx 801356. AE, DC, Visa. 11 rm ⚘ P 🌳 🛁 🎾 former 12thC Benedictine abbey, closed 20 Dec-1 Feb, Sun eve and Mon low season, 660. Rest. ● ♦♦♦ ♿ Joël Robuchon's pupils are becoming famous ; with a special mention to G. Lussac. Spec : *rissolée de langoustines et foie gras en salade, pané de daurade au coulis de tomates, blanc de poulet fermier en vessie,* 210-320.

⛺ ★★Municipal *de la Cascade,* av. A.-Briand (135 pl.), ☎ 86.55.15.44.

Boat-hire : *Héron Cruisers,* B.P. 67, 89700 Tonnerre, ☎ 86.55.25.58.

Recommended : *Jean-Claude Michault,* grower-vendor, Épineuil, 89700 Tonnerre, ☎ 86.55.24.99. A superb red and a delicate rosé.

TOUCY

Auxerre 24, Clamecy 44, Paris 161
A2 ⊠ 89130

SNCF ☎ 86.46.50.50, 86.44.15.48.

Hotel :
Lion d'Or, 37, rue Lucile-Cormier, ☎ 86.44.00.76. Visa. 8 rm P closed 1-21 Dec, Mon eve and Tue, 70. Rest. ♦ ♿ 60-120.

⛺ ★★*Le Pâtis* (50 pl.), ☎ 86.44.10.44.

TOURNUS

Chalon-sur-Saône 27, Lyons 102, Paris 365
C4 ⊠ 71700

ℹ pl. Carnot, ☎ 85.51.13.10.

SNCF ☎ 85.38.50.50, 85.51.07.30.

Hotels :
★★★***Rempart,*** 2-4, av. Gambetta, ☎ 85.51.10.56. 30 rm P 🐕 ♿ 300. Rest. ♦♦ Spec : *pigeonneau à l'ail doux, pêches au poivre vert,* 140-300.
★★★***Sauvage*** (Mapotel), pl. du Champ-de-Mars, ☎ 85.51.14.45. Tx 800726. AE, DC, Euro, Visa. 31 rm P closed 15 Nov-15 Dec. Beautiful residence, 200. Rest. ♦♦ 75-170.
★★***Aux Terrasses*** (L.F.), 18, av. du 23-Janvier, ☎ 85.51.01.74. Visa. 12 rm P closed 5 Jan-5 Feb and Mon, 110. Rest. ♦ ♿ closed Sun eve (low season) and Mon, 100-170.
★***Nouvel Hôtel,*** 1*bis,* av. des Alpes, ☎ 85.51.04.25. Euro, Visa. 6 rm P closed 2-9 Jan, 26 Nov-29 Dec, Wed and Sun eve, 85. Rest. 60-120.

Fleurville, ⊠ 71260 Lugny, 13 km S :
● ★★★***Château de Fleurville*** (Châteaux-hôtels), ☎ 85.33.12.17. AE, DC, Visa. 15 rm P 🌳 🛁 ♿ closed 15 Nov-15 Dec, 260. Rest. ♦♦ 🐕 ♿ closed Mon noon, 90-200.
★***Fleurvil,*** ☎ 85.33.10.65. Visa. 10 rm P ♿ closed 6-15 Jun, 15 Nov-15 Dec, Mon and Tue, 100. Rest. ♦♦ 220-310.

Martailly-lès-Brancion, 13 km SW on the D14 :
★★***Montagne de Brancion,*** ☎ 85.51.12.40. 20 rm P 🌳 🛁 ♿ closed 1 Dec-15 Feb, 200.

⛺ ★★Municipal *le Pas Fleury* (35 pl.), ☎ 85.51.16.58.

Restaurant :
● ♦♦♦ ***Greuze,*** av. Thibaudet, ☎ 85.51.13.52. AE, Visa. closed 3-12 Jul, 19 Nov-4 Dec and Thu. A beautiful house and J. Ducloux's inventive cooking. Spec : *quenelles de brochet, poêlée de grenouilles persillade,* 220-310.

Events : in Aug *Été en Bourgogne (Burgundy Summer Festival) :* religious or classical works, performed in the nave of the abbey or in the cloister ; end May-early Jun, *Salon des Antiquaires* enq

VAL-SUZON

Montbard 58, Auxerre 144, Paris 309
17 km NW of Dijon, C2
☒ 21121 Fontaine-lès-Dijon

Hotel :
★★★***Hostellerie du Val Suzon,*** RN71, ☎ 80.35.60.15. AE, DC, Euro, Visa. 18 rm closed 2 Jan-2 Feb, Wed (Oct-Easter), 250. Rest. ♦♦ closed Wed and Thu noon (Oct-Easter). Meals in the garden weather permitting, 125-220.

VERDUN-SUR-LE-DOUBS

Beaune 22, Mâcon 80, Paris 335
C3 ☒ 71350

mairie, ☎ 85.91.52.52.

SNCF ☎ 85.93.50.50, 85.91.51.05.

Hotels :
★★★***Hostellerie Bourguignonne,*** av. du Pdt-Borgeot, ☎ 85.91.51.45. AE, DC, Euro, Visa. 14 rm closed 22 Dec-8 Feb, and Wed low season, 320. Rest. ♦♦ Excellent, light tasty dishes, 110-210.

Saint-Gervais-en-Vallière, 12 km NW :
● ★★★***Moulin d'Hauterive*** (Relais du Silence, A.R.C.), ☎ 85.91.55.56. AE, DC, Euro, Visa. 16 rm closed 15 Dec-1 Mar, Sun eve and Mon, 280. Rest. ♦♦ 120-250.

★★*Municipal* (170 pl.), ☎ 85.42.55.50.

Aquatic sports : lake, motorboating, water-skiing, ☎ 85.91.52.07.

Boat-hire : *Hobby Voyage,* 8, rue de Milan, ☎ 85.26.60.80. 75009 Paris, *Le Relais,* 64, rue Mazelle, ☎ 85.76.31.60. 57000 Metz.

VERMENTON

Avallon 28, Clamecy 51, Paris 199
24 km SE of Auxerre, A1-2 ☒ 89270

SNCF ☎ 86.46.50.50, 85.53.50.90.

Hotel :
Arcy-sur-Cure, 8 km S :
★***Grottes*** (L.F.), 6, rte Nationale, ☎ 86.40.91.47. closed 10-31 Jan and Wed (low season), 160. Rest. ♦ 60-120.

★Municipal *les Coulemières* (35 pl.), ☎ 86.53.50.01.

Restaurant :
♦ ***L'espérance,*** 3, rue du Gal-de-Gaulle, ☎ 86.53.50.42. AE, DC, Visa, closed 24-30 Dec, Sun eve and Mon. Spec : *escargots en meurette,* 60-130.

Boat-hire : *Burgundy Cruisers,* Accolay, 89460 Cravant, ☎ 86.53.54.55.

VÉZELAY

Avallon 15, Auxerre 51, Paris 225
A2 ☒ 89450

mairie, ☎ 86.33.22.64.

SNCF ☎ 86.46.50.50.

Hotels :
● ★★★***Poste et Lion d'Or,*** ☎ 86.33.21.23. Tx 800949. AE, Visa. 49 rm closed Nov-early Apr and Wed eve (ex summer), 530. Rest. ♦♦ closed Wed and Thu noon (ex nat hols), 120-240.
★***Relais du Morvan,*** pl. du Champ-de-Foire, ☎ 86.33.25.33. Visa. 9 rm closed Jan, Tue eve and Wed, 170. Rest. ♦ 50-120.

Saint-Père-sous-Vézelay, 2 km E :
● ★★★***Espérance*** (Relais et châteaux), ☎ 86.33.20.45. Tx 800005. AE, Visa. 19 rm closed early Jan-early Feb, Tue and Wed noon, 580. Rest. ● ♦♦♦ Marc Meneau is one of France's greatest chefs ; indeed, the country's gastronomical reputation is in part due to his audacious, imaginative cooking : *ambroisie de volaille, turbot rôti au jus de viande, poires et figues chaudes à la cannelle,* 150-450.

Youth hostel : *Croix-Sainte-Marthe,* rte de l'Étang, ☎ 86.33.24.18, 86.33.24.62.

Accommodation for young people : *Centre "Pax Christi",* ☎ 86.33.21.69.

★★*Municipal,* Saint-Père-sous-Vézelay (60 pl.), ☎ 86.33.26.62 ; ★★*l'Hermitage* (33 pl.), ☎ 86.33.24.62.

Festivals and events : 22 Jul *Fête de la Madeleine. Light displays and concerts* in summer.

VILLENEUVE-L'ARCHEVEQUE

Sens 13, Auxerre 44, Paris 135
A1 ☒ 89190

SNCF ☎ 86.86.72.02.

Hotels :
★★***Auberge des Vieux Moulins Banaux*** (L.F.), ☎ 86.86.72.55. Euro. 17 rm closed 15 Nov-15 Mar, Sun eve and Mon, 135. Rest. ♦♦ 55-120.

Vaudeurs, ☒ 89320, 14 km S on the D84 :
● ★★***Vandeurinoise*** (L.F.), rte de Grange-Sèche, ☎ 86.96.28.00. 7 rm closed Feb, 2 weeks in Oct, Tue eve and Wed low season, 200. Rest. ♦♦ 120-200.

VILLENEUVE-SUR-YONNE

Sens 13, Auxerre 44, Paris 135
A1 ☒ 89500

SNCF 86.46.50.50, 86.87.15.44.

Hotel :
★***Hostellerie du Dauphin,*** 14, rue Carnot, ☎ 86.87.18.55. 8 rm closed Nov-Christmas, Feb school hols and Wed low season, 185. Rest. ♦♦ 70-140.

★★*Le Saucil* (100 pl.), ☎ 86.87.00.69.

Boat-hire : *Vivre sur l'Eau,* marina, 89500 Villeneuve-sur-Yonne, ☎ 86.87.31.41.

Recommended : Chocolates and pastries, *Eschbach,* 39, rue Carnot.

Champagne and the Ardennes

A region whose reputation is dominated by its most famous product — champagne — fruit of a second fermentation in the bottle and a skilful blend of different varieties of grape. But Champagne produces red wines, rosés and whites as well, no less palatable for being less well-known.

Champagne is a region of forests — the Ardenne, Saint-Gobain, Villers-Cotterets; lakes — Der Chantecoq is the largest in France — and fertile valleys, dotted with beautiful towns and cities. Langres, with its ramparts and towers dominating the surrounding countryside, was the birthplace of the writer Diderot. The centre of Laon, built on a hill overlooking the great plain of Champagne, has retained its mediaeval streets and character, and boasts a cathedral built in the early Gothic period. The citizens of Troyes have started to painstakingly rebuild a city full of historical treasures dating from the Middle Ages to the Renaissance, the "golden age" of Troyes. The city of Rheims has twice played a central role in the history of France : first in 496 when Clovis was baptised there and founded the Frankish monarchy, and again in 1429 when the valiant Joan of Arc had the Dauphin crowned in Rheims cathedral.

In ages past, Champagne was famous for its great fairs which attracted visitors from all over Europe and even from as far afield as Constantinople. The benches or *"bancs"* that the moneychangers sat on to ply their trade gave their name to our modern banks.

Sightseeing

Facts and figures

Location : *The region stretches between the outcrops of the Ile-de-France in the west and Lorraine in the east, the mountains of the Ardennes in the north and Burgundy in the south.*
Area : *32 978 km².*
Climate : *More temperate in the west (2°-18 °C and 550-700 mm annual rainfall) than in the Ardennes and the Haute-Marne, which are colder and wetter (1 000-1 200 mm rainfall).*
Population : *1 870 695.*
Administration : *Department of the* ***Marne,*** *Prefecture Châlons-sur-Marne; Department of the* ***Haute-Marne,*** *Prefecture Chaumont; Department of the* ***Ardennes,*** *Prefecture Troyes; Department of the* ***Aisne*** *(officially part of the administrative region of Picardy), Prefecture Laon.*

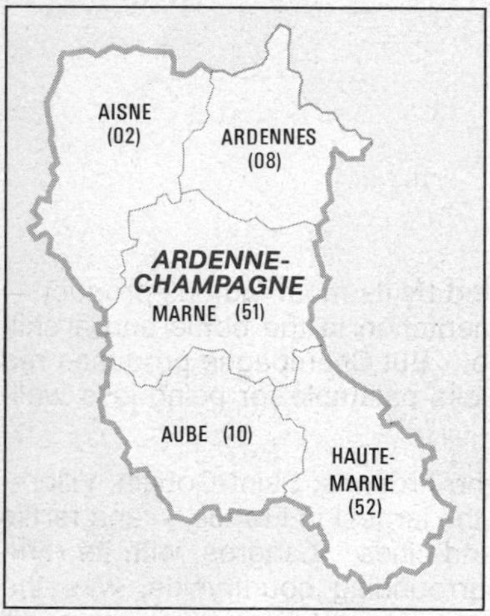

■ ARCIS-SUR-AUBE

B3 / pop. 3 258 (Aube)

The centre of Arcis is the 15th-16thC church; the heart of the town is a shady walk along the banks of the Aube. The 17thC château (now the town hall) stands in a riverside park.

▶ **Lhuître** *(9 km NE)* : the church★ (12thC, 16thC) is among the most beautiful in the region; 16thC stained glass. □

Echelle
0 1 5 10 15 20 km
N
LUX.
Vallée de la Meuse
Givet
Meuse
Fumet
Vallée de la Semois
Hirson
Rocroi
N 51
Monthermé
N 43
CHARLEVILLE-MÉZIÈRES
A 203
SEDAN
Semois
Signy-l'Abbaye
ARDENNES
Meuse
N 43
D 985
ARDENNES
D 947
Longuyon
RETHEL
D 987
D 947
Buzancy
VOUZIERS
N 51
D 980
Aire
REIMS
D 31
Aisne
Verdun
A 4
METZ
N 3
Route du Champagne
MARNE
STE-MENEHOULD
L'EST
Valmy
AUTOROUTE
DE
LORRAINE-VOSGES
Meuse
N 3
PERNAY
Abbaye de l'Epine
CHÂLONS-S-MARNE
Vertus
D 33
N 35
N 44
Marne
N 77
Ornain
Bar-le-Duc
Fère-Champenoise
Abb. des Trois Fontaines
N 4
VITRY-LE-FRANÇOIS
ST-DIZIER
Lhuître
Lac de Der Chantecoq
D 384
D 2
N 67
Vallée de la Marne
Dampierre
Aube
Arcis
Wassy
SEINE
Montier-en-Der
Joinville
N 77
D 400
AUBE
D 960
PARC NATUREL
Brienne-le-Ch.
Vallée de la Blaise
Vignory
Meuse
Ste-Maure
Forêt d'Orient
Pont-Ste-Marie
ROYES
Lac d'Orient
HAUTE MARNE
N 19
BAR S-AUBE
N 19
Colombey-les-2-Eglises
Bouilly
N 71
CHAUMONT
Abbaye de Morimont
VITTEL
Forêt d'Aumont
Bar-s-Seine
D 65
D 417
Aube
N 19
D 429
Nogent-en-Bassigny
Châtel
Chaource
D 443
SEINE
Bourbonne-les-Bains
les Riceys
Mussy
Arc-en Barrois
D 74
N 71
D 965
LANGRES
N 19
1
2
3
4

Don't miss

★★★ : Rheims (B2), Troyes (B4).
★★ : Champagne Road (B2), Langres (C4), Laon (A2).

BAR-SUR-AUBE

B4 / ® / pop. 7 148 (Aube)

Two churches in a hilly region of streams and rivers. One, **St. Pierre,** surrounded by a pretty wooden gallery; inside, 14thC polychrome statue, Virgin with a Posy. ▶ The other, **St. Maclou,** is closed; stroll along the Aube (mill). □

▶ Nearby

▶ **Bayel** *(7.5 km SE on D396) :* in the church, polychrome 15thC Virgin and Child★, a regional masterpiece attributed to the "Master of St. Martha" (→ box). At the Cristalleries de Champagne showroom, overhead view★ of crystal manufacture (founded in 1661; visits), last bastion of a regional craft. ▶ **Clairvaux** *(14 km SE) :* the Cistercian abbey founded by St. Bernard in 1125, rebuilt in the 18thC, is now a prison. ▶ **Trémilly** *(19 km N) :* 18thC château with a Renaissance well *(Easter hols. and 15 Jun.-15 Sep., 10-12 & 2-5; closed Mon.).* □

BOURBONNE-LES-BAINS

C4 / ® / pop. 3 146 (Haute-Marne)

The springs were known to the Gauls and Romans, and the waters are still sought after for the treatment of rheumatism, respiratory infections and the aftermath of broken bones; Romanesque church; Gallo-Roman-remains, thermal spa. □

▶ Nearby

▶ **Coiffy-le-Haut** *(7.5 km SW) :* a wine-producing village with a view★ as far as the Jura mountains. ▶ **Côte des Noues :** (*5 km N,* alt. 425 m, panorama★). ▶ **Morimond** *(NNW) :* vestiges of one of the first four daughter abbeys of Cîteaux (Cistertium, the Latin form of the name, gives rise to "Cistercian") founded in 1115 and razed after the Revolution (1789); its influence throughout Christian Europe was considerable. Return to Bourbonne via the **château de Parnot** *(Apr.-Jun., 10:30-6).* □

BRIENNE-LE-CHÂTEAU

B4 / ® / pop. 4 112 (Aube)

Napoleon studied at the military academy here from the age of 9 (1779) until at 16 he was commissioned as an artillery lieutenant.

▶ The former academy buildings and the 18thC château are still standing; the town centre, demolished in WWII, has been rebuilt in stone; covered market in wood, with tiled roof. ▶ Brienne celebrates its main local product, sauerkraut, with a festival the third weekend in September. ▶ **Napoleon Museum :** war room, miscellaneous documents and memorabilia. ▶ Church of St. Pierre-St. Paul (15th-16thC) : grisaille (monotone grey) stained glass in the 16thC apse. □

▶ Nearby

▶ **Brienne-la-Vieille** *(2 km S) :* church★ (12thC, 16thC); Romanesque doorway from a nearby abbey. ▶ **Rosnay-l'Hôpital** *(9 km N) :* 12thC, 15thC church, crypt; 16thC stained glass, 16th-18thC statuary. ▶ Brienne is in the Eastern Forest (forêt d'Orient) Nature Park (→). □

Weekend tips

The mansions, museums and churches of the old town of Troyes are well worth a day. Detour through the Othe countryside to the south, then turn back NE along the lakes of the Orient and Der-Chantecoq forests. Stopover at Châlons-sur-Marne or Epernay. Next day, visit the Champagne country, with a lunch break at Rheims. Another weekend, visit the Ardennes.

CHÂLONS-SUR-MARNE★

B3 / ® / pop. 54 359 (Marne)

An interesting mixture of ancient and modern architecture in the "dry" (less rainy) region of Champagne.

▶ **Notre-Dame-en-Vaux★★** (B1) : elegant specimen of early 12thC Gothic; stained glass★ from Troyes (although Châlons had its own glass makers); ring of 56 bells. ▶ The **cloister** behind the church, destroyed in the 18thC, was partly rebuilt from 1963 to 1978; rare carved capitals★★; 50 lifelike column-statues★★ *(10-12 & 2-5 or 6; closed Tue.).* ▶ **Cathedral★** (A2) : a neo-Classical façade on the 12thC triple nave and Romanesque tower; 13thC, 14thC and 16thC stained glass★; 12thC baptismal font; numerous tombstones. ▶ **Church of St. Alpin** (B2, pedestrian precinct) grisaille windows right of the entrance.
Also... ▶ **Municipal Museum** (B1, Place Godart) : archaeology, 12th-15thC sculpture, a traditional Champenois interior, paintings, ornithology, Hindu religious statuary★. ▶ **Garinet Museum** (19thC town-dweller's interior); and **Goethe-Schiller Museum** (personal effects of the German poets Johann Wolfgang von Goethe [1749-1832] and Friedrich von Schiller [1759-1805]) in rue Pasteur (B2). ▶ **Church of St. Jean** (C2) : 11thC Romanesque nave. ▶ To

A rich dustbowl

The chalky soil of Champagne is little more than a crust broken by scattered black pine, in contrast to the rich alluvial deposits in the Île-de-France. Nevertheless, in less than half a century modern fertilisers have made Champagne the second most important agricultural region in France. Champagne now holds European records for cereal yields, produces a quarter of French sugar in nine enormous refineries, and grows one-third of European lucerne (dehydrated for cattle fodder). Large tracts are under cultivation for poppyseed, maize, beetroot, and cabbage.

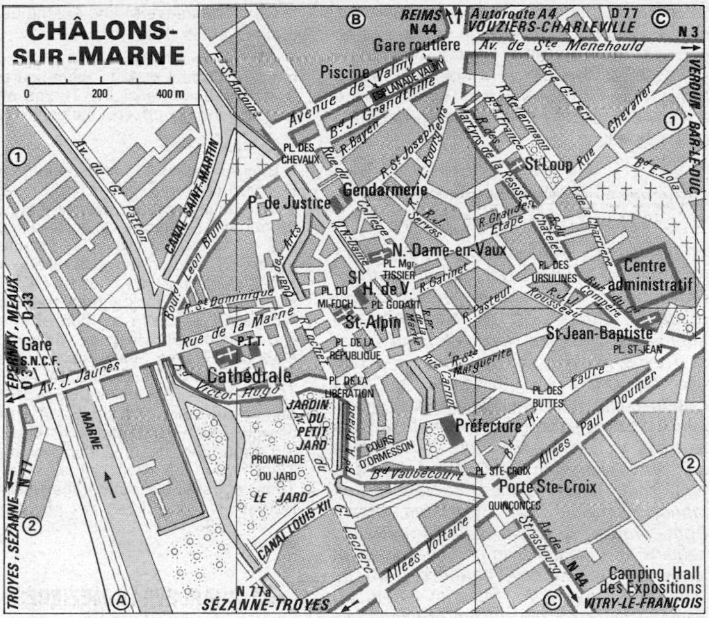

the south, near the civic offices, 13thC mansion of the former Intendants de Champagne (Regional Governors); **St. Croix gateway** (C2) built in 6 weeks (unfinished) to greet Marie Antoinette of Austria on her arrival in France to marry the future Louis XVI. □

▶ Nearby

▸ **Notre-Dame-de-l'Épine★★** *(8 km E on N3)* : a jewel of Flamboyant Gothic (1410-1524) and a site of pilgrimage since the 100 Years' War; elegant choir screen with 14thC Virgin; decorated crossbeam; entombment of Christ, ca. 1500; the choir is Renaissance on the left and Gothic on the right; outside, interesting gargoyles. □

■ The **CHAMPAGNE ROAD★★**
(route du Champagne)

▶ **From Rheims to Vertus *(125 km; full day)***
B2-3 / ® *(see map 1)*

A major attraction around Rheims and Épernay, covering the three regions that represent 80% of the Champagne vineyards : the Montagne de Reims, the Côte des Blancs and the Marne Valley. The fourth region — in the Aube south of Bar-sur-Aube and including Bar-sur-Seine together with 3 200 acres in the departments of Aisne and Seine-et-Marne — makes up a total champagne-producing area of 340 km^2, of which only 250 km^2 are currently planted. This represents 2% of the total vine-growing area of France. The vineyards of Champagne are very fragmented : 120 champagne firms (only 10 are really important) own about 13% of the vineyards. Nevertheless, they account for two-thirds of total production by purchasing grapes from other growers. The remaining one-third comes from about 14 300 smallholdings averaging just under 4 acres in area. Almost one-third of the smallholders make their own wine. After the bad years of 1978, 1980 and 1981, excellent harvests in 1982 and 1983 enabled producers to reconstitute their stocks and stabilise prices. Stocks normally represent 3 years' sales (450-500 million bottles

1. Champagne Road

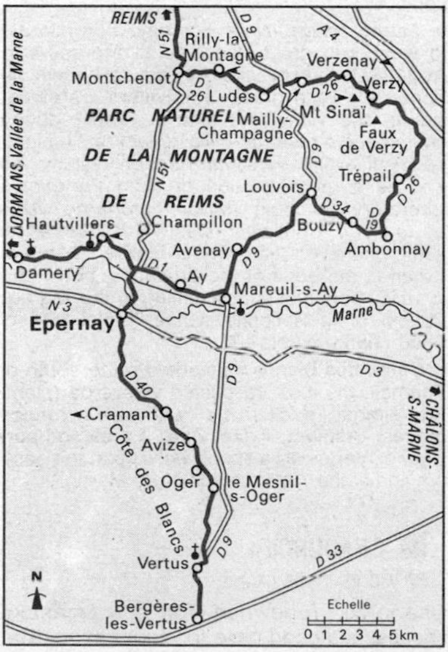

stored in 200 km of cellars dug out of the chalk). Champagne brings in more foreign currency than any other French wine. Even so, 60 % of production is sold in France. More than 10 000 salaried workers are directly or indirectly employed in production and distribution.

The Champagne fairs

In the 12thC, a calendar of trade fairs was devised to take advantage of southern Champagne's location at the trading crossroads of Europe. For several centuries afterwards, two fairs were held every year at Troyes, Provins and Sézanne, and one each at Lagny and Bar-sur-Aube. Merchants came from the British Isles, Germany, Spain, Italy and even Constantinople to trade in leather, wool, precious stones and porcelains from the Orient, hemp and furs from Russia, spices, copper, silken fabrics... Bezants from Byzantium, dinars from Arabia, Austrian thalers, Venetian sequins and Westphalian groschen passed through the money-changers, whose "bench" or "bank" (Fr. banque) *eventually came to stand for the system of exchange.*

▶ **Montagne de Reims :** leaving Rheims, take the road for Épernay; the champagne road is signposted from Mont Chenot. After **Rilly,** on a hill road *(corniche)* above Rheims at the foot of Mount Joli (alt. 274 m), the great names appear one after the other. **Mailly-Champagne :** 13thC church. **Verzenay :** mill, view★. **Verzy :** church with 11thC statue of the Virgin; nearby, twisted beech trees known as "faux de Verzy"; Sinaï Observatory at 288 m, view. **Ambonnay. Bouzy :** produces a light red wine. **Louvois :** park of former château built by a Minister to Louis XIV, later owned by a daughter of Louis XV.

▶ **Marne Valley** *(N of Épernay) :* from east to west, two great vineyards at **Mareuil-sur-Ay** (12thC church), and **Ay** (house known as Henry IV's wine press). **Hautvillers :** prettiest site in the vineyards; with a rebuilt abbey church and a restored building where illuminated mediaeval manuscripts are on display, as well as a reconstruction of Dom Pérignon's laboratory (→ box) *(private property, visits by request).* Continuing westwards, **Damery :** 13thC church★. **Châtillon-sur-Marne :** statue of Urban II, the Pope of the Crusades, born here in 1042. **Dormans** ® : swimming in the Marne; Chapel of la Reconnaissance (burial site of 1 500 unknown soldiers).

▶ **Côtes des Blancs★ :** marked route south of Épernay, the most respected vineyards (planted almost exclusively with Chardonnay grapes) **Cramant, Avize, Oger, Le Mesnil-sur-Oger** ®. **Vertus** ® : a spring wells up at the eastern end of the 12thC church of St. Martin. □

■ CHAOURCE★

B4 / pop. 1 106 (Aube)

Chaource, renowned for a namesake cheese, is a good base for exploration. The town boasts several fine examples of 16thC stained glass from Troyes.

▶ Church★★ : in the crypt a sculpted **Entombment of Christ★★** (1515 eight-figure group) is a superb example of the Troyes style of the period; funerary frescos, statuary. □

▶ Nearby

▶ **Ervy-le-Châtel** *(21 km W on the Saint-Florentin road) :* covered market, old houses, stained glass★ in the church. **Neuvy-Sautour** *(10 km farther on) :* church★ with Renaissance choir and large, ornate cross. ▶ **Bar-sur-Seine** ® *(21 km E) :* church with bas-reliefs, woodwork, 16thC stained glass★; nearby *(100 m)* Renaissance house of brick and carved wood. ▶ **Les Riceys** *(22 km SE) :* a group of three villages and an important vineyard. **Ricey-Bas :** 16thC church★, Troyes Renaissance style, stained glass, 16th-17thC sculpture. **Ricey-Haut-Rive :** 16thC church with stained glass, 15thC pulpit. **Mussy-sur-Seine** *(13 km E, on D17) :* 13thC church★, 14th-15thC statuary, 16thC Pietà (Virgin mourning dead Christ); château (15th, 18thC) now the town hall; several 15th and 16thC houses; Museum of the Resistance (rue Boursault; *Sat. and Sun. pm, May-Oct.*). □

■ CHARLEVILLE-MÉZIÈRES

B1 / ® / pop. 61 558 (Ardennes)

Charleville is an early 17thC town. The poet Arthur Rimbaud (1854-1891) was born and raised here; his grave is in the cemetery. Place Ducale★, urban architecture (Louis XIII-Henry IV) similar to that of the renowned place des Vosges in Paris. Nearby, the Old Mill (Louis XIII); Ardenne Museum, regional folklore, mementoes of Rimbaud *(9-12 & 2-6 ex Mon.).*

▶ **Mézières** was almost entirely rebuilt in red brick after WWII. Church of Notre-Dame-de-l'Espérance★ (15th-16thC Flamboyant Gothic) the black image of the Virgin is the object of an annual pilgrimage; modern stained glass. □

■ CHÂTEAU-THIERRY★

A2-3 / ® / pop. 14 920 (Aisne)

The French Aesop, Jean de la Fontaine (1621-1695) was born here; small museum at 12 Rue La Fontaine *(10-12, 2-2:30-5, 6 or 6:30; closed Tue.).* Through the streets (or up 104 steps) to the 14thC **Porte St. Jean** leading to the promenade of the château overlooking the valley. □

▶ Nearby

▶ **Bois Belleau** *(10 km NW along N3 and D9) :* WWI military cemeteries. ▶ **Essômes** *(3 km S) :* 13th-14thC church. ▶ SE : drive through the **Surmelin Valley.** ▶ **Condé-en-Brie** *(15 km) :* château, with apartments of the Prince de Condé, remodelled in the 18thC *(Jul.-Aug. daily 10-12 & 2:30-6:30; Sun. and nat. hols. only, 2:30-6:30, Easter-Jun. and Sep.-Oct.).* ▶ **Orbais** *(26 km) :* 12th-13thC church (choir★ with triforium and seven rose windows) built by Jean d'Orbais who was one of the builders of Rheims cathedral. ▶ Return to Château-Thierry through Dormans and the valley of the Marne. □

CHAUMONT

C4 / ® / pop. 29 552 (Haute-Marne)

Houses with distinctive staircase towers and corbelled turrets cluster around the keep and basilica. The newer areas are well laid out.

▶ **Basilica of St. Jean :** a mixture of Gothic and Renaissance, with interesting triforium and openwork tower staircase; statuary including polychrome entombment of Christ★ (15thC), Tree of Jesse★ (genealogy of Christ, Troyes 16thC) in St. Nicolas chapel. ▶ Old houses, courthouse; only the 12thC **dungeon** remains from the château of the Counts of Champagne. ▶ **Viaduct★ :** 19thC railway engineering at its best, 654 m long, three stories towering 52 m above the Suize and the road to Châtillon-sur-Seine.

▶ Nearby

▶ **Nogent-en-Bassigny** *(22 km SE through the valley of the Marne and down D107) :* centre for the manufacture of scissors and cutlery. □

COLOMBEY-LES-DEUX-ÉGLISES

C4 / ® / pop. 688 (Haute-Marne)

Since 1979 visitors have been allowed into the four main ground-floor rooms of La Boisserie, the personal residence of the former President of France, General Charles de Gaulle (1890-1970). The books and furniture are in place in the library and in the General's corner study. Visitors are often surprised by the simplicity of the house. De Gaulle is buried in the cemetery around the village church. A memorial cross of Lorraine, 44 m high, overlooks the hills. ▶ Head in the direction of Chaumont to reach the Blaise valley (→ Wassy). □

Lake DER-CHANTECOQ

B3

The region was once an immense oak forest of which only a fragment remains. The name of Der comes from the Celtic world for oak. In 1974, the largest artificial lake in France (48 km^2) was created here to regulate the flow of the Marne and the Seine. Three villages were inundated in the process, but the most interesting buildings were reconstructed along the north shore.

▶ **Sainte-Marie-du-Lac :** Museum-village with traditional wood-faced buildings; church★ at Nuisement, dovecote, smithy, barns, activities Apr.-Oct. ▶ Round trip *(45 km S and SW)* of the churches of the Der. **Montier-en-Der :** former abbey church★ with timber structure reminiscent of early Saxon churches; choir based on that of St. Rémi at Rheims. **Ceffonds :** early 16thC church. **Puellemontier** *(6.5 km NW) :* numerous farmhouses with wood facings; 16thC stained glass in church. **Lentilles★** *(beyond lake Horre) :* pretty wood-faced church with timbered porch and high, steep roof. **Chavanges** *(4 km NW) :* 12thC and 16thC church. **Outines** *(9 km NE) :* church with shingles and studding. □

Champagne

The champagne process, which puts the bubbles in the wine, is a second fermentation that takes place in the bottle. The best champagnes are careful blends of one or more of three authorised varieties of grape (Pinot Noir and Meunier, red; Chardonnay, white). Blanc de Blancs (white from whites), the exception to the rule, is a very pale champagne made from Chardonnay grapes. Dom Pérignon (1638-1715), the cellar master-monk at Hautvillers, is credited with the development of the Champagne process. The details of his experiments are hard to sort out, but it seems that he was the first to blend wines in a systematic fashion, and among the first to use the classic mushroom-shaped cork that keeps the seal despite tremendous pressure in the bottle. The region also produces excellent still wines.

ÉPERNAY

B2-3 / ® / pop. 28 876 (Marne)

Épernay, the heart of the vineyard country around the Montagne de Reims, is where many champagne merchants maintain cellars. The regional museum has an extensive display related to viticulture and wine making.

▶ Church of Notre-Dame (early 20thC neo-Gothic) : 16thC stained glass; interesting regional sculptures. ▶ **Champagne cellars :** Moët et Chandon; Mercier. ▶ Nearby, the Champagne road (→). □

FÈRE-CHAMPENOISE

B3 / pop. 2 518 (Aisne)

Totally destroyed by fire in 1756, much damaged in 1914, and burned out again in 1940, the town has only one church left (13thC tower, 15thC choir).

▶ National Cemetery and War Memorial commemorating the first battle of the Marne (WWI). ▶ **Corroy** *(7 km SSW on D9) :* church dating from 1070; porch. ▶ **St. Gond marsh** *(10 km NNW) :* a 30 km^2 wasteland that saw heavy fighting in 1914 (memorial at **Mondemont**); now partly cultivated. □

FÈRE-EN-TARDENOIS★

A2 / ® / pop. 3295 (Aisne)

A large covered market and an oddly shaped church built in several stages (15th-16thC); 3 km off, the seven round towers of the château de la Fère.

▶ **La Forteresse de la Fère★** *(no entrance fee) :* on a sandstone mound in the forest; the five-arched viaduct topped with a two-story gallery dates from the 16thC; entrance attributed to the sculptor Jean Goujon (1510-1569).

▶ Nearby

▶ Remains of fortresses incorporated into several farmsteads : **Nesles** *(4 km E on D2);* **Armentières** *(13 km W on D310 and D80);* via **Coincy** (beautiful church) and 3 km from **Oulchy-le-Château** : church★ with Romanesque nave, 11thC bell-tower, noteworthy capitals). □

JOINVILLE

C3 / ® / pop. 5 091 (Haute-Marne)

A compact and lively country town with narrow streets and fine Renaissance or neo-Classical houses on a wooded hill overlooking the flowering banks of the river Marne.

▶ **Château du grand jardin★ :** 16thC; rare trees.

▶ Nearby

▶ Near Rupt (via D117 right). **Blécourt★ :** 12th-13thC church in serene Cluniac style; Virgin and Child (copy of 13thC statue stolen in 1965). **Vignory** *(23 km) :* Romanesque church is one of the major 11thC buildings in eastern France; timbered nave, figured capitals, 15th-16thC sculpture (Virgin and Child, Nativity, vision of St. Hubert, altarpiece of Christ's Passion). ▶ **Poissons** *(6 km SE from Joinville on D47)* in the valley of the Rongeant; 16thC church, sculpture. □

LANGRES★★

C4 / ® / pop. 11 359 (Haute-Marne)

A town that invites exploration on foot : seven gates, six towers, ramparts crowned with a sentry walk, view over the country-side where the Marne, the Aube and the Meuse arise.

▶ Place Diderot (named for the philosopher Denis Diderot born here 1713, d. 1784). ▶ **Cathedral★ :** 12thC Burgundian Romanesque with 18thC façade; 14thC Virgin in a Renaissance chapel; pulpit and organ casing from Morimond abbey.
Close by : the chapterhouse, formerly the walled "Ville Capitulaire", former Canon's houses. 20 rue Cardinal Morlot : Renaissance house★ (exterior visits 8am-9pm).▶ **St. Didier Museum :** Gallo-Roman life in the region (13 Roman roads fan out from Langres). ▶ **Museum of the Breuil de St. Germain Mansion :** furniture, ceramics, Diderot memorabilia *(10-12 & 2-5 or 6; closed Tue.).* ▶ Gallo-Roman gateway. □

▶ Nearby

▶ Four reservoirs (19thC feeding the Marne-Saône canal); sailing, especially on Lake Liez. ▶ **Pailly** *(12 km S) :* Renaissance château★. ▶ **Faylé-Billot** *(26 km SE on the Vesoul road)* basket-weaving, craft shops, exhibitions in the basket-weaving school . (École de Vannerie) daily in summer, closed Sun. □

Cuisine in and with champagne

Champagne is used in the preparation of regional delicacies, such as poached pike (brochet) *or braised chicken. Other regional specialities are* andouillettes *(tripe sausages) from Troyes, served sizzling hot with potatoes, fried onions or red beans, and pig's foot à la Sainte-Menehould (first braised then coated with breadcrumbs). Popular dishes include pork and cabbage stew* (la potée champenoise), *breaded ham hock* (jambonneau) *from Rheims, white pudding* (boudin blanc), *and sauerkraut* (choucroute) *from Brienne. The cheeses of Chaource and Thiérache are well known, and local confectionery includes chocolate pebbles* (rocaillons) *from Sedan, pink ratafia biscuits from Rheims, and almond meringues made in Bar-sur-Aube and Wassy.*

LAON★★

A2 / ® / pop. 29 074 (Aisne)

On an isolated hill overlooking the Champagne plain, Laon has some of the finest monuments in northern France. The upper town, a network of narrow mediaeval streets and beautiful houses, will be linked in 1986 to the lower town by a revolutionary French transport system, POMA 2000.

▶ **Cathedral★★★** (B-C2) built in a single stage starting in 1155, except for the 13thC choir. As one of the first Gothic buildings, it introduced many new ideas. The arcaded gallery inspired the one in Notre-Dame-de-Paris; the triangular gables over the porches prefigured those at Chartres; the towers were models for Rheims and others. The carved oxen pay tribute to the beasts that hauled thousands of blocks of stone from quarries in the plain. The four-story nave (118 m from eastern end to doorway, 24 m high) is lit east-west by two symmetrical rose windows and by the openings in the clere-story above the galleries.
The cathedral, chapterhouse, cloister (under repair) and former episcopal palace★ still look much as they did in the Middle Ages. ▶ **Citadel :** (C2) view. ▶ **Porte d'Ardon :** (S, B-C2) 13thC gateway and rampart walk. **Museum** (42 rue G. Ermant; C2) Greek and Roman antiquities★; 12thC chapel of the Templars★. ▶ West through the mediaeval town centre lies the **church of St. Martin★** (A2), a former abbey church built on Cistercian lines (12th-13thC); farther on, the Soissons gateway★. □

▶ Nearby

▶ **Notre-Dame de Liesse★** *(15 km NE on N377) :* pilgrimage site. ▶ West, round trip through the **Saint-Gobain forest★.** Ruined abbeys of Tortoir and St. Nicolas-aux-Bois. **At Saint-Gobain** (13th-14thC church), a sheet-glass and mirror industry was founded at the instigation of Jean-Baptiste Colbert (1619-1683) Minister to Louis XIV. **Coucy-le-Château :** surrounded by ramparts, was guarded by one of the largest mediaeval châteaux, (damaged in WWI; *10-12 & 2-4 or 6; closed Tue. and Wed.).* Return to Laon via : **Abbey of Prémontré,** birthplace of the Premonstratensian Order of White Canons (18thC buildings; magnificent spiral staircase); **Merlieux :** freshwater nature information centre created in 1982, (aquaria, botany trail along the lakes, *Wed., Sat. and Sun. pm).* **Mons-en-Laonnois :** country town with 13th-14thC church. ▶ S, a 25 km tour of the churches of the Laonnois

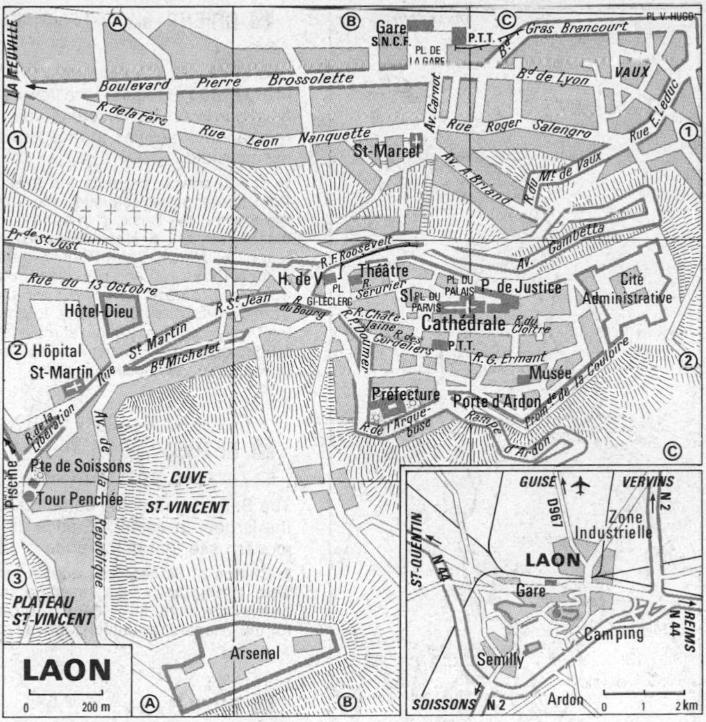

through attractive countryside : **Bruyères** and **Vorges,** both fortified; 11thC **Presles :** 12thC porch; **Nouvion-le-Vineux :** Romanesque bell-tower. ▶ 16 km S of Laon on D967 : the **Chemin des Dames** (Ladies' Road). This narrow crest is followed by D18 from its western crossroads with N2; scene of heavy fighting in WWI; memorial chapel and military cemetery at **Cerny;** la Caverne du Dragon *(signposted),* subterranean fortress and museum; 1 km N of the cavern are the remains of the Cistercian abbey of **Vauclair** (12th-13thC); interesting garden of medicinal plants; small museum of local ceramics *(Apr.-Oct., 8am-10pm).* ▶ **La Fère** ® *(21 km NW) :* Jeanne d'Aboville museum (paintings★). ▶ **Bois-lès-Pargny** *(20 km N) :* 17thC château *(outside visits free; inside visits by request).* □

■ MEUSE Valley★

▶ Round trip from Charleville *(approx 130 km, full day)*

B1 *(see map 2)*

The appearance of factories, cement works and silos in the industrialised Meuse valley has not spoilt the Ardennes forest, which teems with game and has a rich folklore.

▶ 15 km N of Charleville, the crests known as the **Quatre Fils-Aymon** (the four sons of Aymon), brothers reputed to have escaped together from Charlemagne on the legendary steed Bayard. ▶ **Monthermé** ® : summer resort; church of St. Léger, Laval-Dieu : former abbey of White Canons, 12thC church, 18thC wood panelling. **Rock of the tower** *(3.5 km N and 20 min walk round trip) :* view★★ over the Ardennes. **Rock of the Seven Villages** *(3 km S) :* panorama★★ over the river valley. You can drive 18 km down D31 along the river Semoy★ to the Belgian frontier : reedy banks and old mills in an area much appreciated by fishermen and nature lovers. ▶ The valley runs between the **Roches de Laifour** (waterfall) and the ravine of the **Dames de Meuse★** *(1 hr 30 to the top round trip).* ▶ **Revin :** village built across two loops of the Meuse. Nearby, Mont Malgré Tout★ (Mont In Spite of Everything; *30min walk round trip*) : overlooking the town. ▶ After **Fumay** (slate works), the valley widens. ▶ **Haybes.** ▶ **Hierges :** ruins of mediaeval château in a grand setting. ▶ **Chooz :** Franco-Belgian nuclear power station (350 megawatts, 2 billion kWh per year). ▶ **Givet** ® : fortified town at the foot of the stronghold of Charlemont *(Jul.-Aug. 10-12);* the narrow streets are busy during the season; church of St. Hilaire, built by the 17thC military engineer Sebastien de Vauban (1633-1707). ▶ Return to Charleville through the Ardennes forest★ between Vireux and Monthermé. □

■ NOGENT-SUR-SEINE

A3 / ® / pop. 5 103 (Aube)

Meadows, willows, poplars, a mill and, near the quay, a sturdy half-timbered dwelling known as Henry IV's house.

▶ **Church of St. Laurent★ :** 15th-16thC, Renaissance tower; 16thC organ casing; 16th-17thC sculpture and painting. ▶ Rue Gustave

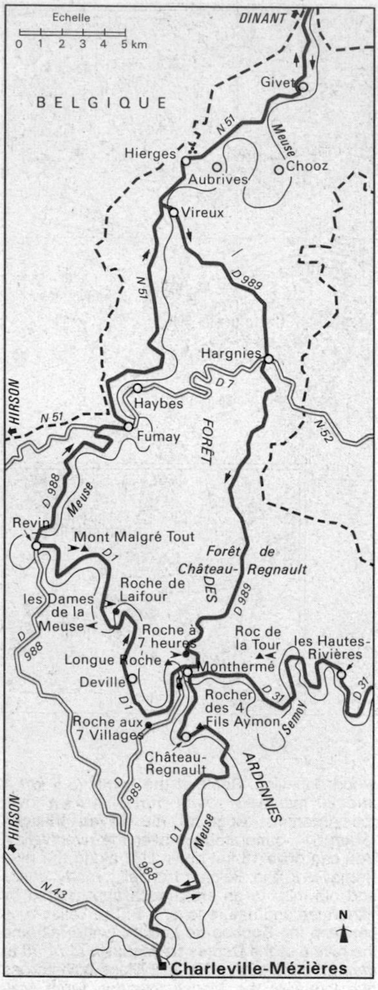

2. Meuse valley

Flaubert leads to the **museum :** works by local sculptors P. Dubois and A. Boucher; Gallo-Roman pottery. □

▶ Nearby

▶ **Le Paraclet** *(6 km SE on the Troyes road) :* site of the convent founded in 1129 by the theologian Peter Abelard, whose beloved Héloise was the first abbess. Parts of the wall still stand, together with the crypts, dovecote and storehouse. The kitchens are incorporated in a wing of the 17thC château *(exterior visit Jul.-Sep.; 2-6 closed Sun).* ▶ **Ferreux** *(3.5 km farther) :* 17thC château, visits by request. ▶ **Pont-sur-Seine** *(8 km E) :* 17th-18thC château *(1 Oct.-31 Nov., Sat., Sun. and hols. 2-5, closed Dec.-Mar.).* ▶ **Château de la Motte-Tilly★ :** 18thC château with superb furnishings★ *(Apr.-Sep. daily; closed Tue. 10-11:30 & 2-6:15).* □

■ ORIENT Lake and Forest★★

B4

The artificial Lake Orient (23 km²) was created in 1966 to regulate the flow of the Seine. It is bordered by an oak forest (13 km²); recreational facilities attract tourists. 30 km scenic route.

▶ The reservoir protects the town of Troyes from flooding and regulates the water level in Paris when the Seine is in spate; small hydro-electric station. ▶ Near **Géraudot :** bird sanctuary. ▶ **Mesnil-Saint-Père :** game reserve 5 km N (boar, red and roe deer; *open Sat. and Sun. 4pm to dusk Apr.-Sep.; 1st and 3rd Sun. from 3pm to dusk Oct.-Mar.).* Information from the Maison du Parc (office) at main forest cross-roads; open daily, fishing (pike), accommodation, sporting and leisure facilities. □

■ RETHEL

B2 / ® / pop. 9 081 (Ardennes)

The Saturday morning cattle market, one of the largest in eastern France, is held on a modern site that is the pride of the town.

▶ **Church of St. Nicolas :** double nave; the left aisle (11th-13thC) was reserved for religious orders, the right, lit by 14thC Gothic windows, for the villagers; beautiful doorway (1511). □

■ RHEIMS★★★

B2 / ® / pop. 181 985 (Marne)

Two key events in France history took place at Rheims (Reims in French). The first was the baptism of Clovis, king of the Franks, in 496AD, which legitimised the monarchy and laid the foundation for a national identity. The second was the coronation of Charles VII in the cathedral on 17 July 1429. This confirmed the success of Joan of Arc in rallying the French to shake off 9 years of English rule, during which France had virtually ceased to exist as a separate entity. Rheims was rebuilt twice during the first half of this century to repair war damage. The growth of Champagne exports since 1970 has enabled the town to expand at a dizzy rate.

▶ **Place Drouet-d'Erlon :** (A1-2) a pedestrian precinct lined with cafés, restaurants, cinemas and shopping arcades; it is the hub of social activity. **Church of St. Jacques :** 13th-16thC, with modern abstract stained glass★ by Vieira da Silva and Joseph Sima. ▶ **Cathedral★★★ :** (B2) 6 650 m² in area, 81.5 m high, 149 m in overall length; the nave is 138.7 m long and 38 m high. Planned by Jean d'Orbais (→ Orbais), building began in 1211 and was mostly completed a century later. The immediate impression is of extreme lightness and elegance : the three arched doorways, the gallery of kings and the delicate openwork towers and flying buttresses are so perfectly proportioned that they appear weightless. Lessons learned from Chartres, begun 20 years earlier, resulted in a brillant fusion of space and light. The perspective leads the eye towards the choir, and the windows appear as integral parts of the ogives, creating a curtain of light around

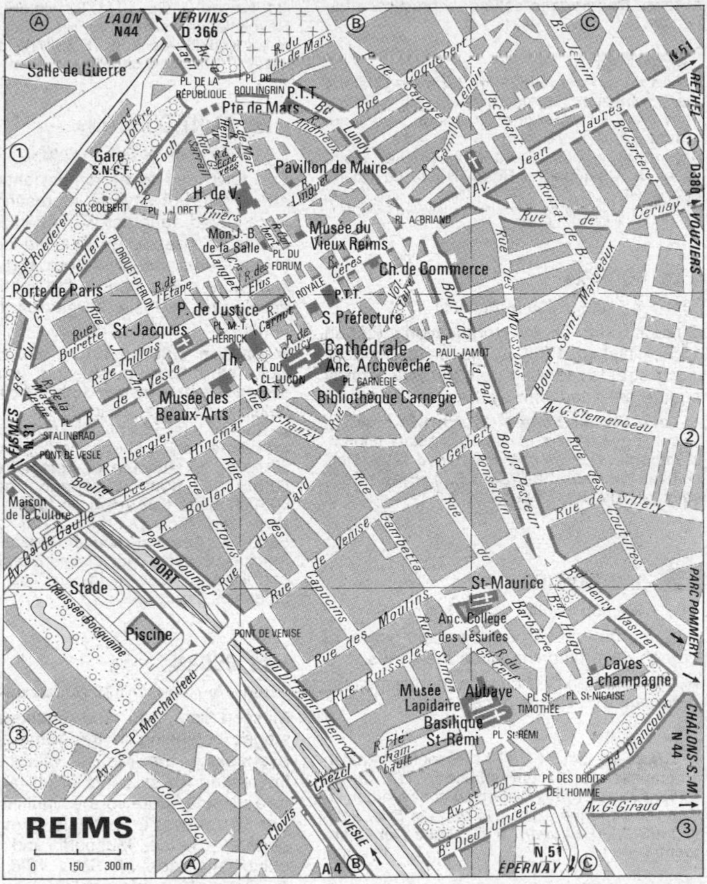

the sanctuary. On the inside western wall★★, superb sculpture (the knight's communion★); outside on the west face, sculptural groups of the Visitation★, the Presentation in the Temple, the Last Judgement, and the famous smiling angel★★ (left doorway), a masterpiece of Champenoise style; ▶ The **Tau Museum :** (B2, right of the cathedral; *10-12 & 2-5 or 6*) formerly the King's coronation residence; treasures and statues★ from the cathedral (Crowning of the Virgin, Goliath). ▶ **Museum of St. Denis :** (A2, 8 rue Chanzy) exceptional collection of 15thC paintings★, drawings★ by the Flemish artist Lucas Cranach the Elder, 19thC paintings, including 20 by Camille Corot★ (→ Île-de-France) and 9 by Eugène Boudin (1824-1898). ▶ **Basilica of St. Rémi★★ :** (BC3) important pilgrimage site (St. Rémi was the bishop who baptised King Clovis); the choir★★ (1162-90) is the earliest example of ogival architecture in Champagne; fine eastern end. ▶ Next door, the former abbey (rebuilt 17th-18thC) now the **archaeological museum** (prehistory to end of Middle Ages; entrance 53 rue St. Simon, BC3) : 16th-19thC weapons, Romanesque archaeology, tapestries★ illustrating the life of St. Rémi.

Also... ▶ Porte mars★ : (A1) superb Roman triumphal arch. ▶ **Salle de Guerre** (War Room) : where the German surrender was signed on 7 May 1945 (Collège Technique, 10 rue Franklin Roosevelt A1; *15 Mar.-11 Nov., 10-12 & 2-6; closed Tue.*). ▶ **Museum of Old Rheims★** : (Vergeur Mansion, 16th, 17th, 18thC; B1) history of the town, documents, illustrations of coronations, furnished rooms, engravings by the German artist Albrecht Dürer (1471-1528) of Christ's Passion and the Apocalypse★ *(2-6; closed Mon. and 25 Dec.)*. Opposite, underground **Roman galleries** (3rdC, place du Forum). Figures by the 18thC sculptor Jean-Baptiste Pigalle surrounding a statue of Louis XV in Place Royale. ▶ **Foujita Chapel** (35 rue du Champs de Mars; B1) frescos by the Japanese artist Tsugouharu Foujita (1886-1968) who was baptised at Rheims. **Church of St. Niçaise :** *(entry via C2)* decorated with Lalique glass, in a housing estate built in the 1920s. ▶ Former Jesuit college (BC-3), vast 17thC ensemble (refectory, kitchens, salons, library). ▶ **Maison de la Culture** (cultural centre) : (A2; rue de Vesle, over the bridge). Round **church of St. Vincent-de-Paul** in the new Quartier de l'Europe. The University is on the edge of town. **Champagne cellars** → practical information. □

▶ Nearby

▶ **Fort de la Pompelle** *(9 km E on the Châlons road)* : museum, German helmets and uniforms from WWI. ▶ **Montagne de Reims :** (regional nature park; *10 km S on the Epernay road*) woods, Saint-Imoges lake, Ardre valley. ▶ Champagne Road (Route du Champagne →). □

■ ROCROI★

B1 / ® / pop. 2 789 (Ardennes)

Guided tours of the fortifications (begun 1555, finished 17thC). The eight perfectly linear streets radiating from the wide central square are lined with slate-roofed houses.

▶ **Lake Vieilles-Forges** *(12 km SE)* : sailing, swimming. **Renwez** *(3 km S)* : 15thC church. **Montcornet** *(1.5 km farther)* : ruined 12th-14thC château *(museum, 2-6 Sat., Sun, Easter-Oct.; daily ex Mon, Jul.-15 Sep.).* □

■ SAINT-DIZIER

C3 / ® / pop. 37 445 (Haute-Marne)

An important crossroad town and typical of French town planning since the 1950s.

▶ "Au Petit Paris" : house in the main street, decorated with shards of ceramics.

▶ Nearby

▶ **Villiers-en-Lieu** *(4 km N)* : Museum of French automobiles. ▶ **Trois-Fontaines★** *(11 km on D16)* : ruins of 13thC Cistercian abbey, outbuildings rebuilt in the 18thC *(15 Jun.-15 Sep. 2:30-7; park open all year).* ▶ S : **Lake Der-Chantecoq** (→). □

■ SAINTE-MENEHOULD

BC2 / ® / pop. 807 (Marne)

The town is known for more than breaded pig's foot (→ box). The lower town of Sainte-Menehould (pron. Sainte-Menou) retains an 18thC urban appearance (town hall, Place du Général Leclerc) in contrast to the village-like upper town clustered around the 12th-14thC church (15thC sculpture, the Dormition of the Virgin). On 21 June 1791, Louis XVI was recognised in the post house (now the Gendarmerie) during his flight from Paris. He was arrested a little farther on at Varennes-en-Argonne. Sainte Menehould was also the birthplace of Dom Pérignon (→ box).

▶ **Municipal museum :** geological collection *(daily from Palm Sunday to 11 Nov., Sat. pm and Sun. rest of year).* □

▶ Nearby

▶ East : **Argonne forest** (→ Lorraine). ▶ **Givry-en-Argonne** ® *(16 km S)* : lakes in the Belval forest. ▶ **Braux-Sainte-Cohière★** *(5.5 km W)* : 16th-17thC château, Regional Museum of the Argonne *(exhibitions and events 20 Jun.-4 Sep., 9-12 & 2-7 closed Tue.).* ▶ **Valmy** *(11 km on)* : site of 1792 victory by French Revolutionary army over invading Prussians. ▶ **La Neuville-au-Pont** *(6 km NW on Vouziers road)* : 14th-16thC church. □

■ SAINT-QUENTIN★

A1 / ® / pop. 65 067 (Aisne)

The town had to be almost entirely rebuilt after WWI, but several interesting buildings were saved, together with an important collection of pastels by Quentin de La Tour (1704-1788), who was born and died here. A 30-acre public park in the centre of town, sailing on Lake Isle, barges on the Somme canal.

▶ **Basilica** (12th-15thC) in the town centre looks stolid from outside but is surprisingly airy and elegant inside; 13thC choir★ with five radiating chapels; magnificent 18thC organ. ▶ Nearby : façade of the 1509 Hôtel de Ville with three gables and a fine bell-tower (ring of 37 bells). ▶ **Museum of Entomology★** in the library : unique European collection of 600 000 butterflies *(daily ex Mon., Apr.-Aug.; Wed. and Thu., Oct.-Mar.; Thu. and Sat. in Sep.).* ▶ **Antoine-Lécuyer Museum** (28 rue Antoine Lécuyer, *daily closed Mon.);* 87 pastel portraits★ by Quentin de La Tour; paintings, tapestries, porcelain. □

■ SEDAN

BC1 / ® / pop. 24 535 (Ardennes)

Massed ramparts and bastions, built in stages beginning in the 15thC, on a rock overlooking the Meuse valley. Extremely interesting for students of military architecture; inside, noteworthy vaulting and timber framework, models from various periods (Sedan Museum and temporary exhibitions *Apr.-14 Sep. 10-6, 15 Sep.-25 Oct. 1:30-6; closed Mon.).* ▶ **Church of Saint Charles,** Place d'Armes, former Protestant church (16thC.). □

▶ Nearby

▶ 30-acre lake to the south : sailing, swimming. ▶ **Bazeilles** *(3.5 km SE)* : rebuit after 1870; small museum; 1730 château de Dorival *(10-12 & 2-6 closed Mon.).* ▶ **Chéhéry** *(10 km S)* : 16thC château du Rocan *(visits).* ▶ **Mouzon** *(17 km SE)* : old country town; Burgundy gateway, remnants of fortifications *(Jun.-Sep., Sat. and Sun. 2-6)* with 13thC Benedictine abbey church (tympanum, galleries and clerestory, choir★ with ambulatory and five radiating chapels). □

■ SEZANNE

A3 / ® / pop. 6 117 (Marne)

Sézanne is one of the largest optical production centres in Europe. In the old town, stroll under chestnut trees overlooking the hillside (Mail des Cordeliers; cloister in the Hospice). In the central square, church with carved doors (restored).

▶ SW, **Traconne Forest★ :** 30 km^2 of hornbeam and oak. **Bricot-la-Ville :** quaint village; ▶ 16 km N : ruined 12thC abbey of Reclus *(Jul.-Aug., 3:30 and 6:30; closed Tue.).*

■ SOISSONS★

A2 / ® / pop. 32 236 (Aisne)

Soissons was largely rebuilt to repair the destruction of the Franco-Prussian War of 1870-1871 and the two world wars. Several admirable buildings have somehow survived.

▶ **Cathedral★★ :** built over 3 centuries, most of it dates from the 13thC; the S transept★ (1177) is the most beautiful part; Adoration of the Shepherds★ by the Dutch painter Peter Paul Rubens (1577-1640); 13thC stained glass in the choir. ▶ Place du Cloître (cloister) with 13thC houses; behind the church, Romanesque remains of St. Pierre-au-Parvis, now a memorial to the Deportation of WWII. ▶ North on the Grand' Place : no. 16 is the 17th-18thC **Barral Mansion** *(visits by request).* ▶ Nearby, the 18thC **Town Hall,** formerly the governor's residence; former abbey church of St. Léger (11thC crypt, 13thC chapterhouse and cloister); in the abbey buildings, **Museum** of Regional Art and Archaeology, 19thC painting★, statuary *(10-12 & 2-5; closed Tue.).* ▶ Across the Aisne *(500 m E from place Alsace-Lorraine) :* ruined **abbey of St. Médard** within a school; 13thC chapterhouse, 11thC crypt, where the tombs of St. Médard and of Clovis's successors Clothaire and Sigisbert were found. ▶ S *(400 m NW of the Paris crossroads) :* 13th-14thC façade★ of the former **abbey of St. Jean-des-Vignes;** cloister, refectory, storehouse (13thC), 16th-18thC abbot's residence *(Mar.-Oct. daily ex Tue., 10-12 & 2-5 or 6; Nov.-Feb., Wed., Sat., Sun. only).*

▶ Nearby

▶ **Septmonts** *(7 km S on D1 then D95 left) :* ruins of mediaeval château. ▶ Near **Condé-sur-Aisne** *(13 km E) :* fort of Condé-Chivres-Val (1877; *8:30-7 pm*). □

The Soissons vase

A story related by Gregory of Tours, 6thC bishop and fore-runner of French historians, has survived as a parable illustrating the change from "Barbarism" to "Civilisation" that took place with the conversion of Clovis to Christianity. During the pillage that followed a battle at Soissons in 486, a Frankish soldier stole a vase belonging to the Bishop of Rheims. Commanded by Clovis to return the booty to its rightful owner, the soldier smashed the vase rather than comply with the order. Clovis's response was to stave in the head of the soldier. Whatever the relevance of the parable may be today, the victory at Soissons was an important event that is taken to mark the end of the Gallo-Roman era and the beginning of the Frankish state. Although Christian civilisation was a Roman importation, Clovis recognised it as the path of the future (his father was a Roman auxiliary in Gaul), and was formally baptised ten years later, thus conferring legitimate status and respectability upon his rule.

■ The THIERACHE Region★

▶ Round trip from Vervins *(75 km, half-day)*
AB1 *(see map 3)*

The peaceful countryside is divided by hedges and dotted with black and white cows, whose milk is used to make Maroilles cheese. Along the banks of the Brune or the Heureau, however, fortified churches with turrets and keeps often rise in the midst of the villages.

Until the 17thC, Thiérache was a frontier that suffered from frequent invasion and pillage. The churches served as refuges for both man and beast, equiped with wells and bread ovens in the buildings themselves. About 50 such buildings still exist from the 12th-15thC. Nine are included in this itinerary; others can be seen near Hirson (near Wimy) and NW of Vervins between Étréaupont and Guise (→ Vervins).

▶ Take the road to Hirson. ▶ **La Bouteille :** rectangular church★ built in sandstone by the Cistercians (ruined abbey of Foigny). ▶ **Plomion :** pink church (16thC) has a square keep with round towers; a chimney leads from the hall of the keep to the roof space, converted into a strongroom. Nearby, at **Jeantes :** the church of St. Martin (façade framed by solid square towers), modern paintings and stained glass by Charles Eyck (1962). ▶ **Dagny :** farm buildings in cob, latticework barns. ▶ **Brunehamel :** ruined 16thC château. ▶ **Parfondeval :** old houses around a brick church. ▶ **Montcornet :** 12th-13thC church with 16thC turrets on the transept and eastern end. ▶ **Vigneux :** church with keep and fortified apse. ▶ **Burelles :** keep replaces the bell-tower; the upper story of the fortified transept could shelter the entire village. ▶ **Prisces :** four-story square keep. ▶ **Gronard :** 16thC church with keep and two round towers; attractive square shaded by lime trees. □

3. Thiérache region

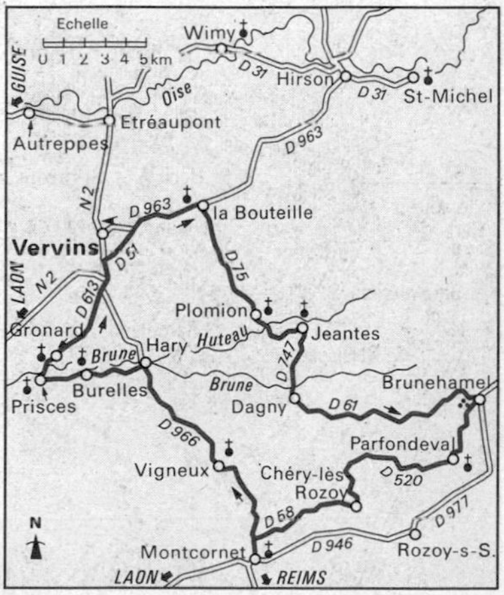

TROYES★★★

B4 / ® / pop. 64 769 (Aube)

Troyes has a rich architectural heritage from the Middle Ages to the Renaissance; mansions, cathedral, churches, and residential quarter are all in good condition. Until the 1970s, much of the half-timbering that gives the town its charm was hidden under plaster; a change in fashion fortunately has brought to light much of the original material.

▶ The **Saint-Jean quarter :** this pedestrian precinct is the centre of life in Troyes. Note : For security reasons all the churches in Troyes and the environs are closed except for the hours of service and the summer season; keys available from the SI, from 16 boulevard Carnot *(near the station)*, or from the caretakers. Guided tours available. ▶ The maze of restored streets and alleys (rues Champeaux, Paillot-de-Montabert, Charbonnet, des Chats) converge on Place Maréchal Foch (B2) and the **Town Hall** (17thC; B1-2). ▶ **Church of St. Urbain**★ (B1, rue Clemenceau) : a 13thC architectural feat whose walls seem no thicker than the stained glass★ (also 13thC), especially in the choir; numerous statues including 16thC Virgin with Grapes★. ▶ **Ste. Madeleine**★ (A1-2) : 12thC nave and transept, Renaissance choir and tower, Flamboyant Gothic choir screen★★ (early 16thC, 10 years in the making) with arches as delicate as lace. Statue of Ste. Marthe★★, a 15thC masterpiece by a master sculptor; in the apse, stained glass★ typical of Renaissance Troyes. ▶ On the other side of Dampierre quay, beyond the infirmary (B1), **Pharmacy-museum**★ *(daily, 10-12 & 2-6, closed Tue. and nat. hols.)*, the **cathedral**★★ (C1) : 4 centuries (1208-1638) of brilliant architectural achievement; 13th-14thC stained glass★ in the choir; 15th-16thC in the nave (including the "Mystical Pressing" 1625 by Linard Gontier, symbolically representing Christ as a grapevine); treasury. ▶ To the right of the Cathedral, **Museum of Modern Art**★★, inaugurated in 1982 in the former episcopal palace : the Lévy Collection of Fauvist paintings, including works by Marinot, La Fresnay, Soutine; sculpture by Degas, Maillol, Picasso, Rodin; African and Oceanic art.

Also... ▶ **St. Jean** (B2) : stained glass★ (Martyrdom of Ste. Agathe). ▶ **St. Pantaléon** (A2) : 16thC Troyes statuary. ▶ Opposite, **Vauluisan Museum**★ **:** mansion with interesting collection including statuary and costumes. **Maison de l'Outil** (B2, Maurois mansion★) : unique collection of woodworking tools maintained by the Compagnons du Devoir, a craft guild with origins in the Middle Ages. ▶ **Library** (Bibliothèque)★ : stained glass by Linard Gontier (life of Henri IV); **Fine Arts Museum** (same building, different entrance; B1) : archaeology, painting, natural history. □

▶ Nearby

▶ To the N and W *(via A1)*. Church of **St. Martin-ès-Vignes** *(1 km N)* : 16th-17thC stained glass★★, **Ste. Savine** *(1.5 km W)* : paintings on wood panels, **Church of St. André-les-Vergers** *(3 km SSW)* : doorway, 16thC altarpiece. ▶ Church★ of **Pont Sainte-Marie** ® *(3 km NE)* : stained glass★. ▶ Barberey-Saint-Sulpice *(7 km NW)* : Louis XIII château *(exterior visits Aug.-15 Sep., 10-12 & 2-6)*. ▶ **Feuges** *(12 km N)* : Christ★ attributed to the Master of Sainte-Marthe (→ Troyes). ▶ **Villemaur-sur-Vanne** *(27 km W)* : bell-tower; carved wood choir-screen★, stalls. ▶ **Bouilly** *(15 km S on N77)* : altarpiece★ (16thC Troyes), Piétà, statue of Ste. Marguerite. ▶ **Isle-Aumont :** Carolingian choir, Romanesque choir ("nailheads" of oriental origin around the outside window) and Gothic choir *(visits Sun. at 3pm)*. ▶ **Rumilly-lès-Vaudes :** church★ (painted altarpiece and

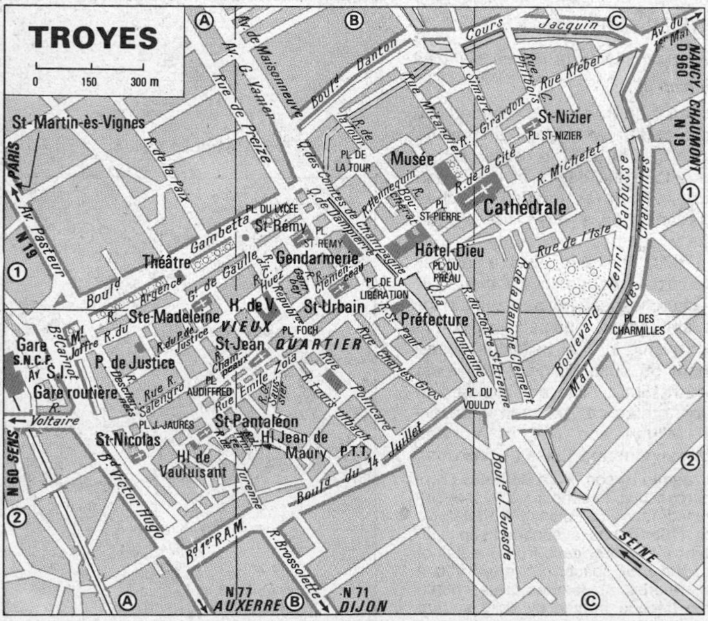

The golden age of Troyes

One-third of all the stained glass in France is in and around Troyes. Most of it dates from the 16thC and early 17thC. Works of art in the churches of Troyes, Châlons and Sens, among others, display the range of religious and secular images that served as the main medium of instruction in the Middle Ages. Brilliant coloured images on a smaller scale can also be seen in village churches, sometimes arranged to form a sequence of geometric panels. Some of the more grisly martyrdoms might not qualify for general viewing today.

stained glass); 16thC Tourelles manor house★ with wooden galleries, now the town hall *(groups only).* □

■ VERVINS

A1 / ® / pop. 2 981 (Aisne)

▶ **Church of Notre-Dame** (13th-14thC) : stone and brick gatetower; inside, painting by Jouvenet, Christ in the House of Simon (1699). ▶ **Town Hall** (17thC). ▶ **Coigny Mansion** (16thC) : where Philip II of Spain and Henri IV signed a treaty to end hostilities in 1598.

▶ Nearby

▶ **Hirson** *(18 km NE) :* an important railway junction; 4 km E, **Benedictine abbey of St. Michel** *(visits by request)* founded 944, rebuilt in 1715 in brick and stone (early Gothic choir, transept with Renaissance triple nave). The valley of the Gland is 30 km^2 of forest stretching to the Belgian frontier. **Wimy** *(8 km W from Hirson) :* fortified church with well, chimney and bread oven. Between Vervins and Guise to the W, follow the Maubeuge road 8 km to Étréaupont. On the left, the Oise valley : fortified churches at **Autreppes, Saint-Algis, Englancourt, Marly-Gaumont** (turrets, façade with loopholes), **Malzy, Beaurain.** ▶ **Guise :** former fief of the powerful Guise family (château★ incorporating the mediaeval citadel, under restoration; *9-12 & 2-5:30, 6 or 7; closed 25 Dec.*). **Vadencourt** *(7 km NW) :* collection of 2 500 traditional tools and implements at the Atelier du Bois (woodworking shop; *Sat. and Sun.*). □

■ VILLERS-COTTERETS★

A2 / ® / pop. 8 402 (Aisne)

Museum, rue Desmoutiers *(pm closed Tue.; Sun. 9-12 & 2-5).* Château *(open daily)* completed in 1535 for François I by Philibert Delorme, 17thC park designed by Le Nôtre (→ Versailles), galleried façade, staircase. At 46 Rue Alexandre Dumas, birthplace of the writer Alexandre Dumas the elder (1803-1870). □

▶ Nearby

▶ **Longpont** *(11 km NE) :* ruins of an abbey consecrated in 1227 in the presence of St. Louis (Louis IX); the 13thC storehouse was turned into a château, rebuilt in the 18thC and restored after 1918 *(10-12 & 2:30-7 closed Thu., Mar.-Oct.; Sat., Sun. and hols., Nov.-Feb.);* 15thC painted panels in parish church, remains of cloister; **Vierzy** *(8 km farther) :* ferme (farm) du Vieux Château (15thC keep, *Jul.-Sep., Sun. pm)* ▶ **Retz Forest** (13 km^2) : mostly beech with oak and hornbeam, red and roe deer, boar, pheasants; the northern part is the most attractive. Marked trails to **Montgobert** (woodworking museum in the château; *Apr.-Oct. 10-12 & 2-6 closed Tue., Sun. 3-7*). ▶ **Soucy :** fortified church. ▶ **Saint-Pierre-Aigle.** ▶ **Cœuvres :** château, salt barns, 12th-15thC church. **La Ferté-Milon** *(10 km S) :* birthplace of the author Jean Racine (1629-1699), ruins of 14thC fortress; church of St. Nicolas with fine Renaissance choir. □

■ VITRY-LE-FRANÇOIS

B3 / ® / pop. 18 290 (Marne)

An important crossroads town, junction of the Marne-Rhine and Marne-Saône canals, rebuilt after WWII on the ground plan used for its creation under François I.

▶ 17th-18thC cathedral with neo-classical interior.

▶ Nearby

▶ 10 km N on the Châlons road and right : **Saint-Amand-sur-Fion :** 12th-13thC church with porch, choir★. Numerous timber-framed farmhouses in the village and on the roads (D60 and D14) to Vitry. □

■ VOUZIERS

B2 / pop. 5 214 (Ardennes)

Birthplace of the historian Hippolyte Taine (1828-1893); burial place of the aviator Roland Garros (1886-1915) who was the first to fly the Mediterranean.

▶ **Church of St. Maurille :** 16thC, with Renaissance triple doorway★.

▶ Nearby

▶ **Grandpré** *(17 km SE) :* 17thC doorway of former château. **Saint-Juvin** *(5 km farther) :* 17thC fortified church. ▶ **Buzancy** *(22 km E on D947) :* 13th-15thC church in Champenois style; Château de la Cour, former residence of the dukes of Lorraine. ▶ **Vision de Belval park** *(30 km NE on D947 then 16 km on D6) :* 2 500 acres of forest; animals living wild *(Apr.-15 Nov. 9 or 10-8 or 9 pm).* □

■ WASSY

C3 / pop. 3 596 (Haute-Marne)

On Sunday 1 March 1562 in a barn near the church, the troops of François de Guise massacred 250 Protestants. This "Wassy massacre" began 35 years of internecine religious warfare throughout France.

▶ 17thC **Town Hall** with astronomical clock.

▶ Nearby

▶ Drive through the valley of the Blaise *(38 km)* to **Juzennecourt.** Château de **Cirey-sur-Blaise** *(private)* with mediaeval keep. □

Architecture

The scarcity of suitable building stone, and the plentiful supply of timber and clay, encouraged timber and cob construction for both rural and urban buildings. With slight regional variations, the technique is as follows : a shallow foundation of crushed brick or limestone supports the framework of oak uprights and cross-beams braced by struts. The spaces between the studs are filled with cob, a malleable mixture of clay, earth and straw spread on small planks of wood. The walls exposed to rain are protected by overlapping weatherboards of split oak or wooden shingles. This type of building may be seen in Troyes, Châlon and Langres.

Wooden stud construction, Aube region

Some of the churches built in this way are still in existence (e.g., Lentilles and Nuisement, → Lake Der-Chantecoq). This form of construction, like the raw earth buildings of the Dauphiné region, can survive for a long time provided the foundations and roof are watertight. The roof is usually finished with flat or channelled tiles and must overhang sufficiently to keep rain off the walls. Timber, sometimes roofed with tiles, was widely used for covered markets (→ Brienne, Fère-en-Tardenois, Chaource), church porches (Bar-sur-Aube) and bell-towers (Villemaur-sur-Vanne → Troyes). ● Chalk, in the form of tufa covered with plaster or planks under

Wooden house, Ardennes

a wide overhang, or cut into building blocks and used with brick door and window frames, is found in the north and west of "dry Champagne". ● To the south, in "wet Champagne" and Brie, houses are frequently built of fieldstone or a mixture of yellow millstone grit and grey pebbles under a projecting roof with a long rear slope. Although farm buildings in Champagne are usually free standing, the fieldstone or yellow sandstone buildings in the Ardennes are placed in a single block so that the warmth of the stables helps to heat the house.

Southern ("wet") Champagne

Brief regional history

BC

More than 1 000 sites dating from between 3000 and 4000 BC have been excavated in the region, and 80 megaliths have been uncovered, 69 of them in the Aube sector. ● Even then, Champagne was a cross-roads and scene of territorial dispute between Danubians and Celts.

Roman Era The arrival of Julius Caesar and the Roman occupation brought peace and prosperity. Invading **Franks** and **Teutons** remained to settle in an uneasy coexistence. When, however, in 451 **Attila the Hun** threatened the region, Visigoths, Franks and Romans were obliged to join forces to defeat Attila at the battle known as the "Champs (fields) Catalauniques" 20 km north of present-day Troyes.

3rd-10thC

The encroachment of Christianity received official sanction when **Clovis,** King of the Franks, was baptised at Rheims in 496. ● At Clovis's death, the kingdom was divided among his three sons, then partitioned further among their heirs. The empire disintegrated after Charlemagne's death in 814, and Champagne became a buffer region, suffering invasions from both east and west, with the **Normans** in 883, and the **Hungarians** in 926 and 954.

10th-13thC The advantages of Champagne's geographical position came to the fore as trading increased during the Middle Ages. The success of the regular Champagne Fairs consolidated the value of the region as a hub of European commerce.

13th-17thC

The Gothic cathedrals built at Troyes, Laon and Rheims were an inspiration to 13thC Christendom. In the 14thC Jean Sans Peur (the Fearless), Duke of Burgundy, decided to annex Champagne to forge a link between his territories in Flanders and Burgundy. To enhance his military strength, he formed an alliance with the English who, in turn, wished to press their claim to the throne of France. The resulting conflict put a stop to prosperity. Rallied around the banner of Joan of Arc, the French managed to expel the English in 1429 and Charles VII was crowned King of France at Rheims. ● The region again flourished until the 16thC, when the Holy Roman Emperor Charles V invaded eastern France. Throughout the latter half of the 16thC, the country was torn apart by the Wars of Religion, which pitted Catholic against Protestant. The Edict of Nantes (1598), which guaranteed freedom of religion to Protestants, resolved the internal conflict, but France was at war with Spain from 1635 until 1643, and Champagne did not see true peace until 1652. ● The coronation of Louis XIV at Rheims in 1654 marked the return of Champagne to French rule.

20thC From the very beginning of WWI, the Front was fixed in Champagne, between the Chemin des Dames and Saint-Mihiel. Despite a determined attack, Germany failed to capture Verdun in 1916, and was forced to retreat. In 1918, Germany once more took the Chemin des Dames and thrust toward Rheims and the Marne, where the advance was repulsed in a horrific battle. In September 1918, when the Allied army freed the Ardennes, the Ardennes-Champagne region emerged devastated by conflict. ● During WWII, the French Front was pushed back to Sedan on 13 May 1940, and Champagne was occupied for 4 years. The invasion caused heavy damage (Rethel, Vitry-le-François, Châlons, Vouziers), and the bombings during and after the Allied landing in 1944 devastated the region.

Practical information

The region

Information : Champagne-Ardennes : *Comité Régional du Tourisme Champagne-Ardenne* (C.R.T.), 2 *bis,* bd Vaubecourt, 51100 Châlons-sur-Marne, ☎ 26.68.37.52. **Aisne :** *Comité Départemental de Tourisme* (C.D.T.) : 1, rue Saint-Martin, 02000 Laon, ☎ 23.23.24.53. **Ardennes** (C.D.T.) : Résidence Arduinna, 8, av. Georges-Corneau, 08000 Charleville-Mézières, ☎ 24.56.06.08. **Aube** (C.D.T.) : Hôtel du Département, 10026 Troyes, ☎ 25.73.48.01. **Marne** (C.D.T.) : 2 *bis,* bd Vaubécourt, 51100 Châlons-sur-Marne, ☎ 26.68.37.52. **Haute-Marne** (C.D.T.) : Hôtel de la Préfecture, 52000 Chaumont, ☎ 25.03.65.00. *Direction Régionale du Temps Libre, Jeunesse et Sports,* 20, rue Simon, 51100 Reims, ☎ 26.05.10.83. *Dir. Rég. des Affaires culturelles,* 5, rue Jéricho, 51022 Châlons-sur-Marne Cedex, ☎ 26.68.29.60.

Bookings : *Loisirs-Accueil* **Ardennes** (enrolments for instruction courses, leisure centres) : 18, av. Georges-Corneau, 08000 Charleville-Mézières, ☎ 24.56.00.63. Tx 840016. Chamco (Tourism). **Marne :** Office de Tourisme de Reims, 3, bd Lundy, 51100 Reims, ☎ 26.88.39.89. Tx 830631.

Maps : *Michelin* « Champagne-Ardennes » n°s 241, 56 and 53, all 1/200 000. *I.G.N.* n°s 103 and 104 at 1/250 000.

S.O.S. : Aisne : SAMU (emergency medical service), ☎ 23.20.45.97 and 17. **Aube :** SAMU, ☎ 15. **Ardennes :** ☎ 24.57.21.21. **Marne :** SAMU, ☎ 17 and 26.06.07.08. **Haute-Marne :** SAMU, ☎ 17. Poisoning Emergency Centre : Paris, ☎ 12.05.63.29. Lille, ☎ 20.54.55.56. Reims, ☎ 26.06.07.08.

Weather forecast : Aisne : ☎ 23.68.84.33. **Aube :** ☎ 25.74.65.00. **Ardennes :** ☎ 24.88.74.91. **Marne :** ☎ 26.88.63.63. **Haute-Marne :** ☎ 25.05.21.12.

Farmhouse gîtes and chambres d'hôtes : enq at the Relais Départementaux. **Ardennes :** Chambre d'Agriculture, 1, av. du Petit-Bois, 08000 Charleville-Mézières, ☎ 24.33.38.66. **Aube :** Chambre d'Agriculture, 2 *bis,* rue Jeanne-d'Arc, 10000 Troyes, ☎ 26.73.25.36. **Marne :** Complexe Agricole du Mt-Saint-Bernard, rte de Suippes, B.P. 1505, 51002 Châlons-sur-Marne. **Haute-Marne :** Hôtel du Conseil Général, 52011 Chaumont Cedex, ☎ 25.03.65.00. **Aisne :** B.P. 116, 02006 Laon.

Farmhouse-inns : Haute-Marne : *Association Pour le Développement Rural,* 26, av. 109e-R.I., 52011 Chaumont, ☎ 25.03.13.35.

Camping : Complete list in pamphlet published by the *Comité Régional de Tourisme.*

Festivals and events : May : *Joan of Arc Festival* in Rheims. **Jun :** *Popular Festival* in Troyes. *International Folk Festival* in Châlons-sur-Marne ; *Jazz Festival* in Rheims. **End Sep** (every 3 years) : *World Marionette Festival* in Charleville-Mézières. **Dec :** *Shepherds' Christmas Festival* in Braux-Sainte-Cohière (Marne).

Markets and rural events : *andouillette market (chitterling sausage)* in Signy-l'Abbaye (Ardennes). Jun : *cheese market* in Rocroi. 3rd weekend in **Sep :** *Sauerkraut days* in Brienne-le-Château (Aube). Oct : (every 2 years) : *cheese market* in Chaource (Aube).

Scenic railway : *« petit train touristique du Vermandois » ;* departure from Saint-Quentin (02100), Saint-Quentin S.I., hôtel de ville, ☎ 23.67.05.00.

National and nature parks : *Parc Régional de la Montagne de Reims :* Maison du Parc, 51160 Pourcy, ☎ 26.59.44.44. *Parc Régional de la Forêt d'Orient* (*Orient Forest ;* including a 5 500-acre lake : fishing, sailing, bathing) : Maison du Parc, 10220 Piney, ☎ 25.41.35.57 and 41.34.90.

Rambling and hiking : Several GRs cross Champagne-Ardennes : G.R. 2 (148 km traversing the Othe region and the length of the Seine Valley) ; G.R. 24 (141 km circuit, starting from Bar-sur-Seine, and crossing the Parc Régional de la Forêt d'Orient) ; G.R. 12, part of the European Walkway n° 3 from the Atlantic to Bohemia ; G.R. 14 (vineyards and forests of Reims Mountain). The G.R. 78 forms a large circuit around Langres, on the plateau. Addresses of associations at the Comités Départementaux de Tourisme (see Information). Topoguides for sale at the *Maison des Sociétés Sportives,* 2, bd Carnot, 10000 Troyes.

Riding holidays : Extensive selection of bridle-paths (weekend, 4-5 days), rallies, instruction courses, stays at riding centres. Enq at the *Association Champagne-Ardenne de Tourisme Équestre,* Crédit Agricole, 08460 Signy l'Abbaye, ☎ 24.35.80.03, and bookings at *Loisirs-Accueil.* For the **Aisne** region : *Comité Départemental du Tourisme.*

Cycling holidays : circuits with specific themes of interest over Reims Mountain (see Natural Parks). Cycling tours and stays around the Der-Chantecoq Lake (*Maison du Lac,* Giffaumont-Champaubert, 51920 Saint-Rémy-en-Bouzemont, ☎ 26.41.62.80 and 87. Weekends in the Langres region (Office du Tourisme, pl. Bel'Air, 52200 Langres, ☎ 25.85.03.32). For further information : *Fédération Française de Cyclotourisme, Ligue Champagne-Ardennes,* 3, rue Vieille-Rome, 10000 Troyes, ☎ 25.43.19.55. Bicycle hire : see C.D.T.

River and canal cruises : from Berry-au-Bac (20 km N of Reims) to Château-Thierry and beyond, by house-boat : *Champagne-Navigation,* rte Nationale, 02190 Berry-au-Bac, ☎ 23.79.95.01, and *Navigation-Champagne-Ardennes,* rue Pasteur, 08130 Attigny, ☎ 24.31.26.74. By canal, traversing the **Haute-Marne,** leaving from Saint-Dizier : *Double Écluse,* port de plaisance (pleasure-boat port), rue Alfred-de-Musset, 52100 Saint-Dizier, ☎ 25.06.10.56.

Golf : two 18-hole courses : château de la Cordelière, 10210 Chaource, ☎ 25.46.11.05, and Rheims in Champagne, château des Dames de France, Gueux, 51140 Jonchery-sur-Vesle, ☎ 26.48.60.40.

Tennis : *Ligue Régionale,* pdt M. Pierre Lorin, 28, av. Eugène-Franquin, 08200 Sedan.

Aquatic sports : sailing and bathing in the Bairon and Vieilles-Forges lakes (Ardennes), the Forêt d'Orient Lake (Aube), nautical sports centres in Tréou-sur-Marne and Monampteuil (Aisne). Motorboating on the Der-Chantecoq Lake (Marne), the four lakes around Langres (Haute-Marne) and in Villeneuve-Saint-Germain (Aisne). Enq : Dir. Rég. du Temps Libre, Jeunesse et Sports (see Information).

Canoeing : *Ligue Champagne-Ardennes de la Féd. Francaise de Canoë-kayak,* 81, rue du Gal-Leclerc, Fagnières, 51000 Châlons-sur-Marne. **Aisne :** *Comité Départemental de Canoë-kayak,* rte de Lesquielles, Vadencourt, 02120 Guise, ☎ 23.61.07.35.

Climbing : principal sites in the Ardennes Mountains, at the spot known as Roc-la-Tour, near Monthermé. In the **Marne** region : Vertus and Grauves cliffs, not far from Épernay. Enq : *Dir. Rég. du Temps Libre, Jeunesse et Sports* (see Information).

Flying, gliding and ballooning : light aircraft, U.L.M., enq at the Charleville-Mézières aerodrome, 08540 Tournes, ☎ 24.33.14.89, and *Troyes Gliding Centre,* B.P. 4074, 10013 Troyes Cedex, ☎ 25.43.39.13. Ballooning : *Club Aérostatique de Champagne,* 42, rue Gambetta, 51100 Reims, ☎ 26.47.81.24. Hang-gliding : four established sites : near Revin (Ardennes), Joigny-sur-Meuse **(Ardennes)** and Bar-sur-Aube (Aube). Information : *Féd. Francaise de Vol Libre,* 73220 Aiguebelle, and *Directions Dép. de la Jeunesse et des Sports* : **Ardennes,** 16, rue Porte-de-Bourgogne, 08000 Charleville-Mézières, ☎ 24.57.22.11 ; **Aube,** Ancien Évêché, 10042 Troyes Cedex, ☎ 25.43.10.65. Parachuting : *Centre de Parachutisme de la Marne,* B.P. 104, 51064 Reims Cedex, ☎ 26.47.88.39.

Hunting and shooting : reserve at *Loisirs-Accueil* in **Ardennes,** *Féd. Dép. des Chasseurs :* **Aisne :** 133, rue Crécy, 02000 Laon, ☎ 23.23.30.89. **Ardennes :** 16, rue Aubilly, 08000 Charleville-Mézières, ☎ 24.56.07.35. **Aube :** 4, rue Preize, 10000 Troyes, ☎ 25.43.82.79. **Marne :** 41, rue Pierre-Bayen, 51000 Châlons-sur-Marne, ☎ 26.65.17.85. **Haute-Marne :** 24, rue Ampère, 52000 Chaumont, ☎ 25.32.07.25.

Fishing : enq at the *Féd. Dép. des Associations de Pêche et de Pisciculture.* **Ardennes :** 52, av. d'Arches, 08000 Charleville-Mézières, ☎ 24.54.34.14. **Aube :** 139, rue Blanqui, 10000 Troyes. **Marne :** 74, rue de Witry, 51250 Sermaize-les-Bains, ☎ 26.41.21.90. **Haute-Marne :** 8, rue de la Convention, 52000 Chaumont, ☎ 25.03.10.78.

Towns

BAR-SUR-AUBE

Chaumont 42, Troyes 52, Paris 217
B4 ⊠ 10200

ℹ hôtel de ville, ☎ 25.27.04.21.

SNCF ☎ 25.27.09.92.

Hotel :
★★***Pomme d'Or,*** 79, fg de Belfort, ☎ 25.27.09.93. Visa. 30 rm Ⓟ closed 1 Dec-6 Jan, 80. Rest. ♿ 85.

⛺ ★★*La Gravière* (43 pl.), ☎ 25.27.12.94.

BAR-SUR-SEINE

Troyes 33, Dijon 120, Paris 200
B4 ⊠ 10110

ℹ mairie, ☎ 25.38.80.35.

Hotel :
★***Barsequanais,*** 6, av. Gal-Leclerc, ☎ 25.29.82.75. 24 rm Ⓟ closed 25 Dec-25 Jan, Sun eve and Mon noon, 180. Rest. ♦ ♿ closed Sun eve and Mon noon, 80-130.

⛺ ★★*La Motte Noire* (65 pl.), ☎ 25.38.86.38.

BERRY-AU-BAC

Rheims 20, Laon 27, Paris 162
A2 ⊠ 02190 Guignicourt

Restaurant :
● ♦♦ ***Cote 108,*** rte de Laon, ☎ 23.79.95.04. AE, DC, Visa Ⓟ closed Sun eve and Mon, 20 Dec-1 Feb. The open country and S. Gourville's excellent cuisine. Spec : *émincé de Bresse aux pleurotes,* 100-280.

BOURBONNE-LES-BAINS

Langres 43, Dijon 111, Paris 312
C4 ⊠ 52400

1 Mar-30 Nov, ☎ 25.90.07.20.

ℹ pl. des Bains, ☎ 25.90.01.71.

SNCF ☎ 25.03.50.50.

Hotels :
★★***Hérard*** (L.F.), 29, Grand-Rue, ☎ 25.90.13.33. AE, DC, Euro, Visa. 43 rm Ⓟ ♿ 160. Rest. ♦ 60-100.
★★***Lauriers-Roses,*** pl. des Bains, ☎ 25.90.00.97. 80 rm ♿ closed 1 Nov-1 Apr, 145. Rest. ♦ 45-85.

⛺ ★★★***Le Montmorency*** (60 pl.), ☎ 25.90.08.64.

BRIENNE-LE-CHÂTEAU

Troyes 40, Bar-le-Duc 70, Paris 198
B4 ⊠ 10500

SNCF ☎ 25.77.80.34.

Hotels :
★***La Croix Blanche,*** 7, av. Pasteur, ☎ 25.92.80.27. DC, Visa. 12 rm Ⓟ closed 17 Dec-17 Jan, 100. Rest. ♦ ♿ closed Sun eve and Mon, 80-130.
★***Voyageurs,*** 30, av. Pasteur, ☎ 25.92.83.61. Visa. 14 rm Ⓟ ♿ 125. Rest. ♦ 40-80.

CHÂLONS-SUR-MARNE

Rheims 45, Troyes 77, Paris 187
B3 ⊠ 51000

ℹ 3, quai des Arts (B1), ☎ 26.65.17.89.

SNCF (A2), ☎ 26.65.18.35.

Car-hire : *Budget,* train + auto, at the station, ☎ 26.65.18.35.

Hotels :
★★★***Angleterre,*** 19, pl Mgr-Tissier (B1), ☎ 26.68.21.51. DC, Euro, Visa. 18 rm Ⓟ 30 Jun-15 Jul, 20 Dec-7 Jan and Sun eve, 260. Rest. ♦♦ closed Sun, 130-260.
★★***Pasteur,*** 46, rue Pasteur (C1), ☎ 26.68.10.00. Visa. 28 rm Ⓟ ♿ 125.
★★***Pot d'Étain,*** 18, pl. de la République (B2), ☎ 26.68.09.09. 25 rm Ⓟ closed 20 Dec-19 Jan, 200.

Épine, 8 km NE, on the N3 :
★★★***Aux Armes de Champagne,***

☎ 26.68.10.43. 38 rm Ⓟ ♨ ✈ ♿ 320, closed 2 Jan-15 Feb. Rest. ● ♦♦ Luxury and comfort enhance the good Champenoise cuisine. Spec : *escargots au champagne, pigeon au Bouzy ;* selected champagnes, 80-270.

Youth hostel : rue Kellermann, ☎ 26.68.13.56 (1 Jul-15 Sep).

⛺ ★★★★*Municipal* (96 pl.), ☎ 26.68.38.00.

Restaurant :
♦ ***Les Ardennes,*** 34, pl. de la République (B2), ☎ 26.68.21.42. Euro, Visa, closed Sun eve, Mon and 28 Jul-26 Aug, 65-145.

CHARLEVILLE-MÉZIÈRES

Rheims 83, Saint-Quentin 119, Paris 225
B1 ⊠ 08000

ℹ 2, rue Mautove, ☎ 24.33.00.17.

SNCF ☎ 24.33.50.50., 24.33.01.08.

Car-hire : *Budget,* train + auto, at the station, ☎ 24.33.91.42.

Hotels :
★★★***Relais du Square*** (L.F.), 3, pl. de la Gare, ☎ 24.33.38.76. Tx 841196. AE, DC, Euro, Visa. 49 rm Ⓟ ♿ Modernised. Good value, 210.
★★***Paris,*** 24, av. Corneau, ☎ 24.33.34.38. 29 rm ✈ ♿ closed 21 Dec-7 Jan, 165.

Youth hostel : 3, rue de Tambours, ☎ 24.57.44.36.

⛺ ★★★*Mont Olympe* (180 pl.), ☎ 24.33.23.60.

Restaurant :
♦♦ ***La Cigogne,*** 40, rue Dubois-Crancé, ☎ 24.33.25.39. Visa. closed Sun eve and Mon, 31 Jul-13 Aug. Spec : *saumon cru aux citrons verts, pâté de truite en brioche,* 60-145.

Recommended : shops in the rue de la République (mall) and pl. Ducale (specialities : game, *andouillettes, boudin blanc et noir*).

CHÂTEAU-THIERRY

Rheims 58, Troyes 110, Paris 96
A2-3 ⊠ 02400

ℹ pl. de l'Hôtel-de-Ville, ☎ 23.52.10.79.

SNCF ☎ 23.83.11.27.

Car-hire : *Budget,* train + auto, at the station, ☎ 23.83.14.08.

Hotel :
★★***Ile de France*** (Inter-Hotel), 2 km on the Soissons road, ☎ 23.69.10.12. Tx 150666. AE, DC, Euro, Visa. 56 rm Ⓟ ♨ closed 23 Dec-31 Jan, 240. Rest. ♦ ♿ 50-150.

⛺ ★★★*Municipal* (20 pl.), ☎ 23.83.25.58.

CHAUMONT

Troyes 94, Dijon 103, Paris 259
C4 ⊠ 52000

ℹ bd Thiers, ☎ 25.03.04.74.

SNCF ☎ 25.03.50.50., 25.03.33.91.

Car-hire : *Budget,* train + auto, at the station, ☎ 25.03.26.10.

Hotels :
★★★***Terminus Reine*** (Mapotel), pl. du Gal-de-Gaulle, ☎ 25.03.66.66. Tx 840920. AE, DC, Euro. 63 rm Ⓟ ♿ 265. A good hotel. Rest. ♦ closed Sun eve from 1 Nov-Easter, 50-120.
★★***Le Grand Val*** (Inter-Hotel), rte de Langres, ☎ 25.03.90.35. AE, DC, Euro, Visa. 64 rm Ⓟ ♿ closed 1 Nov-1 Mar and Sun eve, 180. Rest. ♦ 40-90.
★★***L'Étoile d'Or*** (L.F.), rte de Langres, ☎ 25.03.02.23. Euro, Visa. 15 rm Ⓟ ♿ closed 1 Oct-2 Nov, Sun eve and Mon noon, 180. Rest. ♦ 50-125.

Youth hostel : rue Decres.

⛺ ★★*Municipal* (100 pl.), ☎ 25.32.11.98.

Restaurant :
♦♦ ***La Clé des Champs,*** 33, fg de Buxereilles, ☎ 25.03.48.72 Ⓟ ♿ closed Sun eve and Mon, 80-130.

COLOMBEY-LES-DEUX-ÉGLISES

Chaumont 27, Troyes 68, Paris 232
C4 ⊠ 52330

Hotel :
★★★***Les Dhuits*** (Mapotel), ☎ 25.01.50.10. Tx 840920. AE, DC, Euro. 30 rm Ⓟ ♨ closed 20 Dec-10 Jan, 185. Rest. ♦ ♿ 45-100.

DORMANS

Rheims 38, Châlons-sur-Marne 58, Paris 119
A2 ⊠ 51700

ℹ mairie, ☎ 25.50.21.45.

SNCF ☎ 25.50.21.95.

Hotel :
★***Demoncy*** (L.F.), 10, rue de Châlons, ☎ 25.58.20.86. 10 rm Ⓟ ♨ ✈ closed 24 Jan-1 Mar, 180. Rest. ♦ ♿ closed Mon eve, Tue, 120-210.

⛺ ★★*Essi Plage* (120 pl.), ☎ 25.50.21.45.

ÉPERNAY

Rheims 27, Troyes 111, Paris 143
B2-3 ⊠ 51200

ℹ pl. Mendès-France, ☎ 26.55.33.00.

SNCF ☎ 26.51.39.07.

Car-hire : *Budget,* train + auto, at the station, ☎ 26.51.22.64.

Hotels :
★★★***Berceaux,*** 13, rue des Berceaux, ☎ 26.55.28.84. 25 rm, 220. Rest. ● ♦♦ closed Sun eve. Good classic cooking. Spec : *terrine de ris de veau, tournedos en croûte,* famous champagnes, 115-210.
★★★***Champagne,*** 30, rue Eugène-Mercier, ☎ 26.51.30.22. Tx 830225. AE, Visa. 32 rm Ⓟ ♿ 230.

Champillon-Bellevue, 6 km N on the N51 :
★★★***Royal Champagne*** (Relais et Châteaux), ☎ 26.51.11.51, Tx 830111. AE, DC, Euro, Visa. 16 rm Ⓟ ♨ ♿ 400. Beautiful rooms (bungalows). Rest. ● ♦♦♦ Moët et Chandon's gastronomic stop ; beautiful view over the Champagne country. Spec : *turbot grillé au beurre de corail, poulet au champagne,* 220-310.

Vinay, 7 km S on the N51 :
★★★***Briquetterie,*** 4, rte de Sézanne, ☎ 26.54.11.22. Tx 842007. AE, DC, Euro, Visa. 42 rm Ⓟ ♨ ♿ closed 1-15 Jan, 340. Rest. ♦♦ A gastronomic stop in a charming hostelry, 150-250.

Montmort, ⊠ 51270, 18 km SW on the D51 :
★***Cheval Blanc,*** ☎ 26.59.10.03. 12 rm Ⓟ ♿ closed 15 Feb-15 Mar and Fri, 130. Rest. ● ♦ Pleasant meals in a small village. Spec : *coq au vin,* 60-145.

⛺ ★★★*Municipal* (100 pl.), ☎ 26.55.32.14.

Restaurants :
● ♦♦ ***La Terrasse,*** 5 et 7, quai de la Marne, ☎ 26.55.26.05. Euro, Visa. ♿ closed Tue eve, Wed, 1-15 Feb, 15-31 Jul. Quality fare in an

agreeable setting. Spec : *foie gras de canard,* 50-130.

● ♦ ***Jean Burin,*** 8, pl. Mendès-France, ☎ 26.51.66.60. ♿ closed Sun. Formerly a Parisian, J. Burin has adapted well to the Champagne country, 120-210.

Recommended : *Caves Dom Pérignon-Moët et Chandon (champagne cellars),* 18, av. de Champagne. Visit from 9:30-12 & 2-5:30 ; Sat, 9:30-12 & 2-5:30 ; closed sun & 2-4. *Champagne Avenue,* 15, pl. de la République, B.P. 117, ☎ 26.55.27.39 : regional products shop, champagne tasting bar and panoramic restaurant (Champenois menu).

La FÈRE

Saint-Quentin 23, Rheims 74, Paris 135
A1 ✉ 02800

SNCF ☎ 23.23.23.35.

Hotels :

★★***Relais de Champagne,*** 81, rue de la République, ☎ 23.56.21.39. 24 rm Ⓟ 180. Rest. is recommended ♦♦ closed Sun eve, Mon, Jan and Feb. Spec : *charolais aux girolles,* 220-310.

Vendeuil, 7 km on the N44 :

★★***Auberge de Vendeuil*** (L.F., Relais du Silence), ☎ 23.66.85.22. AE, DC, Visa. 22 rm Ⓟ ♿ 235. Rest. ♦♦ Warm, family atmosphere. Spec : *fricassée de langoustines et St-Jacques au citron vert, papillote de saumon rose à l'ail confit,* 80-200.

FÈRE-EN-TARDENOIS

Château-Thierry 26, Rheims 45, Paris 110
A2 ✉ 02130

SNCF ☎ 23.82.24.50.

Hotel :

★★★★***Hostellerie du Château*** (Gérard Blot) [Relais et Châteaux], ☎ 23.82.21.13. 13 rm and 7 apart. Ⓟ ♿ closed 2 Jan-28 Feb. Attractive residence, close to château and its park, 680. Rest. ● ♦♦♦♦ Gérard Blot welcomes you into his superb establishment, while the talented Patrick Michelon works in the kitchen for your greatest pleasure. Spec : *foie gras chaud aux bigorneaux, brésoles de turbot au foie gras et langoustines,* 220-330.

GIVET

Charleville 55, Saint-Quentin 143, Paris 275
B1 ✉ 08600

ℹ quai Fort-de-Rome, ☎ 24.55.03.54.

SNCF ☎ 24.55.06.04.

Youth hostel : château Mon Bijou, rte des Chaumières, ☎ 24.55.10.60.

Restaurant :

♦ ***Maison Baudouin,*** 2, pl. du 148ᵉ R.I., ☎ 24.55.00.70. AE, Visa ♿ closed Mon, Tue, Wed eve, 19 Aug-8 Sep and Feb school hols. Former 16thC post-house. Good small restaurant, 500 m from the border, 45-160.

JOINVILLE

Chaumont 43, Troyes 93, Paris 243
C3 ✉ 52300

ℹ mairie, ☎ 25.96.13.01.

SNCF ☎ 25.96.14.77.

Hotel :

★★***Poste*** (France-Accueil), pl. de la Grève, ☎ 25.96.12.63. AE, DC, Euro, Visa. 11 rm Ⓟ closed 10 Jan-10 Feb and Thu low season, 130. Rest. ♦ Enjoyable fare ; good value for money. Spec : *poussin aux morilles,* 50-120.

⛺ ★*Petit Bois* (100 pl.), ☎ 25.96.06.64.

LANGRES

Chaumont 35, Dijon 68, Paris 294
C4 ✉ 52200

ℹ pl. Bel'Air, ☎ 25.85.03.32.

SNCF ☎ 25.85.05.21.

Hotels :

★★***Europe*** (L.F.), 23-25, rue Diderot, ☎ 25.85.10.88. AE, DC, Euro, Visa. 28 rm Ⓟ closed 21 Apr-5 May, 28 Sep-20 Oct, Sun eve and Mon noon. Beautiful 17thC house, 170. Rest. ♦ Spec : *truite soufflée au bourgogne blanc,* 50-150.

★★***Cheval Blanc,*** 4, rue de l'Estres, ☎ 25.85.07.00. Euro, Visa. 23 rm Ⓟ closed 2-31 Jan and Wed. Set in a former abbey, 130. Rest. ♦ Spec : *pavé de lotte et son coulis aux poivrons rouges, tournedos aux morilles,* 50-130.

★★***Lion d'Or,*** rte de Vesoul, ☎ 25.85.03.30. Visa. 14 rm Ⓟ closed end Dec-end Jan, Fri eve and Sat noon, 160. Rest. ♦ ♿ 50-150.

★★***La Grange au Prieur*** (L.F.), 2 km, on the Nancy road, ☎ 25.85.10.27. AE, DC, Euro, Visa. 19 rm Ⓟ closed Sun eve and Mon noon, 15 Nov-15 Dec, 70. Rest. ♦ ♿ 50-100.

★***Auberge Jeanne d'Arc,*** 26, rue Gambetta, ☎ 25.85.03.18. 9 rm, closed Mon eve, Tue, 15 Oct-22 Nov, 85. Rest. ♿ 50-100.

⛺ ★★*Navarre* (65 pl.), ☎ 25.85.37.80.

LAON

Rheims 47, Cambrai 95, Paris 138
A2 ✉ 02000

ℹ pl. Parvis (B2), ☎ 23.23.45.87.

SNCF ☎ 23.79.10.79.

🚌 pl. de la Gare, ☎ 23.23.04.13.

Hotels :

★★★***Angleterre,*** 10, bd de Lyon (lower city : C1), ☎ 23.23.04.62. Tx 145580. AE, DC, Euro, Visa. 30 rm Ⓟ ♿ 195. Rest. ♦ closed a week in Dec, 60-170.

★★***Bannière de France,*** 11, rue F.-Roosevelt (B2), ☎ 23.23.21.44. AE, DC, Euro, Visa. 18 rm Ⓟ closed 20 Dec-15 Jan and 1 May. A 1685 post-house, 270. Rest. ♦ Spec : *noix de St-Jacques aux pointes d'asperges, rognons de veau au Bouzy,* 65-170.

★★***Commerce,*** 13, pl. de la Gare (B1), ☎ 23.79.10.38. Visa. 25 rm Ⓟ closed 21 Dec-7 Jan and Sun, 155.

★***Gare,*** 16, av. Carnot (lower city : B1), ☎ 23.23.02.08. 21 rm, closed 23 Dec-2 Jan, Fri, 100.

Youth hostel : area known as Bois-du-Charron, N4, direction Soissons, ☎ 23.23.06.81.

⛺ ★★★*Municipal* (71 pl.), ☎ 23.23.29.07.

Restaurants :

♦♦ ***Chateaubriand,*** 7, pl. Saint-Julien (upper city : B2), ☎ 23.23.46.77 ♿ closed 15 Aug-15 Sep, a week in Apr and Mon (ex nat hols). Spec : *tarte au maroilles,* 80-130.

Étouvelles, 8 km SW :

♦♦ ***Au Bon Accueil,*** 24, rue de Paris, ☎ 23.20.62.09 Ⓟ ♿ closed two weeks in Feb, 120-210.

Recommended : confectioner-caterer *Rojer,* 7, rue Châtelaine. Spec of the town : *pâté de perdreaux en croûte.*

MONTHERMÉ

Sedan 40, Saint-Quentin 133, Paris 242
17 km N of Charleville, B1 ✉ 08800

SNCF ☎ 24.32.11.67.

Hotel :
★★***Franco-Belge*** (L.F.), 2, rue Pasteur, ☎ 24.34.31.20. Visa. 14 rm Ⓟ ♨ ✈ closed 10 Jan-10 Feb, 100. Rest. ♦ closed Sun low season, 40-140.

⛺ ★★*Rapides de Phades* (100 pl.), ☎ 24.53.06.73 ; ★★*Au Port à Diseur* (100 pl.), ☎ 24.53.01.21 ; *Échina « Chez Marius »* (50 pl.), ☎ 24.53.05.56.

NOGENT-SUR-SEINE

Sens 42, Troyes 56, Paris 109
A3 ✉ 10400

SNCF ☎ 25.25.81.61.

Car-hire : *Budget,* train + auto, at the station, ☎ 25.25.81.61, and in Romilly-sur-Seine, 16, voie Herbesace, ☎ 25.24.30.86, or at Romilly station, ☎ 25.24.70.44.

Hotel :
★***Beau Rivage*** (L.F.), 20, rue Villiers-aux-Choux, ☎ 25.39.84.22. Visa. 7 rm ♨ ✈ 110. Rest. ♦ closed Sun eve, and Mon, Fri eve low season, 50-140.
Restaurant :
♦♦ ***La Chapelle-Godefroy*** (3 km E on the N19), ☎ 25.39.88.32. Visa Ⓟ ♨ closed eves. Good food in a mill setting, 120-210.

RETHEL

Rheims 39, Charleville 44, Paris 180
B2 ✉ 08300

ℹ mairie (high season), ☎ 24.39.12.16.

SNCF ☎ 24.39.00.66.

Hotels :
★★***Moderne*** (Inter-Hotel), pl. de la Gare, ☎ 24.38.44.54. AE, DC, Euro, Visa. 25 rm Ⓟ closed 22 Dec-3 Jan, 200. Rest. ♦ ♿ Spec : *côte à l'ardennaise,* 130-190.
★★***Sanglier des Ardennes*** (L.F.), 1, rue Curie, ☎ 24.38.45.19. AE, DC, Euro, Visa. 24 rm Ⓟ 🔔 closed 24 Dec-3 Jan and Sun, 60-110.

RHEIMS

Châlons-sur-Marne 45, Charleville 83, Paris 141
B2 ✉ 51100

ℹ 1, rue Jadart (B1), ☎ 26.47.25.69.

✈ Rheims-Champagne, ☎ 26.07.18.35.

Air France Agency, 26 A, rue de Vesle, ☎ 26.47.17.84.

SNCF (A1), ☎ 26.88.50.50., 26.47.84.30.

🚌 pl. du Forum (B1), ☎ 26.65.17.07.

Car-hire : *Budget,* train + auto, at the station, ☎ 26.40.01.02, extension 1166.

Hotels :
● ★★★★(L) ***Boyer-Crayères*** [Relais et Châteaux], 64, bd Henry-Vasnier (C3), ☎ 26.82.80.80. 16 rm Ⓟ ♨ 🔔 ♿ closed 22 Dec-13 Jan, 1000. Rest. ● ♦♦♦♦ closed Mon and Tue noon. One of the best stopping places in France. Gérard Boyer invites us to a real gourmet feast : *feuilleté de foie gras chaud au beurre de truffes, canard rouennais aux poires et gingembre ;* exceptionally good cellar, 270-350.
★★★***La Paix*** (Inter-Hotel), 9, rue Buirette (A2), ☎ 26.40.04.08. Tx 830974. AE, DC, Euro, Visa. 105 rm Ⓟ ♨ 295. Rest. ♦ *Drouet* ♿ closed Sun. Good dishes, 60-85.
★★***Bristol,*** 76, pl. Drouet-d'Erlon (A1-2), ☎ 26.40.52.25. 40 rm, 180.

Sept-Saulx, 18 km SSE on the Châlons road :
★★★***Le Cheval Blanc*** (Relais du Silence), ☎ 26.61.60.27. Tx 830885. AE, DC, Euro, Visa. 22 rm Ⓟ ♨ 🔔 🎾 closed 15 Jan-15 Feb, 270. Rest. ♦♦ Excellent cuisine by a woman chef. Spec : *rognons à l'aigre doux,* game in season, 140-250.

⛺ ★★★*Airotel de Champagne* (115 pl.), ☎ 26.85.41.22.

Restaurants :
● ♦♦♦ ***Le Chardonnay,*** 184, av. d'Épernay, ☎ 26.06.08.60. AE, DC, Euro, Visa Ⓟ ♿ closed 3 Aug-3 Sep and 20 Dec-10 Jan. Still an excellent cuisine in the Boyer family's birthplace. Spec : *côte de bœuf, confit de canard,* 150-200.
● ♦♦♦ ***Le Florence,*** 43, bd Foch (A1), ☎ 26.47.12.70. AE, DC, Euro, Visa, closed 1-21 Aug, Feb school hols, Sun eve and Mon (1 Nov-Easter). Refinement and quality. Spec : *pigeonneau en terrine au foie gras, turbot braisé au champagne,* 150-250.
♦♦ ***Le Continental,*** 95, pl. Drouet-d'Erlon (A1), ☎ 26.88.01.61. Good traditional dishes from Reims and Champagne. Spec : *foie gras au ratafia,* lobster, 120-210.
♦♦ ***Le Vigneron,*** pl. P.-Jamot (B2), ☎ 26.88.00.31 and 26.47.00.71 ♿ This distinctly Champagne restaurant-museum recreates a wine-grower's home ; classic fare, closed Sat noon and Sun, 27 Jul-19 Aug, 23 Dec-2 Jan, 80-120.

Châlons-sur-Vesle, 8 km W on the Soissons road :
● ♦♦ ***L'Assiette Champenoise,*** ☎ 26.49.34.94. AE, DC, Visa ♿ closed Sun eve, Wed, Feb school hols. Quality country restaurant. Taught by Guérard, J.-P. Lallement has not forgotten his lessons. Light and inspired cuisine, 220-310.

Montchenot, 11 km S on the Épernay road :
● ♦♦ ***Le Grand Cerf,*** ☎ 26.97.60.07. AE, Euro, Visa Ⓟ ♨ 🔔 closed Tue eve and Wed, 8 Aug-1 Sept, 20 Dec-3 Jan. The charm of open country and a good quality cuisine : *escalope de bar au beurre d'étrilles, ris de veau à la fondue d'oignons,* 130-250.
See also Berry-au-Bac.

Tours of champagne cellars : *Piper-Heidsieck,* 51, bd Henry-Vasnier, ☎ 26.85.01.94 ; *Pommery,* 5, pl. du Gal-Gouraud, ☎ 26.05.05.01 ; *Veuve Clicquot-Ponsardin,* 1, pl. des Droits-de-l'Homme, ☎ 26.85.25.68 ; *Taittinger,* 9, pl. Saint-Nicaise, ☎ 26.85.45.35.

Flea-market : pl. du Boulingrin, 1st Sun of the month.

Recommended : charcuterie *Au Cochon sans Rancune,* maison Cœuriot, 47, rue de Vesle (A2). Reims confectioner : *A Dom Perignon,* 13, rue du Cadran-Saint-Pierre (A1). *Petite Friande,* 15, cours J.-B.-Langlet, for chocolates in the form of champagne corks ; *Fossier,* 25, cours J.-B.-Langlet, for biscuits.

ROCROI

Charleville 29, Laon 83, Paris 234
B1 ✉ 08230

ℹ pl. A.-Hardy (high season), ☎ 24.54.10.22.

Hotels :
★★***Commerce,*** pl. Aristide-Briand, ☎ 24.54.11.15. AE, DC, Euro, Visa. 12 rm Ⓟ 🔔 closed 5 Jan-10 Feb, 170. Rest. ♦ closed Mon low season, 55-115.

Auvillers-les-Forges, ✉ 08260 Maubert-Fontaine, 13 km SW on the D877 :
★★★***Hostellerie Lenoir*** (Jean Lenoir) [Relais du Silence], ☎ 24.54.30.11. 21 rm Ⓟ ♨ 🔔 ♿

closed Fri, Jan and Feb, 260. Rest. ● ♦♦♦ Jean Lenoir lives up to his title of Best Chef in France. A great table. Spec : *soufflé de sandre au basilic, gâteau de foie d'oie au miel et jasmin, ris de veau aux champignons des Ardennes,* fine champagne list. (Special price for three days of cooking lessons), 170-240.

⛺ ★★*Les Remparts* (50 pl.), ☎ 24.54.10.22.

SAINT-DIZIER

Bar-le-Duc 24, Chaumont 74, Paris 212
C3 ✉ 52100

ℹ Pavillon du Jard, ☎ 25.05.31.84.

SNCF ☎ 25.05.67.68.

Hotels :
★★★***Le Gambetta,*** 62, rue Gambetta, ☎ 25.56.52.10. AE, DC, Visa. 63 rm Ⓟ ♿ 180. Rest. ♦ closed Sun eve and eves of nat hols, 60-150.
★★★***Soleil d'Or,*** 2 km on the Bar-le-Duc road, ☎ 25.05.68.22. Tx 840946. AE, Visa. 60 rm Ⓟ ♨ ♿ 240. Rest. closed Sat and Sun, 60-80.
★***Picardy,*** 15, av. de Verdun, ☎ 25.05.09.12. 12 rm Ⓟ ♨ closed 17-26 Aug, 130.

Youth hostel : *Centre de Loisirs des Ajoto,* 3 km on the Chaumont road.

SAINTE-MENEHOULD

Châlons-sur-Marne 46, Verdun 47, Paris 220
B-C2 ✉ 51800

ℹ pl. du Gal-Leclerc, ☎ 26.60.85.83.

SNCF ☎ 26.60.80.55.

Hotels :
★★***Saint-Nicolas,*** 36, rue Chanzy, ☎ 26.60.80.59. 18 rm Ⓟ 110. Rest. ♦ ♿ closed Tue, Sun eve low season. Good meals at moderate prices, 60-150.

Givry-en-Argonne, ✉ 51330, 16 km S :
★***L'Espérance,*** pl. de la Halle, ☎ 26.60.00.08. 7 rm Ⓟ ♨ ♿ closed Sun eve, 120. Rest. ♦ 50-120.

⛺ ★★*La Grelette* (50 pl.), ☎ 26.60.80.21.

Restaurant :
Florent-en-Argonne, 8 km NE on the D85 :
★***Auberge la Menyère,*** ☎ 26.60.93.70. Visa ♨ ♿ closed Feb, a week in Aug, Sun eve and Mon. Set in an attractive old house, 80-130.

SAINT-QUENTIN

Laon 46, Valenciennes 70, Paris 155
A1 ✉ 02100

ℹ hôtel de ville, ☎ 23.67.05.00.

SNCF ☎ ① 23.62.34.03.
® 23.62.51.45.

Car-hire : *Budget,* train + auto, at the station, ☎ 23.62.24.03.

Hotels :
★★★***Grand Hôtel,*** 6, rue Dachery, ☎ 23.62.69.77. Tx 140225. AE, DC, Euro, Visa. 41 rm Ⓟ closed 29 Jul-19 Aug and 4-18 Feb, 230. Rest. ♦ ***Le Président,*** closed Sun eve and Mon. A place which deserves and lives up to its reputation, 115-280.
★★***Paix, Albert Ier,*** 3, pl du 8-Octobre, ☎ 23.62.77.62, Tx 140225. AE, Euro, Visa. 82 rm Ⓟ ♿ 260. Rest. ***Le Brésilien,*** 85-120.
★★***France et Angleterre*** (Inter-Hôtel), 28, rue Émile-Zola, ☎ 23.62.13.10, Tx 140986. AE, DC, Euro, Visa. 28 rm Ⓟ 180.

Blérancourt, ✉ 02300 Chauny, 23 km NW on the D6 :
★★★***Le Griffon*** (Châteaux-Hôtels), château de Blérancourt, ☎ 23.39.60.11. AE, DC, Euro, Visa. 24 rm Ⓟ ♨ ♿ closed four days Christmas, three weeks in Feb, Sun eve and Mon, 180. Rest. ♦ 120-210.

Restaurants :
♦♦ ***Au Petit Chef,*** 31, rue Émile-Zola, ☎ 23.62.28.51. AE, Euro, Visa ♿ closed 1-25 Jul, 22-30 Dec, Fri eve and Sun. Spec : *truite farcie au champagne,* 60-135.
♦ ***Le Riche,*** 10, rue des Toiles, ☎ 23.62.33.53. closed Tue eve and Sun, 5-20 Jan, 20 Jul-10 Aug. Spec : *salade du pêcheur,* 60-150.

Neuville-St-Amand, 3 km SE :
● ♦♦ ***Le Château,*** ☎ 23.68.41.82. AE, DC, Euro, Visa Ⓟ ♨ closed Sun eve, Mon, Wed eve, 3-24 Aug, a week at Christmas and Feb hols. Good cooking by the Meyresonne brothers. Spec : fish (delivered directly from Boulogne), *pigeon rôti,* 120-220.

SEDAN

Charleville 22, Verdun 80, Paris 237
B-C1 ✉ 08200

ℹ pl. Turenne, ☎ 24.29.03.28.

SNCF ☎ 24.27.14.84.

Car-hire : *Budget,* train + auto, ☎ 26.84.00.88, at the station, ☎ 24.27.10.64.

Hotels :
★★***Europe,*** 5, pl. de la Gare, ☎ 24.27.18.71. Tx 840133. AE, DC, Euro, Visa. 25 rm Ⓟ ♿ closed 20 Dec-5 Jan and Sun, 180. Rest. ♦ closed Sun, 80-130.
★★***Univers,*** pl. de la Gare, ☎ 24.27.04.35. AE, DC, Euro, Visa. 11 rm Ⓟ closed Sun eve, Aug, 200. Rest. ♦ ♿ 40-100.

⛺ ★★Municipal *Prairie de Torcy* (150 pl.), ☎ 24.27.13.05.

Restaurants :
♦♦ ***Au Bon Vieux Temps,*** 3, pl. de la Halle, ☎ 24.29.03.70. AE, DC, Euro, Visa closed Sun eve, Mon, and Feb. Rich, regional cooking. Spec : *foie gras de canard, tournedos Curnonsky,* 160-230.
♦ ***Chariot d'Or,*** 20, pl. de Torcy, ☎ 24.27.04.87 Ⓟ ♿ closed Sun eve and Mon eve, 50-150.

SÉZANNE

Châlons-sur-Marne 57, Troyes 60, Paris 118
A3 ✉ 51120

ℹ pl. de la République (high season), ☎ 26.80.51.43.

SNCF ☎ 26.80.52.97.

Hotels :
★★***France,*** 25, rue Léon-Jolly, ☎ 26.80.52.52. AE, DC, Euro, Visa. 24 rm Ⓟ 100. Rest. ♦ closed 15 Jan-15 Feb, Tue and Sun eve low season, 80-130.
★★***Croix d'Or*** (L.F.), 53, rue Notre-Dame, ☎ 26.80.61.10. AE, DC, Euro, Visa. 13 rm Ⓟ closed 1-17 Jan, 21-29 Oct and Mon, 120. Rest. ♦ 50-120.

⛺ ★★*Municipal* (65 pl.), ☎ 26.80.57.00.

SOISSONS

Laon 36, Rheims 56, Paris 100
A2 ✉ 02200

ℹ av. Gal-Leclerc, ☎ 23.53.08.27.

SNCF ☎ 23.53.07.45., 23.53.34.05.

Hotels :
★★★***Picardie,*** 6-8, rue Neuve-Saint-Martin, ☎ 23.53.21.93. AE, DC, Euro, Visa. 33 rm Ⓟ ♨ ♿ 260. Rest. ♦♦ closed Sun eve, 120-210.

★★***Motel des Lions,*** rte de Reims, 500 m on the N31, ☎ 23.73.29.83. 28 rm Ⓟ ♨ ♿ 250. Rest. ♦ Good cooking. Spec : *rognons de veau échalotes,* 100-160.
★★***Lion Rouge,*** square Saint-Martin, ☎ 23.53.31.52. Euro, Visa. 33 rm Ⓟ ♨ ♿ 175. Rest. ♦ closed Sun eve, 50-105.

⛺ ★★*Municipal* (100 pl.), ☎ 23.59.12.00.

Restaurant :
♦♦ ***Le Grenadin,*** 19, rte de Fère-en-Tardenois, ☎ 23.53.08.12. closed Sun eve, Mon, Aug, 80-130.

TROYES

Rheims 130, Dijon 152, Paris 165
B4 ⊠ 10000

ℹ 16, bd Carnot, ☎ 25.73.00.36.

✈ *Barberey-Saint-Sulpice,* 5 km N, ☎ 25.72.08.50.

SNCF pl. Mal-Joffre, ☎ 25.72.50.50., 25.72.50.08

Car-hire : *Budget,* train + auto, 24, rue Voltaire, ☎ 25.74.29.41, and at the station.

Hotels :
★★★***Grand Hôtel,*** 4, av. Mal-Joffre (A2), ☎ 25.79.90.90. Tx 840582. AE, DC, Euro, Visa. 100 rm ♨ ♿ 260. Rest. ♦ ***Le Champagne,*** 120-200 ; ***Le Brasero,*** 150 ; ***Brasserie Le Croco,*** 50-100. ***Jardin de la Louisiane,*** 100.
★★★***Royal,*** 22, bd Carnot (A2), ☎ 25.73.19.99. Tx 841015. AE, DC, Euro, Visa. 37 rm closed 15 Dec-6 Jan, 200. Rest. ♦ closed Sun eve and Mon noon, 70-130.
★★★***Poste,*** 35, rue Émile-Zola (B2), ☎ 25.73.05.05. Tx 840994. AE, Visa. 34 rm 280. Rest. ♦ ♿ closed Sun eve. Talented preparation of market-fresh produce. Spec. : *terrine gourmande de foie gras, filet d'agneau rôti à la crème des champignons des bois,* 150-220.
★★***France,*** 18, quai Dampierre (B1), ☎ 25.73.11.95. AE, DC, Euro, Visa. 60 rm Ⓟ ♿ 180. Rest. ♦ 80-130.
★★***Champenois,*** 15, rue P.-Gauthier (A1), ☎ 25.76.16.05. Visa. 28 rm Ⓟ ♨ closed 16 Dec-3 Jan and 5-22 Aug, 155.
Aix-en-Othe, ⊠ 10160, 31 km ESE :
● ★★***Auberge de la Scierie,*** La Vove, ☎ 25.46.71.26. 10 rm Ⓟ ♨ ♿ closed Mon eve and Tue (15 Oct-15 Apr), 1-15 Feb, 180. Rest. ● ♦♦ Excellent cuisine in an 17thC mill. Spec : *andouillette à la fondue de chaource, aiguillette de canard au vinaigre de cerises,* 110-250.

Youth hostel : 5 km, St-Julien-les-Villas, ⊠ 10800, ☎ 25.82.00.65.

Restaurants :
♦♦ ***Le Bourgogne,*** 40, rue Gal-de-Gaulle (A1), ☎ 25.73.02.67 closed Sun and Mon eve, 2 Jul-1 Sep. Good, conventional dishes. Spec : *biscuit aux fruits de mer et aux pistaches, escalope de foie de canard au vinaigre de framboises,* 140-180.
Pont-Sainte-Marie, 3.5 km N :
♦♦ ***Host. de Pont-Sainte-Marie,*** ☎ 25.81.13.09. Tx 840995. AE, DC, Visa ♨ closed Sun eve and Mon, 13 Jan-10 Feb. Enjoyable fare. Spec : *mignardises de la mer au ragoût d'aubergines, feuilleté de filet d'agneau parfumé au gingembre,* 240-300.

Guided tours : enq at ℹ

Recommended : cakes and pastries : *Confiserie de Champagne,* 28, rue Auger (Sainte-Savine). *Auction hall,* 1, rue de la Paix. Handicrafts : *Les Métiers d'Art,* 1, pl. Jean-Jaurès.

VERTUS

Châlons-sur-Marne 30, Rheims 47, Paris 137
20 km of Epernay, B3 ⊠ 51130

SNCF ☎ 26.52.12.31.

Hotel :
★★★***Reine Blanche*** (Inter-Hôtel), 18, av. Louis-Lenoir, ☎ 26.52.20.76. AE, DC, Euro, Visa. 23 rm Ⓟ 280. Rest. 120-225.

Restaurant :
Le Mesnil-sur-Oger, ⊠ 51190, 5 km N :
● ♦♦ ***Le Mesnil,*** 2, rue Pasteur, ☎ 26.57.95.57. AE, DC, Euro, Visa Ⓟ ♿ closed Mon eve and Wed, Feb hols, 10 Aug-4 Sep. The good and copious cooking of Claude Jaillant. Spec : *terrine maison,* game in season, 90-260.

VERVINS

Laon 36, Charleville 72, Paris 172
A1 ⊠ 02140

ℹ pl. du Gal-de-Gaulle (high season), ☎ 23.98.09.92.

SNCF ☎ 23.98.03.54.

Hotels :
★★★***Tour du Roy,*** 45, rue du Gal-Leclerc, ☎ 23.98.00.11. AE, DC, Euro, Visa. 15 rm Ⓟ ♿ Henri IV once stayed here. closed 15 Jan-15 Feb. Henri IV once stayed here, 185. Rest. ● ♦♦ closed Sun eve and Mon noon low season, 15 Jan-15 Feb. A warm welcome and excellent regional cooking. Spec : *gâteau de lapereau aux herbes et mirabelles, jarret de veau à la crème d'artichauts,* 120-300.
★***Cheval Noir,*** 33, av. de la Liberté, ☎ 23.98.04.16. Visa. 15 rm Ⓟ ♿ 180. Rest. ♦ closed Sun eve and Mon noon, 20 Dec-14 Jan, 80-130.

VILLERS-COTTERETS

Soissons 23, Meaux 42, Paris 77
A2 ⊠ 02600

SNCF ☎ 23.96.01.85.

Hotels :
★★★***Régent,*** 26, rue du Gal-Mangin, ☎ 23.96.01.46. Tx 150747. AE, DC, Euro, Visa. 17 rm Ⓟ ♨ ♿ 260.
★★***Commerce,*** 17, rue du Gal-Mangin, ☎ 23.96.19.97. Visa. 7 rm closed Sun eve and Mon, 15 Jan-15 Feb, 130. Rest. ♦ Spec : *fricassée d'escargots forestière, gratin de fruits,* 70-175.
Longpont, 12 km NE through the forest :
★★***Abbaye*** (L.F.), ☎ 23.96.02.44. Euro, Visa. 11 rm ♨ ♿ 180. Rest. ♦ View of the abbey and the forest, 120-210.

Bicycle hire : at Hôtel de l'Abbaye.

VITRY-LE-FRANÇOIS

Châlons-sur-Marne 32, Troyes 74, Paris 183
B3 ⊠ 51300

ℹ pl. Giraud, ☎ 26.74.45.30.

SNCF ☎ 26.74.71.86.

Hotels :
★★***Poste,*** pl. Royer-Collart, ☎ 26.74.02.65. AE, DC, Euro, Visa. 30 rm ♿ 180. Rest. ♦ closed Sun, 20 Dec-2 Jan, Aug, 80-130.
★★***Cloche,*** 34, rue Aristide-Briand, ☎ 26.74.03.84. Euro, Visa. 24 rm Ⓟ ♨ ♿ 190. Rest, 70-85.

⛺ ★★*Municipal la Peupleraie* (70 pl.), ☎ 26.74.11.00.

Corsica

Corsica, an island with the astonishing diversity of a continent : the snowy peaks of Cinto, the palm trees of the capital Ajaccio, the luminous gulf of Porto, the cool forests of Vizzavona and the burning desert of Les Agriates. It is almost as if the gods had decided to give it a little of everything : mountain torrents, rivers and alpine lakes, alpine pastures and deep chestnut groves, scented *maquis* and immense laricio pinetrees, white limestone cliffs and red rocks. The eye travels in an instant from icy slopes to orange groves, from vineyards to the ever-present sea.
Corsica is a mountain in the Mediterranean, bearing traces of human presence and human labor since Antiquity : terraced hillsides, olive groves and sheep-pens abandoned in the *maquis,* which covers two-thirds of the island in a dense, perfumed mantle. It has always served as a hiding place for bandits, outlaws and those bent on the vendettas that have always characterized Corsican society.
From the 11th to the 13th century, Corsica was placed under the authority of the Republic of Pisa, and Tuscan architects and masons erected Romanesque churches and chapels, small and perfectly proportioned. Corsica's most famous son is Napoléon Bonaparte, of Italian descent. The island has its own Romance language, which has been undergoing a revival since the early 1970s as a symbol of the region's cultural identity.
Corsican wines are solid and colorful like the island itself. The food is excellent : sausages, smoked hams and salamis with an Italian influence. Wild boar, goat and lamb are popular, and fish and shellfish are found in abundance. Cheese and dishes prepared with sweet chestnuts round off a cuisine that should not be thought inferior to that of the mainland. Corsican craftsmen, supported by craft associations, produce high-quality pottery, wickerwork, wood sculptures, jewellery, knives and woven garments.

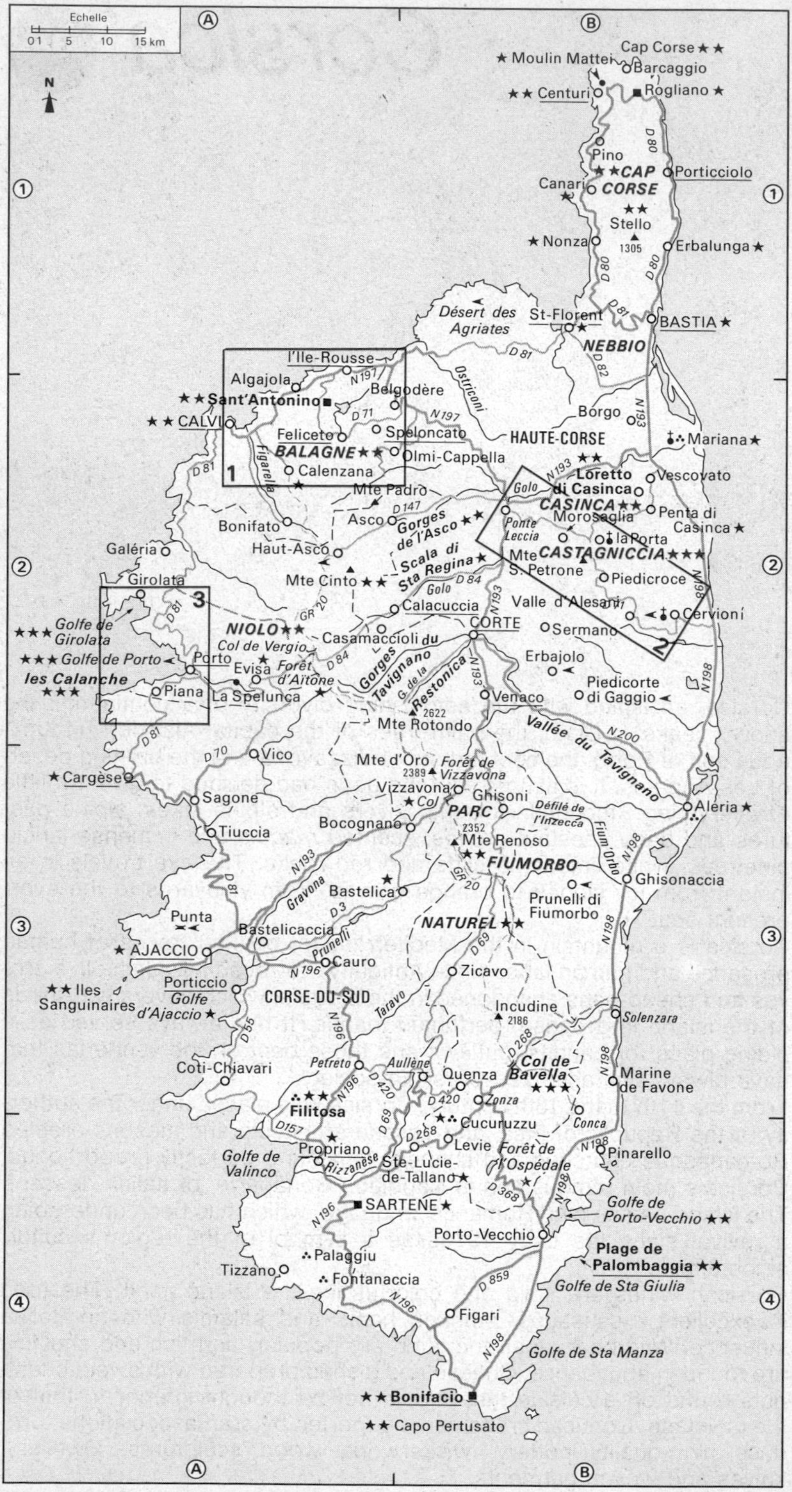
Echelle
0 1 5 10 15 km
N
A
B
1
2
3
4
Cap Corse ★★
Moulin Mattei
Barcaggio
★★ Centuri
Rogliano ★
Pino
★★CAP CORSE
Porticciolo
Canari
★★
Stello
1305
★ Nonza
Erbalunga ★
D 80
D 81
Désert des Agriates
St-Florent
NEBBIO
BASTIA ★
D 82
l'Ile-Rousse
Algajola
N 197
★★ Sant'Antonino
Belgodère
Ostriconi
D 71
★★ CALVI
Feliceto
Speloncato
BALAGNE ★★
Olmi-Cappella
Calenzana
Figarella
Borgo
N 193
HAUTE-CORSE
Mariana ★
★★
Loretto di Casinca
Vescovato
CASINCA ★★
Penta di Casinca ★
Golo
Morosaglia
Ponte Leccia
la Porta
CASTAGNICCIA ★★★
Mte S. Petrone
Piedicroce
Valle d'Alesani
Cervioni
Sermano
Mte Padro
D 147
Asco
Gorges de l'Asco ★★
Bonifato
Haut-Asco
Galéria
Scala di Sta Regina ★
Mte Cinto ★★
D 84
Girolata
★★★ Golfe de Girolata
★★★ Golfe de Porto
les Calanche ★★★
Porto
Piana
Evisa
La Spelunca
GR 20
Calacuccia
NIOLO ★★
Casamaccioli
CORTE
Col de Vergio
Forêt d'Aïtone
Gorges du Tavignano
G. de la Restonica
2622
Mte Rotondo
Erbajolo
Piedicorte di Gaggio
Venaco
Vallée du Tavignano
N 200
N 198
Vico
D 70
★ Cargèse
Sagone
Tiuccia
Mte d'Oro
2389
Forêt de Vizzavona
Vizzavona
★ Col
Ghisoni
PARC
Défilé de l'Inzecca
Aleria ★
Bocognano
2352
Mte Renoso
Fium'Orbo
FIUMORBO
Ghisonaccia
Prunelli di Fiumorbo
Gravona
Bastelica
D 3
Punta
Bastelicaccia
NATUREL ★★
★ AJACCIO
Prunelli
Cauro
N 196
D 69
Zicavo
★★ Iles Sanguinaires
Porticcio
Golfe d'Ajaccio ★
CORSE-DU-SUD
Taravo
Incudine
2186
Solenzara
D 55
D 268
Coti-Chiavari
Petreto
Aullène
Quenza
Col de Bavella ★★★
Marine de Favone
D 420
Zonza
Filitosa
D157
Cucuruzzu
Conca
Golfe de Valinco
Propriano
Rizzanese
Levie
Forêt de l'Ospédale
Pinarello
Ste-Lucie-de-Tallano ★
D 368
SARTENE ★
Golfe de Porto-Vecchio ★★
Porto-Vecchio
Plage de Palombaggia ★★
Palaggiu
Tizzano
Fontanaccia
D 859
Golfe de Sta Giulia
Figari
Golfe de Sta Manza
★★ Bonifacio
★★ Capo Pertusato

Sightseeing

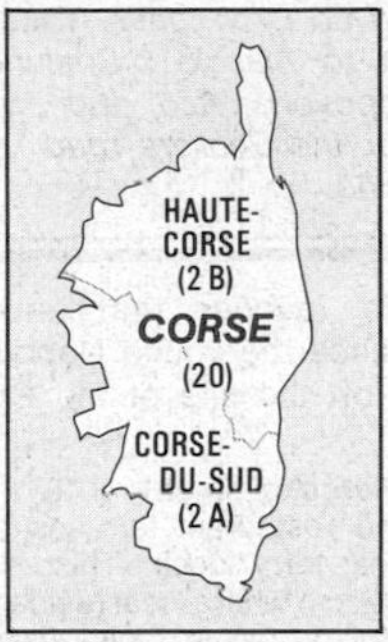

Facts and figures

Location : *82 km from Italy, 180 km from mainland France.*
Area : *8 721 km² (vs. Sardinia, 24 089 km²); max. length 183 km; max. width 83 km.*
Climate : *Mediterranean. Av. temp. > 12 °C : Ajaccio 14.7°, Bastia 15.2°; sea temp. : May 16 °C, Jun. 19°, Jul. 22°, Aug. 23°, Sep. 22°, Oct. 20°.*
Population : *240 178; working : 81 310; towns 125 000 (Ajaccio and Bastia 100 000).*
Administration : *Department of* ***Southern Corsica,*** *Prefecture Ajaccio; Department of* ***Upper Corsica,*** *Prefecture Bastia.*

■ AGRIATES Desert

B1

D81 runs through 30 km of parched landscape that was once the granary of Corsica. Apart from a few houses at **Casta** *(12 km W of Saint Florent)*, a few shepherds' stone huts are the only habitations in the 160 km² Agriates.

▶ From Casta, a difficult road *(12 km, negotiable at low speed)* leads to **Saleccia Beach★★** (restaurant). □

■ AJACCIO★

A3 / ® / pop. 55 000

The colours in the magnificent bay change with the hours and the weather. New white buildings rise above red-tiled roofs and

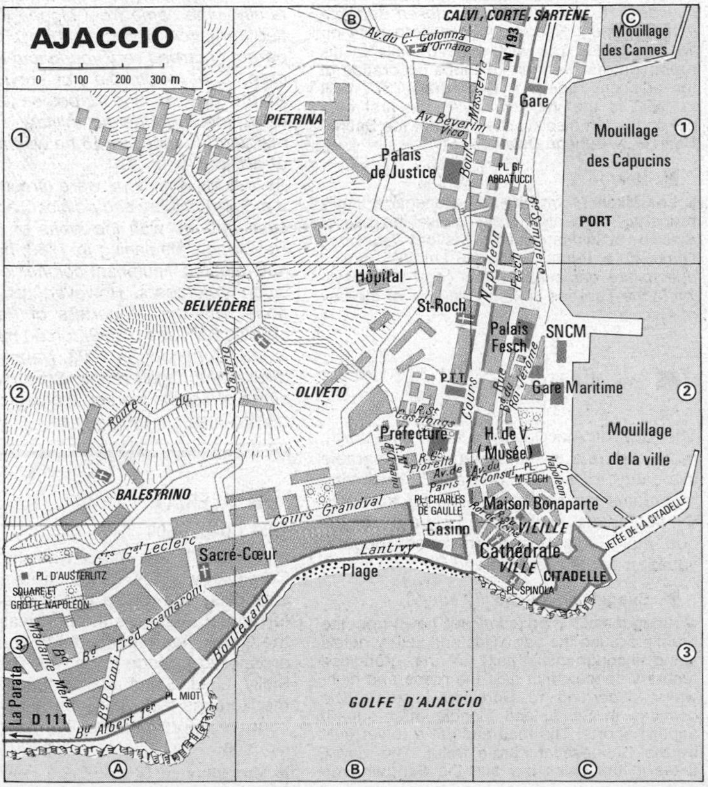

Weekend tips

First visit : Ajaccio by night, the port, Place Maréchal Foch, the old town. Next day, drive to Porto : Piana inlet, bay of Porto (lunch) and La Croix pass. Take the inland road back to Ajaccio : Spelunca gorges, Evisa (stopover), Vico, then via Sagone (quicker) or the Écoliers road : Arbori and Sari d'Orcino.

terra cotta façades that have scarcely changed since the young Napoléon played in a cave on the site of the Place d'Austerlitz.

▶ **Place Maréchal Foch★** (C2) : palm trees, fountain and restaurant terraces a few steps from the car-ferry dock. This is the social centre of Ajaccio where local residents traditionally stop for a *pastis* (anise-flavoured alcoholic drink) before lunch. ▶ In the Town Hall, the **Napoleonic Museum** *(9-12 & 2:30-5:30; 2-5 in winter)* commemorates the Emperor (Napoléon's baptismal certificate and other memorabilia). ▶ Each morning the neighbourhood market bustles with noise and colour as choice Corsican produce (cheese, *charcuterie, beignets,* fritters) is laid out for the day. ▶ **Fesch Palace** (C2) : built in 1827 by Cardinal Fesch (Napoléon's uncle); Imperial Chapel, burial vault of the Bonaparte family. The Fesch Museum★★ *(closed for restoration)* boasts 1 200 paintings covering 5 centuries of Italian art. ▶ The **Bonaparte House★** *(C2; 9-12 & 2-6, summer; 10-12 & 2-5, winter; closed Sun. pm and Mon. am).* Napoléon I was born here on 15 Aug. 1769. The whitewashed walls of his room contrast with the luxurious decoration of the adjacent rooms. ▶ **Cathedral** (C3) : built in 1593 in the Venetian style; the first chapel on the left displays the Virgin of the Sacred Heart★ by Eugène Delacroix.

▶ Nearby

▶ **Les Milelli** *(4 km NW) :* the Bonaparte family property, in an olive grove above the bay of Ajaccio; buildings closed to visitors *(festival in summer).* ▶ **Punta Castle** *(13 km NW; closed due to fire damage) :* 19thC copy of a pavilion in the Tuileries in Paris. View★★ of the bay of Ajaccio. □

■ Bay of AJACCIO★

A3

The bay of Ajaccio, angular in the north, more tortuous in the south, is comparable in beauty to the bay of Naples. Encircling mountains present a majestic backdrop to the sea. Inlets, beaches and natural anchorage make this one of the most popular vacation spots on the island.

▶ Sanguinaires Road *(12 km W)*

▶ Along the cliff road *(corniche),* hewn from the granite around the bay, villas and luxury hotels stand incongruously next to the grandiose funerary chapels that face the roads and highways, according to Corsican custom. The beaches at Scudo and Vignola offer superb aquatic sports. The road ends at a tower built by the Genoese at **Parata Point.** The view★ takes in the entire bay and the **Sanguinaires Islands** beyond. ▶ **Sanguinaires Islands★★** *(motorboats leave from Ajaccio, opposite Place Maréchal Foch; 9 and 2, Apr.-Oct.; 3hr round trip) :* the French author Alphonse Daudet (1840-1897) lived for a year at the lighthouse on the largest of these islets. He left a vivid record of his impressions in his humorous sketches of Provençal life, "Lettres de Mon Moulin". □

▶ Porticcio and the mountain road★ *(83 km round trip, half-day)*

▶ Beyond the airport at **Campo dell'Oro** the southern coast of the Bay of Ajaccio has been extensively developed for tourism.

▶ **Porticcio,** accross from Ajaccio : the focal point of seafront development. ▶ Port of **Chiavari** and **Verghia** beach backed by pine forest. 6 km of narrow road leads to **Castagna Point** (view★). ▶ Leaving the bay, the road plunges into thick *maquis* (heathland → box) with glimpses of the sea★ along the way. ▶ **Coti Chiavari :** a village on the hillside above the bay. ▶ Drive to the TV relay station, where the view takes in the bays of Ajaccio and **Valinco.** ▶ To take the road across the mountains go back 1.3 km on the Ajaccio road then follow D55 *(right)* through a terrain covered with heather, arbutus, filaria and cistus, the combination known to local people as *le maquis dense.* ▶ The passes at Cortone *(625 m),* Chenova *(629 m)* and Bellevalle *(522 m)* offer impressive views. □

Napoléon and Corsica

The Buonaparte (the original Italian spelling) family, who came from Liguria in Italy, settled in Ajaccio during the 16thC. Napoléon's parents married very young and had 13 children, 5 of whom did not survive infancy. At the age of nine Napoléon left Corsica to attend the Brienne military academy in mainland France; by 16 he was a lieutenant of artillery.

At first his ambitions were directed towards a modest military and political career in Corsica. Imbued with the ideas of the French Revolution, beginning in 1789, he had himself elected lieutenant-colonel of the Corsican Volunteers. However, his confrontations with the supporters of Pascal Paoli (1725-1807; see p. 539) forced him to return to the Continent. In 1793, Napoléon's decisive action against the British during the siege of Toulon marked the beginning of his rise to national prominence.

■ ALÉRIA★

B3 / pop. 3 000

In ancient times, Aléria was the capital of Corsica by virtue of its strategic position straddling sea-routes to the eastern Mediterranean. Alalia, as the port was known to the Greeks who founded it in about 565BC, prospered through trade with Greece, Italy, Sicily, Gaul, Spain and Carthage. In 259BC the Romans took Alalia and used it as their base of operations for the colonisation of Corsica.

▶ **Museum★** *(8-12 & 2-7, 2-5 in winter) :* permanent display of archaeological finds from ancient Alalia; funerary relics, weapons and ceramics★ illustrate the importance of the eastern coast of Corsica to economic and military expansion in the ancient world. The entrance ticket also covers the Roman excavations (forum, temple, baths, law courts). □

■ ASCO Valley★★

B2 / ®

▶ Road through the **Asco valley** *(30 km from Ponte Leccia)*

The river Asco winds through the austere but magnificent landscape of the highest mountains in Corsica. Rugged snow-covered peaks exceeding 2 000 m in altitude, pine forest, granite walls channelling the torrent, a low scrub-covered valley, holm oak and alders rising out of a barren plain : such drastic changes within only a few kilometres are typical of Corsica. The Asco valley subsists on a mountain economy based on forestry and livestock; the rich countryside of Balagne provides pasturage during the winter. Formerly, the women of the valley wove goat hair and wool, while the men made wooden buckets, milkpails, spoons, ladles and moulds for the *brocciu* cheese. Asco is the habitat of the bearded vulture, an endangered species with a wingspan exceeding 2.5 m. Wild sheep (moufflons) are protected in a nature reserve in the upper valley.

▶ 2 km along the **Calvi** road, then straight down D47. ▶ **Asco,** at the mouth of the river gorges, the only village in the valley : the area attracts hunters, anglers, botanists and climbers; honey from the region is especially prized. ▶ **Haut-Asco :** skiing from Dec. to Apr.; in summer Haut-Asco becomes a base camp for mountaineers' assaults on **Mount Cinto** *(2 710 m),* the highest peak in Corsica; an easy but time-consuming climb *(6hr up, 4hr down)*; panorama★★. □

Don't miss

★★★ : *Bavella Pass (B3), Les Calanche (A2), Girolata Bay (A2), Porto Bay (A2).*
★★ : *Asco Valley (B2), Balagne (A2), Bonifacio (B4), Calvi (A1), Cape Corse (B1), Casinca (B2), Filitosa (A3-4), Niolo (A2), Regional Nature Park (AB2-3), Porto-Vecchio Bay (B4).*

■ The BALAGNE Region★★

▶ Round trip *(99 km, full day)*

A2 *(see map 1)*

This oil- and wheat-growing region was once the garden of Corsica. Olives, figs and oranges from Balagne were exported via Calvi and Ile-Rousse. Low hills and fertile plains lie between the sea and the mountains. The golden-grey villages cluster around slender bell-towers, and each hillside echoes the next in a landscape enlivened by the distant sea.

Here and there you may pick out traces of abandoned agricultural terraces. Although attempts have been made to resume olive-growing on a commercial basis, livestock and grapevines are the principal resources today. Endowed with a climate in which palms, agave and Barbary figs flourish, Balagne has also succeeded in developing its coastline for tourism. Popular resorts include Calvi, Algajola, Île-Rousse, the marinas at Davia and Sant'Ambroggio and an extensive holiday village at Lozari, stretch-

1. Balagne region

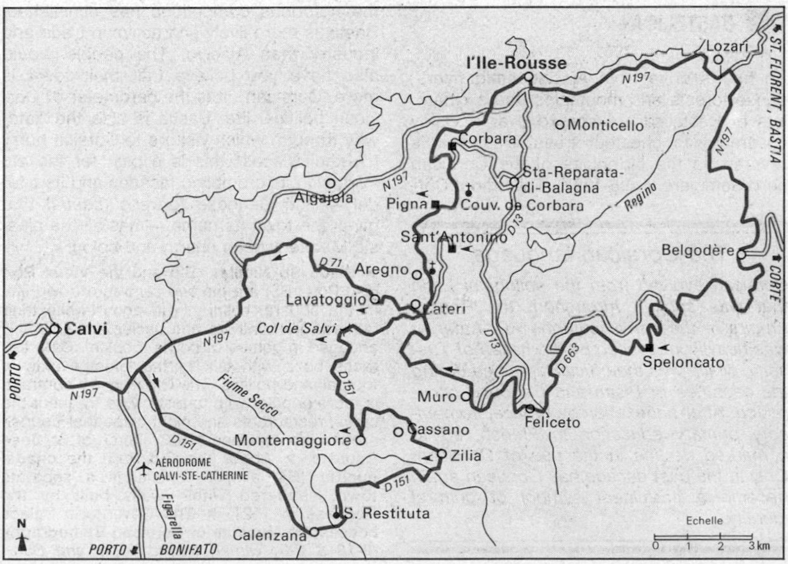

Corsica

ing over 50 acres along a beautiful sandy beach. Handicrafts, too, have been developed in Balagne in recent years through the efforts of promotional associations such as La Corsicada (→ box). At villages such as Pigna and Lumio, peasant crafts have been revived, and attractive items (pottery, weaving, wood and wickerwork) are available.

▶ **Calvi** (→). ▶ **Calenzana** ®, long a base for independence movements, claims to be Corsican at heart, in contrast to neighbouring Calvi, which was the seat of the occupying Genoese. Start of GR20 *(hiking trail).* ▶ **Church of Sta. Restituta** rises above groves of sturdy olives. The frescos★ in the 15thC cenotaph are reminiscent of miniatures. ▶ **Zilia :** view★ over the valley and Montemaggiore. ▶ **Cassano :** in the church, a triptych★ of the Virgin and Child by a local painter, Simonis de Calvi (1505). ▶ **Montemaggiore★ :** imposing Baroque church overlooking Calenzana and Calvi Bay. 1 km N, Romanesque church (12thC) of San Rainiero with walls of black and white granite. ▶ **Sant'Antonino★★** *(2 km right) :* perched high in the hills of Balagne; a maze of narrow streets and steps among façades of dark granite (craftshops, small restaurants) is worth exploring. ▶ **Aregno :** surrounded by orange and lemon trees, with 13thC church of the Trinity★ in Pisan Romanesque style (frescos★). ▶ **Pigna★ :** among olive groves overlooking the bay of Algajola; craftshop *(maison d'artisanat)* run by La Corsicada (pottery). ▶ **Convent of Corbora :** starting point for a 1hr climb to **Monte Sant'Angelo** (alt. 562 m; view★). ▶ **Corbora :** a Moorish-looking village below a ruined castle. ▶ **L'Ile-Rousse** ® : named for its islets of red granite linked to the shore by a jetty, this seaside resort is much appreciated for pleasant weather and a beach of fine sand. ▶ **Belgodère ;** the ruins of an old fort overlook the valley. ▶ **Speloncato** ® : named for the numerous caves *(spilunca)* in the surrounding hillsides. ▶ Superb view★ of Balagne. ▶ Road continues through the villages of Nessa, Feliceto, Muro, Cateri (crafts *on right*) and Lavatoggio. □

■ BASTELICA★

A-B 3 / ® / pop. 796

An hour's drive from Ajaccio amid rivers, dense forests and mountains, the six hamlets of Bastelica are spread over a valley covered with chestnut trees. Bastelica is revered as the birthplace of the Corsican hero Sampiero (1498-1567). This "most Corsican of Corsicans" led a long struggle against the Genoese. □

The Corsican language

Corsican evolved from the colloquial Latin that was spoken throughout the Roman Empire in the early centuries AD. Later, it was heavily influenced by the Italian of Tuscany, which was the official language during the centuries of Pisan and Genoese occupation. After annexation by France, compulsory primary education in French led to a marked decline in the use of Corsican. Only in the past decade has Corsican again become a prominent symbol of cultural identity.

The Pisan churches

From the 11th to the 13thC Corsica was governed by the city-republic of Pisa, which brought architects, sculptors and stone masons from Tuscany. These builders were responsible for most of the Romanesque churches of Castagniccia, Nebbio and Balagne. Pisan sanctuaries in Corsica are recognisable by their small size and perfect proportions. The buildings are roofed with flat stones (teghje)*; the alternation of dry-jointed blocks of limestone, schist or granite gives a beautiful polychrome effect to the walls. Today many churches and chapels are lost in the* maquis. *Of those still accessible the most interesting are : La Trinité at Aregno, La Canonica at Mariana, St. Jean at Carbini, San Michele at Murato and the old cathedral of Nebbio at Saint Florent.*

▶ Nearby

▶ **Prunelli Gorges★** *(14 km by D27 and D3) :* the road runs through Tolla, where the houses overlook a reservoir. Farther on, **Bocca di Mercuio** commands a view of a natural amphitheatre in the mountains. Climb left *(300 m) :* view★ of the dam and the gorges. ▶ **Mount Renoso** *(alt. 2352 m) :* one of the most commanding lookout points in Corsica *(7 hr 30 up, 4-5hr down).* □

■ BASTIA★

B1 / ® / pop. 45000

The two great Corsican towns of Ajaccio and Bastia, facing the sea in opposite directions, once seemed destined to remain rivals forever. But since Bastia was made the administrative centre for Upper Corsica, the notorious competition has diminished. Bastia is more lively and active in trade and industry than Ajaccio. The people would also have you believe that their town is more "Corsican". It is the barometer of Corsican political life. Bastia is also the gateway through which visitors to Corsica hurry to other places; this is a pity, for the old Port, with its crumbling façades and its citadel — the Genoese fortress *(bastia)* that gives the town its name — has all the classic Mediterranean charm and colour.

▶ **Place St. Nicolas** (B2) and the **Vieux Port** (Old Port; B3) are the two centres of town life. In the square, children run about while their fathers, grandfathers and uncles are solemnly engaged in games of bowls *(boules).* Café terraces buzz with talk of the latest events in football and politics. The Old Port, by contrast, is more popular with tourists, who frequent the cafés, restaurants and night clubs that flourish around the imposing 17thC church of St. Jean Baptiste. ▶ Above the Old Port, the **citadel quarter** (B4) almost constitutes a separate town, sheltered within walls built by the Genoese in 1521. ▶ The Governor's Palace houses the **Museum of Corsican Ethnography** *(9-12 & 2-6; winter, closed 5 pm and Sun.;*

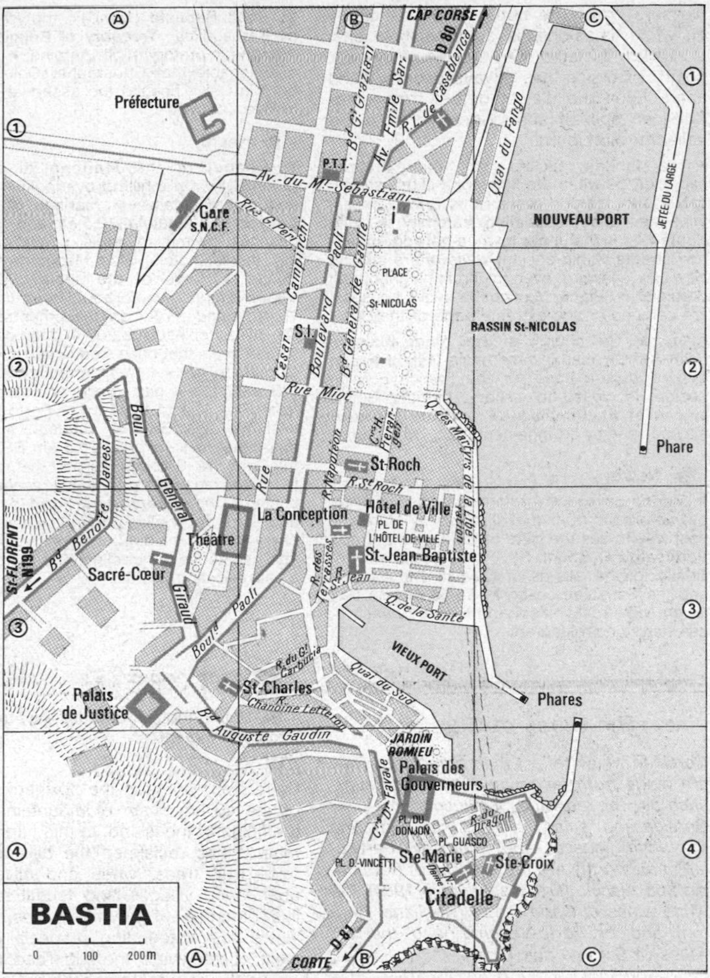

currently undergoing repairs). Among the exhibits is the turret of the submarine Casabianca, which played a crucial role in the liberation of Corsica during WWII. ▶ The **church of Ste. Marie** (built between 1495 and 1604) displays a sculpted-silver Assumption★ (1856). ▶ The nearby **chapel of Ste. Croix** is richly decorated with gilded stucco; the water-blackened image of Christ★ was found floating in the sea in 1428.

Also... ▶ Works of art in the **chapel of the Conception** (B3). **The municipal Library.** □

■ BAVELLA Pass★★★

B3

The Bavella Pass *(alt. 1 243 m)* cuts through the dorsal mountain chain to provide one of the most spectacular landscapes on the island. The granite needles of Bavella rear above a plateau covered with grass and sparsely strewn with windswept pines. To the north stretches the Incudine Massif, whereas to the east, the sea is framed between walls of red rock.

▶ The Bavella Pass is reached by D268 linking Solenzara to Zonza *(39 km).* The road crosses **Larone Pass** (view★★) and winds through the coniferous **Bavella Forest★.** With luck you may glimpse a flock of moufflons on the rocky slopes above 1 000 m. ▶ The *auberge* (inn) on the pass will supply full information about hiking around Bavella; GR20, the main hiking trail, crosses the pass *(red/white markers).* ▶ **Zonza** ® : surrounded by forests, a favourite with trout fishermen. □

■ BONIFACIO★★

B4 / ® / pop. 2 736

Did Ulysses make landfall at Bonifacio, as the Odyssey suggests? No matter whether the legendary voyager took shelter there, today the Marina is a popular harbour for pleasure craft. The upper town, set firmly on white limestone, is an irresistible site. Bonifacio, isolated on the southernmost point of Corsica, has always been a world apart. Even the dialect differs from other Corsican speech and is derived from the Italian of old Liguria.

▶ The **Marina★ :** tucked away in an extraordinary cleft between the limestone cliffs; shops, cafés, and seafood restaurants draw tourists, fishermen and the boating fraternity. ▶ **Ville Haute★★ :** in the upper town, a network of narrow streets within ancient walls offers striking views★★ seaward, even taking in neighbouring Sardinia. ▶ **Place Manichella :** old houses★ are perched on the extreme edge of the cliff.

Also... ▶ The **church of Ste. Marie Majeure** (12th-13thC); marble tabernacle (1465). ▶ The Citadel, now a base for the French Foreign Legion, is closed to visitors, but the Gothic **church of St. Dominique★** and the cemetery may be seen by arrangement *(apply to the SI)*. □

▶ Nearby

▶ **Marine caves★★** *(grottes marines; 45 mins by motorboat from the Quai de la Marine) :* best way to see the cliffs of Bonifacio. ▶ **Cape Pertusato★★** *(5.5 km SE) :* spectacular view of Bonifacio, the islands of Cavallo and Lavezzi and the Sardinian coast. ▶ **Santa Manza Bay** *(6 km NE) :* rocky inlets and isolated beaches, sea views and restaurant. □

The wines of Corsica

Corsican wines reflect their homeland. They are made from recognised grape varieties, such as, for red wine, "nielluccio" in Upper Corsica and "sciacarello" in the south, and for white, muscat and malmsey. Particularly noteworthy are the A.O.C.s of Patrimonio and Ajaccio (first classified in 1984), the white wines of Cape Corse (Rogliano, Centuri) and of Porto-Vecchio, and the red wines of Sartène and Figari.

■ CALVI★★

A2 / ® / pop. 3633

Calvi dramatically combines past and present : the semi-deserted citadel crumbles with age, while the Marina spills over with summer life. The setting of sea, palm trees and broad beach bordered with umbrella pines against the **Cinto Massif** (snow-covered until early summer), make Calvi one of the most popular seaside resorts.

▶ The **Marina** and Rue Georges Clemenceau (running parallel), are the traditional promenades. Restaurants and cafés, vantage points for watching the comings and goings of yachts and fishing boats, keep up a brisk trade until late at night. ▶ The **Citadel,** between the bays of Calvi and Revellata, symbolises almost 5 centuries of Genoese occupation. Walk on the ramparts★, sea views. ▶ **Church of St. Jean Baptiste** (18thC) : triptych★ (15thC) by Barbagelata; **Treasury of Religious Art of Balagne** in oratory of St. Antoine. ▶ It is highly questionable that Christopher Columbus was born in Calvi, despite the assertive inscription in Rue Colombo.

▶ Nearby

▶ **Chapel** of the **Madona di a Serra★** *(6 km SW) :* on a hilltop overlooking Calvi Bay and the mountains. ▶ **Marinas of Saint'Ambroggio** and **Algajola** *(12.5 km and 15 km NE) :* beaches, swimming pools, scuba diving, sailing, tennis, hotels, Club Méditerranée holiday village. ▶ **Cave of the seals★** *(Grotte des Veaux Marins; motorboat from the Marina, 1hr45 round trip) :* on the other side of the Revellata Peninsula, a 200 m-deep cave named for the seals that once frequented it. ▶ **Calvi to Girolata by sea★★** *(daily from the Marina, 9 am, Easter-Oct, full day, lunch at Girolata :* view from Revellata to the Bay of Porto and Piana inlet, via the Bay of Girolata. ▶ **Bonifato amphitheatre★** *(cirque; 20.5 km SE) :* beyond the Calvi Ste.-Catherine airport thef road enters the Calenzana Forest (recently ravaged by fire), ending at the **Auberge de la Forêt** (details available here for walking tours), where the porphyry walls of the natural amphitheatre of Bonifato rise above the treeline. The road turns into a path rejoining GR20. □

■ CAPE CORSE★★

▶ Round trip *(113 km, full day)* from Bastia to Saint Florent

B1

Cape *(cap)* Corse is the northern extremity of the 40 km chain of mountains forming the spine of the island. In this harsh setting, *maquis* has reclaimed the hillsides where once fruit trees, vines and olives grew; abandoned villages and feudal ruins look like outcrops of the mountains. The sea views are astounding, especially on the west coast where the cliff road runs high above the saw-tooth coastline. Cape Corse natives, unlike other Corsicans, have always been drawn to the sea and distant lands, such as South America and the West Indies. Imposing houses *(palazzi)* attest to the profitability of these sojourns abroad. Characteristic of the peninsula are the *marines,* or marinas, once village extensions for fishing and trading, now given over to tourism.

▶ **Bastia** (→). ▶ **Lavasina :** renowned for pilgrimages to the Virgin Mary. From here you can reach **Monte Stello★★** *(4 km by road to Pozzo then a 5hr walk round trip) :* highest point on the cape *(1307 m).* ▶ **Sisco** *(7 km left) :* 17 hamlets surrounded by myrtle, heather, arbutus, chestnut and holm oak; church of St. Martin (reliquary of St. John Chrysostom★★, 13th or 14thC); 15 min walk to the **church of St. Michele★** (Romanesque, 11thC); view★. ▶ Romanesque **church of Santa-Catharina :** oriental-style ceramic decorations. ▶ **Macinaggio :** long a port, now an important marina; **Tomino** *(3.5 km SW) :* panorama★. ▶ **Rogliano★ :** three castles, three churches, eight hamlets, fortified towers clinging to the rock; once a powerful stronghold that controlled all the north of Cape Corse. ▶ **Ersa** (*16 km round trip to* **Tollare★** *and* **Barcaggio★** ®) : a few stone houses isolated on the point facing a small island of green serpentine marble. ▶ **Moulin Mattei :** panorama★ over cape and sea. ▶ **Centuri-Port★★** ® *(5 km right) :* prettiest marina on the peninsula. ▶ **Pino :** a village perched above the sea; narrow road to **Bocca di Santa Lucia★** *(5 km)* and Seneca's Tower *(30 min walk)* : panorama★★. ▶ **Canari★★** on the mountainside; churches of Santa Maria★ (12thC) and St. François. ▶ Pass the disused asbestos mine at Albo to reach **Nonza★ :** an ancient stronghold built on sheer black rock. □

■ CARGÈSE★

A3 / ® / pop. 898

Cargèse, on a granite promontory between the bays of Sagone and Pero, is reminiscent of Greece where, indeed, many of the inhabitants have their origins. The people maintain the cultural and religious traditions of their forebears who fled from Ottoman oppression in the 17thC. Opposite the Catholic church stands an Orthodox church decorated with icons in the Byzantine style.

▶ **Sagone** *(13 km SE)* and **Tiuccia** *(21 km SE)* in the curve of the **bay of Sagone★ :** pleasant resorts on a fine sandy beach. □

■ CASINCA★★

B2

This is one of the most fertile regions of Corsica and one of the most densely populated. Between the sea and the mountains — Monte Sant'Angelo — lie fields of corn, vegetables, citrus, vines and tobacco. □

▶ Tour of **Casinca** *(35 km, narrow roads).*

▶ **Vescovato★** (pop. 2 129), the principal town of this little region, is reached by D237, which branches off 2.5 km SE of **Casamozza.** ▶ Continue through **Venzolasca** to **Loreto-di-Casinca★★** *(detour 16 km round trip on D6)* and **Penta-di-Casinca** and **Castellare-di-Casinca★** ® : exceptionally well-situated villages with typical Corsican architecture. □

■ The CASTAGNICCIA Heights★★★

▶ From Ponte Leccia to the east coast *(76 km, full day)*
B2 *(see map 2)*

A garden fortress in a maze of mountains, Castagniccia is difficult to reach but worth the effort. This was a stronghold of island resistance, where the signal was given for revolt against the Genoese. Pascal Paoli (18thC leader of Corsican independence) was born here. Narrow roads twisting through the rocky landscape offer glimpses of hidden valleys. The chestnut trees that gave Castagniccia its name (bot. Castanea : chestnut) and former prosperity (flour, timber) are still plentiful, but this *arbre à pain* ("bread tree", as it is known locally) is no longer economically important. The villages scattered along the mountain crests today are almost deserted; the villagers have left to work in the plain or on the Continent.

▶ **Ponte Leccia.** ▶ Follow D71 : at Serna Pass, turn left for **Santa-Maria-de-Valle-di-Rostino** *(5 km by road then a 15 min walk) :* pre-Romanesque church (10C) in ruins and **St Tomoso de Pastoreccia** (6 km by road, then a 10 min walk and a pre-Romanesque chapel with 15th-16thC frescos★. ▶ **Morosaglia** (pop. 854) : birthplace of Pascal Paoli (museum : documents, personal effects); his remains are buried in the chapel. ▶ **Porta** *(8 km left) :* Baroque church (1720), bell-tower★; concerts in summer on the Italian-style organ (1780). ▶ **Campana** (pop. 20) : church (Adoration of the Shepherds★★, 17thC school of Seville). ▶ **Campodonico** *(3.5 km right) :* path up Monte San Petrone *(alt. 1 767 m; 5 hr round trip),* panorama★★. ▶ **Convent of Orezza** (ruins) : formerly a centre of Corsican resistance (Paoli met Napoléon here in 1790). ▶ **Piedicroce** (pop. 164) : oldest pipe-organ★ (17thC) in Corsica; *verde di Corsica* (Corsican green), a type of marble found only in this region, was used to decorate the Medici chapel in Florence, Italy. ▶ **Carcheto** (pop. 39) : Baroque bell-tower★. ▶ **Valle d'Alesani** ® (pop. 192) : another stronghold of resistance against the Genoese. A German adventurer had himself proclaimed King Theodore I of Corsica here in the 18thC; church (15thC Sienese painting : the Virgin of the Cherries★★). ▶ **Cervioni** (pop. 1 254) : vineyards, view★ of the eastern plain. ▶ **Chapel of Sta. Cristina** *(1 km to Valle di Campoloro then 45 min walk round trip, rocky path) :*

2. Castagniccia heights

twin Romanesque apses decorated with frescos★ (1473). ▶ Route along the cliff road of Castagniccia★. **San Nicolao** (pop. 867) : terraced village surrounded by orchards, chestnut and olive trees. □

■ CORTE

B2 / ® / pop. 5 446

Corte is a symbol of independence in the heart of the island. From 1755 to 1769 it was Paoli's capital. As the seat of the Corsican university, it embodies the island's cultural identity.

▶ On the Cours Paoli, the main artery of Corte, students debate the latest news in the Rex-Bar. ▶ From Place Paoli walk through the **Old Town** *(Vieille Ville)* to the Place Gaffori (bullet marks on façades are relics of violent fighting during the 18thC war of independence). ▶ The **National Palace** (seat of the independent government of Corsica), the **Citadel** and the **Belvédère★** overlook the Tavignano and Restonica gorges. □

▶ Nearby

▶ **Restonica Gorges★★** *(15 km SW first towards Ajaccio then turn right).* ▶ The gorges are the starting point for several hikes : **Lake Melo** and **Lake Capitello★** (pleasant ; *1hr15 for the former, 2hr for the latter*) ; **Monte Rotondo★** (alt. 2 262 m ; recommended but rather difficult towards the top ; *5hr up, 4hr down*). ▶ **Tavignano Gorges★** (no road ; *6hr30 to the pass*) : wild and splendid country. ▶ **Popolasca** *(20 km NNW ; Bastia road and left on D18)* : a pleasant drive in the countryside around Corte ; the village is overshadowed by red rock needles★ similar to those at Bavella. ▶ **Sermano★** *(23 km E ; Bastia road and right on D41)* : one of the rare villages where Mass is still sung in the old Corsican settings for male voices *(a paghiella)* : chapel of San Nicolao *(15 min walk from the village ;* frescos★). Roads from **Sermano** invite exploration : **Casardo Pass★ ; Zuani** (old houses★) ; **San Cervone Pass★.** □

Boating in Corsica

Corsica is a haven for navigators in every kind of vessel — from yachts to inflatable dinghies. The rocky, jagged coastline invites exploration among inlets and beaches inaccessible to landlubbers. Especially attractive are Cape Corse, the Agriates Desert, the bays of Girolata and Porto, the southern coast of Propriano, and Bonifacio and Porto-Vecchio.
The best-equipped marinas : Ajaccio, Propriano, Porto-Vecchio, Campoloro, Macinaggio, Centuri-Port, Saint Florent, Sant'Ambroggio and Calvi.

■ EVISA★

A2 / ® / pop. 248

Between Corte and Porto, a stopover 830 m high among chestnut trees and swift streams. □

▶ Nearby

▶ **Spelunca Gorges★★** *(3hr walk to Ota)* : leave by the Porto road and turn right past the cemetery wall to arrive at the Geneoese bridge at **Zaglia★** (base of the **Spelunca amphitheatre★★**). ▶ **Aïtone Forest** *(4.5 km on the Corte road to the forester's lodge)* : pine, beech, fir and holm oak (4 200 acres) ; the lodge is the starting point for walks to **Bocca di Salto** *(1hr)* and **Bocca di Cocavera** *(3hr)* ; panorama★★. ▶ **Vico** ® *(21 km SE)* and **Guagno** *(42 km SE)* on D70. Drive over Sevi Pass to **Vico,** then take D23 left to the spa at **Guagno-les-Bains** and **Guagno,** in the heart of the forest ; up to **Orto** and on to **Soccia★.** □

The maquis

Once the refuge of "bandits d'honneur" (→ Vendetta) *and just plain bandits, the* maquis *and forests of stone pine are typical of the Corsican countryside. The* maquis *covers almost two-thirds of the island with dense scrub up to 6 m high that tends to take over cultivated land and burnt forest.*
Many different species combine to make up this mixture : cistus, arbutus, briars, Corsican broom, asphodel, clematis, smilax, holm oak. Napoléon used to say that he could recognise Corsica with his eyes shut, just by the smell of the maquis.
The Corsicans are hoping to perfect a shredder — "the mechanical mule" — in an attempt to recover some of the formerly cultivated land now overrun by the maquis.

■ FILITOSA★★

A3-4

The face of prehistoric Corsica can be seen in the stone warriors of Filitosa. The men who appeared in the Taravo valley as early as 6 000BC were shepherd warriors. Towards 2 000BC the inhabitants of Filitosa had created a structured society and had built strongholds such as Torre and Cucuruzzu. Their crowning achievement was the creation of statues of armed men on which the fame of the region rests. It has been suggested that the indigenous people might have been conquered by the Shardanes (Torréens in Corsican), skilled navigators who plied the Mediterranean. (Filitosa : *8am to sunset ;* better light am).

▶ The **Museum** near the entrance displays excavated artifacts. ▶ 70 m ahead to the right is **Filitosa V★,** most representative of menhirs of this type. ▶ The **oppidum** (town) : a group of fortifications and religious monuments fashioned from large boulders. Above and to the right of the entrance is **Filitosa IX★,** the megalithic masterpiece. ▶ The remains of a **Torréen village** and five menhirs in a quarry are still visible. □

■ FIUMORBO

B3

An isolated stretch that takes its name from the Fiumorbo river. The local people were renowned for their independence and unceasing resistance to foreign occupation.

Hemmed around by mountains and chestnut forests, the villages look across to **Aléria.**

▶ Walk through **Fiumorbo** from **Ghisonaccia** to **Prunelli-di-Fiumorbo★** (*19 km;* pop. 2 050). □

■ GHISONI

B3 / pop. 385

In a deep valley, unlike most Corsican villages, Ghisoni lies below the Verde and Sorba Passes.

▶ 27 km of beautiful road, running between the green serpentine walls of the **Inzecca Pass,** then through the **Strette Pass★,** links Ghisoni to **Ghisonaccia.** Ghisonaccia has thrived since modern cultivation was introduced to the eastern plain. □

■ LEVIE

B4 / pop. 752

The archaeological museum *(9-12 & 2-6, Jun.-Sep.; 10-12 & 2-5 winter)* shows that man lived on the Levie plateau from Neolithic times until the Bronze and Iron Ages; ivory Christ (15thC; *apply to presbytery below church*). □

▶ Nearby

▶ **Cucuruzzu★** *(3.5 km on D268, then 3.5 km right and 700 m on foot; guided tours in season) :* fortified Torréen stronghold (→ Filitosa) from the Bronze Age. View★ to the Bavella needles. ▶ **Sainte-Lucie-de-Tallano** (*8.5 km SW;* pop. 362) : one of the best Corsican wines is produced here. A rare variety of greenstone★ (orbicular diorite) is quarried nearby. ▶ Church (**holy water stoup★** and **marble bas-relief,** 15thC). The **Crucifixion★★** and the **Virgin and Child altarpiece★** are currently in restoration. ▶ **Carbini** (*8 km SE;* pop. 125) : in the Middle Ages a sect called the Giovannali preached and practised communal living here; they were massacred. **Church of San Giovanni★** (12thC). □

■ MARIANA★

B2

Named for Marius who founded it in 92BC during the Roman colonisation of Corsica.

▶ Only a few sections of brick wall remain from Roman times. In the 12thC the Pisans built La Canonica★★ the Romanesque cathedral *(key in café opposite).* ▶ 50m S, remains of an earlier cathedral (4th-10thC) and baptistery decorated with **mosaics★.** ▶ **Church of San Parteo** *(300m SW)* has a noteworthy apse (11thC). □

■ The NIOLO Region★★

A2

Niolo is a region of superlatives. Bounded in the west by the Vergio pass and the upper Golo basin and in the east by the Scala di Santa Regina are the grandest mountains (the Cinto Massif), the biggest river (the Golo), the most extensive pine forests, the highest villages, and the oldest traditions.

Corsican cuisine

The pigs that run wild through the maquis provide the raw material for an excellent charcuterie : prisuttu *(the Corsican version of* prosciutto *ham),* lonzu *(rolled and smoked fillet of pork),* coppa, salciccie *(a kind of salami) and* figatelli *(smoked pork liver sausage). Roast leg of lamb, kid and suckling pig are also very good. Fish dishes include mullet, bream or bass baked or grilled over aromatic herbs, langoustes (small Mediterranean lobster) and other shellfish, as well as* azimu, *the local fish soup.*
Brocciu, *a cheese made from a mixture of whey and whole milk from either ewes or goats, is an important ingredient in Corsican cooking. It adds flavour to soups, cakes, turnovers and fritters, as well as* pasta *dishes, which are widely favoured.*
Noteworthy cheeses are the soft varieties of Calenzana, Niolo and Venaco, and the pressed cheese of Sartène. Corsican ewe's milk is used in the production of 10 % of mainland Roquefort.
The chestnut is eaten in many forms : as flour it makes desserts, cakes and fritters; whole as a vegetable it goes well with boiled fennel. Popular dishes include omelettes flavoured with mint, asparagus tips, mushrooms, or brocciu.

Sheep and goats, always the mainstay of the region, are still more economically important than forestry.

▶ **Calacuccia** (pop. 418) : the main town in the region alongside the reservoir; a base for excursions to the Cinto massif. ▶ **Casamaccioli** (*3 km SW;* pop. 500) : view of the Cinto from the other side of the lake. ▶ **Scala di Santa Regina★** *(10 km NE) :* the Corte road runs through a pass hewn from granite. ▶ **Valdo-Niello Forest★** *(24 km SW to the Vergio pass on the Porto road) :* 46 km² of stone pine, alder and beech; Corsica's largest forest. ▶ **Lake Nino★** *(2hr30 drive)* 14 km along D84 towards Porto, then left on a track joining GR20. ▶ **Monte Cinto★★** *(4hr30 to the glacier edge round trip; 7hr to the top) :* D218 via Lozzi, drive for 10 km, then hike. □

■ OSPEDALE Forest★

B4

Spread above the bay of Porto-Vecchio, this 45 km² pine forest looks on to granite needles.

▶ **Porto-Vecchio** (→) to **Zonza** *(40 km) :* D368 runs through wooded peaks and the Barocaggio-Marghese forest, crossing the Ospedale dam; 800 m past the dam, an unmarked path on the right leads to the **Piscia di Gallo waterfall** *(often dry in summer; 2hr round trip).* □

■ Bay of PORTO★★★

A2 *(see map 3, following page)*

The most beautiful spot is in the bay of

3. Bay of Porto

Beautiful beaches

In July and August empty beaches exist only in the imagination. However, certain parts of the Corsican coast are so difficult to reach by land that they remain the preserve of boating enthusiasts : Saleccia (→ Agriates Desert), Girolata (→ Porto). On Cape Corse, Barcaggio and Nonza beaches are usually quiet even at the height of the season. The most beautiful beaches of fine sand are in the bay of Valinco (→ Propriano) and around Porto-Vecchio (→), but first prize goes to Palombaggia, with its red rocks and umbrella pines. Another superb seascape is the cove at Ficajola, near Piana (→ Porto). On the east coast, the beaches are huge stretches of sand, bordered by hotels and holiday villages; they are particularly suitable for children, since the sea is warm and shallow. Calvi beach (→) has 7 km of sand surrounded by pine forest.

Girolata; farther on, the granite needles and columns of the Calanche rise 300 m above the water.

▶ **Porto** ® : restaurants and hotels deep in the bay and at the end of the valley; climb *(5 min)* the Genoese tower on the promontory to watch the sunset★★; eucalyptus wood along the pebble beach. ▶ **Sea excursions★★** leave Porto for the Calanche *(2hr)* or Girolata *(3hr)*.

▶ From Porto to the Calanche and Capo Rosso *(approx 22 km)*

▶ Drive to the chalet at Roches Bleues *(8 km from Porto),* where you can obtain all the directions you need for walks around the Calanche; **castle** *(60-75 min return, blue markers)*; former **mule track** *(chemin des Muletiers★; 60-90 min return, blue markers).* ▶ **Piana** ® : D624 *(right)* runs down to **Ficajola cove★★** *(4 km),* and D824 runs towards **Capo Rosso** (*9 km*; splendid view★★) and the beach at Arone. ▶ **Lava pass★★** *(1 km S from Piana by D81)* : view over the Calanche and the **bays of Porto and Girolata.**

▶ From Porto to Girolata *(23 km then 4hr walk round trip)*

▶ D81 leaves the red rocks of Bussaglia beach on the left. Beyond Partinello, pebble beach at Caspio. ▶ **La Croix Pass** *(272 m)* : view★★★ of the bays of Porto and Girolata. ▶ From the pass, a mule track leads to a fishing hamlet deep in the bay of **Girolata**; rendez-vous for pleasure craft (inns). □

■ Bay of PORTO-VECCHIO★★

B4

White sand, emerald sea, umbrella pine and cork-oak forests are the setting for the inlets and sun-filled creeks of this bay. Before WWII Porto-Vecchio was a malaria-ridden village. Today, free of malaria, it is a town (pop. 8 103, inflated to 40 000 in summer) whose old streets and Genoese fortifications are steadily being turned into a seaside resort. It is the third largest port on the island and exports locally harvested cork as well as wine. There is an attractive olive grove by the marina *(1 km).*

▶ **Piccovagia peninsula★★** *(28 km round trip)* : closes the southern end of the bay. Take the Bonifacio road (N198) south, and proceed left on V7. **Palombaggia beach★★** : looking over to the Cerbicale Islands. ▶ **Santa Giulia Bay★** *(8 km S)* : Club Méditerranée, and a white sand beach. ▶ **Sogno Bay, Saint Cyprien** and **Pinarello★★** ® beaches *(approx 15 km).* D468 (narrow) leads to creeks and inlets on the northern coast of the bay : holiday villages, campsites and small hotels. ▶ **Torre** and **Arraggio★** *(8 km and 10 km N)* : stone fortresses built during the Bronze Age (2000BC). □

■ PROPRIANO★

A4 / ® / pop. 3 098

On Valinco Bay, kilometres of fine sand border a placid sea, ideal for underwater fishing and aquatic sports. □

▶ Nearby

▶ **Valinco Bay★, north coast : Porto-Pollo** and **Filitosa★★** *(28 km).* Cliff road above the bay; after 14 km, road to the right for Filitosa (→) : prehistoric statues. **Porto-Pollo** ® : a family resort where sailing boats used to load charcoal. ▶ **Valinco Bay★, south coast : Belvédère** and **Campomoro** *(16 km; light best in the evening).* Portigliolo : 1.5 km of sand. Belvédère overlooking the bay. **Campomoro★** : a Genoese watch-tower at the end of the cape. ▶ **Olmeto** *(9.5 km N)* : Prosper Mérimée (1803-1870; author of *Carmen*) featured the town in *Colomba,* a novel that traced the course of a *vendetta.* Nearby, **Fozzano, Santa Maria-Figaniella, Arbellara** and **Viggianello** overlook the bay of Valinco. □

■ QUENZA

B2 / pop. 229

The Bavella needles *(aiguilles)* rear like

fangs above the horizon; to the north lies the Cuscione plateau, among southern Corsica's finest high pastures, and a centre for cross-country skiing, horse riding and hiking; church (carved pulpit and panels, 16thC).

▶ **Aullène** ® *(15 km W)* : church with pulpit whose carving recalls the pirate raids that ravaged the coast until the 18thC. □

■ REGIONAL NATURE PARK★★

AB 2-3

200 km^2 (a quarter of the island) stretching from the Bay of Porto to the forests of Ospedale, this sampler of Corsica's natural assets offers deep creeks, beaches, lakes and rivers, rocks, woods, and mountain heaths. The objective is to protect flora and fauna, but the park is also designed to encourage agricultural development and the prevention of forest fires. Native species include *moufflon*, bearded vulture, osprey, golden eagle and kite. More easily spotted : wild boar, the Corsican nuthatch (which climbs pine trees), pigeon, woodcock and trout.

▶ GR20, see marked route on sightseeing map

▶ Hiking on GR20 is the best and most energetic way to explore the reserve : 200 km from Calenzana (near Calvi) to Conca (above Porto-Vecchio). Eleven equipped lodges and chalets; hotels and private huts near the route. GR20 is passable from mid-Jun. (snow still possible) to the beginning of Nov. Time for the journey : about 15 days. Take proper equipment, including warm clothing and good mountain- or rock-climbing boots. Certain stretches are very difficult and sometimes dangerous. □

Crafts

Corsica has always had to depend on its own resources. Thus evolved a simple, almost rudimentary craftsmanship, derived from function and utility. Local production began to decline only toward the end of the 19thC, when manufactured goods were imported in large quantities from the continent.

Today, Corsican craftsmanship is undergoing a revival, thanks to the efforts of associations such as La Corsicada (Communauté d'Organisation Rurale pour le Service, l'Information et la Création de l'Artisanat de l'Art). The Corsican Centre for Social Advancement provides professional training for craftsmen, and local handicrafts (pottery, wickerwork, woodcarving, jewellery, knives, weaving) are on sale at craftshops (case di l'artigiani) *in Ajaccio, Bastia, Corte, Cargese, Murato, Evisa, Pigna (HQ of La Corsicada), Sartène and Zonza.*

■ SAINT-FLORENT★

B1 / ® / pop. 1 217

Base for pleasure craft and scuba diving; the regional capital of Nebbio along the shoreline deep in a picture-postcard bay★ : Place des Portes, marina, and old town around the Genoese citadel.

▶ **Nebbio Cathedral★** *(1 km; key from the SI on the Bastia road)* : this handsome Romanesque building (early 12thC Pisan) is the only vestige of the city of Nebbio; carved stylised animals on some capitals.

▶ Around Nebbio★★ *(60 km round trip, approx. 4hr)*

▶ The region fans out from the bay of Saint-Florent to a semicircle of mountains on the horizon; vineyards (including those of Patrimonio), orchards and olive groves alternate with pastureland and sheepfolds.

▶ Take D81 towards Calvi; after 5 km, take D62 left. ▶ **Santo-Pietro-di-Tenda :** a red stone church (17thC); 800 m farther on, the ruins of the Romanesque St. Pietro (13thC). ▶ **Sorio.** ▶ **Rapale :** Romanesque church of **San Michele★★;** unusual gate-tower; white and green (serpentine) walls. ▶ **San Stefano Pass★★** *(road right towards Bastia via Lancone Pass★)* : the sea on either side. **Oletta :** known for a Roquefort-like cheese. ▶ **Teghime Pass★★ :** view of both flanks of Cape Corse is even better if you go up to the **Serra di Pigno★★** *(4 km of narrow road; left just after the pass towards Bastia).* ▶ **Patrimonio :** renowned for wine. □

■ SARTÈNE★

A4 / ® / pop. 3 184

The austere mediaeval buildings are typically Corsican; flowered window-boxes and garlands of washing brighten the sombre granite walls in the old town★.

▶ **Church :** cross and chains carried by the Grand Penitent during the penitential procession *(Procession du Catenacciu)* on Good Friday evening; this ritual is often compared to that of Holy Week in Seville. ▶ **Museum of Prehistoric Corsica★** *(10-12 & 2-5 or 6; winter, closed Sat. and Sun.)* : artifacts dating from the early Mediterranean Neolithic (6000BC) to the early Iron Age. ▶ **Panorama★** from the rocky outcrop overlooking the village from the east. □

▶ Nearby

▶ **Belvédère de Foce★** *(5 km E)* : view of the Rizzanèse basin and Valinco Bay. ▶ The **Palaggiu megaliths** *(16 km SW)* : 258 menhirs, the largest single group in the Mediterranean. The road continues to the marina at **Tizzano** *(5 km)* : beach, creeks, scuba diving. ▶ The **Fontanaccia dolmen** *(17 km SSW)* : six vertical stones supporting a horizontal slab 3.40 m long. Nearby : **Rinaiu** (45 menhirs) and **Stantari** (25 menhirs). □

■ TAVIGNANO Valley

B2-3

The Tavignano river winds through rocky gorges between Corte and Aléria before running into the eastern plain. Ancient villages clinging to the northern slopes are linked by cliff roads.

▶ Along the Tavignano *(84 km, leave Corte by D14)*

▶ **Erbajolo** : panorama★★. ▶ **Altiani.** ▶ **Piedicorte-di-Gaggio** : view★. ▶ **Pancheraccia.** Return to Corte by N200 beside the river. □

■ VIZZAVONA★

B3 / ®

Just off the Bastia-Ajaccio road, this hideaway in the heart of the forest consists of a minuscule railway station and a few hotels. As a stopover on GR20, Vizzavona is popular with hikers. ▶ The **forest★,** 3 700 acres of pine and beech, is criss-crossed with walking trails. **Vizzavona Pass** (alt. 1 168 m; *3 km towards Ajaccio*) links the schist region of NE Corsica to the crystalline rocks of the SW. □

▶ Nearby

▶ Excursions on foot ranging from easy strolls to cross-country treks. ▶ Chemin des Ponts *(45 min).* ▶ **Madonuccia** *(1hr).* ▶ **Cascade des Anglais** *(45 min).* ▶ **Punta di u Ceppa** *(1hr30).* **Monte d'Oro★** *(8hr30 round trip).* □

Vendetta

Rough justice was a natural response to the venal and arbitrary decisions officially meted out to the Corsicans by the Genoese. The vendetta *was a predictable reflex on an island where violence was a way of life.*
A vendetta *might originate with an offence or a slight to someone's honour, but it was just as likely to have an economic trigger, such as a dispute over water or pasture.*
Once started, the vendetta *could continue for generations, decimating families. To escape the authorities, avengers often took to the* maquis. "Bandit of honour", *signifying an outlaw of the* vendetta, *was a title often spuriously claimed by common criminals and escaped prisoners.*

■ ZICAVO

B3 / ® / pop. 269

Among mountains covered in beech and chestnut, this large village is a base for hiking and cross-country skiing excursions towards the Coscione and the Incudine ranges.

▶ **Incudine★★** (2 128 m) : vantage point of southern Corsica, accessible by a forest road and GR20 *(4hr30 round trip).* □

Architecture

According to the Corsicans, "three houses and an oven *(tre case e un fornu)* are enough to make a village *(paisolu)*". And the island villages are often very small : perched on rocky peaks, clinging to steep slopes

Near Porto-Vecchio

or buried in valleys, the diminutive clusters of dwellings seem to have grown out of the rocks rather than to have been built by human hands. ● Corsican houses, gradually expanded over generations to accommodate the entire family, are usually several houses in one. In fact, villages rather resemble complex houses, with streets instead of passages, and village squares instead of open space. ● In the north, schist; in the south and centre, granite; around Bonifacio and Saint-Florent, limestone : these are the preferred materials. But the size and shape of the Corsican house is always much the same : three or four stories in a tall, rectangular block. ● Schist cut into fine slabs *(teghje)* is used

Facade embellished by staircase

in the north for roofing, whereas elsewhere pantiles are more common ; a few old houses still have roofs of chestnut shingles *(scandule)* held in place by blocks of granite.

Cape Corse

Brief regional history

6500-ca. 565BC

The first traces of **prehistoric man** in Corsica are relatively recent, dating from the Early Neolithic era. An immigrant, he was principally a hunter-gatherer before progressing to the use of primitive agricultural techniques. ● The **Megalithic period,** ca. 3000-1000BC, saw the arrival of various civilisations, which left traces of their culture in the form of **dolmens** and **menhirs** (stone monuments), forts, and burial vaults. The most interesting are the **menhirs** dating from around 1500BC. Their stylised human forms resemble the stone figures found in the Cyclade Islands.

565BC-455AD

Recorded history in Corsica began with the **Phoceans** (Greeks from Asia Minor) who also founded Marseilles on the mainland. They founded the city of Alalia (modern Aléria), introduced the cultivation of wheat, olives and vines, and established mining and international trade as well as written communication. ● The subsequent **Roman occupation** of Corsica lasted 6 centuries from 260BC, but remains from this period are meagre, apart from the discoveries at **Aléria** and less significant finds at Mariana, Rome's second colony on the island. ● Even fewer traces were left by the conquered inhabitants. This is not surprising, since they were largely shepherd tribes, who supplemented their staple diet by gathering honey and hunting boar.

455-1077

Successive **invasions** (Vandals, Ostrogoths, Byzantines and Lombards) brought anarchy and poverty after the relative security of Roman rule. This turbulent period saw the rise of an aristocracy of native Corsicans. As they fought for land and power, these aristocrats did not hesitate to form alliances with one or other of the foreign powers — namely, **Pisa** or **Genoa** — that were contending for possession of Corsica.

1077-1755

Long after the **Pax Romana,** the **Pax Pisana** — rule by the Italian city-state of Pisa — was established (1077-1284). ● Trade increased greatly during this period and many churches were built (→ box). **Genoa** took over the island after finally defeating Pisa in the naval battle of Méloria (1284). ● The Genoese held sway for 484 years, and founded or fortified the towns of Calvi, Ajaccio, Porto-Vecchio, Bastia and Saint Florent. Watch-towers erected by the Genoese for defense are still in existence on many parts of the coast. ● Faced with both anarchy and Genoese exploitation, the native Coriscans made several attempts to seize control of their destiny. The **Terre du Commun** revolt of 1384, the struggles led by **Sampiero Corso** in 1564 and the War of Independence between 1729 and 1769 (the 40 Years' War) ultimately led to annexation by France, which had already intervened several times, either on her own account (1553) or at the request of Genoa (1737, 1747).

1755 to the present day

In 1755 the Corsicans declared **Pascal Paoli** "General of the Nation"; a new constitution was proclaimed, the economy was reorganised, the University of Corte was founded and education was made compulsory. By 1762, Corsica was practically independent, and again Genoa sought the aid of France to suppress insurrection. ● In 1768, the Genoese ceded their claims on Corsica to the French. On **8 May 1769** French troops defeated the Corsican patriots at **Ponte Nuovo;** Corsica was now united with France, for better or worse. ● Patronised by the monarchy, ignored by the successive governments of the Revolution, the Consulate and the Empire, Corsica thrived only under the July Monarchy (Louis-Philippe, 1830) and the Second Empire (Napoléon III, 1852). A network of roads was created and more land was brought under cultivation. However, population growth (from 150 000 in 1796 to 322 000 in 1936) forced many Corsicans to leave the island, which lacked the resources to feed them. ● **WWI accelerated the outflow.** Depleted of its youth, Corsica failed to modernise agriculture and industry, and instead remained entrenched in outmoded practices. In 1974 the island was divided into two departments : **Haute Corse** (Upper Corsica, pop. 131 574) and **Corse du Sud** (Southern Corsica, pop. 108 604). ● In 1982 Corsica became the first French region to elect a regional assembly.

Practical information

The region

Information : *Fédération régionale des O.F.S.I.,* 22, cours Grandval, 20000 Ajaccio, ☎ 95.51.00.22 ; Paris : *Paris-Corse Accueil,* 3, rue des Lavandières-Sainte-Opportune, 75001 Paris, ☎ (1) 42.36.23.29.

Maps : *Michelin,* nº 90 at 1/200 000. *I.G.N.,* nºs 73 and 74 at 1/100 000.

S.O.S. : Corse-du-Sud : *S.A.M.U.* (Emergency Medical Service), ☎ 95.21.50.50. **Haute-Corse :** *police station,* ☎ 95.33.52.06. *Poisoning emergency centre :* ☎ 95.75.25.25. *Mountain rescue :* ☎ 95.23.30.31. *Diving emergencies,* ☎ 95.21.52.67 and 95.21.37.02.

Weather forecast : Corse-du-Sud : ☎ 95.21.32.71. **Haute-Corse :** ☎ 95.36.04.96.

Air travel : *Air France* and *Air Inter* offer daily flights, as does *T.A.T.* in the high season. There are airports at Ajaccio, Bastia, Calvi and Figari. Enquiries and reservations : *Air Inter,* 12, rue de Castiglione, 75001 Paris, ☎ (1) 45.39.25.25 ; *Air France,* 119, av. des Champs-Élysées, 75008 Paris, ☎ (1) 45.35.61.61 ; *T.A.T.,* 17, rue de la Paix, 75002 Paris, ☎ (1) 42.61.85.85.

Ferries : *S.N.C.M. :* Daily service during high season and twice weekly in winter from Marseilles, Nice, Toulon to Ajaccio, Bastia, Calvi, Ile-Rousse and Propriano. The crossing takes between 5 and 10 hours. Summer crossings should be booked well in advance. Enquiries and reservations : Paris, 12, rue Godot-de-Mauroy, 75009, ☎ (1) 42.66.60.19 ; Marseilles, 61, bd des Dames, ☎ 91.91.90.20 ; Nice, 3, av. Gustave-V, ☎ 93.89.89.89 ; Toulon, C.M.T., 21 et 49, av. de l'Infanterie-de-Marine, ☎ 94.41.25.76 and 94.41.01.76, and in all major railway stations and S.N.C.F. tourist offices.

Rural gîtes and chambres d'hôtes : *Relais Régional des Gîtes Ruraux,* 22, bd Paoli, 20177 Ajaccio, ☎ 95.22.14.60.

Holiday villages : The *Guide de Villages de Vacances et du Naturisme* published by the A.R.T.L. provides a complete list.

Camping : over 100 sites. *Fédération Camping Plein Air,* Pisciatello, ☎ 95.20.00.51.

Religious events : Good Friday, procession in Ajaccio, *Catenacciu procession* in Sartène, *Cerca procession* in Erbalunga, procession in Bonifacio ; **Maundy Thursday,** *Canistrelli procession* in Calvi, and during the rest of the week, religious ceremonies in the great church Uniate de Cargèse. Mass is still sung *a paghiella* (Corsican male voice choir) in Sermano.

Exhibitions and trade fairs : in May, *Ajaccio trade fair ;* May-Jun : *Bastia trade fair.*

Sporting events : *Motoring :* Tour de Corse rally, leaving from Ajaccio (2-6 May). *Ronde d'Ajaccio* (end Jan) and a number of races in summer (Sartène, Propriano, Corte, Bastia-Tehhime). *Sailing :* Giraglia regatta (14 and 15 Jul).

Rural fairs : early Sep, *Niolo fair* in Casamaccioli ; Aug, *Castagniccia fair* at the col de Prato ; May, *St-Pancrace fair* in Sorbo ; mid-May, *Corte fair ;* end August, *fairs* in Zonza and in Renno.

Scenic railways : *S.N.C.F.* lines offer a captivating view of Corsica. Principal towns served : Ajaccio, Corte, Bastia, Ile-Rousse and Calvi. Daily connections between Ajaccio and Bastia. The Balagne tramway serves beaches between Calvi and Ile-Rousse.

Nature park : *Corsican Regional Nature Park,* Maison du Parc, 4, rue du Gal-Fiorella, 20000 Ajaccio, ☎ 95.21.56.54.

Rambling and hiking : the 173 km G.R. 20 crosses Corsica. Topoguide *I.G.N.* du G.R. 20, Michel Fabrikant guides published by Didier Richard in Grenoble.

Riding holidays : 1 000 km trails with gîtes, *Association Régionale du Tourisme Équestre Corse,* Pinetu-Lucciana, 20290 Borgo, ☎ 95.36.03.27.

Aquatic sports : *Corsican Sailing League,* President, M. J. Frigara, fossés de la Citadelle, 20000 Ajaccio, ☎ 95.21.07.79. *Corsican marina,* 24, rue Napoléon, 20200 Bastia, ☎ 95.31.01.15.

Scuba diving : *Fédération Française d'Études et de Sports sous-marins (Divers' Federation),* M. J. Bellan, 25, bd Dominique-Paoli, 20000 Ajaccio, ☎ 95.22.23.78.

Canoeing : Especially in Mar, Apr and May. M. Santonacci, rte des Sanguinaires (Barbicaja), 20000 Ajaccio, ☎ 95.21.39.46.

Potholing and spelunking : *Association Spéléologique Corse,* 2, rue Martinetti, 20000 Ajaccio, ☎ 95.21.68.21.

Climbing-mountaineering : *Associu di i Muntagnoli Corsi,* quartier Santa-Maria, 20122 Quenza, ☎ 95.78.61.25 and in Sollacaro, ☎ 95.74.62.28.

Winter sports : Cross-country skiing in Bastelica, Quenza, Evisa and Zivaco.

Hunting and shooting : *Féd. Dép. des Chasseurs de la* ***Corse-du-Sud,*** 19, av. Beverini, 20000 Ajaccio, ☎ 95.23.16.91. *Féd. Dép. de la* ***Haute-Corse,*** M. D. Mezzadri, résidence Nouvelle-Corniche, Saint-Joseph, 20200 Bastia, ☎ 95.32.25.99.

Fishing : *Féd. Dép. de Pêche et de Pisciculture,* President M. Martini, 7, bd Paoli, Bastia, ☎ 95.31.47.31. *Féd. inter-dép. de Pêche et de Pisciculture,* 13, rue du Dr-Del-Pellegrino, 20000 Ajaccio, ☎ 95.23.13.32.

Towns

AJACCIO

Corte 83, Bastia 153, Calvi 159
A3 ⊠ 20000

ℹ hôtel de ville, pl. Mal-Foch (C2), ☎ 95.21.53.39, 95.21.40.87.

SNCF (C1), ☎ 95.23.11.03.

✈ Campo dell' Oro, 7 km E, ☎ 95.21.07.07. *Air France agency,* 3, bd du Roi-Jérôme, ☎ 95.21.16.36, and at the airport, ☎ 95.21.16.70.

S.N.C.M., quai Lherminier, ☎ 95.21.90.70.

Car-hire : *Budget* train + auto, opposite the marine station, bd Sampiero, ☎ 95.22.38.00, and at the airport, ☎ 95.20.45.33.

Hotels :

★★★★***Campo dell'Oro*** (Mapotel), plage du Ricanto, ☎ 95.22.32.41. Tx 460087. AE, DC, Euro, Visa. 132 rm ⚘ P ♨ ⛱ ▭ ⛳ ♿ private beach, 690. Rest. ♦♦♦ ✾ closed 1 Jan-15 Mar, 150-350.

● ★★★***Costa,*** 2, bd Colomba (B3), ☎ 95.21.43.02. AE, DC, Euro, Visa. 53 rm ⚘ ♨ ⛱ ✾ 300.

● ★★★***Albion,*** 15, av. Gal-Leclerc (A3), ☎ 95.21.66.70. Tx 460084. AE, DC, Euro, Visa. 63 rm P ⛱ 290.

★★★***Napoléon,*** 4, rue Lorenzo-Véro, ☎ 95.21.30.01. Tx 460625. AE, DC, Euro, Visa. 62 rm ♿ 280.

● ★★***San Carlu,*** 8, bd Danielle-Casanova, ☎ 95.21.13.84. AE, DC, Euro, Visa. 44 rm ⚘ ✾ 245.

★★***Spunta di Mare,*** quartier Saint-Joseph (C2), ☎ 95.22.41.42. 64 rm ⚘ P closed mid-Dec - mid-Jan, 260. Rest. ♦ ♿ 120-210.

On the Sanguinaires road :

● ★★★★***Eden Roc*** (Relais et châteaux), ☎ 95.52.01.47. Tx 460484. AE. 34 rm ⚘ P ♨ ⛱ ✾ ▭ closed 30 Sep-4 May, 500. Rest. ♦♦ ✾ Excellent, varied cooking for regular and spoilt customers, with pension or half-pension only, 200-250.

★★★***Cala di Sole,*** ☎ 95.52.01.36. AE, DC, Euro. 31 rm ⚘ P ♨ ⛱ ▭ ⛳ ♿ closed 30 Sep-1 Apr, 345. Rest. pens. ⚘ ✾

⛺ ★★★*Château de Barbicaggia,* rte des Sanguinaires (100 pl.), ☎ 95.52.03.50 ; Pisciatello, 10 km E of Ajaccio : ★★★*U Prunelli* (300 pl.), ☎ 95.20.00.51.

Restaurants :

● ♦♦ ***L'Amore Plattu,*** 8, place du Gal-de-Gaulle, ☎ 95.51.00.53, closed 1-20 Aug, Sun and noon. You must try Marie-Louise Maestracci's delightful little restaurant for the good family style fixed price menu, 140.

● ♦♦ ***Côte d'Azur,*** 12, cours Napoléon (C3), ☎ 95.21.50.24. AE, DC, Visa ; closed Jun-20 Jul and Sun. For "continental" people who do not want to disturb their habits, but also for Corsican gourmets and gourmands, Marc Lamic's specialities : *terrine de poulet aux foies de volailles, cuisse de canard rôtie.* Natural, mild Corsican wines, muscat and malvoisie, 95-200.

♦♦ ***Palmiers,*** 3, pl. Foch (C2), ☎ 95.21.02.45. AE, DC, Visa ; closed mid-Nov-mid-Mar. A fashionable "brasserie" near the port, 120-210.

♦♦ ***Point "U",*** 59 *bis,* rue Fesch (C2), ☎ 95.21.59.92 ♿ closed 15 Mar-15 Apr and Wed. Country cooking and fresh fish, 80-130.

♦ ***Grange,*** 4, rue Notre-Dame (C2), ☎ 95.21.25.32. AE, Visa ; closed 30 Nov-1 Mar and Mon, 80-130.

♦ ***France,*** 59, rue Fesch (C2), ☎ 95.21.11.00. AE, DC, Visa ♿ closed Sun, Nov. A pleasant blend of Corsican and Perigord cooking, 50-150.

On the Sanguinaires road :

♦ ***I Sanguinari,*** at Parata Point, ☎ 95.52.01.70 ⚘ ♿ closed eve low season. In 1863, when he used to come to the biggest "islet", Alphonse Daudet already had good taste. Today, the Corsican cooking is good and simple, the sun is always there and smiles improve many things. Sea urchins (in season), 100-150.

♦ ***Auberge de la Terre Sacrée,*** ☎ 95.52.00.92 ⚘ P ♨ ⛱ ✾ closed 1-30 Oct and Tue. Corsican, good and reasonably priced cooking, 120-150.

Baleone, ⊠ 20167, 8 km NE on the N193 :

♦♦ ***Chez Maisetti,*** ☎ 95.22.37.19. closed Sun. The 65-year-old Pierrette manages this restaurant where the tradition of Corsican family cooking has been maintained : *artichauts au broccio, cabri à la corse grillé,* river trout, *beignets à la farine de châtaignes.* Local wines, 90-200.

See also Cauro and Porticcio.

Events : *Craftsmen's Day* in Jul ; *folklore festival* in Aug.

Casino, bd Lantivy, ☎ 95.21.41.44.

Bicycle hire : Centre commercial Castellani, ☎ 95.22.27.68. *Ets Solvet,* 5, rue Maglioli, ☎ 95.23.20.21 ; airport, ☎ 95.23.23.42.

Recommended : *Casa di l'Artigiani,* Corsican handicrafts, 9, rue Notre-Dame (C2). Wine : *Comte Peraldi,* ☎ 95.22.37.30 ; *Bianchelli,* clos Capitoro, rte de Sartène, Pisciatella. Corsican products : *Y. Leca,* 3, rue Fesch ; *Loviconi Valérie,* 6, rue Fesch.

ASCO and HAUT-ASCO

Corte 42, Bastia 64, Ajaccio 125
A2 ⛷ 1 450 - 1 820 m ⊠ 20276

ℹ mairie d'Asco, ☎ 95.47.82.07.

Hotel :

★***Chalet,*** ☎ 95.47.81.08. 22 rm ⚘ P ⛱ closed 30 Sep-1 Jun. View over the Cinto Massif, 160. Rest. 70-130.

BARCAGGIO

Bastia 47, Calvi 137, Ajaccio 210
12 km NE of Centuri-Port, B1 ⊠ 20275 Ersa

Hotels :

★★***La Giraglia,*** ☎ 95.35.60.54. 24 rm ⚘ P ♨ ⛱ closed 25 Sep-3 Apr, 170. Rest. 80-100.

Centuri-Port, ⊠ 20238 :

● ★***Vieux-Moulin,*** ☎ 95.35.60.15. AE, DC, Visa. 14 rm ⚘ P ♨ ⛱ ⛳ On the harbour ; closed 30 Oct-30 Mar, 145. Rest. ♦ ♿ Spec : *langouste grillée, bouillabaisse,* 85-150.

Restaurant :

♦ ***U Fanale,*** ☎ 95.35.62.72. ♿ closed Wed and 20 Sep-31 May. Situated opposite Giraglia Island. Spec : *soupe de poissons,* Corsican wines, 120-210.

BASTELICA

Ajaccio 41, Corte 62, Sartène 84
A-B3 ⊠ 20119

Hotel :

★★***U Castagnetu,*** ☎ 95.28.70.71. Visa. 15 rm ⚘ P ⛱ ⛳ closed 2 Nov-2 Dec and Tue, 145.

Rest. ♦ The cooking is a foretaste of the mountains : *charcuterie,* grilled blackbird and leg of lamb, 50-120.

Restaurant :
♦ ***Chez Paul,*** ☎ 95.28.71.59. Good simple cooking. Good broccio. Local wines, 40-65.

BASTIA

Corte 70, Calvi 93, Ajaccio 153
B1 ✉ 20200

ℹ 35, bd Paoli, ☎ 95.31.02.04 ; pl. St-Nicolas, ☎ 95.31.00.89.

✈ Bastia-Poretta, 20 km S, ☎ 95.36.03.52.

Air France Agency, 6, av. E.-Sari, ☎ 95.32.10.29, and at the airport, ☎ 95.36.03.21.

S.N.C.M., new port (C1), ☎ 95.31.36.63.

SNCF (A1), ☎ 95.31.20.09.

Car-hire : *Budget* train + auto, RN193, Furiani, ☎ 95.33.09.28, and at the airport, ☎ 95.36.05.56.

Hotels :
★★***Posta Vecchia,*** quai des Martyrs (B2), ☎ 95.32.32.38. Tx 460655. AE, DC, Euro, Visa. 44 rm 260.
★★***Bonaparte,*** 45, bd Gal-Graziani (B1), ☎ 95.34.07.10. AE, DC, Euro, Visa. 24 rm 245.

Pietranera, 2 km N :
★★★***Pietracap,*** rte de San Martino, ☎ 95.31.64.63. AE, DC, Euro, Visa. 22 rm P closed 1 Dec-28 Feb, 360.
★★***Cyrnéa,*** ☎ 95.31.41.71. 20 rm P closed 23 Dec-1 Feb, 170.

Erbajolo, 4 km on the N193, south exit :
★★★***Ostella,*** ☎ 95.33.51.05. AE, Visa. 30 rm P 180. Rest. 80-130.

Biguglia, 10 km S :
★★***Pineto,*** ☎ 95.33.56.04. AE, Visa. 11 rm P closed 10 Oct-1 Apr, 215. Rest. 45-150.

Restaurants :
● ♦♦ ***Chez Assunta,*** 4, pl. Fontaine-Neuve, ☎ 95.31.67.06. AE, DC, Visa. closed 1 Jan-30 Feb, Sun and nat hols. In a redecorated 17thC chapel, Assunta Cianelli is the perfect image of the Corsican cook ; she takes care of everything and even finds time to prepare, on request, fresh pasta, ice-creams and bread. Her husband takes care of fresh fish and *beignets.* Everything is delightful : seafood, *lapin au four,* home made desserts. Local wines, 100-160.
● ♦♦ ***Bistrot du Port,*** rue Posta-Vecchia, ☎ 95.32.19.83. P closed Feb school hols, 30 Sep-30 Oct and Sun. Cosy atmosphere and service in a 1900 style setting. J. Rovinalti's excellent cooking : a rich and wide choice of fish and meat specialities. Local and "Continental" wines, 120-150.
♦♦ ***U Tianu,*** 4, rue Mgr-Rico, ☎ 95.31.36.67. Closed Aug, 80-130.
♦♦ ***La Taverne,*** 9, rue du Gal-Carbuccia, ☎ 95.31.17.87. AE, DC, Visa. closed Mon ; Corsican cooking, 60-130.
♦♦ ***La Cantina di l'Artigiani,*** rue St-Michel, La Citadelle, ☎ 95.31.24.67. closed 1 Nov-1 Dec and Sun. Theatre evenings, 70-100.

Erbalunga, ✉ 20222, 10 km N :
♦ ***Le Pirate,*** ☎ 95.33.24.20. Visa, 120-210.

Bicycle hire : *Locanautic,* 1, rue Cdt-L'Herminier, ☎ 95.31.37.38.

Recommended : *Casa di l'Artigiani,* Corsican handicrafts, 5, rue des Terrasses, ☎ 95.32.65.21.

BOCOGNANO

Ajaccio 40, Corte 43, Bastia 113
A-B3 ✉ 20136

Hotels :
★★***Premier Consul,*** ☎ 95.27.41.51. 13 rm P closed 30 Sep-1 Apr, 140. Rest. ♦ 50-70.

Col de Vizzanova, 20219 Vivario, 9 km NE :
★***Monte d'Oro,*** ☎ 95.47.21.06. 47 rm P Forest setting ; closed Oct-Jun, 100. Rest. 80-130.

BONIFACIO

Sartène 54, Ajaccio 140, Bastia 170
B4 ✉ 20169

ℹ rue Longue, ☎ 95.73.03.48.

Connections with Sardinia, quai J.-Comparetti, ☎ 95.73.01.28.

Hotels :
● ★★★***Solemare,***
☎ 95.73.01.06. 58 rm P closed 30 Sep-1 Apr, 320.
★★★***La Caravelle,*** 11, quai Comparetti, ☎ 95.73.06.47. 30 rm closed Oct-1 Apr 310. Rest. ♦♦ Superb hotel and unforgettable specialities : *chapon farci, sole aux aubergines, canelloni aux poissons,* 200-300.
★★***Résidence du Club Nautique,*** ☎ 95.73.02.11. 10 rm P closed 1 Nov-27 Mar, 260.
★***Étrangers,*** ☎ 95.73.01.09. Visa. 30 rm P closed 15 Nov-20 Mar, 130.

⛺ ★★★*Campo di Liccia* (120 pl.), ☎ 95.73.03.09 ; ★★★*Gurgazo* (135 pl.), ☎ 95.73.05.55.

Restaurants :
● ♦♦ ***Stella d'Oro*** (Chez Jules), 7, rue Doria, ☎ 95.73.03.63. AE, DC, Visa. closed 15 Sep-15 Apr. The golden star of good cooking shines in this pleasant gourmand stopover. Fish specialities, 80-300.

Sant'Amanza Gulf, 6 km on the D58 :
♦ ***U Ceppu,*** ☎ 95.73.05.83. P closed 15 Oct-20 Mar. Tue eve and Wed in Apr, May and Oct. Fresh fish from the gulf could be prepared in a more rigourous fashion, 80-180.

BORGO

Corte 58, Calvi 110, Ajaccio 140
13 km from Bastia, B2 ✉ 20290

Hotels :
★★★***Isola,*** ☎ 95.33.19.60. Tx 460695. AE, DC, Euro, Visa. 70 rm P Private beach ; closed 31 oct-1 Apr, 390. Rest. ♦ 75-100.
★★***La Marana,*** ☎ 95.31.70.81. 240 rm P High season, 180. Rest. 80-130.

Casamozza, 8 km S :
★★★***Chez Walter,*** ☎ 95.36.00.09. 32 rm P 250. Rest. closed Mon, 120-210.
★★***Soleil Levant*** (L.F.), ☎ 95.36.02.25. AE, DC, Euro, Visa. 40 rm P 190. Rest. ♦ 65-150.

CALENZANA

Calvi 12, Corte 100, Ajaccio 172
A2 ✉ 20214

Hotels :
★***Monte Grosso,*** ☎ 95.62.70.15. 10 rm 180.
★***Bel Horizon,*** 4, pl. Prince-Pierre, ☎ 95.62.71.72. 15 rm, closed 30 Sep-31 Mar, 155.

⛺ ★★*Paradella* (150 pl.), ☎ 95.65.00.97 ; ★★*Morsetta* (90 pl.), ☎ 95.62.70.08.

Recommended : *Casa di l'Artigiani,* specially flavored wines, jams, almond-based natural foods. Coopérative de Calenzana-Balagne, ☎ 95.05.09.08.

CALVI

Bastia 93, Corte 96, Ajaccio 160
A2 ⊠ 20260

ⓘ chemin de la Plage, ☎ 95.65.05.87.

✈ Calvi-Sainte-Catherine, 7 km SE, ☎ 95.65.08.09.

⛴ *S.N.C.M.,* quai Landri, ☎ 95.65.02.81. *Corsica Ferries,* ☎ 95.65.10.84.

SNCF ☎ 95.65.00.61. Calvi-Bastia - Calvi-Ajaccio Lines. Summer service to Ile-Rousse.

Car-hire : *Budget,* train + auto, G.I.L., route de l'aéroport, ☎ 95.65.02.15, and at the airport, ☎ 95.65.11.63.

Hotels :
● ★★★***Résidence des Aloès,*** quartier Donateo, ☎ 95.65.01.46. AE, DC, Visa. 26 rm ⚟ Ⓟ ♣ ≋ ✗ closed 1 Oct-1 May, 210.
● ★★★***Balanéa,*** 6, rue Clemenceau, ☎ 95.65.00.45. Tx 460540. AE, DC, Visa. 37 rm ⚟ ♿ 320. Rest. ◆◆ ***l'Abricotier.*** closed 1 Nov-30 Mar, 120-210.
★★★***Grand Hôtel,*** 3, bd Pdt-Wilson, ☎ 95.65.09.74. Tx 460718. AE, DC, Euro, Visa. 58 rm ⚟ ♿ 420.
★★★***L'Abbaye,*** former Franciscan abbey, rte de Santore, ☎ 95.65.04.27. AE. 46 rm ⚟ Ⓟ ♣ ♿ closed 15 Oct-15 Apr, 260.
★★★***Saint-Erasme,*** rte d'Ajaccio, ☎ 95.65.04.50. Tx 460540. AE, DC, Visa. 31 rm ⚟ Ⓟ ♣ ≋ ♿ closed 15 Oct-31 Mar, 230.
★★★***Kalliste,*** 1, av. Cdt-Marche, ☎ 95.65.09.81. 28 rm ⚟ Ⓟ ♣ ♿ closed 30 Sep-1 Jun, 320. Rest. ◆ 75-110.
★★★***Le Magnolia,*** rue Alsace-Lorraine, ☎ 95.65.19.16. AE, DC. 14 rm ⚟ ♣ ✗ 480.
★★***Aria Marina,*** rte d'Ajaccio, ☎ 95.65.04.42. AE. 31 rm ⚟ Ⓟ ≋ closed 10 Oct-1 May, 210.
★★***Corsica,*** 2.5 km S, ☎ 95.65.07.36. AE. 48 rm ⚟ Ⓟ ♣ ≋ ✗ closed 31 Oct-1 Apr, 210. Rest. ◆ 80-130.
★★***La Caravelle,*** rte de Bastia, ☎ 95.65.01.21. 20 rm (bungalows) ⚟ Ⓟ ♣ ≋ ✗ ♿ closed 1 Oct-30 Apr, 185. Rest. Pension only, 85.
★***Galfino,*** ☎ 95.65.08.72. 13 rm ⚟ Ⓟ ♣ ≋ ▭ ♿ half pension, 300.

Δ ★★★*Clos du Mouflon* (80 pl.), ☎ 95.65.03.53 ; ★★★*Bella Vista* (160 pl.), ☎ 95.65.11.76 ; ★★★*Paduella* (74 pl.), ☎ 95.65.06.16 ; ★★★*la Dolce Vita* (200 pl.), ☎ 95.65.05.99 ; ★★★*Campo di Fiori* (24 pl.), ☎ 95.65.02.43 ; ★★★*la Pinède* (240 pl.), ☎ 95.65.02.42.

Restaurants :
● ◆◆ ***Ile de Beauté,*** quai Landry, ☎ 95.65.00.46. AE, DC. ⚟ ✗ closed 20 Sep-1 May and Wed (ex Jul-Aug). One of Corsica's best restaurants where a brilliant chef, supervised by Mr. Baumeil prepares excellent sea-food specialities : *millefeuille de sole, escalope de saumon, fricassée de homard.* On the first floor, ***le Bœuf en Terrasse,*** nice meat specialities, 80-300.
◆◆ ***Comme chez Soi,*** quai Landry, ☎ 95.65.00.59. AE, Euro, Visa. Meat and fish specialities, 80-300.

Bicycle hire : Balagne cycles, Laniella 2, ☎ 95.65.12.44.

CARGESE

Ajaccio 51, Corte 106, Calvi 108
A3 ⊠ 20130

ⓘ rue du Dr-Dragacci, ☎ 95.26.41.31.

Hotels :
● ★★★***Lentisques,*** rte du Pero, ☎ 95.26.42.34. 20 rm ⚟ Ⓟ ♣ ≋ ♿ (bungalows), 100 m from the beach ; closed 30 Sep-30 Apr, 200. Rest. ◆ Pension, 100.
★★***Spelunca,*** ☎ 95.26.40.12. 20 rm ⚟ ♣ ✗ closed 30 Oct-early Apr, 230.
★***Thalassa,*** Pero Beach, 1.5 km N, ☎ 95.26.40.08. 20 rm ⚟ Ⓟ ♣ ≋ ♿ closed 30 Sep-20 May. Family-run hotel. Pension only, 390.

Δ ★★*Torrace* (70 pl.), ☎ 95.26.42.39.

CORTE

Bastia 70, Ajaccio 83, Calvi 96
B2 ⊠ 20250

SNCF ☎ 95.46.00.97.

Hotels :
★★***Sampiero Corso,*** av. du Pdt-Pierucci, ☎ 95.46.09.76. Visa. 31 rm ✗ ♿ closed Oct-Mar, 165.
● ***Auberge de la Restonica,*** at the entrance to the Restonica Gorges, ☎ 95.46.09.58. Visa. 6 rm Ⓟ ♣ ≋ closed Thu low season, 180. Rest. ◆◆ ♿ closed 2 Nov-28 Feb. Spec : *tarte aux herbes, cabri rôti aux herbes,* 80-130.

Santo Pietro de Venaco, ⊠ 20231, 9 km S :
★***Torrent,*** ☎ 95.47.00.18. 25 rm Ⓟ ♣ ♿ 180. Rest. 80-130.

Venaco, ⊠ 20231, 13 km S :
● ★★★***E Caselle,*** ☎ 95.47.02.01. Tx 460145. AE, DC, Visa. 47 rm in bungalows ⚟ ♣ ≋ ▭ ↗ ♿ closed 1 Oct-30 Apr. 280. Rest. ◆ Mountain cabin style, 90-120.

Δ ★★★*Tuani* (35 pl.), ☎ 95.46.11.65.

Restaurant :
Pont de Castirla, 20218 Ponte Leccia, 12 km N :
● ◆◆ ***Chez Jacqueline Costa,*** ☎ 95.47.42.04. On the way to the mountains, honest and sincere family cooking. One menu only with three entrees, home-made *canellonis,* main dish, cheese and dessert, 60. No, you are not dreaming !

Recommended : *Casa di l'Artigiani,* Corsican handicrafts, 13, rue du Colonel-Ferracci.

EVISA

Corte 63, Ajaccio 72, Calvi 99
A2 ⊠ 20126

Hotels :
★★★***U'Castellu,*** ☎ 95.26.20.71. 8 rm Ⓟ ♣ closed low season, 180.
★★***Scopa Rossa,*** ☎ 95.26.20.22. 20 rm ⚟ Ⓟ ♣ ≋ ✗ ♿ closed 1 Nov-10 Feb, 180. Rest. ◆ 80-130.
★***Aïtone,*** route Principale, ☎ 95.26.20.04. 17 rm Ⓟ closed Nov-Dec, 200. Rest. ● ◆◆ The Spelunca valley and its chestnut trees right in front of you. Family style cooking by Toussaint Ceccaldi : *terrines maison, crêpes à la farine de chataîgne,* 50-150.

Col de Vergio, 20224 Calacuccia, 12 km NE :
● ★***Castel de Vergio Albertaccio,*** ☎ 95.48.00.01. 40 rm Ⓟ ≋ closed Oct-Nov, 180. Rest. ◆ ♿ 80-130.

Recommended : *Casa di l'Artigiani* (Apr-Sep and Christmas), ☎ 95.26.22.24.

GALÉRIA

Calvi 33, Porto 50, Ajaccio 133
A2 ⊠ 20245

Hotels :
★★***Fango,*** 4 km W, ☎ 95.62.01.92. 15 rm ⚟ Ⓟ ♨ 🜲 ♿ 140. Rest. 45-60.
★★***Filosorma,*** ☎ 95.62.00.02. 14 rm ⚟ Ⓟ 🜲 closed 5 Oct-15 Apr, 180. Rest. ♦ ✿ ♿ 70-100.

⛺ ★★*Idéal Camping* (67 pl.), ☎ 95.62.01.46.

L'ILE-ROUSSE

Calvi 24, Bastia 69, Ajaccio 155
A1 ⊠ 20220

ℹ av. J.-Calizzi, ☎ 95.60.04.35.

⛴ *S.N.C.M.* at the Tramar agency.

SNCF ☎ 95.60.00.50, L'Ile-Rousse-Calvi : frequent service in summer.

Hotels :
★★★***La Pietra,*** rte du Port, ☎ 95.60.01.45. AE, DC, Visa. 40 rm ⚟ Ⓟ 🜲 closed 1 Nov-31 mar, 330. Rest. ♦♦ ✿ classic dishes, 105-180.
★★***L'Isola Rossa,*** rte du Port, ☎ 95.60.01.32. AE, DC. 20 rm ⚟ Ⓟ ♨ closed 1 Feb-15 Mar, 155.
★***Grillon,*** av. Paul-Doumer, ☎ 95.60.00.49. 16 rm ⚟ Ⓟ 🜲 ✿ ♿ closed 15 Nov-15 Feb, 180. Rest. ♦ 65-130.
★***La Bergerie,*** rte de Monticello, ☎ 95.60.01.28. Visa. 13 rm ⚟ Ⓟ ♨ 🜲 ♿ closed 15 Dec-28 Feb, 200. Rest. ● ♦ closed Sun eve and Mon only Mar-Apr. Moroccan specialities : *tagines de mérou à la juive,* mutton, *brochettes* but also grilled or baked fish, 120-160.

Monticello, 3 km SE :
● ★★***A Pasturella,*** ☎ 95.60.05.65. 12 rm ⚟ 🜲 170. Rest. ♦ ✿ ♿ 80-130.

Algajola, 9 km SW :
★***Plage,*** ☎ 95.60.72.12. 36 rm ⚟ Ⓟ ♨ 🜲 ✿ closed Oct-May, 130. Rest. 60-130.

⛺ Algajola : ★★*Plage* (70 pl.), ☎ 95.60.71.76 ; ★★*Cala di Sole* (120 pl.), ☎ 95.31.68.26.

Restaurants :
♦♦ ***California,*** rte du Port, ☎ 95.60.01.13 ⚟ ♿ closed 1 Dec-1 Feb, Wed. Spec : *langouste,* fish, 80-130.
♦ ***Chez Pancrace*** (Osteria Porte Suprane), Traditional, eve only, 80-130.

Show : folk-group *la Lanterne.*

Recommended : *Clos Petra Rossa,* rue du Gal-Graziani : wines and malmsey.

PORTICCIO

Ajaccio 17, Sartène 80, Corte 85
A3 ⊠ 20166

ℹ ☎ 95.25.05.74.

Hotels :
● ★★★★(L) ***Thalassa Sofitel,*** ☎ 95.25.00.34, Tx 460708. AE, DC, Euro, Visa. 100 rm ⚟ Ⓟ ♨ 🜲 ✿ ▭ ⚲ private beach, water-skiing, diving, 900. Rest. ● ♦♦♦ The great culinary tradition of the Sofitel hotels. F. Dulucq, the chef, successfully blends Corsican specialities and "grande cuisine" : *cassolette d'escargots à la corse, omelette au brucceio à la menthe, andouillette de mérou au jus de persil.* Corsican and "Continental" wines, 200-320.
★★★★***Maquis,*** ☎ 95.25.05.55. Tx 460597. AE, DC, Visa. 20 rm ⚟ Ⓟ ♨ 🜲 A few nicely restored old houses. Private beach, 400. Rest. ♦♦ Excellent home-made *tagliatelles.* Corsican wines, 220-310.
★★***Isolella,*** ☎ 95.25.41.36. 32 rm ⚟ Ⓟ 180. Rest. closed Oct-Apr, 60.

Pisciatello, 6 km NE :
★★***Motel d'Acqua Dolce,*** ☎ 95.20.02.77. 31 rm ⚟ Ⓟ ♨ 🜲 ▭ closed 31 Oct-1 May and Wed, 150.
★★***Le Ranch,*** ☎ 95.20.01.48. 30 rm Ⓟ 190. Rest. ♦ closed Thu, 75-150.

Bastellicaccia, 8 km NE :
★***Les Amandiers de Fontanaccia,*** ☎ 95.20.02.58. 11 rm Ⓟ ♨ 🜲 150.

⛺ ★★★★*Benista* (200 pl.), ☎ 95.20.04.41.

Restaurant :
♦ ***Le Club,*** on the beach, ☎ 95.25.00.42. AE, DC, Visa Ⓟ ♨ ♿ Buffet. Fresh fish. For the pleasure of Corsican and "Continental" people : *charcuterie, terrine de merle, agneau grillé au feu de bois,* bear (in season), 80-170.

Bastellicaccia :
♦♦ ***Auberge Seta,*** ☎ 95.20.00.16. AE, DC. closed 2 Jan-8 Feb and Wed. Spec : *mousse de poisson à la crème de poivrons, agneau de lait grillé au feu de bois,* 90-150.

PORTICCIOLO

Bastia 25, Ajaccio 178
B1 ⊠ 20228 Luri

Hotel :
● ★★★***Caribou,*** ☎ 95.35.00.33. AE, DC, Euro, Visa. 35 rm ⚟ Ⓟ ♨ 🜲 ▭ ⚲ closed 1 Oct-10 Jun. Pension 800. Rest. ♦ ♿ 150-250.

PORTO

Calvi 76, Ajaccio 83, Bastia 135
A2 ⊠ 20150 Ota

ℹ on the rte de la Marine, ☎ 95.26.10.55.

Hotels :
★★★***Kallisté,*** at the Marine, ☎ 95.26.10.30. AE, DC. 62 rm ⚟ Ⓟ 🜲 ✿ closed 10 Oct-30 Mar, 275. Rest. ♦♦ 120-210.
★★★***Flots Bleus,*** at the Marina, ☎ 95.26.11.26. 20 rm ⚟ Ⓟ 🜲 closed 15 Oct-1 Apr, 280. Rest. ♦♦ 70-160.
★★***Capo d'Orto,*** rte de Calvi, ☎ 95.26.11.14. 30 rm ⚟ Ⓟ ✿ ▭ closed Nov-Mar, 180. Rest. ♦ 80-130.
★★***Le Porto,*** rte de Calvi, ☎ 95.26.11.20. AE, DC, Euro, Visa. 30 rm ⚟ Ⓟ 🜲 ✿ closed Oct-Apr, 200. Rest. ♦ 85-130.
★***Bella Vista,*** rte de Calvi, ☎ 95.26.11.08. AE, Euro, Visa. 20 rm ⚟ Ⓟ ♨ 130.

Bussaglia beach, 6 km N :
★***Maquis,*** rte de Calvi, ☎ 95.26.12.19. AE, DC. 6 rm ⚟ closed Nov-15 Dec, 180. Rest. 80-150.

Piana, ⊠ 20115, 11 km SW :
★★★***Capo Rosso,*** ☎ 95.26.12.35. AE, DC, Euro, Visa. 57 rm ⚟ on the sea and gulf Ⓟ ♨ 🜲 ✿ ▭ closed low season, 290. Rest. ♦♦ ⚟ 80-180.

⛺ ★★★*Les Oliviers* (140 pl.), ☎ 95.26.14.49 ; Orsani (Girolata), ★★*E Gradelle* (90 pl.), ☎ 95.26.18.82.

Restaurant :
♦♦ ***Cabane du Berger,*** access by boat only, ☎ 95.27.30.64 ⚟ Grilled *langoustes,* 120-210.

PORTO POLLO

Sartène 33, Ajaccio 60, Corte 135
A3 ⊠ 20140 Petreto Bicchisano

Hotels :
★***Les Eucalyptus,*** ☎ 95.74.01.52. AE, DC, Visa. 24 rm ⚟ ♨ 🜲 ✿ ⚲ closed 1 Oct-1 May. On the Valinco Gulf, 180. Rest. ⚟ ♿ Spec : fish and seafood, 80-130.

Petreto-Bicchisano, 24 km NE :
★***France,*** ☎ 95.24.30.55. Euro. 7 rm 🅿 ♣ ⛱ ✗ closed 3 Nov-1 May, 115. Rest. ♦ ♿ closed 30 Nov-1 Apr. Spec : *terrine de sanglier* and *charcuterie maison,* 100-200.

⛺ ★★*Valinco* (70 pl.), ☎ 95.74.02.12 ; ★★*Alfonsi* (116 pl.), ☎ 95.74.01.80.

PORTO-VECCHIO

Sartène 63, Ajaccio 131, Bastia 143
B4 ✉ 20137

ℹ 2, rue du Mal-Juin, ☎ 95.70.09.58.

Hotels :
★★***Aiglon,*** rte du Port, ☎ 95.70.13.06. 19 rm 🅿 closed 1 Nov-1 Mar, 170.
★★***Roches Blanches,*** at the Marina, ☎ 95.70.06.96. 15 rm ☼ ⛱ ✗ closed 1 Oct-1 May, 170. Rest. ♦ 85-160.
★★***Le Goéland,*** at the Marina, ☎ 95.70.14.15. 21 rm ☼ 🅿 ♣ ⛱ ✗ ♿ Private port, 180.
★★***San Giovanni,*** 2 km rte d'Arca, ☎ 95.70.22.25. Visa. 26 rm 🅿 ♣ ⛱ ✗ ▭ 🎾 ♿ closed 15 Oct-31 Mar, 300. Rest. ♦ 80-145.

On the N coast of the gulf :
★★★***Cala Rossa,*** ☎ 95.70.09.65. Tx 460394. AE, DC, Visa. 50 rm ☼ 🅿 ♣ ⛱ 🎾 ♿ closed 15 Oct-10 May. Private beach. Pension 1 100. Rest. ● ♦♦ ✗ Excellent cooking : *salade tiède de rongets, chapon braisé, cabri rôti, broccio frais.* Buffet, 160-200.
★★★***Ziglione*** (Relais du Silence), rte de Picovaggia, ☎ 95.70.09.83. 32 rm ☼ 🅿 ♣ ⛱ closed end Sep-May, 260.

Trinité de Porto-Vecchio :
● ★★***Stagnolo,*** rte de Cala Rossa, ☎ 95.70.02.07. AE, DC, Visa. 30 rm (bungalows) ☼ 🅿 ♣ ⛱ closed 1 Oct-15 Mar, 260. Rest. ♦ 80-160.

Palombaggia beach, 14 km SE :
● ★★***Le Hameau de Palombaggia,*** ☎ 95.70.03.65. 20 bungalows 🅿 ♣ closed 1 Nov-1 Apr. Weekly accommodation, snacks, 260.

Pinarello, ✉ 20144, 14 km NE :
★★***La Tour Génoise,*** ☎ 95.71.44.39. 28 rm ☼ 🅿 ⛱ closed 1 Oct-1 Jun, 260. Rest. ♦ ✗ 80-130.

⛺ ★★★★*Golfo di Sogno* (500 pl.), ☎ 95.70.08.98 ; ★★★*les Ilots d'Or* (100 pl.), ☎ 95.70.01.30 ; ★★★*la Baie des Voiles* (100 pl.), ☎ 95.70.01.23 ; ★★*Arutoli* (50 pl.), ☎ 95.70.12.73.

Restaurants :
♦♦ ***Troquemuche,*** Quatre-Chemins, rte de Bastia, ☎ 95.70.12.19. Visa ♿ closed Sun. Very good value, 120-210.
♦♦ ***Auberge du Maquis,*** rte de l'Ospédale, ☎ 95.70.20.35. ♿ closed 1 Oct-1 Jun, 120-210.
♦ ***Lucullus,*** 17, rue du Gal-de-Gaulle, ☎ 95.70.10.17. AE, DC, Euro, Visa. ♿ closed 15 Jan-28 Feb, Mon noon and Sun from 1 Oct-1 Jun. Quality regional cooking, 60-160.

Recommended : Sica des Vignerons, on the Bonifacio road, *Domaine de Torraccia,* N198, Lecci, ☎ 95.71.43.50.

PROPRIANO

Sartène 13, Ajaccio 73, Corte 138
A4 ✉ 20110

ℹ 17, av. du Gal-de-Gaulle, ☎ 95.76.01.49.

Car-hire : *Budget* train + auto, Valinco Auto, ☎ 95.76.04.08.

Hotels :
● ★★★***Miramar,*** on the Corniche, ☎ 95.76.06.13. DC. 28 rm ☼ 🅿 ♣ ✗ ▭ closed 31 Oct-1 Apr, 260. Rest. ♦♦ 120-210.
★★***Lido,*** ☎ 95.76.06.37. AE, DC, Visa. 17 rm ☼ 🅿 ♣ by the sea, 180. Rest. ♦♦ Lobster specialties prepared by A. Pittelloni, 100-150.

⛺ ★★★*Le Corsica* (120 pl.), ☎ 95.76.00.57 ; ★★★*Tikiti* (200 pl.), ☎ 95.76.08.32 ; ★★★*Colomba* (100 pl.), ☎ 95.76.06.42.

Restaurants :
♦♦ ***Le Cabanon,*** 14, av. du Gal-de-Gaulle, ☎ 95.76.07.76. AE, DC, Visa. 🅿 ⛱ closed 5 Oct-15 Mar. Corsican specialities, 60-160.
♦ ***Rescator,*** ☎ 95.76.08.46. ♿ Terrace over the port ☼ High season only, 120-210.

Bicycle and scooter hire : Locavelos, Oasis Building.

QUENZA

Sartène 44, Ajaccio 84, Bastia 150
B3 ✉ 20122

ℹ mairie, ☎ 95.78.62.11.

Hotels :
★★***Sole e Monti,*** ☎ 95.78.62.53. 20 rm ☼ closed 15 Sep-1 May, 310.

Aullène, ✉ 20116, 14 km W :
★***Poste,*** ☎ 95.78.61.21. 20 rm ☼ 🅿 ✗ ♿ closed Oct-May, 120. Rest. ♦ Unique menu of regional specialities, 70-90.

SAGONE

Ajaccio 38, Corte 93, Calvi 120
A3 ✉ 20118

Hotels :
★★***Marine,*** on the beach, ☎ 95.28.00.03. AE, DC, Visa. 15 rm 🅿 ♣ ⛱ ✗ ♿ closed 15 Dec-1 Mar, 190. Rest. ♦ 45-170.
★★***Santana,*** ☎ 95.28.00.09. AE, DC, Visa. 45 rm ☼ 🅿 ♣ closed Sep-15 Apr, 180. Rest. ♦ ✗ 80-130.

SAINT-FLORENT

Bastia 23, Calvi 70, Ajaccio 176
B1 ✉ 20217

ℹ at the administration centre, ☎ 95.37.06.04.

Hotels :
★★★***Bellevue,*** ☎ 95.37.00.06, Tx 460296. AE, DC, Euro. 27 rm 🅿 ♣ ⛱ ▭ 🎾 ♿ private beach closed 1 Nov-28 Feb, 380. Rest. ♦♦ Spec : Corsican-style *calamar, cabri aux artichauts,* 80-150.
● ★★***Dolce Notte,*** rte de Bastia, ☎ 95.37.06.65. 25 rm ☼ 🅿 ♣ ⛱ ✗ closed 15 Nov-15 Mar, 290.
★★***Europe,*** pl. des Portes, ☎ 95.37.00.03. 22 rm. closed Nov-Easter, 180. Rest. ♦ 80-130.
★***Centre,*** ☎ 95.37.00.68. 12 rm, 120.

⛺ ★★★*Camp d'Olzo* (60 pl.), ☎ 95.37.03.34 ; ★★★*Kalliste* (170 pl.), ☎ 95.37.03.08 ; ★★*U Pezzo,* rte de la Plage (145 pl.), ☎ 95.37.01.85 ; ★★*Acqua Dolce* (70 pl.), ☎ 95.37.08.63.

Restaurant :
♦ ***La Gaffe,*** on the port, ☎ 95.37.00.12. AE, DC. Shady terrace ♿ closed Mon and 30 Oct-1 Apr, 120-210.

Recommended : *Casa di l'Artigiani,* pl. de la Poste. *Dominique Gentile,* 2 km N, ☎ 95.37.01.54 : delicious muscatel wine. In Patrimonio, 5 km : *Cave Marsifi* and the *Winegrowers' Cooperative* on the road out of the village.

SARTÈNE

Ajaccio 86, Corte 140, Bastia 178
A-B4 ⊠ 20100

ℹ cours Saraneli, ☎ 95.77.15.40.

Hotels :
● ★★**Roches,** ☎ 95.77.07.61. Visa. 66 rm ⚟ Ⓟ ♨ ♘ ♿ 180. Rest. ♦ 70-120.
★★**Villa Piana,** rte Propriano, ☎ 97.77.07.04. DC, Visa. 32 rm Ⓟ ♨ ♘ ✈ ⚲ 200.

⛺ ★★★*L'Avena,* domaine de Zivia, in Tizzano (280 pl.), ☎ 95.77.02.18.

Restaurants :
♦♦ **La Chaumière,** 39, rue Méd.-Cap. Benedetti, ☎ 95.77.07.13. AE, DC, Visa. Ⓟ ♿ closed 2 Jan-2 Mar, Sun low season. Spec : *tripette, cabri en sauce,* Corsican-style piglet, 120-210.

Bains de Caldane, 15 km NE on the D69, D268 and D148 :
♦♦ **Caldane,** ☎ 95.37.00.34. High season only. Very traditional restaurant with copious country-style cooking. Bathing in a natural pool, 80-130.

Recommended : *Casa di l'Artigiani,* rue Bonaparte, ☎ 95.77.02.26. open Apr-Sep and Christmas. *Cellar of the Great Sartenais Wines* on the Propriano road ; *Santa Barba Cooperative Wine-Cellar,* ☎ 95.77.01.05.

SOLENZARA

Sartène 77, Bastia 103, Ajaccio 131
B3 ⊠ 20145 Sari di Porto-Vecchio

ℹ mairie annexe, ☎ 95.57.40.05.

Hotels :
★**La Solenzara,** ☎ 95.57.42.18. Euro. 27 rm ⚟ Ⓟ ♨ ♘ ♿ 180.

Sainte-Lucie de Porto-Vecchio, ⊠ 20144, 12 km S :
★★**U Dragulinu,** plage de Favone, ☎ 95.57.20.30. Visa. 24 rm ⚟ Ⓟ ♨ ♘ closed 30 Sep-1 May, 260. Rest. ♦ 80-130.

Restaurants :
♦♦ **Caravelle,** ☎ 95.57.46.27. AE, DC, Euro, Visa. ♨ ♿ 80-130.

SPELONCATO

Calvi 32, Corte 57, Ajaccio 150
A2 ⊠ 20281

Hotels :
● ★**Spelunca,** ☎ 95.61.31.21. 14 rm ⚟ closed 15 Sep-early Jul, 180. Rest. ♿ Spec : Corsican cooking, 80-130.

Feliceto, 20225 Muro, 12 km SW :
● ★★**Mare e Monti** (L.F.), ☎ 95.61.73.06. AE, DC. 18 rm ⚟ Ⓟ ♨ ♘ closed 1 Oct-1 May, 140. Rest. ♦ ♿ 65-100.

TIUCCIA

Ajaccio 26, Corte 96, Calvi 137
A3 ⊠ 20111 Calcatoggio

ℹ at the Cinarca Hotel.

Hotels :
● ★★★**Cinarca** (L.F.), ☎ 95.52.21.39. 30 rm ⚟ Ⓟ ♨ ♘ closed 30 Sep-30 Apr, 270. Rest. only 1 Jul-31 Aug ✈ 80-130.
★★**La Liscia,** ☎ 95.28.21.40. 46 rm ⚟ Ⓟ ♨ ♘ ▭ ⚲ closed 30 Sep-1 May. Diving and windsurfing school, 220.

Restaurant :
♦ **Les Flots Bleus,** ☎ 95.52.21.65. Visa. 80-130.

VICO

Ajaccio 52, Corte 81, Calvi 121
A3 ⊠ 20160

Hotels :
★★**U Paradisu,** rte du Couvent, ☎ 95.26.61.62. AE, Visa. 24 rm ⚟ Ⓟ ♨ ♘ 160. Rest. 55-90.

Soccia, ⊠ 20125, 18 km NE :
● ★★**U Paese,** ☎ 95.28.31.92. 22 rm ⚟ Ⓟ ♨ ♘ closed 20 Nov-20 Dec, 180. Rest. ♦ 80-130.

ZICAVO

Sartène 60, Ajaccio 63, Corte 81
B3 ⛷ 1 600 m ⊠ 20132

ℹ mairie, ☎ 95.24.40.05.

Hotel :
★**Tourisme,** av. Napoléon, ☎ 95.24.40.06. 15 rm ♨ ♘ ✈ 115. Rest. 45-60.

ZONZA

Sartène 37, Ajaccio 91, Corte 128
B3 ⊠ 20124

Hotels :
★★**Incudine** (L.F.), ☎ 95.78.42.76. Visa. 10 rm ⚟ Ⓟ closed 30 Sep-1 May, 145. Rest. ♦ 70-95.
★**Tourisme,** ☎ 95.78.42.31. AE, Euro, Visa. 10 rm, closed 1 Nov-15 Mar, 110. Rest. ♦ Corsican cooking. Excellent value, fruit from the orchard, 80-130.

Restaurants :
♦ **La Terrasse,** ☎ 95.78.42.42. With 8 rm ⚟ ♨ ♘ ✈ ♿ closed 30 Oct-1 Mar. Spec : Corsican *charcuterie,* 80-130.

Col de Bavella, 9 km NE :
♦ **Auberge de Bavella,** ☎ 95.57.43.87 ⚟ ♨ closed 15 Oct-15 May. Spec : *charcuterie maison,* 50-80.

Recommended : *Casa di l'Artigiani,* ☎ 95.78.44.50. Open Apr-Sep and Christmas.

The Dauphiné Region

In Dauphiné — between mountains and Midi, between Alps and Mediterranean — the green fields and dark forests of the Vercors meet up with the dry mountains and lavender fields of the Diois region. At Chamrousse, Alpe d'Huez and Les Deux Alpes, the winter skier can enjoy mountain scenery and southern sun, or can ski through the snow-covered pasturelands of Vercors and the forests of Chartreuse. In summer, the tourist can hike through villages, hamlets and sheep-folds nestled on high mountain passes, past torrents of clear mountain water where marmots come to drink and play.

The Drôme valley, bathed in a light reminiscent of Tuscany, unfolds its centuries-old villages with their southern beechtrees and oleanders. The Chartreuse Massif climbs towards immense banks of dark pine-trees studded with strange limestone formations. In 1085 Saint Bruno founded the monastery which became the mother house of his order. The monks still make the famous Chartreuse liqueur — yellow and green — which was originally intended for pharmaceutical use, from 130 plants carefully combined according to a secret recipe.

Grenoble, the capital of Dauphiné, is a dynamic city with a high-tech reputation in industry and scientific research, and played a leading role in the great hydroelectric power adventure of the last century. It is characterized by the intellectual ferment of its university campuses and research centers.

The area around Valence produces wines belonging to the great Côtes du Rhône family. Châtillons-en-Diois produces light, fruity, elegant wines which are mostly drunk in the region. Dauphiné's most famous recipe is the *gratin dauphinois,* a delicious dish of potatoes baked with eggs and cheese. But there are all kinds of *gratins,* using macaroni, eggplant, and many other specialities of the region.

Sightseeing

Facts and figures

Location : *The Dauphiné region is the hinge linking the northern and southern Alps, joining Savoie and Italy in the northeast to the Alps of Haute-Provence in the south. In the west, the Dauphiné is bounded by the Rhône.*
Area : *19 219 km².*
Climate : *Except in the extreme south and the lowest valleys, the mountains dictate the weather. The Dauphiné's position between northern and southern Alps is evident in the region's marked temperature changes.*
Population : *1 319 583; Isère : 860 378; Drôme : 361 847; Hautes-Alpes : 97 358.*
Administration : *Department of* ***Isère,*** *Prefecture : Grenoble. Department of* ***Drôme,*** *Prefecture : Valence. Department of* ***Hautes-Alpes,*** *Prefecture : Gap.*

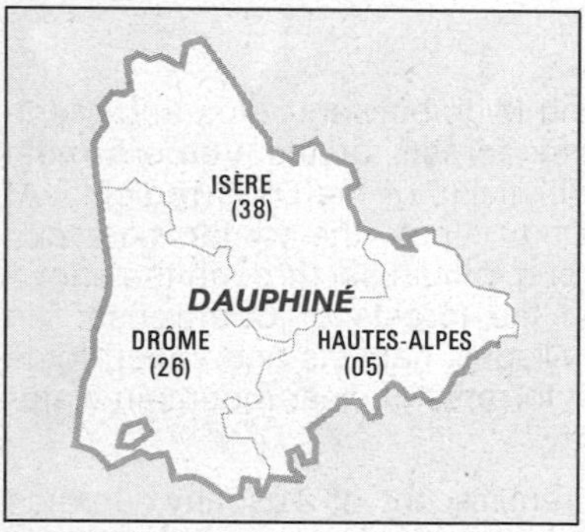

BRIANÇON★

C2 / ® / pop. 11 831 (Hautes-Alpes)

Briançon, formerly the guardian of the valleys, is the highest town in Europe (alt. 1 321 m) and has always been something of a fortress.

▶ Overlooking the modern part of the town (Sainte-Catherine) the **Ville Haute★★** (upper town) has hardly changed since Vauban, Louis XIV's great military architect, surrounded it with ramparts. ▶ The main shopping area, on the other side of the Porte de Pignerol gate, is the **Grand-Rue★,** where the waters of the Grand Gargouille hurtle through the town. ▶ Behind the church of **Notre-Dame,** also built by Vauban (1718) the highest peaks of the Briançonnais are visible. ▶ Visits to the citadel are organised by the TO. Panorama★. ▶ Note the **Pont d'Asfeld★** (1734), bridge with a fifty-six metre span above the river Durance. □

▶ The Briançon region★★.

▶ Briançon, at the heart of a cluster of valleys, is the chief town in the basin of the upper Durance. The sky is almost always clear and sunny for skiing in this area. ▶ **Puy-Saint-Pierre** *(4 km SW)* and **La Croix de Toulouse** *(6.5 km N)* have good views★★ over Briançon and the valley of the Durance. ▶ The **Valley of the Clarée★** *(Névache road, 20.5 km N) :* this is the first of these luminous and uninhabited valleys which are more and more frequent on the

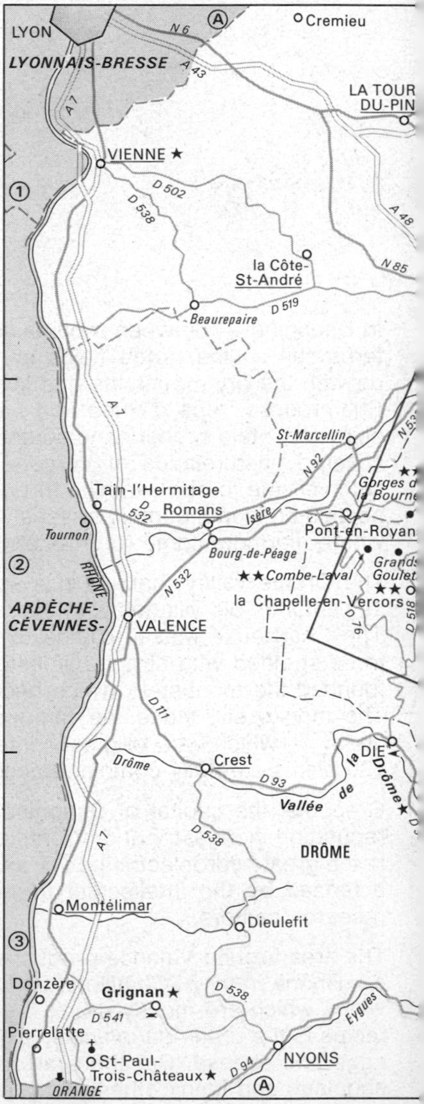

way south. Take a look in passing at the beautiful houses of the Briançonnais; also the churches, which are often decorated with murals★. Beyond **Névache,** the route continues *(9.5 km)* to the chalets of Laval (flowers★). ▶ **Route de Montgenèvre** *(2 km NE to the pass)* : since the turn of the century the sunny slopes of **Montgenèvre** ® have been popular for skiing. And in the past almost all the conquerors of Italy and Gaul, including Caesar, took this historic passage. ▶ **Route de L'Izoard**★★ *(21 km SE to the pass).* The last of the Dauphinois passes on the road to the Grandes Alpes (→ Savoie). The Izoard road leads through to Queyras (→). From the pass the view★★ is superb and the **Casse Desert** looks like a lunar landscape. ▶ **Valley of the Guisane**★ *(28 km NW to the Lautaret Pass).* **Serre-Chevalier** ® is the name given to the associated hamlets of the valley, which have banded together to take advantage of the white gold on the mountain slopes. From **Chantemerle,** a road leads *(12 km)* to the Granon Pass (alt. 2413 m; view★★) and the cable-car to Serre-Chevalier (alt. 2483 m); view over the massif du Pelvoux and the Briançonnais. **Le Monêtier-les-Bains** ® (pop. 970) is a rendez-vous for walkers and mountaineers. □

Don't miss

★★★ : *The Oisans Massif (B2), The Queyras Basin (C2), the Vercors Massif (A-B2).*
★★ : *The Chartreuse Massif (B1), Grands Goulets (A2), Grenoble (B2), the Izoard road (C2).*

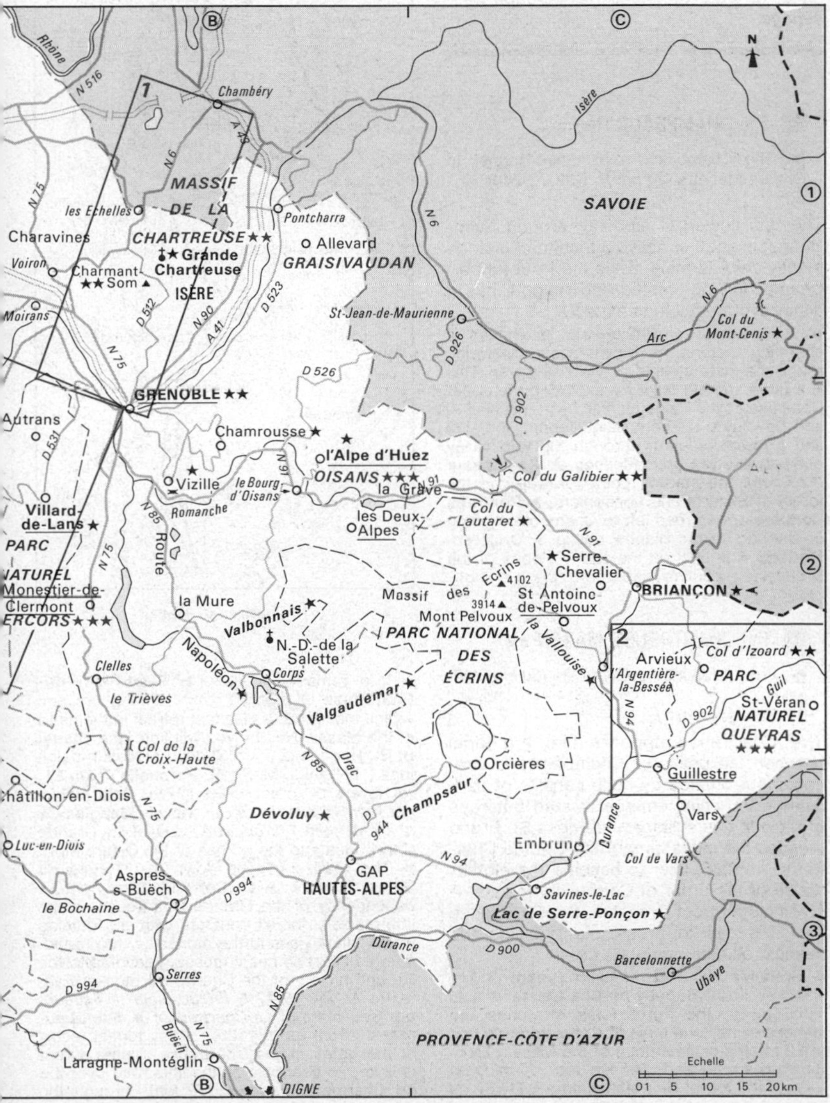

Weekend tips

Visit Grenoble first of all, an hour from Lyons by motorway. See the Musée de Beaux-Arts (Fine Arts Museum) and the old quarters of the town; lunch in the Rue St. Vincent. After a few hairpin bends and over the Porte pass, you're in La Chartreuse, with splendid landscapes and a famous monastery, not open to visitors, but at La Correrie you will learn everything about the monks and their liqueur. On returning to Grenoble, dine at La Bastille overlooking the lights of the town.
The next day see the Vercors Massif : a real mountain trip. From Villars-de-Lans return either by Pont-en-Royans and the Isère Valley or go back the same way through Sassenage.

The **CHAMPSAUR** Region

▶ The Champsaur road, Saint-Bonnet to Orsière-Merlette *(24 km E, D945, D944)*
C3

The Bas (lower) Champsaur around Saint-Bonnet is another active agricultural district, mostly dairy farming, while the Haut (upper) Champsaur, deforested and rugged, has a distinctly mountainous aspect.

▶ **Saint-Bonnet-en-Champsaur** ® makes a charming picture, its brown roofs clustering round the slate steeple of the bell-tower. This is a good starting point for exploring the upper Champsaur, the Valgaudemar (→), Trièves (→) and Dévoluy (→). From Saint-Bonnet, the D23 and a forest road run through the wild valley of **Séveraisette★** up to **Molines-en-Champsaur** *(12.5 km),* the starting point for walks in the forest of Suzerre and Londonière. ▶ **Pont des Corbières;** then road left to Champollion going up the harsh **Drac Blanc★** ravine. ▶ **Orcières-Merlette** ® is built on the sunny slopes of the Drouvet (alt. 2 655 m ; cable car; spring skiing). □

The **CHARTREUSE MASSIF★★**

▶ From Grenoble to Chambéry *(80 km, half-day)*
B1 *(see diagram 1)*

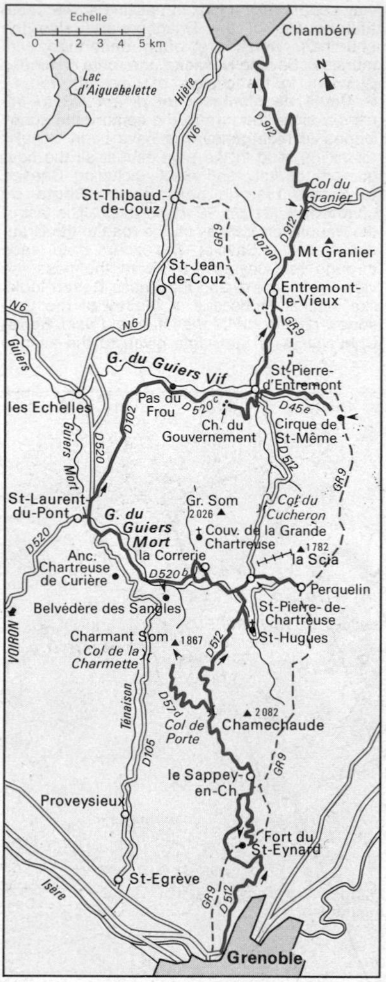

1. Chartreuse Massif

The Chartreuse appears like a citadel between the peaks of Chambéry and Grenoble, surrounded by huge carpets of dark pines from which emerge twisted outcrops of rock. In this solitary wilderness St. Bruno founded the monastery of the Grande Chartreuse in 1085, later to become the mother house of the order of Carthusian monks. A few minutes from Grenoble, the Chartreuse Massif is ideal for cross-country skiing and medium altitude mountain hikes.

▶ **Grenoble** (→) **Fort du Saint-Eynard** *(4 km)* view★★. From **Sappey-en-Chartreuse** ® (alt. 1 000 m) to the Porte Pass stretches the immense limestone table of **Chamechaude** (alt. 2 082 m), the highest point of the Massif. From the pass a road leads *(4.5 km, then 30 mins on foot)* to the top of **Charmant Som★★** (1 867 m) with a remarkable view. ▶ **Saint-Pierre-de-Chartreuse** ® *(right, 1 km)* : among firs and Alpine meadows, a pleasant retreat in the heart of the Massif. Nearby you will find : the **chapel of St. Hugues** *(2.5 km S)* decorated with paintings (1953 by J. M. Pirot); **Perquelin** *(3 km E)* : for lovers of forest walks (GR9); **Scia** *(cable-car then 15 mins on foot)* : view★; **Sangles★★** *(2 km W, then 1 hr on foot)* : view of the Grande Chartreuse and the gorges of the Guiers Mort. ▶ The road continues down the **Gorges du Guiers Mort★★.** ▶ **La Correrie** *(1 km right),* a dependency of the Grande Chartreuse, is the intermediary for all contacts with the outside world, since visits to the monastery are forbidden. La Correrie has a museum devoted to the life and history of the Chartreuse monks *(Easter to 1 Nov., 9-12 & 2-6:30, sale of liqueurs and souvenirs of La Chartreuse).* ▶ **Saint-Laurent-du-Pont** (pop. 4 125) : a tiny tourist resort at the gates of the Chartreuse. Saint-Laurent is linked to Grenoble by the little road over the **La Charmette Pass★★** *(30 km),* through the woods and along the hilltop road (view★); **Voiron** ® (*15 km SW of Saint-Laurent;* pop. 19700) makes skis (Rossignol) and also distills the famous Chartreuse liqueur. (Caves de la Chartreuse, *8-11:30 & 2-6:30, 5:30 Sat., closed Sat. and Sun. 1 Nov.-Easter*). ▶ Beyond Saint-Laurent, take the road through the **Gorges du Guiers Vif★** (see the Pas du Frou★★ promontory). ▶ **Saint-Pierre-d'Entremont** ® (pop. 459; *3 km W) :* view★ and especially, the **Cirque de Saint-Même** *(4.5 km SE) :* two superb waterfalls★ which give birth to the Guiers Vif. ▶ **Granier Pass** (alt. 1164 m, view★★, *chalet-hôtel*).

■ The **DÉVOLUY** Massif★

B3

Amid the harsh scenery of this area, the little oases of Saint-Disdier, Saint-Étienne and the forest of Bois-Rond are the only relief. Le Dévoluy is riddled with underground cavities known as *Chouruns*.

▶ The **pass of Souloise★** to the north, to the east the **Noyer pass★★** and the pass of Potrachon to the south are the entrances to the natural fortress which surrounds **Saint-Étienne-en-Dévoluy** ® (pop. 527) and the winter sports station of **Superdévoluy.** To the NW, the Étroits Pass★★ and *(6.5 km)* **Saint-Disdier,** noteworthy for its 12thC Church★. □

■ VALLEY OF THE **DRÔME★**

▶ From Crest to Cabre Pass *(82 km, approx. 4 hr)*

A3

The valley of the Drôme should be better known. Bathed in a light like that of Tuscany, it is a lovely mixture of Dauphiné and Provence. D93 takes you from Crest to ancient villages with plane trees and rose laurel, reminiscent of the Midi.

▶ **Crest** ® (pop. 7844) is crowned by a superb 12thC keep★ *(visit).* ▶ **Pontaix** (site★). ▶ **Die** ® (pop. 4047) overlooked by the escarpment of the Glandasse, with its famous *Clairette,* a sparkling wine which you will be invited to taste all along the road; cathedral (12th-17thC), museum (Gallo-Roman remains). ▶ 6 km beyond Die road left to **Châtillon-en-Diois** ® where you can see *(10 km N)* the **Cirque d'Archiane★,** a magnificent limestone amphitheatre *(GR93).* 7 km E of Châtillon : the **Gorges des Gas★** near Lus-la-Croix-Haute. ▶ After **Luc-en-Diois** ®, the road crosses the site of **Claps★** (landslide), leaves the Drôme and climbs towards the Col de Cabre pass (alt. 1180 m). □

■ GAP

B3 / ® / pop. 32000 (Hautes-Alpes)

Dauphiné with a touch of the south - a busy, animated crossroads on the holiday trail. Pleasant walks in pedestrian precincts in the shadow of the cathedral (interesting polychrome stonework). The museum contains the mausoleum of de Lesdiguières★, last Constable of France (16th-17thC, by Jean and Jacob Richier). ▶ 15 km S : **Tallard** is overlooked by a 14th-16thC château★. □

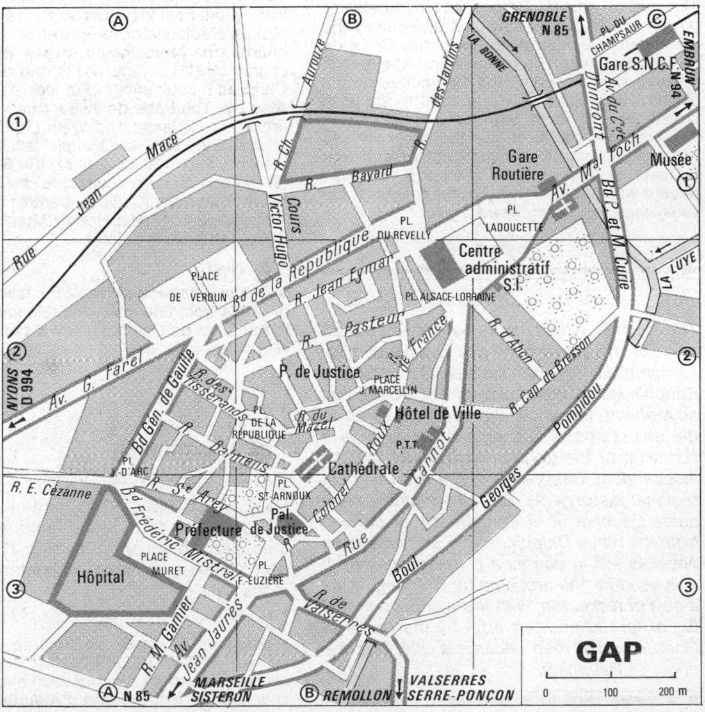

Chartreuse

The secret has been well kept. We know only that 130 plants go into the composition of the famous elixir given to the Charterhouse monks in 1607 and known as Chartreuse. Pinks, absinthe, fir buds and balm are among the ingredients, but the proportions are a secret. Today the Carthusian monks are still active (in Voiron → Chartreuse) around their great stills. Green Chartreuse (55°) and yellow Chartreuse (43°) are made directly from this mysterious mixture, which was originally for medicinal use only.

■ The GRAISIVAUDAN Valley

B-C1

The Graisivaudan, through which the Isère runs today, is a large valley hollowed out by glaciers, and formerly occupied by a lake, which was linked with the Lac du Bourget. This is one of the most fertile regions in the Alps.

▶ To see the majestic mountains of the Chartreuse and Belledonne to best advantage, follow the little roads between Grenoble and Pontcharra at the foot of the two Massifs. ▶ **Chartreuse** (D30) : look for the **Bec du Margain★** *(15 mins on foot)* with a remarkable panorama from Vercors to Mont Blanc and **Saint-Hilaire-du-Touvet,** famous for its funicular railway (1924), with a slope of 83°. ▶ **Belledonne** (D280) : in **Lancey** *(13 km NE of Grenoble)* the Museum of Aristide Bergès and hydroelectric power. For an overall view of Graisivaudan and the Chartreuse Massif go up to the **Croix de Revollat★★** peak. From Laval to **Allevard** ® (thermal spa; museum), the communes on the slope of Belledonne have grouped together to create the station of **Sept Laux★** (alt. 1 350-2 200 m) : the charm of little mountain villages with the facilities of a major summer and winter resort. ▶ 1 km S from Pontcharra : **château Bayard** was the birth place of the knight of the same name (museum, view★). □

Why a Dolphin?

The dolphin which figures on the coat of arms of the province is not the reason for its name. In fact it is the reverse : the title Dauphin led to the choice of the Dolphin as an emblem. We know the title was given to the eldest son of the King of France as a condition of the agreement transferring the independent Dauphiné to France (→ brief regional history). As for the origins of the name Dauphin, it is thought that it derives from the name Dalphinus (the feminine, Delphine, is still in use as a Christian name). It was used for the first time by Guigues IV, as a sort of nickname, with the symbolic meaning of "proud and powerful by the grace of God". Dauphin then became a title, and the origin of Dauphiné.

■ GRENOBLE★★

B2 / ® / pop. 160 000 (Isère)

Grenoble is the capital of the Dauphiné, straddling the junction of the Drac and the Isère rivers. The birthplace of Stendhal, Grenoble is a centre of Dauphiné industry, with an international reputation for metallurgy, electronics, scientific research, and advanced energy research. It was one of the earliest towns to develop hydroelectric power, and it is at the forefront in the fields of tourism and sport (Olympic city 1968).

▶ If you want to see how Grenoble lives, stroll around the **Place Grenette** (B3) and the neighbouring pedestrian precincts to the **Place Victor-Hugo** (B3). ▶ The **Stendhal Museum** (B2; life of the writer) is in the former town hall *(10-12 & 2-6; Feb.-15 Sep., closed Mon.),* with the church of St. André nearby (13thC, tomb of Bayard) and the **Palais de Justice★** (law courts), former Parliament of the Dauphiné, a beautiful Gothic and Renaissance building (see the woodwork★). ▶ **Grenoble Museum★★** *(12-7; closed Tue.) :* active, unexpected, always full of ideas, this is a permanent centre of research. See the famous gallery of contemporary art★, and also the Francisco de Zurbarans★★ (17thC), Philippe de Champaigne and the painters of the 19th and 20thC★ : Corot, Boudin, Renoir, Monet, Bonnard, Picasso. And don't forget the Egyptian room★. ▶ **Fort de la Bastille★★** *(B1, a cable-car runs until midnight) :* from this magnificent spot there is a fine view across Grenoble and the Belledonne. (Restaurant; old car museum); descent possible on foot through Guy-Pape park★ and the Garden of the Dauphins★ *(consult timetables).* ▶ **Dauphinois Museum★** (B2; *10-12 & 2-6; closed Tue.*) installed in an ancient 17thC convent, is the best introduction to the life, art and popular traditions of the province. In the same quarter, the **Merovingian crypt★** (6thC) of the church of St. Laurent (B1) is one of the oldest Christian monuments in France.

Also... ▶ The **hôtel de ville★** (town hall; C3) by architects Novarina and Welti (1967), the Paul Mistral park with its Olympic facilities (sports stadium, speed skating rink), the Perret tower (87 m) and modern sculptures. ▶ The **Maison de la Culture★** (Cultural Centre; 1968 arch. Wogensky). ▶ Ernest Hébert Museum : works of this Dauphinois painter. □

▶ Nearby

▶ **Chamrousse★** ® *(30 km SE) :* favourite haunt of skiers from Grenoble. A cable-car takes you to the Croix de Chamrousse★★ peak (2 225 m) with a fabulous view.

■ MONTÉLIMAR

A3 / ® / pop. 30 200 (Drôme)

Hard or soft, nougat has made the name of this quiet little town world famous. The château des Adhémar (12th-14th-16thC) from which it takes its name is situated on a bluff to the east. □

▶ Nearby

▶ **Puygiron** *(8 km E),* **La Bégude de Mazenc** *(15 km E)* and **Le Poët-Laval** ® *(23 km E)* should be seen for their location and mediaeval character. ▶ **Notre-Dame d'Aiguebelle** *(17 km*

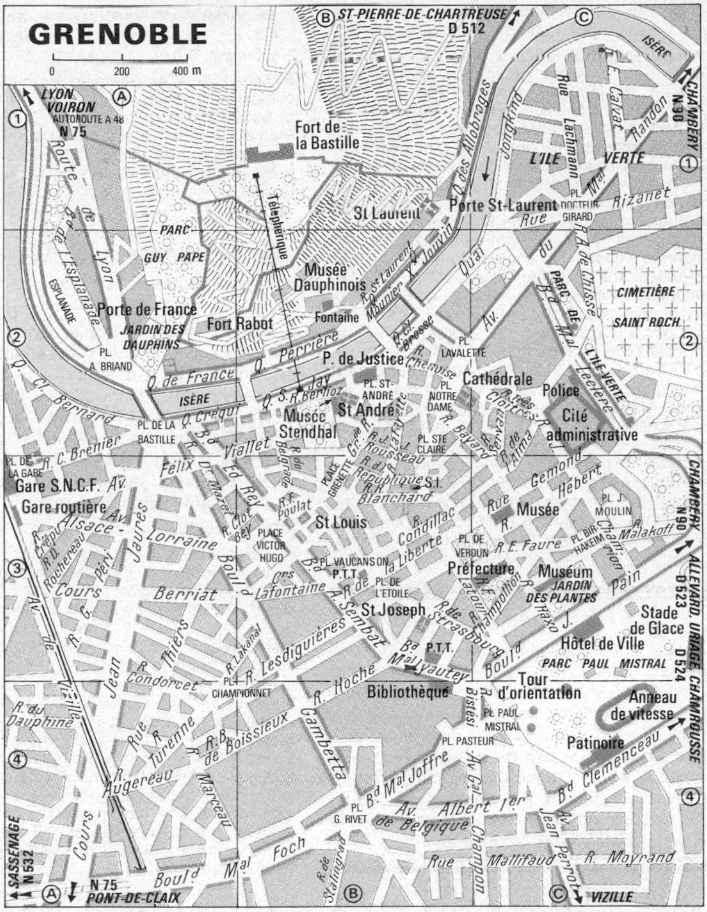

SE) is an ancient Cistercian abbey (12thC). ▶ **Grignan★** ® *(27 km SE)* : Madame de Sévigné wrote most of her famous letters to her daughter, who became Comtesse de Grignan by marriage; visit the château★ (16th-17thC) where she stayed *(8:30-11:30 & 2:30-5:30; closed Tue. and Wed. am; closed Nov.).* □

■ NYONS

A3 / ® / pop. 6 293 (Drôme)

Olives, truffles and jam are the specialities of Nyons, also known for the mildness of its climate. See the Forts★, an area of narrow streets and staircases, and the bridge (14thC) over the Aygues. □

▶ Nearby

▶ SE : The little **Baronnies Massif★** with its principal town **Buis** ®, pokes its limestone crest through a decor of vines, olive trees and fields of lavender. ▶ Discover old fortified villages★ such as : **Sainte-Jalle** *(17 km E)*, **Saint-Auban-sur-l'Ouvèze** *(40 km SE)* and **Verclause** *(35 km NE)*. □

Nougats

Black nougat is an old Provençal delicacy; almonds bound together by lightly caramelised honey and eaten between two wafers. The better-known white Montélimar nougat is a refined cousin : egg white for smoothness, a few pistachios and various flavours are added to make this delicious candy that Montélimar exports all over the world.

■ The **OISANS** Massif★★★

B2

L'Oisans is to the Dauphiné what the Mont Blanc Massif is to the Savoie, a sanctuary for climbers. Apart from the road from Grenoble to the Lautaret pass up the Romanche Valley, only vertiginous paths lead into this fortress of peaks and frozen wastes. □

▶ Valley of the Romanche★★ : from Bourg d'Oisans to the Lautaret pass *(39 km, 2 hr)*

▶ **Le-Bourg-d'Oisans★** ® (pop. 3071) is well known to amateur geologists, who find a wealth of mineral samples in the area. ▶ Anyone who likes crazy little mountain roads, should go up to **Villard-Reculas★, Auris★, Villard-Reymond★** (ascent of Prégentil promontory★★ *40 mins*) and **Villard-Notre-Dame★★** for the view and charming character of these villages. ▶ The road which continues to **l'Alpe d'Huez★** ® (peak *13 km*) is easier. Facing full south, one thousand metres above the Romanche River, the ancient hamlet of **Huez** overlooks the sparkling Meije glaciers. An international winter sports resort, and also an excursion centre : to the Pic du Lac Blanc★★★ *(access by cable-car)* the Dôme des Petits Rousses★★ peaks, and to Lake Besson★. ▶ Hydroelectric reservoir of **Chambon★.** ▶ Right : the D213 goes up *(10 km)* to the **Deux-Alpes** ® ski-resort among the high wastes where you can ski even in summer on the glacier of Mont de Lans (3160 m). ▶ **La Grave★** ® (pop. 453) seems to live only for the Meije★★ peak, shining from all its glaciers above this important mountaineering centre. The cable-car from the Ruillans Pass★★★ (alt. 3200 m) enables you to see this marvel of ice. □

The craftsmen of Queyras

Formerly the peasants carved the tools and utensils needed for daily life, while craftsmen produced remarkable chests decorated with scrollwork, foliage, interlacings and suns. The stone pine they worked in is a soft wood which can be easily carved with a simple knife. Today, the craftsmanship of Queyras maintains the tradition of beautiful furniture and beautiful objects in places such as Saint-Véran and Abriès.

▶ Valleys of Vénéon★★★ and Bérarde *(26 km, leave from 5 km SE of Bourg-d'Oisans, 2 hr)*

▶ This is an area reserved for high mountain guides and mountaineers. ▶ From the hamlet of **La Bérarde** on foot *(1 hr 15, easy)* to the **Plan du Carrelet** (*chalet-hôtel;* wood and stone construction) one of the most beautiful sights in the Écrins Nature Reserve (Parc National des Écrins). □

■ The **QUEYRAS** Upper Valley★★★

C2 *(see diag 2)*

Clear rushing water, rolling pebbles of green and mauve marble, woods of larch and stone pine filtering the southern light; and the slopes are dotted with thousands of flowers. Flora and fauna are all protected within the Regional Park. The Queyras is a country of high villages (all are over 1300 m alt.) with a long tradition of woodworking, where craftsmen still produce toys, furniture and decorated wooden chests. □

▶ From Guillestre to Abriès *(31 km, 2 hr)*

▶ A stopover on the Grandes Alpes route, **Guillestres** ® (pop. 2009) is also the principal town in the Queyras region. 4 km NW : **Mont-Dauphin★,** a fortified city in pink marble, designed by Vauban. 10 km S **Vars** ® : winter sports resort based on several villages strung out along the road to the Vars Pass. ▶ **Château-Queyras★,** a mediaeval fortress (13thC) framed between the two slopes of the valley; 11 km to the Bucher Summit (view★★). 5.5 km NW **Arvieux** ® (pop. 351) : on the road to the Izoard Pass★★, a centre for master-toymakers. ▶ **Aiguilles** (pop. 310) and **Abriès** (pop. 322) : surrounded by forests, for winter skiing and summer walks to high meadows covered with flowers. The road continues *(16 km)* dawdling along with the Guil river to the **Mount Viso★★** viewpoints. □

2. Queyras region

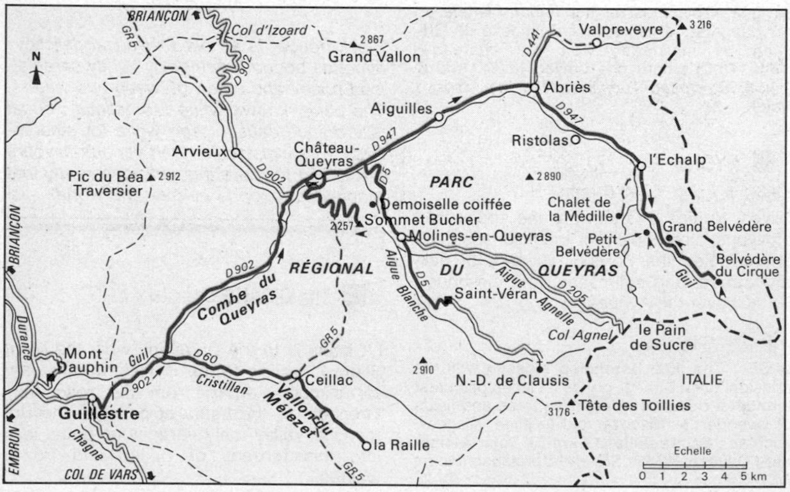

▶ From Guillestre to Ceillac★ *(road 14 km)*

▶ Pines and larches accompany you from the enclosed valley of Cristillan to **Ceillac** (beautiful isolated chapel). Excursion into the Mélezet valley★ (GR5). □

▶ From Château-Queyras to Saint-Véran★★ *(14 km)*

▶ The houses typical of the region first appear at **Molines-en-Queyras** ® (pop. 375) in the valley of the Aigue Blanche. ▶ **Saint-Véran★★** ® (pop. 275) : famous for its European altitude record (1 990-2 040 m) and its houses★ crowned with huge lofts. □

Hydroelectrics

Thanks to hydroelectric power, the mountain regions have long been a scene of industrial activity : mills, sawmills, nail-stamping, etc. But modern exploitation of water power only dates from the second half of the last century. Aristide Bergès was the first (1869) to canalize a fall of water to increase its power; this water turned the turbines of the Lancey paper mill near Grenoble. The invention of the dynamo by Gramme (1871) made the production of electricity possible, and Bergès improved his techniques. Most notably, he had the idea of using lakes as natural reservoirs and increasing their capacity by means of artificial dykes. Thus, hydroelectric power was born.

■ ROMANS-SUR-ISÈRE

A2 / ® / pop. 34 000 (Isère)

Feet have always been the major preoccupation here, and by the 15thC the guild of *sabotiers* and *grolleurs* (clog- and shoemakers) was prospering. Today the town remains the French capital of quality footwear.

▶ From Egypt to the present day, the march of history is retraced in the **Musee de la Chaussure★** (Shoe Museum) which also includes a section on regional ethnography *(closed Tue. and nat. hols.)*. ▶ Don't miss the **collegiate church of St. Barnard★** (12th-13th-14thC) and its Flemish hangings★★ of 1555. □

▶ Nearby

▶ 28 km N, **Hauterives :** where a mystically inclined postman named Cheval (1836-1924) built the **Palais Idéal★** *(visits all year)*, using stones and rocks picked up during a lifetime of rounds. ▶ 23 km NE, **Saint-Antoine** ® : 12th-15thC Gothic church★★; treasure room; 16thC ivory Christ★. □

■ ROUTE NAPOLÉON★

▶ From Gap to Vizille *(86 km, half-day)*
B2

The road taken by the Emperor Napoleon on his return from Elba (March 1815), runs from Golfe-Juan (→ Provence) to Grenoble, and is marked with commemorative plaques and monuments.

▶ **Gap** (→). ▶ **Corps** ®. Hotels and restaurants make this a tourist stopover; at 15 km : **Notre-Dame de la Salette,** the destination of a pilgrimage whose origin stems from an apparition of the Virgin to two young shepherds (1846). West of Corps : the Sautet Dam★ on the river Drac, overlooked by the Obiou (alt. 2 790 m); trip★★ around the lake *(35 km)*. ▶ **La Mure** (pop. 5 913) : industry and commerce and a little tourist train★ to Saint-Georges-de-Commiers *(30 km)*. ▶ **Laffrey** ®, lakes on the Plateau de la Matésine. This is where the Royalist troops, sent to arrest Napoleon, met the Emperor on 7 March 1815 and rallied to his cause. ▶ **Vizille** ® (pop. 7 365) : château★ of the Duke of Lesdiguières (17thC); Louis XIII furnishings and tapestries *(10-12 & 2-5 Jan.-Mar.; 9-12 & 2-7 Apr.-Sep.; closed Mon., Tue.)*. □

■ SERRE-PONÇON Lake★

C3 (Hautes-Alpes)

Today hundreds of little coloured sails brighten this enormous sheet of water *(30 km²)*. The lake's prime function since 1960 has been to regulate the flow of the Durance, irrigating the Alps of Haute-Provence and producing electricity.

▶ Near the enormous dam (viewpoint★★) of packed earth (14 million m³) is the **underground generating plant★** *(visits at 2 and 4, Jun.-Sep.)*. ▶ **Savines-le-Lac** ® (pop. 859) has replaced the old village, now submerged under the lake. ▶ **Embrun** ® (pop. 5 813) has a remarkable church of Notre-Dame★ (Romanesque, end 12thC; treasure room★). 10 km S : ancient abbey★ (12thC) and **forest of Boscodon★★,** pines, spruce and larch. □

Bayard

The chevalier Bayard belongs in the very select Who's Who of great heroes whose exploits have passed into legend. Pierre Terrail, Seigneur de Bayard, was born in 1476 near Pontcharra, in Graisivaudan (→). Very early in life he won distinction for his prowess at arms and his knightly qualities; at the age of 16 he floored one of the best jousters in the kingdom. His military career, in the service of Charles VIII, Louis XII and François 1st, was unequalled. His heroic defense of the bridge over the Garigliano river, alone against 200 Spaniards, is but one feat of arms among many. Bayard is the epitome of the loyal servant and faithful knight.

■ LA TOUR-DU-PIN

A1 / ® / pop. 7 037 (Isère)

The triptych★ in the church is by a pupil of Dürer (1541). 15thC Renaissance house, known locally as the Maison des Dauphins★. □

▶ Nearby

▶ **Bourgoin-Jallieu** *(15 km W).* Museum with 19th-20thC paintings and drawings. One room devoted to tapestries and printing on cloth, specialities of Bourgoin *(11-12 & 2:30-5 Sat.; 2:30-5:30, Mon. and Wed.).* ▶ **La Côte-Saint-André** ® *(36 km NW),* Hector Berlioz Museum in the house where the composer was born *(9-12 & 3-6; Feb. 2-5; closed Mon. and Jan.).* ▶ **Château de Virieu**★ *(12 km SE)* 11thC, a fortress *(summer, 2-6; closed Tue.).* ▶ **Paladru Lake**★ *(20 km SE).* Neolithic man lived around the shores of this emerald lake, now the hunting-ground of wind-surfing enthusiasts from Lyons and the Dauphiné. □

■ The TRIÈVES Region

B2

▶ **Monestier-de-Clermont** ® (pop. 774) is the best starting point for exploring the Trièves, a green land deeply scored by the waters of the Drac and the Ebron. ▶ A pleasant trip by car to **Mens** *(21 km SE)* via the **Pont de Brion**★ (bridge), and from there to **La Mure** *(19 km N)* via the **Accarias Pass**★ or the Sautet Dam★ and Corps *(25 km E)* via the Saint-Sébastien Pass. ▶ From Monestier, you can also reach the upper valley of the Gresse via the Allimas Pass★ *(17 km SW);* view★★ of Mont Aiguille (alt. 2 086 m). □

■ The VALBONNAIS and VALJOUFFREY Valleys★

B2

From La Mure (→ Route Napoléon) the road crosses these two little regions which are in fact the lower and upper reaches of the river Bonne. Dark larch and bright birch clothe the slopes around **La Chapelle-en-Valjouffrey**★ *(24 km);* from here you can reach Le Désert *(8.5 km),* in an amphitheatre★ of snowy peaks. Trips to the **Valsenestre**★ (gorges and forests★). □

■ VALENCE

A2 / ® / pop. 68 000 (Drôme)

Valence is the main market (fruit and vegetables) for the Drôme and the Ardèche regions; it is easy to appreciate the charms of Valence in the narrow streets and alleys of the old town around the cathedral.

▶ The **cathedral**★ (A-B2) is a handsome 12thC Romanesque building well-reconstructed in the 17thC. ▶ Nearby, the **museum** *(2-5:45)* has a remarkable series of 96 sanguines★★ (red ochre crayon sketches) and drawings of Italy by Hubert Robert (1755-75). ▶ North of the

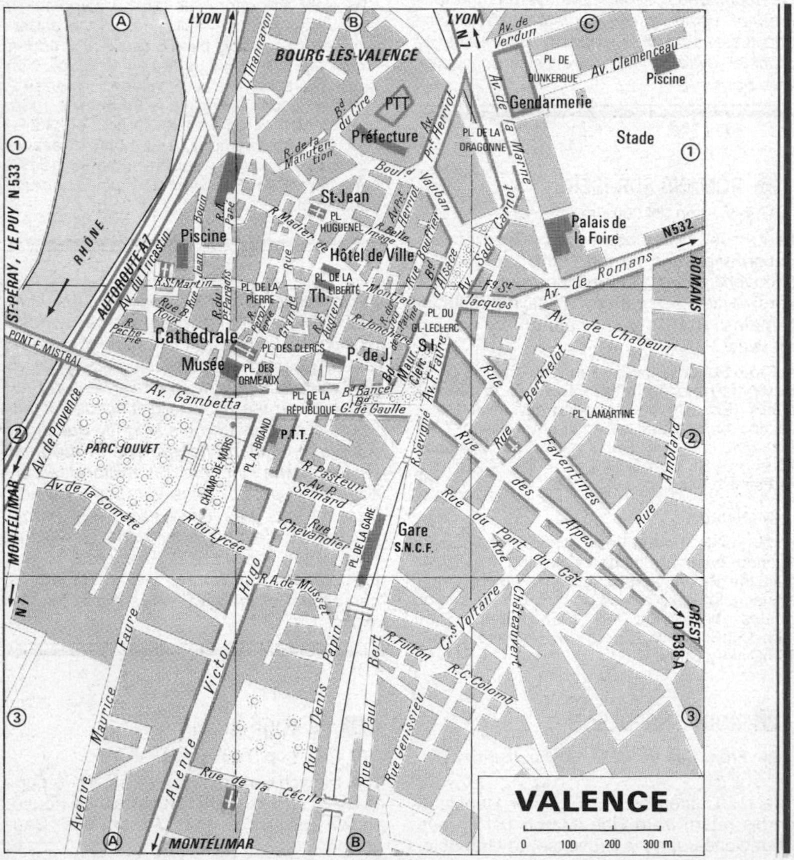

cathedral, the Pendentif is a graceful Renaissance chapel (1548).
Also... ▶ The **Maison Dupré-Latour★,** early 16thC (7, Rue Pérollerie, B1-2) and the **Maison des Têtes★,** Renaissance (57 Grand-Rue, B2). □

▶ Nearby

▶ **Saint-Marcel-lès-Valence** *(7 km NE)* : "La Vieille Auto" museum *(9-12 & 2-7).*

The wines of the Dauphiné

North of Valence, the wines of L'Ermitage and Crozes-Ermitage belong to the great family of Côtes du Rhône. These wines taste strongly of their origins, a flavour of blackberries and hawthorns. Among the reds : Bessards, Croze and Larnage; among the whites, Chante Alouette and Le Clos des Hirondelles (great years : 1945, 49, 54, 57, 61, 67, 71). Also worthy of attention, are the reds of Haut-Comtat around Nyons, solidly structured and generous, and those of the Coteaux du Tricastain, light and fruity. Clairette de Die is a sparkling wine, admired for its freshness and finesse.

■ The **VALGAUDEMAR** Valley★

B2

Valgaudemar is hidden deep in the Massif des Écrins, on the fast-running Séveraisse. Downstream there are fresh meadows where curtains of poplars scintillate in the sunshine. The scenery changes completely with the houses of Villar-Loubière, clinging to the the rock : the valley is suddenly surrounded by bright walls and dark shaded woods as the mountains close in.

▶ From **La Chapelle-en-Valgaudemar** *(18 km along the N85)* climb to the hamlet of Portes to see the view★★ over the Olan Peak. ▶ Continue 9 km to the chalet-hotel of Gioberney, shortly after the Cascade du Voile de la Mariée (Bride's Veil Falls) site★; numerous excursions from the chalet. □

■ The **VALLOUISE** Valley★

C2

The Vallouise leads up to the foot of the highest peaks in the Dauphiné. The villages of the region are typically Dauphinois : around the Romanesque bell-tower, the large stone houses, sometimes adorned with arcades and crowned with wooden storage lofts, are backed against the hillside so that you can walk in on the upper level. □

▶ Vallouise Route★ : from Argentière to Pré de Madame Carle *(24 km)*

▶ The village churches of the Vallouise strike a charmingly rustic note among the houses. Inside they are frequently decorated with frescos (Les Vigneaux, Vallouise), while the doors are equipped with locks★ and ironwork peculiar to this valley. Above the beautiful houses with their large wooden galleries in the village of **Vallouise** (pop. 512) stands the winter sports resort of **Puy-Saint-Vincent** ®. Going up the valley via **Saint-Antoine** ® as far as **Ailefroide** ®, in the middle of the meadows, one passes by numerous hamlets of the commune of **Pelvoux** which are all mountaineering centres.
▶ From the village of **Pré de Madame Carle★** you can climb in 2 hr 30 *(beware of icy surfaces — névé)* to the mountain refuge on the Glacier Blanc (view★★). □

■ The **VERCORS** Massif★★★

Circuit *(142 km, 1 day)*

A-B2 *(see diag 3)*

There are two Vercors : the visible and the invisible. The first, accessible to all, is the country of wide pastures and silent forests. The other Vercors, the invisible one, is the subterranean world carved out by the waters, a hidden world reserved for the speleologist : sink-holes, grottos and chasms (such as the Gouffre Berger) abound. Between the Isère and the Drôme rivers, Vercors is a natural citadel. Near Grenoble, the Montagne de Lans is cattle country, open to tourism (Villard-de-Lans,

3. Vercors Massif

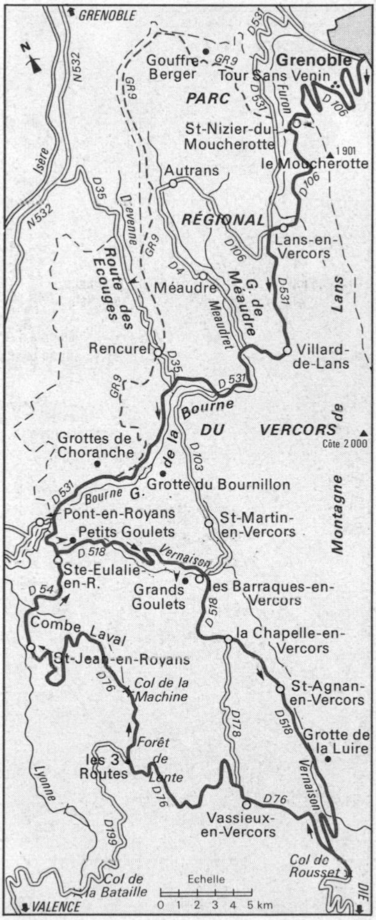

Dauphiné

Autrans), while further south Le Royans and the Vercors proper are less developed. Here it is mainly forest (Forêt de Lente). Vercors has since 1970 been part of a nature reserve (1 350 km²) which safeguards agricultural and pastoral activity while promoting rural tourism under controlled conditions. During the last war, the Vercors was the scene of much Resistance activity.

▶ **Grenoble** (→). **Saint-Nizier-du-Moucherotte** (pop. 515) : a balcony over Grenoble and the Alps which can be reached on skis or on foot. Romanesque church★ (12thC). Viewpoint★★. ▶ **Villard-de-Lans★** ® (pop. 3320) : cradled in pastures and surrounded by forests, a resort which is very popular with children and has an ideal climate. Alpine and cross-country skiing, naturally, but also numerous mountain excursions, including one to the Pas de l'Oeille★★ (cable-car then 1 hr on foot). ▶ **La Balme-de-Rencurel :** right, the dizzy road to Écouges★★. ▶ **Grotte du Bournillon** *(1 km left, then 30 mins on foot)* and **Grottes de Choranche★** *(2.5 km right),* caves with visiting facilities, including the underground lake with astonishing reflections of hollow stalactites ("macaroni"). ▶ **Pont-en-Royans★** ® (pop. 1 119) : houses★ clinging to the rocks above the river Bourne. Stopover before the famous road through the Petits (Small) and **Grands Goulets★★★,** a narrow defile in the grey rocks. The road emerges suddenly into full daylight on the Plateau de Vercors at **Les Barraques-en-Vercors** ®. ▶ **Grotte de la Luire** *(left, 5 mins on foot)* where the Résistance installed a field hospital in 1944. The wounded were massacred by the Nazis. ▶ Leave the road ahead to the **Rousset Pass★★,** opening on to the southern landscape of the Diois, to take the road right to **Vassieux.** National cemetery of Vercors and Resistance museum. ▶ Firs and beeches in the **Lente Forest★★** *(68 km²)* conceal a chaos of limestone cliffs, riddled with grottos, avens and potholes. ▶ Left : the road to the **Bataille Pass★★** (a superb run downhill). The La Machine Pass road leads to **Combe-Laval★★★.** The road clings to the cliff wall 600 m above the spectacular Torrent du Cholet. ▶ **Saint-Jean-en-Royans** (pop. 2700) : specialising in turned and inlaid wood. ▶ From here, rejoin Pont-en-Royans or reach the N532 Romans to Grenoble road. □

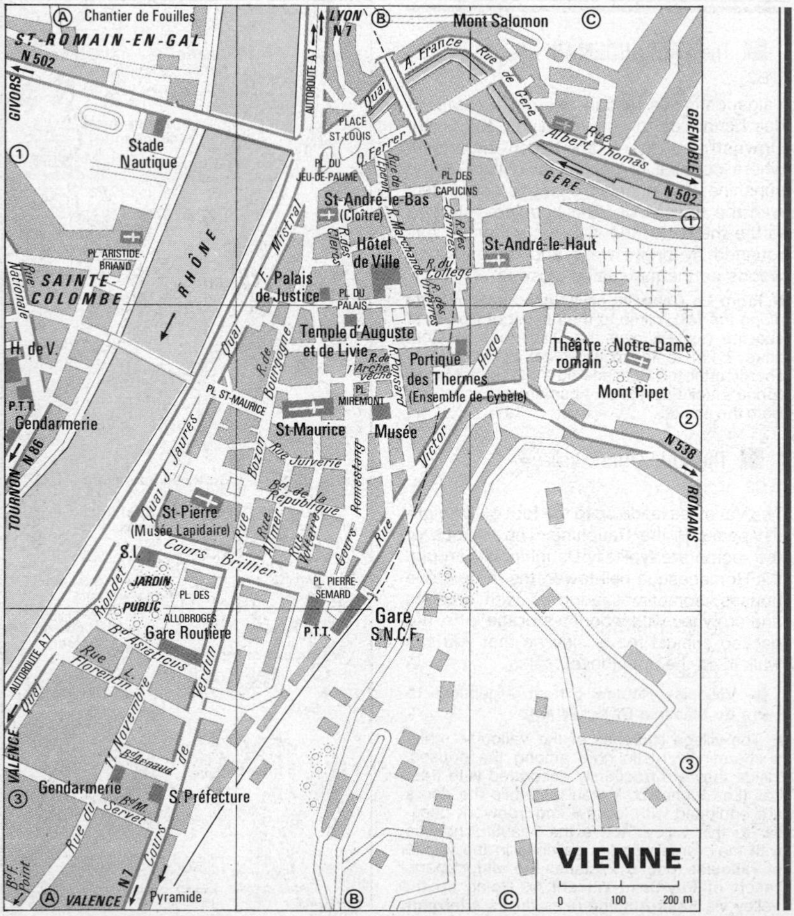

■ VIENNE★

A1 / ® / pop. 29 000 (Isère)

Appearances are deceptive; behind Vienne's grey façade overlooking the river the scenery changes. It is a real pleasure to pursue the narrow streets of the old town in search of times past, when Vienne was one of the major cities of Roman Gaul, and a cradle of the arts under the aegis of its Count Archbishops.

▶ Don't miss the capitals★ in the nave and the cloister★ (Romanesque 12thC) of the church of **Saint-André-le-Bas** (B1), 9th-12thC, housing the musée d'Art Chrétien (museum of Christian art; *same hours as the Lapidaire Museum*) with concerts and a festival of sacred music in June and July. ▶ The **temple of Augustus and Livia**★★ (B2) used to dominate the forum of the Roman town. Built around 25BC, it is remarkably well preserved. ▶ Other interesting classical remains : the portico of the hot baths, with nearby the remains of a temple to the goddess Cybele and a shrine of the Mysteries (today devoted to archaeology). ▶ Backing on to Mont Pipet is a **Roman theatre**★ (C2) unearthed in 1922, which has now regained some of its former glory, staging events and spectacles in the summer. It is one of the largest in Roman Gaul. ▶ **St. Maurice**★ (B2; formerly a cathedral), unites a 12thC Romanesque nave to a Flamboyant Gothic (14th-15thC) façade in lacy stonework (don't miss the sculptured doorways and the tomb★ of the Archbishops; 18thC.). ▶ The **museum** (B2) contains collections of Prehistoric and Gallo-Roman remains and some fine Moustiers ceramics★. ▶ **The church of St. Pierre**★ (A2), one of the oldest Christian sanctuaries in France (6th-12thC), houses the Lapidaire Museum (Stonework Museum; *9-12 & 2-6:30, Apr.-15 Oct.; 10-12 & 2-5, Wed.-Sat.; 16 Oct.-Mar.; closed Tue.).*

Also... ▶ The **Pyramide** (A3), which used to decorate the spine of the Roman circus. ▶ **Saint-Romain-en-Gal**★ (A1), the commercial and industrial quarter of the ancient city (mosaics★). □

Dauphinois cuisine

This is the country of the gratin, *the most famous of the breed being potato-based* Gratin Dauphinois. *There is no room here to list all the possible variations and explain the different points of view of Dauphiné cooks; but here is the recipe considered (by many, if not all!) as the basic starting point : thickly butter a gratin dish and cover it in fine slices of good quality potato. Salt and pepper. Beat a whole egg, and add whole milk. Moisten the potatoes with the mixture and sprinkle with dabs of butter. Cook in a slow oven. Grated Gruyère cheese is optional. The list of possible gratins is unlimited — macaroni, aubergine, crayfish, etc. As for other delicacies, olive trees grow in profusion around Dignes and Nyons. Truffles can be found, during the season, in the Drôme. The local pastry is known as* la pogne, *halfway between a brioche and a tart, and garnished with fruit or squash according to season. Numerous liqueurs including the famous Chartreuse, and* génépi, *are made from the aromatic plant of that name.*

Architecture

On the plateau of Vercors the farms are isolated, as in the valley of the Rhône, while in the south, where sheep farming is traditional, people live in closely-grouped villages. With their protecting ramparts, and perched as they often are, on high ground, these villages look like miniature towns. ● In the Oisans and the Briançonnais regions, the villages are also grouped, while the Chartreuse region and the plateaus of Trièves and Dévoluy are characterised by scattered hamlets as in Savoie. ● Around the Roman bell-tower, usually stone-built with pediments (a distinctive trait of the Dauphiné region), will be found the inevitable town hall, school and cemetery. ● Many villages here, since they are no longer concerned by problems of local defence, have an ancient section perched on a height, and the more modern buildings closer to the rivers and

Briançon area

cultivable land. ● Generally speaking, the builders of the Dauphiné use more stone than their neighbours in Savoie. The houses of Oisans, for example, are built entirely of stone with cut stone doorframes and corners. Wood is used for window frames and gables, with plain vertical planks leaving space for air to circulate through the hayloft. The roof has two slopes, covered with *essendoles* (tiles of split wood), thick slates or stone slabs. ● The architecture in the Briançonnais and Queyras regions is particularly characteristic : large stone houses with two or three floors, sometimes decorated with beautiful arcaded balconies and sundials; on top there is a large upper storey of wood which is the loft. The houses in Saint-Véran are among the most typical.

Dauphiné region

● The houses in the Montagne de Lans, part of the Vercors region are recognisable by their stepped gables, covered with stone slabs to protect the masonry work against snow and rain. Living quarters, stable and barn are all under the same roof (formerly thatched) with two asymmetrical slopes. In the south the influence of the Midi can be seen as slates and flat tiles make way for Roman tiling. ● The rectangular houses of the Chartreuse region, with pyramidal roofs, are typical of the Dauphiné : this sort of roof, inspired by that of the Convent of La Grande Chartreuse, is also found in Graisivaudan and the northern plain. Contrary to other mountain areas, here the living quarters, stable and barn are separated. ● The size of the house and the composition of its walls (cut stone, dry stone or cob) indicate the wealth of the inhabitants; in general, tiles have replaced thatched roofs. Down in the plain the little houses and agricultural buildings are usually of cob, while roofs have only a double pitch. Sometimes one side of the roof overhangs sufficiently to be used as a shelter for reserves of wood, sheaves of corn, crates of cheeses or tools. ● In the walnut producing regions, principally around Grenoble, you can see large drying areas under the eaves, closed off by chestnut wood latticework.

Drôme region farmhouse

Brief regional history

B.C. Starting around 650 B.C. the **Celts,** the ancestors of the Gauls, began to settle in Dauphiné; the best-known tribe was the **Allobroges,** famous for their resistance to the Romans.

121BC-5AD The **Roman occupation** of the Dauphiné lasted 575 years, and Vienne, the capital of the conquered Allobroges, became a rich and brilliant Roman city (commerce, industry).

6th-13thC As the feudal system took hold during the **Middle Ages,** certain seigneurs dominated the others, by force or through suitable alliances. Thus **Guigues le Vieux,** Comte d'Albon, would seem to be the founder of the Dauphiné. His descendants continued his policy of expansion; Guigues IV was the first to bear the title of Dauphin (→ box).

14thC But two centuries later, **Humbert II,** last of the third line of Dauphins, ruined and childless, negotiated the sale of his domains (200 000 florins and a life's income) to the King of France. This was the famous *Transport du Dauphiné.* The agreement stipulated that the Dauphiné should be the province of the eldest son of the King of France, which is why the Crown Prince was known as the Dauphin until the fall of the French monarchy.

15th-17thC The Crown's **newly acquired province** was a **well-administered territory,** with a diversified economy : cattle, arable farming (at altitudes up to 2 000 m), wine, fruit, hemp, wood and wool were the Dauphiné's principle products. ● During the wars of religion (16thC), the Dauphiné was on the whole favourable to the Protestant Reformation. At this point there appeared the formidable and destructive Baron des Adrets and the great Protestant war-chief, **Lesdiguières** (1543-1626).

18thC Politically, the old **Delphinal Council** instituted by Humbert II (14thC) was **transformed into a Parliament** (1453) by the future Louis XI, the only royal Dauphin to have visited his province in order to govern it. The Parliament of Grenoble, as it was known, was to play a major role in the early stages of the French Revolution. ● In 1791 the Dauphiné was divided into three departments : the Isère, the Drôme and the Hautes-Alpes.

19thC This century was marked principally by **economic change,** and by the building of roads and railways (greatly benefitting Valence, on the Paris-Marseilles line). 1869 saw Aristides Bergès' first use of water power, which he called "white coal" *(houille blanche),* to operate a paper mill in Graisivaudan. Grenoble was also to profit from this new energy source, and the developing electrochemical and metallurgical industries, large consumers of electricity, sprang up near generating stations built in the valleys of the Graisivaudan, the Romanche, Maurienne and the Tarentaise.

20thC This spirit of imaginative research and capacity for invention characterises the Dauphiné today. The local character is one of tenacity and resistance; during the last war the **Maquis** (partisans) of Oisans, Chartreuse and Vercors demonstrated this to the full.

Practical information

The region

Information : Dauphiné : *Comité Régional du Tourisme* (C.R.T.), 14, rue de la République, B.P. 227, 38019 Grenoble Cedex, ☎ 76.54.34.36. **Hautes-Alpes :** *Comité Départemental du Tourisme* (C.D.T.), 5 *ter*, rue Capitaine-de-Bresson, 05000 Gap, ☎ 92.53.62.00. **Drôme :** *C.D.T.,* 1, av. de Romans, 26000 Valence, ☎ 75.43.27.12. **Isère :** *C.D.T.*, same address as the *C.R.T. Dir. Rég. Jeunesse et Sports,* 15, rue de la République, B.P. 1145, 38022 Grenoble Cedex, ☎ 76.42.75.90.
In Paris : *Maison* ***Alpes-Dauphiné,*** 2, pl. André-Malraux, 75001, ☎ 42.96.08.56. *Maison de la* ***Drôme,*** 14, bd Haussmann, 75009, ☎ 42.46.66.67. *Maison des* ***Hautes-Alpes,*** 4, av. de l'Opéra, 75002, ☎ 42.96.05.08.

Bookings : *Loisirs-Accueil* ***Hautes-Alpes,*** 16, rue Carnot, 05000 Gap, ☎ 92.51.39.49 and 92.52.14.23. **Gestel,** ☎ 36.14.91.56, code of access : Gestel.

Maps : *Michelin* nos 77, 81, 93 1/200 000 ; *I.G.N.* nos 51, 52, 54, 60 1/100 000, and no 112 (Savoie-Dauphiné) 1/250 000.

S.O.S. : Drôme : *S.A.M.U. (emergency medical service),* ☎ 75.42.44.44. **Hautes-Alpes :** ☎ 17 ; **Isère :** *S.A.M.U.,* ☎ 76.42.42.42. Poisoning Emergency Centre : ☎ 91.75.25.25 in Marseilles.

Weather forecast : Hautes-Alpes : ☎ 92.20.10.00 ; **Drôme :** ☎ 75.01.83.50 ; **Isère :** ☎ 76.51.11.11. *Weather forecast-snow conditions,* **Hautes-Alpes :** ☎ 92.21.07.91, and **Isère :** ☎ 76.51.19.29. *Snow conditions* (24 hr automatic answering service) : ☎ 76.54.30.80.

Rural gîtes and chambres d'hôtes : enq : *Relais Départementaux ;* **Hautes-Alpes :** 8 *ter,* rue Capitaine-de-Bresson, B.P. 55, 05002 Gap Cedex, ☎ 92.51.31.45 ; **Drôme :** bd Vauban, B.P. 121, 26001 Valence, ☎ 75.42.04.00, ext 18 ; **Isère :** *Maison du Tourisme,* 14, rue de la République, 38000 Grenoble, ☎ 76.54.34.36.

Camping : more than 350 camp sites. *F.F.C.C. (national camping federation) regional offices :* **Rhône-Alpes :** 448, av. du Covet, L'Esplanade, 73000 Chambéry, and **Provence-Côte d'Azur :** chemin Bon-Encontre, Les Pins - Logis Neuf, 13190 Allauch.

Cultural events : Apr-May : *International Quartet Festival* at the château de Grignan. **May :** *Fine Arts, Music and Song Festival* in Saint-Antoine-l'Abbaye. **Jun :** *Festival* at the château de Vizille. **Jul :** *Jazz Festival* in Vienne, *Festival of Film Shorts* in Grenoble. **Aug :** *Festival of Sacred Music* in Vienne. **Mid-Dec-end Apr :** *organ recitals* in L'Alpe-d'Huez (every Sat).

Folklore : Apr : *spring festival* in Nyons. **Jul :** *wood-cutter's competition* in Allevard and Lans-en-Vercors, *international folk festival* in Montseveroux. **Aug :** *wood-cutters' festival* in Chamrousse, *world assembly of Dauphinois kinsmen* in Grenoble, *mountain festival* in L'Alpe-d'Huez, *mountain pasture festival* in Gresse-en-Vercors, *festival of* the Saint-Hilaire funicular railway, *beer festival* in Allevard, *threshing festival* in Fressinières.

Sporting events : Mar : *Grand Prix de L'Alpe-d'Huez* (skiing), *Chamrousse 6-hour* (cross-country competition). **Jul :** *International Summer Skiing Grand Prix* in L'Alpe-d'Huez, *pedestrian rally* from Oisans to Bourg-d'Oisans. **Aug :** *Trophée des Écrins* in Venosc, *Speleology* (spelunking) *Film Festival* in La Chapelle-en-Vercors (28 Aug-2 Sep). **Sep :** *International Hang-gliding Film Festival* in Saint-Hilaire. **Oct-Nov :** *6 cyclists' days* in Grenoble.

Fairs and markets : Apr : *International Market of Minerals and Crystals* in Bourg-d'Oisans. **May :** *post-card salon* in Pont-de-Beauvoisin, *scale model show and agricultural fair* in Chapareillan, *antique fair* in Crémieu, *Festival of Artistic Trades and Professions* in Rives. **Jun :** *scale model and miniature show* in Grenoble, *bric-à-brac* in Beaucroissant, *exhibition and market of arms* in the château de la Condamine, Corenc, *artistic trades and professions show* in Beaucroissant. **Jul :** *International Olive Market* in Nyons. **Aug :** *lavender festival* in Lesches-en-Diois. **Sep :** *bric-à-brac* in Vienne, *fair* in Lans-le-Vercors, *antique fair* in Chapareillan, Beaucroissant fair. **Oct :** *honey fair* in Vienne. **Nov :** *Alpexpo* in Grenoble. **Dec :** *motor show* in Grenoble.

Scenic railways : Saint-Georges-La Mure line : runs every Sun from end May to end Sep, enq : *Chemin de Fer de La Mure,* ☎ 76.46.12.51. Saint-Hilaire-du-Touvet funicular railway : daily ex Tue 15 May-15 Oct, enq : ☎ 67.08.00.02. Bréda-Pontcharra-La Rochette line : runs on the first Sun of each month from May to Oct, 1 hr 30 trip (allow approx 6 hours return for day-trip). Enq : M. Vargel, ☎ 76.21.02.10, and M. Portenart, ☎ 76.27.21.56.

National and nature parks : *Parc national des Écrins,* 7, rue du Colonel-Roux, B.P. 142, 05004 Gap Cedex, ☎ 92.51.40.71, and *Maison du Parc,* 05290 Vallouise, ☎ 92.23.32.31. *Parc régional du Vercors,* 38250 Lans-en-Vercors, ☎ 76.95.40.33, and *Maisons du Parc,* 38650 Gresse-en-Vercors, ☎ 76.34.08.40, in La Chapelle-en-Vercors, Chamaloc, Saint-Jean. *Parc régional du Queyras,* rte de la Gare, 05600 Guillestre, ☎ 92.45.06.23.

Rambling and hiking : topoguides G.R. 5-54/541, 549-58/541, G.R. 9/91/93/95, 9/429, G.R. 91, G.R. 94/946. The Briançon Guide Office organises accompanied excursions : tour of the Cerces, tour of Champsaur, tour of the Rochebrune peak, tour in Queyras, tour of Viso and South Oisans ; enq and enrollments, ☎ 92.21.29.48. *Centre d'Information Montagne et Sentiers* (C.I.M.E.S.), ☎ 76.54.34.36.

Riding holidays : *Assn. Régionale* ***Rhône-Alpes*** *de Tourisme Équestre,* 47, av. A.-Briand, 38600 Fontaine, ☎ 76.27.10.61.

Cycling holidays : *Ligue Régionale Dauphiné-Savoie,* hameau d'Allières, 38640 Claix. *Comité Dép. des Hautes-Alpes,* ☎ 92.51.57.45.

Handicraft courses : silk and wood painting, drawing, mosaic work, pottery, porcelain, weaving, wood sculpture, carpentry, book binding, wicker-work and photography : see *Maisons du*

Tourisme in Grenoble and Paris to obtain the list, and the *Ateliers du Canet*, 38590 Saint-Martin-le-Vinoux, ☎ 76.87.61.17, which organise most of these courses.

Other courses : botany and apiculture at the *Maison de la Flore*, near Die, ☎ 75.22.11.82 ; the *Hutte aux Pies Association* organises circuits to discover minerals, plant-life and habitat, ☎ 92.66.25.40 : Instructional courses in mountain bird-watching, observation of mountain wildlife and flora : enq at the *A.N.C.E.E.S.F.*, Maison de la Nature, 05460 Abriès, ☎ 92.45.73.54. The *Maison du Parc des Écrins* proposes summer courses in ornithology, plant-life, botanical fauna, geology and ethnology.

Sailing and wind-surfing : *Féd. Régionale **Dauphiné-Savoie*** **(Isère + Drôme),** M. Duclot, clos des Gentons, 38570 Theys, ☎ 76.54.41.27. *Féd. **Alpes-Provence*** **(Hautes-Alpes),** M. Bouveyron, C.N.M., Pavillon Flottant, quai Rive-Neuve, 13007 Marseille, ☎ 91.33.73.55.

Water skiing : *Ligue Régionale **Dauphiné,*** M. Cortez, 14, rue Charrel, 38000 Grenoble, ☎ 76.23.35.36, and for the **Hautes-Alpes :** *Ligue Régionale Méditerranée*, Mme F. Lion, 8, rte de Cannes, 06650 Opio, ☎ 93.77.31.71.

Canoeing : *Ligue Régionale **Dauphiné,*** M. Thiel, 1, rue du Vercors, 38800 Le Pont-de-Claix.

Potholing and spelunking : *Comité Régional C* **(Isère + Drôme),** 28, quai St-Vincent, 69000 Lyon, ☎ 78.39.71.78, and *Comité Régional D* **(Hautes-Alpes),** Acquaviva, 29, bd Rodocanachi, 13008 Marseille. Also see *Spéléo Club Alpin*, 9, rue Bayard, 05000 Gap, ☎ 92.51.55.14.

Climbing : *Comité Régional de la Féd. de la Montagne pour le **Dauphiné,*** M. Féasson, 15, av. de la Boisse, 73000 Chambéry. The Centre-école d'Embrun organises courses for groups, instructional courses in climbing on ice, a snow school, climbing school : ☎ 92.43.02.75 for all information.

Skiing : *Comité Régional F.F.S.* **Dauphiné (Drôme + Isère),** B.P. 193, 38005 Grenoble Cedex, ☎ 76.46.32.46, and *Comité Régional* ***Alpes-Provence*** **(Hautes-Alpes),** 30, rue Sénac, 13001 Marseille, ☎ 91.48.21.28. Excursions in the *massif des Écrins*, in Oisans, standard races, snow-ski races and summer-skiing down the long slopes of the *massif des Écrins*. Information at *O.T. Montgenèvre*, ☎ 92.21.90.22, and *Cie des guides de l'Oisans*, Serre-Chevalier, ☎ 92.24.74.54. For the Vercors ski crossing, enq at *Comité régional F.F.S.*, rte de Lyon, ☎ 76.47.84.68.

Ice sports : *Féd. Régionale **Dauphiné,*** M. Moyencourt, ☎ 93.81.12.05.

Parachuting : Centre école de Grenoble, 3, pass. du Palais-de-Justice.

Hunting and shooting : enq at the Féd. Dép. **Hautes-Alpes :** quartier Lareton, 05000 Gap, ☎ 92.51.16.25, and imm. Montjoie, chemin Bonne, 05000 Gap, ☎ 92.51.33.62 ; **Drôme,** 60, av. Sadi-Carnot, 26000 Valence, ☎ 75.43.05.36 ; **Isère,** 6, rue St-Francois, 38000 Grenoble, ☎ 76.43.11.01, and 12, rue Montorge, 38000 Grenoble, ☎ 76.46.20.23.

Fishing : enq at the *Féd. Dép. des Féd. de Pêche et Pisciculture*, **Hautes-Alpes :** 18, rue Arène, 05000 Gap, ☎ 92.51.11.40 ; **Drôme :** 3, pl. Dragonne, 26000 Valence, ☎ 75.43.17.98 ; **Isère :** 1, rue Cujas, 38000 Grenoble, ☎ 76.44.28.39.

● Towns

ALLEVARD

Chambéry 35, Grenoble 38, Paris 596
13 km SE of Pontcharra, B1 ✉ 38580

♆ (17 May-24 Sep), ☎ 76.97.56.22.

ⓘ pl. de la Résistance, ☎ 76.45.10.11.

Hotels :
★★***Ermitage,*** av. des Bains, ☎ 76.97.51.41. 50 rm ⚘ Ⓟ ♨ ⛰ ⚲ closed 25 Sep-mid-May, 180. Rest. ♦ ✂ 80-130.
★★***Parc,*** av. Davallet, ☎ 76.97.54.22. 48 rm ⚘ Ⓟ ♨ ⛰ ⚲ ♿ closed mid-May-25 Sep, 180.
★★***Pervenches*** (L.F., Relais du Silence), av. Davallet, ☎ 76.97.50.73. 30 rm ♨ ⛰ ▭ ⚲ ♿ closed 25 Sep-1 Feb, 210. Rest. ♦ ✂ closed Wed and Thu noon, 80-130.

Pinsot, 7 km S on the D525 :
★★***Pic de la Belle Étoile*** (L.F.), ☎ 76.97.53.62. Euro, Visa. 34 rm ⚘ Ⓟ ♨ ⛰ ⚲ ♿ closed 13 Apr-10 May, 12 Oct-9 Nov, Sun eve and Wed, 215. Rest. ♦ ✂ 75-165.

Collet-d'Allevard, 10 km E on the D109 ; ⛷ 1 450-2 100 m :
★★***Plein Ciel,*** ☎ 76.97.52.30. 20 rm ⚘ Ⓟ ⛰ closed May-Nov, 160. Rest. ♦ 70-160.

⛺ ★★*Caravaneige du Collet* (90 pl.), ☎ 76.45.10.32 ; ★★*Clair Matin* (150 pl.), ☎ 76.97.55.19 ; ★★*Idéal Camping* (60 pl.), ☎ 76.97.50.23.

L' ALPE-D'HUEZ

Grenoble 62, Briancon 79, Paris 627
B2 ⛷ 1 860-3 350 m ✉ 38750

ⓘ pl. Paganon, ☎ 76.80.35.41.

Hotels :
★★★★***Ours Blanc*** av. des Jeux, ☎ 76.80.31.11, Tx 320807. AE, DC, Euro, Visa. 34 rm, ⚘ Ⓟ closed Easter-Christmas. Board only, 1 000. Rest. ♦♦ ✂ 165-190.
● ★★★***Chamois d'Or,*** ☎ 76.80.31.32. 41 rm ⚘ Ⓟ ⛰ ✂ closed 25 Apr-15 Dec, 310. Rest. ♦♦ Light fare for ski-bound clients : *friand de saumon, émincé de blanc de Bresse en papillote au beurre de truffe*, 75-200.
★★★***Christina,*** rue Maurice-Rajon, ☎ 76.80.33.32. 30 rm ⚘ Ⓟ ⛰ ⚲ ♿ closed 20 Apr-15 Dec, 260. Rest. ♦ ✂ 120-210.
★★★***Vallée Blanche,*** ☎ 76.80.30.51, Tx 320892. DC, Visa. 41 rm ⚘ Ⓟ ⛰ closed 24 Apr-15 Dec, 480. Rest. ♦ ✂ 125-175.
★★***Alp'Azur,*** rte du Signal, ☎ 76.80.34.02. Visa. 20 rm ⚘ ⛰ closed 15 May-30 Jun, 235.
★★***Chaix,*** rue du Rif-Neil, ☎ 76.80.30.22. AE, DC, Euro, Visa. ⚘ Ⓟ ♿ closed 25 Apr-10 Dec, 260. Rest. ♦ ✂ 120-210.
★★***Outa,*** ☎ 76.80.34.56. DC, Euro, Visa. 11 rm ⚘ ♨ ⛰ closed 1 Jul-31 Aug, 15 Dec end Apr. Rest. ♦♦ 100.

Youth hostel : Marc Sangnier, ☎ 76.80.37.37.

Restaurant :
♦♦ ***La Cordée,*** ☎ 76.80.35.39. AE, Visa, closed 1 Sep-11 Nov, 90-180.

Summer skiing : special connections by helicopter to Deux-Alpes info : S.E.T.A.M. ☎ 76.80.30.30 and Alti-bar, ☎ 76.80.41.15.

ARVIEUX

Briançon 32, Gap 81, Paris 737
21 km NE of Guillestre, C3
⊠ 05350 Château-Ville-Vieille

ℹ La Chalp, ☎ 92.45.75.76.

Hotel :
★★***Borne Ensoleillée,*** ☎ 92.45.72.89. 15 rm P closed 20 Sep-20 Dec, 15 Apr-15 Jun, 200. Rest. ♦ 55-95.

AUTRANS

Grenoble 36, Valence 76, Paris 590
15.5 km N of Villard-de-Lans, B2
1 050-1 610 m ⊠ 38880

ℹ mairie, ☎ 76.95.30.70.

Hotels :
★★***Buffe*** (L.F.), La Côte, ☎ 76.95.33.26. Visa. 18 rm P closed 5 Sep-1 Dec, 20 Apr-20 May, 180. Rest. 50-130.
★★***Poste*** (L.F.), ☎ 76.95.31.03. AE, DC, Euro, Visa. 30 rm closed 15 Oct-15 Dec, 20 Apr-10 May, 150. Rest. 50-160.
★***Feu de Bois,*** ☎ 76.95.33.32. 10 rm P closed low season, 180.

Méaudre, ⊠ 38112, 5.5 km S on the D106 :
★★***Prairie*** (L.F.), ☎ 76.95.22.55, 25 rm P closed Nov, 150. Rest. ♦ ♿ 50-95.

★★★*Joyeux Réveil* (100 pl.), ☎ 76.95.33.44 ; ★★★*Vercors* (63 pl.), ☎ 76.95.31.88.

BEAUREPAIRE

Vienne 30, Grenoble 64, Paris 522
A1 ⊠ 38270

SNCF ☎ 74.84.62.00.

Hotel :
★★***Fiard,*** 23, rue de la République, ☎ 74.84.62.02. AE, DC, Euro, Visa. 21 rm closed 2 Jan-15 Feb and Sun eve low season, 180. Rest. ♦♦♦ ♿ A classical menu of superb quality : *rouelles de lottes au noilly et aux pâtes fraîches, pot-au-feu de pintade aux raviolis du Royans, nougat glacé au coulis de framboises,* 80-200.

★★*Municipal* (50 pl.), ☎ 74.84.64.89.

BOURG-D'OISANS

Grenoble 49, Briancon 67, Paris 614
B2 720 m ⊠ 38520

ℹ quai Girard, ☎ 76.80.03.25.

☎ 76.80.00.40.

Hotels :
★★***Oberland*** (L.F.), B.P. 18, av. de la Gare, ☎ 76.80.24.24. AE, DC, Euro, Visa. 30 rm P closed 30 Sep-15 Dec, 14 Apr-14 May, 205. Rest. 60-165.

La Garde-en-Oisans :
★***Forêt de Maronne*** (L.F.), ☎ 76.80.00.06. 13 rm P closed 20 Sep-20 Dec, 20 Apr-20 Jun, 155. Rest. ♦ ♿ 45-130.

Allemont, 11 km N on the N91 and the D526 :
★***Giniès,*** ☎ 76.80.70.03. 18 rm P 115. Rest. ♦ closed 30 Sep-2 May, 65-130.

★***Tilleuls,*** ☎ 76.80.70.24. 21 rm P closed 1 Oct-25 Apr, 100. Rest. ♦ 80-130.

Le Freney-d'Oisans, ⊠ 38142, 14 km W on the N91 and D25 :
★★***Cassini*** (L.F.), ☎ 76.80.04.10. Visa. 15 rm P closed 2 May-Pencoste, 15 Oct-20 Dec, 160. Rest. 80-130.
★★***Panoramique,*** Mizoen, ☎ 76.80.06.25. 9 rm P closed 30 Sep-30 May, 170. Rest. 80-130.

★★★★*Rencontre du Soleil* (73 pl.), ☎ 76.80.00.33 ; ★★★★*Belledonne* (130 pl.), ☎ 76.80.07.18 ; ★★★★*Cascade* (133 pl.), ☎ 76.80.02.42 ; ★★★*Vernis* (60 pl.), ☎ 76.80.02.68 ; ★★*Piscine* (65 pl.), ☎ 76.80.02.41.

BRIANÇON

Gap 87, Grenoble 116, Paris 681
C2 ⊠ 05100

ℹ Vieux Colombier, ☎ 92.21.08.50, and Centre de Congrès, av. de la République, ☎ 92.21.04.42.

Car-hire : *Budget* train + auto, at the station, ☎ 92.21.00.50.

SNCF ☎ 92.21.03.84, ☎ 92.21.00.50.

Hotels :
★★★***Vauban,*** 13, av. Gal-de-Gaulle, ☎ 82.21.12.11. 44 rm P ♿ closed 12 Nov-20 Dec, 260. Rest. ♦♦ 75-135.
★★***Mont-Prorel,*** 5, rue R.-Froger, ☎ 92.20.22.88. AE, DC, Euro, Visa. 18 rm P 250. Rest. ♦ closed 1-20 Dec, 60-120.

Montgenèvre, 12 km NE on the N94, 1 850-2 800 m, ℹ ☎ 92.21.90.22 :
★★★***Napoléon,*** ☎ 92.21.92.04. 42 rm P closed 30 Apr-15 Dec, 500. Rest. ♦ 120-210.
★★★***Valérie,*** ☎ 92.21.90.02. 20 rm closed 20 Apr-20 Dec, 240. Rest. ♦♦ 120-210.
★★***Alpet,*** ☎ 92.21.90.06. 10 rm P closed 1 Sep-Christmas, Jan-Mar, 25 Apr-1 Jul, 160. Rest. ♦ 80-130.

★★★*Cinq Vallées* (116 pl.), ☎ 92.21.06.27 ; ★★*Municipal* (80 pl.), ☎ 92.21.04.32.

BUIS-LES-BARONNIES

Carpentras 40, Digne 115, Paris 693
B2 ⊠ 26170

ℹ pl. du Champ-de-Mars, ☎ 75.28.04.59.

Hotels :
★★***Oliviers,*** chemin du Menon, ☎ 75.28.08.77. 23 rm P closed Jan and Wed low season, 160. Rest. ♦ 60-100.
★***Lion d'Or,*** ☎ 75.28.11.31. 16 rm P closed 15 Oct-15 Nov, 120.

★★*Municipal* (55 pl.), ☎ 75.28.04.96.

Farmhouse-inn : *Moulin de Cost,* ☎ 75.28.09.82.

Event : lime-tree festival, mid-Jul.

Recommended : Wed market for *picodons* (local goat cheese). *La Savoilane,* 2.5 km, ☎ 75.28.03.39 : sale of cheeses, honey and olive oil.

CHAMROUSSE

Grenoble 29, Chambéry 80, Paris 596
B2 1 450-2 250 m ⊠ 38410 Uriage

ℹ Le Recoin, ☎ 76.97.02.65, and Roche Béranger, ☎ 76.97.20.88.

☎ 76.97.02.06.

Hotels :
★★★***Hermitage,*** Le Recoin, ☎ 76.89.93.21. Visa. 45 rm closed 15 Apr-15 Dec, 550. Rest. ♦ 90-150.
★★***Virage,*** Le Recoin, ☎ 76.89.90.63. 19 rm ♿ closed 1 Oct-10 Dec, 180.
★***Grenouillère,*** ☎ 76.89.90.27. 17 rm closed 25 Apr-15 Dec, 180. Rest. 80-130.

Youth hostel : Le Recoin, ☎ 76.97.01.14 and 76.97.01.31.

La CHAPELLE-EN-VERCORS

Grenoble 62, Valence 63, Paris 607
5 km S of Grands Goulets, A2 ✉ 26420

ℹ pl. de l'Hôtel-de-Ville, ☎ 75.48.22.54.

Hotels :
★★***Bellier,*** ☎ 75.48.20.03. AE, DC, Visa. 12 rm closed 25 Sep-10 Jun, 230. Rest. ♦♦ ♿ Spec : *terrine de grives, poulet aux écrevisses,* 110-195.
★***Nouvel Hôtel,*** ☎ 75.48.20.09. 35 rm closed 6 Oct-3 Feb, 100. Rest. 80-130.

Barraques-en-Vercors, 5 km N on the N518 :
★★***Grands Goulets,*** ☎ 75.48.22.45. Visa. 30 rm ♿ closed Oct-May, 100. Rest. 80-130.

Echevis, ✉ 26190, 10 km N on the N518 :
★★***Refuge*** (L.F.), ☎ 75.48.68.32. 20 rm closed mid-Nov-mid-Dec, 180. Rest. ♦ 80-130.

⛺ ★★*Municipal* (150 pl.), ☎ 75.48.22.54.

CHARAVINES

Grenoble 40, Chambéry 52, Paris 540
13 km NW of Voiron, B1 ✉ 38850

ℹ rte Nationale, ☎ 76.06.60.31.

Hotels :
★★***Lac Bleu*** (L.F.), ☎ 76.06.60.48. 15 rm closed 15 Oct-15 Mar, Mon eve and Tue (ex summer season), 185. Rest. ♦ ♿ 65-135.
★★***Poste*** (L.F.), ☎ 76.06.60.41. Visa. 21 rm ♿ closed 31 Oct-1 Mar, Sun eve and Mon ex Jul-Aug, 180. Rest. ♦ ♿ 65-135.

⛺ ★★*Bord du Lac* (85 pl.), 76.06.60.09.

CHÂTILLON-EN-DIOIS

Valence 79, Grenoble 85, Paris 641
14 km SE of Die, A2-3 ✉ 26410

ℹ rue Reclus, ☎ 75.21.10.07.

Hotels :
★***France*** (L.F.), ☎ 75.21.12.02. 19 rm closed 11 Nov-26 Dec, Fri eve, Sat noon and Sun eve, 90. Rest. 40-70.

Treschenu-Creyers, 11 km NE on the D120 :
★★***Mont-Barral*** (L.F.), hameau des Nonières, ☎ 75.21.12.21. Euro. 24 rm closed 15 Nov-20 Dec, 1 week in Apr and Tue, 140. Rest. ♦ ♿ 60-115.

Luc-en-Diois, ✉ 26310, 12 km S :
★★***Levant,*** ☎ 75.21.33.30. 16 rm closed 1 Oct-1 Feb, 185. Rest. 65-105.

⛺ ★★*Municipal* (133 pl.), ☎ 75.21.10.21.

CORPS-LA-SALETTE

Gap 40, Grenoble 63, Paris 628
B2 ✉ 38970

ℹ rue des Fossés, ☎ 76.30.03.85.

Hotels :
● ★★***Boustigue,*** rte de la Salette, ☎ 76.30.01.03. 19 rm closed 20 Sep-1 Feb and 28 Feb-Whitsun, 195. Rest. ♦ 75-130.
● ★★***Poste*** (L.F.), pl. de la Mairie, ☎ 76.30.00.03. 14 rm ♿ closed 15 Nov-15 Jan, 180. Rest. ♦ 60-160.

Saint-Firmin, ✉ 05800, 11 km SE :
★★***Alpes*** (L.F.), ☎ 92.55.20.02. AE, DC. 26 rm ♿ 180. Rest. 80-130.

⛺ ★★*La Villette* (33 pl.), in Saint-Firmin, ☎ 92.55.23.55.

La CÔTE-SAINT-ANDRÉ

Grenoble 49, Lyons 65, Paris 528
A1 ✉ 38260

Hotel :
★***Europe*** (L.F.), 20, rue de la République, ☎ 74.20.53.10. Euro, Visa. 14 rm closed Oct, 100. Rest. 80-130.

Restaurant :
Mottier, 10 km N on the D71 :
● ♦ ***Les Donnières,*** ☎ 74.54.42.06. AE. ♿ Reservations, closed Wed, Thu, Sun eve, 1-31 Jan and 15 Jul-15 Aug. In this old barn, a limited number of places and J.L. Boland's excellent quality cooking : *gâteau de foie de volailles, noisettes de chevreau,* 90-120.

CRÉMIEU

Lyons 37, Bourg-en-Bresse 59, Paris 500
40 km NE of Vienne, A1 ✉ 38460

ℹ mairie, ☎ 74.90.70.92.

Hotels :
★★***Petite Auberge,*** 7, rue de la Juiverie, ☎ 74.90.75.45. Euro, Visa. 14 rm closed 4 Jan-4 Feb, 1 week in Sep, Sun eve and Mon low season, 180. Rest. ♦ 120-210.
★***Auberge de la Chaite,*** cours Baron-Raverat, ☎ 74.90.76.63. AE, DC, Euro, Visa. 11 rm closed Dec, Mon, 180. Rest. 80-130.

Restaurant :

Villemoirieu, 1.5 km W :
♦ ***Chez Roby,*** Beptenoud, ☎ 74.90.73.90, Tx 380024. AE, Euro, Visa. ♿ closed Sun eve, Mon eve, Tue, 15-30 Dec and 1-15 Aug. Copious, tasty country cooking with farm-fresh produce. Spec : *pintadeau velaisanne, salade lyonnaise et saucisson brioché, gâteau aux foies de volailles,* 70-140.

CREST

Valence 28, Die 37, Paris 590
A3 ✉ 26400

ℹ quai Latune, ☎ 75.75.11.38.

SNCF ☎ 75.75.05.81

Hotels :
★★***Grand Hôtel*** (L.F.), 60, rue de l'Hôtel-de-Ville, ☎ 75.25.08.17. Euro, Visa. 20 rm. closed 2-31 Jan, Sun eve and Mon noon (ex Jul, Aug), 160. Rest. ♦ 60-100.

Grane, 8 km W on the D104 :
★★***Giffon,*** pl. de l'Église, ☎ 75.62.60.64. AE, DC, Euro, Visa. 9 rm. closed Sun eve and Mon, 180. Rest. ● ♦ A pleasant stop-over for the gourmet client. Spec : *salade de caille au chou, ragoût de fruits de mer à la crème d'oursin,* 120-250.
★***Kléber,*** 6, rue Aristide-Dumont, ☎ 75.25.11.69. Euro, Visa. 7 rm closed 1-17 Sep, 2 weeks end Jan, Sun eve and Mon, 105. Rest. ● ♦♦ 65-155.

⛺ ★★*Corinthe* (200 pl.), ☎ 75.75.05.28.

Restaurant :
♦ ***Porte Montségur,*** av. des Trois-Becs, east exit, ☎ 75.25.41.45. AE, Euro, Visa. P ♨ ♿ closed 15-end Feb, and Wed, Mon eve ex Jul-Aug, 60-200.

Les DEUX-ALPES

Briançon 65, Grenoble 74, Paris 640
B2 1 650-3 423 m ✉ 38860

ℹ imm. la Croisette, ☎ 76.79.22.00.

🚌 ☎ 76.80.51.22.

Hotels :
★★★★***La Farandole*** (Relais et châteaux), ☎ 76.80.50.45, Tx 320029. AE, DC, Euro, Visa. 60 rm P ♨ ♿ closed 1 May-22 Jun, 10 Sep-1 Dec, 800. Rest. ♦♦ 160-260.
● ★★★***Mariande*** (L.F.), ☎ 76.80.50.60, Tx 320883. 25 rm P ♨ ♿ closed 1 Sep-21 Dec; 21 Apr-20 Jun, 360. Rest. ♦♦ Cooking with market-fresh produce, 120-210.
★★★***La Bérangère*** (Relais et châteaux), ☎ 76.79.24.11, Tx 320878. AE, Visa. 59 rm P ♿ closed 15 Apr-15 Dec, 450. Rest. ♦♦ Rustic setting, 145-195.
★★★***Marmottes,*** Mont-de-Lans, ☎ 76.79.21.91, Tx 320700. 50 rm P ♿ closed 31 Aug-5 Dec, 1 Apr-22 Jun, 180. Rest. ♦♦ 120-210.
★★***Chalet Mounier,*** Venosc, ☎ 76.80.56.90, Tx 308411. 37 rm P ♨ closed 10 Sep-15 Dec, 15 Apr-25 Jun, 300. Rest. ♿ 95-155.

★★***Provençal,*** ☎ 76.80.52.58. 18 rm P closed 1 May-Nov, 200. Rest. 80-130.

DIE

Valence 65, Gap 95, Paris 627
A2-3 ✉ 26150

ℹ pl. St-Pierre, ☎ 75.22.03.03.

SNCF ☎ 75.22.05.42.

Hotels :
★★***Saint-Domingue*** (L.F.), 44, av. C.-Buffardel, ☎ 75.22.03.80. 26 rm P ♨ closed Nov, 140. Rest. ♦ ♿ 50-80.
★★***Petite Auberge,*** av. Sadi-Carnot, ☎ 75.22.05.91. Visa P ♨ closed mid-Dec-30 Jan, Sun eve and Mon (ex Jul and Aug), 180. Rest. ♦ Spec : *millefeuille de saumon fumé, truite à la clairette,* 80-130.
★★***Relais de Chamarges,*** av. de la Clairette, ☎ 75.22.00.95. 9 rm P ♨ closed Sun eve and Mon, 25 Jan-1 Mar, 130. Rest. ♦ 60-90.

⛺ ★★*Chamarges* (100 pl.), ☎ 75.22.14.13 ; ★★*Essi* (133 pl.), ☎ 75.22.03.03 ; ★★*Piscine* (160 pl.), ☎ 75.22.06.19 ; ★★*Glandasse* (100 pl.), ☎ 75.22.02.50.

Recommended : *Coopérative de Clairette de Die,* av. Clairette, B.P. 9 : wine-tasting on the spot.

DIEULEFIT

Orange 58, Valence 72, Paris 635
A3 ✉ 26220

ℹ pl. de l'Église, ☎ 75.46.42.49.

Hotels :
★★***Chez Nous*** (L.F.), rue Brun-Larochette, ☎ 75.46.40.59. 22 rm P ♨ ♿ closed 20 Nov-2 Feb, 195. Rest. ♦♦ closed Mon eve and Tue. Traditional setting, 50-95.
★★***Levant*** (L.F.), pl. Chateauras, ☎ 75.46.42.30. AE, Visa. 27 rm ♨ closed Jan and Mon low season, 180. Rest. ♦ Provencal regional fare, 80-130.

Poët-Laval, ✉ 26160 La Bégude-de-Mazenc, 5 km W on the N540 :
★★★***Hospitaliers*** (L.F.), ☎ 75.46.22.32. AE, DC, Euro, Visa. 20 rm P ♨ Set in a mediaeval commandery looking out over the entire valley, closed 15 Nov-1 Mar, 400. Rest. 120-210.

⛺ ★★*Municipal* (67 pl.), ☎ 75.46.40.12.

DONZÈRE

Orange 39, Valence 60, Paris 624
16 km S of Montélimar, A3 ✉ 26290

ℹ ☎ 75.51.71.50.

SNCF ☎ 75.51.60.42.

Hotel :
★★★***Roustan,*** 26, Basse-Bourgade, detour Montélimar S, direction Avignon, ☎ 75.51.61.27. Visa. 11 rm P ♨ closed 31 Jan-1 Mar and Wed ex Jul-Aug, 155. Rest. 75-135.

EMBRUN

Gap 38, Digne 97, Paris 706
C3 05200

ℹ pl. Dosse, ☎ 92.43.01.80.

SNCF ☎ 92.43.00.61.

Hotels :
★***Notre-Dame*** (L.F.), av. Gal-Nicolas, ☎ 92.43.08.36. AE, DC, Visa. 15 rm ♨ closed 15 Nov-15 Dec, 100. Rest. 120-210.

Crots, 5 km SW on the N94 :
★★★***Bartavelles,*** ☎ 92.43.20.69, Tx 401480. AE, DC, Euro, Visa. 43 rm P ♨ closed 30 Sep-7 Nov, 245. Rest. ♦♦ 70-170.

Les Orres, 14 km S :
★★***Kornac'haot,*** ☎ 92.44.00.83. Visa. 34 rm P ♨ closed 1 Sep-20 Dec, 155. Rest. 65-130.

Youth hostel : 13 km E on the D39, in Crevoux, ☎ 92.43.18.18. closed 20 Apr-20 Dec.

⛺ ★★★*La Clapière* (446 pl.), ☎ 92.43.01.83 ; ★★★*la Tour* (113 pl.), ☎ 92.43.17.66 ; ★★★*les Tourelles* (100 pl.), ☎ 92.43.15.31 ; ★★*la Madeleine* (83 pl.), ☎ 92.43.14.20 ; ★★*la Vieille Ferme* (100 pl.), ☎ 92.43.32.75.

Restaurant :
♦ ***Lac,*** ☎ 92.43.11.08. closed Oct-May, 80-130.

GAP

Digne 87, Grenoble 103, Paris 668
B3 ✉ 05000

ℹ 5, rue Carnot (B2), ☎ 92.51.57.03.

✈ Gap-Tallard, ☎ 92.54.10.38.

SNCF (C1), ☎ 92.51.50.50, 92.51.00.93, 92.51.24.84.

Car-hire : *Budget* train + auto, Solomaf, Shell station (Galera), Pente d'Embrun, ☎ 92.43.23.15 ; at the station, ☎ 92.50.02.21.

Hotels :
★★★***Grille,*** 2, pl. F. Euzière (B3), ☎ 92.53.84.84. AE, DC, Euro, Visa. 30 rm ♿ closed 1 Dec-1 Jan, 210. Rest. closed Sun eve and Mon, 55-105.
★★***Clos,*** 20 *ter,* av. Cdt-Dumont (C1), ☎ 92.51.37.04. Visa. 42 rm P ♨ closed 25 Oct-5 Nov and Sun eve, 140. Rest. ♦ ♿ 55-100.
★★***Fons Regina*** (L.F.), château de Font-Reyne, 3 km SW on the N85, ☎ 92.53.98.99. AE, DC, Euro, Visa. 22 rm P ♨ 180. Rest. ♦ 60-115.

⛺ ★★★*Alpes Dauphiné* (66 pl.), ☎ 92.51.29.95 ; ★★★*Essi Provence* (83 pl.), ☎ 92.51.57.03 ; ★★*Napoléon* (70 pl.), ☎ 92.52.12.41.

Restaurants :
♦♦♦ ***Roseraie,*** rue de Villarobert, 2 km on the D92, ☎ 92.51.43.08. AE, DC, Euro, Visa. 🅿 ♿ closed Sun eve, Thu and Jan, 90-180.
♦♦ ***Carré Long,*** 32, rue Pasteur (B2), ☎ 92.51.13.10. AE, DC, Euro, Visa. ♿ closed 1-15 May, 1-15 Oct, Sun and Mon, 65-100.

La GRAVE

Briançon 39, Grenoble 77, Paris 642
11 km W of the Lautaret Pass, C2
ℹ ☎ 76.79.90.05. ⊠ 05320

Hotels :
★★***Castillan,*** RN91, ☎ 76.79.90.04. Visa. 43 rm 🅿 closed 21 Sep-20 Dec, 20 Apr-24 May, 150. Rest. ♦ ♿ 60-120.
★★***Meijette*** (L.F.), ☎ 76.79.90.34. 18 rm 🅿 closed 20 Apr-1 May, 1 Nov-15 Feb, 180. Rest. closed Tue (low season), 80-130.

[camping] ★★*Ermitage* (66 pl.), ☎ 76.79.90.33.

GRENOBLE

Chambéry 55, Lyon 104, Paris 567
B2 ⊠ 38000
ℹ 14, pl. de la République (B3), ☎ 76.54.34.36.

✈ Grenoble-St-Geoirs, 29 km NW, ☎ 76.05.71.33.
Air France Agency, 4, pl. V.-Hugo, ☎ 76.87.63.43.

[SNCF] (A3), ☎ 76.57.50.50, 76.47.09.45.

[bus] pl. de la Gare (A3), ☎ 76.87.34.26.

Car-hire : *Budget* train + auto, 3, bd Mal-Joffre, ☎ 76.87.61.84, at the airport and the station, ☎ 76.42.09.45.

Hotels :
★★★★***Park,*** 10, pl. P.-Mistral (C4), ☎ 76.87.29.11, Tx 320767. AE, DC, Euro, Visa. 59 rm 🅿 ♿ closed 24 Dec-2 Jan, 820. Rest. ♦♦ ***la Taverne de Ripaille.*** closed Sun noon, 120-210.
● ★★★***Angleterre,*** 5, pl. V.-Hugo (B3), ☎ 76.87.37.21, Tx 320297. AE, DC, Euro, Visa. 70 rm ♿ 320.
● ★★★***Lesdiguières,*** 122, cours de la Libération, Tx 320306. AE, DC, Euro, Visa. 36 rm 🅿 closed 28 Jul-2 Sep and Christmas hols, 295. Rest. ♦ Hotel training school, 100-140.
★★***Alpes,*** 45, av. F.-Viallet (B2-C3), ☎ 76.87.00.71. AE. 40 rm 🅿 closed end-of-year hols, 155.
★★***Rive Droite,*** 20, quai de France (A2), ☎ 76.87.61.11, Tx 320232. AE, DC, Euro, Visa. 58 rm 🅿 ♿ 260. Rest. 80-130.

Saint-Martin-le-Vinoux, ⊠ 38950, 2 km N on the A48 and N75 :
Pique-Pierre, 1, rue Konrad-Kilian, ☎ 76.46.12.88. Visa. 10 rm 🅿 ♿ closed Sun eve, Mon, Aug, 100. Rest. ♦♦ 100-250.

Meylan, ⊠ 38240, 3 km NE on the N90 :
★★★***Alpha*** (Mapotel Best-Western), 34, av. de Verdun, ☎ 76.90.63.09, Tx 980444. AE, DC, Euro, Visa. 60 rm 🅿 305. Rest. ♦ ***les Saisons*** ♿ 62-100.

Corenc-Montfleury, ⊠ 38700 La Tronche, 3 km N on the D512 :
★★★***Trois Roses*** (Mapotel Best-Western), 32, av. du Grésivaudan, ☎ 76.90.35.09, Tx 980593. AE, DC, Euro, Visa. 50 rm 🅿 ♿ closed 25 Dec-1 Jan, 270.

Bresson, 8 km S on the D5, ⊠ 38320 Eybens :
★★***Chavant,*** ☎ 76.25.15.14, Tx 980882. AE, Visa. 8 rm 🅿 closed Wed, 400. Rest. ● ♦♦♦ J.-P. Chavant maintains the excellent culinary traditions established by his father. Spec : *poissons marinés maison, contrefilet à la compote d'échalotes,* and the authentic, ever-present *gratin dauphinois,* 230-310.

Claix, ⊠ 38640, 10.5 km S on the N75 and D269 :
● ★★***Oiseaux*** (Relais du Silence), ☎ 76.98.07.74, Tx 320871. DC, Visa. 20 rm 🅿 closed Nov-Jan, Fri noon Sat and low season, 180. Rest. ♿ 120-210.

Herbeys, ⊠ 38320 Eybens, 12 km S on the D5 and D112 :
★***L'Aubergeade,*** rte Napoléon, ☎ 76.73.67.52. 7 rm 🅿 closed Sun eve and Mon, 145. Rest. ♦ friendly atmosphere and tasty fare, 50-100.

Varces, ⊠ 38760, 12.5 km S on the N75 :
★★★★***Escale*** (René Brunet) [Relais et châteaux], pl. de la République, ☎ 76.72.80.19. AE, Euro. 12 rm 🅿 ♿ closed 1-30 Jan, 2-9 May, 20-28 Nov, Sun eve and Mon low season, Tue in summer, 300. Rest. ● ♦♦ In this sanctuary of great classical cooking, René Brunet, a disciple of Carême, Escoffier and Nignon has been enchanting us for the last 40 years. Spec : *saumon frais aux aubergines, mousse à la chartreuse locale.* The menus offer good value for money, 150-280.

Échirolles youth hostel, av. du Grésivaudan, "la Quinzaine", ☎ 76.09.33.52.

[camping] ★★*Municipal* (133 pl.), ☎ 76.96.19.87.

Restaurants :
● ♦♦ ***La Poularde Bressane,*** 12, pl. P.-Mistral (C4), ☎ 76.87.08.90. 🅿 closed Sat, 17 Jul-18 Aug. The chef, a former pupil of France's culinary masters, is adept in the art of light gastronomical fare : *mosaïque de légumes, soyeux d'agneau,* 230-310.
♦♦ ***Le Pommerois,*** 1, pl. aux Herbes, ☎ 76.44.30.02. Visa. ♿ closed noon in Aug and Mon. Excellent cooking, 220-310.
● ♦ ***Auberge Bressane,*** 38 *ter,* imp. Beaublache (A3), ☎ 76.87.64.29. ♿ closed Sun. Unpretentious regional cooking. Spec : *poulet de Bresse au vinaigre, gratin d'écrevisses,* 120-210.
♦ ***Rabelais,*** 55, av. Alsace-Lorraine (A3), ☎ 76.46.03.44. Euro, Visa. ♿ 40-110.

Tronche, ⊠ 38700, NE exit, 2 km :
♦ ***Trois Dauphins,*** 24, bd Chantourne, ☎ 76.54.49.73. Visa 🅿 ♿ closed Sat eve, Sun, Jul-Aug, 100-250.

Montbonnot, ⊠ 38330 Saint-Ismier, 7 km NE on the N90 :
♦♦ ***Les Mésanges,*** ☎ 76.90.21.57. Euro ♿ closed Sun eve, Mon, 1 week in Feb and Aug. Good classical cooking : *foie gras maison, gratin de queues d'écrevisses,* 85-190.

Recommended : *Miland,* 17, pl. Grenette : delicious walnut-based sweetmeats.

GRIGNAN

Orange 44, Valence 71, Paris 634
A3 ⊠ 26230

Hotels ;
★★***Sévigné,*** ☎ 75.46.50.97. Euro. 20 rm 🅿 ♿ closed 1 Dec-15 Jan and Mon (low season), 180.

Montségur-sur-Lauzon, 8 km S on the D71 :
★***Auberge du Dauphin,*** ☎ 75.98.11.56. 10 rm 🅿 closed Oct and Tue, 145. Rest. ♿ 55-100.

Recommended : *la Mère Peyrol bakery* for *pain de courge* (bread made from pumpkin dough) and traditional regional atmosphere. Domaine de Grangeneuve, Roussas, 8 km W, ☎ 75.98.50.22.

GUILLESTRE

Briançon 35, Gap 60, Paris 716
C3 ⊠ 05600

ℹ pl. Salva, ☎ 92.45.04.37.

Hotels :

● ★★***Barnières 1*** (L.F.), ☎ 92.45.05.07. 35 rm closed 15 Oct-20 Dec, 180. Rest. ♦ 120-210.

★★***Barnières 2*** (L.F.), ☎ 92.45.04.87. 39 rm closed 1 Oct-20 Dec, May, 220. Rest. ♦ 120-210.

★★***Queyras,*** ☎ 92.45.16.00. 30 rm closed 30 Oct-15 Dec, 15 Apr-15 Jun, 180. Rest. 80-130.

Risoul, 3 km S, 1 850-2 570 m ; ℹ ☎ 92.45.02.60 :

★***Bonne Auberge*** (L.F.), ☎ 92.45.02.40. AE, 36 rm closed 20 Sep-20 Dec, 15 Mar-1 Jun, 140. Rest. ♦ 65.

Youth hostel : *les Quatre Vents,* rte de la Gare, ☎ 92.45.04.32.

⛺ ★★★★*Le Villard* (83 pl.), ☎ 92.45.06.54 ; ★★★*la Rochette* (233 pl.), ☎ 92.45.02.15 ; ★★★*Saint-James-les-Pins* (100 pl.), ☎ 92.45.08.24 ; ★★*Serre Altitude 1000* (100 pl.), ☎ 92.45.00.40.

MONESTIER-DE-CLERMONT

Grenoble 33, Die 64, Paris 598
33 km W of La Mure, B2 ⊠ 38650

ℹ municipal park, ☎ 76.34.06.20.

SNCF ☎ 76.34.08.13.

Hotels :

★***Modern,*** ☎ 76.34.07.35. 21 rm closed Nov-early Feb, 180. Rest. 80-130.

Saint-Paul-lès-Monestier, 1.5 km NW on the D8 :
★★***Sans-Souci*** (L.F.), ☎ 76.34.03.60. AE, Visa. 16 rm closed Jan, Sun eve and Mon, 170. Rest. ♦ 55-160.

Gresse-en-Vercors, 5 km S :
● ★★***Chalet*** (L.F.), ☎ 76.34.02.08. Euro. 31 rm closed 15 Apr-15 May, 30 Sep-15 Dec, 220. Rest. ♦ Regional cooking, 65-165.

Youth hostel : Chichiliane 18.5 km, La Donnière, 38930 Clelles-en-Trièves, ☎ 76.34.43.00.

MONTÉLIMAR

Valence 45, Avignon 82, Paris 508
A3 ⊠ 26230

ℹ Champ-de-Mars, ☎ 75.01.00.20.

SNCF ☎ 75.01.19.00, 75.01.09.88, 75.01.74.99.

Car-hire : *Budget* train + auto, RN7, le Grand Pélican, ☎ 75.01.74.99, and at the station, ☎ 75.01.02.06.

Hotels :

● ★★★★***Parc Chabaud,*** 16, av. d'Aygu, ☎ 75.01.65.66, Tx 345324. AE, DC, Visa. 22 rm closed 24 Dec-1 Feb, 490. Rest. ♦♦♦ closed Sat, Sun, 200-450.

★★***Printemps*** (L.F. ; Relais du Silence), 8, chemin de la Manche, ☎ 75.01.32.63. 16 rm closed 31 Nov-1 Feb, Sun low season, 190. Rest. eve only, 75-150.

★***Pierre*** (L.F.), 7, pl. des Clercs, ☎ 75.01.33.16. 11 rm 100.

Montboucher-sur-Jabron, ⊠ 26740, 5 km E on the D169 :
★★★***Castel,*** château de Montboucher, ☎ 75.46.08.16. AE, DC, Visa. 11 rm 13thC farmhouse. closed 12 Nov-20 Dec and Tue, 360. Rest. eve only ex Sun, 120-180.

Malataverne, ⊠ 26780, 9 km S on the N7 :
★★★***Domaine du Colombier,*** rte de Donzère, ☎ 75.51.65.86. 12 rm closed 15 Jan-1 Mar, 300. Rest. ♦♦ Spec : *paupiettes de lotte,* 120-210.

Saulce-sur-Rhône, ⊠ 26270 Loriol, 18 km N :
★★***Reys de Saulce,*** N7, ☎ 75.63.00.22. AE, Euro, Visa. 18 rm closed 15 Dec-15 Jan, Sun eve (low season) and Mon, 135. Rest. ♦ 55-95.

Mirmande, ⊠ 26270 Loriol, 20 km N :
★★***Capitelle*** (Relais du Silence), ☎ 75.63.02.72. DC, Euro, Visa. 15 rm closed 15 Nov-20 Mar, Tue, 185. Rest. ♦ Dinner only, 50-100.

⛺ ★★★*International* (100 pl.), ☎ 75.01.88.89.

Restaurants :

♦♦ ***Le Palou,*** N7, rte de Marseille, ☎ 75.01.75.68. With rm closed in winter, 80-130.

♦ ***Petit Resto,*** 14, rue Peyrouse, behind the post-office, ☎ 75.51.02.58. Visa. closed Sun noon and Mon. Regional specialities, 80-130.

♦ ***Ardèche,*** av. du Gal-de-Gaulle, ☎ 75.01.81.19. AE, DC. grill, 80-130.

Recommended : *Chabert et Guillot nougat,* 1, rue Ducatez.

NYONS

Orange 42, Gap 106, Paris 657
A3 ⊠ 26110

ℹ pl. de la Libération, ☎ 75.26.10.35.

Hotels :

★★★***Alizés*** (L.F.), 77, av. H.-Rochier, ☎ 75.26.08.11. 22 rm closed Christmas-1 Feb, 280.

● ★★***La Picholine*** (L.F.), promenade de la Perrière, ☎ 75.26.06.21. AE, DC, Euro, Visa. 15 rm 250. Rest. ♦ 70-130.

Aubres, 4 km E :
★★***Auberge du Vieux Village,*** ☎ 75.26.12.89. AE, DC, Euro, Visa. 15 rm 450. Rest. ♦ closed Wed noon, 60-200.

⛺ ★★★*Municipal* (97 pl.), ☎ 75.26.22.39 ; ★★*Saint-Rimbert* (80 pl.), ☎ 75.26.03.81.

Restaurant :

Condorcet, 6 km NE, on the D94 and D70 :
♦♦ ***La Charrette Bleue,*** rte des Alpes, ☎ 75.26.43.03. Euro, Visa. Farmhouse and one-time post-house. Flowered terrace setting, closed Nov, Wed ex Jul-Aug. Spec : *sauté d'escargots aux girofles, carré d'agneau à la crème de thym,* 60-120.

ORCIÈRES

Gap 33, Grenoble 115, Paris 680
C3 1 439-2 650 m ⊠ 05170

ℹ Merlette, ☎ 92.55.70.39.

Hotel :

★***Poste,*** ☎ 92.55.70.04. 31 rm 100. Rest. 80-130.

Youth hostel : *la Fruitière,* les Tourengs, ☎ 92.55.44.30.

PIERRELATTE

Orange 32, Valence 66, Paris 630
23 km S of Montélimar, A3 ⊠ 26700

ℹ Administrative centre, ☎ 75.04.07.98.

SNCF ☎ 75.04.30.54.

🚌 pl. du Champ-de-Mars, ☎ 75.04.24.42.

Hotels :
★★**Centre** (L.F.), 6 pl. de l'Église, ☎ 75.04.28.59. AE, DC, Euro, Visa. 29 rm 🅿 180. Rest. ♦ **les Récollets,** ☎ 75.90.83.10. closed 4-28 Aug, 1 week in Feb school hols, 50-120.
★★**Tom II** (L.F.), av. du Gal-de-Gaulle, ☎ 75.04.00.35. AE, Visa. 13 rm 🅿 closed Sun eve and Mon, 120. Rest. ♦ 60-130.

La Garde-Adhémar, 8 km W on the D358 and D572 :
L'Escalin, ☎ 75.04.41.32. Visa. 6 rm 🅿 closed Feb school hols, Aug, Sun and Mon, 130. Rest. ♦♦ ♿ 90-120.

Saint-Restitut, ✉ 26130 Saint-Paul-Trois-Châteaux, 12 km SE :
★★★**Auberge des Quatre Saisons** (L.F.), ☎ 75.04.71.88. AE, DC. 10 rm closed 12 Nov-8 Dec, 15 Jan-2 Feb, 290. Rest. ♦ **Trente-six Soupières.** Regional fare served in a setting of mediaeval stone vaulting and pediod furniture, 60-190.

Solérieux, ✉ 26130 Saint-Paul-Trois-Châteaux, 14 km E on the D59 and D71 :
★**Ferme Saint-Michel,** rte de la Baume, ☎ 75.98.10.66. 10 rm 🅿 165. Rest. ♦♦ ♿ closed 20 Dec-31 Jan and Sun eve and Mon noon (and eve in winter), 65-110.

Suze-la-Rousse, ✉ 26130 Saint-Paul-Trois-Châteaux, 18 km SE :
★★**Relais du Château** (L.F.), ☎ 75.08.87.07. AE, Euro, Visa. 20 rm 🅿 closed 15 Dec-15 Jan, 190. Rest. ♦ 55-100.

Restaurants :
♦♦ **Relais Côtes-du-Rhône,** 2 km on the N7, exit Bollène, ☎ 75.04.04.86. DC. 🅿 ♿ closed Sat (low season) and Sun eve. For enthusiasts of good meats, 60-80.

La Garde-Adhémar :
♦♦ **Au Tisonnier,** Vieux Village, ☎ 75.04.44.03. closed Sat noon, Sun eve and Mon. Friendly atmosphere. 80-130.

Recommended : 8 km E, *SICA France Truffes,* Valréas road to Saint-Paul-Trois-Châteaux : fresh produce and preserves. *Université du Vin,* courses in œnology, wine-tasting, château de Suze, ☎ 75.04.86.09, 75.04.86.86.

PONT-EN-ROYANS

Valence 45, Grenoble 60, Paris 590
24 km W of Villard-de-Lans, B2 ✉ 38680

Hotels :
★**Beau Rivage,** rue Gambetta, ☎ 76.36.00.63. Visa. 16 rm 🅿 closed 1 Dec-1 Feb and Mon low season, 100. Rest. ♿ 50-100.

Saint-Nazaire-en-Royans, ✉ 26190 Saint-Jean-en-Royans, 9 km W :
● ♦ **Du Royans,** RN532, ☎ 76.48.40.84. Euro, Visa. ♿ closed 22 Sep-22 Oct, 2-18 Jun, Tue eve and Wed. Excellent traditional cooking : *ravioles de Romans, feuilleté de coquilles St-Jacques, filet mignon au poivre vert,* 50-110.

Å ★★*Municipal* (92 pl.), ☎ 76.36.03.09.

ROMANS-SUR-ISÈRE

Valence 18, Grenoble 81, Paris 562
A2 ✉ 26100
ℹ pl. Jules-Nadi, ☎ 75.02.28.72.
SNCF ☎ 75.02.31.75.

Hotels :
★★**Magdeleine,** 31, av. P.-Sémard, ☎ 75.02.33.53. 16 rm ♿ 200.

Bourg-de-Péage, ✉ 26300, 0 km S .
★★**Yan's** (L.F.) ☎ 75.72.44.11. AE. Visa. 25 rm 🅿 ♿ 230.

Granges-lès-Beaumont, ✉ 26600 Tain-l'Hermitage, 5 km W on the D532 :
★**Lanaz** (L.F.), ☎ 75.71.50.56. 8 rm 🅿 ♿ closed 29 Apr-13 May, 3-24 Sep, Ascension and Tue, 100.

Restaurants :
♦♦ **Ponton,** 40, pl. Jacquemart, ☎ 75.02.29.91. ♿ closed 1 week in Feb, 10-26 Jul, Sun eve and Mon. Regional cooking : *ravioles* local style, 120-210.

Pizançon, ✉ 26300, Bourg-de-Péage east exit on the N531 :
● ♦ **Astier,** ☎ 75.70.06.27. closed Sat eve and Sun, 10 Jul-10 Aug. Tradition and quality : *mousse de grives, ravioles,* 100-150.

Granges-lès-Beaumont :
♦♦ **Cèdres,** ☎ 75.71.50.67. AE 🅿 closed 16 Aug-4 Sep, Tue eve and Wed. A highly-reputed restaurant, 90-200.

SAINT-ANTOINE-DE-PELVOUX

Briançon 33, Gap 90, Paris 746
Vallouise, C2 ✉ 05340

Hotels :
★★**Belvédère** (L.F.), ☎ 92.23.31.04. AE, DC. 30 rm 🅿 closed end Oct-18 Dec, 15 Apr-21 May, 190. Rest. ● ♦♦♦ ♿ A very pleasant meal in a remarkable setting, 220-310.

Ailefroide, 5.5 km NW on the D994 :
★**Chalet Rolland** (L.F.), ☎ 92.23.32.01. Euro. 30 rm 🅿 closed 10 Sep-20 Jun, 140. Rest. 50-130.
★**Les Clouzis,** ☎ 92.23.32.07. Visa. 11 rm 🅿 closed 15 Jun-15 Sep, 110. Rest. ♿ 60-80.

Puy-Saint-Vincent, ✉ 05290 Vallouise, 7.5 km S ; 1 400-2 700 m ; ℹ ☎ 92.45.02.60 :
★★**Saint-Roch,** ☎ 92.23.32.79. 12 rm 🅿 closed 15 Apr-20 Jun, 1 Sep-20 Dec, 200. Rest. 80-130.
★**Pendine,** Les Prés, ☎ 92.23.32.62. 32 rm 🅿 closed 13 Apr-12 Jun, 15 Sep-15 Dec, 160. Rest. 60-110.

Å ★★*Ailefroide* (400 pl.), ☎ 92.23.31.07.

SAINT-BONNET-EN-CHAMPSAUR

Gap 15, Grenoble 90, Paris 655
B-C3 ✉ 05500
ℹ ☎ 92.50.02.57.

Hotels :
★★**Crémaillère** (L.F.), ☎ 92.50.00.60. AE, Euro. 20 rm 🅿 closed 1 Oct-1 Feb, 1 Mar-1 Apr, 170. Rest. ♿ 60-120.
★★**Mauberret-Combassive** (L.F.), ☎ 92.50.00.19. AE, DC, Euro, Visa. 27 rm ♿ closed 15 Oct-25 Dec, 20 Apr-1 Jun, 120. Rest. 55-100.

Saint-Julien-en-Champsaur, 6 km SE on the D945 :
★★**Chenêts** (L.F.), ☎ 92.50.03.15. AE, DC, Euro, Visa. 20 rm 🅿 closed 1 Oct-1 Dec, 165. Rest. 55-80.

SAINT-MARCELLIN

Valence 44, Grenoble 55, Paris 571
A2 ✉ 38160
SNCF ☎ 76.38.10.10, 77.52.81.20.

Hotels :
★★★**Savoyet-Serve,** 16, bd Gambetta, ☎ 76.38.04.17. Visa. 60 rm 🅿 ♿ closed Jan, Sun eve and Mon noon (Oct-Jul), 180. Rest. ♦ 120-210.

Saint-Hilaire-du-Rosier, ☒ 38840, 8 km SW on the N92 :
★★★**Bouvarel,** ☎ 76.36.50.87. AE, DC, Visa. 15 rm 🅿 🌳 🏊 closed Jan, Sun eve and Mon (low season), 260. Rest. ♦♦ Good traditional fare, 150-360.

Saint-Lattier, ☒ 38840, 12 km SW on the N92 :
★★★**Chêneraie** (Relais et châteaux), ☎ 76.36.50.67. AE, DC. 7 rm ⚟ 🅿 🌳 🏊 ♿ closed 15 Nov-15 Mar. Mon low season and Sun eve (1 Nov-1 Apr), 280. Rest. ● ♦♦ ***Lièvre Amoureux*** ⚟ 🌳 closed 1 Dec-15 Mar. Talented regional cooking : *lièvre rôti à la broche, ravioles.* Restaurant set in a large park, 130-300.

Saint-Antoine, ☒ 38160, 12 km NW on D27 :
● ♦ ***Auberge de l'Abbaye,*** ☎ 76.36.42.83. AE, Visa. closed 31 Jan-28 Feb and Tue. Spec : *feuilleté d'escargots, filets de sole à l'avocat, magret de canard,* 70-205.

SAINT-PIERRE-DE-CHARTREUSE

Grenoble 29, Chambéry 40, Paris 576
B1 ⛷ 900-1700 m ☒ 38380 St-Laurent-du-Pont

ℹ ☎ 76.88.62.08.

Hotels :
★★★**Beau Site** (L.F.), ☎ 76.88.61.34. AE, Euro, Visa. 33 rm ⚟ 📺 closed 1 Oct-15 Dec and Wed (low season), 230. Rest. ♦ ⊘ 65-130.
★**Nord,** ☎ 76.88.61.10. 19 rm ⚟ 🅿 🌳 closed Oct, 120. Rest. 50-105.

Col du Cucheron, 3.5 km N on the D512 :
★**Chalet du Cucheron** (L.F.), ☎ 76.88.62.06. AE, Euro, Visa. 8 rm ⚟ 🅿 🌳 closed 15 Oct-15 Dec (ex week-end and school hols), 130. Rest. ♦ ⊘ ♿ 60-120.

Col de Porte, ☒ 38700 La Tronche, 10.5 km S on the D512 and D57 :
★★**Col de Porte,** Sarcenas, ☎ 76.88.82.04. 16 rm ⚟ 🅿 🏊 ♿ 260. Rest. ♦ 80-130.

Sappey-en-Chartreuse, ☒ 38128, 13 km S on the D512, ⛷ 1 000-1 350 m :
★★**Skieurs,** ☎ 76.88.80.15, Tx 320245. 18 rm ⚟ 🅿 🌳 🏊 📺 15 Apr-5 May, Oct, 15 days in Nov, Sun eve and Mon (ex school hols), 200. Rest. ♦ ⊘ 80-130.
★**Bon Abri,** ☎ 76.88.81.20. 13 rm ⚟ 🅿 🌳 🏊 closed Easter-Jun, 20 Sep-20 Dec, 100. Rest. 80-130.

St-Hugues youth hostel, ☎ 76.88.62.37.

⛺ ★★*Martinière* (100 pl.), ☎ 76.88.60.36.

SAINT-VÉRAN

Briançon 51, Gap 92, Paris 748
32 km E of Guillestre, C3 ⛷ 2 040-2 560 m
☒ 05490

ℹ ski-lifts, ☎ 92.45.82.21.

Hotels :
★★**Grand Tétras** (L.F.), ☎ 92.45.82.42. Visa. 21 rm ⚟ 🅿 🏊 closed 15 Apr-15 Jun, 15 Sep-19 Dec, 195. Rest. ♦ 50-120.

Molines-en-Queyras, ☒ 05390, 5.5 km N on the D5, ⛷ 1 750-2 450 m ; ℹ ☎ 92.45.83.22 :
★★**Équipe** (L.F.), ☎ 92.45.83.20. AE, DC, Euro, Visa. 22 rm ⚟ 🅿 🌳 closed 20 Apr-7 Jun, 16 Sep-18 Dec, 175. Rest. 45-120.

SAVINES-LE-LAC

Gap 28, Briançon 59, Paris 696
C3 ☒ 05160

ℹ ☎ 92.44.20.44.

SNCF ☎ 92.44.20.34.

Hotels :
★★**Flots Bleus,** pl. de la Marianne, ☎ 92.44.20.89. 20 rm ⚟ 🅿 🌳 🏊 ♿ closed 1 Oct-31 Mar, 200.

Prunières, ☒ 05230 Chorges, 8 km NE :
★★**Preyret** (L.F.), ☎ 92.50.62.29, Tx 405868. AE, DC, Euro. 40 rm ⚟ 🅿 🌳 🏊 ⊘ 📺 🎾 ♿ closed 10 Oct-26 Dec, 7 Apr-1 May, 240. Rest. ⊘ 90-110.

Youth hostel : *les Chaumettes,* ☎ 92.44.20.16. ⚟ sailing and wind-surfing school.

⛺ ★★★*Les Sources* (46 pl.), ☎ 92.44.20.52 ; ★★★*Chaumettes* (50 pl.), ☎ 92.44.20.16 ; ★★*Eygoires* (333 pl.), ☎ 92.44.20.48 ; ★★*Grand Morgon* (80 pl.), ☎ 92.44.22.15. On Prunières : ★★★*le Nautic* (100 pl.), ☎ 92.50.62.49 ; ★★★*Roustourias* (100 pl), ☎ 92.54.62.63.

Restaurant :
♦ ***Relais Fleuri,*** ☎ 92.44.20.32. ⚟ 🅿 closed 30 Sep-15 May and Mon low season, 50-130.

SERRE-CHEVALIER

Briançon 8, Gap 95, Paris 673
C2 ⛷ 1 350-2 660 m ☒ 05330 Saint-Chaffrey

ℹ Saint-Chaffrey-Chantemerle, ☎ 92.24.00.34.

Hotels :
★★**Balme** (Petits Nids de France), Chantemerle, ☎ 92.24.01.89. 28 rm ⚟ 🅿 🌳 🏊 closed May, Oct, Nov, 290. Snack eve.
★**Boule de Neige,** ☎ 92.24.00.16. 10 rm ⚟ closed Easter-hols and Christmas, 100. Rest. Good, rich family fare, 80-130.

La Salle-des-Alpes, ☒ 05240, 2.5 km NW on the N91 :
★★★**Serre-Chevalier,** ☎ 92.24.74.67. 24 rm ⚟ 🅿 ⊘ closed 20 Apr-1 Jul, 10 Sep-20 Dec, 180. Rest. ♦ in winter 80-130.

Villeneuve-la-Salle, ☒ 05240 :
★★**Lièvre-Blanc,** rte de Grenoble, ☎ 92.24.74.05. AE, DC, Visa. 26 rm ⚟ 🅿 🌳 📺 closed 10 Sep-15 Dec, 1 May-20 Jun (ex w.-e.), 295. Rest. 65-165.
★★**Vieille Ferme,** ☎ 92.24.76.44. Visa. 30 rm ⚟ 🅿 🏊 ♿ closed 21 Apr-22 Jun, 8 Sep-21 Dec, 180. Rest. ♦♦ ⊘ 70-140.

Monêtiers-les-Bains, ☒ 05220, 8 km S on the N91 :
★★**Europe,** ☎ 92.24.40.03. AE, DC, Euro. 29 rm 🌳 🏊 closed 30 Sep-15 Dec, 20 Apr-1 Jun, 180. Rest. ♿ 50-120.
★★**Le Choucas** (L.F. ; Châteaux-hôtels, Relais du Silence), 17, rue de la Fruitière, ☎ 92.24.42.73. DC. 13 rm 🌳 closed 15 Apr-15 Jun, 1 Oct-15 Dec, 180. Rest. ♦♦ The vaulted dining-room adds to the charm of simple, carefully prepared dishes in this former farmhouse of the old Monêtiers region, 90-300.

Youth hostel : *le Bez,* B.P. 2, 05240 La Salle-des-Alpes, ☎ 92.24.03.54.

SERRES

Gap 42, Die 65, Paris 672
B3 ☒ 05700

ℹ mairie, ☎ 92.67.03.50.

SNCF ☎ 92.67.00.39.

Hotels :
● ★★**Fifi Moulin,** rte de Nyons, ☎ 92.67.00.01. AE, DC, Euro, Visa. 25 rm ⚟ 🅿 🌳 📺 ♿ closed 15 Nov-beginning Feb school hols and Wed, 150. Rest. ● ♦ Very good, copious meals : Drôme chicken, lamb from the Alps, 65-160.

⛺ ★★★★*Deux Soleils* (75 pl.), ☎ 92.67.01.33 ; ★★★*Les Barillons* (66 pl.), ☎ 92.67.01.16.

TAIN-L'HERMITAGE

Lyons 90, Grenoble 100, Paris 550
18 km N of Valence, A2 ✉ 26600

ⓘ pl. de l'Église, ☎ 75.08.06.81.

SNCF ☎ 75.08.30.43.

Hotels :

★★★**Commerce** (Inter-Hôtel), 69, av. Jean-Jaurès, ☎ 75.08.65.00, Tx 345573. AE, DC, Euro, Visa. 27 rm P ♨ ♘ ♿ closed 15 Nov-15 Dec, 220. Rest. 75-150.

Mercurol, 4 km :
★★**L'Abricotine** (L.F.), rte de Romans, ☎ 75.08.42.00. Euro, Visa. 10 rm ☀ P ♨ ♘ ♿ closed 20 Nov-10 Dec and Sun (low season), 155. Rest. ♦ 40-60.

Saint-Vallier, ✉ 26240, 14 km N :
★**Terminus** (L.F.), 116, av. J.-Jaurès, ☎ 75.23.01.12. AE, DC, Euro, Visa. 11 rm P closed 4-24 Aug, Feb school hols, Tue eve and Wed, 85. Rest. ♦ Excellent dishes served in a rustic setting. Spec : *bavarois de saumon fumé, émincé de volailles aux écrevisses,* 90-250.

⛺ ★★*Les Lucs* (120 pl.), ☎ 75.08.32.82.

La TOUR-DU-PIN

Lyons 55, Grenoble 67, Paris 518
A1 ✉ 38110

SNCF ☎ 74.97.04.34.

Hotels :

★**Dauphiné-Savoie** (L.F.), 2, rue A.-Briand, ☎ 74.97.03.87. Euro. 12 rm. closed 15-31 Oct, 2nd week in Mar, Mon noon, 100. Rest. ♿ 50-105.

Cessieu, 6 km W on the N6 :
★★**Gentilhommière** (L.F.), ☎ 74.88.30.09. AE, DC, Euro, Visa. 6 rm ♨ ♘ closed Sun eve and Mon, 15 Nov-10 Dec, 176. Rest. ♦ ♿ A pleasant stop-over between Lyons and Chambéry, 90-200.

Faverges-de-la-Tour, 10 km E on the N156 and D145 B :
● ★★★★(L) **Le Château** (Relais et châteaux), ☎ 74.97.42.52, Tx 300372. AE, DC, Visa. 40 rm ☀ P ♨ ♘ ⊡ ⚲ closed end Oct-early May, 720. Rest. ♦♦ 175-350.

Abrets, 12 km E on the N6 :
★★**Belle Étoile** (L.F.), 4, rue V.-Hugo, ☎ 76.32.04.97. AE, Euro, Visa. 15 rm P ♨ 120. Rest. ♦ ♿ closed Mon and Sun eve, 60-110.
★**Host. Abrésienne,** rue Gambetta, N75, ☎ 76.32.04.28. 22 rm P closed 20 Sep-12 Oct and Tue, 100. Rest. 80-130.

Nappes, 18 km NE on the N516 and N75, then D40 through Avenières :
★★**Relais des Vieilles Postes** (Relais du Silence), ☎ 74.33.62.99. AE, DC, Euro, Visa. 17 rm P ♨ ♘ ⚲ ♿ closed 1-20 Dec, 1-8 Apr, Sun eve and Mon low season, 195. Rest. ♦ ✂ 100-200.

⛺ ★★*Coin Tranquille,* les Abrets (117 pl.), ☎ 74.32.12.48.

VALENCE

Lyons 100, Grenoble 100, Paris 562
A2 ✉ 26000

ⓘ pl. Gal-Leclerc (B2), ☎ 75.43.04.88.

✈ Valence-Chabeuil, 5 km SE, ☎ 75.44.48.80.

SNCF (B2), ☎ 75.41.50.50, 75.56.33.33.

Car-hire : *Budget* train + auto, 98 *bis,* av. V.-Hugo, ☎ 75.44.50.52, at the station, ☎ 75.44.36.68, and at the airport.

Hotels :

★★★**2000,** av. de Romans (C1), ☎ 75.43.73.01. AE, DC, Visa. 31 rm P ♨ ♘ ♿ 380. Rest. 60-150.
★★**Europe,** 15, av. F.-Faure (B2), ☎ 75.43.02.16. Visa. 26 rm P ♘ Provençal-style furniture, 220.

Bourg-lès-Valence, ✉ 26500, 3 km NE on the N7 :
★★**Seyvet,** 24, av. Marc-Urtin, ☎ 75.43.26.51. DC, Euro, Visa. 34 rm P ♨ ♘ ♿ closed 7-27 Jan, 215. Rest. ♦♦ closed Sun eve and Mon low season, 55-200.

Pont-de-l'Isère, ✉ 26600 Tain-l'Hermitage, 9 km N :
★★**Chabran** (Michel Chabran), ☎ 75.84.60.09. Visa. 12 rm P ♘ closed Sun eve and Mon low season, Mon and Tue noon during the holiday period, 260. Rest. ● ♦♦ Michel Chabran's constant efforts are finally being rewarded and his customers are delighted. The restaurant is being redecorated and the cooking is of the highest standard : *asperges aux truffes fraîches* (in season), *filets de rougets, bœuf au vieil hermitage.* Great Côtes-du-Rhône wines, 160-380.

Chabeuil, ✉ 26120, 11 km E by the D68 on the N538 :
★★**Relais du Soleil** (L.F.), rte de Romans, ☎ 75.59.01.81. 21 rm ☀ P ♨ ♘ closed Christmas and Feb school hols, Mon, 100. Rest. ♦ ✂ 80-130.

⛺ ★★*L'Espervière* (170 pl.), ☎ 75.43.63.01.

Restaurants :

● ♦♦♦♦ **Pic** (Relais gourmand), 285, av. V.-Hugo (A3), ☎ 75.44.15.32. AE, DC. 5 rm P ♨ ♿ closed Aug, 1 week in Feb, Sun eve and Wed. Jacques Pic and his family have now one more asset, his young son Alain. This restaurant is one of the best of France and a comfortable and friendly one : *filet de loup au caviar, pétales d'agneau aux aubergines,* fabulous choice of Côtes-du-Rhône wines, 200-400.

● ♦♦ **Le Saint-Ruff,** 9, rue Sabaterie, ☎ 75.43.48.64. Visa. closed 15 Jul-15 Aug, Sun and Mon. Friendly atmosphere in the old town, 150.

♦ **La Petite Auberge,** 1, rue d'Athènes, ☎ 75.43.20.30. AE, Euro, Visa. ✂ ♿ closed Aug, Sun and Wed eve, 70-145.

♦ **Le Petit Récamier,** 4, rue Châteauvert, ☎ 75.55.20.79. closed Aug, Feb school hols, Sat and Sun. Spec : *salade d'épinards au haddock, foie de veau au vinaigre de miel,* 120-210.

Montmeyran, ✉ 26120, 14 km SE on the N538A :
♦♦ **La Vieille Ferme,** ☎ 75.59.31.64. AE, DC, Visa. P ♨ ♘ closed Sun eve, Tue and Aug, Mon eve. Spec : *terrine de foie de volailles sur petite salade aux lardons,* 120-170.

Guided tours : C.N.M.H.S., all year round, by appointment : enq T.O.

Recommended : *Dragon,* 12, av. de Chabreuil, ☎ 75.43.11.71 : *pognes* and pastries. *Fullana,* 5, av. V.-Hugo, ☎ 75.43.07.62 : charcuterie. *Fereyre,* 21, av. V.-Hugo, ☎ 75.44.24.32 : fish, fowls, game, *foies gras. Giraud,* 5, pl. de la République, ☎ 75.43.05.28 : chocolates and cakes.

VARS

Briançon 47, Gap 72, Paris 727
C3 ⛷ 1 650 - 2 250 m ✉ 05560

ⓘ ☎ 92.45.51.31.

Hotels :
Claux, 3 km S :
★★★***Caribou,*** ☎ 92.45.50.43. Euro. 35 rm P closed 10 Apr-22 Dec. Pension only, 490. Rest. ◆ 155-200.
★★***Escondus*** (L.F.), ☎ 92.45.50.35. 23 rm P closed end Aug-15 Dec, Easter-Jun, 185. Rest. 75-150.
★★***Écureuil,*** ☎ 92.45.50.72. Euro, Visa. 17 rm P closed 15 Apr-30 Jun, 1 Sep-20 Dec, 245.

Youth hostel : *Spoutnik chalet,* 27 rm, 1.5 km S, ☎ 92.45.50.39.

VIENNE

Lyons 30, Grenoble 88, Paris 493
A1 ⊠ 38200

ℹ cours Brillier (A2), ☎ 74.85.12.62.

SNCF (B3), ☎ 74.85.03.17.

Bus pl. des Allobroges (A3).

Hotels :
★★★***Central,*** 3, rue de l'Archevêché (B2), ☎ 74.85.18.38. AE, Visa. 26 rm P ♿ 205.
★★★***Résidence de la Pyramide,*** 40, quai Riondet (A3), ☎ 74.53.16.46. AE. 15 rm P ♿ closed Feb, 1-15 Nov, 250.

Seyssuel, 5 km N on the N7 and D4 :
★★★***Château des Sept Fontaines,*** ☎ 74.85.25.70. AE, DC, Visa. 15 rm P closed 24 Dec-1 Feb, 210. Rest. ◆ ♿ closed Sun eve and Mon, 80-130.

Chonas-l'Amballan, ⊠ 38121 Reventin-Vaugris, 9 km S N7 :
★★***Domaine de Clairefontaine,*** ☎ 74.58.81.52. Visa. 18 rm P ♿ closed 15 Dec-1 Feb, Sun eve low season and Mon noon, 180. Rest. 55-110.

Roches-de-Condrieu, ⊠ 38370, 12 km S :
★★***Bellevue*** (L.F.), 1, quai du Rhône, ☎ 74.56.41.42. 20 rm P ♿ closed 15 Feb-7 Mar, 4-14 Aug, Sat from Oct to Apr and Mon from Apr to Oct, 180. Rest. ● ◆◆ A pleasant stopover on the banks of the Rhône : *filet de sandre au beurre de ciboulette, aiguillettes de canard au porto,* 120-210.

⛺ ★★★*Le Leveau* (200 pl.), ☎ 74.85.23.15.

Restaurants :
● ◆◆◆◆ ***Pyramide*** (Chez Point), 14, bd Fernand-Point (A3), ☎ 74.53.01.96. AE, DC P closed 1-28 Feb, Mon eve and Tue. Book ahead. Mado Point has not always received the appreciation due her for services rendered to great French cooking. She is 85 years old, and often makes a tour of the tables and talking with her is a real delight. Guy Thivard, a faithful pupil of the great Fernand Point, has been doing the cooking for more than 25 years, 330-400.
◆◆ ***Magnard,*** 45, cours Brillier (A2), ☎ 74.85.10.43. AE, DC, Visa. ♿ closed 5-20 Aug, Feb hols, Tue eve and Wed, 75-160.

Guided tours : C.N.M.H.S. (National Monuments Board), 1 Jul-15 Sep daily ex. Tue, Thu and Sun at 3 pm, enq and R.V. : T.O. and S.I. Visits of Saint-Romain-en-Gal archaeological dig on Tue, Thu, Sun at 4 pm ; 1 Apr-30 Oct, Sun at 4 pm, enq ℹ

VILLARD-DE-LANS

Grenoble 34, Valence 69, Paris 588
B2 ⛷ 1 050-2 170 m ⊠ 38250

ℹ pl. Mure-Ravaud, ☎ 76.95.10.38.

Hotels :
● ★★★***Eterlou,*** rte de Grenoble, ☎ 76.95.17.65. AE, DC, Euro, Visa. 24 rm P closed 15 Sep-15 Dec, 15 Apr-15 Jun, 350. Rest. ◆ 110-245.
● ★★★***Paris*** (Mapotel), B.P. 56, ☎ 76.95.10.06, Tx 308448. AE, DC, Euro, Visa. 60 rm P ♿ closed 1 Nov-15 dec, 15 Apr-2 May, 300. Rest. ◆ 90-150.
★★***Pré Fleuri*** (L.F.), av. A.-Pietri, ☎ 76.95.10.96. 18 rm P closed 1 Oct-20 Dec, Easter-Whitsun, 215. Rest. ◆ 70-150.
★★***Villa Primerose,*** ☎ 76.95.13.17. Visa. 18 rm P closed 15 Apr-15 Jun, 15 Sep-20 Dec, 170. Rest. ◆ 1/2 pension only, 55.

Corrençon-en-Vercors, 5.5 km S on the D215 :
★★***Lièvre Blanc,*** Les Magots, ☎ 76.95.16.79. Euro. 19 rm P closed 1 Oct-25 Dec, Easter-1 Jun, 170. Rest. 75-150.

Lans-en-Vercors, 8 km N on the D531 :
★★***Col de l'Arc*** (L.F.), Le Village, ☎ 76.95.40.08. AE, Visa. 22 rm P closed 15 Oct-15 Dec, May, 160. Rest. ◆ 60-100.
★***Val Fleury,*** ☎ 76.95.41.09. 22 rm P closed 20 Sep-Easter, 100. Rest. 80-130.

⛺ ★★★*Font-Noir* (200 pl.), ☎ 76.95.14.77.

Chambres d'hôtes : Les Geymonds, ☎ 76.95.12.77.

VIZILLE

Grenoble 15, Briançon 100, Paris 582
B2 ⊠ 38220

ℹ pl. du Château, ☎ 76.68.13.99.

Hotels :
★★***Parc,*** 25, av. A.-Briand, ☎ 76.68.03.01. AE, Euro, Visa. 28 rm, 140.

Laffrey, 7.5 km S on the Napoleon road :
★***Parc*** (L.F.), ☎ 76.68.12.98. Euro. 11 rm P ♿ closed Oct, 120. Rest. 50-130.

Uriage, ⊠ 38410, 9 km N on the D524 :
★★★***Grand Hôtel,*** ☎ 76.89.10.17. 51 rm P closed 25 Sep-1 May, 180. Rest. ◆ 80-130.
★★***Manoir,*** rte de Premol, ☎ 76.89.10.88. 18 rm P closed 24 Nov-13 Dec, 5-28 Jan, Sun eve and Mon low season, 195. Rest. ♿ 50-145.

Saint-Martin-d'Uriage, 12 km NE on the D524 and D111 :
★***Mésanges,*** ☎ 76.89.70.69. Euro. 37 rm P closed 1 Oct-1 May, ex week-ends and school hols, 170. Rest. ♿ 55-150.

⛺ ★★★*Municipal* (128 pl.), ☎ 76.68.12.39.

VOIRON

Grenoble 29, Chambéry 44, Paris 550
B1 ⊠ 38500

ℹ Voiron Chartreuse, pl. de la République, ☎ 76.05.00.38.

SNCF ☎ 76.05.50.50, 76.05.06.14.

Hotels :
★★★***Castel Anne,*** 73, av. Dr-Valois, ☎ 76.05.86.00. AE, DC, Visa. 12 rm P closed 8-28 Feb, 245. Rest. ◆◆ closed Wed, 90-150.
★Chaumière (L.F.), rue de la Chaumière, ☎ 76.05.16.24. 25 rm P closed 25 Dec-8 Jan and Sat eve, 165. Rest. ◆ closed Sat eve and Sun noon, 55-95.

⛺ ★★★*Porte de Chartreuse* (70 pl.), ☎ 76.05.14.20.

Franche-Comté ●

Franche-Comté means "Free County" : the region's long tradition of independence is the fruit of its struggle to retain its personality under successive waves of foreign invasion, but Franche-Comté's independence is combined with a community spirit characterized by the co-operatives set up by dairy farmers and cheesemakers as early as the 13th century. Exploitation of the region's forests too has always been a communual undertaking. The motto of the winegrowers of Arbois in the 19th century — "We are all in charge" — could well stand for the whole region. In the 16th century, Franche-Comté was, along with Flanders and Spain, part of the empire of Holy Roman Emperor Charles the Fifth. It remained attached to the Spanish branch of the Hapsburg family — with a semi-autonomous parliament in Dole — until 1674 when Richelieu reclaimed Franche-Comté for the Sun King, after an arduous six-month campaign and the great siege of Besançon.

Geographically it is really two regions : the high valley of the Saône is wide, gently rolling country with a certain rustic simplicity, while the Jura is wild, untamed and mountainous with torrents of water, forests of black spruces and slopes made for adventurous skiers.

Besançon, birthplace of Victor Hugo and site of a prestigious music festival, has been producing watches since the end of the 17th century, and despite foreign competition and the need to adapt to new techniques, it is holding its own : in 1980 Besançon workshops and factories produced some 15 million units. Dole is the birthplace of the scientist Louis Pasteur.

Vines have covered the slopes of Revermont since antiquity, and today *A.O.C.* wine is produced in an area covering over 1 200 acres. Other local specialties are kirsch, plum brandy and white brandy or *marc.* Franche-Comté is also the home of many excellent cheeses : Comté, Morbier, Vacherin and Cancoillotte. The lakes and rivers of the region are a paradise for fishermen, providing excellent trout, carp and pike and many other smaller fry.

Sightseeing

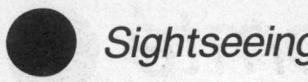

Brief description

Location : *On the Swiss border; the French sector of the Jura and the high plain of the Saône together form most of Franche-Comté.*
Area : *16 271 km*^{2}.
Climate : *plentiful lakes and rivers; frequent rain, especially in autumn, but ample sunshine for vine cultivation. Franche-Comté is generally damp and cool; best season, June to September; severe winters, spring sometimes late; mild summers.*
Population : *1 084 000.*
Administration : *Department of the* ***Haute-Saône,*** *prefecture, Vesoul; Department of* ***Belfort Territory*** *(smallest in France), Prefecture Belfort; Department of* ***Doubs,*** *Prefecture Besançon; Department of* ***Jura,*** *Prefecture Lons-le-Saunier.*

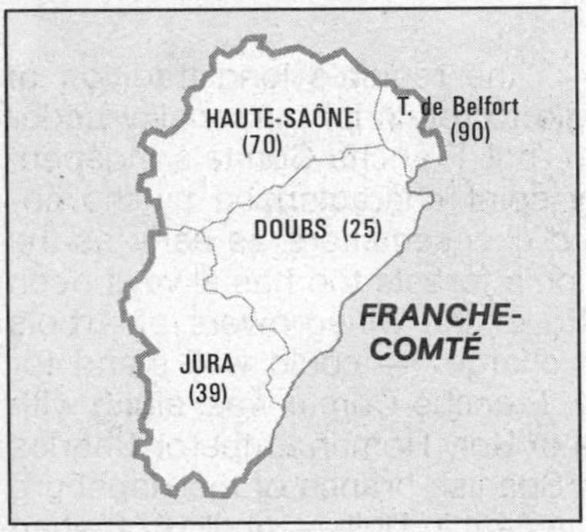

Don't miss

★★★ : Arc-et-Senans (B3), Baume-les-Messieurs (B2), Besançon (B2). Ronchamp (C1), Saut du Doubs (C3), ★★ Dole (A3), Goumois Corniche (C2), Hérisson Waterfalls (B4), Joux Forest (B3), Lison Springs (B3), Loue Valley (B3), Ornans (B2), Lake Vouglans (AB4).

■ ARBOIS★

B3 / ® / pop. 4 160 (Jura)

The river Cuisance threads a passage among the famous vineyards of the Jura before it reaches picturesque Arbois. This town of winemakers and wine lovers makes an appealing stopover. Many cellars offer visits and tastings.

▶ At the northern entry to town, the **family home of Louis Pasteur** (1822-95; inventor of the pasteurisation process)★★ is maintained as if the scientist were expected at any moment

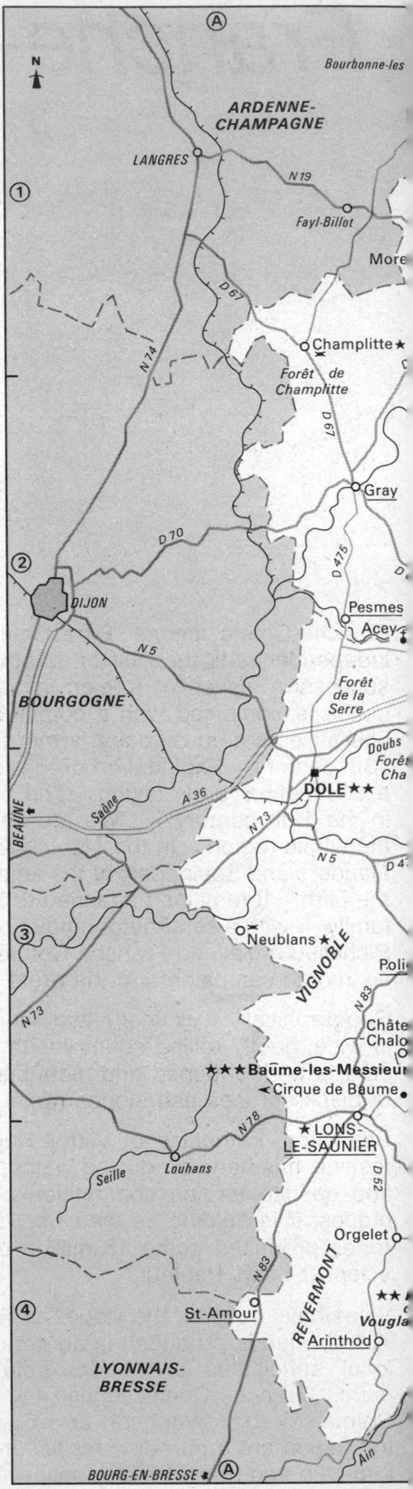

Franche-Comté

Weekend tips

A quick (half-day) look at Besançon along the Loue valley with a detour to Morteau and Saut du Doubs and a stopover at Pontarlier. Next day, Nozeroy and Joux forest, Salins, Arbois (lunch) and Poligny, to Baume-les-Messieurs before climbing back to Dole. Two full days to capture the flavour of the Jura; you will have to come back another time for the northern Franche-Comté.

(9-12 & 2-5; Jun.-Sep.; closed Tue.). ▶ Near the place de la Liberté is the **Musée de la Vigne et du Vin** (wine museum) in the cellars of the town hall *(3-7, Jul.-Aug.; Sat. and Sun. in Jun.; closed Tue.).* The **Sarret-de-Grozon Museum** displays furniture, silverware and porcelain in an 18thC mansion *(same hours as wine museum).* ▶ In front of the church of St. Just (along Rue de Faramand and left) view of the towers of old Arbois from the Capucins bridge. ▶ Lookout points at l'**Ermitage** *(D469 then road right)* and le **Tourillon** *(D107 E; orientation chart).* □

▶ Nearby

▶ **Planches Reculée** valley★★ : in the valley bottom are the two springs of the river Cuisance, one of which forms a waterfall at the exit of the **Planches Caverns**★ (cave flora and fauna; *9-12 & 2-6:30, Jun.-Sep.; 10-12 & 2-6, May-Sep. and spring hols.; Sun., Apr. and Oct.*); lakes form when the water is high. D469 leads to the **Fer à Cheval** ("horseshoe")★★, a natural **amphitheatre** 200 m above the springs. □

■ ARC-ET-SENANS★★★

B3 / ® / pop. 1 300 (Doubs)

The architect Claude-Nicolas Ledoux (1736-1806; forerunner of modern city planning) hoped to create an ideal community at **Salines Royales**★★★ in **Arc-et-Senans.** The plan was never realized but the beginnings are still visible.

▶ The scheme called for a town built in concentric circles around the salt pans *(salines),* but only the buildings required for salt production were completed (1775). The size and organisation of these buildings ranged around the house of the Director suggest the scale of the entire project. Salt water was to be brought by a wooden pipeline from Salins-les-Bains (→), and fuel to be supplied by the Chaux forest. The venture, never profitable, was abandoned in the 19thC. The Salines Royales of Arc-et-Senans now house an International Centre for Future Studies (colloquia, exhibitions, receptions, shows from the Besançon festival), with an important library (specialized in architecture), and a Salt Museum. ▶ NE of the salt pans, the **Chaux forest**★★ covers almost 200 km^2 with oaks, beech, hornbeam, birch and aspen; forest roads lead to Dole (→) and the Doubs valley. □

■ BAUME-LES-DAMES

B2 / ® / pop. 5 696 (Doubs)

Baume-les-Dames was once an abbey reserved for daughters of the nobility. It was founded in the 7thC on the spot where Ste. Odile, the patron saint of Alsace (→ Alsace) is said to have sought refuge from her cruel father in the 6thC.

▶ Although badly damaged during WWII, Baume still has several 16th, 17th and 18thC buildings, as well as the abbey church (access via porch in the Place de la République); church of St. Martin, rebuilt in the 17thC, has a (Louis XIII altarpiece). The town is a centre of tobacco-pipe manufacturing. □

▶ Nearby

▶ **Source Bleue**★ : reach the spring by D21 through the Cuisancin valley, 14 km from Baume via Pont-des-Moulins. ▶ **Glacière Caverns**★★ *(19 km S; 9-6, Easter-30 Nov.);* a natural phenomenon preserves ice formations in the cavern all year round. Nearby, 18thC buildings of the monastery of Grâce-Dieu founded in the 12thC by the monastic reformer St. Bernard of Clairvaux (1088-1153). □

■ BAUME-LES-MESSIEURS★★★

A3 / ® / pop. 174 (Jura)

In a deep valley : old walls covered with climbing plants, roofs bowed by time; flowered cloisters, and memories of Jean de Watteville (see box), one-time abbot who was also a brawler, a libertine and, when it suited, a Muslim.

▶ The **abbey** was founded in the 6thC by the Irish monk St. Columban (→ Luxeuil); a small group from Baume-les-Messieurs (then Baume-les-Moines) founded the renowned abbey of Cluny (→ Burgundy) in the 10thC. The buildings are modest and unadorned. The Romanesque **church**★★ has a 15thC façade; tombstones, Burgundian statuary (15thC), a noteworthy **altarpiece**★★ (scenes from the life of Christ; 16thC Flemish). ▶ **Museum of Crafts of the Jura** in the abbey (*10:30-12:30 & 3-6, Jul. to 15 Sep.;* forge and cooperage). ▶ Natural **amphitheatre of Baume :** (D70-E3 and D70-E1) **Baume caves**★ *(9-12 & 2-6, 30 min earlier Sun. and nat. hols., 15 Mar. to 15 Oct.),* several caverns, small lake. Via Baume to the plateau *(D70 then D4 and D471 to right),* lookout over **Baume rocks**★★★ from the top of the amphitheatre. □

■ BELFORT★

C1 / ® / pop. 52 700 (T.-de-Belfort)

The city's symbol is a huge sandstone lion carved by Frédéric Bartholdi (1834-1904), sculptor of New York's Statue of Liberty. Belfort commands a strategic position between Alsace and Bourgogne, between the Vosges and the Jura. It is an important centre for the production of rolling stock, electronic equipment and other industrial goods.

▶ A system of **fortifications** established by Vauban (1633-1707, military engineer to Louis XIV) proved its worth during three determined sieges in 1814, 1815 and 1870. The **old town**★ (B2, C2) is organised around the Place de la République *(Trois Sièges* monument by Bartholdi) and the Place d'Armes on the left bank of the river Savoureuse, which separates the old town from the new. ▶ Behind the **cathe-**

dral of St. Christophe (C2 ; 18thC wrought iron, wooden panelling), a recently restored area leads up to the **Citadel★★** (C2), where, on the right of the carpark, is a path to the **Lion★★★** 22 m long, 11 m high *(10-12 & 2-5 Apr.-Sep. ; 8-12 & 2-7 Nov.-Mar.).* ▶ The château in the court of honour of the citadel houses the **Art and History Museum★ :** prehistoric artifacts, relief plan of Belfort, regional art, coins, paintings *(8-12 & 2-7 May-Sep. ; 10-12 & 2-5 closed Tue. in winter).* ▶ Back toward the town past **Porte de Brisach★,** erected by Vauban in 1687 (C1). □

■ BELFORT Territory

C1

In 1871, Belfort surrendered to the Prussians after a 103-day siege. In recognition of the heroic resistance shown by the townspeople, it was granted the right to remain French thus becoming the smallest department in France. Today, Belfort is highly industrialised but the landscapes remain largely unspoilt between the Jura S and the Vosges N.

▶ **Malsaucy Lake** *(10 km NW from Belfort) :* facing the Ballon d'Alsace heights (→ Alsace), has been developed as a recreational park (lake shore, sailing, watersports). ▶ **Etueffont** *(15 km NE) :* forge museum with traditional tools, furniture *(2-6 Easter Sun. to 1 Nov.).* **Rougemont-le-Château :** ruins of a Romanesque priory. **Seigneurie lake :** shore park. ▶ **Delle** ® *(SE of Belfort) :* known as the *Petit Sologne ;* like Sundgau just over the border, many fishing lakes ; 16thC houses. □

Lacuzon

Jean-Claude Prost (1607-81), called Captain Lacuzon, personifies Comtois independence. He rallied resistance to the invading armies of the Prince de Condé and his ally, Bernard de Saxe-Weimar. Caves, once used as hideouts, honour the name of this pious merchant from Saint-Claude, who overcame his natural reserve and timidity to lead bands of partisans starting in 1636 and continuing up to the incursions of Louis XIV (see Brief Regional History). For the Comtois people, Lacuzon is a sort of Robin Hood, a passionate and courageous man who resorted to violence out of necessity rather than inclination.

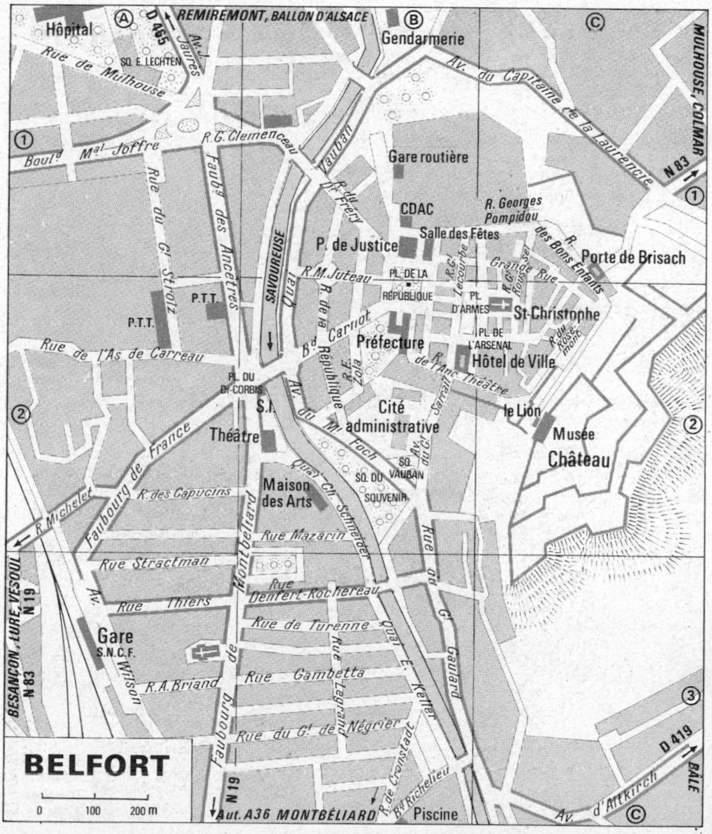

■ Château de **BELVOIR★**

C2

For seven centuries the lords of Belvoir ruled the plain from the 12thC château on the Lomont premontory; several rooms display furniture and mementoes *(10-12 & 2-6:30, daily Jul.-Aug., Sun. and nat. hols. Easter to 1 Nov.).* ▶ Market buildings and old houses in the village. □

■ BESANÇON★★★

B2 / ® / pop. 119 600 (Doubs)

Besançon used to be a city of watchmakers; however, since the advent of quartz mechanisms, precision engineering has in part taken the place of the traditional industry. Much of the elegant architecture of Besançon, abundantly adorned with wrought-iron grillwork, dates from the late 17thC, when Besançon replaced Dole as capital of the Franche-Comté. The novelist Victor Hugo (1802-85) was born in Besançon. The city benefited during the 16thC from the patronage of Nicolas Granvelle (1486-1550), who rose from peasant stock to become a doctor of law and chancellor to the Emperor Charles V. The fortune and power he amassed placed his family among the most influential in the region.

▶ Besançon has pioneered a traffic control system that favours pedestrians and the use of public transport. Leave your car at the Chamars car park (free, but often full) or on the Doubs quay (near the République bridge), then explore the city on foot or by bus. ▶ The hub of activity is the **Grande-Rue,** which is partly a pedestrian mall; nearby, busy market stalls around the **Fine Arts Museum★★★** (B2), which occupies the former corn market; an excellent collection includes paintings by Bellini, Cranach, la Tour, Rubens, Fragonard, Boucher, Greuse, Ingres, Courbet, David, Goya, Matisse and Picasso; archaeological finds; interesting watch and clock-making section *(9-12 & 2-6; closed Tue.).* ▶ Opposite the church of St. Pierre (18thC) are the beautiful façades of the **town hall** (16thC) and the courthouse (Renaissance). ▶ Several mansions from the 16th-18thC stand along the Grande-Rue. ▶ **Granvelle palace★★** (B2; 16thC) : residence of Nicolas Perrenot de Granvelle (see above) and of his son Antoine (1517-86), Cardinal-Prime Minister of the Lowlands, Viceroy of Naples, Minister to Philip II of Spain. ▶ **His-**

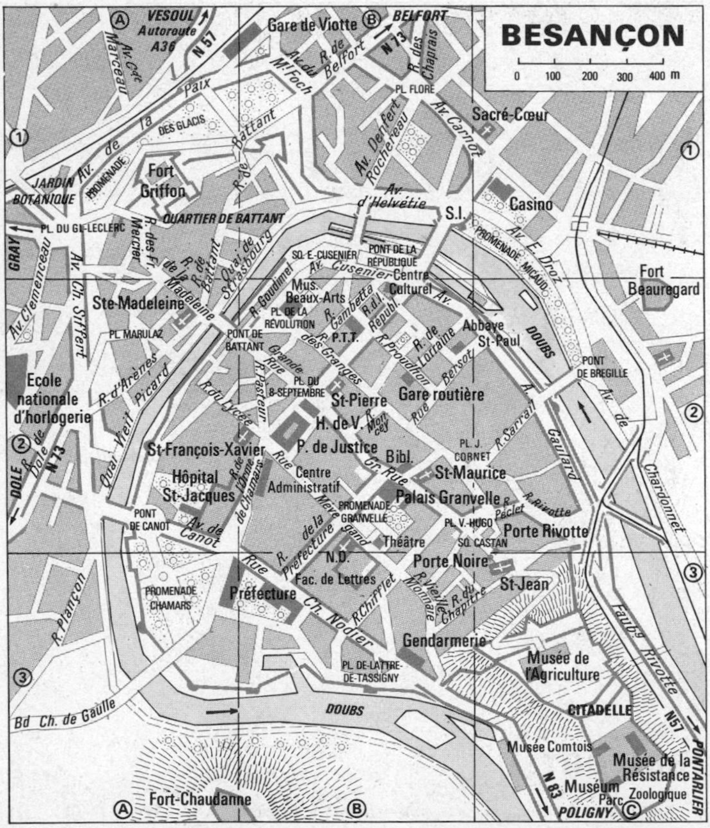

torical Museum★ : Charles V tapestry (17thC), mementoes of Granvelle, Victor Hugo, Proudhon and Fourier (see Brief Regional History; *9:30-12 & 2-6, closed Tue.*). Behind the palace is the Granvelle promenade. ▶ Place Victor-Hugo : birthplaces of the novelist and of the Lumière brothers, Auguste (1862-1954) and Louis (1864-1948) who, in 1895, invented cinematography. ▶ At the end of Grande-Rue : Roman remains including the 2ndC **Porte Noire★** (Black Gate) in front of the **cathedral of St. Jean :** (C3; 12th, 18thC) with an apse at either end of the nave; Virgin with Saints★ (Fra Bartolomeo, 1512); "the rose of St. John" (4thC Roman marble altar); 18thC paintings. ▶ **Astronomical clock★★** (1857-60, restored 1900) 30 000 moving parts, 70 dials, and a parade of mechanical figures *(daily at 9:50, 10:50, 11:50, 2:50, 3:50, 4:50; closed Tue.).* ▶ Noteworthy houses in Rues Rivotte and De Pontarlier and Place J.-Cornet (BC2). ▶ The **citadel★★★,** towering nearly 120 m above the city, was built largely by Vauban (see Belfort). Its sentry walk provides superb **views★★.** Museums : (C3; *9-6:30 or 5:30 in winter; museums closed Tue. and, like the aquarium, 11:30-1:30*). **Comtoise Folk Museum★★★ :** agriculture, crafts, daily life, folklore, furniture, decoration and marionettes; the **Museum of the Resistance and the Deportation** (WWII), and the **Museum of Natural History** occupy neighbouring buildings. The moat has been converted into an **aquarium. Also...** ▶ Municipal **library** (B2, facing Granvelle palace) illuminated manuscripts. ▶ Near the **Prefecture,** 17th and 18thC buildings. ▶ **Battants quarter** (on the right bank of the Doube) mansions and old houses undergoing restoration. ▶ **Micaud promenade** (C1). ▶ On the eastern edge of town, forts offer **splendid views :** Brégille, Chaudanne, Montfaucon, and the lookout at Notre-Dame-de-la-Libération★. □

▶ Nearby

▶ **Osselle Caves★★** *(26 km SW) :* stalactites and stalagmites in several caverns; the caves provided refuge for priests during the Revolution (1789) *(9-12 & 2-6 Apr.-Oct.; 9-7 Jun.-Sep.).* ▶ **Courtefontaine :** Romanesque church. □

■ CHAMPAGNOLE

B3 / ® / pop. 10 070 (Jura)

The steel, furniture and toy industries that maintain the prosperity of Champagnole draw their energy from the river Ain.

▶ **Syam** offers a look at the face of industry during the 19thC at the hamlet of Forges *(5 km SE, D127),* Empire château in Italian style. **Perte de l'Ain★** (N) where the Ain disappears into a crevice, and **Sirod** (12th and 13thC church). S on D279 **Billaude waterfalls★** *(20 mins on foot, difficult climb).* D127 continues to the **Langouette gorges★** and to the **Malvaux gorges** formed by the river Saine. □

■ CHAMPLITTE★

A1 / pop. 1 130 (Haute-Saône)

Château★ (16th-18thC) with **Museum of Folk Arts and Tradition★★★.**

▶ The Albert-Demart museum is named after a shepherd who systematically collected articles and artifacts connected with disappearing **rural customs :** reconstructed interiors, furniture, tools, miscellaneous objects *(9-12 & 2-5; closed Sun. am and Tue.).* □

■ CHATEAU-CHALON★

A3 / pop. 156 (Jura)

The sloping vineyards around château Chalon are renowned for two fine wines : *vin jaune de garde,* deep gold in colour, Is aged in barrels for at least 6 years before being bottled and sold; *vin de paille* (straw), also golden, is a rare dessert wine made from grapes that are left on straw mats to become overripe before being pressed.

▶ The ramparts and the château are now picturesque ruins; the **site★★** overlooks the Seille Valley; treasures of the church include an alabaster panel and a wood carving of Christ. □

▶ Nearby

▶ **Cirque de Ladoye** (natural amphitheatre)★★ *(6 km E, D5) :* lookout over a blind valley. ▶ **Arlay** *(12 km W, D120) :* **château** rebuilt in the 18thC; furnished in Restoration (ca. 1820) style; park; ruins of the mediaeval château overlooking château Chalon *(10-12 & 2-6 in summer, closed Sun. am).* ▶ **Frontenay** *(7 km N) :* château (12thC-18thC) among vineyards *(10-12 & 2-6, Apr.-Oct.).* □

Abbot, adventurer, monk and Mohammedan

The Duke of St. Simon (1675-1765), whose diaries provide a meticulous record of life at the court of Louis XIV, recounts the adventures of Jean de Watteville (1613-1702). When an army officer, lying low after killing an opponent in a duel, he underwent a religious conversion and entered a monastery. Predictably finding monastic life tedious, he was challenged while in the act of escaping over the monastery wall, struck the abbot dead, and was again obliged to take flight. After countless escapades in Spain, he found himself at Constantinople, where he embraced Islam and offered his military expertise to the Grand Turk. He spent several years as pasha and governor of Morea, availing himself of the harem that went with the job. Eventually, however, ordered to fight the Venetians, he instead struck a bargain with them : surrender in exchange for papal absolution for all his past crimes plus the abbotship of Baume. Shriven and shorn, he led the monks as if they were troops, and continued to carry out his military commissions for Louis XIV, living more like a lord than a monk.

■ CLAIRVAUX-LES-LACS

B4 / ® / pop. 1 430 (Jura)

An attractive holiday spot; lakeshore beaches at Clairvaux; aquatic sports at **Etival** *(11 km S D118);* the valley of the Ain and Vouglans Lake (→). □

■ DESSOUBRE Valley★

C2

The river Doubs winds among meadows in this wooded valley, passes through a mill-turned-inn *(auberge)* and a saw-mill, eventually reaching a confluence with the Reverotte.

▶ The lookout at **Roche du Prêtre★★★** (Priest's Rock) *(via D41 or D461)* provides the best view of the **Consolation natural amphitheatre★★**, where the Dessoubres river arises. ▶ Back down on D39 via the old convent of Notre-Dame de Consolation (18thC woodwork), follow the river for about 30 km to Saint-Hippolyte (→ Goumois *corniche* cliff road). □

■ DOLE★★

A3 / ® / pop. 27 950 (Jura)

The Rhône-Rhine canal reflects the red and brown roofs of Dole, clustered around the bell-tower of Notre-Dame. The capital of Comté until superseded by Besançon in 1678, Dole retains much of the past, although it looks ahead to economic and industrial realities. Dole's population is larger than that of Besançon, the department's Prefecture.

▶ From **Place Grévy** (C1) stroll to the **old town★★** : numerous 15th-18thC houses with carved doorways, turrets, courtyards, and wells. ▶ **Church of Notre-Dame★** (B2; 16thC) : a stolid exterior concealing broad and airy nave; 15thC statues, handsome 16thC furniture; Sainte-Chapelle. ▶ **Rue Pasteur★ :** site of the tanner's house where Louis Pasteur (see box) was born on 27 Dec. 1822; museum *(10-12 & 2-6 Apr.-Sep.; closed Tue.).* ▶ The **hospital★★ :** imposing 17thC edifice with balconies, galleries, courtyard, pharmacy. ▶ **Rue des Arênes** (AB2) : **Museum of Archaeology and Painting** *(10-12 & 2-6; closed Tue.).*; in a blind alley (impasse) the **Palais de Justice★** (court house) formerly a Cordeliers' Convent (16thC). ▶ **Place aux Fleurs★ :** view over the rooftops. ▶ **Rue du Mont-Roland** (AB2) : **Froissard mansion★★** (court-yard); former **Carmelite convent★** with ornate wrought iron. ▶ Rue du Collège-de-l'Arc : a former jesuit **college★★** (1582), now a school (Renaissance porch★ at the entrance to the former chapel). ▶ Faubourg de Chalon (D739) : **church of St. Jean** (1964). □

■ ESMOULIÈRES Plateau★

▶ Circuit *(70 km half-day)*

C1 *(see map 1)*

An isolated plateau between the basins of the Saône and the Moselle at the foot of the blue Vosges mountains. Lakes, wild heaths and woodlands are occasionally punctuated by cultivated fields.

▶ The villagers of **Faucogney-et-la-Mer** ® (pop. 750 today) held out to the last against the force of Louis XIV. All were put to the sword in 1674, and the fortified château was razed. Sheets of zinc protect the gables on the sandstone houses. ▶ Beyond **Mélisey** ®, the road leaves the **Ognon Valley** to climb towards **Fresse** (pulpit★ in the church) beside the river Raddon. Left fork : numerous lookouts before **Belfahy** (alt. 870 m; skiing), where the narrow road descends towards the **Saut de l'Ognon★** and **Servance.** ▶ **Croix Pass** (alt. 753 m) : detour to the **Mountain Museum★** in **Château-**

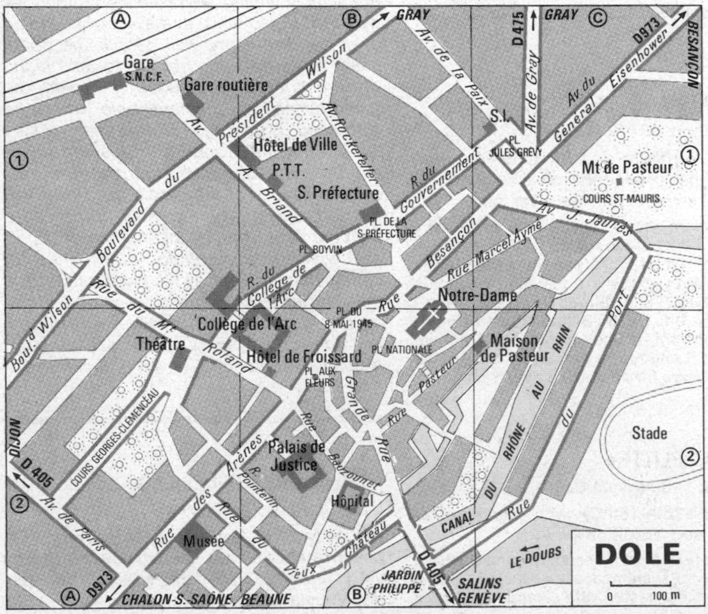

Lambert, a typical village of northern Haute-Saône *(9-12 & 2-6, Easter to 1 Nov. closed. Tue).* 12 km from the pass, the **Ballon de Servanoo** (alt. 1210 m, view★). ▶ After the Mont Fourche Pass, the emptiness of the plateau is apparent : nothing but lakes and the single village of **Esmoulières.** □

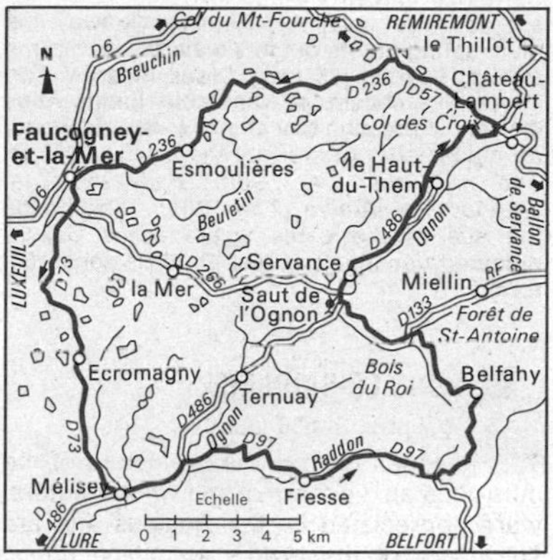

1. Esmoulières plateau

The GOUMOIS Corniche★★

▶ Circuit *(80 km, full day).*

C2 *(see map 2)*

On the high plateaux where Comté is made, green meadows stretch into dark fir forests. The Doubs gorges offer an impressive landscape.

2. Goumois Corniche

▶ **Maîche** ® : a busy dairy and commercial centre, good for summer or winter holidays. Near the church : château where Montalembert (historian and academician, 1810-70) lived. ▶ The road runs down through woods to **Saint-Hippolyte** ® through splendid countryside dotted with a few old houses, then climbs up the course of the Doubs, under cliffs. ▶ On the right bank, the rustic site★ of **Montjoie-le-Château.** ▶ **Vaufrey** a 18thC château and a fountain★ decorated with lions. ▶ **Glère** still has traditional houses, unfortunately close to modern pseudo-chalets. Right to **Indevillers,** typical village surrounded by firs; beyond, a sawmill. ▶ The **Goumois Corniche★★★** (cliff road) runs above the Doubs gorges, forming the frontier with Switzerland (bridge of **Goumois** ® in a remarkable site★).▶ **Charmauvillers :** typical Jura houses. ▶ Near **Combe-Saint-Pierre** (S of **Charquemont** ® : hikes, and the **Cendrée Belvédère** (lookout)★. ▶ **Echelles de la Mort★★★ :** dizzy viewpoint in gorges cut almost 800 m into the plateau *(access via D464, then past the frontier post [tell the border guards you are not going to Switzerland] along a road towards the power station of Refrain; from there 25 mins on foot.).* □

GRAY

A2 / ® / pop. 8313 (Haute-Saône)

Gray sits on the left bank of the Saône, a quiet little town, and an ideal place to stay if you like the countryside and fishing from river banks.

▶ On the heights, the Renaissance **Hôtel de Ville★** (town hall); glazed-tiles gleaming, near the **church of Notre-Dame★** (late Gothic). ▶ Beyond a mediaeval tower, the **château** (18thC) houses a **municipal museum (Baron-Martin★) :** 16th-20thC paintings, engravings★ by Jacques Calot (1592-1635); P.-P. Proudhon (1758-1823) pastels and drawings★; archaeology *(9-12 & 1-6; winter 9-12 & 2-5, closed Tue.).* National Museum of Esperanto *(Wed. and Sat., 3-6).* ▶ **Autrey-lès-Gray** *(11 km NW) :* church frequently remodelled but with Romanesque choir, handsome statuary. □

GY

B2 / ® / pop. 985 (Haute-Saône)

Gy was the official residence of the bishops of Besançon in the Middle Ages, to which the town owes its château. **Hôtel de Ville★** (town hall) in Palladian style; fountain in the form of a classical portico; **church★** 18thC, Neoclassical. □

▶ Nearby

▶ **Monts de Gy Massif :** hiking trail, Captiot chasm, expanse of limestone, view. ▶ **Bucey-les-Gy** *(3 km N) :* Romanesque church; town hall and wash-house dating from 1st Empire (1800-1814). ▶ **Frasne-le-Château** *(9 km NE) :* 16thC château built for Cardinal de Granvelle. □

HÉRISSON Falls★★

B4

At the foot of Aigle peak (alt. 993 m) the Jura presents lakes, waterfalls, and rivers in a pleasant holiday area, with views and walks in all directions.

▶ Follow the course of the Hérisson (a tributary of the Ain) from **Doucier** ® by skirting **Lake Chambly** and **Lake Val** *(from car park, 1h15 on foot to Saut-Girard).* ▶ **Éventail★★★** *(10 mins)* : a 60 m high waterfall; footbridge to the top. 300 m ahead left, another footbridge to the **Lacuzon cave.** ▶ **Grand-Saut waterfall★★ :** 60 m in a single fall; upstream, **Gour Bleu★★** (basin), **Saut Château-Garnier,** and **Saut de la Forge★.** ▶ 30 mins farther to **Saut-Girard,** leading to **Ilay** ®. □

■ JOUX Forest★★

B3

Fir trunks often more than 50 m high make a cathedral of the Joux Forest, one of the finest in France (27 km²; 12 000 trees felled each year). The nearby **forest of Fresse★★** (11.5 km²) is also beautiful. Both are traversed by marked trails.

▶ The **Route des Sapins** (Fir Road) is signposted from Equevillon *(D21, Jura)* to Villers-sous-Chalamont *(D49, Doubs; approx. 30 km).* The road passes by the Glacière firs★★, some of which are 300 years old, to reach an arboretum, then the President Fir *(Sapin Président)*★★ (4 m girth, 44 m high, 300 years old). □

▶ Nearby

▶ N of **Ilay** ®, the D75 looks onto **Motte Lake★, Maclu Lake** and **Narlay Lake★,** all easily accessible. ▶ N of Doucier, **Chalain Lake★★★** has an attractive recreation centre (shore, sailing, fishing, aquatic sports); see it first from the **lookout★★** *(road panel on D39).* □

■ LISON Springs★★

B3

The Lison runs underground for some distance to reappear at this enchanting site, easily reached from the charming village of Nans-sous-Sainte-Anne.

▶ Just beyond the car park, path right to the **Sarrazine cavern★★** *(15 min the Lison resurges in wet weather);* 10 min walk away, the main spring bursts out in a waterfall that forms a lake; beyond *(15 min),* **Creux Billard★ :** an impressive chasm. ▶ **Nans-sous-Sainte-Anne** ® : very interesting **tool shop★★** with old wooden machinery powered by the Lison *(2-6 Sun. and nat. hols., Apr.-Jun.; daily ex. Tue. Jul.-Aug.).* ▶ **Alaise** *(7 km NW) :* said to be the site of the battle where Julius Caesar defeated Vercingetorix (see Brief Regional History). □

■ LONS-LE-SAUNIER★

A3 / ® / pop. 21 800 (Jura)

This peaceful town is the Prefecture of the Jura; it is also a thermal spa whose waters, were appreciated by the Romans and are still used for the town's swimming pools. The word *Saunier* referring to a salt worker or merchant, reflects the earliest industry in the town.

▶ **Place de la Liberté** (B2) : the clock tower marks the start of **Rue du Commerce,** bordered with 18thC arcades; No. 24 is the birthplace of Claude-Joseph Rouget de Lisle (1760-1836), composer of the French National

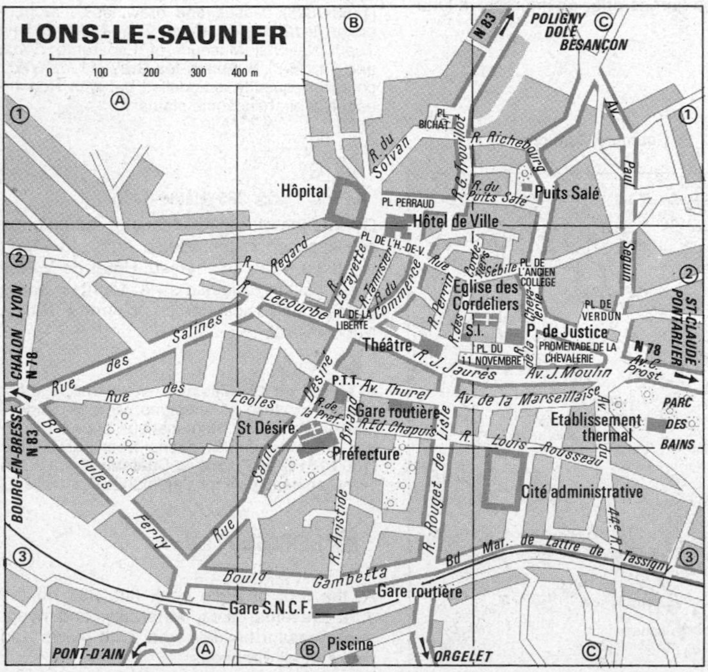

Anthem, the Marseillaise. ▶ Hôtel de Ville (town hall) (B1-2) : **museum** of local prehistory, painting and sculpture *(10-12 & 2-6; closed Tue. and Sat., Sun. am)*. Nearby, behind a magnificent wrought-iron **grille★★**, the 18thC hospital (pharmacy★). ▶ Close to the Prefecture (B2) : **church of St. Désiré★** (Romanesque interior, 18thC vaulting behind a 19thC façade, over an 11thC crypt). ▶ Attractive gardens on the Chevalerie promenade and in the Park des Bains (C2). □

▶ Nearby

▶ **Conliège** *(4 km SW)* : among vineyards; beautiful church (14th-18thC; furnishings). Farther on, **Creux de Revigny.** ▶ **Pin★★** *(5 km N)* : **château** rebuilt in the 15thC (square keep). **L'Étoile** *(W, on the other side of N83)* : recognised for wine; pretty site★ on the hillside, ruins of a mediaeval château. □

■ The LOUE Valley★★

▶ From the Belvédère du Moine-de-la-Vallée to Arc-et-Senans *(approx 100 km full day)*.

B3 *(see map 3)*.

The Loue, one of the most beautiful rivers in the Jura, springs from the high plateaux. Emerging into the day after a long journey underground, the river runs through a valley in which all the landscapes in the region are found. Here, so the local people say, the Vouivre still haunts the caverns.

▶ **Belvédère du Moine★★** : overlooking the valley towards Mouthier and Lods. ▶ **Loue spring★★★** : spurting from a cavern on the flank of a 100 m rock wall to run down the gorges de Nouailles (view from D67). ▶ Several springs and waterfalls add to the Loue before it reaches **Mouthier-Haute-Pierre★** ® : a village among orchards, half in the valley and half on a hill (kirsch). Natural History museum *(daily, 8-11:30 & 1:30-5 closed Wed.)*. Mouthier-Haut : old houses and church (15thC, furnishings). ▶ **Lods** ® *(pronounced Lô)* : houses on the waterside; view from the other bank; forges, old mill; 16thC château; **museum of vines and wine** *(9:30-12 & 2-6:30 Jul.-Sep.)*. ▶ **Vuillafans** : old houses, ruins, an old bridge. ▶ **Ornans** (→), then left, chapel of Notre-Dame du Chêne : pilgrimage site. ▶ **Scey-en-Varais** : ruined feudal castle reflected in the river. **Malbrans** *(4 km N)* : 19thC tileworks. ▶ The road skirts the beautiful **château Cléron★★** (14th-16thC; *2:30-6 15 Jul.-15 Aug.*). ▶ Confluence of the Lison and Loue; Châtillon forges : pretty **sites★**. ▶ **Chenecey-Buillon** : in a loop of the Loue, ruined abbey and feudal ruins; then road rejoins N83. ▶ **Port-Lesney** ® : a delightful stopover beside a peaceful stretch of the Loue, very popular with fishermen. ▶ **Arc-et-Senans★★★** (→).□

■ LUXEUIL-LES-BAINS★

B1 / ® / pop. 10 530 (Haute-Saône)

Luxeuil is a thermal spa (hot radioactive waters, well equipped leisure facilities) in an ancient town with beautiful houses. St. Columban came to Luxeuil from Ireland in the 6thC to establish one of the first monastic communities in the West.

▶ Around Place St. Pierre and Place St. Martin : palatial former abbot's residence (18thC) now the town hall, **Basilica of St. Pierre** : 14thC,

The Jura

Stretching in an arc from Bugey to Alsace, the Jura is a mountainous region of parallel limestone chains (Monts) running NE/SW enclosing high plateaux that were thrown up by alpine folding during the Tertiary era, and hollowed out by subsequent glacial erosion. The eastern (Swiss) flank is steep, but the west is gentler and scored by deep valleys (Revermont, Vignoble). Very wet (lakes, springs, and rivers), occupied largely with stock raising and forestry, harsh in winter and temperate in summer, the Jura's highest point is the Crêt de la Neige (alt. 1 718 m).

3. Loue Valley

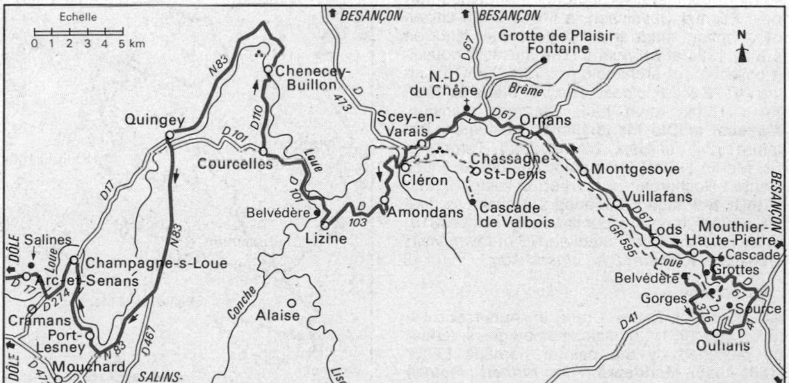

Franche-Comté

16thC choirstalls★; 17thC organ, cloister★. Renaissance house (supposedly belonged to King François I); **Jouffroy mansion★** (15thC) opposite the **Hôtel des Échevins★★** (the aldermen's house), a fortified house of the same period. Jules-Adler Museum : 19thC paintings and drawings *(2-5:30 closed Tue.)*. ▶ At the Municipal Library : **Baumont museum** (historical archives). ▶ **Baths :** elegant 18thC **façade★★.** □

▶ Nearby

▶ **Saint-Valbert** (N4) : beautiful village washhouse and hermitage in a splendid park (animals). **Fougerolles** ® *(9 km)*: kirsch-distilling. Farther on **Distillery Museum★** *(N57, right on D308)* : houses, workshops, interiors *(2-6, 15 May-Oct. closed Tue.)*. □

Franche-Comté cuisine

Cheese in myriad local varieties rules the régional palate, but charcuterie *is also very important. Try the smoked meats and the renowned Morteau sausages known as* Jésus. *The region is a fisherman's paradise : the abundant lake and river fish (trout, carp, pike, char) are prepared* en pauchuse *(with white wine) or* en meurette *(red wine). The chickens of nearby Bresse are prized throughout France, often served with cream sauces or braised* au vin jaune. *In season, game and mushrooms enrich the menu. The gastronomic traditions of the Montbéliard region are similar to those of southern Alsace.*

■ MONTBELIARD

C2 / ® / pop. 33 300 (Doubs)

At the heart of the dense industrial development dominated by Peugeot, château Wurtemberg gives a Germanic look to the city. Until 1793, Montbéliard was a free and independent principality, famous at that time for a breed of cattle and for sausage *(saucisse)*.

▶ **Château★ :** museum commemorates native son Georges Cuvier (1769-1832), founder of the study of comparative anatomy and palaeontology. Étienne Oelmichen, a Montbéliard citizen by adoption, made the first helicopter flight on 4 May 1924 at Arbouans. The museum houses a collection of archaeology : 19th-20thC painting *(10-12 & 2-6, closed Tue.)*. ▶ **Place St. Martin :** 18thC town hall, Beurnier mansion, **Museum of Old Montbéliard :** costumes, furniture; *(2-4 Jul.-Sep., closed Tue.)*; Temple of St. Martin (18thC Protestant church). ▶ Place Denfert-Rochereau : market buildings (16th-17thC). ▶ Peugeot factories : in business (first as a steel foundry) continuously since 1810; entry near the Bonal stadium NE of town *(visits weekdays 8:30 am; 3 hr, closed Aug.)*. □

▶ Nearby

▶ Church of Sacré Cœur in **Audincourt★★** *(6 km SE;* 1951) : mosaic, stained glass, tapestry designed by the painter Fernand Léger (1881-1955). **Mandeure** *(7 km farther) :* Roman theatre. □

■ MONTBENOÎT★

BC3 / ® / pop. 163 (Doubs)

In the 12thC the Lord of Joux offered the upper Doubs Valley to monks as a penitential offering; the monks established the abbey of Montbenoît in the Val du Saugeais, whose villages formed an independent republic, populated largely by Swiss. The area still preserves unique characteristics including dialect. Church : (12th-16thC) statuary, choir **stalls★★** (16thC); **cloister★** (15thC). □

■ MOREY

A1

A peaceful village on the flank of La Roche (view★★) with a public park.

▶ **Chauvirey-le-Châtel** *(10 km N) :* 15thC chapel of St. Hubert (carved stone altarpiece). □

■ MOREZ and tour of the Gorges★

▶ Circuit *(approx 68 km, half-day)*

B4 *(see map 4)* (Jura)

A country of high plateaux, deep gorges, hidden valleys.

▶ **Morez** ® : in a narrow pass along the Bienne (Jourdain museum, Thu. and Fri., Museum of Spectacle Manufacture, *Wed., Thu., Fri., 2-6*). ▶ Before reaching Lézat, leave the **Bienne gorges★** and climb to the turn-off to **La Rixouse :** right road to **Lake Abbaye** *(12 km)*. ▶ Views of the gorges before you reach **Saint-Claude** (→) : detour to the **Queue de Cheval** (horsetail) **waterfall★** and the **Crêt Pourri★** (alt. 1 025 m). ▶ The **Flumen gorges★ :** beyond a tunnel, the *corniche* (cliff road) offers a glimpse of the waterfall before forming a hair-

4. Morez and tour of the Gorges

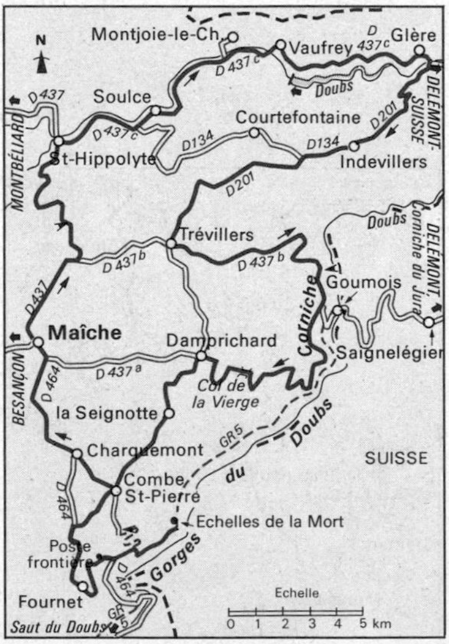

pin bend at the **Chapeau de Gendarme** (policeman's cap), rock formation dating from the Tertiary era. ▶ After **Septmoncel,** leave the road for the Faucille Pass on the right (→). ▶ **Lamoura** ® : on the edge of a winter sports plateau just before the lake pass; on the right, **Crêt Pela** (alt. 1 495 m) in the **Massacre forest★.** ▶ After **Prémanon,** lookout over the Arcets natural amphitheatre. □

■ MORTEAU

C1 / ® / pop. 6 699 (Doubs)

Morteau is a relatively new town rebuilt during the 19thC after a disastrous fire. Numerous watchmakers; visits to the bell foundry *(Rue Louhière, weekdays; closed 1 month in summer).* □

▶ Nearby

▶ Upstream, the Doubs runs through the Coin de la Roche pass *(D437)* at the foot of the village of **Grand'Combe-Châteleu★★** ®, which has many of the traditional *tué* houses (see box); church, Baroque altarpiece. ▶ The **Doubs gorges★★ :** downstream from Morteau, **Villers-le-Lac** ® : watch collection in the France mansion. Take a boat to explore the **Saut** (waterfall) **du Doubs★★★** beyond **lake Chaillexon★★,** or drive *(follow road signs; 25 mins on foot).* □

■ NEUBLANS★

A3 / pop. 383 (Jura)

The **château de Neublans** was built for an 18thC president of the Parliament of Franche-Comté; the stables are almost as beautiful as the house *(no visits).* □

■ NOZEROY★

B3 / pop. 452 (Jura)

Nozeroy is a former stronghold in the middle of an unspoilt plateau crossed by the Serpentine river. Two gateways and part of the ramparts of the 16thC château des Chalon, ruined in the Revolution, still attest to its former grandeur. ▶ 16thC church; old houses in the Grand-Rue. □

▶ Nearby

▶ **Mièges** *(2 km N) :* 16th-17thC church, once part of a priory; rich furnishings, Flamboyant Gothic chapel. ▶ S of Nozeroy, Serpentine waterfalls and the **Source de l'Ain★** *(paths from D283).* □

■ OGNON Valley★

▶ From Lure to Pesmes *(approx 120 km, full day)*
B2

The river Ognon runs down from the Vosges mountains to irrigate a large part of the Franche-Comté, and forms the frontier between the Haut-Saône and the Doubs departments for two-thirds of its course. The pleasant valley is ideal for exploring on foot or by bicycle.

▶ **Lure** (→ Ronchamp). ▶ **Villersexel** ® (B1) : 19thC château *(3-6;* furniture, history). To the west, ruined priory of **Marast** (12thC) and feudal fortress of **Oricourt.** ▶ **Montbozon :** 16thC château. ▶ In the western valley, châteaux of **Bellevaux** *(D209)* and **Sorans** *(N57)* (both 18thC). ▶ Pretty 16thC château at **Buthiers.** ▶ **Voray-sur-l'Ognon :** large **church** with cupola, late 18thC. ▶ **Etuz** ® : colonnaded village **wash-house** (18thC). ▶ **Moncley★★ : château** (18thC) is perhaps the most beautiful in Franche-Comté, surrounded by trees, convex towards the courtyard, concave to the garden side *(Sat. and Sun. 2:30-6:30 15 Apr.-15 Sep.;* furniture, wallpapers★). ▶ **Marnay** ® : old houses near the fortified château and the church (15th-16thC, statuary). **Acey abbey** (founded 12thC; rebuilt 18thC) a Cistercian centre for Gregorian chant. ▶ **Malans :** a feudal fortified farmstead that assumed its present aspect in the 16th and 19thC; 2nd Empire (ca. 1850) furniture *(3-5 closed Tue., 15 Jun.-15 Sep.).* ▶ **Pesmes★** ® : a splendid site over the river where ramparts and château recreate the past; church★ (13th-14thC) furnishings, fine statuary. Chapel of Andelot★ (Renaissance) marble. An attractive setting, with excellent facilities for summer holidays. □

Gustave Courbet

Gustave Courbet was born at Ornans in 1819. He abandoned the study of law to take up painting, and, disdaining the subject matter chosen by recognised artists, switched from Romanticism to Realism. His preferred subjects were daily life, rural poverty and Comtois landscapes. In 1852 he became a supporter of the social theorist Proudhon. He took part in the Commune of Paris (1871) but was ruined when convicted for dismantling the Vendôme column. He went into exile in Switzerland where he died in 1877.

■ ORNANS★★

B2-3 / ® / pop. 4 234 (Doubs)

Home town of the painter Gustave Courbet (→ box) who found much of his inspiration there *(museum in his birthplace, 9h30-12 & 2-6 Apr.-Nov.; closed Tue. the rest of year).* The wooden balconies of the houses overhang the river Loue (view★★ from the Grand Pont), which broadens a little farther into a pond called the Miroir (Mirror). The village is the tourist centre of the valley, but has kept a simple rustic charm; choir stalls and 18thC altarpiece in the church. □

▶ Nearby

▶ Via the Puits Noir ravine *(D67 then right)* to the **Grotte de Plaisir-Fontaine** (cavern). ▶ Farther north *(D67 and D112),* **Foucherans :** rural museum *(Sun. by request, tel. 81.86.73.20);* and **Trépot :** old cheese dairy★ *(2-6, Jun., Jul., Aug.).* ▶ **Poudrey chasm** *(14 km by D492) :* mineral formations, subterranean river, immense subterranean hall (600 m in circumference, 110 m deep) *(May-Sept. 8:30-12 & 1:30-7; Mar., Apr., Oct., Nov., 9-12 & 2-6; closed Wed.).* □

The lion of Sochaux

Belfort has a stone lion, whereas Montbéliard has a lion of a different sort : the Peugeot lion. The Peugeots, originally weavers, have been continuously in business since the early 19thC. A steel foundry opened in 1810 produced first tools then bicycles; in 1899 the Peugeots, in association with Serpollet, produced a three-wheeled car. The Peugeot automobile factory opened in 1897; a second factory, at Sochaux, opened in 1912. Tools, bicycles and cars remain the basis of Peugeot's continuing success.

■ POLIGNY

B3 / ® / pop. 5 182 (Jura)

Poligny is a wine-producing centre located in a blind valley *(reculée)* cutting into the main plateau of the Jura. It is also the acknowledged centre of the Comté cheese industry.

▶ Infirmary *(Hôtel-Dieu)* and 17thC houses around the **church of St. Hippolyte** (15th-16thC) : fine collection of Burgundian statues, 15thC altarpiece, 18thC wood panelling. ▶ National Dairy Industry School (Place du Champ-de-Foire) fosters progress in the regional industry. ▶ Near Champagnole, N5 offers views of the **Culée de Vaux** behind Poligny. □

■ PONTARLIER

B3 / ® / pop. 18 800 (Doubs)

Pontarlier is a commercial and holiday centre of the upper Doubs. The surrounding country-side is more interesting than the town itself, which was rebuilt in the 18thC (commemorative arch); statuary in the church of St. Bénigne; municipal museum *(daily, 2-6, closed Sun.)*, Franche-Comté painting, archaeology. □

▶ Nearby

▶ **Entreportes Pass** *(D47 E)* : rocks, meadows and firs; a popular place for a stroll. ▶ **Fort du Larmont; château de Joux★★** (Arms museum; *9-12 & 2-6:30 Jul.-Aug., 5 pm in Jun.; Sat. and Sun. Apr.-Oct.*) rebuilt by Vauban; Toussaint L'Ouverture (1743-1803), who led the slaves of Santo Domingo in their struggle for freedom, died at Fort de Joux, where he had been imprisoned on the personal orders of Napoleon. The fort overlooks the 200 m deep valley of **La Cluse-et-Mijoux★★.** ▶ Recreation facilities on **Saint-Point lake,** and along the Doubs, especially at **Malbuisson** ®. ▶ **Métabief** ®, **Les Hôpitaux-Neufs** ® and **Jougne** ® *(21 km S)* are winter sports centres near Mont d'Or (alt. 1 463 m). □

■ The REVERMONT Region

A4

As you look over the plain of Bresse towards distant Burgundy, pastures gradually turn into vineyards. Here, on the borders of the Comté, south of Lons-le-Saunier, *D59, D10,* then *D117* thread through a historic landscape.

▶ From **Montaigu,** view★★ over Lons and the surrounding area; house of Rouget de Lisle (see Lons-le-Saunier). Another remarkable view★★ at **La-Croix-Rochette** *(9 km farther on, right).* ▶ Right again, ruins of the fortified château in **Présilly.** ▶ **Orgelet** and **Arinthod** ® : small market towns with arcade houses. ▶ **Saint-Hymetière : Romanesque church★★** on the west side of the village. ▶ W to the Suran valley : **Montfleur** (17thC château, former mediaeval stronghold). ▶ **Andelot-les-Saint-Amour :** 15th-16thC château. ▶ **Gigny :** 10thC **Romanesque church★,** remains of a Cluniac abbey. ▶ **Cressia★ :** 15thC château in an old town, picturesque but less well-situated than ▶ **Saint-Laurent-la-Roche** (view★★). □

■ RONCHAMP★★★

C1 / ® / pop. 3 139 (Haute-Saône)

The **chapel of Notre-Dame du Haut de Ronchamp★★,** although dedicated to peace, has fallen victim to several wars. It was most recently rebuilt in 1955 by the architect Le Corbusier (1887-1965) who created a major work of art here.

▶ The design of the chapel unites elegance, functional aptitude (external choir for pilgrims) and technical expertise (concrete roof shell) to make a beautiful place of meditation *(9-8 Apr.-Oct., 10-4 Nov.-Mar.).* ▶ In the village, where coal was mined until 1958, the **Maison de la Mine★** (mining museum, arts centre; *3-6, May-Sep.*). □

▶ Nearby

▶ Planche des Belles Filles (alt. 1 150 m) downhill and cross-country skiing; view. ▶ **Lure** ® *(12 km W) :* Sub-prefecture located in an 18thC building — sole remainder of the local abbey. □

A brief vocabulary of the Jura

***Affouage :** communal system for sharing firewood, sometimes in proportion to the area of each household's roof.*
***Baroichage :** "Republic" of villages around Pontarlier, founded in the 13thC.*
***Baume :** cave or grotto (Celtic origin).*
***Brési or brésil :** smoked beef, similar to the dried beef of Grisons.*
***Chablis :** dead forest trees to be cut down.*
***Chalet :** a cowherd's or cheesemaker's shelter on an alpine pasture.*
***Châtenage :** enclosed meadow.*
***Chaux :** limestone desert or heath.*
***Cluse :** perpendicular passage between two high mountain valleys.*
***Combe :** high valley running down the axis of a mountain (as in the English "coomb" or "cum", e.g. Cumberland).*
***Couvert :** shingled wooden lean-to covered by the roof overhang.*
***Crêt :** mountain summit.*
***Fouletot :** a goblin who lurks, so they say, under the fir trees.*
***Foyard :** the local name for the beech.*
***Fruitière :** coopérative association of milk*

producers for the manufacture of Comté *cheese, in existence since the Middle Ages; by extension the place where* Comté *is made.*
Garide : *grassy limestone heath.*
Houteau : *the kitchen in traditional rural houses.*
Jésus : *smoked sausage from Morteau.*
Joux : *forest of fir, sometimes interspersed with beech.*
Levée : *ramp giving access to the barn or upper floor of a house in the Jura.*
Morge : *bacterial flora in the crust of Comté.*
Pessière : *forest of spruce (pesses), sharper and darker than fir.*
Planche : *unit for measuring the volume of a treetrunk (33 planches/m^3).*
Poêle : *heated room in the house, serving as bedroom and, for special occasions, dining room.*
Pré-bois : *meadows dotted with clusters of trees.*
Reculée : *a deep notch or blind valley in the Jura caused by the successive collapse of caves or grottos, exposing the river that dug them.*
Rouliers : *men of Grandvaux who used to convoy treetrunks down to the Atlantic ports for ships' masts, and spend the autumn selling their produce from pushcarts throughout France.*
Tavaillons : *wooden panels covering the walls on the exposed face of a house, today replaced by zinc sheeting.*
Tué : *central room of the house, built of wood, forming a chimney hood, where the oven is situated for heating the house, smoking meat, drying forage (the chimney leads through the hayloft); sometimes providing an escape route from the house when snow blocks other exits. The tué goes through the roof via a cut-off pyramid closed by movable shutters.*
Val : *in the Jura landscape, a high valley between two peaks.*
Vouivre : *a mythical winged serpent haunting chasms and water.*
Yorbe : *in the Montbéliard district, a turreted spiral staircase.*

■ Les ROUSSES

B4 / ® / pop. 2 573 (Jura)

A winter sports resort that is also a pleasant spot in summer on a 1 100 m high plateau. Fine view from the church; walks, especially towards the fort (19thC), the **Rousses lake★** and the **Risoux Forest** (partly in Switzerland). Lac Leman (Lake Geneva) is only 24 km away. □

■ SAINT-CLAUDE

B4 / ® / pop. 14 100 (Jura)

Saint-Claude lies along a terrace★ between the Bienne gorges and Tacon. Diamond-cutting and pipe-making (more than 3 million pipes a year) are the main industrial activities.

▶ **Cathedral★ :** 14th-15thC with 18thC façade; vestige of a famous abbey with noteworthy choir stalls★★ and altarpiece★. ▶ **Pipes exhibition** *(left of cathedral; 9:30-11:30 & 2-6:30, Jun.-Sep.);* **display of precious stones** *(next door, same hours).* ▶ Nearby, **church of Saint-Lupicin★** *(12 km W);* **chapel of Saint Romain** (view over the Bièvre Valley; *15 km W*); Morez, and tour of the gorges (→). □

Tobacco pipes

The use of tobacco pipes spread throughout France with tobacco, imported from the New World, beginning in the 16thC and achieving wide popularity by the 18thC. Since 1854, craftsmen at Saint-Claude have turned stems and bowls of briar-root imported from the Mediterranean basin. Measurement, rough-cutting, drilling, trueing, counter-sinking and grinding are the major manufacturing operations in the production of 3 million pipes per year.

■ SAINT-LAURENT-EN-GRANDVAUX

B4 / ® / 1 813 (Jura)

Saint-Laurent (alt. 908 m) is the main settlement of the Grandvaux plateau; zinc has replaced the wooden panels that used to protect the houses from the weather. In times gone by, the *rouliers* (see Brief Vocabulary of the Jura) used to leave here in the autumn to carry local products all over France on their carts; in the spring they returned to work on the land.

Louis Pasteur

Son of one of Napoléon's soldiers turned tanner, Louis Pasteur was born in Dole in 1822. At the age of five, he moved with his family to Arbois, where he returned to spend the rest of his life after completing brilliant studies in Besançon and Paris. He studied fermentation in both wine and beer, and was able to demonstrate that the process was due to the action of microorganisms. He showed that milk could be rendered safe and preserved by heating to 75°C (the process later called "pasteurisation" in his honour). His studies of the silkworm made important contributions to the silk industry. His identification of the staphylococcus and streptococcus germs, together with his development of vaccines for rabies and anthrax, laid the foundations of bacteriology and spared untold suffering. The rigour of his approach, the importance of his discoveries and the breadth of his interests caused Pasteur to be considered, even in his own lifetime, as one of the greatest of scientists and a benefactor of mankind. He died in 1895.

▶ Saint-Laurent is a base for exploring the wooded mountains of the Crête de la Joux-Devant, the Mont Noir forest and the Pic de l'Aigle (→ Hérisson falls). ▶ **Lake Abbaye** *(7 km SW)* : private property; aquatic sports for a fee. ▶ 9 km on the other side of the Savine pass (alt. 991 m), **Morbier** ® : gave its name to a cheese now produced at Morez (→). □

The cheeses of Comté

Comté is an important dairy region (more than 300 000 milk cows) largely relying on the Pie de l'Est *(piebald red and white) and the* Montbéliard *(white flecked with red) breeds. Franche-Comté produces several fine cheeses, of which* comté *is generally acknowledged as the best. Six hundred litres of milk are used for every 50 kg mould of cheese. The milk is partly skimmed, then curdled by heating under pressure ; the curd is reheated, stirred, moulded and pressed. It is then matured for 6 months in cellars maintained alternately at 16-18°C and 10-12°C, during which the rind is rubbed with coarse salt. The finished product is solid, with very few holes, unlike its* Emmenthal *and* Gruyère *cousins. The taste is characteristically nutty.*

Morbier *is much smaller, requiring only 80 litres of milk per cheese. The initial preparation is similar to that of* ***Comté,*** *but the cheese is drained, cut horizontally, then reformed after the addition of a thin layer of wood charcoal. It is then pressed and matured for 2 months.* ***Morbier*** *can be recognised by the fine black line in the middle of the slice.* ***Vacherin,*** *an uncooked, very creamy, soft cheese is produced in the Champagnole region.* ***Cancoillotte,*** *a speciality of the Haute-Saône, is served like cream in a small pot. It is popular for breakfast and is made from pressed curds dried in the cellar, then beaten and mixed with butter and white wine. Processed or* fondue *cheeses (such as* Crème de Gruyère*) are made industrially in the region around Lons-le-Saunier and Dole.*

■ SALINS-LES-BAINS★

B3 / ® / pop. 4 180 (Jura)

On the right bank of the river Furieuse and, until the 19thC, deriving its prosperity from salt. Salt production in turn gave rise to a wood industry. The town's prosperity was defended by the Belin and Saint-André★ forts, the remains of which are visible. The warm springs (spa) and pleasant surroundings attract tourists.

▶ Church of St. Antoine (13thC Cistercian Gothic) overlooks the town. ▶ The main monuments are the Hôtel de Ville (town hall, 18thC) chapel of Notre-Dame-la-Libératrice (17thC) and the infirmary (17thC); **salt springs★★★** comparable to those at Arc-et-Senans (→) *(9-11 & 2:30-5:30 Jun.-15 Sep.; 11:30, 3:30 and 4:30 Easter-Jun.)*; 12thC galleries; old boilers and machinery. ▶ Pretty villages of **Aresches, Fonteny** and **Cernans** (SE). □

■ The valley of the SAÔNE★

B1, A2, B2

The river Saône winds through a wooded valley below the Vosges, where glazed tiles on square-topped bell-towers gleam. The water still serves 18thC wash-houses in agricultural villages, which date largely from the reconstruction following the 30 years' war (18thC). From north to south :

▶ At **Passavant-la-Rochère** (B1) : the oldest glass-blowing works in France, founded in 1475 and still in use *(2:30-5:30 May.-Oct., closed Sun. and Aug.)*. ▶ **Jonvelle :** archaeological and agricultural museum near the Roman baths *(2-6 Apr.-Oct.)*; remains of a 15thC château and 12th-16thC church with Renaissance doorway; bridge. **Jussey :** on the Amance, 18thC church and fountains. **Noroy-les-Jussey :** archaeological excavations. **Blondefontaine** *(6 km NW)* : 18thC octagonal church. ▶ **Faverney :** entombment of Christ (15thC) in the church, formerly part of an abbey, with Romanesque nave, 13thC porch, choir, flamboyant Gothic apse. **Saint-Rémy** *(N)* : regional hospital in the 18thC château. ▶ **Port-sur-Saône** ® (B1) : best stopover in the Saône valley, good leisure facilities. ▶ **Scey-sur-Saône** and **Rupt-sur-Saône :** 18thC churches, mediaeval keep. ▶ **Ray-sur-Saône :** 17th-18thC château in a park (furniture, weapons; *2:30-6:30 Sun. and nat. hols., Easter-30 Sep.)*; church with 16thC furnishings. ▶ SE of **Fresne-Saint-Mamès** (recreation area) : former abbey of La Charité (Louis XVI château); village of **Fondremand :** keep, old houses, 12th-14thC church. ▶ **Gray** (→). □

Jura wines

The slopes of Revermont, facing SSW, were first planted with vines during the Roman era. Cultivation of grapes was spread throughout the Jura during the Middle Ages. Today, vineyards covering more than 1 200 acres produce A.O.C. *white, red and rosé wines, including the* vin jaune *(yellow wines) of Château-Chalon. The five best districts are :* ***Arbois, Arbois-Pupillin, Côtes du Jura, Etoile*** *and* ***Château-Chalon.*** *The grape harvest* (vendange) *is sometimes as late as November for the Savagnin grapes used to make Château-Chalon. High production costs and low yield have made "vin de paille" extremely rare ; after a very long fermentation, only 18 litres are produced for every 100 kg of grapes. The wines of the Jura stand natural champagnisation very well. Good years : 1947, 49, 50, 53, 55, 57, 59, 61, 62, 64, 69, 71, 73, 76, 79.*

In addition to wines, Franche-Comté makes kirsch *(cherry-flavoured liqueur) in the Loue valley and* Fougerolles*, plum brandy in Haute-Saône, and* marc *(distilled from the skins and fruit left after the grape-pressing) in the vine-growing areas.*

VESOUL

B1 / ® / pop. 20 200 (Haute-Saône)

Vesoul, around the curve of La Motte (panorama★) the Prefecture of Haut-Saône, blends thriving modern industry with an old town.

▶ Old houses and mansions grouped around the **church of St. Georges** (Classical style with cupola, 18thC; furnishings, 16thC statues) in a new pedestrian precinct. ▶ Rue des Ursulines, **G. Garret Museum** *(Wed., Sat., Sun. 2-6)*: local archaeology, paintings. ▶ Former hospital (17thC) and fortified mediaeval gateway to the north.

▶ Nearby

▶ W, **Lake Vaivre;** Roman camp of Cita; then *(12 km by D13, left)* the **Baignes forges** (18thC). ▶ S, the Rocher de la Baume and the cave of Solborde. ▶ On a promontory, **château de Filain** (15th-16thC) : handsome Renaissance interiors (overmantels; *visits, Jul.-14 Aug. 2-7; the rest of the year by request, tel. 84.78.33.26*). □

Lake VOUGLANS★★

AB4

The Ain was dammed in 1968 to form the third largest reservoir in France (32 km long, 16 km²). The steep, wooded banks have been left in their natural state, except where two aquatic sports centres have been established.

▶ **La Pyle Bridge** *(D470; 2 km NW)* : pilgrim church of **St. Christophe** (12th-15thC), view over the north of the lake *(take D301 right).* ▶ **Maisod** : near château, a path above the lake. Farther on, the **Regardoir belvédère★★** (lookout). ▶ S of the lake : view of the dam, 103 m high and 420 m wide; the power station produces 235 million kWh per year. □

Watches and grandfather clocks

Watches have been manufactured at Besançon since the early 17thC. Two centuries later, the town was producing nearly 300 000 of the 2.5 million made annually in all the French Jura. After regrouping and modernisation, production reached 15 million units in 1980, in spite of competition from overseas.
Movements for tall-case clocks made in the Franche-Comté were distributed all over France to be cased locally. The name comtoise (i.e., from Comté) was applied first to the mechanism and later to the whole clock. The second half of the 19thC was the golden age for grandfather clocks : painted, carved, inlaid with wood or encrusted with metal; pyramidal (the oldest), upright, or — most often — contoured. Behind the glass, the weights and movement were often decorated to match the dials, which were enamelled or laquered with flowers, royalist or revolutionary symbols, imperial eagles or republican cockerels. Les belles comtoises *are still in production in the Morez region.*

Architecture

The traditional rural house in Comté is simple and robust, adapted to the rugged climate and to the practical requirements of the people. There are three main types, according to region. ● In all cases, the house forms a single, squat block, clustered in villages in the plain and vineyard areas, and scattered in the mountains. Under a single roof you find family accommodation, stabling for horses and cattle, and a barn or hayloft. The family quarters include two main rooms : the *houteau* (kitchen) and the *poêle,* which is a bedroom and, on special occasions, a dining room as well. ● In the high Jura, thick stone walls are pierced by small openings and protected by shingles, wooden panels *(tavaillons)* or sheets of zinc on the exposed side. Family quarters and stables are on the ground floor; the first-floor hayloft is reached by a ramp. The large, overhanging roof is placed at a 45° angle. ● The *tué* (→ Brief Vocabulary of the Jura) in the heart of the house enables the family to live in isolation during the winter. ● The houses on the Saône plain are also cubes with access to the hayloft through the barn in the middle of the façade. Family quarters and stabling lie on either side and the overhanging roof juts over the gable. As in Lorraine (→), the house is set back from the street and the resulting space is used as a yard. ● In the Revermont and especially in the vineyards, a stone staircase, under the overhang, leads from the ground floor cellar to the family quarters above. Barn and stabling protected by a large overhang give directly onto the street. ● Most Comtois villages were devastated during the 30 years' war (18thC); after the French conquest, the churches were rebuilt on the same model as the houses. Thus the square, domed bell-tower is a characteristic silhouette of the region. ● Industries of the past have left numerous interesting and well-preserved architectural relics. ● Urban architecture shows few distinctive characteristics except in details. The mansions (hôtels particuliers) of the 17th-18thC are the most representative of the type.

Farmhouse on the plains

Jura farmhouse

Cross-section of a *«Tué»*

Brief regional history

BC Franche-Comté has always occupied a **strategic position** and even the Gallic Sequanii who lived there were frequently obliged to call for outside help against Germanic invasion. An appeal to Julius Caesar resulted in the establishment of a permanent garrison at Vesontio (modern-day Besançon). ● To shake off the Roman yoke the Sequanii made common cause with the Gaulish chief Vercingetorix, but met with defeat at Alésia in 52AD. Alésia has never precisely identified, but may have been either at Alaise or Salins in Franche-Comté, or in Burgundy. ● Roads and settlements attest to the **mercantile development** of the region, which lay along the north-south axis of the Roman Empire; Vesontio remained an important military base.

1st-11thC Two Greek missionaries, Ferréol and Ferjeux, evangelised the region late in the 2ndC. Their martyrdom by the Roman government failed to prevent the spread of Christianity, and Besançon became a bishopric. ● The **Burgundians,** considered by the Romans to be "the most civilised of the Barbarians", established a kingdom extending from Alsace to Provence and from the Jura to Morvan, starting in 407AD. At the same time, religious hermits in the region began to live communally in small groups, thus creating the first local monasteries. ● **Early in the 6thC, Burgundy fell to the Franks.** The conversion of the Frankish King Clovis stimulated the expansion of Christianity, and the Irish missionary monk Columban made his way to Franche-Comté to found monasteries at modern-day Luxeuil and Baume-les-Messieurs. Despite barbarian invasions throughout the 9th and 10thC, the abbeys remained untroubled centres of learning, where many agricultural improvements originated.

9th-13thC In 843, Charlemagne's empire was divided among his descendants. The allocation to Lothaire of the lands between the Rhine, the Saône and the Rhône was later seized upon by the **German emperors** as the basis of their claims to the territory. In the 10thC, the region was divided : the Jura district formed the county (comté) of Burgundy, while the Saône territories were included within the duchy (duché) of Burgundy. In 1032, the county was ceded to the German emperor, but imperial control grew progressively weaker as the power of the feudal lords increased.

14th-16thC In 1384, Philippe the Bold, who had received the duchy as a settlement from his father King Jean the Good of France, married the heiress to the county and thus **reunited the territories.** He founded a line of Grand Dukes of Burgundy whose power exceeded that of the Kings of France. ● After the death of Charles the Bold, last of the Grand Dukes, in 1477, **King Louis XI seized the Comté.** Fourteen years later, Charles VIII ceded the province to Maximilian, Emperor of Austria who, in 1493, bestowed it on his son Philip the Fair. Philip died young but, by his marriage to Joan the Mad, only daughter of the Spanish rulers Ferdinand and Isabella, left a 6-year-old son, Charles of Austria, who inherited both the Comté and Flanders from his father, ascended to the Spanish throne through his mother, and succeeded his grandfather to become the Emperor Charles V. The Comté prospered under the benevolent rule of Charles, but fared less well under his successors.

17thC

French initiatives begun in 1635 culminated in **conquest by France in 1678.** The Comté has remained part of France ever since. During the long and bitter fighting that preceded the treaty with France, local heros, such as Lacuzon (Jean-Claude Prost, 1607-81) rallied popular strength and came to personify the regional ideal of independence. Under French rule, Besançon replaced Dole as the regional capital. ● The Reformation, preached by Swiss Lutherans, took root around Montbéliard, although Catholicism remained the predominant religion of the territory.

18thC to present

Most of the churches and public buildings in Franche-Comté date from the 18thC, which witnessed concerted efforts to repair the devastating effects of long drawn-out wars. Prosperity increased with peace, and Besançon became an important intellectual and cultural centre. The ancient independent spirit of Comté fostered far-seeing social theorists, including Ledoux (see Arc-et-Senans), Charles Fourier (1772-1837) and Pierre-Joseph Proudhon (1809-65). The linchpin city of Belfort, made impregnable by Vauban as demanded by Louis XIV, offered **heroic resistance** to the sieges of 1814, 1815 and 1870. After the disastrous defeat of the French army by the Prussians at Sedan in 1870, 85 000 French soldiers managed to reach safety in Switzerland under the protection of the forts at Salins, Joux and Larmont. ● Similarly, the geography of the Jura favoured the activities of the Resistance during WWII. The strategic importance of Besançon and Belfort led to fierce fighting along the Doubs during the Liberation. Today, the region thrives on agricultural and pastoral industries, manufacturing, timber and — to a much lesser extent — tourism.

Practical information

The Region

Information : Franche-Comté : *Comité régional de Tourisme* (C.R.T.), pl. de la 1re-Armée-Francaise, 25041 Besançon Cedex, ☎ 81.80.92.55. **Doubs :** *Association départementale du Tourisme,* Hôtel du Département, av. de la Gare-d'Eau, 25000 Besançon, ☎ 81.81.80.80, ext. 380. **Jura :** *Comité départemental du Tourisme jurassien* (C.D.T.), 8, av. du 44e-R.I., 39000 Lons-le-Saunier, ☎ 84.24.19.64. **Haute-Saône :** *C.D.T.,* B.P. 117, 70000 Vesoul Cedex, ☎ 84.75.43.66. **Territoire de Belfort :** *Association départementale du Tourisme,* 3, rue de la République, 90000 Belfort, ☎ 84.21.27.95. In Paris : *Maison de Franche-Comté,* 10, rue du Colisée, 75008 Paris, ☎ 45.62.71.57.

Bookings : *Loisirs-Accueil* (S.L.A.) **Jura** and **Haute-Saône** at the C.D.T.

Maps : *Michelin* nos 66, 70 and 243 1/200 000 ; I.G.N. nos 30, 37, 38 1/100 000.

Local and regional press : *le Comtois, le Bien Public.*

S.O.S. : Doubs : *SAMU* (emergency medical service), ☎ 81.81.13.12. **Jura :** *SAMU,* ☎ 15. **Haute-Saône :** *SAMU,* ☎ 84.75.33.33. **Territoire de Belfort,** ☎ 84.21.15.15.

Weather forecast : Doubs, ☎ 81.50.47.10. **Jura,** ☎ 81.50.47.10. **Haute-Saône,** ☎ 84.93.80.80. **Territoire de Belfort,** ☎ 84.28.26.30.

Farmhouse gîtes and chambres d'hôtes : Doubs : *Relais des Gîtes de France,* Office du Tourisme, 25041 Besançon Cedex, ☎ 81.30.38.18. **Jura :** *Relais des Gîtes Ruraux du Jura,* Service L.A. **Haute-Saône :** L.A., ☎ 84.75.43.66. **Territoire de Belfort :** *Assn. Dép. du Tourisme.*

Camping : approx 120 sites. Enq : C.R.T. Franche-Comté.

Fairs and events : Mid-Mar : *carnival* at Vesoul ; **May :** *Foire Comtoise* in Besançon. Whitsun (Pentecost) : *Fête des Sapins* in Levier ; *Fête des Gentianes* in Russey. **14 Jul :** *crafts day* in Fondremand. **14 Jul-15 Aug :** *Salon des Annonciades* (contemporary regional art) in Pontarlier. **1st fortnight in Aug :** *son-et-lumière* at Château-Chalon. **15 Aug :** *son-et-lumière* at Pesmes, *Fête du Lac* at Vesoul. **1st Sun in Sep :** *Fête du Biou* in Arbois. **1st fortnight in Sep :** *Fair of French wines and gastronomy ;* **2nd fortnight in Sep :** *International Music Festival, Salon of Antique Dealers,* in Besancon.

Wines : *Société de Viticulture du Jura,* av. du 44e-R.I., B.P. 396, 39016 Lons-le-Saunier, ☎ 84.24.21.07, ext 57, publishes a brochure on wines of the Jura and can provide information.

Technical tourism : *Distillery,* 49, rue des Lavaux, 25300 Pontarlier, ☎ 81.39.04.70. Cars Peugeot, Sochaux centre, 25318 Montbéliard, ☎ 81.33.12.34, visits every mornings, 8-12. *Salt springs,* tourism office of Salins-les-Bains, ☒ 39110, ☎ 84.73.81.34. Visits daily : 9-11/2-5 : 30 Jun-Sep (11:30, 3:30, 4:30 Easter-Jun). **Art :** *Glass manufactury* at Passavount-La Rochère, 70210 Vauvillers, ☎ 84.92.44.44. Visits daily : 2:30-5:30, 9 May-27 Jul and 27 Aug-29 Sep ; Exhibition and sale.

Rambling and hiking : G.R. tracks 5, 9, 59, 559, 590, and 595 all cross the Franche-Comté. G.R. topoguides. Instructional rambling and hiking courses : *L.A.* Jura ; *L.A.* Haute-Saône. *The Assn. dép. du Tourisme du* **Doubs** publishes a brochure on GRs in the Montbéliard area. Expeditions on foot in the Jura Massif : *Accueil Montagnard,* La Chapelle-des-Bois, 25240 Mourthe, ☎ 81.69.26.19.

Riding holidays : 18 riding centres and 23 centres for horse hire. Riding holidays organised by the *S.L.A.* Jura and *S.L.A.* Haute-Saône. List of riding centres and gîtes, centres for horse hire, and Doubs blacksmiths : *Assn. dép. du Tourisme du Doubs.*

Cycling holidays : Discover the **Haute-Saône** by bicycle : *L.A. Haute-Saône ;* « 13 Circuits à Vélo » and « Le Guide du Cyclotourisme du **Doubs** » are extremely detailled brochures published by the *l'Assn. dép. du Tourisme du Doubs.*

River and canal cruises : cruises on the Saône River, the Doubs Canal, the canal linking the Rhône and Rhine rivers. Enq : *C.R.T. Franche-Comté ; groupement pour le Tourisme Fluvial,* Chambre régionale de Commerce et d'Industrie du Doubs, 30, av. Carnot, 25043 Besançon, ☎ 81.80.41.11.

Handicraft courses : Enq : *L.A.* Jura and *L.A.* Haute-Saône.

Tennis : *Ligue Régionale,* M. C. Cheval, 25770 Serre-les-Sapins.

Winter sports : Enq : *Office du Tourisme,* pl. de la 1re-Armée-Française, 25041 Besançon Cedex ; *C.D.T.* Jura. Low-cost package tours *(forfaits)* for cross-country or downhill skiing : *L.A.* Jura and *L.A.* Haute-Saône. For all enq concerning ski centres and schools : *Maison de la Franche-Comté* in Paris and *C.R.T.* Franche-Comté.
The *Grande Traversée du Jura* is a continuous cross-country track traversing the Massif. Enq : *Assn. dép. du Tourisme du* Doubs and *C.D.T.* Jura.

Hunting and shooting : Enq : *Fédérations départementales des chasseurs.* **Doubs :** 41, rue H.-Baigue, ☎ 81.53.23.30. **Jura :** 4, cité Foch, ☒ 39000 Lons-le-Saunier, ☎ 84.47.13.16. **Haute-Saône :** 5, rue P.-Curie, 70000 Vesoul, ☎ 84.75.24.43. **Territoire de Belfort :** 6, rue Denfert-Rochereau, 90000 Belfort, ☎ 84.22.28.71.

Fishing : Numerous fishing associations ; enq : *Assn. dép. du Tourisme du Doubs. Haute-Saône : Féd. dép. de la Pêche,* 3, rue de Gerlingen, 70000 Vesoul, ☎ 84.75.28.14.

Towns

ARBOIS

Dole 35, Besançon 49, Paris 401
B3 ⊠ 39600
ⓘ mairie, ☎ 84.66.07.45 (high season).

SNCF ☎ 84.66.07.62.

Hotel :
★★***Paris*** (France-Accueil), 9, rue de l'Hôtel-de-Ville, ☎ 84.66.05.67. AE, DC, Euro, Visa. 18 rm Ⓟ closed 15 Nov-15 Mar, 280. Rest. ● ♦♦♦ ♿ closed Mon eve and Tue ex school hols. With the classic skill of André Jeunet and the light and inventive style of his son Jean-Paul Jeunet, the miraculous happens. Spec : *poulet au vin jaune et morilles, mousseline de brochet, choux de saumon sauvage d'Écosse au jus de foie gras,* 90-280. Œnology lessons on request.

⛺ ★★*Municipal Les Vignes* (100 pl.), ☎ 84.66.14.12.

Restaurant :

Mont-sous-Vaudrey, ⊠ 39380, 17 km NW :
● ♦ ***Auberge Jurassienne,*** rte Léon-Guignard, ☎ 84.81.50.17 Ⓟ ♿ closed 15 Jun-1 Jul and Wed. An enjoyable stopover in relaxing surroundings. Simple but tasty fare : *jambon au Pupillin, côtes de veau aux nouilles,* 80-130.

Recommended : charcuterie (pork-butcher), *Breton,* pl. de la Liberté ; pastry, *Hersinger,* 38, Grande-Rue ; wine retailer, *Henri Maire,* La Boutière, Montigny-les-Arsures.

ARC-ET-SENANS

Besançon 37, Lons-le-Saunier 55, Paris 404
B3 ⊠ 25610
Hotels :
★***Relais*** (L.F.), Grande-Rue, ☎ 81.57.40.60. 11 rm closed 27 Jun-2 Jul/4 Oct-21 Nov, Sun eve and Mon, 100. Rest. ♦ 80-130.

Port-Lesney, ⊠ 39340, 7.5 km SE :
★★***Parc*** (L.F.), ☎ 84.73.81.41. 17 rm Ⓟ ♿ closed early Nov-Easter. 18thC manor, 250. Rest. ♦♦ 80-180.

⛺ ★★*La Halte Jurassienne,* Port-Lesney (30 pl.), ☎ 81.73.82.72.

ARINTHOD

Lons-le-Saunier 37, Bourg-en-Bresse 50, Paris 445
A4 ⊠ 39240
Hotels :
★***Tour,*** ☎ 84.48.00.05. 14 rm Ⓟ 150. Rest. ♦ Good menu, 45-90.

Thoirette, 17 km S :
★***Auberge du Pont,*** ☎ 84.76.80.46. 12 rm Ⓟ closed 1 Nov-28 Feb, 100. Rest. ● ♦ Good, unadorned Franche-Comté. cooking, 60-140.

BAUME-LES-DAMES

Besançon 29, Vesoul 48, Paris 444
B2 ⊠ 25110
ⓘ mairie, ☎ 81.84.07.13 (high season).

SNCF ☎ 81.84.00.25.

Hotels :
★★★***Château d'As,*** ☎ 81.84.00.66. AE, Visa. 10 rm Ⓟ closed Jan-Feb, Sun eve and Mon ex nat hols, 180. With a well-known restaurant. ♦♦ Spec : champagne-braised salmon, *goujonnette de sole au beurre blanc,* 220-310.
★★***Central*** (L.F.), 3, rue Courvoisier, ☎ 81.84.09.64. Visa. 12 rm closed 15-30 Nov, 15-31 Jan and Sun eve from 1 Nov to 31 Mar, 150.
★***Abbaye,*** 8, av. de Verdun, ☎ 81.84.12.13. Visa. 17 rm Ⓟ closed 1 Oct-3 Nov and in winter, Sat eve, Sun, 80. Rest. ♦ ♿ closed Sun noon, 30-70.

Pont-les-Moulins, 6 km S :
★★***Levant*** (France-Accueil), rte de Pontarlier, ☎ 81.84.09.99. AE, DC, Euro, Visa. 15 rm Ⓟ closed 2 Nov-28 Feb, 200. Rest. ♦♦ 70-150.

Hyèvre-Paroisse, 7 km E :
★★★***Ziss,*** ☎ 84.84.07.88. AE, Visa. 21 rm Ⓟ closed 8-30 Oct, 24 Dec-7 Jan and Sat noon (and eve from 1 Nov to 31 Mar), 200. Rest. ♦♦ 45-100.

⛺ ★*De Lonot* (50 pl.), ☎ 81.84.07.13.

BAUME-LES-MESSIEURS

Lons-le-Saunier 17, Dole 54, Paris 424
A3 ⊠ 39210 Voiteur
Restaurant :
♦ ***Grottes,*** ☎ 84.44.61.59 Ⓟ ♿ closed 15 Oct-30 Mar, Wed ex Jul-Aug, 50-100.

BELFORT

Besançon 98, Strasbourg 140, Paris 500
C1 ⊠ 90000
ⓘ pl. Dr-Corbis (A-B2), ☎ 84.28.12.23.

✈ Fontaine, 14 km E, ☎ 84.21.35.35.

SNCF (A3), ☎ 84.21.55.12, 84.28.50.50, 84.28.15.14.

🚌 4, rue Dr-Fery (B1), ☎ 84.28.11.29, and av. Wilson (A3), ☎ 84.28.04.86.

Car-hire : *Budget* train + auto, impasse Pershing (pl. de la Gare ; A3), ☎ 84.22.70.23, at the station, ☎ 84.28.18.35, and airport.

Hotels :
● ★★★***Hostellerie du Château Servin,*** 9, rue Gal-Négrier (B3), ☎ 84.21.41.85. AE, DC, Visa. 10 rm Ⓟ closed Aug, end Feb-early Mar, 300. Rest. ♦♦♦ Spec : *foie chaud au vinaigre de framboises,* 140-350.
★★★***Grand Hôtel du Lion,*** 2, rue G.-Clemenceau (B1), ☎ 84.21.17.00, Tx 360714. AE, DC, Euro, Visa. 82 rm Ⓟ 260. Rest. ♦♦ closed Sat and Sun noon, 1 Nov-30 Mar, 120-210.
★★***Capucins,*** 20, fg Montbéliard (A2), ☎ 84.28.04.60. Visa. Ⓟ closed 15 Dec-15 Jan, Sat and Sun low season, 199. Rest. ♦ 57-150.
★★***Modern' Hôtel,*** 9, av. Wilson (A3), ☎ 84.21.59.45. AE, Visa. 46 rm Ⓟ ♿ closed 21 Dec-7 Jan and Sun low season, 225.
★***Thiers*** (L.F.), 9, rue Thiers (C3), ☎ 84.28.10.24. Visa. 18 rm. closed 11-31 Dec, Sat eve and Sun ex Jul-Aug, 100. Rest. ♦ closed Sat and Sun eves, 80-130.

Restaurants :
♦♦ ***Le Pot-au-Feu,*** 27 *bis,* Grande-Rue (C1), ☎ 84.28.57.84. Euro, Visa ♿ closed 1-20 Aug, 1 week in Jan and in Apr, Sun and Mon, 60-150.

Offemont, 3 km N :
♦♦ ***Le Sabot d'Annie,*** 5, rue Aristide-Briand, ☎ 84.26.01.71. AE, DC, Visa Ⓟ closed Sat and Sun. Spec : *gigot de volailles farci aux pâtes fraîches, blanquette de St-Jacques,* 120-250.

Danjoutin, 3 km S on the N19 *bis :*
♦ ***Pot d'Étain,*** ☎ 84.28.31.95. Visa. Ⓟ ♿ closed 2-15 Jan, 4-22 Jul, Sat noon, Sun eve and Mon. Roger Clevenot's good and personal-

ized cooking is bound to surprise : *filets de sandre frais fumé, filets d'agneau en croûte,* 220-310.

Valdoie, 5 km N :

♦♦ ***Au Bon Accueil,*** ☎ 84.26.18.49. DC, Euro, Visa. 🅿 closed 1-25 Jul, 3-15 Jan, Sun eve and Mon. Spec : *petite terrine des deux truites sauce verte, fricassée de lotte et de homard à la niçoise, aiguillettes d'agneau sauce à la menthe,* 91-250.

Events : château : 15 Jun-15 Jul, summer eves, theatre, concerts ; 16 Jul-31 Aug, Wed. eve, concert.

Recommended : tea room, *Dame Charlotte,* pl. Grande-Fontaine, ☎ 84.28.18.62.

BESANÇON

Belfort 98, Dijon 102, Paris 411
B2 ✉ 25000

ℹ 1, pl. de la 1re-Armée-Française (B1), ☎ 81.80.92.55.

✈ Thise, 7 km NE, ☎ 81.80.40.04.

SNCF (B1), ☎ 81.80.11.58, 81.53.50.50.

🚌 9, rue Proudhon (B2).

Car-hire : *Budget* train + auto, at the station, ☎ 81.80.35.18, and 33, av. Carnot, ☎ 81.88.86.66.

Hotels :

● ★★***Gambetta,*** 13, rue Gambetta (B2), ☎ 84.82.02.33. AE, DC, Euro, Visa. 26 rm, 100.
● ★★***Nord,*** 8, rue Moncey (B2), ☎ 84.81.34.56. AE, DC, Euro, Visa. 44 rm 🅿 ♿ 160.
★★***Franc-Comtois,*** 24, rue Proudhon (B2), ☎ 84.83.24.35. AE. 22 rm 🅿 175.
★★***Moncey,*** 6, rue Moncey (B2), ☎ 84.81.24.77. Euro, Visa. 25 rm, 160.
★★***Terrass'Hôtel*** (L.F.), 38, av. Carnot (B1), ☎ 84.88.03.03. AE, DC, Euro, Visa. 38 rm 🅿 150. Rest. ♦ 52-130.

⛺ ★★★★*Plage de Chalezeule* (110 pl.), ☎ 84.88.04.26.

Restaurants :

● ♦♦ ***Le Chaland,*** Brégille Bridge, Micaud Park (C2), ☎ 84.80.61.61. Visa. 🅿 ♿ closed 1-25 Aug, Feb school hols, Sat noon and Sun. This restaurant, on the bridge of a boat, offers guaranteed fresh fish, 150-300.
♦♦ ***Le Chaudanne,*** 95, rue de Dole (A2), ☎ 84.52.06.13 🅿 ♿ closed Christmas and Feb school hols, Sat, Sun and eves. Spec : *truite au vin jaune, magret de canard au vinaigre de framboises.* Good value, 52-120.
♦♦ ***Tour de la Pelote,*** 39, quai de Strasbourg (B1), ☎ 84.82.14.58. AE, DC. closed 31 Jul-22 Aug, 24 Dec-4 Jan, Sun eve and Mon, 80-130.
♦♦ ***Poker d'As,*** 14, square Saint-Amour, ☎ 84.81.42.49. AE, DC, Visa. closed 8 Jul-5 Aug, 24 Dec-3 Jan, Sun eve and Mon. Spec : fish and seafood, 120-210.

Recommended : tea room, *Vaufrey,* 54, rue des Granges. ☎ 84.81.34.30.

CHAMPAGNOLE

Lons-le-Saunier 34, Besançon 71, Paris 426
B3 ✉ 39300

ℹ hôtel de ville, ☎ 84.52.14.56 (high season).

SNCF ☎ 84.52.04.69.

Hotels :

★★***Parc*** (L.F.), 13, rue P.-Cretin, ☎ 84.52.13.20. AE, DC, Euro, Visa. 18 rm 🅿 ♿ closed 1 Nov-1 Dec and Sun low season, 200. Rest. ♦ 50-120.
★***Franc-Comtois*** (L.F.), 15, rue G.-Clemenceau, ☎ 84.52.04.95. Visa. 14 rm. closed Oct, Sun eve and Mon, 120. Rest. ♿ 42-100.

Restaurants :

♦♦ ***Taverne de l'Épée,*** 2, rue du Pont-de-l'Épée, ☎ 84.52.03.85. Visa. closed Mon and 7-22 Jan, 45-110.
♦♦ ***Belle Époque,*** 57, rue du Mal-Foch, ☎ 84.52.28.86. AE, DC, Euro, Visa. 🅿 closed end Oct-end Jan and Wed, 65-145.

On the Geneva road, 7.5 km.

♦♦ ***Auberge des Gourmets,*** ☎ 84.52.01.64. Visa. 🅿 closed 15-30 Mar and 15 Nov-5 Dec and Sun eve, 120-210.

Guided tours : see ℹ

CLAIRVAUX-LES-LACS

Lons-le-Saunier 22, Pontarlier 77, Paris 429
B4 ✉ 39130

Hotels :

★***Commerce*** (L.F.), pl. du Commerce, ☎ 84.25.80.76. AE, DC, Euro. 21 rm 🅿 ♿ closed Sun eve and Mon, 140. Rest. ♦ closed Sep-Oct, Sun eve and Mon, 45-120.

Bonlieu, 11 km NE on the N78 :

★★***Alpage*** (L.F.), N78, ☎ 84.25.57.53. Visa. 11 rm 🅿 ♿ closed 15 Nov-26 Dec and Mon noon low season, 145. Rest. ● ♦ Quality decor and cooking. Spec : *croustade, truite belle-courtoise, magret de barbarie aux airelles,* 70-150.
★★***Poutre*** (L.F.), ☎ 84.25.57.77. AE, DC. 10 rm 🅿 closed Nov school hols, 1 Dec-1 Feb, Tue and Wed, 170. Rest. ● ♦ How beautiful is the mountain... and how sincere and good is Mr. Moureaux's cooking. Spec : *tournedos aux morilles, crêpes jurassiennes,* 80-200.

Farmhouse gîte : Boissia Village, 3 km on the N78 and D37, ☎ 84.48.34.56.

DELLE

Montbéliard 18, Belfort 19, Paris 496
C2 ✉ 90100

ℹ train station, ☎ 84.36.03.06.

SNCF ☎ 84.36.10.08.

Hotel :

★★***National*** (L.F.), 32, av. Gal-de-Gaulle, ☎ 84.36.03.97. Visa. 14 rm 🅿 closed Mon and Sun eve, 180. Rest. ♦ 120-210.

⛺ ★★*Le Passe-Loup* (150 pl.), ☎ 84.36.01.46.

DOLE

Dijon 48, Besancon 57, Paris 370
A3 ✉ 39100

ℹ 7 pl. Grévy (C1), ☎ 84.72.11.22.

SNCF (A1), ☎ 84.72.81.23, 84.72.16.75.

🚌 av. A.-Briand (A1).

Car-hire : *Budget* train + auto, bus station, ☎ 84.72.43.94 ; train station, ☎ 84.72.81.23, and airport.

Hotels :

★★★***Grand Hôtel Chandioux*** (Mapotel), 2, rue de Besancon (C1), ☎ 84.79.00.66, Tx 360498. AE, DC, Euro, Visa. 33 rm 🅿 260. Rest. ♦♦ ♿ Spec : *ragoût de lotte et écrevisses à l'aligoté blanc,* 120-210.
● ★★***La Chaumière*** (L.F.), 346, av du Mal-Juin (off B2 map), ☎ 84.79.03.45. 18 rm 🅿 closed 15-25 Jun and 15 Dec-15 Jan, Sun low season. A modern hotel in the traditional style, peaceful and comfortable, 200. Rest. ● ♦ closed Sat and Sun low season. Former farm on the

Franche-Comté

edge of the woods, classic cooking. Spec : *biscuit de brochet, filet de bœuf aux morilles à la Jurassienne,* 70-200.
★★***Nouvel Hôtel,*** 2, pl. J.-Grévy (C1), ☎ 84.79.12.11. DC, Visa. 29 rm Ⓟ ♿ closed 24 Dec-1 Feb, 197. Rest. ♦ 60-120.
★***Logis Comtois*** (L.F.), 290, av. de Genève, ☎ 84.72.24.48. Euro, Visa. 13 rm Ⓟ ﾛﾛﾛ closed Nov, Sun eve and Mon noon, 76. Rest. ♦ ♿ 40-80.
Brévans, 2 km NE :
★★***Au Village*** (L.F.), Grande-Rue, ☎ 84.72.56.40. 18 rm Ⓟ ﾛﾛﾛ closed 24 Dec-2 Jan, 180. Rest. ♦ ♿ closed 10-24 Jul, Fri eve and Sat noon (low season), Sun, 80-130.
Parcey, 10 km S on the N5 :
★★***As de Pique*** (L.F.), ☎ 84.71.00.76. AE, Visa. 15 rm Ⓟ ﾛﾛﾛ closed eve 15 Dec to end-Jan, Sun eve and Mon, 180. Rest. ♿ 80-130.

⛺ ★★*Le Pasquier* (100 pl.), ☎ 84.72.02.61.

Guided tours : see ℹ

GRAY

Besançon 46, Dijon 49, Paris 362
A2 ✉ 70100

ℹ 8, rue Victor-Hugo, Chambre de Commerce, ☎ 84.65.20.14, and Ile Sauzay (high season), ☎ 84.65.14.24.

SNCF ☎ 84.65.22.16.

Hotels :
★★***Bellevue*** (L.F.), 1, av. Carnot, ☎ 84.65.47.76. AE, DC, Euro, Visa. 15 rm Ⓟ ﾛﾛﾛ closed 15-31 Dec, Sat eve low season, 113. Rest. ♦ closed Fri eve and Sat low season, 50-73.
★★***Fer à Cheval,*** 4, av. Carnot, ☎ 84.65.32.55. AE, DC, Euro, Visa. 39 rm Ⓟ ﾛﾛﾛ ♿ closed 24 Dec-2 Jan and 4-19 Aug, 170.
Rigny, 5 km NE :
● ★★★***Château de Rigny*** (Demeure de Tradition, Relais du Silence) ☎ 84.65.25.01, Tx 362926. AE, DC, Euro, Visa. 24 rm Ⓟ ﾛﾛﾛ ♿ closed 5-31 Jan. In a 12-acre English-style park with river and small lake, 280. Rest. ♦♦♦ Spec : *salade de lapereau au vinaigre de lavande, cassolette d'escargots au beurre de poivron rouge, noisette d'agneau à l'essence de truffe,* 135-200.
Nantilly, 5 km W :
● ★★★***Relais de Nantilly*** (Relais et Châteaux), ☎ 84.65.20.12, Tx 362888. AE, DC, Euro, Visa. 20 rm Ⓟ ﾛﾛﾛ closed 1 Nov-end Mar, Feb school hols, 400. Rest. ♦♦ closed Sun eve and Mon from Dec to end Mar, 120-210.

⛺ *Municipal* (100 pl.), ☎ 84.65.16.85.

Restaurant :
♦♦ ***Relais de la Prévôté,*** 6, rue du Marché, ☎ 84.65.10.08. AE, DC, Visa. Ⓟ closed Sun eve and Mon ex nat hols. Regional specialities, 80-130.

Guided tours : see ℹ

GY

Besançon 31, Vesoul 37, Paris 382
B2 ✉ 70700

ℹ ☎ 84.32.85.28.

Hotel :
Cheval Noir, ☎ 84.32.81.55. Visa. 10 rm Ⓟ ﾛﾛﾛ closed 23 Dec-2 Jan, Sun eve and Mon, 100. Rest. ♦ 80-130.

LAMOURA

Genève 47, Lons-le-Saunier 78, Paris 483
16 km W of Saint-Claude
B4 ⛷ 1 150 m ✉ 39310 Septmoncel

Hotels :
★★***Dalloz,*** ☎ 84.42.61.45. 27 rm ♿ closed 1 Oct-10 Dec and 15 Apr-15 May, 134. Rest. ♦ 40-90.
★★***Spatule*** (L.F.), ☎ 84.42.60.23. Visa. 25 rm Ⓟ ﾛﾛﾛ closed 25 Sep-15 Dec and 25 Apr-15 Jun, 180. Rest. ♦ ♿ 80-130.

LODS

Pontarlier 22, Besançon 38, Paris 447
Vallée de la Loue, B3 ✉ 25930

Hotel :
Mouthier-Haute-Pierre, ✉ 25920, 3 km E :
★★***Cascade*** (L.F.), ☎ 84.62.19.00. 23 rm Ⓟ ♿ closed 1-21 Dec, 6 Jan-1 Feb, 190. Rest. ♦ 50-150.

LONS-LE-SAUNIER

Dole 52, Besançon 88, Paris 407
A3-4 ⚕ (1 Jun-31 Oct), ☎ 84.24.20.34 ✉ 39000

ℹ 1, rue Pasteur (B-C2), ☎ 84.24.20.63.

SNCF (B3), ☎ 84.24.01.23, 84.47.50.50.

🚌 av. Thurel (B2).

Car-hire : *Budget* train + auto, 13, av. A.-Briand, ☎ 82.24.33.80, and station, ☎ 84.24.01.25.

Hotels :
★★★***Grand Hôtel de Genève,*** 39, rue Jean-Moulin (C2), ☎ 84.24.19.11. AE, DC, Euro, Visa. 42 rm Ⓟ ♿ 300. Rest. ♦ 70-110.
★★***Gambetta*** (L.F.), 4, bd Gambetta (B3), ☎ 84.24.41.18. Euro, Visa. 24 rm Ⓟ closed 24 Dec-2 Jan and Sun low season, 115.
★★***Cheval Rouge,*** 47, rue Lecourbe (B2), ☎ 84.47.20.44. DC, Visa. 18 rm Ⓟ ﾛﾛﾛ closed 5-25 Nov, Sat (low season), 180. Rest. ● ♦♦ closed Tue. Good regional food is a tradition : *escargots aux herbes fraîches, poulet au vin jaune,* 120-210.
Pannessières, 5 km NE :
★★***Hostellerie des Monts Jura,*** ☎ 84.43.10.03. Euro. Ⓟ ﾛﾛﾛ closed 15 Jan-15 Feb, Sun eve and Mon, 100. Rest. ♦♦ 80-170.
Crançot, 10 km NE :
★***Belvédère*** (L.F., Juratel), ☎ 84.48.22.18. AE, DC, Euro, Visa. 9 rm Ⓟ ﾛﾛﾛ closed 10-20 Oct, 1 Jan-2 Feb, Sun eve and Mon low season, 200. Rest. ♦ ♿ Spec : *oreille de goret farcie de gras double aux petits lardons chauds, filet de brochet à l'essence de truffes et beurre blanc,* 62-220.
Saint-Germain-lès-Arlay, 10 km N on the N83 :
★★***Hostellerie Saint-Germain,*** ☎ 84.44.60.91. 10 rm Ⓟ ﾛﾛﾛ closed Nov and Tue, 180. Rest. ♦♦ 70-120.

⛺ ★★★*La Marjorie* (120 pl.), ☎ 84.24.26.94.

Restaurants :
♦***Relais des Trois Bornes,*** 11, pl. Perraud (B1), ☎ 84.47.26.75 Ⓟ closed 1-25 Sep, Fri eve, Sat and Sun eve, 60-90.
Courlans, 6 km E :
● ♦♦ ***Auberge de Chavannes,*** ☎ 84.47.05.52. AE, DC. Ⓟ ﾛﾛﾛ closed Tue and Wed. To guarantee quality, Pierre Carpentier restricts the number of diners. Spec : *gâteau de veau à la brunoise de truffes fraîches, filet de lapin fermier,* 120-250.

Recommended : pastries and sweets, *Barillot,* 22, rue du Commerce, ☎ 84.24.51.80.

LURE

Vesoul 30, Belfort 33, Paris 481
B-C1 ⊠ 70200

ℹ 6, rue de la Font, ☎ 84.62.80.52.

SNCF ☎ 84.30.15.59.

Hotels :
★★***Commerce*** (L.F.), pl. de la Gare, ☎ 84.30.12.63. 24 rm Ⓟ 180. Rest. ♦ ♿ closed Fri eve and Sat (Oct-Feb), 80-130.

Champagney, ⊠ 70290, 15 km E on N19 and D4 :
★***Commerce,*** 4, av. du Gal.-Brosset, ☎ 84.23.13.24. AE, DC, Visa. 25 rm Ⓟ closed 3 weeks in Feb, 2 weeks in Oct and Mon, 100. Rest. ♦ 80-130.

LUXEUIL-LES-BAINS

Vesoul 28, Belfort 52, Paris 372
B1 (Apr-Nov) ⊠ 70300

ℹ 1, rue des Thermes, ☎ 84.40.06.41.

SNCF ☎ 84.40.22.03.

Hotels :
★★★***Beau Site,*** 18, rue des Thermes, ☎ 84.40.14.67. 44 rm Ⓟ ♿ closed 24-30 Dec, Fri eve and Sat from 1 Nov to 1 Apr, 230. Rest. ♦ closed Fri eve and Sat 1 Nov-1 Apr, 60-120.
★★***Thermes,*** rue des Thermes, ☎ 84.40.03.67. 21 rm ♿ closed 30 Sep-1 May, 180.
★★***France,*** 6, rue G.-Clemenceau, ☎ 84.40.13.90. AE, DC, Visa. 20 rm Ⓟ closed 1-31 Jan and Sun eve, 155. Rest. ♦ ♿ 51-120.
★***Ermitage,*** 21, rue Marcel-Donjon, ☎ 84.40.15.64. 24 rm Ⓟ closed 15 Oct-1 Nov, 60. Rest. ♦ 40-80.

Faucogney-et-La Mer, ⊠ 70310, 15 km W :
★***Coq Gaulois*** (L.F.), ☎ 84.49.30.89. Visa. 12 rm Ⓟ ♿ closed Sep and Mar, 70. Rest. ♦ ♿ closed Sun eve and Mon, 40-120.
⛺ ★★★*Stade Maroselli* (100 pl.), ☎ 84.40.02.39.

Restaurants :
♦♦ ***Thermes,*** 4, rue des Thermes, ☎ 84.40.18.94. DC, Visa Ⓟ closed 1-15 Oct, 1 week at Easter school hols and Wed eve and Sun eve (Oct-Apr), 40-180.

Fougerolles, ⊠ 70220, 9 km N :
♦ ***Au Père Rota,*** 8, Grande-Rue, ☎ 84.49.12.11. Ⓟ ♿ closed 21 Feb-3 Mar, 1-7 Jul, 17 Nov-6 Dec, Sun eve and Mon, 110-120.

MAÎCHE

Belfort 60, Besançon 75, Paris 485
C2 ⊠ 25120

Hotels :
★★***Panorama,*** coteau Saint-Michel, ☎ 81.64.04.78. 32 rm Ⓟ closed 5 Nov-26 Dec, 160. Rest. ♦ closed Sun eve and Mon, 1 Oct-Easter ex school hols, 84-168.

Charquemont, ⊠ 25140, 6 km SE :
★★***Poste*** (L.F.), 6, pl. de l'Hôtel-de-Ville, ☎ 81.44.00.20. Visa. 32 rm Ⓟ closed 1-15 Nov, 145. Rest. ♦ ♿ closed Sun eve and Mon noon low season, 50-80.

Damprichard, ⊠ 25450, 7 km E :
★★***Lion d'Or,*** 7, pl. Centrale, ☎ 81.44.22.84. DC, Euro, Visa. 19 rm ♿ closed Oct, 147. Rest. ♦ closed Sun eve low season, 55-108.

Charquemont :
● ♦♦ ***Au Bois de la Biche,*** Le Boulois (N464), ☎ 81.44.01.82. Euro, Visa Ⓟ closed 15 Nov-6 Dec and Mon eve. Good regional dishes and game at this Franche-Comté farm. Spec : *croûte aux moules, poularde au champagne,* Jura wines, 67-140.

Event : horse festival, last Sun in Aug.

MALBUISSON

Pontarlier 16, Besançon 74, Paris 469
B3 900-1 000 m ⊠ 25160

ℹ ☎ 81.69.31.21.

Hotels :
★★★***Lac,*** Grande-Rue, ☎ 81.69.34.80, Tx 360713. DC, Euro, Visa. 53 rm Ⓟ closed 2-13 Dec, 168-234. Rest. ♦♦ ♿ 60-125.
★★★***Terrasse*** (L.F.), ☎ 81.69.30.24. AE, DC, Euro, Visa. 23 rm Ⓟ closed 10 Nov-1 Feb, 200. Rest. ♦♦ 80-188.
★★***Bellevue,*** ☎ 81.69.30.89. DC, Visa. 12 rm Ⓟ closed 30 Nov-20 Dec, 3-18 Jan, 15 Apr-1 May, Mon eve and Tue ex 15 May-15 Sep and winter, 151. Rest. ♦ ♿ 65-200.
★★***Fuvelle,*** 8, Grande-Rue, ☎ 81.69.30.12. 14 rm Ⓟ closed 1 Oct-20 Dec, 15 Apr-15 May, 150. Rest. ***Le Chevreuil,*** closed 8 Nov-15 Dec and Thu, 50-80.
★***Bon Accueil,*** ☎ 81.69.30.58. 16 rm Ⓟ closed 30 Oct-20 Dec and 15-30 Apr, Wed low season, 100. Rest. ♦ 50-130.

⛺ ★★*Les Fauvettes* (300 pl.), ☎ 81.69.31.50 ; Saint-Point, 6 km, ★★*Municipal* (80 pl.), ☎ 81.89.40.18.

Leisure activities : sailing circuit (St-Point Lake), ☎ 81.75.12.50 and 81.69.32.33.

MARNAY

Besançon 21, Dijon 63, Paris 376
Vallée de l'Ognon, B2 ⊠ 70150

ℹ ☎ 84.31.74.42 (high season).

Hotels :
★***Commerce,*** 64, Grande-Rue, ☎ 84.31.74.88. Euro. 16 rm closed 15 Sep-15 Oct, 90. Rest. 40-85.

Cussey-sur-l'Ognon, ⊠ 25860, 16 km NE :
★★***Vieille Auberge*** (L.F.), ☎ 84.57.78.35. Euro, Visa. 10 rm Ⓟ closed Feb school hols, Sun eve and Mon, 140. Rest. ● ♦♦ closed Sun eve and Mon. Varied, unpretentious cooking in a classic setting. Spec : *saumon au gros sel, croûte aux morilles, carré d'agneau aux trois moutardes,* 50-120.

Restaurant :
Étuz, 15 km NE :
● ♦♦ ***La Sablière,*** rte de Cussey-sur-l'Ognon, ☎ 81.57.78.50. AE, DC, Visa Ⓟ ♿ closed 19 Aug-10 Sep, 20 Feb-3 Mar, Sun eve and Thu. Solidly traditional fare : *girolles* and game (in season), 85-200.

MÉTABIEF

Pontarlier 16, Lons-le-Saunier 77, Paris 472
8 km E of Malbuisson, B3 1 000-1 400 m
⊠ 25370 Les Hôpitaux-Neufs

ℹ Les Hôpitaux-Neufs, ☎ 81.49.13.81.

Hotels :
★***Étoile des Neiges*** (L.F.), ☎ 81.49.11.21. Visa. 15 rm Ⓟ closed 15 Apr-15 Jun, 15 Sep-15 Dec, 130. Rest. ***Le Bief Rouge*** ♿ 45-80.

Les Hôpitaux-Neufs, 3 km E :
★***Robbe*** (L.F.), ☎ 81.49.11.05. 21 rm Ⓟ closed 10 Sep-20 Dec and 20 Apr-30 Jun, 110. Rest. ♦ 40-80.
★***Chamois,*** ☎ 81.49.11.18. 18 rm Ⓟ closed end-Apr to end-Jun, 20 Sep-15 Dec, 120. Rest. ♦ 60-130.

Jougne, 3 km S :
★★***Bonjour*** (L.F.), ☎ 81.49.10.45. Visa. 18 rm ⚘ Ⓟ ♨ ⚓ ✂ ♿ closed 15 Sep-23 Dec and 7 Apr-15 Jun, 143. Rest. ♦ ✂ ♿ 55-125.
★★***Deux Saisons,*** ☎ 81.49.00.04. DC, Visa. 21 rm ⚘ Ⓟ ♨ ⚓ ♿ closed 1 Oct-15 Dec, 20 Apr-30 May, 145. Rest. ♦ 47-91.
★★***Poste*** (L.F.), ☎ 81.49.12.37. Visa. 15 rm ⚘ closed 1 Oct-15 Dec and 15 Apr-20 May, 120. Rest. ♦ ✂ ♿ 50-130.
★***Au Col des Enchaux*** (L.F.), ☎ 81.49.10.75. DC, Euro, Visa. 18 rm ⚘ Ⓟ closed 15 oct-15 Dec and 15 Apr-1 Jun, 120. Rest. ♿ 40-120.

MONTBÉLIARD

Belfort 22, Besançon 82, Paris 483
C2 ✉ 25200

Hotels :
★★***Balance,*** 40, rue de Belfort, ☎ 81.91.18.54, Tx 360724. Visa. 41 rm Ⓟ ⚓ 135.
★★***Joffre,*** 34 *bis,* av. du Mal-Joffre, ☎ 81.94.44.64, Tx 360724. Visa. 30 rm ♿ closed 1-15 Aug and 25 Dec-1 Jan, Sun low season, 170.

Restaurant :
♦♦♦ ***Tour Henriette,*** 59, fg Besançon, ☎ 81.91.03.24. AE, DC, Euro, Visa ♿ closed 27 Jul-25 Aug, eves Sun, Mon. Spec : *ris de veau des gourmets, croustade de morilles,* 97-280.

Farmhouse-inn : *La Forge d'Isidore,* 70400 Villers-sur-Saulnot, 13 km on the N83 and D33, ☎ 84.46.35.89.

MONTBENOÎT

Pontarlier 14, Besançon 68, Paris 466
B-C3 ✉ 25650

ⓘ ☎ 81.38.10.32.

Hotel :
Gilley, 8 km N on the D131 :
★***Gare,*** 7, rue de la Gare, ☎ 81.43.30.94. 13 rm Ⓟ ♨ closed 20 Sep-20 Oct and Mon low season, 65. Rest. ♦ 40-80.

Arc-sous-Cicon, 15 km NW :
Farmhouse-inn : *La Masure,* ☎ 81.38.23.23. 7 rm.

MOREZ

Lons-le-Saunier 58, Pontarlier 70, Paris 460
B4 ⛷ 830, 1 028, 1 360 m ✉ 39400

ⓘ pl. J.-Jaurès, ☎ 84.33.08.73.

SNCF ☎ 84.33.01.33.

Hotels :
★★***Poste,*** 1, rue du Dr-Regad, ☎ 84.33.11.03. AE, DC, Euro, Visa. 44 rm ⚘ Ⓟ ♨ ⚓ ♿ closed 15 Nov-20 Dec, 165. Rest. ● ♦♦ closed Mon. Good cooking served without pretention : *jambon de Morteau gratiné, croûte aux morilles,* 58-150.
★★***Commerce,*** 7, rue Lamartine, ☎ 84.33.01.02. Visa. 19 rm ⚘ Ⓟ ⚓ 145.

Morbier, 3 km N :
★***Route Blanche*** (L.F.), 114, Grande-Rue, ☎ 84.33.12.78. 12 rm Ⓟ ⚓ ✂ closed Oct and Sun, 130. Rest. ♦ 40-100.

⛺ ★★*Les Pontets* (70 pl.), Morbier, ☎ 84.34.37.17.

MORTEAU

Pontarlier 31, Besancon 67, Paris 477
C3 ✉ 25500

ⓘ pl. de la Gare, ☎ 81.67.18.53 (high season), and mairie, ☎ 81.67.14.78.
SNCF ☎ 81.53.50.50.

Hotel :
★★***Guimbarde*** (L.F.), 10, pl. Carnot, ☎ 81.67.14.12. Euro, Visa. 20 rm Ⓟ ⚓ ♿ 140. Rest. ♦ closed Oct and Mon noon ex Aug, 50-110.

Farmhouse gîte and farmhouse-inn : rue de la Fruitière, Montlebon, 2 km on the N437. Produce for sale.

⛺ ★★★*Essi* (30 pl.), ☎ 81.67.17.52.

Restaurant :
Grand-Combe-Chateleu, ✉ 25570 3 km SE on the D437 :
♦♦ ***Auberge de la Roche,*** ☎ 81.68.80.05. Visa Ⓟ ♨ ♿ closed 17 Jun-1 Jul, Sun eve and Mon, 70-150.

Recommended : charcuterie, *Rieme,* 42, Grande-Rue, ☎ 81.67.07.05.

MOUTHE

Pontarlier 31, Lons-le-Saunier 76, Paris 459
15 km SW of Malbuisson B3 ⛷ 935 m
✉ 25240

Hotel :
Chatelblanc :
★★***Castelblanc*** (L.F.), ☎ 81.69.24.56. 11 rm ⚘ Ⓟ ♨ ⚓ closed 30 Sep-15 Dec, May-Jun ex nat hols, 224. Rest. ♦ ♿ 50-90.

⛺ ★★*Source du Doubs* (50 pl.), ☎ 81.69.23.57.

Sports : *Ski school and centre* (cross-country and downhill), ☎ 81.69.22.64. La Chapelle-des-Bois, ☎ 81.69.26.19.

NOZEROU

Pontarlier 33, Lons-le-Saunier 51, Paris 443
B3 ✉ 39250

Hotels :
★***Parc,*** pl. des Annonciades, ☎ 84.51.12.86. 22 rm Ⓟ ♨ ♿ 80. Rest. ♦ 58-80.
★***Taverne des Remparts,*** ☎ 84.51.13.44. 10 rm ♨ 80.

ORNANS

Besançon 26, Pontarlier 34, Paris 436
B2-3 ✉ 25290

Hotels :
★★***France*** (L.F.), 51-53, rue P.-Vernier, ☎ 81.62.24.44. DC, Visa. 31 rm Ⓟ ✂ closed 1 Dec-15 Jan, 225. Rest. ♦ closed Sun eve and Mon ex school hols, 61-150.

Bonnevaux-le-Prieuré, 6 km of the D67 and D280 :
★★★***Moulin du Prieuré*** (Moulin-Étape, Châteaux Indépendants, Relais Saint-Pierre), ☎ 81.59.21.47. AE, DC, Euro, Visa ⚘ Ⓟ ♨ ♿ closed 15 Dec-15 Mar, Sun eve and Mon low season, 250. Rest. ♦♦ 95-220.

⛺★★★*Le Chanet* (70 pl.), ☎ 81.62.23.44.

Event : Jul : *Journée de la Brocante* (second-hand goods, bric-a-brac).

PESMES

Dole 24, Besançon 40, Paris 360
A2 ✉ 70140

ⓘ mairie, ☎ 84.31.22.16.

Hotels :
★★***France*** (L.F.), ☎ 84.31.20.05. Euro, Visa. 10 rm ⚘ Ⓟ ♨ ⚓ ♿ closed 20 Oct-8 Nov, 100. Rest. ♦ 60-100.

Aubigney, 7 km N :
★★***Auberge du Vieux Moulin*** (Châteaux et Hostellerie d'Atmosphère, Moulin-Étape),

☎ 84.31.21.16. 7 rm 🅿 ⚘ ✁ 240. Rest. ● ♦♦ The Mirbey sisters prepare good, traditional dishes. Spec : *lapereau en gelée, œufs en meurette*, 100-300.

⛺ ★★*La Colombière* (35 pl.), ☎ 84.31.20.20.

POLIGNY

Lons-le-Saunier 28, Besançon 60, Paris 403
A-B3 ✉ 39800

ℹ Grande-Rue, ☎ 84.37.24.21 (high season).

SNCF ☎ 84.37.20.01.

Hôtels :
Monts-de-Vaux, 5 km SE:
★★★**Hostellerie des Monts de Vaux** (Relais et Châteaux), RN5, ☎ 84.37.12.50, Tx 362952. AE. 10 rm ⚟ 🅿 ⚘ ✁ closed end Oct to end Dec, half-pension, 800. Rest. ♦♦ closed Tue and Wed noon, 150-200.
● ★★**Hostellerie Vallée Heureuse** (L.F.), rte de Genève, ☎ 84.37.12.13. AE, DC, Visa. 12 rm ⚟ 🅿 ⚘ ✁ closed 10-20 Jun and 10-30 Oct, Wed and Thu noon. A beguiling, unpretentious hotel on the banks of a trout-fishing river, 190. Rest. ● ♦♦ closed Tue eve and Wed. Calm and peace ; good, simple food, 80-160.
★★**Paris** (L.F.), 7, rue Travot, ☎ 84.37.13.87. 24 rm 🅿 ▭ closed 3 Nov-3 Feb, 180. Rest. ♦ closed Mon eve and Tue noon low season, 60-180.

Passenans, 11 km SW on the N83 and D57 :
● ★★**Revermont** (Relais du Silence), ☎ 84.44.61.02. Visa. 28 rm ⚟ 🅿 ⚘ ✁ ▭ 🎾 ♿ closed 1 Jan-1 Mar, Christmas Day, Sun eve, Mon low season. A wonderfully peaceful, comfortable hotel set in the midst of a park, 175. Rest. ♦ ✗ closed Sun eve and Mon low season, 63-150.

Recommended : Franche-Comté cheese, *Monts Jura*, rue du Pont-Chorolet ; cheese, butter and honey, *Boichol*, in Tourmont.

PONTARLIER

Besançon 58, Lons-le-Saunier 77, Paris 454
B3 ✉ 25300

ℹ hôtel de ville, B.P. 187, ☎ 81.46.48.33.

SNCF ☎ 81.39.14.88.

Car-hire : *Budget* train + auto, square Wandel, ☎ 81.39.26.66.

Hotels :
★★★**Commerce,** 18, rue du Dr-Grenier, ☎ 81.39.04.09. Euro, Visa. 30 rm 🅿 ⚘ ♿ closed 15 Jan, Mon noon and Sun eve low season, 180. Rest. ♦ 80-130.
★★**Poste,** 55, rue de la République, ☎ 81.39.18.12. AE, DC, Visa. 55 rm 🅿 closed 15 Oct-15 Dec, 180. Rest. ♦♦ ♿ closed Sun eve low season and Mon, 70-100.
★**Morteau,** 26, rue J.-d'Arc, ☎ 81.39.14.83. Visa. 19 rm. closed 15 Sep-7 Oct, 1 week in Mar and Jun, Sat eve and Sun 🅿 ✁ 110. Rest. ♦ 42-80.
★**Centre,** 7, rue du Bastion, ☎ 81.39.18.46. 15 rm 🅿 ✗ closed 1-15 May, 105.

Oye-et-Pallet, ✉ 25160 Malbuisson, 6.5 km S on the D437 :
★★**Riant-Séjour** (L.F.), ☎ 81.89.42.03. Visa. 18 rm ⚟ 🅿 ⚘ ✗ closed 3 Dec-3 Jan, 1 week early Oct, Sun eve and Mon, 220. Rest. ♦♦ ♿ closed Sun eve and Mon, 70-220.

PORT-SUR-SAÔNE

Vesoul 12, Langres 13, Paris 357
B1 ✉ 70170

ℹ mairie, ☎ 84.91.50.18.

Hotels :
★**Pomme d'Or** (L.F.), 1, rue Saint-Valère, ☎ 84.91.52.66. Visa. 9 rm ⚟ 🅿 closed 22 Aug-15 Sep and Mon, 100. Rest. ♦ ♿ 50-80.

Combeaufontaine, ✉ 70120, 12 km W on the N19 :
★★**Balcon** (L.F.), rte de Paris, ☎ 84.92.11.13. AE, DC, Euro, Visa. 26 rm 🅿 ✗ closed 26 Dec-15 Jan and Mon low season, 150. Rest. ♦♦ ♿ 65-160.

⛺ ★★★*Municipal* (130 pl.), ☎ 84.91.51.32.

Restaurant :
Vauchoux, 3 km S :
♦♦♦ **Château de Vauchoux,** ☎ 84.91.53.55. AE, DC, Euro, Visa 🅿 ⚘ ✁ ▭ 🎾 ♿ closed Feb, Mon and Tue. Louis XV stayed in this nice place. Quality fish and seafood, good wines, 130-350.

RONCHAMP

Belfort 21, Vesoul 43, Paris 492
C1 ✉ 70250

ℹ ☎ 84.20.64.70.

Hotels :
★★★**Ronchamp,** 1, rue Neuve, ☎ 84.20.60.35. Visa. 21 rm 🅿 ⚘ ✁ ♿ closed 20 Dec-30 Jan, Sun eve in winter, 165.
★**Pomme d'Or,** rue Le Corbusier, ☎ 84.20.62.12. AE, Euro, Visa. 25 rm 🅿 100. Rest. ♦ ♿ 40-130.

Les ROUSSES

Genève 47, Lons-le-Saunier 66, Paris 470
B4 ⛷ 1 120 m-1 680 m ✉ 39220

ℹ pl. Pasteur, ☎ 84.60.02.55.

Hotels :
★★★**France,** 323, rue Pasteur, ☎ 84.60.01.45. AE, DC, Visa. 34 rm 🅿 ⚘ closed 1-25 Jun and 1 Nov-17 Dec, 240. Rest. ● ♦♦ ♿ Light and inventive cooking. Spec : *raviolis d'escargots*, Bresse fowl, Jura wines, 100-160.
★★**Chamois** (L.F.), Le Noirmont, ☎ 84.60.01.48. Visa. 12 rm 🅿 ✁ closed 15 Apr-15 May and Nov, 164. Rest. ♦ 50-90.
★★**Redoute** (L.F.), N5, ☎ 84.60.00.40. Visa. 26 rm 🅿 closed May and Nov, 160. Rest. ♦ 60-140.
★★**Relais des Gentianes** (L.F.), ☎ 84.60.50.64. 14 rm 🅿 ⚘ ♿ 180. Rest. ● ♦ Good, solid classic cooking fit for hungry skiers. Spec : *truites et poulet au vin jaune, gratin de queues d'écrevisses*, 120-210.
★★**Auberge des Piles** (L.F.), Les Cressonnières, ☎ 84.60.00.44. DC, Visa. 20 rm 🅿 ⚘ ✁ ♿ closed 20 Apr-1 May, Oct, Fri eve and Sat, 160. Rest. ♦ 70-90.

Le-Bois-d'Armont, 10 km NE :
★★**Auberge du Vivier** (L.F.), 70, rte du Vivier, ☎ 84.60.03.40. 12 rm 🅿 ⚘ ✁ closed 26 Apr-10 Jun and 1 Oct-10 Dec, 180. Rest. ♦ 80-130.

⛺ ★★*Les Monts Jura* (70 pl.), ☎ 84.60.01.63.

SAINT-AMOUR

Bourg-en-Bresse 28, Lons-le-Saunier 33, Paris 412
33 km SW of Lons-le-Saunier, A3-4 ✉ 39160

ℹ pl. de la Chevalerie, ☎ 84.48.76.69 (high season), and mairie, ☎ 84.48.74.77.

Hotel :
● ★★**Alliance,** rue Ste-Marie, ☎ 84.48.74.94. DC, Visa. 16 rm 🅿 ⚘ ✁ closed Sun eve and Mon low season. Beautiful 17thC residence, 140. Rest. ♦♦ 41-108.

⛺ ★★*Municipal* (70 pl.), ☎ 84.48.71.68.

SAINT-CLAUDE

Lons-le-Saunier 60, Genève 61, Paris 467
B4 ⊠ 39200

ℹ 1, av. de Belfort, ☎ 84.45.34.24.

SNCF ☎ 84.45.03.05.

Hotels :
★★***Saint-Hubert,*** 3, pl. Saint-Hubert, ☎ 84.45.10.70. Euro, Visa. 30 rm P closed 20 Nov-6 Dec, 135-180.

Martinet, 3 km S :
● ★★***Joly*** (L.F.), ☎ 84.45.12.36. Visa. 16 rm P closed 1 Nov-31 Jan, 180. Rest. ♦♦ ♿ closed Sun eve and Mon low season. A peaceful restaurant ; artful preparation of traditional dishes. Spec : *soufflé de brochet au coulis d'écrevisses, coq au vin jaune d'Arbois*, 68-150.

Villard-Saint-Sauveur, 5 km S :
★***Au Retour de la Chasse*** (L.F.), ☎ 84.45.11.32. AE, DC, Euro, Visa. 12 rm P closed 1-22 Dec, 26 May-7 Jun, Sun eve and Mon, 150. Rest. ● ♦ This modest stopover in a Jura valley offers an array of regional treasures. Spec : *langue de bœuf salée fumée, suprême de canard aux baies de cassis*, 50-180.

⛺ ★★*Le Martinet* (130 pl.), ☎ 84.45.00.40.

SAINT-HIPPOLYTE

Belfort 50, Besançon 81, Paris 496
C2 ⊠ 25190

Hotels :
★★***Bellevue*** (L.F.), rte de Maîche, ☎ 81.96.51.53. 15 rm P closed 2 Jan-20 Feb, Sun eve and Mon noon from 1 Oct to 31 Mar, 100. Rest. ♦ closed Sun eve and Mon noon Nov to end-Mar, 80-130.

Goumois, ⊠ 25470 Trévillers, 22 km SE :
● ★★★***Taillard*** (Relais du Silence), ☎ 81.44.20.75. AE, DC, Euro, Visa. 17 rm P ♿ closed 28 Oct-1 Mar, Wed in Mar and Oct, 140-210. Rest. ♦ Spec : *caquelon de morilles à la crème double, jambon fumé du Tuyé, foie gras de canard frais*, 84-220.

⛺ ★★*Les Grands Champs* (35 pl.), ☎ 81.96.54.53.

SAINT-LAURENT-EN-GRANDVAUX

Lons-le-Saunier 46, Pontarlier 60, Paris 448
B4 ⊠ 39150

Hotels :
★★★★***Moulin des Truites Bleues*** (Châteaux-Hôtels, Moulin-Étape), ☎ 84.34.83.03, Tx 360443. AE, DC, Visa. 20 rm P 250-490. Rest. ♦♦ Spec : Jura-style beef fillet steak, 95-250.

Ilay, 10 km NW :
★***Auberge du Hérisson,*** ☎ 84.25.58.18. 14 rm P closed 15 Oct-31 Mar and Wed, 140. Rest. ♦ Home-made *charcuterie*, fresh trout, 58-90.

Foncine-le-Haut, ⊠ 39460, 16 km NE :
★★***La Terrasse et La Truite*** (L.F.), rue Principale, ☎ 84.51.53.62. 20 rm P A pleasant, unpretentious stopover, 140. Rest. ● ♦♦ ♿ Simple and tasty fare, 50-130.

⛺ ★★*Champ de Mars* (100 pl.), ☎ 84.60.14.13.

SALINS-LES-BAINS

Besançon 45, Lons-le-Saunier 52, Paris 411
B3 ⊠ 39110

ℹ pl. des Anciennes-Salines, ☎ 84.73.01.34.

Hotels :
Val d'Héry, 3 km, ☎ 84.73.06.54. Visa. 7 rm P closed 1 Dec-early Jan, Tue eve and Wed ex Jul-Aug, 180. Rest. ♦♦ 80-130.

Andelot-en-Montagne, 13 km SE :
★***Bourgeois,*** ☎ 84.51.43.77. 15 rm P closed Nov, 100. Rest. ● ♦ Good, simple cooking, 80-130.

Nans-sous-Sainte-Anne, ⊠ 25330 Amancey, 14 km NE :
★***Poste*** (L.F.), ☎ 81.86.62.57. 11 rm P closed 1 Nov-15 Jan, 1-15 Mar and Tue, 90. Rest. ♦ 40-100.

VESOUL

Besançon 47, Belfort 64, Paris 450
B1 ⊠ 70000

ℹ rue des Bains, ☎ 84.75.43.66.

SNCF ☎ 84.75.50.50, 84.15.02.12.

🚌 pl. de la Gare, ☎ 84.75.03.61.

Car-hire : *Budget* train + auto, at the station, ☎ 84.75.02.12.

Hotels :
★★★***Nord,*** 7, rue de l'Aigle-Noir, ☎ 84.75.02.56. AE, DC, Euro, Visa. 36 rm P ♿ 160. Rest. ♦♦ 68-122.
★★★***Relais,*** N19, rte de Paris, ☎ 84.76.42.42. AE, DC, Euro, Visa. 26 rm P closed 21 Dec-12 Jan, Sat and Sun in winter, 250. Rest. ♿ 60-167.
★★***Lion,*** 4, pl. de la République, ☎ 84.76.54.44. AE, Euro, Visa. 19 rm P 148-169.
★★***Vendanges de Bourgogne*** (L.F.), 49, bd Ch.-de-Gaulle, ☎ 84.75.12.09. AE, DC, Visa. 31 rm P 160. Rest. ♦ ♿ 50-80.

Youth hostel : rue Paul-Petitclerc.

⛺ ★★★*Municipal du Lac* (160 pl.), ☎ 84.76.22.86.

Guided tours : see ℹ

VILLERSEXEL

Vesoul 26, Besançon 61, Paris 475
B1-2 ⊠ 70110

Hotels :
★***Commerce,*** rue du 13-Septembre-1944, ☎ 84.20.50.50. DC, Euro, Visa. 15 rm P closed 1-15 Jan, 5-18 Oct and Mon eve, 101. Rest. ♦ 38-104.
★***Terrasse*** (L.F.), ☎ 84.20.52.11. Euro, Visa. 17 rm P closed 19 Dec-2 Jan, 130. Rest. ♦ closed Fri Sun eves low season, 50-120.

⛺ ★★*Du Chapeau Chinois* (55 pl.), ☎ 84.43.04.97.

VILLERS-LE-LAC

Pontarlier 37, Besançon 73, Paris 483
6 km W of Morteau, C3 1 100-1 290 m
⊠ 25130

ℹ rue Bercot, ☎ 81.43.00.98 (high season).

Hotels :
★★***France*** (L.F.), 8, pl. M.-Cupillard, ☎ 81.68.00.06. AE, DC, Euro. 14 rm P closed 1 Nov-31 Jan, 88-200. Rest. ♿ closed Sun eve and Mon, 88-200.
★***Saut du Doubs,*** 1, Terres-Rouges, ☎ 81.68.05.31. Visa. 10 rm P 70. Rest. ♦ ♿ 45-80.

Farmhouse-inn : *La Pierre à Feu*, 9 km on the D447, ☎ 81.43.05.41. *Terrine maison*, smoked ham, lemon tarts.

⛺ ★★*Saut du Doubs* (70 pl.), ☎ 81.43.04.97.

Ile-de-France

When we think of a region, we think of a place united by geography or history, with its own special language and customs. The Ile-de-France is an exception to the rule, since its history, customs and language have merged with those of Paris, and spread throughout the whole country. The destiny of France was played out in the Ile-de-France, in the magnificent castles of Fontainebleau, Compiègne, Provins, Chantilly, Saint-Germain and Versailles. This "garden of the kings" is in fact made up of many smaller regions whose names — Valois, Beauvaisis, Vexin, Brie, Gatinais, Hurepoix — irresistibly evoke royal banners and the pageantry of past years. Despite urban sprawl and agricultural uniformity, they still retain much of their individuality.

Square belltowers in gentle valleys under the everchanging sky, white silos on endless plains of wheat : subtle and harmonious landscapes painted and praised by Racine, La Fontaine, Corot and all the landscape painters. The region is a living museum : Gothic art was born here and there are hundreds of beautiful churches and cathedrals. Ile-de-France was populated early and its clergy benefitted from the generosity of the great lords and the royal family. The magnificent castles of Chantilly, Fontainebleau and Versailles with its magnificent royal apartments and gardens, bring the history of France to life again. The cathedral of Chartres dominates the flat wheat-covered plains of Beauce and the medieval town at its feet. Its stained glass windows mark the apogee of an art which has never yet been transcended, nor even equalled.

Thanks to the royal penchant for hunting, Paris is surrounded by forests : Fontainebleau, Compiègne, Saint-Germain-en-Laye, which attract Parisians in their thousands every weekend. There are interesting walks and hundreds of little paths where lovers of all ages stroll down leafy avenues and breathe in the freshness of these green retreats from the big city.

Sightseeing

ANET★

A2 / ® / pop. 2 430 (Eure-et-Loir)

The damaged but still majestic late Renaissance **château★** of Diane de Poitiers (1499-1566; Henri II's mistress) was the crowning achievement of the architect Philibert Delorme. The most distinguished artists of the time, including Cellini and Goujon, contributed to the decoration. ▶ The one remaining wing was much modified during the 17thC, as was the funerary chapel★ *(Apr.-Oct., 2:30-6:30; Sun. and hols. 10-11:30 & 2:30-6:30; Nov.-Mar., 2:30-6:30; closed Tue.).* □

▶ Eure Valley *(22 km from Anet to Dreux).*

▶ **Ezy-sur-Eure** ® : Gothic bridge. ▶ **Château de Sorel** (ruins) : Renaissance doorway. ▶ On the other bank of the river : disused 12thC abbey of **Breuil-Benoist** in light, golden stone, standing in a huge clearing; Louis XIII abbey manor *(visits on request).* ▶ **Saint-Georges-Motel** : château (also Louis XIII; *no visitors*) hidden in parkland. ▶ **Louye** : church and château. □

ARPAJON

C3 / pop. 8 000 (Essonne)

Heart of the French bean-growing country, marred by traffic, but with beautiful 17thC **covered market**; market-day Friday. □

▶ Nearby

▶ **Courson** *(9 km W)* : château originally built by Guillaume de Lamoignon, first president (1676) of the parliament of Paris. Gardens★, improved in 1920s by Count Ernest de Caraman, following the example of philanthropist Albert Kahn (→ Paris : Gardens), represent the French idea of an English park. *(Apr-Nov pm).* □

▶ Remarde Valley★ *(26 km from Arpajon to Saint-Arnoult).*

▶ Winds among rustic villages and elegant châteaux W of **Arpajon.** ▶ **Château du Marais★** : Louis XVI structure fronted by a mirror-like lake *(Mar.-Nov., Sun. and nat. hols., 2-6:30).* ▶ **Saint Cyr-sous-Dourdan** : fortified farmhouse and 13thC church. ▶ **Rochefort-en-Yvelines** : on a hillside; old houses, town hall in 18thC prison. Château (1900), copy of the Palace of the Legion of Honour in Paris. ▶ **Saint-Arnoult** : Romanesque church modified in 15thC; panelled vaulting; murals. ▶ Dourdan road runs through an oak forest. □

AUVERS-SUR-OISE★

C2 / pop. 5 700 (Val-d'Oise)

A pretty town on a slope above the river Oise, forever associated with the Dutch Impressionist painter Vincent Van Gogh (1853-90) : the room where he died; in the cemetery, his tomb next to that of his brother Theo; monument by Zadkine; the church *(of which there is a painting by Van Gogh in the Jeu de Paume Museum, Paris)* mingles Gothic and Renaissance styles (12th-13th-16thC). □

Weekend tips

Start your "17th Century Weekend" with a trip to Port Royal. Lunch in the Chevreuse valley and end the day at Vaux-le-Vicomte (candle-light tour on summer Saturdays). Versailles is an inexhaustible treasure-house; spend Sunday there. In the town you will find numerous good restaurants. In summer see the "Grandes Eaux" *fountain displays.*

BARBIZON

C3 / ® / pop. 1 270 (Seine-et-Marne)

Village in the forest of Fontainebleau (→), once fashionable among the followers of the landscape painters Théodore Rousseau (1812-67) and Jean-François Millet (1814-75) who used to gather at the Auberge du Père Ganne. Unfortunately, the village is now over-commercialised but the Auberge (now a museum) and Millet's former studio are worth a visit *(Apr.-Oct., 9:30-5:30; closed Tue.)*; small museum in converted barn (formerly Rousseau's *atelier*). The artists' tombs are at **Chailly-en-Bière** ®. □

The BEAUCE Plain

B4

The wide horizons of the Beauce plain roughly correspond to the Midwest cornbelt in the USA, with mechanised farming, straggling villages here and there (the Beauce was never densely populated) and occasional fortified farmsteads. Although wheat silos have replaced windmills, a few mills are still valued for their beauty and as reminders of an earlier way of life. Information : *Association Régionale des Amis des Moulins (A.R.M.) de Beauce, Bois-de-Feugères, Bouville.* □

▶ Around the windmills of Beauce *(130 km approx, full day)*

▶ **Chartres** (→). ▶ **Moulin de Maisons** : mill closed to visitors. ▶ **Denonville fortress** : rebuilt 16thC *(2-6, Jul.-Sep. closed Tue.).* ▶ **Ouarville** : 14thC mill *(Sat. and Sun. pm May-Sep. on request; tel 37-99-56-49).* ▶ **Levesville-la-Chenard** : 15thC mill *(pm on request; tel 37-47-59-97.* ▶ **Moutiers-en-Beauce** : working mill *(pm, tel in advance : 37-47-56-97).* ▶ Between the mills at **Ymonville** *(A.R.M. de Beauce)* and **Bazoche** *(visits daily, contact proprietor M. Mercier, tel. 37.99.78.72)* : **Villeprévost** château *(S of D927),* a fine

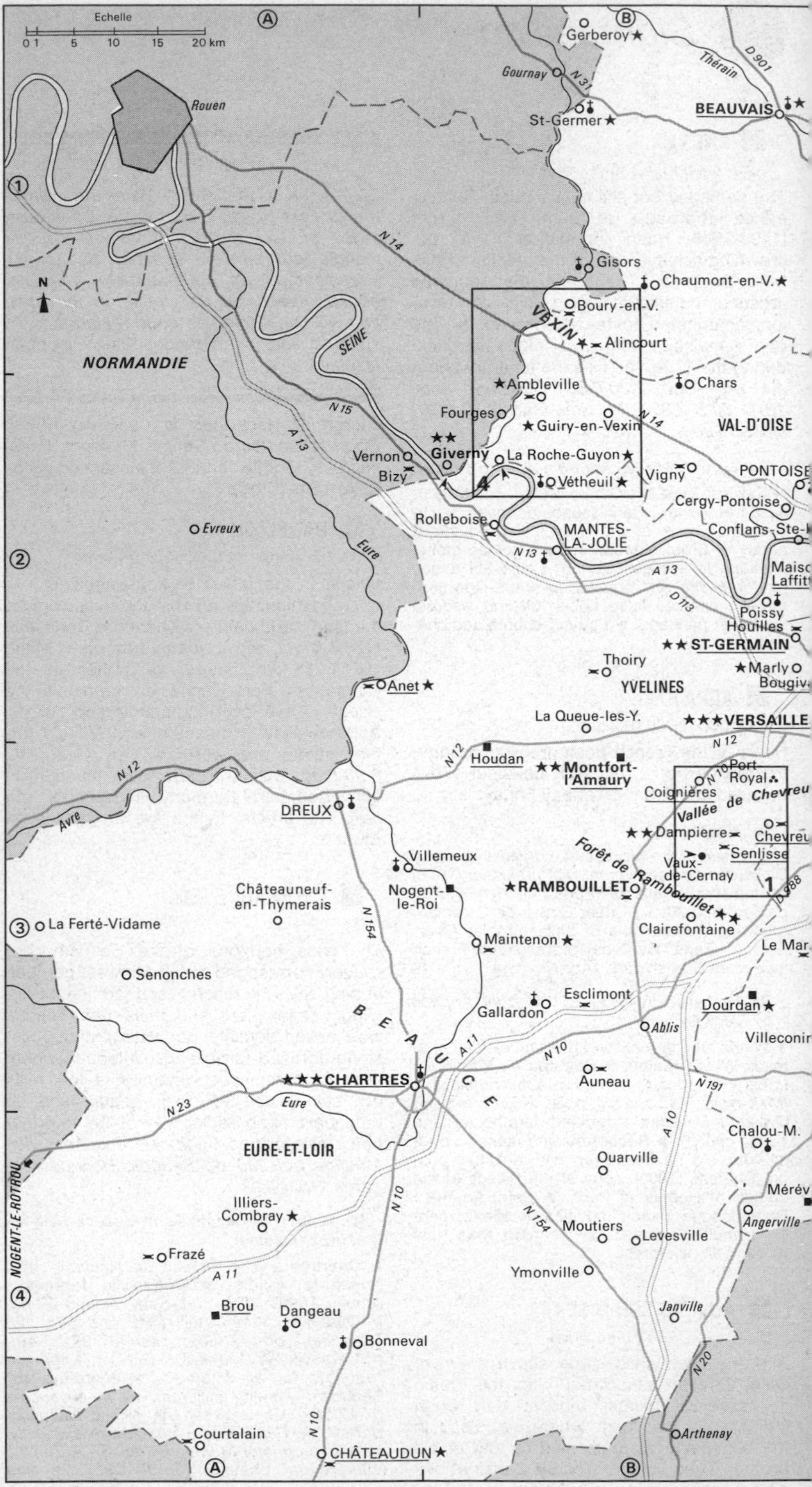
Echelle
0 1 5 10 15 20 km
Rouen
NORMANDIE
SEINE
N 14
N 15
A 13
Eure
Evreux
Gournay
N 31
Gerberoy
St-Germer
BEAUVAIS
Thérain
D 901
Gisors
Chaumont-en-V.
Boury-en-V.
VEXIN
Alincourt
Chars
Ambleville
Fourges
Guiry-en-Vexin
VAL-D'OISE
Giverny
Vernon
Bizy
La Roche-Guyon
Vétheuil
Vigny
PONTOISE
Cergy-Pontoise
Rolleboise
MANTES-LA-JOLIE
N 13
Conflans-Ste-
Maisc Laffit
D 113
Poissy
Houilles
ST-GERMAIN
Thoiry
Marly
Bougiv
YVELINES
Anet
La Queue-les-Y.
VERSAILLE
N 12
Houdan
Montfort-l'Amaury
Port Royal
Coignières
Vallée de Chevreu
DREUX
Avre
Dampierre
Chevreu
Senlisse
Vaux-de-Cernay
Forêt de Rambouillet
Villemeux
Nogent-le-Roi
RAMBOUILLET
Châteauneuf-en-Thymerais
N 154
D 988
La Ferté-Vidame
Clairefontaine
Maintenon
Le Mar
Senonches
Esclimont
Gallardon
Dourdan
Ablis
Villeconir
BEAUCE
A 11
N 10
CHARTRES
Auneau
N 191
N 23
Eure
EURE-ET-LOIR
A 10
Chalou-M.
Ouarville
Mérév
NOGENT-LE-ROTROU
Illiers-Combray
Angerville
Moutiers
Levesville
Frazé
Ymonville
Brou
Dangeau
Janville
Bonneval
N 20
Courtalain
Arthenay
CHÂTEAUDUN

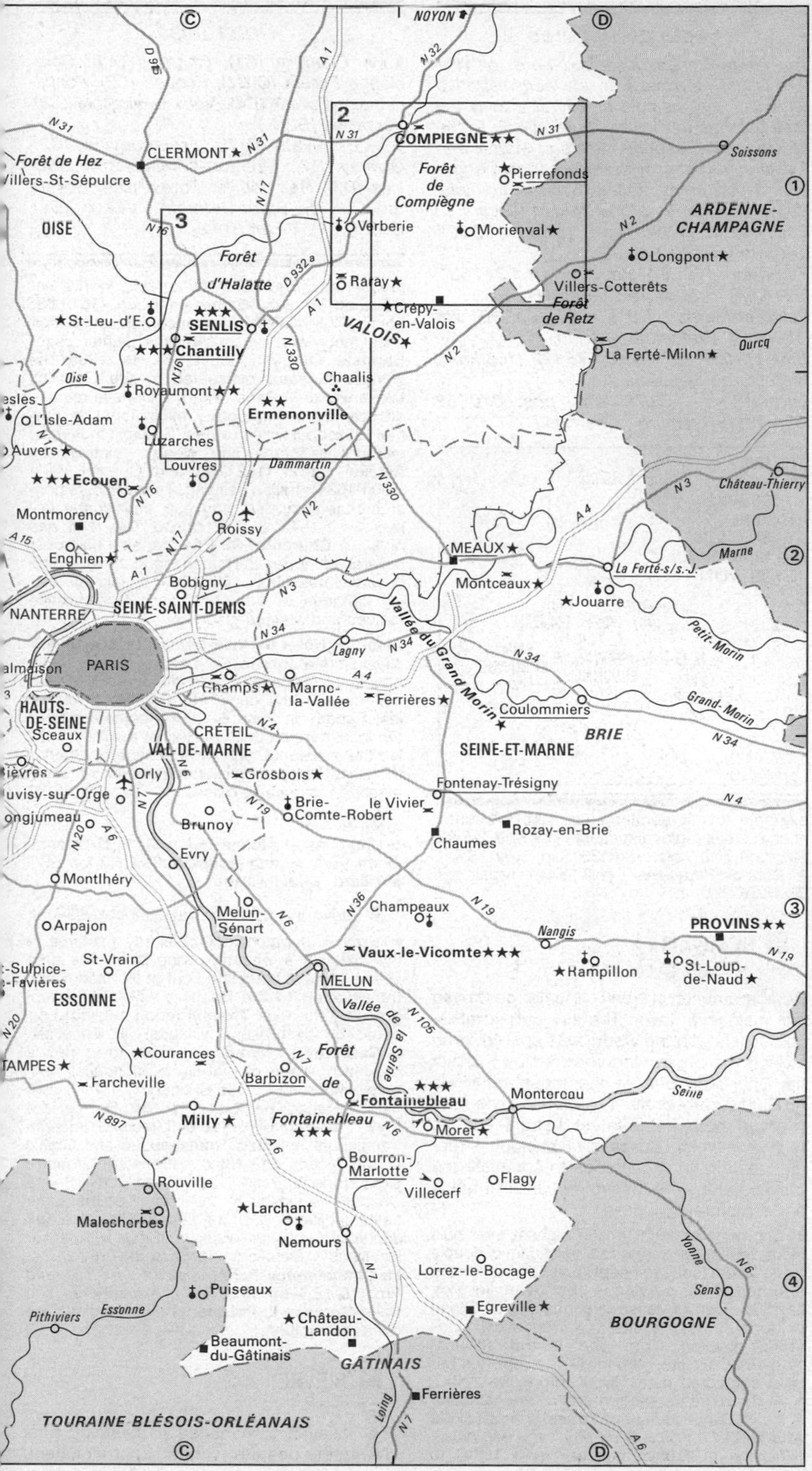
NOYON
COMPIEGNE★★
Forêt de Compiègne
Pierrefonds
Soissons
ARDENNE-CHAMPAGNE
CLERMONT★
Forêt de Hez
Villers-St-Sépulcre
OISE
Verberie
Morienval★
Longpont★
Forêt d'Halatte
Raray★
Villers-Cotterêts
Forêt de Retz
Crépy-en-Valois
VALOIS★
St-Leu-d'E.
★★★ SENLIS
★★★Chantilly
La Ferté-Milon★
Ourcq
Chaalis
Royaumont★★
Oise
L'Isle-Adam
★★ Ermenonville
Luzarches
Auvers★
Louvres
Dammartin
★★★Ecouen
Montmorency
Roissy
Château-Thierry
Enghien★
MEAUX★
Marne
La Ferté-s/s.-J.
Montceaux★
Jouarre
Bobigny
SEINE-SAINT-DENIS
NANTERRE
Petit-Morin
Vallée du Grand Morin
Lagny
PARIS
Champs★
Marne-la-Vallée
Ferrières★
Coulommiers
Grand-Morin
HAUTS-DE-SEINE
Sceaux
CRÉTEIL
VAL-DE-MARNE
SEINE-ET-MARNE
BRIE
Orly
Grosbois★
Fontenay-Trésigny
Brie-Comte-Robert
le Vivier
Brunoy
Rozay-en-Brie
Chaumes
Evry
Montlhéry
Champeaux
Melun-Sénart
Arpajon
Nangis
PROVINS★★
Vaux-le-Vicomte★★★
St-Vrain
MELUN
Rampillon
St-Loup-de-Naud★
ESSONNE
Vallée de la Seine
Forêt de Fontainebleau
★Courances
Barbizon
Farcheville
★★★ Fontainebleau
Montereau
Seine
Milly★
★★★
Moret★
Bourron-Marlotte
Flagy
Villecerf
Rouville
Larchant
Malesherbes
Nemours
Lorrez-le-Bocage
Yonne
Sens
Puiseaux
Egreville★
BOURGOGNE
Pithiviers
Essonne
Château-Landon
Beaumont-du-Gâtinais
GÂTINAIS
Ferrières
Loing
TOURAINE BLÉSOIS-ORLÉANAIS

Facts and figures

The Ile-de-France described here for visitors is not identical with the administrative region of that name : strictly speaking the Oise belongs to Picardy, Eure-et-Loir to the centre ; only Essonne, Seine-et-Marne and Yvelines, together with Paris and its peripheral departments, fall within the administrative boundaries of the Ile-de-France.

***Essonne** : 1 820 km^2, pop. 997 522 (543/km^2). Prefecture : Evry.*

***Yvelines** : 2 284 km^2, pop. 1 211 521 (524/km^2). Prefecture : Versailles.*

***Seine-et-Marne** : 5 915 km^2, pop. 901 593 (150/km^2). Prefecture : Melun.*

***Oise** : 5 857 km^2, pop. 675 172 (103/km^2). Prefecture : Beauvais.*

***Eure-et-Loir** : 5 879 km^2, pop. 370 952 (63/km^2). Prefecture : Chartres.*

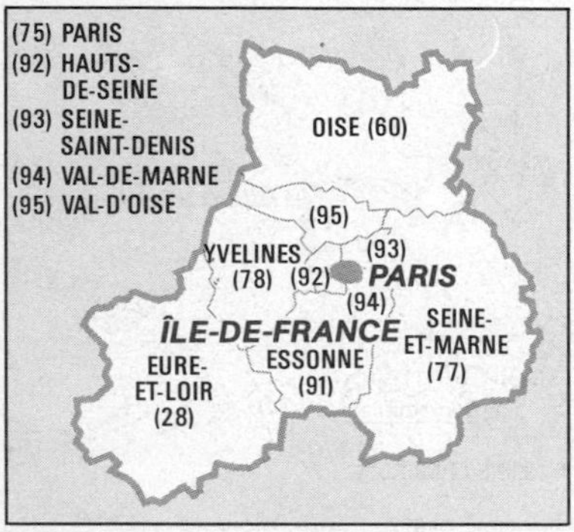

Don't miss

★★★ Chantilly (C1), Chartres (A3), Compiègne Forest (C-D1), Écouen (C2), Fontainebleau Forest (C4), Vaux-le-Vicomte (C3), Versailles (B2).

★★ Beauvais (B1), Ermenonville (C2), Giverny (B2), Montfort-l'Amaury (B3), Provins (D3), Rambouillet Forest (B3), Royaumont (C2), Saint-Germain-en-Laye (B2), Senlis (C1), Vexin (B1-2).

example of a gentleman's 18thC country house ; small regional museum *(10-12 & 2-6:30, Sat. and nat. hols. ; 2-6h30 Sun. ; Jun.-Sep.).* ▶ **Bois-de-Feugères** : mill under repair *(tel 37-47-56-97).* □

■ BEAUVAIS★★

B1 / ® / pop. 54 000 (Oise)

Bombardments in 1940 virtually destroyed this mediaeval town. The airy **cathedral★★** (loftiest choir in the world) was spared, even though the organ was wrecked by a direct hit. This was one of the most ambitious of Gothic cathedrals. The Gothic style here reached both its greatest beauty and its technical limits. Successive bishops struggled in vain for 4 centuries to complete the building, but were thwarted by lack of funds and structural collapses. □

▶ Choir★ (13th-19thC) : the highest ever built (48m vaults), is supported by gigantic double flying buttresses ; transept (finished in 16thC) : adorned with carvings★ by Jean le Pot, ca.1530. Tree of Jesse★ (genealogy of Christ) in north window (16thC). Astronomical clock (1868) copied from one in Strasbourg ; 15th-16thC cloister ; the lower transept (the original cathedral) dates from before the 10thC. ▶ At the extreme eastern end of the cathedral is the **National Gallery of Tapestry and Textile Arts** *(9:30-11:30 & 2-6, ex Mon. and nat. hols.),* exhibition of French tapestry from 15thC to present day. The Beauvais tapestry works, established by Jean-Baptiste Colbert (1619-83 ; Louis XIV's minister of finance), achieved their finest hour with designs by the painter Jean-Baptiste Oudry (1686-1755). In 1939 the workshops were evacuated to the Gobelins textile works in Paris, where they have remained ever since (temporary exhibitions). ▶ Former Episcopal Palace★ (late Gothic) : **museum ;** statuary in stone and wood ; paintings by Antoine Caron (1521-99) and Quentin Varin (1590-1634) ; Italian paintings ; ceramics, regional archaeology, *art nouveau* and contemporary art *(10-12 & 2-6, closed Tue. and nat. hols.).* ▶ **Church of St. Étienne,** also built over several centuries : Romanesque nave, Flamboyant Gothic choir, 16th-18thC tower ; interesting carvings at the north end ; Renaissance statues and stained glass★★.

Also... ▶ **Hôtel de Ville :** 18thC façade. ▶ Voisinlieu : **Maladrerie St. Lazare** (former leper hospital) ; **Marissel :** beautiful church (12thC bell-tower, 13thC choir, 16thC nave). ▶ On the last Sunday in June Beauvais commemorates the local heroine Jeanne Hachette who in 1472 led the resistance against the siege by Charles the Bold, Duke of Burgundy *(following Mon. is a holiday ; museums closed).* □

▶ Nearby

▶ Churches at **Alonne** *(4 km S) ;* ▶ **Therdonne** *(5 km SW) ;* ▶ **Jouy-sous-Thelle★** *(17 km SW).* ▶ **Tillard :** quaint village. □

▶ Drive through the Bray district★ *(65 km)*

▶ **Bray** is a patchwork of shady pastures in the midst of a wheat-growing plain. The area seems to have been lifted out of Normandy and transplanted to the Beauce, where it is kept green by the river **Thérain** (good angling ; bordered by picturesque villages). ▶ **Beauvais.** ▶ **Gerberoy★ :** formerly a walled town, now a delightful village of half-timbered houses covered with roses : 15thC church ; 18thC town hall ; terraced gardens★. ▶ **St. Germer-de-Fly★ :** church of great architectural interest, transitional between Romanesque and Gothic (17thC façade and 18thC bell-tower). Group of eight stone figures★ (17thC) ; the Gothic Sainte Chapelle is similar to the chapel of the same name in Paris. *(Son et Lumière the 1st Sat. Jun.-Sep. ; musical week in Aug.).* ▶ Road to Beauvais : excellent views of the region. At **La Chapelle-aux-Pots** *(museum : 4-7 Tue. and Fri. ; 10-12 Wed. and Thu.),* **Armentières** and **Saint-Germain-la-Poterie,** potters continue the old local tradition. □

■ BIÈVRE Valley

C3

The valley has managed to keep its rural character despite urban encroachment.

Rustic villages, churches and châteaux seem oddly out of place in a 20thC environment.

▶ **Bièvres :** National Photography Museum★ *(10-12 & 2-6);* exhibitions organised by the **Vauboyen Artistic and Cultural Centre** in an old mill (16th-17thC, *2-5, closed Tue.*). ▶ **Jouy-en-Josas,** beautiful statue of the Virgin in the 13th-16thC church ; **Oberkampf Museum★,** manufacture of *toiles de Jouy* (printed textiles ; *Tue., Sat., Sun. and nat. hols., 2-5 ; closed 14 Jul.-30 Sep.*) ; houses of Juliette Drouet (Victor Hugo's mistress) and Léon Blum (1870-1952 ; French premier 1936-37). ▶ **Buc Aqueduct :** built to supply Versailles. ▶ **Val, Moulin-à-Renard, Geneste :** artificial lakes (near the sources of the river Bièvre) with fishing and sailing facilities. □

■ CARNELLE Forest

C2

100 km² of beech (especially in NE) and oak, interspersed with hornbeam and chestnut copses. **Blue pools★ :** follow the GR markers between Noisy-sur-Oise and the prehistoric megalith at Pierre Turquaise. □

▶ On the eastern edge of the forest, **Viarmes :** church (12th-13th-19thC) ; **Asnières-sur-Oise :** town hall château (18thC), charming church (12th-13thC). ▶ Interesting church at **Beaumont-sur-Oise** (12th-16thC) and **château de Nointel** (18thC ; contemporary art centre ; *11-6:30 Sat., Sun. and hols. ; 15 Mar.-15 Nov., 2-6 weekdays*). ▶ More lovely churches at **Belloy-en-France** (14th-16thC) S of Viarmes, and at **Champagne-sur-Oise** (13th-16thC). □

■ CHANTILLY★★★

C1 / ® / pop. 10 200 (Oise)

Chantilly, historically the seat of the Princes de Condé (princes of the royal blood, descended through Charles de Bourbon from a younger son of St. Louis), has two great attractions : the château, in a park on the edge of one of the great forests of France, and the race-course, created by the horse-crazy dandies of the last century.

The thoroughbred horse has reigned supreme ever since in this blue-blooded town : 3 000 thoroughbreds train here each year for many world-renowned races, including the Prix de Diane and the Prix de l'Arc de Triomphe. The 18thC stables★★ have now become the **Live Museum of the Horse★ ;** they are more sumptuous than most human dwellings, which may be less astonishing when you remember that at least one Prince de Condé expressed a desire to be reincarnated as a horse ! A must for horse-lovers (*10:30-6 ; 1-5 in winter ; ex Tue. ;* dressage in costume). □

▶ The great chef Vatel committed suicide when Louis XIV dined at the **Château de Chantilly** and the fish arrived too late to be served. Today the château houses a **collection** of masterpieces★★★ that are displayed in the old-fashioned style preferred by the 19thC owner, the Duc d'Aumale (1822-97). This son of King Louis-Philippe bankrupted himself in his efforts to restore Chantilly to its former splendour, and finally donated the château and its works of art to the Institut de France.

The major Italian painters are represented, together with France's Poussin, Delacroix, and Ingres, and the Flemish Masters. Jewels of the collection include the Fouquet miniatures, the 16thC Clouet portraits and unique illuminated manuscripts *(10:30-6, Apr.-Sep. ; 10:30-5, Oct.-Mar., closed Tue.).* ▶ Two great houses were built on the site by Anne de Montmorency (1493-1567 ; male, despite his name), Constable of France and brilliant soldier who developed his taste as a patron of the arts during a sojourn in Italy. However, only the smaller (built ca. 1560 by Jean Bullivant) survived the Revolution ; the larger was rebuilt during the 19thC by the Duc d'Aumale. ▶ The park includes French gardens by André Le Nôtre (1630-1700), English gardens, the Maison de Sylvie (*Apr.-Nov. ;* pretty 17thC forerunner of the Trianon → Versailles), and the Jeu

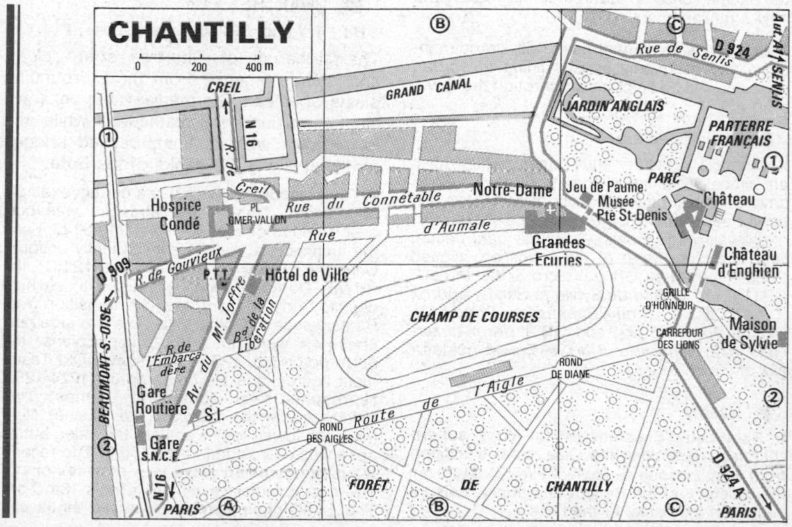

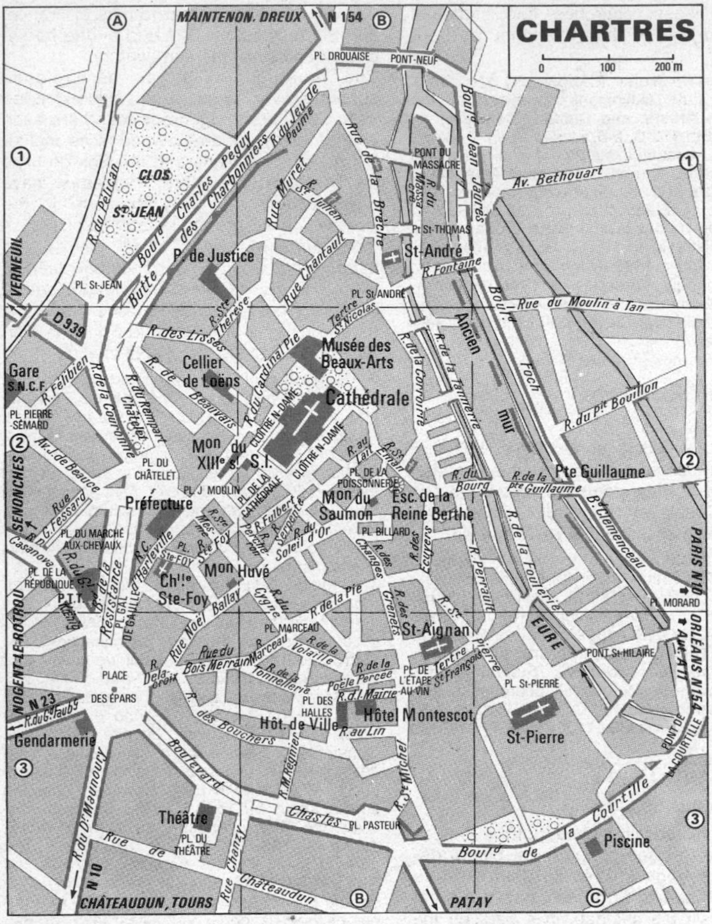

de Paume, once a covered tennis court and now a museum.

▶ Chantilly is an **elegant town,** with grand mansions and handsome houses lining the broad avenues, and bridle paths cut through the town. □

▶ Chantilly Forest★★

▶ Chantilly, Halatte and Ermenonville, form an almost continuous forest. Chantilly alone covers 63 km^2, painstakingly planted and laid out for deer hunting by its princely owners. Lily-of-the-valley still grows wild under oak, beech, lime and pine. Most of the roads are closed to cars, but three GR trails cross the forest : GR11 *(from Maison de Sylvie to Senlis, approx 3 hr);* GR 12 *(from Commelles Pond★ to Halatte Forest, 3 hr);* and GR 1 *(from Luzarches to Ermenonville, 6 hr).* ▶ Forest guides : *ask at the SI.* □

▶ Nearby

▶ **Saint-Leu-d'Esserent** (6 km W) : superb church★ overlooking the Oise, clear transition from Romanesque to Gothic. Pretty view from the cloister★ of the Benedictine priory. Leisure centre on the banks of the Oise. □

■ CHARTRES★★★

B3 / ® / pop. 39 250 (Eure-et-Loir)

The cathedral of Chartres soars clear, sharp and immense from the surrounding plains of wheat. The mediaeval upper town clusters around the cathedral, while the lower town with its hump-backed bridges stretches along the banks of the Eure.

▶ The **cathedral★★★** (B2) is a perfect example of a pilgrim church. The structure was built over a period of only 30 years (1194-1225) and the architectural style is consequently uniform. Only the façade dates from the 12thC; the **Royal Doorway★★★** (1145-1155), which depicts Christ in glory, marks a transition from Romanesque to Gothic style. The two **side porches★★★** were not in the original plans; the north porch (ca. 1200-1225) shows Old Testament figures, and the south porch (1224-1250) represents New Testament themes. Two **towers** frame the façade : the Clocher Neuf (new bell-tower, left) is actually the older, but its spire was only added in the 16thC. The recently restored **stained glass★★★** provides one of the most complete examples of this 13thC art. The 14thC **choir screen** of carved stone can be seen in the treasure room★. 9thC and 10thC crypts beneath the side aisles. The SI is housed in the 13thC Canons' House *(maison des chanoines)*. ▶ The **Enclos de Loëns**★ (storehouse) is now used for exhibitions of stained glass. ▶ The Bishop's Garden overlooks the Eure Valley; the Palace★ (14th to 19thC) is now a **museum** *(10-12 & 2-5; closed Tue.)* : 16thC Flemish tapestries; 16thC Limoges enamel★; paintings (Ste. Lucie★ by Zurbaràn, Molière by Mignard). Regional museum; The Vlaminck Donation; contemporary art exhibitions. ▶ **Upper town**★ : numerous old houses (B2); Maison du Saumon (15thC), Queen Bertha's staircase (16thC), Hôtel de la Caige (15thC), church of St. Aignan (16thC), Hôtel de Ville (17thC), Renaissance house of Claude Huvé, doctor to Henri II. ▶ Lower town : the **Church of St. André** (B1; 12thC) partly destroyed in the 19thC; now disused; formerly the church of the craftsmen of Chartres (concerts). ▶ **Church of St. Pierre*** (C3) : formerly part of a Benedictine abbey from 1700 to 1709; 11thC tower; 12thC and 13thC additions; 14thC and 16thC stained glass★, 17thC convent buildings. Pleasant walk along the **Eure**★ (boats at the *Pont de la Courtille*).

Also... ▶ **Maison Picassiette**★ decorated with colourful shards of porcelain *(primitive painting, 22, rue du Repos, 10-12 & 2-6 ex Tue. in season)*. ▶ **Gardens of the Horticultural Society** north of the town *(8-7:30, Apr.-Oct.)*. □

▶ Nearby

▶ **Meslay** *(6 km SW)* : church (frescos : *Danse Macabre*). ▶ **Gallardon**★ ® *(20 km NE)* : 12thC keep, known locally as "the shoulder"; old houses including one with carved wooden facings (15thC); 13thC church★. ▶ **Auneau** *(25 km E)* : typical village of the region; 14thC castle★ with 11thC keep. □

▶ Along the Eure Valley★ between Chartres and Dreux *(43 km; 2-3 hr)*.

▶ **Jouy** : interesting church doorway (13thC). ▶ **Saint Piat** : mill; sarcophagus (5thC) in the 16thC church★. ▶ **Maintenon**★ ® : Château★ (12th-16th-17thC) that belonged to the Marquise de Maintenon (1615-1719), secretly married to Louis XIV soon after the death of his first wife; attractive canal setting. *(Apr.-31 Oct., 2-6; Sun. and nat. hols. 10-12 & 2-6; 1 Jan.-31 Mar., Sat., Sun. 10-12; closed Tue., 25 Dec. and Jan.)*; Chinese wallpaper★ in the reception rooms. ▶ The Eure branches out at **Nogent-le-Roi** ®; 16thC houses : Flamboyant Gothic and Renaissance church. On the other bank : former abbey of **Coulombs** ®; mill. ▶ **Dreux** (→). □

CHÂTEAUDUN★

A4/ ® / pop. 16 000 (Eure-et-Loir)

A defensive site on a spur formed by the river Loir, reinforced by a feudal château★★ whose foundations plunge sheer to the bottom of the valley.

▶ 12thC **keep** with 15thC timberwork; Flamboyant Gothic Sainte Chapelle with statuary★★ carved in the Loire Valley (late 15thC); main building 15thC with 16thC return wing; kitchens★; tapestries★; *(9:30-11:45 & 2-6 23, Mar.-15 Sep.; 10-11:45 & 2-4, 19 Oct.-22 Mar.)*. ▶ Near the ramparts, Romanesque **church of the Madeleine**★. ▶ To the east, the **church of St. Valérien**★ (late 12thC), vaulting 12thC, bell-tower late 15thC. ▶ Cemetery : façade of 16thC church. ▶ On the opposite bank of the Loir, **church of St. Jean** (11th-12th-15thC). ▶ Houses in the old town rebuilt by Jules Hardouin-Mansart (1647-1708, grandson of the renowned architect François Mansart). **Natural History and Fine Arts Museum. Foulon Grotto** *(10-12 & 2-6, May-Sep.; winter 2-6 only; closed Mon. and 15 Jan.-15 Feb.)*.□

▶ Nearby

▶ **Mémillon** (10 km N) : three châteaux along the Loir *(pm 15 Jul.-15 Sep.)*; the most important dates from the Second Empire (Napoleon III, 1852-70). ▶ **Bonneval** *(14 km on Chartres road)* : 13thC bridge; 12th-15thC abbey, now a psychiatric hospital; church; Gothic houses; local museum. ▶ **Alluyes** *(7 km NW from Bonneval)* : 16thC church with Romanesque apse and Gothic paintings; feudal castle with Renaissance additions (visits by request). ▶ **Dangeau** *(9 km W from Bonneval)* : fine Romanesque church (15th-16thC statues); bridge. ▶ **Courtalain** : along the river Yerre; château (Renaissance) built in 1483 on the site of a mediaeval fortress. ▶ **Cloyes-sur-le-Loir** ®, chapel of Yron, romanesque frescos. □

CHÂTEAU-LANDON★

C4 / pop. 3 000 (Seine-et-Marne)

Overlooking the Fusain Valley. A signposted circuit leads past the sentry-walk *(terrasse des larris)*, the Madeleine Tower and the former *château-mairie* (municipal offices).

▶ The psychiatric hospital was once an abbey (14th-16hC); beneath the ruins of the abbey church is an older church (11thC) with murals. The church of Notre Dame was built in the 10th-14thC. In the centre of town, a Romanesque tower; former Mint. Lovely view down the Loing Valley (→) from the sentry-walk.

Also... ▶ On the other side of the Loing and the N7, ruins of the colossal 13thC château of **Mez-le-Maréchal**★. □

CHEVREUSE Valley★

▶ Round trip starting at Saint-Quentin-en-Yvelines *(approx 35 km; half day)*
B3 *(see map 1)* (Yvelines)

Wooded slopes in the Upper Yvette Valley, villages, châteaux and historic remnants of a period of religious and political confusion.

▶ **Saint-Quentin-en-Yvelines** : the former house of the **Commandery of Villedieu** (Knights Templars) has been converted into a cultural and information centre (cultural centre of the new city of Saint-Quentin-en-Yvelines). ▶ **Mesnil-Saint-Denis** : château de Montmort (16thC), now the civic centre. ▶ **Dampierre**★★ ® : 17thC château built by Hardouin-Mansart for the Duc de Luynes *(2-6 ex Tue., Apr.-15 Oct.)*; gardens★ (André Le Nôtre) irrigated by the river Yvette; festival hall *(Salle des Fêtes)*★ decorated by the painter Ingres (1780-1867). ▶ **17 Bends** *(tournants)* **Road**★ climbs to Port-Royal. ▶ **Senlisse** ® : château; church on the hillside above a stream. ▶ To the west, **Vaux-de-Cernay**★ : lakes and a "sea" of sand, one of the best-known sites in the vicinity of Paris. Walk from the Moulin des Roches to the former Cistercian abbey. ▶ **Choisel : Château de Breteuil** (Louis XIII style); wax museum recalls

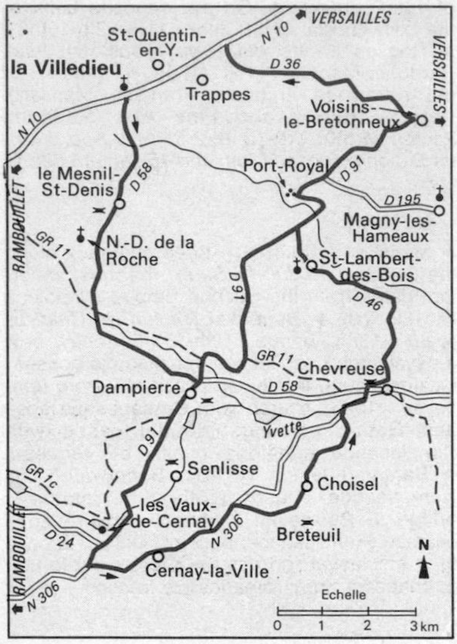

.1. Chevreuse Valley

celebrities who stayed here in the 19thC; park★ (birdlife; *daily 2:30-5:30 or 6; 11-12:30 Sun. and nat. hols.; park open from 10 am*). ▶ **Chevreuse** ® : church (12th-17thC); feudal keep (La Madeleine, 12thC). Racine Road (signposted, 5km) leads to ▶ **Port-Royal**★ *(pm only, 3 persons min.; closed Tue.)* : the abbey, once a hotbed of political intrigue and religious dissension, was suppressed by royal command in 1710. Bones exhumed from the nuns' cemetery during the dissolution were tossed into a common pit; a granite monument near the church of **St. Lambert-des-Bois**★ marks the spot. ▶ The **Granges** (name of the hilltop site) **National Museum,** in the former school building *(Petites Ecoles),* provides an insight into the importance of Jansenism (a 17thC religious movement) in the development of French religious thought. *(10-11:30 & 2:30-5, Sun. 10-11 & 3-5; closed Mon., Tue. and nat. hols.).* ▶ **Magny-les-Hameaux :** the church is adorned with the tombstones from the desecrated abbey. □

■ CLERMONT★

C1/ ® / pop. 8700 (Oise)

A hill, a river, forests all around. ▶ Remarkable 14thC Hôtel de Ville★ (restored 19thC). Church★ (14thC, remodelled 15thC and 16thC) : 16thC sepulchre, stained glass, organs (15th-16thC) □

▶ Nearby

▶ The **forest of Hez**★ stretches west across the plateau with more than 4000 acres of beech and oak. Marsh and Riding Habit Museum at **Sacy-le-Grand.** ▶ To the west, **Agnetz :** church (12th-16thC); south, **Cambronne-les-Clermont :** 12th-13thC church; southwest, **Bury :** church (11th-13thC). In the north, facing Picardy, are the abbey church (13thC) and the farm buildings of St. Martin-aux-Bois★. ▶ **Neuilly-sous-Clermont :** 14thC house and chapel of the Knights Templars, Renaissance residence *(visit on prior request, 1 May-15 Oct.)*; 18thC **château de Verderonne** houses a Magic Museum *(3-6, Sat. and Sun., 15 Apr.-15 Oct., and by appt.).* □

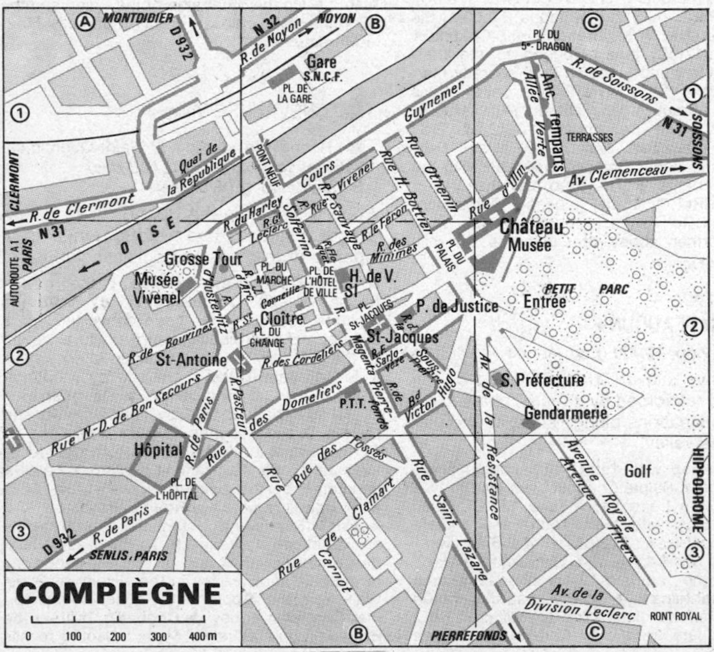

COMPIÈGNE★★

D1/ ® / pop. 43300 (Oise)
(see plan preceding page)

Compiègne was a country retreat for French rulers from the earliest Capets to Napoleon III. The 18thC **château★** built by Jacques and Jacques-Ange Gabriel (father and son architects to Louis XV) is a treasury of I and II Empire art and design (grand apartments); **Museum of Transport and Touring★** will delight car enthusiasts *(9:30-12 & 1:30-5, closed Tue.)*. ▶ The **Allée des Beaux Monts★** leads from the **park★** to the forest (→).

▶ **Hôtel de Ville** (B2; late Gothic, restored) : historical statuettes depicting military costumes and battle plans★ *(9-12 & 2-5 or 6, ex Mon.)*; carillon in the façade. ▶ **Cloister of St. Corneille** (14thC). ▶ **Vivenel Museum** (A2) in 18thC mansion; Greek vases★, statues, enamels *(ex Tue. and nat. hols.)*. ▶ Rue des Lombards (B2) : gabled house (16thC); 18thC covered market designed by Nicolas Ledoux (foremost neo-Classical architect, 1736-1806); 17thC and 18thC mansions; stud farm *(haras)* designed by Gabriel. □

▶ Nearby

▶ **Château Plessis-Brion★,** 16thC pink and black patterned *(1 Jul.-15 Aug.)*, between the river Oise and the Laigue Forest. ▶ Ruins of **Ste. Croix d'Offémont Priory, Saint-Crépin-aux-Bois** early 17thC church. □

COMPIÈGNE Forest★★★

▶ Down the Automne Valley through the forest of Compiègne *(approx 80 km, can be combined with Halatte → Senlis excursion).*
C-D1 *(see map 2)*

Compiègne Forest is among the largest and most beautiful in France, 220 km² including the forests of Laigue, Ourscamps, and the 130 km² of Villers-Cotterêts; fringed by hills providing splendid views (especially to the north), cut by gorges and watered by numerous streams and ponds. The eastern forest is the most interesting for walkers; marked trails. □

▶ **Compiègne** (→). ▶ The Automne Valley★ runs between the Halatte and Retz forests; the road follows the river. ▶ **Verberie :** church (13th-15thC), doorway with beautiful, carved Virgin. ▶ **Saintines :** church with double nave, Romanesque spire, 15thC doorway and polychrome statues. ▶ Twin villages, contrasting churches : **Béthisy-Saint-Pierre** (Romanesque church rebuilt 16thC, former priory 14th-16thC) and **Béthisy-Saint-Martin** (13thC church). ▶ **Orrouy :** Fine Romanesque bell-tower and remarkable Renaissance stained glass; 16thC manor. ▶ **Champlieu :** Gallo-Roman ruins; access difficult. ▶ **Gilocourt :** 13thC and 15thC church. ▶ **Fresnoy-la-Rivière** (13th-15thC church) : on the edge of deep countryside again. ▶ **Morienval :** three bell-towers and the finest Romanesque church in Ile-de-France; in the ambulatory an unknown mason raised the first Gothic vaults in the region; choir stalls; 15thC Christ. □

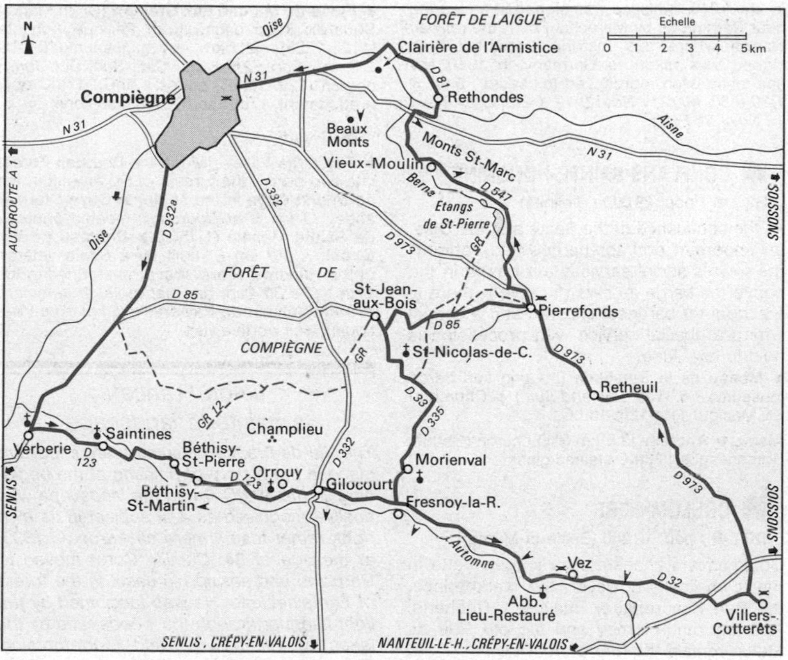

2. Compiègne Forest and the Automne Valley

▶ From Morienval to Pierrefonds : forest road past the ruined priory of St.-Nicolas de Courson, and one of the prettiest villages in the forest, **Saint-Jean-aux-Bois★** ® born from a 13thC Benedictine abbey. ▶ **Lieu-Restauré :** the abbey rising from the ruins was rebuilt in 16thC (hence the name, meaning "restored place"). **Vez,** with 14thC keep : once the capital of the ancient county of Valois. 12th-13thC church, l6thC timberwork, 17thC wood panelling, view. ▶ **Largny-sur-Automne** (fine 12thC church with 16thC porch) is the last village in the valley before the broad fields of Villers-Cotterêts (→) and the Champenois. ▶ **Pierrefonds★** ® : rises out of the woods by the lake. Its colossal walls look like a stage set. The restoration by the 19thC architect Eugene Viollet-le-Duc has been much criticized, but gives an idea of late feudal architecture, designed for both military and residential needs. Delightful for children of all ages. *(10-12 & 2-6, Apr.-Oct.; 10-12 & 2-4:30, Oct.-Mar.; closed Tue.).* ▶ **Etangs de Saint-Pierre** (lakes) near **Vieux-Moulin** ®. ▶ The avenue of Beaux Monts★ was laid out by Napoleon to remind his second wife Marie Louise, Archduchess of Austria, of her childhood home, Schönbrunn palace in Vienna. ▶ The 1918 Armistice was signed in a clearing near **Rethondes** by Maréchal Foch; the railway wagon where this historic document was signed was taken to Germany in 1940 but has since been reproduced (museum : *8-12 & 1:30-6:30, Mar.-11 Nov; 9-12 & 2-5:30 ex Tue., 12 Nov.- 28 Feb.*). □

■ CONFLANS-SAINTE-HONORINE

B2 / ® / pop. 29 000 (Yvelines)

At the confluence of the Seine and the Oise, an important port for barges and lighters; the town's social services are based in the converted barge *Je sers* ("I serve"); there is a school for bargees' children and a chapel where a special service with procession is held in late June.

▶ **Musée de la Batellerie** (boating and barge museum; *3-6, Wed. Sat. and Sun.*). ▶ Church of St. Maclou, 11th-12th-13thC.

Also... ▶ **Andrésy** (2.5 km SW) church (Gothic, Romanesque); 16thC stained glass. □

■ COULOMMIERS

D2 / ® / pop. 12 250 (Seine-et-Marne)

Coulommiers cheese is no longer made in the town itself; however, the marketplace, the Rue Beaurepaire, Rue de la Récherie, Rue Bertrand-Flornoy and the old Rue de Melun remain the hub of activity.

▶ Municipal Park : remains of a **château des Longueville,** by Salomon de Brosse (1571-1624, architect of the Luxembourg Palace in Paris), situated between two arms of the Morin. Small municipal and regional museum in the chapel (Sat. and Sun. pm in summer). ▶ In the upper town, a former **Templars Commandery** houses numerous exhibitions and provides archaeological interest *(pm in summer*). □

■ CRÉPY-EN-VALOIS★

D1 / ® / pop. 12 280 (Oise)

Between the forests of Compiègne and Retz, Crépy-en-Valois retains reminders of its heyday as the former principal city of the Valois (Place Gambetta : sculpted façades, turrets, pediments).

▶ **Church of St. Denis** (12thC and 16thC), restored. ▶ The former **Abbey of St. Arnould** dates from the 11thC, crypt 12thC, cloister 14thC (now the *Musée d'Arts et Traditions Populaires; pm Sat. and Sun.).* ▶ The fortress du Château Royal is now the **Archery Museum★,** honoring a tradition that still flourishes in the region; the museum also contains religious images rescued from defunct or destroyed churches throughout the Valois. *(10-12 & 2-6, Apr.-11 Nov.; Sun., 10-12 & 3-7; closed Tue.).*

Also... ▶ 12thC façade of the **church of St. Thomas** (named for the martyred English Archbishop Saint Thomas-à-Becket). □

■ DOURDAN★

B3 / ® / pop. 8 000 (Essonne)

Capital of the region of **Hurepoix,** traditionally one of the market gardens of Paris.

▶ **Place du Marché aux Grains★** (Grain Market Square); keep dating from Philippe Auguste (1125-1223); salt barn, now a museum *(10-12 & 2-6, Jul.-Sep.; 2-6 Wed., Sat., Sun. Oct.-Jun.);* church (12th-13thC, spires 17thC), 17thC covered market, 17thC and 18thC mansions. □

▶ Nearby

▶ The Orge Valley divides the **Dourdan Forest** into two parts : the forests of St. Arnoult in the north and Ouye in the south. ▶ **Ouye :** former abbey *(3 km S of Dourdan);* moated **château de Sainte Mesme** (17thC). ▶ **Château de Villeconin★** *(10 km E)* built by a Scots veteran of the Hundred Years' War; transformed in the 17thC *(2-6:30 Sun. and nat. hols. in summer).* ▶ **Saint Sulpice-de-Favières★** *(5 km from Villeconin),* well worth a visit. □

Ile-de-France : a painter's landscape

The Ile-de-France assumed an important place in the history of painting at the beginning of the 19thC, when the landscape was finally recognised as a fit subject in its own right, rather than a mere backdrop. In 1830, at the age of 34, Camille Corot moved to Barbizon and set up his easel in the forest of Fontainebleau. He was fascinated by the light filtering through the woods, and by the lakes of Ville-d'Avray and Mortefontaine. The artists who followed - Rousseau, Diaz, Ziem, Troyon, and Millet - eventually became known as the Barbizon School. In 1871 Cézanne and Pissarro settled in Pontoise; Renoir, Monet, Sisley and Dégas worked in Louveciennes and Argenteuil. The landscape movement lasted 10 years, until Cézanne left for Provence and Renoir for Algeria and Italy; Sisley moved to Moret and Monet to Giverny. Sixty years after Corot led the way into the Ile-de-France, Van Gogh committed suicide in front of his easel at Auvers-sur-Oise. Painting had entered the 20th century.

Forests

The numerous forests around Paris owe their existence to the royal predilection for hunting. The forests were formerly maintained as game reserves and most still shelter a large number and variety of game birds and animals. The best known forests are Fontainebleau, Compiègne, Rambouillet and Chantilly, but Saint-Germain, Ermenonville, L'Isle-Adam, Carnelle, Villers-Cotterêts, Halatte, Dreux-Anet, and Hez-Froidmont are pleasant diversions. Foresters from the Office National des Forêts (O.N.F.) *will willingly guide you. The forests deserve their title of* poumons verts *"green lungs" : over a year 1 ha (2.5 acres) of beech filters 80 tons of dust (vs. 30 tons for the same area of spruce).*

■ DREUX

A3 / ® / pop. 33 760 (Eure-et-Loir)

The old town seems unaware of development that has made it the region's most important industrial centre. ▶ The church★ and the belfry★ are the work of two architects from the local Métezeau family (16thC); however, the ▶ Chapelle Royale of the royal Orléans family is much better known; the funerary chapel is a showcase of 19thC academic statuary *(9-12 & 2-dusk).* ▶ Drouais Museum *(2-5, Wed., Sat., Sun.)* □

▶ Nearby

▶ The **forest of Dreux** covers a 30-km² plateau between Anet and Dreux, with oak, hornbeam and conifers. Crossed by GR22 and numerous trails. □

■ ÉCOUEN★★★

C2 / pop. 4 390 (Val-d'Oise)

The sumptuous château of Anne de Montmorency (→ Chantilly) is one of the most important buildings of the 16thC (1538-1555); now the **National Renaissance Museum★★★.** Twenty restored rooms display collections formerly in the Cluny Museum in Paris *(9:45-12:45 & 2-5:15; closed Tue.; free of charge Wed.).* Painted overmantels in the style of Fontainebleau; tapestry depicting David and Bathsheba★★; ceramic flooring by Abaquesne; enamels by Léonard Limosin; sculptures by della Robbia, Goujon and others; park and panorama★.

▶ **Saint Acceul** and **Mesnil-Aubry** *(4 km N)* : stained glass in the parish churches. □

■ ENGHIEN★

C2 / ® / pop. 9 740 (Val-d'Oise)

Lake surrounded by greenery; pedal boats; casino and Rococo villas; all the charm of a turn-of-the-century spa only a short drive from Paris. □

■ ÉTAMPES★

C3 / pop. 19 500 (Essonne)

This large town on the edge of the Beauce plain hides treasures worthy of an Italian Renaissance city-state behind its somewhat suburban façade, including several Gothic churches and the Renaissance mansions of successive royal mistresses.

▶ **Church of St. Basile :** Romanesque façade from the 15th-16thC (*bas-reliefs* illustrating the life of Christ); Renaissance house opposite. ▶ **Notre Dame du Fort** (end 12thC) : doorway reminiscent of Chartres, Romanesque capitals, 16thC stained glass, 11thC crypt. ▶ Numerous Renaissance mansions around the town hall (1514); local museum *(2-5, weekdays; 3-6 Sun. and nat. hols.; closed Mon. and last Sun. of month).* ▶ **Guinette Tower;** 12thC royal keep with four watch-turrets, at the top of the town. Down the main street : **St. Gilles Church** has a Romanesque façade with Gothic nave and bell-tower, 15th-16thC side aisles. ▶ **Church of St. Martin** (12th and 16thC) has a leaning tower.

Also... ▶ **Farcheville★** : imposing 13thC **fortified château** 7 km E (no visitors). □

▶ Round trip South of Etampes *(42 km approx).*

▶ The **Juine** and its tributary the **Chalouette★** cut through the golden plain of Beauce. ▶ **Méréville** ® : lake fed by the Juine; 18thC park, partly subdivided. Near the station and the covered market is Cook's Column, all that remains of the statuary commissioned by Jean-Joseph de Laborde (finance minister to Louis XVI), 18thC proprietor of the Renaissance château. The rest of the sculpture is now at Jeurre (see below). ▶ **Chalou-Moulineux :** the source of the Chalouette river *(fontaine Ste. Apolline);* the 12thC church was a dependency of the neighbouring Templar's Commandery. **Moulineux :** lake reflecting the ruined 12thC church. ▶ **Châlo-St.Mars :** 11thC church, much remodelled. ▶ Return road to Étampes bordered by green fields. □

▶ Round trip North of Étampes *(60 km approx).*

▶ The **Juine Valley★** abounds with châteaux. ▶ **Morigny :** Abbot's Palace (18thC) and 12thC church★. ▶ Fortified farmhouse at **Villemartin.** ▶ **Jeurre★** : park with statuary★ from Méréville *(see above; 10-3, ex nat. hols. and long weekends; closed Wed. and Sat. am).* ▶ On the opposite bank : **Château de Chamarande★** and park by Mansart and Le Nôtre *(park visit only; 10-12 & 2-6, Sat. and Sun.).* ▶ **Gillevoisin** Château : three 17thC buildings. ▶ Lardy : the river flows through the town hall park. ▶ One of the largest dovecotes in France at the **château de Mesnil-Voisin,** a severe Louis XIII building *(2-6 Sun.).* ▶ **Saint-Vrain :** where Mme. du Barry, Louis XV's mistress, was banished on his death; 325-acre safari park with African fauna. *(10-12 Apr.-Sep.; 12:30-5 Oct.-Mar.).* ▶ Junction of the Juine and Essonne rivers; popular with anglers and hunters. ▶ Ballancourt : château du **Grand Saussaye,** two 17thC buildings face-to-face *(2-5, Sun. 15 Mar.-15 Oct.).* ▶ **La Ferté-Alais :** one of the earliest Gothic churches in the region. ▶ Follow the road along the right bank. ▶ **Boutigny-sur-Essonne;** another 12thC church, a mill and the château de Belesbat (17thC; now a hotel-restaurant) ; the river runs through cress beds, a regional specialty. ▶ Return to Étampes through the last stretch of Fontainebleau ; view of the imposing walls of Farcheville★. □

■ FERRIÈRES★

C2 / pop. 1 340 (Oise)

An astonishing steel-and-glass structure in Renaissance style built in 1859 by Joseph Paxton (English architect, 1801-65) for the financier James de Rothschild ; scene of magnificent entertainments and also of negotiations that led to the Franco-Prussian Armistice of 1871. Louis XVI-Impératrice decoration★ by the painter Eugène Lami (1800-90) ; English park★ *(2-7, May - Sep. ; Sun. 2-5, Oct. - Apr., ex Tue.).* □

▶ Nearby

▶ **Forest of Ferrières :** former hunting reserve now crossed by rambling and cycling paths ; angling ; to the south, the **forest of Armainvilliers** and a string of small lakes. □

■ FONTAINEBLEAU★★★

C3 / ® / pop. 18 750 (Seine-et-Marne)

The **château**★★★ was built for the kings of France, who hunted deer, boar, wolf and other game in the forest. François I built the original hunting lodge, but his successors in turn transformed it to suit contemporary tastes : Francois I's gallery, Henri II's ballroom, the apartments of the three queen mothers (Catherine and Marie de Medicis and Anne of Austria), the throne room (Louis XIII ceiling), Madame de Maintenon's apartments, the Louis XV wing, Marie-Antoinette's boudoir. Napoleon refurnished many of the salons ; the courtyard with the famous horseshoe staircase *(La Cour du Cheval Blanc)* is also known as *« La Cour des Adieux »* (the farewell courtyard), for it was here that Napoleon bade farewell to his men when he abdicated in 1814. Forty years later, Napoleon III added a charming theater.

Like Versailles at a later date, Fontainebleau created a decorative style of its own. The first

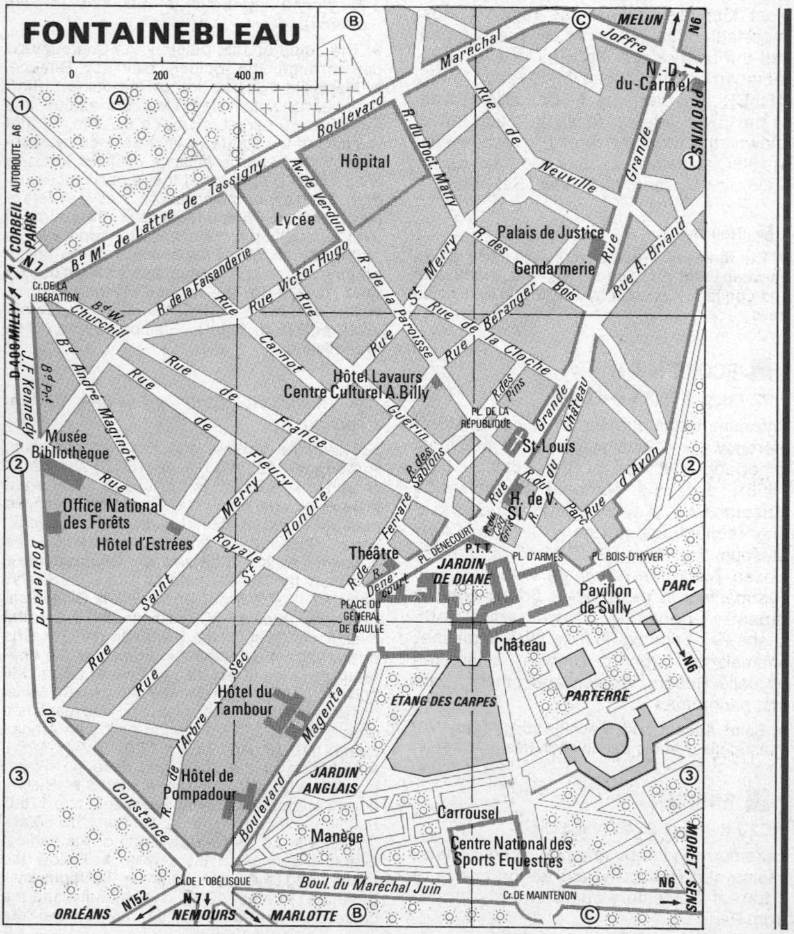

school of Fontainebleau, as the earlier style is known, was influenced by Mannerist tastes introduced by the Italian artists - Il Primaticcio, Rosso, Cellini, to name only three - whom François commissioned to adorn his residence. This style was supplanted by the work of the Flemish craftsmen who, during the reign of Henri IV, inspired the second Fontainebleau school. ▶ Garden of Diana - named for the central statue of the Goddess Diana : **gardens★** arranged in the manner of an English park to the East, and in the formal French style to the west *(visits : gardens and park, sunrise to sunset; château : 10-12:30 & 2-5 or 6, closed Tue.)* □

Also... ▶ Napoleonic Museum of Military Art and History *(2-5:30, ex Sun. and Mon.; closed Sep. and nat. hols.).* ▶ **Hôtel d'Orléans★** (18thC) decorated by pupils of the painter Boucher (1703-70) (visits on request). ▶ Le Vieux Logis, ravishing Ile-de-France house opposite park *(10-12 & 2-4, Apr.-Sep. ex Sun.).* ▶ **Avon church★** (12th-16thC) : tombs of many of the artists and craftsmen who worked on the château. □

■ FONTAINEBLEAU Forest★★★

C4 (Seine-et-Marne)

The 170 km² forest of Fontainebleau has been a renowned hunting ground since the Middle Ages when it was known as Bière. Dramatic rocks, lush vegetation and abundant wildlife attract thousands of nature-lovers, archaeologists, rock-climbers and hikers - familiarly known as *bleausards* - every week. Newcomers can find a guide at the Office National des Forêts, 217 Rue Grande, Fontainebleau.

The oak is found most often, followed by beech, hornbeam, alder and pine. Long, broken sandstone ridges cover a total of about 40 km² and end in bare spurs and plateaux. Depressions are called *gorges, vallées* or *plaines,* according to size. Many of the rocky outcrops contain caves with markings that provoke endless debate among archaeologists. Paths were first marked out in the 19thC when enthusiasm was at its height for the natural landscape beloved by the Barbizon school painters. Today a network of walking and bridle paths is in constant use, and four "quiet zones" have been created. The **forest paths** are marked in blue, the GR in red/white; don't confuse these signs with the orientation marks painted on the rocks for climbers. Among the most famous sites : Denecourt Tower (named for one of the first 19thC enthusiasts), La Solle (above the racecourse), Apremont Gorges near Barbizon (→) and the Franchard Gorges.

Also... ▶ Les Trois Pignons near Milly (→), Chaos de Nemours (→) and La Dame Jehanne near Larchant (→ Nemours). □

■ GRAND MORIN Valley★

▶ From Lagny to Coulommiers *(45 km approx; illuminations in summer)*
C-D 2

The Brie plateau is picturesque valley country with lush vegetation, apple orchards, streams and villages.

▶ **Lagny-sur-Marne** (pop. 18 000) : an old fortified town, now part of the new town of **Marne-la-Vallée** ® : gabled houses in the 15thC covered market, Place de la Fontaine (12thC fountain and Flamboyant Gothic church), and Notre Dame des Ardents★ (unfinished 13thC church of a former abbey). Local museum *(2-6 Wed.-Sun.).* ▶ **Coupvray** is a traditional Brie village, birthplace of Louis Braille (1809-52), the harness-maker's son who, although blind himself from the age of three, invented the alphabet for the blind. **Museum★** *(10-12 & 2-6, Apr.-Sep.; 2-5, Oct.-Mar.; closed Tue.).* ▶ **La-Chapelle-sur-Crécy** : elegant 13thC Gothic collegiate church★. ▶ **Crécy-la-Chapelle★** ®, a fortified island town encircled by the Morin. A pleasant road continues along the left bank as far as **Coulommiers** (→), through **Tigeaux** and **Guérard,** in a bend of the river. □

■ HOUDAN

B3 / ® / pop. 2 975 (Yvelines)

When Houdan was a staging post for the army the wood-fronted houses along the two streets leading to the **church★** were mostly inns. The church, a superb mixture of Flamboyant Gothic and Renaissance styles, has an amusing 16thC fresco. 12thC keep, washhouses on the Vesgre and the Opton rivers. □

■ ILLIERS-COMBRAY★

A4 / ® / pop. 3 450 (Eure-et-Loir)

The writer Marcel Proust (1871-1922) spent his childhood holidays at Illiers with his Aunt Léonie (museum★ *3-5 ex Tue.*), and devotees of his great novel *Remembrance of Things Past* come here to discover Combray, the Vivonne (the Loir), the Pré Catelan, St. Hilaire (church of St. Jacques, 14thC, with painted wood barrel-vault) and the famous *madeleine* cakes from the local bakery, the Pâtisserie Benoist. □

▶ Nearby

▶ **Brou★** ® : old market town between Beauce and Perche; 16thC houses. ▶ Renaissance church at **Yèvres** (wood panelling and classic French furniture). ▶ **Chateau de Frazé** (15thC, much restored; *open Sun. and nat. hols.).* □

■ L'ISLE-ADAM

C2 / pop. 9 480 (Val-d'Oise)

On the Oise, riverbank recreation area; Cabouillet Bridge; Renaissance church; a forest of oak and limetrees. Hilly to the east; pleasant churches at **Presles** (12th-16thC) and **Maffliers** (16thC).

■ JOUARRE★

D2 / pop. 2 700 (Seine-et-Marne)

Jouarre looks down from the Brie plateau to Le Petit Morin, melting into the Marne. The road, dating from the Revolution, divides the buildings of the the Benedictine abbey★.

▶ On one side is the parish church (16thC; remarkable sculptures) and the **Mérovingian crypt** built of Gallo-Roman material (tombs★★

of the founders); on the other side is the Romanesque tower of the abbey church, three superimposed units vaulted in the 16thC, where memorabilia from the abbey are on display. *(10-12 & 2-6, 5 pm Oct.-Mar. weekdays; 11-12 & 2-5 or 6, Sun. and nat. hols.; closed Tue.).* □

▶ Petit Morin Valley★ *(50 km approx)*

▶ **Jouarre.** ▶ The road runs up the central plateau of dairy-farming Brie until it reaches **Rebais,** on Gargantua Hill (view) : 12thC church and abbey buildings (17thC). ▶ Detour to **Doue** ® to see the Gothic choir and 14thC stained glass. ▶ The imposing church at **Verdelot** (15th-16thC) is dedicated to St. Crispin, patron saint of shoemakers (15thC statuettes). ▶ Frescos in the 13th-14thC church at **Bellot** ▶ Return along the right bank via **Saint-Cyr-sur-Morin :** the writer Pierre MacOrlan (1882-1970) lived here from 1924 until his death; (museum; *visits by arrangement, pm*); church 12thC, 14thC and 16thC. □

■ MANTES-LA-JOLIE

B2 / ® / pop. 43 585 (Yvelines)

This town no longer lives up to its name ("Pretty Mantes") : WWII left little of its former beauty, and the banks of the Seine, polluted and concrete-laden, offer little to attract walkers. Nevertheless the **collegiate church★★,** twin of Notre Dame de Paris, is an important example of Gothic art.

▶ Central doorway; chapel of Navarre (14thC); statuettes of the four royal foundresses. Hôtel-Dieu (18thC; hospital). ▶ Saint Maclou Tower. ▶ Maximilian Luce museum (work of local landscape painter; *2-5:30, closed Tue.*). ▶ Pont de Limay (12thC bridge). ▶ **Gassicourt** *(2 km W) :* Romanesque church (12th-13thC) with 13thC stained glass. ▶ Limay : 11th-13thC church, statues★. □

▶ Nearby

▶ **Rosny :** to the west, the Château de Sully (16th-19thC), neo-Classical almshouse; and Singer sewing-machine factory. ▶ To the south, Vaucouleurs Valley : **châteaux of Rosay** (17thC) and **Septeuil** (18thC). ▶ **Mauldre Valley :** 12thC church; **Château d'Epône** (18thC). ▶ **Maule :** château (Louis XIII) and Romanesque-Renaissance church. □

▶ Valleys of the Vexin★ *(65 km approx, half-day).*

Every village has a pretty church and/or a château. ▶ **Mantes.** ▶ The route climbs north on the plateau of Arthies (views). ▶ Romanesque church at **Fontenay-Saint-Père;** pink and white château at **Mesnil.** ▶ **Arthies :** fortress with dovecote. ▶ In July, detour via the **château de Maudétour** (18thC, unfinished). ▶ **Guiry-en-Vexin★** ® : classic 17thC château where J. de Maistre (1753-1821; Catholic political theorist) lived. Local archaeology museum *(tel 3-467-40-31 or 704-31-73).* Renaissance church. ▶ Another 17th-18thC château at **Gadancourt;** church with Romanesque bell-tower. ▶ **Avernes,** by the source of the river Aubette, 13thC and 18thC church. ▶ **Thémericourt :** lovely site, 17thC château and 13thC church. ▶ **Château de Vigny** (Renaissance, 19thC; *Mar.-Nov., Sat., Sun., Mon. and hols.*), ancestral home of the poet Alfred de Vigny (1797-1863). Nearby, château de **Grisy** *(Aug., pm).* ▶ **Longuesse :** Romanesque church, remodelled in 17thC. ▶ **Château de Villette★,** designed by Hardouin-Mansart (1667). The philosopher and encyclopaedist Condorcet (1743-94) lived here *(Sun. and nat. hols., 3-6).* ▶ **Meulan :** a yachting centre on the Seine. ▶ Return along the **Montcient Valley** in the shadow of the 12th-13thC church spires of **Gaillon-sur-Montcient.** □

Safaris start here

African big game roams free in the reserve park at **Thoiry** ® *(9:45-6, Apr.-Oct.; 10-5, Nov.-Mar.), as well as in the wooded park at* **Saint-Vrain** *(10-6, Apr.-Sep.; 12-5, Oct.-Mar.). Don't forget the ornithological reserve at the* **Château de Sauvage,** *or the smaller indigenous wildlife in the forest of Rambouillet at* **Clairefontaine.**

The glory of the cathedrals

Gothic art was sired by invention out of necessity. The need was for larger and lighter churches to accommodate growing populations and to exalt the faith. The invention was the ogive vault, which redistributed the thrust of the classic Romanesque vault, enabling windows and openings to be more easily introduced. This new architectural technique made its first timid appearance in France at Morienval around 1125, in the wake of early developments in Lombardy and England. The architects of the Ile-de-France initiated the series of great cathedrals that were to symbolise the enthusiastic faith of the Middle Ages. All the arts were involved in this creative explosion : Gothic sculpture appeared at Chartres in 1145 and was perfected at Senlis with the invention of the statue column; Chartres alone demonstrates that stained glass achieved its most brilliant expression in the Gothic era : the blues have never been reproduced or repeated elsewhere.

■ MARLY-LE-ROI★

B2 / ® / pop. 17 300 (Yvelines)

The hillside town of Marly once looked down on the 13 pavilions built by Mansart to provide a country retreat for Louis XIV. The pavilions have long since gone, but the grounds have been preserved.

▶ The **park★** plunges down to the Seine; the horse-pond was formerly adorned by the Girardon statues of horses now to be seen in Paris at the junction of the Champs-Elysées and the Place de la Concorde. Near the royal gate, an **outdoor museum** records the history of the village and the estate *(4-6; closed Mon., Tue. and nat. hols.).* Artists such as Sisley, Maillol and Vuillard flocked to Marly in the late 19thC and early 20thC. ▶ The church of St. Vigor is by Mansart. ▶ 18thC mansions around the town hall and the royal kennels. ▶ Port-Marly : Villa Monte-Cristo, the Oriental-Gothic folly where the novelist Alexandre Dumas the elder (1802-70) lived. □

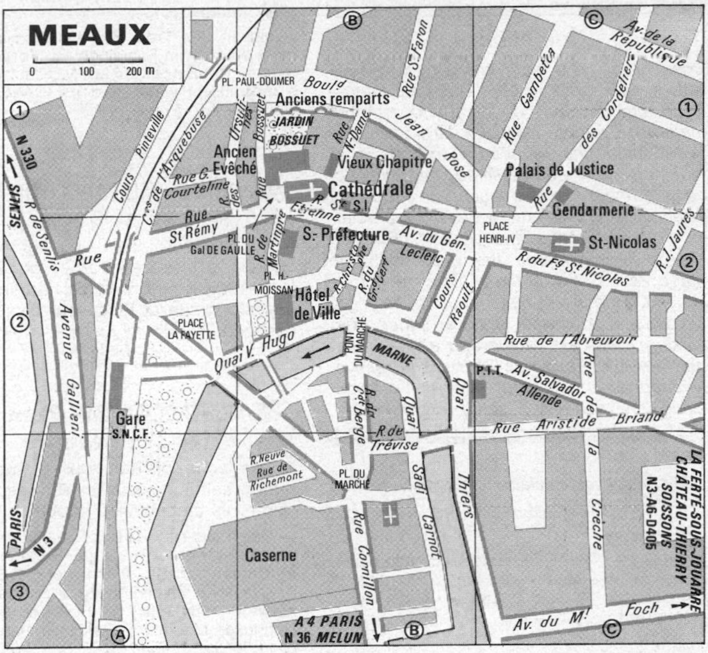

▶ Nearby

▶ **Louveciennes** ® : another aristocratic retreat : 13thC church; 18thC château; Mme. du Barry's pavilion (designed by Ledoux). ▶ **Forest of Marly :** 20 km² of oak, beech and chestnut with many roe deer; explore it along GR1. □

■ MARNE Valley

C2 (Seine-et-Marne)

The area between Nogent and Lagny has still retained its rustic character; the river is dotted with islands, and a canal runs beneath rows of poplars. Parks and a leisure centre are still under construction for the new town of Marne-la-Vallée.

▶ Mme. de Pompadour (1723-64; Louis XV's mistress and advisor) lived at the **Château de Champs★** *(18thC; 10-12 & 1:30-6, 21 Mar.-30 Sep.; 10-12 & 1:30-5 in Nov.; 10-12 & 1:30-4:30, 1 Dec.-20 Feb.; 10-12 & 1:30-4:30, 21 Feb.-21 Mar.; closed Tue. and Wed.).* ▶ See the Menier chocolate factory★ (designed by Gustav Eiffel, 1832-1923) and workers' accommodation at **Noisiel;** a valuable reminder of 19thC industrial architecture and workforce organisation. ▶ **Guermantes★** ® : château, evoking Proust's masterpiece (→ Illiers-Combray) 18thC décor *(2-6, Sat., Sun. and nat. hols., 15 Mar.-15 Nov.).* □

■ MEAUX★

D2 / ® / pop. 45 875 (Seine-et-Marne)

This market town in a loop of the Marne is renowned for Brie and Bossuet : Brie de Meaux is the local variety of the cheese; the celebrated bishop of Meaux, the writer and orator Bossuet (1627-1704), was tutor

New towns

Paris has expanded continuously since the turn of the century. The city has tripled in area, and is now surrounded by a ring of urban development 15 km wide. Beyond this point, the agglomeration has spread in tentacle fashion along the major road, rail and motorway networks. In 1969, five new towns were created 30 km from Paris in an attempt to control the urban sprawl generated by industry and housing. The new towns were planned to incorporate the traditional elements (housing, work, leisure facilities) that tend to be lacking in too many suburban areas. Although the scheme has not been an unqualified success, the new towns of Evry (26 km SW of Paris, A6), Cergy-Pontoise (30 km W of Paris, A15), Melun-Sénart (40 km SE of Paris, A6 and F6), Marne-la-Vallée (13 km E of Paris, A4) and St. Quentin-en-Yvelines (30 km W of Paris, A13 and N10) benefit from a clearly-defined city structure and embody contemporary ideas in architecture and urban planning.

to the Dauphin (later Louis XV), and a leading 17thC intellectual.

▶ The Gothic cathedral★ (end 12th-16thC) is connected to the chapterhouse (13thC; covered staircase 16thC). ▶ The former episcopal palace★ (12thC, 17thC) squares off the courtyard; Bossuet Museum (personal effects, writings) and Briard Museum (the Brie region; *2-6, closed Tue. and nat. hols.*); garden in the form of a bishop's mitre by Le Nôtre; Bossuet's

Brie cheese

Brie cheese is a soft, cow's-milk cheese with a pale, gold colour. The characteristic flavour develops during the one-month maturation period. Between 10% and 35% fail to meet the required standards after maturing and are declassified; they may not be sold under the Brie label. Long a purely local delicacy, Brie is now widely appreciated both in France and abroad. Brie de Meaux is considered the best, with the smoother Coulommiers Brie a close second. Brie from Melun has a stronger flavour and a coarser texture. Other Brie-making towns are Montereau and Nangis; at Dreux, the "Feuille de Dreux" is attractively wrapped in chestnut leaves. Fontainebleau cheese is very creamy, soft and white.

study *(Historical spectacle in summer).* ▶ View from the ramparts. □

▶ Nearby

▶ **Trilport** ® *(5 km E)*: riverside recreation area. **Montceaux-les-Meaux** *(8.5 km E)*: ruins of Catherine de Médicis' château★ in park (visit on request). □

■ MELUN

C3 / ® / pop. 36 220 (Seine-et-Marne)

Melun, like Paris, grew from an island in the Seine into an important industrial centre.

▶ On the right bank, **St. Aspais Church** (late Gothic, 16thC). ▶ On the island, next to the prison, the **church of Notre Dame** (Romanesque, much restored); Vicomté Mansion, Quai de la Courtille : small museum with 19thC landscapes *(10-12 & 2-6; closed Tue., Sun. and nat. hols.)*; Henri Chapu museum (official sculptor of the Third Republic; *3-6, Wed., Thu., Sat.; closed summer*) on the right bank of the river. □

▶ Nearby

▶ Ruins of the **abbey of Lys** *(3 km SW)*, founded by Blanche de Castille (1188-1252, wife of Louis VIII and mother of Louis IX (St. Louis). ▶ 18thC château at **Vaux-le-Pénil**★ *(2 km on Chartrettes road)*; now a museum of Surrealist art (Dali, de Chirico; *usually open Sun. pm; tel (6) 068 61 33*). ▶ 11 km into the Brie plain is the Château de Blandy, an interesting example of feudal architecture *(9 or 10-11:45 & 2-5 or 6; closed Mon., Sat. and Sun. in winter).* ▶ Gothic church at **Champeaux**★ *(11 km NE)*: amusing choir stalls. □

■ MILLY-LA-FORÊT★

C4 / ® / pop. 3 795 (Essonne)

Milly lies in a basin on the edge of the forest of Fontainebleau, where the river École waters cress beds and fields of medicinal plants. The decorations by Cocteau (1959) in the chapel of **St. Blaise des Simples** were inspired by this local specialty of "simples" or medicinal herbs *(Easter-1 Nov : daily ex Tue.; winter, Sat. and Sun. : 10-12 & 2-6).* 15thC **marketplace**★. □

▶ Nearby

▶ **Massif des Trois Pignons**★★ : among the most dramatic in Fontainebleau Forest. ▶ **Château de Courances** *(10 km NE)*: surrounded by a magnificent water-garden★★ *(4-8, Sat. and Sun, and Apr.-Nov.).* □

■ MONTEREAU-FAULT-YONNE

D4 / pop. 19 550 (Seine-et-Marne)

At the junction of the Seine and the Yonne; church of Notre Dame et St. Loup (14th-16thC); Priory of St. Martin (11thC); prehistoric site at Pincevent on the Varennes road. □

■ MONTFORT-L'AMAURY★★

B3 / ® / pop. 2 675 (Yvelines)

At the edge of Rambouillet forest (→) : rather self-consciously picturesque, with tiled roofs and cobbled streets.

▶ Old ramparts; ruins of the Montfort keep (11thC); tower of Anne de Bretagne (15thC). ▶ Church of St. Pierre (end 15th-17thC; Renaissance stained glass). ▶ Former **charnel-house**★ (1584-1608). ▶ Ravel Museum : the composer Maurice Ravel lived here 1921-37 *(9-11:30 & 2:30-5:30 or 6, Sat. Sun. and nat. hols.; Mon. Wed. Thu. : pm).* □

▶ The Forest of Rambouillet

▶ GR1 from Neauphle to St. Léger goes past Ravel's house to the lake near the Baudet Gate; a cycle path runs to Rambouillet (→) past the prettiest **lakes** in the forest. Views of châteaux : ▶ SE, **Les Mesnuls** ® : château (16th-18thC), now a hospital and training centre for physically-handicapped children; ▶ **Château de la Mormaire,** (Louis XIII style; *4 km SW*); ▶ **Château du Rouvray** W of St. Léger; ▶ **Château de Neuville** (16thC), at **Gambais** ®. ▶ The forest villages are now full of weekend cottages : ▶ **Saint-Léger-en-Yvelines** ® is a good excursion centre; ▶ **Grosrouvre** : pretty church on attractive site. □

■ MONTMORENCY

C2 / pop. 20 830 (Val-d'Oise)

A quiet residential town on a hill SE of the forest, once the fief of the Montmorencys, one of the great families of Old France. The philosopher Jean-Jacques Rousseau stayed there; it was a fashionable resort during the Second Empire (mid-19thC).

▶ Hôtel de Ville (end of 18thC); Flamboyant Gothic-Renaissance church (stained glass★). ▶ Rousseau Museum *(2-6, closed Mon.).* □

▶ Nearby

▶ The valley of Montmorency, famed for the cherries grown there, has been transformed by the proximity of Roissy International Airport; the beautiful valley **forest** is nevertheless splendid; views. Numerous trails including GR1 (NW). ▶ SW, **Taverny** church★ : many sculptures★; Renaissance altar piece; four statues of the Virgin; 16thC crucifix; and wood panelling. Former priory *(Sat., Sun. in summer).* □

MORET-SUR-LOING★

D4 / ® / pop. 3 555 (Seine-et-Marne)

A favourite of Impressionist painters.

▶ 14thC gates in town wall; François I house in Hôtel de Ville courtyard; ▶ 15th-16thC house in Rue Grande; ▶ 13th-15thC church; ▶ 15thC main building of Bon St. Jacques almshouse; ▶ damaged 12th-17thC keep *(2:30-6:30, Sat., Sun. and nat. hols., Easter-Oct.)*; ▶ House of Alfred Sisley (1839-99), English Impressionist; ▶ Clémenceau museum on the other side of the Loing Bridge★ (residence of statesman Michel Clémenceau, 1873-1944; *Sat. and Sun. pm*). □

Also... view over the town from Montigny road, ▶ **Saint-Mammès :** excursions on the Seine. Leave from the right bank quay. ▶ Lakes to the south (→ Nemours). ▶ Summer festival *(every Sat.)* : local history depicted by costumed townspeople. ▶ Try the **sucres d'orge** (barley sugar) originally made by local nuns and still a thriving cottage industry in Moret. □

▶ Down the valley of the Loing★ *(40 km approx, half day)*

▶ Sisley's favourite river runs along the edge of the forest parallel to a poplar-lined canal, through a series of charming villages. On the left bank, **Montigny** is crowned by the massive bell-tower of its 11th-16thC church. ▶ **Bourron-Marlotte** ®, turn-of-the-century villas in the forest (W), a second Barbizon (→) for Romanticist and Impressionist painters; attractive Louis XIII château *(visits on request, tel 6-070-90-06)*. ▶ The best view of **Grez-sur-Loing** is from the other bank, near **Montcourt :** mossy 15thC bridge, 12thC keep and 12th-13thC church among thickets. ▶ At **Fromonville** the canal joins the river to form a sort of peninsula. To one side is a small Romanesque church. ▶ The other side of **Nemours** (→) : massive rock outcrops in the woods. ▶ **Portonville** and **Glandelles :** mills, then scattered islets. ▶ **Souppes-sur-Loing :** lake and Romanesque church (13thC). ▶ **Château-Landon**★ (→) : fortified town on a spur overlooking the Fusain; best approach from E. ▶ **Mez-le-Maréchal★ :** impressive 13thC castle ruins. □

NEMOURS

C4 / ® / pop. 11 675 (Seine-et-Marne)

A waterside clearing around a feudal château and a church, between the river Loing and the canal; spoiled by nearby N7.

▶ 16thC church of St. Jean Baptiste : noteworthy radiating chapels; 12th-13th and 15thC château *(10-12 & 2-5:30, Sat., Sun., Mon.; 2-5:30, Wed., Thu., Fri.; closed Tue.)*. ▶ In the forest, **Museum of Prehistoric Ile-de-France★★** *(Sens road, 10-12 & 2-5:30, ex Tue. and nat. hols.)*. ▶ **Rochers Gréau Park★,** 70 acres of rocky forest. □

▶ Forest walks

The SI of Nemours has marked a network of walks around the town (blue markers) that match up with GR13 and lead to interesting sites : natural amphitheatres, a sand "sea", woods and sandstone outcrops. □

▶ Nearby

▶ **Larchant★** ® *(8 km NW)* : a charming village in the Commanderie woods★, part of the forest of Fontainebleau (→). Remains of the pilgrim church★ of St. Mathurin ("for the healing of madmen and fallen women"); various styles from Late Romanesque to Gothic; 14thC doorway★, 15thC statues★ ▶ The wood N of Larchant hides the largest rock outcrop in the forest, including **La Dame Jehanne★,** the highest rock in the vicinity of Paris. ▶ **Egreville★,** picturesque village *(19 km SE)* : 16thC market; 13th-15thC church; 16thC barn and 16th-17thC château once owned by the opera composer Jules Massenet (1842-1912). □

▶ Along the valleys of the Lunain and the Orvanne★ *(65 km approx)*

The two rivers spread out into lakes before mingling with the Loing. ▶ **Nemours.** ▶ **Paley :** a gabled bell-tower. ▶ **Lorrez-le-Bocage :** the Lunain empties into the moat of a theatrical 16thC château; 13thC church. ▶ Church and tithe barn at **Chéroy.** ▶ Take the fork to **Vallery :** unfinished Renaissance château★. ▶ The Orvanne runs past the foot of the **Manor of Diant.** ▶ **Chevry :** Louis XIII château. ▶ Mill-hotel at **Flagy** ® : an ideal stop. ▶ **Château St. Ange :** once the residence of the Duchess of Étampes, François I's mistress. ▶ **Villecerf :** a last look at the Orvanne and the **Moret Lakes★** (→). □

NOGENT-LE-ROTROU

A4 / ® / pop. 13 200 (Eure-et-Loir)

This principal town of the Perche country is an important agricultural market and industrial centre.

▶ The old town, rebuilt in the 15thC, possesses numerous Flamboyant Gothic and Renaissance buildings. ▶ 11th-12thC château, now the **Perche museum** (regional ethnology; *1 May-31 Oct., 10-12 & 2-6; 1 Nov.-30 Apr., 10-12 & 2-5; closed Tue.)*. ▶ Church of Notre Dame (13th-14thC, much restored) : former chapel of the 17thC Hôtel-Dieu (hospital); tomb of Sully (1559-1641; minister to Henri IV) and his wife. ▶ Old houses in rues Bourg-le-Comte and St. Laurent. ▶ Churches of St. Laurent (15th-16thC) and St. Hilaire (same era, 13thC choir). ▶ Nearby; **Cloche Valley★,** NE. □

NOYON★

D1 / ® / pop. 14 850 (Oise)

This industrial centre between canals that run parallel to the Oise river retains numerous monuments despite widespread destruction during WWII. **Cathedral★ :** one of the first in the Gothic style (1145-1200), still surrounded by dependencies (chapterhouse, 16thC library and 13thC cloister).

▶ Noyonnais museum in the Renaissance Episcopal Palace *(10-12 & 2-5 or 6 ex Tue.)*. ▶ Restored Renaissance Hôtel de Ville. ▶ The religious reformer Jean Calvin, born here in 1509, is commemorated by a museum *(Apr.-Nov., 10-12 & 2:30-5; closed Tue.)* and Municipal Museum of Noyonnais *(daily ex. Tue., 10-12 & 2-5 or 6)*.

Also... ▶ Ruined **Abbey of Ourscamps★★** (12th-13thC); Salle des Morts★ (13thC infirmary) is now a chapel; 18thC building. ▶ Franco-American museum in the **Château de Blérancourt** *(14 km SE; tel. 23.39.60.16)*. □

POISSY

B2 / ® / pop. 36 550 (Yvelines)

The town was a royal residence until the

15thC. St. Louis (Louis IX), who was born here, instituted a cattle market that eventually became the biggest in France. The town is now largely supported by the motor industry.

▶ Church of Notre Dame (12thC) : Romanesque bell-towers, remodelled in 13thC, 15thC, and 16thC; restored by Viollet-le-Duc (19thC). St. Louis may have been baptised in the font in 1215; 16thC *Burial of Christ;* statue. ▶ Abbey of Poissy : 14thC building flanked by towers at the entrance; inside : **Toy Museum★** *(9:30-12 & 2-5:30; closed Mon., Tue. and nat. hols.).* ▶ **Villa Savoye★** in the school grounds, designed by the architect Le Corbusier in 1930 *(10-12 & 1:30-5; closed Tue.).* □

▶ Nearby

▶ **Villennes-sur-Seine** *(4.5 km W) :* recreation area on an island in the river. ▶ **Triel :** church★ (12th-13thC, Renaissance porch and apse), stained glass attributed to Jean Le Prince (16thC). □

PONTOISE

B2 / ® / pop. 29 400 (Val-d'Oise)

This ancient stronghold of the Vexin retains its historic charm despite WWII damage and recent urban development nearby. The lower town, along the bank of the Oise, is crowned by the red roofs of houses built by generations of craftsmen. Kings of France who visited Pontoise endowed it with monuments.

▶ Church of Notre Dame (late 16thC, statues 13thC). ▶ **Church of St. Maclou :** primitive Gothic choir (ca. 1140); nave and façade date from 15thC; Renaissance side aisles (see 16thC *Burial of Christ; windows).* ▶ The **Tavet-Delacour Museum** in a turreted mansion dating from the late Gothic period : 16th-18thC sculptures in wood and stone, drawings, Freundlich Collection (works of Otto Freundlich 1878-1943 and others : *10-12 & 2-6; closed Tue. and nat. hols.).* **Pissarro Museum** *(2-6; closed Mon., Tue. and nat. hols.).* □

▶ Along the Viosne Valley *(approx 40 km).*

The river's green banks are marked out by old mills, and every village boasts a church that deserves more than a casual glance; an area popular with weekend cyclists. ▶ Pontoise. ▶ **Montgeroult,** a real citadel *(5 Jul.-10 Aug. and 20 Aug.-10 Oct. ex Thu. and Fri.)* and 13thC church; and opposite, **Courcelles** (Louis XIII manor) by the riverside. ▶ Three churches you should see : **Santeuil★** (Romanesque), **Nucourt★** (Renaissance; 15th-16thC statues), and **Chars★ :** Romanesque façade, Gothic choir, Renaissance tower. ▶ Return via **Marines** (interesting Renaissance doorway); **Moussy** (16thC château, *1 May-15 Oct.*); **Cormeilles-en-Vexin** ® (12thC, 13thC, 16thC church). □

PROVINS★★

D3 / ® / pop. 12 680 (Seine-et-Marne)

This "town of roses" rising, like Chartres, from fields of corn, is a superb, yet little-known relic of the Middle Ages. The 12th-13thC ramparts of the upper town, worthy of the renowned walled city of Carcassonne, enclose exceptional buildings, charming cottages and gardens spilling over with roses. Mediaeval gables and Renaissance doorways recall the days when Provins was the third largest town in France and merchants from all over Europe flocked to the twice-yearly Foires de Champagne (regional fairs) : tour of the monuments *(10-12 & 2-5 or 6, Apr.-Sep.; 2-4:30 low season).*

▶ Upper town : Rue St. Thibault (B1); the Hôtel-Dieu (old infirmary) has a 13thC doorway, a Renaissance stone altarpiece and 13thC font. ▶ Nº 16 : entrance to the vaulted and ornamen-

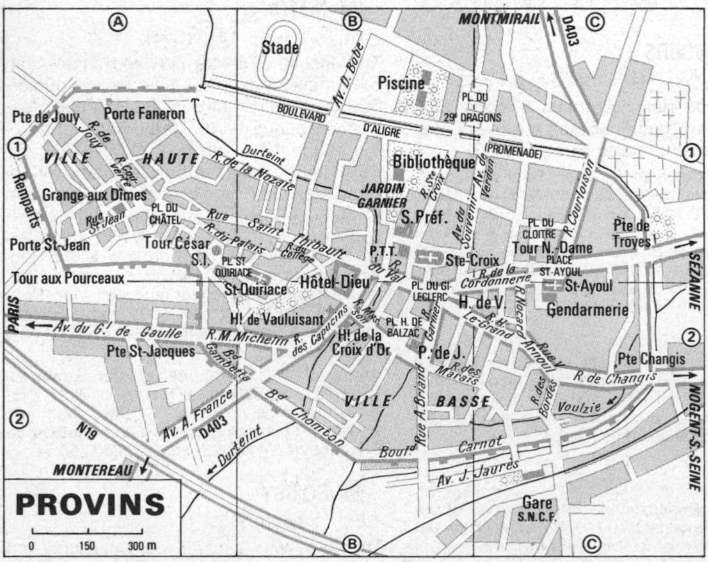

ted **underground passages**★ that run beneath the infirmary *(2-6, Sun. and nat. hols. Easter-1 Nov.)*; Nº 18 : 16thC house; Nº 50 : remains of 12thC birthplace of St. Thibault. ▶ **Church of St. Quiriace :** choir★ (late 12thC), transept and nave 13thC (remodelled), fine north (12thC) and south (13thC) side doorways. ▶ **Caesar's Tower** *(Tour César)*★ is a 44 m-high landmark dating from the 12thC; the base was added by English soldiers during the Hundred Years' War (14thC); 17thC roofs (timberwork and sentry walk★). ▶ rue du Palais : Romanesque house. ▶ Tithe barn★ (end 12thC). ▶ The best preserved **ramparts** run between the St. Jean and Jouy gates. ▶ St. Thibault's ramp leads to the **lower town.** ▶ To the south, 13thC mansions of Vauluisant and Croix d'Or. ▶ In the north, Ste. Croix church (B1; 12thC nave, 16thC choir); **church of St. Ayoul** (C2), a former Benedictine abbey church : 12thC, much rebuilt especially in the 16thC. Romanesque doorway (damaged), 16thC statues, 17thC woodwork. ▶ Tower of Notre Dame du Val : sole remnant of a 16thC collegiate church . □

▶ Nearby

▶ Some of the most beautiful churches in France are hidden in the green countryside around Provins. ▶ **St-Loup-de-Naud**★ *(8 km SW) :* rivals Provins from its walled hilltop; Benedictine church (11th-12thC) with superb doorway★★. ▶ Detour to the fortress of **Sigy** (15th-16th-17thC; *visit by written request*) *en route* to the fortified town of **Donnemarie-Dontilly** *(18 km SW;* oil wells nearby) : early 13thC church★ , cemetery with 16thC wooden gallery. ▶ SW of Donnemarie : imposing Cistercian abbey of **Preuilly** with attached farm. ▶ **Rampillon**★ **:** 13th-14thC church, once a Commandery of the Knights Templar; only one tower remains, but the Twelve Apostles still await the Judgement Day★★. ▶ **Nangis,** former stronghold on the Champagne fair route : fortress (transformed) and Gothic church. ▶ Before returning to Provins, visit the 17thC mill★ at **Chaix,** N of Nangis *(Sun. 3-6, 15 Apr.-30 Sep.)*. □

■ RAMBOUILLET★

B3 / ® / pop. 22 500 (Yvelines)

The **château**★ (mostly 18thC) has often been rebuilt, but the round tower where François I died can still be seen. Louis XVI here established Marie-Antoinette's dairy, the **English gardens** and an experimental farm that was the forerunner of the modern-day sheepfolds of the **Bergerie Nationale**★**,** where you can see the renowned merino stud★ *(10-12 & 2-6 or 5 pm out of season; closed Tue.)*. □

■ RAMBOUILLET Forest★★

B3 (Yvelines)

A royal hunting preserve where packs still hunt; abundant growth of oak, birch and beech, with good access; many streams and ponds★.

▶ GR1 runs right through the forest, and two cycle trails run from Rambouillet to Montfort-l'Amaury (→) and from Montfort to St. Léger-en-Yvelines. The forest population of wild boar, red deer and roe deer can be seen in the animal park at **Clairefontaine** *(pm and all day Sun.; closed Mon. and May-Jun.)*. □

▶ Nearby

▶ **Epernon** (13 km) : timber-framed houses, church in Beauce, regional Gothic, 12thC cellars. ▶ **Château de Sauvage :** ornithological reserve and deer park *(6 km from Epernon)*. ▶ **Le Perray-en-Yvelines** ® : horse-breeding. □

■ ROYAUMONT★★

C2 (Val-d'Oise)

The abbey, founded by St. Louis when he was only 12, became one of the richest in the Ile-de-France *(visits all year round, every day ex. Tue.)*; it is now a cultural centre (concerts★).

▶ Abbey church : 13thC remnants among woods and lakes; Gothic cloister★★ and refectory★★; 18thC abbot's palace built by Ledoux.

Also... ▶ Romanesque, Gothic and Renaissance church at **Luzarches** *(5 km S)*. □

■ SAINT-GERMAIN-EN-LAYE★★

B2 / ® / pop. 40 830 (Yvelines)

The epitome of an affluent residential town : an old château in the forest, good air, fast trains to Paris (40 mins by RER regional express network).

▶ The **château** was one of the principal royal residences; many aristocratic 17thC and 18thC mansions are still in evidence nearby. The château was rebuilt by François I and restored under Napoleon III; 14thC keep, and Sainte Chapelle★ from the reign of St. Louis. **National Antiquities Museum**★★ **:** artefacts from Prehistoric (Brassempouy Venus★★), Celtic (Antreville helmet★ , Bourray deity★), Gallo-Roman (statue of Mercury from Lezoux★, candelabrum from Bavai★, mosaic from St. Romain★), and Merovingian eras *(9:45-12 & 1:30-5:15 ex Tue. and hols.)*. ▶ **Terrace** designed by Le Nôtre overlooking the Seine (view★); the Henri IV pavilion, S, is a remnant of the château where Louis XIV was born. ▶ French Classical church (1776). ▶ In the Arts garden, sculpture by Lobo and **museum :** 16th-17thC satirical Flemish paintings (*The Conjuror* by Hieronymous Bosch); drawings; medicine chest that belonged to Mme. de Montespan (1641-1707), Louis XIV's mistress *(closed for renovation)*. ▶ Almshouse★, founded by Mme. de Montespan, where Maurice Denis (1870-1943) lived; now the **Prieuré Museum**★**,** displaying the works of the Symbolist school and the Nabis; Maurice Denis studio *(10:30-5:30, ex Mon., Tue. and nat. hols)*; monument to Debussy by Maillol. □

■ SAINT-GERMAIN Forest★

B2 (Yvelines)

Although intersected by major roads, this 40 km^2 forest in a bend of the Seine has well-planned walking trails.

▶ **Château du Val** *(3 km NE)*, designed by Mansart (1669). ▶ **Maisons Laffitte** ® *(9 km NE) :* a dormitory town centred on a race-course, Mansart's best-known château★, a model of *Grand Siècle* (17thC) architecture *(9-12 & 2-6; closed Tue. and Sun. am.)*.

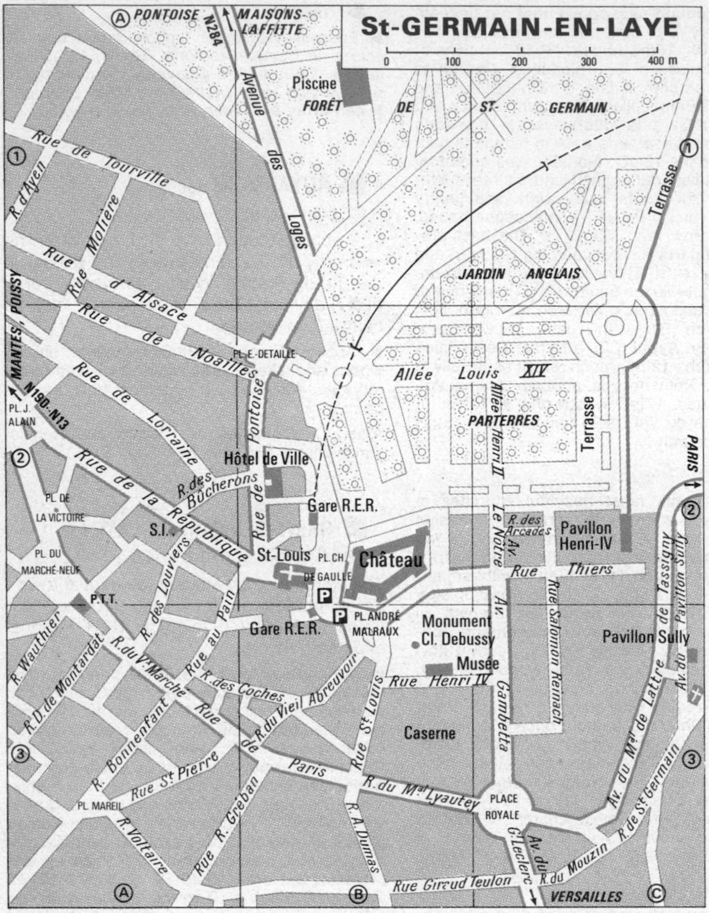

■ SEINE Valley★

▶ Excursion *(30 km approx from Moret to Melun)*
D4-C3

Between Moret (→) and Melun (→) the Seine takes on a festive air and the villages on the forested banks look like turn-of-the-century waterside resorts.

▶ **Moret.** ▶ **Thomery★** ® : reminiscent of the Midi; vineyards everywhere; large low church (12thC-14thC); 17thC château. ▶ **Samoreau,** between the forest and the Brie plain. ▶ **Héricy** ® : green islets in the Seine; charming church with four gables on the bell-tower, typical of Brie. ▶ **Fontaine-le-Port :** similar bell-tower. ▶ After **Melun** (→) : regatta waters around **Seine-Port** and **Morsang-sur-Seine.** □

■ SÉNART Forest

C3

An oak forest with birch and pine towards the centre, now at the heart of the new town of Melun-Sénart; especially attractive in the west near **Champrosay.**

▶ From **Brunoy** ® to the N, by crossing the forest, one arrives at **La Faisanderie :** outdoor sculpture museum and forest information centre in an 18thC pavilion. □

■ SENLIS★★★

C1 / ® / pop. 15 280 (Oise)
See plan on following page

Senlis is a quiet country town where life goes on behind imposing Renaissance and

An Ile-de-France museum

The 17thC château de Sceaux, rebuilt in 1861, was formerly the residence of Colbert (→ Beauvais), finance minister to Louis XIV; it is now the Regional Museum of the Ile de France, with collections and exhibitions that illustrate every aspect of this historic region. Park : Orangerie by Mansart; pavilion by Aurore de Perault; Hanover Pavilion (→ Paris, Suburbs section).

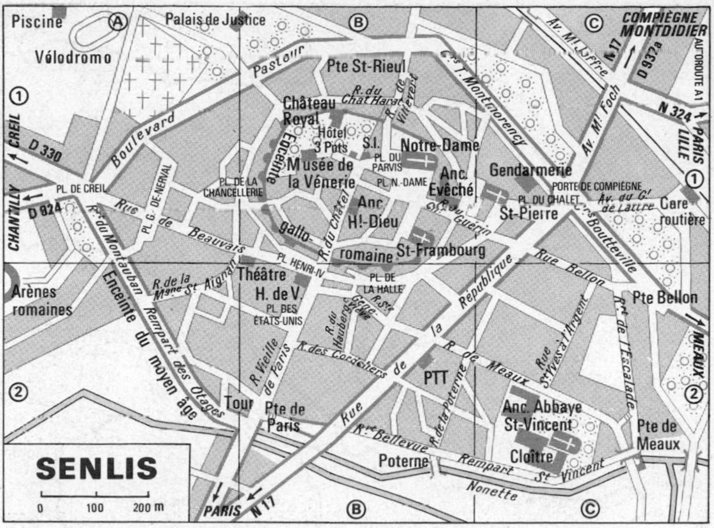

neo-Classical doorways. The town is charming rather than spectacular, although it contains a famous cathedral and Gallo-Roman fortifications with 16 towers.

▶ **Cathedral★★** (B1) : the first in a chain of churches dedicated to the Virgin; the history of Gothic architecture in the Ile-de-France is evident in this 12thC to 16thC construction. The airy 13thC spire★ was often copied; the central doorway★ was the first to be entirely dedicated to the Virgin Mary (end of 12thC); the lateral doorways★ are in Flamboyant Gothic; Flamboyant carvings behind the façades; chapel of the Blessed Sacrament (actually a tiny pre-Romanesque church) with 15thC frescos; 14thC chapterhouse with interesting capitals; 14th-15thC statuary. ▶ In the square, 13th-16thC episcopal palace which now contains the Museum of Art and Archaeology *(10-12 & 2-6 or 6 from Oct.-Mar.; closed Tue. and Wed. am.)*, 16th-18thC houses. ▶ Cathedral forecourt : Hôtel de Vermandois, now a museum of fine arts, *same hours as above.* S., Place St. Frambourg : 12th-13thC church has become a concert auditorium named after renowned pianist Georgy Cziffra *(concerts Sat., Sun. pm. Apr.-Oct.).* ▶ Church of St. Pierre (12thC, 13thC and 16thC); E, library (18thC). ▶ On the other side of the forecourt : 16thC House of the Three Pots (*Trois Pots;* 16thC) and the Château de St. Louis (13th-14thC and 18thC), now a **hunting museum★ (Musée de la Vénerie;** *10-12 & 2-5 or 6, Oct. to Mar.; closed Tue. and Wed. am*). ▶ View of the château and the Gallo-Roman wall from Rue du Chat-Haret (B1). ▶ **Haubergier Museum** (in the former Archbishop's palace, 16thC; B1; archaeology; *same hours as the château*). Numerous old houses, especially Rue du Chatel, Rue de la Treille, Place Gérard de Nerval (A1), Rue de Beauvais, Rue Vieille de Paris (hôtel de ville 1495).

Also... ▶ **Gallo-Roman arena,** *W, (9-6).* ▶ **Abbey de La Victoire★,** commemorating Philippe Auguste's victory over Flemish forces at Bouvines (1214). ▶ Direct road to Mortefontaine (→) through the forest. □

▶ Round trip South of Senlis *(55 km, approx half day)*
C1 *(see map 3)*

▶ **Senlis** ▶ The **forest of Ermenonville★★** has many attractions : lily of the valley growing wild in the spring, play areas for children, picturesque ruins, a museum and parks with reminders of J-J Rousseau and the poet Gérard de Nerval (1808-55). ▶ **Montépilloy :** 12thC fortress on a hilltop. ▶ **Fourcharet :** 13thC monastery barn in a perfect state of preservation. ▶ The ruins of the **Abbey of Châalis★** (13thC) are overgrown and a roost for birds; frescos in the abbey chapel are attributed to Il Primaticcio (ca.1504-70); 18thC buildings by Aubert (architect of the Chantilly stables) house the superb **Jacquemart-André collections★★ :** Egyptian and Roman antiquities, mediaeval sculptures, two paintings by Giotto, and Italian Renaissance art *(park and rose garden; 1:30-6, Mon., Wed., Sat., Sun., Mar.-Nov.; the park★ is open daily ex Tue.).* ▶ The **Mer de Sable** (literally, "sea of sand"), opposite, is a very popular fine-weather leisure area. ▶ Less crowded in **Ermenonville** ® : the **Desert★** (a sandy tract) or the Marquis de Girardin's park, a splendid example of a garden from the Romantic era, dedicated to J-J Rousseau and his ideals of Nature, and ornamented with follies *(daily 10-6, Apr.-Sept.; 1:30-5 rest of year).*

▶ The mystical writer and poet Gérard de Nerval spent his childhood first at Loisy and then at **Mortefontaine** with an uncle, while his parents followed Napoleon's Grande Armée across Europe. Nerval's novel Sylvie seems to come to life in the still-wild valley of the Thève★. ▶ **Vallière park :** another of the Romantic gardens so much admired in the 18thC; glimpses of it among mist-shrouded lakes from GR1. ▶ A delightful road overlooks the **Commelles Ponds★** in the forest of Chantilly (→). ▶ The hunt used to meet at the 19thC Château de la Reine Blanche. ▶ The forest road is the best approach to Chantilly : see the the châteaux, the vast stables, the lakes and the racecourse at a single glance (→). If you have time, follow the forest road rather than the direct route to Senlis : wonderful views over both towns. □

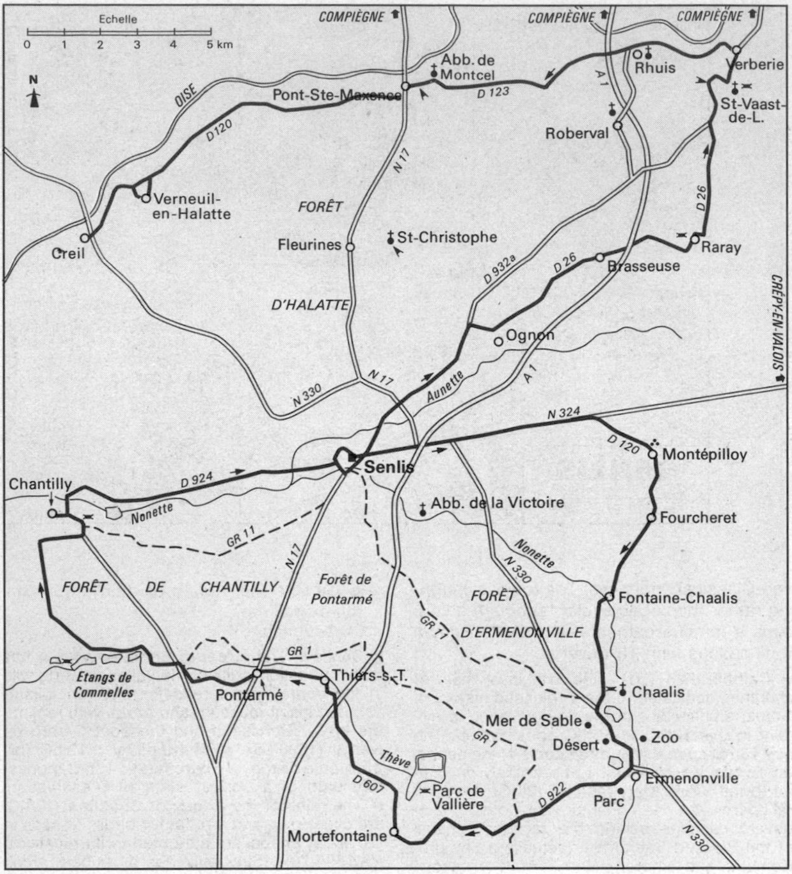

3. The Senlis area

▶ Round trip North of Senlis *(40 km approx, 2-3 hr)*
C1 *(see map 3)*

▶ **Senlis.** ▶ The **forest of Halatte★** together with the forests of Chantilly★ , Pontarmé and Ermenonville formed the great princely hunting ground of the Guise Forest. The tradition lives on, and *la chasse à courre* (literally, "hunting in pursuit", i.e. not waiting for driven game) is still practised in the Valois (→), as is the ancient art of archery. ▶ **Ognon :** park closed to visitors. ▶ **Raray★ :** visit the Italian park *(15 Mar.-15 Nov., Sat. and Sun. pm).* Renaissance château (remodelled in 18thC); remarkable sculpture and carved hunting scenes; location for Cocteau's film *La Belle et la Bête* (Beauty and the Beast). 15th-16thC church and Renaissance manor in the village. ▶ The wide plain is succeeded by valleys and villages with appealing churches. ▶ **St.-Vaast-de-Longmont,** 12thC spire, 16thC. ▶ **Rhuis★ :** three-story bell-tower and early ogive vaulting. ▶ **Abbey of Montcel★** (14th-17thC) : *(daily, 9-12 & 2-6; closed Tue. and Fri.).* ▶ From Montcel to **Fleurines** (Peaux Rouges [Redskins] Valley amusement park); road through deep forest. ▶ Ruined priory of St. Christophe, where Nature has clearly won over Art ▶ **Verneuil-en-Halatte :** Graffiti studio; collection of casts *(Sat., Sun. pm).* □

SENONCHES

A3 / ® / pop. 3 410 (Eure-et-Loir)

▶ 15th-17thC château flanked by square 12thC keep, deep in the forest; 15thC church. ▶ Oak woods★ dotted with ponds to the NW; a paradise for mushroom-pickers. The woods continue into Montecot and Champrond woods. □

▶ Nearby

Thymerais : a regional way-station between Beauce and Perche, ideal for cyclists. ▶ **La Ferté-Vidame** *(12 km W) :* the ancient château of St.-Simon has long since disappeared; the "new" one (18thC) is now in ruins; 17thC church. ▶ **Pontgouin :** on the edge of the Eure *(20 km SE) :* 16thC château, Romanesque and Gothic church, canal locks★ designed by the engineer Sebastien Vauban (1633-1707). ▶ **Courville** *(7 km S-E of Pontgouin) :* 16thC church; wooden barrel-vault; altarpiece★ and **château de Blanville,** Louis XIII style *(visits on* *request).* ▶ **Tillières** *(21 km N)* : Romanesque church. ▶ **Château de Maillebois** *(12 km NE)* defended by the fortified farmstead at **Rouvray** *(visits on request, 15 Apr.-15 Sep.).* □

■ THÉRAIN Valley

▶ From Creil to Beauvais *(45 km)*

B-C1

The river Thérain meanders through Corot country between Creil and Beauvais; almost every village church hides a masterpiece. **Creil** itself is an important industrial centre in the valley of the Oise.

Don't miss the **Gallé-Juillet Museum★,** a late 18thC house built on the ogival basement of the former château; original decor (ceramics, delft-ware, porcelain; *winter : 1-5; summer : 1:30-5:30, ex Tue.*). Take the right bank from **Cramoisy** to **Mello :** 18thC château and Renaissance church. ▶ **Bury :** church (transitional between Romanesque and Gothic). ▶ **Villers-St.-Sépulcre :** superb Burial of Christ★ in polychrome stone in the church. ▶ A forest road cuts through the **Hez beech woods** to Clermont (→). □

■ The VALOIS Region★

C-D1

The rustic wooded Valois has been miraculously preserved among agricultural lands only an hour's drive from the urban encroachment of Paris. This region is richly endowed with classified monuments and Gothic architecture began in its churches. The Valois has always been hunt country where the pursuit of game on foot or on horseback is a passion, and where a number of villages still have archery fields. Don't miss the *Musée de la Vénerie* (hunting with hounds) at Senlis (→), and the Archery Museum at Crépy-en-Valois (→ Archery Festival in May). □

■ VAUX-LE-VICOMTE★★★

C3

This splendid château was built by the celebrated 17thC architects Le Brun, Le Vau and Le Nôtre for Nicolas Fouquet (1615-80; minister of finance under Louis XIV). Not to be outdone, the king employed the same architects to build Versailles, first exiling the over-reaching Fouquet to Brittany before condemning him to life imprisonment. Carriage museum★; kitchens★; Fouquet's small apartments★; **gardens★★,** relaid from Le Nôtre's drawings and now replanned each year to maintain the splendour of the *Grand Siècle (Mar.-end Oct., 10-6 Sun. and nat. hols., closed 1-2 rest of week; 1 Nov.-31 Dec. and Feb., 11-5 Sat., Sun. and nat. hols. Fountains play 2nd and 4th Sat., 3-6; Candlelight visits 1st and 3rd Sat. each month).* □

■ VERSAILLES★★★

B2 / ® / pop. 95 240 (Yvelines)

Imitated, praised and debated (Is it neo-Classical or Baroque?), Versailles is a unique expression of the vitality of French art during the 17th-18thC. Decoration ranges from the grandiose Louis XIV Grands Appartements to the grace of the Louis XV and Louis XVI Petits Appartements. The gardens are simply unrivalled. Four million visitors annually pass through the palace and grounds.

▶ Louis XIV took up residence at Versailles in May 1682 before construction was completed, while Mansart was still overseeing 36,000 labourers and soldiers. Ten thousand residents crowded into the buildings, not counting the servants. The pomp and circumstance which attracted awed attention from the rest of Europe did not hide the reverse side of the coin : overcrowding, disorganisation encouraging intrigues of all sorts, the palace so filthy that the atmosphere often became unbearable. Fortunately, the king and court could always take the air at Marly or another royal retreat *(9:45-5 or 6; closed Mon. and nat. hols.; park daily from sunrise to sunset).*

▶ **West façade,** 580 m long overlooking the park. The central section that housed the royal family projects in front of the wings; the leading sculptors of the period were employed here. ▶ The **château** itself can be visited in four stages : (1) Chapelle★★★ (1689-1710); Grands Appartements★★★ including the Hall of Mirrors *(Salle des Glaces)* and the Salon d'Hercule *(no guides)*; (2) the King's apartments and the Louis XV interiors (guided tour); (3) Museum of French History, 15thC to present day *(no guides)*; (4) Petits Appartements★★★ (Louis XV, Louis XVI and Marie-Antoinette), apartments of Mme. de Maintenon and Mme. du Barry★★, and the Opéra Royal★★★ *(lecture-tours at various times; tel 39.50.58.32.*

▶ The **gardens★★★** by Le Nôtre are classic French formal gardens (derived from Italian design theory); geometric flower-beds and fountains (by Le Brun and Mignard) are in perfect harmony with the architecture of the palace. The **Grandes Eaux,** with an hour-long fountain display, and the Fêtes de Nuit, with nighttime fireworks, bring back a little of the great days at Versailles *(fountains 2 or 3 Sundays each month May-Sep., 4-5; fireworks four times each summer, ask at the SI).* In the **park★** (open to cars) the **Grand Canal★** leads the eye towards the horizon.

▶ **Le Grand Trianon★★** (on your right in the park as you leave the château) built by Mansart in 1687; Louis XIV used to seek rest there : façades in white and pink marble; Empire-style decoration dating from Napoleon, who used to stay there (no guides; guided tour on request Sat. and Sun. in summer). ▶ **Le Petit Trianon★★** (1768) : built by Gabriel, decorated by Guibert for Louis XV and Mme. de Pompadour; favourite residence of Marie-Antoinette, who commissioned the Anglo-Chinese gardens★★ and had built the make-believe rustic hamlet *(2-5 or 6; check by phone, 39.50.58.32.* □

▶ The town

Versailles grew up as a dependency of the château, around three avenues radiating from the Place d'Armes where the Grandes et Petites Ecuries (stables) were located. Built by Mansart in 1685 and recently restored, the Petites Ecuries now house the National School of Architecture, Motorcar Museum and Museum of Ancient Monuments. ▶ The old town evokes the 18thC and 19thC; the heart of the northern section is the **church of Notre Dame,** the oldest in Versailles (1658, by Hardouin-Mansart). ▶ **Lambinet Museum** of local history, especially 18thC *(2-6 ex Mon.).* ▶ The southern section of Versailles housed government ministries in the 18thC; the **Salle du Jeu de Paume** (tennis court), restored to its 1789 condition, will shortly be open to the public. The **St. Louis Cathedral** (1754) overlooks the former palace kitchen garden *(Potager du Roi;* now the National Horticultural School) and the courtyards of the **Carrés St. Louis★** (18thC commercial development). ▶ The **Arboretum de Chèvreloup★** near Roquencourt is an annex of the Jardin des Plantes in Paris *(10 and 2:30, Sat.).* □

■ The VEXIN Region★★

▶ Through the Vexin★★ *(80 km approx, full day)*
B1-2 *(see map 4)*

The Vexin abounds in rich agricultural land and wealthy farms, vineyards along the Seine, and wooded hills; stone spires of numerous Romanesque churches break the skyline. Many of the churches were remodelled during the Renaissance (→ Mantes).

▶ **Vétheuil★ :** looks like a fishing village, with narrow streets leading down to the water; church with early Gothic choir and pre-Renaissance nave and façade. ▶ A sudden bend in the river downstream **(Lavacourt Pool),** often inspired the Impressionist Claude Monet (1840-1926). The chalky banks that enclose the Seine are honeycombed by caves, many of which have been made into attractive dwellings. ▶ **Haute-Isle :** a village of "troglodyte" weekend cottages; there is even a cave-church in the cliff. ▶ **La Roche-Guyon★ :** château built partly into the cliff-face with 12thC keep; main building 12thC to 18thC; stables worthy of Chantilly (→). 14th-15thC church; town hall in the former covered market (18thC); yachting centre. ▶ Continue to **Giverny,** Monet's renovated house★ and replanted gardens★★ : enchanting whatever the time of year *(10-6, Apr.-Oct.).* The Moulin de **Fourges :** on the banks of the **Epte** where the Plantagenets (once the royal house of England) had their châteaux; an ideal base for exploring the Vexin. ▶ **Beaudémont** and **Berthenonville :** ruined châteaux. ▶ In 911 the treaty of **St-Clair-sur-Epte** defined the boundaries of Normandy, the region named for the invading Norsemen who had settled there. ▶ **Dangu :** Gothic and Renaissance church; 16th-17thC statues of the Twelve Apostles; stud-farm. ▶ **Boury-en-Vexin :** château★ by Hardouin-Mansart *(daily ex. Tue. in Jul. & Aug.; Sat., Sun. 2:30-6:30, Easter-15 Oct.).* ▶ Churches at **Montjavoult, Parnes** (Romanesque) and **St. Gervais★** with magnificent Renaissance doorways. ▶ The **Château d'Alincourt,** bristling with towers and turrets, is a medley of styles from the 15thC to 17thC. ▶ **Magny-en-Vexin :** the church, like most of those in the region, veers between late Gothic and early Renaissance. ▶ **Wy :** château de **Maudéjour** *(2-6 daily),* and mediaeval forge and tool museum★ *(9-12 & 2-6:30; closed Sun. am).* ▶ **Omerville★ :** classified site includes 15thC farm and church. ▶ **Ambleville :** château with two beautiful gardens and two façades, one Renaissance, the other neo-Classical. ▶ **Villarceaux :** delightful water-garden; Renaissance manor; 18thC château. ▶ The hilltop road★ ends the trip with views over the Epte and Aubette valleys and the keep at La Roche-Guyon. □

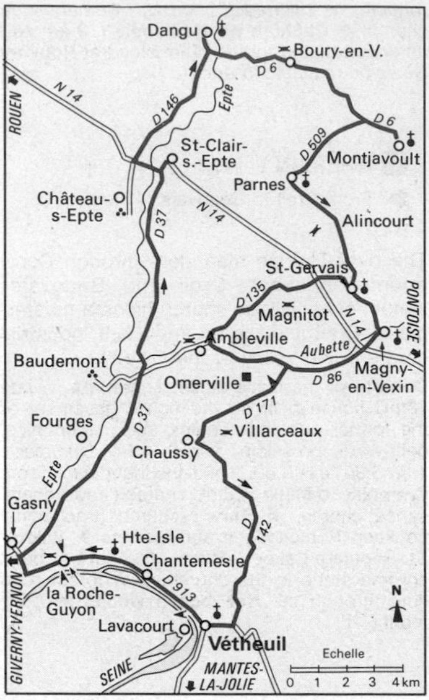

4. Tour of the Vexin region

Architecture

In Seine-et-Marne

In the Beauvais region

The Ile-de-France has suffered more than any other area in France from urbanisation and ill-considered renovation. Nevertheless the region is enhanced by a varied architecture based on local styles and influenced by surrounding areas, including Picardy, Normandy and Beauce. ● The typical Ile-de-France farmhouse is drawn up around a square courtyard closed by a large doorway that sometimes achieves monumental proportions. The construction material varies, from stone and plaster in the Yvelines and Seine-et-Marne to brick or stone in the Oise. Limestone is widely used in the Vexin; timber frames are common near Mantes; the millstone grit used in the Chevreuse Valley becomes sandstone farther south. ● An original architectural form was developed around Meaux-Vaujours to meet the needs of the many local straw-merchants *(pailleux)* who supplied the stables of Paris. The central house is abutted on one side by a vast storage barn, and on the other by lodgings for grooms and carthandlers.

Courtyard and out-buildings

Farm entrance

Brief regional history ●

1st-5thC

The Ile-de-France is more a collection of landscapes than a definite territory, and has always been more of a crossroads than a settlement : a focal point of change and innovation. The population has never been tied to the soil as in, say, the Auvergne, Corsica or Brittany. ● Nevertheless, wealth from the land progressively transformed the **Frankish state** into **modern France** and helped to spread its influence throughout Western civilisation.

In 52BC Labienus, Julius Caesar's lieutenant, drove the Parisii (a Gaulish tribe) from the Grenelle Plain. Retreating to an island in the middle of the Seine, they founded a settlement called **Lutetia.** Towards the middle of the 4thC, this became known as Paris, after its founders. During this period the **Franks** (a Germanic people) colonised the area between the Marne and the Oise rivers. In 451 the Huns, led by Attila, attempted to take Paris, but were deflected by the statecraft of a young shepherdess, later revered as Ste. Geneviève. In 508 the Frankish King **Clovis** chose Paris as the Merovingian capital.

From the Middle Ages...

The duchy of the Ile-de-France became an autonomous feudal territory in 987, when **Hugues Capet** was elected King of France, thus founding a dynasty that ruled the country with only one brief interruption (from the Revolution of 1789 to the end of the Empire, 1814) until the middle of the 19thC. ● The independent existence of the Ile-de-France continued for two centuries while reluctant vassals were brought into line, as the ruins of **feudal keeps** (e.g. Montlhéry, Étampes, Dreux, Pierrefonds) attest. In the 13thC the duchy became synonymous with the French kingdom as a whole.

...to the present day

Over the centuries the Ile-de-France has been vitally involved in French history. ● In the 12thC it witnessed the birth - at St. Denis, Paris, Senlis, Beauvais and Noyon - of **Gothic art.** ● It was the cradle of the northern French tongue (the *langue d'oïl*), which became the official language in 1537. ● The great architecture of châteaux and garden landscapes was developed here in the 17thC and 18thC, at Vaux-le-Vicomte, St.Germain, Chantilly, Fontainebleau, Compiègne, and - above all - at Versailles. ● The visual revolution behind modern art evolved in the villages of Barbizon, Argenteuil, Bougival and Auvers-sur-Oise; Impressionism and Fauvism were both direct products of the quality of light in the Ile-de-France. ● Only the region's situation as a crossroads and a melting-pot for cultural influences could have generated these vigorous historical movements.

The region

Information : Ile-de-France, *Comité régional de Tourisme* (C.R.T.), 19, rue Barbet-de-Jouy, 75007 Paris, ☎ (1) 45.51.09.92. **Essonne :** *Comité départemental du Tourisme* (C.D.T.), 4, rue de l'Arche, 91000 Corbeil-Essonnes, ☎ (1) 60.89.31.32, ext. 254. **Eure-et-Loir :** *C.D.T.*, 7, pl. des Épars, B.P. 67, 28000 Chartres, ☎ 37.21.39.99. **Hauts-de-Seine :** *C.D.T.*, 1, rue Trosy, 92140 Clamart, ☎ (1) 46.42.17.95. **Oise :** *C.D.T.*, 1, rue Villiers-de-L'Isle-Adam, B.P. 222, 60008 Beauvais Cedex, ☎ (1) 44.45.82.12. **Seine-et-Marne :** *C.D.T.*, château Soubiran, av. H.-Barbusse, 77190 Dammarie-les-Lys, ☎ (1) 64.37.19.36. **Seine-Saint-Denis,** *C.D.T.*, 2, av. Gabriel-Péri, 93100 Montreuil, ☎ (1) 42.87.38.09. **Val-de-Marne,** *C.D.T.*, 11, av. de Nogent, 94130 Vincennes, ☎ (1) 40.08.13.00. **Val-d'Oise :** *Union départemental des O.T.S.I.*, B.P. 23, 95290 L'Isle-Adam, ☎ (1) 34.69.09.76. **Yvelines :** *C.D.T.*, préfecture, 78010 Versailles, ☎ (1) 39.51.82.00, ext 2697. *Dir. rég. du Temps libre, Jeunesse et Sports*, 6-8, rue Eugène-Oudiré, 75013 Paris, ☎ (1) 45.84.12.05. *Dir. rég. des Affaires culturelles*, Grand Palais, porte C, av. Franklin-D.-Roosevelt, 75008 Paris, ☎ (1) 42.25.11.40.

Maps : *Michelin* n°s 55, 56, 60, 61, 96, 101,237, 1/200 000. *I.G.N.*, n°s 3, 8, 9, 20, 21, 1/100 000. *Michelin* n° 90, *Environs de Paris*, 1/100 000.

S.O.S. : Eure-et-Loir : *SAMU* (Emergency Medical Service), ☎ 17. *Poisoning Emergency Centre* (Tours), ☎ 47.66.15.15. **Oise** and **Essonne :** *SAMU*, ☎ 17. **Val-d'Oise** and **Yvelines :** *SAMU*, ☎ 15. **Seine-et-Marne :** *SAMU*, ☎ (1) 64.37.10.11. *Poisoning Emergency Centre* (Paris) : **Oise, Essonne, Val-d'Oise, Yvelines, Seine-et-Marne,** ☎ (1) 42.05.63.29.

Weather forecast : Essonne : ☎ (1) 60.84.65.81. **Eure-et-Loir :** ☎ 37.21.28.24. **Oise :** ☎ (1) 44.45.27.90. **Seine-et-Marne :** ☎ (6) 64.37.14.29. **Val-d'Oise :** ☎ (1) 30.31.23.39. **Yvelines :** ☎ (1) 36.32.29.98.

Farmhouse gites and chambres d'hôtes : *Gîtoise, Relais dép. des Gîtes ruraux de l'Oise*, B.P. 222, 60008 Beauvais Cedex, ☎ 44.48.16.87. *Relais dép. des Gîtes ruraux de Seine-et-Marne* : C.D.T. Seine-et-Marne. *Relais dép. des Gîtes ruraux d'Eure-et-Loir,* Chambre d'Agriculture, av. M.-Proust, 28024 Chartres, ☎ 37.34.52.09.

Camping : list of sites at the C.D.T.

Festivals and events : Jan-Apr : Dreux *Auturae Musical.* **Apr :** *Annual Fair of Cheese and Wine* at Coulommiers ; **3rd Sat in month, May-Oct :** *son et lumière*, Meslay-le-Grenet. **Mid-May-early Jun :** *Festival de l'Ile-de-France,* concert-promenades in the châteaux and parks. **May or Jun :** Fontainebleau *Music Festival ;* Provins *Music Festival ;* Meaux *Music Festival ;* Yvelines *Music and Architecture Festival ; fête du muguet (lily-of-the-valley - traditional spring festival)* in Rambouillet ; Royaumont *Music Season.* **May :** *Jazz Festival,* Fontainebleau. **First Sun in Jun :** *rose festival* in Brie-Comte-Robert ; **second Sun in Jun :** *daisy festival* in Vésinet ; **mid-Jun** *Music Festival* in Blandy-lès-Tours ; **last Sun in Jun :** *Bargees, Festival* in Conflans-Sainte-Honorine. **Jun :** *Django Reinhardt Festival* at Samois-sur-Seine, Versailles *Festival, fête de Jeanne Hachette* in Beauvais, *Music Festival* in Meaux, *mediaeval week* in Moret-sur-Loing, *mediaeval games* in Provins. **Beginning Jul to mid-Jul :** *summer festival,* concerts in Chartres, *old-fashioned threshing* in Saint-Victor-de-Buthon (near La Loupe) ; **1 Jul-15 Aug :** *fête des Loges* in Saint-Germain-en-Laye. **Aug :** organ recitals at Chartres Cathedral (odd years) ; **last Sun in Aug :** *harvest festival* in Provins. **Sep :** Versailles *Festival ; fêtes de Nuit ; fair-exhibition* in Mantes-la-Jolie ; *carrot festival* in Croissy-sur-Seine ; *International Cello Festival* in Nemours ; **Oct :** *horse-riding festival* in Rambouillet ; Paris-Versailles *marathon.* **Nov :** *festival du Rire, du Sourire et de l'Humour (laughter, smiles and humour)* in Meaux. **Dec :** *Annual Poultry Contest* at Egreville.

Rambling : GR 1, 2, 11, 12, 13, 14, 14A, 22, 26, 32, 35, 111, 123, 122 cross the Ile-de-France region. *Topoguides* n°s 1, 2, 11, 111, 12, 13, 14A, 14, 32, 35. *I.G.N. maps* n°s 401 (Fontainebleau), 402 (Rambouillet), 403 (Compiègne), 404 (Chantilly), 418 (Val-d'Oise), 413, 419. Brochures suggesting various ramble roads are published by the Essonne, Oise, Seine-et-Marne and Yvelines C.D.T., and the *Assn. dép. de Tourisme pédestre d'Eure-et-Loir,* 7, cloître Notre-Dame, 28000 Chartres. *Délégation régionale de l'Ile-de-France des Sentiers et de la Randonnée pédestre,* 64, rue de Gergovie, 75014 Paris, ☎ (1) 45.45.31.02.

Riding holidays : *A.R.T.E.I.F. : Association Régionale de Tourisme Equestre de l'Ile-de-France,* 15, rue de Bruxelles, 75009 Paris, ☎ (1) 48.74.53.15. **Eure-et-Loir :** *Assn. Randonneurs équestres,* M. Chary : château Javersy, 28300 Cottainville, ☎ 37.31.69.64. **Oise :** C.D.T. Equestre de l'Oise, ☎ 44.45.82.12.

Horse-drawn holidays : *Assn. d'attelage,* M. Decourtie, Villars, Châtillon-en-Dunois, 28290 Arrou.

Cycling holidays : the S.N.C.F. publishes a brochure *"16 Promenades à vélo en Yvelines, Eure, Eure-et-Loir, Oise avec parcours d'approche en train"*, which suggests interesting roads. Enq : ☎ (1) 42.61.50.50. *R.E.R. bicycle hire* in Noiziel-le-Luzard, Saint-Germain-en-Laye, Saint-Rémy-lès-Chevreuse, Courcelles-sur-Yvette, Vincennes, Fontenay-sous-Bois. *S.N.C.F. bicycle hire* in Chartres, Dreux, Esbly, Fontainebleau, Gretz-Armainvilliers, La Ferté-sous-Jouarre, La Loupe, Maintenon, Nogent-le-Rotrou, Rambouillet, Ballancourt, Dourdan, Étampes, Montsoult, Pontoise, *Comité Départemental de cyclotourisme,* 11, rue de Mignières, 28360 Dammarie. The *Comité régional de Tourisme et des Loisirs* and the *Bicy-Club de France* publish a booklet of 10 roads in the Ile-de-France region. The **Yvelines, Essonne** and **Oise** C.D.T. have organised touristic cycling itineraries. The *Bicy-Club de France* organises trips and hires out bicycles. Enq : 8, pl. de la Porte-Champerret, 75017 Paris, ☎ (1) 47.66.55.92.
Cycling tracks : enq : *Direction régionale de l'Équipement,* 21, rue Miollis, 75032 Paris Cedex 15, ☎ (1) 45.67.55.03.

River and canal cruises : *Nautic Croisières,* port de Billancourt, quai du Point-du-Jour, 92100 Boulogne, ☎ (1) 46.21.48.15. *Péniche Amour,* 77920 Samois-sur-Seine, ☎ (1) 64.24.66.99. Canal cruises : *Quiztour,* 19, rue d'Athènes, 75009 Paris, ☎ (1) 48.74.75.30. *B.N.A.L.,* B.P. 27, 60150 Longueil-Annel, ☎ 44.76.18.80.

Children : Amusement parks : *la Vallée des Peaux Rouges,* N of Senlis, in Fleurines, ☎ 44.54.10.66. *Mer de sable* d'Ermenonville, ☎ 44.54.00.96.

Golf : courses in Saint-Quentin-en-Yvelines (18 holes), Villeray (18 holes), Saint-Aubin (18 holes), Chevry (9 holes), Fontainebleau (18 holes), Domont (18 holes), Compiègne (18 holes), Chaussy (18 holes), Chaumont-en-Vexin (18 holes), Chantilly (9 and 18 holes), Fourqueux (3 9-hole rounds), Lamorlaye (18 and 9 holes), Le Coudray (18 and 9 holes), Le Prieuré in Sailly (18 holes), Mortefontaine (18 holes), Ormesson (18 holes), Ozoir-la-Ferrière (18 and 9 holes), Plaisir (9 holes), Rochefort (18 holes), Saint-Cloud (18 holes), Saint-Germain-en-Laye (18 and 9 holes), Saint-Nom-la-Bretèche (18 holes), Seraincourt (18 holes), Versailles (18 holes).

Leisure centres : Créteil, Bois-le-Roi, Buthiers, Brou, Jablines, Saint-Quentin-en-Yvelines, Cergy-Neuville, Moisson, Étampes, Val-de-Seine, Draveil-Juvisy-Vigneux, Souppes-sur-Loing, Le Perray-en-Yvelines, Saint-Leu-d'Esserent.

Aquatic sports : numerous aquatic centres. Enq : *Ligue régionale de Voile,* M. Devesa, B.P. 5, Le Mesnil-le-Roi, 78600 Maison-Laffite, ☎ (1) 39.62.93.53, and C.D.T. In the Oise, windsurfing is allowed on the stretches of water of Canada, Beauvais, Therdonne, Saint-Leu-d'Esserent and Verberie. List of expanses of water available from *C.D.T. Eure-et-Loir.*

Canoeing : *Ligue de Canoë-Kayak,* 87, quai de la Marne, 94340 Joinville-le-Pont, ☎ (1) 48.89.31.34 (Mon and Thu). *Club Bonnevalais,* Moulin du Pont leisure centre, 28800 Bonneval, ☎ 37.47.48.59 or 37.47.56.14. *Piscine des Vauroux,* 28300 Mainvilliers, ☎ 37.21.68.90.

Climbing : most of the climbing roads are in La Ferté-Alais region, Fontainebleau forest, the massif des Trois-Pignons, and the area from Malesherbes to Nemours. Group excursions, discovery and beginners' courses, are organised by the *Club Alpin Francais, Touring Club de France, F.S.G.T.,* 31, av. C.-Vellefaux, 75010 Paris, ☎ (1) 42.01.82.00, and the *Groupe Universitaire de Montagne,* 53, rue du Moulin-Vert, 75014 Paris, ☎ (1) 45.43.48.37.

Flying, gliding and ballooning : *Assn. aéronautique de Coulommiers,* 6, av. C.-Bernard, 77320 La Ferté-Gaucher. *Assn. aéronautique de Meaux,* aérodrome Coulommiers-Voisins, 77120 Coulommiers ; *Centre de vol à voile de Fontainebleau,* aérodrome de Moret-Episy, 77250 Moret-sur-Loing. *Centre aéronautique de Beynes* and the *Centre de jeunesse fédéral de vol à voile de la Région parisienne,* aérodrome, 78650 Beynes. *Assn. aéronautique du Val-d'Essonne,* B.P. 31, 91490 Milly-la-Forêt. *Assn. aéronautique du Val-d'Oise,* aérodrome de Chérence, 95510 Vétheuil. *Centre de parachutisme sportif Paris-Ile-de-France,* 77320 La Ferté-Gaucher.

Fishing : *Féd. dép. des Assn. de Pêche et de Pisciculture,* **Seine-et-Marne :** 13, rue des Fossés, Melun, ☎ (1) 64.39.03.08. **Yvelines :** 19, rue du Dr-Roux, 78520 Limay, ☎ (1) 34.77.58.90. **Eure-et-Loir :** M. Seigneuret, 11, rue des Demoiselles, 28800 Châteaudun, ☎ 37.45.42.40. **Oise :** 10, rue Pasteur, 60200 Compiègne, ☎ (1) 44.40.46.41. **Val-d'Oise :** 19, rue des Coteaux, 95300 Pontoise, ☎ (1) 40.38.39.33. **Essonne :** 10, rue de la Tuilerie, 91100 Corbeil-Essonnes, ☎ (1) 60.75.14.63. *Plaisance sur Seine :* chemin de la Varenne, 77870 Vulaines-sur-Seine, ☎ (1) 64.23.71.87 ; you may have your trout or salmon catch prepared at the adjoining restaurant.

Hunting and shooting : *Féd. dép. des Chasseurs d'Eure-et-Loir : maison de l'Agriculture,* 28000 Chartres, ☎ 37.34.52.09.

● Towns

ANET

Dreux 16, Chartres 50, Paris 80
A2 ✉ 28260

Hotel :

Berchères-sur-Vesgre, ✉ 28560, 8 km E :
● ★★★★(L) ***Château*** (Châteaux-hôtels, Relais du Silence), ☎ 37.82.07.21. Tx 780684. AE, DC, Visa, Euro. 32 rm closed Aug and 24-31 Dec. A Louis XV castle in a 61-acre park, 420. Rest. ♦♦ Spec : *filet de sole Berchère,* 195-250.

Restaurant :

Ezy-sur-Eure, ✉ 27530, 2 km NW :
● ♦♦ ***Maître Corbeau,*** 15, rue M.-Elet, ☎ 37.64.73.29. AE, DC, Visa closed 8 Jan-5 Feb, Tue eve and Wed. Lovely garden, lace and refined service all year for excellent cooking : *canard sauvage aux chanterelles,* 165-280.

BARBIZON

Fontainebleau 10, Étampes 40, Paris 60
C3 ☎ 1 ✉ 77630
ⓘ 41, rue Grande, ☎ (1) 60.66.41.87.

Hotels :

★★★★(L) ***Le Bas Bréau*** (Relais et châteaux), 22, rue Grande, ☎ (1) 60.66.40.05. Tx 690953. AE, Euro, Visa. 19 rm closed beg Jan-mid-Feb. A magnificent floral setting, 825. Rest. ♦♦♦♦ Exceptionally good fare. Spec : *fricassée de queues de langoustines aux courgettes, saumon frais sauvage d'Écosse à la fondue de poireaux et cerfeuil,* 280-500.

● ★★★***Hostellerie la Clé d'Or*** (L.F., Châteaux-hôtels), 73, Grande Rue, ☎ (1) 60.66.40.96. Tx 692131. AE, DC, Euro, Visa. 15 rm closed 15 Nov-15 Dec, Sun eve and Mon ex nat hols, 290. Rest. ♦♦ Spec : *saumon fumé maison,* 140-200.

★★★***Les Pléiades,*** 21, Grande-Rue, ☎ (1) 60.66.40.25. Tx 692131. AE, DC, Euro, Visa. 18 rm 230. Rest. ♦♦ Spec : *fricassée de homard aux pâtes fraîches, magret de canard aux fruits tropicaux, duo de cailles dans leur nid,* 120-250.

● ★★***Les Alouettes*** (L.F.), 4, rue A.-Barye, ☎ (1) 60.66.41.98. 25 rm 180. Rest. 150-300.

Restaurants :

♦♦♦ ***Grand Veneur,*** 63, rue G.-Séailles, on the outskirts of the forest, ☎ (1) 60.66.40.44. AE,

DC, Visa. P ꟿ ♿ closed 24 Jul-24 Aug, Wed eve and Thu. Cooking *à la broche* (kebabs), game, 150-300.

♦ ***La Broche de Barbizon,*** N7, ☎ (1) 60.66.40.76. Visa. ♿ closed 3 weeks in Jan, Wed eve and Thu. Spec : *poulet au feu de bois,* 75-120.

Chailly-en-Bière, ✉ 77960, 1 km N :

♦♦ ***Chalet du Moulin*** (1.5 km on N7), ☎ (1) 60.66.43.42. AE, Visa. P ꟿ ♿ closed Aug, Mon eve and Tue. Set in greenery. Spec : *côtelettes de brochet aux aiguillettes d'anguilles, charlotte de truite rose aux écrevisses,* 180-250.

♦♦ ***Auberge de l'Empereur,*** 27, rte de Paris, N7, ☎ (1) 60.66.43.38. AE, DC, Visa. P ♿ closed 20 Jan-21 Feb, 18-26 Sep, Wed eve, Thu and Sun eve. Attractive garden. Spec : *ris de veau braisé aux truffes,* 70-200.

Arbonne, 5 km :

♦♦ ***Petit Cornebiche,*** 417, rue de la Libération, ☎ (1) 60.66.26.34. Visa. ꟿ ♿ closed 5 weeks in winter, Tue and Wed. Spec : *foie gras, coquilles St-Jacques,* 70-200.

BEAUVAIS

Amiens 60, Rouen 80, Paris 76
B1 ✉ 60000

i 6, rue Malherbe (B2), ☎ 44.45.08.18, and (high season) 1, rue St-Pierre (B2), ☎ 44.45.25.26.

SNCF (C3), ☎ 44.45.91.11.

✈ Tillé, 4 km NE, ☎ 44.45.01.06.

🚌 rue du Warge (B3), ☎ 44.48.08.47.

Hotels :

● ★★★***Chenal*** (Inter-Hôtel), 63, bd Gal-de-Gaulle (C3), ☎ 44.45.03.55. Tx 145223. AE, DC, Euro, Visa. 29 rm P ꟿ 260.

Warluis, ✉ 60430, 7 km SE on the N1 :

★★***Alpes Franco-Suisses,*** ☎ 44.02.01.21. Tx 14906. AE, DC, Visa. 25 rm P ꟿ closed Christmas, 150.

Restaurant :

♦ ***La Crémaillère,*** 1, rue G.-Patin (B1), ☎ 44.45.03.13. Visa. ♿ closed Tue eve and Wed. Spec : *ficelles picardes,* 70-145.

⛺ ★★*Municipal* (100 pl.), ☎ 44.02.00.22.

Guided tours : C.N.M.H.S., Sun from May to Nov → i

Event : *fête de Jeanne Hachette,* last week-end in Jun.

BOUGIVAL

Nanterre 6, Versailles 7, Paris 18
6 km SE of Saint-Germain, B2 ☎ 1 ✉ 78380

SNCF ☎ (1) 39.18.59.92.

Hotel :

● ★★★★***Château de la Jonchère,*** 10, côte de la Jonchère, ☎ (1) 39.18.57.03. Tx 699491. AE, DC, Euro, Visa. 8 rm P ꟿ 700. Rest. ♦♦♦ ♿ Luxurious castle, Napoléon III setting, friendly welcome. Spec : *saumon cuit à la vanille, bar fumé minute au caviar,* 150-250.

Restaurants :

● ♦♦♦♦ ***Le Camélia*** (Jean Delaveyne), 7, quai G.-Clemenceau, ☎ (1) 39.69.03.02. AE, DC, Visa. ♿ closed Sun eve and Mon. Jean Delaveyne is named by his friend "the Bougival sorcerer" and he deserves it as a master of French cooking. Unforgettable specialities : *soyeux d'agneau de chez Fournaise, turbot à l'étouffé aux aromates,* mushrooms in season. Yvonne, his wife, takes care of the flowers, and his son Guy takes care of the customers and the fabulous wines. Just next to it, the annex ***l'Huître et la Tarte.*** On the ground floor, "degustation" of caviar, salmon, etc., wine by the glass. Take away dishes. On the first floor, fast service restaurant, 160-380.

♦♦♦♦ ***Le Coq Hardi,*** 16, quai Rennequin-Sualem, ☎ (1) 39.69.01.43. AE, DC, Visa. closed 15 Jan-15 Feb and Wed. Delightful setting of flowered terrace, gardens, 200-400.

BRIE-COMTE-ROBERT

Melun 18, Provins 56, Paris 30
C3 ☎ 1 ✉ 77170

SNCF ☎ (1) 64.39.50.50.

Hotel :

La Grâce de Dieu, 45, rue Gal-Leclerc, ☎ (1) 64.05.00.76. Visa. 9 rm P ♿ closed Aug, Sun eve and Wed, 100. Rest. ♦ Spec : *choucroute, saumon frais à l'oseille,* 80-110.

BROU

Chartres 38, Alençon 94, Paris 128
A4 ✉ 28160

SNCF ☎ 37.47.00.17.

Hotel :

La Bazoche-Gouët, 28330 Authon-du-Perche, 20 km SW :

L'Étoile, 58, rue J.-Moulin, ☎ 37.49.30.64. Visa. 7 rm P ♿ closed Wed, 65. Rest. ● ♦♦ A warm welcome and dishes with a personal touch. A handy resting place just off the motorway. Bicycle hire, 55-100.

Restaurant :

Unverre, 7 km NW :

♦ ***La Clé des Champs,*** ☎ 37.97.20.36 P ꟿ ♿ closed 1-8 Aug, Feb hols, Christmas, Easter, Mon eve and Tue. Spec : *ris de veau morilles, écrevisses, brochettes St-Jacques,* 50-120.

BRUNOY

Évry 16, Melun 23, Paris 30
Forêt de Sénart, C3 ☎ 1 ✉ 91800

SNCF ☎ (1) 64.39.50.50, (1) 60.46.01.77.

Hotel :

Varennes-Jarcy, 91480 Quincy-sous-Senart, 4 km E :

Moulin de Jarcy, ☎ (1) 69.00.89.20. Visa. 5 rm P ꟿ closed 5-28 Aug, 21 Dec-15 Jan, Tue eve, Wed and Thu, 120. Rest. ♦♦ ♿ closed 6-28 Aug, 24 Dec-15 Jan, Wed and Thu. Simple, family-style dishes at modest prices, 60-140.

CHANTILLY

Beauvais 50, Amiens 91, Paris 48
C1 ✉ 60500

i av. Mal-Joffre (A2), ☎ 44.57.08.58.

SNCF (A2), ☎ 44.57.00.77, 44.57.57.61.

🚌 Next to the S.N.C.F. station.

Hotels :

Gouvieux, ✉ 60270, 3 km E :

● ★★★***Château de la Tour,*** chemin de la Chaussée, ☎ 44.57.07.39. AE, Visa. 15 rm P ꟿ ♿ closed 15 Jul-11 Aug, 260. Rest. ♦♦ 80-200.

● ★***Pavillon St-Hubert,*** ☎ 44.57.07.04. 21 rm P ꟿ ♿ closed 31 Jul-1 Sep, 185. Rest. 80-150.

Lamorlaye, ✉ 60260, 5 km E :

● ★★★***Hostellerie du Lys,*** 7, av. du Rd-Pt-de-la-Reine, ☎ 44.21.26.19. Tx 150298. AE, DC, Euro. 35 rm ꟿ ♿ 260. Rest. ♦♦ 120-170.

Ile-de-France

Restaurant :
♦♦ ***Relais de Condé,*** 42, av. Mal-Joffre, ☎ 44.57.05.75. AE, DC, Visa Former chapel ; closed Mon and Tue, 20 Jan-6 Feb, 15-31 Jul. Good fare and a fine wine selection, 50-200.

Events : horse races *(prix de Diane, prix du Jockey Club).* Jun, *Grande Semaine de Chantilly.*

CHARTRES

Orléans 73, Le Mans 116, Paris 90
A3 ⊠ 28000

ℹ 7, cloître Notre-Dame (B2), ☎ 37.21.54.03.

SNCF (A2), ☎ 37.28.50.50, 37.28.42.61.

(A2), next to the S.N.C.F. station, ☎ 37.21.30.35.

Car-hire : *Budget* train + auto, Z.U.P. de la Madeleine, av. Marcel-Proust, ☎ 37.34.86.84, and at the station, ☎ 37.36.22.61.

Hotels :
● ★★★***Grand Monarque*** (Mapotel), 22, pl. des Épars (A3), ☎ 37.21.00.72. Tx 760777. AE, DC, Euro, Visa. 46 rm Ⓟ 350. Rest. ♦♦♦ The cooking has to reach the high standards of the wines proposed by G. Jallerat and his colleagues' service, 155-240.
● ★★***Jehan de Beauce,*** 19, av. J.-de-Beauce (A2), ☎ 37.21.01.41. 46 rm, closed 15 Dec-15 Jan, 160.

Voves, ⊠ 28150, 24 km SE :
Aux Trois Rois (L.F.), 4, rue des Trois-Rois, ☎ 37.99.00.88. 7 rm, closed Tue eve, Wed and 2-9 Jan, 75. Rest. ● ♦♦ ♿ Weddings and celebrations : delicious local produce, served with the finest wines. Spec : *pâté de saumon aux petits légumes, magret de canard au poivre vert,* 65-120.

Youth hostel : 23, av. Neigre, 68 beds, ☎ 37.34.27.64.

⛺ ★★★*Bords de l'Eure* (250 pl.), rue de Launay, ☎ 37.28.79.43 (open 1 Mar-31 Oct).

Restaurants :
♦♦♦ ***Le Buisson Ardent,*** 10, rue au Lait (B2), ☎ 37.34.04.66. AE, DC Ⓟ closed Aug, Sun and Tue eves and Wed. Pleasant setting. Spec : *salade tiède de raie à l'huile d'olive, saumon fumé,* 70-120.
♦♦ ***Henri IV,*** 31-33, rue du Soleil-d'Or (B2), ☎ 37.36.01.55. DC ♿ closed Mon eve and Tue ex nat hols, 10 Jan-10 Feb. Delicious fare : *blanquette de ris de veau aux cèpes et crème de foie gras, foie de canard chaud aux pommes fruits.* Excellent wine list, 150-250.
♦♦ ***La Vieille Maison,*** 5, rue au Lait (B2), ☎ 37.34.10.67. AE, DC, Euro, Visa ; closed 5-17 Jan, 25 Jun-9 Jul, Sun and Mon eves. Beautiful 16thC vaulted room. Spec : *brouillade de ris de veau et nouilles au foie gras, poulet de ferme truffé sous peau, rôti, lasagnes fraîches au foie gras,* 150-250.

Saint-Prest, 28300 Mainvilliers, 6 km N :
♦ ***La Ferme,*** 75, rue de la République, ☎ 37.22.30.95. Euro, Visa ♿ closed 1 week in Feb, Sun eve (and Mon in Aug). Good traditional cooking, rustic setting, 45-135.

Guided tours : enq ℹ

Craftsmen : workshops of master glass craftsmen : *Ateliers F. Lorin,* 46, rue de la Tannerie, ☎ 37.34.00.42. *Ateliers P. Millous,* 10, rue des Chaises, ☎ 37.28.62.28.

Event : end Oct *Antique Dealers'Fair.*

Auction room : 7, rue Collin-d'Harleville, ☎ 37.36.04.33. Sales every Sun.

Recommended : Confiseries Bazile, 15, rue de la Pie.

CHATEAUDUN

Orléans 48, Tours 95, Paris 132
A4 ⊠ 28200

ℹ 1, rue de Luynes ☎ 37.45.22.46.

SNCF ☎ 37.45.50.50, 37.45.00.54, 37.45.15.15.

Hotels :
★***Rose*** (L.F.), 12, rue Lambert-Licors (B2), ☎ 37.45.21.83. DC, Visa. 8 rm Ⓟ closed 8 Dec-14 Jan, Sun eve and Mon, 110. Rest. ♦♦ Spec : *gourmandise de volailles au cidre,* 70-200.

Cloyes-sur-le-Loir, ⊠ 28220, 12 km SW :
★★★***Hostellerie Saint-Jacques*** (Châteaux-hôtels, France-Accueil), 35, rue Nationale, ☎ 37.98.50.08. AE, DC, Visa. 20 rm Ⓟ closed 15 Nov-30 Jan, Sun eve and Mon, 210. Rest. ● ♦♦ ♿ Fine gastronomy on the banks of the Loir. A former 16thC post-house that maintains an unhurried country spirit. Spec : *charlotte d'asperges au fin jus de langoustines, filet de saint-pierre aux courgettes, sauce framboisée,* 125-235.

Saint-Maur-sur-le-Loir, 28800 Bonneval, 14 km NE on N10 and D360 :
★★★***Château de Mémillon,*** ☎ 37.47.53.81, Tx 780890. 14 apart ♿ Fishing, 500. Table d'hôte, 60-80.

⛺ ★★*Municipal* (100 pl.), ☎ 37.45.05.34 ; Cloyes-sur-le-Loir, ★★★*Parc de Loisirs* (100 pl.), ☎ 37.98.60.63.

Restaurants :
♦♦ ***Caveau des Fouleurs,*** 33, rue des Fouleries (A-B1), ☎ 37.45.23.72. AE, DC, Visa Ⓟ ♿ closed 15 Aug-1 Sep and 15 Feb-1 Mar, Sun eve and Mon. Restaurant built into the cliff-face, 75-150.
● ♦ ***La Licorne,*** 6, pl. du 18-Octobre, ☎ 37.45.32.32. Euro, Visa ♿ closed 23 Dec-23 Jan, 10-20 Jun, Tue eve and Wed. Masterly cooking in a restful setting. Spec : *salade Licorne, filet de bœuf au roquefort, gâteau grand-mère,* 50-120.

Marboue, 7 km N :
● ♦♦ ***Château des Coudreaux,*** ☎ 37.45.53.78. AE, DC, Visa Ⓟ ♿ closed 27 Jan-28 Feb, Tue, Wed, Thu, Fri, Sun eve and Mon noon. Spec : *turbotin braisé au Vouvray, filet de bœuf au chinon et à la moelle,* 115-250.

CHATEAUNEUF-EN-THYMERAIS

Chartres 25, Le Mans 115, Paris 103
21 km S of Dreux, A3 ⊠ 28170

Hotel :
★★***Écritoire,*** 43, rue de Dreux, ☎ 37.51.60.57. 5 rm Ⓟ 18thC post-house, closed 22 Aug-7 Sep, 22 Jan-9 Feb and Tue, 180. Rest. ♦♦ 90-250.

Restaurants :
Saint-Jean-de-Rebervilliers, 4 km N :
♦♦♦ ***Auberge St-Jean,*** ☎ 37.51.62.83. AE, DC, Euro, Visa Ⓟ closed 1-31 Mar, Thu eve and Fri. Lobster and langoustes, 130-170.
♦ ***Le Relais d'Aligre,*** 25, rue J.-Moulin, ☎ 37.51.69.59 ♿ closed 1-22 Sep, 3 weeks in Jan, Mon eve and Thu eve. Traditional cooking, 60-190.

CHEVREUSE

Versailles 16, Étampes 45, Paris 32
D0 ☎ 1 ☒ 78460

Restaurants :

Saint-Rémy-lès-Chevreuse, ☒ 78470, 2.5 km E :
♦♦♦ ***La Cressonnière,*** 46, rte de Port-Royal, ☎ (1) 30.52.00.41. AE, DC, Visa closed Feb hols, Tue and Wed. Refined gastronomy, 135-250.

Gyf-sur-Yvette, ☒ 91190, 7 km E :
● ♦ ***Gril'Beuf,*** F18, exit Centre Universitaire, ☎ (1) 60.19.34.13. Visa ♿ For the decor and the folklore, Slavik has hung oxen from the ceiling. Excellent grilled meats, 70-100.

Châteaufort, ☒ 78530, 8 km NE :
● ♦♦♦ ***La Belle Époque,*** 10, pl. de la Mairie, ☎ (1) 39.56.21.66 Ⓟ ♿ closed Sun eve, 13 Aug-4 Sep, 22 Dec-7 Jan. In his lovely turn-of-the-century inn, Michel Peignaud takes advantage of his numerous trips around the world to spoil his faithful customers ; a preference for Japan and its delicate tastes : *tamis de homard aux algues, raviolis de petits-gris, st-pierre aux feuilles d'épinard, délice glacé à l'orange infante,* 220-310.

CLERMONT-AGNETZ

Beauvais 26, Amiens 66, Paris 77
C1 ☒ 60600

ℹ old town hall, ☎ 44.78.19.70.

SNCF ☎ 44.50.00.59.

Hotels :
★★***Clermotel*** (France-Accueil), N31, Agnetz, ☎ 44.50.09.90. Visa. 30 rm Ⓟ 195. Rest. ♦ ♿ closed 1-15 Jan and Sat from 1 Nov to 28 Feb, 60-140.

Liancourt, ☒ 60140, 10 km SE :
★★***Hostellerie du Parc,*** av. Ile-de-France, ☎ 44.73.04.99. AE, Visa. 14 rm Ⓟ closed 1-24 Aug and Sun eve, 200. Rest. ♦ Spec : fish, 55-150.

COIGNIÈRES

Versailles 18, Chartres 54, Paris 40
13 km NE of Rambouillet, B3
☎ 1 ☒ 78310 Maurepas

Restaurants :
♦♦♦ ***Le Capucin Gourmand,*** 170, RN10, ☎ (1) 30.50.30.06. AE, DC, Euro, Visa ♿ Spec : *salade de lotte, tournedos Capucin,* 200-320.
♦♦♦ ***Auberge d'Angèle,*** 296, RN10, ☎ (1) 30.50.58.23. AE, DC, Visa closed Sun eve. Spec : *noix de coquilles Saint-Jacques et foie gras poêlé, salade de queue de bœuf et saucisson de lapin aux cèpes,* 200-300.
● ♦ ***Le Saint-Georges,*** RN10, ☎ (1) 30.50.10.23. DC, Visa Ⓟ closed Sat noon and Sun eve, Aug. Quality cooking by an excellent cook. Spec : *filets de sole Argenteuil, crabe Fourtin,* 90-160.

COMPIÈGNE

Beauvais 57, Amiens 76, Paris 82
D1 ☒ 60200

ℹ pl. de l'Hôtel-de-Ville (B2), ☎ 44.40.01.00.

SNCF (B1), ☎ 44.83.37.50, 44.83.36.36, 44.83.37.55.

(B1), opposite the S.N.C.F. station.

Car-hire : *Budget* train + auto, at the station, ☎ 44.83.35.75.

Hotels :
● ★★★***Harlay,*** 3, rue de Harlay (B1), ☎ 44.23.01.50. AE, DC, Euro, Visa. 20 rm Ⓟ closed 20 Dec-3 Jan, 230.
● ★★***Royal-Lieu,*** 9, rue de Senlis (not on the A3 map), ☎ 44.20.10.24. AE, DC, Visa. 18 rm Ⓟ ♿ 240. Rest. ♦♦ 140-210.

Elincourt-Sainte-Marguerite, ☒ 60157, 15 km on the D42 :
★★★***Château de Bellinglise*** (Châteaux indépendants), ☎ 44.76.04.76. DC, Euro, Visa. 35 rm Ⓟ closed Sun eve, 340. Rest. ♦♦ ♿ closed Sun eve and Mon, 75-180.

★★*Hippodrome* (100 pl.), ☎ 44.20.28.58.

Restaurants :
♦♦ ***Auberge des Étangs du Buissonnet,*** Choisy-au-Bac (5 km NE), ☎ 44.40.17.41. Visa Ⓟ ♿ closed Sun eve and Mon. Spec : *choucroute de poissons,* 150-250.

Vieux-Moulin, ☒ 60350, 9.5 km SE on N973 and D14 :
♦♦♦ ***Auberge du Daguet,*** 25, rue Saint-Jean, ☎ 44.85.60.72 ♿ closed 15 days in July, Feb school hols and Wed. Beautiful 17thC house ; reasonably priced menu, 130-180.

Guided tours : C.N.M.H.S. (May-Jun, Aug-Oct). Enq : ℹ

Events : end Jul, *International Tourism on Horse-back Rally* ; Oct, *Antique Fair.*

Recommended : *auction room,* 18, rue des Cordeliers, ☎ 440.40.06.16. Cake shop : *les Muscadines,* 1, rue de Solférino, ☎ 44.23.33.64.

CONFLANS-SAINTE-HONORINE

Pontoise 8, Mantes 40, Paris 30
B2 ☎ 1 ☒ 78700

ℹ 23, rue M.-Berteaux, ☎ (1) 39.72.86.51.

SNCF ☎ (1) 39.19.96.09.

Restaurant :
♦ ***Au Bord de l'Eau,*** 15, quai des Martyrs, ☎ (1) 39.72.86.51 closed 4-29 Aug, 3-10 Mar, Mon and eve ex Sat, 90-225.

COULOMMIERS

Meaux 29, Sens 77, Paris 60
D2 ☎ 1 ☒ 77120

ℹ 11, rue du Gal-de-Gaulle, ☎ (1) 64.03.88.09.

SNCF ☎ (1) 64.03.01.61.

Restaurants :
● ♦ ***Central,*** 34-36, pl. du Marché, ☎ (1) 64.03.01.69. AE, DC, Euro, Visa ♿ closed 5 Feb-11 Mar, 19 Aug-4 Sep, Sun, Mon eve and Tue. Varied menu : *fricassée d'encornets à l'américaine, filet de sole princesse beurre angevin,* 120-190.
♦ ***Auberge de Montapeine,*** 72, av. de Strasbourg, ☎ (1) 64.03.09.16. AE, Euro, Visa ♿ closed 15 Aug-8 Sep, Sun eve, Mon and Wed eve. Specialities of the Périgord region, 45-100.

Doue, 77510 Rebais, 9 km NE :
Auberge Saint-Éloi, 1, pl. de Verdun, ☎ (1) 64.03.18.64. Euro, Visa Ⓟ ♿ closed Sun eve and Sep. Good simple fare, 45-100.

CRÉPY-EN-VALOIS

Compiègne 24, Laon 68, Paris 70
D1 ☒ 60800

SNCF ☎ 44.87.14.11, 44.87.16.44.

Ile-de-France

Hotel :
★★***Trois Pigeons*** (L.F.), 2, pl. du Paon, ☎ 44.59.11.21. Euro, Visa. 14 rm Ⓟ closed Feb, Sun eve and Mon ex Jul-Aug, 150. Rest. ♦ Spec : : fish *(ragoût frais de la mer), mêlée de ris de veau et rognons à la périgourdine, pigeonneau à la valoise,* 65-120.

DAMPIERRE-EN-YVELINES

Rambouillet 16, Versailles 18, Paris 36
B3 ☎ 1 ✉ 78720

Hotels :

Senlisse, 3 km S :
★★★***Auberge du Pont Hardi,*** 1, rue du Couvent, ☎ (1) 30.52.50.78. DC, Visa. 5 rm Ⓟ closed Tue eve and Wed, 320. Rest. ♦♦♦ ♿ Spec : *saumon à l'oseille,* 165-250.
Auberge du Gros Marronnier, pl. de l'Église, ☎ (1) 30.52.51.69. AE, DC, Visa. 14 rm Ⓟ ♿ closed 1 Jan-10 Mar, 230. Rest. ● ♦♦ Traditional dishes : *lapin provençal, entrecôte,* 100-150.

DOURDAN

Étampes 18, Chartres 42, Paris 55
B3 ☎ 1 ✉ 91410

ℹ pl. Gal-de-Gaulle, ☎ (1) 64.92.86.97.

SNCF ☎ (1) 64.59.70.46.

R.E.R. (line C) : ☎ (1) 64.59.70.46.

Hotel :
● ★★★★***Hostellerie Blanche de Castille,*** pl. des Halles, ☎ (1) 64.59.68.92. Tx 690902. AE, DC, Visa. 40 rm Ⓟ 280. Rest. ♦♦♦ Spec : *assiette corrézienne au foie gras frais de canard, ragoût de homard à l'américaine,* 180-220.

⛺ ★★★*Les Petits Prés* (150 pl.), ☎ (1) 64.92.80.75.

DREUX

Chartres 35, Rouen 97, Paris 82
A3 ✉ 28100

ℹ 4, rue Porte-Chartraine, ☎ 37.46.01.73.

SNCF ☎ 37.28.50.50.

Hotels :
● ★★***Auberge Normande*** (L.F.), 6, pl. Métézeau, ☎ 37.50.14.51. AE, Euro, Visa. 16 rm Ⓟ 160. Rest. ♦ closed 25 Jul-1 Sep, 90-135.

Vernouillet, ✉ 28500, 2 km SW :
★***Auberge de la Vallée Verte*** (L.F.), 6, rue L.-Dupuis, ☎ 37.46.04.04. Visa. 12 rm, closed Aug, Fri eve, Sun eve and Mon, 115. Rest. ♦♦ ♿ Market fresh produce, 85-150.

Youth hostel : 19, rue Pastre, ☎ 37.42.09.58.

Restaurant :

Montreuil, 28500 Vernouillet, 8 km N :
♦♦♦ ***Gué des Grues,*** ☎ 37.43.50.25. DC, Visa Ⓟ ♿ closed Jan, Mon eve and Tue. Spec : *délice de foie gras aux petits légumes, escalope de saumon au vin rouge,* 150-220.

Auction rooms : 4, rue des Tanneurs, ☎ 37.46.04.22.

ENGHIEN

Pontoise 20, Chantilly 32, Paris 18
C2 ☎ 1 ✉ 95880

(high season : 15 Mar-31 Dec).

ℹ 2, bd Cotte, ☎ (1) 34.12.41.15.

SNCF ☎ (1) 39.64.05.45, ☎ 39.64.62.04.

Hotel :
★★★★(L) ***Grand Hôtel,*** 85, rue Gal-de-Gaulle, ☎ (1) 34.12.80.00. Tx 697842. AE, DC, Visa. 50 rm Ⓟ 505. Rest. ♦♦ 125-200.

Restaurant :
● ♦♦♦♦ ***Duc d'Enghien,*** 3, av. de Ceinture, at the casino, ☎ (1) 34.12.90.00. Tx 697842. AE, DC, Visa closed Sun eve and Mon. To assist Jacques Ducis and his team at the Casino, Michel Kerever and wife Nelly have settled permanently in Enghien (their son has stayed in Liffré) to manage this superb hotel-spa complex. Everything runs well, and the great Michel's inventive cuisine gets everyone's vote. Spec : *raviolis de homard, paupiettes de choux au pigeon et foie gras,* 250-400.

Casino : 3, av. de Ceinture, ☎ (1) 34.12.90.00.

ERMENONVILLE

Senlis 14, Meaux 24, Paris 47
C2 ✉ 60440

ℹ parc Jean-Jacques-Rousseau, ☎ 44.54.01.58.

Hotel :
★***Croix d'Or*** (L.F.), 2, rue Prince-Radziwill, ☎ 44.54.00.04. Visa. 11 rm Ⓟ closed 17 Dec-16 Feb and Fri, 105. Rest. ♦♦ Spec : *calissons de mousse de foie blonds en salades gourmandes, poêlon d'escargots aux cèpes,* 80-150.

⛺ ★★*J.-J.-Rousseau* (200 pl.), ☎ 44.54.00.08.

ÉVRY

Melun 25, Versailles 38, Paris 34
C3 ☎ 1 ✉ 91000

ℹ pl. de l'Agora, ☎ (1) 60.77.36.98.

SNCF ☎ (1) 60.77.31.34.

Hotel :
Grigny, ✉ 91350, 4 km NW :
★★★***Château du Clotay*** (Châteaux-hôtels), 8, rue du Port, ☎ (1) 69.06.89.70. AE, DC, Visa. 10 rm Ⓟ closed Feb school hols, Sun eve and Mon, 450. Rest. ♦♦♦ 140-400.

Restaurant :
Viry-Châtillon, ✉ 91170, 6 km NW :
♦♦ ***La Dariole,*** 21, rue Pasteur, ☎ (1) 69.44.22.40. closed 31 Aug-30 Sep, Sat noon and Sun, nat hols. A pleasant suburban bistro, 150-230.

La FERTÉ-SOUS-JOUARRE

Meaux 20, Rheims 82, Paris 66
D2 ☎ 1 ✉ 77260

ℹ ☎ (1) 60.22.01.49.

Hotel :

Mary-sur-Marne, ✉ 77440 Lizy-sur-Ourcq, 13 km NW :
★★***Le Château Marysien*** (L.F.), ☎ (1) 60.01.71.30. 10 rm Ⓟ ♿ closed Feb, Sun eve and Mon, 160. Rest. ♦♦ 75-150.

⛺ ★★★★*Les Bondons* (100 pl.), ☎ (1) 60.22.00.23.

Restaurants :
● ♦♦ ***Auberge de Condé*** (Relais et châteaux), 1, av. de Montmirail, ☎ (1) 60.22.00.07. AE, DC, Euro, Visa Ⓟ closed 2 weeks in Feb, Mon eve and Tue. Spec : *émincé de canard aux pointes d'asperges, saumon au sauternes,* 200-280.
♦♦ ***Le Relais,*** 3, av. F.-Roosevelt, ☎ (1) 60.22.02.03. Visa Ⓟ closed Wed eve and Thu. Spec : *lotte au coulis de langoustines, raie au muscadet,* 55-110.

FONTAINEBLEAU

Melun 16, Orléans 88, Paris 65
C3 C4 ☎ 1 ✉ 77300

ℹ 38, rue Grande, ☎ (1) 64.22.25.68.

SNCF ☎ (1) 64.39.50.50, 64.22.39.82.

Hotels :

● ★★★★(L) ***Aigle Noir*** (Mapotel), 27, pl. Napoléon-Bonaparte, ☎ (1) 64.22.32.65. Tx 600080. AE, DC, Euro, Visa. 30 rm Ⓟ 785. Rest. ● ♦♦♦ ***Beauharnais*** ♿ Remarkable dishes with market-fresh produce, 200-300.

Recloses, ✉ 77116 Ury, 7 km SW :
★★***Auberge Casa del Sol*** (Relais du Silence, L.F.), ☎ (1) 64.24.20.35. Tx 692131. AE, DC. 10 rm Ⓟ closed Jan, Mon eve and Tue low season, 260. Rest. ♦♦ 120-210.

Samois-sur-Seine, ✉ 77920, 8 km N :
★★★***Le Country Club,*** 11, quai F.-D.-Roosevelt, ☎ (1) 64.24.60.34. Visa. 16 rm Ⓟ 210. Rest. ♦♦ closed Sun eve and Mon, 90-150.

Brolles, ✉ 77590 Bois le Roi, 12 km N :
★★***Hostellerie de la Forêt,*** 67, av. Alfred-Roll, ☎ (1) 60.69.60.31. AE, DC, Euro, Visa. 23 rm 175. Rest. ♦♦ closed Sun eve. Spec : *ragoût de St-Jacques aux truffes, terrine d'anguilles au poivre vert,* 85-120.

Restaurants :

♦♦ ***Chez Arrighi,*** 53, rue de France, ☎ (1) 64.22.29.43. AE, DC, Euro, Visa ; closed Mon and Tue noon. Spec : *blanquette de ris de veau à l'oseille, gigot d'agneau en civet aux oignons confits,* 75-120.

♦♦ ***Le Filet de Sole,*** 5-7, rue du Coq-Gris, ☎ (1) 64.22.25.05. AE, DC, Euro, Visa ♿ closed 30 Jun-1 Aug, Tue and Wed. In former mansion, 100-160.

♦♦ ***Le François-Ier,*** 3, rue Royale, ☎ (1) 64.22.24.68. AE, DC, Euro, Visa. closed Mon eve and Tue from 1 Sep to 15 Jun, 90-220.

Recommended : cake shop *L. Breton,* 21, rue des Sablons.

Auction room : auctioneer, J.-P. Osenat, 5, rue Royale, ☎ (1) 64.22.27.62.

FONTENAY-TRÉSIGNY

Coulommiers 23, Sézanne 66, Paris 52
5 km N of Chaumes, D3 ☎ 1 ✉ 77610

Hotel :

● ★★★★***Le Manoir*** (Relais et châteaux), ☎ (1) 64.25.91.17. Tx 690635. AE, DC, Euro, Visa. 15 rm Ⓟ ♿ closed 15 Nov-15 Apr, 570. Rest. ● ♦♦ closed Tue. Fare for aesthetes and fine palates, in a charming Norman English-style residence set in the middle of a park. Spec : *saumon sauvage mariné à la suédoise, bœuf ficelle,* 120-220.

Restaurant :

Villeneuve-le-Comte, ✉ 77174, 13 km N :
♦ ***La Bonne Marmite,*** 15, rue du Gal-de-Gaulle, ☎ (1) 60.25.00.10 ♿ closed Tue eve and Wed, 3 weeks Feb-Mar and end Aug-early Sep, 120-210.

GALLARDON

Chartres 21, Dreux 37, Paris 75
B3 ✉ 28320

Hotel :

Saint-Symphorien-le-Château, ✉ 28700 Auneau, 6 km W :
● ★★★★(L) ***Château d'Esclimont*** (Grandes Étapes françaises, Relais et châteaux), ☎ 37.31.15.15. Tx 780560. DC, Euro, Visa. 54 rm Ⓟ 50 acre closed 5 Jan-10 Mar, Sun eve and Mon low season, 450-1 650. Rest. ♦♦♦ ♿ A dream setting for a talented young chef. Spec : *petits moules de saumon frais à la crème de citron vert, râble et cuisse de lapereau farci en cocotte,* 195-370.

HOUDAN

Dreux 21, Versailles 41, Paris 63
B2-3 ☎ 1 ✉ 78550

SNCF ☎ (1) 36.46.60.58.

Restaurants :

● ♦♦♦ ***La Poularde,*** N12, 24, av. de la République, ☎ (1) 30.59.60.50. AE, Visa Ⓟ closed 10-20 Feb, Wed eve and Thu. Sylvain, and his father, Pierre Vandenameele, make a close, efficient team, preparing classic and modern dishes : *tourte houdanaise, st-pierre au basilic, brouet de canard au miel,* chocolate cake. Mauricette and her daughter-in-law welcome you, 145-220.

Bazainville, ✉78123, 4.5 km E on the N12 :
● ♦♦ ***Relais du Pavé,*** ☎ (1) 34.87.61.52. Visa. With 8 rm Ⓟ ♿ closed 1 week in Feb and Aug, Mon eve and Tue. Manifestly the restaurant with the greatest flower garden in the region ; over 1 hectare with 200 trees, 696 rose bushes and 1 200 other plants. A superb setting for the fine classic cooking of C. Marguerite : *gourmandise du chanoine, assiette de Monseigneur, symphonie au « dieu des mers »,* 180-250.

Event : *St. Matthew's Fair,* end Sep.

ILLIERS-COMBRAY

Chartres 25, Le Mans 95, Paris 118
A4 ✉ 28120

SNCF ☎ 37.22.01.51.

Hotel :

● ★★***Moulin de Montjouvin*** (L.F.), 2 km on the rte de Brou, ☎ 37.24.32.32. DC, Euro. 19 rm Ⓟ ♿ closed 20 Dec-20 Jan, 29 Jul-10 Aug, and Wed, 150. Rest. ♦ ♿ 60-150.

⛺ ★★Municipal *de Moutjouvin* (30 pl.), ☎ (1) 37.24.00.05.

JUVISY-SUR-ORGE

Évry 9, Versailles 27, Paris 21
6 km S of Orly, C3 ☎ 1 ✉ 91260

SNCF ☎ (1) 69.21.24.14, (1) 69.21.97.98.

R.E.R. (ligne C) : ☎ (1) 69.21.24.14.

Hotel :

★★★***Occitanie*** (Mapotel), 2, rue de Draveil, ☎ (1) 69.21.50.62. Tx 690316. AE, DC, Euro, Visa. 29 rm Ⓟ 350. Rest. ♦ ***le Pays d'Oc*** ♿ 110-170.

Restaurant :

Morangis :
♦ ***Rêve d'Alsace,*** 65, av. E.-Rostand, ☎ (1) 39.09.14.78 Ⓟ closed Mon eve, Sun and nat hols "Nouvelle cuisine", Alsace style. Spec : *tarte à la confiture d'oignons, poissons fins marinés au citron, blanquette de poussins,* 170-250.

LONGJUMEAU

Évry 16, Étampes 31, Paris 21
6 km N of Montlhéry, C3 ☎ 1 ✉ 91160

SNCF ☎ (1) 64.48.81.07.

Hotels :

Saulx-les-Chartreux, 3 km SW :
★★★★***Relais Saint-Georges,*** ☎ (1) 64.48.36.40. Tx 603038. AE, DC, Euro,

Ile-de-France

Visa. 40 rm ⚘ P ♨ ⚲ ♿ closed Aug and Christmas, 300. Rest. ♦♦ 170-210.
★★★**Relais des Chartreux,** ☎ (1) 69.09.34.31. AE, Euro, Visa. 100 rm ⚘ P ♨ ▭ ⚲ ♿ Minibus service to Paris and Orly, 295. Rest. ♦♦ 120-200.

MAINTENON

Chartres 19, Dreux 25, Paris 75
B3 ⊠ 28130

SNCF ☎ 37.27.60.28.

Hotel :
Saint-Denis (L.F., Auberge de France), 5, pl. A.-Briand, ☎ 37.23.00.76. Visa. 13 rm ⚘ P ♨ ⚲ closed Thu eve, Feb and 20 Sep-10 Oct, 150. Rest. ♦ ♿ Local specialities, 80-150.

⛺ ★★★*Les Quinconces* (100 pl.), ☎ 37.23.00.98.

MAISONS-LAFFITTE

Pontoise 18, Mantes 37, Paris 21
B2 ☎ 1 ⊠ 78600

SNCF ☎ (1) 39.62.07.85.

Restaurants :
● ♦♦♦♦ ***La Vieille Fontaine,*** 8, av. Grétry, ☎ (1) 39.62.01.78. AE, DC, Visa ; closed Aug, Sun and Mon ⚘ P ♨ ⚲ ♿ Manon Le Tourneur and François Clerc can now devote their full attention to their beautiful restaurant for their customer's delight. Spec : *cuisses de grenouille à la coque, aumonière de caviar, gigot d'agneau à l'embeurrée de choux et de tomates,* 165-285.
● ♦♦♦ ***Le Tastevin,*** 9, av. Egle, ☎ (1) 39.62.11.67. AE, DC, Visa P ♨ ⚲ ♿ closed 15 Aug-9 Sep, 15 days in Feb, Mon eve and Tue. One of the great restaurants, with impeccable discretion and quality. Spec : *boudins de mer aux écrevisses, noix de St-Jacques au coulis de truffe,* 210-350.
♦♦ ***Le Laffitte,*** 5, av. de St-Germain, ☎ (1) 39.62.01.53. AE, Visa ♿ closed Aug, Tue eve and Wed. Spec : fish dishes, 195-255.

⛺ ★★★★*Airotel International* (200 pl.), ☎ (1) 39.12.21.91.

MANTES-LA-JOLIE

Versailles 44, Rouen 81, Paris 60
B2 ☎ 1 ⊠ 78200

ℹ pl. Jean-XXIII, ☎ (1) 34.77.10.30.

SNCF ☎ (1) 34.77.55.14, (1) 30.92.45.16.

Hotel :

Rolleboise, 78270 Bonnières, 9 km W :
● ★★★***Château de la Corniche*** (Châteaux-hôtels, Relais du Silence), 5, rte de la Corniche, on N13, ☎ (1) 30.93.21.27. Tx 695544. AE, DC, Euro, Visa. 27 rm ⚘ P ♨ ⚲ ▭ ⚲ ♿ closed 27 Jan-15 Mar, Sun eve and Mon from 1 Oct to 30 Apr, 420. Rest. ♦♦♦ Spec : *foie gras de canard au naturel,* lobster, 190-270.

Restaurants :
♦♦♦ ***La Feuilleraie,*** 4, rue Wilson, in Folainville, ☎ (1) 34.77.17.66. Visa ♨ ⚲ ♿ closed Aug, Mon eve and Tue. Spec : *ris et rognons de veau aux champignons,* 170-250.

Bonnières, ⊠ 78270, 12 km NW :
♦♦ ***Hostellerie du Bon Accueil,*** rte de Vernon, ☎ (1) 30.93.01.00. AE, DC, Visa ♿ closed 1 Aug-1 Sep, Feb school hols, Tue eve and Wed. Spec : fish, 240.

Guided tours : collégiale C.N.M.H.S. (Sat, Sun and nat hols), enq ℹ

Event : first Wed in Dec, *onion fair.*

MARLY-LE-ROI

Saint-Germain-en-Laye 4, Versailles 9, Paris 27
B2 ☎ 1 ⊠ 78160

SNCF ☎ (1) 39.58.51.90, (1) 39.58.47.73.

Hotel :
★★★★***Auberge Henri IV,*** 5, pl. de l'Abreuvoir, ☎ (1) 39.58.47.61. AE. 8 rm ⚘ P ⚲ ♿ closed 28 Jul-28 Aug and Feb hols, 250. Rest. ♦♦ closed Sun and Wed eve. Fish specialities, 125-160.

Restaurant :

Louveciennes, ⊠ 78430, 2 km E :
♦♦ ***Aux Chandelles,*** 12, pl. de l'Église, ☎ (1) 39.69.08.40. Visa ; closed 1-21 Jul, Wed, Sat noon and Sun eve, 125-210.

MEAUX

Melun 57, Rheims 96, Paris 53
D2 ☎ 1 ⊠ 77100

ℹ 2, rue Notre-Dame (B1), ☎ (1) 64.33.02.36.

SNCF (A2), ☎ (1) 64.33.11.36, (1) 64.34.06.14.

Car-hire : *Budget* train + auto, at the station, ☎ (1) 64.34.06.14.

Hotels :
● ★★★***Sirène,*** 33, rue Gal-Leclerc (B2), ☎ (1) 64.34.07.80. AE, DC, Visa. 16 rm P ♨ ⚲ closed Feb school hols, 190. Rest. ♦♦ 100-220.
● ★★***Richemont,*** quai de la Grande-Ile (B2), ☎ (1) 60.25.12.10. Euro, Visa. 42 rm ⚘ P ♿ 210. Rest. ♦ 60-110.
Relais Saint-Étienne, 1, pl. Ch.-de-Gaulle, ☎ (1) 64.34.00.26, 64.34.28.18. 10 rm ♿ 115. Rest. ♦ Spec : *foie gras,* 50-200.

Restaurants :

Armentières-en-Brie, 77440 Lizy-sur-Ourcq, 9 km NE :
Auberge du Poisson Couronné, 7, rue de Meaux, ☎ (1) 64.35.50.85. 12 rm P ♨ ♿ closed Nov-Feb and Tue. Former stopover for canal and river craft. Rest. ♦♦ Spec : *confit de lotte aux amandes, émincé de bœuf au coulis landais,* 120-210.

Crécy-la-Chapelle, ⊠ 77580, 15 km :
♦♦♦ ***Auberge du Moulin,*** ☎ (1) 64.36.99.89 ⚘ P ♨ ⚲ ♿ closed Tue eve and Wed, Jan-Mar. Tasty dishes with fresh market produce in this charming mill setting, 150.

Claye-Souilly, ⊠ 77410, 15 km W :
♦♦ ***La Grillade,*** 19, rue J.-Jaurès, ☎ (1) 60.26.00.68. AE, Euro P ⚲ ♿ closed 15-end Feb, 14 Aug-14 Sep, Sun eve and Mon. Spec : *délice de morilles à la ciboulette,* 100-220.

Sound and light show : Fri and Sat from 15 Jun to mid-Jul at 10:30 pm and from 31 Aug to end Sep at 9:30 pm, ☎ (1) 64.34.90.11 or (1) 64.37.19.36.

MELUN

Meaux 57, Sens 66, Paris 57
C3 ☎ 1 ⊠ 77000

ℹ corner av. Thiers and av. Gallieni, ☎ (1) 64.37.11.31.

SNCF ☎ (1) 64.39.50.50, (1) 64.37.15.91, (1) 64.39.18.23.

Hotels :
★★★***Grand Monarque Concorde,*** av. de Fontainebleau, ☎ (1) 64.39.04.40. Tx 690140. AE, DC, Euro, Visa. 50 rm P ♨ ⚲ ▭ 350. Rest. ♦♦ Spec : *saumon fumé maison, turbotin braisé au cidre,* 135-250.

Restaurants :
● ♦♦ ***Auberge Vaugrain,*** 1, rue de la Vannerie, ☎ (1) 64.52.08.23. AE, Visa. 16thC house. Spec : fish and seafood, 100-200.

Pringy, ☒ 77310, 6 km SW :
♦♦ ***Auberge du Bas-Pringy,*** 20, av. de Fontainebleau, ☎ (1) 60.65.57.75. AE, DC, Euro, Visa Ⓟ ♨ ♿ closed Mon eve and Tue, 28 Jul-29 Aug, 10 days end Feb. Spec : *terrine de saumon maison sauce aigrette, entrecôte poêlée à la crème de Brie et de noix,* 49-200.

Moissy-Cramayel, ☒ 77550, 13 km NW :
♦♦ ***La Mare au Diable,*** parc du Plessis-Picard, RN6, ☎ (1) 60.63.17.17 Ⓟ ♨ riding centre. Spec : *salade de Saint-Jacques tiède à l'estragon, choucroute du pêcheur, ris de veau aux morilles et pâtes fraîches,* 120-210.

MÉRÉVILLE

Étampes 16, Chartres 53, Paris 68
B4 ☎ 1 ☒ 91660

Restaurant :
La Poste-de-Boisseaux, 28310 Janville, 12 km SW :
♦♦ ***La Panetière,*** ☎ (1) 38.39.58.26. AE, DC, Visa. Ⓟ ♨ ♿ Good cooking : *velouté d'escargots, carré d'agneau aux herbes,* 150-250.

MILLY-LA-FORET

Fontainebleau 20, Orléans 76, Paris 62
C4 ☎ 1 ☒ 91490

Restaurant :
♦♦♦ ***Le Moustier,*** 41 *bis,* rue Langlois, ☎ (1) 64.98.92.52. Visa ; closed 18 Aug-9 Sep, 22 Dec-6 Jan and Tue. In a 14thC chapel, 130-300.

⛺ ★★★*La Musardière* (120 pl.), ☎ (1) 64.24.52.03.

MONTFORT-L'AMAURY

Versailles 28, Dreux 40, Paris 50
B3 ☎ 1 ☒ 78490

SNCF ☎ (1) 64.86.00.56.

Hotels :
La Queue-en-Yvelines, ☒ 78890, 5 km NW :
Auberge de la Malvina, la Haute-Perruche, ☎ (1) 64.86.45.76. Visa. 5 rm Ⓟ ♨ closed 1st wk Sep, Nov, 200. Rest. ♦♦ closed Wed eve and Thu. Spec : *confit de canard maison, ris de veau aux girolles,* 140-160.

Pontchartrain, ☒ 78670, 9 km NE :
★★★★***Auberge de la Dauberie*** (Châteaux-hôtels), Les Mousseaux, ☎ (1) 64.87.80.57. AE, DC, Visa. 10 rm Ⓟ ♨ ♿ closed Feb, Mon and Tue, 380. Rest. ♦♦♦ 140-240.

Restaurants :
● ♦♦♦ ***Les Préjugés,*** 11, pl. R.-Brault, ☎ (1) 64.86.92.65. AE, DC, Visa Ⓟ ♨ ♿ closed 2-30 Jan and Tue. Spec : *terrine de girolles, pot-au-feu de foie gras, bar au beurre de clémentines,* 175-350.

♦♦ ***Chez Nous,*** 22, rue de Paris, ☎ (1) 64.86.01.62. AE, DC, Visa ♿ closed Oct, 25 Dec, Fri eve, Sun eve and Mon. Menu varies according to the market. Spec : *sauté de gigot à l'ail doux, gratin de framboises,* 150-200.

Les Mesnuls, 3 km SE :
♦♦♦ ***La Toque Blanche,*** 12, Grande-Rue, ☎ (1) 34.86.05.55. AE, DC, Visa Ⓟ ♨ ♿ closed Aug, Christmas, Sun eve and Mon. Spec : *marmite de canard sauce poivrade,* 240.

MORET-SUR-LOING

Fontainebleau 10, Sens 43, Paris 77
D4 ☎ 1 ☒ 77250

ℹ pl. Samois (high season), ☎ (1) 60.70.41.66.

SNCF ☎ (1) 64.24.82.47.

Hotels :
Flagy, 77156 Thoury-Férottes, 12 km SE :
● ★★***Moulin de Flagy,*** 2, rue du Moulin, ☎ (1) 60.96.67.89. AE, DC, Visa. 10 rm Ⓟ ♨ closed 15-27 Sep, 19 Dec-23 Jan, Sun eve and Mon. A converted mill that once belonged to Blanche de Castille (mother of St. Louis), 245. Rest. ● ♦♦ ♿ Dinner by candle-light, with a blazing fire in winter. Refined cuisine at affordable prices. Spec : *truite à l'oseille, filet de bœuf au bleu des Causses,* 80-180.

Bourron-Marlotte, ☒ 77780, 12 km SW :
● ★***La Maison Blanche*** (L.F.), 26, rue Murger, ☎ (1) 64.45.75.58. 10 rm Ⓟ ♨ 100. Rest. ♦ ♿ closed Sun eve and Mon, Sep and one week in Feb. Spec : *compote de lapin aux pruneaux, filet de daurade à la moelle.* A pleasant small, reasonably priced restaurant, 60-120.

Restaurant :
La Genevraye, 77690 Montigny, 10 km SW :
♦♦ ***L'Auberge,*** ☎ (1) 64.45.83.99 Ⓟ ♨ ♿ closed 24 Feb-12 Mar, 8 Sep-1 Oct and Mon eve, Tue, 60-135.

Sound and light show : Sat eves, from 25 Jun to end Aug. Enq and bookings at the T.O.

NANGIS

Melun 26, Troyes 96, Paris 65
D3 ☎ 1 ☒ 77370

ℹ municipal offices, ☎ (1) 64.08.00.50.

SNCF ☎ (1) 64.08.00.68.

Hotel :
★★***Le Dauphin,*** 14, rue du Dauphin, ☎ (1) 64.08.03.57. AE, DC, Visa. 12 rm Ⓟ closed Sun eve, 150. Rest. ● ♦♦ ♿ Spec : *suprême de lotte au coulis de langoustines, foie gras frais maison,* 65-200.

NEMOURS

Melun 32, Orléans 87, Paris 80
C4 ☎ 1 ☒ 77140

ℹ 17, rue des Tanneurs, ☎ (1) 64.28.03.95.

SNCF ☎ (1) 64.28.00.23.

Hotel :
★★***Écu de France,*** 3, rue de Paris, ☎ (1) 64.28.11.54. AE, DC, Euro, Visa. 28 rm Ⓟ closed 2 weeks at Christmas, 195. Rest. ♦♦ ♿ 70-120.

⛺ ★★★*A.C.C.F.* (119 pl.), ☎ (1) 64.28.10.62.

Restaurants :
Bagneaux-sur-Loing, 5 km S :
♦♦ ***Poisson Doré,*** 51, rte de Glandelles, ☎ (1) 64.28.07.03. Visa. 5 rm Ⓟ ♨ closed Tue eve and Wed, 70. Summer dining on the banks of the Loing. Spec : *ris de veau lyonnaise,* 45-130.

♦ ***Auberge des Marronniers,*** 59, rte de Glandelles, ☎ (1) 64.28.07.04. Visa Ⓟ ♿ closed 15-31 Jan, 15-31 Aug, Tue eve and Wed. Spec : *gratin de fruits de mer au vermouth, escalope de saumon à l'oseille,* 65-200.

♦ ***La Glandelière,*** 22, rte de Glandelles, ☎ (1) 64.28.10.20. Visa Ⓟ ♨ ♿ closed Mon eve, Tue and Thu eve, 15-30 Sep, 15-28 Feb. Spec : *foie gras frais maison, gâteau de lotte à la crème,* 55-150.

NOGENT-LE-ROI

Chartres 29, Mantes 50, Paris 85
B3 ✉ 28210

Restaurant :
♦ ***Relais des Remparts,*** 2, pl. Marché-aux-Légumes, ☎ 37.51.40.47. DC, Visa P ♨ ♿ closed 15 Aug-3 Sep, Feb school hols, Tue eve, Wed, Sun eve in winter, 60-130.

NOGENT-LE-ROTROU

Chartres 54, Le Mans 71, Paris 147
A4 ✉ 28400

ℹ rue Gouverneur, ☎ 37.52.22.16.

SNCF ☎ 37.28.50.50.

Hotels :
★★***Dauphin,*** 39, rue Villette-Gâté, ☎ 37.52.17.30. Visa. 26 rm P ♨ closed 30 Nov-1 Mar, Sun eve and Mon low season, 200. Rest. ♦♦ Spec : *turbot petits légumes, jambonneau confit,* 65-180.

Villeray, 61110 Condeau, 11 km :
★★★***Moulin de Villeray*** (Relais et châteaux), Condeau, ☎ 33.73.30.22. Tx 171779. AE, DC, Euro, Visa. 10 rm P ♨ closed Dec, Jan, Tue and Wed noon. Private fishing, heliport, very comfortable rooms, 540. Rest. ♦♦♦ ♿ 180-280.

Event : early Sep, *grande fête du Perche.*

Auction room : 13, rue Abbé-Beule, ☎ 37.52.01.85.

Recommended : *Cosse* cake shop, 35, rue Villette-Gâté.

NOYON

Amiens 60, Rheims 98, Paris 106
D1 ✉ 60400

ℹ pl. de l'Hôtel-de-Ville, ☎ 44.44.02.97.

SNCF ☎ 44.44.00.61.

Hotel :
★★***Saint-Éloi,*** 81, bd Carnot, ☎ 44.44.01.49. Tx 145768. AE, Visa. 31 rm P ♿ closed Sun eve, 155. Rest. ♦ 65-180.

See also Soissons (→ Ardennes, Champagne).

Guided tours : *C.N.M.H.S.*, enq ℹ

PIERREFONDS

Compiègne 14, Soissons 31, Paris 87
D1 ✉ 60350

Hotels :
★***Étrangers,*** 10, rue du Beaudon, ☎ 44.42.80.18. 16 rm P ♨ closed 5 Jan-15 Feb, Sun eve and Mon low season, 120. Rest. ♦ 45-130.

Saint-Jean-aux-Bois, 60350 Cuise-la-Motte, 6 km W :
● ★★★***La Bonne Idée,*** rue des Meuniers, ☎ 44.42.84.09. AE, Visa. 15 rm P ♨ closed 15 Jan-15 Feb, 26 Aug-6 Sep, Tue eve and Wed noon, 220. Rest. ♦♦♦ Spec : *andouillette de sole au beurre de homard, potée d'escargots forestière, aiguillette de canette à la fleur de moutarde.* Reasonable prices, 190-300.

Λ ★★Municipal *de Batigny* (50 pl.), ☎ 44.42.80.83.

POISSY

Pontoise 17, Mantes 30, Paris 28
B2 ☎ 1 ✉ 78300

ℹ 132, rue du Gal-de-Gaulle, ☎ 30.74.60.65.

SNCF ☎ 30.74.17.06.

Restaurant :
♦♦ ***L'Esturgeon,*** 6, cours du 14-Juillet, ☎ 39.65.00.04. AE, DC, Visa ♿ closed 1 week in Jan, Aug and Thu. Spec : *foie gras de canard, caneton aux cerises, turbotin au blanc de poireaux.* On the banks of the Seine, 150-220.

PONTOISE

Mantes 40, Rouen 90, Paris 36
B2 ☎ 1 ✉ 95300

ℹ 6, pl. Petit-Martroy, ☎ 30.38.24.45.

SNCF ☎ 30.32.21.21, 30.32.45.45.

Restaurant :
Cormeilles-en-Vexin, ✉ 95830, 9.5 km :
♦♦ ***Relais Sainte-Jeanne,*** rte de Dieppe, ☎ 34.66.61.56. AE, DC, Visa. P ♨ ♿ closed 15 Aug-6 Sep, Christmas, 1 week Feb school hols, Sun eve and Mon. Spec : *soufflé de foie gras au coulis de truffes, pigeon de ferme en cocotte,* 220-310.

PROVINS

Melun 48, Troyes 76, Paris 90
D3 ☎ 1 ✉ 77160

ℹ tour César (A1), ☎ 64.00.16.65.

SNCF (C2), ☎ 64.00.01.95.

Hotels :
★***Croix d'Or,*** 1, rue des Capucins, ☎ 64.00.01.96. 7 rm ♿ closed Sun eve and Mon, 180. Rest. ♦ closed 1-15 Aug, 1 week in winter, 120-170.

Noyen-sur-Seine, ✉ 77114 Gouaix, 18 km S :
★★***Auberge du Port Montain*** (L.F.), ☎ 64.01.81.05. 10 rm P ♨ closed Jan, 182. Rest. ♦ ♿ 85-250.

Restaurants :
● ♦ ***Aux Vieux Remparts*** (M.C.F.), 3, rue Couverte, Ville-Haute, ☎ 64.00.02.89. AE, Visa. closed 8 Sep-4 Nov, Tue eve and Wed. Spec : *côtelette de volaille à la landaise, râble de lapin rôti au thym et fondue d'oignons,* 60-170.

Lizines, 10 km SW :
♦♦ ***Auberge St-Georges,*** 2, rue St-Georges, ☎ 60.67.32.48 P ♿ closed 1-20 Sep, Wed and eve ex Sat, 45-100.

Guided tours : C.N.M.H.S. by appointment ; enq at ℹ

RAMBOUILLET

Versailles 32, Orléans 90, Paris 52
B3 ☎ 1 ✉ 78120

ℹ ☎ 34.83.11.91.

SNCF ☎ 34.83.01.34, 34.83.84.45.

Hotels :
Gazeran, 4.5 km W :
★***Villa Marinette*** (L.F.), 20, av. du Gal-de-Gaulle, ☎ 34.83.19.01. DC, Visa. 6 rm ♨ closed 20 Aug-10 Sep, 2 weeks in Feb, Tue eve and Wed, 160. Rest. ♦♦ ♿ 90-150.

Saint-Léger-en-Yvelines, 5 km N :
★★★***La Belle Aventure,*** 8, rue de la Croix-Blanche, ☎ 34.86.31.35. 13 rm ♨ closed 17 Aug-1 Sep, Sun eve and Mon, 200. Rest. ♦ 100-200.

Λ ★★★*Le Pont Hardi* (65 pl.), ☎ 30.41.13.81.

Restaurants :
Gazeran, 4.5 km W :
♦♦ ***Au Rendez-vous de Chasse,*** 30, av. du Gal-de-Gaulle, ☎ 34.83.81.49. Visa P ♨ closed Christmas end-of-year hols, Mon and Tue eves. Spec of the Southwest, 150-200.

Le Perray-en-Yvelines, 5 km N :

♦♦♦ ***Auberge de l'Artoire,*** rue de Paris ☎ 34.84.17.91. AE, Visa Ⓟ ♨ ♿ closed 15 Jan-15 Feb and Tue (Oct-May). Classic cooking, 100-250.

Les Bréviaires, ✉ 78610 Perray-en-Yvelines, 8 km NW :

♦♦ ***Auberge des Bréviaires,*** 3, rte du Matz, ☎ 34.84.18.47. AE, Visa Ⓟ ♿ closed 20 Feb-15 Mar, 1 May and Christmas, Wed eve and Thu. Spec : *saumon frais mariné à l'aneth, noisette d'agneau en chevreuil,* 150-200.

SAINT-GERMAIN-EN-LAYE

Mantes 34, Dreux 70, Paris 21
B2 ☎ 1 ✉ 78100

ℹ 1 *bis,* rue République, ☎ 34.51.05.12.

SNCF ☎ 39.73.37.38.

R.E.R. : line A, ☎ 34.51.02.82.

Hotels :

● ★★★★(L) ***Cazaudehore et la Forestière*** (Relais et châteaux), 1, av. du Pdt-Kennedy, ☎ 39.73.36.60. Tx 696055. Visa. 30 rm Ⓟ ♨ ♿ 530. Rest. ● ♦♦♦ closed Mon ex nat hols. Quiet country charm on the edge of the forest. Good, classic cooking. Spec : *bar rôti sur sa peau à l'huile d'olive et à l'aneth, suprême et cervelas de volaille au coulis d'écrevisses,* 220-310.

★★★★(L) ***Pavillon Henri IV,*** 21, rue Thiers (C2), ☎ (1) 34.51.62.62. 42 rm Ⓟ ♨ ♿ Birthplace of Louis XIV, 1 200. Rest. ● ♦♦♦ 320-450.

Le Vésinet, 5 km E :

★★★***Les Ibis,*** île du Grand-Lac, ☎ (1) 39.52.17.41. 20 rm. closed 7 Jul-7 Sep. Ⓟ ♨ on an island, 260. Rest. ♦♦ closed Jul, 120-210.

Orgeval, 8 km NW :

● ★★***Moulin d'Orgeval,*** rue de l'Abbaye, ☎ (1) 39.75.95.74. Visa. 13 rm Ⓟ ♨ closed 22 Dec-7 Feb, 225. Rest. ♦♦ ♿ Spec : *terrine de foies de volailles, coquilles St-Jacques au whisky,* 145-180.

Restaurants :

● ♦♦ ***Pavillon de la Croix de Noailles,*** carrefour de Noailles, 6 km N on N184, ☎ (1) 39.62.53.46. AE, Visa. Ⓟ ♨ ♿ closed 17-27 Feb, Sun eve and Mon in winter. A very good chef in a pleasant restaurant : *bavarois de saumon, aiguillettes de canard au vinaigre de cidre, miel d'acacia,* 100-250.

♦ ***Au 7 Rue des Coches,*** 7, rue des Coches, ☎ (1) 39.73.66.40. ♿ closed 4-27 Aug, Sun eve and Mon. Pleasant setting, 170-240.

Events : July *music festival ;* early Jul-15 Aug : *fête des Loges.*

Recommended : *Dumas Sibenaler,* cakes and pastries, ice-creams, catering, 21, rue du Vieux-Marché, ☎ (1) 34.51.02.07.

SENLIS

Meaux 38, Amiens 100, Paris 51
C1 ✉ 60300

ℹ hôtel des Trois-Pots, pl. du Parvis-Notre-Dame (B1), ☎ 44.53.06.40.

SNCF bus service, ☎ 44.53.00.06.

🚌 (C1)

Hotels :

★★***Hostellerie de la Porte Bellon*** (L.F.), 51, rue Bellon (C2), ☎ 44.53.03.05. 19 rm Ⓟ ♨ closed 20 Dec-20 Jan and Fri low season, 180. Rest. ♦♦ 120-210.

Nogent-sur-Oise, 60100 Creil, 15 km NW :

● ★★★***Sarcus*** (Inter-Hôtel), 7, rue Chateaubriand, ☎ 44.74.01.31. 62 rm Ⓟ ♨ ♿ closed Aug, Sat noon and Sun, 250. Rest. ♦♦ 90-160.

Restaurants :

♦♦ ***Le Formanoir,*** 17, rue du Châtel, ☎ 44.53.04.39. Visa. Former convent (16thC), 140-200.

♦ ***Scaramouche,*** 4, pl. Notre-Dame, ☎ 44.53.01.26. AE, Visa. Ⓟ closed Thu and 16-28 Aug. Pleasant setting, 70-150.

Guided tours : *C.N.M.H.S.* (Sat, Sun and nat hols, Mar-Oct), enq at ℹ

Concerts : in the Franz-Liszt auditorium, former St-Frambourg church.

SENONCHES

Dreux 35, Mortagne 42, Paris 120
A3 ✉ 28250

Hotel :

La Loupe, ✉ 28240, 11 km S :

★***Le Chêne Doré*** (L.F.), 12, pl. de l'Hôtel-de-Ville, ☎ 37.81.06.71. AE, DC. 14 rm Ⓟ closed 22 Dec-31 Jan, Sun eve and Mon, 145. Rest. ♦♦ Spec : *escalope de foie gras chaude percheronne, brouillade d'œufs aux cèpes et foie gras,* 45-140.

VERSAILLES

Chartres 68, Orléans 120, Paris 23
B2 ☎ 1 ✉ 78000

ℹ 7, rue des Réservoirs, ☎ (1) 39.50.36.22, and 45, rue Carnot.

SNCF Versailles-Chantiers, ☎ (1) 39.50.34.95 ; Versailles-Rive-Droite, ☎ (1) 39.51.44.19. **R.E.R.** (Line C), Versailles-Rive-Gauche, ☎ (1) 39.50.08.16.

🚌 pl. Lyautey (B-C3), ☎ (1) 39.50.45.55.

Hotels :

● ★★★★(L) ***Trianon Palace,*** 1, bd de la Reine (C2), ☎ (1) 39.56.34.12. Tx 698863. AE, DC, Euro, Visa. 130 rm Ⓟ ♨ ♿ 770. Rest. ♦♦ 150-250.

● ★★★ ***Bellevue,*** 12, av. de Sceaux, ☎ (1) 39.50.13.41. Tx 695613. AE, DC, Euro, Visa. 25 rm ♿ 280.

★★★***Versailles,*** 7, rue Sainte-Anne, ☎ (1) 39.50.64.65. AE, Visa. 48 rm Ⓟ ♿ 285.

● ★★***Saint-Louis,*** 28, rue Saint-Louis (B3), ☎ (1) 39.50.23.55. Tx 698958. 27 rm ♿ 180.

★★***Angleterre,*** 2 *bis,* rue de Fontenay, ☎ (1) 39.51.43.50. Tx 698311. Visa. 20 rm ♨ ♿ 220.

Saint-Cyr-l'École, ✉ 78210, 5 km W :

● ★★***Aérotel*** (Relais du Silence), 88, rue Dr-Vaillant, ☎ (1) 30.45.07.44. Tx 698160. 26 rm Ⓟ ♿ 220.

⛺ ★★*Municipal* (160 pl.), ☎ 3.951.23.61.

Restaurants :

● ♦♦♦♦ ***Les Trois Marches,*** 3, rue Colbert, ☎ (1) 39.50.13.21. AE, DC, Visa. closed Sun and Mon. ♨ Next to the statue of "The Sun King", a royal setting for the former mansion of the duc de Gramont where Gérard Vié, intelligently prepares high quality, refined cooking. Spec : *flan chaud de foie gras aux huîtres et écrevisses, terrine de céleri au foie gras, sauté d'agneau aux abats, pain au lard maison,* choice of coffees, fine wines, 250-450.

● ♦♦♦ ***La Rôtisserie de la Boule d'Or,*** 25, rue du Mal-Foch, ☎ (1) 39.50.22.97. AE, DC, Visa. closed Sun eve, Mon. Versailles' oldest inn.

Authentic, period decor sets the scene for dishes traditionally prepared by the Sun King's master cooks, 130-300.

● ♦♦ ***Le Potager du Roy,*** 1, rue du Mal-Joffre, ☎ (1) 39.50.35.34. Visa. Good, simple fare in the annex of *the Trois Marches,* 85-125.

● ♦♦ ***Rescatore,*** 27, av. de Saint-Cloud, ☎ (1) 39.50.23.60. AE, Visa. closed Sat noon and Sun. Seafood specialities worthy of any port : *cassoulet de poisson, bouillabaisse,* 145-270.

Guyancourt, ⊠ 78280, 5 km S :

♦ ***Lac Hong,*** rte de la Minière, ☎ (1) 30.44.03.71. Visa. Ⓟ ♿ closed Wed and 13 Aug-8 Sep. Facing Minière ponds, a restaurant where you can taste Mr. Tung's excellent Vietnamese cooking. Spec : *coquelet désossé farci aux 7 parfums, caille grillée aux épices,* 50-70.

Guided tours : enq at ℹ

Market : covered market, several week days.

Versailles Festival : May-Jun and Sep. Historical spectacles and folk festivals, concerts in the town and at the castle, opera and theatre. Enq : ℹ

Recommended : *Guinon,* cake shop and tearooms, 60, rue de la Paroisse, ☎ (1) 39.50.01.84. *Pellisson,* cakes and pastries, ice-creams and catering, 44, rue de la Paroisse, ☎ (1) 39.50.01.63. *Auction room :* hôtel des Chevaux Légers. *Passage des Antiquaires (Antique Dealers) :* 10, rue Rameau, ☎ (1) 39.53.84.96. open Fri, Sat and Sun 10-19h. *Le Grenier :* antiques, folk art, 7, pl. St-Louis, ☎ (1) 39.51.71.70.

The Languedoc Roussillon Region

A region of many personalities, set between the peaks of the Cévennes and the Pyrénées, and the blue Mediterranean, with plains and mountains, plateaus and thriving cities. Languedoc Roussillon is studded with vineyards and salty marshlands, and a wealth of Romanesque buildings, all imbued with the spirit of the south : Catalan and *langue d'Oc* traditions with their special lifestyles, their deep religious feeling and their passion for rugby and bullfighting.

Carcassonne is a city whose past is so strong that it almost overpowers the present. It is in fact two villages, one made up of the acropolis and its fortifications, restored by Viollet-le-Duc, and the other, lower, on the left bank of the Aude. Montpellier is a university town a few kilometres from the sea. France's first medical colleges were established there in the year 1000 after contact with the learned Orient, and in 1289 Pope Nicholas IV created the University of Montpellier. Today the Medical Faculty of Montpellier shares with the Paris Faculty the distinction of being the leading medical university in France. The old part of Perpignan has barely changed since the 18th century, but the dynamism and prosperity of this Catalan town with its festivals and processions and its bustling produce markets and wine trade mark it as belonging very much to the living present.

Almost the whole of the low country is covered with vineyards, but recently the risks of over-production and foreign competition have stimulated local farmers to diversify their crops. Now fruit trees and market-gardens are slowly invading the irrigated parts of the Aude Valley.

Cooking is Provençal, characterised by garlic and olive oil, with delicious sausages and smoked hams, *foie gras* and truffles. The region produces delicious pastries and sweetmeats made from almond paste and flavored with aniseed, pistachio and orange-flower water.

Sightseeing

Weekend tips

The first day will take you from Montpellier, Sète or Béziers into the Hérault Valley; lunch at Ganges; then through the Vis Valley and the natural mountain amphitheatre at Navacelles to Lodève (stopover). Up the Orb Valley on the second day to the Espinouse Range (lunch at Lamalou or Saint-Pons) and the Montagne Noire, before arriving at Carcassonne. Another suggestion : from Narbonne, go right up the valley of the Aude and lunch at Carcassonne; after Quillan, a stopover at Font-Romeu. On day two, after an excursion into Cerdagne, turn back through Conflent towards Perpignan; lunch at Villefranche, then Saint-Michel-de-Cuxa or Saint-Martin-du-Canigou.

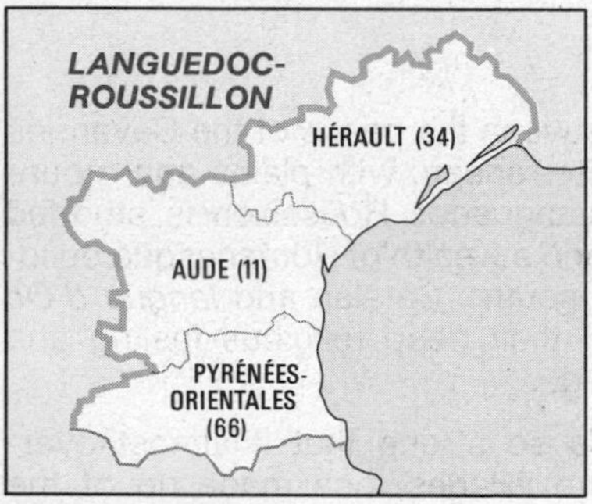

Facts and figures

Location : *on the Mediterranean coast, between the Rhône delta and the Spanish frontier, and including the southern face of the Cévennes Massif and the eastern Pyrénées.*
Area : *16 431 km².*
Climate : *Summer temperatures are high along the eastern Pyrénées and the Mediterranean coast : Perpignan shares the national mean temperature record with Corsica. The area is exceptionally sunny (notably around Font-Romeu and the Cerdagne region). Winters are extremely mild in the lower Pyrénées valleys. Spring comes early in the Corbières region, which has a milder climate than the coastal regions, especially when the cold Tramontane mountain wind is blowing. Further inland, winters are harsh in the Cévennes and the lower tip of the Massif Central; summer here is also cooler than elsewhere. Although there is comparatively little rainfall in the region as a whole, mountain storms occasionally produce disastrous effects.*
Population : *1 321 740 inhabitants, mainly concentrated in the coastal towns.*
Administration : Aude *Department, Prefecture : Carcassonne;* ***Hérault*** *Department, Prefecture : Montpellier;* ***Pyrénées-Orientales*** *Department, Prefecture : Perpignan.*

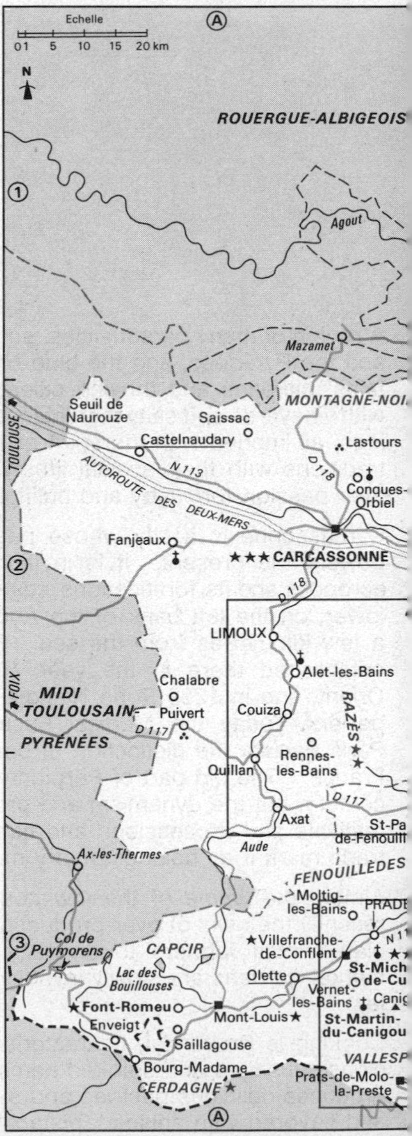

■ AGDE★

C2 / ® / pop. 13 107 (Hérault)

Agde, on the bank of a branch canal from the Hérault, seems far removed from the coast, suspended between an ancient past and the modern seasonal influxes of holiday-makers. The port has seen better days; it was founded as an outpost of the Greek colony of Marseilles.

▶ **Church of St. Étienne★ :** Romanesque, formerly a fortified cathedral; barrel-vaulted interior; 17thC furnishings. ▶ Nearby, **GRASPA Museum :** the local Organisation for Research in underwater Archaeology and Diving exhibits their finds from the seabed *(daily ex Tue. 10-12 & 2-6).* ▶ **Agde Museum :** near Place Gambetta, in a mansion (5, Rue de la Fraternité; *closed Tue.*) : ethnography and regional archaeology, scale model boats. □

Don't miss

★★★ : *Canigou Massif (A3), Carcassonne (A2), Montpellier (C1), Saint-Michel-de-Cuxa (A3).*

★★ : *Cerdagne (A3), Côte Vermeille (B3), Espinouse Range (B1), Fontfroide (B2), Hérault Valley (C1), Narbonne (B2), Navacelles (C1), Perpignan (B3), Pézenas (C1), the Razès Region (A2-3), Saint-Guilhem-de-Désert, Saint-Martin-du-Canigou (A3).*

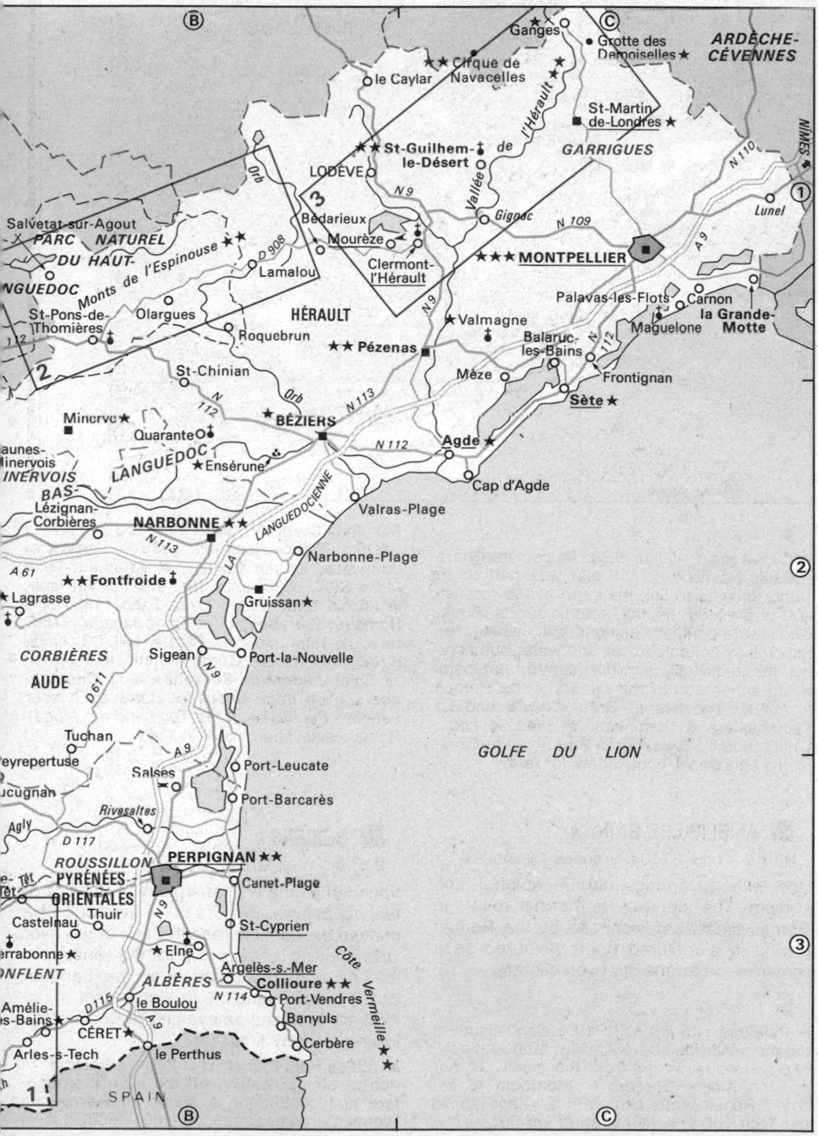

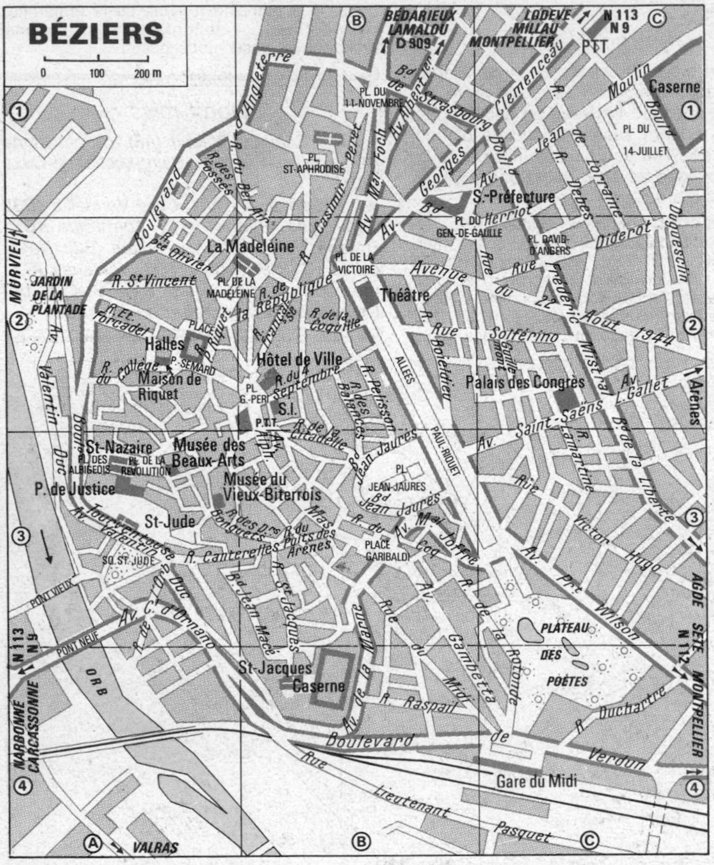

▶ Nearby

▶ **Cap Agde** ® *(7 km SE) :* tourist area on a volcanic promontory; the pier was part of an 18thC scheme to link the cape to the fortified islet of Brescou; marina, aquatic sports, Aqualand leisure park, amusement park, fishing, sea trips (glass-bottomed boat and water bus serving the beaches), seminar centre, naturism. ▶ On either side of the mouth of the Hérault *(4 km S),* beaches at **Grau d'Agde** and **La Tamarissière** ® (naturism). ▶ **Vias** *(4 km) :* 14thC church . **Cassafières Port** *(9 km farther) :* on the Midi Canal, houseboats for rent. □

■ AMÉLIE-LES-BAINS★

B3 / ® / pop. 3713 (Pyrénées-Orientales)

Spa with 20 springs rich in sulphur and sodium. The site was a thermal resort in Roman times, as evidenced by the Roman paving in a restored pool; favoured as a winter resort for the dry even climate. □

▶ Nearby

▶ **Palalda**★ *(1.5 km NE) :* a Catalan village on the mountainside above Amélie; 10thC church; two towers remaining from the castle. Higher up, the **Ample Gorges.** ▶ **Montbolo** *(6 km NW) :* Romanesque church in a village above the Tech Valley. ▶ **Montalba** *(8 km SE)* via the Mondony Gorges★ : from there a 3 hr hike on GR10 to **France Rock** (alt. 1 450 m) : view★ of both sides of the frontier. ▶ **Arles-sur-Tech** *(4 km SW) :* commercial centre of the Vallespir, in an old town wound around the 11th-12thC **Romanesque abbey**★ (sculpted façade, 17thC reredos, 13thC cloister). Farther still, D3 climbs through the **Guéra Gorges**★ (chestnut forest) to **Saint-Laurent-de-Cerdans**★ and **Coustouges** *(24 km from Amélie-les-Bains on a spur between the basins of the Tech and the Muga),* Romanesque church built in 1147. □

■ BÉZIERS★

B2 / ® / pop. 90 000 (Hérault)

Founded as the Roman colony of *Julia Septimania Biterae,* Béziers is on the edge of a plateau overlooking the left bank of the river Orb. The city is the centre for the wine, spirits and related industries of the Languedoc. To understand the true character of the Midi, try to spend an evening at Béziers following a rugby final.

▶ **Allées Paul-Riquet** (B-C 2-3) : a network of narrow streets leading off the main thoroughfare and centred on a statue of Pierre-Paul Riquet, Baron de Bonrépos (1604-1680), a local landowner who conceived and executed the Midi Canal that links the Mediterranean to the Atlantic (by way of the river Garonne) The Allées lead to the **Plateau des Poètes** (C 3-4) : public gardens. ▶ To W, mediaeval streets : **Rue du Quatre-Septembre** (pedestrians only) crosses in front of the **Penitents' Church** (Flamboyant Gothic doorway) and leads to Place Gabriel-Péri and the 18thC **town hall.** ▶ **Cathedral of St. Nazaire** (A3) : rebuilt during the 13th-14thC following the Albigensian Crusade, when the town was sacked (1209); statuary museum in the **cloister; view** over the Orb Valley. ▶ **Fine Arts Museum★ :** in the Fabrégat Mansion (A3), 16th-20thC paintings, Greek vases *(closed Sun. am and Mon.)* ▶ In the former Dominican church, **Museum of the Old Biterrois** (a Biterrois is an inhabitant of Béziers) **and of Wine★ :** (A3, 7 Rue Massol; *closed Mon.*) regional costumes; underwater archaeological finds from near Agde. ▶ **Rue des Canterelles :** lined with ancient houses, leads to the 13thC **Pont Vieux** (Old Bridge; A3). **Church of St. Jacques** (B4) : 12thC apse; terraces offer a view over the cathedral and the numerous Orb bridges, including the aqueduct that carries the Midi Canal.

Also... ▶ **Natural History Museum** (15 Place Pierre-Sémard, A2, *open am ex. Sat. and Sun.*). ▶ **Church of la Madeleine** (B2) : Romanesque, last and vain refuge during the massacre of 1209. ▶ **Basilica of St. Aphrodise** (B1) : pre-Romanesque origins, a cathedral until 760. □

▶ Nearby

▶ On the SW edge of the town, the **locks** of **Fonséranes** compensate for the 25 m difference between the levels of the aqueduct and the Orb. ▶ **Ensérune★** *(12 km SW) :* a fortified hill-top town occupied between the 6thC BC and 1stC AD by Celtiberians; open year round; view★ over the ancient **Montady Pool,** drained during the 13thC; **Museum :** reconstructed burial sites; Greek vases *(closed Tue.).* ▶ **Nissan-les-Ensérune** ® *(3 km S) :* 14thC church : archaeological museum. ▶ **Valras-Plage** ® *(15 km SE) :* at the mouth ot the Orb, a fishing port and a marina : aquatic sports; view from the 7 km-long beach extends from Cape Agde to the Canigou Massif. □

■ The CANIGOU Massif★★★

▶ 2-day tour starting from Prades *(approx 180 km)*
A3 *(see map 1)*

Standing as a sentinel before the eastern Pyrénées, the Canigou Massif is visible

1. Canigou Massif

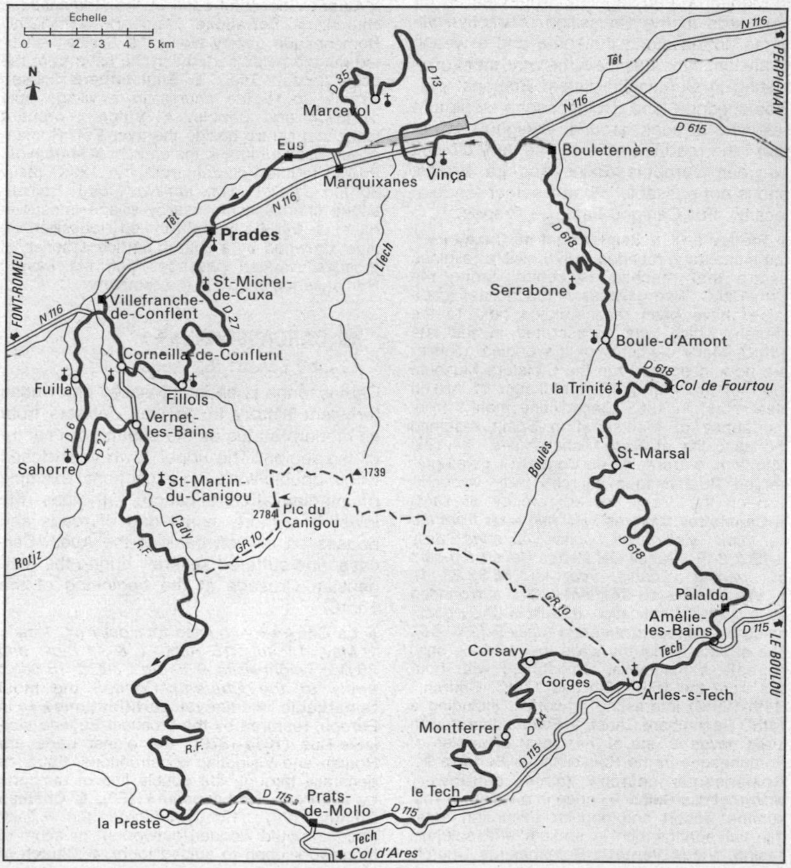

Romanesque Roussillon

The first Catalan religious sanctuaries were founded towards the end of the 8thC by Spanish refugees fleeing the Moorish conquerors. With the establishment of Saint-Michel-de-Cuxa in 974, churches multiplied rapidly in the mountain regions. These churches were usually modest in size, but embellished with cloisters, sculpture, painted doors and occasional murals (Saint-Martin-de-Fenollar). From the second half of the 12thC, Romanesque art flourished in the Languedoc. Roussillon was spared the worst devastation during the Albigensian Crusade and the Wars of Religion (16th-17thC). However, many buildings were wrecked when the Revolution (1789) closed the churches and monasteries, and still others were stripped of Romanesque and pre-Romanesque treasures to enrich museums in the 19th and 20thC.

from far away, especially from the coast. Snow is present practically year-round in the high country. The mountain rises behind the high hills of Aspres, which are covered in Mediterranean vegetation but cleared for vineyards in the Roussillon. Attractive villages dotted along the route and a wealth of ancient churches mark the way, most originating in Carolingian times. Regional pre-Romanesque and Romanesque sculpture reached a peak around Canigou. **Attention :** the road is unsealed and very difficult between Vernet-les-Bains and La Preste, and is not passable in bad weather (enquire locally). For Canigou Peak, → Prades.

▶ **Prades** (→). ▶ **Saint-Michel-de-Cuxa★★★ :** the monastery, founded in 878, was a religious centre that reached its zenith during the 11th-12thC. Two galleries of the cloister (capitals★) have been reconstructed next to the church, which was consecrated in the late 10thC. Many elements of the original cloister are now incoporated in the Cloisters Museum (part of the Metropolitan Museum of Art) in New York. In 1965, Benedictine monks from the abbey of Montserrat in Spain resumed monastic life at Saint-Michel *(visits daily ex. Sun. am).* ▶ **Corneilla-de-Conflent★ :** well-preserved Romanesque church★ with wrought-iron on the doors, carved reredos of 1345. ▶ **Canalettes Caverns :** *(10 min walk from the car park; visit takes approx. 45 mins; daily 9-12 & 2-7).* Grands Canalettes Caverns *(hours of opening variable, info. tel. 68.98.23.11).* ▶ **Villefranche-de-Conflent★** ® : surrounded by a 15thC fortification (rebuilt 17thC) dominated by a citadel; **ramparts** *(daily 9-12 & 2-6).* The streets within the walls (pedestrians only) recreate a mediaeval atmosphere with houses from the 15th, 16th and 17thC. **Church :** (11th-12thC) interesting artwork★, including a 14thC Recumbent Christ. ▶ **Fuilla :** church with three naves is one of the oldest examples of Romanesque in the Roussillon. ▶ **Sahorre** ® : Romanesque church★ (apse, bell-tower). ▶ **Vernet-les-Bains** ® : deep in a valley; a spa, summer resort and popular excursion area; thermal springs rich in sodium and sulphur; casino. **Vieux Vernet :** Romanesque Church, ancient château. ▶ **Saint-Martin-du-Canigou★★** *(45 min walk from neighbouring Casteil, or by jeep from Vernet) :* 1 065 m above sealevel on a peak above precipices; founded in the early 11thC; the church and square bell-tower have been ably restored in the 20thC; cloister (modernised) has beautiful carved capitals★ *(daily at 10, 11, 2, 3, 4 and 5; be present 15 mins before).* ▶ **Goa :** a mediaeval watch-tower 90 mins from Casteil; view★. **La Preste** (alt. 1 130 m) : alkaline, sulphur-bearing, radioactive springs in an extensive bathing establishment on a beautiful site; a good centre for day trips into the mountains, especially towards the **Costabonne Peak** (alt. 2 465 m; view★). ▶ **Prats-de-Mollo** ® : well-kept square, ramparts and 17thC church, dominated by Fort La Garde, with a 13thC tower. Trips into the mountains might include the **Mir Tower** *(2 hr SW;* 13thC watch-tower) and the **Coral Hermitage** *(2 hr 30 S)* rebuilt 17thC; views★. ▶ Beyond the **Baillanouse Pass** reach Arles direct via the **Pas de Loup** or detour through **Montferrer** (Romanesque church; view★ over the Vallespir and Canigou) and the **Fou Gorges★ :** in places no wider than 1 m; *(entrance fee to a wooden footbridge, Easter-end Sep. 9-6).* ▶ **Arles-sur-Tech, Amélie-les-Bains** (→ Amélie). ▶ **Prunet-et-Belpuig :** in the heart of the Aspres, **church of the Trinity** (Romanesque) with 12thC wood Christ; 30 mins to the ruined **château de Belpuig** (view★) and the **Fourtou Pass.** ▶ **Boule-d'Amont :** beautiful apse in the Romanesque church. ▶ **Serrabone :** priory★ 11th-12thC Romanesque gallery along the S side; sculpted marble pulpit separating the nave from the choir *(closed Tue.).* ▶ **Bouleternère :** steep streets up to the church in a village built of brick and pebble. ▶ **Vinça :** orchard (peaches) centre beside the river Têt; Romanesque wrought iron in the church. ▶ **Marcevol :** Priory, fortified church from the 12thC *(daily 30 Jun.-31 Oct.; Sun. am Nov.-Jun.);* Romanesque church in the nearby village (mostly in ruins). ▶ **Eus★ :** typical fortified Roussillon village, crowned by a church astride a series of arcades, vaulted passages and stairways : Romanesque chapel in the cemetery. □

■ CARCASSONNE★★★

A2 / ® / pop. 41 153 (Aude)

Carcassonne is an intact walled city whose turbulent history in no way detracts from its modern status as the commercial centre of the region. The upper town is enclosed within double walls (an exceptional example of mediaeval fortification), whereas the lower is a more recent grid of roads and houses on the left bank of the Aude. Carcassonne suffered severely during the Albigensian Crusade at the beginning of the 13thC.

▶ **La Cité★★★ :** *(guided tour daily ex. 1 Jan., 1 May, 14 Jul., 15 Aug., 1 & 11 Nov. and 25 Dec.; night visits, 9:30 pm 1 Jul. to 15 Sep.; apply to the Château Comtal)* the most remarkable mediaeval **fortifications★★** in Europe, restored by the architect Eugène Viollet-le-Duc (1814-1879); the oldest parts are Roman and Visigothic constructions. Entrance generally through the double line of ramparts by the **Porte Narbonnaise★** (E3). ▶ **Château Comtal★** (E3) : (12thC) reinforces the W flank (reconstructed wooden outworks); museum of stonework open to guided tours. ▶ **Church of**

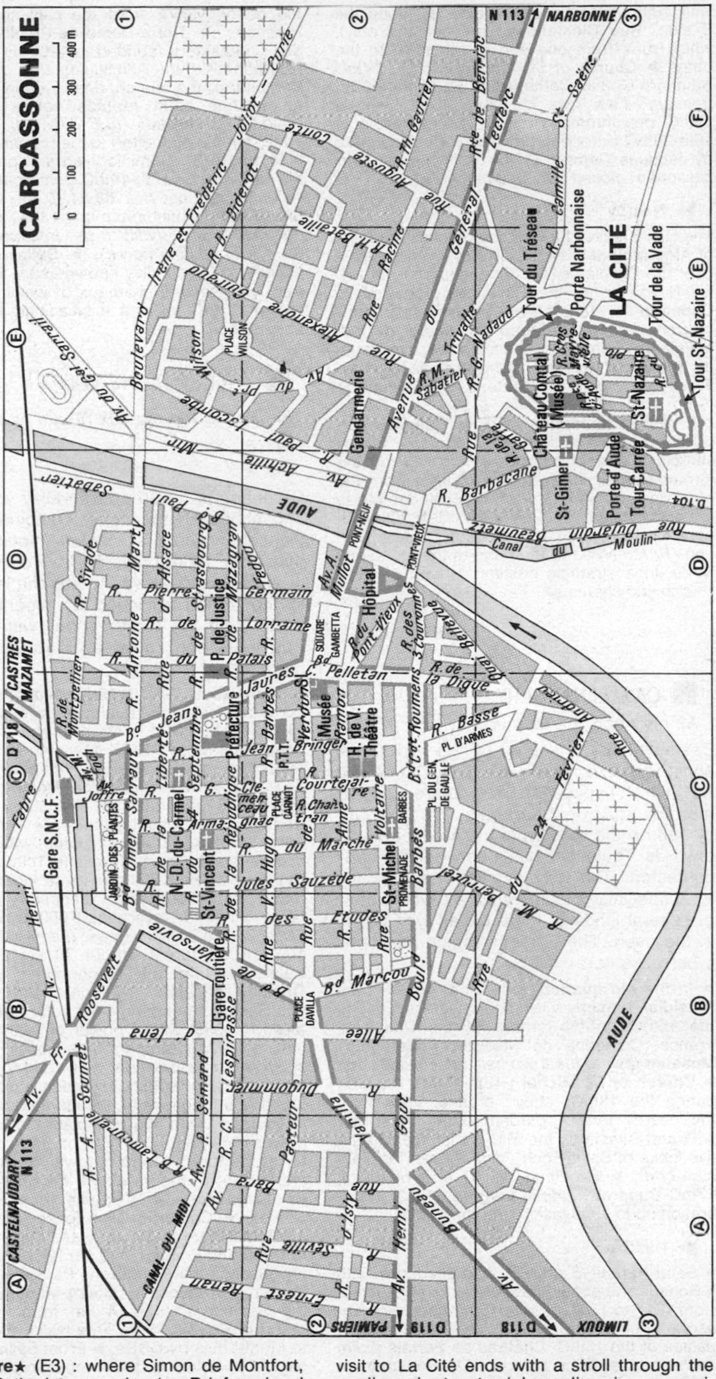

St. Nazaire★ (E3) : where Simon de Montfort, the anti-Catharist crusader (→ Brief regional history) was buried; Romanesque nave, 13thC transept and choir, 14thC statues, 14th-16thC stained glass★. The 360° view from the **St. Nazaire Tower** (behind the church) takes in the Montagne Noire and the Pyrénées. ▶ The visit to La Cité ends with a stroll through the mediaeval streets (abounding in souvenir shops and outlets for regional products) and a tour of the **ramparts.** Fireworks display on 14 Jul. (French National Day). ▶ **Place Carnot** (E2) : centre of the **lower town,** a market square shaded by plane trees and adorned with 18thC fountain of Neptune. ▶ Along the E side, **Rue Clémenceau** (pedestrians only), which runs from one end of the town to the other. ▶ **Church of St. Vincent★** (C1) : 14thC Southern Gothic. **Cathedral of St. Michel** (C2) : treasury; **Fine Arts Museum,** 13thC, with a 14thC polychrome Virgin; (C2; archaeology, 16th-20thC European painting, including works by Jacques Gamelin (1738-1803) born at Carcassonne; *closed Sun. and nat. hols.*). □

▶ Nearby

The GR36 leaves La Cité and reaches the crest of **Alric Mountain** with a hike of 2-3 hr. (view★ over the Corbières, the Pyrenees and the valley N as far as the Cévennes); descent to **Capendu** ® : *(16 km E of Carcassonne).* 14thC church, ruined château of same period. ▶ **Palaja :** *(5 km SE)* in the town hall, a museum of palaeontology and pre-history *(daily from 5 pm to 7 pm).* ▶ **Château de Pennautier** *(6 km NW; daily ex. Tue. & Sun., Jul.-Oct.) :* 17th-18thC furnishings, park. ▶ **Conques-sur-l'Orbiel :** *(8 km N)* fortified village with Gothic church. **Villarzel-Cabardès** *(5 km NE) :* in the former school, an exhibition of finds from the Merovingian cemetery of Mourral-des-Morts *(by appointment; tel. 68.77.02.11).* ▶ **Villegailhenc** *(9 km N) :* regional produce on sale. **Aragon** *(10 km NW) :* at the edge of the Montagne Noire, in a strategic position around a 12thC church and château. □

■ CASTELNAUDARY

A2 / ® / pop. 10 750 (Aude)

Castelnaudary is served by the Midi Canal and the railway, as well as by N113 and A61, which bypass the town centre. The former capital of Lauragais, strategically placed on the road from the Mediterranean towards Toulouse, has often been bitterly contested. This city is renowned for the local speciality of *cassoulet,* a savoury stew of several kinds of meat baked with beans in the oven. The Foreign Legion maintains a barracks here.

▶ In the **old quarter,** 16th-18thC houses; the **Présidial,** formerly a law court, was built during the 16thC on the orders of the Queen of France, Catherine de Médicis; **Archaeology Museum** *(ask at the town hall, tel. 68.23.11.16).* ▶ **Church of St. Michel :** 13th-14thC, restored during the 18thC; choir; organs. **View** from the nearby terrace garden to the Pyrénées. ▶ **Grand Bassin** on the Midi Canal, feeding the five locks of Saint-Roch : also a base for pleasure-craft. ▶ On Pech Hill (N side of town), 17thC **Cugarel windmill** (restored 1962) in operation up to 1919 *(ask at the town hall).* □

▶ Nearby

▶ **Saint-Papoul** *(8 km NE) :* a fortified town with a Benedictine abbey that served as a cathedral from 1317 to 1790; unique 16thC nave, Romanesque choir, 14thC cloister. Former episcopal palace of the 16thC. **Château de Ferrals** *(3 km farther on).* ▶ **Bram** *(16 km SE) :* Roman town of Eburomagus, market centre of the Lauragais, in concentric circles around the church; archaeological exhibition at the town hall *(closed Sat. and Sun.).* ▶ **Montréal** *(23 km SE) :* on an isolated hill-top; 14thC fortified church in meridional Gothic style (18thC organs); from the belfry, view★ from the Cévennes to the Pyrénées. ▶ **Notre-Dame-de-Prouille** *(17 km SE) :* monastery founded in 1206 by St. Dominic (founder of the Dominican religious Order of Preachers); the church, destroyed in the Revolution, has been replaced by a mediocre building. **Fanjeaux** *(3.5 km on) : Fanum Jovis* (temple of Jupiter) to the Romans; stronghold where St. Dominic lived and preached in the early 13thC; 13th-14thC Dominican convent, visits by request *(tel. 68.24.70.16).* Church of Ste. Marie : rebuilt in the late 13thC in Languedoc Gothic style *(visit to the treasury by appt. tel. 68.24.70.05;* view★). ▶ **Salles-sur-l'Hers** *(20 km W) :* in a valley known as the **Piège** (the trap) with several châteaux of which the most recent (17thC) offer a misleadingly mediaeval appearance. □

■ The CERDAGNE Valley★★

▶ Round trip *(approx 50 km by D618 and N116)*

A3

Cerdagne is an attractive valley with views and majestic mountains, combined with a pleasant way of life. The little mountain train that links Mont-Louis to La Tour-de-Carol provides an ideal way to see the landscape in the spring encircled by mountains still white from the winter snow, with budding fruit trees and cattle farms stretching into the distance.

▶ **Mont-Louis** (→). ▶ **Superbloquère :** S of D618 (alt. 1 780 m) a health resort composed of villas in a forest of larch, pine and fir. ▶ **Pyrénées 2000** *(N of D618) :* a winter sports resort offering night-time skiing on the plain of Serrat de l'Ours. ▶ **Calvaire de Font-Romeu :** view★★ over the Sègre Valley. ▶ **Hermitage de Font-Romeu :** near a spring that once attracted pilgrims (*romeu* in dialect); chapel with Baroque decoration; buildings from the 18thC. ▶ **Font-Romeu★** ® (alt. 1 800 m) : winter sports, health resort for children with respiratory diseases, faces full south; averages 3 000 hr of sun per year; 30 km of ski-slopes, numerous ski-lifts; 100 km^2 of forest; about 70 km of marked trails. ▶ Near the neighbouring resort of **Odeillo★** ® : CNRS (National Centre for Scientific Research) experimental solar furnace (installed in 1969) with a power of 1 000 kW thermal, achieving temperatures above 3 500 °C. ▶ From **Targassonne★** ®, a road to Thémis : most powerful solar generating station in the world (2.5 megawatts), inaugurated in 1983; it is equipped with 200 heliostats that adjust the power level and focus light on the giant receptor at the top of an 80 m tower. ▶ Descend to the bottom of the valley via the **chaos** (gorge) **de Targassonne★ :** granite rock formation; views★. ▶ Church of **Ur :** consecrated in 953, a Romanesque trefoil apse and decorated interior. Beyond **Enveigt** ® *(3 km W),* the Carol Valley ascends the Puymorens Pass (→ Midi Toulousain, Pyrénées). ▶ **Bourg-Madame** ® : on the Spanish frontier, 4 km from the health resort of **Osséja;** from here walkers can climb to Mont-Louis by GRE4. ▶ From **Saillagouse** ® (lapidary workshop, jewel mounting) to **Llo★** ® *(2 km E) :* a remarkable site at the entrance to the **Sègre Gorges;** or to **Estavar** *(4 km W) :* Romanesque 12thC church with murals on the edge of the Spanish enclave of Llivia. ▶ After crossing the **Perche Pass** (alt. 1 579 m; view★) return to Mont-Louis. □

CÉRET★

B3 / ® / pop. 6 798 (Pyrénées-Orientales)

A centre of Catalan culture, where avant-garde artists and adherents of Cubism gathered around the composer Déodat de Séverac (1873-1921) and the Catalan sculptor Manolo (1872-1945) in the early years of the century. Céret is also an important agricultural centre, especially for the cultivation of cherries and grapes. The Easter Sunday procession, the Sadana dance festival on the last Sunday in August, and the September bull races show that Catalan traditions are thriving.

▶ In the old town, 18thC **church** with three cupolas and a 14thC portal. This quarter is a series of courtyards shaded by plane trees marking the lines of the ancient ramparts, whose French and Spanish gates still stand. ▶ Place Pablo-Picasso : a former convent of Ste. Thérèse, now the **Catalan Cultural Centre** with a museum, a theatre and dance group; next door is the **St. Roch Crafts Centre.** ▶ **Museum of Modern Art★ :** Cubist paintings. ▶ Place de la Résistance (not far from the bullring) : the **Toreador Monument** designed after a statuette by Manolo. □

▶ Nearby

▶ **Fontfrède Peak** *(12 km S) :* one of the most entrancing sites★ in the region. ▶ Bridge of 1340 *(1.5 km N of town centre, near D115) :* restored in the 18thC. ▶ **Château d'Aubiry :** turn off D115 to visit the wine cooperative *(3 km NE; closed Sun. and Mon.).* ▶ **Le Boulou** ® *(9 km NE) :* church with Romanesque doorway and 17thC altarpiece; thence to the **Perthus Road** via les **Bains-du-Boulou :** spa (sodium bicarbonate) specialising in treatment of liver complaints; church of **Saint-Martin-de-Fenollar★** (11th-12thC, with 12th-13thC paintings), and **L'Écluse** (remains of Roman fortifications, ruins of mediaeval château, Romanesque church). ▶ **Le Perthus** *(14 km SE of Céret) :* a village astride a spur of the same name (alt. 290 m) between France and Spain; on the path of the Carthaginian general Hannibal who crossed the Alps with elephants in 218 BC. From here, a small road climbs *(13 km E)* to the **Ouillat Pass** (936 m), continuing to **Trois Termes Peak** (alt. 1 130 m) : views★★. □

CÔTE VERMEILLE★★

(The Gilded Coast)

▶ Itinerary Argelès-sur-Mer to the Spanish frontier *(approx 30 km, half-day)*

B3

Coastal Roussillon between Argelès and Cerbère, with a rapid succession of creeks, cliffs and ports, is known as the Gilded Coast (Côte Vermeille). The name seems particularly appropriate at sunset, when the light enhances the ochre shades of the predominant schist. Béar, Abeille, Rederis and Cerbère are forelands offering lookouts along the route. The traditional night-time fishing by lamplight has declined in recent years.

▶ **Argelès-sur-Mer** ® : behind crumbling ramparts, a typical village of the plain. ▶ **Argelès-Plage** ® *(3 km on) :* a busy seaside resort. ▶ **Collioure** ® : attractive site and historical charm for an important tourist centre; typical Mediterranean mediaval **fortified city★,** with a port overlooked by a **royal château** (12th-14th-17thC; museum of folk arts and traditions of the Roussillon). Many painters, including Pablo Picasso and Henri Matisse, have been attracted by the exceptionally brilliant light and colour. The tower of the 17thC church formerly served as a lighthouse; the **church** altarpiece★ is considered a masterpiece of Catalan Baroque. ▶ **Port-Vendres** ® *(Porta Veneris :* "gate of Venus" for the Romans) : fortified by the military engineer Sébastien Vauban (1633-1707), still looks like a simple fishing port, even if the harbour is taken over by pleasure craft. At the quayside, fish are sold straight off the boat at the end of the afternoon near the terraced cafés. ▶ **Banyuls-sur-Mer** ® : in a bay★ where orange trees grow, reputed for sweet wines (audiovisual display in the Templars' cellars). **Arago Laboratory** (part of the University of Paris) : marine biological research and aquarium of Mediterranean specimens *(daily 9-12 & 2-6:30).* The sculptor Aristide Maillol (1861-1944) was born in Banyuls; he created the War Memorial on the Île-Grosse rock : his grave at the **Métairie Maillol** *(farm; 4 km S)* is marked by his bronze *The Thinker.* ▶ **Cerbère** ® : last French resort on the coast in a deep bay ringed by mountains. ▶ You can return by the **Balcon de Madeloc** road between Banyuls and Collioure, with view★ through the vineyards, particularly from the 14thC Madeloc Tower. □

The ESPINOUSE Range★★

▶ Round trip *(approx 170 km, full day)*

B1 *(see map 2)*

The Espinouse (prickly) Range is a granite crest linking Larzac (→ Rouergue-Albigeois) and the Montagne Noire (→). The southern face, with torrential streams and steep rocks, is covered with prickly maquis (hence the name) that, lower down, yields first to chestnut trees then to olive groves. The more humid northern face is pastureland. The Orb and Agout valleys demonstrate the difference in terrain. The Haut-Languedoc National Park includes part of the range.

▶ **Lamalou-les-Bains** ® : hot springs★ with temperatures from 16° to 50° beside the river Bitoulet; lookout point at **Notre-Dame-de-Capimont** *(approx. 50 mins climb)* or **château de Saint-Michel** *(approx. 2hr SE).* ▶ Near the confluence of the Jaur and the Orb, you can go down the **Orb Gorges** (→ Saint-Chinian) or up the **Héric Gorges,** visible from Mons-la-Trivalle. ▶ **Olargues** ® : on a promontory in a bend of the Jaur and dominated by a square tower; 15thC bridge. ▶ **Saint-Pons-de-Thomières** ® : near the source of the Jaur (site★) in a natural mountain amphitheatre; the **Haut-Languedoc National Park** is based here. The **church,** first an abbey, then a cathedral until the Revolution, is one of the most imposing fortified churches in the Languedoc; the choir was destroyed when the existing façade was built in the 18thC. Several 15th-17thC houses; archaeological museum in the former Chapel of the Penitents. ▶ **Devèze Cavern★ :** discovered in 1886; open year-round. ▶ **Labastide-Rouairoux :** textile production centre of the Tarn region.

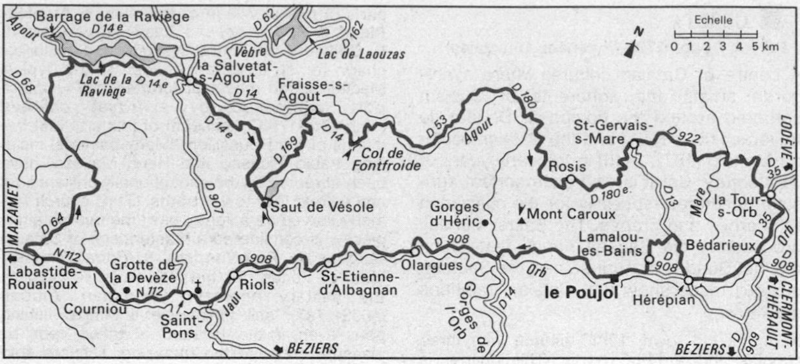

2. Espinouse Range

▶ **Raviège Reservoir :** a dam on the Agout, with a road alongside the lake. ▶ **La Salvetat-sur-Agout** ® : centre for cattle raising and cereal cultivation on the northern face of the Espinouse. ▶ Detour via **Saut de Vésole** (view★) at the foot of a dam of the same name. ▶ Panorama from the **Espinouse** Summit (alt. 1125 m). ▶ **Douch** *(2.5 km SW of D180) :* Natural History Museum *(Jun. to Sep.);* point of departure for a climb *(approx. 40 mins)* up **Mont Carroux★ :** lookout over much of the Languedoc and the Pyrénées; below, the **Héric Gorges.** ▶ East, a path crosses the **Écrivains Combattants** (soldier-writers) **Forest :** pines and firs planted from 1931 onwards in memory of writers who died in WWI. ▶ **Saint-Gervais-sur-Mare :** village and an excursion centre; geology and regional history museum. ▶ A little off the route, **Boussagues :** now a village, formerly a stronghold. ▶ **Bédarieux** ® : near bauxite mines : 15th-16thC church, cultural centre on Abbé-Tarroux Avenue (regional artists; *daily pm Jun.-Oct.*). □

■ GANGES★

C1 / ® / pop. 3533 (Hérault)

At the junction of several mountain valleys (Hérault, Rieutord, Vis), Ganges is one of the gates to the Cévennes. From the 17thC until the advent of synthetic fibres, the town thrived from the manufacture of silk stockings. The hosiery industry - now based on modern textile and chemical production continues to be the mainstay of Ganges. □

▶ Nearby

▶ From Ganges, go down the **Hérault Valley** (→) or go up (pass) to reach the **Vis Valley★** overshadowed on the left by the limestone chain of the Séranne (alt. 953 m) : view★ over the gorges★ from roads winding up to **Saint-Maurice-Navacelles★★.** ▶ Best view of the **natural amphitheatre of Navacelles★★** is from La Baume-Auriol, a farming settlement on the edge of the plateau *(causse).* ▶ In a depression *(approx. 33 km from Ganges)* formed by a loop in the river, **Navacelles :** hamlet and waterfall★. A 2hr hike up the Vis Valley to the **Vissec amphitheatre★;** or a drive via the village of Blandas (views★). □

■ The HÉRAULT Valley★★

▶ Round trip from Lodève *(approx 180 km, full day)*

C1 *(see map 3)*

On the verge of the Larzac plateau and the scrubland marking the hinterland of Montpellier. The softer rocks have been eroded by subterranean rivers and weathered into an unusually beautiful landscape. Man's traces are apparent in the form of Romanesque buildings.

▶ **Lodève** (→). ▶ Priory of **Saint-Michel-de-Grandmont :** just off the route, an 11th-12thC building in an extensive park with prehistoric megaliths and ancient statues *(daily pm ex.*

3. Hérault Valley

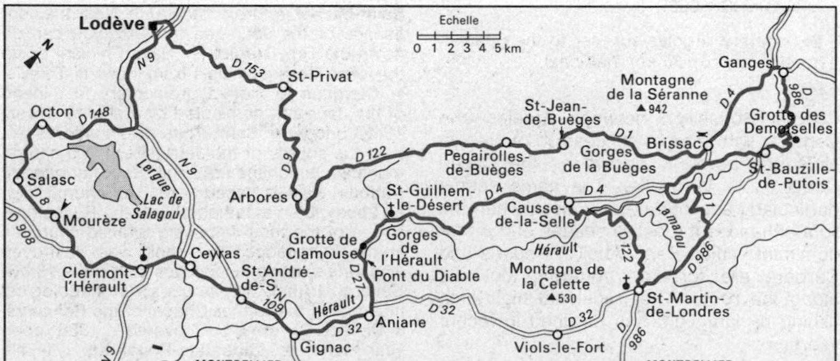

Mon. from 15 Jun.-15 Sep.; Sun. and nat. hols. pm from 15 Mar. to 14 Jun. and from 15 Sep. to 31 Oct.). ▶ **Saint-Jean-de-Buèges :** hike from here down the Buège Gorges. ▶ **Brissac :** a mountain village★ crowned by a ruined 16thC château. Between Brissac and Cazilhac, walk to the **Rubanel Abyss,** a sinkhole more than 100 m deep. ▶ **Cazilhac :** 12th-16thC château *(visits pm).* ▶ **Ganges** (→). ▶ At the exit of a pass between high white cliffs, access to the **Demoiselles Grotto★★,** a pothole in the Thaurac plateau discovered in 1770 *(daily).* ▶ Romanesque chapel of **Saint-Étienne-d'Essensac :** a site typical of the banks of the Hérault. ▶ From the hamlet of **Moscla,** follow the **Arcs Ravine** hollowed out by the Lamalou and running under several natural bridges *(approx. 1hr).* ▶ **Saint-Martin-de-Londres** ® (→). ▶ After leaving the valley, the road rejoins the **Hérault Gorges★,** with chalky walls typical of the Midi region. ▶ **Saint-Guilhem-le-Désert★★** ® : beautiful village squeezed into the narrow Verdus Gorge. **Romanesque church★★,** built to house a supposed fragment of Christ's cross, is a fine example of Languedoc Romanesque (apse★★, statues of Apostles, 12thC altar, remains of cloister). Walk up the **Verdus Gorges** to the **amphitheatre of Infernet★** surrounded by steep cliffs, or visit the **Baume-Cellier Cavern.** ▶ Downstream of Saint-Guilhem, the route crosses the natural basin of the **Foux de Clamouse** ("the bawling fountain"), which cascades into the bed of the Hérault, outlet of a subterranean network draining the waters from the Larzac plateau. The **Clamouse Cavern★★ :** mineral formations *(daily).* ▶ **Gignac** ® : fortified city, parts of whose ramparts and a 13thC keep survive; view★ from the 17thC chapel of **Notre-Dame-de-Grace.** ▶ **Clermont-l'Hérault** ® : once protected by the keep now in ruins; old houses; fortified 14thC church. ▶ **Villeneuvette★ :** a weaving town with a 17thC appearance. ▶ **Mourèze amphitheatre★ :** rocky wilderness surrounding the village named **Mourèze** ® ▶ **Salasc :** museum of folk arts and traditions of the Lodève. ▶ Above **Octon** (ruins of the 15thC château de Lauzières) the road follows the **Salagou Dam** (8 km²; aquatic sports; fishing). □

LODÈVE

B1 / ® / pop. 8378 (Hérault)

At the junction of the Roman road and muletracks, and hemmed in on a terrace overlooking old factories on the river bank, Lodève seemes to hover between its prosperous wood-working, paper-making and weaving past, and an uncertain industrial future to be derived from the recent discovery of uranium nearby. The town used to hold a monopoly on the manufacture of military uniforms. Today a workshop reproduces antique rugs for the Mobilier National (French equivalent of the National Trust).

▶ The dark, narrow streets and grey houses built of stone and basalt are enlivened by carriage doors and wrought-iron balconies. ▶ **Church of St. Fulcran :** fortified, 14thC, 18thC furnishings, 15th-18thC cloister, a cathedral until 1790. The 18thC bishop's palace is now the town hall. The gothic Montifort bridge straddles the Soulandres river, beneath the Saint-Fulcran church. ▶ In the former Carmelite chapel (3, Blvd de Fumel), the **Jacques-Audibert Museum** maintains exhibits on geology and prehistory. □

▶ Nearby

▶ **Gourgas amphitheatre** known as the Bout-du-Monde (World's End)★ : a craggy wooded site *(9 km NE).* S of D25, the **forest of Parlatges.** ▶ **Pas-de-l'Escalette :** the name refers to wooden stairways that formerly marked a passage along the edge of the plateau (view★ over the Lergue Valley). **Le Caylar** *(19 km N) :* at the foot of a rockfall; modern church with 14thC altarpiece. ▶ W by the **Baraque-de-Bral Pass** to **Lunas** ® *(15 km).* ▶ From **Le Bousquet-d'Orb** *(17 km)* down the **Orb Valley** towards Bedarieux (→ Espinouse Range), or up the valley to the **Avène Reservoir,** passing **Joncels Abbey** and the **château de Cazilhac,** built as the valley's main defence in the 13thC, rebuilt during the Renaissance; terraced gardens *(daily pm closed Tue., Wed., Thu., ex. nat. hols. from 10 Jul. to 20 Sep.).* Winding **Orb Gorges★;** thermal spring at **Bains-d'Avène.** □

MINERVE and the MINERVOIS Region★

B2 / ® / pop. 112 (Hérault)

In a landscape of chalky rocks, Minerve has lent its name to the whole calcareous region of the Cévennes foothills, scored with canyons hollowed by the rivers Cesse, l'Argent-Double and Clamoux. Wines from the regional vineyards are widely appreciated.

▶ In the once-fortified **village★,** (ruins of 11th-13thC château) you can visit the little **Romanesque** church (rare altar of 465) and the **Prehistorical and Cathar Memorial Museum** (recalls the dramatic passage of Simon de Montfort through the region in 1210 → box). ▶ Go round the spur on which the village is built to see the two **natural tunnels** dug by the river Cesse *(direct access in summer when the river bed is dry).* □

▶ Tour of the Minervois Region★★ (approx 90 km)

▶ **Bize-Minervois** *(17 km SE) :* a village on the edge of the plain, overlooked by the ruined tower of Boussecos. ▶ At the entry to **Mailhac** *(5 km SW of Bize)* is the archeological depository *(every Sun pm by appointment : tel 68.46.14.05)* with the results of the diggings at the *oppidum* (fortified hilltop) of Cayla. ▶ At **Olonzac** *(9 km W of Mailhac)* the centre of the Minervois wine industry, there is a small archeological museum *(tel 68.91.20.33).* ▶ Go through **Pépieux** *(5 km W of Olonzac)* formerly fortified, and now a wine growing town and **Azille** *(3 km SW of Pépieux;* 14thC church) to reach **Rieux-Minervois** *(6 km W from Azille) :* curious Romanesque church with a heptagonal ground plan; 3 km S : the prehistoric **covered road** of **Saint-Eugène.** ▶ **Laure-Minervois** *(6 km SW of Rieux) :* one of the centers of the Minervois wine industry (traces of fortifications). ▶ **Caunes-Minervois** *(9 km N of Laure)* at the entrance to the **gorges of the Argent-Double★;** an ancient Benedictine abbey in Romano-Gothic style, several well-restored houses of 16th-17thC; nearby, red and rose marble quarries and the hermitage of Notre-Dame-de-Cros. ▶ Return towards Minerve via **Félines-Minervois** *(8 km E of Caunes;* small archeological museum : *M. Marty, tel 68.91.41.79)* and the **gorges of La Cesse★.** □

The **MONTAGNE NOIRE★** (Black Mountain)

▶ Round trip from Saissac *(approx 120 km, full day)*

A2

Between Mazamet and Carcassonne, the broad plateau of the Montagne Noire culminates abruptly at Nore Peak (alt 1 210 m). The northern face, towards the Tarn and the Haut-Languedoc National Park, is more humid and forested with beech, spruce, oak and fir. The mountain descends even more abruptly towards the Aude, in the broad terraces of the historic Cabardès region, with numerous vestiges of the Middle Ages.

▶ **Saissac** ® : a mediaeval city, and a good departure point for excursions; remains of 15th-16thC fortifications below; the 12thC tower in the village is now the **Museum of Old-Time Crafts of Montagne Noire** *(daily 1 Jul. to 15 Sep., or ask at the town hall, tel. 68. 24.40.22)*; view★ to NE of the town. ▶ **Villelongue Abbey** *(8 km S)* : on the banks of the Vernassonne, ruined 13thC church occupied by a farm. **Montolieu** *(4 km E)* : a township of several thousand inhabitants in the 17thC, as the large church suggests. ▶ **Salsigne** *(6 km E)* : gold *(or)* still to be found in the region gives its name to the nearby river Orbiel. ▶ Continuing E, on the left, access to the **lookout★** at **châteaux de Lastours** : village underneath a huge rock on whose four peaks stand the ruins known as Cabaret, Régine Tower, Surdespine and Quertinheux. ▶ **Limousis Cavern★** *(7 km E)* : mineral formations *(daily Jun. to Oct.; Sun. and nat. hols. pm by appt. Oct.-May tel. M. Montagné 68.77.12.65)*. ▶ Through the **Clamoux Gorges★** N to the mountain village of **Pradelles-Cabardès** (view★). ▶ **Mas-Cabardès** *(11 km SW from Pradelles)* : below mediaeval ruins; beyond, ruins of the 16thC **church of St. Pierre-de-Vals** and the fortress of **Miraval-Cabardès** in the upper valley of the Orbiel. ▶ S of **Martys,** a small health resort called **Cuxac-Cabardès.** ▶ From here NW via **Fontiers-Cabardès** (view over the Corbières and the Pyrénées) to the **Alzeau Basin** designed by Riquet (→ Sète) to feed the Midi Canal over the verge of Naurouze; a road runs along the channel as far as the Saint-Ferréol Basin (→ Midi Toulousain-Pyrénées). Cross the **Ramondens Forest** and skirt the **Lampy Reservoir** to arrive at **Saissac** by D4, passing close to the menhir called the **Pierre Levée** (raised stone) **of Picaret.** □

MONT-LOUIS★

A3 / ® / pop. 239 (Pyrénées-Orientales)

Mont-Louis was built as a stronghold by Louis XIV's engineer Vauban to maintain peace in the Pyrénées; now a winter sports and tourist resort. It is located at 1 600 m altitude on a narrow plateau between the Perche and Quillaine passes, in a strategic position for controlling the valleys of the Sègre (→ Cerdagne), the Têt (Conflent) and the Aude (Capcir).

▶ **Citadel** : a classically regular construction; 1736 **church** with late 16thC crucifix. Visits also to the experimental **solar furnace,** which was used from 1952 to 1967. ▶ Outside the fortified enclosure, monument to General Dagobert, an expert in mountain warfare, who repulsed a Spanish invasion of the Roussillon in 1793. □

▶ Nearby

▶ **Planès** *(6 km S)* : 11th-12thC **church★** with three apses in an unusual triangular design. ▶ **Lake Bouillouses** *(14 km NW by a forest road)* : at alt. 2015 m. A 13 million m³ reservoir that regulates the flow of the Têt in summer; ski centre linked to the Domaine de Font-Romeu (→ Cerdagne); numerous forest walks. The lake is surrounded by mountains★ ending to the west at **Carlit Peak** (alt. 2291 m; *4hr climb, guide advisable; panorama★★*). ▶ **Thuès-les-Bains** *(17 km E)* : 42 alkaline, silicate and sulphur-bearing springs in the enclosed Têt valley. From **Thuès-entre-Vals** farther upstream, a path up the **Carança Gorges** to a lake of the same name (alt. 2265 m; *approx. 5 hr 30)*. ▶ From Mont-Louis to **Villefranche-de-Conflent** (→ Canigou Massif) : take the mountain train from La Tour-de-Carol-Perpignan across the Têt Valley (Gisclard bridge and Séjourné viaduct). □

The Cathar tragedy

Adherents of the Cathar sect, influenced by both Western and Eastern religious trends, believed that good resided only in the spiritual world, and that the material world, hence man, was intrinsically evil. They rejected the sacraments of Catholicism and raised a clergy of both men and women, who were known as the "Perfects". The movement, condemned as the Albigensian heresy by the Pope, thrived in the Languedoc under the protection of the Counts of Toulouse. After the Papal Legate to the region was assassinated in 1208, the Anglo-French warrior Simon de Montfort (→ Brief regional history) was delegated to lead a crusade to eradicate the Cathars. This era of religious upheaval ceased in 1229 with the capitulation of the Count of Toulouse to the French crown.

The Medical University of Montpellier

Mediaeval connections with the East through the spice trade enabled Montpellier to attract learned men who brought with them medical knowledge far in advance of what was then known in the West. In about 1000 AD formal medical schools were first established in the city. Grouped into a single faculty in 1221, they were confirmed as the University of Montpellier in 1289 by Pope Nicolas IV. Montpellier still rivals Paris in the brilliance of its medical school. The University maintains a standard of intellectual activity in Montpellier, while also fostering the turbulent spirit of youth and enquiry characteristic of university towns. Many of the most distinguished scientists of France have been educated at Montpellier.

▶ The upper Aude Valley★★ *(57 km N)*

▶ By **La Llagonne** ® (cross-country skiing; 12thC painted wood crucifix in church) and the **Quillaine Pass** (alt. 1715 m; view★) to **Capcir★**, the **upper basin of the Aude.** ▶ At the foot of **Aude Rock** (alt. 2 377 m) and other peaks that are under snow 7-8 months of the year, a winter sports resort and the village of **Angles** (alt. 1 600 m) above the Matemake reservoir (3 km²). ▶ Winter sports also around **Formiguères,** former capital of Capcir. ▶ Leaving the Aude Valley, visit the ruins of the château of Quérigut, then rejoin the Aude at **Usson-les-Bains** (sulphurous and arsenical waters) below the ruins of a château that once controlled the confluence of the Aude and the Bruyante. ▶ Nearby, "potholing and spelunking safaris" in **Laguzon Cavern** *(full day; max. 10 persons; equipment provided : Jul.-Aug. by appointment with M. Bataillon at Usson, tel 68.20.40.33).* Finally, via the **Aude Gorges★** and the **Saint-Georges★ Pass,** framed by wooded hillsides, to Axat, at the gates of the Pierre-Lys Pass (→ Razès). □

■ MONTPELLIER★★★

C1 / ® / pop. 201 067 (Hérault)

The settlement, about 10 km from the coast, began as a trading post on the spice route from the Near East, and later prospered as a stopover on the pilgrimage route to Saint-James of Compostela. Cloth was traded in the city, and the university and renowned medical school were founded in the 13thC. The handsome appearance of Montpellier is due in large part to extensive building and development during the 18thC. The prosperous 19thC wine trade was checked by the vine-louse phylloxera, which devastated French vineyards. Re-establishment of French vines on resistant American root stocks put the wine growers back in business by the mid-20thC. Montpellier today is a dynamic regional capital.

▶ **Place de la Comédie** (C3) : called "L'Œuf" (The Egg), with the 18thC fountain of the Three Graces, is the main meeting place. From the 19thC **theatre** (Comédie) at the S end, the place is prolonged N by the **Esplanade** and the Champs de Mars garden at the foot of the 17thC citadel, and NE (direct pedestrian access) by the new commercial and administrative quarter of **Le Polygone** (hotels, shopping arcades, department stores, town hall). ▶ From the Place, **Rue de la Loge** (C3) joins **Rue Foch** near the Prefecture (B2), forming the main axis through the old city. ▶ The street passes under the 1691 **Arc de Triomphe** (com-

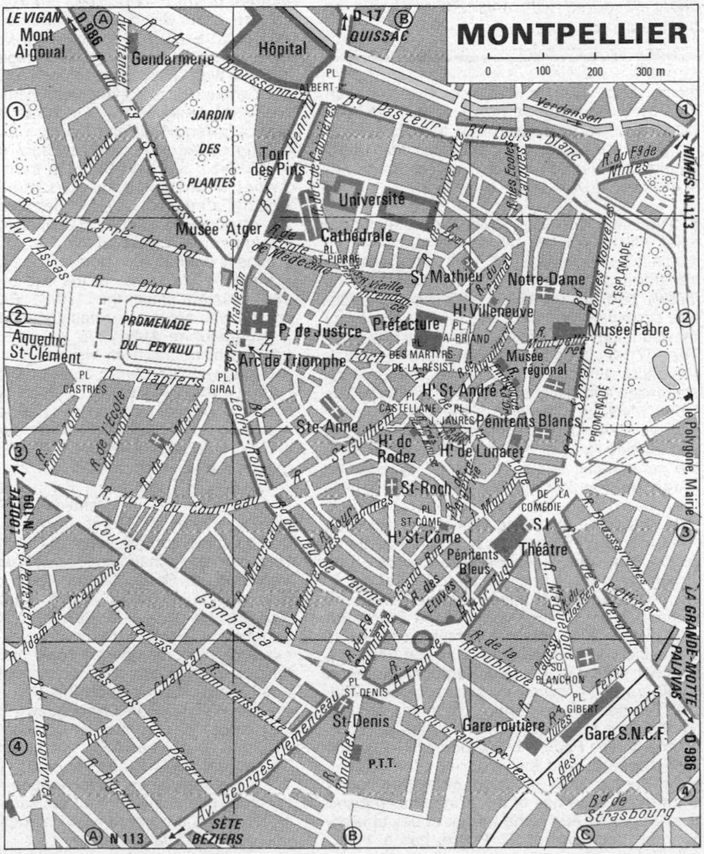

began

The table

The food of Languedoc and Roussillon is essentially the cuisine of the Midi. The regional dishes are quite similar to those of neighbouring Provence. The staple ingredients are olive oil and garlic enlivened by aromatic herbs from the stony heath of the garrigue, *and the plentiful regional wine. Mutton and lamb are the most common meats on the chalky plateaus and narrow valleys of the* causse; charcuterie *is also important, particularly the sausages and smoked ham that are essential ingredients of the* cassoulet *of Castelnaudary. Specialities include* foie gras, *turkey patés, and other preparations flavoured with the rare truffle. In season, game from the* garrigue *is much sought after. Snails are often prepared* en cargolade, *that is, grilled over vine cuttings. Fish is popular along the coast : anglerfish is frequently included in the fish soup* (bourride) *of Sète and the fish stew* (boulinade) *of Roussillon. Mussels and oysters are cultivated in the Thau Lagoon. The region has relatively few cheeses, although the* bleu des Causses *(made from cow's milk) is widely known. The local pastries and sweets are often based on almond paste flavoured with aniseed, pistachio or orange-flower water.*

memorating victories of Louis XIV) to reach the **Peyrou Promenade★** (A2) : 17th-18thC terraces shaded by plane trees around reflecting pools : views to the mountains; the 18thC aqueduct ends in canals that lead to the handsome water-tower of the same era.

▶ The **old town★★** is divided by the central axis, which was laid out in the 19thC. From mediaeval beginnings, it was progressively transformed during the 17th-18thC. Mansions *(hôtels particuliers),* often hidden behind austere carriage entrances, are open to discovery by enquiring pedestrians (plan from the TO). The 17thC buildings show marked Italian influence, with central courtyards, monumental staircases and galleries on the first floors. The more "frivolous" buildings of the following century were adorned with wrought-iron balconies and carving. ▶ S of the major transverse axis, the commercial sector is pierced by **Rue de l'Argenterie** and **Grand-Rue-Jean-Moulin,** both now pedestrian precints; at the crossroads (B3), the 1757 **St. Côme Mansion★,** formerly the College of Surgeons. ▶ From Rue de la Loge, **Rue des Trésoriers-de-France** runs through an equally lively sector (C1-2 : at No. 5, the 17thC **Lunaret Mansion** is the office of the archaeological society) to the **Place Pétrarque** (C2), where a university for senior citizens is maintained in the Nicolas Mansion (No. 2), together with the **Fougau Regional Museum** (ethnography, Occitanian library; *Wed. Thu. pm*). Farther on, the former University quarter has become more residential with the passage of time. ▶ The **Faculty of Medicine** (B1-2) since 1795 has occupied the restored 16thC Abbey of St. Benoit; here too, **Atger Museum :** Italian and French drawings of the 17th-18thC *(closed Sat., Sun. and Aug.);* the former abbey church, now the **cathedral of St. Pierre,** has a 14thC nave and porch but was clumsily restored in the 17th and 19thC. ▶ From the other side of Boulevard Henri IV (beside which stands the Pins Tower, a vestige of the mediaeval fortifications) the **Botanical Gardens★** (Jardin des Plantes), the oldest in France, founded in 1593. ▶ **Fabre Museum★★** (C2; enter from Boulevard Sarrail; *daily ex. Mon.) :* occupies part of the former Jesuit College (18thC), fine art including paintings ranging from regional Primitives to the 20thC, notably important 19thC works. Nearby in rue Montpelliéret, **Cabrières-Sabatier d'Espeyran Mansion :** a museum of the decorative arts of the 18th and 19thC *(guided tours Wed. and Sat.).* □

▶ Nearby

▶ The **University of Montpellier** is now relocated outside the old town; in the new sector, N : accommodation, the stadium, several scientific institutes and clinics, as well as the zoo. ▶ On the edge of town, follies built as country retreats by wealthy citizens during the 17th and 18thC : **châteaux★ de la Piscine** (*3 km W,* formal French Park); **de la Mosson** *(5 km W, 1723);* **de l'Engarran** (*6 km SW,* formal French park); **d'O** (*4 km NW,* beautiful garden); **d'Assas** *(12 km N,* built next to a Romanesque church; *Sat. Sun. pm from Easter to mid-Oct.);* **de Flaugergues** *(3 km E near the E motorway,* French and English gardens with Mediterranean trees; furnishings; wine tastings; *daily pm ex. Mon. from 15 May to 15 Sep.);* **de la Mogère** *(4 km E, park; daily pm from Easter to 15 Oct., Wed. Sat. Sun. and nat. hols. pm from 15 Oct. to Easter).* ▶ **Castries** *(12 km NE) :* the most beautiful **château★** in the region; built in 1565, it was remodelled in the 17thC to house the Languedoc regional government; furniture; parkland designed by Le Notre (→ Île-de-France : Versailles) and fed by a 27 km aqueduct *(daily ex. Mon. and nat. hols. from 1 Apr. to 15 Dec.; Sat. and Sun. pm from 15 Jan. to 1 Apr.).* ▶ **Château d'Agnac** *(12 km S the other side of Fabrègues) :* the Mediterranean Institute for Introduction to French Culture (courses for foreigners). ▶ **Lattès** *(5 km S of Montpellier) :* originally the maritime port for the city, but supplanted by Marseilles at the end of the 15thC and disused since the 17thC; Romanesque church with sculpted grotesques on the façade. ▶ **Maguelonne Abbey** *(16 km via Palavas) :* a fortified bishopric from Merovingian times until the see was tranferred to Montpellier; 11thC church★ (doorway of 1178) on an isolated hilltop surrounded by lakes. ▶ Farther E, **Lake Mauguio :** fishing and waterfowl hunting. ▶ This lake separates the true coastline from the tourist area that stretches as far as the lakes of the Camargue (18 km beach). From W to E, successively : **Palavas-les-Flots** ®, the seaside resort of Montpellier (not attractive) and a fishing port (Museum of Old Palavas and Underwater Archaeology; *daily pm ex. Thu. from Jun. to Sep.);* **Carnon-Plage :** sparkling new marina, but hardly more attractive than Palavas; **La-Grande-Motte★** ®, best-known of Languedoc seaside resorts, is a successful example of contemporary town planning, with 52-acre marina and the commercial centre of Point Zero; **Le Grau-du-Roi** (® → Ardèche, Cévennes) and **Port-Camargues** (→ Ardèche, Cévennes) : marinas and yacht harbours. ▶ **Lunel** ® *(22 km NE) :* at the entry to the Camargue, wine centre (Muscat); public gardens. ▶ **Château de Marsillargues** *(4 km SE) :* in Renaissance style, with Paul Pastre museum of geology, archaeology, ethnology, fine arts *(daily pm ex. Sun.).* □

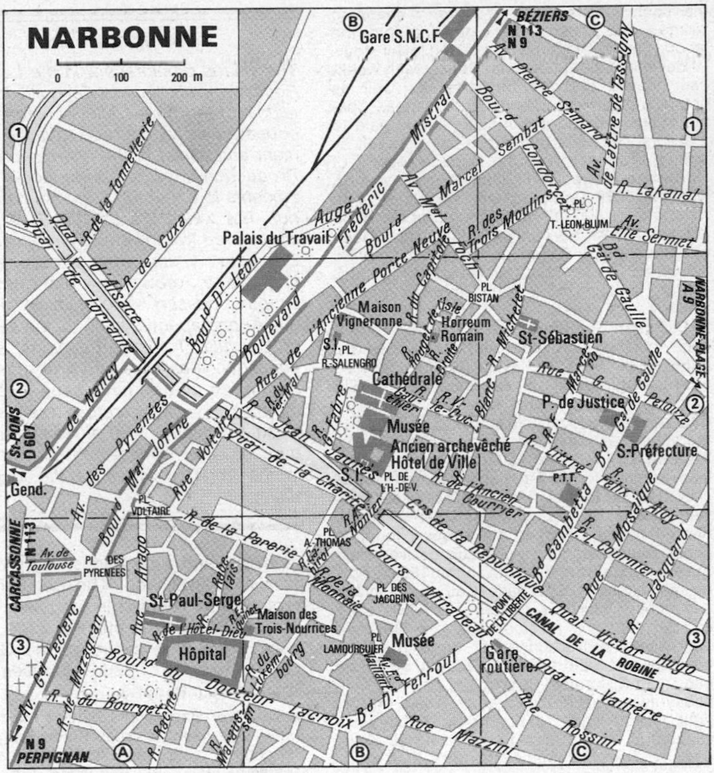

NARBONNE★★

B2 / ® / pop. 42 657 (Aude)

In succession, a Roman, Visigothic and Arab city, essentially Mediterranean. The site is divided by the canalised Robine river. The old town, with its tortuous, narrow streets and mediaeval monuments, is girdled by shady boulevards that are most lively at midday and in the evening, when the residents like to spend an hour or two on the café terraces.

▶ In the centre of town, the former **Archbishop's Palace** (B2) : now the **town hall** and **museums★★** *(daily ex. Mon. from 1 Oct. to 15 May).* The **Gilles-Aycelin Keep** was built in the 13thC on Roman foundations; view over the town *(daily Jul.-Sep.).* In the inner courtyard, the **Archaeological Museum★** (prehistory, Roman neo-Classical staircase), **Fine Arts Museum** and the Archbishop's **Apartments★** fitted out in the 17thC. ▶ Leading from Palace courtyard, the **Passage de l'Ancre,** facing the **Madeleine Courtyard** where the apse of the Cathedral can be seen. At the end of the passage (marked by the anchor that gives the valley its name) cross the 13thC cloister directly into the choir of the **cathedral of St. Just★** (B2). The choir was constructed between 1272 and 1310 in the Gothic tradition of northern France, but the church was never finished (treasury with 15thC Flemish tapestry depicting the Creation★). ▶ N from the Cathedral, near the TO, the **Maison Vigneronne,** a wine museum (exhibitions) occupying a 17thC powder magazine. ▶ In the maze-like old city, **Place Bistan** (B-C2) marks the site of the Roman capital and forum, which can be picked out, with the aid of an explanatory plan, from a few fragments of architecture. **Church of St. Sébastien** (C2) 15th-17thC, built on the presumed birthplace of this early Christian martyr. ▶ Rue Rouget-de-l'Isle, **Horreum** (B2) : an underground warehouse built by the Romans in the 1stC AD. ▶ Along **Rue Droite** (B2) return to the Place de l'Hôtel-de-Ville; the street continues as the pedestrian **Rue du Pont-des-Marchands** and crosses the river Robine by the ancient Roman bridge, of which one arch still stands. View of the old bridge, as well as of the principal mediaeval monuments, from the alleys of Cours Mirabeau (B3).

Also... ▶ In the southern part of the city, 12th-13thC **church of Notre-Dame-de-Lamourguier** (B3) : now a Sculpture and Stonework Museum of Gallo-Roman and early Christian antiquities. **Basilica of St. Paul-Serge** (A3) : 12th-13thC, next to an early Christian cemetery. Nearby in Rue de l'Hôtel-Dieu, the 16thC **Maison des Trois Nourrices** (house of the three wet-nurses), facetiously named for the amply endowed caryatids on the façade. □

▶ Nearby

▶ La **Montagne de la Clape :** a chalky outcropping, covered in vineyards on the lower slopes, separates Narbonne from the sea. To the south, **Gruissan** ® *(15 km) :* charming village★ on a peninsula extending into the lagoons and overlooked by a ruined tower; tourist development at **Gruissan Beach,** with week-end houses perched on stilts, as well as hotels, restaurants, shops and marina. Chapel of **Notre-Dame-des-Auzils** (view★) next to a sailors' cemetery (numerous *ex-votos* left by sailors). Farther north, the seaside resorts of **Narbonne-Plage** and **Saint-Pierre-sur-Mer,** with the l'**Œil Doux Chasm** *(1.5 km N, then foot path for 500 m).* At the mouth of the Aude *(23 km NE of Narbonne),* the fishing village of **Cabannes-de-Fleury.** ▶ **Ouveillan** *(approx. 4.5 km SE; 14 km N of Narbonne) :* 11th-12thC church; remains of a 13thC moated grange, which was a dependency of Fontfroide abbey. ▶ **Lézignan-Corbières** ® *(21 km W) :* on the edge of the Corbières and the Minervois, Museum of Vines and Wine (3, Rue Turgot : wine-tastings *daily*). ▶ **Fabrezan** *(9 km SW of Lézignan) :* memorial museum named for Charles Cros, a local intellectual, poet and photographer *(daily ex. Sat., Sun. and nat. hols.).* ▶ **Lagrasse**★ *(approx. 10 km) :* a mediaeval village, formerly fortified and ably restored; 14thC church of St. Michel, 15th-18thC houses, cobbled streets, artists' studios. Over a hump-backed bridge (1308) to the **abbey**★ founded under Charlemagne, whose successive constructions date from the 10th to the 18thC; now maintained by a Byzantine Catholic religious community, which is restoring it *(visits daily ex. Sun. am and religious hols.).* ▶ Between Lagrasse and Narbonne *(41 km),* cross the river Nielle at **Saint-Laurent. Château de Gaussan :** 13thC, formerly a property of Fontfroide abbey (wine-tasting). A narrow road on the right *(2 km)* leads to **Fontfroide Abbey**★★ **:** situated at the entrance to deep ravines *(visits daily ex. Tue., Oct.-Mar.)* with 12th-13thC cloister and chapterhouse, and various monastic buildings (most recent, 17thC); some of the most beautiful Cistercian architecture in the Midi. ▶ Beside Lake Bages and Sigean, **Peyriac-de-Mer** *(13 km S from Narbonne) :* museum of ornithological specimens from the lake and artifacts excavated from the neighbouring oppidum (hill-fort) of Moulin *(visits by appt. with M. Jouas, tel. 68.32.50.45 or M. Fabre, tel. 68.32.37.43).* ▶ Beyond, **Sigean Safari Park**★ *(visits daily by car).* ▶ Near **Portel-des-Corbières** *(17 km S) :* the ruined church of **Notre-Dame-des-Oubliels** (under restoration). ▶ **Sigean** ® *(21 km) :* archaeological museum of Corbières displaying ceramics from the Pech Maho oppidum (64 Grande-Rue, *by appt. tel. 68.48.20.04).* ▶ **Port-La-Nouvelle** ® *(30 km) :* founded in 1820 as a maritime port for the Midi-Toulousain region; today both a port and an industrial centre (salt pans, cement works, oil storage, heavy cargo, shipping, fishing) as well as a seaside resort stretching along a beautiful sandy beach. □

PERPIGNAN★★

B3 / ® / pop. 120 000 (Pyrénées-Orientales)

The city proudly proclaims its Catalan identity as "Perpinya" on roadsigns at the entrance to town. Built on a plain between a fortified hilltop and the Têt Valley, it is a formal capital and stronghold of the Roussillon. The old town has changed little since the 18thC, but Perpignan is not a museum town. The vitality of bustling streets and markets attests to the prosperous fruit, vegetable and wine trades that provide the main local livelihood. The Catalan spirit is kept alive by festivals in the town. The Sardana is danced at the Place de la Loge twice a week in summer. The Good Friday processions of penitents resemble their Spanish counterparts.

Regional wines

The vine is omnipresent in the Languedoc-Roussillon, starting at Fenouillèdes or the middle of the Aude Valley. In most districts, cooperatives encourage quality improvement and assist in the distribution of wine. Production in the Languedoc-Roussillon amounts to about 60 % of total national output. The wines are as varied as the landscape : red from Hérault, the Minervois and Corbières; whites from Narbonne; sparkling white known as blanquette *from Limoux; dessert wine* (Muscat de Frontignan)*; and apéritifs such as the sweet wine of Banyuls. To lessen regional economic dependence on wine and problems of overproduction, efforts have been made during the past 20 years to return to a more diversified agriculture. Fruit orchards and market gardens have been established, especially in the irrigated areas of the lower Aude Valley.*

▶ The river Basse runs between the flowered banks of a canal to cross **Place Arago** (A-B2), the central square, and leads eventually to the **Castillet**★ (B1) : the handsome fortified gateway built in about 1370 and transformed into a fortress a century later. The gateway is now the **Casa Pairal,** a museum of Catalan folk arts and traditions *(daily except Tue. and nat. hols.);* view from the terraces. ▶ **Place de la Loge**★ (B2) : adorned with a statue of Venus by Maillol; the Place is named for the beautiful Gothic building called the **Loge de Mer,** built in 1388 to serve as the muncipal commodity exchange (Bourse). The **Hôtel de Ville** (town hall) next door was rebuilt during the 16th-17thC; in the courtyard, a statue by Maillol representing the Mediterranean. ▶ **Cathedral of St. Jean** (B1) : built between 1324 and 1507, one of the largest examples of Meridional Gothic architecture; the exterior is undistinguished, but the interior is paved with Pyrenean marble and decorated with superb altar-pieces★, of which the most interesting are those of the main altar (1620), St. Peter (left apse, 15thC) and the Virgin (right apse, ca. 1500). Through the S door into a chapel where a crucifix, revered as the **"Devout Christ"**★★ (German, early 14thC) is kept. ▶ No. 16 Rue de l'Ange, in the 17thC Lazerme Mansion, the **Fine Arts Museum**★ (B2, *closed Tue. and nat. hols.*) : works by the 17thC Perpignan painter Hyacinthe Rigaud, as well as modern paintings and Catalan ceramics. ▶ The **citadel** (B3; entry facing Avenue G. Brutus; *closed Tue.*) : fortifications built by Louis XI of France, Charles V and Philip II of Spain enclosing the former 13th-14thC **Palace of the Kings of Majorca**★**;** in the Court of Honour, the loggia and the "Paradise Gallery" framing the two-storey chapel; exhibitions in the Majorca Hall. **Also...** ▶ **Platanes Promenade** (B1) : designed for strolling, and leading to the **Congress Palace,** with extensive **gardens** remarkable for

their varied vegetation. ▶ **St. Jacques Church** (C2) : 14th-18thC, with altarpiece of Notre-Dame-de-l'Espérance (late 15thC), and Chapel of La Sanch (Precious Blood) supported by the brotherhood that organises the Good Friday procession (Cross of Dishonour, representing the various stages of Christ's Passion, in the cloister). Behind the church, the **garden of La Miranda** on the remains of Mediaeval fortifications. ▶ In the suburb of Saint-Godérique *(1.5 km SE)* is the **Mas St. Vicens :** cultural centre in an old house decorated by the contemporary tapestry designer Jean Lurçat; exhibitions and sale of contemporary ceramics and tapestries *(9-11:45 and 2-6:45 daily).* □

▶ Nearby

▶ **Château-Roussillon** *(6 km E) :* founded in 7thC BC on the road to Perthus and superseded by Perpignan in the 10thC AD; archaeological excavations. ▶ **Cabestany** *(5 km SE) :* church with Romanesque tympanum★ depicting the sleeping Virgin. ▶ **Saint-Cyprien-Plage** ® *(17 km SE) :* together with **Canet-Plage** ® *(13 km E)* is the southernmost point of the development of the Languedoc-Roussillon coast; separated by 9 km of fine sandy beach, both towns have marinas. ▶ **Port-Barcarès**® and **Port-Leucate** *(15 km N, 25 km NE of Perpignan) :* twin resorts that offer numerous diversions; marinas; activities both on the sea front and around Lake Leucate, beyond which the Canigou Massif is visible. **Port-Barcarès :** a seawater treatment centre; casino-nightclub on the steamboat **Lydia**; marine zoo; oyster beds along road to **Leucate.** ® ▶ **Fort de Salses**★ ® *(16 km N) :* a model of 16thC military architecture built by the Spaniards to defend the entry to the Roussillon *(visits daily).* ▶ **Rivesaltes** ® *(9 km N) :* birthplace of the French WWI military leader Marshal Joffre (1852-1931); renowned for Muscat wines (wine-cellars, cooperative), garden produce and apricots. ▶ **Espira-de-l'Agly** *(3 km W) :* Romanesque church with nave ending in twin apses encompassed by a single massive piece of stonework. ▶ **Estagel** *(13 km farther) :* the birthplace of the physician and politician François Arago (1786-1853). ▶ **Millas** *(14 km S of Estagel) :* reached via the Bataille Pass, base also for the **Hermitage of Força-Réal :** view★ over the Têt Valley and the Canigou. **Château de Corbère :** built in the 11thC on a promontory *(6 km from Millas);* **Castelnou**★ *(8 km SE) :* fortified village on a foothill of the Aspres, which is crowned by a 10thC fortress (restored 1875). ▶ **Thuir** *(5 km NE of Castelnou, 13 km SW of Perpignan) :* visits to the Celliers des Aspres, a wine museum. ▶ Priory of **Monastir-del-Camp**★ *(11 km SE) :* believed to have been founded by Charlemagne; 11thC church with 12thC west door and early 14thC cloister. ▶ **Brouilla** *(8 km SE) :* Romanesque church with trefoil choir. ▶ **Saint-Génis-des-Fontaines** *(S of Tech; 3 km from Brouilla) :* church with figured Romanesque lintel datable, by an inscription, to 1020; most of the cloister has been removed to the Philadelphia Museum of Art in the United States. ▶ **Elne** *(10 km NE of Saint-Génis, 14 km S of Perpignan) :* a bishopric from 577 to 1602; upper town partly surrounded by ancient ramparts that are still flanked by towers. 11th-12thC **church**★, formerly a cathedral; the cloister★★ (12th-14thC) is considered one of the most beautiful in France; the south gallery, a masterpiece of sculpture of the Roussillon school *(daily ex. Sun. off season).* □

The Sardana

A traditional Catalan dance, the Sardana, is a popular event in which anyone can join simply by finding a place in the circle. Far from an exhibition of folklore kept up for tourists, this is a living, authentic tradition whose origins probably reach back to the Roman occupation of the Mediterranean basin. The Sardana is accompanied by an orchestra (cobla), *composed generally of eleven musicians led by the tambourine and the strident* flaveol, *a local form of flageolet.*

■ PÉZENAS★★

C1 / ® / pop. 7 519 (Hérault)

Pézenas used to be the site of three annual fairs that attracted traders from all over Europe. The city played an important political role between the 15th and 17thC as the seat of the Languedoc regional government. The Montmorencys, royal governors of the province, and later, Armand de Bourbon, Prince de Conti, made Pézenas into a cultural haven that attracted artists and writers. The playwright Molière (1622-1673) spent several extended periods at Pézenas as "Actor to His Serene Highness the Prince de Conti". Many mansions have survived from that era (arrowed itinerary in the old town). Pézenas offers a wealth of cultural and theatrical activities, especially during the Arts Festival (Mirondela dels arts) in July-August.

▶ At the foot of the hill crowned by Château Montmorency, a pedestrian precinct is the heart of the **old town★★,** centred on the Place Gambetta. Renaissance **Consulaire Mansion** (1693 belfry); nearby, the **Vulliod-St. Germain Museum** (3 Rue Albert-Paul-Alliés; *daily ex. Mon. and Tue.; closed 30 Jun., 1 Jul.; 31 Aug. and 1 Sep.*), mementoes of old Pézenas and Molière's day. ▶ At the entrance to Rue F.-Oustrin, the TO is in the house where Molière lodged with a barber called Gély. Farther on, the 15thC **Lacoste Mansion★,** where Louis XIV stayed; exhibitions in the stables. ▶ Facing the 17thC **church of St. Jean,** the 16thC Commandery of the Order of St. John of Jerusalem (Knights-Templar). ▶ Along **Rue de la Foire,** bordered by beautiful houses, and Rue Émile Zola, to the mediaeval Jewish quarter. ▶ From there via the gate of the Consulaire Prison to **Jean-Jaurès Court,** laid out in 1627 (interesting houses) at the edge of the mediaeval town. ▶ Beyond, the 17thC sections of the town also contain interesting houses, especially **Rue de Conti :** No. 36, **Alfonce Mansion;** see the rear courtyard with two-tiered loggias (concerts and theatrical performances in the summer); also, the **Hostellerie du Griffon d'Or** (Inn of the Golden Griffin), an inn courtyard typical of the period. □

▶ Nearby

▶ **Saint-Thibéry** *(8 km S) :* in a volcanic basalt amphitheatre, a 15th-16thC abbey church; close by, ruins of a **Roman bridge** mark the path of the Via Domitiana (ancient Roman highway) over the Hérault. ▶ **Montagnac** *(6 km E) :* also an important medieaval market; Gothic church. **Lavagnac** *(3 km N);* 17thC château surrounded by mediaeval turrets. ▶ **Valmargne★** *(7 km E) :* 13th-14thC Cistercian **abbey** church and cloister★; 17thC main buildings *(daily pm ex. Tue. from 15 Jun. to 15 Sep., Sun. and nat. hols. pm rest of year);* site. □

■ PRADES

A3 / pop. 6 100 (Pyrénées-Orientales)

Formerly the main centre of the Conflent district, this town paved with pink marble grew around a Gothic church (Romanesque bell-tower in Lombard style; 17thC altar-piece). Setting for the annual Pablo Casals Festival (named for the revered Catalan cellist, 1876-1973); an excellent starting point for climbing Canigou Peak. □

▶ Nearby

▶ **Canigou Peak★★** (try to spend 2 days, sleeping at the Chalet des Cortalets), reached by a difficult, winding forest road *(jeeps for hire at Prades, tel. 68.96.53.38 or Vernet-les-Bains, Villacecque garage, tel. 68-05-51-14)* to 27 km beyond **Cortalets** (alt. 2 200 m; view★), then another 1 hr 45 hike to the summit (alt. 2 785 m; astounding panorama★★); go down directly to Vernet-les-Bains via the **Escale de l'Ours★.** ▶ **Conat** *(6 km W) :* Romanesque church. At the entrance to the wild Nohèdes Valley, the church is perched on one hilltop and the modest village on its neighbour. ▶ **Moligt-les-Bains** ® *(8 km NW) :* thermal springs (sulphur, soda, radioactive waters for the treatment of skin and eye, ear and throat ailments) in the Castillane Gorges; fishing and hunting on the mountain add to resort attractions. □

■ QUILLAN

A2-3 / ® / pop. 4 459 (Aude)

An industrial centre (for the manufacture of laminate surfaces), Quillan is an excellent base for exploring the Corbières and the Aude Valley.

▶ At the foot of mediaeval ruins, with a town hall in the 18thC **Espezel Mansion.** □

▶ Nearby

▶ SE of the town, an interesting drive through the **Fanges Forest★** above the **Pierre Lys Gorges** (→ Razès) among fir trees growing at the 1 000 m mark. ▶ Along D613 and the **Sault Plateau** or from **Axat** *(11 km S)* to the **valley of the Rebenty★;** upstream of Joucou, the **passes★ of the river Joucou,** (road tunnels), **Able** (Moulin d'Able electric power station) and **Niort** (or Sault). ▶ Across the **Portel Pass** (alt. 601 m; view) and through **Nébias** *(9 km W) :* museum of hunting *(daily Jul.-Aug., Sun. and nat. hols. pm by appt. out of season, tel. 68.20.06.13, town hall);* then to **Puivert,** below the ruins of a 12th-13thC **château** *(passable road from D121),* one of the most easily accessible Corbières châteaux, once the haunt of troubadours (→ Provence). From the aviation base at Puivert you can take an air excursion over the Cathar châteaux. ▶ **Chalabre** ® *(8 km N of Puivert) :* social and cultural centre at Les Cèdres; various sporting activities. □

The RAZÈS Region★★

▶ Round trip *(approx 150 km, full day)*
A2-3 *(see map 4)*

In the central Aude Valley, where the western buttresses of the Corbières meet the Pyrenees and encompass the Fenouillèdes (upper Agly Valley), Razès is a region of contrasts. The Pierre-Lys and Galamus Gorges, which carve a passage between the forested limestone crests, contrast with neat vineyard valleys producing *blanquette de Limoux* (→ box). This Roman settlement of *Rhedae* was succeeded as regional capital by Rennes-le-Château, whereas in the 14thC, Alet became the episcopal see; on every peak stand the remains of the apparently inaccessible châteaux that formerly defended the region.

▶ **Quillan** (→). ▶ **Coulza** ® : at the exit from town, near the Aude, the one-time château of the dukes of Joyeuse is today a seminar and congress centre; the mediaeval appearance is tempered by Renaissance elements (courtyard). ▶ **Alet-les-Bains★** ® : best approach to the mediaeval township is along the Saint-Salvayre road; church of Notre-Dame, first an abbey then a cathedral, was destroyed during the 16thC Wars of Religion; visit the **ruins** *(daily, closed Sun.; key at the neighbouring tobacconist)*; the church of St. André was built in the 16thC in meridional Gothic. The Place de la République, with its half-timbered houses, has the appearance of a theatre set. The former convent buildings are now partly occupied by a thermal spa. ▶ Farther on, the road enters a craggy **pass** known as the **Étroit-d'Alet★**, then runs into the fertile basin where the *blanquettes de Limoux* are produced *(visits to cellars, including the producers cooperative, on the Alaigne road)*. ▶ **Limoux** ® : the centre of activity is the Place de la République, surrounded by arcaded houses; nearby, the 14th-16thC church of St. Martin has a Romanesque doorway. On the Avenue de Tivoli (fortifications W of the town) is the **Petiet Museum,** late 19thC decorative arts *(daily ex. Mon. Jul.-Aug., or by appointment at the mayor's office tel. 68.31.01.16)*. ▶ A miraculous spring was the origin of the church of **Notre-Dame-de-Marceille** (pilgrimage site, 17th-18thC interior decoration). ▶ Among vineyards, the fortified church of St. Hilaire : transition between Romanesque and Gothic styles (early 13thC; 14thC cloister). ▶ **Saint-Polycarpe :** 11th-14thC abbey church, also fortified. ▶ **Arques Towers★** (24 m, 13th-14thC) : a well preserved keep *(visits by request to the town hall daily am ex. Fri. and Sun. tel. 68.74.03.37)*. ▶ At the crossroads of D14 and 613, the barely discernible ruins of **château de Blanchefort** (view★). ▶ **Rennes-les-Bains** ® : a spa in **Sals Gorges.** ▶ **Galamus Gorges★★ :** linking the Agly to the Fenouillèdes (lookout at the chapel of St. Antoine). ▶ Downstream from **Saint-Paul-de-Fenouillet,** the Agly runs through the **Clue de la Fou.** ▶ S of **Caudiès-de-Fenouillet,** marking the western boundary of the Roussillon vineyards, the chapel of **Notre-Dame-de-Laval** stands at the entry to **Saint-Jaume Gorge** (ruins of several fortresses, picturesque village of **Fenouillet).** ▶ Above **Lapradelles-Puilaurens** *(4.5 km S by narrow road, then 15 mins walk) :* on a crag, the ruined **château de Puylaurens★** (11th-13thC). ▶ The Aude Valley runs downstream from Quillan into a deep wooded gorge called the **Défilé de Pierre-Lys★★.** □

4. Razès region

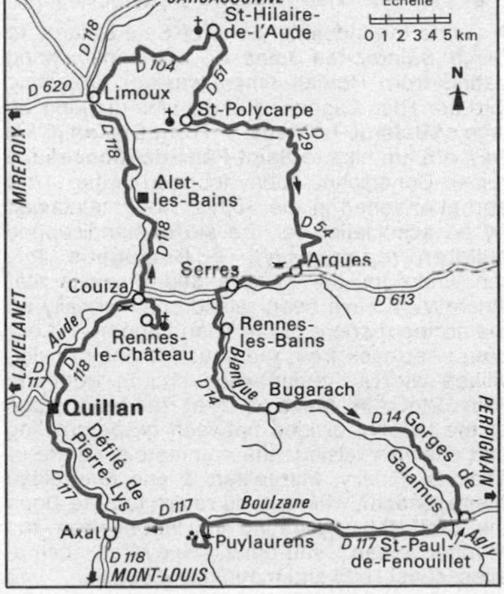

SAINT-CHINIAN

B1-2 / pop. 1 735 (Hérault)

Saint-Chinian, at the mouth of the Nouvre★, hemmed in by high, coppery cliffs, lends its name to a red wine.

▶ On the frontier between the vinegrowing plain and the first foothills of the Cévennes, a good base for exploration. □

Holy week

Holy Week in Roussillon is celebrated almost as fervently as in neighbouring Spain. After the good cheer of Palm Sunday (processions with palm branches), on Wednesday the ceremonies assume a funereal character. The procession at Perpignan is the most remarkable, although impressive Good Friday processions are also held at Arles-sur-Tech, Bouleternères, Bompas and Collioure. Organised since 1416 by the Confrérie de la Sanch (Brotherhood of the Blood), the procession winds through the streets from the church of St. Jacques to the cathedral of St. Jean. At the head, the Regidor, a red-robed Penitent, wears the traditional hood of persons condemned to death; he is followed by Penitents in black, displaying the misteris, wax and wood figures representing the various personages of the Passion, and carrying the Croix des Outrages, a cross adorned with all the instruments of the Passion, but without the Christ. Interesting Easter Day processions, representing Christ's Resurrection, are held at Ille-sur-Têt and Céret.

▶ Nearby

▶ **Villespassans** *(9 km SW)* : museum of mineralogy and archaeology in the town hall *(tel. 68.38.04.53)*. ▶ **Cruzy** *(13 km S)* : museum of prehistory, Gallo-Roman era, *contact M. Fages, tel. 67.89.41.79.* ▶ **Quarante** *(2.5 km SE from Cluzy)* : statuary museum near the 10th-11thC Romanesque church. ▶ **Abbey of Fontcaude** *(10 km E of Saint-Chinian, Sun. pm by appt.)* : abbey founded by the Premonstratensian Order (White Canons) in the 12thC, ruined in 1560 during the Wars of Religion *(daily closed Mon.)*. ▶ From **Cessenon** *(9 km NE)* to the village of **Roquebrun**★ ® (dessert wines), then continue up the **Orb Gorges**★ towards Lamalou-les-Bains (→ Espinouse Range). □

■ SAINT-MARTIN-DE-LONDRES★

C1 / ® / pop. 1 065 (Hérault)

A large village★ on the road from Montpellier to Ganges. The lower village, around the bell-tower and the fountain, suffers a little from being near a main road, but as you climb towards the centre of the village you discover a rare site that time seems to have passed by. The houses form a barrier around the church★, which is a typical example of Languedoc early Romanesque. □

▶ Nearby

▶ **Viols-le-Fort** *(6 km S)* : archaeological museum. ▶ **Les Matelles** *(12 km SE)* : just off D986, museum of the University of Montpellier's Centre for Prehistoric Studies; the region is rich in neolithic traces, dolmens and Gallic hill-forts. ▶ **Saint-Loup-Peak** can be reached by GR60 from Saint-Martin *(or in less than 3hr walk from Cazevielle, 8 km SE)*; at 658 m, the highest point in the region; view★★ over the Cévennes, the Garrigue, the Camargue, the Pyrénées and the sea. Beyond, ruined **château de Monferrand :** formerly a dependency of Maguelone Abbey (→ Montpellier) with a view from a height of 410 m★. ▶ **Notre-Dame-de-Londres** *(7 km NE)* : 15thC **château,** with Renaissance furnishings and paintings *(daily pm Jul.-Sep.; Sun. and nat. hols., pm rest of year)*. □

■ SÈTE★

C2 / ® / pop. 39 345 (Hérault)

Between the lake, the sea and Mont St. Clair, Sète is the major fishing port of the Mediterranean and the second commercial port after Marseilles, developed as a result of the Midi Canal. In the background of the picturesque waterfront, cranes, warehouses and reservoirs, and the pervasive smell of oil suggest the extent of recent industrial expansion in the town.

▶ At the foot of Mont St. Clair, the **Sète Canal** (B3) is bordered by Résistance Quay and General Durand Quay, where fishing-boats and fish restaurants draw crowds. Rue Général-de-Gaulle (pedestrians only) runs into the oldest quarter, near the 17thC **church of St. Louis** (B3), surmounted by a statue of the Virgin. ▶ At the end of General Durand Quay is the fish market, and beyond it the **St. Louis Breakwater** (B-C4), which protects the port and provides a view back over the whole town. ▶ Farther S, 17thC **Fort Saint-Pierre** is cut off from the mountain by the Route de Corniche (cliff road). Today the Fort is occupied by the Theatre of the Sea. ▶ St. Charles Cemetery is a little below the sailors' cemetery (**Cimetière Marin;** A-B4), immortalised by the poet Paul Valéry (1871-1945) and where he himself is buried. The musician Georges Brassens (d. 1982) is buried 3 km farther on in the new cemetery facing the Thau Lagoon. ▶ Just above the Cimetière Marin is the **Paul Valéry Museum**★ *(daily)* : art, archaeology, history; exhibits on water jousting (→ box) and on Valéry and Brassens. ▶ Higher still, **Fort Richelieu,** continuing *(2 km, tiring walk)* to the summit of **Mount-Saint-Clair** (pilgrimage chapel), covered with weekend cottages. View of *les Garrigues,* the Cévennes, the Canigou Massif and the Mediterranean. ▶ Beyond the railway station (C1), Pointe Courte, the fishermen's quarter. □

Water jousting

The tradition of water jousting (les joutes) stretches back to the founding of Sète in the 17thC. Jousts are held during the latter 2 weeks of August. Two boats, each with 10 rowers and a pair of musicians who play the 300-year-old jousting song, are equipped with projecting prows on which the jousters stand, each armed with lance and shield. The uproarious game consists of manœuvering until one of the jousters can land a blow to topple his adversary into the water. Mementoes of past jousts are to be seen in the Museum of Sète. This form of jousting is also practised at Agde, but the water tournaments of Sète are better known.

▶ Nearby

▶ **Frontignan** ® *(7 km NE)* : excellent muscat wine and plenty of opportunities to try it. Fortified **church of St. Paul;** at No. 4 Rue Lucien Salette, **Municipal Museum** (prehistory, Middle Ages, local economy); on the edge of town, a huge oil refinery. □

▶ Tour of Thau Lagoon★ *(approx 50 km)*

▶ Cross the industrial zone of Sète-Balaruc to reach **Balaruc-les-Bains** ®, a thermal spring dating from Roman times (casino) projecting into the Thau Lagoon, and the vine-growing village of **Balaruc-le-Vieux.** ▶ From **Gigean** *(6 km NE)*, a 3 km hike to **Saint-Félix-de-Monceau,** a ruined Benedictine abbey founded in the 11thC and abandoned in the 16thC; now maintained by an association for the aid of handicapped children *(open daily)*. ▶ **Bouzigues** ® : renowned for the oysters and mussels that since WWII have been raised commercially on the northern shore of the Thau Lagoon. ▶ **Loupian :** set back from the coast, a vine-growing village with a Romanesque church from the 11th-12thC. ▶ **Mèze** ® : at the very edge of the lagoon, divided between grape-growing and shellfish-raising; the commercial centre of Thau. ▶ Finally, **Marseillan** ® and **Marseillan Plage** (beach), whence you return to Sète along the sand spit separating the lagoon from the Mediterranean; salt-pans, vineyards, campsites, coast road and magnificent beach. □

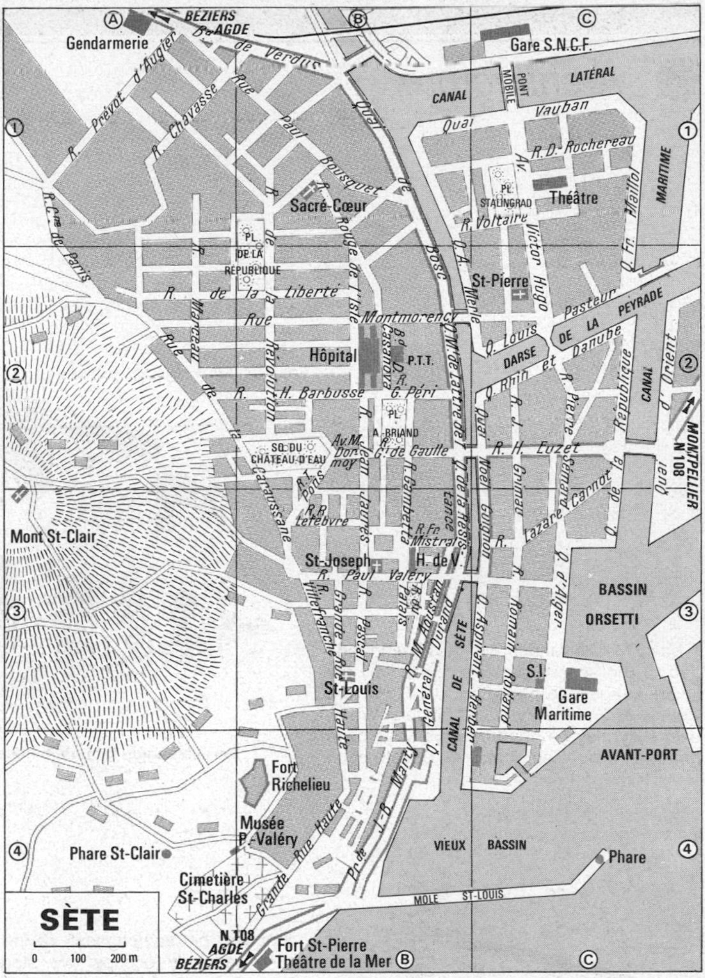

■ TUCHAN

B2-3 / pop. 814 (Aude)

At the intersection of the roads across the Corbières, at the foot of Tauch Mountain, Tuchan is a busy wine centre in the official wine district of Fitou; the village of the same name is situated near the coast. □

▶ Nearby

▶ 3 km E, overlooking the vineyards is the ruined 12thC **château d'Aguilar,** which during the Middles Ages kept watch over the Spanish frontier; the château was abandoned when the frontier was moved to its present position in the 17thC. ▶ Along D12 to **Vingrau** *(10 km SE)* in the Eastern Pyrénées, then to the **Caune** (Cavern) **de l'Arago** *(guided tours in Jul.-Aug.),* where the remains of Tautavel Man dating from 450 000-400 000BC were discovered. The Museum of Prehistory displays important finds excavated on the site *(daily ex. Tue.; closed 1 Jan., Easter Mon. and Whitsun, 1 May and 25 Dec.);* ruined 11thC château, and Cooperative of the Maître Vignerons (Master Wine Makers) of **Tautavel.** ▶ **Château de Padern** *(8 km SW from Tuchan) :* in ruins, once the stronghold at the entrance to the Torgan Gorge★. ▶ From **Cucugnan** ® *(13 km)* climb to the **Grau de Maury** (view★) and the 13th-14thC **château de Quéribus** built on a crag after the Albigensian Crusade. ▶ Above **Duilhac** *(17 km),* the 11th-12thC **château de Peyrepertuse** *(20 mins on foot)* with the château de San-Jordy forms a defensive fortification on the same rocky crest 800 m higher up; view★; the path completes the circuit in approx. 1 hr 30. ▶ **Rouffiac des Corbières** *(2 km) :* château; Romanesque church modified in the 14thC. ▶ **Termes** *(30 km NW)* and **Villerouge-Termenès** *(28 km NW) :* the former has a 12thC keep; the latter is the very picture of a mediaeval village. □

Architecture

Hérault region mountain house

A basic Mediterranean form has been modified to the special problems posed by life in the Languedoc plain, the foothills of the Cévennes and the Pyrenean heights. Wherever they may be, the houses always have gently sloping tiled roofs. ● Construction materials vary from place to place : limestone in coastal regions; sandstone and schist in the Corbières; granite in Cerdagne and the Montagne Noire; drystone construction in the Cévennes (Hérault) and the Pyrenean valleys, although marble is also occasionally seen. Flat stone tiles are common, and stones from the river bed are sometimes used. ● In vineyard areas the houses, or *"campagnes"*, of the vinegrowers generally occupy two storeys above the winery. ● As the altitude increases and vines become rarer, the winery becomes less important, and the houses lose a storey. ● In more warlike times, houses were tightly clustered in defensive villages on the heights. Houses in mountain areas are thus less expansive in appearance than dwellings on the plain.

Catalan house

Wine-growers house *("campagne")*

Brief regional history

The beginning

450 000 years separates us from **Tautavel Man,** the first known inhabitant of the Pyrénées, some of whose bones were found at Tautavel in the Eastern Pyrénées. ● During the **Neolithic Age,** farming settlements developed along the coastal fringe. The numerous **megaliths** in the region date from that period. ● During the 8th-7thC BC (Iron Age), successive waves of migration prompted the inhabitants already settled to construct strongpoints, such as at Ensérune, on easily defended heights. At about the same period, Greek navigators founded several **coastal trading stations,** including Agde. ● **Celts** settled the region in the 4thC BC.

1stC BC - 8thC AD

The Romans arrived in the province of Narbonne in the 2ndC BC; they established colonies of military veterans at Narbonne, Béziers and Carcassonne. ● The region thrived under the **Pax Romana** but, like most of Gaul, eventually succumbed to **Barbarian invasion.** Nevertheless much of Latin culture was maintained during a century of **Visigoth** rule. ● Arabs invading from Spanish strongholds in 719 AD held a substantial territory, including Narbonne and Carcassonne, for the next 40 years.

8th-13thC

The 8thC **Empire of Charlemagne** brought a brief stability, although the nature of the landscape, as much as that of the people, fostered feudal rivalry and separatism. ● Wealth from trade combined with the literary flowering of the **langue d'oc** (the regional tongue supplanted by the langue d'oïl, which a Royal decree designated as the official French language in 1539) encouraged the founding of universities at Toulouse and Montpellier. Many towns and villages also prospered as way-stations on the pilgrimage routes to Saint James of Compostela in Spain. ● The independent spirit of the Languedoc was expressed in a persistent religious movement, **Catharism,** a branch of the Albigensian heresy whose basic tenet proposed that man and the material world were the antithesis of the deity and, hence, inherently base. The movement was ruthlessly suppressed, largely under the leadership of the Anglo-French Simon de Montfort (1208-1265), who rooted the heretics out of every mountain stronghold. Despite the savage eradication of the Cathars, religious dissidence persisted in the region.

13th-17thC

In 1258, the King of France ceded the sovereignty of Catalonia and the Roussillon to the Spanish House of Aragon. ● Resentment of Spanish rule, together with widespread adoption of the **Protestant Reformation,** brought sustained civil unrest, which was quelled only with the personal intervention of Louis XIII of France. ● In the wake of a general revolt against the Spanish government, French troops occupied the entire area from 1642. Thc **Pyrénées Treaty** of 1659 restored Roussillon, together with Cerdagne, to French rule.

17thC to the present

The 1685 Revocation of the Edict of Nantes, which had guaranteed freedom of religion to Protestants, opened the doors to revolts and repressions that caused as much devastation as the Wars of Religion of the previous century. ● The French **Revolution** of 1789 was generally favoured, but the subsequent Napoleonic wars drained men and money. ● In the 19thC, the building of the railway stimulated the economy by providing access to the many spas in the Languedoc-Roussillon. Industrial development and **tourism** have continued the trend to prosperity, and the region is an important agricultural producer, accounting for a substantial part of the national **wine output.**

Practical information

The region

Information : Languedoc-Roussillon : *Comité Régional du Tourisme* (C.R.T.), 12, rue Foch, 34000 Montpellier, ☎ 67.60.55.42 ; **Aude :** *Comité Départemental du Tourisme* (C.D.T.), 39, bd Barbès, 11012 Carcassonne Cedex, ☎ 68.71.30.09 ; **Hérault :** *C.D.T.,* pl. Gaudechot, 34000 Montpellier, ☎ 67.54.20.66 ; **Pyrénées-Orientales :** *C.D.T.,* Palais Consulaire, quai de-Lattre-de-Tassigny, 66005 Perpignan, ☎ 68.34.29.94 and 68.34.29.95. In Paris : *Maison des Pyrénées,* 15, rue Saint-Augustin, 75009, ☎ 42.61.58.18.

Bookings : Aude *Loisirs-Accueil,* 70, rue Aimé-Ramon, 11001 Carcassonne Cedex, ☎ 68.47.09.06.

Maps : *Michelin* nos 83 and 86 at 1/200 000 ; no 240 Languedoc-Roussillon. *I.G.N.* nos 64, 65, 71, 72 at 1/100 000 and no 114 at 1/250 000 Pyrénées-Languedoc.

Local and regional press : *le Midi Libre, la Dépêche du Midi, l'Indépendant* (Perpignan).

S.O.S. : *SAMU* (Emergency Medical Service) : **Hérault,** ☎ 67.63.00.00. For other departments, dial 17 to obtain the local number ; *Poisoning Emergency Centre* for the 3 departments, ☎ 67.63.24.01.

Weather forecast : Aude : ☎ 68.25.10.58 ; **Hérault :** ☎ 66.92.62.12 ; **Pyrénées-Orientales :** ☎ 68.61.07.10. Information on coastal conditions : ☎ 68.61.03.92 ; mountain conditions : ☎ 68.61.30.32.

Rural gîte, chambres d'hôtes and farmhouse camping : Aude, see C.D.T. ; **Hérault,** *Chambre d'Agriculture,* pl. Chaptal, 34076 Montpellier Cedex, ☎ 67.92.88.00, ext. 22 ; **Pyrénées-Orientales,** *Comité de l'Habitat rural,* 30, rue P.-Bretonneau, 66000 Perpignan, ☎ 68.55.33.55.

Camping : approx. 450 sites. Lists available at the C.R.T. or C.D.T.

Youth hostels : *F.J.T.,* 3A, rue du Capitole, 11000 Narbonne, ☎ 68.32.07.15.

Cultural events : Jul, 1st fortnight : *Music Festival* in Béziers. **End Jul :** *Cinema Festival* in Prades and *Dramatic Arts Festival* in Marsillargues. **Jul-Aug :** *Mirondella dels Arts* in Pézenas, *Theatre Festival* in Sète, *Pablo Casals Music Festival* in Prades, *Classical Music Festival* in Perpignan and summer cultural events in Pézenas (theatre and music). **Aug :** *Classical Music Festival* in Hix and *Occitan Festival* in Bédarieux. **Oct :** *Bullfight Films festival.*

Religious events : Good Friday : *processions des Pénitents Noirs* in Arles-sur-Tech, Bouleternère, Collioure ; *procession de la Sanch* in Perpignan. **Easter Sunday :** *processions du Ressuscité* in Céret and Ille-sur-Têt. **Easter Monday :** *pilgrimage* to the marine cemetery of Notre-Dame des Auzils in Gruissan, traditional *aplech* at Notre-Dame de Laval, Caudies-de-Fenouillèdes. **Ascension :** *votive festival* in Gignac. **Jul :** 1 Sun : *Grand Pardon de St-Pierre* in Sète, *International Conference on Religious History of the Midi,* in Farjeaux. **8 Sep :** *Aplech de la Vierge Noire* in Font-Romeu. **Christmas :** Traditional vocal music of the Goigs in Céret, Perpignan and Prats-de-Mollo.

Folklore and traditional events : Feb-Mar : *carnivals* in Quillan, Céret, Argelès, Perpignan, Trouillas, Vinça ; *Fête de l'ours* (Bear Festivals) in Prats-de-Mollo and Saint-Laurent-de-Cerdans. **Jun :** *Festival de la Saint-Jean and the Sardanes* (until Sep) in Perpignan and Montauriol. **Jul :** *Festival de la Cité* in Carcassonne, *International Folk Festival* in Saint-Pons, *National Water Tournament Festival* in Sète. **Aug :** *wine festivals* in Saissac, Narbonne, Lagrasse, Sérignan, Elne ; *muscatel wine festival* in Frontignan ; *water tournaments* in Agde and Palavas ; *international folk fair* in Amélie-les-Bains ; *Féria* in Béziers ; *Festival de la Sardane* in Céret. **Sep :** *wine festival* in Bram. **Oct :** *wine festival* in Béziers ; *chestnut festival* in Saint-Pons ; *wine, fresh fruit and produce festivals* in Perpignan.

Fairs and markets : Apr : *antique fairs* in Montpellier and Perpignan. **Jun :** Castelnaudary *gastronomy fair.* **Jul :** *second hand goods, bric-à-brac and second-hand cars* in Narbonne. **Oct :** *International Vine and Wine Fair* in Montpellier. **Nov :** *St. Martin's Fair* in Perpignan.

Scenic railways : Hérault : *funiculaire de la grotte des Demoiselles,* 3, rue Maguelonne, 34000 Montpellier, ☎ 67.72.74.12, daily and evenings from 10 Jul to 31 Aug. **Pyrénées-Orientales :** The Cerdagne-Villefranche-La Tour-de-Carol line S.N.C.F., Perpignan, ☎ 68.54.50.50, and S.N.C.F. Villefranche-de-Conflent, ☎ 68.05.60.01.

National and nature parks : *parc naturel du Haut-Languedoc,* 12, rue du Cloître, 34220 Saint-Pons, ☎ 67.97.02.10.

Rambling and hiking : topoguides G.R. 36, 6, 7/74, 71, 77, 10. *Féd. Audoise de Tourisme de Randonnée,* 70, rue Aimé-Ramon, 11000 Carcassonne, ☎ 68.47.09.06. M. Ségui, *Assn. de Tourisme de Randonnée Languedoc-Roussillon* (A.T.R.), 14, rue des Logis, Loupian, 34140 Mèze, ☎ 67.43.82.50 ; *Itinérances,* 37, rue Descartes, 75005 Paris, ☎ 43.54.25.28, proposes two 7-day rambles in the Pyrénées, leaving from Mont-Louis. *Club Alpin Français* (C.A.F.), 4, rue de l'Académie, 66000 Perpignan. *C.I.M.E.S.,* 3, sq. Balagué, 09200 Saint-Girons, ☎ 61.66.40.10. Also consult *Guides des Hauts Cantons,* 34390 Olargues, ☎ 67.97.71.27.

Riding holidays : *Assn. Régionale pour le Tourisme Équestre and l'Équitation en Languedoc-Roussillon* (A.T.E.C.R.E.L.), M. Ségui, 14, rue des Logis, Loupian, 34140 Mèze, ☎ 67.43.82.50.

Cycling holidays : *Ligue du Languedoc-Roussillon,* M. Coupet, 24, av. de Figuerolles, 34000 Montpellier.

River and canal cruises : on the Midi canal, from Castelnaudary to Thau Lagoon, on the Rhône canal in Sète and the lateral canal of the Garonne. For boat hire, enq at : *Beaver Fleet,* port Cassafières, 34420 Portiranes, ☎ 67.90.91.70 ; *Blue Line,* Grand Bassin, B.P. 21, 11400 Castelnaudary, ☎ 68.23.17.51, or 3, quai Sud-Ouest, 34340 Marseillan,

☎ 67.77.21.59. *Les Berges d'Oc,* marina, B.P. 36, 34470 Perols, ☎ 67.68.19.65. *Lo Pais,* 18, rue Dom-Vaissette, 34000 Montpellier, ☎ 67.58.77.68.

Courses : œnologie, *Syndicat du Cru Minervois,* bd L.-Bazin, 34210 Olonzac, ☎ 67.91.21.66. Medieval archaeology (15 days), 42, rue Victor-Hugo, 11000 Carcassonne. *L'Institut Méditerranéen d'Initiation à la Culture Française,* B.P. 6039, 34030 Montpellier Cedex, proposes courses for foreigners in French language and civilisation.

Children : tennis and football coaching : Grand Stade, 66750 Saint-Cyprien, ☎ 68.21.24.21. For winter sports, contact : *Assn. Loisirs Montagne,* 1, rue Morse, 34500 Béziers, and Comité Dép. *UFOLEP,* Maison des Sports, 34100 Montpellier, ☎ 67.54.02.02 ; *A.D.P.E.P.,* 24, rue Émile-Zola, 66000 Perpignan, ☎ 68.34.21.37.

Golf : Perpignan-Saint-Cyprien (18 and 9 holes).

Tennis : *Ligue Régionale du Languedoc,* 12, rue Pasteur, 30000 Nîmes.

Motorcycling : enduro, trail-bikes, and scrambling in Amélie-les-Bains, M. Fernandez, ☎ 68.39.04.34, and Moto-club de Corbère-les-Cabanes, ☎ 68.52.72.29.

Sailing and wind-surfing : *Ligue Régionale Languedoc-Roussillon,* 33, rue des Deux-Ponts, 34000 Montpellier.

Water skiing : *Ligue Régionale Midi-Pyrénées,* 91, allée Charles-de-Fitte, 31300 Toulouse.

Diving : *Ligue Régionale Languedoc-Roussillon,* 6, rue Dautezac, 31300 Toulouse. *Club International* in Collioure, ☎ 68.82.06.34. *Redris Club* in Banyuls, ☎ 68.38.31.66. *Les Corailleurs* in Argelès, ☎ 68.81.16.33.

Canoeing : *Ligue Régionale,* moulin de Tarassac, 34390 Mons-la-Trivalle, ☎ 67.97.74.64 ; **Aude :** *Club d'Alet-les-Bains,* ☎ 68.69.90.70 ; **Hérault :** *Lamalou Aquatic Club,* in Lamalou-les-Bains, ☎ 67.95.61.30 ; **Pyrénées-Orientales :** *Base U.D.S.I.S.,* enq *Dir. dép. Jeunesse et Sports,* pl. J.-Moulin, ☎ 68.50.31.29.

Potholing and spelunking : Languedoc-Roussillon is an ideal potholing region which abounds in caves. *Assn. Entente Spéléo du Roussillon,* 4, rue Mailly, 66000 Perpignan ; *Assn. d'Exploration des Grottes,* mairie de Fontrabiouse, 66210, ☎ 68.04.40.51. *Spéléo-Club Alpin,* rue de Substantion, 34000 Montpellier.

Climbing : *Compagnie des Guides du Languedoc-Roussillon* (C.I.J), impasse Petite-Corraterie, 34000 Montpellier, ☎ 67.72.16.19 and 67.27.54.10, and *A.S.P.T.T. (section montagne),* 13, rue Rondelet, B.P. 1063, 34007 Montpellier Cedex, organises climbing excursions every Sun (Saint-Loup, Caroux, Taurac peaks, and climbing school Wed p.m. and Sat).

Winter sports : cross-country skiing in the parc du Haut-Languedoc. Sports activities, 34390 Mons-la-Trivalle, ☎ 67.97.72.85. Also Font-Romeu, ☎ 68.30.02.74 ; at the Centre-École de Matemale, ☎ 68.04.41.48 ; by the *Groupe Excursionniste Pyrénéen,* 66360 Mantet, ☎ 68.05.54.90, and in Valcevollère, ☎ 68.04.52.33 ; *Club Alpin* (mountaineering club), branches in Perpignan, Prades, Canigou and Carcassonne. Also *C.I.M.E.S.,* 3, sq. Balagué, 09200 Saint-Girons, ☎ 61.66.40.10.

Hand-gliding : Aude and **Pyrénées-Orientales** Delta-Club, 28, rue Armand-Izarn, 66000 Perpignan, ☎ 68.67.26.72.

Parachuting : Roussillon Center and School, B.P. 4, 66600 Salses, ☎ 68.89.20.60 or 68.83.04.80 ; upward parachuting, plage des Elmes, 66650 Banyuls-sur-Mer, ☎ 68.88.33.43.

Hunting and shooting : *Ligue Régionale Languedoc-Roussillon,* 12, rue Maury, 34000 Montpellier, ☎ 67.92.95.86, and *Féd. Dép. de la Chasse des Pyrénées-Orientales,* 7, pl. Paul-Bert, Lot. Porte d'Espagne, 66000 Perpignan, ☎ 68.56.70.55.

Fishing : *Halieutique interdépartementale,* mas de Carles-Octon, 34800 Clermont-l'Hérault, ☎ 67.96.11.35. **Aude :** *Féd. Dép. de Pêche et Pisciculture,* 32, rue de Mazagran, 11000 Carcassonne, ☎ 68.25.16.03. **Pyrénées-Orientales :** *Féd. de Pêche,* 3, rue Guillaume-Giltard, 66000 Perpignan, ☎ 68.66.53.52.

Towns

AGDE

Béziers 22, Montpellier 58, Paris 815
C2 ✉ 34300

ℹ rue L.-Bages, ☎ 67.94.29.68 and 67.94.25.86.

SNCF ☎ 67.94.25.86., 67.94.11.65.

Hotels :

La Tamarissière, 4 km S on the D32 :

● ★★★***La Tamarissière*** (Inter-Hôtel), 21, quai Th.-Cornu, ☎ 67.94.20.87. Tx 490225. AE, DC, Euro, Visa. 40 rm closed 15 Dec-15 Mar, 210. Rest. ● ♦♦ closed Sun eve and Mon low season. N. Albano has transformed this family hotel into a fashionable restaurant on the banks of the Hérault estuary. Excellent cooking, 80-300.

Cap-d'Agde, 5 km SE on the D32 ; ℹ ☎ 67.94.08.58 :

★★★***Matago,*** rue du Trésor-Royal, ☎ 67.26.00.05. Tx 480979. AE, DC, Euro, Visa. 88 rm closed 15 Oct-Easter, 260. Rest. ♦♦ ***la Louisiane,*** 120-210.

★★★***Golfe,*** île des Loisirs, ☎ 67.26.87.03. Tx 480709. AE, DC, Visa. 50 rm closed 31 Oct-20 Mar, 295. Rest. ♦ 140-180.

★★★***Saint-Clair,*** pl. St-Clair, ☎ 67.26.36.44. Tx 480464. Visa. 82 rm closed 1 Dec-15 Mar, 335. Rest. ***les Trois Sergents.*** closed Dec, Jan, Sun eve and Mon (ex Jul-Aug), 65-200.

★★***Pins,*** rue Labech, ☎ 67.26.00.11. Tx 480942. AE, DC. 40 rm 290.

Florensac, 9.5 km N :

★★***Léonce,*** 8, pl. de la République, ☎ 67.77.03.05. AE, DC, Visa. 18 rm closed 16 Sep-7 Oct, 28 Jan-16 Feb, Sun eve and Mon, 180. Rest. ● ♦♦ In a new luxurious decor, J.-C. Fabre formerly on the « Maximin » staff will become famous. He has joined the family business to help his parents. Delicious menu, 100-200.

▲ ★★★★*Domaine des Champs Blancs* (103 pl.), ☎ 67.94.23.42 ; ★★★*International* (416 pl.), ☎ 67.94.12.83 ; ★★★*la Clape* (450 pl.), ☎ 67.94.71.23 ; ★★★*l'Escale* (128 pl.), ☎ 67.94.18.16 ; ★★★*Lou Rouquet* (66 pl.), ☎ 67.94.21.82.

Restaurants :
♦♦ ***Pétoulet,*** pl. St-Clair, ☎ 67.26.00.70. Visa ♿ closed end-of-year hols, 120-210.
♦♦ ***Boucanier,*** tour de la Vigie, pl. Agde-Marine, ☎ 67.94.73.76. Closed Oct, Mon and Tue (ex Jul and Aug), 120-210.

Port-Richelieu, 7 km SE on the D32 :
♦ ***Brasero,*** ☎ 67.26.24.75. Visa ⚘ 🅿 ♿ closed Jan-Feb, Tue low season. Spec : *anchois frais au citron, thon grillé à l'aïoli,* 70-120.

Wines : Claude Gaujal, domaine de Pinet, ✉ 34850, 10 km NE.

AMÉLIE-LES-BAINS-PALALDA

Perpignan 38, Prades 60, Paris 944
B3 ✉ 66110

⚕ (spa, ex 25 Dec-10 Jan), ☎ 68.39.02.72.

ⓘ pl. de la République, ☎ 68.39.01.98.

🚌 ☎ 68.39.00.90.

Hotels :
★★★***Reine Amélie,*** 30, bd de la Petite-Provence, ☎ 68.39.04.38. AE, DC, Euro, Visa. 69 rm ⚘ 🅿 ♿ 260. Rest. ♦♦ 95-160.
★★★***Catalogne,*** rte du Vieux-Pont, ☎ 68.39.02.26. Visa. 38 rm ⚘ 🅿 ♨ 🔔 closed 1 Nov-1 Mar, 190. Rest. ♦♦ ♿ 80-140.
★★***Martinet,*** rue Hermabessière, ☎ 68.39.00.64. Visa. 40 rm ⚘ 🅿 ♨ 🔔 ✗ ♿ closed 15 Dec-1 Feb, 170. Rest. ♦ ✗ 60-80.
★★***Ensoleillade*** (L.F.), 70, rue J.-Coste, ☎ 68.39.06.20. 20 rm 🅿 ♨ closed 30 Nov-early Apr, 165.

1 km, rte de la Corniche :
★★***Castel Émeraude*** (Relais du Silence), ☎ 68.39.02.83. Visa. 31 rm ⚘ 🅿 ♨ 🔔 ✗ ♿ closed 30 Nov-1 Feb, 200. Rest. ♦ 60-180.

Arles-sur-Tech, ✉ 66150, 4 km W :
★★***Clycines*** (L.F.), rue du Jeu-de-Paume, ☎ 68.39.10.09. Euro, Visa. 34 rm ⚘ 🅿 ♨ 🔔 closed 31 Dec-15 Jan, 150. Rest. ♦ ♿ closed Mon, 60-170.

⛺ ★★*Gaou* (170 pl.), ☎ 68.39.19.19 ; Arles-sur-Tech : ★★★*la Rive* (100 pl.), ☎ 68.39.15.54 ; ★★★*Vallespir* (100 pl.), ☎ 68.39.05.03 ; ★★*Riuferrer* (150 pl.), ☎ 68.39.11.06.

Restaurant :
♦♦ ***Auberge Saint-Michel,*** La Bastide, ☎ 68.39.41.49. ⚘ 🔔 Spec : *charcuterie maison, cailles aux cèpes,* 90-140.

ARGELÈS-SUR-MER

Perpignan 21, Prades 58, Paris 930
B3 ✉ 66700

ⓘ pl. des Arènes, ☎ 68.81.15.85.

SNCF ☎ 68.81.02.00.

Hotels :
★★***Commerce,*** rte de Collioure, ☎ 68.81.00.33. AE, DC, Visa. 40 rm 🅿 ♨ ▭ closed Jan, Sun eve and Mon in winter, 160. Rest. ♦ 80-115 ; and annex : ***Parc,*** ☎ 68.81.05.52. 23 rm ♨ 🔔 ▭ closed Sep-Jun, 190.
★★***Mouettes,*** rte de Collioure, 3 km, ☎ 68.81.21.69. 24 rm ⚘ 🅿 ♨ ▭ 🎾 ♿ 180. Rest. ♦♦ 120-210.
★★***Cottage*** (L.F.), rue A.-Rimbaud, ☎ 68.81.07.33. DC, Visa. 14 rm ⚘ 🅿 ♨ 🔔 closed 31 Oct-1 Apr, 160. Rest. ♦ closed 31 Oct-1 May, 80-110.

At the beach, 2.5 km E :
● ★★★***Lido*** (Inter-Hôtel), bd de la Mer, ☎ 68.81.10.32. Tx 505220. Visa. 65 rm ⚘ 🅿 ♨ ▭ ♿ closed Oct-15 May, 260. Rest. ♦♦ 80-120.
★★★***Plage des Pins,*** ☎ 68.81.09.05. DC. 49 rm ⚘ 🅿 ♨ ✗ ▭ closed Oct-May, 260. Rest. ♦ ✗ ♿ 80-120.
★★***Golfe,*** rte de Collioure, ☎ 68.81.14.73. 30 rm ⚘ 🅿 closed Oct-Easter, 180.

Racou, 6.5 km :
★***Val Marie,*** ☎ 68.81.11.27. 28 rm ⚘ 🅿 ♨ 🔔 closed 15 Oct-30 Apr, 160. Rest. ♦ closed 30 Sep-20 May, 30-70.

⛺ ★★★★*Arbre Blanc* (132 pl.), ☎ 68.81.26.49 ; ★★★★*Licorne* (137 pl.), ☎ 68.81.15.24 ; ★★★★*Sirène* (320 pl.), ☎ 68.81.04.61 ; ★★★★*Soleil* (750 pl.), ☎ 68.81.14.48 ; 28 sites ★★★ and 80 sites ★★

BALARUC-LES-BAINS

Montpellier 29, Béziers 49, Paris 786
C1 ✉ 34540

⚕ (14 Feb-17 Dec), ☎ 67.48.51.02.

ⓘ av. des Thermes, ☎ 67.48.50.07.

Hotels :
★★***Grand Hôtel,*** 2, av. du Port, ☎ 67.48.50.26. 16 rm, closed 15 Nov-15 Mar, 160.
★★***Pins*** (L.F.), 13, sq. Marius-Bordes, ☎ 67.48.50.15. 20 rm 🅿 ♨ 🔔 ♿ closed 5 Dec-15 Mar, 180.

⛺ ★★★*Mas du Padre* (112 pl.), ☎ 67.48.56.57 ; ★★*Chemin des Bains* (152 pl.), ☎ 67.48.51.41 ; ★★*Pech d'Ay* (163 pl.), ☎ 67.48.50.34.

Restaurant :
♦♦ ***Martinez,*** ☎ 67.48.50.22. 🅿 ♨ 🔔 ♿ closed 15 Jan-15 Mar, Sun eve and Mon (low season), 70-150.

BANYULS-SUR-MER

Perpignan 37, Prades 73, Paris 947
B3 ✉ 66650

ⓘ hôtel de ville, ☎ 68.88.31.58.

SNCF ☎ 66.88.30.64.

🚌 av. du Gal-de-Gaulle, ☎ 68.88.32.26.

Hotels :
★★★***Catalan,*** rte de Cerbère, ☎ 68.88.02.80. Tx 500557. AE, DC. 36 rm ⚘ 🅿 ♨ 🔔 ▭ 🎾 ♿ closed 15 Oct-1 Apr, 330. Rest. ♦ 100-150.
★★***Elmes,*** plage des Elmes, ☎ 68.88.03.12. Euro, Visa. 21 rm ⚘ 🅿 ✗ ♿ closed 30 Oct-20 Mar, 260. Rest. ♦♦ 80-130.
★★***Villa Miramar,*** quartier Miramar, ☎ 68.88.33.85. 6 rm and 2 apt 🅿 ♨ 🔔 closed 1 Oct-15 Apr, 210.

⛺ ★★★*Le Stade* (33 pl.), ☎ 68.88.31.70 ; ★★*Municipal* (80 empl.), ☎ 68.88.00.62.

Restaurant :
♦♦ ***Sardinal,*** 4 *bis,* pl. Paul-Reig, ☎ 68.88.31.14. Euro, Visa. ♿ closed Jan, 15-31 Oct and Sun eve and Mon low season. Spec : *foie gras au vinaigre de Banyuls, suquet, ouillade,* 70-200.

Visit to wine cellar : *Coopérative l'Étoile,* av. Puig-del-Mas, ☎ 68.88.00.10 : daily from 8-12 and 2-5:30.

BÉDARIEUX

Béziers 35, Montpellier 71, Paris 860
9 km NE of Lamalou-les-Bains, B1 ✉ 34600

ⓘ rue St-Alexandre, ☎ 67.95.08.79.

SNCF ☎ 67.95.02.92.

Hotel :
★★***Moderne,*** 64, av. Jean-Jaurès, rte de St-Pons, ☎ 67.95.01.52. AE, DC, Euro, Visa. 28 rm 🅿 closed 15 Dec-20 Jan, 155.

⛺ Les Aires, 6 km W on the D160 : ★★*Camp de Gathinie* (103 pl.), ☎ 67.95.60.81.

Restaurants :

♦ ***Grange,*** ☎ 67.95.68.45. Euro, Visa. 🅿 closed 1 week in Sep, Mon (winter), 50-90.

Lunas, ✉ 34650, 14 km N on the D35 :
♦ ***Manoir du Gravezon,*** ☎ 67.23.81.58. closed 15 Jan-1 Mar, Mon eve and Tue eve (low season), 120-210.

La Tour-sur-Orb, 6 km on D157 :

Farmhouse-inn : *mas de Riols,* ☎ 67.23.10.53.

BÉZIERS

Montpellier 67, Perpignan 93, Paris 825
B2 ✉ 34500

ℹ 27, rue du 4-Septembre (B2), ☎ 67.49.24.19.

SNCF (C4), ☎ 67.62.50.50, 67.28.81.85.

✈ Béziers-Vias, 15 km E, ☎ 67.94.02.80.

🚌 pl. Jean-Jaurès (B3), ☎ 67.28.40.45.

Car-hire : *Budget* train + auto, at the station, ☎ 67.28.26.72 ; and at the airport.

Hotels :

★★★***Impérator*** (Inter-Hôtel), 28, allées P.-Riquet (B2), ☎ 67.49.02.25. Tx 490608. AE, DC, Euro. 45 rm 🅿 ♿ 250.
★★★***Midi*** (Inter-Hôtel), 13, rue de la Coquille (B2), ☎ 67.49.13.43. Tx 490608. AE, DC, Euro, Visa. 31 rm ♿ closed 2 Nov-2 Dec, 280. Rest. ♦♦ ***la Rascasse.*** ♿ closed Sat and Sun noon. Fish specialities, 70-150.
★★★***Europe,*** 87, av. Pdt-Wilson (C3), ☎ 67.76.08.97. Tx 490064. AE, DC, Euro, Visa. 30 rm 🅿 340.
★★***Splendid,*** 24, av. du 22-Août-1944 (B2), ☎ 67.28.23.82. Euro. 26 rm ♿ 130.
★★***Poètes,*** 80, allées P.-Riquet (B2), ☎ 67.76.38.66. Visa. 14 rm 🅿 closed Sat and Sun noon, 200.

Nissan-lez-Ensérune, ✉ 34440, 10 km SE :
★★***Résidence*** (L.F.), 35, av. de la Cave, ☎ 67.37.00.63. 19 rm 🅿 closed Feb, 1 Nov-31 Apr and Sun, 180. Rest. ♦ Eve, guests only, 80-130.

Capestang, ✉ 34310, 15 km E :
★★***Franche-Comté*** (L.F.), 39, cours Belfort, ☎ 67.93.31.21. 15 rm 🅿 140. Rest. ♦ (for people staying overnight) closed noon and Sun, 50-130.

Restaurants :

♦♦♦ ***L'Olivier,*** 12, rue Boëldieu (B2), ☎ 67.28.86.64. AE, DC, Euro, Visa ; closed Sun eve and Mon low season. A new management which looks promising, 120-210.
♦♦ ***Trou Normand,*** 13, allées P.-Riquet (B2), ☎ 67.28.53.01. AE, DC ; closed Sun eve and Mon. *Ragoût de nouilles fraîches aux fruits de mer, confit de canard fait maison,* 70-120.

Wines : Faugères A.O.C., château de la Liquière, at Cabrerolles, ✉ 34480, 12 km N.

Le BOULOU

Perpignan 24, Prades 51, Paris 931
B3 ✉ 66160

⚕ Spa (10 Apr-31 Oct), ☎ 68.83.01.17.

ℹ pl. de la Mairie, ☎ 68.83.15.60.

SNCF ☎ 68.83.15.51.

🚌 pl. de la République, ☎ 68.83.15.59.

Hotels :

● ★★***Grillon d'Or*** (Inter-Hôtel), 40, rue de la République, ☎ 68.83.03.60. Tx 500400. Euro, Visa. 40 rm 🅿 ♿ closed 10 Jan-10 Feb, 15 Nov-15 Dec, 170. Rest. ♦ closed 3 Jan-10 Feb, 45-130.
★★***Sources,*** les Thermes, rte du Perthus, ☎ 68.83.00.81. 64 rm 🅿 ♿ closed 30 Oct-1 Apr, 130. Rest. ♦ 80-130.
★***Canigou,*** rue Bousquet, ☎ 68.83.15.29. 17 rm 🅿 closed Nov-Apr, 180. Rest. ♦ 80-130.
4.5 km SE :
★★★***Relais des Chartreuses,*** rte d'Argelès-sur-Mer, ☎ 68.83.15.88. 10 rm 🅿 ♿ closed 14 Nov-20 Dec, 260. Rest. ♦♦ closed Mon. Book ahead. Moroccan or French cooking, 120-210.
5 km S on the N9 :
★★***L'Écluse,*** ☎ 68.83.15.70, 68.83.16.65. 21 rm 🅿 closed Jan and Moon, Tue, Wed, Thu (low season and Aug), 480. Rest. ♦ *Magret de canard aux cèpes, paëlla,* 120-250.

⛺ ★★*L'Olivette* (190 pl.), ☎ 68.83.00.81 ; ★★*les Oliviers* (85 pl.), ☎ 68.83.12.86.

Casino, rte du Perthus, ☎ 68.83.01.20, 68.83.02.81. Rest. ♦ ☎ 68.83.01.20.

CANET-PLAGE

Perpignan 13, Narbonne 72, Paris 919
B3 ✉ 66140

ℹ pl. de la Méditerranée, ☎ 68.80.20.65.

Hotels :

★★★***Sables*** (Inter-Hôtel), 25, rue de la Vallée-du-Rhône, ☎ 68.80.23.63. Tx 505213. AE, DC, Euro, Visa. 41 rm 🅿 270.
★★***Clos des Pins,*** 34, av. du Roussillon, ☎ 68.80.32.63. AE, DC. 20 rm 🅿 closed 1 Apr-30 Oct, 230.
★★***Althaéa*** (Mapotel), 120, prom. de la Côte-Vermeille, ☎ 68.80.28.59. Tx 505098. AE, DC, Euro, Visa. 48 rm 🅿 closed 1 Nov-1 Apr, 310.
★★***Aquarius,*** 40, av. du Roussillon, ☎ 68.80.25.48. 40 rm 🅿 ♿ 200. Rest. ♦ closed 30 Sep-1 Apr, 60-100.
★★***Font Le Patio,*** B.P. 19, Front-de-Mer, ☎ 68.80.31.04. 70 rm ♿ closed 31 Oct-1 Apr, 180. Rest. (self-service) 50-110.

⛺ ★★★★*Ma Prairie* (260 pl.), ☎ 68.80.24.70 ; 9 sites ★★★ ; 4 sites ★★

CARCASSONNE

Narbonne 61, Perpignan 113, Paris 907
A2 ✉ 11000

ℹ bd Camille-Pelletan (C2), ☎ 68.25.07.04 and 68.25.41.32.

✈ Carcassonne-Salvaza, 3 km W, ☎ 68.25.12.33.

SNCF (C1), ☎ 68.47.50.50, 68.25.60.80.

🚌 bd Sabatier (D1), ☎ 68.25.12.74.

Car-hire : *Budget* train + auto, at the station, ☎ 68.25.60.80, and at the airport.

Hotels :

★★★★***Cité,*** pl. de l'Église (E3), ☎ 68.25.03.34. Tx 500829. AE, DC, Euro, Visa. 54 rm 🅿 ♿ closed 20 Oct-20 Apr, 600. Rest. ♦♦♦ ♿ closed Mon, 120-250.
● ★★★***Terminus*** (Inter-Hôtel), 2, av. Mal-Joffre (C1), ☎ 68.25.25.00. Tx 500198. AE, DC, Euro, Visa. 110 rm 🅿 ♿ 300.
★★★***Donjon*** (Mapotel, L.F.), 2, rue du Comte-Roger (E3), ☎ 68.71.08.80. AE, DC, Euro, Visa. 36 rm 🅿 300. Rest. closed Wed and noon, 100-150.

Languedoc Roussillon

★★★***Montségur,*** 27, allées d'Iéna (B2), ☎ 68.25.31.41. AE, DC, Euro, Visa. 21 rm Ⓟ ✗ ♿ closed 15 Dec-15 Jan, 300. Rest. ♦♦ ***Languedoc,*** 32, allées d'Ién : ♿ closed 15 Dec-15 Jan and Sun and Mon. Regional specialities, 90-220.

★★***Aragon*** (France-Accueil), 15, montée Combéléran (E3), ☎ 68.47.16.31. AE, DC, Euro, Visa. 19 rm ⚘ Ⓟ ✎ 250.

3.5 km S (off map near D3) :
★★★★***Domaine d'Auriac*** (Relais et châteaux), rte de St-Hilaire, ☎ 68.25.72.22. Tx 500385. AE, DC, Euro, Visa. 23 rm ⚘ Ⓟ ≋ ✎ ▭ ⚲ ♿ closed 15-31 Jan, Sun and Mon noon low season, 500. Rest. ● ♦♦♦ Old-fashioned ; good, traditional gourmet cooking, 150-200.

3 km E on the N113 :
● ★★★***Logis de Trencavel,*** 286, av. Gal-Leclerc (off map near F3), ☎ 68.71.09.53. AE, DC, Visa, Euro. 12 rm Ⓟ ≋ closed 10 Jan-10 Feb, 220. Rest. ● ♦♦♦ closed Wed. Rich and inventive cooking of J.-C. Rodriguez (M.C.F.). Spec : *millefeuille lauragеais, poire en rose des vignes,* 90-200.

Capendu, ⊠ 11700, 16 km E :
★★***Top du Roulier,*** rte de Narbonne, ☎ 68.79.03.60. Visa. 30 rm Ⓟ ✎ 130. Rest. ♦♦ ♿ 50-100.

Peyriac-Minervois, ⊠ 11160 Caunes-Minervois, 25 km NW :
★★★***Château de Violet*** (Relais du Silence), rte de Pépieux, ☎ 68.78.10.42. AE, DC, Euro, Visa. 15 rm ⚘ Ⓟ ≋ ✎ ▭ ♿ 500. Rest. ♦♦ 135-200.

Youth hostel : rue du Vicomte-Trencavel, mediaeval town, ☎ 68.25.23.16.

⛺ ★★*Stade Albert Domec* (200 pl.), ☎ 68.25.11.77.

Restaurants :
♦♦ ***Crémade,*** 1, rue du Plo (E3), ☎ 68.25.16.64. AE, DC, Euro, Visa ; closed 1-31 Jan, Sun eve and Mon low season, 60-120.
♦♦ ***Auberge du Pont-Levis,*** mediaeval town (E3), ☎ 68.25.55.23. AE, DC, Euro, Visa. Ⓟ ≋ ✎ ✗ closed Sun eve, Mon, 28 Jan-17 Feb and 29 Jul-11 Aug. Spec : *loup de mer au chou vert et saumon fumé, « dodine » de canard au foie gras et pruneaux,* 100-150.

Guided tours : C.N.M.H.S., ☎ 68.25.04.65 or T.O., ☎ 68.25.07.04 and 68.25.01.66 for the Dépôt Lapidaire. Illuminations in the City on 14 Jul, during the City Festival, info, ☎ 68.47.58.06.

Bicycle hire : *Bourronnet,* 12 *bis,* rue Auguste-Conte, ☎ 68.25.66.64.

CASTELNAUDARY

Carcassonne 41, Toulouse 59, Paris 768
A2 ⊠ 11400

ⓘ pl. de la République, ☎ 68.23.05.73.

SNCF ☎ 68.23.29.56, 68.23.01.46.

🚌 pl. de la République, ☎ 68.23.04.85.

Hotels :
★★★***Palmes et Industries*** (Mapotel), 10, av. Mal-Foch, ☎ 68.23.03.10. Tx 500372. AE, DC, Euro, Visa. 20 rm Ⓟ ♿ closed Jan, 200. Rest. ♦♦ 60-160.
★★***Fourcade,*** 14, rue des Carmes, ☎ 68.23.02.08. AE, DC, Euro, Visa. 14 rm, closed Wed, 130. Rest. ● ♦♦ ♿ Michel Chabit's famous *cassoulet* and for gourmets duck and goose *foie gras,* 50-180.

Saissac, ⊠ 11310, 22 km NE :
★★***Castel de Villemague*** (Châteaux-hôtels, L.F.), on the D103, 6 km W, ☎ 68.60.22.95. Visa. 9 rm ⚘ Ⓟ ≋ ✎ Traditional furnishing ; book ahead during low season, 270. Rest. ♦♦ 80-180.

Farmhouse gîte : Fontiers-Cabardès, *la Canade,* ☎ 68.26.52.65, and Pantouquet, ☎ 68.26.52.83.

⛺ ★★*Municipal* (35 pl.), ☎ 68.23.11.23 ; Saissac : ★★*municipal* (50 pl.), ☎ 68.24.40.22.

Restaurant :
♦♦ ***Auberge,*** 22, cours de la République, ☎ 68.23.15.32. Closed 25 Déc-10 Jan, Mon, 80-130.

CERBÈRE

Perpignan 47, Prades 83, Paris 957
B3 ⊠ 66290

ⓘ 1, av. de la Côte-Vermeille, ☎ 68.88.42.36.

SNCF ☎ 68.88.41.32., 68.88.40.20.

Hotel :
★★***Dorade,*** av. Gal-de-Gaulle, ☎ 68.88.41.93. DC, Visa. 25 rm ⚘ ♿ closed 15 Oct-15 Mar and Wed, 170. Rest. ♦♦ ⚘ ♿ closed 15 Oct-20 Mar, 50-140.

⛺ ★★*Plage del Sorell* (80 pl.), ☎ 68.38.41.64.

CÉRET

Perpignan 31, Prades 55, Paris 938
B3 ⊠ 66400

ⓘ av. G.-Clemenceau, ☎ 68.87.00.58.

SNCF ☎ 68.87.00.14.

Hotels :
★★★***Terrasse au Soleil*** (Relais du Silence), rte de Fontfrède, 1.5 km W, ☎ 68.87.01.94. 18 rm ⚘ Ⓟ ≋ ✎ ▭ ♿ closed 31 Oct-31 Mar, Mon and Tue noon, 360. Rest. ♦♦ closed Mon and Tue noon ex guests, 160-210.
★★***Châtaigneraie,*** rte de Fontfrède, 2 km W, ☎ 68.87.03.19. 8 rm ⚘ Ⓟ ≋ ✎ ✗ ▭ closed 1 Oct-14 May, 350. Rest. ♦ Evening meals for guests only, 120-210.

⛺ ★★★*St-Georges* (60 pl.), ☎ 68.87.03.73 ; ★★*Bosquet de Nogarède* (132 pl.), ☎ 68.87.26.72.

Restaurant :
★★★***Ferme de Céret,*** 15, av. G.-Clemenceau, ☎ 68.87.07.91. AE, DC, Euro, Visa ; closed Nov, Mon and Tue eve, 50-120.

CHALABRE

Quillan 24, Carcassonne 48, Paris 959
8 km N of Puivert, A2 ♥ ⊠ 11230

ⓘ cours Colbert, ☎ 68.69.20.10.

Hotel :
★***France,*** cours Raynaud, ☎ 68.69.20.15. Euro, Visa. 20 rm Ⓟ closed 3 Oct-4 Nov, 80. Rest. ♦♦ 45-120.

⛺ ★★*Municipal* (65 pl.), ☎ 68.69.20.39.

Restaurant :
Sainte-Colombe-sur-l'Hers, ⊠ 11230, 16 km SW by RN620 :
★***Colombières,*** 60, Grande-Rue, ☎ 68.69.21.91. ♿ closed 27 Aug-15 Sep, 50-80.

CLERMONT-L'HÉRAULT

Montpellier 41, Béziers 44, Paris 802
C1 ♥ ⊠ 34800

ⓘ rue René-Gosse (high season), ☎ 67.96.23.86.

SNCF ☎ 67.96.01.43.

Hotels :
★★***Sarac,*** rte de Nébian, ☎ 67.96.06.81. 22 rm Ⓟ closed 15 Dec-15 Jan, Sat and Sun 1 Oct-1 Mar, 100.

Mourèze, 8 km E on the D8 :
● ***Hauts de Mourèze,*** ☎ 67.96.04.84. 10 rm Ⓟ closed 15 Oct-29 Mar, 150.

⛺ ★★*Lac du Salagou* (300 pl.), ☎ 67.96.13.13 ; ★★*les Rivières* (66 pl.), Canet (5 km), ☎ 67.96.75.53.

Farmhouse-inn : Salasc, 15 km W D8 : *Vallée du Salagou,* ☎ 67.96.15.62. Spec : dishes prepared with goat cheese (also sold at the farm).

COLLIOURE

Perpignan 27, Prades 64, Paris 937
B3 ✉ 66190

ⓘ av. C.-Pelletan, ☎ 68.82.15.47.

SNCF ☎ 68.52.05.89.

🚌 ☎ 68.82.18.83.

Hotels :
★★★***Frégate,*** 24, quai de l'Amirauté, ☎ 68.82.06.05. Tx 505072. Visa. 24 rm, 230. Rest. ● ♦♦ Catalan spec, 90-150.
★★★***Casa Pairal*** (Relais du Silence), ☎ 68.82.05.81. Tx 505220. 28 rm Ⓟ closed 1 Nov-1 Apr, 300.
★★★***Madeloc*** (Inter-Hôtel), rue Romain-Rolland, ☎ 68.82.07.56. AE, DC, Visa. 22 rm Ⓟ closed 15 Oct-30 Mar, 250.
★★***Ambeille et Bellevue,*** rte du Port-d'Avail, ☎ 68.82.08.74. 21 rm Ⓟ closed 30 Sep-Easter, 220.
★★***Villa Basque,*** 22, av. de la République, ☎ 68.82.04.82. 26 rm Ⓟ closed 15 Oct-Easter, 200.
★★***Caranques,*** rte de Port-Vendres, ☎ 68.82.06.68. 16 rm closed 11 Oct-1 Apr, 200. Rest. : guests only ; closed 30 Sep-1 Jun.
★★***Bon Port,*** rte de Port-Vendres, ☎ 68.82.06.08. 22 rm Ⓟ closed end Sep-Easter, 180. Rest. ♦ Beautiful view of Collioure, 60-100.
★★***Terrasses,*** rue Jean-Bart, ☎ 68.82.06.52. Euro, Visa. 20 rm 180.
★★***Hostellerie des Templiers,*** 12, quai de l'Amirauté, ☎ 68.82.05.58. Visa. 52 rm closed Nov-Apr, 240. Rest. ♦♦ closed Sun eve and Mon, 80-160.
★***Bona Casa,*** 20, rue de la République, ☎ 68.82.06.62. 6 rm, closed 15 Dec-15 Mar, Mon and Tue eve, 100. Rest. ♦ Two young brothers have enthusiastically taken over the management of their parents' hotel. Good gastronomic menu : *terrine chaude de légumes au coulis de tomates, paupiettes de lapereau farci aux pruneaux, fromage blanc au miel de citron,* 120-160.

⛺ ★★*Girelle* (65 pl.), ☎ 68.81.25.56 ; ★★*Amandiers* (92 pl.), ☎ 68.81.14.69.

Restaurants :
♦♦♦ ***La Balette,*** rte de Port-Vendres, ☎ 68.82.05.07. Ⓟ closed 7 Nov-7 Feb, Sun eve and Mon (ex high season). Enjoy such dishes as *lotte au beurre de poivron rouge, truite de mer saumonée au champagne* or *gratin de fruits de mer,* in this superb setting. Good desserts, 80-300.
♦♦ ***La Marinade,*** 14, pl. de la République, ☎ 68.82.09.76. Euro, Visa. closed Wed and Sun eve, 5 Jan-2 Feb. Spec : *anchois de Collioure, bouillinade du pêcheur,* 90-150.
♦♦ ***Bodega,*** 6, rue de la République, ☎ 68.82.05.60. AE, DC, Visa ; closed Mon eve and Tue (low season), 8 Nov-23 Dec. A former wine and spirits storehouse, featuring such dishes as *bouillabaisse,* red mullet and John Dory, 75-150.
♦ ***Chiberta,*** 18, av. du Gal-de-Gaulle, ☎ 68.82.06.60. Closed Mon eve and Tue (Apr-Jun), 1 Oct-1 Nov, 80-130.

Recommended : *Boutique du Port,* pl. de la République, for real Catalan ladies (espadrilles for dancing the *sardane*). *Roque,* local produce, 40, rue de la Démocratie, ☎ 68.82.04.99. *Bartissol,* pastry, rte de Port-Vendres.

CUCUGNAN

Perpignan 40, Quillan 50, Paris 911
4 km E of Peyrepertuse, B3 ✉ 11350 Tuchan

Restaurant :
♦♦ ***Auberge de Cucugnan,*** rue de l'Auberge, ☎ 68.45.40.84. Ⓟ closed 1-15 Sep, Wed low season, 60-160.

ENVEITG

Font-Romeu 17, Perpignan 106, Paris 1 019
6.5 km NW of Bourg-Madame, A3
✉ 66760 Bourg-Madame

Hotels :
★★***Transpyrénéen*** (L.F. ; Inter-Hôtel), ☎ 68.04.81.05. AE, DC, Euro, Visa. 40 rm Ⓟ closed 5 May-30 Jun, 1 Oct-15 Dec, 180. Rest. 60-160.
★***Mirasol,*** ☎ 68.04.80.16. Visa. 14 rm closed Oct, Mon (low season), 80. Rest. ♦ 40-70.

⛺ ★★★*Robinson* (166 pl.), ☎ 68.04.80.38 ; ★★*Puigmal* (100 pl.), ☎ 68.04.71.83.

FONT-ROMEU

Prades 45, Perpignan 88, Paris 1 000
A3 1 800-2 250 m ✉ 66120

ⓘ av. E.-Brousse, ☎ 68.30.02.74.

SNCF ☎ 68.30.03.12.

🚌 ☎ 68.30.01.28.

Hotels :
★★★***Cimes,*** av. des Écureuils, ☎ 68.30.07.45. AE, Euro. 23 rm closed end Apr-early Jul and winter, 240.
★★***Grand Tetras,*** rue E.-Brousse, ☎ 68.30.01.20. Tx 500802. AE, DC, Euro, Visa. 36 rm Ⓟ closed 1 Oct-15 Dec, 230.
★★***Carlit*** (L.F.), ☎ 68.30.07.45. Tx 500802. AE, Euro. 60 rm closed 5 Apr-15 Jun, 1 Oct-15 Dec, 260. Rest. ♦ 60-120.
★★***Clair Soleil,*** rte d'Odeillo, ☎ 68.30.13.65. Euro, Visa. 31 rm Ⓟ closed 15 Oct-20 Dec and 15 Apr-20 May, 200. Rest. eve only, 70-170.
★★***Orée du Bois,*** av. E.-Brousse, ☎ 68.30.01.40. AE, Visa. 36 rm Ⓟ 185.
★★***Y Sem Bé,*** rue des Écureuils, ☎ 68.30.00.54. 27 rm Ⓟ closed 15 Oct-20 Dec and 27 Apr-1 Jun, 205. Rest. ♦ 80-100.
★★***Pyrénées,*** pl. des Pyrénées, ☎ 68.30.01.49. AE. 37 rm closed 4 Nov-15 Dec and 5 Apr-10 May, 175. Rest. ♦ 40-110.
★★***Bellevue,*** av. Dr-Capelle, ☎ 68.30.00.16. Visa. 68 rm Ⓟ closed Nov and May, 200. Rest. ♦ 80-120.

Odeillo, 3 km SW D29 :
★★***Romarin,*** av. F.-Arago, ☎ 68.30.09.66. 15 rm Ⓟ closed 30 Oct-15 Dec and 20 Apr-20 Jun, 200. Rest. ♦ evening meal guests only 80-130.

Targassonne, 4 km W :
★*Tourane,* ☎ 68.30.15.03. 30 rm ⊰ P ⚲ ✌
100. Rest. ♦♦ 60-90.

Via, 5 km SW :
★★*L'Oustalet,* ☎ 68.30.11.32. Euro, Visa.
29 rm ⊰ P ⚌ ⚲ closed 1 Nov-1 Dec and 1 May-
1 Jun, 180. Rest. ♦ ✌ ᵶ 50-80.

⚑ ★*Le Menhir* (200 pl.), ☎ 68.30.09.32.

Restaurant :
♦♦ *La Potinière,* rue E.-Brousse, ☎ 68.30.11.56.
AE, Euro. ⊰ ᵶ closed 15 May-15 Jun, 15 Sep-
15 Dec, Tue from May-Sep, 70-160.

GANGES

Montpellier 45, Nîmes 64, Paris 757
C1   ⊠ 34190

ⓘ plan des Ormeaux, ☎ 67.73.84.79.

SNCF ☎ 67.73.80.33.

Hotels :
★★*Poste,* 8, plan des Ormeaux, ☎ 67.73.85.88.
26 rm ✌ 155.
★*Caves de l'Hérault,* 14, av. du Jeu-de-Ballon,
☎ 67.73.81.09. Visa. 14 rm ⚌ ⚲ closed 23 Dec-
31 Jan, Fri eve and Sat low season, 140. Rest.
♦ 45-75.

Saint-Laurent-le-Minier, 30440 Sumène, 5 km W
on the D25 :
Chez Christian, ☎ 67.73.86.92, 8 rm, 100.
Rest. ♦ 80-130.

Farmhouse-inn : *Mas de Coulet,* Saint-Bauzille-
de-Putois, 8 km by D986, ☎ 67.73.74.18. With
2 gîtes accommodating 5 persons.

⚑ ★★*Pic Saint-Loup* (50 pl.), Saint-Martin-de-
Londres, ⊠ 34380 ☎ 67.55.00.53.

Restaurant :
♦♦ *La Crèche,* on the road to Frouzet, 18.5 km
S, ☎ 67.55.00.04. AE, DC, Euro. 7 rm ⊰ P ⚌
⚲ ⬚ ⋰ closed Mon and Tue low season,
1 Feb-1 Mar, 150-230.

GIGNAC

Montpellier 30, Béziers 150, Paris 791
C1   ⊠ 34150

ⓘ pl. du Gal-Claparède, ☎ 67.57.58.83.

Hotels :
Aniane, 5 km N on the D32 :
★*Clamouse,* ☎ 67.57.71.63. 10 rm, closed Nov-
15 Dec, 1-15 Mar, Mon eve and Tue low season,
130. Rest. ᵶ 50-100.

Saint-Guilhem-du-Désert, 13 km N on the D27 :
Fonzès, 2, av. Saint-Benoît-d'Aniane,
☎ 67.57.72.01. 11 rm ⊰ glorious panoramic view
⚌ ✌ closed 30 Nov-1 Mar, 130. Rest. ♦ 60-
130.

⚑ ★★*Camp du Pont* (36 pl.), ☎ 67.57.52.40.
Aniane : ★★*Moulin de Siau* (75 pl.),
☎ 67.57.51.08.

Restaurants :
♦♦ *Chez Capion,* 3, bd de l'Esplanade,
☎ 67.57.50.83. AE, DC, Euro, Visa. With rm ;
closed Sun eve and Mon, Feb. Cooking according to the day's market, traditional and tasty,
130-200.

Saint-Guilhem-du-Désert :
♦ *Taverne de l'Escuelle,* 11, rue du Val-de-
Gellone, ☎ 67.57.72.05. With rm ; closed 1 Nov-
1 Apr, 60-130.

La GRANDE-MOTTE

Montpellier 20, Nîmes 44, Paris 754
C1   ⊠ 34280

ⓘ pl. du 1er-Octobre, ☎ 67.56.62.62.

Hotels :
★★★*Quetzal,* allée des Jardins, ☎ 67.56.61.10.
52 rm P ⚲ ⬚ closed 1 Nov-29 Feb, 400.
★★*Europe* (Inter-Hôtel), square Navigarde,
☎ 67.56.62.60. Tx 490206, 34 rm P ⚲ ✌ ⬚
closed 10 Oct-25 Mar, 230.

⚑ ★★★★*L'Or* (300 pl.),
☎ 67.56.52.10 ; ★★★★*Garden* (237 pl.),
☎ 67.56.50.09 ; ★★★★*Lorraine-Aquitaine*
(240 pl.), ☎ 67.56.50.41 ; ★★★★*Lous Pibons*
(200 pl.), ☎ 67.56.50.08.

Restaurants :
♦♦♦ *Alexandre-Amirauté,* terre-plein de la
Capitainerie, ☎ 67.56.63.63. ⊰ P ⚌ ⚲ ✌
closed 10-22 Nov, 6 Jan-22 Feb, Sun eve and
Mon (low season). Spec : *cassolette d'huîtres
aux truffes, assiette « bouille »,* 160-300.
♦ *L'Estrambord,* 18, quai Pompidou,
☎ 67.56.50.50. Closed Tue low season and
10 Jan-28 Feb. Fish specialities for the mostly
"regular" clients, 120-210.

GRUISSAN

Narbonne 14, Carcassonne 72, Paris 858
B2   ⊠ 11430

ⓘ bd Pech-Meynaud, ☎ 68.49.03.25.

Hotels :
★★*Corail* (L.F.), quai du Ponant, ☎ 68.49.04.43.
AE, Visa. 32 rm ⊰ P closed 30 Oct-1 Mar, 200.
Rest. ♦ ᵶ Nice location on the port. Good
service, cuisine improving, 60-130.
★*Plage,* av. des Dunes, ☎ 67.49.00.75. 17 rm
P ✌ ᵶ closed 15 Sep-Easter, 140.

⚑ ★★★*Les Ayguades* (400 pl.),
☎ 68.49.81.59 ; ★★*Municipal* (200 pl.),
☎ 68.49.07.22 ; ★★*Pech-Rouge* (255 pl.),
☎ 68.33.80.88.

Recommended : smoked-fish processing factory (follow the indicating boards at the entrance
of the town).

LAMALOU-LES-BAINS

Béziers 39, Montpellier 80, Paris 870
B1
♨ (t.a.), ☎ 67.95.25.55   ⊠ 34240

ⓘ 24, av. Charcot, ☎ 67.95.64.17.

Hotels :
★★*Belleville,* 1, av. Charcot, ☎ 67.95.61.09.
Visa. 44 rm P ⚌ ⬚ ⋰ ᵶ 150. Rest. ♦ ᵶ 40-100.
★★*Grand Hôtel Mas* (L.F.), av. Charcot,
☎ 67.95.62.22. 40 rm P ⚌ ⋰ ᵶ closed Jan-Feb,
200. Rest. ♦♦ 120-210.
★★*Paix,* rue du Dr-Privat, ☎ 67.95.63.11. Visa.
28 rm P ⚌ ⚲ ᵶ closed end Oct-1 Apr, 135.
Rest. 60-110.

LEUCATE

Perpignan 34, Narbonne 37, Paris 883
B3 ✉ 11370

ℹ ☎ 68.40.91.31 (in summer).

SNCF ☎ 68.45.70.01.

Hotels :
★★***Jouve,*** 39, av. Côte-Rêvée, ☎ 68.40.02.77. Euro, Visa. 7 rm closed 15 Oct-15 Mar, Mon low season, 180. Rest. ♦ ♿ 60-160.

La Franqui, 7 km N :
★★***Plage,*** bd du Front-de-Mer, ☎ 68.45.70.23. 32 rm P closed Oct-Easter, 180. Rest. ♦♦ 50-120.

⛺ ★★★*Port-Leucate* (142 pl.), ☎ 68.40.93.94 ; ★★★*Rives des Corbières* (275 pl.), ☎ 68.86.00.31 ; ★★*Cap Leucate* (450 pl.), ☎ 68.40.01.37 ; ★★*Domino* (33 pl.), ☎ 68.45.70.12.

LÉZIGNAN-CORBIÈRES

Narbonne 24, Carcassonne 38, Paris 871
B2 ✉ 11200

ℹ sq. Marcellin-Albert, ☎ 68.27.05.42.

Hotels :
★★***Tassigny,*** pl. de-Lattre-de-Tassigny, ☎ 68.27.11.51. Visa. 16 rm P ♿ closed 1-15 Sep, 1 week in Feb and Sun eve, 150. Rest. ♦ closed Mon and Sun eve, 50-120.
★***Grand Soleil,*** 32, av. Mal-Foch, ☎ 68.27.01.20. 24 rm P closed Oct, 100. Rest. ♦ 80-130.

Ornaisons, 8 km E :
★★★***Val d'Orbieu*** (Relais du Silence), ☎ 68.27.10.27. AE, DC, Euro, Visa. 18 rm P ♿ closed 1 Dec-20 Mar, 350. Rest. ● ♦♦ In the heart of Corbières vineyards, a quiet and peaceful place : *tarte aux cèpes, foie gras aux raisins,* 145-300.

Youth hostel : *Centre international de Séjour,* 25, rue Marat, B.P. 26, ☎ 68.27.03.34.

⛺ ★★★*La Pinède* (50 pl.), ☎ 68.27.05.08.

LIMOUX

Carcassonne 24, Perpignan 101, Paris 841
A1 ✉ 11300

ℹ prom. Tivoli, ☎ 68.31.11.82 (high season).

SNCF ☎ 68.31.02.17.

Hotels :
★★***Moderne et Pigeon,*** 1, pl. Gal-Leclerc, ☎ 68.31.00.25. AE, DC, Visa. 31 rm P closed 15 Dec-15 Jan, 190. Rest. ♦ ♿ closed Mon low season and Mon noon in Jul-Aug, 50-140.

Couiza, ✉ 11190, 15 km S :
Château des Ducs de Joyeuse, ☎ 68.74.02.80. 35 rm P 16thC fortress of mediaeval style. Interior decoration Renaissance style. Huge fireplaces, 140. Rest. booking necessary, 45-80.

Alet-les-Bains, 18.5 km S :
★***Évêché*** (L.F.), av. N.-Pavillon, ☎ 68.69.90.25. 35 rm P closed 30 Sep-1 Apr, 160. Rest. ♦ 40-130.

⛺ ★★*Du Breil* (50 pl.), ☎ 68.31.13.63 ; Alet-les-Bains : ★★*Charles Clarou* (16 pl.), ☎ 68.69.90.05.

Restaurant :
♦♦ ***Maison de la Blanquette,*** prom. de Tivoli, ☎ 68.31.01.63. Euro, Visa. ♿ closed Wed eve and Oct. Good, simple regional fare, 55-150.

Recommended : *blanquette de Limoux* : *Antech,* domaine de Flassian, ☎ 68.31.15.88 ; *Caudeval,* rte de Carcassonne, ☎ 68.31.02.45 ; *Guinot,* chemin de la Ronde, ☎ 68.31.01.33.

LODÈVE

Montpellier 54, Béziers 64, Paris 815
B1 ✉ 34700

ℹ 7, pl. de la République, ☎ 67 44 07.56.

SNCF ☎ 67.44.30.33.

Hotels :
★★***Croix Blanche,*** 6, av. de Fumel, ☎ 67.44.10.87. 32 rm P closed Dec-Apr, 130. Rest. ♦ Eve only ♿ 40-90.
★★***Nord,*** 18, bd de la Liberté, ☎ 67.44.10.08. AE, Euro, Visa. 19 rm P closed Nov, Sat (low season), 180. Rest. ♦ 40-160.

Saint-Jean-de-la-Blaquière, 16 km SW on the D144 :
★★★***Auberge du Sanglier*** (Relais du Silence), ☎ 67.44.70.51. 10 rm P ♿ closed 1 Nov-15 Mar, 170. Rest. 90-200.

LUNEL

Montpellier 25, Nîmes 31, Paris 741
C1 ✉ 34400

ℹ pl. des Martyrs-de-la-Résistance, ☎ 67.71.01.37.

SNCF ☎ 67.71.11.90.

Hotels :
★★***La Clausade*** (L.F.), 456, av. Col-Simon, ☎ 67.71.05.69. Euro, Visa. 10 rm P ♿ closed 21 Dec-5 Jan, 160. Rest. ♦ closed Sat, Sun and 3 weeks in Aug, 60-120.
★★***Le Palais,*** 12, av. de-Lattre-de-Tassigny, ☎ 67.71.11.39. 26 rm closed 20 Dec-12 Jan, Sun eve and Mon noon low season, 170. Rest. ♦♦ A one-time post-house, now a traditional restaurant of quality, 50-140.

Le Cailar, ✉ 30740, 10 km E :
★★***Sanglier,*** rte d'Arles, ☎ 66.88.05.40. AE, Euro, Visa. 28 rm P ♿ 190. Rest. ♦ 70-150.

⛺ ★★★*Bon Port* (115 pl.), ☎ 67.71.15.65 ; ★★*Municipal* (100 pl.), ☎ 67.71.18.70 ; ★★*Pont de Lunel* (44 pl.), ☎ 67.71.10.22.

MÈZE

Montpellier 34, Béziers 41, Paris 791
13 km SW of Balaruc-les-Bains, C1 ✉ 34140

ℹ 8, rue Massaloup, ☎ 67.43.93.08.

Hotel :
Bouzigues, 5 km E on the N113 :
★★★***Côte Bleue,*** ☎ 67.78.31.42. 32 rm P ♿ closed Feb, 250. Rest. ♦♦ ☎ 67.78.30.87. Closed Tue eve, Wed (ex Jul-Aug), Sun eve and Mon (high season). Book at Mr. Archambaud's to taste the famous oysters of Bouzigues, 130-180.

⛺ ★★*Beau Rivage* (234 pl.), ☎ 67.43.81.48 ; Marseillan, 15 km SW, on D51, ✉ 34340 : ★★★★*les Sirènes* (600 pl.), ☎ 67.94.15.12 ; ★★★★*la Nouvelle Floride* (500 pl.), ☎ 67.94.15.20 ; and 20 sites ★★★/★★

Restaurants :
♦ ***Barbecue,*** 38, rue du Port, ☎ 67.43.84.99. AE, DC, Visa. closed 15-31 Jan, Sun eve and Mon low season, 55-150.

Marseillan, 9 km SW :
◆◆ ***Le Glacier,*** bd V.-Hugo, ☎ 67.77.22.04. ♿ closed Mon. Bistro atmosphere and wonderfully fresh shell-fish, 120-210.

MINERVE

Narbonne 33, Béziers 45, Paris 871
B2 ⊠ 34210 Olonzac

Chambres d'hôtes :
Relais Chantovent, ☎ 68.91.22.96. Euro, Visa. 5 rm closed Feb, Sun eve and Mon (ex Jul-Aug), 100. Rest. ◆ 50-110.

Farmhouse-inn : *domaine du Bois Bas,* ☎ 68.97.14.95. Table d'hôtes, camping and fowl for sale.

MOLITG-LES-BAINS

Prades 7, Perpignan 50, Paris 962
A3 ⊠ 66500 Prades

(all year), ☎ 68.96.10.66.

ⓘ ☎ 68.96.27.58.

Hotels :
★★★★(L) ***Château de Riell*** (Relais et châteaux), ☎ 68.96.20.56.Tx 500705. AE, Visa. 21 rm Ⓟ closed 4 Nov-1 Apr, 700. Rest. ◆◆◆ The gloriously refined setting of this neo-gothic castle is matched by a sumptuous menu : a masterly *ouillade,* succulent desserts and good wines, 210-300.
★★★***Thermal,*** ☎ 68.96.10.66 and 68.05.00.50. Tx 500705. 56 rm Ⓟ closed 31 Oct-1 Apr, 300. Rest. ◆◆ Ⓟ 80-130.

MONT-LOUIS

Prades 36, Perpignan 79, Paris 991
A3 ⊠ 66210

ⓘ ☎ 68.04.21.97.

Hotels :
★★***Clos Cerdan,*** on the N116, ☎ 68.04.23.29. Euro, Visa. 60 rm ♿ closed Nov, 160. Rest. ◆ ♿ 50-90.

La Llagonne, 3 km N on the D118 :
★***Commerce,*** ☎ 68.04.22.04. 31 rm Ⓟ closed 29 Sep-15 Dec and 20 Apr-4 Jun, 210. Rest. ◆◆ ♿ 50-100.
Saint-Pierre-dels-Forcats, 3.5 km S on the D10 and D32 ; 1 570-2 750 m :
★★***Mouli del Riu,*** ☎ 68.04.20.36. 20 rm Ⓟ closed 1 Oct-15 Dec, Wed (low season), 180. Rest. ◆ 80-160.

Les Angles, 10 km NW ; 1 600-2 400 m :
★★***Llaret,*** av. de Balcère, ☎ 68.04.42.02. AE. 28 rm Ⓟ closed Oct-Nov, May, 150. Rest. 70-130.

Restaurant :
Les Angles :
◆◆ ***Remballade,*** rue de la Remballade, old village, ☎ 68.04.43.48. AE, DC, Visa. closed Mon and 1 May-30 Jun and 1 Oct-15 Dec. Cooking over a wood fire in a converted barn, 50-150.

MONTPELLIER

Nîmes 51, Béziers 93, Paris 761
C1 ⊠ 34000

ⓘ 6, rue Maguelone, ☎ 67.58.26.04 ; at the station (C4), ☎ 67.92.90.03, and the Pavillon d'Accueil, rd-pt des Moulins (off map near C4), ☎ 67.65.67.38 (high season).

✈ Montpellier-Fréjorgues, 6, km SE, ☎ 67.65.60.65. *Air France Agency,* ☎ 67.65.43.43. *Air France Agency* in town : 6, rue Boussairolles, ☎ 67.58.81.94.

SNCF (C4), ☎ 67.58.50.50. 67.92.15.16., 67.58.43.06.

rue Jules-Ferry (C4), ☎ 67.92.01.43.

Car-hire : *Budget* train + auto, cour Colin, rue Alexis-Alquié, ☎ 67.64.37.29, at the station, ☎ 67.50.08.54, and at the airport.

Hotels :
★★★★***Métropole*** (Mapotel), 3, rue du Clos-René (C3), ☎ 67.58.11.22. Tx 480410. AE, DC, Euro, Visa. 92 rm Ⓟ 540. Rest. ◆◆◆ ***la Closerie,*** 120-300.
● ★★★***Noailles,*** 2, rue des Écoles-Centrales (C2), ☎ 67.60.49.80. AE, DC, Euro, Visa. 30 rm ♿ closed 20 Dec-13 Jan, 300.
★★★***Domaine des Brousses,*** 4 km E, rte de Vauguières, ☎ 67.65.77.66. AE, DC. 18 rm Ⓟ closed Oct-Apr, 370. Rest. ◆◆ ***le Mas,*** ☎ 67.65.52.27. Delicious, original fare in this former farmhouse, 150-210.
★★★***George V*** (Inter-Hôtel), 42, av. St-Lazare (C1), ☎ 67.72.35.91. Tx 480953. AE, DC, Euro, Visa. 39 rm Ⓟ closed 22 Dec-6 Jan, 280.
★★***Myrtes,*** 10, rue de la Cour-du-Recteur, 5, av. Lepic (B2), ☎ 67.42.60.11. Visa. 30 rm Ⓟ ♿ closed Feb, 200.
★★***Parc,*** 8, rue Achille-Bégé (off map near A1), ☎ 67.41.16.49. 19 rm Ⓟ ♿ 200.

Clapiers, ⊠ 34170 Castelnau-le-Lez ; 8 km on the N113 and D112 :
★★★***Las Couréjas,*** ☎ 67.59.10.93. Euro, Visa. 30 rm Ⓟ closed 19-28 Dec, 15 Jan-10 Feb, 340. Rest. ◆ closed Sun eve and Sat noon (low season), 80-160.

Pérols, ⊠ 34470, 6 km SE :
★★★***Sun Hôtel,*** rte de Carnon, ☎ 67.50.03.04. Tx 480652. AE, DC, Euro, Visa. 77 rm Ⓟ ♿ 370. Rest. ◆◆ 120-210.

Ⲁ ★★★*Montaubérou* (136 pl.), ☎ 67.65.40.60.

Restaurants :
◆◆◆ ***Réserve Rimbaud,*** 820, av. de St-Maur-Quartier des Aubes (off map near C1), ☎ 67.72.52.53. AE, DC, Visa. ♿ closed Sun eve, Mon, 2-10 Jan. Spec : *gigot de mer aux herbes de la garrigue,* 175-230.
◆◆◆ ***Ayamé,*** 20, pl. des Martyrs (B2), ☎ 67.60.40.51. AE, DC, Euro, Visa. ♿ closed 3 Nov-2 Dec, 3-12 Jun, Sun and Mon. Refined Japanese cooking under vaulted ceilings, 120-150.
● ◆◆ **Chandelier,** 3, rue Leenhardt (B4), ☎ 67.92.61.62. AE, DC, Euro, Visa ; closed Sun, Mon noon, 1-30 Aug. Charming restaurant. Quality cooking and interesting menu : *mosaïque de lapereau au foie gras, ragoût de langouste aux herbes en lasagnes,* 90-260.
◆◆ ***Diligence,*** 2, pl. Pétrarque (B2), ☎ 67.66.12.21. ♿ Interesting menus under 15thC vaulted ceilings : *magret de canard au sauternes et aux pistaches, daurade vapeur aux deux poivrons,* 90-160.
◆◆ ***Table de la Reine,*** 8, rue du Bras-de-Fer (C3), ☎ 67.60.62.80. AE, Euro, Visa ; closed Sun and Aug. Spec : *brochette st-pierre,* 80-180.
◆ ***Louvre,*** 2, rue de la Vieille (C3), ☎ 67.60.59.37. Visa. ♿ closed 2 weeks in May, 2 weeks in Oct, Sun and Mon, 80-170.
◆ ***Chez Marceau,*** 7, pl. Chapelle-Neuve (C1), ☎ 67.66.08.09. AE, Euro, Visa ; closed 22 Dec-30 Jan, 1 week in Feb and Sun. Salad luncheons, 40-80.

Castries, ⊠ 34160, 12.5 km :
● ◆◆ ***L'Art du Feu,*** 13, av. du 8-Mai-1945, ☎ 67.70.05.97. AE, Euro, Visa. ♿ closed Wed, 1-31 Aug, Feb school hols. Simple cooking, low prices, 60-120.

Bicycle hire : 6, rue des Écoles-Laïques (C1), ☎ 67.66.05.59., and S.N.C.F. luggage office, ☎ 67.92.15.16., ext 509.

Recommended : *Sorbets de Fréjorgues,* marché Gare, Z.I. des Prés d'Avoine, ☎ 67.58.72.98 ; *Jardin des Glaces* (ice-cream parlour), on the Esplanade, 25, bd Sarrail (C2) ; *Pinto,* 14, rue de l'Argenterie, ☎ 67.60.57.65 ; *le Buron,* polygone shopping centre : cheesemonger.

NARBONNE

Béziers 27, Carcassonne 61, Paris 849
B2 ⊠ 11100

ℹ pl. R.-Salengro (B2), ☎ 68.65.15.60.

SNCF (B2), ☎ 68.62.50.50, 68.32.12.47, 68.32.38.83.

Bus quai Vallière (C3), ☎ 68.32.07.60.

Car-hire : *Budget* train + auto, 32, rue Ancienne-Porte-Neuve, ☎ 68.32.04.65, at the station, ☎ 68.32.14.87.

Hotels :
● ★★★***Résidence,*** 6, rue du 1er-Mai (B4), ☎ 68.32.19.41. Tx 500441. AE, Visa. 26 rm Ⓟ ♿ closed 4 Jan-4 Feb, 260.
★★★***Languedoc*** (Mapotel), 22, bd Gambetta (C3), ☎ 68.65.14.74. AE, DC, Euro, Visa. 45 rm ♿ 250. Rest. ♦♦ closed Jan, Fri eve and Sat low season, 55-150.
★★***Midi*** (L.F.), 4, av. de Toulouse (A3), ☎ 68.41.04.62. Tx 500401. AE, DC, Euro, Visa. 47 rm ♿ closed 15 Dec-15 Jan, Sun (ex Jul-Aug-Sep), 160. Rest. ♦ ♿ closed 20 Dec-31 Jan and Sun, 50-130.
★★***Régent,*** 13, av. de Suffren (C2), ☎ 68.32.02.41. Visa. 15 rm closed 20 Dec-5 Jan, 150.

Youth hostel : pl. R.-Salengro (B2), ☎ 68.32.01.00.

⛺ Coursan : ★★*Municipal* (75 pl.), ☎ 68.33.51.59 ; Narbonne-Plage, 13 km E. : ★★★★*la Falaise* (336 pl.), ☎ 68.49.80.77 ; ★★★★*la Nautique* (40 pl.), ☎ 68.65.48.19 ; ★★★*Languedoc* (170 pl.), ☎ 68.65.24.65 ; ★★★*Mimosas* (100 pl.), ☎ 68.49.03.72 ; ★★★*Soleil d'Or* (212 pl.), ☎ 68.49.86.21 ; ★★*Saint-Solvayre* (100 pl.), ☎ 68.32.08.19 ; ★★*Roches Grises* (130 pl.), ☎ 68.32.04.67.

Restaurants :
● ♦♦♦ ***Réverbère*** (Claude Giraud), 4, pl. des Jacobins (C3), ☎ 68.32.29.18. AE, DC, Visa. ♿ H.-C. Giraud proposes one of the tastiest and least expensive "sample-menus" in France, which changes every month : *homard aux truffes en habit de choux verts, lobe de foie gras vinaigrette de mousserons, pigeonneau à la lie de genièvre.* Good choice of coffees and teas, 150-400.
♦ ***Alsace,*** 2, av. P.-Sémard (C1), ☎ 68.65.10.24. AE, DC, Euro, Visa. ♿ closed Mon eve and Tue low season ; 18 Nov-18 Dec. Spec : *salade de fruits de mer, ragoût de palourdes,* 50-180.
● ♦ ***Le Saint-Germain,*** 22, rue Ancienne-Porte-de-Béziers (B2), ☎ 68.32.51.52. ♿ closed Sun noon and Tue. We must encourage these nice young people lost in the old part of Narbonne. Good and simple cooking, nice *entrecôtes,* 120-210.

Recommended : *Pâtisserie Louvel,* 8, rue du Pont-des-Marchands, ☎ 68.32.03.47.

PALAVAS-LES-FLOTS

Sète 28, Nîmes 59, Paris 769
12 km S of Montpellier, C1 ⊠ 34250

ℹ hôtel de ville, ☎ 67.68.02.34.

Hotels :
★★★***Amérique,*** av. F.-Fabrège, ☎ 67.68.04.39. AE, DC, Euro, Visa. 33 rm Ⓟ ♿ closed 17 Dec-3 Jan, 220.
★★***Mar y Sol,*** 8, bd Mal-Joffre, ☎ 67.68.00.46 and 67.68.02.01., Tx 485082. AE, DC, Visa. 39 rm Ⓟ ♿ 250.
★★***Languedoc,*** 4, rue Carrière, ☎ 67.68.03.45. Euro, Visa. 21 rm bordering the canal ; closed Dec-Jan, 150.

⛺ ★★★*Roquilles* (792 pl.), ☎ 67.68.03.47 ; ★★★*Palavas* (400 pl.), ☎ 67.68.01.28 ; ★★★*Saint-Maurice* (150 pl.), ☎ 67.68.94.61 ; ★★*Montpellier-Plage* (685 pl.), ☎ 67.68.00.91.

Restaurants :
♦♦ ***Maison de l'Huître,*** 3, av. Foch, ☎ 67.68.09.85. AE, DC, Euro, Visa. ♿ closed Mon (30 Sep-30 Mar), 22 Dec-26 Jan. *Bouillabaisse,* shell-fish, fish, 70-140.
♦♦ ***Sphinx,*** quai P.-Cunq, ☎ 67.68.00.21. AE, DC, Visa. ♿ closed 15 Dec-20 Jan. *Bouillabaisse,* fish, 150-250.
♦ ***Le Chalut,*** 15, quai P.-Cunq, ☎ 67.68.00.03. Visa. ♿ *Grillades aux sarments,* 100-200.

PERPIGNAN

Béziers 93, Carcassonne 113, Paris 909
B3 ⊠ 66000

ℹ quai de-Lattre-de-Tassigny (A2), ☎ 68.34.29.94, and on the autoroute Catalane, ☎ 68.21.60.05.

✈ Perpignan-Rivesaltes, 6 km N, ☎ 68.61.28.98.

SNCF (off map near A2), ☎ 68.54.50.50, 68.34.73.11.

Bus 2, bd St-Assiscle, ☎ 68.54.54.66.

Car-hire : *Budget* train + auto, 17, rue du Lt-Pruneta, ☎ 68.34.25.43, at the station, ☎ 68.51.10.44, and at the airport.

Hotels :
★★★***Loge,*** pl. de la Loge (B2), ☎ 68.34.54.84. AE, DC, Euro, Visa. 29 rm. Attractive setting 230.
★★★***Windsor*** (Inter-Hôtel), 8, bd Wilson (B1), ☎ 68.51.18.65. Tx 500701. AE, Visa. 57 rm ♿ closed 1-15 Feb, 300.
★★★***Park,*** 18, bd J.-Bourrat (C1), ☎ 68.35.14.14. AE, DC, Euro, Visa. 67 rm Ⓟ ♿ 200. Rest. ♦ ***le Chapon Fin,*** closed Sat eve and Sun, 90-200.
★★★***Mondial,*** 40, bd G.-Clemenceau (A1-2), ☎ 68.34.23.45. Tx 500920. Visa. 40 rm Ⓟ 220.
★★★***Mas des Arcades,*** av. d'Espagne (off map near A1), ☎ 68.85.11.11. Tx 500176. 128 rm Ⓟ ♿ closed 20 Dec-15 Jan, 280. Rest. ♿ 80-150.
● ★★***Athéna,*** 1, rue Quéya (B2), ☎ 68.34.37.63. AE, DC, Euro, Visa. 35 rm Former private mansion, 170.
★★***Pyrénées,*** 122, av. Torcatis (A1), ☎ 68.61.19.66. 22 rm Ⓟ 130.

Rivesaltes, 10 km N :
★★***Alta Riba,*** av. de la Gare, ☎ 68.64.01.17. DC, Visa. 54 rm Ⓟ ♿ closed mid-Dec-mid-Jan, Sun eve and Mon noon, Fri eve (1 Oct-31 May), 170. Rest. ♦ 50-140.
★***Debèze,*** 11, rue A.-Barbès, ☎ 68.64.05.88. AE, DC, Euro, Visa. 16 rm Ⓟ 160.

Youth hostel, av. de Grande-Bretagne (A1), in the parc de la Pépinière, ☎ 68.34.63.32.

⛺ ★★*La Garrigole* (22 pl.), ☎ 68.34.29.94 ; ★★*Catalan* (80 pl.), ☎ 68.63.16.92.

Restaurants :
● ♦♦ ***François Villon,*** 1, rue du Four-St-Jean (B1-2), ☎ 68.51.18.43. ♿ closed Sun, Mon

and 14 Jul-15 Aug. Thanks to Pierre Charreton, this old 16thC convent has become a fine gastronomic place : *brochette de porc à l'orange sauce diable,* a good menu, 130-250.
● ♦♦ ***L'Apéro,*** 40, rue de la Fusterie (B2), ☎ 68.51.21.14. Euro, Visa. ♿ closed Sun and Mon noon. Creative dishes served in a 1900's setting. Spec : *ouillade de poissons,* 100-130.
♦♦ ***Supion,*** 71, av. du Mal-Leclerc (A1), ☎ 68.34.53.42. AE, DC. Ⓟ ♿ closed Mon. Period decor and a classic menu. Spec : *saumon glacé Béatrice, assiette de St-Jacques aux truffes,* 100-350.
♦♦ ***Festin de Pierre,*** 7, rue du Théâtre (B2), ☎ 68.51.28.74. AE, DC, Euro, Visa. Ⓟ closed Sun noon and Wed (summer), Tue eve and Wed (winter) and Feb. Market-fresh produce and fish in a 15thC house, 120-200.
♦♦ ***La Serre,*** 2 *bis,* rue Dagobert (A3), ☎ 68.34.33.02. AE, DC, Euro, Visa. ♿ closed Sun. Spec : *avocat au gratin, canard au cidre,* 75-130.
♦♦ ***Pizzeria Luigi,*** 11, quai Battlo, ☎ 68.35.15.56. AE, DC, Euro, Visa ; closed Mon eve, Tue and Wed, 20 Dec-5 Jan. It is hard to find better pizzas anywhere else. Other dishes are as good and prices low, 90-130.
♦♦ ***Antiquaires,*** pl. Desprès, ☎ 68.34.06.58. closed Sun eve and Mon ; 1-15 Jul. Fish, turbot in champagne, 100-160.
♦♦ ***Le Lyonnais,*** 95, bd A.-Briand (C3), ☎ 68.67.09.80. Closed Sun eve and Mon. Spec : *émincé de rognons de veau au beaujolais,* 120-210.

Recommended : *Comteroux,* av. d'Espagne, Catalan furniture.

PÉZENAS

Béziers 23, Montpellier 52, Paris 809
C1 ✉ 34120

ⓘ pl. du Marché-au-Blé, ☎ 67.98.11.82.

SNCF ☎ 67.98.12.21.

Hotel :
★★***Genieys*** (L.F.), 9, av. A.-Briand, ☎ 67.98.13.99. AE, DC, Euro, Visa. 20 rm Ⓟ closed 4 Nov-25 Dec, Sun eve, Mon low season, 160. Rest. ♦ ♿ Good, simple fare, 50-200.

Farmhouse-inn, 4, rte de Nizas, 34720, Caux, 8 km NW on D13 E, ☎ 67.98.40.44. Languedoc regional specialities.

Recommended : wines : M. Jany, 34230 Paulhan, 10 km N : château de la Condamine-Bertrand (white wines), comte d'Ormesson, château de St-Ferreol.

PORT-BARCARÈS

Perpignan 21, Narbonne 64, Paris 190
B3 ✉ 66420

ⓘ Sea-front, ☎ 68.86.16.56 and 68.86.10.50, and Suisse and Bordeaux shopping centre, ☎ 68.86.18.23.

Hotels :
★★★***Lydia Playa*** (P.L.M.), la Grande-Plage, ☎ 68.86.25.25. Tx 500837. AE, DC, Visa. 192 rm Ⓟ ♿ closed 30 Oct-20 Apr, 480. Rest. ♦♦ 90-130.
★★***Front de Mer,*** in the village, ☎ 68.86.13.84. 30 rm, closed 1 Nov-20 May, 260.

Barcarès, 3.5 km S :
★★***Casa Blanca,*** 6, bd de la Côte-Vermeille, ☎ 68.86.13.18. Visa. 21 rm Ⓟ closed 30 Sep-1 Apr, 130.

⛺ ★★★*Le Paris* (176 pl.), ☎ 68.86.15.50 ; ★★★*Tamaris* (330 pl.), ☎ 68.86.08.18.

Restaurant :
♦♦ ***Don Quichotte,*** ☎ 68.86.06.57. Ⓟ closed Wed low season, Jan. Fish, *bouillabaisse,* 100-155.

PORT-VENDRES

Perpignan 31, Prades 68, Paris 941
B3 ✉ 66660

ⓘ quai Forgas, ☎ 68.82.07.54.

SNCF ☎ 68.82.00.42.

Hotels :
★★***Tamarins,*** plage des Tamarins, ☎ 68.82.01.24. Visa. 37 rm Ⓟ closed Oct-Easter, 210. Rest. 60-180.
★★***St-Elme,*** 2, quai Forgas, ☎ 68.82.01.07. AE, DC, Euro, Visa. 30 rm Ⓟ 180.
★***Commerce,*** 2, rue Jules-Ferry, ☎ 68.82.00.29. Visa. 28 rm, closed 1 Oct-1 Apr, 180.

⛺ ★★*Clos St-Elme* (20 pl.), ☎ 68.82.00.85 ; ★★*Presqu'île* (162 pl.), ☎ 68.82.11.40.

PRATS-DE-MOLLO-LA-PRESTE

Perpignan 61, Prades 83, Paris 967
A3 ✉ 66230

(1 Apr-1 Dec), ☎ 68.57.21.21.

ⓘ foyer rural, pl. Le Firal, ☎ 68.39.70.83.

Hotels :
★★★***Park d'Estamarius,*** access by the pont d'Espagne, ☎ 68.39.70.04. DC. 77 rm. 12thC commandery Ⓟ ♿ closed 1 Oct-30 Apr. 200. Rest. ♦♦ Mountain river trout, 60-100.
★★***Touristes*** (L.F.), 1, av. du Haut-Vallespir, ☎ 68.39.72.12. AE, DC, Euro, Visa. 44 rm Ⓟ closed 1 Nov-1 Apr, 170. Rest. ♦ 60-140.

⛺ ★★*Can Nadal* (85 pl.), ☎ 68.39.70.89 ; ★★*St-Martin* (75 pl.), ☎ 68.39.73.08.

QUILLAN

Carcassonne 51, Perpignan 74, Paris 961
A2-3 ✉ 11500

ⓘ pl. de la Gare, ☎ 68.20.07.78.

SNCF ☎ 68.20.05.63.

Hotels :
★★★***Chaumière*** (Inter-Hôtel, L.F.), 25, bd Ch.-de-Gaulle, ☎ 68.20.17.90. 18 rm Ⓟ ♿ closed 2 Nov-15 Dec, 200. Rest. ♦♦ 50-250.
★★***Cartier*** (L.F.), 31, bd Ch.-de-Gaulle, ☎ 68.20.05.14. Euro, Visa. 35 rm Ⓟ ♿ closed 15 Dec-15 Mar and Sat noon low season, 200. Rest. ♦ ***les Trois Quilles*** ♿ 50-150.
★★***La Pierre-Lys,*** rte de Carcassonne, ☎ 68.20.08.65. 18 rm Ⓟ closed 18 Nov-10 Dec, 100. Rest. ♦♦ ♿ Spec : *salade "Pierre-Lys", fondue bruxelloise,* 40-150.

Belcaire, 11340 Espezel, 27 km SW :
★***Bayle*** (L.F.), ☎ 68.20.31.05. Euro, Visa. 16 rm Ⓟ ♿ closed 3 Nov-13 Dec, Fri eve and Sat noon low seaon, 130. Rest. ♦ Regional dishes, 50-100.

⛺ ★★★*Les Sapinettes* (90 pl.), ☎ 68.20.13.52.

Table d'hôte : Saint-Julia-de-Bec, on the D609, 6 km SE : *Moulin du Roc,* ☎ 68.20.07.15.

RENNES-LES-BAINS

Quillan 20, Carcassonne 47, Paris 864
8.5 km SE of Couiza, A2 ✉ 11190

(1 Apr-13 Nov), ☎ 68.69.87.01.

ⓘ mairie, ☎ 68.69.87.95.

Hotel :
★***France,*** ☎ 68.69.87.03. 25 rm ⚟ ♿ 180. Rest. 45-180.

ROQUEBRUN

Béziers 30, Narbonne 51, Paris 854
17 km NE of Saint-Chinian, B1-2
✉ 34460 Cessenon

Hotel :
★★***Petit Nice*** (L.F.), ☎ 67.89.64.27. Euro, Visa. 35 rm ⚟ P ♿ closed 15 Dec-15 Mar, 190. Rest. ♦ closed Sat (ex Jun-Sep), 50-150.

⛺ ★★*Le Nice* (40 pl.), ☎ 67.89.61.99.

SAILLAGOUSE

Prades 48, Perpignan 91, Paris 1 003
9 km NE of Bourg-Madame, A3 ✉ 66800

ℹ mairie, ☎ 68.04.72.89 (high season).

SNCF ☎ 68.04.72.88.

Hotels :
★★***Planotel,*** rue du Torrent, ☎ 68.04.72.08. Visa. 20 rm ⚟ P ♿ closed 20 Sep-20 Dec, Easter-1 Jun, 180.
★★***Planes*** (old Cerdane style house), ☎ 68.04.72.08. 23 rm ⚟ P ♿ 180. Rest. ♦♦ Also the Planotel restaurant ♿ closed 15 Oct-15 Dec, 70-160.

Llo, 2 km SE on D33 :
★★★***Auberge Atalaya*** (Relais du Silence, Châteaux-hôtels), ☎ 68.04.70.04. DC. 9 rm ⚟ P closed 5 Nov-20 Dec, 260. Rest. ♦♦ closed Mon and Tue noon. Good mountain dishes, 100-175.

Eyne, 7 km E on the D33 :
★★★***Auberge d'Eyne*** (Châteaux-hôtels), ☎ 68.04.71.12. Visa. 11 rm ⚟ P closed 15 Nov-15 Dec, 260. Rest. ♦♦ Beautiful mountain grange, 80-120.
★★***Roc Blanc,*** Super-Eyne, ☎ 68.04.72.72. AE. 23 rm ⚟ P closed 15 Sep-20 Dec ; mid-Apr, mid-Jun, 200. Rest. ♦♦ 50-80.

Bourg-Madame, ✉ 66760, 9 km SW N116 :
★★***Hostellerie Cerdane,*** bd de Lax, ☎ 68.04.53.16. Visa. 34 rm P 120. Rest. ♦♦ 60-120.
★★***Célisol,*** av. des Guinguettes, ☎ 68.04.53.70. 14 rm P 170.

Youth hostel, rte d'Estavar, ☎ 68.04.71.69.

⛺ ★★★*Cerdan* (50 pl.), ☎ 68.04.70.46 ; ★★*Segré* (80 pl.), ☎ 68.04.74.72.

SAINT-CYPRIEN-PLAGE

Perpignan 15, Prades 57, Paris 926
B3 ✉ 66750

ℹ quai A.-Rimbaud, ☎ 68.21.01.33, and quai de la Pêche, ☎ 68.21.08.14.

Hotels :
★★★***Mas d'Huston,*** golf de Saint-Cyprien, ☎ 68.21.01.71. Tx 500834. AE, DC, Euro, Visa. 50 rm ⚟ P ♿ closed 2 Feb-1 Mar, 460. Rest. ● ♦♦ Enjoyable fare, 100-200.
★★***Belvédère,*** rue P.-Benoît, ☎ 68.21.05.93. 30 rm ⚟ P closed 1 Oct-1 Jun, 200. Rest. ♦ 50-220.
★★***Glycines,*** 2, rue E.-Delacroix, ☎ 68.21.00.11. Visa. 37 rm ⚟ P ♿ closed Oct-Apr, 220. Rest. ♦♦ 70-160.
★★***Lagune,*** B.P. 69, Les Capellans, ☎ 68.21.24.24. 30 rm ⚟ closed 1 Oct-Easter, 390.

⛺ ★★★★*Cala Gogo* (500 pl.), ☎ 68.21.07.12 ; ★★★*Bosc d'En Roug* (660 pl.), ☎ 68.21.11.82 ; 4 sites ★★

SAINT-PONS-DE-THOMIÈRES

Béziers 51, Narbonne 52, Paris 878
B1 ✉ 34220

ℹ pl. du Foirail, ☎ 67.97.06.65 (high season).

Hotels :
★★★***Château de Ponderach*** (Relais et châteaux), rte de Narbonne, ☎ 67.97.02.57. AE, DC, Euro. 12 rm ⚟ P ♿ closed 15 Oct-Easter, 320. Rest. ♦♦♦ Spec : *mousse de poireau truffé, sole en croûte,* 130-300.

Col du Cabaretou, 10 km N on the D907 :
★★***Cabaretou,*** rte de la Salvetat, ☎ 67.97.02.31. 10 rm ⚟ P closed 15 Nov-1 Mar, Wed, 230. Rest. ♦♦ Book ahead, 220-310.

SALSES

Perpignan 16, Narbonne 47, Paris 892
B3 ✉ 66600

ℹ 13, pl. St-Jacques, ☎ 68.38.66.13.

SNCF ☎ 68.38.60.14.

Hotels :
★★★***Relais du Roussillon,*** RN9, ☎ 68.38.60.67. 56 rm P 180. Rest. 80-130.
★★***Relais Castel,*** former road N9, ☎ 68.38.60.26. 30 rm P ♿ closed 15 Sep-15 Jun, 180.

⛺ ★★*La Montagnette* (50 pl.), ☎ 68.38.64.06 ; ★★*le Roussillon* (110 pl.), ☎ 68.38.60.72.

La SALVETAT-SUR-AGOUT

Béziers 72, Narbonne 73, Paris 732
21 km NW of Saint-Pons-de-Thomières, B1 ♥
✉ 34330

ℹ ☎ 67.97.64.44.

Hotels :
★★***Auberge de la Resse*** (L.F.), rte d'Angles, ☎ 67.97.61.98. Visa. 22 rm P ♿ closed Nov-Mar, 180. Rest. ♦ ♿ 60-100.
★***Cros,*** rte de Lacaune, ☎ 67.97.60.21. AE, DC, Euro, Visa. 23 rm P closed 31 Oct-1 May, 100. Rest. ♦ Very good value, 50-130.

⛺ ★★*La Blaquière* (60 pl.), ☎ 67.97.61.29 ; ★★Municipal *des Bouldouires* (100 pl.), ☎ 67.97.62.30 ; ★★*Goudal* (100 pl.), ☎ 67.97.60.44.

Restaurant :
Soulié, 9.5 km S on the D150 :
♦♦ ***Moulin de Vergougniac,*** ☎ 67.97.05.62. P closed Mon eve and Tue, 15 Jan-3 Mar, 90-150.

SÈTE

Montpellier 34, Béziers 53, Paris 791
C2 ✉ 34200

ℹ 22, quai d'Alger (C3), ☎ 67.74.73.00, and pl. A.-Briand (B2), ☎ 67.74.05.86.

SNCF (C1), ☎ 67.48.62.57, 67.48.64.62.

⛴ Moroccan line, 22, quai d'Alger, ☎ 67.74.73.00. Algerian line, at the port, ☎ 67.74.70.55.

Car-hire : *Budget* train + auto, at the station, ☎ 67.74.21.74.

Hotels :
★★★***Grand Hôtel,*** 17, quai Mal-de-Lattre-de-Tassigny (B2), ☎ 67.74.71.77. Tx 480225. AE, DC, Euro, Visa. 51 rm ⚟ ♿ closed 20 Dec-1 Jan, 290. Rest. ♦♦ ***la Rotonde.*** ♿ closed Sun end Sep-Easter, 60-100.

★★***Orque Bleue,*** 10, quai Aspirant-Herber (C3), ☎ 67.74.72.13. AE, DC, Visa. 30 rm ☼ ✂ closed 10 Jan-20 Mar and Sun low season, 345.
★★***Régina,*** 6, bd D.-Casanova (A1), ☎ 67.74.31.41. AE, DC, Visa. 20 rm ✂ closed 5 Nov-20 dec ; 5-20 Jan, 200.
★***Dôme,*** 29, av. V.-Hugo (C1-2), ☎ 67.74.91.78. 16 rm ✂ 150. Rest. ♦ 80-100.

On the corniche, 2 km :
★★★***Impérial*** (Mapotel), pl. E.-Herriot, ☎ 67.53.28.32. Tx 480046. 43 rm 🅿 ♿ 385.
★★***Tritons,*** bd Joliot-Curie, ☎ 67.53.03.98. Visa. 40 rm 🅿 ✂ closed Oct-Apr, 270.
★★***Bosphore,*** la Corniche, ☎ 67.53.05.53. AE, DC. 15 rm 🅿 190. Rest. closed 24 Sep-15 Feb, 60-160.
★★***Sables d'Or,*** pl. E.-Herriot, ☎ 67.53.09.98. Visa. 30 rm ☼ 🅿 ♿ 250.

Frontignan, ✉ 34110, 7 km NE on the N112 :
★★★***Balajan*** (Inter-Hôtel), ☎ 67.48.13.99. Visa. 21 rm 🅿 ♨ ♿ closed 26 Dec-1 Jan, 1 Feb-6 Mar, 290. Rest. ♦♦ closed Mon noon, 70-160.

Youth hostel : rue du Gal-Revest (A2-3), ☎ 67.53.46.68, on the Mt St-Clair, which looks out over the town, the sea and Thau Lagoon ; closed 1 Dec-15 Jan.

⛺ ★★★★*Castellas* (896 pl.), ☎ 67.53.26.24 ; and 4 sites ★★

Restaurants :
● ♦♦ ***La Palangrotte,*** 1, rampe P.-Valéry (B3), ☎ 67.74.80.35. DC. ☼ ♿ closed Mon 15 Jan-15 Feb and Sun low season. The young cook A. Gemignani uses only high quality produce : fresh shell-fish from the Thau lagoon, delicious fish, very light fresh pastas, perfect service, commedia dell'arte decor, 90-200.
♦♦ ***La Rascasse,*** 27, quai Gal-Durand (B3), ☎ 67.74.38.46. AE, DC, Visa. ☼ of the marina. ♿ closed Thu. Book ahead. Menu includes shellfish, 60-180.
♦ ***Alsacien,*** 25, rue P.-Sémard (C2), ☎ 67.74.77.94. Closed Sun eve and Mon, 10 Jun-7 Jul, 23 Dec-3 Jan. For choucroute-lovers ; very good value, 80-200.

Recommended : *Capecchi,* cake and pastry shop, 9, av. Victor-Hugo, ☎ 67.74.57.27.

SIGEAN

Narbonne 21, Perpignan 40, Paris 866
B2 ✉ 11130

Hotels :
★★★***Château de Villefalse*** (Château-hôtel), rte de Narbonne, ☎ 68.48.21.53. DC, Euro, Visa. 19 rm 🅿 ♨ 🌳 📺 ♿ closed Nov-Feb and Tue and Wed noon low season, 300. Rest. ♦♦ Attentively prepared fare, 100-200.

Port-la-Nouvelle, ✉ 11210, 9 km E :
★★★***Méditerranée*** (Mapotel), ☎ 68.48.03.08. AE, DC, Euro, Visa. 32 rm ☼ 🅿 closed 20 Nov-20 Dec, 200. Rest. ♦♦ Regional cooking, 60-140.

⛺ ★★*Municipal* (100 pl.), ☎ 68.48.20.04 ; Port-la-Nouvelle : ★★★*Cap-du-Roc* (109 pl.), ☎ 68.48.00.98 ; ★★★*Côte Vermeille* (334 pl.), ☎ 68.48.05.80.

VALRAS-PLAGE

Béziers 15, Montpellier 72, Paris 830
B2 ✉ 34350

ℹ pl. Cassin, ☎ 67.32.36.04.

Hotels :
★★★***Mira-Mar,*** 1, bd Jean-Moulin, ☎ 67.32.00.31. AE, Euro, Visa. 52 rm ☼ 🅿 closed 30 Sep-15 Mar, 260. Rest. ♦♦ ♿ 70-160.
★★***Plage*** (L.F.), 3, av. St-Saëns, ☎ 67.32.08.37. AE, DC, Euro, Visa. 20 rm, closed 15 Nov-15 dec, 200. Rest. ♦ ♿ 60-180.
★★***Moderne,*** pl. Gal-de-Gaulle, ☎ 67.32.25.86. AE, Euro, Visa. 24 rm 🅿 ♿ closed Oct-1 Jun, 200. Rest. 40-100.

⛺ ★★★★*La Yole* (1 000 pl.), ☎ 67.32.14.47 ; ★★★*Méditerranée* (300 pl.), ☎ 67.32.36.00 ; ★★*Valras* (333 pl.), ☎ 67.32.22.31 ; ★★*le Port* (50 pl.), ☎ 67.32.08.98.

VERNET-LES-BAINS

Prades 12, Perpignan 55, Paris 967
A3 ♥ ✉ 66500 Prades

♨ (year round), ☎ 68.05.52.24.

ℹ 1, sq. Mal-Joffre, ☎ 68.05.55.35.

SNCF ☎ 68.96.09.18.

🚌 ☎ 68.05.52.24.

Hotels :
★★★***Mas Fleuri*** (Relais du Silence), 25, bd Clemenceau, ☎ 68.05.51.94. AE, DC, Visa. 30 rm 🅿 ♨ 🌳 ✂ 📺 ♿ closed 2 Nov-Easter, 310.
★★★***Comte Guifred de Conflent*** (collège d'Application hôtelière - hotel training centre), av. des Thermes, ☎ 68.05.51.37. DC, Visa. 10 rm 🅿 ♨ 🌳 ♿ closed 1 Nov-15 Dec, 230. Rest. 20-130.
★★***Princess,*** rue des Lavandières, ☎ 68.05.56.22. Visa. 23 rm 🅿 🌳 solarium terrace ; closed 1 Nov-31 Mar, 170.
★★***Thalassa,*** bd Clemenceau, ☎ 68.05.55.42. AE, DC, Euro, Visa. 12 rm 🅿 🌳 closed Dec-Mar, 175. Rest. ♦♦ 70-160.
★***Angleterre,*** av. Burnay, ☎ 68.05.50.58. 20 rm ♨ ✂ closed 26 Oct-2 May, 110. Rest. ♿ 65-100.

Casteil, 2.5 km S on the D116 :
★***Molière,*** ☎ 68.05.50.97. Visa. 12 rm 🅿 ♨ 🌳 ✂ ♿ closed 20 Oct-15 Dec, 120. Rest. 40-150.

Sahorre, 66360 Olette, 4.5 km SW on the D27 :
★***Châtaigneraie,*** ☎ 68.05.51.04. 8 rm ☼ 🅿 ♨ 🌳 ♿ closed 1 Oct-Easter, 100. Rest. ♦ closed Tue, 80-130.

⛺ ★★*Camp del Bosc* (110 pl.), ☎ 68.05.54.54 ; ★★*Fontanelle,* Sahorre (50 pl.), ☎ 68.05.53.15 ; ★★*Cady,* Casteil (83 pl.), ☎ 68.05.52.71.

VILLEFRANCHE-DE-CONFLENT

Prades 6, Perpignan 49, Paris 961
A3 ✉ 66500 Prades

ℹ pl. de la Mairie, ☎ 68.96.10.78.

SNCF ☎ 68.96.09.18.

Hotels :
★★***Vauban,*** 5, pl. de l'Église, ☎ 68.96.18.03 or 68.96.14.47. Euro, Visa. 16 rm 🅿 🌳 150.

Olette, ✉ 66360, 10 km SW :
★***Fontaine,*** pl. de la Victoire, ☎ 68.97.03.67. DC, Euro, Visa. 10 rm 🅿 🌳 ♿ closed Jan and Wed (Oct-May), 120. Rest. ● ♦♦ Spec : *magret de canard aux figues, homard au beurre de truffes,* 100-300.

Restaurants :
♦♦ ***Au Grill,*** 81, rue St-Jean, ☎ 68.96.17.65. Euro, Visa ; closed Sun eve, Mon and 11 Nov-10 Jan. Catalan specialities, 60-110.
♦ ***Auberge Saint-Paul,*** pl. de l'Église, ☎ 68.96.30.95. ♿ closed Wed low season and Jan. Regional cooking, 40-110.

The Limousin Region

Land of trees and water — this slightly hackneyed phrase sums up the two outstanding characteristics of Limousin. Water everywhere you look, welling up from thousands of springs, carving out valleys and gorges in its path towards the Loire or the Garonne rivers, irrigating sloping meadows dotted with reservoirs and strings of tranquil mirror-smooth lakes reflecting the sky. Here and there the hiss of the turbines gives way to the creaking of an old moss-covered waterwheel, or the tuneful murmurs of waterfalls and ancient wishing wells reputed to cure a whole host of human ills. Limousin is also a region of trees, thickets, and dense groves, narrow roads bordered with hedgerows and great stands of beeches, oaks and chestnut trees.

The gorges of the Dordogne and Maronne rivers, with their views of high-growing patches of purple heather and yellow broom, welcome the citydweller thirsty for greenery, for Limousin is a mosaic of green : the soft velvety green of its meadows, the sharper green of newly-cut grass, and the deep green of its dense forests, interspersed with the translucent green of fern fronds. Far from the madding crowd the visitor can find a warm welcome at country guesthouses, and wander for a whole day along country tracks without meeting another tourist.

But Limousin has other charms besides rural pleasures. The town of Aubusson, former site of the Royal Tapestry Works, Limoges with its fine porcelain and the ruins of the Saint-Martial Abbey, the Château Pompadour, converted into a stud-farm after the death of the famous Marquise de Pompadour, and the holiday town of Bort-les-Orgues nestling under its high dam and vast man-made lake, all bear out the local tourist board slogan "a discovery awaits you at the end of every path". The local people have another saying — "chabatz d'entrar", or "have done with entering" — another way of bidding you to make yourself at home.

Sightseeing

■ ARGENTAT★

B3 / ® / pop. 3424 (Corrèze)

The old stone bridge crossing the Dordogne has a view over this ancient town which would delight any painter : the ragged lines of low, wooden-porched houses along the quay, the circle of pointed stone or slate roofs, studded with windows, turrets and pepper-pot towers. □

▶ Nearby

▶ 4.5 km SW : see the murals in the church at **Monceaux★.** ▶ The church in **Saint-Chamant** *(6 km NW)* has a 15thC wooden-galleried bell-tower and a Romanesque doorway; from here, continue to the waterfalls at Murel, to **Albussac** (11thC church) and to the **Roche de Vic★** *(636 m peak; panorama★).* □

▶ Round the gorges of the Dordogne and Maronne rivers★★★ *(60 km approx; 2hr3O) See diag 1*

▶ **Argentat.** ▶ Enjoyable drive along the left bank of the Dordogne, reflecting the 14thC **château de Gibanel;** farther on, see the wall belfry of the Romanesque church at **Glény.** ▶ The 85 m high dam at **Chastang** turns the Dordogne into a lake 30 km long; panorama★ from the viewing area close by. ▶ **Servières-le-Château** is a former stronghold with stone-roofed houses nicely set over the gorges of the Glane. ▶ **Saint-Privat :** 13th-16thC church with broad square tower. ▶ From Saint-Julien-aux-Bois, drive down to **Saint-Cirgues-la-Loutre;** you come out high above the gorges of the **Maronne★.** ▶ The **Tours de Merle★** (11th-18thC) were once a fortress in joint ownership; hence the two keeps! *(Jun.-Sep., 10-1 & 2-7; son et lumière show in Jun.-mid-Aug.).* □

1. The Dordogne and Maronne Gorges

Don't miss

★★★Bort-les-Orgues (B2), Dordogne Gorges (B2).
★★Aubazines (B3), Collonges-la-Rouge (B3), Vassivière Lake (B2).

Facts and figures

Location : *in the heart of France, between the Massif Central and the Atlantic coast.*
Area : *16932 km²*
Climate : *influenced by the Atlantic (W and SW winds) and relatively mild except in the east (Plateau de Millevaches), which is more continental.*
Population : *378726*
Administration : Corrèze *Department, Prefecture : Tulle.* ***Creuse*** *Department, Prefecture : Guéret.* ***Haute-Vienne*** *Department, Prefecture : Limoges.*

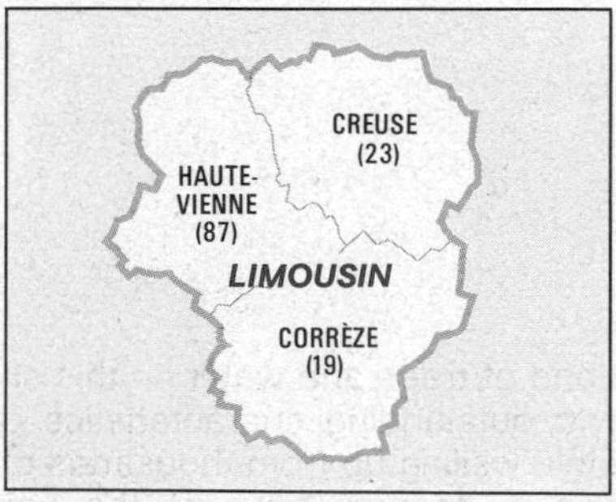

■ AUBUSSON

B1 / ® / pop. 6513 (Creuse)

Famous for its tapestry workshops since the 16thC. Tapestry is everywhere : galleries, exhibitions, workshops, and street names.

▶ On the left bank, visit the **Ecole Nationale d'Art Décoratif** (National School of Decorative Art; *Jul.-Sep., 9-12 & 2-5 ex Sat. pm, Sun. and nat. hols.*), and the **tapestry museum** (Centre Culturel et Artistique Jean Lurçat; *daily ex Tue. am*). ▶ On the right bank, see the **Maison des Vallenet** (16thC mansion), the **Hôtel de Ville** (exhibitions in summer) and near by, the **Maison du Vieux Tapissier★** (15thC; old tapestry workshop; local history; *Jul.-10 Sep., 9:30-12 & 2-6:30*). ▶ From the church (large 1770 tapestry), climb up to the château ruins (panorama★). □

▶ Nearby

▶ **Felletin** *(11 km S) :* bell-tower★ (1451) on the 12-15thC church of Le Moutier; Flamboyant doorway. This town has always been the rival of Aubusson : several workshops, exhibitions *(Jul.-15 Sep.)* in the former church of Notre-Dame du Château (15thC, wooden shingled bell-tower); the diamond cooperative is open to visits *(9-12 & 3-6; closed Sat., Sun. and nat. hols., diamond cutting);* 12thC lantern of the dead in the cemetery; handsome mediaeval bridge and old houses. ▶ **Saint-Maixant,** 12thC

Weekend tips

Enjoy the Saturday morning bustle in Brive-la-Gaillarde (and its market), before lunching early at a speciality restaurant in Varetz; along the valley of the Corrèze, via Tulle to Argentat (stopover). The trip round the Dordogne and Maronne gorges will make a pleasant Sunday morning; after lunch, perhaps at Beaulieu-sur-Dordogne, return to Brive via Collonges-la-Rouge and Turenne.

church and 14thC castle, roofed with chestnut shingles; beautiful park *(Jul.-Oct., 9-12 & 2-6).* □

■ BEAULIEU-SUR-DORDOGNE★

B3 / ® / pop. 1 603 (Corrèze)

On the edge of one of the most beautiful rivers in France, this little city has a famous 12thC **abbey church,** a fine example of Limousin Romanesque art.

▶ The impact of the carved tympanum★★ over the main doorway (a Last Judgement, reminis-

Tapestries

Although Aubusson tapestries have never been as exquisite as those of the Netherlands, the industry has flourished here since the 16thC, and was probably established as early as the 14thC. During the reign of Louis XIV (17thC), the workshops at Aubusson were elevated to the status of Manufactures Royales *(Royal workshops). The abundant output of the 17th and 18thC led to a loss of originality. Designs were frequently copied from paintings and repetition of the same designs brought a decline in creativity. In the 30's, Madame Cuttoli commissioned Aubusson tapestries based on contemporary paintings. In 1937, Jean Lurçat reduced the number of colours in use and created original designs better adapted to weaving techniques. He has been followed by Gromaire, Picart le Doux, Saint-Saëns, Dom Robert and many others who have contributed to the revival of what is now a contemporary form of artistic expression.*

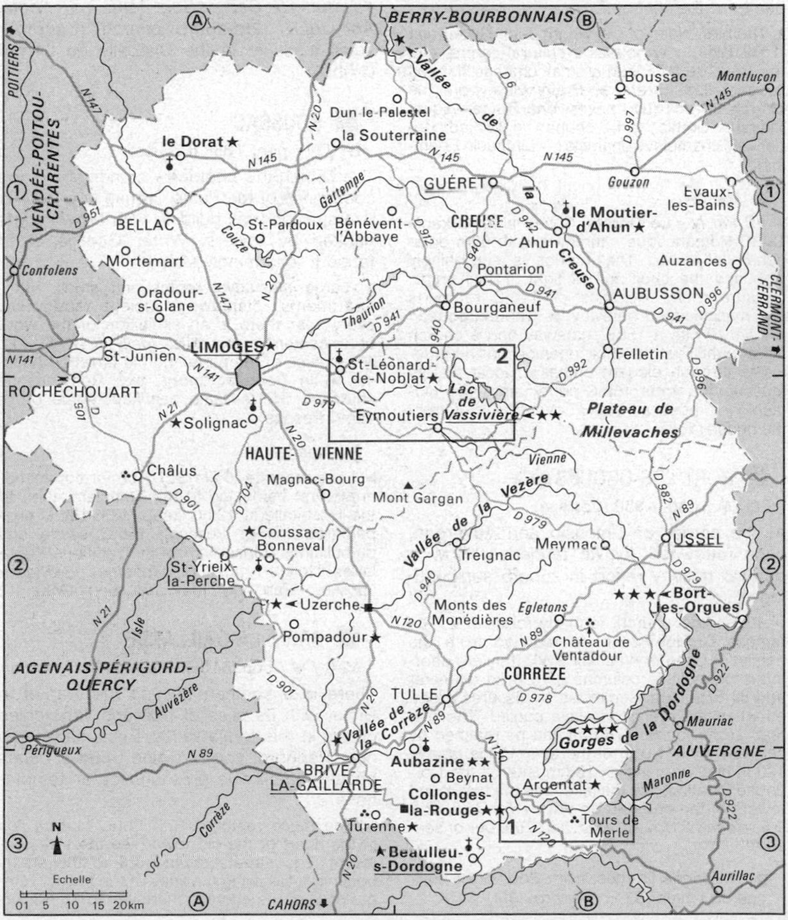

cent of the one at Moissac) tends to distract from the church itself. The nave has large side-aisles with galleries like those in the Auvergne region; see the ambulatory and radiating chapels; don't miss the treasure room★ (12thC Virgin in silvered wood, 10thC reliquary, enamelled 18thC shrine). ▶ Charming old houses around the church, including one from the Renaissance. ▶ By the Dordogne, there is a picturesque chapel with 12thC wall-belfry. □

▶ Nearby

▶ **Queyssac-les-Vignes** *(9 km W-SW)* : fine view of the Dordogne from the tower of an ancient château. From here, proceed to **Curemonte** (12thC church with 16thC cross outside, massive castle with keep and square towers), on a spur above the Sourdoire; on to **Puy d'Arnac** (panorama★ from the church terrace). ▶ To the east is **Reygade** *(13 km, D41);* 15thC Burial of Christ★ in polychrome stone (cemetary chapel); 8 km farther on : **Mercœur,** with an old Gothic church roofed with stone tiles. □

BELLAC

A1 / ® / pop. 5 465 (Haute-Vienne)

On the edge of the Limousin and Poitou regions, with quiet streets on the steep banks of the Vincou.

▶ The birth place of playwright **Jean Giraudoux** (1882-1944) now houses a cultural centre, and the Hôtel de Ville is in a small château flanked by corbelled turrets. ▶ Pretty view from the **church terrace** (two naves, one Romanesque, the other Gothic; 12thC shrine★ in worked copper with champlevé enamels (→ Limousin Enamels). □

▶ Nearby

▶ *12 km N :* **Le Dorat**★ ® has a remarkable 12thC Romanesque church★★ with 60m octagonal bell-tower. The interior is surprisingly high and the choir full of light. 11thC crypt; treasure room. Remains of 15thC ramparts and machicolated gateway. ▶ **Châteauponsac** *(21 km E)* has a 15thC gateway and a church (11th-15thC) with a choir opening on the side-aisles through elegant arches★; local history museum in former 15thC priory; attractive old-fashioned houses; view★ over the city from the bridge (1609). □

BORT-LES-ORGUES★★★

B2 / ® / pop. 4 950 (Corrèze)

At the border of Limousin and Auvergne, once renowned for its tanneries. Now a popular holiday resort in superb surroundings.

▶ 12th-14thC church, formerly fortified. ▶ The famous **Orgues**★ can be reached from the hamlet of Chantéry *(2.5 km SW);* they are enormous phonolithic columns 8-10 m in diameter and 80-97m high, separated by fissures created when the prehistoric lava cooled. The plateau at the top (alt. 769 m) can be reached by car (view★). ▶ North of the town is the **dam★,** 120 m high, forming an 18 km lake on the Dordogne (boating); by the lake, see the five round towers of the **château de Val**★ (15thC; *9-12 & 2-6; closed 2 Nov.-15 Dec. and Tue. out of season*). □

▶ Dordogne Gorges, from Bort to the Barrage de l'Aigle *(83 km; approx 3hr).*

▶ Leave Bort by the Meymac road, which runs close to the Château de Pierrefitte (15thC) and fork left towards the site★ of **Saint-Nazaire** *(1/4hr on foot),* a promontory above the junction of the Dordogne and the Diège; a long detour is subsequently necessary to get round the gorge. ▶ Near **Liginiac** (12thC ironwork on the church door) go to see the **Marèges Dam**★ before moving on to the one at Neuvic-d'Ussel. ▶ At **Neuvic-d'Ussel,** 12th-15thC church, remains of fortifications, Henri Queuille Museum (dedicated to this famous radical thinker and to the Resistance; ethnography collection). ▶ Small Romanesque church in **Sérandon;** here join the **Route Touristique des Ajustants★,** running down into the gorge of the Dordogne and along the right bank. ▶ After **Saint-Projet** (site★, suspended **bridge** between two little tunnels), the Labion gorge leads on to Mauriac. ▶ At La Besse, D105 (on the left) runs back to the Dordogne at the **Barrage de l'Aigle**★ (dam, 90 m high). ▶ Return to Bort via Mauriac (→ Auvergne). □

BOURGANEUF

B1 / ® / pop. 4 030 (Creuse)

The Tour Zizim is one of the three towers of a former Hospitallers' castle (15thC); superb timber-work★; small museum *(daily 15 Jul.-15 Sep.; Sun. and nat. hols. Apr.-Jul.)*; 12th-15thC church ; another small museum in the Chapelle de l'Arrier (17thC). □

BOUSSAC

B1 / ® / pop. 1 868 (Creuse)

The 15th-16thC **château**★ stands above the confluence of the Petite Creuse and Béroux rivers, a long tall building with brown roofs flanked by towers. Writer George Sand found it "charmingly simple".

▶ Large mediaeval rooms and small 18thC apartments, displaying ancient tapestries; every year there is an exhibition of the work of a contemporary artist *(daily 9-12 & 2-7).* ▶ Remains of ramparts and old turretted houses. ▶ In **Boussac-Bourg,** two Romanesque churches; Notre-Dame has kept some of its 12thC frescos. □

▶ Nearby

▶ **Lavaufranche** *(6 km SE)* : former commandery★, first belonging to the Templars, then to the Hospitallers. 12thC keep, 12th-18thC chapel, (remains of frescos), 15thC castle and outbuildings (Musée d'Arts et Traditions Populaires - folk art museum; tapestries; *2-6, daily Jul.-Aug.; Sun. only : May, Jun., Sep., Oct.*). □

BRIVE-LA-GAILLARDE

A2-3 / ® / pop. 54 032 (Corrèze)

There is a southern feel to the market in Brive, with its piles of fruit and vegetables grown in this fertile valley. Because it is so near Périgord, you also find truffles, *cèpes* (mushrooms), *foie gras* and other temptations.

▶ The much restored 12th-14thC **church** lies in the heart of the old town (see the treasure-room). The streets radiate out to the shady boulevard following the lines of the former ramparts; S of the church, charming 15-16thC turretted houses. ▶ A 16thC mansion is now the **Ernest-Rupin Museum** (regional history and art; *10-12 & 2-5 or 6, closed Sun. and nat. hols.*). Close by, the charming Renaissance **Hôtel de Labenche★** (see courtyard). In Rue Charles Teyssier, 13th, 14th and 15thC houses. The Town Hall is now installed in the 17thC buildings★ of a former religious and political movement known as the Doctrinaires. **Edmond-Michelet Museum** (Rue Champanatier; *10-12 & 2-6, closed Sun.*; WWII Resistance and Deportation). □

▶ Nearby

▶ Collonges-la-Rouge (→) and Turenne. ▶ **Valley of the Corrèze★ :** pretty route to Tulle *(29 km)*; detour via **Aubazine** ® to see the Cistercian abbey-church★★ (12thC; inside, 12thC stained-glass, beautiful 12thC decorated oak cupboard with arcatures; 18thC Gothic tomb of St. Etienne★★); in the abbey buildings (16th-18thC), Romanesque chapter *(1 Jun.-15 Sep., daily, ex Mon. 2-5:30; off-season, Sat., Sun. pm)*. From here, go up the Puy de Pauliac (alt. 520 m; panorama★; *drive, then 10 min on foot*). ▶ **Gorges de la Vézère** and the peak of **Puy d'Yssandon** *(NW; 75 km; approx 2hr30)* : drive first to **Donzanac,** a picturesque country town on the banks of the Maumont; turretted houses. In **Alassac,** see the impressive bell-tower keep of the 12thC church. A Gothic bridge crosses the Vézère where it leaves the Gorges, between the château de Lasteyrie (19thC, left bank) and the **château du Saillant.** From **Objat** ®, N to **Saint-Bonnet-la-Rivière** (circular Romanesque church copied from the Holy Sepulchre in Jerusalem) reach **Saint Robert,** to the SE; (see the fine Romanesque choir in the church) and continue to the **Puy d'Yssandon** (355 m peak; château ruins). □

■ CHÂLUS

A2 / pop. 2 094 (Haute-Vienne)

The hills around Chalus are still frequented by *feuillardiers,* the men who prepare the chestnut slats used in barrel-making (these barrels give Cognac its amber colour). The wood is also used for furniture manufacture.

▶ Châlus is built around a sloping square and a circular 18thC keep. Across the Tardoire river there is an older **keep,** the remains of the château de Châlus-Chabrol where Richard the Lion-Hearted was mortally wounded in 1199. ▶ Close by is the **Musée des Feuillardiers,** a museum in an 18thC building *(Sat. and Sun. pm, Easter-end Jun., daily Jul.-Sep.)*. □

▶ Nearby

▶ There is a magnificent 12-14thC fortress★ at **Montbrun** *(daily 9-12 & 2-5 or 7)*. ▶ The **château de Brie★** (16thC; *Apr.-Sep., Sun. and nat. hols. 2-4*) has a fine collection of Louis XVI furniture. □

■ COLLONGES-LA-ROUGE★★

B3 / ® / pop. 379 (Corrèze)

No electricity cables, no telegraph poles and no cars *(Jun.-15 Sep.)*; 15-17thC houses built in red sandstone (hence the name); manors, towers, pepper-pot chimneys, corbelled turrets, the town-gate, a charming covered market with a communal oven, and roofs of slate or stone; all these features make Collonges-la-Rouge the prettiest village in Limousin.

▶ 11th-15thC **church** with tympanum showing the Ascension. Next to it is the **chapel of the penitents** (exhibitions). □

▶ Round the Corrèze Plateau *(50-70 km; approx 2hr30)*

▶ **Collonges.** ▶ Drive to **Meyssac :** another town in red sandstone, full of old houses; 12thC church; pottery workshop. ▶ The handsome Romanesque doorway★ of the church in **Saillac** is protected by a narthex. ▶ **Turenne★** is built entirely in white limestone; until the 18thC, it was an independent Limousin Vicomté; numerous 15th and 16thC houses on the slopes of the hill below the castle★ (14thC square tower, 18thC round tower; *daily 9-12 & 2-7, Mar.-15 Nov.; Sun. 2-5, 16 Nov.-Feb.*); 1 km S : château de Linoir (15thC); 5 km N : exhibition of contemporary ceramics in the outbuildings of the **château de Lacoste** (13th-15thC; *daily, pm)*. ▶ On the road to Noailles, **Grotte de La Fage** (cave; *Apr.-Sep., 2-7; Jul.-Aug. 9-7*). ▶ At **Noailles,** 15th-18thC château, home of a famous French family, next to a Romanesque-Gothic church (12th-18thC). □

Limousin cuisine

As a starter, there is a marvellous soup called Bréjaude, *eaten with rye bread, and so thick with cabbage and other vegetables that your spoon will stand up in it.* Charcuterie *(pork products) occupies an important place :* saucisses, andouille *(chitterling sausage),* boudin *(blood sausage) with chestnuts, not forgetting the* grillons *(pork crackling) prepared when the lard is rendered.*
*Traditional dishes include a variety of stews, slowly simmered on the kitchen fire, and sauced dishes, accompanied by chestnuts or rye pancakes (*galettes, galetons *in Haute-Vienne and* tourtons *in the Corrèze); also try the* potée *(cabbage stew) and the* cassoulet *(pork and beans). The beef of the region is extremely tender and full of flavour. There are few cheeses apart from the* Brach, *a cousin of the Roquefort, since cattle breeding is mostly for meat.*
Deserts include thick home-made cakes : clafouttis *with cherries,* flaugnarde *with apples,* galette Corrézienne, *and the almond cake of the Creuse.*

■ ÉVAUX-LES-BAINS

B1 / ® / pop. 1 906 (Creuse)

This little spa on a granite plateau is a good base for exploring the upper valleys of the Cher and the Tardes. 11th-18thC gate-tower on the church. □

▶ Nearby

▶ Further upstream, **Chambon-sur-Voueize** has one of the most beautiful Romanesque churches★ in the Limousin (11th-12thC, stalls, enclosures and woodwork from the 17thC; reliquary bust★ of Saint Valérie, 15thC); mediaeval hump-backed bridge. □

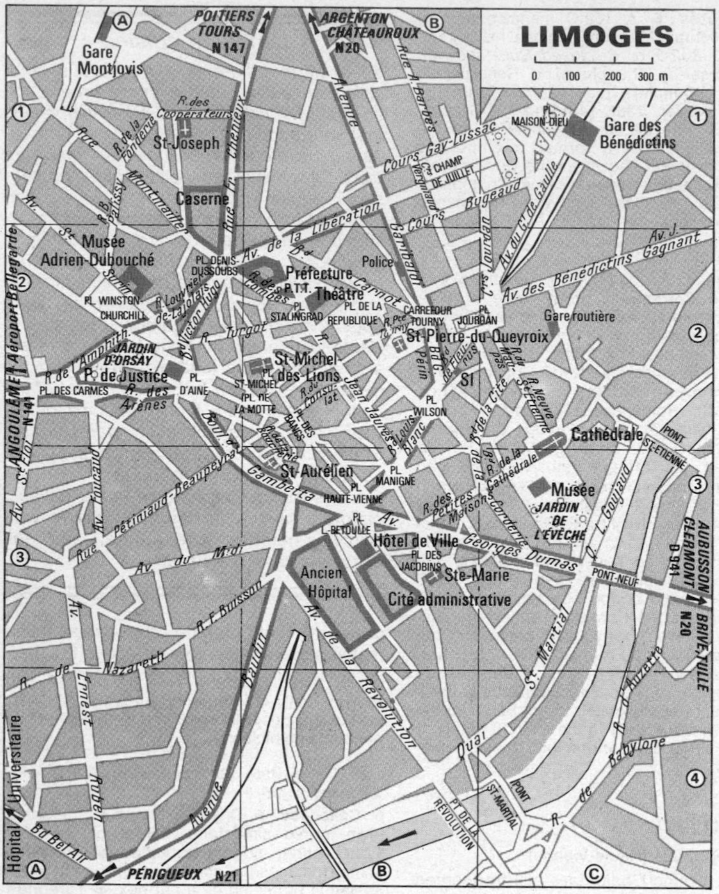

■ GUÉRET

B1 / ® / pop. 16 621 (Creuse)

Close to the valley of the Creuse, bordered by wooded hills to the south. Capital of the Creuse Department.

▶ Next to the Prefecture is the **Hôtel des Moneyroux★** (15th-16thC Gothic). ▶ Almost opposite, the Grande-Rue leads to the heart of **Old Guéret;** picturesque market in the Place Piquerelle *(Thu., Sat.)*. ▶ South of the town, in a public garden, is a former 18thC convent, enlarged in 1905 and now housing the **museum** [*10-12 & 2-5:30 or 6:30; closed Tue.;* Limousin enamels★★, ceramics★ (including Chinese), tapestries, antiques, etc.]. □

▶ Nearby

▶ **Sainte-Feyre** *(7 km SE) :* 18thC château; 2 km further : charming Romanesque church at **La Saunière;** 1 km from the village, see the **château du Thérel** (15th-16thC) roofed with chestnut shingles; further on *(4 km),* is the château de Beaumont (17th-18thC). From here, proceed through **Chaumeix** (regional house with reproduction of a 19thC interior; old tools), to Moutier-d'Ahun (→). □

■ LIMOGES★

A1 / ® / pop. 144 082 (Haute-Vienne)

This, the capital of the French porcelain industry, is too little known. In addition to the attraction of the town itself, the surrounding countryside is delightful.

▶ Parking in the Place de la République (B2); two steps away is the **Crypt of St. Martial★** (4th-9thC), the only remains of a once-famous abbey *(Jul.-Sep. 9:30-12 & 2:30-7)*. ▶ Opposite **St. Pierre du Queyroix** (12th-16thC; handsome tower★; interesting statues) is a marvellous 1900 building entirely covered with porcelain tiling. ▶ Through the pedestrian Rue du Consulat (see the **Cour du Temple★** at N°22, surrounded by 16thC half-timbered buildings), go to the Place des Bancs (market★), and up to the **Rue de la Boucherie★** (B2-3; literally, butcher street). This is the heart of a picturesque district of half-timbered houses; at N°36, visit the **Maison Traditionnelle de la Boucherie** (17thC butcher's house and traditional shop). ▶ Through the Place de la Motte (note ceramic frieze under the cornice of the market building) to the Place d'Aine; behind the Palace of Justice is the beautiful **Jardin d'Orsay★** (A2, 18thC; garden; remains of Roman arena).

▶ See the **Musée National Adrien Dubouché★★;** splendid collection of Limousin, French, European and Asian ceramics (10 000 pieces; *10-12 & 1:30-5:30 or 6, closed Tue.*). ▶ The bell-tower★ of **St. Michel-des-Lions** (B2; 14th-15thC) is very elegant; north of the church, the **Place du Présidial** is lined with fine buildings (17th-18thC; half-timbered houses); see the **Maison Limousine de la Vie Populaire** (local crafts and daily life; *daily ex Sun.*). ▶ Overlooking the right bank of the Vienne river is the former episcopal town known as the Cité, with old houses grouped around the **cathedral★** (C2; 12th-16thC, flanked by a bell-tower copied by many other churches in the Limousin). Enter by the Flamboyant N doorway★; inside, 16thC stained-glass, Renaissance choir-screen★, 14th and 16thC tombs. ▶ In the middle of the **Jardin de l'Evêché** (bishop's garden, C3; 18thC; *9-7*), is the **museum,** with its well-known collection of Limousin enamels★★ *(10-11:45 & 2-5 or 6; closed Tue. ex Jul.-Sep.)*. ▶ From the chevet of the cathedral the ancient houses slope down towards the Vienne and the St. Etienne bridge★ (C2-3; 18thC).

Also... ▶ The **Pont St. Martial★ :** hump-backed bridge (C4; 18thC). ▶ **Hôtel de Ville** (B3; annual porcelain exhibition, *15 Jun.-30 Sep., 9-12 & 2-6*). ▶ Place Denis Dussoubs (A2), elegant late 18thC architecture. ▶ **Gare des Bénédictins★** (railway station, C1; 1929). □

▶ Nearby

▶ **Solignac★** : where St. Eloi founded an abbey in 632; Romanesque abbey church★★ (1143), in Périgord style with cupolas over the nave; fine 15thC stalls. □

▶ Round trip of the Ambazac mountains and the Taurion Valley *(133 km; full day)*

▶ From Limoges, follow the N20 north to **La Crouzille,** once well-known for its uranium mines. **Compreignac** *(6 km W)* : its 12th-15thC church★ is one of the most complete examples of Limousin fortified religious architecture. ▶ The **St. Sylvestre church** has two reliquaries★ (13th and 15thC) from the treasures of the neighbouring **Abbey of Grandmont,** which is now only a heap of ruins near two small lakes★ dug by the monks. ▶ Towards the NW, beyond **Razès,** the artificial **lake of Saint-Pardoux** ® *(15 km from Saint-Sylvestre)* has been made into a leisure centre. ▶ In **Saint-Léger-la-Montagne** *(7 km NE of Saint-Sylvestre)* : 12th-15thC church; 3 km S at the foot of the **Puy de Sauvagnac** (alt. 701 m; *1hr round trip on foot;* panorama★) is the hamlet of **Sauvagnac,** with a 12th-15thC church★ *(guided tours in summer);* old peasant's house open to visitors. ▶ Further N, **Saint-Sulpice-Laurière :** 12th-18thC church built against an 11thC keep. ▶ At **Saint-Goussaud,** SE, there is a statue of the saint in the village church; it is full of holes, as young unmarried villagers stick pins in the statue in the hope that their patron saint will help them find a partner; lantern of the dead; small archaelogy and folklore museum; 1.5 km SE is the **Puy de Jouer** (697 m peak; panorama) on which is the smallest Roman theatre known. ▶ **Châtelux-le-Marcheix★** is built on a promontory above the Taurion river. ▶ 16thC frescos in the church (12th-16thC) of **Saint-Martin-Sainte-Catherine.** ▶ After **Les Billanges** (precious metalwork in the church), cross the Taurion by the **Pont du Dognon** (bridge; site★), and again at **Saint-Martin-Terressus** (view★ over the gorges). ▶ **Ambazac :** 12th-15thC church with two more magnificent pieces from the treasure of the Abbey of Grandmont, a 12thC shrine★★ and a dalmatic (11thC). □

Limousin enamels

Tradition has it that enamel-work was begun in the 7thC at the instigation of St. Eloi, patron saint of metal workers, who was then abbot of Solignac.

There are two techniques : champlevé, *where the enamel is retained in cavities worked into a gold, silver or copper background, and* cloisonné, *where the background is much thinner and the enamel is contained by tiny soldered strips of gold or silver.*

The soil of the Limousin region is rich in the metallic oxides which give enamels their brilliant colour. Uranium salts give yellow; manganese, copper and cobalt give green, blue, pink, etc. Because firewood was plentiful in the area, the enameller's art became highly developed, especially in 12th-14thC; Limoges is on the pilgrim road to Compostela and religious objects and reliquaries were in great demand.

During the 16th and 17thC, a new technique was introduced : painted enamels, largely replacing the difficult, delicate cloisonné. Here, the enamel is built up in layers fired one after the other, resulting in transparent overlays of great beauty. Among the most famous enamellers were Raymond, Courteys, Nouailher, the Pénicaud family and the well-known Léonard Limosin.

MILLEVACHES Plateau

B2 (Corrèze)

Despite its name, this doesn't mean "plateau of the thousand cows"! The name is of Celtic origin, indicating the presence of many streams : the rock and soil formations act as a water reservoir. The bare landscape has a beauty all of its own, with marvellous views, especially when the heather is in bloom.

▶ In the heart of the plateau the village of **Millevaches** (pop. 79) still has a number of thatched houses. □

The MONEDIÈRES MASSIF

B2

The Monedières look like mountains from the south and molehills from the north. They offer a marvellous view over the Limousin, with its black forest land and purple heather.

▶ **Treignac★ :** at the foot of the Massif, on the left bank of the Vézère; Gothic bridge; 15thC church; Marc Sangnier Museum (folk art; *closed Sun.*). □

MOUTIER-D'AHUN★

B1 / pop. 234 (Creuse)

Only the Flamboyant doorway and the Romanesque choir and transept remain of the abbey church. See the remarkable **woodwork★★** (17thC enclosures, stalls, panelling, altarpiece and lectern; *9-12 & 2-7*). 14thC bridge over the Creuse. □

▶ Nearby

▶ **Ahun** *(2 km SW)* was an important town in Gallo-Roman days; in the Middle Ages money was minted here; partially Romanesque church (apse★; 10thC crypt). ▶ 12 km E : **Chénérailles,** in a lovely setting of lakes and woodland (châteaux), a charming mediaeval town; bas-relief★ of 1300 in the church. □

Porcelain

This hard and translucent ceramic, made by the Chinese from the clay deposits of Kao Ling, was known and admired in Europe in the 16thC. The Italians, under the Médicis, and the French ceramicists of Rouen and Saint-Cloud, towards the end of 17thC succeeded in making an artificial "soft paste" porcelain. Finally, a kaolin deposit was discovered near Meissen and the secret was sold to the manufacturers of Sèvres in 1761. Exhaustive search led to the discovery of another deposit at Saint-Yrieux in 1765, when Turgot, Intendant *(administrator) of Limousin, encouraged the further development of the French porcelain industry. The paste from which porcelain is made is a mixture of kaolin, quartz and feldspar, which is slowly dried and then given an initial firing at 950-980°C; this is the "biscuit". It is then covered with liquid enamel and refired at 1400°, to vitrify the paste. Finally, decoration is applied, and fired between 800-950°; these are the principal stages of a process involving some thirty operations.*

POMPADOUR★

A2 / ® / pop. 1474 (Corrèze)

The famous Marquise de Pompadour hardly ever visited the château here, given to her by Louis XV when she received her title in 1745. After her death, the king repurchased the estate and created the stud-farm which still bears her name.

▶ The **château** (18thC façade between machicolated 15thC towers) has terraces which are open to visitors *(9-12 & 2-6; closed pm on race-days).* ▶ The **stud** breeds Anglo-Arabs *(weekdays 3-5; Sun. and nat. hols. 9:30-11:30 & 3-5; closed 21 Feb-15 Jul.)*; horse shows and races in summer. □

▶ Nearby

▶ **Arnac** *(2 km NW)* : 12th-13thC church. ▶ 9 km NW : **Ségur-le-Château★** *(guided tours 15 Jul.-10 Sep.),* on a loop of the Auvézère; several old houses; ruins of a 12th-14thC castle; at **Saint-Eloi-les-Tuileries** *(2 km)* : Les Boins; Gallo-Roman villa *(open Aug.).* ▶ *6 km N,* **Lubersac :** Romanesque church (storiated capitals★); the castle is flanked by three 15thC towers. □

SAINT-JUNIEN

A1 / ® / pop. 11194 (Haute-Vienne)

On the heights of the right bank of the Vienne, facing south, Saint-Junien has a tradition of glove-making that dates from the Middle Ages, now supplemented by the production of leatherwear.

▶ A circular boulevard follows the line of the old ramparts around the centre of town (14thC houses). 12th-13thC **church★;** tomb of St. Junien★★, masterpiece of 12thC sculpture; other sculptures★, remains of 12th-13thC frescos; interesting statues. ▶ Near the 13thC **bridge★,** is the chapel of Notre-Dame-du-Pont (15thC, with charming 13thC statue of the Virgin). □

▶ Nearby

▶ **Valley of the Glane★ :** see the *site Corot* which inspired the great painter *(1 km N and 15 min round trip on foot).* ▶ 15thC **château de Rochebrune** *(10 km W; Palm Sunday-11 Nov., 10-12 & 2-6;* Empire furniture and memorabilia). ▶ **Rochechouart :** view★ from a high hill. Old houses, tower, ramparts and a large late 15thC château★ (façades 17thC), with museum; 16thC frescos★ in one of the rooms *(10-11:30 & 3-6, daily Jul.-15 Sep.; Sat., Sun. and nat. hols. only Palm Sunday-30 Jun. and 16 Sep.-11 Nov.; Sun. pm rest of year).* ▶ **Oradour-sur-Glane** *(13 km NE from Saint-Junien) :* in June 1944, 642 people including 247 children (the entire population of the village), were massacred by the Nazi SS; burned remains of the old village. □

SAINT-YRIEIX-LA-PERCHE

A2 / ® / pop. 8037 (Haute-Vienne)

This is the town that made the fortune of Limoges. At nearby Marcignac *(4 km E),* the first kaolin deposits were discovered in 1765 (→ Porcelain).

▶ The **collegiate church,** or Moûstier★ (13thC), has a sturdy 12thC gate-tower; see the treasure room★. ▶ Close at hand is the Plô Tower (1243). ▶ **Les Palloux :** porcelain museum, near the Arfeuille lake. □

▶ Nearby

▶ **Le Chalard** *(8 km NW) :* almost intact 12thC priory; (interesting church furniture); unusual mediaeval cemetery and a few old houses. ▶ At **Coussac Bonneval★** ® *(11 km E) :* 12thC lantern of the dead and imposing château (14th-18thC; furniture and tapestries of 16th-18thC; *daily 2-6*). □

La SOUTERRAINE

A1 / pop. 5850

This town got its name (meaning "underground") from a very old crypt beneath the church, communicating with an even older burial vault, possibly Gallo-Roman; the church itself is Romanesque, but was over-restored in the 19thC. Interesting 15thC city gate. □

▶ Nearby

▶ 20 km SE, **Bénévent-l'Abbaye** has a remarkable Romanesque church★ (12thC, much restored); walk to Puy de Goth (541 m peak; panorama★). □

TULLE

B2 / ® / pop. 20 642 (Corrèze)

A long string of houses at the bottom of the narrow picturesque valley of the Corrèze.

▶ The 12thC **cathedral★** with its single nave is a very elegant building overlooked by a high bell-tower★ (75 m high; 12th-14thC). ▶ In the cloister★ and the chapter room (remains of 14thC frescos) is the **André-Mazeyrie Museum** (archaeology and art; *9:30 or 10-12 & 2 or 2:30-5 or 6, closed Tue.*). ▶ Opposite the cathedral, the 16thC **Maison de Loyac★** stands on the edge of the old quarter of the town. ▶ Conservatoire des instruments anciens des métiers régionaux (**Conservatory of regional crafts and old tools;** *Mon., Sat., 8:30-12 & 1:30-6 and Wed. am)* in the Rue des Portes-Chanac. ▶ On the opposite side of town is the **Manufacture Nationale d'Armes** (fine collection of weapons; *groups only, by previous request).* □

▶ Nearby

▶ The church at **Saint-Fortunade** *(9 km S)* has a 12thC choir and houses a beautiful 15thC bust reliquary★; 15thC castle, much restored. ▶ *14 km NE :* **Gimel-les-Cascades** is set in a magnificent site★★ in the gorge of the Montane river, which, upstream, breaks into a series of waterfalls (143 m total height; view★ from Vuillier Park, *open Easter-Sep.*); ruins of 16thC château; superb collection in the treasure room★ of the church; *9 km E* from Gimel is **Clergoux** near the artificial lake of La Valette. From here, visit the Renaissance **château de Sédières** (14th-16thC; ethnography museum; *Jul.-Aug., 10-12 & 2-7, closed Tue.*). □

USSEL

B2 / ® / pop. 12 252 (Corrèze)

This old town at the top of a hill is a network of narrow streets with turretted 15th and 16thC houses. See the **Hôtel de Ventadour★,** an elegant building in spite of the rugged granite from which it is built. In front of the school is a large Roman eagle★. Nº 12 Rue Michelet houses the craft collections of the **Musée du Pays d'Ussel** (regional museum; *Jul.-Aug., 10-12 & 3-7*); the art and ethnography collections are in the **chapel of the Pénitents Blancs** in Rue Pasteur *(same hours).* The street leads up to the **chapel of Notre-Dame de la Chabanne** (1640; *10 min*; panorama★). □

▶ Nearby

▶ **Saint-Angel** *(9 km SW)* has a former priory and 12th-14thC granite church, 14thC chapter room and 14thC tower. ▶ *8 km NW,* **Meymac** ® : at the foot of the Plateau de Millevaches (→). Here you can see the church of a former Benedictine abbey, a pretty wooden covered market on granite pillars and a 15thC belfry; on the top floor of the abbey is the Marius-Vazeilles Museum (local collections; *Jul.-Aug., daily ex Tue., 10:30-12 & 3:30-6:30, May-Jun. and Sep.-15 Oct., Sat., Sun. and nat. hols. 3-5*). □

UZERCHE★

A2 / ® / pop. 3 185 (Corrèze)

Built on a promontory in a loop of the Vézère, Uzerche is a ravishing town with an unusual number of turretted elegant 15th-16thC houses.

▶ Superb view of the town, especially at sunrise, from the Eymoutiers road. ▶ Enter the town from the south via Place Marie Colain, the Rue Porte Barachaude (old houses) and the **Porte Bécharie★** (14thC town gate). ▶ The church of **St. Pierre★** is a handsome 12thC Romanesque building with 11thC crypt and an attractive Limousin bell-tower. □

VASSIVIÈRE Lake★★

▶ From Saint-Léonard-de-Noblat to the lake *(70 km; leisurely half-day).*

B2 / *see map 2* (Haute-Vienne)

A 10 km² artificial lake created in 1952 by damming the Maulde river. Hydro-electric generating stations downstream. The lake is remarkably well-equipped and is one of the largest leisure centres in the Limousin, popular with nature lovers as well as with sports enthusiasts.

▶ **Saint-Léonard-de-Noblat** ® (pop. 5 318) has a mediaeval air, with its numerous old houses and 11th-12thC church★ (remodelled, fine Limousin bell-tower★). ▶ The ruins of the **Prieuré de l'Artige** (1165; site★) overlook the confluence of the Vienne and Maulde rivers. ▶ At **Peyrat-le-Château :** see the tall square tower (12thC) of the old castle (15thC); 10 km S, **Eymoutiers :** 15thC choir lit by 15 stained glass windows★ (15th-16thC) in the church; treasure-room. ▶ Scenic route round **Vassivière Lake** ®; the water is said to be extremely pure. □

2. From Saint-Léonard-de-Noblat to Vassivière Lake

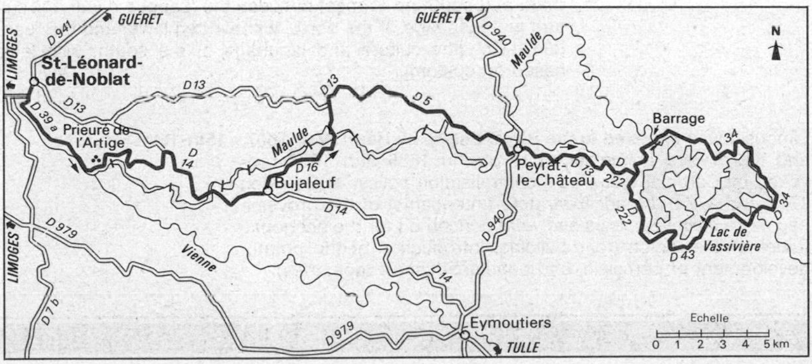

Architecture

Although generations of French masons have come from the Limousin, the regional architecture is not particularly original : in the east, buildings resemble those of the Auvergne (Cantal), and in the south and west those of Quercy and Périgord. ● Timber-built houses are rare outside towns and villages. In the department of the Creuse, walls are usually of granite; riverstone is used in the Dordogne, and sandstone in shades of ochre or red in the Brive valley. Elsewhere, fieldstone with or without facing is the rule. Wood is used for door and window frames everywhere that cut stone cannot be found; in the south, it is also used for balconies and porches. ● Curiously enough, the most northerly part of the region has Mediterranean style roofs with a gentler slope and hollow tiles. Elsewhere, the roofs are steeper, often with four facets, covered by flat tiles, slate or stone. Here and there, especially on bell-towers, there are chestnut shingles. ● There is very little ornamentation : however, weather-vanes became popular after the 17thC, when they ceased to be a seigneurial privilege. Examples of metal 18th and 19thC weather-vanes can still be seen on many Limousin roofs.

NW of Limoges

Brief regional history

Before the Roman conquest The Limousin is a **plentiful source of neolithic remains,** even if they are not as spectacular as those in neighbouring Périgord. ● The native population - the Lemovici - developed from the amalgamation of Ligurian, Iberian and Celtic immigrants.

52BC-10thC The Limousin was part of the Roman province of Aquitaine, and suffered badly during the barbarian invasions which followed the collapse of the Roman Empire. The region was not secured and consolidated until the 7thC, in the reign of King Dagobert. ● Subsequently, the relative isolation of the region left it more or less untouched by the great political upheavals of the period; its peaceful, character existence favoured the spread of **abbeys and monasteries.**

10th-14thC Around the 10thC, the Limousin was **divided into feudal fiefs,** Vicomtés, Seigneuries, or Baronnies, all more or less independent. ● Still part of Aquitaine, Limousin became English after the marriage of Eleanor (1152) to Henry II Plantagenêt. ● It was not definitively reclaimed for France until the reign of Charles V (1374). Even then, it remained a **frontier region** between **northern** and **southern** France, between the "Langue d'Oïl" (the culture and language of the north, with written laws) and the "Langue d'Oc" (the culture and language of the south, with laws based on custom).

15th-18thC Limousin was **annexed to the Royal Estate by Henri IV** in 1607, and there were a number of revolts in 1636 and 1637 provoked by Cardinal Richelieu's centralisation policy. ● Between 1730 and 1774, the administrators (Intendants) of the province had more flexible policies and were concerned for the economic future of the region (road-building, introduction of the potato, development of porcelain, and popularisation of tapestries).

Practical information

The region

Information : *Délégation Régionale au Tourisme* and *Comité Régional de Tourisme* (C.R.T.), 8, cours Bugeaud, 87000 Limoges, ☎ 55.79.57.12. **Corrèze :** *Comité Départemental de Tourisme* (C.D.T.), *Maison du Tourisme,* quai Baluze, 19000 Tulle, ☎ 55.26.46.88. **Creuse :** *Comité Départemental de Tourisme* (C.D.T.), 43, pl. Bonnyaud, 23000 Guéret, ☎ 55.52.33.00. **Haute-Vienne :** *Union Touristique-C.D.T.,* Préfecture, bd Carnot, ☎ 55.77.58.21. In Paris : *Maison du Limousin,* 18, bd Haussmann, 75009 Paris, ☎ 47.70.32.63.

Bookings : *Loisirs-Accueil Haute-Vienne* (S.L.A.), 14, pl. Jourdan, 87000 Limoges, ☎ 55.34.70.11. *Loisirs-Accueil Corrèze* (S.L.A.), quai Baluze, 19000 Tulle, ☎ 55.26.46.88. *Creuse,* 43, pl. Bonnyaud, 23000 Guéret, ☎ 55.52.33.00.

Maps : *Michelin,* nos 72, 73, 75, 76, 1/200 000 ; *I.G.N.,* nos 34, 35, 40, 41, 42, 48, 49, 1/100 000 and nos 107, 110, 111, 1/250 000.

Local and regional press : *Centre-Presse, la Charente Libre, l'Écho du Centre, la Montagne, le Populaire du Centre.*

S.O.S. : Corrèze : *SAMU (emergency medical service),* ☎ 55.26.00.00. **Creuse :** ☎ 17. **Haute-Vienne :** *SAMU,* ☎ 55.33.33. Poisoning Emergency Centre : **Corrèze :** ☎ 56.96.40.80 and 73.91.96.96. **Creuse :** ☎ 73.91.96.96. **Haute-Vienne :** ☎ 56.96.40.80.

Weather forecast : Corrèze : ☎ 55.26.29.99. **Creuse :** ☎ 55.52.52.52. **Haute-Vienne :** ☎ 55.00.11.00.

Farmhouse gîtes, chambres d'hôtes, gîtes for children, farmhouse camping : enq at the C.R.T. and *relais départ.* **Corrèze :** 36, av. du Gal-de-Gaulle, 19000 Tulle, ☎ 55.20.24.54. **Creuse :** 1, rue Martinet, 23000 Guéret, ☎ 55.52.55.75. **Haute-Vienne :** 16, pl. Jourdan, 87000 Limoges, ☎ 55.34.70.11. Bookings at the *S.L.A.*

Holiday villages : see "Practical Holiday Guide" at start of book.

Camping : approximately 200 campsites ; list available at the *C.R.T.* and *C.D.T.*

Festival and events : early May : *choral and orchestral performances* in Limoges. **Jun :** *Departmental Music Festival* in Aubusson ; **Jun-Jul :** *Jean Giraudoux Theatre, Dance and Music Festival* in Bellac. **Jul :** *International Folklore Festival* in Brive ; Vieux Chénérailles *Mediaeval Festival ;* Guéret *Festival.* **Jul-Aug :** *Music Festivals* at St-Léonard Collegiate Church in Aubazine, in Beaulieu-sur-Dordogne, Saint-Robert, Saint-Sétiers, Sédières, Turenne, Ussel and Uzerche ; *International Folklore Festival* in Brive ; *Fortnight of Popular Arts and Traditions* in Davignac ; *festival of concerts* in the Tulle cloister.

Exhibitions and trade fairs : early Jan : *Foire des Rois :* sale of *foies gras* and truffles in Brive. **Apr :** goat fair in Aubazine. **May :** horse fair in Chénérailles ; *Foire de la St-Loup* in Limoges. **Jun :** ham day in St-Mathieu. **Jul :** second-hand and bric-à-brac fair in Argentat, Aubazine and Objat, cheese days in Pageas, *Journée des Feuillardiers et de l'Artisanat du Châtaignier* (chestnut wood work). **Aug :** sheep fair in Féniers. **Sep :** Limousin cattle breeding - international days, pig fair in Bonnat. **Oct :** goat fair in Chénérailles ; chestnut fair in Dournazac. **Dec :** turkey fair in Chénérailles.

Folklore festivals : Jun : « *Bonnes Fontaines* » *Folklore Festival in Cussac.* **Jul :** couronnement du Roi et course de la Bague in St-Léonard-de-Noblat. **Aug :** festival of the mills in Piot. **Oct :** *Fête de Notre-Dame des Petits Ventres* in Limoges.

Technical tourism : Limoges Porcelain : *Bernardaud,* ☎ 55.77.40.80 ; *Haviland,* ☎ 55.79.20.18, by advance appt. Enamel workshops : enq ℹ de Limoges, bd de Fleurus, ☎ 55.32.70.56.

Rambling and hiking : the region is crossed by GRs 33, 4, 41, 44, 46, 440 and 480 (topoguides). **Corrèze :** a topoguide of short rambles is available at the *C.D.T.* **Creuse :** the *Comité Creuse Expansion Tourisme* publishes a remarkable brochure, *Itinéraires Pédestres de Petite Randonnée,* containing indications and descriptions of short hikes and rambles. **Haute-Vienne :** the *C.D.T.* publishes *Fiches-circuits. Pédestres* (leaflets on walking routes).

Riding holidays : Enq and lists of riding centres : *C.D.T. ; Assn. de Tourisme Équestre du Limousin,* A.T.E.L., 19470 Le Lonzac, ☎ 55.98.20.23. *Ligue Équestre du Limousin,* La Jachère, 19100 Brive, ☎ 55.87.46.13. *Assn. Dép. de Tourisme Équestre,* A.D.T.E., Chambre d'Agriculture, 32, av. du Gal-Leclerc, 87000 Limoges, ☎ 55.77.20.27. Courses and excursions : bookings at the *L.A.*

Cycling holidays : a brochure proposing cycle tours in the **Corrèze** is on sale at the *C.D.T.* and the *T.O.* Other enquiries to the *C.D.T.* Cycling holidays and excursions bookings : *S.L.A.*

Handicraft courses : Weaving : enrolments, *L.A. ;* Mme Giletti, Trimoulines, 23130 Chénérailles, ☎ 55.62.36.80. Mme Gilmert, 19320 Marcillac-la-Croisille, ☎ 55.27.83.75. Pottery : M.C. Escaravage, 4, rue St-Étienne-d'Obazine, 19400 Argentat-sur-Dordogne, ☎ 55.28.06.14. Enrolments at the *L.A.* Wood sculpture : enrolments, *L.A. ;* M. J.-P. Ruiz, Maison Rouge, Chabrignac, 19350 Juillac, ☎ 55.25.65.01. Ceramics-modelling : château des Portes, Mainsat, 23700 Auzannes, ☎ 55.67.00.76, and *L.A.*

Other courses : weekend courses in regional cooking for beginners, weekend courses in *cuisine du terroir* (preparation of *foie gras, conserves d'oie*), etc. : enrollments at the *L.A.* **Creuse, Haute-Vienne** and **Corrèze.**

Children : Numerous gîtes for children, proposing specific activities (walks, cycling, etc.). Bookings : *S.L.A.* **Corrèze** and *S.L.A.* **Creuse/Haute-Vienne.** Other enq at the *relais départ. des gîtes ruraux.*

Tennis : *Ligue Régionale du Limousin,* 15, rue Michel-Ange, 87000 Limoges.

Golf : Aubazine (9 holes), Neuvic (9 holes), Limoges (18 holes).

Aquatic sports : several stretches of water suitable for sailing, windsurfing, waterskiing, etc.

Enq at the *C.D.T.* and the *Ligue du Limousin de La Féd. Française de Voile,* 6, rue F.-Coppée, 87000 Limoges, ☎ 55.37.27.90.

Canoeing : Canoe centres in Anzème, Aubusson, Vassivière-en-Limousin, Guéret, Argentat-sur-Dordogne, Beaulieu-sur-Dordogne, Brivezac, Marcillac-la-Croisille, Saint-Priest-de-Gimel, Voutezac. Enq at the *C.D.T. ; Kayak-Club Marchois,* 16, rue du Colonel-Fossey, 23000 Guéret, ☎ 53.52.37.64.

Hunting and shooting : enq at the féd. dép. des chasseurs : **Corrèze :** 1, av. W.-Churchill, 19000 Tulle, ☎ 55.20.08.85. **Creuse :** av. Sénatorie, 23000 Guéret, ☎ 55.52.17.31. **Haute-Vienne :** 43, rue St-Paul, 87000 Limoges, ☎ 55.79.12.62.

Fishing : the region abounds in pure, rapid rivers and streams. Enq at the *féd. dép. des A.P.P.* : **Corrèze,** 12, quai de Rigny, 19000 Tulle, ☎ 55.26.11.65. **Creuse :** *Maison de La Pêche,* 60 *bis,* av. L.-Laroche, 23000 Guéret, ☎ 55.52.24.70. **Haute-Vienne :** 7, rue Banc-Léger, 87000 Limoges, ☎ 55.34.35.89. Fly fishing : enq at the *S.L.A. Creuse.*

● *Towns*

ARGENTAT

Tulle 30, Aurillac 54, Paris 513
B3 ♥ ⊠ 19400

ℹ av. Pasteur, ☎ 55.28.10.91 (high season).

Hotels :
★★***Gilbert*** (L.F.), rue Vachal, ☎ 55.28.01.62. AE, DC, Visa. 30 rm Ⓟ ♨ ⛱ ♿ closed 1 Dec-1 Mar, 220. Rest. ● ♦♦ closed Sat ex Jul-Aug. Fare both copious and varied ; carefully prepared menus, 60-160.
★***Fouillade,*** 11, pl. Gambetta, ☎ 55.28.10.17. 30 rm Ⓟ ♨ ♿ closed Mon From 15 Oct-15 May, 4 Nov-5 Dec ex school hols, 130. Rest. ♦ Pleasant service in a country setting ; traditional family dishes of the Auvergne Region, 45-130.

⛺ ★★*Le Longour* (60 pl.), ☎ 55.28.13.84.

Farmhouse gîte and camping : *Moulin Bas,* ☎ 55.28.00.25. Fishing.

Events : fair on 1st and 3rd Thu each month.

AUBAZINE

Tulle 19, Aurillac 86, Paris 506
15 km E of Brive, A-B3 ⊠ 19190 Beynat

SNCF ☎ 55.25.70.07.

Hotel :
★***Saut de la Bergère*** (L.F.), 2 km E on D48, ☎ 55.25.74.09. Visa. 10 rm Ⓟ ♨ ⛱ closed Feb and Nov school hols, Wed noon low season, 100. Rest. ♦ 38-80.

⛺ ★★★*Centre de tourisme du Coiroux* (143 pl.), ☎ 55.27.21.96.

Bicycle hire : *Centre de Tourisme du Coiroux,* Aubazine, 19190 Beynat, ☎ 55.27.21.96.

AUBUSSON

Guéret 42, Clermont-Ferrand 93, Paris 382
B1 ⊠ 23200

ℹ rue Vieille, ☎ 55.66.32.12 (high season).

SNCF ☎ 55.66.13.28.

🚌 av. des Lissiers, ☎ 55.66.20.32.

Hotel :
★★***France*** (L.F.), 6, rue des Déportés, ☎ 55.66.10.22. AE, DC, Euro, Visa. 25 rm Ⓟ 145. Rest. ♦♦ closed Sun eve and Mon noon from 1 Oct to Easter. Traditional regional cooking, 60-130.

⛺ ★★★*La Croix Blanche* (95 pl.), ☎ 55.66.18.00.

Events : every 2 years, early Sep : *foire aux boudins et au fondu creusois* (fair of boudin sausages and fondu from the Creuse Valley Region).

Recommended : cake and pastry shop : *La Noisettine,* 11, rue des Déportés, ☎ 55.66.10.21 ; spec : *le creusois, noisette aubussonnaise ;* handicrafts : M. Milluy, weaver in Blessac.

BEAULIEU-SUR-DORDOGNE

Tulle 40, Aurillac 65, Paris 523
B3 ♥ ⊠ 19120

ℹ pl. Marbot, ☎ 55.91.09.94.

Hotels :
★★★***Le Turenne,*** 1, bd St-R.-de-Turenne, ☎ 55.91.10.16. AE, DC, Euro, Visa. 21 rm Ⓟ ♨ ⛱ closed 30 Sep-4 May, 235. Rest. ♦ 67-165.
★★***Central Hôtel Fournié*** (L.F.), 4, pl. du Champ-de-Mars, ☎ 55.91.01.34. 33 rm Ⓟ ♨ closed 15 Nov-15 Mar, 160. Rest. ● ♦ ♿ In a big country house. Spec : *foie gras, omelette aux truffes, confit de lapin aux girolles,* 45-150.

Youth hostel : pl. du Monturu, ☎ 55.91.13.82.

⛺ ★★★*Des Iles* (66 pl.), ☎ 55.91.02.65.

Restaurant :
Lostange, ⊠ 19500 Meyssac, 14 km N :
♦♦ ***L'Orée des Bois,*** ☎ 55.25.43.79. AE, DC. ☼ Ⓟ ♨ ⛱ closed 15 Jan-15 Feb and Wed. Very good food, 85-250.

Bicycle hire : at the youth hostel, 1 Apr-30 Oct.

BELLAC

Limoges 41, Guéret 74, Paris 360
A1 ♥ ⊠ 87300

ℹ 1 *bis,* rue Jouvet, ☎ 55.68.12.79.

SNCF ☎ 55.68.00.07.

Hotels :
★★***Les Châtaigniers*** (L.F.), 2 km W, rte de Poitiers, ☎ 55.68.14.82. AE, Euro, Visa. 27 rm Ⓟ ♨ ⛱ ♿ closed Nov-May and Sun low season, 220. Rest. ♦ 70-170.
★***Central*** (L.F.), 7, av. Denfert-Rochereau, ☎ 55.68.00.34. 16 rm Ⓟ closed 1-15 Jan, 15 Sep-10 Oct, Mon, 120. Rest. ♦ 60-120.

⛺ ★★*Les Rochettes* (100 pl.), ☎ 55.68.13.27.

Chambres and table d'hôtes : La Plaine, Blond, ☎ 55.68.82.57. Rouffignac, Blanzac, ☎ 55.68.03.38.

Events : market 1st of month. End Jun : national festival.

Bicycle hire : enq at the ℹ

Recommended : needlework pictures, Mme Lamaut, La Ronze-Blond. Clog-maker : M. Masson, St-Junieu-les-Combes, ☎ 55.68.08.07.

BEYNAT

Tulle 25, Aurillac 78, Paris 512
20 km E of Brive, A-B3 ✉ 19190

Hotel :
★***Touristes*** (L.F.), ☎ 55.85.50.20. Visa. 13 rm Ⓟ 90. Rest. ♦ 45-80.

⛺ ★★★*Centre Touristique de Miel* (90 pl.), ☎ 55.85.50.66.

Bicycle hire : M. Espargelière, ☎ 55.85.50.09.

BORT-LES-ORGUES

Tulle 71, Aurillac 86, Paris 470
B2 ✉ 19110

ℹ ☎ 55.96.02.49.

SNCF ☎ 55.96.82.17.

Hotels :
★★***Central*** (L.F.), 65, av. de la Gare, ☎ 55.96.74.82. DC, Euro, Visa. 25 rm Ⓟ ♿ closed 10 Jan-5 Mar, Mon low season, 160. Rest. ♦ Friendly service and good, reasonably priced fare (book ahead), 50-150.
★***Gare*** (L.F.), av. de la Gare, ☎ 55.96.73.07. AE, DC, Euro, Visa. 27 rm Ⓟ closed Sat noon (winter), 180. Rest. ♦ 80-130.

⛺ ★★*Beau Soleil* (200 pl.), ☎ 55.96.00.31.

Events : market 2nd and 4th Tue each month.

Bicycle hire : M. Combe, 82, av. Gambetta, ☎ 55.96.02.83 (Jun-Sep).

BOURGANEUF

Guéret 33, Limoges 49, Paris 387
B1 ✉ 23400

ℹ Tour Lastic (high season) and at the mairie, ☎ 55.64.07.61.

SNCF ☎ 55.64.00.04.

🚌 ☎ 55.64.00.27.

Hotels :
★★***Commerce*** (L.F.), 12, rue de Verdun, ☎ 55.64.14.55. 16 rm Ⓟ closed 22 Dec-15 Feb, Mon eve and Mon low season, 200. Rest. ♦ Simple, family-style cooking, 50-170.

Saint-Moreil, 13 km SW on D941 and D22 :
● ★★***Moulin de Montalétang*** (L.F., Relais du Silence), ☎ 55.54.92.72. 14 rm Ⓟ ♿ closed 15 Nov-1 Mar and Wed low season, 190. Rest. ♦♦ This converted floumill provides a pleasant setting, 75-210.

⛺ ★★*La Chassagne* (50 pl.), ☎ 55.64.07.61.

Events : market-competition (livestock) on 1st Wed in Oct. Market on 1st and 3rd Wed of the month.

Recommended : cake and pastry shop : M. Lenoir, 21, rue Zizim, ☎ 55.64.06.82. Spec : *pâté de champignons Creusois.*

BOUSSAC

Montluçon 34, Guéret 41, Paris 337
B1 ✉ 23600

ℹ château, ☎ 55.65.07.62.

SNCF ☎ 55.65.00.97.

Hôtels :

Nouzerines, 1 km NW, on D97 :
★★***La Bonne Auberge*** (L.F.), ☎ 55.82.01.18. AE. 8 rm closed Feb hols, 26 Aug-15 Sep and Sat from Sep-Easter, 120. Rest. ♦ 45-100.
Relais Creusois, rte de La Châtre, ☎ 55.65.02.20. Visa. 4 rm closed in winter and 10 days in Jun, Tue eve and Wed ex Jul-Aug, 95. Rest. ♦♦ 77-180.

⛺ ★★*Creuse Nature* (60 pl.), ☎ 55.65.03.34.

Events : fair-competition (liestock) on 3rd Sun in Nov and Mar. Markets : 2nd and 4th Thu each month.

Bicycle hire : ℹ ☎ 55.65.01.09.

Recommended : cake and pastry shop : *Aux Délices,* rue Martin-Nadau, ☎ 55.65.02.05.

BRIVE-LA-GAILLARDE

Tulle 29, Limoges 96, Paris 493
A3 ✉ 19100

ℹ pl. du 14-Juillet (B1), ☎ 55.24.08.80.

✈ Laroche, 5 km W, ☎ 55.87.32.94.

SNCF ☎ 55.74.90.70., 55.74.23.97.

🚌 10, av. du Mal-Leclerc (B3), ☎ 55.24.29.93/94.

Car-hire : *Budget* train + auto, 15 *ter,* rue Dumyrat, ☎ 55.24.09.35, at the station, ☎ 55.23.30.80, and at the airport.

Hotels :
★★★***Truffe Noire,*** 22, bd Anatole-France (B1), ☎ 55.74.35.32. AE, DC, Euro. 35 rm Ⓟ 240. Rest. ♦ ♿ 80-150.
★★★***Chapon Fin,*** 1, pl. de-Lattre-de-Tassigny (B3), ☎ 55.74.23.40. AE, DC, Euro, Visa. 30 rm Ⓟ 205. Rest. ♦♦ 60-110.
● ★★***La Crémaillère,*** 53, av. de Paris (B1), ☎ 55.74.32.47. AE. 12 rm closed Sun eve and Mon, 15-28 Feb., 15-31 Aug, 150. Rest. ● ♦♦♦ closed Sun eve. Traditional recipes from the Corrèze Region served in an elegant setting, 60-180.
★★***Régent*** (L.F.), pl. W.-Churchill (B-C3), ☎ 55.74.09.58. Visa. 24 rm ♿ closed 15 Oct-15 Nov and Mon, 120. Rest. ♦♦ Good fare at reasonable prices, 55-250.

Ussac, ✉ 19270 Donzenac, 5 km N on N20 and D57 :
★★***Auberge de Saint-Jean*** (L.F.), ☎ 55.88.30.20. 13 rm Ⓟ 130. Rest. ♦ ♿ closed Fri eve low season, pension or 1/2 pens., 50-110.

Varetz, ✉ 19240 Allassac, 10 km NW on D152 :
★★★★***Castel Novel*** (Albert Parveaux) [Relais et Châteaux], ☎ 55.85.00.01. Tx 590065. AE, DC, Visa. 28 rm Ⓟ closed end Oct-early May. This charming castle is full of memories of Colette, 1 200. Rest. ● ♦♦♦ The lively Albert Parveaux and his chef, J.-P. Faucher, prepare a pleasant and modern menu. Spec : *foie frais en papillote aux pruneaux confits, baudroie poêlée aux mousserons, crêpes fourrées à la crème de citron,* 165-310. Winter quarters at the Pralong restaurant in Courchevel (2 000 meters).

Objat, ✉ 19130, 20 km NW :
★***Pré Fleuri,*** ☎ 55.25.83.92. AE, DC, Visa. 7 rm Ⓟ closed 10-25 Jan, Mon, 250. Rest. ● ♦♦ ♿ Expert, imaginative regional cuisine : *tourin à l'ail, soupe aux truffes, fricassée de cèpes,* 110-250.

Youth hostel : 56, av. Mal-Bugeaud, ☎ 55.24.34.00.

Restaurants :
♦♦ ***La Belle Époque,*** 27, av. J.-Jaurès (A3), ☎ 55.74.08.75 ♿ closed 1-15 Jul and Sun, 120-210.
♦♦ ***La Périgourdine,*** 15, av. Alsace-Lorraine (C3), ☎ 55.24.26.55. AE, Visa closed 13-20 Mar, 14 Jul-4 Aug, Wed eve and Sun, 75-220.

Events : market 1st and 3rd Tue of each month, 7 Jan, 12 Jun and Ash Wed.

Limousin

Bicycle hire : M. Vergne, 30, av. de Paris, ☎ 55.24.08.51.

Recommended : *Hall des Ventes,* 2 *bis,* rue Lamartine, ☎ 55.74.05.08. Handicrafts : wickerwork, M. Redon, 13, av. Thiers. Decoration, leatherwork : M. Nadal, 15, bd Mal-Lyautey. Weaving : Mme Delord, 40, rue F.-Delmas. Painted furniture : M. Laizeau, 10, av. Bourzat.

COLLONGES-LA-ROUGE

Brive 21, Tulle 45, Paris 513
B3 ⊠ 19500 Meyssac

Hotel :
★★***Relais Saint-Jacques-de-Compostelle,*** ☎ 55.25.41.02. Visa. 12 rm Ⓟ closed 15 Nov-15 Dec, Tue eve and Wed low season, 150. Rest. ◆ 45-145.

LE DORAT

Limoges 53, Guéret 68, Paris 348
A1 ⊠ 87210

ℹ pl. de l'Église, ☎ 55.60.76.81 (high season).

SNCF ☎ 55.60.73.06.

Hotel :
★***Promenade*** (L.F.), 3, av. de Verdun, ☎ 55.60.72.09. 8 rm Ⓟ closed Feb school hols, 1-21 Sep, Sun eve and Mon, 100. Rest. ◆ 80-130.

DUN-LE-PALESTEL

Guéret 27, Limoges 74, Paris 341
18 km NE of La Souterraine, A1 ⊠ 23800

ℹ rue des Sabots, ☎ 55.89.00.75, and at the mairie, ☎ 55.89.01.30.

Hotel :
★***Joly*** (L.F.), ☎ 55.89.00.23. Euro. 15 rm Ⓟ 110. Rest. ◆◆ closed Sun eve and Mon noon ex high season and nat hols, 50-165.

Events : market : 1st and 3rd Thu of the month. Livestock show : last Sat in Sep ; *Fête Populaire* 13 Jul.

Bicycle hire : ℹ

Recommended : cake and pastry shop : M. Delorme, ☎ 55.89.09.70. Spec : *le creusois, croquets aux amandes.*

ÉVAUX-LES-BAINS

Montluçon 25, Guéret 52, Paris 345
B1 ⊠ 23110

⚕ (12 Apr-17 oct), ☎ 55.65.56.77.

ℹ pl. de l'Église, ☎ 55.65.50.90.

SNCF ☎ 55.65.51.38.

Hotels :
★★***Grand Hôtel Thermal,*** Le Vallon des Thermes, ☎ 55.65.50.01. 77 rm Ⓟ closed 20 Oct-31 Mar, 155. Rest. ◆ ♿ 40-175.
★***Chardonnet*** (L.F.), 18, rue de l'Hôtel-de-Ville, ☎ 55.65.51.78. Euro. 28 rm Ⓟ ♿ closed 20 Oct-1 Apr, 155. Rest. ◆ ♿ 44-100.

⛺ ★*Ouche de Budelle* (40 pl.), ☎ 55.65.50.20.

Events : market every Mon.

Recommended : cake and pastry shop : M. Godet, 26, rue de Verdun, ☎ 55.65.52.40.

GUÉRET

Châteauroux 89, Limoges 90, Paris 354
B1 ⊠ 23000

ℹ av. Ch.-de-Gaulle, ☎ 55.52.14.29.

SNCF ☎ 55.52.00.37.

🚌 av. du Dr-Brézard, ☎ 55.52.46.44.

Car-hire : *Budget* train + auto, at the station, ☎ 55.52.40.53.

Hotels :
★★***Auclair*** (L.F.), 19, av. de la Sénatorerie, ☎ 55.52.01.26. AE, DC, Euro, Visa. 33 rm Ⓟ 200. Rest. ◆◆ 50-100.
● ★***L'Univers,*** 8, rue de l'Ancienne-Mairie, ☎ 55.52.02.03. AE, Visa. 7 rm ♿ closed 25 Jun-7 Jul and Mon, 103. Rest. ● ◆◆ Traditional cooking of the Creuse region and warm service. A charming, inexpensive stopover, 45-100.

⛺ ★★★*Pommeil* (103 pl.), ☎ 55.52.07.02.

Restaurant :
◆ ***Boueiradour,*** rue J.-Ducouret, ☎ 55.52.25.86. AE, DC, Euro, Visa, closed Sun eve. Inspired cooking in a friendly atmosphere, 25-100.

Events : fair-competition (livestock) last Sat in Feb ; fair of fatted geese in mid-Dec.

Recommended : cake and pastry shop : *Villechalane-Sionneau,* 1, pl. Bonnyaud, ☎ 55.52.53.31. Spec : *creusois,* « Lacreuse » chocolates.

LIMOGES

Poitiers 119, Bordeaux 220, Paris 396
A1-2 ⊠ 87000

ℹ bd de Fleurus (B2), ☎ 55.34.46.87 (closed Sun and nat hols low season).

✈ Limoges-Bellegarde, 10 km NW, ☎ 55.00.11.84.

SNCF ☎ 55.01.50.50., 55.77.73.24.

🚌 9, rue Charles-Gide (C2), ☎ 55.34.47.77.

Car-hire : *Budget* train + auto, at the station, ☎ 55.79.33.90, and at the airport.

Hotels :
★★★***Richelieu,*** 40, av. Baudin (B3), ☎ 55.34.22.82, ☎ 55.34.33.63. Tx 580705. Visa. 27 rm Ⓟ ♿ 164.
★★***Orléans Lion d'Or*** (L.F.), 9-11, cours Jourdan (B2), ☎ 55.77.49.71. Tx 580011. Visa. 42 rm, closed 24 Dec-Jan, 195. Rest. ◆ closed 1 Dec-mid-Jan and Sat low season, 80-130.
★★***Europe*** (L.F.), 2, pl. Wilson (B2), ☎ 55.34.23.72. Euro, Visa. 23 rm Ⓟ closed 15 Dec-15 Jan and Sat, 100. Rest. ◆ 50-120.
★***Carlin,*** 12, rue Pétiniaud-Dubos, ☎ 55.77.39.75. Visa. 18 rm Ⓟ ♿ 100.
★***Petit Paris,*** 48 *bis,* av. Garibaldi (B1-2), ☎ 55.77.39.82. 18 rm Ⓟ closed 15 Dec-2 Jan, Sat and Sun low season, 130. Rest. ◆ 55-100.

Feytiat. ⊠ 87220, 5 km E :
★★***Le Mas Cerise,*** av. G.-Clemenceau, ☎ 55.00.26.28. AE, DC, Euro, Visa. 15 rm Ⓟ closed 4-17 Aug, Sun eve and Mon, 185. Rest. ◆◆ ♿ closed Sun and Mon. This young cook has been trained by the greatest chefs and is now becoming famous : *salade de lapereau au vinaigre de cidre, confit du mas cerise, marquise au chocolat sauce pistache,* 95-220.

Nieul, ⊠ 87510, 12 km NW on N147 and D35 :
● ★★★***La Chapelle St-Martin*** (Relais et Châteaux), ☎ 55.75.80.17. 10 rm Ⓟ ♿ closed Jan-Feb, 1st week Aug and Mon, 350. Rest. ◆◆◆ A most agreeable setting, 150-230.

⛺ *Vallée de l'Aurence* (190 pl.), ☎ 55.38.49.43.

Restaurants :
◆◆ ***Les Petits Ventres,*** 20, rue de la Boucherie (B2-3), ☎ 55.33.34.02. closed Feb school hols, 1-15 Jul, Sun and Mon noon. Spec of the Limousin Region : *turbot aux pâtes fraîches, confit de canard aux cèpes,* 120-210.

♦♦ ***Versailles,*** 20, pl. d'Aine (A2), ☎ 55.34.13.39. Visa, closed 17 Feb-4 Mar, 4-26 Aug, Sun eve and Mon. Good, inexpensive cooking, 85.
♦♦ ***Cantaut,*** 10, rue Rafilhoux, ☎ 55.33.34.68. AE, DC, closed 21 Feb-2 Mar, Sun noon from 1 May to 30 Sep. Fare for gourmets. Spec : *choux farcis à la mousse de truite, crème de cèpes, filet de rascasse aux olives.* Very good wines, 98-350.

Events : carnival procession, Sun before or after Shrove Tuesday. Fair-exhibition : 2nd fortnight in May at Palais des Expositions. Exhibition of porcelain and enamel : Jul, Aug, Sep. Horse racing : May-Sep. Market, last Thu of month ex in Dec.

Recommended : Doll-making : Mme Sagnat Michèle, 86, av. Garibaldi, ☎ 55.77.69.29. Stained glass, *Galerie du Bouvier,* M. de Comble, 18, rue de la Boucherie, ☎ 55.34.65.64.

MAGNAC-BOURG

Tulle 58, Brive 62, Paris 425
30 km SE of Limoges, on the N20, A1-2
✉ 87380 St-Germain-les-Belles.

Hotels :
★★***Auberge de l'Étang*** (L.F.), ☎ 55.00.81.37. 15 rm Ⓟ ♨ ⛱ ♿ closed 10 Feb-10 Mar, 3rd week in Oct, 180. Rest. ♦ closed Sun eve and Mon low season. Spec : *foie d'oie frais au sauterne, confit de canard aux marrons,* 120-210.
★★***Hôtel du Midi*** (L.F.), ☎ 55.00.80.13. AE, DC, Euro, Visa. 13 rm Ⓟ ♨ closed 15 Jan-15 Feb, 15-30 Nov, Mon low season and nat hols, 150. Rest. 60-150.

⛺ ★★★*Les Écureuils* (30 pl.), ☎ 55.00.80.28.

Restaurant :
♦♦ ***Tison d'Or,*** ☎ 55.71.84.78 Ⓟ closed 3-22 Jan, 15-31 Oct, Tue, Wed low season, 120-210.

MEYMAC

Tulle 52, Limoges 97, Paris 437
B2 ♥ ✉ 19250

ⓘ pl. Bucher, ☎ 55.95.18.43 (high season).

SNCF ☎ 55.95.11.69.

Hotel :
★***Modern'H,*** av. Limousine, ☎ 55.95.10.19. 30 rm Ⓟ ♨ ♿ closed Nov-6 Dec and Sat low season, 120. Rest, 90-120.

Farmhouse-inn : Lestrade, 8 km, ☎ 55.95.19.30. closed Mon-Thu in winter. Spec : crab, stuffed cabbage, poultry and spring lamb.

POMPADOUR

Brive 52, Limoges 59, Paris 455
A2 ✉ 19230 Arnac-Pompadour

ⓘ mairie, ☎ 55.73.30.43.

SNCF ☎ 55.73.30.37.

Hotels :
★★***Auberge de la Marquise*** (L.F.), 4, av. des Écuyers, ☎ 55.73.33.98. AE, DC, Visa. 12 rm Ⓟ 🐕 closed 6 Oct-8 Jun, 175. Rest. ♦ Spec of the Périgord Region, 95-285.
★***Auberge de l'Hippodrome*** (L.F.), ☎ 55.73.35.03. 10 rm Ⓟ ♨ ⛱ 🐕 closed Apr, 100. Rest. ♦ closed Sat 30 Nov-1 May, 80-130.

PONTARION

Guéret 24, Limoges 59, Paris 378
10 km NE of Bourgneuf, B1 ✉ 23250

Hotel :
Saint-Georges-la-Ponge, 12 km E :
● ★***Domaine des Mouillères,*** 2 km N, ☎ 55.66.60.64. AE. 7 rm ⚘ Ⓟ ♨ ⛱ closed Nov and Feb school hols. A warm, comfortable old residence in the woods, 190. Simple, tasty fare for residents only, 92.

SAINT-JUNIEN

Limoges 30, Angoulême 73, Paris 434
A1 ♥ ✉ 87200

ⓘ pl. du Champ-de-Foire, ☎ 55.02.17.93 (high season).

SNCF ☎ 55.02.10.25.

Hotels :
★★***Relais de Comodoliac,*** 22, av. Sadi-Carnot, ☎ 55.02.27.26. Tx 590336. AE, DC, Euro, Visa. 28 rm Ⓟ ♨ ♿ 185. Rest. ♦ 55-150.
★★***Concorde*** (L.F.), 49, av. H.-Barbusse, ☎ 55.02.17.08. AE, Euro, Visa. 26 rm Ⓟ 178.
★***Corot,*** 46, rue L.-Dumas, ☎ 55.02.17.74. 10 rm 🐕 closed 1 Feb-10 Mar, 127. Rest. ♦ ♿ closed Sun eve and Mon, 90-160.

Youth hostel : 13, rue Saint-Amand, ☎ 55.02.22.79.

Chambre d'hôte : Le Goth, ☎ 55.09.80.77. Fishing.

⛺ ★★*Municipal* (90 pl.), ☎ 55.02.34.86.

Events : Fair 3rd Sat each month.

SAINT-LÉONARD-DE-NOBLAT

Limoges 21, Guéret 61, Paris 417
A1 ✉ 87400

ⓘ foyer rural, ☎ 55.56.11.18 (high season).

SNCF ☎ 55.56.00.09.

Hotels :
★★***Grand Saint-Léonard,*** rte de Clermont, ☎ 55.56.18.18. AE, DC, Visa. 15 rm. closed 2-9 May and 15 Dec-15 Jan, 166. Rest. ♦ 🐕 closed Mon and Tue noon low season, 120-210.
★***Modern*** (L.F.), bd Adrien-Pressemane, ☎ 55.56.00.25. Euro, Visa. 8 rm. closed 1 Feb-1 Mar, Sun eve and Mon. Warm welcome, 160. Rest. ♦ 75-160.

Le Châtenet-en-Dognon, 8.5 km N :
★★★***Chalet du Lac,*** ☎ 55.57.10.05. 20 rm ⚘ Ⓟ ♨ ⛱ closed 15 Jan-15 Mar, 250. Rest. ♦ closed Tue eve and Wed, 65-150.

Brignac-Royères, 7 km NW :
★***Beau Site,*** ☎ 55.56.00.56. 11 rm Ⓟ ♨ ⛱ closed Nov hols, 10-25 Feb, Fri, eve and Mon noon low season, 130. Rest. ♦ 46-115.

⛺ ★★*Parc de Vacances de Beaufort* (100 pl.), ☎ 55.56.02.79.

Farmhouse camping : *Le Chalet,* ☎ 55.56.15.05. Produce for sale. Tennis, hiking and rambling.

SAINT-PARDOUX

Limoges 33, Guéret 60, Paris 372
A1 ✉ 87250 Bessines-sur-Gartempe

Hotel :
★★***Couze,*** ☎ 55.76.30.11. 10 rm Ⓟ ♨ ⛱ 🐕 ♿ closed 1-28 Feb and Mon, 134. Rest. ♦ 49-70.

⛺ *Site de Sautop,* on the lake, 4 km (120 pl.), ☎ 55.71.04.40.

SAINT-YRIEIX-LA-PERCHE

Limoges 40, Brive 62, Paris 436
A2 ✉ 87500

ⓘ pl. de l'Église, ☎ 55.75.94.60 (high season).

SNCF ☎ 55.75.00.28.

Hotels :
★***Modern'Hotel*** (L.F.), bd de l'Hôtel-de-Ville, ☎ 55.75.02.86. 10 rm closed 1-30 Oct and 1-15 Jan, 100. Rest. ♦ ♿ closed Sun ex summer, 80-130.

Coussac-Bonneval, 11 km E :
★★***Voyageurs*** (L.F.), ☎ 55.75.20.24. Euro, Visa. 12 rm ♿ closed Jan, Mon low season, 150. Rest. ♦♦ Good traditional fare, 50-160.

⛺ ★★★*Municipal* (50 pl.), ☎ 55.75.08.75.

Restaurant :
La Roche-l'Abeille, ✉ 87800 Nexon, 12 km N on D704 :
● ♦♦ ***Moulin de la Gorce,*** ☎ 55.00.70.66. AE, DC, Visa. Ⓟ ♿ closed 2 weeks in Feb, Sun eve and Mon low season. Pleasant setting in an old 16thC mill. Spec : *lièvre à la royale aux cèpes,* 220-250.

SOLIGNAC

Limoges 12, Tulle 81, Paris 408
A2 ✉ 87110

SNCF Solignac-le-Vigen, ☎ ① 55.00.50.21.

Hotels :
★★***Saint-Éloi*** (L.F.), 66, av. Saint-Éloi, ☎ 55.00.50.11. 10 rm closed Sun eve and Mon, Sep-Jun, 100. Rest. ♦ 80-130.
★***Auberge du Pont Rompu*** (L.F.), ☎ 55.00.51.38. 7 rm Ⓟ 100. Rest. ♦ closed Sun, 80-130.

Restaurant :
♦♦ ***Domaine de Pradepont,*** ☎ 55.00.50.40 Ⓟ closed Sun eve. Pleasant setting, 120-210.

Bicycle hire : enq at the ⓘ

Recommended : wickerwork : M. Bayle, Les Crauzettes.

TULLE

Aurillac 84, Limoges 88, Paris 483
B2 ✉ 19000

ⓘ quai Baluze, ☎ 55.26.59.61 (closed Sun and Mon low season).

SNCF ☎ 55.20.22.54.

🚌 covered market, station, ☎ 55.20.18.45.

Hotels :
★★★***Limouzi,*** quai de la République, ☎ 55.26.42.00. 50 rm Ⓟ ♿ 150. Rest. closed Feb, 1-8 Jul and Sun, 70-180.
★★***Gare*** (L.F.), 25, av. de la Gare, ☎ 55.20.04.04. 14 rm closed 1-15 Sep, 1 week in Fev, 150. Rest. ♦ 50-60.
★★***Toque Blanche,*** 29, rue Jean-Jaurès, ☎ 55.26.75.41. AE, Visa. 10 rm Ⓟ closed 10-30 Jan and Mon from Oct to Mar, 120. Rest. ♦♦ Fine traditional fare and pleasant service. Spec : *veau à l'ancienne, civet de lapin au Cahors,* 70-180.

⛺ ★★★*Bourbacoup* (58 pl.), ☎ 55.26.75.97.

Restaurant :
♦ ***Central,*** 32, rue Jean-Jaurès, ☎ 55.26.24.46. Visa, closed 21 Jul-18 Aug, Sat and Sun eve, 75-220.

Events : market 2nd and 4th Wed each month.

USSEL

Tulle 60, Clermont-Ferrand 86, Paris 439
B2 ✉ 19200

ⓘ pl. Voltaire, ☎ 55.72.11.50 (high season), and 67, av. Carnot, ☎ 55.96.11.32 (high season, closed Sat and Sun).

SNCF ☎ 55.96.14.89., 55.96.24.83.

Hotel :
Saint-Dézery, 4 km on the Clermont road :
★★***Gravades*** (L.F.), ☎ 55.72.21.53. AE, Visa. 20 rm Ⓟ 200. Rest. ● ♦♦ closed Fri eve and Sat noon (low season). Copious fare in a country setting. Careful preparation of both regional and traditional dishes. Spec : *crêpes limousines, truite à l'oseille,* 65-250.

⛺ ★★★*De Ponty* (140 pl.), ☎ 55.72.30.05.

Youth hostel : rue Pasteur, ☎ 55.96.13.17.

Farmhouse gîte camping : 15 km from Ussel on RN89 and RD27 ; *Les Couderches,* St-Étienne-aux-Clos, 19200 Ussel, ☎ 55.94.51.40. Farm produce for sale.

Events : market 1st and 3rd Wed each month, and in mid-Nov.

Bicycle hire : M. Malves, 7, bd V.-Hugo, ☎ 55.72.10.27. M. Bourdain, 2, pl. Victoire, ☎ 55.95.25.76.

UZERCHE

Tulle 31, Limoges 56, Paris 452
A2 ✉ 19140

ⓘ pl. Lunade, ☎ 55.73.15.71 (high season).

SNCF ☎ 55.73.25.49.

Hotel :
★★***Ambroise,*** av. de Paris, ☎ 55.73.10.08. 20 rm Ⓟ closed Nov, Sat and Sun ex Jul-Aug, 100. Rest. ♦ 80-130.

⛺ ★★*La Minoterie* (33 pl.), ☎ 55.73.17.00.

Events : market 20th of each month, early Nov, and mid-Nov.

VASSIVIÈRE lake

Limoges 56, Guéret 60, Paris 413
B2 ✉ 87470 Peyrat-le-Château

Hotels :
● ★★★***Caravelle*** (L.F.), ☎ 55.69.40.97. 22 rm Ⓟ ♿ closed Feb-15 Mar, 180. Rest. ♦♦ 120-210.
★★***Golf du Limousin*** (L.F.), ☎ 55.69.41.34. 18 rm Ⓟ closed end Oct-early Mar, 132. Rest. ♦ 55-108.

⛺ ★★*Le Moulin de l'Eau* (60 pl.), ☎ 55.69.41.01 ; ★★*Les Peyrades d'Auphelle* (135 pl.), ☎ 55.69.41.32.

Lorraine and the Vosges

Battlefields and garrison towns, countryside blackened by industrial smoke and dust, cloudy skies, cold and taciturn people — these are only some of the unjust and unflattering clichés applied to a region which deserves far better. Because of its geographical location Lorraine was the site of some of the fiercest battles of both World Wars, and is still the centre of heavy industry in France. Ever since the time of Joan of Arc, born in the little town now known as Domrémy-la-Pucelle, the inhabitants of Lorraine have earned a reputation for their devotion to the nation and their willingness to work hard for its sake.

And yet Lorraine's country castles and churches, the superb cathedral of Metz, one of the best examples of Gothic architecture in Europe, and the gracious proportions of the Place Stanislas in Nancy, can hold their own against any rival. Lorraine was the cradle of many of the industrial arts in the early 18th century and is still justly renowned for its fine glassware, crystal and earthenware, which attract tourists in search of the painstaking excellence of master craftsmen. The Lunéville château, impregnated with the memory of Stanislas, ex-king of Poland and father-in-law of Louis XV, is an interesting variant on the theme of Versailles. The good Stanislas is reputed to have invented the original *rhum baba* — still a Lorraine speciality — while one of his female cooks is credited with the invention of the ubiquitous *madeleine* cake.

But perhaps the greatest charm of this region lies in its green countryside, its thick forests alternating with ploughed fields and meadows, the famous thermal stations of Bains-les-Bains and Contrexéville, and the peace and tranquillity of Lorraine's national park, created to provide the hardworking population with easy access to nature. The Vosges forest too is another inexhaustible source of pleasure for hikers and weekend walkers. The region also has another source of natural wealth in its inhabitants, who despite the harsh and often bitter destiny of their native land, can offer the tourist eager to communicate with his fellow man, a gift for solid friendship and a tradition of human solidarity.

Sightseeing

Brief description

Location : *NE corner of France between the Parisian basin and the Vosges mountains, which separate it from the Plain of Alsace; the rivers are almost all tributaries of the Meuse and the Moselle, which flow into the North Sea.*
Area : *23 700 km²*
Population : *2 331 000*
Administration : *Department of* ***Meurthe-et-Moselle,*** *Prefecture Nancy; Department of* ***Meuse,*** *Prefecture Bar-le-Duc; Department of* ***Moselle,*** *Prefecture Metz; Department of* ***Vosges,*** *Prefecture Epinal.*

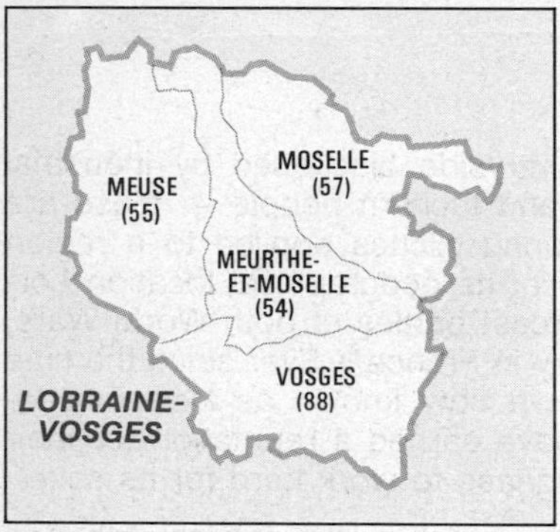

Don't miss

★★★ *Metz (B2), Nancy (B2/3)*
★★ *Dabo (C2-3), Gérardmer (C4), Lunéville (C3), Toul (B3).*

The **ARGONNE** Region★

▶ From Clermont to Beaulieu *(approx 90-120 km, half-day).* A 1-2 *(see map 1 following page).*

Rising 100m from the plains, this wooded massif separating Lorraine from Champagne was an important strategic area during WWI.

▶ **Clermont-en-Argonne :** ® (pop. 1 810) overlooking the Aire valley (view★ from the terrace of the 16thC church), on the site of the château, chapel with 16thC Holy Sepulchre; orientation chart. ▶ Near Rarécourt **fortified house of the valley** (17th-18thC; *6 km S, Jul.-Aug. 10-12 & 2-6:30;* collection of regional ceramics★). ▶ Only shell-holes mark the spot where the village of **Vauquois** once stood. Like

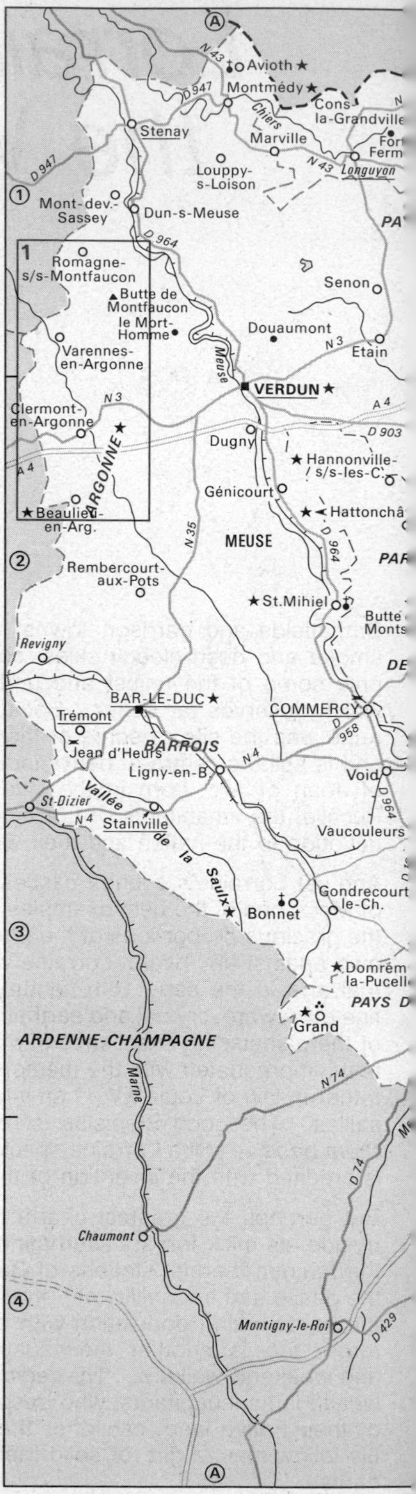

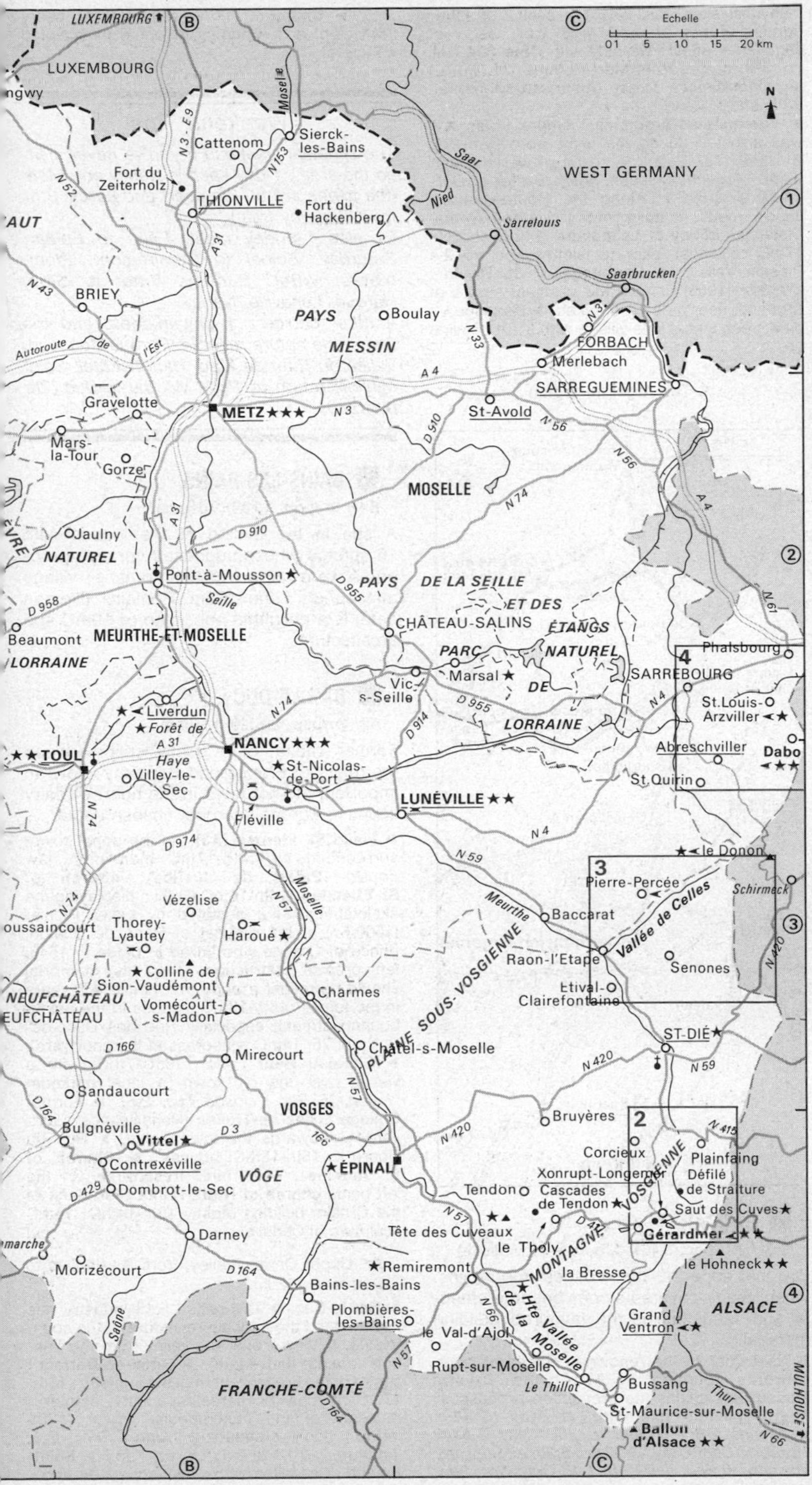
LUXEMBOURG
Echelle
0 1 5 10 15 20 km
N
WEST GERMANY
Cattenom
Sierck-les-Bains
Fort du Zeiterholz
THIONVILLE
Fort du Hackenberg
Saar
Nied
Sarrelouis
Saarbrucken
BRIEY
PAYS MESSIN
Boulay
FORBACH
Merlebach
Autoroute de l'Est
SARREGUEMINES
Gravelotte
METZ ★★★
St-Avold
Mars-la-Tour
Gorze
MOSELLE
Jaulny
NATUREL
Pont-à-Mousson ★
PAYS DE LA SEILLE
ET DES ÉTANGS
Seille
CHÂTEAU-SALINS
Beaumont
MEURTHE-ET-MOSELLE
LORRAINE
PARC NATUREL DE LORRAINE
Marsal ★
Vic-s-Seille
Phalsbourg
SARREBOURG
St.Louis-Arzviller
Liverdun
Forêt de Haye
★★ TOUL
NANCY ★★★
Abreschviller
Dabo ★★
St-Nicolas-de-Port
Villey-le-Sec
St.Quirin
LUNÉVILLE ★★
Fléville
★★ le Donon
Moselle
Meurthe
Schirmeck
Pierre-Percée
Vallée de Celles
Vézelise
Baccarat
Thorey-Lyautey
Haroué ★
Raon-l'Etape
Senones
Colline de Sion-Vaudémont
Etival-Clairefontaine
NEUFCHÂTEAU
Charmes
Vomécourt-s-Madon
ST-DIÉ ★
PLAINE SOUS-VOSGIENNE
Châtel-s-Moselle
Mirecourt
Sandaucourt
VOSGES
Bruyères
Bulgnéville
Vittel ★
Contrexéville
VÔGE
★ ÉPINAL
Corcieux
Plainfaing
Défilé de Straiture
Xonrupt-Longemer
Dombrot-le-Sec
Tendon
Cascades de Tendon ★
Saut des Cuves ★
Darney
Tête des Cuveaux
le Tholy
Gérardmer ★★
MONTAGNE VOSGIENNE
Morizécourt
★ Remiremont
la Bresse
le Hohneck ★★
Bains-les-Bains
Hte Vallée de la Moselle
Plombières-les-Bains
Grand Ventron ★
ALSACE
le Val-d'Ajol
Rupt-sur-Moselle
Le Thillot
Bussang
Thur
MULHOUSE
Saône
FRANCHE-COMTÉ
St-Maurice-sur-Moselle
Ballon d'Alsace ★★
B
C
1
2
3
4

many hill sites, this was the scene of bitter fighting during the 1914-18 war, as vast cemeteries attest; similarly with **Côte 304** (Hill no. 304, across from Mort-Homme, *11.5km E*) and **Montfaucon Crest** (American Memorial, *234 steps,* view★).
▶ **Varennes-en-Argonnes :** where Louis XVI was arrested during his flight from Paris on 21 June 1791; also the scene of wartime carnage. Argonne Museum *(daily, Easter to Oct., 10-12 & 2-6).* ▶ Along the Haute-Chevauchée★ road : a quick detour via the former Cistercian **abbey of Lachalade** (14thC church, 17thC buildings), back to Islettes and up the Biesme Valley. ▶ **Hermitage of St. Rouin :** chapel★ (1955), one of the prettiest sights of Argonne, near a string of lakes. ▶ Beaulieu★ : on a crest, a neat little village with a 13thC wine press. ☐

1. The Argonne region

■ BACCARAT

C 3 / ® / pop. 5 437 (Meurthe-et-Moselle)

On the edge of the Vosges mountains, where the fir-covered slopes become steeper and sandstone is the favoured building material.

▶ Next door to the renowned **Baccarat crystalworks** founded in 1764, the **Crystal Museum**★ explains the production processes; many splendid examples *(1 May-15 Jun, weekends 2-6; 16 Jun.-15 Jul. daily 2-6:30; 16 Jul.-15 Sept. daily 10-12 & 2-6:30, ex Sun. am, Tue.; 16-30 Sep. daily 2-6; 1-15 Oct., Apr. Sun. 2-6).* ▶ **Church :** (1957) with steeple belfry 70m high, and windows mounted in sculpted concrete. ☐

Weekend Tips

The simplest weekend if you've never visited the area : 1 day each in Nancy and Metz (the towns are 60 km apart and barely 3 hr from Paris by train).

Or else : Friday night, Paris to Epinal; Saturday, Epinal to Remiremont, Plombières, Vittel; Sunday, Vittel to Sion, Haroué, Lunéville, Nancy.

Another choice : 1 day in Metz and the 2nd in the nature reserve (Pont-à-Mousson, Vallée du Rupt de Mad, Hattonchâtel, Saint Mihiel); return to Paris via Bar-le-Duc (2hr by train).

■ BAINS-LES-BAINS

B4 / ® /pop. 1792 (Vosges)

A spa in the middle of the woods with 16 springs whose supposed curative properties were known to the Romans; village atmosphere; the "Bain Romain" (Roman bath) is a delightful specimen of 19thC spa architecture. ☐

■ BAR-LE-DUC★

A2/ ® /pop. 20 029 (Meuse)

Former capital of a duchy split between the rulers of France and Germany; now an important market town in the heart of dairy country; Europe's largest cheese depot.

▶ **Place St. Pierre★ (A3) :** in the upper town, surrounded by 14th-17thC mansions; law courts (Palais de Justice); **church of St. Etienne**★ (14th-16thC Gothic) displaying the skeletal figure★★ sculpted by Ligier Richier (1500-67) at the request of René de Châlon, prince of Orange who, killed in battle in 1545, left precise instructions that his memorial should represent a body that had lain 3 years in the tomb. 16th-18thC façades in the neighbouring streets, especially Rue des Ducs-de-Bar (no. 75, 14thC winepress in the courtyard). ▶ **Château Neuf :** (A2; 16th-17thC) with a view★ over the old town, a local **museum** *(1 Jun.-15 Sep.; closed Tue. 2-6).* ▶ Former **Collège Gilles-de-Trèves** (Renaissance courtyard★) : towards the lower town. ▶ Rue du Bourg : 16th-18thC houses. ▶ **Church of St. Antoine :** 14th-15thC frescos. ▶ On the left bank, **church of Notre-Dame :** left bank of the Ornain, building mostly 13th-14thC; 16thC sculpture of Christ★. ☐

▶ Upper Ornain Valley, from Bar-le-Duc to Domrémy *(62 km).*

▶ **Bar-le-Duc.** ▶ Diversified light industry has not changed the agricultural nature of the countryside. ▶ View★ over the valley from the **Tannois** lookout (belvédère). ▶ **Ligny-en-Barrois :** centre of the French lens-making industry; 13th-17thC church with interesting pulpit★, statuary; museum of the Luxembourg Tower (12th-14thC.): local archaeology *(Jun., Sep., 2-6; Jul.-Aug., 10-12 & 2-6; closed Tue.)* ▶ **Saint-Amand :** Gallo-Roman excavations *(open Aug.).*

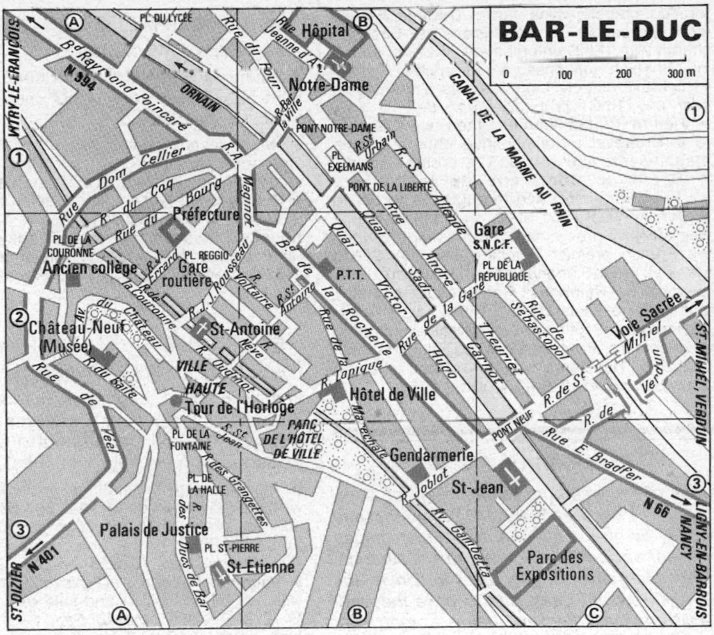

▶ **Bonnet** : *(4.5 km from Houdelaincourt)* 12th-14thC church; polychrome recumbent effigy of Saint Florentin, damaged but interesting paintings of his miracles. ▶ **Gondrecourt-le-Château** : 14thC tower next to old building housing a Horse Museum. □

■ BUSSANG

C4/ ® /pop. 1 920 (Vosges)

Among mountains near the source of the Moselle, where the Théâtre du Peuple (People's Theatre) was founded in 1895; open-air stage where performances are given by the local people *(Sun. in Aug.).* □

▶ Nearby

▶ The Route du Col (Old Pass Road) 4 km E to the source of the Moselle. A narrow forest track climbs to the **Petit Drumont** (*5 km drive then 15 mins on foot;* alt. 1 200 m; splendid view★). ▶ Down the **Moselle Valley★** via **Saint-Maurice** ® (*climb to Tête des Perches, 11 km;* alt. 1 224m; view; *or the Ballon d'Alsace★★, 9.5 km;* → Alsace) and **Le Thillot** ® (side trip to the Ballon de Servance, *1.5 km drive then 10 mins on foot,* alt. 1 216 m, superb view★). □

■ CHARMES

B3/ ® /pop. 5 457 (Vosges)

15thC church, 16thC chapel. Monument de Lorraine : *(3.5km SW)* valley view★.

▶ Nearby

▶ 9km E, **Portieux** glassworks *(visit Tue.-Fri. 9-12; closed 1 month in summer).* ▶ **Châtel-sur-Moselle** *(11 km SE)* : ruins of 15thC fortress razed by Louis XIV, currently being restored; underground passages and small museum *(Sun. and hols., 3-6, Mar.-Oct.).* □

■ COMMERCY

A2/ ® /pop. 7 958 (Meuse)

When Stanislas Leszczynski governed Lorraine in the 18thC (→ Brief Regional History), his cook, it is said, invented the widely appreciated little cakes known as *madeleines de Commercy.*

▶ **Château★** (18thC), destroyed by fire in 1944 and rebuilt, now houses municipal offices; museum with small but choice display (ivories, ceramics; *16 Jul.-2 Sep. 4 p.m daily ex. Tue.; Sun. 3, 4:30*). □

■ CONTREXÉVILLE

B4/ ® /pop. 4 582 (Vosges)

A well-known spa in a peaceful, wooded valley near Vittel (→).

▶ **Bulgnéville** *(6.5km W)* : produces several cheeses including Munster; 16thC entombment of Christ in the church; small museum.

▶ Forest of Darney, from Contrexéville to Vittel *(approx 100km, half-day).*

▶ **Contrexéville.** Through **Dombrot-le-Sec** (14thC statue of the Virgin, 16thC Sainte Anne, 18thC wrought iron) to **Viviers-le-Gras** (pretty fountains), then follow the road that winds at the foot of the hills. ▶ **Morizécourt** : 17thC Benedictine priory *(daily ex. Tue. and Fri. 2-5 in Jul.; Sat. and Sun., Aug.-Sep.).* ▶ **Sérécourt** :

fortified church; mink farm. Through **Flabémont Forest** to ▶ **Monthureux-sur-Saône :** church with 16thC entombment of Christ showing Rhenish influence. ▶ **Bleurville :** small 11th-14thC church, long used as a barn, built over an 11thC crypt *(Jul.-Aug., 9-11 & 1-7).* ▶ Return to Monthureux, then via Claudon to ▶ **Droiteval :** Romanesque church on the magnificent site of a Cistercian abbey. ▶ Detour to **Cristallerie de la Rochère** (→ Franche-Comté) and through the forest to ▶ **Darney** where the state of Czechoslovakia was officially proclaimed at a meeting between the French premier Poincaré and the Czech Masaryk in 1918 (monument; museum in 18thC town hall). ▶ **Relanges :** Romanesque church★ in the style of Cluny (11thC, 16thC nave). **Saint-Baslemont :** 16th-18thC château illustrating development from fortress to elegant residence. ▶ **Thuillières :** austere 18thC château *(Sat., Sun., Mon., 2:30-7).* ▶ **Vittel** (→). □

Joan of Arc

Joan of Arc was born in the village of Domrémy (→) on 6 January 1412. At the age of 13, by now a shepherdess, Joan began to hear voices (St. Michael, Ste. Catherine, Ste. Margaret) urging her to drive the English out of France and to have the Dauphin crowned King at Rheims. Joan kept quiet for 3 years but eventually confided in her uncle, who accompanied her to an audience with Robert de Baudricourt, the royal governor at Vaucouleurs. Undeterred by Baudricourt's incredulous dismissal (he threatened to box her ears and have her exorcised), Joan managed by her sincerity to win support among the people of the region. They gave the girl a horse and equipment, and Baudricourt, won over by her determination, supplied an escort of six men. On 23 February 1429, to the acclamations of the townsfolk, 17-year-old Joan rode out of Vaucouleurs to seek the Dauphin at Chinon. She never saw her native Lorraine again.

DOMRÉMY-LA-PUCELLE★

A3 / pop. 205 (Vosges)

The most famous village in Lorraine, among wooded hills overlooking the Meuse valley.

▶ **Joan of Arc's birthplace** (maison de Jeanne d'Arc) *(daily; 8-12:30 & 1:30-7, Apr.-12 Oct.; 9-12 & 2-5, closed Tue., rest of year).* Typical well-to-do 15thC peasant's house; the museum traces Joan's life (1412-31) and heroic career. ▶ Church : 12thC font where Joan was christened. ▶ Basilica : (1891-1926) at **Bois-Chesnu,** where Joan heard her voices; a popular place of pilgrimage; **view★** over the valley. □

▶ To Vaucouleurs *(22 km N)*

▶ **Goussaincourt :** in the outbuildings of the 16th-18thC château, a museum of peasant life and crafts exhibition. ▶ **Montbras :** château★ (1600) with superb Renaissance façade. □

DUN-SUR-MEUSE

A1 / ® /pop. 749 (Meuse)

A country town, formerly fortified, on a hill 80m above the river; 14thC church with a martial appearance.

▶ **Mont-devant-Sassey** *(6 km) :* 11th-12thC Romanesque church★ showing Rhenish influence, porch★, 11th-16thC statuary, crypt. ▶ **Stenay** ® *(13 km)* another fortified town, now a centre of light industry; a few 17th-18thC houses. Museum of the Stenay Region (archaeology, folk arts and traditions; *9-12 & 2-6:30 daily Jul.-12 Sep.; weekends in May, Jun.*). □

ÉPINAL★

BC 4/ ® /pop. 40 954 (Vosges)

Images d'Epinal, brightly coloured pictures on patriotic, pious or moralistic themes, were distributed throughout France by pedlars during the 18th and 19thC.

▶ **Museum :** (B2) paintings (including 17thC works by Georges de la Tour and Rembrandt) and an exceptional collection of popular art from the 16thC to the present day *(daily ex. Tue. and nat. hols. 10-12 & 2-6 or 5, Oct.-Mar.).* ▶ **Imagerie Pellerin :** *(42 bis quai de Dogneville, via B1)* exhibition and sale of popular art *(8-12 & 2-6 or 7, closed Sat., Sun. and nat. hols.; Sat. 8-10 am Jun.-Sep.).* ▶ Near the Place des Vosges : (B2; arcades, old houses) 13th-14thC **basilica of St.-Maurice;** 11thC tower, reinforced 13thC; late Romanesque and regional Gothic. **Also...** ▶ **Church of Notre-Dame :** (A1; 1958) door with enamelled panels; stained glass★. Library and Rose Garden on left bank of the Moselle (via B1). □

Salt

From time immemorial Lorraine has been a major centre of salt production in France. Traces of large salt mines dating from prehistoric times have been found in Saulnois (→ Marsal). Today, Lorraine remains responsible for half the national production.
In the 19thC, the availability of salt deposits encouraged the development of chemical industries (e.g., chlorine, bicarbonate of soda), which were established mostly between Nancy and Lunéville.

GÉRARDMER★★

C4 / ® /pop. 9 647 (Vosges)

The oldest tourist office in France was founded here in July 1875; pure air and superb countryside (lake, meadows, woods, mountains) make it a pleasant year-round resort where the traditional production of fine linens continues. ▶ Delightful walks by the lake. ▶ In town, **Forestry Museum; Vosges Regional Craftshop.** ▶ More than 300km of marked trails in the forest. □

▶ Vallée des Lacs (the valley of lakes) and the upper Meurthe region *(round trip approx 70km, half-day, see map 2).*

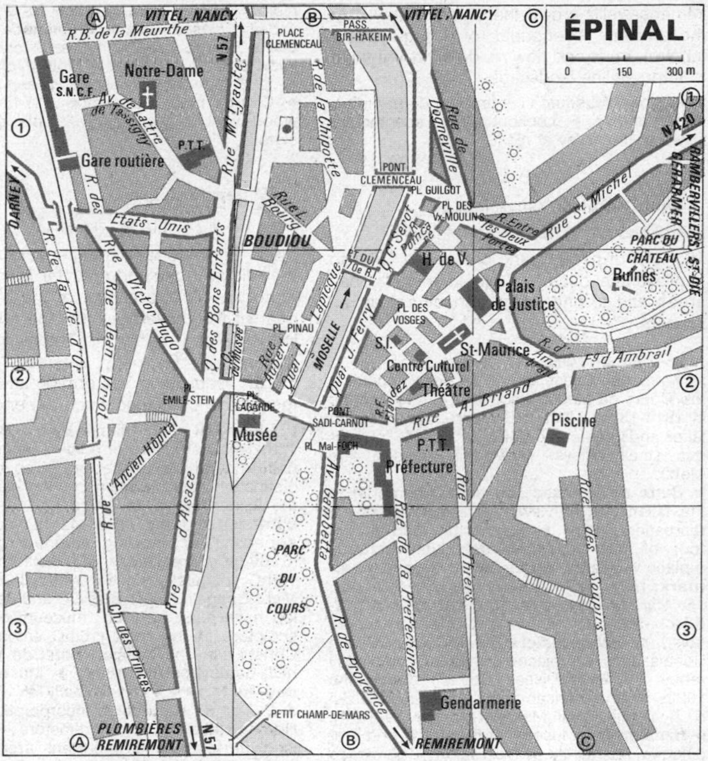

▶ **Gérardmer.** ▶ **Saut-des-Cuves★ :** waterfall. ▶ 2km beyond **Xonrupt-Longemer** ®, a road on the right leads to **Moineaudière :** exhibition and sale of cacti, fossils and minerals★. ▶ One way leads to D417 running above the Vallée des-Lacs : view★★ over **Lakes Retournemer** and **Longemer** from the **Roche du Diable** (devil's rock)★ : exhibition of minerals, *Jun.-Sep.* ▶ From **Le Collet :** ® *(2 km from the*

2. Vallée des Lacs and the Upper Meurthe region

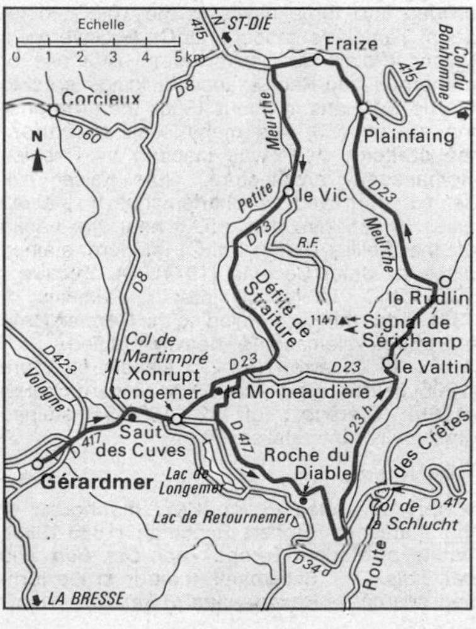

Schlucht pass)★, excursions to Hohneck★★ and the Alpine Garden at Haut-Chitelet (→ Alsace). Return by the Meurthe Valley. Just before Rudlin : the **Rudlin Waterfall** *(45 min walk there and back).* ▶ **Plainfaing** ® and **Fraize :** up the **valley** of the **Petite Meurthe.** ▶ From Vic : forest track to the **Sérichamp Signal** (alt. 1 147 m ; panorama★★). ▶ **Défilé de Straiture :** valley narrows and, in summer, the river disappears under the tumbled rocks. □

▶ Towards Épinal

▶ **Liézey :** *(10 km)* craftshop *(exhibition, sale ; Sun. and school hols., 3-6 ; closed Jan-Mar.).* ▶ After **Le Tholy** ® : great and small **Tendon** ® waterfalls★. □

▶ Tétras road, from Gérardmer to Bussang *(approx 40 km).*

▶ **La Bresse** ® *(14km S of Gérardmer) :* Important winter sports resort ; the road cuts through 100 km² of forest inhabited by red and roe deer, wild boar, woodgrouse and other game. ▶ **Lake Corbeaux :** walled in granite. Proceed to La Vierge pass and, by the forest roads, one arrives at the foot of **Grand Ventron★** (alt. 1 202 m ; *10 mins on foot ;* view★). ▶ From La Chaume, get back on the road which, starting at **Ventron** ®; climbs towards the Oderen Pass. ▶ Before arriving at the summit, turn right on a small road which leads to the Page Pass, then back down towards Bussang (→). □

LONGWY

B1 / pop. 17 482 (Meurthe-et-Moselle)

The second-largest steel production centre in Lorraine is at Longwy-Bas, where immense mills crowd the Chiers Valley. At the ancient stronghold of Longwy-Haut (above), trees and flowers do what they can to improve the landscape.

▶ **Regional Museum :** ceramics and enamels★ from Longwy. ▶ Lookout offers spectacular views of the valley at night.

■ LORRAINE Nature Park★

AB2 and C2/ ® (Meurthe-et-Moselle)

185 km² of nature park, created in 1974 to improve the quality of life in major urban areas and to encourage agricultural development.

▶ Western zone

▶ From the Meuse to the Moselle, including the Côtes de Meuse : scene of heavy fighting in 1914-18; the Plain of Woëvre, covered with lakes and forests; the Côtes de Moselle (numerous small valleys, → Pont-à-Mousson and Metz).
▶ **Butte de Montsec :** American memorial to the fallen (1918); view over Lake Madine; a recreation centre. ▶ Follow the road at the foot of the slopes, where plum orchards replace vineyards. ▶ **Heudicourt** ® : **bird sanctuary** *(N)*★ *(15 Jun.-15 Sep., 10-8 pm; 15 Mar.-14 Jun. and 16 Sep.-15 Nov., 2-6 Mon.-Sat., or 10-6 Sun., nat. hols. and school hols.).* ▶ **Hattonchâtel**★ **:** 14thC church with Renaissance altarpiece★; château completely rebuilt (in "Walt Disney Gothic") during the 1920s by an American donor *(daily, 9-12 & 2-5 or 7);* Louise Cottin Museum (painter, 1907-74).
▶ **Hannonville :** Museum of Rural Arts and Traditions★ (19thC life in the region; *2-6, closed Tue.; Thu. and Sat. 9-12 & 2-6*).

▶ Eastern zone

▶ Forest and lakes (now recreation areas) between Château Salins and Sarrebourg. ▶ **Vic-sur-Seille :** a few old houses, including the 1456 Mint *(Jul.-15 Sep., Wed-Sun., 9-12 & 2-6);* gate and towers of 13thC château. ▶ **Marsal**★ **:** salt was mined here in prehistoric times; Salt Museum★ *(2-6, closed Tue.; Thu. and Sat. 9-12).* **Tarquimpol :** on the edge of Lake Lindre; church with round bell-tower; 1.5 km farther, Château (16th-18thC) Alteville. ▶ **Vision-de-Ste.-Croix Park :** near Stock lake *(daily ex. Mon. from 10 am., Apr.-Nov.).* ▶ **Fénétrange** *(E of park)* : small mediaeval town where a nightwatchman still makes the rounds *(May-Sep., 9pm and 10pm);* old houses, remains of fortifications (15th-16thC door); château (15thC), now Museum of Folk Arts and Traditions. ▶ **Munster** *(N of park, near* ***Albestroff***) : 13th-14thC church★ in pure Gothic style. □

■ LUNÉVILLE★★

C3 / ® /pop. 23 231 (Meurthe-et-Moselle)

The 18thC philosopher Voltaire called this town "the Versailles of Lorraine" in honour of brilliant evenings at the court of Duke Leopold and later of Stanislas Leszczynski.

▶ **Château**★★★ **:** (started in 1702; restored after WWII) laid out like Versailles; unfortunately, the interior decoration has completely disappeared. *Son et lumière* spectacle 'Le Grand Carrousel' in the gardens (*Fri, Sat., Sun., 29 Jun.-16 Sep.).* ▶ **Museum :** local ceramics★, history of the local garrison *(9-12 & 2-5 or 6 daily; closed Tue).* ▶ **Promenade des Bosquets :** large garden in French style *(son et lumière show Jul.-Sep).* ▶ **Motorcycle Museum** *(9-12 & 2-6 daily, closed Sun. and nat. hols).* ▶ **Church of St. Jacques**★ **:** (1745; Regency wood-work★) a perfect example of Rococo style. □

■ METZ★★★

B2 / ® /pop. 118 502 (Moselle)

Metz, an important commercial town since the Middle Ages and now 3hr from Paris by motorway, is the capital of the region and seat of the university. On the edge of the industrialised valley of Thionville, it was annexed to Germany between 1871 and 1918. Rebuilding, restoration and development have continued since the end of WWI.

▶ **Cathedral of St.-Etienne**★★★ : (B2; Gothic) 13th-14thC structure of golden sandstone; the uniformity of the architecture gives it particular distinction; the elevations of the eastern end, the Tour (tower) de Mutte (facing the place d'Armes) and the nave (42 m vaulting) are superb; the glowing stained glass★★★ (6 500 m² in area) dates from the 13th, 15th and 16thC; panels designed by the 20thC artists Marc Chagall, Roger Bissière and Jacques Villon have been installed; museum of religious sculpture in the crypt (16thC entombment of Christ★). ▶ The classical **Hôtel de Ville** (town hall) dates from the 18thC. ▶ **Museum of Art and History**★★ **:** *(B1-2; daily ex. Tue., 9-12 & 2-5 or 6)* in buildings incorporating ancient Roman baths and 15thC grainstore; well-organised museum with important archaeological and mediaeval collections; fine arts; military section. ▶ South of the cathedral : covered market (an episcopal palace begun in 1785 and never finished) past streets leading to the ▶ **Place St. Louis :** mediaeval arcades, 14th-16thC houses with sturdy stone buttresses. ▶ **Church of St. Martin :** (B3; 13th-15thC) on the Roman rampart. ▶ **Esplanade**★ **:** bordered N by the 18thC law court (palais de justice); (A2) offers a pleasant stroll overlooking the Moselle. ▶ **Church of St. Pierre-aux-Nonnains**★ **:** reputedly the oldest in France, occupying a 4thC Roman basilica that was divided into three naves in the 10thC; octagonal Templar's chapel (12thC). ▶ Governor's Palace (Palais du Gouverneur) : (A3) one of numerous neo-Renaissance buildings erected by the Germans in about 1900; the area near the station (B3) has many such structures; the **station**★ itself was inspired by Rhenish Romanesque architecture. Note Kaiser Wilhelm II portrayed as Charlemagne in stained glass. ▶ **St. Maximin :** (C2) near the banks of the Seille, partly 12thC; modern stained glass by Jean Cocteau (1974). **St. Eucaire :** 12th-15thC; interesting interior. Remains of 13th-15thC ramparts including the **German Gate** (porte des Allemands)★, heavily fortified.
Also... ▶ **Theatre**★ (B1-2) : elegant structure (1806) next to the police HQ. ▶ Modern **church of Ste. Thérèse :** (off A2; 1938-54) stained glass by N. Untersteller. □

▶ Nearby

▶ **Scy-Chazelles** *(5 km W) :* the house of the statesman Robert Schuman (1886-1963), "father of Modern Europe" *(Apr.-Oct. Sun. and nat. hols. 2-6).* Schuman's tomb is in the fortified church. ▶ **Rozérieulles** *(3 km on) :* 15thC

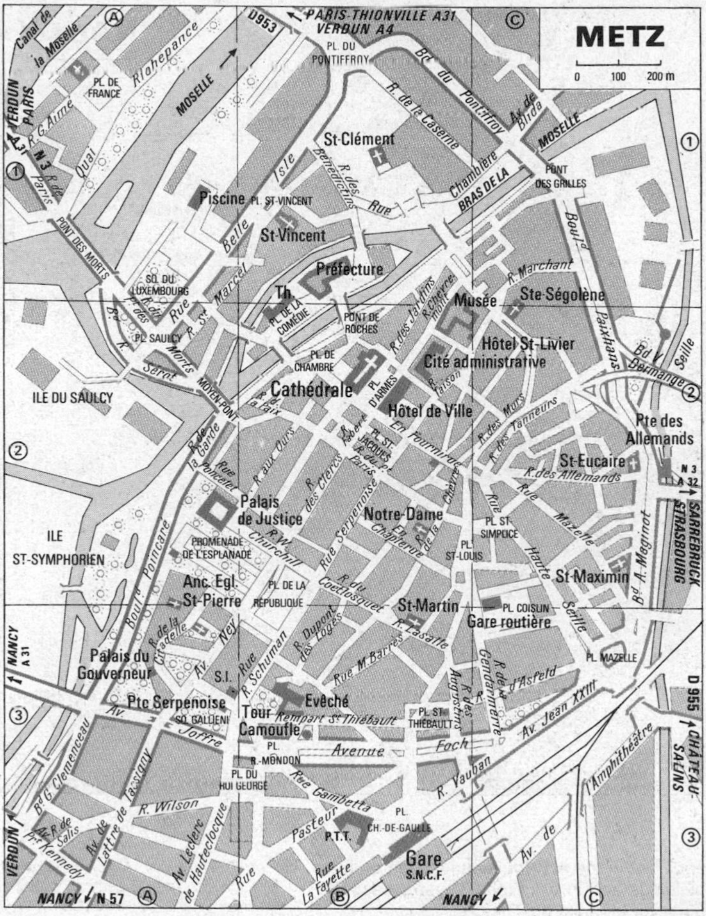

church, old houses, view★ over Metz. ▶ Road up the left bank★ of the Moselle : view of Roman aqueduct at **Jouy-aux-Arches ;** narrow road right to ▶ **Gorze** ® : (site★) old town clustered around an abbey, 17thC buildings, late 12thC church with Romanesque exterior, Gothic interior; small museum of the Gorze region *(Mar.-Oct., Sun., hols.)*. ▶ Lorraine Nature Reserve (parc naturel ; →) : excursion to the **Rupt de Mad Valley,** via **Waville** (13thC church) as far as Jaulny, with 16th-18thC château *(May-Oct. daily 2-6)*. ▶ **Sillegny** *(16 km S)* : 13th-15thC church with frescos from 1540. □

■ MONTMÉDY★

A1 / ® /pop. 2324 (Meuse)

▶ **Upper town★ :** typical 17thC fortifications ; tour the ramparts, moats (now dry) and underground passages (directional arrows) starting at the barracks (SI ; small museum) *(daily 9-6 Feb.-Oct. ; Sun. am rest of year)*. ▶ **Lower town :** Bastien Lepage (local painter) museum in the town hall. □

▶ Nearby

▶ **Avioth** *(8 km N) :* flamboyant Gothic basilica★★ (12thC-14thC), site of pilgrimage every 16 July ; Gothic and Renaissance furnishings★, 14thC stained glass ; the Récevresse (receptacle)★, a small Gothic structure in front of the church, is where pilgrims used to leave offerings. ▶ **Fort at Villy-la-Ferté** *(19 km W) :* western end of the Maginot Line, the defensive barrier erected between the two World Wars to protect French territory from invasion from the east and named after Minister of War André Maginot (1877-1932). *(1:30-5:15 pm, Easter to Oct., Sun. and nat. hols. ; daily Jul.-Aug.)*. ▶ **Marville** *(12 km SE) :* 16th town that prospered from the leather and cloth industries ; unusually large number of 16th-17thC houses with carved façades ; 11th-12thC chapel (often closed) ; cemetery, a museum of 14th-17thC funerary sculpture. □

■ NANCY★★★

B2-3 / ® /pop. 99307 (Meurthe-et-Moselle)
(see plan following page)

A town proud of its history, from the dukes who made it their capital, to Stanislas Leszczynski who made it elegant. Now an important industrial and university town, Nancy has not forgotten its artistic heritage,

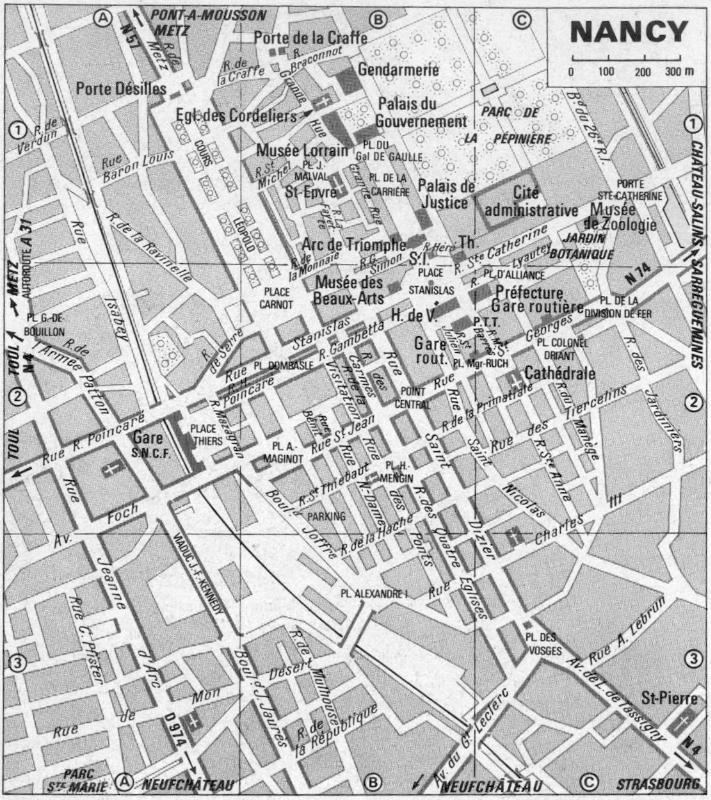

apparent in the Art Nouveau façades on the buildings and in the World Theatre Festival (Festival Mondial du Théâtre).

▶ **Place Stanislas★★★ :** (B2) a magnificent mid-18thC architectural achievement created for Stanislas Leszczynski by Emmanuel Héré, an architect of Nancy; fountains★ by Guibal, a Nîmes sculptor; Jean Lamour, a local craftsman, wrought the gates of gilt iron★★ as well as the baluster of the town hall (hôtel de ville) staircase★ *(audio-guided visits of the reception rooms, evenings 15 Jun.-15 Sep.).* ▶ **Fine Arts Museum :** Italian works, French Classical and contemporary paintings *(10-12 & 2-6, closed Mon, am and Tue.).* ▶ Place Stanislas is linked to **Place de la Carrière** (B1) by a triumphal arch in honour of Louis XV. Former ducal château (16thC), now the **Museum of Lorraine** *(B1; 10-12 & 2-5 or 6, closed Tue. and nat. hols.).* ▶ **Cordeliers' church :** tombs of the dukes of Lorraine; recumbent effigy★ of Philippe de Gueldre (mid-16thC) *(same hours).* **Museum of Folk Arts and Traditions** *(daily ex Mon. 10-12 & 2-5 or 6).* ▶ 16th and 17thC mansions, some in poor repair, in neighbouring streets. ▶ Grande Rue, main street of the old town, leads to the **Craffe Gateway :** (14th-15thC) now a museum of religious sculpture *(15 Jun.-15 Sep., 10-12 & 2-6, closed Tue.).* ▶ Walk back to the town centre through the 60-acre plant nursery **(La Pépinière).** ▶ At the entrance to the **Botanical Gardens** (C1) is the **Zoological Museum :** the tropical aquarium★ is unique in France *(2-6; closed Tue. ex. Jul.-Aug.).* ▶ Through the Place d'Alliance to the Classical **cathedral :** (C2), treasury★ (visits by request). **Also...** ▶ **Church of Notre-Dame de Bonsecours :** avenue Strasbourg (via C3) 18thC tomb of Stanislas Leszczynski; **Museum of the School of Nancy★★ :** (36 Rue du Sergent Blandan, via Avenue Foch, A3; *10-12 & 2-5 or 6; closed Tue.*) major contributions by local artists to the Art Nouveau movement. Several houses exemplify the style; ask for addresses at the museum. **Cristalleries Daum :** (Rue des Cristalleries via C1); crystal-works *(weekday mornings, pm Sat. and Sun);* **Museum of Ironwork★ :** (at Jarville) metallurgy since prehistoric times *(2-5 or 6, closed Tue.).* □

▶ Nearby

▶ **Château de Fléville** *(8 km S on B33 and 1km left) :* Renaissance building with 12thC keep *(Apr.-Oct., Sat., Sun. and nat. hols., 1-7; Jul.-Aug. 2-6 daily).* ▶ **Chartreuse de Bosserville** *(8 km E) :* 17th-18thC convent buildings. Farther on, **Saint-Nicolas-de-Port :** flamboyant Gothic (late 15th-early 16thC) basilica★ : large size emphasises the importance of pilgrimages to the relic (a finger preserved here) of the patron saint of Lorraine; early 16thC stained glass; treasury. ▶ **Haye forest★** *(10 km W on N4) :* zoo★ (mostly local varieties; *9-12 & 2-sunset, closed Mon.*); Automobile Museum *(Jul.-Sep., Sat.-Sun., 2:30-7).* ▶ **Liverdun★** ®, *(15 km NW) :* on a hill in a bend of the Moselle; 16thC gate, late-12thC church. □

The art nouveau school of Nancy

Starting in 1901, Émile Gallé, master glass-blower and cabinet-maker, assembled a group of artists who based their work on flower forms. Stained glass by J. Gruber, metalwork by G. Prouvé, furniture by L. Majorelle and vases by E. Gallé and the Daum brothers attracted considerable interest, but had little influence on the general taste. After half a century of neglect, Gallé vases now fetch substantial prices at antique dealers.

NEUFCHÂTEAU

B3 / ® /pop. 9086 (Vosges)

Rulership of the town was hotly disputed during the Middle Ages by the dukes of Champagne and Lorraine.

▶ On the hill where the ducal château used to stand, the **church of St. Nicolas** (12th-13thC) has two stories to fit the steep slope; it houses a holy sepulchre★ with a group of nine figures (15thC Swabian). ▶ Town hall (Hôtel de Ville) Renaissance (1597), fine Italian staircase. □

▶ Nearby

▶ **Grand**★ *(23 km W) :* despite its name (big), a small village; excavations (continuing for the past century) of a Roman town, including a large amphitheatre *(9-12 & 2-7 or 5 in winter, daily);* basilica has the largest mosaic★★ in France *(daily Apr.-11 Nov., Sat. and Sun. rest of year; closed Feb.);* 15thC church. ▶ **Pompierre** *(11.5 km S) :* church with Romanesque doorway★ (12thC), naive but lively sculpture. □

PLOMBIÈRES-LES-BAINS

BC4 / ® /pop. 2298 (Vosges)

Typical 18th-19thC spa in a deep valley framed by forests.

▶ Street names constitute a directory of famous invalids who have taken the waters at the 30 warm springs; **Bain** *(bath)* **Stanislas** (1736; underground, *visits 3pm Tue., Thu., Sat. in season);* **Bain Romain; Bain National** (Napoleonic era façade, pre-1814); **Thermes** (warm baths) **Napoleon** were built during the Second Empire (Napoleon III, ca. 1855). ▶ Maison des Arcades (1761; SI). ▶ **Louis Français Museum :** Barbizon school painter (→ Ile-de-France) and his associates *(2-6, closed Tue. in season).* ▶ National Park. ▶ **Fontaine Stanislas :** *(4 km SW)* in beech woods. □

PONT-À-MOUSSON★

B2 / ® /pop. 15746 (Meurthe-et-Moselle)

The name is recognized throughout France on drainpipes and manhole covers.

▶ Place Duroc : surrounded by 16th-18thC **arcaded houses,** the town centre. ▶ On the right bank, the 15th-16thC **church of St. Martin :** late 15thC entombment of Christ. Opposite, the Jesuit College : (restored) an important 16thC university, transferred to Nancy in 1768. ▶ The **Premonstratensian** (Prémontres) **abbey**★ : 18thC monastery just to the north, now a cultural centre and the site of international meetings for the plastic arts, music, theatre and contemporary dance *(8:30-12:30 & 2-6:30, closed Sun. am, 20 Dec.-19 Jan.);* Baroque church with three naves, wrought iron baluster★ in the abbey. □

▶ Nearby

▶ **Dieulouard** *(7 km S) :* church (1504), two 15thC statues of the Virgin; from here make a short excursion to **Little Switzerland of Lorraine** (petite Suisse Lorraine) through the Esch valley. □

REMIREMONT★

C4 / ® /pop. 10860 (Vosges)

A busy textile centre, once the site of an abbey for noble ladies that was as exclusive as it was independent.

▶ The main street : (renamed Rue du General De Gaulle) more than 200m of 18thC arcades. ▶ **Charles-de-Bruyères Museum :** *(10-12 & 2-5, 6 or 7, closed Tue. and nat. hols)* regional life and history. **Charles-Friry Museum :** history of the abbey, fine arts *(May-Oct. 2-6, closed Tue.).* ▶ **Abbey church** (13thC, restored 18thC) has an 11thC crypt. Hôtel de Ville (town hall) : adjacent, the former abbess's residence (1752). Nearby, 17th-18thC houses where the ladies of the abbey (canonesses) lived independently without the restraints of vows. □

▶ Nearby

▶ **Tête des Cuveaux**★ : lookout peak *(15 km N, 20mns on foot; alt. 783m, panorama★).* □

SAINT-DIÉ★

C3 / ® /pop. 24816 (Vosges)

This city calls itself "America's godmother," since, in 1507, the first book calling the New World by the name of America was printed here. The pink sandstone buildings were reconstructed after WWII.

▶ **Cathedral :** Classical façade covers a typically Rhenish-Romanesque structure (12thC); the 16thC choir shows the influence of Champagne. A flamboyant Gothic **cloister**★ links it with the **Church of Notre-Dame**★ : (12thC) also Romanesque, from the same source. ▶ Behind, **museum** of Everyday Life in the Vosges mountains *(9-12 & 2-7, closed Mon.).* ▶ Moyo-dé-Soyotte at the **Faing de Sainte-Marguerite** *(2 km S, N415) :* a renovated farm illustrating rural crafts and life. □

Just desserts

The rhum baba, a yeast-cake steeped in rum syrup, was supposedly invented by ex-King Stanislas at Lunéville. Sweet delicacies are extremely popular in Lorraine : chocolate thistles (chardons), *candy pebbles* (cailloux) *in the Vosges, truffles* (truffes) *and "little nothings"* (nonettes); *small butter cakes* (madeleines) *from Commercy, hard candies* (dragées) *in Verdun, fondants* (bergamotes) *and macaroons* (macarons) *from Nancy, and the seedless preserves of whole red currants from Bar-le-Duc.*

■ SAINT-MIHIEL★

A2 / ® /pop. 5 555 (Meuse)

On the banks of the Meuse, seat of an important abbey from Carolingian times, later a 14thC regional capital.

▶ Birthplace of the sculptor Ligier Richier (1507-1567), whose works are the principal attractions in local churches : Fainting Virgin supported by Saint-John★ in **St. Michel** (rebuilt 17thC, 16th-18thC furnishings). The neighbouring **abbey★,** rebuilt at the same time, now houses the municipal offices, Court and Library★. **Church of St. Etienne :** Holy Sepulchre★★ (16thC). □

■ SARREBOURG

C2 / ® /pop. 15 139 (Moselle)

On the edge of the Lorraine plateau, abutting the outcrops of the Vosges, which supplied the pink sandstone for its houses.

▶ **Chapel of the Cordeliers :** (13thC) façade illuminated by a modern stained-glass window★ (Chagall). ▶ **Regional Museum of Sarrebourg :** (13 Avenue de France; *8-12 & 2-6, closed Tue.; closed Sun. am out of season)* 16thC ceramics★. □

▶ Nearby

▶ **Saint-Ulrich** *(4 km NW) :* Gallo-Roman villa *(guided tours 4 and 5 pm Sun. and nat. hols. 15 May-15 Sep., daily Jul.-Aug.).* ▶ **Reding :** *(3.5 km E)* 13thC frescos in chapel of Ste. Agathe. ▶ **Phalsbourg** ® *(16 km E) :* 16thC fortified square; museum of local military history and art on the Place d'Armes (apply to the Mayor's office; *15 Mar.-31 Oct. 2-5; Sun. and nat. hols. 10-12, Wed. and Sat. 9-11).* Veralor crystal-works *(9-12 & 1:30-6; Sat. 9-12).* □

▶ From Phalsbourg to the Donon *(67 km, half-day; see map 3).*

▶ **Phalsbourg.** Enter the narrow Zorn valley at **Lutzelbourg★** ® overlooked by a ruined 12thC château on a spur (view★). A few kilometres upstream, the spectacular barge lift at **Saint-Louis-Arzviller★** cuts out 17 locks *(visit by boat daily Mar.-Nov.).* ▶ **Rocher** (rock) **de**

3. From Phalsbourg to the Donon

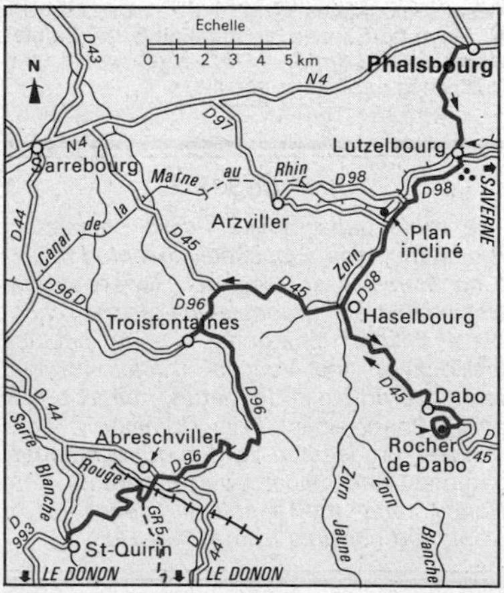

Dabo★★®: (alt. 664 m) provides a superb view that can hardly be bettered - even by climbing the tower. ▶ Just off the road, **Niderviller** and **Vallerysthal** have been producing fine crystal and ceramics since the 18thC. ▶ A little steam train offers trips through the forest at **Abreschviller** ® in a pretty valley watered by the Sarre-Rouge *(Sun. and nat. hols. in Apr., plus Sat. in May, Jun., Sep., daily Jul.-Aug.).* ▶ 18thC abbey church at **Saint-Quirin** is topped by a triple onion dome; from **Turquestein-Blancrupt** ® down the Sarre-Blanche valley to ascend to the Donon. □

■ SARREGUEMINES

C1-2 / ® /pop. 25 178 (Moselle)

Separated from Germany by the river Sarre and famous for ceramics.

▶ Unique collection of ceramics★ from 18thC to present day in the town hall museum *(2-6 ex. Tue. and Wed. 9-12).* ▶ Nearby, very old kiln. □

▶ Nearby

▶ **Frauenberg** *(6 km NE) :* ruined château (14thC). ▶ **Zetting** *(7 km SE) :* 15th-16thC church; Romanesque round bell-tower; stained glass; furnishings. ▶ **Heckenransbach** *(9 km SW) :* fortified cylindrical bell-tower★ (10thC). □

■ SAULX Valley★

Stainville to Mognéville and Bar-le-Duc *(41 km, approx. 2hr).* A3

Neat stone houses alongside a tributary of the Marne that has provided power for local industries since the Middle Ages.

▶ **Stainville** ® : 16thC château. ▶ **Bazincourt** ® *(6 km) :* château (1534; *Sun. and nat. hols. am in Jul.; last 2 wks of Aug. and Sep.; am daily first 2 wks Aug. and Sep).* ▶ **Rupt-aux-Nonnains** ® : pretty stone bridge (1775). ▶ **Haironville :** two châteaux almost face-to-face, La Varenne★ (16thC; *15 Jul.-end Aug., 10-12 & 2-6*) in a beautiful park, and La Forge (1735). **Ville-sur-Saulx :** paper mills, now disused, were active in 1348, château (1555) and outbuildings *(Easter-31 Oct. ex Tue., Wed.).* ▶ Beyond **Lisle-en-Rigault :** the road skirts the park of the **Château de Jean d'Heurs★** (18thC, restored 19thC, *visits summer by appt., tel. 29.71.30.52*). ▶ **Couvonges :** Romanesque church★ (11th-13thC) with overhanging roof. ▶ **Mognéville :** church (13th-15thC) with magnificent 15thC carved wood altarpiece★. ▶ Return to Bar-le-Duc along the same road as far as **Beurey** then via **Trémont-sur-Saulx** ®. □

■ SENONES

C3 / pop. 3 506 (Vosges)

The 18thC capital of the principality of Salm, which Voltaire said a snail could walk around in one day. The town grew up around a Benedictine abbey, today occupied by a textile factory.

▶ **Château** of the Princes of Salm, **abbey** and town hall form a fine if austere 18thC architectural group; at the foot of the abbey staircase★ is a small **museum** of local history; in summer *(Sun. 11:30 am),* re-enactment in period costume of the changing of the guard. □

▶ Round trip of the Donon and the Celles Valley *(approx 80 km, half-day; see map 4).*

▶ **Senones.** ▶ The road runs up the Rabodeau Valley into the forest; pretty drive to the Donon pass★ (→ Alsace) then down to Raon-l'Étape. ▶ **The Plaine Valley** (also known as Celles Valley) has magnificent fir forests on the slopes. ▶ From **Vexaincourt,** charming drive to **Maix Lake.** ▶ The sawmill *(scierie)* at **Hallière** *(open in summer)* continues a traditional valley trade. ▶ From **Celles-sur-Plaine** up to **Pierre Percée** at the foot of a ruined 11thC château (view★) ▶ Beyond the lake, which supplies part of the needs of the French electricity company (E. D. F.), the road joins the Meurthe Valley at Raon-l'Étape. ▶ **Etival-Clairefontaine :** 12thC abbey; tourist train to Senones. ▶ **Moyenmoutier :** (between Etival and Senones) beautiful 18thC church (choir stalls). □

4. Donon and the Celles Valley

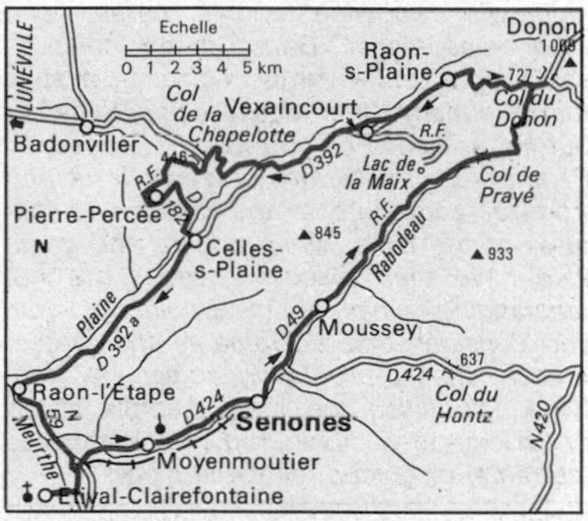

■ SION-VAUDÉMONT Hill★

B3 ® (Meurthe-et-Moselle)

Limestone crescent emerging from flat, rich earth. One end of the crescent is the site of a very old pilgrimage to the Virgin; at the other is the ruined château of the counts of Vaudémont, dukes of Lorraine.

▶ **Views** over the countryside from the orientation chart behind the convent (archaeological and missionary museum). ▶ Signal de Vaudémont *(3 km S) :* another orientation chart and view. ▶ **Vaudémont :** ruined 11thC fortress. □

▶ Nearby

▶ **Thorey-Lyautey** *(6 km W) :* château built in 1928, currently being converted into a museum. ▶ **Vézelise :** *(8 km N)* 16thC houses, church with Renaissance stained glass, covered markets (1599). ▶ **Haroué** *(11 km NE) :* château★ of the princes of Beauvau-Craon, one of the masterpieces of 18thC architecture in Lorraine *(15 Mar.-15 Nov., 2-6).* ▶ **Mirecourt :** *(17 km S)* famous for skilled musical-instrument makers (museum in the municipal offices, *Mon.-Fri., 9-12 & 2-5*); covered markets contemporary with those at Vézelise; the bell-tower of the church (13th-15thC) is shut in by houses. □

■ THIONVILLE

B1 / ® /pop. 41 448 (Moselle)

Capital of a vast industrial agglomeration stretching along the Moselle to Metz and invading neighbouring valleys, this iron- and steel-working city was hard hit by the early-1980s steel crisis.

▶ Thionville was a favourite residence of Charlemagne, and later became an important fortress. Still evident are 16thC arcaded houses, bastions, a bell-tower and the **Tour aux Puces** (tower of fleas; so-called from a grisly legend about a princess, captive in the tower, who was bitten to death)★ (11th-12thC; local history museum, *May.-Sep., 10-12 & 2-6, Oct.-Apr., 2-6; closed Mon.*). ▶ **Château de la Grange★ :** at the north exit from town (furniture★; *Sat., Sun., hols., 2:30-5:30*). □

▶ Nearby

▶ You can visit several sectors of the Maginot Line : **Zeiterholz** *(9 km NW,* near Entrange; *1st and 3rd Sun. in Jun., Jul., Aug., 2-5:30);* **Immerhof** (near Hettange-Grande, *2nd and 4th Sun*); **Hackenberg★** *(20 km, near Veckring)* the most important position *(Sat., Sun. from 2 pm).* ▶ **Rodemack** *(15 km N) :* remains of 14thC ramparts★ and a Baillif's House *(Sep.-Jun., daily ex Mon., 3-7);* **Roussy-le-Bourg :** two large châteaux (15th and 18thC) and further N, the château de Praisch (17thC., park). **Sierck-les-Bains** ® : where the river Moselle narrows into a gorge; ruined 11thC château high on the rocks *(9:30-12 & 1:30-7 closed Mon. am; view★).* □

■ TOUL★★

B3 / ® /pop. 17 752 (Meurthe-et-Moselle)

Overflowing 17thC fortifications, this ancient episcopal seat stretches along the Moselle, which is in the course of being "depolluted" to meet European standards.

The **cathedral★★** (13th-14thC) Gothic style of Champagne with flamboyant Gothic façade★★ (late 15thC); view from the cloister★. The cathedral symbolised the town's historic independence as one of the Three Bishoprics (see Brief Regional History) that existed outside the jurisdiction of either Lorraine or France until 1648. ▶ **Church of St. Gengoult★ :** (13th-15thC) close in style to the cathedral but with an even more elegant 16thC cloister. ▶ In the former infirmary (Maison Dieu, 16th-17thC) the local **museum** is currently undergoing restoration. □

▶ Nearby

▶ **Pierre-la-Treiche** *(8 km E) :* picnic spot on the banks of the Moselle. ▶ **Bruley** *(6 km NW) :* with its neighbours, among the last vine-growing areas of central Lorraine; they produce "Gris de Toul," a very dry white wine. ▶ **Écrouves :** 12th-13thC Romanesque church. □

■ VAUCOULEURS

A3 / pop. 2 511 (Meuse)

Little remains of the château where Robert de Baudricourt, royal governor of the region, dismissed Joan of Arc after threatening to box her ears (see box). The chapel still stands (rebuilt in 1924, except for the 13thC crypt).

▶ The **French Gateway** (La Porte de France) : where Joan set out for Chinon, was rebuilt in the 17thC; a few other towers remain from the old ramparts. ▶ 18thC church. ▶ **Johannique museum,** Place de la Mairie with Joan of Arc room; Joan prayed in front of the image of Christ (then in a country chapel) before setting out on her mission in 1429. *(Jul.-Aug., 9-12 & 2-6 and on request from the town hall rest of the year).* ▶ **Gombervaux** *(4 km farther)* : ruins of 14thC feudal **château** with gate keep. □

Beer, wine and spirits

Not long ago, almost every regional town had its own brewery and there were great brews to be discovered. In recent years, take-overs, amalgamations and closures have reduced the brewing industry to a few vast factories whose beer is consistent but little else. Wines from the Côtes de Toul (rosé, called «grey» [gris] *locally) and the* Côtes de Moselle *near Metz (white) are dry, fruity and perfumed, delicate and fine.If you are not driving, try an* eau-de-vie, *one of the fruit-flavoured spirits that rival those of Alsace and Haute-Saône : cherry* (kirsch), *raspberry* (framboise), *purple plum* (quetsche), *sloe* (prunelle), *bilberry* (myrtille), *pear* (poire) *and especially the little golden* mirabelle *plum with its incomparable perfume.*

VERDUN★

A2 / ® /pop. 24 120 (Meuse)

This name is forever-written on the blackest pages of history, even though German and French troops alike showed heroic courage and self-denial. The successive battles from Feb. 1916 to Oct. 1917 killed more than 800 000 men.

▶ **Cathedral★ :** (11th-12thC, frequently restored) at the top of the town; Rhenish-Romanesque (Romanesque crypt; flamboyant Gothic cloister★; treasury). Next door, 18thC bishop's residence. ▶ Renaissance **Hôtel de la Princerie** (residence of the clergyman second in importance to the bishop)★ : museum *(May-Sep., 10-12 & 2-6, closed Tue.).* ▶ Administrative offices and law courts are in a 17thC abbey. ▶ **Porte Chaussée :** facing the bridge over the Meuse, a vestige of the 14thC ramparts. ▶ On the right bank, Town Hall (1623). ▶ The **Citadel,** which stands on top of 7 km of underground tunnels, has been turned into a War Museum *(8-12 & 2-4:30 or 7 according to the season; closed 15 Dec.-28 Feb.).* □

▶ Battlefield of **Vaux-Douaumont** *(marked tour of 31 km; forts open 8-6 or 8-7, 1 Feb.-15 Dec.).*

Leave Verdun by the Etain road (N3) then take the left fork to **Fort-de-Vaux.** ▶ Through Fort-de-Souville (destroyed) you reach the site of Fleury, a ruined village (memorial museum *closed 15 Dec.-15 Jan.*). ▶ Passing alongside the **National Cemetery** (Cimetière National; 15 000 graves) to **Fort-de-Douaumont** above the site of a lost village of the same name. ▶ Return to the **Ossuaire de Douamont,** last resting-place for 130 000 unidentified soldiers *(open all year).* ▶ **The Bayonet Trench** (La tranchée des Baïonnettes) where two entire infantry companies were buried alive during fierce bombardment. Back to Bras-sur-Meuse, thence to Verdun. □

▶ Nearby

▶ **Dugny-sur-Meuse** *(8 km S)* : Romanesque church, bell-tower crowned with a wooden gallery. ▶ **Génicourt** *(10 km upstream on the other bank)* : church with fortified bell-tower; 16thC furnishings, frescos and stained glass. ▶ **Étain** ® *(20 km NE)* : entirely rebuilt after 1918, still has a 14th-15thC church with flamboyant Gothic choir★★ (modern stained glass★). □

Cuisine in Lorraine

In Lorraine, grandfathers traditionally ask : "Who do you love best, Maman or Papa?" The traditional teasing answers : "I love bacon best!" People in Lorraine love bacon; they are also very fond of cream and butter and eggs. That's how they invented the quiche *(whose original name, which nobody uses any more, is* fiouse*). Depending where you are, the tart may be enlivened with mushrooms, chives, onions or any of a dozen additions. The* migaine *is often poured into other kinds of pastry delicacies through a hole in the crust during the baking. A regional speciality is the* tourte, *a pie made with short pastry enclosing a mixture of roughly equal parts of minced pork and veal, marinated overnight with red wine, onions, parsley and other seasonings. Bacon is an indispensable ingredient in* potée Lorraine, *a stew that, like many other local recipes, is hearty but not as heavy as you might suppose. Pike, perch, freshwater crayfish, trout and frogs all contribute to the tastes and textures of the table, while poultry and game also have their place. Cheeses are not outstanding, which is disappointing when you consider that Lorraine is the largest French cheese-producing region by tonnage. To finish the meal, sample a tart or an* eau-de-vie *flavoured with* brimbelles *(currants) or golden* mirabelle *plums.*

VITTEL★

B4 / ® /pop. 6 440 (Vosges)

A renowned resort created in 1854 for the treatment of metabolic disorders, including liver and kidney ailments, by a lawyer from Toulouse. It is now a popular centre for rest and relaxation, notably among top-class athletes; parks, golf, race-course, country walks.

▶ Church of St. Rémy : (12thC, remodelled 15th-16thC). ▶ **Water-bottling factory :** almost 3.5 million bottles daily *(visits 9-11 & 2-4, closed Sat., Sun., and nat. hols.).* □

▶ Nearby

▶ Excursions on foot or by car among the woods and lakes of the Faucille mountains. ▶ → Contrexéville and Neufchâteau. □

Architecture

Farmhouse in the Metz region

Isolated houses are relatively rare in Lorraine and the architecture is generally uniform. In every village, houses aligned along the main street (Grand'Rue) resemble one another except for minor details. They are often terraced and of the same height, so that you might almost think that the houses in a row were covered by a single long roof. ● The houses are set back some metres from the road behind a yard *(usoir)* where firewood, farm implements and midden are traditionally kept. Middens for the most part disappeared some 20 years ago

Lorraine village

except in the Xaintois and certain regions in the Moselle. ● Walls are usually of fieldstone faced with rough plaster. In a few regions, the abundance of fine limestone is reflected in entire houses built of this material. ● The regular openings are framed with limestone or sandstone. A door and a window (sometimes sharing the same frame) usually open into the kitchen-living room, whereas a second door of similar size leads to the stable and cowshed. A much larger door opens on the barn. According to village custom, these doorways to the farm sheds are either topped with lintels fashioned from heavy wooden beams, or rounded off with stone arches.

Upper floors are equally regular. The grainstore is usually above the kitchen; a casement door above the stables permits access to the fodder store. There is usually a skylight or bull's eye above the barn door to light the loft. ● The grooved terracotta tiles that used to cover the shallow roof (20-30° maximum) are now commonly replaced by industrial tiles. Survival of the old-fashioned tiles from the Roman

Bar-le-Duc region

era is hard to explain when the adjacent regions for centuries have adopted other roofing materials. ● In the Vosges, isolated farms differ slightly from this general outline; the rear roof descends a little lower, accentuating the squat outline. The western gables are protected from the rain by wooden shingles, fibro-cement or even metal sheeting.

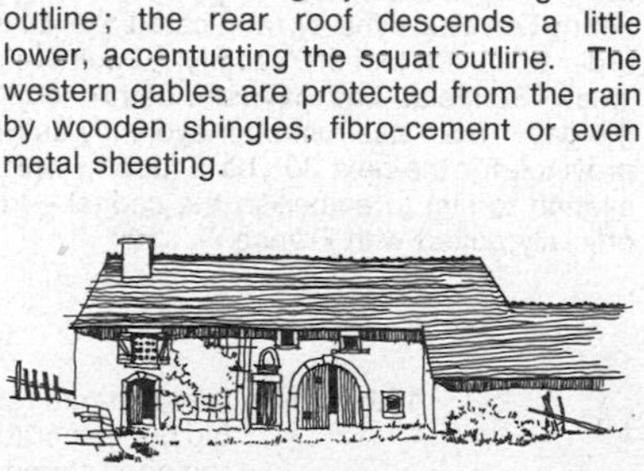
Vosges farmhouse

Brief regional history

Prehistory and Roman times When the Romans invaded Lorraine they found it inhabited by two Celtic peoples centred mainly around modern-day Metz and Toul. ● Here and there, iron was already being smelted, salt-mines were in production, and trade was growing with Belgium and Burgundy. The Roman organisation of roads and cities encouraged economic development.

6th-10thC A territory now roughly corresponding to Lorraine was allotted to Thierri, one of the four sons of Clovis, King of the Franks in the 6thC. The early capital of Rheims was superseded by Metz; the country prospered. In the 8thC, the Emperor Charlemagne often visited **Austrasia,** as it was then designated, stopping at Metz, Remiremont, Thionville and other cities. **Lothaire II,** 9thC King of the Franks, lent his name to the region extending from the upper Saône to the mouth of the Rhine; "Lorraine" is derived from Lotharingia (lotharii regnum = Lothar's kingdom). A Duchy corresponding more or less to modern-day Lorraine was created during the 10thC reign of the Holy Roman Emperor Otto I.

10th-14thC Ruled by the Saxon dynasty, Lorraine was divided among the dukedom and the three independent bishoprics of Metz, Verdun and Toul, together with several counties, led by that of Bar. In 1301 the **Count of Bar** became vassal of the King of France for all his territory west of the Meuse.

14th-18thC 50 years later Bar was reunited with the Duchy of Lorraine; but France still had designs on this rich border state. Wars with Spain, royal marriages, and skirmishes provoked by Cardinal Richelieu increased France's control over Lorraine. In 1648, the three independent bishoprics were definitively attached to the French crown. In 1738, François III, founder of the Habsbourg-Lorraine dynasty, abdicated the dukedom of Lorraine in order to accept that of Tuscany. Louis XV appointed his father-in-law, **Stanislas Leszczynski,** dethroned King of Poland, to fill the gap. Stanislas ruled benevolently as Royal Governor of the province for the next 30 years, during which he used the funds allotted to him to embellish the capital. In 1766, Lorraine was officially united with France.

18th-20thC Lorraine has remained a focus of dispute by virtue of its strategic but vulnerable position between France and Germany. The region suffered extensively during the Franco-Prussian war of 1870-1871 and the two world wars.

Practical information

The region

Information : Meurthe-et-Moselle : *Association Départementale du Tourisme,* 4, rue Lyautey, B.P. 65, 54002 Nancy, ☎ 83.35.61.20, ext. 511. **Meuse :** *C.D.T.,* Préfecture, 55012 Bar-le-Duc, ☎ 29.79.00.02. **Moselle :** *C.D.T.,* Préfecture, 57000 Metz, ☎ 87.30.81.00. **Vosges :** *C.D.T.,* rue Gilbert, 88008 Épinal Cedex, B.P. 332, ☎ 29.82.49.93. In Paris : *Maison de l'Alsace et des Vosges,* 39, Champs-Élysées, ☎ 42.56.15.94.

Maps : *Michelin,* n°s 57 and 62 (1/200 000). *I.G.N.,* n°s 10, 11, 12, 23, 30, 31 and 311, Lorraine Natural Park region (1/100 000).

Local and regional press : *l'Est Républicain, le Républicain Lorrain, la Liberté de l'Est.*

S.O.S. : *SAMU* (Emergency Medical Service) : **Meurthe-et-Moselle,** ☎ 83.32.85.79. **Moselle,** ☎ 87.62.27.11. **Vosges,** ☎ 29.34.34.34. Poisoning Emergency Centre : **Meurthe-et-Moselle, Moselle,** ☎ 83.32.36.36.

Weather forecast : Meurthe-et-Moselle, Meuse, Moselle, ☎ 83.29.49.15. **Vosges,** ☎ 29.35.15.15.

Rural gîtes and chambres d'hôtes : enq at the *Relais Départementaux des Gîtes Ruraux ;* **Meurthe-et-Moselle,** 5, rue de la Vologne, 54520 Laxou, ☎ 83.96.49.58. **Meuse :** Préfecture, 55012 Bar-le-Duc Cedex, ☎ 29.79.48.10. **Vosges :** 13, rue Aristide-Briand, B.P. 405, 88010 Épinal Cedex, ☎ 29.35.50.34. *Relais du Tourisme Rural de la Moselle,* Maison de l'Agriculture, 64, av. André-Malraux, 57045 Metz Cedex, ☎ 87.63.13.25.

Holiday villages : see practical holiday guide.

Camping : more than 100 camping sites. Lorraine : *Délégation Régionale de la Fédération Française de Camping-Caravaning,* M. Jean Mourot, École Buzy, 55400 Étain, ☎ 54.55.57.88.

Cultural events : Apr : *Festival de Science-Fiction et de l'Imaginaire* in Metz. **May :** *World Theatre Festival* in Nancy. **End Jun :** *Cultural Festival* (music in Fénétrange). *Festival international de l'image* in Épinal. **Oct :** *Jazz Festival* in Nancy. **Nov :** *International Contemporary Music Festival* in Metz. *International Super-8 Film Festival* in Metz.

Traditional Festivals and Folklore : Feb : *Carnaval* in Vic-sur-Seille. **Apr :** *Daffodil Festival* in Gérardmer (only if the Easter hols are before 25 Apr). *Fête des Champs-Golots* in Épinal, Wed before Easter (children float illuminated boats in the gutters). **Jun :** *Fête et Tradition,* in Manonville, *Fête des Côtes de Meuse* (wine festival) in Vigneulles-lès-Hattonchâtel. **Jul :** *Cottage cheese and rural traditions festival* in Sarrebourg, *Fête de la Myrtille* (bilberry festival) in Dabo. **Aug :** *Féerie Lumineuse* (light display) on Gérardmer Lake (14-15), *Fête de la Mirabelle* (Darney, Metz, Vigneulles-lès-Hattonchâtel).

Fairs, exhibitions and markets : Mar : *Spring Fair* in Bar-le-Duc. **Apr :** *Antique Dealers' Salon, Minerals Market, International Forestry Fair* in Nancy. **Jun :** *International Fair* in Nancy (1st fortnight). **Jul :** *Horse Festival* in Vigneulles-lès-Hattonchâtel. **Sep :** *Agricultural Fair* in Verdun, *Antique Dealer's Salon* in Bar-le-Duc. **Oct :** *Jazz Festival* in Nancy. **Nov :** *Antique Dealers' Salon, International Aviculture Exhibition* in Metz ; *Ornithology Exhibition* in Épinal.

Scenic railways : Moselle : *Associations du Chemin de Fer Touristique d'Abreschwiller,* ☎ 87.03.70.09. From Easter to early Oct, 1 service on Sat, 6 services on Sun and nat hols, special supplementary services 1 Jul-31 Aug from Mon to Sat and on request all year round. **Vosges :** Rabodeau, gare de Senones, ☎ 29.57.60.32. Organiser : M. Jean Hubert, at Yutz, ☎ 82.56.07.87. Services on Sat, Sun and nat hols Jun-Sep. Trains can be reserved for groups and special outings.

Technical tourism : *Cristallerie de Baccarat* (Crystal works), N59, 54120 Baccarat, ☎ 83.72.10.01. *Bergère de France,* 91, rue Ernest-Bradfer, 55020 Bar-le-Duc, ☎ 29.79.01.01. *Fine porcelain and enamel,* 4, rue de la Faïencerie, 54400 Longwy, ☎ 82.24.30.94.

Rambling and hiking : topoguides G.R.5, G.R.7, G.R.14/141, G.R.53. Enq concerning indicated trails and forest walks : *C.R.T. Lorraine-Vosges, Assn. parc naturel régional de Lorraine,* B.P. 35, 54700 Pont-à-Mousson, ☎ 83.81.11.91, *Assn. parc naturel régional des Vosges du Nord,* château de la Petite-Pierre, 67290 Wingen-sur-Moder, ☎ 88.70.46.55 ; O.T.S.I. de la Montagne, which publishes local maps and guides, and *Assn. des Accompagnateurs de Moyenne Montagne,* ☎ 29.63.17.50. Signposted trails : list can be obtained from *Vita,* 1, rue Vernet, 75008 Paris, ☎ 47.23.72.02. Enq concerning shelters : local SI, *Club Pédestre Vosgien,* 27, rue de la République, 54000 Nancy, ☎ 83.27.40.53, and *Amis de la Nature,* 28, rue des Soupirs, 88000 Épinal, ☎ 29.82.37.63. *Grande Traversée des Vosges* (major trail across the Vosges Mountains) : M. André Richard, Remiremont, ☎ 29.62.13.41. Also health walks (forest trails), rambles and hiking from Gérardmer ; enq ⓘ

Riding holidays : list of riding centres can be obtained from the *Assn. Régionale de Tourisme Équestre Lorrain,* 22, rue François-de-Neufchâteau, 88000 Épinal, ☎ 29.82.21.70.

Cycling holidays : numerous possibilities — Tour of the Vosges, Randonnée des Grandes Sources (excursions) and proficiency certificate for the Hautes-Vosges : enq : M. Carsani, 41, rue de la Xanée, 88200 Remiremont, ☎ 29.62.51.54, SI, local bicycle dealers.

River and canal cruises : *Meuse Nautic :* Enq : Dun-sur-Meuse.

Instructional courses : Vosges spinet piano, traditional dance, guitar ; enq : *Maison de la Culture,* 1, bd Saint-Dié, 88400 Gérardmer, ☎ 29.63.11.96 (early Jul-mid-Aug).

Children : farmhouse holidays, Menil-Colline-des-Granges, 88160 Le Thillot, ☎ 29.25.03.00 ; children participate in farm activities. Home d'enfants de La Bresse, 88250, ☎ 29.25.43.70.

Golf : Nancy (18 holes) ; Combles (9 holes), 9 km

from Bar-le-Duc ; Cherisey (9 holes) ; Vittel (18 and 9 holes).

Tennis : *Ligue Régionale,* pdt André Daillot, 25, rue de Rigny, 54000 Nancy.

Sailing and wind-surfing : sailing circuit in Moselle (100 km) ; enq *Dir Dép. Jeunesse, Sports et Loisirs,* 57036 Metz, ☎ 87.75.41.55. Centre-École du lac de Madine, ☎ 29.89.03.59. Meuse : *Dir. Dép. Jeunesse et Sports,* ☎ 29.79.48.55.

Water skiing : Meurthe-et-Moselle : Fontenoy, ☎ 83.43.62.15 ; Pont-à-Mousson, ☎ 83.81.06.90. **Meuse :** Madine Lake, ☎ 29.89.32.50 ; Dun-sur-Meuse, ☎ 29.80.90.38 ; Saint-Mihiel, ☎ 29.89.03.59 ; Bonzée, ☎ 29.87.31.98 ; **Moselle :** Metz-Metz-Campagne, ☎ 87.75.65.21, and Thionville-Sierck, ☎ 82.53.33.18.

Diving : Meuse : Madine Lake, ☎ 29.89.32.50 ; Contrisson and Mouzay, ☎ 29.79.48.55, ext. 321 ; Sommedieue, ☎ 29.87.60.45. **Moselle :** diving is possible in all the larger stretches of water (→ sailing). **Vosges :** Corbeaux Lake, ☎ 29.61.11.29.

Canoeing : *Comité de Canoë-Kayak,* 18, rue de Champagne, 55800 Revigny-sur-Ornain, ☎ 29.70.61.95. *Association Golbéenne Sports et Loisirs Canoë-Kayak,* 8, rue d'Épinal, 88190 Golbey, ☎ 29.34.34.62.

Climbing-mountaineering : instructional courses, excursions, climbing school : *Club Alpin Français,* 5, rue Saint-Julien, 54000 Nancy, ☎ 83.32.37.73, and O.T. de Gérardmer, ☎ 29.63.08.74, La Bresse, ☎ 29.61.11.29.

Skiing : most ski resorts are in the Vosges Mts, offering cross-country, down-hill skiing, or Nordic-style-ski-treks. Enq : Vosges : 13, rue A.-Briand, 88000 Épinal, ☎ 29.35.50.34 ; Centre-École de Longemer, ☎ 29.63.10.76. Centre-École de Mauselaine, ☎ 29.63.33.23 ; Centre-École (cross-country) des Bas-Rupts, 88400 Gérardmer, ☎ 29.63.12.06 (high season), 29.63.13.87 (low season). Meurthe-et-Moselle : *Club Vosgien,* 27, rue de la République, 54000 Nancy, ☎ 83.27.40.53. Ski jump in Bussang, T.O., ☎ 29.61.50.37.

Flying, gliding, parachuting, ballooning : numerous air clubs for gliding : *Aéro-Club* (A.C.) *de l'Est,* ☎ 83.29.43.63 and 83.29.34.58 ; *A.C. de Blainville,* ☎ 83.29.50.42 ; *A.C. de Haute-Moselle,* ☎ 83.47.33.54, *Ailes Mosellanes,* 57000 Metz, B.P. 701, *A.C. de Sarrebourg ;* Dieuze, Sarreguemines and Thionville : enq S.I. and T.O. *Parachuting : A.C. de Doncourt,* ☎ 83.29.58.78, *Ailes Mosellanes* (see above), *A.C.* de Dieuze, Sarrebourg, Sarreguemines, Thionville : enq S.I. and T.O. Flights in light aircraft, beginners' courses and first flights at all air clubs. *Hang gliding :* Thionville : *A.C. de Basse-Moselle,* Thionville-Yutz Airfield and *A.C. de Sud-Meusien,* ☎ 29.79.23.72 or 29.78.56.06 ; base Marville, Monturédy, ☎ 29.80.01.11 ; Plagny-la-Blanche-Côte, ☎ 29.89.46.67. *Ballooning : A.C. de la Mortagne,* ☎ 83.73.27.21, *A.C. Bassin de Briey,* ☎ 83.29.58.78, and Lorraine Aéronautic Club, ☎ 29.36.31.85.

Hunting and shooting : Féd. Dép. : **Meurthe-et-Moselle :** 1, rue St-Dizier, 54000 Nancy, ☎ 83.32.33.21. **Meuse :** 4, rue Henri-Dunant, 55000 Bar-le-Duc, ☎ 29.79.03.31. **Moselle :** 2, rue Chèvremont, 57000 Metz, ☎ 87.75.11.74. **Vosges :** 11, rue Charlet, 88000 Épinal, ☎ 29.31.10.74.

Fishing : enq at Féd. Dép. de la Pêche. **Meuse :** 2, rue Saint-Maur, 55100 Verdun, ☎ 29.86.15.70. **Moselle :** 5, rue de la Monnaie, 57580 Remilly, ☎ 87.64.60.72. **Vosges :** 18, av. du Mal-de-Lattre-de-Tassigny, 88000 Épinal, ☎ 29.35.08.89.

● Towns

ABRESCHWILLER

Lunéville 56, Strasbourg 71, Paris 607
C3 ⊠ 57560

ℹ mairie, ☎ 87.03.70.32.

SNCF ☎ 87.03.70.28.

Hotels :
★★***Cigognes*** (L.F.), 92, rue Jordy, ☎ 87.03.70.09. 29 rm Ⓟ 180. Rest. ♦♦ 55-125.

Turquestein-Blancrupt, 10 km S :
● ★★***Kiboki*** (L.F., Relais du Silence), ☎ 87.08.60.65. 15 rm Ⓟ ♿ closed Feb and 1-15 Oct, 130. Rest. ♦ closed Tue, 30-100.

BACCARAT

Épinal 41, Nancy 60, Paris 434
C3 ⊠ 54120

ℹ résidence du Centre, ☎ 83.72.13.37.

SNCF ☎ 83.75.10.39.

Hotels :
★***Renaissance*** (L.F.), 31, rue des Cristalleries, ☎ 83.75.11.31. AE, DC, Euro, Visa. 18 rm, closed 15 Jan-15 Feb and Sat (low season), 150. Rest. ♦ ♿ 40-110.

Raon-l'Étape, ⊠ 88110, 9 km SE :
★★***Eau Vive*** (L.F.), rue J.-B.-Demenge, ☎ 29.41.44.68. 12 rm Ⓟ closed 31 Oct-1 Feb, 180.

Farmhouse-inn : *Ferme de Prébois,* 2, rte de Bayon, ☎ 83.75.13.75. Table d'hôte. Spec : *quiche lorraine, poulet aux raisins, pastourelle.*

Recommended : *Cie des Cristalleries de Baccarat* (Crystal works), rue des Cristalleries, ☎ 83.75.12.47.

BAINS-LES-BAINS

Épinal 30, Vesoul 50, Paris 372
B4 ⊠ 88240

1, av. du Dr-Matthieu, ☎ 29.36.32.04.

ℹ pl. du Bain-Romain, ☎ 29.36.31.75.

SNCF ☎ 29.36.30.22.

Hotels :
★★***Promenade*** (L.F.), 8, av. du Colonel-Chavane, ☎ 29.36.30.06. 33 rm Ⓟ closed 1 Nov-1 Mar, Mon low season, 150. Rest. ♦♦ 60-140.
★***Central,*** 5, rue du Gal-de-Gaulle, ☎ 29.36.30.20. 36 rm Ⓟ closed 30 Nov-15 Apr, 100. Rest. ♦ 80-130.

▲ ★★*Les Pins* (50 pl.), ☎ 29.36.33.51.

BAR-LE-DUC

Verdun 57, Châlons-sur-Marne 70, Paris 263
A2 ✉ 55000

ℹ hôtel de ville (B2), ☎ 29.79.11.13.

SNCF (C2), ☎ 29.79.21.98.

🚌 pl. Reggio (A2), ☎ 29.79.34.35.

Car-hire : *Budget* train + auto, 13, rue de la Gare, ☎ 29.79.09.10, and at the station, ☎ 29.79.21.98.

Hotels :
★★★***Ducs,*** parc Bradfer (C3), ☎ 29.79.32.66. DC, Euro, Visa. 26 rm P ♨ ♘ ♿ 230. Rest. ♦ 60-210.
● ★★***Metz et Commerce*** (B2), 17, bd de La Rochelle, ☎ 29.79.02.56. Euro. 51 rm P ♨ 160. Rest. ♦ ♿ closed Sun eve (low season), 50-160.

Trémont-sur-Saulx, 9.5 km SW :
● ★★***Source*** (L.F.), ☎ 29.70.45.22. Euro. 16 rm P ♨ ♘ closed 10-24 Feb, 4-25 Aug, Sun eve and Mon, 180. Rest. ♦♦ 60-160.

Restaurants :
● ♦♦ ***La Meuse Gourmande*** (A2), 1, rue François-de-Guise, ☎ 29.79.28.40. AE, DC, Euro, Visa ⚘ P ♨ ♘ ♿ closed 18 Aug-3 Sep, 3-21 Jan, Sun eve and Mon. In the old town, gastronomic stop in a former monastery. Regional cuisine : *quiche lorraine, blanquette d'escargots,* 70-170.

Bazincourt, 14 km S :
♦ ***Auberge des Chasseurs,*** ☎ 29.78.60.48. ♨ closed Wed, 80-130.

Stainville, ✉ 55500, 15 km S :
● ♦ ***La Petite Auberge,*** ☎ 29.78.60.10. Closed Fri eve, Sat, Sun eve, 21 Jul-12 Aug. Excellent fare ; fresh, refined dishes such as *sole meunière* and *coquilles Saint-Jacques.* A worthwhile stopover for sophisticated palates, 120-210.

Rupt-aux-Nonains, ✉ 55170, 17.5 km S :
♦ ***Les Tonnelles,*** ☎ 29.70.21.02. ♨ 80-130.

Events : Mar (2nd Tue) : *spring fair.* Sep : *Antique Dealers' Salon* (1st week) and *currant* (every 2 years) ; Nov (1st Tue) : *autumn fair.*

Recommended : *Auction hall,* 40, quai V.-Hugo (B2), ☎ 29.79.20.64. *Aux Ducs de Bar,* for currant jam, 72, bd de La Rochelle (B2), ☎ 29.79.01.38. High quality pull-overs from the manufacturer : av. Gambetta (C3).

La BRESSE

Colmar 54, Épinal 60, Paris 420
C4 ⛷ 630-1 350 m ✉ 88250

ℹ 21, quai Iranées, ☎ 29.25.41.29.

Hotels :
● ★★★***Vallées*** (L.F., France-Accueil), 31, rue P.-Claudel, ☎ 29.25.41.39. Tx 960573. AE, DC, Euro, Visa. 60 rm + 60 aprts ⚘ P ♨ ♘ ▭ ⚲ ♿ 320. Rest. ♦ 70-180.
★★***Lac des Corbeaux,*** 2.5 km on the rte de la Schlucht, ☎ 29.25.41.17. DC, Euro, Visa. 18 rm ⚘ P ♨ ♘ ♿ 130. Rest. ♦ 40-70.

Farmhouse-inn : *la Retelere,* ☎ 29.25.52.10. Accommodation in summer only. Appetising fare ; farm produce for sale.

⛺ ★★*Les Écorces* (150 pl.). ☎ 29.25.41.29.

Restaurant :
♦ ***Auberge du Pêcheur,*** Vologne, ☎ 29.25.43.86. AE, DC, Euro, Visa ⚘ P ♨ ♘ closed 1 week early May, 25 Jun-7 Jul, 1-15 Dec, Tue eve and Wed, 45-90.

BUSSANG

Belfort 43, Épinal 61, Paris 450
C4 ⛷ 641-1 220 m ✉ 88540

ℹ 7, rue d'Alsace, ☎ 29.61.50.37.

SNCF ☎ 29.61.50.21.

Hotels :
★★***Sources*** (L.F.), rte de la Source, 2 km NE on the D89, ☎ 29.61.51.94. DC, Visa. 9 rm ⚘ P ♨ ♘ ✗ 150. Rest. ♦♦ 55-125.
★★***Tremplin*** (L.F.), rue du 3e-R.T.A., ☎ 29.61.50.30. AE, DC, Visa. 20 rm P ✗ closed 30 Sep-30 Oct and Mon ex school hols, 160. Rest. ♦ ♿ 45-110.

⛺ ★★*Larcenaire* (58 pl.), ☎ 29.61.51.74 ; ★★*Deux-Rivières* (35 pl.), ☎ 29.61.50.36.

CHARMES

Épinal 26, Nancy 44, Paris 324
B3 ✉ 88130

Hotels :
★***Central*** (L.F.), 4, rue des Capucins, ☎ 29.38.02.40. DC, Euro, Visa. 10 rm P ♨ closed 1-15 Dec, 15-30 Jan, Sun eve and Mon, 170. Rest. ♦♦ ♿ 60-180.
★***Dancourt*** (L.F.), 6, pl. de l'Hôtel-de-Ville, ☎ 29.32.80.80. Visa. 10 rm ♘ closed 1-15 Jan, 1-15 Jul, Fri and Sat noon, 130. Rest. ♦ Spec : *mille feuille de coquilles Saint-Jacques au vermouth, noisettes d'agneau aux cinq baies,* 60-190.

⛺ *Municipal* (70 pl.), ☎ 29.32.85.85.

CLERMONT-EN-ARGONNE

Verdun 30, Bar-le-Duc 49, Paris 235
A2 ✉ 55120

Hotels :
Bellevue (L.F.), rue de la Libération, ☎ 29.87.41.02. DC, Euro. 16 rm P ♨ ♘ closed 25 Dec-10 Jan, 15-28 Feb and Wed, 100. Rest. ♦♦ closed Wed ex Jul-Aug, 20 Dec-10 Jan. Spec : *terrine de foies de volaille, lotte à l'oseille,* 50-130.

Beaulieu-en-Argonne, ✉ 55250 Seuil-d'Argonne, 12 km S :
★***Abbaye,*** ☎ 29.70.72.81. 10 rm ⚘ ♘ ✗ closed 15 Dec-18 Feb, Sun eve (1 Oct-1 Apr), 95. Rest. ♦ ♿ 45-90.

Restaurant :
Futeau, 10 km SW :
Orée du Bois, à Courupt, ☎ 29.88.28.41. With 3 rm ⚘ ♘ closed Jan, Sun eve and Tue, 60-160.

COMMERCY

Bar-le-Duc 38, Verdun 53, Paris 267
A2 ✉ 55200

ℹ mairie, ☎ 29.91.02.18.

SNCF ☎ 29.91.01.03.

Hotel :
★★***Stanislas*** (L.F.), 13, rue René-Grosdidier, ☎ 29.91.12.36. Euro, Visa. 32 rm ♿ closed Christmas, 150. Rest. ● ♦ ✗ closed Mon noon. Pleasant hotel restaurant, regional dishes, 80-150.

CONTREXÉVILLE

Épinal 48, Nancy 76, Paris 329
B4 ⚕ May-Sep, ☎ 29.08.03.24. ✉ 88140

ℹ galeries du parc thermal (spa galleries), ☎ 29.08.08.68, and mairie, ☎ 29.08.09.35.

SNCF ☎ 29.08.01.42.

Hotels :

● ★★★ ***l'Établissement,*** cour d'Honneur, ☎ 29.08.17.30 and 29.08.01.31. AE, DC, Visa. 29 rm P closed 22 Sep-10 May, 280. Grill-room ♦♦ ***Relais Stanislas,*** 110-145.

★★★***de la Souveraine,*** parc thermal (spa), ☎ 29.08.09.59 and 29.08.13.79. AE, DC, Visa. 31 rm P Built for the Shah of Iran in 1905. Closed 18 Sep-10 May, 255. Rest. (see *Établissement* above).

★***Beauséjour*** (L.F.), 204, rue Ziwer-Pacha, ☎ 29.08.04.89. Visa. 31 rm closed 1 Oct-20 Apr, 125. Rest. ♦ 60-80.

▲ ★★★*Municipal* (80 pl.), ☎ 29.08.15.06.

DABO

Sarrebourg 21, Strasbourg 49, Paris 447
C2-3 ☒ 57850

ℹ 19, pl. de l'Église, ☎ 87.07.40.04.

Hotel :

★***Au Rocher,*** ☎ 87.07.40.14. 10 rm P closed Oct-Mar, 100. Rest. ♦♦ Spec : *choucroute, truite aux morilles,* 80-300.

Local events : *marathon and drum-majorettes festival* (May). *Fox festival* (Aug). *« Bois Bourgeois »* (Burger's wood) festival (Nov).

DUN-SUR-MEUSE

Verdun 33, Sedan 47, Paris 275
A1 ☒ 55110

ℹ mairie, ☎ 29.80.90.55.

Hotel :

★***Commerce*** (L.F.), ☎ 29.80.90.25. DC, Euro. 11 rm P closed 25 Dec-31 Jan, Sun eve and Mon, 120. Rest. ♦ 50-110.

▲ ★★*Lac Vert* (110 pl.), ☎ 29.80.90.38.

ÉPINAL

Nancy 70, Vesoul 85, Paris 360
B-C4 ☒ 88000

ℹ 13, rue de la Comédie (B2), ☎ 29.82.53.32.

✈ Épinal-Mirecourt, 40 km NW, ☎ 29.37.01.99.

SNCF ☎ 29.82.41.51.

pl. de la Gare (A1), ☎ 29.82.54.82.

Car-hire : *Budget* train + auto, 31, av. de Beaulieu, in Golbey, ☎ 29.34.45.54 ; at the station, ☎ 29.35.13.69.

Hotels :

★★★***Ducs de Lorraine*** (B1), 16, quai du Colonel-Sérot, ☎ 29.34.39.87. Tx 960573. AE, DC, Euro, Visa. 10 rm P closed Sun eve, Mon, 250. Rest. ♦♦♦ Spec : *œufs de caille aux morilles et foie d'oie, filet de bœuf canaille,* 85-220.

★★***Mercure*** (A2), 13, pl. E.-Stein, ☎ 29.35.18.68. Tx 960277. AE, DC, Euro, Visa. 41 rm P 350. Rest. ♦♦ ***Mouton Blanc.*** Spec : *salade d'huîtres aux œufs de caille, boudin de cailles aux épinards,* 90-190.

Golbey, ☒ 88190, 4 km N on the N57 :

★★***Côte Olie,*** ☎ 29.34.28.28. Tx 961011. AE, DC, Euro, Visa. 24 rm P 240. Rest. ♦ ***la Mansarde*** closed Sun, 80-180.

Recommended : *Auction Hall,* 10, av. Gal-de-Gaulle, ☎ 29.82.54.08.

ÉTAIN

Verdun 20, Metz 47, Paris 286
A1 ☒ 55400

Hotel :

★***Sirène*** (L.F.), 22, rue Prud'homme-Havette, ☎ 29.87.10.32. Euro, Visa. 30 rm P closed Jan, 150. Rest. ♦ 60-130.

Restaurant :

Senon, ☒ 55230 Spincourt, 9 km N :

♦♦ ***La Tourtière*** (A.R.C.), ☎ 29.85.41.80. P closed Tue eve and Wed low season, 45-150.

FORBACH

Sarreguemines 20, Metz 60, Paris 384
C1 ☒ 57600

ℹ hôtel de ville, ☎ 87.85.02.43.

SNCF ☎ 87.85.50.50.

Car-hire : *Budget* train + auto, at the station, ☎ 87.85.33.71.

Hotel :

★★***Berg,*** 50, av. St-Rémy, ☎ 87.85.09.12. 21 rm P 150.

Restaurants :

● ♦ ***Chez Lucullus,*** 35, rue de Verdun, ☎ 87.87.62.40. DC, Euro, Visa closed Sat noon and Sun ex nat hols. Simple and good dishes : *terrine maison, ris de veau aux morilles, fish, 40-120.*

Rosbruck, ☒ 57800 Freyming-Merlebach, 4 km :

♦♦ ***Albert-Marie,*** 1, rue Nationale, ☎ 87.04.70.76 P closed Aug, Sun eve, Mon. Spec : seafood and poultry from the Bresse area, 100-210.

GÉRARDMER

Saint-Dié 30, Épinal 41, Paris 430
C4 666-1 113 m ☒ 88400

ℹ pl. des Déportés, ☎ 29.63.08.74.

SNCF ☎ 29.63.08.76.

Hotels :

● ★★★***Bas-Rupts*** (Relais du Silence, M.C.F.), 4 km SW, ☎ 29.63.09.25 and 29.63.15.29. Tx 960992. AE, DC, Visa. 18 rm P 400. Rest. ● ♦♦ Booking required. In an elegant chalet, M. Philippe's light cuisine. Spec : *pot-au-feu de la mer, feuilleté de soles,* 90-250.

★★★***Grand Hôtel Bragard,*** pl. du Tilleul, ☎ 29.63.06.31. Tx 960964. AE, DC, Euro, Visa. 58 rm P 490. Rest. ♦♦♦ ***Grand Cerf.*** closed 1 Nov-10 Dec, 120-210. Grillroom ♦♦ ***le Darou.***

★★★***Réserve,*** esplanade du Lac, ☎ 29.63.21.60. Tx 961509. AE, DC, Euro, Visa. 32 rm P closed 15 Nov-20 Dec, 380. Rest. ♦♦ Spec : *asperges et saumon tiède sauce aigrelette, filet de bœuf à la graine de moutarde,* 70-180.

● ★★***Croisette,*** 2, bd de Colmar, ☎ 29.63.24.10. AE, Euro, Visa. 32 rm P closed 15 Oct-10 Dec, 180. Rest. ♦♦ 50-145.

★★***Lacotel,*** facing the lake, ☎ 29.63.38.23. Visa. 50 rm P closed 1 May-15 Oct, 200. Rest. ♦ 50-130.

★★***Relais de la Mauselaine*** (L.F.), La Rayée, ☎ 29.63.05.74. 15 rm P At the foot of the ski-slopes. Closed 1 Oct-15 Dec, 15-31 Mar, 210. Rest., 50-140.

Les Bas-Rupts, 4 km S by D486:

★★***Chalet du Lac*** (L.F.), rte d'Épinal, ☎ 29.63.38.76. 11 rm. P closed Oct, Fri low season, 170. Rest. ♦ *Coq au riesling,* 120-210.

Col de Martimpré, 5 km on the Saint-Dié road : ★★**Bonne Auberge** (L.F.), ☎ 29.63.19.08. Tx 961408. AE, DC, Euro, Visa. 11 rm closed 6 Nov-15 Dec, Tue eve and Wed (low season, 185. Rest. ♦ 70-120.

Granges-sur-Vologne, ✉ 88600 Bruyères, 13 km NW : ★★**Lorraine,** 6, rue de-Lattre-de-Tassigny, ☎ 29.57.40.65. AE, DC, Euro, Visa. 23 ch. closed Fri eve, 140. Rest. ♦♦ 50-140.

Ⅹ ★★★★*Ramberchamp* (266 pl.), ☎ 29.63.03.82 ; ★★*Bas-Rupts* (50 pl.), ☎ 29.63.37.15 ; ★★*Myrtilles* (65 pl.), ☎ 29.63.21.38 ; ★★*Granges Bas* (100 pl.), ☎ 29.63.12.03 ; ★★*Ruisseaux* (70 pl.), ☎ 29.63.13.06 ; ★★*Sapins* (70 pl.), ☎ 29.63.15.01.

Restaurants :
♦♦ ***Auberge de Lorraine*** (L.F.), 4, bd de St-Dié, ☎ 29.63.09.82. With 8 rm closed Sun eve and Mon low season, 25 Oct-25 Nov, 80-130.

Les Bas-Rupts :
♦♦ ***A la Belle Marée,*** ☎ 29.63.06.83. AE, DC, Visa. closed 3 weeks Jan, 23 Jun-5 Jul, Sun eve, Mon ex Jul-Aug and nat hols. Fish and shellfish straight from the ocean, 45-140.

Coach excursions : 2 to 4 daily excursions in the Vosges : S.T.A.H.V., rue de la 3e-D.I.A., ☎ 29.63.01.45.

Casino : daily May-Sep : Thu, Sun (low season).

Bicycle hire : *Picart Cycles,* 16, bd Ketsch, and *Chipot Cycles,* 4, rue des Vosges.

Recommended : local produce for sale at *la Réserve,* ☎ 29.63.21.60.

Events : Apr : *daffodil festival ;* 14 Aug : *fireworks.*

LIVERDUN

Nancy 16, Metz 56, Paris 309
B2 ✉ 54460

SNCF ☎ 83.49.47.87.

Hotel :
★★★***Vannes et sa Résidence,*** 6, rue Porte-Haute, ☎ 83.24.46.01. AE, DC, Visa. 11 rm closed 1 Feb-8 Mar, Mon and Tue noon, 450. Rest. ● ♦♦♦ The young chef makes real efforts. Spec : *salade maraîchère de pigeons de Bresse et son petit jardin, rognon de veau aux amandes et pignons avec ses fèves en vinaigrette,* 135-280.

Ⅹ ★★★*Municipal* (166 pl.), ☎ 83.49.43.78.

Restaurant :
♦♦ ***Golf Val Fleuri,*** rte Villey-St-Étienne, ☎ 83.24.53.54. Euro, Visa. closed 2 Jan-1 Feb and Wed (ex Jun-Sep). Spec : *marmite d'Océan cardinal et petits légumes, blanc de volailles et ris de veau au fumet de cidre doux,* 100-170.

LONGUYON

Verdun 48, Metz 69, Paris 314
A1 ✉ 54260

SNCF ☎ 82.39.42.57.

Hotel :
★★**Lorraine** (Inter-Hôtel), 6, pl. de la Gare, ☎ 82.39.50.07. AE, DC, Euro. 15 rm, closed 6 Jan-8 Feb, 195. Rest. ● ♦♦ ***le Mas*** closed Mon (ex Jul-Sep). Best wine waiter of France, G. Tisserant is also a good cook, dishes according to season : *langoustine en feuilleté a la julienne de légumes.* Small and great wines, 80-210.

Restaurant :
Beuveille, ✉ 54620, 8 km SE on the D18 :
♦♦ ***La Grillade,*** ☎ 82.89.75.06 closed Mon eve, Tue, 15-31 Aug, Feb. Pleasant little inn, 40-160.

LORRAINE Nature Park (East)

C2

ⓘ *maison du Sel,* in Marsal (→), ✉ 57170 Château-Salins, ☎ 87.01.16.75 ; hôtel de la Monnale (→) Château-Salins (→).

Farmhouse gîte and table d'hôte :
Cirey-sur-Vezouze, ✉ 54480, SE on the D7 : *Relais de la Vigne,* ☎ 83.42.52.66 Riding, fishing. An attractive menu of regional specialities : meals on request only.

Dieuze, ✉ 57260 : *Ferme du Moulin Bas,* Guebling, ☎ 87.01.51.37 : gîte and camping ; farm produce for sale.

LORRAINE Nature Park (West)

A-B2

ⓘ B.P. 35, 54703 Pont-à-Mousson Cedex, ☎ 83.81.11.91 ; in La Croix-Saint-Clément, Ancy-sur-Moselle, 57310 Ars-sur-Moselle ; in Saint-Mihiel (→) ; at the *Maison des Arts et Traditions rurales* in Hannonville-sous-les-Côtes (→), 55210 Vigneulles-lès-Hattonchâtel, ☎ 29.87.32.94 ; in Bouzée at the *Base de plein air* (leisure centre), 55160 Fresnes-en-Woëvre, ☎ 29.87.31.98.

Hotels :
Heudicourt, ✉ 55210 Vigneulles-lès-Hattonchâtel :
★★***Lac de Madine*** (L.F.), ☎ 29.89.34.80. Euro, Visa. 33 rm closed 2 Jan-28 Feb and Mon low season, 180. Rest. ♦ 60-120.

Ⅹ alongside Madine Lake : ★★*les Aires* (100 pl.), ☎ 29.89.32.50 ; ★★*les Passoms* (201 pl.), ☎ 29.89.32.50.

Restaurant :
Bouconville-sur-Madt, ✉ 55300 Saint-Mihiel :
♦♦ ***Deux Cheminées,*** ☎ 29.90.42.79. Euro, Visa, closed Mon eve and Tue, Feb school hols. Spec : *turbotin à l'anchois, pistil de safran ; agneau aux fèves et purée d'ail,* 95-180.

Bicycle hire : M. Viardot, Mandres-aux-Quatre-Tour, ☎ 83.52.20.62.

Recommended : *Centres for promotion of local produce* in Vigeulles-les-Hattonchâtel and at the Foyer rural in Saint-Maurice-sous-les-Côtes.

LUNÉVILLE

Nancy 35, Metz 93, Paris 409
C2-3 ✉ 54300

ⓘ pl. du Château, ☎ 83.74.60.70.

Hotels :
★★★***Pages,*** 8, rue Chanzy, ☎ 83.74.11.42. AE, Visa. 27 rm 170. Rest. ♦ Grill, pizzas, 80-130.
● ★★***Voltaire,*** 8, av. Voltaire, ☎ 83.74.07.09. AE, DC, Euro, Visa. 10 rm closed sun eve and Mon, 240. Rest. ♦♦ 60-160.

Ⅹ ★★*Les Bosquets* (36 pl.), ☎ 83.73.37.58.

Restaurants :
♦♦ ***Georges de la Tour,*** 18, rue de Lorraine, ☎ 83.73.44.04. AE, Visa. closed Feb school hols, 15-31 Aug, Tue eve and Wed. Spec : game (in season), fish, 55-170.

Rehainviller, 3 km S on the D31 :
♦♦♦ ***Château d'Adoménil,*** ☎ 83.74.04.81. AE,

DC, Euro, Visa. closed Sun eve, Mon, Feb school hols. Elegance and comfort surround good classic cooking. Spec : *flan d'huîtres à la crème de poireaux, pigeonneau en pot-au-feu,* 185-290.

Réchicourt-la-Petite, ✉ 54370 Einville, 235 km N :
Ferme-Auberge du Grand-Moulin, ☎ 83.72.93.78, closed Nov-Easter. Spec : *terrine de foies de volailles, charcuterie maison,* fresh fruit pastry, 70-100.

Son et lumière : ☎ 87.34.06.55 (Jul-Sep).

METZ

Nancy 57, Strasbourg 162, Paris 330
B2 ✉ 57000

porte Serpenoise (A3), ☎ 87.75.65.21.

✈ Metz-Frescaty, 6 km SW, ☎ 87.65.41.11.

Air France Agency, 2-4, in Chaplerue, ☎ 87.74.33.10.

SNCF ☎ 87.36.50.50.

pl. Coislin (C2-3), ☎ 87.75.26.62.

Car-hire : *Budget* train + auto, *Gardin Location,* 6, pl. Gal-de-Gaulle, ☎ 87.75.55.43, at the airport and at the station, ☎ 87.66.82.22.

Hotels :
★★★***Royal Concorde,*** 23, av. Foch (B3), ☎ 87.66.81.11. Tx 860425. AE, DC, Euro, Visa. 73 rm 580. Rest. ♦ ***le Caveau,*** 120-210.
★★***Central,*** 3 *bis,* rue Vauban (B3), ☎ 87.75.53.43. Tx 930281. Euro, Visa. 72 rm 250.
★***Lutèce*** (L.F.), 11, rue de Paris (A1), ☎ 87.30.27.25. DC, Euro, Visa. 21 rm closed 20 Dec-20 Jan, 130. Rest. closed Sat, Sun and nat hols, 60-100.

Rugy, ✉ 57640 Argancy, 11 km N on the D1 :
★★***La Bergerie*** (Relais du Silence), ☎ 87.64.82.27. Visa. 22 rm 200. Rest. ♦♦ 100-130.

Gorze, ✉ 57130 Ars-sur-Moselle, 20 km SW :
★***Lion d'Or*** (L.F.), ☎ 87.52.00.90. DC, Euro, Visa. 10 rm closed 1-10 Feb and Mon, 130. Rest. ♦♦ Spec : *filets de truite au brouilly et moëlle de bœuf, 60-190.*
Youth hostel : pl. du Pontiffroy (B1), ☎ 87.30.44.02. *Relais d'Amélécourt,* Maison de l'École in Liocourt (30 km S).

★★★★*Municipal de Metz* (150 pl.), ☎ 87.32.42.49.

Restaurants :
♦♦♦ ***Ville de Lyon,*** 7, rue des Piques, ☎ 87.36.07.01. AE, Euro, Visa. closed 27 Jul-26 Aug, Sun eve and Mon. Spec : *brioché de ris de veau avec sa gelée au Xérès, panaché de poissons à la purée de poireaux,* 80-160.
● ♦♦ ***La Dinanderie,*** 2, rue de Paris (A1), ☎ 87.30.14.40. AE, Euro, Visa. closed 3 Aug-3 Sep, end-of-year hols, Feb school hols, Sun and Mon. Inventive, resourceful cooking : *filets de sole à la crème de persil, pieds de porc farcis en chemise,* 150-210.

Noisseville, ✉ 57117, 9 km NE :
Relais de la Poste, 25, rue Principale, ☎ 87.76.61.78, closed 10-20 Jan, Sun, Mon and Tue eve. Spec : *escalope de foie gras aux pommes, pintade à la mirabelle,* 50-120.

Ars-sur-Moselle, ✉ 57130, 10 km SW by D6 :
♦♦ ***Auberge de la Gare,*** ☎ 87.60.62.03. AE, DC, Euro, Visa. Pleasant fare, 85-120.

Corny-sur-Moselle, ✉ 57680 Novéant, 13 km SW on the N57 :
♦♦ ***Gourmet Lorrain,*** 28, rue de la Moselle, ☎ 87.52.81.56, closed Thu and Sun eve, 120-210.

Sainte-Barbe, ✉ 57530 Courcelles-Chaussy, 13 km NE on the D954 :
♦♦ ***Mazagran,*** ☎ 87.77.01.11. AE, Visa. closed 16 Aug-10 Sep, Tue eve and Wed. Spec : *cassolette d'escargots à l'anis, filets de sole Valéry,* 85-220.

Local events : *carnival and cavalcade* (Mar).

Recommended : *fleamarket* : 1st and 3rd Sun of each month. Chocolates : *Pierre Kœnig,* 11, rue Pasteur (B3).

MONTMÉDY

Verdun 48, Charleville 64, Paris 258
A1 ☎ 55600

Hotels :
Mady, 8, pl. R.-Poincaré, ☎ 29.80.10.87. 15 rm closed Feb, Mon, 100. Rest. ♦♦ 80-130.

Damvillers, ✉ 55150, 22 km S :
★***Croix Blanche*** (L.F.), 7, rue Carnot, ☎ 28.85.60.12. AE, DC, Visa. 9 rm, closed Feb, Mon and Sun eve (low season) 125. Rest. ♦ 50-110.

NANCY

Metz 57, Strasbourg 145, Paris 294
B2-3 ✉ 54000

14, pl. Stanislas (B2), ☎ 83.35.22.41.

✈ Nancy-Essey, 4 km NE, ☎ 83.29.56.90.

SNCF 3, pl. Thiers (A2), ☎ 83.56.50.50.

pl. Colonel-Driant (C2), ☎ 83.32.23.58 ; 56, pl. Mgr Ruch (C2), ☎ 83.32.34.20.

Car-hire : *Budget* train + auto, at the station, ☎ 83.32.72.50, and at the airport.

Hotels :
● ★★★★***Grand Hôtel de la Reine*** (Concorde, Relais et Châteaux), 2, pl. Stanislas (B2), ☎ 83.35.03.01. Tx 960367. AE, DC, Euro, Visa. 52 rm and 2 apt This superb 18thC residence is a protected historic monument, 800. Rest. ***Stanislas*** ● ♦♦♦ 140-280.
★★★***Astoria Albert Ier*** (Inter-Hôtel), 3, rue de l'Armée-Patton (A2), ☎ 83.40.31.24. Tx 850895. AE, DC, Euro, Visa. 136 rm 265.
★★★***Europe,*** 5, rue des Carmes, ☎ 83.35.32.10. AE, DC, Euro, Visa. 80 rm 250.
★★★***Frantel,*** 11, rue R.-Poincaré (A-B2), ☎ 83.35.61.01. AE, DC, Euro, Visa. 112 rm 420. Rest. ♦♦ closed 14 Jul-1 Sep, nat hols, Sat noon and Sun. Spec : *le chausson de brouet de saint-pierre aux radis, le mignon de bœuf au vin de Bruley,* 100-220.

Méréville, ✉ 54850 Messein, 12 km S :
★★★***Maison Carrée*** (L.F.), ☎ 83.47.09.23. AE, Euro, Visa. 23 rm 175. Rest. ♦♦ Classic cooking in a rustic setting, 80-170.

Custines, ✉ 54670, 13 km N :
★★***Ile,*** 48 *bis,* rue de Metz, ☎ 83.49.39.56. Visa. 34 rm closed year end hols, and Jun, 180.

★★*Municipal,* Villers-lès-Nancy (460 pl.), ☎ 83.27.18.28.

Restaurants :
● ♦♦♦ ***Capucin Gourmand*** (Gérard Veissière), 31, rue Gambetta (B2), ☎ 83.35.26.98. Visa. closed Aug, Sun and Mon. Booking required. In a "School of Nancy" classified setting, among Majorelle furniture and blown glass-pieces, Gérard Veissière likes to introduce exotic

flavours : *pigeonneau en Kefta, salades de grenouilles fraîches au gingembre* ; nice cellar, 200-320.

● ♦♦ ***Gentilhommière,*** 29, rue des Maréchaux (B1), ☎ 83.32.26.44. AE, DC, Euro, Visa. closed 1st week in Feb, Aug, Sat, Sun and nat hols. Good modern cooking. Spec : *loup aux artichauts, turbot aux concombres,* 160-230.

● ♦♦ ***Gastrolâtre,*** 39, rue des Maréchaux (B1-2), ☎ 83.35.07.97. closed Sun, Mon, 1 week in Feb, Christmas, 1-7 Jan. P. Tanesy creates an enjoyable light cooking in a pretty turn-of-the-century setting. Spec : *cervelas de grenouilles, choux farcis aux langoustines,* lobster, oysters, 120-210.

♦ ***Jéricho,*** 25, rue de Jéricho, fg Malzéville, ☎ 83.29.47.85. Euro, Visa. Ⓟ ⚘ ⚲ ♿ closed Sat, Sun, eve, 6-31 Jul. Good, simple, genuine Lorraine cooking. Spec : *chauyottes en salade, fiouse (pie) lorraine, lard paysan grillé.* Gris côtes de Tour wine, 80-130.

♦ ***Nouveaux Abattoirs,*** 4, bd Austrasie (not on the map), ☎ 83.35.46.25 Ⓟ ♿ closed Aug, Sat, Sun, 1 week end year and nat hols. For those who enjoy good meat dishes, 60-150.

Champenoux, ⊠ 54280 Seichamps, 15 km on the N74 :

♦♦ ***Lion d'Or,*** 48, rue St-Barthélemy, ☎ 83.31.61.23. AE, DC, Euro, Visa. Ⓟ ♿ 80-250.

Guided tours : the old town : 15 Jul-15 Sep at 10 am and 5 pm ; departure and enq ⓘ ; evenings : Jun-Sep at 9 pm ; departure and enq : ⓘ

Recommended : for macaroons and bergamotes, *Maison Aptel,* 21, rue Gambetta (B2). Chocolates, *Michel Lalonde,* rue Here. *Foies gras* and fine *charcuterie, Caraux-Caderlet,* 52, rue Stanislas (B2). Auction halls : 23, rue Gustave-Simon (B1-2), ☎ 83.32.00.76, and 107, rue du Sgt-Blandan (not on the map), ☎ 83.28.13.31.

PHALSBOURG

Strasbourg 57, Nancy 99, Paris 395
C2 ⊠ 57370

Hotels :

★★***Erckmann-Chatrian*** (L.F.), 14, pl. d'Armes, ☎ 87.24.31.33. AE, Visa. 18 rm Ⓟ ⚲ closed Oct, Mon and Tue noon, 160. Rest. ♦ ♿ closed Mon, 45-160.

Lutzelbourg, ⊠ 57820, 4 km S :

★★***Vosges,*** 149, rue Ackermann, ☎ 87.25.30.09. 22 rm Ⓟ ⚘ ⚲ ♿ on the riverside, closed 13 Jan-17 Mar, Wed ex Jul-Aug, 180. Rest. ♦♦ 45-150.

Youth hostel : *Château d'Einhartzhausen,* ☎ 87.07.13.72. closed 1 Nov-1 Apr.

⛺ ★★*Le Vieux Château* (50 pl.), ☎ 87.24.13.72.

PLAINFAING

Colmar 38, Épinal 56, Paris 477
18 km SE of Saint-Dié, C3 ⊠ 88230 Fraize

Hotels :

★★***Vosges-Alsace,*** col du Bonhomme, ☎ 29.50.32.61. AE, DC, Euro, Visa. 13 rm Ⓟ ⚲ ♿ closed 15 Oct-15 Nov, 180. Rest. ♦ 40-100.

Anould, 6 km W :

★***Poste*** (L.F.), pl. de Montluçon, ☎ 29.57.11.14. Visa. 10 rm ⚟ ⚘ ⚲ Ⓟ ♿ closed Sep-10 Oct, 130. Rest. ♦♦ closed Mon, 80-130.

Farmhouse gîte : *domaine du Grand Maly,* at Mandray, 10 km N, ☎ 29.58.01.74. Fishing, farm produce for sale.

Farmhouse-inn : *les Grands Prés,* ☎ 29.50.83.48 ⚟ Spec : *terrines, pâté lorrain, volailles, tartes aux framboises, mirabelles, foie gras confits* (in autumn).

PLOMBIÈRES-LES-BAINS

Épinal 30, Vesoul 48, Paris 380
C4 ⚕ May-Nov, ☎ 29.66.02.17 ♥ ⊠ 88370

ⓘ rue Stanislas, ☎ 29.66.01.30.

SNCF ☎ 29.66.00.29.

Hotels :

★★★***Grand Hôtel,*** 2, av. des États-Unis, ☎ 29.66.00.03. 115 rm Ⓟ ⚘ ⚲ ⚲ ♿ closed Oct-Apr, 220.

★★***Acacias*** (L.F.), 25, av. Louis-Français, ☎ 29.66.00.01. 44 rm ⚟ Ⓟ ⚘ ⊡ ♿ closed Oct-Apr, 100.

★★***Rosiers*** (L.F.), av. Val-d'Ajol, ☎ 29.66.02.66. 22 rm ⚟ Ⓟ ⚘ ⚲ closed 30 Oct-Easter, 170. Rest. ♦ ⚲ ♿ 50-110.

★***Commerce*** (L.F.), 16, rue de l'Hôtel-de-Ville, ☎ 29.66.00.47. Visa. 45 rm ⚘ ⊡ closed 30 Sep-1 May, 130. Rest. ♦ 50-120.

★***Touring*** (L.F.), av. Louis-Français, ☎ 29.66.00.70, 23 rm ⚟ Ⓟ ⚘ ♿ closed 1 Nov-1 Apr, 100.

4 km :

● ★★***Fontaine Stanislas,*** ☎ 29.66.01.53. 19 rm ⚟ Ⓟ ⚘ ⚲ closed 1 Oct-31 Mar, 200. Rest. ♦♦ ⚲ 65-120.

⛺ ★★*Municipal,* Ruaux, 4 km W (50 pl.), ☎ 29.66.00.71. *Farmhouse-camping "Étang des Prêtres",* La Crousette (3 km), ☎ 29.66.03.84.

Farmhouse gîte : 15 km : *les Cinq Sols,* ☎ 29.66.03.46. Farm produce for sale. Fishing ⚲ Rambling and hiking.

Ballooning : *Club aérostatique de Lorraine,* ☎ 29.36.31.85.

Recommended : *glace plombieres* Chez Pierre Brunello, 15, rue Liétard, ☎ 29.66.01.52. Brandies and spirits at *Ferme Chaussat.* Embroidery *maison Dié,* rue du Chevalier-de-Boufflers.

PONT-A-MOUSSON

Nancy 31, Metz 32, Paris 325

B2 ⊠ 54700

ⓘ 52, pl. Duroc, ☎ 83.38.06.90.

SNCF ☎ 83.56.50.50.

Hotel :

★★***Européen,*** 156, av. de Metz, ☎ 83.81.07.57. 19 rm Ⓟ ⚘ closed 4-25 Aug, 100. Rest. ♦ 80-130.

Restaurant :

Belleville, ⊠ 54940, 13 km :

● ♦♦ ***Bistroquet,*** ☎ 83.25.90.12 Ⓟ closed Jan, Aug, Sat noon, Sun eve and Mon. Booking required. In a 1900's decor, the good cooking of Jean Ponsard. Spec : *panaché de la mer, pigeon cocotte aux échalotes,* 170-240.

REMIREMONT

Épinal 27, Vesoul 64, Paris 414
C4 ⊠ 88200

ⓘ 2, pl. H.-Utard, ☎ 29.62.23.70.

SNCF ☎ 29.62.54.87.

Hotels :

★★***Chanoinesses*** (L.F. ; Inter-Hôtel), 14-16, fg du Val-d'Ajol, ☎ 29.62.27.46. Tx 960277. AE, DC, Euro, Visa. 30 rm Ⓟ ⚲ 215. Rest. ♦♦ ⚲ ♿ 70-140.

★★***Poste,*** 67, rue Ch.-de-Gaulle, ☎ 29.62.55.67. AE, DC, Visa. 21 rm, closed 17-

31 Aug, 15 Dec-10 Jan, 220. Rest. ♦♦ ♿ closed Fri eve and Sat (low season), 50-130.

Saint-Nabord, 5 km :
★★**Relais de Belcour** (L.F.), rue de Turenne, ☎ 29.62.06.27. 18 rm Ⓟ closed end-of-year hols, 100.

⛺ ★★*La Demoiselle* (44 pl.), ☎ 29.62.23.60.

Rural gîte : *Ferme Couval,* Olichamp-la-Demoiselle, 5 km SSW : booking required, farmhouse-inn, ☎ 29.62.28.86. Spec : *andouille du Val-d'Ajol, fumé des Hautes-Vosges ;* farm produce for sale. Ferdrupt, on the route des Forts, *Chez Marie,* ☎ 29.25.95.22. Snacks : mountain-cured ham, munster cheese, bilberry tart, *saucisse au cumin.*

Recommended : *Charcuterie Claude Thiébaut,* opposite Volontaire statue : cooked meats and sausages. *Pâtisserie B. Thiews,* under the Arcades : local spec, *toiles des Vosges,* 14, rue de la Courtine.

RUPT-SUR-MOSELLE

Épinal 39, Mulhouse 70, Paris 426
12 km S of Remiremont, C4 ✉ 88360

ℹ rue de l'Église, ☎ 29.24.34.09.

Hotels :
★★**Prégouttes,** ☎ 29.24.35.09. DC, Euro, Visa. 12 rm Ⓟ closed Sun eve, 180. Rest. ♦ 50-150.
★**Centre** (L.F.), 28, rue de l'Église, ☎ 29.24.34.73. AE, DC, Euro, Visa. 11 rm Ⓟ closed 7-28 Jan, Sun eve and Mon low season, 210. Rest. ♦ 60-200.

⛺ ★★*Le Pont de Maxonchamp* (33 pl.), ☎ 29.24.37.12.

SAINT-AVOLD

Metz 45, Nancy 73, Paris 369
C2 ✉ 57500

ℹ mairie, ☎ 87.92.10.07.

SNCF ☎ 87.92.07.27.

Restaurants :
♦♦ **Neptune,** ☎ 87.92.27.90. AE, DC, Euro, Visa. Ⓟ ♿ closed 8 Aug-8 Sep, Sat noon, Sun eve, Mon. Spec : *noisettes de chevreuil aux airelles* (in season), *gratin de mirabelles,* 140-270.

Carling, ✉ 57490, 7 km N :
♦ **La Choucroutière,** 176, rte Principale, ☎ 87.93.64.64. DC, Visa. Ⓟ ♿ closed Feb school hols, 28 Jul-13 Aug, Thu eve. Assortment of *choucroutes,* sea-food and game when in season. Alsatian wine, 50-150.

SAINT-DIÉ

Épinal 50, Strasbourg 90, Paris 460
C3 ✉ 88100

ℹ 32, rue Thiers, ☎ 29.56.17.62, and (high season) Chalet d'Accueil, entrance to the Ste-Marie-aux-Mines Tunnel, ☎ 29.57.22.66.

SNCF ☎ 29.56.10.00.

🚌 pl. St-Martin, ☎ 29.56.18.65.

Car-hire : *Budget* train + auto, 3, quai Jeanne-d'Arc, ☎ 29.56.25.19 ; at the station, ☎ 29.56.44.07.

Hotels :
★★**France,** 1, rue Dauphine, ☎ 29.56.32.61. AE, DC, Visa. 11 rm Ⓟ 230.
★★**Vosges et ★Commerce,** 53-57, rue Thiers, ☎ 29.56.16.21. AE, DC, Visa. 30 rm Ⓟ ♿ 220.

⛺ ★★*La Vanne* (50 pl.), ☎ 29.56.23.56.

Farmhouse gîte : *la Charriole,* Les Hautes-Fosses, Taintrux, 9 km, ☎ 29.56.36.83. Spec : *cabri à l'oseille, gigot au four à pain, canard aux herbes, cochon de lait farci.*

Restaurant :
● ♦ **Le Tétras,** 4, rue d'Hellieule, ☎ 29.56.10.12. AE, DC, Euro, Visa. ♿ closed Fri eve, Sat and 30 Sep-30 Oct, 1 week Feb. A tradition of steady menus : game when in season, *tarte au miel et aux amandes,* 70-190.

SAINT-MAURICE-SUR-MOSELLE

Belfort 39, Épinal 57, Paris 446
45 km SW of Bussang, C4 ✉ 88560
560-1 250 m

ℹ pl. du 2-Octobre-1944, ☎ 29.25.12.34, and mairie, ☎ 29.25.11.21.

Hotels :
★★★**Relais des Ballons,** rte Bénélux-Bâle, ☎ 29.25.11.09, 17 rm Ⓟ closed 7-21 Oct and Mon noon, 200. Rest. ♦ ***l'Auberge,*** 80-130.
★★**Au Pied des Ballons** (L.F.), 1, rte du Ballon-d'Alsace, ☎ 29.25.12.54. DC, Euro, Visa. 30 rm Ⓟ ♿ closed 15-30 Nov, 140. Rest. ♦ closed Mon eve low season, 50-190.

⛺ ★★★*Les Deux Ballons* (130 pl.), ☎ 29.25.11.26.

SAINT-MIHIEL

Bar-le-Duc 33, Metz 66, Paris 303
A2 ✉ 55300

ℹ pl. des Halles, ☎ 29.89.04.50.

SNCF ☎ 29.89.00.07.

Hotel :
★**Régence,** rue Basse-des-Fossés, ☎ 29.89.01.05. Euro, Visa. 35 rm. closed Christmas hols, Fri eve (1 Nov-1 Mar) Ⓟ 140. Rest. ♦♦ 50-130.

⛺ ★★*Base de Plein Air* (43 pl.), ☎ 29.89.03.59.

Restaurant :
Bannoncourt, 10 km N on D34 :
♦♦ **La Clé des Champs,** ☎ 29.90.11.67. closed 1 Dec-1 Mar Ⓟ 80-130.

SARREBOURG

Strasbourg 70, Nancy 74, Paris 426
C2 ✉ 57400

ℹ chapelle des Cordeliers, ☎ 87.03.11.82.

SNCF ☎ 87.03.50.50.

Hotel :
★★**France** (L.F.), 3, av. de France, ☎ 87.03.21.47. Euro, Visa. 52 rm Ⓟ 220. Rest. ♦ closed Sat and Sun eve, 1-15 Nov, 80-180.

Restaurant :
♦♦ **Mathis,** 7, rue Gambetta, ☎ 87.03.21.67. AE, DC, Euro, Visa. Ⓟ ♿ closed Sun eve and Mon. Spec : *foie gras de canard cuit au torchon fait maison, fricassée de sandre et nouillettes maison à l'alsacienne,* 90-180.

SARREGUEMINES

Metz 69, Strasbourg 104, Paris 394
C2 ✉ 57200

ℹ rue de la Poste, ☎ 87.98.52.32.

Hotel :
★★★**Alsace** (Mapotel), 10, rue Poincaré, ☎ 87.98.44.32. Tx 860582. AE, DC, Euro, Visa. 28 rm Ⓟ 280. Rest. ♦♦♦ ***Ducs de Lorraine.*** Light traditional cooking. Seafood specialities, 100-250. Brasserie ♦ ***Taverne,*** 80-130.

Restaurants :
♦♦♦ ***Vieux Moulin,*** 135, rue de France, ☎ 87.98.22.59. AE, DC, Euro, Visa. Ⓟ Alongside the river. Closed, Tue and Wed. Spec : *truite au riesling, filet de sole poivre vert, ballotine de canard au foie gras,* 120-210.
● ♦♦ ***St-Walfrid,*** 58, rue de Grosbliederstroff, ☎ 87.98.43.75 Ⓟ closed Jan, Aug, Sun and Mon. Spec : *lotte à l'ail, filet de bœuf aux deux moutardes,* 90-250.

Event : *carnaval and cavalcade* (mid-Feb).

SIERCK-LES-BAINS

Metz 45, Verdun 105, Paris 358
B1 ☒ 57480

Hotel :
★***Central,*** 6, quai des Ducs-de-Lorraine, ☎ 82.83.71.14. 14 rm Ⓟ closed Fri and 25 Aug-10 Sep, 100. Rest. ♦ 80-130.

⛺ ★★*Municipal* (100 pl.), ☎ 82.83.82.15.

Restaurant :
● ♦♦♦ ***La Vénerie,*** 10, rue Porte-de-Trèves, ☎ 82.83.72.41. AE, DC. Ⓟ ♿ closed 25 Jan-1 Mar and Mon. Excellent cooking. Spec : *gratin de cuisses de grenouilles, panaché de turbot et de St-Jacques au safran,* 100-200.

SION

Nancy 37, Épinal 52, Paris 329
B3 ☒ 54330

Hotel :
★***Notre-Dame,*** colline de Sion, ☎ 83.26.91.82. 16 rm Ⓟ ♿ closed 15 Nov-1 Mar, 120. Rest. ♦ 50-150.

STENAY

Sedan 34, Verdun 46, Paris 241
A1 ☒ 55700

Hotel :
Inor, 7 km N :
★★***Faisan Doré,*** rue de l'Écluse, ☎ 29.80.35.45. Euro, Visa. 13 rm Ⓟ ♿ closed Fri noon low season, 185. Rest. ● ♦♦ ♿ On bank of the Meuse river, nice and cool. Spec : *sanglier aux morilles, canard aux mirabelles,* 40-160.

⛺ ★★*Municipal* (200 pl.), ☎ 29.80.30.31.

Le THILLOT

Belfort 44, Épinal 50, Paris 439
C4 ☒ 88160

ⓘ mairie, ☎ 29.25.00.59.

SNCF ☎ 29.25.00.67.

Hotel :
★★***Perce-Neige*** (L.F.), col des Croix, ☎ 29.25.02.63. AE, DC. 20 rm Ⓟ closed 1 Nov-20 Dec, 160. Rest. ♦ 55-110.

Farmhouse gîte : 3 km on the N486 : *le Prey,* chapelle des Vées. Cross-country and downhill skiing.

THIONVILLE

Metz 29, Verdun 87, Paris 340
B1 ☒ 57100

ⓘ 16, rue du Vieux-Collège, ☎ 82.53.33.18.

SNCF ☎ 82.56.50.50.

🚌 pl. du Luxembourg, ☎ 82.53.84.75.

Car-hire : *Budget* train + auto, *Gardin Locations,* 5, rue St-Pierre, ☎ 82.53.71.71 ; at the station, ☎ 82.56.23.25.

Hotels :
● ★★★***Horizon*** (Relais et châteaux), 50, rte Crève-Cœur, 3 km NW, ☎ 82.88.53.65. AE, DC, Visa. 10 rm Ⓟ ♿ closed 25 Dec-20 Feb, 500. Rest. ♦♦ closed Sat noon and 10 Dec-16 Mar, 170-260.
★★***Portes de France*** (L.F.), 1, pl. Gal-Patton, ☎ 82.53.30.01. AE, DC, Visa. 21 rm Ⓟ closed 2-25 Aug, 24 Dec-2 Jan, 190.

Youth hostel : pl. de la Gare, ☎ 82.53.38.80.

⛺ ★★*Municipal* (45 pl.), ☎ 82.53.03.75.

Restaurant :
♦♦ ***Auberge du Crève-Cœur,*** ☎ 82.88.50.52. Ⓟ ♿ closed Sun eve and Mon. Since 1899, wine-growers have been coming here for the good cooking. Spec : *porcelet en gelée, mirabelles flambées,* 120-210.

Le THOLY

Épinal 30, Saint-Dié 40, Paris 419
10 km W of Gérardmer, C4 ☒ 88530

ⓘ mairie, ☎ 29.61.81.18.

Hotels :
★★***Grande Cascade*** (L.F.), 24, rte du Col-de-Bonnefontaine, ☎ 29.33.21.08. Tx 850743. AE, DC, Visa. 20 rm Ⓟ ♿ closed 25 Oct-5 Dec, 130. Rest. ♦ 50-200.
★★Gérard (L.F.), 1, pl. Gal-Leclerc, ☎ 29.61.81.07. Tx 961408, AE, DC, Euro, Visa. 20 rm Ⓟ closed 1-31 Oct, 180. Rest. ♦ ♿ 50-100.

Julienrupt, ☒ 88120 Vagney, 5 km SW :
★★***A la Vallée de Cleurie,*** ☎ 29.61.10.00. DC, Visa. 15 rm Ⓟ ♿ closed 25 Sep-25 Oct and Wed eve, 155. Rest. ♦ 60-150.

Tendon, ☒ 88460 Docelles, 8 km NW :
★★***Au Repos des Cascades*** (L.F.), under the village, ☎ 29.66.24.80. Tx 960277. DC, Euro, Visa. 13 rm. Ⓟ ♿ 170. Rest. ♦ 80-120.

⛺ ★★★★*De Noir Rupt* (35 pl.), ☎ 29.61.81.27.

Farmhouse gîte and camping : Blanfaing, 3 km on the N11 and D417, ☎ 29.61.80.45. Fishing. Berlingouth-Bonvacôte, 3 km on the N417, farmhouse-inn, ☎ 29.61.84.82.

TOUL

Nancy 23, Bar-le-Duc 61, Paris 290
B3 ☒ 54200

ⓘ parvis de la Cathédrale, ☎ 83.64.11.69.

SNCF ☎ 83.43.10.30.

🚌 porte de France, ☎ 83.43.01.29.

Hotel :
★★***Europe,*** 35, av. V.-Hugo, ☎ 83.43.00.10. 21 rm Ⓟ closed 1-15 Feb, 210.

Restaurants :
● ♦♦ ***Dauphin,*** rte de Villey-Saint-Étienne, ☎ 83.43.13.46. Ⓟ closed Sun eve and Mon, 20 Sep-10 Oct. Elegant stop and C. Vohmann's excellent cooking. Spec : *foie gras aux mirabelles séchées, turbot au Côtes-de-Toul ;* local wines, 80-210.
♦♦ ***Belle Époque,*** 31, av. Victor-Hugo, ☎ 83.43.23.71. closed Sat noon, Sun eve and Mon, 1-18 Jan, 1-24 Jul. Spec : *escalope de lotte à la ciboulette et nouilles fraîches, escalope de sandre et turbot à la petite sauce d'herbes, panaché des cinq poissons à la vapeur,* good desserts, 120-210.

Recommended : *Vin gris (rosé)* from Toul, *Gabriel Demange,* 4, rue du Chêne, Bruley (5 km NW ; ☎ 83.43.20.96).

Le VAL-D'AJOL

Épinal 44, Vesoul 45, Paris 377
12 km S of Plombières, C4 ⊠ 88340

ℹ 2, rue du Devau, ☎ 29.66.66.30.

Hotel :
★★***Résidence*** (L.F.), 5, rue des Mousses, ☎ 29.30.68.52. Tx 960573. AE, DC, Euro, Visa. 60 rm P ♿ closed 20 Nov-20 Dec, 175. Rest. ♦ 50-180.

Farmhouse gîte and inn : *St-Vallier,* Les Haies, vallée de Girmont, ☎ 29.66.38.37 and 29.66.62.77. Spec : *omelette au lard, jambon de montagne* and *andouille du Val-d'Ajol.*

Ⲁ ★★*Les Cigognes* (35 pl.), ☎ 29.30.66.51.

VENTRON

Gérardmer 26, Épinal 57, Paris 444
C4 630-1 100 m ⊠ 88310 Cornimont

Hôtels :
● ★★★***Buttes,*** Ermitage du Frère Joseph, ☎ 29.24.18.09. 30 rm P ♿ closed 15 Nov-20 Dec, 250. Rest. ♿ 85-170.
● ★★***Ermitage*** (L.F.), annex of *Les Buttes,* ☎ 29.24.18.29. 50 rm P ♿ closed 15 Oct-15 Nov, 250. Rest. 65-80.

Gîtes and farmhouse-inns :
La Chaume du Grand Ventron, ☎ 29.25.52.53/29.24.17.61. At 1 200 m altitude. Spec : *fumé de Laboyaure, omelette des Chaumes, saucisse fumée aux tofayes* (potatoes stuffed with onions and smoked bacon).
La Zimette, rupt du Moulin ☎ 29.24.18.20. Spec : *fumé* and *terrine maison, coq au riesling.*
Skiing, fishing, tennis.

VERDUN

Metz 78, Reims 120, Paris 261
A2 ⊠ 55100

ℹ pl. de la Nation, ☎ 29.84.18.85.

SNCF ☎ 29.86.25.65.

pl. Vauban, ☎ 29.86.02.71.

Hotels :
● ★★★***Coq Hardi,*** 8, av. de la Victoire, ☎ 29.86.00.68. Tx 860464. AE, DC. 39 rm ♿ closed 23 Dec-1 Feb, 460. Rest. ♦♦ closed Wed. Spec : *terrine d'écrevisses au sabayon rose, canard au vinaigre de framboises, mirabelles flambées au caramel,* 135-260.
★★★***Bellevue,*** 1, rd-pt du Mal-de-Lattre-de-Tassigny, ☎ 29.84.39.41. Tx 860464. AE, DC, Visa. 72 rm P ♿ closed 15 Oct-1 Apr, 300. Rest. ♦ (set menu only), 70-150.
★★***Montaulbain,*** 4, rue Vieille-Prison, ☎ 29.86.00.47. 10 rm 170.
★★***Poste et Pergola*** (L.F.), 8, av. Douaumont, ☎ 29.86.03.90. Visa. 23 rm, closed 20 Jan-20 Feb, 100. Rest. ♦♦ Good basic fare, 80-130.

Youth hostel, pl. André-Maginot, Belleville, ☎ 29.86.64.58 and 29.84.43.47.

Ⲁ ★★★*Les Breuils* (90 pl.), ☎ 29.86.15.31.

Excursion : on the Meuse on *le Tibre,* 112 pl. river launch. Enq : ℹ

Recommended : *Dragées Braquier,* ☎ 29.84.30.00 ; chocolate cannon-balls (they really explode) ; the factory in Coulmier is open to visitors.

VITTEL

Épinal 43, Nancy 70, Paris 334
B4 ☎ 29.08.00.00 ⊠ 88800

ℹ palais des Congrès, ☎ 29.08.12.72.

SNCF ☎ 29.08.02.24.

Hotels :
★★★***Angleterre,*** rue de Charmey, ☎ 29.08.08.42. AE, DC, Visa. 62 rm P ♿ closed 15 Dec-15 Jan, 260. Rest. ♦ ♿ 90-160.
★★***Beauséjour,*** 160, av. des Tilleuls, ☎ 29.08.09.34. Euro. 37 rm P closed 1 Oct-30 Apr, 230. Rest. ♦ ♿ 70-125.
★★***Castel Fleuri,*** rue de Metz/rue Jeanne-d'Arc, ☎ 29.08.05.20. 42 rm P closed 15 May-21 Sep, 230. Rest. ♦ 60-90.
★★***Orée du Bois*** (L.F.), race course turning on the D18, ☎ 29.08.13.51. Tx 960573. AE, Visa. 30 rm P closed Mon, 185. Rest. ♦ ♿ closed Sun eve (1 Nov-30 Apr), 50-130.
★★***Le Chalet*** (L.F.), 6, av. G.-Clemenceau, ☎ 29.08.07.21. 10 rm P closed Oct, Sun eve (ex hotel), Sat (low season), 1 week in Jan, 180. Rest. Spec : *soufflé chaud à la mirabelle,* 80-210.

Ⲁ★★★*Municipal* (130 pl.), ☎ 29.08.02.71.

Restaurant :
♦♦ ***L'Aubergeade,*** 265, av. des Tilleuls, ☎ 29.08.04.32. AE, DC, Visa. P ♿ closed Sun eve, Mon, 1-10 Jan, 1-10 May, 1-10 Oct. Spec : *filet d'agneau en feuilleté, blanc de turbot à la vapeur au pinot noir,* 110-270.

Casino : all games, ☎ 29.08.12.35.

XONRUPT-LONGEMER

Saint-Dié 28, Épinal 46, Paris 435
C4 700-1 225 m ⊠ 88400 Gérardmer

ℹ Gérardmer, ☎ 29.63.08.74.

Hotels :
★★★***Saut des Cuves,*** in Saut-des-Cuves, ☎ 29.63.30.46. AE, DC, Visa. 27 rm P closed 3 Nov-15 Dec, 235. Rest. ♦ 60-250.
★★***Lac de Longemer*** (L.F.), 100, rue Longemer, ☎ 29.63.37.21. AE, DC. 18 rm P closed 15 Nov-15 Dec, 200. Rest. ♦ 50-170.
★★***La Vallée,*** rte de la Schlucht, ☎ 29.63.37.01. 12 rm P closed 15 Nov-1 Dec, 100. Rest. ♦ Family-style eating. Spec : *truite au bleu, potée,* succulent tarts, 40-100.

Le Collet, 9 km SE :
● ★★★***Le Collet,*** rte de la Schlucht, ☎ 29.63.11.43. Tx 961408. AE, DC. 23 rm P closed 15 Nov-15 Dec, 220. Rest. ♦♦ 55-170.

Youth hostel : *la Roche du Page,* ☎ 29.63.07.17.

Ⲁ ★★*Belle Vue* (35 pl.), ☎ 29.63.13.30 ; ★★*Domaine de Longemer* (210 pl.), ☎ 29.63.07.30 ; ★★*Eau Vive* (42 pl.), ☎ 29.63.07.37 ; ★★*Orée du Bois* (40 pl.), ☎ 29.63.29.82 ; ★★*Chaumière* (35 pl.), ☎ 29.63.13.30 ; ★★*Vologne* (70 pl.), ☎ 29.63.07.24 ; ★★*Jonquilles* (220 pl.), ☎ 29.63.34.01 ; ★★*les Pergis* (70 pl.), ☎ 29.63.20.36 ; ★★*Sorbiers* (33 pl.), ☎ 29.63.36.04 ; *Verte Vallée* (90 pl.), ☎ 29.63.21.77.

Gîte and farmhouse-inn : *de Balveurche,* rte du col de la Schlucht, ☎ 29.63.26.02. Spec : *choucroute, tourte* and munster cheese (sold at the farm). Centre for nordic-style cross-country skiing.

The Lyonnais and Bresse Regions

The city of Lyons, with a population second only to Paris — and thanks to the TGV or High-Speed train, a mere two hours from the capital — has dominated life and landscape in this region since the Roman conquest of Gaul. Its influence is felt far beyond the borders of the three *départements* described in this chapter and the relatively new name of "Lyonnais" covers an enormous disparity of natural regions, historical identities and economic development.

To the east is the department of Ain, made up of a number of smaller regions which were attached to the House of Savoy before coming under the sway of the Kings of France in the 17th century. To the west the Forez region has flourished for over one hundred years in the shadow of the enormous industrial and economic complex of Saint-Étienne. To the north is Beaujolais, still living on the excellent tradition and reputation of its vineyards, where every year around October the new wine is bottled and sent to restaurants and wine cellars all over the world. To the south are the Pilat Mountains marking the northern borders of Vivarais.

And yet despite this seeming disparity, the city of Lyons, city of rivers, provides a link forging the parts into a single whole, adding the human dimension and retaining its links with the industrial empire of bygone days. Lyons, whose cooking is reputedly the finest in France and, many would claim, the world, is full of surprises for the tourist. It may have lost its silkweavers and the army of small craftsmen chased out by the factory owners after the bloody uprisings of the early 19th century, but it has kept its old panoramas and invented new ones. The enterprising tourist will discover the old Roman town of Lugdunum beneath its modern trappings, and by wandering through its streets and visiting its many museums, will be able to enjoy the busy cultural life of a city which has been an important crossroads of civilization for some 2000 years.

Sightseeing

AMBÉRIEU-EN-BUGEY

BC1-2 / pop. 10 470 (Ain)

A small town beneath Mount Luisandre *(NE)* amid countryside popular with anglers for trout and grayling. □

▶ Nearby

▶ **Ambronay** *(4 km N)* : Benedictine abbey with Gothic cloister★, monks' cells, gargoyle-emblazoned door (13thC) *(closed Sun., Jul.-Aug. & Mon. rest of year)*. ▶ E on a ridge of **Mt Luisandre, Allymes** (alt. 809 m, panorama★), 13th-16thC **château** and ancestral home of the counts of Savoy. ▶ **Saint-Sorlin-en-Bugey** *(S via Lagnieu, near the river Rhône)* : "city of roses", Romanesque and Gothic church of the Madeleine (15thC fresco; summer concerts). □

Facts and Figures

Location : *an artificial designation for the region between Auvergne and the Jura Mountains, the Lyonnais region straddles a swath cut by the river Rhône. The three administrative areas (*départements*) are : Eastern and Western Loire (4 800 km², corresponding to the former designation of Forez; Rhône, the country's smallest department (3 215 km²) after Paris, and Ain (5 836 km²), a mosaic of small landholdings.*
Climate : *Mediterranean in the Beaujolais and Bresse; in low-lying areas and around Lyons, fog and overcast skies are common. The forested mountains have wet, brisk weather, harsh in winter on Mount Pilat and in the upper reaches of the Jura — which may have snow until May.*
Population : *Ain, 429 300; Loire, 747 600; Rhône, 1 464 300. Density : 192/km² — among the highest in France, with the urban population more than 50% of the total.*
The Lyons-St. Étienne region extends from Firminy in the west to the confluence of the Rhône and the Ain in the east; 90% of the region's population — more than 2.64 million — lives in this urban band.

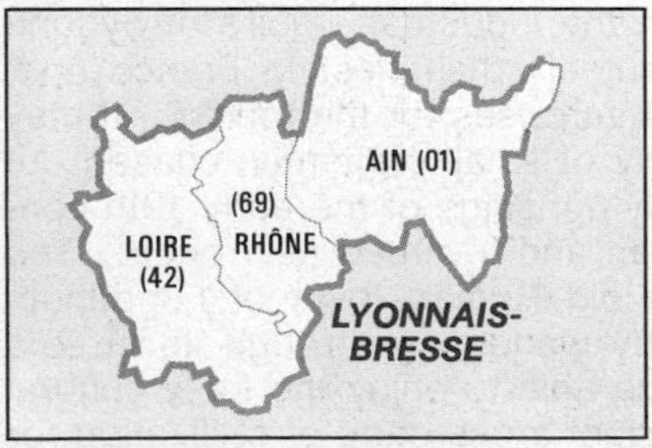

Weekend tips

Lyons (→ box, Burgundy) : 2 hrs by TGV (Train Grande Vitesse : high-speed train) from Paris. First day, city tour : Fourvière and the old city (morning) : a museum or two and a stroll through the passageways (traboules) of Lyons (afternoon); a visit to Tête d'Or Park (evening). Second day : half-day or day trip to Mont d'Or and Rochetaillée; or Beaujolais, Bresse, or Dombes and Pérouges. From the Saint-Étienne region : visit Forez Plain or drive to Mount Pilat. At Divonne or in the Gex area : Faucille Pass, Valserine and Valromey (preferably between May and late Oct.).
On any trip, plan to dine at one of the superb regional restaurants.

AMBIERLE★

A1 / pop. 1 596 (Loire)

Among the Roanne vineyards, a hillside market town around a Gothic church★.

▶ Church : **stained-glass windows★,** Gothic choir stalls, 15thC Burgundian-Flemish School triptych depicting **Christ's Passion★.** ▶ **Forez Regional Museum :** Alice Tavern *(10-12 & 2-5, 6 or 7 according to season; closed Tue. except Jun.-Aug.),* reconstructed 18thC and 19thC interiors★★. □

▶ Roanne District

▶ **Saint-Haon-le-Châtel** *(S) :* walled market town★ (12th-15thC); ramparts, clock tower, gate, former hospital, church, 15thC château, Renaissance house, wine cellar *(open Sun. pm).* ▶ **Renaison** ® *(2 km E) :* château de Boisy *(15th-16thC).* Follow the Renaison Valley to Tache Dam *(6 km).* ▶ **Saint-André-d'Apchon** ® : Renaissance stained glass in church (12th-15thC); Château des d'Albon (Renaissance). ▶ **Saint-Alban-les-Eaux** ® : mineral springs. ▶ **Lentigny** ® : pop. 1 311. ▶ **Crozet★** *(N) :* walled market town; Romanesque keep : panorama; houses, some timbered; local history museum. ▶ **La Pacaudière** *(1 km) :* 16thC houses. □

Don't miss

★★★ : Lyons (B2), ★★ : La Bastie d'Urfé (A2), Beaujolais region (AB1-2), Bourg-en-Bresse (B1), Charlieu (A1), Pérouges (B2), Valmorey (C1).

L'ARBRESLE

B2 / ® / pop. 4 909

In one of the Brévenne valleys, this industrial centre preserves vestiges of the Savigny monks' buildings (see below).

▶ 13th-16thC church (Gothic stained glass); Renaissance houses; 11thC château ruins. ▶ Historical museum (Rue P.-Sémard : *Sun. pm).* ▶ **La Tourette Convent★★** *(1 km S via Eveux) :* designed by the architect Le Corbusier (1887-1965) for Dominican nuns (1957-59 : *drive-through private park; Sunday visits to church, advance written permission needed for other days).* □

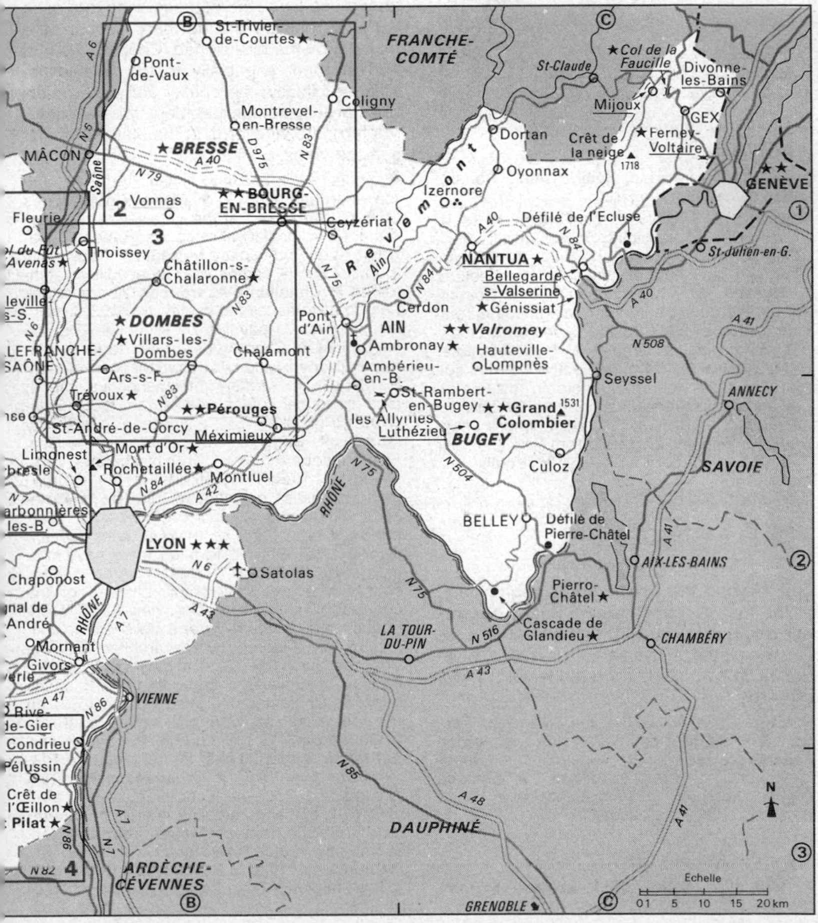

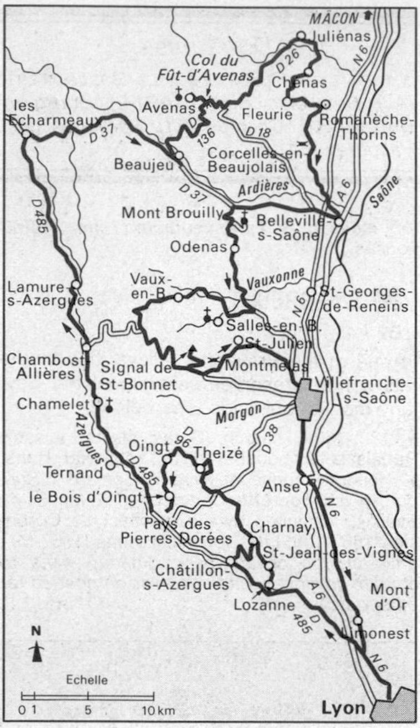

1. Beaujolais region

▶ Nearby

▶ By the Tarare road, **Bully** : 14thC Renaissance castle and ramparts.

▶ **Saint-Bel** *(S by N89)* : 12thC ruins. ▶ **Saint-Pierre-la-Palud** : mining museum *(1 Mar.-30 Nov., Sat., Sun, hol., 2-6).* ▶ **Savigny** *(2 km W)* : museum of mediaeval architecture. ▶ **Nuelles** *(N)* : two churches, one Romanesque, the other (more interesting) Gothic (outside staircases). ▶ E by the Lyons road : lookout *(3 km, left).* ▶ **Lentilly** ®. ▶ **Charbonnières-les-Bains** ® *(15 km)* : attractive thermal spa (park), centre for rheumatology, traumatology and cardiac rehabilitation. ▶ N, **Dardilly** ® : museum open daily in the house where Jean-Baptiste Vianney, a priest from Ars (→ near Trévoux), was born in 1786. ▶ **Ecully** ® : (pop. 18 467). □

■ La BASTIE-D'URFÉ★★

A2

Just beyond the **Astrée lakes region,** and at the foot of the Madeleine Peaks (**Pierre-sur-Haute** panorama★), the mediaeval castle, renovated in Italian Renaissance style during the 16thC, is the architectural jewel of Forez.

▶ Guided tour *(9:15-12 & 2-5:45, closed Tue. tel. 77.97.54.68)*; courtyard with **equestrian gallery;** painted chapel; "honeycombed" sleeping quarters; "nymphs' grotto". ▶ Gazebo *(pavillon d'amour)* : Renaissance-style round temple in adjacent grounds. □

▶ The Astrée region

▶ **Boen** ® *(7 km NE)* : 18thC château. ▶ **Pommiers**★ *(12 km N of Boen)* : mediaeval fortified town; fortified priory, Romanesque church, 15th-16thC frescos, local history museum on the ramparts. ▶ **Saint-Germain-Laval** ® *(4 km from Pomiers)* : Gothic/Renaissance houses; museum in town hall. ▶ **Sail-sous-Couzan** : overlooked by ruined **château de Couzan**★ on a 650-m peak. ▶ **Montverdun** *(S)* : 12th-16thC church on an isolated volcanic ridge. ▶ **Chalain-d'Uzore** : 14th-16thC castle, formal gardens *(1 Apr.-1 Nov., 8-12 & 2-6).* ▶ **Champdieu** *(3 km farther)* : ramparts, fortified 14thC★, Romanesque priory (13thC nave, crypt, cloister). □

■ The BEAUJOLAIS Region★★

260 km round-trip from Lyons *(at least a full day)*

AB1-2 *(see map 1)*

Vineyards, pastures and forests in countryside traced by tributaries of the river Saône. Essentially mountain country isolated by two large valleys (the Loire in the West), Beaujolais has remained essentially rural with three distinct natural regions : the granite peaks crowned by **Mount Saint-Rigaud** (alt. 1 012 m), where forestry is the staple industry; E, between 600 m and 200 m above sea-level, the compact **vineyard area** 8 km across (in the northern section, the major growths of Juliénas, Chénas, Fleurie) and, around, especially to the Beaujolais-Villages; finally, the chalky soil called **pierres dorées** (golden pebbles), where pastures turn into vineyards at the elevations that suit the vines.

▶ **Lyons** (→). ▶ **Dardilly** (→ near l'Arbresle) and the Azergues Valley★. ▶ **Civrieux-d'Azergues** ®. ▶ N, **Chazay**★ : at the gateway to the pierres dorées, mediaeval ramparts (Baboon Gateway); Rural Architecture Museum. ▶ **Lozanne** ® (pop. 1 704) : N, château de Gage, valley watchtower. ▶ **Châtillon-d'Azergues**★ : on a hillock next to a Romanesque castle; two 10thC chapels, one with a painting by Hippolyte Flandrin (→ Lyons). ▶ **Charnay** *(3 km N)* : fortified castle; mullioned windows; Romanesque church. ▶ **Alix** *(3 km farther)* : Romanesque church façade; feudal château de Marzé. ▶ **Le Bois-d'Oingt** (pop. 1 465) : château de Tanay (15thC). ▶ **Bagnols** *(SE)* : porticoed houses, Romanesque church, Gothic château (fireplace). ▶ **Theizé** : concerts in the church; manor houses; museum in Clos de la Platelière. ▶ **Oingt**★ : ruins of fortress. ▶ **Ternand**★ : right bank of the Azergues *(36 km from Lyons),* Gaulish fortified town on a promontory; mediaeval village (historic site★); church fresco★, 6thC crypt; château of the count-archbishops of Lyons (view from Tarare Peaks road). ▶ **Saint-Vérand** : two Gothic châteaux, one restored by the architect Eugène Viollet-le-Duc (1814-1879), in a park★. ▶ **Sainte-Paule** : mediaeval church. ▶ **Létra** : castle ruins. ▶ **Chamelet** : fortified market town on the outskirts of vineyards and pastures. ▶ **Chambost** : Gothic church. ▶ **Lamure-sur-Azergues** ® (pop. 1 065) W : château de Pramenoux (15th-18thC). ▶ **Echarmeaux Pass** (alt. 720 m) : at Poule-les-Echarmeaux, in a pine forest (hiking and rambling trails). ▶ **Chénelette** : at the foot of **Mount Tourvéon** (alt. 953 m, panorama). ▶ **Beaujeu**★ ® (pop. 2 013) : old houses; temple of Bacchus (wine-tastings); folk art museum (19thC dolls, reconstruction of an interior; *Easter to 1 Nov., closed Tue. & am* *in winter).* ▶ **Fût d'Avenas Pass** (alt. 762 m) : vineyard panorama★. ▶ **Avenas :** Carolingian altar in modest church. ▶ Down to the valley via Chiroubles and the Saint-Amour and Moulin-à-Vent **vineyards :** Romanesque churches at **Juliénas** ® (cellars, tithe barn), **Chénas** ® and **Fleurie** ®. ▶ **Romanèche-Thorins :** zoo *(daily)* and Trades Museum *(Sun. and hols.; Easter-1 Nov.).* ▶ **Château de Corcelles :** 16th-17thC *(Sat., Sun.).* ▶ **Belleville-sur-Saône** ® (pop. 6580) : 12thC walled enclave *(bastide)* of the lords of Beaujeu; old pharmacy. ▶ **Mont Brouilly :** vineyard panorama from summit (alt. 485 m). ▶ **Odenas :** château de **La Chaize** *(1 km away)* built by Mansart, formal gardens by Le Nôtre (the foremost designer of the 17thC, → Ile-de-France, Versailles) *(temporarily closed).* ▶ **Blaceret** ®. ▶ **Salles-en-Beaujolais** ® : Romanesque cloister in former priory★. ▶ **Saint-Bonnet Pass** (alt. 660 m) : panorama reached by hill paths★. ▶ **Château de Montmelas :** 19thC restoration by Viollet-le-Duc. ▶ Return to Lyons via Limonest (→ Mont d'Or). □

■ BELLEGARDE-SUR-VALSERINE

C1 / ® / pop. 11 787 (Ain)

An industrial centre at the confluence of the Rhône and Valserine rivers, overshadowed to the N by the **Grand Crêt d'Eau** (crest) (alt. 1 624 m); panorama★★ over Mont Blanc (Alps) and Lake Léman (Switzerland), Lakes Annecy and Bourget (Savoy); trail *(4-hr hike one-way).* □

▶ Nearby

▶ S by D25 and Billiat : **Génissiat Dam★** *(14 km) :* France's largest hydroelectric station (1.8 million kWh) after Donzère-Mondragon *(no visits).* ▶ E towards Gex (→) and Geneva, the **Ecluse Gorge★** *(10 km).* ▶ W towards Valromey (→ near Hauteville-Lompnès), the road climbs the eastern rim (view★) from the **Retord Plateau** (alt. 1 200-1 300 m); S, Crêt du Nu (alt. 1 351 m). ▶ N via N84 toward Nantua (→) : **Perte** (disappearance) of the river **Valserine★** *(3 km).* ▶ Beginning at Châtillon-de-Michaille *(5 km),* the road overlooks the gorge and river Sémine to *(12 km)* **Saint-Germain-de-Joux** ®. ▶ From there, N via **Giron** (winter sports resort), **Fauconnière★** (natural amphitheatre) and, via Belleydoux, Orval combe. □

▶ Valserine Valley from Bellegarde to Mijoux *(37 km, D991)*

▶ **Pont-de-Pierres :** 80-m arched bridge. ▶ **Chalam Crest★** (alt. 545 m) : looking on to Chezery-Forens (17thC church, abbey buildings). ▶ The road climbs beyond **Sous-Balme Gorge★;** to the right, the **Jura Crest :** (over 1 700 m) Reculet, Crêt de la Neige and, N, Colomby-de-Gex and Mont-Rond (→ near Gex) (more than 3 hrs climb); views★★. ▶ **Lelex** ® : winter resort (alt. 900 m, pop. 203) : semi-precious stones, cheesemaking. ▶ Mijoux (→ near Gex). □

■ BELLEY

C2 / ® / pop. 8 372 (Ain)

Birthplace of the gastronomist Jean-Anthelme Brillat-Savarin (1755-1826), author of *The Physiology of Taste* (pub. 1825), still considered the gourmet's bible. The poet Alphonse Lamartine (1790-1869) attended secondary school in Belley.

Lyons regional cuisine

From Lyons to Bresse and Bugey by way of the Dombes, food is an art and a science. The raw materials are superb : poultry, butter, cheese, freshwater fish, mushrooms, and wine.

Traditional regional cooking does not tamper with basic flavour. As the French say, "Let things taste as they are". François Rabelais (ca. 1490-1553), author and physician at the Lyons hospital (Hôtel-Dieu), *acknowledged the region's culinary traditions in his exuberant satirical chronicles of sensory pleasure.*

The city of Lyons alone has about 30 renowned restaurants. The Dombes area, the Rhône Valley and Forez boast many others of international repute. Gastronomic tours are organized by TO at Vienne, Pérouges and Saint-André-de-Corcy. Regional home-style dishes include the sausages known as rosette *and* Jésus, *potted pork* (cru) *and* pâté *in pastry crust; salads made with the mushroom known as* pied de mouton *(sheep's foot), with dandelion, sippets and herring, or with dandelion and coddled eggs; poached mousse of pike* (quenelles de brochet) *with a hot butter sauce; tripe known as "sapper's apron"* (tablier de sapeur); *pig's tail; "chicken in half-mourning" with slices of truffle under the skin; cardoons with marrow; and sundry tasty snacks taken at any time of day with a glass of Beaujolais. Specialties of Forez and Bugey include freshwater crayfish* (écrevisse), *duck braised in red wine, and roast game.*

▶ Cathedral : Gothic choir and transepts; building finished in the 19thC. Bishop's palace (late 18thC). Brillat-Savarin's birthplace (62 Grande-Rue). ▶ Seminary museum, Rue Sainte-Marie, reopening scheduled for 1986. □

▶ Nearby

▶ Vignoble bugiste - tasting cellars - ▶ **Pierre-Châtel Gorge★** *(S, 8 km) :* cut by the Rhône, site of a namesake mediaeval fortress, enlarged in the 19thC. ▶ Road follows the **Bugey Peaks** (alt. 700-1 000 m) : Château de Peyrieu; ruined Château de Cordon. ▶ **Glandieu Waterfall★.** ▶ Château de Groslée. ▶ **Lhuis★ :** overlooking the Rhône; Gallo-Roman traces; church with Romanesque apse. ▶ **Massignieu** Lake *(E, 6 km),* leisure centre. □

■ BOURG-EN-BRESSE★★

B1 / ® / pop. 43 675 (Ain)

A gourmet's delight, as well as an art and architecture centre of the first order.

▶ Church (1505-1536) : among the finest examples of Flamboyant Gothic; choir **rood-screen★ :** choir stalls★, Renaissance stained glass; sculpted **tombs★;** altarpiece (Flemish Renaissance : Seven Joys of the Virgin★). ▶ **Ain Museum★★★ :** in the three monastery cloisters regional folk art and traditions, reconstructed interiors *(1 Oct.-31 Mar., 9-12 & 2-5; 1 Apr.-30 Sept., 2-6:30).* □

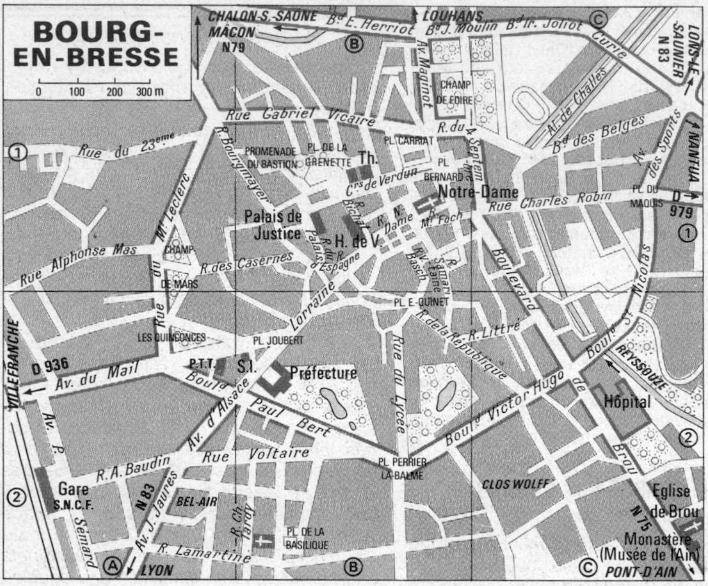

The BRESSE Region★

"Saracen chimneys route" *(approx. 130 km NNW of Bourg; full day)*

B1 *(see map 2)*

Mixed forest and pastureland, renowned for blue cheese (visits to cheese factories) and chicken. Bresse was placed under the crown by Henry IV in 1601. Many of the regional **timber-built farmsteads** date back to that era. The chimneys of these farmsteads — ornamented in Mediterranean style and known as "Saracen" chimneys to the local people — are a distinctive feature of the landscape.

▶ Leave Bourg via N83 : at **Saint-Étienne-du-Bois** *(12 km)* take the first road E through Treffort Wood. ▶ **Treffort-Cuisiat :** Gothic church (furnishings); 15th-16thC houses; covered market. ▶ **Cuisiat :** chapel of Notre-Dame-de-Montfort (13th-14thC). ▶ **Meillonas** *(S) :* pottery centre (18thC). ▶ **Verion :** church partly Renaissance (unusual for Ain), 17thC triptych. ▶ **Coligny** ® : 15th-16thC church. ▶ **Courtes** *(18 km from* Coligny) : forest farm★ (Romanesque-style square chimney hood, folklore museum). ▶ **Vernoux** *(N) :* Grand Colombier farms. ▶ **Saint-Trivier-de-Courtes**★ *(guided tours, ask at the SI),* farms at Tremblay (three-storied chimney) and Grandval (Romanesque-style chimney hood). ▶ **Pont-de-Vaux** ® (pop. 2 050) : Chintreuil Museum (paintings by a student of the 19thC landscape painter Camille Corot), Gothic church; Baroque school façade; mediaeval and Renaissance houses. ▶ **Reyssouse :** chimney topped by brick cross at Reyssouse Farm. ▶ **Chevroux :** Mont Farm (exterior staircase); Bourbière Farm (16thC chimney hood). ▶ Via Bâgé-le-Châtel, **Saint-André-de-Bâgé :** 11thC Romanesque church, octagonal bell-tower. ▶ **Pont-de-Veyle :** old wall. ▶ **Saint-Cyr-sur-Menthon :** N, Planons Farm★ (wooden gallery, fireplace, furnishings). ▶ From Bourg on N79 : **Logis-Neuf** (*N,* Confrançon ®). ▶ **Vonnas** ® *(5 km SE;* pop. 2 500). ▶ **Montrevel-en-Bresse** (NE; pop. 2 000) recreation area 1 km W; Sougey Farm★★ (one of the finest Bressan interiors in the region). ▶ **Foissiat :** Tiret Farm (brick chimney rebuilt early 20thC). ▶ Return to Bourg via Viriat (church). □

CEYZERIAT

B1 / ® / pop. 1 982 (Ain)

Base for hiking excursions at the foot of the Rèvermont foothills of the Jura.

▶ Revermont and the Ain gorges *(E, about 95 km, 5-hr round trip)*

▶ Via Hautecourt-Romanèche *(10 km) :* view from **Hautecourt peak** over Allemant lake and dam. ▶ N, via **Cize,** follow D59b ridge road (views). ▶ At **Thoirette,** cross to the left bank and climb towards **Coiselet Dam.** ▶ Return to D18 and head for Nantua, passing by **Oignin** reservoir (at upper end, Charmine Falls). ▶ **Izernore :** Gallo-Roman excavations with three columns from the temple of Izarnodurum; museum in village. ▶ Return to Ceyzeriat via **Berthiand Pass** (views) and the landmarks visible from **Serrières** bridge over the Ain. □

CHARLIEU★★

A1 / ® / pop. 4 380 (Loire)

Romanesque Benedictine **abbey** ruins, 15thC **cloister,** chapter house, **narthex**★ (a masterpiece of 12thC Burgundian sculpture). The ancillary buildings (15thC and Renaissance) are private property *(July, Aug., Sept., 9-12 & 2-7; 1 Apr.-30 June, closed Tue.; 1 Oct.-30 Nov. and 1 Feb.-31 Mar., closed Tue. and Wed.).* Painted Renaissance choir stalls can be seen in the parish church.

▶ Stonework museum : **ornamentation** from the abbey. ▶ 500 m from abbey, former **Cordeliers' convent :** 14th-15thC cloister★. □

▶ Nearby

▶ N, to see the Brion Romanesque churches (→ Burgundy). ▶ W, via **Pouilly-sous-Charlieu** ® *(5 km,* pop. 2 973). **La Bénisson-Dieu★** *(5 km farther) :* abbey church (12thC nave, 15thC bell-tower, glazed-tile roof). □

DIVONNE-LES-BAINS

C1 / ® / pop. 4 783 (Ain)

Cold-water mineral springs used to treat nervous disorders.

▶ Spa situated at the feet of the highest peaks in Jura (le Crêt d'eau, le Crêt de la neige, 1 723 m) in a 74-acre **park** with recreational facilities, including golf, casino, lake. □

The DOMBES plateau★

Starting from Villars-les-Dombes (see below), from Bourg (→) or from Trévoux (→).

B1-2 *(see map 3 following page)*

A plateau dotted with ponds, popular with waterfowl hunters and anglers; also a preserve for migrating birds, including grey and tufted heron, duck, the barnacle goose, coot and buzzard.

▶ **Villars-les-Dombes** ® (pop. 2 832) : ruined Romanesque castle; 14th-15thC church. 1 km S, 54-acre **bird sanctuary★★** *(daily)* next to a 515-acre preserve closed to the public; more than 2 000 animals and birds of 400 species, including all indigenous species of the Dombes and tropical birds; aquarium, vivarium. ▶ **Chalamont** *(14 km E) :* sandy moors and reeds at the foot of the highest peak in the Dombes (alt. 334 m, view); Gothic houses, Plantay "tower". ▶ **Meximieux, Pérouges** ® (→). ▶ Toward Lyons, **Montluel★** ® (pop. 5 604) : fortified city; ramparts, cloister, old streets, 15th-17thC mansions; Notre-Dame-des-Marais Collegiate church; chapel of St. Barthélémy (13thC); hospital apothecary (painted ceiling). ▶ **Miribel** ® (pop. 7 111). ▶ **Les Echets** ®. ▶ **Mionnay** ®. ▶ **Saint-André-de-Corcy** ®. ▶ **Trévoux** ®; Ars-sur-Formans, Jassans-Riottier (→ near Trévoux ®). ▶ **Châtillon-sur-Chalaronne★** ® (pop. 2 687) : floral town; ramparts (Villars Gateway); 15thC covered market; 11thC castle ruins. ▶ **Saint-Paul-de-Varax** *(14 km from Villars) :* Romanesque church (sculpted doorways★); Jourdan Museum of painting. ▶ Return to **Villars** via Notre-Dame-des-Dombes Abbey. □

FEURS

A2 / ® / pop. 8 103 (Loire)

A Gallo-Roman city on a strategic crossroads.

▶ Gothic church, ornamented portals (Renaissance panels). **Gallo-Roman Museum★;** Assier Park, reconstructed villa (mosaics; *2-6*). □

▶ Nearby

▶ N, via **Balbigny** ® (pop. 2 469), **Saint-Marcel-de-Félines** *(17 km) :* 16thC château, rooms decorated with paintings *(22 Apr.-1 Nov., Sun., Mon., hols. 2-6, daily).* ▶ **Panissières** *(15 km NE;* pop. 2 944) : base for mountain hikes. ▶ **Montrond-les-Bains** ® *(11 km S;* pop. 3 194) : mineral-water spa; 11th-16thC castle ruins *(Jul.-Aug., Sat., Sun., hols., 2-6);* Renaissance church. □

2. Bresse region

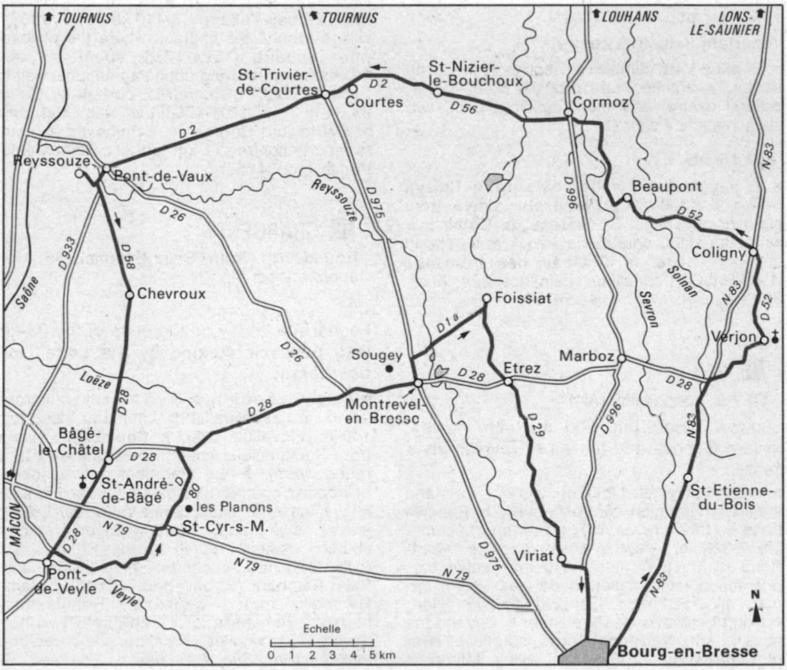

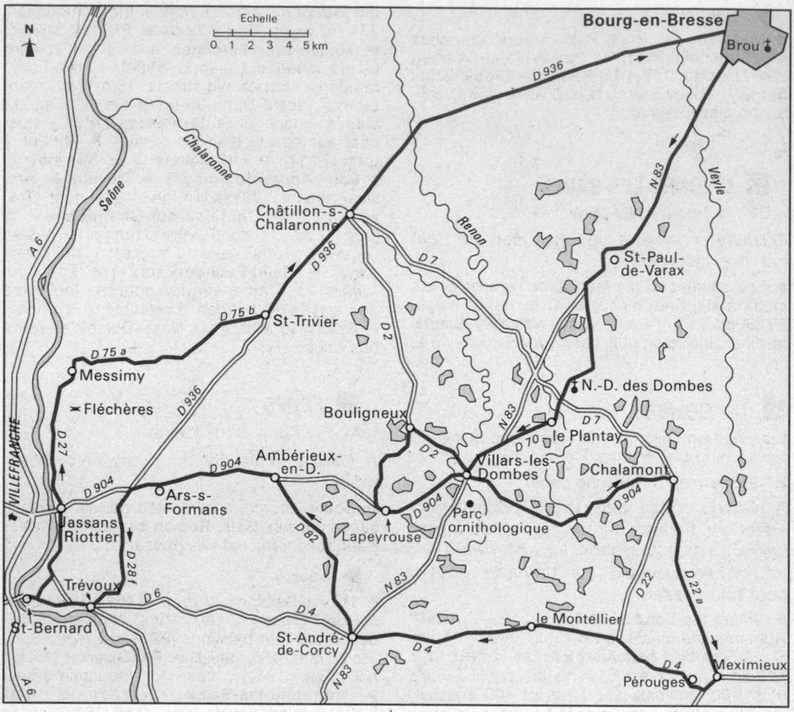

3. Dombes plateau

FIRMINY

A3 / ® / pop. 24 356 (Loire)

Important industrial centre.

▶ **Firminy-Vert** complex★ : collaborative project by the architect Le Corbusier (1887-1965); cultural centre, apartment building, pool, two stadiums and a church. □

▶ Nearby

▶ E, **Feugerolles** : feudal château★. ▶ **Unieux** (NW pop 8 309 ® **Le Pertuiset**) : view★ from suspension bridge. S, **château de Cornillon**★ with 13th-16thC church, on a rock at a bend in the river Loire. ▶ **Château des Bruneaux** (16th-18thC.), panelling, paintings *(24 Mar.-30 Sept., Sat., Sun., hols., 2-6:30).* □

GEX

C1 / ® / pop. 4 869 (Ain)

Summer resort (alt. 600 m) with views★ toward Geneva and the Alps; English-style garden.

▶ W, **Le Pailly** (alt. 1 200 m) : winter sports and summer recreation centre; view★. ▶ **Faucille Pass** ® *(12 km N, via N5) :* winter sports centre (alt. 1 328 m); view to Mont Blanc. ▶ **Mont-Rond** *(3 km SW);* (alt. 1 540 m) : cable car; orientation table. **Colomby-de-Gex** (*8 km farther;* alt. 1 691 m) : overlooking countryside; walking trails over pasturelands. ▶ Beyond the pass *(3 km),* Valserine Gorge, source of river of same name; in Valserine Valley, **Mijoux** ® (winter-sports centre), as at **Lélex** ®. ▶ E, Divonne-les-Bains (→). ▶ S, via the Geneva road, **Ferney-Voltaire**★ ® (*10 km;* pop. 6 400) : village around the château where the philosopher Voltaire (1694-1778) spent his last 18 years before dying during a triumphal visit to Paris in 1778 : memorabilia, portrait by Quentin de la Tour (1704-1788) *(Jul.-Aug., Sat. pm).* ▶ SW toward Bellegarde, **Echenevex** ® : winter-sports centre; 11 km farther : **Saint-Genis-Pouilly** (pop. 4 655). □

GRANGENT★

Round trip from Saint-Etienne *(55 km, approx. 2 hr)*

A3

Feudal site, today on the edge of the 23-km long reservoir created by the **Loire Gorges Dam**★.

▶ **Saint-Etienne** (→). ▶ S via the left bank, road left toward **Essalois :** 12thC **château,** view from 150 m above the river. ▶ **Chambles :** view★ from Romanesque church tower (flanked by a round keep). ▶ **Le Pertuiset :** atmosphere of popular country pastimes (→ near Firminy). ▶ Via the right bank, **Saint-Victor-sur-Loire :** site★; swimming, boating; Romanesque church; château rebuilt at the Renaissance (cultural centre, concerts). ▶ N, **Saint-Just-Saint-Rambert** (*5 km;* pop. 10 646) : Saint-Rambert, ruined ramparts; Renaissance houses; Romanesque church★ with two bell-towers (Carolingian, Romanesque); regional museum *(Sat., Sun., hols. pm).* □

HAUTEVILLE-LOMPNÈS

C1 / ® / pop. 4 905 (Ain)

Summer resort at alt. 800 m in the heart of Bugey; well known for climate (rest centres, functional reeducation).

▶ Round trips from Haut-Bugey and Valromey★★ *(68 km, at least a half-day).*

▶ **Albarine Gorges★** : Albarine Waterfall *(4 km);* **cliffs** rising 500 m above the road. ▶ At Tenay *(take the Chambéry road left)* : **Cluse des Hôpitaux★★** (gorge); ruined feudal château de Rossillon. ▶ **Artemare** ® : continue left towards **Valromey★★;** alpine flora. **Cerveyrieu Waterfall★** and cross-country skiing in winter; on left, Luthézieu (®, Artemare). ▶ **Ruffieu** (alt. 730 m) : attractive scenery, via **Rochette Pass** (alt. 1 119 m; view★★ to Mont Blanc) to Hauteville. □

LYONS★★★

B2 / ® / pop. 418 476 (Rhône)

See plan on following pages

Two rivers, one calm, the other spirited; two hills, Fourvière "begging", and La Croix-Rousse "working" — according to the French historian Jules Michelet (1798-1874). Ever since Man came to live here 600 years before the Roman occupation (see *Brief regional history*), the territory has been expanded by means of the rivers. In the High Middle Ages, the Saône and Rhône converged slightly W of the present Place des Terreaux, which explains the original Celtic name of *Condate* (confluence). Canabae, one of the two islands to the S, was already inhabited when, in 43BC, Julius Caesar's officers founded Lugdunum on the summit of the western hill. The high ground was gradually abandoned in the 3rdC and 4thC in favour of l'Ile Saint-Jean below, now the site of "Old Lyons".

A merchant colony flourished between the two rivers, alongside one of the oldest religious foundations in the country — the abbey of St. Martin, known as Ainay since the 11thC.

The history of Lyon can be traced in the present city layout : the original settlement W to E in Fourvière; the mediaeval and Renaissance city on the right bank of the Saône; 17th-18thC development between the rivers; and Croix-Rousse, dating from the 19thC, on the left bank of the Rhône and within the industrial suburbs that are home for two-thirds of the area's residents. Eighty-five percent of the city's annual total of 5 million visitors are not tourists; they come for the range of events held all year round at Eurexpo, Lyon's new centre for exhibitions at Chassieu *(6 km)* (→ ®). □

▶ Old Lyons★★

AB2-3 and A4

▶ From **Place Bellecour** cross **Bonaparte Bridge** (B3) opposite the eastern end of the cathedral of St. Jean. ▶ Enter Old Lyons, the most extensive (61 acres) grouping of 15thC and Renaissance buildings in France. ▶ Avenue Adolph-Max, in the same direction as the bridge, towards the **St. Jean Quarter,** restored, together with the neighbouring districts, some years ago and now closed to vehicles. ▶ Rue Adolph-Max : passes the former archbishop's palace, now the municipal library *(closed Aug.);* at the end of the street, cable-car station. ▶ **Manécanterie** (former house of the cathedral cantors) : early Romanesque frieze-ornamented façade; first floor, cathedral treasury *(entry from the cathedral)* : mediaeval Limoges enamels, ivory, 12thC Byzantine works of art. ▶ **St. Jean cathedral★** (A3) : formerly the Seat of the Primate (chief bishop) of Gaul; Romanesque; façades finished in Flamboyant Gothic; portals with 368 15thC sculpted insets. ▶ In the nave, four 32-m-high vaulted bays; ornament★ in choir, apse and side chapels (chapel of the Bourbons; chapel of the Annunciation); stained glass★, much of it 13thC (apse); in left transept, 17thC astronomical clock★. ▶ N, **excavation** of primitive church★. ▶ S of cathedral, **St. Georges Quarter★ :** Place de la Trinité (square); **Café du Soleil,** a former convent later used for *Guignol* (Punch and Judy) performances. Enter at No. 2 Rue St. Georges to reach oval courtyard★ of the Maison du Soleil; proceed by the signposted passageways *(traboules)* to Gourguillon. ▶ **Rue St. Georges** (A3) : shop signs, Gothic windows, artisans' workshops here and in adjacent Rue du Doyenné (interesting courtyard at No. 32). ▶ **Rue St. Jean** (A3, N) : mediaeval thoroughfare; No. 37, Chamarrier Mansion. ▶ Farther, **law courts** with 19thC colonnade★, opening on to Saône Quay. ▶ **Viste Mansion** (Nos. 29-27) : Gothic portal. ▶ Passageway at No. 19 links to Rue des Trois-Marie (Renaissance houses). ▶ **Place de la Baleine :** No. 5, HQ for the Old Lyons Urban Renewal Association. ▶ No. 24 Rue St. Jean, Laurencin Mansion *traboule* joins up with No. 1 Rue du Bœuf. ▶ **Place du Gouvernement :** Gothic façade, Governors' Assembly; upstairs, raised courtyard, gallery★, covered well. ▶ No. 11 Rue St. Jean : Gothic courtyard, passageway and ornamented door★. ▶ **Place du Change** (B2) : Renaissance drapery market; 18thC gallery. Opposite, **Thomassin Mansion :** enter through courtyard★. ▶ **Rue Lainerie :** staircase at No. 18; **Mayet-de-Beauvoir Mansion★** (No. 14) : Gothic façade. ▶ **Place St. Paul** (A2) : Laurent Mourguet grew up at No. 2 (→ box *Guignol*). ▶ **St. Paul church :** octagonal lantern tower; Flamboyant Gothic chapel; sculpted animals at eastern end; frieze depicting angel-musicians (3rd chapel on right). ▶ Return to St. Jean via **Rue de la Juiverie** (A2) : No. 4, **Paterin Mansion** (Henri IV) staircase, galleries, arcades. ▶ No. 8 **Buillioud Mansion** : gallery on squinches★, a major architectural expression of the Renaissance. ▶ Nos. 22-23, Dugas Mansion (Lion House). ▶ At intersection with Rue de la Loge, **montée du Change** (stairway); view★. ▶ **Rue de Gadagne :** No. 12, mansion of same name with **Edouard-Herriot Museum** and **Marionette Museum★** *(entrance at No. 14, 10:45-6; closed Tue.)* worldwide theatre★, including Mourguet. ▶ **Place du Petit-Collège** (Garillan steps). ▶ **Rue du Bœuf** (A3; *traboule* at No. 1) : No. 19, **L'Outarde d'Or** (famous "golden bustard" shop sign); No. 16, passage to **Crible House★★** (17thC); turreted staircase. ▶ At **corner of Rue de la Bombarde** (restored Renaissance covered staircase★), sculpture of bull (the *bœuf* of the street). ▶ Place St. Jean : cable-car. □

▶ Fourvière★
A3

▶ **Basilica forecourt** *(parvis)* : 130 m above Old Lyons; on the site of a Romanesque church, the 1870 edifice overlooks the city. ▶ Access to the **basilica** via 300 steps; orientation table *(daily Mar.-Oct.; Sat., Sun. rest of year)*; **view★** over Lyons, the Auvergne region, the Alps from Mont Blanc to Ventoux in clear weather. ▶ **View★★** from left terrace of church, site of the first forum of the Roman city of Lugdunum.

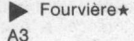

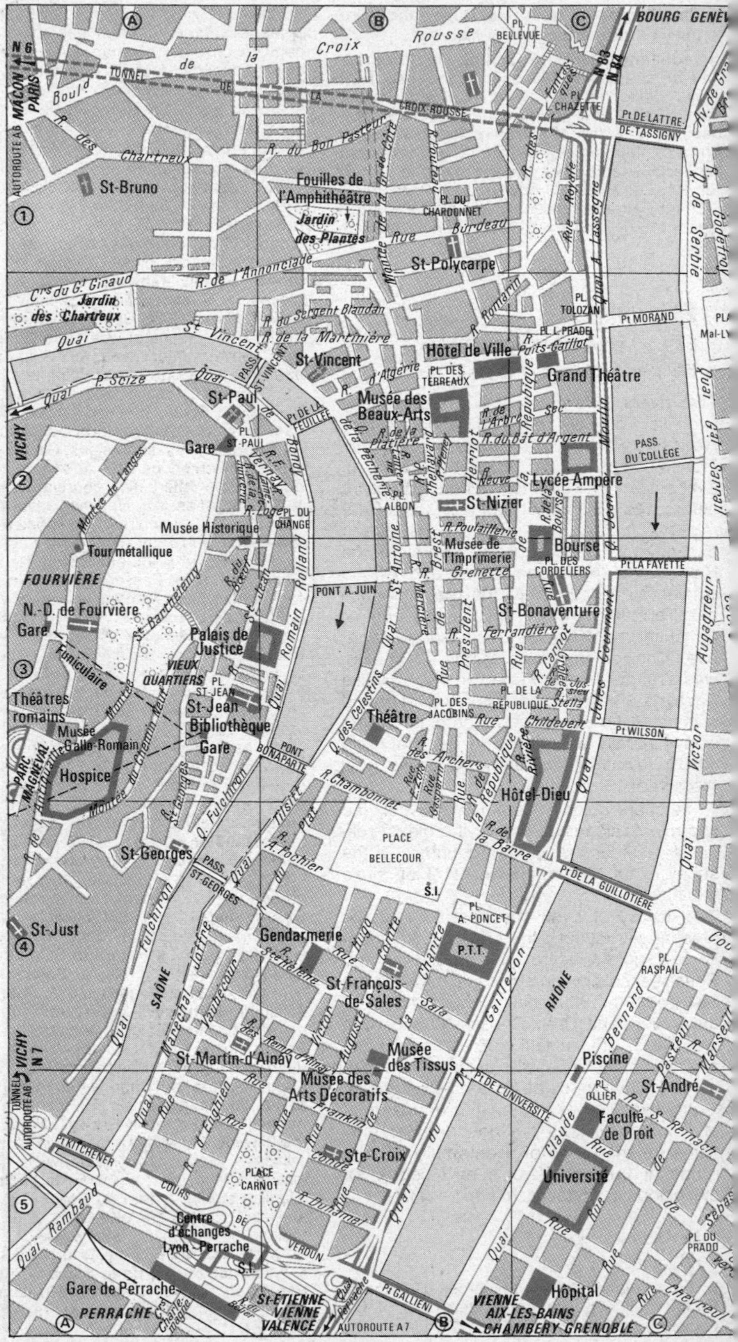

▶ **Gallo-Roman Museum**★★ : 17 Rue Cléberg *(9:30-12 & 2-6; closed Mon., Tue.; optional guided tours)* built in 1975 on the hillside site of Lugdunum; chronicles regional history from the Neolithic Era to the High Middle Ages; Gallo-Roman inscriptions, Gallic calendar from Coligny, the Claudian tablet★★ (plea presented by the Emperor Claudius to the Roman Senate), epitaphs, treasure from Vernaison, Cremieu, La-Côte-Saint-André, statuary★, sarcophagi, everyday objects, restored **mosaic**★★★. ▶ From museum windows, the

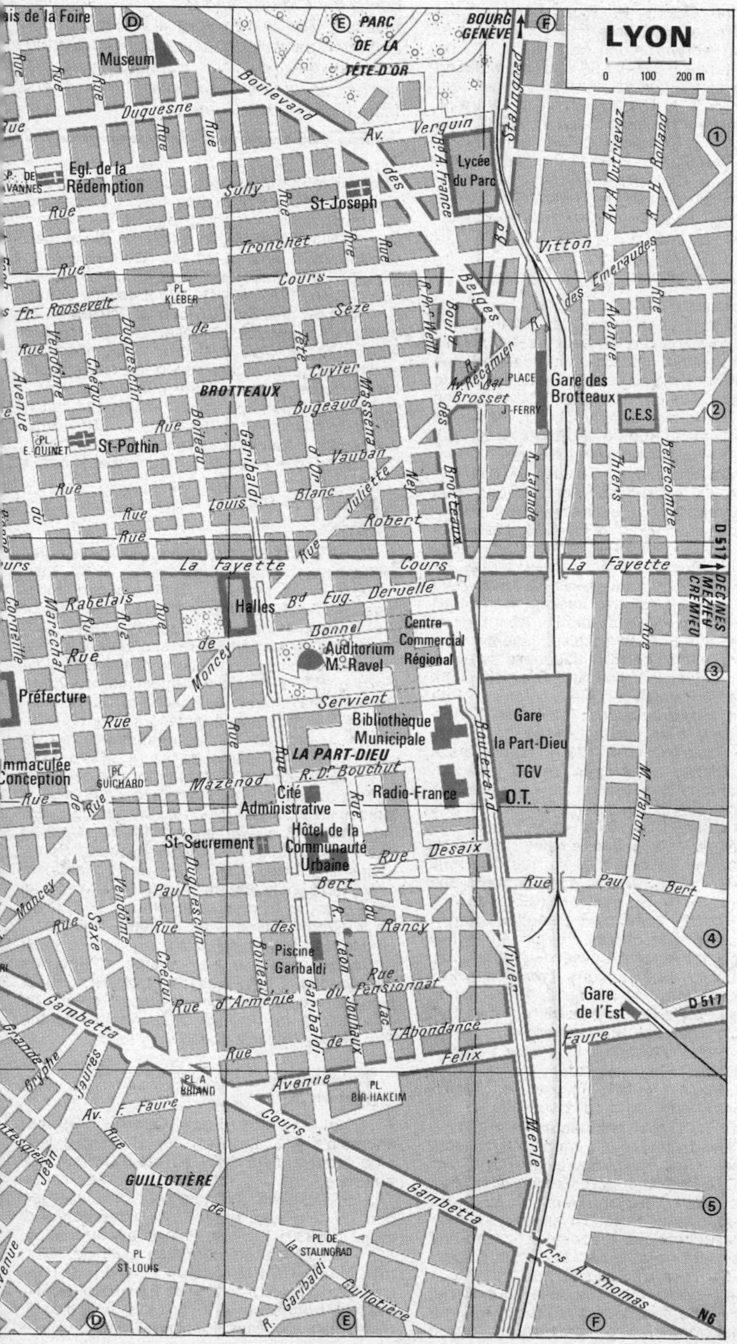

Roman **theatre★ excavations** are visible *(entrance at 6 Rue de l'Antiquaille; closed Sun., hols. am in summer, Sat., Sun. rest of year).* ▶ The **Grand Théatre :** the oldest in France (15BC) and one of the largest (10 500 spectators after enlargement under the Emperor Hadrian); access by a side staircase (view★), where Roman paving (about 80 m) slopes towards the Odeon. ▶ Right, site of the ruined **Temple of Cybele** (most important in the Roman world), among other finds. ▶ The **Odeon★** (capacity 3 000) : an auditorium dating from the same period as the Temple; restored paving★. ▶ The ancient city grew up on the plateau; early ruins abound in the **St. Just Quarter** around **St. Irénée Church** (5thC crypt) and at Choullans, where the aqueducts (→ Mornant) that provided city water for 300 years terminated. ▶ Return via Saône Quay through the **Duchère Quarter :** view; Firemen's Museum *(9-12 & 2-6, Sat. 9-12).* □

▶ The Museums of Presqu'île★★★

BC2-3-4

▶ Europe's largest pedestrian mall (2 km between Perrache Station and the Town Hall) parallels the *Métro* (underground transport) line and simplifies visits to central Lyons. ▶ At the SE corner of **Place Bellecour** (B4; TO), the tower of the former Charity Church overlooks flower stalls along **Rue de la Charité.** ▶ No. 30, **Decorative Arts Museum★★** (B5) (same hours as Historical Museum of Textiles → below) : more than 200 exceptional works in furnished rooms on three floors (goldsmiths' work, porcelain, pendulum clocks). ▶ No. 34, **Historical Museum of Textiles★★★** (Villeroy Mansion; *10-12, 2-5:30; closed Mon., hols; ticket includes visit to Decorative Arts Museum next door) :* Coptic tapestries, weaving from 4thC Egypt up to contemporary fabrics from Lyons; Byzantine and Persian textiles, Oriental carpets, 18thC furnishing silks, Japanese screens, Chinese costumes, Italian and Spanish cloth. ▶ Rue des Ramparts-d'Ainay crosses **Rue Auguste-Compte** (antiques), then **Rue Victor-Hugo,** a pedestrian precinct. ▶ At the S end, **Perrache Trade Centre** (A1), a controversial modern building. ▶ **Ainay★** (A4) : restored Carolingian church with Romanesque features remaining from a monastery founded in the 6thC, active until the 18thC; gate tower, side tympanum, capitals. ▶ **Saône Quay :** view over Old Lyons and Fourvière. ▶ Via the Célestins Theatre (B3; 19thC), **Place des Jacobins** and Rue Mercière to **St. Nizier★** (B2) : townspeople's church; 15thC tower (another 19thC); Flamboyant Gothic interior; Virgin and Child by the sculptor Antoine Coysevox (1640-1720), born in Lyons. ▶ **Place des Terreaux** (B2) : fountain★ by Frédéric Bartholdi, 19thC sculptor of New York's Statue of Liberty; **Town Hall** (façade clock tower; 18thC interior decoration; Edouard Herriot Museum). **St. Pierre Palace :** former abbey; 18thC **cloister★,** statuary★ by Auguste Rodin (1840-1917), Aristide Maillol (1861-1944), and Antoine Bourdelle (1861-1929), now the **Fine Arts Museum★★★** *(9-12 & 2-6:30; closed Tue.),* most important museum in France, after the Louvre in Paris, for late-19thC and 20thC art; French art; also important Italian, Spanish, Flemish and Dutch works. ▶ S towards Bellecour, parallel streets : **Rue de la République** (pedestrian street) and Rue Président Herriot (luxury shopping); opposite the Commercial Building and the **Stock Exchange** (*Bourse,* C3), Rue de la **Poulaillerie,** No. 13, Printing and Banking Museum★ (Couronne Mansion; Gothic courtyard★; *closed Mon., Tue.)* : important industries in Lyons since the Renaissance (the first book printed in French rolled off the press of Barthélémy Buyer, Rue Mercière, in 1476). ▶ **Place des Cordeliers :** church of St. Bonaventure : Gothic; 17thC Aubusson tapestries. ▶ **Hospital** (*Hôtel-Dieu;* 1741; C3-4) : 325-m façade on the Rhône, now the **Public Hospice Museum★★,** entrance, Place de l'Hôpital *(1-4:30, closed weekends and hols.) :* history of city hospitals and medicine through works of art and objects for the most part from the demolished Hôpital de la Charité (tapestries, Flemish and Italian primitive paintings, pharmacy jars, 17th-18thC woodwork, Louis XIII **pharmacy★,** exhibition on the history of the medical profession at Lyons.

The passageways of Lyons

The traboules, *covered passageways giving access from one street to another through courtyards and buildings, are a unique feature of Lyons. No fewer than 100 honeycomb the Old City and the slopes of Croix-Rousse. The entrance to a* traboule *often is hidden behind a building doorway. During the last century certain* traboules *were the scene of violent uprisings by workers* (canuts) *from the silk mills.*

▶ La Croix-Rousse

BC1-2

▶ **Place des Terreaux** (B2) : at No. 6, enter the *traboule* running to the Church of St. Polycarpe (17thC), through courtyards and buildings. ▶ **Place Sathonay :** near the site of the Gallic Settlement of Condate; farther on, **Trois-Gaules Amphitheatre,** site of early Christian martyrdoms; excavations at the Botanical Garden (B1). ▶ Rue de l'Annonciade to **Place Rouville** (A2) : view. ▶ **Church of St. Bruno :** Baroque architecture and decoration★ (18thC). ▶ Boulevard de la **Croix-Rousse** towards square of same name *(direct by Métro from Town Hall) :* centre of activity for quarter. ▶ N by Rue du Mail to **Rue d'Ivry** (second on right) : **Maison des Canuts** (No. 10), two facing buildings housing a workshop and the *Cooptis* (Weavers' Cooperative) display *(closed Sun.);* Lyons supported 15 000 weavers *(canuts)* in 1930, today only 300 maintain the trade and all belong to this workers' cooperative. ▶ E, Blvd. de la Croix-Rousse ends at **Place Bellevue :** boulder left from the last Ice Age. ▶ Go back down towards Place des Terreaux by **Rue des Fantasques** (C1, views★); or from St. Sébastien stairway to the right of **Place Colbert,** go in at No. 9 to stroll by *traboule* right to the Place de la Comédie (theatre). □

▶ Left Bank of the Rhône

DE-1 *(drive)*

▶ N of the **Brotteaux Quarter, Guimet Museum★** (D1; 28 Blvd. des Belges; *closed Mon., Tue. and am daily).* ▶ **Tête d'Or Park** (E1, entrance N of D1) : 350 acres of trees centuries old, lake with islands, zoo, botanical garden, 19-acre **rose garden.**) ▶ **Villeurbanne** ® (pop. 118 330; E of Brotteaux railway station, F2) : **Place de la Libération** built in 1934; new **Modern Art Museum** (11, rue du Dr Dollard, *pm., closed Tue.*). ▶ **La Part-Dieu** (E3-4) : view★★ from tower of Crédit Lyonnais (bank); pedestrian walkways, fountains; Maurice Ravel

auditorium★; commercial centre, library, radio & television broadcasting centre. ▶ **Medical Quarter** *(1 km S of Guillotière Bridge,* C5) : **Edouard Herriot Hospital.** ▶ **Vénissieux** (pop. 64 982; *SSE of map*) : Motor Museum at Berliet factory. ▶ **Gerland** *(2 km S of map) :* modern architectural development. □

▶ Nearby

▶ **Saint-Rambert** *(5 km N) :* on a mid-river island; site of **L'Ile Barbe,** former abbey; 12thC bell-tower remaining; Renaissance pavilion; boat trips (Saint-Rambert Port). ▶ **Fontaines-sur-Saône** ® (*12 km N;* pop. 7 129). ▶ **Rochetaillée-sur-Saône**★ ® *(2-km climb) :* fortress★ (restored in the 19thC) of the count-archbishops of Lyons, now a unique Motor Museum★★ *(closed 25 Dec., 1 Jan.).* □

MONTBRISON★

A2 / ® / pop. 13 650 (Loire)

Once the principal town of the Loire and capital of the Lords of Forez, who surveyed the city from their château situated on a volcanic outcrop.

▶ On the circular road along the former ramparts, **Barrière Tower** (also known as Baron-des-Adrets). ▶ **Collegiate** mediaeval church of Notre-Dame d'Espérance★ (13th-15thC). ▶ At the eastern end, the Chamber of Diana, late 13thC Gothic vaulting, poorly restored in the 19thC; adjoining museum *(10-12 & 2-5; Jun.-Sep., 2-6, closed Tue.)* of Gallo-Roman archaeology (city gate panels), mediaeval sculpture. ▶ Town Hall in former Cordeliers' Convent (15th-18thC); law courts in former Visitation Convent (18thC). ▶ **Old houses** (some 15thC) around modern church of St. Pierre. ▶ **Musée de la Poupée**★ (Doll Museum) : **Allard Museum** of mineralogy, ornithology *(2h30-6).* □

▶ Nearby

▶ NW, **Chalmazel** winter sports centre. ▶ S, **Moingt :** Romanesque church; Gallo-Roman archaeology. ▶ By the Saint-Etienne road : **Saint-Roman-le-Puy** *(8.5 km;* pop. 2 423) : a basalt peak (panorama★) supporting a fortified priory (Romanesque and 15thC church; fresco fragments, 10thC nave, crypt★). ▶ **Sury-le-Comtal** (*12 km;* pop. 4 207) : 18thC château★; woodwork, fireplaces, ceilings *(Easter-15 Oct., Sun., Mon. and hols., 2-6).* N, **Motor Museum :** 50 models of 1930-37. □

The MONT-D'OR LYONNAIS★

▶ Round trip from Lyons *(55 km, approx 3 hr)*

B2 / ® Lyons, unless mentioned below

▶ **Lyons** (→). ▶ Paris road. ▶ **Champagne-au-Mont-d'Or** ® : on the right by a footpath over the hills, **Saint-Didier :** a large village, two châteaux, one Renaissance, the other with Henry II courtyard. ▶ **Limonest** ® (pop. 2 244) : on mountainside; footpaths begin at alt. 400 m; village nature museum. ▶ Head towards Mount Verdun. On the right after 4 km, **Saint-Fortunat.** Climbing towards the pass : right, 18thC château de la Barollière. ▶ **Mount Verdun** (alt. 625 m) French Army base *(no visits);* **view** from pass. ▶ **Poleymieux** (alt. 500 m; pop. 1 364) : museum of folk arts and crafts *(closed Mon.).* N, **Croix-Rampeau** road *(1.5 km) :* orientation table (alt. 463 m); view★ (clear weather) from

Guignol theatre

The marionette was created at Lyons in the early 19thC by Laurent Mourguet (1769-1841). Guignol — *Mr. Punch French-style — embodies the* canut, *the Lyons silk weaver. Bantering, mocking and philosophical,* Guignol *theatre projects the local workers' slang, outlook, dress and character. Among* Guignol's *principal partners are* Madelon *(Judy), his stingy, screechy, quarrelsome and intractable wife, and his friend* Gnafron, *always the tipsy, mawkishly sentimental, pompous moralizer. The* Guignol *presentations make much of local and national politicians as well as other public figures.*

Meije to Puy de Dôme. S, **Electricity Museum** *(closed Tue.)* in the birthplace of André-Marie Ampère, with 18 visitor-operated basic electrical experiments. ▶ In the valley, **Albigny-sur-Saône** ® (*8 km;* pop. 2 653). ▶ **Mount Thou** (alt. 609 m) : views, summit closed to public. ▶ Below, near the Saône, **Couzon** ® (pop. 2 476) : church with 12thC bell-tower; quarries for the Lyons building stone. ▶ **Mount Cindre** ® (alt. 469 m) : television relay tower; 14thC hermitage; **view**★ (from adjacent banks of the Saône entering Lyons 300 m below. ▶ **Saint-Cyr** ® (pop. 4 914) : 13thC château tower; Lyons Regional Museum of Criminology *(at the police academy; written requests in advance).* ▶ **Saint-Rambert** (→ Rochetaillée-sur-Saône). ▶ **Collonges** ® N *(4 km);* pop. 2 832) : location of one of the most renowned restaurants in France. □

MORNANT

B2 / ® / pop. 3 463 (Rhône)

In a small valley broached by the 30-arch Roman **Gier aqueduct**★ serving Lyons; ruins visible around Orliénas and Beaunant, among other sites; an arch N of Mornant. Gothic church : woodwork; 15thC Madonna in priory. **Riverie**★ *(8 km NW) :* mediaeval market town on promontory; site★; crafts centre. □

NANTUA★

C1 / ® / pop. 3 639 (Ain)

Ancient lookout at a mountain pass, on a 3-km-long lake, Nantua was a religious centre before it became a summer resort and a centre of gastronomy.

▶ **Church :** Romanesque; doorway★; interior, Renaissance altar, woodwork, painting by Eugène Delacroix (1799-1863), Martyrdom of St. Sebastian★. ▶ S *(2-hr walk round trip),* view from **Mont d'Ain**★ (alt. 1 127 m) to the fir-covered lakeshore *(500 m),* large leisure centre. □

▶ Nearby

▶ E, the Geneva road through the **Cluse** follows the northern shore of **Lake Sylans** (ancient glaciers) for 2 km. ▶ Left on D95, via Charix, **Lake Genin** *(16 km from Nantua) :* site★ (alt. 830 m). ▶ N via the Saint-Claude road, **Oyonnax** ® *(16 km)* (pop. 22 804) : comb and eyeglass manufacturing, reorganized since WWII for plastics manufacture *(plant visits);*

Museum of Combs and Plastics *(10-12 & 3-6, Jul.-Aug.; closed Sun., hols.; 2-5 Tue., Sat. rest of year). (8 km farther)* **Dortan** the capital of chess in a pass below a ruined château; boxwood artisans' workshops. ▶ SW, via the Lyons road, **Cerdon Caverns** *(23 km)*: handsome entrance to 800 m track. ▶ Vineyard producing a sparkling rosé wine: le cerdon. □

■ NOIRÉTABLE

A2 / ® / pop. 1 998 (Loire)

On the border of Forez and the Livradois, medium-altitude (alt. 700 m) resort. Attracts hikers and anglers for trout. Gothic church. □

▶ Nearby

▶ **Notre-Dame-de-l'Ermitage** *(7 km SW;* alt. 1 100 m). ▶ **Cervières★** *(3 km N)*: ancient market town; ruined ramparts; Renaissance houses; 15th-16thC church; lime tree. ▶ Via Champoly *(10 km NE)*, ruined **château d'Urfé★** (1-hr walk; alt. 936 m; view of Alps in clear weather. ▶ **Saint-Just-en-Chevalet** ® *(18 km;* pop. 1 798) in Aix Valley: ruined castle; 15thC church on knoll. ▶ S, D101 passes through Ermitage Woods and Loge Pass (alt. 1 243 m) before entering the **Forez Peaks.** ▶ **Chalmazel** *(28 km;* pop. 670): winter sports resort (alt. 867 m); 13th-16thC château *(school hols.: daily, 10-12 & 2-6; termtime: Sundays only, 10-12 & 2-6; closed All Saints - Easter).* ▶ Via **Béal Pass★** (alt. 1 390 m; *10 km W*) and the high Forez Peaks road, **Pierre-sur-Haute★** (alt. 1 634 m; *1h30 walk)*: panorama★★. ▶ Via N89 from Saint-Étienne, **Hôpital-sous-Rochefort** *(21 km)* 12th-16thC church, ruins of fortified priory (15th-16thC). W, near **Saint-Laurent-Rochefort**: Gothic church, castle and 12thC chapel on a cliff. □

■ PÉROUGES★★

B2 / ® / pop. 658 (Ain)

This mediaeval village of weavers, which has provided the scenery for numerous films, situated 70 m above the plain has been completely restored, since 1911. A fortified city with houses built up to the ramparts, fortified church, palace, 15th-16thC craftsmens' workshops along **Rue des Rondes★** and the central square.

▶ Avoid the summer tourist peak and Sun. ▶ **Place du Tilleul**: Museum of Folk Arts and Traditions; the weaver's workshop reflects the time when hemp was the only regional crop *(closed Wed.).* □

▶ Nearby

▶ **Meximieux** ® *(2 km E;* pop. 4 254): sculptured choir stalls in church; château du Monteiller (restored 11thC keep). ▶ **Saint-Maurice-de-Gourdans** ® *(13 km S;* pop. 1 157): Gothic paintings in church nave. ▶ 20 km S via D65, Loyettes ® (pop. 1 178). □

■ Mount PILAT★

AB3

Like a pyramid rising sharply 1 000 m above the Gier and the Rhône, Mount Pilat, with massive crests *(chirats)* at about 1 400 m, supports a naturally wooded regional park

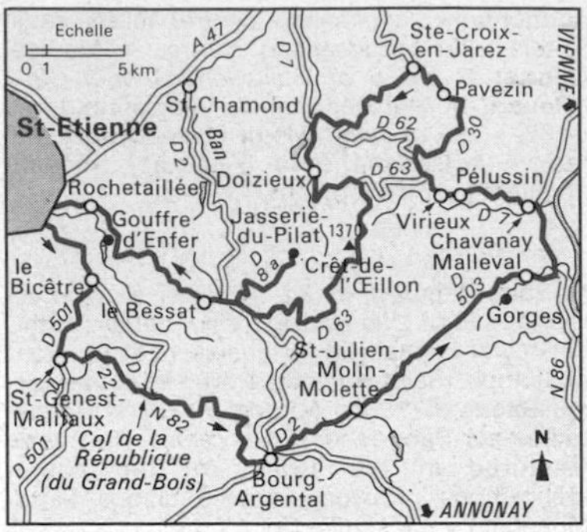

4. Tour of Mount Pilat

— ash, chestnut, beech and pine — with few pastures. 200 km of rivers and streams run off the mountain, which is a haven for wildlife including boar, fox, civet and deer, predatory birds and butterflies. Designated a nature park in 1974 (600 km^2 including 280 km^2 coniferous forest), Mount Pilat, with ski slopes and 300 km of hiking trails, is the open-air playground for Lyons-Saint-Étienne. □

▶ From Saint-Étienne to the Rhône Valley

▶ Via **Le Bessat** and **Pélussin** *(57 km)*: **Rochetaillée** (→ Saint-Étienne). ▶ **Le Bessat** ® (pop. 214): mountain resort. ▶ After the Chambouret Cross, left 7 km to **Pilat Farmstead**: view of Perdrix Crest (alt. 1 434 m). ▶ **Œillon Crest Pass**: orientation table at summit★ (alt. 1 365 m; 1-hr round trip). ▶ **Pélussin** (pop. 2 930): lookout over the Rhône Valley; old town; disused mill (Virieu). ▶ N, **Saint-Croix-en-Jarez**: 13thC Charterhouse abandoned at the French Revolution. ▶ **Chavanay** ®: 10 km E on the Rhône; pop. 1 858. ▶ N, **Condrieu** ® (pop. 3 158): old houses; river port; Croix-Regis zoo (2 km upriver); renowned vineyards.

▶ By **Republique Pass** (alt. 1 145 m) and Bourg-Argental *(65 km).* ▶ Detour via **Saint-Genest-Malifaux** (pop. 2 384): cottage industry of braid trimmings. **Marlhes**: folk arts and traditions in the Eau and Béate Houses *(14 Jul.-15 Sept., Sun. and hols., 3-6:30).* ▶ **Saint-Sauveur-en-Rue**: Vialle gateway; church (Descent from the Cross); fortified **Rue House.** ▶ **Bourg-Argental** ® (pop. 3 302): Town Hall in feudal château; church with Romanesque portal; **silk museum** at park office (reconstructed weaver's workshop). ▶ **Saint-Julien-Molin-Molette**: megalith. ▶ **Malleval**: mediaeval village★ on a crag above gorges, waterfall. □

■ PONT-D'AIN

B1 / ® / pop. 2 224 (Ain)

The most frequented part of the valley (popular with trout and grayling anglers), where the Dombes and Bugey meet, Pont-d'Ain lies below the ruined 15thC château where Louise de Savoie (mother of François I) was born; Renaissance staircase; grounds. □

▶ Nearby

▶ E *(6 km)*, **Jujurieux**: a town of 15 châteaux, including the château de la Tour des Echelles, French gardens★ *(Sat., Sun. Jul.-Sep.).* ▶ Via the Nantua road, **Poncin** (*8 km;* pop. 1 204) : 13thC castle; on the right bank of the Ain, Colombière Cavern. ▶ Farther on, via the Veyron Valley and S, **Préau Pass★** and ruined château de Châtillon. □

ROANNE

A1 / ® / pop. 49 638 (Loire)

A one-time Loire River port superseded in the 19thC by the canal to Briare, an industrial centre for metallurgy, armaments, tyres and textiles, with an equal reputation for fine food.

▶ 200 m from the Town Hall, **Joseph Déchelette Museum** (Rue Anatole-France, *10-12 & 2-6; closed Tue.*) : archaeology, painting, regional ceramics. ▶ Saint-Étienne Church : Renaissance stained glass, near 11thC ruined keep. ▶ Surrounding area abounds in Gallic and Gallo-Roman sites. □

▶ Nearby

▶ Via N7 from Lyons : l'**Hôpital-sur-Rhins** *(10 km).* ▶ **Saint-Symphorien-de-Lay** : 15thC church, Renaissance carving★; summer exhibits at 17thC Mansard House. ▶ Climb to **Pin-Bouchain Pass** (alt. 764 m) : S via back roads, 27 km from Roanne **château de l'Aubépin★** (Gothic and Renaissance; *access to park only*).

▶ Villerest Dam *(S)*

▶ A 40-km round trip through uninhabited countryside that gradually recedes under the waters of the Villerest Dam. ▶ **Villerest★ :** fortifications high on the left bank; 12th-16thC church, Gothic and Renaissance houses. ▶ **Perron Waterfall.** ▶ **Saint-Jean-Saint-Maurice :** view. ▶ **Saint-Maurice★** *(12 km) :* 12thC stronghold on a mountain peak (view from keep); gateway, ramparts, 13thC painted murals in church, Roman bridge pilings. ▶ Continue to the upper end of the gorge in a broad loop via **Ménars** and **Saint-Polgues;** cross the Loire at **Fragny Bridge** *(13 km from Saint-Maurice; site★).* ▶ Back through the valley★ on the right bank. □

SAINT-BONNET-LE-CHÂTEAU★

A3 / pop. 2 089 (Loire)

A lace-making town, formerly fortified, some walls still intact; 16thC double gate. ▶ **View★** over Forez Plain and the Lyonnais mountains. ▶ Gothic and Renaissance **houses.** ▶ Collegiate church (15th-16thC) : Renaissance doorway, Gothic fresco in crypt; mummified remains. ▶ Hospital chapel : Baroque furnishings, altarpiece. ▶ **Usson-en-Forez** (*13 km SW;* pop. 1 358) :

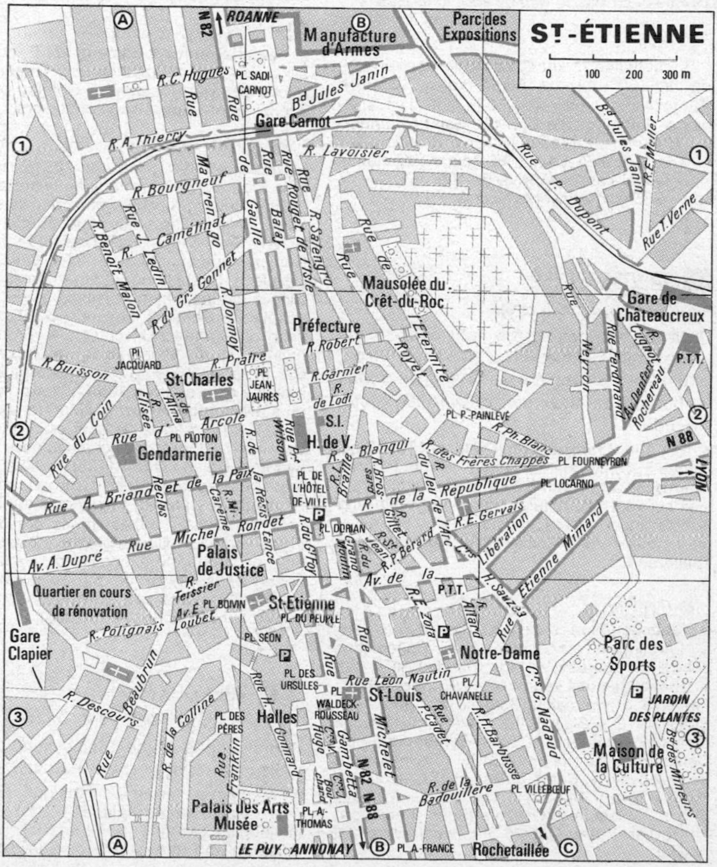

summer resort (alt. 944 m), angling; church with three 15thC naves). □

SAINT-ÉTIENNE

A2-3 / ® / pop. 206 688 (Loire)
See plan on preceding page

At the foot of Mt. Pilat (→) on a slope ranging from 700 m to 500 m alt., crossed by the high Furan Valley, Saint-Étienne started to grow in the 16thC; industry has continued to expand for the past 150 years in metallurgy, arms, tools and milling machinery. A "green city", Saint-Étienne enjoys 2 000 hours of sunshine annually (more than half the year) and an active cultural life.

▶ The N-S road *(6 km)* leads to the **Town Hall** (square★) and historic quarter (mediaeval church, restored in the 19thC), around the **Place du Peuple** (B3), bright with flower-stalls. ▶ S, the **Palais des Arts** houses the Museum of Art and Industry★★ and the Mining Museum : zoology, weaving, armour, contemporary painting★, sculpture, prints, drawings *(10-12 & 2-5; closed Tue. and Wed. am).* ▶ Museum of Old Saint-Étienne (No. 13 Rue Gambetta; B3). ▶ Near the Palais des Arts, **Jardin des Plantes** (Botanical Garden; C3) : view from terraces of Cultural Centre. ▶ Return by way of the Town Hall and Arms Museum (19 Rue J.-C. Tissot, *visit by appt. only* B2). □

▶ Nearby

▶ **Rochetaillée** *(7 km E) :* old village overlooking (alt. 800 m) the Furan Valley; **Gouffre d'Enfer** (lake) created by 50-m-high dam spillway. ▶ **Valley of the Gier** (E). **Saint-Chamond** ® (*12 km;* pop. 40 571) : naval shipyards *(closed Sat., Sun.);* ruins of Roman aqueduct; 9thC feudal castle. ▶ **Rive-de-Gier** ® (*22 km;* pop. 15 850) : glassworks *(visits).* □

SAINT-GALMIER

A2 / ® / pop. 3 796 (Loire)

On a hill overlooking the right bank of the Loire, Saint-Galmier is a well-known spa, where the effervescent water sold as *Badoit* is bottled at the rate of 43 500 hectolitres/day.

▶ 16th-17thC **ramparts;** toll gate. ▶ 15th-16thC **church :** 16thC statue, Virgin of the Pillar★; altarpiece, Virgin with a Bird. ▶ Hospital in former convent (altarpiece, cloister); Gothic and Renaissance **houses;** museum. ▶ 1 km away on the bank of the Coise, 16th-17thC manor of **Teillières★.** □

▶ Nearby

▶ **Veauche** (*6 km S;* pop. 5 707) : church, partly Carolingian (decoration★). ▶ Benedictine abbey of **Jourcey,** priory founded in 1130. ▶ **Chazelles-sur-Lyon** (*10 km NE;* pop. 5 047) : Museum of Hatmaking *(closed am and Tue., Sun., 10-12 & 2-6);* 15thC tower, only vestige of military outpost. ▶ **Saint-Symphorien-sur-Coise** (*7 km farther;* pop. 3 267) : escarpment occupied since Celtic times, still a mediaeval fortified town; 10th-15thC buildings. ▶ **Pomeys** *(2 km) :* Museum of Oceania (South Pacific; at La Neylière; *daily May-15 Sep. week-ends rest of year*). □

SEYSSEL

C1-2 / ® / pop. 831 (Ain)

Two communities on each side of the Rhône, the smaller in the Ain, the other in Haute-Savoie, linked by a suspension bridge. Museum of wood *(pl. de la République).*

▶ W, **Le Grand-Colombier★★** (alt. 1 531 m) : accessible by car on mountain road starting at Anglefort *(5 km S);* before the summit, view from **Fenestrez★** over the **Culoz** Basin (pop. 2 630); nearby, château de Mont-Ferrand. In the distance, Lake Bourget, Revard, Chartreuse. □

TARARE

A2 / ® / pop. 10 935 (Rhône)

43 km from Lyons, weavers' houses line the main street of a town that flourished in the late 18thC by making muslin and cotton goods; Tarare still thrives from the manufacture of curtain materials and synthetics.

▶ Commercial Court in a 17thC Capuchin Friary; textile and natural sciences museums *(temporarily closed);* 16thC tower. ▶ Hikes among the woods, streams and waterfalls of the nearby mountains. Every five years (those ending in 0 and 5) : fête de la Mousseline. □

▶ Nearby

▶ **Pontcharra-sur-Turdine** (*6 km E;* pop. 1 833) silk centre. ▶ S, picturesque **Toranchin Valley★.** SE, Clévy chapel : Gothic; pilgrimage site. ▶ **Saint-Loup,** village of flowers. □

▶ Tarare Peaks *(N via D8)*

▶ **Sauvage Pass** (*8 km;* alt. 723 m). ▶ **Amplepuis** (pop. 5 055) : formerly an important textile centre; sewing-machine museum; castle ruins (tower built in the year 1 000, Roman bridge). ▶ NW, **Saint-Victor-sur-Rhins★** *(6 km) :* partly Romanesque church. ▶ E, Pilon Pass, **Ronne :** cromlech (prehistoric stone monoliths encircling a mound); menhir (single stone megalith) adapted to Christian devotion. ▶ NE, **Cublize :** echo phenomenon in church. ▶ From Amplepuis to Cours, "Pines Road". ▶ **Thizy★** ® (alt. 560 m; pop. 3 699; 3 200 at Bourg-de-Thizy) : a textile centre in the 18thC; tile-roofed village on a **promontory★** overlooking Trambouze Valley (view★); mediaeval quarter, 11thC church decorated with frescos; château once occupied by Mme. Roland (1754-1793), a member of the moderate republican party (Gironde) during the Revolutionary period, to whom is attributed the cry : "Oh liberty! What crimes are committed in thy name!" ▶ **Cours-la-Ville** (pop. 5 095; alt. 560 m) : formerly a centre for manufacturing cotton bedspreads. W, the Beaujolais region via **Pavillon Pass,** alt. 683 m); NE, the Brion and Roanne regions (→ Charlieu). □

TRÉVOUX★

B2 / ® / pop. 5 055 (Ain)

Former capital of the principality of Dombes, a pleasure-craft port on the river Saône.

▶ Mediaeval streets; mansions facing the river; **Government Palace.** ▶ Old **pharmacy** in hospital grounds. ▶ Town Hall : historical **museum and library** (Trévoux newspaper collection★; Jesuit dictionary. ▶ 11th-12thC **fortified castle :** view from octagonal tower. □

▶ Nearby

▶ **Ars-sur-Formans** ® *(9 km NE) :* pilgrimages to the former presbytery of a popular 19thC priest, Jean-Baptiste Vianney (1786-1859): basilica *(Mar.-Sep.).* ▶ Toward Ambérieux (rose gardens), road crosses the TGV high-speed train line. □

▶ Saône Valley, upstream

▶ **Saint-Bernard :** château belonged to the early 20thC painter Maurice Utrillo. ▶ **Jassans-Riottier** ® (pop. 3380) : Romanesque church. ▶ Via Fareins *(14 km) :* 17thC **château de Fléchères★** in a deer park *(Sat., Sun., hols., Jul.-Sep.).* ▶ **Montmerle-sur-Saône** ® *(21 km;* pop. 2023). ▶ **Thoissey** ® *(35 km;* pop. 1421) : old pharmacy in former hospital. □

VILLEFRANCHE-SUR-SAONE

B1-2 / ® / pop. 29066 (Rhône)

Walled town founded in the 12thC by the lords of Beaujeu; 15thC capital of Beaujolais (→), today a centre for the cotton industry and the wine trade.

▶ **Rue Nationale** (N6) bordered for 3 km by **14th-16thC houses :** Nos. 83, 142, 144, 196 (Renaissance, former Town Hall), 202, 793, 831 (former prison). ▶ Church 12th-16thC : adjacent paved area. □

YZERON★

AB2 / ® / pop. 590 (Rhône)

Small resort 30 km from Lyons, at medium altitude (alt. 700 m) on a crag (orientation map behind church; excursions; mountain-climbing); during the 19thC an important production centre for velvet (150 looms in a village of 800 people). **Châteauvieux** (2.5 km) : farms, megaliths, ruined Roman aqueduct. □

▶ Lyonnais Mountains

▶ **Luère Pass** *(10 km NE;* alt. 714 m) : view★. ▶ Below, **Pollionnay★** (pop. 1088) : 15thC fortified house, Renaissance church, square tower on Romanesque château *(exhibitions in summer).* ▶ W via Duerne *(8 km),* at alt. 830 m, **Sainte-Foy-l'Argentière** *(15 km;* pop. 1188) in Brévennes Valley★. ▶ Farther N, **Haute-Rivoire★.** ▶ S, **Saint-Martin-en-Haut** ® *(8 km;* alt. 736 m; pop. 2969) : traces of Roman roads, ruined château de Rollefort *(1.5 km).* ▶ **St. André Peak** *(5 km farther,* alt. 937 m, footpath) : highest point in the Lyonnais Mountains (panorama). □

Architecture

The past is reflected by rural and domestic architecture rather than by great monuments in Lyons, Forez and Bresse : long, low Dombes farmhouses with pebble-dashed earthen walls; Beaujolais houses built of *pierres dorées* (the limestone pebbles called "golden" because of the high content of yellow ochre), with Mediterranean-style tile roofs; the farm outbuildings of Pilat and Madeleine, thatched like the

Farmhouse in the Dombes region

House in the Beaujolais region

cheesemakers' cabins of the Auvergne; country houses in the Loire Basin, with high walls enclosing a courtyard or timbered gallery. ● These sturdy, freestanding buildings share a family likeness that can be traced back to the Roman villa, an ample one-story structure covered by a spreading red-tile roof. ● Another kind of rural dwelling resembles more the traditional buildings of Champagne and Comté : the timber-faced balconied house of Bresse. ● The Saracen chimneys of Bresse mostly date back to the 16th-17thC; about 60 can still be seen N and NW of Bourg (→ Bresse tour). These chimneys are built in a manner that goes back to Mediterranean and Oriental roots, with whitewashed openwork brick "hoods". Their closest counterparts can be seen in the Algarve and Sicily. The style appears to have been introduced to Bresse by Italian

House in the Bresse region

craftsmen during the Renaissance, when the region was governed by the counts of Savoy.

Brief regional history ●

6thC BC-4thC AD The valley had known at least 2000 years of human habitation and trade **(the tin and amber road)** before the first Roman colonists settled at Lugdunum (Lyons) in 43 BC. The site was a convenient centre for the administration of the **Roman colonies;** a road network spread, and the city was made the capital of Gaul in 16 BC. ● The population soon reached 100000. **Early Christians** sought protection at Lyons in 177, but many of them were martyred : 18000 von 197 AD; the victory of Septimus Severus over Albinus, brought about the destruction of the city and the massacre of its 18,000 inhabitants. During the reign of the Roman Emperor Diocletian (284-305), Lugdunum was eclipsed in political importance by Arles, Trèves and Vienne.

5th-14thC At the dissolution of Charlemagne's Frankish Empire, the region of Lyonnais was incorporated into the kingdom of Provence, and later intergrated, along with Burgundy, into the Holy Roman Empire. The establishment of church buildings affiliated with Cluny Abbey caused Romanesque art to flourish in the region. ● Lyons continued to expand as an important **trading centre;** the townspeople resisted attempts by the Church to interfere in commerce, and banded together to form the first municipality (1240) in France, which received the formal **protection of the French Crown** in 1275.

15th-16thC At the beginning of the 15thC, refugees from civil wars in the Italian city republics fled to Lyons, where they introduced the **silk industry.** When, in 1463, Louis XI granted Lyons the privilege of four free fairs per year, **Florentine merchant bankers** opened branches of their Geneva operations at Lyons in 1466, and **Germain printers** set up shop on Rue Mercière in 1473. ● By the 16thC Lyons had outdistanced Paris in wealth and population; the city stock market — the oldest in France — was opened in 1506, by which time more than 100 publishers were in business. The Protestant **Reformation** found ready acceptance. ● In this independent atmosphere occurred the first recorded **workers' strike** — by printers in 1539-1542. Protestants began to suffer reprisals during the 1540s, and many were forced to flee to Geneva and other sympathetic refuges in 1551.

17th-18thC The first workers' organizations were formed at the Lyons silk mills in the 18thC. **Coal mines** were put into commercial production in the **Saint-Étienne area** in 1759. ● From the eve of the Revolution onwards, invention and innovation were flourishing in the Lyonnais region : the first balloon ascent was made at Brotteaux in 1784, shortly after the *pyroscaphe* — precursor of the steamship — had been successfully launched on the Rhône.

19thC-Present Invention and industry continued to thrive with Joseph-Marie Jacquard's loom of 1804, based on the same punched-card principal used in computers today. The Jacquard loom revolutionized textile weaving (and hence the clothing and related industries) throughout the world. Violent workers' revolts in the 1830s led many mill owners to abandon mechanized city plants and re-establish weaving centers in the countryside where labour was plentiful and cheap. ● Metal-working thrived by virtue of the ample fuel supply in the Saint-Étienne region. ● During WWII, Lyons was the "capital" of the Resistance movement.

Practical information

The region

Information : *Comité Régional de Tourisme (C.R.T.),* 5, pl. de la Baleine, 69005 Lyon, ☎ 78.42.50.04. C.D.T. **Rhône,** 69223 Lyons Cedex 2, ☎ 78.42.25.75 ; C.D.T. **Loire-Forez,** 5, pl. Jean-Jaurès, 42021 Saint-Étienne Cedex 1, ☎ 77.33.15.39 ; C.D.T. **Ain,** 2, rue Guichenon, B.P. 78, 01002 Bourg-en-Bresse Cedex, ☎ 74.23.66.66. — U.D.S.I. du Rhône et T.O. Lyon-Communauté, pavillon du Tourisme, pl. Bellecour, 69002 Lyons, ☎ 78.42.25.75.

Bookings : *Loisirs-Accueil Loire,* 5, pl. Jean-Jaurès, 42021 Saint-Étienne Cedex 1, ☎ 77.33.15.39. *Loisirs-Accueil Ain,* info. C.D.T. Ain.

Maps : *Michelin* n°s 91 and 93 (Lyons region), and n°s 73, 74 and 76 1/200 000. *I.G.N.* n°s 112, 109, and 111 1/250 000 ; n° 13 *(of the Pilat area)* 1/50 000 (nature parks collection).

S.O.S. : *SAMU* (Emergency Medical Service), ☎ 78.54.51.55 and 78.53.81.11 ; *Poisoning Emergency Centre,* ☎ 78.54.14.14 ; *Groupement des ambulanciers rhodaniens,* ☎ 78.54.81.92.

Weather forecast : Ain, ☎ 74.38.21.58 ; **Loire,** ☎ 77.36.56.08 ; **Rhône,** ☎ 78.26.73.74. *Snow conditions,* ☎ 12.66.54.26. *Road conditions :* **Rhône,** ☎ 78.54.33.33 ; **Ain,** ☎ 74.22.82.11.

Rural gîtes : enq at the **Ain** departmental relais : 1, pl. Clemenceau, 01000 Bourg-en-Bresse, ☎ 74.21.42.08. **Loire :** 43, av. Albert-Raimond, 42270 Saint-Priest-en-Jarez, ☎ 77.79.15.22. **Rhône,** 4, pl. Gensoul, 69002 Lyons, ☎ 78.42.65.92.

Holiday villages : see Practical Holiday Information.

Camping : limited possibilities, fewer than 150 sites for the region. Enq at the C.D.T.

Festivals : end May : Villerest festival ; **end Jun and early Jul :** Divonne-les-Bains. **Jul :** *« Estivades » (summer festival)* in Sail-sous-Couzan. **Early Sep :** Lyon-La Part-Dieu, *international marionnette festival,* followed by a *Light Festival* (exclusively for under 13 year-olds). **Sep :** *Berlioz* in Lyons ; *music festivals* in Saint-Victor-sur-Loire **(May-Jun** and **Nov-Dec** week-ends). In Ambierle and Charlieu in the Loire, in **summer :** enq to the Festival Committee.

Religious events and ceremonies : 4 Aug : *pilgrimage at the Basilica of Saint Curé d'Ars.* **8 Sep :** *pilgrimage of the Brouilly mountain wine-growers.* **24 Dec :** Pérouges, *lantern procession and Midnight Mass.*

Folklore : end Jan : *« vague » de Villefranche-sur-Saône (festival of the army conscripts) ;* **May-Jun,** Gex region, *bird festival.* **End Jun :** Villefranche, *Beaujolais festival.* In **summer,** in the Ain region, *Festival.* **Mid-Jul :** Montrond-les-Bains, Saint-Germain-Laval, *mediaeval festivals ;* Amplepuis, *folk festival* 1 week-end in Oct : *festival de la fourme (local cheese)* in Montbrison. **Oct :** *wine festival* in the Ain region (Ceyzériat, St-Trivier-de-Courtes).

Fairs : Mon after Shrove Tuesday, Roanne *torch fair.* **Apr :** *spring fair* in Haute-Rivoire ; **second fortnight :** *handicrafts fair* in Ambierle. **End Apr-early May :** *Forez wine days* in Boen. **End May :** *"the grand curio fair"* in Lyons *(a thrice-yearly bric-à-brac and second-hand fair).* **Early Nov :** *fair of « vins bourrus » (unsophisticated country wines)* in Saint-Haon-le-Vieux. In Beaujolais, *Fleurie and Le Bois-d'Oingt wine fair.* **Second Sun in Dec :** *wine sales* at the Beaujeu Almshouse.

Sporting events : End of Jan, cross-country skiing, Great Croissing of Haut-Bugey (departure from Le Poizat). **Mar :** Lyon-Charbonnières, *car rally.* **Early Jul :** *col de la République, cycling days.* **Jul-Aug :** *water tournaments* in Condrieu.

Exhibitions and trade fairs : *Lyons,* see Eurexpo calendar (info S.E.P.E.L, ☎ 72.22.33.44.). *Exhibition-fairs* in Montbrison on **Ascension Day ;** in Saint-Étienne during the **first fortnight in May** *(salon de l'Arme)* and the **second fortnight in Sep ;** in Roanne, **May,** in Bourg, during the **second fortnight in Dec.** *Salon de la Gastronomie* at Bourg in **Oct.**

Scenic railways : *Ligne d'Anse* (info. Lyons T.O.), *small train at Villerest.*

National and nature parks : parc naturel régional du Pilat, moulin de Virieu, 2, rue Benay, 42410 Pélussin, ☎ 74.87.65.24.

Rambling and hiking : the region is traversed by the G.R. trails 32, 7, 72, 73, 76 between Bourgogne and Cévennes ; 760 (tour of Beaujolais) ; G.R. 3, the Forez Mountains ; G.R. 59 (Bresse and Bugey) ; G.R. 9 and alternative trails (*G.T.J. :* major crossing of the Jura ; 200 km ; *G.T.A. :* major Alpine crossing, from the Rhône to the Riviera). Rambling and hiking programs are organised by the *Ligue du Lyonnais,* 43, bd L.-Guérin, Vénissieux, *Assn. des groupes de randonneurs de la Loire* (at the C.D.T.), the *Comité départ. de tourisme pédestre du Rhône* (C.D.T.). Also see the *Féd. de Moyenne-Montagne,* 4, Grande-Rue-de-la-Guillotière, 69007 Lyons, ☎ 78.72.02.69.

Riding holidays : *A.R.A.E.,* M. Buriane, 46, rue Léon-Lamazière, Saint-Étienne ; main office : 4, rue André-Malraux. F.E.F., Ligue Rhône-Alpes, 28, pl. Bellecour, 69002 Lyon, ☎ 78.37.33.68.

Horse-drawn holidays : departure from Sainte-Catherine (Lyonnais mountains), ☎ 78.81.81.94 ; in the **Ain** region, in Ceyzériat : Cheval-Bugey, ☎ 74.30.01.21. Equestrian farm at Malagretaz, ☎ 74.30.81.19.

Cycling holidays : *Fédération française de cyclotourisme : Ligue du Lyonnais,* 49, rue Pasteur, 69300 Caluire ; *Ligue du Forez,* 11, rés. Fontquentin, Roanne ; *C.D.T.* Bourg-en-Bresse. Excursions organised in the Pilat region (*C.D.T.,* in Saint-Étienne, and *maison du Parc,* in Pélussin), the Beaujolais area (leaving from Villefranche) ; cycle tour of the **Loire :** *M. Frasse,* Pouilly-sous-Charlieu ; in the **Ain** region : *Cyclobressan* (train + vélo) at the Montbrison and Villars-les-Dombes railway stations.

Young people : *Direction départementale du Temps libre, Jeunesse et Sports :* **Rhône,**

26, rue de la Baisse, 69100 Villeurbanne, ☎ 78.84.33.08 ; **Ain,** 3, rue des Casernes, 01012 Bourg-en-Bresse, ☎ 74.23.44.66 ; **Loire,** 9, rue Claude-Lebois, 42000 Saint-Étienne, ☎ 77.37.33.33. *C.R.I.J.* du Lyonnais : 9, quai des Célestins, 69002 Lyons, and Miribel-Jonage park and leisure centre, chemin de la Bletta, 69120 Vaulx-en-Velin. *Atitra (Crous),* 59, rue de la Madeleine, 69007 Lyons, ☎ 78.72.55.47. *OOCAJ,* 11, rue de la République, 69000 Lyon.

Tennis : Ligue régionale, Les Granges-Béons, Jasseron, 01250 Ceyzeriat.

Golf : in the **Rhône :** Villette-d'Anthon (Golf-Club des Îles de Lyons ; 27 holes), St-Symphorien-d'Ozon (9 holes) ; in the **Ain,** Divonne-les-Bains (18 holes) ; Cottet (15 holes). In the **Loire :** Craintilleux (9 holes), Champlong (9 holes).

Canoeing : Féd. française, 17, rte de Vienne, 69007 Lyon, ☎ 78.61.28.06 ; *Ligue du Lyonnais,* 56, rue du Perron, 69600 Oullins ; *Comité départ. :* **Ain,** based at Longeville-Ambronay, 01500 Ambérien-en-Bugey ; **Loire,** M. Morel, 1, chemin de la Vieille-Ferme, 42700 Firminy.

Climbing, mountaineering : especially in the **Ain** region (Revermont, Bugey, Valserine) : *Maison des Sociétés,* bd Juliot-Curie, 01000 Bourg-en-Bresse, ☎ 74.23.29.43, M.J.C. de Bellegarde, ☎ 50.48.13.31. Climbing section of the *C.A.F. :* 38, rue Thomassin, 69002 Lyons ; 26, rue Marengo, Saint-Étienne, 1, montée de l'Abbaye, 01130 Nantua, ☎ 74.76.52.58.

Potholing and spelunking : in particular, in the Colomby-de-Gex, Bugey and Revermont chasms **(Ain) ;** *Departmental Committees :* 29, rue Michelet, Oyonnax ; and *Maison des Sociétés,* Bourg-en-Bresse ; **Rhône,** 28, quai Saint-Vincent, 69001 Lyons, at the *Féd. Nat. de spéléologie,* ☎ 78.39.43.30 ; M. Krupa Daniel, 16, rue du Cimetière, 42100 Saint-Étienne.

Skiing : Ain : 15 fully-equipped resorts, 900 km of cross-country ski trails : enq C.D.T. and *Assn. Départementale du ski de fond de l'Ain.* **Loire :** *Assn. dép. pour le développement du ski nordique,* M. Charrondière, Les Noës, 42370 Renaison ; *Comité Forez* de la F.F.S., 2, rue Étienne-Dolet, 42000 Saint-Étienne, ☎ 77.32.42.53.

Flying, gliding, hang-gliding : *Union des aéro-clubs Rhône-Alpes,* aérodrome de Lyon-Bron, ☎ 78.26.81.09. *Assn. aéronautique de Bellegarde,* ☎ 50.77.90.83. Hang-gliding : *Club du Rhône,* 66, chemin du Boisset, 69600 Oullins ; *Assn. de Vol libre,* 01130 Nantua ; *Club du Pays gessien,* 01170 Gex ; *Université-club,* 34, rue Francis-Baulier, 42000 Saint-Étienne.

Fishing : numerous stretches of water, 1st category for fishing : rivers in Ain (trout, granyling) ; the thousand lakes of the Astrée region (Forez) in the 1st or 2nd category ; organised fishing holidays (Saint-Paul-de-Varax). Departmental Federations of fishing associations : 10, allée de Challes, 01000 Bourg-en-Bresse, ☎ 74.22.38.38 ; 10, quai Augagneur, 69003 Lyon, ☎ 78.60.81.05 ; 2, rue d'Arcole, 42000 Saint-Étienne, ☎ 77.32.14.99. In the **Rhône :** *Féd. des groupements de pêcheurs sportifs* (fishing competition in sheltered waters in the Ain River), 5, rue Jules-Verne, 69740 Genas.

Hunting and shooting : *Fédération de chasseurs :* **Ain,** 57, rue de la République, 01000 Bourg-en-Bresse, ☎ 74.22.25.02 ; **Loire,** 8, pl. de l'Hôtel-de-Ville, 42000 Saint-Étienne, ☎ 77.25.25.96 ; **Rhône,** 11, rue Childebert, 69002 Lyon, ☎ 78.42.69.09.

Towns

ANDRÉZIEUX-BOUTHÉON

Roanne 66, Lyons 76, Paris 458
16 km NE of St-Étienne, A3 ✉ 42160

SNCF ☎ 77.55.04.46.

Restaurant :
♦ ***Chapon Doré,*** pont de la Loire, ☎ 77.55.05.53. P closed Sun eve, Mon and Aug, 80-130.

Farmhouse-inns : St-Just-St-Rambert, 3 km S, *Les Faux,* ☎ 77.23.01.58. *La Bergerie,* Cordeyron, ☎ 77.52.38.19.

ANSE

Villefranche 6, Lyons 26, Paris 442
B2 ✉ 69480

ⓘ mairie, ☎ 74.67.03.84.

Hotel :
★★***Saint-Romain*** (L.F.), rte de Graves, ☎ 74.68.05.89. AE, DC, Euro, Visa. 22 rm P ♿ closed Sun eve (1 Nov-28 Apr), 170. Rest. ♦ Fish specialities, 60-150.

L'ARBRESLE

Lyons 25, Roanne 61, Paris 457
B2 ✉ 69210

ⓘ pl. de la République, ☎ 74.01.12.44.

SNCF ☎ 74.01.02.06.

Hôtels :
★★***Le Lion d'Or,*** 4, rue Centrale, ☎ 74.01.00.16. 12 rm P 150. Rest. ♦ 40-70.

Civrieux-d'Azergues, 69380 Lozanne, 10 km NE :
★★***La Roseraie,*** ☎ 78.43.01.78. DC, Visa. 10 rm P closed from Mon to Fri ex Jul-Aug, 165. Rest. ♦ Spec : *caneton aux pêches, gratin forézien,* 60-150.

⛺ ★★★*Municipal* (100 pl.), ☎ 77.01.11.50.

Restaurant :
♦ ***Le Vieux Four,*** 6 km NW, on the RN7, ☎ 74.01.02.67. AE, DC, Visa. P ♿ closed 4-30 Jan, Wed eve and Thu, 50-100.

ARS-SUR-FORMANS

Villefranche 9, Lyons 36, Paris 441
B1-2 ✉ 01480 Jassans-Riottier

ⓘ mairie, ☎ 74.00.71.84.

Hotels :
★★***Regina,*** ☎ 74.00.73.67. 33 rm P ♿ closed 1 Dec-15 Mar and Nov, 150. Rest. ♦ closed Wed low season, 65-120.
★***Basilique*** (L.F.), ☎ 74.00.73.76. 60 rm P closed Nov-Apr, 150.

Son et lumière : Jul-Sep.

BALBIGNY

Roanne 30, Lyons 77, Paris 422
9 km N of Feurs, A2 ✉ 42510

ⓘ mairie, ☎ 77.28.14.12.

SNCF ☎ 77.28.11.84.

Restaurant :
♦ ***Le Midi,*** pl. de l'Église, ☎ 77.65.43.01. Ⓟ ⅏ closed Mon, Tue and Wed (1 Oct-1 Mar), 70-150.

BEAUJEU

Villefranche 26, Mâcon 35, Paris 433
A-B1 ☒ 69430

ⓘ mairie, ☎ 74.04.80.84.

Hotel :
★***Anne de Beaujeu*** (L.F.), 28, rue de la République, ☎ 77.04.87.58. 7 rm Ⓟ closed 15 Dec-20 Jan, 1 week in summer, Sun eve and Mon low season, 130. Rest. 60-120.

Recommended : *le Temple de Bacchus,* ☎ 77.04.81.18, and sale of wines at the Almshouse on the 2nd Sun in Dec.

BELLEGARDE-SUR-VALSERINE

Nantua 18, Annecy 41, Paris 508
C1 ☒ 01200

ⓘ rue de la République, ☎ 50.48.03.56. closed Sun and Mon.

SNCF ☎ 50.48.04.74.

Car-hire : *Budget* train + auto, at the station, ☎ 50.48.04.74.

Hotels :
★★★***La Belle Époque*** (L.F.), 10, pl. Gambetta, ☎ 50.48.14.46. AE, Euro, Visa. 10 rm Ⓟ closed 3-20 Jul, 20 Nov-5 Dec, Sun eve, Tue, 200. Rest. ♦ 100-200.
★★***Central et Colonne*** (L.F.), 1, rue J.-Bertola, ☎ 50.48.10.45. AE, DC, Euro, Visa. 28 rm Ⓟ closed 15 Oct-15 Nov, 150. Rest. closed Sun eve and Mon, 60-120.

Lancrans, 3 km :
★***Sorgia,*** ☎ 50.48.15.81. 22 rm Ⓟ closed 15 Sep-8 Oct, 5-15 Jan and Mon noon and Sun eve low season, 110. Rest. 50-120.

Ochiaz, 5 km :
● ★***Auberge de la Fontaine,*** rte de Genissiat, ☎ 50.48.00.66. AE, DC, Euro, Visa. 7 rm Ⓟ closed 5 Jan-5 Feb, 1-7 Sep, Sun eve and Mon, 130. Rest. ♦ Spec : *mousseline de truite sauce Périgueux, foie gras frais de canard,* 95-200.

Eloise, 5 km SE, on the N508. (left bank of the Rhône-Hte-Savoie) :
● ★★***Le Fartoret*** (Relais du Silence), ☎ 50.48.07.18. DC, Visa. 42 rm Ⓟ 250. Rest. ♦♦ Spec : *compote de lapin aux herbes,* 60-150.

Ⅹ ★★★★*Crêt d'Eau* (70 pl.), ☎ 50.48.23.70.

BELLEVILLE-SUR-SAÔNE

Mâcon 25, Lyons 45, Paris 420
B1 ☒ 69220

ⓘ 50, rue de la République, ☎ 74.66.11.16.

SNCF ☎ 74.66.32.11.

Hotels :
★★***Gare,*** 43, rue du Mal-Foch, ☎ 74.63.34.68. 30 rm, 180.
★***Le Beaujolais,*** 49, rue du Mal-Foch, ☎ 74.66.05.31. 11 rm Ⓟ closed Dec, Tue eve and Wed, 90. Rest. ● ♦♦ Spec : *gratin de courges, andouillettes, coq au vin,* 70-130.

Taponas, 3 km NE :
★★***Sablons,*** ☎ 74.66.34.80. Visa. 15 rm Ⓟ 180. Rest. ♦ closed Tue low season, 60-150.

Montmerle, ☒ 01090, 3 km S (left bank) :
★★***Rivage*** (L.F.), ☎ 74.69.33.92. AE, DC, Euro, Visa. 11 rm Ⓟ closed 15 Nov-15 Dec, 190. Rest. ♦ closed Wed, 60-200.

Thoissey, ☒ 01140, 12 km NE :
● ★★★★***Chapon Fin*** (Relais et Châteaux), ☎ 74.04.04.74, Tx 305728. Visa. 25 rm Ⓟ closed early Jan-early Feb and Tue low season, 360. Rest. ♦♦♦ Spec : *chaud-froid de volaille, crêpes Parmentier,* 160-320.

Restaurants :
St-Jean-d'Ardières, ☒ 69220, 3 km NW on N6 :
♦♦ ***Maison des Beaujolais,*** ☎ 74.66.16.46. Visa. Ⓟ closed Jan, Wed eve and Thu, 60-90.

Montmerle, ☒ 01090, 3 km S (left bank) :
♦♦ ***Castel de Valrose,*** 12, bd de la République, ☎ 74.69.30.52. AE, DC, Visa. Ⓟ closed 5-26 Jan, Sun eve and Mon. Spec : *ragoût de queues d'écrevisses, noix de ris de veau en papillotes, filet de loup au coulis d'épinards,* 110-230. With 5 rm, 150-220.

Ⅹ ★★★★*Municipal* (440 pl.), Montmerle, 3 km S, ☎ 74.69.34.40.

BELLEY

Chambéry 36, Bourg-en-Bresse 75, Paris 502
C2 ☒ 01300

ⓘ hôtel de ville, ☎ 79.81.29.06.

Hotels :
★★***Manicle,*** 2, bd du Mail, ☎ 79.81.01.56. 15 rm Ⓟ closed 14-25 Jul,14-26 Oct, Sun eve and Mon, 160. Rest. 55-130.

Benonces, ☒ 01470 Serrières-de-Briort, 28 km NW :
★★***Auberge de la Terrasse*** (L.F.), ☎ 79.36.73.56. Euro, Visa. 10 rm Ⓟ closed 2 Jan-22 Mar, 180. Rest. ♦ closed Mon, 70-160.

Farmhouse-inns : *l'Auberge,* hameau de Boissieu, 4 km, ☎ 79.81.35.74. Spec : *coq au vin, gratin dauphinois, gigot.* Ordonnaz, 19 km NW on the D32, ☎ 79.36.42.38 or 79.36.42.39.

Recommended : *Distillerie de l'Étoile,* 44, rue Ste-Marie : brandies and liqueurs. Syndicat des vins du Bugey, bd du 133e-R.I., ☎ 79.81.30.17 : list and enq about the vineyards.

Le BESSAT

Saint-Étienne 18, Annonay 30, Paris 528
11 km N of the col de la République, A3
☒ 42660 St-Genest-Malifaux

1 170-1 430 m

ⓘ ☎ 77.20.40.61.

Hotels :
★★***France*** (L.F.), ☎ 77.20.40.99. 33 rm Ⓟ closed 1-15 Sep, Apr and end-of-year hols, 130. Rest. ♦ 40-90.
★***La Fondue,*** ☎ 77.20.40.09. 12 rm closed Dec-Feb, 180. Rest. 80-130.

BOEN

Saint-Étienne 53, Lyons 86, Paris 440
A2 ☒ 42130

SNCF ☎ 77.24.09.03.

Hotels :
Saint-Germain-Laval, ☒ 42260, 12 km N :
★***Touristes,*** rue Nationale, ☎ 77.65.41.08. 13 rm Ⓟ closed Feb and Tue, 120. Rest. ♦ 45-100.

Farmhouse-inns : *le Mazet,* St-Georges-en-Conzan, 12 km SW, ☎ 77.24.80.95. Farm-produced *charcuterie, patcha* and fruit tarts. *Le Vieux Moulin,* Veaux 42990 Saint-Georges-en-Couzan, ☎ 77.24.23.32, 77.24.21.24.

Event : end Apr-early May, Forez wine days, ☎ 77.24.23.32.

Recommended : *Cave coopérative des Côtes du Forez,* Trelins, RD8, ☎ 77.24.00.12.

BOURG-ARGENTAL

Saint-Étienne 28, Le Puy 77, Paris 545
A-B3 ♥ ⊠ 42220

ℹ rue de la République, ☎ 77.39.60.40 (high season), and mairie.

Hotel :
★★**France** (L.F.), pl. du 11-Novembre, ☎ 77.39.60.28. 20 rm P closed Feb, Sun eve and Mon, 180. Rest. 120-210.

BOURG-EN-BRESSE

Lyons 62, Lons-le-Saulnier 62, Paris 427
B1 ⊠ 01000

ℹ 6, av. Alsace-Lorraine, ☎ 74.22.49.40, and bd de Brou (high season), ☎ 74.22.27.76.

SNCF (A2) ☎ 74.21.13.31.

Car-hire : *Budget* train + auto, 3, rue Jean-Morgon, ☎ 74.23.34.00, and at the station, ☎ 74.21.50.52.

Hotels :
● ★★★**Prieuré,** 49-51, bd de Brou, ☎ 74.22.44.60. AE, DC, Visa. 15 rm P ♿ 450.
★★★**France,** 19, pl. Bernard (B1), ☎ 74.23.30.24, Tx 330740. AE, DC, Euro, Visa. 52 rm P 240. Rest. ♦ closed 18 Nov-2 Dec, Sat noon and Sun, 120-210.
★★★**Logis de Brou,** 132, bd de Brou (C2), ☎ 74.22.11.55. AE, DC, Visa. 30 rm P 230. Rest. 50-120.
● ★★**Chantecler** (Relais du Silence), 10, av. de Bad-Kreuznach, ☎ 74.22.44.88, Tx 380468. AE, DC, Euro, Visa. 28 rm P ♿ 210. Rest. ♦ closed Sat noon, 70-130.
★★**Terminus,** 9, rue A.-Baudin (A2), ☎ 74.21.01.21, Tx 380844. AE, DC, Euro, Visa. 51 rm P 180. Rest. ***l'Albatros.*** closed 5-19 Jan, 70-130.
★★**Mail,** 46, av. du Mail, ☎ 74.21.00.26. DC. 11 rm P closed 2-17 Jan, 23 Dec-14 Jan, Sun eve and Mon, 140. Rest. ♦♦ ♿ 70-175.
★★**Ariane,** bd Kennedy, ☎ 74.22.50.88. Euro, Visa. 29 rm P ♿ closed Christmas school hols, 200. Rest. closed Sun and nat hols, 90-130.
★**Le Revermont,** 19, rue Ch.-Robin, ☎ 74.22.66.53. AE, Euro, Visa. 15 rm. closed Sat eve and Sun. A pleasant, extremely comfortable hotel with a welcoming little bar, 100. Rest ● ♦♦ Simple, copious fare ; good, unsophisticated cooking, specially recommended for enthusiasts of frogs' legs, 40-100.

Confrançon, ⊠ 01130 Polliat, 17 km NW :
★★★**Auberge la Sarrasine** (Relais du Silence), ☎ 74.30.25.65, Tx 375830. 10 rm P ♿ closed Jan, Wed and Thu noon, 270. Rest. ♦♦ 130-180.

Youth hostel : *Centre culturel le Penessuy,* ☎ 74.22.03.53.

⛺ ★★★★*Challes* (125 pl.), ☎ 74.22.27.79.

Restaurants :
● ♦♦♦ **Auberge Bressanne,** Brou, ☎ 74.22.22.68. AE, DC, Visa. P ♿ closed Mon eve and Tue. A delicious rendition of the famous Bresse poultry dishes in this top-quality establishment, not, however, confined to regional traditions, as seen by such tasty, original dishes as the *gâteau de foies blonds de volaille à l'ancienne,* 100-180.
♦♦ **Chalet de Brou,** 168, bd de Brou, ☎ 74.22.26.28. ♿ closed 1-15 Jun and 20 Dec-20 Jan, Thu eve and Fri, 50-180.

Saint-Just, ⊠ 01250 Ceyzériat, 3 km E :
♦♦♦ **La Petite Auberge,** ☎ 74.22.30.04. Visa. closed early Jan-early Feb, Mon eve and Tue. Book ahead for eve meals. Spec : *foie gras maison, filet de bœuf aux morilles et échalotes confites,* 90-190.

CEYZÉRIAT

Bourg-en-Bresse 8, Nantua 32, Paris 435
B1 ♥ ⊠ 01250

Hotels :
★★**Mont-July** (L.F.), ☎ 74.30.00.12. 19 rm P closed 30 Oct-2 Mar, Thu low season, 180. Rest. ♦ 80-130.
★**Relais de la Tour,** rue J.-Bernier, ☎ 74.30.01.87. Euro, Visa. 7 rm ♿ closed 10 Oct-10 Nov, Mon, 140. Rest. ♦ closed Sun eve and Mon low season, 60-170.
★**Balcon** (L.F.), rue Jérôme-Lalande, ☎ 74.30.00.16. 10 rm P closed 15 Nov-31 Dec, Tue eve and Wed low season, 250. Rest. 60-150.

CHARBONNIÈRES-LES-BAINS

Lyons 8, Saint-Étienne 59, Paris 463
B2 ♆ (year round) ⊠ 69260

ℹ spa centre, ☎ 78.87.02.70.
SNCF ☎ 78.92.17.28

Hotels :
★★★**Domaine des Pins** (P.L.M. ; E.T.A.P.), 4-6, rte de Paris, ☎ 78.87.83.14, Tx 330060. AE, DC, Euro, Visa. 82 rm P ♿ 270. Rest. ♦♦ Good meals, 100-150.
● ★★**Beaulieu,** 19, av. du Gal-de-Gaulle, ☎ 78.87.12.04. AE. 42 rm P ♿ 160.

Restaurant :
● ♦ **Gigandon,** 5, av. Gal-de-Gaulle, ☎ 78.87.15.51. AE, Visa. closed Aug, 1 week in winter, Sun eve and Mon. Beautiful restaurant on the road out of Lyons. A big variety of well-prepared, refined dishes to be enjoyed in a calm, relaxed atmosphere, 70-180.

Pollionnay, 69290 Craponne, 7 km W :
♦ **Terrasse,** ☎ 78.48.12.06. closed 16 Aug-3 Sep and Mon. Noon only, 80-130.

CHARLIEU

Roanne 19, Mâcon 77, Paris 405
A1 ⊠ 42190

ℹ rue A.-Farinet, ☎ 77.60.12.42 (high season).

Hotel :
★★**Relais de l'Abbaye** (L.F.), La Montalay, Le Pont-de-Pierre, ☎ 77.60.00.88. AE, Euro, Visa. 27 rm P 205. Rest. ♿ 50-130.

⛺ ★★★*Municipal* (100 pl.), ☎ 77.60.09.47.

CHÂTILLON-SUR-CHALARONNE

Bourg-en-Bresse 24, Lyons 54, Paris 420
B1 ♥ ⊠ 01400

ℹ Champ-de-Foire, ☎ 74.55.02.27 (high season).

Hotels :
★★★**Chevalier Norbert,** av. Clément-Desorme, ☎ 74.55.02.22. AE, DC, Euro, Visa. 33 rm P ♿ 150. Rest. ♦♦ closed Jan and Mon low season.

Spec : *goujonette de turbot à la mousse de cresson,* game during the hunting season, 120-170.

★★*La Tour* (L.F.), pl. de la République, ☎ 74.55.05.12. 12 rm Ⓟ closed 10 Feb-15 Mar, Sun eve and Wed, 160. Rest. 70-170.

⅄ ★★★★ *Le Vieux Moulin* (165 pl.), ☎ 74.55.04.79.

Restaurant :

♦♦ ***Auberge de Montessuy,*** 2 km SE, rte de Marlieux, ☎ 74.55.05.14. Euro, Visa. closed 28 Sep-11 Oct, Jan, Mon eves and Tue. Spec : *mousse de brochet, grenouilles,* 60-160.

CHENAS

Mâcon 17, Lyons 62, Paris 411

☒ 69840 Juliénas

Restaurant :

♦♦ ***Robin,*** Les Deschamps, ☎ 85.36.72.67. AE, DC, Visa. Ⓟ closed 1 Feb-15 Mar, Wed and eves ex Sat. Spec : *andouillette aux fines herbes,* 130-170.

Recommended : cave du *domaine des Brureaux,* ☎ 85.36.72.67. Cave du château de Chénas, ☎ 74.04.11.91.

COLIGNY

Mâcon 45, Bourg-en-Bresse 45, Paris 418
21 km N of Bourg-en-Bresse, B1 ☒ 01270

Hotel :

Le Moulin-des-Ponts, 7 km on the RN83 :

★★***Solnan*** (L.F.), ☎ 74.51.50.78. AE, DC. 20 rm Ⓟ closed 2 Jan-1 Feb and Sun eve and Mon low season, 175. Rest. ♦ Spec : *feuilleté de grenouilles à la crème de ciboulette,* 120-200.

Restaurant :

● ♦♦ ***Le Petit Relais,*** ☎ 74.30.10.07. AE, DC, Euro. closed Feb school hols, 4-22 Jun, Tue eve and Wed. Spec : the day's fresh-caught fish, 80-200.

CONDRIEU

Vienne 11, Lyons 40, Paris 503
B2-3 ☒ 69420

ⓘ pl. du Marché, ☎ 78.85.53.48.

Hotel :

● ★★★★***Host. Beau Rivage*** (Relais et Châteaux), ☎ 74.59.52.24, Tx 308946. AE, DC, Euro, Visa. 24 rm Ⓟ ♿ closed 5 Jan-15 Feb, 330. Rest. ♦♦ Spec : *escalope de turbot homardine, suprême de Bresse Albufera,* 160-250.

Restaurant :

Chavanay, ☒ 42410 Pélussin, 7 km SW of Condrieu :

♦♦ ***Alain-Charles,*** ☎ 74.87.23.02. Euro, Visa. ♿ closed 2nd fortnight in Aug, Sun eve and Mon low season. Spec : *pâté chaud de canard aux truffes, loup grillé au beurre blanc,* 60-150.

⅄ ★★★*Belle Rive* (180 pl.), ☎ 74.59.51.08.

DIVONNE-LES-BAINS

Geneva 19, Nantua 65, Paris 506
C1 (t.a.), ☎ 50.20.06.70. ☒ 01220

ⓘ pl. des Bains, ☎ 50.20.01.22.

SNCF ☎ 50.20.07.27.

Hotels :

● ★★★★***Château de Divonne,*** rte de Gex, ☎ 50.20.00.32, Tx 309033. Visa. 25 rm Ⓟ closed 5 Jan-12 Mar, 600. Rest. ♦♦♦ 190-320.

● ★★★★(L) ***Golf et Grand-Hôtel,*** ☎ 50.20.06.63, Tx 385716. AE, DC, Euro, Visa. 145 rm Ⓟ ♿ 600. Rest. ♦♦ ***le Pavillon*** (high season), ♦♦ ***la Terrasse,*** 120-250.

● ★★***Bellevue-Marquis*** (L.F.), ☎ 50.20.02.16. AE, DC, Euro, Visa. 17 rm Ⓟ closed 1 Dec-1 Mar, Mon and Tue noon, 170. Rest. ♦ *Marquis* 100-190.

★★***Mont-Blanc-Favre,*** Arbère, ☎ 50.20.12.54. 18 rm Ⓟ closed 30 Oct-1 Apr, 170. Rest. Pension only in season, 90-260.

★★***Les Coccinelles,*** rte de Lausanne, ☎ 50.20.06.96. Euro. 18 rm Ⓟ closed 24 Dec-31 Jan, 150.

★★***Jura,*** rue d'Arbère, ☎ 50.20.05.95. 24 rm Ⓟ closed mid-Nov-mid-Dec, 170.

★***Divona,*** ☎ 50.20.00.91. 22 rm Ⓟ closed 20 Oct-20 Mar, 120.

★***Le Provençal*** (L.F.), 9, rte de Genève, ☎ 50.20.01.87. AE, DC, Euro, Visa. 12 rm closed 1-8 Jul, 15 Oct-15 Nov, 9-12 Feb, Tue and Wed noon, 80. Rest. ♦♦ 100-210.

Restaurants :

Grilly, 2 km :

♦♦ ***Auberge de Grilly,*** ☎ 50.20.71.63. closed Sun eve and Mon. Spec : *brioche de foie gras frais, truffe de sole au crépy,* 220-310.

Farmhouse inn : *la Combette,* in Vesancy, 3 km SW, ☎ 50.41.64.17. Spec : *foies gras, confits* and *magrets.*

Col de la FAUCILLE

Geneva 28, Nantua 75, Paris 487
C1 1 000-1 550 m ☒ 01170 Gex

Hotels :

★★***La Couronne,*** ☎ 50.41.32.65. Visa. 23 rm Ⓟ closed 15 Apr-15 May and Nov, 160. Rest. ♦ ♿ 70-140.

★★***Petite Chaumière,*** ☎ 50.41.30.22. Visa. 34 rm + 8 rm (annex) Ⓟ closed May and Oct to mid-Dec, 160. Rest. ♦ 70-170.

FERNEY-VOLTAIRE

Geneva 7, Nantua 54, Paris 508
C1 ☒ 01210

Car-hire : *Budget* train + auto, la Résidence, ☎ 50.40.67.87.

Hotels :

★★★★***Ferney-Genève*** (Frantel), av. du Jura, ☎ 50.40.77.90, Tx 309071. AE, DC, Euro, Visa. 122 rm Ⓟ ♿ 400. Rest. ♦♦ ***le Voltaire*** ♿ 130-300.

★***Bellevue,*** 5, rue Gex, ☎ 50.40.58.68. 12 rm closed 15 Oct-15 Nov, 140. Rest. closed Sat and Sun eve, 40-110.

Restaurant :

♦♦♦ ***Le Pirate,*** av. de Genève, ☎ 50.40.63.52. AE, DC, Euro, Visa. Ⓟ♿ closed 14 Jul-7 Aug, 21 Dec-5 Jan, Mon noon and Sun, 160-300.

FEURS

Saint-Étienne 38, Lyons 68, Paris 431
A2 ☒ 42110

ⓘ pl. Antonin-Drivet, ☎ 77.26.31.52, and château d'Assier, ☎ 77.26.05.27 (summer).

SNCF ☎ 77.26.04.56.

Hotel :

Commerce, 2, rue de la Loire, ☎ 77.26.05.87. AE, Visa. 12 rm Ⓟ closed 1-17 Feb, 1 week end Jun, Tue eve and Wed, 190. Rest. 60-100.

⅄ ★★★*Municipal* (380 pl.), ☎ 77.26.43.41.

Restaurant :

♦♦♦ ***Chapeau Rouge,*** 21, rue de Verdun, ☎ 77.26.02.56. AE, DC, Euro, Visa. Ⓟ ♿

closed 1-8 Jul, Feb school hols, Tue eve and Wed. Spec : *terrine de crustacés, cassolette de ris de veau aux morilles,* 60-170.

Bicycle hire : 3, pl. Geoffroy-Guichard.

FIRMINY

Saint-Étienne 12, Le Puy 66, Paris 531
A3 ✉ 42700

SNCF ☎ 77.56.12.37.

Hotels :
★★★***Firm'Hôtel,*** 37, rue J.-Jaurès, ☎ 77.56.08.99. AE, DC, Euro, Visa. 20 rm, 170. Rest. ♦ closed Sun eve and 1-20 Aug, 50-90.
★★★***Pavillon,*** 4, av. de la Gare, ☎ 77.56.00.45. AE, DC, Euro, Visa. 22 rm Ⓟ 220. Rest. ♦♦ closed Sun eve. Famous cellar, 60-90.

Youth hostel : Le Pertuiset, 5 km NE, ☎ 77.35.72.94.

Restaurants :
♦ ***La Réserve,*** 8, rue de la Gampille, in La Tardive, via the Chaney bridge, ☎ 77.56.01.45. AE, DC, Visa. ♨ ♿ 70-150.

Le Pertuiset, 5 km NE, ✉ 42240 Unieux :
♦♦ ***Verdier-Riffat,*** ☎ 77.35.71.11. AE, DC, Euro, Visa. Ⓟ ♨ ♿ closed Feb, Tue eve and Wed. Spec : *truite farcie,* 60-170.

FLEURIE

Mâcon 21, Lyons 58, Paris 416
B1 ✉ 69820

Restaurant :
♦♦ ***Auberge du Cep,*** ☎ 74.04.10.77. AE, Visa. ♨ closed Dec, Sun eve and Mon low season. Good fare : *mousseline chaude de sandre,* 200-300.

⛺ ★★★*Grappe fleurie* (50 pl.), ☎ 74.69.80.07.

Recommended : *cave coopérative des Grands Vins de Fleurie,* daily, ☎ 74.04.11.70.

GEX

Geneva 17, Nantua 57, Paris 498
C1 ✉ 01170

ℹ rue A.-Reverchon, ☎ 50.41.53.85.

Hotels :
★★***Parc,*** av. des Alpes, ☎ 50.41.50.18. Visa. 20 rm Ⓟ ♨ closed 20 Nov-early Feb, 180. Rest. ♦ ♿ 100-230.
★★***Roseraie,*** 218, rue de Gex-la-Ville, ☎ 50.41.56.44. Euro. 10 rm Ⓟ ♨ closed Sat eve and Sun, 140. Rest. ♦ 90-190.

Échenevex, 4 km S :
● ★★★***Auberge des Chasseurs,*** ☎ 50.41.54.07. 12 rm Ⓟ ♨ ♿ Beautifully furnished. closed 1 Nov-31 Mar, Sun eve and Mon, 220. Rest. ♦♦♦ 90-180.

Thoiry, ✉ 01630 St-Genis-Pouilly, 11 km S :
★★***Motel International,*** ☎ 50.42.02.72. AE, DC, Euro, Visa. 42 rm Ⓟ 165. Rest. ♦ closed Sun eve and Mon noon, 50-120.

Youth hostel : 482, rte de l'Etraz, ☎ 50.41.55.80.

Restaurants :
♦ ***Le Florimont,*** 6 km N, ☎ 50.41.53.34. With 10 rm Ⓟ ♨ closed Oct and Tue, 120-210.

Chevry, 7 km S on the D84 :
♦♦ ***Auberge Gessienne,*** rte Nationale, ☎ 50.41.01.67. closed Sun and Mon, 3 weeks in Feb, 2 weeks in Aug. Delicious cooking in an old converted farmhouse. Spec : *quenelles de brochet, gratin de queues d'écrevisses, gratin dauphinois,* good wines, 80-180.

GIVORS

Vienne 12, Lyons 22, Paris 485
B2 ✉ 69700

SNCF ☎ 78.73.06.46, 78.73.05.48.

Hotels :
★★***Gare,*** 6, pl. Pasteur, ☎ 78.73.02.42. 14 rm Ⓟ closed Sun eve, 150.

Grigny, ✉ 69520, 2 km N :
● ★★★***Les Sources*** (Relais du Silence), 43, rue A.-Sabatier, ☎ 78.73.05.61. AE, Euro, Visa. 10 rm Ⓟ ♨ closed Sun eve and Mon (in winter), 260. Rest. ♦♦ ♿ closed Sun eve and Mon noon in summer, 80-130.

Restaurants :

Loire-sur-Rhône, 4 km SE :
♦♦ ***Camerano,*** 35, rte Nationale, ☎ 78.73.20.07. Euro, Visa. Ⓟ ♨ closed Aug, Sun eve and Mon. Spec : *matelote d'anguille, lavaret à la crème,* 80-150.

St-Romain-en-Gal, ✉ 69560 Ste-Colombe :
♦♦ ***Chez René,*** N86, ☎ 74.53.19.72. AE, DC, Visa. ♿ closed 4-17 Mar, 5-25 Aug, Sun eve and Mon ; open Mon noon nat hols, 75-160.

HAUTEVILLE-LOMPNÈS

Belley 33, Bourg-en-Bresse 52, Paris 479
C1-2 ✉ 01110

850-1 195 m

ℹ mairie, ☎ 74.35.39.73.

Hotels :

Luthézieu, ✉ 01260 Champagne, 15 km SE :
● ★★***Vieux Tilleul,*** ☎ 74.87.64.51. 12 rm Ⓟ ♨ closed Jan, Tue eve and Wed low season, 100. Rest. ♦ Spec : *lavaret à l'oseille, poulet aux écrevisses,* 120-210.

Artemare, ✉ 01510 Virieu, 22 km SE :
★★***Hostellerie du Valroney*** (L.F.), ☎ 74.87.30.10. 30 rm Ⓟ 180. Rest. ♦ 80-130.
★***Jacquier,*** ☎ 79.87.31.60. 24 rm Ⓟ closed 15 Oct-15 Nov, 100. Rest. closed Wed, 80-130.

JASSANS-RIOTTIER

Lyons 35, Bourg-en-Bresse 48, Paris 440
6 km NE of Trévoux, B2 ✉ 01480

Hotels :
★★***La Bonne Auberge,*** ☎ 74.60.95.40. 16 rm Ⓟ closed 1 week in Feb and Sun, 100. Rest. 80-130.
★***Les Sports (Marcel),*** in Fareins, ☎ 74.67.83.60. Visa. 7 rm closed Tue eve, Wed and Oct, 75. Rest. 80-130.

⛺ ★★★***Idéal-Camping*** (400 pl.), ☎ 74.60.95.44.

Restaurant :
♦ ***Auberge Bressanne,*** in Beauregard, ☎ 74.60.93.92. AE, Visa. Ⓟ ♿ closed Tue eve and Wed, and 2 weeks in Nov or Dec, 60-180.

JULIÉNAS

Mâcon 17, Lyons 52, Paris 412
21 km NE of Belleville-sur-Saône, B1 ✉ 69840

Restaurants :
★***Le Coq au Vin,*** ☎ 74.04.41.98. AE, DC, Euro, Visa. 7 rm Ⓟ closed 15 Jan-15 Feb and Wed, 130. Rest. ♦ ♿ 40-100.
★***Chez la Rose*** (L.F.), ☎ 74.04.41.20. Euro. 12 rm Ⓟ closed Tue and 8-16 Jan, 100. Rest. ♦ 70-100.

Recommended : *Wine cellar de la Vieille-Église,* château du Bois-de-la-Salle, ☎ 74.04.42.61 :

beaujolais wines. *Wine cellars du domaine des Brureaux,* ☎ 85.36.72.67. *Cellier du château de Chénas,* ☎ 74.04.11.91.

LAMURE-SUR-AZERGUES

Villefranche 30, Lyons 52, Paris 450
A1 ✉ 69870

SNCF ☎ 74.03.02.80.

Hotels :

★***Commerce,*** ☎ 74.03.05.00. Visa. 10 rm P ♿ closed 1 Jan-3 Mar, Tue eve and Wed, 80. Rest. ♦ closed from Mon to Fri ex Jul-Aug, 50-125.

★***Ravel*** (L.F.), ☎ 74.03.04.72. AE, Visa. 10 rm P closed 5-30 Nov and Fri low season, 120. Rest. ♿ 55-125.

Claveisolles, 5 km N on D9 :
★***Koller,*** ☎ 74.03.07.71. 12 rm P closed 2 Nov-1 Feb and Fri low season, 100. Rest. ♿ 50-100.

Poule-les-Écharmeaux, 10 km N :
★***Nations,*** au col des Écharmeaux, ☎ 74.03.64.85. 20 rm P closed 15 Nov-15 Dec, 100. Rest. ♦ 80-130.

LIMONEST

Villefranche 18, Roanne 78, Paris 454
13 km NW of Lyons, B2 ✉ 69760

Hôtel :

★★***Platane,*** 36, Grande-Rue, ☎ 78.35.12.10. 16 rm closed Sun eve and Mon P 130. Rest. ♿ 60-120.

Restaurant :

♦ ***Puy d'Or*** (L.F.), 25, rte du Puy-d'Or, 3 km S on the D42, ☎ 78.35.12.20. AE, Euro, Visa. With 7 rm P closed 4-30 Oct, Tue eve and Wed, 80-140.

LYONS

Chambéry 98, Grenoble 104, Paris 463
B2 ✉ 69001 to 69009 (arrondissements)

ℹ pl. Bellecour (B4), B.P. 2254, 69214 Lyon Cedex 2, ☎ 78.42.25.75 ; La Part-Dieu, in the station ; in Perrache, exchange centre.

✈ *Satolas* (25 km E), ☎ 78.71.92.21 ; *Lyons-Bron,* ☎ 78.26.81.09. *Air France Agencies,* 10, quai J.-Courmont, 69002, ☎ 78.42.79.00 ; 17, rue V.-Hugo, 69002, ☎ 78.92.48.11, and Satolas airport, ☎ 78.71.96.20.

SNCF Perrache and La Part-Dieu, ☎ 78.92.50.50, 78.92.50.70.

🚌 *Perrache exchange centre,* ☎ 78.42.27.39.

Car-hire : *Budget* train + auto, 11, rue des Émeraudes, 69006, ☎ 78.52.85.57 ; Satolas airport, ☎ 78.71.95.38 ; Perrache station, ☎ 78.37.14.23, and La Part-Dieu station, ☎ 78.33.37.19.

Hotels :

Bellecour-Terreaux quarters (69001 and 69002) :
● ★★★***Royal*** (Mapotel), 20, pl. Bellecour (B4), ☎ 78.37.57.31, Tx 310785. AE, DC, Euro, Visa. 90 rm, 560. Rest. ♦ 80-90.

● ★★★***Carlton,*** 4, rue de Jussieu (C3), ☎ 78.42.56.51, Tx 310787. AE, DC, Euro, Visa. 90 rm, 340.

★★★***Beaux-Arts,*** 75, rue du Pdt-Herriot (B3), ☎ 78.38.09.50, Tx 330442. AE, DC, Euro, Visa. 80 rm, 320.

★★***Moderne,*** 15, rue Dubois (B3), ☎ 78.42.21.83. 31 rm P ♿ 210.

★★***Globe et Cecil*** (Inter-Hôtel), 21, rue Gasparin (B3), ☎ 78.42.58.95, Tx 305184. AE, DC, Visa. 65 rm ♿ 225.

★***Saint-Vincent,*** 9, rue Pareille, ☎ 78.28.67.97. 31 rm closed Sun eve, 140.

Perrache quarter (69002) :
★★★***Terminus-Frantour,*** 12, cours de Verdun (A5), ☎ 78.37.58.11, Tx 330500. AE, DC, Euro, Visa. 140 rm P ♿ 480.

★★★***Tourinter,*** 3, rue M.-A.-Petit, ☎ 78.92.81.61, Tx 380401. AE, DC, Visa. 60 rm P ♿ 320. Rest. ♦ closed Sat and Sun eves in winter and Aug, 120-210.

★★★***Bristol,*** 28, cours de Verdun (B5), ☎ 78.37.56.55, Tx 330584. AE, DC, Euro, Visa. 130 rm ♿ 240.

★★***Savoies,*** 80, rue de la Charité (B5), ☎ 78.37.66.94. 46 rm P ♿ closed 24-31 Dec, 230.

La Part-Dieu (69003) :
★★★★***Frantel,*** 129, rue Servient (E3), ☎ 78.62.94.12, Tx 380088. AE, DC, Euro, Visa. 245 rm P ♿ 500. Rest. ♦♦♦ ***l'Arc-en-ciel,*** closed 13 Jul-19 Aug, Sun and Mon noon, 80-200.

Les Brotteaux (69006) :
★★★***Roosevelt,*** 25, rue Bossuet, ☎ 78.52.35.67, Tx 300295. AE, DC, Euro, Visa. 87 rm P ♿ 300.

★★***Britania,*** 17, rue du Pr.-Weil (E2), ☎ 78.52.86.52. 22 rm P 180.

Préfecture-Guillotière :
★★***Helder,*** 38, rue de Marseille (C5), ☎ 78.72.09.39, Tx 306411. AE, DC, Visa. 120 rm P 220.

Monchat-Montplaisir (69008) :
★★★***Laennec,*** 36, rue Seignemartin, ☎ 78.74.55.22, Tx 310917 Visa. 14 rm P 250.

★★★***Lyon-Est,*** 104, rte de Genas, 69003, ☎ 78.54.64.53. 42 rm P 180.

Saint-Paul quarter (69005):
★★***Phénix,*** 7, quai de Bondy (B2), ☎ 78.28.30.40. AE. 36 rm 220.

Sainte-Foy-lès-Lyons, ✉ 69110, 6 km SW :
★★***Les Provinces,*** 10, pl. Saint-Luc, ☎ 78.25.01.55. 14 rm P 150.

Villeurbanne, ✉ 69100, E and SE suburbs :
★★***Congrès,*** pl. du Cdt-Rivière, ☎ 78.89.81.10, Tx 370216. AE, DC, Euro, Visa. 132 rm P ♿ 225. Rest. ♦ closed Sun, 120-210.

★★***Athéna-Zola,*** 163, cours Émile-Zola, ☎ 78.85.32.33. 100 rm P ♿ 180. Rest. ♦ closed Sat and Sun, 60-120.

★★***Athéna-Tolstoï,*** 90, cours Tolstoï, ☎ 78.68.81.21. Visa. 140 rm P ♿ 170. Rest. ♦ closed Sun, 60-120.

Meyzieu, ✉ 69330, 8 km E of Villeurbanne :
● ★★★***La Régence,*** 35, rue Saulnier, ☎ 78.31.40.04. AE, DC, Visa. 19 rm closed Aug, 240. Rest. 50-160.

★★★***Le Président,*** RN517, ☎ 78.31.52.25, Tx 305857. AE, DC, Euro, Visa. 100 rm, 230. Rest. 80-125.

★★***Le Mont Joyeux*** (L.F.), av. V.-Hugo, ☎ 78.04.21.32. AE, DC, Euro, Visa P ♿ closed Sun eve, 170. Rest. ♦♦ closed 3 Jan-3 Feb, Sun eve and Mon, 60-130.

Bron, ✉ 69500, 10 km E, exits N6 A43 :
★★★***Dau Ly,*** 28, rue de Prévieux, ☎ 78.26.04.37. 22 rm P 230.

Saint-Priest, ✉ 69800, 11 km SE :
★★***Central,*** 18, rue A.-Briand, ☎ 78.20.26.62. 24 rm closed 3 weeks in Aug, 80-140.

Miribel, ✉ 01700, 14 km NE :
★★***Les Délices*** (L.F.), ☎ 78.55.30.53. Euro. 17 rm P 160. Rest. ♦ closed noon from Mon to Sat, Sun eve and Mon in summer, 70-110.

Youth hostels : Vénissieux (2 km), 51, rue Roger-Salengro, ☎ 78.76.39.23, and *Maison des Jeunes*, 101, rue des États-Unis, 69008.

Restaurants :
Town centre :
● ♦♦♦ ***Léon de Lyon*** (J.-P. Lacombe), 1, rue Pleney, 69001 (B2), ☎ 78.28.11.33. Visa. closed 23 Dec-8 Jan, Sun, Mon noon and nat hols. A stop at Jean-Paul Lacombe's is a must. Modern and, of course, Lyonnais cooking which varies according to produce availability. Spec : *filets de rougets sauce au foie du rouget, sauté d'agneau, saladiers de lyonnaiseries, gras double, cervelle de canut.* Nice cellar, Georges Dubœuf Beaujolais, « Mère Richard » cheeses, 130-300.
● ♦♦♦ ***Orsi*** (Relais Gourmand), 3, pl. Kléber (D2), ☎ 78.89.57.68, Tx 305965. AE, DC, Visa ♿ closed Aug, Sun. Fabulous meals served by long-gowned young maidens. The heights of perfection at unbelievably reasonable prices (set menu : 140 F, service included). Specialities : *saumon cru mariné au citron vert, crêpes fourrées aux fraises, coulis de framboises,* 170-250.
● ♦♦♦ ***La Tour Rose,*** 16, rue du Bœuf, 69005 (A3), ☎ 78.37.25.90. AE, DC, Euro, Visa ⚘ closed Sun. Spec : *saumon mi-cuit au fumoir, noisette d'agneau, jardinière d'artichauts liée au foie gras et basilic,* 150-300.
● ♦♦♦ ***Vettard,*** 7, pl. Bellecour (B4), ☎ 78.42.07.59. AE, DC, Visa ♿ closed Sun, 22 Jul-22 Aug. The former French President, Edouard Herriot's favorite « cantine ». J. Vettard has renewed the setting and the cooking. Spec : *paupiette de loup, saumon au beurre de citron,* 170-350.
● ♦♦♦ ***Nandron*** (Relais Gourmand), 26, quai Jean-Moulin (C2), ☎ 78.42.10.26. AE, DC, Euro, Visa ⚘ closed 25 Jul-24 Aug, Feb school hols, Fri eve and Sat. A well-known establishment on the banks of the Rhône River. Classical Lyonnais cooking and more recent creations. Spec : *quenelles de brochet, ris de veau aux truffes,* 150-300.
● ♦♦♦ ***Bourillot,*** 8, pl. des Célestins (B3), ☎ 78.37.38.64. AE, DC, Visa ⛵ ♿ closed Jul, 22 Dec-2 Jan, Sun and nat hols. An excellent price-quality ratio for the cooking of C. Bourillot (M.O.F.). Spec : *rognons de veau aux navets, saumon frais à la fondue d'aubergines,* 120-210.
● ♦♦ ***La Mère Brazier,*** 12, rue Royale, ☎ 78.28.15.49. AE, DC, Visa ♿ closed 27 Jul-25 Aug, Sat noon and Sun. Spec : *quenelle au gratin, fonds d'artichaut au foie gras,* 160-200.
● ♦♦ ***La Voûte (Chez Léa),*** 11, pl. A.-Gourju (B3), ☎ 78.42.01.33. AE, DC ♿ closed 10-28 Jul and Sun, 80-200.
● ♦♦ ***Chez Gervais,*** 42, rue P.-Corneille (D2), ☎ 78.52.19.13. closed Jul, Sat noon, Sun and nat hols. Classical and inventive cooking of Germain Lescuyer. Spec : *gratin d'écrevisses, volailles au vinaigre,* 120-210.
♦♦ ***Le Nord,*** 18, rue Neuve (B2), ☎ 78.28.24.54. AE, DC, Visa. closed Aug, Sat, and Sat and Sun in Jun and Jul, 70-180.
♦♦ ***Tante Alice,*** 22, rue des Remparts-d'Ainay (B4), ☎ 78.37.49.83. AE. closed 20 Jul-25 Aug, 24 Dec-2 Jan, Fri eve and Sat, 60-130.
♦♦ ***Bistrot de Lyon,*** 64, rue Mercière (B3), ☎ 78.37.00.62. Visa. closed 23 Dec-8 Jan and nat hols. 1900's setting, Lyonnais specialities by J.-P. Lacombe and J.-C. Caro, 150-210. Adjacent is ***Bar du Bistrot*** open eves ex Sun.
♦ ***La Tassée,*** 20, rue de la Charité (B4), ☎ 78.37.02.35. DC, Visa ♿ closed 24 Dec-3 Jan and Sun, 80-170.
♦ ***Le Comptoir du Bœuf,*** 3, pl. Neuve Saint-Jean, 69005, ☎ 78.37.25.90. closed Sun. *Tour Rose* wine bistro, 95-130.
♦ ***Chevallier,*** 40, rue du Sergent-Blandan (B2), ☎ 78.28.19.83. Visa ⛵ 28 Aug-26 Sep, 10 days in Feb, Tue and Wed, 75-150.
♦ ***Garet,*** 7, rue Garet (C2), ☎ 78.28.16.94. closed 3-13 Feb, Aug, Sat and Sun, 80-130.

Perrache quarter (brasseries) :
♦♦ ***Alsacienne,*** 20, pl. Carnot (A4-5), ☎ 78.37.44.47 ♿ closed Aug, 70-120.
♦♦ ***La Mère Vittet,*** 26, cours de Verdun (B5), ☎ 78.37.20.17. Open day and night, 120-210.
♦♦ ***Georges,*** 30, cours de Verdun (B5), ☎ 78.37.15.78. AE, DC, Visa. closed 1 May, 70-90.
♦ ***Le Pasteur,*** 83, quai Perrache, ☎ 78.37.01.04. Visa. closed Sat, Sun and Aug. A single menu, but one which changes daily, 80-130.

Left bank of the Saône :
♦♦♦ ***Cazenove,*** 75, rue Boileau, 69006, ☎ 78.89.82.92, Tx 305965. AE, Visa ♿ closed Aug, Sat and Sun, 180-210.
♦♦ ***Pavillon du Parc,*** parc de la Tête-d'Or (E1), ☎ 78.89.56.16. AE, DC, Visa. closed eves and Mon during low season (15 Oct-15 Mar), Sun eve, 1 May and 23-30 Dec, 100-190.
♦♦ ***La Pastourelle,*** 51, rue de la Tête-d'Or (E2), ☎ 78.24.90.89. AE, DC, Visa. closed Aug, Sat noon, Sun and nat hols, 100-150.
♦ ***La Bonne Auberge (Chez Jo),*** 48, av. F.-Faure (E4), ☎ 78.60.00.57. AE, DC, Visa. closed Aug, Sat eve and Sun, 80-120.
♦ ***La Grille*** (A.R.C.), 106, rue S.-Gryphe (C5), ☎ 78.72.46.58 ♿ closed Sat, Sun and 1-28 Aug, 90-130.
♦ ***Marc,*** 12, rue Mazenod (D3-4), ☎ 78.60.05.52, 80-130.
♦ ***Chez Rose,*** 4, rue Rabelais (D3), ☎ 78.60.57.25. AE, DC, Euro, Visa ✈ ♿ closed 2-25 Aug, Sun and nat hols, 90-140.

Right bank of the Saône :
♦♦♦ ***Roger Roucou (Mère Guy),*** 35, quai J.-J.-Rousseau, ☎ 78.51.65.37. AE, DC, Visa 🅿 ♨ ⛵ ♿ closed Aug, Feb school hols, Sun eve and Mon, 160-400.

Tassin-la-Demi-Lune, ⊠ 69160, 2 km E :
♦♦ ***Le Chateaubriand,*** 12, av. Mal-Foch, ☎ 78.34.15.64. AE, DC, Euro, Visa 🅿 ♿ closed Sat, Sun eve, Wed eve, 3 weeks in Aug. Superb, beautifully served dishes in a large house set in parklands, 70-200.

Rillieux-la-Pape, ⊠ 69140, 7 km NE :
● ♦♦ ***Larivoire,*** chemin des Iles, ☎ 78.88.50.92. AE, DC, Visa 🅿 ♨ ♿ closed 1-25 Feb, 1-7 Sep, Mon eve and Tue. The fashionable rendez vous for Lyonnais who do not want to go any great distance. At the stove is B. Constantin, a disciple of Bocuse. Spec : *huîtres chaudes gratinées, fricassée de volaille au vinaigre, gibiers,* 120-220.

Champagne-au-Mont-d'Or, ⊠ 69410, 7 km NW :
● ♦♦ ***Les Grillons,*** 18, rue D.-Vincent, ☎ 78.35.04.78. AE, DC, Euro, Visa 🅿 ♨ ⛵ closed Nov, Sun eve and Mon. Attractive restaurant in a beautiful bourgeois home ; novel dishes. Spec : *mousseline de saumon au coulis de crustacés, gâteau de foies.* A charming stopover, 90-180.

Collonges-au-Mont-d'Or, ⊠ 69660, 12 km N on the D433 and D51 :
● ♦♦♦♦ ***Paul Bocuse,*** ☎ 78.22.01.40. When we ask him, "Who does the cooking when you are away ?" Paul Bocuse replies : "The same people who do it when I am present !" That means Roger Jaloux (M.O.F.), assisted by Christian Bouvarel. What a lively person and what a reply to his detractors. This year he has enlarged his kitchen, bought an IBM 36 and recruited a highly-

talented cook (M.O.F.) as manager. Good Collonges cooking with its classical dishes. Spec : *soupe V.G.E., loup en croûte, poularde en vessie.* Not to forget the "boss's" beaujolais, and "Mère Richard" cheeses, plus the charm of Raymonde Bocuse's discrete efficiency, 220-310.

Mont Cindre, ☒ 69450 St-Cyr-au-Mont-d'Or, 14 km N :
♦♦ ***Ermitage,*** ☎ 78.47.20.96. AE, Euro, Visa ⚟ 🅿 ♧ ⛰ ♿ closed 6 Jan-1 Mar, Tue and Wed, 70-185.

Events : 2nd fortnight in Mar, International Fair, enq : Eurexpo, 69683 Chassier, ☎ 78.22.23.34 ; end May, "curio fair" (bric-à-brac and second-hand goods), in the Saint-Jean quarter, enq : *Renaissance du Vieux-Lyon,* 5, pl. de la Baleine, 69005, ☎ 78.37.16.04. *Grand illuminations of the town :* 8 Dec.

River and canal cruises : visits with commentary : "Lyons between the Saône and Rhône", daily at 9 a.m. and 2 p.m. (duration of the trip, 3 hr), enq : *France Croisières fluviales,* 4, quai Rambaud, 69002, ☎ 78.37.42.66.

Silk manufacture : *Maison des Canuts-Cooptis,* 10, rue d'Ivry (La Croix-Rousse) ; *Bloch-Lazarus,* 54, rue du Pdt-Herriot ; *Clarence,* 24, rue des Archers ; *Nuance,* 4, rue Childebert ; *Moriss,* rue de l'Ancienne-Préfecture.

Shopping, antique dealers : rues Auguste-Comte and Victor-Hugo (between Bellecour and Perrache) ; *Brocante Stalingrad :* 115, bd de Stalingrad, Villeurbanne (daily).

Caterers : *Halles de La Part-Dieu* (all the best shops for foodstuffs). *Le Comptoir du Bœuf,* pl. Neuve-St-Jean, 69005 : dishes and produce with Chavent's label. *Bocuse-Bernachon,* 49, rue de Sèze, 69006.

Cakes and pastries, chocolates : *Bernachon,* 42, cours F.-Roosevelt, 69006. *Casati,* 31, rue Ferrandière, 69002. *Pignol,* 17, rue Emile Zola, 69002, ☎ 78.37.30.67.

Marché de la Création : quai Romain-Rolland, 69005 (every Sun a.m.).

MEXIMIEUX

Bourg-en-Bresse 35, Lyons 39, Paris 454
B2 ☒ 01800

SNCF ☎ 74.61.05.89.

Hotels :
★★★***La Mère Jacquet,*** Pont de Chazey, 3 km E, ☎ 74.61.94.80. Visa. 10 rm 🅿 ♧ 🎾 ♿ closed Dec and Sun eve, Mon, 225. Rest. 110-300.
★★***Claude Lutz*** (L.F.), 17, rue de Lyon, ☎ 74.61.06.78. Visa. 16 rm 🅿 ♧ closed 13 Oct-4 Nov, 1 week in Feb, 15-23 Jul, Sun eve and Mon, 170. Rest. ● ♦♦ Claude Lutz is a disciple of Paul Bocuse, as is immediately apparent. Spec : *civet de turbot au gamay du Bugay, magret de canard aux pommes,* 100-200.

Saint-Maurice-de-Gourdans, ☒ 01800, 10 km S :
● ★★***Relais Saint-Maurice,*** rte de Meximieux, ☎ 74.61.81.45. Visa. 10 rm closed 2 weeks in Sep, 3 weeks in Jan and Sat, 180. Rest. ♦ 60-190.

Restaurant :
Loyettes, ☒ 01980, 16 km S :
● ♦♦ ***Antonin (La Terrasse),*** rte Lt-Delaye, ☎ 74.32.70.13. AE, Visa ⚟ ♿ closed Sun eve and Mon. A rendez vous favoured by the Lyonnais for its cooking of produce fresh from the market. Spec : *petite pêche Bretonne, courgettes frites,* 100-210.

Farmhouse-inn : Saint-Maurice-de-Gourdans, 10 km S, ☎ 74.61.82.44.

MIJOUX

Geneva 37, Nantua 84, Paris 478
C1 ☒ 01410 Chézery Forens

Hotels :
★★***Les Egravines,*** ☎ 50.41.30.65. Visa. 16 rm ⚟ 🅿 ⛰ closed 13 Apr-28 Jun, 1 Sep-20 Dec, 190. Rest. ♦ 70-90.
★★***Vallée et Valserine*** (L.F.), ☎ 50.41.32.13. Visa. 25 rm 🅿 ⛰ ♿ closed 24 Apr-1 Jun and winter, 180. Rest. ♦ 50-120.

Lélex, 8 km S :
● ★★***Crêt de la Neige*** (L.F.), ☎ 50.20.90.15. Euro. 30 rm ⚟ 🅿 ♧ ⛰ ▭ 🎾 closed 15 Apr-29 Jun and winter, 140. Rest. ♦ ✻ ♿ 60-120.

MONTBRISON

Saint-Étienne 36, Lyons 95, Paris 456
A2 ☒ 42600

ℹ pl. de l'Hôtel-de-Ville, ☎ 77.58.20.44.

Hotels :
★★***Lion d'Or*** (L.F.), 14, quai des Eaux-Minérales, ☎ 77.58.34.66. AE, Euro, Visa. 18 rm 🅿 150. Rest. ♦♦ closed Sun eve, 45-60.
★★***L'Escale*** (L.F.), 27, rue de la République, ☎ 77.58.17.77. 18 rm, 180. Rest. ♦ closed Sun. Set menus only, 80-130.

⛺ ★★★*Municipal* (85 pl.), ☎ 77.58.08.30.

MONTLUEL

Lyons 23, Bourg-en-Bresse 44, Paris 471
B2 ☒ 01120

ℹ pl. des Augustins, ☎ 78.06.20.46.

SNCF ☎ 78.58.01.21.

Hotels :
★★***Le Petit Casset,*** La Boisse (3 km), ☎ 78.06.21.33. 11 rm 🅿 ♧ ⛰ ♿ 220.
★★***Chez Nous,*** Sainte-Croix (5 km), ☎ 78.06.17.92. Euro, Visa. 16 rm 🅿 ♧ ⛰ closed 2nd fortnight in Aug, Feb and Fri, Sun, 160. Rest. ♦ 70-180.
★★***Plage,*** rue Neuve, Thil, ☎ 78.06.23.99. Euro, Visa. 15 rm 🅿 ♧ ⛰ closed 10-31 Jan and Fri, 160. Rest. ♿ 60-100.

MONTROND-LES-BAINS

Saint-Étienne 27, Lyons 68, Paris 442
A2 ☒ 42210

⚕ 15 May-1 Oct, ☎ 77.54.40.04.

ℹ mairie, ☎ 77.54.42.77.

SNCF ☎ 77.54.42.65.

Hotel :
★★★***La Poularde*** (Relais Gourmand), ☎ 77.54.40.06. AE, DC, Visa. 14 rm 🅿 closed 2-16 Jan and Mon eve, 320. Rest. ● ♦♦♦ ♿ closed Mon eve and Tue noon. An institution. Solid and good cooking. Spec : *chartreuse de l'océan, beurre aux pistils de safran, lit blanc d'écrevisses au manioc,* 140-300.

Restaurant :
♦♦ ***Le Vieux Logis,*** 4, rte de Lyon, ☎ 77.54.42.71. Visa ♿ closed 2 weeks in Feb, 2 weeks in Jun, Sun eve and Mon. Set menus only, 70-180.

MORNANT

Lyons 23, Saint-Étienne 35, Paris 482
B2 ☒ 69440

Hotels :
★★***Poste*** (L.F.), 5, pl. de la Liberté, ☎ 78.44.00.40. AE, DC, Visa. 12 rm 🅿 ♧ 120.

Rest. ♦ ♿ closed Sun eve and Mon noon, 50-140.

Ste-Catherine, ✉ 69440, 18 km SW on the D63 : ★**Beauséjour** (L.F.), ☎ 78.81.80.83. Visa. 13 rm ♨ ♿ closed Tue, 100. Rest. 50-90.

Restaurant :
Ravel, 4 km E :
♦♦ **Acacias,** ☎ 78.48.73.06. Visa Ⓟ ♨ ♿ closed 15 Jan-15 Feb and Tue. Spec : *soufflé de brochet aux écrevisses.* By reservation only, 90-160.

NANTUA

Bourg-en-Bresse 56, Lyon 96, Paris 483
C1 ✉ 01130

ℹ 2, rue du Dr-Mercier, ☎ 74.76.50.05 (summer).

Hotels :
★★★**France,** 44, rue du Dr-Mercier, ☎ 74.75.00.55. AE, DC, Visa. 19 rm Ⓟ ♨ closed Nov-20 Dec and Fri ex school hols, 280. Rest. ● ♦♦♦ 95-180.
★★**Lyon** (L.F.), 19, rue du Dr-Mercier, ☎ 74.75.17.09. Visa. 18 rm Ⓟ closed 1st fortnight in Jun, Nov, Sun eve (ex Jul-Aug) and Mon, 140. Rest. ♦♦ 70-150.
★★**Lac,** 15, av. de la Gare, ☎ 74.75.00.12. AE, DC, Euro, Visa. 18 rm Ⓟ closed 15 Nov-15 Dec, 130. Rest. ♦ ♿ closed Wed, 70-135.

Saint-Germain-de-Joux, ✉ 01490, 13 km E : ★★**Reygrobellet** (L.F.), ☎ 50.59.81.13. DC, Visa. 10 rm Ⓟ closed 1 Oct-11 Nov, 1 week early Mar, Tue eve and Wed, 180. Rest. ♦ ♿ 70-170.

⛺ ★★★★*Le Signal* (80 pl.), ☎ 74.75.02.09. Saint-Germain-de-Joux, *Municipal* (70 pl.), ☎ 50.59.81.51.

Restaurant :
♦ **Auberge du Lac,** at Lake Génin, ☎ 74.76.08.30. With 5 rm Ⓟ closed Mon and 15 Oct-1 Dec, 120-210.

NOIRÉTABLE

Roanne 47, Saint-Étienne 80, Paris 413
A2 ✉ 42440

ℹ mairie, ☎ 77.24.70.12.

SNCF ☎ 77.24.72.49.

Hotel :
★★**La Chaumière,** rue de la République, ☎ 77.24.73.00. Visa. 28 rm Ⓟ ♨ ♿ closed Nov-15 Mar, 180. Rest. ♦ 50-160.

Restaurant :
Saint-Julien-la-Vêtre, 5 km on the N89 :
♦♦ **L'Aquarium,** ☎ 77.24.90.72 Ⓟ closed Jan and Wed (ex summer), 120-210.

Farmhouse-Inn : *Les Sapins,* Cervières, 5 km N, ☎ 77.24.71.94 : *patcha, truite aux amandes, potée.*

OYONNAX

Nantua 16, Bourg-en-Bresse 49, Paris 476
C1 ✉ 01100

ℹ 83, rue A.-France, ☎ 74.77.20.86.

Hotel :
★★**Buffard** (L.F.), pl. de l'Église, ☎ 74.77.86.01. Euro, Visa. 28 rm Ⓟ ♨ ♿ 150. Rest. ♦ closed mid-Jul-mid-Aug, Fri eve, Sat and Sun eve, 60-100.

Restaurant :
♦♦ **Paris,** 79, rue A.-France, ☎ 74.77.01.50. Visa. closed 31 Jul-25 Aug, 25-28 Dec, 3 days Easter and Sun, 80-170.

PÉROUGES

Bourg-en-Bresse 37, Lyon 39, Paris 455
B2 ✉ 01800 Meximieux

Hotels :
● ★★★★**Host. du Vieux-Pérouges,** pl. du Tilleul, ☎ 74.61.00.88. Visa. 25 rm Ⓟ ♨ closed Wed, Thu noon ex summer, 630. Rest. ♦♦ 125-240.
★★**Relais de la Tour,** ☎ 74.61.01.03. 7 rm. closed Jan-Feb, 180. Rest. ♦ 80-130.

Event : 24 Dec, "lantern procession" and Midnight Mass.

PONT-D'AIN

Bourg-en-Bresse 19, Nantua 35, Paris 446
B1 ✉ 01160

ℹ 17, rue St-Exupéry, ☎ 74.39.05.84 (summer).

Hotel :
★★**Alliés** (L.F.), 1, rue Brillat-Savarin, ☎ 74.39.00.09. Visa. 18 rm Ⓟ closed 16 Dec-15 Jan, 26 May-2 Jun, Thu and Fri noon (ex Jul-Aug and 1-15 Sep), 180. Rest. ♦ 80-120.

⛺ ★★★*Municipal* (250 pl.), ☎ 74.39.05.23.

Restaurant :
♦ **Terminus,** ☎ 74.39.07.17 Ⓟ closed Mon eve and Tue, 40-200.

PONT-DE-VAUX

Mâcon 22, Bourg-en-Bresse 38, Paris 383
B1 ✉ 01190

ℹ 2, rue du Mal-de-Lattre, ☎ 85.37.30.02 (high season).

Hotels :
★★**Commerce,** 5, pl. Joubert, ☎ 85.30.30.56. AE, DC, Euro, Visa. 11 rm Ⓟ closed 24 Nov-18 Dec, Tue and Wed (ex eves low season), 180. Rest. ♦♦ ♿ 80-180.
★★**Raisin,** 2, pl. Michel-Poisat, ☎ 85.30.30.97. AE. 7 rm Ⓟ closed 2 Jan-6 Feb, Sun eve and Mon, 130. Rest. ♦ ♿ 50-130.
★★**Reconnaissance** (L.F.), 9, pl. Gal-Joubert, ☎ 85.30.30.55. Euro, Visa. 11 rm Ⓟ closed 12-26 Oct, 24 Dec-6 Jan, 130. Rest. ♦ ♿ closed Sun eve and Mon low season, 60-160.

⛺ ★★★*Les Peupliers* (160 pl.), ☎ 85.37.31.01.

RENAISON

Roanne 11, Saint-Étienne 89, Paris 383
A1 ✉ 42370

Hotel :
★**Jacques Cœur,** rte de Vichy, ☎ 77.64.25.34. AE, Visa. 10 rm. closed 15 Feb-1 Mar, Sun eve and Mon, 210. Rest. ♦ ♿ 90-210.

Restaurants :
Saint-André-d'Apchon, 2.5 km S on the D8 :
● ♦♦ **Le Lion d'Or,** ☎ 77.65.81.53. With 6 rm. closed 16-30 Jul, Jan, Sun eve and Mon. Original inventions from a chef trained by Bocuse and Alain Chapel. Spec : *goujonnette de sole au piment doux,* 120-210.

Saint-Alban-les-Eaux, 5 km S :
♦ **Saint-Albanais,** ☎ 77.65.84.23 ♿ closed 28 Jul-15 Aug and Wed, 80-140.

RIVE-DE-GIER

Saint-Étienne 22, Lyons 37, Paris 500
B2-3 ✉ 42800

SNCF ☎ 77.75.00.20.

Hotels :
★★★***Hostellerie la Renaissance*** (Relais et Châteaux), 41, rue A.-Marel, ☎ 77.75.04.31, Tx 370241. AE, DC, Euro, Visa. 10 rm Ⓟ closed 15 days in Feb, Sun eve and Mon low season, 240. Rest. ● ♦♦♦ Spec : *biscuit de rascasse et rouget, choux farci au beurre de caviar,* 150-400.

Restaurant :
Génilac :
♦♦ ***Au Feu de Bois,*** Le Sardon, ☎ 77.75.61.70. Visa. With 11 rm Ⓟ closed Sat and end-of-year hols, 10-31 Aug, 40-120.

ROANNE

Vichy 74, Lyons 86, Paris 392
A1 ⊠ 42300
ℹ cours de la République, ☎ 77.71.51.77 and 77.71.42.48.

✈ Roanne-St-léger, ☎ 77.68.83.55.

SNCF ☎77.71.11.46., 77.71.25.01.

🚌 ☎ 77.72.28.66.

Car-hire : *Budget* train + auto, at the station, ☎ 77.71.42.14.

Hotels :
★★★★***Frères Troisgros*** (Relais et Châteaux, Relais Gourmand), pl. de la Gare, ☎ 77.71.66.97, Tx 307507. AE, DC, Visa. 24 rm Ⓟ ♿ closed 4-20 Aug, Jan, Tue and Wed noon, 600. Rest. ● ♦♦♦♦ Pierre Troisgros and his son Michel are "fighters". The "duo" is perfectly experienced. The young team works a lot and a visit to their ultra-modern kitchen is a must. Nice cellar with large choice of Bourgogne wines. Shop. Pleasant bar. Spec : *salade de bulots aux haricots verts à la crème, foie gras à la rhubarbe sauce caline,* 190-350.
★★★***Grand-Hôtel*** (Inter-Hôtel), 18, cours de la République, ☎ 77.71.48.82, Tx 300573. AE, DC, Euro, Visa. 48 rm Ⓟ ♿ closed 22 Dec-3 Jan, 220.

Le Coteau, ⊠ 42120, right bank :
★★***Artaud*** (L.F., Inter-Hôtel), 133, av. de la Libération, ☎ 77.68.46.44, Tx 900394. Euro, Visa. 18 rm Ⓟ closed Sun, 150. Rest. ♦♦ closed 5-25 Jul and Sun ex nat hols. Spec : *marquise de fruits de mer aux pâtes fraîches, gigot de poulette farçi cuit en papillote et ses mousselines,* 60-200.
★★***Terminus,*** 15, cours de la République, ☎ 77.71.79.69. 51 rm Ⓟ ♿ 185.
★★***Central,*** 20, cours de la République, ☎ 77.71.65.88. AE, Visa. 32 rm ♿ closed Sun eve and end-of-year hols, 160.

Riorges, ⊠ 43640, 3 km W on the D31 :
★★***Le Marcassin,*** rue Jean-Plasse, ☎ 77.71.30.18. Visa. 10 rm Ⓟ closed 1-22 Aug, Feb school hols and Sat, 150. Rest. ● ♦♦♦ ♿ closed Sun low season, 90-180.

St-Germain-Lespinasse, ⊠ 42640, 12 km NW :
★★★***Relais de Roanne,*** RN7, ☎ 77.71.97.35. AE, DC, Visa. 30 rm Ⓟ ♿ 190. Rest. ● ♦♦ closed 2-29 Jan, 70-180.

Lentigny, ⊠ 42155, 9 km SW on the D53 :
★★★***Ferme Napoléon,*** Le Ruizor, ☎ 77.63.11.11. Visa. 7 rm Ⓟ closed Sun eve and Mon, 200. Rest. ♦♦♦ ♿ 160-340.

L'Hôpital-sur-Rhins, ⊠ 42132 St-Cyr-de-Favières, 10 km S on D43 :
★★***Favières*** (L.F.), ☎ 77.64.80.30. Visa. 16 rm Ⓟ closed Jan and 15 Aug, Fri eve and Sat, 160. Rest. ♦♦ Interesting recommended meals at reasonable set-prices, 90-170.

Youth hostel, rue Chassain-de-la-Plaise, ☎ 77.68.09.79.

⛺ ★★★*Municipal* (80 pl.), ☎ 77.31.12.82.

Restaurants :
● ♦♦ ***Côté Jardin,*** 10, rue B.-Malon, ☎ 77.72.81.88. Visa ♿ closed Sat noon and Sun, 1 week in Jan. Near the hôtel de ville, a restaurant inspired by the example of its famous neighbours, the Troisgros brothers ; excellent quality at reasonable prices. Spec : *cassolette d'escargots et d'œufs de caille, soufflé d'oursins et St-Jacques à la coque, filet de magret de canard au beurre d'orange,* 70-120.
♦♦ ***L'Astrée,*** 17 *bis,* cours de la République, ☎ 77.72.74.22. AE, DC, Visa Ⓟ ♿ closed Sat noon and Sun, 18-31 Aug, 23 Dec-6 Jan. Spec : *boudin d'écrevisses, saumon fumé,* 80-130.
♦♦ ***Taverne Alsacienne,*** pl. de la Paix, ☎ 77.71.21.14. closed mid Apr-mid May, Oct and Mon, 80-130.
♦♦ ***L'Escargot,*** 12, rue A.-France, ☎ 77.71.30.75. Visa. closed Mon and Aug, 40-100.

Le Coteau, ⊠ 42120, right bank :
● ♦♦♦ ***Auberge Costelloise,*** 2, av. de la Libération, ☎ 77.68.12.71. closed 20 Jul-20 Aug, Sun eve and Mon. Daniel Alex's good cooking, reasonable prices, 80-200.

Recommended : *Pralus,* chocolate-confectioner, 8, rue Ch.-de-Gaulle.

ROCHETAILLÉE-SUR-SAÔNE

Lyons 15, Villefranche 22, Paris 455
B2 ⊠ 69270 Fontaines-sur-Saône

Hotels :
★***Paris*** (L.F.), 2, rue Henri-Bouchard, ☎ 78.22.33.62. 10 rm Ⓟ 180. Rest. ♦♦ ♿ Spec : *quenelles aux fruits de mer,* 120-210.

Couzan-au-Mont-d'Or, right bank :
★***Tonnelles,*** 26, rue Gabriel-Péri, ☎ 78.22.17.05. 8 rm Ⓟ closed Wed, 100. Rest. ♦ 80-130.

Fontaines-sur-Saône, left bank :
★***Terrasse,*** 12, quai Simon, ☎ 78.22.36.86. 11 rm Ⓟ 180. Rest. closed 2 weeks in Aug, 120-210.

Restaurant :
Albigny-sur-Saône, ⊠ 69250 Nevelle, right bank :
♦ ***Les Isles,*** 1, av. Gal-de-Gaulle, ☎ 78.91.30.88 Ⓟ ♿ closed Wed (Sep-Jul). Spec : game (in season), *lotte à l'armoricaine,* 60-140.

SAIL-LES-BAINS

Vichy 44, Saint-Étienne 110, Paris 367
35 km NW of Roanne, A1
⊠ 42310 La Pacaudière

⚕ mid May-Sep, ☎ 77.64.30.81.

Hotel :
● ★★ ***Grand-Hôtel,*** in the spa park-grounds, ☎ 77.64.30.81. AE. 32 rm Ⓟ closed Sep-May, 220. Rest. ♦ 50-120.

⛺ ★★*Municipal* (70 pl.), ☎ 77.64.30.85.

SAINT-ANDRÉ-DE-CORCY

Lyons 24, Bourg-en-Bresse 38, Paris 456
13 km E of Trévoux, B2 ⊠ 01390

SNCF ☎ 78.81.11.62.

Hotels :
St-Marcel, 3 km N :
★★★***Manoir des Dombes,*** ☎ 78.81.13.37. AE, DC, Visa. 18 rm Ⓟ 300.

Mionnay, 4 km S :
★★★★(L) ***Alain Chapel*** (Relais et Châteaux), ☎ 78.91.82.02, Tx 305605. AE, DC. 13 rm Ⓟ

closed Jan and Mon ex nat hols, 750. Rest. ● ♦♦♦♦ closed Mon and Tue noon ex nat hols. Alain Chapel's creative talent for preparation brillantly executed every day. His team is experienced, the cooking excellent. One cannot discuss it, just enjoy it religiously, 300-420.

Echets, ✉ 01700, 7 km S :
★★★★***Douillé,*** RN83, ☎ 78.91.80.05. Visa. 8 rm Ⓟ closed 5-29 Aug, 4-16 Feb, Mon eve and Tue, 300. Rest. ♦♦♦ Spec : *fricassée de volaille à la crème, assiette du pêcheur*, 130-250.
★★★***Le Sarto,*** RN83, ☎ 78.91.90.02, Tx 305141. AE, DC, Euro, Visa. 13 rm Ⓟ ♿ closed Sun eve and Mon, 190. Rest. ♦♦♦ closed Sun eve and Mon eve, 100-200.
★★***Marguin*** (L.F.), rte de Strasbourg, ☎ 78.91.80.04. AE, DC, Visa. 9 rm Ⓟ closed 2-16 Jan, 1-15 Sep, Tue eve and Wed, 160. Rest. ● ♦♦♦ ♿ A fortunate apprentice of Bocuse, Jacques Marguin cooks with talent and the assistance of his wife. Spec : *pintadeau citron vert, poulet à la crème*. A fine and extensive cellar of burgundies, 110-220.

SAINT-CHAMOND

Saint-Étienne 12, Lyon 47, Paris 510
A2-3 ✉ 42400

SNCF ☎ 77.22.02.28.

Hotels :
★★***Ambassadeurs,*** 28, av. de la Libération, ☎ 77.22.02.80. 19 rm, 180. Rest. ♦ 80-130.
★***Chemin de fer,*** 27, av. de la Libération, ☎ 77.22.00.15. 11 rm closed Aug. Rest. ♦ closed Sat eve and Sun eve, 120-210.
★***Lion d'Or,*** bd Delay, ☎ 77.22.01.38. 15 rm Ⓟ closed Sat, Sun eve and Mon, 180. Rest. ♦ 120-210.

L'Horme, ✉ 42152 :
★★***Vulcain,*** rue du Puits-Gillier, ☎ 77.22.17.11, Tx 370425. AE, Visa. 30 rm Ⓟ ♿ 205.

Farmhouse-inn : *les Grillons*, St-Paul-en-Jarez, ☎ 77.22.25.19. Spec : *soufflé de foies de volaille aux quenelles, gratin maison.*

SAINT-ÉTIENNE

Lyons 59, Le Puy 78, Paris 522
A2-3 ✉ 42000

ℹ 12, rue Gérenter (B2), ☎ 77.25.12.14 ; 5, pl. Jean-Jaurès, ☎ 77.33.15.39.

✈ 15 km NW, ☎ 77.55.03.91 and 77.36.54.79.

SNCF ☎77.37.50.50, 77.32.43.79.

Car-hire : *Budget* train + auto, at the station, ☎ 77.33.03.94, and at the airport.

Hotels :
★★★★***Grand-Hôtel,*** 10, av. de la Libération (B-C2), ☎ 77.32.99.77, Tx 300811. AE, DC, Euro, Visa. 44 rm ♿ 500. Rest. ♦♦♦ ***Gillet,*** ☎ 77.32.04.90, 120-210.
★★★***Terminus du Forez,*** 31, av. Denfert-Rochereau (C2), ☎ 77.32.48.47, Tx 330683. AE, DC, Euro, Visa. 66 rm Ⓟ 180. Rest. ♦ closed Sun, 70-130.
★★★***Astoria,*** rue H.-Dechaud (not on the C3 map), ☎ 77.25.09.56, Tx 330949. AE, DC, Euro, Visa. 33 rm Ⓟ 210.
★★***Cheval Noir,*** 11, rue Gillet (B2), ☎ 77.33.41.72. AE, DC, Euro, Visa. 46 rm closed 4-25 Aug, 130.
★★***Touring Continental,*** 10, rue F.-Gillet (B2), ☎ 77.32.58.43. 25 rm Ⓟ closed 20 Jul-20 Aug, 140.

Restaurants :
● ♦♦ ***Pierre Gagnaire,*** 3, rue G.-Teissier, ☎ 77.37.57.93. AE, DC, Visa ♿ closed 9 Aug-9 Sep, Feb school hols, Sun and Mon noon. Pierre Gagnaire deserves being part of our jury. His remarkable cooking is making him more and more famous. To make your gourmand feast perfect, choose among the dishes inspired by market-fresh produce. Spec : *marinade de thon blanc, rougets de roche, fricassée de homard aux champignons sylvestres, confit de lièvre à l'Hermitage.* Wide choice of gourmand desserts. A "hi-tech" setting and a stylish service, 145-310.
♦♦ ***Le Chantecler,*** 5, cours Fauriel (not on the C3 map), ☎ 77.25.48.55. AE, DC, Euro. closed Aug, Sat and Sun, 75-150.

Saint-Priest-en-Jarez (4 km N) :
♦♦♦ ***Le Clos Fleuri,*** 76, av. A.-Raimond, ☎ 77.74.63.24. AE, DC, Visa Ⓟ ♿ closed Sun eve and Mon, 95-220.

Guided tours : enq C.D.T. and ℹ

Recommended : *Weiss*, chocolate confectioner, 18, av. Denfert-Rochereau ; *Chocolaterie des Princes*, 23, rue de la République.

SAINT-GALMIER

Saint-Étienne 22, Lyons 60, Paris 452
A2 ✉ 42330

ℹ av. G.-Cousin, ☎ 77.54.06.08 (high season), and mairie, ☎ 77.54.00.05.

SNCF ☎ 77.56.61.34.

Hotel :
★***Voyageurs,*** pl. de l'Hôtel-de-Ville, ☎ 77.54.00.25. 12 rm Ⓟ closed 16 Dec-16 Jan, 1-15 Aug and Fri eve, Sat, 100. Rest. 80-130.

Restaurants :
♦♦ ***Auberge du Parc,*** bd du Dr-Cousin, ☎ 77.54.01.57. closed Wed, 120-210.
♦ ***Poste,*** 31, rue Nationale, ☎ 77.54.00.30. closed 2nd fortnight in Jul, mid-Jan-mid-Feb, Wed eve and Thu, 120-210.

SAINT-JUST-EN-CHEVALET

Roanne 30, Saint-Étienne 80, Paris 326
18 km NE of Noirétable, A2 ✉ 42430

ℹ mairie, ☎ 77.65.00.62.

Hotel :
★***Poste*** (L.F.), ☎ 77.65.01.42. 15 rm Ⓟ closed Tue low season, 100. Rest. ♦ 120-210.

⛺ ★★*Municipal* (70 pl.), ☎ 77.65.00.62.

SALLES-EN-BEAUJOLAIS

Mâcon 38, Lyons 42, Paris 443
11.5 km NW of Villefranche, B1-2
✉ 69830 St-Georges-de-Reneins

Hotel :
★★★***Host. Saint-Vincent,*** ☎ 74.67.55.50. AE, DC, Visa. 28 rm Ⓟ ♿ 180. Rest. ♦ 90-160.

Restaurants :
♦♦ ***La Benoîte,*** ☎ 74.67.52.93. Euro Ⓟ closed 15-31 Jul, 15 days in Feb, and Wed, 50-120.

Blaceret, 2 km E :
♦♦ ***Le Beaujolais,*** ☎ 74.67.54.75. AE, DC, Euro, Visa. closed Feb, 1-7 Oct, Mon and Tue, 80-140.

Recommended : Beaujolais wine-tasting : *la Tassée du Chapitre.*

SEYSSEL

Belley 30, Annecy 39, Paris 530
C1-2 ✉ 01420

ℹ mairie, ☎ 50.59.26.56 (summer).

Hotel :
★★***Rhône*** (L.F.), quai du Gal-de-Gaulle, ☎ 50.59.20.30. AE, DC, Euro, Visa. 15 rm ⚟ Ⓟ closed 15 Nov-15 Feb, Sun eve and Mon noon low season, 240. Rest. ♦♦ ***Herbelot,*** 90-240.

Recommended : *Clerc et Varichon,* ☎ 50.59.23.15 : wine-tasting and sales, visits on request.

TARARE

Roanne 43, Lyons 43, Paris 468
A2 ⊠ 69170

ⓘ 6, pl. de la Madeleine, ☎ 74.63.06.65.

SNCF ☎ 74.63.01.81.

Hotels :
★★***Europe*** (L.F.), 17, rue de la République, ☎ 74.63.02.81. 20 rm Ⓟ closed 30 Sep-1 Nov, Sun eve and Mon, 100. Rest. ♦ 80-130.
★★***Git'otel*** (L.F.), RN7, ☎ 74.63.44.01. AE, DC, Euro, Visa. 33 rm ⚟ Ⓟ ♿ 190. Rest. ♦♦ ***Auberge de la Grange Cléat.*** closed Sun, 40-100.
★★***Chez la Mère Paule,*** 2 km W, ☎ 74.63.14.57. Visa. 14 rm Ⓟ closed 1-23 Sep, Feb school hols, Tue eve and Wed, 130. Rest. ♦ ♿ 50-150.

Pontcharra-sur-Turdine, ⊠ 69490, 5.5 km E :
★★***France,*** 27, rue Michelet, ☎ 74.63.72.97. 12 rm Ⓟ ♿ closed Wed low season and Nov, 180. Rest. 80-130.

⛺ ★★★*Municipal* (40 pl.), ☎ 74.63.26.80.

Restaurant :
● ♦♦ ***Jean Brouilly,*** ☎ 74.63.24.56. With 10 rm Ⓟ ꙮ closed 8-23 Aug, Sun and Mon. Spec : *huîtres en homardière, ris de veau braisé aux poivrons,* 120-210.

THIZY

Roanne 22, Lyons 70, Paris 414
A1 ⊠ 69240

ⓘ 28, rue Jean-Jaurès, ☎ 74.64.03.84.

Hotel :
★★***La Musardière*** (L.F.), 12, rue du Bois-Semé, ☎ 74.64.03.15. 10 rm Ⓟ ꙮ ♿ closed Sun eve and Mon noon, 180. Rest. ♦ 80-130.

TRÉVOUX

Lyons 28, Bourg-en-Bresse 51, Paris 448
B2 ⊠ 01600

ⓘ 26, Grande-Rue, ☎ 74.00.17.46.

SNCF ☎ 74.00.08.18.

Restaurant :
♦ ***Gare*** (L.F.), ☎ 74.00.12.42. With 7 rm ꙮ closed Jul, Mon eve and Tue, 80-130.

⛺ ★★★*La Petite Saône* (200 pl.), ☎ 74.00.14.16.

VILLARS-LES-DOMBES

Bourg-en-Bresse 28, Lyons 34, Paris 365
B1 ❤ ⊠ 01330

ⓘ ☎ 74.98.06.29 (high season).

SNCF ☎ 74.98.04.32.

⛺ ★★★ *Les Autières* (240 pl.), ☎ 74.98.00.21.

Restaurants :
♦ ***Le Col Vert,*** rue du Commerce, ☎ 74.98.00.33. AE, DC, Euro, Visa. closed Sun eve and Mon, 60-130.
♦ ***Tour,*** pl. du Nord, ☎ 74.98.03.21. Euro, Visa closed All Saints' Day, Feb school hols, Tue eve and Wed, 70-120.

Bouligneux, 4 km :
● ♦♦ ***Auberge des Chasseurs,*** ☎ 74.98.10.02. Visa. Ⓟ ꙮ ♿ closed 2 weeks in Aug, Feb, Tue eve and Wed, 140-210.

Maison de l'artisanat et du tourisme de l'Ain (at the entrance to the bird sanctuary), ☎ 74.98.05.90.

VILLEFRANCHE-SUR-SAÔNE

Lyons 31, Mâcon 41, Paris 436
B1-2 ⊠ 69400

ⓘ 290, rue de Thizy, ☎ 74.68.05.18. *Union Interprofessionnelle des Vins du Beaujolais,* 210, bd Vermorel, ☎ 74.65.45.55 : for all enq concerning the vineyards, wines and tasting facilities.

SNCF 113, pl. de la Gare, ☎ 74.65.27.16.

Hotels :
★★★***Plaisance,*** 96, av. de la Libération, ☎ 74.65.33.52, Tx 340777. AE, DC, Euro, Visa. 68 rm Ⓟ ♿ 24 Dec-2 Jan, 240. Rest. ♦♦ ***Fontaine Bleue.*** closed Sun low season, 120-210.
★★***Paris-Nice,*** 573, rte d'Anse, ☎ 74.65.36.95. 12 rm Ⓟ closed 15 Dec-15 Jan and Sun, 120.

Chervinges, 3 km E :
★★★★***Château de Chervinges*** (Châteaux-Hôtels), ☎ 74.65.29.76, Tx 380772. AE, DC, Visa. ⚟ Ⓟ ꙮ 750. Rest. ♦♦ closed Sun eve and Mon, 140-250.

⛺ ★★★*Municipal* (125 pl.), ☎ 74.65.33.48.

Restaurants :
♦♦♦ ***Auberge du Faisan Doré,*** Le Pont-de-Beauregard, 2 km N, ☎ 74.65.01.66. Ⓟ ꙮ closed Aug, Sun eve and Mon, 120-210.

Farmhouse-inn : *la Bicheronne,* Fareins, 7 km NE, ☎ 74.67.81.01 : *tarte au fromage, poulet à la crème.*

Guided tours : the Beaujolais regions, in summer, enq : ⓘ

VONNAS

Mâcon 19, Lyons 66, Paris 412
24 km W of Bourg, B1 ❤ ⊠ 01540

Hotel :
● ★★★★*Georges Blanc* (Relais et Châteaux ; formerly *la Mère Blanc ;* L.F.), ☎ 74.50.00.10, Tx 380776. AE, DC, Visa. 31 rm Ⓟ ꙮ ♿ closed 2 Jan-10 Feb, 400. Rest. ● ♦♦♦♦ closed Wed and Thu, open Thu eve high season. Every year, a few new details are added to improve the comfort of this small paradise. The cellar can be seen from the dining-room : the competent Georges Blanc is always bettering the quality of his regional and light dishes. Spec : *bar à la marinière, poulet au vinaigre, grenouilles des Dombes,* superb cellar. Flower bouquets made by Jacqueline Blanc. Nearby home products shop, 210-360.

⛺ ★★★★*Municipal* (50 pl.), ☎ 74.50.02.75.

YZERON

Lyons 28, Saint-Étienne 52, Paris 483
A-B2 ⊠ 69510 Thurins

ⓘ ☎ 78.81.01.52 (high season).

Hotels :
★***Cheval Blanc*** (L.F.), ☎ 78.81.02.63. 12 rm Ⓟ ꙮ closed Nov, Tue eve and Wed, 180. Rest. ♦♦ 120-210.

Saint-Martin-en-Haut, ⊠ 69850, 8 km SW :
★***Soleil,*** ☎ 78.48.60.05. 10 rm, 100. Rest. 80-130.

The Maine and Anjou Regions

Unlike their counterparts in Touraine, the stately manors and châteaux of the Anjou region have deserted the banks of the River Loire to hide away instead in the countryside around Angers, in romantic parks or melancholy splendor beside the region's tiny lakes. At the palace of Lude on summer evenings, jousting matches, pavanes and minuets illuminated by a thousand lights bring the past to life again; during the day the tourist can confirm Maine's claim to possess the largest number of inhabited châteaux and manor houses in France, as he peers down country lanes to discover signs of life.

But alongside this past full of historical associations and imaginary deeds of valor, there is another more concrete reality — the countryside itself and its regional differences : the Loire Valley full of orchards and flower gardens, the sunny charm of local vineyards and dark brooding stretches of mushroom beds. The vineyards of Layon produce wine as mild as the landscape itself, before giving way to the bristling hedgerows and narrow paths of Mauges and Le Choletais where Royalist and Republican armies laid bloody ambushes for each other in the days of the Revolution. Further on is the Vendée, a landscape of heather and gorse, alternating with rich meadowland and peacefully grazing herds of cattle.

The town of Angers on the Maine river is famous for its produce market — fruit, vegetables and local wine — and boasts possession of the Apocalypse tapestry, woven between 1373 and 1380, as well as a museum displaying its modern counterpart, Jean Lurçat's Song of the World, woven from the master's sketches between 1957 and 1966.

To the North, between Brittany and Normandy, the Maine region has all the charm of the traditional French countryside : thick groves alternating with wheat fields and dark pine forests. Black and white cows and plump piglets forage peacefully in the shade of apple trees in bloom. With its signposted tracks and country roads, and its miles of tranquil waterways and locks, Maine is perfect for tourists who are allergic to crowds.

Sightseeing

Facts and figures

***Location** : in western France, Anjou is joined to the Armorican Massif to the West ("Anjou Noir", or Black Anjou) and the Parisian Basin in the East ("Anjou Blanc", or White Anjou, and the Vale of Anjou). A distinction is also made between Bas (lower) Maine with its heavy Armorican soil, and Haut (upper) Maine, with its lighter soil more typical of the Parisian Basin.*

***Area** : Anjou : 7218 km²; Maine : 11456 km².*

***Population :** 1451873 inhabitants.*

***Climate** : The Vale (Val) of Anjou has an especially warm, dry climate, ideal for delicate crops. Mediterranean plants, such as magnolias and palm trees are to be found here. Maine has a somewhat harsher, moist climate.*

***Administration :** Department of **Maine-et-Loire,** Prefecture Angers. Department of **Mayenne,** Prefecture Laval. Department of **Sarthe,** Prefecture Le Mans.*

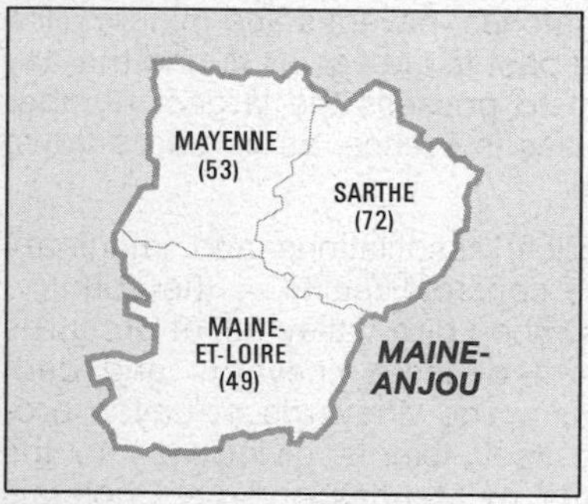

Don't miss

★★★ : Angers (A3), Fontevraud (B4), Le Mans (B2), Saumur (B3).

★★ : Bercé Forest and valley of the Loir (C2), Corniche Angevine (A3), Évron (B1), Le Plessis Bourré (A2-3), Sainte-Suzanne (B1).

■ The **ALPES MANCELLES★**

▶ From Saint-Léonard-des-Bois to Mont des Avaloirs *(20 km, 2 hr).*

B1

The "Alpes Mancelles" turn out to be a mountain area, not very extensive, but wild and charming. Here the Sarthe meanders

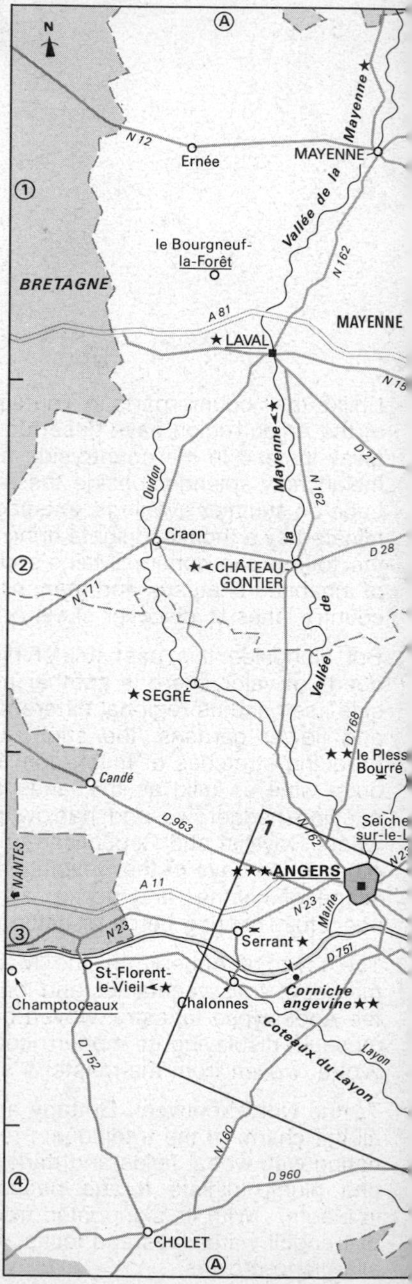

at its pleasure through deep granite gorges amid gorse and broom.

▶ **Saint-Léonard-des-Bois★** ® *(20 km SW from Alençon → Normandy;* pop. 512) : overlooked by rocky escarpments, on a bend in the river; numerous walks (GR 36 & 36A), especially in the **Vallée de Misère★** *(1hr45 on foot round trip).* ▶ **Saint-Céneri-le-Gérlei★** *(D146, 5 km N),* equally appealing with its old bridge and older Romanesque church (14thC fresco★). ▶ **Mont des Avaloirs★** *(D144 for 12.5 km then 2 km right)* : highest point in the west of France (alt. 417 m); view★★. ▶ A worthwhile complement to this walk is the **Corniche du Pail★** *(leave from Pré-en-Pail ®, 5 km NW of Mont des Avaloirs),* through the valley of the Mayenne, with views of the Normandy hills. □

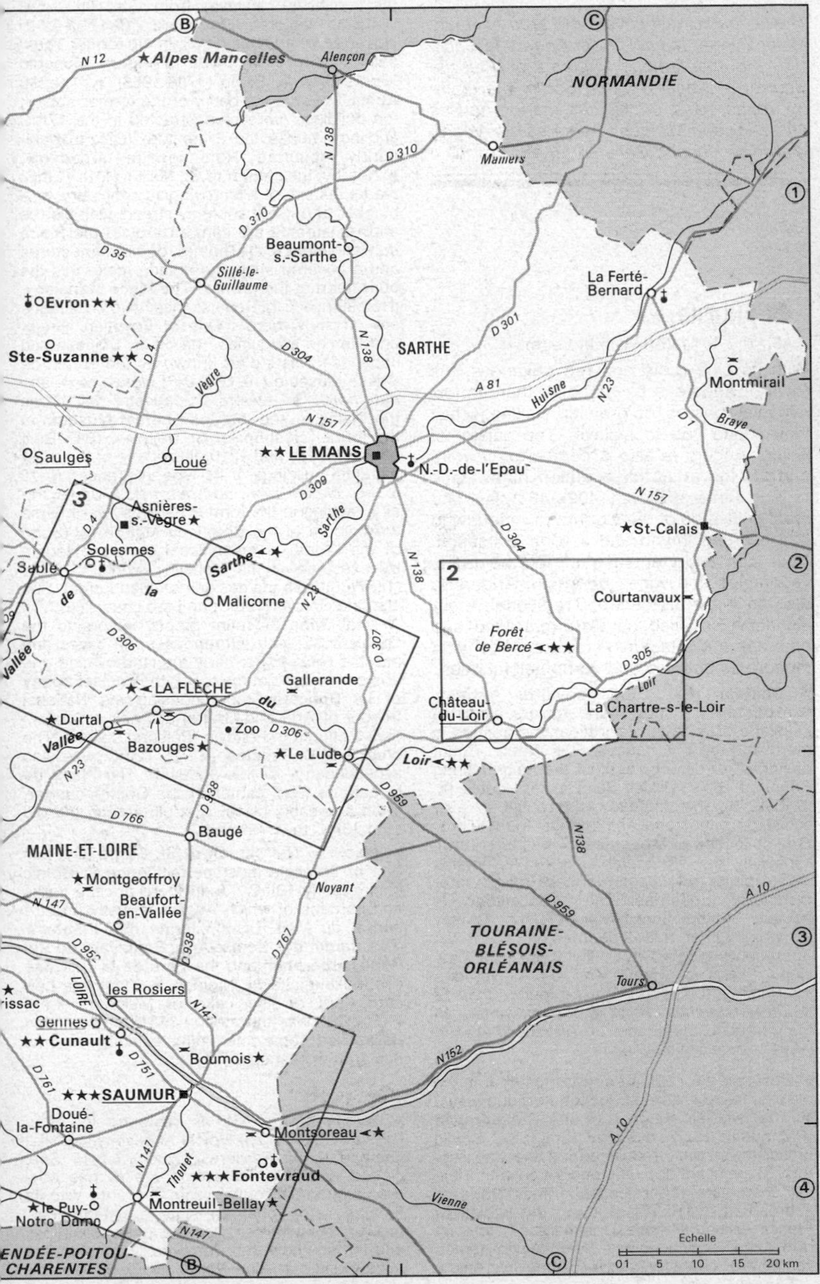

Weekend tips

From Angers there are two outstanding tours which take in most of the region. The first (the Loire and the Coteaux de Layon) takes you up the Loire to the white town of Montsoreau, a good place for lunch before going on to Fontevraud and Montreuil-Bellay along the minor roads of the Layon valley.

The second circuit covers the area of Haute Maine (Upper Maine); from Angers to Sablé (→), via the famous château of Plessis-Bourré (→ Angers). From Sablé, the country roads pass by hidden manor houses and secluded villages; Asnières-sur-Vègre, Malicorne (lunch), Gallerande, etc.

■ ANGERS★★★

A3 / ® / 141 143 (Maine-et-Loire)

With its blue roofs and red chimneys, the town of Angers is far friendlier than its formidable fortress of grey crystalline schist would lead you to believe. The capital of Anjou, Angers is also a centre for flowers and for the arts; this tradition dates back to King René of Sicily (1409-1480), last and most cultivated of the Counts of Anjou, who had a green thumb and a wide education. Today an important market for the fruits, vegetables and wines of Anjou, Angers is also an industrial centre. Traditional Angevin activities such as slate-quarrying and umbrella manufacture now co-exist with modern electronics and computer facilities.

▶ **Château** (B2) : This powerful fortress, flanked with 17 huge round towers, was the keystone of a chain of fortifications erected in the 11thC by the famous Fulk Nerra, Count of Anjou, for defence against the neighbouring Count of Blois. Under Saint Louis (Louis IX, 1215-1270), the château was rebuilt in grey schist on sandstone and granite foundations. **Fine collection of tapestries★★★** (14th-17thC), especially the **"Apocalypse"★★★,** a notable masterpiece which influenced many later mediaeval tapestries. The "Apocalypse" is housed in the specially-built Long Gallery (→ box). Other fine tapestries in the Royal Apartments (Logis Royal; Tenture de la Passion★ , end of 15thC) and the Governor's Apartments (Logis du Gouverneur); *(9:30-12 & 2-6 in summer, 10-12 & 2-5 in winter).* In the courtyard the chapel of Yolande d'Aragon (15thC, Angevin vaulting★). □

▶ Between the château and the cathedral, the old city; narrow, quiet streets, stately doorways. ▶ The two tall steeples of the **Cathedral of St. Maurice** (B-C2; beautiful 12th-13thC Gothic architecture) were rebuilt during the last century. Magnificent doorway decorated with Biblical characters (door leaves 17thC) leads to a broad nave (16.38m across, the widest of French cathedral naves), illuminated, left, by rare 12thC stained glass. The heavily-domed vaults are characteristic of Angevin (Anjou) architecture. An astonishing St. Christopher with a dog's head can be made out in the superb stained glass of the choir (13thC); rich treasure-room *(apply to the sacristan; closed Tue.).* ▶ Small sculpted figures decorate the **Maison d'Adam** (C2), a charming 15thC bourgeois house. ▶ The **Logis Louis Barrault** dates from the same period; Caesar Borgia (15thC - son of Pope Alexander VI) and Marie de Médicis (Henri IV's queen, 1573-1642) stayed here. Today it houses a **Fine Arts Museum;** works of the primitives, canvases from 17th-18thC incl. Watteau, Lancret, Fragonard *(10-12 & 2-6; closed Mon. and nat. hols.).* In the former Toussaint Abbey, new **David d'Angers Museum** (works of P.-J. David, 1788-1856). ▶ The **St. Aubin Tower** is the belfry of the former abbey; the buildings were reconstructed in the 17thC and now house the Prefecture (C3); magnificently sculpted Romanesque arcades★. ▶ Nearby, the **church of St. Martin** (11th-12thC) marks the site of a Merovingian sanctuary. ▶ A number of pedestrians-only streets with bistros and restaurants are centred around the **Place du Ralliement** (C2). Theatre, department stores and a covered shopping arcade make this the busy heart of the town. ▶ **The Pincé Mansion★** (Hôtel Pincé, C2), Renaissance : two collections are on show here : One of Egyptian, Greek and Roman antiquities, the other, Chinese and Japanese objets d'art known as the Turpin de Crissé Museum *(10-12 & 2-6; closed Mon. and nat. hols.).* ▶ Lovers of tapestry will cross the Maine to see the **Jean Lurçat Museum** in the former **Hospital of St. Jean★★** (B1). Built between 1180 and 1210, this is one of the most beautiful buildings of its type in France *(10-12 & 2-6; closed Mon. and nat. hols.).* Under the airy vaulting in the former patients' ward flame the colours of the **Chant du Monde★★** (Song of the World), a magnificent ten-piece tapestry executed at the Gobelins works in Paris (1957/66) from the designs of Jean Lurçat. See also the cloister (12thC) and the chapel (13thC). A small **wine museum** greets visitors to the Greniers St. Jean (storehouses), in caves dug into the rock. ▶ Formerly the land-owning and aristocratic area of the town; the ancient **abbey of Le Ronceray** (now housing the National School of Arts and Crafts) still has a Romanesque church in Poitevin (Poitiers) style. ▶ The **church of La Trinité★** (B1/2), 12thC, was also a dependency of this abbey. ▶ The **Place de la Laiterie** (B1), center of the Doutre quarter, is an agreeable place to stroll, among the old 15th-18thC town houses.

▶ **Also...** ▶ The **church of St. Serge** (C1) has one of France's most perfect Angevin Gothic choirs (early 13thC). Then there are the parks and gardens of which Angers is justly proud : **Jardin du Mail** (DC-2), **Jardin des Plantes★** (D2), **Jardin des Beaux-Arts, Boulevard du Roi René, Arboretum** and the **Parc de la Garenne** overlooking lake **St. Nicolas.** ▶ West, the **Leisure park** on the Lake of Maine (1 km²). ▶ Finally, near the station (B3) the **Parc des Haras** has some interesting exhibition rooms and craft workshops. □

▶ Nearby

▶ **Avrillé** *(5 km NW)* is restoring its moulins caviers (→ box), typical Angevin windmills; château de la Perrière (17thC; *Jul.-15 Sep. closed Wed.*). ▶ **Trélazé** *(8 km E)* has covered a good part of the roofs of France with its famous slate. Today the slate is mined underground, but you can visit the old excavations and the see how the "Perreyeux", the old slate miners, lived. ▶ **Les Ponts de Cé** *(8 km S) :*

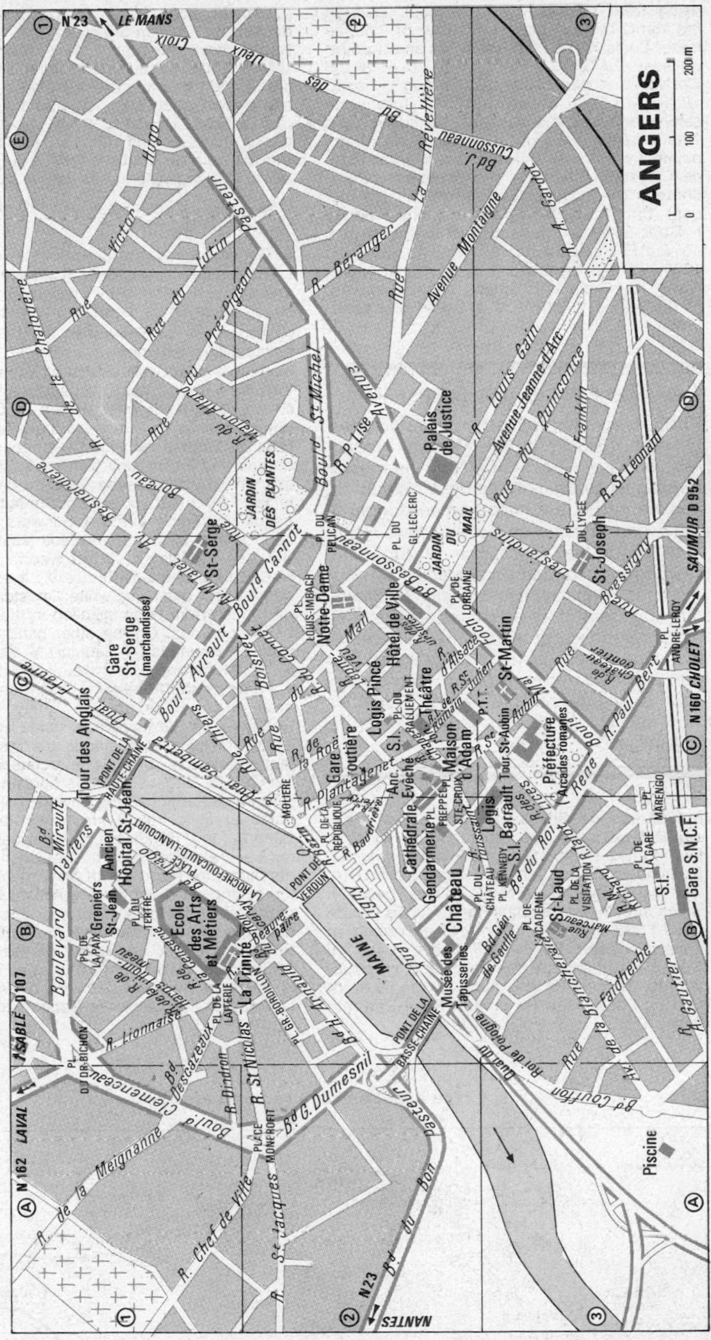

Musée des Coiffes (Bonnet museum; *daily 3-6 Jul.-Aug.; Sat. and Sun. Sep.-Oct.).* □

▶ The châteaux of Anjou *(within 24 km of Angers)*

▶ **Château du Plessis-Macé★** *(13 km NW)* : 15thC, Angevin to the last detail *(10-12 & 2-6 13 Jul.-Sep.; 1:30-6 Mar.-Jun. and Oct.-Nov.; closed Dec.-Feb.).* ▶ **Château du Plessis-Bourré★★** *(17 km N)* : double towers and walls rising from the water in the moat. Built in the 15thC by Jean Bourré, Minister of Finance under Louis XI, as both a fortress and a country seat *(10-12 & 2-7 Apr.-Sep., 10-12 & 2-5 Oct.-Mar; closed Wed. ex Jul.-Aug.; closed 15 Nov.-15 Dec.).* Superb 18thC furniture in the salons and see the beautiful ceiling★★ (end 15thC) in the Salle des Gardes (Guardroom), painted with humorous and sometimes indecent scenes illustrating proverbs and fables. **château de la Hamonière** *(4 km N)* : an elegant 15thC and Renaissance country house *(15 Jul.-Sep.).* ▶ **château de Montgeoffroy★** *(24 km E)* : all elegance and classic harmony, 1775; wooden panels and Louis XVI furniture, signed by the most famous cabinet makers of the period. *(9:30-11:30 & 2:30-6:30 Easter-1 Nov.).* □

The Apocalypse tapestry

This exquisite tapestry was created between 1373-80 by the Parisian weaver Nicolas Bataille from designs by the painter Hennequin de Bruges who drew his inspiration from various illuminated manuscripts of the period. The subject matter follows closely texts of the Apocalypse of St. John, reproduced here and accompanied by photographs. Originally the tapestry (168m by 5m) consisted of seven pieces, each showing a personage of importance followed in two superposed ranks by fourteen scenes with alternate red and blue backgrounds. Four of the personages remain, together with 68 whole scenes and five large fragments.

▶ **Château de Brissac** *(15 km SE)* at **Brissac-Quincé :** just like Montgeoffroy, Brissac has remained in the family which built it, which explains its lived-in feeling. Rebuilt from 1614, with two large round 15thC towers between which stretches a beautiful Renaissance façade *(9:30-11:20 & 2:15-4:15 or 5:45 according to season; closed Tue. ex Jul.-Sep.; closed 16 Nov.-6 Feb.;* soirées musicales and introduction to the arts of the hunt). 4 km N from Brissac : cavier mill (→ box) at **Saint-Saturnin** *(D751; by appt. tel. 41.91.93.03).* ▶ **Château de Serrant★** *(16km SW)* : is a true work of the Renaissance although it took three centuries (16th-18thC) to complete it. Its walls of brown schist and white tufa are reflected in the moats and a melancholy lake. *(9-11:30 & 2-5:30 Palm Sun.-1 Nov.; closed Tue. ex Jul.-Aug).* Staircase★, furniture and 16thC tapeistries, tomb of the marquis de Vaubrun (1675). 3 km SW : a mill in working order *(visits daily in summer).* □

▶ Loire - Layon★ *(circuit 177 km, one day, see map 1).*

▶ Gentle curves and peaceful views take the Loire dreamily through Anjou between vineyard and orchard, fringed by smiling villages. This circuit takes us as far as Montsoreau.

▶ **Angers.** ▶ **Le Thoureil★;** the Loire here is an eyefilling expanse of water. En route you may have visited the church of **Saint-Rémy-la-Varenne** (Roman apse, Angevin vaulting in the chapel★) or the former **Abbey of Saint-Maur** (6thC). 6km W of Thoureil is the beautiful **Château de Montsabert** (15thC), an echo of Montsoreau (→). ▶ Through **Gennes** ® (view★ from Church of Saint-Eusèbe; dolmen de la Madeleine★ *1 km S*) you reach **Cunault,** Romanesque church★★ 12thC. Binoculars needed to see details of the marvellous sculptures on the 223 capitals★★. 13thC wooden reliquary. ▶ **Chênehutte-les-Tuffeaux** ® : lives up to its name, with gleaming white limestone houses and mushroom beds installed in the cool dark of the quarries. On the other bank : the **Château de Boumois** (→ Saumur). ▶ **Saumur** (→). ▶ At **Montsoreau** (→) you leave the Loire. ▶ **Fontevraud-l'Abbeye** (→) has recently recovered much of its ancient dignity. **Montreuil-Bellay** (→). ▶ **Le Puy-Notre-Dame :** whose collegiate buildings are among the most consistent specimens of Angevine architecture of the 13thC. The Virgin's girdle is housed here; the relic supposedly has the power to alleviate the pains of childbirth. 9 km N is **Doué-la-Fontaine** ® (pop. 6 855), the city of roses, sending out several million rose bushes each year. The amphitheatre hewn out of an ancient quarry is the setting in Jul. for the Journée de la Rose. At the gates of the town, other quarries accommodate the **Zoo des Minières** *(8-7 Jul.-15 Sep.; 9-12:30 & 2-6:30 remainder of year).* On the D960, tower *sur cavier* (→ box; La Fourchette; *last Sun. in month ex Dec.*). 6 km NW of Doué-la-Fontaine, at **Louresse-Rochemenier,** a lit-

1. The Angevine Loire and the Layon hills

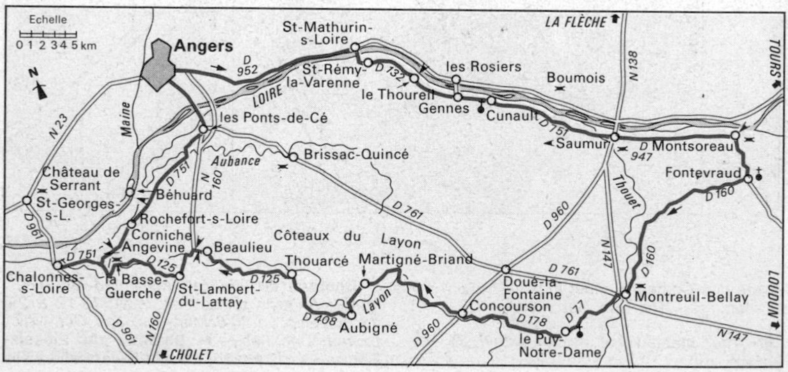

tle underground country museum *(every day ex Mon. in summer; Sat. and Sun. in winter).* ▶ **Vallée du Layon★** (Layon Valley) : many picturesque sights, famous wine producing area. ▶ **Martigné-Briand** is a village of wine growers, specialists in round well-structured whites. ▶ **Thouarcé,** then **Beaulieu-sur-Layon,** where the local cellars welcome visitors and the orientation table *(W exit)* shows you the vineyards of Layon dotted with châteaux. ▶ **Manoir de la Basse-Guerche** (15thC) in a bend of the Layon. ▶ **Corniche Angevin** (→) over the Loire. □

BAUGÉ and the BAUGEOIS region

B3 / ®® / pop. 3906 (Maine-et-Loire)

In this little region of forests and gorse (Chandelais★, Monnaie, Chambiers), nothing is simple. The bell-towers are built in spirals, and they still play with bias bowls, which don't run straight either (→ box).

▶ **Baugé** ® : a peaceful little town with charming old houses. In the château (15thC), museum of weapons and ceramics *(Jun.-Sep.)* and lovely spiral staircase. See also the pharmacy in the Hôpital St. Joseph and the famous Croix d'Anjou in the chapel of the Incurables. □

▶ Nearby

▶ **Le Vieil-Baugé** *(1.5 km SW),* **Pontigné** *(5 km E)* and **Mouliherne** *(13.5 km SE)* have spiral, helicoidal or corkscrew bell-towers on their beautiful 12th-13thC churches (murals in Pontigné★). ▶ **Breil** *(25 km SE)* has an operational watermill (Moulin au Jau, *3-7 Sat. and Sun.*). ▶ **Beaufort-en-Vallée** *(15 km SW) :* in the middle of the rich game preserves *Varennes* of the Val d'Anjou, a center of arable farming and flower growing; ruins of a 14th-15thC château; 15th-16thC church with Renaissance bell-tower. □

BEAUMONT-SUR-SARTHE

B1 / ® / pop. 1938 (Sarthe)

An old Roman keep, mounting guard over the right bank of the river which twists between the islets. ▶ La Motte-à-Madame is a beautiful walk with views★ over the valley. A peaceful little town like so many in the Sarthe. □

▶ Nearby

▶ 2.5 km E : ancient Benedictine priory of **Vivoin** (13thC chapter; exhibitions, concerts). ▶ **Fresnay-sur-Sarthe** ® *(12 km NW;* pop. 2692) : on a slope overlooking the river; Roman church of Notre-Dame (Renaissance main door★). Museum of regional headdresses *(every day Jul.-Aug. Sun. Mar.-Jun. and Sep.)* in fortified gateway of château (garden★). ▶ 21 km W of Beaumont, forest and lake leisure centre at **Sillé-le-Guillaume** ®. □

BERCÉ Forest★★

▶ Circuit through the Bercé Forest and the valley of the Loir *(93 km 3 hr).*
C2 *(see map 2)*

The oak forests of Bercé are without doubt the most beautiful in France; tall trunks like cathedral pillars accompanied by a few beech trees, in the central and eastern parts

2. Bercé Forest

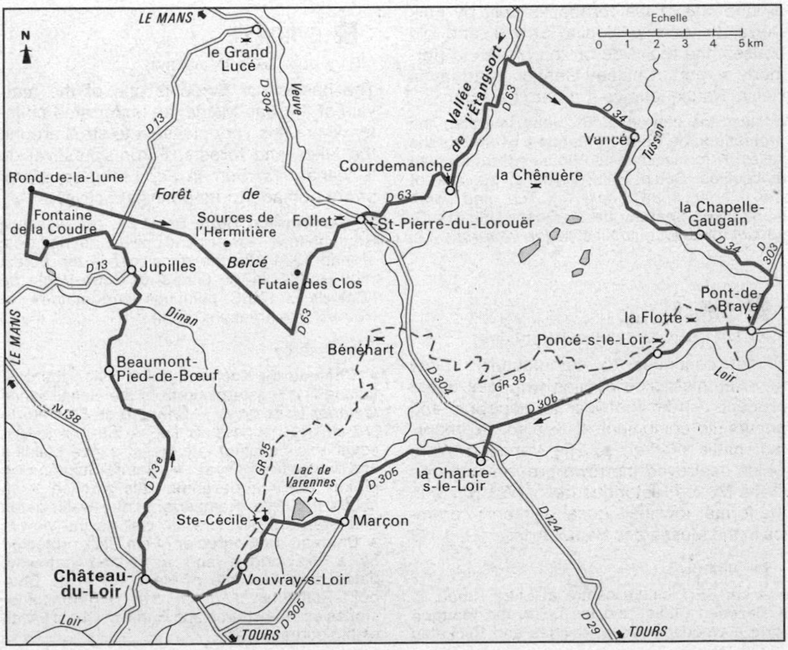

of these 54 km^2 of forest, remnant of the formerly vast forest of Mans. The western side is sandier and covered with pines.

▶ **Château du Loir** (pop. 589) : you will search in vain for any château here ! ▶ **Vallon de l'Yre :** leading to **Beaumont-Pied-de-Boeuf,** where amateurs of weapons and uniforms will be intrigued by the Sentinelle museum *(Easter-Sep., Sun. pm; 14 Jul.-30 Aug., 2-7 daily).* ▶ **Jupilles :** at the edge of the forest, woodworking crafts *(Easter-30 Jun., 8 Sep.-1 Nov., Sat., Sun. 2:30-6; 1 Jul.-7 Sep., daily ex Mon.).* ▶ **Fontaines de la Coudre :** in pretty surroundings. ▶ **Sources de l'Hermitière :** among oaks and beeches. ▶ **La Futaie des Clos :** magnificent and venerable oaks, some reaching over 40 m in spite of gales. ▶ **Saint-Pierre-de-Lorouër :** via Courdemanche and the valley of the **Étangsort** -- green hedges, poplars and willows bordering a pretty river. ▶ At **Vancé** and **Pont de Braye** you return to the imperturbable Loir flowing among cow-pastures and meadows. ▶ **Poncé-sur-Loir :** the sculptured vaulting of the Renaissance staircase in the château (1542) is a real marvel; gardens★ and dovecote★ . The ethnographic museum of Maine is housed in the château *(10-12 & 2-6 ex Sun. am Apr.-11 Nov.).* 500 m from the château : the **Moulin de Paillard,** craft centre of Poncé (pottery, glass-blowing, woodwork, weaving, wrought-iron; *9-12 & 2-6 closed Sun.).* ▶ **La Chartre-sur-le-Loir** ® (pop. 1 791) : produces an excellent white wine, Jasnières, greatly appreciated by Henri IV and many less illustrious connoisseurs. □

■ CHÂTEAU-GONTIER★

A2 / ® / pop. 8 352 (Mayenne)

You should come to this old city in Chouan country on Thursdays, when the calf sales are in full swing. Château-Gontier grew up around one of the fortresses built by Fulk Nerra. Its narrow sloping streets and old houses, the quayside on the Mayenne (formerly a port, Château-Gontier is today a Relais Nautique) give it great character.

▶ Near the **church of St. Jean** (murals), the **promenade du Bout-du-Monde★** overlooks the valley. A former mansion houses the **museum** (antiquities, Dutch 17thC painting, statue★ of Ste. Marthe 15thC; *daily, ex Tue. and Jan.).* ▶ 7km SW, **Château de St. Ouen,** 15th-16thC, square tower★ Louis XII style *(no visitors).* □

■ CHOLET

A4 / ® / pop. 56 528 (Maine-et-Loire)

Cholet continues to manufacture dainty handkerchiefs side by side with less dated products : from footwear to electronic and pneumatic equipment. It is also an important cattle market. ▶ The Vendéen Wars which destroyed the town are remembered in the Musée Historique *(tel. 41.62.20.78)* in the former townhall. Local painters; ceramics in the Musée des Beaux Arts. □

▶ Nearby

▶ 4 km SE : leisure centre at **Lake Ribou.** ® ▶ Between Cholet and the Loire, the **Mauges** form a wooded area of ravines and thicketed valleys. This little cockpit was evidently made for ambushes and was the scene of many dramatic episodes during the Wars of Vendée. ▶ 24 km NE : **Chemillé** grows medicinal plants (garden in the Parc de la Mairie). ▶ 19 km NNW : **Beaupréau,** an imposing 15th-18thC château burned by the Blues in 1793 and rebuilt during the Restoration. □

■ La CORNICHE ANGEVINE★ (The Angers cliff road)

▶ From Angers to Chalonnes-sur-Loire *(29 km, 2 hr).*
A3

SW of Angers between Rochefort and Chalonnes, the road leaves the banks of the Loire to take to the heights along the cliff. The valley of the Loire can now be seen to its full extent. The Loire continues on its way between the islands under the peaceful gaze of little towns and pretty manors, while the manicured slopes of the vineyards promise a *quart de Chaume* full of character and *coteaux de Leyon* of substance and body.

▶ **Angers** (→); leave by the D111. ▶ **Bouchemaine.** ▶ **Savennières** (church★ part 10thC) remembers its windmills; **La Possonnière** still turns; *(Sun and nat. hols. Apr.-15 Dec.)* while in the middle of the river **Béhuard★** huddles around the church (15thC) which watched over the sailors on the Loire; Musée de la Poupée *(tel. 41.54.53.97).* ▶ Here is **Rochefort-sur-Loire** ® (pop. 1 819) with watchtowers on its houses; the famous **Corniche Angevine★** and **La Haie-Longe** (view★). ▶ Finally **Chalonnes-sur-Loire** (pop. 5 358) invites you to stroll along its quays in the old port. 5 km SW, **Saint-Laurent-de-la-Plaine,** museum of ancient crafts *(9-12 & 2-6 Apr.-Oct.).* □

■ ÉVRON★★

B1 / pop. 6 774 (Mayenne)

The basilica of Évron is one of the marvels of the Bas-Maine, an underrated country where it is very pleasant to stroll around the lakes and forests. Évron's Festival de la Viande *(1st Sun. in Sep.)* renders appropriate homage to its principal activity.

▶ The **Basilica Notre-Dame★★** possesses a Romanesque tower and nave dating from around 1000 AD; the remainder is the purest High Gothic; in the **chapel of Notre-Dame de l'Épine★ :** 13thC paintings and statue★ of Notre-Dame (treasure room). □

▶ Nearby

▶ **Château du Rocher★** (5 km NW) : the east facade is a masterpiece from the Renaissance *(exterior visits only).* ▶ **Château de Foulletorte** *(10 km W) :* access as far as the grill to discover this beautiful late Renaissance building and water-filled moat. ▶ **Sainte-Suzanne★★** *(7 km SE) :* a delightful little fortified town above the Erve. Ramparts, sentry walk, gates and keep are all there, as well as the view★. ▶ **Château de Montecler** *(4 km SW),* protected by a drawbridge and a vaulted gateway, dates from the time of Henri IV. ▶ **La Chapelle-Rainsouin** *(11 km SW);* 16thC tombstones★ in the church and Burial of Christ★ with eight figures (1522). □

La FERTÉ-BERNARD

C1 / ® / pop. 10 053 (Sarthe)

Lush meadows with the river Huisne branching crazily through them.

▶ The most interesting thing in La Ferté is its Renaissance choir★★ (1500-96) in **Notre-Dame des Marais.** A fortified gateway, old houses (Rues d'Huisne and Carnot) and the market buildings (1536) are also worthy of interest. ▶ *15 km SE,* the 15thC **château de Montirail★** *(daily ex Tue., Jul.-15 Sep.; Sun., hols., Mar.-30 June, 16 Sept.-1 Nov.)*; view. ▶ 16 km S, **Vibraye** ® and the forest of the same name (5 000 acres) with its well-stocked lakes. ▶ 14 km SW : **Tuffé** with its lake and little tourist train *(Sun. and nat. hols., Jul.-Sep.).* □

Produce of Maine and Anjou

There is no lack of gastronomic specialities in this region. Various forms of potted meat - rillettes - *are produced, especially around Le Mans and Connerré.* Rillettes *are usually made from pork, but also from goose or rabbit. Le Mans' famous capons are gastronomic rivals of the* poulardes - *fatted pullets - of La Flèche.*

Excellent Reinette *apples come from the Sarthe, Montfort-le-Rotrou and Le Mans (the Maine-et-Loire Department is in fact France's leading apple producer).*

Freshwater fish - eel, pike, gudgeon - are prepared in typical local style, such as roulade d'anguille *(with eel), and various fish* pâtés, *and fried dishes.*

The cattle of Maine-Anjou produce very succulent beef, and cul-de-veau à l'angevine *is a celebrated regional dish.*

La FLÈCHE★

B2 / ® / pop. 16 421 (Sarthe)

Generations of soldiers have passed out of Le Prytanée de La Flèche, the celebrated school for officers' sons; but this small town is neither rigid nor military in appearance. In a bend in the Loir near a dam and two ancient mills, La Flèche is an important regional market for the fruit producers of Maine; and, discreetly hidden away, the town's printing presses turn out millions of *Livres de Poche,* France's most popular line in paperbacks.

▶ Near the bridge (view★) : the much rebuilt **château des Carmes** (15thC) is now the town hall. ▶ **Le Prytanée★** was formerly a Jesuit college, founded by Henri IV and with Descartes among its alumni. It is a masterpiece of the Baroque, consisting of enormous 17thC buildings and a chapel★ *(9:30-12 & 2-5).* ▶ 3.5 km SE at **Tertre-Rouge★** there is a most unusual zoo : its founder, J. Bouillault, is a friend of every animal there, from elephant to crocodile; interesting museum on regional fauna *(9:30-7 in summer; 10-dusk in winter).* □

FONTEVRAUD-L'ABBAYE★★★

B4 / ® / pop. 1 850 (Maine-et-Loire)

The originality of its architecture, the presence of so much history, and the extraordinary Franco-British dialogue which developed there make Fontevraud one of the high places of Western civilisation, another Vézelay (→). Founded in the 11thC by Robert d'Arbrissel, a preacher famous throughout Brittany and Anjou, Fontevraud consisted of five monasteries, of which three still exist; Grand-Moûtier, with the abbey church, St. Benoît, immediately E of the first, and St. Lazare, originally for the sick and leprous. Used as a prison from the time of Napoléon until 1964, Fontevraud is undergoing a rebirth; currently under restoration, it is now a cultural and convention centre under the aegis of the Historic Monuments Department. It welcomes symposia, organises concerts, spectacles, exhibitions, courses and activities for young people : studios for arts and crafts, archaeological sites...

▶ The **abbey church★★** is a superb Romanesque building from the first half of 12thC *(9-12 & 2-6 Apr.-Sep.; 10-12 & 2-4 Oct.-Mar.).* In the great single nave, decorated capitals★ adorn the enormous pillars. The Plantagenets, Counts of Anjou and later Kings of England, greatly favoured the abbey, and many of the family were buried there, including Henry II, his wife Eleanor of Aquitaine, their famous son Richard the Lion-Hearted *(Coeur de Lion),* and Isabel of Angoulême, wife of his younger brother King John. Of the effigies of the family, these four are all that remain, magnificent examples of 13thC sculpture★★. ▶ See also the great 16thC cloister, the **chapterhouse** with its 16thC frescos portraying various personalities of the day (restored), the **Romanesque refectory,** vaulted with ogives at the beginning of 16thC, and the famous 12thC **kitchens,** with fish-scale tiling and a multitude of chimneys. At the entrance to the abbey is the **church of St. Michel★** (12th-15thC), where numerous works of art from the abbey can be seen. □

LAVAL★

A1 / ® / pop. 53 766 (Mayenne)

Mayenne is a region strongly attached to its traditions, but Laval, its capital, has often tended to be non-conformist. Here were born Ambroise Paré (1509-90), often called "the father of modern surgery", Henri Rousseau, the customs officer and renowned naïf painter, Alfred Jarry, precursor of Surrealism, and Alain Gerbault, solo yachtsman. Laval is a pretty town, with its older houses firmly grouped around a solid château on one bank of the Mayenne river, opposite newer buildings on the other side.

▶ Discover the **old town,** with its 16thC houses cantilevered out over the road and its classic 18thC town mansions; around the **Place de la Trémoille** (B2), stroll along the Rue des Orfèvres, and down the Grande-Rue (see the house of the Grand Veneur★, Renaissance) to the **Pont Vieux** (Old Bridge; 13thC) over the Mayenne. ▶ At the back of the Place is the **Nouveau** (New) **Château,** now the Law Courts

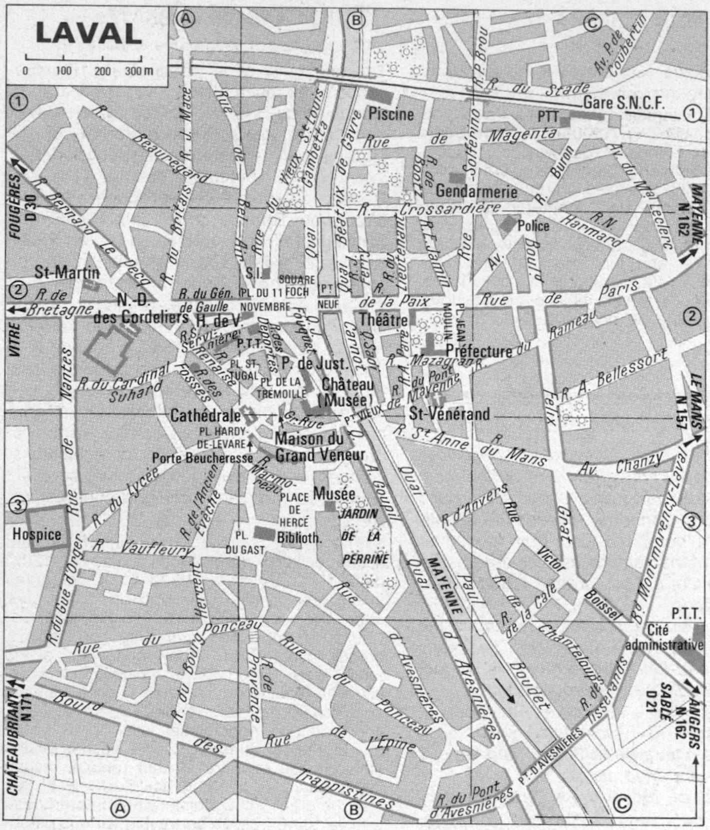

(Palais de Justice), not in fact very new, as they date from 1540; beautiful Renaissance façade. ▶ The **Vieux** (Old) **Château★,** home of the Counts of Laval, is a severe and forbidding building with an enormous 12thC keep topped by a wooden gallery; very pleasant apartments on the courtyard side, decorated Renaissance style with large richly carved windows *(daily Apr.-mid Sep.; pm only rest of year; closed Tue.).* ▶ From the ramparts you look over the roofs of the old town; a staircase runs down to the **Romanesque chapel★** (12thC) where the workmanship of the capitals is well worth seeing. ▶ In the main apartments visit the Salle d'Honneur (wooden vaulting), with 15thC murals and regional sculptures 14th-16thC; on the ground floor an interesting collection of **naïf paintings,** centred around a work by Douanier Rousseau. ▶ In the keep, 36m high, there is an astonishing **framework of oak and chestnut beams★★;** local historical material, masterpieces by craftsmen and builders of the period. ▶ Excellent view of the château from the **Jardin de la Perrine★** (B3), a terraced garden over the river.

Also... ▶ B2-3 : the **cathedral's** Romanesque nave has been roofed with primitive ogives (1185); Aubusson tapestries (17thC); at the main altar, an altarpiece in white stone and polychrome marble (1640); large triptych★ of St. John (wooden panels, school of Antwerp 16thC) etc. ▶ Near the cathedral, the 15thC **Beucheresse Gate** is a remnant of Laval's old fortifications. ▶ In the **church of St. Vénérand** (B2) : stained glass★ of 1521 showing the Passion. ▶ **Notre-Dame des Cordeliers** (A2) : six marble altars★, 17thC. ▶ **St. Martin★** (A2; *closed*) : Romanesque, end of 11thC. ▶ To the south (C4) : on the banks of the Mayenne, **Notre-Dame d'Avesnières** (11th-12thC) : noteworthy apse★. ▶ 2 km N : **Notre-Dame de Pritz,** Carolingian origins; murals★ from 11th-16thC and painted 13thC calendar. □

▶ Nearby

▶ **Church of Clermont Abbey** *(15 km NW);* pure lines of Cistercian architecture. ▶ **Château de Montjean** *(16 km SW);* a ruined lakeside fortress. ▶ **Cossé-le-Vivien** *(18 km SW),* ceramics and symbolic sculptures by Robert Tatin in the museum *(daily).* □

■ Le LUDE★

B2-3 / ® / pop. 4 895 (Sarthe)

On certain summer nights, the Loir is ablaze with light. On its banks, pavanes and stately minuets are danced, Henri IV caracoles on a snow-white horse, and Mme de Sévigné steps delicately ashore from her barge. The whole town takes part in the glories of an evening on the Loir, in the noble setting of the château and its gardens. The quality of the presentation has contributed largely to the reputation of this little low-roofed town in the Sarthe. A favourite spot for fishermen. Local industry : dairy produce and furniture.

▶ Deep, dry moats protect the **château** and its four enormous towers, though their crenels and machicolations are now no more than decoration. The north façade is Gothic, while the south façade dates from 1520-1530 (François I), with Italian Renaissance medallions and delicate sculptures. Overlooking the Loir, the harmonious Louis XIV façade in white stone unites the two. Take a walk along the terrace above the river *(daily 3-6, Apr.-Sep.)*. □

■ Le MANS★★★

B2 / ® / pop. 150 331 (Sarthe)

The reputation of Le Mans rests on a thrilling 24hr car race, jars of potted meat and delicious apples. It is all too easy to forget that this capital of Maine has seen enough history to be well provided with churches, museums, Gallo-Roman remains, and, of course, a noble cathedral. Fairs, exhibitions, trade and big business in the form of powerful banks, insurance companies and the car industry (Renault) have all combined to make this a city worthy of its past; and important planning initiatives are under way to make sure that the city's inheritance is not allowed to dwindle.

▶ The magnificent **cathedral of St. Julien★★★** *(8-12 & 2-7)* rises nobly above the Place des Jacobins, where the city's Friday market is

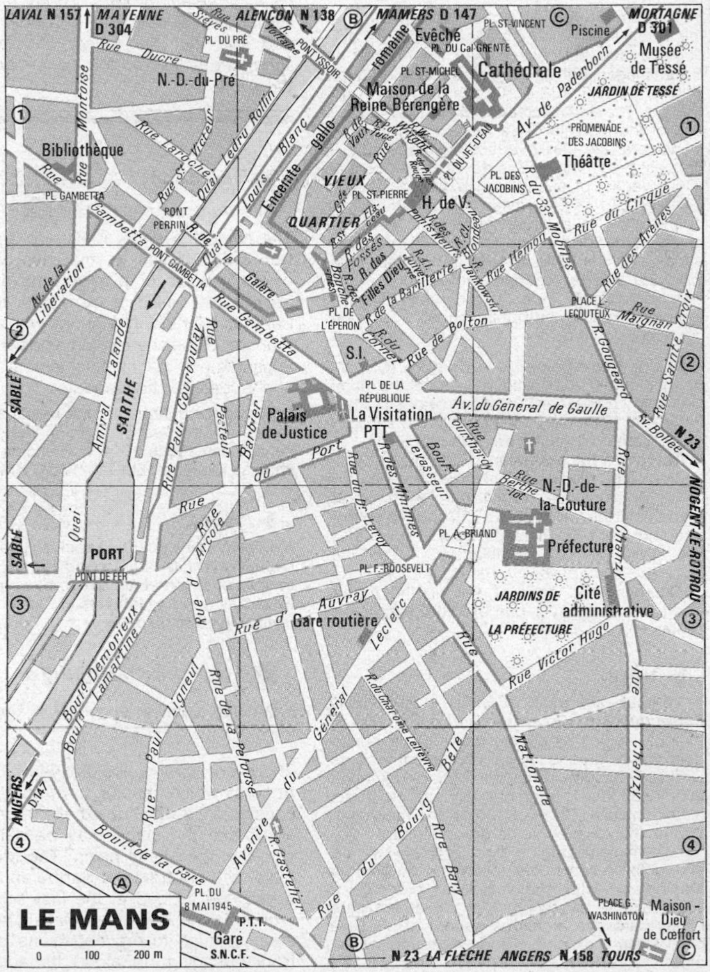

held. The cathedral's nave and façade are Romanesque (11th-12thC), while the transept and choir are Gothic. On the south side, the statues round the doorway★★ (12thC) recall those of the Royal Door at Chartres. The choir★★★ (1217-1254) is a masterpiece of Gothic architecture; superb stained glass★★ (14th-15thC) illuminates the interior; painting★ from the end of the 14thC in the apsidal chapel; in the baptismal chapel, the tombs★★ of Charles IV of Anjou and Guillaume du Bellay (1491-1543, warrior and diplomat). ▶ Facing the cathedral : restored Renaissance **Grabatoire Mansion★.** ▶ SW of the cathedral : **Vieux Mans** (the old town), with its antique dealers and craftsmen, offers a vivid reminder of the Middle Ages and the Renaissance. ▶ Many ancient buildings : Rue de la Reine Bérengère (B1), N° 9, Renaissance house, N° 11-13, **Maison de la Reine Bérengère,** 15thC, devoted to the history, art and popular traditions of Maine; temporary exhibits of arts and crafts from around the world *(9-12 & 2-6, closed Mon. and Mar.).* ▶ Opposite : 15thC **Maison des Deux Amis.** ▶ Nearby : Rue des Chanoines, remains of the **Priory of St. Martin** (6th-9thC), crypt and artists' workshops *(daily Jul.-15 Sep. closed Sun.).*

▶ The **Grande-Rue,** the direct continuation of the Rue de la Reine Bérengère, is also bordered by fine old houses; see the Maison du Pilier Rouge, (16thC), **Maison d'Adam et Eve★** (N° 69); N°s 86, 108 & 105 are also worth noticing. ▶ The **Gallo-Roman fortress** (3rd-4thC) is one of the marvels of Le Mans; with its eleven towers, the part overlooking the Sarthe is the best preserved. ▶ The **de Tessé Museum★** (C1) : variety of shows and exhibitions, good paintings *(9-12 & 2-6, closed nat. hols.);* the star of the show is a large plaque of *champlevé* enamel (c.1150) showing Geoffroi Plantagenet, ancestor of the Kings of England. Italian primitives are well represented, notably the 14thC school of Sienna (Pietro Lorenzetti★); French, Spanish, Flemish and Dutch schools; gallery of contemporary art.

Also... ▶ **Notre-Dame-de-la-Couture** (C3; *8-7 daily*) : former abbey church; note the semicircular★ choir (11thC), the doorway★ (13thC), Virgin★ by Germain Pilon (16thC), the shroud★ of St. Bernard (oriental silk, 6th or 7thC).
▶ **Church of the Visitation,** 1730, dependency of the 18thC convent. ▶ **Notre-Dame-du-Pré** (B1) : Romanesque, 11th-12thC. ▶ **Place St. Pierre** (B1), the town hall of 1760 and the **collegiate church of St. Pierre-la-Cour** (11th-14thC), now given over to exhibitions *(2-7 Tue.-Sat, entry Rue des Fossés-St. Pierre)* and concerts.
▶ **Church of St. Joan of Arc,** in the former Coëffort hospital (C4), end of 12thC (capitals★, beams★). □

▶ Nearby

▶ **24-hour race-track** *(6 km S to Automobile Museum). Tertre Rouge, Mulsanne* and *Arnage,* famous landmarks on the course, are household words among motor racing enthusiasts. Ordinarily open to traffic, the track circuit measures 13.26 km. The famous day and night race is held in June. On the D139, at the main entry to the track, is an underground entrance to the permanent Bugatti circuit (4.24 km, car and motorcycle schools, tests) and **Automobile Museum★★** with 150 vehicles : old cars to 1914, steam, electric and petrol driven cars, racing cars, the *monstres sacrés* of 1920-49, cars which took part in the 24 Hours, cycles, motorcycles *(9-12 & 2-7, Easter-15 Oct.; 9-12 & 2-6, 16 Oct.-Easter; closed Tue.).* ▶ The **abbey of l'Épau★** *(4.5 km E/SE from Le Mans) :* founded in 1229 by Bérengère (Berengaria), wife of Richard the Lion-Heart, restored in the 15thC after a fire; chapterhouse, cellar, kitchen, refectory. The queen's tomb is in the church, with a 13thC effigy. *(9:30-12 & 2-6; closed Thu. 15 Sep.-15 Apr.).* Near the abbey : the **Bois de Changé,** 2.5 km² of leisure park. ▶ **Domaine de Pescheray** *(24 km E),* agricultural museum, animal park, "Knowledge of Trees" instructional trail *("Connaissance des Arbres"; 10-7 Apr.-Oct., closed Mon.; 12 till dusk, Wed., Sat. & Sun., Nov.-Mar.).* □

The Le Mans 24-Hours Race

In 1923 the organisers of the Automobile Club de l'Ouest, Gustave Singher and Georges Durant, arranged the first of these famous trials for car manufacturers. The first year, the winning car - a Chenard and Walcker - covered 2,209 km at an average of 92 kph, while the track record was won by a Bentley (107 kph). Today the famous Hunaudières straight *is taken at over 300 kph, but the noise, the colour, the lights, the smell and the excitement are still the same.*

■ MAYENNE

A1 / ® / pop. 14 298 (Mayenne)

The name Mayenne applies to an administrative department, a small river with many of the aspects of a mighty torrent, and a quiet town which is rarely in the news. Perhaps that's why visitors who don't like tourism come here; Mayenne's principal advantage is that is has almost no traffic and is ideal for houseboats.

▶ Above the right bank : the **basilica of Notre-Dame,** (12thC early Gothic) restored after serious damage in 1944. ▶ Remains of ancient château rebuilt in 15thC. ▶ 17thC Hôtel de Ville. □

▶ Nearby

▶ **Lassay** *(19 km NE) :* a real fairy tale fortress (15thC) with five large round towers *(2:30-6:30 in season; son-et-lumière★ eves every Fri., Sat., May-Sep.)* ▶ **Jublains** *(10 km SE),* Roman fortifications *(closed Tue.).* □

■ Valley of the **MAYENNE★**

▶ From Laval to Angers *(115 km, half-day)*
A1

There are forty locks between Laval and Angers, which makes it a poor river for commercial traffic but excellent for pleasure craft; and the same may be said for the whole of the Maine basin. The Mayenne is quite different from the Sarthe and the Loir; it has dug its bed in the last schistic outcrop from the Armorican Massif, with banks steep enough to prevent towns or villages from springing up along its edges. Bas-

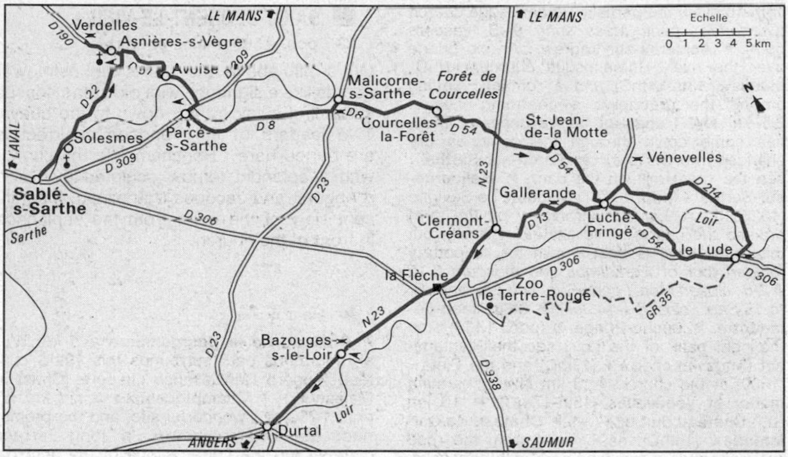

3. Tour of Upper Maine

Maine, which the Mayenne waters from north to south, was formerly the poor country of the Chouan insurrectionists, nothing but heath and scrub. Today, lush meadows and forage crops feed the area's pigs and cattle.

▶ Laval (→) ▶ **La Trappe du Port-du-Salut** is the home of the famous cheese of the same name, made today in a dairy next to the abbey. ▶ **Château-Gontier** (→). ▶ Several handsome manor-houses standing well back from the river : **Escoubière Manor** (16thC); **château du Percher,** between Gothic and Renaissance; **château du Bois-Mauboucher** (15th-17thC). ▶ **Le Lion-d'Angers** ® (pop. 2775) : occupies a picturesque site on the right bank of the Oudon; see the church of St. Martin (nave 11thC, paintings 15thC). Le Lion is known for horse-breeding; 1 km E, the **National Stud of l'Isle Briand** is open to visitors *(2-5).* ▶ Le Plessis-Macé (→ Angers). □

■ MONTREUIL-BELLAY★

B4 / ® / pop. 4331 (Maine-et-Loire)

One of the most picturesque sites in Anjou, on a little hill above the right bank of the Thonon. Two fortified gateways and part of the ramparts still surround the town.

▶ They say that the fearless Duchess de Longueville (1619-79), sister of the Grand Condé (Louis II de Bourbon, the brilliant general), rode her horse up the staircase of the **château;** the edifice in question was a rugged fortress in the 11thC, metamorphosed during the 15thC into a superb residence. Remarkable **kitchen★** with a central hearth *(10-12 & 2-6 Apr.-Oct.; 10-12 & 2:30-6:30 Jul. & Aug.; closed Tue.).* ▶ At the foot of the château : remains of the Priory of Nobis (12th, 14th & 17thC). ▶ On the edge of the forest of Cizay : the **abbey of Asnières** *(8 km N)* is in ruins, but the choir★★ of the church (1210-20) is one of the most perfect specimens of 13thC Angevin Gothic *(10-12 & 2-6 Jul.-Aug.; closed Tue.).* □

■ MONTSOREAU★

B4 / ® / pop. 454 (Maine-et-Loire)

On the edge of Anjou and Touraine, the epitome of the discreet Loire town. Nothing is missing; the white wine (coteaux de Saumur) is full and perfumed, and the château overlooks the river.

▶ The **château** (15thC) was the earliest in Anjou to evolve from the mediaeval fortress to a more courtly residence; Grand Staircase★; *Goums* museum (North African tribal levies in the French Army) *(9-12 & 2-7, Apr.-Sep.; 9-12 & 2-5, Oct.-Mar.; closed Tue.).* ▶ 2.5 km NW : **Moulin de la Herpinière** (mill) at Turquant *(15 Mar.-15 Oct.; closed Mon. ex Jul. & Aug.).* □

■ SABLÉ-SUR-SARTHE

B2 / ® / pop. 12721 (Sarthe)

An imposing château in severely classic style overlooks this modest town, which has given its name to a famous form of biscuit *(sablés).* The town occupies both banks of the Sarthe. In the Island Quarter *(Quartier de l'Ile),* see the church of Notre-Dame (1891); 15th-16thC stained glass. Pleasant gardens above the river. □

▶ Exploring the Haut-Maine, trip from Sablé-sur-Sarthe to Durtal *(96 km, half-day, see map 3)*

▶ The Sarthe and the Loir (→ also Forêt de Bercé) meander peacefully through the pastureland of the Haut-Maine in the department of the Sarthe, a landscape full of woods and meadows, with little-known villages and hidden manors. ▶ **Solesmes** ® : Benedictine abbey, rebuilt in 1833, on the banks of the Sarthe; source of a world-famous series of Gregorian Chant recordings. See especially the **Saints of Solesmes★★,** marvellous sculptures of

15th-16thC in the partially Romanesque church *(Gregorian chant, Mass sung 9:45, vespers 5pm).* ▶ **Asnières-sur-Vègre★ :** An old bridge over the river, Romanesque church (11thC; murals★ 13th-14thC) and a romantic setting among the greenery; a charming village. 2.5 km NW : **château de Verdelles★,** 1490, has come down through the centuries unchanged *(no visitors).* ▶ **Parcé-sur-Sarthe :** see the great mill on the dam. ▶ **Malicorne-sur-Sarthe** ® (pop. 1 773) : Madame de Sévigné (1626-96; renowned chronicler of the era) praised the charm of its château (17thC), but this small town is best known for its pottery *(guided tour of workshops and museum 8-12 & 2-6; closed Mon.; open Sun. and Easter hols. to 15 Sep.; closed 1-14 Jul.).* ▶ **Saint-Jean-de-la-Motte.** ▶ **Luché-Pringé** ® (pop. 1 433) : on the right bank of the Loir; see the Plantagenet (Angevin) choir★★ (13thC) and the Pietà★ (1500) in the church. ▶ 3 km NW : charming **manor of Vénevelles** (16th-17thC). ▶ 10 km SE : **Château du Lude** (→). ▶ **Château de Gallerande★** (15thC), easily seen from the road *(no visitors)* in a romantic park with peacocks. ▶ **La Flèche** (→). ▶ **Bazouges-sur-le-Loir★** ® (pop. 1 313) : from the bridge over the river, the old wash-houses, the 16thC château and the mill make a charming picture *(Tel. 43.94.30.67).* ▶ **Durtal :** a peaceful town on the Loir; waterfront, mills, 15th-17thC château. S : the **forest of Chambiers** (13 km^2 of oak and pine), pleasant walks. □

The moulins caviers

In addition to the smock-mill, which has a conical wooden roof turning to the wind, and the post-mill, where the entire mill turns, there exists also in Anjou a local variant, in which the post-mill is mounted on a masonry base which is vaulted to make cellars for storage. Its silhouette is easily recognisable : from the stone and earth foundations, a conical tower rises into the sky, carrying the mechanism and the four great sails. Two beams, which also serve as a ladder, are used to turn the mill. Unlikely as it may seem, the moulins-caviers *of Anjou are alive and well; an association,* Les Amis des Moulins, *sees to their restoration. Several are already back in use. For information (in French) : tel. 41.88.82.23.*

■ SAINT-CALAIS★

C2 / ® / pop. 4 779 (Sarthe)

The river Anille (it means 'tendril') twines prettily past the moss-covered stones and flowered gardens of this important agricultural market town on the edges of Maine and the Vendômois.

▶ The **church of Notre-Dame :** handsome Renaissance façade★ (1522). ▶ Ruins of 11thC château on the hill. ▶ 11 km S : **château de Courtanvaux,** 15th-16thC, restored in 1815 *(free entry to the park; tours every day ex Tue. at 10, 11, 2, 3, 4, 5, 6 May-Sep.; Sun. and nat. hols. Oct.-Apr.; in season,* exhibitions of art, theatre and music, "Summer Evenings at the Château de Courtanvaux"). □

■ SAINT-FLORENT-LE-VIEIL★

A3 / pop. 2 500 (Maine-et-Loire)

On a hill above the Loire the bell-tower stands like a signpost, with old stone houses streaming away from it down to the quays. Two leaders of the Vendéen insurrection are buried here : Bonchamp, in the church with a splendid tomb★ sculpted by David d'Angers, and Jacques Cathelinau. Magnificent view of the Loire from the esplanade in front of the church. □

▶ Nearby

▶ **Château de la Bourgonnière** *(5.5 km W) :* an enormous park surrounds this 19thC château; superb Renaissance chapel★ (Christ in Majesty★). ▶ **Champtoceaux★** ® *(21 km W;* pop. 1 252) ® : wonderful site, and the promenade de Champalud★★, a long terrace overhanging the Loire, is one of the principal sights of Anjou. The local white wine has considerable merit. ▶ **Liré** *(12 km W) :* birthplace of poet Joachim du Bellay, "the French Ovid" (1522-1560). There is a little museum devoted to him in the village *(closed Mon.).* □

The wines of Anjou

Tradition has it that the vineyards of Anjou were introduced by the Gauls. In any case, they have been largely honoured by royalty, and the Plantagenets, Lords of Anjou and Kings of England, always remained faithful to the wines of their homeland. The whites are made from the Chenin Blanc *grape or the* Pineau de la Loire, *and the reds from the* Cabernet Franc *and to a lesser extent the* Gamay. *As for the rosés, they are made principally from* Cabernet Franc *and* Cabernet Sauvignon *grapes.*

***Whites :** the wines from the right bank of the Loire* (coteau de Savennières) *are dry, firm and vigorous, while those from the left bank* (crus de Layon) *are full-bodied, plump and fruity. The* coteaux de l'Aubance *are drier than those of Layon with an excellent earthy taste. Among the whites we must also mention the* coteaux de Saumur, *light and dry, vigorous and perfumed; some of these wines are transformed into sparkling wine; the best carry the mention* "Tête de cuvée". *For a long time the "great" wine of Anjou was the white, but the reds and rosés are now gaining ground.*

*Among the **rosés** the* Rosé d'Anjou *is distinguished from the* Cabernet d'Anjou, *the former being lively and fruity (demi-sec and dry) and the latter, like the* Cabernet de Saumur, *fine and delicate.*

*The **reds,** principally* coteaux de Saumur ("grand cru": Champigny) *are substantial and full-bodied.*

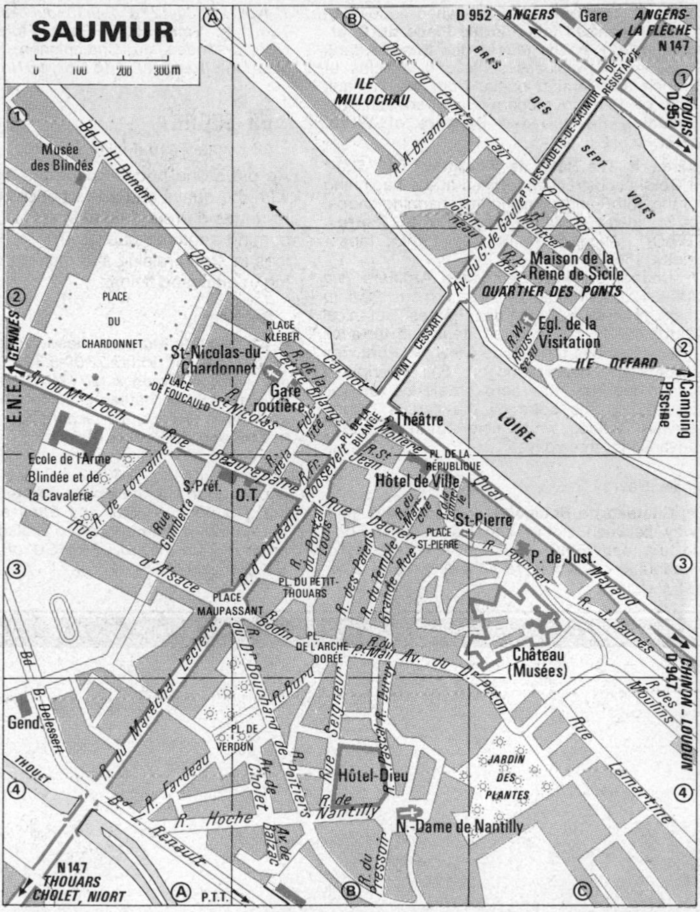

■ SAUMUR★★★

B3 / ® / pop. 33 953 (Maine-et-Loire)

"The pearl of Anjou" owes its renown in great part to the horse : the famous Cadre Noir cavalry school, renowned throughout the equestrian world, is based here, and has schooled generations of horsemen and their mounts. The town has other claims to fame, however : its white wines, vigorous and perfumed, the mushrooms of the area and, perhaps least known of all, its carnival mask factory, which exports laughter all over Europe.

▶ The **château** (C3) rises proudly over the grey slate roofs and the light-filled landscape of the Loire. Rebuilt at the end of the 14thC and remodelled a number of times since, it has four towers at the corners crowned with machicolations *(daily 9-6:30 Jul.-Sep.; 9-11:30 & 2-6 Apr.-Jun. and Oct.-Nov.; 9:30-11:30 & 2-5; closed Tue. Nov.-Mar.; Jul. and Aug., evening tours 8:30-10.30).* ▶ As its name indicates, the Tour du Guet (watchtower) has a splendid outlook over the valleys of the Loire and the Thouet. ▶ There are two museums in the château : the **Decorative Arts Museum** occupies the first floor of the two restored wings. Beautiful collections of objets d'art from the Middle Ages and the Renaissance (chests, enamels, tapestries; the Bal des Sauvages, c.1500) and a rare collection of 17th-18thC ceramics (Delft, Rouen★, Nevers, Moustiers) and French soft paste porcelains. On the second floor, the **Museum of the Horse** traces the history of equitation in France and abroad; collections★ of saddles, bits, stirrups etc. ▶ On leaving the château, there is a pleasant walk along the hilltop **Rue des Moulins** (C4). ▶ The **church of Notre-Dame de Nantilly** (B4) is a fine Romanesque building (12thC), both powerful and severe; it houses a remarkable collection of tapestries★★ (16th-17thC) from the Loire, Tournai, Flanders, Brussels and Aubusson; note particularly the Tree of Jesse★ (N. transept). ▶ **Cavalry Museum** (A2-3) displays the history of the famous French cavalry officers' training school, founded in 1768. The school now teaches the tactics and strategy of tank warfare *(visit on prior request).* In 1972 the Ecole Nationale d'Equitation (National Riding School) was founded in the Terrefort woods where the celebrated **Cadre Noir** has its headquarters. Don't miss the renowned equestrian and mechanised tattoo in the **Place du Chardonnet** (A2). ▶ The **Musée des Blindés** (tank museum; A1) includes some 150 vehicles of French and foreign origin, from the Renault tank of 1918 to modern armoured vehicles, including the dreaded Panzers of WWII. *(9-11:30 & 2-5:30).*

Also... ▶ The **Hôtel de Ville** (town hall; B3) : a Gothic construction fortified at the beginning of the 16thC and including the charming chapel of St. Jean★, 13thC. ▶ **Church of St. Pierre★** (B3-C) : Angevin Gothic, 12th-13thC; tapestries★ 16thC.
▶ **Chapel of Notre-Dame des Ardillers** *(via A1) :* 17thC, fronted by an enormous 20.6 m diam. rotunda. ▶ **Jardin des Plantes** (Botanical Gardens; B-C4) : flowered steps and terraces of vines across the hillside (view). ▶ **Pont des Cadets-de-Saumur** (Bridge : C1; inscription) commemorates the heroic defence of the bridges on the Loire by the cadets of the Cavalry school, which held up the German advance for three days. □

▶ Nearby

▶ **Château de Boumois★** *(6.5 km NW) :* midway between Gothic and Renaissance, built in tufa (end 15thC-early 16thC); collections of weapons, dovecote *(10-12 & 2-6, Palm Sun.-1 Nov.; 9:30-12 & 2-6:30 Jul.-Aug.; closed Tue.).* ▶ **Saint Hilaire-Saint Florent** *(2 km NW) :* Musée du Champignon (Mushroom Museum; *10-12 & 2-6 15 Mar.-15 Nov.*). □

■ SEGRÉ★

A2 / pop. 7 416 (Maine-et-Loire)

An old stone bridge spans the Oudon, and with the quays and a few houses of character lends a great deal of charm to this unassuming regional capital. The area specialises in stock raising and multiple crop farming in enclosed fields. □

▶ Nearby

▶ **Château de Mortiercrolles★** *(10 km N) :* built at the end of 15thC *(2:30-5:30 closed Tue., Jul.-Aug.).* ▶ **Craon** ® *(20 km N) :* has a beautiful late-18thC château in white stone *(garden and park, 9-5 or 9-7 according to season).* ▶ **Château de Raguin** *(8.5 km S) :* early 17thC *(May-Sep.).* ▶ Châteaufort de **Pouancé** ® *(25 km; Jul.-Aug., 9:30-12 & 2-6).* ▶ Mill-lovers should go to see the **Moulin d'Angrie,** still turning, *(18 km SW; Sat. and Sun.)* and the mill at **Challain-la-Potherie** which is also in running order *(16 km SW; mill 2 km SW of the village; Sat. pm, Jun.-15 Sep.).* □

Architecture

The traditional houses of Maine and Anjou are distinguished more by the diversity of materials employed than by their characteristics, which are more or less homogenous from one area to another. ● A rural house is usually a simple rectangle of approx. 9 m by 5.5 m. ● In the Val d'Anjou (Maine blanc) as in Touraine, tufa is most commonly used. It is easy to work and encourages the creation of moldings, cornices, fillets and carved window surrounds which add to the dignity of the buildings. ● In contrast with the Anjou blanc of the limestone region - and this applies to Maine also - is the Anjou noir of the schist region. This material is most used in the wooded and enclosed areas such as Mauges, Craonnais, and Segréen. But this distinction between white and black is not, of course, a cut and dried difference; the two materials are frequently employed outside their regions of origin (tufa in Laval, Château-Gontier and south of the Mayenne). ● At the crossroads of Brittany, Normandy, and the Pays de Loire, Mayenne is a geologically disparate region. Granite is found in the North, but you will find blue limestone in the Lavalais, and grey schist around Renazé. During the last century brick was much used in Mayenne. To further complicate matters, in both Sarthe and Mayenne you will find timber-framed houses with rock, brick or earth infill. ● In Maine as in Anjou, roofs are usually double pitched, with large overhangs; the gables frequently overlap as a protection against wind. Slate from Trélazé or the old quarries of Javron and Segré is used throughout Anjou and to a large extent in Mayenne, where you also find around Sainte-Suzanne the flat rectangular or rounded tiles common in the Sarthe. ● A roof with four faces (Mayenne, Anjou) marks a well-to-do house, and frequently has a pedimented porch. In Anjou as in Touraine access to the loft is either by ladder or by a staircase supported against the baking oven. Bas Maine and Haut Maine differ in the size of the land holdings; in Mayenne, large holdings are more frequent, with austere granite buildings set round a courtyard or in parallel lines. Sarthe, with a less favourable soil, has smaller farms, and their buildings often shelter accommodation and work areas under the same roof of flat tiles.

6. Tufa built house

4. House in Anjou

7. Master's house in the Mayenne region

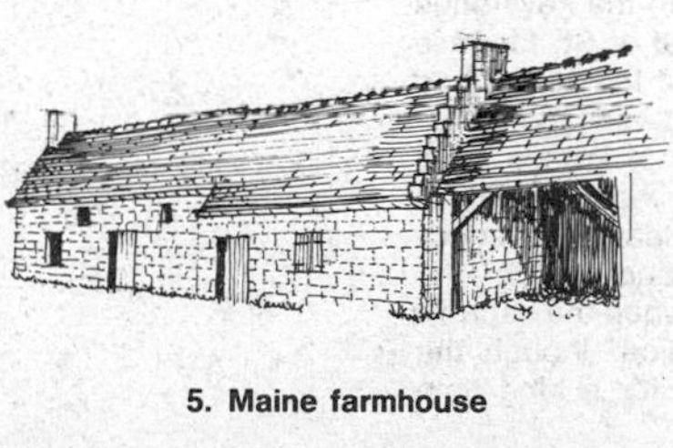

5. Maine farmhouse

Brief regional history

Up to the Roman Conquest

Traditionally, the first men in Maine and Anjou are supposed to have appeared in the **Palaeolithic** (Saulges Caves) and **Neolithic** periods respectively. ● Maine and Anjou, corresponding to the Gallic regions of Aulerques and Andécaves, enter history with Caesar's conquests. ● From this point on, **Vindinium** (Le Mans) and **Noviodunum** (Jublains) became important crossroads, while Angers - former capital of the Andécaves - developed into **Juliomagus,** a substantial Roman city with heated baths, a theatre and an amphitheatre.

9th-11thC

During the 9th century, Maine and Anjou were invaded by the **Normans** and the **Bretons.** ● During the second half of the 9thC the **Count of Angers,** Robert the Strong, fought off the Normans and bequeathed the County of Angers to his son Robert, briefly king of France. He in turn installed a viscount, **Ingelger,** who founded the first Angevin dynasty. Maine too became an hereditary county in 955 (Hugues 1st), but its overlordship was disputed by the Dukes of Normandy and the Counts of Anjou. ● The greatest of the region's mediaeval overlords was without doubt **Fulk Nerra** (970-1040), who waged unremitting war on his neighbours well into his old age. With his son **Geoffroi Martel,** he extended Anjou to cover Mauges (→ Cholet), Saumur, part of Touraine, Vendôme and Maine. He is reputed to have been violent, greedy, ambitious and unscrupulous, with sudden accessions of Christian humility (leading him on one occasion to make a penitential pilgrimage to Jerusalem) and to shower churches and convents with endowments. He built some twenty fortresses in Anjou and Touraine.

12th-14thC

Marriages and alliances played an essential role in the ascent of the House of Anjou. One of its sons, **Geoffroi V the Handsome** (1113-1151), who carried a sprig of broom in his hat *(genêt,* hence *plante à genêt),* married Matilda, daughter of Henry I of England. Their descendants took the name of Plantagenet, and the son, Henry, married Eleanor of Aquitaine in 1152. Two years later he acceded to the throne of England as Henry II Plantagenet. ● Anjou then became part of an empire which included England, Normandy, Brittany, Aquitaine and Gascony. ● The 12thC was also the great epoch of **Angevin architecture,** (church at Cunault, abbey of Fontevraud). In 1130, the first ogive vault appeared in the tower of St. Aubin at Angers. Angevin ingenuity was to devise a new approach to the problem of vaulted structures, the domed **Angevin** (or Plantagenet) **vault,** with the keystone of the diagonal arches higher than the keystones of the wall arches. The vaulting in the cathedral of St. Maurice in Angers (1150) is an excellent example. ● But the vassal had grown more powerful than his overlord; faced with the formidable strength of the Plantagenets, the Capets of France cut a poor figure. Political struggle between the two houses was to continue throughout the Hundred Years' War, leaving a legacy of strife to succeeding generations of English and French. The first French success of note occurred in 1205, when the capable **Philippe Auguste** regained possession of Anjou, though the suzerainty remained an object of hot dispute for a long time afterward.

15th-17thC Thus, Anjou did not enter the French camp for good until 1481. ● Before that, the region had been given in appanage by Louis IX (Saint Louis) to his younger brother **Charles,** who was however more interested in his Italian adventures. Subsequently it was given as a Duchy to Louis I of Anjou, the younger son of Jean le Bon (John the Good). The crown of Anjou was thus borne from the 13th-15thC by Capets of direct descent, and thereafter by the Valois dynasty. ● The last of the Dukes of Anjou was **"Good King René"** (1409-80), who had many other titles including the kingships of Sicily and Naples. He was also Count of Provence, and although extremely active in improving and embellishing Angers, preferred the sunshine of Aix to the soft airs of Anjou - or such is the reason given for his philosophical retreat south when Louis XI decided to repossess Anjou for the Crown of France. The dynasty of Valois-Anjou did in fact make Angers a centre of art and education; the famous series of hangings known as the **Tapisseries de l'Apocalypse** was completed as early as 1376; they can still be seen today in the Château of Angers (→). ● Maine, also attached to the Crown in 1481, was the appanage of a number of royal princes between the 16th-17thC, and in the 18thC became a Duchy once more. From 1560-98, Anjou was devastated by the **Wars of Religion,** until **Henri IV** ('Paris is worth a Mass') put an end to trouble with the Catholic "Holy League", by promising his son César to Françoise de Lorraine, daughter of the Duke of Mercoeur, the League's last hope for a Catholic king. The Edict of Nantes (1598), which gave freedom of worship to Protestants, was signed a few days later.

18th-19thC In 1793 Anjou was one of the principal theatres of war during the **uprising of the Vendée,** a Catholic and Royalist insurrection against the Revolutionary Convention which had taken power in Paris, and which in February of that year had voted for mass conscription. From spontaneous beginnings, the movement quickly became organised into a "Catholic Royal Army" (the Whites) some 40,000 strong. It was headed not only by nobles (d'Elbée, La Rochejaquelin, Charette) but also by commoners (Cathelineau, Stofflet). During Laval's campaign in the Bas-Maine, the royalist partisans were for the first time nicknamed **"Chouans",** from the call of the tawny owl *(le chathuant)* which they adopted as a rallying cry. After capturing a number of towns (including Angers) in surprise attacks, the Whites were defeated by the Republican armies (the Blues) at Cholet, Le Mans and Savenay (Dec. 1793). Guerilla resistance continued until the offensive launched by Hoche in 1796. ● After losing the Mayenne region in the north (Bas-Maine; Sarthe constituting the Haut-Maine) and the Vienne region to the south, the Angevin kingdom was reduced in size to the department of **Maine-et-Loire.**

20thC In June 1940 the Cadets from Saumur's military school put up a spirited resistance to advancing German troops on the bridges of the Loire. ● Since then, like the neighbouring regions around Orléans and Tours, the Vale of Anjou has settled into more peaceful agricultural activities; flowers, vegetables, wine and fruit do particularly well here because of the mild climate. Maine and Anjou are also stock farming regions (cattle, pigs, sheep, goats and poultry). The cattle markets - Craon, Château-Gontier and Cholet - are the principal points of assembly for the little towns in the region. ● Angers and Le Mans are the leading industrial centres of the area; Angers, formerly a slate and umbrella producer, has now added electronics to its manufacturing capacities, while Le Mans is, suitably enough, a specialist in both insurance and automobile production (Renault).

Practical information

The region

Information : Maine-et-Loire : *Comité Départemental du Tourisme* (C.D.T.), B.P. 852, 49008 Angers Cedex, ☎ (1) 41.88.23.85. **Mayenne :** *C.D.T.*, Chambre d'Agriculture, 9, rue de l'Ancien-Évêché, 53000 Laval, ☎ (1) 43.53.27.40. **Sarthe :** *C.D.T. and D.D.T.*, Hôtel du Département, 41, rue Dr-Leroy, 72040 Le Mans Cedex, ☎ 43.84.96.00.
In Paris : *Maison de la Sarthe,* esplanade de la gare Montparnasse, 75015, ☎ (1) 43.22.74.99.

Bookings : *Loisirs-Accueil Mayenne,* 9, rue de l'Ancien-Évêché, B.P. 723, 53002 Laval Cedex, ☎ 43.49.35.40.

Maps : *Michelin* n°s 60 and 63 1/200 000 and nº 232 Pays de Loire. *I.G.N.* nºs 17-19-25 and nº 106 Val de Loire 1/100 000.

S.O.S. : Maine-et-Loire : *S.A.M.U.*, Emergency Medical Service, ☎ (1) 41.48.44.22. **Sarthe :** *S.A.M.U.*, ☎ (1) 43.23.23.23. *Poisoning emergency centre :* Angers, ☎ (1) 41.48.21.21.

Weather forecast : Maine-et-Loire, ☎ (1) 41.48.54.77. **Mayenne,** ☎ (1) 43.53.43.82. **Sarthe,** ☎ (1) 43.84.30.26.

Farmhouse gîtes and chambres d'hôtes : *Relais départementaux des Gîtes ruraux :* cf. *C.D.T.* and Village de Gîtes de Cavire, ☎ (1) 41.89.19.80.

Camping : approximately 150 sites. Farmhouse camping and ferme-auberge accommodation : see *C.D.T.* for lists.

Scenic railways : Connerré-Plan d'eau de Tuffé-Prévelles-Bonnétable line (18 km) : M. Blanchard, ☎ (1) 43.28.65.03. M. Terrieux, ☎ (1) 43.21.47.59. M. Lecomte, ☎ (1) 43.29.06.17 : train-hire possible. Semur-en-Vallon : 1st Sun May-end Sep, ☎ (1) 43.93.07.50. Sillé-le-Guillaume, around the big lake at Sillé-Plage (20 km). Week-ends, Easter-30 Sep, Jul, Aug every day, ☎ (1) 43.97.04.36.

Technical tourism : *Cointreau S.A.*, carrefour Molière, St-Barthélemy-d'Anjou, 49800 Trélazé, ☎ (1) 41.43.25.21, open days at 10 and 2:30.

Visits to wine-cellars : *Conseil interprofessionnel des Vins d'Anjou et de Saumur,* 21, bd Foch, 49000 Angers, ☎ (1) 41.87.62.57.

Cultural events : end Mar in Champagné : *Fêtes des Lances* (historical reconstitution). **First fortnight May :** *Painting and Sculpture Exhibition* in Lassay. **May :** *Music Festival* in Laval. **Jun :** *Regional Art Exhibition* in Ernée. **Jun-Jul :** *Anjou Festival* in Saumur. **Jul-Aug :** *Nuits de Mayenne* in Sainte-Suzanne ; Abbey of l'Epau, *Festival of Music, exhibition.* **Jul-Sep :** *Cultural evenings* at the Vivoin priory ; *Evening performances* at the château de Lassay, ☎ (1) 43.04.72.33, (1) 43.04.74.33, and at the château du Lude, ☎ (1) 43.94.62.20. **First Sunday in Sep :** *Festival of the old trades,* at Laigné-en-Belin.

Folklore : mid-Jul : *Rose days* in Doué-la-Fontaine. **End Jul :** *Gathering of Anjou headdresses* in La Ménitré. **Mid-Aug :** *St-Fiacre festival* Château-Gontier, *Chanzeaux folk festival, Harvest festival* in Angrie, Saint-Denis-d'Orques.

Fairs and markets : mid-Feb : *Wine Fairs* in Chalonnes-sur-Loire, Saumur. **End Mar :** *Spring Fair* in Le Mans, *Meat Fair* in Évron.

Sporting events : Whitsun : *Bais-Hambers motor and motorcycle races.* **Apr :** *Le Mans Motorcycle Grand Prix de France.* **Mid-May :** *Motorcycle 24 heures* in Le Mans. **End Jul :** *"Carrousel du Cadre Noir" (equestrian demonstration)* in Saumur. **Early Sep :** *Stock-car racing* in Le Mans. **Mid-Sep :** *World Go-cart Championship* in Le Mans, *Fortnight of the horse* in Saumur, *Horse races* in Craon. **Early Oct :** *Trucks 24 heures* in Le Mans.

Rambling and hiking : topoguides. G.R. 35-36-3-235-365. Enq at the *Délégation dép. de la Féd. Nat. de Randonnée Pédestre :* François Cormier, 14, rue Éd.-Dunas, 72000 Le Mans, ☎ (1) 43.81.78.95.

Riding holidays : Enq at *Assn. Dép. du Tourisme équestre,* B.P. 852, 49008 Angers Cedex.

Cycling holidays : Circuits organised by the *C.D.T.* along the banks of the Erve, through the Loir valley and in the Baugeois, with lodgings in chambres d'hôtes. French Railways *(S.N.C.F.),* one of the organisers of this operation, offers a 30 % reduction on certain trains. *Voyages Conseil,* bd de Coubertin, 49000 Angers, ☎ (1) 41.68.19.33.

River and canal cruises : A 250 km network on the Maine, the Mayenne, the Oudon and the Sarthe. **Info. :** *Grouped Booking Service of the Bassin de la Maine,* B.P. 2207, 49022 Angers Cedex, ☎ (1) 41.88.99.38. River cruises : "Sablésien", quai National, 72300 Sablé, ☎ (1) 43.95.14.42. Navigation in flat-bottomed barges : Brilhaut Plaisance, 137, rue de Bretagne, 53000 Laval, ☎ (1) 43.69.19.00.

Children : *Leisure Centres* de Belle Beille, ☎ (1) 41.48.59.22. Le Hutreau, ☎ (1) 41.66.66.46. St-Gabriel, ☎ (1) 41.68.11.55. *Organised activity centre,* lac de Maine, ☎ (1) 41.48.08.36. *Outdoor centres :* mairie d'Angers, ☎ (1) 41.88.98.92. *Poney-Club* de la Bonde, Changé, ☎ (1) 43.40.10.01 (from 4 years).

Tennis : *Ligue régionale Centre,* pdt M. Back, Chargelegue, c/o F.F. Tennis.

Golf : Arnage-Le Mans (18 holes) ; Angers-Saint-Jean-des-Mauvrets (9 holes) ; Laval-Le Jariel (9 holes).

Canoeing : lac de Maine, ☎ (1) 41.48.57.01 ; Saumur, ☎ (1) 41.51.03.06 ; Seiches-sur-Loir, ☎ (1) 41.50.20.27 ; Laval, ☎ (1) 43.56.08.65 ; Mayenne, ☎ (1) 43.04.19.37 ; Daon, ☎ (1) 43.07.14.10 ; La Flèche, ☎ (1) 43.94.00.26 ; Saint-Calais, ☎ (1) 43.35.20.05, and see *C.D.T. Sarthe.*

Water skiing : Champtoceaux, ☎ (1) 41.83.52.48. Ingrandes-sur-Loire, ☎ (1) 41.41.40.05. Rochefort-sur-Loire, ☎ (1) 41.41.80.24. Château-Gontier, on the Mayenne, with a 31 acre stretch of water, ☎ (1) 43.07.97.24. Daon, mairie, ☎ (1) 43.07.14.10. Arnage, mairie, ☎ (1) 43.21.10.06.

Sailing, wind-surfing : enq at *Délégation Dép. du Temps Libre, Jeunesse et Sports :* **Maine-et-Loire,** Cité administrative, 49043 Angers Cedex, ☎ (1) 41.66.21.32. **Mayenne,** 26, rue Mortier, Laval, ☎ (1) 43.53.51.81. **Sarthe,** rue Chanzy, 72000 Le Mans, ☎ (1) 43.84.97.84.

Motoring : Instructional courses for seasoned drivers, courses for motorists and motorcycle riders, enq *Automobile-Club de l'Ouest* (A.C.O.), Circuit des 24 Heures, 72040 Le Mans Cedex, ☎ (1) 43.72.50.25.

Mountaineering : *Club Alpin* (C.A.F.), 17, rue Marengo, 72000 Le Mans (excursions in the nearby Mancelles "Alpes").

Hang-gliding : Angers-Avrillé airport, ☎ (1) 41.34.61.57 ; Union aéronautique des Mauges, Cholet, ☎ (1) 41.62.30.43 ; aéro club de Saumur-Terrefort, ☎ (1) 41.50.20.27 ; aérodrome Laval-Entrammes, ☎ (1) 43.53.71.30.

Fishing : enq at the mairies, at the *S.I., C.D.T.*, and at the Maine-et-Loire *Fédération de Pêche et Pisciculture,* 12, rue Grandet, 49000 Angers, ☎ (1) 41.87.57.09.

Hunting and shooting : enq at the *Féd. dép. des chasseurs.* **Maine-et-Loire :** 9, rue L.-Gain, 49000 Angers, ☎ (1) 41.88.25.04. **Mayenne :** 30, rue Mazagran, 53000 Laval, ☎ (1) 43.53.09.32. **Sarthe :** 1, rue Bruyère, 72000 Le Mans, ☎ (1) 43.82.21.46.

● Towns

ANGERS

Nantes 89, Poitiers 133, Paris 289
A3 ⊠ 49000

ℹ pl. Kennedy (C2), ☎ (1) 41.88.69.93, and railway station, main hall (B3), ☎ (1) 41.87.72.50.

SNCF (B3), ☎ (1) 41.87.76.60, (1) 41.88.43.18.

✈ Angers-Avrillé, 4 km NW, ☎ (1) 41.34.61.57.

🚌 pl. de la République (B2), ☎(1).88.59.25.

Car-hire : *Budget* train + auto, 2, av. Gal-Patton (A1), ☎ (1) 41.48.53.17, and at the station, ☎ (1) 41.87.76.60.

Hotels :
★★★***Anjou*** (Mapotel), 1, bd Mal-Foch (C3), ☎ (1) 41.88.24.82. Tx 720521. AE, DC, Euro, Visa. 51 rm Ⓟ 330. Rest. ♦♦ ⛒ ***la Salamandre,*** closed Sun, 80-200.
★★★***Progrès*** (Inter-Hôtel), 26, rue Denis-Papin (B3), ☎ (1) 41.88.10.14. Tx 720982. AE, DC, Euro, Visa. 41 rm ♿ 230.
★★★***France*** (France-Accueil), 8, pl. de la Gare (B3), ☎ (1) 41.88.49.42. Tx 720895. AE, DC, Euro, Visa. 57 rm ♿ 340. Rest. ♦ ***les Plantagenêts,*** closed 23 Dec-6 Jan, Sat and Sun noon, 65-100.
● ★★***Iéna,*** 27, rue Marceau (B3), ☎ (1) 41.87.52.40. 22 rm, 180.
● ★★***Saint-Julien,*** 9, pl. du Ralliement (C2), ☎ (1) 41.88.41.62. AE, Visa. 34 rm ⛒ 160.
★★***La Boule d'Or,*** 27, bd Carnot, ☎ (1) 41.43.76.56. Tx 720930. Visa. 33 rm Ⓟ 140. Rest. ♦♦ ♿ 45-125.
★★***Lac de Maine***, 3 km on the D111, exit "lac de Maine", ☎ (1) 41.48.02.12. Tx 721111. AE, DC, Euro, Visa. 79 rm Ⓟ ♿ closed 26 Dec-6 Jan, 280. Rest. ♦♦ ***le Diffen*** ♿ closed Sun, 65-210.

Saint-Sylvain-d'Anjou, ⊠ 49480, 5 km NE :
★★***La Fauvelaie*** (L.F.), rte de l'Épervière, ☎ (1) 41.43.80.10. 9 rm Ⓟ ♿ 95. Rest. ♦♦ ♿ closed 4-24 Aug and Sun eve, 50-160.

Youth hostel, rue Darwin, 2 km NW, ☎ (1) 41.48.14.55.

⛺ ★★★***Lac de Maine*** (165 pl.), ☎ (1) 41.73.05.03.

Restaurants :
● ♦♦♦ ***Le Vert d'Eau,*** 9, bd Gaston-Dumesnil (A2), ☎ (1) 41.48.52.31. AE, DC, Euro, Visa Ⓟ ♿ closed Sun eve, Mon, nat hols and Aug. A must for enthusiasts of Loire wines. Regional cooking : *paupiettes de sandre, ris de veau braisé,* 120-250.
● ♦♦ ***Le Quéré*** (Paul Le Quéré), 9, pl. du Ralliement (C2), ☎ (1) 41.87.64.94. AE, DC, Visa ; closed Fri eve and Sat, Feb school hols and 1-24 Jul. As one of Robuchon's team, Paul Le Quéré is a remarkable cook. Light and simple cooking : *coquillages au crémant de Loire.* Martine Le Quéré is your competent guide for wines, 140-220.
● ♦♦ ***Le Toussaint,*** 7, rue Toussaint (B2), ☎ (1) 41.87.46.20. AE, DC, Visa ⛒ closed 13 Aug-8 Sep, end-of-year and Feb school hols, Sun and Mon. A pleasant meal, just across from the cathedral, 100-200.
♦♦ ***L'Entracte,*** 9, rue Louis-de-Romain (C2), ☎ (1) 41.87.71.82 Ⓟ closed 15 Jul-end Aug, Sat and Sun eve, 120-210.
♦♦ ***Le Logis,*** 17, rue Saint-Laud (C2), ☎ (1) 41.87.44.15. AE, DC, Euro ; closed 15 Jul-20 Aug, Sat eve, Sun (May-Oct), Sun (Oct-May) and nat hols. Delicious fish specialities, 100-140.

Saint-Sylvain-d'Anjou :
★★***Auberge d'Eventard*** (L.F.), ☎ 41.43.74.25. AE, DC, Euro, Visa. 10 rm Ⓟ closed 2-19 Jan, 9 Sep-1 Oct, Sun eve and Mon, 145. Rest. ♦♦ ⛒ ♿ Spec : *tiède de coquille St-Jacques au vinaigre de Xérès,* 120-210.

Recommended : *le Petit St-Antoine,* charcutier, rue St-Aubin ; *Maison du vin de l'Anjou,* 5 *bis,* pl. Kennedy (C2) : enq and wine-tasting. Salesroom, 12, rue des Arènes, ☎ 41.88.63.89, and Sat *flea-market,* pl. Imbach.

BAUGÉ

Angers 38, Tours 68, Paris 260
B3 ⊠ 49150

ℹ mairie, ☎ 41.89.12.12.

SNCF ☎ 41.67.50.50.

Hotel :
★***Boule d'Or*** (L.F.), 4, rue du Cygne, ☎ 41.89.82.12. 14 rm ⛒ closed 1-31 Jan, Sun eve and Mon, 170. Rest. ♦ ♿ 60-250.

⛺ ★★*Municipal* (100 pl.), ☎ 41.89.14.79.

Gîte à la ferme : *Claire-Fontaine,* in Vieil-Baugé (D61), ☎ 41.89.20.74.

Bicycle hire : Nouchet, ☎ 41.89.24.85.

Le BOURGNEUF-LA-FORET

Mayenne 34, Rennes 59, Paris 293
19 km NW of Laval, A1 ⊠ 53410 Port-Brillet

Restaurant :
● ♦♦ ***La Vieille Auberge*** (L.F.), ☎ 43.37.71.12. With 8 rm, 100 ♿ closed 20-30 Sep, Jan, Sun and eve on nat hols. Good, simple cooking. Spec : *pied de veau ravigote, langue de bœuf sauce piquante,* 80-130.

CHAMPTOCEAUX

Nantes 31, Angers 63, Paris 351
20 km W of Saint-Florent-le-Vieil, A3
⊠ 49270 Saint-Laurent-des-Autels

ⓘ mairie, ☎ 40.83.52.31.

Hotel :
★★***Côte*** (L.F.), 2, rue du Dr-Giffard, ☎ 40.83.50.39. 28 rm Ⓟ closed 1 Oct-1 Apr and Fri low season, 180. Rest. ♦ 80-130.

Restaurant :
● ♦♦ ***La Forge,*** 1 *bis,* pl. des Piliers, ☎ 40.83.56.23. AE, Euro, Visa Ⓟ closed Sun eve, Tue eve and Wed. Next to the castle, local dishes : *salade de moules glacées safranée, marguerite de saumon au champagne et poivrons doux, magret de canard aux cerises,* 110-160.

La CHARTRE-SUR-LE-LOIR

Tours 40, Le Mans 44, Paris 215
C2 ⊠ 72340

ⓘ centre municipal de Gérondie, 20, rue Carnot, ☎ 43.44.40.04.

SNCF ☎ 43.44.40.42.

Hotels :
★★***France*** (L.F.), 20, pl. de la République, ☎ 43.44.40.16. Visa. 32 rm Ⓟ closed 15 Nov-15 Dec. Fishing in a private lake, 180. Rest. ♦ 55-220.
★***Cheval Blanc*** (L.F.), ☎ 43.44.40.01. Visa. 12 rm Ⓟ closed 15 Jan-15 Feb, Mon. Fishing in a private lake, 120. Rest. ♦ 50-120.

CHÂTEAU-GONTIER

Laval 30, Angers 46, Paris 284
A2 ⊠ 53200

ⓘ mairie, ☎ 43.07.07.10.

SNCF ☎ 43.07.10.95.

Hotels :
★★★***Parc*** (L.F.), 46, av. Joffre, ☎ 43.07.28.41. Euro, Visa. 23 rm Ⓟ ♿ closed 15 Dec-5 Jan, Sun, 180.
★★***Brasserie*** (L.F.), 2, av. Joffre, ☎ 43.07.10.80. Euro, Visa. 21 rm ♿ closed 15 Dec-10 Jan and Sun, 120. Rest. ♦♦ 70-210.
★***Cerf*** (L.F.), 31, rue Garnier, ☎ 43.07.25.13. DC, Euro, Visa. 22 rm Ⓟ ♿ 100.

Bazouges, 1.5 km N :
★★***Mirwault,*** ☎ 43.07.13.17. AE, DC, Euro, Visa Ⓟ ♿ closed 1 Jan-1 Mar, Fri and Sat noon low season, 180. Rest. ♦♦ Spec : *salade de St-Jacques* et *de ris de veau aux cèpes, fricassée d'anguilles,* 50-160.

⛺ ★★*Municipal du Parc* (100 pl.), ☎ 43.07.35.60.

CHÂTEAUNEUF-SUR-SARTHE

Angers 31, Le Mans 76, Paris 274
31 km N of Angers, A3 ⊠ 49330

ⓘ mairie, ☎ 41.42.10.22.

Hotel :
Cheffes, 8 km S :
● ★★★***Château de Teildras*** (Relais et châteaux), rte de Juvardeil, ☎ 41.42.61.08. Tx 722268. Visa. 11 rm Ⓟ closed 15 Nov-1 Apr. 16thC property, 400. Rest. ♦♦ ♿ closed Tue noon. Spec : *sandre à l'oseille, bar aux petits légumes,* 220-250.

CHOLET

Nantes 61, Angers 61, Paris 349
A4 ⊠ 49300

ⓘ pl. de Rougé, ☎ 41.62.22.35.

SNCF ☎ 41.62.31.35, 41.62.35.33.
Car-hire : *Budget* train + auto, at the station, ☎ 41.62.31.34.

Hotels :
At the Ribou lake, 5 km SE on the D20 :
★★★***Belvédère,*** ☎ 41.62.14.02. AE, DC, Visa. 8 rm Ⓟ closed end Jul-end Aug, nat hols and Sun eve, 210. Rest. ♦♦ 120-210.
★★***Europe,*** 8, pl. de la Gare, ☎ 41.62.00.97. AE, DC, Euro, Visa. 21 rm Ⓟ 195. Rest. ● ♦♦ (James Baron), closed Sat noon. A deserved promotion for James Baron, new member of our great chefs jury. Light and personalized excellent cooking : *foie gras poêlé à la compote d'aubergines au miel, rouget au gingembre ;* wines are Geneviève Baron's business, 90-260.
★★***Poste,*** 26, bd G.-Richard, ☎ 41.62.07.20. AE, Euro, Visa. 56 rm Ⓟ 210. Rest. ♦♦ ♿ closed 1-21 Aug, Sat eve and Sun (ex nat hols), 60-160.
★★***Vieux Chouan,*** 77, av. Leclerc, ☎ 41.46.10.99. 18 rm Ⓟ 180.

Nuaillé, 49340 Trémentines, 7.5 km NE :
★★***Relais des Biches*** (Inter-Hôtel), pl. de l'Église, ☎ 41.62.38.99. AE, DC, Visa. 13 rm Ⓟ ♿ 205. Rest. ♦♦ closed Sun, 65-155.

Saint-Macaire-en-Mauges, ⊠ 49450, 12 km NW :
★★***La Gâtine,*** 4, rue de Vendée, ☎ 41.55.30.23. 13 rm closed 14 Jul-15 Aug, 110. Rest. ♦ closed Sun eve and Mon, 50-155.

⛺ ★★★★*Lac de Ribou* (186 pl.), ☎ 41.62.47.04.

Farmhouse gîte and tables d'hôtes : *la Roullière,* 16 km, 49710 Le Longeron, ☎ 41.46.54.20 River fishing and riding.

Restaurant :
5.5 km W :
♦♦ ***Château de la Tremblaye*** (Châteaux-hôtels), rte des Sables-d'Olonne, ☎ 41.58.40.17 Ⓟ closed 1-21 Aug, Sun eve and Mon. Quality cooking in a 19thC castle : *enroulade de saumon sauce soufflée, blinis de rivière aux écrevisses, aiguillette et gigot de caneton au vinaigre de framboise,* 65-170.

Festivals and fairs : Mid-Lent carnival ; Fair-exhibition end Sep.

CONNERRÉ

Alençon 68, Tours 81, Paris 183
25 km E of Le Mans, B2 ⊠ 72160

ⓘ mairie, ☎ 43.89.00.66.

SNCF ☎ 43.29.00.08.

Hotels :
★***Gare,*** ☎ 43.89.00.02. 12 rm Ⓟ closed 10 Oct-1 Nov, 10-20 Jan and Fri, 120. Rest. ♦ 55-110.

Thorigné-sur-Dué, 4 km SE :
★★***Saint-Jacques,*** pl. du Monument, ☎ 43.89.95.50. DC, Visa. 10 rm Ⓟ ♿ closed 20 Jun-1 Jul, 6 Jan-4 Feb, Sun eve and Mon, 200. Rest. ♦ 60-160.

⅄ ★★*Municipal* (200 pl.), ☎ 43.29.00.66.

Restaurant :

♦♦ ***Tanto Lóonio,*** 58, rue de Paris, ☎ 43.89.00.24. Visa Ⓟ ♿ closed 2-17 Feb, 2-12 Aug, Mon eve and Tue, 70-130.

CRAON

Laval 30, Angers 56, Paris 308
A2 ⊠ 53400

ℹ rue Pantigny, ☎ 43.06.14.33.

SNCF ☎ 43.06.14.33.

Hotels :

★★***Boule d'Or*** (L.F.), pl. du 11-Novembre, ☎ 43.06.10.01. AE, DC, Euro, Visa. 21 rm, 150. Rest. 40-150.

Château de Craon (Château-Accueil), ☎ 43.06.11.02. 6 rm Ⓟ closed 15 Sep-Jun. 18thC castle in a 99-acre park, reservations, 400.

Restaurants :

♦♦ ***Ancre d'Or,*** 2, av. Promenade-Ch.-de-Gaulle, ☎ 43.06.14.11 Ⓟ closed Mon eve and Tue eve, Sun eve low season, 80-130.

2.5 km :

♦ ***Ferme-auberge la Borderie,*** ☎ 43.06.26.67 ♿ closed 5 days Christmas and Wed. Spec : *charcuterie, galettes,* pancakes ; warm welcome. Book for week-ends, 30-50.

DOUÉ-LA-FONTAINE

Angers 41, Poitiers 92, Paris 316
B3-4 ⊠ 49700

ℹ pl. de l'Hôtel-de-Ville, ☎ 41.59.18.53.

Hotels :

★★***France*** (L.F.), 17, pl. du Champ-de-Foire, ☎ 41.59.12.27. Visa. 18 rm, closed 23 Dec-18 Jan, Sun eve and Mon, 140. Rest. ♦ 45-140.

★***Dagobert*** (L.F.), 14, pl. du Champ-de-Foire, ☎ 41.59.14.44. AE, Visa. 20 rm Ⓟ ♿ closed 6 Jan-15 Feb, Fri eve and Sat low season, Mon high season, 120. Rest. 45-130.

⅄ ★★*Municipal* (70 pl.), ☎ 41.59.14.47.

La FERTÉ-BERNARD

Le Mans 49, Alencon 56, Paris 164
C1 ⊠ 72400

ℹ mairie, ☎ 43.93.04.42.

SNCF ☎ 43.93.00.47.

Hotels :

★***St-Jean,*** 13, rue R.-Garnier, ☎ 43.93.12.83. Visa. 16 rm 145.

★***Perdrix,*** 2, rue de Paris, ☎ 43.93.00.44. AE, DC. 10 rm Ⓟ 100. Rest. ♿ closed Tue, 65-160.

⅄ ★★*Belle Étoile* (66 pl.), ☎ 43.93.04.42.

Events : *Folklore* in Jul.

La FLÈCHE

Le Mans 41, Angers 47, Paris 241
B2 ⊠ 72200

ℹ 23, pl. du Marché-au-Blé, ☎ 43.94.02.53, and Maison du Tourisme, ☎ 43.94.49.82.

SNCF ☎ 43.94.00.71.

Hotels :

● ★★★***Relais Cicéro*** (Châteaux-hôtels), 18, bd d'Alger, ☎ 43.94.14.14, Tx 720015. AE, DC, Visa. 20 rm Ⓟ ♿ closed 15 Dec-15 Feb, 280. Rest. ● ♦♦ Quality fare on tables laden with flowers, 100-150.

★***Quatre Vents,*** 11, rue du Marché-au-Blé, ☎ 43.94.00.61 Ⓟ 15 rm. closed Feb and Sun (low season), 100.

⅄ ★★★*Municipal* (100 pl.), ☎ 43.94.55.90 ; free camping at the *parc animalier du Tertre Rouge,* ℹ ☎ 43.94.04.55 ; *Municipal* (53 pl.), in Bazouges-sur-le-Loir, 7 km W, ☎ 43.94.30.20.

Restaurant :

Bazouges-sur-le-Loir, 7 km W :

♦♦ ***Croissant,*** ☎ 43.45.32.08 Ⓟ closed 15 Jan-15 Feb, Sun eve and Mon, 80-130.

FONTEVRAUD-L'ABBAYE

Tours 61, Angers 69, Paris 306
B4 ⊠ 49590

ℹ mairie, ☎ 41.51.71.21.

Hotel :

★***Croix Blanche,*** 7, pl. des Plantagenêts, ☎ 41.51.71.11. 19 rm Ⓟ ♿ closed 15-30 Nov, 150. Rest. 40-130.

Restaurant :

♦ ***Abbaye,*** 8, av. des Roches, ☎ 41.51.71.04 Ⓟ ♿ closed 7 Oct-1 Nov, 10 Feb-1 Mar, Tue eve (winter) and Wed, 50-85.

FRESNAY-SUR-SARTHE

Alençon 20, Le Mans 38, paris 235
12 km NW of Beaumont-sur-Sarthe, B1
⊠ 72130

ℹ mairie, ☎ 43.97.23.75.

SNCF ☎ 43.97.20.33.

Hotel :

★★***Ronsin*** (L.F.), 5, av. Ch.-de-Gaulle, ☎ 43.97.20.10. AE, DC, Visa Ⓟ 12 rm. closed Sun eve and Mon noon (low season), 175. Grill-room, pizzeria, 50-115.

⅄ ★★★*Sans-Souci* (100 pl.), ☎ 43.97.32.87.

GENNES

2.5 km NW of Cunault, B3 ⊠ 49350

ℹ mairie, ☎ 41.51.81.30.

Hotels :

● ★★***Naulets d'Anjou,*** 18, rue Croix-de-Mission, ☎ 41.51.81.88. 20 rm Ⓟ ♿ closed Nov-end Apr. Art workshops, 190. Rest. ♦ closed Mon, 60-160.

★★***Loire*** (L.F.), rue des Cadets-de-Saumur, ☎ 41.51.81.03. 11 rm Ⓟ closed 27 Dec-8 Mar, Mon eve and Tue. Former post-house, 200. Rest. ♦ ♿ 50-150.

⅄ ★★*Du District* (170 pl.), ☎ 41.51.81.30.

LAVAL

Angers 73, Rennes 74, Paris 278
A1 ⊠ 53000

ℹ pl. du 11-Novembre, ☎ 43.53.09.39.

✈ Laval-Entrammes-Beausoleil, ☎ 43.53.73.15.

SNCF ☎ 43.53.21.50, 43.53.35.82.

Car-hire : *Budget* train + car, at the station, ☎ 43.53.21.00.

Hotels :

★★***Ouest,*** 3, rue Jules-Ferry (B2), ☎ 43.53.11.71, Tx 721028. AE, DC, Euro, Visa. 30 rm Ⓟ 160. Rest. ♦ ♿ 50-75.

★★***Impérial,*** 61, av. R.-Buron (C1), ☎ 43.53.55.02. AE, DC, Visa. 32 rm Ⓟ ♿ closed 4-10 and 16-28 Aug, 24-31 Dec, 165.

★***Gerbe de Blé,*** 83, rue V.-Boissel (C3), ☎ 43.53.14.10. AE, DC, Visa. 12 rm closed 6-27 Jan, 4-19 Aug, Sun eve and Mon, 170. Rest. ● ♦♦ Simple, quality dishes ; traditional and modern cooking. Loire wines, 120-220.

Gîtes d'étapes and chambres d'hôtes : *ferme la Véronnière,* in l'Huisserie, 9 km on the D112, 53260 Entrammes, ☎ 43.98.02.96 ; *ferme du Grand Vaugeron,* in la Bazouge-de-Chemère, 19 km on the N157 and D152, 53170 Meslay-du-Maine, ☎ 43.01.21.15.

Restaurants :

● ♦♦ ***Bistro de Paris,*** 67, rue Val-de-Mayenne, ☎ 43.56.98.29. Visa. ♿ closed Aug, Feb hols, Sat noon and Sun. Book ahead. Guy Lemercier's tasty cooking : *ris de veau aux ravioles de poivrons, filet de bœuf aux citrons et groseilles,* Loire wines, 70-200.

♦ ***La Rousine,*** 333, rte de Tours, ☎ 43.53.03.10. Visa. Ⓟ closed 3-25 Aug, Feb school hols, Sun eve and Mon. Enjoyable fare 60-150.

Le LION-D'ANGERS

Laval 52, Nantes 87, Paris 291
22 km NW of Angers, A3 ⊠ 49220

ℹ mairie, ☎ 41.91.30.16, and 14, pl. du Champ-de-Foire, ☎ 41.91.83.19 (high season).

Hotel :

★***Voyageurs,*** 2, rue du Gal-Leclerc, ☎ 41.95.30.08. 13 rm, closed 10-16 Oct, mid-Jan-10 Feb, 150. Rest. closed Sun eve and Mon (ex holidays), 40-120.

⛺ ★★*Municipal* (100 pl.), ☎ 41.91.31.56.

LOUÉ

Laval 50, Alençon 61, Paris 228
28 km W of Le Mans, B2 ⊠ 72540

Hotel :

★★★***Ricordeau*** (Relais et châteaux), rue de la Libération, ☎ 43.88.40.03. Tx 722013. AE, DC, Euro, Visa. 22 rm Ⓟ closed Jan, Sun eve and Mon, 355. Rest. ● ♦♦♦ The chef of this former post-house on the banks of the Vegré knows how to receive with style : *tête de veau, poulet poêlé aux petits légumes,* 150-250.

⛺ ★★Municipal *de la Vègre* (35 pl.), ☎ 43.27.40.18.

Traditional fair : *poultry fair* early Dec.

Le LUDE

Le Mans 44, Tours 52, Paris 247
B2-3 ⊠ 72800

ℹ pl. F.-de-Nicolay (high season) and 8, rue du Bœuf (low season), ☎ 43.94.62.20.

Hotels :

★★***Maine*** (L.F.), 24, av. de Saumur, ☎ 43.94.60.54. Euro, Visa. 24 rm Ⓟ closed Christmas-20 Jan, Mon (high season, ex hotel), Sat and Sun eve (low season), 190. Rest. ♦ 60-110.

Luché-Pringé, 10 km NW :

● ★★***Port des Roches*** (L.F.), 4 km E on the D13, ☎ 43.45.44.48. DC. 15 rm Ⓟ closed Sun eve and Mon, 180. Rest. ♦ 60-110.

⛺ ★★★★*Municipal* (400 pl.), ☎ 43.94.67.70 ; ★★*Municipal* (60 pl.), in Luché-Pringé, 10 km NW, ☎ 43.94.43.25.

Son et lumière : *château du Lude* (Thu, Fri, Sat, from Jun to Sep), a gorgeous pageant with 350 characters, 300 fountains, and a fireworks display, enq : ☎ 43.94.62.20.

MAMERS

Alençon 25, Le Mans 45, Paris 195
C1 ⊠ 72600

ℹ 9, rue Ledru-Rollin, ☎ 43.97.60.63.

Hotel :

★★***Bon Laboureur*** (L.F.), 1, rue P.-Bert, ☎ 43.97.60.27. AE, DC, Euro, Visa. 10 rm. closed 2-22 Jan, Fri eve and Sat noon (low season), 180. Rest. ♦ ♿ Small, pleasant restaurant, 45-180.

⛺ ★★*Municipal* (50 pl.), ☎ 43.97.68.30.

Le MANS

Tours 82, Angers 88, Paris 203
B2 ⊠ 72000

ℹ 40, pl. de la République (B2), ☎ 43.28.17.22 ; sq. Jacques-Duboiss, ☎ 43.24.84.88.

✈ Le Mans-Arnage, 7 km S, ☎ 43.84.00.43.

SNCF (A4), ☎ 43.24.96.10, 43.24.74.00, 43.24.59.50.

Car-hire : *Budget* train + auto at the station, ☎ 43.24.44.74.

Hotels :

★★★***Concorde*** (Concorde), 16, av. du Gal-Leclerc (B3), ☎ 43.24.12.30. Tx 720487. AE, DC, Euro, Visa. 68 rm Ⓟ 310. Rest. ♦♦ 130-230.

★★★***Moderne,*** 14, rue du Bourg-Belé (B4), ☎ 43.24.79.20. 32 rm Ⓟ ♿ 260. Rest. ♦♦ Spec : *nage de langoustines, dos de turbot aux poireaux, saumon frais à la moelle et au chinon,* 120-210.

★★***Escale,*** 72, rue Chanzy (C3), ☎ 43.84.55.92. AE, DC, Euro, Visa. 49 rm Ⓟ ♿ closed 20 Dec-5 Jan, 155.

★★***Chantecler,*** 50, rue de la Pelouse (A4), ☎ 43.24.58.53. 36 rm Ⓟ ♿ 184. Rest. closed Sat eve, Sun and 20 Dec-1 Jan, 60-150.

★★***Saumon,*** 44, pl. de la République (B2), ☎ 43.24.03.19. 40 rm Ⓟ ♿ closed end-of-year hols, 150.

★★***Galaxie,*** 39, bd de la Gare (A4), ☎ 43.24.99.50. Euro, Visa. 47 rm, closed Christmas vacation, 180.

4 km E on the N23 :

● ★★***Pommeraie,*** rte de l'Éventail, ☎ 43.85.13.93. 35 rm Ⓟ 130.

Restaurants :

♦♦ ***La Grillade,*** 1 *bis,* rue C.-Blondeau (B-C1), ☎ 43.24.21.87. AE, Visa. ♿ closed Sun eve. Spec : *aiguillettes de canard au poivre vert,* 70-180.

♦ ***L'Adresse,*** 1, rue du Rempart, ☎ 43.28.55.77. A good, small restaurant, 80-130.

Arnage, 7 km S on the N23 :

● ♦♦♦ ***Auberge des Matfeux,*** rte d'Angers, ☎ 43.21.70.71. Ⓟ ♿ closed 15-30 Jul, Jan, Sun eve and Mon. Rich setting, excellent refined and flavourful cooking : *filet de sandre grillé et sa sauce aux herbes du jardin, fricassée de poulette de la ferme au vinaigre de cidre,* 120-230.

Guécélard, 72230 Arnage, 16 km SW :

♦♦ *Botte d'Asperges,* 49, rue Nationale, ☎ 43.21.12.03. Closed 1-15 Jul, 1-15 Feb, Wed eve and Thu. Spec : *filet de barbue aux crevettes,* 80-130.

Recommended : *Auction hall,* rue des Ursulines, ☎ 43.24.47.07, and *Grenier à Sel,* 20, rue Wagram, ☎ 43.28.80.38. *Charcuterie la Truie qui File,* 25, pl. de la République, ☎ 43.28.43.36. :

for traditional *rillettes* (potted meats). *Pâtisserie Pasquier*, 33, rue Gambetta, ☎ 43.28.05.37., for delicious frosted cakes.

MAYENNE

Laval 30, Alençon 61, Paris 284
A1 ☒ 53100

ℹ pl. du 9-Juin-44, ☎ 43.04.19.37.

SNCF ☎ 43.04.11.12.

Hotels :
● ★★***Grand Hôtel*** (L.F.), 2, rue A.-de-Loré, ☎ 43.04.37.35. 29 rm Ⓟ closed 24 Dec-8 Jan, 180. Rest. ♦ 80-130.
★★***Croix Couverte*** (L.F.), 1.5 km rte d'Alençon, ☎ 43.04.32.48. AE, DC, Euro, Visa. 11 rm Ⓟ 140. Rest. ♦♦ ♿ closed 25-31 Dec and Sun eve, 60-160.

⛺ ★★*Municipal* (100 pl.), ☎ 43.04.21.01.

Chambres d'hôtes : *ferme Grappay*, Brécé, 20 km NW on the N12 and D5, 53120 Gorron, ☎ 43.04.63.65.

MONTREUIL-BELLAY

Angers 53, Poitiers 80, Paris 315
B4 ☒ 49260

ℹ mairie, ☎ 41.52.33.86.

SNCF ☎ 41.52.30.10.

Hotel :
● ★★***Splendid,*** with annex (L.F.), 13, rue du Dr-Gaudrez, ☎ 41.52.30.21. 40 rm Ⓟ closed 10-25 Jan, Sun eve (low season), 220. Rest. ♦ 60-150.

⛺ ★★★*Airotel des Nobis* (100 pl.), ☎ 41.52.33.66.

Restaurant :
♦♦ ***Porte Saint-Jean,*** 432, rue Nationale, ☎ 41.52.30.41. Ⓟ closed 3 wks Jan, 2 wks Nov-Dec, Mon eve and Tue. Menu acc. to season and market : *sandre à l'oseille, saumon au beurre rouge*, 120-210.

MONTSOREAU

Tours 56, Angers 64, Paris 301
B4 ☒ 49730

ℹ mairie, ☎ 41.51.70.22.

Hotel :
● ★★***Le Bussy*** (L.F.), ☎ 41.51.71.76. Visa. 19 rm Ⓟ ♿ closed 15 Dec-31 Jan, Tue (ex Jul-Aug), 225. Rest. ♦♦ ***Diane de Méridor*** ☎ 41.51.70.18. Spec : fish from the Loire served with Saumur wine, 65-95.

Gîte à la ferme : *château de Parnay*, ☎ 41.38.10.85. Fishing within 500 m.

⛺ ★★Municipal *de l'Isle Verte* (160 pl.), ☎ 41.51.76.60.

Restaurant :
♦♦ ***La Loire,*** ☎ 41.51.70.06. Euro, Visa. With 7 rm, 65 Ⓟ ♿ closed 15 Jan-3 Mar, Thu eve (low season) and Fri, 50-100.

POUANCÉ

Laval 51, Angers 60, Paris 329
24 km W of Segré, A2 ☒ 49420

ℹ mairie, ☎ 41.92.45.86, and rue Porte-Angevine, ☎ 41.92.45.86 (high season).

Hotel :
★★***Cheval Blanc,*** rte de Segré, ☎ 41.92.41.16. Visa. 14 rm, 140. Rest. ♦ ♿ closed Mon low season 55-120.

⛺ ★★*Municipal* (50 pl.), ☎ 41.92.43.97.

ROCHEFORT-SUR-LOIRE

Cholet 45, Nantes 80, Paris 313
20 km SW of Angers, A3 ☒ 49190

ℹ mairie, ☎ 41.78.70.24, and "Grand Cour" (high season).

Hotel :
★★***Grand Hôtel*** (L.F.), 30, rue R.-Gasnier, ☎ 41.78.70.06. Visa. 8 rm Ⓟ closed 15 Jan-15 Feb, last week in Jun, Sun eve and Mon (low season), 120. Rest. ♿ 60-115.

⛺ *Municipal* (150 pl.), ☎ 41.78.70.24.

LES ROSIERS-SUR-LOIRE

Saumur 15, Angers 30, Paris 290
3.5 km NW of Cunault, B3 ☒ 49350 Gennes

ℹ mairie, ☎ 41.51.80.04.

Hotel :
● ★***Val de Loire*** (L.F.), pl. de l'Église, ☎ 41.51.81.03. Euro. 11 rm Ⓟ ♿ closed 1-28 Oct, Sun eve (ex high season) and Mon, 130. Rest. ♦ Regional cooking, 45-135.

⛺ ★★*Du District* (100 pl.), ☎ 41.51.80.04.

Restaurants :
● ♦♦♦ ***Jeanne de Laval,*** 54, rue Nationale, ☎ 41.51.80.17. AE, DC, Visa. With 15 rm, 240 Ⓟ closed 20 Nov-28 Dec, 4-12 Mar, Sun eve (ex high season) and Mon (ex nat hols). Albert Angereau's famous *beurre blanc* is now prepared by his son Michel and is a delicious garnish for Loire fish. Anjou wines, 140-250.
♦♦ ***Toque Blanche,*** ☎ 41.51.80.75. Visa ; closed 1-7 Sep, Feb school hols, Tue eve and Wed. Book ahead, 50-125.

SABLÉ-SUR-SARTHE

Laval 42, Le Mans 48, Paris 252
B2 ☒ 72300

SNCF ☎ 43.95.00.79.

Hotel :
Solesmes, 3 km NE :
★★★***Grand-Hôtel*** (France-Accueil), ☎ 43.95.45.10. Tx 722903. AE, DC, Euro, Visa. 30 rm closed Feb, 275. Rest. ♦♦ ♿ closed Sun eve low season. Spec : *salade de saumon sauvage, sandre mousse d'oseille, noisettes d'agneau à la purée d'ail*, 75-200.

⛺ ★★★*Municipal* (133 pl.), ☎ 43.95.42.61.

Restaurant :
Saint-Denis-d'Anjou, 53290 Grèz-en-Bouère, 10 km :
♦♦ ***Roi René,*** 4, Grande-Rue, ☎ 43.70.52.30 1 rm, 200 Ⓟ closed mid-Jan-Feb, Tue eve and Wed, 65-140.

SAINT-CALAIS

Le Mans 45, Blois 64, Paris 186
C2 ☒ 72120

ℹ rue Ch.-Garnier, ☎ 43.35.00.36.

Hotel :
★***Angleterre;*** 9, rue Guichet, ☎ 43.35.00.43. 13 rm Ⓟ closed 10-23 Jun, 25 Dec-15 Jan, Sun eve and Mon (ex nat hols), 145. Rest. 50-135.

⛺ ★★Municipal *du Lac* (100 pl.), ☎ 43.35.04.81.

Folklore in Sep.

SAINT-LÉONARD-DES-BOIS

Le Mans 50, Laval 75, Paris 211
19 km SW of Alençon, B1 ⊠ 72590

ℹ mairie, ☎ 43.97.23.75.

Hotel :
★★★***Touring*** (Mapotel), ☎ 43.97.28.03. Tx 722006. AE, DC, Euro, Visa. closed 10 Dec-1 Feb, 255. Rest. ♦♦ closed Fri eve and Sat from 15 Nov to 15 Mar. Spec : *écrevisses du vivier sautées au jasnières,* 65-160.

⛺ ★★*Municipal* (66 pl.), ☎ 43.97.28.10.

SAULGES

Laval 37, Le Mans 60, Paris 255
20 km NW of Sablé, B2 ⊠ 53340 Ballée

Hotel :
● ★★***Ermitage*** (L.F.), ☎ 43.01.22.28. Euro, Visa. 22 rm closed Sun eve and Mon (ex Jul-Aug and nat hols), 130. Rest. ♦♦ Skilfully prepared dishes, 70-145.

⛺ ★★*Municipal* (35 pl.), ☎ 43.01.22.23.

SAUMUR

Angers 52, Tours 66, Paris 300
B3 ⊠ 49400

ℹ 5, rue Beaurepaire, ☎ 41.51.03.06.

SNCF av. David-d'Angers, ☎ 41.50.40.55.

pl. St-Nicolas, ☎ 41.51.27.29.

Car-hire : *Budget* train + car, at the station, ☎ 41.50.31.25.

Hotels :
★★***Roi René,*** 94, av. du Gal-de-Gaulle, ☎ 41.67.47.03. 39 rm 260. Rest. ♦ closed Sat noon, 120-210.
★★***Londres,*** 48, rue d'Orléans, ☎ 41.51.23.98. 26 rm 180.
★***Croix Verte,*** 49, rue de Rouen, ☎ 41.67.39.31. Euro, Visa. 18 rm closed 20 Dec-31 Jan, 150. Rest. ♦ closed Fri eve and Sun eve, 45-85.

Chênehutte-les-Tuffeaux, 49350 Gennes, 8 km NW :
● ★★★★***Le Prieuré*** (Relais-châteaux), ☎ 41.50.15.31. 34 rm closed Jan-Feb, 900. Rest. ● ♦♦♦ René Travessac is fond of beautiful things. Regional dishes by P. Doumercq and J.-N. Lumineau. Spec : *médaillons de lotte aux palourdes et safran, confit de lapereau au layon.* Good wines. 220-350.

⛺ ★★★*Municipal* (150 pl.), ☎ 41.50.45.00.

Farmhouse gîte : *la Poitevinière,* 8 km N on the N147, 49680 Neuillé, ☎ 41.52.55.08. This riding centre offers 3 ch. d'hôtes and a table d'hôte. Riding at the farm 5 km.

Restaurants :
♦♦ ***Gambetta,*** 12, rue Gambetta, ☎ 41.51.11.13. AE, DC, Visa ; closed 20 Dec-10 Jan, 11-20 Mar, Sun eve and Mon. Spec : *matelote d'anguilles, coq au saumur, soufflé maison.* Good wines, 80-125.
♦ ***Escargot,*** 30, rue du Mal-Leclerc, ☎ 41.51.20.88. Visa. closed 3 weeks in Nov, 2 weeks in Feb, Tue eve and Wed ex early May-end Sep, 65-110.

SEICHES-SUR-LE-LOIR

Saumur 45, Le Mans 70, Paris 270
19 km NE of Angers, A3 ⊠ 49140

ℹ mairie, ☎ 41.80.00.37.

Hotel :
● ★***Saint-Jacques,*** Matheflon, 2 km N, ☎ 41.76.20.30. 10 rm closed 8-15 Oct, 15 Jan-8 Feb, Sun eve and Mon, 100. Rest. ♦ 45-60.

SILLÉ-LE-GUILLAUME

Le Mans 33, Alençon 37, Paris 230
B1 ⊠ 72140

SNCF ☎ 43.20.10.41.

Hotel :
★***Bretagne*** (L.F.), 1, pl. de la Croix-d'Or, ☎ 43.20.10.10. 14 rm closed 20 Dec-20 Jan, Sun eve and Mon low season, 90. Rest. ♦ 50-120.

⛺ ★★★*Les Mollières* (133 pl.), ☎ 43.20.16.12.

Chambres d'hôtes and farmhouse-inn : *Abbaye de Champagne* (12th-13thC residence), 8 km S of Rouez on the D45, ☎ 43.20.15.74. within 10 km. Riding. Farm produce for sale (eggs and poultry).

VIBRAYE

Le Mans 45, Alençon 72, Paris 170
16 km N of Saint-Calais, C2 ⊠ 72320

Hotels :
★★***Auberge de la Forêt*** (L.F.), 38, rue G.-Goussault, ☎ 43.93.60.07. AE, DC, Visa. 7 rm closed Jan, Sun eve and Mon. A pleasant stop-over in a vast park, 100. Rest. ♦ 55-100.
★***Chapeau Rouge*** (L.F.), pl. de l'Hôtel-de-Ville, ☎ 43.93.60.02. Euro, Visa. 12 rm closed 15-30 Aug, Feb, Sun eve and Mon, 100. Rest. 50-170.

⛺ ★★*Municipal* (85 pl.), ☎ 43.93.60.27.

The Midi Toulousain and Pyrénées Regions

The Garonne runs its course between the lush Armagnac and the outwardly austere Ariège regions. Here, cliffs and peaks rise up abruptly above green valleys, serving as foundation stones for look-out castles and churches echoing the untamed color of the surrounding stone.

Traces of human society dating back as far as 300,0000 or 400,000 years have been discovered in Haute-Garonne, and on the walls of the famous Ariège caves are paintings done by Paleolithic hunters. Many centuries later the caves provided welcome shelter for people fleeing the violence of the Wars of Religion and the Cathar tragedy. Other traces of prehistoric art have been found here, too — animals sculpted from deer antlers, clay figurines and, at the end of the Paleolithic area, the beginnings of a geometrical and abstract art with in some places stylized human figures.

In the 12th and 13th centuries, the troubadours sang the joys of courtly love in the *Langue d'Oc* (the southern French tongue), beginning a transformation of the unsophisticated habits of the day into something finer and more poetic. But the Albigensian crusades sounded the deathknell for this form of literary expression and the troubadours and their language died out.

Where the Garonne makes a final hair-pin turn and chooses the Atlantic coast, midway between the Atlantic and the Mediterranean, is Toulouse, whose extraordinary location has proved its fortune. The "pink city", so named after the color of its brick, is an economic and intellectual capital whose dynamism and character make it the natural capital of the whole region between the Pyrénées and the foothills of the Massif central. Once the capital of the Haut-Languedoc kingdom, it is now the spokesman for the *Langue d'Oc* culture and works hand in hand with its sister cities to revive the language and literature of this second branch of French culture and civilization.

Sightseeing

Facts and figures

Location : *the central portion of the Pyrénées, the upper valley of the Garonne and the valleys that fan out from the plateau of Lannemezan to the Gers.*
Area : *17 456 km²*
Climate : *A variety of micro-climatic conditions; the numerous valleys each have differing degrees of sunshine and exposure to prevailing winds, which come from the Atlantic; in autumn, the south-easterly Autan is strongly felt in the middle valley of the Garonne. Winters can be colder and dryer than in the Paris region.*
Population : *approx 1 189 000.*
Administration : *the three departments belong to the Midi-Pyrénées economic region.* ***Ariège,*** *Prefecture : Foix.* ***Haute-Garonne,*** *Prefecture : Toulouse.* ***Gers,*** *Prefecture : Auch.*

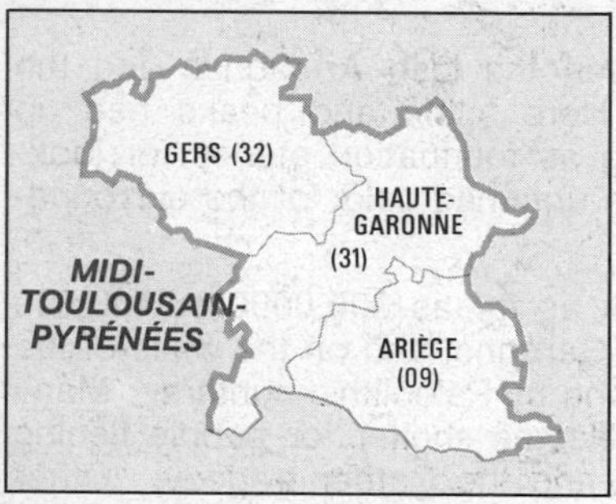

Weekend Tips

Starting from Saint-Gaudens, the first day will cover from Montmaurain to Aurignac, Martres-Tolosanne and Salies-du-Salat (lunch); continue via Saint-Girons and the Gorges de Ribaouto to the valley of Bethmane and Castillon-en-Couserans; stop here for the night. The next day, visit Saint-Béat, lunch at Luchon and on to Saint-Bertrand-de-Comminges and Montréjeau.
From Foix, there is a different route running through Tarascon-sur-Ariège and the Grotte de Niaux, Vicdessos, Aulus-les-Bains and Masat, where you have lunch. Take the road to Verte, the Bastide-de-Sérou and the Mas-d'Azil; stopover at Foix, Varilhes or Saint-Jean-de-Verges. Return to Toulouse through Lavelanet, Montségur, Bélesta, Mirepoix (lunch) and Villefranche-de-Lauragais.

■ AUCH★★

A1-2 / ® / pop. 25 540 (Gers)
See plan on following page

The interesting part of this old town is on

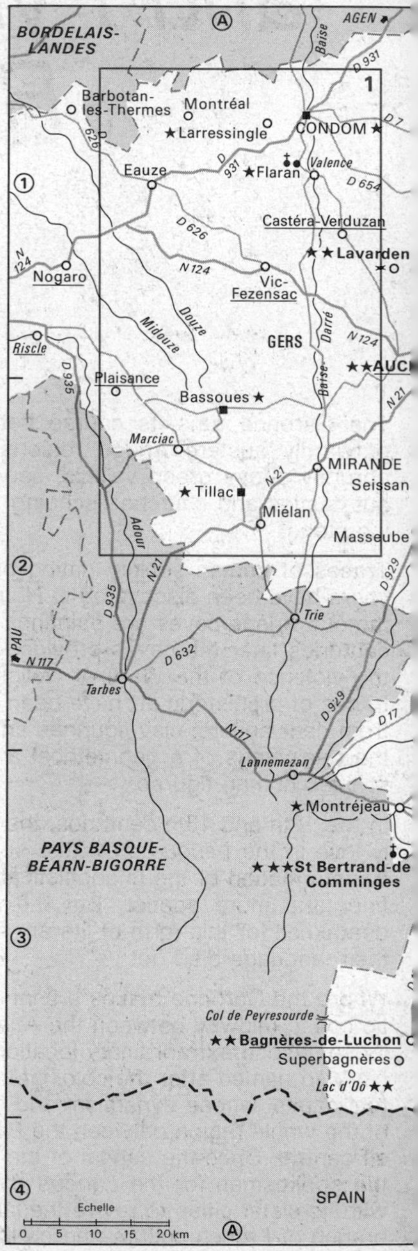

the hill overlooking the Gers. Here you will find the Hôtel de Ville, the Allées d'Étigny, the cathedral, shops selling regional produce, and the Hôtel de France, one of the best gastronomic addresses in the region.

▶ The **cathedral**★ (B1) has a late 17thC French-Classical façade (fine wrought iron gates), but is in fact a Gothic 15th-16thC building; exceptional stained glass★, mostly by Arnaud de Moles, ca. 1513. Carved stalls★★ in the choir,

Don't miss

★★★ : *Saint-Bertrand-de-Comminges (A3), Toulouse (C2),* ★★ : *Auch (B1), Bagnères-de-Luchon (A3), Lombrives Caves (C3), Lavardens (A1), Mas-d'Azil Caves (B3), Montségur (C3), Oô Lake (A3), Saint-Lizier (B3).*

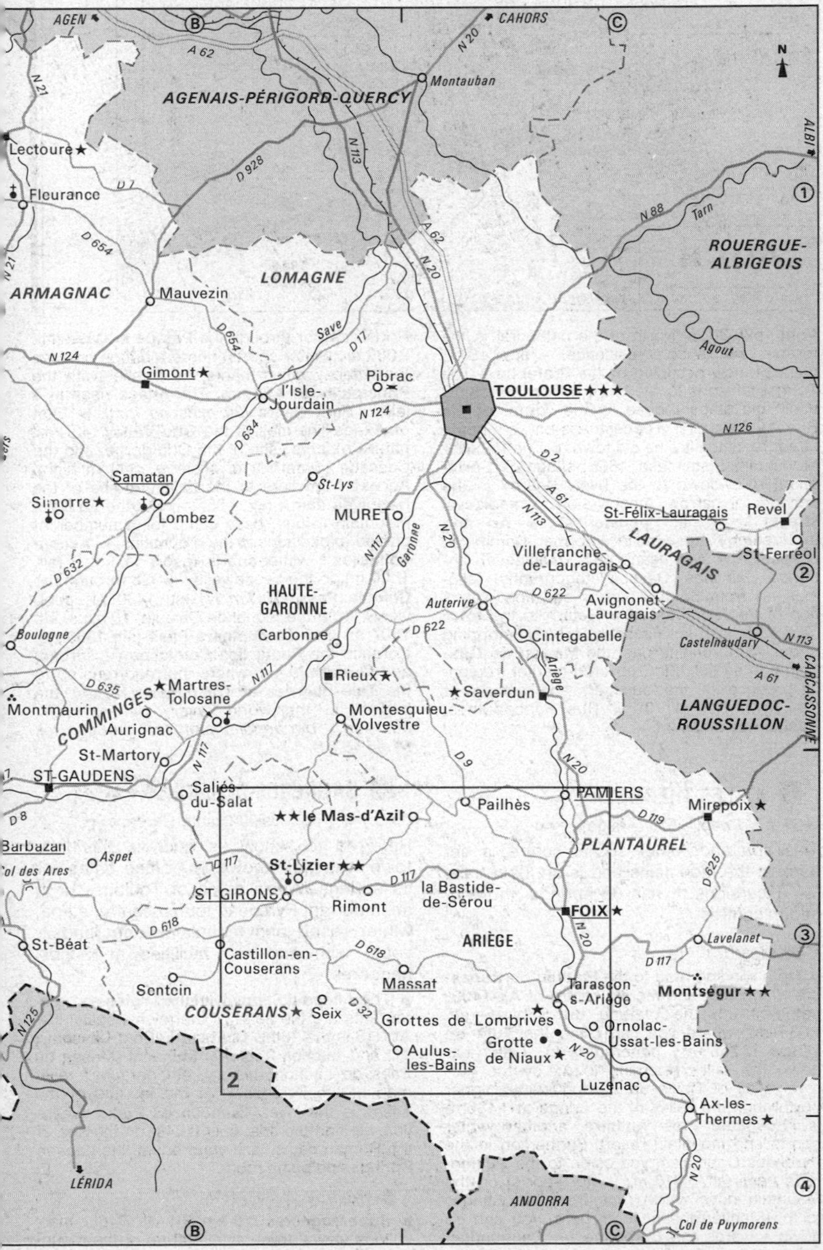

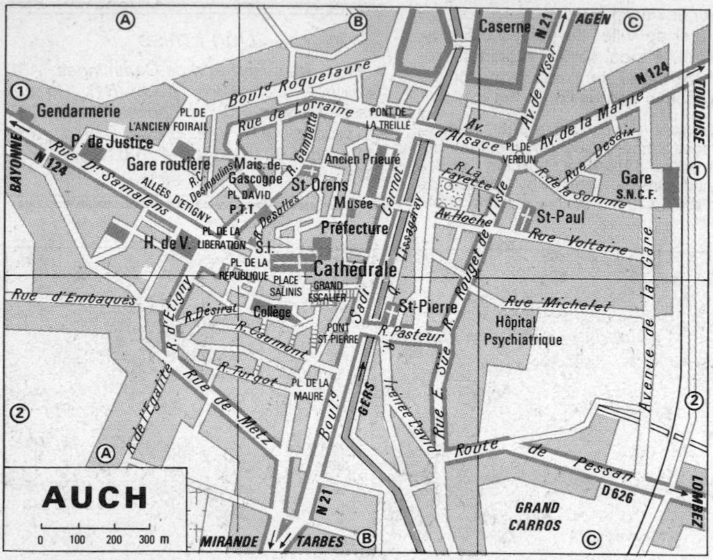

from 1520-30. ▶ North of the cathedral is the former archbishop's residence, a fine 18thC mansion now occupied by the **Prefecture.** The Tourist Office is located in a handsome 15thC brick and timber house on the corner of the Rue Dessoles (B1), a pedestrians-only shopping street running into the old town. ▶ The Escalier Monumental (staircase, 1666; statue of d'Artagnan) runs down to the river. Nearby is the network of narrow, steeply-sloping mediaeval streets known as **"pousterles".** ▶ **Art and archaeology museum** in a former Dominican chapel, Rue Daumesnil (B1; mediaeval antiques, paintings, Gascon ethnography, religious art from South America and fine collection of Peruvian vases). ▶ Return to the town centre along Rue Gambetta, a busy shopping street, (B1), running past the **Maison de Gascogne** in an old 18thC covered market (regional produce in the summer) and ending at the Town Hall (1770). ▶ Rue Pagodéontés, **Resistance Museum.** □

■ AX-LES-THERMES★

C3 / ® / pop. 1 510 (Ariège)

This spa and winter sports centre is set back in the mountains and is an ideal base for excursions. It has 60 springs and four health centres. □

▶ Nearby

▶ Up a winding road to the **Plateau du Bonascre** *(8 km SW)* and the ski centre of **Ax-1400;** cable-car to the plateau du Saquet (alt. 2 030 m), where you can climb the **Tute de l'Ours** (2 255 m; panorama★★). Cable-car down the valley returning to Ax by the narrow valley of Défilé du Berduquet. ▶ Higher up through the valley of the Ariège at 1 436 m is **l'Hospitalet-Près-l'Andorre,** another winter sports and mountain resort. Further on in the Pyrénées Orientales, you come to the **Puymorens Pass** (alt. 1 915 m; winter sports) on the mountain ridge which runs from the Atlantic to the Mediterranean. From here, you can go down towards the **Cerdagne** (→ Languedoc-Roussillon) or through the **Pas de la Case** (alt. 2 085 m; winter sports) : here a bridge crosses the Ariège, which marks the frontier with the **Principality of Andorra.** The Ariège rises in a lake : **Font Nègre** *(30 mins on foot).* ▶ East of Ax-les-Thermes is the **Orlu Valley** (43 km² nature reserve; site of the Orlu gorge, and the Cascade (waterfall) of Nioles★, 300 m high). Access from here to the delightful site of the **Naguilles dam★** (alt. 1 864 m) and the En Beys mountain refuge, base camp for a number of guided expeditions in the mountains. ▶ **Ascou-Pailhères :** winter-sports resort 11 km E (alt. 1500 m), in the Lauze valley. ▶ Go through the **Chioula Pass** (*10 km N;* alt. 1430 m; good view★ from the Signal de Chioula, *10 mins,* alt. 1507 m) and the **Marmare Pass** (alt. 1360 m), to reach the **Route des Corniches★** (cliffroad) and **Lordat** *(29 km)* where the road runs up to the **Talc quarries at Trimouns★** *(12 km),* the largest in the world *(every pm ex Sun., Jul.-Aug.; by appointment for groups, tel. 61.64.48.01).* □

■ BAGNÈRES-DE-LUCHON★★

A3 / ® / pop. 3 600 (Haute-Garonne)

Referred to simply as **Luchon,** this little town was well known in Roman times for its springs. Within reach of Toulouse, it is an important Pyrenean tourist centre, a spa, winter resort and mountaineering rendezvous, with excellent facilities at Superbagnères.

▶ The **Allées d'Étigny** with their cafés and restaurants are the heart of the town's social life. At N18 is the 18thC **Château Laffont-Lassalle;** TO and **Luchon Regional Museum** (Musée du Pays de Luchon; history, ethnography; relief map of the Pyrénées). At the far end of the Allées is the lovely **Quinconces Park★** where you will find the spa, built (1848) on the site of the Roman baths, with vaporarium, the Lepape Springs and pump room. □

▶ Nearby

▶ **Superbagnères** *(19 km SW on D46)* : marvellous view★ from (alt. 1 800 m) of the mountain chain, from the Crabère in the east, to the Arbizon in the west, including the Massif de la Maladeta. Down below : the **Lys Valley★**, which actually means "valley of the avalanches" (Lis) is a wooded valley leading to the Cascade (waterfall), the Gouffre (chasm) and the **cirque d'Enfer★** (natural amphitheatre). ▶ Along the **valley of La Pique★** you come to the **Hospice de France** (*10.5 km;* alt. 1 360 m site★) near the Cascade du Parisien; excursions to the Port de Vénasque (alt. 2,486 m), superb views★★ over the Spanish border to the **Pic d'Aneto** (alt. 3 404 m), the highest peak in the Pyrénées. ▶ Finally the One Valley is the north-west passage to the **Oueil Valley★** (you can climb Mont Né★ to Bordères lake★), and to the **Larboust Valley★** (**Saint-Aventin,** village with charming Romanesque church) and to the **Val d'Oô★.** From here, you arrive at the Val d'Astau (valley) and climb on foot to the **Lake Oô★★** surrounded on all sides by jagged peaks; the Lake Espingo empties into it in a 273 m waterfall. The Peyresourde Pass (alt. 1 570 m) leads to the Aure Valley (→ Basque Country, Béarn, Bigorre). □

The BASTIDES of ARMAGNAC★

▶ Round trip *(approx 300 km, 2 days)*
A1-2 *(see map 1)*

Solid fortified towns with covered markets and arcades, unpretentious country châteaux, little churches; all hidden in the soft countryside of the Gers. Spring is the ideal season for visiting this charming region, unless you prefer the colours of autumn, when the vineyards are a blaze of russet.

▶ **Condom** (→). ▶ **Valence-sur-Baïse** ®, a 13thC *bastide* (→ p. 793) which still has its old church (14thC) and its arcaded square. The church at **Flaran★** is more interesting, with chapter and cloister of the former Cistercian abbey, founded in the 12thC. ▶ **Cassaigne** is today a centre of Armagnac production; the bishops of Condom formerly had their country residence in the château (traditional kitchen and 18thC Armagnac cellars). ▶ The episcopal residence at **Larressingle★** is older still, fortified in the 13thC, but today a peaceful and charming little village, the size of a pocket handkerchief (sale of Armagnac and Gascon produce). ▶ The little *bastide of* **Fourcès★** was an 11thC stronghold; it is built in concentric circles round a tiny village square (15thC castle). ▶ **Montréal** ® was founded in 1255; the **Gallo-Roman villa of Séviac** and the mosaics discovered there *(every day in summer; guided tours, tel 62.28.43.18)* are reminders of the importance of northern Armagnac in Roman days. ▶ **Éauze** ®, on a hill overlooking the Gélise, was the most important Gallo-Roman town in its district, eventually becoming a bishopric. The southern Gothic cathedral was built at the end of the 15thC. On the arcaded square is a house known as the Maison de Jeanne d'Albret (Henri IV's mother). Armagnac production; equestrian centre. ▶ Between **Castelmore** (supposed birth place of Dumas' hero d'Artagnan) and Lupiac, there is an old windmill on the Ténarèze hills which has been restored; view. ▶ Coming from Fustérouau, there is an excellent view of the **château de Termes d'Armagnac**, a tall keep (36 m high, 14thC) overlooking the valley of the Adour. ▶ The *bastide* of **Plaisance** ® is a peaceful town in the centre of the plain. ▶ **Beaumarchès,** another *bastide,* (solid bell-tower with 16thC stone carving) is higher up; the road continues along a ridge with good views. ▶ **Marciac** is a characteristic late 13thC bastide; near the arcaded square, you can see the high bell-tower (17 m) of the southern Gothic church (14th-16thC) and another bell-tower belonging to a disaffected convent. 80-acre lake for aquatic sports. ▶ Through **Villecomtal** to the **Puntous de Laguian,** view★ of the Pyrénées. ▶ **Miélan** ®, former *bastide,* not far from a dammed lake on the Osse. ▶ The little village of **Tillac★,** older than the *bastides* is built on both sides of a short central street closed by two gates. ▶ **Bassoues★** has one of the most beautiful keeps in the Gers (14thC; 38 m) overlooking the remains of a castle belonging to the former bishops of Auch. Don't miss the central square where the houses with their wooden arcades front an old covered market spanning the road. ▶ The attractive little town of **Montesquiou** is built on a promontory overlooking the Osse (remains of 13th-14thC fortifications remains). ▶ **Isle-de-Noé** ® is a little fishing centre at the junction of the Grande and Petite Baïse (17thC château). ▶ **Barran :** remnants of fortifications and unusual spiral bell-tower on the 15thC church (note stalls of same period in the choir). Arcades and wood-built covered market. ▶ **Lavardens★★ :** a fortified village dramatically situated on a spur with a large 17thC château. ▶ **Castéra-Verduzan** ® is a small spa specialising in mouth and gum ailments. ▶ **Terraube :** 14thC fortified village; fine château from a later period. ▶ The collegiate church★ of **La Romieu** was built in 1317 on the pilgrim *(roumiou)* road to Compostela. It had its own fortified wall around the church, flanked by two towers with a fine 14thC cloister, which formerly had two floors. □

CONDOM★

A1 / ® / pop. 7 840 (Gers)

This town has clustered up around its abbey-turned-cathedral since mediaeval

1. The Bastides of Armagnac

Armagnac

Approximately 350 km^2 of vineyard stretch across the north and west of the Gers and overflow into the Departments of the Lot-et-Garonne and the Landes. Production from Bas Armagnac (110 km^2) is considered superior by connoisseurs; next come Ténarèze (110 km^2 in the heart of the region) and Haut Armagnac.

Armagnac is distilled from an indifferent local white wine. However, only wine made from specified varieties of grape (Folle Blanche, Jurançon and St. Emilion) may be distilled. The characteristic golden colour comes from prolonged aging in oak barrels. Armagnac can be drunk after four years in the barrel, but eight or ten years are required to give it a smooth yet vigorous fullness.

times. Condom is now a vigorous agricultural market town, with a brisk trade in armagnac.

▶ The old **cathedral★** in the town centre was rebuilt at the beginning of the 16thC (Flamboyant doorway, cloister and 18thC furniture). ▶ In the outbuildings of the former bishop's residence is the small but interesting **Armagnac Museum** *(daily ex Sun., and Mon. and nat. hols. out of season).* ▶ Strolling around the old town, you will find a number of handsome 17th and 18thC houses. □

■ From **COUSERANS** to **PLANTAUREL**

▶ Round trip *(approx 240 km, 2 to 2 1/2 days)*

B-C3 *(see map 2)*

The foot-hills of the Pyrénées, with their wooded cover and uneven terrain, promise delightful discoveries. Since prehistoric times men have lived in these mountains, where there are numerous caves containing traces of sophisticated symbolic and figurative art. The caves at Niaux and Mas d'Azil, open to visitors, are in this respect the most important in the region.

▶ **Saint-Girons** (→). ▶ **Rimont** ® is a former 14thC *bastide,* rebuilt after WWII; monument to the Martyrs of the Resistance.
The **caves of Mas d'Azil★★** are among the most beautiful in the Pyrénées. They were inhabited during the Upper Palaeolithic period, 40 000 to 10 000 BC; prehistoric collection in the cave, prehistory museum close by; reproductions and photographs of the wall paintings *(daily Jul.-Sep.; Sun. and nat. hols. and daily pm Apr.-Jun.).* The village was an early seat of Protestantism; the church was restored in the 18thC; several typical houses. ▶ **Serres-sur-Arget** lies in the heart of the valley of the Barguillère (or Arget) where the **Route Verte★** runs up to the **Marrous Pass★** (alt. 990 m). Past the foot of the **Tour Laffont,** a former lookout post with a view★ over the Pyrénées, to the top of **Portel** (alt. 1 485 m; similar view★) and the road to the Crouzette (alt. 1 240 m). ▶ Run down through the **valley of the Arac,** a winding defile★ lined with red rocks. ▶ **Massat** ®: 17thC church and chapel of Ave Maria (16thC). ▶ The **Port Pass★** (alt. 1 250 m) leads to the Saurat Valley. The caves at **Bédeilhac** were also inhabited in prehistoric times: 14 000 year-old paintings and rock carvings; the lower cave has revealed numerous worked flints and clay models *(daily Jul.-10 Sep., visits every 30 mins, 10-11:30 & 2-6; Easter-Jun. and early Sep.-early Oct., at 3 pm and 4:30 ex. Tue.).* ▶ **Tarascon-sur-Ariège** ®, set between high mountains, is the industrial centre of the valley (electro-metallurgy). The church was rebuilt in 17thC; 14thC doorway. The **caves of Lombrives★★,** 3.5 km SE, are, at more than 17 km deep, the largest in Europe and the most visited; fine rock formations; underground lake

2. From Couserans to Plantaurel

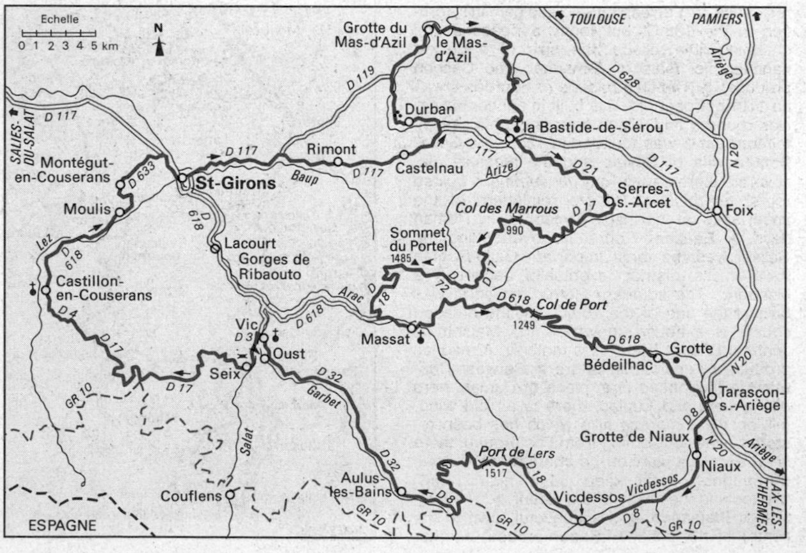

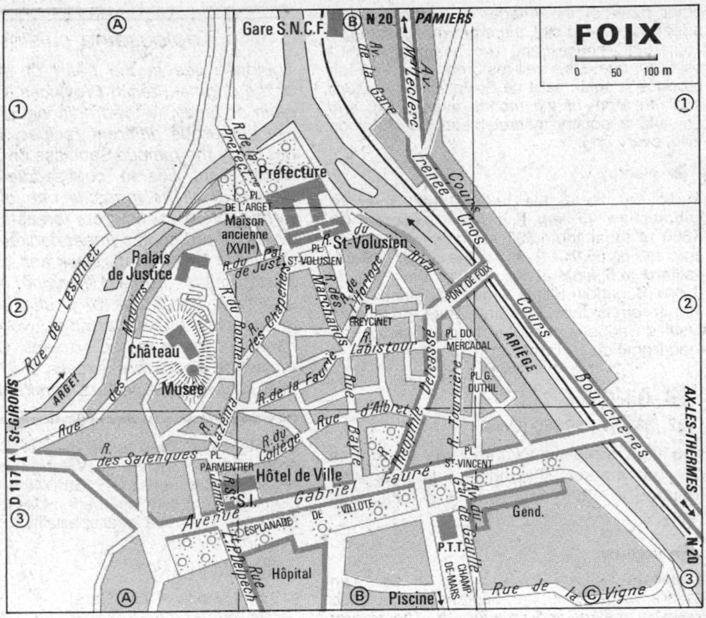

(10-12 & 2-5, Palm Sun.-31 May, 30 Sep.-31 Oct., daily 10-7, Jun.-Sep.). Further on, you come to the hot spa of **Ornolac-Ussat-les-Bains** ®; here the water emerges at 38°C. ▶ At the entrance to **Niaux** is the Musée Paysan (farmers' museum; *daily 10-6 Easter and Jun.-Sep.)* : tools and everyday objects from the old days in the area. **Niaux caves★** *(daily Jul.-Sep., visits every 45 mins, tel. 61.05.88.36; Oct.-Jun., daily at 11, 3 and 4:40; 20 people max per visit, 8:30-11:30 & 1:30-5:15; advance booking recommended, tel. 61.05.88.37).* Magdalenian era drawings★ (10-14 000 BC). On the opposite side of the valley, the cave of **La Vache Alliat** was also inhabited during the same period *(daily Jul.-Sep., visits every 30 mins 10-11:30 & 2-6; Easter-Jun. and early Sep.-early Oct., daily ex Tue. at 3:30 and 5 pm).* ▶ Industrial area of **Vicdessos** and **Auzat** (aluminium) at the foot of Montcalm; ruins of the château of Montréal. ▶ Across the Port de Lers and the Agnès Pass : mountain **valley of the Garbet★.** ▶ At **Aulus-les-Bains** ® (spa with calcium, iron and sulphate waters; new treatment buildings 1983) : facilities for excursions on foot and horse-back into the mountains; craft workshops; see the Cascade d'Arse nearby. ▶ Beyond **Seix** ®, the road climbs to the Core Pass (alt. 1 395 m) descent into the **Bethmale Valley★.** The church at **Ayet,** close by, has beautiful woodwork. ▶ See the Romanesque chapel of calvary★ (12th-13thC) at **Castillon-en-Couserans** ®; the château of Coumes is open in summer by appointment. ▶ The church of Notre-Dame de Tanesaygues at **Audressein** is decorated with 15th-16thC frescos; visit the clog maker. □

■ The Upper **COUSERANS** Valleys★

B3

The Couserans, a historically rich area traditionally covering eighteen valleys, runs up to the Spanish border. This charming maze of valleys can be explored by a network of ancient paths. Castillon-en-Couserans (former capital of the area), Oust and Aulus-les-Bains are good starting points (→ From Couserans to Plantaurel).

▶ The **Riberot Valley,** edged by the Bordes forest, leads to the **Massif du Valier reserve** (88 km²; panorama from the top of the mountain, alt. 2 838 m). ▶ Along the **Haut Salat Valley★,** past Conflens, you come to the **Pause Pass,** (views★) and to the tungsten mines at **Salau;** 11thC Romanesque church in the village. ▶ Finally, the **Ustou Valley★,** one of the most interesting, branches off the Salat Valley at the foot of the ruins of the **château de Lagarde;** traditional cheese-making. □

■ FOIX★

C3 / ® / pop. 10 060 (Ariège)

Whether you are coming from Toulouse, Saint-Girons, or Ax-les-Thermes, Foix looks like an enormous rock bristling with towers, at the foot of which run the Ariège and the Arget rivers. The annual "Journées Médiévales" are held in July (historic parade and mediaeval spectacle, market, craftsmen; one week duration) - the best time to buy regional products and craftwork.

▶ There are two bridges across the Ariège linking the N20 with the heart of the town. The **château★** des Comtes de Foix (A2; *daily ex the first Mon. in Sep., tel. 61.65.56.05*) has three towers, of which the most conspicuous is the 42m high 15thC keep. At its foot, the **Ariège museum** exhibits prehistory, history and ethnography collections; view★ from the centre tower *(daily, 1 May-30 Sep., 10-12 & 2-6:30; 1 Oct.-30 Apr., 10-12 & 2-6).* ▶ The **church of St. Volusien** (B2) presently being restored, has undergone numerous transformations (11th-14th-17thC). Fine presbytery visible from the other bank of the Ariège. ▶ In the twisting streets of the old city, there are many timbered 15th-16thC houses and two beautiful (19thC) covered markets, well-restored, where fresh produce is sold : halle de St-Volusien : *1st, 3rd and 5th Mon. of the month, every Wed. and Fri.* and a poultry market (near the Hôtel de Ville, *every Fri.*). □

▶ Nearby

▶ To the north, the **underground river of Labouiche★** *(5 km)* has been explored for 3 800 m (boat trip 1 500 m; *daily in summer, enq. tel. 61.65.04.11*). ▶ To the south : **Montgaillard** *(4.5 km)*; at the foot of the *Pain de Sucre* (Sugarloaf Hill) is a ruined château. 8 km further on is the old 13thC **Pont du Diable** (Devil's Bridge) across the river Ariège, on the road from Foix to Tarascon. □

GIMONT★

B2 / ® / pop. 2 950 (Gers)

The high street in Gimont runs through a covered market; this ancient *bastide* was founded in 1322; *foie gras* is a local specialty. □

▶ Nearby

Mauvezin *(13 km N)* is proud of its town square, larger than the Capitole in Toulouse (covered market and arcades). ▶ The former *bastide* at **Cologne** *(7 km from Mauvezin)* has a similar arcaded square round a central 14thC market. Between Cologne and L'Isle-Jourdain ® *(10 km E from Gimont)* is the St. Cricq Lake (aquatic sports); another lake at **L'Isle-Jourdain** itself. Also the arcaded square, covered market, the 15thC castle tower and the collegiate church (1785). □

The LAURAGAIS Region

C2

The Lauragais, between the Massif Central and the Pyrénées, is where Aquitaine meets the Midi. In spite of its low altitude (190 m) the watershed at Narouze (Aude) between the Mediterranean and Aquitaine basins is marked by distinct changes in vegetation. This is where the Canal du Midi is joined by the feeder canal from the Bassin de St. Ferréol (memorial to Riquet, the canal engineer).

▶ **Avignonet-Lauragais,** near the canal and close to three well-stocked lakes, has a 15thC church; Paul Riquet centre can be reached by the rest area of Port Lauragais (A61), the Midi Canal or the RN113. There one follows the history of the Midi Canal and a sculpture fountain which illustrates the system of water supply. Permanent and temporary exhibitions and audiovisual displays complete this. ▶ **Revel** ® (winter resort); a former *bastide* (1342), now a food production and craftwork centre (furniture, marquetry; workshop visits). Arcades around the central square; temporary exhibitions are held in the covered market, which is crowned by a tower dating from the Revolution. Many leisure facilities : fishing, sailing, canoe/kayak, equitation, cycling, potholing, hang-gliding etc. (large artificial lake at Saint-Ferréol *(3 km SE)*. ▶ **Saint-Félix-Lauragais** ®, charming site : 14thC church, covered market and old streets clustered inside the remains of the fortifications; 12th-13thC castle with 14thC keep *(open daily ex Wed.)*; artificial lake at Enclas. ▶ **Villefranche-de-Lauragais,** 12thC *bastide*, 13th-14thC Southern Gothic church with wall-belfry. *Cassoulet* (pork and bean stew) is a local speciality. □

Toulousaine cuisine

Toulouse lies at the heart of the largest of the original French Provinces. Cassoulet, *plain or fancy, is the traditional dish. There are numerous different recipes. Don't forget to try the famous* Saucisse de Toulouse, *made from coarse cut saddle of pork. Goose in all its forms is one of the star turns :* foie gras, magrets *(breasts of goose or duck) and* confits *(meat cooked and preserved in its own fat). Duck and truffles are also popular - truffles, like wine, have good and bad years. Lots of poultry and game in season : thrush, partridge, wood-pigeon, hare, and more rarely, ortolans. Of course, the white beans are excellent. The ewe's-milk cheeses are no less admirable.*

LAVELANET

C3 / ® / pop. 8 430 (Gers)

On the Cathar pilgrimage road to Montségur, this former capital of the Olmes area is a lively little textile town. □

▶ Nearby

9 km W on a rocky outcrop are the remains of the **château de Roquefixade** (12th-13thC); a heliograph system made it possible to communicate from here with the fortresses of Montgaillard, Montségur and Puivert. ▶ **Monts d'Olmes** (alt. 1 400-2 100 m) winter sports resort *(21 km SW; season Dec.-Mar.)*; St. Barthélemy Peak (alt. 2 348 m). ▶ **Montségur★★** *(12 km S; difficult 30 min climb from the car-park)*; the last stronghold of the Cathar religious movement, finally captured after a ten month siege in 1244; the 210 men and women who refused to renounce their "heresy" were burnt alive... Exceptional view★ from the ruins (alt. 1 215 m). Oddly enough, they show none of the usual characteristics of military architecture found in other fortresses in the region. In the little tile-roofed village below, there is a small archaeological and prehistory museum *(near the town hall; daily May-Sep. or by appt. tel. 61.01.10.27)*. ▶ Further on, through the **Gorges du Lasset, Fougax-et-Barrineuf** (access road to the **Gorges de la Frau★**) and past the intermittent fountain at **Fontestorbes,** the road runs down to **Bélesta** "world capital of natural horn combs". Walks in the forest of Bélesta. ▶ Down in the **valley of the Hers, L'Aiguillon** and **La Bastide-sur-l'Hers** also specialise in horn comb production; visit the premises of Laffont de La Bastide *(15 people max.; tel. 61.01.11.01)*. □

LECTOURE★

B1 / pop. 4 420

To see Lectoure at its best, you should come from Fleurance; the old houses seem to huddle inside their mediaeval protective walls.

▶ From the **Promenade du Bastion★,** you can

see most of the Pyrénées in fine weather. ▶ The former **cathedral** (it was demoted to church during the Revolution) combines Southern Gothic (13thC nave) with Northern Gothic (14thC choir). The bishop's palace (16th-18thC) is today the **town hall :** portraits of great men born in the region; **Antiquities Museum★** *(daily).* In 1540, 3rd-4thC altars for ritual bull sacrifices were discovered on the site of the cathedral choir; local excavations have produced many remains from Gallo-Roman civilisation in the northern Gers. □

▶ Nearby

▶ Artificial lake at **Trois Vallées,** *(3 km SE).* ▶ The 13thC **château de Gramont★** *(14 km E in the Lot-et-Garonne; daily ex Tue. Apr.-Oct.; closed mornings Apr.-Jun. and 16 Sep.-Oct.),* was remodelled in the Renaissance; furniture and terraced gardens. ▶ **Saint-Clar** *(15 km SE) :* an elegant Gascon *bastide;* remains of a 16thC château of the kings of Navarre and another (17thC) belonging to the bishops of Lectoure; sale of regional produce. ▶ 3 km SE above the valley of the Arratz is the 13thC **château d'Avezan,** rebuilt in 17thC *(daily 10-6, guided tours in summer).* ▶ **Fleurance** ® *(11 km SE) :* a *bastide* founded in 1280; 14th-15thC church in Southern Gothic, with three fine 16thC stained glass windows★ by Arnaud de Moles, not far from the town square (arcades, covered market in stone). □

LOMBEZ

B2 / pop. 1 240 (Gers)

Lombez, like Lectoure, was formerly a bishopric, which explains the large cathedral in so small a village.

▶ This fine brick 14th-15thC church has a fortress-like appearance relieved only by the elegant five-storied octagonal bell-tower in Toulousain style; old stained-glass and fine recumbent Christ from a 15th-16thC Burial of Christ; treasure room. □

▶ Nearby

▶ 3 km NE of Lombez is **Samatan** ®, an agricultural centre of some importance (market). ▶ **Simorre** *(17 km SW)* has the most beautiful fortified church★ in Gascony (14thC; stalls and stained-glass 16thC). ▶ **L'Isle-en-Dodon** *(14 km S, in the Haute Garonne)* is a winter and country-holiday resort (equitation, cycling holidays, fishing and shooting); 14thC church, automobile museum *(closed Mon.).* □

MIRANDE

A2 / ® / pop. 4 150 (Ariège)

A *bastide* founded in 1285 with central square and streets laid out on a grid pattern; one of the most typical in SW France.

▶ Near the arcaded **square,** the 15thC fortified **church** has an unusual bell-tower straddling the street. ▶ Beside it, **museum** *(daily; if closed, apply to SI next door) :* collection of minor masters, from Italian primitives to 19thC French painters, old ceramics and Gascon glazed pottery. □

MIREPOIX★

C3 / ® / pop. 3 580 (Ariège)

This 13thC *bastide* is straight out of the Middle Ages, with its regular street plan and houses almost intact. Market days are Thursday and Saturday; picturesque cattle market on the second and fourth Monday each month. Mediaeval Week in July.

▶ The half-timbered houses on the **Place Centrale** are built over one of the largest arcaded squares in the Midi Toulousain. ▶ The **cathedral** was begun in the 13thC, but the present vaulting dates from 1867; the 60 m bell-tower is a prominent landmark. ▶ The **Tour Ste. Foy** is a remnant of the 12th-13thC fortress of Lévis-Mirepoix; this family also owned the **château de Caudeval** *(9 km E* in the Aude, dating from 12th, 14th and 17thC); museum : artillery and Roman remains *(daily mid-Jul.-end Aug.).* □

NOGARO

A1 / ® / pop. 2 400 (Gers)

Nogaro is well known to sports enthusiasts : in spring and autumn numerous motorcycle and car races are held on the Circuit Paul-Armagnac. Hang-gliding is also popular. ▶ 12thC collegiate church (doorway). □

▶ Nearby

▶ **Barbotan-les-Thermes** ®, 26 km N, is a spa (calcium, magnesium and sulphur waters; *season Apr.-Nov.)* specialising in the treatment of rheumatism and circulatory disorders. Fishing, *Courses Landaises* (dodging a charging heifer by skillful footwork) and wood-pigeon *(palombe)* shooting are among the favourite activities; lovely park; a fortified gateway forms the porch of the Romanesque church. □

PAMIERS

C3 / ® / pop. 15 190 (Ariège)

The town was named by the Count of Foix on his return from the Crusades (12thC), in memory of Apamea on the banks of the Orontes, where he acquired a number of holy relics. Pamiers is today the major commercial and industrial centre of the department.

▶ One of the castles of the Counts of Foix used to stand on the **Butte du Castella;** view★ over the Pyrénées and the plain of Toulouse. ▶ The **cathedral of St. Antonin,** remodelled in the 18thC, has a 12thC doorway and a 14thC Toulousain bell-tower. ▶ The church of **Notre-Dame-du-Camp** was also rebuilt (17th-18thC) and has preserved an imposing 14thC fortified façade. □

▶ Nearby

▶ **Varilhes** *(9 km S;* country holidays), where the valley of the Ariège widens out, has numerous old half-timbered houses. ▶ **Vals** *(13 km E)* has an unusual church built into the rock; it dates from Carolingian times (8th-10thC) and is decorated with 11thC Romanesque frescos; small archaeological museum in a neighbouring house. ▶ **La Bastide-de-Mazères** *(17 km NE)* was built to a grid pattern in 1252 and still has its old covered market where, each December, the best goose and duck *foie gras* are judged. Annual *fête des fleurs* (flower festival) at the end of May. ▶ **Saverdun** ® *(13 km N)* was one of the key towns of the County of Foix in the 12thC and a centre of the Reformation during the Wars of Religion (second half of the 16thC). The upper town was formerly defended by a feudal castle (Tour Gaston Phoebus; view) while the lower town was surrounded by defensive walls. Regional information and sale of produce (food and crafts) at the Maison de l'Ariège. ▶ The old fortified town of **Saint-Ybars** *(29 km NW)* has a lively poultry market on the fourth Wednesday of each month. □

■ SAINT-BERTRAND-DE-COMMINGES★★★

A3 / ® / pop. 230 (Haute-Garonne)

On an isolated knoll overlooking the valley of the Garonne. Archaeological research and the existing historic monuments combine to make this little town the most renowned art and history site in the central Pyrénées.

▶ The **cathedral of Ste. Marie★,** in the heart of the upper town, was built in several stages : 11th-12thC nave with bell-tower keep and Romanesque doorway; 14th-15thC choir and rich **furnishings★★** (note the Renaissance stained-glass, the choir-screen, the stalls, the 15thC bishops' tombs, the mausoleum of St. Bertrand (15thC), the curiously positioned organs and the 16thC Flemish tapestries); treasure room★ in the former chapter, and cloister★ with one Gothic and three Romanesque galleries. ▶ Don't miss the **Gallo-Roman museum★** *(closed in '86 for restoration)* in the former Benedictine (Olivetan) chapel. Numerous 15th-16thC houses within the upper town. ▶ The **lower town★,** sacked by the Vandals in 408, is built on the site of the Gallo-Roman town of *Lugdunum Convenarum;* excavations have revealed the remains of the theatre, the forum, the baths, a Roman basilica, and a 4thC Christian basilica. ▶ 2 km away, on the banks on the Garonne, **Valcabrère** was built in the late Middle Ages using material from the ruins of the Gallo-Roman city; the **church of St. Just★,** somewhat apart from the town, was the first cathedral of the diocese of Comminges (rebuilt in the 11th-12thC). □

▶ Nearby

▶ The **Gargas Caves** (*6 km NW,* Hautes Pyrénées) are famous for their rock formations and a large number of prehistoric hand prints; these show hands missing parts of one or two fingers; their significance is unknown. ▶ **Barbazan** ® *(5 km E)* is a spa with calcium sulphate waters *(season May-Sep.);* beautiful park★, small natural lake, fishing and walks in the mountains. ▶ **Saint-Béat** ® (where stands the house which gave E. Rostand the inspiration for the balcony scene between Cyrano de Bergerac and Roxane, *20 km S*), is a pleasant resort (trout fishing and mountain hikes), built on both banks of the Garonne with a marble bridge in the middle (marble and onyx quarries nearby, from which certain sections of Versailles originated). Pretty Romanesque church reconstructed by the Beaux-Arts : treasury★ (tympanum) and ruins of 14th-15thC castle (view). The chair-lift at Mourtis *(10 km E)* goes to the top of the **Tuc de l'Étang** (alt. 1 816 m) with a view★ of the central Pyrénées. □

■ SAINT-GAUDENS

B3 / ® / pop. 12 229 (Haute-Garonne)

Saint-Gaudens is built on a hill-side overlooking the Garonne. Industrial activity includes gas production from the St. Marcet field and the manufacture of paper pulp. Tourist and leisure activities : shooting, fishing and horse riding. Artificial lake. Calf sale every Thursday (the local breed is milky white).

▶ 11th-12thC **church** modelled on St. Sernin in Toulouse. The largest carillon of the Midi-Pyrénées and tapestries of Aubusson of 18thC. Behind it is the SI and the **museum** *(closed)* with prehistory, history, religious art and ethnography collections. View★ over some 180 km of the Pyrénées from **Boulevard Jean-Bepmale. Comminges Museum** : local folklore *(daily ex. Sun. 8:30-12 & 2-6).* □

▶ Nearby

▶ **Montréjeau★** ® *(14 km W) :* a 13thC *bastide* founded by King Philippe III in 1272. Situated at the junction of the Neste and the Garonne (view★), it has become a tourist and resort town; international folklore festival the week of 15 Aug. ▶ 18 km NW, noteworthy remains of the **Gallo-Roman villa Montmaurin★** (4thC; museum; *closed Tue. and Wed.*). From here you can reach the **Save gorges** and *(9 km)* the former *bastide* at **Boulogne-sur-Gesse** ® (13thC; 15thC church; arcaded square) which is now a holiday town (artificial lake). ▶ 8 km S is the former spa of **Encausse-les-Thermes.** ▶ **Aspet** *(15 km SE)* (Saracen tower, Henri IV fountain) : a pleasant town set among wooded valleys (mediaeval tower, music festival in July); mountain walks to the caves (incl. that of Gouillon) and the **Portet d'Aspet** (pass at 1 069 m; view★). □

■ SAINT-GIRONS

B3 / ® / pop. 7 720 (Ariège)

A little market town at the junction of a number of roads and valleys, seat of the local administration.

▶ The **church of St. Valier** has a crenellated wall-belfry over its façade; 16thC bridge near the church of St. Girons, named after a martyr put to death by the Visigoths. Visit to the cheese-producers Faup and Temp Lait *(every am ex Sat. and Sun.).* ▶ **Saint-Lizier★★** *(2 km N;* festival of classical music in Sep.) is the Gallo-Roman city of *Lugdunum Consaranorum;* the capital of Couserans in the Middle Ages (remains of fortifications). The 12thC cathedral, with 14thC ogive vaulting and a Toulousain bell-tower, is decorated with 12th and 14thC frescos; the cloister★ (end 12thC) had an additional story added in 15thC; treasure room★ *(daily 15 Jun.-15 Sep., 10-12 & 2:30-6:30, tel. 61.66.16.22).* **Notre-Dame-du-Siège,** in the upper town, is also a cathedral; 12thC chapter, fine view of the Pyrenees. Old half-timbered houses in the narrow streets. ▶ Above the town are the **gorges of Ribaouto★.** □

■ SAINT-MARTORY

B2-3 / pop. 1 170 (Ariège)

A little town on the Garonne on the site of a Gallo-Roman city. ▶ An 18thC bridge links the town to the suburb on the right bank, by the **château de Montpezat** (15th-16thC; restored). □

▶ Nearby

▶ 5 km W, remains of the former abbey of **Bonnefont;** parts of the cloister are in Saint-Martory; the remainder grace the Cloisters Museum in New York; on the site, you will see

Sauvetés, castelnaux and bastides

The first sauvetés appeared in the 11thC. They were little communities founded by religious orders to clear the land and bring it under cultivation. At almost the same period, the castelnaux *began to spring up near the feudal castles, creating another form of agricultural township. The* bastides *were introduced into the region in the 13thC to reassemble and control the population after the Albigensian Crusades and the extermination of the Catharist heretics had "purged" the region (first half of 13thC - p. 652); two successive kings, Philippe III and IV, followed this policy, aided by a number of feudal lords and princes of the Church. Many of these* bastides *were symbolically sponsored by important cities throughout Christendom, hence the names : Barcelone, Boulogne, Cologne, Grenade, Fleurance, Plaisance, Valence... and even Montréal, which has no connection with its Canadian counterpart.*

parts of the wall, the dovecote and a 16thC door. ▶ The spa at **Salies-du-Salat** ® *(6 km S; season May-Sep.)* is characterised by extremely salty water gushing from a cristalline salt deposit 200 m down. The town is built at the foot of a hill on which are the ruins of the castle of the Counts of Comminges (11th-13thC). **Montsaurès** *(2 km),* Templars' commandery. From here, you can go up the **Arbas Valley** and, beyond Labaderque *(23 km),* on foot to the **Gouffre (chasm) de la Henne Morte,** 446 m deep. ▶ Through the transverse valley of **Boussens** ® (menhirs at **Mancioux,** *4.5 km*) to **Martres-Tolosane**★ ® *(10 km).* The circular layout of this little mediaeval city (14thC Gothic church), is especially interesting. Handworked ceramics, produced since the 18thC (visit studios). ▶ **Alan** *(8 km NW from Martres-Tolosane),* with château of the bishops of Comminges (famous carving of a cow over the door to the staircase tower). ▶ **Aurignac** ® *(5 km W from Alan, 12 km NW from Saint-Martory)* gave its name to the prehistoric Aurignacian period; Cro-magnon man lived in these regions some 30000 years ago; prehistory museum *(Wed.-Sat., Jul.-Aug.; or by appt. with the town hall, tel. 61.19.90.08;* view★ from the ruins of a keep (ca. 1240) on a neighbouring rock. ▶ **Rieux-Volvestre** *(31 km NE from Saint-Martory)* in a bend of the Arize, is a former episcopal city which is now a holiday resort; 13th-14thC cathedral (Toulousain bell-tower and remarkable bishop's treasury★); brick houses from the 15th, 16th and 17thC; *fête of the Papagaï* (archery contests) on first Sun. in May. □

■ TOULOUSE★★★

C2 / ® / pop. 354 290 (Haute-Garonne)

See plan following pages

Toulouse has developed in concentric circles around its site on a wide bend in the Garonne. The Roman *castrum* and the city of the Visigoths gave way to the towns of the Middle Ages and the Renaissance, later enclosed by a circle of boulevards; around these grew new rings, outlined by the Canal du Midi and the motorways. More recently still, new towns such as Le Mirail and Colomiers have sprung up on the outskirts. During the periods of the city's greatest historical importance, (12th, 13th, 16th and 18thC), Toulouse was enriched by the construction of many remarkable buildings. After a quiescent period in the 19thC, Toulouse has achieved a place in the front rank of French cities during the second half of the 20thC. The intellectual impetus of the university (founded in 1229) has burgeoned not only in scientific research but in its industrial application (aerospace, electronics, data processing, chemistry, biology, agronomy, etc.), while the artistic traditions of the town have been reborn in the creation of a number of art and music festivals; Toulouse now shares with Bordeaux the burgeoning of the Great Southwest. It is lively and animated in the evenings.

▶ The **Place du Capitole**★ (D2; cafés, restaurants and famous bookshops) is the living heart of the town. One side of the Place is bordered by the **Capitole**★★ (1750-53) which was the assembly hall of the municipal magistrates *(Capitouls)* and today houses the city's administrative offices, together with one of France's most renowned theatres *(to visit the historic parts of the building ex. Tues., Sat., Sun. and nat. hols. tel. 61.22.29.22, ext 3412).* Behind the Capitole building is the **keep** (D2), which formed part of the Capitole itself in the 16thC. It now houses the Tourist Office; pleasant gardens. ▶ The church of **Notre-Dame-du-Taur** (D2) was built in the 14thC in Southern Gothic style; its fortified façade has a wall-belfry which inspired many churches throughout the Midi. ▶ The **basilica of St. Sernin**★★ (an important stop on the road to St-Jacques de Compostelle; D1-2; 11th-12thC) is dedicated to the saint who evangelised Toulouse, becoming its first bishop in the 3rdC. It is the church of a former Benedictine abbey and is 115 m long : during the Romanesque period only Cluny (in Burgundy) was larger. See the chevet★ with its radiating chapels, the 12th-13thC spire★ which was the model for so many "Toulousain" bell-towers, and the Romanesque Miégeville gate★ facing the Rue du Taur. Inside, note the 11thC altar, the stalls (1670) and the tomb of St. Sernin, in an 18thC sculptural setting. ▶ On the square the **Saint-Raymond Museum,** in a former 16thC college, specializes in archaeology from prehistory to the Carolingian period *(closed Tue., Sun. a.m. and nat. hols.).* ▶ **The Jacobins convent**★★ *(Couvent des Jacobins; C3; daily ex Sun. am;* music festival in summer) was founded by St. Dominique to coun-

Toulousain bell-towers

Since the 12thC the bell tower of St. Sernin in Toulouse, with triangular mitres crowning the openings in its octagonal upper stories, has been the model for bell-towers throughout the region. The style is seen to perfection on the Jacobins convent church (Toulouse, 13thC). Toulouse is also the origin of another architectural characteristic of the Midi : the wall-belfry (Notre-Dame-du-Taur), also found in a large number of fortified 13th and 14thC churches.

teract the Cathar heresy. It has been recently restored. Note the double nave (13th-14thC) and the palm leaf-ribbed vaulting; see the cloister, the chapter, and the chapel of St. Antonin (decorated with 14thC frescos). The bell-tower (no spire) of 1294 is considered one of the most perfect examples of Toulousain Gothic. Reliquary containing the remains of Saint Thomas Aquinas, brought back from Italy in the 14thC. ▶ The church of **Notre-Dame-de-la-**

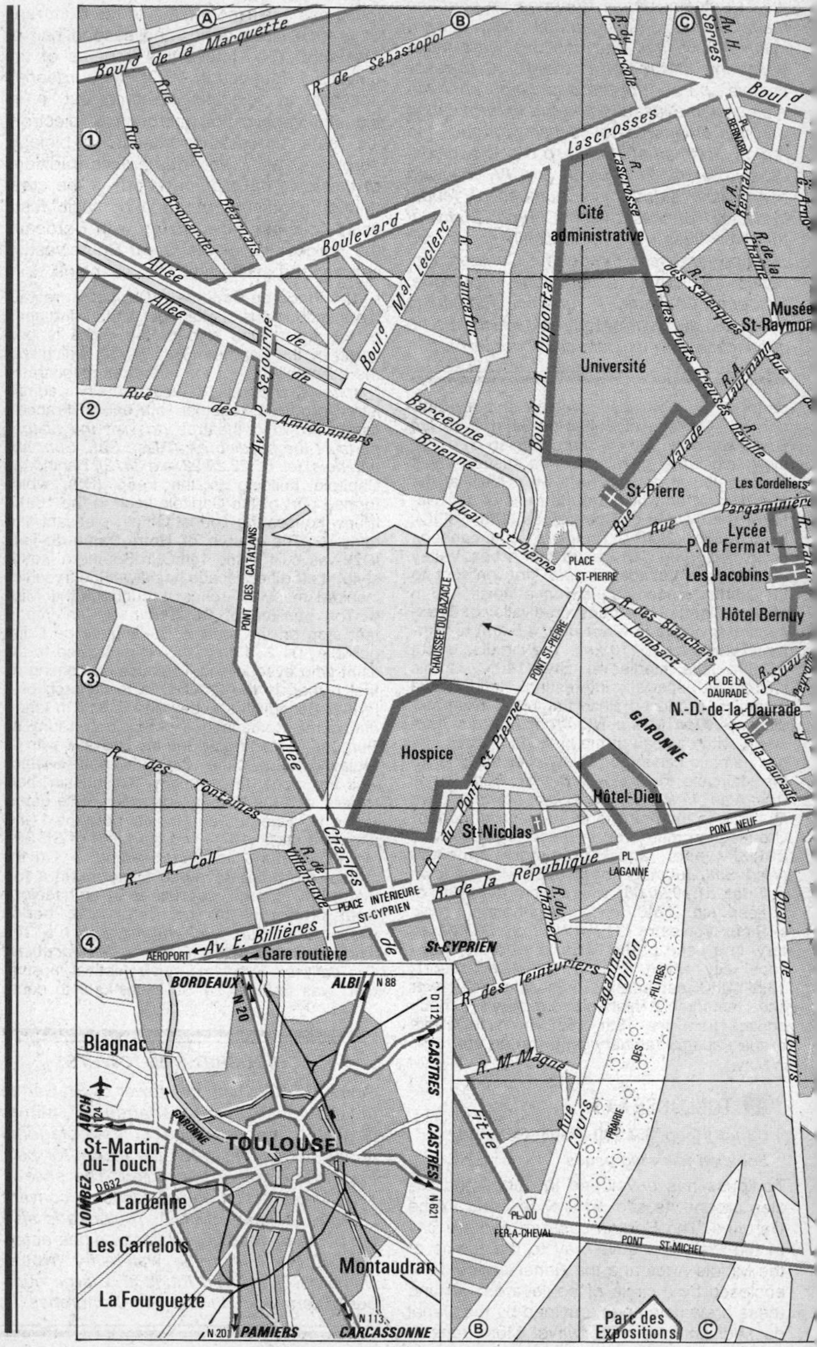

Daurade (C3), rebuilt in the 18thC, takes its name from the gilded mosaics which decorated the original 5thC sanctuary; many column capitals from the Romanesque building are exhibited in the Augustins museum. ▶ **Notre-Dame-de-la-Dalbade** (D4) is a fine specimen of Southern Gothic (16thC; the enamelled terracotta tympanum on the façade dates from 1070). The church takes its name from the lime rendering which was used for the walls of the

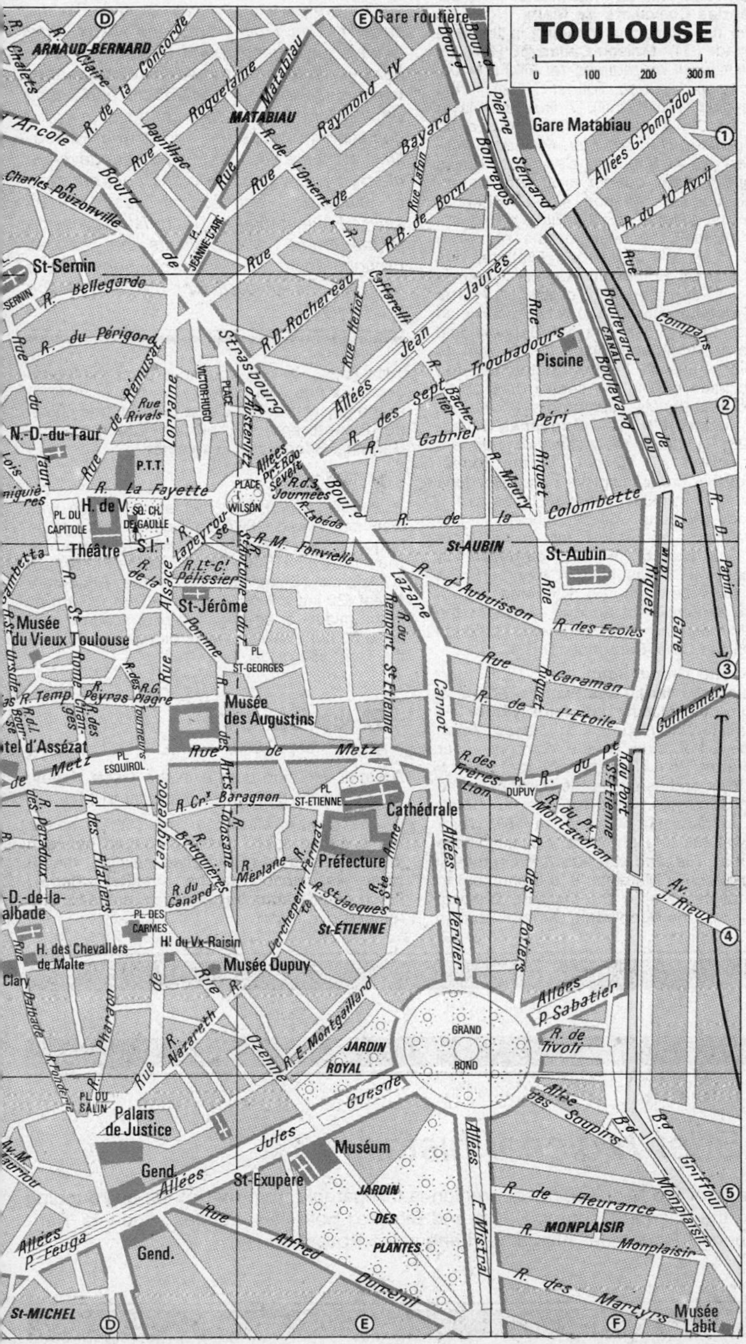

first church on this site. ▶ The **old quarter★★** to the south of the Capitole has hardly changed since wealthy merchants in the dye and grain trades built magnificent brick houses here between the 16th and 18thC; see the **Hôtel de Berring** (16thC) Rue Gambetta; **Hôtel d'Assézat★** (D3; 1555; Museum of Medecine; *open Tue.*), Rue de Metz; **Hôtel de Clary** and **Hôtel des Chevaliers de Malte, Hôtel de Pierre** two fine mansions standing in the Rue de la Dalbade (D4); **Maison Callas,** 50 Rue des Filatiers (D4; *visit on request, tel. 61.53.14.00, for public open-days enq. Tourist Office*); in the **Hôtel du May** (16th-17thC), 7 Rue du May: **Museum of Old Toulouse★** (D3; *Musée du Vieux-Toulouse; Thu. pm Mar.-May and Oct.-Nov.; every pm ex Sun. Jun.-Sep.).* Don't miss the antique dealers' quarter around la Daurade, or the regional craftshop, 42 Rue Pharaon (D4). The Rue de Metz and the Place d'Esquirol (D3) run through the heart of the old town from the river; the Rues des Filatiers, des Changes and St. Rome run into the Place du Capitole, and are pedestrian precincts. ▶ The **Rue d'Alsace-Lorraine** (D2-3) was constructed in the last century between the Capitole and the **Place du President-Wilson** (D-E2) with its surrounding cafés. ▶ Further to the SE, the **Place Occitane** (E3) is the centre of a newly renovated area (hotels, restaurants, boutiques, lively in summer). ▶ The **Augustins Museum★★** (D3; 21 rue de Metz, *daily ex Sun. am and Tue.; Wed. till 10 pm*), in the former convent of that order, displays rich collections of sculpture from palaeochristian times to the present day (Romanesque capitals★), 16th to 19thC paintings and a recent organ (concerts in the church). ▶ The **cathedral of St. Étienne★** (E3) was built in two parts on different axes between the 12th and 15thC. There are a number of antique shops in the vicinity, and also the oldest house in Toulouse (13thC, 15 rue Croix-Baragnon, D-E3).

Also... ▶ **The Grand Rond** (E4); 18thC garden; nearby, the **Jardin des Plantes** (botanical garden) and the **Musée d'Histoire Naturelle★** (Natural History Museum; E5; *closed Tue.*). ▶ On the other side of the Garonne river (access via the Pont Neuf (new bridge); view★ over the town and as far as the Pyrénées), the Faubourg St. Cyprien (B4) includes the **Hôtel-Dieu-St. Jacques** (13thC) and an 1830 brick **water tower** housing photographic exhibitions (*every pm ex Tue. and nat. hols.).* ▶ On the hill **(La Colline)** above Matabiau is a monument to a battle fought here by the invading Duke of Wellington and the Napoleonic General Soult in 1814 (view). ▶ NW from the town, the **Ponts Jumeaux** (the twin bridges) were built in 1780 at the junction of the Canal du Midi, the Canal de Bienne and the branch Canal to the Garonne. Good walks in summer. □

The birth of art

The most interesting of the numerous prehistoric paintings and engravings found in the Pyrénées are those in the Ariège. These first expressions of mankind's artistic instincts are particularly well-displayed in the caves at Les Trois-Frères and Niaux. Clay models have been found at Tuc d'Audoubert, while animals carved in reindeer horn were discovered at Mas-d'Azil and many other sites. Progressive changes in living conditions towards the end of the Palaeolithic era were accompanied by the development of a new geometric and abstract style of expression, enriched at Mas-d'Azil by stylised human figures. Pictorial expression in the Ariège Valley reflects the changes brought about by new technology in the Neolithic era, in particular the introduction of pottery.

▶ Nearby

▶ **Pibrac** *(17 km W)*: mediaeval church with wall belfry and 1967 basilica (pilgrimage in honor of Germaine Cousin, who lived here in the 17thC); 1540 Renaissance château. ▶ Approx 15 km beyond is the **Bouconne forest** (20 km²). ▶ **Villemur-sur-Tarn** *(33 km N)* in the middle of an irrigation pilot scheme covering 30 km²; sailing, walks along the banks of the Tarn; vineyards. □

■ VIC-FÉZENSAC

A1 / ® / pop. 3990

A small vacation centre in the Osse Valley, famed for its bullfights; festivals in May.

▶ The **church,** altered in the 15thC., has a Romanesque apse; nearby, wedged between the houses, a 14thC fortified building; handsome *Assumption* in the **hospital chapel;** 2 km N at **Marambat**: ruined chateau and remains of rampart. □

● Brief regional history

The history of the Midi Toulousain region is inseparable from that of the surrounding regions: the Basque Country, Béarn and Bigorre; Bordelais, Landes; Agenais, Périgord, Quercy; Rouergue, Albigeois; Languedoc-Roussillon (→).

Architecture ●

House in the Gers region

Toulousain farm

Throughout the Midi Toulousain, the design of the houses changes the nearer they are to the Pyrénées. The typical southern roof with hollow tiles and two or four slopes is common throughout the Gers and the Toulouse region as well as in the lower valleys of the Garonne and the Ariège. ● Farmers, market-gardeners and vine-growers have houses adapted to their specific needs; in Armagnac the wine cellar is generally a part of the farmhouse itself. ● Stone is not much used in the Gers and disappears almost completely around Toulouse, where brick is the principal building material; brick is also used in traditional Gersois construction, usually to fill in a timbered framework, while a stone foundation protects the house from damp. In the highest mountain valleys, where houses are frequently grouped in hamlets or villages, the usual material is sandstone, schist or granite, or even stones from the river bed, depending on availability. Here, the symmetry of design is often sacrificed. The slate or stone covered roofs are more steeply sloped; the architecture resembles that of other Pyrenean valleys.

Simple mountain house ("maison-bloc")

Practical information

The region

Information : Midi-Pyrénées, *Délégation régionale au Tourisme,* 12, rue Salambô, B.P. 2166, 31022 Toulouse Cedex, ☎ 61.47.11.12. **Ariège :** *Conseil départemental du Tourisme* (C.D.T.), 14, rue Lazéma, 09000 Foix, ☎ 61.65.29.00 ; **Haute-Garonne,** *C.D.T.*, Administrative centre, 31, rue de Metz, 31066 Toulouse, ☎ 61.33.43.69, and *Maison de la Haute-Garonne,* ☎ 61.81.69.46, aire de Port-Lauragais, autoroute A61 des Deux-Mers ; **Gers :** *C.D.T.,* B.P. 69, 32000 Auch, ☎ 62.05.37.02. In Paris : *Maison du Gers et de l'Armagnac,* 16-18, bd Haussmann, 75009, ☎ 47.70.39.61 ; *Maison des Pyrénées,* 15, rue St-Augustin, 75008, ☎ 42.61.58.18. In Lille : *Maison de Midi-Pyrénées,* 57-59, rue Faidherbe, 59800, ☎ 20.06.15.06.

Bookings : *Loisirs-Accueil Haute-Garonne,* 31, rue de Metz, 31066 Toulouse, ☎ 61.33.43.69 and *Gers,* Maison des Agriculteurs, rte de Tarbes, 32003 Auch Cedex, ☎ 62.63.16.55.

Maps : *Michelin* n°s 82 and 86 1/200 000 and n° 235, Midi-Pyrénées ; *I.G.N.* n°s 63, 64 and 71 1/100 000.

Local and regional press : *la Dépêche du Midi, Sud-Ouest, la Croix du Midi.*

S.O.S. : Ariège : ☎ 17. **Haute-Garonne :** ☎ 17. **Gers :** *S.A.M.U., Emergency Medical Service,* ☎ 62.05.33.33. Poisoning Emergency Centre, Toulouse, ☎ 61.49.33.33.

Weather forecast : Ariège : ☎ 61.66.28.22. **Haute-Garonne :** ☎ 61.71.02.76. **Gers :** ☎ 62.63.07.22.

Rural gîte and chambres d'hôtes : *Relais départementaux,* **Ariège :** *Association des Gîtes de France,* 14, rue Lazéma, 09000 Foix, ☎ 61.65.01.15. **Haute-Garonne :** 31, rue de Metz, 31066 Toulouse, ☎ 61.33.43.69. **Gers :** chambre d'agriculture, rte de Tarbes, 32003 Auch Cedex, ☎ 62.05.36.36, poste 395-390.

Holiday villages : see practical holiday information.

Camping : 572 sites. Enq : C.D.T. and *Point Information Camping,* B.P. 2000, 31017 Toulouse, ☎ 61.47.11.12, for immediate information on possibilities in the region and elsewhere in France.

Festivals : May : *Journées intercontemporaines (concerts by contemporary music ensemble)* in Auch, *Spring Festival of Popular Arts and Traditions* in Launac. **May-Jun :** *Festival d'Auch et de Gascogne, Rencontres sans Paroles* in Auch, *Grand Fénétra* in Toulouse. **Jun :** *Documentary Film Festival* in Luchon, *Week of Organ Music* in Toulouse, *Journées gasconnes* in Valence-sur-Baïse, *Pyrotechnics Festival* in Auch. **Jul :** *Théâtre en Pays d'Auch, Musical evenings* in Armagnac, *theatre and concerts* at Flaran Abbey. *Festival de Messidor* at Vendemiaire. **Jul-Aug :** *Music Festival* in St-Bertrand-de-Comminges. **Sep :** *International History Conferences,* in Valence-sur-Baïse and *Lectoure international festival* in St-Lizier (classical music). **Nov :** *International Painting Exhibition* in Lavelanet. *Festival de piano aux Jacobins* in Toulouse.

Religious event : Christmas in Vals, in the Carolingian stone church, with a real manger, Occitan Christmas.

Local festivals and folklore : May : *flower festival* in Mazères, *Festival de Bandas y Penas,* in Condom. **Jun :** *fête des brandons (torch festival)* in Luchon. **Jul :** *Journées médiévales de Gaston Phœbus* in Foix, *Folk Festival* in La Bastide-de-Sérou, *popular and artistic festivals* in Luchon, *mediaeval pageant* in Mirepoix. **Aug :** *Sentein Folk Festival, Festival international d'Art populaire* in Geix, *flower festival* in Luchon, *Annual Folk Festival* in Montréjeau. **Sep :** Festival of Foix.

Fairs and markets : Apr-May : Toulouse *Fair* and *foire au Salé* (salted goods) ; *Fair-Exhibition* in Auch. **Jun :** *foire aux eaux-de-vie d'Armagnac* (Armagnac brandy fair) and, **in Aug,** *Animal Fair* in Éauze. **Oct :** *Automobile Show, Garlic Fair* and, **in Nov,** exhibition organised by the Toulouse antique dealers.

Sporting events : Easter : *Grand Prix automobile* (F2) in Nogaro. **Whitsun :** *Grandes Corridas* in Vic-Fézensac (bull-fights). **Aug :** *horse races* in Nogaro.

Rambling and hiking : topoguides, G.R. 65, 652, 653 (Santiago de Compostela "St-Jacques-de-Compostelle" pilgrimage route), 7, 10. Enq : *Délégation régionale Midi-Pyrénées-Sud de la F.F.R.P.,* M.G. Ville, 11, rte de Grenade, 31700 Blagnac ; *Comité dép. de R.P.,* 14, rue Lazéma, 09000 Foix, ☎ 61.65.29.00. *C.I.M.E.S. :* Délégation dép. **Ariège :** 3, square Balagué, 09200 Saint-Girons, ☎ 61.66.40.10. **Haute-Garonne :** M. Évrard, rés. les Ormes, bât. G3, 31320 Castanet-Tolosan, ☎ 61.81.77.69. **Gers :** *Délégation des Sentiers G.R.,* 32700 Lectoure, ☎ 62.68.76.98, and château de Saint-Cricq, 32100 Auch, ☎ 62.05.27.17.

Riding holidays : *Transpyrénéenne* and *Grande Traversée ("great crossing") des Pyrénées :* enq at *C.I.M.E.S.* and *Maison des Pyrénées.* Chevauchée des Deux-Mers : enq and enrolments *Loisirs-Accueil in* Gers. L'Armagnac en roulotte : *les Attelages d'Armagnac,* domaine de Cézaou, 47170 Mézin, ☎ 53.65.70.61.

Cycling holidays : *Féd. française de Cyclotourisme, Ligue des Pyrénées,* 1, allée de l'Estérel, 31770 Colomiers, ☎ 61.78.77.29.

Children : les *Directions dép. Jeunesse et Sports :* **Ariège,** av. de Lérida, 09000 Foix, ☎ 61.65.09.25 ; **Haute-Garonne :** cité administrative, bd Armand-Duportal, 31000 Toulouse, ☎ 61.23.31.05 ; **Gers :** 9, rue d'Espagne, 32000 Auch, ☎ 62.05.44.99, organise sporting activities for children and young people.

Golf : Luchon (9 holes) ; Toulouse-Palmola (18 holes) ; Golf-club de Toulouse (18 holes) ; L'Isle-Jourdain (9 holes) ; la Bastide-de-Serron (9 holes).

Aquatic sports : Sailing : *Ligue Midi-Pyrénées,* 54, rue des Sept-Troubadours, 31000 Toulouse, ☎ 61.62.19.65. Water skiing : *Ligue Midi-*

Pyrénées, 17, rue Daydé, 31200 Toulouse, ☎ 61.23.92.48.

Diving : *Groupe d'activités sous-marines,* 6 bis, rue Kennedy, 31000 Toulouse, ☎ 61.78.64.64, and *Féd. franç. d'Études et Sports sous-marins :* Comité régional, 6, rue d'Autezac, 31000 Toulouse, ☎ 61.42.17.64.

Canoeing : *Comité dép. de Haute-Garonne,* 54, rue des Sept-Troubadours, 31000 Toulouse, ☎ 61.41.08.48, and *Ligue régionale,* 4, rue du Château-de-l'Hers, ☎ 61.20.13.96 ; Canoeing section, A.S.P.T.T. Ariège, 09000 Foix, ☎ 61.65.05.06, and C.I.M.E.S.

Potholing-spelunking : Ariège : *Comité dép. de Spéléo,* M. Christian Billiard, « Clarac » Boulon, 09000 Foix. **Haute-Garonne :** *Comité dép. de Spéléo,* 54, rue des Sept-Troubadours, 31000 Toulouse. *Maison des Gouffres,* Herran-Labaderque.

Winter sports : *Comité régional Pyrénées-Est,* 1, rue de la Charité, 31000 Toulouse, ☎ 61.62.89.15 ; *Pyrénées Club de France,* 29, rue du Taur, 31000 Toulouse, ☎ 61.21.11.44. The principal winter sports are cross-country skiing and nature-discovery hikes on snow-shoes. Enq : *A.D.S.F.A. au C.D.T. Ariège,* ☎ 61.65.29.00. *Club Alpin* (C.A.F.), M. Brionne, 8, chemin de Caussou, 09000 Montgaillard, ☎ 61.65.38.65, and *U.C.P.A.* 40, rue de la Concorde, 31000 Toulouse, ☎ 61.62.63.18.

Hang-gliding : *Aigles de Cabaillère,* 17, rue Bayle, 09000 Foix, ☎ 61.65.01.73.

Parachuting : *Ligue des Pyrénées* (F.F.P.), 87, rte de Narbonne, 31400 Toulouse, ☎ 61.53.74.06.

Gliding : air-clubs in Saint-Girons-Antichan, ☎ 61.66.11.00, and Pamiers, ☎ 61.68.60.60, for gliding, light aircraft, for beginners and first flights, contact M. Andriou in the Haute-Garonne, 6, pl. Gilbert-Privat, 31100 Toulouse, ☎ 61.40.51.82.

Hunting and shooting : Ariège : *Féd. dép.,* 50, av. Gal-Leclerc, 09000 Foix, ☎ 61.65.04.02. Game : quail, hare, boar and wild goat. To organise full- or half-day hunting, contact *Sologne Ariégeoise,* Montégut-Plantaurel, 09210 Varilhes, ☎ 61.92.24.12. **Haute-Garonne :** *Féd. dép.,* 2, rue Jolimont, 31000 Toulouse, ☎ 61.48.49.66. Enq in **Gers** at *Loisirs-Accueil* which organises week-end pigeon hunts.

Fishing : Ariège : *Féd. dép. des Assn. de Pêche et de Pisciculture,* 26, av. de Barcelone, 09000 Foix, ☎ 61.65.12.82. **Haute-Garonne :** *Assn. Pêche et Pisciculture,* 5, pl. Wilson, 31000 Toulouse, ☎ 61.21.18.65, *Club Français des Pêcheurs à la Mouche,* quartier la Fount, 31130 Balma, ☎ 61.24.27.81. **Gers :** *Féd. dép. des Assn. Pêche et Pisciculture,* 75, bd Sadi-Carnot, 32000 Auch, ☎ 62.05.15.95.

Towns

AUCH

Agen 71, Toulouse 78, Paris 797
A1-2 ⊠ 32000

ⓘ pl. de la Cathédrale (B1), ☎ 62.05.22.89.

✈ Auch-Lamothe, 5 km N, ☎ 62.63.03.89.

SNCF (C1), ☎ 62.05.60.95 - 62.05.00.46.

🚌 cité administrative (A1), ☎ 62.05.06.37.

Hotels :

★★★***France*** (André Daguin) [Mapotel, Relais gourmand], 2, pl. de la Libération (A1), ☎ 62.05.00.44, Tx 520474. AE, DC, Euro, Visa. 30 rm decorated by Jo Daguin Ⓟ 570. Rest. ● ♦♦♦♦ closed Jan, Sun eve and Mon. The opulent and generous Gascon cooking is prepared in a friendly and happy atmosphere by André Daguin admirabily assisted by his son Arnaud, a promising young man : tasting of duck and goose *foie gras, grandes soupes bœuf de Bazas,* bull meat, desserts with a theme, great wines and armagnacs. Wines and take away products shop, 230-350.

★★***Poste***, 5, rue C.-Desmoulins (A1), ☎ 62.05.02.36. Tx 531918. AE, Euro. 27 rm Ⓟ ♿ 200. Rest. ♦♦ closed 15 Oct-Easter, 50-100.

Robinson, 2 km S :

★★★***Robinson,*** rte de Tarbes, ☎ 62.05.02.83. Euro. 26 rm Ⓟ ♨ 🏊 180.

Restaurants :

♦♦ ***Le Neuvième,*** 2, pl. de la Libération (A1), ☎ 61.05.00.44. AE, Euro, DC, Visa, closed Sun eve and Mon (low season). The *hôtel de France* bar is a nice place for a quick meal until midnight : *cassoulet, garbures, daubes,* 120-160.

♦♦ ***Claude Laffitte,*** 38, rue Dessoles, ☎ 61.05.04.18. Closed 1-15 Feb, Sun eve and Mon (low season). In his Gascogne style inn, the lively C. Laffitte keeps very busy with his regional products shop and his bar, 80-260.

Sainte-Christie-d'Auch, ⊠ 32390, 13 km N on the N21 :

● ♦♦ ***Relais de Cardenau,*** ☎ 61.65.51.80. Visa, AE. ♿ closed Mon. Terrace. Spec : *aiguillette de canard, fricassée de pintade,* 60-250.

Market : Wed morning, Thu and Sat.

Recommended : *foie gras, armagnacs,* spiced fruits : *Caves de l'Hôtel de France,* 2, rue d'Étigny. *Maison de la Gascogne,* rue Gambetta. *Pork Butchery Claude Laffitte,* rue Dessoles. *Caperan,* 8, rue d'Étigny, ☎ 61.05.07.69 : gascon dollars. *Pork Butchery des Trois Mousquetaires,* 10, rue Dessoles, ☎ 61.05.33.66.

AULUS-LES-BAINS

Saint-Girons 33, Foix 77, Paris 833
BC-3 ⊠ 09140

ⓘ allée des Thermes, ☎ 61.66.94.59, and mairie, ☎ 61.66.93.55.

Hotels :

★★***Beauséjour*** (L.F.), ☎ 61.96.00.06. 30 rm ⚘ Ⓟ ♨ 🏊 ⚒ ♿ closed Sep-Jun, 180. Rest. ♦ ⚒ 70-80 eve.

● ★***France,*** ☎ 61.96.00.90. AE. 30 rm ⚘ Ⓟ ♨ 🏊 closed 10 Oct-20 Dec, 130. Rest. ♦ ⚒ 50-150.

Bicycle hire : at ⓘ 15 Jun-20 Sep.

AURIGNAC

Saint-Gaudens 22, Toulouse 76, Paris 785
14 km W of Martres-Tolosane, B2-3 ⊠ 31420

Hotel :
★★***Cerf Blanc,*** rue St-Michel, ☎ 61.90.95.76. 11 rm Ⓟ closed Mon, 180. Rest. ● ♦ ♿ The Picard family are now settled in their beautiful house with nice terrace. Spec : *blanc de turbot aux morilles, râble de lapereau farci aux rognons de veau à l'estragon,* 70-210.

AX-LES-THERMES

Foix 42, Quillan 53, Paris 834
C3 ⊠ 09110

ℹ ☎ 61.64.24.83. 720-2 300 m.

ℹ av. Delcassé, ☎ 61.64.20.64.

SNCF ☎ 61.64.24.72.

Car-hire : *Budget* train + auto, at the station, ☎ 61.64.20.72.

Hotels :
★★★***Royal Thermal*** (Mapotel), esplanade de Couloubret, ☎ 61.64.22.51. Tx 530955. AE, Euro, Visa. 64 rm Ⓟ 300. Rest. ♦ ♿ 100-160.
★★***Chalet*** (L.F.), av. de Turell, ☎ 61.64.24.31. Tx 520594. 10 rm closed 12 Nov-20 Dec, 3-24 Jan, 190. Rest. ♦ 50-105.
★★***Sicre et Espagne,*** 2, av. du Dr-Gomma, ☎ 61.64.22.95. Visa. 68 rm Ⓟ ♿ closed Nov-Jan, 210. Rest. ♦ 50-100.
★★***Perles et Castelet,*** 3 km NW, ☎ 61.64.24.52. Tx 530955. AE, Visa. 28 rm Ⓟ ♿ closed Dec-12 May, 170. Rest. ♦♦ closed Tue eve and Wed ex school hols, 80-180.

Unac, ⊠ 09250 Luzenac, 9 km NW :
★***Oustal,*** ☎ 61.64.48.44. 7 rm Ⓟ closed 11 Nov-15 Mar and Mon, 140. Rest. ♦♦ Simple, tasty fare in a rustic setting. Spec : *salade méli-mélo aux petites seiches et poivrons grillés, écrevisses à ma façon, pescajouve aux pommes,* 100-200.

⛺ ★★★*Luzenac le Castella* (100 pl.), ☎ 61.64.47.53 ; ★★*En Rameil* (60 pl.), ☎ 61.64.22.85.

Casino, ☎ 61.64.20.20 and 61.64.22.93.

BAGNÈRES-DE-LUCHON

Saint-Gaudens 46, Tarbes 89, Paris 843
A3 ⊠ 31110

(1 Apr-20 Oct), ☎ 61.79.03.88.

ℹ 18, allées d'Étigny, ☎ 61.79.21.21.

SNCF ☎ 61.79.00.85, 61.79.03.36.

Car-hire : *Budget* train + auto, at the station, ☎ 61.79.03.36.

Hotels :
★★★***Corneille,*** 5, av. A.-Dumas, ☎ 61.79.36.22. Tx 520347. AE, DC, Visa. 58 rm Ⓟ closed 20 Oct-1 Apr, 550. Rest. ♦♦ 60-200.
● ★★***Loisirotel,*** 29, allées d'Étigny, ☎ 61.79.00.40. 53 rm Ⓟ closed 10 Oct-10 Dec, 200. Rest. ♦♦ 50-130.
★★***Bains*** (Inter-Hôtel), 75, allées d'Étigny, ☎ 61.79.00.58. Tx 521437. AE. 53 rm Ⓟ ♿ closed 20 Oct-20 Dec, 230. Rest. ♦♦ 75-100.
★***Deux Nations*** (L.F.), 5, rue V.-Hugo, ☎ 61.79.01.71. 27 rm Ⓟ 120. Rest. ♦ 55-100.

⛺ ★★★*Val de l'Air* (80 pl.), ☎ 61.79.10.02 ; ★★*Beauregard* (133 pl.), ☎ 61.79.30.74 ; ★★*la Lanette,* Montauban-de-Luchon (210 pl.), ☎ 61.79.00.38.

BARBAZAN

Saint-Gaudens 13, Tarbes 59, Paris 812
5 km E of Saint-Bertrand-de-Comminges, A3
ℹ ☎ 61.88.30.06. ⊠ 31510

Hôtels :
★★★***Aristou*** (L.F.), rte de Sauveterre, ☎ 61.88.30.67. AE, Euro, Visa. 8 rm Ⓟ 250. Rest. ♦♦ 70-170.
★★***Panoramique*** (Relais du Silence), hameau de Burs, ☎ 61.88.35.23. 20 rm Ⓟ ♿ 250. Rest. ♦ In the open country and facing the Pyrénées mountains, a comfortable hotel where good food is served : *foie gras au torchon, délice de soles à l'oseille, côte de bœuf,* 50-100.

Sauveterre-de-Comminges, 4 km E :
● ★★★***Host. des Sept Molles*** (Relais et châteaux), hameau de Gesset, ☎ 61.88.30.87. Tx 530171. AE, Visa. 19 rm Ⓟ ♿ closed 1 Nov-15 Dec and Tue low season, 400. Rest. ♦♦♦ Traditional gastronomy. Spec : *foie gras chaud aux myrtilles, saumon sauvage aux pointes d'asperges, sabayon de Jurançon.* Book ahead, 125-200.

BARBOTAN-LES-THERMES

Mont-de-Marsan 40, Auch 72, Paris 728
A1 ⊠ 32150

(1 Feb-31 Dec), ☎ 62.69.52.09.

ℹ pl. d'Armagnac, ☎ 62.69.52.13.

Hotels :
★★★***Bastide Gasconne*** (Relais et châteaux), ☎ 62.69.52.09. 43 rm Ⓟ and pigeon aviary, closed 1 Nov-1 Apr, 390. Rest. ♦♦♦ Spec : *fricassée d'escargots, pintadeau au lard fumé et au margaux, crêpes fourrées à l'armagnac.* Good wines, 200-300.
★★★***Château de Bégué*** (Relais du Silence), 2 km SW, ☎ 62.69.50.08. 25 rm Ⓟ closed Oct-2 May, 260.
★★***Cante Grit,*** ☎ 62.69.52.12. 23 rm Ⓟ closed 1 Nov-15 Apr, 250. Rest. ♦♦ 100-200.

Cazaubon, 3 km SW :
★★★***Bellevue*** (Châteaux-Hôtels), 19, rue J.-Cappin, ☎ 62.09.51.95, Tx 521429, AE, DC. 27 rm Ⓟ ♿ closed Dec-Feb, 330. Rest. ♦ 100-230.

⛺ ★★★*L'Uby* (200 pl.), ☎ 62.09.53.91.

CASTÉRA-VERDUZAN

Auch 25, Agen 59, Paris 793
7 km SE of Valence-sur-Baïse, A1 ⊠ 32410

(1 May-31 Oct), ☎ 62.28.53.41.

ℹ ☎ 62.68.10.66 (summer).

Hotels :
★★***Ténarèze,*** Grand-Rue, ☎ 62.68.10.22. 22 rm ♿ closed Feb, 150. Rest. 50-130.
★★***Florida,*** Grand-Rue, ☎ 62.68.13.11. 22 rm, closed 11 Nov-3 Dec, 130. Rest. ● ♦♦ Family atmosphere and cooking. *Foie gras* and *magret* prepared with taste, 55-180.

CONDOM

Agen 40, Auch 44, Paris 740
A1 ⊠ 32100

ℹ pl. Bossuet, ☎ 62.28.00.80.

SNCF ☎ 62.28.15.36.

Hotels :
★★***Logis des Cordeliers*** (Relais du Silence), ☎ 62.28.03.68. 21 rm Ⓟ ♿ closed 15 Nov-15 Dec, 260. Rest. ♦♦♦ closed Fri low season. The former management has taken over this dream place, 200-340.

Valence-sur-Baïse, ⊠ 32310, 8 km S :
★★***Ferme de Flaran,*** rte de Condom, ☎ 62.28.58.22. AE, Euro, Visa. 15 rm Ⓟ closed Nov, Sun eve and Mon, 190. Rest. ♦♦ ♿ Good regional dishes, 60-100.

⛺ ★★★*Municipal* (75 pl.), ☎ 62.28.17.32.

Recommended : *Château de Roquebèrc,* rte de Nérac : *foie gras, magrets, confits. Château de Cassaigne,* 6.5 km SW : tour of an armagnac "chai" (storehouse)

ÉAUZE

Auch 52, Mont-de-Marsan 52, Paris 743
A1 ✉ 32800

ℹ pl. de la Mairie, ☎ 62.09.85.62.

SNCF ☎ 62.09.82.59.

Hotels :
Armagnac, 1, bd Saint-Blaucat, ☎ 62.09.88.11. Euro, Visa. 12 rm closed 1-15 Mar and Sun, 90. Rest. ♦ 45-90.

Gondrin, ✉ 32330, 12 km NW :
★***Le Pardaillan,*** ☎ 62.29.12.06. Euro, Visa. 11 rm ♿ On the border of the Gondrin lake (swimming), 120. Rest. ♦♦ Pleasant service, regional spec, 40-200.

Bourrouillan, 32370 Manciet, 15 km SW D931/D153 :
Moulin du Comte, ☎ 62.09.06.72. AE. 10 rm ♿ closed early Jan-end Feb, 150. Rest. ♦♦ 50-170.

⛺ ★★*Pouy Plage* (20 pl.), ☎ 62.09.86.00.

Recommended : *Floc* (grape juice and armagnac) *de Gascogne,* Syndicat des Producteurs, 9, pl. d'Armagnac. *Chevalier Gascon,* 60, rte de Nogaro. *Marquis de Caussade,* rte de Cazaubon, with son et lumière in the chai (wine and spirits store-house), 1 Jul-15 Sep.

FLEURANCE

Auch 24, Agen 47, Paris 781
B1 ✉ 32500

ℹ mairie, ☎ 62.06.10.01.

SNCF ☎ 62.06.10.92.

Hotels :
★★★***Fleurance,*** rte d'Agen, ☎ 62.06.14.85. 25 rm ♿ closed 15 Dec-15 Jan, 230. Rest. ♦♦ closed Mon ex Jul-Aug, 105-200.
★★***Relais,*** rte d'Auch, ☎ 62.06.05.08. 25 rm closed 21 Jan-mid-Feb, 165.

Market : on Tue.

Recommended : *Cantan pork butchery,* 43, rue A.-Cadéot, ☎ 62.06.10.36.

FOIX

Carcassonne 81, Toulouse 83, Paris 792
C3 ✉ 09000

ℹ 45, cours Gabriel-Fauré (A-B3), ☎ 61.65.12.12.

SNCF (B1), ☎ 61.65.07.62, 61.65.27.00.

Car-hire : *Budget* train + auto, at the station, ☎ 61.65.27.00.

Hotels :
★★★***Pyrène,*** rue Serge-Denis, le Vignoble, 2 km SE, ☎ 61.65.51.12. AE, Euro, Visa. 12 rm ♿ closed 20 Dec-5 Jan, 190.
● ★★***Audoye Lons*** (L.F.), 4, pl. G.-Duthil (C2), ☎ 61.65.52.44. 35 rm ♿ 200. Rest. ♦♦ closed Sat low season, 55-105.

Saint-Paul-de-Jarrat, ✉ 09260, 7 km S on the N20 and D117 :
● ★★***Charmille*** (L.F.), ☎ 61.64.17.03. Visa. 10 rm closed 20 Dec-1 Mar and Mon, 160. Rest. ♦♦ Spec : *foie gras, magret de canard,* freshwater crayfish, 100-210.

Farmhouse gîte and inn : *Cantegril,* St-Martin-de-Caralp, 09000 Foix, 7 km NW, ☎ 61.65.15.43. Riding centre, trout fishing.

⛺ ★★*Municipal* (300 pl.), ☎ 61.65.11.58.

Restaurants :
♦♦ ***Phoebus,*** 3, cours I.-Cros (B1-C2), ☎ 61.65.10.42. Euro, Visa ♿ closed Jul, Sun eve and Mon. Spec : *aile d'oie au sang, aiguillettes de canard au poivre vert, poissons,* 60-110.
♦ ***XIXe Siècle,*** 2, rue Delcassé (B2), ☎ 61.65.12.10. ♿ closed Feb-15 Mar and Sat (low season). Spec : *cassoulet au confit, foie gras maison,* 55-130.

Funfair : 1st, 2nd, 3rd Mon of the month.

Market : on Fri, on allées de Villotte.

Recommended : *Rouch pork butchery,* pl. Volusien. *Bakery Hebrard,* 18, rue Lafaurie. *Antiquary Foix,* 23, rue Lafaurie.

GIMONT

Auch 26, Toulouse 53, Paris 732
B1-2 ✉ 32200

Hotel :
● ★★★***Château Larroque*** (Relais et châteaux), ☎ 62.67.77.44. Tx 531135. AE, Visa. 15 rm ♿ closed 1 Jan-1 Feb, 385. Rest. ● ♦♦♦ A dream setting and André Fagedet's rich Gascogne region cooking, 120-210.

⛺ ★★*Municipal* (50 pl.), ☎ 62.67.70.02.

Farmhouse-inn : *En Sarrade,* ☎ 62.67.76.14. Spec : stuffed fowl, wood pigeon.

Recommended : *foies gras : Ducs de Gascogne,* rte de Mauvezin.

L'ISLE-JOURDAIN

Toulouse 35, Auch 43, Paris 713
B2 ✉ 32600

ℹ mairie, ☎ 62.07.14.39, and Maison du Lac, ☎ 62.07.03.84 (summer).

Hotel :
★★★***Lac,*** 1 km W on the N124, ☎ 62.07.03.91. Visa. 25 rm 190. Rest. ♦♦ Spec : *foie frais aux pommes,* 50-170.

⛺ ★★*Municipal* (53 pl.), ☎ 62.07.14.39.

LAVELANET

Foix 27, Carcassonne 66, Paris 814
C3 ✉ 09300

ℹ foyer municipal, ☎ 61.01.22.20.

Hotel :
★★★***Espagne,*** 20, rue J.-Jaurès, ☎ 61.01.00.78. Visa. 23 rm 170. Rest. ♦ 50-120.

Farmhouse gîte : Raissac, 09300 Lavelanet, 3 km W, ☎ 61.01.12.88. Fishing, farm produce for sale. Book ahead.

Bicycle hire : *Villanova Cycles,* 13, rue du Marché-Couvert, ☎ 61.01.03.14.

MARTRES-TOLOSANE

Saint-Gaudens 29, Toulouse 61, Paris 770
B2 ✉ 31220 Cazères-sur-Garonne

Hotels :
★★***Castet,*** rue de la Gare, ☎ 61.90.80.20. DC, Visa. 18 rm closed 10-30 Oct and Mon (Oct-May), 130. Rest. ♦ Spec : *foie frais aux pommes,* 50-120.

Boussens, 31360 Saint-Martory, 5 km SW :
★★***Lac,*** ☎ 61.90.01.85. 12 rm closed 25 Nov-27 Dec, 135. Rest. ♦♦ ♿ closed Sun eve low season. Good family cooking, 50-160.

⛺ ★★★*Le Moulin* (50 pl.), ☎ 61.90.86.40 ; at Boussens, ★★★*du lac* (30 pl.), 61.90.02.25.

MASSAT

Saint-Girons 28, Foix 46, Paris 828
B-C3 ⊠ 09320

Hotel :
● ★★★***Trois Seigneurs*** (L.F.), ☎ 61.96.95.89. 25 rm ♿ closed Nov-Mar, 190. Rest. ♦♦ 50-200.

MIÉLAN

Tarbes 34, Auch 39, Paris 807
A2 ⊠ 32170

Hotel :
★★***Lac,*** ☎ 62.67.51.59. 10 rm P ♿ Bathing in the lake, closed Jan and Wed low season 150. Rest. ♦ 60-200.

⛺ ★★★*Lac* (70 pl.), ☎ 62.67.51.76.

MIRANDE

Auch 25, Toulouse 103, Paris 793
A2 ⊠ 32300

ℹ 13, rue de l'Évêché, ☎ 62.66.68.10.

Hotel :
★★***Europ'Hôtel Maupas,*** 2, av. d'Étigny, ☎ 62.66.51.42. Euro. 20 rm P closed 20 Dec-10 Jan, Feb school hols and Sat, 130. Rest. ♦♦ ♿ 60-150.

⛺ ★★★*Île du Pont* (100 pl.), ☎ 62.66.64.11.

Restaurant :
L'Isle-de-Noé, 9 km N :
♦***Auberge de Gascogne,*** ☎ 62.64.17.05 ♿ closed 5 Nov-10 Dec and Wed, 50-105. With 7 rm.

Recommended : *les Producteurs Gascons,* rte d'Auch : *foies gras* and *confits.*

MIREPOIX

Foix 34, Carcassonne 47, Paris 796
C3 ⊠ 09500

Hotel :
★★***Commerce*** (L.F.), 20, cours Dr-Chabaud, ☎ 61.68.10.29. Euro, Visa. 32 rm P closed Jan, 1-15 Oct, 165. Rest. ♦ closed Sat low season, 50-140.

⛺ ★★*Municipal* (64 pl.), ☎ 61.68.10.41.

Farmhouse gîte : *Mazerette,* ☎ 61.68.15.25 riding and lake, hiking and bicycle tracks.

Farmhouse-inn : *Balestie,* Malegoude, 5 km NE, ☎ 61.68.12.15. With rm. Riding centre, fishing.

MONTRÉAL

Agen 55, Mont-de-Marsan 65, Paris 745
10 km W of Larressingle, A1 ⊠ 32250

ℹ pl. de l'Hôtel-de-Ville, ☎ 62.28.43.18.

Hotel :
★***Gare,*** 3 km S on the D29, ☎ 62.28.43.37. AE, DC, Euro, Visa. 5 rm P ♿ closed Jan, Thu eve and Fri low season. In the old station, 110. Rest. ♦♦ Spec : *garbure gasconne, salmis de palombe, poulet grillé à l'échalote* and good regional fare, 70-140.

MONTRÉJEAU

Saint-Gaudens 14, Auch 76, Paris 856
A3 ⊠ 31210

ℹ pl. Valentin-Abeille, ☎ 61.95.80.22, and mairie, ☎ 61.95.84.17.

SNCF ☎ 61.95.80.29.

Hotel :
★★***Lecler*** (Inter-Hôtel), 4, av. de St-Gaudens, ☎ 61.95.80.43. AE, DC, Euro, Visa. 22 rm P ♿ closed 5 Nov-15 Dec, 160. Rest. ♦ 60-100.

Youth hostel : rte de Tarbes, N117.

⛺ ★★*Midi-Pyrénées* (100 pl.), ☎ 61.95.86.79 ; ★★*Hortensias* (33 pl.), ☎ 61.95.80.22.

MURET

Toulouse 21, Auch 75, Paris 729
B-C2 ⊠ 31600

ℹ av. St-Germier, ☎ 61.51.03.53.

SNCF ☎ 61.51.00.38.

Hotels :
Vernet, 38810 Venergue, 10 km SE :
★★***Clair Logis,*** RN20, ☎ 61.08.50.44. AE, Visa. 15 rm P ♿ closed 15-30 Jan, 130. Rest. ♦ ♿ closed Wed and Sun eve, 40-220.

Noé, ⊠ 31410, 13 km S :
★★***Arche de Noé,*** pl. de la Bastille, ☎ 61.87.40.12. Visa. 26 rm P ♿ 160. Rest. ♦♦ Spec : *petits rouleaux de sole en ragoût, cailles farcies au foie gras, magret aux cèpes sauce fine champagne,* 50-160.

NOGARO

Mont-de-Marsan 42, Auch 62, Paris 747
A1 ⊠ 32110

Hotels :
★***Dubroca,*** rue d'Artagnan, ☎ 62.09.01.03. Euro, Visa. 12 rm P ♿ closed 1 Dec-5 Jan, Sat and Sun low season, 120. Rest. ♦ 50-160.

Luppé-Violles, 9 km SW on the N124 :
● ★★★***Relais de l'Armagnac,*** ☎ 62.09.04.54. 10 rm P closed Jan and Mon (ex Jul-Aug), 210. Rest. ● ♦♦ Good regional cooking, 100-210.

Flying school : circuit Paul-Armagnac, ☎ 62.09.02.49 and 62.09.02.08.

Recommended : *Armagnacs Michel Faure,* Z.I., ☎ 62.09.02.50.

ORNOLAC-USSAT-LES-BAINS

Foix 20, Saint-Girons 62, Paris 812
3.5 km SE of Tarascon-sur-Ariège, C3
⊠ 09400 Tarascon-sur-Ariège

☎ 61.05.63.62.

Hotels :
★★***Parc,*** ☎ 61.05.74.74. AE. 60 rm P closed Nov-1 Apr, 175. Rest. ♦ 50-60.
★***Villa des Roses,*** ☎ 61.05.63.39. AE. 27 rm P closed 3 weeks in Nov and 3 weeks in Jan, 170. Rest. ♦♦ Spec : *cassoulet,* 50-180.

PAMIERS

Foix 19, Toulouse 64, Paris 773
C3 ⊠ 09100

ℹ pl. du Mercadal, ☎ 61.67.04.22.

SNCF ☎ 61.67.00.85.

Car-hire : *Budget* train + auto, at the station, ☎ 61.67.00.85.

Hotels :
● ★★***France*** (L.F.), 13, rue de l'Hospice, ☎ 61.60.20.88. Visa. 32 rm P ♿ 180. Rest. ♦ closed Sun low season, 60-140.
★★***Parc*** (L.F.), 12, rue Piconnières, ☎ 61.67.02.58. 12 rm, closed Nov, 150. Rest. ♦ 60-110.

Chambres and table d'hôtes : *la Faurie,* 4 km RN20, ☎ 61.67.02.75. Fishing.

⛺ ★★*Municipal* (100 pl.), ☎ 61.67.12.24 ; ★★*Parc du Château,* Varilhes, 9 km S (100 pl.), ☎ 61.60.71.17.

Recommended : *sweets Laurent,* 28, rue des Jacobins, ☎ 61.67.01.65 ; for water ices.

PLAISANCE

Tarbes 44, Auch 55, Paris 766
13 km SE of Riscle, A1 ✉ 32160

ℹ 4, rue Ste-Quitterie, ☎ 62.69.44.69.

Hotel :
★★***Ripa Alta*** (L.F.), pl. de l'Église, ☎ 62.69.30.43. AE, Euro, Visa. 15 rm Ⓟ ♨ closed 1 Nov-15 Dec, Sun eve and Mon, 200. Rest. ● ♦♦ Some of the best cooking of SW region from the inventive Mr Coscuella, inspired by the seasons and market produce : *poulet à l'armagnac, piballes.* Nice cellar, 70-230.

Ⲁ ★★*L'Arros* (33 pl.), ☎ 62.69.30.28.

REVEL

Carcassonne 44, Toulouse 53, Paris 762
C2 ✉ 31250

ℹ pl. Ph.-de-Valois, ☎ 61.83.50.06.

Hotel :
★★***Lac*** (Inter-Hôtel), ☎ 61.27.66.55. AE, DC, Visa. 39 rm ⚘ Ⓟ ♨ ⚲ closed 24 Dec-6 Jan, 170. Rest. ♦ ♿ 60-200.

Restaurant :
♦♦ ***Lauragais,*** av. de Castelnaudary, ☎ 61.83.51.22 Ⓟ ♨ ♿ Regional cooking in a rustic setting. Spec : *foie gras à l'ancienne, cassoulet au confit d'oie,* 100-205.

RISCLE

Tarbes 52, Auch 70, Paris 529
A1 ✉ 32400

SNCF ☎ 62.69.70.25.

Hotel :
Ségos, 18 km W (and 9 km S Aire-sur-l'Adour) :

★★★★***Domaine du Bassibé*** (Relais et châteaux), ☎ 62.09.46.71. Tx 531918. AE, DC, Euro, Visa. 9 rm ⚘ Ⓟ ♨ ⚲ ▭ closed 15 Oct-1 May, Sun eve and Mon noon low season, 570. Rest. ♦♦♦ Spec : Excellent traditional cooking : *confit aux cèpes, tripes de mouton à l'armagnac,* 120-200.

Ⲁ *Le Pont de l'Adour* (68 pl.), ☎ 62.69.70.10.

SAINT-BÉAT

Bagnères-de-Luchon 20, Saint-Gaudens 32, Paris 830
B3 ✉ 31440

Hotel :
Cierp, 5 km O :
★***La Bonne Auberge,*** ☎ 61.79.54.47. 5 rm ⚲ closed Oct and Wed (low season), 120. Rest. ♦ 75-150.

ST-BERTRAND-DE-COMMINGES

Saint-Gaudens 17, Tarbes 61, Paris 816
A3 ✉ 31510

Hotel :
★***Comminges*** (L.F.), ☎ 61.88.31.43. 13 rm ⚘ ⚲ ⚒ closed Oct-Easter, 250. Rest. ♦ Eve only, 70-180.

Ⲁ ★★*Es Pibous* (66 pl.), ☎ 61.88.31.42.

SAINT-FÉLIX-LAURAGAIS

Castres 37, Toulouse 43, Paris 758
10 km W of Revel, C2 ✉ 31540

Hotel :
★★★***Auberge Poids Public*** (L.F.), ☎ 61.83.00.20. Visa. 13 rm ⚘ Ⓟ ♨ ⚲ closed 6 Jan-7 Feb and Sun eve, 215. Rest. ● ♦♦♦ closed Sun eve from 15 Oct to 15 Mar, 6 Jan-7 Feb. A good gourmet address. B. Augé is a fine cook who keeps high standards : *civet d'anguille, canelle aux figues.* Regional wines, 50-180.

SAINT-GAUDENS

Tarbes 65, Toulouse 90, Paris 797
B3 ✉ 31800

ℹ pl. du Mas-St-Pierre, ☎ 61.89.15.99.

SNCF ☎ 61.89.16.07.

Car-hire : *Budget* train + auto, at the station, ☎ 61.89.16.07.

Hotels :
★★***Esplanade*** (L.F.), 7, pl. du Mas-St-Pierre, ☎ 61.89.15.90. 12 rm ⚘ Ⓟ ♿ 120.

Villeneuve-de-Rivière, 5 km W, on the N117 :
★★★***Cèdres*** (Relais du Silence, Châteaux-hôtels), ☎ 61.89.36.00. 20 rm Ⓟ ♨ ⚲ ⚐ 265. Rest. ♦♦♦ Enjoy André Clausse's inventive cooking in this manor once owned by Mme de Montespan, 90-190.

Ⲁ ★★★*Belvédère* (96 pl.), ☎ 61.89.15.76.

SAINT-GIRONS

Foix 44, Toulouse 91, Paris 800
B3 ✉ 09200

ℹ pl. des Capots, ☎ 61.66.14.11.

SNCF ☎ 61.66.01.13.

Hotels :
● ★★★***Eychenne*** (Mapotel), 8, rue P.-Laffont, ☎ 61.66.20.55. AE, Euro, Visa. 48 rm Ⓟ ♨ ⚲ closed 21 Dec-1 Feb, 300. Rest. ● ♦♦♦ Good regional dishes in this former posthouse : *foie de canard aux raisins, confit de canard aux cèpes,* 75-200.
★★★***La Truite Dorée*** (L.F.), 28, av. de la Résistance, ☎ 61.66.16.89. 15 rm Ⓟ ♨ ⚲ ⚒ ♿ closed 15 Oct-15 Dec, 260. Rest. ♦ Family inn. Very good carte with wide choice of trout dishes, 70-110.
★★***Mirouze*** (L.F.), 19, av. Gallieni, ☎ 61.66.12.77. Euro. 25 rm Ⓟ ♨ ⚲ closed 21 Dec-1 Jan and Sat (low season), 150. Rest. ♦ 50-80.

Lorp-Sentaraille, ✉ 09190 St Lizier, 5 km NW :
★★***Horizon 117*** (L.F.), ☎ 61.66.26.80. Tx 530955. AE, Euro, Visa. 20 rm Ⓟ ♨ ⚲ closed 15 Oct-1 Nov and Sun eve low season, 170. Rest. ♦♦ ♿ 60-135.

Youth hostel : parc de Palétés, ☎ 61.66.06.79.

Ⲁ ★★★*Palétés* (50 pl.), ☎ 61.66.06.79.

SALIES-DU-SALAT

Saint-Gaudens 22, Toulouse 76, Paris 785
B3 ✉ 31260

ℹ bd J.-Jaurès (high season) and mairie, ☎ 61.90.53.26.

Hotel :
★★***Grand Hôtel*** (L.F.), 3, av. de la Gare, ☎ 61.90.56.43. 26 rm Ⓟ ♨ ⚲ ⚒ closed 15 Sep-2 Jun, 160. Rest. ♦ 50-105.

SAMATAN

Auch 35, Toulouse 48, Paris 733
2 km NE of Lombez, B2 ✉ 32130

Hotel :
★***Maigné,*** ☎ 62.62.30.24. 15 rm ♨ ⚲ closed 20 Sep-20 Oct, 100. Rest. ● ♦♦ Regional cooking : *foie gras, cassoulet,* 250-350.

Marché au gras : Mon (Nov-Apr).

SAVERDUN

Pamiers 15, Toulouse 49, Paris 758
12 km S of Cintegabelle, C2 ☒ 09700

SNCF ☎ 61.60.33.60.

Hotel :
★★★***Larlenque,*** 2 km S on the N20, ☎ 61.60.30.20. 17 rm Ⓟ closed 15 Oct-15 Nov, 180. Rest. ♦♦ closed Sun eve, Mon, Tue noon low season, 60-105.

Farmhouse-inn : *l'Ours,* ☎ 61.60.41.02. Riding centre. Book ahead.

SEISSAN

Auch 19, Toulouse 82, Paris 753
6 km N of Masseube, A2 ☒ 32260

⛺ ★★★*Laverdure* (85 pl.), ☎ 62.66.21.76.

Restaurant :
♦♦ ***Samaran,*** rue du Marché, ☎ 62.66.20.32. ♿ closed 1-15 Sep and Mon. Spec : *cous d'oie farcis, magret aux pêches, confit de poularde,* 50-160.

SEIX

Foix 62, Toulouse 109, Paris 818
18 km S of Saint-Girons, B3 ☒ 09140

Hotels :
Oust, 2 km NE :
● ★★★***Poste,*** ☎ 61.66.86.33. 28 rm Ⓟ closed 1 Nov-Easter, 220. Rest. ♦♦ Spec : *soufflé de truites aux écrevisses, pigeon à la crème d'ail, magret à l'orange, gâteau de foie gras au porto et aux truffes, papillote de saumon aux cèpes, marquise au café et chocolat.* Good wines, 75-200.

Pont de la Taule, 5 km S :
★***Deux Rivières*** (L.F.), ☎ 61.66.83.57. 11 rm Ⓟ closed winter ex week-ends and school hols, and 20 Sep-30 Oct, 60. Rest. ♦♦ ♿ 45-120.

Restaurant :
♦♦ ***Haut Salat,*** ☎ 61.66.88.03. closed winter (ex school hols), 80-130. With rm.

⛺ ★★★★*Haut Salat* (127 pl.), ☎ 61.66.81.78.

TARASCON-SUR-ARIÈGE

Foix 16, Saint-Girons 88, Paris 808
C3 ♥ ☒ 09400

ⓘ av. V.-Pilhes, ☎ 61.05.63.46.

SNCF ☎ 61.05.62.61.

Hotels :
★★***Poste*** (L.F.), 16, av. V.-Pilhes, ☎ 61.05.60.41. AE. 30 rm closed 15-3 Nov, 170. Rest. ♦ 60-120.
★***Confort,*** 3, quai A.-Sylvestre, ☎ 61.05.61.90. 14 rm closed 24 Dec-3 Jan, 175.

See also Ornolac-Ussat-les-Bains.

⛺ ★★*Pré Lombard* (100 pl.), ☎ 61.64.61.94.

TOULOUSE

Auch 78, Foix 83, Paris 709
C2 ☒ 31000

ⓘ donjon du Capitole (D2), ☎ 61.23.32.00.

✈ Toulouse-Blagnac, 7 km NW, ☎ 61.71.11.14. *Air France agency,* 2, bd de Strasbourg, ☎ 61.62.84.04.

SNCF (F1) ☎ 61.62.50.50, 61.63.11.88, 61.62.85.44.

🚌 68, rue P.-Sémard (E1), ☎ 61.48.71.84.

Car-hire : *Budget* train + auto, at the station, ☎ 61.63.71.71, 61.62.50.50, and at the airport, ☎ 61.71.11.14, poste 598.

Hotels :
★★★***Caravelle*** (Mapotel), 62, rue Raymond-IV (F1), ☎ 61.62.70.65. Tx 530438. AE, Euro, Visa. 30 rm 320.
★★★***Progrès*** (Inter-Hôtel), 10, rue Rival (D2), ☎ 61.23.21.28. Visa. 33 rm Ⓟ ♿ 200.
● ★★★***Grand Hôtel de l'Opéra,*** 1, pl. du Capitole (D2), ☎ 61.21.82.66, Tx 521998. AE, Euro, Visa. 49 rm ♿ 700. Rest. ● ♦♦♦ ***les Jardins de l'Opéra.*** closed Sun eve and Mon. D. Toulousy has just left Auch to raise the cooking at the *Opéra* to very high standards. Pleasant and cosy setting, 150-200.
★★***Victor Hugo*** (Inter-Hôtel), 26, bd de Strasbourg (D2-E1), ☎ 61.63.40.41. AE, Visa. 32 rm ♿ 200.

Mirail, ☒ 31100, 3.5 km SW on the D23 :
★★★***Diane,*** 3, rte de St-Simon, ☎ 61.07.59.52, Tx 530518. AE, Euro, Visa. 33 rm Ⓟ ♿ 330. Rest. ♦♦♦ closed nat hols, Sat noon and Sun. Fish specialities. Good desserts and regional wines, 120-170.

Saint-Jean, ☒ 31240, 4 km NE on the N88 :
★★★***Horizon 88,*** rte d'Albi, ☎ 61.74.34.15. DC, Visa. 38 rm Ⓟ ♿ 250. Rest. ♦ closed Feb, Aug, Sat noon and Sun, 60-170.

Montrabé, ☒ 31130, 6 km E :
★★★***Val Rose,*** ☎ 61.84.76.58. 14 rm Ⓟ Discothèque. Park with centuries-old trees, 180. Rest. ♦ 100-205.

Saint-Martin-du-Touch, 6 km W :
★★★***Airport,*** 176, rte de Bayonne, ☎ 61.49.68.78. Tx 521752. AE, DC, Euro, Visa. 48 rm Ⓟ ♿ 240.

Ramonville, 7 km SE on the N113 :
★★★***Chaumière*** (Inter-Hôtel), 102, av. Tolosane, ☎ 61.73.02.02. Tx 520646. AE, Euro, Visa. 43 rm Ⓟ ♿ 280. Rest. ♦ 80-200.

Tournefeuille, ☒ 31170, 8.5 km E :
★★★***Les Chanterelles*** (Relais du Silence), 277, chemin Ramelet-Moundi, ☎ 61.86.21.86. 10 rm Ⓟ ♿ 250.

Vieille-Toulouse, 9 km S :
★★★***La Flânerie,*** rte Lacroix-Falgarde, ☎ 61.73.39.12. Visa. 12 rm Ⓟ 360.

Villeneuve-Tolosane, ☒ 31270, 13 km SE :
★***Promenade,*** 22, allée des Platanes, ☎ 61.92.04.45. AE, Visa. 10 rm ♿ 120. Rest. ♦ closed Wed (31 Aug-1 May), 60-120.

Youth hostel : 125, av. Jean-Rieux (F5), ☎ 61.80.49.93.

⛺ ★★★*Pont de Ruppé* (162 pl.), ☎ 61.70.07.35. ★★*La Bouriette* (100 pl.), ☎ 61.49.64.46.

Restaurants :
● ♦♦♦♦ ***Vanel (Lucien Vanel),*** 22, rue Maurice-Fonvielle (E3), ☎ 61.21.51.82. AE, Euro. Closed 26 Jul-26 Aug, Sun and Mon noon. The marvellous choice proposed by Lucien Vanel is without fault as is his divine and creative cooking. Wide choice of dishes. Spec : *tarte aux moules, escargots, foies de lapin, soufflé de grenouilles, barbu à la crème, saint-honoré...* Great wines, brandies, armagnacs, liqueurs, 200-300.
● ♦♦♦ ***Belle Époque,*** 3, rue Pargaminières (C2), ☎ 61.23.22.12. AE, DC, Visa ♿ closed 24 Dec-2 Jan, Sat noon, Sun and nat hols. The very imaginative P. Roudgé will surprise you : *sole de ligne en goujonnette, ravioles de truffes au céleri, magret de canard.* The number of calories are indicated on the carte, for diet sake, but not yet reimbursed by the social security, 180-310.

● ◆◆◆ **Darroze,** 19, rue Castellane (E2), ☎ 61.62.34.70. AE, Visa. ⊿ ✻ ᕻ closed Sat noon, Sun and nat hols. The Darroze family is still successful as ambassador of the Landes region cooking : *délice de salade au foie gras, foie gras frais aux raisins, pigeon fermier en cocotte.* Fine bordeaux wines and armagnacs, 110-220.

● ◆◆◆ **Émile,** 13, pl. St-Georges (E3), ☎ 61.21.05.56. AE, Euro, Visa. closed Sun, Mon, 12 Aug-1 Sep, 23 Dec-5 Jan. F. Ferrier is an expert on fish dishes. More than 200 different recipes in the year : *lisette au vinaigre de cidre, sole à la fondue de courgettes.* For traditional dishes : excellent *cassoulet,* 150-220.

● ◆◆◆ **Ubu Club,** 16, rue St-Rome, ☎ 61.23.26.75. AE, DC, Euro. Toulouse's "chic" in restaurant. Faded lights, excellent cooking : grilled or poched fish, *foie gras, magret.* Service until 2 a.m, 180-200.

◆◆◆ **Séville,** 45, rue des Tourneurs (D3), ☎ 61.21.37.97. Good fish specialities and superb pastries, 110-200.

● ◆◆ **Bouchon Lyonnais,** 13, rue de l'Industrie (E2), ☎ 61.62.97.43. AE, Euro, Visa. closed 10-30 Jul, Sat and Sun. In his pleasant "bouchon", L. Orsi keeps the good tradition of Lyonnaise cooking for the greatest delight of his Toulousain customers : *saladier lyonnais, cervelas beaujolais,* not to forget his fish specialities : *assiette de la mer, mérou sauce vierge,* 80-185.

● ◆◆ **La Marmite en Folie,** 28, rue P.-Painlevé, ☎ 61.42.77.86 ░ ᕻ closed Sat noon, Sun and Mon noon. Mr Brandelin's cooking is steadily progressing for his customers' greatest delight : *foie gras aux câpres et au sauternes, salade tiède de rougets et pétoncles,* good desserts, served In an arbour, 90-180.

● ◆◆ **Le Van Gogh,** pl. St-Georges, ☎ 61.21.03.15. Closed Sun. A good quality restaurant, traditional Toulouse and Quercy regional cooking supervised by P. Lannes. Piano-bar in evenings, 140-220.

◆◆ **Dominique Laval,** 9, rue Gabriel-Péri (D2), ☎ 61.62.70.44. AE, Visa ᕻ closed 1-20 Aug, Christmas, Sat noon and Sun. Spec : *salade de langoustines, salade de pâtes fraîches aux crustacés, matelote d'anguille aux poireaux,* 80-150.

◆◆ **Belvédère,** 11, bd des Récollets (not on the D5 map), ☎ 61.52.63.73. ⸙ closed Aug, Sun and nat hols. Good regional cooking, 100-210.

◆◆ **Cassoulet,** 40, rue Peyrolières (C3), ☎ 61.21.18.99. Closed Mon, 30 Jun-15 Jul, 2-10 Jan. Spec : *magret de canard à la charlotte de courgettes,* 80-150.

◆◆ **Le Bleu Marine,** 4, rue A.-Bernard, ☎ 61.22.78.08. Fresh sea food, musical atmosphere, 60-170.

◆◆ **Rôtisserie des Carmes,** 11, pl. des Carmes (D4), 38, rue des Polinaires, ☎ 61.52.73.82 ℗ ᕻ closed Sat. A good, small restaurant with a 1900's setting, 60-170.

● ◆ **Le Colombier,** 4, rue Banard, ☎ 61.62.40.05. AE, Visa ᕻ closed Sat and Sun, 1 week at Christmas and Easter, 3 weeks in Aug. For amateurs of G. Lasso's authentic *cassoulet,* 65-160.

● ◆ **Chrisfloz,** 26, av. Saint-Exupéry, ☎ 61.53.12.86. closed 1-26 Aug. Pleasant woman's cooking by P. Pezet : *émincé de bar aux choux braisés, jarret de porc confit,* 100-180.

● ◆ **Maréchale,** 18, rue Mage, ☎ 61.52.21.16 ᕻ closed Sat, Jun, Mon noon. A surprising menu which is often changed, 70-90.

◆ **La Belle Chaurienne,** pl. Héraclès, allée de Barcelone (A2), ☎ 61.21.23.85. A barge turned into a restaurant specialising in *cassoulet,* 120-210.

◆ **La Braisière,** 42, rue Pharaon, ☎ 61.52.37.13. closed Sat, Sun. Warm atmosphere in country setting, around a chimney : *moules farcies, côte de bœuf,* 100-200.

Blagnac, 6 km NW :

◆◆◆ **Pujol,** 21, av. Gal-Compans, ☎ 61.71.13.58. Visa ℗ ░ closed Feb school hols, 3 weeks Aug, Sat and Sun eve. For foie gras enthusiasts, 150-210.

◆◆ **Horizon,** Airport, ☎ 61.71.02.75. AE, DC, Visa ⸙ Regional cooking, 90-190.

Lacourtensourt, ✉ 31140 Aucamville, 8 km N :

◆◆ **La Feuilleraie,** ☎ 61.70.16.01 ℗ ░ ☐ Spec : *ris de veau aux morilles, fricassée aux cèpes,* 90-205.

Vigoulet-d'Auzil, ✉ 31320, 12 km SW :

● ◆◆◆ **Tournebride,** ☎ 61.73.34.49. AE, DC ⸙ ℗ ░ ⊿ ᕻ closed 10-30 Jan, 10-30 Aug, nat hols, Sun eve and Mon. The marvellous view over the Pyrénées makes us better appreciate the Nouys' good cooking. Successful combination of classical and market produce cooking : *émincé de veau, steak au pot, perdreau en croûte.* Fine wines and armagnacs, 160-200.

La Barthe-sur-Lèze, 31120 Portet sur Garonne, 15 km W :

●◆ **Le Poëlon,** ☎ 61.08.68.49. closed Aug, 1 week Jan, Sun eve, Mon, Tue eve. Excellent value for J.-C. Antébon's cooking. Market produce : *blanquette de lotte, émincé de magret à l'orange,* 100-200.

Villematier, 31340 Villemur sur Tarn, 24 km N :

● ◆ **La Braise,** ☎ 61.35.35.64 ℗ ░ ⊿ ᕻ closed 15 Jul-14 Aug, 15 Jan-1 Feb, Sun eve, Mon and Tue. A former farmhouse where the Bertin family delights us with *foie gras chaud au verjus, loup en habit vert d'anis.* Côteaux du Frontonnais, 100-230.

Recommended : *Maison régionale des Artisans créateurs (regional handicrafts centre),* 42, rue Pharaon, ☎ 61.52.49.96 ; *Xavier,* 6, pl. V.-Hugo, ☎ 61.21.53.26, et *le Coup de Torchon,* 22, pl. Dupuy, ☎ 61.63.76.49 : cheese-makers.

VIC-FÉZENSAC

Auch 30, Agen 68, Paris 768
A1   ✉ 32190

Hotels :

● **D'Artagnan,** pl. de la Mairie, ☎ 62.06.31.37. DC. 10 rm, closed Mon, 80. Rest. 80-150.

Saint-Jean-Poutge, ✉ 32570, 8 km SE :

● ★★**Baise,** ☎ 62.64.62.11. AE, Euro, Visa. 18 rm ℗ ⊿ ✻ closed 1-30 Oct, 8 days May and Mon, 130. Rest. ◆◆ ✻ ᕻ Good menu : *salmis de palombes, cœurs d'oie fourrés au foie gras,* 50-90.

⋏ ★★*Municipal* (33 pl.), ☎ 62.06.30.08.

Normandy

Normandy is no longer the home of the Norsemen, those blond, blue-eyed Vikings who roamed the world in wooden-prowed boats, although their descendants continue to wrest a living from the sea. The sea plays an important role in this region, with its 600 kms of coastline, beaches and cliffs framing the vast estuary of the Seine.

Normandy, shaped by history and geography into a single cultural entity, is an intensely agricultural region, with medium-sized farms scattered throughout a landscape of alternating forest and meadow land, with fruitful orchards and excellent dairy produce. It is also the historic land of the great abbeys and châteaux, the manor houses described by novelists such as Flaubert and Maupassant, the seascapes of Boudin and Monet's vision of the Rouen cathedral metamorphosed by light. This is a Normandy to discover and explore, with its inviting seaside or country beauty spots sitting calmly side by side with the economic bustle and dynamism of its two capitals — Rouen and Caen — and the industrial and port complex of Le Havre-Rouen.

Peasant women in lace head-dresses on their way to the village market, and the once-common Percheron horses are now very rarely glimpsed. But although the personality of Normandy may be more muted than that of Brittany or Alsace, you can sense behind the tranquil façade of everyday life what it means to belong in Normandy, what it means to belong to a single community on a single land, a unity enriched and softened by the age-old generosity of its inhabitants. Fishing villages, traces of the Viking past in the Cotentin peninsula, the quaint half-timbered houses of the Auge region, the American Film Festival and summer casino in fashionable Deauville — all make up the rich mosaic of Normandy, while to the extreme west Mont-Saint-Michel rises up out of the flat salty marshlands of the bay, bearing the heavy crown of its mediaeval abbey, and its streets thronged since the 11th century with pilgrims, merchants and sightseers.

Sightseeing

Weekend tips

Two days in Normandy : Les Andelys, Rouen, Honfleur, Deauville, Caen (stop-over), the D-Day Landing Beaches, Mont-Saint-Michel and Alençon. It can be done, but it's better not to be too ambitious. Start with a quick visit to Rouen and the valley of the Seine; stop-over in Le Havre. Next day : Étretat, Fécamp, Rouen. Alternatively, still starting from Rouen : Marais Vernier, Honfleur, Deauville (stop-over), the Auge region, Caen. Starting from Alençon : the Argentan region, La Suisse Normande (Swiss Normandy stop-over), Caen; alternatively Perche, the Ouche region (stop-over), Neubourg, Évreux, Vernon, the valley of the Seine, Rouen.

Don't miss

★★★ : *Auge Region (B2), Caen (B2), D-Day Landing Beaches (A1-2 B2), Honfleur (B1), Mont-Saint-Michel (A2), Rouen (C1), lower valley of the Seine (BC2-3).*

★★ : *Alençon (B3), Bayeux (A2), the Cotentin Coast (A1), Normandy-Maine Regional Park (B3), Perche (B-C3), La Suisse Normande (Swiss Normandy) (B2).*

■ ALENÇON★★

C3-4 / ® / pop. 32 530 (Orne)

See plan on following page

Commercial and administrative centre of the rich Sarthe countryside, this lace-making town retains the aristocratic air of a one-time ducal city; now also an important centre for the manufacture of household appliances.

▶ Across from the **Prefecture**★ (B1; 1630) is the Rue St. Blaise ending in a pedestrian precinct by the church of **Notre-Dame**★ (B2; 16thC porch★). At No. 50 is the birthplace *(closed Tue.)* of Thérèse Martin (1873-97), canonised St. Thérèse in 1927. The neighbouring 15thC Maison d'Ozé houses the SI as well as a local museum. Rue du Pont-Neuf (B2) : lace-making school (École Dentellière, visits on request). ▶ Church of St. Léonard (B2), Flamboyant Gothic, the centre of **old Alen-**

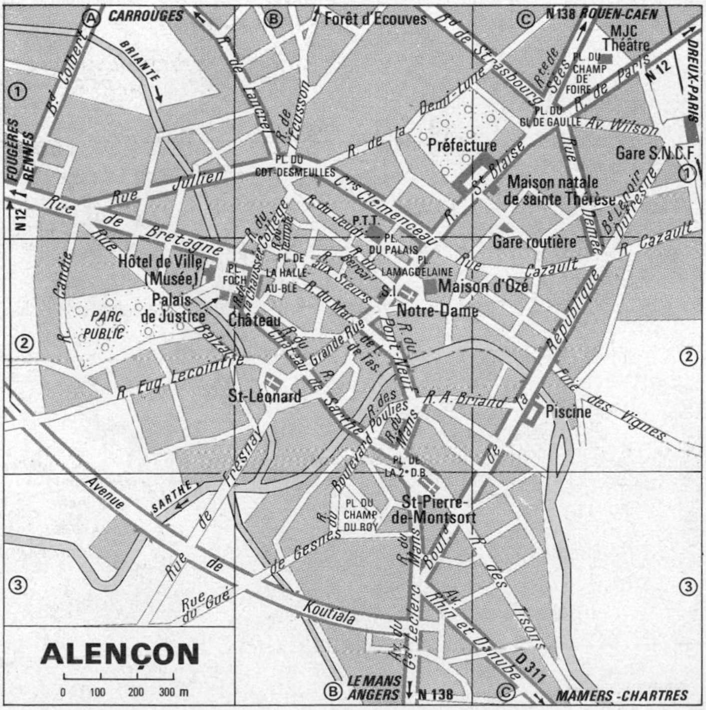

çon. ▶ Place Foch (A-B2) : the 1783 Hôtel de Ville (town hall) stands near the 14th-15thC Ducal Castle (Château des Ducs). The **Musée des Beaux-Arts et de la Dentelle**★ (Fine-Arts and Lace-making Museum, A1 ; *closed Mon.*) is installed in the former Jesuits' college (1620). □

▶ Nearby

▶ **Saint-Céneri-le-Gérei**★ *(14 km SW) :* on the edge of the "Alpes Mancelles" (hills, really) in a loop of the Sarthe ; 14thC frescos in the Romanesque church. ▶ **Perseigne Forest** (50 km^2, *SW*) and **Écouves Forest** (75 km^2, *NW*) are both part of the Normandy-Maine Nature Park *(parc naturel);* both shelter red and roe deer and wild boar (→ Bagnoles de l'Orne). ▶ **Sées** ® *(22 km N) :* seat of a bishopric, 13th-14thC Gothic cathedral★★ (14th-15thC stained glass★, 19thC spires); museum of sacred art ; episcopal palace (1778); remains of the 18thC **abbey of Notre-Dame-de-la-Place.** □

■ Les ANDELYS★

D2 / ® / pop. 8 210 (Eure)

The town includes **Grand Andely** (church of Notre-Dame★, 12th-15thC, with Renaissance organ-casing) and **Petit Andely.**

▶ Church of St. Sauveur★ (11thC) with 14thC wooden porch; Hospice St. Jacques (infirmary); 1784 dome. ▶ **Château Gaillard★★ :** an exceptional view★ over the Seine; the fortress, once the pride of the 12thC English King Richard the Lion-Heart, was captured by Philippe Auguste in 1204; it is now in ruins *(daily ex Tue. and Wed. am).* □

■ ARGENTAN

C3 / ® / pop. 18 000 (Orne)

In a rich cattle-farming region, the town was rebuilt after WWII. Remains of the 14thC château and 12thC keep; Gothic and

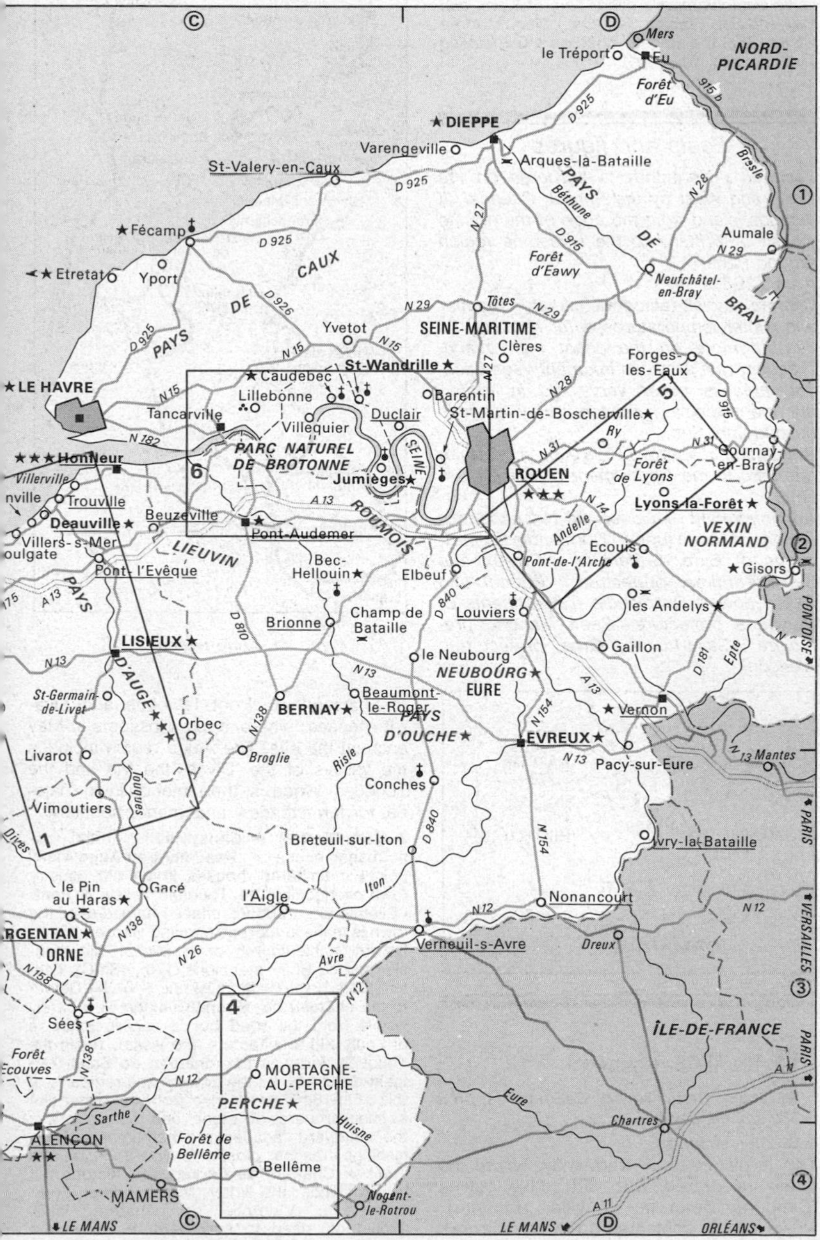

Normandy

Renaissance church of St. Germain; 16thC stained glass in church of St. Martin. ▶ Birthplace of the painter Fernand Léger (1881-1955). ▶ Benedictine abbey *(2 Rue de l'Abbaye)* where the nuns make lace (point d'Argentan). □

▶ Nearby

▶ Numerous **châteaux** and **manor houses★★** from various periods, including the **château du Pin★** *(15 km E;* 1728) : site of a stud-farm founded in 1714 *(free guided tours; harness horse demonstrations every Thu. at 3 pm, end May-end Sep.; racing Sep.-Oct.).* Near Mortrée *(16 km SE)* : the graceful **château d'O★** *(closed Tue.; am only Nov.-Apr.).* □

Facts and figures

Location : *Normandy is bordered on the North and West by the English Channel; it extends inland from the edge of the granite massif of Brittany to the limestone region around Paris.*
Area : *29 896 km².*
Climate : *moist, temperate climate; summer and winter temperatures differ relatively little, but more on the coast than inland. Frequent rain provides luxuriant vegetation. The area is never very cold in winter, but the swimming season rarely extends beyond Jun.-Sep.*
Population : *approx 3 008 000; more than one-third in the Department of Seine-Maritime.*
Administration : *includes the two economic regions of Haute (upper) Normandie (Departments of* ***Eure,*** *prefecture : Évreux and* ***Seine-Maritime,*** *prefecture : Rouen) and Basse (lower) Normandie (Departments of* ***Calvados,*** *prefecture : Caen,* ***Manche,*** *prefecture : Saint-Lô and* ***Orne,*** *prefecture : Alençon).*

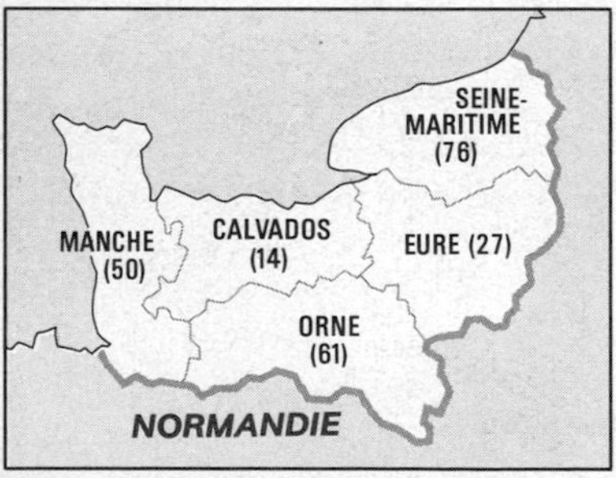

The **AUGE** Region★★★

▶ From Deauville to Cabourg *(approx 180 km, full day)*

BC2-3 *(see map 1)*

This is picture-book Normandy, where the coast is dotted with attractive towns (Cabourg, Deauville-Trouville, Honfleur); where inland, contented cows provide milk for Camembert, Pont l'Évêque and Livarot cheeses; where apple blossoms in May enchant the eye. The Auge region includes the valleys of the Dives, the Vie and the Touques. Wood is the usual building material for farmsteads★ and manor houses★.

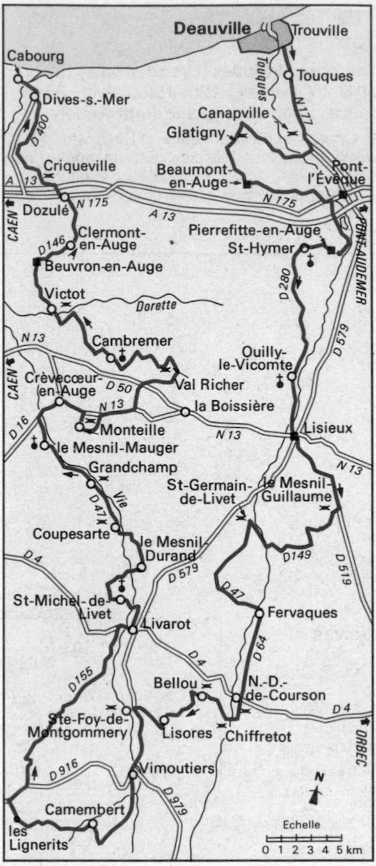

1. **Auge region**

▶ **Deauville** (→). ▶ **Canapville** ® : 15thC rustic manor house. ▶ **Beaumont-en-Auge** viewpoint★ : timbered houses in an old country town overlooking the Touques Valley. ▶ **Pont-l'Évêque** ® : a superb cheese named after the town is made in the surrounding villages; Flamboyant Gothic church of St. Michel; Montpensier and de Brilly mansions (17th, 18thC); half-timbered houses. ▶ **Lisieux** (→). ▶ Detour to the **château de Mesnil-Guillaume★ :** barely visible from the road but a superb example of Louis XIII architecture *(no visits);* rejoin the Touques Valley at the **château de Saint-Germain-de-Livet★★ :** the towers and ramparts of this 15th-16thC castle rise from the water like a checkerboard of stone and glazed brick; the courtyard façades are half-timbered (furnishings, frescos; *closed 15 Dec.-end Jan. and Tue.).* ▶ **Château de Fervaques :** historic but less romantic; the writer Chateaubriand (François-René, Vicomte de Chateaubriand, 1768-1848) used to stay here. ▶ Leave the

Touques Valley at **Moutiers Hubert** (**Chiffretot manor,** 17thC) and drive past **Bellou Manor★,** (17thC, half-timbered). Near **Lisores :** Bougonnière farm *(terme),* with a small Fernand Léger Museum (→ Argentan; *closed Wed.*). ▶ **Vimoutiers** ® : Place de la Mairie : statue of Marie Harel, a local farmwoman who perfected the making of Camembert cheese. ▶ **Camembert :** in the late 19thC, Marie Harel made her cheese at the Beaumoncel farm. ▶ **Livarot** ® *(on the Vie)* lends its name to another well-known cheese; also a major butter producer *(visits of cheese-making).* ▶ **Coupesarte :** 16thC timber-built manor house★. **Grandchamp :** unusually tall half-timbered building. ▶ **Crèvecoeur-en-Auge :** a fortified site from the 11thC; restoration undertaken by the industrialist Schlumberger family; includes museums of Norman Architecture and Petroleum Research *(in Apr., May, Jun. and Sep., closed Wed.; in Feb., Mar., Oct., Nov., Sat. and Sun.; open daily, 12-8 pm Jul.-Aug.; closed Dec. and Jan.).* ▶ Beyond the ruins of the former **Val Richer abbey,** the classic 17thC **château de la Roque Baignard.** ▶ **Cambremer :** the heart of cider country; visits to farms displaying the sign *"cru* (crop) *de Cambremer".* ▶ Important stud farm at the **château de Victort★** (16thC). ▶ **Beuvron-en-Auge★** ® : craft-centre; historic village (Place de la Halle) sometimes called "the cider capital" *(festival in Nov.).* **Clermont-en-Auge :** view★ over the Auge Valley. ▶ You reach the coast at Dives-sur-Mer and Cabourg (→ Deauville). □

■ BAGNOLES-DE-L'ORNE★

B3 / ® / pop. 780 (Orne)

One of the major spas in western France, situated in the valley of the river Vée. Casino on the lake and, in the middle of the warm springs park (Parc Thermal), a rocky gorge covered with fir trees. □

▶ Nearby

▶ **Andaines Forest :** (40 km²) ideal area for walking, riding, cycling or driving. ▶ **Carrouges** ® *(23 km E)* : fine 15th-17thC château★ *(closed Tue.;* antique furnishings). On the edge of the estate, a 15th house is the Normandy-Maine Nature Park HQ★★ : the 234 km² park includes the forests of Andaines, Écouves (in the Orne Department) Perseigne, and Sillé (in the Sarthe Department); numerous recreational facilities, including cross-country hikes, horse-riding, rock-climbing, canoeing, kayaking, sailing. ▶ **Domfront** ® *(19 km W)* : view★ from the ruins of the 11thC keep, surrounded by a fine park; below, the church of Notre-Dame-sur-l'Eau (11thC). □

Norman place-names

The common endings of many Norman place-names reflect their origins as Viking or Norse settlements : bec : stream; beuf : house; crique : church; fleur : bay; ham : dwelling; hague, hogue : hill; mare : lake or pond; tot : homestead, home. Ville, one of the commonest endings, is derived from the farm estates (villas) of the Gallo-Roman era; later, it was often joined to the purely Norman name of a land-owner. As for Langrune (land groen : green land), it is a synonym for Greenland.

■ BAYEUX★★

B2 / ® / pop. 15 240 (Calvados)
(see plan following page)

The fame of the tapestry (in fact an embroidery) tends to make one forget that Bayeux is charming in its own right.

▶ **Cathedral of Notre-Dame★★** (B2) : a fine example of Norman Gothic (13thC); two towers on the façade, 15thC lantern tower★ topped in the 19thC. ▶ The former episcopal buildings

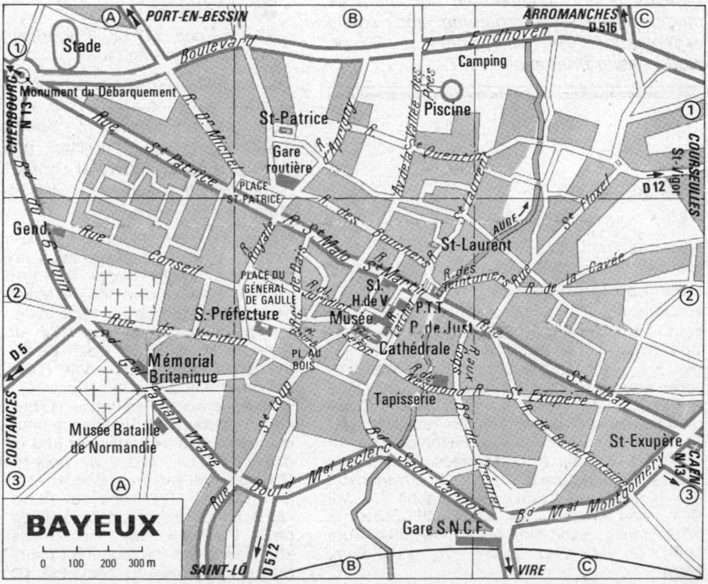

(B2) are now occupied by the town hall, the Law Courts (Palais de Justice; ceiling from the Renaissance chapel), and the **Baron-Gérard Museum★** (paintings ranging from Italian Primitives to Impressionists and local artists; lace and decorative arts; *16 Mar.-30 Sep., 9 to 7; Oct.-15 Mar., 10-12 & 2-6:30).* ▶ The William the Conqueror Cultural Centre (Centre Culturel Guillaume le Conquérant; B2-3) houses the **Bayeux Tapestry** (linen)★★★ (see box; *same hours as the museum*), once wrongly attributed to William's consort Queen Matilda. Fifty-eight scenes covering a length of 70 m tell the story of William's conquest of England in 1066; the embroidery was done in about 1077 in England. ▶ Old houses★ in the town centre. ▶ Place aux Pommes (B2) : on one side of the river Aure (good view) is the Centre Normand de la Dentelle au Fuseau (bobbin lace centre; *closed Sun. in summer, Sun. and Mon. rest of year);* on the other, Clock Workshop (lace-making). **Also...** ▶ Memorial museum of the battle of Normandy★ (Musée Mémorial de la Bataille de Normandie; A3; *daily Apr.-Oct.; 9:30-7 Jul.-Aug.; Sat. and Sun. in winter).* □

The Bayeux tapestry

Locally known as "La Telle du Conquest" (the conquest cloth), the Bayeux Tapestry is an embroidery of woolen threads on a linen ground, 69.55 m long and 50 to 55 cm wide. The sequence of 58 scenes relates the history of the Norman conquest of England from the decision of the childless English king, Edward the Confessor, to name his cousin William, Duke of Normandy, as his heir, through the broken oath of loyalty by William's English rival Harold, to William's victory over Harold at Hastings on 14 October 1066. The scenes are bordered by a frieze of animals and fabulous beasts; the tapestry is an incomparable document of mediaeval warfare, costume and social organisation. The embroidery is Saxon work, dating from about 1077.

■ BERNAY★

C2 / ® / pop. 10 950 (Eure)

An important cattle-rearing centre and market town that originally developed around an 11thC abbey.

▶ Next to the abbey **church★,** the *logis* (17thC) houses a museum of ceramics, furniture, paintings *(closed Tue. and am low-season ex Wed.);* it overlooks a public garden. ▶ Half-timbered **houses★** in many streets, especially Rue G.-Folloppe; No. 15 is the Musée de la Charrette (museum of daily life in the 19thC; *closed Mon.*). ▶ **Plasnes** *(6 km N) :* ornithological park *(Sat. & Sun. pm).* ▶ D133 leads through the pleasant **Charentonne Valley.** ▶ Promenade des Monts (walk, view). **Beaumesnil** *(14 km SE) :* one of the finest Louis XIII châteaux in existence; exhibition of book-binding from 16thC on *(May-Sep. 2:30-6 Fri., Sat., Sun., Mon).* □

■ The **BESSIN** Region

A B-2

West of Caen lies the traditional Normandy of meadows and hedges with the spires of Bayeux cathedral in the distance. This is rich dairy country; Isigny has been famous for dairy produce since the 17thC. The farmsteads are beautiful buildings : double archways lead into a courtyard in front of the main building, often dating from the 15th or 16thC, and sometimes flanked by a tower. The subsoil of the southern Bessin is granitic. The English Channel *(la Manche)* coast is a wall of limestone cliffs broken by small coves that shelter little ports (→ D-Day Landing Beaches). □

■ The **BRAY** Region

D 1

This low-lying, cattle-farming area between the plateaux of Picardy, the Caux region and the Vexin is the "dairy of Paris".

▶ **Forges-les-Eaux** ® : is a spa launched by Louis XIII (1601-43), his wife Anne of Austria and Cardinal Richelieu; three springs are named after them. In the park, a bus has been converted into a museum of model horse-drawn carriages *(pm in season).* The ceramics museum (Musée de la Faïence) in the town hall *(daily 10-11:30 & 2-5 ex Mon., hols.)* illustrates local production during the 19thC. ▶ **Neufchâtel-en-Bray** ® : cheese *(bondon);* the town was rebuilt after WWII; church of Notre-Dame (13th-16thC); J. B. Mathon and A. Durand museum in a 16thC house (folk art; *pm in season, Sat. and Sun. out of season).* ▶ **Mesnières-en-Bray** *(5 km NW) :* Renaissance château★ *(Sat. and Sun. pm).* ▶ **Saint-Saëns :** good starting point for exploring the 65 km² **Eawy Forest★** (beech). □

■ CAEN★★★

B2 / ® / pop. 117 120 (Calvados)
(see plan following page)

The capital of Lower Normandy was rebuilt in a few decades after WWII, which miraculously spared its ancient churches. Today, the favourite city of William the Conqueror is a thriving industrial centre. The Orne canal provides access to the sea for the shipment of goods.

▶ **Castle★★** (B1; founded by William the Conqueror) : wartime destruction exposed the mediaeval walls. From flowered terraces, views★ over the town and the Maison des Quatrans★ (14th-16thC). The base of the 12thC keep has also been exposed. ▶ The chapel of St. Georges (12th-15thC; Caen Battle Memorial); the Échiquier de Normandie (14thC; formerly the great hall of the ducal palace) and the former Governor's Residence (17th-18thC) have been restored. The Residence houses the **Normandy Museum★★** (history and ethnography; *daily ex Tue. and nat. hols.*); **Fine Arts Museum** (Musée des Beaux Arts)★★ (Italian and Flemish Primitives to 19thC paintings; *same hours*) in a modern building. ▶ **Church of St. Pierre★★** (B2) : the 78 m spire (rebuilt after 1944) was the model for many Breton and Norman bell-towers; Renaissance apse; the

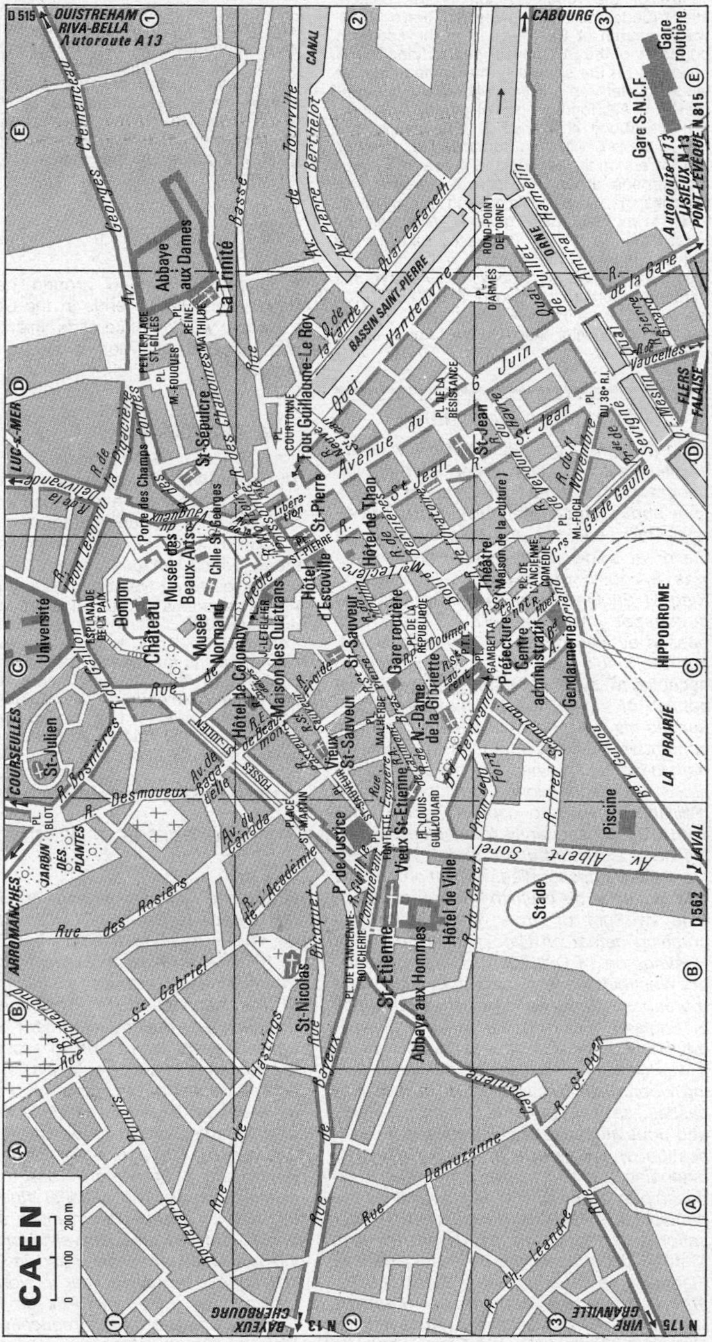
CAEN
0 100 200 m
OUISTREHAM RIVA-BELLA Autoroute A13
CABOURG
Gare routière
Gare S.N.C.F.
Autoroute A13 LISIEUX N 13 PONT-L'ÉVÊQUE N 815
HIPPODROME
LA PRAIRIE
Piscine
Stade
Université
Château
Donjon
Musée des Beaux-Arts
Musée de Normandie
Abbaye aux Dames
La Trinité
St-Pierre
Hôtel d'Escoville
Hôtel de Than
St-Sauveur
Vieux St-Sauveur
Hôtel de Colomby
Maison des Quatrans
St-Sépulcre
Tour Guillaume-Le Roy
St-Jean
Théâtre
Préfecture
Centre administratif
Gendarmerie
Gare routière
N.-Dame de la Gloriette
Vieux St-Etienne
St-Etienne
Abbaye aux Hommes
Hôtel de Ville
St-Nicolas
St-Julien
BASSIN SAINT-PIERRE
CANAL
ORNE
ARROMANCHES
COURSEULLES
LUC-s-MER
BAYEUX CHERBOURG N 13
VIRE GRANVILLE N 175
FLERS FALAISE
LAVAL D 562

Hôtel d'Escoville★ (mansion) is of the same period (B2; TO). ▶ Rue St. Jean leads to the Flamboyant Gothic church of St. Jean (15thC; C2); Boulevard Maréchal Leclerc (C2), at the centre of the rebuilt sector, is the busiest street (pedestrian zone). **Rue St. Pierre** (*westward;* church of St. Sauveur) is the southern boundary of the St. Sauveur quarter (fine 13thC buildings on the square of the same name); it leads to the Men's Abbey **(Abbaye aux Hommes)★★** (A2; founded by William the Conqueror); the abbey church of St. Étienne★★ is a fine example of Norman Romanesque, with two bell-towers on the façade and a beautiful apse; the gardens around the chevet (eastern end) enhance the 18thC buildings; in the **Hôtel de Ville** (town hall; *daily guided visits*), Nature Museum★ *(Wed. pm).* Opposite, ruins of the Old St. Étienne (13th-16thC).
Also... ▶ (The Ladies' Abbey; C1) **Abbaye aux Dames★,** founded by Queen Matilda in 1062; the church of La Trinité★ (11th; 12thC, remodelled 19th) rivals that of the Abbaye aux Hommes. □

William the Conqueror

Born at Falaise ca. 1027, William was the illegitimate son of Duke Robert I and Arlette, daughter of a furrier. His gifts of leadership and endurance enabled him to overcome this handicap, and he proved one of the great soldier-statesmen of his day. He was a cousin of Edward the Confessor, King of England, who had chosen him as successor. At this period, the crown passed by election to one of the royal line, and the king's own choice was subject to acceptance by the Saxon witangemot, *or council of elders. William had further enhanced his claim by forcing the other major contender, Harold Godwinson, to swear an oath in his favour when a shipwreck had enabled the neighbouring Count of Ponthieu (William's vassal) to capture Harold. This oath was subsequently repudiated as having been extracted under threat. When Edward the Confessor died, William proceeded to make good his claim to the throne of England by right of arms; after inflicting a crushing defeat on Harold at the battle of Hastings on 14 Oct. 1066, he was crowned at Westminster on Christmas Day, and thereafter introduced important innovations in England, including the famous Doomsday Book. The first written property census, it was drawn up for taxation purposes, listing woods, fields, mills, towns, houses and castles, as well as cattle, estimated yields and population. He also introduced a modification of the prevailing feudal system by extending the direct sovereign-vassal relationship to minor landholders as well as the principal nobility. William supported the educational system of his day : with his wife Matilda, daughter of the powerful Count of Flanders, he founded some thirty abbeys, among them the Abbaye aux Femmes (Women's Abbey) and the Abbaye aux Hommes (Men's Abbey) in Caen, where he was buried in 1087.*

▶ Nearby

▶ D-Day circuit (→).
▶ **Tilly-sur-Seulles** *(25 km W) :* rebuilt since WWII; museum of the Battle of Tilly in the chapel of the Vale *(Sat., Sun., nat. hols. pm).* ▶ **Villers-Bocage** ® *(26 km SW) :* lively cattle market on Wednesdays. ▶ **Saint-Pierre-sur-Dives** ® *(31 km SE) :* country market every Monday; Gothic church and chapter, conservatory of cheese techniques. Château at **Vendeuvre** *(6 km farther S) :* 18thC; international museum of miniature furniture★ and masterpieces by guild craftsmen in the orangery; *pm Jun.-15 Sep.*). □

■ The CAUX Region

C1

A limestone plateau around Le Havre, Rouen and Dieppe ends at the Channel in a vertical wall of white cliffs. Inland, valleys and curtains of trees protect the fertile farmland. □

■ CHERBOURG★

A1 / ® /pop. 30110 (Manche)

The best way to arrive at Cherbourg by land is to follow the Avenue de Paris, which seems as if it will run right into the Channel. A huge dyke 3.7 km long protects the roadstead, which includes commercial and passenger ports as well as a military arsenal.
▶ The panorama★ is remarkable from the **Fort du Roule** (B3; Liberation museum; *closed Tue. from Oct. to Apr.).* ▶ Near the lively town centre, behind the theatre (B2), are the cultural centre and the **Thomas Henry Museum★** (paintings of the Italian and Dutch schools, portraits by Millet (→ box; *closed Tue.*). ▶ The quays along the Bassin du Commerce (commercial port B2-3) and the outer port lead to

The horses of Normandy

Organised horse-breeding in Normandy dates back to the 14thC, when Philippe VI de Valois founded a stud near Domfront. In 1665, Jean-Baptiste Colbert (Louis XIV's Prime Minister) centralised the management of the national studs in Normandy and encouraged the development of sires. Later, trotters were bred to accommodate the demands of racing enthusiasts. Draught-horses, notably the powerful Percheron, have almost disappeared since the advent of mechanisation on roads and farms. The Japanese, however, are interested in developing a Percheron cross to improve trotting breeds. The national studs (haras) at Saint-Lô and Le Pin maintain some 200 and 80 stallions, respectively. Horse-breeding is particularly widespread in Orne and Calvados. The racing year in Normandy is crowned by the Grand Prix de Deauville. Race-meetings are held frequently at Caen, Lisieux, Rouen, Argentan, Saint-Lô, and Graignes, among other centres.

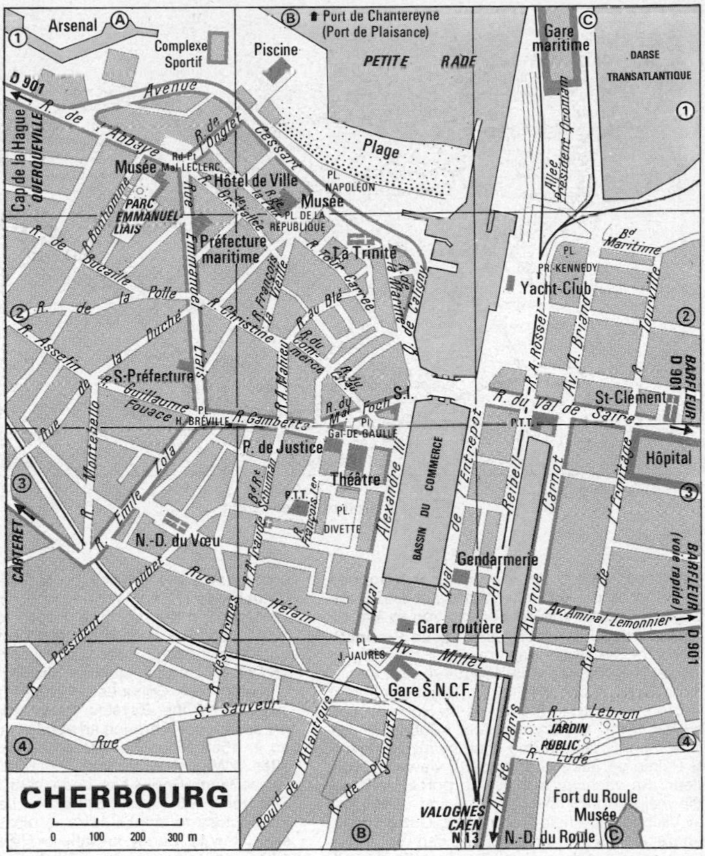

Normandy

the Place de la République (A2); nearby are the church of La Trinité (15thC), the town hall (Hôtel de Ville) and the beach. ▶ At the edge of the **Emmanuel Liais Park★** (A2) (created by the naturalist and astronomer, 1826-1900, after whom it is named; exotic plants), the Natural History Museum (A1; *closed Tue. and nat. hols., May-15 Sep.; pm rest of year*). ▶ **The Arsenal** (France's first nuclear submarine, Le Redoutable, was launched there in 1967) and the military port (A1) are accessible only to French citizens. ▶ **Tourlaville** *(14 km E)* : château and park★ → Cotentin circuit (end). □

■ The **COTENTIN** Peninsula★★

▶ Round trip *(approx 210 km, full day)*
A1-2 *(see map 2)*

The Cotentin Peninsula is where you may still find traces of the Vikings who first settled Normandy. The capes, inlets and headlands rival those of the coast of Brittany; the gentle climate of the Val de Saire favours market gardening. The GR223 follows the coast for part of the way.

▶ **Cherbourg** (→) ▶ **Nacqueville :** 16thC **château** surrounded by an English park *(Easter-Oct., 2-5 closed Tue.)*. ▶ **Landemer :** a seaside resort charmingly placed at one end of the wild, rocky coast that runs to Cape La Hague. The GR233 leads to Castel-Vendon Rock (site★). ▶ The D45 follows the **presqu'île de la Hague★★** (peninsula). ▶ **Omonville-la Rogue★ :** this fishing-port is one of the prettiest villages in the Cotentin. ▶ From **Auderville,** you can drive to **Cape La Hague★** *(1.5 km N)* and the small port of **Goury** (view★ of Gros du Raz reef and lighthouse). ▶ Along the coast : **Ecalgrain Bay★, Nez de Voidries★** (point) and **Nez de Jobourg★★;** out to sea lies the Channel Island of Alderney (île d'Aurigny). ▶ Jobourg heath supports a nuclear fuel-processing plant (information bureau; *pm 15 Jun.-15 Sep.*). From **Beaumont,** walk to the lookout *(belvédère)* at **Pierre-Pouquelée** *(approx 20 mins from D318; easier access from D403)*; panorama★ of the wild bay of Vauville and the protected area of the **Mare de Vauville** (barrens).

▶ **Siouville-Hague :** a salt-water therapy centre. ▶ **Diélette :** small port and seaside resort. Flamanville *(2.5 km SW)* : a **nuclear power station** provides electricity for Caen and part of Brittany; viewpoint and information center *(visits, tel., 33.20.10.55)*. The villages of **Flamanville** have maintained their traditional character. The château★ is a fine classical construction; park★ with palms. ▶ **Bricquebec** ® : remodelled 14thC **château;** museum in the

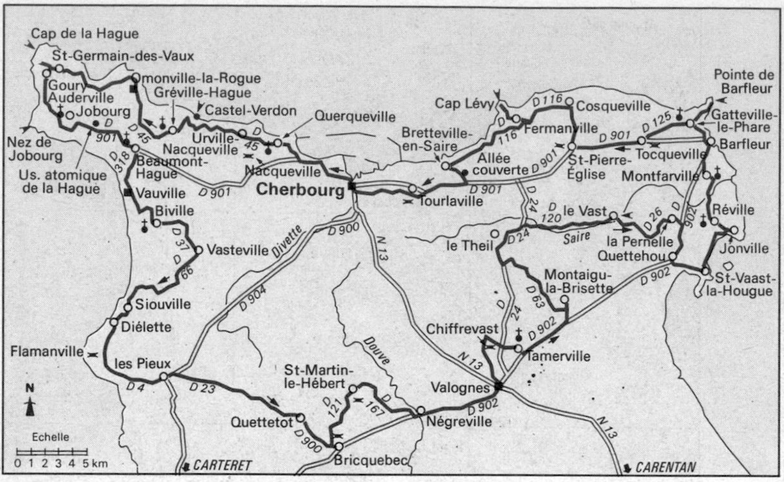

2. Cotentin peninsula

clocktower *(ask at the town hall).* ▶ **Valognes** (→). ▶ A detour through Chiffrevast and **Montaigu-la-Brisette** (church) brings you to **Val de Saire★ :** delightful countryside. ▶ **La Pernelle :** view★ of the whole eastern coast of the peninsula. ▶ **Saint-Vaast-la-Hougue** ® : renowned for oysters, faces the Ilot de Tatihou (citadel), linked by a dyke to the fort at La Hougue, built by the 17thC military architect Vauban. ▶ **Réville :** 11thC church and churchyard cemetery. ▶ Pointe de Saire *(2.5 km SE) :* view★. ▶ **Barfleur** : a yachting and fishing port★, formerly the main port for the Cotentin, and once used by Vikings and Anglo-Normans. ▶ **Gatteville-le-Phare :** view★★; from here, you can reach Barfleur point (lighthouse). ▶ **Tocqueville :** family home of Alexis de Tocqueville (1805-59), the author of "Democracy in America"; 15th-18thC château. ▶ **Fermanville :** view★ from Cape Lévy. ▶ **Tourlaville :** 16thC château; park★. □

■ COUTANCES★

A2 / ® / pop. 13 440 (Manche)

The original settlement was named for the Roman Emperor Constantine. One corrupted form of the name, "Cotentin", came to include the entire peninsula, whereas a second form was confined to the town. Today, Coutances blends the 20thC and the Middle Ages.

▶ The main churches were built along the major N S street : St. Nicolas (16th-17thC); the **Cathedral★★,** with its two towers, a masterpiece of 13thC Gothic; the church of St. Pierre, topped with an octagonal tower. Behind the town hall, the Morinière mansion houses a small museum of ceramics, painting and sculpture *(closed Wed.)*; it opens on to the attractive public garden. □

▶ Nearby

▶ To the W, around the Sienne estuary : **Regnéville-sur-Mer** *(11 km SW) :* small port and seaside resort; **Tourville** *(9 km W) :* birthplace and namesake of an unlucky admiral under Louis XIV (Manoir de la Vallée). **Agon-Coutainville** *(12 km W) :* one of the most popular resorts in the region. ▶ **Pirou** *(18 km NW) :* 12thC castle remodelled in the 17thC (*10-6:30 Jul.-Aug.; pm rest of year; closed 15 Dec.-15 Jan.*; in summer, display of modern tapestry, "The Conquest of Puglia and Sicily", inspired by the Bayeux Tapestry. ▶ **Lessay** *(21 km N) :* grew around an abbey church founded in 1050; Romanesque **church★★** restored after WWII; an important cattle-market (Foire de la Sainte-Croix) has been held here every Sep. for 1 000 years. Farther N : **La Haye-du-Puits,** close to **Mont Castre;** a pleasant excursion (view★). **Cerisy-la-Salle** ® *(14 km E) :* the 17thC **château** is now an international conference centre (Centre International de Rencontre; *visits by request : Thu. and Sun. pm, Jul.-Aug.; closed Tue.*). Ruined **Abbey of Hambye★** *(22 km SE) :* founded in 1145; worth a visit; conservatory of liturgical ornaments *(closed Wed. out of season).* □

■ DEAUVILLE★

C2 / ® / pop. 4 770 (Calvados)

The horse-racing, the *planches* (the famous boardwalk along the seafront) and the proximity to Paris have made Deauville the most popular seaside resort in Normandy.

▶ The **Promenade des Planches** runs the length of the 3 km beach; **Port-Deauville** (A1) is a marina and yacht harbour at the mouth of the Touques. **Gardens★,** weekend houses and luxury hotels line the **Boulevard Eugène Cornuché** (A1-2), while on the edge of town are the race-course and the golf club; elegant houses on the slopes of **Mont-Canisy** (*5 km from town centre;* view★). □

▶ Deauville to Honfleur *(16 km)* the flowered coast

▶ **Trouville** ® is a less exclusive resort than Deauville; comfortable middle-class houses stand on the hill looking out to sea. Facilities include a casino, a seawater therapy (thalassotherapy) centre and a bustling port. The **Eco-**

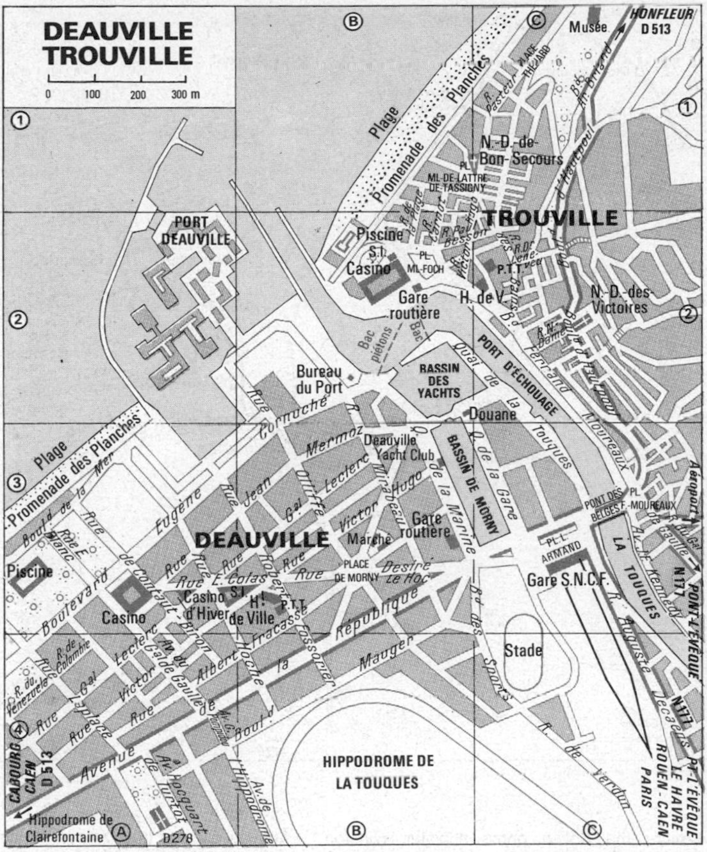

logical Aquarium★ features marine reptiles *(daily Apr.-Sep.; pm Oct.-Mar.)*; museum at the Villa Montebello (drawings, watercolours, 19thC paintings; *Sat. and Sun. pm Easter-15 Jun.; daily pm ex. Tue. in summer*). ▶ Honfleur (→). □

▶ Deauville to Cabourg *(18 km)*

▶ **Bénerville** and **Blonville-sur-Mer** ® : popular extensions of Deauville beaches. ▶ **Villers-sur-Mer** ® : invigorating walk along the sea wall. **Houlgate** ® : approx 2hr drive along the Falaises des Vaches Noires (Black Cow Cliffs)★. ▶ Butte de Caumont *(1 km S)* : a column commemorates William the Conqueror's embarkation in 1066 from ▶ **Dives-sur-Mer** ® : 14th-15thC church; 15th-16thC timbered market. **Cabourg** ® : the town fans out from the main square, where the Grand Hotel and the Casino look towards the sea; turn-of-the century "Norman" country houses. □

■ The D-DAY LANDING BEACHES★★

▶ Round trip from Caen *(approx 353 km, 2-3 days)*

AB2

On 6 June 1944 **Operation Overlord** was launched on the D-Day Landing Beaches, which were code-named Utah, Omaha, Sword, Juno and Gold. Thousands of soldiers died in the fighting, and many towns were destroyed. The suggested itinerary takes you to the beaches as well as through the quiet, friendly Norman countryside of churches, châteaux and manor houses.

▶ **Caen** (→). ▶ **Merville-Franceville-Plage** ® : a long beach runs as far as the mouth of the Orne; museum of the Melville Battery (artillery) in a former German pillbox (daily Jun.-Sep.). Between **Ranville** ® (British cemetery) and **Bénouville** is the Pegasus Bridge over the Orne and its canal; the double bridge was captured intact on the night of 5-6 June (Paratroop museum; *daily ex. Tue., Apr.-Oct.*). **Ouistreham-Riva-Bella** ® : 12th-13thC **church** at Ouistreham; 2 km beach at Riva-Bella; museum recording the French battalion that liberated the town *(daily Jun.-Oct.; Sat. and Sun., Palm Sun.-Jun.)* ▶ **Colleville Montgomery :** associated with the British Field-Marshal Montgomery (1887-1976), who commanded the 21st Army on D-Day; his family originated in Normandy. ▶ **Hermanville-sur-Mer :** centre of operations for **Sword Beach.** ▶ **La Délivrande** ® : very old pilgrimage to the Virgin (19thC basilica). ▶ **Courseulles-sur-Mer** ® : Marvels of the Sea Museum; shellfish; the Canadian sector, **Juno**

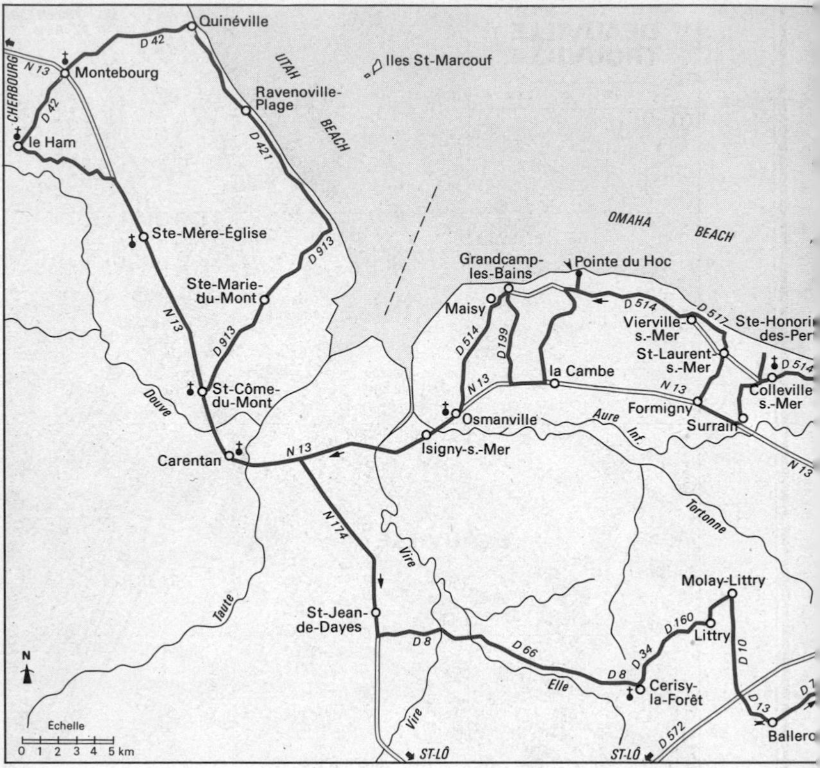

3. D-Day

Beach; the British prime minister Winston Churchill, the commander of the Free French Forces General Charles De Gaulle, and the British monarch King George VI landed between Courseulles and Graye-sur-Mer on 12-16 June 1944 to survey operations. ▶ **Ver-sur-Mer** *(2 km from the coast) :* Romanesque belltower★ marking the eastern end of **Gold Beach.** After **Asnelles-sur-Mer :** panorama★ of the site of Arromanches and the remains of Port Winston where more than 1 000 000 Allied soldiers landed. ▶ **Arromanches** ® : fishing harbour among the man-made harbours built for the Landings (D-Day museum★). ▶ From **Longues-sur-Mer** you can reach the tumbled rocks of Le Chaos★. ▶ **Port-en-Bessin-Huppain** ® : small fishing harbour in a cove. ▶ Beyond **Colleville-sur-Mer :** the **American Cemetery★** (9 385 graves) overlooking **Omaha beach,** one of the most bitterly contested battlefields of 6 June 1944. ▶ Detour through **Formigny** back 500 years in history : the French liberated Normandy from the English here in 1450, ending the 100 Years' War. ▶ Between **Saint-Laurent** and **Vierville-sur-Mer** ®, the Maritime boulevard★, halfway up the cliffs, returns to Omaha Beach. ▶ 15 min walk from the D514 : **Pointe du Hoc★,** an important German position still kept as it looked after the battle. Detour from here to the dramatically situated German cemetery at **La Cambe** (21 000 graves). ▶ **Grandcamp-Maisy** ® : a seaside resort and scallop-fishing port. ▶ **Isigny** : dairy produce (milk, cream, butter) and butterscotch are the specialties here at the edge of rich dairy-farming country (the valleys of the Aure, the Tortonne, the Elle and the Vire). ▶ **Carentan** ® : Gothic church; milk; processing plant). ▶ **Sainte-Marie-du-Mont :** 11th-15thC church; remains of 15thC castle; **Utah Beach** where American troops also landed; Landing Museum *(daily from Easter-1 Nov. Sun. and nat. hols. in winter);* La Madeleine and the Varreville dunes were the main landing points; the beach stretches more than 20 km past **Quinéville.** ▶ **Montebourg :** liberation was particularly difficult; the 14thC church was spared in the fighting ▶ **Sainte-Mère-Église :** one of the main American landings; the start of the Freedom Road (Voie de la Liberté) is marked by the "O" sign in front of the town hall; paratroop museum (Musée des Troupes Aéroportées; *Sun. and nat. hols in winter; daily from Easter to 1 Nov.).* ▶ **Musée de la Ferme du Cotentin** (Farm Museum) set in a typical regional farm (N13; guest rooms; *daily Jul.-Aug.; closed Tue. Easter-Jul. and in Sep.; Sat. and Sun. pm in Oct.*). ▶ **Cerisy-la-Forêt :** on the edge of a large forest (22 km^2), former abbey church★★ (late 11thC); museum *(Sun. and nat. hols. pm 15 Mar.-Jul.; daily ex. Sun. am in summer).* ▶ **Molay-Littry** ® : Musée de la Mine★ (mining museum) recalls the creation of a coal mine here in 1743 *(daily ex. Wed. Apr.-Oct.; all day Sun. and pm Tue.-Sat. rest of year);* château de Molay *(approx 2.5 km) :* 18thC structure now a hotel). ▶ The **château de Balleroy★★** one of the purest examples of Louis XIII style, built (1626-36) by François Mansart, with a park designed by Le Nôtre (→ also Ile-de-France :

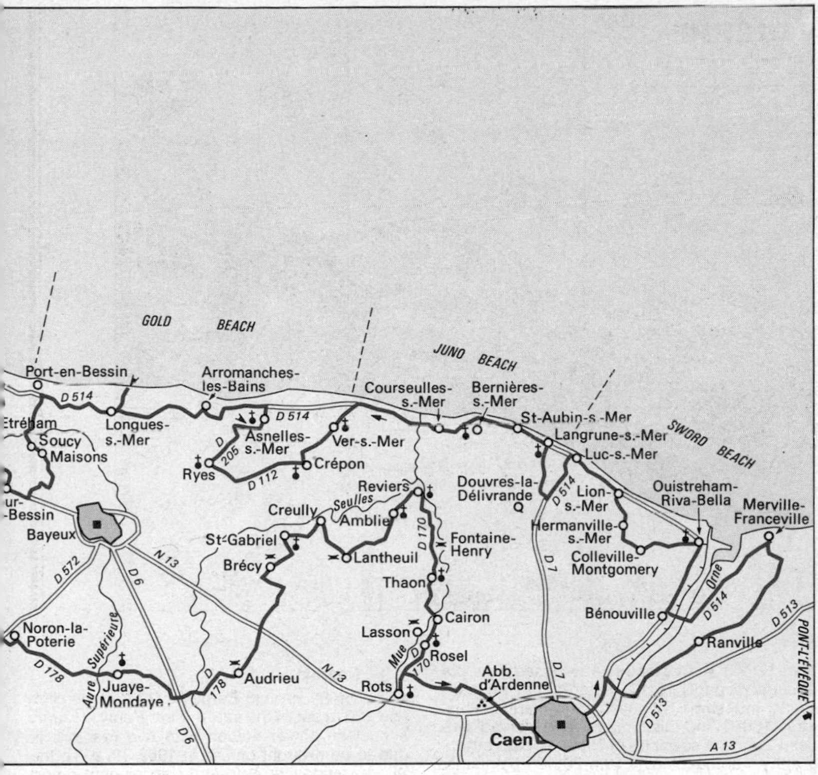

ng beaches

The abbeys of Normandy

The oldest of the many abbeys in Normandy date back to the 6th and 7thC. Mont-Saint-Michel in fact was founded in 708. A spate of building occurred in the 11th and 12thC; William the Conqueror and his wife Matilda are credited with some 30 foundations. Some abbeys, such as Jumièges and Hambye, are picturesque ruins, whereas others, such as Saint-Evroult, have almost disappeared. Many were remodelled in the 17thC (Bernay, Le Bec-Hellouin, Saint-Wandrille), or completely rebuilt in the 19thC (La Grande Trappe). Some abbey churches are as big as cathedrals (Fécamp, the Abbaye aux Hommes at Caen). The earliest abbeys were models of Norman Romanesque art and architecture, which spread to England during the English occupation of Western France. The style was transformed in the late 12thC by the development of the ogival vault, which gave rise to the Gothic style.

Versailles); Museum of Ballooning (*closed Wed.*; international balloonists meet in Jun.) ▶ **Noron-la-Poterie** : pottery on the banks of the Drôme. ▶ **Audrieu** ® : 18thC château with a well-known hotel-restaurant. ▶ **Brécy** : terraced gardens★ at the 17thC château (*Jan.-Oct.; closed Wed.*). ▶ **Creully** : 12th-16thC fortified castle★ overlooking the valley of the Seulles; from the Canadian cemetery near **Reviers,** you can go up the pretty valley of the Mue. ▶ **Château de Fontaine-Henry★ :** Renaissance, beautiful, with carved decoration (*pm ex. Tue. and Fri., Jun.-15 Sep.; Wed., Sat., Sun. and nat. hols in spring and autumn; Sun. and nat. hols. rest of year*). ▶ **Thaon★ :** disused 11thC church in rustic setting on the river Mue; ask for the key in the house next door. □

■ DIEPPE★

D1 / ® / pop. 36 490 (Seine-Maritime)

Popular with the English, who cross the channel to shop in the Dieppe supermarkets. The deep harbour has made the city an important port since the Middle Ages. Overtaken by Le Havre, it is still the fifth largest port in France. 1.5 km of pebble beach; casino.

▶ The Henri IV and Duquesne quays (B1-2) in the fishing and passenger harbours are the main centres of activity, together with the **Grande Rue** (A2; partly pedestrian, market every Sat.), linking the port to the château via the picturesque place du Puits Salé. A short distance away are the churches of St. Jacques (A2, 13th-16thC flamboyant Gothic and Renaissance decoration) and St. Rémy (A2;

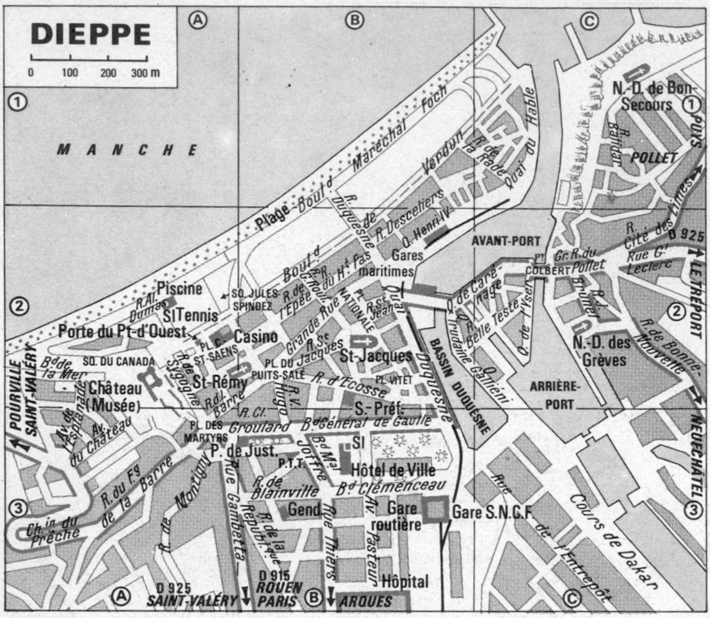

16th-17thC). ▶ **Château★** (A2; *closed Tue. out of season;* partly 15thC, restored) has an interesting **museum★** of the town's maritime history (16th-17thC pilot maps) and carved ivories★, once a specialty of Dieppe; also ethnography, archaeology, 19th-20thC paintings.

Painters and writers

Romantic writers and Impressionist painters have found Normandy an inexhaustible inspiration. Maupassant was born in the Château de Miromesnil (→), Gustave Flaubert (1821-1880) was born in Rouen; Claude Monet lived and died at Giverny, and Jean-François Millet (1814-1875) was born near Cherbourg. Victor Hugo has a tragic association with Normandy : his daughter and her husband were drowned while on their honeymoon at Villequier. Monet painted several studies of Rouen cathedral (example, Musée du Jeu de Paume in Paris), and of coastal cities, including Honfleur, Le Havre and Dieppe. The Normandy coast also inspired Eugene Boudin (1825-98) a fore-runner of Impressionism, Frédéric Bazille (1841-70), Camille Corot (1796-1875; → Ile-de-France : Barbizon), Camille Pissarro (1830-1903), Johann Barthold Jongkind (1819-91) and many others.

▶ Panorama★ from the Boulevard de la Mer, above the château. ▶ 2 km W of the town is the War Museum (Musée de la Guerre), commemorating the Canadian Landings in 1942 *(daily ex. Mon., Easter-Oct.).* □

▶ Nearby

▶ To the E : around **Berneval** *(11 km)* the cliffs rise 100 m out of the sea. ▶ Near **Penly** *(15 km) :* a nuclear power station with two reactors is due to be brought on line in 1989-90. ▶ To the W : **Varengeville** ® *(8 km) :* an elegant resort with beautiful gardens on a wooded plateau; superb panorama★ from the church and cemetery (stained glass, tomb of the painter Georges Braque (1882-1962); **Parc des Moutiers★ :** planted in 1900, with the charm of an English private park *(daily Easter-Dec.);* farther off : **Manoir d'Ango** (16thC), beautiful dovecote. ▶ **Sainte-Marguerite-sur-Mer** ® *(12.5 km) :* a Canadian beach-head in 1942. ▶ **Arques-la-Bataille** *(7 km SE) :* the name ("battle") celebrates a famous victory of Henry IV in 1589; remains of a 12thC castle of the dukes of Normandy; church (16th-17thC) with Renaissance choirscreen★; eastwards, State-owned forest. ▶ **Château de Miromesnil** *(6 km SW) :* birthplace of the novelist Guy de Maupassant (1850-93) (17thC; *May-Oct. pm; closed Tue.*). □

■ ÉVREUX★

D23 / ® / pop. 48 650 (Eure)

Capital of the department of the Eure, although built on the river Iton; rebuilt after WWII; manufacture of electrical equipment and accessories for the automobile industry. ▶ The **cathedral** (B1; 12th-17thC), with a post-war spire, has a rich collection of 13th-16thC stained glass★. Municipal museum★ in the former bishopric dating from 1481 (archaeology, history, ceramics, paintings; *closed Sun. am and Mon.*). Stroll along the ramparts★ by the Iton, between the cathedral and the Tour de l'Horloge (15thC clocktower, 44 m high).

Also... ▶ **St. Taurin :** former abbey **church** (11th-15thC; A1); shrine★ of the patron saint with 13thC enamels. □

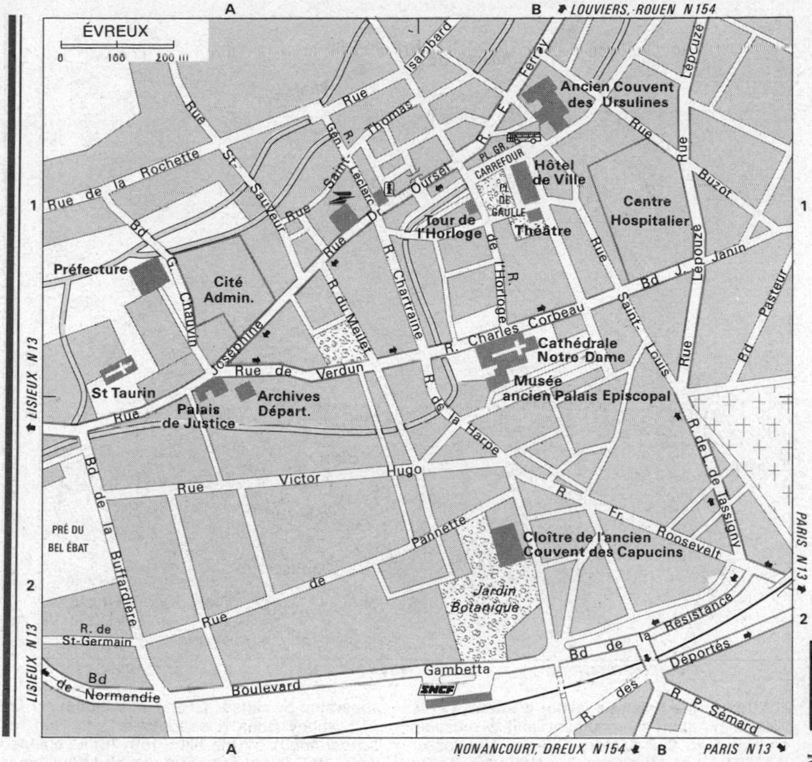

Nearby

▶ **Acquigny★** ® *(18 km N on N154)* : Château Renaissance, situated at the junction of the Iton and Eure Valleys. ▶ **Louviers** ® *(22 km N)* : a former textile centre on the left bank of the Eure; 12th-13thC church of Notre-Dame★ with flamboyant Gothic porch★; a few half-timbered houses; historical museum, place Ernest-Thorel *(pm; closed Tue.)*. ▶ **La Couture-Boussey** *(26 km SE)* : museum of wind instruments and a local tradition of manufacturing recorders, flutes, oboes, clarinets *(pm; closed Tue.)*. ▶ **Pacy-sur-Eure** ® *(18 km E)* : antique shops, weekend houses. ▶ Near **Miserey** *(7 km E on N13)* : monument commemorating the first balloon-crossing of the Atlantic (Aug. 1978). □

FALAISE★

B3 / ® / pop. 8 820 (Calvados)

Just after Ante on the Caen road — or better still, from the Mont Myrrha★ lookout *(15 min from C9)* — you can see at a glance the strategic importance of Falaise, a stronghold of the dukes of Normandy and largely destroyed in the fighting of August 1944.

▶ **Castle★** where William the Conqueror was born in 1027 controls the terrain; a solid, rectangular 12thC keep is linked by a curtain wall to the 13thC Talbot tower *(daily ex. Tue. in summer; closed Mon. and Wed. in winter; closed in Oct.)*. The town hall (Hôtel de Ville, 1784) the church of La Trinité (13th-16thC; Renaissance porch★) and the churches of St. Gervais (11th-16thC) and Notre-Dame (*SE*; Romanesque) survived the fighting around the "Falaise pocket" in Aug. 1944. ▶ **Soumont-Saint-Quentin** *(12 km N)* : farm converted into a museum of regional agriculture *(pm in season; Sat. and Sun. out of season; closed in winter)*. 2.5 km NE from Soumont, the **château d'Assy★** (1788) is a perfect example of classical style. □

FÉCAMP★

C1 / ® / pop. 21 700 (Seine-Maritime)

A Benedictine town twice over : once for the former abbey and once for the Benedictine liqueur originally invented by the monks, rediscovered by Alexandre Le Grand and still manufactured at Fécamp. The town no longer maintains a Newfoundland fishing fleet; the main industry today is fish and food processing.

▶ **Church of La Trinité★★** (B2) : 12th-13thC former abbey church the size of a cathedral (Renaissance additions, including the enclosures of the choir chapels); the municipal offices occupy the 18thC abbey buildings. Close by are the ruins of a 10th-11thC castle of the dukes of Normandy. ▶ Rue A. Legros (B2) : museums and arts centre (fine arts, archaeology, history, folklore; *closed am in winter, and Tue.*). ▶ Just ahead are the **Benedictine Distillery and Museum★** with a rich collection of mediaeval art objects (A1-2; *daily Easter-11 Nov.*; tastings). ▶ On the cliffs N, the chapel of Notre-Dame-du-Salut (A-B1; 13th-14thC; panorama). □

Nearby

▶ Near **Bénouville** *(16 km SW; GR21)* : the cliff valley of Le Curé and the Belval Needle;

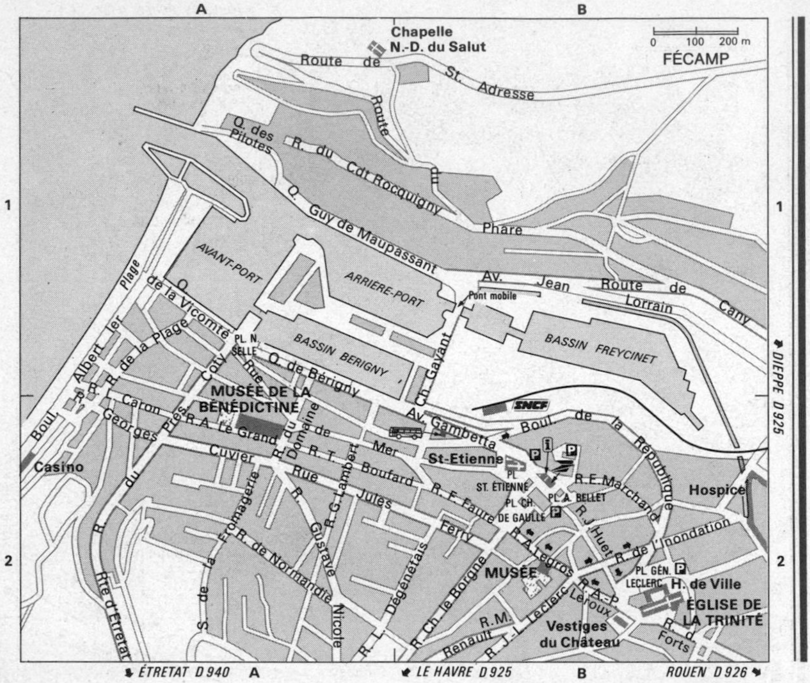

at 20 km : the **Falaises** (cliffs) **d'Étretat**★★ ®. Falaise d'Amont : monument and a museum dedicated to the aviators Charles Nungesser (1892-1927) and François Coli (1881-1927) who died in the first attempt to cross the North Atlantic by air (8 May 1927) *(Sat. and Sun. in spring; daily in summer).* In town, 12th-13thC church of Notre-Dame. ▶ **To the E** : the seaside resorts of **Saint-Pierre-en-Port, Les Grandes Dalles** and **Les Petites Dalles** are separated by cliffs★ (GR21). ▶ **Valmont** *(11 km E) : abbey ruins (closed Wed. and Sun. ex school hols)*; on the hill : 15th-16thC château with 11thC keep *(Sat., Sun. pm and Wed. pm in summer)*; recreational area farther on. ▶ **Château de Bailleul**★ *(12 km SE; daily Easter-Nov. 1)* : Renaissance building (art objects, paintings) in parkland. □

Norman gastronomy

Normandy is in the fortunate position of having ample agricultural resources as well as access to the sea. Normandy butter is widely appreciated, as is crème fraîche *(clotted cream). Thirty-two different varieties of cheese are produced on Norman farms. The local beef is particularly tender, and the salt meadows* (prés-salés) *are ideal for raising succulent lamb. In the kitchen, preparations Norman-style* (à la Normande) *imply the use of cream either alone or blended with cider or* calvados *(apple brandy from the Calvados region).* Andouilles de Vire *(chitterling sausage),* tripes à la mode de Caen *(tripe braised in cider),* poulet Vallée d'Auge *(chicken cooked with onions, cider or* calvados, *and cream),* canard à la Rouennaise *(duck in its own juices) and Mont-Saint-Michel's* omelette de la Mère Poulard *(soufflé omelette) are other specialties. Numerous varieties of fish (especially sole), are caught along the coast, and small grey shrimp at Honfleur.*

FLERS

B3 / ® / pop. 19 405 (Orne)

Once a linen-weaving town that, in the 19thC, turned to processing cotton imported from the United States; textiles are still an important industry. ▶ **Automobile Museum,** place saint-Jean. ▶ **Château**★ : 16th-18thC; moat; regional museum of Bocage-Normand, history and ethnography *(Easter-15 Oct. pm).* □

▶ Nearby

▶ **Cerisy-Belle-Étoile** *(8 km NW) :* at the foot of Mont de Cerisi (260 m), panorama; feudal ruins; rhododendrons in May-Jun.). ▶ Beyond **Condé-sur-Noireau** *(12 km N from Flers) :* **Château de Pontécoulant** (16th-18thC), regional museum (furniture, weapons; *daily ex Tue.; closed in Oct.*); fine park. □

GISORS★

D2 / ® / pop. 8 860 (Eure)

Gisors was one of the most important fortresses on the river Epte, designed to keep a watchful eye on the French Vexin region in the days of the dukes of Normandy. ▶ Within the **castle** walls★ *(closed 15 Dec. to 1 Feb.)* the 11thC keep towers over the

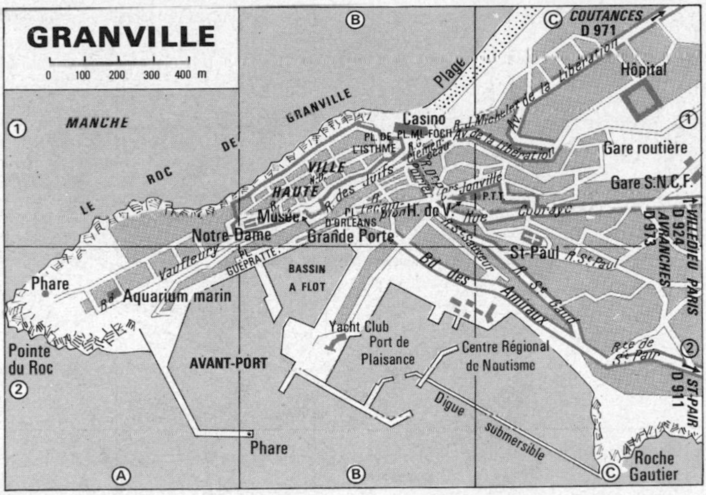

fortifications and gardens *(admission free).* ▶ **Church of St. Gervais-St. Protais★** (13th-16thC) : restored after the destruction of 1940, flamboyant Gothic doorway, Renaissance decoration. □

■ GRANVILLE★

A3 / ® / pop. 15 015 (Manche)

A healthy climate and a fine site have made Granville one of Normandy's most popular seaside resorts since the 19thC; it is also a busy port for commercial, fishing and pleasure craft.

▶ The **upper town★** (A1, antique shops); the fortifications date from 1720. The Logis du Roi (King's Lodge), behind the Grande Porte, is now the Museum of old Granville covering history, folklore and the sea *(daily in season ex Tue.; Wed. pm, Sat. and Sun. rest of year)*; church of Notre-Dame (A1; 15th-18thC); Marine Aquarium (*daily, Palm Sunday-1 Nov.*, shellfish fairyland and mineral palace). ▶ View★ from the Point of the Roc; a path★ runs down to the port. □

▶ Nearby

▶ **Chausey Islands★ :** more than 300 islets at low tide, fewer than 50 at high tide *(reached from Grande-Île),* these are the only French Islands in the Channel. ▶ The **Abbey of Lucerne** *(12 km SE)* has buildings dating from 1164 and later, some remodelled in the 17th and 18thC *(daily).* ▶ **Villedieu-les-Poêles** ® *(28 km E) :* a metalworking tradition revealed in the variety of metal souvenirs and other goods on sale; bell foundry *(visits of a copper workshop);* musée de la Poêlerie; Lacemaker's house (museum of cooking ware; Cours du Foyer, *Jun.-15 Sep.*); **church of Notre-Dame :** a 15thC dependency of the Order of the Knights of Malta; every four years in June there is a ceremony for dignitaries of the order (1987), alternating with a flower festival (1989). ▶ **Carolles-Plage** (beach) and **Carolles-Bourg** (town) ® *(11 km) :* 12th-13thC church, view★ from Pignon Butor and the Cabane Vauban to the bay of Mont-Saint-Michel. ▶ **Avranches** ® *(34 km) :* view★ to Mont-Saint-Michel from the Jardin des Plantes★ (botanical garden). The museum in the former episcopal palace, Place St. Avit, displays precious manuscripts★ (8th-16thC) from Mont-Saint-Michel abbey; examples also of Norman folklore and crafts *(daily ex. Tue., Easter and Sep.).* The monument to General George Patton (1885-1945) stands in a square that is now United States territory. ▶ Beyond Avranches, D75 runs beside salt meadows; views of Mont-Saint-Michel. □

■ Le HAVRE★

C2 / ® / pop. 198 760 (Seine-Maritime)

A lively seaport enhanced by the forest of Montgeon and the hills of Sainte-Adresse, Mont Gaillard and Graville, their natural beauty compensating for the cold 20thC architectural style of Auguste Perret who redesigned the city after WWII. Founded on the Seine estuary in the 16thC by François I, Le Havre is a port second in importance only to Marseilles.

▶ The **Place de l'Hôtel de Ville** (town hall square; B2; 72 m bell tower) is linked by Avenue Foch (A2) to the Ocean Gate (Porte Océane), symbolised by two L-shaped structures that separate it from the sea. ▶ **Church of St. Joseph★** (A2) : an immense building with a bell-tower 106 m high; more attractive from the inside. ▶ The light-filled **André Malraux Fine Arts Museum** has a rich collection of 16th-20thC paintings★ (several works by Boudin, → box; *closed Tue. and nat. hols.*). ▶ Much of the Natural History Museum has been rehoused in the former courthouse (Palais de Justice, 18thC; B3; rebuilt on Place du Vieux Marché at the foot of Rue Notre-Dame; *10-12 & 2-6, closed Tue. and hols.* ▶ **Cathedral of Notre-Dame** (1574-1630; B3), one of the city's oldest monuments. ▶ At Place Gambetta : cultural centre★ **(Espace Culturel Oscar Niemeyer)** (B2, partly underground; exhibition halls, shopping arcade, theatre; inaugurated 1981). ▶ The Bassin du Commerce (B2; international trade centre, 1982) separates the Bourse (stock exchange) from the Île-Saint-François, formerly the main unloading dock;

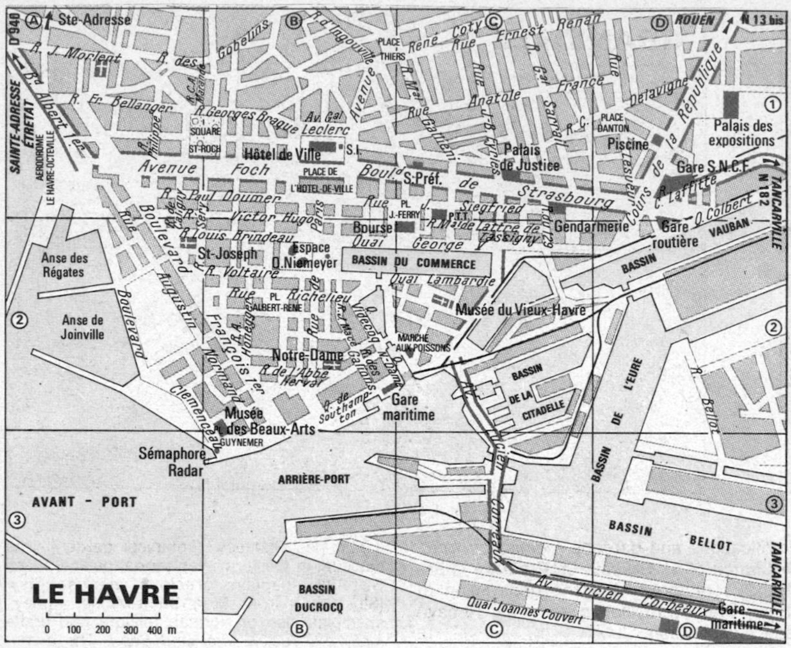

16th-17thC church of St. François and **Old Le Havre Museum** (Musée de l'Ancien Havre; B2; *closed Mon., Tue. and nat. hols.*; history and navigation).

Also... ▶ **Boat trip around the port★** *(Easter-15 Sep.; embark at the yacht harbour,* A2) including the harbour basins and the François I lock, 400 m long. ▶ **Sainte-Adresse** is an elegant part of town between the beach and the hill, crowned by the chapel of Notre-Dame-des-Flots (Our Lady of the Waves, view★); lookout at Cape la Hève★. ▶ Archaeological museum in a former priory (11thC nave and transept) in **Graville,** to the E *(closed Mon., Tue.).* □

▶ Nearby

▶ **Harfleur** *(6 km E) :* a port founded by the Romans, superseded by Le Havre. The areas around the church of St. Martin (15th-16thC; spire★) and the town hall (Hôtel de Ville, 1650) recall the mediaeval English occupation of Western France; Museum in Harfleur Priory *(10-12 & 3-6, Sun.; pm ex Mon., Tue. and hols.).* ▶ View★ of the oil refinery and Seine estuary from the terrace of the **château d'Orcher** above Gonfreville *(9 km; pm ex Tue., Thu., Sat., Jul.-Sep.).* ▶ **Havre-Antifer** *(22 km N) :* oil port built in 1973-1975 and protected by a dyke projecting 3 500 m from the cliff. □

Lace-making

The fashion for lace became a craze in the latter half of the 16thC with the widespread importation of lace from Venice. The Prime Minister, Jean-Baptiste Colbert, decided to counter the drain of funds by creating a French lace industry. In 1665 Alençon began lace production on an industrial scale. In the 18thC, an Alençon lace-maker, Mme. La Perrière, perfected a pattern that consisted of a network of very fine hexagonal stitches scattered with tiny flowers. The 19thC gave rise to the exaggerated lace head-dresses, or Normandy bonnets, worn by well-to-do farmers' wives and townswomen at festivals. Alençon, Argentan and Bayeux still maintain the lace-making tradition; craft courses are available in Bayeux.

HONFLEUR★★★

C2 / ® / pop. 8 530 (Calvados)

The historic port of Honfleur is clearly centuries older than Le Havre, on the other side of the Seine estuary.

▶ **Vieux Bassin★★** (old port; B-C1) : lined with houses of wood and slate; in front of it, the Lieutenance (C2) is a ruined 16thC castle. **Old Honfleur Museum★** (Musée du Vieux Honfleur) in the church of St. Étienne (14th-15thC) and the 16thC house next door (C2; ethnography, folk art, local shipping; *closed weekdays out of season).* ▶ The unique church of **Ste. Catherine★★** (15thC, B2) was built of wood, except for the foundations, by the port's master shipwrights at the end of the 100 Years' War; two parallel naves; separate bell-tower; annex of the Boudin Museum (**Musée Eugène Boudin★,** → box, B2; *closed Tue. and am out of season ex Sat. and Sun., and in Jan.*) 60 paintings and pastels by the painter, plus works by Impressionists and modern painters who stayed in Honfleur; Norman costumes and headdresses. ▶ The farm of St. Siméon (*route A. Marais,* A1) a meeting place for the Impressionists, now a luxury hotel. ▶ View★ from the

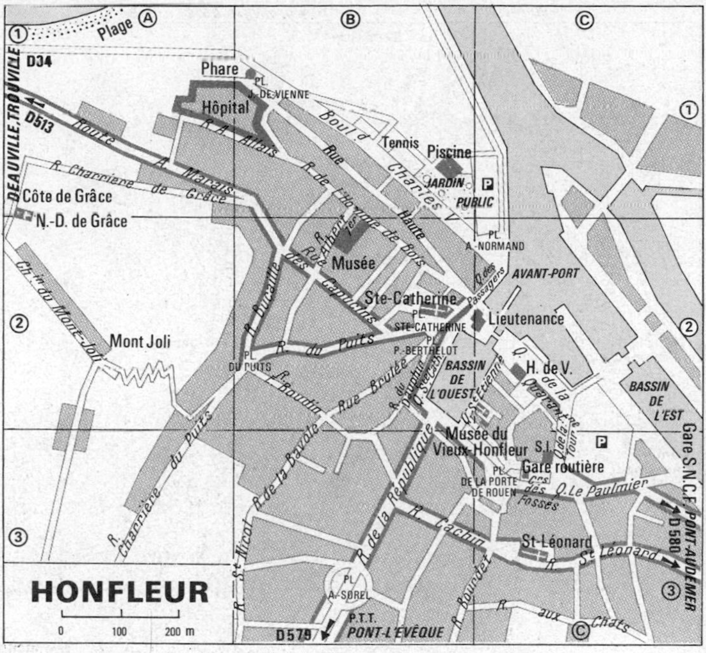

chapel of Notre-Dame-de-Grâce (A1-2; 1615) over the **Côte de Grace★** and the Seine estuary. ▶ **Saint-André d'Hébertot** *(16 km S)* : pleasant moated 17th-18thC château. □

■ LISIEUX★

C2 / ® / pop. 25 820 (Calvados)
(see plan following page)

Lisieux recalls Ste. Thérèse, a young Carmelite nun (→ Alençon) who lived here; she was canonised in 1927. Formerly a town of great architectural beauty whose half-timbered houses were burnt in 1944, it is now essentially a city of pilgrimage to the cathedral and basilica.

▶ **Cathedral St. Pierre★** (A-B1) : a superb example of Norman Gothic (12th-13thC); nearby gilt-decorated law court (Palais de Justice) in a Louis XIII former episcopal palace. ▶ **Church of St. Jacques** (B1, flamboyant Gothic, 1496-1501). ▶ The pilgrimage to Ste. Thérèse includes the **chapel of Carmel** (B2) where her relics are venerated, a slide show (diorama de Ste. Thérèse) and the basilica (B2; 1954; *son et laser spectacle every eve. at 9:30, 25 May-30 Sep.*). ▶ Her childhood home is at Les Buissonnets *(via B1)*. ▶ **Museum of Old Lisieux** (38, boulevard Pasteur, A1; *closed Tue.*) in a handsome 16thC house. ▶ **Orbec★** ® *(20 km SE)* : numerous old houses★, municipal museum in the old manor house (Vieux Manoir) *(pm ex Tue. in summer; Sat. pm rest of year)*. □

■ MONT-SAINT-MICHEL★★★

A3 / ® / pop. 80 (Manche)

The souvenir-sellers who crowd the Grand-Rue right up to the abbey steps continue a tradition begun by the hucksters who accosted pilgrims to Mont-Saint-Michel in the Middle Ages. The architectural beauty and the long history of the fortified abbey draw huge crowds; avoid the high season (mid-summer to early autumn). The monastery was desecrated during the Revolution and converted into a prison during the 19thC. The buildings today are once more maintained in monastic serenity. Salt-meadow lamb and *omelette de la mère Poulard* (Mme. Poulard's omelettes) are the local specialties.

Mont-Saint-Michel Bay

The bay measures 22 km across the mouth from Cancale to Grandville and runs 23 km inland. The rising tide covers the immense stretch of sand at high speed; at low tide, the sea is about 12 km from the shore-line. Efforts have been made since the Middle Ages to reclaim the land. The Dol Marshes were dried out little by little, and during the last century, attempts were made to repeat the process around Mont-Saint-Michel itself. The unexpected result was a build-up of mud flats in the reclaimed area. The Ministry of the Environment has studied the site and strenuous efforts are being made to control silting, principally by the destruction of the Roche-Torin dyke, which obstructs the natural flow of the current.

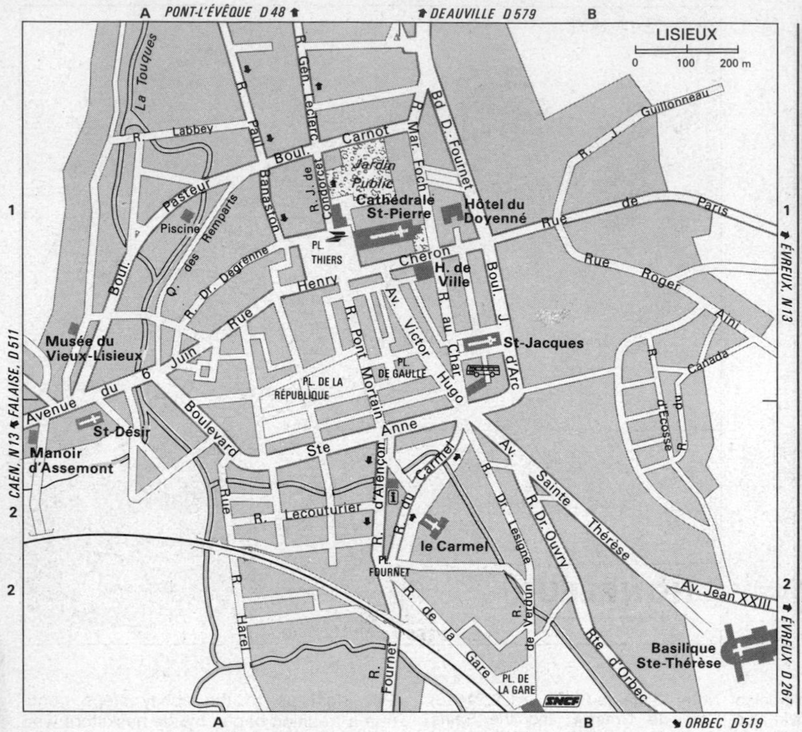

▶ The tour of the **Abbey★★★** *(daily; closed at 4 pm in winter)* starts with the Romanesque abbey church★★; the first few arches of the nave are missing; flamboyant Gothic choir, crypt★; magnificent, delicate Gothic cloister with fine coupled columns; *merveille★★* ("marvel"; 1203-28) : three vast Gothic halls one above the other contain the almshouse and storehouse, the guests' hall and knights' hall, and a refectory and cloister on the same level; to the W, the terraced garden and a few trees. ▶ In the Grand-Rue★, parallel to the **rampart walk★★,** is the 11th-16thC parish church. Two museums : the Mont-Saint-Michel Historical Museum (Musée Historical du Mont) and the Historical Museum (Musée Historique) *(Mar.-Oct., 9-12:30 & 1:30-6:30)* : slide-shows, historic memorabilia, outstanding collection of clock mechanisms. ▶ **Sea Museum** (Musée de la Mer, rue Principale; more than 200 old boat models). ▶ You can walk around the outside of the Mont in 30 mins, but check the times of the tides first. □

■ MORTAIN

A-B3 / ® / pop. 3 040 (Manche)

Devastated during August 1944, the town was rebuilt with local granite. The site of the town is enhanced by the ravines and waterfalls of the Cance Valley.

▶ Church of St. Evroult : 13thC. ▶ **Blanche Abbey** (12thC; *1 km N; Sun. pm and daily ex Tue. Jul.-Sep.).* ▶ Above the town, to the SE, the **chapel of St. Michel** is a lookout point 314 m high★. ▶ **Mortain Forest** *(GR22)* : part of the Normandy-Maine Nature Park. □

▶ Nearby

▶ **Barenton** *(10 km SE)* : the Logeraie, an apple and pear cider museum *(Jul.-Aug., closed Mon.).* ▶ **Bellefontaine** *(6 N) :* leisure centre at the Village Enchanté *(Easter-1 Nov.).* ▶ **Saint-Michel-de-Montjoie** *(22 km NW) :* in the heart of the granite region; quarries, visits; museum *(daily 15 Jun.-15 Oct.; Sat. and Sun. pm Easter-15 Jun.).* □

■ The NEUBOURG Plateau★

D2

This plateau between the Risle and Iton rivers, centred on the town of **Neubourg** ®, is among the richest agricultural areas in upper Normandy; picturesque country churches and several fine châteaux.

▶ **Beaumont-le-Roger** ® *(8 km SW from Neubourg) :* a pretty site on the right bank of the Risle; ruins of 13thC priory★; 14th-15thC church of St. Nicolas; **Beaumont Forest.** ▶ **Brionne** ® *(15 km NW of Neubourg) :* keep, panorama; the **Maison de Normandie** sells handicrafts *(closed Tue., Wed.).* ▶ **Château du Champ de Bataille★** *(4.5 km NW from Neubourg) :* early 18thC; furnished rooms; exhibitions *(Easter-1 Nov.);* also, golf for beginners, cultural events, old-fashioned games and drives in horse-drawn vehicles. ▶ **Harcourt** *(9 km NW of Neubourg) :* feudal castle★, horse trials

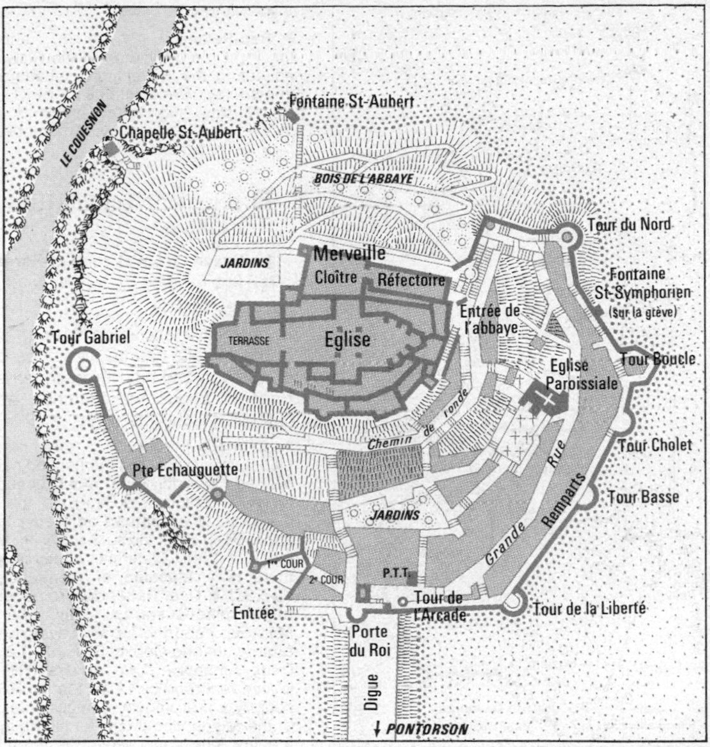

Mont-Saint-Michel

in mid-Jun., 11.5 acre arboretum with exotic trees *(pm, closed Tue. in season, weekdays out of season and Nov.-Mar.).* □

■ The **OUCHE** Region★

C2-D3

The land in this forested cattle-raising region is less rich than in the neighbouring areas. The local rivers are the Iton and the Risle.

▶ **L'Aigle** ® : the "nail and bolt capital", thanks to its long-established main industry; 15th-16thC church of St. Martin with flamboyant Gothic tower; "June-44" museum in the Château (1690; designed by Jules Hardouin-Mansart, → Versailles). ▶ **Breteuil-sur-Iton** ® : surrounded by water diverted from the river in the 11thC to form a defensive moat; only a few sections of wall are left on the eastern edge of the forest of Breteuil; **bird sanctuary.** ▶ **Francheville :** Musée de la Ferronnerie (wrought-iron museum) *(8 km SW; Sat. and nat. hols. pm; Sun. am).* ▶ **Conches-en-Ouche** ® : on a hill in a loop of the river Rouloir; 16thC stained glass★ in the 15th-16thC **church of Ste. Foy★;** public garden in the grounds of the feudal castle; cultural centre (Maison des Richesses de l'Eure, 17thC, half-timbered); the manor house (Maison des Seigneurs) now houses a wrought-iron works *(closed Wed.).*

▶ **La Ferrière-sur-Risle :** leisure centre at Risle Valley Park, 2 km away *(Apr.-Sep.).* ▶ **Verneuil-sur-Avre** ® : at the southern limit of the Ouche region, offers strolls on the site of the former ramparts; flamboyant Gothic tower★ on the church of the Madeleine (16thC); Romanesque church of Notre-Dame; 12thC tower, houses of wood and brick (15th-18thC). □

■ The **PERCHE** Region★★

▶ Round trip *(approx 150 km, full day)*

C3-4 *(see map 4)*

This is the home of the Percheron horse, once eagerly sought for its unique combination of strength and speed, but rare in these days of mechanized farming and transport; meadows, manor houses, lakes, and large forests of oak and beech pierced by the GR22.

▶ **Mortagne-au-Perche** ® : a market town in the Percheron hills, which can be seen from the gardens of the town hall; 15th-16thC flamboyant Gothic church; 12th-16thC city gate (Porte St. Denis) with Percheron museum. ▶ **Forest of Réno-Valdieu** (16 km^2) : named for a 12thC Carthusian monastery (charterhouse); beech and oak up to 40 m high. ▶ **Chapelle Montligeon :** pilgrimage basilica. ▶ **La Vove** manor house : well restored 15th-17thC buildings *(Apr.-Oct.).* ▶ After **Nocé,** pass Courboyer manor (late 15thC) on the way to **Colonard.** ▶ Drive through the forest (24 km^2; La Herse lake; view★ from La Perrière on the

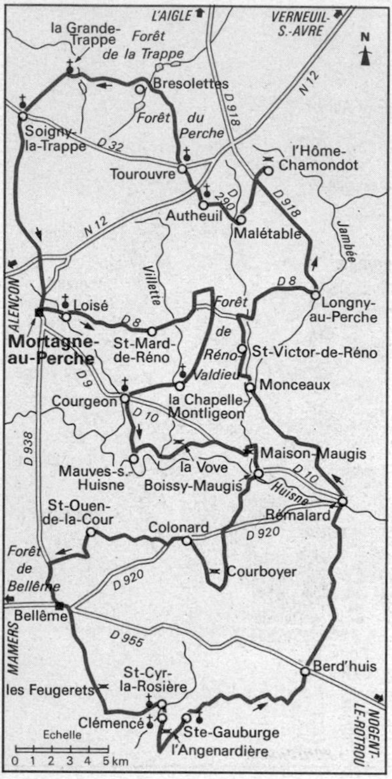

4. Perche region

western edge) and down to **Bellême** ®, where the town clusters around the church and a 15thC fortified gateway. ▶ Château des Feugerets, **Saint-Cyr-la-Rivière :** 17thC terracotta entombment of Christ in the church; Angenardière manor and **Sainte-Gauburge :** folk art and traditions at the Musée Percheron in the church; *pm in season*). ▶ **Rémalard.** ▶ **Longny-au-Perche** ® : 15th-16thC church of St. Martin; Chapel of Notre-Dame-de-Pitié★ in the cemetery (Renaissance sculpture, doorways★). ▶ **Tourouvre** ® : church with 1892 stained glass commemorating local families who emigrated to Canada in the 17thC. ▶ On the other side of the **forests of Le Perche and La Trappe** (21 km²) : **Abbey of La Grande Trappe,** cradle of the strict Cistercian rule (total silence); the monks are better known as Trappists. It was rebuilt in 1884-90; information centre; lakes. □

■ PONT-AUDEMER★

C2 / ® / pop. 10 160 (Eure)

Charming town threaded among canal branches of the River Risle. ▶ **Church of St. Ouen★ :** 11th-13thC choir, oddly unfinished 15th-16thC nave (Renaissance stained glass★); **half-timbered houses★** in the streets and alleys off the Rue de la République; 17thC auberge du Vieux Puits★ (inn of the Old Well, 17thC). □

▶ Nearby

▶ **Bec-Hellouin★** *(24 km SE) :* abbey built in the 11thC on a tributary of the Risle; desecrated during the Revolution, subsequently reoccupied by Benedictines; 15thC Tower of St. Nicolas and 18thC buildings in a park *(closed Tue.);* close by, Automobile museum *(Apr.-Nov., closed Tue.).* □

■ Round trip of **Les QUATRE VALLÉES★** (Four Valleys)

▶ Leave from Lyons-la-Forêt *(approx 162 km, full day)*

D2 *(see map 5)*

An attractive excursion through the valleys of the Andelle and its tributaries the Lieure, the Crevon and the Héron, together with the forest of Lyons and churches, abbeys and châteaux along the way.

▶ **Lyons-la-Forêt★** ® : quiet resort in the Lieure valley; covered market and half-timbered houses; possibly the most beautiful beech forest in France (11 km²). In the middle of the forest, the **château de Fleury-la-Forêt** *(by appt. Sat., Sun., hols. 2-6:30).* ▶ **Mortemer :** the 12th-13thC Cistercian abbey is in ruins but there is a **museum of monastic life** *(daily 10-6:30).* ▶ Near **Radepont :** ruins of the **Abbey of Fontaine-Guérard★** (13thC; *pm ex Mon., Mar.-Sep.*) and the former **Levasseur spinning factory** in neo-Gothic Style. ▶ **La Côte des Deux Amants★** (Two Lovers' Hill) recalls a legend recorded by 12thC Marie de France, the country's first known woman writer : the king of the region would only let his daughter marry a suitor who could prove his strength by carrying her at a run to the top of the hill. Raoul succeeded, but collapsed and died on reaching the summit; Caliste, his disappointed burden, immediately perished from grief. View over the junction of the Andelle and the Seine. ▶ **Pont de l'Arche :** on the left bank of the Seine, at the foot of the forest, flamboyant Gothic church (16thC). **Bonport** *(1.5 km) :* ruins of an abbey founded by Richard the Lion-Heart in 1190. ▶ **Boos :** near Rouen airport, has a beautiful 16thC dovecote with noteworthy brick-work decoration. ▶ **Martainville★ :** 15th-16thC **château** houses a museum of Norman folk art *(closed Tue., Wed.).* ▶ **Ry :** famous as the setting of Flaubert's novel "Madame Bovary" (→ box). The Galerie Bovary, in an old cider-mill, uses mechanical figures to illustrate passages from the novel *(Sat., Sun., Mon. and nat. hols., Easter-Oct.);* carved wooden church porch. ▶ **Vascœuil :** the historian Jules Michelet (1798-1874) lived in the 14th-16thC château (cultural centre with exhibitions of documents and memorabilia, *Apr.-Oct.; Sat., Sun. and weekdays pm).* ▶ **Bois Héroult :** 18thC château with gardens in the French formal style. ▶ **Forges-les-Eaux** (→ Bray Region). ▶ **Sigy-en-Bray :** in the upper Andelle valley; abbey church of 12th-13thC and 18thC. ▶ **Château de Merval** (17thC) : English park open for visits *(daily; closed am in winter).* □

■ ROUEN★★★

D2 / ® / pop. 105 080 (Greater Rouen, 400 000) (Seine-Maritime)

See plan following pages

The fourth-largest port in France, with installations stretching almost 20 km down-

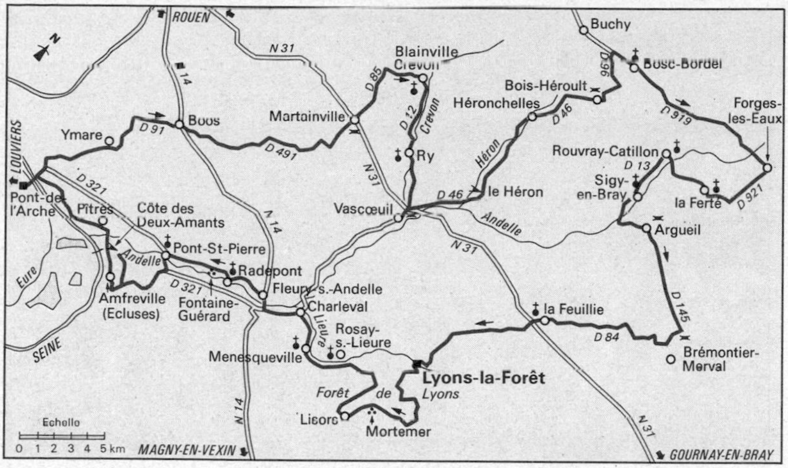

5. Les Quatre Vallées (the four valleys)

stream on the Seine, it is also a beautiful city. The old quarters have been restored and pedestrian malls have been established. The exceptional grouping of historic monuments and half-timbered houses will make you want to know more about the 10thC Viking Rollo, William the Conqueror, Joan of Arc (→ Lorraine), the poet Pierre Corneille (1606-1684), Flaubert (→ box), and other famous people associated with this city. This exceptionally dynamic cultural, and artistic centre only 1hr30 from Paris, has recently built a new administrative complex on the left bank, but the old town remains the historic heart of Rouen.

▶ The best way to grasp the lay of the land is to view the city from a lookout★★ at Bonsecours (basilica and Ste. Catherine hill, F5, *3 km SE*), Canteleur *(4 km W)* or the streets leading to the University at Mont-Saint-Aignan or Bois-Guillaume *(5 km N)*. In town, the principal monuments are within easy reach of the central car-parks. ▶ **Place du Vieux Marché**★★ (B2; remodelled 1978-79) : this centuries-old market square is where Joan of Arc (Sainte Jeanne d'Arc) was burned at the stake in 1431; the exact spot is marked by a tall cross near the church★ entrance. The church itself (1979) is embellished with 16thC stained glass★★ from the former church of St. Vincent. In the square, No. 33 is the Jeanne d'Arc museum (wax museum; *9:30-6:30; closed Mon. in winter*); several half-timbered façades in the square were restored or reassembled from other areas of town. In the nearby Rue de la Pie (A2) is the birthplace of Pierre Corneille (No. 4; *closed Tue. and Wed. am; Fri., Jan., Nov., Dec. and nat. hols.*); Place de la Pucelle, Hôtel (mansion) Bourgthroulde (16thC; B3) : in the courtyard is a bas-relief representing the "Field of the Cloth of Gold" where Henry VIII of England and François I of France held a 16thC summit meeting. ▶ The **Rue du Gros Horloge** (clock)★★ (B2), a lively pedestrian street, leads through the Gros Horloge★ archway : clock; 1390 belfry; small Renaissance pavilion and Louis XV (18thC) fountain *(Palm Sunday-Oct. closed Tue. and Wed. am)*. Nearby, the former 17thC town hall (Hôtel de Ville). ▶ The **Palais de Justice**★★ courthouse (B2; early 16thC), restored to its Gothic beauty after the damage of WWII; during the restoration an interesting 11thC monument with Hebrew graffiti was uncovered. ▶ **Cathedral**★★★ (C3) : begun in the late 12thC, the main fabric was completed by 1250; the flamboyant Gothic decoration (towers★, façade★) dates from the late 15thC-early 16thC; metal spire, 19thC. Inside, Renaissance stained glass★, flamboyant Gothic staircase in N transept; guided tour of the choir★★ *(daily Easter hols. and Jul.-Aug.; Sat., Sun. pm rest of year)* 13thC stained glass, 13th-16thC funerary monuments. ▶ Opposite the cathedral entrance : former Finance Office (Bureau des Finances★, 1502; C3), now the TO. ▶ Rue St. Romain (C3) takes you to the other flamboyant Gothic masterpiece of Rouen : the **church of St. Maclou**★★ (C3; 1437-1581) with curved, five-doored porch; lacy spire and stained glass; Renaissance doors in the façade and northern doorways. On the square, half-timbered houses. ▶ Rue Martainville, l'Aître (cloister) St. Maclou★ (C-D3) 16th-17thC ossuary, now the Fine Arts School (École des Beaux-Arts). ▶ Interesting strolls through Rue Damiette (antique shops) and the Rue Eau de Robec (C-D2; No. 185, National Museum of Education; *pm; closed Mon. and Sun.*). ▶ **Church of St. Ouen**★★ (C-D2) : nearly as imposing as the cathedral, with an outstanding flamboyant Gothic lantern-tower and stained glass; the town hall is in the former abbey (18thC; C-D2). ▶ Pass by Rue Thiers and instead detour through the pedestrian Rue de l'Hôpital and Rue Ganterie to reach the **Fine Arts Museum** ★★★ (C2; *closed Tue., Wed. am and nat. hols.*) : Flemish primitives, Italian, Spanish and French 17th-18thC paintings; masterpieces by Caravaggio, Velázquez, Ingres, Delacroix, Géricault and Duchamp-Villon; Impressionists. Close by, at 1 Rue Faucon the former Hôtel d'Hocquevillé★★ (17thC) houses the new **Faïence museum,** a collection including 6000 pieces of French and foreign ceramics and glassware *(10-12 & 2-6, ex. Tue. and Wed. am)*. ▶ In the former church of St. Laurent, the **Le Secq des Tournelles Museum**★★ (C2; *same*

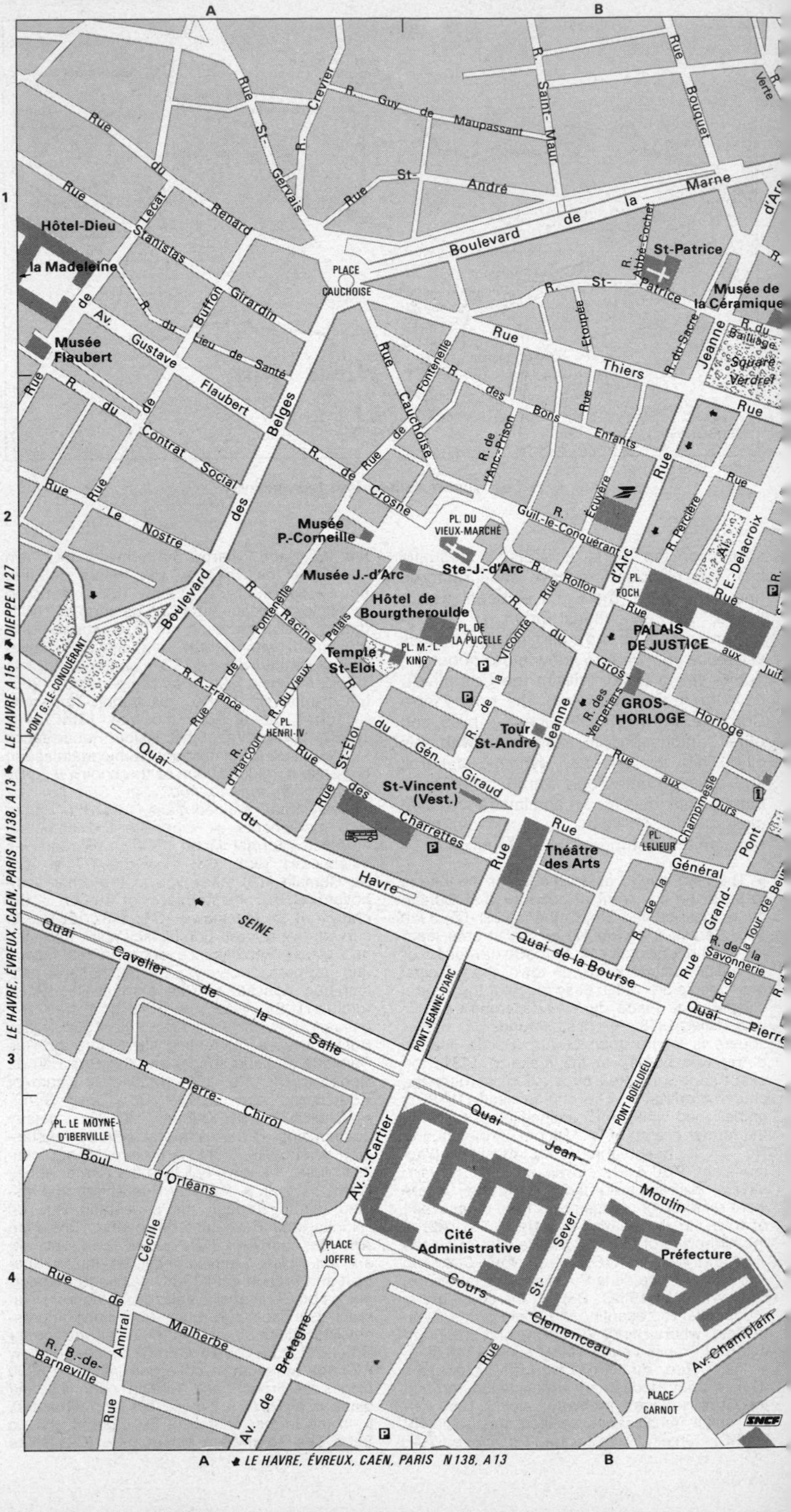

A
B
1
2
3
4
Hôtel-Dieu
la Madeleine
Musée Flaubert
Musée P.-Corneille
Musée J.-d'Arc
Hôtel de Bourgtheroulde
Temple St-Eloi
St-Patrice
Musée de la Céramique
Square Verdrel
PALAIS DE JUSTICE
GROS-HORLOGE
Tour St-André
St-Vincent (Vest.)
Théâtre des Arts
Ste-J.-d'Arc
PL. DU VIEUX-MARCHÉ
PL. DE LA PUCELLE
PL. M.-L. KING
PL. HENRI-IV
PL. FOCH
PL. LELIEUR
PLACE CAUCHOISE
SEINE
Quai du Havre
Quai de la Bourse
Quai Cavelier de la Salle
Quai Jean-Moulin
PONT JEANNE-D'ARC
PONT BOIELDIEU
PONT G.-LE-CONQUÉRANT
Cité Administrative
Préfecture
PLACE JOFFRE
PLACE CARNOT
PL. LE MOYNE-D'IBERVILLE
Boul. d'Orléans
Cours Clemenceau
Av. Champlain
Av. J.-Cartier
Av. de Bretagne
Rue de Malherbe
R. Pierre-Chirol
Boulevard de la Marne
Boulevard des Belges
Rue Jeanne d'Arc
Rue Thiers
Rue du Gros-Horloge
Rue aux Ours
Rue du Général Giraud
Rue des Charrettes
Rue Grand-Pont
Rue Cauchoise
Rue de Crosne
Av. Gustave Flaubert
Rue du Renard
R. Guy de Maupassant
Rue St-André
Rue St-Gervais
R. Crevier
R. Saint-Maur
Rue Bouquet
Rue Verte
R. Stanislas Girardin
R. du Lieu de Santé
Rue du Contrat Social
Rue Le Nostre
R. Racine
R. de Fontenelle
R. des Bons Enfants
R. de l'Anc.-Prison
R. Guil.-le-Conquérant
R. Rollon
R. du Vieux Palais
R. A.-France
R. d'Harcourt
R. St-Eloi
R. de la Vicomté
R. des Vergetiers
Rue Champmeslé
R. St-Patrice
R. Abbé-Cochet
R. du Sacre
Écuyère
Étoupée
R. Percière
Al. E.-Delacroix
R. du Bailliage
Rue aux Juifs
R. de la Savonnerie
R. de la Tour de Beurre
Quai Pierre
Rue St-Sever
Rue Cécile
Rue Amiral
R. B.-de-Barneville
Rue Lecat
Buffon
SNCF
LE HAVRE, ÉVREUX, CAEN, PARIS N 138, A 13
LE HAVRE A 15
DIEPPE N 27

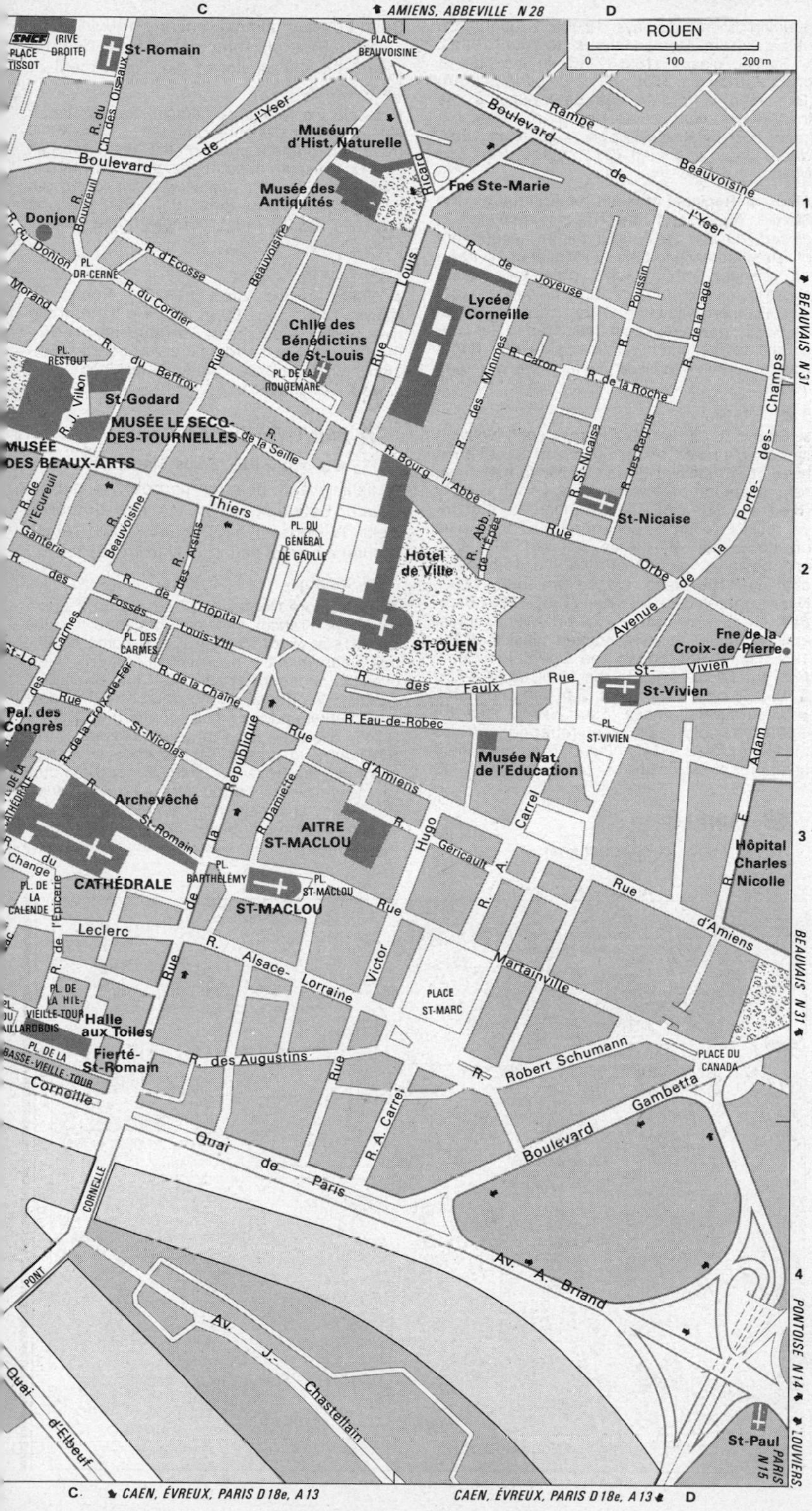
C
D
AMIENS, ABBEVILLE N 28
ROUEN
0
100
200 m
SNCF (RIVE DROITE)
PLACE TISSOT
St-Romain
PLACE BEAUVOISINE
R. du Ch. des Oiseaux
Boulevard de l'Yser
Boulevard de Beauvoisine
Rampe
Muséum d'Hist. Naturelle
Musée des Antiquités
Fne Ste-Marie
R. Ricard
R. Bouvreuil
Donjon
R. du Donjon
PL. DR-CERNE
R. d'Ecosse
R. Beauvoisine
R. du Cordier
Morand
R. de Joyeuse
R. Poussin
R. de la Cage
Rue Louis
Lycée Corneille
Chlle des Bénédictins de St-Louis
PL. DE LA ROUGEMARE
PL. RESTOUT
R. du Beffroy
R. des Minimes
R. Caron
R. de la Roche
R. des Champs
R. J. Villon
St-Godard
MUSÉE LE SECQ-DES-TOURNELLES
MUSÉE DES BEAUX-ARTS
R. de la Seille
R. Bourg l'Abbé
R. St-Nicaise
R. des Requis
R. de l'Ecureuil
Thiers
St-Nicaise
PL. DU GÉNÉRAL DE GAULLE
R. Abb. de l'Epée
Rue Orbe
R. de la Porte-des-Champs
Ganterie
R. Beauvoisine
R. des Arsins
Hôtel de Ville
R. des Fossés Louis-VIII
R. de l'Hôpital
Avenue de la Porte-des-Champs
Fne de la Croix-de-Pierre
PL. DES CARMES
R. des Carmes
ST-OUEN
Rue St-Vivien
St-Lô
R. de la Chaîne
R. des Faulx
St-Vivien
Pal. des Congrès
Rue St-Nicolas
R. de la Croix-de-Fer
R. Eau-de-Robec
PL. ST-VIVIEN
Rue de la République
Musée Nat. de l'Education
R. Adam
Rue d'Amiens
R. Damiette
R. Carrel
Archevêché
R. St-Romain
AITRE ST-MACLOU
Hugo
R. Géricault
Hôpital Charles Nicolle
R. du Change
PL. DE LA CALENDE
CATHÉDRALE
PL. BARTHÉLEMY
PL. ST-MACLOU
ST-MACLOU
Rue d'Amiens
R. de l'Epicerie
Leclerc
R. Alsace-Lorraine
Rue Victor
Rue Martainville
PLACE ST-MARC
PL. DE LA HTE-VIEILLE-TOUR
Halle aux Toiles
Fierté-St-Romain
PL. DE LA BASSE-VIEILLE-TOUR
R. des Augustins
R. Robert Schumann
PLACE DU CANADA
Corneille
Rue
Boulevard Gambetta
Quai de Paris
R. A. Carrel
CORNEILLE
PONT
Av. A. Briand
Av. J. Chastellain
Quai d'Elbeuf
St-Paul
BEAUVAIS N 31
PONTOISE N 14
LOUVIERS, PARIS N 15
CAEN, ÉVREUX, PARIS D 18e, A 13
CAEN, ÉVREUX, PARIS D 18e, A 13
1
2
3
4

opening hours) displays 12 000 wrought-iron objects from Roman times to the 19thC. ▶ Stained glass★ (16th-17thC) in the **church of St. Patrice** (ca. 1535; B1). Rue Jeanne d'Arc (B-1-2-3) runs from the right bank quays to the train station, near the Jeanne d'Arc tower, the keep, built by King Philippe Auguste in 1207, where Joan was tried (C1; *closed Thu. and Nov.*). □

Also... ▶ Regional Museum of Antiquities, the Middle Ages, and the Renaissance★ (C1; *closed Thu. and nat. hols.*) in the former convent of Ste. Catherine (1630). ▶ Museum of natural sciences, ethnography, prehistory (same address; *closed Sun. am, Mon., Tue.*). ▶ Gustave Flaubert was born in the hospital (Hôtel-Dieu; A1), now a museum dedicated to the writer and to the history of medicine (his father was a surgeon) *(closed Sun., Mon. and nat. hols.)*. □

▶ Nearby

▶ **Elbeuf** ® *(20 km S)* : former linen-weaving centre; churches of St. Jean and St. Étienne have 16thC stained glass; in the former town hall, Museum of Natural and Local History *(Wed. and Sat. 2-6)*. The GR2 leads to the Orival rocks★ (*4 km N;* panorama over the valley of the Seine). ▶ **Clères** *(22 km N)* : zoo and botanical garden around the 15th-19thC château (11thC keep; *closed Nov.-early Mar.*). Nearby, Automobile Museum (1892-1955; *8am-8pm daily*). ▶ **Yvetot** ® *(36 km NW)* : almost entirely rebuilt, modern stained glass★ in the 1955 church; European and Oriental ivories★ from the Middle Ages to the 19thC *(8:30-11:30 & 1:30-5; closed Mon. am, Sat. pm and Sun.)*. ▶ **Allouville-Bellefosse** *(6 km SW of Yvetot)* : 1 000 year-old oak tree (chapel), nature museum *(10-12 & 2-7; closed Tue.)*, treatment centre for birds, victims of coastal pollution. □

SAINT-LÔ

A2 / ® / pop. 24 790 (Manche)

Saint-Lô was almost entirely rebuilt after 1944, but the old ramparts still enclose the town. It is the capital of the Department of La Manche.

▶ Inside the ramparts★ administrative district (A1), the Notre-Dame church (A1) : 15th-16thC (restored), outdoor pulpit on the left. Town hall (A-B1) : museum of paintings and 16thC tapestries★ *(daily ex Tue. Jul.-Aug.; closed am out of season)*. ▶ **Stud-farm** (B1) : 200 stallions *(daily 15 Jul.-15 Feb.)*, harness-horse display *(Thu. in Aug. 10am)*. □

▶ Nearby

▶ **Valley of the Vire**★ (GR221). **Roche de Ham**★ *(13 km S)* : 100 m above a bend in the river; picturesque site of **La Chapelle-sur-Vire** (pilgrimage). Not far from here, **Angotière :** 16th-18thC château (site, park, furnishings; *pm; closed Tue. and Jul.*). □

SAINT-VALERY-EN-CAUX

C1 / ® / pop. 5 810 (Seine-Maritime)

A fishing and boating harbour, a pebble beach between cliffs, a half-timbered Henri IV house (1540), a little town rebuilt around a chapel dating only from 1963. □

▶ Nearby

▶ Just before **Conteville** *(7 km W)*, EDF (Électricité de France) information centre for the **power station of Paluel,** due to come on line this year (exhibit on nuclear power; view over the construction site). ▶ **Cany-Barville** ® *12 km SW)* : Renaissance church; 18thC covered market and town hall; **château de Cany**★ (1646, designed by François Mansart; furniture; *Jul.-Aug. closed Fri. and 4th Sun. in Jul.*). ▶ **Veules-les-Roses** ® *(8 km E)* : at the mouth of the smallest non-tributary river in France, the Veule; charming walk along the river and through the streets. Several farms and interesting **villages**★ on the Caux plateau : **Blosseville**

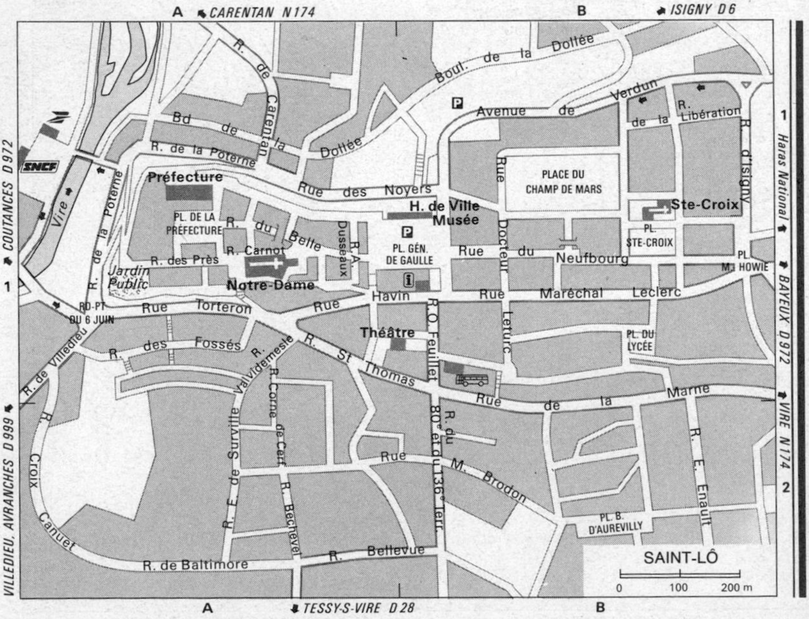

(stained glass in the church); **La Chapelle-sur-Dun** (17thC château); **Ermenouville** (17thC château); **Canville** and **Bretteville** (half-timbered houses); and **Gruchet-Saint-Siméon. Luneray** *(16 km SE from Saint-Valery)* : shops; European Traditional Jazz festival *(May-Jun.)*. **Bourg-Dun** ® *(14.5 km E)* : 12th-16thC church★. □

■ The **Lower SEINE** Valley★★★

▶ Round trip *(approx 235 km, 2 days)* C-D1-2 *(see diag 6)*

The Vikings understood the value of the river Seine as a route inland. Since the Middle Ages, it has never lost its importance as a means of transport for the products of agriculture and industry. Industrial development has not spoilt the countryside. Forests flourish at La Lande, Roumare, Mauny, Brotonne (Regional Park) and the Marais Vernier (polders). Between Rouen and Honfleur, the only two bridges are those of Brotonne and Tancarville at the mouth of the river; ferry plies the waters at Jumièges.

▶ **Rouen** (→). ▶ Pass quickly through the bland suburbs of Petit and Grand Quevilly to arrive at the "house in the fields" (Maison des Champs) bought by the father of the playwright Pierre Corneille so that his delicate son could benefit from country air; the house at **Petit Couronne** preserves memorabilia, furniture, and a thatched bakery; *closed Thu. and Nov.*).

▶ Remains of the 11thC **castle of Robert le Diable** (Robert the Devil, father of William the Conqueror) over the village of Moulineaux; the castle houses a Viking museum *(daily Mar.-Nov.; Sun. only, Nov.-Mar.; closed Jan.)*; view★ of the Seine. ▶ **La Bouille** : stop-over at the foot of the cliffs. ▶ **Jumièges★★** : undoubtedly the most romantic Norman abbey; founded in the 7thC, rebuilt in the 10thC, now only a splendid ruin; stonework museum in the 18thC abbey buildings *(closed Tue. and Wed. in winter)*. ▶ **Notre-Dame-de-Bliquetuit** : starting point for a trip around **Brotonne Park** *(8 km)*; several half-timbered houses★, including a farm with a dovecote, near the exit towards the Pont (bridge) de Brotonne★ (1 280 m long; 1977; toll). On the other side of the bridge, head towards **Caudebec** ® (excellent restaurant); church of Notre-Dame★★ (flamboyant Gothic, noted pipe-organ) and mediaeval Templar building (Old Caudebec museum, *Sat. and Sun. Easter-30 Sep.; daily Jul.-Aug.*). ▶ **Sainte-Gertrude :** 16thC church, half-timbered houses, watermill. ▶ Drive (site★) to **Villequier** : Victor Hugo museum *(daily ex. Tue., 15 Mar.-30 Sep.; closed Mon., Tue. in winter, Nov. and Jan.)*. Between Norville and Saint-Maurice : **château d'Etelan** (late 15thC, restored; cultural events; *15 Jul.-end Aug. pm, closed Tue.*); view of the Seine and the Brotonne forest from the park. A detour through **Notre-Dame-de-Granvenchon** provides views of the valley and **Port-Jérôme.** ▶ **Lillebonne :** a theatre remains from the Roman town; 13thC keep; local archaeological museum *(pm ex. Tue.; closed Sat. and Sun. in winter)*. ▶ **Tancarville★** ® : château (14th-18thC) with restaurant, art gallery, cabinet-maker's workshop, equestrian centre, and museum. **Tancarville bridge★** (1 410 m long, toll) built 20 years before the Brotonne bridge. Off the Pont-l'Évêque road, **Saint-Samson-de-la-Roque :** lighthouse, view★ of the Seine estuary as far as Le Havre. ▶ 44 km^2 of marshy plain at the foot of a cliff, drained since the 17thC, bordered by the village of **Marais Vernier★★** : exceptionally attractive half-timbered farmsteads, houses and yards (1 May, cattle branding). The road along the dyke, built by 16thC Dutch engineers in the region of Henri IV, leads to **Quillebeuf** : once an important river port; Grande Rue★ (pedestrian). The best route to **Sainte-Opportune-la-Mare** is along the high, narrow road that provides a **view★** of the Marais Vernier and the **Grande-Mare** (bird sanctuary; mallards) : In Sainte-Opportune, Maison de la Pomme (apple sales in season); the Place de l'Église (church square) is also the meeting-place for visits to the Mannevilles Nature Park (go properly-equipped to deal with mud, bogs and vipers; half-day, or full day including the Marais Vernier; *information from the Brotonne Park Information Office, tel. 35.91.83.16*). ▶ **Vieux Port★ :** weekend cottages contrast with the farms of the Marais Vernier. **Bourneville :** the **Musée des Métiers** is a crafts centre (pottery; courses; exhibition and sale; *pm ex. Mon. Apr.-Dec.; Sat. and Sun. pm Jan.-Mar.*).

6. Lower Seine valley

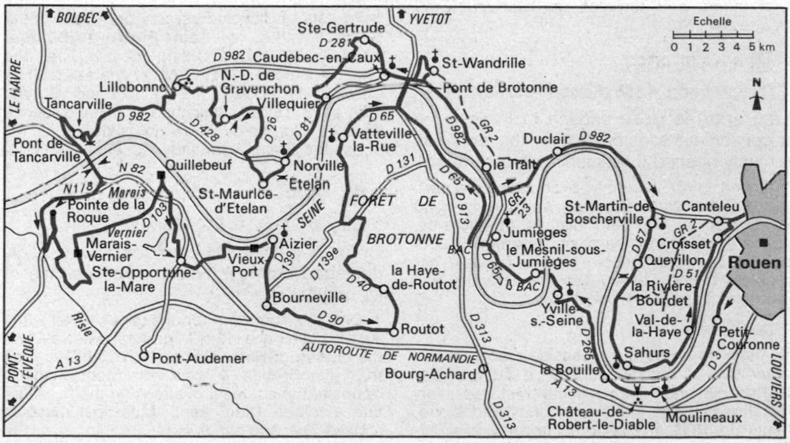

▶ Two giant yews★ stand in front of the church at **La Haye-de-Routot;** nearby is a restored breadoven (old utensils, fancy breads; *pm ex Mon., Jul.-Aug.; Sat. and Sun., spring and autumn*); clog-maker's workshop *(pm; closed Mon. and Tue.).* La Haye-de-Routot is the starting point for two footpaths (6 km and 11 km, respectively) through the regional park. **Brotonne forest★** (68 km²; beech), then Pont de Brotonne. ▶ **Saint-Wandrille :** the abbey★★, founded in the 7thC, is occupied by Benedictines *(Sun. and hols. 11:30, 3pm and 4; 3 and 4 weekdays);* ruins of 13th-14thC church; 14th-15thC cloister; the actual church (noted for Gregorian chant) is a 13thC barn. ▶ **Le Trait :** between the naval shipyards and the thermal power centre at Yainville, HQ of the **Brotonne Nature Park** (three different hikes leave from here on weekdays). The Park★ extends on both sides of the Seine (42 km²) with the aim of protecting the rural environment, cultural heritage, and agriculture and crafts of the region. ▶ **Saint-Martin-de-Boscherville :** former **abbey** church of **St. Georges★★** (12thC) is the finest abbey building left in the valley. □

■ La SUISSE NORMANDE★★

B2-3

This oddly-named area (Norman Switzerland) lies to the east of the Bocage region.

Tourist route of the Suisse Normande. ▶ The GR36 follows the Orne between Thury-Harcourt and Putanges. ▶ At **Thury-Harcourt** ® : ruined château, park and garden of the château d'Harcourt★ *(visit Sun. and nat. hols., Easter-1 Nov.),* 2.5 km W, a narrow loop of the river Hom★. ▶ Near Acqueville *(10 km E) :* **château de la Motte** (1600; *park open daily*). ▶ **Clécy** ® : on a bend in the Orne, the main town in the area; lookouts at Le Pain de Sucre (Sugarloaf Hill, NE), L'Eminence (SW), La Croix de la Faverie (S) and Butte Saint-Clair (E); Placy manor (16thC; Antiquities Museum; *pm Jul.-15 Sep., Sun. out of season*); "Suisse Normande Miniature", miniature railway museum *(Jun.-mid-Sep.; Sun. pm out of season).* ▶ Near Condé, **chateau de Pontécoulant** *(closed Mon., Tue. and Oct.).* Picturesque sites between **Pont d'Ouilly** ® and the Rabodanges dam; junction of the Rouvre, Oëtre rock★, St. Aubert gorge, and the lake at **Putanges-Pont-Ecrepin. Rabodanges :** 17thC château with moats and terraced gardens *(Jul.-Oct., closed Sat., Sun.).* □

■ Le TRÉPORT

D1 / ® / pop. 6 555 (Seine-Maritime)

Le Tréport is close enough to Paris to be a convenient seaside resort; the port has recently opened to vessels of large draught.

▶ Church of St. Jacques : overlooking the port, has a Renaissance doorway and fine hanging keystones. ▶ The port (fishing, restaurants, souvenirs) ends at the casino swimming pool on the seafront; pebble beach. A cable car runs up to the Calvary Terrace (Calvaire des Terrasses) : view★ of the cliffs. □

▶ Nearby

▶ **Mers-les-Bains** ® : a seaside resort on the other side of the river Bresle. ▶ **Eu** ® *(4 km SE)* an old brick town recently restored : former hospital and château of brick and stone, begun in 1578 and restored under Louis Philippe (1773-1850) *(Apr.-Oct.; closed Tue.);* nearby church of St. Laurent (12th-13thC), a 15thC entombment of Christ. The **Eu forest** covers 94 km²; the best part is upstream from **Blangy** ® along the Bresle valley. □

■ VALOGNES★

A1-2 / ® / pop. 6 960 (Manche)

Rebuilt since WWII, Valogne has recovered its pre-war aristocratic atmosphere.

▶ 16thC church of St. Malo (rebuilt); old mansions; Beaumont mansion (*daily pm ex. Wed., Jul.-15 Sep.;* Louis XV (ca. 1750; furniture); Cider Museum (16thC house, *15 Jun.-30 Sep. ex Wed. and Sun. am);* museum of spirits *(Eau-de-vie)* and Old Trades, Hôtel de Thieuville (17th, 19thC). □

▶ Nearby

▶ **Saint-Sauveur-le-Vicomte** ® *(15 km S) :* small museum of the writer Barbey d'Aurevilly (1808-1889) in the château *(closed Tue.).* ▶ **Barneville-Carteret** ® *(30 km SW) :* small port **(Carteret)** with beach; seaside resort at **Barneville** S of the Gerfleur estuary. ▶ 7 km of dunes to **Port Bail** ®, a resort and fishing harbour. □

■ VERNON★

D2 / ® / pop. 23 460 (Eure)

Capital of the Vexin region of Normandy, and too close to Paris to have a truly Norman atmosphere, Vernon is nevertheless a good excursion centre for the Seine, Epte and Eure valleys.

▶ Church of Notre-Dame in the town centre; fine 13th-14thC building with early 19thC mausoleum; half-timbered houses (15thC) nearby. ▶ Near the Tour des Archives (Archives Tower, 12thC); wood and stone buildings (15th-17thC) housing the **Poulain Municipal Museum** (paintings, including two by Monet (Île-de-France : Giverny); sculpture and local history; *closed Tue., Wed. and nat. hols*). ▶ Ruins of a mediaeval bridge and the château des Tourelles (13thC) at Vernonnet on the other bank. ▶ **Château de Bizy** (19thC) : stables and outbuildings (18thC) on the road to Pacy-sur-Eure, in a park (Napoleonic memorabilia; *Apr.-Oct. ex. Fri.).* □

▶ Nearby

▶ Forests of Bizy and Vernon, right bank of the Seine; walks. ▶ **Saint-Pierre-de-Bailleul** *(10 km NW) :* pelt-farming *(closed Tue. and Thu.).* ▶ **Gaillon★** *(14 km NW) :* château built by Cardinal d'Amboise (Minister to Louis XII, late 15th-early 16thC); launched the Renaissance style in Normandy; now in restoration, will house the Upper Normandy Museum. □

■ VIRE

B3 / ® / pop. 14 540 (Calvados)

On a beautiful site, the town was badly damaged during WWII, and retains little of its original charm.

▶ Only the Tour de l'Horloge (clock tower; *Jul.-Aug.*), built on a 13thC fortified gateway and the **church of Notre-Dame** (13th-15thC) are left from historic Vire. ▶ View from Mont Besnard, opposite the château, overlooking the river Vire and a ruined 12thC keep. Municipal museum *(closed Tue. and nat. hols.).* □

Architecture

Cotentin peninsula house

The Norman countryside means half-timbered houses in apple orchards to most people. ● The *masure* (the farm enclosure incorporating the various buildings) of the Caux region is typical : on a foundation of black flint (brick or stone in other regions) is laid an oaken framework of horizontal beams and vertical studding; the window and door openings are placed asymmetrically : *colombes* (smaller planks) are placed vertically or diagonally in the framework. The gaps are filled with cob, a mixture of clay and straw sometimes reinforced with chipped brick or stone. ● In the Caen plain, where the houses are usually clustered together, Caen limestone is used for construction. This stone was exported to England for the construction of many religious buildings. ● In western Normandy, houses have one or two stories, with the gable walls to the side. The door and window openings are more symmetrical than elsewhere. North of Cotentin, pink granite, and farther south, grey granite, are used for the walls. Schist, known as "Pont-de-la-Mousse slate", is found around Thury-Harcourt.

Fortified house in the Perche region

Auge region house

Brief regional history

Up to the Roman era

Little is known about the pre-Stone Age inhabitants of the Normandy region. ● During the **Bronze Age,** trade relations were established with the British Isles (tin from Cornwall, gold from Ireland). ● In the **Iron Age,** the Celtic Gauls enter history; the Unelli tribe was defeated by one of Caesar's lieutenants in 56BC. The "Pax Romana", established at the beginning of the Christian era, led to the emergence of prosperous Gallo-Roman cities, among them *Juliobona* - present-day Lillebonne. Large agricultural estates were developed at this period.

3rd to 10thC

In the 3rd century a separate northwestern Roman province was created which included present-day Normandy. Its capital was at *Rotomagus* (Rouen). As early as 260, Rouen was the seat of the first Norman bishopric. ● During the centuries that followed, the Franks got the upper hand of other invaders. ● With the foundation of the **first Norman abbeys,** the land began to be cleared for agriculture. The succeeding Merovingian and Carolingian dynasties continued this policy, and the abbeys became important cultural centres. ● **From 820 on, Vikings from Denmark** and Norway began their raids (→ box).

911-1204

By the 10thC, the new invaders were strong enough to force the Frankish King Charles to acknowledge the Viking Rollo's overlordship of Normandy; he received the title of Duke, and agreed to be baptised (**Treaty of Saint-Clair-sur-Epte,** 911). In 1066, Duke William successfully asserted his claim to the English throne (→ box). ● In Normandy itself Benedictine and Cistercian monks reformed the Norman abbeys and perfected Norman Romanesque architecture during the 11th and 12thC. The Abbaye aux Hommes (Men's Abbey) in Caen, founded by William, is the prototype of this style. Henry II, Duke of Normandy and son of Geoffroy V of Anjou, succeeded to the throne in 1154, and married Eleanor of Aquitaine after Louis VII of France repudiated her. The English Crown thus acquired its vast land holdings which stretched from the borders of Brittany to the Pyrénées. These possessions were later bitterly disputed, both legally and by force, during the period of the Hundred Years' War (14th-15thC).

1204-1346

During this period Philippe Auguste (Philippe II, 1180-1223) won possession of all Normandy but the Channel Isles *(Isles Normandes).* In 1315 the Rouen Parliament was given special privileges by the **Charte aux Normands** (The Normans' Charter). ● The abbey of Mont-Saint-Michel, the Cathedrals of Coutances and Bayeux, the bell-tower of Saint-Pierre at Caen and the new cathedral at Rouen all date from this epoch, a rich heritage of Gothic architectural achievement.

1346-1450 The Hundred Years' War

After a number of preliminary skirmishes, Edward III landed his troops at Saint-Vaast-la-Hougue (1346), a few miles north of the Utah beach landings almost exactly 600 year later. Edward went on to win an important victory at Crécy. Ten years later, he inherited the Cotentin peninsula from the Count of Harcourt, and captured Jean le Bon, (John the Good, one of France's least-successful and least-popular kings) at the battle of Poitiers, holding him prisoner in London. ● In 1364 Jean's son, Charles V, succeeded him, and re-established French influence in the strategic but unruly Norman region, as well as in most of the centre and southwest. After his death in 1380 his successors were unable to keep the dukedom out of the hands of the English aristocracy, themselves descendants of the Norman invaders of England. **English rule was consolidated** by the victory of Agincourt under Henry V (1415), and an alliance with the independant dukedom of Burgundy. All of Normandy with the exception of Mont-Saint-Michel was reoccupied, and Rouen became the capital of the Duke of Bedford, the English Regent. ● With the resurgence of French national spirit under Joan of Arc, the English were forced to retreat, and in 1449 Charles VII was able to make a solemn entry into Rouen; **the victory of Formigny** near Bayeux (1450) consolidated his hold on Normandy.

1469-18thC

The end of the Hundred Years' War saw the rise of the bourgeoisie and an increase in urbanisation. ● Norman ports prospered as the Normans rediscovered their taste for overseas exploration. ● During the second half of the 16thC Protestantism spread throughout the region, and when the Edict of Nantes was revoked by Louis XIV (1685), many Norman Protestants went into exile. ● In the early years of the 18thC, Norman agriculture expanded to feed the growing Paris population; traditional **textile manufacture** gave way to a flourishing cotton goods industry in Rouen, Elbeuf and Louviers; **lace** too became popular (Argentan). From 1763, British domination in Canada and India saw the Norman ports diminish in importance, while the cotton industry declined as the British textile production was industralised. ● Normandy held aloof from the French Revolution, giving little support to either revolutionaries or royalists.

19thC to the present day

In the early 19thC the British naval blockade against Napoléon paralysed the Norman ports, but the **textile industry found profitable domestic markets.** ● In 1843 the Paris-Rouen railway was inaugurated; Paris-Cherbourg followed in 1858; the first steamship line to the United States had begun in Cherbourg in 1847. The railway contributed largely to the development of the **resort towns** on the Normandy coast (Dieppe, Deauville, Étretat, Le Tréport), which boomed during the Second Empire (1852-70) and were made more famous still by numerous writers and artists (→ box). ● Although Normandy paid heavily in loss of life during WWI, the region itself and its towns were relatively unharmed (the Belgian Government-in-exile was accommodated in Sainte-Adresse, a fashionable resort area of Le Havre). WWII caused far more serious damage; the German occupation of June 1940 was followed by the dramatic **Canadian raid on Dieppe in 1942,** and the almost total destruction of Saint-Lô, Caen, Lisieux, Falaise, Argentan, Le Havre, Rouen and Évreux as the price of the **Allied landings in June 1944.** ● One of the benefits of the subsequent reconstruction was industrial modernisation, and intensive new technologies (electronics and petrochemical industries) now play a major part in the economy of this historic region, together with new energy sources (Seine-Maritime and La Manche nuclear power stations). The 1984 commemoration of the WWII Allied landings saw the visit of United States President Ronald Reagan, the British Prime Minister, Margaret Thatcher, President François Mitterrand of France and other dignitaries.

Practical information

The region

Information : *Comité Inter-régional de Tourisme* (C.I.T), 46, av. Foch, bât. E, 27000 Évreux, ☎ 32.31.03.03. **Calvados** : *Comité Départemental de Tourisme* (C.D.T.), pl. du Canada, 14000 Caen, ☎ 31.86.53.30. **Eure** : *Comité Départemental de Tourisme de l'Eure* (C.D.T.), Chambre de Commerce, 27000 Évreux, ☎ 32.38.21.61. **Manche** : *Office Départemental de Tourisme* (O.D.T.), préfecture, B.P. 419, 50009 Saint-Lô, ☎ 33.57.52.80. **Orne** : *Comité Départemental de Tourisme* (C.D.T.), 60, rue St-Blaise, B.P. 50, 61002 Alençon Cedex, ☎ 33.26.18.71. **Seine-Maritime** : *Comité Départemental de Tourisme* (C.D.T.), B.P. 666, 76008 Rouen Cedex, ☎ 35.88.61.32.

Maps : *Michelin* 1/200 000 : nº 231 (Normandie), nºs 54, 55, 59, 60. *I.G.N.* nºs 3, 6, 7, 8, 18 1/100 000. *I.G.N.* nº 102 (Normandie-série rouge), 1/250 000.

S.O.S. : **Calvados,** ☎ 15 ; **Eure** : SAMU, Emergency Medical Service, ☎ 15 ; **Orne** : SAMU Alençon, ☎ 33.26.65.65. **Manche** : S.M.U.R. Saint-Lô, ☎ 33.05.28.48 ; **Seine-Maritime,** ☎ 15. Poisoning Emergency Centre : Rennes, ☎ 99.59.22.22 ; Rouen, ☎ 35.88.44.00.

Weather forecast : **Calvados** : Caen-Carpiquet, ☎ 31.74.74.74 ; Deauville-Saint-Gatien, ☎ 31.88.84.22. **Eure,** ☎ 32.39.20.96. **Manche,** ☎ 33.44.45.00 ; **Orne,** ☎ 33.29.37.97. **Seine-Maritime,** ☎ 35.21.04.19 ; Marine and coastal forecast, ☎ 35.21.16.11 ; **Manche-Haute-Normandie,** ☎ 35.80.22.48.

Gîtes ruraux and chambres d'hotes : gîtes d'étapes for hikers, gîtes d'enfants : enq at the *Relais Départementaux des Gîtes Ruraux* at the following addresses : **Calvados,** 4, promenade de Mme-de-Sévigné, 14039 Caen Cedex, ☎ 31.84.47.19. **Eure** (booking, ☎ 31.82.71.65), 5, rue de la Petite-Cité, 27000 Évreux, ☎ 32.39.53.38. **Manche,** Channel, préfecture, 50009 Saint-Lô, ☎ 33.57.52.80 ; lodgings in villages : Bellefontaine, Moidrey, Saint-Jean-de-la-Rivière, Saint-Laurent-de-Terregatte et Ver. **Orne,** 60, rue St-Blaise, B.P. 50, 61002 Alençon Cedex, ☎ 33.26.18.71. **Seine-Maritime,** Chambre d'Agriculture, chemin de la Bretèque, B.P. 37, 76230 Bois-Guillaume, ☎ 35.60.48.60.

Holiday villages : see practical holiday information.

Camping : lists at the departmental C.D.T. and ⓘ Farmhouse camping, list of sites provided by the departmental Chambers of Agriculture.

Cultural events : **May-Jun** : Eure Dept. *in flower* ; **May-Jun-Jul** : *Summer Festival* in the Seine-Maritime region. **May-Sep** : Bagnoles-de-l'Orne Festival. **Jul-Aug** : Mont-St-Michel *Music Festival* ; Rouen, *organ recitals in St-Maclou.* **Sep** : Deauville, *Festival of American Cinema.*

Exhibitions and trade fairs : **Mar** : Caen, *spring fair.* **End Apr-early May** : Rouen *fair.* **May** : Cherbourg, *gastronomical fair.* **Jun** : Caen, *salon of antiques and bric-à-brac.* **Sep** : Caen *fair.* **Oct** : Rouen, *salon of antiques.*

Sporting events : **end Apr** : Rouen, *24 hr nautical motor-sports.* **May** : Cherbourg, *international regattas.* **Jul-Aug** : Deauville, *horse races* ; **last Sun in Aug** in Deauville : *Grand Prix de Deauville (horse racing).*

Pilgrimages : **Whitsuntide Mon** in Bernay, *procession des confréries de Charité* ; in Honfleur, *Grand pilgrimage of the sailors to Notre-Dame de Grâce* ; in Préaux, *fête des Charitons.* **End May** in Rouen, *Joan of Arc Festival.* **Jun** in Fécamp : *Trinity Fetes and pilgrimage of Precious Blood.* **In May, Jul and Sep** : *pilgrimages to the Mont-St-Michel.* **Last week-end in Sep** in Lisieux : *Grandes fêtes de Sainte-Thérèse.*

Other events : **May** : in Étretat, *Grand Norman Festival* ; in Le Havre, *Days of the Sea.* **Jun** : in Balleroy, *Day of the balloons.* **Jul** : in Domfront, *International Folklore Festival* ; in Deauville, *Bridge Festival.* **Aug** : in Yport, *Festival of Painting and the Sea* ; **15 Aug** : in Dieppe, *Carnaval des Mitouries.* **Sep** : in Lessay, *Millenial Ste-Croix fair,* horse fair ; in Bellême, *mycology days* ; **1st Sun in Sep** and **2nd Sun in Oct** : in Haras-du-Pin : *horse races, procession. Apple Fair* : **early Nov** in Pont-d'Ouilly and **Oct** in Vimoutiers. **11 Nov** : in Lieurey, *Herring Fair* ; **Nov** : in Dieppe, *Herring Fair* ; in Beuvron-en-Auge, *Cidre Festival.* **6 Dec** : in Évreux, *St-Nicolas Fair.*

Rambling and hiking : the region is traversed by the G.R.2, 21, 22 *bis,* 23, 25, 211, 221, 223 and 225. Topoguides are available for the G.R.21/211/212, 22, 22/22b, 221/221 A and B, 22, 223 and 26.

Riding holidays : *Association Régionale de Tourisme Équestre de Haute-Normandie,* 268, rue Jules-Ferry, 76480 Duclair, ☎ 35.64.50.73. *Association Régionale de Tourisme Équestre de Basse-Normandie,* 60, rue St-Blaise, B.P. 50, Alençon Cedex, ☎ 33.26.18.71.

Holidays in horse-drawn caravans : departure from Tessé-la-Madeleine near Bagnoles-de-l'Orne ; enq : Jean Dinard, B.P. 6, Tessé-la-Madeleine, 61140 Bagnoles-de-l'Orne, ☎ 33.37.00.56. *Les Roulottes du Valdoré,* rte de Manerbe, 14340 Cambremer, ☎ 31.31.14.97. M. de Cressac, manoir d'Auvillars, Hotot-en-Auge, ☎ 31.79.28.86. Excursions in horse-drawn buggies, enq : *S.I.V.O.M.* du Val d'Orne, 15, rue de Condé, 14220 Thury-Harcourt, ☎ 31.79.61.61.

Cycling holidays : S.N.C.F. "Train-Vélo" service : 9 stations in Normandy : Bayeux, Caen, Lisieux and Vire (14) ; Bueil, Vernon (27) ; Villedieu-les-Poêles, Granville, Pontorson (50) ; Argentan (61) ; Dieppe, Le Tréport (76). Cycling tour of Calvados, enq at the *Union Cyclotouriste Divoise,* 20, rue P.-Canton, 14160 Dives-sur-Mer, ☎ 31.91.05.08.

Handicraft courses : **Calvados** : lace-making with a spindle, polished tapestry work in Bayeux, pottery in Brucourt and Neuvron-la-Poterie, wool-spinning in Marolles, weaving at Beaumont-en-Auge, Saint-Laurent-du-Mont, Villy-Bocage, photo at Beaumont-en-Auge. **Eure** : weaving and tapestry-making in Saint-Denis-le-Ferment near Gisors ; weaving, pottery, torchis at the

Maison des métiers de Bourneville near Pont-Audemer. **Manche :** the workshops of Val de Saire ; courses in manual and technical employment at Cherbourg and Saint-Pierre-Église. **Orne :** furniture and decorative chair restoration in Mortrée. **Seine-Maritime :** ornamental gardening in Dieppe, wood sculpture in Rouen, marionettes in Saint-Romain-de-Colbosc. Enq at the C.D.T.

Tennis : enq at the ⓘ

Golf : 8 18-hole courses, in Cabourg, Deauville, Le Vaudreuil, Granville, Dieppe, Étretat, Le Havre, Rouen ; 6 9-hole courses : Houlgate, Agon-Coutainville, Brehal, Cherbourg, Fontenay-sur-Mer, Bagnoles-de-l'Orne. *Beginners' Golf Centre,* château du Champ-de-Bataille, 27110 Le Neubourg, ☎ 32.35.27.66.

Aquatic sports : enq at the C.D.T. and T.O. Sailing-boat's stays at the *Centre Régional de Nautisme de Granville,* B.P. 124, 50400 Granville, ☎ 33.50.18.95. Boats for hire for holiday cruises, *Lesjesqueux Voile,* 3, rue Clément-Desmaisons, 50400 Granville, ☎ 33.50.18.97.

Canoeing : Calvados : *Comité Départemental Stade Nautique,* av. Albert-Sorel, 14000 Caen, ☎ 31.86.04.12. **Eure :** *Direction de la Jeunesse et des Sports,* Cité administrative, 27023 Évreux, ☎ 32.39.52.09. **Manche :** sports' association *Elle et Vire* at Condé-sur-Vire ; *Nautical Club* of Carentan ; *Loisir et Tourisme* at Hambye ; *Loisir et Plein Air* at Saint-Hilaire-du-Harcouët ; Regional and Nautical Centre at Granville ; North Cotentin sea Kayak club.

Potholing and spelunking : enq : *M.J.C.,* av. Aristide-Briand, 27000 Évreux, ☎ 32.39.16.24.

Climbing : rock-climbing in the parks in Suisse normande (Clécy) ; in the **Eure** region, near Les Andelys and on the Deux-Amants coast. Enq : *Club Alpin Français,* 190, rue Beauvoisine, 76000 Rouen, ☎ 35.71.21.97.

Flying, gliding and parachuting : gliding at the aéroclub Caen-Carpiquet, ☎ 31.73.12.00 ; on the Eraine mountains in Falaise, ☎ 31.90.06.54 ; at the aéroclub Jean-Mermoz in Clécy, ☎ 31.69.07.21. Parachuting in Évreux, *Aéro-club de l'Eure,* Fauville, ☎ 32.33.13.86 ; in Dieppe, *Parachute-Club,* Saint-Aubin-sur-Scie, ☎ 35.84.81.97. In the Cotentin region, Cherbourg, Lessay, Saint-Lô, Granville and Avranches airclubs ; in the **Seine-Maritime** region, Boos, Dieppe, Caen-Carpiquet, Eu, Le Havre, Rouen, Saint-Romain-de-Colbosc, Saint-Valéry-en-Caux airclubs.

Hunting and shooting : *Fédération Départementale des Chasseurs :* **Calvados :** rue des Compagnons, la Folie-Couvrechef, 14000 Caen, ☎ 31.95.41.74. **Eure :** 75, rue de Pannette, 27000 Évreux, ☎ 32.33.09.76. **Seine-Maritime :** 216, rte de Neufchâtel, 76420 Bihorel, ☎ 35.60.35.97.

Fishing : *Fédération Départementale des Associations de Pêche et de Pisciculture :* **Calvados :** 120, bd Mal-Leclerc, 14300 Caen, ☎ 31.86.06.97. **Eure :** 34, pl. Louis-Gillain, 27500 Pont-Audemer, ☎ 32.41.04.47. **Manche :** 24, rue de la République, 50120 Equeurdreville-Hainneville, ☎ 33.53.25.63. **Orne :** 8, rue du Collège, 61000 Alençon, ☎ 34.26.10.66. **Seine-Maritime :** *la Belle Gaule de Rouen et de Normandie,* M. Beaulès, rue Louis-Brune, 76000 Rouen. Week-end salmon fishing and fly-fishing school in Ducey, ☎ 33.48.52.26.

Normandy

● Towns

L'AIGLE

Alençon 59, Chartres 80, Paris 140
C3 ⊠ 61300

ⓘ pl. F.-de-Beina, ☎ 33.24.12.40 (high season).

SNCF ☎ 33.24.35.32.

Hotel :

● ★★★**Dauphin** (Mapotel), pl. de la Halle, ☎ 33.24.43.12, Tx 170979. AE, DC, Euro, Visa. 24 rm Ⓟ 300. Rest. ◆ Pleasant setting. Spec : *langouste au porto, rognons à la moutarde,* 100-260.

⛺ ★★*Municipal* (65 pl.), ☎ 33.24.32.79.

Restaurant :

◆◆ ***Auberge St-Michel,*** rte de Paris, ☎ 33.24.20.12. Euro, Visa. Ⓟ ♿ closed Feb, Wed eve and Thu, 60-130.

ALENÇON

Laval 90, Chartres 115, Paris 191
C4 ⊠ 61000

ⓘ Maison d'Ozé, pl. Lamagdelaine (B2), ☎ 33.26.11.36.

SNCF ☎ 33.67.50.50.

Car-hire : Budget train + auto, at the S.N.C.F. station, ☎ 33.29.38.37.

Hotels :

● ★★★***Grand Cerf,*** 21, rue St-Blaise (B1), ☎ 33.26.00.51, Tx 170296. AE, DC, Euro, Visa. 33 rm ⚘ ≈ ♿ closed 15 Dec-15 Jan, 220. Rest. ◆◆ Ⓟ ⚘ closed Sun low season, 60-200.

★★***Gare*** (L.F.), 50, av. du Pdt-Wilson (C1), ☎ 33.29.03.93. AE, Euro, Visa. 22 rm Ⓟ ⚘ closed Sun, 23 Dec-7 Jan, 190. Rest. ◆ 40-100.

Arçonnay, 72610 Saint-Paterne, 4 km S on the N 138 :

★***Host. du Château de Maleffre*** (Châteaux-hôtels), ☎ 33.31.82.78. Euro, Visa. 13 rm ⚟ Ⓟ ⚘ ≈ ♿ closed Xmas hols. Castle surrounded by a moat, 240. Table d'hôte, 110.

Saint-Denis-sur-Sarthon, ⊠ 61420, 11 km W :

● ★★***La Faïencerie*** (Châteaux-hôtels), ☎ 33.27.30.16. 18 rm Ⓟ ⚘ ≈ A royal porcelain factory in a 100-acre park. Closed mid-Nov-Easter, 250. Rest. ◆ closed Tue, 75-105.

Youth hostel : 61250 Damigni, 3 km N, ☎ 33.29.00.48 ; annex in Saint-Céneri-le-Gérei, same tel.

⛺ ★★★*Municipal de Guéramé* (75 pl.), ☎ 33.26.34.95.

Restaurant :

◆◆ ***Petit Vatel,*** 72, pl. du Cdt-Desmeulles (B1), ☎ 33.26.23.78. AE, DC, Euro, Visa Ⓟ closed Wed and Sun eve, 15-31 Aug, Feb school hols, 90-200.

Recommended : *Augnet cake and pastry shop,* 39, Grande-Rue, ☎ 33.26.00.47.

Les ANDELYS

Rouen 39, Beauvais 63, Paris 92
D2 ⊠ 27700

ⓘ rue Philippe-Auguste, ☎ 32.54.08.33.

Hotels :

★★***Chaîne d'Or*** (L.F.), 27, rue Grande, ☎ 32.54.00.31. Visa. 12 rm ⚟ Ⓟ ⚘ ≈ ⊘ closed Jan, Sun eve, Mon (summer), 190. Rest. ◆◆ Terrace overlooking the Seine (15 Mar-15 Oct), 60-180.

★***Paris,*** 10, av. de la République, ☎ 32.54.00.33. 8 rm Ⓟ ⚘ ⛱ closed Feb, Christmas and Wed, 120. Rest. ◆ 50-120.

⛺ ★★★*L'Ile des Trois Rois* (100 pl.), ☎ 32.54.23.79.

Bicycle hire : *Cycle Tanton,* rue M.-Lefebvre, ☎ 32.54.26.25.

ARGENTAN

Caen 57, Le Mans 94, Paris 195
C3 ⊠ 61200

ⓘ pl. du Marché, ☎ 33.67.12.48.

SNCF ☎ 33.67.50.50.

Car-hire : *Budget* train + auto, garage du Croissant, bd Carnot, ☎ 33.67.42.19, and at the station, ☎ 33.67.50.50.

Hotels :
● ★★*Renaissance* (L.F.), 20, av. de la 2e-D.B., ☎ 33.67.16.11. AE, DC, Euro, Visa. 14 rm Ⓟ closed Sun, 200. Rest. ◆◆ ***la Renaissance*** and ***la Marmite,*** closed Sun, 100-200.

Fontenai-sur-Orne, 4.5 km SE :
★★***Faisan Doré*** (L.F.), ☎ 33.67.18.11. 20 rm Ⓟ ⚘ ⛱ closed Sun eve, 210. Rest. ◆ ♿ 55-105.

ARROMANCHES-LES-BAINS

Caen 30, Cherbourg 102, Paris 275
B2 ⊠ 14117

ⓘ pl. du Musée (high season), ☎ 31.22.36.45.

Hotels :
★★***Marine*** (L.F.), 1, quai du Canada, ☎ 31.22.34.19. AE, Visa. 22 rm ☼ Ⓟ closed 15 Nov-1 Mar, Wed, Thu, 175. Rest. ◆ 60-150.
★***Normandie,*** 5, pl. du 6-Juin, ☎ 31.22.34.32. Visa. 21 rm ☼ Ⓟ closed early Nov-1 Feb, 105. Rest, 70-120.

AUMALE

Amiens 45, Rouen 71, Paris 124
26 km E of Neufchâtel-en-Bray, D1 ♥ ⊠ 76390

ⓘ mairie, ☎ 35.93.40.50.

Hotels :
★★***Mouton Gras*** (L.F.), 2, rue de Verdun, ☎ 31.93.41.32. AE, DC, Visa. Ⓟ ⚘ ✗ 105. Rest. ◆◆ Regional cooking in a 17thC house, closed Mon eve, Tue, 16 Aug-10 Sep, 60-120.
★***Dauphin,*** 27, rue St-Lazare, ☎ 35.93.41.92. AE, Visa. 10 rm Ⓟ ⛱ closed 15 Dec-28 Jan, 130. Rest. ◆ closed Sun eve and Mon, 50-150.

⛺ ★*Municipal* (60 pl.), ☎ 35.93.40.50.

Bicycle hire : Étang du Marais, Mme Bourdet, ☎ 35.93.42.27.

AVRANCHES

Rennes 75, Caen 101, Paris 342
A3 ⊠ 50300

ⓘ rue Gal-de-Gaulle, ☎ 33.58.00.22.

SNCF ☎ 33.58.00.77 - 33.58.04.14.

Hotels :
● ★★***Croix d'Or,*** 83, rue de la Constitution, ☎ 33.58.04.88. Visa. 30 rm ☼ Ⓟ ⚘ ⛱ ♿ closed mid-Nov-mid-Mar, 300. Rest. ◆◆ 70-200.
★★***Auberge St-Michel,*** 7, pl. Gal-Patton, ☎ 33.58.01.91. Euro, Visa. 22 rm Ⓟ ⚘ closed 23 Nov-4 Jan, Sun eve and Mon, 170. Rest. ◆ Spec : *filets de sole normande, ris de veau aux pâtes fraîches,* 60-160.
★***Bellevue*** (L.F.), 2, pl. Gal-Patton, ☎ 33.58.01.10. Visa. 20 rm Ⓟ ✗ closed Mon and Tue noon, 20 Dec-1 Apr, Oct (ten days). Flowered terrace, 110. Rest. ◆ 40-85.

Pontaubault, 7 km S of Avranches :
● ★★***Motel des Treize Assiettes*** (L.F.), Le Val St-Père, ☎ 33.58.14.03, Tx 170537. Visa. 36 rm Ⓟ ⚘ ⛱ ✗ ♿ closed 15 Nov-15 Mar and Wed low season, 130. Rest. ◆ 45-120.

Youth hostel : Genêts, ⊠ 50530 Sartilly, 10 km W, ☎ 33.58.02.91.

Flight over Le Mont-Saint-Michel : *aéroclub des Greves du Mont-Saint-Michel,* ☎ 33.58.02.91.

BAGNOLES-DE-L'ORNE

Alençon 48, Laval 61, Paris 233
B3 ⊠ 61140

♨ (Apr-Sep).

See also Tessé-la-Madeleine.

ⓘ pl. de la Gare, ☎ 33.37.05.84 (high season).

SNCF ☎ 33.37.14.12 - 33.37.80.04.

Car-hire : *Budget* train + auto, at the S.N.C.F. station, ☎ 33.37.14.12.

Hotels :
● ★★★***Lutetia-Reine Astrid*** (Châteaux-hôtels), bd Paul-Chalvet, ☎ 33.37.94.77. AE, DC, Visa. 34 rm ⚘ ⛱ ♿ closed Nov-Mar, 260. Rest. ◆◆ 90-220.
★★★***Capricorne,*** allée Montjoie, ☎ 33.37.96.99, Tx 170525. AE, DC, Euro, Visa. 24 rm Ⓟ ⚘ ⛱ ✗ closed 1 Nov-1 Apr. Set in a park, 320. Rest. ◆◆ Eve, hotel guests only, 120.
★★***Beaumont*** (L.F.), 26 bd Lemeunier-de-la-Raillère, ☎ 33.37.91.77. Visa. 38 rm Ⓟ ⚘ ⛱ ✗ closed Oct-Apr, 235. Rest. ◆◆ 70-150.
★★***Grand Veneur,*** 6, pl. de la République, ☎ 33.37.86.79. 23 rm Ⓟ ♿ closed Oct-25 Apr. Friendly atmosphere, 220. Rest. ◆ 70-120.

⛺ ★★★*Intercommunal de la Vée* (133 pl.), ☎ 33.37.25.36.

Casino : *du Lac,* 1 May-30 Sep, ☎ 33.37.01.88.

BARNEVILLE-CARTERET

Cherbourg 37, Caen 113, Paris 353
A2 ⊠ 50270

ⓘ Barneville, pl. du Dr-Auvret, ☎ 33.54.90.58 (high season), Carteret, av. de la République, ☎ 33.54.84.80 (high season).

⛴ *Carteret ferry service,* ☎ 33.54.87.21, in summer for the Channel Islands (30 mn for Jersey).

SNCF summer service, Carteret station, ☎ 33.53.81.13.

Hotels :
★★***Marine*** (L.F.), 11, rue de Paris, ☎ 33.53.83.31. DC, Visa. 34 rm ☼ Ⓟ closed 1 Nov-1 Mar, 220. Rest. ◆ closed Mon low season. Regional dishes, 65-225.
★★***Les Isles,*** 7, bd Maritime, ☎ 33.04.90.76. AE, DC, Euro. 35 rm ☼ Ⓟ ⚘ ⛱ 230. Rest. ◆ closed 15 Nov-15 Jan, 70-170.

⛺ ★★*Bocage* (130 pl.), ☎ 33.53.86.91 ; ★★*Bosquets* (240 pl.), ☎ 33.54.73.62.

Guided tour of the Côte des Iles (flood-lit churches and manors) in Jul-Aug. Enq ⓘ

BAYEUX

Caen 27, Cherbourg 92, Paris 268
B2 ⊠ 14400

ⓘ 1, rue des Cuisiniers (B2), ☎ 31.92.16.26.

SNCF (B3), ☎ 31.92.80.50.

🚌 pl. St-Patrice and pl. de la Gare (B1).

Car-hire : *Budget* train + auto, Esso petrol station, bd d'Eindhoven, ☎ 31.92.05.96.

Hotels :

● ★★★***Lion d'Or*** (L.F. ; Relais du Silence), 71, rue St-Jean (C2), ☎ 31.92.06.90. AE, Visa. 30 rm Ⓟ closed 20 Dec-20 Jan. A beautiful big hotel built in 1770, 260. Rest. ● ♦♦ A quiet place in the town centre. Good Normandy region cooking : *andouille chaude à la Bovary, filets de sole homardine, grenadin au Pommeau,* 70-190.

● ★★***Argouges*** (Châteaux-hôtels), 21, rue St-Patrice (B1), ☎ 31.92.88.86. AE, DC, Euro. 2 rm Ⓟ 18thC townhouse, 150.

★★***Le Bayeux,*** 9, rue Tardif, ☎ 31.92.70.08. 30 rm Ⓟ ♿ closed 3 Nov-15 Mar, 230.

★★***Luxembourg*** (L.F.), 25, rue des Bouchers (B2), ☎ 31.92.00.04, Tx 171663. AE, DC, Visa. 31 rm Ⓟ 170. Rest. ♦ 75-250.

Tilly-sur-Seulles, ⊠ 14250, 12 km S :

★***Jeanne-d'Arc*** (L.F.), ☎ 31.80.80.13. 14 rm Ⓟ ♿ closed 1-15 Oct, 1-16 Feb, Mon, Sun eve, 150. Rest. ♦ 60-100.

Audrieu, ⊠ 14250 Tilly, 12 km SE :

★★★★***Château d'Audrieu*** (Relais et châteaux), ☎ 31.80.21.52. Visa. 22 rm Ⓟ ♿ closed 1 Dec-1 Mar and Thu. 18thC Castle and 25 ha park, 880. Rest. ● ♦♦♦ The cooking is up to the setting, 195-300.

Molay-Littry, ⊠ 14330, 14 km W :

★★★***Château du Molay*** (Châteaux-hôtels, Mapotel), rte d'Isigny, ☎ 31.22.90.82. 40 rm Ⓟ ♿ closed 1 Jan-24 Feb. 18thC mansion, 18 ha park, 470. Rest. ♦♦♦ Regional dishes, refined cooking, 120-220.

Youth hostel : rue des Cordeliers.

⛺ ★★★*Municipal* (150 pl.), ☎ 31.92.08.43.

Event : 14 Jul-31 Aug, *Bayeux Folklore Festival.*

Guided tours : the old town in summer, accompanied by C.N.M.H.S. guides. Enq ℹ

Bicycle hire : *Family Home,* 39, rue Gal-de-Dais, ☎ 31.92.15.22.

BEAUMONT-LE-ROGER

Rouen 51, Caen 96, Paris 134
13 km SW of Neubourg, D2 ⊠ 27170

ℹ mairie, ☎ 32.44.23.88.

SNCF ☎ 32.45.21.03.

Hotel :

● ★★***Lion d'Or,*** 91, rue St-Nicolas, ☎ 32.45.48.08. AE, Visa. 10 rm Ⓟ closed 19 Dec-11 Jan, 29 Jul-10 Aug, Mon eve and Tue, 140. Rest. ♦ 60-90.

Restaurant :

♦♦ ***Paris sur Risle,*** rue St-Nicolas, ☎ 32.45.22.23. Visa. Ⓟ ♿ closed Sun eve, Mon, Thu eve, Fri, Aug, 1 week Sep, 20 Dec-10 Jan. Spec : *ris de veau aux morilles, canard au cidre, lotte aux poireaux,* 65-150.

BELLÊME

Alençon 41, Chartres 75, Paris 168
C4 ⊠ 61130

ℹ hôtel de ville, ☎ 33.73.02.21.

Hotel :

★***Boule d'Or,*** pl. du Gal-Leclerc, ☎ 33.73.10.32. Visa. 9 rm Ⓟ closed Mon, 55. Rest. ♦ 45-70.

⛺ ★★*Municipal* (25 pl.), ☎ 33.73.02.21.

Event : end Sep, *Mycology Days.*

Handicraft courses : wicker- and cane-work, weaving, theatre ; enq *Centre d'initiation à l'artisanat d'art.* Le Porche, rue Ville-Close, ☎ 33.33.12.53.

BERNAY

Rouen 58, Alençon 87, Paris 160
C2 ⊠ 27300

ℹ ☎ 32.43.32.08.

SNCF ☎ 32.43.01.25 - 32.43.17.11.

Hotel :

★***Angleterre*** (L.F.), 10 rue Gal-de-Gaulle, ☎ 32.43.12.59. AE, DC, Euro, Visa. 23 rm Ⓟ 120. Rest. ♦ ♿ *Truite cheval blanc,* 75-200.

⛺ ★★★*Municipal* (83 pl.), ☎ 32.43.30.47.

Restaurant :

♦♦ ***Trois Vals,*** rte de Rouen, ☎ 32.43.21.54. Euro, Visa, closed 16 Aug-10 Sep, Tue eve and Wed, 90-140.

BEUZEVILLE

Deauville 24, Rouen 66, Paris 184
C2 ⊠ 27210

ℹ mairie, ☎ 32.57.72.10.

Hotel :

Corneilles, ⊠ 27260, 12 kms :

● ★***Auberge du Président,*** 70, rue de l'Abbaye, ☎ 32.57.80.37. 14 rm 95. Rest. ♦♦ ♿ Spec. : *sole farcie, hermitage, omelette aux giroles,* 50-150.

Event : mid-Aug : *concerts at St-Hélier Church.*

BLONVILLE-SUR-MER

Lisieux 32, Caen 38, Paris 212
4 km SW of Deauville, C2 ⊠ 14910

ℹ allée des Villas, ☎ 31.87.91.15 (high season).

SNCF ☎ 31.87.92.24.

Hotels :

★★★***Grand Hôtel,*** ☎ 31.87.90.54, Tx 170385. AE, DC, Visa. 23 rm Ⓟ ♿ Direct access to the beach, closed 15 Nov-15 Dec, 2 Jan-15 Feb, Wed eve and Thu, 580. Rest. ♦♦ ***la Brocherie.*** closed Wed eve, Mon, Tue noon and Thu, 95-230.

★★***Mer*** (L.F.), 93, av. de la République, ☎ 31.87.93.23. 20 rm Ⓟ ♿ closed 1 Oct-1 Apr, 200.

⛺ ★★*Blonville Camping* (400 pl.), ☎ 31.87.92.46 ; ★★★*Lieu Bill* (100 pl.), ☎ 31.87.97.27.

BRETEUIL-SUR-ITON

Évreux 32, Alençon 86, Paris 127
11 km N of Verneuil-sur-Avre, C-D3 ⊠ 27160

ℹ mairie, ☎ 32.32.82.45.

Hotels :

★★★***Le Mail*** (Relais du Silence, Châteaux-hôtels), rue Neuve-de-Bémecourt, ☎ 32.29.81.54. Euro, Visa. 13 rm Ⓟ ♿ closed Sun eve to Tue (15 Nov-30 Mar), 400. Rest. ♦♦ Spec : *boudin blanc d'écrevisse, ris de veau aux 3 épices et raisins de Corinthe,* 125-220.

★***Lion d'Or*** (L.F.), 66, rue G.-Clemenceau, ☎ 32.29.81.09. Visa. 14 rm Ⓟ 135. Rest. ♦ closed Sun eve and Mon low season. Spec ; *truite à la normande, mousse au chocolat,* 50-100.

⛺ ★★*Camp fleuri* (33 pl.), ☎ 32.32.76.99.

Normandy

BRICQUEBEC

Cherbourg 22, Saint-Lô 69, Paris 353
A2 ☒ 50260

Hotel :
● ★★***Vieux Château*** (L.F. ; Châteaux-hôtels), 4, cours du Château, ☎ 33.52.24.49. Euro, Visa. 22 rm 🅿 closed 20 Dec-1 Feb. Mediaeval residence with a 14thC keep, 220. Rest. ♦♦ Spec : *moules au fumet, rognons de veau au cidre,* 50-125.

BRIONNE

Rouen 43, Caen 88, Paris 145
C2 ☒ 27800

ℹ pl. de l'Église, ☎ 32.40.80.37 (1 Jul-1 Sep).

SNCF ☎ 32.44.80.22.

Hotels :
★★***Logis de Brionne*** (L.F.), 1, pl. Saint-Denis, ☎ 32.44.81.73. Euro, Visa. 17 rm 🅿 closed 22 Dec-21 Jan, Sun eve and Mon noon, low season Mon and Fri eve, 160. Rest. ♦ 60-150.

La Rivière-Thibouville, ☒ 27550, 6 km S :
● ★★***Soleil d'Or*** (L.F.), Grande-Rue, ☎ 32.45.00.08. Euro, Visa. 12 rm 🅿 ♿ closed Wed, 25 Jan-10 Mar, 240. Rest. ♦♦ Spec : *truite Soleil d'Or,* 60-190.

CABOURG

Deauville 20, Caen 24, Paris 225
B2 ☒ 14390

ℹ Jardins du Casino, ☎ 31.91.01.09.

SNCF gare de Dives-Cabourg, ☎ 31.91.00.74.

Hotels :
★★★★★***Grand Hôtel P.L.M.,*** prom. Jardins-du-Casino, ☎ 31.91.01.79, Tx 171364. AE, DC, Visa. 70 rm over the sea 🅿 650. Rest. ♦♦♦ 130-200.

★★***Paris,*** 39, av. de la Mer, ☎ 31.91.31.34. Visa. 23 rm, 175.

⛺ ★★★*Camping Plage* (283 pl.), ☎ 31.91.05.75 ; ★★★*la Prairie* (433 pl.), ☎ 31.91.03.05 ; ★★★*Vert Pré* (350 pl.), ☎ 31.91.41.68.

Events : Jul, *regatta of the thousand sails ;* mid-Aug, *antique salon ;* end Aug, *festival of William the Conqueror, procession of floats.*

Casino, ☎ 31.91.11.75.

CAEN

Cherbourg 120, Le Mans 151, Paris 240
B2 ☒ 14000

ℹ pl. St-Pierre (D2), ☎ 31.86.27.65.

✈ Caen-Carpiquet, 6 km W, ☎ 31.73.18.00. *Air France Agency,* 143, rue St-Jean, ☎ 31.85.41.26.

SNCF (E3), ☎ 31.83.50.50.

🚌 (E3).

Car-hire : *Budget* train + auto, S.N.C.F. station, ☎ 31.83.70.47 and 31.83.40.00, and Caen-Carpiquet airport.

Hotels :
★★★★***Relais des Gourmets,*** 15, rue de Geôle (C2), ☎ 31.86.06.01, Tx 171657. AE, DC, Euro, Visa. 32 rm 🅿 ♿ 260. Rest. ♦ ♿ ***l'Escale.*** closed Sun eve. Spec : seafood, 130-180.

★★★***Moderne*** (Mapotel), 116, bd Gal-Leclerc (C2), ☎ 31.86.04.23, Tx 171106. AE, DC, Euro, Visa. 56 rm 🅿 ♿ 340. Rest. ● ♦♦ ***les Quatre Vents.*** closed Sun eve from 25 Oct to 31 Mar. Spec : *brochette de lotte au pistil de safran et grains de caviar, noisette d'agneau au miel et petits légumes,* 75-180.

★★★***Dauphin,*** 29, rue Gémare, ☎ 31.86.22.26 🅿 closed 15 Jul-13 Aug, 300. Rest. ● ♦♦♦ Light and simple cooking of Robert Chabredier : *ris de veau aux pommes, huîtres frémies au beurre rouge,* 200-300.

★★***Rotonde*** (L.F.), pl. de la Gare (E3), ☎ 31.82.24.25. AE, DC, Euro, Visa. 33 rm closed 20 Dec-3 Jan, 165. Rest. ♦ closed Sat noon and Sun eve, 45-80.

⛺ ★★*Municipal* (133 pl.), ☎ 31.73.60.92.

Restaurants :
● ♦♦♦ ***Échevins,*** 36, rue Écuyère (C2), ☎ 31.86.37.44 ♿ closed 29 Jun-15 Jul, Sun and Mon noon. Two types of cooking ; the rich and traditional one : *saucisson de canard aux lentilles ;* the lighter one : *millefeuille de saumon au cerfeuil, St-Jacques aux endives,* 130-250.

● ♦♦ ***Bourride,*** 15-17, rue du Vaugueux, ☎ 31.93.50.76. AE, DC, Visa. closed 16-31 Aug, 5-21 Jan, Sun, Mon. Mr Bruneau proposes a small number of spec's carefully chosen : raw fish, *papillote de truffes,* 150-350.

♦♦ ***Alcide,*** 1, pl. Courtonne (D2), ☎ 31.93.58.29. closed Jul and Sat, 50-90.

Bénouville, ☒ 14970, 8 km NE :
● ♦♦♦ ***Manoir d'Hastings*** (Claude Scaviner), av. de la Côte-de-Nacre, ☎ 31.44.63.14 and 31.44.62.43 🅿 closed 1-15 Feb, 1-15 Oct, Sun eve and Mon. A beautiful place near "Pegasus bridge" the famous Second World War site, where Claude Scaviner, prepares light Normand cooking of great quality : *jambon et blanquette de pommes de terre, filet de rouget barbet en civet de bigorneaux.* Home and regional produce shop, 200-350.

Visit of the town : C.N.M.H.S. guides and lecturers ; enq ℹ

Events : Mar : *spring fair.* Jun : *antique salon.* Sep : *Caen fair ; horse races.*

Recommended : *Boutique du Manoir* (see rest. above) : take-away dishes, wide choice of Normandy produce.

CARENTAN

Cherbourg 50, Caen 70, Paris 310
A2 ☒ 50500

ℹ pl. Valnoble, ☎ 33.42.05.87 (high season).

SNCF ☎ 33.42.04.00.

Car-hire : *Budget* train + auto, at the S.N.C.F. station, ☎ 33.42.04.00.

Hotels :
● ★***Auberge Normande*** (L.F.), bd de Verdun, ☎ 33.42.02.99. AE, DC, Visa. 8 rm ♿ closed 10-25 Oct, 15 Jan-1 Feb, Sun eve and Mon, 100. Rest. ♦ Spec : *jambonnette de canard au cidre,* 60-175.

★***Commerce et Gare,*** 28, rue du Dr-Caillard, ☎ 33.42.02.00. AE, DC, Euro, Visa. 16 rm 🅿 closed 1-10 Oct, 22 Dec-22 Jan, Sun eve and Fri in winter, 155. Rest. ♦♦ 60-155.

⛺ ★★★*Haut Dick* (104 pl.), ☎ 33.42.16.89.

CARROUGES

Alençon 29, Laval 59, Paris 210
B3 ☒ 61320

ℹ hôtel de ville, ☎ 33.27.20.38/33.27.20.49.

Hotel :
★*St-Pierre* (L.F.), pl. de la Mairie, ☎ 33.27.20.02. Visa. 7 rm Ⓟ closed Christmas week, Feb, 23-30 Jun, 115. Rest. ♦ closed Tue eve and Wed. Prizewinner for regional cooking in 1984 for : *saumon poché à l'oseille, gâteau St-Pierre,* 60-120.

CAUDEBEC-EN-CAUX

Rouen 36, Le Havre 49, Paris 167
C2 ♥ ✉ 76490

ⓘ mairie, ☎ 35.96.11.12.

Hotels :
★★★*La Marine,* 18, quai Guilbaud, ☎ 35.96.20.11. 33 rm ♿ 240.
★★★*Manoir de Rétival,* rue St-Clair, ☎ 35.96.11.22. AE, DC. 12 rm Ⓟ ♿ closed Oct-Mar, 350.
★★*Normandie* (L.F.), 19, quai Guilbaud, ☎ 35.96.25.11. AE, Visa. 15 rm Ⓟ closed Feb, 150. Rest. ♦♦ closed Sun eve, 50-130.

Event : last week-end in Sep or 1st week-end in Oct, *cider festival.*

Bicycle hire : *Cycles Joël Soudais,* rue de la Vicomté, ☎ 35.96.24.77.

CERISY-LA-SALLE

Saint-Lô 20, Granville 38, Paris 323
A2 ✉ 50210

ⓘ mairie of N.-D.-de-Cenilly, ☎ 33.46.92.10.

Hotel :
Montpinchon, 1.5 km SW :
● ★★★*Hostellerie du Château de la Salle* (Relais et châteaux), ☎ 33.46.95.19. AE, DC, Visa. 10 rm Ⓟ closed 4 Nov-21 Mar, 400. Rest. ● ♦♦ closed 3 Nov-27 Mar. An authentic old residence, for comfort, relaxation, and all the refined pleasures of the gastronomical arts. Spec : *petits filets de nos prairies.* Good value, 110-250.

CHERBOURG

Caen 120, Rennes 210, Paris 360
A1 ✉ 50100

ⓘ 2, quai Alexandre-III (B2-3), ☎ 33.43.52.02.

✈ Maupertus, 12 km E, ☎ 33.53.57.04.

⛴ Ferry terminal (C1). *Townsend Thoresen,* ☎ 33.44.20.13, all year round for Portsmouth (Great Britain). *Sealink,* ☎ 33.53.24.27. Apr-Oct for Weymouth (Great Britain). *Irish Continental Line,* ☎ 33.44.28.96, Apr-Sep for Rosslare (Ireland). *Carteret Ferry Service,* ☎ 33.54.87.21, in Carteret, in summer for Guernesey.

SNCF (B4), ☎ 33.53.54.70, 33.44.31.11, 33.20.47.73.

🚌 (B3).

Car-hire : *Budget* train + auto, at the S.N.C.F. station, ☎ 33.20.34.57 and 33.44.31.11.

Hotels :
★★*Louvre,* 2, rue Henri-Dunant (B1), 33.53.02.28, Tx 171132. Visa. 42 rm Ⓟ ♿ 240.
★*Moderna,* 28, rue de la Marine (B2), ☎ 33.43.05.30. 24 rm 160.

Youth hostel : Social and cultural centre, 109, av. de Paris, ☎ 33.44.26.31.

Restaurants :
♦♦ *Vauban,* 22, quai Caligny (B2), ☎ 33.43.14.17. AE, Visa. ♿ closed all saints'day and nat hols. 50-130.

♦ *Le Plouc* (Chez Pain), 59, rue Au-Blé, ☎ 33.53.67.64. Euro, Visa ♿ closed Sat noon and Sun. Good cooking in a charming atmosphere, 100-150.

Events : May : *gastronomical competitions, international regattas.*

CLÉCY

Flers 21, Caen 37, Paris 246
B3 ✉ 14570

ⓘ mairie, ☎ 31.68.72.84.

Hotels :
★★★*Hôtellerie du Moulin du Vey* (Châteaux-hôtels), ☎ 31.69.71.08. AE, DC, Visa. 19 rm Ⓟ closed 1-24 Dec, Fri (15 Nov-1 Apr), 230. Rest. ♦♦♦ closed Fri (Winter). Spec : *langouste grillée, terrine d'anguille sauce aux câpres,* 100-230.
★★*Site Normand* (L.F.), rue Notre-Dame, ☎ 31.69.71.05. AE, DC. 12 rm Ⓟ closed 15 Jan-1 Mar and Mon low season, 180. Rest. ♦ 70-160.
Pont-d'Ouilly, ✉ 14690, 12 km SE :
● ★★*Auberge Saint-Christophe,* (L.F.), 2 km N by D23 (L.F.), ☎ 31.69.81.23. AE, Euro, Visa. 7 rm Ⓟ closed 2-18 Feb, 6-25 Oct, Sun eve and Mon low season, 180. Rest. ♦♦ 70-150.
★★*Commerce* (L.F.), rue de Falaise, ☎ 31.69.80.16. 16 rm Ⓟ closed 10 Oct-31 May, Sun eve and Mon, 110. Rest. 50-120.

⛺ ★★*Moulin du Vey* (100 pl.), ☎ 31.69.71.47.

Horse hire : *l'Étrier de la Suisse normande,* La Lande, 3 km S, ☎ 31.69.70.06.

CONCHES-EN-OUCHE

Évreux 18, Rouen 60, Paris 120
D3 ✉ 27190

ⓘ mairie, ☎ 32.30.20.41.

SNCF ☎ 32.30.23.17.

Hotel :
★*Grand'Mare* (L.F.), 13, rue Croix-de-Fer, ☎ 32.30.23.30. Visa. 12 rm Ⓟ closed 15 Jan-15 Feb, Mon noon and Tue low season, 120. Rest. ♦ 60-140.

COURSEULLES-SUR-MER

Caen 18, Saint-Lô 55, Paris 262
B2 ✉ 14470

ⓘ 54, rue de la Mer, ☎ 31.97.46.80 (high season).

Hotel :
★★*Belle Aurore* (L.F.), ☎ 31.37.46.23. AE, DC, Visa. 8 rm Ⓟ closed Mon, 3 Jan-1 Feb, 150. Rest. ♦♦ ♿ 65-140.

⛺ ★★★★*Champ de Course* (291 pl.), ☎ 31.97.99.26.

Restaurant :
♦♦♦ *Pêcherie,* 6, pl. du 6-Juin, ☎ 31.37.45.85. AE, DC, Visa ♿ Seafood, 50-200.

Horse hire : *Club hippique des Trois Vallées,* av. Libération, ☎ 31.97.82.04.

Bicycle hire : *garage du Port,* rue Mal-Foch, ☎ 31.97.97.21.

COUTAINVILLE-PLAGE

Granville 34, Saint-Lô 40, Paris 343
A2 ✉ 50230 Agon-Coutainville

ⓘ pl. du 28-Juillet-1944, ☎ 33.47.01.46 (high season).

Hotels :
★★★***Neptune,*** promenoir Jersey, ☎ 33.47.07.66. AE, DC. 11 rm ⚘ ♿ closed 3 Nov-15 Mar, 250.
● ★★***Hardy*** (L.F.), pl. du 28-Juillet-1944, ☎ 33.47.04.11. AE, DC, Euro, Visa. 13 rm closed 6 Jan-8 Feb and Mon, 180. Rest. ♦♦ ♿ Spec : seafood, 70-220.

COUTANCES

Saint-Lô 27, Avranches 47, Paris 330
A2 ✉ 50200

ℹ Les Unelles, ☎ 33.45.17.79.

SNCF ☎ 33.45.17.54.

Hotels :
★★***Grand Hôtel*** (L.F.), pl. de la Gare, ☎ 33.45.06.55. Visa. 28 rm Ⓟ 200. Rest. ♦ closed Christmas and Sun (winter), 60-150.

Trelly, ✉ 50660 Quetreville sur Sienne :
● ★★***Verte Campagne,*** at the Chevalier hamlet (1.5 km on the D539), ☎ 33.47.65.33. Visa. 8 rm ♿ closed 15 Nov-15 Dec, 15 days in Feb, Sun eve and Mon low season. 18thC farm, 200. Rest. ♦♦♦ 105-160.

Guided tours : C.N.M.H.S. from 3 Jul to 5 Sep at the cathedral (ex Sat and Sun morning).

DEAUVILLE

Caen 43, Le Havre 75, Paris 207
C2 ✉ 14800

ℹ pl. de la Mairie (B3), ☎ 31.68.21.43 (closed Sun low season).

✈ Deauville-Saint-Gatien, 7 km E, ☎ 31.88.31.28.

SNCF (C3), ☎ 31.83.50.50, 31.88.28.80, 31.88.50.48.

Car-hire : *Budget* train + auto, at the S.N.C.F. station, ☎ 31.88.28.80.

Hotels :
● ★★★★(L) ***Royal,*** bd Cornuché (A3), ☎ 31.88.16.41, Tx 170549. AE, DC, Euro, Visa. 303 rm ⚘ Ⓟ ♿ closed Oct-Apr, 1 280. Rest. ● ♦♦♦ Simple good cooking by the talented and imaginative P. Moraine : *petite nage de langoustines au citron vert, andouillette de saint-pierre beurre rouge moutarde, rognon de veau au gingembre,* 170-220.
★★★★(L) ***Normandy,*** 38, rue Jean-Mermoz (A3), ☎ 31.88.09.21, Tx 170617. 300 rm ⚘ ♿ 1 150. Rest. ♦♦♦ closed 2 Jan-14 Feb, 170-220.
★★★***Golf,*** Mont Canisy, 3 km S, ☎ 31.88.19.01, Tx 170448. AE, DC, Euro, Visa. 165 rm ⚘ Ⓟ closed 30 Sep-30 Apr, 500. Rest. ♦♦ Nice cooking in the golfers' paradise, 145-170.
★★***Continental,*** 1, rue Désiré-Le Hoc (B3), ☎ 31.88.21.06. AE, DC, Visa. 49 rm Ⓟ ♿ closed 15 Nov-15 Mar, 210.
★★***Nid d'Été*** (L.F.), 121, av. République (A4), ☎ 31.88.36.67. AE, DC, Euro, Visa. 24 rm ♿ closed Dec-mid-Feb, Sun eve and Mon low season, 220. Rest. ♦♦ 55-120.
★★***Patio,*** 180, av. de la République (A4), ☎ 31.88.25.07. 11 rm ♿ 200.
★★***Saratoga,*** 1, av. du Gal-de-Gaulle, ☎ 31.88.24.33. 8 rm closed 3 Jan-3 Feb, 165. Rest. ♦♦ closed Mon eve, Tue in low season. Excellent market produce cooking by Linda Lorasse : *daurade de saumon aux épinards, aiguillettes de canard aux pommes,* 105-205.

Tourgéville, 4 km :
★★★★(L), ***Club 13,*** chemin de l'Orgueil, ☎ 31.88.63.40, Tx 171189. AE, Visa. 25 rm Ⓟ ♿ closed 1 Jan-1 Mar. G.-L. Dubouchereon's Normandy countryside, 750. Rest. ♦♦♦ ♿ 60-200.

Canapville, 6 km SE :
★★***Hostellerie de l'Aubergeade*** (L.F.), ☎ 31.64.15.63. Visa. 13 rm Ⓟ ♿ 225. Rest. ♦ closed 15 Nov-Easter and Wed low season, 60-170.

⛺ ★★★*Clairefontaine,* Tourgéville, 5 km S (260 pl.), ☎ 31.88.14.06.

Restaurants :
● ♦♦ ***Ciro's,*** prom. des Planches (A3), ☎ 31.88.18.10. AE, DC, Euro, Visa ⚘ Ⓟ closed eve Sep-Jun. C. Girault manages this fashionable meeting place on the "Planches" : shell-fish, seafood, fresh fish and grilled meat. Selected wines, 135-210.

Saint-Gatien, ✉ 14130 Pont l'Évêque, 7 km E :
● ♦♦♦ ***Restaurant de l'Aéroport,*** ☎ 31.88.38.75. Ⓟ closed Tue eve and Wed and end Dec-end Jan. An aeroclub atmosphere in front of a fire place, where fish is king : *st-pierre aux cèpes, turbot au champagne,* 80-220.

See also Trouville.

Events : Jul : *world bridge festival ; international dog show, horse races and polo.* End Aug : *yearling sales.* Sep : *Festival of American Cinema.* Oct : *Paris-Deauville vintage car rally.*

Casino : rue E.-Blanc, ☎ 31.88.29.55. ♦♦ ***Les Ambassadeurs.- Grill-room*** Ⓟ closed 16 Sep-15 Mar (ex w-e). Banco ! Let's start the party, the green carpet is nearby. You have to break the bank first as the prices are high for this light cooking : caviar, salmon, *foie gras,* champagne. If you have not made a "hit", the grill is a quieter place, 200-305. *Casino d'hiver,* 93, rue E.-Nicolas, ☎ 31.88.29.91. Rest. ***la Malibran,*** closed 15 Mar-15 Sep.

Boat hire : at the port, ☎ 31.88.67.32.

DIEPPE

Rouen 61, Le Havre 105, Paris 200
D1 ✉ 76200

ℹ bd Gal-de-Gaulle (B3), ☎ 35.84.11.77.

⛴ ferry terminal, quai Henri-IV (B2). *Sealink,* for Newhaven (Great Britain) all year round, ☎ 35.82.24.87.

SNCF (B2), ☎ 35.84.20.71, 35.84.15.00, 35.84.28.92.

Car hire : *Budget* train + auto, at the S.N.C.F. station, ☎ 35.84.28.92.

Hotels :
★★★***Présidence,*** bd de Verdun (B2), ☎ 35.84.31.31, Tx 180865. AE, DC, Euro, Visa. 89 rm ⚘ Ⓟ ♿ 310. Rest. ♦♦ Spec : *ris de veau braisé, pot-au-feu en croûte* (autumn, winter), 150-180.
★★★***Aguado,*** 30, bd de Verdun (B2), ☎ 35.84.27.00. 56 rm ⚘ ♿ 300.
★★***Relais Gambetta*** (L.F.), 95, av. Gambetta (A3), ☎ 35.84.12.91. AE, DC, Visa. 10 rm Ⓟ closed Oct, 160. Rest. ♦ closed Mon eve and Tue low season, 60-160.

Youth hostel : rue L.-Fromager-Janval, Saint-Aubin-sur-Scie, 2 km, ☎ 35.84.85.73.

⛺ ★★*Pré St-Nicolas* (165 pl.), ☎ 35.84.11.39.

Restaurants :
♦♦ ***Marmite Dieppoise,*** 8, rue St-Jean (B2), ☎ 35.84.24.26. Visa, Euro. closed 22 Jun-6 Jul, 21 Dec-4 Jan, Sun eve, Mon and Thu eve. Spec : *marmite dieppoise, choucroute du pêcheur,* 60-140.
♦ ***Sully,*** 97, quai Henri-IV (B2), ☎ 35.84.23.13. Euro. closed 15 Nov-15 Dec, Tue eve and Wed, 50-120.

Events : 15 Aug : *fête des mitouries ("mid August festival"), carnival.* Nov : *herring fair.*

Casino : 3, bd de Verdun, ☎ 35.82.33.60.

Recommended : *Ratel,* chocolates and sweets, 115, Grande-Rue, ☎ 35.84.22.75.

DIVES-SUR-MER

Caen 25, Deauville 19, Paris 224
B2 ⊠ 14160

SNCF Dives-Cabourg station, ☎ 35.91.00.74.

⛺ ★★*Tilleuls* (266 pl.), ☎ 31.91.25.21.

Restaurants :
♦♦ ***Guillaume le Conquérant,*** 2, rue Hastings, ☎ 31.91.07.26. AE, DC, Euro, Visa closed 15-30 Nov, Tue eve and Wed ex Jul-Aug and nat hols. 17thC half-timbered post-house. Fish specialities, 110-250.

Beuvron-en-Auge, ⊠ 14430, 13 km S :
● ♦♦ ***Paré d'Auge,*** ☎ 31.79.26.71. AE, Visa. closed Mon eve, Tue eve, Wed eve. Mme Engel is a sincere and competent cook. Varied cooking : *terrine de poissons, turbot au vinaigre de cidre,* 80-160.

Bicycle hire : S.N.C.F. station, train + vélo, ☎ 31.91.00.74.

DOMFRONT

Laval 60, Alençon 61, Paris 252
B3 ⊠ 61700

ℹ rue Fossés-Plissons, ☎ 33.38.53.27 (high season).

SNCF ☎ 33.38.65.10.

Hotel :
★★***Poste*** (L.F.), 15, rue Foch, ☎ 33.38.51.00. AE, DC, Euro. 29 rm Ⓟ closed 15 Jan-25 Feb, Sun eve and Mon low season, 170. Rest. ♦ closed Mon, 60-160.

Farmhouse gîtes and chambres d'hôtes : Jumèges, 7.5 km S on the D982 and D143, le Cornihout, ☎ 33.91.84.07. Farm produce for sale.

Event : Jul : *international folk festival.*

DUCLAIR

Rouen 20, Le Havre 65, Paris 160
C-D2 ⊠ 76480

ℹ hôtel de ville, ☎ 35.37.50.06.

Hotel :
★★***Poste*** (L.F.), ☎ 35.37.50.04. AE, Euro, Visa. 20 rm closed 2-24 Feb, 1-15 Jul, school hols, Nov and Sun eve, 150. Rest. ♦♦ closed Sun eve and Mon, 50-150.

Restaurant :
● ♦♦♦ ***Le Parc,*** 721, av. Pdt-Coty, ☎ 35.37.50.31. AE, DC, Euro, Visa Ⓟ closed Sun eve and 15 Dec-15-Jan. First class classical cuisine in a calm, pleasant setting on the banks of the Seine. Spec : *sabayon d'huîtres tièdes, filet de sole aux concombres, canard aux croquettes de camembert,* 65-200.

ELBEUF

Rouen 20, Caen 116, Paris 130
D2 ⊠ 76500

ℹ Chambre de Commerce, 28, rue Henry, ☎ 35.77.02.16/35.77.03.78.

SNCF ☎ 35.81.02.52.

Hotel :
★***Nouvel Hôtel,*** 13, rue J.-Jaurès, ☎ 35.81.01.02. 17 rm Ⓟ closed 9-19 May, Aug, Sun and nat hols, 125.

Restaurant :
♦ ***Naudin,*** 1, rue du Mal-Gallieni, ☎ 35.77.06.94. Visa, closed Sat eve, Sun, Feb school hols, 1-25 Aug. Old-fashioned bistro, pleasant service, 90-140.

ÉTRETAT

Le Havre 28, Rouen 86, Paris 218
C1 ⊠ 76790

ℹ pl. de la Mairie, ☎ 35.27.05.21 (high season).

SNCF ☎ 35.43.50.50.

Hotels :
★★★***Dormy House Golf Hotel,*** rte du Havre, ☎ 35.27.07.88. 27 rm Ⓟ closed 5 Nov-Mar, 300. Rest. ♦♦ 100-150.
★★***Falaises,*** bd René-Coty, ☎ 35.27.02.77. 24 rm 190.
★★***Welcome,*** 10, av. de Verdun, ☎ 35.27.00.89. Visa. 21 rm Ⓟ closed Feb and Wed, 220. Rest. ♦♦ 70-150.
Donjon (Châteaux-hôtels), chemin St-Clair, ☎ 35.27.08.23. 7 rm Ⓟ 260. Rest. ♦♦ closed Wed. Spec : seafood, *canard au sang,* 90-180.

Ecrainville, ⊠ 76110, 13 km SE on the D39 and D139 :
Château de Diane (Châteaux-hôtels), ☎ 35.27.76.02 and 35.42.64.19. 22 rm Ⓟ closed Tue, Wed and Thu ex Aug and Sep, 350-500.

⛺ ★★★*Municipal* (120 pl.), ☎ 35.27.07.67.

Restaurants :
♦♦ ***Aiguille Creuse,*** pl. Gal-de-Gaulle, ☎ 35.27.04.21 Ⓟ closed Dec, Feb, Tue low season, 100-200. With 7 rm, 155.
♦ ***Roches Blanches,*** terrasse Eugène-Boudin, ☎ 35.27.07.34. Euro, Visa closed 6 Jan-5 Feb, 29 Sep-23 Oct, Tue, Wed and Thu low season, 60-140.

Event : May, *grand Normandy festival.*

Casino : ☎ 35.27.00.54.

Bicycle hire : *Total petrol station,* av. George-V, ☎ 35.27.03.47.

EU

Dieppe 31, Rouen 92, Paris 165
D1 ⊠ 76260

ℹ 41, rue Paul-Bignon, ☎ 35.86.04.68.

Hotels :
★★★***Pavillon de Joinville*** (Relais du Silence), rte du Tréport, ☎ 35.86.24.03. Euro, Visa. 20 rm Ⓟ 340. Rest. ♦♦ ***la Ferme Modèle,*** ☎ 35.50.01.44, 100-240.
★★***Relais*** (L.F.), 1, pl. Albert-Ier, ☎ 35.86.14.88. 14 rm Ⓟ closed 26 Aug-16 Sep, 1-15 Feb, 210. Rest. ♦♦ closed Feb, Sun eve and Mon, 50-100.

⛺ ★★★*Municipal* (70 pl.), ☎ 35.86.20.04.

Bicycle hire : *Cycles Régnier,* 133, chaussée de Picardie, ☎ 35.86.20.99.

ÉVREUX

Rouen 55, Le Mans 153, Paris 103
D2 ⊠ 27000

ℹ rue du Dr-Oursel (B1), ☎ 32.38.21.61.

SNCF (B3), ☎ 32.38.50.50, 32.38.53.33.

Car-hire : *Budget* train + auto, at the S.N.C.F. station, ☎ 32.33.22.75.

Hotels :
★★★**Normandy,** 37, rue Ed.-Feray (C1), ☎ 32.33.14.40. AE, DC, Visa. 27 rm 🅿 270. Rest. ♦♦ closed Sun and Aug. Spec : *ragoût de lotte, soufflé chaud au Grand Marnier,* 110-200.
● ★★**France** (L.F.), 29, rue St-Thomas (B1), ☎ 32.39.09.25. DC, Visa. 14 rm 🅿 closed Mon, 195. Rest. ♦♦ Spec : *terrine des 4 saisons et son coulis de tomate au Xérès, côtelettes de lapereau sauce périgourdine avec croquettes de salsifis,* 120-260.

⛺ ★★*Municipal* (100 pl.), ☎ 32.39.43.59.

Event : 6 Dec, *St-Nicolas fair.*

Bicycle hire : *Cycles Martin,* rue Gal-Leclerc, ☎ 32.39.17.08.

FALAISE

Caen 34, Alençon 67, Paris 216
B3 ✉ 14700

ℹ 32, rue G.-Clemenceau, ☎ 31.90.17.26.

Gare routière, ☎ 31.86.55.30.

Hotel :
★★**Normandie,** 4, rue Amiral-Courbet, ☎ 31.90.18.26. 28 rm, 180. Rest. ♦ closed Sun, 50-110.

⛺ ★★★★*du Château* (66 pl.), ☎ 31.90.16.55.

Restaurant :
♦ **La Fine Fourchette,** 52, rue G.-Clemenceau, ☎ 31.90.08.59. Euro, Visa 🅿 ♿ closed 1-15 Feb, Tue eve and Wed eve. Fish specialities, 60-155.

Bicycle hire : ℹ

Recommended : *distillery Rambert,* "Guillaume de Normandie" calvados, ☎ 31.90.13.33.

FÉCAMP

Le Havre 40, Rouen 71, Paris 214
C1 ✉ 76400

ℹ sea-front (A1), ☎ 35.29.16.34, and pl. Bellet (B2), ☎ 35.28.20.51.

SNCF (B2), ☎ 35.28.03.11.

Hotels :
★★**Angleterre,** 91 à 95, rue de la Plage (A1), ☎ 35.28.01.60. AE, DC, Visa. 30 rm 🅿 closed 20 Nov-27 Dec, 200.
★**Martin,** 18, pl. Saint-Étienne (B2), ☎ 35.28.23.82. Euro, Visa. 7 rm closed 15 Feb-3 Mar, Sun eve and Mon, 110. Rest. ♦ Spec : *morue fraîche au cidre,* 60-120.

Youth hostel : rte du Cd-Rocquigny, côte de la Vierge, ☎ 35.72.06.45, and 13, rue de l'Inondation (in summer).

⛺ ★★*Renéville* (350 pl.), ☎ 35.28.20.97.

Restaurant :
♦♦ **Maritime,** 2, pl. Nicolas-Selles (B2), ☎ 35.28.21.71. AE, DC, Euro, Visa. Grills and seafood in a marine setting, 70-160.

Events : Jun : *Trinity festival, Pilgrimage of His Precious Blood.* Jul : *sea festival ; music festival* at the Benedictine abbey.

Bicycle hire : *Folliot Sports,* arcades du Théâtre, ☎ 35.28.45.09.

La FERTÉ-MACÉ

Alençon 46, Laval 66, Paris 227
8 km NE of Bagnoles-de-l'Orne, B3
✉ 61600

ℹ 11, rue de la Victoire, ☎ 33.37.10.97. closed Oct.

SNCF ☎ 33.37.20.21.

Car-hire : *Budget* train + auto, garage Peugeot, rte de Bagnoles, ☎ 33.37.16.33.

Hotels :
★★**Auberge du Clouet,** ☎ 33.37.18.22. Visa. 7 rm 🅿 closed 1-15 Jan, 1-15 Oct. Flower-laden terrance, 155. Rest. ♦ Farm produce, closed Sun eve and Mon from 10 Oct-31 Mar, 50-80.

Saint-Michel-des-Andaines, 5 km W :
★★**Bruyère** (L.F.), ☎ 33.37.22.26. Euro, Visa. 20 rm 🅿 closed 1-16 Jan, Sun eve and Mon, 140. Rest. ♦ 60-120.

FLERS

Argentan 45, Caen 57, Paris 238
B3 ✉ 61100

ℹ pl. Gal-de-Gaulle, ☎ 33.65.06.75.

SNCF ☎ 33.65.74.79.

Car-hire : *Budget* train + auto, at the S.N.C.F. station, ☎ 33.75.70.00. and rte de Caen, in Saint-Georges-des-Groseilliers, ☎ 33.65.25.98.

Hotel :
★★**Galion,** 22, rue de la Gare, ☎ 33.65.03.45. Visa. 11 rm 🅿 ♿ closed Sat eve and Sun, 140.

Restaurant :
♦♦♦ **Relais Fleuri,** 115, rue Schnetz, ☎ 33.65.23.89. ♿ closed Sat eve and Sun, 20 Jul-20 Aug. Spec : *terrine de foie truffé du chef, choucroute du pêcheur,* 120-200.

FORGES-LES-EAUX

Rouen 42, Amiens 70, Paris 114
D1 ✉ 76440

ℹ parc de l'Hôtel-de-Ville, ☎ 35.90.52.10.

SNCF ☎ 33.98.50.50/33.90.50.45.

Hotels :
★★★**Continental,** av. des Sources, ☎ 35.09.80.12. AE, DC, Euro, Visa. 50 rm 🅿 ♿ 220. Rest. ♦♦♦ **le Cardinal** Spec : *rillettes de saumon au citron vert,* 120-200.
★**Paix** (L.F.), 17, rue de Neufchâtel, ☎ 35.90.51.22. 5 rm, closed 20 Dec-10 Jan, 105. Rest. ♦ closed Sun eve and Mon low season. Spec : *barbue au cidre,* 90-145.

⛺ ★★*La Minière* (120 pl.), ☎ 35.90.53.91.

Event : July : *salon des Arts Plastiques ; horse festival.* Nov : *Tournoi des Voix d'Or* at the casino.

Casino : av. des Sources, ☎ 35.90.52.67.

Bicycle hire : ℹ

GISORS

Beauvais 32, Rouen 58, Paris 70
D2 ✉ 27140

ℹ pl. Carmélites, ☎ 32.55.20.28. closed Tue.

SNCF ☎ 32.55.01.30.

Hotels :
★★**Moderne** (L.F.), pl. de la Gare, ☎ 32.55.23.51. Euro, Visa. 33 rm 🅿 ♿ closed 15 Jul-10 Aug, 21 Dec-9 Jan, 215. Rest. closed Sun eve and Mon, 50-200.

Bazincourt-sur-Epte, 3.5 km N :
★★★**Château de la Rapée** (Relais du Silence, Châteaux-hôtels), ☎ 32.55.11.61. AE, DC, Visa. 10 rm 🅿 closed 20 Jan-1 Mar, 16-30 Aug and Wed, 360. Rest. ♦♦ Spec : *foie gras de canard pistaches, suprême de poulette farcie en ballottine,* 110-200.

GOURNAY-EN-BRAY

Beauvais 30, Rouen 50, Paris 94
D2 ⊠ 76220

ℹ 4, Porte-de-Paris, ☎ 35.90.28.34.

SNCF ☎ 35.90.00.09.

Hotels :
★★***Cygne*** (L.F. ; Inter-Hôtel), 20, rue Notre-Dame, ☎ 35.90.27.80. AE, DC, Euro, Visa. 29 rm Ⓟ 🐕 ♿ 200. Rest. 60-120.

Bézancourt, 9 km SW :
★★***Château du Landel,*** ☎ 35.90.16.01. 17 rm Ⓟ ♨ 🏊 🎾 closed Nov-Mar, 250. Rest. ♦ 80-150.

GRANDCAMP-MAISY

Caen 57, Cherbourg 71, Paris 298
10 km NE of Isigny, A2
⊠ 14450 Grandcamp-les-Bains

ℹ ☎ 31.22.61.66.

Hotels :
★★***Du Guesclin*** (L.F.), 4, quai Crampon, ☎ 31.22.64.22. Visa. 25 rm ⁂ Ⓟ ♿ closed 15-25 Oct, 15 Jan-1 Feb, 160. Rest. 40-110.
★***Grandcopaise,*** 84, rue Aristide-Briand, ☎ 31.22.63.44. AE, DC, Visa. 17 rm, closed 20 Dec-4 Jan and Mon low season, 90. Rest. 40-105.

⛺ ★★*Joncal* (300 pl.), ☎ 31.22.61.44.

Restaurant :
♦♦ ***La Marée,*** quai Chéron, ☎ 31.22.60.55. DC, Visa. ♿ Spec : *soufflé de coquilles St-Jacques,* 70-190.

GRANVILLE

Rennes 101, Caen 107, Paris 349
A3 ⊠ 50400

ℹ 15, rue G.-Clemenceau (B1), ☎ 33.50.02.67.

⛴ Chausey and Jersey Islands, enq ☎ 33.50.77.45.

SNCF (C1), ☎ 33.50.05.45.

🚌 cours Jonville (B2) and pl. de la Gare (C1), ☎ 33.50.66.66.

Car-hire : *Budget* train + auto, Roussel garage, rte de Villedieu, ☎ 33.50.11.92.

Hotels :
★★***Bains,*** 19, rue Clemenceau (B1), ☎ 33.50.17.31. AE, DC, Euro, Visa. 56 rm 🏊 ♿ closed 1 Jan-1 Feb, 280. Rest. ♦♦ ***la Potinière.*** closed Sun eve and Mon, 75-145.
● ★***Normandy Chaumière*** (L.F.), 20, rue P.-Poirier (B1), ☎ 33.50.01.71. AE, DC, Euro, Visa. 7 rm 🐕 closed 10-27 Oct, Christmas and 1 Jan, Tue eve and Wed, 150. Rest. ♦ Spec : *entrecôte Marie Harel, lotte à la fondue normande,* 70-135.

Bréville-sur-Mer, ⊠ 50290 Bréhal, 4 km NE on the D971 :
★★★***Mougine des Moulins à Vent,*** ☎ 33.50.22.41. 7 rm ⁂ Ⓟ ♨ 🏊 295.
● ★★***Auberge des Quatre Routes*** (L.F.), au Bourg on CD135, ☎ 33.50.20.10. DC, Visa. 7 rm 🐕 closed 1 Oct-30 Mar, 120. Rest. ♦ closed 15-31 Dec, 15-31 Mar, Tue eve and Wed, 40-85.

Saint-Pair-sur-Mer, ⊠ 50380, 4 km S :
★***Grand Hôtel de France,*** pl. de Gaulle, ☎ 33.50.19.03. 19 rm ⁂ closed Nov, 100. Rest. ♦ ♿ closed Tue. Regional specialities, 40-130.

⛺ ★★*La Vague* (100 pl.), ☎ 33.50.29.97.

Restaurant :
♦♦ ***Phare,*** 11, rue du Port (B1), ☎ 33.50.12.94. AE, DC, Euro, Visa. ⁂ Ⓟ 🏊 ♿ closed 15 Dec-20 Jan, 15-22 Sep, Wed eve and Thu. Spec : *andouillette de turbot au beurre blanc, papillote de saint-pierre au fenouil,* 60-120.

Guided tours : enq ℹ

Events : Feb : *Grand Carnaval.* Jul : *pardon des corporations de la mer* and *fête de la Libération.*

Recommended : *Louis Lapie,* 26, rue du Port *(fresh lobster).*

Le HAVRE

Rouen 88, Caen 108, Paris 205
C2 ⊠ 76600

ℹ pl. de l'Hôtel-de-Ville (B1), ☎ 35.21.22.88. closed Sun low season.

✈ Octeville, 6 km NW, ☎ 35.46.09.81.

⛴ *Normandy Ferries,* rte du Môle-Central (not on the D3 map), ☎ 35.26.57.26, car-ferries for Southampton. *Irish Continental Line,* same address, ☎ 35.26.57.26, for Rosslare. *Townsend-Thoresen,* quai de Southampton (B2), ☎ 35.21.36.50, for Portsmouth.

SNCF (D1), ☎ 35.43.50.50, 35.24.01.76.

🚌 4, rue C.-Laffite (CD1), ☎ 35.26.67.23.

Car-hire : *Budget* train + auto, 161, bd de Strasbourg, ☎ 35.22.53.52, and at the station, ☎ 35.26.41.40.

Hotels :
★★★***Bordeaux,*** 147, rue L.-Brindeau (B2), ☎ 35.22.69.44, Tx 190428. AE, DC, Euro, Visa. 31 rm 🏊 ♿ 315.
★★***Foch,*** 4, rue de Caligny (A1-2), ☎ 35.42.50.69. AE, Euro, Visa. 33 rm Ⓟ 🏊 🐕 ♿ 200.
★★***Monaco,*** 16, rue de Paris (B2), ☎ 35.42.21.01. AE, DC, Euro, Visa. 10 rm ⁂ closed 15 Feb-1 Mar, 1-15 Sep, 210. Rest. ♦♦ closed Mon ex Jul and Aug. Classic dishes. Spec : *canard au vinaigre de Xérès,* 70-200.
★★***P.N.F. Parisien,*** 1, cours de la République (D1), ☎ 35.25.23.83. 22 rm Ⓟ ♿ 85-180.
★***Voltaire,*** 14, rue Voltaire (B2), ☎ 35.41.30.91. Visa. 24 rm Ⓟ 🏊 130.

⛺ ★★★★*Forêt de Montgeon* (266 pl.), ☎ 35.46.52.39.

Restaurants :
Sainte-Adresse, ⊠ 76310 :
♦♦♦ ***Nice Havrais,*** 8, pl. Frédéric-Sauvage, ☎ 35.46.14.59. AE, Euro, Visa. 🏊 closed 1-31 Sep and Sun. Dining-room looking over the sea. Spec : *turbotin au vinaigre de framboises, casserole de crustacés au whisky,* 75-240.
♦♦ ***Manche,*** 18, bd Albert-Ier, ☎ 35.41.20.12. AE, DC, Euro, Visa. ⁂ ♿ closed Jul, Sun eve, Mon. In this boat decor restaurant, fish spec : *sole grillée aux courgettes,* oysters, shellfish.

Events : May : *Days of the Sea.* June : *Street festival.* July : *international regatta,* 1st Sun after 15 Aug : *Flower festival.*

Flying, gliding, etc : *"Jean Maridor" Havre Aeroclub,* ☎ 35.48.35.91.

HONFLEUR

Le Havre 57, Caen 63, Paris 192
C2 ⊠ 14600

ℹ 33, cours des Fossés (C3), ☎ 31.89.23.30 (high season).

SNCF (off the C3 map), ☎ 31.09.04.92.

🚌 pl. de la Porte-de-Rouen (C3), ☎ 31.89.28.41.

Normandy

Hotels :

● ★★★★***Ferme Saint-Siméon*** (Relais et châteaux), rue Adolphe-Marais (A1), ☎ 31.89.23.61. Tx 171031. 21 rm 830. Rest. ♦♦♦ closed 2 Jan-15 Mar. A great restaurant on the Normandy coast. Modern cooking, fresh fish. Spec : *navarin de homard, râble de lapereau, feuilleté aux pommes,* 250-420.
★★★***Hostellerie Lechat,*** 3, pl. Ste-Catherine (B2), ☎ 31.89.23.85. AE, DC, Euro, Visa. 26 rm. closed Wed and Thu noon low season, 330. Rest. ♦♦ closed from 15 Nov to 15 Mar ex weekends and hols. Spec : fish, shellfish, 90-200.
★★***Belvédère*** (L.F.), 36, rue E.-Renouf (C3), ☎ 31.89.08.13. Visa. 10 rm closed 15 Nov-15 Dec, 7-20 Jan, 180. Rest. ♦♦ closed Mon noon low season. Spec : *huîtres au beurre rouge, côte de veau au camembert,* 75-120.
★***Grande Cour*** (L.F.), Equemauville-Côte de Grâce (not on the A2 map), ☎ 31.89.04.69. AE, Visa. 13 rm Ⓟ closed Dec and Jan, 170. Rest. ♦ Ⓟ ♿ closed Wed, 60-130.

⛺ ★★★★*La Briquerie,* Equemauville, 3.5 km S (133 pl.), ☎ 31.89.28.32.

Restaurant :

♦♦ ***Écluse,*** 2, quai de la Quarantaine (C2), ☎ 31.89.18.09. AE, Visa. closed 15-28 Feb, 15-30 oct and Mon low season. Superb meats, 70-150.
♦♦ ***Absinthe,*** 10, quai de la Quarantaine, ☎ 31.89.39.00. AE, Visa. ♿ closed 12 Nov-20 Dec, Mon eve, Tue in low season. In this gourmet stop you are welcomed by a former head waiter of the Troisgros brothers. Spec : *filet de barbue au cidre, rognon de veau au calvados,* 110-200.

Farmhouse-inn : *Aux Templiers,* 6 km on the N813 and D62, in the quarter of the Église Penne de pie, ☎ 31.89.06.44. closed winter (ex Sun noon with booking). Spec : *poule à l'estragon.*

Guided tours : C.N.M.H.S., enq ℹ (high season).

Events : Whitsun, *Benediction of the Sea, Pilgrimage of the Sailors.* Jul. : *artists' salon, music festival.*

Bicycle hire : M. Grégory, 12, quai Lepaulmier, ☎ 31.89.34.66.

Recommended : *la Panetière,* 30, rue Montpensier, offers 18 kinds of bread.

HOULGATE

Caen 28, Le Havre 89, Paris 221
C2 ⊠ 14510

ℹ bd des Belges, ☎ 31.91.33.09, closed Oct, Sat pm and Sun, and rue d'Axbridge, ☎ 31.91.06.28, 15 Jun-30 Sep.

SNCF ☎ 31.91.22.41.

Hotels :

★★***Centre,*** 31, rue des Bains, ☎ 31.91.18.15. 22 rm ♿ closed Oct-Mar, 180.
★***Auberge de la Ferme des Aulnettes,*** rte de la Corniche, ☎ 31.91.22.28. 9 rm Ⓟ closed from end Nov to end Mar, 120. Rest. ♦ closed Mon eve and Tue low season, 100-180.
★***Ferme du Lieu-Marot,*** 21, rte de la Vallée, ☎ 31.91.19.44. Visa. 11 rm Ⓟ 200. Rest. ♦♦ closed Wed low season and Oct. Spec : *civet de lapin au cidre,* 85-150.
★***Hostellerie Normande*** (L.F.), 11, rue Émile-Deschanel, ☎ 31.91.22.36. AE, DC, Euro, Visa. 16 rm closed 2-31 Jan, Mon eve and Tue, 150. Rest. ♦♦ 80-150.

⛺ ★★*Plage* (65 pl.), ☎ 31.91.61.25.

Casino, rue Henri-Dobert, ☎ 31.91.60.94.

Recommended : *Exmelin* farm in Gonneville, 3.5 km at the D142 and D24 intersection, direction Dozulé. Daily sale of cider, calvados, honey, butter, cream, pont-l'évêque cheese and jams.

IVRY-LA-BATAILLE

Dreux 24, Évreux 35, Paris 80
D3 ⊠ 27540

Hotel :

● ★★***Au Grand Saint-Martin*** (L.F.), 9, rue d'Ezy, ☎ 32.36.41.39. Visa. 10 rm closed Jan, 250. Rest. ♦ closed Sun eve and Mon. Spec : *magret de canard à la façon d'Ivry,* 150-220.

⛺ ★★★★*Isles* (140 pl.), ☎ 32.64.55.77 ; ★★*Détente et Loisirs* (80 pl.), ☎ 32.64.02.68.

Restaurant :

♦♦♦ ***Le Moulin d'Ivry,*** 10, rue Henri-IV, ☎ 32.36.40.51. AE, Visa. ♿ closed Sun eve and Mon, 15-22 Oct, Feb. Spec : *savarin d'écrevisses,* 120-200.

JULLOUVILLE

Avranches 22, Saint-Lô 64, Paris 357
A3 ⊠ 50610

ℹ ☎ 33.61.82.48.

Hotels :

● ★★***Casino*** (L.F.), ☎ 33.61.82.82. Visa. 57 rm Ⓟ closed 15 Sep-1 May, 160. Rest. ♦ Spec : *timbales de langoustes,* 75-160.

Carolles-Bourg, 3 km S :
★***Relais de la Diligence,*** rue Division-Leclerc, ☎ 33.61.86.42. DC, Visa. 34 rm Ⓟ 21 Sep-29 Oct, 3-14 Mar, Sun eve and Mon, 90. Rest. ♦♦ Spec : *feuilleté de moules à la crème de safran, rognon de veau entier au saumur, 65-180.*

Restaurant :

♦♦ ***Village,*** ☎ 33.61.94.99. Visa. Ⓟ ♿ closed Mon. Spec : *moules au curry, huîtres chaudes aux bigorneaux,* 50-115.

LISIEUX

Caen 49, Alençon 91, Paris 174
C2 ⊠ 14100

ℹ 11, rue d'Alençon (B2), ☎ 31.62.08.41.

SNCF (B2), ☎ 31.62.00.34, 31.62.14.52.

🚌 kiosque, pl. Thiers (A1), ☎ 31.62.49.95.

Car-hire : *Budget* train + auto, S.N.C.F. station, ☎ 31.83.70.47.

Hotels :

● ★★★***Mapotel de la Place,*** 67, rue H.-Chéron (B1), ☎ 31.31.17.44. Tx 171862. AE, DC, Euro, Visa. 33 rm Ⓟ ♿ closed Sun eve, 3 Nov-Easter, 290.
● ★★***Bretagne*** (L.F.), 30, pl. de la République (A2), ☎ 31.62.09.19. AE, Euro, Visa. 14 rm Ⓟ closed Feb, 220. Rest. ♦ ♿ closed Sun eve and Mon low season, 50-200.
● ★★***Coupe d'Or*** (L.F.), 49, rue Pont-Mortain (A1), ☎ 31.31.16.84. AE, DC, Euro, Visa. 18 rm Ⓟ 230. Rest. ♦♦ closed 20 Dec-20 Jan and Sat low season, 80-180.
★★***Normandie*** (L.F. ; Inter-Hôtel), 11 *bis,* rue au Char (B1), ☎ 31.62.16.05, Tx 170269. AE, DC, Euro, Visa. 70 rm Ⓟ ♿ closed Oct-Apr, 215. Rest. ♦ 50-155.

Farmhouse gîte : *Le Bois Hurey,* Leaupartie, in Cambremer, 15 km on the N13 and D85, ☎ 31.63.01.99.

⛺ ★★*Municipal* (100 pl.), ☎ 31.62.00.40.

Restaurants :
♦♦ ***Ferme du Roy,*** 122, bd Herbet-Fournet, 2.5 km, ☎ 31.31.33.98. Visa. Ⓟ closed 15 Dec-15 Jan, Sun eve and Mon. Spec : *gâteau de sole, andouille flambée au calvados,* 150-200.
♦♦ ***Parc,*** 21, bd Herbet-Fournet (B1), on the rte de Deauville, ☎ 31.62.08.11. AE, Visa. Ⓟ closed Tue eve and Wed, 20 Nov-13 Dec. Spec : *huîtres chaudes aux six saveurs,* 70-220.

Manerbe, 7 km NW :
♦♦ ***Pot d'Étain,*** ☎ 31.61.00.94. AE, Visa. closed Nat hols, 1 week Sep, Tue eve and Wed, 90-180.

Ouilly-du-Houley, ⊠ 14590 Moyaux, 9 km NW on the D510 and D262 :
♦ ***Paquine*** ☎ 31.63.63.80. closed 15 days Sept, 24-31 Dec, Tue eve and Wed, 100-200.

Recommended : *Père Jules,* rte de Dives, ☎ 31.79.20.53. Cider.

LIVAROT

Caen 47, Alencon 72, Paris 192
18 km S of Lisieux, C2 ⊠ 14140

Hotel :
★★***Vivier*** (L.F.), pl. de la Mairie, ☎ 31.63.50.29. Visa. 11 rm Ⓟ closed 20 Dec-25 Jan and Mon, 220. Rest. ♦ 50-100.

Recommended : *Graindorge,* cheese specialist, ☎ 31.63.50.02. *Calvados cider brewery,* ☎ 31.63.50.53.

LOUVIERS

Évreux 22, Rouen 30, Paris 108
D2 ⊠ 27400

ⓘ 10, rue Mal-Foch, ☎ 32.40.04.41.

SNCF ☎ 32.38.50.50, 32.40.01.50.

Car-hire : *Budget* train + auto, 28, rue du 11-Novembre, ☎ 32.40.33.94.

Hotels :
★***Rouen,*** 11, pl. Ernest-Thorel, ☎ 32.40.01.83. Euro, Visa. 23 rm Ⓟ closed 10-31 Aug, 1 week Jan and Sun, 140. Rest. ♦ 70-100.

Vironvay, 1.5 km E :
● ★★★***Saisons,*** rte des Saisons, ☎ 32.40.02.56. DC, Euro, Visa. 15 rm Ⓟ closed Jan, 19-26 Aug, 300. Rest. ♦♦ closed Sun eve and Mon. Grilled lobster, 90-180.
★★***Hostellerie de la Poste,*** 11, rue Quatre-Moulins, ☎ 32.40.67.50. Visa. 16 rm, closed Sun eve and Mon, Aug, 215. Rest. ♦ Spec : *magret de canard au miel et citron vert,* 50-110.

Saint-Pierre-du-Vauvray, ⊠ 27430, 5 km N :
● ★★★***Hostellerie Saint-Pierre*** (Relais du Silence, Châteaux-hôtels), ☎ 32.59.93.29. DC, Visa. 14 rm Ⓟ 380. Rest. ♦♦ closed Tue eve and Wed. Spec : *arlequin de pâtes fraîches aux filets de sole,* 140-270.

Connelles, ⊠ 27430 Saint-Pierre-du-Vauvray, 8 km NE (left bank) :
★★★***Moulin de Connelles,*** D19, ☎ 32.59.82.54. AE, Visa. 30 rm Ⓟ closed 15 days Dec, 15 days Feb, 370. Rest. ♦♦ closed Sun eve and Mon low season. Spec : *sole soufflée, huîtres chaudes gratinées au champagne,* 130-300.

Restaurant :
♦♦ ***Clos Normand,*** 16, rue de la Gare, ☎ 32.40.03.56. closed Sun. Spec : *terrine de lapin au poivre vert,* 90-180.

Acquigny, 5 km S :
♦♦ ***L'Hostellerie,*** 1, rue d'Évreux, ☎ 32.50.20.05. Euro, Visa. Ⓟ closed from 1-20 Aug, 15 days Feb, Sun eve and Mon. Spec : *blanquette de ris de veau à l'oseille,* 85-200.

LUC-SUR-MER

Caen 16, Bayeux 28, Paris 259
9 km E of Courseulles, B2 ⊠ 14530

ⓘ mairie, ☎ 31.97.32.71.

Hotels :
★★***Beau Rivage,*** 1, rue Charcot, ☎ 31.96.49.51. Visa. 25 rm Ⓟ closed 30 Sep-15 Mar, 190. Rest. ♦ 60-150.
★★***Marsouin*** (L.F.), 2, rue Charcot, ☎ 31.97.32.08. Tx 170234. AE, DC, Euro, Visa. 15 rm, closed 15 Nov-10 Jan, Sun eve and Mon low season, 200. Rest. ♦ 70-160.

LYONS-LA-FORET

Les Andelys 20, Rouen 36, Paris 103
D2 ⊠ 27480

ⓘ mairie, ☎ 32.49.60.87. closed Sun and Mon.

Hotels :
● ★★★***La Licorne*** (L.F.), pl. Isaac-Berserade, 32.49.62.02. AE, DC, Euro, Visa. 22 rm Ⓟ closed 15 Dec-20 Jan, Sun eve and Mon low season, 275. Rest. ♦♦ Spec : *saumon cru à l'aneth au beurre de tomate, magret de canard au vinaigre de cidre,* 110-190.
★★***Le Grand Cerf,*** pl. de la Halle, ☎ 32.49.60.44. Euro. 10 rm closed 15 Jan-15 Feb, 200. Rest. ♦♦ 150-200.
★★***Domaine Saint-Paul,*** rte de Forges-les-Eaux, ☎ 32.49.60.57. 20 rm Ⓟ closed 15 Nov-15 Mar, 240. Rest. ♦♦ Spec : *truite au bleu à la crème amandine,* 75-125.

⛺ ★★*St-Paul* (40 pl.), ☎ 32.49.60.87.

Event : Whitsun : *Handicraft Days.*

Bicycle hire : ⓘ

MERVILLE-FRANCEVILLE-PLAGE

Caen 19, Deauville 26, Paris 231
B2 ⊠ 14810

ⓘ ☎ 31.91.21.18.

Hotels :
● ★★***Chez Marion*** (L.F.), ☎ 31.24.23.39. AE, DC, Euro, Visa. 18 rm Ⓟ closed 1 Jan-9 Feb and 3 weeks Oct, 260. Rest. ● ♦♦ closed Mon eve and Tue, 110-200.

Ranville, ⊠ 14860, 7 km SW on the D223 :
★★***Moulin du Pré,*** rte de Gonneville, ☎ 31.78.83.68. 10 rm Ⓟ 180. Rest. ♦♦ Jocelyne Hoetz' clever cooking. Good traditional Normandy dishes, 150-240.
★★***Auberge des Platanes*** (L.F.), 12, rue Gal-de-Gaulle, ☎ 31.78.68.48. 7 rm Ⓟ closed 1 Nov-1 Mar, 180. Rest. ♦ 95-160.

⛺ ★★★***Le Point du Jour*** (150 pl.), ☎ 31.91.30.31. At Ranville : ★★*Relais des Sportifs* (93 pl.), ☎ 31.91.29.05.

MONTMARTIN-SUR-MER

Granville 20, Saint-Lô 37, Paris 340
10 km SW of Coutances, A2 ⊠ 50590

ⓘ mairie, ☎ 33.47.54.54.

Hotels :
★★***Au Bon Vieux Temps,*** ☎ 33.47.54.44. 20 rm, 155. Rest. ♦ 50-160.

Hauteville-sur-Mer, 3 km SW :
★★***Plage*** (L.F.), ☎ 33.47.52.33. Visa. 14 rm 🅿 160. Rest. ♦ closed 15 Sep-1 Oct, Tue, Wed and Thu noon low season. A good spot for fresh regional produce, 80-150.

Quettreville-sur-Sienne, 5 km SE :
★★***Château de la Tournée*** (L.F.), ☎ 33.47.62.91. 10 rm 🅿 150. Rest. ♦♦ closed Mon, 15 Sep-1 Oct, Feb. Spec : *escargots en feuilletage, gratin de lotte,* 50-190.

Restaurant :
Hauteville-sur-Mer :
♦ ***Dunes,*** ☎ 33.47.51.14. DC, Visa. closed Sun eve and Mon in winter. Across from the sea-front. Spec : *turbot mousseline, filet de bar à l'oseille.* Good value, 80-165.

Le MONT-SAINT-MICHEL

Avranches 22, Rennes 66, Paris 370
A3 ⊠ 50116

ℹ *Corps de Garde des Bourgeois,* at the entrance to Le Mont, ☎ 33.60.14.30 (high season).

SNCF ☎ 33.60.00.35.

Hotels :
● ★★★***Digue*** (L.F.), at the Digue (the dyke), 2 km S, ☎ 33.60.14.02. Tx 170088. AE, DC, Visa. 35 rm, closed 15 Nov-23 Dec, 2 Jan-20 Mar 🅿 220. Rest. ♦ closed 20 Oct-28 Mar, 50-160.
● ★★★***La Mère Poulard,*** ☎ 33.60.14.01. AE, DC. 27 rm closed 1 Oct-31 Mar, 690. Rest. ♦♦♦ Spec : *langouste rose grillée et flambée Mère Poulard, carré d'agneau de pré-salé, omelette "Mère Poulard" flambée,* 165-425.
★★★***Manoir de la Roche Thorin*** (Relais du Silence), Courtils, ☎ 33.58.41.41, Tx 170380. AE, DC, Euro, Visa. 12 rm 🅿 closed 4 Nov-28 Mar, 300. Rest. ♦♦ eve only, closed Tue. Spec : *agneau de pré-salé,* 120-160.
★★***St-Aubert*** (L.F.), at the Dyke, 2 km S, ☎ 33.60.08.74. 27 rm 🅿 closed Nov-Mar, 170.
★★***Mouton Blanc,*** ☎ 33.60.14.08. 26 rm closed 15 Nov-15 Feb. Rest. ♦♦ 60-100.
Beauvoir, ⊠ 50170 Pontorson, 4 km S :
★***Gué de Beauvoir,*** ☎ 33.60.09.23. 🅿 21 rm. closed 15 Nov-Easter, 170.

Ⓐ ★★*Mont-St-Michel* (300 pl.), ☎ 33.60.09.33 ; ★★*Gué de Beauvoir,* Beauvoir (30 pl.), ☎ 33.60.09.23 ; ★★*Sous les Pommiers* (100 pl.), ☎ 33.60.09.45.

Restaurant :
♦ ***Les Terrasses Poulard,*** Grande-Rue, ☎ 33.60.14.09. AE, Visa. on the bay, 50-120.

Guided tours : C.N.M.H.S. (high season), enq : *almshouse,* ☎ 33.60.14.14.

Events : May, *Saint Michael's festival of Spring ;* Jul, *pilgrimage ;* Jul-Aug, *festival of the musical hours ;* Sep, *autumn pilgrimage.*

MORTAGNE-AU-PERCHE

Alençon 38, Chartres 80, Paris 155
C3 ⊠ 61400

ℹ pl. Gal-de-Gaulle, ☎ 33.25.04.22 (high season).

🚌 ☎ 33.25.19.11.

Hotel :
★★***Tribunal*** (L.F.), 4, pl. du Palais, ☎ 33.25.04.77. Euro, Visa. 15 rm 🅿 closed 22-29 Dec. The charm of a 17thC home, 160. Rest. ♦♦ Spec : *foie frais maison au sauternes, jambonnette de volaille Tribunal,* 60-120.

Ⓐ ★★*Municipal* (66 pl.), ☎ 33.25.04.35.

Events : Lent : *Boudin fair. Mortagne music festival* in June.

Recommended : smoked boudin (black sausage) at the *charcuterie Maurice Batrel,* 52, pl. du Gal-de-Gaulle, ☎ 33.25.16.43.

MORTAIN

Avranches 36, Rennes 90, Paris 277
A-B3 ⊠ 50140

ℹ 1, rue du Bourg-Lopin (summer), and mairie, ☎ 33.59.00.51.

Hotels :
★★***Poste,*** 1, pl. des Arcades, ☎ 33.59.00.05. Euro, Visa. 29 rm 🅿 160. Rest. ♦♦ closed 20 Dec-5 Jan, Fri eve and Sat, 55-110.
● ★***Cascades*** (L.F.), 16, rue du Bassin, ☎ 33.59.00.03. 14 rm. closed 3-18 Mar, 30 Sep-16 Oct, 130. Rest. ♦♦ closed Sun eve and Mon. Spec : *terrine maison, truites au vermouth,* 40-130.

Le NEUBOURG

Évreux 24, Rouen 38, Paris 130
C2 ⊠ 27110

ℹ mairie, ☎ 33.35.17.33.

SNCF ☎ 33.35.00.40.

Hotels :
★★***Grand Saint-Martin*** (L.F.), rue de la République, ☎ 33.35.04.80. 8 rm 🅿 closed Jun and Sep, Thu, 185. Rest. ♦ 60-100.
★★***Rôtisserie du Soleil d'Or*** (L.F.), 29, pl. du Château, ☎ 33.35.00.52. Visa. 8 rm 🅿 closed winter, Sun eve and Mon, 100. Rest. ♦ 55-130.

Foie gras markets : mid-Nov-mid-Dec.

NEUFCHÂTEL-EN-BRAY

Rouen 45, Beauvais 62, Paris 138
D1 ⊠ 76270

ℹ mairie, ☎ 35.93.22.96 (summer), ☎ 35.93.00.85 (winter).

SNCF ☎ 35.93.00.95.

Hotel :
★***Lion d'Or,*** 17-19, pl. Notre-Dame, ☎ 35.93.00.01. 22 rm 🅿 closed Jan, 100. Rest. ♦ closed Fri low season. Spec : *lotte à l'américaine, contrefilet au poivre vert,* 50-95.

Ⓐ ★★★*Sainte-Claire* (100 pl.), ☎ 35.93.03.93.

Bicycle hire : ℹ

NONANCOURT

Évreux 29, Alençon 96, Paris 97
D3 ⊠ 27320

ℹ ☎ 32.58.10.35.

SNCF ☎ 32.58.00.62.

Hotel :
● ★***Grand Cerf*** (L.F.), 17, rue Grande, ☎ 32.58.15.27. AE, DC, Euro, Visa. 7 rm 🅿 closed Sun eve and Mon. 17thC post-house, 135. Rest. ♦♦ Spec : *ris de veau aux morilles,* 60-120.

ORBEC

Caen 69, Alençon 77, Paris 167
C2 2-3 ⊠ 14290

ℹ mairie, ☎ 31.32.73.73.

Hotels :

★★***France*** (L.F.), 152, rue Grande, ☎ 31.32.74.02. Visa. 29 rm Ⓟ ♨ ⚲ ✈ closed 1 week Oct, 15 Dec-15 Jan, 210. Rest. ♦♦ Spec : *truite à l'orbecquoise, tête de veau chaude sauce ravigote,* 60-130.

Meulles, 8 km SW :

★★★***Hostellerie du Château de Montfort,*** ☎ 31.32.91.66. 20 rm Ⓟ ♨ ⚲ ▭ ♿ 200. Rest. ♦♦ closed Tue. Spec : *turbot à l'oseille,* 70-120.

Restaurant :

♦♦ ***Au Caneton,*** 32, rue Grande, ☎ 31.32.73.32. A highly-reputed restaurant in a traditional 17thC Norman building. Closed Feb, Oct, Mon eve and Tue. Spec : *gratin de langouste aux épinards, jambon Michodière,* 190-300.

Recommended : *Camembert Lanquetot,* 8, rue de Vimoutiers, group visits to the factory, ☎ 31.32.80.02, and the *Ferme Nathalie Legros,* chemin des Monts, upon leaving Orbec, on the rte de L'Aigle : sales every afternoon of cider, calvados, rabbits, fruits and cheeses (ex. Sun and Mon). *Le Buisson,* sale of calvados in Saint-Germain-la-Campagne, ✉ 27230 Thiberville, ☎ 32.44.71.11, 5 km N.

OUISTREHAM-RIVA-BELLA

Caen 14, Saint-Lô 70, Paris 251
B2 ✉ 14150

ⓘ pl. Alfred-Thomas, ☎ 31.97.18.63.

Hotels :

● ★★***Univers*** (L.F.), ☎ 31.97.12.16. AE, DC, Visa. 28 rm ⚘ Ⓟ closed 20 Dec-2 Jan, 200. Rest. ♦♦ ***la Broche d'Argent.*** ♿ closed Sun eve (daily Jul-Aug). Spec : *barbue aux huîtres, filet de sole normande,* 65-205.

● ★***St-Georges*** (L.F.), 51, av. Andry, ☎ 31.97.18.79. Visa. 21 rm ⚘ Ⓟ ♨ closed 5 Nov-1 Feb, 140. Rest. ♦ 50-150.

⛺ ★★★*Les Pommiers* (283 pl.), ☎ 31.97.12.66 ; ★★*Municipal* (366 pl.), ☎ 31.97.13.48.

Casino : ☎ 31.97.18.54.

Boat hire : *Serra Marine,* marina, ☎ 31.97.17.54.

Bicycle hire : M. Andasse, 77, av. Foch.

PACY-SUR-EURE

Évreux 18, Rouen 63, Paris 84
13 km SW of Vernon, D2 ✉ 27120

ⓘ mairie, ☎ 32.36.03.27.

SNCF ☎ 32.36.13.03.

Hotels :

★★***Étape,*** 1, rue Isambard, ☎ 32.36.12.77. Visa. 10 rm ⚘ Ⓟ ♨ ⚲ ♿ closed 2 Jan-2 Feb, Tue eve and Wed, 160. Rest. 75-150.

Douains, 6 km NE on the D181 and D75 :

★★★***Château de Brécourt*** (Relais et châteaux), ☎ 32.52.40.50 and 32.52.41.39. Tx 172250. AE, DC, Euro, Visa. 20 rm Ⓟ ♨ ⚲ ⚘ ♿ 550. Rest. ♦♦ 140-280.

Restaurant :

♦♦ ***La Mère Corbeau,*** pl. de la Gare, ☎ 32.36.98.49. Visa. Ⓟ ♿ closed Tue, eve and Wed. Spec : *foie frais de canard maison,* 70-210.

PONT-AUDEMER

Le Havre 48, Évreux 68, Paris 168
C2 ✉ 27500

ⓘ pl. Maubert, ☎ 32.41.08.21.

SNCF ☎ 32.41.01.20.

Hotels :

● ★★***Vieux Puits,*** 6, rue N.-D.-du-Pré, ☎ 32.41.01.48. Visa. 14 rm Ⓟ ♨ ⚲ ✈ ♿ closed 15 Dec-15 Jan, 30 Jun-10 Jul, Mon eve and Tue. 17thC Norman home, 300. Rest. ♦♦ Spec : *andouillette de mer grillée au beurre blanc, tarte de l'auberge,* 140-220.

Campigny, 3 km S on the D180 :

● ★★★★***Petit Coq aux Champs*** (Relais et châteaux), la Pommeraye, ☎ 32.41.04.19, Tx 172524. AE, DC, Euro, Visa. 12 rm ⚘ Ⓟ ♨ ⚲ ▭ ♿ Normandy-style thatched roof. Half-pension oblig, 1 700. Rest. ♦♦♦ Spec : *paletot de Barbarie en aiguillettes au cidre, saumon frais aux orties,* 185-300.

Corneville-sur-Risle, 6 km E :

● ★★★***Cloches de Corneville*** (L.F.), rte de Rouen, ☎ 32.57.01.04. AE, Euro, Visa. 12 rm Ⓟ ♨ ✈ 260. Rest. ♦♦ ♿ closed 1-20 Dec, 1-15 Mar and Wed. Spec : *terrine de foies de volaille au calvados, poulet de Loué à la roumoise,* 80-120.

Restaurants :

♦ ***La Frégate,*** 4, rue de la Seule, ☎ 32.41.12.03. AE, DC, Visa, closed Tue eve, Wed, 3 weeks Feb, 2 weeks end-Jul. Spec : *sandre au basilic, magret de canard au cidre,* 105-165.

Conteville, ✉ 27210 Beuzeville, 10 km NW :

● ♦♦ ***Auberge du Vieux Logis,*** ☎ 32.57.60.16. AE, DC, Euro, Visa. ♿ closed Wed eve and Thu, 15 Jan-20 Feb, 10 days end-Sep. Spec : *foie frais de canard, salade de ris de veau aux langoustines, étuvé de sole aux primeurs, mignons de veau aux cornes d'abondance,* 140-220.

PONT-L'ÉVÊQUE

Caen 47, Le Havre 64, Paris 196
C2 ♥ ✉ 14130

ⓘ mairie, ☎ 31.64.12.77.

SNCF ☎ 31.64.10.69.

Hotels :

★★***Lion d'Or*** (L.F.), 8, pl. du Calvaire, ☎ 31.65.01.55. AE, DC, Euro, Visa. 25 rm Ⓟ closed 15 Dec-25 Jan, Wed ex Jul-Aug, 165. Rest. ♦ 100-180.

Saint-Martin-aux-Chartrains, 4 km NW :

★***Auberge de la Truite*** (L.F.), ☎ 31.64.06.10. 6 rm Ⓟ ♨ 160. Rest. ♦ closed Sun eve and Mon low season, 1 Feb-15 Mar, 50-170.

Quetteville, 10 km NE :

★★***Auberge de la Hauquerie,*** rte de Pont-l'Évêque (N175), ☎ 31.64.14.46. Visa. 8 rm ⚘ Ⓟ ♨ ⚲ ♿ closed 8 Jan-8 Feb and Thu, 260. Rest. ● ♦♦♦ The best in fine original cooking by Mme Carlos Lombard ; wonderful sauces, carefully adapted to each client's whims and appetite. A peaceful winter dining-room, 70-130.

⛺ ★★★*Cour de France* (333 pl.), ☎ 31.64.17.38.

Restaurants :

♦♦ ***Auberge de la Touques,*** pl. de l'Église, ☎ 31.64.01.69. Euro, Visa. ⚘ Ⓟ ♨ ⚲ ♿ closed 15 Nov-20 Dec, Mon eve and Tue. Spec : *barbue aux pommes, magret de canard Bacchus,* 80-140.

Breuil-en-Auge, 8 km S :
● ♦♦♦ ***Auberge du Dauphin,*** ☎ 31.65.08.11. Visa. closed 1-30 Oct, Tue eve and Wed. Winning culinary creations in a traditional Norman inn setting. Spec : *sauté de cèpes aux spaghettis, fleurs de courgettes farcies au homard,* 75-200.

Recommended : calvados *le Père Magloire,* Éts Debrisse-Dulac, ☎ 31.64.12.87. Pierrefitte-en-Auge, 5 km S : *Auberge des Deux Tonneaux,* Norman-style snacks.

PONTORSON

Avranches 22, Rennes 57, Paris 322
A3 ✉ 50170

ⓘ mairie, ☎ 33.60.00.18.

SNCF ☎ 33.60.00.35.

Hotel :
● ★★***Montgomery*** (L.F.), 13, rue du Couesnon, ☎ 33.60.00.09. Tx 171332. AE, DC, Euro, Visa. 33 rm Ⓟ Exceptional furnishings, closed 20 Oct-23 Mar, 180. Rest. ♦♦ Spec : *pâté de saumon et brochet chaud, petit sauté de pigeon et ris de veau,* 60-215.

PONT-SAINT-PIERRE

Rouen 21, Évreux 45, Paris 106
10 km NE of Pont-de-l'Arche, D2 ✉ 27360

SNCF ☎ 32.49.70.57.

Hotel :
★★★***Hostellerie la Bonne Marmite*** (L.F.), 10, rue René-Raban, ☎ 32.49.70.24. AE, DC, Euro, Visa. 9 rm Ⓟ closed 20 Feb-15 Mar, Fri and Sat noon, Sun eve low season. Rest. ♦♦ closed 25 Jul-13 Aug ♿ Spec : *suprême de turbot aux petits légumes, civet de homard,* 75-200.

Restaurant :
♦♦ ***Auberge de l'Andelle,*** ☎ 32.49.70.18. Visa. Ⓟ ♿ closed Sun eve, Mon, 18 Aug-6 Sep and Christmas. Spec : *coulibiac de l'Andelle, filets de sole sauce ambassade,* 70-200.

PORT-BAIL

Cherbourg 45, Saint-Lô 58, Paris 348
8 km SE of Barneville-Carteret, A2 ✉ 50580

ⓘ mairie, ☎ 33.54.88.30.

Carteret Ferry Service, ☎ 33.54.87.21, in Carteret ; in summer for Jersey.

Hotel :
★***Galiche*** (L.F.), 13-15, pl. Éd.-Laquaine, ☎ 33.04.84.18. Euro, Visa. 12 rm Ⓟ ♿ closed Feb and Mon low season. Rest. ♦ 45-135.

⛺ ★★★*du Vieux Fort* (100 pl.), ☎ 33.54.81.99.

PORT-EN-BESSIN

Caen 36, Cherbourg 95, Paris 277
B2 ✉ 14520

Hotel :
★***Marine,*** quai Letourneur, ☎ 31.21.70.08. 17 rm Ⓟ closed 25 Nov-1 Feb, 100. Rest. ♦ 100-180.

⛺ ★★*La Prairie* (185 pl.), ☎ 31.21.70.06.

Restaurant :
● ♦♦ ***La Foncée,*** 12, rue Lefournier, ☎ 31.21.71.66. AE, DC, Euro, Visa. ♿ closed 23 Dec-3 Jan, 17-26 Feb, 15 days Oct, Tue eve, Tue and Wed low season. Former byre in a peaceful pastoral setting. Inventive cooking, market produce, fish, 90-170.

Colleville-sur-Mer, 8 km W on the D154 :
Farmhouse-inn and gîtes : *Loucel,* ☎ 31.22.40.95. Spec : *pâtés,* home-made tarts and cider.

ROUEN

Le Havre 88, Caen 124, Paris 140
D2 ✉ 76000

ⓘ pl. de la Cathédrale (C3), ☎ 35.71.41.77.

✈ Boos, 11 km SE, ☎ 35.80.22.52.
Air France Agency, 15, quai du Havre, ☎ 35.98.24.50.

SNCF (C1), ☎ 35.98.50.50, 35.70.16.34 or 35.70.25.28.

🚌 rue des Charrettes (A-B3), ☎ 35.71.81.71.

Car-hire : *Budget* train + auto, 13, pl. Joffre, ☎ 35.03.01.11, and at the S.N.C.F., station, ☎ 35.71.76.85.

Hotels :
★★★★(L) ***Frantel,*** rue Croix-de-Fer (C3), ☎ 35.98.06.98. Tx 180949. AE, DC, Visa. 125 rm Ⓟ ♿ 450. Rest. ♦♦ ***Tournebroche.*** closed Sun. Spec : *salade du marché à la gelée de lapereau et aux écrevisses,* 70-180.
● ★★★***Dieppe*** (Mapotel), pl. Bernard-Tissot (C1), ☎ 35.71.96.00. Tx 180413. AE, DC, Euro, Visa. 44 rm, 320. Rest. ♦♦ ***les Quatre Saisons.*** Spec : *canard rouennais à la presse,* 140-210.
★★***Cathédrale,*** 12, rue St-Romain (C3), ☎ 35.71.57.95. 23 rm 220.
★★***Grand Hôtel du Nord,*** 91, rue du Gros-Horloge (B2), ☎ 35.70.41.41. Tx 771938. Visa. 64 rm Ⓟ ♿ 180.
★***Havre,*** 27, rue Verte (B1), ☎ 35.71.46.43. 8 rm. Rest. ♦ closed 15 Jul-15 Aug, Fri eve, Sat and Sun eve. Good dishes, 100.

Mesnil-Esnard, 5 km SE :
★★***St-Léonard*** (L.F.), 38, rue Gambetta, ☎ 35.80.16.88. 17 rm Ⓟ ♿ closed 15-31 Jul, 170. Rest. ♦ closed Mon, 70-180.

Grand-Quevilly, 6 km SW :
★★★***Sorétel*** (France-Accueil), av. des Provinces, ☎ 35.69.63.50. Tx 180743. AE, DC, Euro, Visa. 45 rm Ⓟ ♿ 230. Rest. ♦♦ closed Sat noon, Sun eve, 50-150.

Montigny, 76380 Canteleu, 8 km W :
★★★***Atlas,*** ☎ 35.36.05.97. AE, Euro, Visa. 22 rm Ⓟ ♿ 185. Rest. ♦♦ closed 1-21 Aug, Fri and Sat noon. Spec : *st-pierre aux morilles, feuilleté de barbue,* 70-130.

Youth Accomodation Center : 17, rue Diderot, ☎ 35.72.06.45.

Restaurants :
♦♦♦ ***Couronne,*** 31, pl. du Vieux-Marché (B2), ☎ 35.71.40.90. AE, DC, Visa, closed Sun eve. Spec : *salade de foie gras marinée au porto, suprême de barbue aux choux,* 100-250.
● ♦♦ ***Gill,*** 60, rue St-Nicolas, ☎ 35.71.16.14. AE, DC, Visa. ♿ closed 4-20 Jan, last week in Aug-15 Sep, Sun and Mon noon. G. Tournadre, a young cook trained at *Taillevent* is destined to a brilliant success. Light and inspired cooking : *delicat cervelas de crustacés, ravioles de langoustines, pintade aux girolles,* 130-230.
♦♦ ***Dufour,*** 67 *bis,* rue St-Nicolas (C3), ☎ 35.71.90.62. AE, Visa. closed Aug, Sun eve and Mon. Spec : fish dishes, *sole au vieux bordeaux,* 180-200.
♦♦♦ ***Le Beffroy,*** 15, rue Beffroy, ☎ 35.71.55.27. AE, Euro, Visa. ♿ closed Sun and Mon and Aug. Good cooking, prepared in traditional Norman style, 100-230.

♦♦ ***Petits Parapluies,*** 46, rue Bourg-l'Abbé (D2), ☎ 35.88.55.26. AE, Visa, closed Sat noon, Sun, 1-21 Aug, nat hols. Exceptional service. Spec : *émincé de lotte, aiguillettes de canette, foie gras maison,* 100-220.
♦♦ ***Reverbère,*** 9, pl. de la République, ☎ 31.07.03.14. Visa, closed 4-20 Aug, Sun. One main dish entitles you to the full meal : fish, shellfish, meat or poultry, 100-210.

Guided tours : enq ℹ

Events : Apr-May : *24hr nautical motor-racing ;* end May : *fetes of Joan of Arc.* Jul-Aug : *organ recitals* in St-Maclou.

Recommended : *Hardy,* charcutier-traiteur, 22, pl. du Vieux-Marché. *Le Bouchon Normand,* pl. du Vieux-Marché, a wine bar.

SAINT-AUBIN-SUR-MER

Caen 18, Saint-Lô 61, Paris 256
7 km E from Courseulles, B2 ☒ 14750

ℹ rue Pasteur, ☎ 31.97.30.41 (high season).

Hotel :
★★***Clos Normand*** (L.F.), promenade Guynemer, ☎ 31.97.30.47. Tx 170234. AE, DC, Euro, Visa. 29 rm P closed 30 Sep-25 Mar, 170. Rest. ♦ ♿ 70-130.

⛺ ★*Municipal* (40 pl.), ☎ 31.97.30.24.

SAINT-GERMAIN-DES-VAUX

Cherbourg 29, Saint-Lô 107, Paris 390
A1 ☒ 50440 Beaumont-Hague

Hotel :
Port-Racine, 2 km E :
● ★★***Hôtellerie l'Erguillère*** (L.F.), ☎ 33.52.75.31. 10 rm P ♿ closed 1 Jan-15 Mar, Sun eve and Mon low school hols, 195. Rest. ♦ 115-180.

SAINT-HILAIRE-DU-HARCOUET

Avranches 27, Rennes 76, Paris 291
A3 ☒ 50600

ℹ pl. de l'Église, ☎ 33.49.15.27, and mairie, ☎ 33.49.10.06.

Hotels :
● ★★***Cygne*** (L.F.), 67, rue Waldeck-Rousseau, ☎ 33.49.11.84, Tx 171445. AE, DC, Euro, Visa. 45 rm P ♿ closed 24 Dec-3 Jan, 200. Rest. ♦♦ Spec : *feuilleté d'escargots aux cèpes, escalope de lotte au calvados et petits légumes,* 60-170.
★★***Lion d'Or*** (L.F.), 120, rue de la République, ☎ 33.49.10.82. 19 rm P 170. Rest. ♦ closed Oct, Feb, school hols, Sun eve low season and Mon. Spec : *ris de veau à l'ancienne,* 50-120.

⛺ ★*Sélune* (33 pl.), ☎ 33.49.12.67.

Farmhouse-inn rm available : *Dorière,* in Saint-Laurent-de-Terregate, 15 km W on the N176 and D582, ☎ 33.48.41.30. At the lakeside. Fishing. Spec : *galette fourrée au jambon.*

Recommended : *Calvados Gilbert,* Milly, 6.5 km NE, ☎ 33.49.00.63 : visit of storehouses and tasting.

SAINT-LÔ

Caen 63, Cherbourg 78, Paris 303
A2 ☒ 50000

ℹ 2, rue Havin (B1), ☎ 33.05.02.09.

SNCF (A1), ☎ 33.57.50.50, 33.05.11.68.

🚌 (B1-2), ☎ 33.05.65.25.

Car-hire : *Budget* train + auto, 29, rue Valuire, ☎ 33.57.77.69, and at the station, ☎ 33.57.60.06.

Hotels :
★★***Gare et Marignan*** (L.F.), pl. de la Gare (A1), ☎ 33.05.15.15. Euro. 18 rm P closed 7-22 Feb, 220. Rest. ♦♦ Spec : *soupe de petits-gris aux orties, coquilles St-Jacques à la coque,* 50-260.
★★***Terminus*** (L.F.), 3, av. Briovère (A1), ☎ 33.05.08.60. Euro, Visa. 15 rm P closed 21 Dec-7 Jan, 160. Rest. ♦ ♿ closed Sun, 45-65.
★★***Voyageurs,*** 5, av. Briovère (A1), ☎ 33.05.08.63. AE, DC, Euro, Visa. 15 rm P 190. Rest. ♦♦ Brasserie, closed 15 Dec-15 Jan, Sun eve and Mon low season. Seafood specialities ; good value, 50-120.
● ★***Crémaillère,*** pl. de la Préfecture (A1), ☎ 33.57.14.68. Euro, Visa. 12 rm closed 1-21 Feb, Sat, 140. Rest. ♦ Spec : seafood, *poëlon de tripes.* Reasonably-priced, quality fare, 60-110.

Tessy-sur-Vire, ☒ 50420, 18 km S :
● ★***France*** (L.F.), ☎ 33.56.30.01. Euro, Visa. 14 rm P closed 1-15 Feb, 110. Rest. ♦ closed Sun eve and Mon noon low season. Good fare. Spec : *timbale du pêcheur, filets de st-pierre aux herbes,* 40-125.

⛺ ★*Municipal* (33 pl.), ☎ 33.57.57.01.

Event : Aug-Sep : *presentation of horses and teams at the national stud-farm.*

Flying : pilots school, enq ☎ 33.57.17.80.

SAINT-PIERRE-SUR-DIVES

Caen 31, Alencon 88, Paris 203
B2 ☒ 14170

ℹ 17, rue St-Benoît (high season).

SNCF ☎ 31.20.74.01.

Hotel :
★***Gare,*** 47, bd Colas, ☎ 31.20.74.22. Visa. 20 rm P ♿ 85. Rest. ♦ 40-135.

Events : Jun, *Dressage competition. Rural market* on Mon.

SAINT-SAUVEUR-LE-VICOMTE

Cherbourg 35, Saint-Lô 55, Paris 340
A2 ☒ 50390

ℹ mairie, ☎ 33.41.60.26.

Hotel :
★***Auberge du Vieux-Château*** (L.F.), ☎ 33.41.60.15. Euro, Visa. 10 rm P closed winter, 90. Rest. ♦♦ 65-150.

⛺ ★★*Vieux Château* (33 pl.), ☎ 33.41.60.26.

SAINT-VAAST-LA-HOUGUE

Cherbourg 30, Saint-Lô 68, Paris 350
A1 ☒ 50550

ℹ quai Vauban, ☎ 33.54.41.37 (high season), and mairie, ☎ 33.54.42.52.

Hotel :
★★***France et Fuchsias*** (L.F.), ☎ 33.54.42.26. DC, Visa. 20 rm P closed 2 Jan-15 Feb and Mon ex school hols, Tue noon, 210. Rest. ♦♦ Spec : *homard au calvados, pâté de lotte sauce gribiche,* 70-150.

SAINT-VALÉRY-EN-CAUX

Dieppe 32, Rouen 60, Paris 198
C1 ☒ 76460

ℹ pl. de l'Hôtel-de-Ville, ☎ 35.97.00.63.

SNCF ☎ 35.97.08.43.

Normandy

Hotels :
★★*Les Terrasses,* on the beachfront, ☎ 35.97.11.22. Euro, Visa. 12 rm closed Jan and Fri low season, 220. Rest. ♦ 75-130.
★*Bains,* pl. du Marché, ☎ 35.97.04.32. 14 rm closed 1 Dec-15 Feb, 150. Rest. ♦ closed Sun eve and Mon low season, Tue high season, 60-150.

Veulettes-sur-Mer, ☒ 76450 Cany-Barville, 10 km W :
★★*Frégates* (L.F.), ☎ 35.97.51.22. 16 rm Ⓟ closed 23 Dec-10 Jan and Mon low season, 145. Rest. ♦♦ Spec : *terrine de turbot au basilic, filet de barbue à la graine de moutarde,* 100-190.

Cany-Barville, 12 km S on the D925 :
Manoir de Barville, ☎ 35.97.79.30. Euro, Visa. 4 rm Ⓟ closed Jan, Mon eve and Tue, 150. Rest. ● ♦♦ Pleasant cooking in a delightful British-style mansion. Spec : *filet de sole à la rhubarbe et au miel, coussin de turbot au foie gras,* 70-160.

Le Bourg-Dun, ☒ 76740, 15 km E :
Auberge du Dun (L.F.), rte de Dieppe, ☎ 35.83.05.84. 6 rm Ⓟ closed 15 Oct-2 Nov, 15-28 Feb, Sun eve and Mon, 80. Rest. ● ♦♦ A gifted chef ensures the preparation of highest quality fare ; excellent value. Spec : *assiette du pêcheur, crêpe au praliné,* 80-200.

Youth hostel, ☎ 35.97.03.98.

Ⲁ ★★★*Mouettes,* Veules-les-Roses, 8 km E (100 pl.), ☎ 35.97.61.98 ; ★★*Municipal* (133 pl.), ☎ 35.97.05.07.

Restaurants :
♦♦ ***Port,*** 18, quai d'Amont, ☎ 35.97.08.93. Visa. closed 1-15 Sep, Mon and Thu eve. Marine style. Spec : fish, grills, *turbot au brouilly et aux morilles,* 90-200.

Veules-les-Roses, ☒ 76980, 8 km E :
● ♦♦♦ ***Galets,*** 3, rue Victor-Hugo, ☎ 35.97.61.33. AE, DC, Visa, closed Tue eve, Wed and Feb. Gilbert Plaisance (M.C.F) is well-named ; a beautiful house and excellent cooking. Spec : *assiette langouste marinée avec crème de caviar au citron, escalope de turbot sautée au dés de foie gras, homard aux pâtes fraîches et son coulis, salade lotte vinaigrette de cidre et cresson, cœur d'entrecôte sauté aux trois poivres,* 180-420.

SÉES

Alençon 22, Caen 100, Paris 183
C3 ☒ 61500

ⓘ at the hôtel de ville, ☎ 33.28.74.79 (high season).

SNCF ☎ 33.27.80.37.

Hotels :
★*Cheval Blanc* (L.F.), 1, pl. St-Pierre, ☎ 33.27.80.48. Visa. 9 rm closed 15 Oct-8 Nov, 1-15 Mar, Fri and Sat low season, 85. Rest. ♦ ♿ closed Fri, Sat low season, 35-120.

Gacé, ☒ 61230, 24 km N on the N138 :
★★*Host. les Champs* (Châteaux-hôtels), rte d'Alençon-Rouen, ☎ 33.35.51.45. DC, Euro, Visa. 14 rm Ⓟ ♿ closed 15 Jan-15 Feb, Tue and Wed noon (ex season), 270. Rest. ♦♦ 90-180.
★★*Château le Morphée* (Châteaux-hôtels), 2, rue de Lisieux, ☎ 33.35.51.01. Visa. 10 rm Ⓟ closed 15 Dec-15 Jan. Beautiful 19thC residence with hundred-year-old trees, 240.

Ⲁ ★★*Le Clos Normand* (33 pl.), ☎ 33.27.98.08.

Son et lumière : at the cathedral (high season).

TANCARVILLE

Le Havre 30, Caen 77, Pris 175
C2 ☒ 76430 Saint-Romain-de-Colbosc

Hotel :
★★*Marine,* at the foot of the bridge, ☎ 35.39.77.15. Visa. 10 rm Ⓟ closed 16 Aug-7 Sep, Feb school hols, Sun eve, Mon, 170. Rest. ♦ ♿ Spec : *fricassée de sole et langouste, sole cuite à la vapeur d'algues,* 120-200.

Restaurant :
Saint-Vigor-d'Ymouville, 8 km W on the N182 :
♦♦♦ ***Dubuc,*** ☎ 35.20.06.97. AE, DC, Visa Ⓟ ♿ closed 4-26 Aug, 9-16 Mar, Sun eve and Mon. Spec : *salade du Hode, brouillade de homard, filets de sol Dubuc,* 160-245.

TESSÉ-LA-MADELEINE

Alençon 50, Laval 63, Paris 235
2 km SW of Bagnoles-de-l'Orne, B3
☒ 61140 Bagnoles-de-l'Orne

Hotels :
★★*Celtic* (L.F.), 14, rue Albert-Christophe, ☎ 33.37.92.11. AE, Euro, Visa. 28 rm Ⓟ ♿ closed Dec-15 Jan, 250. Rest. ♦♦ 85-180.
★★*Nouvel Hôtel* (L.F.), 8, av. Albert-Christophe, ☎ 33.37.81.22. 30 rm Ⓟ closed 30 Apr-24 Jun, 190. Rest. ♦ 60-110.
★*Clos Joli,* 6, bd Labbé, ☎ 33.37.86.33. 33 rm Ⓟ ♿ closed 30 Sep-25 Apr, 120. Rest. ♦ 65-80.
★*Domaine des Buards,* 16, rue des Buards, ☎ 33.37.81.91. 21 rm Ⓟ closed low season, 100. Rest. ♦ 80-130.

Cultural centre : at the castle.

THURY-HARCOURT

Caen 26, Argentan 50, Paris 265
B2 ☒ 14220

ⓘ pl. St-Sauveur, ☎ 31.79.70.45.

SNCF ☎ 31.79.72.48.

Ⲁ ★★★★*Vallée du Traspi* (106 pl.), ☎ 31.79.61.80 ; ★★★*Bords de l'Orne* (70 pl.), ☎ 31.79.70.78.

Restaurant :
Boulon, 10 km NE :
♦ ***La Bonne Auberge,*** ☎ 31.79.37.60. ♿ closed 1-22 Sep, Mon to Tue ex public hols. Norman spec : *tripes, tergoule (riz au lait), cidre au tonneau,* 40-80.

Bicycle hire : ☎ 31.79.60.79 and 31.79.72.23.

Le TRÉPORT

Dieppe 30, Rouen 91, Paris 170
D1 ☒ 76470

ⓘ esplanade de la Plage, ☎ 35.86.05.69. Closed Tue and Sun.

SNCF ☎ 35.86.23.44.

Hotels :
★★*Picardie,* pl. P.-Sémard, ☎ 35.86.02.22. Visa. 30 rm Ⓟ closed 8 Dec-19 Jan, Sun eve and Mon low season, 180. Rest. ♦♦ ♿ Spec : *pot-au-feu de poisson,* 75-180.
★*Rex,* 50, quai François-Ier, ☎ 35.86.26.55. 17 rm Ⓟ 185. Rest. ♦ closed Fri, 15 Dec-15 Jan, 50-140.

Youth hostel : 25, av. des Canadiens, ☎ 35.86.23.47.

Ⲁ ★★★★*Municipal* (300 pl.), ☎ 35.86.35.47.

Casino, esplanade de la Plage, ☎ 35.86.35.45.

TROUVILLE-SUR-MER

Caen 43, Le Havre 74, Paris 206
C2 ⚓ ☒ 14360

ℹ pl. Mal-Foch (B2), ☎ 31.88.36.19 (high season).

✈ Saint-Gatien, 7 km E.

SNCF ☎ 31.83.50.50, 31.88.28.80, 31.88.50.48.

Car-hire : *Budget* train + auto, at the S.N.C.F. station, ☎ 31.88.28.80.

Hotels :
★★★***St-James,*** 16, rue de la Plage, ☎ 31.88.05.23. AE, Visa. 14 rm, 260. Rest. ♦ 120.
● ★★***Carmen*** (L.F.), 24, rue Carnot (B2), ☎ 31.88.35.43. AE, DC, Euro, Visa. 16 rm closed 4 Jan-4 Feb and Tue, 240. Rest. ♦♦ closed Mon eve and Tue. Spec : *huîtres pochées à la mousseline d'échalote, matelote du chef,* 60-150.
★★***Reynita,*** 29, rue Carnot, ☎ 31.88.15.13. AE, DC, Euro, Visa. 24 rm closed 31 Dec-6 Feb, 170.
★★***Amienoise,*** 5, rue Bon-Secours (B1), ☎ 31.88.12.23. 12 rm ♿ closed 11 Nov-15 Feb, 210.

Touques, ☒ 14800 Deauville, 3 km SW :
★★★***Amirauté,*** on N834, ☎ 31.88.90.62. Tx 171665, AE, DC, Euro, Visa. 121 rm Ⓟ ♿ 510. Rest. ♦♦ 130-150.

Villerville, ☒ 14113, 8 km NE :
★★★***Manoir du Grand Bec,*** ☎ 31.88.09.88. 10 rm Ⓟ 300. Rest. ♦ 125-250.

⛺ ★★*Hamel* (100 pl.), ☎ 31.88.15.56 ; ★★★★*le Haras,* Touques, 3 km SW (250 pl.), ☎ 31.88.44.84.

Restaurants :
♦♦♦ ***La Régence,*** 132, bd F.-Moureaux (C2), ☎ 31.88.10.71. AE, DC, Euro, Visa. ♿ closed Wed eve and Thu low season. Seafood specialities, 130-180.
● ♦♦ ***Le Bar des Planches "Galatée",*** on the beachfront, ☎ 31.88.15.04 ♿ closed 11 Nov-1 Apr and Wed low season. On the boardwalk, facing the sea, Mr. Vola proposes his straightforward cooking. Well prepared fresh fish. Some creations : *foie de canard, profiterolles fourrées, glaces à la menthe.* Good value, friendly atmosphere and pleasant service, 100-205.
♦♦ ***Aux Landiers,*** ☎ 31.88.00.39. closed 15-30 Jun, Tue Wed and Thu, 90-160.
● ♦ ***Les Vapeurs,*** 160, bd F.-Moureaux, ☎ 31.88.15.24 ♿ closed 5 Jan-5 Feb, 15 Nov-5 Dec, Tue eve, Wed. Authentic 1950 setting for Normandy coast establishment "day and night in any season, same prices, food cooked with butter, to the minute". Try the shrimps cooked live, Bouchot mussels, fresh fish from Port-en-Bessin. Friendly atmosphère, low prices, 80-135.

See also Deauville

Casino : pl. Mal-Foch (B3), ☎ 31.88.76.09.

VALOGNES

Cherbourg 20, Saint-Lô 58, Paris 340
A1-2 ☒ 50700

ℹ pl. du Château, ☎ 33.40.11.55 (high season).

SNCF ☎ 33.57.50.50.

Hotels :
★***Agriculture*** (L.F.), 16-18, rue Léopold-Delisle, ☎ 33.40.00.21. 36 rm Ⓟ 135. Rest. ♦ closed 1 week end-Jun, Sun eve and Mon. Oyster specialities, 70-140.

Quinéville, ☒ 50310 Montebourg, 15 km E :
★★***Château de Quinéville,*** ☎ 33.41.21.50. 13 rm Ⓟ 220. Rest. ♦♦ closed Feb, 60-90.

VARENGEVILLE-SUR-MER

Dieppe 8, Rouen 63, Paris 201
D1 ☒ 76119

Hotels :
★★***Terrasse*** (L.F.), Vastérival, ☎ 35.85.12.54. Euro. 28 rm Ⓟ closed Oct-15 Mar. In a pine forest, 170. Rest. ♦♦ 55-100.

Sainte-Marguerite-sur-Mer, 3 km W :
★***Sapins,*** ☎ 35.85.11.45. 25 rm Ⓟ closed Dec and Jan, 85. Rest. ♦ 60-125.

⛺ ★★*Municipal,* Quiberville (300 pl.), ☎ 35.83.01.04.

VERNEUIL-SUR-AVRE

Chartres 56, Rouen 87, Paris 116
D3 ☒ 27130

ℹ pl. de la Madeleine, B.P. 110, ☎ 32.32.03.94.

SNCF ☎ 32.32.14.90.

Hotels :
● ★★★***Hostellerie le Clos*** (Relais et châteaux), 98, rue de la Ferté-Vidame, ☎ 32.32.21.81. Tx 172770. AE, DC, Euro, Visa. 12 rm Ⓟ ♿ 320. Rest. ♦♦ closed 10 Dec-end Jan and Mon. Spec : *escalope de saumon sauvage à la ciboulette,* 120-250.
● ★★***Saumon*** (L.F.), 89, pl. de la Madeleine, ☎ 32.32.02.36. Tx 172770. Euro, Visa. 22 rm Ⓟ 200. Rest. Regional cooking, 45-150.

Balines, 3.5 km E :
★★***Le Moulin de Balines*** (Châteaux-hôtels), ☎ 32.32.03.48. Euro, Visa. 7 rm Ⓟ ♿ closed Mon. A restored mill in a 10-hectare park, fishing in the neighbouring ponds and rivers, 180. Rest. ♦♦ Spec : *cassolette de lotte sauce aux langoustines, gigot d'agneau en croûte sauce aux petits rognons,* 100-160.

⛺ ★★★*Vert Bocage* (50 pl.), ☎ 32.32.26.79.

Restaurant :
♦♦ ***Grand Sultan,*** 30, rue Poissonnerie, ☎ 32.32.13.41. closed Aug and Mon, 45-85.

VERNON

Évreux 31, Rouen 63, Paris 82
D2 ☒ 27200

ℹ passage Pasteur, ☎ 32.51.39.60.

SNCF ☎ 32.51.01.72.

Hotels :
● ★★★***Évreux,*** 7, pl. d'Évreux, ☎ 32.21.16.12. AE, DC, Euro, Visa. 20 rm Ⓟ closed Sun, 285. Rest. ♦♦ ♿ 150-210.
★★***Strasbourg,*** 6, pl. d'Évreux, ☎ 32.51.23.12. Euro, Visa. 24 rm Ⓟ 150. Rest. ♦ ♿ closed 24 Dec-10 Jan, Sun eve and Mon, 85-155.

Youth hostel : 28, av. de l'Ile-de-France, ☎ 32.51.55.23.

⛺ ★★*Fosses Rouges,* Saint-Marcel (82 pl.), ☎ 32.51.59.86.

Restaurant :
● ♦♦ ***Beau Rivage,*** 13, av. Mal-Leclerc, ☎ 32.51.17.27. AE, Euro, Visa. ♿ closed 1-15 Oct, Sun eve, Mon. A pleasant stop during the week-end. Spec : *lotte Beau Rivage,* 65-150.

Chambray, ☒ 27120 Pacy-sur-Eure, 18 km SW :
♦♦ ***Le Vol au Vent,*** 1, pl. de la Mairie, ☎ 32.36.70.05. DC, Euro, Visa. closed 2 Jan-

4 Feb. Spec : *huîtres chaudes en sabayon de cidre, feuilleté de ris de veau aux morilles,* 135-190.

Recommended : *cake and pastry shop,* 45, rue Carnot.

VIERVILLE-SUR-MER

Saint-Lô , Caen 50, Paris 290
13 km NW of Port-en-Bessin, B2

⊠ 14710 Trévières

ⓘ mairie, ☎ 31.22.40.30.

Hotel :
★***Casino,*** bd de Jauvigny, ☎ 31.22.41.02. Visa. 13 rm ⚟ Ⓟ closed 3 Jan-10 Feb, 110. Rest. ♦ 60-150.

Chambres d'hôtes : *Manoir de l'Hormette* (Château-Accueil), Trévières, 9 km S on the D517 and D30, ☎ 31.22.51.79. 17thC farm-house, 180.

VILLEDIEU-LES-POELES

Avranches 22, Caen 78, Paris 321
A3 ⊠ 50800

ⓘ pl. des Costils, ☎ 33.61.05.69 (high season).

SNCF ☎ 33.61.00.30.

Hotel :
● ★★***Saint-Pierre et Saint-Michel*** (L.F.), ☎ 33.61.00.11. 24 rm Ⓟ closed Fri, 26 Dec-5 Jan. Classical setting, 150. Rest. ♦ ***Délices Pompadour*** ♿ 40-100.

Chambres and table d'hôte : *le Bois Mozand,* Percy, 9.5 km N on the D999, ☎ 33.61.23.62. Produce for sale.

⛺ ★★★*Pré de la Rose* (100 pl.), ☎ 33.61.02.44.

Restaurant :
♦♦ ***Crêperie des Chevaliers,*** 6, pl. des Chevaliers-de-Malte, ☎ 33.61.07.94. Euro, Visa. closed 15 Nov-15 Jan and Mon low season. Spec : *galette de sarrasin, cider.* A worthwhile stop, 40-70.

VILLERS-BOCAGE

Bayeux 25, Saint-Lô 35, Paris 268
26 km SW of Caen, B2 ⊠ 14310

Hotel :
● ★★***Trois Rois*** (L.F.), ☎ 31.77.00.32. AE, Euro, Visa. 15 rm Ⓟ closed 1-28 Feb, end week Jun, Sun eve and Mon, 190. Rest. ♦ ♿ Remarkable cooking and quality service in a pleasant atmosphere, 70-180.

Farmhouse gîte and inn : *Craham,* Cahagnes, in Caumont-l'Éventé, 12 km W on the D71, ☎ 31.77.58.34.

VILLERS-SUR-MER

Caen 35, Le Havre 83, Paris 215
C2 ⊠ 14640

ⓘ pl. Mermoz, ☎ 31.87.01.18 (high season), and at the mairie, ☎ 31.87.00.54.

SNCF ☎ 31.83.50.50, 31.87.40.25.

Hotels :
★★★***Bonne Auberge*** (L.F.), 1, rue Mal-Leclerc, ☎ 31.87.04.64. 26 rm ⚟ Ⓟ closed Oct-Mar, 310. Rest. ♦♦ Fish and seafood dishes, 105-180.
★★***Frais Ombrages*** (L.F.), 38, av. Brigade-Piron, ☎ 31.87.40.38. 13 rm Ⓟ closed 15 Nov-31 Jan and Tue, Wed low season, 230. Rest. ♦ Spec : *moules normandes, escalope de veau normande,* 80-120.

VIRE

Caen 60, Laval 105, Paris 270
B3 ⊠ 14500

ⓘ square de la Résistance, ☎ 31.68.00.05.

SNCF ☎ 68.04.08.

Hotels :
★★***France*** (L.F.), 4, rue d'Aignaux, ☎ 31.68.00.35. Euro, Visa. 20 rm Ⓟ ♿ closed 1-15 Jan and nat hols, 190. Rest. ♦ 40-110.
● ★***Cheval Blanc*** (L.F.), 2, pl. 6-Juin-1944, ☎ 31.68.00.21. 23 rm, 220. Rest. ♦♦♦ closed Fri eve and Sat noon low season. Light, refined Normandy cooking. Spec : *marée du jour, canard au pamplemousse,* 70-235.

⛺ ★*La Piscine* (33 pl.), ☎ 31.68.00.05.

Restaurant :
♦♦ ***Pomme d'Or,*** Rouillours, 3 km SE on the D524, rue A.-Touyonne, ☎ 31.68.07.71. AE, DC, Euro, Visa. Ⓟ ♿ closed 23 Feb-19 Mar, 28 Jul-13 Aug, Sun eve and Mon. Spec : *salade gourmande, fricassée de homards aux petits légumes,* 70-180.

YPORT

Le Havre 35, Rouen 77, Paris 214
8 km SW of Fécamp, C1 ⊠ 76111

ⓘ pl. J.-P.-Laurens, ☎ 35.27.32.19.

SNCF ☎ 35.98.50.50.

Hotel :
★★***Sirène*** (L.F.), 3, bd Alexandre-Dumont, ☎ 35.27.31.87. AE, DC, Euro, Visa. 10 rm ⚟ Ⓟ closed Sun, Mon low season, 120. Rest. ♦ 45-130.

Youth hostel : 9, rue E.-Foy, ☎ 35.27.32.06.

⛺ ★★*Municipal* (65 pl.), ☎ 35.27.33.56.

Events : Jul : *traditional market and jumble sale.* Mid-Aug : *sea and painting festival, with auction of paintings executed during the day.*

YVETOT

Rouen 36, Le Havre 51, Paris 176
C1 ⊠ 76190

SNCF ☎ 35.95.14.87.

Car-hire : *Budget* train + auto, at the S.N.C.F. station, ☎ 35.95.02.69.

Hotel :
★★***Le Havre,*** pl. des Belges, ☎ 35.95.16.77. 41 rm Ⓟ ♿ closed 24 Dec-2 Jan, 200. Rest. ♦♦ closed Sun, 17 Dec-16 Jan, 90-170.

Youth hostel, ☎ 35.95.15.54.

Farmhouse gîte : *le Carreau,* in Flamanville, 7 km NE on the N29, ☎ 35.96.85.57. Farm produce for sale.

⛺ ★*Clos Normand* (35 pl.), ☎ 35.95.14.54.

Bicycle hire : M. Chombart, rue Bellenger, ☎ 35.95.08.40.

Picardy and the North

The North — the name evokes tranquil, misty horizons, meandering rivers and a sky perpetually covered with scudding clouds. Images that can easily suggest monotony. And yet the "flat country" lying between the Paris and the Anglo-Norman basins, and immortalized in the songs of Jacques Brel, includes the most varied regions. The south is characterized by the hard underlying soapstone of the Paris basin where the Artois hills rise 100 or 200 metres up from the plain, and further south still are vast limestone plateaus indented with the green valleys of Vimeu, Ponthieu and Santerre. To the north, beyond the chalky ledges of the Artois peaks with their wooded valleys, the chalk strata sinks deeper under sand and clay to form lower and damper ground — this is the true "flat country" whose only relief is provided by the hills of Flanders. The fertile plateaus of the south with their damp valleys and farmhouses huddled together in villages contrast with the wide northern plains sectioned by groves of trees and hedgerows and dotted with isolated farmhouses. The south is thinly populated along the traditional invasion route from the East. But everywhere are the characteristic windmills adding a touch of poetry and fantasy to the landscape.

Perhaps the best time to visit the Pays du Nord is during one of the many festivals, when the people dance together around wickerwork effigies representing their beloved and legendary "giants"; the Festival of Dunkirk just before Lent and the Festival of Gargantua in Bailleul are among the most important.

The bustling towns and ports of the region — many of which were devastated by the battles of the Second World War — have their share of famous churches and abbeys, such as the huge cathedral of Amiens, the largest in France, a true masterpiece of Gothic art. Calais, the largest passenger port in France, is also noted for its lace industry introduced from England at the beginning of the 19th century. Coal, textiles and steel were the traditionnal mainstays of the region's economy, and Lille, Roubaix and Valenciennes have for centuries been important manufacturing centers. Slagheaps and colliery lifting gear still mark the land in which Zola set his *Germinal.* Today, the North is — sometimes reluctantly — shedding its smokestack image, and whitecoated technicians and electronics assembly lines are beginning to replace the ruddy glare of blast furnaces seen from the autoroute.

Sightseeing

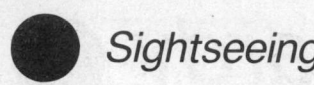

Facts and figures

***Area :** 18 803 km².*

***Population :** 4 477 509.*

***Climate :** temperate; prevailing winds W and NW, with wet winter and spring. Summer is usually fine, and despite the inevitable cloudy periods, the average maximum temperature is 21 °C. In autumn the weather is changeable, but temperatures remain mild.*

***Administration :** the two departments of **Nord** and **Pas-de-Calais** form a single administrative region, the capital of which is Lille. The **Somme** belongs to the region of Picardy, which also includes the departments of **Oise** and **Aisne,** with the regional capital at Amiens.*

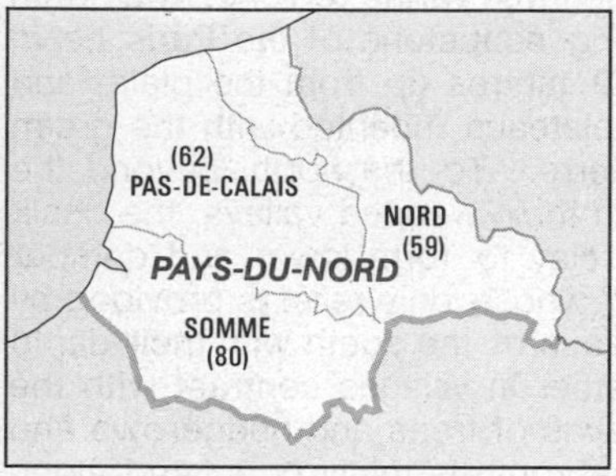

Don't miss

★★★ : Amiens (B3), Arras (B2), Corniche de la Côte d'Opale (A1), Lille (B1), ★★ : Abbeville (A2), Bavay (C2), Bergues (A1), Boulogne (A1), Cassel (B1), Crêtes du Sacrifice (B2), Douai (B2), Rue (A2), Saint-Omer (A1), Saint-Riquier (A2), and Saint-Valéry-sur-Somme (A2).

AIRE-SUR-LA-LYS★

B1 / ® / pop. 9 535 (Pas-de-Calais)

In rich and fertile country; some of its streets still keep their 17th-18thC appearance.

▶ **Grand'Place** (Main Square) : **Hôtel de Ville** (town hall) with classic French belfry and carillon (1717-1721). On a corner of the square, the charming Flemish Renaissance **Baillage**★ (1604; Baillif's Court) formerly housed the city militia. ▶ **Collegiate church of St. Pierre**★ is one of the largest Renaissance and Flamboyant Gothic buildings in Flanders; inside : 1663 organ-casing and statue of Our Lady, the city's patron saint. ▶ 17thC Baroque **church of St. Jacques.** □

AMIENS★★★

A-B3 / ® / pop. 131 330 (Somme)
(see plan on following page)

Amiens is the capital of Picardy and has been a prosperous textile town since the Middle Ages, with a reputation for fine velvet dating back to the 17thC. At the end of

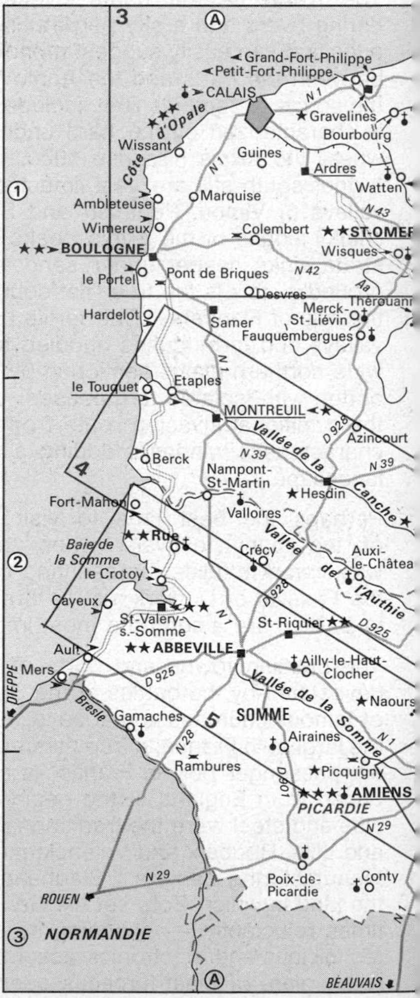

WWII, 60 % of of the town was in ruins and has since been been extensively rebuilt : the **Tour Perret** (tower, 104 m ; C3) dominating the skyline, the **Maison de la Culture** (cultural center ; B2) in a bold mixture of concrete and glass, and the broad university campus on the southern edge of town, are all evidence of the town's successful architectural revolution.

▶ In the city centre, the **Notre Dame Cathedral★★★** (C2) : 145 m long, 70 m wide at the transept with 43-m high vaulting, the largest cathedral in France with 126 pillars and a spire reaching 112 m into the sky.
The main façade has three great **doorways★** decorated with statues and **bas-reliefs** sculpted between 1225-1230 ; the central door shows Christ surrounded by the Apostles ; the statue of "Le Beau Dieu" — Christ in serenity — is the focus of this immense biblical sculpture. Inside the cathedral are the 13thC bronze funeral effigies of the founding bishops. Note the rosette

Weekend tips

If you approach from the south, first visit the cathedral at Amiens ; spend the night in Boulogne (see the illuminations in the old town). The next day watch the fishermen unloading and sorting fish in the port. Head for Calais along the Côte d'Opale ridge road, over the Boulonnais hills and across two promontories. From Saint-Omer climb towards the typically Flemish town of Cassel, before arriving at Lille. The following day choose between two excursions : through the regional nature reserve of Saint-Amand and the Avesnois, or through the beautiful towns of Douai and Arras to the famous ridges at Vimy and Notre-Dame-de-Lorette (Crêtes du Sacrifice).

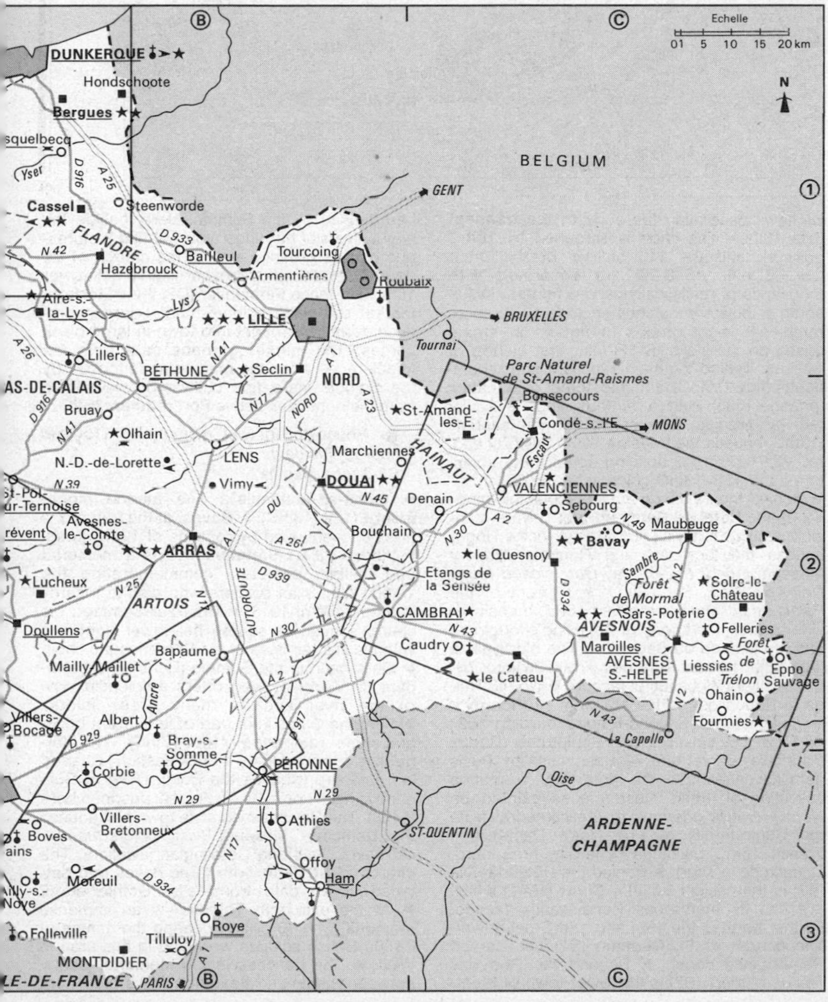

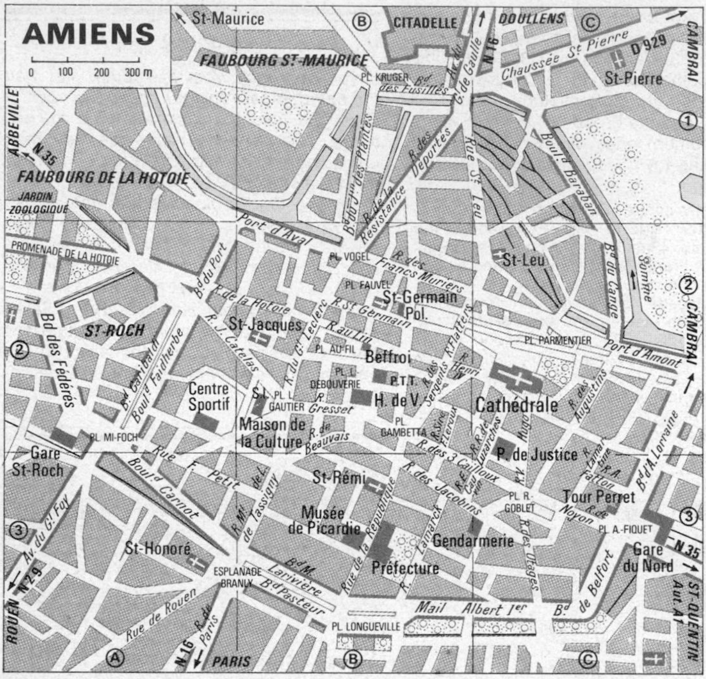

windows decorating the ends of the **transept** (late 13thC). The **choir** is screened by 18thC grillwork and the 110 stalls★ of the choir (carved oak, 1508-20) are decorated with thousands of realistically-carved figures. In the south ambulatory the choir enclosure★ is decorated with eight groups of figures in stone, based on the life of St. Firmin, first bishop of Amiens. Behind the main altar is a fine recumbent effigy (15thC) and the tomb of a canon (priest) (1628) with a famous angel★ sculpted by Nicolas Blasset. A former sacristy (19thC) houses the treasure room *(visit by appt tel. 22.91.27.31)*, containing some thirty sculptures and 12th-13thC goldsmiths work.

▶ Behind the *Palais de Justice* (court building; C2-3), the **Hôtel de Berny** (former private mansion; Louis XIII style; no. 36 Rue Victor Hugo) houses the local Art and Regional History Museum *(10-12 & 2-6, May-Oct; closed Mon; Nov-Apr, Wed., Sat., Sun.)*. ▶ In front of the *Palais de Justice* are two fine 16thC mansions, side-by-side, the **Logis du Roi** (King's lodgings) and the **Maison du Sagittaire.** The old **theatre** (late 18thC) in the Rue des Trois Cailloux (B-C3) has kept its beautiful façade. ▶ No. 48 Rue de la République is the **Museum of Picardy★** in a sumptuous Second-Empire building (B3; *10-12 & 2-6, closed Mon*). Sculptures (Rodin, Bourdelle, Barye) and vast canvases by Puvis de Chavannes. On the first floor a unique collection of 16thC masterpieces painted on wood★ (votive offerings to the cathedral from the Confraternity of Puy Notre Dame) and French 18thC paintings (Chardin, Fragonard, Quentin de la Tour). ▶ Behind the Hôtel de Ville (B2) is the ancient **Bailiff's Court** (1541) which still has its marvellous Renaissance façade. Further north is the 15th and 18thC bell-tower. The **church of St. Germain** (B2) has carved Renaissance doors. ▶ Beyond the Rue des Francs-Muriers (B2) is the lower town of Saint-Leu flanked by the Somme. Here, beside the new university buildings, you will find picturesque houses grouped around the **church of St. Leu** (C2; 15thC; Flamboyant Gothic bell-tower 16thC). In Place Parmentier (C2) the **waterfront market** still sells regional market-garden produce, formerly brought into town in large black barges. The **market gardens** date from the Middle Ages when the many islands formed by the Somme were first cultivated; view them from the right bank above **Port d'Amont** (B2). □

▶ Round trip of war memorials★ *(150 km approx, full day)*
B2-3 *(see map 1)*

▶ **Sains-en-Amiénois :** fine **funeral monument★** (12th-13thC). ▶ **Boves,** at the foot of the hillside, overlooked by remains of 12thC **keep.** ▶ Above **Villers-Bretonneux** ® is a **memorial** and military cemetery commemorating the 10,000 Australian soldiers who died in Picardy in the spring of 1918. ▶ **Bray-sur-Somme :** the church's massive square bell-tower contrasts with the slender lines of the Romanesque choir. ▶ On a bend in the Somme (Curlu), the belvédère de Vaux★ (tower) offers a splendid view of the river and its many green islets. ▶ **Péronne** ® has kept part of its ancient brick-and-stone **ramparts★** (16th-17thC). The **fortress** is surrounded by a brick bastion; Charles le Téméraire (Charles the Bold), Duke of Burgundy, held Louis XI of France prisoner here (1468). The Renaissance style town hall houses the **Danicourt Museum** *(visit on request)* : old coins, Gaul and Carolingian jewellery. The **church of St. Jean,** with three naves and flattened chevets, dates from the last Gothic period. ▶ At the exit from **Thiepval** is an immense **memorial** with 16 pillars, bearing the names of 73 000 British soldiers who died in this area in WWI. ▶ The trenches in the **memorial park★** between **Hamel** and **Beaumont** have been kept

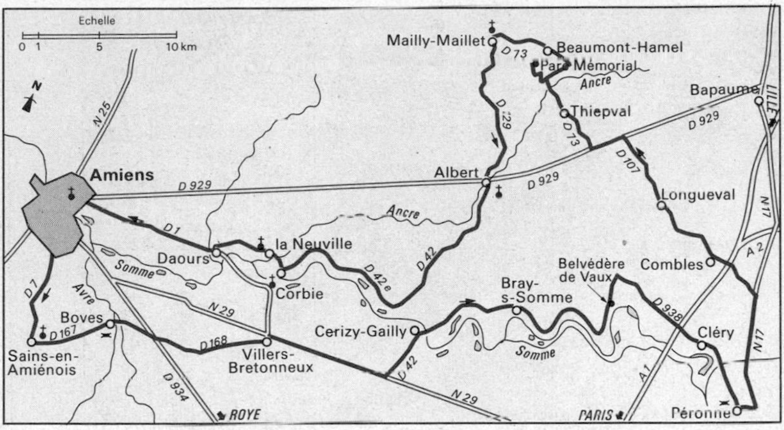

1. Round trip of war memorials

in their original state, illustrating army life in WWI; a monument representing a caribou commemorates the Newfoundland (Canadian) regiment which fought here in 1916. ▶ **Mailly-Maillet** has a 16thC church with a beautiful Flamboyant Gothic doorway. ▶ **Albert** : the town hall with its Flemish belfry was rebuilt, as was the **basilica Notre-Dame-de-Brebières,** in brick and white stone. The 11thC statue of *La Vierge aux Brebis* (The Holy Mother with the lost sheep) is said to have worked miracles and is a frequent object of pilgrimage. ▶ **Corbie** : the former abbey church (16th-18thC) is now the **church of St. Pierre★,** unfortunately reduced to the nave and the façade. Inside : 14th and 15thC statues★. The former **collegiate church of St. Étienne** (11th-13thC) has lost its transept and side aisles but retains a beautiful 13thC doorway dedicated to the Virgin. ▶ La Neuville (a suburb, 2 km W) : the 16thC **church** has a handsome carved tympanum★ over its doorway, representing the "Entry of Christ" into Jerusalem; inside, 12thC baptismal fonts. ▶ **Amiens** (→). □

Windmills

For inhabitants of northern France, windmills symbolize their efforts to make use of the forces of nature, and scores of them are still outlined against the sky in Flanders and Artois. Many are near the coast, but few of these still work. They fall into two categories : the pivot mill where the whole structure turns on a vertical shaft to face the wind, and the solid tower in stone or brick where only the roof turns. Windmills can be cylindrical, square or octagonal, built of brick, wood or stone; all create romantic silhouettes across the flat plains of the north.

▶ Visit to a subterranean refuge★★ *(20 km, half day)*
A2-3 *(see map 5)*

▶ **Bertangles** has a fine stone **château** in French Regency style (1730). The wrought-iron entrance gate★ is decorated with hunting scenes *(15 Jul-15 Sep, daily, pm only).* ▶ Finely carved "Burial of Christ" (15thC) in 13th-16thC church at **Villers-Bocage** ®. ▶ **Naours★** is an ancient earth-and-plaster village with a vast network of **subterranean refuge★★** in the neighbouring plateau, formerly used during the Norman invasions of 9thC, and subsequently during the Wars of Religion (16thC) and the 30-Years' War (17thC). This subterranean area was developed over the centuries and now comprises 2 km of hand-hewn galleries with air vents leading to the plateau 30 m above. 3000 people were able to shelter here; it is now a folklore **museum** *(open daily).* □

■ ARRAS★★★

B2 / ® / pop. 41 740 (80 000 with suburbs) (Pas-de-Calais)

Arras expanded rapidly after WWII and is today a large modern town. During the Middle Ages it was an important centre of weaving and the cloth trade. In the 17th and 18thC the civic dignitaries built a fine city centre; its handsome architecture has been carefully preserved.

▶ **La Grand'Place★★★** (C2) and the **Place des Héros★★★** constitute the most perfect example extant of 17th and 18thC Flemish architecture in France. Both are surrounded by tall narrow houses of brick and stone with ornate gables. The street-level arcades are supported on sandstone pillars. Behind the pillars are trap doors leading down to the **cellars** *(les boves)* which are several stories deep and were used as hiding places during various wars. A very colourful market is held each Saturday in both squares. ▶ The **Hôtel de Ville** (B-C2) has a 75-m high **belfry★** (excellent chimes) surmounted by the Lion of Arras. The main building dates from early 16thC. Guided tour of the underground passages starts in the basement; display cases from the museum's archaeological section and audiovisual spectacle (20 centuries of history in Arras). ▶ The **cathedral★** (18thC; D12) is a huge building in Neo-Classical style. Inside : enormous statues of saints from the Pantheon; 17thC head of Christ in wood (left arm of the transept); fine "Christ Scourged" (wood; 17thC) in the ambulatory. The former 18thC **Benedictine abbey of**

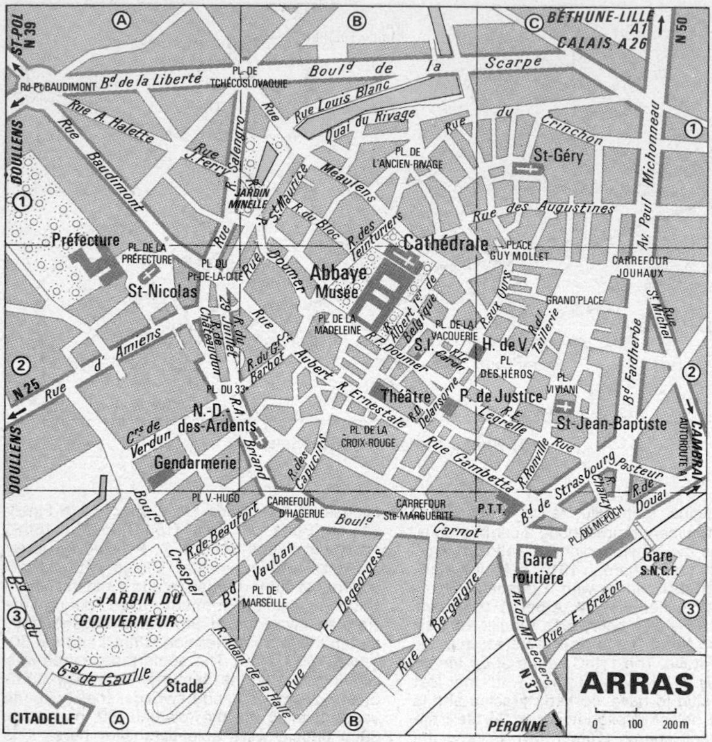

St. Vaast next to the cathedral now houses the **Fine Arts Museum★** (B2; *10-12 & 2-5:30 daily ex Tue.*) : mediaeval sculpture; 16th-18thC paintings (triptychs by Bellegambe, 16thC, northern schools of 18thC); 19thC French paintings (Corot, Delacroix, Daubigny, Chassériau). ▶ In the Place du Théâtre opposite the 18thC **theatre** is the **Ostel des Poissoniers** (Fishermans' Guild Building), a narrow Baroque structure of 1710 decorated with carved sirens and fish. □

▶ Les Crêtes du Sacrifice ("Crests of Sacrifice")★★ *(40 km from Arras to Olhain)*

▶ **Mont-Saint-Éloi** *(8 km NW from Arras)*, on a strategically-placed hill overlooking the Scarpe valley, was the scene of violent fighting in 1915 and 1940. On the summit, imposing remains of the famous **abbey**, founded by St. Éloi in the 7thC. ▶ **Vimy Ridge** *(8 km NE)* was a key position attacked in April 1917 by Canadian troops. The 74,000 Canadians who died in France are commemorated here, and from the massive **memorial★** there is an extensive view over the plain of Lens and its coal mines. To the south, on the wooded slope of the hill, a network of **trenches** has been preserved for visitors. ▶ **Notre-Dame-de-Lorette★★** *(10 km NW from Vimy)* : on this desolate site is a **national cemetery** with 20,000 tombs; eight ossuaries contain the remains of 26,000 unidentified soldiers; on the first floor of the main **ossuary** between the lantern tower (view) is a small memorial museum. Below and opposite on the Souchez road is a **museum-diorama of the battlefields** *(Apr-Nov, daily pm only; Jun-Jul-Aug, 10-6, ex Sun am)*. ▶ **Olhain** ® *(14 km NW)* : leisure centre in the forest; feudal **château★** (13th-15thC) on a romantic site in the middle of a lake. *(15 Apr.-15 Oct., pm only Sun. and nat. hols.)*. □

■ AUTHIE Valley★★

▶ From Doullens to Le Touquet *(110 km approx, full day)*
A-B2 *(see map 4)*

The Authie River winds through the Picardy plain along a green valley of meadows and marshes, with small woods and cultivated areas near the numerous hamlets. Houses are of brick (sometimes whitewashed), usually with well-stocked flower gardens.

▶ **Doullens** ® : citadel by Vauban surrounding the stone bastions of Francois I's castle. **Hôtel de Ville :** early 15thC square **bell-tower;** opposite, **church of Notre Dame** with noteworthy stone Burial of Christ (1583); nave of former **church of St. Peter** (13th-15thC). **Lombart Museum** (Poulbot lithographs; Egyptian and Far Eastern antiquities; *2-5:30 Thu. and Sun.*). ▶ **Lucheux★,** on the border between Artois and Picardy : **castle ruins** of the counts of St. Pol (12th-16thC; 13thC Hall of Justice; *daily 9-6*). In the village : 12th-14thC **gate-tower;** 12thC **church** with fine storiated capitals. ▶ **Auxi-le-Château,** in the valley : Flamboyant Gothic **church;** vaulting with remarkable carved keystones. ▶ **Le Boisle :** a traditional basket-weaving centre on the left bank of the Authie. ▶ The D119 runs past the impressive 17thC doorway of the former **Dommartin Abbey;** ruins of 12thC abbey church; 17thC buildings. ▶ **Tortefontaine** *(1 km)* : pretty 12thC

Romanesque church. ▶ **Argoules,** on the left bank : 16thC church and brick manor-house. ▶ Former Cistercian **abbey of Valloires★★** (12thC), close to the Authie valley : reception room, chapter room, chapel and sacristy have magnificent wood panelling *(10-12 & 2:30-6:30, daily Mar-Oct).* ▶ Leaving **Nampont-Saint-Martin,** below the D85E, picturesque 15th-16thC fortified house; moats filled from the Authie river. ▶ D102 leads to **Fort-Mahon** ® : miles of beach. ▶ **Berck-sur-Mer** ®, climate especially suitable for treatment of bone diseases : 13th-16thC **church** in town centre. On the Le Touquet road, Bagatelle Amusement Park (55 acres). ▶ **Saint-Josse,** 10 km NW of Berck : **church** with 15thC choir; 16thC shrine★ of 5thC hermit St. Josse and triptych illustrating his life. ▶ **Le Touquet** (→ La Canche Valley). □

■ The **AVESNOIS** Area★★

▶ From Quesnoy to Cambrai *(175 km approx, 1 day)*
C2 *(see map 2)*

The Avesnois is an area of green fields and hedges. Along the way you will find water mills still turning in the valleys, charming churches, numerous oratories scattered through the countryside and pretty flowered villages.

▶ **Le Quesnoy★★** ® : 13thC **ramparts★** with leisure centre at their foot. The 1585 town hall had a large Neo-Classical tower added in 1700 : carillon; concerts. ▶ 2 km E, little 13thC feudal **château de Potelle** with large moats *(exterior visit only).* ▶ **Bavay★★ :** slate-roofed houses huddled round the 18thC **Hôtel de Ville,** flanked by a 17thC belfry. This peaceful town was the metropolis of the Gallo-Roman province of Belgium, crossroads for seven major Roman highways. Excavations after WWII revealed the **remains★★** of ancient Bagacum (2ndC; small museum with rich collection of daily objects; *weekdays 9-12 & 2-5; closed Tue; Sun and nat. hols. 9:30-12 & 2-7 or 5 out of season*). ▶ 4 km NW, **Bellignies** has a **museum** of objects carved in local marble *(Apr.-Sep. 2-5).* ▶ **Maubeuge** ®, a major industrial centre in the valley of the Sambre : In the north, the beautiful **Porte de Mons★** (Mons Gate; 1685). On the left bank of the Sambre the **church of St. Pierre** is a remnant of Vauban's fortifications; bell-tower with lovely sounding of bells; concerts on Sunday. The former chapter of Canonesses (end 17thC) is now a regional **museum :** paintings by Van Dyck and Coypel *(daily, 2-5 or 4 out of season; closed Tue).* The 17thC **Jesuit College** is a fine example of Baroque architecture. By the west wall is a multiple-species **Zoo** *(daily May-Sep. 10-6; Oct.-Apr. 1:30-5).* **Sars-Poteries** ® : since the Middle Ages an important earthenware and ceramic centre, turning to glassware in 19thC. Fascinating glass museum★ (Musée du Verre; *2-7, Sat, Sun nat. and school hols.*). **Felleries** *(3 km S)* traditionally a barrel-making centre; pleasant **museum** in an old mill *(2:30-6:30 Sun. and nat. hols., Apr.-Jun. and Sep.-Nov.; daily Jul.-Aug.).* ▶ **Solre-le-Château★** ® : remarkable collection of old buildings in the town; late 16thC **Hôtel de Ville;** the **Gothic church** (end 16thC) has a turreted gate-tower; the spire is topped by an onion dome. Inside : 18thC organ case, 16thC stained glass, treasure room in the Sacristy. ▶ **Liessies** ® on the Greater Helpe river : 16thC **parish church;** 15th-17thC statues; religious artifacts and goldsmiths' work from the former abbey. South of the village : **château de la Motte** (18thC, now a hotel). ▶ On the other side of Liessies there are good views over the artificial lake of **Val Joly.** ▶ **Eppe-Sauvage** has two fine 16thC triptychs in its **church.** ▶ As the valley of the Helpe gets broader, marshes and lakes start to appear. 16thC, **priory** at **Moustier-en-Fagne** (fagne = marsh). At the entry to the village is a charming 16thC **manor house** in brick and stone. ▶ **Ohain** has a 16thC chapel with a very beautiful wooden statue★ of Christ scourged; **Trelon** (3 km N) is a former glass-making centre; **Musée du Verre** (Glass Museum) and workshop *(daily Easter-15 Oct.).* ▶ **Fourmies★** ® became an important textile centre last century. **Ecomusée★★** (museum) in a former cotton mill showing the social and working life of the textile workers in 19thC *(daily 9-12 & 2-6 May-Oct.).* A number of lakes in the nearby woods have been converted for

2. Avesnols - Cambrésis - Valenciennois regions

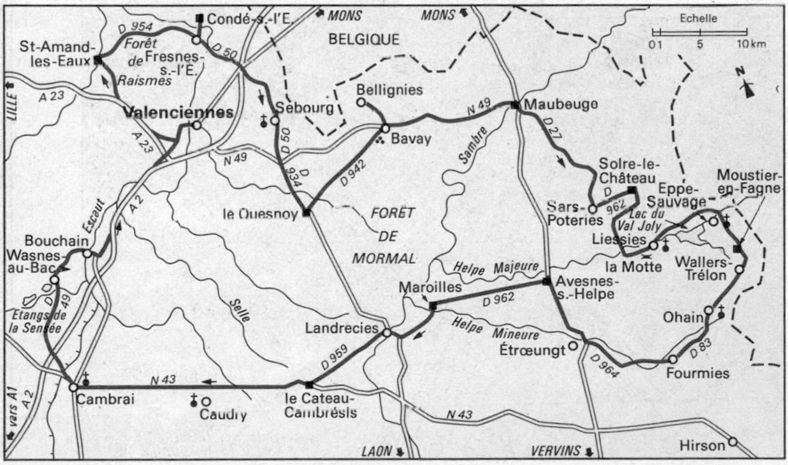

leisure use. ▶ **Avesnes-sur-Helpe** ® : Remains of Vauban-style fortifications; elegant town hall (Neo-Classical); parish **church of St. Nicolas★** with imposing gate-tower; inside : beautiful Louis XV altarpieces partially painted by Louis Watteau.

▶ **Maroilles** ® : on the banks of the Helpe, well known for its cheeses, originally produced by the monks of a Benedictine abbey founded in the 7thC; this was destroyed in the French Revolution and only the outbuildings exist (17thC tithe barn, or *grange dimière*). ▶ 3 km N, across the Sambre, is the vast **Forêt de Mormal★** (Mormal Forest), the largest in the north of France with 22,500 acres; marked paths and numerous picnic places. ▶ **Le Cateau** is on the boundary between pastoral Avesnois and arable Cambrésis. The former **palace** of the Archbishops of Cambrai is today a **museum★** *(Wed.-Sat. 3-6; closed Mon. and Tue.; Sun. 10-12 & 2-6)* with works by two painters from the region, Auguste Herbin and Henri Matisse (born in Le Cateau 1869). In the main square the 17thC **Hôtel de Ville** has a charming 1705 bell-tower. The **church of St. Martin** (1635) is a good example of Baroque architecture. ▶ **Caudry** has a modern church containing the shrine★ of Ste. Maxellende. **Cambrai** (→). □

■ BERGUES★★

B1 / ® / pop. 4 490 (Nord)

This is one of the most picturesque towns in French Flanders, its numerous canals and neat houses surrounded by powerful-looking fortifications.

▶ There are four gates to the town in the **outer walls★★;** the most beautiful is the **Porte de Cassel★** (17thC; to the south), with the royal sun of Louis XIV in its pediment. From the same period on the north side is the **Couronne d'Hondschoote★,** a large system of defensive works ringed by moats. ▶ In the town centre is a **belfry★** crowned by the Lion of Flanders; pretty carillon (concerts). ▶ Behind St. Martin's church is a 17thC Baroque **Mont-de-Piété** (pawnshop), now the municipal museum : fine collection of 16th and 17thC Flemish paintings, and the celebrated "Joueur de Vielle"★ by Georges de la Tour *(daily 10-12 & 2-5; closed Fri).* ▶ 10 km S, **Esquelbecq** ® is a typical Flemish country town with its paved main square lined with old houses and its enormous triple-naved church (16thC); the **château★** still looks like a feudal fortress in spite of the wide 17thC windows; nine pepperpot towers, stepped gables, high watch-tower and wide moats filled by the Yser River *(2-6, daily, 15 Apr.-15 Oct.).* □

■ BOULOGNE-SUR-MER★★

A1 / ® / pop. 47 650 (Pas-de-Calais)

Julius Caesar set out from here in 55 BC to invade England; 17 centuries later Napoléon tried to repeat the performance. During the last century Boulogne began to develop a deep-sea fishing fleet and is now the major French and E.E.C. **fishing port★.** It is also the leading French fish-processing centre.

▶ The modern port was built on the ruins left after WWII. In the **upper town★★★ :** rectangular mediaeval ramparts with **château** at NE corner, overlooked by the enormous dome of the **Notre Dame Basilica** (C2) built between 1827-66; 11thC Romanesque **crypt** with painted pil-

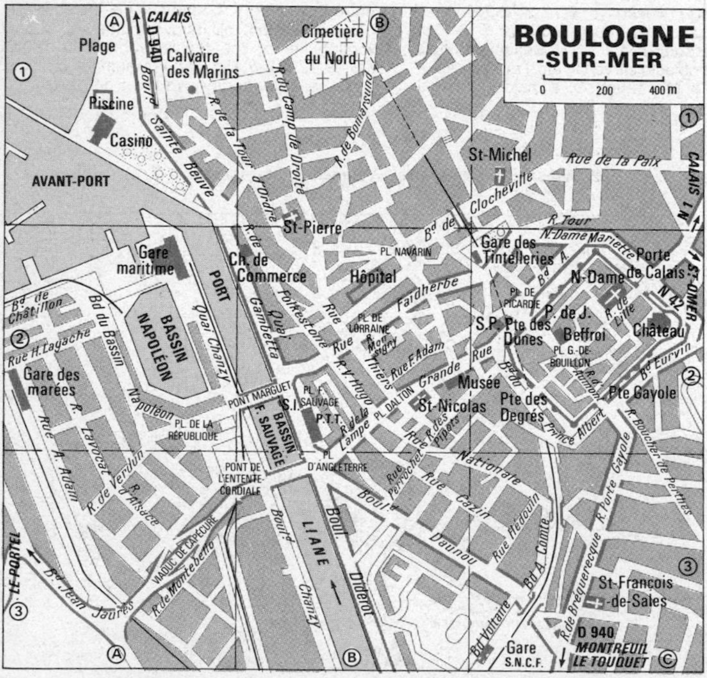

lars; remnants of 3rdC Roman temple. Treasure room of the Basilica in one of the underground rooms. ▶ In the centre of the upper town : 18thC **Hotel de Ville** (brick with stone facing) contrasts with the 12th-13thC square **bell-tower** (C2). Opposite the town hall, the impressive **hôtel Desandrouin★**, ca. 1780 in Neo-Classical style; Napoléon stayed here on several occasions. Nearby is the former 17th and 18thC **Annonciades Convent,** now the Municipal Library. ▶ In the Grande Rue (B2-C2) : **Musée des Beaux Arts★★** (Fine Arts Museum) at no. 34, housed in a former 18thC seminary; fine collection of Greek vases★★ and Egyptian antiquities *(9:30-12 & 2-6:30, Wed.-Sun).* Farther down the Grand Rue, the **Church of St. Nicolas** (B2), 17th-18thC, has a Neo-Classical façade. □

▶ Côte d'Opale Corniche★★★ (cliff road; *50 km from Boulogne to Calais*).
A1 *(see map 3)*

▶ **Wimereux** ® : good view of the port of Boulogne and the Colonne de la Grande Armée from the seafront dyke. ▶ **Ambleteuse** was once a naval base protected by Fort Mahon (17thC). ▶ On the left, along the road to Cape Gris-Nez is a former blockhouse, now a **Museum of The Atlantic Wall;** military equipment *(daily).* **Cape Gris-Nez★★** (from the Gaelic 'Craig Ness', rocky cape); this is where the English Channel meets the North Sea. From this windy promontory 45 m above the waves, you can see the port of Boulogne *(left),* **Cape Blanc-Nez** *(right)* and the English coast opposite. ▶ **Audinghen :** fine modern church. ▶ **Wissant,** extensive beach between Gris-Nez and Blanc-Nez. **Cape Blanc-Nez★★★,** the highest point on the cliffs (134 m). Sharp winding road with good view★ of the English cliffs and the coast towards Calais. Below, monument to Latham, who tried in vain to fly the Channel. ▶ **Sangatte** is a proposed starting place for the tunnel under the Channel. ▶ **Blériot Plage** (beach) : named after Louis Blériot, the first airman to fly the Channel; he landed in Dover, England, on 25 July 1909. ▶ **Calais** (→). □

■ CALAIS

A1 / ® / pop. 77 000 (Pas-de-Calais)

For centuries Anglo-French rivalry centred around Calais. Today its proximity to England has made it the most important passenger port in France. Largely rebuilt since WWII, Calais has developed an important industrial centre. Lace-making, introduced from England at the beginning of the 19thC, is now complemented by the production of other textiles.

▶ To the north, the **old town** is an island surrounded by canals and harbour basins. The only remnant of its past is the 13thC **watchtower** *(tour de guet),* used as a lighthouse until 1848, and the **church of Notre Dame,** begun in 13thC but finished in 16thC under English supervision. This is the only church in France in Perpendicular Gothic, a style developed exclusively in England during the reign of the Tudors.

Kermesses and carnavals

Traditional festivities are either kermesses *(non-religious festivals) or* ducasses *(Saint's day festivals). Processions and cavalcades, fanfares and chorales play a part in both. The folklore of the region includes giant wickerwork figures and dancing through the streets. The most popular and the most famous carnivals are : Dunkerque and Bailleul (Fête de Gargantua), before Lent; Cassel and Aire-sur-la-Lys set their giants dancing on Easter Monday. Summer carnivals are celebrated nearly everywhere : at Douai the giant Gayant and his family have been feted every July since 1530.*

3. Côte d'Opale Corniche road

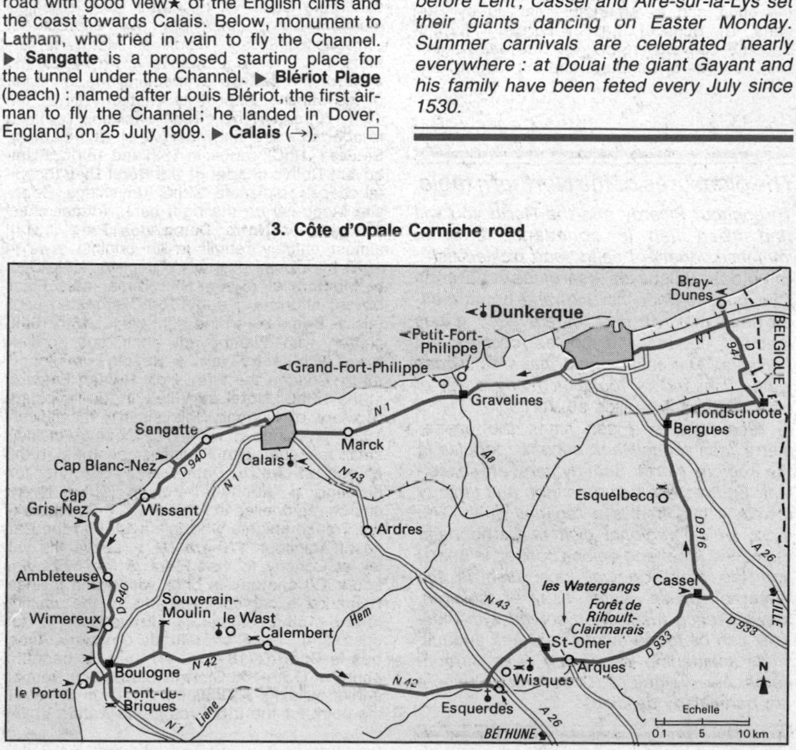

▶ The **Courgain** quarter : 1848 lighthouse, 58 m high with a marvellous view *(daily, Jul-Aug.)*; on the other side of the basin is **Fort Risban,** defending the port entry. ▶ In the Rue Richelieu, the **Musée des Beaux Arts et de la Dentelle★** (Fine Arts and Lace Museum; *10-12 & 2-5 daily; closed Tue; tel. 21.97.99.00*) : 19th and 20thC sculptures and lace history room on the ground floor; 1st floor, rich collection of paintings especially 16th-19thC Dutch and Flemish schools. ▶ **Hôtel de Ville,** built at beginning of 20thC in Flemish Renaissance style, with 75-m belfry (chimes). On the esplanade, the famous **Monument des Bourgeois de Calais** (Calais merchants)★★, by Rodin, 1895. ▶ Opposite the town hall in St. Pierre park, German blockhouse, now the **Musée de la Guerre** (War Museum; *daily, 10:30-5:30 ex Tue., Jun.-Sep. tel. 21.96.62.40*). □

■ CAMBRAI★

B2 / ® / pop. 35 270 (Nord)

From a distance the three towers of Cambrai are visible on the right bank of the Escaut : the belfry, the cathedral and the church of St. Géry. Unlike the brick periphery, the centre of town is built of white limestone.

▶ In the Grand'Place, the **Hôtel de Ville** (1786) is crowned by a bell-tower on either side of which are two famous mechanical figures, Martin and Martine (1512), who mark the hours by hammering a large bell. To the west, the **church of St. Géry** has a 76-m tower; a Neo-Classic building of early 18thC with fine Baroque choirscreen (1635), 18thC woodwork in the choir and a remarkable canvas by Rubens, "The Burial of Christ". ▶ Further N, former **Beguine convent** (16thC; 24 Rue des Anglaises), remains of ramparts and the ruins of the **château de Selles** (13thC; prisoners' graffiti). ▶ South of the town hall is the Rue de la Victoire : to the right, 15th-18thC **belfry;** in the square farther on, the **Maison Espagnole★,** an old half-timbered house with slate gable (late 15thC; SI) and the **chapel of the Grand Séminaire** (1692 : fine Baroque façade). ▶ Opposite, the **cathedral of Notre Dame** (18thC) is decorated at each end of the transept with *trompe l'œil grisailles* from 1760; in the apsidal chapel, fine monument to Fénelon by David d'Angers (1826). ▶ In the Rue-de-l'Épée is the **municipal museum** (18thC mansion); 12th, 16th and 17thC sculptures, 16th and 17thC Dutch and Flemish paintings, 19th and 20thC French paintings *(10-12 & 2-5; closed Tue)*. □

The pleasures of the Northern table

Throughout Picardy and the North you will find fresh fish in abundance and an immense variety of salted and pickled fish : roll-mops, pilchards *(sardines),* harengs saur *(smoke-dried herring) and* bouffi *(salted and smoked). Lots of* crevettes grises *(shrimp),* coques *and* moules *(cockles and mussels). The eel is king of the area's fresh water fish and is found in many sorts of* pâté *such as* Anguilles au Vert.
In recent years a sea plant, the passe-pierre *(sea fennel) has become popular in the region. North Sea oysters are excellent. Endives are very common and chicory mixed with coffee is a regional habit. The most typical regional dish is* Carbonnade Flamande *(beef and onions cooked in beer); and the most original local dish is the* Waterzoï *(fresh water fish, or chicken, stew). French fries, often served with mussels, can be found everywhere and* andouillettes *(chitterling sausages) from Armentières, Arras, Cambrai, Douai and elsewhere are particularly delicious.*

■ CANCHE Valley★★

▶ From Le Touquet to Doullens *(130 km approx, full day)*
A-B2 *(see map 4)*

The Canche River runs lazily across the Artois plateau, through a countryside of meadows, marshes, peat-bogs and poplar groves.

▶ **Le Touquet** ® : a seaside-and-health resort at the mouth of the Canche, with elegant villas set back from the seafront among pines and birches. ▶ **Étaples★,** a fishing port with low houses painted in cheerful colours, has been the inspiration of numerous artists. A 17thC salt warehouse is now the archaeological museum *(daily, 1 Jul-15 Sep; Wed and Sun out of season; closed Tue)*. ▶ **Montreuil-sur-Mer★★** ® : once a coastal town — on the edge of the plateau overlooking the left bank of the Canche. Rebuilt by Vauban (17thC), the 12th-16th and 17thC **citadel★** *(closed Tue)* and **ramparts★★** are still intact (view). **Church of St. Saulve** (11thC), rebuilt in 13th and 16thC. Flamboyant Gothic **chapel of the Hôtel-Dieu** (hospital chapel) : splendid 17thC furnishings. Opposite Montreuil on the right bank, former **charterhouse of Notre Dame des Prés** (1314), almost entirely rebuilt in its original style in 1870 by a pupil of the architect Viollet-le-Duc. ▶ **Montcravel** (5 km N) : remarkable Flamboyant **church★ :** early 16thC storiated capitals. ▶ **Brimeux,** on the right bank : 15th-16thC church with Flamboyant choir and fortified tower with sentry-walk. ▶ **Hesdin★** ® : founded by Charles the Fifth, Holy Roman Emperor in the 16thC; **Hôtel de Ville★** in former palace of Mary of Hungary (his sister); magnificent 1629 bay-window, with 1702 coping; inside : small museum with Flemish tapestries. 16thC **church of Notre Dame,** with Baroque furnishings. ▶ **Auchy-lès-Hesdin** (5 km NW) : church remodelled in 16th and 17thC; tombs of the French knights who fell in 1415 at the Battle of Agincourt *(10 km N)*. ▶ Leave the valley at Conchy to visit **Flers** *(5 km NE) :* fine Louis XVI **château** in brick with stone facings. Remarkable carved keystones to the vaulting in the 15thC chapel. ▶ **Frévent** ® (1 km upstream) : 18thC **château de Cercamp. Avesnes-le-Comte** (18 km W) has a beautiful **church★** (15th-16thC), with 12thC choir from an earlier building. ▶ **Doullens** ® *(15 km S) :* starting point for the trip through the **Authie Valley** (→). □

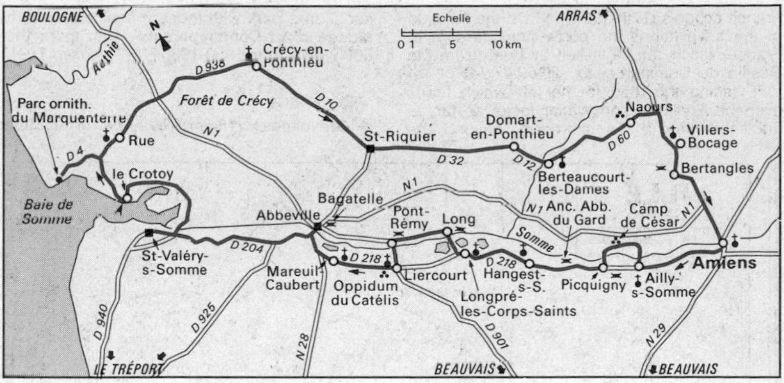

4. Canche and Authie valleys

CASSEL★★

B1 / pop. 2 220 (Nord)

Above the flat plain of Flanders, Mont Cassel rises 175 m to give a wide view across the country.

▶ In 1914-15 the French forces commander Maréchal Foch made his HQ here, and in 1940 the British army tenaciously defended this strategic position before falling back on Dunkirk. On the top of Mont Cassel is an equestrian statue of Maréchal Foch and a picturesque 18thC wooden mill★. Cassel is a charming city with narrow sloping **streets** and flights of steps★★. ▶ In the Grand'Place opposite the town hall is the elegant stone façade of the **Hôtel de la Noble Cour★;** a fine Renaissance doorway leads into a history-and-folklore museum : parchments, ceramics, Flemish furniture, Louis XV wood panelling *(daily, 2-6 Jun.-Sep.; Sun. only Apr.-May).* Nearby the **Hôtel d'Halluin** with fine Louis XVI façade. ▶ The **Collegiate church of Notre Dame** is a massive triple-naved building in Flemish Gothic.

DOUAI★★

B2 / ® / pop. 42 580 (Nord)

Douai, in the heart of the industrial north is the capital of the coal country as well as a university town. Its bell-tower — immortalized by the painter Corot — has the largest carillon in Europe (62 bells). *Gayant,* the most well-known and oldest of the giants of the north, plays a special part in local folklore.

▶ On the Place d'Armes, the beautiful **maison du Dauphin★** (SI) typifies the aristocratic appearance of the town in 18thC. Nearby is a famous square **bell-tower★★** (late 14thC) crowned by the Lion of Flanders (late 15thC). Carillons are rung Sat, Sun and nat. hols. **Hôtel de Ville★** (15thC) : Gothic council room, storerooms (still called the Cloth Hall in reference to the 15thC textile industry) and the aldermen's chapel. ▶ Behind the town hall the Rue de l'Université runs in front of the 17thC **Mont-de-Piété** (pawnshop; fine classical façade), and leads to the 18thC theatre in Louis XVI style. ▶ Opposite the theatre is the **hôtel d'Aoust** (18thC). ▶ The Rue des Foulons leads back toward the town hall; note the **hôtel de la Tramerie** (17thC) in Louis XIII style. ▶ On the quays along the river Scarpe, running S-N through the city, is the **Palais de Justice,** formerly the seat of the Parlement de Flandres and rebuilt in the 18thC (façade in Louis XVI style); the great Salle du Parlement★ (1714) is decorated with superb Louis XV panelling. Nearby, **church of St. Pierre** (18thC). ▶ West of the town centre on the other side of the Scarpe is a former charterhouse, whose 17th-18thC buildings surround a 16thC Flemish Renaissance-style mansion, now a **museum★★** *(10-12 & 2-5; closed Tue) :* unique collection of Flemish primitives including the famous **polyptych of the Trinity★** (1510; J. Bellegambe), the Immaculate Conception (1526) and St. Étienne and St. Jacques (1541 by Jan Van Scorel); fine collection of Italian Renaissance canvases (Veronese, Carraccio); 17thC Dutch and Flemish schools, 17th-19thC French schools. □

DUNKERQUE★

B1 / ® / pop. 73 120 (Nord)

Until the 7thC the land now occupied by the town was covered by the sea. It was only in the 11thC that the name of Dunkerque (the French spelling : church of the dunes) appeared in the archives. Until WWII Dunkirk had kept the appearance of a 17th-18thC Flemish port. Today it is an ultra-modern port whose waterside factories, naval shipyards and high chimneys are totally contemporary.

▶ Near Place Jean Bart is a **bell-tower★** (15thC) with 48 bells (concerts). Opposite, the 15th-16thC **church of St. Éloi** has a French Classical façade. ▶ A little street between **St. Éloi** and the town hall leads to the Place du Général de Gaulle and the **Musée des Beaux Arts** *(10-12 & 3-6; closed Tue) :* ceramics, Dutch and Flemish schools (16th-17thC),

French schools (17th-19thC). ▶ On the far side of the town hall is the port★ (third largest in France) which can be visited by boat (from the Bassin du Commerce, *tel. 20.69.47.14*) or on foot, taking the road to the left which leads over the Trystram and Watier locks as far as the lighthouse. ▶ To the north, beyond the canal, in a park with modern sculptures, is the **Musée d'Art Contemporain★,** with more than 600 works from 1950-1980 *(10-7 ; closed Tue).* □

▶ Nearby

▶ **Gravelines★** *(16 km SW)* : The **fortifications**

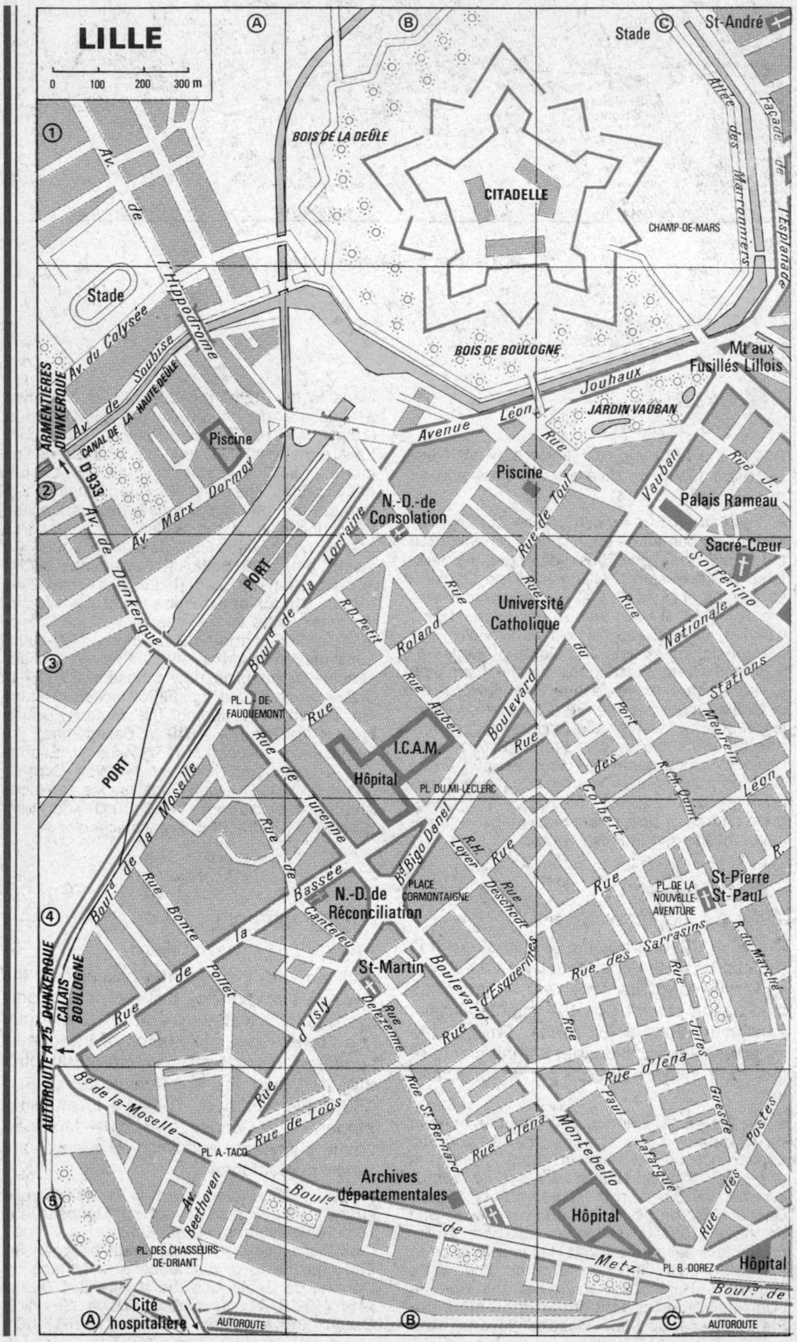

inspired by Vauban are perfectly preserved. From the Grand'Place with its belfry you come to the **arsenal,** which now houses art exhibitions. The **church of St. Willibrod** (Flamboyant Gothic with late Renaissance doorway) contains a magnificent collection of 17thC woodwork (confessionals and organ casings).

▶ **Grand-Fort-Philippe** and **Petit-Fort-Philippe** *(2 km NW) :* these two little townships on either side of the Aa River, named after Spain's King Philippe II, were rebuilt in Flemish style after WWII, and are now fishing centers and seaside resorts. □

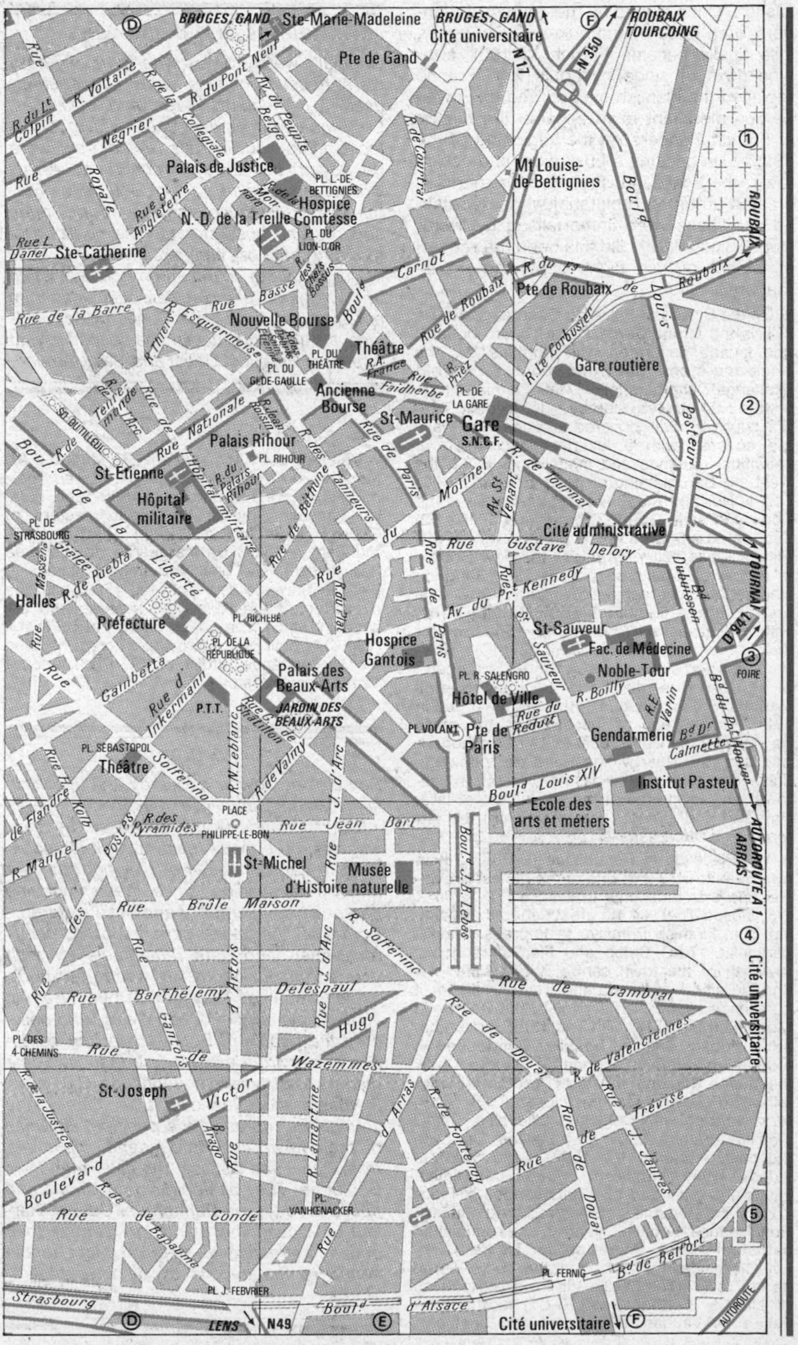

■ LILLE★★★

B1 / ® / pop. 168 420 (total urban area : 1 050 000) (Nord)
(see plan preceding page)

In the Middle Ages the city was surrounded by the river Deule, which is why its name first appears (11thC) as "L'Isle" ("the island"). Once owned by the counts of Flanders, then ruled by the dukes of Burgundy, Lille finally became French in 1667 after nine days of siege by Louis XIV. France replaced the Flemish market, and this prosperous merchant town became the capital of French Flanders. At the beginning of the 19thC Lille became a busy wool and cotton town; the textile industry's rapid expansion created an urban proletariat whose wretched conditions were immortalised by Victor Hugo. Since WWII Lille has been the regional capital of this highly-populated industrial area.

▶ On the S. side of Place du Général de Gaulle (E2) is the **Grand'Garde** (18thC guard-house); fine façade decorated with trophies. E., the brick-and-stone **ancienne bourse★★** (old exchange); characteristic 17thC Flemish architecture : 24 houses, side-by-side, forming interior courtyard with covered arcades; the walls are covered with a luxuriant decoration of caryatids, garlands and medallions. ▶ To the west, the Baroque **church of St. Étienne** (1696; D2). ▶ North of the **Place Gal-de-Gaulle** is the Louis XVI style **Grand Théatre** (ca. 1910; E2) and the **new Bourse** (same period), with 17thC Flemish-style belfry. Opposite the new Bourse is a row of pilastered houses, the Rang de Beauregard, characteristic of late 17thC Lille architecture. ▶ E., **church of St. Maurice★** (E2) with five naves and ornate 14th-15thC tower; inside : works by Van Oost (17thC); polychrome wood statue (16thC), "Christ Scourged". ▶ In the Rue de Paris is the **hospice Gantois** (E3), founded in 15thC and enlarged in 17thC. At the end of the street is the **porte de Paris** (Paris Gate), built in 17thC in honour of Louis XIV. Nearby, the **Hôtel de Ville** (E3), finished in 1933; at the base of the 140 m bell-tower are sculptures of the two giants of Lille, Phynaert and Lydéric; fine view from the top *(open Sun. am Easter-end Sep.).*

▶ W., Place de la République (D-E3) : **Palais des Beaux Arts★★★,** one of the richest provincial fine arts museums in France *(10-12:30 & 2-5; closed Tue);* all the great schools of painting from Flemish Primitive to Impressionist, in particular 17thC Dutch and Flemish schools. ▶ North of the town centre, **Vieux Lille★★★** (the old city) has been under restoration for a number of years : see especially the Rue de la Monnaie (Mint; E1); 17th and 18thC brick-and-stone houses and the **hospice Comtesse★★,** founded in 13thC by Jeanne de Flandres, now the **Musée Régional d'Arts et Traditions Populaires★** (Folk Art Museum; *closed Tue*); kitchen decorated with Delft and Lille tiles, 17thC Flemish furniture, Louis XV panelling. Opposite the main entrance, the 15thC Salle des Malades★ with magnificent boat-shaped timber vaulting is extended by 17thC chapel. ▶ Place Louise de Bettignies (E1) : restored Flemish Renaissance houses. Nearby, the unfinished **cathedral Notre Dame de la Treille** (19th-20thC); inside : miraculous statue of "La Vierge de la Treille" (The Treille Virgin) a protectress of Lille. ▶ Further west (B-C1) is the **citadel★★** by Vauban, the largest and best preserved in France *(Sun. pm, guided tours by the SI).* ▶ Near the **church of St. André** (C-D1; 18thC Jesuit-style) at the intersection of Rue Royale and Rue Princesse is the birthplace of Charles de Gaulle (no. 9 Rue Princesse, small **museum;** *closed Tue*). □

Belfries and bell-towers

Originally watch-towers where the city bells were housed, belfries were subsequently used to safeguard maps and treasures. Over the centuries they became symbols of local rights and liberties. Often they were destroyed but always rebuilt; at Arras, Douai and Dunkirk, as in Boulogne, Bergues and Béthune they overlook huge squares and busy streets. The carillons of the city belfries compete with the bells of neighbouring churches on holidays when both religious and secular peals can ring out over the town. The Concerts de Carillons *attract large audiences, especially at Avesnes, Bergues, Douai and Saint-Amand.*

▶ Nearby

▶ **Villeneuve-d'Ascq** ® *(8 km E)* : **Musée d'Art Moderne du Nord★★** *(daily 10-7; closed Tue);* good collection of works from 1900-1940, notably canvases by all the great masters of Cubism. ▶ **Seclin★** ® *(12 km S)* : **hospital★** founded in 13thC by Marguerite de Flandres (still in use). The brick-and-stone buildings in Flemish Baroque date from the 17thC with the exception of the *salle des malades* and the chapel (15thC). The parish **church of St. Piat★** (13thC) is built on a Merovingian crypt housing the sarcophagus (3rdC) of St. Piat under a 12thC memorial stone. □

The giants

Some ninety towns in Picardy and the North field "Giants", immense wickerwork figures which run and dance, propelled by their wearers, on popular feast days. It is impossible to name them all or to work out their family relationships, since these imposing personalities intermarry and have children... Some of the older generation of giants recall men who were remarkable for their prodigious strength or their fabulous exploits, such as "Gayant de Douai", *born in 1530, in memory of Jehan Gelon who delivered the people of Douai some four centuries earlier from a band of brigands. Some giants recall legends;* Jehan de Calais, *or* Phynaert *and* Lydéric *of Lille. Finally, the youngsters represent the principal activities of their town, like* Cafougnette, *the miner from Denai and* Batisse, *the fisherman from Boulogne. They all appear on religious and public holidays : in Dunkerque, Cassel, Bailleul or Douai, the giants go among their people, retreating to sleep at night to the sound of fanfares, lit by displays of fireworks.*

RUE★★

A2 / pop. 3170 (Somme)

Rue was a seaport in the high Middle Ages and is now the principal town of the **Marquenterre area,** a broad coastal plain reclaimed from the sea, between the estuaries of the Somme and the Authie rivers. Its fields and meadows are interspersed with water-filled ditches, lakes and marshes, and provide refuge for many bird species.

▶ Quadrangular 15thC belfry on the **Hôtel de Ville.** On the north side of the parish church is the **St. Esprit★★ Chapel** (15th-16thC) : richly carved doorway★; inside : marvellously delicate vaulting★ with pendant knobs. Entry from the narthex★ to the two treasure rooms★; upper room decorated with delicately carved biblical scenes; in lower room, vaulting with foliage and animals; early 16thC Virgin and Child. In the **parish church,** rebuilt in 19thC, beautiful 16thC oak stalls★. **Marquenterre** *(7 km W, along coast)* : noteworthy bird sanctuary★. □

SAINT-OMER★★

A1 / ® / pop. 15415 (Pas-de-Calais)

This quiet country town on the edge of French Flanders and Artois grew up around the 7thC Benedictine monastery founded by Omer and his companions, who drained, canalised and cultivated the marshes.

▶ On the Place de l'Hôtel de Ville, the old **Bailliage** (bailiff's court) has a fine Louis XVI façade. Going towards the Basilica of Notre Dame, you pass the **Musée d'Histoire Naturelle H. Dupuis,** in a fine 18thC town house *(closed Tue).* ▶ The beautifully proportioned **basilique Notre Dame★★★** has a 13thC choir and transept, 14thC nave and an imposing tower, decorated with a network of vertical blind arches, dates from 15thC.
This former cathedral is rich in works of art★ : see the astronomical clock of 1558. ▶ The Rue des Tribunaux leads from the Basilica past the **Palais de Justice** (17thC episcopal palace) to the Place Victor Hugo : see the monumental doorway of the **hôtel Sandelin**; inside : **Musée des Beaux-Arts★★** (Fine Arts; *10-12 & 2-5; closed Tue);* woodwork and furnishings from 18thC; Mediaeval art, including the Cross of St. Bertin★, masterpiece of a 12thC goldsmith's work; collection of Dutch and regional ceramics; paintings from Dutch and Flemish schools of 16th-17thC. □

▶ Nearby

▶ **Arques** *(3 km SE)* is well known for its fine crystal ware. The **old boat-lift at Fontinettes** is open to visitors; its construction in 1898 replaced a series of five locks which barges had to pass through on their way from the Aa to the Lys rivers. Today an enormous single lock has replaced the boat-lift. ▶ The **Benedictine Abbey of St. Paul** has been installed for a century in the vast 18thC chateau of **Wisques** *(6 km SW from Saint-Omer).* ▶ In **Eperlecques forest** *(15 km NW of Saint-Omer),* the world's biggest blockhouse was built in 1943-44 to house V2 rockets for the bombardment of England, but never became operational *(Wed, Sat and Sun. pm, Apr. mid-Jun. and mid-Sep.-mid-Nov.; daily mid-Jun.-mid-Sep.).* □

SOMME Valley★★

▶ From Amiens to Saint-Valéry-sur-Somme *(110 km approx, full day)*
A2-3 *(see map 5)* (Somme)

The valley of the Somme is very flat and abounds in lakes and water meadows. The numerous branches of the river are well-stocked with fish, eels and other fresh-water life. Meadows, woods and cultivated fields stretch endlessly.

▶ **Ailly-sur-Somme** clusters around a modern church with a roof in the form of a large sail. ▶ **Picquigny★** on the left bank of the Somme nestles under the ruined **château★** of the Vidames of Amiens. Below and opposite is the **collegiate church of St. Martin,** with nave and transept from 13thC and choir and tower of 15thC. ▶ The 18thC buildings of the **Abbaye du Gard** (abbey), founded in the 12thC are undergoing restoration. ▶ **Hangest-sur-Somme** is a little town surrounded by lakes and watercress beds. In its 12th-16thC church there is 18thC woodwork from the abbey. ▶ 8 km S, **Airaines★** has a Romanesque church with a baptismal font (11thC) decorated with curious squatting figures. In the other church in the village (Flamboyant Gothic) there is a remarkable 16thC carved "Burial of Christ". ▶ **Long,** on a hillside overlooking the left bank of the Somme : church with 16thC bell-tower; 18thC château of pink brick and white stone, in a park by the river.

▶ At **Pont Rémy,** the 15thC château, on an island in the Somme, has been restored in 19thC Romantic Gothic. ▶ **Liercourt :** Flamboyant Gothic church topped by an elegant gabled belfry; ▶ **Abbeville★★** ® : rebuilt around a town hall with a square white stone belfry. **Church of St. Vulfran★ :** fine 16thC Flamboyant Gothic building; 18thC choir; beautiful statuary around the three doorways★; original 16thC central door★ carved with scenes from the life of the Virgin. In the 13thC belfry and adjoining 15thC building is the Boucher de Perthes **Museum★ :** ornithological and prehistoric collections, local ceramics, mediaeval sculptures and 16thC paintings *(2-6; closed Tue. May-Sep.; Wed., Sun. and school hols. out of season).* On the left bank of the Somme at 264 Chaussée d'Hocquet is the **Manufacture Royale des Rames,** built at the beginning of 18thC by the Dutch Van Robais family, who were encouraged by Colbert (Louis XIV's Minister of Finance) to start cloth production in Abbeville. ▶ On the Paris road is the **Château de Bagatelle★★,** built around 1750 by Abraham Van Robais; period furniture and fine wood panelling inside *(2-6:30; closed Tue. Jul.-Sep.).* ▶ **Saint-Riquier★★** (10 km NE), has an imposing **abbey church★★** in the best Flamboyant Gothic style; richly decorated 17thC façade. Inside : 17thC furnishings in the choir; splendid Renaissance baptistery in the left transept; above the sacristy, at the end of the right transept, the abbot's private chapel is now the treasure room★; interesting murals on the afterlife. The abbey buildings, now a cultural centre, house the **Musée de la Vie Rurale** (Museum of Rural Life : *10-12 & 2-6 daily; Jun.-Sep.; 2-6, Sat. and Sun., Apr., May and Oct.).* 16thC **belfry**

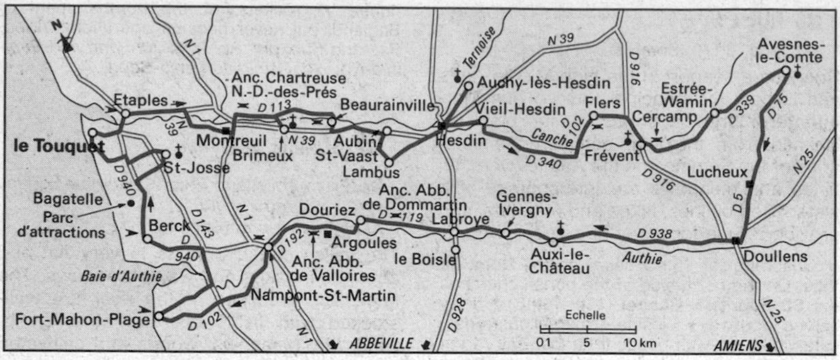

5. Somme Valley

in the square, and, farther on, the early 18thC Hôtel-Dieu (hospital), with a richly decorated chapel. ▶ **Saint-Valéry-sur-Somme★★** ® is a little port at the mouth of the river, with a long shady promenade★ on the dyke along the estuary, giving a good view of the bay. The ramparts of the **upper town★★** start beyond the lighthouse at the end of the dyke. Inside the fortifications is the **church of St. Martin★** (14thC) with chequered walls of flint and sandstone (Renaissance Triptych in the left nave). ▶ All that remains of the former **abbey of St. Valéry** is the 18thC château down in the valley. □

■ VALENCIENNES★

C2 / ® / pop. 40 275 (Nord)

At the heart of the industrialized valley of the Escaut, Valenciennes is the capital of Hainaut and a stronghold which has seen many wars. Over the centuries the town has always had a marked taste for the arts and has been the birthplace of many artists.

▶ Behind a 19thC façade the **church of St. Géry** has preserved its nave and choir in purest Gothic. On the north side, the **square Watteau** has a fountain★ in memory of this famous Valenciennois painter, designed in 1827 by Carpeaux, a native of Valenciennes.

▶ Close by, the **church of St. Nicolas :** pretty 18thC façade; inside : superb 17thC organ casing. In the adjacent buildings, formerly the **Jesuit College★,** is the **municipal library** with a collection of valuable manuscripts, in particular the *Cantilène de Ste. Eulalie,* one of the first documents written in the French tongue (881).

▶ East of the town centre, along the Watteau Blvd. is the **municipal museum★ :** 15th-17thC Flemish paintings; Rubens room; 18thC Valenciennes painters Watteau and Pater; 19thC Carpeaux *(10-12 & 2-5; closed Tue).* □

▶ Nearby

▶ **Saint-Amand-les-Eaux★** ® *(10 km NW) :* only thermal spa in the region; on the edge of a large forest, now the **Regional Nature Reserve,** with marked paths, an ornithological reserve and animal park. There are beautiful remnants of the former Benedictine abbey, notably the elegant Flemish Baroque entrance; the 17thC **échevinage★** (town council pavilion), Baroque façade of **abbey church** (ca. 1640), richly sculptured tower★ with lovely chimes (concerts). The tower now houses the municipal **museum,** 18thC ceramics *(daily, 10:30-12:30; closed Tue. and mornings daily, Oct.-Mar.).* □

[redacted]

Architecture

Somme region

The need for protection from the wind features prominently in the architecture of the northern countries. This applies just as much to small houses as to larger dwellings, which are often built on the side of a hill, protected by a windbreak of trees or grouped round a small courtyard in the case of a farm and its outbuildings. Wood, tile and slate shingles are very common as a protection against the elements. This is usually found on the gable walls, the most exposed parts of the building. ● Brick is the usual building material in the north, although cob and wood facings are found in some older buildings, while stone is used in the Avesnois (Bavay blue stone). In regions where there was sufficient stone of building quality (e.g. Lille), it was used for foundations and lower walls, so that there were three coloured elements in the façade : foundations, walls and roof. The exposed gable walls frequently make use of both brick and stone. ● Brick of varied colours is used, especially in Flanders, to make geometrical patterns on the exposed or visible parts of the building (yellow and red brick, for example). In the country around the Somme River, decorative patterns are achieved by blending pebbles, stones and mortar, or by varying the brick arrangement. ● In the north the houses are often single-storey, usually rectangular, buildings. The layout is based on the main room, which is directly accessible from street level or by small steps. Formerly the interior was designed so that from one side of the living room, the bakehouse led to the bedrooms; on the other side, the living room led directly into the stables and farm buildings.

Boulonnais region

Avesnois region

Brief regional history

1stC BC to 3rdC At the beginning of this period, the population was composed of **Celtic tribes** living in numerous villages; the Romans called the area **Belgium.**

4thC to 6thC In the 4thC **Christianity** started to spread throughout the region; during this period, the Franks continued their westward expansion, establishing large communities in the unpopulated northern areas; later this barrier was to define the linguistic frontier between Flemish and French-speaking peoples.

7thC to 10thC By the 7thC numerous **abbeys** had been founded; as centres of learning and trade, they attracted growing numbers of local inhabitants. ● In the 8thC Charlemagne subdivided his kingdom into domains administered by counts. After the **Norman invasions** of the 9thC, the power of these regional landholders increased at the expense of the central royal power; this was the early outline of the feudal system.

10thC to 12thC As security returned, agricultural activity expanded in the North : forest clearances, marsh drainage and more extensive cultivation of wheat. An active **urban upper class** appeared : belfries and ramparts symbolized the liberties won by town councils. A brilliant artistic life developed in the great cities, and **Gothic art** began to spread.

13thC to 14thC In 1191, **Philippe Auguste** united Artois to the crown of France; at the battle of Bouvines (1214), he put an end to southward expansion by the Count of Flanders. ● In 1304, **Philippe le Bel** pushed French influence into Flanders itself. At the beginning of the **Hundred Years' War,** the Treaty of Brétigny (1360) gave the victorious English the region around Calais and Ponthieu.

15thC to 16thC In 1420 the Treaty of Troyes recognized the rights of the King of England over Picardy and the Boulogne area. After the reconquest lead by Joan of Arc, the King of France transferred the sovereignty of these two northern provinces to the **dukes of Burgundy** (Treaty of Arras; 1435), as a reward for their loyalty. Under the influence of the luxurious court of Burgundy the towns of Flanders, Artois and Hainaut became centres of artistic achievement. ● **Charles le Téméraire** (the Bold), last Grand Duke of Burgundy, died in 1477. His only daughter married Maximilian of Austria, bringing him all the Burgundian states in her dowry. In the 16thC, the "North Countries" passed from the Austrian Habsburgs to the **Habsburgs of Spain.** ● François I of France, held in check by Charles the Fifth of Austria (1529), succeeded in reconquering Calais from the English (1536).

17thC to 18thC **Louis XIV** pursued an expansionist policy in the north : France regained **Artois** by the Treaty of the Pyrenees (1659), **Wallonia** (southern Flanders; Lille, Douai) at the Treaty of Aix-la-Chapelle (1668), **Hainaut** by the peace of Nijmegen (1678). The Treaty of Utrecht (1713) definitively fixed the northern **frontiers** of France.

19thC to 20thC The discovery of coal deposits, near Douai at the end of the 18thC, and in the Pas-de-Calais in 1847, attracted heavy **industry** to the north of France. The two **world wars** were particularly destructive in this area, and a number of towns had to be rebuilt. Today the northern industrial belt is adapting with difficulty to changes in energy development.

Practical information

The region

Information : Nord-Pas-de-Calais : *Comité régional de Tourisme (C.R.T.),* Palais Rihour, pl. Rihour, 59002 Lille Cedex, ☎ 20.30.81.00. *Délégation régionale au Tourisme,* 57, rue de Béthune, 59000 Lille, ☎ 20.57.99.99. **Nord :** *Comité départemental de Tourisme (C.D.T.),* 14, sq. Foch, 59000 Lille, ☎ 20.57.00.61 and 20.57.00.62. **Pas-de-Calais :** *Comité départemental de Tourisme (C.D.T.),* 44, Grand-Rue, 62200 Boulogne-sur-Mer, ☎ 21.31.98.58. **Somme :** *Comité départemental de Tourisme (C.D.T.),* 21, rue Ernest-Cauvin, 80000 Amiens, ☎ 22.92.26.39. In Paris : *Maison du Nord-Pas-de-Calais,* 18, bd Haussmann, 75009, ☎ 47.70.59.62.

Bookings : *Loisirs-Accueil Somme,* 21, rue Ernest-Cauvin, 80000 Amiens ☎ 22.92.26.39.

Maps : *Michelin* n°s 51, 52, 53 1/200 000. *I.G.N.* n° 101 1/250 000 ; n°s 1, 2, 4 1/100 000.

Local and regional press : *Voix du Nord, Nord-Eclair, le Courrier Picard.*

S.O.S. : Nord, *SAMU* (emergency medical service), ☎ 20.54.22.22 ; **Pas-de-Calais,** *SAMU,* ☎ 21.21.51.51 ; **Somme,** *SAMU,* ☎ 22.91.33.33. *Poisoning Emergency Centre* (Lille), ☎ 20.54.55.56.

Weather forecast : Nord : ☎ 20.97.93.11. **Pas-de-Calais :** ☎ 21.30.68.00. **Somme :** ☎ 22.89.44.47.

Rural gites, chambres d'hôtes, farm camping : Nord : *Relais départemental des Gîtes ruraux du Nord, C.D.T.* **Pas-de-Calais :** *Association départementale des Gîtes ruraux de France,* 44, Grande-Rue, 62200 Boulogne-sur-Mer, ☎ 21.30.32.51. **Somme :** *Relais départemental des Gîtes ruraux de France,* 21, rue Ernest-Cauvin, 80000 Amiens, ☎ 22.92.36.39.

Holiday villages : see practical holiday information.

Camping : approx 200 sites, mostly on the Opal Coast. List of sites available at the *Comités départementaux de tourisme.*

Festivals and events : Shrove Sun, Mon and Tue (before Ash Wed) : *Uischerbende Procession* in Dunkerque. **Feb :** *winter carnival* in Bailleul. **Easter Mon :** *Ronde des Géants* (tour of the Giants), in Cassel, Aire-sur-la-Lys. **End-Apr :** *watercress fair* in Lécluse. **May :** Amiens *carnival.* **Mid-May :** *tobacco fair* in Lille. **Jun :** *fair-exhibition* in Amiens. **End-Jul :** *fish festival* in Boulogne. **End-Aug :** *mediaeval festival* in Boulogne, *garlic fair* in Béthune. **First Mon in Sep :** *grande braderie* (big jumble, or garage, sale) in Lille. **Early Sep :** *fête de l'andouille* (chitterling sausage fair) in Aire-sur-la-Lys. **15-30 Sep :** *Festival de la Bêtise* in Cambrai.

Other Festivals : Mar : *International Festival of Short and Documentary Films* in Lille. **May :** *Les Provinciales du Théâtre* in Villeneuve-d'Ascq. **May-Jun :** Valenciennes *Spring Cultural Festival.* **Jul-Aug :** *Opal Coast Festival* and *Picardy Coast Festival.*

Rambling and hiking : Nord-Pas-de-Calais : G.R. trails 120, 121, 121A, 122 traverse the region, as does the G.R. of the Thiérache region : *Fédération régionale des Associations de Randonnée (F.R.A.R.),* 157, bd de la Liberté, 59000 Lille, ☎ 20.57.35.24. Short walks and rambles : *Comité d'Aménagement rural du Ternois (CART),* 1, pl. de Verdun, B.P. 41, 62130 Saint-Pol-Ternoise, ☎ 21.03.22.86. *Maison de la Thiérache,* rte nationale, 59219 Etroeungt, ☎ 27.61.19.21. *Comité d'Aménagement rural du Boulonnais,* 3, rue de l'Église, 62240 Desvres. **Somme :** *Association des Gîtes d'Étape de Picardie,* 9, rue Allart, B.P. 0342, 80003 Amiens Cedex, ☎ 22.92.64.64. The **Somme** Department is traversed by G.R. 123, 124 and 125. Enq : *Délégation départementale de la F.F.R.P.* G.N.S.G.R., 26, rte de Mareuil, 80250 Ailly-sur-Noye.
S.N.C.F. : train + ramble : during spring and summer, the railroad proposes a number of train trips scheduled to allow rambles and hikes in the Picardy region, with approximately 20 % reductions in train fares. The **Somme** C.D.T. publishes brochures on the Region which are available at the S.I. and C.D.T. The *Comité départemental de la Randonnée pédestre,* B.P. 0409, 80004 Amiens Cedex, organises excursions for groups of 10-25 persons. Bookings required at least three weeks in advance.

Riding holidays : the **Nord-Pas-de-Calais** region offers 800 km of marked bridle paths. *A.R.T.E.* **Nord-Pas-de-Calais :** S. Bacquaert, 8, pl. Liexranc, 59700 Marcq-en-Barœul, ☎ 20.72.56.07. F.F.A.R. : 156, bd de la Liberté, 59800 Lille, ☎ 20.57.35.23. **Somme :** numerous riding clubs (enq : **Somme** S.I. and C.D.T.).

Cycling holidays : *Ligue régionale des Flandres de la Fédération francaise de Cyclotourisme,* 77, rue de Soubise, 59140 Dunkerque. *Fédération régionale des Associations de Randonneurs,* 157, bd de la Liberté, 59800 Lille, ☎ 20.57.35.23 (bicycle hire). *Ligue picarde de Cyclotourisme,* M. J.-P. Lavieville, 29, rue Croix-Saint-Firmin, 80000 Amiens, ☎ 22.92.20.08. *Bicycle hire :* S.I., rue J.-Catelas, 80000 Amiens, ☎ 22.91.79.28.

River cruises : boat hire : *Escaut-Yachting,* port du Bassin-Rond, 59000 Hordain, ☎ 27.44.70.15. *Base des Prés du Hem,* Armentières, ☎ 20.77.43.99. River boating licences are not required for either of these centres.

Handicraft courses : Nord : *Maison de la Thiérache,* 7, rue Maurice-Hédor, 59219 Etroeungt, ☎ 27.61.19.21, offers courses in wrought-iron art and stone sculpture. Handicraft courses in the Mormal region (pottery, weaving, ceramics, and more). Information at the *Syndicat intercommunal de Tourisme de l'Ouest avesnois,* hôtel de ville, 59350 Le Quesnoy, ☎ 27.49.12.16.

Golf : Nord-Pas-de-Calais : Bondues (9 and 18 holes), Villeneuve-d'Ascq (18 holes), Marcq-en-Barœul (9 holes), Marly (18 holes), Wimereux (18 holes), Neufchâtel-Hardelot (18 holes), and at Touquet (9 holes and two 18 holes). **Somme :** Quervieu (7 km from Amiens) and Nampont-Saint-Martin (2 × 9 holes).

Aquatic sports : *Ligue Flandre-Artois de la Fédération française de Voile,* 16, rue Molière, 62200 Saint-Martin-lès-Boulogne, ☎ 21.31.48.66. *Comité départemental de Voile* **(Somme),** M. Gagny, av. du Gal-Leclerc, 80270

Airaines, ☎ 22.26.01.08. Speed-sailing : the extensive Opal Coast beaches are ideal for this sport. **Somme** speed-sailing clubs at Somme Bay, Marquenterre and Fort-Mahon.

Canoeing and kayaking : *F.R.A.R.*, 157, bd de la Liberté, 59800 Lille, ☎ 20.57.35.23. *Ligue Flandre-Artois de Canoë-Kayak*, M. B. Macke, 67, av. Kennedy, 59000 Lille, ☎ 20.52.60.03. *Direction départementale de la Jeunesse et des Sports*, 126, rue d'Amiens, B.P. 190, 62021 Arras Cedex, ☎ 21.23.48.11, organises canoeing courses for beginners. Canoes can be hired for a one-and-a-half day trip down the Ternoise River : *Association la Ternoise en fleurs*, M. Paprouki, 62130 Hernicourt-Sautricourt, ☎ 21.03.18.07.

Hunting and shooting : in the **Nord-Pas-de-Calais** region it is possible to hunt on the plains or in the woods, or to shoot waterfowl. Enq : *Féd. dép. des chasseurs.* **Nord :** 69, rue Faidherbe, 59000 Lille, ☎ 20.51.41.66. **Pas-de-Calais :** 26, rue Jeanne-d'Arc, B.P. 289, 62004 Arras, ☎ 21.23.20.67. **Somme :** 12, rue de Dijon, 62000 Amiens, ☎ 22.91.28.32.

Fishing : the best fishing areas are in the **Pas-de-Calais** region. Enq : *fédérations départementales de pêche et de pisciculture.* **Nord :** 10, rue de la Marne, St-Souplet, 59360 Le Cateau, ☎ 27.84.09.46. **Pas-de-Calais :** 2, résidence de France, rue É.-Zola, 62400 Béthune, ☎ 21.01.18.21. **Somme** (C.D.T. publishes a leaflet listing fishing sites, type of catch and tariffs).

● Towns

ABBEVILLE

Amiens 45, Rouen 99, Paris 163
A2 ⊠ 80100

ℹ 26, pl. de la Libération, ☎ 22.24.27.92.

SNCF ☎ 22.24.00.25.

Car-hire : *Budget* train + auto, at the station, ☎ 22.24.00.25.

Hotels :
★★***France,*** 19, pl. du Pilori, ☎ 22.24.00.42. Tx 871836. AE, DC, Euro, Visa. 76 rm Ⓟ ♿ 170. Rest. ♦ 60-150.
★***Le Condé,*** 14-16, pl. de la Libération, ☎ 22.24.06.33. 7 rm closed 16 Aug-6 Sep, Christmas school hols and Sun, 70. Rest. ♿ 50-120.

⛺ ★★*Le Relais du Ponthieu* (15 pl.), ☎ 22.24.29.78.

Restaurants :
● ♦♦ ***L'Escale en Picardie,*** 15, rue des Teinturiers, ☎ 22.24.21.51. AE, DC, Euro, Visa ♿ closed Feb school hols, Aug, Sun eve and Mon. Excellent fresh fish, 200-310.
♦ ***Au Châteaubriant,*** 3, rue des Lingers, ☎ 22.24.08.23. Euro, Visa closed 15 Sep-4 Oct, Sun and Mon. Spec : *quiche picarde*, 50-140.

Epagnette, 80580 Pont-Rémy, 3 km SE :
♦♦ ***La Picardière,*** 101, route de Paris, ☎ 22.24.15.28. AE, DC, Euro, Visa Ⓟ ♿ closed Tue eve and Wed, 50-135.

AIRE-SUR-LA-LYS

Saint-Omer 19, Lille 57, Paris 236
B1 ⊠ 62120

ℹ mairie, ☎ 21.39.07.22 (high season).

SNCF ☎ 21.39.07.09.

Hotel :
● ★★★***Hostellerie des Trois Mousquetaires*** (L.F.), château de la Redoute, RN43, ☎ 21.39.01.11. Visa. 12 rm Ⓟ closed 15 Jan-15 Feb, Sun eve and Mon, 250. Rest. ♦♦ 60-200.

⛺ ★★*De la Lys,* bassin des Quatre-Faces (44 pl.), ☎ 21.39.03.62.

AMIENS

Arras 63, Boulogne 122, Paris 148
A-B3 ⊠ 80000

ℹ rue J.-Catelas (B2), ☎ 22.91.79.28.

SNCF (C3), ☎ 22.92.50.50, 22.91.95.30.

🚌 rue Vallée, ☎ 22.92.27.03.

Agence Air France, 30 *bis*, bd de Belfort (C3), ☎ 22.92.37.39.

Car-hire : *Budget* train + auto, at the station, ☎ 22.91.77.77, and 6, rue de l'Oratoire, ☎ 22.91.31.21.

Hotels :
★★★***Carlton Belfort,*** 42, rue de Noyon (C3), ☎ 22.92.26.44. Tx 140754. AE, DC, Euro, Visa. 36 rm 300. Rest. ♦♦ ♿ closed Sun in Jul and Aug, 90-160.
★★★***Univers,*** 2, rue de Noyon (C3), ☎ 22.91.52.51. Tx 145070. AE, DC, Euro, Visa. 41 rm ♿ 235.
● ★★***Paix,*** 8, rue de la République (B2-3), ☎ 22.91.39.21. 26 rm Ⓟ ♿ closed 15 Dec-25 Jan, Sun and nat hols, 165.
★★***Normandie,*** 1 *bis*, rue Lamartine (C2-3), ☎ 22.91.74.99. 26 rm Ⓟ 130.

⛺ ★★*L'Étang Saint-Pierre* (100 pl.), ☎ 22.44.54.21.

Restaurants :
● ♦♦ ***Petit Chef,*** 8, rue J.-Catelas (B2), ☎ 22.92.24.23. Closed 15-30 Jul, 1 week in Feb, Sun eve and Mon. Delicious regional dishes, *flamiches* (puff-pastry tarts) and *ficelles* (thin loaves of bread), 120-210.
♦♦ ***Joséphine,*** 20, rue Sire-Firmin-Leroux (B2), ☎ 22.91.47.38. Visa ; closed 4-31 Aug, Feb school hols, Sun eve and Mon. Spec : fish, 85-180.
♦ ***Mermoz,*** 7, rue J.-Mermoz, ☎ 22.91.50.63. Closed Feb school hols, Jul, Sat eve and Sun eve. Spec : fish, 120-210.

Villers-Bocage, ⊠ 80260, 11 km N :
♦ ***Le Bocage,*** 13, rue des Charrons, ☎ 22.93.70.94. Euro, Visa Ⓟ ♿ closed Jul, Feb school hols and Wed, 50-90.

Guided tours : ℹ (on request).

Boats rental : *Europyachting,* 172, rue Delpech, ☎ 22.95.34.40.

Auction hall, 17, rue de la République, ☎ 22.91.54.64.

ARDRES

Calais 17, Lille 87, Paris 280
A1 ⊠ 62610

Hotels :
● ★★★***Grand Hôtel Clément*** (Relais du

Silence), 91, pl. Mal-Leclerc, ☎ 21.82.25.25. AE, DC, Euro, Visa. 18 rm 🅿 ⚘ ⛱ 🚫🐕 closed 15 Jan-15 feb and Mon (ex nat hols), 240. Rest. ● ◆◆ ♿ closed Mon and Tue noon (Oct-Mar). Since 1917, the Coolen family treats the gourmands. At present, the young François proposes modern cooking : *petits choux farcis de langoustines au beurre nantais, paupiettes de ris de veau blanc,* 100-280.

★★**Relais** (L.F.), bd C.-Senlecq, ☎ 21.35.42.00. AE, Euro, Visa. 11 rm ⚘ ⛱ 🚫🐕 ♿ closed Nov-Mar, Tue, 210. Rest. ◆◆ Spec : *beignets de filet de daurade,* 60-170.

⛺ ★★*Vivier,* Bois-en-Ardres (27 pl.), ☎ 21.35.45.08.

Restaurant :

Brêmes, 1.5 km W on D231 :

◆◆ ***La Bonne Auberge,*** rte de Guines, ☎ 21.35.41.09. AE, Euro, Visa. With 8 rm 🅿 ⚘ ⛱ 🚫🐕 closed 2 Dec-2 Jan, Sun eve and Mon, 50-160.

ARMENTIÈRES

Lille 19, Dunkerque 59, Paris 237
B1 ⊠ 59280

SNCF ☎ 20.77.12.11.

Restaurants :

◆◆ ***La P'tite Auberge,*** 4, bd Faidherbe, ☎ 20.77.09.66. AE, DC, Euro, Visa ; closed Tue, Sun eve and 15 Aug-15 Sep. Good value, 90-225.

◆ ***Au Commerce,*** 70, rue Nationale, ☎ 20.77.15.03. Visa. Open daily at noon, Fri and Sat eve, closed Wed, Sun and Aug. Three good set menus, 50-150.

Leisure activities : *Base des Prés du Hem,* a 270-acre natural park, including a 108-acre lake, ☎ 20.77.43.99.

ARRAS

Lille 52, Calais 117, Paris 178
B2 ⊠ 62000

ℹ 7, pl. du Mal-Foch, ☎ 21.51.26.95.

SNCF (C3), ☎ 21.73.50.50, 21.21.00.42.

🚌 rue du Dr-Brassant (C3), ☎ 21.21.28.40.

Car-hire : *Budget* train + auto, 75, av. de Cambrai, ☎ 21.73.26.26, and at the station, ☎ 21.21.00.42.

Hotels :

★★★***L'Univers,*** 3, pl. Croix-Rouge (B2), ☎ 21.71.34.01. AE, Euro. 36 rm 🅿 ⚘ ⛱ ♿ A splendid setting in an ancient monastery 🚫🐕 270. Rest. ◆◆ 70-180.

★★***Chanzy*** (L.F.), 8, rue Chanzy (C2), ☎ 21.71.02.02. AE, DC, Euro, Visa. 23 rm 🅿 165. Rest. ◆◆ In this institution, the DeTroy brothers maintain one of the finest wine cellars in France. Spec : *filet mariné mère Jean, turbot aux poireaux,* 75-220.

★★***Les Grandes Arcades,*** 8, Grand'Place (C2), ☎ 21.23.30.89. AE, Euro, Visa. 22 rm, 110. Rest. ◆ Pleasant service in a Flemish setting ; gourmet dishes at modest prices. Spec : *pintadeau aux pêches,* 50-150.

St-Nicolas-lès-Arras, 62223 St-Laurent-Blangy :

★★★***Le Régent,*** 5, rue A.-France, ☎ 21.21.51.09. Visa. 11 rm closed Aug, 220. Rest ◆◆◆ closed Sun eve and Mon ex hols, 125-300.

Youth Hostel, 59, Grand-Place (C2), ☎ 21.21.07.83.

⛺ ★★*Municipal,* 138, rue du Temple (50 pl.), ☎ 21.21.55.06.

Restaurants :

● ◆◆ ***Ambassadeur*** (station buffet), pl. Foch (C3), ☎ 21.23.29.80. AE, DC, Euro, Visa. 🚫🐕 ♿ closed Sun eve. Spec : *harengs à la flamande, sorbet genièvre,* 90-160.

◆◆ ***Victor Hugo,*** 11, pl. V.-Hugo (A2-3), ☎ 21.23.34.96. AE, DC, Euro, Visa. 🅿 ⛱ ♿ closed Aug, Sun eve and Mon. Spec : seafood, 120-270.

Beaurains, ⊠ 62217, 3 km S on the N17 :

◆◆ ***L'Auberge,*** 31, rue P.-Curie, ☎ 21.71.59.30. AE, DC, Euro, Visa. 🅿 ♿ closed eve. Goods grills in a rustic setting, 55-150.

Guided tours : on request ; commentary by staff from *l'Association de sauvegarde des sites et des monuments d'Arras,* 2, rue des Jongleurs, ☎ 21.51.36.50.

Market : Twice weekly at the foot of the belfry.

AVESNES-SUR-HELPE

Valenciennes 49, Saint-Quentin 66, Paris 205
C2 ⊠ 59440

ℹ mairie, ☎ 27.61.11.22.

SNCF ☎ 27.61.10.09.

Hotels :

★***Terminus,*** 15, av. de la Gare, ☎ 27.61.17.79. AE, DC, Euro, Visa. 17 rm 🅿 closed Fri and Sun eve, 170. Rest. ◆ 60-170.

Maroilles, 59550 Lardrecies, 12 km W :

★***Moulin de l'Abbaye*** (L.F.), rue du Moulin, ☎ 27.84.72.15. AE, Visa. 7 rm 🅿 ⚘ ⛱ closed Mon (low season), Jan, 150. Rest. ● ◆◆ Cooking equal to its setting. Spec : *flamiche, turbotin au beurre blanc,* 60-200.

Farmhouse gîtes : *ferme du Foyau,* ☎ 27.61.14.87, Marboux, 8 km W.

⛺ ★★*Municipal,* Champ-de-Mars (40 pl.), ☎ 27.61.11.22.

Restaurants :

● ◆◆ ***La Crémaillère,*** 26 pl. du Gal.-Leclerc, ☎ 27.61.02.30. AE, DC, Euro, Visa. ♿ closed Mon eve, Tue, Jan and 1-15 Jul. Good fare reasonably-priced. Spec : *goujonettes de sole, canard aux mille épices,* 80-160.

◆◆ ***La Grignotière,*** 5, av. de la Gare, ☎ 27.61.10.70. AE, DC, Visa ; closed Mon and Tue eve, end Jun-12 Jul and 15-31 Dec. Spec : fish, 60-200.

Dourlers, 6 km N on the N2 :

● ◆ ***Auberge du Châtelet,*** Les Haies, Charmes, ☎ 27.61.06.70. AE, DC, Visa. 🅿 ⚘ ♿ closed 16 Aug-15 Sep, 2-10 Jan, Sun eve and Wed. The Carlier family proposes an unbeatable menu, 180-200.

BAILLEUL

Lille 30, Dunkerque 44, Paris 248
12 km NW of Armentières, B1 ⊠ 59270

ℹ Monts de Flandre, hôtel de ville, ☎ 28.43.07.11.

SNCF ☎ 28.43.08.47.

Hotels :

La Pomme d'Or, 27, rue d'Ypres, ☎ 28.43.11.01. DC, Euro, Visa. 7 rm 🚫🐕 closed Aug, 165. Rest. ◆◆ Very good value, 180-200.

Boeschepe, ⊠ 59299, 7 km NW on the D10 and 318 :

★***Mont-Noir*** (L.F.), le Mont-Noir, ☎ 28.42.51.33. Tx 110672. AE, DC, Euro, Visa. 7 rm 🅿 ⚘ ⛱ closed early Jan-early Feb and Fri. Country inn, 125. Rest. ◆◆ 85-140.

BERCK-SUR-MER

Boulogne 42, Arras 99, Paris 209
A2 ⊠ 62600

ℹ mairie annex, rue Casimir-Périer, ☎ 21.09.01.20, and kiosk, pl. de l'Entonnoir, ☎ 21.09.07.85 (Jul-Aug).

SNCF ☎ 21.80.50.50.

Hotels :
★★***Comme Chez Soi,*** 44, pl. de l'Entonnoir, ☎ 21.09.04.65. Visa. 19 rm 🅿 ⛱ closed 15 Dec-15 Jan, Feb school hols and (low season) Sun eve and Mon, 190. Rest. ♦ 50-140.
★★***Florida,*** 5, rue du Dr-Menard, ☎ 21.09.15.21. 12 rm ⛱ ✂ 230. Rest. ♦ 60-80.

⛺ ★★*L'Alouette* (104 pl.), ☎ 21.09.04.64 ; ★★*Ami-Ami* (153 pl.), ☎ 21.09.05.55 ; ★★*Bois Magnier* (310 pl.), ☎ 21.09.06.48 ; ★★*la Guinguette* (150 pl.), ☎ 21.09.04.22 ; ★★*International* (180 pl.), ☎ 21.09.13.33.

Restaurants :
♦ ***Auberge du Bois,*** 149, av. du Dr-Quettier, ☎ 21.09.03.43. AE, DC, Euro, Visa. 🅿 ♿ closed Jan and Wed low season. Good and simple cooking, 60-160.

Merlimont, 8 km N :
♦♦ ***Hostellerie Georges,*** 139, rue d'Étaples, ☎ 21.94.70.87. 🅿 ⚘ closed Mon eve, Tue low season and Jan, 120-210.

Events : 15 Aug : *horse races.* End-Oct : Berck *6 hour, speed-sailing competition.*

BERGUES

Boulogne 42, Arras 99, Paris 209
B1 ⊠ 59380

ℹ belfry (high season) and mairie, ☎ 28.68.60.44.

SNCF ☎ 28.68.65.77.

Hotels :
★★★***Motel 25,*** La Croix Rouge, Socx, ☎ 28.68.79.00. AE, DC, Euro, Visa. 41 rm ⛱ ♿ closed Sun eve, 250. Rest. ♦♦ 50-110.

Bollezeelle, ⊠ 59470 Wormhout, 14 km SW :
● ★★***Hostellerie Saint-Louis*** (L.F.) 47, rue de l'Église, ☎ 28.68.81.83. AE, DC, Euro, Visa. 🅿 ⚘ ⛱ ✂ closed 15 Jan-15 Feb, Sun eve and Mon, 220. Rest. ♦♦ Spec : fish, 90-200.

⛺ ★★*Vauban* (90 pl.), ☎ 28.68.65.25.

Restaurants :
♦♦ ***Au Cornet d'Or,*** 26, rue Espagnole, ☎ 28.68.66.27. Visa. 🅿 closed 15 Jun-15 Jul and Mon. Spanish home (protected architectural monument). 🅿 Spec : *ris de veau au roquefort, crépinette de saumon frais au cerfeuil,* 85-140.
♦ ***Le Pont Tournant,*** 59380 Bierne, ☎ 28.68.61.66. Visa. ☀ 🅿 ⚘ ⛱ closed Thu eve, Fri, Sun eve and Jul, 65-180.

Esquelbecq, 10 km S :
♦♦ ***Le Relais du Château,*** 11, Grand-Place, ☎ 28.65.62.87. Closed Jan. Dishes of the Southwestern region ; good value, 120-210.

BÉTHUNE

Arras 33, Lille 39, Paris 213
B1-2 ⊠ 62400

ℹ 34, Grand-Place, ☎ 21.68.26.29.

SNCF ☎ 21.57.29.00., 21.01.35.35.

Car-hire : *Budget* train + car, at the station, ☎ 21.01.35.35.

Hotels :
★★***Bernard et Gare*** (L.F.), 3, pl. de la Gare, ☎ 21.57.20.02. DC, Euro. 32 rm 🅿 130. Rest. ♦ closed Sun eve, 60-150.
★★***Vieux Beffroy,*** 48, Grand-Place, ☎ 21.68.15.00. 65 rm ⛱ 180. Rest. ♦♦ 120-210.

Nœux-les-Mines, ⊠ 62290, 6 km S :
★★***Les Tourterelles,*** 374, rte Nationale, ☎ 21.66.90.75. AE, Euro, Visa. 15 rm 🅿 ⛱ closed Sun eve and nat hols, 210. Rest. ♦ 65-200.

Beuvry, ⊠ 62660, 4 km E on the Lille road :
● ★★★***France II,*** RN41, ☎ 21.57.34.34, Tx 110691. AE, DC, Euro, Visa. 56 rm 🅿 ⚘ ♿ 255. Rest. ♦♦ Spec : fish, *coq à la bière,* 85-180.

Riding gîte and table d'hôtes : *ferme Carvin,* ☎ 21.54.05.66, ⊠ 62350, Saint-Venant, 14 km NW

⛺ ★★*Municipal,* Beuvry (80 pl.), ☎ 21.57.02.01.

Restaurant :
♦♦ ***Au Départ,*** 1, pl de la Gare, ☎ 21.57.18.04. closed Sat eve, Sun eve and Aug. Good classic cooking, 210-320.

BOULOGNE-SUR-MER

Dunkerque 77, Arras 120, Paris 300
A1 ⊠ 62200

ℹ pl. F.-Sauvage (B2), ☎ 21.31.68.38.

⛴ *Sealink, S.N.C.F.,* gare maritime, B.P. 27, 62201 Boulogne-sur-Mer Cedex, ☎ 21.30.25.11. *P & O Ferries,* quai Chanzy, ☎ 21.31.78.00. *Hoverspeed,* International Hoverport, B.P. 201, 62203 Boulogne-sur-Mer Cedex, ☎ 21.30.27.26.

SNCF (C3), ☎ 21.80.50.50, 21.80.44.44.

Car-hire : *Budget* train + auto, 74, bd Daunou, B.P. 144. 62202 Boulogne-sur-Mer Cedex, ☎ 21.30.59.45, at the station, ☎ 21.31.89.94, and at the Hoverport.

Hotels :
★★***Métropole,*** 51, rue Thiers (B2), ☎ 21.31.54.30. Visa. 29 rm ⚘ closed 20 Dec-7 Jan, 230.
★★***Faidherbe,*** 12, rue Faidherbe (B2), ☎ 21.31.60.93. AE. 35 rm ☀ 🅿 ♿ 220.
● ★***Plage,*** 124, bd Sainte-Beuve (A1), ☎ 21.31.45.35. 10 rm ☀ closed 20 Dec-28 Jan, 85. Rest. ♦ closed Sun eve and Mon, 60-130.

Youth hostel : 32, rue Porte-Gayole (C3), ☎ 21.31.48.22.

⛺ ★★★*Moulin Wibert,* rte de Wimereux (130 pl.), ☎ 21.31.40.29.

Restaurants :
● ♦♦♦ ***La Liégeoise,*** 10, rue A.-Monsigny (B2), ☎ 21.31.61.15. DC, Euro, Visa ; closed Sun eve, Fri. Alain Delpierre is a good disciple of Robert Bardot, Spec : *salade de homard, feuilleté d'œufs pochés aux queues de langoustines, pot-au-feu de pigeon,* 90-260.
● ♦♦ ***La Matelote,*** 80, bd Sainte-Beuve (A1), ☎ 21.30.17.97. Euro, Visa. ☀ closed Sun eve and Tue, 15-30 Jun and 23 Dec-15 Jan. T. Lestienne continues to offer excellent fare at reasonable prices. Spec : *soupe d'huîtres et bigorneaux, dés de gigot d'agneau à la menthe poivrée,* 140-190.
♦♦ ***La Charlotte,*** 11, rue du Doyen, ☎ 21.30.13.08. Visa. closed Sun, 75-150.

Pont-de-Briques, ⊠ 62360, 5 km S :
● ♦♦ ***Hostellerie de la Rivière,*** 17, rue de la Gare, ☎ 21.32.22.81. With 9 rm, 80. Closed Aug, Feb school hols, Sun eve and Mon. A restaurant which is on the rise... but the prices remain reasonable. Spec : *soupe d'escargots à la crème d'ortie, ris de veau aux salsifis,* good cellar, 90-160.

Marquise, ☒ 62250, 13 km NE :
● ♦♦♦ ***Grand Cerf,*** 34, av. Ferber, ☎ 21.92.84.53. DC, Euro, Visa Ⓟ ♨ ♿ closed Sun eve, Mon and Feb. J.-F. Lemercier invites you to a gourmet's holiday. Spec : *tian nicois et ses pastilles d'agneau, escalope de saumon au gros sel, nougat glacé au coulis de fraise,* good wine list, 135-265.

Casino : bd Ste-Beuve, ☎ 21.31.50.95.

Sports and leisure activities : *Yacht-Club Boulonnais,* 234, bd Ste-Beuve, ☎ 21.31.80.67 ; *Opal Coast Scuba Club,* ☎ 21.31.47.01 ; *Boulogne Riding Club,* ☎ 21.31.82.38.

Event : 6 Dec, Saint-Nicolas Day.

Market : Food and flowers, Wed and Sat, pl. Dalton, am.

Auction hall, 12, rue du Pot-d'Étain, ☎ 21.31.39.51.

BRUAY-EN-ARTOIS

Arras 36, Lille 47, Paris 213
B2 ☒ 62700

ℹ pl. de l'Europe (closed am and Sat), ☎ 21.26.47.46.

SNCF ☎ 21.26.40.30.

Restaurants :
♦♦ ***Le Constant,*** pl. du Cercle, ☎ 21.62.32.00. Euro, Visa ; closed Sun eve and Mon eve. Pleasant setting. Spec : *filet de bœuf au salpicon de champignon, salade de magret de canard au foie gras,* 60-250.

Olhain, ☒ 62150 Houdain, 8 km SE :
♦ ***Auberge du Donjon,*** ☎ 21.27.93.76. Visa. Opposite the castle of Olhain Ⓟ closed Mon eve, Tue and Aug. Superb wines. *A la carte* only, 200-250.

CALAIS

Boulogne 43, Lille 112, Paris 297
A1 ☒ 62100

ℹ 12, bd Clemenceau, ☎ 21.96.62.40.

✈ Calais-Dunkerque, 8 km E., ☎ 21.96.62.40.

⛴ *Sealink S.N.C.F.,* Transmanche Terminal, ☎ 21.96.70.70. *Townsend Thoresen Car-Ferries,* Car-Ferry Terminal, 62226 Calais Cedex, ☎ 21.97.21.21. *Hoverspeed,* International Hoverport, 62226 Calais Cedex, ☎ 21.96.67.10.

SNCF ☎ 21.96.61.04.

🚌 16, rue Caillette, ☎ 21.36.45.65.

Car-hire : *Budget* train + auto, 20, pl. d'Armes, ☎ 21.97.05.60, at the station, ☎ 21.96.61.04, at the ferry port and at the Hoverport, ☎ 21.97.65.64.

Hotels :
★★★***Meurice,*** 5, rue Éd.-Roche, ☎ 21.34.57.03. AE, DC, Visa. 40 rm Ⓟ ♨ ♿ 200. Rest. ♦♦ ***la Diligence,*** 70-150.
★★***Richelieu,*** 17, rue Richelieu, ☎ 21.34.61.60. AE, Euro, Visa. 15 rm Ⓟ 220.

⛺ ★★*Municipal* (256 pl.), ☎ 21.97.99.00, ext 388.

Restaurants :
♦♦ ***Le Channel,*** 3, bd de la Résistance, ☎ 21.34.42.30. AE, DC, Euro, Visa ; closed Sun eve, Tue and 1 Dec-10 Jan. Generous classical cooking. Spec : *turbot poché hollandaise, tournedos aux girolles,* 60-200.
♦♦ ***La Côte d'Argent,*** Calais beach, ☎ 21.34.68.07. AE, DC, Euro, Visa Ⓟ closed Sep and Mon eve. Spec : seafood, 50-200.

♦♦ ***La Sole Meunière,*** 1, bd de la Résistance, ☎ 21.34.43.01. AE, Euro, Visa ♿ closed 20 Dec-20 Jan, 18-25 Jun, Sun eve and Mon, 55-175.

Casino : *Touquet's,* 57, rue Royale, ☎ 21.34.64.18.

CAMBRAI

Lille 64, Amiens 78, Paris 177
B2 ☒ 59400

ℹ 48, rue de Noyon, ☎ 27.78.26.90.

SNCF ☎ 27.81.22.42.

Hotels :
★★★***Beatus,*** 718, av. de Paris, ☎ 27.81.45.70, 27.81.45.71. Tx 820211. AE, DC, Euro, Visa. 26 rm Ⓟ ♨ ♿ 250.
★★★***Château de la Motte-Fénélon*** (Châteaux-hôtels), pl. du Château, ☎ 27.83.61.38. Tx 120285. AE, DC, Visa. 33 rm Ⓟ ♨ ♿ 230. Rest. ● ♦♦♦ 100-300.
★★***Poste,*** 58, av. de la Victoire, ☎ 27.81.34.69. Visa. 33 rm Ⓟ ♨ 195.

Ligny-en-Cambrésis, ☒ 59191, 10 km SE :
★★★***Château de Ligny*** (Relais et châteaux), ☎ 27.85.25.84. 9 rm Ⓟ ♨ closed Jan, 1 week in Nov and Mon, 400. Rest. ♦♦♦ 160-210.

Restaurants :
● ♦♦ ***L'Escargot,*** 10, rue Gal-de-Gaulle, ☎ 27.81.24.54. AE, Visa ♿ closed Mon, Dec and Jan. An extensive selection of conventional dishes. Spec : *andouillettes* (chitterling sausage), snails, 60-160.
♦ ***La Chaumière,*** 5, av. Michelet, ☎ 27.81.34.22. AE, Visa. closed Aug, Sat noon and Sun (ex nat hols). Spec : *turbot à l'oseille, ris de veau aux morilles.* Booking advisable, 75-120.

Saint-Hilaire, ☒ 59292, 12 km E, on the Solesmes road :
♦ ***Le Gourmet,*** 17, rue Pasteur, ☎ 27.37.05.99. Visa Ⓟ ♨ ♿ closed Sun eve and Wed, 55-140.

Bauvois-en-Cambrésis, 12 km SW, on the Cateau road :
♦♦ ***La Buissonnière,*** 92, rue Watremez, ☎ 27.85.29.97. Visa Ⓟ ♨ closed Sun eve, Mon, Feb school hols and 1-24 Aug. Spec : *gratin de lotte et langoustines homardine, filet de sandre au riesling, crêpes soufflées au coulis de framboise,* 80-140.

CRÉCY-EN-PONTHIEU

Abbeville 19, Arras 72, Paris 182
A2 ☒ 80150

Hotel :
★***La Maye*** (L.F.), 13, rue St-Riquier, ☎ 22.23.54.35. Euro, Visa. 11 rm Ⓟ closed Mon and Feb school hols, 90. Rest. 50-80.

Restaurant :
♦ ***Le Canon d'Or,*** 10, rue du Gal-Leclerc, ☎ 22.23.51.14. AE, DC, Euro, Visa. With 7 rm, 160 Ⓟ closed Sun eve in winter. Picardy regional specialities, 45-140.

Le CROTOY

Abbeville 21, Boulogne 73, Paris 184
A2 ☒ 80550

ℹ digue J.-Noiret (high season), ☎ 22.27.81.97.

Hotel :
★★***La Baie,*** ☎ 22.27.81.22. 14 rm ♨ closed 10-31 Jan, 180. Rest. 100-150.

⛺ ★★★*Le Pré Fleuri* (70 pl.), ☎ 22.27.81.53 ; ★★*la Ferme du Tarteron* (150 pl.),

☎ 22.27.80.20 ; ★★*la Prairie* (250 pl.), ☎ 22.27.02.65 ; ★★*la Roseraie* (100 pl.), ☎ 22.27.80.31.

DOUAI

Lille 38, Saint-Quentin 65, Paris 193
B2 ⊠ 59500

ℹ belfry, rue de la Mairie, ☎ 27.87.26.63.

SNCF ☎ 27.88.86.04, 27.88.41.27.

Car-hire : *Budget* train + auto, at the station, ☎ 27.88.41.27.

Hotel :
● ★★★***La Terrasse*** (L.F.), 8, terrasse St-Pierre, ☎ 27.88.70.04. AE, Visa. 30 rm 265. Rest. ● ♦♦♦ E. Hanique and his wife persevere in their quality. Spec : *filets de rouget aux morilles, canard braisé aux câpres, feuillantine de pomme en chaud-froid,* 65-240.

Restaurants :
♦♦ ***Au Turbotin,*** 1, rue de la Massue, ☎ 27.87.04.16. AE, Euro, Visa ♿ closed Sun, eve preceding nat hols and Mon, 22 Jul-20 Aug, 60-250.
♦♦ ***Aux Comtes de Flandre,*** 72, rue de la Boucherie, ☎ 27.98.25.89. AE, DC, Visa closed Mon and Tue eve, 55-200.

Guided tours : Jun-Oct. Enq : ℹ

Events : *fêtes de Gayant,* 1 two weeks in Jul (folklore processions, concerts, evening recitals of church chimes).

DOULLENS

Amiens 30, Lille 87, Paris 178
B2 ⊠ 80600

ℹ 10, rue Marjolaine, ☎ 22.77.09.28.

Hotel :
★***Aux Bons Enfants*** (L.F.), 23, rue d'Arras, ☎ 22.77.06.58. Euro, Visa. 8 rm Ⓟ 115. Rest. ♦♦ ♿ closed Sat, 55-160.

Restaurants :
♦♦ ***Le Sully,*** 45, rue d'Arras, ☎ 22.77.10.87. Visa. With 8 rm Ⓟ ♿ closed 1-15 Jan and end Jun-12 Jul, Mon low season, and Wed high season, 60-100.

Pommera (62), 7 km NE on the Arras road :
● ♦♦ ***La Faisanderie,*** rte Nationale, ☎ 21.48.20.76. AE, DC, Euro, Visa Ⓟ ♿ closed Sun eve, Mon, 15 days in Aug and Feb school hols. In an old farm, one of the best restaurants in the region. Spec : *fondue de homard riz sauvage, marinière de poulette bressanne au chablis,* 80-280.

DUNKERQUE

Calais 43, Lille 73, Paris 291
B1 ⊠ 59140

ℹ belfry, rue Clemenceau, and sea wall in Malo-les-Bains (high season), ☎ 28.66.79.21 and 28.63.61.34.

SNCF ☎ 28.66.54.11.

✈ Calais-Dunkerque, 28 km SW, ☎ 21.97.90.66.

Sealink A.L.A., Ferry Boats, Maritime Terminal, West port, 59279 Loon-Plage, ☎ 28.66.80.01. *Sally Viking Line,* ☎ 28.68.43.44.

Car-hire : *Budget* train + auto, 2 *bis,* rue du Chemin-de-Fer, ☎ 28.65.23.80, and at the station, ☎ 28.66.50.50.

Hotels :
★★★***Borel*** (Inter-Hôtel), 6, rue l'Hermite, ☎ 28.66.51.80. Tx 820050. AE, DC, Euro, Visa. 40 rm. On the port, 245.
★★★***Europ' Hotel*** (Mapotel), 13, rue du Leughenaer, ☎ 28.66.29.07. Tx 120084. AE, DC, Euro, Visa. 130 rm Ⓟ 235. Rest. closed Sun, 80-130.
● ★★***Hirondelle,*** 48, av. Faidherbe, Malo-les-Bains, ☎ 28.63.17.65. 33 rm 120. Rest. ♦ closed 15 Aug-7 sep, Sun eve and Mon, 40-120.
Au Bon Coin, 49, av. Kléber, Malo-les-Bains, ☎ 28.69.12.63. AE. 4 rm, closed end-of-year hols, 170. Rest. ● ♦ ♿ Seafood. Very good value, 55-120.

⛺ ★★★*Municipal* (500 pl.), ☎ 28.69.26.68.

Restaurants :
♦♦ ***Ducs de Bourgogne,*** 29, rue de Bourgogne, ☎ 28.66.78.69. AE, DC ♿ closed eve ex by reservation, 50-170.
♦♦ ***Le Mareyeur,*** 83, rue Henri-Terquem, ☎ 28.66.29.07. Tx 120084. AE, DC, Euro, Visa ; closed Sun eve and Mon. Seafood. Reasonably-priced menu, 85-150.
♦ ***Richelieu*** (train station buffet), pl. de la Gare, ☎ 28.66.52.13. AE, Visa ♿ closed Sun eve. Proof that a wait at the station can be worth-while ! 40-150.

Teteghem, 6 km on the D204 :
● ♦♦♦ ***La Meunerie,*** 174, rue des Pierres, ☎ 28.26.01.80. AE, DC, Euro, Visa closed Mon, Sun eve and 22 dec-29 Jan. A superb, 19thC restored mill ; the fare is a match for this delightful setting, 140-400.
♦♦ ***Le Vieux Tuilé,*** 43, rue de la Mairie, ☎ 28.26.07.70. AE, Euro, Visa ♿ closed Sun eve, 80-200.

Yacht club *de la mer du Nord,* ☎ 28.66.79.90.

FORT-MAHON-PLAGE

Abbeville 35, Boulogne 55, Paris 200
A2 ⊠ 80790

ℹ pl. Bacquet, ☎ 22.27.70.75 (high season).

Hotel :
★***Victoria,*** pl. Mal-de-Lattre-de-Tassigny, ☎ 22.27.71.05. 17 rm, 110. Rest. 60-150.

⛺ ★★★*Soleil* (100 pl.), ☎ 22.27.70.06 ; ★★★*le Royon* (175 pl.), ☎ 22.23.40.30 ; ★★*Camp de Robinson* (200 pl.), ☎ 22.27.71.43.

FOURMIES

Saint-Quentin 61, Lille 116, Paris 200
C2 ⊠ 59610

ℹ pl. Verte, ☎ 27.60.40.97 (closed Sun and Mon).

SNCF ☎ 27.60.19.55.

Hotel :
★★***Providence,*** 12, rue Ed.-Verpraet, ☎ 27.60.06.25. AE, DC, Euro, Visa. 18 rm Ⓟ closed Aug, Sat and Sun eve, 150. Rest. ♦♦ ♿ 50-140.

⛺ ★★*Les Étangs des Moines* (111 pl.), ☎ 27.60.04.32.

Leisure activities : theatre, rue St-Louis.

Jumble (garage) sales : St. Nicolas Day, 1st Sun in Dec ; in summer, last Sun in Jul.

FRÉVENT

Arras 39, Boulogne 86, Paris 193
B2 ♥ ⊠ 62270

Hotels :
★★***Amiens*** (L.F.), rue Doullens, ☎ 21.04.25.43. Euro, Visa. 10 rm Ⓟ closed Sat low season, 100. Rest. 50-150.

Monchel-sur-Canche, 7 km NW :
● ★***Vert Bocage,*** rue de Flers, ☎ 21.47.36.75. Euro. 9 rm ※ 🅿 ⁂ ⛱ ✈ 200. Rest. ♦♦ ♿ Spec : *coquilles St-Jacques,* 45-180.

⛺ ★★★*Les Longuigneules,* 75, rue du Gal-de-Gaulle (110 pl.), ☎ 21.04.38.79.

HAM

Saint-Quentin 20, Amiens 67, Paris 135
B3 ⊠ 80400

SNCF ☎ 23.81.00.16.

Hotels :
● ★★***France,*** 5, pl. de l'Hôtel-de-Ville, ☎ 23.81.00.22. Euro, Visa 16 rm 🅿 ✈ ♿ closed 1-25 Aug, Feb school hols, 190. Rest. ● ♦♦ closed Sun eve and Mon. Serious classical cooking. Spec : *panaché de poissons au beurre blanc, entrecôte au gratin,* 120-210.
★***Valet,*** 58, rue de Noyon, ☎ 23.81.10.87. Visa. 21 rm 🅿 ⛱ closed end Dec, 145. Rest. closed Sat, Sun and nat hols, 40-50.

HARDELOT

Boulogne 15, Arras 110, Paris 237
A1 ⊠ 62152 Neufchâtel-Hardelot

Hotels :
★★★***Écusson,*** 443, av. François-Ier, ☎ 21.83.71.52. AE, DC, Euro, Visa. 20 rm. closed 30 Jan-1 Mar and 15 Nov-1 Dec, 190. Rest. ♦ ♿ closed Tue noon, Wed and Sun eve low season, 80-160.
★★***Régina,*** av. François-Ier, ☎ 21.32.81.88. DC. 40 rm 🅿 ⛱ ♿ closed 10 Dec-5 Feb, 195. Rest. ♦ ✈ closed Sun eve and Mon. Spec : *coquilles St-Jacques à la crème, saumon fumé,* 60-110.

HAZEBROUCK

Saint-Omer 22, Lille 42, Paris 239
B1 ⊠ 59190

ℹ hôtel de ville, ☎ 28.41.88.00.

SNCF ☎ 28.41.94.33.

Hotel :
La Motte-au-Bois, 5 km S :
★***Auberge de la Forêt,*** ☎ 28.41.80.90. AE, Visa. 15 rm 🅿 ⛱ closed Mon eve and Feb, 150. Rest. ♦ 60-190.

Farmhouse gîte and table d'hôtes : *Ferme de la Rabaude,* ☎ 28.41.91.28, Longue-Croix, 8 km NW passing through Hondeghem.

Restaurant :
Longue Croix, 8 km NW, passing through Hondeghem :
● ♦ ***Auberge de la Longue-Croix,*** rte de Staple, ☎ 28.41.93.34 🅿 ⁂ ✈ closed eve on Sun, Mon and nat hols, Tue, early Dec-Jan, 23 Jun-2 Jul. Booking indispensable. Spec : *carbonade de lotte à la flamande, bar au beurre d'huîtres, gratin de pommes et son sorbet au genièvre,* 120-200.

HESDIN

Abbeville 35, Lille 89, Paris 233
A2 ⊠ 62140

ℹ hôtel de ville, ☎ 21.06.84.76.

SNCF ☎ 21.06.88.21.

Hotels :
★★***Flandres*** (L.F.), 22, rue d'Arras, ☎ 21.86.80.21. AE, Visa. 14 rm 🅿 ⁂ ⛱ closed 18 Dec-15 Jan, 200. Rest. ♦ Good fare. Spec : *coq à la bière,* fish, 50-150.

Marconne-lès-Hesdin, ⊠ 62140 :
★★***Trois Fontaines,*** 16, rte d'Abbeville, ☎ 21.86.81.65. AE, Euro, Visa. 10 rm 🅿 ⁂ ⛱ ♿ 170. Rest. ♦ 60-150.

⛺ ★★*Municipal* (140 pl.), ☎ 21.86.80.24.

LENS

Arras 18, Lille 34, Paris 203
B2 ⊠ 62300

SNCF ☎ 21.28.25.01.

Car-hire : *Budget* train + auto, at the station, ☎ 21.28.10.65.

Hotel :
★★***France,*** 2, pl. de la Gare, ☎ 21.28.18.10. Euro, Visa. 23 rm 🅿 135. Rest. ♿ closed Sun eve, 50-180.

Restaurants :
♦ ***Chez Robert,*** 13, rue de Paris, ☎ 21.28.07.29. AE, DC, Euro, Visa ♿ closed 1 wk in Feb, 1-24 Aug and Sun, 70-160.

Vernelles, ⊠ 62980, 7 km NW :
♦ ***Le Socrate,*** ☎ 21.26.24.63 🅿 ⁂ ♿ closed Sun and Mon eve. Good value, 80-130.

Douvrin, ⊠ 62138, 10 km N :
♦♦ ***La Licorne,*** 1, pl. Thomas, ☎ 21.79.95.25. Euro, Visa ♿ closed Mon, Sun eve and 4 Aug-3 Sep. Spec : dishes prepared in butter and fresh cream sauces ; good wine cellar, 40-130.

LILLE

Amiens 115, Bruxelles 116, Paris 219
B1 ⊠ 59800

ℹ ☎ Palais Rihour, pl. Rihour, B.P. 205, 59002 Lille Cedex (D-E2), ☎ 20.30.81.00.

✈ Lesquin, 8 km SE, ☎ 20.95.92.00.
Air France, 10, rue Jean-Roisin (E2), ☎ 20.57.67.90.

SNCF (E2), ☎ 20.74.50.50, 20.06.26.99.

🚌 pl. Buisses (F2), ☎ 20.06.01.33.

Car-hire : *Budget* train + auto, at the station, ☎ 20.06.80.41, and at the airport.

Hotels :
● ★★★***Carlton*** (Mapotel), 3, rue de Paris (E2), ☎ 20.55.24.11. Tx 110400. AE, DC, Euro, Visa. 70 rm, 385.
★★★***Bellevue,*** 5, rue J.-Roisin (E2), ☎ 20.57.45.86. Tx 120790. AE, Visa. 80 rm ♿ 365.
★★★***Royal,*** 2, bd Carnot (E2), ☎ 20.51.05.11. Tx 820575. AE, DC, Euro, Visa. 102 rm ♿ 380.
★★***Grand Hôtel Central,*** 51, rue Faidherbe (E2), ☎ 20.06.31.57. 32 rm, 165.
★★***Univers,*** 19, pl. des Reignaux (E2), ☎ 20.06.99.69. 56 rm ⛱ ♿ 240.
★★***Monte-Carlo,*** 17, pl. des Reignaux (E2), ☎ 20.06.06.93. Visa. 41 rm ♿ 185.
★***Brueghel,*** 3-5, parvis St-Maurice (E2), ☎ 20.06.15.53. Tx 135855. Euro, Visa. 80 rm ⛱ ✈ 175.

Faches-Thumesnil, 5 km S, near Lesquin Airport :
● ★★***Air Hôtel,*** 405, av. Mal-Leclerc, ☎ 20.96.04.39. AE, Visa. 13 rm 🅿 ⁂ 150. Rest. ♦ closed Sat noon, Mon eve and Tue eve, 70-220.

Youth hostel : 1, av. J.-Destrée, ☎ 20.52.76.02.

Restaurants :
● ♦♦♦ ***Paris*** (Loïc Martin), 52 *bis,* rue Esquermoise (D2), ☎ 20.55.29.41. AE, DC ; closed Sun eve and early Aug-early Sep. It is a real pleasure to stop at Loïc Martin's very enjoyable res-

taurant. He watches over all and helps his chef G. Chomoley in preparing honest and generous dishes according to the market. Spec : *queues de langoustines au chou beurre blanc au soja, chausson de saumon fumé minute ;* special prices on 1981 bordeaux, selection of armagnacs and eaux-de-vie, 170-300.

● ♦♦♦ ***Le Flambard,*** 79, rue d'Angleterre (D1), ☎ 20.51.00.06. AE, DC ; closed Sun eve, Mon, 2-9 Jan and 2 Aug-4 Sep. 17thC setting and 20thC cooking here make for a happy marriage. Talent and imagination abound, and Robert Bardot is well worthy of joining our jury of great chefs. Spec : *profiterolles de foie gras, navarin de turbot, sole à la vapeur d'ail, pot-au-feu d'oie,* 190-370.

● ♦♦♦ ***La Devinière,*** 61, bd Louis-XIV (F3), ☎ 20.52.74.64. AE, DC, Visa ; closed Sat noon, Sun and 1-20 Aug. B. Waterlot keeps his promise of quality cooking : *œuf coque de petits escargots, canard rôti.* Nice cellar, 190-320.

♦♦♦ ***La Belle Époque,*** 10, rue de Pas (D2), ☎ 20.54.51.28. AE, DC, Euro, Visa ; closed Sun eve. A 1900's setting for *la nouvelle cuisine.* Excellent wine selection, 250-300.

● ♦♦ ***Le Hochepot,*** 6, rue du Nouveau-Siècle, ☎ 20.54.17.59. Visa. ♿ closed Sun eve. Typical Flemish setting. Remarkable choice of coffees and gins, 70-150.

● ♦♦ ***L'Huîtrière,*** 3, rue des Chats-Bossus (E2), ☎ 20.55.43.41. Closed Sun eve and 21 Jul-31 Aug. The oysters and shellfish are a non-stop delight, but also the Bresse chicken and Pauillac lamb, 210-320.

● ♦♦ ***Le Varbet,*** 2, rue du Pas, ☎ 20.54.81.40. Closed Sun, Mon and hols, 1 Jul-1 Aug. The calm discrete atmosphere highlights the excellent cooking of Mr. Vartanian. Spec : *pinces de crabes aux fruits, marinade de bœuf cru au cumin, feuilleté de fraises gratiné aux amandes,* 120-200.

♦♦ ***Charlot II,*** 26, bd J.-B.-Lebas (E4), ☎ 20.52.53.38. AE, DC, Euro, Visa. ♿ closed Sat noon, Sun eve, Mon, Easter and 15 Jul-31 Aug. Spec : seafood, 90-220.

♦♦ ***Le Club Clément-Marot,*** 16, rue de Pas (D2), ☎ 20.57.01.10. AE, DC, Euro, Visa ; closed Sun eve, Mon, early Aug-early Sep and 1 week in winter, 100-180.

♦♦ ***Le Compostelle,*** 4-6, rue Saint-Étienne (D2), ☎ 20.54.02.49. AE, DC, Euro, Visa. Ⓟ ♿ closed Sun eve (and noon high season). Light cooking in a 16thC hotel. Spec. : *filet de lieu à la poêle, gâteau aux noix,* 105-250.

♦♦ ***Le Lutterbach,*** 10, rue Faidherbe (E2), ☎ 20.55.13.74. closed 15 Jul-15 Aug. Spec : *choucroute,* fish, 80-130.

♦♦ ***La Provinciale en Ville,*** 8, rue des Urbanistes (E1), ☎ 20.06.50.79. AE, Visa. ♿ closed Sun eve, Mon and 15 Jul-15 Aug. Exclusively regional cooking, 110-160.

♦ ***Le Capucin Gourmand,*** 138, rue de Wazemmes, ☎ 20.57.23.70. Closed Sun eve, Mon and Aug. Seafood, along with specialities of the Southwest. Good value, 120-210.

♦ ***Lino,*** 1, rue des Trois-Couronnes, ☎ 20.31.12.17. Visa. Ⓟ closed Sun eve, Mon and 15 Aug-15 Sep. Italian food, 100-150.

♦ ***Le Samovar,*** 42, rue de la Monnaie, ☎ 20.55.39.56. AE, DC ; closed Sat noon, Sun. Russian specialities, 80-200.

In the Lille area :

Lambersart, ☒ 59130, 3 km NW :

♦♦ ***La Laiterie,*** 138, av. de l'Hippodrome, ☎ 20.92.79.73. AE, DC, Visa. Ⓟ ♿ closed Sun eve, 95-250.

Marcq-en-Barœul, 4.5 km NE :

● ♦♦ ***Le Septentrion,*** parc du château Vert-Bois, 1.5 km, ☎ 20.46.26.98. Ⓟ ♿ closed Sun and Mon eve. G. Lelaurain defends good regional cooking. Spec : *potje vleish, waterzoï de poulet fermier,* 30-80.

Villeneuve-d'Ascq, 4 km E :

♦♦ ***Le Chantilly,*** 98, av. de Flandre, ☎ 20.72.40.30. AE, DC, Euro, Visa. Ⓟ ♿ closed Sun eve and Mon. Good, classic cooking, 80-150.

♦♦ ***La Vieille Forge,*** 160, rue Lannoy-au-Recueil, ☎ 20.05.50.75. AE, DC, Euro, Visa. Ⓟ ♿ closed Wed eve, 100-200.

Marquette, 5 km N :

♦ ***Auberge Saint-Arnoult,*** 178, rte d'Ypres, ☎ 20.51.69.61. closed Aug, Feb school hols, Mon, Tue and Sun eve. An extensive menu and a remarkable wine cellar, 85-150.

Hem-lez-Lille, ☒ 59510, 6 km E :

Auberge de l'Hempempont, 5, rue de Croix, ☎ 20.75.64.32. Ⓟ closed 20 Jul-14 Aug and Sun eve, 80-130.

Prémesques, ☒ 59840, 10 km W :

● ♦♦♦ ***Armorial,*** château de Prémesques, 1055, rte Nationale, on the D933, ☎ 20.08.84.24. DC, Visa. Ⓟ ♿ closed Sun and Tue eve, Wed, 2 weeks early Aug and 3 weeks end Jan. P. Lepelley (S.R.F.) renews his cooking. Spec : *chevreuil au cassis* (in season), *zéphir Rose-Marie aux pruneaux,* 180-320.

Guided tours : ℹ

Markets : Sun am, Wazemmes market ; Sun eve, flea-market. Animal market, rue Littré.

Auction halls : 14, rue des Jardins, ☎ 20.06.10.14 ; auction Sat pm ; 2, rue Ste-Anne, ☎ 20.06.25.81 ; auction Mon pm.

MAUBEUGE

Valenciennes 39, Saint-Quentin 58, Paris 241
C2 ☒ 59600

ℹ porte de Bavay, av. du Parc, ☎ 27.62.11.93.

SNCF ☎ 27.62.30.61.

Car-hire : *Budget* train + car, at the station, ☎ 27.62.30.61.

Hotel :

★★***Grand Hôtel,*** 1, pte de Paris, ☎ 27.64.63.16. AE, DC, Visa. 31 rm Ⓟ ♿ 215. Rest. ♦♦ Good value, 65-220.

⛺ ★★★*Municipal* (93 pl.), ☎ 27.62.25.48.

MERS-LES-BAINS

Abbeville 37, Beauvais 94, Paris 168
A2 ☒ 80350

ℹ rue J.-Barni, ☎ 35.86.06.14 (Jun-Sep).

Hotels :

★★***Bellevue,*** espl. Gal-Leclerc, ☎ 35.86.12.89. AE, DC, Euro, Visa. 25 rm. closed 5 Nov-15 Dec, 180. Rest. ♦ closed Sun, 70-110.

★***Les Charmettes,*** espl. Gal-Leclerc, ☎ 35.86.76.79. Visa. 18 rm, 100. closed Oct-Mar. Rest. ♦ Spec : fish, 60-120.

⛺ ★★★★*Rompval* (135 pl.), ☎ 35.86.25.40 ; ★★*la Falaise* (150 pl.), ☎ 35.86.22.14.

MONTREUIL-SUR-MER

Boulogne 38, Lille 114, Paris 207
A2 ☒ 62170

ℹ pl. de la Poissonnerie, ☎ 21.06.04.27 (high season), and mairie, ☎ 21.06.01.33.

SNCF ☎ 21.80.50.50.

Hotels :
● ★★★★***Château de Montreuil*** (Relais et châteaux), 4, ch. des Capucins, ☎ 21.81.53.04 Tx 135205. AE, DC, Euro, Visa. 14 rm Ⓟ ꙮ ⛵ ✈ ♿ closed 2 Jan-15 Feb, 430. Rest. ● ♦♦ ✈ ♿ closed Thu noon. C. Germain's quality cooking is making itself known. Spec : *mousseline d'huîtres à la ciboulette, magret de canard à l'ail doux, mousse brûlée,* 120-280.
★★***Central,*** 7, rue du Change, ☎ 21.86.16.04. 14 rm. AE, Euro, Visa Ⓟ ✈ closed end-Dec to end-Jan, 200. Rest. ♦ 60-180.

Saint-Aubin, 10 km W :
★***Auberge du Cronquelet,*** rue de Montreuil, ☎ 21.94.60.76. Visa. 8 rm Ⓟ ꙮ ⛵ closed 20-31 Dec, Feb school hols, 120. Rest. ♦ closed Wed. *Terrine aux foies de volailles, pêle-mêle de poissons à l'estragon,* 100-150.

Youth hostel : *la Hulotte* (toward Citadelle), ☎ 21.06.10.83.

⛺ ★★★*Fontaine des Clercs* (76 pl.), ☎ 21.06.07.28.

Restaurants :
♦ ***Le Darnetal,*** 1, pl. Darnetal, ☎ 21.06.04.87. AE, DC, Euro, Visa ♿ closed Mon eve and Tue, 10 days in Jun, Oct, Jan, 60-180.

La Madeleine-sous-Montreuil, 2.5 km W :
● ♦♦ ***Auberge la Grenouillère,*** ☎ 21.06.07.22 Ⓟ ꙮ closed Feb, Tue eve and Wed low season. Three bedrooms to more fully appreciate the welcome, the cooking and the wine cellar of the Gauthiers. Spec : *pot-au-feu du pêcheur, tarte aux fruits chauds,* 150-210.

PÉRONNE

Cambrai 37, Amiens 51, Paris 139
B3 ✉ 80200

ⓘ 31, rue St-Fursy (after 3 pm), ☎ 22.84.42.38.

SNCF ☎ 22.84.00.35.

Hotel :
★★***Les Remparts*** (L.F.), 21, rue Beaubois, ☎ 22.84.01.22. 16 rm ⚘ Ⓟ ꙮ ⛵ ✈ ♿ closed 1-27 Aug, 175. Rest. ● ♦♦ ♿ Spec : *ficelle picarde, anguille fumée,* 55-120.

⛺ ★★★*Port de Plaisance* (90 pl.), ☎ 22.84.19.31.

Restaurant :
♦♦ ***La Quenouille,*** 4, av. des Australiens, ☎ 22.84.00.62. Visa Ⓟ ꙮ ⛵ closed Jun, Sun eve and Mon, 95-130.

Le QUESNOY

Valenciennes 18, Cambrai 33, Paris 220
C2 ✉ 59530

ⓘ mairie, ☎ 27.49.12.16. *S.I./O.T.,* Chalet, rte de Ghissignies.

SNCF ☎ 27.49.12.10.

Hotels :
★★***Hostellerie du Parc*** (L.F.), 7, rue Victor-Hugo, ☎ 27.49.02.42. Euro, Visa. 7 rm Ⓟ ꙮ ⛵ ✈ 130. Rest. ● ♦♦ ♿ closed Sun eve and Mon. Spec : *brochette de lotte au whisky et poivre rose, flamiche au maroilles,* 60-140.

Locquignol, ✉ 59530, 8 km NW :
★★★***Hostellerie de la Tovraille*** (Châteaux-hôtels), rte de Maroilles, ☎ 27.49.05.55. 9 rm Ⓟ ꙮ ⛵ 260. Rest. ♦♦♦ 220-310.

⛺ ★★★*Municipal du lac Vauban* (180 pl.), ☎ 27.49.10.07.

Leisure activities : Port Rouge Pond, Lake Vauban (canoeing), Fer à Cheval Pond.

ROUBAIX

Lille 12, Amiens 127, Paris 230
B1 ✉ 59100

ⓘ hôtel de ville, 17, Grand-Place, ☎ 20.70.70.02.

SNCF ☎20.73.45.45.

Hotels :
★★★***PLM-Grand Hôtel,*** 22, av. J.-B.-Lebas, ☎ 20.73.40.00. Tx 132301. AE, DC, Euro, Visa. 92 rm, 285.

Croix, ✉ 59170, 2 km W :
★★***Flandres,*** 59, rue Holden, ☎ 20.72.35.01. Tx 131339. AE. 31 rm ⛵ ♿ closed 9-23 Aug, 160.

Restaurants :
● ♦♦ ***Le Caribou,*** 8, rue Mimerel, ☎ 20.70.87.08 Ⓟ closed Sat noon, Mon and 9 Jul-25 Aug. Quality fare in a lovely house. Spec : *petit ragoût de langouste au safran,* some exceptional wines, 210-320.
♦♦ ***La Calanque,*** 58, rue de l'Épeule, ☎ 20.70.49.46. Closed Sun and Mon, eve Tue-Thu, Sat noon, 1 week in Jul and Aug. Spec : fish, 120-210.
♦♦♦ ***Les Hauts de Barbieux/La Chaudrée,*** 31, rue Paul-Lafargue, ☎ 20.26.29.05. Visa ꙮ ♿ closed Mon and Aug, 90-250.

Lys-lès-Lannoy, ✉ 59390, 5 km SE :
♦♦ ***Auberge de la Marmotte,*** 5, rue J.-B.-Lebas, ☎ 20.75.30.95. Euro, Visa Ⓟ ♿ closed Tue, Sun eve, Wed, Feb school hols, 29 Jul-31 Aug, 70-180.

ROYE

Amiens 42, Arras 74, Paris 112
B3 ✉ 80700

SNCF ☎ 22.87.00.12.

Hotel :
★★***Nord*** (L.F.), 1, pl. de la République, ☎ 22.87.10.87. 7 rm, 100. Rest. ♦ closed 15 Jul-5 Aug, 15 Feb-5 Mar, Tue eve and Wed, 120-210.

Restaurant :
● ♦♦♦ ***La Flamiche,*** 20, pl. de l'Hôtel-de-Ville, ☎ 22.87.00.56. AE, DC, Visa ♿ closed 14 Dec-13 Jan, Sun and Mon. Solid accent on the new. Interesting menus, reasonably-priced *à la carte.* Spec : *rémoulade de turbot au céleri et aux noix, pigeonneau rôti crème d'ail,* 135-200.

SAINT-AMAND-LES-EAUX

Valenciennes 14, Lille 39, Paris 215
C2 ✉ 59230

♨ early Mar to mid-Dec.

ⓘ abbey tower, ☎ 27.48.67.09.

SNCF ☎ 27.48.57.56.

Hotel :
★★***La Tour,*** 19, rue Thiers, ☎ 27.48.45.31. AE, Euro, Visa. 18 rm, closed Aug, 150-170.

⛺ ★★★★*Mont des Bruyères,* A.C.N.F., 806, rue Basly (100 pl.), ☎ 27.48.56.87.

Restaurants :
♦♦ ***Auberge de la Forêt,*** rte de Raismes, 4 km S, ☎ 27.25.51.98. Visa Ⓟ ✈ ♿ closed Sun and eve of nat hols. Spec : game, grills and seafood, 200-250.
♦ ***Brasserie Alsacienne,*** 23, Grand-Place, ☎ 27.48.50.62. Visa ♿ closed Mon, Sun eve, and Aug. Spec : *choucroute au champagne, beignets de lotte sauce rouge, rognons de veau au genièvre.* Interesting cellar, 55-150.

SAINT-OMER

Calais 40, Lille 64, Paris 261
A1 ⊠ 62500

ℹ hôtel de ville, ☎ 21.98.40.88, and 52, rue Carnot, ☎ 21.38.31.66.

SNCF ☎ 21.38.30.22.

Hotels :
★★***Bretagne*** (L.F.), 2, pl. du Vainquai, ☎ 21.38.25.78. Tx 133290. AE, DC, Visa. 33 rm Ⓟ 190, closed 15-28 Aug and 2-10 Jan, Sun and nat hol eves, Sat. Rest. ♦♦ Spec : seafood, 60-200.
★★***Saint-Louis,*** 25, rue d'Arras, ☎ 21.38.35.21. Euro, Visa. 20 rm Ⓟ closed 25 Dec-1 Jan, 150.

Tilques, 6 km NW on the N43 :
● ★★***Le Vert Mesnil*** (France-Accueil), rue du Château, ☎ 21.93.28.99. Tx 133360. AE, DC, Euro, Visa. 40 rm Ⓟ ♿ 240. Rest. ♦♦ 70-150.

Lumbres, ⊠ 62380, 12 km SW :
★***Auberge du Moulin de Mombreux,*** ☎ 21.39.62.44. AE, DC, Euro, Visa. 6 rm Ⓟ closed 20 Dec-1 Feb, Mon and Sun eve, 135. Rest. ● ♦♦♦ Spec : *la nage de Saint-Jacques parfumée au basilic, la royale de Saint-Jacques au caviar, aneth et citron, le suprême de volaille aux concombres et à la tomate fraîche,* 120-250.

Restaurants :
♦♦♦ ***La Truye qui File,*** 8, rue des Bleuets, ☎ 21.88.41.34. Tx 160600. Visa ♿ closed Aug, Sun eve and Mon ex nat hols, 80-180.
♦♦ ***Le Cygne,*** 8, rue Caventou, ☎ 21.98.20.52. Euro ♿ closed Sat noon, Tue and 10-31 Dec. Good value, 65-130.

SAINT-POL-SUR-TERNOISE

Arras 34, Boulogne 85, Paris 212
13 km N of Frévent, B2 ⊠ 62130

ℹ hôtel de ville, ☎ 21.03.04.98.

SNCF ☎ 21.03.02.55.

Hotel :
★★***Lion d'Or*** (L.F., France-Accueil), 68-74, rue d'Hesclin, ☎ 21.03.12.93. AE, DC, Euro, Visa. 35 rm ♿ 175. Rest. ● ♦♦ ☎ 21.03.10.44. Closed Sun eve (ex school hols and high season). Good regional fare : *flan d'anguilles, gratin de moules, jambon de pays braisé,* 65-180.

SAINT-VALÉRY-SUR-SOMME

Abbeville 20, Boulogne 93, Paris 183
A2 ⊠ 80230

ℹ 23, rue de la Ferté (high season), ☎ 22.27.93.50.

Hotels :
★***Les Pilotes,*** 62-68, rue de la Ferté, ☎ 22.60.80.39. Visa. 22 rm, closed Feb, 160. Rest. ♦♦ 40-220.

Le Hourdel, ⊠ 80410 Cayeux-sur-Mer, 10 km NW :
Le Parc aux Huîtres, ☎ 22.26.61.20. AE, DC, Euro, Visa. 7 rm closed 1 Dec-15 Jan, Tue eve and Wed (low season), 90. Rest. ♦ 60-150.

Riding gîtes : Deramecourt, ☎ 22.27.51.45, Estrebœuf, 5 km S Delabie-Colin, ☎ 22.30.20.58, Friville-Escarbotin, 15 km SW.

⛺ ★★★★*La Croix l'Abbé* (200 pl.), ☎ 22.27.51.46 ; ★★*la Garenne* (200 pl.), ☎ 22.26.81.97.

SECLIN

Lille 12, Valenciennes 45, Paris 207
B1 ⊠ 59113

SNCF ☎ 20.90.11.54.

Hotels :
★★★***Auberge du Forgeron*** (L.F.), 17, rue Roger-Bouvry, ☎ 20.90.09.52. AE, Visa. 20 rm Ⓟ closed Aug, 200. Rest. ● ♦♦ ♿ closed Sat eve and Sun. Good cooking midway between tradition and novelty. Spec : *pied de porc farci, paupiette de saumon fumé,* 70-220.
★★★***Au Tournebride,*** 59, rue Sadi-Carnot, ☎ 20.90.09.59. AE, Euro, Visa. 10 rm Ⓟ ♿ closed 15 Jul-15 Aug and Sat, 250. Rest. ♦♦ Specialities from the Landes region ; seafood, 65-160.

Restaurants :
Annœulin, ⊠ 59112, 7 km SW :
♦♦ ***Le Charolais,*** 9, rue J.-B.-Lebas, ☎ 20.85.69.44. AE, Visa closed 10-30 Aug, Mon, Tue and Sun eves. Very good value, 65-160.

Pont-à-Marcq, ⊠ 59710, 7 km SW :
♦♦ ***La Perdrix,*** 188, rue Nationale, ☎ 20.34.51.51. Visa Ⓟ closed Sun-wed, 80-150.

SOLRE-LE-CHÂTEAU

Maubeuge 18, Cambrai 68, Paris 219
C2 ⊠ 59740

ℹ mairie, ☎ 27.61.61.14.

Hotels :
Sars-Poteries, ⊠ 59216, 5 km SW :
● ★★***Auberge Fleurie,*** 61, rue Gal-de-Gaulle, ☎ 27.61.62.72. 11 rm Ⓟ closed 28 Dec-2 Jan, 180. Rest. ♦♦ ☎ 27.61.62.48. closed 15-31 Aug, Feb and Mon. Good set menu, 130-220.

Liessies, 7 km S :
● ★★***Château de la Motte,*** ☎ 27.61.81.94. 10 rm Ⓟ closed 20 Dec-30 Jan, 160. Rest. ♦ advance notice required, 70-120.

Restaurants :
♦♦ ***La Potinière,*** Grand-Rue, ☎ 27.61.64.55. Visa ♿ closed last week in Dec, 1-10 Mar, Sun eve and Mon. Good value, 50-120.

Dimechaux, 5 km NW :
● ♦♦ ***La Mère Maury,*** rte de Solre, ☎ 27.67.80.49. AE, DC, Visa Ⓟ ♿ closed 16 Aug-10 Sep. A lovely inn and D. Versavel's inventive cooking. Spec : *filet de turbot au basilic, magret de canard aux poires poivrées,* 150-200.

Le TOUQUET

Amiens 105, Lille 132, Paris 220
A2 ⊠ 62520

ℹ hôtel de ville, ☎ 21.05.27.55, and Palais de l'Europe, ☎ 21.05.21.65.

SNCF ☎ 21.80.50.50.

🚌 pl. du Marché-Couvert, ☎ 21.05.22.99.

Car-hire : *Budget* train + auto, at the airport, ☎ 21.05.03.99.

Hotels :
★★★★***Westminster,*** av. du Verger, ☎ 21.05.19.66. Tx 160439. AE, DC, Euro, Visa. 145 rm Ⓟ ♿ closed 15 Nov-15 Mar, 570. Rest. ♦ closed Mon eve and Tue (ex Jul and Aug), 140-180.
★★★***Côte d'Opale,*** 99, bd de la Mer, ☎ 21.05.08.11. AE, DC, Euro, Visa. 28 rm ♿ closed 1 Jan-15 Mar, 290. Rest. ♦♦ 100-250.
★★★***Manoir Hôtel*** and ***Golf Club,*** av. du Golf,

3 km S, ☎ 21.05.20.22. Tx 135565. AE, Euro, Visa. 44 rm ℗ ♿ closed early Jan-14 Mar, 520. Rest. ♦♦ 130-350.
★★**Plage,** bd de la Mer, ☎ 21.05.03.22. Visa. 26 rm closed 15 Nov-15 Mar, 195.

Farmhouse gîtes and table d'hôtes : *ferme du Bout de Haut,* Cormont, 15 km NE, ⊠ 62630 Étaples.

Restaurants :
● ♦♦♦ ***Flavio-Club de la Forêt,*** 1, av. du Verger, ☎ 21.05.10.22. closed 1 Nov-15 Mar (ex week-ends in Dec) and Wed, off season. Flavio is always at the peak of his art. Spec : lobster, fish, excellent cellar, 320-450.
♦♦ ***Le Chalut,*** 7, bd J.-Pouget, ☎ 21.05.22.55. Euro, Visa ♿ closed Tue eve and Wed, Dec and Jan, 100-250.
♦ ***Bistrot de la Charlotte,*** 36, rue St-Jean, ☎ 21.05.32.11. Euro, Visa. closed Jan and Wed. Booking required. Excellent value, 70-90.

Institut de thalassothérapie, sea-water health cures, ☎ 21.05.10.67.

Casinos : *Casinos de la Forêt,* pl. de l'Hermitage, ☎ 21.05.08.76 (high season). *Casino des Quatre Saisons,* 26, rue St-Jean, ☎ 21.05.15.53 and 21.05.16.99.

TOURCOING

Roubaix 4, Lille 13, Paris 234
B1 ⊠ 59200

ℹ Grand-Place, ☎ 20.26.89.03.

SNCF ☎ 20.76.30.59.

Restaurants :
● ♦♦ ***La Saucière,*** 189, bd Gambetta, ☎ 20.26.67.90. Visa ♿ closed Sat noon and Sun, 1 Aug-7 Sep, Feb school hols. Excellent fare at very reasonable prices. Spec : *mousseline de loup,* selection of desserts, 190-210.
♦♦ ***Le Plessy,*** 31, av. Lefrançois, ☎ 20.25.07.73. Visa ; closed Mon and Aug. Reasonable prices, 75-150.
♦ ***Le P'tit Bedon,*** 5, bd de l'Égalité, ☎ 20.25.00.51. AE, Visa closed Mon, 15-30 Jul, 1-15 Sep. Excellent value, 115-150.

Halluin, 8 km NW :
♦♦ ***Auberge du Loisel,*** 599, chemin du Loisel, ☎ 20.94.72.81. AE, Visa ℗ closed Feb school hols, Easter, Aug, Wed eve and Sun, 65-200.

VALENCIENNES

Lille 51, Bruxelles 102, Paris 206
C2 ⊠ 59300

ℹ 1, rue Askièvre, ☎ 27.46.22.99.

SNCF ☎27.46.64.82.

Bus pl. du Hainaut.

Car-hire : *Budget* train + car, station, ☎ 27.46.20.15.

Hotels :
★★★***Grand Hôtel*** (Mapotel), 8, pl. de la Gare, ☎ 27.46.32.01. Tx 110701. AE, DC, Euro, Visa. 96 rm, 260. Rest. ♦♦ Famous for its choucroute, 60-170.
★★★***Auberge du Bon Fermier,*** 64-66, rue de Tamars, ☎ 27.46.68.25. AE, Visa. 10 rm 350. Rest. ♦♦♦ Regional dishes in the historical setting of a 17thC post-house. Spec : *goyère valenciennoise, langue Lucullus, cochon de lait à la broche, sanglier,* 90-200.
★★***Notre-Dame,*** 1, pl. Thellier-de-Poncheville, ☎ 27.42.30.00. 40 rm ♿ 150.

Sebourg, ⊠ 59990 Saultain, 11 km E :
★★***Au Jardin Fleuri,*** ☎ 27.26.53.44. Visa. 12 rm ℗ closed 15 Aug-9 Sep, 25 Jan to 5 Feb, 120. Rest. ♦♦ closed Sun eve. Inexpensive set menus, 70-120.

Restaurants :
● ♦♦ ***L'Alberoi, Buffet de la Gare,*** pl. de la Gare, ☎ 27.46.86.30. AE, DC, Euro, Visa ♿ closed eve Sun and nat hols. New decor. Spec : *langue de Valenciennes Lucullus, andouillette de Cambrai rôtie,* 100-200.

Raismes, ⊠ 59590, 6 km NW :
♦♦ ***La Grignotière,*** 6, rue J.-Jaurès, ☎ 27.36.91.99. Visa ♿ closed Sun eve, Mon ex nat hols and Aug. Spec : *escalope de saumon de Norvège au cresson,* 90-150.

Quievrechain, ⊠ 59920, 12 km NE :
♦♦ ***Le Petit Restaurant,*** 182, rue J.-Jaurès, ☎ 27.45.43.10. Euro, Visa ℗ closed Mon and Aug. Spec : fish, 60-200.

WIMEREUX

Boulogne 8, Lille 120, Paris 306
A1 ⊠ 62930

ℹ pl. Albert-Ier (high season), and mairie, ☎ 21.32.46.29.

SNCF ☎ 21.32.43.11.

Hotels :
★★★***Atlantic,*** digue de la Mer, ☎ 21.32.42.02. Visa. 11 rm ℗ ♿ closed Feb, 200. Rest. ♦♦ closed Sun eve and Mon low season. Spec : fish and shellfish, 150-200.
★★***Centre,*** 78, rue Carnot, ☎ 21.32.41.08. Euro, Visa. 25 rm ℗ closed Sun eve and Mon Nov-Mar, 3-17 Jun, 24 Dec-17 Jan, 150. Rest. ♦ closed Sun eve and Mon from Nov to Mar. Excellent value. Spec : fish, 60-190.

⛺ ★★*Olympic Camping* (110 pl.), ☎ 21.32.45.63.

Provence, Côte d'Azur

Astonishing Provence, which juxtaposes the pink flamingoes of the Camargue and the giant reservoirs of industrialized Fos. Old and new mingle harmoniously throughout the region, and technicians at the Cadarache Nuclear Research Center go home at night to thousand-year-old villages perched on the slopes of the Lubéron. Patiently and lovingly, Provence pieces together the puzzle of its past : Mistral and three-holed fipple flute, cowherds and bull-branding, oil presses and mediaeval trades and crafts. The hilltop villages are coming to life again, grey stone rising up amidst the pinetrees and green oaks. Provence remains true to its origins without compromising its future — a region where life is good, an innovative and inventive culture which keeps one eye on its fascinating past.

The Provence of poets and painters, of Giono, Picasso and Bonnard, still exists — fountains distill eternity under avenues of beechtrees and lavender still grows in profusion on the high plateaux. The Ventoux and Vaucluse mountains are full of honey and truffles, and man-made quarries resemble temples of the gods, abandoned under a sky as blue as that of Greece. The festivals of Aix-en-Provence, Arles and Avignon draw crowds from all over the world to enjoy music and poetry in the perfect climate of the region, or simply to sit in outdoor cafés watching the world go by. Provence's children have dark, laughing faces crowned with unruly black hair, and everywhere you sense the underlying presence of a different culture, once subordinate to the north, but now coming back into its own.

The Côte d'Azur or Riviera, with its palmtrees, beaches and sparkling sea is a favorite holiday spot for French and foreigners alike, and despite its popularity retains much of its charm and beauty. Tourists stroll along the wide Promenade des Anglais in Nice where the sun shines almost all year round, and Cannes with its luxury hotels in the Croisette, its world-famous film festival and elegant restaurants, forms a sparkling and luxurious façade for the old Roman town of Canois perched on the Sucquet hill behind it.

Sightseeing

AIX-EN-PROVENCE★★★

B2-3 / ® / pop. 124 500 (Bouches-du-Rhône)
See plan page 890

Aix seems to embody the noblest aspects of Provençal civilisation. Much of the architecture is derived from the 17th and 18thC, including 198 mansions built for the regional parliamentary councillors, squares and avenues shaded by plane trees and mossy fountains. In July and August, when the city is given over to an international arts festival, the streets seem to be in a state of permanent celebration. A *pastis* (aniseed-flavoured alcoholic drink) on the terrace of the *Deux Garçons* café is practically a rite of initiation for newcomers.

▶ The **Cours Mirabeau**★★ (A-B2) : with attractive cafés and brasseries, bookshops and confectioners, this is one of the great avenues of the world.
17th and 18thC mansions line the avenue; the influence of Italian Baroque is evident. No. 38, **Maurel de Pontevès Mansion**★ (1647); No. 55 is the house where the painter Paul Cézanne (1839-1906) spent his childhood. ▶ **Place d'Albertas**★★ (A2) : 18thC mansions and a fountain provide a gracious setting for summer concerts. ▶ Nearby, at 6 Rue Espariate, **Boyer d'Éguilles Mansion**★ (1675) is a natural history museum *(10-12 & 2-6, closed Sun.)*. ▶ **Place Richelme** (A1) : shaded by plane trees, site of the centuries-old morning fruit and vegetable market. ▶ **Place de l'Hôtel-de-Ville** (A1) : flower market *(Tue., Thu., Sat. am)*. The 17thC Hôtel de Ville (town hall, courtyard★, Méjanes library, St. John Perse Foundation *9-12 & 2-5; sat. 12-5*) stands next to the 16thC **Tour de l'Horloge** (clock tower)★ with four figures representing the seasons. ▶ **Museum of Old Aix**★ (A1) in the Estienne de St. Jean Mansion *(10-12 & 2-5 or 6 in summer; closed Mon and Feb.)*. Next door at No. 17 Rue Gaston de Saporta, the **Châteaurenard Mansion**★ : 1650; monumental staircase★. ▶ Towards the cathe-
monumental staircase★. ▶ Towards the cathe-
dral past the **Musée des Tapisseries** (Tapestry Museum)★ : 17th-18thC Archbishop's palace and display of Beauvais tapestries★ (→ Ile-de-France) of same period *(10-12 & 2-5, 2:30-6:30 in season; closed Tue., Jan. and some nat. hols.)*. The courtyard is the setting for major festival events *(festival office, tel 42.23.37.81)*; gate★. ▶ **St. Sauveur cloister**★★ : Romanesque late 12thC. ▶ **Cathedral** of **St. Sauveur**★★ (A1) : decoration and architecture of every period from the 5th to the 18thC are represented; the Gothic building (1285-1350) incorporates the nave of an earlier Romanesque church (south aisle). The panels★ of the door (1510), the 5thC sarcophagus of St. Mître (first bay in right side-aisle) and the Merovingian baptistery★ (second and third bays) are noteworthy, as is the triptych of the **Burning Bush** (Buisson Ardent)★★★ by Nicolas Froment

Don't miss

★★★ *Aix-en-Provence and Mont Sainte-Victoire (B2), Arles (A2), Avignon (A2), Les Baux-de-Provence and the Alpilles (A2), the Hyères Islands (C3) (Ile de Porquerolles and Ile de Port-Cros), the Abbey of Sénanque (B2), the Abbey of Thoronet (C3) and the Grand Canyon of Verdon (C2).*

★★ *La Camargue (A2-3), Cannes (D2), the* Clues *(narrow valleys) of Haute-Provence (D2), the gorges of Daluis and Cians (C1), Estorel (C-D2), Fontaine-de-Vaucluse (A2), Gordes (B2), Lérins Islands (D2), Lubéron (B2), Marseilles (B3), Les Maures (C3), Menton (D2), Monaco (D2), Nice and the Riviera (D2), Sainte-Croix Lake (C2), Saint-Maximin-la-Sainte-Baume (B3), Saint-Paul-de-Vence (D2), Saint-Tropez (C3), the Abbey of Silvacane (B2), Tinée Valley (C-D1), Turini Forest (D2), Vaison-la-Romaine (A-B1), Ventoux (B1), Vésubie Valley (D2), Villeneuve-les-Avignon (A2).*

Facts and figures

Situation : *N, the Alps of the Dauphiné; E, the Italian frontier; W, the Rhône and the Languedoc; S, the Mediterranean.*
Area : *26 135 km^2.*
Climate : *Mediterranean, with wide divergencies according to altitude and exposure; heavy rain in spring and autumn; mild winters on the Côte d'Azur; cool nights; hot, dry summers. The dry, cold mistral wind blows down the Rhône valley as far as Fréjus.*
Population : *3 860 139; Alpes-de-Haute-Provence 119 068; Alpes-Maritimes 881 198; Bouches-du-Rhône 1 724 199; Var 708 331; Vaucluse 427 343.*
Administration : *Department of* ***Alpes-de-Haute-Provence,*** *Prefecture Digne; Department of* ***Alpes-Maritimes,*** *Prefecture Nice; Department of* ***Bouches-du-Rhône,*** *Prefecture Marseilles; Department of* ***Var,*** *Prefecture Toulon; Department of* ***Vaucluse,*** *Prefecture Avignon.*

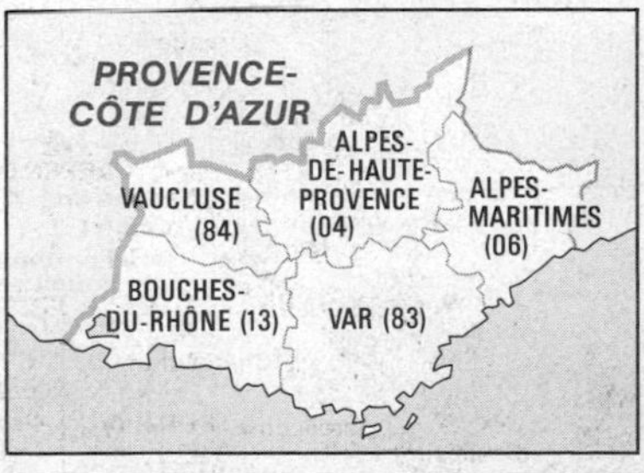

(1476, right wall of nave). Typical of Provençal painting at that period, the work includes elements of Flemish Realism as well as Italian Renaissance influences in perspective and landscape. ▶ The cathedral is in the oldest part of the city. The **springs** at Aix (Établissement Thermal, A1) have been in use since Roman times. The **Vendôme Pavilion** (1667) was built as a provincial residence for the Cardinal de Vendôme; the painter Jean-Baptiste Van Loo (1684-1745) lived and worked there (furniture and Provençal works of art, *10-12 & 2:30-5, 6:30 in season; closed Tue. and last 2 weeks of Jun.).* ▶ Through the streets of old Aix to the **Place des Prêcheurs** (B1) where fragrant *herbs of Provence* complement the fruit and vegetables in the market★ *(Tue.,*

Calissons d'Aix

In Provençal dialect, carnissouns *or* calissouns *are lozenge-shaped sweets made from a mixture of ground sweet almonds and melon preserve with the addition of fruit syrup. The paste is rolled flat, covered with rice paper, given a white glaze, cut into shape and sold by good confectioners. In the past,* calissons *were distributed in the churches on certain feast days, which goes to show that virtue may bring its own reward.*

Thu., Sat. am); antiques and bric-à-brac stands in the neighbouring place de Verdun.
▶ **Church of Ste. Marie-Madeleine** (B1) : (18th-19thC) interesting for its works of art. The 15thC **Annunciation Triptych★★** (centre panel renowned for the Virgin's smile) is in the left side-aisle. ▶ Return to the Cours Mirabeau and take **Rue du Quatre-Septembre** (B2) where the **Paul-Arbaud Museum** and Library have much to offer admirers of Provençal ceramics★; documents about the Félibrige society (founded by Frédéric Mistral and others to preserve Provençal culture) and Provence *(2-5; closed Sun. and nat. hols.).* The 18thC **Gaumont Mansion★** at 3 Rue Joseph Cabassol (A2), now houses the Darius Milhaud Conservatory of Music and Dance. ▶ **The Place des Quatres-Dauphins** (four dolphins)★ (B2) : with old mansions and fountain (1667), an especially attractive square.
▶ **Granet Museum★★** (B2) : in the former Priory of the Knights of Malta (1675) displays aristocratic taste of the late 17thC *(10-12 & 2-5, or 6 in summer; closed Tue. and nat. hols.);* the Provençal painter Granet (1775-1849) is amply represented; the collection of French works from the 16th to the 19thC includes examples by Clouet, La Tour, Largillière and Ingres (Ingres' **portrait of Granet★★**), Flemish and Dutch works (Rubens, Frans Hals, Rembrandt); German school (**portrait** of the English King Henry VIII's Chancellor **Sir Thomas More★** attributed to Mabuse); Italian schools (Guercino, Coreaggio, Giordano); recently-opened Cézanne room.

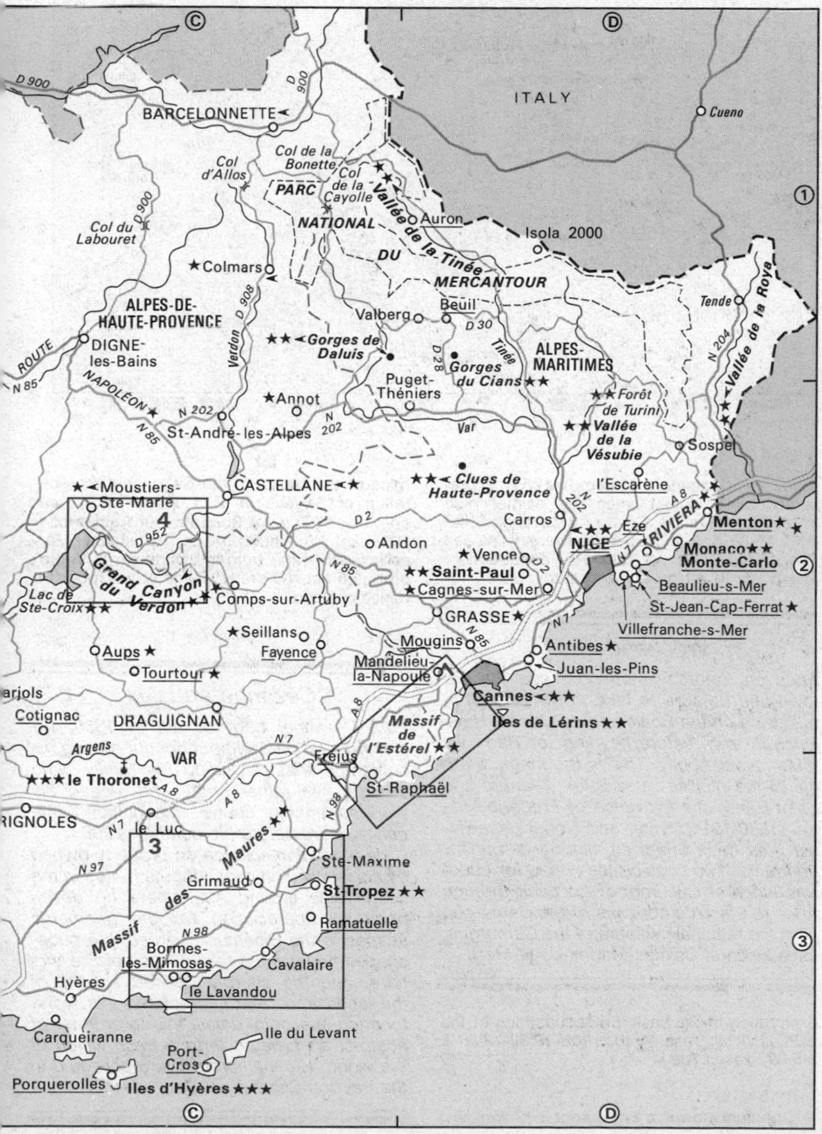

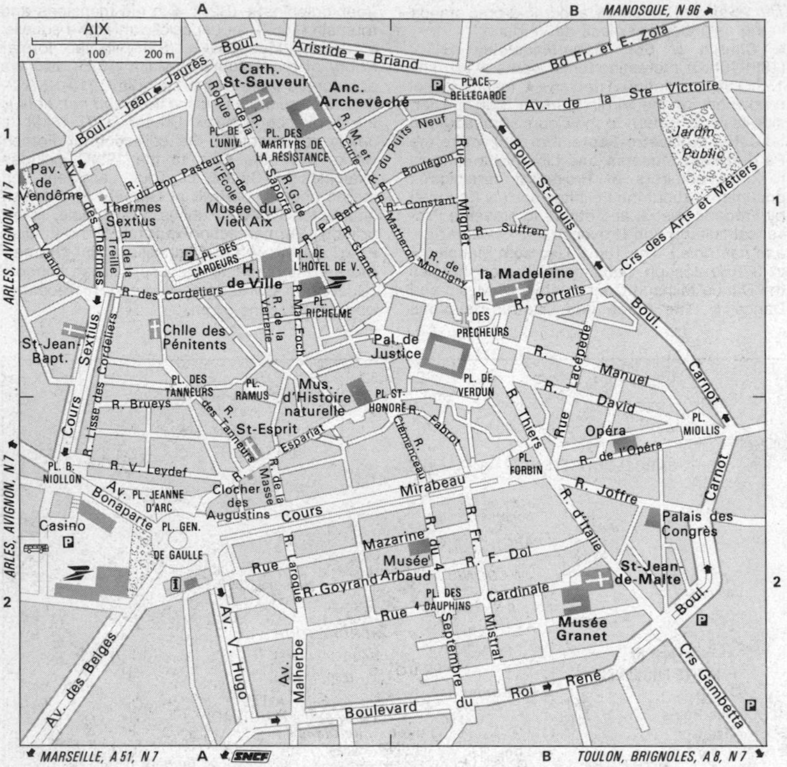

Also... ▶ **Cézanne's studio** (via A1) : preserved as it looked when the painter died in 1906 (memorabilia, Centre for Cézanne Studies; *10-12 & 2-5, 2:30-6 in season; closed Tue. and nat. hols.).* ▶ **Vasarely Foundation★** : *(4 km W)* an art gallery and study centre for exploration of the basic preoccupations of the painter Victor Vasarely (b. 1908) *(9:30-12:30 & 2-5:30; closed Tue.).* □

Weekend tips

Arles on Saturday morning : see the old town and be sure to take in the market in full swing on the Boulevard des Lices. Have lunch in town before heading for Baux via Montmajour Abbey. This is the magic triangle of the Alpilles : Les Baux, Glanum and Saint-Rémy, the Provence of Frédéric Mistral (1830-1914), writer and Nobel prizewinner. Les Baux offers an alluring detour for gourmets. Two possibilities : head for Lubéron (lunch at Cucuron) or go back through Arles to the wide horizons of the Camargue (visit the regional museum of the Camargue, have lunch at Saintes-Maries-de-la-Mer).

▶ Nearby

▶ **Oppidum** (town) **d'Entremont** : *(3 km N)* : ruins of the capital of the Celto-Ligurian federation of Salyens *(9-12 & 2-5 or 6 in season; closed Tue.).* ▶ **Roquefavour Aqueduct ★** *(13.5 km W)* : built in 1847 to supply Marseilles with water from the Durance. ▶ **Ventabren** *(3.5 km N)* : pretty village at the foot of a ruined château. □

Cézanne and Aix

Paul Cézanne, born at Aix in 1839, remained a prophet without honour among his contemporaries, including his family, who thought him rather crazy and judged his work as amateur daubs. Recognition came only 2 years before his death in 1906.

He worked in solitude on property owned by his family or in peasant huts rented in the countryside around Aix, where he developed an appreciation for the geometric shapes in the Bibémus quarries, the cube-shaped houses, the heavy mass of Ste Victoire, and the sharply defined solidity of the landscapes that characterise his work. Ignoring anecdotal detail, this forerunner of abstract art brought forth a fresh vision of the world. His memorabilia are collected in the Pavillon Cézanne at Aix.

▶ Mont Sainte-Victoire★★ *(59 km round trip, half-day).*

Sainte-Victoire★★ forms a backdrop to Aix. The mountain is spectacular, the light is beautiful and it is easy to see why Cézanne was drawn to the site. ▶ **Aix** (leave via C2); take the Cézanne Road (D17). ▶ **Le Tholonet :** (site★) a favourite excursion for the people of Aix; 18thC château, roads lined with plane trees. ▶ From D17, signposted paths lead towards Sainte-Victoire and the **Cengle plateau,** a limestone table S of the mountain. ▶ **Puyloubier :** ruins of a mediaeval château. ▶ **Pourrières.** ▶ Take D23 N then, after 7 km, the Vauvenargues road (D223, D10) down into the upper valley of the Infernet★. ▶ **Château de Vauvenargues :** (16th-17thC) isolated on a peak, belonged to Pablo Picasso (1881-1973), who is buried in the garden. ▶ **Les Cabassols :** the easiest path (GR9) to Sainte-Victoire leaves from here; 1hr30 to the priory, then 10 mins to the **Croix de Provence★★** *(alt. 945 m)* where you can see from the Dauphiné Alps across to Esterel. ▶ **Bimont Dam** (*1.2 km left,* lake reflecting the mountain★; 30 mins on foot to the Zola dam. ▶ D10 runs past the foot of the 16thC **château de Saint-Marc-Jaumegarde.** □

ANNOT★

C2 / ® / pop. 1 062 (Alpes-de-Haute-Provence)

Known to geologists for sandstone eroded into unusual shapes, which add interest to walks in the vicinity.

▶ **Old town★ :** picturesque (alt. 705 m), with narrow streets, vaulted passages, courtyards with 100-year-old plane trees; Romanesque church with Renaissance bell-tower. ▶ The **Toutes Aures Road★** leads to **Lake Castillon** (→ Castellane), *19 km SW* through the **Clues de Rouaine** and **Vergons.** ▶ **Daluis Gorges★★** (→) 15 km NW. □

ANTIBES and JUAN-LES-PINS★

D2 / ® / pop. 63 248 (Alpes-Maritimes)

Juan-les-Pins is famous for a summer jazz festival. There is a superb beach deep in the bay, with all the pleasures of aquatic sports and shore activities. Antibes (*Antipolis* to the Greeks) is an ancient city; its colourful streets overlook the sea. Like neighbouring Nice, Antibes is a city of flowers, especially roses, which it exports all over Europe.

▶ **Avenue Amiral-de-Grasse :** along the ancient ramparts between sea and town (view★) past the principal monuments. ▶ **Church of the Immaculate Conception :** Romanesque eastern end and Classical (17thC) fabric. ▶ **Château Grimaldi :** rebuilt in the 16thC; in 1946, Picasso lived here; his paintings can be seen in the **Picasso Museum★** *(8-12 & 3-6 or 7 in summer; closed Tue., nat. hols. and Nov.).* Drawings, engravings, lithographs and ceramics make up the first-floor display inspired by the Mediterranean. The château also houses archaeology, a painted Descent from the Cross★ (1539) and contemporary art (still life by Nicolas de Staël). ▶ The **Archaeological Museum :** displays artifacts from ancient Antipolis *(9-12 & 2-6 or 7 in summer; closed Tue. and Nov.).* □

▶ Nearby

▶ **Marineland** *(1 km N),* amusement park and marine zoo. ▶ **Biot★** ® *(8 km N) :* charming inland hill village; potters, glass-blowers; regional history museum. SE of the village, **Fernand Léger Museum★★ :** works of the painter (1881-1955) who lived at Biot. The collections illustrate Léger's development *(10-12 & 2-5, 2:30-6:30 in summer; closed Tue.).* ▶ **Sophia Antipolis** *(8 km NW) :* a sociological research centre where modern architecture is blended with the pines and holm oak of the **Valbonne** ® plateau. □

▶ Cap d'Antibes★ ® *(12 km round trip) :*

▶ On this peninsula separating Antibes from Juan-les-Pins, the privacy of luxurious residences is guarded behind thick screens of vegetation. ▶ Antibes. ▶ **Point Bacon :** view of the Nice area. ▶ **Butte de la Garoupe :** lighthouse *(10-12 & 2-5 or 6 in season);* chapel of **Notre-Dame-de-Bon-Port** (13th-16thC), collection of marine *ex-votos,* 14thC icon from Sebastopol. Panorama★★ (orientation chart). ▶ **Thuret Gardens★ :** exotic shrubs and trees acclimatised by the 19thC naturalist for whom the garden is named *(8-12 & 1-5; closed Sat., Sun. and nat. hols.).* ▶ **Napoléon Museum of the Navy** in a former gun battery with a sea view *(10-12 & 2-5, 3-7 in summer; closed Tue. and Nov.).* ▶ **Juan-les-Pins;** 2 km beach of sand, pine forest. □

APT★

B2 / ® / pop. 11 560 (Vaucluse)

Between the Lubéron and the Vaucluse, a typical Provençal small town. Ringed by boulevards lined with plane trees, with old towers, vestiges of ramparts, fountains, and a colourful and aromatic Saturday morning market. Local industries : crystallised fruit; ochre production.

▶ **Place de la Bouquerie :** beside the Calavon, the centre of town activity. ▶ **Church of Ste. Anne :** formerly a cathedral and a record of the city's religious history; 7th and 11thC crypts, Romanesque fabric, chapel of St. Anne with reliquary, treasury, 16thC Italian Annunciation★, 15thC Primitive painting★. ▶ **Museum** in an 18thC mansion : archaeology, ceramics (local specialty), chemist's jars★, popular religious art *(9-12 & 2-6, Apr.-Sep.; 10-12 & 2-5, Oct.-Mar.; closed Tue.).* □

▶ Nearby

▶ **Roussillon★** ® *(13 km NW) :* gold and red like the surrounding cliffs and ochre quarries. ▶ **Rustrel Colorado★** *(10 km NE) :* huge ochre quarry; worth the 2hr walk needed to see it all (GR6). ▶ **Canyon d'Oppedette★** *(20 km NE) :* canyon walls up to 120 m high in sight of D201. ▶ **Simiane-la-Rotonde** (*24 km NE,* Hautes-Alpes) : a hilltop village; the *rotonde* is the keep remaining from a 12th-13thC castle. ▶ **Saignon★** *(4 km S) :* houses cluster 500 m up beside a huge rock; view over Apt; popular site for hikers going to the Claparèdes Plateau and Bories (see box). □

ARLES★★★

A2 / ® / pop. 50 772 (Bouches-du-Rhône)

Arles is a delightful town, alive with traditions centred around the bulls and white horses of the nearby Camargue (→). On

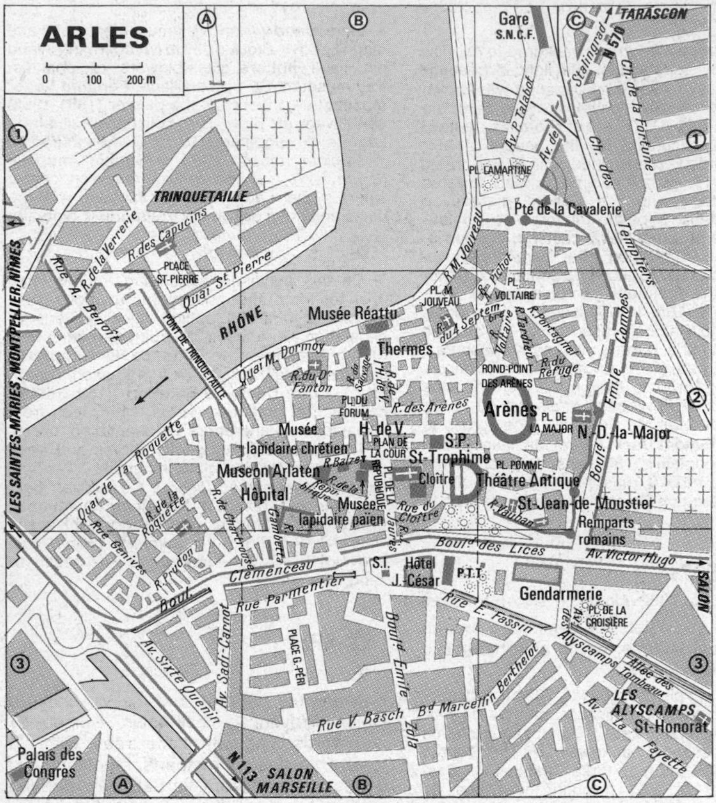

the banks of the Rhône, Arles was once the metropolis of Roman Gaul. Today its picturesque streets annually host the Festival of Dance and the International Photography Conventions.

▶ **Boulevard des Lices** (B-C3) : the focus of town life, with plane trees, cafés and bustling markets on Wednesday and Saturday mornings. ▶ **Place de la République** (B2) : the obelisk was originally in the centre of the Roman Circus. ▶ **Church of St. Trophime★★** (B2) : a synthesis of Romanesque and Classical art, reminiscent of Glanum (→). The richly ornamented doorway★★ (2nd half of 12thC) contrasts with the simple interior; note the high, exceptionally narrow nave; 1614 Adoration of the Magi (right aisle), French painting in the right transept (late 16thC), and 17thC Annunciation★★ (left transept).▶ **St. Trophime cloister★★** : similar concern with architectural equilibrium and harmonious decoration and carving. The church and cloister make Arles a major landmark in Romanesque art *(8:30-12:30 & 2-7, Jun.-Sep., 6:30 Oct.; 9-12:30 & 2-5:30 Nov., 4:30 Dec.; Jan. and Feb., 5:30 Mar.; 8:30-12 & 2-6 Apr., 7pm May; closed 1 Jan., 1 May and 25 Dec.)*; the same hours and a single admission ticket cover the arena (Arènes), the Roman Theatre, the Museums of Pagan and Christian Art, the Arlaten ethnographic museum, the Réattu Museum, the Roman baths and the Alyscamps (cemetery). The cloister was built in two stages (12th and 13th-14thC); there are two Romanesque and two Gothic galleries; figures inspired by classical reliefs on the pillars; figured capitals★; museum of religious art in the north gallery; temporary exhibitions in the chapterhouse. ▶ **Town hall★** (B2, late 17thC) : incorporating a belfry with a 16thC statue of the Roman god Mars; note the flattened vault★ in the entrance hall and behind, on the Plan de la Cour, the former civic offices (1500) and the Viguier Mansion (1200 and 15thC). ▶ **Museum of Pagan Art★★** *(Musée Lapidaire Païen)* (B2) : in the former church of Ste. Anne (17thC, Meridional Gothic survival), Gallo-Roman antiquities excavated around Arles; note, in the nave, the so-called sarcophagus of Phaedra and Hippolytus★ (2nd-3rdC); in the apse, two statues of dancers★ (1stC BC). ▶ **Museum of Christian Art★★** *(Musée Lapidaire Chrétien)* (B2) : said to be the finest in the world after the Vatican. In a 17thC Jesuit chapel, sarcophagi from the two early Christian burial grounds of Alyscamps and St. Genès; a unique display of 4thC Arlesian craftmanship and creativity. Under the museum, entrance to the **cryptoportiques★** : subterranean galleries beneath the forum gates where grain was stored. ▶ **Arlaten Museum★** (B2) : in the Castellane-Laval★ mansion; early 16thC building; Roman portico★ in the courtyard. Frédéric Mistral created the museum and later enriched it with the money he received for the Nobel Prize in 1904. It examines life in and around Arles : furniture, costumes, festivals, legends, trades, music, the Rhône, the Camargue *(closed Mon.*

out of season). ▶ **Roman Theatre★** (B-C2) : the size alone (seating for 7 000 spectators) demonstrates the importance of Arles as a Roman port. It was built during the reign of Augustus (1stC BC). Many of the magnificent decorations are now in the Museum of Pagan Art; a statue know as the Venus of Arles, found here, is now in the Louvre. **Circus★★** (C2) (amphitheatre) : well preserved because, during the Middle Ages, it was converted into a fortress; 200 houses and a church were built in the enclosure. Three 12thC towers remain from the fortification period. The circus, built around 80AD, at 136 m by 107 m is slightly larger than the one at Nîmes; it had seating for 25 000 spectators. ▶ The **Baths of Constantine** (B2) : were originally much larger; the semicircular apse★ enclosed one of the pools. ▶ **Réattu Museum★ :** beside the Rhône in the former 14th-16thC priory of the Knights of Malta (B2); in addition to displaying 17th and 18thC works from around Arles, and almost the complete work of Jacques Réattu (1760-1833, local artist), the museum is acquiring contemporary works of art directly connected with the region; room XII contains about 60 **drawings★ by Picasso** from early 1971, which he presented to the town; the photographic section includes work by the greatest French and foreign photographers. ▶ The **Alyscamps★** (C3) : for almost 15 centuries, first Pagans, then Christians from around Arles and farther afield looked forward to burial here; coffins accompanied by a sum of money — the *mortellage* or burial fee — were shipped on the Rhône, so great was the spiritual reputation of this necropolis. Today there remains only an alley bordered by tombs leading to the ruined church of **St. Honorat★,** a Romanesque sanctuary with 5thC origins much reduced from its earlier dimensions; octagonal Romanesque **bell-tower★★,** worth a visit.

Also... ▶ The **ramparts** (C2) date in part from the 1stC BC. ▶ **Notre-Dame-de-la-Major** (C2) : Romanesque nave, Gothic choir and apse; 17thC façade. ▶ **St. Jean-du-Moustier** (C2) : Romanesque apse★, and **St. Blaise** (12th-14thC) nearby. ▶ 2 km S of the town centre, near the industrial zone, the drawbridge across the Arles canal at Port-de-Bouc is the re-erected **Pont de Langlois** from Vincent Van Gogh's (1853-1890) painting of 1888. □

▶ Nearby

▶ **Montmajour Abbey★★** *(6 km NE) :* on a pine-shaded butte overlooking rice fields, the abbey is an anthology of architectural forms from the 11th to the 13thC. Van Gogh made many drawings of the abbey during his stay in Arles *(9-12 & 2-5, or 6 in season; closed Tue., Nov. and some nat. hols.).* The unfinished church★ dates from the mid-12thC; only two of the five bays originally planned were built. The crypt★ is built into the hill-side; the 12th-13thC cloister★★ is extremely beautiful; commanding keep (1369); the partly underground chapel of St. Pierre★ dates from the foundation of the monastery in the early 11thC. ▶ The small *(Petite)* and great *(Grande)* **Crau plains** *(N and E of Arles) :* separated by the Alpilles, mark the "sacred triangle", that is the Provence of writers such as Frédéric Mistral and Alphonse Daudet (1840-1897). The Petite Crau is cultivated for fruit and vegetables; the Grande Crau, fertile in the north between Arles and Salon, lower down is mostly stones and pebbles from the former delta of the Durance. □

AUPS★

C2 / ® / pop. 1 652 (Var)

Ancient plane trees, old streets, wrought-iron bell-towers, fountains, ramparts and gates : Aups is a charming inland Provençal town. The local specialty is honey, and the Midi accent is strong.

▶ **Church of St. Pancrace :** Provençal Gothic with a renaissance doorway. ▶ Chapel of the former Ursuline convent : **Simon Ségal Museum** of modern paintings (school of Paris; *Easter and 15 Jun.-15 Sep.).* □

▶ Nearby

▶ Main attractions are the **Grand Canyon du Verdon** (→) *(23 km N)* and **Lake St. Croix** (→ Moustiers-Sainte-Marie). ▶ The less known **villages of the upper Var** can be explored from Aups. ▶ **Tourtour★** ® *(10 km SE) :* view★★ over to Saint-Raphaël, old châteaux and regional fossil museum. ▶ **Villecroze** ® *(8 km SE)* : still mediaeval; the name refers to the caves dug into the cliffs. ▶ **Salernes** *(10 km S) :* manufacture of hexagonal red floor tiles, called *tomettes;* several fountains. ▶ **Entrecasteaux** *(18 km S) :* mediaeval, proud of its garden by André Le Nôtre, the 17thC designer of the park of Versailles (→), 17thC château, and the quality of locally produced rugs and olive oil. ▶ **Carcès** ® *(26 km S) :* a hillside village and a lake, surrounded by pines, that feeds Toulon. ▶ **Cotignac** ® *(15 km SW) :* good wine, a beautiful site, a pleasant square. ▶ **Cascade de Bresque★** *(6 km NE of Cotignac)* waterfall 42 m high. □

AVIGNON★★★

A2 / ® / pop. 91 474 (Vaucluse)

Avignon, a maze of ramparts, machicolated towers, belfries and palaces, is the sort of city seen in ancient woodcuts of mediaeval tapestries. The formidable palace-fortress was built for the Popes who, during a century of residence in Avignon (1309-1403) gave the town its monumental appearance. When the Popes returned to Rome, the palaces of the cardinals and archbishops remained; they were built in pairs, one palace in Avignon and another at Villeneuve, so that a prelate under pressure could retreat occasionally from the stresses of the Papal court. Famous both for the Pont d'Avignon (the bridge of the song) and for papal history, Avignon today is the setting for an international festival, which is an important annual event in European theatre; the magnificent courtyards and buildings serve as stages for the performances.

▶ **Palais des Papes★★★** (B1) : fortress and palace, a beautiful example of 14thC Gothic. The main fabric is the work of two successive pontiffs, Benedict XII (originally a Cistercian monk) and Clement VI (first a Benedictine). The northern part, the Palais Vieux, shows the Cistercian taste for simplicity and austerity, where as the Palais Neuf to the South, with ogive vaulting instead of simple wooden ceilings, tends to more sumptuous display *(guided tours at fixed times).* The palace is unfurnished but has beautiful painted murals. **The Requien Museum** (natural history, *closed Sun., Mon.*

and nat. hols., 9-12 & 2-6). ▶ **Palais-Vieux :** Consistory Hall and chapel with frescos★ by Matteo Giovanetti (1348); the Grand Tinel or banquetting hall with frescos by the 14thC Sienese painter Simone Martini, who also decorated the cathedral doorway; the St. Martial chapel, also with frescos★ by Giovanetti; the Robing Room and the Pope's bedroom★, beautifully painted, and finally the Stag Room★, with frescos★ of rustic and hunting scenes reminiscent of Flemish tapestries.

▶ **Palais-Neuf :** Pontifical chapel★ and Great Audience Chamber★ adorned with frescos depicting the Prophets★ (Giovanetti 1353).

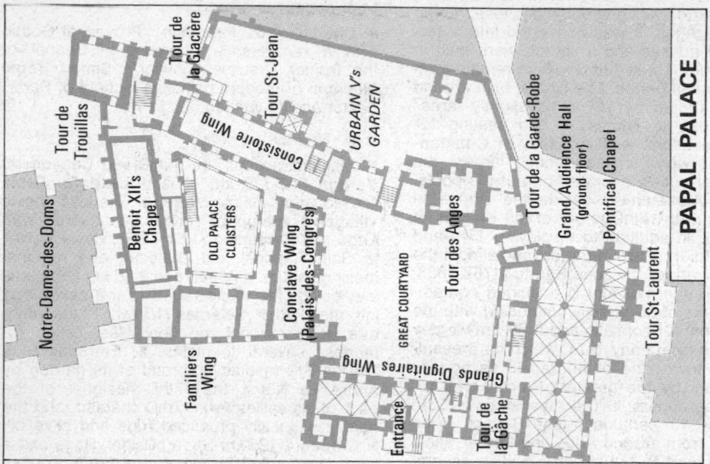

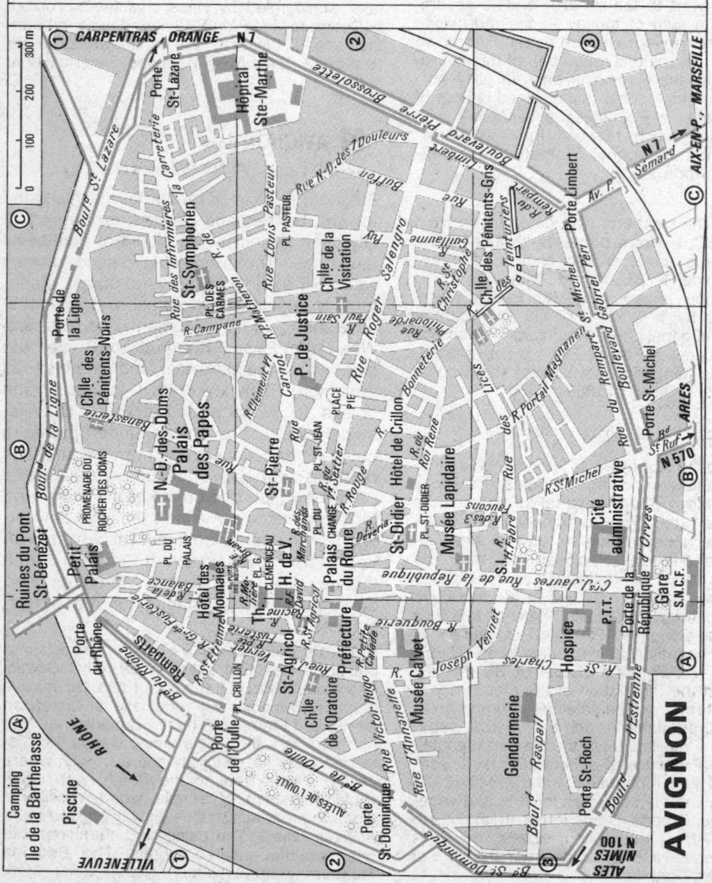

▶ **Place du Palais**★ (B1) : the heart of the city ▶ **Cathedral of Notre-Dame-des-Doms** (B1), remodelled, is still a good example of Provençal Romanesque (tomb of Pope John XXII★, 1345; 12thC marble throne★). ▶ From the **Rocher** (rock) **des Doms** and its gardens : view over the Rhône, St. Bénézet bridge and the Villeneuve fortifications. ▶ **Petit Palais**★ (B1) : formerly the Archbishop's residence (14th-15thC), today the setting for paintings, sculptures and other works of art★★ from the Middle Ages and the Renaissance *(9:15-11:50 & 2-6; closed Tue., hols.)*. A major exhibit is the Campana di Cavelli **collection of Italian Primitives**★★ (14th-15thC) : Virgin Enthroned, by an anonymous Master (1310); Virgin and Child★★ by Sandro Botticelli; Holy Conversation★★ by Vittore Carpaccio. Among the sculptures : the 15thC tomb of Cardinal de Lagrange★★ is strikingly realistic; recumbent effigy of Antoine de Comps (1495). ▶ **Hôtel des Monnaies**★ (the Old Mint), 1619 Italian Baroque, opposite the Papal Palace).

▶ Le Pont d'Avignon of song fame was actually the **Pont St. Bénézet**★ (A-B1) : the Avignonnais in fact used to dance under its arches in restaurants on the midstream Barthelasse Island. Legend has it that the bridge was built by St. Bénézet in the 12thC. Only 4 arches are left out of 22; on the second pier stands the Romanesque and Gothic chapel of St. Nicolas. ▶ The **Place de l'Horloge** (Clock Tower Square, Place Clémenceau, B2) was the Roman forum; a popular meeting place surrounded by cafés and restaurants, it is the scene of much fringe activity during the annual summer festival. Close by, in the **Balance quarter,** well restored 17thC houses★ and modern buildings well adapted to the surroundings. ▶ The **town hall** (Hôtel de Ville) : (B2) rebuilt in the last century (14th-15thC clock tower, where jacks mark the hour); **Church of St. Agricol**★ **:** (A2) Gothic (14th-15thC) building with numerous works of art (near the sacristy, altarpiece★, 1525). ▶ **Calvet Museum**★★ **:** (A2) exhibitions in an 18thC mansion *(9-12 & 2-6; closed Tue. and some nat. hols.)*. Noteworthy exhibits include : 14th-15thC wrought-iron★; Greek sculpture (woman arranging her hair★, 4thC BC); paintings from French and other schools (Louis le Nain★, Géricault★, Chassériau★; Corot★ and Manet★); also works by Joseph Vernet (born in Avignon 1714), Hubert Robert and Soutine. ▶ **Rue des Teinturiers** (clothdyers)★ : (C3) attractive street running along an arm of the Sorgue; you can still see the water-wheels used during the 18th and 19thC in the production of Provençal prints inspired by Indian textiles.

Also... ▶ **Old Avignon** is full of mansions and churches.

▶ **De Crillon Mansion**★ (B2; 17thC) : one of the most beautiful in the city. ▶ **Fortia de Montréal Mansion :** less ornate, 1637. ▶ In the **chapel**★ of the former Jesuit College (1645; Baroque) is the **Lapidary Museum** (B2) : Venus de Pourrières★; and Tarasque de Noves★, a man-eating lion fashioned during the 2nd Iron Age *(9-12 & 2-6; closed Tue. and some nat. hols.)*. ▶ **Church of St. Didier**★ (B2) : one of the largest Meridional Gothic churches (1359), altarpiece of Notre-Dame-du-Spasme★ (1478), so-called from her anguished expression, first chapel on right; 14thC frescos★, first chapel on left. ▶ **Roure Palace**★ (B2) : Gothic, late 15thC with delicate Flamboyant Gothic doorway★. ▶ **Church of St. Pierre**★ (B2) : Meridional Gothic, Renaissance doors★. ▶ NE, the **Banasterie** (basketweaving) quarter : many 17th and 18thC houses. ▶ **St. Symphorien** (C1) : 15th-17thC; 16thC statuary. **Aubanel Museum** (B-C1 : place des Carmes) : in a former private mansion, memorabilia of Théodore Aubanel, founder of Félibrige (printing equipment and rare books from 13thC to present; *guided tours 9-11; closed Sat., Sun., hols. and Apr.)* ▶ **Chapel of the Visitation** (C2) : 1632, fine carving. ▶ **Chapel of the Black Pénitents**★ (B1) : named for a religious brotherhood; 1739 Baroque architecture with white and gold wood panelling. ▶ Many fine houses in **Rue du Vieux-Sextier** (B2, Nos. 10, 20, 22-24 and 33), **Rue Joseph-Vernet** (A2-3, Nos 58, 64, 83 and 87), **Rue Petite-Fusterie** (A2, Nos. 17, 19), **Rue St. Étienne** (A1, Nos. 17, 18, 22-24). ▶ **Jean Vilar House** (8 Rue de Mons) : theatre library. ▶ **Vouland Museum** (17 Rue Victor-Hugo) : French furniture, regional ceramics, decorative art *(10-1 & 3-6 in summer, Fri. until 8, 2-5 rest of year; closed Sat., Sun. and Mon.)*. □

▶ Nearby

▶ **Montfavet** ® *(5 km E)* : 14thC Meridional Gothic church★. ▶ **Châteaurenard** ® (*10 km S;* Bouches-du-Rhône) : with Cavaillon, the most important fruit and vegetable centre in Provence; ruined 14thC feudal château only a few minutes' walk from the church; view★ *(10-12 & 2-6; closed Dec. and Jan.)*. □

▶ Villeneuve-lès-Avignon★★ ® (*2.5 km NW* Gard)

Villeneuve and Avignon, altough separated by the river Rhône as well as by administration boundaries, have always had a close, if stormy, relationship. At one time the Pope's entourage maintained country retreats at Villeneuve; today the Avignonnais cross the river to find peace and quiet on the slopes of the Petit Montagné or at Belle Croix, protected from the Mistral wind (→ box) and the morning mists in the valley.

▶ At the head at the St. Bénézet bridge is **Philip the Fair's Tower**★ (1293), which was intended to keep Avignon at bay *(10-12:30 & 3-7:30 Apr.-Sep.; 10-12 & 2-5 rest of year; closed Feb.; same hours for other monuments)*. ▶ Access to the tower runs in front of the **Municipal Museum**★ : a 17thC mansion housing the **Coronation of the Virgin**★★ (1453), a masterpiece by Engerrand Charonton (born c. 1410), a founder of the school of Avignon painters. The Piétà of Avignon (copy only, original in the Louvre, Paris) is attributed to him. ▶ **Church of Notre-Dame** (14thC) : with single nave, has 14thC polychrome ivory Virgin★★ in the sacristy; cloister of same period. ▶ **Rue de la République :** Nos. 1, 3 and 53, Cardinals' houses. ▶ **Val de Bénédiction Charterhouse**★★ (1356) *(9-12 & 2-6:30, closed Tue. and Feb.)* : monastery founded by Pope Innocent VI, which in 1973 became the International Centre of Research, Creation and Animation. In the 14thC church is the **mausoleum of Innocent VI**★★ (same period); main cloister with the monks' cells; Papal chapel with frescos★ by Matteo Giovanetti (International Summer Conferences take place there parallel to the Avignon Festival). ▶ **Fort St. André**★ *(9-12 & 2-6:30, closed Tue. and Feb.)* : built in the 14thC by order of John the Good and Charles V to overlook Avignon; massive walls and towers, fortified gate★ with two cylindrical towers, a superb example of mediaeval architecture (inside, graffiti scratched by prisoners, an oven marked out for bread). ▶ **Notre-Dame de Belvezet**★ : 12thC Romanesque chapel, worth seeing; the Italian gardens of the former Benedictine abbey make a delightful stroll (view★ over Avignon). □

BANDOL

B3 / ® / pop. 6 713 (Var)

320 days of sunshine every year, a gentle climate and wooded hills that give shelter from the Mistral; palms and eucalyptus along the Promenade near the Marina. Bandol is known for red wine. Leisure facilities, including theatre, crafts and exibitions on the tiny Bendor islet a few hundred metres from shore (boat leaves Bandol on the half-hour).

▶ **Museum of Wines and Spirits :** 8 000 bottles from 50 countries *(10-12 & 2-6 in summer; closed Wed.).* □

▶ Nearby

▶ **Sanary-Bandol** *(3 km NE) :* tropical gardens and zoo *(8-12 & 2-6, 7 pm in summer; closed Sun. am).* ▶ Above **Le Beausset** ® *(10 km N),* the Romanesque chapel of **Notre-Dame-du-Vieux-Beausset** *(14 km NE) :* (collection of *ex-votos*); coast view. ▶ To the W of Beausset, **Le Castellet** ® *(10 km N) :* fortified village on a rocky outcrop (panorama★; Paul Ricard car circuit). ▶ **La Cadière-d'Azur** ® *(3 km SW from Castellet) :* wine-making village set back from the coast. □

BARCELONNETTE

C1 / ® / pop. 3 314 (Alpes-de-Haute-Provence)

Barcelonnette is superbly situated among orchards and meadows surrounded by mountains. The name commemorates the Spanish origins of the family that founded this town in the 13thC. Some of the inhabitants, who emigrated to seek their fortune during the 19thC, managed to establish a monopoly on the cloth trade to Mexico. Having prospered, they returned to build magnificent villas that can still be seen on the Avenue de la Liberation. □

▶ Nearby

▶ **Le Sauze** ® *(6 km S)* and **Super-Sauze** ® (alt. 1 700 m) : winter sports resort on the north slope of the Fours Pass (alt. 2 314 m). ▶ **Pra-Loup** ® *(8.5 km SW) :* skiing on the Pégieu slopes *(2 479 m).* ▶ Three magnificent **mountain roads**★★ go from Barcelonnette towards the Midi : D908 crosses the **Allos Pass**★ (alt. 2 240 m) ®, and runs through the high pastures (view★ over the Verdon Valley); D902 runs through the Bachelard gorges and climbs through the **La Cayolle Pass**★ (alt. 2 327 m) with views over the Var and Bachelard valleys; the third, the highest road in Europe, is the **Route de la Bonette**★★★ (→), beginning at Jausiers *(8 km NE from Barcelonnette)* and climbing through difficult countryside to an altitude of 2 802 m; from here, a 10 min walk to the top of La Bonette (alt. 2 862 m; magnificent view as far as Pelvoux). □

BARJOLS

C2 / ® / pop. 2 016 (Var)

With fountains playing in shady squares, Barjols epitomises the Provençal town. The manufacture of tambourines and a three-hole flute, called the *galoubet,* is traditional here; the instruments are played at local festivals. Every 4 years, the *Tripettes* (tripe) Festival, in which an ox is blessed then slaughtered and roasted for consumption by the townspeople, recalls pagan and Christian traditions. □

▶ Nearby

▶ **La Verdière** *(17 km NW) :* below a château★ on a spur; the old fortress was rebuilt in the 17th-18thC; plasterwork decoration, carving *(guided tours 2-5).* □

The Mistral

Inseparable from life in provence, the Mistral wind brings both good and ill to the land over which it sweeps at speeds up to 190 km/h. Even when the rest of France is under the most dismal weather, the Mistral keeps the Provençal skies clear of clouds while providing an invigorating antidote to the relentless heat of summer. The low, sturdy houses (mas), *their roofs weighted with stones, the long rows of cypress and the rush screens bear witness to the wind's influence on the local landscape.*

Flying tiles and uprooted trees are mild nuisances compared to the forest fires that break out whenever the mistral sweeps from the Massif Central in the North down the Rhône valley to the Mediterranean. Thousands of acres of forestland are lost every year through fires started by a careless cigarette or shard of glass and whipped into an inferno by the unceasing wind. Nevertheless, the mistral's arrival is generally greeted with satisfaction, especially when the first gusts are felt during the day (according to provençal tradition, when it rises at night it never lasts long). For local inhabitants and visitors alike, anything that guarantees good weather can't be all bad.

LES BAUX and the ALPILLES★★★

A2 / ® / pop. 433 (Bouches-du-Rhône)

The white peaks and olive- and almond-clad valleys of the Alpilles were the background to the Provençal "courts of love", where troubadors vied for the prize of a kiss and a peacock's feather in singing the praises of their ladyloves. At Les Baux-de-Provence, an immense pile of stone rising above dense scrub is crowned by a ruined château and ghost town *(la ville morte).* Right next door, the still-inhabited village is a living museum of the Middle Ages.

▶ Enter the town on foot from the car park along the **Rue Porte-Mage** (Three Kings Gate). The most interesting houses, dating from the Renaissance, have simple ground floors and first-floor windows with fluted pilasters clearly inspired by Classical architecture. ▶ **Manville Mansion**★ **:** now the Town Hall; 1572 Renaissance façade. ▶ The **Brion Mansion** houses the Louis Jou Foundation (art works in paper). ▶ The **Porcelets** (Piglets) **Mansion** (1569) : now the **Museum of Modern Art** *(9:30-12 & 2-6:30, Easter-Oct. ex. Wed. in winter).* ▶ **Place**

St. Vincent★ : Provençal elms and a 12thC church set in the rock. ▶ **White Penitents' Chapel :** 17thC cliffside chapel with frescoes by the Provençal painter Yves Brayer (b. 1907). ▶ **Rue du Trencat★ :** hewn from the rock, leads to the ghost village and château. ▶ To the right, Tour-de-Brau Mansion : 14th-15thC house, now the **Archaeological and Lapidary Museum** displaying articles excavated at the village. ▶ Views★★ from the S end of the promontory (monument), and from the 13thC **keep★**, the most intact part of the château. ▶ **Queen Jeanne's Pavilion★** *(15 min walk W from the village) :* Renaissance building that was copied by Mistral for his tomb at Maillane. ▶ **Val d'Enfer** (Hell Valley) : 30 to 45 min walk NW through the Vallon de la Fontaine to a gorge full of strangely shaped rocks and riddled with caverns. In this fantastic setting, **La Cathédrale d'Images★** (audiovisual show). □

▶ Nearby

▶ **Fontvieille** ® *(9 km SW) :* the main industry is quarrying the building stone known as Arles limestone; to the S of the town a small **museum** dedicated to **Daudet,** who wrote a large part of his humorous sketches of Provençal life, *Lettres de Mon Moulin,* here *(9-12 & 1:30-5:30);* view★ over the Alpilles. ▶ **Saint-Gabriel★** *(6 km N of Fontvieille) :* 12thC Romanesque **chapel** displaying typical Provençal taste for the Classical Roman style (façade★, doorway★). □

■ Étang de BERRE
(Berre Lagoon)

▶ Round trip from Martigues *(112 km, half-day)*

A-B3

The Berre Lagoon gives a confusing impression of heavy industry and unspoilt nature, modern military installations and Greek fortifications, a large modern airport and a Roman single-span bridge that was a triumph of engineering in its day. In less than half a century, petrochemical development has transformed the area from a fishing and farming economy to one of the key industrial centres of Europe, which serves as a conduit for much of the oil supplied by the Middle East to Switzerland and Germany. Small towns and villages nevertheless preserve their rural charm despite the encroachment of 20thC technology.

▶ **Martigues** ® (pop. 42 039) a fishing town on the edge of the Étang de Berre, now contained within an industrial complex. Martigues is divided by canals into three sections, each of which has a 17thC church. Ferrières *(north bank) :* **museums** in the former Customs House *(Caserne des Douanes),* archaeological and ethnographic collections, Provençal painters including Félix Ziem (1821-1911) and Francis Picabia (1879-1953) *(10-12 & 2:30-6:30 Wed.-Sun., Jul.-Aug.; 4:30-6:30 closed Mon. and Tue. rest of year).* ▶ **Caronte motorway viaduct★** *(3.5 km N) :* the **chapel of Notre-Dame-des-Marins** (view★); *(5 km W)* **Port-de-Bouc** (chemical industries) extends on both sides of the Caronte canal, protected by a 17thC fort designed by Vauban, and the oil port of Lavera *(visits by request to the BP Oil Refinery, P.O. Box 1, 13117 Lavera).* ▶ On the right, **Saint-Mitre-les-Remparts :** intact 15thC fortifications. ▶ **Saint-Blaise** *(3 km NW) :* **excavations** reveal eight successive layers of human occupation from the 7thC BC to the 14thC. **Chapel of St. Blaise★ :** Romanesque 12thC next to a 17thC hermitage. 100 m away, **Greek** (3rdC BC) **ramparts** just behind early Christian vestige; small museum. ▶ **Istres** ® (pop. 30 360) : between the Berre Lagoon and the Crau plain, has been an aircraft testing ground since before WWI. Old Istre : museum displaying archaeological finds and a reconstructed old-time Provençal kitchen★ *(2:30-6; closed Tue.).* ▶ **Fos-sur-Mer★** *(10 km S) :* a mediaeval township overlooking the metallic industrial landscape (ramparts, Romanesque church, view★). ▶ **La Fossette** *(8 km NW from Fos) :* information centre for the industrial and port complex *(9-12 & 1-5; closed Sun. and nat. hols.).* ▶ **Miramas-le-Vieux :** surrounded by a mediaeval wall on a rocky plateau (view★). ▶ **Saint-Chamas.** ▶ **Cornillon-Confoux** *(4.5 km NE) :* on a promontory with a fine view of the lagoon. ▶ Left of the road, Flavian's Bridge, built by a Roman of that name in the 1stC AD. ▶ 2 km N from the crossroads of D10 and D21 : **Lançon orientation chart★.** ▶ **Vitrolles :** overlooked by a sheer rock, a village enclosed by a large industrial complex. ▶ **Marignane :** an industrial town (pop. 31 213) with the largest French international airport after Paris, serving Marseilles, but which also possesses a museum *(enq. at TO).* □

■ BRIGNOLES

C3 / ® / pop. 10 894 (Var)

Brignoles, in the heart of the Var region, has two faces : a mediaeval town that makes its living from regional agricultural produce and, at the foot of the hill, a new township that has developed as the largest French centre for the extraction of bauxite (the ore from which aluminium is derived). Brignoles is also the marketing centre for wines from the Var and Provence.

▶ **Place Carami :** from this centre of social life, a maze of alleyways leads uphill to the heart of the old town. ▶ **Church of St. Sauveur :** Meridional Gothic. ▶ **Palace of the Counts of Provence,** 13thC summer residence of the provincial rulers, now the **Brignoles District Museum :** sarcophagus of Gayole★, late 2nd-early 3rdC tomb illustrating transition from pagan to Christian symbols; earliest Christian monument from Gaul; reconstruction of an 18thC Provençal kitchen★ *(10-12 & 3-5:30 in summer; 10-12 & 3-5 in winter; closed Mon. and Tue.; if closed tel 94.69.00.26, ext. 247).* □

▶ Nearby

▶ The **abbey of La Celle** *(2.5 km SW) :* was notorious for the easy virtue of the nuns, whose habit was nothing more than a black silk ribbon worn on a dress of the latest fashion; a writer of the day declared : "You could only tell them apart by the colour of their petticoats and the names of their lovers". The realistic 15thC image of Christ in the Romanesque church has given rise to a local proverb : *Laï coumo lou bouan Diou de la Cello* (ugly as the Good Lord of La Celle). ▶ **Montagne de la Loube★** *(14.5 km SW to the no-entry road, then 3.5 km on foot, 2hr round trip) :* limestone rocks in fantastic shapes; view★★ from the Alps to the sea. □

■ CAGNES-SUR-MER★

D2 / ® / pop. 35 426 (Alpes-Maritimes)

A landscape of roses and mimosa, dark

cypresses and silvery olive trees bathed in the dazzling Mediterranean light. The painter Auguste Renoir (1841-1919) spent his last days here; contemporary artists flock to the annual Cagnes Art Festival. The settlement includes Le Haut-de-Cagnes, with a mediaeval château; Cagnes-Ville, the modern business centre; and Le Cros-de-Cagnes ®, a fishing port and seaside resort.

▶ **Haut-de-Cagnes** ® : easily reached on foot by the Bourgade slope *(montée).* ▶ The fortified enclosure dates from the 13thC. ▶ Church of **St. Pierre :** two naves, one early Gothic, the other 17thC. ▶ **Château-Museum :** built as a fortress in the 14thC by Rainier I of Monaco, transformed into a residence in 1620; behind the austere façade, an elegant arcaded **interior courtyard★★** from the Renaissance. In the 1st Floor Festival Hall, the *Fall of Phaëton*★, by the 17thC Italian Carlone, is a masterpiece of illusionist painting *(10-12 & 2:30-7, Jul.-Sep.; 10-12 & 2-6, ex. Tue. out of season; closed 15 Oct.-15 Nov.).* Exhibitions include the Olive Museum★, the Suzy Solidor donation★ (40 portraits of a popular French singer by well known 20thC painters); Museum of Modern Mediterranean Art★ : exhibitions in rotation of works by Chagall, Dufy, Vasarely and others; view★ from the tower. **Notre-Dame de la Protection :** above the valley, 14th-17thC chapel with 16thC frescos. ▶ **Musée du Souvenir★** *(follow the signs E of Cagnes) :* at Collettes, the property where Renoir spent his last 12 years. The decoration of the house has been preserved as Renoir knew it; paintings in the house, sculpture in the garden *(2-6 in summer; 2-5 in winter; closed Tue., nat. hols. and 15 Oct.-15 Nov.).* □

▶ Nearby

▶ The **Var Corniche★** (cliff road) *(12 km N on D118) :* leads to the IBM Study and Research Centre (designed by the architect Marcel Breuer, b. 1902) and *(14 km)* to **La Gaude** ®, known for wine; **Saint-Jeannet** *(3.5 km N of La Gaude) :* citrus orchards and vineyards on a hillside (site★) at the foot of a peak called the **Baou** *(1hr on foot, marked path;* panorama★★). ▶ **Villeneuve-Loubet** ® *(3.5 km W of Cagnes) :* overlooked by a mediaeval château; Museum of Culinary Art in the house where the famous chef Auguste Escoffier (1847-1935) was born *(2-6; closed Mon. and nat. hols.).* ▶ **Marina-Baie des Anges** *(3 km SW) :* yacht harbour with cafés, restaurants and luxurious buildings in a complex designed by the contemporary architect André Minangoy. □

■ La CAMARGUE★★

▶ Round trip from Arles *(91 or 134 km, full day)*

A2-3

La Camargue is a marshy delta that has been preserved largely in its natural state by virtue of decrees in 1928 and 1970 designating the region as a nature park. Extending from Arles (→) between the two arms of the Rhône (Grand Rhône to the E, Petit Rhône W) is a 750 km^2 alluvial plain. The Camargue stretches westward as far as the Costière de Nîmes (→ Cévennes). The land has been built up by alluvial deposits from the river Rhône, but as the same time eroded by the encroachment of the sea. In fact, there are two Camargues : a lagoon wilderness and a vast agricultural tract. Protected flora and fauna in the nature park include the *saladelle* (the blue mascot flower of the *gardians,* the cowboys of the Camargue), beaver, badger, heron, flamingo, wild duck and egret. This is also where the cream-coloured Camargue horses (born bay, they lighten in their fourth year) and black bulls are bred.

In the Haute Camargue, sheep-rearing is the traditional livelihood, although it has become less important since draignage and irrigation projects undertaken after WWII have facilitated large-scale agricultural development in the region.

▶ **Arles** (→). ▶ Take D570 SW (road to Saintes-Maries). ▶ On the left, **mas du Pont de Rousty :** an enormous sheepfold converted into the **Camargue Ecomuseum★** provides a comprehensive introduction to life in the region *(10-12 & 2-6:30 ex Tue., Wed.);* 3.5 km of trails wind among features typical of a Camargue sheep farm. ▶ **L'Albaron** *(right) :* formerly defended from its 13th-16thC tower. ▶ **Aigues-Mortes★★** *(right, D38C, 19 km) :* (→ Cévennes). ▶ **Pont de Gau :** on the shore of Lake Ginès, **Muséon camarguen** (documents, photographs, films; *9-12 & 3-7, 1 Jul.-30 Sep.*). Nearby, a **bird sanctuary** (8 to sunset).

▶ **Boumian Wax Museum :** dioramas of Camargue life *(10-12 & 2-7).* ▶ **Les Saintes-Maries-de-la-Mer** ® (*Li Santo* in Provençal) : a fishing village with vast beaches that attract crowds of summer holidaymakers. The name of the settlement originates from a local legend that Mary (mother of the apostle James the Less and supposedly the sister of the Virgin), Mary Salome (mother of James the Greater and John), Mary Magdalen and various companions (→ Saint Maximim-la-Sainte Baume), including an Egyptian servant called Sarah, fetched up safely at the site in a boat that had been set adrift from the shore of Palestine. The village is the focus of three huge annual pilgrimages, including the gathering of European Gypsies each May. Girls in Arles costume and *Gardians* from the Camargue take part in the colourful celebrations, where *farandoles* are danced, calves are branded and young men brave the bulls. **Church★ :** heavily fortified (12th-15thC) with a fresh-water well for use in time of siege. **Baroncelli Museum :** recounts Camargue life and traditions *(9-12 & 2-6; closed Wed. and Oct.).* ▶ **Sea dyke** (Digue de Mer) *(15 km, or 30 km as far as Salin-de-Giraud) :* the traditional village promenade (not right to the end) of Les Saintes; boat trips on the Petit Rhône. ▶ Take D85A N; just before the Cacharel farmstead, the track to Méjanes *(12 km)* offers vantage points for wildlife observation beside the lakes. ▶ Returning to D570, after 14 km take D37 right to **Méjanes.** The farmstead *(1.5 km right)* maintains a large herd *(manade)* of bulls (calf-branding, *fêtes taurines,* horses and an electric railway along Lake Vaccarès). ▶ Villeneuve crossroads : return directly to Arles (left) or continue via Salin-de-Giraud. The road runs beside **Lake Vaccarès** (views★).

▶ **Salin-de-Giraud :** a late-19thC village founded for harvesting sea-salt. The rows of identical houses bring to mind the housing estates of the industrial North of England. **Plage de Piemançon** *(12 km SE, D36D) :* the vast beach is dangerous for swimming. ▶ Return via D36, past *(600 m on your right)* **château de l'Armellière★** (1607). □

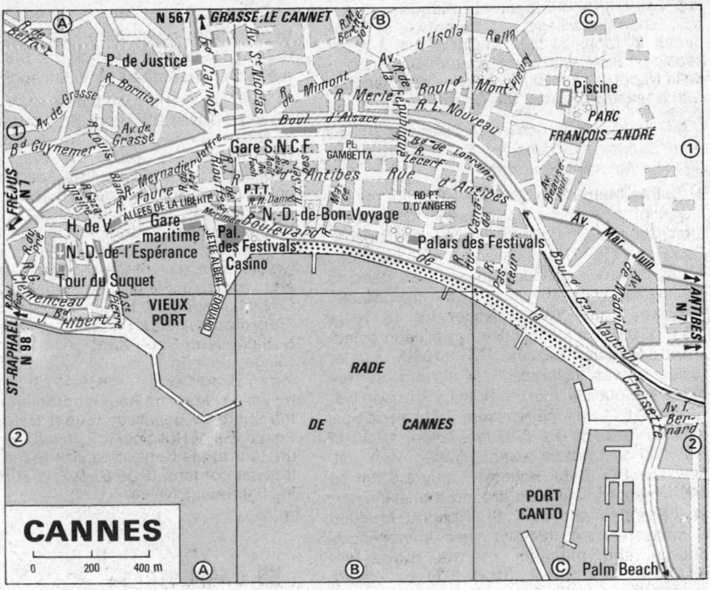

CANNES★★

D2 / ® / pop. 72 787 (Alpes-Maritimes)

The face of modern Cannes is glamorous and sophisticated, with luxurious hotels in picture-postcard scenery providing the setting for renowned international festivals of film, music, yachting, and other elements of the good life. Old Cannes (named for the reeds, Latin *cannae,* that abound in the region) was a Roman trading post and later a fishing port strongly fortified against pirate raids.

▶ Everybody in Cannes — whether permanent resident or festival celebrant — heads for the **Croisette★★** (B1-C2) : the boulevard dividing the beach (partly private) from ranks of hotels, art galleries and exclusive shops. ▶ The **Old Port** (Vieux Port) (*W,* A1-2) : yachts, fishing boats, flower market, alleyways, and the controversial new ultramodern Festival and Congress Palace. ▶ Farther W, the **Suquet :** popular name for Mont Chevalier, site of the earliest settlement of Cannes; church of **Notre-Dame-de-l'Espérance** (A1), meridional Gothic with lifelike 15thC statue of St. Anne★; **view★** from the terrace to the left, or from the **Suquet Tower** (A1), a watchtower built against the possibility of Saracen raids. ▶ **Castre Museum :** in the former château of the abbots of Lérins, superb presentation of Mediterranean archaeology and American, Oriental and African ethnographic collections *(10-12 & 2-5, 3-7 in summer; closed Mon. and Nov.-15 Dec.).* ▶ At the far end of the Blvd. de la Croisette (via C2) is the **headland** of the same name : a cross *(croisette)* used to stand there; **Port Canto,** the **Palm Beach** casino, brilliant flowers, sea views and sunsets. □

▶ Nearby

▶ **Le Cannet** ® *(3 km N) :* linked to Cannes by Boulevard Carnot (A1); the painter Pierre Bonnard (1867-1947) used to stay there. ▶ **Super-**

La Côte d'Azur

The name of Stephen Liégeard means little today. He was a turn-of-the-century poet who wrote a book entitled Côte d'Azur — *Azure Coast. Book and author are long-forgotten, but the title, the world over, instantly conjures up visions of glamorous summer life.*

Cannes : along the Avenue Isola Bell (B-C1) to the **Observatory,** with a panorama from the snowy Alps along the Côte d'Azur to Esterel and Italy; in really clear weather, as far as Corsica. ▶ Continue along the **Hill Road** (Chemin des Collines)★ to the **Saint-Antoine Pass** (view of Cannes). ▶ **Mougins★** ® *(7.5 km N) :* an old village with a renowned restaurant among trees and flowers; next to Autoroute 8, *Musée de l'Automobiliste* (Motorist Museum; *daily 10-7).* ▶ **Notre-Dame de Vie** *(2.5 km SE) :* 12thC chapel (site★, view★). ▶ **Vallauris** *(6 km NE) :* an ancient local tradition of pottery was rediscovered in the 1950s by artists such as Édouard Pignon (b. 1905) and Pablo Picasso (see the *Man with a Sheep* overlooking the market in the Place Paul Isnard). A former priory, converted into a château in the 16thC, is now the **municipal museum,** with works by the painter Alberto Magnelli (1888-1971) and prizewinners at the International Biennial Exhibition of Ceramic Art *(10-12 & 2-5; closed Tue.).* The priory chapel is the **National Picasso Museum** *(10-12 & 2-5, 2-6 in season; closed Tue. and nat. hols.).* □

▶ Tanneron Massif★ *(55 km round trip; 2hr)*

▶ A mimosa-covered hill W of Cannes. ▶ **Cannes** *(Fréjus exit, A1) :* follow N7 to the Logis-de-Paris crossroads, then right along D237, D83 and D37. ▶ **Lake Saint-Cassien** ®. ▶ To the right, before Tanneron, the **chapel of Notre-Dame de Peygros** (view★ over Grasse and Esterel). ▶ **Auribeau-sur-Siagne★** *(8 km NE) :* charming village. ▶ **Descent★★** to **Mandelieu** ® (pop. 14333) which forms a huge seaside resort with **La Napoule** ®. Château de la Napoule : a mixture of styles and periods, with a leaning towards the Orient.

▶The Iles de Lérins★★ *(regular departures from Cannes ; 15 mins for Sainte-Marguerite, 30 mins for Saint-Honorat).*

▶ **Sainte-Marguerite** *(3.3 km by 950 m) :* a haven of pine and eucalyptus★★ for relaxing after Cannes. The island was once a prison ; Fort Royal (1635, remodelled by the ubiquitous 17thC military engineer Vauban) was used to confine the enigmatic "Man in the Iron Mask", who was Louis XIV's prisoner for 16 years (1687-1703) ; his identity has never been established ; Marshall Bazaine (1811-1888), a later resident, was disgraced for having surrendered without a fight in the Franco-Prussian war of 1870-1871. Marine Museum : archaeological exhibits *(9:30-12 & 2-6:30 in season, 10:30-12 & 2-4:30 or 5 out of season, closed Mon. and Nov.-Dec.).* ▶ **Saint-Honorat :** only 1.5 km by 400 m ; enchanting walk around the island★★ ; at the end of the 4thC St. Honorat founded a monastery on the site ; neo-Romanesque church and museum at the monastery *(9:40-4:40 in summer, 10:40-3:30 in winter).* The earlier fortified monastery★ (6th-15thC), rising out of the sea, still has a beautiful two-story cloister. On the E point, chapel of La Trinité★ : Byzantine design. □

■ CAP FERRAT★

▶ Round trip *(10 km, 3hr)*
D2

Luxuriant gardens harbour sumptuous villas in this residential retreat. Nevertheless, the peninsula of Saint-Jean-Cap-Ferrat is more than a resort for the rich : it also protects the naval roadstead of Villefranche.

▶ The Cap Ferrat road leaves the coastal *corniche* (→ Riviera) at Pont St. Jean, 8.5 km NE of Nice. ▶ **Villa-Museum Île de France★ :** at the narrowest part of the peninsula, bequeathed to the Fine Arts Academy in 1934 by Baroness Ephrussi de Rothschild, in magnificent gardens laid out in French, Spanish, Florentine, English and Japanese styles *(4-6, 3-7 in summer ; closed Mon. and Nov.).* Collections typical of a turn-of-the-century patron of the arts : furniture, Flemish tapestries ; paintings by Coypel, Fragonard, Hubert Robert ; exceptional French porcelains★ (Vincennes, Sèvres, Saxe). ▶ **Saint-Jean-Cap-Ferrat** ® : a former fishing village, near to Nice and Monte-Carlo ; painting by Jean Cocteau (1889-1973) in the Registry Office ; **Maurice Rouvier promenade★** along the shore to Beaulieu ; **tourist trail★** from the Pointe Saint-Hospice *(45 mins).* ▶ Complete the tour of the Cap with a visit to the **zoo** in the tropical gardens *(9:30-6 ; 9-7 in summer),* and the **lighthouse** (view). □

■ CARPENTRAS★

A2 / ® / pop. 25886 (Vaucluse)

The former capital of the Papal State *(Comtat)* of Venaissin remained the property of the popes until 1791 (the Revolution). Numerous monuments ; colourful Friday market ; a caramel candy, called *berlingot,* is made in the town.

▶ **Hospital** (Hôtel-Dieu) (B2) : 18thC building, with a beautiful pharmacy★ decorated with blue

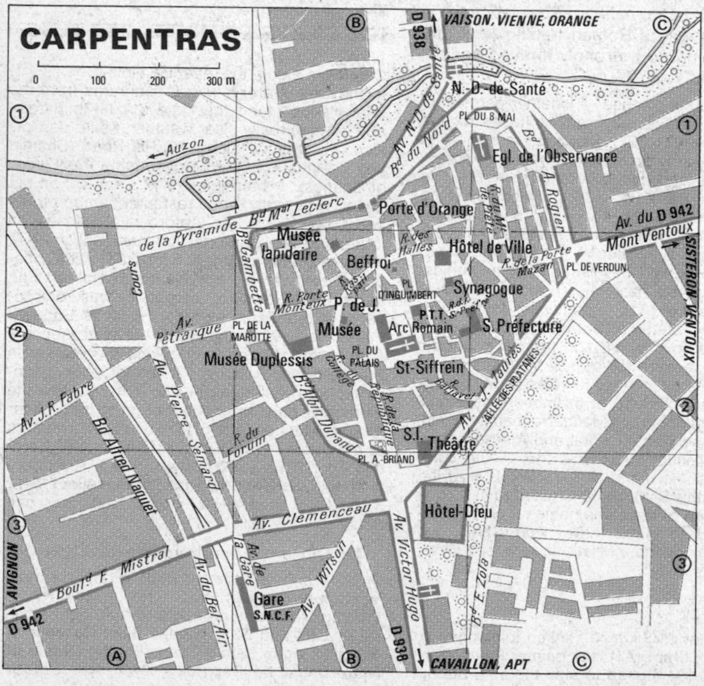

Provençale cuisine

Unlike the menus touted by tourist-trap restaurants, traditional Provençal cooking has nothing to do with pizza or hamburgers. In Provence, meat is most frequently eaten as a daube, *beef braised with garlic, bay or cloves and vegetables. In earlier days, the main meal of the day was often a thick vegetable soup made from fresh vegetables in summer, and dried beans or peas in the winter. The aromatic* soupe au pistou *is made with summer vegetables and vermicelli, to which is added* pistou, *a paste of garlic, basil, cheese and olive oil.*
Vegetables are the traditional staple diet, whether served as gratins, *in salads, or stuffed with meat.*
On the coast, excellent soups and stews are made with rock fish — scorpion fish, gurnard, galinette, *sea bream, anglerfish, red mullet, sea dace — which often have more bones than flesh and are therefore unsuitable for grilling of baking. The* bouillabaisse *— fish in a fragrant emulsion of broth, olive oil and herbs — is the best known of these soups. The* bourride *is made from white fish only — grey mullet, John Dory, turbot — and served with* aïoli, *a creamy* mayonnaise *liberally laced with crushed garlic.*

and white ceramics *(9-11:30, Mon., Wed., Thu.; groups by request at TO).* ▶ **Cathedral of St. Siffrein** (B2) : late Gothic (1405-1519); on the S doorway★ (Flamboyant Gothic), a sculpture known as the *boulo di gari* (rats gnawing a round object), the meaning of which is unknown. Fine marble in the chapels★; note the stained glass in the choir (left, primitive 15thC painting★; 17thC organ loft); in the treasury, 11thC Limoges enamel crozier. ▶ **Courthouse** (B2, 1640) : façade is a reduced copy of the façade of the Farnese palace in Rome; 17thC interior★. ▶ Festivals are held at the **Place d'Inguimbert,** where a Roman **triumphal arch** (1stC AD) can be seen. ▶ **Synagogue** (B2) : the oldest in France (15thC, rebuilt 18th and 20thC); wood panelling, liturgical objects. ▶ **Rue des Halles★ :** an attractive street with covered arcades (B2). ▶ **Porte** (Gateway) **d'Orange** (B1) : sole remnant of the fortifications built in the latter 14thC. ▶ **Duplessis Museum** (B2) : in an 18thC mansion, paintings; same building, **Comtadin Regional Museum :** regional mementoes and artifacts, including bells from herds and flocks that used to be driven through the town to seasonal pastures *(10-12 & 2-6 or 4 in winter; closed Wed.);* and the **Inguimbertine Library :** autograph scores of Johann-Sebastian Bach, Robert Schumann and Johannes Brahms *(9:30-12 & 2:30-7 ex. Sat. pm, Sun., and Mon. am).*
Also... ▶ **Sobirats Museum** (B2) : works by local primitive painters; *(hours as for Duplessis Museum).* ▶ **Archaeological Museum** (B2) : artifacts from the Iron Age to the Middle Ages; *enquire at the Inguimbertine Library.* ▶ **Poetry Museum :** in the Ombrages park, *tel. 90.63.19.49.* □

▶ Nearby

▶ Today the **Comtat Venaissin,** once under Papal authority, is a vast garden, where banks of tall rushes mark out the irrigation system. Muscat and Chasselas grapes, Golden Delicious and Star King apples, strawberries, tomatoes and melons ripen in the sun in the shelter of cypresses. ▶ **Château de Tourreau** *(10 km NW from Carpentras) :* 18thC folly; interesting *ex-voto* in the chapel. ▶ **Pernes-les-Fontaines :** named for the 33 fountains that ornament its streets and squares; Ferrande tower (13thC, murals★); 12thC Church of Notre-Dame; the Notre-Dame Gate★ (1548). ▶ **Venasque** *(11 km SE) :* on a spur★ overlooking the Comtat; Romanesque church of Notre-Dame with a primitive Crucifixion★ (1498, school of Avignon). Nearby, the baptistery★ in fact is a little cruciform 11thC church; the apparent baptismal font was an imaginative invention by the 19thC restorers; Merovingian tombstone★. □

■ CASSIS★

B3 / ® / pop. 6 318 (Bouches-du-Rhône)

Pleasure craft outnumber fishing vessels in this port flanked by the Gardiole heights to the W and the Cap Canaille cliffs to the E. The white wine of Cassis is pleasant.

▶ **Archaeological museum** in the mayoral offices *(3-5 Wed., plus Fri. in season).* ▶ La Grande-Mer Beach : the **Promenade des Lombards** gives a good view of the bay. ▶ The main attractions of Cassis are the **Calanques** (inlets) at **Port Miou, Port Pin★** and **En-Vau★★** *(access by boat, 45 mins, leave from St. Pierre quay, or on foot, 1hr20 to En-Vau by marked trails);* a third route by the **Gardiole Pass** *(6 km NW on D559, then narrow road for 3 km★; 1hr on foot to En-Vau inlet).* ▶ **Corniche des Crêtes** (Crests Road)★★ : tourist road between Cassis and La Ciotat *(19 km SE)* along D41A, following the limestone chain of La Canaille, which falls sheer into the sea (cliffs 400 m high in places). Panoramas from Mont de la Saoupe★★, Cap Canaille★★ and the Semaphore. □

■ CASTELLANE★

C2 / ® / pop. 1 460 (Alpes-de-Haute-Provence)

A typical Provençal town in the shadow of a limestone outcrop 184 m high. The Grand Canyon of Verdon is only 12 km away from the cafés in place Marcel Sauvaire, the main square.

▶ The streets of the old town wind to the Lions Fountain and the 12thC **church of St. Victor.** By the rue St.Victor, one arrives at the belfry which tops a mediaeval gate. Behind the modern parish church, a **sign-posted path★** leads to the **chapel of Notre-Dame du Roc** having skirted the remains of a 14thC keep dominated by a fine pentagonal tower (ruins of feudal town, view★ over the Napoléon bridge and the Grand Canyon of Verdon). □

▶ Nearby

▶ **Senez** *(19 km NW) :* reached by the Route Napoléon (→), which crosses the **Lèques Pass** (alt. 1 146 m, view★) and the spectacular **Clue de Taulanne★;** Flemish and Aubusson tapestries★ in the former cathedral of Senez (Provençal Romanesque, early 13thC). □

▶ Round the lakes★★ *(25 km, 1hr)*

▶ N on D955. ▶ At the **Blache Pass,** a little road to Blaron (D402 on the left) gives a magnificent view★ over Lake Castillon. ▶ **Barrage**

de Castillon : a 1 200-acre lake on the Verdon. ▶ Along the Demandolx road (views★★), then D102 *(tricky in places)* to the **Chaudanne Dam,** an electricity generating station. □

■ CAVAILLON

A2 / ® / pop. 20 830 (Vaucluse)

Cavaillon is renowned for the quality of the melons grown here. However, the real economic importance of this sleepy-looking town is best understood at the sight of the traffic jam around the gates of the M.I.N. *(Marché d'Intérêt National)* market, where thousands of tons of fruit and vegetables are shipped throughout France.

▶ Ornate decoration on the **Roman triumphal arch** (Place François Tourel) contrasts with its simple basic form. A 15 min walk from the arch to the **chapel of St. Jacques** (12th-17thC) among cypress and almond trees on the hill above the village (view★). ▶ **Church of St. Véran :** late 12thC five-sided apse★, 14thC cloister★; exuberant 17thC decoration in the chapel. **Archaeological Museum** in the chapel (1755) of the former hospital : prehistory, Gallo-Roman remains *(10-12 & 2-6 spring and summer, 10-12 & 3-5 out of season; closed Tue).* ▶ Regional **Jewish Museum** of the Comtadin : in the former bakery of the **synagogue★**, 18thC regional art *(10-12 & 2-6, closed Tue.).* ▶ **Regalon Gorges★** *(13.5 km SE, 1hr on foot, inaccessible in wet weather).* □

■ La CIOTAT

B3 / ® / pop. 31 727 (Bouches-du-Rhône)

Giant cranes, blue sparks from the arc-welders and the clang of metal-beating are forcible reminders that the town is a naval shipyard for 11 months of the year. To the north, palm trees and villas around the resort area at a beach that holds records for sunshine.

▶ Naval and crafts museum *(1 Jun.-30 Sep. 4-7; closed Tue., Thu. and Sun.).* ▶ **Church of Notre-Dame-de-l'Assomption :** above the quay; Descent from the Cross (1615). ▶ Excursions to **Île-Verte** *(30 mins by boat from the old port),* to the **Figuerolles Inlet★** *(1.5 km SW),* and to the chapel of **Notre-Dame de la Garde** *(2.5 km SW),* view★ over the bay. ▶ **Les Lesques** *(8 km E)* : family resort; Tauroentum Museum on the foundations of a Roman villa of the 1stC AD. □

■ The CLUES of HAUTE-PROVENCE★★

▶ Round trip from Vence *(137 km, full day)* D2

Clues are narrow passages carved by rivers through the limestone foothills of the Alps; they create a spectacular landscape in the wild heathland and desert plateaux over an area of about 70 by 30 km N of Grasse.

▶ **Vence** (→). ▶ Follow D2 across the **Vence Pass** (extended view★ of the coast). ▶ **Coursegoules** *(1 km to the right)* : on a rocky spur; church with altarpiece★ of St. John the Baptist (1500) attributed to Louis Bréa (1458-1523; eldest of the three Bréa painters). ▶ Drive through the **upper Loup Valley★; Gréolières** ®, at the foot of the Barres-du-Cheiron : Romanesque church with altarpiece of St. Étienne★ (1480) and Virgin and Child★ (14thC). ▶ The road crosses the **Clue de Gréolières★.** ▶ **Gréolières-les-Neiges** ® (alt. 1 450 m; *11 km on the right*) : skiing just 1hr by car from Nice. ▶ **Les Quatre-Chemins. Thorenc** *(3 km left)* : rural hotels and villas. ▶ **Bleine Pass★** *(on D5)* : alt. 1 439 m, among rocks and firs. ▶ **Clue de St. Auban★★ :** The road winds between cliffs honeycombed with caves. ▶ **Briançonnet :** houses built from the stones of the old Roman town (many inscriptions); altarpiece★ (restored) by Louis Bréa in the church. ▶ **Clue du Riolan★ :** the river plunges through a gap. ▶ **Sigale :** a picturesque setting for a stronghold. ▶ **Aiglun★** *(8 km right on D10)* and the **Clue d'Aiglun★★ :** like a sword-cut in the mountain. ▶ **Roquesteron :** continue on D1 to the **Clue de Bouisse.** The road winds from one hilltop village to another above the valleys of the Bouyon and the Var : **Bouyon★, Le Broc★, Carros★★** ® and **Gattières** ®, among vines and olive trees resonant with cicadas. □

■ COLMARS-LES-ALPES★

C10 / ® / pop. 314 (Alpes-de-Haute-Provence)

Forts and ramparts, towers, and walls pierced with loopholes in a mountain setting (alt. 1295 m). **Fort de Savoie★** (uphill) and Fort de France (downhill) used to guard the town from surprise attack. Today the village represents a style that has hardly changed since the 17thC. □

▶ Nearby

▶ Colmars is a good base for exploring the valley of the Verdon (200 km of marked trails; *maps available at SI*), N towards **Allos,** and S to **Lake Castillon** (→ Castellane); near **Beauvezer** ® *(5.5 km SW from Colmars),* hike in the **St. Pierre Gorges★** *(D252 SE then 2hr on foot).* ▶ From Colmars, a mountain road (D2) SE via the **Champs Pass★** (alt. 2 095 m), **Saint-Martin-d'Entraunes,** to the **Daluis Gorges★★** (→). □

■ DALUIS Gorges★★

▶ Round trip from Puget-Théniers *(83 km, half-day, C1)*

Above a white-pebbled river the road crosses red and green ravines and canyons and dives through tunnels to provide astounding views of a unique landscape.

▶ **Puget-Théniers :** Old town★ on the right bank of the Roudoule; church with wooden statuary★ (16th-18thC); in the courtyard, sculpture Action Enchaînée★, by Aristide Maillol (1861-1944), surrounded by elms and palm trees. ▶ N202 W to **Entrevaux★ :** fortified bridge, ramparts, high citadel (views★) in a town straight out of an old engraving; it has hardly changed since the 18thC. Former cathedral (part of the defences) : works of art, including a 17thC altarpiece★. ▶ D902 right, through **Daluis** into the red schist **gorges★★** where the river Var flows. ▶ **Guillaumes :** ruined château. ▶ **Valberg★ :** (alt. 1 700 m) frescos in Notre-Dame-des-Neiges, church dating from WWII. Walk to the **Valberg Cross** *(20 mins;* view★★); road to **Péone** *(8.5 km NW)* in an alpine setting. Valberg is a winter sports resort, like nearby **Beuil★** above the Cians. ▶ The **Cians Gorges★★ :** the upper gorge is red schist, the lower, limestone. D28 snakes between them, passing two picturesque villages : **Rigaud** on the right; **Lieuche** among black schist 5 km on the left (the church has a 1479 altarpiece★ of the Annunciation★ by Louis Bréa). ▶ **Pont de Cians :** bridge at the

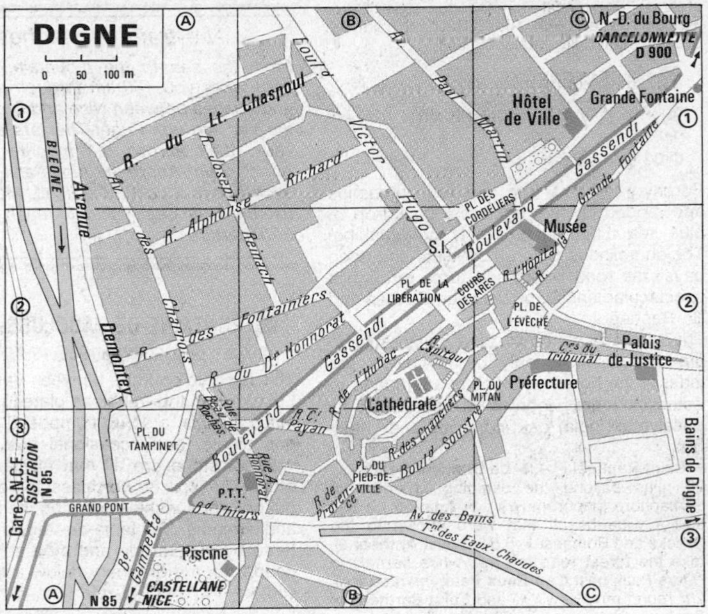

junction with the Var where D28 rejoins N202. ▶ **Touët-sur-Var**★ *(2 km E) :* like a Tibetan village on the rock face, a labyrinth of covered arcades and alleyways, with the river rumbling under the nave of the church. □

■ DIGNE-LES-BAINS

C1 / ® / pop. 16391 (Alpes-de-Haute-Provence)

Digne : a tourist stopover on the Route Napoléon (→), an excursion centre for the Alps of Provence, a rapidly-expanding thermal spa where you can assuage your rheumatism and respiratory problems, and the centre of the August lavender harvest.

▶ The people of Digne pass their leisure hours under the place trees on **Boulevard Gassendi** (B2; statue of the philosopher Pierre Gassendi, known as Gassendi, 1592-1655, born in nearby Champtercier). ▶ **Municipal Museum** (C2) : archaeology, mineralogy and paintings (portraits by Franz Pourbus the Younger, 1569-1622; local artists; *10-12 & 2-6; closed Mon.*). **Cathedral** of **Notre-Dame du Bourg**★ (via C1) : 13thC; among Provence's finest Romanesque churches (remains of 14th-16thC mural). The home of Alexandra David-Neel (off map, A3) now a Tibetan cultural centre *(visits 3-5 or by appt. with Mlle Peyronnet, the writer-traveller's secretary, tel. 92.31.32.38).* Tibetan art shop, and a Tibetan festival is planned for July. Geological centre (exhibitions; *9-12 & 2-5 weekdays*). □

▶ Nearby

▶ **Geological Park :** encompasses 760 km^2 around Digne; instructional courses and excursions; *information from the SI.* ▶ **Courbons**★ *(6 km N)* . Romanesque and Gothic church (view★). ▶ Between Durance and Verdon, *clues* (→ Clues of Haute Provence) carved deep into the limestone : **Clues de Barles**★ *(16 km N)* and *(35 km N)* the **Fanget Pass** (view★), leading to **Seyne-les-Alpes,** a winter-sports and summer-holiday centre in a fine mountain site. ▶ **Clue de Chabrières**★ ®, 18 km S of Digne. □

■ DRAGUIGNAN

C2 / ® / pop. 28194 (Var)

When Baron Haussmann (1809-1891; France's greatest town planner) was prefect of the Var Region, he planned the roads and promenades S of the old town that give a spacious perspective to modern Draguignan. In 1974 the prefecture was transferred to Toulon.

▶ **Boulevard Clemenceau** is the main artery. ▶ **Museum :** behind the theatre, local archaeology, ceramics (Moustiers) and 17th-20thC paintings *(9-12 & 2-6; closed Mon., Sun. and nat. hols.).* The **library,** in the same building, possesses a rare 14thC illuminated manuscript of the great poem of chivalric lore, the *Roman de la Rose.* ▶ Farther on, Place du Marché, with fountains and plane trees, and the self-contained **old town,** where the clock tower (Tour de l'Horloge) has replaced the old keep. □

▶ Nearby

▶ **Le Malmont**★ *(6 km N) :* panorama and orientation chart. ▶ By the D49 which climbs to Ampus, passing by the restored Romanesque church of Châteaudouble and its ruined château, or by the **Châteaudouble Gorges**★ one arrives at **Comps-sur-Artuby** ® *(32 km N) :* new buildings spill into the plain; the 13thC chapel of St. André★ looks over the old village from on top of a rock. ▶ **Bargème**★ *(9 km NE) :* inside a fortified wall at an altitude above 1000 m. Higher still, Château des Pontevès. ▶ Other interesting **villages of the Var**★ around Draguignan : **Callas** *(14 km NE),* **Bargemon** ® *(20 km NE);* **Lorgues** *(13 km SW);* and **Les Arcs** *(10 km S).* ▶ **Chapel of Ste. Roseline** (*4 km NE* of Arcs) : Provençal Romanesque style; Baroque altarpiece★ with 16thC Descent from the Cross in high relief; stained glass. □

■ The ESTEREL Massif★★

▶ Round trip from Saint-Raphaël *(76 km, half-day)*

C-D2 *(see map 1)*

Porphyry eroded into needles, pyramids and ragged chunks against a backdrop of blue sea : Esterel is simply breathtaking. The shoreline is tattered by inlets and deep bays; the road twists and turns through a spectacular landscape between Cannes and St. Raphaël.

The forest of umbrella pine, vulnerable to fire and disease, only partly covers the massif; the Forestry Office is attempting to establish more vigorous species such as eucalyptus, holm oak, cork oak and chestnut.

▶ **Saint-Raphaël** (→). ▶ **Le Dramont Beach** ® : 20 mins beyond the camping ground, the Semaphore (panorama★★). ▶ **Agay** ® : a bay and a wide beach that were known to the Greeks and Romans. ▶ 5.5 km past **Anthéor** ®, take the forest road left *(red/white barrier)* to l'Ours Peak past **Cap Roux Peak** *(marked trail, 2hr round trip;* view★★) and **Saint-Barthélemy Rock** where the view★ *(30 min round trip)* over the roadstead of Agay is spectacular. ▶ Turn right at the Mourrefrey crossroads. ▶ View★ of the expanse of the bare massif, and another view★★ along the coast to Cannes and the Îles Lérins. ▶ **Notre-Dame Pass** is the starting point for several marked trails, including up the **Ours Peak** *(1hr30 round trip),* as far as the television transmitter (view★★★ over the sea and the Alps). ▶ Junction with N7, and return along the **Corniche d'Or** among colours that are even more intense at sunset; inlets, bays and resorts on the way : **La Napoule** (→ Cannes); **Théoule-sur-Mer** ®; **La Galère** ® : **Miramar; Le Trayas.** ▶ From Agay the road leads to **Valescure** ® : villas behind pine plantations removed from the bustle of Saint-Raphaël. ▶ Another Esterel lookout is **Mont Vinaigre** *(18 km N from Saint-Raphaël through Fréjus; then 30 min round trip).* □

Le train des pignes

From the sea to the mountain, a holiday train takes you 150 km through the valleys and villages between Nice and Digne. Along the Var, through Puget-Théniers and Entrevaux, then across the mountain through Annot, Saint-André-les-Alpes and Barrême, each halt is a holiday in itself. Many hikers use the Train des Pignes to reach their base of departure.

■ FONTAINE-DE-VAUCLUSE★★

A2 / ® / pop. 606 (Vaucluse)

This is scrub country, between Ventoux and Lubéron, on the Vaucluse plateau. The aromatic *maquis,* a scrub composed of numerous plants, and occasional huts and low walls of stone are all that the land has to offer. The soil is worthless for cultivation, but brilliant sunshine lights up the fast rivers and streams. Fontaine-de-Vaucluse is watered by the Sorgue and by a spring rising deep from the greenery below a formidable cliff.

▶ **Church of St. Véran :** minor Provençale Romanesque style. Petrach Museum (undergoing reorganisation) commemorates the Italian poet Petrarch, who lived at Fontaine de Vaucluse from 1337 to 1353). ▶ The **Fontaine Road** climbs up the right bank of the Sorge, fringed with cafés and souvenir shops. On the right, the **Norbert Casteret Museum :** speleology *(9-12 & 2-6 in summer; pm in winter) :* and the **Vallis Clausa paper mill★ :** hand-made paper on sale *(9-12:30 & 2-6; Sun. 10:30-12:30 & 2-6; Summer 9-7).* **Musée des Restrictions** (WWII memorabilia; *1-6:30 ex Mon.*). ▶ The **Fontaine-de-Vaucluse★★** is the outlet of a subterranean river draining the water from the limestone plateaux of Vaucluse. In winter and spring the flow reaches 150000 litres per second; the rest of the year, the water level remains steady at the bottom of a rocky basin.□

1. Esterel Massif

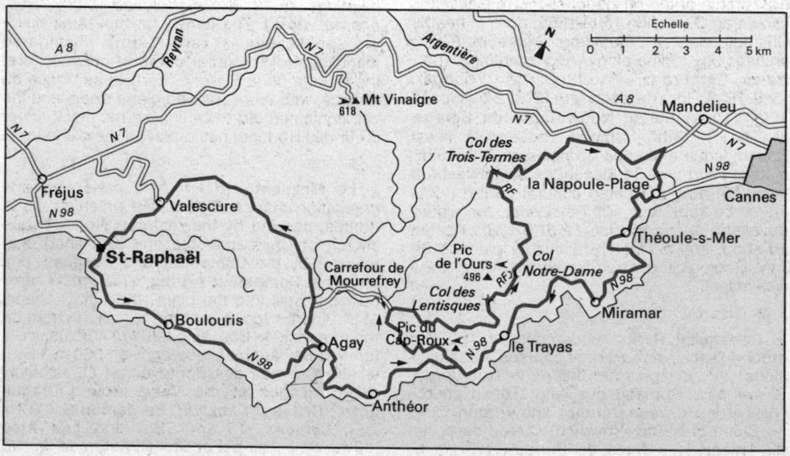

FORCALQUIER

B2 / ® / pop. 3790

The high plateau around Forcalquier runs as far as Lure Mountain (→), the Provençal Olympus. The land abounds in lavender and thyme, truffles and honey but the way of life is austere and solitary; small farms look like miniature fortresses and shepherds guide their flocks from pasture to sparse pasture along dusty tracks. Forcalquier, "town of 4 Queens" — the 4 daughters of Raymond Béranger and Béatrix de Savoie all became queens in the 13thC —, slightly larger than other villages in the area, holds monthly fairs *(1st Mon. of the month)* and a weekly market where lambs are the major item of trade.

▶ **Church of Notre-Dame-de-Provence** (orientation table and panorama★) : austere Romanesque lines that set off the Gothic doorway. With a pretty fountain in its forecourt and a covered way which leads to the old Jewish quarter and the synagogue. ▶ **Convent of the Cordeliers★ :** summer exhibitions and concerts (13thC; *May, Jun. 2:30-6:30; Jul., Aug. 10-12 & 2:30-6:30, closed in winter*). ▶ **Museum :** religious art, Provençal furniture and archaeological material *(daily ex weekends, 3-4).* ▶ Attractive houses in the old town (rue des Cordeliers, du Collège, rue Béranger, rue du Palais). ▶ **Cemetery★ :** clipped yews. □

▶ Nearby

▶ **Notre-Dame-de-Salagon** *(4 km S) :* once a priory; Renaissance building and 12thC church (figured★ and Corinthian capitals, *daily 2-6*). ▶ **Château de Sauvan** (at Mane, *5.5 km S; daily 3-6 ex Sat.*) : Classical French 18thC architecture, 100-year-old trees. ▶ **Saint-Michel-l'Observatoire** *(11 km SW) :* **observatory★** 2.5 km N of village, established in 1938 *(3pm Wed. and 9:30 1st Sun. of month, Apr.-Sep.).* ▶ **Banon** *(25 km NW) :* tall, narrow houses standing stiffly on the hillside, surrounded by ramparts; Le Banon is also the name of a goat cheese, powdered with herb savory, that is delicious with red Gigondas wine. ▶ **Lurs** *(11 km E)* . a mediaeval village where an International Conference on Graphic Arts is held each year. ▶ **Ganagobie Priory★★** *(18 km NE) :* on the edge of a plateau covered with holm oak and *maquis;* 12thC Romanesque church; note the doorway★ and mosaics★ of Eastern inspiration in the sanctuary *(9:30-11:30 & 2:30-4:30, 5:30 out of season).* View★ over the Durance from the **plateau de Ganagobie.** ▶ **Mées rocks★** *(25 km N of Forcalquier) :* a curious rock formation locally known as the "Penitents". □

FRÉJUS

C3 / ® / pop. 32698 (Var)

A town founded by Julius Caesar in 49 BC, and later allocated by his successor Augustus in the form of land grants to retired military veterans. Fréjus enjoys a rich architectural legacy both from the Roman era and from its later prosperity as the seat of a bishopric.

▶ **Cathedral★ :** (C1-2) : early Provençal Gothic; Renaissance panels★ in the doors *(apply to the porter),* vigorous ogival vaulting in the nave; 1450 altarpiece★ over the sacristy door. ▶ The octagonal **baptistery★★** dates from the 5thC; the late 12thC **cloister★** is picturesque with its garden and well. ▶ **Archaeological Museum :** in the cloister, Gallo-Roman art and artifacts excavated in Fréjus, including mosaics★, head of Jupiter★ (1stC BC), Diana in pursuit★ *(baptistery, cloister and museum : 9:30-12 & 2-6, 4pm in winter; closed Tue. and some nat. hols.).* ▶ The Roman ruins display painstaking construction, but lack the luxurious features that characterised building in the later days of the Empire. **Amphitheatre★ :** *(Les Arènes,* A1, *9:30-12 & 4-6, or 4 pm in winter; closed Tue.)* 114 m by 82 m; held more than 10000 spectators. **Theatre and Aqueduct** (C1); **Porte d'Orée** (C2), apparently the remains of the entrance to the public baths. □

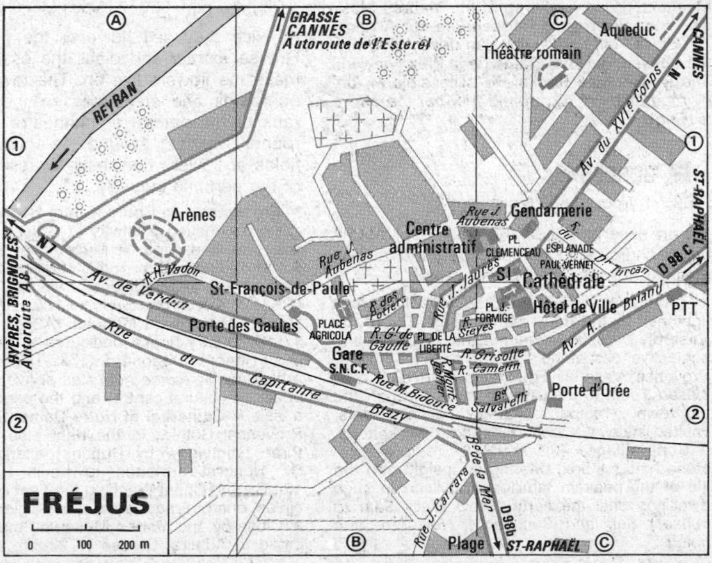

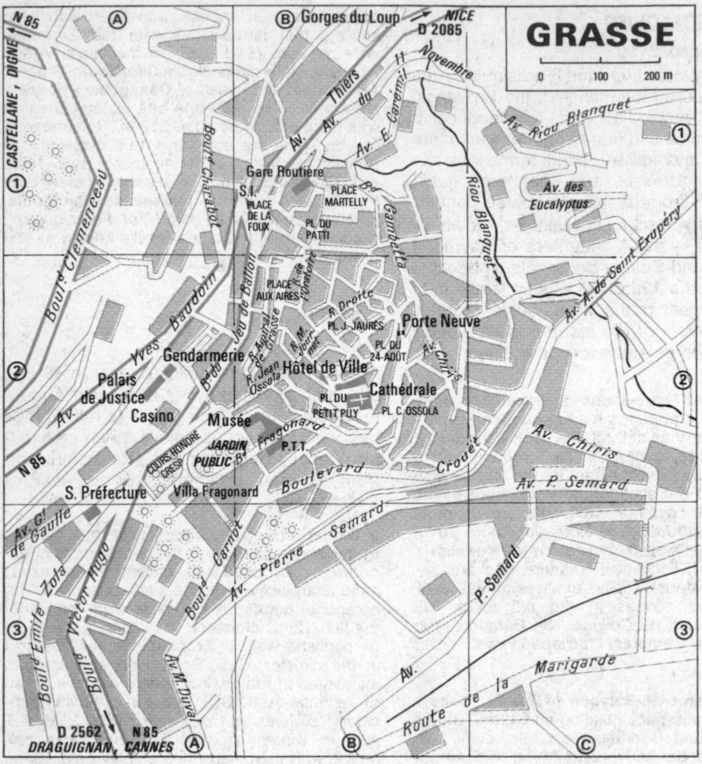

▶ Nearby

▶ Mementoes of colonial troups stationed at Fréjus : the memorial **Buddhist pagoda** *(2 km N from the centre)* erected by Vietnamese in 1919; and the **mosque** *(4 km NW)* built by **Sudanese** serving in the French Army. ▶ **Zoo** and **Esterel Safari Park :** *(5 km N) :* only a windscreen between you and lions. ▶ **Roquebrune Mountain** *(W) :* an outcrop of the Maures Massif. From picturesque **Roquebrune-sur-Argens** *(11 km W from Fréjus)* you can drive 1.5 km to the **Convent of Notre-Dame de la Pitié** (view★). The **Roquebrune Rocks** are accessible *(4 km by road then 2hr hike round trip, but the effort is tiring).* □

■ GORDES★★

B2 / ® / pop. 1 607 (Vaucluse)

On an escarpment of the Vaucluse mountains, church and château perched above massed houses and almond trees.

▶ **Château★** (11th-16thC) : a feudal fortress lightened by the Renaissance style. Site of the **Vasarely Didactic Museum :** the "personal and subjective" part of the painter's work (→ Aix-en-Provence, Vasarely Foundation) *(10-12 & 2-6; closed Tue.).* ▶ Pleasurable stroll through the old town : ramparts, narrow paved streets, vaulted stairways, boutiques, craft workshops. ▶ **Borie village★** *(3.5 km SW) :* restored dry-stone huts (→ box) offering an insight into the life of the peasant families who lived in such dwellings until the early 19thC *(daily 9am to sunset; Sat. and Sun. only, Nov.-Jan. and hols.).* □

▶ Nearby

▶ **Sénanque Abbey★★★** *(4 km N →).* ▶ **Moulin des Bouillons** *(5 km S)* : stained glass museum★ *(10-12 & 4-6).* □

■ GRASSE★

D2 / ® / pop. 38 360 (Alpes-Maritimes)

At Nice they sell flowers; the people of Grasse extract and distill the essences to make the flowers live on. The town climbs on ramps and staircases around the top rank of the natural amphitheatre that surrounds Cannes. Around the town are the fields of flowers that make Grasse the hub of the perfume industry.

▶ **Promenade du Cours** (Cours Honoré-Cresp, A2) : the focus of activity in Grasse, terraced over the landscape. ▶ **Museum of Provençal Art and History** (B2) : 18thC mansion displaying popular arts and traditions of eastern Provence *(10-12 & 4-5 or 6 in summer; closed Sat. and Nov.).* ▶ **Fragonard Museum** (A2) : a beautiful 17thC country house dedicated to the painter Jean-Honoré Fragonard (1732-1806) and his artistic family *(same hours as above);* the villa is also a cultural centre, and the park is worth a visit. ▶ **Cathedral of Notre-Dame** (B2) : early Provençal Gothic; in the right side aisle are three paintings★ by Rubens; altarpiece★ of St. Honorat attribued to Louis Bréa (late 15thC), and Christ Washing the Feet of the Disciples, one of Fragonard's rare religious works. ▶ Close by, the **Marine Museum :** mainly dedicated to Admiral Grasse (1722-88), a hero of the American War of Independence who prevented Hood from relieving Cornwallis at Yorktown and landed at Chesapeake Bay to reinforce La Fayette (models★; *2:30-5, closed Sat., Sun.*). ▶ The perfume houses in Grasse are open to visitors. **Maison Fragonard :** international perfume museum at 20 Boulevard Fragonard (B2). □

▶ Nearby

▶ **Cabris**★ ® *(6 km W)* : view★ to the sea. 300 m W of the Cabris Cross, a Celtic table stone; Ligurian remains (summit of the Ondides). ▶ **Saint-Cézaire-sur-Siagne** ® *(16 km SW)* : a feudal village overlooking the Gorges; orientation chart, view★. **Saint-Cézaire Caverns** *(3 km NE)* : stalactites *(10:30-12 & 2:30-6 in season, 2:30-5:30 rest of year; closed Nov.-Mar.)*. ▶ 15 km NW through the **Siagne Gorges** to **Mons**★ **:** on a spur, fountains, picturesque streets and a superb view from the Place St. Sébastien. □

▶ Around the Loup Gorges★ *(39 km, 3hr)*

▶ **Grasse.** ▶ NE on D2085, then left on 2210. ▶ **Le Bar-sur-Loup** ® : 16thC château, attractive village; church with Dance of Death★, remarkable 15thC painting on wood; also, 15thC doors; altarpiece★ by Louis Bréa (late 15thC). ▶ D6 to the **Loup Gorges**★★ and Courmes Waterfall — a vertical cleft where enormous caverns ("cauldrons") have been hollowed out by the water. ▶ At **Bramafan,** turn left on D3. ▶ **Gourdon**★★ **:** several artists have chosen to live in this village eyrie above the Gorges. Château : (13th-17thC) a museum, painting collection includes the Legend of Ste. Ursula★ (school of Cologne, 1500) and *naïf* works including a portrait by Henri Douanier Rousseau (1844-1910) *(11-1 & 4-7, Jul.-15 Sep.; 10-12 & 2-7 ex. Tue., 16 Sep.-Jun.)*; gardens★, subalpine flowers. ▶ Return to Grasse by D3 or cross the **Caussols Plateau** by D12 NW. □

■ HYÈRES

C3 / ® / pop. 41 739 (Var)

Hyères, oldest resort on the Côte d'Azur and a centre for aquatic sports and sailing, is distinguished by flowers and palm trees broad avenues lined with turn-of-the-century buildings, several Moorish-style residences, 35 km of beach, and a good dozen marinas. The old quarter of the city lies on the slopes of Castéou hill, where feudal fortifications look down to the modern development and the roadstead.

▶ **Church of St. Louis**★ (B1) : 13thC Italianate. ▶ W of Place Clémenceau, a skein of old streets and the market in the **Place Massillon.** ▶ **Place St. Paul** (B1) : lookout★; 11th-16thC church with interesting *ex-votos* and a Provençal *crèche.* ▶ In Rue Paradis, an eye-catching (13thC, restored) **Romanesque house**★. ▶ Over the roofs, the crenellated keep and towers of the ruined **château** (A1, *20 min walk from the car park,* view★).
Also... ▶ **Saint-Bernard Park :** Mediterranean flora at the foot of the ruins, view★. ▶ **Municipal Museum** (B-C2) : archaeolgy, local painters *(10-12 & 3-6, Sat. and Sun. am only; closed Tue.)*. ▶ **Notre-Dame de Consolation**★ *(3 km S)* : built in 1955 by the architect Vaillant, the sculptor Lambert-Rucki and the glazier Gabriel Loir (view★). ▶ **Olbius Riquier gardens**★ (via B2) : 15 acres of palms, dates, eucalyptus, cactus, agave, plus aquatic birds and a small zoo. □

▶ Nearby

▶ **Giens Peninsula** *(12 km S to the Fondue Tower)* : an island linked to the mainland by roads on a double isthmus divided by salt marshes.▶ **Giens** ® is a seaside village with a ruined château (view★★). ▶ The **Fondue Tower** is a departure point for Porquerolles (→ Hyères Islands). □

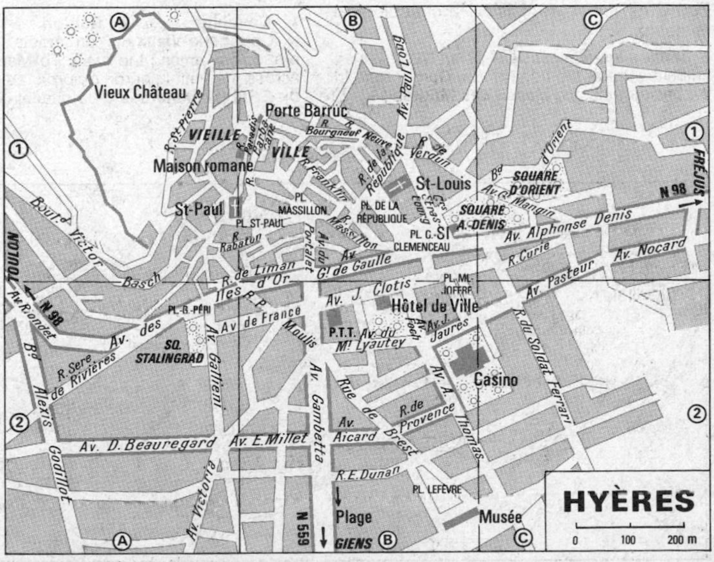

HYÈRES Islands★★★

C3 (Var)

Greeks and Romans settled on these islands that, during the Renaissance, were known as "the Golden Isles". The archipelago only a short distance from the sophistication of the Côte d'Azur has remained a wild and unspoilt shore forest.

Access to the islands → practical holiday information. □

▶ Ile de Porquerolles★★★ ®

The westernmost and largest island (7.5 km by 2 km). On the N side, pine, heather and myrtle fringe the beaches. The S shore is steeper, and the interior is a pine forest; delightful strolls with glimpses of the sea. ▶ **Village** on the shore below 16thC fort Ste Agathe. Walk to the **lighthouse**★ *(2.7 km S)*, the **semaphore**★ *(3 km E)*, or to **Point Grand Langoustier**★ *(5.5 km W)*. □

▶ Ile de Port-Cros★★★ ®

Rising 207 m above the sea level, where Aleppo pine, eucalyptus, mastic, arbutus, myrtle and heather mingle their scents and colours; you may spot a blue merlin or a peregrine falcon. The island is now a National Park, with protection for flora and fauna. ▶ Round the edge of the bay is the village of Port-Cros, with a few colourful houses and an old fort. ▶ Marked trails to various points including **Palu Beach**★ *(1hr30 round trip)* along the Botany Trail; **Solitude Valley**★ *(1hr20 round trip)*; **Port Man**★ *(3hr40)*. □

▶ Ile de Levant

A narrow, rocky spine, 8 km by 1.2 km, is occupied by a nudist colony at Heliopolis and... the French Navy. □

Le LAVANDOU

C3 / ® / pop. 4 275 (Var)

A yacht harbour and seaside resort, protected by Cap Bénat, with a view across to Port-Cros and Levant islet; archaeological museum.

▶ **Bormes-les-Mimosas**★ ® *(2 km NW)*: like an amphitheatre at the edge of the Dom forest. In the background, the **Massif des Maures** (→). □

Perfume and patronage

16thC Grasse was a well established glove-making centre when a fashion arose for perfumed gloves. Abundant flower gardens enabled the city to profit from both sides of the craze. The perfume industry thrived into the 18th and 19thC, and is the mainstay of Grasse today. At first, the flowers were simply distilled. In the mid 18thC, development of the process permitted more thrifty extraction of essences by means of oils and fats. 19thC extraction processes used solvents that could be evaporated to leave a solid residue of perfume and vegetable wax. One ton of jasmine flowers yields 3 kg of an aromatic residue called the concrète. *When oils (60 % of weight) are removed by alcohol treatment, the remaining* absolue de concrète *is the ultimate essence of the flower's perfume.*

The LUBÉRON Heights★★

▶ Through the Lubéron *(74 km from Cavaillon to Céreste; full day)*
B2 *(see map 2)*

Provençal flora and fauna have maintained their natural equilibrium on the Lubéron Heights, for which reason the whole area is now a Regional Nature Park. The ridge is best explored on foot, along the numerous marked trails; many villages on both the N and S flanks make good starting points. Although country towns on the southern slopes still prosper from their traditional occupations, many smaller villages on the poorer N face were abandoned; some are now taking a new lease on life with the summer influx of artists and craftsmen.

▶ **Cavaillon** (→). ▶ **Robion.** ▶ **Maubec.** ▶ **Oppède-le-Vieux**★ : an artists' and writers' colony among the ruins. To Mérindol SSE across the Petit Lubéron *(approx. 14 km, 4hr30 by GR6)*. ▶ **Ménerbes**★ : a citadel on a sheer

2. Lubéron region

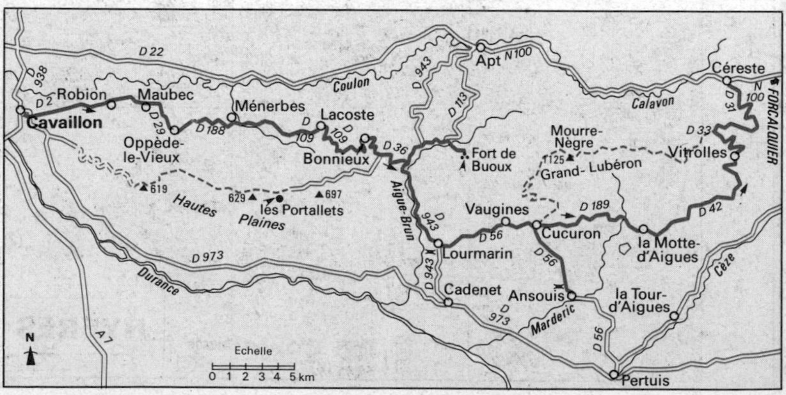

Santons

In the Provençal dialect, santoun *means "little saint". These naïf little figures were first produced when the Revolution of 1789 closed the churches. A Marseilles artist evidently had the idea of making terracotta figurines, depicting not only the biblical characters but also the people of the community : shepherds, knife-grinders, blacksmiths, millers, the village simpleton, and so on. Each family could use the figures to make a Nativity scene. A Santons Fair is held at Marseilles each December, and the figures are widely exported.*

rock; from here to Mérindol, S across the Petit Lubéron *(approx. 13 km, 4hr30).* **Notre-dame de Lumières** *(7 km NNE of Ménerbes) :* a place of pilgrimage; some of the *ex-votos*★ in the 17thC chapel are masterpieces of *naïf* art. ▶ **Lacoste :** the imposing ruins of the Marquis de Sade's château frown down. ▶ **Bonnieux**★ ® : from the terrace by the old church, view★ across the Apt; in the new church, four 16thC painted panels★; Rue de la République, Bakery Museum *(tel 90.75.88.34).* ▶ **Saint-Symphorien** *(2 km left from the crossroads) :* the slender Romanesque bell-tower emerges above the oaks. ▶ 1.5 km father, road right to **Fort de Buoux**★ *(path, 1hr30 round trip) :* fortified since the 13thC (remains of ramparts and old village, view★). ▶ D943 enters the Lourmarin coomb on the right : this is the only passage through the Lubéron range. ▶ **Lourmarin**★ **:** the château, part 15thC-part Renaissance, welcomes artists, writers and researchers *(9-11:45 & 2:30-5:45, or 4:45 out of season; closed Tue., Oct.-Apr.);* the apartements are decorated with Provençal antiques and ceramics, as well as several 15th-16thC Italian paintings; two monumental fireplaces★. ▶ **Vaugines :** starting point for the N crossing of the Lubéron *(approx. 18 km to Apt, 5hr15, GR9).* ▶ **Cucuron** ® : model for Daudet's *Cucugnan* (→ Fontvieille); Romanesque and Gothic church; remains of château and ramparts; museum of Lubéron archaeology and rural life; tel. 90.77.25.02. From Cucuron, a forest trail *(10 km, cars not allowed)* runs to the crest of Grand Lubéron (**Mourre Nègre,** alt. 1125 m, view★★). ▶ **Ansouis**★ *(4.5 km SE of Cucuron) :* remains of fortresses and 17thC château *(2:30-6:30; closed Tue.);* extraordinary village museum of undersea life *(2-6 or 7 in summer).* ▶ **Cabrières d'Aigues :** departure point for NNW crossing of the Grand Lubéron *(approx. 12 km, 4hr, GR92).* ▶ **La Motte-d'Aigues.** ▶ **Grambois** *(5 km SE) :* 1519 triptych★ in the church. ▶ **Vitrolles.** ▶ **Céreste.** ▶ **Carluc**★ *(3.5 km NE) :* **priory** founded early in the 11thC. ▶ **Rellanne** *(10 km NE of Carluc) :* museum of rustic tools. □

The LURE Mountain★

B1

The Lure is a 30 km extension of the Ventoux, a spine ending almost sheer above the valley of the Durance. The 1826 m Signal de Lure is the highest point *(15 min on foot, leaving D53/D113 33 km SW from Sisteron →);* on clear days you can see for 150 km. □

MANOSQUE★

B2 / ® / pop. 19123 (Alpes-de-Haute-Provence)

Manosque has changed radically from the 19thC village where sheep were driven through the streets morning and night as they went to and from the hill pastures. With the establishment of a nuclear research centre at Cadarache *(no visitors),* Manosque has become the principal town in the department.

▶ **Porte Saunerie**★ **:** 14thC gateway to the Rue-Grande (pedestrian zone). ▶ **Church of St. Sauveur :** wrought-iron bell-tower★ (1725). **Notre-Dame de Romigier :** Renaissance doorway★; 12thC Virgin and Child★ in black wood. ▶ Two pleasant walks : **Mont d'Or** *(1.5 km NE from the town centre)* and **Toutes-Aures Hill,** also called Saint-Pancrace *(2 km SW);* views. □

▶ Nearby

▶ **Valensole Plateau :** E, on the other side of the Durance a string of attractive villages : **Valensole** *(21 km E from Manosque);* **Riez** *(35 km E),* with 4thC baptistery★, and 35 million year old fossil wading bird★ in the Provençal Nature Museum *(1 Jul.-15 Sep., 10-12 & 2:30-6:30; 16 Sep.-30 Jun. daily ex Tue., Wed.; Jan.-15 Feb., 2:30-6:30).* □

MARSEILLES★★

B3 / ® / pop. 878689 (Bouches-du-Rhône)
See plan following page

Marseilles, founded almost 26 centuries ago by the Greeks, has always seemed to be a sort of autonomous territory involved more with international trade than with life in Provence. In fact, the biggest port in the Mediterranean is more aptly symbolised by the oil refineries at Fos than by the distinctive local accent.

▶ La **Canebière** (C2-D1-2), with hotels, shops and travel agencies that give it the somewhat stereotyped appearance of city main streets, is the shop-window of Marseilles. ▶ The **Bourse** (C2), the oldest Chamber of Commerce in France, founded by Henri IV in 1599, now the **Marine Museum,** illustrating the history of the town through its maritime associations (remarkable model ships★; *10-12 & 2-6; guided tour Wed. 3 pm; closed Tue.).* Behind the Bourse, the **Marseilles Historical Museum**★★ **:** 2000 years of city history, remains of the Greek port★, illustration of daily life long ago, library and exhibition hall *(12-7; closed Sun. and Mon.).* ▶ The **Old Port** (Vieux Port)★ (B-C2) : today full of pleasure craft, but near the **Port Quay** (17thC town hall façade), the **Roman Docks Museum**★ (B2) : on the site of ancient warehouses, glazed jars, undersea discoveries *(10-12 & 2-6:30; closed Tue. and Wed. am).* ▶ **Diamantée Mansion**★ **:** (Renaissance) houses the **Museum of Old Marseilles**★ (B2; popular art and traditions, *santons*★; 10-12 & 2-6:30; closed Tue. and Wed. am). ▶ To the rear, the 18thC **public infirmary** (Hôtel-Dieu). ▶ **Church of St. Laurent :** pure Provençal Romanesque (A2), sharing the end of the quay with 17thC **Fort Saint-Jean,** which used to control entry into the Vieux Port. Next to the green and white stonework of the 1893 Romano-Byzantine **cathedral** is the **old cathedral**★ (B1) : one of the finest examples of Proven-

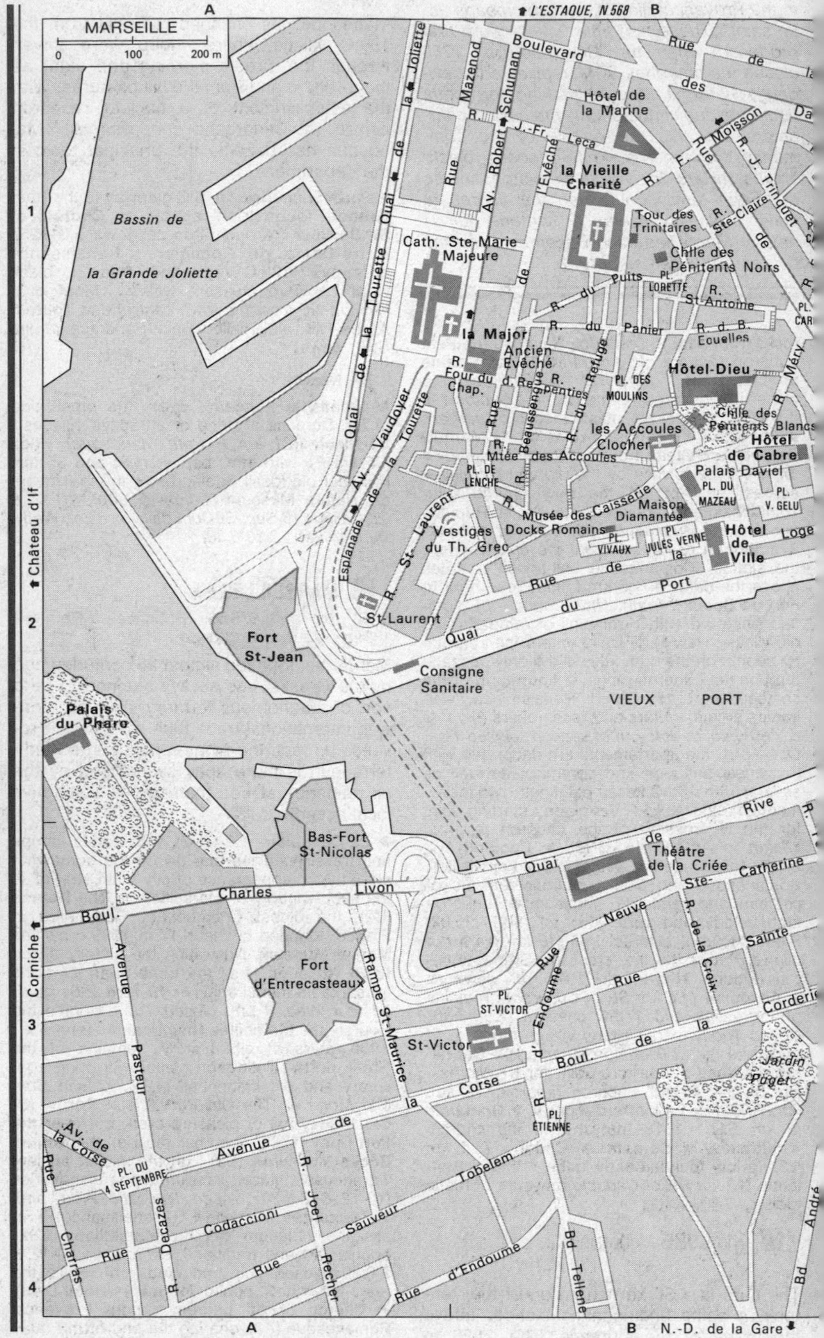
MARSEILLE
0
100
200 m
A
L'ESTAQUE, N 568
B
Bassin de la Grande Joliette
Boulevard des Dames
Rue de la Joliette
Quai de la Tourette
Rue Mazenod
Av. Robert Schuman
R. J.-Fr. Leca
Hôtel de la Marine
la Vieille Charité
Tour des Trinitaires
Chlle des Pénitents Noirs
Cath. Ste-Marie Majeure
la Major
Ancien Evêché
R. Four du Chap.
R. du Panier
PL. LORETTE
R. Ste-Claire
Rue Moisson
R. J. Trinquet
R. du Refuge
R. Beaussenque
Hôtel-Dieu
PL. DES MOULINS
Chlle des Pénitents Blancs
les Accoules Clocher
Hôtel de Cabre
Palais Daviel
PL. DU MAZEAU
PL. V. GELU
PL. DE LENCHE
Av. Vaudoyer
Esplanade de la Tourette
R. St-Laurent
Vestiges du Th. Grec
Musée des Docks Romains
Maison Diamantée
PL. VIVAUX
PL. JULES VERNE
Hôtel de Ville
Rue de la Loge
St-Laurent
Fort St-Jean
Quai du Port
Consigne Sanitaire
VIEUX PORT
Palais du Pharo
Bas-Fort St-Nicolas
Rive Neuve
Théâtre de la Criée
Quai de
Rue Ste-Catherine
R. de la Croix
Rue Sainte
Boul. Charles Livon
Fort d'Entrecasteaux
Rampe St-Maurice
PL. ST-VICTOR
St-Victor
Rue d'Endoume
Rue de la Corderie
Jardin Puget
Boul. de la Corse
Avenue Pasteur
Av. de la Corse
PL. DU 4 SEPTEMBRE
Avenue de
R. Joel Recher
Rue Codaccioni
Sauveur Tobelem
PL. ÉTIENNE
Bd Tellene
Rue d'Endoume
R. Decazes
Rue Charras
Bd André
Château d'If
Corniche
N.-D. de la Garde
1
2
3
4

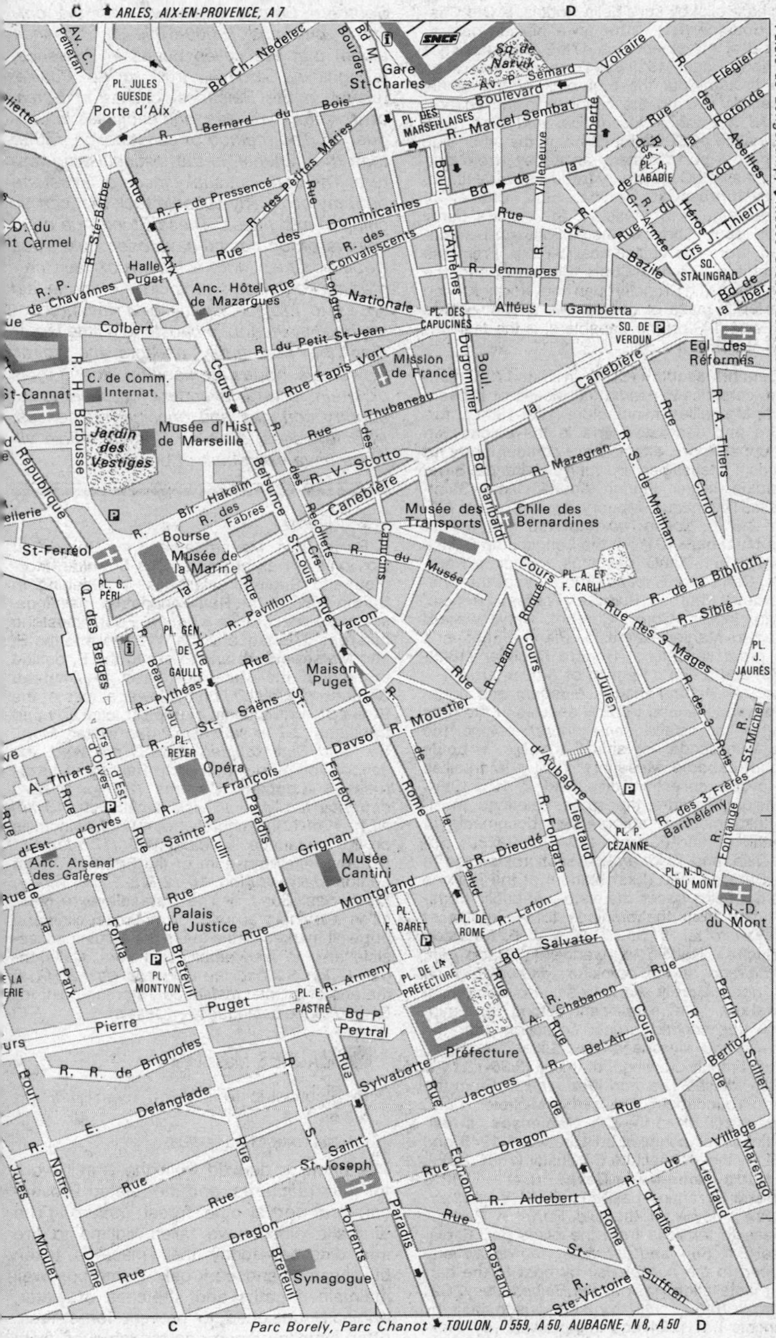
C
ARLES, AIX-EN-PROVENCE, A 7
D
Palais de Longchamp, Musée Grobet Labacie
Av. C. Pelletan
PL. JULES GUESDE
Porte d'Aix
Bd Ch. Nedelec
Bd M. Bourdet
SNCF
Gare St-Charles
Sq. de Narvik
Av. P. Semard
Boulevard Voltaire
Liberté
R. Flégier
R. des Rotonde
R. des Abeilles
R. Bernard du Bois
PL. DES MARSEILLAISES
R. Marcel Sembat
R. des Petites Maries
Boul. d'Athènes
Villeneuve
Bd de la Liberté
PL. A. LABADIE
Coq
R. F. de Pressencé
R. Ste-Barbe
Rue d'Aix
Rue des Dominicaines
R. des Convalescents
Rue St-Bazile
R. de G. Armée
Rue du Héros
Crs J. Thierry
SQ. STALINGRAD
Bd de la Libér.
D. du Mt Carmel
Halle Puget
R. P. de Chavannes
Anc. Hôtel de Mazargues
Rue Nationale
Longue
R. Jemmapes
PL. DES CAPUCINES
Allées L. Gambetta
SQ. DE VERDUN
Egl. des Réformés
Colbert
R. du Petit St-Jean
Dugommier
Boul.
Mission de France
Rue Tapis Vert
Thubaneau
R. H. Barbusse
C. de Comm. Internat.
St-Cannat
Cours Belsunce
La Canebière
Rue Curiol
R. A. Thiers
Jardin des Vestiges
Musée d'Hist. de Marseille
Rue des Récollets
R. V. Scotto
R. Mazagran
R. S. de Meilhan
République
R. Bir-Hakeim
R. des Fabres
Canebière
Musée des Transports
Bd Garibaldi
Chlle des Bernardines
Bourse
Musée de la Marine
St-Ferréol
Q. des Belges
PL. G. PÉRI
Crs St-Louis
R. Capucins
R. du Musée
Cours
PL. A. ET F. CARLI
R. de la Biblioth.
R. Sibié
Rue des 3 Mages
PL. J. JAURÈS
R. Pavillon
PL. GÉN. DE GAULLE
Rue Beauvau
Rue Vacon
Maison Puget
Rue de Rome
R. Jean Roque
Cours Julien
R. des 3 Rois
R. St-Michel
R. Pythéas
St-Saëns
R. Moustier
Cours d'Aubagne
R. Davso
St-Ferréol
Crs H. d'Est. d'Orves
R. PL. REYER
Opéra
A. Thiars
R. François
Paradis
R. Lulli
R. Grignan
Musée Cantini
R. Dieudé
R. Fongate
Lieutaud
PL. P. CÉZANNE
R. des 3 Frères Barthélémy
R. Fontange
PL. N.-D. DU MONT
N.-D. du Mont
Rue Sainte
d'Est.
Anc. Arsenal des Galères
Rue de la Paix
Fortia
Palais de Justice
Rue Breteuil
Rue Montgrand
PL. F. BARET
la Palud
PL. DE ROME
R. Lafon
Bd Salvator
PL. MONTYON
R. Armeny
PL. DE LA PRÉFECTURE
PL. E. PASTRÉ
Puget
Bd P. Peytral
Pierre
Rue Chabanon
Rue Bel-Air
Cours
R. Perrin-Solliers
Berlioz
Préfecture
R. R. de Brignoles
Sylvabelle
Rue Jacques
Rue
Boul.
E. Delanglade
R. Notre-Dame
Jules Moulet
Rue St-Saint-
St-Joseph
Rue Edmond Rostand
Dragon
Rue de Village
Marengo
R. de Lieutaud
d'Italie
R. Aldebert
Rue Rome
Torrents
Synagogue
Rue Dragon
Paradis
R. Ste-Victoire
Suffren
1
2
3
4
Parc Borely, Parc Chanot
TOULON, D 559, A 50, AUBAGNE, N 8, A 50

çal Romanesque art; ask the porter to show the cherub-adorned chapel of St-Lazare★, the Romanesque altar★ (1175), and the white ceramic bas-relief by Luca della Robbia. ▶ **Old Charity Hospice** (B1) : now an exhibition centre; typical of the sumptuous 17thC Baroque style of Pierre Puget (1620-1694); recent restoration has brought out the rose-pink of the stone, especially around the cupola★ in the chapel; *(10-12 & 2-6:30; closed Tue. and Wed. am).* ▶ **Basilica of St. Victor** (B3) : on the other side of the old port, formerly an abbey; from outside, the 11thC sanctuary (rebuilt several times) looks fortress-like; inside, 5thC Chapel of Notre-Dame-de-Confession, St. Victor's burial crypt, early Christian inscriptions and sarcophagi from the catacombs *(3-6).* ▶ From the Canebière (D2) the **Cours Belsunce** and the **Rue d'Aix** (C1) run through the North African quarter, a maze of *casbah*-like shops. ▶ **Rue St. Ferréol,** S off the Canebière, is the fashionable street of the city.

▶ **Cantini Museum★** (CD3) : in a late 17thC mansion, ceramics★, nearly 600 pieces of Provençal or Marseilles manufacture (17th-18thC); furniture and decorative arts in the salons; on the upper floors, examples of contemporary art trends : Messagier, Hartung, Vieira da Silva, Germain Richier, Pignon, Adami, César, Saint-Phalle, Télémaque, Monory, among others *(10-12 & 2-6:30; closed Tue. and Wed. am).* ▶ **Fine Arts Museum★** (D1) : in the Longchamp Palace (1870), 15th-20thC paintings including Perugino, Carraccio, Rubens (Adoration of the Shepherds★), Pourbus, Ruisdaël, Watteau, Tiepolo, David, Ingres, Corot, Courbet, Dufy, Vuillard and two Marseilles artists, Pierre Puget, and the great caricaturist Honoré Daumier (1809-1879) and a fine collection of African art.
Also... ▶ **Natural History Museum** and aquarium with local and tropical species in the right wing of the palace *(same hours);* behind, the **Zoo** with school for animal trainers. ▶ **Louis Grobet-Labadié Museum★** *(D1)* a Marseilles art-lover's collection displayed in his 19thC mansion; furniture, tapestries, paintings, musical instruments★, autographed documents of Beethoven and Paganini (*10-12 & 2-6:30; closed Tue. and Wed. am);* a section installed in the Gare de l'Est (East station) at the Marché des Capucins traces the history of public transportation from the omnibus to the métro of today; *info tel. 91.55.10.19.* ▶ **J. F. Kennedy Corniche★** leading to Avenue du Prado *(left, at the end of the* corniche; *immediately on the right)* **Borély Park : an archaeological museum★** in a magnificent setting for Egyptian★ (the second largest collection after the Louvre) and Mycenaean antiquities, ceramics, 18thC French drawings, statuary *(9:30-12:15 & 1-5:30; closed Tue. and Wed. am).* ▶ From the Prado roundabout, Boulevard Michelet, right, leads *(1 200 m)* to the **Cité Radieuse★,** a residential tower complex built between 1945 and 1952 by the architect Le Corbusier (1887-1965). ▶ **Notre-Dame-de-la-Garde** (B4) : 19thC Romano-Byzantine basilica (gilded Virgin; *ex-votos★;* view★ of the Old Port). ▶ **Port★ :** access to terraces from the place de l'Esplanade (B1; *Sun. and nat. hols., the ocean jetty is open to the public*) visit by boat to the harbour installations *(ask at the Belges Quay,* C2; *approx. 1hr30 round trip)* the prison built by François I in 1524 and immortalised by Alexandre Dumas in his novel, *The Count of Monte Cristo.* On another island of the **Frioul Archipelago,** the former **Caroline Hospital,** lazar house and quarantine centre, forms a handsome early 19thC architectural ensemble.□

Bories

Southern Europe is strewn with the dry-stone buildings (5 000-6 000 in Provence alone) that are called bories *in Provence,* nuraghi *in Sardinia,* trulli *in La Pouille,* talayot *in the Balearics,* casitas *in Spain,* orris *in the Pyrenees, and* capitelles *in Languedoc. The method of construction, rather than the material, is the distinguishing feature. The* borie *is usually made of limestone but may be of any suitable rock that can be chipped into flakes. These Stone Age equivalents of log cabins have been built since Neolithic times, with a false roof vault created by corbelling : each circle of stone laid so as to project slightly over the preceding one; at the top, a capstone a little larger than the rest firmly anchors the spiral. Nowadays,* bories *are used for storing tools or grain, drying lavender, for sheepfolds, country cottages and principal residences. At a few sites, such as Gordes, whole villages have been built of* bories.

▶ Nearby

▶ By the Ave. Mazargues and the Chemin du Roi, one arrives at the famous **Sormiou, Morgiou** and **Sugiton** calanques. ▶ Opening in Spring 1986 of the **Rau Foundation** (paintings, sculpture, decorative arts). ▶ Four limestone outcrops, L'Estaque to the W, L'Etoile to the E, and Marseilleveyre and Puget to the S, outline the rim of the Marseilles basin. ▶ **Château Gombert** *(9 km NE) :* on the lower slopes of the **Etoile Chain;** museum of popular local arts and traditions *(3-7 in summer, 2-6 in winter, Mon., Sat. and Sun.; guided tours 3 pm Wed. ex. school hols.);* in the church, Raising of Lazarus★. ▶ **Loubière Caverns** *(2.5 km NW) : entrance fee, 45 min visit.* ▶ **Allauch** *(13 km NE) :* 16th-17thC church; four 17thC windmills on the esplanade. ▶ **Aubagne** ® *(17.5 km E) :* HQ and small museum of the French Foreign Legion *(daily ex Mon. 10-12 & 3-7, 6 in winter, Wed., Sat., Sun.).* ▶ **The Marseilleveyre Massif** is a training ground for mountain climbers, but well marked paths make the summit accessible also to less ambitious hikers. **Callelongue** (*7 km S along the Corniche via* A2-3) : at the end of an inlet *(calanque);* starting point for GR98b to the *calanques* (→ Cassis). □

■ MAURES Massif★★

▶ Round trip from Saint-Tropez *(126 km, full day)*

C3 *(see map 3 page 908)*

The name is derived from the Greek word for dark *(amauros)* and the related Provençal term for a pine forest *(mauro).* The umbrella pines have fallen victims to fire and disease; today their place is taken by chestnut and cork-oak. Numerous well maintained paths and stretches of water, originally designed to prevent forest-fires, offer rambling itineraries far removed from the seasonal traffic-jams of the *corniche.*
▶ **Saint-Tropez** (→). ▶ **Cogolin** ® : specialises in the manufacture of briar pipes and wool carpets *(guided tour of the carpet factory,*

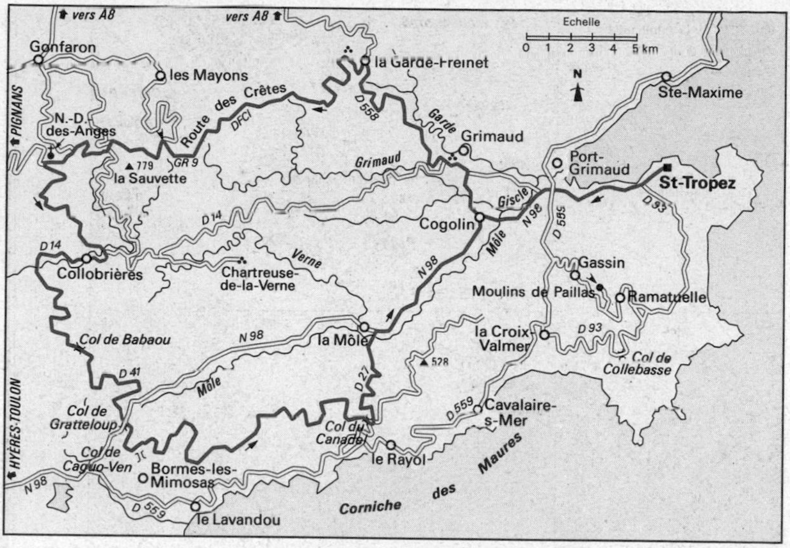

3. Maures Massif

weekdays, 98 Blvd. Louis-Blanc). ▶ **Grimaud★** ®, and, farther up, **La Garde-Freinet :** both with ruined châteaux and superb view★. From **Freinet,** take the **Crest Road★★** (left, DCFI), through beautiful countryside as far as the landmark television relay station, which shares the site★ with a tiny **hermitage, Notre-Dame-des-Anges,** possibly of Merovingian origin; still a pilgrimage site; view from the Alps almost to Corsica. ▶ The road runs down the Vaudrèches valley to **Collobrières,** where the delicious local specialties are chestnut preserve and crystallised fruits; good white wine. **Charterhouse of La Verne★ :** *(12 km E; road in poor repair in places)* 12th-18thC ruins of brown and green stone merging with the chestnut woods; kitchens and bakehouse, cloisters; restaurant in summer). ▶ Over the **Babaou Pass** down to the **Gratteloup Pass** (superb drive, views★). ▶ At the **Caguo-Ven Pass,** take the unmarked asphalt road left, which snakes above the coastline to the **Canadel Pass;** here continue left (D27) towards Cogolin and Saint-Tropez, or turn right to rejoin the Corniche. □

▶ Corniche des Maures★ *(26 km from Lavandou to La Croix-Valmer; 1hr, much longer in summer)*

▶ Tourist country softened by eucalyptus and mimosas, pinewoods and gardens, sun and sand, windsurfing, waterskiing, spectacular sites and views. ▶ **Le Lavandou** (→); **Saint-Clair** ®; **Aiguebelle** ®; **Cavalière** ® (beach★); **Pramousquier; Canadel-sur-Mer; Le Rayol** ® (site★); **Cavalaire** ® (beach★); **La Croix-Valmer** ®. □

■ MENTON★★

D2 / ® / pop. 25 449 (Alpes-Maritimes)

Menton boasts next to no winter, tropical vegetation including orange and lemon trees, and flowers everywhere. The mountains act as a barrier to the prevailing wind and you can tan on beautiful beaches most months of the year. Cultural activities organized by the town range from the Chamber Music Festival to the Biennial International Art Show, not to forget the "Fête du Citron" (Lemon Festival), and other delights. The old town is a maze of narrow streets, dark passages, and crooked steps.

▶ Along the sea front, the **Soleil Promenade★** (A-B2) with cafés, restaurants and shops. ▶ In the fortifications, the **Jean Cocteau Museum★,** arranged according to the artist's instructions with mosaics, tapestries and other works of art *(10-12 & 9-6 in summer; 10-12 & 3-5:30 in winter; closed Mon., Tue. and nat. hols.).* ▶ From the **Bonaparte Quay** (C1), a monumental stairway leads to the **Parvis** (courtyard) **St. Michel★★** and the **church of St. Michel★** (Baroque interior, altarpieces★ and organ lofts★). A few steps to the left of the church, the chapel of the **Pénitents-Blancs★** adorned with garlands of flowers in stucco; concerts during the Chamber Music Festival. ▶ **Rue St. Michel** (C1), the Place aux Herbes and the nearby market are all equally irresistible in their charm.

Also... ▶ **Municipal Museum** (B1) : local history, folk arts, and archaeology including the skull of "Menton Man" from the Late Palaeolithic period and female statuettes★ of the same period *(10-12 & 3-6 in summer; 10-12 & 4-5:30 in winter; closed Mon., Tue. and nat. hols.).* ▶ At the **Town Hall,** marriages are celebrated in a registry office★ decorated by Cocteau *(9-12 & 3-6 in summer; 9-12 & 2-6 in winter; closed Sat., Sun. and nat. hols.).* ▶ **Biovès Gardens★** (A1-2) : palm trees, lemon trees, flowers and fountains, *Belle-Epoque* Europe Palace, a cultural centre. ▶ **Carnolès Palace Museum★** (via A2) : 18thC former summer residence of the princes of Monaco, now an art museum surrounded by splendid gardens (Italian, French and Flemish paintings; *10-12 & 3-6 in summer, 10-12 & 2-5:30 in winter; closed Mon., Tue. and nat. hols.).* ▶ Above the church of St. Michel, the old **cemetery :** view★. ▶ **Exotic Botanical Gardens★; Colombières Gardens★** (via C1). □

▶ Nearby

▶ **Gorbio** *(8 km NW),* **Sainte Agnès** *(11 km*

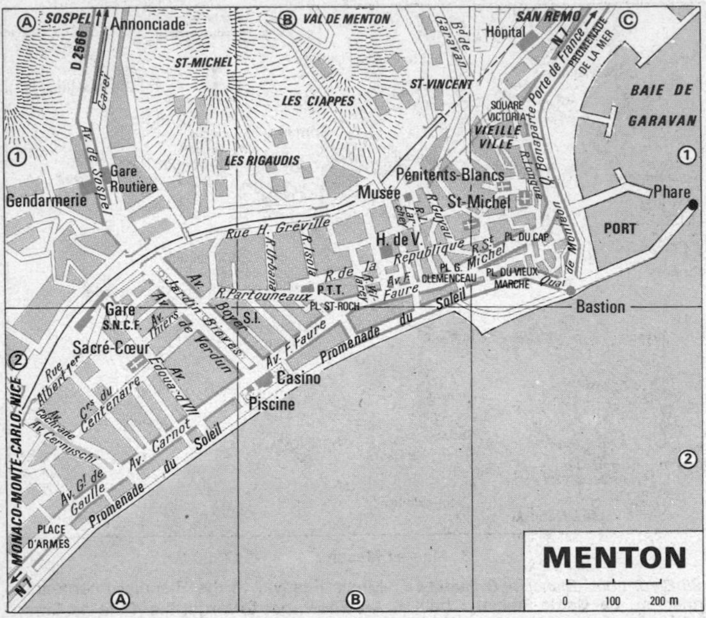

NW), **Castellar** *(7 km N);* old villages★ among olive and pine trees, with the charm of Old Provence. ▶ **L'Annonciade** *(5.5 km NNW) :* 17thC monastery among cypress and eucalyptus (view★). ▶ **Sospel★** ® *(21 km N along D2566 through the* **Carel Valley** *and the Castillon Pass)* in the Alps, old bridge, church with painting of the Virgin by François Bréa (fine example of school of Nice). **Braus Pass★ :** SW of Sospel *(22 km to Escarène)* by D2204. Turini Forest★★ (→) N of Sospel; and *(25 km)* the Turini Pass via the **Piaon Gorges★** and **Bévera Valley★.** ▶ **Roquebrune-Cap-Martin★** *(5 km W; →* Riviera). □

■ Principality of **MONACO★★**

D2 / ® / pop. 27 000
See map following page

Although there are no visible frontier posts of Customs, this tiny sovereign State (475 acres) maintains a character of its own, which encompasses casinos, festivals, motor racing, and the rich and tanned at play. Towards the turn of the century, Monte-Carlo emerged as a fashionable resort. Many buildings still reflect the *Belle-Époque;* newer additions are equally stylish but in a different way. Old Monaco sits above Monte-Carlo : a fairy-tale city with Palace and smartly turned-out Guards.

▶ **Princely Palace★** (B3) : 16th-17thC, with a few mediaeval vestiges. The ceremony of changing the guard takes place on the square daily 5 mins before noon; in the Courtyard of Honour★, 16th-17thC frescos; furniture, fine rugs, portraits in the Throne Room and apartments *(9:30-12:30 & 2-6:30; closed Oct.-Jun.);* **Napoleonic Museum** and **Archives of Monaco :** many personal effects of Napoleon, historic documents of Monaco *(9:30-12 & 2-6:30 Jul.-Sep.; 10-11:30 & 4-5:30 Oct.-Jun.; closed Mon.).* ▶ In the Old Town, 1884 neo-Romanesque **cathedral :** paintings of the

Two armed monks

Monaco was settled by Greeks, Romans and even earlier peoples, but current history opened in the 13thC with the advent of the Grimaldi dynasty. At that time, Italy was divided by the rivalry between Guelphs and Ghibellines. In 1297 Francesco Grimaldi, a Guelph, was expelled from Genoa; accompanied by his men disguised as monks, he wrested the fortress of Monaco from Genoese Ghibellines. Francesco failed to hold the fortress, but in 1308 one of his Grimaldi relatives bought the seigneury of Monaco from Genoa. Since then, the Grimaldi arms have featured two monks brandishing swords in honour of the exploits of François La Malice (Francis the Rogue, as he is remembered).

School of Nice★, including Louis Bréa's **St. Nicolas altarpiece★★** (1500) and **Pietà** donated by **Curé Teste★.** ▶ Through the **St. Martin Gardens★ (B3)** to the **Oceanographic Museum★★,** founded in 1910 by Prince Albert I (aquarium★★, specimens of aquatic fauna; *9 or 9:30-7,9 in Jul.-Aug.);* view★★ from the terrace. ▶ **Historical Museum of the Princes of Monaco :** wax figures depicting the Grimaldi family history *(9-6).* **Chapel of the Miséricorde :** 17thC recumbent★ Christ by the Monegasque artist Bosio. ▶ **La Condamine** (B2) ® : at the foot of the rock; the most luxurious port in the Mediterranean. ▶ **Monte-Carlo** ® : residential towers, hotel complexes, Congress Auditorium, casinos, the renowned **Hôtel de Paris,** where rubbing the knee of the equestrian statue in the hall is said to bring luck at the casino; **Museum of Dolls and Automatons★★** (Princess Grace Avenue, C1), a charming mansion designed by Charles Garnier (1825-1898,

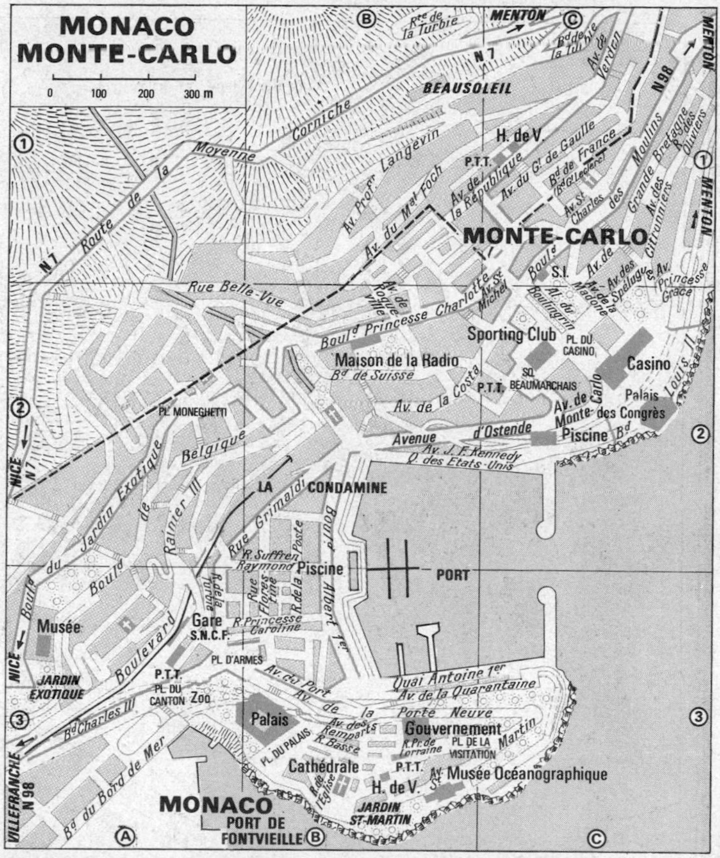

architect of the Paris Opéra) in a rose garden★ (100 19thC working automata, 600 18th-19thC dolls; *10-12:15 & 2:30-6:30; closed some nat. hols.*).

Also... ▶ **Exotic Gardens★★** : overlooking Fontvieille, 6 000 species of semi-desert plants and flowers *(9-6, Oct.-Apr.; 9-9, May-Sep.)*. **Observatory Grotto** : rock formations in a cavern inhabited more than 200 000 years ago; excavated artifacts in the nearby **Museum of Prehistoric Anthropology★** (A3) include the "Grimaldi Venus" a stone-age statuette. □

Moustiers ceramics

Ceramic glazes known as "Faïence" (after Faenza in Italy where they were invented) were introduced at Moustiers in 1679 by Pierre Clérissy. Legend has it that this son and grandson of potters obtained the secret of a brilliant blue glaze from an itinerant monk. For more than a century thereafter, Moustiers thrived on the process. In the 18thC, high-fired multicoloured glazes copied from Spanish ware gave a further boost to the industry. As fashions changed, the trade declined and, in 1874, died out. The tradition was revived again, however, in the 1920s, and flourishes to this day.

■ MOUSTIERS-SAINTE-MARIE★

C2 / ® / pop. 575 (Alpes-de-Haute-Provence)
Beautiful site★ for this town renowned for a ceramic industry that has flourished since the 17thC.

▶ **Museum of Faïence** (ceramics)★ : superb examples of local production *(9-12 & 2-7, Jun.-Aug.; 10-12 & 2-6 rest of year; closed Tue., Nov.-Mar.)*. ▶ **Church** : Lombard Romanesque bell-tower★. **Chapel of Notre-Dame de Beauvoir★** : 12th-14thC. □

▶ Nearby

▶ **Grand Canyon of Verdon★★★** (→). **Lake Sainte-Croix** *(5 km S)*★★.

■ NESQUE Gorges★

B2

17 km E of **Carpentras** (→) D942 climbs to the **gorges★★,** their cliffs riddled with caves. At the highest point (734 m) the road passes the **Cire Rock,** a concave cliff-face 400 m high. At the exit from the gorges is **Sault,** between the **Ventoux** (→) and **Lure Mountain** (→). **Albion Plateau** *(7 km SE)* : missile base (no visitors!). □

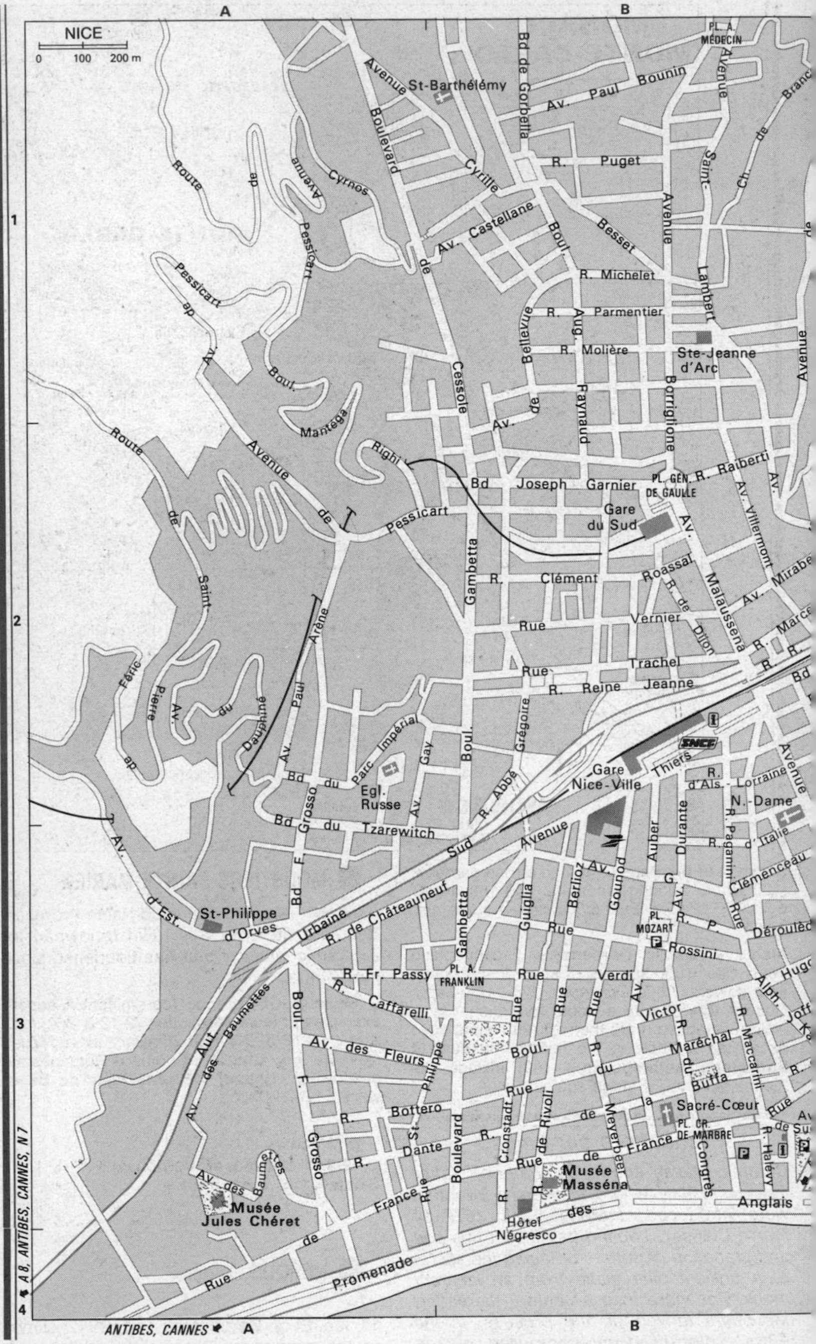

■ NICE★★

D2 / ® / pop. 338 486 (Alpes-Maritimes)

Historic site, capital of the Côte d'Azur, and luxurious resort : Nice, a city of French and Italian heritage, is the setting for innumerable carnivals, festivals and exhibitions.

▶ **Place Masséna** (C3) : laid out in 1815 in the Italian style, with arcades, gardens, fountains, bronze horses. W, palms in the Albert I Gardens (C3); E, past the fountains, the Paillon Promenade, where a car park and shopping centre are discreetly hidden by terraced gar-

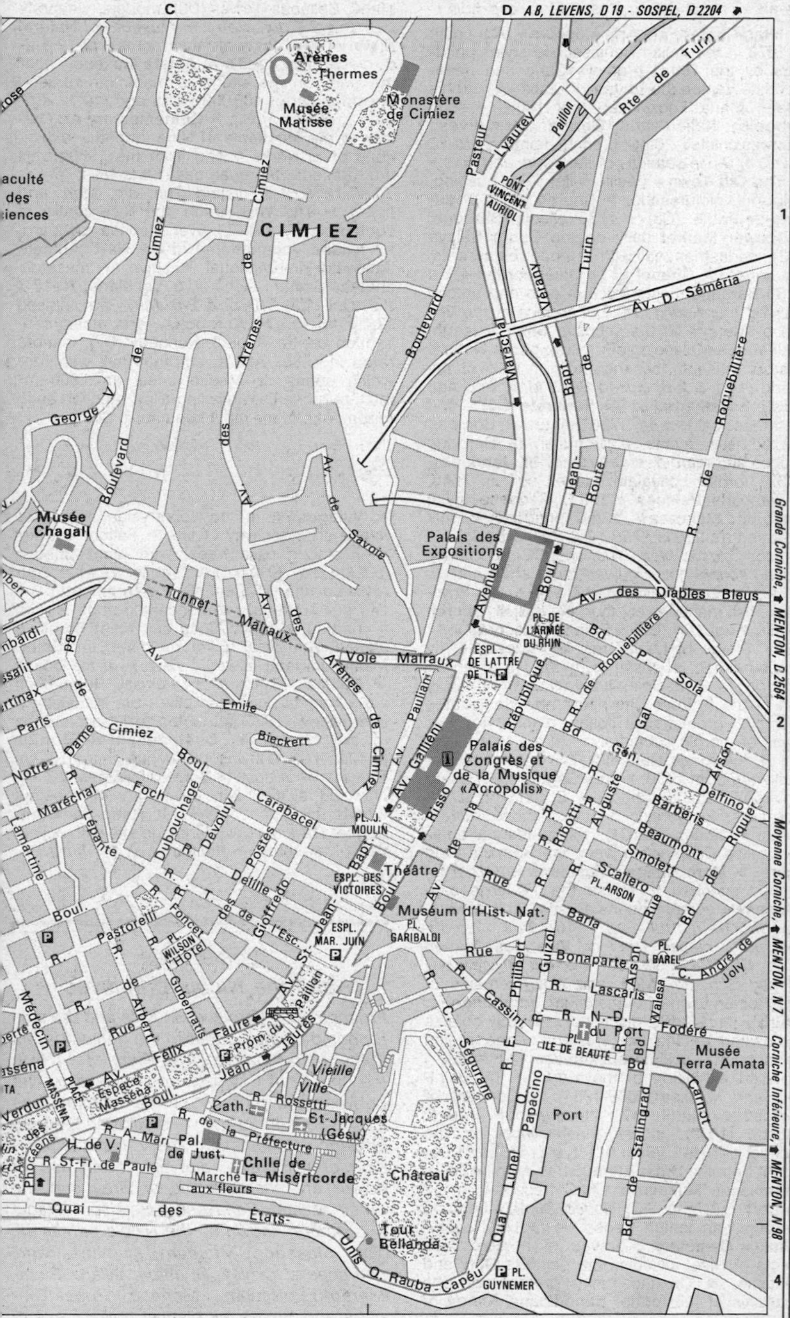

dens; continue towards the Congress Hall and the Flea Market. From Place Masséna, N, department stores on **Jean-Médecin Avenue** (B2-C3), are always busy as is the pedestrian precinct of **Rue Masséna** and **Rue de France** (fish restaurants and pizzerias). ▶ **Promenade des Anglais**★ (A-B3) : fringed with gay-90s *(Belle-Époque)* façades of hotels, cafés and restaurants. ▶ **Masséna Museum**★ (B3) : late 19thC Italian-style mansion; Empire-style salons; primitive Niçois painters★★ (altarpiece of St. Michel, school of Bréa); the 16thC Kiss of Peace reliquary★ in enamelled silver, Niçois folklore and history, Provençal ceramics, jewels★ *(10-12 & 2-5; closed Mon. and hols.).*

▶ **Jules-Chéret Fine Arts Museum★** (A3) : built in 1878 in the Italian Renaissance style; paintings by the 18thC brothers Carle and Jean-Baptiste Vanloo (portraits★ of Louis XV and his queen Maria Leczinska), 17th-18thC French schools; Italian and German primitives; Impressionists; 20thC French painters *(10-12 & 2-5, or 3-6 in season; closed Mon. and hols.).* ▶ **The Old Town★** (Vieille Ville) : E4, bustling, colourful, picturesque. ▶ **Church of St. François-de-Paule** (C3) : 1733 Niçois Baroque. ▶ **Flower Market** daily on the Cours Saleya (C3) : pedestrian mall with seafood restaurants, boutiques. ▶ **Chapel of la Miséricorde★★** : a 1736 Baroque masterpiece in gold and stucco *(guided tours only);* 1420 altarpiece of the Virgin of Mercy★ in the sacristy. **Shell Museum** (Galerie de Malacologie) : annex of the Natural History Museum, seashells★ from all over the world *(11-1 & 2-6, closed Sun., Mon. and nat. hols.).* ▶ **Cathedral of Ste Réparate** (C3) : 1650 neo-Classical façade, 1730 bell-tower, dome of glazed tiles. Inside, a profusion of Baroque stucco and marble. ▶ **Church of St. Jacques★** (C3) : former collegiate chapel, built in 1640. ▶ **Lascaris Palace★** : 17thC Genoese style, restored; staircase★, 18thC pharmacy★, folk arts and traditions *(9:30-12 & 2:30-6 or 6:30 in season; closed Mon., Tue. and Fri.; open daily during school hols.; guided tours at 10 and 3).* ▶ Along Rue Droite to the **Place St. François** : fish market every morning (C3). ▶ **Church of St. Augustin** (C3) : Baroque decoration★; 16thC Pietà★ by Louis Bréa. ▶ **Château★★** *(by steps near St. Augustin or by the lift D3 at the end of the États-Unis Quay)* almost nothing is left of the fortress, the name now designates the hill; promenade, Italian pines, view★★, ruins of the old cathedral. ▶ At the foot of the hill N, the **Place Garibaldi** (D3) : yellow ochre buildings from 1750. ▶ **Rue Ségurane** (D3) and environs : antique shops. ▶ E, the **Port** (D3) : car ferries for Corsica, boat excursions, restaurants. ▶ **Cimiez Hill** (C1) : the residential quarter, called *Cemenelum* when the Romans lived there. ▶ **Marc Chagall Museum★★** (C2) : designed specially to house the 17 large canvasses★★ comprising the artist's "Biblical Message" *(10-7, Jul.-Sep.; 10-12 & 2-5:30, Oct.-Jun.; closed Tue.).* ▶ **Villa des Arènes** (C1; *10-12 & 2:30-6:30, 2-5 out of season; closed Sun. am, Mon. and Nov.)* remains of the Roman town of Cemenelum, **amphitheatre, baths★** (2nd-3rdC); display of everyday objects excavated on the site; history of the region (inscriptions, sculpture). **Matisse Museum★** : detailed exhibition of the work of the painter Henri Matisse (1869-1954). ▶ **Convent of Cimiez** : church with "troubadour Gothic" façade (1850); inside, masterpieces of the School of Nice : Virgin of Pity★ (1475) and Descent from the Cross attributed to Antoine Bréa. **Franciscan Museum** : 17thC frescos★ in the oratory *(10-12 & 3-6; closed Sun.);* charming garden with lemon trees; view★. ▶ Nearby, **Cimiez Cemetery** : graves of notable residents of Nice, including the painters Dufy and Matisse. ▶ On the rocky promontory, the **church★** of the former **Benedictine Abbey of St. Pons.**

Also... ▶ **R Russian Orthodox Church** (A2) : pink brick, pale grey marble, and vivid ceramic tiles (1912). ▶ **Law School** (Faculté de Droit; les Baumettes, via A3) : Chagall mosaic on the first floor. ▶ **Vieux-Logis Priory** (A1) : reconstruction of a 14th-16thC interior; kitchen★ *(4-6 summer, 3-5 winter, Wed., Thu., Sat. and first Sun. of each month).* ▶ **Naval Museum** : in 16thC Bellanda Tower (D3), models, weapons *(10-12 & 2-7 Jun.-Sep.).* ▶ **Museum of Natural History** (D3) : casts of mushrooms★ *(9-12 & 2-6; closed Tue.).* ▶ **Terra Amata Museum** : near the port, on the site of a mammoth-hunters' encampment of 400 000 years ago *(10-12 & 2-6 or 7; closed Mon.).* ▶ **Contemporary Art Gallery of the Museums of Nice** : monthly exhibitions of artworks dating from the 1960s until the present *(59 quai des États-Unis, D-E4; 10:30-12 & 2-6; closed Sun. am, Mon. and hols.).* ▶ The **Villa Arson** (the Nice centre of contemporary art), 20 Ave. Stephen Liégeard. ▶ **Musée International d'Art Naïf Anatole Jakovsky** (International Primitive Art museum, château Sainte-Hélène, Ave. Val Marie, *10-12 & 2-5, Oct.-Apr.; 10-12 & 2-6, May-Sep.; closed Tue., hols.).* ▶ **Acropolis,** arts/music/convention centre, 1 espl. Kennedy (D2), inaugurated in 1985; Agora, entrance hall with roof which opens; le Méditerranée, an 1 800 m^2 multi-purpose hall; bowling alley; Apollon auditorium, one of the most beautiful in Europe. □

▶ Nearby

▶ **Villages★★** in the countryside near Nice evoke an older way of life. ▶ **Falicon** *(10 km N)* : among olive trees, with **Mont Chauve** *(6.5 km NW, 30 min round trip,* view★★). ▶ **Tourette-Levens** *(17.5 km N).* ▶ **Aspremont** *(6 km W from Tourette)* : in concentric rings around a château. ▶ **Mont Alban** and **Mont Boron** *(E and NE from Nice, 10 km round trip),* and **Saint-Michel plateau** *(8 km)* : views★ of the coast. ▶ **Contes** *(18 km N)* : originally Roman, on a spur among pine and olive; Ste Madeleine★ altarpiece★ (1525) attributed to François Bréa in the church. ▶ **Châteauneuf-de-Contes** *(4.5 km W)* : 11thC Romanesque church; *2 km to ruins of village.* ▶ **Berre-des-Alpes** *(27 km N)* : on a mountain covered with chestnut woods (site, panorama★). ▶ **Notre-Dame-de-Laghet** *(14 km NE)* : pilgrimage site with collection of *ex-votos.* ▶ **Peillon★★** ® *(17 km NE)* :

Louis Bréa and the Niçois primitives

Frescos and altarpieces in Nice and the surrounding country attest to the genius of this 15thC Niçois painter. The Pietà of 1475 in the church at Cimiez marks a dividing line between the naïf art of the Middle Ages and the advent of the sophisticated Sienese influence. Schematic drapery, facial expression of spirituality, and the telling use of colour are characteristic of Bréa and the other artists (Canavesio, Balaison, Nadal and others) known as the Niçois primitives. The Masséna Museum at Nice, and churches at Cimiez, Roubion, Villars, Saint-Martin-d'Entraunes, Monaco, Puget-Théniers and Sospel all display brilliant examples of the school. Superb frescos can be seen in the churches at Peillon, Coaraze, Venanson, Saint-Etienne-de-Tinée, Auron, Lucéram, Cians, Roure, Roubion, Valdeblore, Saint-Dalmas, Entraunes, Saorge, Cagnes and Vence.

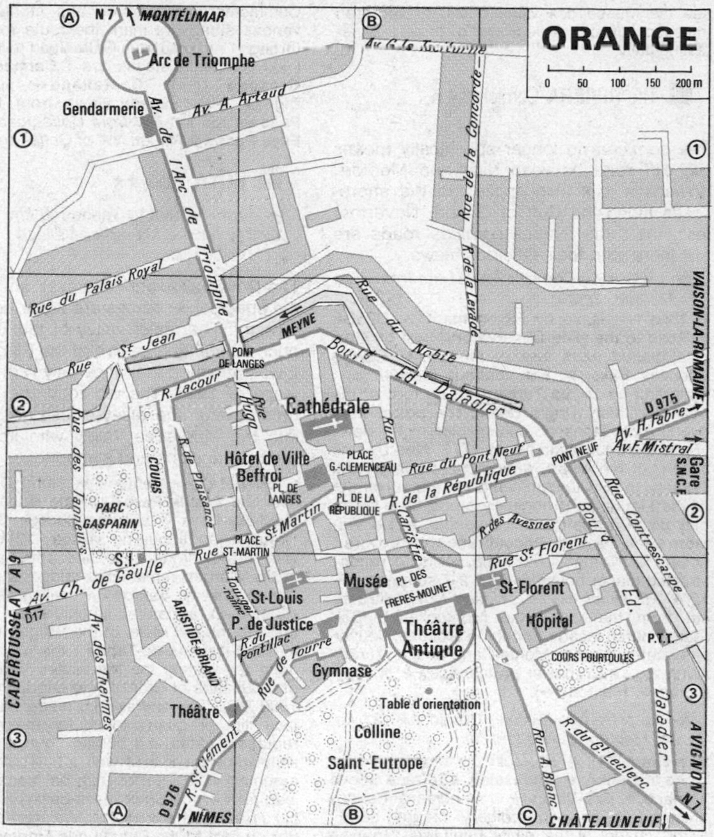

straight out of the Middle Ages, a real eyrie on a rock; 15thC frescos★ by Jean Canavesio in the Chapel of the White Penitents. ▶ **Peille**★ *(12 km of Peillon)* : Gothic houses, stairways and vaulted passages, views over the bay. ▶ At the end of the **Paillon Gorges**★ (D21), **L'Escarène** ® *(25 km NNE)* : view of the old town from the bridge over the Paillon (17thC Baroque church). ▶ **Riviera Corniches**★★ (→). ▶ **Vésubie Valley**★★ (→). □

■ ORANGE★

A1 / ® / pop. 27 502 (Vaucluse)

On the motorway south, Orange is the gateway to the Midi, symbolised by the Roman arch at the entrance to the town. Buyers and sellers come from all over Provence to the Thursday market in the Cours Aristide Briand, redolent with honey from the Ventoux, truffles from Vaison, olives from Nyons, Tricastin lavender, thyme and rosemary, not to mention the fruits of the Comtat. Orange also boasts the best-preserved Roman theatre in existence, which is the setting for the annual international operatic festival known as the *Chorégies*.

▶ The **theatre**★★★ (B3) was built in the 1stC BC during the reign of Augustus. The stage wall (Louis XIV called it the "finest wall in the Kingdom") is the only complete one still standing and is classified the 9th monument in the world *(daily 9-6:30 ex performance days; info TO)*. W of the theatre, the forum and temples. ▶ **Municipal Museum** (B3) : Roman stonework, plan★ of the area in 77AD, history of Orange, and fine arts including numerous work by the English painter and engraver Sir Frank Brangwyn (1867-1956) *(8:30-7, Apr.-Sep.; 9-12 & 2-5, Oct.-Mar.)*. ▶ Old **Cathedral** (B2) : 12thC Provençal Romanesque remodelled in the 16thC. ▶ **Triumphal Arch**★★ (A1) : probably built in 20BC; the decoration includes trophies, a frieze of warriors★★, two battle scenes★★, chained captives symbolizing the defeat of the Gauls. ▶ Saint Eutrope hill (B3) : a public park (view★) where the château of the Princes of Orange used to be. □

▶ Nearby

▶ **Mornas** ® *(11 km N)* : at the foot of a high cliff, plane trees, fortified gates, and a ruined château★. ▶ **Bollène** ® *(22 km N)* : typical Provençal city with plane trees and old houses; collegiate Church of St. Martin (12th-16thC); museum (coins, drawings by Picasso and Chagall; *9-12 & 2-7, Apr.-Sept.; in winter 3-6, closed Tue.*). ▶ **Sérignan-du-Comtat** *(8 km NE)* : where the entomologist Jean-Henri Fabre (1823-1915) lived and studied; his house and grounds are now a museum *(9-11:30 & 2-4, 2-6 in summer; closed Tue. and hols.)*. ▶ **Château-neuf-du-Pape** ® *(10 km S)* : ruined 14thC château; the famous local wine is a real "Papal indulgence", especially when well aged. Also see the Musée des vieux outils du vigneron (museum of old winegrower's tools); wine-tasting daily. □

The **RIVIERA** Corniches★★

D2

The *corniche* no longer specifically means the cliff road between Nice and Menton; nowadays it is also applied to the shore-roads along the Gulf of Genoa. Nevertheless, the three famous *corniche* roads are still there with their fabulous views.

▶ La Grande Corniche★★ *(31 km from Nice to Menton, 2hr30)*

▶ **Nice** (→) leave by F2 on map). ▶ D2564. ▶ Road to the **Nice Observatory,** built by Garnier *(guided tours, ask at the SI).* ▶ Quatre Chemins Pass. ▶ **Eze lookout** (belvédère) : panorama★★. ▶ **La Turbie :** at the foot of the Tête de Chien (Dog's Head), the promontory overlooking Monaco; spectacular night view; Niçois Baroque church★ of 1777. Nearby, the Trophy of the Alps★, a monument built by the Romans in 5BC to commemorate the surrender of the Ligurians. It originally stood 50 m high, only 35 m are left; small museum. ▶ **Le Vistaëro**★★ ® : view. ▶ **Roquebrune**★ ® : covered street, 12thC mediaeval keep, visits to reconstructed manor house *(9-12 & 2-7 summer, 10-12 & 2-5 winter ex. Fri.; closed Nov.)*; streets cut from the rock (Rue Montcollet★); Baroque church façade, shopping arcades, souvenirs, crafts. Walk to Monte-Carlo beach *(1hr30)* along the Le Corbusier promenade★★ on **Cap Martin.** ▶ **Menton** (→).

▶ La Moyenne (Middle) Corniche★ *(31 km from Menton to Nice, 1hr30).*

▶ **Menton** (→). ▶ N7. Join the Moyenne Corniche at **Cabbé.** ▶ **Beausoleil,** a terrace above Monaco. ▶ **Eze-Village**★ ® : medieaval houses crowded in an extraordinary craggy site★; 14thC chapel of the White Penitents (Spanish Smiling Christ, 1258); exotic garden with incomparable view *(8 or 9 to sunset).* The Frédéric-Nietzsche Path (named after the philosopher, 1844-1900, who lived here for a time) leads to **Eze-sur-Mer** *(25 min).* ▶ **Villefranche Pass** (view of Nice). ▶ **Nice** (→). □

▶ L'Inférieure (Lower) Corniche★ : *(35 km from Nice to Menton, 4hr).*

▶ **Nice** (→ leave by F4 on map). ▶ **Villefranche-sur-Mer**★ ® : one of the most beautiful roadsteads in the Mediterranean; still intact 18thC town★ with ancient streets chopped by steps and vaulted passages (see the Rue Obscure★). Chapel of St. Pierre★ : (17thC) entirely redecorated by Jean Cocteau in 1957 *(9-12 & 2:30-7 summer; 9-12 & 2-4:30 winter; 9-12 & 2-6 spring and autumn; closed Fri. and 15 Nov.-15 Dec.).* Citadel★ : (late 15thC) containing the Volti Museum★ : numerous sculptures and red-chalk drawings by a local artist *(10-12 & 3-7 Jun.-Sep.; 11-12 & 2-5 Oct.-May; closed Sun. am, Wed. and Nov.).* ▶ **Eze-sur-Mer** ®. ▶ **Cap d'Ail** ® : attractive houses, flowers, trees; Cap d'Ail trail *(1hr walk round trip)* view★. ▶ **Monaco**★★ (→). ▶ **Menton** (→). □

The **ROUTE NAPOLÉON**★

C2-B1

This is the route taken by Napoléon in 1815 on his return from exile on the island of Elba, from **Golfe-Juan** ®, where he disembarked, to Grenoble (→ Route Napoléon, Dauphiné). Commemorative plaques and monuments at various stopovers mark the route for 180 km through Provence from Golfe-Juan to **Sisteron**★ (→). The main stages are : **Cannes**★★ (→), **Grasse**★ (→), **Castellane**★ (→), and **Digne**★ (→). Superb views from the **Pilon Pass**★★ *(35 km NW from Golfe-Juan)* and the **Faye Pass**★★ *(44 km NW of Golfe-Juan).* □

ROYA Valley★★

▶ From Sospel to Tende *(40 km, 3hr, plus full day for the Merveilles Valley).*

D1

The Roya valley attracts kayak enthusiasts; the principal resources are water power and forestry. The upper valley of the Roya was once a hunting preserve of the King of Italy; it was attached to France only with the plebiscite of 1947. The old road to Turin also runs through the valley whose gorges open into the Merveilles Valley with its strange prehistoric signs and symbols.

▶ **Sospel**★ (→ Menton). ▶ Along D2204 and over the **Brouis Pass**★, to the Roya between **Breil-sur-Roya** ® and the **Saorge Gorges**★ **:** Breuil is an appealing village; 18thC church with 17thC organ case and 1500 altarpiece. In the Gorges remarkable bridge of the Nice-Cuneo railway. **Saorge**★★ **:** village beautifully situated in a natural amphitheatre. ▶ Road through the red rocks of the **Bergue Gorges**★. ▶ **Saint-Dalmas-de-Tende :** the usual starting point for visiting the **Merveilles Valley**★, site of thousands of Bronze Age engravings (1800-1500 BC). The engravings, made on the rock face flint or quartz tools, for the most part represent cattle and human figures, and possibly were associated with a bull cult and/or a mountain cult. The trip can be made by hired jeep *(ask at the SI)* or, (less easily) in a private car *(10 km W across the Minière Valley, then 3hr on foot to the Refuge des Merveilles, base for the next day's exploration of the valley; the engravings are difficult to find without a guide. Even in summer, take warm clothing; up to the end of June and starting again in October, snow may cover the engravings).* The valley itself, walled by mountains, carpeted with flowers and dotted with lakes, is beautiful. ▶ **La Brigue** *(2.5 km E of Saint-Dalmas)* : among orchards in the Levens valley, green schist houses with emblazoned arcades and lintels. Church of St. Martin : (12th-13thC) Lombard Romanesque bell-tower, altarpiece of Ste Marthe★ (School of Nice), Nativity★ by Louis Bréa, and Notre-Dame des Neiges★, 1507 triptych. ▶ **Notre-Dame des Fontaines** *(4 km E from La Brigue)* : forceful 15thC frescos★★. ▶ **Tende** ®. □

SAINT-MAXIMIN-LA-SAINTE-BAUME★★

B3 / pop. 5 552 (Var)

According to legend, St. Maximin was one of the party that disembarked at Saintes-Maries-de-la-Mer (→ La Camargue); he was supposedly buried here some 30 years later.

▶ **Basilica of Ste Madeleine**★★ **:** (1295-1532) a blend of soaring Gothic and the simpler, sober Provençal style. Inside, beautiful organ★ by Jean-Esprit Isnard (1773); concerts; altarpiece of Christ's Passion★ (1520) by a Venetian painter; gold-embroidered cope of St. Louis of Anjou (13thC bishop of Toulouse; choir screen★ (1691); in the crypt, a Gallo-Roman funerary vault of 4th-5thC. ▶ The former **Royal Monastery★** (13th-15thC), N of the basilica, now the College for Contemporary Exchanges which organises activities essentially concerned with music. Exquisite 15thC **cloister★** *(9-11:30 & 2:30-6)*; concerts, recitals, exhibitions in season. ▶ Near the basilica, the town has largely kept its original checkerboard pattern, with here and there small squares and fountains. Houses with arcades (14thC), Rue Colbert, Rue des Arcades : site of former Jewish *ghetto.* □

SAINT-RAPHAËL

C-D3 / ® / pop. 24 310 (Var)

With Fréjus Bay backed by the magnificent Esterel peaks, the site has been a vacation resort since Roman times.

▶ The seafront promenade and the old port are always lively : palms, restaurants, cafés. ▶ **Templars' Church :** 12thC Provençal Romanesque. ▶ **Archaeological Museum :** Roman artifacts recovered from the sea bed *(10-12 & 3-6 ex. Tue. and nat. hols., 15 Jun.-15 Sep.; 11-12 & 2-5 ex. Sun. and nat. hols. in winter).* ▶ **Fréjus** (→); 3 km W. ▶ **Saint-Aygulf** ® *(8 km SW) :* beach fringed by eucalyptus and pine. □

SAINT-RÉMY-DE-PROVENCE★

A2 / ® / pop. 8 439 (Bouches-du Rhône)

Classical ruins, and memories of Frédéric Mistral, the greatest of Provençal poets, who was born and lived in a neighbouring village. More remote yet still-vivid reminders of Nostradamus (1503-1566; seer or charlatan?) the physician-astrologer who was born in the Rue Hoche. Flowers, sun, a fountain, a *pastis* at the café : this is Provence.

▶ The town centre is the **Place de la République.** ▶ **Church of St. Martin :** 14thC bell-tower★. ▶ **Alpilles Regional Museum :** N of the church, in the Mistral de Mondragon mansion★ (1550), folk art and traditions; exhibitions on Mistral and Nostradamus *(Apr.-Oct., 10-12 & 2-6 ex. May; Sat., Sun., Mon., and Ascension Day only; in winter, Sat. and Sun., 10-12 & 2-4).* ▶ **Sade Mansion :** (15th-16thC) excavations from Glanum; marble portraits of Octavia and Julia★ (wife and daughter, respectively, of the Emperor Augustus). Rue Hoche : birthplace of Nostradamus *(guided tours, every hour).* □

▶ Nearby

▶ **Glanum★★** *(1 km S) :* site of a spring sacred to a healing spirit of the Celto-Ligurians (5thC BC), later a Greek settlement (3rdC BC), then a Roman city. When invading Barbarians destroyed Glanum in the 3rdC, only a mausoleum and memorial arch, known locally today as Les **Antiques,** were left standing. The **Commemorative Arch★,** displaying elements of Greek influence, celebrates the Roman conquest of the Gauls. The **Mausoleum★★** is somewhat later (1stC AD), and was built in memory of the two grandsons whom Caesar Augustus had named as his heirs but who died prematurely. ▶ Opposite the Antiques, an alleyway leads to the **monastery** of **Saint-Paul-de-Mausole★★ :** a nursing home where the Impressionist painter Vincent Van Gogh (1853-1890) spent the final year of his life. Church★ : (Romanesque, late 12th, 18thC façade) a scaled-down version of the great Provençal churches; elegant bell-tower★ and cloister★. Close by, the **ruins of Glanum :** *(9-12 & 2-6; 10-12 & 2-5 out of season; closed Tue.)* two houses★ from the Greek period, Roman baths, forum, and (right at the S end) the spring★ that gave rise to the town. ▶ **Maillane** *(7 km NW) :* birthplace and home of Frédéric Mistral; the house he built when he married is now a museum (original décor; *10-12 & 2-6 or 5 in season, closed Mon.).* □

SAINT-TROPEZ★★

C3 / ® / pop. 6 248 (Var)

Once a paradise for painters (Signac, Matisse, Bonnard, Marquet, Dunoyer de Segonzac) and a writers' retreat (Colette, Maupassant), Saint-Tropez is today the summer haunt of a cosmopolitan mixture of tourists and intelligentsia, whose seasonal hedonism tends to obscure the fact that Saint-Tropez is a seaport whose origins date from time immemorial. "Saint Tropez" himself was probably a Roman officer named Torpes, who was martyred as a Christian under Nero (Pisa; 68AD) and whose headless body, set adrift in a boat, washed up on the shore. Every year, on May 16th and 17th a procession known as a *bravade* is held to commemorate the saint, whose bust is paraded around the town to the sound of muskets and blunderbusses freely discharged by the *bravadeurs,* the local menfolk dressed in endearingly disparate versions of the traditional French naval uniform. However, St. Torpes was not alone in arriving by sea : corsair raids and Moorish invasions plagued the coastline for centuries and the seamen of Saint-Tropez were frequently called upon to repel attacks. In 1637 the town fleet routed a force of 21 Spanish galleons, providing the occasion for another *bravade,* held annually on June 15th.

▶ On the heights overlooking the gulf, *(E)* the **citadel★** (14th-16thC) and the **Marine Museum** (models★, marine archaeology; *12-6; closed Thu. and some nat. hols.).* Splendid view from the keep★★. ▶ **Museum of l'Annonciade★★ :** in an ancient chapel, works of prominent painters who spent time at Saint-Tropez; the view from the windows seems to reflect the paintings (Signac, Van Dongen, Matisse, Derain, Vuillard, Braque, Marquet; *10-12 & 3-7, Jun. Sep.; 10-12 & 2-6, Oct.-May; closed Tue. and Nov.).* □

▶ Nearby

▶ **Beaches : La Bouillabaisse** *(1 km W);* **Graniers** *(2 km E);* **Tahiti** *(4 km SE),* leading to **Pampelonne** *(5 km long).* ▶ Chapel of Ste Anne *(1 km S) :* shaded by umbrella pines; view. ▶ **Ramatuelle★** ® *(11 km S) :* typical Provençal village, houses huddled at random above vineyards. ▶ **Paillas Mills** (moulins)★ *(2 km W) :* panorama★★. ▶ 2.5 km farther, **Gassin★.** ▶ **Les Marines de Cogolin** ® *(4 km W of Saint-Tropez) :* residential area and marina. ▶ **Port-Grimaud★** ® *(6 km W) :* built from scratch in 1964, is a "fake" Mediterranean village to which the passage of time has lent a certain authenticity; culverts and canals, narrow streets and colourful "fishermen's houses" add to the effect; less frantic than Saint-Tropez. □

SAINTE-BAUME Massif★★

▶ From Aubagne to Saint-Maximin *(48 km, 3hr)*
B3

"Bauomo" is a Provençal dialect for cave; "Sainte-Baume" is the "holy cavern" where St. Mary Magdalen supposedly repented her misdeeds (→ Saint-Maximin and Les-Saintes-Maries-de-la-Mer, Camargue). The *massif* and green plateau are forested with beech, sycamore, yew, oak and lime, above a carpet of flowers.

▶ **Aubagne** (→ Marseilles, nearby). ▶ **Gémenos** ®. ▶ **Saint-Pons Park★ :** by the swift river Sauge; nothing remains of the abbey except the Romanesque church. ▶ **Espigoulier Pass :** (alt. 728 m) view of Marseilles and the Sainte-Beaume Massif. ▶ **Sainte-Baume Hostelry : a** spiritual retreat open to all, not far from Mary Magdalen's cave. A forest path★★ leads to the cave *(45 mins),* at the foot of a steep escarpment. To reach **Saint-Pilon** (alt. 998 m), go back to the Oratory cross-roads : from there, 40 mins. At the chapel on the peak, the view★★ makes the climb worthwile. Many other walks. ▶ **Nans-les-Pins** ® : summer resort village. ▶ **Saint-Maximin-la-Sainte-Baume** (→). □

SAINTE-MAXIME

C3 / ® / pop. 7364 (Var)

When the Provençal saints aren't in the mountains, they're on the beaches : Saint-Raphaël, Saint-Tropez and now Saint-Maxime : a seaside resort facing south across the bay to Saint-Tropez.

▶ **Saint-Donat Park** *(10 km N) :* **Museum of Gramophones and Mechanical Music★** with exhibits ranging from Edison's first phonograph to quadraphonic systems *(10-12 & 3-6:30, Easter-15 Oct.).* □

SALON-DE-PROVENCE★

A2 / ® / pop. 35845 (Bouches-du-Rhône)

Best known for a flying school, Salon is an old merchant town that has prospered with the expansion of the communications network. The town has spread from its original base on the slopes around the château, down across the plain.

▶ **Rue de l'Horloge** runs straight across the old town, from the fountain in the **Place Crousillat** to the château. On the left it passes **Rue Nostradamus,** where the physician-astrologer (→ Saint-Rémy-de-Provence) wrote his prophecies *(daily ex Tue. 10-12 & 3-7).* ▶ The **Château de l'Emperi★** (12th-16thC) has a noteworthy Courtyard of Honour★; exhibitions on French military history from Louis XIV to WWI *(10-12 & 2:30-6:30, 2-6 Oct.-Mar., closed Tue. and hols.).* ▶ **Church of St. Michel** (left of the esplanade) : 13thC, remarkable doorway★ that is part-Gothic (columns, capitals) and part-Romanesque (archivolt, tympanum). ▶ **Rue du Bourg Neuf** runs down to the machicolated town gate. **Town Hall★ :** dating from Louis XIV. ▶ 400 m E, **Regional Museum of Salon and Crau :** in an 18thC Provençal mansion (wild-life; *10-12 & 2-5, weekdays).* ▶ Collegiate **Church of St. Laurent★** *(N of town) :* Provençal Gothic; in the fourth chapel on the left, the tomb of Nostradamus; 16thC Virgin★ in alabaster). □

SANARY-SUR-MER

B3 / ® / pop. 11689 (Var)

A pink and white town protected from the *mistral* by surrounding hills; palms and sandy beach. □

▶ Nearby

▶ The **Gros Cerveau** *(13 km N) :* view★★. ▶ **Ollioules** and **Mount Caume** *(22 km NE) :* flowers, a Romanesque church; through the **Ollioules Gorges** to **Evenos★** an old village on a rocky peak. The little road to **Mount Caume** zigzags up to two forts at the peak (alt. 801 m; view★). ▶ **Ile des Embiez** *(10 min crossing from Brusc, 6 km S from Sanary) :* a sports, cultural and tourist complex developed by Paul Ricard, the *pastis* manufacturer and motor-racing sponsor; Sea Observatory : aquariums *(9-12 & 2-6, closed some nat. hols.).* ▶ **Notre-Dame-du-Mai★** *(13 km SE from Sanary) :* on **Cap Sicié,** right on the sea (alt. 358 m); *ex-votos★*; view★★. ▶ **Six-Fours-Les Plages** ® *(5 km SE) :* fort *(2 km N)* overlooking Toulon roads; St. Pierre : 17thC Romanesque and Gothic; 16thC painting of the Virgin★ *(Sat. and Sun pm in season; Sat. only out of season).* ▶ **Notre-Dame-de-Pépiole★** *(5 km E) :* a charming site near a 10th or 11thC wood of pine and cork-oak. □

SEILLANS★

C2 / ® / pop. 1609 (Var)

A fortified village on the slopes of Mount Auzières. Charming town, château; enjoyed by the composer Charles Gounod (1758-1823) and the surrealist painter Max Ernst (1891-1976). **Notre-Dame-de-L'Ormeau** *(1 km SE; ask at the SI) :* carved and painted 16thC altarpiece of the Tree of Jesse (geneology of Christ); *ex-votos.*

▶ **Fayence** ® *(7.5 km SE) :* a village of craftsmen on the edge of the Plans de Provence; 18thC neo-Classical church; hang-gliding centre nearby (view★). □

SÉNANQUE Abbey★★★

B2

In the austere valley of the Sénancole, Cistercian monks built the last of the abbeys know as the "three sisters of Provence" (the other two are Silvacane (→) and Thoronet). Sénanque is one of the purest examples of 12thC Cistercian architecture, with elegant lines that would make any further decoration superfluous.

▶ Founded in 1148, Sénanque today is a cultural centre (concerts of ancient music, temporary exhibitions) and institute for Saharan studies *(10-12 & 4-6, 7 in season).* ▶ Visits to the dormitory, the **cloister★,** the chapterhouse, the monks' hall, and the **church★.** ▶ In the **refectory,** audiovisual introduction to Cistercian life; **former kitchens** (17thC) present an introduction to Romanesque symbolism. ▶ Farmstead : **museum of the Sahara** *(10-12:30 & 2-7; tel. 90.70.02.05).* □

SILVACANE Abbey★★

One of the rare Cistercian foundations not

concealed in a forest or solitary valley. The area, however, was never much frequented, isolated as it was in a reed marsh (*silva cannarum* = forest of reeds).

▶ The overall plan is typical of the monasteries of the Order *(10-12 & 2-5 or 6 in season; closed Tue. and hols.)*. ▶ As at Sénanque and Thoronet, the **church★** is very beautiful. The cloister (latter 13thC) is Romanesque but has ogival vaults at three corners. □

▶ Nearby

▶ **Pertuis** ® *(18 km E)* : vestiges of the Middle Ages (rampart, tower, château); in the church, a 16thC triptych. ▶ **La Tour-d'Aigues** *(6 km NE of Pertuis)* : among the ruins of a 16thC château (monumental door★); in the church, painted Christ, Italian 15thC. ▶ **Meyrargues** ® *(16 km SE from Silvacane)* : mediaeval château converted into a hotel. ▶ **Peyrolles-en-Provence** *(6 km E)* : amid orchards and vineyards; 18thC château, now the town hall. 9 km NE from Peyrolles, the Durance runs through the **Mirabeaux Pass★.** ▶ **Rognes** *(9 km SE from Silvacane)* : quarries; church with collection of carved wooden altarpieces★ (late 15th-18thC). □

■ SISTERON★

B1 / ® / pop. 6 572 (Alpes-de-Haute-Provence)

Sisteron is the gateway between Provence and the Dauphiné; flat roofs, a citadel, limestone cliffs eroded over the centuries, and an ageless bridge over the Durance just before the latter widens into a lake.

▶ The **citadel★** (12th-16thC), on a limestone ridge, crowns the site *(8-7, Palm Sunday to 1 Nov.; arrowed itinerary)*; magnificent view from the height. ▶ **Church of Notre-Dame :** 12thC Provençal Romanesque, with Lombard influences in the doorway and the E end; attractive capitals on the pillars in the nave; two French primitive paintings (early 16thC) in the second chapel on the left. Left of the church, an arrowed path leads through the old town. ▶ Little known **Museum of Old Sisteron :** local archaeology; *ask at the SI.* □

▶ Nearby

▶ **Vilhosc** *(6 km E)* : remains of 11thC priory; early meridional Romanesque crypt. ▶ **Château-Arnoux** ® *(14 km SE)* : above **Lake Escale** on the Durance; early 16thC château. ▶ Excursions into the Upper **Vançon Valley,** wooded and deserted *(23 km NE, D3).* □

■ TARASCON★

A2 / ® / pop. 11 024 (Bouches-du-Rhône)

A boundary between Provence and the royal territories of France : haunt also of the *tarasque,* a mythical monster half-crocodile and half-lion, vanquished by St. Martha (sister of Mary Magdalen → La Camargue) whose presumed relics repose here.

▶ **Château★★** (completed in the 15thC) poised on a rock rising out of the Rhône, one of the most beautiful feudal buildings in the country; a frontier post between Tarascon and Beaucaire, outposts of the territories of Provence and France respectively. The crenellated walls and grim exterior hide an interior of great elegance; the château was both fortress and princely residence *(guided tours at 10, 11, 2, 3 and 4; plus 9 and 5 in season; closed Tue. and hols.).* ▶ The cool interior courtyard★ is shaded by the graceful Flamboyant Gothic royal lodgings. ▶ The **Collegiate Church** (12th-17thC) maintains relics of St. Marthe★ which have made it a revered site of pilgrimages. The S door★ is Romanesque. Inside, interesting paintings. ▶ Tombs★ of Jean de Cossa (15thC) and St. Marthe (17thC marble mausoleum) in the crypt. Stroll in **Rue des Halles** (15thC houses); see the *Tarasque* at the SI. □

▶ Nearby

▶ **Boulbon** *(7 km N)* : a rustic hamlet against the tree-covered massif of the **Montagnette,** dominated by a ruined château; in the cemetery, the 12thC Romanesque **chapel of St. Marcellin★.** ▶ **Abbey of St. Michel-de-Frigolet** *(11.5 km NE)* : founded in the 10thC, in the heart of the Montagnette, fragrant with wild thyme; the abbey is maintained by the Order of White Canons *(guided tours, 9-12 & 2-7).* Only the Romanesque church of St. Michel remains from the old Priory; in the 19thC abbey church, superb woodwork★ frames 14 paintings by Mignard. On sale at the monastery (and concocted in the abbey pharmacy) is the Elixir du Révérend Père Gaucher, which was immortalized in a novel by Daudet (→ Fontvieille). ▶ **Barbentane** ® *(15 km NE from Tarascon)* : guarded by two fortified gates, the château★ exemplifies Provençal classicism; 18thC interior decoration★ *(10-12 & 2-6, Easter-All Saints' Day; closed Wed. ex. Jul.-Sep.; Sun. only in winter, same hours).* □

■ THORONET Abbey★★★

C3 / ®

Thoronet, third of the "three sisters" (→ Sénanque, Silvacane), is a perfect 12thC example of the 20thC architectural dictum, "Less is More". The perfect proportions, masterly stonework and the use of light, illustrating the principles of the Cistercian Order, more than compensate for the absence of embellishment.

The monastery buildings were erected between 1160 and 1175; the clean lines of the Romanesque church★ are complemented by the powerful form of the cloister★ (access through N aisle).

▶ **Cabasse** *(7 km SW)* : hidden in the green Issle valley; prehistoric menhirs and dolmens; carved wooden altarpiece★ (1543) in the 16thC church of St. Pons. □

■ TINÉE Valley★★

▶ From Pont de la Mescla to Saint-Étienne-de-Tinée *(53 km, 4 hr)*

C-D1

The river Tinée arises in the Bonette Pass, site of the highest road in Europe. The valley springs to life each winter with the advent of the skiing season.

▶ **Pont de la Mescla** *(39 km N from Nice on N202)*. ▶ D2205 runs along the bottom of the **Mescla Gorges★**. ▶ **La Tour** *(right, 7 km)* : chapel of the White Penitents (1491). ▶ **Clans** *(6.5 km, right)* : church with 12thC frescos, altarpiece of the school of Nice. ▶ **Ilonse★** *(11 km, left)*. ▶ **Saint-Sauveur-sur-Tinée** : the valley's shopping centre and departure point for numerous excursions. ▶ 4 km W, road to **Roure★** : 16thC St. Laurent altarpiece★, Niçoise Assumption (1560). **Roubion★** *(12 km W)* : 12thC ramparts and gates. ▶ **Beuil** *(24 km W)* : (→ Daluis gorges★★). ▶ D2205 runs through the **Valabres Gorges★**. ▶ **Isola** : Romanesque bell-tower, within hearing of the **Louch waterfalls★** (100 m high); 17 km E through the **Chastillon Valley★** to **Isola 2000** ®, a ski resort in a superb natural amphitheatre; Italy is only 5 km away. ▶ **Saint-Étienne-de-Tinée** ® : amid pastures and streams, a base for excursions (Lake Rabuons★, *4hr*); church with Romanesque bell-tower★, 15thC frescos in the chapel of St. Sebastien, museum of religious art in the chapel of St. Michel. ▶ **Auron★** ® *(7 km S;* alt. 1 608 m) : the principal winter resort of the Alpes-Maritimes department; **cable-car** from **Las Donnas★** *(closed May, Jun., Oct., Nov.)*, Alpine panorama★★. ▶ **Bonette Peak★★★** *(26 km NW; →* Barcelonette). □

■ TOULON★

B3 / ® / pop. 181 405 (Var)
See plan following page

Toulon, with its magnificent harbour roads★★, ranks with Portsmouth, San Diego and Yokohama as one of the world's great naval ports. Although the trim French naval uniform with pomponed beret is no longer mandatory for sailors on shore leave, the town is steeped in the tradition of the *Royale,* as the French navy is nicknamed. Toulon is ringed by white limestone mountains studded with pine trees. The architecture in the newer quarters is resolutely modern; the old town still holds a daily market★ in the Cours Lafayette.

▶ **Stalingrad Quay** (B2) : beside the Old Basin *(Darse Vieille),* busy cafés isolated from the rest of town by buildings on the Avenue de la République. ▶ The Maritime Offices mark the beginning of the naval installations. ▶ Near the very handsome monumental gate (formerly the principal entry to the arsenal), the **musée de la Marine★** (Naval Museum, A2) : models★, paintings, figure-heads and other reminders of the city's maritime heritage *(10-12 & 1:30-6; closed Tue. and hols.)*. ▶ The **Maritime Arsenal** : the early hub of Toulon, still a busy naval shipyard. ▶ **Rue d'Alger** (B2) : once the hot-spot of old Toulon; the nearby streets are still colourful, although perhaps more restrained than numerous popular songs about Rue d'Alger would suggest. ▶ (B2) **Cathedral of Ste Marie** : an odd mixture of Classical (1696 façade) and Romano-Gothic (interesting paintings, including works by Puget, Vanloo, Mignard). ▶ **Cours Lafayette : market★,** "wild thyme, a bit of saffron and a net of figs for five francs..." as a traditional song relates. **Museum of Old Toulon** (No. 69; *1-6, Mon., Wed., Sat.*). ▶ **Church of St. François-de-Paule:** curved Italian Baroque façade (1744); gilded wood statue of the Virgin★ (1660). ▶ **Le Mourillon and Cap Brun** (B-C4; *7.5 km round trip*). At the far end of Le Mourillon promontory, the **Royal Tower★** : (16thC) naval museum; panorama★. **Boulevard Dr. Cunéo** (B4) leads to the little port of **Mourillon★** ®, overlooked by the fort of St. Louis★. Farther on, beaches and residential area of Cap Brun.

Also... ▶ **Toulon Museum** (A1) : natural history, art, archaeology (Oriental room, paintings by Carraccio, Brueghel, David, Vanloo, Denis, Vlaminck; *10-12 & 2-6; closed nat. hols.*). □

▶ Nearby

▶ **Chateauvallon** *(7 km NW)* : arts and cultural centre★ among pines, olive trees and rocks. ▶ **Evenos★** (→ Sanary). □

▶ Mount Faron★★ *(18 km round trip; marked road one-way only; access by cable-car daily ex. Mon. am; B1)*

▶ Mount Faron : pine woods on a limestone mountain 542 m above Toulon. ▶ On the left, Beaumont Tower : **National Memorial to the WWII landings** *(débarquement)* in Provence *(9-6 summer; 9-11:30 & 2-5:30 winter);* panorama★★, orientation charts. ▶ Farther on, **Zoo** and **Fort de la Croix-Faron** (view★). □

▶ Around the roadstead★ *(la Rade) (1-2hr by boat, leave from Stalingrad Quay, B2; by car, 17 km to Saint-Mandrier, approx 2hr)*

▶ Leave Toulon by A1. ▶ **La Seyne-sur-Mer** ® : dockyard town; Panoramic Marine Museum (marine fauna and flora; *10-12 & 3-7 summer; 10-12 & 2-6 winter; closed Fri.; Sat. and Mon. am; Nov.*). **Fort de Balaguier** : naval museum, galleys and convict hulks; unique view★★ of the roadstead *(10-12 & 3-7 summer; 10-12 & 2-6 ex. Mon. and Tue. winter)*. ▶ **Tamaris** and **Les Sablettes** : seaside resorts. ▶ **Saint-Mandrier** : fishing port, pleasure craft deep in a bay; view★ of the roadstead. ▶ **Cap Sicié** (→ Sanary). □

■ TURINI Forest★★

▶ From l'Escarène to the Turini Pass *(26 km, 3hr)*

D2

A complete change of scenery just half an hour's drive from the sea and the palms; 35 km^2 of chestnut, beech, maple, spruce, and 30 m-high larches between the Vésubie and Bévera valleys.

▶ **L'Escarène** (→ Nice, nearby). ▶ D2566 to **Lucéram★** : a mediaeval town on an escarpment between two ravines. Church : Romano-Gothic, 18thC Italian rococo decoration; altarpiece of St. Marguerite★ (1500) attributed to Louis Bréa; another of St. Antoine★ (1480) attributed to Canevasio; in the treasury★, St. Marguerite and the Dragon★, silver statuette of 1500. ▶ **Chapel of St. Grat** *(1 km S)* and **chapel of Notre-Dame-de-Bon-Cœur** *(2 km NW)* : both with frescos. ▶ **Peïra Cava★,** ® : year-round resort, view★★. ▶ The road climbs through the Turini Forest★★ to the crossroads at **Turini Pass** ® (alt. 1 607 m). ▶ **Aution★** *(4 km NE)* : memorial to the war dead of 1793 and 1945; **La Pointe des Trois-Communes** *(3 km)* : superb view★★. D70 W of the Pass to the **Vésubie Valley★★** (→) via the **Sainte-Élisabeth Gorges.** SE, D2566 to **Sospel★** (→ Menton). □

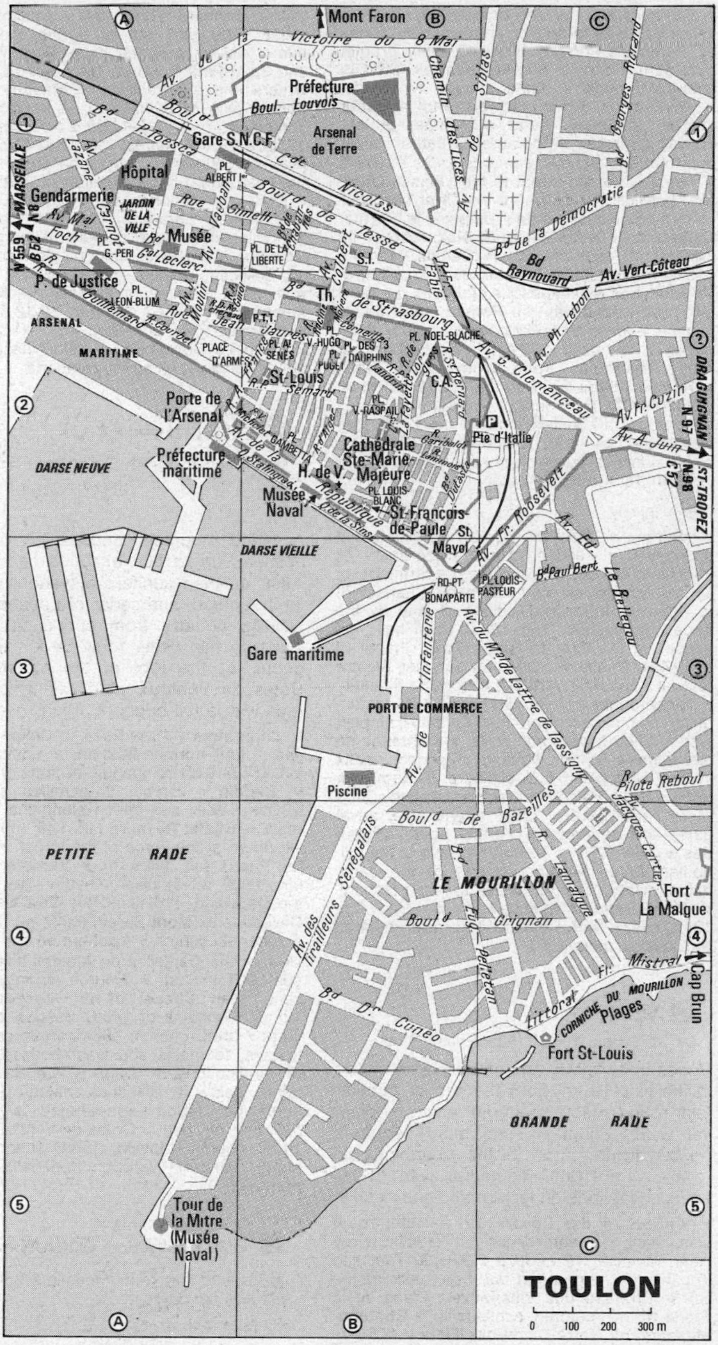

■ VAISON-LA-ROMAINE★★

A1 / ® / pop. 5864 (Vaucluse)

Four in one : a mediaeval town on the prehistoric settlement; a modern one on the Roman city. The green waters of the river Ouvèze run under a single-span Roman bridge. Today Vaison-la-Romaine is a typical Provençal town with flowers, sun, plane trees and a Tuesday market.

▶ Much of the Roman city is hidden by the modern town; in the **Puymin Quarter** *(9-5* *or 6 in season*) : the Villa of Messius, once the estate of a well-to-do Roman townsman. Close by, Pompey's Portico : a walled public promenade 52m × 64m. ▶ **Roman Theatre★** (20AD) : entered through a tunnel on the N hillside. ▶ **Museum** : excavated art and artifacts (marble statues★, head of Venus, athlete crowning himself with laurel wreath★, silver bust of a nobleman★; *same hours as Puymin*). ▶ Along a Roman street to the **Villasse Quarter** : basilica, house where the silver bust was unearthed, House of the Dolphin. ▶ Former **Cathedral of Notre-Dame-de-Nazareth★** : an interesting example of Provençal Romanesque; parts (6th-7thC apse) date from Merovingian times; Romanesque **cloister★** on the N side *(same hours as the Roman monuments; a single admission ticket covers both)*. ▶ **Chapel of St. Quenin★** *(300 m N)* : similar blend of eras; triangular apse from late 12thC. ▶ **Roman bridge** leads to the **mediaeval town** (13th-14thC); This quarter is gradually being restored. 15thC church; ruins of the 12thC château of the Counts of Toulouse. *Les Choralies*, a choral festival takes place every 3 years (next in 1986), 1st fortnight in Aug. □

▶ Nearby

▶ **Valréas** ® *(25 km N)* : an administrative anomaly : a section of the Department of Vaucluse surrounded by the Department of Drôme formed as an enclave by Charles VII to prevent further acquisitions of land by the popes at Avignon. 15th-18thC town hall; old houses in the Grande Rue; 17thC Chapel of the White Penitents. Open-air summer theatre festival in the courtyard of the Hôtel de Simiane. ▶ **Richerenches** *(7 km SW)* : a 12thC rectangular commandery of the Knights-Templar, with fortified towers and walls. ▶ **Dentelles de Montmirail★** *(S of Vaison)* : jagged peaks inviting hikers and rock-climbers. ▶ **Séguret★** ® *(9 km SW of Vaison)* : attracts artists and craftsmen; 12thC church, steep streets, mediaeval gates and ramparts. ▶ Farther south, **Gigondas** ® *(16 km SW of Vaison)* : source of the full-bodied Côtes-du-Rhône wines of the same name (plenty of opportunities for wine-tasting). ▶ **Notre-Dame d'Aubune★** *(6 km S)* : 9th-10thC chapel with Romanesque tower inspired by Classical models. □

■ VENCE★

D2 / ® / pop. 13 428 (Alpes-Maritimes)

Roses and violets, orange and lemon trees in the hills 10 km from the sea. A popular year-round resort sheltered inside mediaeval walls. Fountains and shady squares (Place du Peyrat★) in the charming old town★. 11th-18thC cathedral with 15thC satirical carvings on lectern and choir stalls.

▶ **Chapel of the Rosary** (St. Jeannet road) was designed and decorated (1947-51) by Henri Matisse *(10-11:30 & 2:30-5:30 Tue. and Thu.; open more often Jul.-Sep.; ask at the SI)*. ▶ **Château des Villeneuve** : Place de la Frêne, 15thC restored, exhibitions. ▶ **Château-Museum of Notre-Dame-des-Fleurs** *(2.5 km W)* : perfume and liqueur museum *(10-12:30 & 2-6 in summer; 2:30-5:30 in winter; closed Sun. am.)*. □

▶ Saint-Paul-de-Vence★★ ® *(3.5 km S)*

▶ A fortified mediaeval town whose attractions were rediscovered by the painters Paul Signac (1863-1935), Amedeo Modigliani (1884-1920), Pierre Bonnard (1867-1947), Chaim Soutine (1893-1943) and others during the 1920s; numerous art galleries have since flourished and **Saint-Paul** ® is now the haunt of painters, writers and entertainers. ▶ **Maeght Foundation★★** *(NW of Saint-Paul)* : a living centre of contemporary art *(10-12:30 & 3-7 summer; 10-12:30 & 2:30-6 winter; tel. 93.32.81.63)*; exhibitions, concerts and performances throughout the year; important collection of 20thC art★★ exhibited in rotation. ▶ The village of Saint-Paul is extremely attractive : studios, workshops, art galleries, antique dealers. **Auberge de la Colombe d'Or** (Place Général de Gaulle) : the art collection makes this renowned inn and restaurant a museum in itself. ▶ **Municipal Museum** *(9-12 & 3-7 summer; 10-12 & 2-6 winter; closed Tue. and Sun. am)*. ▶ Church of St. Charles Borromée★ : 18thC Italian; 1740 bell-tower. ▶ **Stroll** on the ramparts. □

■ The VENTOUX★★

▶ Round trip from Carpentras *(76 km, full day)*

B1

A varied mountain landscape : olive and holmoak up to 800 m, beech and oak to 1 600 m, then conifers of various sorts — larch, spruce, and cedar of Lebanon. Good walking country from spring to autumn; skiing in the winter (only 60 km from Avignon). At the foot of the mountain, the Côtes de Ventoux yield dry white wines, reds with a full bouquet, fresh rosés.

▶ **Carpentras** (→). ▶ D974 to **Crillon-le-Brave** *(left 2 km)*, former fiefdom of Louis de Crillon (1543-1615) companion-at-arms of Henri IV. ▶ **Bédoin** : church, 14-panelled altarpiece. ▶ Oak, cedar and beech along the mountain road. ▶ **Chalet Reynard** (alt. 1 460 m) : a small ski resort at the verge of the forest. ▶ **Tempêtes Pass★** (alt. 1 829 m). ▶ **Ventoux Peak★★** (alt. 1 909 m) in clear weather you can see the Dauphiné, Provence, the Vivarais and the Cévennes. ▶ **Mont Serein** (*right*, alt. 1 428 m) : another ski centre. ▶ **Lookout on the N slope** : view of the Dentelles de Montmirail★ (→ Vaison la Romaine). ▶ Source (spring) du Grozeau, then **Chapel of the Grozeau** (11th-12thC) : remains of 14thC frescos. ▶ **Malaucène** : 14thC church, 18thC organ case★, old houses, fountains and wash-houses, remains of fortifications. ▶ D938 to **Le Barroux** *(on right)* : below Renaissance château (1539) with somewhat feudal appearance. ▶ **Caromb** *(2.5 km on left)* : Côtes-de-Ventoux wines; 14thC church (triptych, 15thC school of Avignon); ramparts; wrought-iron belfry. ▶ **Carpentras** (→). □

■ Grand Canyon of VERDON★★★

▶ Round trip from Moustiers-Sainte-Marie *(92 km, full day)*

C2 *(see map 4)*

An axe-blow through the plateau, with sheer cliffs and green waters that appear to stand still; the grandest of the old-world canyons, running NS along the alpine folds, turning lower down to run EW through Provence. Over the 21 km from Rougon to Pont d'Aiguines, the Verdon has cut a series of

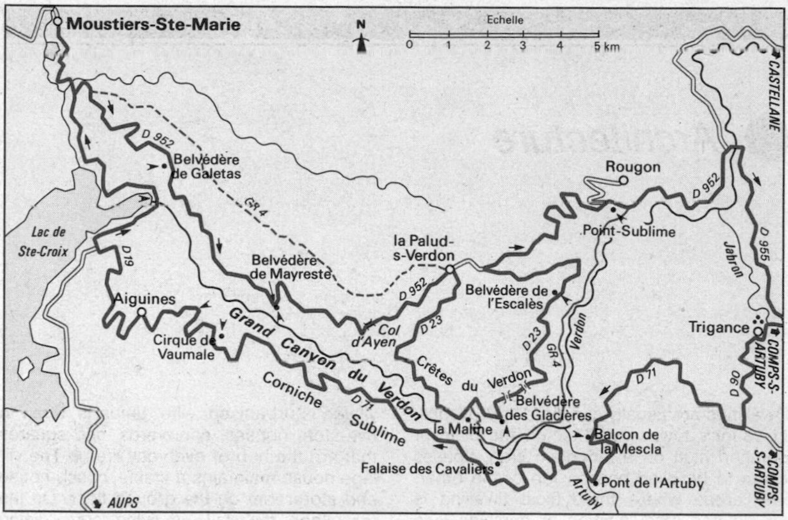

4. Grand Canyon of Verdon

gorges 400-700 m in depth with a drop of 146 m and a slope varying from 4° to 14°.

▶ **Moustiers-Sainte-Marie**★ (→). ▶ D952 climbs above Lake Sainte-Croix (view★). ▶ **Mayreste Lookout**★★ : 150 m right. Lookout at **Ayen Pass** (alt. 200 m). ▶ **La Palud-sur-Verdon** ® : in the village, take the **Crest** (Crêtes) **Road** right (D23)★★★ ; succession of extraordinary views. ▶ **Chalet-de-la-Maline :** GR4 starts for Point Sublime *(6hr actual walking time, 8-9hr with halts; for inexperienced hikers, it is advisable to go with a guide : the walk is demanding, and the weather unpredictable, especially in spring and in periods of heavy rain, but there are memorable sites and views; only 6 paths are open to the public without danger; stay on the paths, neither cross nor bathe in the river; take appropriate footwear, warm clothing, food and torch).* ▶ Lookouts at **Glacières**★★★ ; **l'Escalès**★★★. ▶ **Point Sublime**★★★ ® : on the right *(5 mins)*, lookout overlooking the entrance to the Grand Canyon. ▶ **Rougon** *(3 km N) :* high, near feudal ruins (view★ of entrance to Canyon). ▶ **Couloir Samson Lookout**★ *(1.2 km, right) :* GR4 emerges; junction of the Baou and the Verdon. ▶ **Trigance** ® : overlooked by a château now converted into a hotel. ▶ **Balcons de la Mescla**★★★ : left bank of the Verdon where it joins the Artuby; view. ▶ D71 follows the canyon along the **Corniche Sublime**★★★, from one breath-taking view to another; W, **La Falaise des Cavaliers**★★ : restaurant; site overlooking green waters 300 m below. ▶ The rest of the trip is beautiful : **Baucher Cliff**★★, **Vaumale amphitheatre**★★, ending above **Lake Sainte-Croix**★★ (→ Moustiers-Sainte Marie). □

■ VÉSUBIE Valley★★

▶ From Nice to Saint-Martin-Vésubie *(64 km, full day)*

D2

A trip to the Alpine heartland above Nice : from the sparkling seascape of the Promenade des Anglais to high pastures surrounded by firs, mountains, waterfalls and craggy peaks. The Vésubie valley is the gateway to the Mercantour National Park (700 km^2), one of the richest nature Parks in Europe : southern mountain flora, alpine fauna including *chamois, moufflon* (wild sheep), boar, marmot, eagle, Siberian ibex.

▶ **Nice** (→). ▶ N98 SW for 7 km, then N202 up the Var Valley to **Plan-du-Var** *(30 km from Nice).* ▶ D2565 to the multicoloured walls of the **Vésubie Gorges**★. ▶ **Saint-Jean-la-Rivière. Utelle**★ *(9 km left) :* fortified village perched above the Vésubie; Church of St. Véran (Gothic) with an Annunciation★ (15thC school of Nice) and a 17thC carved altarpiece of Christ's Passion. 6 km SW from the village is the **panorama of Madonna of Utelle**★★★ **:** a pilgrimage site since 850. ▶ **Lantosque**★ ®. ▶ **Roquebillière :** often rebuilt in the wake of floods and landslides; excursion to the **Gordolasque Valley**★★ *(18 km,* D171), waterfalls, attractive village of Belvédère★. ▶ **Saint-Martin-Vésubie** ® : an excursion centre in the heart of this Alpine landscape. ▶ **Le Boréon**★ *(8 km N from Saint-Martin) :* surrounded by woods and pastures; waterfall★, departure point for **Mercantour National Park**★★. ▶ **Madonna of Fenestre**★ *(13 km NE) :* a magnificent mountain amphitheatre★★. ▶ **Venanson**★ *(4.5 km S) :* view; frescos in the chapel of St. Sébastien. ▶ **The Valdeblore Road**★ W leads *(25 km)* to the Tinée Valley★★ (→) via **La Colmiane** (winter sports; chairlift to Colmiane Peak, panorama★★); **Saint-Dalmas** (11thC Romanesque church); **La Bolline :** a cosy summer resort; **Rimplas**★ *(2 km right)* on a rock crest. □

Architecture

Dwellings are usually clustered in Provence. In country towns, whether on the plain or perched high on a mountain crag, houses seem to be piled one on top of the other. The areas where the typical dwelling is an isolated *mas, bastide* or *domaine* (see below) are the exceptions to the general rule. ● The pattern is derived from the idea that there is safety in numbers. A tight cluster of buildings could be more easily defended from invasion than a trail of scattered houses. The earliest settlements were Celto-Ligurian strongholds. ● The Romans

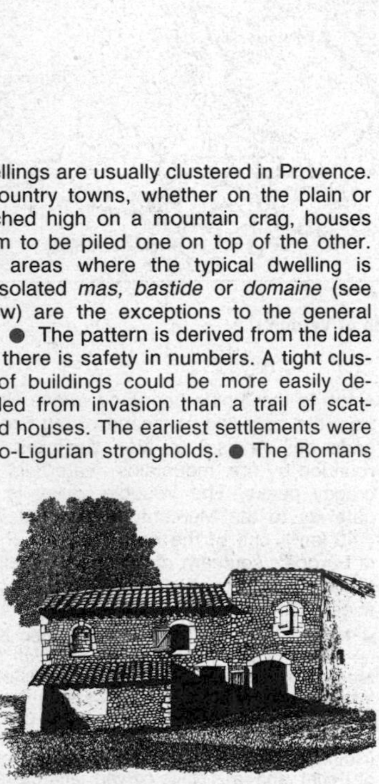

Provençale house

built more dispersed villas, with large homesteads surrounded by outbuildings near springs, rivers or highways. The 10thC fortified village showed characteristics very similar to those of Provençal villages of today : tall terraced houses and narrow streets. In the 19thC, villages began to spread down from the rocky peaks to be nearer roads and cultivated land. ● Today the countryside is dotted with neo-rustic Provençal country cottages, although admirers from colder parts of France, as well as some Provençal natives, have started to restore and rehabilitate real villages that have fallen into disrepair. ● The Provençal village is urbanised, with ramparts, three to five-story houses, courtyards, and squares that are the hub of everyday life. ● The village house maintains a stable, coach-house and storeroom on the ground floor. On the first floor, the *salle* is living-room, dining room and kitchen in one. On the upper floors are the bedrooms, topped by a loft, with a projecting pulley-beam. The house is essentially a feminine domain, whereas the men have the freedom of the square, the *café* and the *boule* (bowling) ground.

An isolated dwelling is called a *mas, bastide* or *domaine*. The *mas* is a smallholding with a patch of land; the house usually has two stories in the plain and three in the hills. ● A *domaine,* immediately distinguishable from a *mas* by its size, is a farmstead on a large estate. The building includes the farmhouse, staff quarters, and workshops or outhouses. This sort of building is an outstanding feature of the plains of the Crau, the Camargue and the Haut Var, as well as the Albion and Valensole plateaux.

● The *bastide,* typically found near towns on the western coast and around Aix, is traditionally a well-to-do city-dweller's house, combining rustic pleasures (fine gardens, decorations) with the means of livelihood, such as agricultural holdings and workshops. ● For the *mas,* construction materials and techniques vary according to means and locality. Whether walls are built of field stone, stones from riverbeds (as in the Crau and the Durance valley), or cob (Alpilles, Vaucluse, Camargue), they are always faced with *crépi* (rough-cast plaster or mortar) and a mixture of sand, lime and crushed terra-cotta. According to the proportions used, the finished wall may be pink (mostly old tile), or orange or mauve (local sand). The exceptions are in the alpine foothills, where the houses are faced with stone. ● Irregularly spaced door and win-

Hillside village street

dow openings are framed in stone and have brightly painted shutters. ● *Bastides* and *domaines* are built of stone, with wrought-iron for balconies, door-knockers and balustrades, as well as door and window-frame mouldings. Unlike the *mas,* these houses have windows placed symmetrically either side of the door. ● Except for occasional houses with stone roofs (Lure Mountain) and thatched cabins in the Camargue, the Provençal roof is covered with round tiles, which are made at Marseilles, Aubagne, Arles, Lambesc, or Auriol.

● In the 18thC, Italian masons introduced the *génoise* or *génévoise,* a now characteristic cornice of two to four rows of hollow tiles set under the edge of the roof to keep rain-water from the façade. ● Drystone or masonry vaulting is frequently seen in Provence in preference to wooden ceilings covered with plaster; it lessens fire risk and is a good form of insulation in both grand and humble buildings.

● Similarly, the handsome *maloun,* the red or brown flooring tiles may be square, triangular, hexagonal *(tomettes)* or even octagonal. ● Annexes include the wine cellar (vaulted and facing N, a most important building in this land of vineyards); the cocoonery under the eaves for the breeding of silkworms; the sheep-pen (integral or separate) and the dovecote, also typical of rural houses. ● A uniquely Provençal feature is the *cabanon,* a shed or shack built to serve as a temporary habitation or a storage hut, but often used for uproarious gatherings as a refuge from domestic order. The *cabanon* and the *borie* (→ box) today serve much the same purpose.

● The *cabanon* of the Camargue is a temporary shelter for *gardians* (cowherds), shepherds or fishermen. The framework is of elm, with reed wattle and lime mortar for the walls and plaited rushes for the roof. An inclined cross is placed at the northern *(mistral)* end, for protection against nameless dangers.

Camargue cabin *(cabane)*

Brief regional history

7thC BC-5thC AD

The Phocean Greeks founded the city of **Massalia** (Marseilles) around 600BC, but it was the **Romans** who **developed Provence.** Arles, Frèjus, Glanum and Orange were Roman settlements in the region then called **Provincia,** whose inland areas were renowned for the quality of the olive oil and corn they produced, and whose coastal towns thrived by ship-building.

5th-15thC

After the fall of the Western Roman Empire in 476, Provincia was invaded by Visigoths, Burgundians and Ostrogoths in rapid succession. Finally, the **Franks peacefully annexed** the region and created a territory of Provence, which was integrated with Burgundy under the administration of counts and viscounts. ● **William the Liberator,** a count who had earned his epithet by recovering a provençal fort from the Saracens, took the title of *marquis de Provence* in 972 and instituted the first dynasty of the Counts of Provence. ● Provence remained a distinct entity during succeeding centuries, passing by marriage to the **Counts of Catalonia,** and later to the house of Anjou. **Charles du Maine** bequeathed Provence to King Louis XI of France in 1481.

15th-17thC

Under the terms of the **Provençal Constitution,** the two states were to unite on equal terms, and Provence was to retain its rights and privileges. ● The central authorities lost no opportunity to weaken the autonomy of the region and, in fact, since the 16thC, the political history of Provence has been a rearguard action against **administrative centralisation.** ● During the 16th and 17thC, the agriculture of Provence changed radically; although sheep and corn remained the basis of the economy, **vineyards** and mulberries spread as the wine and silk industries developed. Land was cleared to accommodate a growing population, and shipbuilding made inroads on the forests. Other important industries were tanning, paper-making, textiles and pottery, including roofing tiles. ● By 1660, **Toulon** was the **largest naval port** in the Mediterranean but in the following century, **Marseilles** outstripped it, prospering from soap-making and tallow-rendering. In 1720, the Plague struck : Marseilles alone lost half its population (38 000 dead) and Provence as a whole lost 100 000 people.

1790 to the present

The political reorganisation that followed the French Revolution **eliminated Provence** as an administrative entity; the departments of **Bouches-du-Rhône, Var** and **Basses-Alpes** were created in 1790, and the following year **Vaucluse** was fashioned from the former Papal States; **Alpes Maritimes** came into being in 1793 and, finally, **Savoy** and **Nice** were **annexed to France in 1860** in exchange for Napoléon III's support for Italian independence. In 1861 France bought Menton and Roquebrune from the Prince of Monaco.

● The opening of the PLM (Paris-Lyons-Marseilles) railway, together with the choice of Nice as the favourite winter resort of the English leisure classes towards the end of the 19thC established Provence-Côte d'Azur as one of the most desirable holiday destinations in the world, which it remains today.

Practical information

The region

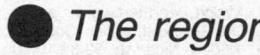

Information : *Comité régional du Tourisme Provence-Alpes-Côte d'Azur* (C.R.T.) : 22A, rue Louis-Maurel, 13006 Marseille, ☎ 91.37.91.22. *C.R.T. Riviera-Côte d'Azur,* 55, prom. des Anglais, 06000 Nice, ☎ 93.44.50.59. **Alpes-de-Haute-Provence :** *Chambre départementale du Tourisme,* rd-pt du 11-Novembre, Maison du Tourisme, 04000 Digne, ☎ 92.31.29.26. **Alpes-Maritimes :** *C.D.T.,* same address as Riviera-Côte d'Azur C.R.T. **Bouches-du-Rhône :** *C.D.T.,* 6, rue du Jeune-Anacharsis, 13001 Marseille, ☎ 91.54.92.66. **Var :** *C.D.T.,* 1, bd Foch, 83300 Draguignan, ☎ 94.68.58.33. **Vaucluse :** *Chambre départementale du Tourisme,* pl. Campana, quartier de la Balance, B.P. 147, 84008 Avignon Cedex, ☎ 90.86.43.42.

Bookings : *Loisirs-Accueil Bouches-du-Rhône,* domaine du Vergon, 13370 Mallemort, ☎ 90.59.18.05. *Vaucluse-Tourisme-Hébergement,* hall of the Avignon train station ; a hotel reservation centre for the department, France and abroad. Info, ☎ 90.85.56.68 ; reservations, ☎ 90.82.05.81.

Maps : *Michelin* nos 81, 84, 77, 83, 93 and 245 (Provence-Côte d'Azur), 1/200 000 ; *I.G.N.* no 115 1/250 000 and 52, 54, 59, 60, 61, 66, 67, 68 1/100 000.

S.O.S. : Alpes-de-Haute-Provence : ☎ 17. **Alpes-Maritimes :** ☎ 93.92.55.55. **Bouches-du-Rhône, Var** and **Vaucluse :** *SAMU* (emergency medical service) : ☎ 91.49.91.91. *Poisoning Emergency Centre :* Marseilles, ☎ 91.75.25.25.

Weather forecast : Alpes-de-Haute-Provence : ☎ 92.64.17.47. **Alpes-Maritimes :** mountain conditions, ☎ 93.72.31.33. **Bouches-du-Rhône :** ☎ 42.09.09.09. **Var :** coastal forecast, ☎ 94.46.90.11 ; mountain conditions : ☎ 94.64.17.47. **Vaucluse :** ☎ 90.86.55.48 (road conditions), ☎ 90.82.69.00 (snow conditions in winter, schedule of events in summer).

Rural gîtes and chambres d'hôte : enq at relais départementaux : **Alpes-de-Haute-Provence,** ☎ 92.31.52.59, and **Alpes-Maritimes** at the C.D.T. **Bouches-du-Rhône :** domaine du Vergon, 13370 Mallemort, ☎ 90.59.18.05. **Var :** 1, bd Foch, 83300 Draguignan, ☎ 94.68.55.43, ext 223. **Vaucluse :** chambre dép. du Tourisme, ☎ 90.85.45.00 and 90.86.43.42.

Camping : approx 1 250 campsites. Enq : T.O. and C.D.T.

Festivals and cultural events : Jan : *International Record and Music Publications Festival* (Midem) in Cannes ; concerts in Menton. **Feb :** *Television Festival* in Monaco. **Apr :** *Festival of Unusual Films* in Digne ; *Festival of Young Soloists* in Antibes. **May :** *International Cartoon Festival* in Aix-en-Provence ; Apt *Music Festival ;* Cannes *International Cinema Festival (usually May).* **Jun :** Aix *en musique ; Festival du Café-Théâtre* in Cannes ; *Religious Music Festival ; Biennale of engraving* at the Museum alternates with *Symposium of Street Sculpture* in Nice. *Cinema Festival* (Lumière brothers' pioneering silent films) in La Ciotat. **Jul :** Aix *International Music Festival ; Arts Festival* — music, photography, dance — in Arles ; *Jazz Festival* in Antibes-Juan-les-Pins, Nice and Salon ; *International Folk Festival* at Château-Gombert in Marseilles ; *Chorégies (choral festival)* in Orange. **Mid-Jul :** *Christian art festival* in Digne ; *Festival of Early Music* in Sénanque-Gordes ; *"Nights of the Citadel"* in Sisteron ; *International Dance Festival* in Châteauvallon ; *New Orleans Jazz Festival* in Saint-Raphaël ; *Jazz Festival* 13 Jul in Digne ; *Nuits du Pian,* concerts in Menton ; *Festival of the Théâtre du Pont d'Olive,* Brignoles ; *Festival* in Vaison-la-Romaine. **Aug :** *Dramatic Arts Festival* in Avignon ; Menton *Music Festival ; "Musical Weeks"* in the Lubéron region ; *"Musical Encounters"* in Saint-Rémy-de-Provence ; Sisteron *Art and Music Festival ; Piano Festival* in La Roque-d'Anthéron. **Sep :** *Young Cinema Festival* in Hyères ; *September Music Festival* in Menton ; *Musical Autumn* in Digne. **Oct :** *International history and archeology meetings* in Antibes : *"Mediaeval Days"* in Brignoles ; *VIDCOM (video and communications exhibition)* in Cannes. **Dec :** *International Marionette Festival* in Cannes ; *International Religious Music Festival* in Marseilles ; *Italian Film Festival* in Nice ; *Cartoon Festival* in Hyères ; Monaco *International Circus Festival.*

Fairs and folklore : Jan : *fête des tripettes* (tripes ; held Feast of St-Marcel) in Barjols. **Feb :** plant fair in Draguignan ; *"Candlemas" fete* in Marseilles ; *lemon fete* in Menton ; *carnival* in Nice. **Mar :** Marseilles *International Fair ; bric-à-brac fair* in Sainte-Maxime ; *spring fair* in Grans. **May :** *bric-à-brac fair* in Avignon ; *rose fete* in Grasse ; **24 and 25 :** *Pilgrimage of the Gypsies* to Les Saintes-Maries-de-la-Mer ; *horse fair* in Eyguières. **Jun :** *carreto zamado* (Saracen-style chariot races) in Barbeurane ; *olive fair* in Draguignan ; *Mediterranean Horse Show* in Marseilles ; *broom-flower festival* in Roquebrune-Cap-Martin ; *St-Peter's Fete* (patron saint of fishermen) in Menton, Cassis and Toulon ; *Santon Fair* in Valensole. **Aug :** *leather fair* in Barjols ; *wine fete* in Cogolin ; *Lavender Fete* in Digne ; *Jasmine Fete* in Grasse ; *traditional high-country farmer's and craftsmens' fair* in Aups ; *pilgrimage* from Saint-Symphorien to Vernegues. **Sep :** *Horse Fair* in Le Luc ; *livestock fair* in Salon. **Oct :** *Pilgrimage of the Gypsies* to Saintes-Maries-de-la-Mer ; *chestnut fete* in Les Mayons. **Nov :** *chestnut fete* in Isola. **Dec :** *Santon Fair* (clay or carved wood nativity figures) in Marseilles ; *provencale midnight mass* in Allauch, in Séguret (arrive early) ; *shepherds' fete* in Les Baux, *santon fairs* in Toulon and Solliès-ville ; *the path of the cribs* in Menton.

Sporting events : Apr : hike up mont Faron ; *International Tennis Open* in Monaco. **May :** *Grand Motorcycle Prix de France* in Le Castellet ; *Formula 1 Grand Prix* in Monaco ; *Terre de Provence Rally* (Fri, Sat, Sun). **Jun :** *Old Ports crossing* in varied craft in Marseilles. **Jul :** *Formula 1 Grand Prix* in Le Castellet. **Sept :** *Bol d'Or* (production motorcycle race) in Le Castellet.

Scenic railways : *Pignes train,* from Nice to

Digne, *Chemins de Fer de Provence,* 52, rue Dabray, 06100 Nice, ☎ 93.88.28.56.

River cruises : on the Rhône, aboard *le Cygne :* info and reservations, quai de la Ligne, 84000 Avignon, ☎ 66.59.45.08, 1 May-14 Aug and at S.I. ; *Hermès :* info, ☎ 90.82.65.11, and VTY at the station, ☎ 90.85.56.68.

National and nature parks : *Mercantour National Park,* 23, rue d'Italie, 06000 Nice, ☎ 93.87.86.10 ; *Maison du Park,* La Sapinière, 04000 Barcelonnette, ☎ 92.81.21.31 ; *Port-Cros National Park,* 50, av. Gambetta, 83400 Hyères, ☎ 94.65.32.98. *Camargue Nature Park,* Le Mas de Pont-de-Rousty, 13200 Arles, ☎ 90.97.10.93. Map *I.G.N.* 303, *Lubéron Nature Park,* pl. Jean-Jaurès, 84400 Apt, ☎ 90.74.08.55.

Rambling and hiking : the region is traversed by G.R. tracks 4, 5, 6, 9, 52, 56, 91, 92, 97 (topoguides). The *Didier-Richard* maps, 1/50 000 n°s 1, 9, 19 are also very useful (alternative trails and shelters). List of member associations of the *Féd. francaise de la Randonnée pédestre* at the *comité régional P.A.C.A.,* 123, allée des Temps-Perdus, 84300 Cavaillon, ☎ 90.71.26.05. **Alpes-de-Haute-Provence :** *Assn. dép. des Relais et Itinéraires* (A.D.R.I.), 14, bd V.-Hugo, 04000 Digne, ☎ 92.31.37.70. **Alpes-Maritimes :** *Comité dép. de la Randonnée pédestre,* M. Resse, Villa Taéma, Montaleigne, 06700 Saint-Laurent-du-Var ; *Sentiers Amitié Montagne,* 70, bd Perrier, 06110 Le Cannet, ☎ 93.45.16.43. **Bouches-du-Rhône :** *Comité dép. de la Randonnée pédestre,* 16, rue de la Rotonde, 13001 Marseille ; I.G.N. 269 for the Calanques (B.d.R.) ; *Excursionnistes Marseillais,* 33, allées Léon-Gambetta, 13001 Marseille ; *Excursionnistes provencaux,* 8, rue du Littera, 13100 Aix-en-Provence, ☎ 42.21.03.53. **Var :** *Comité dép. du Var de la F.F.R.P.,* 3, imp. Baudin, 83000 Toulon ; *Excursionnistes toulonnais,* 26, rue d'Alger, 83000 Toulon. *Assn. Lei Caminaire,* Le Valat-Seillans, 83440 Fayence, ☎ 94.76.06.04. **Vaucluse :** *Comité départemental,* 63, av. C.-Franck, 84000 Avignon. *Cimes et Sentiers du Haut-Comtat,* Centre culturel A Cœur Joie, av. C.-Geoffrey, 84110 Vaison-la-Romaine. The *Chambre dép. de Tourisme* publishes a brochure with map indicating rambling and hiking possibilities in the department.

Riding holidays : map 1/50 000 « En Haute-Provence », n°s 14, 19 and 24, Ed. Didier-Richard. Var and Alpes-Maritimes : *Assn. régionale pour le Tourisme Équestre et l'Équitation de Loisirs,* Arte Proca, 19, bd V.-Hugo, 06130 Grasse, ☎ 93.42.62.98. Vaucluse, Bouches-du-Rhône, Alpes-de-Haute-Provence : *Assn. régionale pour le Tourisme équestre,* Maison du Docteur, 13810 Eygalières, ☎ 90.95.90.57.

Horse-drawn holidays : hire-location : M. Moyne, domaine St-Sauveur, 84320 Entraigues, ☎ 90.83.16.26. M. Pavon, le Clos des Princes, 84660 Maubec, ☎ 90.71.90.29 and 90.71.70.91.

Cycling holidays : Var and Alpes-Maritimes : *Comité dép. de Féd. francaise de cyclo,* 259, chemin rural 133, quartier d'Ouicarde, 83500 La Seyne. *Comité Dép. du Cyclotourisme des Alpes-de-Haute-Provence,* M. Exubis, 22, av. de St-Véran, La Cassette, 04000 Digne. *Comité dép. du Cyclotourisme des Bouches-du-Rhône,* M. Maillet, 15, lotissement de la Trevaresse, 13540 Puyricard, ☎ 42.92.13.41. *Comité dép. de Cyclotourisme du Vaucluse,* M. Gouttebaron, 2, rue Lavoisier, 84000 Avignon.

Handicraft courses : painting, drawing : *Académie internationale d'Été,* villa Paradisio, 21, bd de Cimiez, 06000 Nice, ☎ 93.81.64.06 ; pottery, weaving, spinning : *Centre culturel,* domaine de l'Étoile, 293, av. Pessicart, 06000 Nice, ☎ 93.84.48.12. Wood working : *L'Escarène,* Assn. Peira Cava (information centre), ☎ 93.91.57.97. Weaving : O. Miquau, La Gipote, Les Jaisons, 06530 Peymenade, ☎ 93.66.06.13. Wood, earthernware, leather, silk, crafts, etc. : M. Goutelle, palais Couperin, 15, rue Guiglia, 06000 Nice, ☎ 93.88.13.70 ; *Neiges et Merveilles,* 06430 St-Dalmas-de-Tende, ☎ 93.04.62.40 ; *C.A.M.A.S.,* 6, av. des Poilus, 06140 Vence, ☎ 93.58.03.01. *A.D.A.C.,* domaine de la Garde, rte de Berre, 13150 Éguilles, ☎ 42.92.43.33. *Art et handicrafts,* Mme Mercier, 30, bd Michelet, 13008 Marseille, ☎ 91.77.07.50. *Artisanat Club Mazarin,* 30, rue Cardinale, 13100 Aix-en-Provence, ☎ 42.38.46.60. Alpes-de-Haute-Provence : A.R.T.I.S.A.R.T., 7, bd Mirabeau, 04100 Manosque, ☎ 92.87.56.11. Further enq at C.D.T. and C.R.T.

Other courses : cooking for beginners : *École du Moulin* (under direction of leading chef Roger Verge), Moulin de Mougins, Notre-Dame-de-Vie, 06250 Mougins, ☎ 93.75.78.24. *Académie nicoise de Cuisine,* restaurant l'Academia, 15, rue A.-Mari, 06300 Nice, ☎ 93.62.35.00. Introduction to gastronomy, info at C.D.T./S.L.A. Bouches-du-Rhône. Geology courses from Jul to Sep at Digne (info T.O.).

Youth activities : *Assn. Langues vivantes et Aventures,* Pierrefeu, 06910 Roquestéron, ☎ 93.08.56.15 (language courses, craftwork, excursions). *Vacances Bleues,* 20 *bis,* av. G.-Clemenceau, 06000 Nice, ☎ 93.88.01.13 (tennis and riding courses). ARC, 71, av. des Tuilières, 06800 Cagnes-sur-Mer, ☎ 93.07.28.71 (canoeing). *Aroeven,* Rectorat, 06081 Nice Cedex, ☎ 93.81.45.96 (road from Nice to Digne).

Tennis : Enq at T.O.

Golf : 18-hole courses in Aix-en-Provence, Les Milles, Antibes-Biot, Cannes-Mougins, La Londe-Valcros, Mandelieu-La Napoule, Peille-Mont-Agel, Saint-Raphaël-Valescure and Valbonne ; 9-hole courses in Sainte-Maxime-Beauvallon and Tende-Vievola.

Aquatic sports : numerous marinas and inland stretches of water. Enq at T.O. and C.D.T.

Scuba diving : *Centre international de Plongée,* 2, ruelle de Moulins (port), 06000 Nice, ☎ 93.55.59.50. *Féd. de Plongée,* 24, quai de Rive-Neuve, 13007 Marseille, ☎ 91.33.99.31.

Canoeing : *Comité dép. des Bouches-du-Rhône,* 142, av. J.-Vidal, 13008 Marseille, ☎ 91.73.30.93. *Comité dép. des Alpes-Maritimes,* la Vignerette, quartier la Tour, 06700 St-Laurent-du-Var, ☎ 93.07.82.15. *Jeunes-Canoë-Kayak d'Avignon,* 66, rue des Tireuses-de-Soie, ☎ 90.87.52.47. Ligue Alpes-Provence, ☎ 66.89.83.10.

Potholing and spelunking : *Délégation régionale Provence-Alpes-Côte d'Azur,* M. Acquaviva, 29, bd Rodocanachi, 13008 Marseille. *Comités dép. : Alpes-de-Haute-Provence,* M. Languille, quartier de Trégastel, 04220 Sainte-Tulle, ☎ 92.78.20.89. Bouches-du-Rhône : M. Carol, F4, rés. Bayonne, 13800 Istres. Var : M. Tainton, Le Pont-d'Arroun, 83110 Sanary.

Climbing-mountaineering : *F.F.M.,* 15, av. J.-Médecin, 06000 Nice (list of clubs). *C.A.F. :* same address, ☎ 93.87.75.41, Section Ubaye : mairie, 04400 Barcelonnette, ☎ 92.81.04.73. *Féd. de la Montagne,* 12, rue Fort-Notre-Dame, 13007 Marseille. Vaucluse : C.D.T. and O.T.

Winter sports : downhill skiing, ski treks, cross-country skiing : *F.F.M.*, 15, av. J.-Médecin, 06000 Nice. *F.F.S.*, Comité régional de Ski Côte d'Azur, 39, rue Pastorelli, 06000 Nice, ☎ 93.80.65.77. *AGRAM (Assn. des guides et accompagnateurs des Alpes méridionales) :* office in Saint-Martin-Vésubie, ☎ 93.03.21.28, 93.03.20.73 ; Isola 2000, ☎ 93.23.10.50 ; Tende, ☎ 93.04.60.90 ; Saint-Jeannet, ☎ 93.59.53.38 ; Valberg, ☎ 93.02.52.34. For the Haute-Ubaye region, guide office in Barcelonnette, T.O., ☎ 92.81.04.71.

Gliding : *Ligue du Sud-Est de vol à voile,* M. Gianti, Le Collet-de-Christine, 83440 Les Tourettes-Fayence, ☎ 93.20.97.22. *Union aérienne Sisteron-Durance* at Van Meilh, 04200 Sisteron, ☎ 92.61.27.45.

Parachuting : *Ligue Provence de Parachutisme,* 8, rue Venture, 13006 Marseille, ☎ 91.33.38.69. *Ligue Côte d'Azur de Parachutisme,* B.P. 8, Le Cannet-des-Maures, 83340 Le Luc, ☎ 94.60.72.83. *Centre inter-clubs,* aérodrome Avignon-Pujant, ☎ 90.25.19.20.

Hang-gliding : *Ligue du vol à voile libre du Sud-Est,* 30, rue Guiglia, 06000 Nice, ☎ 93.88.52.19. *Ligue de Provence,* Le Garagaï, domaine de Roques-Blanches, 13777 Venelles, ☎ 42.57.76.67.

Flying in ultra-light aircraft : *Centre de Provence-Côte d'Azur de vol ultra-léger,* 83129 La Mole, ☎ 94.49.57.71. *Centre national de Formation U.L.M.*, Rustrel, 84400 Apt, ☎ 90.74.30.00. Délég. Ref. S.E. Aérodrome Trets.

Hunting and shooting : enq at the *Féd. dép. des chasseurs,* **Alpes-de-Haute-Provence :** 79, bd Gassendi, 04000 Digne, ☎ 92.31.02.43. **Alpes-maritimes :** P.A.L., 7 M.I.N., St-Augustin, 06042 Nice Cedex, ☎ 93.83.82.39. **Bouches-du-Rhône :** quartier Maliverny, 13540 Puyricard, ☎ 42.92.16.75. **Var :** 7, bd G.-Péri, 83300 Draguignan, ☎ 94.68.03.13. **Vaucluse :** rés. Thiers, rue R.-Salengro, 84000 Avignon, ☎ 90.82.51.99.

Fishing : *Féd. dép. de la Pêche.* **Alpes-Maritimes :** 20, bd V.-Hugo, 06000 Nice, ☎ 93.03.24.09. **Alpes-de-Haute-Provence :** 79, bd Gassendi, 04000 Digne, ☎ 92.31.57.14. **Bouches-du-Rhône :** 30, bd de la République, 13100 Aix-en-Provence, ☎ 42.26.59.15. **Var :** B.P. 104, 83170 Brignoles, ☎ 94.69.05.56. **Vaucluse :** *Maison de l'Agriculture,* 40, bd G.-Péri, 84000 Avignon, ☎ 90.86.62.68.

Towns

AIX-EN-PROVENCE

Avignon 75, Nice 176, Paris 753
B2-3 ✉ 13090

☎ 42.26.01.18.

ℹ 2, pl. Gal-de-Gaulle (A2), ☎ 42.26.02.93.

✈ Marseille-Marignane, 27 km NW, ☎ 42.89.90.10.

Air France Agency : 2, rue Aude, ☎ 42.26.26.21.

SNCF (A2), ☎ 42.27.51.63, 42.26.02.89.

rue Lapierre (A2), ☎ 42.27.17.91.

Car-hire : *Budget* train + auto, at the station, ☎ 42.26.12.50.

Hotels :
● ★★★★***Pigonnet*** (PLM), 5, av. du Pigonnet (A2), ☎ 42.59.02.90. Tx 410629. AE, Euro, Visa. 50 rm Charming residence, 520. Rest. ♦♦♦ ***le Patio*** closed Sun eve 1 Nov-31 Mar. Traditional fare served in a garden setting, 100-140.
● ★★★***Augustins,*** 3, rue de la Masse, ☎ 42.27.28.59. 29 rm closed 20 Dec-15 Jan, 400.
● ★★★***Manoir*** (Relais du Silence), 8, rue d'Entrecasteaux (A1-2), ☎ 42.26.27.20. Tx 44189. AE, Visa. 43 rm closed 15 Jan - 15 Feb. A charming historical building with a 16thC cloister and historic furnishings, 370.
★★★***Nègre-Coste,*** 33, cours Mirabeau (A2), ☎ 42.27.74.22. Tx 440181. AE, Euro, Visa. 37 rm 350.
★★★***Paul Cézanne,*** 40, av. Victor-Hugo (A2), ☎ 42.26.34.73. AE. 44 rm closed 1-20 Jan. Quality hotel ; traditional furnishings, 450.

Celony, 3 km NW on the N7 :
★★★★***Mas d'Entremont,*** montée d'Avignon N7, ☎ 42.23.45.32. 14 rm closed 1 Nov-15 Mar. Attractively furnished ; patio, 380. Rest. ♦♦♦ closed Sun eve and Mon noon, 130-170.

Beaurecueil, 10 km E on the N7 and D58 :
★★★***Mas de la Bertrande,*** Le Maistre, ☎ 42.28.90.09. AE, Euro, Visa. 10 rm closed 15-25 Feb, 380. Rest. ♦♦ closed Sun eve and Mon. Good meals, 160-230.
★★***Relais Ste-Victoire*** (L.F.), ☎ 42.28.91.34. AE, Euro, Visa. 8 rm closed Feb, Sun eve and Mon, 200. Rest. ♦♦ Large selection of refined dishes. Spec : home-smoked salmon, 160-300.

Roquefavour, 12 km W on the A8 and D64 :
★★***Arquier*** (L.F., Relais du Silence), ☎ 42.24.21.97. Visa. 18 rm An expansive riverside park ; closed 15 Jan-15 Feb, Mon low season, 200. Rest. ♦♦ Dining in a garden. Spec : *coquilles St-Jacques au noilly, gigolette de volaille à la tapenade,* 100-170.

Youth hostel, av. Marcel-Pagnol, quartier Jas-de-Bouffan, ☎ 42.20.15.99.

★★★★*Arc-en-ciel* (80 pl.), ☎ 42.26.14.28 ; ★★★★*Chantecler* (240 pl.), ☎ 42.26.12.98.

Restaurants :
● ♦♦ ***Caves Henri IV,*** 32, rue Espariat (A2), ☎ 42.27.86.39. Visa closed 5-26 Aug, Feb school hols, Sun and Mon. Splendid 16thC vaulted cellars. Spec : *terrine de lapereaux et pleurotes en gelée de vin blanc au romarin, vapeur de saumon frais et petits légumes à l'estragon,* 150-300.
● ♦♦ ***Aux Semailles,*** 15, rue Brueys (A2), ☎ 42.27.23.44 closed Sun and Mon noon. Three delighful, intimate dining-rooms make up this charming restaurant. Spec : *mignonnette de sole au gingembre, entremet glacé au café et son coulis au caramel,* 130-200.
♦♦ ***La Brocherie,*** 5, rue Fernand-Dol, ☎ 42.38.33.21. AE, DC, Euro, Visa Seasonal produce cooked by A. Barbarant : *gâteau de lapin en gelée, dorade rose grillée, loup en croûte, bourride, bouillabaisse,* 90-150.
♦♦ ***Vendôme,*** 2 *bis,* av. Napoléon-Bonaparte (A2), ☎ 42.26.01.00. AE, Euro, Visa closed Sep-Jun, Tue eve and Wed. Attractive terrace, 170-270.
● ♦ ***Clam's,*** 22, cours Sextius (A1), ☎ 42.27.64.78 closed Wed, 15 Jul-Aug.

Friendly restaurant, sea produce. Spec : seafood steamed in seaweed hot oysters, raw sea-perch, 120-120.

Le Jas-de-Bouffan, 3 km W on the D10 :
● ♦♦ ***Les Nutons-Castellino,*** rte de Berre, ☎ 42.59.55.00. AE, Visa Ⓟ ♨ ♿ closed Wed. Simple and rustic. Spec : meat grilled over a wood fire, *mérou à l'aioli, bouillabaisse,* 65-140.

Puyfond, 7 km on the N96 and D13 :
♦♦ ***Puyfond,*** quartier Rigoulon, ☎ 42.92.13.77 Ⓟ ♨ closed Feb, Mon and Tue, Wed, Thu, Fri and Sat noons, Sun eve. Book ahead. Enchanting Provençal farmhouse with regional specialities, 150-180.

Casino, pl. Jeanne-d'Arc, ☎ 42.26.30.33.

Recommended : calissons d'Aix (local sweets). *Confiserie Vendôme,* 27 *bis,* rue du 11-Novembre, ☎ 42.23.42.96.

ANDON

Grasse 34, Castellane 36, Paris 834
33 km NW of Grasse, C2 ✉ 06750 Caille

L'Audibergue, 1 195-1 642 m

Hotel :
★***Auberge d'Andon,*** ☎ 93.60.45.11. Visa. 15 rm Ⓟ ♨ ♿ closed 1 May-1 Jun, 1 Nov-15 Dec, 170. Rest. 85-110.

Farmhouse-inn and table d'hôte : *domaine du Castellaros,* les Quatre-Chemins-de-Thorenc, ☎ 93.60.00.25/93.60.00.37. Riding.

ANNOT

Castellane 32, Digne 70, Paris 815
C2 ✉ 04240

ⓘ pl. du Revely, ☎ 92.83.22.09.

Hotel :
★★***Grac*** (L.F.), pl. du Germe, ☎ 92.83.20.02. AE. 23 rm ♨ closed 1 Nov-31 Mar, 130. Rest. ♦ ♿ closed Wed (Apr, May, Oct). Enjoyable fare. Spec : *civet de sanglier à l'ancienne, truite maison (porto, crème fraîche et amandes),* 70-140.

⛺ ★★*La Ribière* (53 pl.), ☎ 92.83.21.44.

ANTIBES

Nice 23, Aix 58, Paris 916
D2 ✉ 06600

ⓘ pl. Gal-de-Gaulle, ☎ 93.33.95.64.

SNCF ☎ 93.33.75.66.

Car-hire : *Budget* train + car, at the station, ☎ 93.33.63.51, and 42, av. R.-Soleau, ☎ 93.33.66.83.

Hotels :
● ★★★***Royal,*** bd Mal-Leclerc, ☎ 93.34.03.09. AE, DC, Visa. 43 rm Ⓟ ♿ closed 30 Oct-1 Jan, 380. Rest. ♦♦ ***le Dauphin*** closed Wed low season, 100-250.
★★★***Josse,*** 8, bd James-Wyllie, ☎ 93.61.47.24. Tx 470673. Visa. 29 rm Ⓟ ♿ closed 15 Nov-15 Dec, 15-31 Jan, 400. Rest. ♦♦ closed 1 Nov-31 Jan and Wed, 80-120.
★★★***Mas Djoliba,*** 29, av. de Provence, ☎ 93.34.02.48. Tx 461686. AE, DC, Visa. 14 rm Ⓟ ♨ Beautiful 3 000 m² garden ; well situated between the town centre and the beach, 350. Rest ♦ ♿ closed noon, 100-120.
★***Auberge Provençale*** (L.F.), 61, pl. Nationale, ☎ 93.34.13.24. AE, Euro, Visa. 6 rm, closed 25 Oct-15 Nov, 1-5 May, Sun eve and Mon, 250. Rest. ♦♦ ♿ Terrace and attractive furnishings. Light, original dishes, 75-200.

Biot, ✉ 06410, 7 km N :
★***Arcades,*** 16, pl. des Arcades, ☎ 93.65.01.04. 11 rm 220. Rest. ● ♦ closed Nov-Dec, Sun and Mon. Friendly café-gallery in a 15thC house, art and gastronomy go well together. Provençal country cooking : *aioli, sardines farcies, raviolis,* 120-210.

Cap d'Antibes :
● ★★★★(L) ***Résidence du Cap,*** 161, bd Kennedy, ☎ 93.61.09.44. 40 rm Ⓟ ♨ closed 20 Oct-Mar. Refinement and comfort in a small, palm-tree surrounded palace, 260. Rest. ♦♦♦ 120-210.
★★★★(L) ***Grand Hôtel,*** bd Kennedy, ☎ 93.61.39.01. Tx 470763. 100 rm Ⓟ ♨ closed mid-Oct to Easter. Superb palace with 20-acre grounds, overlooking the sea, 400. Rest. ♦♦♦ ***Cap Eden Roc,*** 200-310.
★★★***Gardiole,*** chemin de la Garoupe, ☎ 93.61.35.03. Tx 470915, 20 rm ♨ ♿ closed Nov-Jan. Charming hotel set among pine trees, 300. Rest. ♦♦ Good Provençal ambiance and cooking, 120-180.

⛺ ★★★★*Embruns* (50 pl.), ☎ 93.33.33.35 ; ★★★★*Frênes* (110 pl.), ☎ 93.33.36.52 ; ★★★★*Mimosas* (17 pl.), ☎ 93.33.52.76 ; ★★★*Camp Rossignol* (88 pl.), ☎ 93.33.56.98.

Restaurants :
♦♦♦♦ ***La Bonne Auberge*** (Relais et châteaux), N7, quartier de la Brague, ☎ 93.33.36.65. Tx 470989. AE, Visa. Ⓟ closed 12 Nov-20 Dec, 10 days in Mar. Classic-style *grande cuisine,* with a Provençal flair ; ingenious desserts *(gratin de fraises des bois),* 300-400.
♦♦ ***La Marguerite,*** 11, rue Sadi-Carnot, ☎ 93.34.08.27. Visa ♿ closed Sun eve, Mon and Tue noon from 15 Jun to 15 Sep. Elegant restaurant, 220-430.
♦♦ ***L'Écurie Royale,*** 33, rue Vauban, ☎ 93.34.76.20. AE, DC, Euro, Visa Ⓟ closed 20 Nov-30 Dec, Sun eve, Mon and Tue noon low season. Quality fare, 130-200.

Cap d'Antibes :
♦♦♦ ***Cabestan,*** 46, bd Garoupe, ☎ 93.61.77.70. AE, DC, Euro Ⓟ ♨ ♿ closed Mon noon and Tue noon (Jul-Aug) and Mon eve and Tue low season. Good meals, 150-280.
● ♦♦ ***Bacon,*** bd Bacon, ☎ 93.61.50.02. AE Ⓟ ♿ closed 15 Nov-31 Jan, Sun eve and Mon. Magnificent view over Anges Bay. Superb *bouillabaisse* and succulent steamed fish. Good wines, 220-500.
♦ ***Maryland,*** traverse des Nielles, ☎ 93.61.47.46. Closed Oct-Mar. Family astmosphere and traditional Provençal dishes, 80-130.

Biot, ✉ 06410, 7 km N :
● ♦♦♦ ***Auberge du Jarrier,*** 30, passage de la Bourgade, ☎ 93.65.11.68. AE, DC, Euro, Visa ♨ closed 18 Nov-18 Dec, 2-6 Mar, Mon eve and Tue low season and Tue and Wed noon (Jun, Jul, Aug). Seasonal produce served in a dream setting : *filet de loup à la crème d'huîtres et aux cèpes, aiguillette de canard au vinaigre de framboises, millefeuille chaud aux poires caramélisées,* 140-250.
♦♦ ***Café de la Poste,*** rue Saint-Sébastien, ☎ 93.65.00.07. Closed Wed, Dec-Jan. Superb inland regional cooking. Spec : *ravioles d'écrevisses cuites dans leur étuvée de légumes,* 120-210.

Casino : *California Bowling Club,* rte de Grasse, ☎ 93.33.23.45.

Bicycle hire : *Chez Chenu,* bd Dugommier, ☎ 93.33.89.75, and at the station, ☎ 93.33.63.51.

Recommended : Provençal market in the old town.

APT

Avignon 52, Digne 91, Paris 732
B2 ⊠ 84400

ⓘ pl. de la Bouquerie, ☎ 90.74.03.18.

SNCF ☎ 90.74.00.85.

Hotels :
★★**Le Ventoux** (L.F.), 67, av. V.-Hugo, ☎ 90.74.07.58 P ♿ 13 rm. closed Dec-Jan, 180. Rest. ♦♦ 60-150.
★★**Aptois,** 6, cours Lauze-de-Perret, ☎ 90.74.02.02. 26 rm P closed 15 Feb-15 Mar, 150.

Youth hostel : *Regain,* in Saignon, 7 km SE, ☎ 90.74.39.34, open Christmas and Easter seasons, 15 Jun-1 Oct.

⛺ ★★*Les Cèdres* (55 pl.), ☎ 90.74.14.61.

Restaurant :
Saint-Martin-de-Castillon, ⊠ 84630, 12 km E :
♦♦ *La Source,* rte de Viens, ☎ 90.75.21.58 closed 4 Jan-12 Feb, Sun eve and Mon. Several aviaries in the garden. Spec : *gourmandise du jardin, chevreau au beurre d'amandes,* 120-210.

Event : Jul-Aug handicrafts festival.

ARLES

Nîmes 30, Marseilles 91, Paris 729
A2 ⊠ 13200

ⓘ 35, pl. de la République (B3), ☎ 90.96.29.35.

SNCF (C1), ☎ 90.96.38.21.

Car-hire : *Budget* train + car, 4, bd Victor-Hugo, ☎ 90.96.75.23, and at the station, ☎ 90.96.01.58.

Hotels :
★★★★**Jules César** (Relais et châteaux), bd des Lices (B3), ☎ 90.93.43.20. Tx 400239. AE, DC, Euro, Visa. 60 rm P closed early Nov-22 Dec. A 17thC Carmelite monastery with attractive gardens, 600. Rest. ● ♦♦♦ **Lou Marquès,** ☎ 90.96.35.72. Original cooking with excellent ingredients. Spec : *bouillabaisse de baudroie, anguilles en marinière, gigot d'agneau de lait des Alpilles.* Good desserts, 140-250.
● ★★★**Arlatan,** 26, rue du Sauvage (D2), ☎ 90.93.56.66. AE, DC. 46 rm P One-time private mansion of the counts of Arlatan de Beaumont. Charming setting with original stone-work and beams, and antique furnishings, 400.
★★★**Villages du Soleil,** mas de Véran, quartier Fourchon, 3 km S, ☎ 90.96.50.68. Tx 401450. AE, DC, Visa. 72 rm P ♿ closed 2-23 Jan, 315. Rest. ♦ 80-130.

4.5 km N on the D35 and secondary road (V.O.) :
★★★**Mas de la Chapelle** (Châteaux-hôtels), ☎ 90.96.73.43. 12 rm P closed Feb, Sun eve low season. Exceptional setting for a glorious 16thC residence with 1/2 pension, 630. Rest. ♦♦♦ 140-220.

Raphèle, 4 km SE on N453 :
★★★**Auberge de la Fenière** (Relais du Silence), ☎ 90.98.45.34. Tx 441237. AE, Euro, Visa. 25 rm P ♿ Old Provençal farm-house in the heart of the Crau region, 370. Rest. ♦♦ closed 1 Nov-20 Dec, Sat noon low season and noon from Pentecost to 1 Nov, 125-190.

Chambre d'hôte : Mas du Grand Gageron, ☎ 90.97.00.09.

⛺ ★★*Bienheureuse* (70 pl.), ☎ 90.98.45.28 ; ★★*City* (100 pl.), ☎ 90.93.08.86 ; ★★*Rosiers* (100 pl.), ☎ 90.96.02.12.

Restaurants :
● ♦♦ **Vaccarès,** 9, rue Favorin (1st floor), pl. du Forum (B2), ☎ 90.96.06.17. Closed 20 Dec-20 Jan, 15-30 Jun, Sun and Mon ex nat hols. Terrace. The characterful, balanced, inventive and light cooking of Bernard Dumas. Spec : *petit sauté d'agneau au pistou, brouffado des mariniers du Rhône, filet de sangre à la poutargue,* 120-210.
♦ **Hostellerie des Arènes,** 62, rue du Refuge (B2), ☎ 90.96.13.05. Euro, Visa ; closed 15-30 Jun, 15 Dec-31 Jan, Tue eve and Wed low season. Reasonably-priced food in Provençal surroundings, 65-100.

AUBAGNE

Marseilles 17, Nice 180, Paris 794
B3 ⊠ 13400

SNCF ☎ 42.03.44.84.

Car-hire : *Budget* train + car, 79, av. de la République, ☎ 42.70.08.19.

Hotels :
★★★**Manon des Sources,** rte d'Éoures, ☎ 42.03.10.31. AE, Visa. 20 rm P 300. Rest. ♦♦ ♿ 170-300.

Géménos, ⊠ 13420, 5.5 km E on the D2 :
★★★★**Relais de la Madeleine,** pont de l'Étoile, exit from the A52 motorway, ☎ 42.82.20.05. Visa. 20 rm P 18thC farmhouse in the middle of a park ; closed 1 Nov-15 Mar, 390. Rest. ♦♦ 150-220.
Parc, vallée de St-Pons (D2), ☎ 42.82.20.34. Euro, Visa. 15 rm P Covered in greenery, 150. Rest. 65-200.

⛺ ★★★*Claire Fontaine* (66 pl.), ☎ 42.03.02.28.

Restaurant :
Géménos :
♦♦ **Fer à Cheval,** pl. de la Mairie, ☎ 42.82.21.19. AE, DC, Euro, Visa ; closed Sat and Sun eve, Aug, end-of-year hols and eve low season, 100-150.

AUPS

Digne 84, Aix 93, Paris 854
C2 ⊠ 83630

Hotels :
★**Auberge de la Tour,** rue de l'Abbé-Aloïsi, ☎ 94.70.00.30. 24 rm P ♿ Delightful Provençal home and garden, 200. Rest. ♦ 90-150.

Moissac-Bellevue, 7 km NW on the D9 :
★★★**Le Calalou,** ☎ 94.70.17.91. Tx 461885. AE, Euro, Visa. 39 rm ♿ closed 15 Dec-15 Mar and Mon eve from 15 Oct to 15 Mar, 350. Rest. ♦♦ ♿ 100-160.

⛺ ★★★*Les Prés* (90 pl.), ☎ 94.70.00.93 ; ★★★*International Camping* (51 pl.), ☎ 94.70.06.80.

Recommended : Truffle market : Nov-Feb on Thu at 10:30.

AURON

Barcelonnette 65, Nice 98, Paris 802
Vallée de la Tinée, C-D1
⊠ 06600 Saint-Étienne-de-Tinée

1 602-2 415 m

ⓘ immeuble la Ruade, ☎ 94.23.02.66.

Hotels :
● ★★★**Pilon,** ☎ 93.23.00.15. Tx 470300. AE, Visa. 30 rm P ♿ Skating rink, closed 15 Apr-25 Jun, 1 Sep-20 Dec, 420. Rest. ♦ Grills at the swimming-pool in summer (noon). Winter : eve only, 120-200.

★★★***Savoie,*** ☎ 93.23.02.51. AE, DC, Euro, Visa. 28 rm, 22 apts ⚟ 🅿 closed 18 Apr-18 Jun, 11 Sep-17 Dec, 270. Rest. ♦ ✇ 90-150.

AVIGNON

Valençe 125, Marseilles 100, Paris 690
A2 ✉ 84000

ℹ 41, cours J.-Jaurès (B3), ☎ 90.82.65.11 ; hotel service, ☎ 90.82.05.81.

✈ Avignon-Caumont, 8 km SE, ☎ 90.31.20.39. See also Nîmes (Ardèche-Cévennes region).

SNCF (A-B3), ☎ 90.82.56.29, 90.82.62.92, 90.82.50.50.

Car-hire : *Budget* train + car, 4, av. du Blanchissage, ☎ 90.82.43.10, and at the station, ☎ 90.82.62.92.

Hotels :
★★★★***Europe,*** 12, pl. Crillon (A1-2), ☎ 90.82.66.92. 53 rm 🅿 ♨ ⛱ 500. Rest. ♦♦ ***Vieille Fontaine.*** closed 21 Jan, 1 week in Aug and Nov, Sun and Mon noon, 150-210.
★★★***Cité des Papes,*** 1, rue J.-Vilar (B2), ☎ 90.86.22.45. AE, DC, Visa. 65 rm ♿ closed mid-Dec to end-Jan, 265.
★★**Central,** 31, rue de la République (B3), ☎ 90.86.07.81. Euro, Visa. 29 rm ♨ ⛱ ♿ 250.
★★***Palais des Papes,*** 1, rue Gérard-Philipe (B1-2), ☎ 90.82.47.31 or 90.86.04.13. AE, Euro, Visa. 25 rm ✇ ♿ closed 1 Dec-15 Jan and Mon, 260. Rest. ♦ 105-200.

Villeneuve-lès-Avignon, ✉ 30400, in the Gard region, 2 km NW :
● ★★★★(L) ***Le Prieuré*** (Relais et châteaux), pl. du Chapitre, ☎ 90.25.18.20. Tx 431042. AE, DC, Euro, Visa. 26 rm and 9 apts 🅿 ♨ ⛱ ☐ 🎾 ♿ Period furnishings in a very comfortably renovated setting, 900. Rest. ♦♦♦ ✇ Highly-reputed dining-room. Spec : *foie gras de canard, cuisse de lapereau,* 180-260.
● ★★★***La Magnaneraie,*** 37, rue du Camp-de-Bataille, ☎ 90.25.11.11. AE, Euro, Visa. 21 rm 🅿 ♨ ⛱ ☐ 🎾 ♿ Elegantly furnished, beautiful 15thC dwelling, 400. Rest. ♦♦ Spec : *noisettes d'agneau* « Tante Lucie », 135-210.
★★★***Hostellerie du Vieux Moulin,*** rue du Vieux-Moulin, ☎ 90.25.00.26. AE, DC. 22 rm ⚟ 🅿 closed Nov and Wed, 265. Rest. ♦♦ 90-140.
● ★★***L'Atelier*** (L.F.), 5, rue de la Foire, ☎ 90.25.01.84. AE, Euro, Visa. 19 rm, closed 20 Dec-5 Feb. Pleasant 16thC setting, with patio, 210.
● ★★***Résidence des Cèdres*** (L.F.), 39, bd Pasteur, ☎ 90.25.43.92. Visa. 25 rm ⚟ 🅿 ♨ closed Sun low season, 200. Restaurant grill-room, 60-70.
★★***Coya,*** rte de Nîmes, ☎ 90.25.52.29. 23 rm 🅿 ♿ Certain rooms look over the papal palace and the Rhône river, 200.

Le Pontet, 3 km NE :
★★★***Agassins,*** N7, ☎ 90.32.42.91. Euro, Visa. 26 rm 🅿 ♨ ⛱ ☐ ♿ closed 2 Jan-28 Feb, 450. Rest. ♦♦ closed Sat noon and Sun eve, 120-230.
★★★***Auberge de Cassagne*** (Relais du Silence), rte de Vedenne, ☎ 90.31.04.18. Tx 432997. 15 rm 🅿 ♨ ⛱ ✇ ☐ 🎾 ♿ Wonderful gardens, 350. Rest. ♦♦ ✇ Spec : *émincé de lapereau et d'agneau aux petits légumes farcis, escalope de foie gras poêlée aux saveurs exotiques,* 180-320.

Les Angles, ✉ 30400 Villeneuve-lès-Avignon, 5 km W :
★★***Le Petit Manoir,*** chemin de la Pinède, ☎ 90.25.03.36. 40 rm 🅿 ♨ ⛱ ☐ 🎾 ♿ closed Mon low season, 100. Rest. ♦♦ ✇ 80-130.

Montfavet, ✉ 84140, 5.5 km E :
● ★★★★***Les Frênes*** (Relais et châteaux), av. des Vertes-Rives, ☎ 90.31.17.93. Tx 431164. AE, Euro, Visa. 18 rm 🅿 ♨ ⛱ ☐ ♿ closed 1 Nov-1 Mar. Delightful setting, with traditional-style furnishings, 800. Rest. ♦♦♦ Peace, comfort and hospitality around the swimming-pool. Transalpine inspired cooking : *gnocchi verdi au gorgonzola, lapereau à l'ail doux.* New Châteauneuf wines, 130-300.

Morières-lès-Avignon, ✉ 84310, 9 km E on the N100 :
★★***Le Paradou*** (L.F.), av. L.-Blum, ☎ 90.22.35.85. Tx 432700. AE, Euro, Visa. 30 rm 🅿 ♨ ☐ 🎾 200. Rest. ♦ ♿ closed Sun eve, 90-130.

Noves, ✉ 13550, 13 km S on the N571 and D28 :
★★★★***Auberge de Noves*** (Relais et châteaux), ☎ 90.94.19.21. Tx 431312. AE, DC, Euro, Visa. 22 rm ⚟ 🅿 ♨ ⛱ ☐ 🎾 ♿ closed 3 Jan-3 Mar. Splendid Provencal farmhouse, 880. Rest. ● ♦♦♦♦ closed Wed noon. The Lalleman family inn is set in the open Provence countryside. Good cooking : *huîtres gratinées au châteauneuf-du-pape, salmis de pigeon au gâteau d'échalotes.* Nice cellar, 170-400.

⛺ ★★★★*Municipal du Pont* (300 pl.), ☎ 90.82.63.50 ; ★★★*Bagatelle* (360 pl.), ☎ 90.86.30.39 ; ★★*Les Deux Rhônes* (50 pl.), ☎ 90.85.49.70.

Restaurants :
● ♦♦♦ ***Hiély-Lucullus,*** 5, rue de la République (B2), ☎ 90.86.17.07. AE ; closed 15 Jun-5 Jul, 24 Dec-8 Jan, Mon and Tue. Book ahead. P. Hiély's wonderful and unique menu. Perfect, light Provençal cooking : *daube d'agneau et aubergines en gelée, pieds paquets provençale.* Fresh young red Châteauneuf wines, 250-450.
● ♦♦♦ ***Brunel,*** 46, rue de la Balance (B1), ☎ 90.85.24.83 ✇ closed winter school hols, Sun and Mon from Oct to Mar, Sun from Apr to Sep. Family-run dining-room ; a short, excellent menu. Spec : *huîtres chaudes gratinées au curry, salade d'artichauts et tapenade,* 180-320.
♦♦♦ ***Le Vernet,*** 58, rue J.-Vernet (A2), ☎ 90.86.64.53 ♨ closed 1 Nov-26 Dec, Sat noon ans Sun low season. Contemporary cooking in a pleasant 18thC private mansion. Several menus, 210-320.
♦♦ ***Auberge de France,*** 28, pl. de l'Horloge (B2), ☎ 90.82.58.86. Closed 4-20 Jan, mid-Jun to 1 Jul, Wed eve and Thu. Regional dishes, 80-130.
♦♦ ***Les Trois Clefs,*** 26, rue des Trois-Faucons (B3), ☎ 90.86.51.53. Visa ✇ ♿ A small, flower-decorated restaurant, offering a warm welcome and inventive cooking which varies according to the season and market offerings, 100-120.
♦ ***Le Saint-Pierre,*** 10, pl. St-Pierre, ☎ 90.82.74.22. Closed Sun (ex during festival), Oct-May. On a quiet square located in the heart of old Avignon, 80-130.

Les Angles :
♦♦ ***Auberge Dou Terraie,*** av. de la 2e-Division-Blindée, ☎ 90.25.49.26. AE, DC, Euro, Visa 🅿 closed 15-30 Jun, Mon eve, Tue eve, Wed and Thu, 100-165.

Montfavet :
● ♦ ***La Ferme Saint-Pierre,*** 1551, av. d'Avignon, ☎ 90.87.12.86. AE, Euro, Visa 🅿 ♨ ⛱ ♿ closed 10 Aug-1 Sep, 21-29 Dec, Sat and Sun. Country-style cooking : *terrine de lapin, tapenade, anchoïade,* 95-140.

Events : early Feb : *Antiques Show ;* mid-July to mid-Aug : *drama and dance festival ;* enq, 8 *bis,* rue de Mons, ☎ 90.82.67.08 ; end Nov : *St-André Fair.*

Bicycle hire : List at S.I.

Recommended : *Simple Simon,* Tea-room, 20, rue de la Petite-Fusterie (A1), ☎ 90.86.62.70. Brunch, delicious cakes in a pleasant setting.

BANDOL

Toulon 17, Aix 68, Paris 826
B3 ⊠ 83150

ℹ allées Vivien, ☎ 94.29.41.35.

SNCF ☎ 94.29.41.51.

Hotels :
★★★★(L) ***Ile Rousse*** (P.L.M.), bd Louis-Lumière, ☎ 94.29.46.86. Tx 400372. AE, Euro, Visa. 55 rm Private beach. Louis XV and Louis XVI setting, 750. Rest. ♦♦♦ ***Les Oliviers.*** Fish and Provencal specialities, 170-260.
● ★★★***Délos Palais,*** Bendor Island (7 min by boat), ☎ 94.29.42.33. Tx 400383. AE, DC, Euro, Visa. 55 rm closed 15 Dec-15 Feb, 450. Rest. ♦♦ 130-200.
● ★★★***Soukana,*** Bendor Island, ☎ 94.29.46.83. 50 rm closed 15 Nov-1 Mar, 290.
★★★***Pieds dans l'Eau,*** Bandol Bay, ☎ 94.74.05.82. Tx 400366. Visa. 45 rm 270. Rest. ♦♦ (half-pension obligatory during high season), 90-100.
★★***La Réserve,*** rte de Sanary, ☎ 94.29.42.71. DC, Visa. 16 rm closed 2 Dec-15 Jan, 28 May-6 Jun, 205. Rest. ♦♦ closed Sun eve and Mon low season. Spec : *gratin de turbotin, agneau des Alpilles,* 90-200.
★★***Brunière*** (L.F.), av. L.-Lumière, ☎ 94.29.52.08. 17 rm 270.
★★***Galets,*** 0.5 km, montée Voisin, Toulon road, ☎ 94.29.43.46. Visa. 22 rm closed 31 Oct-25 Mar, 200. Rest. ♦ 85-230.
★★***Golf Hôtel,*** plage de Renécros, ☎ 94.29.45.83. 24 rm closed mid-Oct to Easter, 300.
★★***Ker Mocotte*** (L.F.), rue Raimu, ☎ 94.29.46.53. Tx 400383. 19 rm. Former villa of respected French actor, Raimu converted into a hotel closed Oct-end Feb, 270. Rest. ♦ 100-130.

Les Lecques, ⊠ 83270 Saint-Cyr-sur-Mer, 10 km NW on the N559 :
★★★***Grand Hôtel,*** ☎ 94.26.23.01. 58 rm closed Nov-Mar, 400. Rest. ♦♦ 120-210.

Ⲁ ★★Municipal *de Capelan* (133 pl.), ☎ 94.29.43.92 ; ★★*Vallongue* (90 pl.), ☎ 94.29.49.55.

Restaurants :
♦♦♦ ***Auberge du Port,*** 9, allées J.-Moulin, ☎ 94.29.42.63. AE, Visa closed 15-31 Jan, Sun eve and Mon low season. Spec : fish and shellfish, 170-250.
♦ ***La Grotte Provencale,*** 21, rue Dr-L.-Marçon, ☎ 94.29.41.52. Visa. closed Tue eve and Wed (from Jul to mid-Sep). Affordable, set menus, 70-130.

Casino, 24, rue de la République, ☎ 94.29.40.88.

BARCELONNETTE

Gap 69, Briançon 84, Paris 737
C1 ⊠ 04400

ℹ av. de la Libération, ☎ 92.81.04.71.

Hotels :
★★★***Grande Épervière,*** 18, rue des Frères-Arnaud, ☎ 92.81.00.70. AE, DC, Euro, Visa. 10 rm and 9 studio apts closed 15 Nov-10 Dec and Mon low season, 200. Rest. 60-130.

Le Sauze, 5 km SE on the D209 :
★★★***Alp' Hotel*** (Relais du Silence), Enchastrayes, ☎ 92.81.05.04 or 92.81.13.33. Tx 420437. AE, Visa. 24 rm and 11 apts closed May and Nov, 300. Rest. ♦ 60-190.
★★***Équipe,*** Enchastrayes, ☎ 92.81.05.12. 24 rm closed 15 Apr-25 Jun, 5 Sep-15 Dec, 170. Rest. ♦ 70-90.

Pra-Loup, 8.5 km SW on the D902 and D109 :
★★★***Airelles,*** ☎ 92.84.13.24. 20 rm closed Sep-10 Dec, end Apr-10 Jul, 230.
★★***Bergers*** (L.F.), ☎ 92.84.14.54. AE. 35 rm closed 20 Apr-30 Jun and 1 Sep-15 Dec. Full board only in winter, 270. Rest. ♦ 65-105, alt-rest.

Super-Sauze, 10 km SE on the D9A :
★★★***Pyjama,*** ☎ 92.81.12.00. 14 rm closed May-1 Jul, 1 Sep-15 Dec, 250.
★★***Ourson,*** ☎ 92.81.05.21. 20 rm closed 20 Apr-30 Jun, 1 Sep-15 Dec, 200. Rest. ♦ 60-80.

Ⲁ ★★★*Plan de Barcelonnette* (45 pl.), ☎ 92.81.08.11 ; ★★★*Tampico* (80 pl.), ☎ 92.81.02.55 ; ★★*Peyra* (50 pl.), ☎ 92.81.04.71 ; ★★*la Chaup,* le Sauze (60 pl.), ☎ 92.81.02.82.

Restaurants :
♦ ***La Mangeoire,*** pl. des Quatre-Vents, ☎ 92.81.01.61. Euro, Visa ; closed 1 Jan-1 Feb, 1-10 Jun, Sun eve and Mon. Simple, enjoyable restaurant, set in a one-time sheep enclosure. Honest cooking prepared by a young chef, 65-130.

Uvernet-Fours, 4 km S on the D902 :
♦♦ ***Passe-Montagne,*** rte de la Cayolle, ☎ 92.81.08.58. AE closed Wed, May, 1-20 Dec. Spec : *feuillantine de St-Jacques aux morilles fraiches, papillote de ris de veau aux concombres en ragoût,* 85-150.

BARJOLS

Draguignan 45, Aix 64, Paris 823
C2 ⊠ 83670

Hotel :
★***Pont d'Or,*** rue E.-Payan, ☎ 94.77.05.23. Visa. 16 rm closed 1 Dec-15 Jan, 140. Rest. closed Sun eve and Mon from 1 Oct to 31 May, 65-130.

Event : Sunday closest to 16 Jan (Feast of St-Marcel) : *Fête des Tripettes* (tripes).

Les BAUX-DE-PROVENCE

Arles 19, Avignon 30, Paris 718
A2 ⊠ 13520

ℹ impasse du Château, ☎ 90.97.34.39.

Hotels :
★★★★(L) ***Oustàu de Baumanière*** (Raymond Thuillier ; J.-A. Charial, chief chef ; Relais et châteaux), ☎ 94.54.33.07. Tx 420203. AE, DC, Euro, Visa. 25 rm Riding club ; closed 15 Jan-1 Nov, wed and Thu noon low season. Large Provencal farmhouse at the foot of the Baux castle, 660. Rest. ● ♦♦♦♦ The 88 year old grandfather can be proud of his grandson and vice versa. The pupil has been well trained. New and "clever" dishes remarkably prepared by the chef : *gâteau de lapin, terrine de légumes* (from the garden), *agneau des Alpilles,* Baux and Côtes-du-Rhône wines. Take-away shop, 350-500.
● ★★★★***Cabro d'Or*** (Relais et châteaux), Val d'Enfer, ☎ 90.54.33.21. Tx 401810. AE, DC, Euro, Visa. 22 rm closed

15 Nov-20 Dec, Tue noon and Mon low season. Traditional Provençal farmhouse, 600. Rest. ● ♦♦♦ Good fare and superb service, 190-300.
★★★*La Benvengudo,* vallon les Arcoules, ☎ 90.54.32.54. 18 rm closed 1 Nov-1 Feb. A well-furnished Provencal farmhouse on a splendid site, 340. Rest. ♦♦ closed Sun eve and noon. Spec : *champignons farcis à l'estragon, loup grillé au fenouil,* 140-210.
★★★*Mas d'Aigret,* ☎ 90.97.33.54. AE, Euro, Visa. 17 rm closed 3 Jan-15 Mar. At the foot of the castle ruins, 200. Rest. ♦ Plain fare ; closed Thu low season, 100-150.

Restaurant :
♦♦♦ ***La Riboto de Taven,*** ☎ 90.97.34.23. AE, Visa closed 6 Jan-24 Feb, Sun eve and Mon. Pleasant meals in magnificent surroundings. Spec : *huîtres de Bouzigues tièdes en feuillantine, agneau des Alpilles,* 220-270.

BEAULIEU-SUR-MER

Nice 10, Menton 20, Paris 945
2 km N of St-Jean-Cap-Ferrat, D2 ✉ 06310

ℹ pl. de la Gare, ☎ 93.01.02.21.

SNCF ☎ 93.01.00.16.

Car-hire : *Budget* train + car, at the station, ☎ 93.01.00.16.

Hotels :
● ★★★★(L) ***Réserve,*** 5, bd du Gal-Leclerc, ☎ 93.01.00.01. Tx 470301, 50 rm closed 1 Dec-10 Jan, 1 380. Rest. ● ♦♦♦ Tradition and quality : Gilbert Picard's superb cooking in a one-hundred-year old institution of the Côte d'Azur, 285-450.
★★★★(L) ***Métropole*** (Relais et châteaux), 15, bd du Gal-Leclerc, ☎ 93.01.00.08. Tx 470304. AE, DC, Euro, Visa. 50 rm and 3 apts Beautiful villa dating from the turn of the century ; private beach ; closed 1 Nov-20 Dec, 700. Rest. ♦♦♦ Expensive, but highest quality. Spec : *soupe de poissons de roche, filet de rouget à la pulpe d'olive,* 350-400.
★★★★***Carlton,*** 7, av. E.-Cavell, ☎ 93.01.14.70. Tx 970421. AE, DC, Euro, Visa. 33 rm closed 1 Nov-27 Dec, 700. Rest. ♦♦♦ 150-180.
★★★***Don Gregorio,*** 3-5, bd du Mal-Joffre, ☎ 93.01.12.15. Tx 970444. AE, Euro, Visa. 70 rm closed Nov-Feb, 450.
★★★***Résidence*** (Relais du Silence), av. Albert-Ier, ☎ 93.01.06.02. Tx 470250. AE, Visa. 21 rm closed 1 Oct-Jan, 650.
★***France,*** 1, montée des Orangers, ☎ 93.01.00.92 16 rm, closed Nov-Jan, 180. Half-pension obligatory, 65.
★***Select Hôtel,*** 1, montée des Myrtes, ☎ 93.01.05.42. 20 rm closed 20 Oct-20 Dec, 160.

Restaurants :
♦ ***La Pignatelle,*** 10, rue Quincenet, ☎ 93.01.03.37. AE, Visa closed 20 Nov-26 Dec and Wed. Family-style, 60-140.
♦ ***African Queen,*** port de Beaulieu, ☎ 93.01.10.85. AE, DC, Visa Terrace and attractive view. Quality seafoods, 105-195.

Casino : 8, av. Blundell-Maple, ☎ 93.01.00.39.

Le BEAUSSET

Toulon 17, Marseilles 47, Paris 822
10 km N de Bandol, B3 ✉ 83330

ℹ mairie, ☎ 94.90.41.39 (in season).

Hotel :
★★***La Cigalière,*** rte du Camp, 1.5 km N on N8, ☎ 94.98.64.63. Visa, 16 rm closed 1-15 Oct and Wed, 250. Rest. ♦♦ 85-120.

Restaurant :
● ♦♦ ***L'Estagnon,*** ☎ 94.98.62.62. AE, DC closed Nov and Mon. Well-restored old oil-mill. Simple regional cooking served by Régis Hermite. Spec : *pieds paquets, gigot à la broche, écrevisses sautées,* 95-160.

BOLLÈNE

Orange 25, Avignon 52, Paris 640
23 km N of Orange, A1 ✉ 84500

ℹ pl. de la Mairie, ☎ 90.30.14.43.

SNCF ☎ 90.30.20.02.

Hotels :
★★★***Belle Écluse,*** 42, rte de Suze, ☎ 90.30.15.14. AE, DC, Euro, Visa. 18 rm closed Nov-15 Feb, 200. Rest. ♦ 80-180.
★★***Mas des Grès,*** rte de St-Restitut, ☎ 90.30.10.79. AE, Visa. 13 rm closed 1-15 Jan, 2-8 May, Sun eve and Mon, 160. Rest. ♦ closed 1-15 Oct, 85-200.

Δ ★★★★*Le Barry* (100 pl.), ☎ 90.30.13.30 ; ★★*le Lez* (70 pl.), ☎ 90.30.16.86.

Event : Jun : *popinjay fete* (parrot fair).

BONNIEUX

Avignon 47, Aix 48, Paris 728
12 km SW of Apt, B2 ✉ 84480

ℹ mairie, ☎ 90.75.80.06 (high season).

Hotels :
● ★★★***Le Prieuré*** (Châteaux-hôtels), ☎ 90.75.80.78. 10 rm closed 5 Nov-14 Feb. Attractive setting : former 17thC convent, 350. Rest. ♦♦ closed Tue and Wed noon. Good meals, 110-160.
6 km SE on the D36 and D943 :
● ★★★***L'Aiguebrun,*** domaine du château de la Tour, ☎ 90.74.04.14. 8 rm closed Jan-Mar. A gracious dwelling under beautiful trees, 320. Rest. ♦♦ closed Mon noon. Pleasant fare. Spec : *figues fraîches à la crème de fenouil,* other desserts, 150-210.

Δ ★*Vallon* (50 pl.), ☎ 90.75.86.14.

BORMES-LES-MIMOSAS

Toulon 40, Fréjus 60, Paris 879
5 km NW of Le Lavandou, C3 ✉ 83230

ℹ rue J.-Aicart, ☎ 94.71.15.17.

Hotels :
● ★★★***Safari,*** rte du Stade, ☎ 94.71.09.83. Tx 404603. AE, Euro, Visa. 33 rm closed 15 Oct-1 Apr. Splendid view over Lavandou Bay, 400. Rest. Grill eve only ex Sun, 130-200.
★★★***Le Palma,*** N559, ☎ 94.71.17.86. AE, Euro, Visa. 20 rm 320. Rest. ♦♦ closed Sun eve and Mon, 1 Jan-1 Feb, 130-260.
★★***Paradis,*** mont des Roses, ☎ 94.71.06.85. 20 rm closed 15 Oct end-Mar, 200.
Cabasson, 8 km S on the D41 :
★★★***Palmiers,*** ☎ 94.64.81.94. 20 rm 440. Rest. ♦♦ 100-150.

Δ ★★★★*Domaine la Favière* (1 200 pl.), ☎ 94.71.03.12 ; ★★★*Manjastre* (120 empl.), ☎ 94.71.03.28 ; ★★*le Grand Batailler* (116 pl.), ☎ 94.71.08.41 ; numerous sites ★★

Restaurant :
● ♦♦ ***La Tonnelle des Frères Gedda,*** pl. Gambetta, ☎ 94.71.34.84 closed Oct-1 Apr and noon (ex week-ends and Apr). For lovers of very good Provençal cooking. Spec : *favouilles farcies aux pinces de crabes, daube provencale,* 130-250.

Casino : rue Carnot, ☎ 94.71.15.28.

BREIL-SUR-ROYA

Menton 36, Nice 60, Paris 993
21 km S of Tende, D1 ♥ ✉ 06540

SNCF ☎ 93.04.40.15.

Hotel :
★★***Relais des Salines*** (L.F.), rte de Tende, ☎ 93.04.43.66. 15 rm Ⓟ closed 2 Nov-1 Mar, 180. Rest. ♦♦ A captivating backwoods inn with plain, good cooking, 120-210.

BRIGNOLES

Toulon 50, Marseille 64, Paris 815
C3 ✉ 83170

ℹ pl. St-Louis, ☎ 94.69.01.78.

SNCF ☎ 93.69.11.95.

Hotels :
★★★***Le Mas de la Cascade,*** 2.5 km S on the D554, ☎ 94.69.07.85. Euro. 10 rm Ⓟ closed 20 Jan-20 Feb, Tue eve and Wed low season, 300. Rest. ♦♦ 110-250.
★***Univers,*** 11, pl. Carami, ☎ 94.69.11.08. AE, DC, Euro, Visa. 12 rm Ⓟ closed Jan, 100. Rest. ♦ Provençal specialities ; good value, 70-200.
★***Hostellerie St-Louis,*** 6 km W on the N7, ☎ 94.69.09.20. Visa. 5 rm Ⓟ ♿ closed Jan, 180. Rest. ♦♦ 65-140.

La Celle, 3 km S on the D554 :
★★★***Abbaye de La Celle,*** ☎ 94.69.08.44. 31 rm Ⓟ ♿ closed Jun, 320. Rest. 80-100.

⛺ *Municipal* (100 pl.), ☎ 94.59.11.86.

La CADIÈRE-D'AZUR

Toulon 22, Marseille 46, Paris 821
9 km N of Dandol, B3 ✉ 83740

ℹ rd-pt R.-Salengro, ☎ 94.29.32.56 (high season).

Hotel :
★★★***Hostellerie Bérard,*** av. G.-Péri, ☎ 94.29.31.43. AE, Visa. 40 rm Ⓟ closed 1 Nov-7 Dec, 250. Rest. ♦♦ Inexpensive set menus. Spec : *biscuit de loup au champagne,* pastries, 125-250.

CAGNES-SUR-MER

Nice 13, Cannes 21, Paris 922
D2 ✉ 06800

ℹ 26, av. Renoir, ☎ 93.20.61.64.

SNCF ☎ 93.20.66.11.

Car-hire : *Budget* train + car, at the station, ☎ 93.20.50.72, and La Pénétrante road, ☎ 93.20.30.40.

Hotels :
● ★★★***Cagnard*** (Relais et châteaux), rue Pontis-Long, ☎ 93.20.73.21. Tx 462223. AE, DC, Euro, Visa. 19 rm Ⓟ ♿ closed 1 Nov-15 Dec and Thu noon. Charming Provençal residence with big flower-laden terraces overlooking the sea, 850. Rest. ♦♦ Excellent service and mouth-watering fare, 270-350.
★★★***Hamotel*** (Inter-Hôtel), rte de la Colle, hameau du Soleil, ☎ 93.20.86.60. Tx 470623. AE, Euro, Visa. 33 rm Ⓟ ♿ closed 10 Nov-15 Dec, 280.
★★***Collettes,*** chemin des Collettes, ☎ 93.20.80.66. 13 rm Ⓟ closed 1 Nov-15 Dec, 220.
★★***Savournin,*** 17, av. A.-Renoir, ☎ 93.20.60.58. AE, Visa. 31 rm Ⓟ closed 1 Oct-1 Dec, 290.

Le Cros-de-Cagnes, ✉ 06170, 2 km SE :
★★★***Motel Horizon,*** 111, bd de la Plage, ☎ 93.31.09.95. AE, Euro, Visa. 44 rm Ⓟ ♿ closed 10 Nov-20 Dec, 325.
★★***Beaurivage,*** 39, bd de la Plage, ☎ 93.20.16.09. Visa. 21 rm Ⓟ 160. Rest. ♿ 65-100.
★★***Serre,*** 22, bd de la Plage, ☎ 93.20.10.54. 26 rm Ⓟ closed early Oct-early Dec, 160. Rest. closed Wed, 80-90.

⛺ ★★★★*Oasis* (100 pl.), ☎ 93.20.75.67 ; ★★★★*Panoramer* (83 pl.), ☎ 93.31.16.15 ; ★★★*Camp' Otel du Club* (40 pl.), ☎ 93.20.91.19.

Restaurants :
Le Haut-de-Cagnes :
♦♦ ***Josy-Jo,*** 8, pl. du Planastel, ☎ 93.20.68.76 ♿ closed 20 Dec-20 Jan and Sun. Charming little restaurant, with the simple fare of sunny climates : *soupe de poissons du pays, foie de veau grillé au charbon de bois,* 130-210.
♦ ***Peintres,*** 71, montée de la Bourgade, ☎ 93.20.83.08. AE, Euro, Visa ♿ closed Wed, 100-180.

Le Cros-de-Cagnes, 2 km SE :
● ♦♦ ***Chez Loulou,*** 91, bd de la Plage, ☎ 93.31.00.17 ♿ closed 1st Fri Jul-1st Mon Sep, Sat eve and Sun. J. Maximin's favorite gourmet stop. Friendly service and fresh, good honest cooking : grilled or roasted meat and fish, 120-210.

CANNES

Nice 34, Toulon 128, Paris 909
D2 ✉ 06400

ℹ Palais des Congrès, la Croisette (B2), ☎ 93.39.24.53, and at the station, ☎ 93.99.19.77.

✈ Nice-Côte d'Azur, 25 km NE, ☎ 93.72.30.30. *Air France Agency,* 2, pl. du Gal-de-Gaulle, ☎ 93.39.39.14.

⛴ Lérins Islands Line, ☎ 93.39.11.82.

SNCF (B2), ☎ 93.99.50.50, 93.99.50.51 and 93.47.01.01.

Car-hire : *Budget* train + car, at the station, ☎ 93.99.33.00, and 1-3, rue A.-Chaude, ☎ 93.99.44.04.

Hotels :
● ★★★★(L) ***Gray d'Albion,*** 38, rue des Serbes (B2), ☎ 93.68.54.54 and 93.99.04.59. Tx 470744. AE, Euro, Visa. 187 rm ♿ Private beach, 1 350. Rest. ● ♦♦♦♦ ***Royal Gray.*** closed 1 Feb-15 Mar, Sun eve low season and Mon. The young Jacques Chibois has grown. Thanks to his mastery and the exceptional quality of his cooking, he is now part of our grand jury : *suprême de dorade royale, galette de ris de veau au xérès.* M. Guénard's desserts are superb : *millefeuille aux pommes sautées sauce caramel.* Wide choice of wines. Buffet on the beach, until 3 am at Jane's, 220-310.
★★★★(L) **Carlton,** 58, bd de la Croisette (C2), ☎ 93.68.91.68. Tx 470720. AE, DC, Euro, Visa. 337 rm Ⓟ ♿ Magnificent view of the sea ; private beach and old-fashioned charm, 1 200. Rest. ♦♦♦ Good meals, 200-300.
★★★★(L) ***Grand Hôtel,*** 45, bd de la Croisette (B1), ☎ 93.38.15.45. Tx 470727. AE, Visa. 76 rm Ⓟ ♿ Beach, 1 300. Rest. ♦♦ ***Lamour*** 140-300.
★★★★(L) ***Majestic,*** 14, la Croisette (C2), ☎ 93.68.91.00. Tx 470787. AE, DC, Euro, Visa. 262 rm Ⓟ ♿ closed 1 Nov-15 Dec. Luxurious old-style hotel with magnificent garden and private beach, 125. Rest. ♦♦♦ 160-300.

★★★★(L) ***Montfleury,*** 25, av. Beauséjour (C1), ☎ 93.68.91.50. Tx 470039. AE, DC, Euro, Visa. 185 rm 🅿 ♨ 🏊 📺 🎾 ♿ closed 10 Dec-20 Jan. In the heart of a 10-acre park overlooking the Bay of Cannes, 1 020. Rest. ◆◆◆ 160-250.

★★★★(L) ***Martinez*** (Concorde), 73, la Croisette (C2), ☎ 93.68.91.91. Tx 470708. AE, DC, Euro, Visa. 400 rm ⚟ 🅿 🏊 📺 ♿ Private beach ; closed 20 Nov-20 Jan, 1 500. Rest. ● ◆◆◆ ***l'Orangeraie.*** Under the inspired administration of the Concorde chain and the director R. Duvauchelle, the revitalised hotel is now a sumptuous palace. A. Duparc gives us the privilege of his light cooking : *dorade au plat, fondant de foies de volailles,* excellent desserts, low calorie menus, 200-300. Buffet on the beach. ● ◆◆◆ ***La Palme d'Or.*** Christian Willer and his team deserve the golden palm of the restaurant's name for their fine cooking, 250-400.

★★★***Beau Séjour*** (Mapotel), 5, rue des Fauvettes, ☎ 93.39.63.00. Tx 470975. AE, DC, Euro, Visa. 46 rm 🅿 ♨ 📺 ♿ closed 1 Nov-15 Dec, 460. Rest. ◆◆◆ 🚫🐕 90-130.

★★★***Acapulco,*** 16, bd d'Alsace (B1), ☎ 93.99.16.16. Tx 470929. AE, Euro, Visa. 59 rm 🅿 ♨ 📺 500. Rest. ◆◆ closed 15 Nov-22 Dec, 90-130.

★★★***Clarice,*** 48, bd Alexandre-III (C2), ☎ 93.43.07.55. Visa. 30 rm 🅿 ♨ 🏊 closed 10 Oct-20 Jan, 300. Rest.◆ 🚫🐕 ♿ 80-130.

★★★***Embassy,*** 6, rue de Bône (B1), ☎ 93.38.79.02. Tx 470081. AE, Euro, Visa. 60 rm 🅿 ♨ 🏊 ♿ 550. Rest. ◆◆ closed Mon and Tue noons, 110-180.

★★★***Paris,*** 34, bd d'Alsace (B1), ☎ 93.38.30.89. Tx 470995. Euro, Visa. 48 rm 🅿 ♨ 🚫🐕 📺 ♿ closed 1 Nov-20 Jan, 500.

★★***El Puerto,*** 45, av. du Petit-Juas (B1), ☎ 93.68.39.75. 22 rm 🅿 ♨ 🏊 🚫🐕 closed 1 Oct-15 Dec, 280. Rest. closed Mon, 80-130.

★★***Modern,*** 11, rue des Serbes (B1), ☎ 93.39.09.87. 19 rm, closed 11 Nov-22 Dec, 300.

★★***Roches Fleuries,*** 92, rue G.-Clemenceau (A1), ☎ 93.39.28.78. 24 rm ⚟ 🅿 ♨ 🏊 🚫🐕 closed 15 Nov-27 Dec, 220.

★***Madeleine,*** 18, av. St-Jean, ☎ 93.39.90.72. 8 rm ♨ closed Nov, 80. Rest. 80-230.

Restaurants :

◆◆◆ ***Croquant,*** 18, bd Jean-Hibert (A2), ☎ 93.39.39.79. AE, Euro ♿ closed 15 Nov-1 Dec, Sun eve and Mon. Marvellous preparation of highest quality dishes. Spec : *fricassée d'escargots aux cèpes, cuisson de canard en petits confits,* 105-240.

◆◆◆ ***Rescator,*** 7, rue du Mal-Joffre (A1), ☎ 93.39.44.57. Visa ⚟ 🏊 ♿ closed Mon low season. Light and inventive cooking with emphasis on fresh fish : *salade tiède de rougets, blanc de saint-pierre au beurre de tomate,* 140-280.

● ◆◆ ***Reine Pédauque,*** 6, rue Mal-Joffre (A1), ☎ 93.39.40.91 ♿ closed 27 Jun-16 Jul, Mon. Everything is going pretty well in this good restaurant : *mousseline de rascasse, filet d'agneau,* 120-320.

● ◆◆ ***Pompon Rouge,*** 4, rue E.-Négrin (A1 ; no phone), closed Nov-15 Dec, Sun and Mon. There is no telephone in this restaurant, a very fashionable point, and one which helps maintain a hectic climate amrongst the "chic" and gourmand customers who know this place well : *foie gras G. Vié, friture,* delicious specials, 200-310.

● ◆◆ ***La Coquille,*** 65, rue F.-Faure, ☎ 93.39.26.33. AE, Euro, Visa ⚟ ♿ closed 24 Nov-14 Dec. Little terrace. A preferred choice of our editors. Always a pleasant welcome by *patron* and staff, with service and cooking quality to match. Spec : excellent *bouillabaisse,* and, for smaller appetities, *bourride ;* shellfish and fish (brought to the table *before* preparation, too). Good white and rosé wines. Reasonably priced, 80-200.

◆◆ ***Bistingo,*** 1, jetée A.-Édouard, casino, Palais des Festivals (A1), ☎ 93.39.01.01. Tx 970327. AE, DC, Visa ♿ Pleasant terrace. Quality fare. Spec : *huîtres chaudes aux poireaux, baron de lapereau aux pâtes fraîches,* 110-130.

◆◆ ***Au Mal Assis,*** 15, quai St-Pierre, ☎ 93.39.13.38. AE, DC, Euro, Visa ; closed 15-20 Dec. On the port facing the yachts. The seats are comfortable ! Fresh fish, 65-100.

◆◆ ***Festival,*** 52, la Croisette (C2), ☎ 93.38.04.81. AE, DC ⚟ ♿ closed 26 Nov-26 Dec, Feb school hols. Light, inventive dishes ; rapid service. The terrace among the most sought-after dining areas on the boulevard, 130-200.

◆◆ ***Mirabelle,*** 24, rue Saint-Antoine (A1), ☎ 93.38.72.75. AE, Visa ♿ closed Tue, 1-21 Dec. An enchanting dining-room where preparation is light and imaginative, the desserts sumptuous, 120-250.

◆◆ ***Poêle d'Or,*** 23, rue des États-Unis (B1), ☎ 93.39.77.65. AE, Visa ; closed Nov and Mon. A good stopover, 140-300.

◆◆ ***Monsieur Madeleine,*** 12, bd Jean-Hibert (A2), ☎ 93.39.72.22. Visa ⚟ 🚫🐕 Superb view of the bay ; closed Jan and Thu ex Jul-Aug. Excellent set menu, 70-150.

◆◆ ***Mère Besson,*** 13, rue des Frères-Pradignac (B1), ☎ 93.39.59.24. AE, Visa ♿ closed Sun. New Dutch management but tradition of Provençal cooking has been kept, 130-150.

◆◆ ***Embuscade,*** 10, rue St-Antoine, le Suquet (A1), ☎ 93.39.29.00. AE ; closed Mon, 15 Nov-27 Dec. Varied menus. Spec : *soupe de poissons, magret de canard,* 120-210.

◆◆ ***Le Ragtime,*** 1, la Croisette, ☎ 93.68.47.10. AE, DC, Euro, Visa ; closed Sun low season. The latest 1925 american-style restaurant/piano-bar. Very good, 85-250.

◆ ***Bec Fin,*** 12, rue du 24-Août (B1), ☎ 93.38.35.86. AE, DC, Visa ♿ closed Sun, 20 Dec-20 Jan. Spec : *daurade grillée au fenouil, petite friture,* 60-110.

◆ ***Monaco,*** 15, rue du 24-Août (B1), ☎ 93.38.37.76 ♿ closed Nov and Sun, 60-100.

◆ ***La Cigale,*** 1, rue Florian, ☎ 93.39.65.79. closed 15 Nov-15 Dec and Wed. For regular customers, simple, good and cheap, 80-170.

◆ ***Le Mâchon,*** 15, rue St-Antoine, ☎ 93.39.62.21. Times are changing, *le Mâchon* is still there, not as fashionable but with candlelight, pretty girls serving salads and grilled meat, 120-210.

◆ ***Petite Maison,*** 4, rue Marceau (B1), ☎ 93.39.31.98. AE, Visa ♨ ♿ closed Mon and Tue noon. Simple, traditional cooking, in a charming setting for dining by candlelight, 90-170.

◆ ***L'Entrecôte,*** 21, rue des Frères-Pradignac, ☎ 93.39.59.91. AE, Visa ♿ For homesick Parisians : same menu as at Porte Maillot restaurant, plus a 1925 piano atmosphere in evenings, 60-120.

◆ ***Mireille,*** 3, rue du Batéguier (B1), ☎ 93.39.06.28 ♿ closed Tue and noon (high season). Good, simple and inexpensive, 80-130.

Son et lumière : Jul, on the nearby islands.

Events : Jul : *international folk festival.* Sep : *vintage car festival, pleasure craft festival.* Dec : *international theatre festival.*

Casinos : *les Fleurs,* 5, rue des Belges, ☎ 93.68.00.33. *Palm Beach,* la Croisette, ☎ 93.43.91.12. *Municipal,* jetée A.-Édouard, ☎ 93.38.12.11.

Bicycle hire : *Cycles Rémy,* 22, av. des Hespérides, ☎ 93.43.44.66, and at the station ; also : 5, rue Alleis, ☎ 93.39.46.15.

Recommended : *l'Étagère,* 22, rue V.-Cousin, ☎ 93.38.27.17, a pleasant wine-bar with daily specials and alot of atmosphere. *Cannoline,* 16, rue Venizelos, ☎ 93.39.08.19. *Maiffret,* chocolates, crystallized fruits, 31, rue d'Antibes, ☎ 93.39.08.29. *Bruno,* 50, rue d'Antibes, ☎ 93.39.26.63. *Angelica,* 74, rue d'Antibes, ☎ 93.39.30.13. Cheese : *Robert Ceneri,* la Ferme Savoyarde, 22, rue Meynardier. Pastry : *Rohr,* 63, rue d'Antibes. Bakery : *Martinez,* rue Meynardier.

Le CANNET

Grasse 15, Nice 31, Paris 907
3 km N of Cannes, D2 ✉ 06110

ℹ 2, bd Carnot, ☎ 93.46.74.00, and av. Campon, ☎ 93.45.34.27.

Hotel :
★★★***Grande-Bretagne,*** bd Sadi-Carnot, ☎ 93.45.66.00. Tx 470918. AE, DC, Visa. 34 rm closed 7 Nov-15 Dec, 480.

⛺ ★★★*Grand Saule* (117 pl.), ☎ 93.47.07.50 ; ★★★*Ranch* (136 pl.), ☎ 93.46.00.11.

Restaurant :
♦ ***Marinette,*** 11, rue Rebuffel, ☎ 93.38.89.46 closed 15 Jul-30 Aug, Thu, Fri and Sat ; noon only in a terrace garden ; good, simple fare, 100-130.

Recommended : *la Théière,* tea-room (a former wine-press site).

CARPENTRAS

Avignon 24, Aix 89, Paris 685
A2 ✉ 84200

ℹ 170, allées Jean-Jaurès (B2), ☎ 90.63.00.78.

SNCF (B3), ☎ 90.63.02.60.

Hotels :
★★★***Univers,*** pl. A.-Briand (B3), ☎ 90.63.00.05. Visa. 25 rm 180. Rest. ♦♦ ☎ 90.63.30.13. Closed Sat low season, 40-110.
★★***Fiacre,*** 153, rue Vigne (C2), ☎ 90.63.03.15. Euro, Visa. 17 rm In an 18thC mansion, 230.
★★***Safari*** (L.F.), av. J.-H.-Fabre (off map near A3), ☎ 90.63.35.35. Tx 432770. AE, DC, Euro, Visa. 42 rm and 14 bungalows 215. Rest. ♦ closed 23 Dec-4 Jan and Sun eve low season, 65-140.

Monteux, 4 km SW on the D942 :
★★★***La Genestière,*** ☎ 90.62.27.04. Tx 432770. AE, Euro, Visa. 20 rm 300 Rest. ♦♦ 100-190.

⛺ ★★*Villemarie* (70 pl.), ☎ 90.63.09.55.

Restaurant :
● ♦♦ ***Le Saule Pleureur,*** quartier Beauregard, ☎ 90.61.01.35 closed 3 wks in Mar, 2 wks in Nov, Tue eve and Wed. Michel cooks good dishes made of regional produce : *salade de loup à la vinaigrette d'orange, rognons de veau au miel de lavande,* 80-320.

CARQUEIRANNE

Hyères 10, Toulon 14, Paris 853
12 km SW of Hyères, C3 ✉ 83320

ℹ mairie, ☎ 94.58.60.78.

Hotels :
★★***Plein Sud,*** av. du Gal-de-Gaulle, ☎ 94.58.52.86. 17 rm closed 1 Nov-15 Dec, 210.
★★***Richiardi,*** port des Salettes, ☎ 94.58.50.13. DC, Euro, Visa. 10 rm closed Nov-6 Dec, 235. Rest. ♦ closed Tue low season, 70-140.

⛺ ★★★★*Le Beau Vézé* (150 pl.), ☎ 94.57.65.30 ; ★★★*les Arbousiers* (100 pl.), ☎ 94.58.56.56.

CARROS

Nice 25, Grasse 41, Paris 942
16 km NE of Vence, D2 ✉ 06510

Hotel :
4 km SW on the D1 :
★★***Hostellerie Lou Castelet*** (L.F.), les Plans de Carros, ☎ 93.29.16.66. AE, Visa. 22 rm closed 31 Oct-1 Dec and Mon, 200. Rest. 60-150.

CARRY-LE-ROUET

Aix 40, Paris 774
27 km W of Marseilles, B3 ✉ 13620

ℹ 6, bd des Moulins, ☎ 42.45.00.08.

SNCF ☎ 42.45.01.03.

Hotels :
★***Tuilière,*** rte de Sausset, ☎ 42.45.02.96. Visa. 20 rm closed Fri (15 Oct-1 Apr), 180. Rest. closed 15 Dec-15 Jan, 70-130.

Sausset-les-Pins, ✉ 13960, 4 km W :
★★***Plage,*** av. du Port, ☎ 42.45.06.31. AE, Visa. 11 rm closed 15 Nov-15 Dec, Sun eve and Mon, 200. Rest. ♦ Fish specialities, 140-250.

⛺ ★★★★*Caravaning Lou Souleï* (700 pl.), ☎ 42.45.05.12.

Restaurants :
● ♦♦♦ ***L'Escale*** (Relais Gourmand), ☎ 42.45.00.47 closed Nov-early Mar, Mon noon (Jul-Aug). A terrace ablaze with flowers and a large dining-room. Provence wines, 220-310.

Sausset-les-Pins :
♦♦ ***Les Girelles,*** rue F.-Mistral, ☎ 42.45.26.16. Visa. closed 2 Jan-28 Feb, Sun eve and Mon (ex 1 Jul-31 Aug). Seafront terrace. Fresh grilled fish. A reasonably-priced, unostentatious menu, 80-170.
♦ ***La Jetée,*** résidence du Port, ☎ 42.45.07.61 closed 15 Oct-1 Mar and Wed, 100-150.

CASSIS

Marseilles 23, Toulon 44, Paris 803
B3 ✉ 13260

ℹ pl. Baragnon, ☎ 42.01.71.17.

SNCF ☎ 42.01.01.18.

Hotels :
★★★***Jardins du Campanile,*** 8, rue Auguste-Favier, rte de Marseille, ☎ 42.01.84.85. AE, Visa. 30 rm closed 31 Oct-1 Apr, 360. Rest. closed 20 Jun-10 Sep, 100-200.
★★★***Plage Bestouan,*** Bestouan Beach, ☎ 42.01.05.70. Tx 441287. AE. 29 rm closed mid-Oct to mid-Mar, 300. Rest. ♦♦ 120-150.
★★★***Rade,*** 1, av. des Dardanelles, ☎ 42.01.13.54, 42.01.02.97. AE, Euro, Visa. 27 rm closed 15 Nov-1 Mar, 250.
★★★***Roches Blanches,*** rte des Calanques, ☎ 42.01.09.30. AE, Visa. 36 rm Large Provençal residence overlooking the sea, closed 15 Nov-15 Feb, 380.
★★***Golfe,*** quai Barthélemy, ☎ 42.01.00.21. 30 rm closed Nov-Mar, 190-200.
★★***Liautaud,*** 4, rue Victor-Hugo, ☎ 42.01.75.37. Visa. 32 rm closed Nov-20 Dec, 200. Rest. 80-135.

⛺ ★★*Cigales* (300 pl.), ☎ 42.01.71.17.

Restaurants :
● ♦♦♦ ***Presqu'île,*** quartier Port-Miou, rte des Calanques, ☎ 42.01.03.77. AE, Visa closed 2 Jan-7 Mar, Sun eve and Mon ex

Jul-Aug. A gourmet feast between sky and sea : shellfish, oysters, fish, 170-300.
♦♦ ***Chez Gilbert,*** 19, quai des Baux, ☎ 42.01.71.36. DC, Visa ♿ closed 15 Dec-15 Feb, Sun eve, Tue low season, Tue noon high season. Well-prepared fish including good *bouillabaisse,* 140-220.

Casino : av. Lerich, ☎ 42.01.78.32.

CASTELLANE

Digne 54, Grasse 63, Paris 800
C2 ✉ 04120

ℹ rue Nationale, ☎ 92.83.61.14.

Hotel :
★★★***Commerce,*** pl. de l'Église, ☎ 92.83.61.00. 46 rm Ⓟ ♿ closed 15 Nov-25 Mar, 205. Rest. ♦ 60-130.

Ⓐ ★★★★*Internatonal* (80 pl.), ☎ 92.83.66.67 ; ★★★★*le Verdon* (421 pl.), ☎ 92.83.61.29 ; 6 camp sites ★★★ with a total of more than 600 pl.

Le CASTELLET

Toulon 20, Marseilles 45, Paris 824
10 km N of Bandol, B3 ♥
✉ 83330 Le Beausset

Hotels :
★★★***Castel Lumière,*** Le Portail, ☎ 94.90.62.20. AE, DC. 5 rm ♿ closed 2-30 Nov, 250. Rest. ♦♦ closed Tue low season, 130-220.
★***Castel Sainte-Anne,*** Sainte-Anne-du-Castellet, ☎ 94.90.60.08. Visa. 20 rm Ⓟ ♿ closed 15 Oct-1 Apr, 230. Rest. 100-170.

Ⓐ ★★★*Le Castillon* (150 pl.), ☎ 94.90.60.33 ; ★★*Auberge d'Arbois* (155 pl.), ☎ 94.90.70.51.

Restaurant :
♦♦ ***Lou Mestre Pin,*** pl. du Jeu-de-Paume, ☎ 94.90.60.27. Euro, Visa ♿ closed Wed, Feb school hols and 25 Dec. Quality fare at reasonable prices. Spec : pastries, 90-160.

CAVAILLON

Avignon 27, Arles 44, Paris 705
A2 ✉ 843000

ℹ rue Saunerie, ☎ 90.71.32.01.

SNCF ☎ 90.71.04.40, 90.71.23.98.

Hotels :
2 km on the N538 :
★★★***Christel,*** 2 km on the N538, ☎ 90.71.07.79. Tx 431547. AE, DC, Euro, Visa. 109 rm Ⓟ ♿ 250. Rest. ♦ closed Sat noon and Sun noon low season, 90-100.
★★***Toppin,*** 70, cours Gambetta, ☎ 90.71.30.42. AE, DC, Euro, Visa. 32 rm Ⓟ closed 20 Dec-10 Jan, 190. Rest. 40-140.

Ⓐ ★★★*Hippodrome* (150 pl.), ☎ 90.71.11.78.

Restaurants :
♦♦ ***Fin de Siècle,*** 46, pl. du Clos, ☎ 90.71.12.27. DC ; closed 1-20 Sep and Wed. Spec : *foie gras, salade de courgettes crues au saumon cru, feuilleté d'écrevisse,* 65-250.
● ♦ ***Nicolet,*** 13, pl. Gambetta, ☎ 90.78.01.56. DC, Visa Ⓟ closed 9-24 Feb, 1-15 Jul, Sun and Mon. Everything is home-made : bread, cakes and pastries, *sorbets, assiette du pêcheur, noisette d'agneau au caviar d'aubergine,* 100-250.

CAVALAIRE-SUR-MER

Fréjus 43, Toulon 61, Paris 900
C3 ✉ 83240

ℹ square de-Lattre-de-Tassigny, ☎ 94.64.08.28.

⛴ Line for Porquerolles, and daily service to Port-Cros, ☎ 94.64.08.04.

Hotels :
★★★***Alizés,*** promenade de la Mer, ☎ 94.64.09.32. 18 rm Ⓟ ♿ closed 18 Nov-15 Jan, 220. Rest. ♦ 90-150.
★★★***Calanque,*** rue de la Calanque, ☎ 94.64.04.27. 33 rm Ⓟ ♿ closed end Sep to end Apr, 380. Rest. ♦ 120-210.
★★***Bel Ombra,*** rue des Maures, ☎ 94.64.04.68. 27 rm Ⓟ closed Oct-Easter, 240 with pension. Rest. ♦ Pension only, 70.

Ⓐ ★★★★*La Baie* (480 pl.), ☎ 94.64.08.15 ; ★★★★*Bonporteau* (240 pl.), ☎ 94.64.03.24 ; ★★★★*La Pinède* (180 pl.), ☎ 94.64.11.14 ; ★★★*Cros du Mouton* (160 pl.), ☎ 94.64.10.87.

CHÂTEAU-ARNOUX

Digne 25, Aix 92, Paris 720
14 km SW of Sisteron, B1 ✉ 04160

ℹ rte Nationale, ☎ 94.64.02.64.

Hotels :
● ★★★★***Bonne Étape*** (Pierre and Jany Gleize ; Relais et châteaux), chemin du lac, ☎ 94.64.00.09. Tx 430605. AE, Euro, Visa. 11 rm + 7 apts Ⓟ closed 3 Jan-mid-Feb, last week Nov, Sun eve and Mon low season, 650. Rest. ● ♦♦♦ At the beginning of the meal, Arlette, Pierre and Jany Gleize wish you "the best appetite in the world". Just like one of Giono's novels : the mountain, lavender and the sea : *roulade de lapereau à l'Hysope, pâté de saint-pierre au fenouil, agneau de Sisteron,* fresh cod, *jambon cru d'agneau* and local wines, 200-350.

Saint-Auban, ✉ 04600, 2 km SW on the N96 :
★★***Villiard,*** ☎ 94.64.17.42. Euro. 20 rm Ⓟ closed Sat and Sun in winter, 270.

Aubignocs, ✉ 04200, 3 km N on the N85 :
★★***Relais Alpes-Côte d'Azur,*** ☎ 94.64.06.16. AE, Euro. 12 rm Ⓟ closed 10-30 Nov, Sun eve and Wed, 95. Rest. ♦ 75-120.

Ⓐ ★★*Des Salettes* (200 pl.), ☎ 94.64.02.40.

Restaurants :
♦ ***Le Barasson,*** RN96, ☎ 94.64.17.12. Visa Ⓟ closed Sun eve and Mon. Spec : *côte de veau aux morilles, écrevisses à la mode du chef, gibiers,* 60-140. With 12 rm, 180.
♦ ***La Casa Mia,*** av. du Gal-de-Gaulle, ☎ 94.64.18.94 Ⓟ closed Oct, 15 days in May and Mon. Simply delicious pizzas, 100.

CHÂTEAUNEUF-DU-PAPE

Avignon 18, Carpentras 24, Paris 529
10 km S of Orange, A1 ✉ 84230

ℹ ☎ 90.83.71.08.

Hotel :
2 km SE on the D17 :
● ★★***Host. Château des Fines Roches,*** ☎ 90.83.70.23. 7 rm Ⓟ 400. Rest. ● ♦♦♦ ♿ closed Mon. One menu only to discover the Estevenins' good regional cooking, 160-180.

Restaurant :
● ♦♦ ***La Mule du Pape,*** pl. de la Fontaine, ☎ 90.83.73.30 closed Mon eve and Tue, Sun eve low season. The vineyard is in the dining-room and your glasses are filled with good wine to enhance the Provencal dishes. Spec : *caillette vauclusienne, biscuit de rouget au pastis,* 80-170.

Event : Jul : musical evenings.

Recommended : wine-cellar visits : list at T.O.

La CIOTAT

Marseille 32, Toulon 37, Paris 806
B3 ✉ 13600

ℹ 2, quai Ganteaume, ☎ 42.08.61.32.

SNCF ☎ 42.83.08.63.

Car-hire : *Budget* train + car, 10, av. Grimelli, ☎ 42.83.46.88.

Hotels :
★★★***Ciotel,*** corniche du Liouquet, 6 km NE, ☎ 42.83.90.30. Tx 441390. AE, DC, Visa. 42 rm P closed mid-Oct to early Apr, 600. Rest. ♦♦ 145-190.
★★***Provence Plage,*** La Ciotat-Plage, 3, av. de Provence, ☎ 42.83.09.61. AE, Visa. 20 rm P closed 2-31 Jan, 170. Rest. 70-200.

⛺ ★★★*Saint-Jean* (90 pl.), ☎ 42.83.13.01 ; ★★*Castel Joli* (100 pl.), ☎ 42.83.50.02 ; ★★*Oliviers,* at Le Liouquet (533 pl.), ☎ 42.83.15.04 ; ★★*Sauge* (230 pl.), ☎ 42.83.47.65.

COGOLIN

Sainte-Maxime 13, Toulon 60, Paris 870
3 km S of Grimaud, C3 ✉ 83310

ℹ pl. de la République, ☎ 94.56.36.52, and Marines de Cogolin, ☎ 94.56.03.70.

Hotel :
★★***Coq'Hôtel,*** pl. de la Mairie, ☎ 94.56.12.66. AE, Euro, Visa. 18 rm P closed Nov, 250. Rest. closed Wed in winter, 65-130.

Restaurants :
♦♦ ***Lou Capoun,*** 39, rue Marceau, ☎ 94.54.44.57. P ♿ closed Sun eve, Wed, 80-220.

Les Marines de Gogolin, 6 km E on the N98 :
♦♦ ***Port-Diffa,*** les Trois Ponts sur la Giscle, Cogolin-Plage, ☎ 93.56.29.07. AE P ♿ closed 6 Jan-5 Mar. Moroccan specialities. Inexpensive set menu, 140-210.

La COLLE-SUR-LOUP

Grasse 19, Nice 19, Paris 926
3 km SW of Saint-Paul-de-Vence, D2 ✉ 06480

Hotels :
★★★★***Hostellerie de l'Abbaye,*** rte de Grasse, ☎ 93.32.66.77. AE, Visa. 19 rm P ♿ 12thC abbey, 650. Rest. ♦♦ 160-350.
★★★***Marc Hély*** (Relais du Silence), 535, rte de Cagnes, ☎ 93.22.64.10. 14 rm P ♿ closed 15 Nov-10 Feb. View of Saint-Paul-de-Vence. Agreeable setting, 330. Rest. eve only for hotel guests.

⛺ ★★★*Pinèdes* (70 pl.), ☎ 93.32.98.94 ; ★★★*Vallon Rouge* (27 pl.), ☎ 93.32.86.12.

Restaurants :
♦♦♦ ***Belle Époque,*** rte de Cagnes, ☎ 93.20.10.92. AE, DC, Visa P ♿ closed 5 Jan-15 Feb and Mon (ex nat hols). Spec : *foie gras de canard à l'ail doux, fricassée de poulet au vinaigre de cerises,* 110-160.
♦ ***Strega,*** rte de Cagnes, ☎ 93.22.62.37. Visa P ♿ closed Sun eve and Mon, 6 Jan-27 Feb, 130-200.

COLMARS-LES-ALPES

Barcelonnette 44, Digne 71, Paris 816
C1 ✉ 04370

ℹ Hôtel des Postes, ☎ 92.83.41.92.

Hotels :
★★***Chamois,*** ☎ 92.83.43.29. 26 rm P closed Easter-20 May and 15 Oct-23 Dec, 160. Rest. ♦ 60-100.

Beauvezer, ✉ 04440, 5.5 km S on the D2 :
★★***Verdon*** (L.F.), ☎ 92.83.44.44. 26 rm P closed 1 20 Dec and Sun eve low season, 170. Rest. ♦ 80-130.

COMPS-SUR-ARTUBY

Draguignan 32, Grasse 60, Paris 827
28 km S of Castellane, C2 ✉ 83840

Hotels :
★***Bain*** (L.F.), ☎ 92.76.90.06. Visa. 17 rm P closed 12 Nov-20 Dec, 150. Rest. ♿ 60-150.

Trigance, 10 km NW :
★★★***Château de Trigance*** (Relais et châteaux), ☎ 92.76.91.18. 8 rm P closed 21 Jan-21 Mar and Wed low season. 12thC fortified castle at the entry to the Verdon Gorges, 360. Rest. ♦♦ 120-210.

COTIGNAC

Draguignan 36, Toulon 70, Paris 839
15 km SW of Aups, C2 ✉ 83850 Carces

ℹ 10, cours Gambetta, ☎ 94.04.61.87.

Hotel :
● ★★★***Hostellerie Lou Calen,*** 1, cours Gambetta, ☎ 94.04.60.40. DC, Euro, Visa. 17 rm P closed Oct-25 Mar, 170-350. Remarkable cooking ; glorious garden. Rest ♦♦ closed Thu low season, 80-180.

Recommended : farmers' wine cooperative, *Vignerons de Cotignac,* ☎ 94.04.60.04.

La CROIX-VALMER

Fréjus 37, Toulon 62, Paris 880
6 km NE of Cavalaire, C3 ✉ 83420

Hotels :
★★★***Mer,*** La Ricarde, SW on the N559, ☎ 94.79.60.61. 31 rm P ♿ Splendid Provencal establishment, 350. Rest. ♦♦ 80-120.
★★★***Parc,*** av. G.-Sellier, 1 km E on the D93, ☎ 94.79.64.04. Visa. 33 rm P closed 15 Oct-1 Apr, 300.

Gigaro, 5 km SE, at Cavalaire Bay :
★★★***Soulelas,*** ☎ 94.79.61.91. Tx 970032. AE, Euro, Visa. 40 rm P ♿ closed 31 Oct-1 Mar. Stunning view of the Levant Islands, 620. Rest. ♦♦ 125-210.
★★★***Moulin de Paillas,*** ☎ 94.79.71.11. 30 rm P closed 1 Oct-1 May. Private beach, 500. Rest. ♦♦ Excellent cooking supervised by R. Guth : *carré d'agneau grillé, assiette des prés sauce verdurette et son œuf poché.* Delicious desserts made by a former Lenôtre pupil, 70-170.

⛺ ★★★★*Sélection Camping* (240 pl.), ☎ 94.79.61.97.

DIGNE-LES-BAINS

Gap 87, Aix 110, Paris 745
C1 ✉ 04000

(Mar-Dec), ☎ 92.31.06.68.

ℹ Rond-Point (A3), ☎ 92.31.42.73.

SNCF off map, A3, ☎ 92.31.00.67.

(A3), ☎ 92.31.50.00.

Hotels :
★★★***Grand Paris,*** 19, bd Thiers (A-B3), ☎ 92.31.11.15. AE, DC, Visa. 27 rm + 5 apts P closed 4 Jan-Feb. Modern comfort in this magnificent establishment in the middle of town. Tastefully luxurious, 310. Rest. ♦♦♦ Quality fare. Spec : *escalope de truite aux poivrons rouges, mignonette d'agneau,* 125-260.

★★★**Ermitage Napoléon** (Inter-Hôtel), bd Gambetta (off map, A3), ☎ 92.31.01.09. AE, DC, Euro, Visa. 60 rm Ⓟ 🌳 🔔 ♿ closed Feb, 280. Rest. ♦♦ 90-170.

⛺ *Municipal* (186 pl.), ☎ 92.31.04.87.

Fairs and markets : Wed and Sat a.m. ; brocante fairs in Jul, Aug ; crafts fairs in Jul.

DRAGUIGNAN

Fréjus 29, Toulon 81, Paris 864
C2 ✉ 83300

ⓘ 9, bd Clemenceau, ☎ 94.68.63.30.

SNCF ☎ 94.68.01.13.

Car-hire : *Budget* train + car, 4, av. du 4-Septembre, ☎ 94.68.58.00, gare des Arcs, ☎ 94.73.30.09, and quartier de la Foux, in Trans-en-Provence, ☎ 94.68.60.96.

Hotels :
★★★**Col de l'Ange** (Inter-Hôtel), rte de Lorgues, 3 km on the D557, ☎ 94.68.23.01. Tx 970423. AE, DC, Euro, Visa. 30 rm ⚘ Ⓟ 🌳 🏊 ♿ with 1/2 pension, 285. Rest. ♦♦ closed Jan, 100-200.
★★**Parc,** 21, bd de la Liberté, ☎ 94.68.53.84. Euro. 20 rm Ⓟ 🌳 closed 15 Dec-15 Jan, 220. Rest. ♦ closed Sun eve in winter, 60-130.

⛺ ★★**De la Foux** (133 pl.), ☎ 94.68.18.27.

Restaurants :
♦♦ **La Calèche,** 7, bd G.-Péri, ☎ 94.68.13.97. Euro, Visa ♿ closed Sun and Mon in summer, eve ex Sat in winter. Spec : *foie gras, ris de veau.* Good value, 60-150.

Ampus, ✉ 83111, 14 km NW on the Lake Sainte-Croix road :
♦ **Fontaine d'Ampus,** ☎ 94.70.97.74. closed 10 Jan to mid-Feb and Mon noon. Spec : *fromage de chèvre cuit sur de la menthe fraîche.* Good value, 80-150.

Bargemon, ✉ 83620, 20 km NE :
● ♦♦ **Maître Blanc,** rue J.-Jaurès, ☎ 94.76.60.24 ♿ closed Dec-Jan and Wed. Lunch only in low season. According to the day's market, mood and inspiration : *coq en croûte, porcelet en daube,* 55-100.

Recommended : specialities of Provence : *René Eugène,* Le Seyrar, ☎ 94.68.05.93. Trout, crayfish : *Alain Guiran,* ☎ 94.68.02.55.

L'ESCARÈNE

Sospel 22, Menton 44, Paris 956
21 km N of Nice, D2 ✉ 06440

SNCF ☎ 93.79.50.02.

Hotels :
★**Host. du Castellino,** ☎ 93.79.50.11. 10 rm ⚘ Ⓟ 🌳 🔔 ✗ closed 20 Sep-1 Nov and Mon. Beautiful site, 140. Rest. ♦ Spec : *cassoulet, confit de canard,* 80-190.

Peillon, 10 km S on the D21 and D121 :
● ★★**Auberge de la Madone** (L.F.), ☎ 93.79.91.17. 19 rm ⚘ Ⓟ 🌳 🔔 ✗ closed 15 Oct-15 Dec and Wed. A pleasant hotel surrounded by an olive grove, 315. Rest. ♦♦ Good local dishes. Spec : *la charlotte aux sanguines et basilic, terrine de foies de volailles à la confiture d'oignons,* 75-170.

Restaurant :
♦♦ **Logis de la Garde,** Blausax, ☎ 93.79.51.03 Ⓟ 🌳 🔔 ♿ closed 15 Jul-14 Aug, Tue and Wed. Spec : stock fish *(estocaficada), kebab de gigot flambé,* 130-210.

ÈZE

Monaco 7, Menton 12, Paris 946
12 km NE of Nice, D2 ✉ 06360

ⓘ at the mairie, ☎ 93.41.03.03.

SNCF ☎ 93.01.54.34.

Hotels :
● ★★★★(L) **Château Eza,** rue de La Pise, ☎ 93.41.12.44. 8 rm Ⓟ 🔔 closed 4 Nov-28 Mar, 3 000. Rest. ● ♦♦ One cannot talk about the *Château Eza ;* it has to be visited, specially after A. Rochat has renovated it. Aufrère is a young and excellent chef. Spec : *ravioles de lapin à l'italienne, filets de dorade à l'anchoïade,* 220-360.
● ★★★★(L) **Cap Estel,** on the waterfront, ☎ 93.01.50.44. Tx 470305. Euro. 48 rm ⚘ Ⓟ 🌳 🔔 🏊 closed 1 Nov-1 Feb. Private beach. Park planted with coconut palms. Half-pension only, 1 570. Rest. ♦♦♦ ✗ 240-350.
★★★★**Château de la Chèvre d'Or** (Relais et châteaux), rue du Barri, Moyenne-Corniche, ☎ 93.41.12.12. Tx 970839. AE, DC, Visa. 6 rm and apts 🔔 🏊 closed Feb and Wed. Exceptional setting, 1 500. Rest. ♦♦♦ Quality fare : *huîtres chaudes au champagne, soufflé chaud framboise,* good wines, 275-400.
★★**Hermitage,** Grande-Corniche, ☎ 93.41.00.68. 11 rm ⚘ 🔔 ✗ closed Sun eve and Mon, 28 Jun-9 Jul, 1-29 Dec. A pleasant Provencal stopover, 180. Rest. ♦ 80-130.

Cap-d'Ail, ✉ 06320, 4 km E :
★★**Miramar,** 126, av. du 3-Septembre, ☎ 93.78.06.60. Visa. 27 rm ⚘ Ⓟ closed 1 Dec-2 Jan, 180. Rest. closed Wed, 80-130.

⛺ ★★*Nationale 7,* Grande-Corniche (50 pl.), ☎ 93.01.81.64.

Restaurants :
♦♦ **Richard Borfiga,** pl. Ch.-de-Gaulle, ☎ 93.41.05.23. AE, DC, Euro, Visa ; closed 13 Jan-15 Feb, Mon in winter. Spec : *flan de lotte, loup au basilic,* 150-300.
♦♦ **Nid d'Aigle,** 1, rue du Château, ☎ 93.41.19.08. ⚘ 🔔 closed Thu, 12 Nov-22 Dec. An attractive setting, a warm welcome, and good, very moderately-priced meals, 60-130.
♦ **Bergerie,** Grande-Corniche, ☎ 93.41.03.67 Ⓟ ♿ closed Wed, 15 Oct-15 Jan. An attractive flowered terrace setting makes the grills and hot *tarte tatin* taste even better ! 150-175.

FAYENCE

Grasse 27, Fréjus 34, Paris 814
7 km E of Seillans, C2 ✉ 83440

ⓘ pl. Léon-Roux, ☎ 94.76.20.08.

Hotels :
● ★★★**Moulin de la Camandoule,** chemin N.-D.-des-Cyprès, 3 km SW on the D19, ☎ 94.76.00.84. 12 rm ⚘ Ⓟ 🌳 🔔 🏊 closed 15 Dec-1 Apr. Wonderfully restored old oil-extraction mill, 290. Rest. ♦♦ closed 1 Oct-1 Apr and Tue, ex Jul-Aug, 100-145.

Seillans, 7.5 km on the D19 :
★★★**Deux Rocs,** pl. Font-d'Amont, ☎ 94.76.87.32. 15 rm 🔔 closed 2 Nov-28 Mar. Old Provencal farmhouse, 200. Rest. ♦♦ ✗ closed Tue and Thu noon, 70-160.
★★★**France,** pl. du Thouron, ☎ 94.76.96.10. 26 rm ⚘ Ⓟ 🌳 🔔 🏊 ♿ closed Jan and Wed low season, 290. Rest. ♦♦ Classic cooking : *escargots de Bourgogne, civet de lapin,* 150-200.

Montauroux, 10 km E :
★★**Marjolaine,** quartier des Laouves, ☎ 94.76.43.32. Visa. 17 rm ⚘ 🌳 🔔 ♿ closed 5 Jan-8 Feb and Wed, 185. Rest. ♦ 90-150.

Lac de St-Cassien, 83810 Callian, 6 km NE : ★***Auberge du Puits Jaubert,*** ☎ 94.76.44.48. Euro, Visa. 8 rm closed 9 Jan-12 Feb, 150. Rest ♦♦ closed Tue. Pleasant setting. Spec : *saumon soufflé, soupière chaude de crustacés en croûte,* 85-160.

Farmhouse-gîte :
Saint-Paul-en-Forêt, 7.5 km on the D563 : *Trestaure,* ☎ 94.76.15.56. Regional farm produce.

⛺ ★★★*Lou Cantaire* (35 pl.), ☎ 94.76.23.77 ; Montauroux, ★★★*les Chaumettes* (120 pl.), ☎ 94.76.43.27.

Restaurant :
♦♦ ***France,*** pl. de la République, ☎ 94.76.00.14. DC ♿ closed 15 Nov-22 Dec, 9-31 Jan, Wed eve and Thu. Classic cooking : *écrevisses, gigot grillé aux herbes,* reasonable prices, 45-120.

FONTAINE-DE-VAUCLUSE

Carpentras 21, Avignon 30, Paris 705
A2 ☒ 84800 L'Isle-sur-la-Sorgue

ℹ pl. de l'Église, ☎ 90.20.32.22 (high season).

Hotel :
● ★★***Parc*** (L.F.), ☎ 90.20.31.57. AE, Visa. 12 rm closed 2 Jan-15 Feb. Attractive park, 180. Rest. ♦♦ closed Wed, 80-130.

Youth hostel : chemin de la Vignasse, ☎ 90.20.31.65.

⛺ ★★*Les Prés* (50 pl.), ☎ 90.20.31.79, 90.20.32.38.

Restaurant :
♦♦ ***Le Château,*** Petite-Place, ☎ 90.20.31.54. Euro closed Feb and Tue. Remarkable view of the Sorgue River. Traditional fare. Spec : *soufflé de truite aux écrevisses, magret de canard au poivre vert,* 65-240.

FONTVIEILLE

Avignon 30, Aix 73, Paris 718
10 km NE of Arles, A2 ☒ 13990

ℹ mairie, ☎ 90.97.70.01.

Hotels :
● ★★★★***Regalido*** (Relais et châteaux), rue Frédéric-Mistral, ☎ 90.97.60.22, 90.97.62.01. AE, Euro, Visa. 13 rm ♿ closed 30 Nov-15 Jan, 620. Rest. ● ♦♦ closed Mon and Tue noon. Book ahead. Alphonse Daudet would certainly have liked to stop here : *gratin de moules, tranche de gigot en casserole à l'ail,* 90-240.
★★★***A la Grâce de Dieu,*** 90, av. de Tarascon, ☎ 90.97.71.90. AE, DC, Visa. 10 rm closed 15 Oct-15 Mar, 250. Rest. ♦♦ Good, simple meals, 100-150.

Farmhouse gîte : *mas de Suspiron,* ☎ 90.97.30.50. Horseback riding.

⛺ ★★★*Municipal* (150 pl.), ☎ 90.97.78.69.

Restaurant :
♦♦ ***Le Patio,*** 117, rte du Nord, ☎ 90.97.73.10. Visa ♿ closed 5 Jan-5 Feb, Tue eve and Wed. Enjoy Provençal specialities and grills cooked over a wood fire in this restaurant set in a one-time sheep enclosure, 90-170.

FORCALQUIER

Digne 49, Aix 66, Paris 774
B2 ☒ 04300

ℹ pl. Bourguet, ☎ 92.75.10.02.

Hotels :
★★***Charembeau*** (L.F.), ☎ 92.75.05.69. 11 rm ♿ closed Nov-Jan, 100. Rest. ♦♦ closed Sun eve and Mon. Spec : *côte de veau aux morilles, ragoût de coquilles Saint-Jacques,* 90-120.

Mane, 3.5 km S on the N100 :
★★★***Mas Saint-Luc,*** campagne de la Laye, ☎ 92.75.05.06. 6 rm ♿ closed Dec-Mar, 220. Rest. ● ♦♦ Happiness in a big park on the water. Nice, rich cooking : *caille au foie gras et raisins, saumon farci, canard à l'orange.* Var and Luberon wines, 90-140.

Saint-Étienne-les-Orgues, ☒ 04230, 12 km N on the D12 :
★★***Saint-Clair*** (L.F.), chemin de Serre, ☎ 92.76.07.09. 27 rm ♿ closed 15 Nov-20 Dec, 3-24 Jan. In the open fields, 160. Rest. 70-120.

FRÉJUS

Draguignan 29, Cannes 40, Paris 874
C3 ☒ 83600

ℹ bd de la Libération, Fréjus-Plage, ☎ 94.57.48.42 (summer), and pl. du Dr-Calvini (C2), ☎ 94.51.53.87.

✈ Fréjus-Saint-Raphaël, 2 km S, ☎ 94.51.04.07.

SNCF (B2), ☎ 94.51.30.53.

Car-hire : *Budget* train + car, 1070, av. de-Lattre-de-Tassigny, ☎ 94.51.33.00.

Hotels :
Fréjus-Plage, 2 km SE :
★★★***Ligure,*** 1074, av. Mal-de-Lattre-de-Tassigny, ☎ 94.53.63.63. AE, DC, Euro, Visa. 64 rm ♿ 310.
★★***Oasis,*** rue H.-Fabre, ☎ 94.51.50.44. Visa. 27 rm ♿ private beach, closed 22 Oct-1 Feb, 120. Rest. ♦♦ bd d'Alger, ☎ 94.51.06.72 closed 22 Oct-1 Dec, Sun eve and Mon low season, 80-150.
★★***Auberge du Vieux Four*** (C2), 57, rue Grisolle, ☎ 94.51.56.38. AE, DC, Euro, Visa. 8 rm closed Feb hols, 20 Sep-20 Oct, Sun and Mon eve, 180. Rest. ● ♦♦ The Angevine sweetness and a vaulted cellar under the hot sun of the coast. Spec : *escalope de saumon frais braisé à l'oseille, foie gras.* Bandol and Côte-de-Provence wines, 145-230.

Le Colombier, 3 km NE on the D4 :
★★★★***Loisirotel,*** rte de Bagnols, ☎ 94.51.45.92. AE, DC, Visa. 60 rm ♿ closed 31 Oct-15 Apr. Bungalows in the middle of an enormous pine plantation, 425. Rest. ♦♦ 120-200.

Saint-Aygulf, 7 km S on the N98 :
★★★***Catalogne,*** av. de la Corniche-d'Azur, ☎ 94.81.01.44. AE, Visa. 32 rm closed 15 Oct-1 Apr, 320. Snack in summer.

Youth hostel : *Domaine de Bellevue,* rte de Cannes, ☎ 94.52.18.75.

⛺ 6 ★★★★, 7 ★★★ and 8 ★★ : big capacity.

Restaurants :
♦♦ ***Les Potiers,*** 135, rue des Potiers (B2), ☎ 94.51.33.74 ♿ closed 1 week in Feb, 15 Nov-20 Dec, Wed and Sat noon, in Jul-Aug eve only. Spec : *marbré de saumon et saint-pierre sauce cresson, ris de veau aux champignons sauvages,* 80-160.

Fréjus-Plage, 2 km SE :
♦ ***Le Trou Normand,*** 611, av. V.-Hugo, ☎ 94.95.05.37. AE, DC, Visa ; closed Wed, Jan, 80-120.

La GAUDE

Nice 21, Grasse 35, Paris 932
9 km E of Vence, D2 ☒ 06610

Hotel :
★★***Hermitage,*** chemin de l'Hermitage, ☎ 93.24.40.05. 10 rm Ⓟ ♣ ⛱ closed 20 Oct-20 Dec and Fri noon, 220. Rest. ◆◆ closed Fri. Spec : *paupiette de sole farcie sauce écrevisses, filet de bœuf en croûte aux morilles,* 90-160.

GIGONDAS

Orange 18, Avignon 39, Paris 679
14 km SW of Vaison-la-Romaine, A1
⊠ 84190 Beaumes-de-Venise

ℹ pl. du Portail, ☎ 90.65.85.46 (Easter-Oct).

Hotels :
★★***Les Florets*** (L.F.), rte des Dentelles, 1.5 km E, ☎ 90.65.85.01. DC. 15 rm Ⓟ ⛱ closed 2 Jan-25 Feb, Tue eve low season and Wed, 180. Rest. ◆◆ Spec : *pieds paquet, soupière marine,* 80-120.
★★*Montmirail* (L.F.), ☎ 90.65.84.01. 46 rm Ⓟ ♣ ⛱ 📺 ♿ closed Dec-15 Mar, 240. Rest. ◆ closed Mon, 90-150.

Recommended : wine : *La Maison du Gigondas,* pl. de la mairie.

GOLFE-JUAN

Grasse 21, Nice 27, Paris 915
2.5 km W of Juan-les-Pins, D2
⊠ 06220 Vallauris

ℹ 84, av. de la Liberté, ☎ 90.63.73.12.

SNCF ☎ 93. 63.71.58.

⛴ Lerins Islands Line, ☎ 93.63.81.31.

Hotels :
★★★***Petit Trianon,*** 18, av. de la Liberté, ☎ 93.63.70.51. 14 rm ☼ Ⓟ closed 20 Oct-20 Dec, 320.
★★★***Résidence les Jasmins,*** RN7, ☎ 93.63.80.83. Tx 970935. AE, DC, Visa. 37 rm Ⓟ ♣ 📺 ♿ closed Nov, 280. Rest. ◆◆ closed Nov-Mar, 80-120.
★★***Crijansy*** (L.F.), av. J.-Adam, ☎ 93.63.84.44. 23 rm Ⓟ ♣ ⊘ ♿ closed 15 Oct-23 Dec, 200. Rest. ◆ 80-130.

Restaurants :
◆◆ ***Tétou,*** bd des Frères-Roustan, ☎ 93.63.71.16 ☼ (seafront) ♿ closed 15 Oct-20 Dec, Mar and Wed. Excellent *bouillabaisse,* 360-400.
◆◆ ***Chez Christiane,*** at the port, ☎ 93.63.72.44. AE, Visa. ☼ ♿ closed 11 Nov-22 Dec, Mon eve and Tue and eve in winter. Good fish restaurant ; attractive terrace, 65-200.

GORDES

Carpentras 34, Avignon 38, Paris 718
B2
⊠ 84220

Hotels :
★★★***La Mayanelle*** (Relais et châteaux), ☎ 90.72.00.28. AE, DC, Euro, Visa. 10 rm ☼ Ⓟ ⛱ closed 2 Jan-1 Mar. Stunning view of the Lubéron Range, 250. Rest. ● ◆◆ closed Tue. Spec : *canard aux olives, omelette « du Comtat »,* 150-200.
★★★***Gordos,*** rte de Cavaillon, ☎ 90.72.00.75, 90.72.05.65. 15 rm ☼ Ⓟ ♣ ⛱ 📺 closed 1 Nov-15 Mar, Sun eve, 250.
★★***Auberge de Carcarille*** (L.F.), 2.5 km E on the D2, ☎ 90.72.02.63. 11 rm Ⓟ ♣ ⊘ 📺 ♿ closed 20 Nov-30 Dec and Fri, 180. Rest. ◆ 50-120.

Joucas, 6 km E on the D2 and D102 :
★★★★***Le Mas des Herbes Blanches*** (Mapotel), rte de Murs, ☎ 90.72.00.74. Tx 432045. AE, Euro, Visa. 14 rm ☼ Ⓟ ♣ ⛱ 📺 ♿ closed 1 Dec-1 Mar. A stone farmhouse in an enchanting spot opposite the Lubéron Range, 570. Rest. ◆◆ 155-240.
★★***Hostellerie des Commandeurs*** (L.F.), ☎ 90.72.00.05. Visa. 12 rm Ⓟ ♣ ⛱ closed Jan-Feb and Wed, 140. Rest. ● ◆ Simple, honest cooking. Spec : *fricassée de volaille au vinaigre de vin, loup au fenouil,* 60-115.
Les Bories, rte de Sénanque, ☎ 90.72.00.51. 4 rm ☼ Ⓟ ♣ ⛱ ⊘ closed Dec, 280. Rest. ● ◆◆◆ ⊘ closed Wed and eve. Book ahead. A little paradise lost in the middle of fields of lavender. Inspired cooking. Spec : game in season, *bourride de baudroie, nougat glacé au coulis d'abricot,* 150-210.

⛺ ★★*Les Garrigues de Fontanille* (100 pl.), ☎ 90.72.02.66.

GRASSE

Cannes 17, Nice 42, Paris 918
D2
⊠ 06130

ℹ pl. Foux (B1), ☎ 93.36.03.56.

SNCF ☎ 93.70.05.53.

🚌 (B1)

Car-hire : *Budget* train + car, bd Leclerc, ☎ 93.70.17.07.

Hotels :
★★***Bellevue*** (L.F.), 14, av. Riou-Blanquet (C1), ☎ 93.36.01.96. 30 rm ☼ ♣ ♿ closed Nov, 240. Rest. ◆ ⊘ 80-130.

Le Plan-de-Grasse, 4 km SE :
★★***Arômes*** (L.F.), 115, RN85, ☎ 93.70.42.01. 7 rm Ⓟ ♣ ♿ closed 1 Nov-1 Feb, 145. Rest. ◆◆ closed Sat noon in Jul-Aug. Spec : *tournedos aux cèpes, escalope de veau « à l'Holstein »,* 70-160.

Cabris, ⊠ 06820, 5 km W on the D4 :
★★***L'Horizon*** (L.F., Relais du Silence), ☎ 93.60.51.69. AE. 18 rm ☼ ♣ ⛱ ⊘ closed 15 Oct-1 Mar, 225. Rest. ◆ closed Wed, 70-130.

Peymeinade, ⊠ 06530, 5 km SW on the D2562 :
★★★***Poste,*** ☎ 93.66.07.77. DC, Visa. 20 rm ☼ Ⓟ ♣ 📺 ♿ closed 2 Jan-15 Mar, 150. Rest. ◆◆ closed Wed, 70-110.

Magagnosc, ⊠ 06520, 5 km NE on the D2085 :
Petite Auberge, 105, av. A.-Renoir, ☎ 93.36.20.34. Visa. 5 rm ☼ Ⓟ closed 1-31 Jul, Feb school hols and Wed, 370. Rest. Pension and 1/2 pension only, 60-110.

Plascassier, 6 km SE on the D4 :
★★***Tourmaline,*** quartier Masseboeuf, ☎ 93.60.10.08. 7 rm ☼ Ⓟ ⛱ closed Nov, 180. Rest. ◆◆ closed Wed. Spec : *rillettes de saumon, ris de veau aux morilles,* 120-210.
★***Mouliniers*** (L.F.), chemin de Masseboeuf, ☎ 93.60.10.37. 10 rm ☼ Ⓟ ♣ ⛱ closed 1-20 Jan, 130. Rest. ♿ 60-110.

Opio, 06650 Le Rouret, 6.5 km E on the D7 :
★***Mas des Géraniums,*** 7, rte de Nice, ☎ 93.77.23.23. 7 rm ☼ Ⓟ ♣ ⛱ ♿ closed Oct-Jan. With pension, 180. Rest. closed Sun eve. Spec : *canard aux figues, rouget à l'opidoise,* 70-140.

Spéracèdes, 06530 Peymeinade, 8 km W :
Soleillade, rue des Orangers, ☎ 93.66.11.15. 10 rm ⊘ ♿ closed Oct-Easter, 180. Rest. ◆ ♿ closed 15 Oct-15 Nov and Wed. Spec : quail, duck, *civet de lapin,* game, 60-150.

Le Bar-sur-Loup, ⊠ 06620, 9 km NE :
★★★***Réserve,*** pont du Loup, 3 km N, ☎ 93.59.32.81. AE, DC, Visa. 15 rm ☼ Ⓟ ♣ 📺 240. Rest. ◆ 60-150.

Pegomas, ⊠ 06580, 10 km S Mouans-Sartoux road :
★★**Bosquet,** quartier du Château, ☎ 93.42.22.87. 18 rm P closed 1 Nov-1 Dec, 190.
Saint-Vallier-de-Thiey, ⊠ 06460, 12 km NW :
★★**Hostellerie le Préjoly,** pl. Rougière, ☎ 93.42.60.86. AE, DC, Euro, Visa. 20 rm P closed Dec-1 Jan, Tue, 280. Rest. ♦ Spec : *terrine de rouget à la crème de basilic, civet de lapereau « grand-mère », loup farci en croûte,* 70-215.
Roquefort-les-Pins, ⊠ 06330, 13 km E :
★★★**Auberge du Colombier,** N85, ☎ 93.77.10.27. Tx 461942. AE, Visa. 15 rm P closed 10 Jan-10 Feb, 400. Rest. ♦♦ closed Tue low season, 150-185.
Mouans-Sartoux, ⊠ 06370 :
★★**Relais de Sartoux,** rte de Valbonne, ☎ 93.60.10.57. Tx 461942. AE, Visa. 12 rm P closed 2 Jan-10 Feb and Wed ex Jul-Aug-Sep, 280. Rest. Spec : *chou farci en papillote à la mousse de foie gras, saint-pierre aux petits légumes,* 90-155.

Λ ★★★*Pont de la Paoute* (127 pl.), ☎ 93.09.11.42 ; Le Bar-sur-Loup : ★★*Gorges du Loup* (33 pl.), ☎ 93.42.45.06 ; Peymeinade : ★★*Pinède* (66 pl.), ☎ 93.36.84.35.

Restaurants :
♦♦ **Chez Pierre,** 3, av. Thiers (B1), ☎ 93.36.12.99. Closed Nov, Sun eve and Mon. Superb pastries, 60-120.
Le Val de Cuberte, 1.5 km SW on the D3 :
♦♦ **Val de Cuberte,** ☎ 93.42.01.82 P closed 15 Nov-15 Dec, Tue and Wed, 80-130.
Magagnosc, ⊠ 06520, 5 km NE on the D208 :
♦♦ **Chantecler,** ☎ 93.36.20.64 closed 1-30 Nov and Wed. Spec : *lapereau aux cèpes, volaille aux morilles,* 120-185.
Spéracèdes :
♦♦ **Bastide du Clos d'Entoure,** rte de Cabris, ☎ 93.60.53.87 P closed Fri. Pleasant dining-room ; meals also served in a garden. Spec : *magret de canard aux pêches, ris de veau aux morilles,* 90-150.
Valbonne, ⊠ 06560, 9 km E :
♦♦ **Caves de St-Bernardin,** 8, rue des Arcades, ☎ 93.42.03.88. Closed Sun and Mon, 1 Dec-17 Jan. Pleasant meals. Spec : *scampi* in tartar sauce, *lasagne,* good desserts, 120-210.

Recommended : in Opio, olive oil at *Roger Michel's mill,* ☎ 93.77.23.03.

Guided tours : 1 Jun-15 Sep, enq i

GRÉOLIÈRES

Grasse 29, Nice 49, Paris 846
26 km NW of Vence, D2
⊠ 06620 Le Bar-sur-Loup

1 425 1 800 m

i ☎ 93.09.20.20.

Hotel :
Gréolieres-les-Neiges, 18 km N :
★★**Alpina,** ☎ 93.59.70.19. 9 rm P closed 20 Apr-15 Jun, 15 Sep-20 Dec, 190. Rest. closed Wed (summer only), 50-150.

Chambre d'hôte : 200 m from the village, *mas du Colombier,* ☎ 93.59.96.45.

GRÉOUX-LES-BAINS

Aix 50, Dijon 62, Paris 787
B2 ⊠ 04800

(1 Feb-23 Dec), ☎ 92.74.22.22.

i 10, pl. de l'Hôtel-de-Ville, ☎ 92.78.01.08.

Hotels :
★★★**Crémaillère,** rte de Riez, ☎ 92.74.22.29. Tx 420357. Visa. 54 rm P closed 15 Dec-15 Feb, 270. Rest. ♦♦ 110-230.
★★**Grand Jardin,** av. des Thermes, ☎ 92.74.24.74. Euro, Visa. 80 rm P closed 10 Nov-mid-Mar, 180. Rest. ♦ 60-150.
★★**Villa Borghese** (Mapotel, Relais du Silence), av. des Thermes, ☎ 92.78.00.91. Tx 401513. AE, Euro, Visa. 70 rm P closed Dec-Feb, 350. Rest. ♦♦ 110-190.
★**Lou San Peyre,** av. des Thermes, ☎ 92.78.01.14. AE, Euro, Visa. 45 rm P closed 25 Nov-25 Feb, 200. Rest. ♦♦ 90-155.

Λ ★★★*Les Cygnes* (180 pl.), ☎ 92.78.08.08 ; ★★*Municipal* (66 pl.), ☎ 92.78.00.62 ; ★★*la Pinède* (76 pl.), ☎ 92.78.05.47.

Casino, av. des Thermes, ☎ 92.78.03.23.

GRIMAUD

Sainte-Maxime 13, Toulon 63, Paris 868
C3 ⊠ 83310 Cogolin

i ☎ 94.43.26.78.

Hotels :
★★**Boulangerie,** rte de Collobrières, 3 km W on the D14, ☎ 94.43.23.16. 10 rm P closed 1 Oct-1 Apr. Attractive setting. Half-pension obligatory during high season, 440. Rest. ♦♦ 95-130.
Port-Grimaud, 6 km E :
★★★★**Giraglia,** pl. du 14-Juin, ☎ 94.56.31.33. 48 rm P closed Oct-Dec, 960. Rest. ♦♦ closed Tue (Jan-Mar), 170-310.
★★★**Port,** ☎ 94.56.36.18. 20 rm P 385.

Λ ★★★★*Automobile Club de France,* Saint-Pons-les-Mûres (246 pl), ☎ 94.56.30.08 ; ★★★★*la Plage* (450 pl.), ☎ 94.56.31.15 ; ★★★★*les Mûres* (700 pl.), ☎ 94.56.16.97 ; 7 sites ★★★ (2 400 pl).

Restaurants :
● ♦♦♦ **Les Santons,** rte Nationale, ☎ 94.43.21.02. AE, DC, Euro closed 15 Oct-15 Mar and Wed ex noon high season. A varied menu in one of the region's best restaurants. Spec : *nage de poissons au safran, baron d'agneau aux herbes,* 250-350.
♦♦ **Le Gacharel,** 7, rue du Gacharel, ☎ 94.43.24.40. Closed Wed, 15 Oct-15 Mar, eve only (Jul-Aug). Regional dishes. Spec : *noisette d'agneau sauce au romarin, médaillon de lotte au curry et au coriandre frais,* 85-200.
Port-Grimaud :
♦♦ **L'Amphitrite,** Grande-Rue, ☎ 94.56.31.33. P closed Mon, Tue in winter and 6 Oct-1 Jan, 120-210.

Farmhouse-inn and gîte : *la Croix,* rte de Grimaud, in Port-Grimaud, ☎ 94.43.21.81.

HYÈRES

Toulon 18, Aix 99, Paris 857
C3 ⊠ 83400

i Denis Garden (B1), ☎ 94.65.18.55.

✈ Toulon-Hyères, 4 km S, ☎ 94.57.41.41.

high season, 6 trips daily from Fondue Tower (Giens peninsula) to Porquerolles (30 min), ☎ 94.58.21.81 ; from port d'Hyères 1 daily trip to Port-Cros in summer and 4 weekly trips in low season, ☎ 94.57.44.07.

SNCF ☎ 94.57.79.60.

pl. G.-Clemenceau (B1), ☎ 94.65.21.00.

Car-hire : *Budget* train + car, 1, rue du Soldat-Ferrari (C2), ☎ 94.65.63.80, at the station, ☎ 94.57.79.60, and at the airport, ☎ 94.57.41.09.

Hotels :

★★★***Paris,*** 20, av. de Belgique (B1), ☎ 94.65.33.61. Euro. 32 rm 200.

Hyères-Plage, 5 km SE :

★★***Méditerranée*** (L.F.), 8, av. de la Méditerranée, ☎ 94.58.03.89. 15 rm, closed 15 Oct-1 Feb and Tue low season, 200. Rest. ♦ ♿ 60-165.

Giens, 12 km S on the D97 :

★★★***Provençal,*** 2, pl. de l'Église, ☎ 94.58.20.09. Euro. 50 rm with terrace or balcony closed 25 Oct-20 Mar. 5-acre park, 485. Rest. ♦♦ ♿ 125-260.

★★★***Riviera Résidence,*** ☎ 94.58.21.24. 46 rm ♿ closed 30 Sep to end May. 1/2 pension only, 300.

★★★***Relais du Bon Accueil*** (Relais du Silence), ☎ 94.58.20.48. 10 rm closed 5 Nov-15 Dec, 295. Rest. ♦ 80-205.

2 sites ★★★★ ; 12 sites ★★★, big capacity.

Restaurants :

♦♦ ***Le Delfin's,*** pl. Clemenceau (B1), ☎ 94.65.04.27. AE, Euro. Visa, closed 15 Jan-15 Feb. Spec : fish, 75-130.

♦♦ ***Le Tison d'Or,*** 1, rue Galliéni (A2), ☎ 94.65.01.37. AE, DC, Euro, Visa ♿ closed Sun eve and Mon. Spec : *jambonnette de caneton aux vieux bourgogne, œufs pochés en meurette,* 100-150.

♦ ***Chez Marius,*** 1, pl. Massillon (A1), ☎ 94.65.08.93. Visa, closed 5 Jan-5 Feb, Sun eve and Mon, Mon noon in season. Reasonably priced, 60-100.

6 km on the N98 :

♦♦♦ ***La Vieille Auberge Saint-Nicolas,*** ☎ 94.66.40.01. closed Jan and Mon low season. Spec : fish, 250-350. With 11 rm.

Recommended : vases, jewelry : *Le Lavandir,* 10, rue Portalet, ☎ 94.35.52.86.

L'ISLE-SUR-LA-SORGUE

Carpentras 17, Avignon 23, Paris 700
9 km W of Fontaine-de-Vaucluse, A2

✉ 84800

ℹ pl. de l'Église, ☎ 90.38.04.78.

Hotels :

★★***Les Névons*** (L.F.), ☎ 90.20.72.00. AE, Visa. 26 rm ♿ closed 15 Dec-16 Jan, 230.

Velleron, ✉ 84740, 6 km N on the D938 :

★★★***Hostellerie de la Grangette,*** ☎ 90.20.00.77. AE, Visa. 17 rm 345. Rest. ♦♦ 120-310.

★★★*La Sorguette* (165 pl.), ☎ 90.38.05.71.

Event : Jul, Sorgue festival.

ISOLA 2000

Barcelonnette 92, Nice 94, Paris 829
6.2 km NE of Valberg, D1

✉ 06420 Saint-Sauveur-sur-Tinée

2 000-2 603 m.

ℹ Maison d'Isola, ☎ 93.02.70.50.

Hotels :

★★★★***Chastillon,*** ☎ 93.23.10.60. Tx 970507. AE, DC, Euro, Visa. 54 rm and 3 apts ♿ closed 20 Apr-15 Dec. Half pension, 660.

★★***Druos,*** ☎ 93.23.12.20. Tx 461175. AE, Visa. 40 rm ♿ closed mid-Sep to mid-Dec, end Apr-early Jul, 370. Rest. ♦ 45-90.

Les ISSAMBRES

Fréjus 13, Toulon 83, Paris 884
10 km NE of Sainte-Maxime, C3

✉ 83380

ℹ parc des Issambres, ☎ 94.96.92.51.

Hotels :

★★***La Quiétude,*** parc des Issambres, ☎ 94.96.94.34. Euro. 20 rm closed 15 Oct-5 Feb, 180. Rest. ♦ 60-190.

San-Peire-sur-Mer, 3 km SW on the N98 :

★★***Le Provençal,*** ☎ 94.96.90.49. Visa. 28 rm closed 8 Oct-1 Apr, 240. Rest. ♦ ♿ Patio. Spec : *bouillabaisse,* 95-170.

★★***La Réserve,*** pointe des Issambres, N98, ☎ 94.96.90.41. Visa. 6 rm ♿ closed end Sep-end Mar, Wed, 200. Rest. ♦♦ Good simple fare in a pine glade : *escargots pistou, marmite du pêcheur (bouillabaisse),* 100-225.

★***La Cigale,*** Issambres Creek, on the N98, ☎ 94.96.91.15. Visa. 7 rm closed Oct-Easter and Thu. Half-pension only, 180. Rest. ♦♦ ♿ Spec : *bouillabaisse, foie gras* (duck and goose) *au naturel,* 140-300.

2 sites ★★★★, 4 ★★★ and 3 ★★

ISTRES

Arles 41, Marseilles 57, Paris 750
A3

✉ 13800

ℹ all. Jean-Jaurès, ☎ 42.56.91.25.

SNCF ☎ 42.55.01.21.

Hotels :

★★★***Mirage,*** rue des Anciens-Combattants, ☎ 42.56.02.26. Tx 400983. DC, Visa. 28 rm ♿ 250. Rest. ♦♦ closed Fri eve and Mon low season, 60-150.

★★***Aystria-Tartugues,*** chem. de Tartugues, ☎ 42.56.44.55. 10 rm 180.

★★***Baumes,*** 26, rue de la Pierre-du-Pébro, ☎ 42.55.02.63. 10 rm 140.

★***Castellan,*** pl. Ste-Catherine, ☎ 42.55.13.09. 17 rm ♿ 170.

JUAN-LES-PINS

Cannes 9, Nice 24, Paris 918
D2

✉ 06160

ℹ bd Ch.-Guillaumont, ☎ 93.61.04.98.

SNCF ☎ 93.61.12.40.

Car-hire : *Budget* train + car, at the station, ☎ 93.61.12.40.

Hotels :

★★★★(L) ***Juana,*** La Pinède, av. G.-Gallice, ☎ 93.61 08.70. 42 rm ♿ Private beach ; closed end-Oct to end-Mar. Half-pension, 400. Rest. ● ♦♦♦ ***la Terrasse.*** Will, courage and persistence are Alain Ducasse's main features. After a terrible and tragic plane crash, and a lengthy reeducation, he has returned to the management of his restaurant. We are happy and proud to include him among the young chefs of our jury. His nice market-fresh produce cooking is as simple and refined as ever. Wonderful vegetables and fish : *st-pierre rôti au fenouil,* 320-450.

★★★★(L) ***Belles Rives,*** bd du Littoral, ☎ 93.61.02.79. Tx 470984. AE. 42 rm ♿ Private beach, closed 1 Oct-1 Apr. Superb view of the bay, 1 000. Rest. ♦♦♦♦ 300-450.

★★★★(L) ***Helios,*** 3, av. Dautheville, ☎ 93.61.55.25. Tx 970906. AE, DC, Visa. 70 rm Private beach, closed 15 Oct-26 Mar, 1 350. Rest. ♦♦♦ ***Le Relais*** ♿ 245-300.

★★★★***Beauséjour,*** av. Saramartel, ☎ 93.61.07.82. Tx 470673. AE, DC. 30 rm closed end Sep-Easter, 780. Rest. ♦♦ closed Mon, 100-210.
★★★***Mimosas,*** rue Pauline, ☎ 93.61.04.16. 35 rm closed 1 Oct-20 Mar, 385.
★★★***Sainte-Valérie,*** rue de l'Oratoire, ☎ 93.61.07.15. AE, DC, Visa. 32 rm Private beach, closed Nov-Easter. 1/2 pension, 310. Rest. ♦♦ 80-130.
★★***Auberge de l'Esterel,*** chemin des Îles, ☎ 93.61.86.55. 16 rm closed 15 Nov-15 Dec, 180. Rest. ● ♦♦ closed Sun eve and Mon. Meals served in a garden. Good value; relaxed atmosphere. Spec : *salade tiède de caille, noix de Saint-Jacques grillées à l'huile de noisette,* 60-180.
★★***Hôtel du Palais des Congrès,*** 4, av. des Palmiers, ☎ 93.61.04.29. 18 rm closed 25 Oct-1 Feb, 260.

Restaurants :
♦♦ ***Perroquet,*** av. G.-Gallice, ☎ 93.61.02.20. AE, Visa ; closed 1 Dec-15 Jan and Wed ex Jul-Aug, 90-200.
♦ *Lou Capitol,* av. de l'Amiral-Courbet, ☎ 93.61.22.44. closed 15 Dec-30 Jan and Wed low season. Good regional dishes, 60-150.

Casino : *Eden Beach,* bd Baudouin, ☎ 93.61.00.29.

LAMBESC

Aix 21, Apt 38, Paris 732
12 km SW of Silvacane Abbey, B2 ⊠ 13410

Hotel :
Mallemort, ⊠ 13370, 15 km NW on the N7 and D16 :
★★★★***Moulin de Vernègues,*** ☎ 90.59.12.00. Tx 401645. AE, DC, Visa. 38 rm An old flour mill in a magnificent park, 750. Rest. ♦♦♦ Gastronomical fare, 200-280.

Overnight gîte : *Barbebelle,* Rognes, 7 km E on the D15, ☎ 42.50.22.12. A small 18thC castle.

Restaurant :
♦♦♦ ***Moulin de Tante Yvonne,*** rue Benjamin-Raspail, ☎ 42.28.02.46. Book ahead. 15thC oil-extraction mill, closed 15 Jul-31 Aug, Sun eve, Mon and Tue. Fine regional fare, 220-360.

LANTOSQUE

Sospel 42, Nice 49, Paris 884
45 km N of Nice, D2 ⊠ 06450

Hotels :
★★***Ancienne Gendarmerie*** (L.F.), Le Rivet, ☎ 93.03.00.65. Tx 460000. AE. 10 rm closed Mon noon, 320. Rest. ♦♦ Spec : fish, 105-185.
La Bollène Vésubie, 2 km N on the D73 and D70 :
★★***Parc,*** ☎ 93.03.01.01. AE. 42 rm closed 15 Oct-17 Apr and Mon low season, 230. Rest. 60-105.
★★***Sapinière,*** ☎ 93.03.01.05.14 rm 100.

Le LAVANDOU

Toulon 41, Sainte-Maxime 42, Paris 880
C3 ⊠ 83980

ℹ quai G.-Péri, ☎ 94.71.00.61.

Les Iles d'Or, trips to Port-Cros and Levant Island, daily in summer and 3 times weekly in winter, ☎ 94.71.01.02.

Car-hire : *Budget* train + car, La Salamandre, rue A.-Renoir, ☎ 94.64.85.31.

Hotels :
★★★***Auberge la Calanque,*** 62, av. du Gal.-de-Gaulle, ☎ 94.71.05.96. AE, DC, Euro, Visa. 39 rm closed 2 Nov-1 Feb. At the port. Rm with terrace, 300. Rest. ♦♦ Spec : *crème de moules « Calanques »,* desserts, 150-200.
★★***Beau Rivage,*** bd du Front-de-Mer, ☎ 94.71.11.09. Visa. 24 rm closed 15 Oct-1Apr. Half-pension only, 300.
Saint-Clair, 3 km on the N559 :
★★★***Orangerie,*** pl. de St-Clair, ☎ 94.71.04.25. AE, Visa. 20 rm including some with kitchenette. closed 30 Sep-1 May, 295.
★★★***Belle Vue*** (Relais du Silence), bd du Fort-des-Maures, ☎ 94.71.01.06. AE, Visa. 19 rm closed 15 Oct-early Apr, 180-360. Rest. ♦♦ 100-150.
La Fossette-Plage, 3 km on the N559 :
★★★★***Hôtel 83,*** ☎ 94.71.20.15. Visa. 28 rm closed 30 Sept-1 Apr, 680. Rest. ♦♦ 140-200.
Aiguebelle, 5.5 km on the N559 :
● ★★★***Roches Fleuries,*** 1 av. des Trois-Dauphins, ☎ 94.71.05.07. Tx 403997. AE, DC, Euro, Visa. 48 rm closed 16 Oct-15 Apr. A delightful setting ; hotel overlooking the sea, with swimming pool nestled in rocks. 1/2 pension, 1 000. Rest. ♦♦ 100-160.
★★***Plage,*** 14, rue des Trois-Dauphins, ☎ 94.05.80.74. 52 rm closed 5 Oct-Easter, 280. Rest. 80-130.
Cavalière, 8 km E on the N559 :
★★★★***Club,*** plage de Cavalière, ☎ 94.05.80.14. Tx 420317. AE, DC, Visa. 32 rm closed mid-Oct to end Apr. Most attractive setting. Private beach. Half-pension, 1 500. Rest. ● ♦♦♦ A. Gigant's highly inventive cooking. Spec : *loup en croûte, nougat glacé au chocolat et à la crème de miel.* Reasonably priced for the coast, 160-250.

⛺ ★★★★*Les Mimosas* (185 pl.), ☎ 94.05.82.94 ; ★★★*Pramousquier* (180 pl.), ☎ 94.05.83.95.

Restaurants :
● ♦♦♦ ***Au Vieux Port,*** quai G.-Péri, ☎ 94.71.00.21. AE, Visa closed 1 Oct-18 Apr. Excellent fish. Spec : *moules fourrées sauce homard, noisettes de baudroie aux écrevisses et petits légumes,* 175-230.
♦♦ ***La Serpe,*** plage d'Aiguebelle, ☎ 94.05.81.49. AE, Visa closed Sep-Jun, 170-260.
♦ ***Denise et Michel,*** 6, rue Patron-Ravello, ☎ 94.71.12.81 closed 30 Oct-1 Apr, Mon and Thu noon low season, 70-100.

LEVENS

Cannes 54, Digne 136, Paris 833
23 km N of Nice, D2
⊠ 06670 Saint-Martin-du-Var

Hotel :
★★***Vigneraie,*** rte de Saint-Blaise, ☎ 93.79.70.46. Visa. 20 rm closed Oct to mid-Jan, 150. Rest. ♦ 50-90.

Le LUC

Draguignan 28, Toulon 53, Paris 841
23 km E of Brignoles, C3 ⊠ 83340

ℹ pl. de Verdun, ☎ 94.60.74.51 (high season), and mairie, ☎ 94.60.88.21.

Hotels :
★★***Hostellerie du Parc,*** 12, rue J.-Jaurès, ☎ 94.60.70.01. AE, Visa. 12 rm closed 28 Apr-8 May and 12 Nov-12 Dec, Mon eve and Tue, 250. Rest. ♦♦ Spec : *brouillade aux truffes, carré d'agneau,* 130-200.

Le Cannet-des-Maures, 2 km E :
★***Mas du Four*** (L.F.), quartier de la Grande-Bastide, 2.5 km on the N7, ☎ 94.60.74.64. DC, Visa. 10 rm 🅿 ♨ ⛱ ⊟ ⚲ ♿ closed 15 Jan-15 Feb, Sun eve and Mon low season, 170. Rest. ♦ ✧ 65-130.

Restaurant :
Le Thoronet, 11 km N :
♦♦ ***Relais de l'Abbaye,*** Les Bruns, 3 km NW on the D84, ☎ 94.73.87.59 ⚘ 🅿 ♨ ⛱ closed Mon and Tue high season, Mon-Fri low season. Pleasant setting. Spec : *tripes à la niçoise, délice de mousse de foie de canard aux raisins, pigeon farci aux morilles,* 130-150.

⛺ ★★★*Le Provençal* (110 pl.), ☎ 94.60.80.50.

Recommended : Fri : Provençal market.

MANDELIEU-LA-NAPOULE

Fréjus 35, Nice 38, Paris 900
7 km W of Cannes, D2 ⊠ 06210

ℹ av. de Cannes, ☎ 93.49.14.39.

SNCF ☎ 93.49.95.13.

Hotels :
★★★★***Ermitage du Riou*** (Mapotel), bd H.-Clews, ☎ 93.49.95.56. Tx 470072. AE, Euro, Visa. 42 rm ⚘ 🅿 ♨ ⛱ ⊟ ♿ Beautiful Provencal building opposite the port, 940. Rest. ♦♦ closed 3 Nov-21 Dec, 100-230.
★★***Sant'Angelo,*** 681, av. de la Mer, ☎ 93.49.28.23. 33 rm ⚘ 🅿 ♨ ⛱ 210.

⛺ ★★★★*L'Argentière* (100 pl.), ☎ 93.49.95.04 ; ★★★*Plateau des Chasseurs* (150 pl.), ☎ 93.49.25.93 ; ★★★*Cerisiers* (160 pl.), ☎ 93.47.22.25 ; ★★★*Roc Fleuri* (150 pl.), ☎ 93.93.08.71.

Restaurants :
● ♦♦♦♦ ***Oasis*** (Louis Outhier), rue Jean-Honoré-Carle, ☎ 93.49.95.52. Tx 461389 ♨ closed Mon eve, Tue and 5 Nov-15 Dec. This pleasant, restful and gourmand place deserves its name. Louis Outhier's cooking is greatly inspired from Southeast Asian flavours, but his restaurant remains one of the greatest in France : *foie gras au gingembre, homard aux heures thaïlandaises, aiguillettes de canard à l'armagnac,* 340-450.
♦♦ ***Brocherie II,*** at the port, ☎ 93.49.80.73. Visa 🅿 closed 5-25 Jan, Mon eve and Tue low season. A single menu : shellfish platter, fish. Excellent value for money, 150-200.

MANOSQUE

Aix 53, Digne 58, Paris 772
B2 ⊠ 04100

ℹ ☎ 92.72.16.00.

SNCF ☎ 92.72.08.04.

Hotels :
★★***Sud,*** av. du Gal-de-Gaulle, ☎ 92.87.78.58. AE, Euro, Visa. 35 rm ♨ ♿ 200.
★★***François Ier,*** 18, rue Guilhempierre, ☎ 92.72.07.99, 92.72.14.34. Euro, Visa. 25 rm, 150.

La Fuste, ⊠ 04210 Valensole, 7 km E on the D907 and D4 :
★★★★***Hostellerie de la Fuste*** (Relais du Silence), ☎ 92.72.05.95. AE, Euro, Visa. 9 rm ⚘ 🅿 ♨ ⛱ Beautiful farmhouse with Provincal furnishings, in a large park, closed 12 Nov-17 Dec, Sun eve and Mon ex nat hols and 30 Jun-15 Sep, 950. Rest. ● ♦♦♦ In the heart of Durance, a beautiful terrace under plane trees. Daniel Jourdan plays with the subtleties of Provençal cooking : *agneau, truite Jean Giono, canard au miel de lavande,* 175-350.

★★***La Rose de Provence,*** rte de Sisteron, ☎ 92.87.56.28, 92.72.02.69. AE, Euro, Visa. 16 rm ⚘ 🅿 ♨ ⛱ 250. Rest. ♦ ♿ closed Sun and Mon eve. Spec : *filet de bœuf en brioche sauce Périgueux, ris de veau braisé aux morilles, côte de veau « Pojarski »,* 125-210.

⛺ ★★★*Municipal* (110 pl.), ☎ 92.72.28.08.

Restaurant :
♦ ***André,*** 21 *bis,* pl. du Terreau, ☎ 92.72.03.09. Euro, Visa ♨ closed Jun, Sun eve (winter only) and Mon, 65-105.

MARSEILLES

Nice 188, Lyons 315, Paris 778
B3 ⊠ 13000

ℹ 4, la Canebière (C2), 13001, ☎ 91.54.91.11.

✈ Marseilles-Marignane, 26 km NW, ☎ 42.89.90.10.
Air France Agency, 14, la Canebière (C2), 13001, ☎ 91.54.92.50, and 331, av. du Prado (off map, C3), ☎ 91.71.11.00.
Airport bus terminal, pl. V.-Hugo, 13003.

⛴ Corsica, quai de la Joliette (A1), 13002, ☎ 91.91.90.66.

SNCF Saint-Charles (D1), ☎ 91.08.50.50, 91.95.10.00, 91.08.84.12.

🚌 *Messagerie des autocars,* pl. V.-Hugo (D1), 13003, ☎ 91.08.09.53.

Car-hire : *Budget* train + car, 36, av. Charles-Nédelec (D1), 13003, ☎ 91.90.88.67, at the station, ☎ 91.50.83.85, 182, av. de la Valbarelle, 13011, ☎ 91.44.96.49, and at the airport. (→ Marignane.)

Hotels :
★★★★(L) ***Petit Nice*** (Relais et châteaux), anse de Maldormé, opposite 160, Kennedy coastal road (off map, A4), 13007, ☎ 91.52.14.39. 14 rm + 6 apts ⚘ 🅿 ♨ ⛱ ⊟ ♿ closed Jan, 950. Rest. ♦♦♦♦ ⚘ ✧ closed 2 Jan-8 Feb, Mon. Very high standard cooking, very high prices too, 250-300.
★★★★(L) ***Vieux Port*** (Sofitel), 36, bd Charles-Livon (A3), 13007, ☎ 91.52.90.19. Tx 401270. AE, DC, Euro, Visa. 222 rm ⚘ 🅿 ⊟ ♿ 850. Rest. ● ♦♦ ***Les Trois Forts*** ⚘ closed Aug. Expertly-prepared regional fare. Spec : *filets de rouget aux deux herbes de poivron, râble de lapereau farci aux écrevisses, nouilles fraîches aux heures,* 250-300. Rest. ***le Jardin.*** Rapid service, 130-150.
★★★★***Beauvau*** (P.L.M.), 4, rue Beauvau (C2), 13001, ☎ 91.54.91.00. Tx 401778. AE, DC, Euro, Visa. 72 rm ⚘ 520.
★★★★***Frantel,*** rue Neuve-Saint-Martin (C2), 13001, ☎ 91.91.91.29. Tx 401886. AE, Euro, Visa. 200 rm ⚘ 🅿 ♿ 550. Rest. ● ♦♦ ***l'Oursinade,*** closed 27 Jul-24 Aug and Sun. A good Lyonnais chef cooks Provençal regional dishes : *fricassée de soles et rougets barigoule, roussettes en timbale, côtes de veau tapenade,* 85-250.
★★★***Palm-Beach*** (Concorde), 2, prom. de la Plage, Prado Bay (off map, C4), 13008, ☎ 91.76.20.00. Tx 401894. AE, DC, Euro, Visa. 161 rm ⚘ 🅿 ♨ ⛱ ⊟ ♿ 530. Rest. ♦♦♦ ***la Réserve.*** Good fish served on a seafront terrace, 120-300. Rest. ***les Voiliers :*** grill, 80-130.
★★★***Castellane,*** 31, rue du Rouet (D4), ⊠ 13006, ☎ 91.79.27.54. AE, Visa. 55 rm 🅿 ♿ 300.
★★★***Grand Hôtel de Genève,*** 3 *bis,* rue Reine-Élisabeth (C2), 13001, ☎ 91.90.51.42. Tx 440672. DC, Visa. 45 rm and 4 apts ⛱ ✧ 260.
★★★***Résidence Bompard,*** 2, rue des Flots-Bleus, just off the coast road, 13007 (off map, A4), ☎ 91.52.10.93. Tx 400430, AE. 47 rm 🅿 ♨ ⛱ ♿ 300.

★★***Européen,*** 115, rue de Paradis (C2), 13006, ☎ 91.37.77.20. 40 rm closed Aug, 230.
★★***Martini,*** 5, bd Gustave-Desplaces (C1), 13003, ☎ 91.64.11.17. AE. 40 rm Ⓟ ♿ 230.
★★***Le Président,*** 12, bd L.-Salvator, ☎ 91.48.67.29. Tx 430301. Visa. 18 rm Ⓟ 200.

Youth hostels : 47, av. Joseph-Vidal, imp. du Dr-Bonfils, 13008, ☎ 91.73.21.81, and château de Bois-Luzy, 13012, ☎ 91.49.06.18.

⛺ ★★*Bonneveine* (200 pl.), ☎ 91.73.26.99 ; ★★*les Vagues* (200 pl.), ☎ 91.73.04.88 ; ★★*Moricelli* (100 pl.), ☎ 91.40.09.88 ; ★★*Calanque Blanche* (67 pl.), ☎ 91.73.67.73.

Restaurants :
● ♦♦♦ ***Maurice Brun,*** 18, quai Rive-Neuve (B2), 13007, ☎ 91.33.35.38. Book ahead ; closed Sun and Mon. This restaurant is a local institution with its single, unchanging *menu dégustation,* sampling Provencal gastronomical fare which has been served up here for the past 4 decades ! 210-320.
♦♦♦ ***Max Caizergues,*** 11, rue G.-Ricard (CD3), 13006, ☎ 91.33.58.07. AE, Visa closed Sat noon, Sun and 13 Jul-16 Aug. The heights of culinary professionalism in this large dining-room ; all dishes are of a consistently exemplary quality. Spec : *homard au pistou, foie chaud à la menthe,* 150-250.
● ♦♦ ***Calypso,*** 3, rue des Catalans (C2), 13007, ☎ 91.52.64.00. closed Sun, Mon and Aug. The twin of the restaurant ***Michel,*** with fresh fish at crazy prices, 210-320.
● ♦♦ ***Michel-Aux Catalans,*** 6, rue des Catalans (C2), 13007, ☎ 91.52.64.22. Visa closed Tue, Wed and Jul. The day's catch, served with the same mastery as at the ***Calypso*** (same family). Spec : *bourride* and *bouillabaisse,* 300-400.
● ♦♦ ***Miramar,*** 12, quai du port (B2), 13002, ☎ 91.91.10.40. AE, Euro, Visa closed Sun, 3-26 Aug and 23 Dec-9 Jan. A good restaurant in the old port, where sure value like this is too often the exception ! Spec : *bourride et vraie bouillabaisse,* 150-220.
● ♦♦ ***Caruso,*** 158, quai du Port (B2), 13002, ☎ 91.90.94.04. AE ♿ closed Sun eve and Mon, 10 Aug-10 Sep. Marseilles folklore, Italian cooking and a view on the old port, 180-300.
♦♦ ***Tire-Bouchon,*** 11, cours Julien (D2), 13006, ☎ 91.42.49.03. Closed Sun, Mon, and 10 Jul-30 Aug. 1900's setting and copious traditional cooking, 125-240.
● ♦ ***Fonfon,*** 140, vallon des Auffes (coastal road ; off map, A4), 13007, ☎ 91.52.14.38. AE, Visa ♿ closed Sat, Sun, Oct and 23 Dec-2 Jan. An excellent bistro, where the fish is fresh-caught and simply prepared : grilled over a wood fire, or served in a *bouillabaisse,* 220-310.
● ♦ ***Chez Angèle,*** 50, rue Caisserie (B2), 13002, ☎ 91.90.63.35. ♿ closed 14 Jul-7 Aug, Sun eve and Mon. Warm family atmosphere with a "Midi" accent, 80-100.
● ♦ ***Le Chaudron Provençal,*** 48, rue Caisserie (B2), 13002, ☎ 91.91.02.37. AE, Visa, Ⓟ ♿ closed nat hols. An abundance of relatively inexpensive fresh fish dishes. Priority is given to local wines, 220-250.
● ♦ ***La Pêcherie,*** chemin Littoral, 13016, 8 km NW, ☎ 91.46.24.33. AE Ⓟ ♿ closed Sun eve. The new port restaurant ; predictably, fish is favored here, 100-250.
● ♦ ***Georges Mavro,*** 2, la Canebière (C2), ☎ 91.33.00.94. AE, DC ; closed Sat and Sun (Jul and Aug), Sun and Mon noon (1 Sep-30 Jun). Nice, modern cooking on la Canebière. Fashionable and expensive, 200-270.

♦ ***Cousin-Cousine,*** 102, cours Julien (D2), 13006, ☎ 91.48.14.50. AE, Visa ; closed Sun and Mon, 15-28 Feb, 1-15 Oct. The fresh-caught fish is recommended, 100-150.
♦ ***La Ferme,*** 23, rue Sainte, ☎ 91.33.21.12. Closed Aug, Sat noon, Sun and nat hols. Spec : *moules en godets, filet de bœuf à la cervelle,* 120-210.
♦ ***La Folle Époque,*** 10, pl. F.-Barret, ☎ 91.33.17.26. ♿ closed Sun, 80-130.

Recommended : chocolates and *calissons* (local sweets) : *Chocolaterie Puyricard,* 315, corniche Kennedy, 13007, ☎ 91.31.31.32.

MARTIGUES

Marseilles 40, Arles 52, Paris 775
15 km S of Istres, A3 ✉ 13500

ℹ quai Paul-Doumer, ☎ 42.80.30.72.

SNCF ☎ 42.81.40.57.

Hotel :
★★★***Saint-Roch,*** moulin de Paradis, old Port-de-Bouc road, ☎ 42.80.19.73. AE, Euro, Visa. 37 rm Ⓟ ♿ 300. Rest. ♦♦ 90-180.

⛺ ★★★*Le Cap* (150 pl.), ☎ 42.80.73.02 ; ★★★ *le Mas* (166 pl.), ☎ 42.80.70.34 ; 7 sites ★★ (more than 1 300 pl.).

MENTON

Nice 27, Cannes 63, Paris 963
D2 ☎ 93 ✉ 06500

ℹ Palais de l'Europe, av. Boyer (A2), ☎ 93.57.57.00.

Old Port, quai Napoléon-III (C1), Menton-Monaco line, ☎ 93.35.51.72.

SNCF (A2), ☎ 93.35.87.89.

av. Sospel (A1), ☎ 93.35.93.60.

Car-hire : *Budget* train + car, at the station, ☎ 93.35.73.61, and 2, av. Boyer, ☎ 93.28.28.54.

Hotels :
★★★***Napoléon,*** 29, porte de France (C1), ☎ 93.35.89.50. Tx 470312. AE, DC, Euro, Visa. 40 rm Ⓟ ♿ Ideally situated at Garavan Bay. Closed 1 Nov-20 Dec. 1/2 pension only, 700. Rest. ♦♦ 130-240.
★★★***Méditerranée,*** 5, rue de la République (B1), ☎ 93.28.25.25. Tx 461361. AE, Visa. 90 rm Ⓟ ♿ closed Sun and Mon noon, 350. Rest Snacks ♿ 75-140.
★★★***Princess et Richemond,*** 32, av. Gal-de-Gaulle (A2), ☎ 93.35.80.20. Tx 470673. AE, DC, Visa. 45 rm Ⓟ opposite the seafront ; terraces and sun-deck ; closed 3 Nov-20 Dec, 300.
★★***Chez Mireille-l'Hermitage,*** 20, av. Carnot and prom. du Soleil (A2), ☎ 93.35.77.23. AE, Visa. 21 rm Ⓟ ♿ A good, unadorned hotel, closed Tue low season, 300. Rest. ♦♦ 100-210.
★★***Dauphin,*** 28, bd du Gal-de-Gaulle (A2), ☎ 93.35.76.37. 30 rm Ⓟ ♿ closed 25 Oct-20 Dec, 260. Rest. ♦ closed eve and Sat. Meals served in a garden, 60-130.
★★***Magali,*** 10, rue Villarey (B1), ☎ 93.35.73.78. 43 rm Ⓟ closed Nov, 200.
★★***Orly,*** 27, porte de France (C1), ☎ 93.35.60.81. 24 rm Ⓟ ♿ closed 25 Oct-20 Dec, 250. Rest. ♦ closed Tue low season. Dining in a garden, 70-120.
★★***Stella Bella,*** 850, promenade du Soleil (A2), ☎ 93.35.74.47. Visa. 26 rm Ⓟ ♿ closed 20 Oct-20 Dec and Mon, 230. Rest. 80-130.
★***Santons*** (L.F.), colline de l'Annonciade (A1), ☎ 93.35.94.10. AE, Visa. 10 rm Ⓟ closed 15 Nov-15 Dec, 180. Rest. ♦♦ Good, simple fare.

Spec : *feuilleté de saumon au châteauneuf-du-pape blanc, ris de veau aux mousselines de volaille et champignons,* 100-300.

Castillon, 12 km N on the D2566 :
★★★**Bergerie,** ☎ 93.04.00.39. 15 rm ⚟ 🅿 ♨ ⛱ ♿ closed 30 Sep-31 Mar. Delightful residence with old-fashioned furnishings, 280. Rest. ♦♦ 95-150.

Youth hostel : Saint-Michel Plateau, ☎ 93.35.93.14.

⛺ ★★*Municipal* (172 pl.), ☎ 93.35.81.23 ; ★★*St-Maurice* (50 pl.), ☎ 93.35.79.84.

Restaurants :
♦♦ ***Roc Amadour,*** 1, sq. Victoria (C1), ☎ 93.35.76.04. AE, Euro, Visa ⚟ 🅿 ♿ closed Mon noon. Simple, traditional dishes. Spec : *salade Roc Amadour (rôtie de bûchettes de chèvre, foie gras sur salade), tian de sardine à la polente.* Beautiful terrace, 90-180.
♦♦ ***Francine,*** 1-3, quai Bonaparte (C1), ☎ 93.35.80.67. AE, Euro, Visa ♿ closed 14 Nov-15 Dec, Mon noon. One of the best sea food restaurants in Menton. Spec : *loup grillé au fenouil, langouste à la normande, filet de saint-pierre à la crème d'estragon,* 120-250.
♦ ***Chez Germaine,*** 46, prom. du Mal-Leclerc (A1), ☎ 93.35.66.90. 🅿 ♿ closed Mon. Good, plain cooking at modest prices, 80-130.

Monti, 5 km N on the D2566 :
● ♦♦ ***L'Artisan Gourmand,*** 25, rue des Marins, ☎ 93.35.74.21. Closed 25 Nov-27 Dec and Sun. Vegetarian. In the old city, a festival of tastes and flavours with only fresh vegetables of the region : *omelette forestière, bagna caouda,* 80-130.
♦♦ ***Pierrot et Pierrette,*** pl. de l'Église, ☎ 93.35.79.76. ⚟ closed 3 Dec-15 Jan and Mon, 100-200. With 3 rm, 165.

Casino : *du Soleil,* av. Félix-Faure, ☎ 93.57.11.31. Night-club.

MONTE-CARLO

Menton 9, Nice 18, Paris 958
(Principality of Monaco)
D2 ⊠ Principality of Monaco

ℹ Direction Tourisme et Congrès, 2A, bd des Moulins (C1), ☎ 93.30.87.01.

SNCF (A3), ☎ 93.50.60.47, 93.30.74.00.

Car-hire : *Budget* train + car, at the station, ☎ 93.30.25.53, and 3, av. Gal-Leclerc, Beausoleil, ☎ 93.78.78.42.

Hotels :
★★★★**Beach Plaza,** 22, av. Princesse-Grace (C1), ☎ 93.30.98.80. Tx 479617, AE, Euro, Visa. 320 rm ⚟ 🅿 ♨ ⛱ ▭ ♿ Private beach. Splendid view of the sea and Monaco, 1 125. Rest. ♦♦♦ 140-250.
★★★★(L) ***Hermitage,*** sq. Beaumarchais (C2), ☎ 93.50.67.31. Tx 479432. AE, DC, Euro, Visa. 252 rm ⚟ 🅿 ♨ ▭ Beautiful late 19thC façade. Charming winter garden, 1 400. Rest. ♦♦♦♦ ***la Belle Époque*** ✠ ♿ Sumptuous baroque-style dining-room. Spec : *saumon cru aux courgettes, viennoise de saumon au confit de poireaux,* 200-300.
★★★★(L) ***Paris,*** pl. du Casino (C2), ☎ 93.50.80.80. Tx 469925. AE, DC, Euro, Visa. 260 rm ⚟ 🅿 ♨ ▭ ♿ 1 600. Rest. ♦♦♦ ***Salle Empire*** ⚟ ✠ 300-500. ♦♦ ***Grill-room,*** closed Mon. Roof-top dining with view of the coast, 120-210. Discotheque and cabaret.
★★★★(L) ***Loews-Monte Carlo,*** av. Spélugues (C1-2), ☎ 93.50.65.00. Tx 479435. AE, Euro, Visa. 636 rm ⚟ 🅿 ♨ ✠ ▭ ♿ 1 700. Rest. ♦♦♦ ***l'Argentin*** ✠ closed noon and 3 Oct-7 Dec. Excellent grilled meats ; pleasant "hacienda" setting, 220-310. ♦♦♦ ***Le Foie Gras*** ✠ closed mid-Nov-20 Dec. Traditional cooking, 220-310. ♦♦ ***Le Pistou*** ✠ Provençal dishes, 220-310. ♦ ***Café de la Mer,*** 120-210.
★★★★(L) ***Mirabeau,*** 1-3, av. Princesse-Grace (C1). ☎ 93.25.45.45. Tx 479413. AE, DC, Euro, Visa. 100 rm ⚟ 🅿 ▭ ♿ 1 100. Rest. ● ♦♦♦ ***la Coupole*** ✠ The fine and delicious cooking of a professional, Yves Garnier : *millefeuille de rouget à la sauce légère,* 165-350.
★★★**Balmoral,** 12, av. de la Costa (B2), ☎ 93.50.62.37. Tx 479436. AE, DC, Euro, Visa. 68 rm ⚟ ⛱ ✠ Established hotel facing the port, 420. Rest. ♦♦ closed Sun eve, Mon and nat hols, 60-130.

Monte-Carlo Beach, 06190 Roquebrune-Cap-Martin, 2.5 km NE :
● ★★★★(L) ***Monte-Carlo Beach,*** av. du Bord-de-Mer, ☎ 93.78.21.40. 46 rm ⚟ 🅿 ⛱ ▭ ⚲ closed mid-Oct to 26 Mar. Period façade and spectacular view over Monaco and the sea, 1 100. Rest. ♦♦ 120-320.

Restaurants :
● ♦♦♦ ***Dominique Le Stanc,*** 18, bd des Moulins (C1), ☎ 93.50.63.37. AE, DC, Visa ♿ closed Sun and Mon. It is the latest future great chef who has settled on the coast. Grand style, blue, beige decor, superb collection of old toys. Light cooking by D. Le Stanc inspired by his masters Chapel, Haerberlin, Senderens : *petites courgettes rondes au homard et truffe, filets de rouget pochés aux olives et basilic, cerises poêlées à la menthe fraîche sur une glace vanille.* Excellent choice of Alsatian wines. Prices are high... the casino is nearby, 180-400.
♦♦♦ ***Bec Rouge,*** 11, av. de Gde-Bretagne (C1), ☎ 93.50.97.48. AE, DC, Euro, Visa 🅿 ♿ closed 2 weeks in Jan, 2 weeks in Jun and Sun. Elegant setting. Spec : *bavaroise de saumon au basilic, gratin de langouste, pot-au-feu de la mer,* 170-220.
♦♦ ***Rampoldi,*** 3, av. des Spélugues (C1-2), ☎ 93.30.70.65. AE, DC, Visa ; closed Nov. Meeting place for the Monte-Carlo fashionable set. Italian specialities, 250-270.
♦♦ ***Toula,*** 20, bd de Suisse (B2), ☎ 93.50.02.02. AE, DC, Visa ♿ closed mid-Dec to mid-Jan and Mon. Superb Italian cooking and good wines, 350-400.
♦♦ ***Calanque,*** 33, av. Saint-Charles (C1), ☎ 93.50.63.19. AE, DC, Visa ; closed 15 Mar-15 Apr and Sun. Wonderfully fresh fish and shellfish, 160-250. Snacks after 11 p.m., 80-130.
● ♦ ***Sam's Place,*** 1, av. H.-Dunand, ☎ 93.50.89.33. Closed Sun. Nice cooking, prices are reasonable for Monte-Carlo, 80-140.
♦ ***Polpetta,*** 2, rue de Paradis (B1), ☎ 93.50.67.84. 🅿 closed Feb and Tue. Elegant trattoria with excellent pasta, 80-150.

Events : Jul-Aug : *International Fireworks Festival.*

Casino : pl. du Casino, ☎ 93.50.69.31.

MOUGINS

Grasse 11, Nice 32, Paris 908
6 km N of Cannes, D2 ⊠ 06250

ℹ pl. du Village, ☎ 93.90.15.15.

Hotels :
● ★★★★**Moulin de Mougins** (Roger Vergé), quartier Notre-Dame-de-Vie, 2.5 km on the D3, ☎ 93.75.78.24. Tx 970732. AE, DC, Visa. 5 rm 🅿 ♨ ⛱ ♿ closed Mon and Thu noon, 15 Feb to end Mar and 15 Nov-3 Dec, 1 000. Rest. ● ♦♦♦♦ An extremely pleasant 16thC mill in the heart of Provence where Denise and Roger Vergé wel-

come you. A gourmand stop-over where the "sunny" cooking remarkably prepared by Serge Chollet leads you to perfect happiness : *petits artichauts violets à la barigoule, blanc de loup au vin de Bourgogne, rougets au pistou.* Very good desserts and wines, 370-600.

● ★★★**Clos des Boyères,** 89, chemin de la Chapelle, ☎ 93.90.01.58. AE, DC, Euro, Visa. 36 rm 🅿 ⚘ ☀ ▭ ⚲ closed 1 Nov-1 Feb, 500. Rest. ♦♦ closed Wed low season, 80-150.

★★★**Mas Candille,** bd Clément-Rebuffel, ☎ 93.90.00.85. Tx 462131. AE, DC, Euro, Visa. 25 rm ⚶ 🅿 ⚘ ☀ ▭ closed 4 Nov-20 Dec and 3 weeks during Jan-Feb. Pretty terrace gardens, 500. Rest. ♦♦ An old Provençal style farmhouse with antique furniture. Cooking prepared by C. Taffarels, a former cook at *Moulin de Mougins : courgette fleur, fricassée de lotte aux pâtes fraîches,* 150-250.

⛺ ★★★*Les Lentisques* (133 pl.), ☎ 93.90.00.45.

Restaurants :

● ♦♦♦ **Relais de Mougins** (Relais Gourmand), pl. de la Mairie, ☎ 93.90.03.47. Visa ♿ closed 11 Nov-18 Dec, Sun eve and Mon ex Jul-Aug and nat hols. The elaborate cooking of the team of André Surmain who is a great professional ; interesting menus. Spec : salmon, turbot, *lotte, volaille* (poultry) *poêlée au foie gras,* 160-400.

♦♦♦ **Amandier de Mougins,** pl. du Cdt-Lamy, ☎ 93.90.00.91. ⚶ closed 2 Jan-12 Feb, Wed and Sat noon. The same management as the *Moulin* above. Excellent cooking inspired by R. Vergé. Good wine selection. "Roger Vergé" cooking school, 220-310.

● ♦♦ **Bistrot de Mougins,** pl. du Village, ☎ 93.75.78.34. closed 30 Nov-15 Jan, Tue and Wed low season. Friendly service ; good, inexpensive meals. Regional dishes : *tourte aux blettes, beignets d'aubergines,* 100-150.

♦♦ **Ferme de Mougins,** 10, av. Saint-Basile, ☎ 93.90.03.74. AE, DC, Euro, Visa 🅿 ⚘ ♿ closed 15 Nov-20 Dec, 15 Feb-15 Mar, Mon and Thu noon ex Jul-Aug. A background of lush greenery and flowers. Good food served with delicious wines from Provence, 140-350.

♦♦ **France,** pl. du Cdt-Lamy, ☎ 93.90.00.01. ⚘ closed Sun eve and Mon, Jan. Charming service and simple, tasty food, 125-200. With rm.

♦♦ **Feu Follet,** pl. de la Mairie, ☎ 93.90.15.78. ⚶ ⚘ ♿ closed 3-23 Nov, 4-21 Mar, Sun eve and Mon low season, 75-120.

MOUSTIERS-SAINTE-MARIE

Digne 48, Aix 86, Paris 793
C2 ✉ 04360

ℹ ☎ 92.74.67.84.

Hotel :

★**Relais,** ☎ 92.74.66.10. 15 rm. closed 1 Dec-1 Mar, 160. Rest. 75-160.

ℹ ★★★*Saint-Jean* (110 pl.), ☎ 92.74.66.85 ; ★★*le Moulin* (100 pl.), ☎ 92.74.66.66 ; ★★*Saint-Clair* (175 pl.), ☎ 92.74.67.15.

Restaurant :

♦♦ **Les Santons,** pl. de l'Église, ☎ 92.74.66.48. AE ⚶ ☀ ♿ closed Mon eve and Tue low season, 5 Jan-20 Feb. The best stop-over in the area ; an enchanting place and dishes full of Provençal flavour, 135-220.

NANS-LES-PINS

Marseilles 41, Aix 42, Paris 800
12 km SW of Saint-Maximin-la-Sainte-Baume
B3 ✉ 83860

ℹ ☎ 92.78.95.91.

Hotel :

● ★★★★**Domaine de Châteauneuf** (Relais et châteaux), 3.5 km on the D00 and N500, ☎ 94.78.90.06. Tx 400747. AE, Euro, Visa. 34 rm ⚶ 🅿 ⚘ ☀ ▭ ⚲ closed 31 Oct-21 Mar, 550. Rest. ♦♦ ♿ 165-285.

⛺ ★★★**Ste-Baume** (90 pl.), ☎ 94.78.92.68.

NICE

Cannes 34, Marseilles 188, Paris 934
D2 ✉ 06000

ℹ av. Thiers (B2), ☎ 93.87.07.07 ; 5, av. Gustave-V (D2), ☎ 93.87.60.60.

✈ Nice - Côte-d'Azur, 7 km SW, ☎ 93.72.30.30. *Air France Agency* : 7, av. Gustave-V, ☎ 93.83.91.00.

⛴ Lines for Corsica (C4), ☎ 93.89.89.89.

SNCF (B2-3), ☎ 93.88.29.54, 93.87.50.50, 93.88.89.93.

🚌 prom. du Paillon, ☎ 93.85.61.81.

Car-hire : *Budget* train + car, 34, rue Auber, ☎ 93.37.29.51, at the station, ☎ 93.88.89.91, and at the airport, ☎ 93.72.36.50.

Hotels :

★★★★(L) **Negresco,** 37, prom. des Anglais (B4), ☎ 93.88.39.51. Tx 460040. AE, DC, Euro, Visa. 150 rm ⚶ ♿ Empire and Napoléon III atmosphere (classified historic monument), 1 500. Rest.

● ♦♦♦♦ **Chanteclerc.** Jacques Maximin's restaurant remains the real gourmand attraction of the Côte d'Azur and even of France. A meal at *Chanteclerc* is superb, like a pilgrimage and worth the trip. Wonderful, light cooking and traditional Niçoise flavoured cooking. Exceptional choice of desserts, 300-600.

★★★★(L) **Beach Regency,** 223, prom. des Anglais (A4), ☎ 93.83.91.51. Tx 461635. AE, Euro, Visa. 322 rm ⚶ 🅿 ▭ ♿ 850. Rest. ♦♦♦ **Rendez-vous,** 145-200.

★★★★(L) **Méridien,** 1, prom. des Anglais (B4), ☎ 93.82.25.25. Tx 470361. AE, DC, Euro, Visa. 314 rm ⚶ ▭ 650. Rest. ♦♦ **l'Estacade** ⚶ ♿ 180-280.

★★★★**La Pérouse,** 11, quai Rauba-Capeu (D4), ☎ 93.62.34.63. Tx 461411. AE, DC, Euro, Visa. 65 rm ⚶ ⚘ ☀ ▭ 600. Rest. ♦♦ grillroom, closed 15 Sep-1 Jun, 80-100.

★★★★**Westminster** (Concorde), 27, prom. des Anglais (B4), ☎ 94.88.29.44. Tx 460872. AE, Visa. 110 rm ⚶ ♿ 850. Rest. ♦♦ **Il Pozzo,** closed 1 Nov-15 Dec, 155-230. **Le Farniente,** 120-210.

★★★**Ambassador,** 8, av. de Suède (B3), ☎ 93.87.75.79. Tx 460025. AE, Euro, Visa. 45 rm ⚶ 🐕 ♿ closed 15 Nov-15 Feb, 500.

★★★**Malmaison** (Mapotel), 48, bd V.-Hugo (B3), ☎ 93.87.62.56. Tx 470410. AE, DC, Euro, Visa. 46 rm 🅿 300. Rest. ♦♦ 90-130.

★★★**Résidence du Petit Palais,** 10, av. E.-Bieckert (C2), ☎ 93.62.19.11. 23 rm ⚶ ⚘ ☀ ♿ 180. Rest. ♦ 🐕 80-130.

★★**Durante,** 16, av. Durante (B3), ☎ 93.88.84.40. 28 rm 🅿 ⚘ ☀ 🐕 closed 27 Oct-2 Dec, 250.

★**Gourmet Lorrain,** 7, av. Santa-Fior (B1), ☎ 93.84.90.78. AE, Visa. 15 rm ⚘ ☀ 200. Rest. ♦♦ closed Sun eve, Mon, 1 week in Jan and Aug. Carefully prepared dishes, which vary with the market and seasons, 75-170.

★**Oasis,** 23, rue Gounod (B3), ☎ 93.88.12.29. 31 rm 🅿 ⚘ ☀ closed 20 Oct-20 Dec. Pension only, 170. Rest. 🐕 50-75.

★**Ann-Margaret,** 1, av. Saint-Joseph, ☎ 93.96.15.70. AE, Visa. 29 rm 🅿 ⚘ ☀ ▭ 200.

Youth hostel : rte forestière du Mont-Alban, ☎ 93.89.23.64.

Restaurants :

♦♦♦ ***Âne Rouge,*** Old Port, 7, quai des Deux-Emmanuels (D3), ☎ 93.89.49.63 ♿ closed 14 Jul-1 Sep, Sat eve, Sun. Reliable dishes. Spec : *loup farci au beurre d'écrevisse, saint-pierre mascareigne,* 150-300.

♦♦♦ ***La Poularde, Chez Lucullus,*** 9, rue Deloye (C3), ☎ 93.85.22.90. AE, DC, Euro, Visa ; closed 10 Jul-18 Aug and Wed. Good, classic fare. Spec : *rouget à la sauvage, suprême de sole « Lucullus »,* good pastries, 150-320.

♦♦ ***Bistrot de la Promenade,*** 7-9, prom. des Anglais, ☎ 93.81.63.48. Closed Sun. Restaurant-ice cream parlour, 100-150.

♦♦ ***Saint-Moritz,*** 5, rue du Congrès (B3), ☎ 93.88.54.90. ♿ closed 7 Jan-7 Feb and Thu. Mountain-resort style atmosphere, 180-210.

♦♦ ***Coco Beach,*** 2, av. Jean-Lorrain, ☎ 93.89.39.26. AE, DC, Euro, Visa. ♿ closed Sun and Mon noon. Expensive but worth it ; excellent grilled fish and a superb *bouillabaisse,* 250-300.

♦♦ ***Aux Gourmets,*** 12, rue Dante (A3), ☎ 93.96.83.53. AE, DC, Visa ; closed Sun eve and Mon. Classic dishes ; good value, 105-145.

♦♦ ***Chez les Pêcheurs,*** 18, quai des Docks (D3), ☎ 93.89.59.61. AE. ♿ closed 1 Nov-15 Dec, Tue eve and Wed. Spec : fish, 140-250.

♦♦ ***Le Grand Pavois, Chez Michel,*** 11, rue Meyerbeer (B3), ☎ 93.88.77.42. ♿ closed Jul-10 Aug and Mon. Good shellfish and excellent *bouillabaisse,* 120-210.

♦♦ ***Dalilou,*** 1, rue Penchienatti (D3), ☎ 93.85.61.55. AE, Visa. ♿ closed Sun. Authentic Niçois cooking : *tripes au basilic, gratin de morue, petits choux farcis,* 65-120.

♦♦ ***Rive Gauche,*** 27, rue Ribotti (D3), ☎ 93.89.16.82. Closed Sun and Mon, Aug. Cozy, simple restaurant with rustic menu, 80-130.

♦ ***La Merenda,*** 4, rue de la Terrasse (C3) ♿ closed Sat eve, Sun and Mon, Feb and Aug. Authentic Nice-style preparation, 80-160.

Saint-Pancrace, 8 km N on the D914 :

● ♦♦♦ ***Rôtisserie de Saint-Pancrace,*** ☎ 93.84.43.69. Visa. 🅿 ♿ closed 5 Jan-5 Feb and Mon. On the hinterland heights, a nice family inn set in a big park, 220-300.

Saint-Martin-du-Var, ✉ 06670, 15 km N on the N202 :

● ♦♦♦ ***Auberge de la Belle Route,*** rte de Digne, ☎ 93.08.10.65. 🅿 ♿ closed 15 Feb-15 Mar, Sun eve and Mon. In his old Provencal inn, J.-F. Issautier is starting to become famous. His menus are more accessible : *marinière de l'océan sauce pistou, feuillantine de loup aux poivrons doux.* Transport price is charged on local wines, 220-350.

Casino-club, 2-4, rue Saint-Michel, ☎ 93.80.55.70.

Bicycle and motorcycle hire : *Arnaud,* 4, pl. Grimaldi, ☎ 93.87.88.55 ; *Moto Rent,* 3, rue Barralis, ☎ 93.88.08.68 ; *Nicea,* 12, rue de Belgique, ☎ 93.82.42.71.

Recommended : candied fruits : *Henri Auer,* 7, rue Saint-François-de-Paule. Olive oil : *Alziari,* 14, rue Saint-Francois-de-Paule. Ice-creams : *l'Entremets,* centre commercial, 15, bd Delfino, ☎ 93.56.06.92.

ORANGE

Avignon 31, Nîmes 55, Paris 660
A1 ✉ 84100

ℹ av. Gal-de-Gaulle (A3), ☎ 90.34.70.88.

SNCF (C2), ☎ 90.34.01.44, 90.34.17.82.

🚌 av. F.-Mistral (C2), ☎ 90.34.15.59.

Car-hire : *Budget* train + car, at the station, ☎ 90.34.17.82.

Hotels :

★★★***Arène*** (L.F., Relais du Silence), pl. de Langes (B2), ☎ 90.34.10.95. Tx 431195. AE, Euro, Visa. 30 rm ♿ closed 31 Oct-7 Dec, 240.

★★★***Louvre et Terminus,*** 89, av. F.-Mistral (C2), ☎ 90.34.10.08. Tx 431195. Visa. 34 rm 🅿 ♿ closed 15 Dec-15 Jan, 230. Rest. ♦♦ closed Sun, 65-120.

★★***Glacier*** (L.F.), 46, cours A.-Briand (A3), ☎ 90.34.02.01. 29 rm ♿ closed 20 Dec-1 Feb and Sun eve, Mon noon low season, 170.

Mornas, ✉ 84420 Piolenc, 11 km NW :

★★***Le Manoir*** (L.F.), N7, ☎ 90.37.00.79. AE, DC, Euro, Visa. 25 rm 🅿 closed 15 Nov-8 Dec, 15 Jan-1 Feb, Sun eve low season, 190. Rest. ♦♦ ♿ 75-150.

⛺ ★★*Saint-Eutrope* (80 pl.), ☎ 90.34.09.22 ; *le Jonquier* (105 pl.), ☎ 90.34.19.83 ; Mornas, ★★*Beauregard* (100 pl.), ☎ 90.37.02.08.

Restaurants :

♦♦ ***Le Pigraillet,*** colline Saint-Eutrope (B3), ☎ 90.34.44.25. AE, DC. 🅿 ♿ closed 5 Jan-11 Feb, Sun eve and Mon, 110-170.

♦♦ ***Le Provençal,*** 27, rue de la République (C2), ☎ 90.34.01.89. Euro, Visa. ♿ closed Wed. Spec : *compote de lapereau aux pruneaux, caneton sauvage au gros plant,* 75-170.

Events : Jul, Aug : *Chorégies* (Choral Festival).

La PALUD-SUR-VERDON

Castellane 25, Digne 68, Paris 813
20 km SE of Moustiers-Sainte-Marie, C2 ✉ 04120

ℹ mairie, ☎ 92.74.68.02.

Hotels :

★★***Gorges du Verdon*** (L.F.), ☎ 92.74.68.26. AE. 35 rm 🅿 ♿ closed 30 Sep-10 May, 200. Rest. ♦ Provençal cooking, 45-120.

★★***Provence,*** ☎ 92.74.68.88. 15 rm 🅿 ♿ closed 15 Nov-15 Mar, 150. Rest. ♦ 70-120.

Point-Sublime, Rougan, 7.5 km E on the D952 :

★***Auberge du Point Sublime,*** ☎ 92.83.60.35. Euro. 15 rm 🅿 ♿ closed 10 Oct-1 Apr, 100. Rest. 50-160.

⛺ ★★*Municipal* (100 pl.), ☎ 92.74.68.02.

PEIRA-CAVA

Sospel 32, Nice 40, Paris 975
40 km N of Nice, D2
1 432-1 600 m ✉ 06440 L'Escarène

ℹ ☎ 93.91.57.22.

Hotels :

Turini Pass, 8 km on the D2566 :

★★***Trois Vallées*** (Relais du Silence), ☎ 93.91.57.21. AE, DC, Euro, Visa. 22 rm 🅿 ♿ closed 15 Nov-15 Dec. A charming chalet in the country, 230. Rest. ♦♦ Spec : *crêpes aux champignons, poulet aux écrevisses,* 50-130.

★★***Chamois,*** ☎ 93.91.57.42. 11 rm 🅿 closed Nov, 100. Rest. 50-170.

PERTUIS

Aix 20, Apt 35, Paris 750
18 km E of the Silvacane abbey, B2 ✉ 84120

ℹ pl. Mirabeau, ☎ 90.79.15.56.

SNCF ☎ 90.79.10.43.

Hotels :

★★★***Sevan*** (L.F., Mapotel), av. de Verdun, ☎ 90.79.19.30. Tx 431470. AE, DC, Euro, Visa. 36 rm 🅿 closed 1 Jan-1 Mar, 350. Rest. ♦♦ Spec : *marmite des pêcheurs au safran, magret de canard et son feuilleté gourmand,* 100-150.

★★***L'Aubarestiëro*** (L.F.), pl. Garcin, ☎ 90.79.14.74. AE, DC, Euro, Visa. 13 rm Ⓟ ♨ ✈ Provençal ambiance, 150. Rest ♦♦ 70-250.

Meyrarques, ✉ 13650, 8 km S :
● ★★★***Château de Meyrargues,*** ☎ 90.57.50.32. AE. 14 rm ☀ Ⓟ ♨ ⛰ closed 1 Nov-1 Feb, Sun eve and Mon. Fortified castle overlooking the Durance Valley, 330. Rest. ♦♦♦ 170-270.

Cucuron, ✉ 84160 Cadenet, 12 km NE :
★★***L'Étang*** (L.F.), pl. de l'Étang, ☎ 90.77.21.25. Euro. 8 rm ⛰ closed 28 Oct-5 Nov, 20 Dec-10 Jan, Wed low season, 160. Rest. ♦ Spec : *feuilleté de saumon chaud, pieds paquets marseillais,* 90-150.

⛺ *Municipal* (200 pl.), ☎ 90.79.10.98.

PORQUEROLLES Island

C3 ✉ 83400 Hyères

⛴ the island is linked by ferry to Giens Peninsula (half-hourly during high season ; 5 trips daily during low season), ☎ 94.58.21.81 ; to Cavalaire (3 trips weekly during high season), ☎ 94.64.08.04 ; to Hyères (6 trips weekly during high season), ☎ 94.54.44.07 ; to Toulon, ☎ 94.92.96.82, and to Le Lavandou, ☎ 94.71.01.02.

Hotels :
● ★★★***Mas du Langoustier,*** ☎ 94.58.30.09. Visa. 48 rm ☀ ♨ ⛰ 🎾 closed 25 Sep-8 May. Stunning site (pension only), 400. ♦♦ Rest. Spec : *feuilleté de loup, bavarois de truite saumonée,* 150-170.
★★***Ste-Anne,*** ☎ 94.58.30.04. 15 rm ♨ ⛰ closed 4-14 Jan, 15 Nov-22 Dec. Pension only, 270. Rest. ♦ closed Wed low season, 80-170.

Restaurant :
♦♦ ***Orée du Bois,*** ☎ 94.58.30.57. Visa ♿ closed 15 Nov-1 Feb, 70-250.

PORT-CROS Island

C3 ✉ 83145

⛴ the island is linked by ferry to Le Lavandou, ☎ 94.71.01.02 (numerous daily trips during high season ; 4 trips weekly during low season) ; to Cavalaire, ☎ 94.64.08.04 (1 trip daily during high season) ; to Hyères, ☎ 94.57.44.07 (1 trip daily during high season, and 4 trips weekly during low season).

Hotel :
● ★★★***Manoir,*** ☎ 94.05.90.52. 24 rm ☀ ♨ ⛰ ✈ closed 15 Oct-Easter. Pension only. Book well in advance. 1/2 pension, 860 ; pension, 1 000.

RAMATUELLE

Sainte-Maxime 18, Toulon 80, Paris 881
10 km S of Saint-Tropez, C3 ✉ 83350

Hotels :
● ★★★***Hostellerie du Baou,*** ☎ 94.79.20.48. Tx 462152. AE, DC, Visa. 36 rm ☀ Ⓟ ⛰ 📺 closed 15 Nov-15 Dec, 600. Rest. ♦♦ Between the sea and the countryside, a luxurious hotel. Jean-Denis Sennequier (the son of Toto of St-Tropez) supervises with his wife a restaurant of great standing. The excellent cooking of the young chef Frerard : *moules en gaspacho, piccatas de veau aux langoustines,* local fish, 200-300.
★★★***Saint-André,*** Tahiti beach, ☎ 94.97.21.54. 30 rm ☀ Ⓟ ♨ ⛰ closed 30 Sep-1 Apr, 275.

⛺ 4 sites ★★★★ (1 400 pl.).

ROQUEBRUNE-CAP-MARTIN

Monaco 8, Nice 20, Paris 950
4 km SW of Menton, D2 ✉ 06190

ℹ hôtel de ville, ☎ 93.35.60.67 ; esplanade Jean-Giono, ☎ 93.57.99.44 (high season).

SNCF ☎ 93.35.00.95.

Hotels :
★★★★(L) ***Vistaëro,*** Grande-Corniche, ☎ 93.35.01.50. Tx 461021. AE, DC, Euro, Visa. 26 rm ☀ Ⓟ ♨ ⛰ 📺 closed 31 Oct-early Apr, 1 100. Rest. ♦♦♦ Good meals. Spec : *filets de rougets à la tomate fraîche et au basilic, mignonnette d'agneau à la fleur de thym,* 180-365.
★★★***Victoria et de la Plage,*** 7, prom. du Cap-Martin, ☎ 93.35.65.90. Tx 470673. AE, DC, Euro, Visa. 30 rm ☀ Ⓟ closed 1 Nov-1 Feb, 420.
★***Reine d'Azur,*** 29, prom. du Cap-Martin, ☎ 93.35.76.84. 18 rm ☀ ♨ ✈ closed mid-Oct-1 Feb. Half-pension only, 150.
★***Westminster*** (L.F.), 14, av. Louis-Laurens, ☎ 93.35.00.68. 30 rm ☀ Ⓟ ♨ ⛰ ✈ closed 10 Nov-5 Feb, 200. Rest ♦ ✈ 60-100.

⛺ ★★★*Toraca* (40 pl.), ☎ 93.35.62.55 ; ★★*Babastrol* (30 pl.), ☎ 93.35.74.58.

Restaurants :
♦♦♦ ***Roquebrune,*** 100, av. J.-Jaurès, lower coast road, ☎ 93.35.00.16. AE, DC, Euro, Visa ; closed 6 Nov-6 Dec, 8-18 Jan, Wed and Thu noon. Pleasant terrace ; well-prepared quality fare, 200-250. With 1 rm, 300.
♦♦♦ ***Hippocampe,*** 44, av. W.-Churchill, ☎ 93.35.81.91 ☀ Ⓟ ✈ closed May, Oct and Jan, Mon and noon low season. Superb view of the bay ; skilled, attentive cooking, 110-240.
♦♦ ***Les Lucioles,*** 12, av. Poincaré, ☎ 93.35.02.19. Visa ☀ Ⓟ ♨ closed Nov-Mar, Thu and Fri noon. Tasty dishes served on a charming terrace overlooking the port, 115-140.
♦♦ ***Grand Inquisiteur,*** 18, rue du Château, ☎ 93.35.05.37. AE ⛰ ✈ closed 3 Nov-25 Dec, 10-20 Mar, Sun eve and Mon. Reserve noon. Light approach, 110-200.

ROUSSILLON

Apt 11, Avignon 48, Paris 728
98 km E of Gordes, B2 ✉ 84220 Gordes

Hotels :
● ★★★***Mas de Garrignon*** (Relais du Silence), 2 km N, ☎ 90.75.63.22. AE, Euro, Visa. 8 rm ☀ Ⓟ ♨ ⛰ 📺 ♿ Delightful setting, 500. Rest. ♦♦♦ ✈ closed Sun eve, Mon noon and 15 Nov-27 Dec. Book ahead, 160-250.
★★***Résidence des Ocres*** (L.F.), ☎ 90.75.60.50. Visa. 15 rm ☀ Ⓟ ♨ ⛰ closed Feb and 15-30 Nov, 200.

⛺ ★★*Arc-en-ciel* (35 pl.), ☎ 90.75.67.17.

Restaurants :
● ♦♦ ***David,*** pl. de la Poste, ☎ 90.75.60.13. DC, Visa ☀ closed Mon, Jan-Mar and Tue low season. Classic fare prepared by a true professional. An unrivalled view of the valley and cliffs, 90-140.
♦♦ ***La Tarasque,*** rue R.-Casteau, ☎ 90.75.63.86. Visa ⛰ closed 5-23 Mar, Wed. Inexpensive set menus, 100-245.

SAINT-ANDRÉ-LES-ALPES

Digne 43, Grasse 84, Paris 788
21 km N of Castellane, C2 ✉ 04170

ℹ rue Principale, ☎ 92.89.02.46.

Hotels :
★★***Lac et Forêt*** (L.F.), ☎ 90.89.07.38. AE, DC, Euro, Visa. 30 rm ☀ Ⓟ ⛰ ♿ closed 16 Dec-Easter, 200. Rest. ♦ Regional cooking, 40-130.

★**Grand Hôtel,** pl. de la Gare, ☎ 90.89.05.06. 24 rm 🅿 ⚘ closed 1 Oct-1 May, 90. Rest. ♦ 40-150.
★**Closeraie Bagatelle,** rte d'Allos, ☎ 90.89.03.08. 10 rm 🅿 ⚘ closed 1 Dec-20 Apr, 140. Rest. Simple, tasty and inexpensive, 50-125.

Saint-Julien-du-Verdon, 8 km S :
★**Le Pidanoux** (L.F.), ☎ 90.89.05.87. 17 rm 🅿 ⚘ closed 15 Dec-15 Mar, 110. Rest. Regional cooking, 50-80.

Ⓐ ★★*Les Iscles* (200 pl.), ☎ 90.89.02.29.

SAINT-CÉZAIRE-SUR-SIAGNE

Cannes 30, Nice 55, Paris 931
16 km W of Grasse, D2 ✉ 06780

ⓘ pl. Ch.-de-Gaulle (high season), 2.5 km on the St-Vallier road.

Hotel :
★★**Claux de Taladoire,** rte de Saint-Vallier, 2.5 km N, ☎ 93.60.20.09. Visa. 22 rm 🅿 closed Oct and Jan, 130. Rest. 55-150.

SAINTE-CÉCILE-LES-VIGNES

Montélimar 45, Avignon 47, Paris 652
16 km NE of Orange, A1 ✉ 84290

Restaurant :
♦♦ **Le Relais,** 50 av. J.-Jaurès, Orange road, ☎ 90.30.84.39 closed 15 Feb-15 Mar, Sun eve and Mon. Spec : fish, *ris de veau aux morilles*, 80-200.

Recommended : wine cellar visit, *Coopérative Cécilia*, cours Pourtalet, ☎ 90.30.83.25.

SAINTE-MAXIME

Cannes 61, Toulon 73, Paris 880
C3 ✉ 83120

ⓘ prom. S.-Lozière, ☎ 94.96.19.24.

Hotels :
★★★★**Belle Aurore,** 4, bd Jean-Moulin, ☎ 94.96.02.45. 18 rm 🅿 closed 15 Oct-15 Mar. Private beach, 600. Rest. ♦♦♦ 165-350.
★★★★**Résidence Brutus,** bd de la Mer, ☎ 94.96.13.55. Tx 970080. AE, Visa. 49 rm closed 3 Nov-15 Mar, 400.
★★★**Calidianus,** bd J.-Moulin, ☎ 94.96.23.21. 27 rm 🅿 Pleasant ambiance, 320.
★★★**Muzelle Montfleuri,** 4, av. Montfleuri, ☎ 94.96.19.57. 31 rm 🅿 ♿ closed 15 Oct-15 Mar, 320. Rest. ♦♦ 90-100.
★★**L'Ensoleillée,** 29, av. J.-Jaurès, ☎ 94.96.02.27. 29 rm closed 1 Oct-1 Apr, 180. Rest. ♦ closed 10 Oct-1 May, 70-90.

Guerrevieille, 2 km SW :
★★**Marie-Louise,** ☎ 94.96.06.45. 14 rm 🅿 ♿ closed 15 Oct-15 Feb, 245. Rest. ♦ ♿ closed 30 Sep-15 Mar, Tue eve and Wed. Spec : *daube à la provençale*, 70-150.

Beauvallon, 4.5 km W on the N98 :
★★★★**Golf Hôtel,** ☎ 94.96.06.09. Tx 470480. AE, Visa. 85 rm 🅿 ♿ Private beach, 280. Rest. ♦♦♦ 120-210.

Plan-de-la-Tour, 9.5 km NW on the D25 and D74 :
★★★**Ponte Romano,** rte de Grimaud, ☎ 94.43.70.56. Euro, Visa 🅿 closed 10 Oct-31 Mar. Pleasant setting, beautiful Provençal style house, 400. Rest. ♦♦♦ ♿ 200-250.
★★**Mas des Brugassières,** rte de Grimaud, ☎ 94.43.72.42. 10 rm 🅿 ♿ closed Jan, 300.

Farm camping : *le Couloubrier*, rte de Plan-de-la-Tour, ☎ 94.96.23.36.

Restaurants :
♦♦ **L'Esquinade,** at the port, ☎ 94.96.01.65 closed 5 Nov-20 Dec and Wed ex Jul-Aug. Spec : fish, grilled *langouste*, 250-400.
♦♦ **La Gruppi,** av. Ch.-de-Gaulle, ☎ 94.96.03.61 closed Mon low season. Facing the sea. Spec : reasonably-priced fish and shellfish ; excellent service, 140-200.
♦♦ **Le Bistrot du Jardin,** av. Jean-Jaurès Bar, piano-bar in a flowered garden ; buffet, 80-130.
♦ **La Réserve,** pl. V.-Hugo, ☎ 94.96.18.32. Closed 15 oct-15 Mar, 20 Apr-20 May. Inexpensive regional meals, 80-160.

Les SAINTES-MARIES-DE-LA-MER

Arles 38, Nîmes 53, Paris 767
A3 ✉ 13460

ⓘ av. Van-Gogh, ☎ 90.97.82.55.

Hotels :
★★★★**Auberge Cavalière,** N510, ☎ 90.47.84.62. Tx 440459. AE, Euro, Visa. 18 rm 🅿 ♿ 600. Rest. ● ♦♦♦ Refined, grand classic fare. Spec : *millefeuille d'artichaut aux filets de cailles à la crème, petit ragoût de lapin à la senteur de thym*, 140-210.

4 km on the D38 :
★★★★**Mas de la Fouque,** 4 km on the D38, ☎ 90.47.81.02. AE, Euro, Visa. 12 rm 🅿 ♿ closed early Nov-28 Mar. A delightful natural setting overlooking the Camargue coastal range, 1 100. Rest. ● ♦♦♦ The day's catch and steaks grilled at pool-side ; dining to the lilt of gypsy guitars, 185-250.
★★★**Pont des Bannes,** rte d'Arles, ☎ 90.47.81.09. 20 rm 🅿 ♿ closed 15 Oct-Mar. Typical Camargue range-rider cabins converted into bungalows, 400. Rest. ♦♦ 80-150.
★★★**Étrier Camarguais,** chemin Bas-des-Launes, ☎ 90.47.81.14. AE, DC, Euro, Visa. 33 rm 🅿 ♿ closed 1 Nov-1 Apr, 350. Rest. ♦♦ 130-175.
★★★**Boumian,** rte d'Arles, ☎ 90.47.81.15. 28 rm 🅿 ♿ Ranger atmosphere on the hotel patio ; closed 2 Jan-28 Feb, 280. Rest. ♦♦ Spec : *noix de Saint-Jacques au jus de truffe, tranche de foie gras à la chiffonnade de choux*, 90-200.
★★★**Mas des Roseaux,** rte d'Arles, ☎ 90.47.86.12. 14 rm 🅿 ♿ closed Oct-Apr, 400.
★★★**Mas du Clarousset,** rte de Cacharel, ☎ 90.47.81.66. 10 rm 🅿 ♿ With 1/2 pension, 710. Rest. ♦♦ Book ahead ; closed Wed ex nat hols, 120-250.
★★**Host. du Pont de Gau,** 5 km N on the Arles road, ☎ 90.47.81.53. AE, Visa. 9 rm closed 5 Jan-15 Feb, Wed low season, 175. Rest. Spec : *salade de St-Jacques tiède à la vinaigrette de truffes*, 60-130.

Youth hostel : former Pioch-Patet school.

Gîte and table d'hôtes : *Mazet du Maréchal-Ferrant*, ☎ 90.97.84.60.

Ⓐ ★★★*La Brise* (1 600 pl.), ☎ 90.97.84.67 ; ★★*le Large* (350 pl.), ☎ 90.97.87.26.

Restaurant :
● ♦♦ **Le Brûleur de Loups,** av. Gilbert-Leroy, ☎ 90.97.83.31. AE closed 15 Nov-15 Mar, Tue eve and Wed ex Aug and Sep. Pleasant surroundings and inexpensive menu. Louis XVI style at the range-riders'. Spec : *salade d'artichaut et crevettes à l'huile de noisettes, piccata de veau aux coquilles St-Jacques*, 115-200.

SAINT-ÉTIENNE-DE-TINÉE

Barcelonnette 58, Nice 91, Paris 795
Vallée de la Tinée, D1 ✉ 06660

ⓘ 1, rue des Communes-de-France, ☎ 93.02.41.96 (high season).

Hotel :
★***Pinatelle,*** bd d'Auron, ☎ 93.02.40.36. 14 rm ♿ closed 1 Oct-1 Dec. Pension, 320. Rest. 80-120.

SAINT-JEAN-CAP-FERRAT

Nice 10, Menton 23, Paris 944
D2 ⊠ 06230

ℹ 59, av. D.-Semeria, ☎ 93.01.36.86.

Hotels :
★★★★(L) ***Cap Ferrat,*** bd Gal-de-Gaulle, ☎ 93.01.04.54. Tx 470184. AE, DC, Euro. 66 rm 🅿 ♿ Private beach, closed 7 Oct-26 Apr, 700. Rest. ◆◆◆ Refined cooking, 300-350.
★★★★(L) ***Voile d'Or,*** port de Saint-Jean, ☎ 93.01.13.13. Tx 470317. 50 rm 🅿 ♿ closed 1 Nov-1 Mar. Extraordinary view on the port. Elegant rooms and sauna, 930. Rest. ◆◆◆◆ Superb choice of new and traditional dishes. Spec : *royale de loup St-Jeannoise, suprême de volaille « Jacqueline », ragoût de poireaux aux truffes,* 220-300.
● ★★***Clair Logis,*** allée des Brises, ☎ 93.01.31.01. Visa. 18 rm 🅿 closed mid-Nov to mid-Dec. Charming residence, 280.
★★***Brise Marine,*** 58, av. Jean-Mermoz, ☎ 93.01.30.73. 15 rm closed 1 Nov-1 Feb, 380. Rest. eve only, 80-130.

Restaurants :
◆◆ ***Les Hirondelles,*** 36, av. Jean-Mermoz, ☎ 93.01.30.25. Visa 🅿 ♿ closed 31 Oct-28 Feb, Sun and Mon. Delightful restaurant with a terrace. Fine fish, 175-350.
◆◆ ***Petit Trianon,*** bd Gal-de-Gaulle, ☎ 93.01.31.68. AE, DC, Euro, Visa ♿ closed Wed eve and Thu, 15 Oct-Mar. Good menu ; traditional and regional fare : *mousseline de rascasse, poulet aux écrevisses,* 180-220.
◆◆ ***Provençal,*** 2, av. Denis-Semeria, ☎ 93.01.30.15. Visa ; closed Tue, 1 Nov-30 Dec. Splendid view of the coast. Good fish, 150-270.
◆◆ ***Cappa,*** pl. du Village, ☎ 93.01.03.07. Closed Wed and mid-Oct to mid-Dec. Fish well-prepared and excellent fish soup, 120-210.

SAINT-MARTIN-VÉSUBIE

Sospel 53, Nice 65, Paris 901
59 km E of Valberg, D1 ⊠ 06450 Lantosque

ℹ pl. Félix-Faure, ☎ 93.03.21.28 (high season).

Hotels :
★★***Bonne Auberge,*** allée de Verdun, ☎ 93.03.20.49. 33 rm 🅿 ♿ closed 10 Nov-20 Dec, 190. Rest. ◆ closed Wed (1 Oct-30 May), 70-90.
★★***Edward's et Châtaignerale,*** ☎ 93.03.21.22. 50 rm 🅿 closed mid-Sep to end Jun. Pension only, 200.

⛺ ★★*Saint-Joseph* (50 pl.), ☎ 93.03.20.14.

Recommended : *Villa Saint-Charles,* ☎ 93.03.20.14 : farm produce for sale (and camping).

SAINT-PAUL-DE-VENCE

Nice 20, Grasse 22, Paris 930
D2 ⊠ 06570

ℹ Maison Tour, rue Grande, ☎ 93.32.86.95.

Hotels :
★★★★(L) ***Mas d'Artigny*** (Relais et châteaux), chemin des Salettes, on the La Colle road, ☎ 93.32.84.54. Tx 470601. 52 rm and 29 apts, 25 with private pool. 🅿 Luxury complex in a 20-acre park, 1 030. Rest. ◆◆◆ Gastronomical fare. Spec. : *pascalines d'agneau façon du berger, millefeuille aux fruits de saison,* 210-350.
● ★★★***Hameau,*** 528, rte de La Colle, ☎ 93.32.80.24. 16 rm 🅿 ♿ Huge orchard garden hugging the hills ; closed 1 Nov-1 Feb, 350.
★★★***Colombe d'Or,*** pl. Gal-de-Gaulle, ☎ 93.32.80.02. Tx 970607. AE, DC, Euro, Visa. 24 rm 🅿 A justifiably famous hotel, frequented by a number of great artists ; closed 5 Nov-18 Dec, 650. Rest. ◆◆◆ ♿ Spec : *salmis de volailles aux morilles, carré d'agneau de Sisteron,* 120-250.
★★★***Orangers,*** quartier les Fumerates, ☎ 93.32.80.95. AE. 10 rm 🅿 closed Nov-Feb. A ravishing flower garden, 320.
★★★***Aubergo dou Souleù,*** rte de La Colle, ☎ 93.32.80.60. AE, DC, Euro, Visa. 7 rm 🅿 closed Jan-15 Feb, 320. Rest. Classic dishes in a beaufiful inn with terrace. Classic cooking, 115-230.

Restaurants :
◆◆ ***Oliviers,*** rte de La Colle, ☎ 93.32.80.13. AE, DC, Visa. 🅿 ♿ closed Dec-Feb. Provencal inn with terrace. Spec : *soupe au pistou, daurade,* barbecued meats, 250-300.
◆◆ ***Morateur,*** 98, rue Grande, ☎ 93.32.81.91. ♿ closed early Nov-18 Dec, Sun eve and Mon low season, 90-200.

SAINT-RAPHAËL

Cannes 43, Toulon 96, Paris 877
C3 ⊠ 83700

ℹ pl. de la Gare, ☎ 94.95.16.87.

SNCF ☎ 94.95.16.90, 94.95.18.91, 94.95.13.89.

Car-hire : *Budget* train + car, at the station, ☎ 94.95.24.57, 94.95.67.41.

Hotels :
★★★***Beau Séjour,*** prom. du Pdt-Coty, ☎ 94.95.03.75. DC, Visa. 38 rm closed 31 Oct-20 Mar, 330.
★★***Excelsior,*** bd F.-Martin, ☎ 94.95.02.42. AE, DC, Euro, Visa. 40 rm 360. Rest. ◆◆ Spec : *bouillabaisse, rognons à la dijonaise,* 75-150.
★***Nouvel Hôtel,*** 6, rue H.-Vadon, ☎ 94.95.23.30. 10 rm, closed 15 Oct-15 Mar, 180. Rest. ◆ Spec : fish, 120-210.

Boulouris, 5 km SE on the N98 :
★★★***La Potinière*** (Relais du Silence), ☎ 94.95.21.43. Visa. 25 rm 🅿 ♿ closed 6 Nov-20 Dec. Rooms with terraces overlooking the garden. Pleasant setting, 400. Rest. ◆◆ ♿ closed Thu noon (1 Oct-31 Mar). Spec : *petite marmite du pêcheur, cœur de filet aux morilles en terrine,* 110-180.

Valescure, 5 km NE on the D37 :
● ★★★***Golf Hôtel de Valescure*** (Mapotel), rte du Golf, ☎ 94.52.01.57. Tx 46105. AE, DC, Euro, Visa. 40 rm 🅿 ♿ closed 15 Oct-20 Dec, 6 Jan-30 Mar, 500. Rest. ◆◆◆ Spec : *corbeille de poissons du pays* and Provençal menu, 130-200.
★★★***San Pedro*** (Châteaux-hôtels), av. Cl.-Brooke, ☎ 94.52.10.24. Tx 461360. AE, Euro. 27 rm 🅿 ♿ closed 30 Oct-Easter, 550.

Le Dramont, 7 km E on the N98 :
● ★★★***Sol E Mar,*** ☎ 94.95.25.60. 47 rm 🅿 closed 15 Oct-27 Mar, 400. Rest. ◆◆ 100-250.

Agay, 9 km E on the N98 :
★★***Beau Site,*** Camp Long, ☎ 94.82.00.45. Visa. 25 rm 🅿 closed 3 weeks in Jan. Half-pension, 220. Rest. ◆ 80-130.

Anthéor, 13 km NE on the N98 :
★★***Les Flots Bleus,*** ☎ 94.44.80.21. Visa. 19 rm 🅿 ♿ closed 15 Oct-Mar, 150. Rest. ◆ closed Mon ex Jul-Aug. Spec : *soupe de poisson.* Reasonably priced, 70-100.

★★*La Réserve d'Anthéor,* Corniche d'Or, N98, ☎ 94.44.80.05. AE, DC, Euro, Visa. 13 rm P Private beach, closed 10 Oct-1 Feb, 180. Rest. ♦♦ Spec : fish, 70-150.

Youth hostel : *la Véronèse,* Le Trayas, 20 km E on the N98, ☎ 94.44.13.34.

Ⲁ *Saint-Raphaël* (town and district) : 7 sites ★★★★ and 6 ★★★

Restaurant :

♦♦♦ ***La Voile d'Or,*** 1, bd Gal-de-Gaulle, ☎ 94.95.17.04. AE, DC, Visa. ♿ closed Wed and 20 Nov-25 Dec. Spec : *bourride raphaéloise, marinade d'anchois,* 130-200.

Event : Feb : *corso des mimosas* (mimosa fete).

SAINT-RÉMY-DE-PROVENCE

Avignon 21, Arles 25, Paris 709
A2 ⊠ 13210

ℹ pl. Jean-Jaurès, ☎ 90.92.05.22.

Hotels :

★★★★***Château des Alpilles*** (Châteaux-hôtels), on the D31 (former Grès road), ☎ 90.92.03.33. Tx 431487. AE, DC, Euro, Visa. 17 rm P Charming 19thC castle, stop-over for writers and politicians of the period ; closed 15 Nov-15 Mar, 650. Rest. ♦ Poolside grillroom, 100-210.

★★★***Vallon de Valrugues,*** chemin de Canto Cigalo, ☎ 90.92.04.40. Tx 431677. Visa. 34 rm P ♿ closed 3 Nov-1 Mar, 420.

★★★***Antiques,*** 15, av. Pasteur, ☎ 90.92.03.02. 27 rm P Riding club, closed 1 Nov-25 Mar, 260.

★★★***Château de Roussan,*** rte de Tarascon, ☎ 90.92.11.63. 12 rm P Handsome 18thC mansion, closed 20 Oct-20 Mar, 480.

★★***Canto Cigalo,*** chemin de Canto Cigalo, ☎ 90.92.14.28. 20 rm P Perfect calm ; closed Nov-Mar, 200.

★★***Van Gogh,*** 1, av. Jean-Moulin, ☎ 90.92.14.02. 18 rm P ♿ closed 1 Nov-1 Mar, 180.

★★***Chalet Fleuri*** (L.F.), 15, av. F.-Mistral, ☎ 90.92.03.62. 12 rm P closed 1 Nov-15 Mar, Tue noon, 180. Rest. Provencal cooking, 70-120.

Gîte and table d'hôte : *Montplaisir,* ☎ 90.92.12.91.

Ⲁ ★★★*Pégomas* (66 pl.), ☎ 90.92.01.21 ; ★★*Montplaisir* (76 pl.), ☎ 90.92.22.70 ; ★★*les Platanes* (33 pl.), ☎ 90.92.07.63.

Restaurants :

♦ ***Jardin Frédéric,*** 8 *bis,* bd Gambetta, ☎ 90.92.27.76. Closed Tue, 1 Nov-15 Jan. Inexpensive set menus, 80-130.

Verquières, ⊠ 13670, 10 km NE :

● ♦♦ ***Le Coupe-Chou,*** pl. de l'Église, ☎ 90.95.18.55. P closed Mon and Tue ex nat hols. Few places only. Young chef to be encouraged. Spec : *galantine de gigot d'agneau, flan de lapereau.* Superb and unique menu for 110 F.

SAINT-TROPEZ

Toulon 69, Cannes 75, Paris 878
C3 ⊠ 83990

ℹ quai J.-Jaurès, ☎ 94.97.41.21.

SNCF ☎ 94.97.01.88.

Hotels :

★★★★(L) ***Byblos,*** av. P.-Signac, ☎ 94.97.00.04. 130 rm, 19 apts P closed 4 Nov-28 Mar. Enchanting Provencal houses which make up a "hotel village", 2 000. Rest. ♦♦♦ ***les Arcades.*** Pleasant restaurant by the side of the swimming-pool, 210-320.

★★★★***Résidence de la Pinède,*** plage de la Bouillabaisse, ☎ 94.97.04.21. Tx 470489. AE, DC, Euro, Visa. 35 rm and 5 apts P ♿ closed 15 Oct-15 Mar. Private beach ; aquatic sports. Spacious rooms, 1 500. Rest. ♦♦♦ 280-350.

★★★★***La Maison Blanche,*** pl. des Lices, ☎ 94.97.52.66. Tx 970456. AE, DC, Visa. 8 rm 950.

● ★★★***Le Levant,*** rte de Sallins, ☎ 94.97.33.33. 94.97.36.59. AE, Visa. 28 rm P closed 14 Oct-23 Mar, 550. Rest. grill-room, 170.

★★★***Les Bergerettes,*** rte des Plages, D93, ☎ 94.97.40.22. AE, Visa. 29 rm P closed 15 Oct-Easter, 500. With grill.

● ★★★***Le Mas de Chastelas,*** 3.5 km on the Cassin road, chemin de Bertaud, ☎ 94.56.09.11. 31 rm, 10 apts P closed early Oct-early Apr. Former silkworm farm situated in vineyards, 800. Rest. ♦♦♦ eve only (noon meal for hotel guests). Lunch at pool-side (res. only), delicious cold dishes. Spec : *raviolis de poissons, noisette de veau au citron vert,* excellent desserts, 220-310.

★★★***La Tartane,*** 3 km on the Salins road, ☎ 94.97.21.23. Visa. 12 rm P closed 5 Nov-15 Mar, 520. Rest. snacks (noon only) ♿ 160-200.

★★★***La Figuière,*** rte de Tahiti Beach, ⊠ 83350 Ramatuelle, ☎ 94.97.18.21. 42 rm P ♿ closed Oct-Palm Sunday. A renovated farmhouse which provides a delightful ambiance, 500. With grill.

★★★***Résidence des Lices,*** av. A.-Grangeon, ☎ 94.97.28.28. Visa. 35 rm P ♿ closed 15 Oct-1 Apr, 400.

★★★***Tahiti Beach,*** Le Pinet, ☎ 94.97.18.02. DC, Visa. 19 rm P closed Oct-Mar, 800. Rest. ♦♦ 120-200.

★★★***Le Yaca,*** 1, bd d'Aumale, ☎ 94.97.11.79. Tx 461516. AE, Euro, Visa. 23 rm closed 15 Oct-Mar, 900.

★★***Lou Cagnard,*** rue P.-Roussel, ☎ 94.97.04.24. 19 rm P closed 15 Nov-24 Dec, 250.

★★***Auberge des Vieux Moulins,*** rte des Plages, 83350 Ramatuelle, ☎ 94.97.17.22. AE, DC, Visa. 7 rm P closed 15 Sep-Apr, Wed (May-Jun), 450. Rest. ♦♦ closed Wed (Jun) and noon. Provencal specialities served around this old house's fountain, 150-200.

Restaurants :

● ♦♦♦ ***Le Chabichou,*** av. Foch, ☎ 94.54.80.00 ♿ closed 15 Oct-31 Mar. Michel Rochedy, with his light and delicate cooking has created the great restaurant that was missing in this city. His customers from Courchevel will not feel out of place. Spec. : *ravioles de homard, suprême de pigeonneau en grillade, purée douce d'ail nouveau avec son tourton au jus de girolles,* 200-300.

♦♦♦ ***Leï Mouscardins,*** 16, rue Portalet, at the far end of the port, ☎ 94.97.01.53. Visa closed 2 Nov-1 Feb. Well-known restaurant. Spec : *bourride provençale, bouillabaisse,* 240-310.

● ♦♦ ***La Ponche,*** pl. Revelin, ☎ 94.97.09.29. ♿ closed 15 Oct-1 Apr. Still luxurious and fashionable. Uncomplicated cooking : *petits farcis, blanquette de lotte,* 80-150.

● ♦♦ ***Le Bistrot des Lices,*** 3, pl. des Lices, ☎ 94.97.29.00. Visa closed noon high season. Piano bar and terrace. Celebrities' meeting place. Good and varied cooking, 160-300.

♦♦ ***Chez Camille,*** quartier de Bonne-Terrasse, ☎ 94.79.80.38 P ♿ closed Oct-Mar and low season. Spec : *bouillabaisse* and fish, 140-270.

◆◆ ***Le Girelier,*** quai J.-Jaurès, on the port, ☎ 94.97.03.87. AE, DC, Euro, Visa ☼ closed 12 Nov-10 Jan and eve from 10 Jan-1 Apr. Spec : grilled fish, *croustade de fruits de mer,* 90-150.
◆◆ ***Les Maures (Chez Dédé),*** 4, rue Dr-Boutin, ☎ 94.97.01.50. DC ♿ closed 30 Sep-30 Mar. Attractive setting. Fish and shellfish specialities, 100-200.
◆◆ ***Lou Revelen,*** La Ponche, 4, rue des Remparts, ☎ 94.97.06.34. AE, DC, Visa. Spec : regional dishes *(pâtes fraîches aux langoustines, sardines farcies).* Inexpensive, set menus, 80-220.
◆◆ ***Bistrot de la Marine,*** port, ☎ 94.97.04.07. AE, DC, Visa ♿ closed Wed low season, Jan. Facing the yachts, a quiet restaurant which serves authentic regional cooking, 120-150.
● ◆ ***La Ramade,*** rue du Temple, ☎ 94.97.00.15. Owner Pierrot fishes at dawn and late in the evening ; thus, his delicious fish, grilled *aux sarments de vignes, aïoli, bourride,* 120-210.
◆ ***L'Escoundu,*** 3, rue du Clocher, ☎ 94.54.83.50. Closed 28 Oct-20 Mar, Wed eve. Excellent quality fare and extremely reasonable prices at this new restaurant, 90-130.

Events : May 16-18 : *Fête de la Bravade ;* 15 Jun : *Bravade des Espagnols ;* 26 Jul : *Sainte-Anne's Fair,* pl. des Lices ; end Aug to early Sep : *Antiques Salon.*

Recommended : wines : *R. Sumeire,* château Barbeyrolles-Gassin, ☎ 94.56.33.58. *Sénéquier,* a famous café at the port, a real must, ☎ 94.07.00.90. Wine bar : 13, rue des Fermiers, ☎ 94.97.46.10. Piano bar : *le Yaca,* jazz, ☎ 94.97.17.24.

SALON-DE-PROVENCE

Aix 36, Arles 41, Paris 724
A2 ⊠ 13300

ⓘ 56, cours Gimon, ☎ 90.56.27.60.

SNCF ☎ 90.56.01.15, 90.56.04.05.

Hotels :
★★***Midi,*** 518, allées de Craponne, ☎ 90.53.34.67. Tx 401056. Euro, Visa. 25 rm Ⓟ ♿ closed Dec, 250. Rest. ◆ eve only, 80-130.
★★***Vendôme,*** 34, rue du Mal-Joffre, ☎ 90.56.01.96. DC, Visa. 22 rm Ⓟ ♨ 150.

5 km NE on the Val-de-Cuech road (D16) :
★★★★***Abbaye de Sainte-Croix*** (Relais et châteaux), ☎ 90.56.24.55. Tx 401247. AE, DC, Euro, Visa. 25 rm ☼ Ⓟ ♨ 🔔 ▭ ⚲ ♿ 9th-12thC abbey situated on a spur of the Alpilles mountains, with a view over the Crau region ; closed 31 Oct-1 Mar, 550. Rest. ● ◆◆◆ closed Mon noon. A dream place in an enchanting setting... Inventive cooking by J.-P. Caris : *daubes,* grilled meats and fish, 175-250.

6 km SW on the D19 :
★★★***Devem de Mirapier,*** ☎ 90.55.99.22. 16 rm Ⓟ ♨ 🔔 ▭ ♿ closed 20 Dec-5 Jan, 300. Rest. ◆ closed Tue, 120-210.

La Barben, ⊠ 13330 Pélissanne, 8 km SE :
● ★★***Touloubre*** (Relais du Silence, L.F.), ☎ 90.55.16.85. AE, Visa. 16 rm Ⓟ ♨ 🔔 closed 15 Nov-1 Dec, 250. Rest. ◆◆ ♿ closed Sun eve and Mon. Spec : *bourride de lotte, filet de bœuf aux morilles,* 100-250.

Gîte, rm and table d'hôte : Vernègues, 10 km on the D16 and D22, *mas de Gance,* ☎ 90.59.15.06., 90.59.14.32.

⛺ ★★★*Nostradamus* (83 pl.), ☎ 90.56.08.36.

Restaurants :
● ◆◆ ***Robin,*** 1, bd Clemenceau, ☎ 90.56.06.53. AE, Euro 🔔 closed Sun eve and Mon, Feb. Francis Robin, president of the "Soleil" cooks, sets the example in his Louis XVI decor : *civet de homard, assiette de pêcheur au safran,* 150-350.
◆◆ ***La Brocherie des Cordeliers,*** 20, rue d'Hozier, ☎ 90.56.53.42. Visa ; closed hols, Sat noon and Sun. Spec : *magret de canard aux myrtilles, sauté de Saint-Jacques à la ciboulette,* 80-300.

SANARY-SUR-MER

Toulon 12, Marseilles 54, Paris 829
B3 ⊠ 83110

ⓘ Jardins de la Ville, ☎ 94.74.01.04.

SNCF ☎ 94.91.50.50.

Hotels :
★★***Bains,*** allées d'Estienne-d'Orves, ☎ 94.74.13.47. AE, VIsa. 34 rm ☼ Ⓟ ♨ 220. Rest. ◆ closed Nov-15 Mar and Mon, 85-160.
★★***Roc Amour,*** bd de la Falaise, 3 km on the Bandol road, ☎ 94.74.13.54. 20 rm ☼ Ⓟ ♨ 🔔 ♿ closed 15 Nov-1 Mar (ex Christmas : 15 days), 200. Rest. ◆ Half-pension obligatory in high season, closed Mon low season. Spec : *collier de St-Jacques en brochette,* 70-240.
★***Parc,*** av. de l'Europe-Unie, ☎ 94.25.80.08. Visa. 40 rm ☼ Ⓟ ♨ ♿ closed 30 Sep-22 Mar, 200.

Six-Fours-les-Plages, 4 km E on the N559 :
★★***Isly*** (L.F.), 101 *bis,* rue de la République, ☎ 94.25.43.68. AE, DC, Euro, Visa. 20 rm Ⓟ ♨ 🔔 ⚘ 180.

⛺ ★★★★*Les Girelles* (220 pl.), ☎ 94.74.13.18 ; ★★★*Mogador* (240 pl.), ☎ 94.74.10.58 ; ★★★*Val d'Aran* (270 pl.), ☎ 94.29.56.18.

Restaurants :
◆ ***La Sartan,*** bd de l'Avenir, ☎ 94.74.37.40. Closed Thu. Spec : *feuilleté de moules aux poireaux, baudroie à la blanquette de légumes.* Reasonably priced, 35-100.

Six-Fours-les-Plages :
● ◆◆ ***Auberge St-Vincent,*** pont de Brusc, ☎ 94.25.70.50 Ⓟ closed Sun eve low season. V. Sciré makes commendable efforts for his clients : *coquillages en vivier, sole aux trois senteurs de Provence, loup aux olives.* Bourgogne and Beaujolais wines, 70-160.

SISTERON

Digne 39, Gap 58, Paris 706
B1 ⊠ 04200

ⓘ av. P.-Arène, ☎ 92.61.12.03.

SNCF ☎ 92.61.00.60.

Hotels :
★★★***Grand Hôtel du Cours,*** pl. de l'Église, ☎ 92.61.04.51. AE, DC, Euro, Visa. 44 rm. closed 15 Nov-15 Mar, 250.
★★***Chênes*** (L.F.), rte de Gap, ☎ 92.61.15.08. AE, Euro, Visa. 22 rm, closed 15 Oct-31 Dec, 180. Rest. ◆ Family-style meals, 60-120.

Restaurant :
Mison-les-Armands, 10 km NW :
◆ ***Central,*** ☎ 92.61.06.63. Visa ♿ closed Mar, 45-115.

⛺ ★★*Municipal* (200 pl.), ☎ 92.61.19.69.

SOSPEL

Menton 22, Nice 43, Paris 980
22 km N of Menton, D2 ❦ ⊠ 06380

SNCF ☎ 93.04.00.17.

Hotel :
★★***Étrangers*** (L.F.), 7, bd de Verdun, ☎ 93.04.00.09. Tx 970439. Euro, Visa. 35 rm closed 25 Nov-30 Jan. A good, simple hotel inland from Menton, 210. Rest. ♦ 65-140.

⛺ ★★*Les Merveilles* (66 pl.), ☎ 93.04.04.66.

Restaurant :
Breil-sur-Roya, 12 km N :
♦ ***Auberge du Col de Brouis,*** ☎ 93.04.41.75 Ⓟ closed Mon and 1 Nov-1 Jun, 60-120. With 9 rm.

TARASCON

Arles 18, Avignon 23, Paris 711
A2 ☒ 13150

ℹ av. République, ☎ 90.91.03.52.

SNCF ☎ 90.91.08.22.

Hotels :
★★***Provençal,*** 12, cours A.-Briand, ☎ 90.91.11.41. 22 rm Ⓟ closed 15 Oct-15 Mar, 150. Rest. ♦ Spec : *bourride, pieds paquets marseillais,* 50-120.
★★***Moderne,*** bd Itam, ☎ 90.91.01.70. 31 rm Ⓟ 180. Rest. ***le Mistral*** ♿ closed 16 Jan-10 Feb and Sat. Spec : *daube provençale,* 55-90.
★★***Saint-Jean***, 24, bd V.-Hugo, ☎ 90.91.13.87. AE, DC, Euro, Visa. 12 rm closed 15 Dec-15 Jan, 180. Rest. ♿ closed Wed low season. Provençal cooking. Spec : *terrine de rascasse au poivre rose, gigot d'agneau des Alpilles en croûte,* 65-120.

Youth hostel : 31, bd du Rhône, ☎ 90.91.04.08.

⛺ ★★*Camp Tartarin* (33 pl.), ☎ 90.91.01.46 ; ★★*Saint-Gabriel* (44 pl.), ☎ 90.91.19.83.

TENDE

Menton 57, Nice 83, Paris 1 020
D1 ☒ 06430

Hotel :
★***Centre,*** 12, pl. de la République, ☎ 93.04.62.19. AE, Visa. 17 rm Ⓟ 120.

Youth hostel : extension of chemin de Ste-Catherine, ☎ 93.04.62.74.

THÉOULE-SUR-MER

Saint-Raphaël 36, Nice 41, Paris 902
10 km SW of Cannes, D2 ☒ 06590

ℹ pl. Gal-Bertrand, ☎ 93.49.97.75.

SNCF ☎ 93.49.96.17.

Hotels :
★★★***Saint-Christophe,*** 47, av. de Miramar, ☎ 93.75.41.36. Tx 470878. AE, DC, Euro, Visa. 40 rm Ⓟ closed 15 Oct-15 Mar. Private beach, 555. Rest. ♦♦ 100-195.
★★★***Tour de l'Esquillon,*** Miramar, ☎ 93.75.41.51. AE, Visa. 25 rm Ⓟ Private beach, closed mid-Oct to early Feb, 450. Rest. ♦ ♿ 150-200.
★★***Corniche d'Or,*** 10, bd de l'Esquillon, Miramar, ☎ 93.75.40.12. Visa. 31 rm Ⓟ closed Oct-Easter, 280. Rest. ♦ 70-150.
★★***Mas Provençal,*** ☎ 93.75.40.20. AE, DC, Visa. 24 rm Ⓟ ♿ closed end Oct-early Mar, 400. Rest. ♦ closed end Sep-20 Mar, 80-110.

La Galère, 2 km on the N98 :
★★★★***Guerguy la Galère,*** ☎ 93.75.44.54. 14 rm Ⓟ closed 30 Nov-2 Feb, 600. Rest. ♦♦ Set in an orange grove facing the Lérins Islands. Spec : *filet de loup, bourride,* 200-300.

TOULON

Marseilles 64, Nice 153, Paris 839
B3 ☒ 83000

ℹ 8, av. Colbert (B1), ☎ 94.22.08.22.

✈ Toulon-Hyères (Le Palyvestre), 21 km E, ☎ 94.57.41.41.

⛴ ☎ 94.41.25.76. Regular service to Corsica during the high season.

SNCF (A1), ☎ 94.91.50.50, 94.22.90.00, 94.22.39.19.

🚌 bd. P.-Toesca, near the train station (A1).

Car-hire : *Budget* train + car, 15, pl. du 11-Novembre, ☎ 94.03.37.37, and at the station, ☎ 94.22.29.11.

Hotels :
★★★***Grand Hôtel,*** 4, pl. de la Liberté (B1), ☎ 94.22.59.50. AE, DC, Euro, Visa. 45 rm Ⓟ ♿ 320.
★★★***Frantel,*** bd Amiral-Vence, at the Mont-Faron cable car (off map, B1), ☎ 94.24.41.57. Tx 400347. AE, DC, Euro, Visa. 93 rm Ⓟ ♿ Splendid view of Toulon and the off-shore ship anchorage, 420. Rest. ● ♦♦♦ ***la Tour Blanche,*** closed Sat noon, Sun low season, and end-of-year hols. Regional dishes, menu made around one main dish : *jambon à l'os tapenade, bourride,* 120-200.
★★★***Corniche,*** 1, littoral F.-Mistral, le Mourillon (C4), ☎ 94.41.35.12. AE, DC, Euro, Visa. 22 rm 350. Rest. ♦♦ closed Feb, Sun eve and Mon. Spec : fish, 120-210.

La Garonne, ☒ 83220 Le Pradet, 11.5 km E on the N559 and D86 :
● ★★***Le Vieux Moulin*** (Relais du Silence), La Garonne Beach, ☎ 94.21.72.43. 17 rm Ⓟ closed Jan-Feb, 190. Rest. ♦♦ closed Sun eve and Mon low season, 75-150.

Les Oursinières, 12 km E on the N559 and D86 :
● ★★★***L'Escapade,*** ☎ 94.21.72.76. 16 rm Ⓟ 390.

Restaurants :
♦♦ ***Le Dauphin,*** 21 *bis,* rue J.-Jaurès (A2), ☎ 94.93.12.07. Closed Jul, Feb hols, Sat, Sun and nat hols. Relatively inexpensive for the region, 120-150.
♦♦ ***La Calanque,*** 25, rue Denfert-Rochereau (A2), ☎ 94.92.28.58. Closed Feb hols, 1 week in Sep, Sun eve and Mon. Expensive *à la carte* dining, but reasonable set menu. Classic cooking. Spec : *sole soufflée en mousseline, filet de turbot sabayon au fenouil,* 120-210.
♦♦ ***La Madeleine,*** 7, rue des Tombades (B2), ☎ 94.92.67.85. DC, Visa ; closed Jun, Tue eve and Wed. Spec : *gratin de moules aux mousserons, cuisse de canard aux foies de volailles,* 80-160.
♦♦ ***La Ferme,*** 6, pl. L.-Blanc (B2), ☎ 94.41.43.74. Closed Sun, Aug. Spec : *salade mer, foie de veau aux raisins,* pastries. Set menu is a good value, 120-210.

Le Mourillon :
♦♦♦ ***Le Lutrin,*** 8, littoral F.-Mistral (B4), ☎ 94.42.43.43. AE, DC, Euro, Visa. ♿ closed Sat. Spec : *foie gras frais du Lutrin, papillotes de rascasse sur fond de légumes frais,* 105-200.
♦♦ ***La Vigie,*** 57, littoral F.-Mistral (C4), ☎ 94.41.37.92. Visa. Ⓟ closed 10 Jan-6 Feb, Sun eve (ex Jul and Aug) and Wed, 95-170.

Solliès-Toucas, ☒ 83210 Solliès-Pont, 18 km NE :
● ♦♦ ***Le Lingousto,*** N554, ☎ 94.28.90.26. AE, DC, Visa. Ⓟ ♿ closed Jan-Feb-Mar, Sun eve

and Mon. A new choice every two weeks. Good Provençal flavour : *turbot au piment doux et gousses d'ail, huîtres pochées au pistou,* 160-250.

Events : Jul : *Antiques show, St. Peter's fete ;* Sep : *Regatta week ;* Oct : *trade fair.*

Recommended : Flea market Sun a.m.

TOURTOUR

Draguignan 20, Toulon 93, Paris 862
10 km SE of Aups, C2 ☒ 83690 Salernes

ℹ mairie, ☎ 94.70.57.20.

Hotels :

● ★★★★***Bastide de Tourtour*** (Relais et châteaux), rte de Draguignan, ☎ 94.70.57.30, Tx 970827. AE, DC, Visa. 26 rm closed Dec-Jan. Splendid view on the Haut-Var region ; delightful surroundings, 420-820. Rest. ♦♦♦ closed Mon and Tue low season. Good fare. Spec : *st-pierre aux poireaux, selle d'agneau,* 110-250.

★★***Host. les Lavandes,*** 1.5 km E on the D51, ☎ 94.70.57.11. 16 rm closed 1 Oct-31 Mar. Handsome Provençal residence in a pine grove. Half-pension obligatory, 270.

★★***Petite Auberge*** (Relais du Silence), 1.5 km SE on the D77, ☎ 94.70.57.16. DC, Euro, Visa. 11 rm closed Feb and Tue, 185. Rest. 80-110.

★★***Auberge St-Pierre,*** 3 km E on the D51, ☎ 94.70.57.17. 15 rm closed 15 Oct-1 Apr, 260. Rest. ♦♦ closed Thu. Family-grown produce, 120-160.

Restaurant :

● ♦♦ ***Les Chênes Verts,*** 2 km W on the Villecroze road, ☎ 94.70.55.06. closed 1 Jan-15 Feb, Tue eve and Wed. Book ahead. One of the most beautiful spots on the Var heights ; fresh and varied cooking : *truffes, turbot au champagne, canette rôtie au thym,* 200-300.

VAISON-LA-ROMAINE

Carpentras 28, Avignon 47, Paris 671
A1 ☒ 84110

ℹ pl. de l'Abbé-Sautel (B1), ☎ 90.36.02.11.

Hotels :

★★★***Beffroi,*** rue de l'Évêché, haute ville (B2), ☎ 90.36.04.71. AE, DC, Euro, Visa. 21 rm closed 15 Nov-15 Mar, 300. Rest. ● ♦♦ closed Mon and Tue noon. A ravishing 16thC setting (gardens and hillside terrace). Classic cooking : *millefeuille d'escargots, mignon de porc aux oignons,* 100-160.

★★***Logis du Château*** (L.F.), les Hauts de Vaison (off map, A2), ☎ 90.36.09.98. Tx 431389. AE, DC, Euro, Visa. 40 rm closed 31 Oct-15 Mar, 210. Rest. ♦♦ 75-150.

Rasteau, 7.5 km W on the D69 :

★★***Bellerive*** (L.F., Relais du Silence), ☎ 90.46.10.20. 20 rm closed 2 Jan-1 Mar, 230. Rest. ♦ 80-210.

Séguret, 9.5 km SW on the D88 :

★★★***Domaine de Cabasse*** (Relais du Silence), ☎ 90.46.91.12. Visa. 10 rm closed 1 Oct-15 Mar, 280. Rest. ● ♦♦ Half-pension only in high season. Excellent and clever cooking by N. Latour. One menu only. Spec : *aubergine à l'estrassade, crespeou comtadin, lapin à la pébrade,* 100-140.

★★***La Table du Comtat,*** ☎ 90.36.91.49. 8 rm closed 15 Jan-1 Mar, Tue eve and Wed, 300. Rest. ● ♦♦ Book ahead. In the open country and among the vineyards ; regional cooking. Spec : *filet de rouget à la crème de romarin, côte d'agneau à l'étuvée de légumes et foie gras,* 175-300.

Youth hostel : 9.5 km SW on the D88, *le Bresquet,* rte de Sablet, 84110 Séguret.

⛺ ★★*Moulin de César* (140 pl.), ☎ 90.36.00.78.

Events : Jul : *festival,* at the ancient amphitheatre ; Aug : *Provençal festival* in Séguret (9.5 km).

Recommended : Côtes-du-Rhône Villages wine-cave visit, Rasteau, 7.5 km W, ☎ 90.46.10.43.

VALRÉAS

Orange 35, Avignon 65, Paris 643
14 km W of Nyons, A1 ☒ 84600

ℹ pl. A.-Briand, ☎ 90.35.04.71.

Hotel :

★★***Grand Hôtel*** (L.F.), 28, av. Gal-de-Gaulle, ☎ 90.35.00.26. 18 rm closed 15 Dec-15 Jan, Sun and Sat eve low season, 200. Rest. ♦ 60-150.

⛺ ★★*La Coronne* (135 pl.), ☎ 90.35.03.78.

Restaurant :

Visan, ☒ 84820, 9 km S on the D976 :

● ♦♦ ***Les Troubadours,*** le Château, ☎ 90.41.92.55. closed 1 Oct-1 Apr, Mon and Tue (ex nat hols). The successful partnership of R. Jacquemet, cook and P. Desportes, music-hall artist, set in a 12thC castle. Good Lyonnais cooking : *tourte au jambon, cervelas en brioche.* Côtes-du-Rhône wines, low prices. Amazing puppet show, 120-210.

Events : *Nuit du Petit Saint-Jean* (23 Jun), Jul-Aug : *theatre festival.*

VENCE

Nice 22, Grasse 25, Paris 930
D2 ☒ 06140

ℹ pl. Gd-Jardin, ☎ 93.58.06.38.

Hotels :

★★★★(L) ***Château du Domaine Saint-Martin*** (Relais et châteaux), Coursegoules road via the D2, ☎ 93.58.02.02. 15 rm and 10 villas Splendid residence overlooking the sea and inland Provence ; closed Nov-Mar, 1 500. Rest. ♦♦♦ Rich, traditional fare. Spec : *ragoût de pâtes fraîches aux truffes, carré d'agneau provençale,* good wines, 280-450.

★★★***Floréal,*** 440, av. Rhin-et-Danube, ☎ 93.58.64.40. Tx 461613. Visa. 43 rm closed Jan, 360.

★★***Muscadelles,*** 59, av. Henri-Giraud, ☎ 93.58.01.25. 14 rm closed 20 Oct-20 Nov, 250. Rest., 50-85.

★***Closerie des Genêts,*** 4, imp. Marcellin-Maurel, ☎ 93.58.33.25. AE, DC, Euro, Visa. 10 rm 140. Rest. ♦ closed 12 Nov-20 Dec, Sun eve and Mon (ex Jul-Aug), Sat eve low season. Good, simple, inexpensive fare ; delicious fish soup, 60-130.

Tourrette-sur-Loup, ☒ 06490, 5 km SW :

★★***Auberge Belles Terrasses,*** rte de Vence, ☎ 93.59.30.03. 16 rm 180. Rest. 60-100.

⛺ ★★★*Domaine de la Bergerie* (310 pl.), ☎ 93.58.09.36.

Restaurants :

♦♦ ***Auberge des Seigneurs,*** pl. du Frene, ☎ 93.58.04.24. Closed Mon and 15 Oct-1 Dec. 14thC Provençal inn. Traditional regional meals and good wines, 110-160. With 10 rm.

♦♦ ***Farigoule,*** 15, rue Henri-Isnard, ☎ 93.58.01.27. Closed Fri ex high season and 15 Nov-15 Dec. Pleasant Provençal inn with garden. Tasty, inexpensive regional dishes, 65-80.
♦♦ ***Auberge des Templiers,*** 39, av. Joffre, ☎ 93.58.06.05. ♨ ♿ closed 15 Dec-20 Jan, 1-10 Jul, Sun eve and Mon. Spec : *panaché de poissons aux petits légumes, carré d'agneau au poivre vert,* 100-200.
♦♦ ***Portigues,*** 6, rue Saint-Véran, ☎ 93.58.36.31. Closed Sun. Pretty dining-rooms, 120-210.

Gattières, ⊠ 06150, 10 km NE on the D2210 :
♦♦ ***Auberge de Gattières,*** pl. du Pré, ☎ 93.08.60.05. P ♨ ♿ closed Wed. Spec : *mousseline chaude de truite à la crème de ciboulette, suprême de canette aux zestes d'orange,* 120-230.

VILLECROZE

Draguignan 21, Toulon 87, Paris 856
8 km SE of Aups, C2 ⊠ 83690 Salernes

ⓘ mairie, ☎ 94.70.63.06.

Hotels :
★★***Esparrus,*** on the N560, ☎ 94.70.70.80. 14 rm ⚘ P ♨ ✗ ⊡ ♿ 180. Rest. closed Mon low season, 80-130.
★★***Vieux Moulin,*** rte de Barbebelle, ☎ 94.70.63.35. 10 rm ⚘ P ♨ ✗ closed 30 Sep-1 Apr. Old oil-extraction mill, 160.

⛺ ★★★*Le Ruou* (100 pl.), ☎ 94.70.67.70 ; ★★★ *les Cadenières* (80 pl.), ☎ 94.70.60.31.

Restaurant :
♦♦ ***Au Bien-Être,*** quartier des Cadenières, ☎ 94.70.67.57. ⚘ P ♨ ♿ closed Wed. Spec : *salade forestière au foie gras frais, terrine de saumon à l'estragon,* 90-180.

Events : 15 May, "storehouses in the street".

VILLEFRANCHE-SUR-MER

Nice 6, Menton 24, Paris 940
4 km NW of Saint-Jean-Cap-Ferrat, D2
⊠ 06230

ⓘ square F.-Binon, ☎ 93.80.73.68.

SNCF ☎ 93.80.71.67.

Hotels :
★★★***Versailles,*** bd Princesse-Grace-de-Monaco, ☎ 93.01.89.56. Tx 970433. AE, Visa. 50 rm ⚘ P ♨ ⊡ ♿ View on the off-shore ship anchorage ; closed 20 Oct-20 Dec, 400. Rest. ♦♦ ✗ Spec : *salade de coquille St-Jacques aux pointes d'asperges, escalopes de loup braisé au vin rouge,* 140-210.
★★★***Welcome*** (Mapotel, Châteaux-hôtels), 1, quai Courbet, ☎ 93.55.27.27. Tx 470281. AE, DC, Euro, Visa. 32 rm ⚘ ♿ closed 4 Nov-22 Dec. 17thC convent ; spectacular site, with view on the ship anchorage and fishing port, 600. Rest. ♦♦ ***le Saint-Pierre*** ✗ Good seafood, 120-350.
★★★***Olivettes,*** 17, av. Léopold-II, ☎ 93.01.03.69. AE, Visa. 19 rm ⚘ P ♨ 400.
★★***Flore,*** av. du Mal-Joffre, ☎ 93.56.80.29. 18 rm ⚘ P ♨ ♿ closed Nov, 210. Rest. closed 1 Nov-15 Dec, 60-120.
★★***Auberge du Coq Hardi*** (L.F.), 8, bd de la Corne-d'Or, ☎ 93.01.71.06. 20 rm ⚘ P ♨ ⊡ closed Nov. Charming little hotel with view on the ship anchorage, 220. Rest. ♦ Good, simple cooking, 70-135.

Restaurants :
● ♦♦♦ ***Massoury,*** av. Léopold-II, ☎ 93.01.93.43. AE, DC, Visa ; closed 18 Dec-31 Jan, Wed. In his beautiful "Riviera" villa, P. Seibt is slowly becoming famous. Excellent service, good cooking : *caviar d'aubergine et mousse de poivrons doux, saint-pierre à la crème au basilic.* Great painters' exhibition on the walls, 175-350.
● ♦♦ ***Campanette,*** 2, rue Baron-de-Brès, ☎ 93.01.79.98. Closed Nov and Sun. An enchanting restaurant at the end of a tiny street ; fish specialities and good local wines, 120-210.

VILLENEUVE-LOUBET

Nice 16, Grasse 23, Paris 923
2 km W of Cagnes-sur-Mer, D2 ⊠ 06270

ⓘ ☎ 93.20.20.09.

Hotel :
At the beach, 5 km S :
★★★***La Pétanque,*** on the N98, ☎ 93.20.07.05. 30 rm and 10 studios P ♨ ✗ Private beach, 180.

⛺ ★★★★*Parc des Maurettes* (116 pl.), ☎ 93.20.91.91 ; ★★★★*Vieille Ferme* (47 pl.), ☎ 93.33.41.44 ; ★★★*Hippodrome* (72 pl.), ☎ 93.20.02.00.

Recommended : wine : Bellet A.O.C. *Chez Pradel,* ☎ 93.20.81.71.

[redacted]

The Rouergue and Albigeois Regions

Here the last foothills of the Massif Central roll gently to a stop. The Midi is just a stone's throw away. The whole region is characterized by the contrast between north and south, the cool greenness of the highlands mingling with a light that is already Mediterranean. Two regions in fact, with striking similarities and just as many differences : the accent of Auvergne and the singing tone of the south — rural Aveyron and industrial Tarn. Their histories are dissimilar too : "poor and pious Rouergue" has always been the land of tradition, while the Albigeois region has cradled all the major religious heresies and the great movements of the working class.

And yet these green countries of southern France share the same astonishing landscape of rocky, limestone plateaus known as *"causses"*, ryefields and gorges dotted with rivers, lakes and ponds. A landscape of many contrasts, from the dry and arid *causse* to sunny valleys, from sheep to vineyards, from red and black gorges to melancholy swamps. The architecture of the region shows the same diversity : the Middle Ages have left their mark and their masterpieces, from the Abbey of Conques to the cathedral of Albi, and each village has some treasure to show, something to offer the visitor in search of the past — Cordes, perched on a hilltop overlooking the Cérou valley, offers its Gothic houses in a perfect state of repair, and its 13th-century church. The windswept, stony plains of Larzac with isolated flocks of sheep and lonely shepherds is the home of Roquefort cheese, set amidst a landscape of magnificent rugged peaks with the twisted shapes of ruined castles. It is also a land of archeological treasures — prehistoric dolmens and menhirs — fortified farmhouses and lookout points. The leather industry of Millau, now fallen on hard times, once sent luxury gloves all around the world ; Laguiole, set in the high pasturelands of the Aubrac mountains, still possesses a knife industry — Laguiole knives are hand-made, each one unique, solid, sturdy and beautiful to look at.

Today the region offers all kinds of active holidays — pottery, weaving, ceramics, video, dance, trekking. Each year there are new courses to take, with villages and craftsmen outdoing each other to create new and exciting formulas.

Sightseeing

Don't miss

★★★ : *Albi (A3), Aubrac mountains (C1), Conques (B1), Cordes (A3), Larzac plateau (C3).*
★★ : *Les Bourines, La Couvertoirade (C3), Dourbie gorges (C3), Espalion (B1), Lot gorges, Valley (B1-C2), Montpellier-le-Vieux (C2), Najac (A2), Salles-la-Source (B2), Sauveterre-de-Rouergue (B2), Sidobre (B4), Sylvanès (C3), Villefranche-de-Rouergue (A2).*

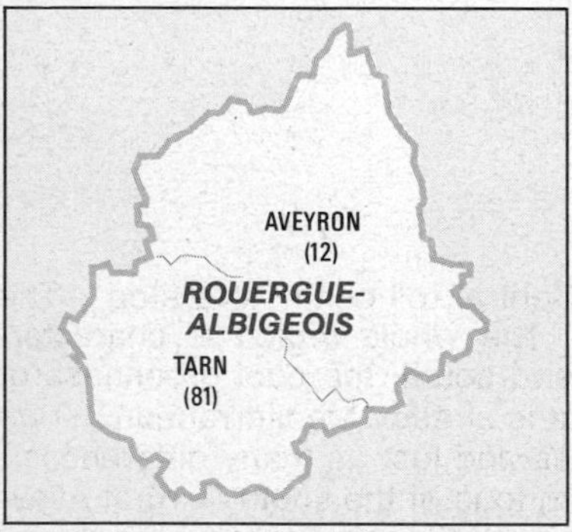

Weekend tips

The decision is simple : from Albi to Conques, through Cordes, Najac, Villefranche-de-Rouergue, Villeneuve and Peyrusse-le-Roc, with a choice between two fine restaurants : the Grand-Écuyer at Cordes, and La Charmille at Villefranche.

■ ALBI★★★

A3 / ® / pop. 48 021
See plan following page

Albi is called *la ville rouge* (the red town) because of its brickwork. Every shade of brick — pink, ochre, red, brown — is represented. The old centre of town, where administration and commerce are concentrated, is like an outdoor museum brought to life by the daily activity.

As early as the Middle Ages, Albi expanded along both banks of the Tarn. The town is now an important industrial centre for agribusiness, textiles, glass, construction, chemicals, and engineering.

▶ **Place du Vigan** (C2) : the main square linking the old town to newly developed areas to the E, with post office, shops, banks, hotels, restaurants and cafés. On either side of the square, the *lices* (boulevards) Pompidou and Moulin mark the line of former ramparts. ▶ To reach the cathedral, go down Rue de l'**Hôtel de Ville** (Renaissance town hall, 16thC; B2) or Rue Timbal (No. 12, **Reynès Mansion,** same period; now the Chamber of Commerce; half-timbered **Enjalbert House**★ with carved decoration). ▶ Between the pedestrian streets of Mariès and Ste. Cécile, **church of St. Salvi** (B2) : 12thC Romanesque, remodelled in the 15thC; triangular cloister reached by marked

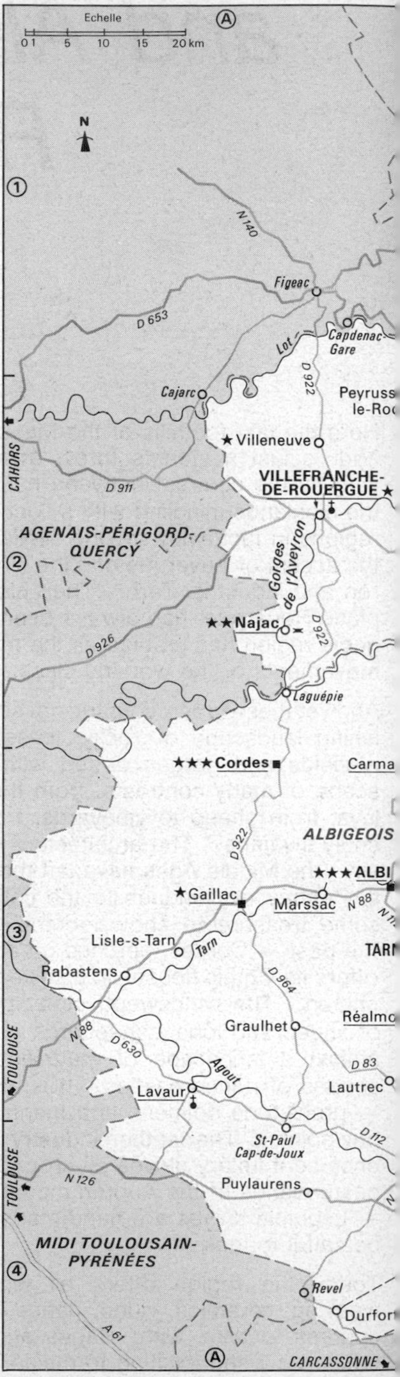

passages through the surrounding buildings. ▶ **Cathedral of Ste. Cécile**★★★ (A-B2) : an outstanding example of southern Gothic, built between 1282 and the late 14thC, single brick nave, turrets, 78 m bell-tower; Flamboyant Gothic canopy added to the southern entrance in 1535; **inside**★, 16thC Italian Renaissance paintings, 15thC French fresco of the Last Judgment (western wall), stained glass from the 14th-16thC; choir screen★ and enclosure★

(ca. 1500) showing Burgundian influence. ▶ N of the cathedral, the **Palais de la Berbie** (former bishops' palace); 13thC, 14thC, 15thC) overlooks the river Tarn from 17thC terraced gardens: reception rooms; **Toulouse-Lautrec Museum** displaying many works (including posters) by the painter Henri de Toulouse-Lautrec (1864-1901), son of the Count of Toulouse-Lautrec, who was especially renowned for his scenes of Parisian life; contemporary art; archaeology *(daily; closed Tue., 1 Oct.-Easter, and 1 Jan., 1 May, 25 Dec.).* ▶ S of the cathedral, mediaeval Albi of narrow streets and old houses; House of Vieil Alby at the corner of Rue Puech-Béranger and Rue de la Croix Blanche. Nearby, **birthplace of Toulouse-Lautrec** in the 18thC Bosc Mansion (No. 14 Rue Toulouse-Lautrec (B2-3, furniture, memorabilia, early works, terraced gardens; in summer, temporary exhibitions on various themes in the painter's work with pictures coming from museums abroad and complementing the museum's own collection; *Easter-Oct., 10-12 & 2-6; Jul.-Aug., 9-12 & 2-6; winter, 2-5 tel. 63.54.21.81).* No. 12 next door was home to the navigator Jean-François Galaud de Lapérouse (1741-1788), born in Albi: **wax museum** (history of Albi; *daily ex. Mon. in Jul.-Aug.; pm only Sep.-Jun.*). At present (between 1985-1987), a final bicentenary trip.

Also... ▶ **Rue de la Grande-Côte** (B1-2) leads down to the **Pont-Vieux** (11thC bridge) crossing the Tarn to the Madeleine quarter. ▶ From the other bridge (Pont du 22 Août), **view**★★ over the old town, the river Tarn, and the tall façades of the Madeleine district on the opposite bank. □

Facts and figures

Location : *the Rouergue extends from the Lot Valley to the Tarn Gorges, while the Albigeois mainly represents the middle basin of the Tarn.*

Area : *14551 km^2.*

Climate : *very hot in summer. Winter : mild and rainy in the Albigeois, more severe in the Rouergue with heavy rain.*

Population : *637500.*

Administration : Aveyron, *Prefecture : Rodez;* ***Tarn*** *Department, Prefecture : Albi.*

▶ Nearby

▶ **Castelnau-de-Lévis** *(9 km NW)* : 12th-15thC castle with 50 m tower overlooking a picturesque village★. ▶ View of Albi and the surrounding country from the chapel of **Notre-Dame-de-la-Drèche** *(5 km N).* ▶ **Lescure** *(5 km NE)* : 14thC church and Romanesque chapel of St. Michel *(500 m S).* □

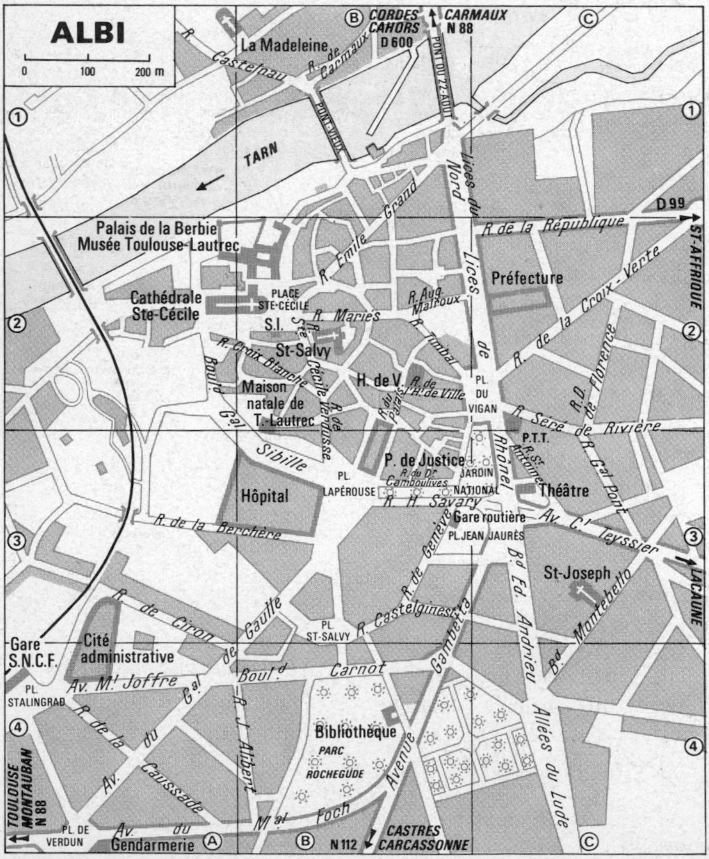

AMBIALET★

B3 / ® / pop. 400 (Tarn)

Ambialet is a mediaeval stronghold on a rocky peninsula★★ created by a twist in the river Tarn.

▶ From S to N along the crest : **castle** ruins; a small Romanesque **church,** cemetery, above the bridge; square **tower** of ruined church; at the point, former monastery of **Notre-Dame-de-l'Auder** which includes a very beautiful primitive Romanesque church (missionary museum). □

▶ Nearby

▶ **Valence-d'Albigeois** *(11 km N) :* 13thC *bastide* town. ▶ **Villefranche-d'Albigeois** *(10 km SW) : bastide* founded in 1239. ▶ **Rassisse★** (® → Réalmont) *(13 km S) :* reservoir in the Dadou valley. ▶ **château de Paulin** *(12 km SE) :* 10thC ruins above the **Oulas gorge★.** ▶ Return to the Tarn valley via **Saint André** (15thC castle, restored) and continue to **Trébas** *(15 km E from Ambialet;* pleasant surroundings). □

AUBRAC Mountains★★★

C1

The Aubrac is a region of undulating meadows. Leave the car and follow the cattle trails, visit the inns *(auberges),* and explore on foot. In the winter, take your skis to enjoy the snow fields.

▶ Isolated towns come to life on fair-days. ▶ **Laguiole** ® : among upland pastures; manufacture of pocket-knives and cheese; Haut Rouergue museum of local crafts; ski-runs. Cattle markets are the main local activity; view over the Aubrac and Cantal hills from the church (1659). ▶ **Saint-Urcize :** regional cattle-fair in mid-Oct; Romanesque church in Auvergne style with wall-belfry; 15thC polychrome stone Christ; old houses. ▶ **Nasbinals★** (® → Ardèche, Cévennes) : quiet resort in pastureland; Romanesque church. ▶ Among woods, **Aubrac★★** ® : former priory of the Knights-Hospitallers, who protected pilgrims on the road to Conques or Rocamadour; square tower (1353); Gothic façade on the almshouse; Romanesque church (13th-15thC); a pleasant resort. ▶ **Saint-Chély-d'Aubrac** ® : more southern than Auvergnat; 15thC church; humpbacked bridge, pilgrim cross. ▶ **Bonnefon :** fortified storage tower (15thC). □

CASTRES★

B4 / ® / pop. 46 880 (Tarn)

Once a Roman camp *(castrum,* hence the name); the natural advantage of the river Agout and an active cloth industry since the 14thC make Castres a busy town.

▶ **Place Jean-Jaurès :** the heart of the town has a southern look with plane trees and café-terraces; open on one side to the Agout, lined with timber-faced and balconied houses. From the other side of the square, pedestrian **Rue Victor-Hugo** leads to Church of **Notre-Dame de la Platé** (18thC; decoration). ▶ **Cathedral of St. Benoît** (1677-1718) : Southern Gothic; 18thC paintings; Romanesque tower from the original abbey. ▶ Opposite, in the former **bishop's palace** (architect, Mansart; 1666; → Versailles), town hall and **Goya Museum★** *(Jul.-Aug., daily, 9-12 & 2-6; Sep.-Jun., daily except Mon., 9-12 & 2-6)* works by the Spanish painter Francisco de Goya (1746-1828); other Spanish paintings of 15th-17thC; Hispano-Moorish ceramics; next door, **Jaurès Museum** *(same hours) :* exhibit on the socialist politician and writer Jean Jaurès, born in Castres in 1859 (assassinated in Paris in 1914). Outside, between the Agout and the town hall : **garden★** by André Le Nôtre (→ Versailles). ▶ 16th-17thC buildings; No. 12 Rue Frédéric-Thomas (B1) : Toulousain Renaissance brick and stone 16thC **Nayrac Mansion.** □

▶ Nearby

▶ To the S, foothills of the **Montagne Noire** (black mountain; views★) covered by the forests of Montaud, Fontbruno and Hautaniboul, in the **Parc Naturel du Haut Languedoc** (Upper Languedoc Nature Reserve). ▶ **Escoussens** *(7 km SW of Labruguière) :* former Roman town; Renaissance château. ▶ **Dourgne** *(16 km SW from Castres) :* a base for exploring the Montagne Noire; 16thC church; fountain. ▶ **Sorèze** *(24 km SW of Castres) :* grew around an abbey founded by the Frankish King Pepin the Short (714-768); 15thC fortified remains of abbey church; 16th-18thC abbey with a religious school; park; archaeological museum in the Maison du Parc Régional (HQ of the regional nature reserve; *Jul.-Aug. daily, 9-12 & 3-7*); houses with overhanging upper stories. **Durfort** *(3 km S of Sorèze) :* coppersmiths. Farther up the Sor Valley, **Malamort waterfall.** ▶ **Saint-Férréol reservoir** *(6 km away) :* built in the 17thC to feed the Midi canal; aquatic sports. □

Southern Gothic

Gothic architecture came relatively late to the south, where Romanesque art had flourished. The growing influence of the northern territories over the independent-minded southern states is illustrated by the fact that a northern architect, Jean Deschamps, was placed in charge of cathedral building (Rodez and Narbonne; 1270 onwards), where he introduced the pure Gothic style that had first been developed in Île-de-France in the mid-12thC. The new style soon assumed a southern character, seen in the cathedral at Albi. The main features are : a wide nave roofed by a single vault, a polygonal choir, fortress-like walls supported by buttresses, and narrow windows to keep out the fierce heat and bright sun. In this dissenting region, the walls symbolised the power of the Church, and the single nave its unity.

Le causse COMTAL (plateau)★

▶ round trip N of Rodez *(approx. 53 km; half-day)*

B2

A *causse* is a plateau marked by underground rivers, springs, caves, waterfalls and ravines. Wheat and sheep-farming in this agricultural area enriched first the Counts of Rodez, and later the citizens. Numerous Romanesque churches, chapels, manors, fortified store-houses and farmsteads were built over the centuries.

▶ **Rodez** (→). ▶ **Aboul :** commandery of the Hospitallers; Renaissance manor; Romanesque church. ▶ **Bozouls**★ ® : site at the edge of the Dourdou canyon; mediaeval village on the left bank, modern town on the right; old sandstone church★; view★. ▶ **Rodelle★★ :** on a spur over the Dourdou (site★), castle, Romanesque-Gothic church (16thC Pietà★). ▶ **Muret-le-Château★ :** 15thC residence of the bishops of Rodez. ▶ **Villecomtal** *(N of Muret) :* 13thC red sandstone walled town. ▶ **Cruou Valley★** leads to Marcillac. D27, runs EW across the plateau past many châteaux and manor-houses. ▶ **Tindoul de la Vayssière :** largest sink-hole in the region. ▶ Return to Rodez. □

CONQUES★★★

B1 / ® / pop. 404 (Aveyron)

Conques clusters around an abbey church, on a hillside above the Ouche gorges.

▶ **Ste. Foy :** one of the great pilgrim churches, in the architectural tradition of St. Martin in Tours, St. Sernin in Toulouse and St. Martial in Limoges; the **tympanum★★★** is a major achievement of Romanesque art, a personal interpretation of the Last Judgement by an anonymous artist of genius : the well-preserved polychrome carvings suggest the original appearance of great mediaeval sanctuaries. Inside, statuary depicting the Annunciation, probably by the same sculptor; 15thC painting on the sacristy walls. ▶ **Museum** in the former monks' refectory. **Treasury★★** has remained intact over centuries : goldsmiths' work from the 11th to the 16thC; **Majesté de Ste Foy★★★** (reliquary depicting the saint enthroned, 10thC; wood covered with gold, enamel and precious stones). A second treasury, opened in the summer of 84, comprises antique furniture, pictures and other ancient relics. ▶ **Village★★.** □

CORDES★★★

A3 / ® / 1 044 (Tarn)

This town over the river Cérou is protected by four walls; founded in 1222 as Cordoue and, like its Spanish namesake Cordoba (Cordoue in French), associated with the leather industry (13th-14thC); mediaeval Gothic houses, many now art galleries, craftshops and souvenir stalls (better out of season; craft courses; ancient and contemporary music).

▶ The main street★ **(Rue Droite) :** from the Ormeaux gate to the Rous gate, lined with **14thC houses, Maison du Grand Ecuyer** (restaurant), **Maison du Grand Veneur** (carved hunting scene on second story) and **Maison du Grand Fauconnier** (town hall and museum; *Sun. and nat. hols. pm, Palm Sunday to last Sun. in Oct.).* ▶ Timbered **market** on stone pillars (1350); well (85 m deep). ▶ **Church of St. Michel :** mauve sandstone; 13thC eastern end; façade and bell-tower 13th-15thC. ▶ At the Rous gate (painted doors), the **Charles Portal Museum :** history of Cordes, *libré ferrat* (chained Bible) on which city officials took their oath *(daily Apr.-Oct.; Sun. pm rest of year).* ▶ **Views★** from La Bride terrace, near the covered market, and from the sentry walk on the S rampart. □

▶ Nearby

▶ **Les Cabannes** *(1 km W) :* Gothic church. ▶ **Cayla** *(7 km SW) :* 15th-17thC **château** *(daily ex. Fri. am).* ▶ **Vaour** *(17 km W) :* ruined Knights-Templar Commandery; dolmen *(3 km);* view from relay-station *(5 km).* **Grésigne national forest★** (33 km^2; oak and hornbeam); marked paths; panoramas.

▶ Valley of the Vère, from Cordes to Bruniquel *(approx. 40 km; half-day)*

▶ **Cordes.** ▶ **Cahuzac-sur-Vère;** in the valley★, country holidays, vineyards. ▶ **Vieux :** Gothic church (murals). Le Verdier : dovecote; dolmen just off the road. ▶ **Castelnau-de-Montmiral** *(4 km SW overlooking the valley) :* 14th-15thC houses; church with 15thC silver-gilt cross. ▶ **Puycelsi★ :** fortified village on the right bank of the Vère (view); Gothic houses, 15th-16thC church. ▶ **Larroque :** red cliffs; caves. ▶ **Bruniquel** (→ Agenais, Périgord, Quercy). □

DECAZEVILLE

B1 / ® / pop. 9 200 (Aveyron)

Once the capital of the Rouergue mining industry.

▶ **Lassalle open-cast mine★ :** gigantic amphitheatre now open to tourists. ▶ Nearby, **Aubin : Rouergue Department Museum★ of Mining** *(daily, Jun.-Sep., 10-12 & 3-6; low season, Sat. and Sun., 3-6);* Romanesque and Flamboyant Gothic **church★** (15thC statues★; Romanesque Christ). ▶ Church of Notre-Dame de Decazeville : Stations of the Cross★ by the 19thC symbolist painter Gustave Moreau. □

▶ Nearby

▶ **Bournazel** *(12 km S of Aubin) :* château★; northern wing, 1545; Renaissance façade of eastern wing, 1554 *(exterior visits only).* ▶ **Belcastel★** *(15 km S, by the Aveyron gorge) :* castle, keep; galleried houses; Gothic bridge; mill; tomb and 15thC sculptures in the church. ▶ **Clairvaux★** *(16 km NE from Belcastel) :* red sandstone; Romanesque church, rebuilt in the 18thC; 17thC furnishings. □

DOURBIE Gorge★★

▶ From Nant to Millau *(32 km; approx. 3 hrs)*

C3

Less well known than the Tarn and Ardèche gorges, but just as spectacular.

▶ The river Dourbie runs from the Aigoual mountains into the Tarn through a narrow canyon between Nant and Millau. ▶ **Les Cuns :** church roofed with fish-scale stone shingles. ▶ **Cantobre★ :** site★; village built into a mushroom-shaped rock; Romanesque church.

The leather industry

Tanning and leatherwork are traditional industries in Millau; at the turn of the century, high-fashion gloves were exported all over the world from the town and surrounding villages. By the 1950s, output was more than 4 million pairs of gloves per year, but production has declined as a result of changing fashion, despite the ready supply of fine leather in this sheep-farming region.

▶ **Saint-Véran★** : on a narrow cliff road in a fold of the plateau; ruins of Montcalm fortress. ▶ **La Roque Sainte-Marguerite**; at the mouth of the Riou Sec ravine from which you can reach the rocks of Montpellier-le-Vieux (→); 17thC château (dovecote; Romanesque church) overlooks a hump-backed bridge and an old mill. ▶ Continue to Millau (→) between eroded cliffs giving way to gardens and poplars towards the end of the journey. □

GAILLAC★

A3 / ® / pop. 10 650 (Tarn)

On a loop of the Tarn near the Abbey of St. Michel (founded 7thC), Gaillac has been renowned for wine (red, white, sparkling) since the Middle Ages.

▶ **Place d'Hautpoul** and **Place de la Libération** (Friday market) form the centre of town. **Pierre de Brens Mansion** (ca. 1500; brick, flanked by mediaeval tower) : museum of folklore, wine and vineyards *(visit at 4 pm in summer except Sun. and Mon.; ask at the TO).* ▶ **Church of St. Pierre** : southern Gothic. At nearby **Place Thiers** (lined with old houses) : **Griffoul fountain** (16th or 17thC). ▶ By the Tarn, **abbey church of St. Michel** : 12th-13thC, restored 17thC, 13thC statue of Virgin and Child.
Also... ▶ **Foucaud Park** : *(S on the Graulhet road)* terraced gardens down to the Tarn; 17thC **château de Huteau**; municipal art and history museum *(daily pm ex. Tue., Apr.-Oct.; Wed., Sun. pm Nov.-Mar.).* ▶ Natural history **museum** at Place Philadelphe Thomas *(every day by request, tel. 63.57.36.31).* □

▶ Nearby

▶ **Alguelèze** : *(9 km E)* aquatic sports on the bank of the Tarn. ▶ **château de Mauriac** : *(9 km N)* 15thC fortress with Renaissance courtyard *(daily pm May-Sep., Sun. and nat. hols. pm rest of year;* exhibitions). □

GRAULHET

A3 / ® / pop. 13 650 (Tarn)

Industrial town on the river Dadou with a long tradition of tanning and leatherwork; the leading European producer of fine leathers. □

▶ Nearby

▶ **Lézignac** *(3 km NW)* : remains of 16th-17thC **château.** ▶ **Briatexte** *(7 km W)* : walled town founded in 1290; arcaded square. ▶ **Lautrec** *(15 km SE)* : gates and remains of fortifications on a hill; church (15th-17th and 18thC) with altarpiece from former collegiate church of Burlats (→ Sidobre and Lacaune mountains); 24 carved stalls; archaeology museum *(daily Jul.-Sep.);* limestone cellars. □

LARZAC Plateau★★★

▶ Round trip from Millau to Le Caylar *(40 km; half-day necessary for good approach)*

C3

The Larzac plateau, where blue Roquefort cheese is made from ewe's milk, is rich in archaeological and architectural remains. The windswept region is dotted with triple-vaulted sheepfolds, traces of Templar and Hospitaller commanderies, fortified farmsteads and villages.

▶ **Millau.** ▶ Long scenic drive along the edge of the plateau. ▶ **Grande Jasse** : sheep-farm 15 km from Millau on N9; information about Larzac : introduction to the region. ▶ **Sainte-Eulalie-de-Cernon** : walled town, long the capital of Larzac; 15thC ramparts; church and château remodelled in the 17thC. ▶ **La Couvertoirade★★** : 15thC fortifications built by the Hospitallers, a defensive outlook for 17th-18thC houses and mansions recalling the prosperous wool trade with nearby Lodève (→). ▶ **Le Caylar** : mediaeval village structure. ▶ View★ over the stony landscape of the Larzac plateau. ▶ Now, the deserted and most Mediterranean part of the plateau. ▶ **Escalette Pass★★** and road 200 m above the Lergue Valley down to the Hérault plain (→).
Also... ▶ **Durzon Valley** (→ Nant), **Sorgues Valley** (→ Saint-Affrique) and **Cernon Valley** (→ Roquefort). □

LAVAUR

A3 / ® / pop. 8 264 (Tarn)

One-time stronghold on the banks of the Agout river, best seen from the Bishop's Palace gardens *(Jardins de l'Évêché).*

▶ **St. Alain Cathedral** (13th-14thC) : in southern Gothic style; Flamboyant Gothic doorway topped by a tower; Romanesque tower with a 17thC Jack-o'-the-clock (mechanism and bell, 1523); inside church polyptych of Christ's Passion (late 16thC). ▶ In former chapel, **Vaurais Museum** (archaeology and local history; *Tue., Thu., Sat. and Sun. pm, 3rd Sun. in May-30 Sep.; Wed. Sat. and Sun. pm rest of year*). ▶ In Grand'-Rue : **Church of St. François** (14th-15thC). ▶ No. 7 Rue du Père Colin : **Maison du Vieux Lavaur** (museum of regional ethnography; *daily pm, 15 Jul.-30 Aug., or by appt. with Mr. Camelin, tel. 63.58.03.65*).

▶ Nearby

▶ **Ambres** ® *(5 km N),* above the junction of the Dadou and Agout rivers; church; panorama. ▶ **Giroussens** ® *(10 km NW),* former pottery centre on the right bank of the Agout; pleasant surroundings, château, 16thC church. □

LÉVEZOU Lakes

▶ From Rodez to Millau via Montjaux *(78 km; very windy road in the second half of the trip; full day)*

B2

The high plateau of Lévezou separates north and south Rouergue. In the north, the landscape is similar to Auvergne: moist, wooded and mountainous, whereas the dry limestone country in the south is more Mediterranean. In the south, the roofs are covered with curved tiles; stone shingles are used in the north. The Lévezou is a heathland with grazing for sheep and tracts under intensive cultivation. The lakes provide excellent fishing and sailing.

▶ **Rodez** (→). **Pont-de-Salars** ® : in the Viaur

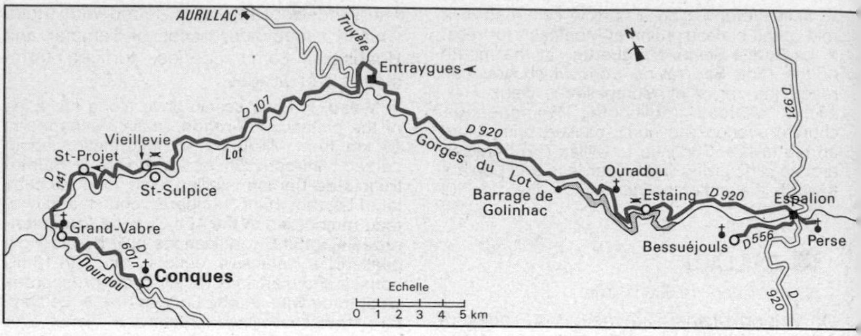

1. Lot Gorges

valley, once a stopover between Rodez and Millau, today a lakeside resort. ▶ **Salles-Curan** ® : former stronghold above **Lake Pareloup** (28 km circumference), around the 15thC castle of the bishops of Rodez, now a hotel; Gothic houses, 15thC church (carved stalls). ▶ Rather than seeing the third lake farther south, explore the picturesque villages of the area, situated on the edge of the plateau. ▶ **Bouloc** ® : on the ridge-line. ▶ **Saint-Beauzély★ :** stopover on the road to Rodez until the 18thC; old houses, 16thC château. ▶ **Combéroumal★ :** W from the village, former priory of the order of Grandmont; the austerity of the monastic rule is reflected by the architecture. ▶ Head back to another mediaeval village, **Castelnau-Pégayrols★ :** overlooking the **Muze gorge,** around the castle of the counts of Lévezou and two Romanesque churches; the dour grey sandstone underlines the fortress outlook of the village; church of St. Victor, in the centre of the village, once belonged to a priory of the same name; the other (11th-12thC), in the cemetery, was the parish church. ▶ **Montjaux★★ :** (site) the streets down to the church are lined with old houses of a pretty pink, with climbing plants, architectural details and Gothic or Renaissance windows ; small 16th-17thC château; pink sandstone church roofed with blue tiles (façade and dome remodelled; inside, capitals). ▶ Opposite, view over **Marzials :** terraced mediaeval fortress. ▶ From Montjaux, to **Millau** (*26 km →*) via the Tarn valley (→) or Saint-Affrique (*23.5 km →*); or go back towards Salles-Curan *(12.5 km)* via **Les Canabières :** Romanesque church and cemetery cross decorated with a Pietà. □

■ LOT Gorges★★

▶ Round trip from Conques to Espalion *(55 km; half-day)*

B1 *(see map 1)*

North of Conques, the river Lot runs through wooded gorges frequented by campers and anglers. Farther downstream, it joins the Truyère at Entraygues and continues past Estaing to broaden out after Espalion.

▶ **Conques.** Drive down the Dourdou valley. ▶ **Grand-Vabre** ® : 15th-16thC church; Pietà. ▶ **Saint-Projet :** views over the Lot and Auze gorges. ▶ **Saint-Sulpice :** hamlet opposite **Vieillevie.** ▶ **Entraygues** ®★ : at the junction of the Lot and the Truyère in a vine-growing valley (rosé wine); mediaeval bridges over the river; 13th-17thC château on the peninsula; once a busy port for lighterage between the plateau and Bordeaux. Entraygues : the houses have a mediaeval appearance (Rue Basse); on the edge of town, Pontet chapel (16th-17thC; statues). ▶ The **Golinhac Dam** has turned the gorge into a lake bordered by chestnut trees. ▶ **Estaing★** ® : in a bend of the Lot (Gothic bridge★); the d'Estaing family was powerful from the 15th to the 18thC; château; 15thC church (outside, Gothic crosses; inside, 15thC Christ, 17thC altarpieces); 15th-16thC château, now a convent *(visits)*; 16th-18thC houses; town hall in 16thC Cayron mansion; balconied houses; bridges over the river Caussane. **Ouradou** *(1 km N)* : Gothic statues★ in the **chapel.** ▶ The valley broadens at **Espalion★★** ® : view from the Pont-Vieux★ (bridge, late 15thC) to the Renaissance château and the tanners' houses. ▶ **Rouergue Regional Museum** in the former prison (evolution of thought; *exhibitions in summer; tel. 65.68.12.86*). Josephe Vaylet Museum in converted church : folk art, prehistory, ceramics *(15 Jun.-15 Sep., daily, 10-12 & 2-7; out of season, by request, tel. 65.44.69.18.)*. ▶ Outside the town, church of **Perse★★** *(1 km S) :* pink and white, with blue slate roof, inspired by Conques; doorway with rustic treatment of the Apocalypse; left, reused Adoration of the Magi; figured capitals; false ogival vaulting; retouched 12thC paintings (concerts in summer). ▶ **Bessuéjouls★** *(3 km W on the left bank) :* church with Romanesque chapel under the bell-tower (primitive decoration). □

■ LOT Valley★★

▶ From Espalion to La Canourgue *(57 km; poor road; half-day)*

B1-C2

At this point, the valley of the Lot divides the dry, cold, volcanic Aubrac (→) massif from the high plateaus of the Lozère.

▶ **Espalion** (→). ▶ On the left, **Flaujac :** fortified hamlet. ▶ **Saint-Côme-d'Olt★ :** encircled by ramparts, centred on a Flamboyant Gothic church (bell-tower, carved doorway); town hall in 15thC château. On a volcanic outcrop to the S, **Roquelaure★ :** feudal château remodelled in the 17thC; chapel (16thC Pietà). ▶ **Castelnau Dam :** makes a reservoir of the Lot gorges. ▶ **Saint-Geniez-d'Olt** ® : an orchard valley, formerly a centre of the cloth trade; on the left bank, former convent (14thC; 16thC triptych) among 17th-18thC mansions. On the right bank, mediaeval town. ▶ The villages lining the river are composed of beautiful houses built of red sandstone with slate roofs. ▶ **La Canourgue** (→ Ardèche, Cévennes). □

■ MAZAMET

B4 / ® / pop. 13340 (Tarn)

At the foot of the Montagne Noire, on the banks of the Arnette, Mazamet is the European centre for processing sheepskin; also a dairy centre.

▶ Place de l'Hôtel de Ville; 18thC church of St. Sauveur. ▶ Near the Caserne carpark : **Fuzier Museum** : Cathars, local history *(daily ex. Sun. and Mon.).* □

▶ Nearby

▶ On the road to Carcassonne : **Plo de la Bise,** lookout over the town and the hamlet of Hautpoul. ▶ **Montagnès** *(7 km farther)* : reservoir surrounded by woods. ▶ **Hautpoul** *(4 km S)* : on a rocky spur, ruined 15thC church of St. Sauveur; two castles destroyed in 1212 by Simon de Montfort, remains of fortifications. Upstream, **Arnette Gorge.** ▶ **Château d'Aiguefonde** *(8 km W)* : 16thC, rebuilt in the 18thC. ▶ Near **Saint-Amans-Soult** ® *(10 km E)* : park, château of Soult-Berg, birthplace of Maréchal Soult (1769-1851, served under Napoléon), who is buried in the village church (octagonal bell-tower with 16thC spire). ▶ **Thoré Valley★** leads to Labastide-Rouairoux (Languedoc-Roussillon →). ▶ **Anglès** ® *(27 km NE)* : between Lakes St. Peyres and Raviège; 15thC château de Monségou. □

■ MILLAU

C2 / ® / pop. 22250 (Aveyron)

Pink-tiled roofs and the Mediterranean trio of sheep, olives and vineyards signal the approach to the deep south. Millau, unlike other towns in the Rouergue, has a strong Protestant tradition. In earlier times the town was a glove-making centre.

▶ The mediaeval town is marked by the belfry (view); the centre of the old quarter is Place du Maréchal Foch (pedestrian precinct) with arcaded galleries and fountain in Empire style; corn-market (school); 18thC town hall with archaeological museum (Millau was an important pottery town in Roman times; *daily except Sun., 10-12 & 2-5; Jul.-Aug., 10-12 & 3-7, visitors to sites of excavation; out of season, daily except Mon. and Tue.; Jul.-Aug., daily except Tue.*); 17thC Counter-Reformation church; the Tauriac Mansion contains a glove museum. Centre of Leather and Skin-tanning *(28 Jun.-7 Sep., 10-12 & 3-7 daily except Sun.).* **Also...** ▶ 18thC **wash-house** on Boulevard de l'Ayrolle. Tarn Gorges (→ Cévénnes). Dourbie gorges (→). □

▶ Nearby

▶ **Compeyre** *(8 km)* : **château de Cabrières** (12th and 14thC).

■ MONTPELLIER-LE-VIEUX★★

C2

Legend has it that this jumble of rocks overlooking the Dourbie is a dead city, buried among pines, oaks and arbutus. A marked path leads you to the most interesting sections *(2 or 3 hrs round trip; avoid very hot weather; maps of the site available from the auberge [inn] at Maubert).* From Douminal, view over the Causses down towards Peyreleau★ on the Tarn and Jonte rivers (→ Cévennes), at the junction of three causses. You can see in succession the Jonte gorges, the Capluc rock at the mouth of the Tarn gorges (→) and Sauveterre peak (→). □

Local vocabulary

babissou : *mountain mushroom.*
buron : *in the Aubrac, summer shelter for the shepherds, where cheese is made.*
cabecou : *small goat-cheese.*
cantales : *in the Aubrac, chief shepherd in charge of the buron and cheese-making.*
jasse : *sheepfold in the Larzac.*
laguiole : *shepherd's horn-handled knife, invented more than a century ago by Mr. Clamels of the village of that name.*
megisserie : *sheepskin tanning.*
oustal : *house in Rouergue region.*
pages : *landowner in Rouergue.*
rougier : *valley in the soft sandstone at the foot of the causses; the glistening red stone is characteristic of the landscape and houses.*
raisine : *jam made with autumn fruits.*

■ NAJAC★★

A2 / ® / pop. 820 (Aveyron)

This stronghold of the Counts of Toulouse was destroyed by Simon de Montfort during the Albigensian Crusade (early 13thC), later rebuilt by Alphonse de Poitiers, brother of St. Louis (Louis IX). The castle (illuminated in summer) is silhouetted at the end of the single street, on a spur in a narrow loop of the Aveyron river.

▶ The original town was crowded between the castle and the church; the present village was the suburb. **Place des Arcades★ :** at the base of the Najac promontory, the long street winds up to the castle; **Gothic houses;** 1344 fountain; **castle★★** *(Apr.-Sep., 10-12 & 2-5 except Jun. 2:30-6 and Jul.-Aug., 2:30-7 every afternoon),* rebuilt in 1253 after a Cathar "heretic" rebellion; Gothic church on the cliff edge built with fines exacted by the Inquisitors (15thC statues; view★).
Also... ▶ **Gothic bridge** and former lepers' hospital on the **Laguépie Varen** road; views. □

■ NANT★

C3 / pop. 970 (Aveyron)

This village at the entrance to the Dourbie valley (→) developed around a Benedictine abbey. The monks drained the marshy Durzon valley to make fertile vineyards and meadows, "the garden of Aveyron".

▶ Arcaded 17thC market on the **Place du Marché★★;** pleasant stroll along the Dourbie river; 16thC **bridge;** Romanesque abbey **church★** (mid-12thC) : each pillar is flanked by eight columns (capitals★★); old houses in neighbouring streets. □

Wayside crosses and Pieta groups

Religious art in Rouergue reached a peak with the development of a school of sculpture in the 15thC. Country churches harbour many of these minor masterpieces of regional art. The entombment of Christ, descent from the cross (Pietà), and related themes from Christ's Passion are portrayed in polychrome stone throughout the area. In the mountain uplands, carved wayside crosses reflect a vigorous faith.

▶ Nearby

▶ **Durzon valley★** *(6 km SW; explore on foot) :* cultivated valley in the Larzac plateau (→) ; trout-stream. **Saint-Martin-du-Vican** (site) : Romanesque chapel. Foux du Dourzon : resurgence of the river. ▶ **Saint-Jean-du-Bruel** ® *(8 km E) :* between the Larzac plateau and Mount Aigoual (→), the chestnut woods and dark stone of the Cévennes (→) appear. S, **château d'Algues** (view★). □

PEYRUSSE-LE-ROC★

A2 / pop. 375 (Aveyron)

A natural stronghold overlooking the Audierne gorge that was one of the earliest towns in Rouergue, by virtue of its strategic position and its silver mines.

▶ At one time Peyrusse boasted a population of 3 000, but cheap silver from Latin America and the consolidation of the French state forced Peyrusse into a decline balanced by the rise of Villefranche, which was better placed for communications. From the 17thC onwards the population of Peyrusse continually dwindled.

▶ Drive down the Diège valley towards **Capdenac** ® *(12 km NW) :* once a citadel **(Capdenac-le-Haut),** it is now an industrial town on the plain **(Capdenac-Gare).** □

PUYLAURENS

A4 / ® / pop. 2 780 (Tarn)

The seat of a Protestant college that flourished from 1565 until the 1685 Revocation of the Edict of Nantes. The Wednesday agricultural market dates back to the 12thC. From the hilltop site, view over the Cévennes and the Pyrénées.

▶ **church :** Romanesque choir, 1675 nave, bell-tower rebuilt in 1900; wooden covered market. □

▶ Nearby

▶ **château de Magrin** *(10 km NW) :* 12th-16thC; Pastel Museum explaining development and trade; Albi art since the 16thC *(Easter, Pentecost, Sun. in Jul., daily in Aug.; tel. 63.75.63.82).* ▶ **château de Montgey** *(13 km NW) :* Romanesque tower, 16th-18thC buildings *(Sun. pm).* □

RABASTENS

A3 / ® / pop. 3 835 (Tarn)

Rabastens, on the banks of the Tarn, was the summer residence of members of the Toulouse parliament.

▶ Near the bridge (view), southern Gothic church of **Notre-Dame du Bourg★** (13th-14thC) : fortified bell-tower; Romanesque doorway with figured capitals showing New Testament scenes (inside, 15thC murals over-restored in the 19thC). ▶ 16th-18thC houses and mansions. □

▶ Nearby

▶ **Saint-Sulpice-la-Pointe** ® *(8 km SW) :* near the junction of the Agout and Tarn rivers : church (rebuilt ca. 1880) with fortified brick façade (14thC Toulouse style). ▶ **château de Saint-Géry★** *(4.5 km NE;* 14th-18thC) : on the right bank of the Tarn; furniture from Louis XIII to the Restoration (1814) *(Sun. and nat. hols. pm, Easter-1 Nov.; daily pm Jul.-Aug.; or by appt. tel. 63.33.70.43).* ▶ **Lisle-sur-Tarn** ® *(9 km NE) :* a 12thC *bastide* (walled town) amid vineyards (Gaillac wines); arcaded square; old houses★; Gothic church (13thC Romanesque doorway; Toulouse-style bell-tower). **Raymond Lafage Museum :** paintings, local archaeology, history *(Sun. am, or by request for groups).* View★ of the town from the bridge over the Tarn. ▶ **Salvagnac** *(12 km N) :* 15thC château; restored mill. □

RÉALMONT

A3 / ® / pop. 2 550 (Tarn)

A *bastide* founded in 1270 on the Blima river, now a pleasant resort.

▶ Church (15th-17thC; Baroque altarpiece) on the shady town square. ▶ 13 km SE, ruined **château de Montredon** (12thC). 17 km SE, 14thC Gothic church of **Notre-Dame-de-Ruffis.** To the E, the **Dadou Valley.** □

RODEZ★

B2 / ® / pop. 26 350 (Aveyron)

A grey and pink town in a bend of the Aveyron river that is the capital of one of the most important rural departments of France.

▶ In mediaeval times, Rodez was divided into an episcopal city and a city ruled by the Counts of Rodez. Traces of the division are still apparent in the pedestrian precinct. **Cathedral★★** (B-C3) : red sandstone structure built over 3 centuries; a masterpiece of religious architecture that was also an integral part of the town's defences; the fortress-like appearance was relieved by the later addition of a central Flamboyant Gothic upper section★ topped with a Classical pediment (inside, 16thC chapel enclosure; 15thC choir screen; 17thC carved walnut organ-casing; several Gothic **altarpieces★,** including a Descent from the Cross). ▶ The **Episcopal Palace** (rebuilt in the 19thC) has a 17thC staircase copied from Fontainebleau (→ Île-de-France). The **Chanoines' quarter** (C2-3, around the Place de la Cité), contains several mansions : Rues Embergue, Bonald, Touat, Bosc and Penavayre. In the rival **Bourg quarter** (C3-4), former domaine of the Counts of Rodez and the merchants : see the Maison de l'Annonciation (16thC, Place du Bourg); the French Classical **Prefecture building★;** the Maison d'Armagnac (Place d'Olmet; façade embellished with sculpted medallions). ▶ Church of St. Amans (C4) : rebuilt in 1758; partly Romanesque interior. ▶ **Fenaille museum** (C3) : in two mansions (14th and 16thC), mediaeval and Renaissance : sculptures, 17 statue-menhirs★ and other archaeological finds from southern Rouergue

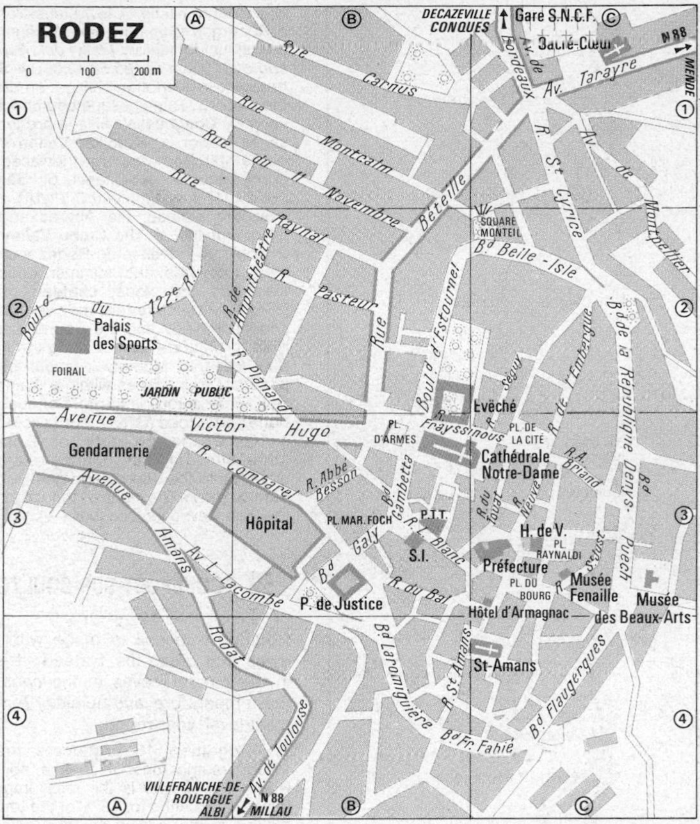

(15 Jun.-15 Sep. 10-12 & 2:30-5:30, closed Sun., Mon. and nat. hols.; out of season, groups only by request tel. 65.68.02.27). Former **Jesuit college★ : chapel** with interesting decoration *(ask at SI).* **Stud-farm★** *(past Place du Foirail, via A2)* in a former charterhouse, 17th-18thC *(visits by request tel. 65.68.68.04, preferably during the winter season).* □

▶ Nearby

▶ On the plateau south of Rodez, two pretty villages : ▶ **Sainte-Radegonde★ :** around a Renaissance house and a church★ fortified to shelter the whole village (13thC, fortified 14th-15thC, 13thC frescos). ▶ **Inières★ :** brownish-pink houses around a 15thC church-keep★ (polychrome stone Annunciation★, 16thC). ▶ **Palanges Forest** *(15km E from Rodez) :* oaks and pines. ▶ Handsome houses on the edge of the plateau north of the forest. **Montrozier★ :** 15th-16thC château. **Anglars :** 16thC polychrome stone entombment of Christ. ▶ Two fortified farmsteads : **Les Bourines★★,** which belonged to the Hospitallers of Aubrac (→); and **Galinières★,** property of Bonneval abbey (richest in the region until the Revolution). □

▶ From Rodez to Conques★★ *(37 km, half-day)*

B2-1 *(see map 2)*

Handsome architecture in the Comtal plateau, beautiful villages, a museum, valleys, a gorge, and finally, Conques.

Country cooking

Charcuterie *of all kinds: ham from Najac and Naucelle, sausage from Lacaune,* paté, *cracklings and hashed meat* (fricandaux); *chicken, goose, turkey and duck from Lévezou; mushrooms; trout; river-shrimp (they may only be caught once a year, but there is no law against shrimp-farming); lamb and mutton from the plateaus : these are the local specialities.*

Aligot, *originally from the Aubrac, is a meal in itself, and simple to make : you need only mix mashed potatoes with Laguiole cheese* (tomme fraîche). Truffade *is a variation on the theme : thin slices of cheese melted over fried potatoes.* Tripou *is a regional dish of stuffed mutton tripe braised with white wine, tomatoes and seasonings. More Mediterranean,* aïgo boulido *is a soup made with garlic and sippets.*

The numerous regional wines are the perfect accompaniment to these copious dishes : Tarn's reds and rosés, dry white from Entraygues (vin de Fel), *rosé from Estaing, and Marcillac red (rough, usually consumed young).*

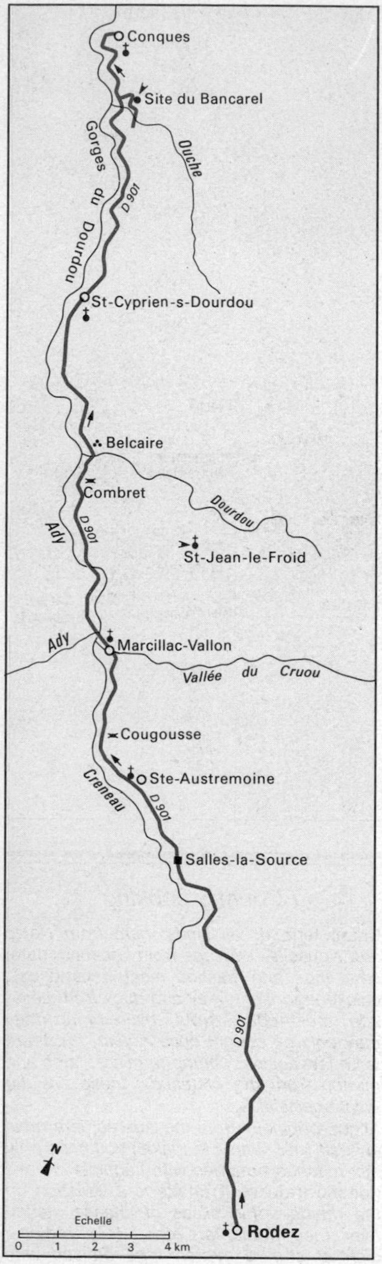

2. From Rodez to Conques

▶ **Rodez.** ▶ château de Fontanges : 16thC, now a hotel. ▶ The **Comtal Plateau** (→) is dotted with châteaux : **Floyrac** (17thC) and **Onet** ® (15th-16thC). ▶ Road through the Faby gorge (resurgence). ▶ **Salles-la-Source★★** ® : one of the prettiest villages in Aveyron by a waterfall on the edge of the plateau (site★); actually three villages one above the other, each with its church and castle. A few steps from a cave is a Rouergue Departmental Museum★ in a former spinning factory *(daily, Jul.-Aug.; low season by request tel. 65.68.12.86).* ▶ **Sainte-Austremoine★ :** another village on the edge of the plateau; Romanesque church★ (15thC Calvary). ▶ **Cougousse :** village around a Renaissance manor. ▶ **Marcillac-Vallon★** ® : centre of the Marcillac wine area; terraced hillsides★, pretty church. ▶ Chapel of **Saint-Jean-le-Froid★** *(4 • km N) :* 16thC Pietà; panorama★ over the plateau, the Aubrac and the Cantal mountains. ▶ The **Cruou Valley★** leads to Bozouls (→) : well-to-do Rodez merchants had their vineyards and summer houses in this area. On the slope, **château de Combret** (17thC). ▶ **Belcaire fortress** overlooks the junction of the Ady and the Dourdou. ▶ Pleasant road to **Mouret★** *(6 km)* along the upper Dourdou valley. At Mouret★ : feudal fortress composed of four castles within a single defensive wall. This detour leads to Conques along the ridge; poor road (GR62), but spectacular views. ▶ Once the property of Conques, the 16th-18thC mill at Sagnes stands at the entrance to the Dourdou gorges. ▶ Site in **Bancarel★ :** from the right of the village entrance, the best view over Conques (→). □

■ ROQUEFORT-SUR-SOULZON★

C3 / ® / pop. 880 (Aveyron)

Roquefort cheese is made with milk from ewes that graze the plateau; it is matured in the natural caves of the *causse,* where the temperature and humidity remain at the ideal level year-round.

▶ Altogether, 13 producers make about 16,000 metric tons of cheese per year; the Roquefort Société is the most important producer, accounting for 75 % of the total. Cheesemaking is the leading pastoral industry of the Aveyron, which supplies 90 % of the milk for Roquefort cheese; the rest is imported from Corsica (→).

▶ Several cheese **cellars** are open to the public (take warm clothing). Archaeological Museum *(daily, 9-11 & 12-6).* □

▶ Nearby

▶ **Saint-Jean-Saint-Paul★ :** *(8 km S) :* fortified village. ▶ The **Cernon Valley** runs at the foot of the Larzac plateau (→). ▶ From Roquefort to Sainte-Eulalie 25 km through old villages fortified by the Hospitallers (who succeeded the Templars) : **La Bastide-Pradines** and **Mélac★, Lapanouse-de-Cernon, Sainte-Eulalie-de-Cernon★** (→ Larzac). □

■ SAINT-AFFRIQUE

C3 / ® / pop. 9 188 (Aveyron)

The Sorgues river separates the mediaeval city at the foot of the Caylus rock from the new district that developed around the 19thC railway station. Linking the two : a 14thC bridge (Pont-Vieux★). □

▶ Nearby

▶ **Vabres-l'Abbaye :** *(4 km SW) :* the seat of a bishopric until the Revolution; Renaissance houses, French Classical mansions; the former cathedral was rebuilt in the 18thC (organ★). ▶ **Saint-Izaire** *(16 km W) :* where bishops and canons maintained summer residences on the Dourdou. ▶ The **Sorgues Valley★** leads to the heart of the Larzac plateau *(50 km upstream from Saint-Affrique to La Couvertoirade, on D7)* : invites exploration by bicycle, off the tourist routes. ▶ **Saint-Affrique.** ▶ **Lapeyre :** Gothic bridge at village entrance; mediaeval streets; re-used Romanesque tympanum on the doorway of a house *(le château);* another Romanesque tympanum★ on the cemetery church (tomb of the poet Byron's daughter). ▶ On the opposite bank : **château de Montalègre** (16thC). ▶ **Versols :** fortified village around a 15thC keep. ▶ **Saint-Félix-de-Sorgues :** commandery of the Hospitallers; a Gothic bridge leads to the hamlet of **Saint-Caprazy★** (former priory). ▶ A pleasant road to **Nonenque Abbey,** where noble Rouergue families once consigned their unmarriageable daughters *(no visits).* ▶ **château de Latour :** 15thC; fortifications. ▶ **Marnhagues :** Romanesque church. ▶ **Cornus :** in a fold of the Larzac plateau (→) : Protestant church. ▶ To N, view over Larzac and Cévennes regions from the rocks at **La Tour d'Aiguillon.** ▶ To S, **source of the river Sorgues★,** near a 15thC keep; the **Mas Raynal sinkhole** opens at the foot of the **Guilhaumard plateau★ :** spectacular. ▶ Up to the Larzac plateau : corn fields, stone walls and eroded rocks. **La Couvertoirade** (→ Larzac plateau). □

■ SAUVETERRE DE ROUERGUE★★

B2 / ® / pop. 793 (Aveyron)

A beautiful *bastide* (walled town →), hardly altered since its foundation 7 centuries ago, with all the classic elements of the *bastides* of SW France (chequerboard layout, arcaded square, fortifications, church-keep). ▶ 16thC carved cross; museum. □

▶ Nearby

▶ This area of the lower Ségala (→) is wild, difficult to reach and fragmented by countless ravines and gorges. ▶ A centre for the Resistance during WWII : **Villelongue** museum-chapel in the **Lézert gorge** (memorabilia of the writer André Malraux, 1901-76). ▶ The painter Toulouse-Lautrec (→ Albi) spent his childhood at the **château du Bosc,** near the Viaur gorges *(13 km SE)* : museum *(10-12 & 2-6).* □

■ SEGALA Region

B2

Ségala is an isolated region between the Aveyron and the Viaur, a high plateau on the fringe of the Massif Central mountains. Once a poverty-stricken area whose inhabitants lived on little but rye-bread and chestnuts, Ségala is now prosperous farmland, thanks to the railway, the Viaur viaduct and the advent of fertilizers. This was among the first regions in France to offer farm holidays to city-dwellers. □

■ SÉVÉRAC-LE-CHÂTEAU

C2 / ® / pop. 2 838 (Aveyron)

Sévérac : view★ from the rocky outcrop in a valley between the Lévezou and the *causses.*

▶ The old town, on top of a butte (hill) crowned by a ruined **castle,** has a resolutely mediaeval air. The fortress was rebuilt in the 17thC. The steep narrow streets are lined with 15th-16thC shops. □

■ SIDOBRE and the LACAUNE Mountains★★

▶ From Castres to Mazamet *(approx. 170 km; full day)*

B4 *(see map 3 following page)*

North of the Montagne Noire (Black Mountain) and the Espinouse mountains on the western edge of the Cévennes, the Sidobre Plateau is separated from the Lacaune mountains by the Agout Valley. The granite plateau is strewn with rocks in fantastic shapes and positions. The Lacaune region includes the plateau, a cold, monotonous tableland between 700 m and 1 000 m altitude, and higher up, the wooded slopes of the mountain, contrasting with the surrounding Mediterranean landscapes.

▶ **Castres** (→). ▶ **Burlats :** ruined Benedictine priory; near the Agout river, Romanesque house. ▶ **Roquecourbe :** 14thC bridge over the Agout; covered arcades around the square. ▶ Farther up the river, in a loop called Sacaradelle, pinnacle of the **Sainte Juliane hill :** traces of a Celtic sanctuary; a ruined Cathar cemetery destroyed during the 12th-13thC. ▶ From **Lacrouzette** ®, a stone-working town, explore rock formations★ including the balancing rock of **Peyro Clavado★,** as well as **Lake Merle** *(4 km SE).* Along D58 : good views of the valley and the **Agout gorge★.** ▶ **Château de Ferrières :** rebuilt 15th-16thC; Upper Languedoc Protestant Museum (historic documents; *daily 15 Jun.-15 Sep.; Sun. and nat. hols. pm out of season; group visits to the furnished apartments by request, tel. 63.74.03.53*). Maison du Luthier (lute-maker) : organised by the upper Languedoc Nature Reserve; a lute-maker's workshop, hand printing shop, ethnographic museum *(visits by request, ask at the château);* concerts in season. ▶ Beyond Vabre, up the winding **Gijou Valley★** on the north flank of the Lacaune plateau : **château de Lacaze** (rebuilt 18thC); mediaeval ruins of **Viane** castle; **Gourp-Fumant,** a natural site near Gijounet. ▶ **Lacaune :** 17thC southern Gothic church, 14thC fountain, 18thC château de Calmels. ▶ Through **Montroucous Forest** to the **Bassine Pass** (alt. 885 m). ▶ **Brassac** ® : on either bank of the Agout; two bridges (one 14thC Gothic), ruined ramparts, 17thC château with two towers by the river's edge. ▶ **Vialavert** *(2 km W) :* Sept-Faux trembling rock. 2 km S from **Saint-Salvy :** Balme Rocks. ▶ Through the Rialet and the Vintrou to the **Arn** (or Banquet) **gorges,** leading down to Mazamet (→). □

■ SYLVANÈS★★

C3 / pop. 117 (Aveyron)

The Abbey of Sylvanès, one of the finest examples of Cistercian architecture in the

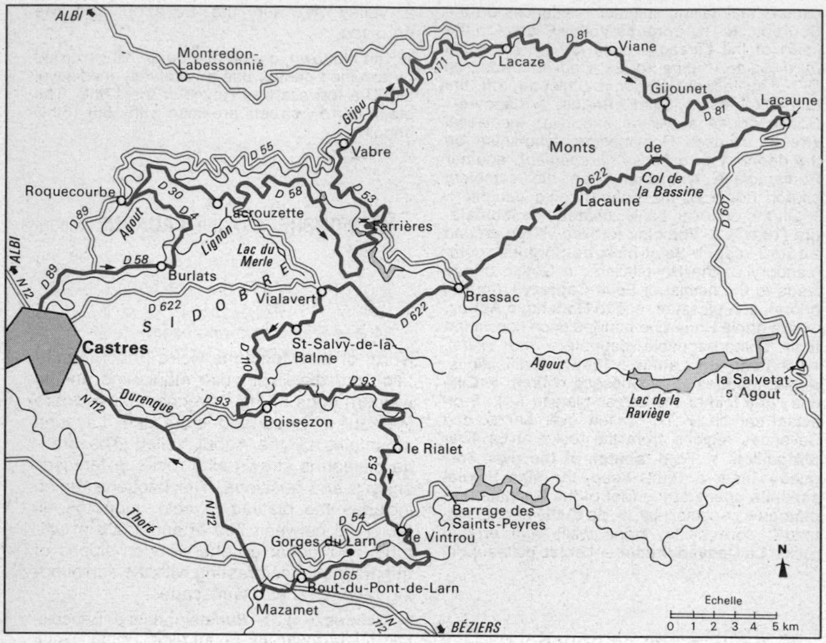

3. Sidobre

south of France, is set in a valley between the Lévezou and Lacaune mountains, on the borders of the Rouergue and Albigeois regions.

▶ The abbey was founded in 1138 by a lord in repentance for a lifetime of brigandage. The **church,** with its single wide nave, was the model for many others in the south. It is now an important cultural centre (concerts, exhibitions, seminars). The abbey buildings are not open to visitors. ▶ **Bains-de-Sylvanès :** a thermal spa built in the 17th-18thC by the monks. □

■ TARN Valley★

▶ From Millau to Saint-Sernin *(140 km; difficult roads; full day)*

B3 (Tarn)

The Tarn valley offers more than just its famous Gorges; between the Camarès and Albigeois regions, the river runs through schist walls, accompanied part of the way by the viaducts and tunnels of a ghost railway that was abandoned before it ever came into service.

▶ **Peyre :** houses huddled against the cliff. ▶ Valleys and gorges, alternating vines and walnut trees. ▶ The valley broadens at **Saint-Rome-de-Tarn :** remains of fortifications and Renaissance houses; ruined castle of Auriac. ▶ The **Pouget-Truel** power station is fed by the Lévezou dams; other dams on the Tarn. ▶ **Brousse-le-Château★** ® : site overlooking the junction of the Tarn and the Alrance (Gothic bridge); village and fortified castle restored by a youth group; Romanesque-Gothic church, once a halt for pilgrims to Compostela. ▶ **Coupiac :** 15thC château in a bend of the river; good view of the Tarn and the old village of Lincou; re-used tympanum on the church. ▶ **Plaisance** ® : on an outcrop above the Rance river, opposite rival **Curvalle;** church★ from former Benedictine abbey, modified in the 15thC (carved decoration). ▶ **Saint-Sernin-sur-Rance★** ® : former stronghold on a hillside between two valleys; half-timbered houses, 15th-16thC mansions; carved ornamentation in the Gothic church. □

■ TRUYÈRE Gorge★

▶ From Entraygues to Thérondels *(50 km, twisting road, half-day)*

B1

The Truyère river winds between two lava plateaus from the Cantal volcano (Tertiary Era); hydroelectric dams have not spoilt its beauty.

▶ **Couesque Dam :** 15 km² reservoir fed by the Goul and Truyère rivers. ▶ **Pons :** Gothic church. ▶ **Rouens :** panorama over the Couesque reservoir and **Vallon★,** crowned by the ruins of a 13thC castle. ▶ **Mur-de-Barrez★ :** a boundary marker between Carladès Plateau and the Bromme valley (view★). In the 17thC Mur belonged to the Grimaldi family, Princes of Monaco; note the ogival door on the clock tower; old houses flanked by towers on the square and along the Grand'Rue; church with Romanesque capitals, Gothic doorway, 17thC furnishings. ▶ **Brommat :** church with 15thC arcaded bell-tower, 17th-18thC statues; 15thC priory. Hydroelectric complex (three dams and two generating stations). ▶ **Albinhac :** 15thC manor; attractive houses; 1478 Gothic church (Annunciation on the doorway, key-stone vaulting, carved coats of arms, bas-relief of

Death★, 16thC polychrome wood statue of St. Martin, maternal figure of Ste. Anne). ▶ **Laussac :** site★; 11thC Romanesque chapel. ▶ **Sarrans Dam :** built in the 1930s, one of the biggest in France; 35 km² reservoir. ▶ **Thérondels :** northernmost village in the Rouergue; the church blends Romanesque and Flamboyant Gothic (compare the capitals). ▶ If time permits, return via **Orlhaguet :** Romanesque church★ converted in the 15thC into a fortress; collection of 16thC wayside crosses★. **Mels★ :** painted walnut altarpiece, a sort of 15thC strip cartoon. **Bès-Bédène★★ :** an abandoned village in a superb setting; Gothic church and bridge, communal oven, old houses. □

■ VIAUR Viaduct

A3

Past **Tanus** ® *(16km NE of Carmaux),* Viaur viaduct★ : built in 1897-1902 by Paul Bodin, a spectacular feat of French railway engineering, linking Rodez to Albi across the Viaur Valley (late 19thC ironwork).

▶ **Viaur gorges** (walk from Tanus bridge) and **Las Planques** hamlet (Romanesque church; 17thC frescos). ▶ **Bastide of Pampelonne** *(16.5 km from Tanus)* and 12thC **château de Thuriès** above the dam. ▶ NW from Carmaux, **Monestiés-sur-Cérou** (16thC church; 15thC sculptures in the Chapel of St. Jacques) and Roucarié reservoir. □

■ VILLEFRANCHE-DE-ROUERGUE★★

A2 / ® / pop. 13 869 (Aveyron)

Mediaeval silver mines assured the prosperity of this 13thC *bastide,* fortified in the 14thC. Ancient houses have largely been preserved and are now being restored. The town is a centre of activity for the western half of the department.

▶ The regular street-plan is still evident; **Cornières Square★★** is surrounded by arcaded houses, many richly ornamented; best seen on market-day *(Thu.)* or Fair-day on the 22nd of the month, when the square is cleared of cars. ▶ The gate-tower of the **collegiate church of Notre-Dame★★** is integrated into the covered arcades; 58 m high, it rivals the tower in Rodez (→). The church was built over 3 centuries, starting in 1260, from apse to façade (inside, 15thC stalls). ▶ **chapel of the Black Penitents★★ :** 17thC Baroque decor; choir stalls from Loc-Dieu, by André Sulpice, a 15thC sculptor *(Jul.-Aug., 9:30-12 & 2:30-6:30).* ▶ **Cabrol Museum :** in a Louis XV mansion, material relating to local personalities; antiquities *(same hours as the chapel).* ▶ The 15thC **Charterhouse★★ :** a great monument of the Rouergue, founded in 1451 by a rich local merchant and his wife, and completed in only 8 years (under restoration; *guided tours Jul.-Aug. 9:30-12 & 2:30-6; unaccompanied visits rest of year);* the large cloister was surrounded by the monks' cells; the small cloister★★ is a Flamboyant Gothic structure; the chapel (stalls by André Sulpice) shelters the monumental tomb★ of the founders; 16thC stained glass in the chapterhouse; in the refectory : Flamboyant Gothic pulpit from which the Bible was read aloud during meals. □

▶ Nearby

▶ **Loc-Dieu** Cistercian abbey : on the borders of Rouergue and Quercy; over-restored and converted into a château in the 19thC; cloister★ similar to that at Villefranche *(Jul.-Aug. 10-12 & 3-6:30, closed Tue.).*

▶ Round trip north of Villefranche *(approx. 70 km, half-day)*

▶ The **Villeneuve plateau** begins outside Villefranche : oak woods, crumbling stone walls, sturdy dovecotes and turreted houses. ▶ The road around **Villeneuve★** ® gives a good view of the layout as well as the remains of the fortifications. The 11thC geometrical plan was based on an arcaded triangular central area : 14th-16thC houses, grain measures under the arcades; 11thC **church** modelled on that of the Holy Sepulchre in Jerusalem, according to the donor's wishes when he left on a pilgrimage to the Holy Land; modified in the 14thC (14thC frescos, stalls, 15thC Christ). ▶ **Foissac** ® : caverns; traces of men and animals that lived there in the Bronze Age. *(Jun.-Sep., 10-11:30 & 2-6, except Jul.-Aug., closes at 6:30; out of season by request tel. 65.64.77.04, for groups.).* ▶ Opposite Saint-Pierre-Toirac, the banks of the Lot (→). ▶ **Salvagnac :** feudal castle; the Romanesque church was its chapel. ▶ Near **Lacapelle-Balaguier** the landscape becomes typical of the plateau (dolmens; 15thC bell-tower keep of **Sainte-Croix**). ▶ **Toulonjac :** a suburb of Villefranche; built around the 15thC castle and Gothic church; bell-tower similar to that at Villefranche (inside, 16thC statues). □

Architecture

● The numerous styles of houses in the Rouergue reflect the geography of the locality, surrounded by the regions of Auvergne, Quercy and Languedoc. Houses are built of red sandstone in the Marcillac and Camarès valleys; of limestone in the Larzac, Rodez

House on the causse

and Villefranche plateaus; of schist around Conques and the Ségala area; and of granite near the Aubrac. ● The varied regional agriculture also influences the architecture : vine-growers' houses in the valleys; triple-vaulted stone farmhouses and elongated sheepfolds *(jasses)* in Larzac; less primitive farmhouses on the Causse Comtal; and shepherds' shelters *(burons)* in the Aubrac, built to withstand cold and snow. ● Brick is the usual construction material in the Tarn region; the oldest and poorest habitations are half-timbered. Dovecotes are often noteworthy for their size and beauty. The small riverside towns are built to withstand

House in Rouergue

flooding : Gaillac, Rabastens, Lisle-sur-Tarn and Castres are among the best examples. The Aveyron is an isolated region off the usual tourist route, where architecture has remained traditional. Rural houses with typical stone roofs and exterior staircases are still common. ● The roofs are steep, with two or four faces, almost always covered in rounded blue, grey or silvery shingles and pierced by elaborate dormer windows.

A "buron"

Brief regional history

Prehistory to Roman era

Neolithic herdsmen and farmers left numerous menhirs and dolmens (→ Brittany, Menhirs/Dolmens) in the region (→ Occitania, Midi-Toulousain). ● Since the time when the settlement now known as Rodez was the capital of the Celtic **Ruteni,** the Rouergue has kept the same outline, enclosing three different climates, three types of terrain and agriculture appropriate to each. The Romans incorporated the Albigeois district into the administrative region of Narbonne. Millau became an important pottery centre during the **Gallo-Roman period.**

10thC

The great **Benedictine abbeys** of Conques, Nant and Saint-Antonin played a major role in the development of the area; many villages grew around priories affiliated with one or other of these abbeys. The townships of Espalion and Estaing prospered alongside bridges on the pilgrim road to **Conques** and the Spanish shrine of Compostela.

12thC

The **Cistercian monks,** who succeeded the Benedictines at Conques, concentrated on the areas around Bonneval, Sylvanès, Loc-Dieu and Beaulieu, while the warrior-monks of the orders of St. John of Jerusalem and St. John of Malta assumed control of the Larzac and Aubrac regions.

13th-16thC

The brilliant court of the Count of Rodez was the centre of Occitanian culture, protected by treaty from the ravages of Simon de Montfort's crusade against the Catharist Albigensians (→ Cathars, Languedoc-Roussillon). ● Ceded to the Plantagenet kings of England with the Treaty of Brétigny (1360), Rouergue became embroiled in the **Hundred Years' War.** ● Later, the Rouergue was incorporated into the Protestant kingdom of Navarre but remained Catholic, with little interest in the ideas of the 16thC Protestant Reformation. However, the southern part of the region, including Millau and Saint-Affrique elected **Protestantism** just as the Albigeois and the Cévennes, and thus became estranged from the northern sector centred around Rodez.

16thC to the present day

In the 15thC, châteaux and churches were rebuilt as peace returned. ● As power became centralised at Paris during the 16thC, the Rouergue diminished in importance. By the 19thC the region was a backwater. The late 19thC arrival of the railway made it easier for inhabitants of Rouergue to emigrate, which they did in great numbers both within France (to Paris) and abroad (to South America).

The **Albigeois region,** farther south, fared differently thanks to its traditional crafts and by the efforts of Protestant industrialists who had built up local **industry** since the 18thC: coal at Carmaux, cloth at Castres, processing sheepskins at Mazamet, tanning at Millau and Graulhet, all of which thrive to this day. ● The **industrial revolution** made Decazeville and Albi-Carmaux the principal industrial centres of the Midi. They were later complemented by the Creusot steelworks at Saut-du-Tarn and Saint-Juery. In the late 19thC the socialist politician, philosopher and historian **Jean Jaurès** (1859-1914) led the workers in a series of epic struggles for their rights; the strike of 1896 is commemorated at the worker-controlled glass factory of Carmaux.

Practical information

The region

Information : Haute Garonne : *Comité régional de Tourisme* (C.R.T.), 12, rue Salambô, 31200 Toulouse, ☎ 61.47.11.12. **Aveyron :** *Comité départemental de Tourisme* (C.D.T.), 33, av. V.-Hugo, 12000 Rodez, ☎ 65.68.11.43. **Tarn :** *Comité départemental de Tourisme* (C.D.T.), hôtel du département, 81014 Albi Cedex, ☎ 63.54.65.25. In Paris : *Maison du Tarn*, 34, av. de Villiers, 75017, ☎ (1) 47.63.06.26.

Bookings : *Loisirs-Accueil Tarn*, hôtel du département, 81014 Albi Cedex, ☎ 63.54.65.25, ext. 508.

Maps : *Michelin*, n°s 79, 80, 82, 83 at 1/200 000 ; *I.G.N.*, n°s 57, 58, 64, 65 at 1/100 000.

S.O.S. : Aveyron : *S.M.U.R.*, ☎ 18. **Tarn :** *S.A.M.U. (Emergency Medical Service)*, ☎ 63.54.99.99. *Emergency poisoning centre* (Toulouse), ☎ 61.49.33.33.

Weather forecast : Aveyron, ☎ 65.60.05.33.

Rural gîtes, chambres d'hôtes, children's gîtes : Aveyron : *A.P.A.T.A.R.* (Reservation and information service), 50, bd du 122^e R.I.,12006 Rodez Cedex, ☎ 65.68.11.38. **Tarn :** *l'Assn. Tarnaise de Tourisme en espace rural*, Maison des Agriculteurs, B.P. 89, 81003 Albi, ☎ 63.54.39.81, publishes a guide which lists rural gîtes, farmhouse camping, farms with riding facilities, children's gîtes and farmhouse-inns.

Holiday villages : → Practical holiday information.

Camping : list of camp-sites at the C.D.T. : *Camping Club du Rouergue*, 6, rue de l'Abbé-Bessou, 12000 Rodez, ☎ 65.68.06.96.

Farmhouse camping : *A.P.A.T.A.R.*, 50, bd du 122e R.I., 12006 Rodez Cedex, ☎ 65.68.11.38.

Cultural events : early Jun : *Photography Week* in Albi, *music festival* in Rodez. **Jul :** *Cultural Week* in Rodez, *Theatre Festival* in Albi, *International Guitar Event* in Castres, *Summer Festival* in Rodez (2nd fortnight), *Music Festival* in Cordes. **Aug :** *Rouergue Music Festival* in Villefranche-de-Rouergue ; *International Folklore Festival* in Pont-de-Salars ; *International 9.5 mm Amateur Cinema Festival* and *Music Festival* in Albi. **Sep :** *J.-S. Bach Festival* in Mazamet.

Sporting events : last week-end in Sep : *100 km (on foot)*, Millau. **Mid-Sep :** *Albi Automobile Grand Prix.*

Other events : Jun : *hunting festival* in Lavaur ; *St-Jean festivals* in numerous districts. **Jul :** *wine festival* in Lisle-sur-Tarn ; **14 Jul,** *Grand Fauconnier festival* in Cordes. **Aug :** *grain threshing festival* in La Salvetat-Peyralès ; **1st Sun Apr and 15 Aug :** *fouace festival* in Najac ; *pink garlic fair* in Lautrec ; *summer festival* in Salles-Curan. **Sep :** *horse fair* in Montredon-Labessonnié. **Oct :** *chestnut and sweet cider festival* in Sauveterre ; *antiques fair* in Albi.

Scenic railways : *Chemin de fer touristique du Tarn*, in Saint-Lieux-lès-Lavaur (81), from Easter to Oct, Sun and nat hols ; Sat, Sun and Mon from 14 Jul to 31 Aug. Enq : A.C.O.V.A., B.P. 2040, 31018 Toulouse Cedex, ☎ 61.47.44.52.

Technical tourism : *Roquefort*, Société anonyme des Caves et des Producteurs réunis, 1, av. F.-Galtier, ☎ 65.60.23.05.

National and nature parks : *parc naturel du Haut-Languedoc*, enq : 13, rue du Cloître, B.P. 9, 34220 Saint-Pons-de-Thomières, ☎ 63.97.02.10 ; *Maisons du Parc* in : Brassac-sur-Agout, Dourgne, Fraisse-sur-Agout, La Salvetat-sur-Agout, Montredon-Labessonnié, Murat-sur-Vèbre, Rieu-Montagné, Roquebrun, Saint-Gervais-sur-Mare, Soreze et Vabre. *Relais du Parc*, hôtel de ville, 81260 Brassac, ☎ 63.74.01.29, and at the S.I. situated on the outskirts of the park.

Rambling and hiking : the G.R. 6, 65 (path traditionally taken for Santiago de Compostela), 62, 62 A, 36, 71, 71 A, 71 B, 71 C, 46, 416, 763 (topoguides) run through the region. For further enq : *Féd. interdépartementale des Sentiers de Pays*, bd Clemenceau, 12400 Saint-Affrique, ☎ 65.49.30.50 ; *Féd. de la Randonnée pédestre* : C.N.S.G.R. - Délégation Aveyron, 1, rue du Barry, 12100 Millau ; Sentiers de l'Aubrac : *Assn. Rencontre Randonnée Soulages-Bonneval*, 12210 Laguiole ; Sentier des 3 Vallées-Decazeville : *Assn. les Randonneurs du Bassin*, B.P. 25, 12300 Decazeville.

Riding holidays : enq C.D.T. and C.R.T.

Cycling holidays : 7-day tour of **Aveyron.** Enq at the Aveyron C.D.T. and O.T. ; *Assn. pour la Promotion du cyclisme en Aveyron*, Lédergues, 12170 Réquista, ☎ 65.70.21.19.

Handicraft courses : pottery (La Capelle, Montbazens, Naussac, Salvagnac-Saint-Loup, Saint-Geniez-d'Olt, Puylaurens, Saint-Cyprien), weaving (Montbazens, Cordes, Labastide-Rouairoux, Saint-Cyprien), wood sculpture (Gelles, Salvagnac-Saint-Loup, Entraygues, La Salvetat-Peyralès, Carmaux), engraving and screen printing (Parisot), wrought iron (Montbazens, Lacalm), copper enamelling (Marsal), stone sculpture (Cordes). See **Tarn** and **Aveyron** C.D.T. Bookings : *Loisirs-Accueil Tarn.*

Tennis : *Ligue régionale Pyrénées*, M. C. Bimes, rés. la Palmeraie, immeuble le Vendée, 226, av. St-Exupéry, 31400 Toulouse.

Golf : Pont-de-l'Arn, 81660 Mazamet (9 holes).

Aquatic sports : Nautical centres in Salles-Curan, Arvieu, Saint-Rome-de-Tarn, Rieu, Montagné (Nages), La Borde-Basse (Castres), Aiguelèze. Enq at the C.D.T.

Canoeing : *Comité départemental de Canoë-Kayak*, M.J.C., rue St-Cyrice, 12000 Rodez, ☎ 65.67.01.13.

Potholing and spelunking : *Comité dép. de Spéléologie*, Michel Ferrières, rue J.-Moulin, 12000 Rodez, ☎ 65.67.23.25.

Winter sports : 3 resorts in the Aubrac mountains, situated at between 1 000 and 1 400 m ; alpine and cross-country skiing : Brameloup, Laguiole, Aubrac. Enq : C.D.T. and S.I. du Haut-Rouergue, in Espalion, ☎ 65.44.05.46.

Hang-gliding : Millau Delta, M. Jullien, 12640 Rivière-sur-Tarn, ☎ 65.60.86.22.

Hunting and shooting : enq at the *Féd. dép. des chasseurs.* **Aveyron :** 23, bd de la République, 12000 Rodez, ☎ 65.42.53.48. **Tarn :** 8, rue Louis-Amboise, 81000 Albi, ☎ 63.54.12.23.

Fishing : enq at the *Féd. dép. des A.P.P.* **Aveyron :** 52, rue de l'Embergue, 12000 Rodez, ☎ 65.68.17.23. **Tarn :** 17, bd du Mal-Foch, 81100 Castres, ☎ 63.59.68.40.

Towns

ALBAN

Albi 29, Millau 84, Paris 735
B3 ☒ 81250

Hotel :
★★***Au Bon Accueil,*** 49, av. de Millau, ☎ 63.55.81.03. AE. 15 rm closed 8 Jan-4 Feb and Mon noon ex Jul-Aug, 150. Rest. ♦ Spec : *daubes cuites à l'ancienne, chevreuil,* 65-145.

ALBI

Toulouse 76, Rodez 78, Paris 707
A3 ☒ 81000

ℹ pl. Ste-Cécile (B2), ☎ 63.54.22.30.

SNCF (A4), ☎ 63.54.50.50, 63.54.17.16, 63.54.74.10.

✈ Sequestre, 3 km SW, ☎ 63.54.45.28.

🚌 pl. J.-Jaurès (B-C3), ☎ 63.54.58.61.

Car-hire : *Budget* train + car, at the station ☎ 63.54.50.50.

Hotels :
● ★★★★***Grand St-Antoine*** (Mapotel), 17, rue St-Antoine (C3), ☎ 63.54.04.04. Tx 520850. AE, DC, Euro, Visa. 56 rm Ⓟ 560. Rest. ● ♦♦ Spec : *saumon frais à l'oseille, pigeonneau désossé aux baies roses,* 100-250.

★★★★***La Réserve*** (Relais et châteaux), on the RN606, 2 km from Cordes, ☎ 63.60.79.79. Tx 520850. AE, DC, Euro, Visa. 20 rm Ⓟ closed 1 Nov-1 Apr, 600. Rest. ♦♦♦ ♿ Spec : *papillote de sandre à l'aneth, daube d'agneau à l'albigeoise,* 130-250.

● ★★★***Grand Hôtel du Vigan*** (Inter-Hôtel), 16, pl. du Vigan (B-C2), ☎ 63.54.01.23. Tx 530328. AE, Euro, Visa. 37 rm Ⓟ ♿ 230. Rest. ♦ and grill-room ♿ closed 15-31 Dec. Spec : *tripes à l'albigeoise,* 60-175.

★★★***Moderne Pujol*** (L.F.), 22, av. Col.-Teyssier (C3), ☎ 63.54.02.92. AE, Visa. 21 rm Ⓟ closed Fri eve and Sat, 230. Rest. ♦ ♿ closed Feb school hols, 21 Jun-15 Jul, Fri eve and Sat. Spec : *foie gras frais aux fruits, soupière aux pâtes fraîches et morilles,* 110-200.

★★***Grand Hôtel d'Orléans,*** pl. Stalingrad, ☎ 63.54.16.56. Tx 521605. AE, Euro, Visa. 64 rm ♿ closed 21 Dec-7 Jan, 210. Rest. ♦ facing the station ; closed Sun. Spec : *jarret de porc haricots, ris de veau financière,* 50-125.

● ★***Vieil Alby*** (L.F.), 25, rue Toulouse-Lautrec (B2), ☎ 63.54.14.69. Euro, Visa. 9 rm, closed 28 Apr-7 May, 15-30 Sep, 24 Dec-7 Jan, Sun eve and Mon, 100. Rest. ♦ 40-155.

Labastide-Dénat, 81120 Réalmont, 9 km SE :
★***Sun Club*** (Motel), ☎ 63.56.65.34. 9 rm 180

Youth hostel, 13, rue de la République, ☎ 63.54.20.67.

⛺ ★★*Caussels* (100 pl.), ☎ 63.60.37.06.

Restaurant :
♦ ***Auberge Saint-Loup,*** 26, rue du Casteviel (A2), ☎ 63.54.02.75. Closed Mon and Oct. Spec : *radis au foie salé, gras double à l'albigeoise,* 80-130.

Gîte, riding centre at the farm : *la Coste,* 81350 Valderiès, ☎ 63.55.11.88, 8 km from Albi on the RN603. Young people over 13 years welcome. Tennis 4 km away ; riding courses.

Bicycle hire : *Rey-Sport,* 41, bd Soult, ☎ 63.54.08.33.

Recommended : *Léo Vrenken,* 7, rue de la Piale, ☎ 63.54.47.96 : flower arrangement. *Michel Belin,* 4, rue Laurent-Camboulive, ☎ 63.54.18.46 : cakes and chocolates. *La Berbi,* 17, pl. Ste-Cécile, ☎ 63.54.13.86 : tea-room.

AMBIALET

Albi 25, Millau 96, Paris 732
B3 ☒ 81430 Villefranche-d'Albigeois

Hotels :
★★***Pont*** (L.F.), ☎ 63.55.32.07. AE, Visa. 13 rm Ⓟ closed 30 Nov-1 Mar, 135. Rest. ♦ Spec : *assiette de canardises, cuisses de canard aux parfums des bois, filet de sandre au pouilly,* 60-100.

Marsal, 8 km W :
★***La Bonne Auberge,*** ☎ 63.55.15.05. 10 rm Ⓟ 100. Rest. 60-100.

⛺ ★★*Pont de Courris* (30 pl.), ☎ 63.55.32.25 ; ★*la Fédusse* (50 pl.), ☎ 63.55.32.10.

Recommended : *la Bastide d'Albignac,* in Valence-d'Albigeois, 11 km N on the D74 : *foies, confits* and *rillettes de canard,* ☎ 63.56.42.43.

BARAQUEVILLE

Villefranche-de-Rouergue 43, Albi 60, Paris 628
19 km SW of Rodez, B2 ☒ 12160

SNCF ☎ 65.69.01.52.

Hotel :
● ★★★***Ségala Plein Ciel,*** ☎ 65.69.03.45. Euro, Visa. 47 rm Ⓟ ♿ closed Jan and Mon, Fri eve and Sun low season, 210. Rest. ♦ 70-150.

Chambres d'hôtes : *le Moulinou,* ☎ 65.69.02.68. Riding centre, trout fishing, farm produce for sale.

Events : in Naucelle, *Sigala festival,* the 3rd Sun in Jul, and *Tripou festival,* the 2nd Sun in Nov.

BOZOULS

Rodez 22, Séverac-le-Château 41, Paris 589
B2 ☒ 12340

Hotels :
● ★★***Le Belvédère,*** rte de Saint-Julien-de-Rodelle, ☎ 65.44.92.66. Euro, Visa. 9 rm Ⓟ closed Feb school hols and Mon eve low season, 120. Rest. ♦♦ Spec : *ris d'agneau persillé, magret de canard grillé sur braise,* 60-120.

★***La Route d'Argent,*** la Rotonde, ☎ 65.44.92.27. Euro. 21 rm Ⓟ closed 15 Dec-8 Jan, 100. Rest. ♦ closed Fri eve low season, 40-120.

BRASSAC

Castres 24, Albi 66, Paris 754
23 km SW of Lacaune, B3 ☒ 81260

Hotels :
★***Balcon,*** 10, pl. Saint-Blaise, ☎ 63.74.00.12. 24 rm Ⓟ closed 24 Dec-2 Jan, 100. Rest. ♦ 60-110.

Anglès, 16 km SE :
★***Auberge de la Souque,*** 4 km SE, ☎ 63.70.98.53. 12 rm Ⓟ ♨ closed 11 Nov-15 Mar, 90. Rest. ♦ 50-110.

Riding centre : *la Roussarié,* rte d'Anglès, ☎ 63.70.97.32. Full board ; open to young people from 13 years ; horsemanship, excursions.

BROQUIÈS

Rodez 57, Albi 62, Paris 666
Tarn Valley, B3 ⊠ 12480

Hotels :
★***Le Pescadou*** (L.F.), 2.5 km S, on the St-Izaire road, ☎ 65.99.40.21. 14 rm ⚘ Ⓟ ♨ ♘ ♿ closed Oct-Easter (eve), 110. Rest. ♦ 40-100.

Brousse-le-Château, 8.5 km W :
● ★***Relays du Château*** (L.F.), ☎ 65.99.40.15. Euro, Visa. 14 rm ⚘ Ⓟ ♘ ⚘ closed 15 Dec-15 Jan, Fri eve and Sat noon, 100. Rest. ♦ ♿ A good small restaurant, 50-75.

CAMARÈS

Millau 53, Albi 78, Paris 683
C3 ⊠ 12360

Hotel :
● ★★***La Demeure du Dourdou,*** ☎ 65.99.54.08. 11 rm ⚘ Ⓟ ♨ ♘ closed 1 Oct-31 Mar, 195. Rest. ♦ 60-125.

⛺ ★★Municipal *le Champ Clos* (50 pl.), ☎ 65.99.51.93.

CAPDENAC-GARE

Figeac 6, Rodez 59, Paris 590
12 km NW of Peyrusse-le-Roc, A2 ⊠ 12700

ℹ bd Paul-Ramadier, ☎ 65.64.74.87.

SNCF ☎ 65.64.80.00.

Hotel :
Saint-Julien-d'Empare :
★★***Auberge de la Diège*** (L.F.), ☎ 65.64.70.54. Euro, Visa. 15 rm Ⓟ ♨ ▨ closed 15 Dec-15 Jan, 145. Rest. ♦ closed Fri eve and Sat low season, 65-200.

⛺ ★*Municipal* (53 pl.), ☎ 65.64.70.13.

CARMAUX

Albi 16, Rodez 62, Paris 685
A3 ⊠ 81400

ℹ pl. Gambetta (high season), ☎ 63.76.76.67.

SNCF ☎ 63.76.50.23.

Hotels :
Monestiés, ⊠ 81640, 8 km NW :
● ★***A l'Orée du Bois*** (L.F.), ☎ 63.76.11.72. 8 rm ⚘ closed 20 Dec-15 Jan, 90. Rest. ♦ Spec : *soupe de campagne, daube de sanglier,* 50-100.

Mirandol-Bourgnounac, ⊠ 81190, 13 km N :
★***Voyageurs,*** ☎ 63.76.90.10. 11 rm ♘ closed end Aug-mid-Sep, 65. Rest. ♦ closed eve low season, 40-85.

Tanus, 81190 Mirandol-Bourgnounac, 16 km NE :
★★***Voyageurs*** (L.F.), ☎ 63.76.30.06. AE, Euro, Visa. 14 rm Ⓟ ♨ ⚘ closed 1-15 Nov, Feb school hols and Fri ex Jul-Aug, 135. Rest. ♦♦ ♿ Excellent cooking. Spec : *civet de porcelet, ris d'agneau provencale,* 60-130.

⛺ ★★*La Croix du Marquis* (35 pl.), ☎ 63.76.52.71 ; Mirandol-Bourgnounac : ★★★*les Clots* (50 pl.), ☎ 63.76.92.78.

CASTRES

Albi 42, Toulouse 71, Paris 733
B4 ⊠ 81100

ℹ pl. de la République, ☎ 63.59.92.44.

SNCF ☎ 63.59.01.66, 63.59.22.00.

✈ Labruguière, 8 km SE, ☎ 63.35.49.58.

🚌 near the jardin du Mail.

Hotels :
● ★★★***Grand Hôtel,*** 11, rue de la Libération, ☎ 63.59.00.30. AE, Euro, Visa. 40 rm Ⓟ closed 15 Dec-15 Jan, 250. Rest. ● ♦♦ ⚘ closed 15 Jun-15 Sep and Sat. Spec : *blanquette de lotte aux poireaux, tournedos aux morilles,* 60-125.
★★***Occitan*** (L.F.), 201, av. du Gal-de-Gaulle, ☎ 63.35.34.20. 30 rm Ⓟ ⚘ closed 1-15 Aug, 20 Dec-2 Jan, Sat and Sun, 200.

Lacrouzette, 81210 Roquecourbe, 16 km NE :
★***Relais du Sidobre*** (L.F.), 8, rte de Vabre, ☎ 63.50.60.06. 26 rm ⚘ ♘ closed 15 Dec-1 Jan, 190. Rest. ♦ ♿ 55-90.

Massaguel, 81110 Dourgne, 17 km SW :
★***Auberge des Chevaliers,*** pl. de la Fontaine, ☎ 63.50.32.33. 7 rm Ⓟ ♘ ⚘ closed Wed and Oct, 70. Rest. ♦ 80-120.

⛺ ★★*Le Gravieyras* (35 pl.), ☎ 63.59.56.49.

Restaurants :
♦♦♦ ***La Caravelle,*** 150, av. de Roquecourbe, ☎ 63.59.27.72. AE, DC, Euro, Visa ⚘ Ⓟ closed Sat and 15 Sep-15 Jun. Spec : *salade tiède aux foies de porc et à la lie de vin, cassoulet au confit d'oie,* 55-180.
♦♦ ***Au Chapon Fin,*** 8, quai Tourcaudière, ☎ 63.59.06.17. AE, DC, Visa ♿ closed 7-31 Jul, Feb school hols, Sun eve and Mon. Spec : *terrine de poisson sauce grelette, filet de canard au vinaigre de framboises, feuilleté de saumon,* 55-130.

Verdalle, 81110 Dourgne, 15 km SW :
♦ ***La Ripaille,*** ☎ 63.50.32.51 ♿ closed 15 days Mar, 15 days Oct, Wed and Thu noon. A Tarnais cook's delightful cooking : *écrevisses en buisson, magret,* 80-130.

Bicycle hire : *Éts Tabarly,* 38, pl. Soult, ☎ 63.59.20.64. *Éts Esclasan,* Corbière, ☎ 63.59.85.13.

CONQUES

Rodez 37, Aurillac 57, Paris 603
B1 ⊠ 12320 Saint-Cyprien-sur-Dourdou

Hotels :
● ★★★***Sainte-Foy,*** rue Principale, ☎ 65.69.84.03. 20 rm Ⓟ ♨ ♘ closed 15 Oct-1 Apr ex Nov 1st hols, 130. Rest. ♦♦ ⚘ closed Sun. Good small restaurant, 85-120.

Grand-Vabre, 6 km :
★★***Aux Gorges du Dourdou,*** ☎ 65.69.83.03. Euro, Visa. 18 rm ♨ closed Dec-Jan, 125. Rest. ♦ closed Wed (low season), 40-160.

⛺ ★★*Beau Rivage* (60 pl.), ☎ 65.69.82.23.

CORDES

Albi 25, Montauban 71, Paris 683
A3 ⊠ 81170

ℹ maison du Grand Fauconnier (high season), ☎ 63.56.00.52, and mairie, ☎ 63.56.00.40.

Hotels :
● ★★★***Grand Écuyer,*** rue Voltaire, ☎ 63.56.01.03. AE, DC, Visa. 15 rm ⚘ ♘ closed 15 Oct-early Apr, 320. Rest. ● ♦♦♦ closed Mon

(Nov-Apr). The excellent chief Y. Thuries is seconded by Jean Bendine, formerly at the Negresco. Spec : *gratin de lapereau, minute de barbue gratinée.* Fabulous desserts. Special gourmet menu, *dessert douceur,* 120-260.
★★***Parc*** (L.F.), Les Cabannes, 1 km ☎ 63.56.02.59. Visa. 15 rm Ⓟ ♨ closed 3 Jan-15 Feb, Sun eve and Mon (1 Oct-1 Jun). 160. Rest. ● ♦♦ Honest and good country cooking. Spec : *lapin aux choux, canard Lapeyrade, foie gras,* 80-150.

⛺ ★★★*Le Moulin de Julien* (130 pl.), ☎ 63.56.01.42.

CRANSAC

Figeac 33, Rodez 37, Paris 617
7 km SE of Decazeville, B1 ⊠ 12110 Aubin

♨ (Apr-Oct), ☎ 65.63.09.83.

ⓘ mairie, ☎ 65.63.03.55.

SNCF ☎ 65.63.00.70.

Hotel :
★★***Parc,*** rue du Gal-Artous, ☎ 65.63.01.78. 30 rm Ⓟ ♨ ♿ closed 15 Oct-15 Apr, 170. Rest. ♦ 50-110.

⛺ ★★*Municipal* (35 pl.), ☎ 65.63.03.55.

DECAZEVILLE

Rodez 37, Aurillac 68, Paris 612
B1 ⊠ 12300

ⓘ 15, av. Cabrol, ☎ 65.43.06.27, and pavillon du Tourisme, pl. Wilson (high season), ☎ 65.43.18.36.

SNCF ☎ 65.43.11.81.

Hotels :
★★***Pontier*** (L.F.), 71, av. P.-Ramadier, ☎ 65.43.04.04. Visa. 25 rm Ⓟ ♨ 160. Rest. ♦ ♿ 55-160.
★★***France,*** pl. Cabrol, ☎ 65.43.00.07. Euro, Visa. 24 rm Ⓟ ♿ 155. Rest. ♦ closed Mon, 60-100.

ENTRAYGUES

Rodez 47, Saint-Flour 95, Paris 595
B1 ⊠ 12140

ⓘ 30, Tour-de-Ville, ☎ 65.44.56.10.

Hotels :
★★***Truyère*** (L.F.), ☎ 65.44.51.10. Tx 530366. Euro. 26 rm Ⓟ ♨ ♿ closed Jan-Mar, Sun eve and Mon low season, 200. Rest. ♦♦ closed Mon noon low season, 60-150.
★★***Deux Vallées*** (L.F.), ☎ 65.44.52.15. 18 rm Ⓟ 145. Rest. ♦ ♿ closed Sat low season, 40-70.
★★***Lion d'Or,*** ☎ 65.44.50.01. Euro. 40 rm Ⓟ ♨ 140.

⛺ ★★*Val de Saures* (200 pl.), ☎ 65.44.53.31 ; ★★*Roquepailhol* (70 pl.), ☎ 65.44.56.79.

ESPALION

Rodez 30, Millau 79, Paris 578
B1 ⊠ 12500

ⓘ mairie, ☎ 65.44.05.46.

SNCF ☎ 65.44.05.38.

Hotels :
★★***Moderne,*** 27, bd Guizard, ☎ 65.44.05.11. Euro, Visa. 32 rm Ⓟ ♨ closed 15 Nov-15 Dec, 6-31 Jan, 180. Rest. ● ♦ closed Sun eve, Mon noon. Copious, richly varied fare. Spec : *truite aux lardons, tripous, terrine de lapin,* 65-180.
★★***Central,*** av. de la Gare, ☎ 65.44.05.25. 26 rm ♨ ♿ closed Jan-Mar, 160.

⛺ ★★*Roc de l'Arche* (130 pl.), ☎ 65.44.02.49 ; Saint-Côme-d'Olt, *Belle Rive* (70 pl.), ☎ 65.44.07.09.

Recommended : *Charcuterie Combacon,* rue Droite, ☎ 65.44.06.26.

ESTAING

Conques 40, Figeac 75, Paris 849
B1 ⊠ 12190

ⓘ rue F.-d'Estaing (high season), ☎ 65.44.70.03.

Hotels :
★★***Aux Armes d'Estaing*** (L.F.), quai du Lot, ☎ 65.44.70.02. Visa. 47 rm Ⓟ closed Nov-Feb, 105. Rest. ♦ 40-100.
● ★***Raynaldy*** (L.F.), ☎ 65.44.70.03. 16 rm Ⓟ ♨ closed 1 Oct-1 Apr, 80. Rest. ♦ 40-80.

⛺ ★★*La Chantellière* (100 pl.), ☎ 65.44.70.92.

GAILLAC

Albi 22, Cahors 89, Paris 684
A3 ⊠ 81600

ⓘ pl. de la Libération, ☎ 63.57.14.65.

SNCF ☎ 63.57.00.23.

Hotels :
★★***Occitan,*** av. G.-Clemenceau, ☎ 63.57.11.52. AE, Visa. 13 rm Ⓟ closed 9-16 Feb, 215.
Técou, 8 km SE :
● ★***Auberge des Barthes*** (L.F.), ☎ 63.33.02.43. Visa. 7 rm Ⓟ ♨ closed end Oct-early Apr and Mon, 150. Rest. ♦ 50-75.

⛺ ★★*Le Lido* (30 pl.), ☎ 63.57.18.30.

Restaurant :
♦♦ ***Le Vigneron,*** 122, av. St-Exupéry, 1.5 km, ☎ 63.57.07.20 Ⓟ ♿ closed 15 Aug-15 Sep, 1-15 Jan, Sun eve and Mon ex in summer, 60-150.

Events : *wine festival,* 2nd Sun in Aug.

Recommended : *Comité Interprofessionnel des Vins de Gaillac,* abbaye Saint-Michel, ☎ 63.57.15.40. *Coopérative de vinification de Técou,* 8 km SE, ☎ 63.57.14.06.

GRAULHET

Albi 37, Toulouse 58, Paris 703
A3 ⊠ 81300

Hotel :
★★***Grandgousier*** (L.F.), 6, pl. Jourdain, ☎ 63.34.50.32. Euro, Visa. 21 rm Ⓟ closed 1-20 Aug and Sun eve, 165. Rest. ♦ 50-180.

LACAUNE

Castres 47, Montpellier 126, Paris 712
B3 ⊠ 81230

ⓘ pl. du Gal-de-Gaulle (high season), ☎ 63.37.04.98.

Hotels :
★★***Fusiés*** (Inter-Hôtel, L.F.), 2, rue de la République, ☎ 63.37.02.03. AE, DC, Euro, Visa. 60 rm Ⓟ ♨ ♿ closed 20 Dec-20 Jan, Fri eve and Sun eve from 15 Nov to 31 Mar, 175. Rest. ♦♦ ♿ M. Fusiés is backed up by chef P. Carpentier. Spec : *feuilleté de truite à l'oseille, magret de canard aux pommes golden,* 70-150.
★***Glacier*** (L.F.), 4, pl. de la Vierge, ☎ 63.37.03.28. AE, Visa. 23 rm ♨ closed 20 Jan-20 Feb and Fri eve low season, 120. Rest. ♦ ♿ Regional cooking. Good value. Spec : *salade tiède aux ris de veau et cèpes, crépinette de mérou au jus de truffe, confit de canard à la fondue d'oignons et aux baies roses,* 55-100.

Nages, 81320 Murat-sur-Vèbre, 13 km SE : ★*L'Escapade* (L.F.), alongside Laouzas lake, 3 km S, ☎ 63.37.40.51. 12 rm 🅿 ♨ 🍴 80. Rest. ♦ 50-160.

Recommended : *charcuteries : P. Calas,* rue de la Mairie, ☎ 63.37.00.20 ; *Sablayrolles,* 5, rue Pasteur, ☎ 63.37.02.45.

LAGUIOLE

Espalion 24, Rodez 56, Paris 554
Monts d'Aubrac, C1 ✉ 12210

⛷ 1 000 m

ℹ ☎ 65.44.32.49 and 65.44.35.64 ; *Syndicat des Communes de l'Aubrac aveyronnais,* rue du Valat, ☎ 65.44.35.56.

Hotels :
★★*Lou Mazuc* (Michel Bras), ☎ 65.44.32.24. AE. 13 rm ♿ 340. Rest. ● ♦♦♦ closed Sun eve and Mon ex Jul-Aug, 6 Oct-25 Mar. Quietly and with much talent and modesty, well supported by his wife Ginette, his mother who serves *aligot* and grilled sausages, and his father who tells stories Michel Bras is becoming one of France's greatest cooks. His flavourful light cooking is a real delight : *tarte chaude aux cèpes, poissons pochés à l'aïgo boulido, lapin aux truffes,* 70-230.
★★*Auguy,* av. de la Pépinière, ☎ 65.44.31.11. Visa. 36 rm 🅿 ♨ closed 7-15 Mar and 15 Nov-15 Dec, 180. Rest. ♦ closed Sun eve and Mon ex May-Sep and school hols, 65-145.

⛺ ★★*La Roseraie* (50 pl.), ☎ 65.44.31.91.

Recommended : *Pierre Calmels,* cutlery, ☎ 65.44.30.03. Coopérative fromagère *Jeune Montagne :* laguiole cheese and *aligot.*

LAVAUR

Toulouse 37, Albi 48, Paris 713
A3 ✉ 81500

ℹ mairie, ☎ 63.58.06.71 (off season), and 22, Grand-Rue (high season), ☎ 63.58.02.00.

SNCF ☎ 63.58.01.19.

Hotels :
★*Central* (L.F.), 7, rue Alsace-Lorraine, ☎ 63.58.04.16. Visa. 10 rm 🐕 closed Mon low season, 120. Rest. ♦ 40-100.

Saint-Lieux-lès-Lavaur, 10 km NW on D87 and D631 :
● ★★*Château de St-Lieux,* ☎ 63.57.60.87. 14 rm 🅿 ♨ 🍴 ♿ 180. Rest. ♦ 55-140.

Giroussens, 10 km NW, on the D87 and D38 : *L'Échauguette,* ☎ 63.57.63.65. 4 rm ⁂ ♨ closed 1st fortnight in Feb, 15 days in Sep, and Mon, 190. Rest. ♦♦ Spec : *ris de veau frais aux morilles, pâtisseries maison,* 100-170.

Events : *hunting festival, dog fair* on the 1st Sun in Jun.

LISLE-SUR-TARN

Albi 31, Toulouse 45, Paris 693
A3 ✉ 81310

SNCF ☎ 63.33.36.48.

Hotel :
★*Princinor,* on the N88, ☎ 63.33.35.44. 11 rm 🅿 ♨ 🍴 ♿ closed Jan and Mon low season, 100. Rest. ♦♦ 80-160.

Restaurant :
♦♦ *Le Romuald,* 6, rue du Port, ☎ 63.33.38.85. Visa ♿ closed Sep, Mon and Tue, 45-120.

Farmhouse-inn : *le Noyer Blanc,* domaine du Noyer Blanc, ☎ 63.57.54.58 🅿 ♨ Spec : *charcuteries, cabecous de chèvre du Noyer Blanc.*

Bicycle hire : *Tonuitti,* lake ☎ 63.33.38.96.

MARCILLAC-VALLON

Rodez 18, Decazeville 26, Paris 590
B2 ✉ 12230

Hotel :
Nuces :
★*Gare* (L.F.), ☎ 65.72.60.20. AE, Euro, Visa. 7 rm 🅿 ♨ closed 1-15 Dec, 15-28 Feb and Sun eve, 95. Rest. ♦ ♿ Spec : *marmite du pêcheur aux nouilles fraîches, truite à la poitrine salée vinaigrée, canette sauce aux foies de volailles,* 55-155.

Restaurant :
Salles-la-Source, 6.5 km S :
Auberge de la Cascade, ☎ 65.71.82.97. Good small restaurant, 50-80.

MARSSAC-SUR-TARN

Albi 10, Gaillac 11, Paris 673
A3 ✉ 81150

SNCF ☎ 63.55.44.81.

Hotel :
★*Poste,* ☎ 63.55.40.26. 19 rm 🅿 ♨ ♿ 100. Rest. ♦ closed Fri eve, 50-80.

⛺ ★★*Cévennes-Languedoc* (50 pl.), ☎ 63.55.40.31.

Chambres d'hôte : *la Sietge,* rte de Labastide-de-Levis, ☎ 63.57.70.00.

Restaurant :
● ♦♦♦♦ *Francis Cardaillac,* RN 88, ☎ 63.55.41.90. AE, DC, Visa ⁂ 🅿 ▭ ♿ closed 3-24 Jan, Sun eve and Mon. Born in the region, Francis Cardaillac knows it by heart. Same customers come regularly to his inn on the banks of the Tarn river. Ever-renewed, inspired cooking : *flan de brochet, tourte au pigeon.* Large choice of desserts. Good local wines, 110-280.

MAZAMET

Carcassonne 47, Albi 60, Paris 751
B4 ✉ 81200

ℹ rue des Casernes, ☎ 63.61.27.07.

SNCF ☎ 63.61.19.00.

Hotels :
★★★*Le Grand Balcon,* sq. G.-Tournier, ☎ 63.61.01.15. 25 rm, 190. Rest. ♦ closed 27 Jul-27 Aug and Sun. Inventive cooking by J.-L. Condamines. Spec : *escargots du Causse en pot au coulis de tomates, coq au gaillac vieux,* 90-240.
★★*Jourdon* (L.F.), 7, av. A.-Rouvière, ☎ 63.61.56.93. Visa. 11 rm 🐕 195. Rest. ♦ closed Sun, 55-200.

Pont-de-l'Arn, ✉ 81660, 2 km on D54 :
● ★★★*Château de Montlédier* (Relais et châteaux), ☎ 63.61.20.54. AE, DC, Visa. 10 rm ⁂ 🅿 ♨ 🍴 closed Jan and Mon. 13thC castle, 10-acre park, golf and tennis 2 km away, 390. Rest. ● ♦♦ Eve only. Spec : *filets de truite coulis d'écrevisses, jambonnette de volaille forestière,* 150-200.
★★*La Métairie Neuve,* Pont-de-l'Arn, ☎ 63.61.23.31. DC, Visa. 7 rm 🅿 ♨ 🍴 closed 1-15 Aug, 20 Dec-10 Jan and Sat, 230. Rest. ♦♦♦ 65-300.

Saint-Amans-Soult, ✉ 81240, 10 km E :
★*Château de la Nouvelle* (L.F.), ☎ 63.98.33.68. AE. 9 rm 🅿 ♨ 🍴 🐕 ▭ closed 1 Nov-1 Apr, 200. Rest. Eve only ex Sun, 65-115.

⛺ ★★★*La Lauze* (60 pl.), ☎ 63.61.24.69 ; Saint-Amans-Soult : *Essi* (35 pl.), ☎ 63.98.30.43.

MILLAU

Rodez 71, Nîmes 166, Paris 631
C2 ✉ 12100

ℹ pl. des Arcades (A-B1), ☎ 65.60.02.42.

SNCF (A1), ☎ 65.60.11.65, 65.60.02.65.

🚌 in front of the S.N.C.F. station (A1).

Car-hire : *Budget* train + car, at the railway station, ☎ 65.60.11.65, and at the bus station, ☎ 65.60.01.66.

Hotels :
● ★★★***International,*** 1, pl. de Tine-av. J.-Jaurès (B1), ☎ 65.60.20.66. AE, Euro. 110 rm P & 340. Rest. ♦♦ closed Jan, Sun eve and Mon low season. Spec : *salmis de col-vert aux baies de genièvre, ris d'agneau aux queues d'écrevisses, escalope de saumon sauvage à la menthe fraîche,* 80-200.
★★★***La Musardière*** (Relais et châteaux), 34, av. de la République (A1), ☎ 65.60.20.63. AE, DC, Visa. 12 rm P closed 10 Nov-mid-Mar. One-time private mansion, 400. Rest. ● ♦♦♦ closed 15 Nov-1 Apr and Mon (ex Jul). Regional cooking with a modern touch. Spec : *charcuteries aveyronnaises, salmis de canard col-vert,* 75-220.
★★***La Capelle,*** 7, pl. de la Fraternité (B1), ☎ 65.60.14.72. Visa. 46 rm & closed Oct-Apr ex Easter hols, 140.

Creissels, 2 km on the St-Affrique road :
● ★★ ***Château de Creissels,*** ☎ 65.60.16.59. AE, DC, Euro, Visa. 30 rm P closed Feb, Fri and Sat noon low season. A glorious 12thC castle, 155. Rest. ● ♦♦ Inventive cooking at moderate prices. Spec : *civet de mouton, poularde à la tomme fraîche,* 60-200.

Bois-du-Four, ✉ 12780 Saint-Léons, 20 km N :
★★***Relais du Bois-du-Four,*** ☎ 65.61.86.17. 27 rm P closed 15 Nov-1 Mar, Tue eve and Wed low season, 120. Rest. ♦ 40-110.

⛺ ★★★★*Millau Plage* (250 pl.), ☎ 65.60.10.97 ; ★★★*Millau-Cureplat* (250 pl.), ☎ 65.60.15.75 ; ★★*Saint-Lambert* (135 pl.), ☎ 65.60.00.48. Aguessac, 7 km N : *Municipal* (70 pl.), ☎ 65.60.80.15.

Restaurants :
♦♦ ***Buffet de la Gare,*** pl. de la Gare (A1), ☎ 65.60.09.04. AE, Euro, Visa. & closed Feb, 10 days in Oct and Tue. "One of France's five best buffets", with a 1925 decor and flowered terrace. Spec : *marmite du pêcheur, trénel* and *coufidou, foie gras de canard aux raisins,* 55-200.
♦♦ ***Capion,*** 3, rue J.-F.-Alméras (B1), ☎ 65.60.00.91. Closed 2-29 Jan, Sun eve (ex from 1 May to 1 Nov) and Mon. Spec : *compote de lapereau, confit de cuisse de canard aux cornichons.* Good value, 65-150.
♦♦ ***La Braconne,*** 7, pl. Mal-Foch (B2), ☎ 65.60.30.93. AE, Visa. & closed Dec, Sun eve and Mon. 13thC vaulted room, 80-100.

Chambres d'hôtes and farmhouse-inn : *ferme-auberge de Jassenove,* Larzac plateau, ☎ 65.60.71.80. Inexpensive farm produce : *crêpes au roquefort, gigot, lièvre à la broche. Auberge du Sanglier,* Segonnac, 12660 Saint-Georges-de-Luzencon, 7 km SW, ☎ 65.62.38.40. 12 rm P & Regional spec : *omelette au roquefort, trénels, charcuterie.*

Event : *minerals market,* mid-Jul.

Recommended : leather-work and glovemaker, *André Sales,* 13, av. J.-Jaurès (B1) and 8, pl. du Mandarous (B2), ☎ 65.61.01.55. *St Jacques,* pastries, 4, pl. du Mandarous (B2), ☎ 65.60.04.03.

NAJAC

Albi 54, Cahors 85, Paris 644
A2 ✉ 12270

ℹ mairie, ☎ 65.65.80.94.

SNCF ☎ 65.65.71.83.

Hotels :
● ★★***Belle Rive*** 2 km NW on the D39, ☎ 65.65.74.20. 40 rm P & closed 15 Oct-1 Apr, 150. Rest. ♦ 50-125.
★★***Miquel l'Oustal del Barry*** (L.F.), pl. du Bourg, ☎ 65.65.70.80. Visa. 21 rm P & closed 3 Nov-23 Mar and Mon in Mar, Apr ex nat hols, 155. Rest. ● ♦ Spec : *cochonailles du terroir, feuilleté de foie gras de canard aux asperges vertes du pays,* 85-150.

Youth hostel : Base de Plein Air, ☎ 65.65.71.15.

⛺ ★★★★*Le Paysseyrou* (100 pl.), ☎ 65.65.72.06.

NAUCELLE

Albi 48, Villefranche-de-Rouergue 51, Paris 642
33 km SW of Rodez, B2 ✉ 12800

SNCF ☎ 65.69.21.29.

Hotels :
★★***Voyageurs,*** pl. de l'Hôtel-de-Ville, ☎ 65.47.01.34. Euro. 15 rm closed 1-15 Nov and Mon ex Jun-Aug, 105. Rest. ♦ & 40-80.
★★***Hostellerie du Viaduc du Viaur,*** ☎ 65.69.23.86. 10 rm P closed 1 Oct-1 May, 370. Rest. ♦♦ & 65-135.

Sauveterre-de-Rouergue, 7 km NW :
★★***Auberge du Sénéchal*** (L.F.), ☎ 65.47.05.78. AE, DC, Euro, Visa. 15 rm closed 31 Oct-1 May, 130. Rest. ♦ 50-180.

Castelpers, 12170 Réquista, 12.5 km SE :
★★***Château de Castelpers,*** ☎ 65.69.22.61. Euro. 8 rm P closed 1 Oct-1 Apr, 230. Rest. ♦ closed Tue, 80-145.

⛺ ★★*Le Valadier* (30 pl.), in Sauveterre-de-Rouergue, ☎ 65.47.05.36.

Events : *Sigala festival,* the 3rd Sun in Jul, and *Tripou festival,* the 2nd Sun in Nov.

PEYRELEAU

Millau 21, Rodez 75, Paris 570
Tarn Gorges, C2 ✉ 12720

Hotel :
★★★***La Muse et le Rozier,*** ☎ 65.62.60.01. AE, Euro, Visa. 38 rm closed early Oct-end Mar, 320. Rest. ● ♦♦♦ Modern decor in a renovated feudal residence on the banks of the Tarn. Spec : *foie de canard frais, selle d'agneau farcie à la fleur de thym,* 110-220.

⛺ ★★*Les Peupliers* (35 pl.), ☎ 65.62.61.33.

PONT-DE-SALARS

Rodez 33, Millau 53, Paris 642
B2 ✉ 12290

ℹ mairie, ☎ 65.46.84.27.

Hotel :
★★***Voyageurs*** (L.F.), ☎ 65.46.82.08. Euro, Visa. 33 rm P closed end Oct, 15 Dec-1 Feb, Sun eve and Mon low season, 180. Rest. ♦♦ Lavish menus, 55-200.

⛺ ★★★*Le Lac et la Source* (200 pl.), ☎ 65.46.84.86.

PUYLAURENS

Castres 22, Albi 53, Paris 730
A4 ☒ 81700

Hotel :
★***Grand Hôtel Pagès*** (L.F.), sq. Ch.-de-Gaulle, ☎ 65.75.00.09. AE, DC, Euro. 21 rm ♿ closed Sat (low season), 120. Rest. ♦ 50-150.

Restaurant :
♦♦ ***La Gousse d'Ail,*** rte de Revel, ☎ 65.75.01.93. Ⓟ ♨ 🌳 ♿ closed 1 Jan-8 Feb, Mon and Tue noon. Spec : *feuilleté d'escargots gris à la fleur de thym, cassolette de queues d'écrevisses, tournedos au fumet de truffes et foie gras,* 55-135.

RABASTENS

Lavaur 22, Toulouse 37, Paris 707
A3 ☒ 81800

ⓘ 6, pl. Saint-Michel (high season) or mairie, ☎ 63.33.70.18.

SNCF ☎ 63.33.72.14.

Hotels :
★★***Pré Vert*** (L.F.), 54, promenade des Lices, ☎ 63.33.70.51. 13 rm Ⓟ ♨ closed 15-31 Dec and Sun eve low season, 220. Rest. ♦♦ 50-125.

Saint-Sulpice-la-Pointe, ☒ 81370, 8 km SW :
★***Auberge de la Pointe*** (L.F.), ☎ 63.57.80.14. AE, DC, Visa. 8 rm Ⓟ ♨ closed Feb and Wed low season, 95. Rest. ♦ ♿ Spec : *fricassée d'escargots aux mousserons, pâté de crabe au Ricard, saumon frais mariné aux herbes,* 50-155.

⛺ ★★★*Les Auzerals* (45 pl.), ☎ 63.33.70.36 ; in Saint-Sulpice, ★★*la Borio Blanco* (35 pl.), ☎ 63.57.81.19.

RÉALMONT

Albi 20, Toulouse 75, Paris 726
A3 🐓 ☒ 81120

Hotels :
● ★★***Noël*** (M.C.F.), rue de l'Hôtel-de-Ville, ☎ 63.55.52.80. AE, Visa. 14 rm Ⓟ ♨ 🚫 closed Feb, Sun eve and Mon from Oct to May, 180. Rest. ♦♦ ♿ Spec : *boudin noir au vinaigre, tournedos aux morilles, ris de veau à l'orange et au citron,* 110-250.

Montredon-Labessonnié, ☒ 81360, 15 km SE :
★***Hostellerie du Parc*** (L.F.), ☎ 63.75.14.08. 15 rm Ⓟ ♨ closed 15 Jan-28 Feb, Sep and Mon ex Jul-Aug, 100. Rest. ♦ 50-90.

Mont-Roc-Teillet, 81120 Réalmont, 25 km NE :
★***Cantegrelh*** (L.F.), barrage de Rasisse, ☎ 63.55.70.37. AE, Visa. 9 rm Ⓟ 🌳 100. Rest. ♦ closed Fri. Spec : *sandre au vin rouge et cèpes séchés, ballotine de canard aux petits légumes et pêches,* 75-160.

⛺ ★★*La Bâtisse* (65 pl.), ☎ 63.55.50.41.

RIEUPEYROUX

Rodez 38, Albi 54, Paris 644
21 km W of Rodez, B2 ☒ 12240

Hotel :
● ★★***Commerce*** (L.F.), rue de l'Hom, ☎ 65.65.53.06. Euro. 28 rm Ⓟ ♨ 🌳 ⛾ closed mid-Dec-mid-Jan, Sun eve and Mon low season, 110. Rest. ● ♦ Local cooking at agreeable prices. Spec : *foie gras, confits* and *pâtisserie maison,* 45-110.

RODEZ

Albi 78, Brive-la-Gaillarde 157, Paris 609
B2 ☒ 12000

ⓘ pl. Foch (B3), near the cathedral, ☎ 65.68.02.27.

SNCF (C1), ☎ 65.42.08.03.

✈ Rodez-Marcillac, 10 km NW, ☎ 65.68.52.53.

Car-hire : *Budget* train + car, at the station, ☎ 65.68.50.50, and at the airport.

Hotels :
★★★***Tour Maje*** (Inter-Hôtel), bd Gally (B3), ☎ 65.68.34.68. AE, Euro, Visa. 48 rm 🌳 ♿ 225.
★★★***Parc,*** pl. d'Armes (B3), ☎ 65.68.11.22. AE, Euro, Visa. 22 rm 🌳 🚫 closed 21 Dec-6 Jan, Sat and Sun (15 Oct-15 Mar), 210.
★★★***Biney,*** 7, bd Gambetta (B3), ☎ 65.68.01.24. Euro, Visa. 28 rm Ⓟ ♨ 🌳 closed 21 Dec-6 Jan. Calm, modern hotel, 175.

Onet-le-Château, 3.5 km N on D601 :
● ★★★***Hostellerie de Fontanges,*** ☎ 65.42.20.28. Tx 521142. AE, Euro, Visa. 45 rm Ⓟ ♨ ⛾ 🎾 235. Rest. ● ♦♦ Modern complex in authentic 16thC setting, terrace. Spec : *foie gras, confits, magrets,* 55-185.

Gages-le-Haut, ☒ 12630, 12 km E :
★***Relais de la Plaine,*** ☎ 65.42.29.03. 22 rm Ⓟ ♨ closed end Sep-mid-Oct and Sun ex Jul-Aug, 120. Rest. ♦ 45-100.

⛺ ★★★★*Layoule* (70 pl.), ☎ 65.67.09.52.

Restaurants :
● ♦♦♦ ***Le Saint-Amans,*** 12, rue de la Madeleine (C4), ☎ 65.68.03.18 ♿ closed Feb, Sun eve and Mon. Calm, music in modern air-conditioned decor ; *feuilleté de langoustines aux petits légumes, médaillon de veau au marcillac,* 95-175.
● ♦♦ ***Le Régent,*** 11, av. Durand-de-Gros (off map through C1), ☎ 65.67.03.30. AE, DC, Euro, Visa ; closed 1-15 Jul and Sun. Reasonably priced set menu and excellent cooking : *foie gras,* local wines, 60-200.

ROQUEFORT-SUR-SOULZON

Millau 24, Lodève 65, Paris 655
C3 ☒ 12250

Hotel :
● ★★★***Grand Hôtel,*** ☎ 65.59.90.20. AE, Visa. 16 rm Ⓟ 🌳 closed 1 Oct-31 Mar, Sun eve and Mon ex Jul-Aug, 300. Rest. ♦♦ 80-160.

SAINT-AFFRIQUE

Millau 31, Albi 82, Paris 662
C3 ☒ 12400

ⓘ bd de Verdun (high season), ☎ 65.99.09.05.

SNCF ☎ 65.99.01.66.

Hotel :
★★***Moderne*** (L.F.), 54, av. A.-Pezet, ☎ 65.49.20.44. Euro, Visa. 38 rm Ⓟ 🌳 closed 15 Nov-15 Mar, 175. Rest. ♦ ♿ closed Mon ex summer, 55-150.

⛺ ★★*Municipal* (50 pl.), ☎ 65.99.05.54.

Farmhouse-inn : *Pinsac,* Les Costes, Gozon, 15 km NW, ☎ 65.99.14.17. Closed Sep. Spec : roasts cooked over a wood-fire, pastries.

Chambres d'hôtes : *le Relais des Raspes,* St-Victor-et-Melvieu (15 km N), ☎ 65.62.51.88.

SAINT-CHÉLY-D'AUBRAC

Espalion 21, Rodez 52, Paris 565
Monts d'Aubrac, C1 ☒ 12470

⛷ 1 250 m

Hotels :
★***Voyageurs,*** ☎ 65.44.27.05. 14 rm 🌳 🚫 closed 1 Dec-1 Apr, 90. Rest. ♦ A good small restaurant, 40-65.

Aubrac, 8 km NE :
● ★★**Moderne** (L.F.), ☎ 65.44.28.42. 27 rm Ⓟ closed early Oct-mid-May ex Feb hols and Easter, 160. Rest. ♦ 45-95.

SAINT-GENIEZ-D'OLT

Sévérac-le-Château 24, Rodez 46, Paris 603
C2 ⊠ 12130

ℹ salle des Cloîtres (high season), ☎ 65.70.43.32.

Hotels :
● ★★**Poste** (L.F.), 3, pl. Neuve, ☎ 65.47.43.30. AE, DC, Euro, Visa. 50 rm Ⓟ closed 15 Dec-end Jan, Mon low season, 160. Rest. ♦ 50-150.
★★**France** (L.F.), ☎ 65.70.42.20. AE, Visa. 42 rm Ⓟ ♿ closed 1 Dec-31 Jan, 135. Rest. ♦ Good value, 50-90.

⛺ ★★★*Municipal* (150 pl.), ☎ 65.70.40.43.

SAINT-JEAN-DU-BRUEL

Millau 48, Lodève 59, Paris 680
C3 ⊠ 12230 La Cavalerie

Hotel :
★★**Midi** (L.F.), ☎ 65.62.26.04. 20 rm Ⓟ closed 11 Nov-22 Mar, 125. Rest. ● ♦♦ ♿ Excellent local cooking from the Papillon family ; terrace overlooking the Dourbie. Spec : *boudin de saumon de fontaine, cépettes et beurre d'herbes, tourte chaude de canard,* 45-130.

⛺ ★★*Claparède* (30 pl.), ☎ 65.62.26.16.

Recommended : *Charcuterie Papillon* (delicious *pâtés au canard, aux grives, au sanglier,* etc), ☎ 65.62.26.26.

SAINT-SERNIN-SUR-RANCE

Lacaune 30, Albi 50, Paris 694
21 km E of Alban, B3 ⊠ 12380

Hotels :
● ★★**Carayon** (L.F., Inter-Hôtel), ☎ 65.99.60.26. AE, Euro, Visa. 23 rm Ⓟ closed Sun eve and Mon low season, 160. Rest. ● ♦♦ Beautiful view of Rance valley, quiet and comfort. Spec : *écrevisses du vivier, saumon frais en brioche,* 55-165.

Plaisance, ⊠ 12710, 10 km NW :
★**Les Magnolias,** ☎ 65.99.77.34. Euro, Visa. 15 rm, closed Feb, Nov 1st and Mon, 140. Rest. ● ♦ Regional cooking with a modern touch. Superb setting (16th-17thC), 55-155.

⛺ ★★*Bellevert* (30 pl.), ☎ 65.99.61.72.

SALLES-CURAN

Rodez 40, Albi 77, Paris 644
B2 ⊠ 12410

ℹ mairie, ☎ 65.46.31.73.

Hotels :
● ★★**Hostellerie du Levézou** (Châteaux-hôtels), ☎ 65.46.34.16. 18 rm Ⓟ closed 20 Oct-1 Apr. Splendid feudal residence, 220. Rest. ● ♦♦ closed Sun eve and Mon low season. Spec : *foies gras, côte de bœuf à la braise, toupine de pied de porc,* 100-200.

Bouloc, 9 km E :
Les Griffouls, ☎ 65.46.35.18. 10 rm closed winter, 80. Rest. ♦ Family-style regional cooking, 45-65.

⛺ ★★★★*Beau Rivage* (80 pl.), ☎ 65.46.36.33 ; ★★★*Base Nautique Pareloup* (65 pl.), ☎ 65.46.36.74 ; ★★*les Vernhes* (30 pl.), ☎ 65.46.33.62.

Farmhouse-inn : *la Baraque,* ☎ 65.46.35.92. Book ahead. Spec : *charcuteries.*

SÉVÉRAC-LE-CHÂTEAU

Millau 32, Saint-Flour 109, Paris 600
C2 ⊠ 12150

ℹ rue des Dunes (high season), ☎ 65.46.67.31. and mairie, ☎ 65.46.62.63.

SNCF ☎ 65.71.61.19.

Hotels :
★★**Moderne et Terminus,** Sévérac-Gare, ☎ 65.46.64.10. 20 rm Ⓟ ♿ closed 27 Sep-1 Nov, 22 Dec-2 Jan, 21 Feb-2 Mar, Fri eve and Sat, 145. Rest. ♦ 50-120.
★**Causses,** av. Aristide-Briand, Sévérac-Gare, ☎ 65.71.60.15. AE, Euro, Visa. 13 rm Ⓟ ♿ closed Oct and Sun eve low season, 140. Rest. ♦ closed Sun and Mon low season, 50-100.

⛺ ★★Municipal *les Calquières* (125 pl.), ☎ 65.46.64.82.

VILLEFRANCHE-DE-ROUERGUE

Cahors 61, Albi 72, Paris 620
A2 ⊠ 12200

ℹ prom. Guiraudet, ☎ 65.45.13.18.

SNCF ☎ 65.45.03.16.

Hotels :
● ★★**Lagarrigue,** pl. B.-Lhez, ☎ 65.45.01.12. Euro. 22 rm closed Feb and Sun ex Dec-Mar, 225. Rest. ♦♦ 55-130.

Martiel :
★★**Les Dolmens,** rte de Cahors, ☎ 65.45.12.52. 23 rm Ⓟ closed Nov-early Mar, 150.

⛺ ★★★*Le Teulet* (100 pl.), ☎ 65.45.16.24.

Restaurant :
● ♦♦ **La Charmille,** 8, rue Ste-Émilie-de-Rodat, ☎ 65.45.36.60. closed Tue eve and Wed. Chef R. Le Brech successfully blends Aveyron and Breton cooking. Calm elegant setting. Spec : *chausson de magret "Charmille", pâtes fraîches aux truffes, millefeuille de cuisses de grenouilles au confit de poireaux.* Excellent wine-list, 70-180.

Chambres d'hôtes and farmhouse-inn : *le Murat,* Saint-Salvadou, ☎ 65.45.80.69, 15 km on the D111 then D605 A. Riding centre. Games room for children. Farm produce for sale.

VILLENEUVE

Figeac 25, Cahors 63, Paris 609
A2 ⊠ 12260

Hotels :
★**Poste,** ☎ 65.45.62.13. 14 rm Ⓟ closed 15 Dec-15 Jan, 95. Rest. ♦ 40-60.

Foissac, 12 km N :
★★**Relais de Fréjéroques** (L.F.), ☎ 65.64.62.80. Euro. 16 rm Ⓟ closed Sat and Sun low season, 105. Rest. ♿ 40-95.

Savoy

Savoy or Savoie, a region of alpine lakes, glaciers and snowy peaks, shares with its Swiss and Italian neighbors the hordes of skiers and mountain climbers, the brilliant wildflowers and hardy animals, chamois, marmots and eagles which thrive at high altitudes. Chamonix is one of the most famous ski resorts in the world — the opening of the Mont-Blanc tunnel in 1965 has helped make it the uncontested capital of skiing and alpine sports in France. But the region has many other ski resorts which are almost as well-known : Les Arcs, La Plagne, Courchevel, Tignes/Val d'Isère. Savoy's history too was linked to its Alpine neighbors, and the region knew many centuries of independence before it came under the sway of the French crown.

The Savoy of the 1980s has adjusted well to the modern era, with its investment in nuclear energy and advanced technology, its healthy and outdoors image, its pure alpine waters which are even more famous than its delicious wines, its winter sports, its sheer falls and outcrops of rock which attract the most seasoned climbers and its deep valleys over which soar modern disciples of Icarus with their multicoloured wings.

Savoy also offers the more tranquil, everyday joys of its villages and hamlets : meadows and running water, the deep blue of the gentian, the silent ballet of the jackdaw. There are flourishing markets and deep forests, creamy Reblochon cheese from Grand-Bornand, wooden crosses on country tracks, the little wooden figurines of the Devils of Bessan repeated in church frescos, the sybilline mottos of ornamental sundials, and the special architecture of the houses, with their wooden galleries and balconies for drying wood and clothes in the winter season. In places you will see the characteristic *greniers* — isolated store houses where fodder for the livestock, the family's Sunday clothes and sometimes their important papers used to be kept to guard against fire.

Sightseeing

AIX-LES-BAINS★

A2 / ® / pop. 23 500 (Savoie)

See plan following page

More than 2 000 years ago, the Romans (masters of the art of the hot bath) built baths at Aix. Since the 16thC this resort has been a rendezvous of the famous, who forgot their rheumatism as they took part in the parade of fashionable life against a backdrop of sumptuously flowered parks and the mirrorlike waters of the Lac du Bourget, made famous by the Romantic poet Lamartine.

Life in Aix centres around the park and its greenery, the Thermes, the Palace of Savoy and the new casino.

▶ The **Hôtel de Ville**★ (town hall; C2) occupies the ancient château (1513; Renaissance staircase★). The nearby **Temple of Diana** (2ndC or 3rdC) houses prehistoric and Gallo-Roman antiquities. ▶ In the middle of the Place des Thermes is the Arch of Campanus (3rdC or 4thC). The **Thermes Nationaux** (1860, modernized in 1972) include the remains of the Roman baths and the hot springs. ▶ The **Museum of Dr. Faure**★ (C2) has a rich collection from the 19thC and 20thC (Corot, Degas, Cézanne, Pis-

Don't miss

★★★ : Lake Annecy (A2), Lake Bourget (A2), Chamonix-Mont-Blanc (B2), Grandes Alpes Route (B2-3), Lac Léman (Lake Geneva) (A-B1). ★★ : Annecy (A2), The Beaufortain region (B2), The Chablais region (B1), The Faucigny region (B1), Megève (B2), Saint-Gervais (B2), Vanoise Massif (B3).

sarro, Vuillard, Sisley, watercolours by Rodin. Lamartine is not forgotten : furniture from the apartment occupied by the poet at the Perrier *pension,* souvenirs and documents. Porcelain, regional and foreign ceramics *(9-12 & 2-6; Sun. 10-12 & 4-6; closed Sat. pm and Sun. in winter).* ▶ Between the *petit port* (beach★) and the *grand port,* the **Boulevard du Lac★★** (by A1) is the general meeting place for an evening stroll. And in the background are the **abbey of Hautecombe** and the Dent du Chat ("Cat's Tooth") peak. □

▶ Nearby

▶ **Abbey of Hautecombe★★** (→ Lake Bourget) : boat excursion leaving from the Grand-Port. ▶ **Tresserve** *(2 km S)* on the mountain crest overlooking the lake : monument to Lamartine who in 1817 composed his famous poem "Le Lac" here. □

▶ Circuit of Mont Revard★ *(45 km, D913 and 912)*

▶ **Mont-Revard** ® : a 20 km² fir-covered plateau SE of Aix, overlooking Le Bourget. Numerous walks in search of the *martagon* or Turk's cap lily, or more simply looking for mushrooms, blackcurrants and wild strawberries or the *rose du Revard* (a variety of thistle). ▶ **La Féclaz** is the winter sports resort of the inhabitants of Chambéry. This smoothly undulating plateau, bordered by forests, is a beautiful suntrap. The cable car from Oriandaz goes up to 1560m, with a beautiful view over Mont Blanc, Lake Bourget, the Dents du Nivolet and the Revard mountain. ▶ From Déserts, a road and a path take you to the **Croix du Nivolet** (alt. 1 457m; view). □

■ ALBERTVILLE

A2 / ® / pop. 17 530 (Savoie)

To replace the fortified city of Conflans (worth a visit for its own sake) King Charles Albert (1798-1849) had a new town planned

Weekend tips

A few steps from the station at Chamonix, the téléphérique *(cable-car) of the Aiguilles du Midi opens the way to the high mountains. Lunch in Chamonix. In the afternoon the train from Montenvers winds past peaks and crests up to the famous Mer de Glace (Ice Sea). Spend the night at Lavanché. The next day discover Les Grands Montets and the Col (Pass) des Montets with its nature reserve.*

Facts and Figures

Location : *In the SE corner of France, Savoie has frontiers in the north and east with Switzerland and Italy. To the west it is bounded by the Rhône and the Guiers and in the south by the mountains (Belledonne, Grandes Rousses) that separate it from the Dauphiné region.*
Area : *10 428 km²; 50 km wide between Geneva and the Haute Chablais; 150 km long from Léman to Galibier.*
Climate : *A mountain climate, varying with altitude and orientation. The vegetation and crops show the differences clearly. For example, vines grow in the warm region beside Lac Léman (Lake Geneva), but on the high peaks the climate is arctic.*
Population : *753 000 (Haute-Savoie 447 795; Savoie 305 118).*
Administration : *Department of* ***Haute-Savoie :*** *Prefecture Annecy; Department of* ***Savoie :*** *Prefecture Chambéry.*

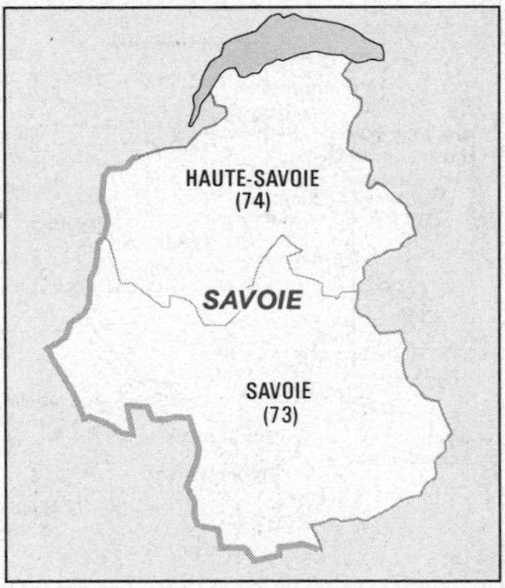

Reblochon

Reblochon was once a fromage de dévotion *(tithe or votive cheese), which the peasants of Savoie used to give each year to the Carthusian monks who came to bless their fields. It is a soft, uncooked cheese made from cows' milk and lightly pressed. It is a speciality of the Aravis region (Grand-Bornand). Matured in cold damp cellars for about 4 weeks, the cheese is then washed and presented on round sheets of wood. It contains 50% of fat, has a mild, creamy taste and a smooth texture, and should be a pinky yellow with a smooth crust that dimples to the touch. The best season is the end of June to the end of November. The name comes from* reblochage, *which means "second milking".*

and built in 1845 to which he gave his name. At the entrance of the Val d'Arly, Albertville is essentially a major highway intersection.

▶ **Conflans★,** on a hill overlooking the junction of the Isère and the Arly, is a typical small military town from the Savoie of earlier times. Numerous craftsmen have given new life to old shops in the ancient Grand' Rue. 17thC pulpit★ in the church. In a charming square, the Maison Rouge* (16thC Gothic) houses a Savoyard museum. From the Terrace of La Roche there is a view over the valley of the Isère. ▶ **Route du Fort du Mont★** *(11 km E)* panorama★★ over the whole valley of Savoie, the Tarentaise region, Mont-Blanc, etc. □

■ ANNECY★★

A2 / ® / pop. 49 773 (Haute-Savoie)

The lakeside town. The calm, clear waters of Lake Annecy are set against a marvellous backdrop of mountains. The swift currents of the Thiou swirl under the bridges of the old town. This quarter is now a pedestrian precinct at the foot of the château. The quiet streets are bordered by arcades and often decked with flowers. Faithful to the Savoyard tradition of metalwork, Annecy is an important industrial centre (ball-bearings and razors) with a nuclear research centre discreetly hidden in the urban landscape.

▶ The **lakeside★★** and old Annecy are the greatest attractions : Champ de Mars (C2); Pont des Amours★; Public Gardens★; Quais du Thiou, a canal into the lake from which the boat trips start. ▶ The **old town★★** (market★ *Tue., Fri. and Sun. am*) : **church of St. François** (B3, 1652); **church of St. Maurice** (15thC) : funerary fresco★ of 1458 and a Descent from the Cross by P. Pourbus the Elder. In the Thiou river is the **Palais de l'Isle** (B3, 12th-14thC), formerly a prison, today the home of temporary exhibitions *(entrance free)*. ▶ Follow the canal and bear R to the **Cathedral of St. Pierre** (B3) dating from 1535. St. François de Sales, the major figure in Annecy's history, was Bishop here. With St. Jeanne de Chantal (1572-1641), he founded the first monastery of the Visitation. Beside the cathedral, the former **Episcopal Palace** (1784) occupies the site of the house where Jean-Jacques Rousseau met Madame de Warens (1729) whom he was to remember lovingly (see p. 990). ▶ The **château★** (B3, 12thC), rebuilt after several fires, now contains the **Historical Museum of Annecy and Haute-Savoie :** archaeology, ethnography and architecture *(10-12 & 2-6, closed Tue.)*.

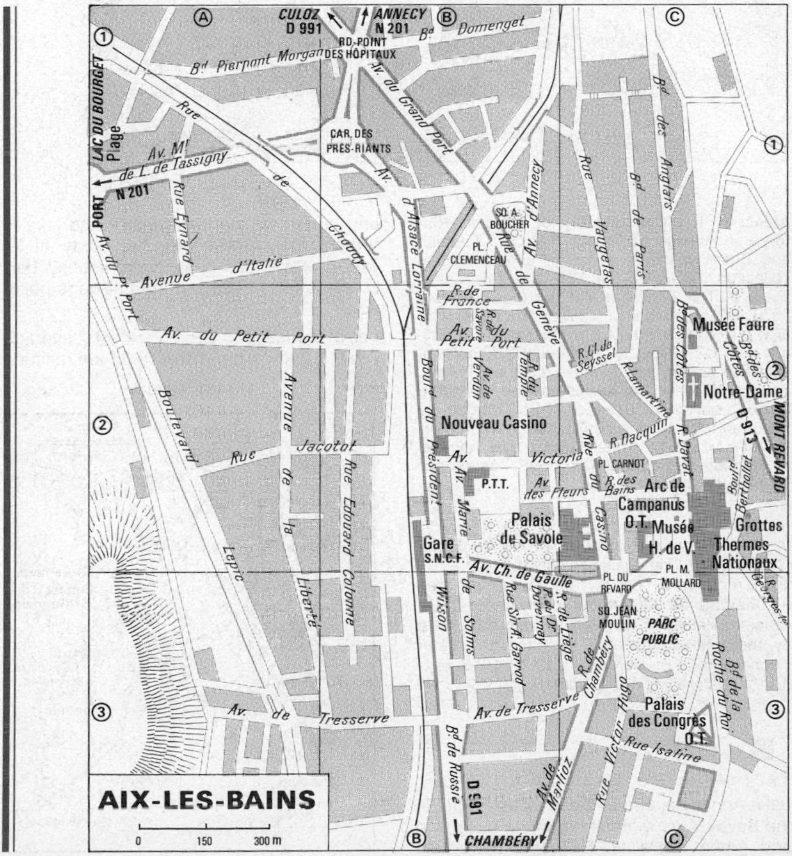

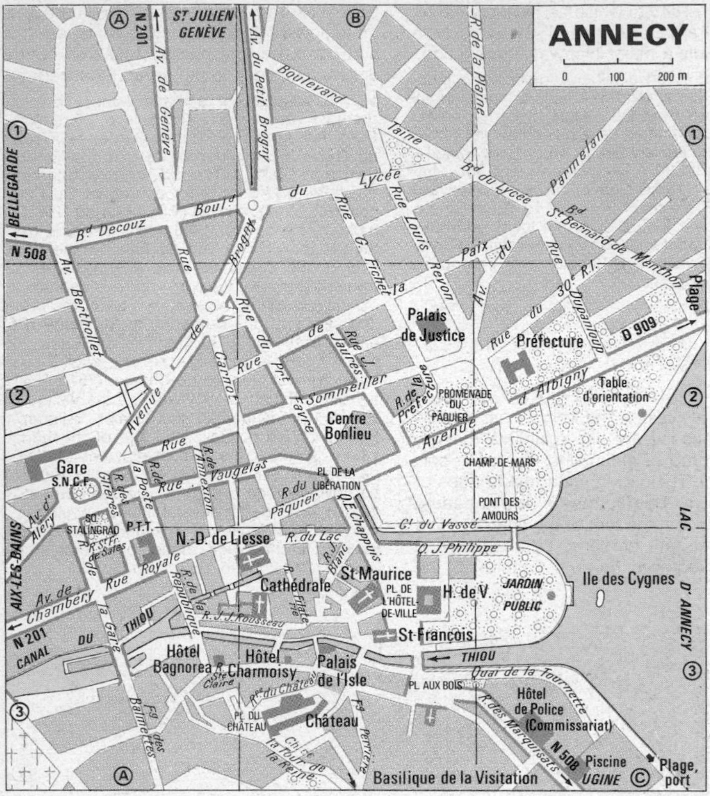

Also... ▶ The **Conservatory of Art and History★** in Avenue de Trésun (via C3 : Flemish and Dutch paintings and the Payot mountain collection, *14 Jul.-15 Sep., 10-12 & 2-6, closed Tue.*). ▶ The **Palais de Justice** (Law Courts; 1978; C2); the work of Maurice Novarina, who also built the church of Ste. Bernadette d'Albigny (via C2; 1965). ▶ **Bonlieu** (B2) : cultural activities centre, with theatre, galleries, library, Tourist Office. ▶ The **Basilica of the Visitation** (via B3), built in 1930 : relics of St. François de Sales and St. Jeanne de Chantal; view★. Permanent exhibition of the Paccard **bell foundry** at **Annecy-le-Vieux** *(2,5 km NE; weekdays 10-12 & 3-6:30, Sun. 3-6:30).* □

▶ Nearby

▶ Lake Annecy (→); the **Gorges du Fier★** *(11.5 km W),* with galleries clinging to the cliff wall; remarkably narrow gorges *(entry fee).* ▶ **Château de Montrottier** (13th and 14thC); varied collections; bas-reliefs in bronze cast by the lost-wax method by Hans and Peter Vischer (1520) of Nuremberg *(9-12 & 2-6, Jul.-Aug. ; Easter-Oct. closed Tue.).* □

Lake ANNECY★★★

A2 *(see map 1)* (Haute-Savoie)

Lake Annecy is one of the loveliest spots in the Savoy Alps, with its mountain backdrop and green shoreline. Hallowed by artists and writers of the last century, the lake is today widely praised for the purity of its water, which has been preserved by herculean efforts to save it from sewage pollution.

Lake statistics : Length 14 km, average width 1.2 km, circumference 35 km, altitude

1. Lake Annecy

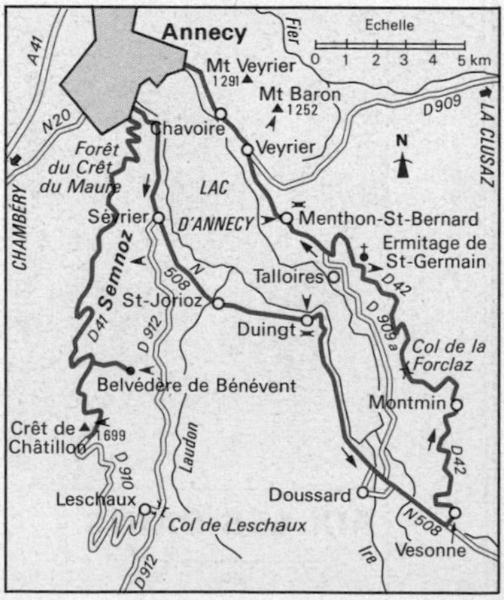

446 m, max depth 82 m at the Boubioz spring.

Fish : trout, angler fish, perch, char (*omble chevalier,* a local delicacy), carp, rudd, roach, pike and other freshwater fish. □

▶ Around the lake.

▶ **By boat :** Best way to explore it. Information and departure from the Quais du Thiou in Annecy.

▶ **By road** *(39 km; 56 km with detour by the La Forclaz Pass).* ▶ **Sévrier** ® : pleasant country retreat at the foot of Semnoz mountain. ▶ **Saint-Jorioz** ® : for summer holidays. ▶ **Duingt★** ® : by the rocky straits near Talloires separating the *Grand Lac* from the *Petit Lac.* The château on its green island makes a splendid tableau for the visitor with a camera. Above is a 15thC château. ▶ **Doussard** ® : with a forest road up the **Combe d'Ire★,** enlivened by streams that sparkle through the woods. This little valley is today swallowed up in the game reserve of Bauges, where roe deer, chamois, rock partridge, black grouse, marmot and Corsican wild sheep are protected. ▶ Beyond Doussard, continue along **La Forclaz Pass★★,** with superb views over the lake. ▶ **Talloires** ® : pleasure for both eyes and palate. The most beautiful sight on the lake and a major gastronomic rendez vous. ▶ **Menthon-Saint-Bernard★** ® : More family oriented than the neighbouring resort; château (13th-15thC) girdled with walls and turrets *(2-6 Sun. and Thu. Jun.-Sep.).* Tomb of the historian Taine (d. 1893) on the N face of the Chère Rock. ▶ **Veyrier,** surrounded by orchards is dominated by **Mont Baron,** the SE extremity of the Montagne de Veyrier. From the summit, magnificent view over the lake, the Semnoz, the Dent du Chat, the Massif des Bauges, the glaciers of the Maurienne; Mont-Blanc to the East. □

▶ Le Semnoz *(18 km to the Crêt de Châtillon)*

▶ The last link in the chain of the Bauges mountains, at the very gates of Annecy, **Le Semnoz★★** gives yet another view of the lake and of the country around Albens. ▶ Numerous paths to lookout points threading through the beautiful forests of the **Crêt du Maure★.** ▶ Climb up to the **Crêt du Chatillon★★** *(15 mins);* view of the Alps from Mont-Blanc to the Chartreuse Massif. □

The BAUGES Mountains★

A2

Above the Savoie valley between Lake Bourget and Lake Annecy, the mountains known as Les Bauges raise their natural fortifications to more than 1 500 m around a high plateau. Fir, spruce and beech woods alternate with beautiful pastureland; enormous walnut trees grow in the valleys. Formerly the *Baujus* (the inhabitants of Bauges) spent the winter making studs and wooden dishes that were mockingly known as "Bauges silverware". Bauges includes the *canton* of Châtelard and a national nature reserve of more than 50 km^2.

Wildlife

Take your binoculars to the high pastures on the upper edge of the forest, and of course to the National Park of the Vanoise (Parc National de la Vanoise), where there is a good chance of seeing various Alpine fauna : ibex, marmot, and the rarer chamois and blue hare.

Alpine ibex : *there were fewer than 50 of these mountain goats in Savoie when the Parc de la Vanoise was created in 1963. Heavily built with superb bowed horns.*

Chamois : *smaller than the ibex, very shy, a real nomad, off at the gallop at the approach of man. May be seen on the upper edges of the Alpine pastures, or perched on rocky outcrops.*

Marmot : *a ball of reddish fur trotting from one burrow to another, mostly in the high pastures. This pretty rodent lives in families or communities and goes into hibernation at the onset of winter.*

Chough and eagle : *the chough, connoisseur of picnic leftovers, is a little yellow-beaked crow often seen gliding around the area's peaks. Several pairs of eagles have reappeared in the park.*

Blue hare : *white in winter and blue-grey in summer, he is the king of camouflage, and doubly difficult to observe in the mountain pastures that are his habitat.*

The BEAUFORTIN Region★★

▶ Albertville to Beaufort *(20 km, full day)*

B2

Between Mont Blanc and the Tarentaise, a land of wide pastures, forests, mountain hikes and long distance cross-country skiing, against the backdrop of Mont-Blanc and La Vanoise mountains. The villages (Beaufort, Arèche, Boudin) are quite unspoilt.

▶ The D925 goes right up the beautiful **valley of the Doron★.** ▶ **Villard-sur-Doron :** with a little road climbing towards the **Signal de Bisanne★★** (panoramic view). ▶ **Beaufort★** ® has given its name to the region and also to an excellent cheese made in the village co-opera-

Beaufort cheese

This relative of Gruyère is made in the Beaufortin and Tarentaise regions from whole cow's milk. There are two varieties : summer Beaufort from the Alpine pastures and winter Beaufort produced in the valley farms. It is a moulded, firm, cooked cheese, very pale yellow, smooth-textured with holes. It is round, with a concave crust - this distinguishes it from the gruyères - and each cheese weighs from 40 to 60 kilos. It matures for six months in a damp cellar at low temperature. The cheese co-operative in the village of Beaufort is open to visitors.

tive *(visitors welcome).* With narrow streets and overhanging roofs, Beaufort is a typical example of an old-fashioned Savoyard village. It's a good base for exploration by car : **Hauteluce** *(12 km N)* to see the lake and the Girotte dam★; the **Des Saisies Pass** *(20 km NW; alt. 1 633m)* with skiing facilities; the **Roselend dam**★ *(15 km E)* in an immense and rocky waste; to Bourg-Saint-Maurice *(40 km from Beaufort)* by D902, which runs down the valley of the Torrent des Glaciers★. □

■ Lake BOURGET★★★

A2 *(see map 2)* (Savoie)

Since the poet Lamartine sang its praises at the beginning of the 19thC, Lake Bourget has been a continous source of pleasure to visitors. This mysterious and magical lake lies between the rugged slopes of the Mont du Chat and the Chambotte.

The lake : 18 km long; 1.5 to 3 km wide; max depth 145 m, area 45 km², alt. 231 m; N, the lake is linked to the Rhône by the Canal de Savières.

2. Lake Bourget

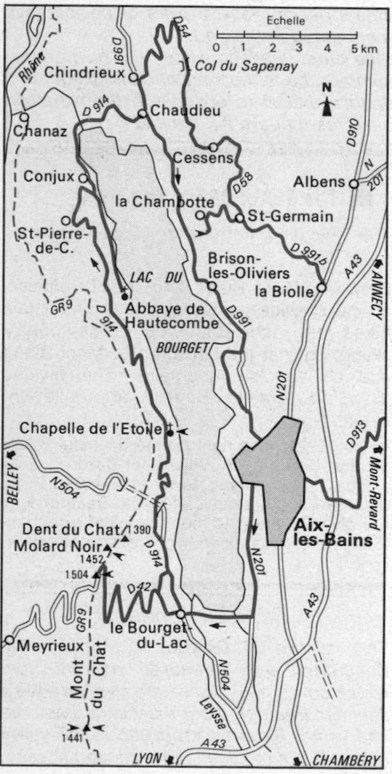

Fish : trout, char, pike, perch and gudgeon. □

▶ Round the lake

▶ **By boat**

Leave from the Grand Port d'Aix-les-Bains; excursions during the season to the Abbey of Hautecombe.

▶ **By car** *(52 km; 71km by the Sapenay Pass and the Chambotte).* ▶ **Le-Bourget-du-Lac** ®, favourite residence of the Counts of Savoy. This yachting and holiday centre was formerly an important port, linked with Lyons by a steamer service. Visit the church of the old priory (11th-13th-15thC) for its sculptures★★ from a rood-screen (Life and Passion of Christ), 15thC cloister and Italian park *(3-7 pm in summer).* ▶ From Bourget D42 climbs *(14 km)* to the **Mont du Chat★.** GR9 crosses the crest of this peak : a marvellous walk, especially towards the **Molard Noir**★★ *(1hr return, alt. 1 452 m)* panoramic view★★. ▶ **Chapelle de l'Etoile** *(on right, 5 mins on foot);* view★★ over the lake. ▶ **Abbaye de Hautecombe**★★ *(4 km right)* isolated in a magnificent site on the W bank of the lake. This abbey contains the tombs of the Princes of the House of Savoie. It was founded in 1125 by St. Bernard and Count Amédée III. The Benedictines of Solesmes have occupied it since 1922. Entirely restored during the 19thC by artists from Piedmont, the church is noted for its profusion of marbles, stucco, paintings and statuary. A beautiful Pieta★ *(cassette-guided visit 9:30-11:30 & 2:30-5:30; mass in gregorian chant 9:15 Sun., 9:30 wk; tel 79.63.26.12).* ▶ After **Conjux,** the road crosses the Canal de Savières at **Portout.** This canal links the lake to the Rhône and runs across the Chautagne marsh, full of rushes and poplars. ▶ At **Chaudieu** there is a choice between the lakeside road (D991) or the magnificent panoramic views from the route over the **Sapenay Pass** *(D991 N to Chindrieux, then right and left on D56).* ▶ At Saint-Germain D991B leads to the peak of the **Chambotte** (restaurant), superb view★★ over the Lac du Bourget. □

■ The CHABLAIS Region★★

B1

Rising in broad steps over Lac Léman (Lake Geneva), this outcrop of the Alps is a complicated landscape of limestone crests and deep valleys. A distinction is usually made between the Bas (lower) Chablais and the Haut (upper) Chablais. The Bas Chablais has slopes planted with vines (the famous Crépy), with chestnut woods along the south bank of Lac Léman (→). Between Évian and the valley of the Dranse d'Abondance lies the Gavot region, forming a broad plateau of woodland and pasture ideal for country walks (GR5). The Haut Chablais around Morzine (→) is segmented by three deep valleys of forest and pastureland. ▶ Thonon (→) and Évian (→) are ideal bases from which to discover this region.□

▶ Circuit around the three passes★ *(52 km, half day)*

▶ **Thonon** (→). ▶ Follow D26 to the SE, overlooking the Gorges of the Dranse. The road quickly enters the lovely **valley of Bellevaux,** wooded with beech and fir. ▶ From the hamlet of Jambaz the D236 leads on to the upper valley (Vallon de la Chèvrerie★) : numerous walks, lake, former Charterhouse (Carthusian monastery). ▶ Return via the Col (Pass) de Jambaz and the Terramont and Cou passes. □

▶ **Gorges de la Dranse;** from Thonon to Morzine *(33 km, 2hr)*

▶ **Thonon** (→). ▶ D902 takes you past the **Gorges du Pont du Diable;** a maze of potholes *(entry fee)* and ruins of the Cistercian Abbey of **Notre-Dame d'Aulps** (12th-13thC). ▶ **Morzine** (→). □

▶ The **Abondance Valley★;** from Thonon or Évian to the Pas de Morgins *(Swiss frontier; 42 km, approx 3hr)*

▶ From Thonon or Évian *(D21),* rejoin D22 which climbs through the wooded gorges of the **Dranse d'Abondance.** This is one of the valleys of Chablais where the chalets have best preserved their original character. Note the warm red patina of the spruce walls and the beautifully fretted balconies. ▶ **Abondance** ® (pop. 1 300) : summer and winter resort in a charming location. The old abbey (founded 1128) was an influential religious centre throughout the Middle Ages. The cloister (14thC) has frescos★ illustrating the life of the Virgin *(9-12 & 2-6).* ▶ **La Chapelle d'Abondance** ®, small ski village. ▶ **Châtel★** ® (alt. 1 235 m), the last village in the valley. You can ski at **Super-Châtel** (alt. 1 647 m) surrounded by alpine pasturelands (many good walks). Cable-car from here up the **Pic de Morclan** (alt. 1 970 m; panoramic view★★). □

■ CHAMBÉRY★

A2 / ® / pop. 55 000 (Savoie)

Chambéry was the capital of Savoie when it was a sovereign state, with the rank of County and later Duchy. Proud of its ancient title, this town was the home of Jean-Jacques Rousseau and the seat of Savoie's Senate. Chambéry still has an aristocratic flavour, clearly visible in the elegance of the porticos from the austere château to the famous Fontaine des Éléphants. The Place St. Léger, heart of the pedestrian precinct, is surrounded by houses with the warm colour of Italian buildings.

▶ La **Fontaine des Éléphants** (B2) is a useful reference point. Christened the 'Quatre-Sans-Culs' (the bottomless four) by the Chambériens, the fountain (1838) honours the memory of the Comte de Boigne (1741-1830) who brought back a fortune from the Indies and devoted it to the town. Among his major achievements is the street (B2) that bears his name. Flanked with porticos, this is the main shopping street of Chambéry. ▶ At the **Place St. Léger★** spend some time getting lost in the *trajes* — the labyrinth of alleys and vaulted passages that creates a secret network through the courtyards and apartment buildings adjoining the Place and the Rue de Boigne. The **château★** (B2; now the prefecture) is the former dwelling of the Dukes of Savoie. Parts of it date back to 14th and 15thC but the accommodation dates from the 18th and 19thC. ▶ The **Sainte-Chapelle** (15thC) with stained glass from the 16thC is particularly admired *(guided tour of the old town : 15 Jun.-15 Sep., Sat. 3:30; departure inner courtyard of the château; Jul.-Aug., evening visit at 9 pm ex. Sun.;* Carillon de la Sainte-Chapelle (chimes), *concerts Wed. at 6:30 and Sat. at 11:30 and 6:30).*

Also... ▶ **Savoisien Museum** (B2) in the former Franciscan convent; excavation finds from lakeside sites round Bourget, history of Chambéry, ethnography, collection★ of Savoie primitives in a gallery of the cloister *(10-12 & 2-6; closed Tue.).* ▶ **Cathedral of St. François de Sales** (B2) : the former church of the Franciscan convent, 15thC Gothic; *trompe-l'oeil* painting of 1848; Louis XIII buffets in the sacristy★; treasure room with 10thC Byzantine diptych★ *(3-5 Sat., Jun.-Sep.).* ▶ **Fine Arts Museum** (B1) : Italian paintings★ 14th-18thC including 'Portrait of a Young Man' by Uccello, 'Children at Play' attributed to Titian; Dutch, Flemish and German schools; French painting of 17th and 18thC *(10-12 & 2-6, closed Tue.).* ▶ **Lémenc church** (15thC) is built over a crypt that is partially Merovingian (Burial of Christ 15thC). ▶ **Les Charmettes** *(2 km on C2) :*

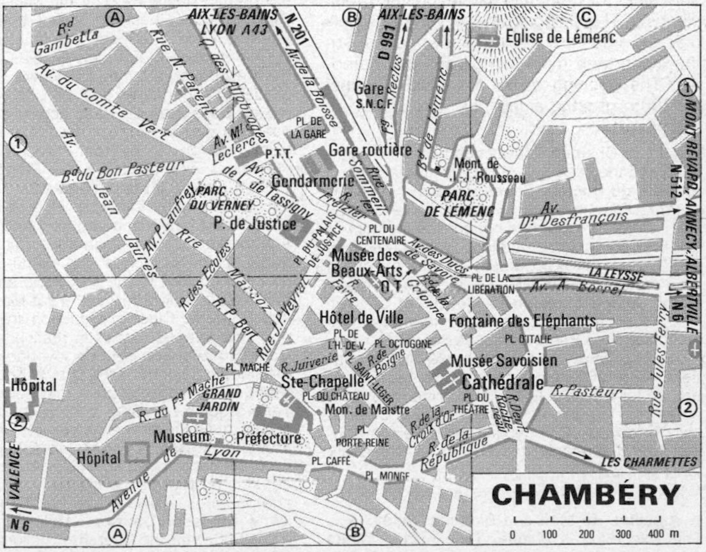

Regional flora

June and July are the best months for discovering the great variety and richness of alpine flora. Many colourful species are to be found above the treeline, over 2 200m : golden globe-flowers, intense blue gentians, delicate violets, white anemones, the silver suns of carline thistles, the violet flowers of the soldanelle, *pansies and asters, and vivid red rhododendrons. In particular look out for the wonderful martegon lily or Turk's cap, with purple-streaked pink flowers.*

the country house of Madame de Warens, where Jean-Jacques Rousseau lived from 1736 to 1742. He describes their idyll in unforgettable terms in book 6 of his "Confessions" *(10-12 & 2-6, Apr.-Sep. ; 10-12 & 2-4:30, Sun. and Wed. Oct.-Mar. ; other days ex Tue. 2-4:30).* □

▶ Nearby

▶ **Challes-les-Eaux** ® *(6 km SE) :* a mineral spa specialising in the treatment of respiratory ailments ; excursion to **Mont-Saint-Michel★** *(9.5 km E and 20 mins on foot;* view.) ▶ **Saint-Pierre-d'Albigny** *(2.6 km E) :* among the vines. ▶ 3.5 km NE you can visit the **château de Miolans★★** (10th-14thC), magnificently sited on a rock above the valley. This is an excellent example of mediaeval military architecture *(10-11:30 & 2:30-5:30, Apr.-Sep., closed Sun. am).* **Lake Aiguebelette★** ® *(27 km W) :* at the foot of the Montagne de l'Epine ; several summer resorts, ideal for fishing and boating excursions. □

■ CHAMONIX-MONT-BLANC★★★

B2 / ® / pop. 9 000 (Haute-Savoie)

Chamonix is the uncontested capital of French skiing and mountain climbing. Between Mont-Blanc and the Brévent, it is unrivalled for mountain excursions and rock climbing. The skiing areas, served by numerous ski lifts, are world renowned as are the celebrated mountain guides of Chamonix. The opening of the Mont-Blanc tunnel in 1965 greatly aided the expansion of this resort.

▶ Life in Chamonix is dictated by the mountains and the seasons. Activity is greatest along the **Rue du Docteur-Paccard** and in the neighbouring Place de Saussure and Place de Balmat ; these three names honour the memory of the first conquerors of Mont Blanc (1786 and 1787). Their great adventure and the history of the conquest of the alpine peaks are recorded in the **Alpine Museum** in the centre of town *(daily, 2 or 3-7).* ▶ Other resorts in the Chamonix Valley : **Les Houches** ®, **Les Bossons** ®, **Les Praz, Les Tines, Le Lavancher** ® and **Argentière** ®. ▶ 300 km of paths have been signposted for walking. A map of summer mountain walks may be obtained from the TO in Chamonix. To go up the mountain with a guide contact the Compagnie des Guides in Chamonix or Argentière. □

▶ Principal excursions *(see map 3)*

▶ **Aiguilles du Midi** and **Blanche Valley★★★.** This excursion is unique. Take warm clothes

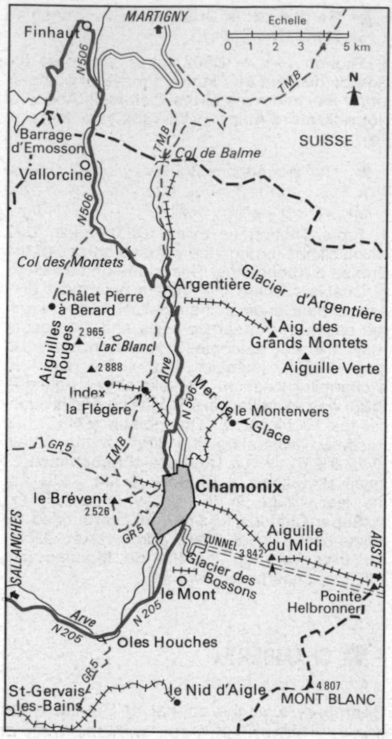

3. The Mont Blanc massif

and sunglasses. The cable-car goes up to the Aiguilles du Midi (alt. 3 790 m; panoramic view★★★). Continue up to the Helbronner Peak (alt. 3 452 m) by cable-car from the Blanche Valley. Italy is accessible from here, by the road down to Cormayeur. ▶ **Le Brévent** (alt. 2 525 m) : access by ski lift and cable-car. Panoramic view★★★ over the Massif du Mont-Blanc and the Chamonix Valley. ▶ **Les Grands Montets★★★ :** the most beautiful skiing region in Chamonix (and France) ; alt. 3 297 m. Access from Argentières by ski lift. View★★★ over the glacier of Argentières and the Chamonix valley. ▶ **Les Bossons★★ :** easy access to the most beautiful glacier in the massif, either by ski lift from the top or by foot through the forest *(40 mins);* ice grotto. ▶ **La Flégère★★** (alt. 1 894 m) by ski lift and then as far as the Index (alt. 2 385 m) by cable-car. View★★ over the Massif du Mont-Blanc and particularly over the Aiguille Verte. ▶ **Le Prarion★★** (alt. 1 967 m) : leave from Houches by cable-car ; allow 35 mins on foot to the top. Panorama★★ over the Massif du Mont-Blanc. ▶ **La Mer de Glace** (Ice Sea)★★. Classic excursion from Chamonix. This famous glacier is reached by **railway from Montenvers.** Site★★ overlooked by the formidable column of the Dru. ▶ **Tour of Mont-Blanc★★** on foot : allow a minimum of 6 days. Take equipment and a *Topo-guide* ("Topographical Guide of the Sentier de Grande Randonnée"). ▶ **Balme Pass★** (alt. 2 204 m) : leave from the cable-car 3 km NE of Argentière, then 20 mins on foot to the frontier pass. Flowers★ and pastures. View★★ over the Chamonix Valley. ▶ **Emosson Dam★★ :** 18 km N of Chamonix (N506 ; see the church in Vallorcine on the

The wines of Savoie

As Henri Bordeaux, novelist and member of the Académie Française, once said : "These are great wines, subtle and sometimes treacherous." To begin with the whites : Apremont, Abymes, Chignin, Montmélian, dry and fruity. Marignan, Marin, Ripaille, dry and open. The Roussette, fine and heavily perfumed. Roussette de Seyssel and Crépy, light, dry and diuretic. Ayze, pétillant *or sparkling, recommended as an* apéritif. *Finally, the reds : Gamay, full-bodied, fairly fruity; Mondeuse, purple-red with a bouquet of strawberry, raspberry and violet. Good years : 1955, 57, 61, 67, 69, 71, 76, 78, 79, 81.*

road) to the Swiss frontier, then a small road to the left via Finhaut. From the dam, a view★★ of the Aiguille Verte, Mont-Blanc and the Valais Alps. ▶ **Col des Montets*** 12 km N of Chamonix (N506) : see the nature reserve of the Aiguilles Rouges★★ (nature museum, flora, ecology trail). ▶ **Bérard Valley★.** *(path to the left approx. 2 km after the Col des Montets) :* a pretty 2hr walk to the Chalet de Pierre-à-Bérard. □

La CLUSAZ★

A2 / ® / pop. 1 695 (Haute-Savoie)

In the heart of the Aravis, La Clusaz is the largest summer and winter resort in this part of the Alps. The village, clustered around its Byzantine-looking bell-tower, is surrounded by larch woods and Alpine pastures. Highly recommended for walks. ▶ In the background is the impressive wall of the Aravis. □

▶ Nearby

▶ **Vallon des Confins★** *(5.5 km E) :* along this valley runs the little road to Fernuy at the foot of the Aravis escarpment. ▶ **Thônes** ® and the **valley of Manigod★** *(round trip of 32 km; W).* Thônes is one of the centres of Reblochon production. This is a delicious farm cheese with a creamy texture, the speciality of the Aravis region *(market Sat. am).* 3 km NW is the cemetery of Glières where 105 Resistance fighters from the Plateau de Glières were buried (Jan.-Mar. 1944). From Thônes, follow D12 S then D16 via Manigod and the La Croix-Fry Pass★. ▶ **Borne Valley★** towards **Bonneville** *(23 km N).* Beyond Saint-Jean-de-Sixt, take D12, which runs through the defile of Etroits★ then after Petit-Bornand, the Gorge of Éveaux★. From **Le Petit-Bornand** ® there is a pleasant excursion *(6.5 km)* to Paradise★. ▶ The **Route de la Colombière towards Cluses** *(3.3 km NE) :* in Saint-Jean-de-Sixt take D4 through the austere valley of **Chinaillon** (old village★) and beyond la Colombière Pass you will reach the valley of the Reposoir. See also **Le Grand-Bornand** ®, source and origin of Reblochon (market★ Wed. am) and the **Chartreuse du Reposoir,** founded in 1151, occupied today by Carmelites; buildings and cloister 15thC. ▶ **Road from the Aravis★★ to Flumet** *(19 km SE) :* without doubt the most beautiful drive in the region. Plan to arrive at the Aravis Pass (alt. 1 498 m) at the end of the afternoon for the view★★ over the Massif du Mont-Blanc in all its glory. The landscape opens out from the **Croix de Fer★★** (alt. 1 649 m; *2hr on foot round trip*). Once the rocky barrier of the Aravis has been crossed, the road goes down into the gorges of the Arondine★, cutting through the rocks. □

COURCHEVEL★

B3 / ® (Savoie)

This is the leading resort in the region of the Trois Vallées ("Three Valleys" : Saint-Bon, Doron-des-Allues and Doron-de-Belleville). The valleys are interlinked by an immense network of ski lifts centred on Courchevel. There are three levels at Courchevel : 1 550 m, 1 650 m., and 1 850 m; the ski lifts all connect with the lowest level. □

▶ Nearby

▶ **La Saulire★★** (alt. 2 693 m) : access by ski lift and cable-car leading from Courchevel 1850. 40 mins on foot to the summit. Panoramic view★★. ▶ **Doron de Belleville :** the most remote of the three valleys. There is skiing at **Les Menuires** (alt. 1700 m) and **Val-Thorens** (® → Saint-Martin-de-Belleville); this last resort (2 200 m) is equipped for summer skiing on the Glacier de Péclet. At **Saint-Martin-de-Belleville** ®, the village in the valley, see the church of St. Martin for its large Baroque altarpiece and the chapel of Notre-Dame de la Vie (Romanesque) for its numerous works of art (Christ★, painting of the German school 1502). ▶ **Doron des Allues.** The central of the three valleys with the second largest winter sports resort (on a par with **Méribel** ®; alt. 1 600 m) in the area. In the summer Méribel is a good excursion base. From Méribel and its satellite resort of **Méribel-Mottaret** you can go by cable-car to La Saulire★★, and from there down to Courchevel. □

ÉVIAN-LES-BAINS★★

B1 / ® / pop. 6 133 (Haute-Savoie)

Beautifully situated on the edge of Lac Léman (Lake Geneva), with an air of old-fashioned charm in the grand hotels and casino, Évian is a great spa with a venerable reputation. Modernisation is nonetheless gradually eroding the town's old-world allure; it has become famous as a bathing, sailing and sports centre as well as for the original Évian water. The busy social and cultural life, the activity in the pedestrians-only streets, the flowered parks and gardens, the beautiful lake front★★ and the white boats all give the season in Évian an air of permanent festivity.

▶ In the **church** (14th-19thC), bas-relief of the Virgin (15thC); the **Palais des Congrès** (conference building, 1956) constructed by Novarina and decorated by Quinet; near the port : the English garden★. □

▶ Nearby

▶ **Château de Larringes** *(10 km SSW);* the château itself (14thC) is not open to visitors, but the view over Lac Léman and Mont-Blanc is superb. ▶ **Lakes of La Beunaz** and **Bernex** *(11 km SE).* **La Beunaz** (® → **Saint-Paul-en-Chablais**) is a pretty summer resort and **Bernex** is a winter sports centre and a good excursion base (easy ascent of the Dent d'Oche (alt. 2 225 m). ▶ **Thollon** ® and the **Plateau des Mémises★★** *(11 km* E) : **Thollon** (alt. 992 m) is the starting point of the cable-car for the Plateau des Mémises (alt. 1 600 to 2 000 m). Lookout point over the lake and a nice family resort. □

■ The FAUCIGNY Region★★

B1

Razor-edged crests, gigantic barriers of stone in twisted shapes and the splendid Fer à Cheval (Horseshoe) amphitheatre, give Le Faucigny a special place in the heart of the limestone region of the French Alps. The valley of the Arve from Sallanches to Bonneville, and that of the Giffre, its principal tributary, are the major axes of this area. Regional architecture is seen to best advantage in the high valleys. As in the Chablais region, chalets here are built into the slope ; the inhabited part has solid stone walls, while the barn or *fenière* either forms a separate floor or is located under the roof.The *fenière* is usually a wooden structure covered with vertical planks of fir. □

▶ The Valley of the Arve, from Bonneville to Sallanches *(31 km by N205, 3hr)*

▶ **Bonneville** ® (pop. 8 087) is the former capital of the Faucigny region. Resistance Museum *(Wed. and Sat., 2:30-6).* 8 km W : **La Roche-sur-Foron** ® (pop. 6 818) is the major agricultural market of the region ; remains of ramparts and of the first château (1016). ▶ Between Bonneville and Cluses try a detour *(5 km farther)* via **Mont Saxonnex★** ® : a very pleasant holiday resort built on a broad terrace above the valley of the Arve (view★). ▶ **Cluses** (pop. 15 900) is a screw-making and metal-working centre, both Savoyard specialties. ▶ Beyond Cluses, the road runs through a narrow gorge *(cluse)* to which the town owes its name. ▶ At **Balme**

The produce of Savoie

Savoie produces many cheeses of renown, among them Reblochon *and* Beaufort. *The lakes are still unpolluted and full of fish : pollan, char, salmon-trout and freshwater* lotte. *The liver of the* lotte *is a local delicacy. There are also pike, perch and* gravanche *(fished only in Dec.). The pure mountain air is excellent for curing meat (ham and dry-cured* saucisson*). Look out for a very special spiced sausage called* pormonier. *Many varieties of mushroom :* mousserons, cêpes, morilles. *The* gratin de pommes de terre savoyard *differs from its Dauphinois cousin in that it is made without milk (potatoes, cheese and stock). The local pastries are very light ; try the* gâteau de Savoie.

(4 km) a road runs up to the winter sports resorts of **Les Carroz-d'Arâches** ® *(9 km)* and **Flaine** ® *(24 km),* built (1974) in reinforced concrete sections in an immense valley leading into the **Désert de Platé.** This is a large limestone plateau of 15 km^2, accessible by cable-car. □

▶ The Valley of the Giffre *(24 km from Taninges to the Fer-à-Cheval amphitheatre, 2 hr)*

▶ From Cluses, go on to Taninges and take D907 towards Samoëns. ▶ **Samoëns** ® and Sixt were formerly renowned for masons and stoneworkers whose craft school was the oldest in France. After working the land during fine weather, stonemasons from the valley of the Giffre would hawk their skills throughout Savoie and beyond. Sculpted lintels, Doric columns, crosses, oratories and fluted stoups for holy water bear witness today to the mastery of the artisans from this valley. In Samoëns, the little capital of Haut-Faucigny, ancient houses cluster around the totem of the

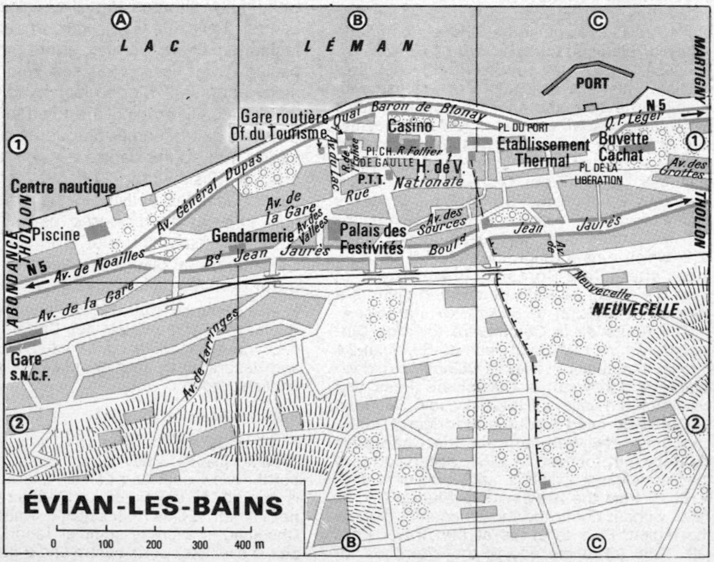

market place, a huge lime tree planted in 1438 *(market Wed.)* Flowers are everywhere, and there is a pretty Alpine garden created by Marie-Louise Jay, born in Samoëns, who with her husband, Ernest Cognacq, founded *La Samaritaine,* a well-known chain of French department stores. Don't miss the robust 16thC church. As well as a winter sports resort, **Samoëns** is also a marvellous excursion centre. (**La Rosière,** *6 km N;* view★★ of Mont-Blanc). ▶ At the exit from the village, see the waterfall of Nant d'Ant★, and the Gorges de Tines★. ▶ **Sixt-Fer-à-Cheval** is also a pleasant winter sports resort. All that is left of its abbey is a Gothic church and a 17thC building that is now a hotel (dining room★). ▶ The **Fer-à-Cheval amphitheatre★★,** surmounted by the Pic de Tanneverge, forms a gigantic semicircle of limestone cliffs, where in the month of June some 30 waterfalls can be seen. ▶ Go on foot *(50 mins)* to the rocky site of Fond-de-la-Combe★. □

Four-star skiing

Of course this is not an official classification but the choice is that of a number of Savoyard mountain specialists. After each resort is the name of the skiing region followed by the highest altitude reached by various forms of ski lift.

Chamonix : *Les Grands Montets (3721 m).*

Les Arcs : *L'Aiguille Rouge (3000 m).*

La Plagne : *Bellecôte (3250 m).*

Courchevel : *La Saulire (2700 m).*

Tignes/Val d'Isère : *La Grande Motte (3459 m).*

The most beautiful hors-piste *(off-trail) skiing (be sure to take a guide) : Aiguille du Midi-Vallée Blanche; Les Grands Montets; via the Pas de Chêvre, La Mer de Glace to Chamonix.*

The GRANDES ALPES Route★★★

B2-3 *(see map 4)*

This road crosses the eastern Alps from north to south and is the most attractive in the Savoie and the Dauphiné regions. From Lac Léman to the La Cayolle Pass (D902), nearly 700 km of hairpin bends, *corniche* roads and deep gorges; spectacular views.

▶ The high point is the crossing of the passes between Bourg-St. Maurice and La Cayolle Pass. ▶ **Iseran Pass★★** (alt. 2270 m) : gateway to the Tarentaise and the Haute-Maurienne (view of the glacier peaks of Albaron and Charbonel). **Galibier Pass★★** (alt. 2640 m) : view of rock wall and sparkling glaciers (Les Écrins, La Meije). ▶ **Lautaret Pass★** (alt. 2058 m) : between Grenoble and Briançon. ▶ **Izoard Pass★★** (alt. 2361 m) and its famous **Casse Déserte,** with tawny needles of rock looking like a lunar landscape. ▶ Finally, **La Cayolle Pass** (alt. 2326 m) or, even more spectacular, the **Route de la Bonette★★★** (alt. 2802 m), which leads to one of the most beautiful circular panoramas of the southern Alps. □

4. The Grandes Alpes route

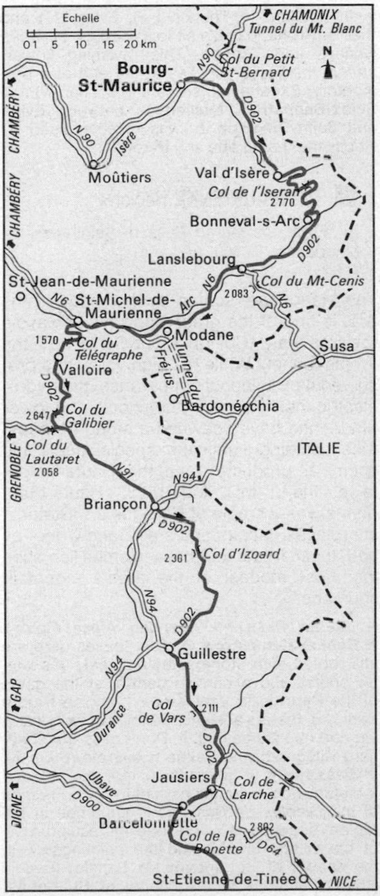

Lac LÉMAN (Lake Geneva)★★★

A-B1

In the heart of the Alps there are two rivieras, one French and one Swiss, linked by great white boats flying the Cross of Savoie or the Cross of Switzerland. Thirteen times longer than Lake Bourget, Léman (580 km^2, 72 km long, max 13 km wide, 310 m deep) has a microclimate that tends to prolong summer into late autumn. A blend of blue, green and white where this inland sea meets the mountains, the pleasures of country walks, fishing, the beach... and just messing about in boats. ▶ On the French side, Thonon (→) and Évian (→) are the two social, sporting and health poles of this peaceful little world.

Local costume

The women's costumes worn in the high Alpine valleys have no equal in cut and colour. They vary from one valley to the next, but all have the same accessories; a multicoloured shawl and a gold or silver cross suspended from a metal heart by a black velvet ribbon. The costume of the Tarentaise region is characteristic : a black dress and a black embroidered apron striped with bright colours, a wimple of white lace and a black headdress known as a frontière. *The headdress, embroidered and laced with gold, has three distinctive points, one over the forehead and the other two over the temples. Today these traditional Savoyard costumes are only worn on festival days and for traditional celebrations.*

▶ Cruises

▶ From a simple crossing to a complete tour of the lake (approx. 10 h), visiting all the resorts on both French and Swiss sides. Ask at the embarkation points in Thonon and Évian. □

▶ The south bank of the lake *(D25 and N5)*

▶ In addition to Thonon (→), Évian (→) and their environs, pay a visit to **Yvoire★★** between Geneva and Thonon. This ravishing flower-strewn mediaeval city lies at the end of a promontory. **Excenevex** (shore and scenery★) and **Sciez-Bonnatrait. Meillerie★,** between Évian and **Saint-Gingolph** ®, was much praised by Rousseau, Lamartine and Byron. □

■ The MAURIENNE Region★

▶ From the Iseran Pass to Saint-Jean-de-Maurienne *(87 km, full day)*
A-B3

The Maurienne, scored by the valley of the Arc, is one of the great highways of Savoie towards Italy (Col du Mont-Cenis and the Fréjus tunnel). While the high valley has preserved its traditional appearance, the hydroelectric installations in the middle and lower Maurienne have spawned a string of industries including aluminium, special steels and chemical products. Like the Haute-Tarentaise, the 17thC and 18thC Haute-Maurienne was a cradle of Baroque art. Statues, altarpieces, pulpits and stalls, and works by both local artists and Italians embellish even the most modest of the area's mountain churches.

▶ **Iseran Pass** (→ Grandes Alpes Route). ▶ **Bonneval-sur-Arc★** ® : the houses here are still roofed with stone slabs *(lauzes)*; this winter sports and excursion centre, at the gates of the Parc de la Vanoise★★ (Vanoise Nature Park, →), fosters ancient traditions of woodcarving and cheesemaking. ▶ Don't miss the shepherd villages of the **Vallée d'Avérole** *(6 km S).* ▶ **Bessans** ® is a cradle of popular art and a district rich in traditions (costumes). Frescos of the *Diables de Bessans* in churches in the region, sculpted in wood. See the sculptures★ of the village church and the paintings★★ in the chapel of St. Antoine. ▶ **Lanslevillard** ® (15thC paintings in the chapel of St. Sebastian), **Lanslebourg** ® and **Termignon** together constitute the resort of **Val-Cenis.** Route N6 from Mont-Cenis towards Italy (pass, lake, view★★). ▶ **Modane** ® is an important railway junction, industrial centre and customs inspection post; access to the Fréjus tunnel. ▶ **Saint-Michel-de-Maurienne** ® : route (D902) from the Télégraph Pass★ towards **Valloire★** ® (typical village; see the decoration★ of the church; winter sports resort) and the Galibier Pass★★. ▶ **Saint-Jean-de-Maurienne** ® (pop. 10 420), former capital of Maurienne; **cathedral** (stalls★, ciborium★ and 15thC cloister; pre-Romanesque crypt). ▶ From Saint-Jean : access to winter sports resorts of **La Toussuire** ® (alt. 1 690 m) and **Corbier** (alt. 1 560 m) and the loop road★★ to the **Glandon Pass★** *(63 km D926 and 927)* via **Saint-Jean-d'Arves** and the La Croix de Fer Pass★★ (alt. 2 068 m). □

■ MEGÈVE★★

B2 / ® / pop. 5 375 (Haute-Savoie)

Since the 1920, the queen of French winter sports resorts, Megève is fashionable but retains its Savoyard charm and offers excellent social and sporting activities; children are particularly welcome here. The sunny slopes of Mont d'Arbois, Rochebrune and the Jaillet provide marvellous skiing and offer a wide choice of walks in summer. See the Place de l'Eglise and the Calvary with figures sculpted in wood. □

▶ Nearby

▶ Pleasant views served summer and winter by cable-car : **Mont d'Arbois★★** ® (alt. 1 833 m); **Croix des Salles★★** (alt. 1 705 m); **Rochebrune-Super-Megève★** (alt. 1 754 m). From all three sites there are magnificent views over the Massif du Mont-Blanc. ▶ To the SW of Megève, by the N212, the **Arly Valley,** a high valley of prairies and pines studded with ski villages : **Praz-sur-Arly** ®, **Flumet** ® (view★ from the bridge of old wooden houses), **La Giettaz** ®, **Notre-Dame-de-Bellecombe** ®, **Crest-Voland** ®. Passing through the beautiful Arly gorges, one arrives at **Ugine,** centre of the valley and renowned for its special steel. □

■ MORZINE★

B1 / ® / pop. 2 650 (Haute-Savoie)

The tourist capital of the Chablais region (→), with its chalets distributed around the junction of six valleys, a very popular medium-altitude excursion centre and ski resort. The ski slopes here are linked to those of Avoriaz by cable-car and road. □

▶ Nearby

▶ The classic car trip★★ *(29 km)* leads around **Montrond Lake★** and **Avoriaz** ®, the first winter sports resort to ban cars. Highly original architecture; roofs and façades covered with red cedar shingles. ▶ From Morzine to Samoëns, 20 km via the spectacular **Ranfolly Pass★★** (alt. 1 650 m; view★★; restaurant). ▶ 7 km SE of Morzine is the winter sports resort of **Les Gets** ®. ▶ 8 km N, ruins of the Cistercian abbey of **Notre-Dame-d'Aulps** (12th-13thC). □

■ SAINT-GERVAIS-LES-BAINS★★

B2 / ® / pop. 4 800 (Haute-Savoie)

Skiing, with a network of lifts linked to

those of Megève and Chamonix, a streetcar named Mont-Blanc, mountaineering and mountain schools, a climate particularly suited to children : Saint-Gervais also has a thermal spa (Fayet), the original source of its renown. The resort is very well situated on a plateau above the valley of the Arve at the exit from the pretty valley of Montjoie. ▶ See the **church of Notre-Dame-des-Alpes** (1938; architect Novarina, stained glass by Cingria; fresco by Monier). □

▶ Nearby

▶ **Le Bettex** and **Mont d'Arbois★★** *(8 km SW and cable-car)* : satellite resort of Saint-Gervais, Le Bettex is also a marvellous viewpoint for Mont-Blanc and Les Aravis. Summer or winter, the cable-car goes up to Mont d'Arbois★★; from here another cable-car descends to Megève. ▶ **Tramway du Mont-Blanc** (leaves from Fayet or Saint-Gervais). Although somewhat eclipsed by the cable-cars, the TMB offers a fine introduction to the High Alps : **Voza Pass** (alt. 1 653 m) and the **Nid d'Aigle** (Eagle's Nest)★ (alt. 2 386 m) : from here it is a 30 minute climb to the glacier of Bionnassay. ▶ **Saint-Nicolas-de-Veroce** *(9 km SSE)* occupies an extraordinary site opposite Mont-Blanc. Go up to Le Planey *(1.5 km)* or the plateau of la Croix *(3km by car)*; view★★ over the Montjoie Valley and Mont-Blanc. ▶ **Les Contamines-Montjoie** ® *(9 km S)* : a summer and winter resort in the Montjoie valley★. The road continues *(4 km)* to the **chapel of Notre-Dame de la Gorge,** a place of pilgrimage and a typical example of Savoyard Baroque. Starting point for the tour of Mont-Blanc on foot (→ Chamonix). □

■ Le SALÈVE★

AI

Le Salève is a huge mass of limestone (alt. 1 380 m) that towers above Geneva. Although it is on French territory, it is very much the stamping ground of Swiss mountaineers (the mountaineering term *varappe* comes from one of the routes across the Salève).

▶ The **route de Crête★★** (D41) is easily accessible via Cruseilles or Annemasse. View★★ over Geneva and the lake, particularly from the orientation table of the Treize-Arbres. ▶ **Annemasse** ® (pop. 23 655) is an important economic centre of the Haute-Savoie. ▶ 1.5 km E of **Cruseilles** are the leisure resources of the **Dronières Park** (20 acres of water). □

■ SALLANCHES

B2 / ® / pop. 8 448 (Haute-Savoie)

One of the best sunset views★★ of Mont-Blanc. This little town was entirely rebuilt after a great fire in 1840. The facilities of Mont-Blanc-Plage (shore) attract numerous summer visitors. □

▶ Bassin de Sallanches★

▶ Between two valleys of the Arve, the Bassin de Sallanches seems to have been created to provide views of Mont-Blanc. ▶ Little roads down the mountain offer changing views of the massif and the Aravis, including the chain of the Fiz, spreading over the Plateau d'Assy.

▶ **Cordon** *(4 km SW)* is a charming village; near Nant-Cruy, see the chapel of Médonnet (panorama★★). ▶ **Combloux★** ® *(8 km S)* is a pretty summer and winter holiday resort famous for its view★★ of Mont-Blanc. ▶ **Plateau d'Assy** ® *(11.5 km E)* : the trip★★ across the plateau in view of Mont-Blanc is a marvel. Facing South with its back to the Fiz, the Plateau d'Assy stretches across the shoulders of the mountain chain and is highly reputed for its climate (numerous sanatoriums and family houses). The **church of Notre-Dame-de-Toute-Grâce★★** marks an important point in the contemporary renewal of sacred art. Designed by the architect Novarina (1937), consecrated in 1950, this church has been decorated by many famous artists : on the façade is a mosaic by Fernand Léger, inside is a tapestry by Lurçat, stained glass by Roualt and Bazaine, works by Chagall, Bonnard, Matisse, and a Christ by Germaine Richier. ▶ From the Plateau d'Assy there is a difficult road★★ around **Plaine-Joux** and the Lac Vert (Green Lake), which reflects Mont-Blanc. □

■ The TARENTAISE★

▶ Trip from Moûtiers to Val-d'Isère *(59 km, half to full day)*

B2

The Tarentaise, formed by the upper valley of the Isère between Conflans (Albertville) and Val d'Isère, owes its name to the ancient *Darentasia,* today's Moûtiers, which was the principal town. The Romans were not the only ones to use this link between Aosta and the Rhone Valley. They were followed by founders of monasteries, upland settlers, pedlars and seasonal migrants who flocked to the valley of the Isère. In modern times it has become a centre for "white coal" (Tignes dam, Isère-Arc diversion) and the electrochemical industry (Moûtiers), in addition to being a winter sports resort (Courchevel, La Plagne, Les Arcs, Tignes).

▶ **Moûtiers** ® (pop. 4 868) is the gateway to the Trois Vallées, (→ Courchevel). Cathedral (11th-15thC; sculptures and wooden panelling) and the Museum of the Académie de Val d'Isère in the former archbishop's palace, now devoted to local history. 6 km SE : **Brides-les-Bains** ®, a watering place specialising in the treatment of obesity. ▶ **La Léchère** *(6 km NW),* spa reputed for treatment of circulatory problems. ▶ **Aime** (pop. 2 472). Man has been living on this site since prehistoric times, as attested by the collections in the archaeology museum *(9-12 & 2-6, Jul.-Aug.; closed Tue).* Built on the remains of a Gallo-Roman site and a 5th-6thC church, the ancient **Basilica of St. Martin★★** is the best example in Savoie of early Romanesque (11thC) architecture. Fragments of frescos from 11th-12thC. ▶ 18 km SE : **La Plagne** ® (1 980 m) a big winter sports resort; access by cable-car to the Grande Rochette★★ (alt. 2 505 m; view) and the slopes of the Bellecôte (2 994 m, view★★). ▶ After Bellentre, a road to the right leads to the pretty **valley of Ponturin★** and the villages around the summer and winter resort of **Peisey-Nancroix** (alt. 1 300 m). From here explore the Bellecôte and Pourri mountains. ▶ **Bourg-Saint-Maurice** ® (pop. 5 729) occupies a strategic position on a valley crossroads. 'The Bourg', as they say in Savoie, with the resort of **Les Arcs** ®, also has its ski-centres farther up the mountain : Arc 1600, Arc 1800 and Arc 2000, which have superb views★★ over the massifs of Beaufortin and Mont-Blanc. North, D902 goes to Le Cormet de Roselend and **the Beaufortin** (→). 31 km NE (route★★ N90) : the **Petit-Saint-Bernard Pass** (alt. 2 188 m), which was historically a very important military and commercial pass to the Aosta Valley. View★ of the Italian slopes of Mont-Blanc (panorama★★★ from the **summit of Lancebranlette,** alt. 2 928 m ; *4 hr round trip*). ▶ D902 now goes back up to the Haute-Tarentaise, where the villages perch on bluffs above the road. ▶ **Barrage de Tignes★★** (1953 ; vaulted dam), the key construction in the Haute-Isère electrification project (more than 1 billion kWh). The original village of Tignes, swallowed up by the resulting lake, was rebuilt on the left bank of the Isère. ▶ 5 km SW round a smaller lake is the winter sports centre of **Tignes** ® (2 100 m), also an excursion centre for trips into the Vanoise (cable-car from the Grande Motte★ alt. 3 450 m ; summer skiing). **Val d'Isère** (→). □

■ THONON-LES-BAINS★

A1 / ® / pop. 28 200 (Haute-Savoie)

A flowery town sitting on a terrace overlooking Lac Léman. This captivating town was the historic capital of the Chablais region (→). Its waters have long been sought by those with kidney problems. Geneva and Lausanne are just a boat trip away and on the Plage de Ripaille (shore) are excellent sailing facilities.

▶ The **Place du Château★** offers a fine view of the lake and the Swiss shore. Nearby : the Anthoinoz Garden, the **English Garden★,** and the Art and Leisure Centre (architect Novarina, 1966). ▶ From the Place, a funicular provides transportation to **Rives,** the port of Thonon, still retaining a few pretty houses from earlier times. ▶ **The Chablais Museum** (history ; popular art ; excavation finds), is in the 17thC château de Sonnaz *(10-12 & 3-6, 1 Jul.-15 Sep., closed Sun.)*. ▶ The **church of St. Hippolyte** (15th-17thC) made famous by St. François de Sales during his mission to the Chablais (1594-98) to bring the country back to Catholicism ; see the decoration★ of the vault (stucco and paintings) by Italian artists of the 17thC. Neo-Gothic **Basilica of St. François de Sales,** Chemin de Croix★ by Maurice Denis. □

▶ Nearby

▶ **Château de Ripaille★** *(1.5km, access from Rives and the Quai de Ripaille).* It is not certain that the expression "faire ripaille" (to feast) comes from the many fêtes and galas that were given there, but the former residence of the House of Savoie (15thC) abounds in charm, in spite of the numerous remodellings it has suffered. Kitchens★ of the Charterhouse (Carthusian monastery) installed 17th-18thC ; original equipment *(10-12 & 2-6, Apr.-Oct., closed Mon.)*. ▶ **Château des Allinges** *(6.6 km S)*; ruins of two châteaux (11th-14thC) on the peak ; a chapel from the end of the 11thC with a Romanesque fresco★ ; view★ over Lake Léman and the Jura mountain region. ▶ Fortified **Château of Avully** (14th and 15thC : *May-Sep., 10-12 & 2-6*). □

■ THORENS-GLIÈRES

A1-2 / pop. 1 376 (Haute-Savoie)

In the heart of the tiny valley of Bornes this modest summer resort was the home of St. François de Sales (born 21 Aug 1567). The **Chapelle de Sales** (1 km E) marks the site of the château where he was born. His family moved subsequently to the nearby **Château de Thorens** (15thC) : souvenirs of the saint, a collection of pictures and furniture *(9-12 & 2-6, Apr.-Nov.)*.

▶ 14 km E : the **Plateau des Glières** is remembered for one of the most heroic episodes of the Resistance in 1944. ▶ On the Glières Pass (alt. 1 440 m) is an explanatory panel giving details of the military operations involved. Memorial monument. □

■ VAL D'ISÈRE★

B3 / ® / pop. 1 344 (Savoie)

This is where the experts ski, over varied slopes ranging in altitude from 1 800 m to 3 750 m. The nearby Vanoise Nature Park and the Iseran Pass make this a favourite centre for summer excursions.

▶ **Rocher de Bellevarde★★** (alt. 2 826 m) and the **Tête du Solaise★★** (alt. 2 551 m) : both reached by cable-car ; magnificent views. □

■ VANOISE Massif★★

B3

A happy outcome of the difficult marriage between tourism and nature. The **National Park** between Arc and Isère includes the Massif de la Vanoise. The first park of this type created in France (1963), it covers 530 km², and is surrounded by an outer park of 1 450 km², which attracts tourists from the Maurienne and Tarentaise regions. With its Italian neighbour, the Gran Paradiso, this park pursues the objectives of preserving and protecting alpine flora and fauna and without doubt constitutes one of the most charming initiations to nature study. Ibex, chamois, marmot and blue hare live peacefully here among an extraordinarily rich variety of flowers, especially during June and July. The park is ideal for hikers. □

▶ **Pralognan-la-Vanoise★** ® (pop.569) is the best departure point for exploring the park. Surrounded by fir trees and running water at the foot of the Grand Marchet, which looks as if it alone were holding back the sparkling icefields of the Vanoise. It is not uncommon to see summer visitors suddenly scramble from their cars to focus binoculars on the peaks : a troop of chamois has come into view.

The **Maison du Parc et du Tourisme** de Pralognan provides all the necessary information for excursions, including details of mountain refuges and overnight lodgings, guided trips and mountain schools with guides from the national park. ▶ **GR55,** which leads from the upper station of Mont Bochor★ cable-car, (alt. 2 023 m) is the best path for visiting the park. ▶ The charming **Doron du Champagny Valley★** can be reached from Bozel, 14 km NW of Pralognan ; this is another excellent way into the park. ▶ Other entrances : Peisey-Nancroix, Tignes (→ Tarentaise), Val d'Isère (→), Bonneval, Bessans, Lanslevillard (→ Maurienne). □

Architecture

The typical Savoyard village is only rarely a single group of dwellings. Usually it consists of several hamlets, two to eight or even more, spread around the village centre astride the main road, with houses placed to derive maximum benefit from the sunshine. On the mountain shoulders and plateaux, houses are gathered around the village bell-tower. Formerly, the public fountain, the communal oven and the *fruitière* (co-operative dairy) were meeting places for people living in these rather scattered villages. ● In Savoie the houses must above all give protection from the cold. Buildings are massively constructed and openings are always small. Wooden galleries and balconies are essential features in this rural architecture; they enable wood to be dried and allow a certain amount of domestic activity to take place out of doors. ● The roofs differ greatly : wooden tiles *(ancelles* or *tavaillons)* or grey *ardoises* (slates) in the north, whereas in the south, in the Tarentaise and Maurienne, the roofs are predominantly stone tiles *(lauzes).* ● Walls are of locally available wood or stone, depending on resources. In general, wood is used more widely in the north; the chalets of the Haut Genevois, the Haut Chablais and Haut Faucigny have larch or fir trunks laid horizontally on a stone foundation; farther south, stone is used more. There is mixed construction in wood and stone in the Beaufortin, but stone houses are usual in the Tarentaise and the Maurienne, where wood is used only for balconies and gables. ● The cross (seen in Haut-Chablais), the sundial and a greater or lesser degree of re-

Wooden walls

Stone walls

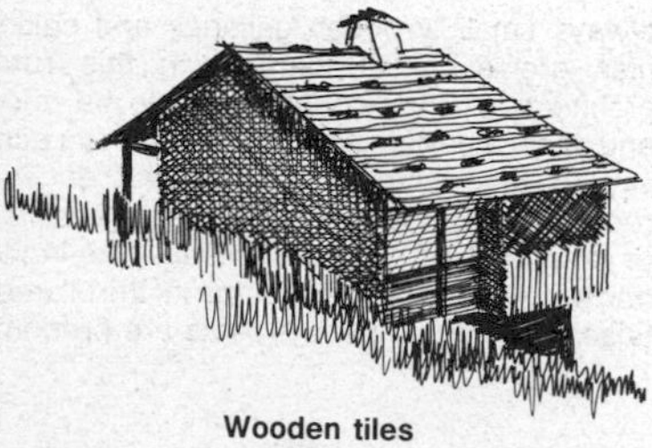
Wooden tiles

finement in the fretwork of the balustrades constitute the exterior ornamentation. ● The interior of the traditional house is generally quite plain. It is essentially composed of two main rooms : the *poêle* or communal room and the *outo* or guest room. Further bedrooms may be added around this nucleus. ● In regions lacking firewood (principally the Haute Tarentaise), men and animals used to live in the same building, since the animals provided a source of appreciable heat during the winter. In this case there would sometimes be summer accommodation on the first floor. ● A separate barn is a frequent accessory to the Savoyard house. This is characteristic of mountain regions and is found as often in the Pyrenees as in Scandinavia. It is a very simple little construction built from timbers, roughly squared off and resting on cornerstones to fend off damp and rats. The building was used to store food supplies (wheat, barley) away from possible fire risk, hence its isolation. Linen, clothes and even family papers were stored there. The Chablais, the Faucigny and Les Bornes are the regions where these buildings are most frequently found nowadays. ● Regional architecture appears in its most traditional form in the high valleys; but apart from the broad characteristics dictated by soil, climate and agricultural needs, there is no standardised architecture in Savoie. Even from one valley to another, differences can be very marked. In the same valley, even in the same village, there will be obvious variations. Perhaps the most typical Savoyard villages are the following : Abondance, Bessans, Bonneval, Grand-Bornand, Morzine, Salvagny, Samoëns, Sixt.

Savoyard "grenier"

Brief regional history

Up to the 8thC BC

The discovery of tools, mostly in the Tarentaise and Maurienne areas, shows that **shepherd tribes** from the north of Italy inhabited Savoie from the Bronze Age onward. ● During the Iron Age, the Gauls appeared. From the mouth of the Isère to the banks of the Valance, their communities were more or less united and known as the **Allobroges.** Conquered by Rome (122-118BC), the country of the Allobroges seems to have been from this time on a natural communications link between the valleys of northwestern Italy and the valleys around the Rhône, in spite of the difficulties of terrain. The **highway from Vienne to Milan** runs through the region; Aix (Aquae) and the valley of the Rhône, already much used by shipping, were both flourishing at this time.

9th-12thC

Subject to Lothair (843), later to Burgundy (888), Savoie fell under the nominal authority of the Holy Roman Empire in 1032. At this time, the first representative of the **House of Savoy** appears in the person of **Humbert aux Blanches Mains,** a native of the Vienne region. This dynasty was to Savoie what the Capets were to France. From county to duchy to royalty, this family created a sovereign state of rich and complex character, based on political and economic exploitation of its position at the crossroads of Europe. By dint of shrewd marriages and political alliances, the Blanches Mains eventually ruled both northern and southern slopes of Savoie, "the gatekeepers of the Alps". ● The 11th-12thC also saw the rapid spread of important monastic orders (Cistercians, Carthusians).

13th-14thC

From the reign of Amédée IV to Amédée VIII Savoie grew steadily in power. The Counts of Savoie owned Turin and Geneva, and the passes of Mont-Cenis and Petit St. Bernard, where there were hospices or inns for the benefit of travellers, made Savoie the cross-roads for the **constant traffic** into Italy from Champagne, the Germanic countries and the South of France. Small but well governed, Savoie took its place in the affairs of the great European states.

15th-16thC

The Emperor Sigismund made **Amadeus VIII** the Duke of Savoie in 1416, and statesmanship and wisdom made this Prince without doubt the greatest of his dynasty. Under his reign and during the reigns that followed, Chambéry, Annecy and their abbeys became centres of artistic activity and rivals in elegance. ● The Dukes of Savoie, owners also of Nice and Piedmont (1429) began to play off **France against the Hapsburg Empire,** a game that sometimes brought rewards and sometimes losses. It was in fact because of this power that the Duchy was invaded by François I of France (1536), and the Bernese laid waste the Chablais, an area that, converted to Protestantism, passed directly under the control of Calvin. After his subsequent victory over France at Saint-Quentin (1557), Duke Emmanuel-Philibort was able to restore the state of Savoie; however, since Chambéry was too close to France for comfort, the Duke transferred his capital to Turin. Henceforth **Piedmont was of greater importance than Savoie,** in spite of the impression of riches created by mines, fairs and flourishing commercial life.

17th-18thC

By the 17thC, Savoie was thoroughly imbued with **French culture.** Honoré d'Urfé (social commentator, 1567-1625) stayed at Chambéry; St. François de Sales (→ Annecy), an exemplary Savoyard, enriched French literature with his "Introduction to the Devout Life" (1608). In the confrontation between France and Austria, Savoie played its hand with varying results. Louis XIV invaded on two occasions; but by the Treaty of Utrecht (1713) **Duke Victor-Amédée II** found himself in the winning camp; he received the crown of Sicily, which he soon exchanged for that of Sardinia. At the head of his **Sardinian States,** this Prince began to instigate reforms that were well ahead of their time. ● At that time, 90 out of 100 Savoyards lived from the land; life became less precarious with the introduction of the potato (1750), maize (1780), and communal lands for sheep grazing. The introduction of **watch-making** in Faussigny made full use of the ingenuity and manual dexterity that northern Savoyards had always possessed, and that is exemplified today in the screw-cutting industry of the Haute-Savoie. ● The **first ascent of Mont Blanc** was made in **1786;** in 1792, Savoie was occupied by the forces of the French Revolution, and rechristened the Department of Mont-Blanc.

19th-20thC

By the **Treaty of Paris** (1815), King Victor Emmanuel of Italy recovered his Sardinian domains together with Savoie. The laws in force before 1792 were re-established and the province settled into what has been called the **Buon Governo,** a conservative era with rigorous morals and severe police controls. ● In 1848, however, the King granted a constitution (Le Statuto) that allowed for the creation in Turin of two chambers of Parliament. Savoie was to be represented in terms of its physical importance and not its historical stature. This led to widespread discontent, with grievances ranging from the omnipresence of the Piedmontais in the administration to the use of Savoyard taxes to benefit foreigners, and the refusal to create a French-language University at Chambéry. ● At this period the liberal party was reborn. People looked more and more to the France of Napoleon III. In 1858, the Italian statesman **Cavour** (1810-61) and **Napoleon III** agreed that in exchange for French aid to drive the Austrians out of Italy, France would receive Savoie and Nice. At the plebiscite of 23 and 24 April 1868, the Savoyards voted massively for **union with France.** ● Thus impoverished Savoie was joined to rich France. After a period of setback stemming from lack of investment and strong commercial competition, the province, divided into the **two departments** of Savoie and Haute-Savoie, became integrated with the development of France : the railway was extended across the Alps to Fréjus (1872), the road network was improved and tourism began to grow; heavy industry made its appearance with hydroelectricity ("white coal").

Practical information

The region

Information : Savoie : *Comité Régional de Tourisme* (C.R.T.) Savoie-Mont-Blanc, 9, bd Wilson, 73100 Aix-les-Bains, ☎ 79.88.23.41. **Haute-Savoie-Mont-Blanc :** *Association Touristique Départementale,* 56, rue Sommeiller, B.P. 348, 74012 Annecy, ☎ 50.51.32.31. *Association Départementale de Tourisme de Savoie,* 4, rue du Château, 73000 Chambéry, ☎ 79.85.12.45.

Bookings : *Loisirs-Accueil Savoie (L.A.),* 5, rue du Château, 73000 Chambéry, ☎ 79.85.01.09. Paris : *Maison de Savoie,* 16, bd Haussmann, 75009, ☎ 42.46.59.26/27/28.

Maps : *Michelin,* nº 92 1/200 000. *I.G.N.* 1/100 000 (green series), nºs 45 and 53. *I.G.N.* 1/250 000 (red series), nº 112.

S.O.S. : Savoie : *SAMU* (Emergency Medical Service), ☎ 79.69.25.25. **Haute-Savoie :** ☎ 17. *Poisoning Emergency Centre :* Grenoble, ☎ 76.42.42.42.

Weather forecast : Savoie, ☎ 79.61.58.55. **Haute-Savoie,** ☎ 50.53.03.40.

Rural gîtes and chambres d'hôtes : *Loisirs-Accueil Savoie ; Relais Départemental des Gîtes Ruraux,* 52, av. des Iles, 74010 Annecy, ☎ 50.57.82.40 ; *Service Tourisme rural,* 5, rue du Château, 73000 Chambéry. Numerous possibilities (children's gîtes, rural hostels, country inns, gites d'etapes, alpine chalets, rural campsites).

Holiday villages : see practical holiday information.

Camping : for a list and classification of sites and information about rural and farmhouse campsites, enq at the *C.R.T. Savoie-Mont-Blanc* and at the *Assn. Touristique Dép. Haute-Savoie-Mont-Blanc.*

Festival and events : Early Apr : *International Festival of Music* in Évian. **Early May :** open week at the Lake Léman European Centre. **End May :** *Antiques Salon* in Chambéry. **Early Jun :** *International Animated Film Festival* in Annecy. **Mid-Jul :** *Maurienne Festival* in Saint-Jean-de-Maurienne. **End Jul :** *fete of the Bellevilles Valley guides. International Festival of Folklore Dance* in La Clusaz. **Early Aug :** *livestock fair* in Saint-Martin-de-Belleville ; **1st Sun in Aug :** *lake festival* in Annecy. **Mid-Aug :** *procession at the Prés-Plans chapel ; guides' fete* in Les Arcs ; *mountain costume fete* in Peisey-Nancroix. **Early Sep :** *Aix-les-Bains-Lac du Bourget Music Festival,* in Bourget-du-Lac ; *Beaucroissant Fair* in Grignon. **Mid-Sep :** *Savoie fete* in Chambéry. **End Sep :** *local fair* in Annecy. **Early Oct :** *Antiques Salon* in Aix-les-Bains. **Early Dec :** *1st Snow Elimination Trials* in Val-d'Isère.

Sporting events : Mid-Apr : *International Car Rally* at Annemasse. **Mid-May :** *International Golf Week* at Évian. **Early Jun :** *International Rowing-Regatta* at Évian. **Late Jun :** *French Marathon Campionships* at Annecy. **Late Jul :** *National Horse-riding Competition* at Talloires.

Scenic railways : *Alpazur,* Genève-Digne-Nice, daily end May to end Sep. Enq : S.N.C.F. *Breda Scenic Railway :* from Poncharra-La Rochette, 2 return trips daily, approx once weekly from Jun to Sep. Enq : M. Vargel, ☎ 76.48.55.61.

National and nature parks : *Direction du parc national de la Vanoise,* 135, rue du Dr-Julliand, B.P. 105, 73003 Chambéry Cedex, ☎ 79.62.30.54, for lists of shelters and overnight gîtes, topoguides and maps of the park.

Rambling and hiking : *I.G.N. maps* 1/50 000 and 1/25 000. *Didier-Richard* in Grenoble publishes maps of the various massifs. GR5 (Haute-Savoie), GR5-55 (Savoie), GR9 and GR96 topoguide, along with GTA nº 15. Lists of shelters and gîtes d'étapes are available at the *Gîtes Ruraux de Savoie* and the *Club Alpin Français.* The "Great Crossing of the Alps" (G.T.A.) consists of nine routes, from Lake Léman to Menton. Enrollment at the Centre-école Chaudemaison, 67, Cervières, 05100 Briançon, ☎ 92.21.01.87.

Riding holidays : all enquiries concerning riding centres and activities should be addressed to the *Comité Départemental Savoie pour le Tourisme Équestre, l'Équitation de loisirs et sportive* (C.D.S.T.E.), Maison des Sports, 6, montée Valérieux, 73000 Chambéry, ☎ 79.69.69.69.

Handicraft courses : weaving (Les Arcs) ; stained glass (Val-d'Isère) ; pottery (La Norma) ; silk painting (Montchavin) ; wickerwork (Séez) ; copper enamelling (Séez) ; woodwork (Lanslebourg), etc. Enq : *Assn. Dép. de Tourisme de Savoie.*

Other courses : *numerous sports courses :* summer ski courses in Val-d'Isère, Tignes, Les Ménuires ; tennis in Méribel, Val-Thorens, Courchevel ; canoeing in Lanslebourg ; riding in Val-d'Isère ; martial arts in Courchevel ; competition running in Courchevel and Méribel ; archery in Montchavin and Valmorel, etc. ; *cultural courses :* dance, music, theatre in Val-d'Isère, Courchevel and Les Arcs ; photography in La Norma, Les Ménuires and Montchavin ; *mountain discovery courses* in Champagny, Peisey-Nancroix and Val-d'Isère ; other more novel courses such as micro-computer work in Lans-le-Villard, bridge and *nouvelle cuisine* in Les Arcs, etc. Enq : *Assn. Dép. de Tourisme de Savoie* ☎ 79.85.12.45.

Golf : Aix-les-Bains (18 holes) ; Annecy (18 holes) ; Bourg-Saint-Maurice (18 holes) ; Chamonix (9 holes) ; Évian (18 holes) ; Megève (18 holes) ; Méribel (9 holes) ; Tignes (9 holes).

Tennis : *Ligue régionale,* pdt M. Antoine Lovera, 143, rue des Alliés, 38100 Grenoble.

Aquatic sports : the Savoie-Mont-Blanc C.R.T. publishes a brochure listing stretches of water in the Savoie region.

Canoeing : list of schools and clubs, and enq at the *Assn. Dép. de Tourisme de Savoie.*

Mountaineering : list of shelters and enq at the *Assn. Dép. de Tourisme de la Savoie.*

Winter sports : *cross-country skiing :* the *Assn. Dép. de Tourisme de la Savoie* offers numerous courses.

Hunting and shooting : *Féd. Dép. des Chasseurs*

de Savoie, 15, rue Nivolet, 73000 Chambéry, ☎ 79.62.04.61. *Féd. Dép. des Chasseurs de Haute-Savoie,* 9 *bis,* av. Berthollet, 74000 Annecy, ☎ 50.57.14.27.

Fishing : *la Féd. Dép. des Assn. de Pêche et de Pisciculture de la Savoie,* plage de la Glière, 73240 Saint-Genix-sur-Guiers, ☎ 76.31.61.53, publishes the list of affiliated associations, along with a map of stretches of water : perch, pike, trout, fresh-water char, carp.

● Towns

ABONDANCE

Thonon 28, Annecy 102, Paris 607
B1 ⛷ 950-1800 m ⊠ 74360

ⓘ mairie, ☎ 50.73.02.90.

Hotels :
★★***Bel Air*** (L.F.), Richebourg, ☎ 50.73.01.71. 22 rm [P] closed 20 Apr-20 May, 180. Rest. ♦ closed Wed low season, 80-130.
★***Touristes,*** ☎ 50.73.02.15. 28 rm [P] closed 15 Sep-15 Dec, 15 Apr-15 Jun, 220. Rest. 100-170.

AIGUEBELETTE-LE-LAC

Chambéry 21, Grenoble 59, Paris 553
A2-3 ⊠ 73610 Lépin-le-Lac

ⓘ pl. de la Gare, Lépin-le-Lac, 5 km W, ☎ 79.36.00.02.

Hotels :
Saint-Alban-de-Montbel, 7 km NW :

★★***St-Alban Plage,*** ☎ 79.36.02.05. 20 rm [P] ♿ closed 1 Oct-Easter, 245.

Novalaise, ⊠ 73470, 7 km N :
★★***Novalaise-Plage,*** ☎ 79.36.02.19. 16 rm [P] closed 1 Nov-1 Apr, Mon eve and Tue low season. Alongside the lake (private beach), 210. Rest. ♦ 55-160.

⛺ Novalaise : ★★*le Grand Verney* (83 pl.), ☎ 79.36.02.54 ; ★★*les Chavannes* (117 pl.), ☎ 79.36.02.82.

AIX-LES-BAINS

Chambéry 16, Annecy 34, Paris 567
A2 ⊠ 73100

⛲ year-round, ☎ 79.35.38.50.

ⓘ pl. M.-Mollard (C2), ☎ 79.35.05.92.

✈ Chambéry-Aix-les-Bains, 6 km SW, ☎ 79.61.46.00.

⛴ regular daily service from the Grand-Port : *Cie de Navigation du Lac du Bourget,* ☎ 79.35.05.19, 79.61.45.75, 79.61.42.40. Supp. service on Sun for mass (Gregorian chant) at Hautecombe Abbey. Excursion to the Rhône, via the north of the lake and the Savières canal : Mon-Fri (Jul-Aug) and Mon (Jun-Sep) : departure Grand-Port 2:45 pm and return 6:15 pm.

SNCF (B2), ☎ 79.35.03.87.

🚌 pl. Clemenceau (B1), ☎ 79.35.09.33.

Car-hire : *Budget* train + car, at the station, ☎ 79.35.14.30, and at the airport.

Hotels :
★★★***International Rivollier,*** 18, av. Ch.-de-Gaulle (B2-3), ☎ 79.35.21.00. 62 rm. Tx 320410. AE, DC [P] ♿ 225. Rest. ♦♦♦ 70-140.
★★★***Manoir*** (L.F., Relais du Silence), 37, rue George-I[er] (C3), ☎ 79. 61.44.00. 72 rm [P] closed 23 Dec-1 Feb, 300. Rest. ♦♦ 120-210.
★★***Dauphinois*** (L.F.), 14, av. de Tresserve (B3), ☎ 79.61.22.56. 84 rm [P] ♿ 205. Rest. ♦ closed Sun eve and Mon (Nov-Mar), 70-135.
★★***Lille,*** Grand-Port (3 km NE), ☎ 79.35.04.22. 18 rm. AE, DC, Visa [P] ♿ closed Jan-Feb, 230. Rest. ♦ closed Wed. Remarkable dishes. Spec : fresh-water char cooked in champagne, 100-250.
★★***Pastorale*** (L.F.), 221, av. du Grand-Port, ☎ 79.35.25.36. 30 rm. AE [P] closed 15 Feb-1 Apr, 230. Rest. ♦♦ closed Sun eve and Mon, 70-135.

Grand-Port, 3 km NE :
★★***Davat,*** 21, chemin des Bateliers, ☎ 79.35.09.63. 20 rm [P] closed 2 Nov-20 Mar, 225. Rest. ♦ closed Tue. Classic cooking : stuffed quail, *délice de foie de canard, gratin de queues d'écrevisses,* 75-170.

Pugny-Chatenod, 5 km E :
★★***Clairefontaine*** (L.F.), rte du Revard, ☎ 79.61.47.09. 19 rm. Euro, Visa [P] closed 15 Oct-25 Mar, 190. Rest. ♦ 65-140.

Ruffieux, ⊠ 73310 Chindrieux, 21 km N of Aix on D991 :
★★★***Château de Collonges*** (Relais du Silence), ☎ 79.62.27.38. 10 rm. AE, Visa [P] ♿ closed Jan, 335. Rest. ♦♦ closed Sun eve and Mon low season, 120-210.

⛺ ★★★ *Sierroz* (300 pl.), ☎ 79.61.21.43 ; ★★ *Elvire* (100 pl.), ☎ 79.61.07.91

Casino : palais de Savoie (B2).

ALBERTVILLE

Annecy 45, Chambéry 49, Paris 610
A2 ⊠ 73200

ⓘ pl. de la Gare, ☎ 79.32.04.22.

SNCF ☎ 79.32.49.83.

🚌 Val-d'Arley buses, ☎ 79.31.61.14.

Car-hire : *Budget* train + car, at the station, ☎ 79.32.40.50.

Hotels :
★★★***Million*** (Philippe Million ; Relais et châteaux), 8, pl. de la Liberté, ☎ 79.32.25.15. AE, DC, Visa. 29 rm [P] ♿ closed 25 Apr-10 May, 25 Sep-10 Oct, 300. Rest. ● ♦♦♦ No need to spend a lot to appreciate Philippe Million's cooking. His beautiful place is a recommended stop : *marinade de poisson à la feuille de choux, raie à l'estragon aux langoustines.* Nice desserts, 130-380.

Grisy-sur-Isère, ⊠ 73460 Frontenex, 15 km SW :
★★***Tour de Racoret*** (Relais du Silence), ☎ 79.37.91.59. AE, Visa. 10 rm [P] closed 7 Oct-1 Mar, 270. Rest. ♦ 120-190.

Queige, ⊠ 73720, 12 km :
★***Auberge des Roches,*** rte de Beaufort, ☎ 79.38.02.18 [P] 14 rm, closed 10-30 Apr, 5 Nov-15 Dec 120. Rest. ● ♦ Simple, tasty fare to meet all budgets, 50-90.

⛺ ★*Adoubes* (134 pl.), ☎ 79.32.06.62.

Restaurants :
Saint-Vital, ☒ 73460 Frontenex, 10 km SW :
♦ ***Au Vieux Pressoir,*** ☎ 70.38.64.07 closed Sun eve and Mon, 60-150.

Recommended : *Parat,* chocolates, 39, rue de la République. *Aminthas,* cheese shop, 71, rue de la République.

AMPHION-LES-BAINS

Thonon 6, Annecy 80, Paris 585
3,5 km from Évian, B1
☒ 74500 Évian-les-Bains

ℹ rés. de la Rive, ☎ 50.72.00.63 (high season).

excursions, tour of the lake : enq at the S.I. or *Cie générale de Navigation* c/o Office des Baigneurs in Évian, ☎ 50.75.27.53.

Hotels :
★★***Plage,*** ☎ 50.72.00.06. 38 rm closed 25 Sep-20 May, 180. Rest. ♦ 80-130.
★★***Amiral,*** rue du Lac, ☎ 50.70.00.36. 13 rm. closed Oct-May, 130. Rest. ♦ 70-100.

Publier, 1.5 km S :
★★***Chablais,*** ☎ 50.75.28.06. 25 rm closed 1 wk at Easter, 2 wks in Oct and Sun low season, 160. Rest. 55-120.

★★★★*La Plage* (86 pl. ; caravaning in winter), ☎ 50.70.00.46 ; ★★*Grand Pré* (32 pl.), ☎ 50.70.00.45.

ANNECY

Geneva 57, Lyons 137, Paris 550
A2 ☒ 74000

ℹ 1, rue J.-Jaurès, Bonlieu, ☎ 50.45.00.33.

SNCF (A2), ☎ 50.45.52.44.

✈ Meythet, 4 km NW, ☎ 50.57.53.42.
Air France Agency, rés. l'Araucaria, 5, allée des Platanes.

Compagnie des Bateaux du lac d'Annecy, ☎ 50.51.08.40 : tour of the lake with stops in the small villages : duration 1 hr 30.

Car-hire : *Budget* train + car : at the station, ☎ 50.45.03.63, and at Annecy airport.

Hotels :
● ★★★★***Tresoms,*** 3, bd de la Corniche (not on the C3 map), ☎ 50.51.43.84. 44 rm closed 15 Nov-1 Mar, 500. Rest. ♦♦♦ 120-210.
★★★***Splendid,*** 4, quai Chappuis (B2), ☎ 50.45.20.00. Tx 385233. Visa. 53 rm closed 24 Dec-2 Jan, 280. Rest. ***la Taverne,*** 120-210.
★★***Allobroges*** (L.F.), 11, rue Sommeiller (B2), ☎ 50.45.03.11. AE, Euro, Visa. 55 rm 220.

★★*Belvédère* (250 pl.), ☎ 50.45.48.30 ; ★★*Pré d'Avril* (50 pl.), ☎ 50.23.64.46 ; ★★*Petit-Port* (100 pl.), ☎ 50.23.45.25.

Restaurants :
♦♦♦ ***Auberge de Savoie,*** 1, pl. St-François (B3), ☎ 50.45.03.05 closed mid-Jun-mid-Jul, Tue eve and Wed low season. Spec : *terrine de brochet, aiguillettes de canard au coing,* 135-230.
● ♦♦ ***Le Boutae,*** 10, rue Vaugelas (A-B2), ☎ 50.45.62.94. AE, Euro, Visa closed Feb school hols, 1-16 Aug, Sun and Tue eve. Spec : *saumon à l'oseille,* fish from the lake, 70-100.
♦♦ ***Belvédère,*** chemin du Belvédère, ☎ 50.45.04.90 closed 3 wks in Apr, Nov, Sun eve and Mon. Dishes prepared with all the subtlety and experience of a great chef ; excellent service, enhanced by an unrivalled view over the lake. Saltwater fish specialities, 120-310.
♦♦ ***Salino,*** 13, rue Jean-Mermoz, at Annecy-le-Vieux, ☎ 50.23.07.90. AE, Euro, Visa closed a week in Feb, 17 Jun-10 Jul, Wed and Sun eve. Spec : *gigot de lotte dans sa fondue acidulée, pigeon de Bresse rôti sauce salmis,* 130-250.

Recommended : *le Fréti* cheese shop, 73, rue Carnot ; *Debauge,* pl. St-Maurice for the chocolates called "roseaux d'Annecy" ; antiques, *M. Forain,* rue du Pâquier, ☎ 50.45.15.17.

ANNEMASSE

Geneva 8, Annecy 51, Paris 550
A1 ☒ 74100

ℹ hôtel de ville, ☎ 50.92.53.03.

SNCF ☎ 50.37.00.72.

Car-hire : *Budget* train + car, 57, av. de la Gare, ☎ 50.38.50.09.

Hotels :
★★★***Central Hôtel,*** 2, pl. de l'Hôtel-de-Vile, ☎ 50.38.27.06. 28 rm. 225.

Bons-en-Chalais, ☒ 74890, 15 km NE :
★***La Couronne,*** Grand'Rue, ☎ 50.43.11.17. 12 rm closed 20 Dec-1 Feb, Sun eve and Mon, 200. Rest. ● ♦♦ Attractive fare served in a charming inn with a delightful garden ; the owner, Pierre Mignan, prefers real quality to the superficially spectacular, 60-210.

Les ARCS

Bourg-St-Maurice 12, Chambéry 113, Paris 674
B2 ☒ 73700 Bourg-Saint-Maurice

1 600-3 000 m

ℹ Maison des Arcs : 1 600 m, ☎ 79.07.73.73, at 1 800 m, ☎ 79.07.26.00, and S.I., ☎ 79.07.04.92. In Paris : 83, bd du Montparnasse, ☎ (1) 42.22.15.30 ; 98, bd du Montparnasse, ☎ (1) 43.22.43.32 ; rue de la Pompe, ☎ (1) 45.53.80.75.

Hotels :
★★★***Cachette Pierre Blanche,*** Arc 1 600, ☎ 79.07.73.73. Tx 980016. AE, DC, Visa. 78 rm, closed 15 Apr-1 Jul, 1 Sep-17 Dec, 380. Rest. Hotel-Club, Flat rate only, ski-lifts included.
★★★***Trois Arcs,*** Arc 1 600, ☎ 79.07.78.78. Visa. 48 rm closed 17 Apr-17 Dec. Half pension, 600. Pens, 680. Rest. ♦♦ 80-130.
★★★***Golf,*** Arc 1 800, ☎ 79.07.25.17. Tx 980404. Visa. 300 rm in summer closed 30 Apr-25 Jun and 15 Sep-15 Dec, 360. Rest. ♦♦♦ ***le Green,*** 120-400.

ARGENTIÈRE

Geneva 91, Annecy 104, Paris 624
8 km NE of Chamonix, B2
☒ 74400 Chamonix-Mont-Blanc

1 253-3 271 m

Hotels :
★★***Bellevue,*** 274, rue Charlet-Stratton, ☎ 50.54.00.03. AE, Visa. 17 rm closed 20 May-20 Jun and Oct-Nov, 300.
★★***Dahu,*** 325, rue Charlet-Stratton, ☎ 50.54.01.55. AE, Euro, Visa. 22 rm closed 17 Oct-15 Dec and 15 May-15 Jun, 180. Rest. ♦ closed Wed (15 Sep-15 Oct), 45-150.
★★***Grands Montets,*** 340, chem. des Arberons, ☎ 50.54.06.66. Euro, Visa. 41 rm closed 20 Dec and 5 May-1 Jun, 310.

Montroc-sur-Argentière, 2 km N :
★★★***Becs Rouges,*** ☎ 50.54.01.00. 24 rm closed 30 Apr-15 Jun, 15 Sep-15 Dec, 260. Rest. ♦♦ 90-175.

Plateau d'ASSY

Chamonix 32, Annecy 80, Paris 609
B1-2 ⊠ 74480

ℹ av. Dr-Arnaud, ☎ 50.58.80.52.

Hotel :
★★***Tourisme,*** ☎ 50.58.80.54. 15 rm closed 25 Oct-10 Nov and Wed, 100.

AVORIAZ

Chamonix 86, Annecy 109, Paris 604
B1 ⊠ 74110 Morzine

1 800-2 275 m

ℹ Maison d'Avoriaz, ☎ 50.74.02.11.

Hotels :
★★★***Dromonts,*** 1 800 m, ☎ 50.74.08.33. AE, DC, Euro, Visa. 40 rm 750. Rest. ♦♦ closed 15 Apr-15 Dec, 200-300.
★★***Hauts-Forts,*** ☎ 50.74.09.11. 50 rm closed 20 Apr-10 Dec, 560. Rest. ♦♦ 120-210.

BEAUFORT-SUR-DORON

Albertville 20, Chambéry 69, Paris 630
B2 ⊠ 73270

ℹ pl. de la Mairie, ☎ 79.31.23.40.

Hotels :
★***Roche,*** ☎ 79.31.20.16. 17 rm closed Nov, 70. Rest. ♦ 80-130.

★Municipal *de Domelin* (100 pl.), ☎ 79.31.20.44.

BONNEVAL-SUR-ARC

Val-d'Isère 30, Chambéry 45, Paris 704
B3 ⊠ 73480 Lanslebourg-Mont-Cenis

1 800-3 250 m

ℹ ☎ 79.05.08.08.

Hotels :
● ★★***Bergerie,*** ☎ 79.05.94.97. Euro, Visa. 22 rm closed 1 May-15 Jun, 20 Sep-15 Dec, 145. Rest. ♦ 55-70.
★***Glacier des Évettes*** (L.F.), ☎ 79.05.94.06. 19 rm closed 1 Nov-10 Dec, 180. Rest. 120-210.

Bessans, 6 km N :
★***Mont Iseran,*** pl. de la Mairie, ☎ 79.05.95.97. 20 rm closed 25 Apr-25 Jun and 1 Oct-20 Dec, 120. Rest. 50-65.

Restaurant :
♦♦ ***Pré Catin,*** ☎ 79.05.95.07. Euro ; closed 5 May-27 Jun, 29 Sep-18 Dec and Mon, 50-80.

BONNEVILLE

Annecy 41, Chamonix 56, Paris 570
A1 ⊠ 74130

ℹ rue Carroz, ☎ 50.97.20.64.

SNCF ☎ 50.97.00.15.

Restaurant :
● ♦♦♦ ***Sapeur et Vivandière,*** pl. de l'Hôtel-de-Ville, ☎ 50.97.20.68. AE, DC, Visa closed Sun eve (low season), Mon, end Aug-beg Sep, end Dec-beg Jan. A well thought-out menu, carefully prepared dishes. Reasonable prices in a friendly atmosphere. Spec : *turbot aux cèpes,* 75-200.

Le BOURGET-DU-LAC

Aix-les-Bains 9, Chambéry 11, Paris 562
A2 ⊠ 73370

ℹ pl. des Marronniers (high season), ☎ 79.25.01.99.

boats for Aix-les-Bains : enq at the *Cie de Navigation du lac du Bourget,* ☎ 79.35.05.19.

Hotels :
● ★★★★***Ombremont*** (Relais et châteaux), RN504, rte du Tunnel, ☎ 79.25.00.23. Tx 980832. AE, DC, Euro, Visa. 20 rm closed 15 Nov-2 Feb, 560. Rest. ● ♦♦♦ closed Sat noon ex Jul-Aug and Mon noon, 150-250.
★★***Port,*** lake, ☎ 79.25.00.21. 30 rm closed Jan and Thu. Beside the lake, 195. Rest. ♦ 85-140.

Le Caton, 2.5 km NW :
★***La Cerisaie,*** ☎ 79.25.01.29. Euro, Visa. 10 rm closed 1 Nov-beg May, 140. Rest. ♦ Chalet setting. Fish, *feuilleté d'escargots à la mousse d'ail,* 55-160.

★★★*Ile aux Cygnes* (267 pl.), ☎ 79.25.01.76.

Restaurants :
● ♦♦♦ ***Le Bateau Ivre,*** ☎ 79.25.02.66 Restaurant with terrace in a former barn ; delightful setting and service ; closed 11 Nov-beg May and Tue. Subtle, refined cooking. Spec : *pigeon farci et rôti sauce pleurotes,* 145-400.

At the entrance to the Mont-du-Chat tunnel :
♦♦ ***Auberge Lamartine,*** rte du tunnel du Chat, Bourdeau, ☎ 79.25.01.03 closed 1 Dec-25 Jan, Sun eve and Mon, 150-220.

BOURG-SAINT-MAURICE

Chamonix 83, Chambéry 101, Paris 662
B2 ⊠ 73700

800-1 600 m

ℹ pl. de Castex, ☎ 79.07.04.92.

SNCF ☎ 79.07.00.74.

Car-hire : *Budget* train + car, at the station, ☎ 79.07.15.70.

Hotels :
★★***Host. Petit Saint-Bernard,*** 2, av. du Stade, ☎ 79.07.04.32. AE, DC, Visa. 24 rm closed May-Jun, Oct-Nov, 150. Rest. ♦ 60-80.
★***Petite Auberge,*** le Reverset, ☎ 79.07.05.86. 13 rm closed Apr-May, Oct, 180. Rest. 80-130.

★★★★*Vallée Haute Renouveau* (37 pl.), ☎ 79.07.18.07.

Restaurants :
♦ ***Édelweiss,*** pl. de la Gare, ☎ 79.07.05.55 closed Jun, 1-15 Nov, 40-120.
♦ ***Val d'Isère,*** pl. de la Gare, ☎ 79.07.12.59. AE, Euro, Visa closed 2 May-2 Jun and Oct-Nov, 80-150.

BRIDES-LES-BAINS

Annecy 77, Chambéry 79, Paris 640
6 km SE of Moûtiers, B2-3
⊠ 73600 Moûtiers-Tarentaise

(mid-Apr-end Oct), ☎ 79.55.23.44.

ℹ rue Leray, ☎ 79.55.20.64.

Hotel :
★★★***Savoy,*** ☎ 79.55.20.55. 40 rm closed 1 Oct-10 May, 250. Rest. ♦♦ 80-130.

Casino : ☎ 79.55.23.07. In the warm spring park.

Les CARROZ-D'ARACHES

Chamonix 51, Annecy 73, Paris 596
13 km SE of Cluses, B1 ⊠ 74300 Cluses

1 150-1 850 m

ℹ ☎ 50.90.00.04.

Hotels :
★★★***Arbaron,*** ☎ 50.90.02.67. Tx 385281. 30 rm ⚘ Ⓟ ♨ ⛱ closed 15 Apr-15 Jun, 25 Sep-15 Dec, 310. Rest. ♦♦ ✂ only half-pension or pension, 105-145.

★★***Croix de Savoie*** (L.F.), Le Pernant, ☎ 50.90.00.26. Visa. 19 rm ⚘ Ⓟ ♨ ⛱ ✂ closed 15 Apr-15 Jun, 5 Sep-15 Dec, 200. Rest. ♦ 80-110.

CHALLES-LES-EAUX

Albertville 14, Annecy 55, Paris 567
6 km SE of Chambéry, A2 ⊠ 73190

⚕ ☎ 79.85.20.04.

ⓘ av. Chambéry, ☎ 79.25.10.13.

Hotels :
★★★***Château de Challes,*** ☎ 79.85.21.45. AE, Visa. 75 rm Ⓟ ♨ ⛱ ⛆ ⚲ ♿ closed 30 Nov-1 Feb, 180. Rest. ♦♦ ✂ 75-160.
★★***Château de Trivier*** (Châteaux-hôtels), ☎ 79.85.07.27. 30 rm Ⓟ ♨ ⛱ ♿ 300. Rest. ♦ Good, simple fare, 75-170.

⛺ ★★★*Savoy* (88 pl.), ☎ 79.70.40.81 ; ★★*Mont-Saint-Michel* (100 pl.), ☎ 79.85.20.73.

Casino : ☎ 79.85.20.07.

CHAMBÉRY

Grenoble 55, Lyons 98, Paris 561
A2 ⊠ 73000

ⓘ 24, bd de la Colonne (B1), ☎ 79.33.42.47.

✈ Chambéry-Aix-les-Bains, 8 km NW, ☎ 79.61.42.77.

SNCF (C1), ☎ 79.62.93.50.

Car-hire : *Budget* train + car, 15, quai de la Rize, ☎ 79.33.28.09, 79.33.04.12, at the station, ☎ 79.62.31.02, and at the airport.

Hotels :
★★★***Grand Hôtel Ducs de Savoie,*** 6, pl. de la Gare (B1), ☎ 79.69.54.54. Tx 320910. AE, DC, Visa. 55 rm Ⓟ ♨ ♿ closed 15-30 Jul, 450. Rest. ♦♦ closed Sun, 90-250.
★★***Pervenches*** (L.F.), les Charmettes, 2 km SE, ☎ 79.33.34.26. 13 rm ⚘ Ⓟ ⛱ ✂ closed Feb school hols, 16 Aug-10 Sep, 100. Rest. ♦ closed Wed and Sun eve, 80-130.

Restaurants :
● ♦♦♦ ***Roubatcheff,*** 6, rue du Théatre (B-C2), ☎ 79.33.24.91. AE, Visa ♿ closed 10 Jul-10 Aug, Sun eve and Mon. Unusual and exotic ; the fare is predictably Russian, like the name of the restaurant : the Caucasus in the French Alps ! Spec : *fondant de saumon frais, panaché de rouget et bar au pinot rouge,* 120-300.
● ♦♦ ***Vanoise,*** 6, place de la Gare, ☎ 79.69.02.78. Ⓟ⛱ closed Sun. Pierre Lenain is a great chef. Spec. : *huîtres chaudes aux épinards, lotte au lard et choucroute,* 95-250.
♦♦ ***Tonneau,*** 2, rue Saint-Antoine (B1), ☎ 79.33.78.26. AE, Euro, Visa. Terrace ♿ closed 5-25 Aug, Mon and Tue. Traditional and regional dishes, 50-100.
♦ ***Le Sporting,*** 88, rue Croix d'Or (B2), ☎ 79.33.17.43. AE, Euro, Visa ♿ For enthusiasts of meats and Savoie wines, 50-90.

Guided tours : ⓘ and C.N.M.H.S., ☎ 79.33.42.47.

Recommended : *Michaud* for ices, cakes and pastries, 5, bd du Théâtre (near the Elephants fountain).

CHAMONIX-MONT-BLANC

Geneva 80, Annecy 93, Paris 624
B2 ⛷ 1 035-3 842 m ⊠ 74400

ⓘ pl. de l'Église, ☎ 50.53.00.24.

✈ buses for Geneva airport, 90 km.

SNCF ☎ 79.53.12.98.

Car-hire : *Budget* train + car, at the station, ☎ 79.53.00.44.

Hotels :
★★★★***Auberge du Bois Prin,*** 69, chemin de l'Hermine, Les Moussoux, ☎ 79.53.33.51. AE, Euro, Visa. 11 rm ⚘ Ⓟ ♨ ⛱ closed 5 May-13 Jun and 6 Oct-18 Dec, 750 Rest. ♦♦ ♿ closed Wed eve low season. Reservations necessary to sample this excellent cooking, 130-220.
★★★★***Mont Blanc,*** pl. de l'Église, ☎ 79.53.05.64. Tx 385614. AE, Euro, Visa. 54 rm ⚘ Ⓟ ♨ ⛆ in summer ⚲ closed 15 Oct-15 Dec, 580. Rest. ***Matafan*** ♦♦ 130-180.
★★★***Albert Iᵉʳ,*** 119, imp. du Montenvers, ☎ 79.53.05.09. Tx 380779, 34 rm ⚘ Ⓟ ♨ ⛆ ⚲ ♿ closed 21 Apr-16 May and 6 Oct-29 Nov, 370. Rest. ♦♦♦ ✂ 110-240.
★★★***Sapinière-Montana,*** 102, rue Mummery, ☎ 79.53.07.63. 30 rm ⚘ Ⓟ ♨ ✂ closed Oct-15 Dec and 15 Apr-15 May, 230. Rest. ♦ closed May, Oct-Nov, 120-220.
★★***Hermitage et Paccard,*** rue des Cristalliers, ☎ 79.53.13.87. Tx 385417. AE, DC, Visa. 29 rm ⚘ Ⓟ ♨ ⛱ ♿ closed 2 May-1 Jun, 1 Oct-15 Dec, 290. Rest. ♦♦ 90-120.

Les Bossons, 3.5 km SW :
★★***L'Aiguille du Midi,*** 479, chemin Napoléon, ☎ 79.53.00.65. 50 rm ⚘ Ⓟ ♨ ⛆ ⚲ ♿ closed 20 Sep-20 Dec, 220. Rest. ♦ ✂ 80-150.

Le Lavancher, 6 km NE :
● ★★***Gentianes*** (L.F., Relais du Silence), RN 506, ☎ 79.54.01.31. Tx 385022. 14 rm ⚘ Ⓟ ♨ ⛱ ✂ closed 20 Apr-1 Jun, 28 Sep-20 Dec. Half pension in season, 260. Rest. ♦ 80-100.
● ★★***Beausoleil*** (L.F.), ☎ 79.54.00.78. 17 rm ⚘ Ⓟ ♨ ⛱ ⚲ closed 20 Sep-20 Dec, high season pension or half pension, 220. Rest. ✂ 60-120.
● ★***Beauséjour,*** ☎ 79.54.00.76. 11 rm ⚘ ♨ ⛱ closed 8 May-15 Jun and 30 Sep-20 Dec. Pens., 300. Half-pens., 260. Rest. ♿ 40-80.

⛺ ★★★*Les Deux Glaciers* (80 pl.), ☎ 79.53.15.84 ; ★★*les Drus* (70 pl.), ☎ 79.53.18.05 ; ★★*Mont Blanc-Les Rosières* (120 pl.), ☎ 79.53.10.42.

Restaurants :
♦♦ ***Bartavel,*** 26, cours du Bartavel, ☎ 79.53.26.51. AE, Euro, Visa ; closed 12 Nov-15 Dec, end May-early Jun, Sun eve and Mon. Specialities from the Quercy region, 70-200.
♦ ***Le Chouca,*** 206, rue Paccard, ☎ 79.53.03.23. AE, DC, Visa ; closed 10 days in Jun, 10 in Nov, Mon low season. Mountain atmosphere, 80-120.
♦ ***Brasserie des Alpes,*** 148, rue Dr-Paccard, ☎ 79.53.15.25. Closed Mon. Spec : *fondue, escalope soufflée au fromage,* 80-130.
La Potinière, pl. Balmat, ☎ 79.53.02.84, 80-130.

Casino : ☎ 79.53.07.65.

CHÂTEL

Thonon 39, Annecy 114, Paris 618
B1 ⛷ 1 200-2 080 m ⊠ 74390

ⓘ ☎ 50.73.22.44.

Hotels :
★★★***Macchi,*** ☎ 50.73.24.12. 32 rm ⚘ Ⓟ ♿ closed 15 Apr-25 Jun, 1 Sep-20 Dec, 230. Rest. ♦♦ 65-110.

La Chapelle-d'Abondance, ⊠ 74360, 5.5 km NW :
★★***Chabi,*** ☎ 50.73.50.14. Visa. 22 rm ⚘ Ⓟ ♨ ⛱ closed 15 Apr-28 Jun and 1 Sep-20 Dec, 210. Rest. ♦ 80-130.

★***Alpage*** (L.F.), ☎ 50.73.20.26. 24 rm 🄿 ≋ closed 15 Apr-15 Jun, 15 Sep-15 Dec, 100. Rest. ⊘ 80-130.

⛺ ★★★*L'Oustalet* (100 pl.), ☎ 50.73.21.97.

La CLUSAZ

Annecy 32, Albertville 40, Paris 568
A2 ⛷ 1 100-2 600 m ⊠ 74220

ℹ pl. de l'Église, ☎ 50.02.60.92.

Hotels :
● ★★★***Aravis 1500*** (L.F.), Les Étages, ☎ 50.02.61.13. 18 rm ⚟ 🄿 ≋ ⚘ ☐ ♿ closed 20 Apr-1 Jul, 31 Aug-15 Dec, 290. Rest. ♦♦♦ 65-100.
★★***Vieux Chalet,*** Les Tollets, ☎ 50.02.41.53. 7 rm 🄿 ⊘ closed 15 Jun-4 Jul, 13 Oct-8 Nov, 190. Rest. ♦♦ closed Tue, Wed and Thu low season, 75-190.
★★***Aravis*** (L.F.) Village, ☎ 50.02.60.31. 41 rm ⚟ ≋ ⚲ ♿ closed Easter-22 Jun and 4 Sep-17 Dec, 220. Rest. ♦ ♿ 55-120.
★★***Christiania*** (L.F.), ☎ 50.02.60.60. 30 rm 🄿 ≋ ⊘ ♿ closed 18 Sep-18 Dec, 20 Apr-30 Jun, 210. Rest. ♦♦ ♿ 65-110.

Youth hostel : *le Marcoret,* rte du Col de Croix-Fry, B.P. 47, ☎ 50.02.41.73.

⛺ ★★★*Plan du Fernuy* (33 pl.), ☎ 50.02.44.75.

Restaurants :
♦ ***Dallian,*** ☎ 50.02.41.24. 80-130.
♦ ***Braise,*** closed 15 May-15 Jun, 15 Sep-15 Nov. Spec : pizzas cooked in a wood oven, 60-130.

COMBLOUX

Chamonix 35, Annecy 65, Paris 605
5 km NE of Megève, B2 ⛷ ⊠ 74920

ℹ Pavillon savoyard, rte Nationale, ☎ 50.58.60.49.

Hotels :
★★★★***Ducs de Savoie,*** le Bouchet, ☎ 50.58.61.43. AE, Visa. 50 rm ⚟ over mont Blanc 🄿 ≋ ⚘ ☐ ♿ closed 15 Apr-8 Jun, 22 Sep-20 Dec. 360. Rest. ♦♦ 90-120.
★★★***Aiguilles de Warens*** (L.F.), Basseville, ☎ 50.58.70.18. AE, Visa. 34 rm 🄿 ≋ closed 15 Apr-20 Jun, 300. Rest. ⊘ ♿ closed 18 Sep-21 Dec, 90-110.
★★***Cœur des Prés,*** ☎ 50.58.70.55. Tx 385550. 35 rm ⚟ 🄿 ≋ ⚘ ♿ closed 15 Apr-1 Jun, 15 Sep-20 Dec, 210. Rest. ♦ ⊘ ♿ 50-130.

Les CONTAMINES-MONTJOIE

Chamonix 34, Annecy 96, Paris 618
8.5 km S of Saint-Gervais, B2
⛷ ⊠ 74190 Le Fayet

ℹ pl. de la Mairie, ☎ 50.47.01.58.

Hotels :
★★★***La Chemenaz,*** les Hameaux du Lac, ☎ 50.47.02.44. 38 rm ⚟ 🄿 ≋ ⚘ ☐ ♿ closed 15 Apr-15 May, 1 Oct-15 Dec, 290. Rest. ♦ 70-110.
★★***Chamois,*** ☎ 50.47.03.43. 17 rm ⚟ 🄿 ≋ closed 15 Apr-1 Jul, 1 Sep-15 Dec, 220. Rest. ♦ closed in summer, 80-105.

COURCHEVEL

Albertville 51, Chambéry 97, Paris 658
B3 ⊠ 73120

⛷ Le Pras 1 300 m, Courchevel 1 550 m, Moriond 1 650 m, Courchevel 1 850 m (cable-car providing access to the Méribel Valley), and summer resort : 1 600-3 000 m.

ℹ ☎ 79.08.03.29.

Hotels :
● ★★★★***Pralong 2000*** (Relais et châteaux), rte de l'Altiport, Courchevel 1850, ☎ 79.08.24.82. Tx 980231. AE, DC, Visa. 72 rm ⚟ 🄿 ⚘ ☐ closed 10 Apr-20 Dec, 1 540. Full or half pension only. Rest. ● ♦♦♦ ***le Paral*** ♿ closed noon and Mon. Spec : *consommé de crabes aux queues de langoustines, truffes en papillote de choux, filet de morue à la lie de vin,* 220-240.
● ★★★★***Carlina Courchevel 1850*** (Relais et châteaux), ☎ 79.08.00.30. Tx 980248. AE, DC, Euro, Visa. 53 rm ⚟ 🄿 ⚘ closed 15 Apr-18 Dec. Pension only, 1 400. Rest. ● ♦♦ ⊘ Spec : *foie gras, fricassée de saint-pierre aux Saint-Jacques,* 180-225.
★★★★(L) ***Byblos des Neiges*** (Relais et châteaux), le Jardin Alpin, ☎ 79.08.12.12. Tx 980580. AE, DC, Visa. 69 rm 🄿 ☐ Rich people from St-Tropez can now maintain their tan all year long in this superb palace. Half or full pension only, 1 700-3 400. Rest. ♦♦♦ ***les Arches,*** A new team for a "cuisine nouvelle", 230-390.
★★★★***Annapurna,*** in Super-Pralong, ☎ 79.08.04.60. Tx 980324. AE, Euro, Visa. 68 rm ⚟ 🄿 ⚘ ☐ closed 15 Apr-15 Dec, 1 860. Rest. ♦♦ ⊘ ♿ Spec : *escalope de loup de mer aux huîtres et au champagne, noisette d'agneau Edouard VII,* 230-350.
★★★***Airelles,*** le Jardin Alpin 1850, ☎ 79.08.02.11, Tx 980190. 42 rm ⚟ 🄿 ⚘ ⊘ closed 20 Apr-15 Dec, 560. Pension only. Rest. ♦♦ 120-210.
★★★***Caravelle,*** le Jardin Alpin 1850, ☎ 79.08.02.42. Tx 980821. DC, Visa. 47 rm ⚟ 🄿 ⚘ ☐ ♿ closed 1 May-1 Dec, 580. Half-pension only. Rest. ♦♦ 75-165.
★★★***Pomme de Pin,*** Les Chenus, Courchevel 1850, ☎ 79.08.02.46. 36 rm, closed Easter-20 Dec ; mountain setting, terrace, Pens. or half-pens. only, 900. Rest. ● ♦♦ ***le Bateau Ivre.*** The Jacobs father and son love cooking fish and shellfish : *salade de langoustines,* 220-450.
★★★***Crystal 2000,*** rte de l'Altiport, ☎ 79.08.28.22. Tx 309170. Visa. 51 rm. closed 10 Apr-20 Dec. At the foot of the slopes. Half-pension only, 890. Rest. ♦♦ A satellite of the Pralong 2000, same comfort and very good quality cooking, 115-155.

Restaurant :
♦♦ ***La Bergerie,*** Courchevel 1850, ☎ 79.08.24.70. Closed 15 Apr-15 Dec, 60-250.

Classical music series : every Wed 6 pm (28 Dec-15 Apr) at the auditorium, ☎ 79.08.01.61 ; summer rehearsal space for young musicians.

CREST-VOLAND

Albertville 27, Annecy 56, Paris 605
6 km S of Flumet, A-B2
⛷ 1 134-1 500 m ⊠ 73590 Flumet

ℹ ☎ 79.31.62.57.

Hotel :
★★***Aravis,*** le Cernix, ☎ 79.31.63.81. 17 rm ⚟ 🄿 ≋ ⚘ closed 15 Apr-1 Jul, 1 Sep-20 Dec, 140. Rest. ♦ 70-100.

DOUSSARD

Albertville 26, Chambéry 68, Paris 568
19 km S of Annecy, A2 ⊠ 74210 Faverges

ℹ mairie, ☎ 50.44.30.45.

Hotels :
★★★***Marceau,*** ☎ 50.44.30.11. AE, Visa. 18 rm ⚟ 🄿 ≋ ⚘ ⚲ ♿ closed 1 Nov-1 Feb, hols, 280. Rest. ♦ 90-200.

Chaparon, 4 km N :
★★**Châtaigneraie,** (L.F.), ☎ 50.44.30.67. Tx 385417. AE, Euro, Visa. 26 rm closed 1 Nov-1 Feb, Sun eve and Mon low season, 220. Rest. ♦ ♿ 60-160.

⛺ ★★★*La Serraz* (133 pl.), ☎ 50.44.30.68 ; ★★★*le Lac Bleu* (216 pl.), ☎ 50.44.30.18.

DUINGT

Albertville 33, Chambéry 61, Paris 549
12 km SE of Annecy, A2 ✉ 74410 Saint-Jorioz

ℹ mairie, ☎ 50.68.67.07.

Compagnie des bateaux du lac d'Annecy : Dep to Annecy, 11:26-3:20 pm-4:07 pm-5 pm (end May-end Oct).

Hotel :
★★**Auberge du Roselet** (L.F.), ☎ 50.68.67.19. 17 rm closed 15 Oct-15 Feb. Private beach, 220. Rest. ♦ 80-180.

ÉVIAN-LES-BAINS

Geneva 42, Annecy 84, Paris 588
B1 ✉ 74500

☎ 50.75.04.26.

ℹ pl. de la Porte-d'Allinges (B1), ☎ 50.75.04.26.

Cie générale de Navigation (C1), boat service to Lausanne across Léman lake (Lausanne) ; enq Office des Baigneurs, ☎ 50.75.27.53.

SNCF ☎ 50.75.25.26.

Car-hire : *Budget* train + car, at the S.N.C.F. station, ☎ 50.26.44.84.

Hotels :
★★★★**Royal Club Évian,** south shore (C2), ☎ 50.75.14.00, Tx 385759. AE, DC, Euro, Visa. 200 rm ♿ closed 15 Dec-15 Feb, 1 480. Rest. ♦♦♦♦ 85-230.
● ★★★**Verniaz et ses Chalets** (Relais et châteaux), rte d'Abondance (C2), ☎ 50.75.04.90. Tx 385715. 45 rm closed Dec-Jan, 750. Rest. ● ♦♦ Nice restaurant in the quiet countryside : lake fish and sea shellfish, roasted and grilled meats, 135-265.
★★**Bourgogne,** 73, rue Nationale (B1), ☎ 50.75.01.05. AE, Euro, Visa. 9 rm ♿ closed 2 Nov-20 Dec, 250. Rest. ♦♦ closed Tue eve and Wed low season. Spec : *foie gras d'oie, filets de truite,* 110-200.

⛺ ★★*Braconnay de Grande Rive* (100 pl.), ☎ 50.75.01.17.

Restaurant :
♦♦♦ **Toque Royale** (casino), château de Blonay, ☎ 50.75.03.78. Eve only, 210-400.

FLAINE

Chamonix 66, Annecy 79, Paris 611
24 km SE of Cluses, B1 ✉ 74300 Cluses

1 600-2 480 m

ℹ ☎ 50.90.80.01.

Hotels :
★★★**Totem,** ☎ 50.90.80.64. 54 rm closed 22 Apr-15 Dec, 410. Rest. ♦♦ 150-220.
★★**Aujon,** ☎ 50.90.80.10. 120 rm ♿ closed 1 May-15 Dec, 330. Rest. 80-130.

Restaurant :
♦♦ **Kry's Eye,** ☎ 50.90.82.83. Euro, Visa ♿ closed 25 Apr-1 Jul, 1 Sep-20 Dec, 70-160.

FLUMET-VAL-D'ARLY

Albertville 21, Annecy 50, Paris 600
A-B2 1 000-1 800 m ✉ 73590

ℹ ☎ 79.31.61.08.

Hotel :
★★★**Hostellerie le Parc des Cèdres,** rue des Aravis, ☎ 79.31.72.37. 24 rm closed 15 Apr-25 May, 1 Oct-15 Dec, 230. Rest. ♦♦ 80-130.

Les GETS

Thonon 37, Annecy 86, Paris 597
B1 1 172-1 850 ✉ 74260

ℹ rte Nationale, ☎ 50.79.75.55.

Hotels :
★★★*La Marmotte* (L.F.), ☎ 50.79.75.39. 45 rm ♿ closed 15 Apr-30 Jun, 31 Aug-20 Dec, 310.
★★**Alpina,** ☎ 50.79.73.76. 29 rm closed 15 Apr-1 Jul, 9 Sep-20 Dec, 170. Rest. pension only, 70-90.

La GIETTAZ

Albertville 27, Chambéry 76, Paris 605
6 km N of Flumet, A-B2
1 100-1 900 m ✉ 73590 Flumet

ℹ ☎ 79.31.70.36.

Hotels :
★★**Relais des Aravis** (L.F.), ☎ 79.32.91.78. 27 rm closed 20 Apr-29 Jun, 15 Sep-20 Dec, 170. Rest. ♦ 80-160.
★**Vernes** (L.F.), le Plan, ☎ 79.32.92.68. Euro. 15 rm closed 20 Apr-15 Jun, 15 Sep-20 Dec, 110. Rest. 50-60.

Le GRAND-BORNAND

Annecy 32, Albertville 46, Paris 581
6 km N of La Clusaz, A2
950-1 850 m ✉ 74450

ℹ pl. de la Mairie, ☎ 50.02.20.33.

Hotels :
★★**Amborzales** (L.F.), Le Chinaillon, ☎ 50.27.02.50. 13 rm closed 20 Apr-30 Jun, 1 Sep-15 Dec, 140.
★★**Cortina** (L.F.), Le Chinaillon, ☎ 50.27.00.22. 30 rm closed 20 Apr-1 Jul, 1 Sep-15 Dec, 200. Rest. ♦ 80-200.
★★**Croix-Saint-Maurice** (L.F.), ☎ 50.02.20.05. 21 rm ♿ closed 20 Apr-20 Jun, 15 Sep-20 Dec, 175. Rest. ♦ ♿ 50-60.
★★**Saytels,** chef-lieu, ☎ 50.02.20.16. AE, Euro, Visa. 29 rm ♿ closed 15 Apr-1 Jul and 15 Sep-15 Dec, 240. Rest. ♦ ♿ Spec : *Raclettes, fondues,* carefully prepared meals, 60-110.

⛺ ★★★*L'Escale* (50 pl.), ☎ 50.02.20.69 ; ★★★*le Borne* (100 pl.), ☎ 50.02.22.45.

Market : the famous *reblochon* cheese market on Wed mornings.

Les HOUCHES

Geneva 72, Annecy 85, Paris 616
8 km SW of Chamonix, B2 ✉ 74310
1 113-1 900 m

ℹ ☎ 50.55.50.62.

Hotels :
★★**Christ-Tal,** la Griaz, ☎ 50.54.50.55. Visa. 25 rm closed 14-30 Apr (ex nat hols) and 1 Oct-20 Dec, 190. Rest. 60-150.
★★**Piste Bleue,** rte des Chavants, ☎ 50.54.40.66. 25 rm closed 15 Apr-20 Jun, 15 Sep-20 Dec, 180. Rest. ♦ for hotel guests only, 55-65.

⛺ ★★★★*Air Hôtel du Bourgeat* (35 pl.), ☎ 50.54.42.14 ; ★★★*le Petit Pont* (100 pl.), ☎ 50.54.41.30 ; ★★*le Clair de Lune* (50 pl.), ☎ 50.54.41.84.

Restaurants :
♦ ***Boîte à Sel,*** pl. du Téléphérique, ☎ 50.54.41.95. Closed May-15 Jun, Oct-15 Dec, 80-130.
♦ ***Fouffion,*** rés. du Goûter, ☎ 50.54.46.68. Visa ♿ closed 1 week Sep, Wed low season. Regional dishes, 40-125.

LANSLEBOURG-MONT-CENIS

Briançon 87, Chambéry 124, Paris 685
B3 1 500-2 800 m ☒ 73480

ℹ Maison du Val-Cenis, ☎ 79.05.23.66.

Hotels :
★★★***Alpazur*** (L.F., Inter-Hôtel), ☎ 79.05.93.69. AE, Euro, Visa. 24 rm P closed 13 Apr-10 Jun, 20 Sep-20 Dec, 225. Rest. ♦♦ ♿ 90-200.
★★***Relais des Deux Cols*** (L.F.), ☎ 79.05.92.83. 30 rm P closed 12 Apr-28 May, 25 Sep-20 Dec, 180. Rest. ♦ ♿ 60-100.

Lanslevillard, 3 km E :
★★***Prais*** (Relais du Silence), Val-Cenis, ☎ 79.05.93.53. DC, Euro. 30 rm. P closed 25 Apr-20 Jun, 10 Sep-15 Dec, 170. Rest. ♦ 60-150.

★ *Municipal* (133 pl.), in Lanslevillard, ☎ 79.05.90.52.

Youth hostel : hameau des Champs, ☎ 79.05.90.96.

La LÉCHÈRE

Albertville 21, Chambéry 68, Paris 629
6 km NW of Moûtiers
B2-3 ☒ 73260 Aigueblanche

(early Apr-end Oct), ☎ 79.24.11.33.

ℹ av. de l'Isère, ☎ 79.55.51.60.

Hotel :
★★★***Radiana,*** ☎ 79.22.61.61. 80 rm. Euro, Visa. P ♿ closed Nov-1 Feb, 290. Rest. ♦♦ 65-100.

MEGÈVE

Chamonix 36, Annecy 60, Paris 610
B2 1 113-2 040 m ☒ 74120

ℹ rue de la Poste, ☎ 50.21.27.28 and 50.21.29.52.

Hotels :
★★★★(L) ***Mont Blanc,*** ☎ 50.21.20.02. Tx 385854. AE, Euro, Visa. 65 rm P ♿ closed 15 Apr-23 May, 1 250. Rest. ***les Enfants Terribles,*** ♦♦ 150-200.
★★★***Au Vieux Moulin,*** rue Ambroise-Martin, ☎ 50.21.22.29. Tx 385532. 33 rm P closed 30 Sep-15 Dec, 15 Apr-15 May. Half-pension, 360. Rest. ♦♦ 80-140.
★★★***Castel Champlat,*** ☎ 50.21.25.49. 20 rm P closed 1 Sep-20 Dec, 15 Apr-20 Jul, 460. Rest. ♦♦ dinner only, 120-215.
★★★***Coin du Feu,*** rte de Rochebrune, ☎ 50.21.04.94. Visa. 23 rm ♿ closed 15 Apr-1 Jul, 10 Sep-15 Dec, 450. Rest. ♦♦ dinner only, 100-120.
★★***Gai Soleil*** (L.F.), 343, rue du Crêt-du-Midi, ☎ 50.21.00.70. Visa. 20 rm P closed 15 Apr-15 Jun, 20 Sep-12 Dec, 210. Rest. ♦ 60-90.
★★***Saint-Jean*** (L.F.), 87, boucle des Mouilles, ☎ 50.21.24.45. 15 rm P closed 15 Apr-1 Jul, 15 Sep-15 Dec, 280. Rest. ♦ 70.

Mont d'Arbois :
★★★★(L) ***Chalet du Mont d'Arbois*** (Relais et châteaux), rte du Mont d'Arbois, ☎ 50.21.25.03. Tx 309335. 12 rm P closed 14 Apr-14 Jun, 850. Rest. ♦♦♦ 230-400.

★★***Ferme Duvillard,*** ☎ 50.21.14.62. 19 rm P closed 15 Sep-30 Dec, 15 Apr-15 Jun, 255. Rest. ♦♦ 125-210.

★★ *Caravaneige municipal* (60 pl.), ☎ 50.21.14.60 ; ★★ *Gai Séjour* (60 pl.), ☎ 50.21.22.58.

Restaurants :
♦♦ ***Au Capucin Gourmand,*** rue du Crêt-du-Midi, ☎ 50.21.01.98. AE, Visa ♿ closed 25 Apr-22 Jun, 30 Sep-19 Dec and Mon low season, 140-250.
♦♦ ***Le Prieuré,*** pl. de l'Église, ☎ 59.21.01.79. AE, Visa ♿ closed 15 Apr-12 Jul, 10 Sep-20 Dec. Savoie tavern, regional cheeses, 135-160.
♦ ***Chalet,*** ☎ 60.21.00.43. closed 15 Apr-15 Jun, 15 Sep-15 Dec. Spec : *braserade, raclette,* 110-215.

Mont d'Arbois :
♦♦ ***Le Chalet dans les Arbres,*** ☎ 50.21.39.36. Visa. P ♿ In a charming wooden chalet, closed 10 Apr-1 Jul, 15 Sep-15 Dec and Thu, 90-150.

Casino : ☎ 50.21.25.11.

MENTHON-SAINT-BERNARD

Albertville 37, Chambéry 58, Paris 558
9 km SE of Annecy
A2 ☒ 74290 Veyrier-du-Lac

ℹ ☎ 50.60.14.30 (high season).
Compagnie des bateaux du lac d'Annecy : excursion around the lake (duration 1 hr 30) : enq, ☎ 50.51.08.40.

Hotel :
★★★***Palace Hôtel,*** ☎ 50.60.12.86. Tx 385292. AE, Visa. 93 rm of lake and mountain P ♿ closed 1 Oct-1 Jun, 560. Rest. ♦♦ 130-160.

★★ *Le Clos Chevalier* (55 pl.), ☎ 50.60.22.81 ; ★★ *le Clos Don Juan* (72 pl.), ☎ 50.60.18.66.

MÉRIBEL-LES-ALLUES

Annecy 89, Chambéry 91, Paris 652
B2 1 550-2 700 m ☒ 73550

ℹ ☎ 79.08.60.01.

Hotels :
★★★★***Altiport Hôtel,*** ☎ 79.00.52.32. Tx 980456. AE, Visa. 42 rm P closed 15 Apr-30 Jun, 31 Aug-15 Dec. Half-pension only, 350. Rest. ♦♦ 180-240.
★★★***Grand-Cœur et Arolaz*** (Relais et châteaux), ☎ 79.08.60.03. AE, DC, Visa. 24 rm and 10 apts P closed 20 Apr-1 Jul, 31 Aug-15 Dec, 1 080 half-pension. Rest. ♦♦ 160-250.
★★***Orée du Bois*** (Relais du Silence), rd-pt des Pistes, ☎ 79.00.50.30. Visa. 32 rm P closed 20 Apr-1 Jul, Sep-15 Dec, 300. Rest. ♦ 90-100.

MODANE

Briançon 65, Chambéry 101, Paris 662
B3 1 050-2 750 m ☒ 73500

ℹ pl. Replaton, ☎ 79.05.22.35.

SNCF ☎ 79.05.05.22.

Car-hire : *Budget* train + car, at the station, ☎ 79.05.10.09.

Hotel :
★★***Perce-Neige***, 14, av. Jean-Jaurès, ☎ 79.05.00.50. 18 rm ♿ closed 20-31 Nov, 1-15 May, 185. Rest. ♦ 55-135.

MONTMÉLIAN

Chambéry 15, Grenoble 10, Paris 575
A2-3 ⊠ 73800

ℹ ☎ 79.84.05.42.

Hotels :
★***Central*** (L.F.), 1, rue Dr-Veyrat, ☎ 79.84.07.24. 25 rm 🅿 ⅏ closed Oct, 3-18 Jan and Mon eve low season, 140. Rest. ✂ 60-140.

⛺ ★*Escale Camping*, Sainte-Hélène-du-Lac (33 pl.), ☎ 79.84.04.11.

MONT-SAXONNEX

Chamonix 51, Annecy 57, Paris 580
9.5 km W of Cluses, B1 ⊠ 74130 Bonneville

ℹ mairie, ☎ 50.98.30.39.

Hotel :
★***Jalouvre,*** ☎ 50.96.90.67. 15 rm ⁂ 🅿 ⅏ closed 5-24 May, 22 Sep-1 Nov, 110. Rest. ✂ ♿ 80-130.

MORZINE

Évian 40, Annecy 93, Paris 604
B1 ⛷ 1 000-2 274 m ⊠ 74110

ℹ pl. Crusaz, ☎ 50.79.03.45.

Hotels :
● ★★★***Dahu,*** Mas-Métoud, ☎ 50.79.11.12. Euro, Visa. 26 rm ⁂ 🅿 ⅏ ⛱ closed 15 Apr-30 Jun, 1 Sep-15 Dec, 300. Rest. ♦ 110-120.
★★★***Airelles,*** ☎ 50.79.15.24. Tx 385178. AE, Euro, Visa. 50 rm ⁂ 🅿 ⅏ ⊡ closed 10 Sep-15 Dec, 15 Apr-15 Jun, 320. Rest. ♦♦ 80-130.
★★★***Carlina,*** av. Joux, ☎ 50.79.01.03. Tx 385596. AE, DC, Euro, Visa. 22 rm 🅿 ⅏ closed 15 Apr-30 Jun, 1 Sep-15 Dec. Half-pension or pension, 780. Rest. ♦♦ 150-180.
★★★***Tremplin,*** ☎ 50.79.12.31. Tx 385620. 40 rm ⁂ 🅿 ⅏ ⛱ ♿ closed 29 Mar-28 Jun, 30 Aug-20 Dec, 350. Rest. ♦♦ 160-200.
★★***Alpina,*** les Bois-Venants, ☎ 50.79.05.24. 18 rm ⁂ 🅿 ⅏ ⛱ ♿ closed 15 Apr-25 Jun, 10 Sep-20 Dec, 230. Rest. ♦ ✂ 70-85.
★***Ours Blanc,*** les Bois-Venants, ☎ 50.79.04.02. 20 rm ⁂ 🅿 ⅏ ⛱ closed 15 Apr-25 Jun, 6 Sep-15 Dec, 180. Rest. 80-125.

⛺ ★★★*Le Fornay* (60 pl.), ☎ 50.79.15.59.

Youth hostel : *Beau Site,* B.P. 11, ☎ 50.79.14.86.

NOTRE-DAME-DE-BELLECOMBE

Annecy 53, Chambéry 74, Paris 602
2.5 km S of Flumet, A-B2
⛷ 1 134-1 500 m ⊠ 73590

ℹ ☎ 79.31.61.40.

Hotel :
★★***Bellevue*** (L.F.), ☎ 79.31.60.56. 23 rm ⁂ 🅿 ⅏ closed 20 Apr-15 Jun, 10 Sep-18 Dec, 200. Rest. ♦ 60-80.

Le PETIT-BORNAND-LES-GLIÈRES

Annecy 44, Albertville 52, Paris 582
A1-2 ⊠ 74130 Bonneville

⛷ 700-2 000 m

ℹ mairie, ☎ 50.03.50.90.

Hotel :
★***Terminus,*** ☎ 50.03.50.05. 16 rm 🅿 110. Rest. closed Mon noon, 50-70.

⛺ ★★*Les Marronniers* (60 pl.), ☎ 50.03.52.05.

La PLAGNE

Bourg-St-Maurice 31, Chambéry 109, Paris 669
B2 ⛷ 1 970-2 700 m ⊠ 73210 Aime

ℹ ☎ 79.09.02.01.

Hotels :
★★★***Christina,*** ☎ 79.09.28.20. Tx 980266. 58 rm ⁂ 🅿 ⛱ closed 20 Apr-20 Dec, 260. Rest. ♦♦ 120-210.
★★★***Graciosa,*** ☎ 79.09.00.18. 14 rm ⁂ 🅿 ⛱ closed 25 Apr-5 Dec, 500. Rest. ♦♦ ✂ 125-220.

Restaurant :
♦♦ ***Tire-Bouchon,*** ☎ 79.09.11.79. Closed 25 Apr-1 Jul, 25 Aug-5 Dec. Spec : fish and live shellfish, *sole pochée au cidre, truite soufflée à la mousse de poissons*, 120-210.

PRALOGNAN-LA-VANOISE

Albertville 55, Chambéry 101, Paris 662
B3 ⛷ 1 470-2 360 m ⊠ 73710

ℹ Maison du Parc, ☎ 79.08.71.68.

Hotel :
★★***Grand Bec*** (L.F.), ☎ 79.08.71.10. 39 rm ⁂ 🅿 ⅏ ♿ closed 20 Apr-2 Jun, 15 Sep-15 Dec, 220. Rest. ♦ ✂ 55-95.

⛺ ★★*Le Chamois* (200 pl.), ☎ 79.08.70.77.

Restaurants :
♦ ***Seillons,*** imm. Chasse-Forêt, ☎ 79.08.72.32. Closed 20 Apr-15 Jun, end Sep-15 Dec, 20-100.
♦ ***Varappe,*** imm. Chasse-Forêt, ☎ 79.08.72.10. ♿ 40-60.

PRAZ-SUR-ARLY

Albertville 26, Annecy 55, Paris 615
4.5 km SW of Megève, B2
⛷ 1 000-1 800 m ⊠ 74120 Megève

ℹ rue Nationale, ☎ 50.21.90.57.

Hotels :
★★★***Quatre As,*** ☎ 50.21.90.11. 13 rm ⁂ 🅿 ⅏ ✂ closed Nov and May, 220. Rest. ♦♦ 70-140.
★★***Mont Charvin*** (L.F.), ☎ 50.21.90.05. 31 rm ⁂ 🅿 ⅏ 🎾 closed 15 Apr-31 May, 1 Nov-20 Dec, 200. Rest. ♦ ✂ 75-180.

⛺ ★★*Chantalouette* (33 pl.), ☎ 79.21.90.25.

Restaurant :
♦ ***Cannibal's,*** rte Nationale, ☎ 79.21.91.94 ⁂ 🅿 ⛱ closed Wed low season, 75-85.

Mont REVARD

Aix-les-Bains 21, Chambéry 26, Paris 588
A2 ⊠ 73100 Aix-les-Bains

⛷ 1 270-1 500 m

Hotel :
★***Chalet Bouvard*** (L.F.), ☎ 79.61.51.43. 30 rm ⁂ 🅿 ⅏ ✂ ♿ closed 10 Oct-15 Dec, 20 Apr-30 May, 200. Rest. 60-120.

La ROCHE-SUR-FORON

Bonneville 8, Annecy 33, Paris 566
8 km W of Bonneville, A1 ⊠ 74800

ℹ pl. Andrevetan, ☎ 50.03.36.68.

SNCF ☎ 50.03.20.62.

Restaurant :
♦♦ ***Marie-Jean,*** Vozerier-Amancy, 2 km E, rte de Bonneville, ☎ 50.03.33.30 ⅏ ⛱ closed 3 weeks Aug, 1 week spring, Sun eve and Mon. Old house. Spec : *soupe de pêches blanches aux langoustines*, 120-200.

SAINT-CERGUES

Thonon 25, Annecy 54, Paris 559
10 km S of Douvaine, A1 ☒ 74140 Douvaine

ℹ ☎ 50.43.51.89.

Hotel :
★★***France*** (L.F.), ☎ 50.43.50.32. Euro, Visa. 22 rm Ⓟ closed 15 Oct-1 Dec, Sun eve and Mon low season, 150. Rest. ♦ 70-160.

SAINT-GERVAIS-LES-BAINS

Chamonix 21, Annecy 87, Paris 605
B2 ☒ 74190 Le Fayet

900-1 950 m

May-Sep, ☎ 50.78.23.47.

ℹ av. du Mt-d'Arbois, ☎ 50.78.22.43.

SNCF ☎ 50.78.21.67.

Car-hire : *Budget* train + car, at the station, ☎ 50.78.12.87.

Hotels :
★★★***Arbois-Bettex,*** Le Bettex, ☎ 50.93.12.22. DC, Visa. 27 rm of Mont Blanc Ⓟ closed 20 Apr-1 Jul, Sep-20 Dec, 305. Rest. ♦♦ 110-125.
★★★***Carlina,*** 95, rue du Rosay, ☎ 50.93.41.10. AE, Euro. 34 rm Ⓟ near the cable car ; closed 15 Apr-15 Jun, 1 Oct-20 Dec, 300. Rest. ♦♦ 100-200.

⛺ ★★*Les Domes de Miage* (90 pl.), ☎ 50.93.45.96.

Restaurant :
♦ ***Four,*** 1364, av. du Mont-Paccard, ☎ 50.78.14.16. AE, Visa Ⓟ ♿ closed five weeks (autumn) and Tue ex school hols. Spec : *fondues, raclettes, charbonnades,* 90-120.

SAINT-GINGOLPH

Thonon 26, Annecy 101, Paris 605
17 km E of Évian, B1 ☒ 74500 Évian-les-Bains

ℹ ☎ 50.76.72.28.

Hotel :
★★***Ducs de Savoie*** (L.F.), ☎ 50.76.73.09. Euro, Visa. 14 rm Ⓟ ♿ closed Jan, Mon eve and Tue low season, 115. Rest. ♦ ♿ 90-130.

SAINT-JEAN-DE-MAURIENNE

Chambéry 71, Grenoble 108, Paris 632
A3 ☒ 73300

ℹ pl. de la Cathédrale, ☎ 79.64.03.12.

SNCF ☎ 79.64.18.87.

Car-hire : *Budget* train + car, at the station, ☎ 79.64.17.00.

Hotel :
★★***Saint-Georges,*** 334, rue de la République, ☎ 79.64.01.06. AE. 23 rm Ⓟ 160.

⛺ ★*Municipal* (64 pl.), ☎ 79.64.28.02.

SAINT-JORIOZ

Albertville 36, Chambéry 58, Paris 546
9 km S of Annecy, A2 ☒ 74410

ℹ pl. de la Mairie, ☎ 50.68.61.82.

Hotels :
★★***Châtaigniers*** (L.F.), Machevaz, ☎ 50.68.63.29. Tx 385417. Euro. 55 rm Ⓟ ♿ sauna, closed 1 Oct-25 Apr, 185. Rest. ♦ 70-150.
★***Semnoz*** (L.F.), hameau de Monnetier, ☎ 50.68.60.28. Visa. 33 rm Ⓟ ♿ closed Oct-1 May, 130. Rest. ♦ 60-95.

⛺ ★★★*Europa Camping* (150 pl.), ☎ 50.68.51.01 ; ★★★*International lac d'Annecy* (133 pl.), ☎ 50.68.67.93 ; ★★*les Roseaux* (66 pl.), ☎ 50.68.66.59.

SAINT-JULIEN-EN-GENEVOIS

Geneva 9, Annecy 35, Paris 538
A1 ☒ 74160

ℹ ☎ 50.49.30.61.

SNCF ☎ 50.49.00.44.

Restaurants :
♦♦ ***Diligence et Taverne du Postillon,*** rue de Genève, ☎ 50.49.07.55. Closed 30 Dec-10 Jan, 1-20 Jul, Sun eve and Mon. Spec : *turbot aux algues dans sa carapace de sel, pigeonneau fermier cocotte,* 110-295.

Présilly, 7 km S :
♦♦♦ ***Abbaye de Pomier,*** N201, ☎ 50.04.40.64. DC, Visa Ⓟ 12thC former charterhouse, closed Tue eve and Wed, 180-250.

SAINT-MARTIN-DE-BELLEVILLE (Les Menuires-Val-Thorens)

Albertville 62, Chambéry 100, Paris 661
B3 1 810 - 2 885 m ☒ 73440

ℹ ☎ 79.08.20.12 ; Les Menuires, ☎ 79.08.20.12 ; Val-Thorens, ☎ 79.08.21.08.

Hotels :
★★★***L'Oisans,*** la Croisette, Les Menuires, ☎ 79.00.62.96. Tx 980084. AE, Visa. 20 rm Ⓟ closed 18 Apr-9 Dec, 500. Rest. ♦♦ eve only, 80-100.
★★★***Val Chavière,*** Val-Thorens, ☎ 79.00.00.33. Tx 980572. Visa. 42 rm Ⓟ ♿ closed 1 May-5 Nov. Pension, 350. Rest. ♦♦ 120-210.
★★***Sherpa,*** Val-Thorens, ☎ 79.00.00.70 and 50.67.76.29. 40 rm Ⓟ ♿ closed 5 May-10 Dec, 270. Rest. ♦ 125-220.

⛺ ★★*Caravaneige* (50 pl.), ☎ 79.00.60.58.

SAINT-MICHEL-DE-MAURIENNE

Briançon 69, Chambéry 84, Paris 645
A3 ☒ 73140

Hotel :
★★***Savoy*** (L.F.), 25, rue du Gal-Ferrié, ☎ 79.56.55.12. AE, Visa. 22 rm Ⓟ ♿ closed 20 Jun-10 Jul, Sun eve and Mon low season, 220. Rest. ♦ 55-145.

SAINT-PAUL-EN-CHABLAIS

Thonon 11, Annecy 92, Paris 590
9 km SE of Évian, B1
☒ 74500 Évian-les-Bains

Hotel :

La Beunez, 4 km SE :
★★***Bois Joli*** (Relais du Silence), ☎ 50.73.60.11. DC. 24 rm ♿ closed 15 Nov-15 Dec, 1-15 Mar, 200. Rest. ♦ closed Tue, 80-130.

SAINT-PIERRE-D'ENTREMONT

Chambéry 25, Grenoble 50, Paris 568
25 km S of Chambéry, A2 ☒ 73670

ℹ ☎ 79.65.81.90.

Hotel :
★***Château de Montbel*** (L.F.), ☎ 79.65.81.65. Euro, Visa. 10 rm Ⓟ closed 1 Nov-15 Dec, Sun eve and Mon low season, 150. Rest. 55-90.

⛺ ★★*Cozon* (33 pl.), ☎ 79.65.80.02.

SALLANCHES

Chamonix 28, Annecy 75, Paris 597
B2 ⊠ 74700

ℹ quai de l'Hôtel-de-Ville, ☎ 50.58.04.25.

SNCF ☎ 50.58.00.30.

Car-hire : *Budget* train + car, 44, av. de Genève, ☎ 50.58.11.32.

Hotels :
★★★***Chamois d'Or,*** Cordon, ☎ 50.58.05.16. AE, Visa. 30 rm of the Mont-Blanc chain closed 15 Sep-20 Dec, 15 Apr-26 May, 300. Rest. ♦♦ 80-120.
★★★***Sorbiers*** (L.F.), 17, rue de la Paix, ☎ 50.58.01.22. 36 rm 240. Rest. ♦♦ closed Sun and Mon noon low season, 65-150.

⛺ ★★★★*Mont Blanc Village* (130 pl.), ☎ 50.58.43.67 ; ★★*Relais de la Vallée Blanche* (90 pl.), ☎ 50.58.04.25 ; ★★*Miroir du Mont Blanc* (120 pl.), ☎ 50.58.14.28.

Restaurant :
♦ ***Chesery,*** rte de Megève, ☎ 50.58.10.16 closed Oct, 1-15 May and Mon low season. Spec : *fondues, raclettes* and seafood, 70-120.

SAMOËNS

Chamonix 63, Annecy 85, Paris 596
B1 720-2 125 m ⊠ 74340

ℹ bus station, ☎ 50.34.40.28.

Hotels :
★★★***Glaciers,*** ☎ 50.34.40.06. 50 rm closed 15 Apr-1 Jun, 15 Sep-18 Dec, 270. Rest. ♦ 85-140.
★★★***Neige et Roc,*** ☎ 50.34.40.72. 33 rm closed 15 Sep-15 Dec, 15 Apr-1 Jun, 220. Rest. ♦ 70-150.
Morillon, 74400 Taninges, 5 km W :
★★***Sauvageon,*** ☎ 50.90.10.25. Euro, Visa. 14 rm closed 15 Apr-15 May, 15 Oct-15 Nov, and Mon low season, 130. Rest. 75-150.

⛺ ★★*Le Giffre* (200 pl.), ☎ 50.34.41.92.

Restaurant :
♦ ***Louisiane,*** ☎ 50.34.42.83. Closed May, Sep-Nov ex week-ends, 80-130.

SEEZ

Val-d'Isère 28, Chambéry 104, Paris 665
3 km NE of Bourg-Saint-Maurice, B2
⊠ 73700 Bourg-St-Maurice

ℹ hôtel de ville, ☎ 79.27.98.08 and 79.07.00.65.

Hotel :
★★***Malgovert*** (L.F.), ☎ 79.07.02.05. 20 rm closed Oct-22 Dec, 1 May-15 Jun, 180. Rest. ♦ 60-100.

Youth hostel : *la Verdache,* Longefoy, ☎ 79.07.10.61.

⛺ ★*Le Reclus* (108 pl.), ☎ 79.07.05.75.

SERVOZ

Albertville 54, Annecy 92, Paris 611
14 km SW of Chamonix, B2
⊠ 74310 Les Houches

ℹ ☎ 50.47.21.68.

Hotels :
★★***Chamois*** (L.F.), ☎ 50.47.20.09. DC, Euro, Visa. 7 rm + chalet closed 15 days in Apr, 15 days end Nov, 190. Rest. ♦ 60-160.
★***Cimes Blanches*** (L.F.), le Mont, ☎ 50.47.20.05. 10 rm closed 15 Apr-10 May, 8 Sep-22 Dec, 100. Rest. 60-70.

⛺ ★★★*La Plaine Saint-Jean* (200 pl.), ☎ 50.47.21.87.

SÉVRIER

Albertville 40, Chambéry 54, Paris 542
5 km S of Annecy, A2 ⊠ 74410 Saint-Jorioz

ℹ ☎ 50.46.40.56.

Hotels :
★★***Beauregard*** (Inter-Hôtel), rte d'Albertville, ☎ 50.46.40.59. Tx 370679. Euro, Visa. 32 rm 260. Rest. ♦ closed Sun eve (1 Nov-1 Apr), 60-110.
★★***Riant Port,*** ☎ 50.46.41.08. Tx 514141. DC, Euro, Visa. 36 rm closed 25 Sep-10 Oct, 23 Dec-1 Mar. Riding, sailing, water-skiing, 180. Rest. ♦ 80-120.

⛺ ★★★*Au Cœur du Lac* (100 pl.), ☎ 50.48.46.45 ; ★★★*le Panoramic* (133 pl.), ☎ 50.46.43.09.

Restaurant :
♦ ***Auberge du Bessard, L'Oasis,*** ☎ 50.46.40.45. Closed Nov-15 Mar, 60-90.

TALLOIRES

Annecy 13, Chambéry 62, Paris 562
A2 ⊠ 74290 Veyrier-du-Lac

ℹ pl. de la Mairie, ☎ 50.60.70.64.

Hotels :
● ★★★★***Abbaye*** (Relais et châteaux), rte du Port, ☎ 50.67.40.88. 32 rm over the lake closed 15 Dec-15 Jan, 700. Rest. ● ♦♦♦ closed 1 Jan-1 May and Wed. Spec : : *fricassée de caïon, chausson de truite,* 220-310.
★★★★(L) ***Auberge du Père Bise*** (Relais et châteaux), rte du Port, ☎ 50.60.72.01. Tx 385812. AE, Visa. 34 rm closed 20 Dec-20 Jan, 16 Apr-4 May, 1 000. Rest. ● ♦♦♦♦ The great tradition of the Bise family : silverware, Baccarat crystal, piano-bar and home creations : *mousse de foie, gratin de queues d'écrevisses* (in season), *pâté chaud sauce poivrade.* Cellar as great as the prices are high, 350-480.
★★★***Beau Site,*** ☎ 50.60.71.04. 38 rm closed 30 Sep-20 May. Private beach, 185. Rest. ♦♦ 120-210.
★★★***L'Hermitage-Domaine des Primevères*** (Relais du Silence), ☎ 50.60.71.17. Tx 385196. AE, DC, Euro, Visa. 50 rm closed 31 Oct-1 Mar (ex 15 apts open all year round), 350-620. Rest. ♦♦ 120-200.
★★★***Cottage,*** ☎ 50.60.71.10. 34 rm closed 15 Oct-15 Mar, 715. Rest. ♦♦ 170-280.

⛺ ★★★*Le Lanfonnet* (166 pl.), ☎ 50.60.72.12 ; ★★*Au Cœur des Prés* (890 pl.), ☎ 50.23.04.66 ; ★★*l'Horizon* (120 pl.), ☎ 50.60.75.36.

THOLLON-LES-MEMISES

Thonon 20, Annecy 95, Paris 600
14 km E of Évian, B1
1 000-1 983 m ⊠ 74500 Évian-les-Bains

ℹ mairie, ☎ 50.75.25.87.

Hotel :
★★***Gentianes,*** ☎ 50.70.92.39. Visa. 22 rm closed 20 Apr-1 Jun, 20 Sep-15 Dec, 165. Rest. ♦ 45-130.

THÔNES

Annecy 20, Albertville 36, Paris 569
A2 ⊠ 74230

ℹ ☎ 50.02.00.26.

Hotel :
★★***Midi,*** pl. de l'Hôtel-de-Ville, ☎ 50.02.00.44. AE, Visa. 22 rm Ⓟ closed 11 Nov-15 Dec, 160. Rest. ♦ closed Mon eve and Tue off season, 60-150.

⛺ ★★*Le Tréjeux* (70 pl.), ☎ 50.02.06.90 ; ★★*les Grillons* (48 pl.), ☎ 50.02.06.63.

Market : Sat am.

THONON-LES-BAINS

Geneva 33, Annecy 81, Paris 580
A1 ⊠ 74200

♨ year-round, ☎ 50.26.17.22.

ⓘ pl. de l'Hôtel-de-Ville, ☎ 50.71.00.51.

⛴ at Rives port : *Cie générale de Navigation sur le lac Léman ;* enq : Office des Baigneurs, ☎ 50.71.14.71.

SNCF ☎ 50.71.31.98.

🚌 pl. des Arts.

Car-hire : *Budget* train + car, at the station, ☎ 50.71.12.93.

Hotels :
★★★***Savoie et Léman,*** 40, bd Carnot, ☎ 50.71.13.80. Tx 385905. AE, Euro, Visa. 35 rm ⚘ Ⓟ ⚘ closed Sep, Sat eve and Sun ex Jul-Aug, 310. Rest. ♦♦ ✗ 65-110.
★★***Duché de Savoie*** (L.F.), 43, av. Gal-Leclerc, ☎ 50.71.40.07. 15 rm ⚘ Ⓟ ⚘ ✗ closed Nov-Jan, 180. Rest. ♦ 80-130.
★***Ombre des Marronniers*** (L.F.), 17, pl. de Crête, ☎ 50.71.26.18. Euro, Visa. 22 rm ⚘ ⚘ ✗ closed 4 Nov-4 Dec, 140. Rest. closed Mon ex Jun-30 Sep, 60-120.

Armoy, 7 km SE :
★★***Carlina*** (L.F.), ☎ 50.73.94.94. 18 rm ⚘ Ⓟ ⚘ ⚘ closed Jan, Mon, 155. Rest. ♦ 70-125.
★***Écho des Montagnes,*** ☎ 50.71.32.01. 64 rm Ⓟ ⚘ ✗ closed Dec-Jan, 150. Rest. closed Mon eve and Tue low season, 65-105.

⛺ ★★*Camp de Morcy* (80 pl.), ☎ 50.71.32.65 ; ★★*le Lac Noir* (66 pl.), ☎ 50.71.12.46 ; ★★*St-Disdille* (733 pl.), ☎ 50.71.14.11.

TIGNES

Bourg-St-Maurice 30, Chambéry 131, Paris 692
B2-3 ⛷ 2 100-3 500 m ⊠ 73320

ⓘ ☎ 79.06.15.55.

Hotels :
★★★***Ski d'Or*** (Relais et châteaux), Val-Claret, ☎ 79.06.51.60. 21 rm ⚘ ♿ closed May-15 Dec. Half-pension, 1 000. Rest. ♦♦ 200-250.
★★★***Curling,*** Val-Claret, ☎ 79.06.34.34. Tx 980039. AE, Euro, Visa. 35 rm ⚘ Ⓟ ⚘ closed 5 May-1 Jul, 31 Aug-25 Oct, 480.
★★***Campanules,*** lac de Tignes, ☎ 79.06.34.36. Visa. 36 rm ⚘ ⚘ Pens. and half pens., 310. Rest. ♦ closed 3 May-1 Jul, 31 Aug-1 Dec, 80-110.

⛺ *Le Chantel* (400 pl.), ☎ 79.06.15.55.

Restaurants :
♦♦ ***Caveau,*** le Val-Claret, ☎ 79.06.52.32. Closed 15 May-1 Nov. Spec : *terrine de saumon, filet de turbot au riesling,* 130-220.
♦ ***La Poutrerie,*** le Val-Claret, ☎ 79.06.32.64. Closed 15 May-15 Oct. Spec : *fondues* and *raclettes,* 70-140.

Summer sports : trignathlon which includes a ski race, mountain cycle, scrambling, wind-surf across the lake : this new competition is individual and international. Medical certificate is compulsory.

La TOUSSUIRE

Chambéry 89, Grenoble 126, Paris 650
16 km SW of Saint-Jean-de-Maurienne
A3 ⊠ 73300

⛷ 1 300-2 230 m

Hotel :
★★★***Airelles*** (L.F.), ☎ 79.56.75.88. Visa. 31 rm ⚘ Ⓟ ⚘ closed 20 Apr-30 Jun, 8 Sep-15 Dec, 150. Rest. ♦ 65-160.

Youth hostel : ☎ 79.56.72.04 or 79.56.71.52.

⛺ ★★*Caravaneige du Col* (62 pl.), ☎ 79.83.00.80.

VAL-D'ISÈRE

Albertville 85, Chambéry 132, Paris 693
B3 ⛷ 1 850-3 230 m ⊠ 73150

ⓘ ☎ 79.06.10.83, and *Centre des sports,* ☎ 79.06.10.83.

Hotels :
★★★★***Christiania,*** ☎ 79.06.08.25. 45 rm ⚘ Ⓟ ⚘ ♿ closed 5 May-5 Dec, 455. Rest. ♦♦♦ ✗ 135-230.
★★★***Altitude,*** ☎ 79.06.12.55. Visa. 30 rm ⚘ Ⓟ ⚘ ✗ ⚘ closed 5 May-30 Jun, 25 Aug-1 Dec, 540. Rest. ♦ 90-150.
★★***Bellevue,*** ☎ 79.06.00.03. 23 rm ⚘ Ⓟ ⚘ closed 10 May-29 Jun, 15 Sep-15 Nov, 270.

⛺ ★★*Les Richardes* (75 pl.), ☎ 79.06.00.60.

Restaurants :
♦♦ ***Brussels,*** ☎ 79.06.01.58. closed 1 May-1 Dec. Terrace in the heart of Val, 130-230.
♦♦ ***Goitschel'Lodge,*** ☎ 79.06.02.01. AE, DC, Visa ; closed 8 May-1 Jul, Sep-1 Nov. Spec : *saumon cru tahitienne, aiguillettes de canard aux pêches, cailles aux pêches de vigne.* With a warm welcome from Marielle, 150-210.
♦ ***Arolay,*** Le Fornet, ☎ 79.06.11.68. closed May-Jun, Sep-20 Dec. Spec : *braserade, fondue* and *raclette,* 50-80.
♦ ***Le Bar Jacques,*** ☎ 79.06.03.89 ♿ closed 9 May-24 Jun, 1 Sep-30 Oct. A friendly atmosphere, Lyonnais specialities and Beaujolais wines. Serv. until 4 a.m., 100-210.

VALLOIRE

Briancon 52, Chambéry 101, Paris 662
A-B3 ⛷ 1 430-2 430 m ⊠ 73450

ⓘ in the square, ☎ 79.56.03.96.

Hotels :
★★★***Grand Hôtel de Valloire et du Galibier*** (Inter-Hôtel), ☎ 79.59.00.95. Tx 980553. AE, DC. 43 rm ⚘ Ⓟ ⚘ ♿ closed 15 Apr-15 Jun, 15 Sep-18 Dec, 270. Rest. ♦ 70-200.
★★***Christiania*** (L.F.), le Tigny, ☎ 79.59.00.57. Visa. 26 rm Ⓟ ⚘ ⚘ closed 15 Apr-20 Jun, 10 Sep-15 Dec, 170. Rest. ♦ ✗ 60-90.

Touraine, the Blésois and Orléanais Regions

The light of the Val de Loire is different from that of the surrounding Ile-de-France and Normandy regions. Leonardo da Vinci, guest of Francois I, drew the royal château of Amboise bathed in an ephemeral pink light overlaid with a triumphant patina of gold. In his Notebook he wrote of his concern to "render the light accurately".

Along the embankments built to contain floods — for there have been some very devastating ones — stand little houses in white tufa, which still house bargees and market-gardeners. The region is the "garden of France", and fruit, vegetables and flowers thrive on the rich alluvium deposited by the Loire and its tributaries. The soft, chalky tufa conditions the character of the Loire region and creates an underground world of cave villages, wine cellars, and underground chicory and mushroom beds. The white stone was also hewed out of the earth to build cathedrals, royal châteaux and great buildings of state.

For most people, the Loire valley is above all the valley of châteaux. Tourists "do" the Loire châteaux, rather as they "do" the Greek islands, visiting three or four a day. Chambord, a fairy castle nestling amidst woods and ponds, shares the stage with Blois and its fabulous staircase, Chaumont with its feudal past, Chenonceaux stretching effortlessly across the river Cher, and Azay-le-Rideau, set like a diamond in the waters of the Indre. All eloquent witnesses to the Renaissance in arts and letters which once flowered along the banks of the Loire.

But Touraine is more than castles — it is also a whole other world of lonely manor houses in leafy forests, bubbling streams and peaceful villages sleeping in the shadow of their Romanesque and Gothic churches, dense forests where lords and their subjects once hunted fierce packs of wolves, the earthenware factories of Gien and the strange cave villages scattered throughout the region.

Sightseeing

Don't miss

★★★ : *Azay-le-Rideau (A2), Chambord (B2), Chenonceaux (B2), Saint-Benoît-sur-Loire (C1), Tours (A2).*

★★ : *Amboise (A2), Beaugency (B1), Blois (B2), Chaumont (B2), Cheverny (B2), Chinon (A2), Indre Valley (A2), Langeais (A2), Loches (A2), Loir Valley (A-B1), Sully-sur-Loire (C1), Vendôme (B1), Villandry (A2).*

AMBOISE★★

A2 / ® / pop. 11 415 (Indre-et-Loire)

In 1516 François I invited Leonardo da Vinci, "the greatest genius of all time", to Amboise. With him he brought the Mona Lisa...

▶ The **château★★** d'Amboise, terraced high above the river, is flanked by two enormous round towers : the Tour des Minimes beside the Loire once had a spiral ramp for horsemen. On the left, the **chapel of St. Hubert** (1493) is a Gothic jewel. A stone slab covers a tomb reputed to be that of Leonardo da Vinci. The **Logis du Roi** (*King's Lodge ;* late Gothic, end 15thC) was built by Charles VIII, who died there. Gothic and Renaissance furniture and Aubusson tapestries in the Louis 12th-François Ist wing. The young François spent his youth and the first three years of his reign here, giving magnificent balls, tourneys and masquerades. See the **gardens** *(low season, 9-12 & 2-6:30; in season, 9-6:30; Son et Lumière, inf. tel 47.57.09.28).* ▶ The Rue Victor Hugo (old houses) leads to the **Manor of Le Clos Lucé★** *(9-7 1 Jun.-15 Sep.; rest of year, 9-12 & 2-7).* This is where Leonardo da Vinci spent the last three years of his life (d. 1519). Da Vinci was painter, sculptor, architect, engineer, mathematician, anatomist, writer and musician, and this 15thC manor recalls the period when this great savant drew the plans of the first aeroplane and the first automobile. In the basement are scale models of **machines★** based on his sketches, put together by I.B.M. ▶ The town itself offers an excellent Sunday morning market and a number of leisurely walks : down the Rue de la Concorde (16thC houses); around the foot of the château; and the pedestrian precinct of **Rue Nationale,** where local specialities such as *rillettes,* goat cheese and pastries tempt the passer-by. ▶ You arrive eventually at the **church of St. Denis★** (Angevin 12thC) with its figured capitals and a 16thC effigy★, possibly of La Belle Babou, mistress of François I.

Also... ▶ Historical collections in the Hôtel de Ville (Town Hall). ▶ Post Museum *(Musée de la Poste),* transport through the ages *(9:30-12 & 2-6:30; Apr.-Sep. 10-12 & 2-5; Oct.-Mar. closed Tue.).* □

▶ Nearby

▶ **Amboise Forest** *(S of town);* covering the plateau between the Loire and the Cher. Marked paths through the park of La Moutonnerie. ▶ The **Chanteloup Pagoda** *(2.5 km SE, on the edge of the forest)* reflects the taste of the period for Chinese curios *(1 Jan.-31 Mar., 9-5, closed Mon.; 1 Apr.-15 Sept., 9-8, closed Mon. am; 16 Sept.-11 Nov., 9-6, closed Mon. am; 12 Nov.-31 Dec., 9-5, closed Mon.).* ▶ **Château-Renault** ® *(22 km N) :* 12th-18thC. 11 km W : church of **Saint-Laurent-en-Gâtines,** in a former 15thC manor. □

AZAY-LE-RIDEAU★★★

A2 / ® / pop. 2 915 (Indre-et-Loire)

One of the most beautiful châteaux in the Loire Valley, surrounded by trees and reflected in its lake.

▶ As with many other châteaux in the region, Azay was a replacement for a small fortress, the first appearance (1518) of the Italian Renaissance in Touraine and one of the first examples of the precedence of comfort over security. The corner turrets and machicolations are purely decorative. *(9:15-12 & 2-6:30, Palm Sunday-30 Sep.; 9:15-12 & 2-5, Oct.-15 Nov.; 9:15-12 & 2-4:45, 16 Nov.-Palm Sunday, closed nat. hols. Son et Lumière info, tel 47.61.61.23 and at the château tel 47.43.32.04).* Paintings, furniture and 16thC tapestries make the interior a veritable Renaissance museum. Note the kitchens and the straight flights of stairs★, an innovation for the period. ▶ The village church has an interesting Carolingian façade★. □

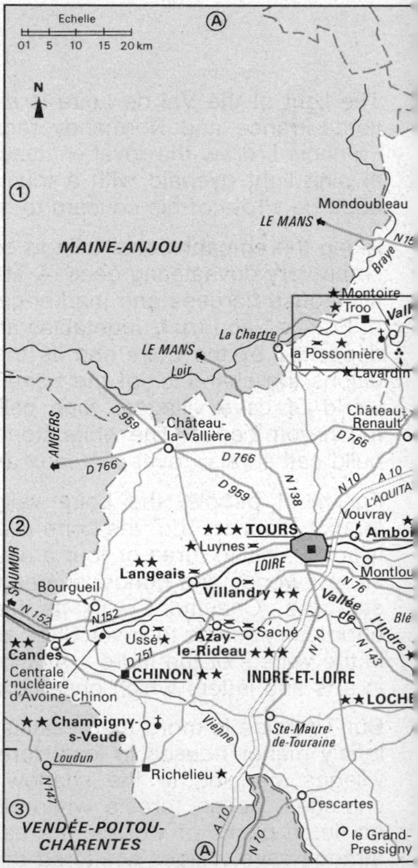

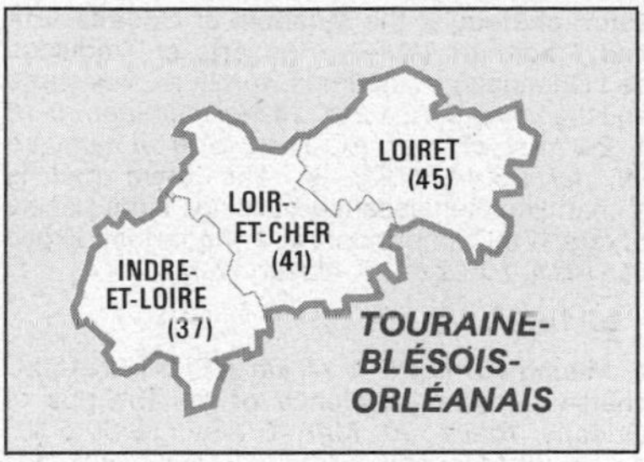

Weekend tips

Near Chambord and Cheverny, the lesser known châteaux around the Sologne : Villesavin, Troussay, Beauregard and Fougères (→ Cheverny). Lunch at Cheverny or Blois and spend the night at Vendôme (→). The next day see the delighful villages in the Loir valley (→) : Montoire (lunch), Lavardin and Trôo.

Facts and figures

Location : *The Orléanais, the Blois region and the Touraine region belong to what is usually called the Val de Loire (Loire Valley). A distinction is made between the Val d'Orléans, the Val de Loire proper (between Orléans and Tours) and the Val de Touraine. All told, a 300 km strip, three to twelve km wide, with neighbouring regions around the tributaries of the Loire.*
Area : *19 180 km*^{2}.
Climate : *Proverbial for its gentle climate; the Atlantic ocean makes for mild winters and temperate summers. The temperature rarely falls below 10 °C (50 °F). Indian summers are a reality here; the autumn is an ideal season for visiting the Val de Loire.*
Population : 1 252 476; Loiret 490 189; Loir-et-Cher 296 200; Indre-et-Loire 478 601.
Administration : Loiret Department, Prefecture : Orléans; **Loir-et-Cher** Department, Prefecture : Blois; **Indre-et-Loire** Department, Prefecture : Tours.

Touraine, Blésois, Orléanais

▶ Nearby

▶ **Château de l'Islette★** *(2.5 km NW)* probably built by the craftsmen from Azay, which would explain a certain similarity. ▶ **Saché★** ®: 16thC manor, renovated in the 19thC, famous for the writer Honoré de Balzac (1799-1850) who stayed here on many occasions, to write *Le Père Goriot* and other famous novels. The writer's room has been preserved as he left it. *(9-12 & 2-6, 15 Mar.-Sep.; 9-12 & 2-5, Oct.-14 Mar.; closed Wed., Dec. and Jan.).* Also see stabiles and mobiles installed by Calder on a hill around his house. Before arriving, watermills at Pont-de-Ruan on the Indre. ▶ **Villaines-les-Rochers** *(6.5 km S),* a village of harness makers and potters; basket weaving has been traditional here since the 9thC. □

■ BEAUGENCY★★

B1 / ® / pop. 7 339 (Loiret)

Legend has it that the Devil himself offered the 22 arched bridge★ across the Loire to the town of Beaugency in exchange for the soul of the first being to cross it. As it happens, this was a cat; and the people of Beaugency are still nicknamed *chats* (cats). Other colourful mediaeval characteristics of the town are more realistically dated from the Hundred Years' War between England and France.

▶ The **Tower of St. Firmin** (16thC), the **keep★** (11thC), the **church of Notre Dame** (12th-17thC, organs★), the former abbey and the château form an unusually beautiful group. ▶ In the 15thC **château** is the **Museum of Orleans Arts and Traditions** (Musée des Arts et Traditions de l'Orléanais): costumes, furniture, vineyards and the Loire *(9-12 & 2-6, 16 Mar.-30 Sept.; 9-12 & 2-4 rest of year ex Tue.; Son et Lumière inf. tel 38.44.55.23).* ▶ The **town hall** is a charming Renaissance building; eight panels of rare 17thC embroidery★. ▶ **Aquarium,** exotic fish *(daily 10-12 & 2-6, closed Wed.).* □

▶ Nearby

▶ **Meung-sur-Loire** ® *(7 km NE)*: 13th-18thC château, former residence of the Bishops of Orléans *(daily 30 Mar.-1 Nov., 8:30-5:30; 1 Jan.-29 Mar. and 2 Nov.-31 Dec., weekends only, 9-5).* **St. Liphard** (11th-16thC) is a cruciform church unusual for the region. ▶ **Cléry-Saint-André** *(12 km NE).* Louis XI was so fond of Cléry that he chose the town's fine 15thC Flamboyant Gothic basilica★ *(8-5, 6:30 in summer)* as his place of burial; visit the vault and the Renaissance chapel of St. Jacques★. ▶ 11 km SW: **the nuclear power stations of Saint-Laurent-Nouan** (A and B); public information office (diagrams, models, viewing platform; *daily 9-8; to visit tel 54.87.75.66).* □

■ BLOIS★★

B2 / ® / pop. 49 422 (Loir-et-Cher)

Wolves no longer howl at the gates of the town, whose Celtic name (Bleiz) meant "wolf"; but the forests they haunted are still there. Between the Sologne and the Beauce, built of white stone and blue slate, Blois is an important market for corn, wine,

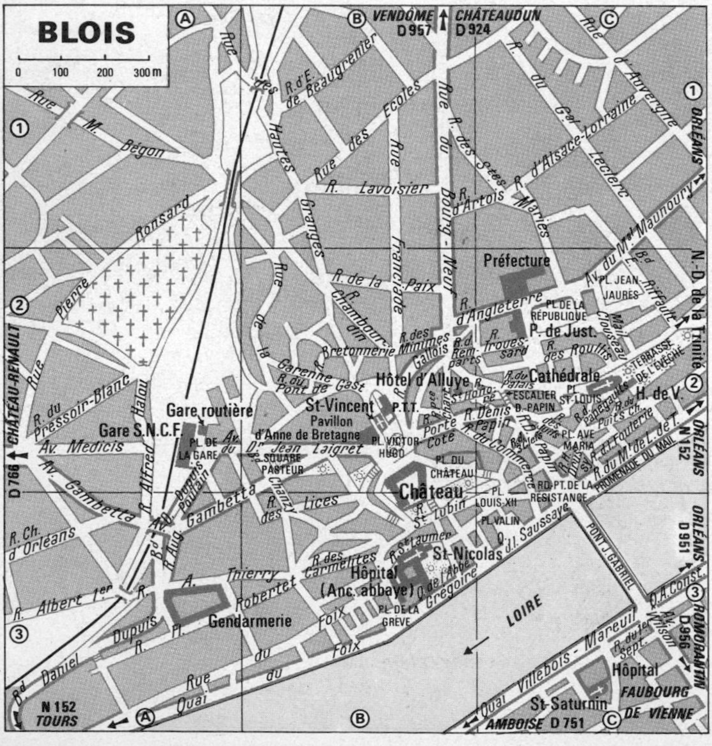

strawberries and asparagus. Cocoa used to come up river from Nantes; today the town is still pervaded by the delicious scent from the Poulain chocolate factories.

▶ **The château★★★** (B2) is a marvellous résumé of French architecture from the Middle Ages to the Neo-Classical period *(9-6:30, Easter and Jun.-Aug.; 9-12 & 2-6:30, 15 Mar.-May and Sep.; 9-12 & 2-5, Jan.-14 Mar. and Oct.-Dec.; Son et Lumière inf. at SI, tel 54.74.06.49).* ▶ Entry to the Court of Honour is through the Louis XII wing (1498), late Gothic. **Fine Arts Museum :** 16th-19thC paintings, and **archaeological museum** *(1 Jan.-30 Jun., Mon. and Wed. only, 9-12 & 2-5:30; 1 Jul.-31 Aug., 2-5:30; 1 Sep.-31 Dec., 9-12 & 2-5:30, closed Wed.).* ▶ On the right, the François I wing (1515 Renaissance) and the dazzling octagonal tower of the **Grand Escalier★★★** (Grand Staircase). In this wing see the Queen's apartments, with Catherine de Medici's Renaissance furniture and tapestries; on the floor above, the apartments of Henri III were the scene of the dramatic assassination of the Duke of Guise (1588). ▶ The **Grand Salle des Etats★** (State Room) (13thC) between the two wings is a reminder of the former fortress on this site. ▶ Opposite the entrance, the **Gaston d'Orléans wing★** in Neo-Classical style was built by François Mansart (1635). ▶ In the **Rue St. Lubin** at the foot of the château there are still some picturesque wooden houses, in spite of the destruction of 1940. ▶ The 12th-13thC **church of St. Nicolas** is a happy marriage of Romanesque and Gothic styles. Nearby, in the Jacobin convent **Natural History Museum** *(daily, 2-6, ex. Mon.).* ▶ The **old town★** *(visits 1 Jul.-31 Aug., 10-3, ex. Wed and Sun.)* between the château and the cathedral (C2) is now a pedestrian precinct lined with old Renaissance houses★ : Rue de la Fontaine des Elus, Rue du Puits Châtel, Rue des Papegaults, Rue des Juifs etc. ▶ The **St. Louis cathédral** was rebuilt in Gothic style after the terrible hurricane of 1678; see the crypt of St. Solenne, 10thC and 11thC. ▶ Behind the cathedral, the **gardens★** of the former Bishops' residence (18thC, Hôtel de Ville) make a magnificent walk above the Loire.

Also... ▶ **Hôtel d'Alluye★** (private mansion; B2; 1508). **Anne de Bretagne's pavilion★** (B2; 15thC.). ▶ **Basilica-Notre Dame de la Trinité** (via C2) 1937, chime of 48 bells★, concerts. ▶ **Church of St. Saturnin** (C3), 15th-17thC with 16thC cemetery housing a **stonework museum** *(10-12 & 2:30-5:30 daily ex. Mon. and Tue., 15 Mar.-Oct.; 10-12 & 2-5 Wed, Sat. and Sun. rest of year).* ▶ **Poulain chocolate factory** *(summer 8:45, 10, 1:30, 2:45; winter 10, 2:45; prior notice required; tel. 54.78.39.21).* □

▶ Nearby

▶ **Saint-Denis-sur-Loire :** château (14th-18thC; *exterior visit in summer, 9-12 & 2-6; closed Sun.).* ▶ **Ménars** ® *(8 km NE) :* Antoinette Poisson (1721-64), better known as La Marquise de Pompadour, bought the **château★** in 1760 and had it enlarged by Gabriel and Soufflot. Louis XIV and XV furniture; magnificent gardens★ above the Loire. ▶ **Cour-sur-Loire★** *(10 km NE) :* 15thC château *(visit by request, tel 54.46.81.04),* 15th-16thC church. ▶ **Suèvres** *(13 km NE) :* old houses running down to the Loire; two interesting churches, St. Lubin and St. Christophe (both 12thC, remodelled). ▶ **Mer :** château de Chantecaille (15th-17thC; *visit 1 Apr.-1 Nov., 3-5, closed Thu.).* ▶ **Château de Talcy★** *(28 km NE)* rebuilt in 1520, the château has a remarkable 18thC interior complete with furnishings★ from the French Regency (1715-1723) to the Directoire (1795-99) *(9-11:15 & 2-6, Apr.-Sep.; 10-11:15 & 2-4:30, 1 Oct.-31 Mar.; closed hols.).* 10 km NW Romanesque church of **Saint-Leonard-en-Beauce.** □

▶ The châteaux around Blois★★★ *(Round trip 92 km; 2 days)*

▶ Renaissance châteaux in a setting of woods and lakes; **Chambord** (→), **Villesavin** and **Cheverny** (→), **Beauregard, Fougères** (→ Cheverny) and **Chaumont** (→). Stopover at **Cour Cheverny** ® or return to Blois. □

▶ **The Blois Forest★** *(23 km round trip)*

▶ **Blois.** ▶ D766 to **Molineuf.** 1 km SW, **church of St. Secondin** (11th-16thC) and ruins of **château de Bury** *(500 m).* ▶ **Orchaise,** well known for its wines, picturesque cave. ▶ Return to Blois via **Saint-Lubin-en-Vergonnois.**

▶ Along the Loire★★ *(58 km from Blois to Tours, 2 hr)*

▶ Between the two towns the Loire has a *route touristique★★* on each bank. We recommend the right bank (N152), with magnificent views of Chaumont (→) and Amboise (→). □

The wines of Touraine

Rabelais sang the praises of the red and white wines of Touraine. Vouvray is probably the best known, a dry, demi-sec or sweet white wine. On the opposite side of the Loire, Montlouis is another dry or demi-sec white, which is drinkable earlier than Vouvray and ages well. Other A.C. wines (white and rosé) : Touraine-Amboise, Touraine-Mesland, Touraine-Azay-le-Rideau and Touraine. All go very well with fish and white meat. As for the reds, Chinon, as Rabelais well knew, can be drunk young like Bourgueil. Chinon is full-bodied and ages well, while Bourgueil is a hardier and more sinewy wine which can take fifteen to twenty years in the bottle. Good years : 1945, 47, 55, 57, 64, 66, 69, 70, 71. The Orléanais and the Blésois : red, white and rosé from the Coteaux de Giennois and the Orléanais (Gris-Meunier, Cheverny, Coteaux du Vendômois and Châteaumeillant). Try Jasnières, a well known dry white from the Coteaux du Loir (communes of Lhomme and Chartre-sur-le-Loir).

■ BOURGUEIL

A2 / ® / pop. 4 185 (Indre-et-Loire)

Wine tasting in a cellar near Chevrette *(2 km N,* wine museum, *10-12:30 & 2-6 or 7:30 in summer).* ▶ In the village, the **church of St. Germain,** 12thC Angevin choir★ and former **abbey** (18thC Prior's residence, cloister gallery (1472), abbey château (17thC), storerooms★ 13thC). □

▶ Nearby

▶ 5 km S, **Château des Réaux** (15th-18thC), transformed into a château-accueil. ▶ 5 km E, **Restigné,** remarkable 11th-12thC church★. □

■ CHAMBORD★★★

B2 / ® / pop. 206 (Loir-et-Cher)

The château de Chambord is one of the marvels of the French Renaissance, marking the ambitious start of the reign of François I and the first signs of the architectural megalomania which ultimately led to the construction of Versailles. François I's liking for this residence is perhaps explained by his penchant for hunting.

▶ Chambord was a former hunting lodge, rebuilt from 1519. While based on the plan of a feudal château, with a four-towered central keep and enclosing wall, the central keep is actually inspired by Saint Peter's in Rome which was thus, for the first time, adapted to civil architecture. Characteristically, the façades are very simple, almost classical, while the "keep" is profusely decorated with chimneys, windows, spires and pinnacles, a sort of aerial village appearing above the trees in the park and symbolising "the ideal city" *(daily ex. hols. 9:30-12 & 2-5, 6 or 7 according to season;* C.N.M.H.S. (Historical Monuments Board) guided tours and Son et Lumière, *tel 54.20.31.32).* ▶ The **Grand Escalier** (Grand Staircase)★★★ with its double spiral crowned by the famous lantern, is a marvel of Renaissance ingenuity. There are no less than 440 rooms but the most interesting are the chapel, the guard rooms and the **terraces★★**, together with the apartments of Louis XIV and François I. ▶ The château is surrounded by a magnificent **park★** of 55 km^2 where the court could watch the hunt from the terraces. The park is now a national wild life reserve and only part of it is open to the public; viewing platforms have been set up to watch the deer and wild boar feeding in the early morning or late evening. The GR3 runs through the park. □

■ CHAUMONT-SUR-LOIRE★★

B2 / ® / pop. 842 (Loir-et-Cher)

High walls and enormous towers surrounding the top of the highest hill overlooking the Loire.

▶ This ancient feudal fortress (10thC) blends late Gothic (Amboise Tower and west side, 1465-81) and Renaissance styles (the three other towers and the S and E buildings and chapel). Three of the great ladies of French history stayed here, sometimes unwillingly : Catherine de Medici (1519-89) and her rival, Diane de Poitiers (1499-1566), wife and mistress respectively of Henri II; and Madame de Staël (1766-1817), when exiled from Napoleon's court. *(9:30-11:45 & 2:15-5:45, Apr.-Sep.; 9:45-12 & 2-4, 1 Oct.-31 Mar.).* ▶ The courtyard has a splendid view north over the valley. 15th-16thC furniture and works of art in the apartments. Remarkable **stables★.** □

■ CHENONCEAUX★★★

B2 / ® / pop. 361 (Indre-et-Loire)

It was Diane de Poitiers who proposed a five arched bridge across the Cher as a project for architect Philibert Delorme. However on the death of Henri II Catherine de Medici forced her to exchange Chenonceaux for Chaumont (→) and had the same architect build the great gallery on the bridge.

The rich table of the Val de Loire

Fruit and vegetables are the speciality of the Touraine and Orléanais regions. The Loire provides excellent salmon, carp (à la Chambord), *shad (with mushrooms) and other river fish. Pork and poultry provide the many forms of* andouillette, andouille *(chitterling sausages) and* rillettes *(potted meat), black or white* boudin *(blood sausage),* noisette de porc *(with prunes) and poultry (with* girolle *mushrooms). In the Sologne there are pheasant, boar, and lark and game patés and wild mushrooms...*
Country bread, goat cheese and red wine are the traditional staples of the Tourangeaux *(inhabitants of Touraine). Goat cheese comes in a variety of shapes and sizes. In the Orléanais they produce other delicious cheeses : Saint-Benoît, Cendré d'Olivet and Patay.*
In the French equivalent of the Gingerbread House, le parquet était de croquet, *in other words, the parquet floors were made of a delicious crunchy almond biscuit, only rivalled in popularity by* Pithiviers *(from the town of the same name),* macarons *(from Cormery),* "Gateaux Royaux" *(from Amboise and Loches) and other local specialities.*
Confectionery in the Val de Loire still clings to the traditional recipes : pruneaux *(prunes) de Tours, crystallised fruit, quince marmalade from Orléans, barley sugar and much more.*

▶ The **château** itself was built in 1515. The great **keep** in the foreground belongs to a former fortified manor which was destroyed to build the château *(9-7, 16 Mar.-15 Sep.; 9-6:30, 16-30 Sep.; 9-6, Oct.; 9-5, 1-15 Nov.; 9-12 & 2-4:30, 16 Nov.-15 Feb.; 9-5:30, 16-28 Feb.; 9-6, 1-15 Mar. No guides; boat trips on the Cher, children's facilities, Jul.-Aug.; restaurant and self-service 15 Feb.-15 Nov.; Son et Lumière : at the Time of the Ladies of Chenonceaux, 10 pm, Jul.-mid Sep.; tel 47.29.90.07).* ▶ A magnificent alley of plane trees leads up to the château. See the Guardroom **(Salle des Gardes;** 16thC **tile work★)** with fine Flemish tapestries; see also the **chapel,** and the bedrooms of Diane de Poitiers and François I. Magnificent Renaissance, 17th and 18thC paintings (Van Loo, Il Primaticcio, Rubens...) and marvellous furniture. ▶ You can also visit the kitchens and a wax museum (4 centuries of history, *separate ticket)* and walk in the **park.** □

■ The CHER Valley★

▶ From Vierzon to Tours *(112 km, half-day)*
B2

On the edge of the Sologne and in Touraine, the Cher is a slow-running river moving through peaceful countryside dotted with manors, châteaux, attractive towns and rows of poplars.

▶ **Vierzon** (→ Berry). ▶ **Mennetou-sur-Cher★** ® : A mediaeval country town with ramparts and old houses. The church has a 13thC square choir. ▶ Charming road along the left bank through **Saint-Loup** (see 13thC frescos in the church). ▶ **Villefranche-sur-Cher;** Romanesque capitals in the church . ▶ **Selles-sur-Cher,** clustered around Notre-Dame-la-Blanche★ (12th-19thC) and the former abbey (17thC, small museum, *visits by request tel 54.97.40.19*). The moated château is an ancient feudal fortress transformed in the time of Henri IV *(9:30-12 & 2-6, Jul.-15 Aug.; Sat., Sun. and pm only out of season; closed 12 Nov.-Easter)*. ▶ **Châtillon-sur-Cher;** panel★, school of da Vinci, in the church . ▶ **Noyers-sur-Cher** where the Canal du Berry joins the river; 13thC church with Angevin vaulting. ▶ **Saint-Aignan★** ® (pop. 3680) with old houses, Romanesque and Gothic Collegiate church (12th, 13th and 14thC murals in the crypt) and a château rebuilt in the reign of François I *(external visit only)*. **Beauval, ornithological park** *(10-nightfall)*. ▶ 5 km N, through Monthou-sur-Cher is the **Château du Gué-Péan★** (16th-17thC), a ravishing building hidden among oak trees *(9-6:30, 15 Mar.-15 Sep.; 9-6, 16 Sep.-15 Nov.; 10-5 rest of year)*. ▶ **Montrichard★** ® (pop. 3786) : The hillsides overlooking this ancient little town are honeycombed with caves where the white wine of Touraine goes through the champagne process (visit and wine tasting). Old houses with wooden facings in the Rue Nationale. Jeanne de France and the future Louis XII were married in the **church of St. Croix** (12thC). See also the **church of Nanteuil★** (12th, 13th and 15thC) and the **fortress★.** Richard Cœur-de-Lion (Richard the Lion Heart) was imprisoned in the enormous 12thC keep *(9:30-12 & 2:30-6:30 15 Jun.-5 Sep.; hols., Sat. and Sun. only rest of year)*; fine view from the top. ▶ 7.5 km NE, the former **abbey of Pontlevoy,** founded in 11thC, with 13th-15thC church housing beautiful 17thC altarpieces. Convent buildings 17thC. *(1 Jun.-15 Sep., 10:30-12 & 2:30-6:30, closed Mon.)*. ▶ 12 km SW, **château de Montpoupon★** one of the most graceful early Renaissance buildings in Touraine; Musée de la Vénerie (Hunting Museum) *(23 Mar.-31 Apr., 2-6; 1 May-14 Jun., 10-12 & 2-6; weekends and hols. only; 15 Jun.-30 Sep., 10-12 & 2-6 daily ex. weekends and hols.)*. ▶ **Chissay-en-Touraine,** 15th-17thC château. **"Or" strawberry liqueur distillery** *(visits Easter-end Sep.)* □

CHEVERNY★★

B2

Apart from Brissac, Cheverny is the only château on the Loire still belonging to the family that owned it at the beginning of the 16thC. It was completed in 1634 and is a transition between Renaissance and Louis XIV styles.

▶ The principal point of interest is the splendid **interior decoration★★** dating from the reign of Louis XIII and still in its original state *(9-6:30 in season; 9:30-12 & 2:15-5 or 6:30 remainder of year)*. Note the sumptuous furnishings of the *Chambre du Roi* (King's Bedroom), hung with magnificent tapestries. The **Cheverny Museum** maintains the old traditions of the hunt, with more than 2500 trophies. □

▶ Nearby

▶ **Château de Villesavin★** *(8 km NE)* : on the right bank of the Beuvron, right next to **Bracieux** ® *(10 km NE)*, this château, the marble fountain basin and the medallions on the left wing show the influence of the Florentine craftsmen who built this charming Renaissance structure in 1537. The **kitchens★** (the first for grills, the second for baked or roasted dishes and washing up, and the third as a cold room) illustrate the lifestyle of the period. Dovecote and old cars *(daily 10-12 & 2-nightfall; closed 20 Dec.-20 Jan.)*. ▶ **Château de Troussay★** *(3 km SW)* : this Renaissance country house is a perfect example of the small estates in Sologne (→) at that time *(Easter school hols. : 10-12:30 & 2:30-6:30; between Easter school hols. and summer school hols. : Sun. and nat. hols. only, same hours; summer school hols. : daily to 7; from then to 11 Nov : Sunday and nat. hols. only, 10-12:30 & 2-5)*. ▶ **Château de Beauregard★** *(9 km NW)*. This fine Renaissance building, enlarged 17thC, has a famous **portrait gallery★** of 363 "celebrities" of the period. Note also the Delft **tiling★** showing an army of the time of Louis XIII on the march, the oak panelling and the paintings in the *Cabinet des Grelots★* (literally, "cow-bell room" *9:30-12 & 2-6:30 Apr.-Sept.; 9:30-12 & 2-5 ex Wed. rest of year; closed 15 Jan.-15 Feb.)*. ▶ **Fougères-sur-Bièvre★** *(11.5 km SW)* : a beautiful example of military architecture at end 15thC *(2 Jan.-31 Mar., 10-11:15 & 2-3:30, closed Tue. and Wed.; 1 Apr.-30 Sep., 9-11 & 2-6, closed Tue., Wed.; 1 Oct.-31 Dec., 10-11:15 & 2-3:30)*. Beyond **Contres** ® *(9 km S)*, the village of **Chémery** *(19 km SW)* contains a château dating from the 13th, 15th and 16thC *(daily, 10-dusk; closed Tue.)*. □

CHINON★★

A2 / ® / pop. 8673 (Indre-et-Loire)
See plan on following page

The old town is a lively reminder of the Middle Ages, where the streets have hardly changed since the day in March 1429 when Joan of Arc passed through them on her way from Domrémy to meet the Dauphin (heir to the throne) and change the destiny of France.

▶ **Rue Haute-St. Maurice** and its continuation, **Rue Voltaire** (B2) are lined with picturesque buildings from the 15th, 16th and 17thC. Here and in the **Grand-Carroi★★** is the heart of the old city. ▶ No. 44, the Maison des États Généraux (15thC) houses the **Vieux-Chinon museum** *(10-12 & 2-5, Sep.-May; 10-12 & 3-7, Jun.-Aug.; 2-6, Sep.-Dec.; closed Tue. and Jan.)*. ▶ The ruined **château★★** was composed of three fortresses separated by deep moats and mounted on a rocky spur *(9-12 & 2-5, or 6 in season; 9-6, Jul.-Aug.; closed Wed., Dec., Jan.; Son et Lumière, mid Jun.-mid Sep.; Tue. and Fri., live performances; visit to the underground passages some Sats. Jul.-Aug. 9 pm)*. ▶ In the east, the remains of Fort St. Georges. The **Pavillon de L'Horloge** (Joan of Arc Museum) leads to the **château du Milieu** (12th-14thC), scene of the first meeting between Joan of Arc and the Dauphin, when the 18-year-old Joan was able to recognise the future Charles VII, despite his anonymous appearance, in the midst of 300 knights (March 9th, 1429). A bridge over the moat links this château to the **château du Coudray** (13thC keep★) on the west of the promontory (view★). ▶ The famous **echo★** is ten minutes away on foot *(signposted)*.
Also... ▶ The bridge and the **Quai Danton** (A3) : superb view over the town. ▶ **Church of St.**

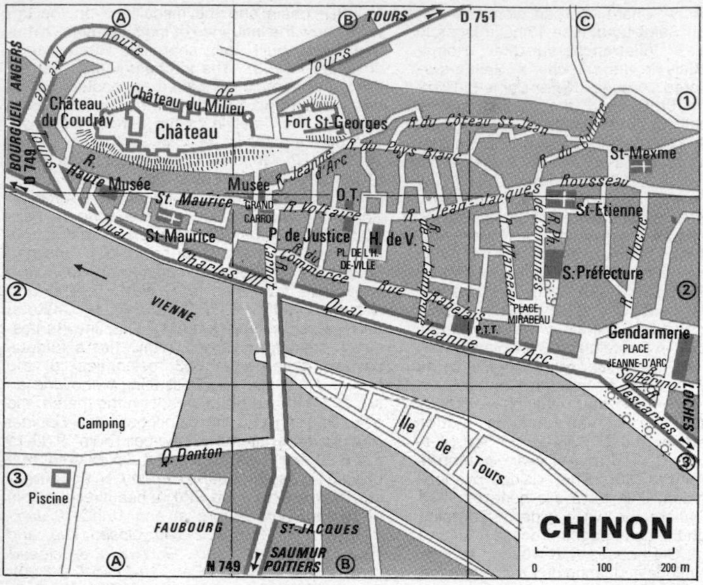

Maurice★ (A2, 12thC), in purest Angevin style. ▶ **Church of St. Etienne** (C1-2), Flamboyant Gothic 15thC). ▶ **Church of St. Mexme** (C1), former Collegiate church of 10thC (11th and 15thC towers), 15 mins on foot up to **Chapel of St. Radegonde,** a troglodyte sanctuary (6th-12thC with 12thC fresco). Close by, Animated museum of wine and barrel-making *(1 Apr.-30 Sep., 10-12 & 2-6, closed Feb.).* □

▶ Nearby

▶ **"Train 1900",** steam train from Chinon to Richelieu *(1 hr, 15 km),* food and wine halt by request at Ligré-Rivière *(regular service Sat. and Sun., 15 May-end Sep.).* ▶ **Avoine Nuclear power station** *(12 km NW)* : Chinon A (gas-graphite) and Chinon B (enriched uranium); *(requests for visits at least 2 weeks in advance : Centrale de Chinon, B.P. 23, 37420 Avoine, tel 47.93.04.50; visit to Chinon B site, tel 47.93.20.40).* ▶ **Château du Rivau** *(11.5 km SE)* : 13th-15thC., period furniture, exhibitions of painting *(10-12 & 2-7, 15 Mar.-Oct.).* ▶ **Champigny-sur-Veude**★ *(15 km SE)* : the **chapel**★★ of the old château is a Renaissance gem with marvellous **stained glass**★★ (1538-61), *(9-12 & 2-6, Apr.-15 Oct.; 16 Oct.-3 Nov., closed weekends and hols.).* □

▶ Rabelais territory *(17 km round trip SW, 2 hr).*

▶ **Chinon.** ▶ **La Devinière,** a simple late-15thC building, the former estate of the Rabelais family. François was born there around 1494. All his literary place names are derived from the neighbourhood and in "Gargantua" he made it the scene of the Picrocholine War. Museum of the writer's life and work *(9-12 & 2-6, or 5 out of season; ex Wed. Dec., Jan.).* ▶ **Seuilly.** Benedictine abbey where one of Rabelais' heroes gave battle to his enemies. □

▶ La Vienne upstream from Chinon *(34 km round trip, 1 hr).*

▶ **Chinon.** ▶ **Cravant-les-Coteaux.** 1 km N, in the old town, church with Carolingian elements; small archaeological museum *(2:30-6; closed Tue.).* ▶ **L'Isle Bouchard :** on the left bank, church of St. Maurice (14th-15thC) with carved 16thC pulpit★ and Romanesque ruins of the church of St. Léonard★ (end 11thC; capitals★★). On the right bank, the church of St. Gilles (11th-12thC). ▶ **Tavant,** late 11thC church, crypt decorated with remarkable Romanesque paintings★★ *(1 Mar.-30 Nov., 10-12 & 2-6:30).* □

▶ La Vienne downstream from Chinon *(16 km round trip, 1 hr 30).*

▶ **Candes-Saint-Martin,** in one of the loveliest **sites**★★ in the Val de Loire. 13thC church★★, fortified in the15thC, on the site of the house where St. Martin died (397). ▶ Close by : Fontevrault l'Abbaye and Montsoreau★★ (→ Maine-Anjou). □

■ GIEN★

C2 / ® / pop. 16784 (Loiret)

One of the first royal châteaux, Gien is the start of the sumptuous route through the Val de Loire. The town was rebuilt after WWII in traditional regional style using cut stone and glazed pink brick.

▶ The **château**★ (1484) can be seen above the old town, with its façade of red and black brick

Gien pottery

The beautiful Gien ceramics draw their inspiration from allegories, proverbs, riddles, and military scenes... They first appeared in 1820, at a period when antiquity was the fashion. The Manufacture de Gien, the largest ceramics works in France, covers some 15 acres W of the town.

in geometrical patterns. It houses the **Musée International de la Chasse** ★★ (International Shooting Museum); paintings by François Desportes (1661-1743) *(9:15-11:45 & 2:15-6:30 or 5:30 out of season)*. ▶ Nearby, the **church of Ste. Jeanne-d'Arc**★ (1954) in brick, with 15thC bell-tower. ▶ Place de la Victoire, the **Manufacture de Gien** (ceramics works) houses an interesting **museum** *(9-11:45 & 2-5:45; factory visit on request, no children under 12)*. □

▶ Nearby

▶ **Château de la Bussière** *(13 km NE)* : 15th-16thC, beside a lake; Musée des Pêcheurs★ (fishermen's museum; *9-12 & 2-6; on request, ex Sun. out of season; closed Mar.)*. ▶ **Briare** ®® *(11 km SE)* : canal-bridge★ (1890) over the Loire; Automobile museum (1895-1960). ▶ **Ouzouer-sur-Trezee,** château de Pont-Cherron (19thC), Gallo-Roman mosaics *(1 Apr.-15 Sep., 2-6, closed Tue.)*. □

Le GRAND-PRESSIGNY★

A3 / ® / pop. 1 185 (Indre-et-Loire)

This little village on the edge of the Touraine is known principally for its prehistoric finds. Near the ruined château (12thC keep★) the new Renaissance château houses a remarkable **Prehistory Museum**★ *(9-12 & 2-6, or 5 out of season; closed Wed. and Dec.-Jan.)*. □

▶ Nearby

▶ **La Guerche** *(7 km SW)* : château★ built by Charles VII on the edge of the river *(10-12 & 2-7, Jul.-Aug., ex Sun. am; closed Tue. out of season; closed Dec.-Mar.)*. ▶ **Descartes** *(11.5 km NW)*, further down the captivating **valley of the Claise**★ **:** birthplace of famous French thinker and philosopher René Descartes (1596-1650); small museum *(2-6:30 closed Tue.)*. □

The INDRE Valley★

▶ From Loches to Azay-le-Rideau *(54 km, 4 hr)*
A2

A luminous valley typical of the Touraine where the Indre runs quietly between two walls of tufa, the beautiful white stone used to build so many of the houses in the Val de Loire. Loches (→) and Azay-le-Rideau (→) are high points of mediaeval and Renaissance architecture respectively.

▶ **Loches.** ▶ **Azay-sur-Indre** (site★ and château, which belonged to La Fayette, hero of the American War of Independence). ▶ **Reignac** (château, dairy and mill). ▶ **Cormery,** known for its macaroons and the Benedectine abbey founded in the 8thC; St. Paul tower★ (11thC); refectory★ (13thC); kitchens and storerooms etc. *(visit 3 pm Jun.-Sep.; closed Sun. and nat. hols.)*. ▶ Further on, the **château de Couzières** (15th-17thC). **Montbazon** ® : a formidable rectangular keep★ (12thC; *1 June-15 Sep., daily 10-10; 15 Oct.-31 Jan., 1 Mar.-31 May, Sat., Sun., hols. 10-6; Mon., Tue., Thu., Fri., 10-2*). ▶ **Artannes-sur-Indre,** a picturesque grouping of château, church and mill. ▶ As far as **Saché** (→ Azay-le-Rideau) the itinerary retraces one of Balzac's famous novels, *Le Lys dans la Vallée*. □

In the steps of Balzac

Balzac's writings reveal a lifelong devotion to his native Touraine, where the Château de Saché provided a refuge for the harassed author. A large part of his work describes towns in the Loire Valley : Orléans, Vouvray, Blois, Moncontour, Saumur and especially Tours.

LANGEAIS★★

A2 / ® / pop. 4 142 (Indre-et-Loire)

The château de Langeais was erected in a single operation around 1465; in this severe feudal fortress, Charles VIII of France married Anne, Duchess of Brittany, on 16 December 1491, thus paving the way for the cession of Brittany to France.

▶ A visit to the **apartments**★★ will take you straight into the Middle Ages; only the original inhabitants are lacking in this lordly setting. Magnificent **tapestries collection**★★ *(15 Mar.-30 Jun., 9-12 & 2-6:30; July-Aug., 9-6:30; 1-30 Sep., 9-12 & 2-6:30; 1 Oct.-2 Nov., closed at 6; 3 Nov.-14 Mar., closed at 5; 15 Mar.-30 Sep., closed Mon. am non-hols.; 1 Oct.-14 Mar., closed Mon. non-hols.)*. □

▶ Nearby

▶ **Cinq-Mars-la-Pile** ® *(5 km E)* : overlooked by the ruins of a feudal château with huge moats★; interesting historical associations with Richelieu and Louis XIII *(10-12 & 2-6 or dusk Mar.-11 Nov.; closed Mon. ands hols.)*. □

LOCHES★★

A2 / ® / pop. 7 019 (Indre-et-Loire)
See plan on following page

The beauty of Loches's trim white houses, set in the idyllic countryside of the Indre, contrasts sharply with the sinister reputation of its fortress, where those unwise

The kings of the Val de Loire

The seat of royalty was transferred to the Touraine region when the English captured Paris during the Hundred Years' War, and the Plantagenet Kings of England ruled most of France. But Touraine, Berry, Poitou and the Blésois remained faithful to the House of Valois, and in 1422 Charles VII was proclaimed King at Mehun-sur-Yèvre. With the advent of Joan of Arc, the reconquest of the Val de Loire was the first step in the restoration of the French kingdom and Charles VII established himself in the provinces which had supported him. Louis XI and Charles VIII could subsequently have taken up residence in Paris, but preferred the charms of the Touraine. The glow of royalty faded from the Val de Loire with Henri IV and the Protestant question .... Paris was worth a Mass, as he said.

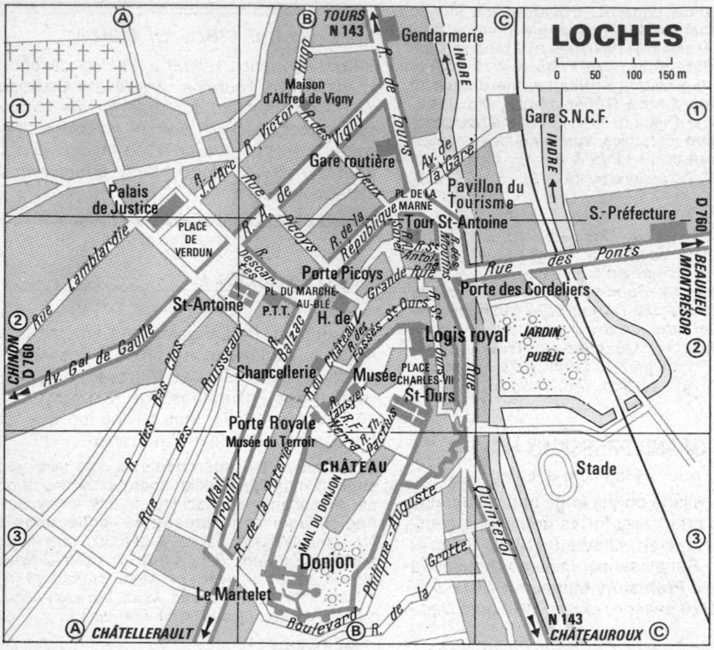

enough to displease the kings of France were once imprisoned in damp dungeons.

▶ The **Porte des Cordeliers★** (B2, 15thC) leads to the Grande Rue; on the right, the Renaissance **Hôtel de Ville★** and the 15thC **Porte Picoys★.** ▶ The Rue du Château (fine Renaissance houses) climbs to the **Cité Médiévale★★** (mediaeval town) with its impressive 13thC towers and ramparts. Behind the **Porte Royale★** (Royal Gate) is the Regional Museum (Musée du Terroir); paintings by the Vendéen artist Lansyer *(Easter-end Sep., 9-11:45 & 2-6; Mar., Oct., 9-11:45 & 2-5; Nov.-end Feb., 9-11:45 & 2-4; closed Fri.).* ▶ **Church of St. Ours★★,** 12thC Romanesque, with two octagonal pyramids between the towers, covering the nave. ▶ The **château★★** was inhabited by Charles VII, Louis XI, Charles VIII and Louis XII. The Old Wing (Vieux Logis; Mediaeval) is easily distinguished from the Nouveau Logis (New Wing) of the Renaissance. **Triptych★★** (1485, school of Jean Fouquet), **effigy of Agnès Sorel★**, the beautiful favourite of Charles VII *(15 Mar.-30 Sep., 9-12 & 2-6; 1 Jun.-31 Aug. 9-6; 1 Oct.-14 Mar., 9-12 & 2-5; closed Wed., Dec., Jan.).* ▶ The 11th-15thC **keep★★** is a fine example of the fortifications of the period, with dungeons dug deep into the rock. ▶ **Tour of the ramparts★★** *(opens, closes, 1/2 hr after château).* □

▶ Nearby

▶ **Beaulieu-lès-Loches** *(1 km E)* : 11th-15thC abbey church (12thC bell-tower★). ▶ **Bridoré** *(15 km SE)* : with a 14th-15thC fortress. ▶ **Loches Forest★** *(7 km E)* : perfect for walks and bicycling; former **Chartreuse du Liget,** founded 1178 *(9-12 & 2-6 or 7, exterior only).* ▶ **Montrésor** *(17 km E)* : Renaissance **church★** (1519) with contemporary **tombs★;** fortified Louis XII - style **château★** *(Apr.-Oct., 9-12:30 & 2-6:30).* ▶ **Nouans-les-Fontaines** *(26 km E)* : in 13thC church, **Descent from the Cross** by the school of Jean Fouquet (15thC). □

The troglodytes

In the Touraine, around Vendôme and south of the Sarthe, the soft white limestone tufa bordering the river proved ideally suited for carving out semi-subterranean dwellings; even chapels and manors have been partially dug into the rock. These days cellars and terraces are often complemented by a house built against the cliff face. In this vine-growing country, tufa cellars are naturally used for storing wine; many of them are open for wine-tasting (Amboise, Montlouis, Vouvray...). The valleys of the Loire, the Loir, the Indre and the Cher have the best examples of troglodyte dwellings. See especially the village of Trôo (→ Valley of the Loir).

The **LOIR** Valley★★

▶ From Vendôme to La Chartre-sur-le-Loir *(40 km, 3 hr)*
A-B1 *(see map 1)*

The Loir (on no account confuse this peaceful little river with the far greater Loire), runs from the Ile-de-France to Anjou through rich meadows and lines of poplars. The surrounding vineyards, gardens, chalky hillsides and white, creeper-covered houses represent the epitome of rural tranquility.

▶ **Vendôme** (→). ▶ **Villiers-sur-Loir.** 1.5 km SW : **château de Rochambeau** (16th-18thC). ▶ **Gué-du-Loir;** captivating site★. ▶ **Montoire-sur-le-Loir★** ® (pop. 4 431) : an angler's paradise; Renaissance houses and town hall; **murals★★** (12th-13thC) in the chapel of St.

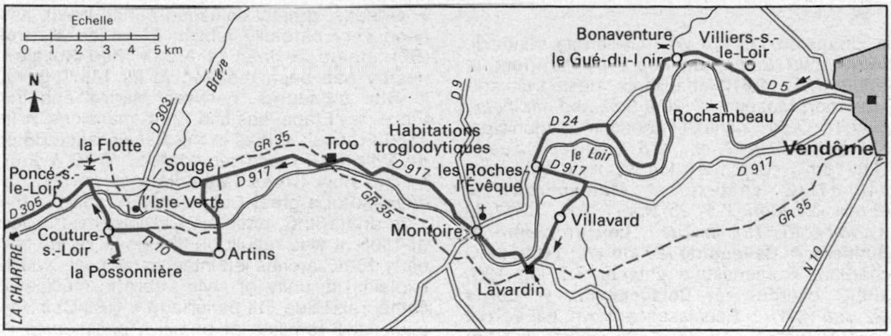

1. River Loir near Vendôme

Gilles *(1 Oct.-28 Feb., 9:30-7; closed Tue., 1 Mar.-30 Sept., 9:30-7; daily)*. On the hill, ruins of 12th-14thC château. 2.5km SE, **Lavardin★** ® is overlooked by the romantic ruins of the château of the Counts of Vendôme; 11th-12thC keep★ (visits by request *9-7 in summer*). In the village, the Romanesque church of St. Genest has murals★ from the 12th to 16thC. ▶ **Trôo★** is partially dug into the side of the hill. Passages, narrow streets and *Caforts* (galleries) dug into the rock form an impenetrable maze. Go to see the Church of St. Martin★ (12thC), and on the edge of the plateau near a feudal motte (view★) the "Puits-Qui-Parle" (echoing well). There is also a fossil cave. ▶ On the left bank, ▶ **Saint-Jacques-des-Guérets :** 12thC church with paintings★ of the same period. ▶ **Manor of La Possonnière★,** Renaissance, where the poet Ronsard was born in 1524. ▶ Poncé-sur-le-Loir and La Chartre-sur-le-Loir (→ Maine-Anjou). □

■ MONTARGIS

C1 / ® / pop. 17 629 (Loiret)

The numerous parallel branches of the Loing, with their attendant bridges, have gained for Montargis the somewhat grandiose title of "la Venise du Gâtinais" (the Venice of the Gâtinais); despite this exaggeration, the town is undeniably attractive and is a popular fishing and hunting centre.

▶ The local speciality is **"pralines"** (chocolates or sweets, usually almond flavoured), sold in all shapes and sizes. Pralines are still sold in the restored building where they were invented. ▶ Next door is the **church of the Madeleine** (12thC nave, 16thC choir★). **Girodet Museum** in the town hall, in large part devoted to this local painter *(9-12 & 1-5:30; closed Mon.)*. □

▶ Nearby

▶ **Chapelon** *(15 km W)* : Gaillardan Windmill, 15thC *(3-6 Sun., May-Sep.)*. ▶ **Pithiviers** ® *(45 km NW)* : 9 812 inhabitants, steam train and Transport Museum *(2 :30-6 Sun. and nat. hols., May-16 Oct.)*; Kanaka collection in Municipal Museum *(10-12 & 2-6; closed Tue.)*; 12th-16thC church. 19 km NE from Pithiviers, 14th-17thC château at **Malesherbes** ® *(2 Nov.-24 Mar., 2-5; 25 Mar.-1 Nov., 10-11:30 & 2:30-6:15; closed Tue.)*; **Leisure centre at Buthiers.** ▶ **Bellegarde** *(23 km W)* : 14th-18thC château, Romanesque church. 7.5 km NW, 13thC church★ at **Boiscommun.** ▶ **Lorris** *(22 km SW)* : Renaissance town hall★, old covered market and 12th-13thC church. ▶ **Châtillon-Coligny** : outbuildings of the famous Admiral de Coligny's (1519-72) family château (12thC keep★, Renaissance well★). ▶ **Ferrières-en-Gâtinais** *(12 km N)* : 11th-15thC church★. ▶ **Domaine des Barres Arboretum** *(20 km S)* : 10 000 trees of 3 500 species *(visits by request, tel 38.47.60.20)*. □

■ ORLÉANS★

B1 / ® / pop. 105 589 (Loiret)

Like all the towns on the Loire, Orléans is best seen from the river. On 7 May 1489, Joan of Arc made her triumphal entry into the town after the English had been driven out. Since then, the Fête de Jeanne d'Arc on the 7th and 8th of May has remained one of the high spots of the town's year. Orléans has always been a thriving commercial town and, to the north, now has an industrialised zone, in addition to its traditional business in corn, potatoes, vegetables, Loire wines and local nursery produce. Across the Loire is a new ecologically oriented town, **Orléans-La-Source.** In addition to its widely-known Botanical Gardens, it has managed to surround its offices and factories with woods and greenery.

The school of the Loire and the Renaissance

After the Hundred Years' War, the second half of the 15thC proved a period of growth and well-being. A return to more orderly ways allowed security to be gradually sacrificed to comfort; the châteaux became progressively less military and took on the role of country estates. The school of the Loire (Plessis-lès-Tours, Gien, Clos-Lucé, Azay-le-Rideau) is marked by the introduction of Italian designs (Charles VIII brought back a number of artists from his campaigns in Italy), and the conservatism which adhered to traditional concepts. This first French Renaissance period ended with the Pavia Campaign (1525) and was succeeded by a more intellectual phase reflecting the ideas of humanist architects, whose inspiration was drawn first from the Italians and later, more directly, from classical antiquity.

▶ Orléans, greatly damaged during WWII, has been very carefully rebuilt. **Place du Martroi** (B2), statue of Joan of Arc. ▶ **Rue Royale★** nearby has been restored to its 18thC glory. ▶ **Rue d'Escures,** between Martroi and the Place de l'Etape, has fine 17thC mansions. ▶ In 1560 François II died in the Renaissance **Hôtel de Ville** (B2, much remodelled, *10-12 & 2-6*). ▶ The **Holy Cross Cathedral★** is an unusual example of a great Gothic church rebuilt in the 17th and 18thC, after the Calvinist destruction of 1568. It was rebuilt on the model of the two early 16thC arches left intact in the nave, which explains its unity of style - rare in mediaeval cathedrals. See the panelling★★ (18thC) in the choir; the remains of primitive sanctuaries in the crypt (4th and 9th-11thC); interesting treasure room. ▶ The **gardens★** of the former Bishops residence are charming. ▶ **Fine Arts Museum★★** (B2), in the Place de la Cathédrale, has an incomparable collection of 17th-18thC portraits★★ (French school), and a series of pastels★★ and busts★ signed Houdon, Pigalle and Germain Pilon. Don't miss St. Thomas★ by Velázquez and L'Ombre★ by Rodin.

Also... ▶ **Church of St. Aignan** (C3) : late 10thC crypt★. ▶ **Hôtel Cabu★** (B2), charming Renaissance building housing the History Museum *(10-12 & 2-5 or 6; closed Tue.)*. ▶ The **house of Joan of Arc** (dioramas), Place Gen. de Gaulle (B2). ▶ **Notre-Dame de Recouvrance★** (A2), 16thC, stained glass★ in the Apse. ▶ **Charles Péguy Museum,** 11 Rue du Tabour *(1:30-6; closed Tue.)*. □

▶ Nearby

▶ **Olivet** ® *(4 km S)* : fishing, canoeing, restaurants and cafes along the delightful banks of the Loiret. ▶ **Parc Floral de la Source★★** (floral park) *(8 km SE)* : in season, enchanting displays of tulips, iris, roses, dahlias and chrysanthemums; fountains, animals and attractions in the Park, where the Loiret surfaces *(9-6, Apr.-11 Nov.; 2-5 Jan.-Mar. and 12 Nov.-Dec.*; greenhouse restaurant). ▶ **Tigy** *(29 km SE)* : Museum of Old Rural Crafts *(2:30-6:30 Sun., 15 Apr.-15 Oct.; on request the rest of year)*. ▶ **Saint-Denis-de-l'Hôtel** *(16 km E)*, house of Maurice Genevoix *(Easter-30 Sep., Fri., Sat., Sun., 10-12 & 3-6)*. ▶ **Châteauneuf-sur-Loire** ® *(25 km E)* : In the château park, arboretum, giant rhododendrons★; Museum of Loire Rivercraft and of Old Châteauneuf *(10-12 & 2-6 Jul.-Aug., pm on request rest of year)*. ▶ **Forest of Orléans★,** NE of town; more than 340 km², mostly pines and oaks; signposted walks, picnic areas and guided tours *(info at SI)*. Ecological Museum, Forêt des Loges, at **Nibelle** *(Mar.-Nov.)*. □

■ RICHELIEU★

A3 / ® / pop. 2 496 (Indre-et-Loire)

Once a little village, then transformed at Cardinal Richelieu's behest into a planned town to provide accommodation for his court near his huge château, now almost entirely destroyed. One of the most beautiful towns in French classical style (17thC). 28 mansions, all alike, border the Grande-Rue linking two symmetrical squares. Covered market with exceptional 17thC timber structure★. ▶ **Richelieu Museum** in the Hôtel de Ville *(10-12 & 2-6, Jul.-Aug.; 10-12 & 2-4 rest of year; closed Tue., weekends, hols. out of season)*; ▶ Château **park★** (1 000 acres, *admission free*). ▶ Tourist railway (→ Chinon). □

SAINT-BENOÎT-SUR-LOIRE★★★

C1 / ® / pop. 1 925 (Loiret)

The abbey spire here is rich in symbolism. The site has been a place of pilgrimage since the time of the druids; in the Middle Ages the relics of Saint Benedict, the "Father of Western monasticism" were transferred here; under Charlemagne the cultural influence of the Benedictine abbey spread throughout the Christian world.

▶ **The abbey church**★★★ (1067-1218) is one of France's most remarkable Romanesque buildings; in front of the façade is an enormous square tower, forming the porch. Don't miss : the **capitals**★★ in the porch, the 13thC **sculptures**★ by the north doorway and the balanced proportions of the choir (4th-5thC mosaic), and the 11thC **crypt**★ containing the relics of St. Benedict *(7 am-10 pm ex during services, no guides; guided tour on written request; Gregorian chant; mass Sun. and religious feastdays, 10h45, wkdays 11h45).* □

▶ Nearby

▶ **Germigny-des-Prés** *(5.5 km NW)* : little church★★ dating from Charlemagne (806 except 11thC nave) superb 9thC mosaic★★ (l'Arche d'Alliance) in E. apse *(8-8).* □

The SOLOGNE Region★

▶ Round trip *(119 km, half-day)*
B2 *(see map 2)*

The Sologne is a region of woods, heaths and lakes in a loop of the Loire, south of Orléans. It is a paradise for anglers and hunters, but less so for walkers since much of the land is enclosed or private property.

2. Sologne

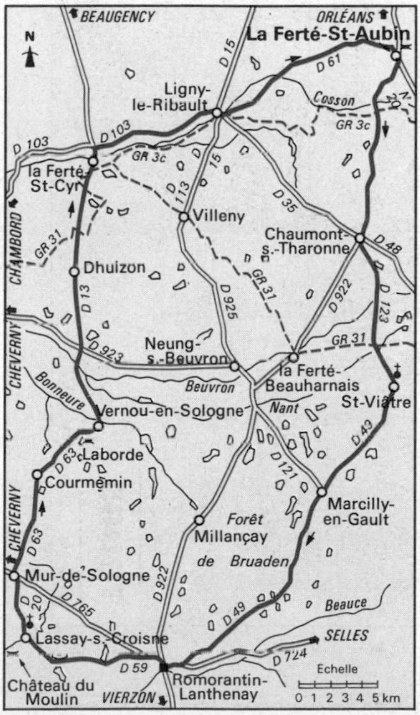

The Sologne was once a region of marshes and fevers and was only drained after the Second Empire; the rivers were dredged, one-third of the lakes were filled in, and the woods-were replanted. Today almost half the 5 000 km^2 of the Sologne is cultivated land : maize, fruit (especially strawberries), and vegetables (especially asparagus). There are also numerous game farms.

To avoid continually running up against the "No Entry" signs which are numerous in this part of the world, it is worth buying the map of the area, La Carte de la Sologne *(I.G.N., 1/100 000), showing all footpaths and bridle-paths together with details of leisure facilities and accommodation.*

▶ **La Ferté-Saint-Aubin** ® (pop. 5 498) : low wood-faced brick houses round the château in Louis XIII style; typical of the Sologne. ▶ 6 km E, the **Domaine Solognot du Ciran** *(book beforehand, tel : 38.65.90.93)* : good description of the Sologne countryside; portrayal of past lifestyles. ▶ **Ligny-le-Ribault.** ▶ **La Ferté-Saint-Cyr.** ▶ **Dhuizon.** ▶ **Château de Labord.** ▶ **Courmemin,** 13thC church. ▶ **Mur-de-Sologne;** 3 km NW : château de la Morinière (16thC). **Gy-de-Sologne,** straize agricultural museum; *(visit 15 Mar.-15 Nov., 10-11:30 & 3-6:30; closed weekends).* ▶ **Château du Moulin** *(9-11:30, & 2-6:30 Mar.-15 Nov.),* charming 15thC manor with wide moats fed by the Croisne; fine furniture and tapestries (15th-17thC). ▶ **Romorantin-Lanthenay** ® (pop. 18 187) : a large market town; almost the only important centre in the region. Ancient houses★, gardens and the various arms of the Sauldre make this a charming town. Sologne Museum★ in the town hall; life, folklore, crafts etc. *(1 Oct.-31 Mar., weekdays 10-11:30 & 2-5, Sat. 10-11:30 & 2-5:30, Sun. and hols. 11-12 & 2-5:30; 1 Apr.-30 Sept., Mon., Wed., 9:30-11:30 & 2-5:30, Thu., Fri., Sat., 10-11:30 & 2-5:30; Sun. and hols. close at 6; closed Tue.).* Rue de la Résistance, 16thC building (the Chancellory, Hôtel Saint-Pol). Remnants of former royal château (15th-16thC). Motor Racing Museum, 29-31 Fbg. d'Orléans *(1 Oct.-31 Mar., Mon. 11-12 & 2-5, Wed., weekends 11-12 & 2-7, Thu., Fri. 11-12 & 2-6; 1 Apr.-30 Sept., Mon. 10-12 & 2-5, Wed., Sat. 10-12 & 2-7, Thu., Fri. 10-12 & 2-6).* Archaeological Museum, Carroir-Doré *(tel 54.76.22.06).* 17.5 km E : **Château de la Ferté-Imbault,** 16th-17thC. *(1 Aug.-30 Sep., Mon., Fri., weekends 2-2:45 & 3:30-4:45).* ▶ **Saint-Viâtre** *(25 km NE of Romorantin)* : four 16thC painted panels★ in the church. □

SULLY-SUR-LOIRE★

C1 / ® / pop. 5 825 (Loiret)

Sully is a pleasant little country town facing the Loire, known for its château with water-filled moats and popular as a hunter's rendez-vous.

▶ **The château**★★ is linked to the memory of the indefatigable Sully, the great minister of Henri IV. It was he who rebuilt the **"Petit Château"** at the beginning of 17thC, at right angles to the 14thC mediaeval château, overlooking the Loire *(daily 10-11:45 & 2-4:45; changeable hours-check ahead; closed Dec.-Feb.)*; magnificent **beams**★★ in the keep. ▶ Place de la Halle, Renaissance house from Henri IV period. ▶ Stained glass windows in church of **Saint-Ythier** (16thC.). □

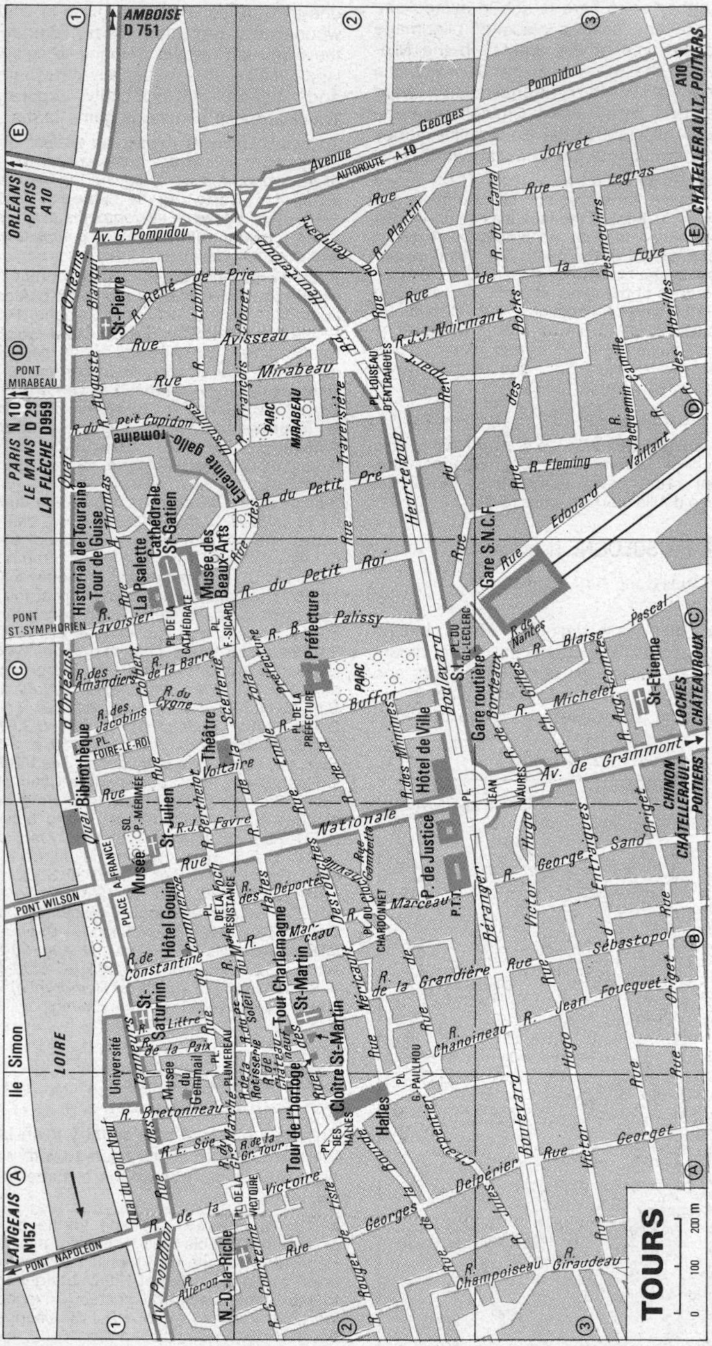
TOURS
0 100 200 m
LOIRE
Ile Simon
AMBOISE D 751
ORLÉANS PARIS A10
PARIS N 10 LE MANS D 29 LA FLÈCHE D959
PONT MIRABEAU
PONT ST-SYMPHORIEN
PONT WILSON
PONT NAPOLEON
LANGEAIS N152
A10 CHÂTELLERAULT, POITIERS
LOCHES CHÂTEAUROUX
CHINON CHÂTELLERAULT POITIERS
Avenue Georges Pompidou
AUTOROUTE A 10
Av. G. Pompidou
Quai d'Orléans
St-Pierre
Rue Avisseau
Rue Mirabeau
PARC MIRABEAU
Enceinte gallo-romaine
Historial de Touraine Tour de Guise
La Psalette
Cathédrale St-Gatien
Musée des Beaux-Arts
R. du Petit Pré
R. du Petit Roi
Préfecture
PARC Buffon
Gare S.N.C.F.
Gare routière
Hôtel de Ville
P. de Justice
P.T.T.
Bibliothèque
Théâtre
St-Julien
Musée
Hôtel Gouin
St-Saturnin
Université
Musée du Gemmail
Tour Charlemagne
St-Martin
Cloître St-Martin
Tour de l'horloge
Halles
N.-D.-la-Riche
St-Etienne
Boulevard Heurteloup
Rue Nationale
Av. de Grammont
Boulevard Béranger
Rue Victor Hugo
R. Jean Fouquet
R. Fleming
Rue Jolivet

TOURS★★★

A2 / ® / pop. 136 483 (Indre-et-Loire)

A city of rich merchants, who built the elegant Renaissance and Neo-classic mansions, Tours today is a centre of light industry, research and data processing. The old quarters of the town have been renovated and many are pedestrian precincts. This is a tourist centre for those visiting the châteaux of the Loire, but it is also the scene of important International Fairs in May and September and a world-famous Music Festival held in the Grange de Meslay *(last Fri. and weekend in June and 1st Fri. and weekend in July).*

▶ **Place Jean-Jaurès** (C3) with its café-terraces, flowers and fountains is the centre of social activity under the watchful eye of the Caryatids on the Hôtel de Ville (1905). ▶ At No. 19 Rue Émile-Zola is the **Hôtel Mame** (18thC), a town mansion with an exhibition of furniture, tapestries and old books *(2:30-6 or 6:30, Apr.-13 Sep.).* ▶ The **cathedral quarter** (C1) is an island of calm; a gigantic **cedar of Lebanon★** shades the courtyard of the former Archbishop's residence (17th-18thC) which houses the **Musée des Beaux-Arts** (Fine Arts Museum)★★ *(9-12:45 & 2-6, ex Tue. and nat. hols.).* A remarkable succession of salons decorated with wood panelling and silk wall coverings from Tours evokes French taste from Louis XIV to Louis XVI. French, Flemish and Italian schools are well represented : the museum's masterpieces are 'Christ au Jardin des Oliviers'★★, the 'Résurrection' by Mantegna, a Rubens, and Rembrandt's 'Flight into Egypt'. **Public garden★.** ▶ **The cathedral of St. Gatien★★** shows the evolution of Gothic style from 13thC (choir) to 15th-16thC (façade), terminating in the Renaissance lanterns on the two towers. See the 13th-14thC stained glass★★. ▶ Close by, the **cloister of La Psalette★** (15th-16thC, frescos) where Balzac located several chapters of his *Curé de Tours.* To the north, the **Tour de Guise** (C1) is one of the remnants of the royal château built in 1160 by Henry II of England. The château, now restored, houses the **Historial de Touraine** (leather museum created by the Grévin Museum of Paris : *summer 9-9; spring, fall 9-12:30 & 2-7; winter 2-6; no tickets sold 1 hr before closing).* ▶ Along the Rue Colbert to the **Place Foire-le-Roi** lined with 15thC gabled houses. At no. 8, **Hôtel Babou de la Bourdaisière★,** Renaissance. ▶ The **church of St. Julien★** (13thC Gothic) originally belonged to an abbey; its cellars are today the **Touraine Wine Museum** *(9-12 & 2-6; closed Tue.).* Above the Chapter★ *(temporary exhibitions)* is the **Musée du Compagnonnage★** (Craft Guild Museum) where you can see the pieces created by craftsmen to prove their mastery of various trades *(9-12 & 2-6; closed Tue.).* ▶ Nearby in Rue Jules-Favre are the **Palace of Commerce★** (1759), the remains of the Renaissance Hôtel de Semblançay and the Fontaine de Beaune★ (1511). ▶ Rue du Commerce (B1), the **Hôtel Gouin★,** Renaissance mansion, housing the **Touraine Archaeological Museum** *(9-12 & 2-5 or 6; closed Fri., Dec., Jan.).* ▶ Now you come to **Vieux Tours★★** (Old Tours), rich in old houses and mansions. Magnificently restored and transformed into a pedestrian precinct, this is an area to see in the daytime for its gabled façades and half timbering; in the evening the cafés and restaurants come to life. Don't miss the **Place Plumereau★,** centre of the old mediaeval quarter, the **Rue Briçonnet★** and the **Rue Paul-Louis-Courier★.** In the neighbourhood, **Gemmail Museum** (AB-1), exhibiting stained glass compositions lit from behind *(10-12 & 2-6:30, Apr.-15 Oct.; closed Mon.).* ▶ In the Halles (Market) quarter, the Tour de l'Horloge and the Tour Charlemagne (the clock-tower and Charlemagne's tower) (B2) are the only remains of the 12th-13thC **Basilica of St. Martin,** with origins dating from the 5thC. Beside them stands the new Basilica (1887-1924).

Also... ▶ **The gardens★ :** Jardins de l'Archevêché (C1), the Préfecture (C2), the Prébendes, and the **Jardin Botanique★** (Gardens of the Archbishopric, the Prefecture, the Prebendary and the Botanical Gardens; animals and exhibitions in the latter). In the new quarter along the banks of the Cher (via C3) is the **Promenade du Lac★** (Olympic swimming pool, sailing). □

▶ Nearby

▶ **St. Cosme Priory★** *(3 km W)* : ruins of 11th, 12th and 15thC church where poet Pierre de Ronsard is buried *(9-12 & 2-5 or 6; closed Wed. out of season, closed Dec.-Jan.).* 1.5 km SE, **château de Plessisy-lès-Tours :** exhibition on Louis XI who built it (1463) and died there in 1483. *(10-12 & 2-5, Apr.-Dec.; closed Tue. and nat. hols.).* ▶ **Luynes** ® *(12 km W)* : 13th-15thC château★ *(no visitors).* ▶ **Château de la Roche-Racan** *(26 km NW)* : lovely early-17thC château, interesting works of art in the **church of St. Paterne-Racan** *(2 km NW).* ▶ **Château-La-Vallière** *(33 km NW)* : to the south, woods and lake, picturesque ruins of **château de Vaujours.** 7 km W, **Marcilly-sur-Maulne :** late 16thC château. ▶ **Grange de Meslay★** *(9 km NE)* : this 1220 tithe barn is the setting for the Touraine Music Festival which attracts internationally famous performers from all over the world. (→ ®). 2 km S, **Parçay-Meslay;** 12thC murals in the church. ▶ **Vouvray** ® (*9 km E,* right bank of the Loire) and **Montlouis-sur-Loire** ® (*12 km E,* left bank) both produce white wines of repute (wine-tasting in the cellars). □

USSÉ★

A2

Charles Perrault (1628-1703; author of "Mother Goose" and other stories) is said to have drawn his inspiration for the tale of the Sleeping Beauty from Ussé. This fairytale castle gleams too white ever to have been involved in war and overlooks an enchanting green countryside at the junction of the Indre and the Loire. The tall trees and the lakes in the park add to its charm.

▶ Ussé was built in the 15thC, and is halfway between a mediaeval castle and a Renaissance château. It stands on the site of a former fortress. The **chapel★** has Flamboyant Gothic architecture and Renaissance decoration *(9-12 & 2-6 or 7 according to season, 15 Mar.-Sept.).* ▶ South of Ussé is the **Forest of Chinon★,** more than 50 km² of oaks and pines (picnic areas). □

VENDÔME★★

B1 / ® / pop. 18 218 (Loir-et-Cher)

See plan on following page

Vendôme is a charming old town bedecked

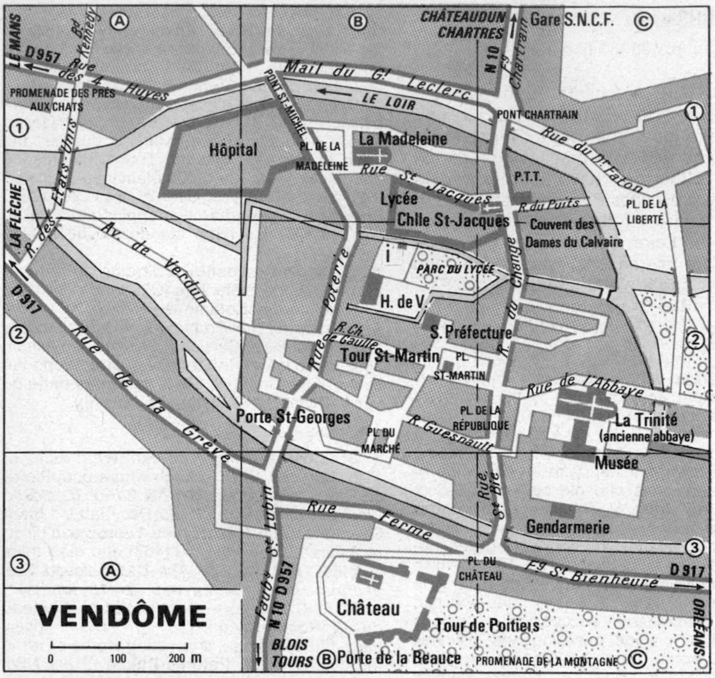

with bell-towers and pointed slate roofs, and situated at the foot of a steep hill crowned by the massive ruins of a feudal château. Round the town run the arms of the Loire flowing quietly past the wash houses and gardens.

▶ The **Tour St. Martin** (B2), 15th-16thC, marks the centre of Vendôme, a pedestrian precinct. ▶ **La Trinité★★** (C2). The original abbey was founded in the 11thC by Geoffroi Martel, Count of Anjou, after seeing three fiery lances plunge into a fountain (according to the legend). All architectural styles from 11th to early 16thC are represented; the façade★★ is a masterpiece of Flamboyant Gothic; the magnificent bell-tower is a vestige of the feudal abbey. Inside, note the Romanesque capitals★★ of the transept crossing and the 12thC stained glass★ Virgin and Child in an apsidial chapel. ▶ The buildings of the former Benedictine abbey stand on the south side of the Church and house a **museum** of Vendômois religious art, with murals from the valley of the Loir and a section on traditional trades *(daily 9-11:30 & 2-5:30; 1 Jan.-30 Apr., Oct.-Dec., open at 10; closed Tue.)*. ▶ The **public garden** (C2) has a good view over the town.

Also... ▶ **Church of the Madeleine** (1474). ▶ **Porte St. Georges★** (14th-16thC) between two large round towers. ▶ See the **château of the Counts of Vendôme** (12th-15thC) whose ruins crown the *Montagne* (in fact a modest hill), now arranged as a garden (views★); remains of the Collegiate church of St. Georges *(daily 9-12 & 2-6; closed Tue. ex July, Aug.; Dec.-Feb., Sun. only 2-6)*. □

▶ Nearby

▶ **Areines** *(3 km NE)* : interesting murals in the church. ▶ **Mondoubleau** ® *(28 km NW)* : ruins of 10th-11thC château, Bré-Barré menhir; 7 km NE : **château de St. Agil** (13th-16th-18thC; *visit park*); 11km NE **Arville** : former Templar Commandery *(visit by request tel 54.80.91.74)*, fortification walls and 12thC church. ▶ **Sargé-sur-Braye** *(24 km NW)* : 11th-15thC church with 14th-16thC murals, château de Radrets, 14th, 16th, 18thC *(15 June-15 Sep., weekends 2:30-6:30)*. ▶ **Valley of the Loir★★** (→). □

■ VILLANDRY★★

A2 / ® / pop. 742 (Indre-et-Loire)

Relaid according to the designs of du Cerceau, the Renaissance **gardens★★★** of Villandry are as famous as the château : a marvellous herb and vegetable garden, box hedges which twine endlessly in astonishing symbolic patterns round the formal French flowerbeds and on the terrace the fountains, basins and cascades.

▶ The courtyard has a wide view over the Cher and the Val de Loire. The three 16thC buildings are among the last of the great Renaissance creations in Touraine; classical influence is already noticeable in the 1532 reconstruction by Jean le Breton, François I's Secretary of State, who supervised the building of Blois, Chambord and Chenonceaux. The interiors were modified in 18thC with the addition of new windows. All that remains of the original fortress is the keep. *(Palm Sun.-12 Nov., 9-6; gardens 9-dusk)*. ▶ The village itself, with old houses bordering its quiet streets, makes a pleasant walk (Romanesque church 11th-12thC). ▶ 2.5 km E : **fossilising caves** (heavily mineralised water) at **Savonnières** ® *(8 Feb.-31 Mar., 1 Nov.-20 Dec., 9-12 & 2-6; 1 Apr.-30 Sep., 9-7)*. □

Architecture

The Touraine, Blésois and Orléanais inevitably call to mind the magnificent string of châteaux along the Loire and its tributaries. ● During the Renaissance and above all in the 18thC, the bourgeoisie, civil servants and merchants built elegant mansions in the towns (Blois, Tours). Like the churches and châteaux of the area, the houses are of tufa, a fine white limestone from the hillsides. ● However the Val de Loire also possesses a charming rural architecture in tune with the character of the countryside. ● The use of tufa for more humble buildings dates only from the last century; previously, brick and stone coated with plaster (still used in the north of the region) were the usual building materials. It is the same with the roofs : Angers slate, until then reserved exclusively for châteaux, began to be used for smaller buildings in the 19thC. It is the combination of blue slate and white stone which creates the cheerful and luminous character of the region. ● Traditional houses are oriented S or SE to protect them from the prevailing winds. Doors are in two halves : the lower half in solid wood and the upper glazed in small squares. Windows are tall and narrow. In both Touraine and the Orléanais, dormer windows continuing the line of the wall are frequently found; they are often decorated. Whether in brick or stone, the chimney stacks are of imposing dimensions. External stairs against the gable wall lead to the red tiled first floor or loft, and are sometimes built over the bread oven which resembles a little semi-circular tower.

3. Tufat buil-house

4. Dovecote, or "fuie", in the Loire Valley

● Farms in Touraine tend to be built on two stories, forming an open courtyard in conjunction with the outbuildings. ● Another very characteristic element of architecture in the Val de Loire is the *fuie* or dovecote. This may be circular, square or hexagonal and may be attached to the farmhouse or separate. ● The *lubites* are isolated little houses which were used by the vinegrowers. Their walls are generally of rocks and plaster with stone reinforcements at the corners. ● In the Blésois you may see brick used with rocks and plaster or with cut limestone. ● Brick is also a typical material in the Sologne; beginning in the 19thC, it has replaced the cob which was used to fill in timber-framed structures. ● In this region farm buildings stand separated around the courtyard; the barn is usually the tallest of them. ● Finally, in the Gâtinais, traditional construction frequently includes walls made of lumps of flint known as *têtes de chat,* bedded in limestone mortar, while the lintels are of millstone grit.

5. Typical Sologne house

Brief regional history

Up to 1200 BC At the end of the Neolithic Period a Mediterranean people, the **Ligurians,** overran Brittany and the Loire (Liger) to which they gave their name.

1200 BC-4thC AD The **Celts** came from central Europe, colonising the Val de Loire (Loire Valley) between 1200 and 800 BC. They founded Orléans and Blois and established a port and a town built on piles at Tours, which controlled trade on the Loire and the Cher. In 52BC **Julius Caesar** arrived with his legions; thenceforth the Angevins, Bretons and Tourangeaux lived with the Pax Romana, Roman gods, Roman baths, forums, theaters and aqueducts in their towns. ● Christianity was introduced in the first centuries AD, **Saint Martin of Tours** (316-97) being its most popular exponent.

4th-8thC During this period of **Barbarian** and later Arab invasion, the great abbeys in the Val de Loire struggled to preserve Christian teachings and fragments of Greek and Roman **knowledge.** ● In **448** Clovis and the Germanic Merovingians began their **conquest of Gaul** and established themselves in the Val de Loire. In 451 the Huns were repelled at Bordeaux and in 731 the Arabs fought their way to the gates of Tours, before their defeat at Poitiers by Charles Martel.

8thC-1453 The reign of **Charlemagne** was one of stability. Bishop Theodulfe founded the first University at Orléans and established free schooling. ● When the Count of Anjou, **Henry Plantagenet,** became King of England (his mother was descended from William the Conqueror), the Val de Loire became the scene of a struggle between the Plantagenets and the Capetians. Philippe Auguste came off best (Azay-le-Rideau 1189); the peace lasted for a century, only to be followed by the **Hundred Years' War** between France and England (1337-1453).

1453-1589 The appearance of **Joan of Arc** and the establishment on the throne of the House of Valois ended the Hundred Years' War; the Kings of France remained in the Val de Loire. ● Under **Louis XI,** trade was revived; he started the **silk** industry at Tours and, like his father Charles VII, relied on merchants and craftsmen rather than feudal lords as his **administrators.** The beautiful town houses *(hôtels particuliers)* in Blois and Tours were built by these civil servants, as were Chenonceaux, Villandry, Azay-le-Rideau and the Blésois châteaux. ● 1494 to 1559 saw a continual French presence in the Italian peninsula; as a result many Italian artists and artisans came to work in France, and the Italian Renaissance took root along the Loire. ● The **wars of religion** between Catholics and Protestants subsequently broke out in the Loire Valley and were only partially resolved when the Protestant Henri IV was converted to Catholicism, and moved the seat of government to **Paris.**

Practical information

The region

Information : *Comité Régional du Tourisme,* (C.R.T.), 10, rue du Colombier, B.P. 2412, 45000 Orléans, ☎ 38.62.68.48. **Indre-et-Loire :** *Comité Départemental du Tourisme* (C.D.T.), 16, rue de Buffon, 37032 Tours Cedex, ☎ 47.61.61.23, ext 2160 or 2161. **Loiret :** *C.D.T.,* 3, rue de la Bretonnerie, 45000 Orléans, ☎ 38.66.24.10. **Loir-et-Cher :** *C.D.T.,* 11, pl. du Château, 41000 Blois, ☎ 54.78.55.50 and 54.78.47.43.

Bookings : *Loisirs-Accueil :* **Loir-et-Cher,** same address as C.D.T. ; **Loiret,** same address as C.D.T., ☎ 38.62.04.88.

Maps : *Michelin* nº 64 1/200 000. *I.G.N.* nºs 20 and 26 1/100 000.

S.O.S. : Indre-et-Loire : *SAMU,* ☎ 47.28.15.15. **Loir-et-Cher :** *SAMU, Emergency Medical Service,* ☎ 54.78.78.78. **Loiret :** *SAMU,* ☎ 38.63.33.33. *Poisoning Emergency Centre :* Tours, ☎ 47.66.15.15.

Weather forecast : Indre-et-Loire, ☎ 47.54.54.43 ; **Loir-et-Cher,** ☎ 54.78.77.50 ; **Loiret,** ☎ 38.88.44.83.

Rural gîtes and chambres d'hôtes : Indre-et-Loire : *Chambre d'Agriculture,* 38, rue A.-Fresnel, 37170 Chambray-lès-Tours Cedex, ☎ 47.27.56.10. **Loir-et-Cher :** *C.D.T.* **Loiret :** *C.D.T.* and *Relais des Gîtes Ruraux,* ☎ 38.66.24.10.

Camping : more than 200 camp-sites. C.D.T. **Indre-et-Loire, Loir-et-Cher, Loiret.**

Scenic railways : Gare de Richelieu, 37120 Richelieu, ☎ 47.58.36.29. *Ligne Chinon-Richelieu-Champigny-Ligré-la-Rivière* with sampling of local produce ; from mid-May to end Sep : 1 round-trip Sat, 2 round-trip Sun *Marcilly-sur-Maulne,* 37330 Château-la-Vallière, ☎ 47.24.07.95 and 47.24.04.46. Sun and nat hols : 1 May-end Sep. *Pithiviers :* O.T., 45300 Pithiviers, ☎ 38.30.50.02. *Blanc Argent,* a small train which traverses the Sologne. Info. C.D.T.

Musical events and festivals : end Jun-early Jul : *Touraine Music Festival* in La Grange-de-Meslay, Langeais *International Music Days.* **Jul-Aug :** *Summer in Loir-et-Cher,* concerts. **End Nov-early Dec :** *International Music Week* in Orléans. Mid-Oct-mid-Mar : *Musical week-ends* in Montbazon, château d'Artigny. **Throughout the year, every other Sat Oct-Mar :** *Concerts of chimes at N.-D.-de-la-Trinité* in Blois.

Fairs and events : Jan : *Vouvray wine fair.* **Feb :** *Wine fairs* in Bourgueil, Azay-le-Rideau, Montlouis. **Mar :** *paper fair* in Orléans. **Apr :** *Bourgueil wine fair.* **May :** *andouillette fair* (chitterling sausages) in Mennetou-sur-Cher ; *Rhododendron festival* in Châteauneuf-sur-Loire. **Jun :** Chinon *flower show ; Folklore* in Saint-Jean-de-la-Ruelle ; *dog fair* in Mur-de-Sologne. **Jul :** *garlic fair* in Bourgueil and on Saint Anne's Day **(26 Jul)** in Tours ; *peasant market* in Loches ; **End-Jul :** *Vintage car races* at Blois. **Aug : 1st Sun,** *donkey fair* in Savonnières ; *World Folklore Festival* in Montoire-sur-Loir. **Sep :** *Wine harvest Chapterhouse* in Chinon ; *melon festival* in Amboise ; *festival du pâté à la citrouille* in Millançay. **End Oct :** *Sologne gastronomy festival* in Romorantin ; *apple fair* in Azay-le-Rideau.

Rambling and hiking : Topoguide nº 3 ; 3/32, 31. I.G.N. map of the Sologne region, 1/100 000, for information concerning access means, activities, unusual excursions and sites, sports groups and accommodation possibilities, enq : *Tourisme-Accueil Loiret :* see C.D.T. *Tourisme-Accueil Loir-et-Cher :* see C.D.T. *Comité Touraine de la Randonnée Pédestre,* S.I. St-Avertin, 29, rue de Rochepinart, 37170 Chambray-lès-Tours, ☎ 47.27.01.72.

Riding holidays : *Tourisme-Accueil du Loiret, Loir-et-Cher, Indre-et-Loire,* see C.D.T. *Association régionale de Tourisme équestre du Val de Loire-Centre,* B.P. 7, 36600 Valençay.

Cycling holidays : *Comité Départemental d'Indre-et-Loire,* Centre municipal des Sports, 37000 Tours. *Association Culturelle de la Touraine du Sud,* ☎ 47.94.91.24. *Tourisme-Accueil du Loiret,* du *Loir-et-Cher :* see C.D.T. *Train + bike :* S.N.C.F. stations and Tours, ☎ 47.61.46.46.

River and canal cruises : canoe trip down the Loire and Vienne rivers, canoe excursions on the Loiret : *Dir. Dép. du Temps Libre.* Holidays in houseboats or inflatable motorised dinghies : *Tourisme-Accueil du Loiret :* C.D.T. Trips in barge-caravans : round-trip Chinon-Monsoreau : *O.T. Chinon,* pl. de l'Hôtel-de-Ville, 37500 Chinon, ☎ 47.93.17.85. *Tourisme-Accueil Loir-et-Cher.*

Handicraft courses : weaving (Amboise), ceramics, drawing, painting (Gatinais), *Tourisme-Accueil Loiret,* see C.D.T.

Golf : Ballan-Miré (18 holes) ; Sully-sur-Loire (18 holes) ; Donnery-Orléans (9 holes).

Sailing and wind-surfing : Stretches of water : Tours and Saint-Avertin, lac du Rillé, lac de Chemillé-sur-Indrois, lac de Loire, Montrichard, le Plessis Dodin : C.D.T. **Indre-et-Loire ;** Cerdon : C.D.T. **Loiret ;** Châtres-sur-Cher, Salbris : C.D.T. **Loir-et-Cher.**

Hunting and shooting : *C.D.T. Loir-et-Cher* and *Loiret ; Féd. Départ. des Chasseurs,* 9, imp. Heurteloup, 37012 Tours Cedex, ☎ 47.05.65.25. Battues, hunting with game dogs, duck and water-fowl : *Loisirs-Accueil Loir-et-Cher. Fox-hunting, Nov-end Mar,* ☎ 47.43.49.45.

Fishing : *Fédérations Départementales de Pêche,* 25, rue C.-Gilles, 37000 Tours, ☎ 47.05.33.77 ; 36, Grande-Rue, Avaray, 41500 Mer, ☎ 54.81.04.28.

Towns

AMBOISE

Tours 25, Châteauroux 104, Paris 221
A2 ⊠ 37400

ℹ quai Gal-de-Gaulle, B.P. 233, ☎ 47.57.09.28.

SNCF ☎ 47.57.03.89.

Hotels :
★★★**Amboise** (Novotel), 17, rue des Sablonnières, ☎ 47.57.42.07. 82 rm P ♿ 260. Rest. Grill 80-130.
★★★**Belle Vue** (L.F.), 12, quai C.-Guinot, ☎ 47.57.02.26. Visa. 30 rm ♿ closed 15 Nov-15 Dec and Sun eve low season, 200. Rest. ♦ ***le Monseigneur,*** 80-130.
● ★★**Lion d'Or,** 17, quai C.-Guinot, ☎ 47.57.00.23. Visa. 23 rm P closed 2 Nov-30 Mar, 210. Rest. ♦ 100-170.
★★**Auberge du Mail** (L.F.), 32, quai du Gal-de-Gaulle, ☎ 47.57.60.39. AE, Visa. 12 rm P closed 1 Jan-15 Feb, Mon eve and Tue, 180. Rest. ♦ Spec : *foie confit au vouvray,* 95-175.

Chargé, NE on the D751 :
★★★**Château de Pray** (Châteaux-hôtels), ☎ 47.57.23.67. AE, DC, Euro, Visa. 16 rm P closed 31 Dec-10 Feb, 320. Rest. ♦ 120-150.

⛺ ★★Municipal *de l'Ile-d'Or* (520 pl.), ☎ 47.57.23.37.

Youth hostel, *Centre Ch.-Péguy,* Entrepont, Ile-d'Or, ☎ 47.57.06.36.

Restaurants :
♦ ***Bonne Étape,*** La Briqueterie, 2 km on the D751, ☎ 47.57.08.09. AE, Euro, Visa P ♿ closed Tue eve, 75-140.

Neuillé-le-Lierre, 37380 Monnaie, 16 km :
♦♦ ***Auberge de la Brenne,*** rue de la Gare, ☎ 47.52.95.05. AE, Visa P ♿ closed 20 Jan-20 Feb, 13-20 Oct, Sun eve and Mon. Spec : *charcuterie tourangelle, géline de Touraine,* 60-130.

Events : *Renaissance evening spectacle* at the castle in Jul and Aug ; *wine fair* Apr and Aug.

Recommended : *Pâtisserie le Fournil,* pl. du Château, ☎ 47.57.04.46.

AZAY-LE-RIDEAU

Tours 28, Chatellerault 94, Paris 262
A2 ⊠ 37190

ℹ 26, rue Gambetta, ☎ 47.43.34.40 (high season), and mairie (low season), ☎ 47.43.32.11.

Hotels :
★★**Grand Monarque** (L.F.), pl. de la République, ☎ 47.43.30.08. 30 rm P closed 20 Nov-1 Mar, 290. Rest. ♦ 120-240.

3 km N :
Château de Gerfaut (Château-accueil), ☎ 47.43.30.16. 3 rm P closed Aug, Dec-May, 260.

⛺ ★★Municipal *du Sabot* (184 pl.), ☎ 47.43.32.72.

Restaurants :
● ♦ ***Le Muscadin,*** 10, rue A.-Riché, ☎ 47.45.23.96. Closed Tue eve and Wed low season, 15-30 Nov, 15-30 Jan. A modest restaurant, with a charming decor. Spec : *magret de canard au xérès, saucisson chaud au bourgueil,* 120-210.

Saché, 7 km SE :
♦♦ ***Auberge du XIIe s.,*** ☎ 47.26.86.58. AE, DC, Visa P ♿ closed 20 Jan-28 Feb, Tue, Wed low season. Spec : game during season, 180-200.

Son et lumière : Whitsun-Sep, tour of the castle accompanied by guides in Renaissance costumes, enq ℹ

BEAUGENCY

Orléans 25, Tours 87, Paris 151
B1 ⊠ 45190

ℹ 28, pl. Martroi, ☎ 38.44.54.42 (high season).

SNCF ☎ 38.44.50.28.

Hotels :
★★★**Abbaye,** 2, quai de l'Abbaye, ☎ 38.44.67.35. Tx 780038. AE, DC, Euro, Visa. 18 rm P 450. Rest. ♦♦♦ 155-220.
★★**Écu de Bretagne** (L.F.), pl. du Martroi, ☎ 38.44.67.60. AE, DC, Euro, Visa. 26 rm P closed 23 Jan-1 Mar, 230. Rest. ● ♦♦ ♿ Friendly, country-style gourmand stopover on the castle road. Spec : *cul de lapereau au miel, noisette de porc aux pruneaux,* 70-150.

Tavers, 3 km W on RN152 :
★★★★**Tonnellerie** (Châteaux-hôtels), 12, rue des Eaux-Bleues, ☎ 38.44.68.15. DC, Euro. 26 rm P ♿ closed 5 Oct-Apr, Tue and Wed in May, 350. Rest. ♦ 140-180.

Youth hostel, 152, rue de Châteaudun, ☎ 38.44.61.31.

⛺ ★★*Municipal* (130 pl.), ☎ 38.44.50.39 ; Saint-Laurent-Nouan, 9 km S : ★★*Amitié* (60 pl.), ☎ 54.87.01.52.

Les BÉZARDS

Montargis 23, Orléans 69, Paris 138
16 km NE of Gien, C2
⊠ 45290 Nogent-sur-Vernisson

Hotels :
● ★★★★(L) ***Auberge des Templiers*** (Relais et châteaux), ☎ 38.31.80.01. Tx 780998. AE, DC, Visa. 28 rm P ♿ closed 15 Jan-15 Feb, 750. Rest. ● ♦♦♦ Spec : game during season, *fricassée de rognons et pieds de veau en barbouille,* good wines, 230-430.
★★★★**Château des Bézards,** ☎ 38.31.80.03. Tx 780335. AE, DC, Euro, Visa. 43 rm P 390. Rest. ♦♦ Cooking and setting are of the same standard. Spec : *ris de veau tiède en salade, pot-au-feu de la mer,* 100-280.

BLOIS

Orléans 59, Angers 152, Paris 181
B2 ⊠ 41000

ℹ 3, av. Jean-Laigret (B2), ☎ 54.74.06.49.

SNCF (B2), ☎ 54.74.20.50, 54.78.01.07.

✈ Blois-Le Breuil, 16 km NW, ☎ 54.20.17.68 and 54.20.17.64 (airports' refreshment bar).

Car-hire : *Budget* train + car, 148, av. Maunoury, La Chaussée-Saint-Victor, ☎ 54.78.42.85, and at the S.N.C.F. station, ☎ 54.78.83.49.

Hotels :
★★**Grand Cerf** (L.F.), 40, av. Wilson (C3), ☎ 54.78.02.16. 14 rm P closed Feb and Fri low season, 180. Rest. 45-180.
★★**Hostellerie de la Loire,** 8, rue Mal-de-Lattre-de-Tassigny (C2), ☎ 54.74.26.60. AE,

DC, Visa. 17 rm ⚘ closed 15 Jan-15 Feb, 2nd week in Jun, 225. Rest. ♦♦ ♿ closed Sun. Spec : *filet de sandre au beurre rouge*, 85-220.

Cellettes, 41120 Les Montils, 8 km S :
Château de Lutaine (Château-accueil), rte de Seur, ☎ 54.70.40.25. 10 rm, 1 apt Ⓟ ♨ ♿ closed 1 Nov-Easter. Fishing, 450.

Chitenay, 11.5 km :
★★***La Clé des Champs,*** ☎ 54.44.22.03. 10 rm Ⓟ ♨ closed 3 Jan-3 Feb, Mon and Tue, 180. Rest. ♦♦ Spec : *coquilles Saint-Jacques au vouvray*, 120-210.

Ouchamps, 41120 Les Montils, 16 km :
★★★***Relais des Landes*** (Relais du Silence, Châteaux-hôtels), ☎ 54.44.03.33. Tx 751454. AE, DC, Euro, Visa. 18 rm ⚘ Ⓟ ♨ ♿ closed 2 Nov-25 Mar, 430. Rest. ♦♦ ♿ closed Wed. Fresh produce, simple but tasty fare, 135-185.

Mer, ✉ 41500, 16 km NE :
★***Les Calanques*** (L.F.), 21, rue S.-Hême, ☎ 54.81.00.55. 11 rm Ⓟ ♨ closed 15 Dec-15 Jan, Wed and Sun eve, 225. Rest. ♿ Spec : fish, seafood, 90-150.

Youth hostel, *les Groyets*, ☎ 54.78.27.21.

⛺ ★★★★*Base du Lac de Loire,* Vineuil, 4 km E (250 pl.), ☎ 54.78.82.05 ; ★★★*Municipal de la Loire* (80 pl.), ☎ 54.74.22.78.

Restaurants :
♦♦ ***La Péniche,*** moored on the banks of the Loire, prom. du Mail (C2), ☎ 54.74.37.23. AE, Euro, Visa ⚘ Spec : *ragoût d'escargots aux girolles, blanquette de la mer*, 120-180.

Ménars, 41500 Mer, 8 km :
♦ ***L'Époque,*** 23, rte Nationale, ☎ 54.46.81.07. Euro, Visa Ⓟ ♿ closed 19 Feb-5 Mar, Tue eve and Wed in winter, Wed high season. Spec : *foie gras frais maison, pétales de St-Jacques riz pilaf*, 60-160.

Guided tours : le Vieux-Blois, Jul and Aug, ex Wed and Sun *son et lumière at the castle. Tourist flights over the castle and region*, ☎ 54.20.17.68. *Circuits touristiques*, enq : *S.D.T.*

Events : *2nd International festival of contemporary theater* (Jun) with street animation.

Bicycle hire : *Blot*, 3, rue Henri-Drussy, ☎ 54.78.02.64. *Sapta*, av. de Châteaudun, ☎ 54.78.42.22.

BOURGUEIL

Tours 45, Angers 63, Paris 278
A2 ✉ 37140

ℹ mairie, rue Picard, ☎ 47.97.70.50.

Hotel :
★***Thouarsais,*** pl. Hublin, ☎ 47.97.72.05. 30 rm ♨ closed Feb, New-Year's Day and Sun eve low season, 155.

Farmhouse gîte and chambres d'hôtes, *Clos du Vigneau*, Saint-Nicolas-de-Bourgueil, 6 km W, ☎ 47.97.75.10.

Wines : visit of the *Caves de la Dive Bouteille* and adjoining museum : daily 1 Feb-30 Nov and *Wine fairs* early Feb and early Apr.

BRACIEUX

Blois 18, Orléans 53, Paris 183
B2 ✉ 41250

Hotel :
★***Cygne*** (L.F.), 20, rue Roger-Brun, ☎ 54.46.41.07. Visa. 18 rm Ⓟ closed 15 Jan-10 Mar and Wed, 200. Rest. 50-120.

⛺ ★★Municipal *des Châteaux* (90 pl.), ☎ 54.46.41.84.

Restaurant :
● ♦♦ ***Relais,*** 1, av. Chambord, ☎ 54.46.41.22. AE, DC, Visa ♿ closed 17 Dec-25 Jan, Tue eve and Wed. Reserve in advance. Rustic decor. Spec : *terrine de homard breton, carpe à la Chambord*, and local wines, 170-250.

Farmhouse gîte, *la Baguenodière*, Tour-en-Sologne, 3 km W, ☎ 54.46.45.33.

BRIARE

Bourges 80, Orléans 89, Paris 227
C2 ✉ 45250

ℹ pl. de la République, ☎ 38.31.24.51 (high season).

SNCF ☎ 38.31.24.68.

Hotel :

Ousson, ✉ 45710, 7 km SE :
★***La Chaumière,*** pl. de l'Église, ☎ 38.31.45.66. Euro, Visa. 7 rm ⚘ Ⓟ ♨ ♿ closed 1 week in Sep, 180. Rest. ♦ closed Wed ex Jul-Aug. Spec : *omelette aux truffes, tournedos aux airelles*, 45-100.

⛺ ★★*Le Martinet* (80 pl.), ☎ 38.31.24.50 ; ★★*les Combles* (66 pl.), ☎ 38.31.20.08.

CHAMBORD

Blois 18, Orléans 45, Paris 175
B2 ✉ 41250 Bracieux

ℹ pl. St-Michel, ☎ 54.20.34.86.

Hotels :
★★***Saint-Michel*** (L.F.), ☎ 54.20.31.31. Visa. 38 rm ⚘ Ⓟ ♨ closed 12 Nov-22 Dec, 260. Rest. ♦ 75-150.

Saint-Dyé-sur-Loire, 41500 Mer, 5 km S :
★★***Manoir du Bel Air,*** ☎ 54.81.60.10. 40 rm ⚘ Ⓟ ♨ ♿ closed 15 Jan-15 Feb, 250. Rest. ♦♦ Spec : *rillettes de saumon, cailles aux cèpes*, 65-150.

Guided tours : at the porte Royale, C.N.M.H.S., ☎ (1) 42.74.22.22. and 42.78.19.47, and high season tour of the castle by night, before the evening spectacle, May-Sep : ℹ C.N.M.H.S. and ☎ 54.46.31.32.

CHÂTEAUNEUF-SUR-LOIRE

Orléans 25, Bourges 102, Paris 134
C1 ✉ 45110

ℹ pl. A.-Briand, ☎ 38.58.44.79 (high season).

SNCF ☎ 38.58.42.07.

Hotels :
● ★★***Capitainerie*** (L.F.), 1, Grande-Rue, ☎ 38.58.42.16. Euro, Visa. Ⓟ ♨ closed 1 Jan-15 Feb and Tue (ex during high season), 205. Rest. ♦♦ ♿ 70-150.

Fay-aux-Loges, 9.5 km NW :
★***Poisson d'Argent*** (L.F.), 2, rue Gal-de-Gaulle, ☎ 38.59.56.28. AE, DC, Euro, Visa. 11 rm Ⓟ closed Sun eve, 85. Rest. ♦ ♿ *sandre aux petits légumes*, 40-150.

⛺ ★★*Essi* (66 pl.), ☎ 38.89.42.46.

Restaurant :
● ♦ ***Auberge des Fontaines,*** 1, rue des Fontaines, ☎ 38.58.44.10. Closed Sun eve and Sep. Booking required. Rustic setting and simple fare : *rillettes de lapin, rognons de veau à la moutarde*, 120-210.

CHÂTEAU-RENAULT

Tours 30, Le Mans 86, Paris 198
A2 ⊠ 37110

ℹ parc Vauchevrier, ☎ 47.56.54.43 (high season).

SNCF ☎ 47.56.50.13.

Hotels :
★★★***Écu de France*** (L.F.), 37, pl. Jean-Jaurès, ☎ 47.29.50.72. AE, DC, Visa. 9 rm Ⓟ closed 20-30 Dec, 1-15 Feb Sun eve and Mon noon (ex during high season), 190. Rest. ♦♦ ♿ 55-110.
★***Lion d'Or,*** 166, rue de la République, ☎ 47.29.66.50. DC, Visa. 10 rm Ⓟ closed Sun eve and Mon, 145. Rest. ● ♦ A small menu, comprised of market fresh produce. Spec : *ragoût de St-Jacques sauce corail, salade de ris de veau au kiwi, vinaigre de framboise,* 60-145.

Farmhouse gîte, *la Ruellerie,* Auzouer, 7 km S, ☎ 47.56.99.03.

⛺ ★★Municipal *de Vauchevrier* (110 pl.), ☎ 47.56.54.43.

CHAUMONT-SUR-LOIRE

Blois 17, Tours 41, Paris 200
B2 ⊠ 41150 Onzain

ℹ mairie, ☎ 54.20.98.41.

Hotels :
★★★***Château*** (L.F.), 2, rue du Mal-de-Lattre-de-Tassigny, ☎ 54.20.98.04. AE, DC, Euro, Visa. 15 rm Ⓟ closed 15 Nov-15 Mar, 270. Rest. ♿ 60-130.

Onzain, 2 km :
● ★★★★***Domaine des Hauts-de-Loire*** (Relais et châteaux), ☎ 54.20.72.57. Tx 751547. AE, Euro, Visa. 30 rm Ⓟ ♿ closed 1 Dec-15 Mar, 880. Rest. ♦♦♦ Spec : *mousse de persil à l'huile de noisette, filet de sandre au beurre d'échalote,* 190-300.
★★***Château des Tertres*** (Châteaux-hôtels), rte de Monteaux, ☎ 54.20.83.88. AE, Visa. 14 rm Ⓟ closed 3 Nov-22 Mar, 240.

Rilly-sur-Loire, 4 km :
★★***Château de la Haute Borde,*** ☎ 54.20.98.09. Euro. 18 rm Ⓟ ♿ closed 15 Nov-15 Mar, Sun eve, 185. Rest. ♦ ♿ closed Mon, 50-125.

Candé-sur-Beuvron, ⊠ 41120, 6 km E :
★★***Host. de la Caillère,*** rte des Montils, ☎ 54.44.03.08. AE, DC, Visa. 5 rm, closed 15 Nov-15 Dec, Sun eve from 15 Oct to Easter and Wed, 180. Rest. ♦♦ Spec : *salade de raie, St-Jacques, foie gras aux capres et soja, brochet aux morilles et pinot noir,* 105-200.

⛺ ★★*Essi* (60 pl.), ☎ 54.46.98.65.

CHENONCEAUX

Tours 35, Châteauroux 89, Paris 224
B2 ⊠ 37150 Bléré

ℹ 1 *bis,* rue du Château (high season), ☎ 47.29.94.45.

SNCF ☎ 47.29.90.64.

Hotels :
★★★***Bon Laboureur et du Château,*** 6, rue du Dr-Bretonneau, ☎ 47.23.90.02. AE, DC, Euro, Visa. 29 rm Ⓟ ♿ closed mid-Dec-mid-Feb, 290. Rest. ♦♦ 90-180.
★***La Renaudière,*** 24, rue du Dr.-Bretonneau, ☎ 47.23.90.04. Euro, Visa. 12 rm Ⓟ ♿ 180. Rest. ♦ 60-125.

CHINON

Tours 49, Poitiers 96, Paris 283
A2 ⊠ 37500

ℹ 12, rue Voltaire (B2), ☎ 47.93.17.85.

SNCF ☎ 47.93.11.04.

Hotels :
● ★★***Diderot,*** 4, rue Diderot (not on the C2 map), ☎ 47.93.18.87. 20 rm Ⓟ pleasant 18thC house, closed 15 Dec-15 Jan, 260.
★★***Gargantua*** (Châteaux-hôtels), 73, rue Haute-St-Maurice (A1-2), ☎ 47.93.04.71. AE, Euro, Visa. 11 rm Ⓟ closed Jan and Feb, 210. Rest. ● ♦♦ closed Thu low season. As indicated by the name (Gargantua being a genuine "giant" of French litterature), this is an ideal stop-over for hearty eaters. A 15th-20thC residence with a mediaeval setting and rustic fare : *omelette Gargamelle, matelote d'anguilles, écrevisses du mont Louis,* 90-140.

Beaumont-en-Véron, 37420 Avoine, 5 km NW :
Château de Danzay (Châteaux-hôtels), ☎ 47.58.46.86. Visa. 5 rm Ⓟ closed 30 Oct-1 Apr. A private residence which receives visitors, 900.
★★***Giraudière*** (L.F., Relais du Silence), ☎ 47.58.40.36. AE, DC, Euro, Visa. 25 rm Ⓟ ♿ closed 15 Nov-1 Mar, 260.
Manoir de Montour (Château-Accueil), ☎ 47.58.43.76. 2 rm and 2 apts Ⓟ Set in a 17th-18thC sericulture establishment, 210.

Marçay, 7 km on the D116 :
★★★★***Château de Marçay*** (Relais et châteaux), ☎ 47.93.03.47. Tx 751475. AE, DC, Visa. 40 rm and 3 apts Ⓟ ♿ closed 4 Jan-15 Mar, 990. Rest. ♦♦ ♿ Spec : *œufs coque purée de morilles, petit sauté d'abats nobles au chinon,* 195-300.

Youth hostel, rue Descartes (C3), ☎ 47.93.10.48.

⛺ ★★*Municipal* 150 pl ; (A3), ☎ 47.93.08.35.

Restaurant :
● ♦♦ ***Au Plaisir Gourmand,*** 2, rue Parmentier, ☎ 47.93.20.48. closed 6-21 Jan, Sun eve and Mon. The young Rigollet couple has just settled into this beautiful house in old Chinon, with a fine menu for our gourmand delight. Spec : *feuilleté de pointes d'asperges à la ciboulette, sandre de Loire au vieux vouvray,* 100-200.

Wines : *tours of cellars :* Dumont ; Plouzeau ; château de Ligré ; Clos de l'Écho : ℹ

Fairs and markets : *Chapitre de la St-Vincent* end Jan ; *Chapitre de la Fleur* early Jun ; *Salon des Antiquaires* mid-Jul.

CONTRES

Blois 21, Châteauroux 77, Paris 201
B2 ⊠ 41700

Hotel :
★★***France*** (L.F.), 37, rue Pierre-Henri-Mauger, ☎ 54.79.50.14. 42 rm Ⓟ ♿ closed Feb and Fri low season, 190. Rest. ♦ 60-190.

Restaurant :
♦♦ ***Botte d'Asperges,*** 52, rue P.-H.-Mauger, ☎ 54.79.50.49. Visa ; closed 2-31 Jan and Mon. A country restaurant, 60-160.

Farmhouse gîte and chambres d'hôtes, *La Presle,* Oisly, 6 km SW, ☎ 54.79.52.69.

COUR-CHEVERNY

Blois 13, Châteauroux 87, Paris 194
B2 ⊠ 41700 Contres

ℹ 4, av. de la République, ☎ 54.79.95.63.

Hotels :
● ★★***Saint-Hubert*** (L.F.), rue Nationale, ☎ 54.79.96.60. Euro, Visa. 20 rm Ⓟ ✈ ♿ closed 5 Dec-15 Jan and Tue low season, 140. Rest. ♦ ✈ ♿ closed Tue, 75-170.
★★***Trois Marchands*** (L.F., France-Accueil), pl. de l'Église, ☎ 54.79.96.44. AE, DC, Euro, Visa. 40 rm Ⓟ 🌳 closed 15 Jan-1 Mar, 220. Rest. ♦ Spec : fish and game, 90-200.

Cultural events : *nightime festivals* at Cheverny, on the theme of hunting (Jul-Aug).

La FERTÉ-SAINT-AUBIN

Orléans 21, Blois 54, Paris 152
B-C1-2 ⊠ 45240

SNCF ☎ 38.91.50.04.

⛺ ★★*Municipal* (40 pl.), ☎ 38.91.55.90.

Restaurants :
♦♦ ***Écu de France,*** 6, rue Gal-Leclerc, ☎ 38.76.52.20. Ⓟ closed 15 Sep-1 Oct, Feb and Thu. Lunch only and Sat eve, 80-130.
♦♦ ***Ferme de la Lande,*** 2.5 km NE on the Marcilly road, ☎ 38.76.64.37. Visa. Ⓟ 🌳 ♿ closed Mon. Spec : *nage de petits coquillages à l'étuvée de légumes, filet de sole de Petit Bateau et ses huîtres cuites à la vapeur,* 120-180.

GIEN

Orléans 64, Bourges 76, Paris 154
C2 ♥ ⊠ 45500

ⓘ rue Anne-de-Beaujeu, ☎ 38.67.25.28.

SNCF ☎ 38.67.01.18.

Hotels :
★★***Rivage*** (L.F.), 1, quai de Nice, ☎ 38.67.20.53. AE, DC, Visa. 29 rm ⁂ Ⓟ closed 10 Feb-3 Mar, 215. Rest. ♦ View on the Loire river, quality service : pike (in season), *magret de canard aux échalotes,* 70-215.
★★***Sanotel,*** 21, quai Sully, ☎ 38.67.61.46. Tx 780777. Visa. 46 rm ⁂ Ⓟ 🌳 ♿ 205.

Restaurant :
♦ ***Loire,*** 18, quai Lenoir, ☎ 38.67.00.75. ✈ ♿ closed 1-10 Sep, Feb, Tue eve and Wed, 60-95.

⛺ ★★*Municipal* (135 pl.), ☎ 38.67.12.50.

Le GRAND-PRESSIGNY

Poitiers 63, Tours 67, Paris 303
A3 ♥ ⊠ 37350

Hotels :
★***Savoie Villars*** (L.F.), pl. Savoie-Villars, ☎ 47.94.96.86. Euro, Visa. 8 rm Ⓟ 🌳 ✈ closed 15 Jan-15 Mar, Tue eve and Wed low season, 150. Rest. 50-155.
Espérance, Le Carroir des Robins, ☎ 47.94.90.12. AE, Visa. Ⓟ 🌳 ✈ ♿ closed 6 Jan-6 Feb, 140. Rest. ♦ Spec : *galantine de faisan, coussin de loup à la crème de cerfeuil,* 55-220.

LAMOTTE-BEUVRON

Orléans 36, Blois 59, Paris 167
B-C2 ⊠ 41600

SNCF ☎ 54.88.01.13.

Hotels :
★***Tatin*** (L.F.), 5, av. de Vierzon, ☎ 54.88.00.03. Euro, Visa. 8 rm Ⓟ 🌳 closed 15 Jan-20 Feb, 15-25 Nov, Sun eve and Mon, 155. Rest. ♦ Spec : the famous *tarte tatin,* 60-150.
★***Monarque,*** 2, av. de l'Hôtel-de-Ville, ☎ 54.88.04.47. 13 rm Ⓟ 🌳 ♿ closed 16-26 Aug, Feb, Tue eve and Wed, 180. Rest. ♦ Sologne regional cooking, 80-180.

Rabot, 7 km NW :
★★***Bruyères,*** ☎ 54.88.05.70. DC, Euro, Visa. 50 rm Ⓟ 🌳 ⊟ ✈ ♿ A 270-acre property ; skeet shooting, hunting grounds, 12-acre lake, private fishing, 190. Rest. ♦ 45-100.

Nouan-le-Fuzelier, 8 km S :
★★***Charmilles,*** rte de Pierrefitte-sur-Sauldre, ☎ 54.88.73.55. Visa. 14 rm Ⓟ 🌳 ✈ ♿ closed 15 Jan-15 Mar, and Mon (Oct-Dec). 250.
★***Moulin de Villiers,*** ☎ 54.88.72.27. 20 rm ⁂ Ⓟ 🌳 ✈ closed 1 Jan-15 Mar, 1-15 Sep, Tue eve and Wed (Nov-Dec). 10-acre lake, private fishing, 150. Rest. 60-125.

Chaumont-sur-Tharonne, 10 km W :
★★★***Croix Blanche*** (Relais du Silence), 5, pl. Mottu, ☎ 54.88.55.12. AE, DC, Euro, Visa. 15 rm Ⓟ 🌳 ✈ ♿ closed 3 Jan-7 Feb, 24 Jun-4 Jul and Wed. 1/2 pension, 300. Rest. ♦♦ A creative menu with game, mushrooms, *foie gras,* 150-350.

Restaurants :
Nouan-le-Fuzelier :
♦♦ ***Le Dahu,*** 14, rue de la Mare, ☎ 54.88.72.88. AE, Euro, Visa Ⓟ 🌳 ♿ closed 10 Feb-20 Mar, 16-20 Jun, Tue eve and Wed low season. Spec : *feuilleté d'asperges au beurre de ciboulette, barbue aux moules et à l'orange, canard sauvage aux pêches,* 80-180.

Souvigny-en-Sologne:
● ♦ ***La Perdrix Rouge,*** rue du Gâtinais, ☎ 54.88.41.05. Visa Ⓟ ♿ closed Mon eve, Tue, 15-26 Jan, 26 Feb-26 Mar. Excellent cooking, one of the highlights being the *noix de coquilles Saint-Jacques "Perdrix Rouge",* prepared by Dominique and Jean-Noël Beurienne. A worthwhile stop-over in Sologne, 65-220.

⛺ ★★★*La Grande Sologne,* Nouan-le-Fuzelier, 7 km S (70 pl.), ☎ 54.88.70.22 ; ★★*Municipal* (66 pl.), ☎ 54.96.85.80.

LANGEAIS

Tours 25, Angers 83, Paris 258
A2 ♥ ⊠ 37130

ⓘ mairie (high season), ☎ 47.96.71.62.

SNCF ☎ 47.55.82.19.

Hotels :
★★***Hosten,*** 2, rue Gambetta, ☎ 47.96.82.12. DC. 12 rm, closed 15 Jun-10 Jul, 15 Jan-5 Feb, Mon eve and Tue, 220. Rest. ♦ ***le Langeais*** ♿ 130-180.

Cinq-Mars-la-Pile, 5 km E, rte de Tours at Langeais :
Château de Cinq-Mars (Château-accueil), ☎ 47.96.40.49. 3 rm ⁂ Ⓟ 🌳 closed 15 Oct-1 Apr, 260.

LOCHES

Tours 42, Châteauroux 70, Paris 258
A2 ⊠ 37600

ⓘ pl. de la Marne (B1), ☎ 47.59.07.98.

SNCF (C1), ☎ 47.59.00.44.

🚌 (B2), 3, rue de Tours, ☎ 47.59.06.23.

Hotels :
● ★★***France,*** 6, rue Picois (B2), ☎ 47.59.00.32. Visa. 22 rm Ⓟ closed 8-15 May, 3 Jan-10 Feb, Sun eve and Mon noon, 160. Rest. ♦ ♿ 45-100.
★★***Le George Sand,*** 39, rue Quintefol, ☎ 47.59.39.74. AE, DC, Euro, Visa. 17 rm ⁂ Former 17thC post-house, 160. Rest. ♦♦ 55-120.

Farmhouse gîte and chambres d'hôte : *la Cloutière,* Perrusson, 2 km S, ☎ 47.59.00.62.

Riding gîte : domaine de Marolles, Génillé, 10.5 km E, 37400 Montrésor, ☎ 47.59.50.01.

Events : *Country market :* craftsmen and traditional trades (mid-Jul) ; Fair-exhibition (Easter) ; *Festival of the forest* (mid-Aug).

Recommended : *Couturier,* master pastry-chef, 24, rue de la République (B2), ☎ 47.59.06.47, and *Néret,* master pastry-chef, 7, rue Picois (B2), ☎ 47.59.06.31.

LUYNES

Tours 13, Angers 97, Paris 246
A2 ✉ 37320

Hotel :

★★★★(L) ***Domaine de Beauvois*** (Relais et châteaux, Grandes Étapes Françaises), rte de Cléré, ☎ 47.55.50.11. Tx 750204. Visa. 40 rm closed 15 Jan-15 Mar, 935. Rest. ♦♦ Delightful Touraine cooking, 120-300.

MALESHERBES

Melun 46, Orléans 62, Paris 83
C1 ✉ 45330

i rue Pilonne, ☎ 38.34.81.94.

SNCF ☎ 38.34.60.49.

Hotel :

★***Écu de France*** (L.F.), 10, pl. du Martroi, ☎ 38.34.87.25. AE, Visa. 13 rm P 120. Rest. ♦ closed Thu, 45-160.

★★★*Municipal* (90 pl.), ☎ 38.34.85.63.

MENNETOU-SUR-CHER

Bourges 50, Blois 58, Paris 214
B2 ✉ 41320

SNCF ☎ 54.98.00.08.

Hotel :

★★***Lion d'Or*** (L.F.), 2, rue Marcel-Bailly, ☎ 54.98.01.13. DC, Euro, Visa. 20 rm P closed 15 Jan-15 Feb and Mon, 180. Rest. 60-130.

MEUNG-SUR-LOIRE

Orléans 18, Blois 40, Paris 145
B1 ✉ 45130

SNCF ☎ 38.44.31.10.

Hotel :

★***Saint-Jacques,*** 60, rue du Gal-de-Gaulle, ☎ 38.44.30.39. Euro, Visa. 12 rm P closed 20 Jan-4 Feb, 12-28 Oct and Mon, 110. Rest. 50-130.

★★*Municipal* (66 pl.), ☎ 38.44.44.98.

Concerts : in Jun, at the collégiale Saint-Liphard.

MONDOUBLEAU

Blois 60, Le Mans 63, Paris 163
28 km NW of Vendôme, B1 ✉ 41170

Hotel :

★★***Grand Monarque*** (L.F.), 2, rue Chrétien, ☎ 54.80.92.10. Euro, Visa. 10 rm P closed 23 Dec-14 Jan, Sun eve and Mon, 130. Rest. ♦ 60-155.

★★Municipal *des Prés Barrés* (40 pl.), ☎ 54.80.90.73.

Restaurant :

Droué, ✉ 41270, 14 km NE :

♦♦ ***Le Faisan Doré,*** 26, rte de Vendôme, ☎ 54.80.50.51 closed 15-31 Dec and eve. Touraine regional cooking and a surprising and delicious Canadian meal in the pure tradition of Québec : *coquilles St-Jacques, tourte "mer-forêt", coupe "Faisan Doré",* 45-95.

MONTARGIS

Sens 51, Orléans 71, Paris 115
C1 ✉ 45200

i pl. du Patis, ☎ 38.98.00.87.

SNCF ☎ 38.85.40.55.

pl. A.-Briand, ☎ 38.85.08.26.

Hotels :

● ★★***Lyon,*** 74, rue A.-Coquillet, ☎ 38.85.30.39. Visa. 22 rm P 160. Rest. ♦♦ closed Sun eve and Mon, 60-200.

★★***La Gloire,*** 74, av. du Gal-de-Gaulle, ☎ 38.85.04.69. 19 rm, closed Tue eve and Wed, 1 Jan-25 Feb, 15-25 Aug, 180. Rest. ● ♦♦ Excellent value for money particularly, such treasures as Mr. Joly's *aile de volaille dans sa feuille de chou,* and pastry selection, 120-210.

★★★Municipal *de la Forêt* (100 pl.), ☎ 38.98.00.20.

Restaurants :

♦♦ ***Chez Pierre,*** 57, rue Jean-Jaurès, ☎ 38.93.27.39. AE, DC, Euro, Visa 55-125.

Amilly :

● ♦♦ ***Auberge de l'Écluse,*** rue des Ponts, ☎ 38.85.44.24. Visa P closed 20 Dec-10 Jan, 22-30 Aug, Sun eve and Mon. Excellent dishes prepared by J.-L. Giraud : *vinaigrette de mâche et de foie de canard, sandre gratinée,* 65-200.

Recommended : *Pralines Mazet,* 43, rue du Gal-Leclerc. *Relais du Miel Villeneuve,* RN, 7.5 km S, ☎ 38.85.32.02.

MONTBAZON

Chinon 41, Poitiers 94, Paris 248
13 km S of Tours, A2 ✉ 37250 Veigné

i ☎ 47.26.03.31.

SNCF ☎ 47.26.00.26.

Hotels :

★★★★(L) ***Château d'Artigny*** (Relais et châteaux), rte d'Azay-le-Rideau, ☎ 47.26.24.24. Tx 750900. Visa. 55 rm and 6 apts P closed 1 Dec-10 Jan, 995. Rest. ♦♦♦♦ 180-300.

★★★★***Domaine de la Tortinière*** (Relais du Silence, Châteaux-hôtels), ☎ 47.26.00.19. Tx 750806. Euro, Visa. 21 rm P closed 15 Nov-1 Mar, 410. Rest. ♦♦♦ closed Mon and Tue noon, 1 Mar-1 Apr, 15 Oct-15 Nov, 190-300.

Veigné, 5 km on the N10 and D37 :

★★★***Moulin Fleuri*** (Châteaux-hôtels, L.F.), ☎ 47.26.01.12. AE, Visa. 10 rm P closed Mon, 1-20 Feb and 15-30 Oct, 140. Rest. ♦♦ Alain Chaplin's pleasant regional cooking. Low prices. Exceptional choice of Touraine wines. Spec : *assiette gourmande de la ferme, sole farcie,* 80-170.

★★*Municipal* (100 pl.), ☎ 47.26.06.43.

MONTLOUIS-SUR-LOIRE

Tours 12, Blois 48, Paris 235
A2 ✉ 37270

i pl. de l'Hôtel-de-Ville, ☎ 47.45.03.06.

SNCF ☎ 47.50.80.77.

★★★*Municipal* (250 pl.), ☎ 47.50.81.90.

Restaurant :

● ♦♦ ***Relais de Belle Roche,*** 14, rue de la Vallée, near the château de la Bourdaisière, ☎ 47.50.82.43. AE, DC, Visa. P closed 1-31 Mar, Tue eve and Wed. Unusual dining-room, set in a former cellar. Spec : *ris de veau braisé au montlouis, estouffade de gésiers de canard,* good local wines, 45-110.

MONTOIRE-SUR-LE-LOIR

Vendôme 19, Blois 44, Paris 191
A1 ✉ 41800

ⓘ mairie, ☎ 54.85.00.29.

Hotel :
● ★★**Cheval Rouge** (L.F.), 1, pl. Mal-Foch, ☎ 54.85.07.05. Euro, Visa. 17 rm 🅿 closed 26 Jan-27 Feb, Tue eve and Wed, 160. Rest. ♦ ♿ 80-220.

Restaurant :
Lavardin, ✉ 41800, 2 km SE :
♦♦ ***Auberge Paysanne,*** ☎ 54.85.02.72. ♿ closed Thu, 70-140.

⛺ ★★Municipal *des Reclusages* (40 pl.), ☎ 54.85.02.53.

MONTRICHARD

Blois 33, Tours 43, Paris 214
B2 ✉ 41400

ⓘ (high season) ☎ 54.32.05.10, and mairie, ☎ 54.32.00.46.

SNCF ☎ 54.32.03.09.

Hotels :
★★★**Bellevue** (L.F., Inter-Hôtel), 16, quai du Cher, ☎ 54.32.06.17. AE, DC, Euro, Visa. 29 rm ♿ closed 15 Nov-21 Dec, Mon eve, Tue (low season), 240. Rest. ♦♦ 75-180.
★★★**Tête Noire** (L.F.), 24, rue de Tours, ☎ 54.32.05.55. Visa. 38 rm 🅿 closed 3 Jan-7 Feb and Fri (Oct-15 Mar), 240. Rest. ♦♦ 60-180.
★★★**Château de la Ménaudière** (Châteaux-hôtels), ☎ 54.32.02.44. Tx 751246. AE, DC, Visa. 25 rm 🅿 12 acres closed 1 Dec-1 Mar, Sun eve and Mon low season, 380. Rest. ♦♦ 140-200.

Monthou-sur-Cher :
Château du Gué-Péan (Châteaux-hôtels), ☎ 54.71.43.01 and 54.71.46.09. Tx 750382. Private castle which receives guests, 20 rm 🅿 135 acres 370. Meals, 120-210.

⛺ ★★*Municipal l'Étourneau* (40 pl.), ☎ 54.32.10.16.

Restaurant :
♦♦ ***Le Gril du Passeur,*** 2, rue du Pont, ☎ 54.32.06.80. Euro, Visa. ♿ closed 1 Dec-15 Mar and Tue eve. Spec : *navarin de coquilles St-Jacques,* 80-120.

ORLÉANS

Chartres 73, Bourges 106, Paris 119
B1 ✉ 45000

ⓘ pl. Albert-Ier (B1), ☎ 38.53.05.95, and C.D.T., 3, rue de la Bretonnerie, ☎ 38.66.24.10.

✈ Bricy, 16 km NW, ☎ 38.43.23.60.

SNCF (B1), ☎ 38.86.32.81, 38.62.56.65.

Car-hire : *Budget* train + car, station, ☎ 38.62.60.61.

Hotels :
★★★★(L) ***Sofitel,*** 44-46, quai Barentin (A3), ☎ 38.62.17.39. 110 rm 🅿 ♿ 480. Rest. ♦♦ ***la Vènerie,*** 120-210.
● ★★★**Cèdres** (Inter-Hôtel), 17, rue du Mal-Foch (A1), ☎ 38.62.22.92. Tx 760912. AE, Euro, Visa. 35 rm 250.
★★★**Saint-Aignan,** 3, pl. Gambetta (A1), ☎ 38.53.15.35. AE, Euro, Visa. 27 rm 🅿 225.
● ★★**Marguerite** (L.F.), 14, pl. du Vieux-Marché (A2), ☎ 38.53.74.32. 25 rm, 140.

Saint-Jean-de-la-Ruelle, ✉ 45140, 2 km W :
★★★**Auberge de la Montespan** (Châteaux-hôtels), 31, av. G.-Clemenceau, ☎ 38.88.12.07. Visa. 8 rm 🅿 closed 20 Dec-1 Feb, 350. Rest. ♦♦♦ ♿ 130-185.

Olivet, ✉ 45160, 4 km S :
★★**Rivage** (Relais du Silence), 635, rue de la Reine-Blanche, ☎ 38.66.02.93. AE, DC, Euro, Visa. 21 rm 🅿 closed Feb, 220. Rest. ♦ closed Sun eve (1 Nov-30 Mar). Spec : *salade de langouste aux mangues fraîches, agneau de lait à la crème d'ail,* 100-140.

Youth hostel : 14, fg Madeleine, ☎ 38.62.10.48.

⛺ ★★*Municipal* (80 pl.), in Olivet, ☎ 38.63.53.94.

Restaurants :
● ♦♦♦ ***Crémaillère*** (Paul Huyart), 34, rue N.-D.-de-Recouvrance (B2), ☎ 38.53.49.17. AE, DC. ♿ closed Aug, 1 week in Feb, Sun eve and Mon. In his beautiful comfortable restaurant where he has been installed since 1966, Paul Huyart does not forget his Breton origins. Fresh fish and perfect *"cuisson minute".* Spec : *salade de tourteaux, bar rôti sauce au vin, pâtes fraîches à l'encre, turbot sauce homard,* 130-280.
● ♦♦ ***Les Antiquaires,*** 2-4, rue Au-Lin (C2), ☎ 38.53.52.35. AE, Visa. ♿ closed Aug, 1 week in Feb, Sun and Mon. Spec : river fish, 100-220.
● ♦♦ ***Le Lautrec,*** 26, pl. du Châtelet, ☎ 38.54.09.54. AE, Euro, Visa. ♿ closed 15-28 Feb, 15-31 Jul and Sun. Rich and good Tarn region cooking in a 1900-style setting. Wide choice of *foie gras, confit, mique* prepared by Bruno Bonlais, nice choice of armagnacs, 100-160.
♦♦ ***La Poutrière,*** 8, rue de la Brèche (B3), ☎ 38.66.02.30. AE, DC, Euro, Visa. 🅿 closed 1-7 Mar, Sun eve and Mon. Spec : *minute de bar et de saumon sauce citronnette, bœuf ficelle au raifort,* 120-220.
♦♦ ***Le Bigorneau,*** 54, rue des Turcies (A2), ☎ 38.68.01.10. AE, DC, Visa. ♿ closed 2 weeks in Feb and Jul, Sun, Mon and nat hols. Spec : fish and seafood, 120-180.

Olivet, ✉ 45160, 4 km S :
♦♦♦ ***Quatre Saisons,*** 351, rue de la Reine-Blanche, ☎ 38.66.14.30. Visa. 🅿 ♿ closed Jan-15 Mar. Spec : *pot-au-feu de fruits de mer,* grilled perch, 90-180.
♦♦ ***Madagascar,*** 315, rue de la Reine-Blanche, ☎ 38.66.12.58. 🅿 ♿ closed 20 Jan-22 Feb, Sun, Tue and Wed in winter, Wed high season, 80-170.
♦♦ ***Manderley*** (Inter-Hôtel), 117, sentier des Prés, ☎ 38.66.19.85. AE, DC, Euro, Visa. 🅿 ♿ closed Sun eve and Mon, 80-125.

Recommended : *Lenormand,* charcuterie, 318 fg Bannier, 45400 Fleury-les-Aubrais ; *Martin-Pouret,* traditional-style vinegar, 236, fg Bannier, 45400 Fleury-les-Aubrais ; *Chocolaterie Royale,* 53, rue Royale, 45400 Fleury-les-Aubrais ; *Morin, pâtisserie,* 209, rue de Bourgogne.

Guided tours : full-day tour of Orléans, Orléans-Beaugency, etc., C.D.T. Canal excursions, enq ⓘ

Events : *Fair-exhibition* in Apr ; *Festival of Jeanne d'Arc,* early May ; *Horticulture shows* at the parc d'Orléans-La Source ; *Foire à la paperasse et aux antiquités* early Mar ; *Salon des Antiquaires,* end Nov.

PITHIVIERS

Orléans 43, Chartres 73, Paris 82
C1 ✉ 45300

ⓘ Mail Ouest, ☎ 38.30.50.02.

SNCF ☎ 38.30.00.62.

Hotel :
★★**Chaumière** (L.F.), 77, av. de la République, ☎ 38.30.03.61. 8 rm, closed 15 Dec-10 Jan and Mon, 160. Rest. ♦ 47-110.

Youth hostel : 2, rue Madeleine-Rolland, ☎ 38.30.02.04.

⛺ ★★*Pré au Sage* (40 pl.), ☎ 38.30.04.21.

Restaurant :
♦♦♦ ***Péché Mignon,*** 48, fg Paris, ☎ 38.30.05.32. AE, DC, Visa Ⓟ closed 15 Jan-15 Feb, Sun eve and Tue. Spec : *savarin d'écrevisses, feuilleté de St-Jacques au confit de poireaux, sandre aux primeurs,* 80-180.

RICHELIEU

Chinon 21, Tours 60, Paris 295
A3 ☒ 37120

ℹ mairie, ☎ 47.58.10.13 and 47.58.13.62 (high season).

Hotel :

9 km SE on the D749 :
★★★**Château de Milly** (Châteaux-hôtels), Razines, RD749, ☎ 47.58.14.56. AE, DC, Euro, Visa. 15 rm 37 acres closed 31 Oct-15 Apr, 345. Rest. ♦ 135-230.

⛺ ★★*Municipal* (35 pl.), ☎ 47.58.10.13.

ROMORANTIN-LANTHENAY

Poitiers 54, Tours 60, Paris 295
B2 ☒ 41200

ℹ pl. Paix, ☎ 54.76.43.89.

SNCF ☎ 54.76.06.51.

Hotels :
★★★**Lion d'Or** (Relais et châteaux), 69, rue G.-Clemenceau, ☎ 54.76.00.28. Tx 750990. AE, DC, Euro, Visa. 10 rm Ⓟ ♿ closed 5 Jan-13 Feb, 430. Rest. ♦♦♦ Former posthouse, beautifully restored. Spec : *ris de veau braisé aux pamplemousses, langoustines rôties aux épices douces,* 200-330.
★★★**Le Colombier** (L.F.), 10, pl. du Vieux-Marché, ☎ 54.76.12.76. AE, DC, Euro, Visa. 10 rm Ⓟ closed 13 Jan-11 Feb, 15-22 Sep, 160. Rest. ● ♦♦ ♿ closed Mon. Old beamed ceiling, flower-filled terrace, and a wonderful choice of excellent, refined dishes such as : *sandre au beurre d'oseille, papillote de saint-pierre à la crème de gingembre,* 70-180.

SAINT-AIGNAN

Blois 39, Châteauroux 64, Paris 219
B2 ☒ 41100

ℹ ☎ 54.75.13.31 and 54.75.22.85 (high season).

SNCF ☎ 54.75.20.14.

Hotel :
★★**Saint-Aignan** (L.F.), 7-9, quai J.-J.-Delorme, ☎ 54.75.18.04. 23 rm Ⓟ closed 15 Dec-1 Feb, Sun eve and Mon, 240. Rest. ♦ 60-180.

⛺ ★★★*Municipal* (200 pl.), ☎ 54.75.15.59 and 54.75.04.58.

Restaurant :
♦ ***Relais de la Poste,*** 3, rue de l'Ormeau, ☎ 54.75.23.47. closed 1-28 Feb and Mon low season. Spec : *tripes au sauvignon, rognons au gamay,* 45-85.

SAINT-BENOÎT-SUR-LOIRE

Orléans 35, Bourges 90, Paris 144
C1 ☒ 45110 Châteauneuf-sur-Loire

Hotel :
★★**Labrador** (L.F.), 7, pl. de l'Abbaye, ☎ 38.35.74.38. 22 rm Ⓟ ♿ closed Jan, 185.

SAINTE-MAURE-DE-TOURAINE

Tours 37, Poitiers 69, Paris 272
A2 ☒ 37800

ℹ rue du Château (high season), ☎ 47.65.66.20, and mairie, ☎ 47.65.40.12.

Hotel :
★**Gueulardière** (L.F.), 10, rte Nationale, ☎ 47.65.40.71. AE, DC, Euro, Visa. 15 rm Ⓟ closed 20 Jan-3 Feb, 15-30 Oct, Sun eve (Oct-Mar) and Mon, 155. Rest. 50-150.

Farmhouse gîte and chambres d'hôtes : *domaine la Gapillière,* 18 km, ☎ 47.65.01.27.

Buggy hire : *Joseph Visag,* « Vaugourdon », Saint-Épain, ☎ 47.65.49.86.

SALBRIS

Bourges 50, Orléans 56, Paris 187
C2 ☒ 41300

SNCF ☎ 54.97.00.05.

Hotels :
★★★**Parc** (L.F.), 8-10, av. d'Orléans, ☎ 54.97.18.53. Tx 751164. AE, DC, Euro, Visa. 27 rm Ⓟ 220. Rest. ♦♦ closed 13 Jan-16 Feb, 70-250.
★**Sauldraie,** 1 km N20, 81, av. d'Orléans, ☎ 54.97.17.76. Euro, Visa. 12 rm Ⓟ 10 acres ♿ closed 20 Mar-3 Apr, 10-25 Sep and Tue, 160. Rest. ♦ 60-100.

⛺ ★★★Municipal *de Sologne* (65 pl.), ☎ 54.97.06.38.

SULLY-SUR-LOIRE

Orléans 42, Bourges 82, Paris 155
C1 ☒ 45600

ℹ pl. Gal-de-Gaulle, ☎ 38.35.22.21.

SNCF ☎ 38.35.21.02.

Hotels :
● ★★**Pont de Sologne,** 21, rue Porte-de-Sologne, ☎ 38.36.26.34. DC. 24 rm Ⓟ closed 21 Dec-13 Jan, 170. Rest. ♦ ♿ 80-160.
★★**Poste** (Inter-Hôtel), 11, fg St-Germain, ☎ 38.36.26.22. AE, Euro, Visa. 27 rm Ⓟ closed 15 Jan-3 Mar, 180. Rest. ♦ ♿ 70-210.

⛺ ★★*Essi* (133 pl.), ☎ 38.36.23.93.

Events : *Musical festival* in Jul. *Fête de St-Hubert* last Sun in Oct.

TOURS

Le Mans 82, Orléans 112, Paris 234
A2 ☒ 37000

ℹ pl. du Mal-Leclerc, ☎ 47.05.58.08.

SNCF (C3), ☎ 47.61.46.46, 47.20.23.43.

✈ Saint-Symphorien, 7 km NE, ☎ 47.54.21.45. *Agence Air France,* 8-10, pl. de la Victoire, ☎ 47.05.08.16.

🚌 pl. Mal-Leclerc (C2-3), ☎ 47.05.30.49.

Car-hire : *Budget* train + car, station, ☎ 47.66.36.69 and 47.05.38.01.

Hotels :
★★★★**Méridien,** 292, av. de Grammont (not on C3 map), ☎ 47.28.00.80. Tx 750922. AE, DC, Euro, Visa. 125 rm and 6 apts Ⓟ ♿ 450. Rest. ♦♦ 100-195.
★★★**Bordeaux** (L.F.), 3, pl. Mal-Leclerc (C2), ☎ 47.05.40.32. Tx 750414. AE, DC, Euro, Visa. 52 rm ♿ 270. Rest. ♦♦ 100-200.
★★★**Grand Hôtel,** 9, pl. Mal-Leclerc, ☎ 47.05.35.31. Tx 750105. AE, DC, Euro, Visa. 79 rm Ⓟ ♿ closed 10 Dec-9 Jan, Sat and Sun eve low season, 300.

★★★**Central,** 21, rue Berthelot (B-C1), ☎ 47.05.46.44. Tx 751173. AE, DC, Euro, Visa. 42 rm Ⓟ ♨ ⛰ ♿ 230.
★★★**Univers,** 5, bd Heurteloup (C2), ☎ 47.05.37.12. Tx 751460. AE, DC, Euro, Visa. 91 rm Ⓟ ⛰ ♿ 325. Rest. ♦♦ ♿ 90-180.
● ★★**Castel Fleuri,** 10, rue Groison, ☎ 47.54.50.99. 14 rm Ⓟ ⛰ ♿ closed Sun (Nov-Mar). Rest. ● ♦♦ ***les Jardins du Castel,*** ☎ 47.41.94.40 Ⓟ ♨ ⛰ closed 2-31 Jan. In the discrete charm of a comfortable house, quality at reasonable prices. Delightful garden, pleasant in summer. Spec : *huîtres gratinées au bacon, rouget en papillote, canard au chinon,* 140-200.

Joué-lès-Tours, ✉ 37300, 4 km SW by D86 and D207 :
★★★**Château de Beaulieu** (Relais du Silence, Châteaux-hôtels), rte de l'Épend, ☎ 47.53.20.26. Visa. 17 rm ⚘ Ⓟ ♨ ⛰ 18thC manor, 350. Rest. ♦♦ ♿ 135-260.
★★**Chantepie,** 6, rue Poincaré, ☎ 47.03.06.09. Euro, Visa. 20 rm Ⓟ ♨ ⛰ closed 26 Dec-15 Jan, 200.

Rochecorbon, 37210 Vouvray, 3 km NE :
● ★★**Fontaines St-Georges** (L.F.), 6, quai de Loire, ☎ 47.52.52.86. AE, DC, Euro, Visa. 15 rm Ⓟ ♨ ⛰ ♿ 230.

Youth hostel, parc Grandmont, ☎ 47.28.15.87.

⛺ ★★*Municipal Péron* (62 pl.), ☎ 47.61.81.24.

Restaurants :
● ♦♦ ***Bistrot 17,*** 17, pl. de la Victoire, ☎ 47.39.61.72 ♿ closed Aug, Sun. Classy bistrot. Refined Touraine cooking : *terrine de ris de veau et canard au marc de Touraine, suprême de barbue au sabayon de vouvray,* 135-200.
● ♦♦ ***Tuffeaux,*** 19, rue Lavoisier (C-D1), ☎ 47.47.19.89 ⚘ ♿ closed 1-25 Jan, 10-20 Aug, Sun and Mon. Spec : *blanc de turbot sauce au vin de Layon et melon, pigeonneau farci en sa feuille de chou,* 150-260.
♦♦ ***Rôtisserie Tourangelle,*** 23, rue du Commerce (B1), ☎ 47.05.71.21. AE, DC, Euro, Visa ⛰ closed 14 Jul-5 Aug, Sun eve and Mon. Spec : *sandre au sabayon de vouvray, aiguillette de canard au fumet de bourgueil,* 130-270.

Saint-Cyr-sur-Loire :
♦♦ ***Poêle d'Or,*** 9, quai des Maisons-Blanches, ☎ 47.54.03.62. AE, Visa ⚘ closed Aug, Tue eve and Wed. Delicious regional cooking, good wines and desserts, 120-200.

Rochecorbon, 37210 Vouvray, 3 km NE :
♦♦ ***L'Oubliette,*** 34, rue des Clouets, ☎ 47.52.50.49. Euro, Visa ♿ closed 2-20 Jan, 1 week early Nov, Sun eve and Mon. Spec : *sandre, ris de veau aux pleurotes,* 90-180.
♦ ***Lanterne,*** 48, quai de la Loire, ☎ 47.52.50.02. Visa ⚘ Ⓟ ♨ ♿ closed Sun eve and Mon, 10 Jan-28 Feb. Spec : *petite friture sauce tartare, magret de canard aigre-doux à l'orange,* 55-150.

Exhibitions and trade fairs : *Foire à l'ail et au basilic,* Jul. *Fair-Exhibition,* early May. *West European Agricultural Fair,* Sep.

Bicycle hire : *M. Barat,* 156, rue Giraudeau, ☎ 47.61.03.58, and *Grammont-Motocycles,* 93, av. de Grammont, ☎ 47.66.62.83.

Recommended : Stuffed prunes : *Sabat,* 76, rue Nationale, and *Poirault,* confectioner, 31, rue Nationale. Antiques : *Comparaison,* pl. Plumereau, ☎ 47.61.42.34, and *l'Échiquier,* 74, rue Colbert, ☎ 47.66.69.81.

VENDÔME

Blois 32, Le Mans 77, Paris 172
B1 ✉ 41100

ℹ tour Saint-Martin, rue Poterie (B2), ☎ 54.77.05.07.

SNCF (C1), ☎ 54.77.20.40.

Hotels :
● ★★**Saint-Georges,** 14, rue Poterie (B2), ☎ 54.77.25.42. AE, DC, Euro, Visa. 37 rm Ⓟ ♿ 245. Rest. ♦ ♿ closed 1-30 Nov, Sat noon and Sun eve, 70-200.

La Ville-aux-Clercs, 41160 Morée, 16 km :
● ★★**Manoir de la Forêt** (L.F., Châteaux-hôtels), ☎ 54.80.62.83. Visa. 21 rm ⚘ Ⓟ ♨ ⛰ 200. Rest. ♦ closed Sun eve and Mon in winter, 95-190.

⛺ ★★★*Municipal* (200 pl.), ☎ 54.77.00.27.

Restaurant :
● ♦ ***Chez Annette,*** 194 *bis,* fg Chartrain (not on C1 map), ☎ 54.77.23.03. AE, Visa ♿ closed Thu and Christmas school hols. A well-known, ideally situated stopping place for motorists. Rustic setting, with dishes such as the classic slice of beef and a subtle *brochet au beurre blanc,* 55-100.

VILLANDRY

Tours 20, Angers 97, Paris 254
A2 ✉ 37300 Joué-lès-Tours

Hotel :
Savonnières, ✉ 37510, 2.5 km E :
★★★**Cèdres** (Relais du Silence), ☎ 47.53.00.28. Tx 752074. Euro, Visa. 37 rm Ⓟ ♨ ⛰ ▣ ♿ 410. Rest. ♦♦ ☎ 47.53.37.58. Spec : *poulet aux écrevisses, pétale de sandre à la mousse d'oseille,* 120-250.

VOUVRAY

Tours 10, Blois 49, Paris 233
A2 ✉ 37210

Hotels :
★★**Grand Vatel** (L.F.), rue Brulé, ☎ 47.52.70.32. AE, DC, Visa. 7 rm Ⓟ ♨ 🐕 closed 20 Nov-28 Dec, Sun eve from 1 Nov to 31 Mar, and Mon, 185. Rest. ♦ ♿ 75-180.

Vernou-sur-Brenne, 5 km E :
★★**Perce-Neige,** 13, rue A.-France, ☎ 47.52.10.04. AE, Euro, Visa. 15 rm Ⓟ ♨ ⛰ closed Feb, Sun eve and Mon low season, 210. Rest. ♦♦ 100-170.

Event : Fair for tourists, mid-Aug.

Visits of cellars : *Vallée Coquette,* ☎ 47.52.75.03 ; *Viticulteurs du Vouvray,* château de Vaudenuits, ☎ 47.52.60.20 ; *la Caillerie,* ☎ 47.52.78.75 ; *Vallée de Vaux,* ☎ 47.52.93.22.

Recommended : *Hardouin,* charcutier, 9, rue du Commerce, ☎ 47.52.73.37.

The Vendée, Poitou and Charentes Regions

The softness of the Charentes countryside, with its nimbus of light and luminous mist, has always fascinated the traveller. But Poitou is full of paradoxes, and today's travellers, like many before them, tend to hurry through the softly rolling hills and high-growing stands of heather and brushwood, dotted with fertile pastures and marshlands, on their way to the Atlantic coast.

Poitou is an agricultural region and every pore of its being is tuned to the Ocean from which it derives a great part of its wealth, for without the great waterways leading to the sea, Poitou would lose half its solid prosperity. Here, from the most mediocre of local wines, experts distil the most perfect of spirits : cognac. The gentle landscape is dotted with places of interest : estuary ports, old relays, inns and farms, where the traveller can break his journey like the pilgrims of Compostela so many years ago, until he reaches the coast with its clear sky, enormous beaches, villages sparkling in the sun, and wide foreshores where fish farming flourishes and migratory birds add to the richness of the habitat.

The art of the region is imbued with the legendary, as is apparent in the joyous figures found on the great church portals, and in the mysticism which inspired the frescos of Romanesque churches. Manor houses and châteaux bear witness to the wealth of the countryside and the taste and spirit of its inhabitants. This refinement is equally well expressed in the gently-simmered dishes for which the region is famous. Its wine, seafood, snails, sausages and salami, hearty meat dishes and wide variety of cheeses — including 50 varieties of *chabichou* goat's milk cheese — make Poitou an exciting visit for tourists who appreciate good living and the joys of the table.

Sightseeing

■ L'AIGUILLON-SUR-MER

A2 / ® / pop. 2 152 (Vendée)

An oyster and mussel producing town on the estuary of the Lay. □

▶ Nearby

▶ **La Faute-sur-Mer** ®, seaside resort leading to the **Pointe d'Arçay,** where there is a 1 200 acre bird sanctuary - and a naturist area *(no cars).* ▶ **Saint-Michel-en-l'Herm** *(to the N, rte de Luçon)* is the site of a former abbey partly rebuilt in the 17thC *(10-12 & 3-5 in season).* ▶ **La Tranche-sur-Mer** ® *(13 km W) :* immense beach sheltered behind dunes and pines; the soft climate favours bulb growing *(flower season Easter-Jun.)*; boat trips in summer; 2 km away, **phare** (lighthouse; *open to visitors*) on the Pointe du Grouin-du-Cou (panorama). □

Facts and figures

Location : *Between the Loire river (N), the Gironde river (S), Limousin (E) and the Atlantic (W; 550 km of coast).*
Area : *33 190 km².*
Climate : *One of the sunniest regions in France (over 2 000 hr of sun p.a. : nearly as much as Ajaccio Bay); avg. temp. Jul.-Aug. : 18-23 °C.*
Population : *2 051 000.*
Administration : *Department of **Charente;** Prefecture : Angoulême. Department of **Charente-Maritime;** Prefecture : La Rochelle. Department of **Deux-Sèvres;** Prefecture : Niort. Department of **Vendée;** Prefecture : La Roche-sur-Yon. Department of **Vienne;** Prefecture : Poitiers.*

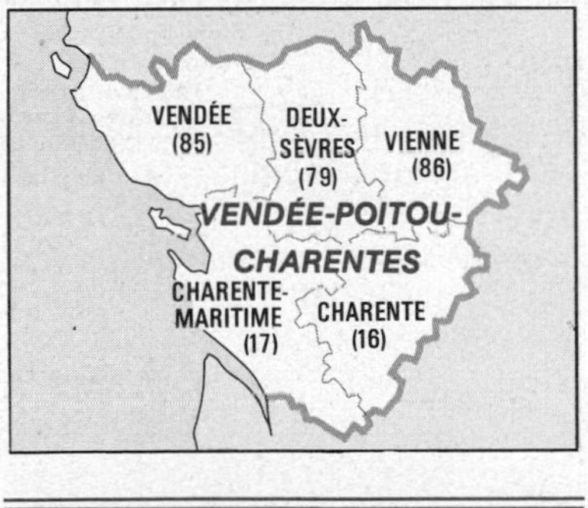

■ AIRVAULT★

C1 / ® / pop. 3 847 (Deux-Sèvres)

Remarkable Romanesque church of St. Pierre (narthex★) on the Place du Minage; half-timbered houses in surrounding streets; folk art museum in neighbouring 13thC buildings *(daily Jul.-15 Sep., 2-6; Sun. and nat. hols. out of season, 2-5).* □

Don't miss

★★★ : Aulnay (B2), Poitiers (C1), La Rochelle (B2), Saint-Savin (C1), Saintes (B3).
★★ : Chauvigny (C1), the Marais Poitevin (marshes) (AB2), Ile d'Oléron (A2), Ile de Ré (A2), Rochefort (B3), Talmont (B3), Thouars (B1), Ile d'Yeu (A1).

▶ Valley of the Thouet *(13 km S and 7 km N; 2 hr)*

▶ **Airvault :** at the southern exit from the town is the Romanesque Vernay Bridge (11 arches, 12thC). ▶ **Saint-Loup-Lamairé,** famous for its goat's milk cheese; Louis XIII château with Gothic keep and moats *(exterior visit only)*; Gothic and Renaissance houses in town (staircase★ of the Auditoire). ▶ **Gourgé :** Romanesque church; bridge used by pilgrims to Compostela; nearby, château de la Roche-Faton (15th-16thC). ▶ North of Airvault *(6.5 km)* **Saint-Généroux★ :** 13thC bridge and one of the oldest churches in France (9thC, much restored in the 19thC). □

▶ Round trip along the banks of the Dive *(25 km W; 2 hr)*

▶ **Saint-Jouin-de-Marnes :** large fortified Romanesque church★; façade, Angevin vaulting in the nave, stalls. ▶ **Moncontour** (86), on the opposite bank : massive 12thC keep, rebuilt in the 15thC. ▶ Near Marnes, manor house of **Retournay** (15thC). □

■ Île d'AIX★

(Aix Island)

B2 / pop. 173

From La Fumée Point, a 20 to 30 minute

Weekend tips

Travel by air or fast train (4 hrs from Paris) to La Rochelle in time for dinner on Friday night. After dark, walk around the town and see the Vieux-Port (old port), the Rue Chaudrier and the flood-lit town hall.
Early Saturday morning, take the boat from La Pallice and spend the day on the Île de Ré (island; → ®; lunch at La Flotte, Saint-Martin or Ars); return to La Rochelle at the end of the afternoon (maybe spend the evening in Châtelaillon → ®).
On Sunday, tour the Marais Poitevin (marshes; →) : boat-trip before having lunch in Coulon, Arçais or Niort; in the afternoon, visit the abbey of Maillezais, the bird sanctuary at Saint-Denis-du-Payré, Marans; dinner in Esnandes → ® (mussels are the speciality here) before returning to La Rochelle.

boat-trip will take you to this small island (320 acres, 3 km at its longest; *no cars*) : the only means of transportation are on foot, bicycles or horse-drawn carriages.

▶ Inside the surrounding wall, the village has only three streets, lined with low houses draped with hollyhock; at the end of the main street, opposite the church (Pre-romanesque crypt), is a **mother-of-pearl** workshop *(closed nat. hols.)*. ▶ On the Rue Napoléon, two museums : the **Maison de l'Empereur** where Napoleon spent his last nights in France in July 1815 *(Apr.-Oct., 10-12 & 2-6, closed Tue.)*; and the **African Museum** (ethnography and zoology; *same hours, closed Wed.)*. □

■ ANGLES-SUR-L'ANGLIN★

C1 / pop. 465 (Vienne)

Beautiful site★, with a nice bridge over the Anglin, near the water wheel of a mill; impressive mediaeval fortresses (illuminations, *early Aug.*). Some of the women here keep up the needlework tradition : Angles has even given its name to a certain kind of stitch : *jours d'Angles*. □

▶ Nearby

▶ Romanesque church in **Vicq**★ (12thC; *to N*). ▶ Gorges of the Anglin Valley *(to S)*. ▶ Through the Gartempe Valley, prehistoric caves around **Saint-Pierre-de-Maillé,** and château de la Guittière on the edge of a cliff. □

■ ANGOULÊME★★

C3 / ® / pop. 50 151 (Charente)

On a bend in the Charente, Angoulême is set on a hill-top, still surrounded by ramparts. A commercial and industrial centre, one of the principal towns of western France.

▶ The Hôtel de Ville (town hall) was built in the 19thC (13thC style) on the site of the castle of the Counts of Angoulême, of which two towers remain : the **Tour de Lusignan** (late 13thC) and the **Tour de Valois** (late 15thC). ▶ Walk through **Old Angoulême** (houses from the Renaissance to Louis XIV) to reach the cathedral (via Place Louvel) or the Esplanade Beaulieu (via Rue Beaulieu) overlooking the **Jardin Vert** (gardens; view). The **cathedral**★ (12thC) has a storiated façade★★ of great interest. The north transept is topped by a 60 m high Romanesque bell-tower★. ▶ Left of the cathedral façade, the former bishops' residence is now a **Fine Arts Museum** (painting, porcelain, history, African art, ethnology, *closed Tue.*). ▶ **Musée de la Société archéologique** (Museum of the Archaeological Society), 42, 44 Rue de Montmoreau. ▶ Most interesting : walk along and around the **ramparts.** ▶ In the old town, restoration projects. □

▶ Eaux-Claires Valley *(32 km round trip; half-day)*

▶ From **Puymoyen** *(4 km S;* 13thC church), go down into the **Eaux-Claires Valley** and visit the prehistoric habitations; **Le Verger Mill,** where vellum is still produced by traditional methods *(demonstrations, daily visits)*. ▶ **Mouthiers-sur-Boëme :** prehistoric habitations, Romanesque church, Renaissance château. ▶ **La Couronne :** vestiges of the former abbey (ruins of the Romanesque abbey church and cellars from the 13thC; 18thC buildings; *visit on request*). ▶ **Château de L'Oisellerie** (Renaissance). ▶ Romanesque church at **Saint-Michel-d'Entraygues**★ *(5 km from Angoulême),* built in an octagonal design (restored in the 19thC). ▶ Nersac : **Fleurac Mill,** traditional paper-making *(instruction)*. □

▶ Charente Valley *(85 km round trip; half-day)*

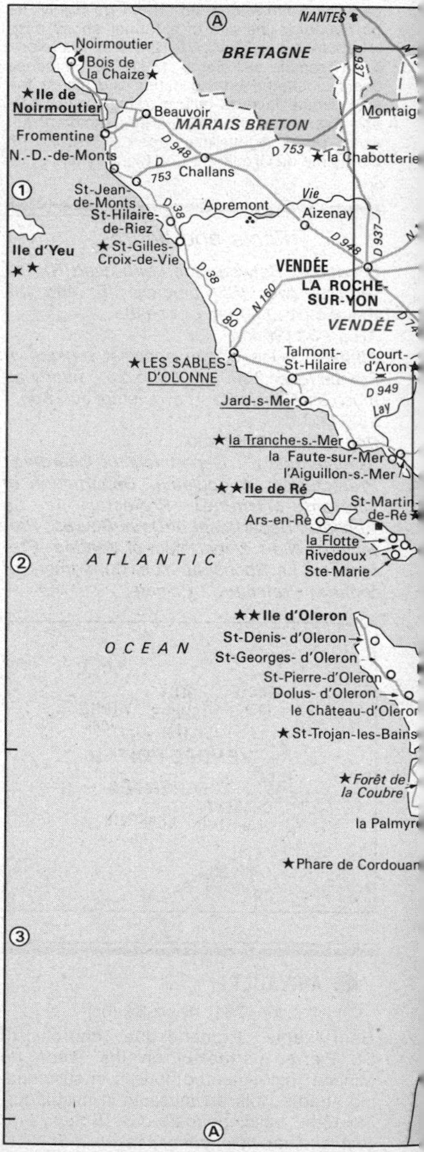

▶ **Château de Balzac** (home of Guez de Balzac, 17thC). ▶ **Asnières-sur-Nouère** ®: Romanesque church. ▶ **Saint-Cybardeaux :** 1.5 km N, Gallo-Roman theatre at **Les Bouchauds**★ (1stC; *admission free, guided visits : SI*). ▶ **Marcillac-Lanville :** beautiful rural architecture. ▶ **Saint-Amant-de-Boixe :** one of the great Romanesque churches★ of the area (12thC; choir rebuilt 15thC; Gothic murals); right of the façade, remains of cloister (12th-14thC). ▶ Return via N10. □

AUBETERRE-SUR-DRONNE★

C3 / ® / pop. 404 (Charente)

Built in the form of an amphitheatre, this village of white buildings and tiled roofs on the road to Compostela resembles the towns of Navarre in Spain, also on the pilgrim route.

▶ At the foot of the castle ruins (14th-15thC) is **Saint John's church** (12thC) cut into the white limestone rock that gives the village its name. ▶ In the upper town, beyond the Renaissance **Chapter-house,** all that remains of the pilgrim **church of St. Jacques** is the imposing storiated façade★. □

▶ Nearby

▶ **Chalais** *(11 km W),* renowned for its fairs : visit the Talleyrand **Château** (14th-18thC) and the church **(Romanesque doorway).** □

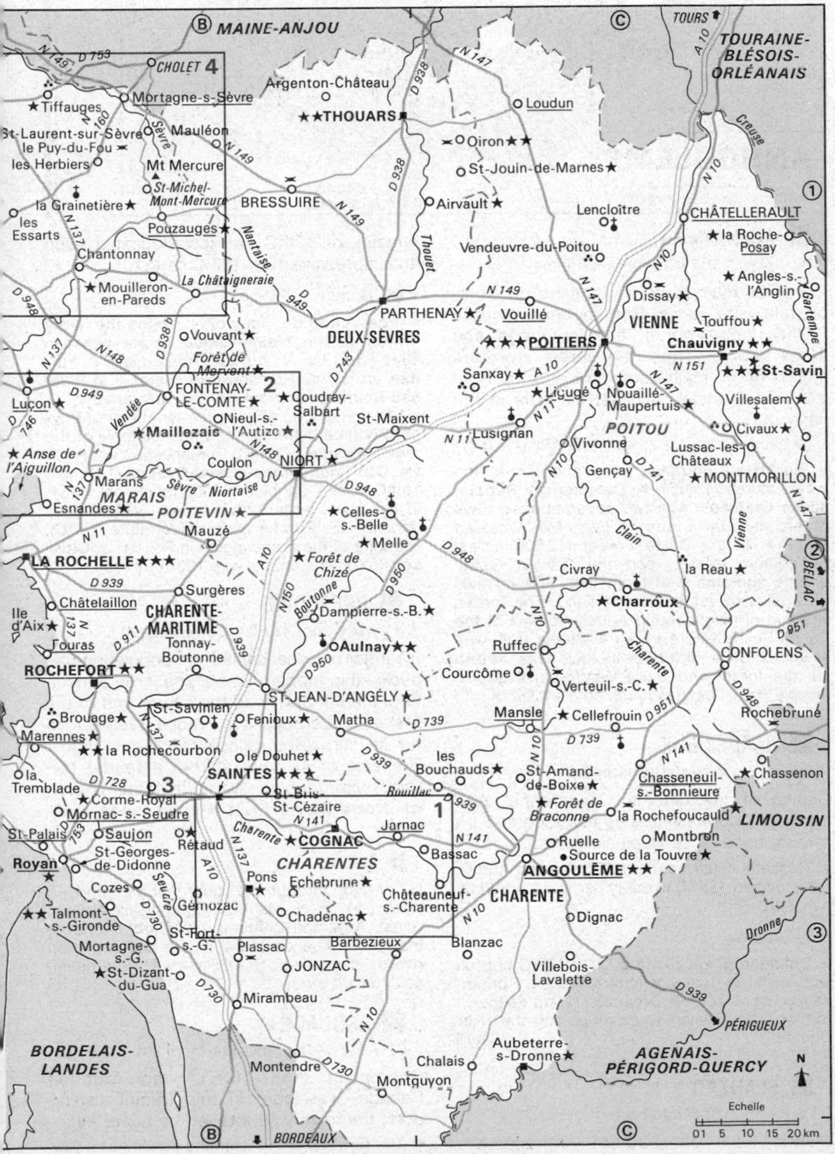

Vendée, Poitou, Charente

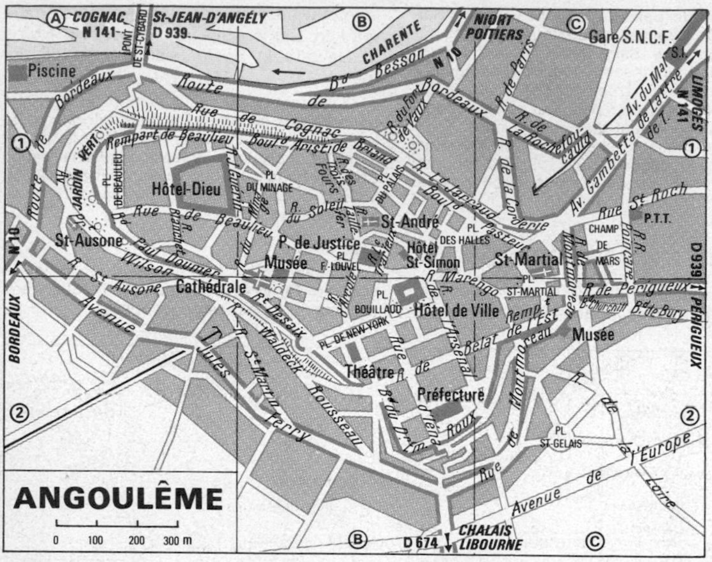

■ AULNAY★★★

B2 / pop. 1 505 (Charente-Maritime)

Along the main route to Santiago de Compostela, the large Romanesque church (12thC) looms out of the yew trees and stone tombs. Note the three storiated arches of the main doorway★ and the right transept doorway; sculpted capitals in the nave. □

▶ Round trip of the Boutonne *(65 km; 3 hr)*

▶ **Nuaillé-sur-Boutonne** *(S)* : doorway in the small church (13thC). ▶ **Dampierre : Renaissance château★** with two superimposed rows of arcades, by a stream *(Nov.-Mar.; closed Thu.)*. ▶ In the **Chizé Forest** (12 500 acres, remarkable trees : see the "Seven Oaks" group), **zoorama** with more than 600 animals on a 60 acre estate *(closed Tue.)*. The forest, like that of neighbouring Aulnay, is part of the Val de Sèvre Nature Park (→ Marais Poitevin). ▶ **Brioux,** once known for its mule fairs; return via the forest and **Saint-Mandé-sur-Brédoire** (simple Romanesque church on a knoll). □

■ BARBEZIEUX

B3 / ® / pop. 5 404 (Charente)

Capital of the Grande Champagne area (→ Cognac box), a trading town located on a route used since Neolithic times.

▶ Rochefoucauld **castle** (reconstructed 15thC, restored late 19thC) is today partly occupied by a museum. □

▶ Nearby

▶ **Condéon** *(8 km S, via D731)* : 12thC church with multifoil doorway (characteristic Romanesque decoration). ▶ **Brossac** *(12 km farther)* : former Gallo-Roman spa overlooking the river Double. □

■ BLANZAC

C3 / pop. 978 (Charente)

Market town of southern Angoulême : remains of 12thC La Rochefoucauld keep and impressive 12th-13thC church. □

▶ Nearby

▶ Poet Alfred de Vigny often visited the "Ivory Tower" of the **Maine-Giraud** estate between 1827-63 *(3 km N; private; visits daily)*. ▶ Farther on, 12thC Romanesque church★ at **Plassac-Rouffiac** overlooking the vineyards. ▶ E, via **Pérignac** (church), the former abbey of **Puypéroux** on a beautiful site : fine example of the region's earliest (11thC) Romanesque art. ▶ SE via D10, **Montmoreau-Saint-Cybard** *(13 km)* : 15thC castle on bluff *(visits to chapel only)*; in the town, large 12thC church with multifoil doorway. S, **Porcheresse** church (late 11thC), with one of the first cupolas in Poitou; at **Cressac,** Templars' chapel with 12thC frescos. □

■ BRESSUIRE

B1 / ® / pop. 19 502 (Deux-Sèvres)

A former regional capital; its population has declined in modern times. The large agricultural market here was the site of one of the first slaughterhouses in France. Well-known for its fairs *(Aug.)* since the Middle Ages. Remains of 48 towers from a **feudal fortress** with double walls. 12th-14thC **church of Notre-Dame** with Renaissance belltower. □

▶ Nearby

▶ Long trip through the country of the Vendéen wars (→). ▶ N, via **Voultegon** (Gallo-Roman ruins), **Argenton-Château** ® *(17 km)* overlooking the confluence of the Ouère and Argenton rivers; church of St. Gilles with interesting sculpted doorway. □

■ BROUAGE★

B2 / pop. 476 (Charente-Maritime)

Champlain (1567-1635), who founded Canada, was born in this former fishing port; the town was fortified by Louis XIII.

▶ The **fortified wall★** is in fine condition; a tour

of the sentry walk *(1.6 km)* will show you the town gates, the produce market, the former arsenal, forges and the underground ports *(son et lumiere some summer nights).*

▶ Tour of the marshes *(35 km N; 28 km S; 4 hr)*

▶ To the S, **Marennes** ® (pop. 4549) : panorama★ from the bell-tower (15thC; 78 m high) over the marshes now converted to oyster farms; in the village : oyster diorama *(in summer);* château de La Gataudière (18thC, *10:30-12 & 2:30-6, Jun.-Oct.; Sun. and hols., Nov.-May, 2-5, on request*) via the yacht harbour to the oyster port of **La Cayenne** *(4 km; organised visit of the parks).* ▶ West of Marennes : **Chapus Point** (oyster port); offshore is **Fort Louvois** (17thC), accessible by causeway *(submerged at high tide);* oyster museum *(closed Tue.).* □

CHARROUX★

C2 / pop. 1552 (Vienne)

Octagonal **lantern-tower★** on the 11thC church in a Carolingian abbey partially destroyed during the religious wars. **Collection of precious stones** from the abbey's portal, kept in the 14th and 15thC buildings *(closed Oct. and Tue. off season).* Close by : a number of half-timbered Gothic houses. □

▶ Nearby

▶ **Civray** *(11 km),* on the right bank of the Charente : remarkable storiated façade★★ on the 12thC church; octagonal bell-tower at the transept crossing. ▶ **Sommières-du-Clain** *(15 km N) :* château de Vareilles (French Classical style). ▶ **La Reau Abbey★** *(14 km NE) :* in the middle of the countryside, mediaeval ruins (12thC; burnt during the Hundred Years' War); some constructions were rebuilt in the 15th and 18thC *(10-12 & 2:30-5:15 in summer; closed Tue.).* ▶ On the road to Poitiers : **Usson** Church (Romanesque doorway). □

CHÂTELLERAULT

C1 / ® / pop. 36870 (Vienne)

Ancient port on the Vienne; splendid bridge; one of Poitou's most important commercial centres.

▶ **Rue Bourbon,** the main street until recent years, is now for pedestrians only : No. 162, former home (16thC) of philosopher Descartes (museum : *closed Tue. and some nat. hols.).* ▶ On the quay : **Chéron de la Martinière Museum** in the castle ruins (local history and craftwork, Nevers faïence; Rue Godeau-Lerpinière, *2-6, closed Tue., Sun. and hols.*). ▶ **Henri IV bridge** (late 16thC) opens onto the Châteauneuf district : upstream, the armaments factory is now partially taken over by an **automobile museum★** *(closed Tue. out of season).* □

▶ The Châtellerault region (Châtelleraudais)

▶ **Ingrandes** *(N via N10) :* church (partially Carolingian). ▶ **Les Ormes** *(17 km) :* 18thC château. ▶ To the NE, **Oyré :** Romanesque church, pillared arcade (inside : late 15thC murals). ▶ S, through the Vienne Valley, **Ozon :** former Templar commandery (frescos). ▶ SW, through the Clain Valley, **Vieux-Poitiers** *(10 km) :* Gallo-Roman ruins near the supposed site of the Saracen defeat in 732 (Moussais-la-Bataille; *excavations in progress*). ▶ Via La Triche-rie, **Beaumont :** Romanesque church; ruins of 10th-11thC keep. □

▶ Hills to the N and W *(60 km; half-day)*

▶ Via **Châtellerault Forest** (3750 acres), Romanesque church at **Colombiers.** ▶ To the NW via **Thuré :** Massardière manor (14th-15thC), and **Scorbé-Clairvaux** château (15th-17thC). ▶ To the N via Saint-Gervais-les-Trois-Clochers : **Marmande Butte,** hill with ruined 14thC keep (40 m high; panorama). Return via **La Motte-d'Usseau** castle (15thC). □

CHAUVIGNY★★

C1 / ® / pop. 6684 (Vienne)

On this steep promontory are the ruins of five enormous fortified castles that once guarded the route to Berry.

▶ The **baronial castle** (or Bishop's), is the first encountered climbing up the hill (large square keep; 12thC); higher up, Harcourt Castle (13th-15thC), followed by Montléon (12th-15thC), Gouzon (with 11thC keep), and finally, the Flins Tower. ▶ The **church of St. Pierre★★** (11th-12thC) has remarkable storiated capitals★. ▶ Near the entry, a stairway leads to the **museum and panorama** *(daily Jun.-Sep.; Sun. pm out of season).* □

▶ The Vienne Valley *(43 km; half-day)*

▶ North via **Bonnes** (two Romanesque churches on the left bank) : **Touffou** castle★ *(8 km; Jul.-Aug.; closed Mon. out of season and winter),* in a park overlooking the Vienne; group of attractive 12th-15thC buildings. ▶ South, along the right bank : small partially Carolingian church at **Saint-Pierre-les-Eglises** *(2 km)* housing the oldest murals in Poitou; cemetery; Merovingian sarcophagi. ▶ Cross the river at Valdivienne *(7 km);* 3 km S of Bonneuil, **Morthemer★ :** large castle, Gothic pentagonal keep and adjoining Romanesque church with crypt. ▶ **Civaux** ® *(5 km farther) :* archaeological dig (Gallo-Roman temple) around the church ® (Carolingian apse); 200 m away : Merovingian necropolis★ with several thousand tombs. Nuclear power plant under construction. ▶ On the right bank, **Cognons Tower :** ruins of a Romanesque square keep. ▶ **Lussac-les-Châteaux** ® *(6 km S)* surrounded by **caves** inhabited as early as the Magdalenian era : Marche Cave (engraved flagstones) and Fadets Cave; 18thC pavilion and park of the château where Madame de Montespan was born. □

COGNAC★

B3 / ® / pop. 23000 (Charente)

Cognac was once a small-craft port on the Charente, protected by a fortress where François I was born in 1494. When brandy *(brandevin)* was invented in the middle of the 17thC, the image of the city was changed radically by the wine and spirit warehouses opened along the quays. Here, Dutch and English traders produced the "burntwine" for export. Over the years, the walls of the sidestreets have become covered with a black veneer of mould; this is an effect of alcoholic fumes.

▶ Every visit to Cognac starts with a tour of the cellars *(closed Sat. and Sun. out of season)* and of **Valois Castle** (cellar, *Jul.-Aug., 10-6; Jun., Sep., 10-12 & 2-6 ex. Tue.*). ▶ E, a large **wooded park★** in a bend of the Charente river.

About cognac

Strangely enough, the wines of the principal cognac-producing areas (Charente and Charente-Maritime, along with their islands) are of mediocre quality; but distilled, they become the best-known French eau-de-vie. *The vineyards cover only a small area : less than 250 000 acres, compared to more than 750 000 acres before the vast destruction of vines by phylloxeræ (1876-1882).*

The vine-growing areas most highly regarded are those of Grande Champagne *(between Cognac, Jarnac and Barbezieux), those surrounding them* (Petite Champagne), *as far as Pons and Jonzac, and the* Borderies *(N of the Charente); these vines are cultivated with the greatest care. On the neighbouring clay-soils, the growths of lesser quality are, in descending order : Fins Bois, Bons Bois and Bois Ordinaires (coastal and island vineyards); in the E, the vineyards are confined to the first escarpments of the Limousin, and in the S, to the area of Bordeaux, near Blayais.*

Of the 250 million bottles produced annually, about 4/5 are destined for export (in value equal to one third of the region's exports).

Cognac is aged in oak barrels, which give it its rich colour. There are three gradings : after 30 months of ageing, it merits three stars (★★★); after four and a half years, it is labeled VSOP (or ★★★★); and after ten years, it is called Royal or Napoléon.

Pineau, a popular local aperitif, seems to have been invented quite accidentally. White or red, it is produced from diluted fresh grape *must mixed with cognac. Pineau is always drunk chilled.*

▶ Hôtel de Ville : **Cognac and Local Traditions Museum** *(1-30 Jun., 10-12 & 2-6; 1 Jul.-30 Sep., 10-6; Oct.-May, open pm; closed Tue.).* ▶ In the old town, see the **half-timbered houses,** and the partially Romanesque church of St. Léger. □

▶ Nearby : *visit the vineyards and storehouses; information : TO*

▶ To the N, **Richemont,** among the smaller estates *(guided visits Sat., Sun., Jul.-Aug.)* : two castles and church (pre-Romanesque crypt). ▶ Romanesque church at **Cherves,** and Renaissance château in Chenel. ▶ To the SW, **Ars Castle★,** church and panorama in **Montils.** ▶ **Saint-Fort-sur-le-Né** (® in Cierzac, *1 km*) : prehistoric site (the most beautiful dolmen in the entire Angoulême region). □

▶ Tour of the Champagne Cognac vineyards *(round trip, 145 km; one day)*

B3 *(see map 1)*

▶ To the W, the Charente Valley *(N41, then D24)* : along the right bank to the mill at Saint-Laurent. ▶ **Merpins :** ruins of Condate Roman spa; archaeology repository *(Jun.-Aug.).* ▶ **Chaniers :** attractive islands of La Baine; in the village : Romanesque church (see the chevet). ▶ **Port-Hublé :** former inland port where barges were loaded with wheat. ▶ The trip can be made by boat from Cognac as far as Saintes (→). ▶ Chermignac, Thénac and Tesson (→ Saintes, nearby). ▶ Gémozac (→ Talmont, nearby). ▶ Pons (→). ▶ **Echebrune :** Romanesque church (portal ★★). ▶ **Archiac :** feudal remains, panorama. ▶ Via Ambleville and **Lignières-Sonneville** (façade of Romanesque church; moated castle), **Bouteville :** ruins of castle (17thC), Romanesque church, panorama. ▶ **Châteauneuf-sur-Charente :** leisure activities on the river; Romanesque church★ (beautiful façade and triple nave). ▶ **Saint-Même-les-Carrières :** prehistoric site, quarries worked since the Roman epoch. ▶ **Bourg-Charente :** bridge over the river (view); on the right bank : Renaissance château; on the left bank : Romanesque and Gothic church. ▶ 2 km away : dolmen. ▶ Former church of **Châtres,** isolated in a valley (cupolas, Saintonge Romanesque façade). ▶ **Château de Garde-Epée :** 15thC dovecote. □

■ CONFOLENS

C2 / ® / pop. 3 320 (Charente)

In an attractive site on the Vienne river, Confolens is known for its international folklore festival in August *(week of the 15th, from Fri. to Mon.).*

▶ Downstream from the **15thC bridge,** the

1. Tour of the Champagne Cognac vineyards

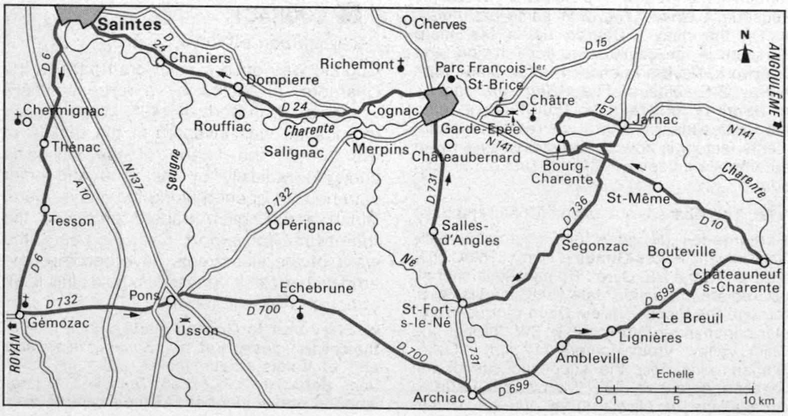

Vienne and Goire rivers meet; ruins of a keep; half-timbered houses; narrow lanes. Along the right bank of the Vienne, Romanesque **church of St. Barthelemy** (11thC). ▶ **La Fontorse :** curious fountain. □

▶ The Confolens area (Confolentais; *E and SE; 65 km; full day)*

▶ **Esse :** church (13thC); megaliths. ▶ **Lesterps** (pronounced : Létère) : Romanesque gate-tower (12thC, 43 m). ▶ **Brigueil :** Fête de la Rosière, famous Easter celebration involving election of most virtuous local maiden; mediaeval granite buildings. ▶ Etagnac : **Rochebrune castle** (11th-16thC) surrounded by moats; mementos of Napoleonic times *(10-12 & 2-6, Palm Sunday-11 Nov.).* ▶ **Chassenon** *(4 km S)* : Roman ruins of *Cassinomagus* (1st-2ndC; Easter-Nov.). ▶ **Chabanais** ®, rebuilt in 1946; 16thC bridge. ▶ **Exideuil :** Chétardie château; partially Romanesque church; to the S : Pressac château. □

COUBRE Forest★

A3

▶ Round trip from Royan on the Arvert Peninsula *(65 km; full day)*

Not until the 18thC was an effort made to halt the progress of the dunes created by the strong winds and wild currents between the Gironde estuary and the straits of the Charente archipelago. The pine groves of the Royan region covering these dunes (64 m high at the Gardour signal) are today traversed by foot-and bridle-paths. The marshes have now been partially drained : the straight seashore to the W, wild and dangerous, is mostly frequented by naturists who come for the sun.

▶ **La Grande Côte** *(9 km from Royan)* : rocky coast beyond the dunes; view from the lighthouse at Cordouan. ▶ **La Palmyre** ® in the pines : Bonne Anse Bay (beach, aquatic sports); zoological park★ (African animals; *open all year*). ▶ Coubre Lighthouse (*20 km;* 60 m high, panoramic terrace, 300 steps). ▶ **Côte Sauvage :** accessible only by paths, except 30 km along the Espagnole Point *(bathing dangerous).* ▶ **Ronce-les-Bains** *(35 km),* sea-side resort in the middle of a forest : sheltered beach near the straits of Maumusson; on the straits, beautiful beach of Galon-d'Or *(3 km farther).* ▶ **La Tremblade** ® (38 km; pop. 4 687) : large oyster farms; small maritime museum; "inter-island" cruises and visits to the oyster-beds leave from the port at the end of the jetty *(in summer).* ▶ **Étaules :** oyster museum (at the SI, *in summer*). ▶ **Mornac-sur-Seudre** ® : artisans' village; partly Romanesque church. ▶ **Breuillet :** church with Saintonge style façade. ▶ Return via **Saint-Sulpice** (another Romanesque church). □

ESNANDES★

B2 / pop. 1 370 (Charente-Maritime)

This white village by the cliffs of Aunis and the home of the mouclade (mussels with cream), is probably as well known for its miles of mussel pens, as it is for its Romanesque church fortified in the 15thC (doorways★ on the façade).

Oyster farming in the Marennes-Oléron basin

The Seudre estuary and the shoals round the Oléron island make this the greatest oyster-producing area in Europe, and perhaps in the world in terms of quality. The 2 500 concessions provide a living for 25 000 people, and an annual yield of 40 000 tons (half of France's production). Guided tours of the farms leave from the ports of Chapus, Bourcefranc and Marennes; from La Tremblade and Etaules; and, of course, from Le Château-d'Oléron. The educational museums in Fort-Louvois, Marennes, Etaules and La Tremblade are also worth visiting.

▶ The whole region, similar in many aspects to the Camargue (→), is frequented by migratory birds (→ L'Aiguillon-sur-Mer). □

FONTENAY-LE-COMTE★

B2 / ® / pop. 16 650 (Vendée)

The town is divided into two different areas on each side of the Vendée river. ▶ On the right bank is an aristocratic district (houses dating from Renaissance to Classical times) : tower of **Notre-Dame** (15th-16th; inside : Renaissance chapel and Romanesque crypt); in front of the church is the **Vendée Museum;** nearby : beautiful buildings along Rue du Pont aux Chèvres and **Place Belliard.** ▶ Via Rue de la Fontaine, **Quatre-Tias fountain** (Renaissance). ▶ On the left bank, the town is typified by the busy Rue de la République; parallel, is **Rue des Loges :** older houses (some of them half-timbered) leading to the Gothic and Renaissance **church of St. Jean,** in the district of the same name. Towards the W exit, along the right bank : **château of Terre-Neuve★** (rich collections, ceilings and fireplaces; *daily 9-12 & 2-5*). □

▶ Nearby

▶ Round trip through the Mervent Forest (→).
▶ Via the Niort road, former **abbey of Nieul-sur-l'Autize** *(10 km)* : Romanesque cloister★★ and chapter room. ▶ 3 km farther, **Oulmes :** church (partially 11thC). □

FOURAS

B2 / ® / pop. 3 297 (Charente-Maritime)

Sea-side resort and fishing port; Napoléon left from here in July 1815 on his way to the island of Aix.

▶ Beautiful pine and holm oak forest (15 acre Casino Park) overlooking Semaphore beach.
▶ Tour of the 15thC **fort** (regional museum) *(in season : 3-6, daily; winter : Sun. and nat. hols.)*
▶ **Fumée Point** (*3 km;* departure place for Aix Island). □

Les HERBIERS

B1 / ® / pop. 12 494 (Vendée)

In the heart of the hilliest region of Vendée,

this is a livestock market town, and a centre of the shoe and furniture industries.

▶ A **Gothic church** with Romanesque bell-tower, and another 15thC **church** in **Petit-Bourg** *(S)*, survived the burning of the town during the Vendée wars in 1794. □

▶ Nearby

▶ N, via the road to Cholet : **Mont des Alouettes★** (alt. 231 m ; orientation table ; panorama). The windmill vanes were used for signalling in 1793 during the Vendée Wars. ▶ **Le Puy-du-Fou** (peak ; *11 km S;* part of **Epesses**) : Renaissance château partially burnt down during the Vendée Wars *(daily 9-6 ; late evening shows in summer ;* interesting **Ecomuseum**). ▶ Via La Roche-sur-Yon road *(6 km SW) :* **Grainetière Abbey** *(2 km S;* 12th-15thC) ; cloister★ *(daily Jul.-Aug. ; Sun. pm out of season).* ▶ N of crossroads, **La Tricherie** Lake : leisure centre. □

JARNAC

B3 / ® / pop. 4 917 (Charente)

Great cognac producer *(visit the cellars),* and home town of President François Mitterrand (1916) ; Romano-Gothic crypt in the church. □

▶ Nearby

▶ **Bassac** *(8 km) :* partially Romanesque abbey★ *(3-6).* ▶ **Vibrac** ® *(11 km) :* Renaissance church. From **Vibrac** to **Angeac :** road with 6 Roman bridges. □

JONZAC

B3 / ® / pop. 4 873 (Charente-Maritime)

Rich in prehistoric sites (e.g. caves in Heurtebise) and buildings from the time of pilgrimages to Compostela, this former Protestant stronghold has become an important market for cognac *(Petite Champagne),* pineau and Charentes butter. □

▶ Nearby

▶ **Champagnac** *(5 km SE) :* Romanesque church remodelled during the Gothic period ; another Romanesque church at **Fontaines-d'Ozillac** (doorway arches★). ▶ 12 km W on the Pons to Blaye road : **Plassac Château★** (18thC) in a park *(exterior visit only; pineau tasting).* ▶ 4 km S, remains of the former **abbey of La Tenaille :** Saintonge façade ; 18thC buildings. □

LOUDUN

C1 / ® / pop. 8 448 (Vienne)

Overlooking the town, the "Square Tower" (11th-12thC) provides a panorama.

▶ In the lower town, **Ste. Croix Church** (11thC choir) converted into a covered market. ▶ Above, Gothic and Renaissance **church of St. Pierre.** ▶ East of the butte, on the **Rue de Martray,** is a **regional museum** (with African collection) and the former Carmelite Gothic and Renaissance church of St. Hilaire ; mediaeval city gate. To the S, **La Chaussée : Maison de l'Acadie** (Acadia House, books, documents about history of Loudunaise families who emigrated to Acadia in the 17thC ; *by appt., tel. 98.15.96*). □

LUÇON★

B1-2 / ® / pop. 9 500 (Vendée)

Large agricultural market town on a hill at the edge of the drained marshes.

▶ Gothic **cathedral** (13th-14thC) with Classical façade and 85 m spire ▶ To the S, a Renaissance cloister★ inside the episcopal palace. ▶ Behind the town hall is a landscaped park *(topiary of scenes from La Fontaine's Fables),* the **Jardin Dumaine★.** □

▶ Nearby

▶ **Mareuil-sur-Lay** *(10 km N) :* bell-tower of Romanesque church★ ; ruins and keep of Renaissance castle. ▶ Saint-Cyr-en-Talmondais *(13 km W) :* ornamental fireplaces, tapestries, prehistoric and antique collections in the **La Court-d'Aron Château** *(daily Jun.-Sep., 9-12 & 2-5) ;* **flower shows** in park *(May-Oct.) ;* **Curzon** *(2 km S) :* Romanesque crypt.★ □

LUSIGNAN

C2 / ® / pop. 2 855 (Vienne)

Castle of the Counts (panorama from Blossac promenade), built, according to legend, in one night by the fairy Mélusine. A number of Crusader "Kings" of Jerusalem were born here.

▶ Set back from the fortified site, the Romanesque church★ (bell-tower) with its Gothic gate-tower was badly damaged during the Hundred Years' War between France and England. Bertrand de Got was prior there until he became Pope Clement V ; he was the Pope who transferred the papacy to Avignon (1309), and subsequently suppressed the Order of Templars (1312). □

MAILLEZAIS★★

B2 / ® / pop. 939 (Vendée)

11thC abbey built on an islet in the middle of a marsh (still at that time the Bay of Poitou). The abbey's mission was to drain and improve the surrounding lands.

▶ The imposing remains of the **church** (Romanesque choir, Gothic walls in the nave with ogival windows)★ overlook an immense esplanade ; S, former **monastic buildings** (13th-14thC), built in a square : the dormitory, monks' refectory, Rabelais' "dungeon" and the kitchen with its octagonal ventilation tower, now a lapidary museum *(daily 9-12 & 2-7, 8 in summer).* ▶ Boat cruises leave from the port on the Autize, at the foot of the terrace. ▶ In the village centre, a Romanesque **church** heavily restored in the 19thC (12thC façade ; 13thC cross in cemetery). □

MARAIS POITEVIN★★

(Poitou Marshes)

▶ Round trip, passing through 3 departments, from Niort *(205 km ; full day ; save at least 2 hours for a boat trip from Coulon, La Garette, Arçais, Saint-Hilaire-la-Palud, Magné, Damvix or Maillezais)*

AB2 *(see map 2 following page)*

N of Niort is the former bay of Poitou, now traversed by the river Sèvre, which floods

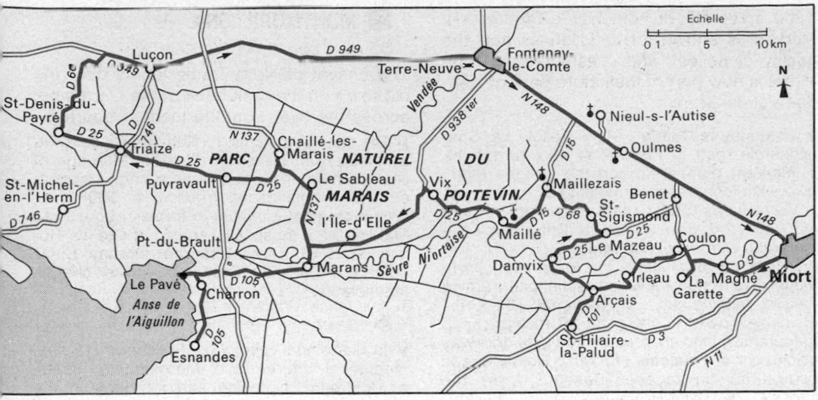

2. Marais Poitevin (Poitou marshes)

the area in winter and spring. The abbey has worked since the Middle Ages to reclaim the land; 150 000 acres have been reclaimed, primarily since the 17th-18thC, by the use of techniques developed in the Low Countries by the Dutch. The area, which covers some 600 km² is incorporated in the **Val-de-Sèvre Regional Nature Park.** Upstream between Niort and Damvix are the "wet" marshes, comprising some 37 000 acres known as "Green Venice" *(La Venise Verte),* a web of canals under a roof of poplars and beeches; primarily devoted to mixed horticulture, with the farmers moving about by boat. Downstream approx. 100 000 acres of drained marshlands intersected by a network of dyked canals; these are essentially cattle pastures.

▶ **Niort** (→). ▶ **Magné :** gateway to the "wet" marshes; Romanesque and Renaissance church. ▶ **Coulon** ® *(11 km),* along the right bank of the Sèvre : a former sailors' village, principle centre for excursions through "Green Venice" *(also from La Garette, 3 km S).* ▶ **Arçais** *(10 km from Coulon) :* small port at the foot of the château. ▶ **Saint-Hilaire-la-Palud** *(4 km S) :* "capital of the wild marshes"; boat trips and excursions on foot. ▶ **Le Mazeau** and Saint-Sigismond, between "wet" marshes and reclaimed land. ▶ Maillezais (→). ▶ **Maillé :** small port on the Jeune Autize; façade of Romanesque church. ▶ **Vix** was once an island; archaeological remains from Gallo-Roman times. ▶ **L'Ile-d'Elle :** major agricultural centre (dairy co-operative). ▶ **Marans** (17) ® (pop. 4 307) : along canalised section of the Sèvre, former grain port now devoted to pleasure craft; leisure park; museum in Hôtel de Ville; at S exit, ruins of Gothic church. ▶ N, beyond Sableau, the Five Abbots' Channel (dug in the Middle Ages) before reaching *(direction Luçon)* the "Dutch ring" (17thC). ▶ **Chaillé-les-Marais :** at the foot of a 15 m cliff, once the river bank. ▶ Via Triaize, **Saint-Denis-du-Payré :** bird sanctuary *(daily in season, 9-5).* ▶ Luçon (→); Nalliers; Fontenay-le-Comte (→); Nieul-sur-l'Autize, Oulmes (→ Fontenay, Nearby). ▶ Return via **Benet :** Renaissance doorway of Romanesque church. □

■ MATHA

B2 / pop. 2 303 (Charente-Maritime)

Crafts centre from which horse-back and horse-drawn caravan excursions are organised; important cereal, wine and dairy market *(visits to distilleries and co-operative dairy).*

▶ Fortified gate in Gothic town walls. ▶ Large Gothic church with Romanesque façade★ and raised Gothic choir in the **Saint-Hérie** quarter. □

■ MELLE★

BC2 / ® / pop. 4 575 (Deux-Sèvres)

Former stopover for Compostela pilgrims, once renowned for its sanctuaries, inns and mule fairs.

▶ Underground **Loubeau** silver mines *(1 km S of town; Jul.-Aug., 2-6).* ▶ Three large Romanesque churches : in lower town, **St. Hilaire★★** with impressive apsidial chapels, equestrian statue above side doorway, interior decoration (cornices, arches over inner doorway); **St. Savinien** (early 12thC) houses a music festival in May-Jun. ▶ N, church of **St. Pierre** (12th-13thC). □

▶ Nearby

▶ **Lezay** *(11 km NE) :* goat, calf and cheese fairs. ▶ **Celles-sur-Belle** *(7 km NW) :* Gothic church with multifoil arches★ over doorway incorporated into narthex★. ▶ **Javarzay** *(15 km SE) :* Renaissance château in park *(Oct.-Apr., by appt.)* and partially Romanesque church. ▶ 2 km farther, **Chef-Boutonne :** well known for goose preserves; feudal mound, ancient buildings. □

■ MERVENT Forest★

▶ Round trip from Fontenay *(64 km; full day)*

B1-2 (Vendée)

One of the densest and most beautiful forests in Western France, covering

6 000 acres NE of Fontenay-le-Comte (→). Mervent is known for its wildness and the quality of its oak and chestnut trees. The forest is now part of the nature park of Vendée-Val-de-Sèvre. □

▶ **Fontenay-le-Comte** (→). ▶ Follow La Chataigneraie road to Pissotte *(4 km),* turn right. ▶ **Mervent dam,** 8 km, on the Vendée river; lake 9 km long, reservoir holding 8.5 million m^3. ▶ Via Oulières road, **Gros-Roc zoological park** *(13 km; 10-6, 5 in winter).* ▶ Citardière Château *(ext. visit only).* **Mervent★** ® *(17 km) :* former fortified town above the Mère river; from the terrace of now-vanished castle, panorama★ *(beach, bathing etc.).* ▶ **Vouvant★** *(31 km) :* Mélusine Tower (13thC) and 30 m high keep (panorama); in town, ornamented side doorway of church. ▶ **Foussais** *(40 km) :* Romanesque sculptures on façade (Descent from the Cross★). ▶ Saint-Hilaire-des-Loges (*48 km;* → nearby Fontenay-le-Comte). □

■ MONTENDRE

B3 / ® / pop. 3 383 (Charente-Maritime)

A park surrounds the well-restored keep (12thC); viewpoints over the pines of Tout-y-Faut *(S)* and Bussac *(SE)* heaths. □

▶ Towards the Double river

▶ Via **Montlieux-la-Garde** *(12 km SE)* feudal ruins; **Montguyon** ® *(19 km) :* known for international folklore festival *(mid-Jul.);* vestiges of château (12th-15thC) superb keep rising above trees. ▶ 2 km N, Pierre-Folle dolmen. □

■ MONTMORILLON★

C2 / ® / pop. 7 541 (Vendée)

The chevet of Notre-Dame looms over the old town on the right bank of the Gartempe, across the river from the modern quarter.

▶ The apse of the church (12th-14thC), decorated inside with **frescos★** (Mystical Marriage of Ste. Catherine), is built over a crypt decorated with Romanesque frescos. ▶ 500 m S, **archaeological museum** in former Augustinian Maison-Dieu (hospital); storied frieze in Romanesque **St. Laurent church;** strange 12thC building in park, the **Octogone,** former chapel-mausoleum. □

▶ Nearby

▶ In Gartempe Valley *(S) :* **Plaisance** *(12 km),* mediaeval church and Merovingian vaults. ▶ Upstream, canoeing and kayaking in the **Gorges d'Enfer.** ▶ To SE, lantern of the dead at Moussac *(via D117);* **Bourg-Archambault** castle (*13 km;* 13th-15thC), still inhabited. ▶ NE, lantern of the dead at **Journet** *(11 km);* Romanesque abbey church in **Villesalem** (arches★ of side doorway), classical monastic buildings. □

■ NIORT★

B2 / ® / pop. 60 230 (Deux-Sèvres)

Formerly a cloth and leather centre, the city has developed into a major centre of the insurance business (more than half the inhabitants are employed in service industries).

▶ Standing above the Vieux-Ponts (Old Bridges), two enormous square towers, at-

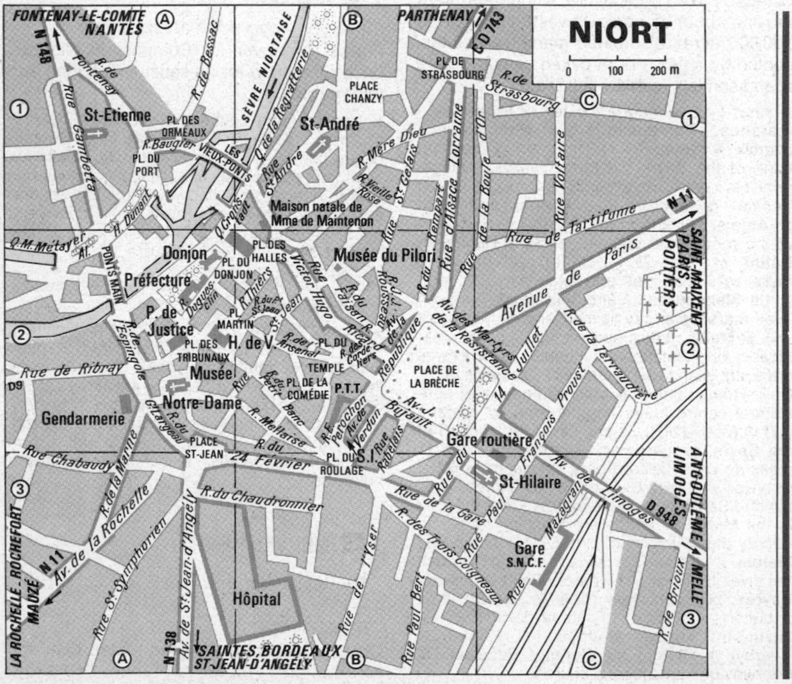

tached by a modern wall, are the remains of the ramparts of the château built by Henry II Plantagenet (12thC).

tached to the Romanesque **keep★** house an interesting **museum★** of arts and local customs *(daily 9-12 & 2-6, 5 in winter; closed Tue.)*. ▶ From the bridges via **Rue du Pont** (old houses) to the **Hôtel du Pilori** (former town hall). Renaissance building housing numismatic and archaeological museum *(daily 9-12 & 2-6, 5 in winter; closed Tue.)*. ▶ **Rue St. Jean** (pedestrian); half-timbered houses, leading to **church of Notre-Dame** (tapestries), and the Hôtel de Ville. ▶ Natural History and **Fine Arts Museums★** (paintings; *daily ex. Tue., in Jul.-Aug.; out of season, closed Tue. Sat., Sun.*). ▶ 70 m spires of St. André near the **Jardin des Plantes** (botanical gardens), terraced above the Sèvre (viewpoints). □

▶ Nearby

▶ Round trip of the Poitou Marshes (→). ▶ N, the Sèvre and Egray valleys: via **Echiré** *(8 km)*, Taillée Château (15thC) and Romantic ruins (12th-13thC) of **Coudray-Salbart★,** above the Sèvre *(Mar.-Oct., 9-12 & 2-7, closed Tue.)*. ▶ Via the road to Secondigny, **Champdeniers** *(12 km)*; Romanesque church and crypt. ▶ Return via **Egray** Valley: Romanesque church of **Sainte-Ouenne** remarkably well-restored; fortified 15thC manor at Gazeau. □

■ NOIRMOUTIER Island★

A1 / ® / pop. 8 482 (Vendée)

A large flat island (average altitude 8 m, 15 000 acres), reached by boat from Pornic, driving through the marshes at low tide via the Gois causeway, or any time via the toll bridge. There are in fact two islands, connected by the isthmus of Tresson, in the centre of semi-disused salt marshes. Known for its mild climate and sunshine; mimosa bloom in mid-Feb., Mediterranean trees grow in the Chaize woods. (The population of the island increases dramatically in Jul./Aug. (best visited out of season; *round trip by car, half-day*).

Only N part of the island is touristically interesting. ▶ Beyond the cultivated dunes (pine groves) of **Barbâtre** (beautiful beaches), is the salt-marsh region. ▶ **La Guerinière** *(to W)*: museum of arts and local traditions *(Apr.-Oct.)*. ▶ **Noirmoutier-en-l'Ile,** fishing port on a 2 km wide channel: Romanesque keep on the Place d'Armes; 18thC mansions; museum (exceptional collection of English faïence; *Jun.-Sep., closed Tue.)*; E of esplanade, St. Philibert church, ruins of monastery founded in 7thC and destroyed by the Normans (Romanesque choir, Merovingian crypt). ▶ 2 km farther are the beaches of Dames and Souzeaux with a lighthouse tower emerging from the holm oak of the **Chaize** Woods★. ▶ 5 km W, **L'Herbaudière**: sardine port which has become an important leisure centre. □

■ Île d'OLÉRON★★ (Oléron Island)

A2 / ® / pop. 16 841

The 3 km toll viaduct from Chapus Point runs to France's largest Atlantic island (175 km², 30 km NW-SE). Flat, like Aix and the Île de Ré, with massive dunes (30 m) on W coast, covered with pine and holm oak. The mild climate encourages exceptional flower growth *(mimosa festival in Feb.)*. This "island of perfumes" was always more given to farming than fishing — Pliny the Elder praised its vineyards. But oyster farming has grown considerably in the last 50 years and is now a larger industry (at Le Château) than fishing (from La Cotinière). □

▶ Round trip of the island *(full day)*

▶ **Le Château,** oyster-farming centre, at the foot of citadel (17thC, seriously damaged in 1945; small oyster museum; *guided tours of oyster parks*). ▶ **Dolus**: attractive white houses. ▶ **Boyardville**: military port established by Napoleon; at the foot of wooded **Saumonards** dunes, beautiful beach (naturists). ▶ **Saint-Georges,** among the vines: doorway★ of Romanesque church (only historic monument on island). ▶ Via **Saint-Denis** (beach and sailing), **Chassiron** Lighthouse *(afternoons only, off season; panorama)*. ▶ Bird sanctuary on cliffs of N coast. ▶ **Domino: Sables-Vigniers** beach and dunes. ▶ **La Cotinière** fishing port. ▶ **Saint-Pierre**: lantern of the dead (13thC) near bell-tower (viewpoint); on the same street, Eleanor of Aquitaine Museum *(15 Jun.-15 Sep., closed Sun., 10-12 & 2:30-6:30)*. ▶ Through the beautiful **forests★** of **Remingeasse** and **Vert-Bois** to **Grand-Village**: small Oléron Museum *(in season)*. ▶ **Saint-Trojan**: one of the country's great coastal spas, on the edge of 5 000 acres of forest★; fishing and pleasure-craft port; small train *(in summer)* to **Gatseau** Point on the straits of Maumusson (beaches). □

■ PARTHENAY★

B1 / ® / pop. 11 666 (Deux-Sèvres)

Former fortified town, now a major meat market *(fairs Wed. am)*.

▶ Via the steep cobbled **Rue de la Vaux,** lined with old houses★, approach the **upper town,** formerly fortified; enter through the Porte de l'Horloge (13thC): ruins of **mediaeval churches** and view points from terraces of the former fortress. ▶ Via Niort road *(2 km)* to **Parthenay-le-Vieux:** church★ (12thC) with Poitevin façade. □

▶ Nearby

▶ **Secondigny** *(14 kmW)*: church 11thC; octagonal tower, capitals in the nave. ▶ Via Fontenay-le-Comte road, **Fenioux**: Romanesque church (ornamentation, octagonal bell-tower★, chevet). ▶ S of Parthenay *(E of Niort road)*: churches in **Allonne** and **Saint-Marc-la-Lande** (Flamboyant Gothic and Renaissance façade). ▶ Via Bressuire road *(N)*: Tennessus fortified castle (14thC; *Sat., Sun., hols., 2:30-6:30*). □

■ POITIERS★★★

C1 / ® / pop. 82 884 (Vienne)

The former religious, university and political capital of Poitou is still, architecturally and in terms of monuments, one of the most exciting cities in France.

▶ From **Place du Maréchal-Leclerc** (B2) take the pedestrian Rue Gambetta, at the corner of the theatre: **St. Porchaire church** (16thC; Romanesque gate-tower). ▶ Via Rue P. Guillon, 16thC City Magistracy (Hôtel de l'Echevinage). ▶ **Palais de Justice** (the law courts) is in the former palace of the Counts of Poitou (Maubergeon tower; large Gothic hall whose **gabled wall**

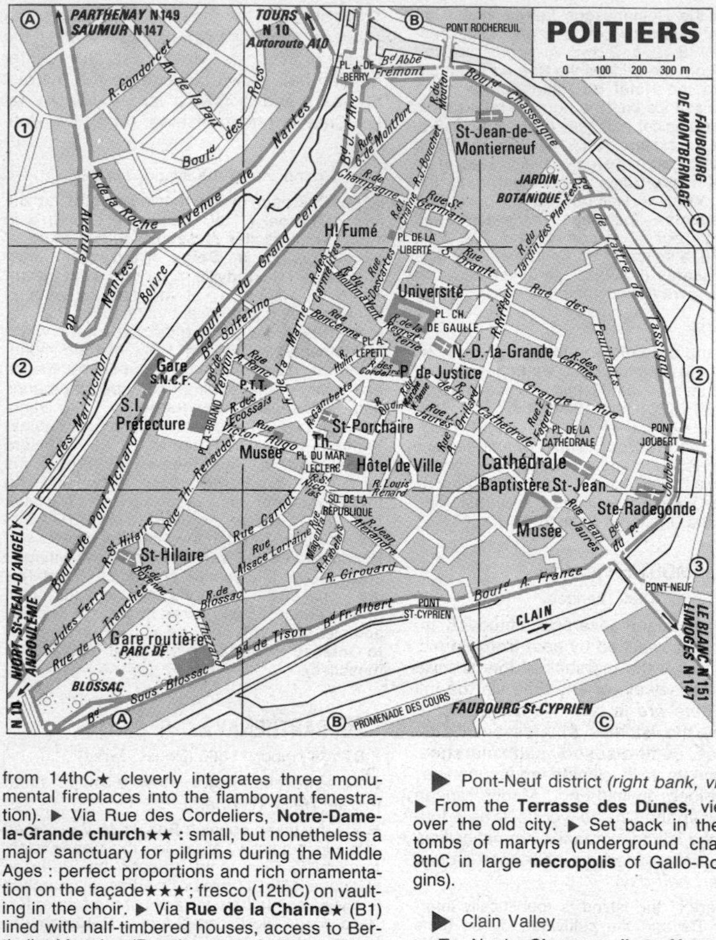

from 14thC★ cleverly integrates three monumental fireplaces into the flamboyant fenestration). ▶ Via Rue des Cordeliers, **Notre-Dame-la-Grande church★★ :** small, but nonetheless a major sanctuary for pilgrims during the Middle Ages : perfect proportions and rich ornamentation on the façade★★★ ; fresco (12thC) on vaulting in the choir. ▶ Via **Rue de la Chaîne★** (B1) lined with half-timbered houses, access to Berthellot Mansion (Renaissance); further, to right, **St. Jean-de-Montierneuf church** (C1 ; 11th-14thC, much restored) : high Gothic apse. ▶ Return to Notre-Dame-la-Grande through the botanical gardens (C1).

▶ Via Grande-Rue (mansions and houses, 15th-17thC) reach the immense Romanesque **cathedral :** 13thC doorways★ ; façade and towers finished in the 15thC ; vast nave lit by stained glass windows (13thC); modern choir stalls. ▶ **Ste. Radegonde Church★ :** gate-tower ; apse and crypt (11thC) house the tomb of Ste. Radegonde (587). ▶ **St. Jean Baptistry★★,** one of France's oldest Christian monuments (14thC); Merovingian archaeological museum; Romanesque fresco *(closed Wed. in winter).* ▶ **Ste. Croix Museum★★ :** classical and mediaeval archaeology and fine arts (mainly paintings★ ; *closed Tue.*).

▶ From Place Leclerc (B2), S, Renaissance mansion of Jehan Beaussé; further on, former Jesuit school; 17thC chapel *(closed Aug.),* to reach Rue Carnot. ▶ Church of **St. Hilaire-le-Grand★★** (11th-12thC), of imposing dimensions (nave and choir); can be viewed at night : illuminated absidial chapels. ▶ Nearby, former Deanery (Renaissance). ▶ **Parc de Blossac** (park; 18thC design) on former ramparts : view over the Clain Valley. □

▶ Pont-Neuf district *(right bank, via C3)*

▶ From the **Terrasse des Dunes,** viewpoint★ over the old city. ▶ Set back in the hillside, tombs of martyrs (underground chapel from 8thC in large **necropolis** of Gallo-Roman origins). □

▶ Clain Valley

▶ To N via **Chasseneuil** ®, **Vayres** manor (dovecote ; *Jul.-Sep. pm, closed Tue.*) and **Dissay Castle★** *(15 km),* circled by moats (15th-18thC ; *pm, closed Wed.*). □

▶ Round trip of abbeys *(130 km, full day)*

▶ To S, sites inhabited since prehistoric era (caves in Saint-Benoît-Ligugé region). ▶ **Saint-Benoît** *(4 km ;* ® → Poitiers), Romanesque abbey church. ▶ **Ligugé** ® : famous Benedictine abbey (Gregorian chant) founded by St. Martin (mid-4thC), of which only a Renaissance building remains; large archaeological dig★. ▶ **Nouaillé-Maupertuis★★ :** Romanesque church and large group of monastic buildings (bell-tower-keep, choirscreen and stalls, crypt). ▶ Via Nieul-l'Espoir, château de **Chambonneau** (Renaissance). ▶ **Saint-Maurice-la-Clouère :** church (Romanesque side doorway, 14thC; fresco). ▶ **Gençay :** ruins of Gothic castle; la Roche-Magné château (Order of Malta museum). ▶ Romanesque church in **Champagné-Saint-Hilaire.** ▶ N10 at the Chaunay turning : take the return road. ▶ Romanesque churches in **Brux** and **Vaux,** then **Couhé.** ▶ **Vivonne** ® : ruins of Gothic castle ; church (12th-16thC); footpaths. ▶ **Château-Larcher :** remains of château and church *(son et lumière some summer evenings);* 13thC lantern of the dead in cemetery. ▶ N, small roads lead to numerous megaliths. ▶ Return to Poitiers possible via **Fontaine-le-Comte** *(Niort road)* : Romanesque church★ of former abbey. □

▶ Round trip of the Boivre Valley *(W; 56 km; half-day)*

▶ **Norée Grottos** *(4 km)*. ▶ Site of **Montreuil-Bonnin** Castle, built by Richard the Lion-Hearted; Romanesque church. ▶ Forest drive. ▶ Renaissance monuments in **Lavausseau.** □

PONS★

B3 / ® / pop. 5 364 (Vienne)

In what has become one of the best cognac vineyard regions, the old town was built around a castle terrace (view over Seugne Valley). Superb keep★ (late 12thC).

▶ In the lower town, the road goes past the **church of St. Vivien** (Romanesque façade) through one of the city gates. From here, a vaulted passage★ connects the former **Pilgrims' Almshouse** to what was once the church of St. Martin. ▶ Renaissance **château of Usson**★ *(2 km; ext. visit only, Jul.-15 Sep.)*. □

▶ Round trip of Saintonge Romanesque church façades *(47 km; could take a day)*

▶ Via D142 *(SE)* : **Avy★, Fléac-sur-Seugne, Marignac★, Chadenac** (façade★★), **Jarnac-Champagne★, Lonzac** (Renaissance church), **Coulonges, Pérignac★, Echebrune** (doorways★★) and **Biron★.** ▶ Follow part of the Cognac round trip (→ Nearby Cognac). □

POUZAUGES★

B1 / ® / pop. 5 792 (Vendée)

An excellent centre *(hiking trails)* in the Vendée hills, in a beautiful site★ beneath the woodlands of La Folie (alt. 280 m). In the village : Romanesque and Gothic church and ruins of a 13thC keep.

▶ **Pouzauges-le-Vieux** *(1 km S)* : small isolated Romanesque church★ decorated with 13thC paintings. ▶ **Puy Crapaud** *(3 km)* : panoramic terrace (alt. 290 m; orientation table). □

ILE DE RÉ★★
(Ré Island)

A2 / ® / pop. 11 396

28 km long, and 3 to 5 km wide, this is in fact two islands connected by the narrow isthmus of Martray (a few dozen metres). Vineyards and vegetable fields encircle a large lagoon (Le Fiers d'Ars), former salt marshes now partially converted to oyster farming *(visits to oyster parks from villages of Rivedoux, Loix, Ars, Les Portes)*.

▶ The ferry from La Pallice comes to Sablanceaux Point. ▶ After **Rivedoux,** to the right in the distance is the 17thC La Prée Fort; ruins of Romanesque and Gothic **abbey of Châteliers.** ▶ **La Flotte :** fishing and pleasure port. ▶ **Saint-Martin** *(10 km)* : citadel constructed by Vauban still serves as a prison; the port, once commercial, now used by pleasure craft; remains of old fortifications and city gates; ruins of church (15thC); Renaissance Clerjotte mansion converted into naval and folklore museum *(10-1 & 3-6; Wed. and Sun. pm only out of season)*. ▶ **La Couarde** *(15 km)* : beach and flowered streets; then Isthmus of Martray (Loix road). ▶ **Ars** *(23 km)* by the broad expanse of the Fier d'Ars (lagoon); Romanesque church façade★ beneath bell-tower painted black to serve as a sea-mark; large yacht harbour. ▶ **Phare des Baleines** ("Whale" Lighthouse, 57 m, 250 steps) near Conche (naturist beach). ▶ **Les Portes** *(visits to oyster beds)* on the edge of Trousse-Chemise Woods. □

ROCHEFORT★★

B2 / ® / pop. 27 716 (Charente-Maritime)

Built between 1666 and 1670, Rochefort was originally a military establishment equipped with a strong arsenal. A veritable town within the town, conceived by Fernand Blondel, the place was run for more than a century using prisoners sentenced to forced labour. The ramparts later gave way to large avenues and promenades, including the Jardin de la Marine. Masterpiece of this ensemble and unique testimony to 17thC industrial architecture : the 17thC Corderie Royale★ (royal rope-makers), perfectly restored, houses today the International Centre of the Sea; permanent and temporary exhibitions, visits to the monument, conferences and symposia; *(museum open in summer daily 10-6)*.

▶ From the Cours Roy-Bry to the W (SI building), via Ave. Général de Gaulle going down towards Porte de Soleil : **Fine Arts Museum** *(1:30-5:30, closed Sun., Mon. and nat. hols.;* archaeology, painting, Far Eastern art, ethnography). ▶ The avenue crosses **Rue Pierre-Loti,** named after the writer (1850-1923) whose birthplace (No. 141, on right) is now a **museum★** *(1 Oct.-31 Mar., 10-12 & 2-5, closed Sun. am, Mon. am and Tue.; 1 Apr.-30 Sep., closed Mon. am and Sun. am)*. ▶ Near the Charente River : **Navy Museum★** *(daily ex. Tue., 10-12 & 2-6)* : models of ships built in Rochefort. □

▶ Nearby

▶ **Martrou** bridges : lifting bridge (1966) carrying the road : upstream, former transporter bridge (1890). ▶ Via La Renaissance, **Échillais** *(4.5 km)* : Romanesque façade★ on the church. ▶ **Saint-Jean-d'Angle** *(14 km)* : Gothic church and castle; 5 km E, **Pont-l'Abbé-d'Arnoult★ :** craftwork centre (museum); fortified gate; façade of Romanesque church★. ▶ Via Saint-Symphorien : "Donjon" at **Broue** (11th-12thC keep; *3 km W*) on hillock among marshes; viewpoint. ▶ After the Cadeuil crossroads, to the E, **Le Gua :** Romanesque church. ▶ **L'Eguille :** oyster port on the Seudre. □

La ROCHEFOUCAULD★

C3 / ® / pop. 3 328 (Charente)

Large castle (11th-16thC) on the right bank of the Tardoire : Romanesque keep (35 km) on the S façade (partially collapsed 1960).

▶ Access to courtyard *(on request)* : 2 wings with three floors of **covered galleries★;** S aisle : superb staircase. ▶ In town : cloister (15thC) of former **Carmelite convent.** ▶ Old half-timbered houses, late 13thC church. □

▶ Nearby

▶ Trip through Rancogne woods, valleys of the Tardoire and Bandiat : **Rancogne Grottos**

(5 km) and Renaissance château (dovecote). ▶ **Prehistoric Fontechevade Cave.** ▶ **Montbron** site ® : château (12th-15thC), chapel of the Leper hospital, some old houses. ▶ **Marthon :** feudal fortress. ▶ **Pranzac :** lantern of the dead. ▶ **Queroy Grottos** *(visits).* ▶ To W, **Braconne Forest★** (10 000 acres) and its *fosses* (pits). ▶ To N, Romanesque churches of **Coulgens, Sainte-Colombe, Saint-Amant-de-Bonnieure.** ▶ N, **Cellefrouin★** *(18 km) :* Romanesque church, lantern of the dead in the cemetery★. □

■ La ROCHELLE★★★

B2 / ® / pop. 78 231 (Charente-Maritime)

A commercial town since 11thC, La Rochelle became a fishing port in the 19thC, then a heavy industry centre; today it is also a pleasure port. Because it was razed by Cardinal Richelieu in the 17thC, little remains of the city from before that period.

▶ The Chaîne and St. Nicolas towers guard the entrance to the **Vieux-Port★★** (old harbour; B3; fishing; in summer departure point for boat tours in summer). ▶ In NW corner, 14thC **Grosse Horloge** (Great Clock) **Gate★** gives access to the town built in the French Classical period (see below). ▶ Opposite is the **Bassin à flot,** the centre of the fishing harbour *(wholesale fish market, early am until 10).* ▶ Standing back from Quai Duperré, **St. Sauveur Church :** 15thC square bell-tower. ▶ **Tour de la Chaîne** (Chain Tower, late 14thC) : the chain was drawn across the harbour mouth to close the port at night *(1 Apr.-30 Sep., 9-12 & 2-6 ex Tue.).* ▶ Via Rue Sur-les-Murs, 15thC **Tour de la Lanterne★** (Lantern Tower) : the lantern on the octagonal spire once served as a lighthouse (*mid-Apr.-Sep.;* panorama). ▶ **Mail** Promenade : 800 m walk along beach. ▶ N at right angles : **Charruyer Park★ :** more than 1 km long at the foot of the ramparts built by Vauban. ▶ **Tower of St. Nicolas★ :** once a fortress (early 14thC : 35 m keep; visits to different levels), view★ from the terrace. ▶ Towards Minimes Port, *la ville en bois* (the city of wood); wonderful **aquarium★.** ▶ Via Grosse-Horloge Gate (B3) and Place Fromentin, take **Rue du Palais,** lined with beautiful doorways★ (and see the parallel streets, notably **Rue de l'Escale★**). ▶ Going uphill to the left : **Hôtel de la Bourse** (Exchange; 18thC; courtyard★), and above, the Palais de Justice (law courts, late 18thC); the street continues into **Rue Chaudrier,** also lined with doorways, to Place de Verdun (B2) : cathe-

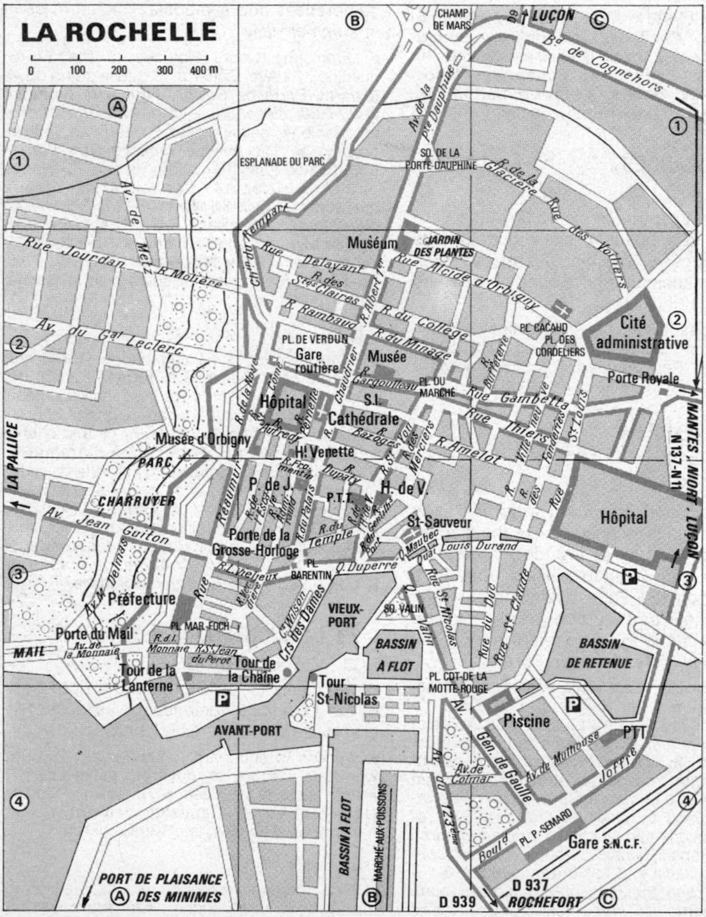

dral (arch. Gabriel; 18thC). ▶ To the right, Rue des Augustins : Renaissance house reputedly the former residence of **Diane de Poitiers** (Henri II's mistress). ▶ Still further up on the right : No. 10 Rue Fleurian, SI and **Musée du Nouveau Monde** (New World Museum). ▶ S from Place de Verdun, **Orbigny Museum★** (2 Rue St. Côme; *closed Sun. am and Tue.)* : history and ceramics. ▶ N of Place de Verdun, via Rue Albert-Ier, Jardin des Plantes (botanical garden) and **Lafalle Museum★★** *(closed Sun. am and Mon.)*; oceanography. ▶ E of Place de Verdun, Rue Gargoulleau : **Fine Arts Museum★** *(closed Sun. am and Tue. currently in restoration)* : mainly paintings. ▶ From Place du Marché, turn right on **Rue des Merciers★** (16th-17thC houses), to the **Hôtel de Ville** (town hall; Gothic and Renaissance) : courtyard **façade★★**; historic collections. ▶ Return to the Vieux-Port via the pedestrian precinct. □

▶ Nearby

▶ **La Pallice** ® *(5 km W)* : departure point for the Ile de Ré (→). ▶ SE via the new quarter of Périgny to the industrial centre of **Aytré** ® : from there via Surgères road to **La Jarne** (Romanesque church, and **Burzay Château** (18thC). ▶ Towards Rochefort, the seaside resorts of **Angoulins** and **Châtelaillon★** ® : magnificent 4 km beach : viewpoints★ from esplanade and site of Vieux-Châtelaillon; visit oyster parks by tractor-drawn trailer. □

■ La ROCHE-POSAY

C1 / ® / pop. 1 404 (Vienne)

On a high hill, remains of a fortress (12thC keep; *visits*) and bell-tower of Romanesque church (11thC) on site★ inhabited since the Palaeolithic era.

▶ On plateau at the foot of the hill, **thermal spa** : can be reached from the old city via a gateway in the ramparts (12th-14thC). □

▶ Nearby

▶ **Coussay-les-Bois** *(6 km NW)* : Romanesque church and close by Vervolière Castle (15thC). ▶ **Château de la Guerche★** *(15 km N)*, built by Charles VII on the banks of the Creuse *(closed Tue. and Sun. am in winter)*. □

■ La ROCHE-SUR-YON

A1 / ® / pop. 48 156 (Vendée)

Created by Napoleon, in a checkerboard pattern, the town is centred on the Place d'Armes (called the "Place Napoléon" due to the equestrian statue of Napoléon). The city now harbours the Prefecture of the Vendée.

▶ E of **Place Napoléon,** Empire façade of the church of St. Louis. ▶ Via Place du Marché (Market Square), crafts museum, place de la Vieille Horloge *(daily 9-12 & 2-5)*. ▶ Opposite the square via Rue Clemenceau (SI), the municipal **Historical Museum** (temporary exhibitions, modern painting; *Wed., Sat.*). ▶ S of the Prefecture park is one of the largest **stud farms★** in France *(15 Jul.-15 Feb.; by appt., visits preferably during winter season, closed am)*. N of the city : Moulin-Papon Lake *(sailing, canoeing, bathing forbidden)*. □

■ ROYAN★

B3 / ® / pop. 18 125 (Charente-Maritime)

Established in the 19thC around an old port, and known for its small bays with beaches and its numerous parks, Royan was rebuilt after the damage suffered in 1945, and is now the largest seaside resort between La Baule and Biarritz.

▶ More than 4 km of ocean frontage between **Pontaillac★** and **Vallières** Point (St. Georges) : panorama★. ▶ In centre, sardine fishing port and yacht marina, then **Grande-Conche★** beach facing the sea front. ▶ Farther back, the modern city is laid out on either side of the Blvd A. Briand, which leads to **covered market.** ▶ To the E, **park★,** residential area and garden. ▶ To the W, modern buildings : Casino, Palais des Congrès (Conference Centre) and **church of Notre-Dame★,** entirely in reinforced concrete with 65 m spire. ▶ Beyond is the **Foncillon** residential quarter. ▶ Via Ave. de Pontaillac to the Hôtel de Ville (town hall; **museum**) *(in season; Mon., 1:30-5; Wed. and Fri., 10-11:30*

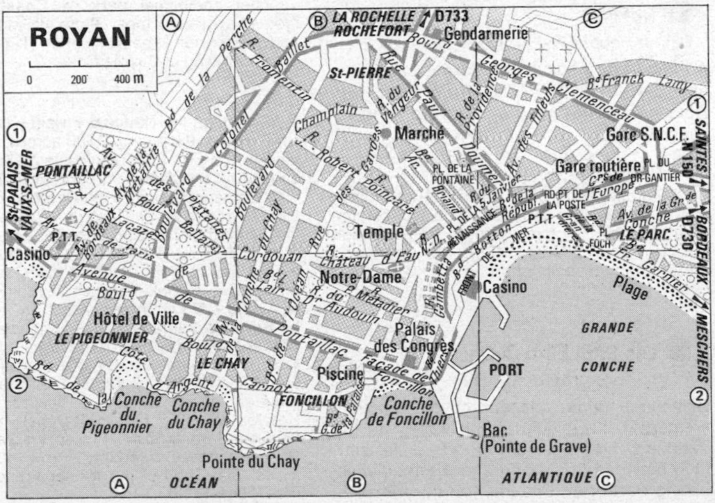

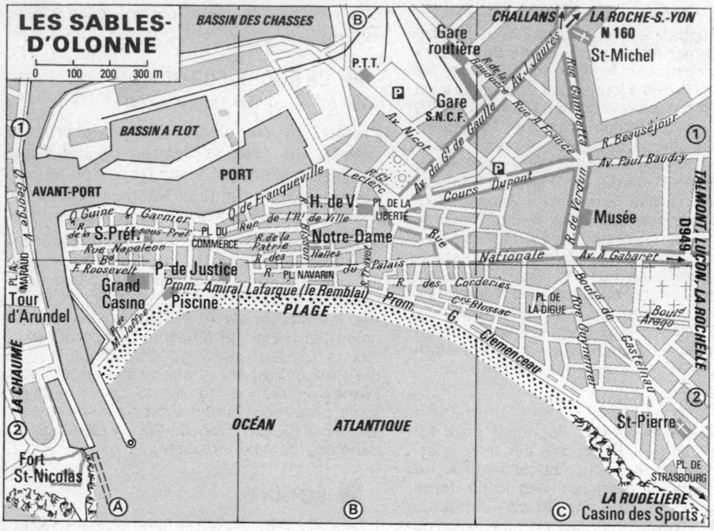

& 1:30-5; out of season; Mon., Wed. and Fri., 1:30-5). □

▶ Nearby

▶ To NW, **Vaux-sur-Mer :** Romanesque church and Nauzean Bay. ▶ **Saint-Palais★** ® : resort; Maine-Gaudin amusement park. ▶ To SE, **Saint-Georges-de-Didonne** ® : more than 2 km of beach★. ▶ Forests of Suzac★ and Meschers (→ Nearby Talmont). ▶ Via the rte. de Saintes, **Médis** *(6 km)* : airport, Romanesque church. ▶ **Saujon** ® *(11 km)* : thermal spa (neuropsychiatry centre). ▶ 6 km N, former abbey of **Sablonceaux★** (13thC) : domes, bell-tower, Romanesque cellars). ▶ **Sea excursions :** to Saint-Georges, Meschers and Talmont (→); Renaissance and 17thC **Courdouan Lighthouse★** *(5 hr round trip, visits to the lower two floors of the tower).* □

■ RUFFEC

C2 / ® / pop. 4766 (Charente)

An important agricultural market for Poitou and the Angoulême region. Church with Romanesque façade★ and several Renaissance houses. □

▶ Nearby

▶ **Courcôme** *(8 km SW)* : 11th-12thC church★. ▶ To S, **Verteuil★ :** terraced Renaissance château above the river bank; Romanesque church (Burial of Christ, 16thC). ▶ **Lichères :** small Romanesque church★. ▶ **Mansle :** church (12th-16thC). □

■ Les SABLES-D'OLONNE★

A1 / ® / pop. 16657 (Vendée)

Built on a dune, this attractive town was created in the middle of the 19thC as the Vendée's first seaside resort. It is situated between the strand and the mediaeval fishing port of La Chaume, on the narrows. The recent (1978) decision to create the artificial Chasses Harbour has now made Les Sables-d'Olonne one of the most frequented yachting venues on the Atlantic coast.

▶ **Notre-Dame-de-Bon-Port** church (17thC) is the only historic monument of Les Sables. ▶ **La Chaume** (ferryman at the corner of Quai Guiné) : partially Romanesque church, Gothic tower; near the fort (18thC), pilgrims' church of **St. Nicolas** (12thC), now a cultural centre (after recent restoration); nearby, small maritime museum (Taverne de l'Olonais). ▶ Returning to Les Sables, follow the **Remblai** from the Grand Casino to the Rudelière district *(2 km) :* left, via Rue Guynemer, former abbey of **Ste. Croix,** now a **regional museum** and museum of contemporary art, one of the very first in France *(closed Mon., Oct. and am Nov.-Jun.);* close by, Marine Zoo (Rue Chanzy). ▶ Via La Rudelière (Casino des Sports), Le Tanchet **zoological park.** ▶ **Coastal road★** *(corniche)* passes near **Puits d'Enfer** *(3 km),* and the former Orbestier abbey (12thC; *5 km)* before arriving at **Cayola** Cove. □

▶ Nearby

▶ N, through the **National Forest★** *(1 km after La Chaume;* 9 km long, 3300 acres of pine and oak growing on the dunes) : **Ile d'Olonne,** bird sanctuary. ▶ **Olonne-sur-Mer** *(5 km) :* church with Romanesque choir. ▶ **Château de Pierre-Levée★** *(5 km via La Roche road;* 18thC) : park visit only (menhir). ▶ **Talmont-Saint-Hilaire** ® *(13 km E) :* ruins of castle (11th-16thC; *daily 9-12 & 2-6*); before reaching town, **automobile museum★** (100 old vehicles in running order). ▶ **Avrillé** *(10 km)* in region rich in megaliths : **Le Bernard dolmens** (SE), among which is that of Frébouchère★, one of the largest in France. ▶ From Talmont via L'Aiguillon road : **Jard-sur-Mer** ® *(7 km) :* 2 km W, **Lieu-Dieu Abbey,** founded in the 12thC by Richard the Lion-Hearted (cellars; 17thC lodgings); **Saint-Vincent-sur-Jard** ® *(2 km E) :* on the sea *(1 km),* G. Clemenceau's "shanty", now a museum *(visits, May-Oct.)* of the former French statesman (1841-1929). □

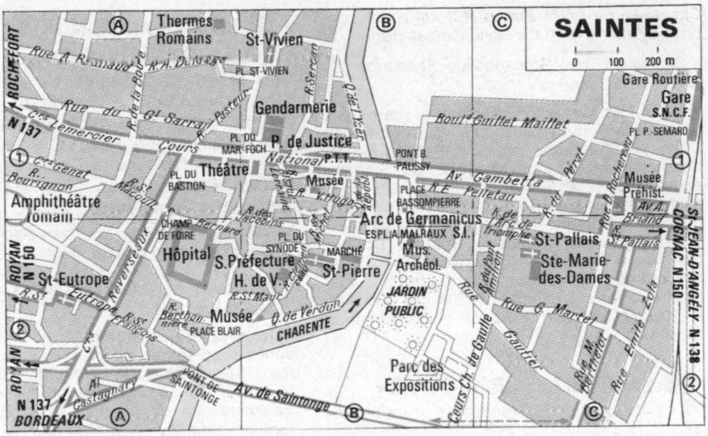

■ SAINTES★★★

B3 / ® / pop. 27 486 (Charente-Maritime)

This town has become both a large regional market and a craftwork and industrial centre. In terms of monuments and museums it is one of the richest towns in France.

▶ Esplanade A. Malraux (SI; B2) : archaeological museum★★ (partly outdoor). ▶ Near the water, **Germanicus' Arch**★ (erected in 19AD in honour of the Roman Emperor Tiberlus, and restored in the 19thC by Mérimée, Inspector of Historical Monuments, author of "Carmen"). ▶ Via the Rue de l'Arc-de-Triomphe, **St. Pallais church** (12th-13thC) and, nearby, **Abbaye aux Dames** (C2) : Ste. Marie church★★ (11th-12thC, restored in 1938; doorways★★, façade, "pinecone" belltower★); further back, the abbey buildings (17thC) where the music festival (→ ®) takes place. ▶ Prehistory museum in Ave. Gambetta. Higher up, near the station, is a **stud farm** *(visits)*. ▶ Via Bernard Palissy Bridge the **Cours National** runs up towards the theatre and the boulevard on the former ramparts. ▶ Past St. Vivien Church (N), remains of the **Roman baths.** ▶ S, on Rue Victor-Hugo : **Fine Arts Museum**★ *(closed Tue.*, paintings, ceramics from Saintonge). ▶ **Archaeological dig** (information from Archaeological Museum, *tel. 46.74.20.97*). ▶ **Church of St. Pierre**★ (12th-17thC), former cathedral rebuilt after Protestant destruction : 15thC façade doorway★. ▶ **Dupuy-Mestreau Museum**★★ (B2) : history, regional arts and traditions *(Apr.-Oct., at 3 and 5, closed Mon.)*. ▶ **St. Eutrope Church**★ (11thC; A2; choir, radiating chapels★★ in the apse), enlarged in the 15thC (bell-tower★) and again in the Renaissance, built over a **crypt**★★★ housing the 3rdC tomb of the first bishop of Saintes. ▶ Imposing ruins of **Roman amphitheatre** *(NE;* site★★) where some of the Festival performances take place on summer nights. □

▶ Round trip to the E *(40 km; half-day)*

▶ Along the Charente River : **Port-Hublé,** then Chaniers (*8 km;* round trip of Cognac vineyards). **La Chapelle-des-Pots,** historical crafts centre where the green ceramic glazes of Saintonges *(Verts de Saintonges)* were created. ▶ **Saint-Bris-Saint-Cézaire :** Maison de la Mérine (local arts and traditions), and zoological garden. ▶ Former **abbey of Fontdouce** (12th-17thC) : archaeological dig; concerts and shows in summer. □

▶ Round trip of Charente Valley *(N; 65 km; half-day min.)*
B2-3 *(See map 3)*

▶ **Le Douhet** *(11 km)* : doorway★★ of Romanesque church; **château** (17thC; *daily in season; closed am and Mon.)*: underground vaulted hall (11thC), Renaissance dovecote, tiled tower (17thC), park, ruins of the Roman aqueduct that brought water to Saintes. ▶ **Écoyeux :** Romanesque church with fortified façade (15thC). ▶ **Saint-Hilaire-de-Villefranche.** ▶ **Granjean :** Briacq★ (Saintonge arts and traditions). ▶ **Fenioux :** doorway★ arches of Romanesque church; lantern of the dead (12thC; stairway to the top). ▶ **Saint-Savinien** (→) : cross the Charente. ▶ Via **Saint-Porchaire** (Romanesque and Gothic church), to 15th-17thC **Rochecourbon Château**★★, 2 km away in a splendid park (prehistoric caves, French gardens★); monument ("Château of the Sleeping Beauty") saved from ruin by writer Pierre Loti; halls decorated with paintings, timbered roof★; prehistoric museum in the keep (15thC; *9:30-6:30, closed Wed. out of season*). ▶ Return toward the Charente : **Crazannes** Château (15th-18thC; Gothic keep, *ext. visit only*) and **Panloy** château (18thC; *in season*). ▶ **Port-d'Envaux :** former wine port, stopover for river cruisers. ▶ Overlooking the Charente, ruins of 15thC castle; on right bank,

3. Charente valley

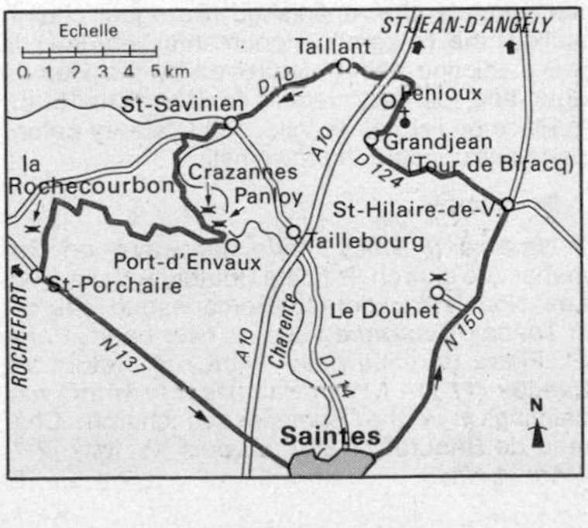

Chaussée de Saint-James *(1.2 km road)* supposedly dating from the Gallo-Roman period. □

▶ Roman and Romanesque Saintonge *(S; 70 km; full day)*

▶ D737, **Les Arènes** *(7 km)* : right of road, ruins of a Gallo-Roman sanctuary. ▶ **Chermignac** *(7 km W)* : "Hosanna" cross. ▶ **Rétaud** : richly decorated pentagonal chevet★ on Romanesque church. ▶ **Rioux** : château; church★, akin to the one in Rétaud. ▶ Small but very charming Romanesque churches in **Saint-André-de-Lidon, Thaims★, Grézac, Corme-Écluse★.** ▶ Saujon (→ Royan, Nearby). ▶ **Saint-Romain-de-Bénet** (Romanesque church), then former abbey of Sablonceaux (→ Royan). ▶ Church at **Corme-Royal** : Romanesque façade★. □

■ SAINT-GILLES-CROIX-DE-VIE★

A1 / ® / pop. 6339 (Vendée)

Two small former fishing ports on either side of the *Havre de Vie* (estuary of the river Vie) gave birth to what is today Saint-Gilles : a pleasant seaside resort as well as a fishing and pleasure craft port.

▶ N, the **Corniche Vendéenne★** (coastal road) runs as far as Sion beach *(4 km)*, part of Saint-Hilaire-de-Riez ® (see paintings in church of same name). □

▶ Round trip of Vie and Jaunay Rivers *(approx 40 km; half-day)*

▶ **Commequiers** *(12 km)* : ruins of moated 13thC castle; 2 km SW, Pierre-Folle dolmen. ▶ **Apremont★** : ruins of Renaissance château *(visits in season)* overlooking the valley road; water tower in the upper village *(access to panoramic terrace)*. ▶ Through Coex, **La Chaize-Giraud** *(13 km farther)* : Romanesque façade★ on the church. ▶ Return past the park of **Beaumarchais Château** (17thC; *no visits*). ▶ Via Les Sables road : **Brétignolles-sur-Mer** (rocks, beaches : La Parée★). Before arriving in Saint-Martin-de-Brem, 500 m to the left, partially destroyed church of **St. Nicolas-de-Brem** (12thC). □

■ SAINT-JEAN-D'ANGÉLY★

B2 / ® / pop. 9530 (Charente-Maritime)

Formerly capital of lower Saintonge, later a wine port for the Boutonne River, this small town shows many traces of its tumultuous past.

▶ Through the **Porte de l'Horloge** (Clock Gate, 14thC; bell-tower), to **Pilori Fountain★** (Renaissance). ▶ S, **Audouin-Dubreuil Museum.** ▶ At the foot of the unfinished Baroque church (called **"the Towers"** : monumental façade★), is a Benedictine abbey destroyed by the Huguenots and partially rebuilt in the 17th-18thC. ▶ Place de l'Hôtel-de-Ville, 18thC **abbey colonnade** surrounding the town hall. □

▶ Nearby

▶ **Varaize** *(8 kmE)* : side doorway★ on Romanesque church. ▶ In the Boutonne Valley *(W)*, **Les Nouillers** : domed Romanesque church. ▶ **Tonnay-Boutonne** : site on river bank; Porte St. Pierre (fortified gate; 14thC). ▶ Return via **Landes** *(11 km NW of Saint-Jean)* : 14thC wall paintings★ in the Romanesque church. Château de **Beaufel** *(2 km)*, a Louis XV folly *(2-7, 1 Apr.-1 Nov.)*. □

■ SAINT-JEAN-DE-MONTS

A1 / ® / pop. 5611 (Vendée)

This resort was created by the promoter Merlin, who built a façade of apartment houses that today stretch for several miles along the seashore. A seaside boulevard runs along the dune to Demoiselles Beach. Known for its safety, the area is also famous for its shrimp.

▶ Nearby, museums at Saint-Hilaire-de-Riez, Grenouillères and Orouet, 6 km S. □

▶ Round trip of Breton marshes *(70 km; half or full day)*

▶ **Notre-Dame-de-Monts** ® : at the end of the dunes road to the beach, view of Yeu Island (Ile d'Yeu). ▶ **La Barre-de-Monts :** art and local traditions museum, "Davianol" Discovery Centre (recreation of a typical 19thC farm) and a former water tower with a room which enjoys a panoramic view. ▶ **Fromentine** ® : departure point for Île d'Yeu. ▶ **Beauvoir-sur-Mer** ®; formerly on the shore *(today, 4 km away)* : partially Romanesque church; road towards Noirmoutiers (covered at high tide; *see hours posted*). ▶ **Boulin :** island in the marshes. ▶ Through Bois-de-Céné : former abbey of **Ile-Chauvet** *(SW)*. ▶ **Challans** ® (pop. 13060) : famous duck market, in the heart of a breeding area. Leisure area. ▶ **Sallertaine :** restored Romanesque church. **Rairé :** one of two working **windmills** (18thC) in the Vendée, the other being at Châteauneuf *(visits)*. ▶ Return via Le Perrier or Soullans (craftwork). □

The pilgrim road to Compostela

Religious buildings sprang up along the roads to Compostela in Northern Spain from the beginning of the 11thC. This was part of the Church's homage to St. Jacques, (Santíago in Spanish), Patron Saint of the Christian armies then engaged in reconquering Spain from the Moslems. Pilgrims converged on Compostela from all over Europe. The routes were quite precise, and were adorned not only with churches and convents (more than 300 in Poitou and Saintonge), but also with almshouses, hospitals and resting places of all sorts. The principal routes from the north of France, Normandy, England and Ireland crossed Poitou and Saintonge in the direction of Bordeaux and the Gironde Estuary. For nearly two centuries the Saintes region was travelled each year by half-a-million people going either way. Along the pilgrim roads all services ranging from information to protection were offered. There was even a guidebook, written by a monk from Parthenay. Along the most frequented route, from Châtellerault to Bordeaux (via Poitiers, Saintes, Pons and Blaye), the stopover town of Aulnay only started to lose importance at the beginning of the Renaissance with the decline of the pilgrimage.

Regional cuisine

La Rochelle is a special shrine for the gourmet, but in fact the entire region has a solid gastronomic reputation. Some of the delights available : oysters (from Marennes or Oléron), mussels (from Aiguillon Bay), shrimp (from the Vendée beaches), prawn (from the Cotinière), éclade *(mussels flambée on a bed of pine needles),* mouclade *(mussels in cream or white wine), eels, fried or in a soup (*bouilliture*), snails from Niort or the Charente and lobster (large or "baby"). Other entrées include melon served with* pineau, *ham and sausages, and hare pâté from the Vendée. Fish dishes : stuffed carp, trout, river pike, sardines, salmon, shad from the Gironde; and the* chaudrée, *a typically Charente version of fish soup (with wine).*
Among the poultry : Bressuire fatted hen, Barbezieux capon, Challans duck (known as Canard Nantais*) and goose prepared with chestnuts. The meats are plentiful as well : ribs of beef* à la parthenaise, *white veal from Chalais, pig's head soup. Vegetables include :* mojettes *(beans) from the marshes, salad with walnut oil, and* far *(stuffed lettuce). There are fifty types of* chabichou *(goat's milk cheese from the region). Among the cakes and sweets :* angélique *from Niort, cheesecake (white cheese and eggs, baked), sugar-preserved chestnuts,* duchesse de l'Angoumois *(chocolate), as well as* nougatine *and the macaroons of Vivonne and Poitiers.*

■ SAINT-MAIXENT-L'ÉCOLE

B2 / pop. 9 358 (Deux-Sèvres)

Primarily a market town, most renowned for its military (infantry) school founded 100 years ago.

▶ Via Châlon Gate, walk across the town : numerous Renaissance and 17thC mansions and houses. ▶ **St. Maixent Church★ :** former cathedral remodelled in Renaissance style (17thC) after being sacked by the Protestants (11thC doorway, 15thC transept and bell-tower, pre-Romanesque crypt). ▶ 7thC crypt under the neighbouring church of St. Léger. □

▶ Round trip of Vonne and l'Hermitain *(60 km, 4-5 hr)*

▶ Via Parthenay road *(N)* : right, **Exireuil** Butte (viewpoint). ▶ Pond and ruins of Châteliers Abbey. ▶ **Ménigoute :** small Flamboyant chapel. ▶ **Sanxay :** along a hillside in a small valley (40 acres), Roman ruins★ (amphitheatre, temple, baths). ▶ S, beyond the highway (Seuil de Poitou) and the N11 : **Pamproux,** attractive village. ▶ Megaliths along Exoudun road. ▶ **La Mothe-Saint-Héray :** 15thC church; orangery★ and two Louis XIII pavilions, last remnants of a château. ▶ Return via Sainte-Eanne *(4 km N)* or the **Hermitain Forest★** (viewpoint). □

■ SAINT-SAVIN★★★

C1 / pop. 1 058 (Charente-Maritime)

On the Gartempe River, (13thC bridges★) this fishing centre is known for its **church** (abbey founded in the Carolingian era; magnificent 15thC spire, 94 m).

▶ The broad vault of the **nave★★** and the crypt are decorated with **murals★★★** (11th-13thC) restored 1968-74, showing scenes from the Old Testament. □

▶ Gartempe Valley *(15 km to S; 2hr)*

▶ **Antigny :** 12thC church and lantern of the dead (with altar). ▶ Boismorand Gothic and Renaissance château. ▶ Along the side of the valley, La Roche Windmill. ▶ **Jouhet★ :** 15th-17thC murals in the funeral chapel. ▶ **Pruniers :** Renaissance château overlooking the river. ▶ Montmorillon (→). □

■ SAINT-SAVINIEN

B2 / ® / pop. 2 376 (Charente-Maritime)

Port on the Charente, departure point for organized river cruises (mostly to Saintes and Cognac). This large village is also a hiking and horse-back excursion centre; also trips in horse-drawn carriages.

▶ On the side of the limestone plateau, stone is still quarried and taken away on river barges. *(Quarries open to the public; guide necessary).* ▶ On the plateau : Gothic chapel of an Augustinian convent; **Romanesque church façade.** ▶ Nearby : trip through Charente Valley (→ Saintes, Nearby). □

■ SURGÈRES

B2 / ® / pop. 6 491 (Charente-Maritime)

This small town has kept several monuments inside its castle precinct (11th-14thC) : Romanesque doorway; Romanesque church with broad façade★ and octagonal bell-tower; public garden.

▶ Cooperative dairy (begun in 1888; *am Mon.-Fri.*); entomological museum. □

■ TALMONT-SUR-GIRONDE★★

B3 / ® / pop. 79 (Vendée)

Tiny village with only one small street (full of flowers) : terrace with viewpoint★ over the Gironde; Romanesque church★★★.

▶ Minuscule church situated on the cliff edge, showing the skills of mediaeval builders : carved doorway★; rustic nave; apse★★ ornamented like the prow of a ship. The cliff was reinforced to hold up this edifice. □

▶ Nearby

▶ Via Pons road : Romanesque churches in **Arces** and **Cozes; Gémozac★** ® : 13thC choir; château in a park, with wine-tasting in the cellars, ®. ▶ **Meschers** ® *(6 km N) :* grottos (called *trous*) opened in cliffs *(visits)* and *conches* at Nonnes★ (beach). ▶ Upstream from the estuary *(S, 33 km; half-day) :* **Barzan** *(2 km to right of hill),* **Fâ Mill,** remains of a

Gallo-Roman circular temple. ▶ Drive through vineyards. ▶ **Mortagne-sur-Gironde :** at the foot of a hill, port on the Rive, now used for pleasure boating; 800 m upstream, dug into the cliff, St. Martial hermitage (3rdC?). ▶ **Saint-Dizant-du-Gua :** "blue fountains" in the park of the Château de Beaulon. ▶ **Saint-Thomas-de-Conac :** village with a number of craftsmen's workshops. □

■ THOUARS★★

B1 / ® / pop. 11 913 (Deux-Sèvres)

Set on a plateau surrounded by the Thouet river, the town can be entered from the St. Jean district (Loudun to Bressuire road) and the southern access road (below : 15thC bridge).

▶ On the isthmus, French Classical **château** with Cours d'Honneur★ (Grand Courtyard); from the **terrace** (Flamboyant Gothic funeral chapel), viewpoint★. ▶ Follow the **Rue du Château,** lined with ancient houses, to **St. Médard church** (Romanesque : arched doorway★), facing the SI in a 16thC house. ▶ The old town was built on the plateau behind the church : 12th-13thC **Prince-de-Galles** (Prince of Wales) **Tower;** Renaissance **President-Tyndo** mansion, **Prévost's Gate★** (13th-14thC). ▶ Return to the modern part of town and follow Rue de La Trémoille : 100 m to the right, Hôtel de Ville (town hall) in 17thC building of former **St. Laon Abbey;** in its 12th-15thC church is a chapel with Head of Christ Crucified★. ▶ Farther down, small **museum** *(daily; in summer, 10-12 & 2-6; in winter, 2-4)* : prehistory, archaeology, regional crafts, mementos of the Vendéen Wars (18thC). □

▶ Nearby

▶ On a bend of the Thouet *(S),* the *Cirque* (natural amphitheatre) of **Missé** *(4 km).* ▶ **Pommiers** waterfalls *(3 km W).* ▶ **Tourtenay** *(12 km NE) :* only troglodyte dovecote in France; small agrarian tools museum *(no visits).* ▶ **Oiron** *(12 km E);* **Château★★** (16th-17thC) in French landscaped park *(closed Mon. and Tue.);* the left wing is considered a masterpiece of Renaissance architecture (open gallery★); inside : guardroom (coffered ceiling, 16thC frescos), grand stairway, banquet hall, king's bedroom (Louis XIII ceiling★), Cabinet des Muses★ (paintings). Gothic, Flamboyant and Renaissance **church★ :** 16thC tombs★, altar-pieces. □

■ The VENDÉE WARS

Two tours through the area, involving the principal sites of the 18thC religious and political struggle that raged throughout the Vendée. Places important in the life of the French statesman Clemenceau (1841-1929) are also included. □

▶ Round trip from Bressuire *(265 km; 2 days)*

AB1 *(See map 4)*

▶ N of Bressuire, La Roche-Jacquelein and La Durbie manors (15th-16thC), followed by **Les Aubiers** and, some distance from the road, the ruins (since 1793 fire) of manor-farm of **La Durbelière.** ▶ **Mauléon** ® (pop. 8 498; known as Châtillon-sur-Sèvre during the Revolution) : Romanesque doorway★ of La Trinité church : ruins of feudal castle. ▶ **Saint-Laurent-sur-Sèvre** ® : site★; one of the basilicas houses

4. Battle sites of the Vendée Wars

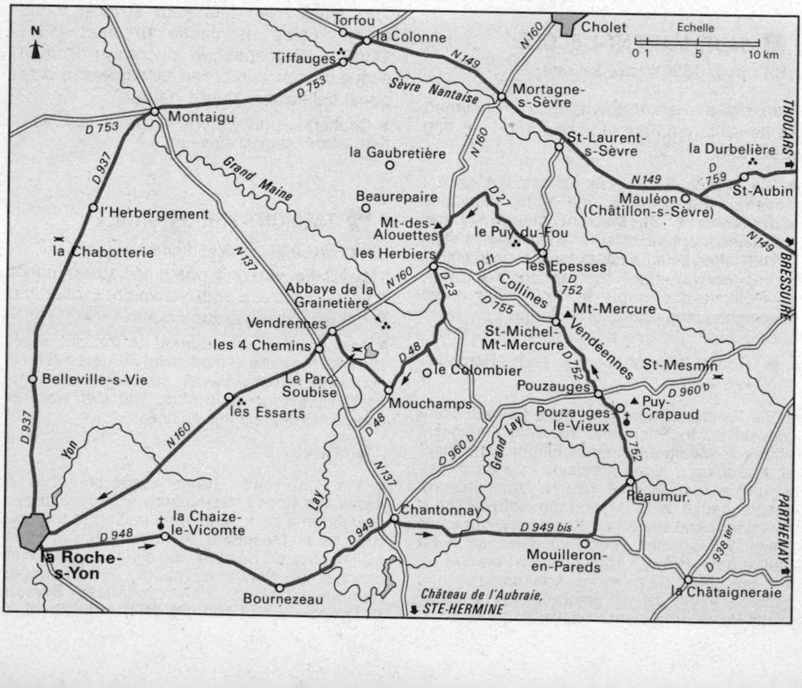

the tomb of Grignon de Montfort (1716). ▶ **Mortagne-sur-Sèvre** ® (pop. 5 359): terraced gardens on the old city wall; ruins of 14th-15thC castle long occupied by the Royalists in the Vendée Wars; large granite church (partially 12thC). ▶ **Torfou Crossroads :** monument to the victory of the royalist Vendéens (Whites) over the Revolutionary army (Blues), in September 1793. ▶ **Cholet** (*15km E* → Maine-Anjou) : scene of the bloodiest encounters during the Vendée Wars. ▶ **Tiffauges :** imposing ruins of the castle★ (13th-15thC), a battle site but also connected with Gilles de Retz, the Bluebeard of legend, reputed also to have been Joan of Arc's comrade-in-arms; site★ *(May-15 Sep., 9-12 & 2-6 daily; out of season Sun. and nat. hols. only).* ▶ **Montaigu :** horse-back excursion centre in the Maine Valley; Museum of the Northern Vendée. ▶ **La Chabotterie :** Renaissance style 17thC château. ▶ La Roche-sur-Yon (→). ▶ **La Chaize-le-Vicomte :** Romanesque church. ▶ **Chantonnay** (pop. 7 479), where d'Elbée massacred 6 000 Revolutionery troops (Blues) in Sep. 1793. ▶ N, via Les Roches-Baritaud (15thC castle), site of **Mouchamps** *(14km)* and **Coulombier farm** *(4 km farther);* Clemenceau's tomb. ▶ S of Chantonnay, via the Grand-Lay gorges and the **Angle-Guignard** reservoir *(6km long),* L'Aubraie château (16thC), where Clemenceau spent part of his childhood; then, **Sainte-Hermine** *(19 km) :* château (17thC); monument to Clemenceau. ▶ The route continues as follows : **Mouilleron-en-Pareds :** birthplace of Clemenceau and Maréchal de Lattre de Tassigny; two museums. ▶ **Cheffois :** 7 km N, **Réaumur** (manor of the physicist of the same name; fortified church; château). ▶ **La Châtaigneraie.** ▶ **Saint-Pierre-du-Chemin** *(6 km farther),* one of the highest points in the region (alt. 230 m ; panorama★). ▶ **La Forêt-sur-Sèvre :** château burned during the Vendée Wars (rebuilt in the 19thC). □

▶ Round trip from Mortagne-sur-Sèvre *(185km; full day)*

▶ Mont des Alouettes, then **Les Herbiers** (→). ▶ La Grainetière, Le Parc-Soubise (→ Les Herbiers, nearby). ▶ **Les Essarts** (pop. 3 672) : 11thC crypt decorated with frescos from the church; ruins of castle (11th-16thC) in park★. ▶ La Roche-sur-Yon (→). ▶ Chantonnay (→ above) ▶ **Saint-Prouant** *(11 km) :* **La Pellissonnière Château** (*2 km N;* 16th-17thC). ▶ **Château de Saint-Mesmin** (14th-16thC), site of intense fighting between Vendéens and Revolutionary forces (1796). ▶ Former abbey of **Beauchêne,** 13th-15thC chapel. ▶ **Cerizay** (pop. 4 881), industrial centre (gloves, shoes, automobiles), seriously damaged during WWII. □

■ VENDEUVRE-DU-POITOU

C1 / pop. 2 154

Romanesque and Gothic church (side doorway). ▶ **Tours Mirandes★** *(1 km N) :* largest archaeological site (1st-2ndC) in western France. ▶ **Roches Château** (*1 km SE;* 15th-16thC).

▶ Nearby

▶ **Avanton** *(8 km S) :* Renaissance château; 14thC church. ▶ Ruins of castle *(2 km SE)* built by Admiral Bonnivet, favourite of François I. ▶ **Marigny-Brizay** *(6 km E) :* in a well-known vine-growing area; **Colombiers,** tiny Romanesque church. ▶ **Lencloître** *(10km N) :* Romanesque church★ (façade fortified in 15thC). □

■ ILE D'YEU★★

(Yeu Island)

A1 / ® / pop. 4 896 (Vendée)

This island of granite and shale, 30km off the Vendée coast, rises 35m above the water at its highest point. Though it enjoys a very mild climate (frost is unknown on the island), its nearly 6 000 acres remain barren of flowers due to the strong Atlantic winds. Nonetheless, the islanders do grow some early vegetables. The main activity remains fishing or related occupations; most of the population lives around Port-Joinville, one of the great trawling harbours in France, and disembarcation point from the continent. □

▶ The trip around the island *(15 km; can be made on foot (6hr) or bicycle (3hr); departures for the mainland are determined by high and low tides)*

▶ **Port-Joinville :** small museum, one room of which is dedicated to Maréchal Pétain, who died on the island in 1951 : his tomb can be seen in the cemetery on the road to Fort Pierre-Levée, where he was in captivity; *(no visits).* ▶ Grand Phare (lighthouse; *3.5 km;* panorama★). ▶ N, many megaliths (mostly dolmens) on the road to the creeks. ▶ On the **Côte Sauvage** (western coast), ruins of **Vieux-Château** (old castle; site★★), now restored; view from the keep. ▶ From there, footpath along the fjord to **Port de la Meule** (lobstermen), rocks and grottos, and to the Bight of Vieilles : view towards the Corbeaux Lighthouse. ▶ Return via **Saint-Sauveur** (Romanesque church) and **Ker Chalon** beach (aquarium nearby). □

Brief regional history

Up to the Roman conquest

Like his Périgord neighbour, the Lascaux caveman lived in the Clain, Vienne and Anglin Valleys (ca. 15 000BC); but the Angoulême region (Eaux-Claires and Rancogne Valleys) was not inhabited until Neolithic man appeared there around 12 000BC. ● The later **Megalithic** civilisation (6000-4000BC) left many dolmens and covered passages in Upper and Lower Poitou. Their routes are easily traced today, in the coastal Vendée region from Aquitaine to Armorica. ● The most important wave of **Celts** settled in the Clain Valley around 600BC (**La Tène** period); and it was the **Pictons** who first confronted, in 56BC, the Roman legions of **Crassus.** ● The future Poitou and Saintonge regions were lined with roads from **flourishing cities** (like *Mediolanum Santonum,* which would become Saintes), as early as the 1stC AD. This was the flowering of Roman Aquitaine, when the Imperial Legate resided in Poitiers.

From early Christianity to the birth of the County of Poitou

In the 4thC, one of the great bishops, **Hilaire,** spread the Christian faith around Poitiers; and one of his disciples, Martin, founded an abbey in Ligugé in 370. Within the next hundred years, the **Visigoths** occupied the area, setting up their capital in Toulouse. ● **Clovis'** victory at Vouillé in 507 effectively ended the invasion. ● The Duchy of Aquitaine was gradually built up from counties, including Poitou, established in the 7thC. ● Around this time, the **Islamic armies** invaded the region on their way northward. Charles Martel halted their progress near Poitiers in 732. ● But the Carolingian Renaissance was stifled by **Scandinavian invasions.** These gave the local nobility the chance to fortify their domains, building numerous keeps, and also, from the 10thC, religious establishments.

The roads to Compostela and the Hundred Years' War

From the **11thC,** abbeys and collegiate churches sprang up along the routes of the Compostela **pilgrims.** The political powers conceded more and more terrain to the Church, here represented by the **Cluniacs** (→ Burgundy). The immense areas confided to religious organisations were steadily improved. ● In 1152, this development was halted by the beginning of three centuries of strife : repudiated by Louis VII (King of France), **Eleanor of Aquitaine** married Henry II Plantagenet, who was later to become King of England. ● For the next three centuries the rival houses of Valois and Plantagenet fought for control of Aquitaine and its dependencies. At the death of Eleanor in 1204, **Philippe-Auguste** annexed Poitou for France (although the Angoulême region was not recovered until the reign of Philippe IV, a century later). ● The beginning of the **Hundred Years' War** is officially dated 1337; this long period of bloodshed was marked by the **defeat of Jean II** (John the Good) at Poitiers. It was later confirmed by the **Treaty of Brétigny** (1360), which gave the English all of the Aunis, Saintonge and Angoulême regions; this was followed by the campaigns of **Du Guesclin** who, until 1380, managed to contain France's adversaries around Bordeaux. ● Strangely enough, this was a time of **economic prosperity;** northern European merchants, descending upon the region for salt and wine, ensured the growth and prosperity of La Rochelle, the future Protestant stronghold. ● In 1422 **Charles VII** undertook the reconquest of the kingdom, then almost entirely in English hands beginning from Poitiers. But the war dragged on until the victory at **Castillon** in 1453.

The Renaissance and the French Classical period

A new era began for Poitou at the end of the 15thC. The discovery of the New World, as well as commerce with the western islands and later Canada, brought growing prosperity in which the Northern Europeans participated. And thanks to the Dutch, the Poitou region embraced the **ideas of the Reformation** at an early stage. ● Calvin himself taught in Angoulême and the Poitiers region; but the area was torn by religious disputes, which remained unsettled until the Edict of Nantes (1598) gave the Protestants **places of refuge,** among them La Rochelle. ● Nonetheless, **Louis XIII** laid siege to the city in 1627, and in October of the following year it capitulated, only to be razed to the ground by the king's troops. ● The same century saw the invention of **cognac distillation,** the founding of **Rochefort** in 1665 by Colbert, and the **Revocation of the Edict of Nantes** (1685), which forced many Protestants to emigrate. ● During the next century the era of the **Administrators** (Blossac in Poitiers and Châtellerault, Reverseaux in Saintes) was marked by widespread urban development. La Rochelle was not alone in its prosperity; Rochefort, Niort, and Angoulême also expanded rapidly.

From the Vendée Wars to the present day

The Constitutional Assembly created the Department of the Vendée in 1791. Two years later, the region rose in revolt against the forced military **conscription** voted by the Revolutionary Government in Paris. **"The Years of Terror"** began in March **1793** and continued until 1796, leaving dead Charette and Stofflet, the last two great leaders of the Vendée. Napoléon's "pacification" was not truly effective until the beginning of the Empire. ● In the middle of the 19thC, with the introduction of **sea-side resorts** and the planting of vegetation to stabilise the dunes, the wealthy middle classes from Bordeaux began to frequent the casino at Royan (1847). ● On the nearby coast, the Portuguese **oyster** made its appearance and La Rochelle came back to life as a fishing centre. **Phylloxeræ** destroyed the vineyards (1876-1882), but a new source of income was soon found : dairy produce. In 1888, the first French **agricultural cooperative** opened at Surgères. ● The cities of Rochefort, Royan and La Rochelle were the last pockets of German resistance at the end of **WWII,** and sustained heavy damage. ● Reconstruction was accompanied by major **public works :** leasehold housing construction began in 1955 under the initiative of Guy Merlin; bridges were built between the islands and the mainland and across the estuaries; and the "Aquitaine" highway was inaugurated, linking the region to Paris and the motorway network.

Architecture

In the Poitou region

In the north of the region the dominant roofing material is tufa; moving south, the slates of the Loire are replaced by the characteristic tiles of Aquitaine. ● The attractive island houses have whitewashed exteriors, brightened by painted shutters and colourful flowers. ● Poitou is a rural region with widely separated houses; a *commune* often

Near Confolens

comprises sixty or more isolated dwellings. ● The house in the Vendée (in fact, lower Poitou), is a long one-storeyed rectangular building of granite or schist, with attached stables and out-houses; the upper windows give access to storage areas under the roofs, reached from the outside by ladder. The front door, set in the centre of the façade, opens onto a corridor leading to the main rooms. The gently sloped four-sided roof is covered with gutter-tiles, generally

Marshland house, or *bourrine*

placed directly on the beams. Note the size of the honey-combed cornice and the unusual ridge-tiles. ● The Charente house is similarly symmetrical and single-storeyed; limestone is the usual building material, and whitewashed exteriors are rare. A low wall runs round the small flower garden in front of the house, in which there is often a well.

In the Charente region

Practical information

The region

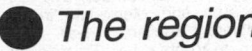

Information : *Comité Régional au Tourisme* (C.R.T. Vienne, Charente, Charente-Maritime, Deux-Sèvres), 2, rue Sainte-Opportune, B.P. 56, 86002 Poitiers Cedex, ☎ 49.88.38.94. Tx 790448 ; *Comité départemental de Tourisme (C.D.T.)* : **Vendée :** C.D.T., 8, pl. Napoléon, 85000 La Roche-sur-Yon, ☎ 51.05.45.28 ; **Charente,** C.D.T., 27, pl. Bouillaud, 16021 Angoulême Cedex, ☎ 45.92.24.43. Tx 791607 ; **Charente-Maritime,** 11 *bis*, rue des Augustins, B.P. 1152, 17008 La Rochelle Cedex, ☎ 46.41.43.33 ; **Deux-Sèvres,** 74, rue Alsace-Lorraine, 79000 Niort, ☎ 49.24.76.79 ; **Vienne,** 11, rue V.-Hugo, 86000 Poitiers, ☎ 49.41.58.22. Tx 792091. Paris : *Maison Poitou-Charentes,* 4, av. de l'Opéra, 75001, ☎ (1) 42.96.01.88. Tx 120496.

Bookings : *Loisirs-Accueil* : **Charente,** pl. Bouillaud, 16021 Angoulême, ☎ 45.92.24.43 ; **Charente-Maritime,** 11 *bis*, rue des Augustins, 17000 La Rochelle, ☎ 46.41.43.33 ; **Vendée,** 8, pl. Napoléon-Bonaparte, 85000 La Roche-sur-Yon, ☎ 51.62.08.24 ; **Vienne,** 11, rue V.-Hugo, 86000 Poitiers, ☎ 49.41.58.22.

Maps : *Michelin* n°s 67, 68, 71 and 72 1/200 000 ; *I.G.N.* n°s 107 and 110 (red series, tourist maps) 1/250 000 ; for the islands, *I.G.N.* n°s 502 (Noirmoutier) and 505 (Oléron) 1/50 000, n° 504 (Ré) 1/40 000 ; n° 503 (Yeu) 1/20 000.

Local and regional press : *La Charente Libre, Sud-Ouest, Ouest France, la Nouvelle République du Centre-Ouest, la France-la Nouvelle République, Courrier de l'Ouest, Presse Océan, l'Éclair.*

S.O.S. : *SAMU* (Emergency Medical Service), Poitiers, ☎ 49.88.33.34 ; La Roche-sur-Yon, ☎ 51.37.61.34.

Weather forecast : Charente-Maritime, ☎ 46.41.11.11, 46.38.29.20, 46.93.13.13, 46.85.06.00 ; **Vendée,** ☎ 51.32.01.80 ; **Deux-Sèvres,** ☎ 49.24.11.11 ; **Charente,** ☎ 45.82.21.25.

Rural gîtes and chambres d'hôtes : Relais dép. **Charente :** C.D.T., pl. Bouillaud, 16021 Angoulême, ☎ 45.92.24.43. **Charente-Maritime :** 2, av. de Fétilly, B.P. 540, 17023 La Rochelle Cedex, ☎ 46.67.34.74. **Deux-Sèvres :** 70, rue Alsace-Lorraine, 79000 Niort, ☎ 49.24.00.42. **Vienne :** 11, rue V.-Hugo, 86000 Poitiers, ☎ 49.41.58.22. **Vendée :** 124, bd A.-Briand, 85000 La Roche-sur-Yon, ☎ 51.62.33.10.

Farmhouse-inns, holidays villages, camping : bookings at the above-mentioned organisations.

Festivals and concerts : Jan (last week-end) : *International Cartoon Show* in Angoulême. **Mar :** *Angourama,* photo festival and « diaporama ». **Apr :** *Police film festival* in Cognac. **Mar-May :** *spring music festival* in Poitiers. **May :** *jazz festival* in Angoulême ; *May cultural festival* in Bressuire. **May-Jun :** *Théâtre du Silence* in La Rochelle. **Jun :** *Saint-Savinien Music Festival* in Melle ; *Rose festival,* Poitiers roseraie. *International Contemporary Art Meetings* (until Jul) in La Rochelle. **Jul :** *Val de Charente festival ; early music,* in Saintes, *Jeux santons* (folklore), shows in the arena. **Aug :** *rural festivities* in Gencay (Vienne). **Oct :** *Musical Meetings* in Poitiers.

Son et lumière : Jun-Aug : Le Puy-du-Fou (Vendée, info, ☎ 51.57.65.65), Les Sables-d'Olonne. **Jul-Sep :** Cognac, La Rochefoucauld (Fri and Sat, end Jun-early Aug), Coulon (summer eve). **Aug :** Angles-sur-l'Anglin. Evening shows in Brouage, Coulon (boatmen's festival the 15th), La Roche-Courbon, and at the sources of the Trouve (near Angoulême).

Local festivals and folklore : Feb : *wine festival* in Loudun (folklore celebrations, sometimes in Nov), Mimosa festival in Saint-Trojan (Oléron). **Apr :** *flower show and pageant* in La Tranche-sur-Mer. **Easter :** *rose festival* in Brigueil (Charente). **May :** *folklore* (cavalcade) in Parthenay, *Festival of the Sea* (end May) on the île d'Yeu. **Jun :** Rochefort Carnival (pageant), *traditional festival* in Xanton-Chassenon (Vendée), *Irais Procession* (2nd Sun) in Airvault ; *cavalcade of St. John's Day,* flowered floats, at Mirebeau ; *reconstitution of the battle of 1356 in which Jean le Bon was captured by the Black Prince* at Nouaillé-Maupertuis. **Jun-Oct :** *horticulture show* in La Court-d'Aron (Vendée). **Jul-Aug :** *peasant festivities* organized by the inhabitants of Cherves (Vienne). **Jul :** *sea festivals* in Royan ; *flower festival* at Les Sables-d'Olonne. *Records Festival,* Aubigny. Montguyon *International Folk Festival* (mid-Jul ; Charente-Maritime). **Aug :** *threshing festival* (1st or 2nd Sun) in Cozes, *historical reenactment* (1st fortnight), in La Flotte-en-Ré, Confolens *international folk festival* (mid-Aug ; Charente), *folklore (*end Aug-early Sep) in Gémozac, *Agricultural Olympics,* La Limouzinière. **Sep :** *festival of the rosebush* (early Sep) in La Mothe-Saint-Héray, *festival of the piglet* in Ranton (Vienne), tour of the ramparts in old automobiles.

Sporting events : May : Montignac-sur-Charente, *canoe rally ;* La Rochelle, *international sailing week ;* Poitiers, *international fencing competition ;* La Rochelle, *international sailing meetings* in **Jul-Aug ;** *International Atlantic Fishing Week and cruise-race,* in **Aug ;** *Côte de lumière marathon,* Saint-Jean-de-Monts ; *grand pavois (ships in full bunting),* in **Sep.**

Horse racing : Jun and Sep, in Barbezieux, Châtellaillon, Gémozac, Ternac, Montendre, La Palmyre. **Jul-Aug :** Cow running in Saint-Georges-de-Didonne ; Horse and greyhound races, La Roche-Posay.

Fairs : all year round : in Challans, **Tue morning** (duck fair) ; Parthenay, **Wed morning** (butcher's meats). **Feb :** Jaunay-Clan *wine fair* (Vienne). **Mar :** *wine fair* in Thouars. **Apr :** Lezay *goat fair.* **Jun :** *young goose fair* in Javarzay (Deux-Sèvres) ; *gastronomy fair* in Saint-Maixent ; *sheep fair* in Montmorillon (Vienne) ; *wool fair* (mid-Jun), in Champagné-Saint-Hilaire (Vienne). **Aug :** *La Saint-Louis,* at Mirebeau ; *cheese fair* (1st Sat and Sun), in Saint-Maixent ; *Saboureau fair,* in Bressuire ; Argenton-Château *dog fair* (last Sun) ; *peasant festival* and *"festival of the unmarrieds"* in La Génétouze (Charente-Maritime). **Sep :** *grape-harvest festival* in Burie ; *Saint Michael's Fair* in Vivonne.

Scenic railways : Oléron, small train from Saint-Trojan to Gatseau Point *(Easter-Sep, 7 km return) ;* Mervent, Pierre-Brune *tortillard* (2 km). Scenic train from Le Puy-du-Fou *(Sat, Sun, hols, 1 Jun-mid-Oct).* Scenic train of la Sandre, 16, pl. de l'Église, 17600 Saujon, ☎ 46.02.40.06. Lambon : a small circuit around a lake, ☎ 49.09.80.17.

Rambling and hiking : *G.R.4* Méditerranée-Océan ; *G.R.36* Channel-Pyrénées ; *G.R.48* (E of the Charente) ; *G.R.360* of Romanesque Saintonge ; *G.R.364* Vienne-Vendée. Topoguides for all rambles.

Riding holidays : *Association régionale (A.R.T.E.),* M. Josquin, La Vivandière, 79330 Saint-Varent, ☎ 49.67.52.75 ; or colonel Cabaret, Brigueil, Charente ; *Ligue Poitou-Charente de la fédération équestre française (F.E.F.),* Poursay-Garnaud, 17400 Saint-Jean-d'Angely ; *comités départementaux :* at the La Rochelle T.O., and 9, bd Clemenceau, 85300 Challans. Also, information at the C.D.T.'s.

Horse-drawn holidays : Sainte-Hermine, in the Vendée region ; in the Charente-Maritime region (enq at the La Rochelle O.D.T.) in Aulnay *(Relais de Saintonge),* Matha *(Le Marquisat),* Saint-Savinien, Haimps (near Matha), Aubigny, 79390 Thénezay (*la Chevalerie du Thonet),* ☎ 49.98.26.29.

Cycling holidays : *Relais départemental du Tourisme rural,* La Rochelle (→ package-deal holidays) ; *Direction départementale de l'Agriculture,* pl. de la Vendée, La Roche-sur-Yon ; *les Comités départementaux de cyclotourismes* (Barbezieux, Bourneuf, 17220 La Jarrie, Thouars, La Roche-sur-Yon).

Boating and sailing holidays : on the Charente, house-boat hire (Charente : C.D.T. and *Sté Quiztour*) ; ocean holidays (house-boat hire in Royan). Inter island and river cruises, *R.D.P.E.* La Rochelle, ☎ 46.42.61.48, and C.D.T.

Handicraft courses : *A.J.* in Poitiers and Saint-Pierre-de-Maillé ; *F.O.L.* in Poitiers and La Roche-sur-Yon ; *U.P.C.P.* in Vouillé, 79230 Prahecq, ☎ 49.75.67.71, Pouzaugues centre. Embroidery, lace-making (Angles-sur-l'Anglin, Ménigoute) ; ceramics (Ars-en-Ré, Mornac-sur-Seudre) ; decoration (La Rochefoucauld) ; wood tooling (Poitiers) ; pottery (Saint-Jean-de-Monts, Challans, île de Ré) ; sculpture (Esse, Charente) ; tapestry (hameau des Forges, and Chantecorps, Deux-Sèvres) ; weaving (Moncontour, Château-Larcher, Chantecorps and Ménigoute in the Deux-Sèvres region), Soullans (near Challans), Saint-Jean-de-Monts, La Tranche-sur-Mer, Mornac-sur-Seudre, Talmont-sur-Gironde ; basket-making (L'Isle-Jourdain). Info : O.D.T. and C.D.T.

Young people : *C.I.J.-Poitou,* 64, rue Gambetta, Poitiers, B.P. 176, ☎ 49.88.64.37 ; *C.D.I.J.-La Rochelle,* 14, rue des Gentilshommes, B.P. 1005, 17007 La Rochelle Cedex, ☎ 46.46.16.99.

Golf : Angoulême (9 holes) ; Poitiers (9 holes) ; Roiffé (18 holes) ; Royan-Saint-Palais (9 holes) ; Saintes (9 holes).

Tennis : *Ligue régionale,* pdt M. J. Lision, 33, av. de Verdun, 79000 Niort.

Aquatic sports : list of marinas, sailing schools and inland stretches of water at the O.D.T.

Speed-sailing : Notre-Dame and Saint-Jean-de-Monts, Saint-Gilles-Croix-de-Vie.

Canoeing : *Ligue Poitou-Charente,* 9, av. C.-Coulomb, 16800 Soyaux, ☎ 45.92.06.98 ; A.J. d'Angoulême, courses in the Vienne region, info at C.D.T.

Potholing and spelunking : *Comité régional,* 20, rue des Cressonnières, 16000 Angoulême, ☎ 45.92.19.95 ; *Comité départemental,* 221, rue de La Tour-d'Auvergne, Angoulême.

Fishing : *Fédérations départementales des A.P.P. :* 31, rue de Bellevue, Angoulême ; 43, av. Eugène-Normandin, La Rochelle ; rue Galucher, 79000 Niort, ☎ 49.73.94.06 ; 17, rue La Fayette, B.P. 179, 85007 La Roche-sur-Yon Cedex ; 14, rue Jean-Jaurès, Poitiers.

Sea fishing : *Amicale rochelaise de pêche sportive,* 26 *bis,* rue Thiers, La Rochelle, ☎ 46.41.15.07 ; *Royan Maritime service,* voûtes du Port, ☎ 46.05.69.49.

● Towns

L'AIGUILLON-SUR-MER

Luçon 21, La Rochelle 50, Paris 445
A2 ⊠ 85480

ℹ mid-Jun-mid-Sep, ☎ 51.56.43.87.

Hotel :

● ★★***Port,*** 2, rue Bellevue, ☎ 51.56.40.08. Visa. 33 rm ✻ 🅿 ♨ ▭ ✓ closed 15 Nov-15 Mar, 180. Rest. ♦ Seafood, 60-150.

⛺ ★★★*Bel Air* (200 pl.), ☎ 51.56.44.05.

AIRVAULT

Poitiers 51, Niort 64, Paris 350
C1 ♥ ⊠ 79600

ℹ mairie, ☎ 49.64.70.13.

SNCF ☎ 49.64.70.63.

Hotel :

★★***Vieux Relais,*** ☎ 49.64.70.31. Euro. 12 rm 🅿 ♨ ▭ closed 1st fortnight in Oct, 1 week in Feb, Mon, 160. Rest. ♦♦ ♿ 50-180.

ANGOULÊME

Périgueux 85, Bordeaux 116, Paris 446
C3 ⊠ 16000

ℹ hôtel de ville (B2), ☎ 45.95.16.84, and pl. de la Gare, ☎ 45.92.27.57.

SNCF ☎45.92.86.77.

Car-hire : *Budget* train + car, 22, av. Gambetta, ☎ 45.95.23.37, and railway station, ☎ 45.92.20.34.

Hotels :

● ★★★***France*** (Inter-Hôtel), 1, pl. des Halles (B1), ☎ 45.95.47.95. Tx 791020. AE, Euro, Visa. 47 rm ✻ 🅿 ♨ ▭ ♿ 250. Rest. ♦♦ ✕ ♿ closed 23 Dec-2 Jan and Sat, 100-130.

Roullet, ⊠ 16440, 10 km SW :

★★★***Vieille Étable,*** les Plantes, ☎ 45.66.31.75. AE, Euro, Visa. 13 rm 🅿 ♨ ▭ ✓ ♿ closed mid-Feb-mid-Mar, 185. Rest. ♦ ✕ Spec : *magret de canard,* 55-180.

Asnières-sur-Nouère, 16290 Hiersac, 12 km NW :

★★★★***Moulin de Maine-Brun,*** ☎ 45.96.92.62.

Tx 791053. AE, DC, Visa. 20 rm 🅿 closed 1 Nov-15 Jan, Sun eve, 430. Rest. ♦♦ 140-250.

Youth hostel : Ile de Bourgines, ☎ 45.92.45.80.

⛺ ★★★*Ile de Bourgines* (70 pl.), ☎ 45.92.83.22.

Restaurants :
♦♦ ***Chamade,*** 13, rampe d'Aguesseau, ☎ 45.38.41.33. AE, DC, Euro, Visa. ♿ closed 1-25 Aug, a week in Feb, Sun and Mon noon, 130-250.

Nersac, ⊠ 16440, 10 km W :
♦♦ ***Auberge du Pont de la Meure,*** rte de Hiersac, ☎ 45.90.60.48. AE, DC, Euro, Visa closed Aug, Fri eve and Sat, 70-150.

Recommended : *pâtisserie Au Palet d'Or,* 1, pl. Fr.-Louvel, ☎ 45.95.00.73.

Guided tours : *C.N.M.H.S.* (in Jul-Aug daily ex Sun), at the *O.M.T.*

AUBETERRE-SUR-DRONNE

Chalais 10, Angoulême 46, Paris 492
C3 ⊠ 16390

ⓘ pl. Ludovic-Trarieux, ☎ 45.98.50.33.

Hotel :
★★***Périgord,*** ☎ 45.98.50.11. 8 rm 🅿 closed 15-31 Dec, 90. Rest. ♦ closed Sun eve and Mon low season, 50-130.

⛺ ★★*Dronne* (50 pl.), ☎ 45.98.50.33.

BARBEZIEUX-SAINT-HILAIRE

Angoulême 33, Bordeaux 84, Paris 478
B3 ⊠ 16300

ⓘ 3, bd Chanzy (Jul-Aug), ☎ 45.78.02.54, and mairie, ☎ 45.78.20.22.

Hotel :
● ★★***Boule d'Or*** (Inter-Hôtel), 9, bd Gambetta, ☎ 45.78.22.72. AE, Euro, Visa. 28 rm. Pension (only high season), 150. Rest. ♦♦ 45-140.

BEAUVOIR-SUR-MER

Noirmoutier 22, Nantes 60, Paris 437
A1 ⊠ 85230

ⓘ 15 Jun-15 sep, ☎ 51.68.71.13, and mairie, ☎ 51.68.70.32.

Hotel :
★***Touristes*** (L.F.), rte du Gois, ☎ 51.68.70.19. AE, DC, Euro, Visa. 20 rm 🅿 ♿ closed end Nov-early Dec, 160. Rest. closed in Jan. Spec : seafood, 50-150.

Organised visits : the marshlands in a buggy or gig (enq at the *T.O.*).

BRESSUIRE

Cholet 45, Angers 82, Paris 356
B1 ⊠ 79300

ⓘ pl. de l'Hôtel-de-Ville, ☎ 49.65.10.27.

SNCF ☎ 45.65.00.06.

Hotel :

Cerizay, ⊠ 79140, 14 km W :

★★***Cheval Blanc,*** 33, rue du 25-Août, ☎ 49.80.05.77. Euro, Visa. 25 rm 🅿 ♿ closed 20 Dec-6 Jan and Sat (ex Jul-Aug), 210. Rest. ♦ 40-90.

Youth hostels : Centre d'accueil de Pugny (15 km), 79320 Mont-Coutant, ☎ 49.72.73.64 ; in Cerizay, *F.J.T.*, allée du Midi.

Events : festival (May cultural festival) ; fairs.

CHALLANS

Les Sables-d'Olonne 43, Nantes 60, Paris 432
A1 ⊠ 85300

ⓘ 4, rue Gambetta (high season), ☎ 51.93.19.75. Closed Sun.

Hotels :
★★***Rocotel,*** 9, bd de la Gare, ☎ 51.93.07.48. AE, DC, Visa. 21 rm 🅿 closed Sun and nat hols, 250. Rest. ♦ ***le Dauphin*** Spec : *marée vendéenne aux blancs de poireau, Saint-Jacques aux pommes,* 150-180.

Restaurant :
♦♦ ***Gîte de Tourne-Pierre,*** rte de Soullans (3 km), ☎ 51.68.14.78. 🅿 closed Sep, Oct, 2 weeks in Mar and Fri eve-Sat noon, 90-220.

Guided tours : in the Brittany marshlands (enq at the *T.O.*).

Events : duck market on Tue morning.

CHANTONNAY

La Roche-sur-Yon 33, Nantes 73, Paris 401
B1 ⊠ 85110

ⓘ pl. de la Liberté (Jul-Aug, closed Sun), and mairie, ☎ 51.94.46.51.

SNCF ☎ 51.94.30.14.

Hotel :
★★***Moulin Neuf*** (3 km S), ☎ 51.94.30.27. 49 rm 🅿 closed 21-28 Dec and first week in Feb, 180. Rest. ♦ 40-90.

⛺ ★★*Les Asphodèles,* le Moulin-Neuf (40 pl.), ☎ 51.94.46.51.

CHASSENEUIL-SUR-BONNIEURE

Angoulême 33, Limoges 70, Paris 448
C3 ⊠ 16260

SNCF ☎ 45.39.50.09.

Hotel :

Nieuil, 16270 Roumazières, 8 km NE :
● ★★★★***Château de Nieuil*** (Relais et châteaux), ☎ 45.71.36.38. 14 rm 🅿 ♿ closed 12 Nov-26 Apr, 550. Rest. ● ♦♦ closed Wed noon ex hotel guests. One of the greatest "châteaux-hotels". Luce Bodinaud's good cooking. Spec : *farci charentais, tournedos sauce pineau,* 160-200.

CHÂTELAILLON-PLAGE

La Rochelle 12, Niort 62, Paris 468
B2 ⊠ 17340

ⓘ Municipal park, closed Sat low season and Sun ex Jul-Aug, ☎ 46.56.26.97, and mairie, ☎ 46.56.22.24.

SNCF ☎ 45.35.10.72.

Hotels :
★***Océan,*** 121, bd de la République, ☎ 46.56.25.91. Visa. 24 rm ♿ closed 15 Feb-15 Mar and Sun eve-Mon low season, 170. Rest. ● ♦♦ A real family boarding house. Very good cooking : fish, seafood, Charentes ham, 50-250.
★***Jeanne d'Arc,*** 12, rue Musset, ☎ 46.56.20.01. 23 rm 🅿 closed 20 Dec-4 Jan, Sat and Sun during low season, 135. Rest. ♦ ♿ Spec : *filet de sole Jeanne d'Arc, rognon au porto,* 50-100.

⛺ ★★★*Clos des Rivages* (50 pl.), ☎ 46.56.26.09, and a dozen camp-sites ★★ (1 000 pl.).

CHÂTELLERAULT

Poitiers 35, Tours 72, Paris 306
C1 ⊠ 86100

ⓘ bd Blossac, ☎ 49.21.05.47, closed Mon low season and Sun.

SNCF ☎ 49.21.00.24.

Car-hire : *Budget* train + car, *l'Orée du Bois,* RN10 S, ☎ 49.21.30.90, and S.N.C.F. railway station, ☎ 49.21.02.35.

Hotels :
★★★***Moderne*** (Mapotel), 74, bd Blossac, ☎ 49.21.30.11. Tx 791801. AE, Euro, Visa. 39 rm ♨ ♿ 250. Rest. ◆◆ ***la Charmille,*** closed Tue and 15 Jan-15 Feb, a week in Oct, 150-270.
★★***Croissant,*** 19, av. Kennedy, ☎ 49.21.01.77. AE, Euro, Visa. 20 rm, closed 23 Dec-6 Jan and Sun eve and Mon, 160. Rest. ◆ ♿ Spec : *paupiette de moules sauce roquefort, sandre à l'étuvée de poireaux satranée, paletot de volaille à la vapeur aux noisettes de ris de veau,* 50-175.
★★***L'Escale,*** 17, av. d'Argenson (N exit on the RN10), ☎ 49.21.13.50. Euro, Visa. 32 rm 🅿 ♨ ♿ 180.

Chambres and tables d'hôte : *château de Saint-Bonnet,* Sérigny, 86230 Saint-Gervais, 25 km E, ☎ 49.86.01.55. 5 rm 🅿 ♨ 🔔 ✗ closed 1 Oct-31 May, 350.

Youth hostel : *le Chillou d'Ozon* (all year round), exit W towards Chauvigny (20 km NW), ☎ 49.21.29.22.

⛺ ★★*Municipal* (65 pl.), ☎ 49.21.94.02.

Restaurants :
Naintré, ⊠ 86530, 9 km S :
● ◆ ***Grillade,*** ☎ 49.90.03.42. Visa. ♿ closed Sun eve, Mon, 10-30 Jan, 10-20 Nov. Under a thatched roof, good traditional Charentais cooking, nice grilled meats, *daube de bœuf,* eels, 65-130.

Events : *Saint-Roch festival* (Sun after 15 Aug) ; *exhibition-fair* in Sep.

Leisure activities : cultural centre ; *parc de loisirs* des Petites Minaudières (9 km E).

CHAUVIGNY

Poitiers 23, Montmorillon 26, Paris 336
C1 ⊠ 86300

ⓘ pl. du Champ-de-Foire (Jul-Aug, closed Sun afternoon) and mairie, ☎ 49.46.30.21.

Hotels :
● ★★***Lion d'Or*** (L.F.), 8, rue du Marché, ☎ 49.46.30.28. 27 rm 🅿 closed Sat low season and 15 Dec-15 Jan, 190. Rest. ◆ ♿ Spec : *aiguillette à l'ail,* 60-130.
● ★***Beauséjour,*** 20, rue Vassalour, ☎ 49.46.31.30. Euro, Visa. 20 rm 🅿 ♨ ♿ closed 25 Dec and New Year's Day, 110. Rest. closed Sun, 40-70.

⛺ ★★★*La Fontaine* (100 pl.), ☎ 49.46.31.94.

Visits with guide : upper town in Jul-Aug (enq at the S.I.).

COGNAC

Saintes 26, Angoulême 44, Paris 480
B3 ⊠ 16100

ⓘ pl. J.-Monnet, closed Sun, ☎ 45.82.10.71.

SNCF ☎ 45.82.25.90.

⛴ cruises on the Charente river : towards Jarnac and Angoulême, and Saintes and Rochefort, information and tickets at the S.I.

Hotels :
★★★***François Ier*** (Inter-Hôtel), pl. François-Ier, ☎ 45.32.07.18. AE, Euro, Visa. 31 rm 🅿 🔔 ♿ 190.
★★★***Pigeons Blancs,*** 110, rue J.-Brisson, ☎ 45.82.16.36. AE, DC, Visa. 6 rm 🅿 ♨ 🔔 ✗ ♿ closed 1-15 Jan and Sun, 250. Rest. ☼ ✗ Spec : *foie gras frais de canard au pineau, filet de sole à la vapeur de cognac,* 85-200.
★★***Moderne*** (L.F.), 24, rue E.-Mousnier, ☎ 45.82.19.53. 39 rm 🅿 ♨ 🔔 ♿ closed 15 Dec-15 Jan, 170.
★★***L'Auberge,*** 13, rue Plumejeau, ☎ 45.32.08.70. Euro, Visa. 25 rm, closed 25 Dec and New Year's Day, 180. Rest. ◆ closed Sat. Spec : *brochette de coquilles St-Jacques à la vapeur de cognac, sole au champagne,* 60-120.

Saint-Laurent-de-Cognac, 5 km W :
● ★★★***Logis de Beaulieu*** (L.F. ; Châteaux-hôtels), ☎ 45.82.30.50. Euro, Visa. 21 rm ☼ 🅿 ♨ 🔔 closed 2nd fortnight in Dec, 390. Rest. ◆◆ ***l'Alambic.*** Spec : *pot-au-feu du pêcheur,* 90-200.

Saint-Fort-sur-le-Né, ⊠ 16660 Cierzac :
★★★***Moulin de Cierzac,*** ☎ 45.83.61.32. AE, Visa. 10 rm 🅿 ♨ 🔔 closed Feb and Mon low season, 330. Rest. ♿ This 17thC beautiful house is a peaceful gastronomic stop : *crème d'huîtres aux pétoncles, selle d'agneau à la crème d'ail.* Good cognacs, 100-280.

Restaurant :
◆ ***Coq d'Or,*** 33, pl. François-Ier, ☎ 45.82.02.56. AE, DC, Euro, Visa ; closed 18 Aug-8 Sep, Sun and Fri eve in winter. Spec : *foie de canard aux pommes et au pineau,* 60-160.

Visits : audioguided tour of Old Cognac (enq at the S.I.) ; visits of certain industrial establishments (*Saint-Gobain,* etc.). Visits of Hennessey wine and spirits storehouse and musée de la Tonnellerie : rue de la Richonne, ☎ 45.82.52.22. 5 km E, in Gensac-la-Pallue, 16130 Segonzac, visit of *Prince H. de Polignac Cognac* storehouses, Pavillon du Laubaret, N141, ☎ 45.32.13.85 (from Apr to end Sep). Visit of the *Martell* storehouses, pl. Ed.-Martell, ☎ 45.82.44.44.

Spectacles : son et lumière at the François-Ier castle.

Fairs : in May and in Nov.

CONFOLENS

Bellac 36, Angoulême 63, Paris 407
C2 ♥ ⊠ 16500

ⓘ pl. des Marronniers, ☎ 45.84.00.77, closed Oct, Sun and nat hols.

Hotel :
★★***Auberge de la Belle Étoile*** (L.F.), rte d'Angoulême, ☎ 45.84.02.35. 14 rm 🅿 ♨ ✗ closed Oct, 1st week in Feb and Mon low season, 140. Rest. ◆ Spec : Confolens-style *cèpes* (fine, delicate mushrooms), 50-120.

⛺ ★★*Municipal* (70 pl.), ☎ 45.84.01.97.

Event : *International Folk Festival* in Aug.

COULON

Niort 11, La Rochelle 59, Paris 419
10 km W of Niort, B2 ♥ ⊠ 79510

ⓘ pl. du Colombier, mid-Jun-mid-Sep, ☎ 49.35.94.74, and mairie, ☎ 49.25.90.26.

Hotels :
★★***Au Marais,*** 46, quai Louis-Tardy, ☎ 49.25.90.43. Visa ☼ 🔔 closed Sun eve and Mon low season, 160. Rest. closed 25 Dec, New Year's Day. Fish specialities, 60-150.

★***Central,*** pl. de l'Église, ☎ 49.35.90.20. Euro, Visa. 11 rm closed 15 Sep-15 Oct, 15 Feb-8 Mar and Sun eve-Mon, 90. Rest ♦ Spec : *sandre au beurre blanc, bouquet maraîcher,* 60-150.

⛺ ★★*Venise Verte* (100 pl.), ☎ 49.25.90.36.

Aquarium of Venise Verte : river fish, 8-10, pl. de l'Église *(Apr-Nov daily 10-12:30, 2:30-7, on request,* ☎ *49.35.90.31).*

DIGNAC

Angoulême 17, Bergerac 86, Paris 463
17 km S of Angoulême, C3 ✉ 16410

Restaurant :
Vouzan-Maison-Neuve, 8 km :
♦♦ ***Orée du Bois,*** ☎ 49.60.72.61. 🅿 ♨ closed 2 weeks in Nov and Mon low season. Spec : *bloc de foie gras maison, cagouille à la charentaise,* 100-150.

La FAUTE-SUR-MER

Luçon 22, Les Sables-d'Olonne 49, Paris 446
1 km from L'Aiguillon, A2
✉ 85460 L'Aiguillon-sur-Mer

ℹ rd-pt Fleuri, Jul-Aug, ☎ 51.56.45.19.

Hotel :
★★***Les Chouans,*** 1, rd-pt Fleuri, ☎ 51.56.45.56. Visa. 22 rm, closed 16 Oct-19 Dec and Mon, 200.

⛺ ★★★*Club Franca* (100 pl.), ☎ 51.56.40.62 ; and 10 campsites ★★ (500 pl.).

Restaurants :
♦ ***La Crinière,*** 6, rue du Port-des-Yachts, ☎ 51.56.43.44. 🅿 ♿ closed Mon eve and Tue low season, 23 Feb-11 Mar and 1-21 Oct. Spec : *sole à l'orange, crottin chaud aux noix, huîtres gratinées aux amandes,* 50-200.
♦ ***Les Délices de la Mer,*** rd-pt Fleuri, ☎ 51.56.47.62. Visa ; closed 10 Dec-10 Jan and Wed. Spec : *pot-au-feu de la mer, homard grillé,* 60-120.

FONTENAY-LE-COMTE

La Rochelle 49, Cholet 76, Paris 409
B2 ✉ 85200

ℹ quai du Poey-d'Avant, closed Mon low season and Sun, ☎ 51.69.44.99.

🚌 pl. de Verdun.

Hotel :
★★***Rabelais,*** rte de Parthenay, ☎ 51.69.86.20. AE, DC, Euro, Visa. 35 rm ⚘ 🅿 ♨ ▭ 220. Rest. 50-120.

Youth hostel : *F.J.T.*, rue des Gravants.

⛺ → Mervent.

Restaurant :
♦♦ ***Chouans Gourmets,*** 6, rue des Halles, ☎ 51.69.55.92. AE, Euro, Visa ⚘ closed Feb school hols, 1st fortnight in Jul and Sun eve-Mon. Fish specialities, 70-140.

FOURAS

Rochefort 14, La Rochelle 27, Paris 478
B2 ✉ 17450

ℹ pl. Bujeau and av. du Casino, ☎ 46.88.60.69.

⛴ *R.D.P.E. :* crossings for the île d'Aix (departure from the *pointe de la Fumée,* 3 km), ☎ 46.88.60.50.

Hotel :
● ★★★***Résidence du Parc,*** rue du Bois-Vert, ☎ 46.84.61.26. 17 rm 🅿 ♨ ⛰ ♿ closed Oct-Easter, 320.

⛺ ★★*Le Cadoret* (600 pl.), ☎ 46.84.02.84.

FROMENTINE

Noirmoutier 21, Nantes 60, Paris 446
At the foot of the Noirmoutier bridge, A1
✉ 85550 La Barre-de-Monts

ℹ sea terminal, ☎ 51.68.52.32 (summer), and mairie, ☎ 51.68.52.31.

⛴ for the île d'Yeu (1:10), ☎ 51.68.53.65.

⛺ ★★★*Le Grand Corseau* (450 pl.), ☎ 51.68.52.87 ; and three sites ★★ (more than 1 000 pl.).

Restaurant :
♦ ***L'Océan,*** 2, av. de l'Estacade, ☎ 51.68.50.04. Euro ; closed 15 Nov-15 Jan and Tue low season, 50-100.

Les HERBIERS

Cholet 25, La Roche-sur-Yon 40, Paris 374
B1 ✉ 85500

ℹ centre du Lavoir, Jul-Aug, ☎ 51.67.18.39.

Hotel :
★***Le Centre,*** 6, rue de l'Église, ☎ 51.67.01.75. AE, Euro, Visa. 8 rm. closed 1-16 Aug, 15-30 Dec, Fri eve and Sat in low season, 90. Rest. ● ♦♿ One of the famous spots of the Vendée wars and of good gastronomy : fish specialities, 50-120.

Son et lumière : Cinescenie at Le Puy-du-Fou castle (10 km) mid-Jun-Aug ; enq and bookings at the *mairie des Épesses,* ☎ 51.57.65.65.

JARD-SUR-MER

Les Sables-d'Olonne 20, La Rochelle 80, Paris 470
7 km S of Talmont-Saint-Hilaire, A1 ✉ 85520

ℹ pl. de la Liberté, ☎ 51.33.40.47.

Hotel :
★★***Parc de la Grange*** (L.F.), rte de l'Abbaye, ☎ 51.33.44.88. AE, DC, Euro, Visa. 55 rm 🅿 ♨ ⛰ ▭ 🎾 ♿ closed 1 Oct-31 Mar, 220. Rest. ● ♦♦ An English chef in the heart of Vendée country. Spec : *crabes farcis, magret de canard aux pommes,* 70-120.

⛺ ★★★*La Coquille* (35 pl.), ☎ 51.33.42.67 ; ★★★*les Écureuils* (190 pl.), ☎ 51.33.42.74 ; and 9 ★★ sites.

JARNAC

Cognac 15, Bordeaux 112, Paris 454
B3 ♥ ✉ 16200

ℹ pl. du Château, closed Sun and nat hols, ☎ 45.81.09.30.

SNCF ☎ 45.81.07.09.

⛴ cruises on the Charente river (information at the ℹ).

Hotels :
★***Terminus*** (L.F.), av. Carnot, ☎ 45.81.07.04. AE, DC, Euro, Visa. 12 rm 🅿 ♨ closed 15 Dec-15 Jan, 110. Rest. ♦ closed Sat low season. Spec : *escargots à la charentaise,* 50-120.

Fleurac, 10 km NE :
● ★★★***Château de Fleurac*** (Châteaux-hôtels), ☎ 45.81.78.22. 18 rm 🅿 ♨ ⛰ ♿ closed 1 Nov-15 Dec and Sun eve, Mon low season, 300. Rest. ♦♦ ⚘ Spec : *crabe gratiné au champagne,* 110-160.

Vibrac, 11 km SE :
● ★★***Les Ombrages*** (L.F.), ☎ 45.97.32.33. 10 rm 🅿 ♨ ⛰ ⚘ ▭ 🎾 closed Christmas and Feb school hols and Sun eve-Mon in winter, 130. Rest. ♦ ♿ 60-110.

⛺ ★★*Municipal* (200 pl.), ☎ 45.81.18.54.

Restaurants :

◆ ***Château,*** 15, pl. du Château, ☎ 45.81.07.17. Euro, Visa ; closed 17 Aug-7 Sep, Feb school hols and Sat noon, Sun eve and Mon. Charente specialities, prepared with cognac and pineau, seafood, 70-135.

Bourg-Charente, 6 km W :

◆◆ ***La Ribaudière,*** ☎ 45.81.30.54. AE, Visa ⚘ 🅿 ♨ closed Feb school hols and Sun eve, 60-140.

Visit of the *Courvoisier* storehouses, pl. du Château, ☎ 45.81.04.11.

Fair on the 1st Sat of the month.

JONZAC

Saintes 49, Angoulême 60, Paris 513
B3 ⊠ 17500

ⓘ mairie, ☎ 46.48.04.11.

SNCF ☎ 46.48.00.36.

Hotel :

★★***Le Club,*** 8, pl. de l'Église, ☎ 46.48.02.27. Visa. 15 rm 🔔 ✈ closed 2nd fortnight in Feb, 140.

Restaurant :

◆◆ ***Vieux Logis,*** Clam (6 km), ☎ 46.48.15.11. Euro, Visa 🅿 ♨ ▭ ♿ closed 18 Nov-13 Dec, Mon low season, 50-180.

LOUDUN

Châtellerault 49, Tours 72, Paris 314
C1 ✤ ⊠ 86200

ⓘ hôtel de ville, ☎ 49.98.15.96.

SNCF ☎ 49.22.00.32.

Hotel :

★★***Roue d'Or*** (L.F.), 1, av. d'Anjou, ☎ 49.98.01.23. Euro, Visa. 16 rm 🅿 closed Feb school hols and Sat-Sun low season, 120. Rest. ◆ Simple cooking. Spec : *poulet poitevin, tête de veau, contrefilet aux cèpes*, 60-130.

LUÇON

La Roche-sur-Yon 32, La Rochelle 51, Paris 433
B1-2 ⊠ 85400

ⓘ 7, pl. Leclerc, ☎ 51.56.36.52.

SNCF ☎ 51.56.01.49.

Hotels :

★★***Le Bordeaux***, 14, pl. des Acacias, ☎ 51.56.01.35. AE, Visa. 24 rm ✈ 240. Rest. ● ◆◆ ♿ closed Sun eve and Mon. Simple but tasty fare, low prices. Spec : *jambon de canard fumé maison, panaché de poisson à la royale, escalopine de magret de canard au miel*, 65-120.

Sainte-Hermine, ⊠ 85210, 16 km NE :

★***Relais de la Marquise,*** ☎ 51.30.00.11. Euro. 12 rm 🅿 closed in Oct, end-of-year, Sun eve in winter and Fri eve-Sat, 120. Rest. ◆ ✈ Spec : *saumon grillé au beurre d'anchois*, 60-130.

Fair : during the holiday of 15 Aug.

LUSIGNAN

Poitiers 24, Niort 47, Paris 360
C2 ✤ 86600

ⓘ ☎ 49.43.31.36.

SNCF ☎ 49.43.31.26.

Hotel :

★***Promenades*** (L.F.), 19, av. de Poitiers, ☎ 49.43.31.35. 10 rm 🅿 ♨ ♿ 220. Rest. ◆ ♿ Spec : *coquelet au gamay, escargots farcis*, 60-100.

⛺ ★★*Vauchiron* (100 pl.), ☎ 49.43.30.08.

LUSSAC-LES-CHÂTEAUX

Montmorillon 12, Poitiers 36, Paris 357
C2 ⊠ 86230

ⓘ ☎ 49.48.42.77.

SNCF ☎ 49.48.40.35.

Hotels :

Pont-de-Lussac, 2 km W on the N147 :

★★***Connestable Chandos*** (L.F.), ☎ 49.48.40.24. Euro. 7 rm 🅿 🔔 closed 7-14 Oct, 11 Feb-4 Mar and Mon, 125. Rest. ♿ Spec : *fruits de mer, coquilles St-Jacques, civet de sanglier*, 70-175.

Civeaux, 6 km NW :

★★***Cascade,*** ☎ 49.48.45.04. 21 rm ⚘ 🅿 ♨ ✈ ♿ closed Feb, 10 days in Nov and Fri low season, 150. Rest. ◆ Traditional cooking, 60-160.

MAILLEZAIS

Fontenay-le-Comte 15, Niort 29, Paris 436
B2 ⊠ 85420

ⓘ le Bourg, ☎ 51.87.23.01.

⛺ ★★★*L'Autize* (36 pl.), ☎ 51.00.70.79.

Barge trips in the marshlands ; tickets sold at the abbey entrance.

MANSLE

Angoulême 26, Poitiers 84, Paris 419
17 km S of Ruffec, C2 ⊠ 16230

Hotel :

Saint-Groux, 3 km NW :

● ★★***Trois Saules*** (L.F.), ☎ 45.20.31.40. Euro, Visa. 10 rm 🅿 ♨ 🔔 ♿ closed 3-11 Nov, Feb school hols, Sun eve and Mon noon low season, 100. Rest. ◆ 40-120.

MARENNES

Rochefort 22, Saintes 40, Paris 488
B2 ⊠ 17320

ⓘ pl. de la Poste, ☎ 46.85.04.36. mid-Jun-mid-Sep, closed Sun afternoon, or ☎ 46.85.25.55.

Hotels :

★***Commerce et Poste,*** rue de la République, ☎ 46.85.00.09. Euro, Visa. 14 rm, closed Feb, 120. Rest. Spec : *huîtres gratinées*, 40-120.

France, 8-10, rue de la République, ☎ 46.85.00.37. 14 rm 🅿 closed Oct and Sun eve, Mon ex Jul-Aug, 120. Rest. Seafood spec : 40-85.

Bourcefranc-le-Chapus, ⊠ 17560, 5 km NW :

● ★★***Les Claires*** (Relais du Silence), ☎ 46.85.08.01. Tx 792055. AE, DC, Euro, Visa. 18 rm ⚘ 🅿 ♨ 🔔 ▭ 🎾 ♿ 250. Rest. ◆◆ 120-240.

Youth hostel : bd de la Mer, Marennes-Plage.

⛺ Two sites ★★ (total of 200 pl.).

Visit : oyster beds.

MELLE

Poitiers 46, Saintes 72, Paris 391
B-C2 ⊠ 79500

ⓘ pl. Bujault (bus station) and mairie, ☎ 49.27.00.23.

Hotel :

★***Central,*** 5, pl. R.-Goussard, ☎ 49.27.01.11. 14 rm 🅿 ✈ closed 2nd fortnight in Sep and Sat, 60. Rest. eve only for guests, 40-65.

Event : Saint-Savinien music festival (Jun-Sep).

MERVENT

La Rochelle 60, La Roche-sur-Yon 64, Paris 411
10 km N of Fontenay-le-Comte, B1-2
✉ 85200 Fontenay-le-Comte

ℹ le Vieux Château, ☎ 51.00.20.97, closed Mon low season.

Hotels :
★***Auberge de la Forêt*** (3 km NE), ☎ 51.00.21.09. Visa. 9 rm 🅿 closed 25 Dec-15 Jan and Mon low season, 145. Rest. 60-120.
★***Ermitage de Pierre-Brune***, ☎ 51.00.25.53. 18 rm 🅿 ♿ closed 15 Nov-8 Mar, 135. Rest. 55-135.

⛺ ★★★*Chêne-Tord* (80 pl.), ☎ 51.00.20.63.

MESCHERS-SUR-GIRONDE

Royan 11, Saintes 42, Paris 512
5 km N of Talmont, B3 ✉ 17132

ℹ pl. de Verdun, ☎ 46.02.70.39, 15 Jun-15 Sep.

⛺ ★★★*Côte de Beauté* (330 pl.), ☎ 46.05.26.93 ; and 6 sites ★★

Restaurant :
♦♦ ***Grottes de Matata,*** bd de la Falaise, ☎ 46.02.70.02. Visa. closed 1 Oct-31 Mar, Sun eve and Mon, 90-160.

MONTBRON

Angoulême 30, Limoges 72, Paris 458
14 km SE of La Rochefoucauld, C3
✉ 16220

ℹ pl. de l'Hôtel-de-Ville, Jul-Aug, closed Sun, ☎ 45.70.61.71.

Hotel :
★★★***Hostellerie Sainte-Catherine*** (Châteaux-hôtels), 3 km S, ☎ 45.70.60.03. 18 rm 🅿 230. Rest. ♦♦ ♿ Spec : *coquelet sauce champagne, rognons perigourdins,* 50-180.

⛺ ★★*La Piscine* (50 pl.), ☎ 45.70.60.09.

MONTENDRE

Saintes 62, Bordeaux 62, Paris 518
B2 ✉ 17130

ℹ av. de la République, ☎ 46.49.46.45 (high season), and mairie, ☎ 46.49.20.84.

SNCF ☎ 46.49.40.04.

Hotel :
★★***Deux Gares et Pins,*** 20, av. de la Gare, ☎ 46.49.43.57. Visa. 14 rm 🅿 ♿ 145. Rest. ♦ 60-135.

⛺ ★★★*Forêt* (45 pl.), ☎ 46.49.20.17.

MONTGUYON

Jonzac 34, Bordeaux 64, Paris 510
B3 ✉ 17270

ℹ mairie, ☎ 46.04.10.19.

Hotel :
★***Poste*** (L.F.), 18, av. de la République, ☎ 46.04.19.39. Euro, Visa. 18 rm 🅿 ♿ 110. Rest. ♿ 40-70.

Event : *international folk festival* in mid-Jul.

MONTMORILLON

Poitiers 48, Limoges 84, Paris 362
C2 ✉ 86500

ℹ av. F.-Tribot, ☎ 49.91.11.96, closed mornings low season and Sat-Sun.

SNCF ☎ 49.91.00.60.

Hotel :
★★***France,*** 2, bd de Strasbourg, ☎ 49.91.00.51. AE, Euro, Visa. 25 rm, closed 1 Jan-1 Feb and Sun eve-Mon, 195. Rest. ● ♦♦ ♿ 90-210.

⛺ ★★★*L'Allochon* (80 pl.), ☎ 49.91.02.33.

Guided tours : conducted by official C.N.M.H.S. guides, Jul-Aug ex Tue ; information at the ℹ

MORNAC-SUR-SEUDRE

Royan 13, Marennes 23, Paris 504
B3 ✉ 17113

ℹ ☎ 46.22.70.97.

Hotel :
Chaillette, ✉ 17890, 4 km N :
● ★★★***La Brousse,*** ☎ 46.36.60.93. 16 rm 🅿 closed 8 Sep-Jun, 440 with half-pension. Rest. ♦ half-pension only.

Restaurant :
♦ ***La Gratienne,*** rte de Breuillet, ☎ 46.22.73.90. 🅿 closed 15 Apr-7 May, 15-30 Dec and Wed-Thu ex Jul-Aug. Open only during the week-end in Jan, Feb and Mar, 85-140.

Visits : villages of craftsmen (courses).

MORTAGNE-SUR-SÈVRE

Cholet 10, Nantes 56, Paris 359
10 km SW of Cholet, B1 ✉ 85290

ℹ rue Nationale, ☎ 51.90.60.01.

Hotel :
● ★★***France*** (L.F.), 4, pl. Dr-Pichat, ☎ 51.67.63.37. AE, DC, Euro, Visa. 25 rm 🅿 ♿ closed Sat, 240. Rest. ♦♦♦ ***la Taverne.*** Excellent, 60-170.

⛺ ★★*La Romaine* (40 pl.), ☎ 51.67.60.45.

Restaurant :
La Verrie, 85130 La Gaubretière, 6 km S :
♦ ***La Malposte,*** pl. Ch.-de-Gaulle, ☎ 51.91.56.14 🅿 ♿ closed 28 Jul-15 Aug, 10-25 Feb and Mon, 120-210.

NIORT

Rochefort 60, Poitiers 74, Paris 407
B2 ✉ 79000

ℹ pl. de la Poste (B2), ☎ 49.24.18.79. closed Sun.

✈ Niort-Souché airport (6 km E), ☎ 49.24.02.89.

SNCF ☎ 49.24.24.77., 49.24.13.20.

🚌 pl. Saint-Hilaire.

Car-hire : *Budget* train + car, S.N.C.F. railway station, ☎ 49.24.13.20.

Hotels :
★★★***La Brèche,*** 8, av. Bujault (B2), ☎ 49.24.41.78. AE, DC, Euro, Visa. 49 rm ♿ closed 24 Dec-7 Jan, 200.
★★★***Grand Hôtel,*** 32, av. de Paris (C2), ☎ 49.24.22.21. AE, Euro, Visa. 40 rm 🅿 ♿ 350.
★★***Paris,*** 12, av. de Paris (C2), ☎ 49.24.93.78. 🅿 38 rm, closed 12-28 Jul and 23 Dec-6 Jan, 170.

Saint-Rémy ✉ 79410, 6 km N :
★★***Relais du Poitou,*** ☎ 49.73.43.99. 22 rm 🅿 150. Rest. ♦ closed Mon. Spec : *turbot tahitienne,* 80-130.

La Crèche ✉ 79260, 10 km NE :
● ★★★***Motel des Rocs*** (Relais du Silence), ☎ 49.25.55.28. AE, DC, Euro, Visa. 51 rm 🅿 ♿ 260. Rest. ♦♦ 100-250.

⛺ ★★★*Parc des Loisirs* (150 pl.), ☎ 49.79.05.33.

Restaurants :

● ♦♦ ***Relais Saint-Antoine,*** pl. de la Brèche, ☎ 49.24.02.76. AE, Euro, Visa ; closed 5-25 Jul, 1 week in Feb and Sat. The talented T. Fichet's light and personalized cooking : *rouleau printanier au saumon cru d'Écosse, petit pavé de foie gras de canard aux oranges glacées, ris de veau braisés aux morilles,* 70-310.

♦♦ ***Tuilerie,*** Bessines, rte de La Rochelle (5 km), ☎ 49.73.52.93. AE, DC, Euro, Visa. Ⓟ ♨ 🍽 ▭ 🎾 ♿ closed Aug and Sun eve, 100-300.

● ♦ ***La Poêle d'Or,*** 26, rue P.-F.-Proust, ☎ 49.28.04.58. AE, Euro, Visa. ♿ closed Sat and Sun eve. True cooking from the Vendée bocage, copious and of high quality. Spec : *sole pochée au muscadet, magret de canard au bleu du Poitou,* 60-120.

♦ ***La Belle Étoile,*** 115, quai M.-Métayer (2.5 km W on the A2), ☎ 49.73.31.29. Ⓟ closed 1-22 Aug, Sun eve and Mon. Spec : *feuilleté d'huîtres en habit net,* fish, 70-150.

Beauvoir-sur-Niort, ⊠ 79360, 17 km S :

● ♦ ***Voyageurs,*** 32, pl. de l'Hôtel-de-Ville, ☎ 49.09.70.16. AE, DC, Euro, Visa. 🍽 ♿ closed Feb school hols and Wed. J.-C. Batiet loves his region and its cooking : *lumas* (snails), *fricassée, gratin d'anguilles, andouillette au muscadet,* home-made *confit* to take away, nice local wines, 90-200.

Market : Thu, Sat.

Auction house, 322, rue du Mal-Leclerc, ☎ 49.24.65.85.

Recommended : *la Maison du Fromage,* 19, rue St-Jean. Pedestrian streets in center of town.

Ile de NOIRMOUTIER

La Roche-sur-Yon 78, Nantes 82, Paris 459
A1 ⊠ 85330 Noirmoutier-en-l'Ile

ℹ 1, rte du Pont, 85630 Barbâtre, ☎ 51.39.80.71., closed Sun low season ; quai Jean-Bart, Noirmoutier-en-l'Ile, ☎ 51.39.12.42 (high season).

🚌 ☎ 51.39.04.72.

⛴ boat service between Pornic and le *bois de la Chaize* (plage des Dames).

🚗 acces via the La Barre-de-Monts bridge (tolls) ; passage du Gois (→ Beauvoir-sur-Mer), 2 hours before and 2 hours after low tide.

Hotels :

★★★***Général d'Elbée,*** pl. du Château, ☎ 51.39.10.29. AE, DC, Visa. 33 rm 🍽 ▭ ♿ closed Oct-Mar, 360. Rest. ♦♦ 70-140.

★★★***Saint-Paul,*** bois de la Chaize, ☎ 51.39.05.63. Visa. 48 rm ♨ 🍽 🎾 ♿ closed Oct-Apr, 300. Rest. ♦♦ 🍴 100-150.

★★★***Punta Lara,*** bois des Éloux, la Guérinière, ☎ 51.39.11.58. AE, DC, Visa. 60 rm ⚟ Ⓟ ♨ 🍽 ▭ 🎾 closed 15 Oct-30 Mar, 540. Rest. ♦♦ 160-220.

● ★★***Les Prateaux*** (Relais du Silence), bois de la Chaize, ☎ 51.39.12.52. Tx 911733.13 rm Ⓟ 🍽 🍴 ♿ closed 1 Oct-14 Mar, 250. Rest. ♦♦ 🍴 ♿ 150-310.

★★***Fleur de Sel*** (L.F.), rue des Saulniers, ☎ 51.39.21.59. Euro, Visa. 23 rm Ⓟ 🍽 🍴 ♿ closed 12 Nov-25 Dec, 6-15 Jan, 260. Rest. ♦ ♿ closed Sun eve and Mon from Nov to Mar. Spec : *moules du gois gratinées, suprême de bar à la maraichine,* 75-180.

⛺ ★★★*Les Onchères,* Barbâtre (610 pl.), ☎ 51.39.81.31, and numerous sites ★★ (more than 2 000 pl.).

Restaurant :

♦ ***Le Grand Four,*** 1, rue de la Cure, ☎ 51.39.12.24. Visa. 🍽 🍴 ♿ closed 5-28 Jan and Wed ; Tue eve and Wed off-season. Spec : *terrine de saumon au vert, filet de bar aux épinards,* 70-130.

NOTRE-DAME-DE-MONTS

Noirmoutier-en-l'Ile 25, Nantes 74, Paris 455
7 km NW of Saint-Jean-de-Monts, A1
⊠ 85690

ℹ mairie, ☎ 51.58.84.97.

Hotel :

★★***Plage*** (L.F.), 2, av. de la Mer, ☎ 51.58.83.09. AE, Euro, Visa. ⚟ Ⓟ 🍽 closed Sun eve, Mon low season, 200. Rest. ♦ Spec : *bar poché au beurre rouge,* 65-150.

⛺ ★★★*Le Grand Jardin* (180 pl.), ☎ 51.58.87.76 ; ★★★*le Bois Soret* (180 pl.), ☎ 51.58.84.01, and approx 10 sites ★★ (approx 700 pl.).

Restaurant :

♦♦ ***Pier'Plot,*** rte de Saint-Jean-de-Monts, ☎ 51.58.86.48. AE, Euro. Ⓟ noon only from 1 Oct to end Feb, closed Wed low season, 70-150.

Ile d'OLÉRON

Marennes 9.5, Saintes 49, Paris 496
A2 ⊠ for localities

🚗 via the Chapus toll bridge.

⛴ Ronce-les-Bains-Saint-Trojan (summer) and La Rochelle-Boyardville ; enq *R.D.P.E.,* La Rochelle.

LE CHÂTEAU ⊠ 17480

ℹ pl. de la République, ☎ 46.47.60.51.

Hotel :

★***Le Mail,*** ☎ 46.47.61.40. Visa. 16 rm ♿ closed 1 Nov-1 Feb and Tue, 90.

⛺ ★★★*Montravail* (130 pl.), ☎ 46.47.61.82.

Visits : oyster beds.

LA COTINIÈRE ⊠ 17310 Saint-Pierre-d'Oléron

Hotels :

★★★***Le Vivier,*** ☎ 46.47.10.31. Visa. 8 rm ⚟ ♨ ♿ closed Nov-Jan and Sun eve-Mon low season, 300. Rest. ♦♦ 🍴 Spec : *filet de bar aux huîtres, feuilleté de langoustines,* 100-220.

★★★***Motel Ile de Lumière,*** ☎ 46.47.10.80. 45 rm ⚟ Ⓟ ♨ 🍽 ▭ 🎾 ♿ closed Oct-Mar, 380.

DOLUS ⊠ 17550

ℹ ☎ 46.57.34.12 (summer) and 46.75.32.84.

Hotels :

★★★★***Grand Large,*** La Remigeasse, ☎ 46.75.37.89. Tx 790395. 28 rm ⚟ Ⓟ ♨ 🍽 ▭ 🎾 closed Nov-Mar, 1 150. Rest. ♦♦ 170-300.

★★★***Les Pins,*** le Vert-Bois, ☎ 46.75.34.98. AE, DC, Visa. 21 rm ⚟ Ⓟ ♨ 🍽 ▭ 🎾 closed 15 Sep-24 Juin, 500. Rest. ♦ 🍴 180-220.

⛺ ★★★*Ostrea* (200 pl.), ☎ 46.47.62.36. ; ★★★*la Remigeasse* (80 pl.), ☎ 46.75.31.11. ; ★★★*l'Océan* (80 pl.), ☎ 46.75.31.70.

SAINT-GEORGES ⊠ 17190

ℹ Boyardville, ☎ 46.47.04.76.

Hotel :

★★***Bains,*** Boyardville, ☎ 46.47.01.02. AE, DC, Euro, Visa. 10 rm ⚟ Ⓟ closed 15 Sep-May, 160. Rest. ♦ 65-235.

⛺ ★★★★*Signol,* Boyardville (330 pl.), ☎ 46.47.01.22 ; ★★★★*Rex,* Domino (450 pl.), ☎ 46.76.55.97 ; ★★★★*le Suroît* (250 pl.), ☎ 46.47.07.25 ; ★★★*la Désirade* (150 pl.), ☎ 46.76.54.43.

Restaurant :
♦♦ ***Trois Chapons,*** 14, rte de Saint-Pierre, ☎ 46.76.51.51. AE, Euro, Visa 🅿 ⛱ ♿ closed 15 Dec-15 Jan, Mon eve and Tue ex summer and school hols, 95-250.

SAINT-PIERRE 17310

ⓘ pl. Gambetta, ☎ 46.47.11.39., Jun-Aug.

Hotels :
★★***Square,*** 4, pl. Denfert-Rochereau, ☎ 46.47.00.35. 30 rm 🅿 ⛱ closed 30 Nov-14 Mar, 190. Rest. ♦ 85-300.
★★***Atlantic,*** la Ménounière, ☎ 46.47.07.09. 20 rm 🅿 ♿ closed 1 Oct-1 Apr, 180. Rest. ♦ ♿ 55-95.

⛺ ★★★*Les Cercelles* (70 pl.), ☎ 46.47.19.24.

SAINT-TROJAN-LES-BAINS ✉ 17370

ⓘ bd P.-Wiehn and carrefour du Port, ☎ 46.76.00.86., closed Sun and Wed low season.

Hotels :
★★★***Les Cleunes,*** ☎ 46.76.03.08. 49 rm 🅿 ⛱ closed 5 Nov-20 Mar and Mon low season, 250.
★★***Forêt,*** 16, bd P.-Wiehn, ☎ 46.76.00.15. 44 rm 🅿 ⛱ ♿ closed 15 Oct-31 Mar, 180. Rest. ♿ 60-90.
★★***L'Albatros,*** 11, bd du Dr-Quineau, ☎ 46.76.00.08. 13 rm 🅿 ⛱ ♿ closed Oct-Feb, 180. Rest. ♿ 60-120.

Event : *mimosa festival,* end Feb-early Mar.

PARTHENAY

Bressuires 32, Niort 42, Paris 374
B1 ✉ 79200

ⓘ Palais des Congrès, ☎ 49.64.11.88.

SNCF ☎ 49.64.04.35.

Hotel :
★★***Nord*** (L.F.), 86, av. du Gal-de-Gaulle, ☎ 49.94.29.11. Euro, Visa. 13 rm 🅿 closed 20 Dec-10 Jan and Sat, 125. Rest. ♿ ♦ Spec : *chevreau à la gâtinaise,* 45-135.

⛺ ★★★*Municipal* (90 pl.), ☎ 49.94.39.52 ; Verruyes (16 km S) : ★★★*la Fragnée* (65 pl.), ☎ 49.63.21.37.

Events : *livestock fair* Wed morning ; *folklore festivities* early May ; shows at the Palais des Congrès (theatre).

POITIERS

Tours 101, Nantes 176, Paris 335
C1 ✉ 86000

ⓘ rue des Grandes-Écoles, ☎ 49.41.21.24, and (high season pm), pavillon de la Gare, same tel.

✈ aéroport de Biard (4 km W), ☎ 49.58.27.96 or 49.41.65.07 ; *Air France Agency,* 11 *ter,* rue des Grandes-Écoles, ☎ 49.88.89.63.

SNCF (A2) ☎ 49.41.22.88., 49.58.23.89., 49.58.29.53.

🚌 *Rapides du Poitou,* ☎ 49.46.27.45 ; *S.T.A.O.,* ☎ 49.41.11.88 ; *Tourisme Verney,* 2, rue Victor-Hugo.

Car-hire : *Budget* train + car, 95, bd du Grand-Cerf (opposite the station, A2), ☎ 49.58.24.20, at the station, ☎ 49.58.22.88, and at the airport.

Hotels :
★★★★***France*** (Mapotel), 28, rue Carnot (B3), ☎ 49.41.32.01. AE, Euro, Visa. 86 rm ⛱ ♿ 360. Rest. ♦♦ ♿ Spec : *saucisson chaud à la poitevine,* 70-95.
★★★***Royal Poitou,*** 215, rte de Paris (5 km N), ☎ 49.01.72.86. AE, Euro, Visa. 32 rm 🅿 ♿ 260. Rest. ♦♦ closed Sat noon and Sun in winter. Spec : *gratin de langouste au champagne, sole aux cèpes,* 70-200.
● ★★***Europe,*** 69, rue Carnot (B3), ☎ 49.88.12.00. Visa. 50 rm 🅿 ⛱ ♿ 250.

Saint-Benoît, ✉ 86280, 4 km S :
★★***Chalet de Venise,*** 6, rue du Square, ☎ 49.88.45.07. 10 rm 🅿 ⛱ closed Jan, 22-31 Oct, Sun eve and Mon, 160. Rest. ♦ Spec : *terrine de pâté de lièvre, chevreau poitevine,* 55-170.

Chasseneuil-du-Poitou, ✉ 86360, 8 km N :
★★★***Relais de Poitiers,*** ☎ 49.52.90.41. Tx 790502. AE, Euro, Visa. 99 rm ♿ 275. Rest. ♦♦ ♿ Spec : *foie gras frais de canard, blinis de saumon au citron vert,* 70-140.

Ligugé, 86240, 9.5 km S :
● ★★★***Bois de la Marche,*** RN10 S exit S from Poitiers, ☎ 49.53.06.36. Tx 790133. AE, Euro, Visa. 47 rm 🅿 ⛱ ♿ 255. Rest. ♦♦ 75-170.

Youth hostel : 17, rue de la Jeunesse.

⛺ ★★*Districal,* Saint-Benoît, 4 km S (65 pl.), ☎ 49.88.48.55.

Restaurants :
● ♦♦ ***Armes d'Obernai,*** 19, rue A.-Ranc (B2), ☎ 49.41.16.33. Euro, Visa ♿ closed 15 Feb-5 Mar, 1-15 Sep and Sun eve-Mon. Spec : *choucroute de poisson,* 65-200.
♦♦ ***Maxime,*** 4, rue St-Nicolas, ☎ 49.41.09.55. AE, DC, Euro, Visa ♿ closed Sat noon and Sun, 70-180.
♦♦ ***Auberge de la Cigogne,*** 20, rue du Planty (off map near B1), ☎ 49.61.61.47 ♿ closed 1-21 Aug, Sun-Mon, 120-210.
♦ ***Cul de Paille,*** 3, rue Th.-Renaudot, ☎ 49.41.07.35. closed Aug and Sun, 70-120.

Guided tours : conducted by official *C.N.M.H.S.* guides, in Jul-Aug daily 10 and 3 ; enq at the S.I. (hôtel de ville).

PONS

Saintes 22, Bordeaux 96, Paris 494
B3 ✉ 17800

ⓘ hall du Donjon, 15 Jun-15 Sep, ☎ 46.94.00.04.

SNCF ☎ 49.91.30.25.

Hotel :
★★***Auberge Pontoise,*** 23, av. Gambetta, ☎ 46.94.00.99. Euro, Visa. 22 rm 🅿 ♿ closed 20 Dec-19 Jan, 13-26 Apr and Sun eve-Mon (ex summer), 200. Rest. ♦ ♿ Spec : *feuilleté d'huîtres au beurre rouge, lamproie au vin de Bordeaux et blancs de poireaux.* 85-230.

POUZAUGES

Bressuire 28, Nantes 81, Paris 384
B1 ✉ 85700

ⓘ pl. du Calvaire, ☎ 51.91.82.46 (high season), ☎ 51.57.01.37.

SNCF ☎ 51.57.02.67.

Hotels :
★★★***Chouannerie,*** 27, rue A.-Delaveau, ☎ 51.57.01.69. AE, DC, Visa. 9 rm 🅿 ♿ closed 2 weeks in Feb, 1-15 Aug, 190. Rest. ♦ ☎ 51.91.33.96. Closed Sun eve and Mon noon, 60-200.
● ★★***Bruyère*** (L.F. and Relais du Silence), ☎ 51.91.93.46. 30 rm 🅿 ⛱ ♿ 210. Rest. ♿ ♦ Spec : *escalope de bar au cresson,* 40-135.

Ile de RÉ

La Rochelle 5, Nantes 151, Paris 476
A2 ✉ see localities

Car-ferry day and night, leaving from La Pallice

(15 mn crossing ; wait of up to 4 hours during peak season) ; enq : *R.D.P.E.* (Régie départementale des Passages d'Eau), ☎ 46.42.61.48.

ℹ bureau central : **La Flotte** (open till midnight high season), quai Sénac, ☎ 46.09.60.38.

Visit of oyster beds : departures from Rivedoux, Loix, Ars, les Portes (enq at the S.I.).

ARS ✉ 17590

ℹ ☎ 46.29.46.09.

⛺ ★★*Soleil* (140 pl.), ☎ 46.29.41.74 ; *Essi* (140 pl.), ☎ 46.29.44.73.

Recommended : visit of oyster beds, oyster farmers' cooperative, ☎ 46.29.44.24.

LE BOIS-PLAGE ✉ 17850

ℹ rue des Barjottes, ☎ 46.09.23.26.

Hotel :

★★***Les Gollandières,*** ☎ 46.09.23.99. AE, DC, Visa. 32 rm Ⓟ ♨ ⛱ 📺 ♿ closed 4 Nov-1 Mar and Sun eve, 250. Rest. ♦ 80-150.

⛺ ★★★★*Antioche* (120 pl.), ☎ 46.09.23.86 ; ★★★*Interlude* (180 pl.), ☎ 46.09.18.22.

Recommended : *Ile de Ré Wine-grower's Cooperative* (cognac, pineau), ☎ 46.09.23.09.

LA FLOTTE ✉ 17630

ℹ quai Sénac, ☎ 46.09.60.38.

Hotels :

★★★***Richelieu,*** ☎ 46.09.60.70. Visa. 30 rm ⚘ Ⓟ ♨ ⛱ 📺 ⚲ ♿ closed Jan, 500. Rest. ♦♦ The first class cooking of the Ile de Ré whose reputation has spread far beyond the island itself ; a gourmand festival of seafood. Spec : *marguerite de coquilles Saint-Jacques, huîtres chaudes aux petits légumes,* 160-300.

★★***Le Belle Rive,*** 10, cours F.-Faure, ☎ 46.09.60.02. AE, DC, Visa. 22 rm ♿ closed 15 Nov-15 Dec, 210. Rest. Spec : *éclade de moules,* 50-120.

SAINT-MARTIN ✉ 17410

ℹ hôtel de Clerjotte, ☎ 46.09.20.06 (high season).

Hotel :

★★***Colonnes,*** quai Job-Foran, ☎ 46.09.21.58. AE, Euro, Visa. 30 rm ⚘ closed 1 week in Oct and 15 Dec-2 Feb, 185. Rest. ⚘ ♿ closed Wed, 65-120.

⛺ ★★*Sainte-Thérèse* (200 pl.), ☎ 46.09.21.96.

Restaurant :

♦ ***Saint-Hubert,*** at the port, ☎ 46.09.20.38 ⚘ closed 15 Oct-Feb. Spec : *bar braisé,* 120-210.

SAINTE-MARIE ✉ 17740

ℹ rue de la République, ☎ 46.30.22.92.

Hotel :

● ★★★***Atalante,*** ☎ 46.30.22.44. AE, DC, Euro, Visa. 65 rm ⚘ Ⓟ ♨ ⛱ 📺 ⚲ ♿ 400. Rest. ✂ Spec : *sole maritaise,* 80-200.

Restaurant :

♦ ***Auberge de la Chauvetière,*** 1, rue de la Beuretière, ☎ 46.30.21.56. Closed 6-20 Feb and Wed. A former chef of Richelieu's and a trainee of the Troisgros brothers prepares good sea specialities : *mouclade, sole rochelaise,* 120-210.

⛺ ★★★*La Cadorette* (60 pl.), ☎ 46.30.22.59.

Bicycle hire : Ars, Le Bois-Plage, La Couarde, La Flotte, Saint-Martin.

Sail-boat hire : La Flotte, Saint-Martin.

ROCHEFORT-SUR-MER

La Rochelle 32, Saintes 40, Paris 465
B2 ✉ 17300

⚕ (closed Jan)

ℹ av. Sadi-Carnot (A3), ☎ 46.99.08.60.

SNCF ☎ 46.99.01.95 and 46.99.00.26.

🚌 pl de Verdun, ☎ 46.99.23.67.

Car-hire : *Budget* train + car, S.N.C.F. railway station, ☎ 46.99.01.95.

Hotel :

★★***Remparts,*** 43, av. C.-Pelletan, ☎ 46.87.12.44. AE, DC, Visa. 63 rm Ⓟ ♿ 250. Rest. 50-150.

Soubise, ✉ 17780, 7 km SW :

★★***Soubise,*** 62, rue de la République, ☎ 46.84.93.36. AE, Euro, Visa. 23 rm Ⓟ ♨ closed 15 Oct-15 Nov, Sun eve and Mon ex Jul-Aug, 120. Rest. ● ♦♦ A bastion of Saintonge culinary traditions maintained by Liliane Benoît. Spec : *goujonettes de sole et de langoustines aux pâtes fraîches, émincé de magret et son foie tiède,* 100-180.

Restaurants :

♦♦♦ ***Marais,*** 10, rue Lesson, ☎ 46.99.47.13. AE, Euro, Visa ; closed 2nd week in Feb, 3rd week in Jun, 2nd half of Nov and Sun. 85-170.

♦ ***Tournebroche,*** 56, av. du Gal-de-Gaulle (B3), ☎ 46.99.20.19. AE, Euro, Visa ; closed 1-15 Jul and 15-28 Feb, Sun and Mon, 60-150.

La ROCHEFOUCAULD

Angoulême 22, Limoges 81, Paris 444
C3 ♥ ✉ 16110

ℹ 41, rue des Halles, Jun-Oct, ☎ 45.20.07.45.

Hotel :

★★***La Vieille Auberge,*** 13, fg la Souche, ☎ 45.62.02.72. AE, Euro, Visa. 28 rm Ⓟ ♨ closed Jan, 160. Rest. ♦ ♿ closed 3-23 Jan and Mon noon, 45-100.

Riding gîte, rooms and table d'hôtes : M. Goueset, in Pransac, 9 km S, ☎ 45.70.31.17.

La ROCHELLE

Saintes 70, Nantes 146, Paris 471
B2 ✉ 17000

Marinas : *les Minimes* (3 000 pl.) and le *Vieux-Port.*

ℹ 10, rue Fleuriau (B2), ☎ 46.41.14.68., closed Sun ; *Accueil de France,* at l'O.D.T., 11 *bis,* rue des Augustins, ☎ 46.41.43.33. Tx 790712.

✈ aéroport de Laleu (4 km), ☎ 46.42.18.27. *Air France Agency,* 23, rue Fleuriau, ☎ 46.41.65.33.

⛴ ferry service to the île de Ré (departure from La Pallice), excursions and cruises (including on the Charente river) : *R.D.P.E.,* ☎ 46.36.61.48.

SNCF ☎ 46.41.34.22, 46.41.09.91, 46.41.15.98., 46.41.09.06.

🚌 cours des Dames (B3), ☎ 46.41.35.33.

Car-hire : *Bugdet* train + car, *Villemonteil Location,* 11, av. Gal-de-Gaulle, ☎ 46.37.46.84 ; *S.N.C.F.* railway station, ☎ 46.41.34.22, and airport.

Hotels :

● ★★★***Yachtman,*** 23, quai Valin (B3), ☎ 46.41.20.68. Tx 790762. AE, DC, Euro, Visa. 40 rm Ⓟ ⛱ 📺 ♿ 370. Rest. ♦ ***Roof,*** 80-130, and ♦♦ ***Yachtman,*** 90-300.

● ★★★ ***Brises,*** chemin de la Digue-de-Richelieu, ☎ 46.43.89.37. Visa. 46 rm ⚘ Ⓟ ♨ closed 15 Dec-20 Jan, 370.

★★★***France et Angleterre*** (Mapotel), 22, rue Gargoulleau (B2), ☎ 46.41.34.66. AE, DC, Euro, Visa. 76 rm Ⓟ ♨ ⛱ ♿ 280. Rest. ♦♦ ***le Richelieu.*** closed 15 Dec-15 Jan, Sun and Mon noon, 100-220.

★★★**Champlain,** 20, rue Rambaud (B2), ☎ 46.41.23.99. Tx 790717. AE, DC, Euro, Visa. 37 rm Ⓟ ♿ closed mid Dec-28 Feb, 000.
● ★★**François Ier** (Relais du Silence), 13-15, rue Bazoges (B2), ☎ 46.41.28.46. Visa. 34 rm Ⓟ ♿ 180.
★★**Saint-Jean-d'Acre** (Inter-Hôtel), 4, pl. de la Chaîne, ☎ 46.41.73.33. AE, Euro, Visa ♿ 49 rm, 230. Rest. ♦ ***Au Vieux Port.*** closed 15-31 Jan and Fri in winter, 70-200.
★★**Le Rochelois,** 66, bd W.-Churchill, ☎ 46.43.34.34 Ⓟ ♿ 200. Rest. Pension or half-pension, 65-100.
★**Pré Vert,** 43, rue St-Nicolas, ☎ 46.41.24.43. AE, Euro, Visa. 19 rm, closed 1st week in Nov, 3rd week in Jan and Sun eve (1 Nov-31 Mar only), 140. Rest. ● ♦ ♿ Spec : *anguille au cassis, merlu aux queues de langoustines,* 50-130.
Youth hostels : *Minimes* international youth centre (at the marina), and *A.J. de L'Houmeau,* Lagord (N suburb).

⛺ Aytré (4 km SE) : ★★★*Richelieu* (100 pl.), ☎ 46.44.19.24.

Restaurants :
● ♦♦♦ **Serge,** 46, cours des Dames (B3), ☎ 46.41.18.80. AE, DC, Euro, Visa ♿ closed mid-Jan-mid-Feb and Sun low season. La Rochelle cooking *par excellence ;* Serge Coulon is a great character in the port and the champion of fish cooking : *fruits de mer, soupe de poisson, embeurrée de poisson,* 90-300.
● ♦♦♦ **Richard Coutanceau,** plage de la Concurrence, ☎ 46.41.48.19 Ⓟ private beach ; closed Mon eve, Sun. This restaurant is getting more and more famous. Fresh fish is cooked masterfully : *blanc de turbot et bigorneaux à la crème de curry, homard breton rôti légumes croquants,* 220-310.
♦♦♦ **Marmite,** 14, rue Saint-Jean (A3), ☎ 46.41.17.03. AE, DC, Euro, Visa ♿ closed 2nd fortnight in Jan and Wed, 135-280.
♦♦ **Flots,** 1, rue de la Chaîne (B3), ☎ 46.41.32.51. Closed 25 Jan-3 Mar and Mon. Spec : *homard grillé ; bouillabaisse,* 90-185.
● ♦ **Bar André,** 5, rue Saint-Jean (A3), ☎ 46.41.28.24. AE, DC, Euro, Visa ; closed Mon low season. A popular seafood restaurant ; tables called over the microphone and tickets distributed for them, an enormous bank of oysters, 120-150.

Aytré, ⊠ 17440 (4 km SE) :
♦♦ **Maison des Mouettes,** rte de la Plage, ☎ 46.44.29.12. AE, Euro, Visa Ⓟ ♿ closed 1 Feb-4 Mar and Mon ex nat hols, 95-300.

Dompierre (8 km E) :
♦♦ **Vieux Noyer** (Châteaux-hôtels), 64, rue du Gal-de-Gaulle, ☎ 46.35.31.32. AE, DC, Euro, Visa. With 5 rm Ⓟ ♿ closed 20 Jan-19 Feb and 22 Sep-1 Oct and Mon eve-Tue ex Jul-Aug, 70-160.

Guided tours : conducted by official *C.N.M.H.S.* guides, Jul-Aug, all year upon demand at 10 and 2:30 ; visits of the town in a buggy (→ ⓘ in all cases) ; visit of the roadstead by boat : *Guilloteau,* ☎ 46.41.41.98.

Events : May, *Pageant and International Sailing Week ;* Jun-Jul : *contemporary art encounters* and *theatre festival ;* end Aug-early Sep, *exhibition-fair ;* Sep : *bunting and bedecking of boats.*

Visit of towers, ☎ 46.41.09.37.

Recommended : *Maison des Artisans,* 14, rue Bletterie.

Bicycle hire : train + bike, at the station.

Hire of sail and motor boats : *Loca-boat,* ☎ 46.42.44.24.

La ROCHE-POSAY

Châtellerault 23, Poitiers 49, Paris 314
C1 (end Apr-early Oct) ⊠ 86270
ⓘ cours Pasteur, ☎ 49.86.20.37., closed Sun.

Hotels :
● ★★★★**Relais du Château,** at the casino, ☎ 49.86.20.10. AE, Visa. 13 rm Ⓟ closed Oct, 300. Rest. ♦♦ Dinner only ; closed Tue, 60-130.
★★**Esplanade,** ☎ 49.86.20.48. Euro, Visa. 25 rm Ⓟ closed Dec-Feb, 125. Rest. ♦ Spec : *ris de veau à l'antonignaise,* 55-150.
★**Parc,** av. des Fontaines, ☎ 49.86.20.02. 80 rm Ⓟ closed 30 Sep-2 May, 160. Rest. 45-55.

⛺ ★★★*Municipal* (200 pl.), ☎ 49.48.48.32.

La ROCHE-SUR-YON

Nantes 65, La Rochelle 83, Paris 414
A1 ⊠ 85000
ⓘ galerie Bonaparte, pl. Napoléon, ☎ 51.36.00.85.
✈ aérodrome Couzinet (6 km NE), ☎ 51.37.46.03.
SNCF ☎ 51.37.28.50.
Bus pl. Napoléon, ☎ 51.62.18.23.

Car-hire : *Budget* train + car, S.N.C.F., railway station, ☎ 49.62.50.50.

Hotel :
★★★**Napoléon,** 50, bd A.-Briand, ☎ 51.05.33.56. Euro, Visa. 29 rm Ⓟ closed end-of-year hols, 235.

Youth hostel : bd Arago.

Restaurant :
♦♦ **Rivoli,** 31, bd A.-Briand, ☎ 51.37.43.41. AE, Euro, Visa ♿ closed 2-23 Aug, Sat eve and Sun. Spec : *foie gras de canard maison, filet de sole aux courgettes et au basilic,* 70-150.

ROYAN

Saintes 38, Bordeaux 129, Paris 505
B3 ⊠ 17200
ⓘ Palais des Congrès (B2), ☎ 46.05.70.34 and 46.05.65.02 ; pl. de la Poste (C1), ☎ 46.05.04.71.
✈ aérodrome de Médis (5 km E), ☎ 46.05.34.54.
Ferry for Le Verdon (Gironde) : *Trans-Gironde,* ☎ 46.05.23.03 and 46.38.59.91.
SNCF ☎ 46.05.20.10, 46.05.62.32 ; in summer : 46.05.08.61.
Bus (C1), ☎ 46.05.03.81.

Car-hire : *Budget* train + car, rte des Saintes, ☎ 46.05.54.75 ; S.N.C.F. railway station, ☎ 46.05.62.32.

Hotels :
★★★**France** (Inter-Hôtel), 2, rue Gambetta (B2). ☎ 46.05.02.29. AE, Euro, Visa. 32 rm Ⓟ closed ♿ 270. Rest. ♦ 18 Dec-1 Feb and Mon (ex Jul-Aug), 70-150.
★★★**Hermitage,** 56, Front-de-Mer (B2), ☎ 46.38.57.33. AE, Euro, Visa. 25 rm closed 15 Oct-15 Feb, 230. Rest. ♦ 60-120.
★★★**Les Embruns,** 18 *bis,* bd Garnier (C12), ☎ 46.05.02.17. AE, DC, Euro. 24 rm Ⓟ closed 1 Oct-1 Apr, 230.
★★★**Grand Hôtel,** 195, av. de Pontaillac (A2), ☎ 46.38.00.44. 55 rm Ⓟ closed 1 Oct-1 May, 300.
● ★★**Goelands,** 4, av. de l'Ermitage (A1), ☎ 46.39.01.50. 20 rm Ⓟ ♿ closed Oct-Apr, 180.
★★**Résidence de Saintonge,** allée des Algues

(A2), ☎ 46.39.00.00. 40 rm 🅿 ⚘ closed Oct-Mar, 230. Rest. ♦ ***le Pavillon Bleu*** 60-130.
★★**Beau Rivage,** 9, façade de Foncillon (B2), ☎ 46.38.73.11. 22 rm ⚘ ♿ 250.
★★**Bellevue** (Denise), 122, av. de Pontaillac, ☎ 46.38.06.75. Visa. 25 rm 🅿 ⚘ ♿ closed mid Mar-mid Nov, 210.

Nauzan beach, 17640 Vaux-sur-Mer :
★★★**Résidence de Rohan** (Relais du Silence), rte de St-Palais, ☎ 46.38.00.75. 22 rm 🅿 ⚘ ♿ closed 2 Nov-1 Apr, 430.

⛺ ★★★*Clairefontaine* (300 pl.), av. Louise, ☎ 46.38.08.11, Médis (6 km NE) ; ★★★*Clos Fleuri* (100 pl.), ☎ 46.05.62.17.

Restaurants :
♦♦ ***Chalet,*** 6, bd Grandière (C1), ☎ 46.05.04.90. AE, DC, Visa ♿ closed 2 Jan-1 Mar and Wed ex Jul-Aug, 85-250.
♦♦ ***Squale,*** 102, av. Semis (not on the C2 map), ☎ 46.05.51.34. Visa ; closed Tue and Mar. Spec : *coquilles St-Jacques aux épinards,* 110-200.
♦ ***Près des Flots,*** 57, bd de la République, ☎ 46.05.12.13. AE, Visa ♿ closed Thu, 40-75.

Bicycle hire : enq at the ℹ

Recommended : visit to wine-grower's cellars, *château de Didonne,* 7 km E, ☎ 46.05.05.91.

RUFFEC

Angoulême 43, Poitiers 66, Paris 401
C2 ❤ ⊠ 16700

ℹ mairie, ☎ 45.31.05.42.

SNCF ☎ 45.31.00.40.

Hotels :
Villegats, RN10, S :
★★★**Charentais,** ☎ 45.31.40.32. AE, Visa. 13 rm 🅿 ⚘ 220. Rest. ♦♦ ***Chez Georges,*** 60-170.
Verteuil-sur-Charente, ⊠ 16510, 6 km S :
● ★**La Paloma** (L.F.), ☎ 45.31.41.32. Visa. 10 rm 🅿 ⚘ closed 25 Oct-5 Nov, 20 Feb-3 Mar and Mon, 150. Rest. ♦ 50-100.

Youth hostel, rue Raoul-Hédiard.

⛺ ★★*Les Ormeaux* (50 pl.), ☎ 45.31.00.68.

Restaurant :
Condac, 3 km E :
♦ ***Moulin Enchanté,*** ☎ 45.31.04.97 ♿ closed Mon, Tue, Wed, 60-80.

Riding gîte, rooms and table d'hôtes : *le Petit logis du Breuil Vigier,* Bernac, ☎ 45.31.07.55.

Les SABLES-D'OLONNE

La Roche-sur-Yon 36, Nantes 91, Paris 450
A1 ⊠ 85100

ℹ rue du Mal-Leclerc, ☎ 51.32.03.28., closed Sun low season.

⛴ summer ferry service to the île d'Yeu.

SNCF ☎ 51.32.00.20.

🚌 *Transvendéens,* ☎ 51.32.08.27 ; *Citroën,* ☎ 51.32.02.28.

Car-hire : *Budget* train + car, S.N.C.F. station, ☎ 51.32.01.20.

Hotels :
★★★**Atlantic,** 5, prom. Godet, ☎ 51.95.37.71. Tx 710474. AE, DC, Euro, Visa. 30 rm ♿ 495. Rest. ***le Sloop,*** 105-230.
★★**Beau Rivage,** 40, prom. Clemenceau, ☎ 51.32.03.01. AE, DC, Euro, Visa. 28 rm closed Dec-mid-Jan, 30 Sep-10 Oct and Sun eve-Mon low season, 230. Rest. ● ♦ A restaurant that does well, especially in season : beautiful fish, 100-280.
★**Merle Blanc,** 59, av. A.-Briand, ☎ 51.32.00.35. 31 rm ⚘ closed 30 Sep-20 Mar, 150.

Youth hostel : la Chaume (semaphore) in Jul-Aug.

⛺ ★★★★*Les Roses* (215 pl.), ☎ 51.95.10.42 ; Olonne : ★★★*l'Orée* (270 pl.), ☎ 51.33.10.59 ; ★★★*la Loubine* (130 empl.), ☎ 51.33.12.92.

Restaurants :
♦♦ ***Chez Loulou,*** rte Bleue, La Chaume, ☎ 51.32.00.22. 🅿 closed Oct and Tue. Spec : *chaudrée charentaise,* 80-130.
♦♦ ***Au Capitaine,*** 5, quai Guiné, ☎ 51.95.18.10. AE, DC, Euro, Visa ; closed end Sep-end Oct, 12-26 Dec, 3-12 Mar, Sun eve ex Jul-Aug and Mon. Spec : *bar aux algues,* 110-180.
♦♦ ***Relais de Cayola,*** baie de Cayola (7 km S on the coastal road), ☎ 51.95.11.16. AE, DC, Visa 🅿 ♿ closed mid-Nov-Jan and Mon eve-Wed low season, 50-130.

Bicycle hire : train + bike, at the station.

SAINT-GEORGES-DE-DIDONNE

Royan 3, La Rochelle 75, Paris 508
B3 ⊠ 17110

ℹ bd Michelet, Feb-Sep, ☎ 46.05.09.73.

Hotel :
★**Colinette,** ☎ 46.05.15.75. 25 rm closed 15 Nov-Feb, 140. Rest. closed Sun eve and Mon low season, 40-110.

Youth hostel : 23, av. de Cordouan, Apr-Nov.

⛺ ★★★★*Le Bois Soleil,* forêt de Suzac (350 pl.), ☎ 46.05.05.94 ; ★★★*Idéal-Camping nº 1* (400 pl.), ☎ 46.05.29.04.

Bicycle hire : enq at the *T.O.*

SAINT-GILLES-CROIX-DE-VIE

Les Sables-d'Olonne 30, Nantes 78, Paris 448
A1 ⊠ 85800

ℹ espl. du Quai (high season), ☎ 51.55.05.07 and 51.55.03.66, closed Sun and Mon ex Jul-Aug, and mairie, ☎ 51.55.01.57.

SNCF ☎ 51.62.50.50.

🚌 ferry service to the île d'Yeu (Jul-Aug).

Hotel :
★★**Embruns,** 16, bd de la Mer, ☎ 51.55.11.40. Visa. 23 rm closed Nov and Sat low season, 120. Rest. ♦ Spec : *sole farcie,* 60-150.

⛺ ★★★★*Le Pas Opton,* le Fenouiller (140 pl.), ☎ 51.55.11.98 ; Givrand : ★★★★*Domaine de Beaulieu* (210 pl.), ☎ 51.55.59.46 ; ★★★*Europa* (170 pl.), ☎ 51.55.32.68.

Restaurant :
♦♦ ***Jean Bart,*** Grande-Plage, ☎ 51.55.06.19., closed Jan, Sun eve and Mon, 120-210.

Bicycle hire : enq at the ℹ

SAINT-HILAIRE-DE-RIEZ

Saint-Gilles-Croix-de-Vie 5, La Roche-sur-Yon 47, Paris 445
A1 ⊠ 85270

ℹ Pays de Riez, mairie, ☎ 51.54.40.58, and in Sion, pl. Henri-Renaud, ☎ 51.55.08.64.

Hotel :
★★**L'Atlantique,** 173, av. de la Corniche, ☎ 51.55.09.25. 20 rm, closed Sep-May, 160.

⛺ ★★★★*Les Biches* (350 pl.), ☎ 51.54.38.82 ; ★★★*Riez à la Vie* (250 pl.), ☎ 51.54.30.49 ; ★★★*les Grandes Roselières* (90 pl.), ☎ 51.55.11.74 ; ★★★*la Parée Preneau* (100 pl.), ☎ 51.54.33.84 ; ★★★*la Parée des Joncs* (150 pl.), ☎ 51.54.32.92 ; ★★★*les Écureuils* (230 pl.), ☎ 51.54.33.71 ; ★★★*les Chouans*

(200 pl.), ☎ 51.54.34.90 ; and 30 sites ★★ (approx 3 000 pl.).

SAINT-JEAN-D'ANGELY

Saintes 27, Angoulême 65, Paris 444
B2 ⊠ 17400

ⓘ hôtel de ville, ☎ 46.32.04.72.

SNCF ☎ 46.32.01.01.

Hotel :

★★***Paix*** (L.F.), 5, av. du Gal-de-Gaulle, ☎ 46.32.00.93. 16 rm Ⓟ closed 15 Nov-28 Feb, 190. Rest. ♿ closed Sat, 55-90.

SAINT-JEAN-DE-MONTS

Noirmoutier 32, Nantes 79, Paris 448
A1 ⊠ 85160

ⓘ Palais des Congrès, ☎ 51.58.00.48., closed Sun low season.

bd du Mal-Leclerc.

Hotels :

★★***Plage,*** 1-3, espl. de la Mer, ☎ 51.58.00.35. AE. 52 rm Ⓟ closed 9 Sep-15 May, 230. Rest. 100-170.

★★***Chez Tante Paulette*** (L.F.), 32, rue Neuve, ☎ 51.58.01.12. AE. 41 rm closed 11 Nov-1 Mar, 145. Rest. ♿ 50-95.

Orouet (6 km) :

★★***Chaumière,*** ☎ 51.58.67.44. AE, DC, Euro, Visa. 17 rm Ⓟ ♿ closed 26 Sep-1 May, 200. Rest. ♦ 45-140.

Youth hostel : rue Milcendeau.

⛺ ★★★★*Les Pins* (140 pl.), ☎ 51.58.17.42 ; ★★★★*l'Abri des Pins* (220 pl.), ☎ 51.58.83.86 ; ★★★★*le Bois Masson* (500 pl.), ☎ 51.58.62.62 ; ★★★★*les Amiaux* (380 pl.), ☎ 51.58.22.22 ; ★★★★*la Yole* (165 pl.), ☎ 51.58.67.17 ; ★★★*le Clarys-Plage* (140 pl.), ☎ 51.58.10.24 ; ★★★*Aux Cœurs Vendéens* (120 pl.), ☎ 51.58.84.91.

SAINT-LAURENT-SUR-SÈVRE

Cholet 12, Nantes 62, Paris 361
B1 ⊠ 85290 Mortagne-sur-Sèvre

Hotels :

★★***Hermitage,*** 2, rue de la Joucance, ☎ 51.67.83.03. 17 rm Ⓟ closed Sun low season, 180. Rest. ♦ Spec : *grillade aux sarments de vigne*, 65-120.

La Trique, 3 km N :

● ★★★***Baumotel*** (Châteaux-hôtels), ☎ 51.67.88.12. Euro, Visa. 20 rm Ⓟ ♿ 290. Rest. ♦♦ ***la Chaumière.*** ♿ Excellent pastry chef, formerly with Lenôtre. Spec : *foie gras frais maison, rognons de veau au vinaigre de cidre*, 55-210. ***Le Vendéen*** (grill).

SAINT-PALAIS-SUR-MER

Royan 5.5, La Rochelle 77, Paris 511
B3 ⊠ 17420

ⓘ ☎ 46.22.11.09 ; mairie, ☎ 46.22.10.64.

SNCF ☎ 46.22.12.66.

Hotels :

● ★★★***Villa Nausicaa,*** 1, prom. de la Plage, ☎ 46.23.14.78. 11 rm Ⓟ closed Wed low season, 300. Rest. ♦♦ 80-140.

● ★★***Primavera,*** ☎ 46.23.20.35. 36 rm Ⓟ ♿ closed Nov-25 Dec and Wed (Oct-Apr), 300. Rest. ♦♦ 75-150.

★★***Plage,*** 1, pl. de l'Océan, ☎ 46.23.10.32. Visa. 22 rm closed 20 Oct-Easter, 180. Rest. ♦ 60-100.

★★***Téthys,*** 60, av. de la Corniche, ☎ 46.38.31.00. 23 rm Ⓟ closed 15 Sep-1 Jun, 180. Rest. ♦ ♿ For hotel guests only, 50-110.

Nauzan creek *(conche) :*

★***La Biche au Bois,*** ☎ 46.39.01.52. 9 rm ♿ closed 30 Sep-30 Mar and Wed (30 Mar-30 May), 105. Rest. ♦ 40-110.

⛺ ★★★*Le Logis* (900 pl.), ☎ 46.22.20.23 ; *Domaine de Bernezac* (100 pl.), ☎ 46.22.11.42 ; *les Deux Plages* (200 pl.), ☎ 46.22.11.42 ; *le Puits de l'Autre* (400 pl.), ☎ 46.22.20.31 ; *Marcel Taburiaux* (120 pl.), ☎ 46.38.00.71 ; and eight sites ★★

Restaurant :

Le Grallet, 17920 Breuilhet :

♦♦ ***La Grange,*** ☎ 46.22.72.64. Ⓟ closed Sep-Jun, 160-210.

SAINTES

Royan 38, Bordeaux 116, Paris 470
B3 ⊠ 17100

ⓘ espl. A.-Malraux, ☎ 46.74.23.82.

cruises on the Charente river : enq at the *S.I.*

SNCF ☎ 46.92.04.19.

cours Reverseaux (W).

Car-hire : *Budget* train + car, ☎ 46.93.21.81 ; S.N.C.F. railway station, ☎ 46.92.50.50.

Hotels :

★★★***Bois Saint-Georges*** (Relais du Silence), D137 (direction Royan), ☎ 46.93.50.99. 21 rm Ⓟ ♿ 380. Rest. ♦♦ ♿ closed Mon noon. Spec : *turbot à la crème de langoustine*, 93.

★★★***Commerce*** *(Mancini),* rue des Messageries, ☎ 46.93.06.61. Tx 791012. AE, DC, Euro, Visa. 42 rm, 230. Rest. ♦♦♦ Spec : *escalope de bar aux huîtres*, 60-220.

★★***Avenue,*** 116, av. Gambetta, ☎ 46.74.16.85. AE, Visa. 15 rm Ⓟ closed Mon low season, 180. Rest. ***Brasserie Louis*** ♿ 60-110.

★★***Bosquets,*** rte de Rochefort (2 km), ☎ 46.74.04.47. Euro, Visa. 35 rm Ⓟ ♿ closed 23 Dec-2 Jan, 170. Rest. ♦ ***les Restaurants Jardins,*** ☎ 46.74.11.80. ♿ 70-90.

Youth hostel : 6, rue Pont-Amilion, ☎ 46.92.14.92.

Restaurant :

6 km on the Rochefort road :

♦♦ ***La Vieille Forge,*** ☎ 46.92.98.30. Ⓟ closed 5-25 Jun, 10 days in Oct, and Tue, 120-210.

Visits : conducted by official *C.N.M.H.S.* guides, daily from 15 Jun to 15 Sep (enq at the *S.I.*).

Events : Jul, *early music festival,* followed by the *Jeux santons* (local folklore festivities).

Bicycle hire (enq at the S.I.) and horse hire (enq at the stud farm).

Recommended : visit of the Paul Bossuet cellar and storehouses, logis de Folle-Blanche, Senonches, 17610 Chaniers (7 km E from Saintes).

SAUJON

Royan 11, Saintes 26, Paris 494
B3 (Jun-Sep) ⊠ 17600

ⓘ pl. du Gal-de-Gaulle, Jul-Aug, closed Sun, ☎ 46.02.83.77.

✈ aérodrome de Médis (→ Royan).

SNCF station on the Royan-Paris line, ☎ 46.02.80.39.

Hotels :

★★***Commerce,*** 7, rue de Saintonge, ☎ 46.02.80.50. 19 rm Ⓟ closed Dec-Jan, Sun eve and Mon low season, 180. Rest. ♦ 50-120.

★★***Auberge du Moulin,*** Le Chay, ☎ 46.02.83.25. 16 rm Ⓟ ♿ closed 15 Sep-Whitsun, 140. Rest. ♦♦ Spec : *moules au pineau, poulet aux fruits de mer*, 50-90.

Châlons, 8 km N :
● ★★★***Moulin de Châlons*** (Châteaux-hôtels), ☎ 46.22.82.72. AE, Euro. 14 rm P closed 25 Sep-10 May and Tue, 260. Rest. ♦ ♿ 120-250.
★★***La Galiote,*** ☎ 46.22.81.94. 11 rm closed Tue eve and Wed, 200. Rest. 90-130.

SURGÈRES

Rochefort 26, Niort 34, Paris 440
B2 ⊠ 17700

ℹ sq. du Château, ☎ 46.07.20.02, Jun-Sep, closed Sun.

SNCF ☎ 46.07.00.69.

Car-hire : *Budget* train + car, S.N.C.F. railway station, ☎ 46.07.00.69.

Hotel :
★***Ronsard,*** pl. du Château, ☎ 46.07.00.63. Visa. 11 rm P closed Feb, Fri eve and Sat, 120. Rest. ♦ 50-125.

TALMONT-SAINT-HILAIRE

Les Sables-d'Olonne 13, La Roche-sur-Yon 29, Paris 443
A1 ⊠ 85440

ℹ hôtel de ville, ☎ 51.33.20.42.

Hotels :
Boule d'Or, 3, rue du Château, ☎ 51.90.60.23. Euro. 12 rm P closed 20 Dec-20 Jan, 60. Rest. closed Sun eve and Mon, 55-120.
La Guittière port :
★★***Parcs,*** ☎ 51.90.61.64. AE, Euro. 21 rm P private beach ; closed 20 Jan-20 Feb, 170. Rest. ♦ 45-145.

⛺ Numerous campsites ★★ (approx 800 pl.).

TALMONT-SUR-GIRONDE

Royan 16, Saintes 35, Paris 517
B3 ⊠ 17120 Cozes

ℹ mairie, ☎ 46.90.80.97.

Hotels :
Le Caillaud port :
★***L'Estuaire,*** ☎ 46.90.73.85. Visa. P closed 15 Oct-15 Mar and Tue eve-Wed (ex Jul-Aug), 125. Rest. ♦ 55-125.
Les Monards (5 km) :
Auberge des Monards, ☎ 46.90.78.00. 3 rm P closed Thu (Oct-Apr), 200. Rest. ♦♦ 65-130.
Restaurant :
♦♦♦ ***Les Flots,*** Le Caillaud, ☎ 46.90.70.45. AE, Euro, Visa. P ♿ closed Oct-15 Jun, in season open only eve. Booking required, 150-200.

THOUARS

Bressuire 29, Châtellerault 69, Paris 327
B-C1 ♥ ⊠ 79100

ℹ pl. Saint-Médard, ☎ 49.66.17.65.

SNCF ☎ 49.66.00.13.

Hotel :
★★***Château*** (L.F.), rte de Parthenay, ☎ 49.66.18.52. Euro, Visa. 20 rm P closed Sun eve, 140. Rest. ♦ 50-80.

Youth hostel, 5 bd du 8-Mai.

⛺ Several campsites ★★ (approx 200 pl.).

Guided tours conducted by official *C.N.M.H.S.* guides, Jul-15 Sep 3 times weekly (enq at the *S.I.*).

La TRANCHE-SUR-MER

Luçon 32, La Rochelle 62, Paris 454
A2 ⊠ 85360

ℹ pl. de la Liberté, ☎ 51.30.33.96.

⛴ Inter-island cruises in summer.

Hotels :
● ★★***Le Rêve,*** 8, rue Launis, ☎ 51.30.34.06. Euro. 40 rm P closed 4 Nov-end Mar, Sun eve and Mon low season, 170. Rest. ♦ 60-120.
● ★***Océan*** (L.F.), 49, rue A.-France, ☎ 51.30.30.09. 56 rm P closed 25 Sep-1 Apr. Half-pension 160, pension 210. Rest. ♦ 80-120.
La Grière (2 km E) :
★★***Cols Verts,*** ☎ 51.30.35.06. Euro. 35 rm ♿ closed Oct-1 Apr and Mon, 210. Rest. ♦ 70-170.

⛺ ★★★★*Baie d'Aunis* (160 pl.), ☎ 51.30.37.36 ; ★★★*Cottage Fleuri* (160 pl.), ☎ 51.30.34.57. Longeville, ⊠ 85560, 11 km N : ★★★★*De Jarny* (200 pl.), ☎ 51.33.42.21 ; ★★★★*Fief du Bonair* (100 pl.), ☎ 51.33.31.09 ; ★★★*les Dunes* (125 pl.), ☎ 51.33.32.93 ; ★★★*le Clos des Pins* (120 pl.), ☎ 51.33.30.33.

Event : *international horticulture show* in Apr-May.

Bicycle hire : enq at the *O.T.*

VIVONNE

Poitiers 19, Niort 63, Paris 354
13 km E of Lusignan, C2 ♥ ⊠ 86370

ℹ mairie, ☎ 49.43.41.05.

Hotel :
★***La Treille*** (L.F.), 10, av. de Bordeaux, ☎ 49.43.41.13. AE, DC, Euro, Visa. 4 rm P ♿ closed 10-25 Jan, Feb hols and Wed low season, 65. Rest. ♦ Spec : *bouilliture d'anguilles,* 60-150.

VOUILLÉ

Poitiers 17, Thouars 52, Paris 341
18 km SW of Vendeuvre, C1 ⊠ 86190

Hotel :
★★★***Domaine de Périgny*** (Relais et châteaux), 4 km SE, ☎ 49.51.80.43. AE, Euro, Visa. 39 rm P ♿ closed 15 Jan-28 Feb. A magnificent hotel complex, which offers calm and relaxation along with good cooking, 440. Rest. ● ♦♦♦ Spec : *cervelas de brochet aux pistaches, millefeuille de petits-gris à la coriandre,* 100-250.

Ile d'YEU

A1 ⊠ 85350

ℹ Port-Joinville ferry terminal, ☎ 51.58.32.58.

⛴ 1 to 4 trips daily from Fromentine (1 hr 10), ☎ 51.68.53.65.

Hotel :
Port-Joinville :
★★***Flux Hôtel,*** 27, rue Pierre-Henry, ☎ 51.58.36.25. 15 rm P ♿ closed Jan-Feb, 165.

⛺ ★★*Marais de la Guerche* (200 pl.), ☎ 51.58.37.60.

Recommended : *Spay,* tuna presented in all possible ways, including smoked, ☎ 51.58.36.10.

Alphabetical place-names index

The index of place-names mentionned in the guide includes two sets of page-numbers: Sightseeing in blue; Practical Information in red; also in red are the names of departments and the regions of the guide.

A

B

C

D

H

M

N

O

P

Paris

P (continued)

Q

R

S

T

U

V